November 3–7, 2014
Orlando, Florida, USA

Association for
Computing Machinery

Advancing Computing as a Science & Profession

MM'14

Proceedings of the 2014 ACM Conference on Multimedia

Sponsored by:
ACM SIGMM

Supported by:
FX PAL, NFS, Symantec, UCM, Google, IBM Research, Microsoft Research, NASA, Yahoo! Labs, and Yandex

Association for
Computing Machinery

Advancing Computing as a Science & Profession

The Association for Computing Machinery
2 Penn Plaza, Suite 701
New York, New York 10121-0701

ISBN: 978-1-4503-3063-3 (Digital)

ISBN: 978-1-4503-3426-6 (Print)

Additional copies may be ordered prepaid from:

ACM Order Department
PO Box 30777
New York, NY 10087-0777, USA

Phone: 1-800-342-6626 (USA and Canada)
+1-212-626-0500 (Global)
Fax: +1-212-944-1318
E-mail: acmhelp@acm.org
Hours of Operation: 8:30 am – 4:30 pm ET

Printed in the USA

Message from the General Chairs

Welcome to ACM Multimedia 2014 in Orlando! As in the past, this year's conference is being organized as a full week of events from November 3rd to November 7th, 2014. The 3-day main conference is preceded by eight tutorials and followed by 12 workshops on current topics in multimedia computing, communications, and applications.

Orlando, nicknamed "The City Beautiful," is one of the busiest American cities for conferences and conventions. The city's famous attractions and vibrant downtown make Orlando the most visited American city, with approximately 50 million tourists a year. The greater Orlando metropolitan area has a population of over two million residents, with a rapidly growing technology industry of more than 2,600 companies. It serves as the divisional headquarters for many major companies such as Siemens, Mitsubishi, Lockheed Martin, L-3 Communications, SAIC, and Electronic Arts. The city is home to the University of Central Florida, currently the 2nd largest university in the United States. The Central Florida Research Park, located adjacent to the university, is the 7th largest research park in the country. Metro Orlando is also home to the simulation procurement commands for the U.S. Army, Navy, Air Force, Marines, and Coast Guard. Forbes magazine lists Metro Orlando among the "Best Places for Business and Careers." Entrepreneur Magazine rates Orlando as the "Number One City for Entrepreneurs." BusinessWeek featured Metro Orlando among its picks of "global hot spots" in its issue titled "What makes a Winner: The Competition Issue." Orlando is one of the three communities in the world to be featured.

Since the founding of ACM SIGMM in 1993, ACM Multimedia has been the worldwide premier conference and a key world event to present scientific achievements and innovative industrial products in the field of multimedia. At ACM Multimedia 2014, we celebrate its twenty-second iteration with an extensive program consisting of technical sessions covering all aspects of the multimedia field in the forms of oral and poster presentations, tutorials, panels, exhibits, demonstrations, and workshops, bringing into focus the principal subjects of investigation, competitions of research teams on challenging problems, and also an interactive art program stimulating artists and computer scientists to come together to take contemporary art to a new level with multimedia interaction.

We are happy that we were able to maintain registration fees at about the same levels as in 2011, the last time the conference was held in the U.S. This is possible with the generous financial support from our many sponsors of the conference. In particular, we are indebted to our host, the University of Central Florida, who provided substantial financial contributions in the early stage to give us a solid basis for organizing a successful conference. It is also our privilege to acknowledge the generous support of Symantec, our Platinum sponsor; FXPAL and Google, our Gold sponsors; and IBM, Microsoft Research, NASA Florida Space Grant Consortium, Yahoo Lab, and Yandex, our Silver sponsors.

ACM Multimedia has a long tradition of financially supporting student participation. We are thankful for a grant from US National Science Foundation, which with additional fund from SIGMM has allowed us to continue this tradition by providing substantial number of student travel grants. We have also organized a lunch for the Doctoral Symposium to give the students the opportunity to meet and interact with leaders of the research community. ACM SIGMM also provided special funds for us to organize the 'Women's Research Meeting' lunch, an annual SIGMM event started by Klara Nahrstedt in 2010 to strengthen the social networking among junior and senior female researchers and to work on increasing the participation of women in the SIGMM community.

Organizing a conference with the magnitude of ACM Multimedia requires a large number of enthusiastic volunteers. We have truly enjoyed working with an outstanding group of colleagues in the organization committee, who have generously contributed their time and effort for over two years. This conference would not have been possible without their dedication and hard work.

We thank all those who contributed to the organization of the outstanding technical programs through a highly selective review process: Technical Program Committee Chairs Alan Hanjalic, Apostol Natsev, and Wenwu Zhu; Workshop Chairs Andreas Mauthe, Max Muhlhauser, and Hari Sundaram; Technical Demo Chairs Shu-Ching Chen, Stefan Gobel, and Carsten Griwodz; Interactive Art Exhibit Chairs Andrea Cavallaro and Cheryl Cabrera; Tutorial Chairs Hermann Hellwagner and Wei Tsang Ooi; Industry Exhibit Chairs Minoru Etoh and Dulce Ponceleon; "High-Risk High-Reward Papers" Chairs abdulmotaleb El Saddik, Rainer Lienhart, and Balakrishnan Prabhakaran, "Multimedia Grand Challenge Papers" Chairs Changsheng Xu and Cha Zhang, Open Source Competition Chairs Andreas Girgensohn and Lynn Wilcox; Research Panel Chairs Wolfgang Klas and Chang Wen Chen; Industrial Panel Chairs, Borko Furth and Ivica Rimac; and Author's Advocate Chair Pablo Cesar.

We also thank all those who worked tirelessly behind the scenes to make sure everything running smoothly: Web Chair Alex Aved; Local Arrangement Chairs Mainak Chatterjee and Cliff Zou; Finance and Registration Chairs Tai Do, Ning Jiang, and Ming Li; Proceedings Chairs Wallapak Tavanapong and Ying Cai; Publicity and Social Media Chair Grace Ngai; Travel Grant Chairs Danzhou Liu and Junghwan Oh; Sponsorship Chairs Hassan Foroosh and Mark Liao; and History Preservation Chairs Duc Tran and Roy Villafane.

We want to thank former ACM SIGMM Chair Klara Nahrstedt, former SIGMM Director of Conference Mohan Kankanhalli, current SIGMM Chair, Shih-Fu Chang, and current SIGMM Director of Conference Nicu Sebe for their advice and help in all stages of the organization of the conference. Last, but not least, we gratefully acknowledge Sheridan Printing Company for their help with the preparation of the conference proceedings.

It was our great honor to accept the responsibility of Conference General Chairs. We hope that you will find ACM Multimedia 2014 to be a stimulating, informative, and enriching experience. We are sure that you will also find time to enjoy the beautiful city of Orlando with the many entertainment options.

Kien A. Hua Yong Rui Ralf Steinmetz
ACM Multimedia 2014 General Chairs

Report from the Technical Program Chairs

It is our pleasure to introduce to you the Technical Program of the *ACM International Conference on Multimedia 2014*. While we built this year's program upon the best practices from previous editions of the conference, we also introduced several adjustments with the goal to define the set of submission areas to reflect the current and emerging research directions in the multimedia field and to improve the quality of the review process and the feedback provided to the authors.

Papers were submitted to 14 areas: *Big and Broad Multimedia*, *Deep Learning for Multimedia*, *Emotional and Social Signals in Multimedia*, *Media Transport and Delivery*, *Multimedia and Society*, *Multimedia and the Crowd*, *Multimedia Art, Entertainment and Culture*, *Multimedia HCI and QoE*, *Multimedia Search and Recommendation*, *Multimedia Security, Privacy and Forensics*, *Multimedia Systems and Middleware*, *Multimodal Analysis and Description, Music*, *Speech and Audio Processing in Multimedia*, and *Social Media and Collective Online Presence*. This set of areas resulted from revising and expanding the areas from previous years, and based on the discussion within the Technical Program Committee (TPC) that aimed at highlighting new and emerging research directions (e.g., big and broad multimedia, multimedia and society, QoE), promising new technical approaches not traditionally covered at ACM Multimedia (e.g., deep learning), and reaching out to related communities with complementary expertise (e.g., emotional and social signals). At the same time, some areas were discontinued, either due to the sub-standard number of submissions over the past several years (e.g. multimedia authoring and collaboration) or due to the fact that some technologies and platforms have become mainstream and need no special emphasis any more (e.g. mobile and multi-device).

For each area, a team of Area Chairs (ACs) was appointed to handle the paper review process. In total, 38 ACs were appointed. The sizes of the teams were defined based on the anticipated number of submissions per area. Consequently, the teams ranged from two to seven ACs. The TPC consisted of both experienced and junior ACs. Also, some ACs were new to the ACM Multimedia venue, with the intention to broaden the ACM Multimedia community and open it up to related communities. ACs were given autonomy to define the Call for Papers (CfP) for their areas, select reviewers, assign papers to them (either manually or through a bidding process), assess papers based on their reviews, and provide initial acceptance recommendation as input for the TPC meeting.

The activities of the ACs were steered at the meta level by the following guidelines defined by the TPC Chairs to maximize the program quality:

- The conference must preserve its unique multimedia character in order to stand out among related scientific venues and attract highest-quality submissions.
- The papers were handled in a double-blind fashion and for each paper a minimum of three reviews were required.
- The CfPs for different areas were defined so as to minimize overlap among areas, optimally highlight the focus of individual areas, and maximize the overall topic coverage of the conference program. For this purpose, ACs were requested to share their CfPs with other ACs, and to collaboratively resolve any overlap or ambiguity issues. This resulted in several area-CfP adjustments.
- ACs were also requested to share their lists of reviewers so as to maximize the level of expertise per area and to make the lists non-overlapping in order to control the review load per reviewer (a reviewer was allowed to participate in multiple areas only with the explicit agreement of the reviewer and the corresponding ACs).

- ACs were instructed to administratively reject improperly formatted papers and to move papers to other tracks if they believed there was a better fit for the paper. This required the agreement of ACs from both the outgoing and the receiving area.
- Conflict of Interest (CoI) handling: ACs were allowed to submit at most one full paper and one short paper to their own area. Since the submission system (EasyChair) only allowed the ACs to have access to papers and reviews in their own track, any submission by ACs were moved to a separate meta track, which included only papers with conflicts of interest. All of these papers were handled by another qualified AC, either from the same area or from another area. If the papers co-authored by ACs passed the threshold for discussion during the TPC meeting, the discussion was led by the handling AC and the author-AC was asked to leave the room.

An elaborate ***EasyChair Paper Management Guidelines*** document was written containing instructions for the ACs on how to implement the TPC Chair's guidelines and how to navigate the submission management system (EasyChair). This Guidelines document will be made available to the SIGMM Director of Conferences to share with future TPCs of the ACM Multimedia conference. As an aside, we would strongly suggest to future TPCs to explore alternative conference management systems as EasyChair presented a number of challenges over the course of this process.

Regarding the paper submission and review process,

- There was no pre-submission of abstracts. This led to a simplification of the submission process, and given the large number of submissions, we feel it did not negatively influence the paper submission process.
- Submission of full and short papers were separated from each other, with short papers being submitted only after the full paper submission had been closed. This improved the ease of managing different types of submissions, and allowed authors to more easily plan for both full and short papers, if desired. This may be a possible explanation for the noticeable increase in the number of submissions this year.
- For full papers, we organized a two-stage review process, and authors were invited to submit a rebuttal based on the first stage reviews. The reviewers were then instructed to consider the rebuttal, to revise their reviews accordingly, and to enter discussion with each other aiming to improve review consensus on each paper. The results of the second round reviews and discussion were then summarized by the ACs into meta reviews, which included tentative ACCEPT/REJECT/BORDERLINE recommendations, to be discussed and finalized during the TPC meeting.
- Compared to 2013, the full paper submission deadline was moved back to the end of March, while keeping the two-stage review process. Despite the significantly shortened review period, all full papers received at least three reviews on time (some as many as six!). We really appreciate the effort by our ACs and reviewers and thank them for the great job they did!
- Following the successful experience from 2013, an Author's Advocate (AA) role was created to provide authors with an independent channel to express concerns about the quality of the reviews for their papers, and to engage into a discussion with ACs on how to handle these concerns. The AA received requests for mediation for a total of 22 of the full papers (8%). The AA reviewed all the cases and successfully handled them in a collaborative effort with the ACs in charge of the corresponding papers. As a result of the mediation, 4 new reviews were generated and 14 other reviews were revised. The mediation from the AA happened

before the TPC meeting, so the material serving as input for the discussions during the meeting did not include any low-quality review.

- We received 300 full and 397 short papers by the corresponding submission deadlines, or in total 697 papers. After removing improperly anonymized or otherwise invalid papers, 286 full and 393 short papers remained and entered the regular review process. The latter numbers served as the reference for computing the acceptance rate.
- Based on the first review results for full papers (after notification), 14 papers were withdrawn by the authors and removed from the system, leaving 665 papers in the review processing pipeline: 272 full papers and 393 short papers. This is the number that served as input for TPC meeting. The table below gives a distribution of these papers across areas.

Area	Full papers	Short papers
Big and Broad Multimedia	10	8
Deep Learning for Multimedia	23	21
Emotional and Social Signals in Multimedia	16	29
Media Transport and Delivery	18	15
Multimedia and Society	11	13
Multimedia and the Crowd	7	8
Multimedia Art, Entertainment and Culture	19	19
Multimedia HCI and QoE	20	38
Multimedia Search and Recommendation	56	80
Multimedia Security, Privacy and Forensics	10	23
Multimedia Systems and Middleware	17	25
Multimodal Analysis and Description	43	75
Music, Speech and Audio Processing in Multimedia	8	18
Social Media and Collective Online Presence	14	21

Decisions on full and short papers were made at the two-day TPC meeting held at Google Inc. in Mountain View, CA, USA on 18-19 June 2014. Two TPC Chairs and 28 ACs attended the meeting. While not all ACs were requested to be present, it was required that all areas are represented in the meeting. AC-teams per area were requested to agree on their recommendations on all papers in the area before the meeting so the representing AC(s) can lead the discussion for the entire area. On the first day, full papers were handled, and on the second day the short papers together with the discussion on awards nominees. We accepted 55 full and 117 short papers, leading to acceptance rates of 19.2% and 29.8% for full and short papers, respectively.

The discussion on both full and short papers was conducted per area, leaving the ACs the opportunity to nominate the papers from their area into the pool of accepted papers. The discussion was at all times plenary, enabling ACs from any area to comment on any paper being discussed from the point of view of their individual expertise, experience, or rating criteria. The discussion went over all areas, and covered all papers flagged for discussion from each area by the ACs, as well as all papers scoring above a certain threshold in terms of their average review score. This way, we made sure to discuss both high-scoring and borderline papers as well as any controversial papers (with large review score discrepancy or with discrepancy between the scores and recommendations from the ACs). The discussion on the papers was intensive, taking into account all the information collected per paper, including reviews, the scores, the authors' rebuttals, the initial recommendations by the ACs (in the form of a meta review) and the reviews performed by other ACs during the meeting.

After the meeting the TPC Chairs finalized the program by grouping the accepted papers into sessions, and the ACs finalized the meta reviews to include extra information based on the TPC meeting discussion. The sessions were formed based on research topics and do not necessarily reflect the submission areas. After notification, all accepted full papers were shepherded to make sure that the revised papers adequately addressed reviewers' concerns and the authors implemented any changes promised in their rebuttals.

The TPC has done everything in their power to ensure that the technical program of the conference is of the highest possible quality. This would not have been possible without the commitment of the Area Chairs and the reviewers. We would like to thank them for their rigor and engagement, and we look forward to having a strong and engaging technical program in Orlando, FL!

We hope you enjoy the program!

Alan Hanjalic
Delft University of Technology
The Netherlands

Apostol (Paul) Natsev
Google Inc.
USA

Wenwu Zhu
Tsinghua University
PR China

Table of Contents

Session: Action, Activity, and Event Recognition

Session Chair: Cees Snoek *(University of Amsterdam)*

Session: Music, Speech and Audio

Session Chair: Cynthia Liem *(Delft University of Technology)*

Session: Deep Learning for Multimedia

Session Chair: Apostol Natsev *(Google Inc.)*

Doctoral Symposium 1

Session Chair: Oge Marques *(Florida Atlantic University)*

Doctoral Symposium 2

Session Chair: Christian Breiteneder *(Vienna University of Technology)*

Open Source Software Competition 1

Session Chair: Andreas Girgensohn *(FXPAL)*

Open Source Software Competition 2

Session Chair: Lynn Wilcox *(FXPAL)*

Art Exhibit

Session Chair: Cheryl Cabrera *(University of Central Florida)*

Demos 1: Searching and Finding

Session Chair: Shu-Ching Chen *(Florida International University)*

Demos 2: Senses and Sensors

Session Chair: Stefan Göbel *(Technische Universität Darmstadt)*

Demos 3: Systems

Session Chair: Carsten Griwodz *(Simula Research Laboratory)*

Posters Session 1

Session Chair: Duc Tran *(University of Massachusetts at Boston)*

Posters Session 2

Posters Session 3

Session Chair: Roy Villafane *(Andrews University)*

Tutorials

Workshop Summaries

MM 2014 Conference Organization

General Chairs:	Kien A. Hua *(University of Central Florida, USA)* Yong Rui *(Microsoft Research, China)* Ralf Steinmetz *(Technische Universität Darmstadt, Germany)*
Technical Program Committee Chairs:	Alan Hanjalic *(Delft University of Technology, Netherlands)* Apostol (Paul) Natsev *(Google, USA)* Wenwu Zhu *(Tsinghua University, China)*
Author's Advocate:	Pablo Cesar *(CWI, Netherlands)*
High-Risk High-Reward Papers Chairs:	Abdulmotaleb El Saddik *(University of Ottawa, Canada)* Rainer Lienhart *(Augsburg University, Germany)* Balakrishnan Prabhakaran *(University of Texas at Dallas, USA)*
Multimedia Grand Challenge Chairs:	Changsheng Xu (*Chinese Academy of Sciences, China)* Cha Zhang *(Microsoft Research, USA)*
Technical Demo Chairs:	Shu-Ching Chen (*Florida International University, USA*) Stefan Göbel *(Technische Universität Darmstadt, Germany)* Carsten Griwodz *(Simula Research Laboratory, Norway)*
Industrial Exhibit Chairs:	Minoru Etoh (Mick) *(NTT DoCoMo, Japan)* Dulce Ponceleón *(IBM Research, USA)*
Interactive Art Exhibit Chairs:	Andrea Cavallaro *(Queen Mary University of London, UK)* Cheryl Cabrera *(University of Central Florida, USA)*
Panel Chairs:	Wolfgang Klas *(University of Vienna, Austria)* Chang Wen Chen *(State University of New York at Buffalo, USA)*
Industrial Panel Chairs:	Borko Furth (*Florida Atlantic University, USA)* Ivica Rimac *(Bell Labs / Alcatel-Lucent, USA)*
Open Source Competition Chairs:	Andreas Girgensohn (*FX Palo Alto Laboratory, Inc., USA)* Lynn Wilcox *(FX Palo Alto Laboratory, Inc., USA)*
Doctoral Symposium Chairs:	Laszlo Böszörmenyi *(University of Klagenfurt, Austria)* Christian Breiteneder *(Technical University of Vienna, Austria)* Oge Marques *(Florida Atlantic University, USA)*
Tutorial Chairs:	Hermann Hellwagner *(University of Klagenfurt, Austria)* Wei Tsang Ooi *(National University of Singapore, Singapore)*

Workshops Chairs: Andreas Mauthe *(University of Lancaster, UK)*
Max Mühlhäuser *(Technische Universität, Germany)*
Hari Sundaram (*University of Illinois at Urbana Champaign, USA)*

Web Chair: Alex Aved *(U.S. Air Force Research Lab, USA)*

Local Arrangements Chairs: Mainak Chatterjee *(University of Central Florida, USA)*
Cliff Zou *(University of Central Florida, USA)*

Finance and Registration Chairs: Tai Do *(Microsoft, USA)*
Ning Jiang *(Institute for Systems Biology, USA)*
Ming Li *(California State University, USA)*

Sponsorship Chairs: Hassan Foroosh *(University of Central Florida, USA)*
Mark Liao *(Academia Sincia, Taipei, Taiwan)*

Travel Grant Chairs: Danzhou Liu *(NetApp, USA)*
JungHwan Oh *(University of North Texas, USA)*

Proceedings Chairs: Ying Cai *(Iowa State University, USA)*
Wallapak Tavanapong *(Iowa State University, USA)*

History Preservation Chairs: Duc Tran *(University of Massachusetts in Boston, USA)*
Roy Villafane *(Andrews University, USA)*

Publicity and Social Media Chair: Grace Ngai *(Hong Kong Polytechnic University, S.A.R. China)*

MM 2014 Area Chairs

Big and Broad Multimedia:	Nuria Oliver *(Telefonica, Spain)* Vivek Singh *(MIT, USA)* Alan Smeaton *(Dublin City University, Ireland)*
Deep Learning for Multimedia:	Marc'Aurelio Ranzato *(Facebook, USA)* Kai Yu *(Baidu, China)* George Toderici *(Google, USA)*
Emotional and Social Signals in Multimedia:	Hatice Gunes *(Queen Mary University of London, United Kingdom)* Hayley Hung *(Delft University of Technology, Netherlands)* Bjorn Schuller *(TU Munich, Germany)*
Media Transport and Delivery:	Carsten Griwodz *(University of Oslo, Norway)* Baochun Li *(University of Toronto, Canada)*
Multimedia and Society:	Jenny Benois-Pineau *(University of Bordeaux, France)* Wallapak Tavanapong *(Iowa State University, USA)*
Multimedia and the Crowd:	Kuan-Ta Chen *(Academia Sinica, Taiwan)* Martha Larson *(Delft University of Technology, Netherlands)*
Multimedia Art, Entertainment and Culture:	Teresa Chambel *(University of Lisbon, Portugal)* Frank Nack *(University of Amsterdam, Netherlands)*
Multimedia HCI & QoE:	Marc Cavazza *(Teesside University, United Kingdom)* Touradj Ebrahimi *(EPFL, Switzerland)*
Multimedia Search and Recommendation:	Xian-Sheng Hua *(Microsoft Research, USA)* Qi Tian *(University of Texas San Antonio, USA)* Shuicheng Yan *(National University of Singapore, Singapore)* Hector Yee *(Google, USA)*
Multimedia Security, Privacy and Forensics:	Gerald Friedland *(ICSI Berkeley, USA)* Mohan Kankanhalli *(National University of Singapore, Singapore)*
Multimedia Systems and Middleware:	Jiangchuan Liu *(Simon Fraser University, Canada)* Roger Zimmermann *(National University of Singapore, Singapore)*

Multi-modal Analysis and Description:
Alex Hauptmann *(Carnegie-Mellon University, USA)*
Benoit Huet *(Eurecom, France)*
Xuelong Li *(Chinese Academy of Sciences, China)*
Ansgar Scherp *(Kiel University and Leibniz Information Center for Economics, Germany)*
Mubarak Shah *(University of Central Florida, USA)*
Cees Snoek *(University of Amsterdam, Netherlands)*
Rong Yan *(Square, USA)*

Music, Speech and Audio Processing in Multimedia:
Xavier Anguera *(Telefonica, Spain)*
Cynthia Liem *(Delft University of Technology, Netherlands)*

Social Media and Collective Online Presence:
Peng Cui *(Tsinghua University, China)*
Lexing Xie *(Australian National University, Australia)*

MM 2014 Program Committee

Alberto Abad
Sheikh Ahamed
Lffat Ahmed
Luca Maria Aiello
Ceyhun Akgül
Albert Ali Salah
Francesc Alias
Tim Althoff
Noam Amir
Mostafa Ammar
Kristina Andersen
Oya Aran
Shervin Ardeshir
Pradeep Atrey
Yannis Avrithis
Sileye Ba
Lamberto Ballan
Sabina Barakovic
Vittorio Baroncini
Alessio Bazzica
Emmanuelle Beauxis-Aussalet
Georgios Bebis
Ali C. Begen
Nathalia Beloff
Nadia Berthouze
Marco Bertini
Subhabrata Bhattacharya
Giulia Boato
Victor Boer
Olga Bondarenko
Lubomir Bordev
Damian Borth
Nicolas Boulanger-Lewandowski
Jeffrey Boyd

Alessandro Bozzon
Francois Bremond
Alexia Briasouli
Kjell Brunnstrom
Yaroslav Bulatov
Felix Burkhardt
Ian Burnett
Carlos Busso
Daragh Byrne
Deng Cai
Antonio Camurri
K. Selcuk Candan
Yu Cao
Mark Cartwright
Pablo Cesar
Gary Chan
Surendar Chandra
Guillaume Chanel
Carl Chang
Shih-Fu Chang
Fred Charles
Vincent Charvillat
Gal Chechik
Trista Chen
Tao Chen
Minghua Chen
Kuan-Ta Chen
Songqing Chen
Berlin Chen
Wen-Huang Cheng
Elaine Chew
Ed Chi
Sumit Chopra
Wei-Ta Chu

Ching-Hua Chuan
Chloé Clavel
Kathy Clawson
Mark Claypool
Matthew Cooper
Nuno Correia
Eduardo Coutinho
Marco Cristani
Peng Cui
Kevin Curran
Kerstin Dautenhahn
Larry Davis
Piet de Groen
Fernando de La Torre
Giorgio De Michelis
Giovanni De Poli
Afshin Dehghan
Alberto Del Bimbo
Cheng Deng
Giusy Di Lorenzo
Klaus Diepold
Jana Dittmann
Christian Dittmar
Sidney Dmello
Michael Dorr
Zhiyao Duan
Alan Dunning
Pinar Duygulu Sahin
Serge Egelman
Sebastian Egger
David Eigen
Hazım Kemal Ekenel
Dan Ellis
Sabu Emmanuel

Herman Engelbrecht
Gorka Epelde Unanue
Julien Epps
Dumitru Erhan
Slim Essid
Georg Essl
Sebastian Ewert
Tiago Falk
Giulia Fanti
Benoit Favre
Wu-Chi Feng
Karel Fliegel
Soren Forchhamer
Piero Fraternali
Jason Freeman
Jonathan Freeman
Enrique Frias-Martinez
Andrea Frome
Raymond Fu
Takuya Fujishima
Luciano Gamberini
Xinbo Gao
Kevin Gao
Chenqiang Gao
Yue Gao
Zan Gao
Jason Gauci
David Geerts
Bo Geng
Bogdan Ghita
Andreas Girgensohn
Stefan Goebel
Emilia Gomez
Andrew Gordon

Masataka Goto
Luke Gottlieb
José Goutierez
Guillaume Gravier
Carsten Griwodz
Peter Grosche
Lei Guo
Michael Gurevich
Pal Halvorsen
Raffay Hamid
Yahong Han
Mei Han
Jungong Han
Allan Hanbury
Philippe Hanhart
Lynda Hardman
Jonathon Hare
Xiaofei He
Junfeng He
Mohamed Hefeeda
Dirk Heylen
Andrew Hines
Jason Hockman
Steven C.H. Hoi
Richang Hong
Tobias Hossfeld
Cheng-Hsin Hsu
Winston Hsu
Yao Hu
Yuheng Hu
Ke Hu
Gang Hua
Zixia Huang
Jiwu Huang
Zi Huang
Qingming Huang
Thomas Mensink

Chung-Lin Huang
Benoit Huet
Mark Hughes
Inseok Hwang
Haroon Idrees
David Imseng
Omer Inan
Bogdan Ionescu
Panos Ipeirotis
Ignasi Iriondo
Yuri Ivanov
Christian Jacquemin
Giulio Jacucci
Alejandro Jaimes
Lucjan Janowski
Mostafa Javed
Omar Javed
Dinesh Babu Jayagopi
Rongrong Ji
Jia Jia
Shen Jialie
Yu-Gang Jiang
Wei Jiang
Lu Jiang
Ajita John
Maritza Johnson
Gareth Jones
Dhiraj Joshi
Lina Karam
Stefan Katzenbeisser
Koray Kavukcuoglu
Gabriella Kazai
Aisling Kelliher
Lyndon Kennedy
Salman Khokhar
Ben Knapp
Wei Pan

Peter Knees
Hiroki Kobayashi
Yiannis Kompatsiaris
Pavel Korshunov
Dejan Kostic
Alex Krizhevsky
Eleni Kroupi
Antonio Kruger
Dragan Kukolj
Shiro Kumano
C.-C. Jay Kuo
Gregorij Kurillo
Vivek Kwatra
Zhenzhong Lan
Nicholas D. Lane
Jakob Larsen
Rasmus Larsen
Martha Larson
Neal Lathia
Patrick Le Callet
Jeongkyu Lee
Sune Lehmann
Riccardo Leonardi
Bruno Lepri
Alexander Lerch
Thomas Leung
Mark Levy
Miachel Lew
Baoxin Li
Xi Li
Zhifeng Li
Ming Li
Xirong Li
Huan Li
Haibo Li
Hongzhi Li
Mukesh Saini

Mark Liao
Cynthia Liem
Yu-Ru Lin
Suzanne Little
Feng Liu
Jingen Liu
Yong-Jin Liu
Fangming Liu
Jiangchuan Liu
Si Liu
Xueliang Liu
Zheng Liu
Xueliang Liu
Zicheng Liu
Dong Liu
Luoqi Liu
Xiaoqiang Lu
Huchuan Lu
Lie Lu
Jiebo Luo
Jordi Luque
Mathias Lux
Zhigang Ma
Kevin Ma
Mathew Magimai Doss
Stephane Marchand-Maillet
Jose Martinez
Andreas Mauthe
Ketan Mayer-Patel
Stephen Mckenna
Gary McKeown
Andre McPherson
Remi Megret
Tao Mei
Nasir Memon
Deyu Meng
Mohammad Soleymani

Bernard Merialdo
Michele Merler
Florian Metze
Rada Mihalcea
Yue Ming
Prasenjit Mitra
Vicki Moulder
Emily Mower-Provost
Yadong Mu
Sudhir Mudur
Henning Mueller
Meinard Mueller
Vittorio Murino
Klara Nahrstedt
Alok Nandi
Paolo Nesi
Edith Ngai
Chong-Wah Ngo
Bingbing Ni
Feiping Nie
Oliver Nina
Jasminko Novak
Junghwan Oh
Igor Olaizola
Eckehard Olbrich
Sean O'Malley
Eng-Jon Ong
Wei Tsang Ooi
Omar Oreifej
Vincent Oria
Nicola Orio
Jörg Ott
Daniel Overholt
Katsunori Oyama
Manohar Paluri
Yanwei Pang
Bryan Pardo
Alexandre Passos
Geoffroy Peeters
Catherine Pelachaud
Yuxin Peng
Fernando Pereira
Fernando Perez-Gonzalez
Andrew Perkis
Stavros Petridis
Dinh Phung
Fabio Pianesi
Massimo Piccardi
Claudio Pinhanez
Antonio Pinheiro
Hamed Pirsivash
Ronald Poppe
Reid Porter
Kishore Prahallad
Michael Pucher
Guojun Qi
Daniele Quercia
Alexander Raake
Zafar Rafii
Nitendra Rajput
Sanjay Rao
Judith Redi
Ulrich Reiter
Martin Rerabek
Elisa Ricci
Gaël Richard
Michael Riegler
Andreas Riener
Stevan Rudinac
Bahjat Safadi
Albert Ali Salah
Imran Saleemi
Dasarathi Sampath
Jose San Pedro
Jitao Sang
Emre Sargin
Shin'Ichi Satoh
Markus Schedl
Peter Schelkens
Nicu Sebe
Doree Seligmann
Subhabrata Sen
Pierre Sermanet
Joan Serrà
Mubarak Shah
Cyrus Shahabi
David A. Shamma
Shiguang Shan
Sgshan Shan
Xiaowei Shao
Ling Shao
Jialie Shen
Jacky Shen
Jianbing Shen
Yi Shen
Prashant Shenoy
Fuming Shih
Shervin Shirmohammadi
Jon Shlens
Erez Shmueli
Börkur Sigurbjörnsson
Gwendal Simon
Athanassios Skodras
Lea Skorin-Kapov
Paris Smaragdis
Mingli Song
Khurram Soomro
Nitish Srivastava
Jacopo Staiano
Eckehard Steinbach
Arkadiusz Stopczynski
Ramanathan Subramanian
Av Subramanyam
Sainbayar Sukhbaatar
Aixin Sun
Lingfen Sun
Yaniv Taigman
Jinhui Tang
Dacheng Tao
Wallapak Tavanapong
Tony Thomas
Bruce Thomas
Christian Timmerer
Steve Tjoa
George Toderici
Giorgos Tolias
Wei Tong
Naoko Tosa
Khiet Truong
Michael Carl Tschantz
Alexey Tsymbal
Mika Tuomola
George Tzanetakis
Andreas Uhl
Jasper Uijlings
Marian Ursu
Gonzalo Vaca-Castano
Michel Valstar
Jan van Gemert
Martin Varela
Sudheendra Vijayanarasimhan
Tuomas Virtanen
Yan Wang
Xinxi Wang
Yi Yang
Linjun Yang
Wojciech Zaremba
Eric Zavesky

Gualtiero Volpe
Stefanos Vrochidis
Yi Wang
Meng Wang
Qi Wang
Hanzi Wang
Xiaogang Wang
Zhi Wang
Fei Wang
Xiaoyu Wang
Jingdong Wang
Meng Wang
Ye Wang
Ju-Chiang Wang
Jingbin Wang
Xiangjun Wang
Zhiyong Wang
Jing Wang
Leon Watts
Robert Wechsler
Lynn Wilcox
Johnny Wong
Chuck Wooters
Marcel Worring
Chuan Wu
Wanmin Wu
Min Wu
Fei Wu
Zhong Wu
Lingxi Xie
Changsheng Xu
W. Yan
Tom Yan
Weiqi Yan
Ming Yang
Fei Yang
Weilong Yang
Yi-Hsuan Yang
Kuiyuan Yang
Guangnan Ye
Yangli Hector Yee
Woon Seung Yeo
Jude Yew
Junyong You
Ehsan Younessian
Shoou-I Yu
Meng Yu
Yuan Yuan
Xiaotong Yuan
Titus Zakharia
Massimo Zancanaro
Zhengjun Zha
Zheng-Jun Zha
Lijun Zhang
Longfei Zhang
Shiliang Zhang
Yongdong Zhang
Lei Zhang
Liang Zheng
Huiyu Zhou
Will Zhou
Hanning Zhou
Wengang Zhou
Jinfeng Zhuang
Michael Zink

MM 2014 Grand Challenge Program Committee

Chairs: Changsheng Xu *(Chinese Academy of Sciences)*
Cha Zhang *(Microsoft Research)*

Program Committee: ***New York City 360o Challenge:***
Yuan-Chi Chang *(IBM Research)*
John R. Smith *(IBM Research)*
Liangliang Cao *(IBM Research)*

MSR-Bing Image Retrieval Challenge
Xian-Sheng Hua *(Microsoft Research)*
Ming Ye *(Microsoft Bing)*

VideoLectures.NET Challenge
Gaber Cerle *(VideoLectures.NET)*
Vasileios Mezaris *(CERTH)*

Emotional Response to Multimedia Content Grand Challenge
Christel Chamaret *(Technicolor)*
Philippe Guillotel *(Technicolor)*
Patrick Pérez *(Technicolor)*
Christophe Diot *(Technicolor)*

Machine Learning for Computational Photography
Qing Zhang *(Huawei)*

MM 2014 Doctoral Symposium Committee

Chairs: Laszlo Böszörmenyi *(Klagenfurt University, Austria)*
Christian Breiteneder *(Vienna University of Technology, Austria)*
Oge Marques *(Florida Atlantic University, USA)*

Program Committee: Vincent Charvillat *(University of Toulouse, France)*
Marco Cristani *(Università degli Studi di Verona, Italy)*
Dubravko Culibrk *(University of Novi Sad, Serbia)*
Xavier Giró-i-Nieto *(UPC, Barcelona, Catalunya, Spain)*
Pål Halvorsen *(University of Oslo and Simula Research, Norway)*
Hayley Hung *(Technical University of Delft, The Netherlands)*
Hari Kalva *(Florida Atlantic University, USA)*
Mohan S. Kankanhalli *(National University of Singapore, Singapore)*
Ralf Klamma *(RWTH Aachen University, Germany)*
Harald Kosch *(Passau University, Germany)*
Stephane Marchand-Maillet *(University of Geneva, Switzerland)*
Liam Mayron *(Florida Institute of Technology, USA)*
Pier Luca Montessoro *(University of Udine, Italy)*
Klara Nahrstedt *(University of Illinois, USA)*
Arnold Smeulders *(University of Amsterdam, The Netherlands)*
Ooi-Wie Tsang *(National University of Singapore, Singapore)*
Andreas Uhl *(Salzburg University, Austria)*
Svetha Venkatesh *(Deakin University, Australia)*

Panelists: **Session 1**
Laszlo Böszörmenyi *(Klagenfurt University, Austria)*
Christian Breiteneder *(Vienna University of Technology, Austria)*
Xavier Giró-i-Nieto *(UPC, Barcelona, Catalunya, Spain)*
Session 2
Vincent Charvillat *(University of Toulouse, France)*
Hayley Hung *(Technical University of Delft, The Netherlands)*
Oge Marques *(Florida Atlantic University, USA)*
Arnold Smeulders *(University of Amsterdam, The Netherlands)*
Wallapak Tavanapong *(Iowa State University, USA)*

MM 2014 Technical Demos Program Committee

Chairs: Shu-Ching Chen *(Florida International University, U.S.A.)*
Stefan Göbel *(Technische Universität Darmstadt, Germany)*
Carsten Griwodz *(Simula Research Laboratory, Norway)*

Program Committee: Ramazan Aygun *(University of Alabama in Huntsville, USA)*
Fernando Boronat *(Polytechnic University of Valencia - IGIC Institute, Spain)*
Yu Cao *(University of Massachusetts Lowell, USA)*
Richard Chbeir *(University of Bourgogne in Dijon, France)*
Kuan-Ta Chen *(Academia Sinica, Taiwan)*
Chao Chen *(Capital One Bank, USA)*
Min Chen *(University of Washington Bothell, USA)*
Songqing Chen *(George Mason University, USA)*
Ching-Hua Chuan *(University of North Florida, USA)*
Mario Montagud Climent *(Universitat Politècnica de València (UPV), Spain)*
Simon Clippingdale *(NHK Science & Technical Research Laboratories, Japan)*
Cyril Concolato *(Telecom ParisTech, France)*
Tim Dutz *(TU Darmstadt, Germany)*
Wolfgang Effelsberg *(University of Mannheim, Germany)*
Jianping Fan *(University of North Carolina at Charlotte, USA)*
William Grosky *(University of Michigan-Dearborn, USA)*
Yang Guo *(Bell Labs, USA)*
Michael Gutjahr *(Tu Darmstadt, Germany)*
Zifang Huang *(Western Union Digital, USA)*
Wolfgang Huerst *(Utrecht University, Germany)*
Mohan Kankanhalli *(National University of Singapore, Singapore)*
Ashfaq Khokhar *(Illinois Institute of Technology, USA)*
Seon Ho Kim *(University of Southern California, USA)*
Johannes Konert *(Technische Universität Darmstadt, Germany)*
Ying Li *(IBM T.J. Watson Research Center, USA)*
Lin Lin *(American National Standards Institute, USA)*
Zhu Liu *(AT&T Research Labs, USA)*
Dianting Liu *(University of Miami, USA)*
Hongli Luo *(Indiana University - Purdue University Fort Wayne, USA)*
Robin Mellecker *(The University of Hong Kong, Institute of Human Performance, China)*
Tao Meng *(University of Miami, USA)*
André Miede *(Hochschule für Technik und Wirtschaft des Saarlandes, Germany)*
Nilesh Patel *(Oakland University, USA)*
Nicholas Race *(Lancaster University, United Kingdom)*
Nabil Sarhan *(Wayne State University, USA)*
Ishwar Sethi *(Oakland University, USA)*
Mei-Ling Shyu *(University of Miami, USA)*
Leonel Sousa *(Universidade de Lisboa, Portugal)*
Yonghong Tian *(Peking University, China)*
Gareth Tyson *(Queen Mary, University of London, United Kingdom)*
Zhen Wen *(IBM T.J. Watson Research Center, USA)*

Technical Demo Program Committee (continued):

Viktor Wendel *(TU Darmstadt, Germany)*
Chuan Wu *(The University of Hong Kong, China)*
Jianhua Yan *(Amazon, USA)*
Chengcui Zhang *(The University of Alabama at Birmingham, USA)*
Tong Zhang *(HP Labs, USA)*
Qiusha Zhu *(SENZARI, USA)*

MM 2014 Open Source Software Competition Organization Committee

Chairs: Andreas Girgensohn *(FX Palo Alto Laboratory)*
Lynn Wilcox *(FX Palo Alto Laboratory)*

Program Committee: Jerome Berclaz *(Microsoft, USA)*
Surendar Chandra *(Datrium, USA)*
Huizhong Chen *(Stanford University, USA)*
Michael Cutter *(University of California at Santa Cruz, USA)*
Laurent Denoue *(FXPAL, USA)*
Luis Francisco-Revilla *(The University of Texas at Austin, USA)*
Gang Hua *(Stevens Institute of Technology, USA)*
Lyndon Kennedy *(Yahoo Labs, USA)*
Thommen Korah *(Microsoft, USA)*
Qiong Liu *(FXPAL, USA)*
Les Nelson *(Palo Alto Research Center, Inc., USA)*
Wei Tsang Ooi *(National University of Singapore)*
Timo Pylvanainen *(Microsoft, USA)*

MM 2014 HRHR Program Committee

MM 2014 Sponsor & Supporters

Sponsor:

Platinum Supporters:

Gold Supporter:

Silver Supporters:

Medical Case Retrieval

Mario Taschwer
Institute of Information Technology (ITEC)
Alpen-Adria-Universität Klagenfurt, Austria
mario.taschwer@aau.at

ABSTRACT

The proposed PhD project addresses the problem of finding descriptions of diseases or patients' health records that are relevant for a given description of patient's symptoms, also known as medical case retrieval (MCR). Designing an automatic multimodal MCR system applicable to general medical data sets still presents an open research problem, as indicated by the ImageCLEF 2013 MCR challenge, where the best submitted runs achieved only moderate retrieval performance and used purely textual techniques. This project therefore aims at designing a multimodal MCR model that is capable of achieving a substantially better retrieval performance on the ImageCLEF data set than state-of-the-art techniques. Moreover, the potential of further improvement by leveraging relevance feedback of medical expert users for long-term learning will be investigated.

Categories and Subject Descriptors

H.3.3 [**Information Storage and Retrieval**]: Information Search and Retrieval; I.5.2 [**Pattern Recognition**]: Design Methodology; H.4.2 [**Information Systems Applications**]: Types of Systems—*decision support*; J.3 [**Life and Medical Sciences**]: medical information systems; I.2.6 [**Artificial Intelligence**]: Learning

General Terms

Algorithms; Design; Experimentation; Measurement; Performance

Keywords

biomedical information retrieval; multimodal information retrieval; ImageCLEF medical tasks

1. PROBLEM DESCRIPTION

Medical case retrieval (MCR) is the problem of finding descriptions of diseases or patients' health records (document corpus) that are relevant for a given description of patient's symptoms (query), as decided by medical experts. MCR is a major building block of clinical decision support systems [15] employing the paradigm of case-based reasoning [3], where the "most similar" medical cases need to be retrieved for a given symptom description before diagnosis and treatment can be proposed by the system. Moreover, MCR is also a relevant problem in medical education and research, because it allows to select interesting cases for students and to generate data sets for studies meeting case-based criteria.

Case and symptom descriptions are multimedia documents, typically consisting of structured text and medical images. Designing an automatic MCR system applicable to general medical data sets (as opposed to data sets in narrow medical domains, see [3]) still presents an open research problem. The ImageCLEF evaluation campaign[1] [19] issued a yearly MCR challenge between 2009 and 2013, leading to a general biomedical data set of about 75,000 documents (case descriptions) and 35 queries (symptom descriptions) in 2013. The moderate retrieval performance of the best MCR runs submitted to ImageCLEF 2013 and their purely textual techniques emphasize the need for further research regarding multimodal MCR techniques [9].

This PhD project aims at developing an MCR model that is able to substantially improve retrieval performance on the ImageCLEF MCR data set upon state-of-the-art retrieval systems. Moreover, in the context of case-based reasoning, the proposed MCR model should support long-term learning from the relevance feedback of medical expert users.

2. STATE OF THE ART

The narrow research field of medical case retrieval (MCR) can be positioned at the intersection of three larger areas of artificial intelligence research: *multimedia information retrieval* provides techniques to index and retrieve multimedia documents; *knowledge representation* research produces models to capture medical expert knowledge; and *computer vision* methods specialized to medical images are needed to extract discriminative features and detect semantic concepts. Corresponding domain-specific research fields are predominant subjects of medical informatics [14].

From these research areas, multimedia IR (information retrieval) is the most relevant one for the proposed PhD topic. We categorize its relevant techniques into four groups: *text retrieval* (classical IR), *visual retrieval* (content-based image and video retrieval), *data fusion* (combining several

[1] `http://www.imageclef.org/`

MM'14, November 3–7, 2014, Orlando, FL, USA.

http://dx.doi.org/10.1145/2647868.2654856.

IR systems or information sources), and *relevance feedback* (learning from users to improve IR).

Text retrieval research has developed various IR models during the last four decades. The most prominent ones are the *vector space model* [26], the *probabilistic model* [23], language models [18], and divergence from randomness [2]. The latter has been found to be the most effective model on a biomedical data set [1].

A fundamental limitation of text retrieval systems is the mismatch of words used to express the same concepts in the query and in the document collection, known as the *vocabulary problem* in IR. It has been addressed by several techniques in IR research. For MCR, query expansion [5] and relevance feedback [25] are most relevant, as they allow to inject medical expert knowledge into the retrieval process.

In the context of this work, **visual retrieval** is mainly concerned with content-based image retrieval (CBIR) [8]. Typically, the user of a CBIR system expects semantic similarity of images – depending on the user's context and application domain –, which is hard to express in terms of digital image properties. This discrepancy is known as the *semantic gap* [27]. It is still an open problem in many application domains of CBIR, including the medical domain [34]. A review of CBIR in medical applications and its clinical benefits is given by Müller et al. [20].

The core techniques of the CBIR process include: feature extraction, visual signature building, and applying similarity measures to visual signatures. Due to the wealth of *image features* and *similarity measures* proposed in the literature [8], extensive experimental comparisons on different data sets, including medical ones, are valuable [10, 12]. Whereas global features (describing an entire image) are often used directly as *visual signatures*, pattern recognition techniques are applied to local features (describing an image region) to build the signature. In an attempt to reduce the semantic gap, visual signatures can be represented in terms of *semantic concepts* detected in the image or video [21, 28]. The IRMA code [17] provides a visual signature for diagnostic images based on coarse semantic categories.

Combining text and visual retrieval leads to the more general problem of **data fusion** [31]. The objective is to combine several information sources to improve retrieval effectiveness, either at the feature level (early fusion) or at the decision level (late fusion). An overview of late fusion techniques based on ranks or scores of individual result lists as well as proposals for linear score combination and score normalization are given by Wu [32]. A recent comparison of late fusion techniques on the ImageCLEF 2013 MCR data set showed that linear score combination of text and image retrieval is superior over individual retrieval [13]. Rahman et al. [22] successfully applied fusion techniques to multimodal biomedical image retrieval.

Relevance feedback (RF) is not only a technique to overcome the vocabulary problem in text retrieval, but it also addresses the semantic gap problem in visual retrieval [8, 33]. As it works by incorporating interactive relevance judgments from users during the search process, it may provide a useful approach to learn from medical expert users of an MCR system. Whereas *short-term learning* affects the current query only, *long-term learning* aims at improving retrieval for future queries [7] and provides a more promising avenue for MCR. Because expert users typically label only a few results suggested by the system, advanced RF approaches make use of *semi-supervised learning* [6].

Medical **knowledge representations**, particularly ontologies or controlled vocabularies [24] (e.g. UMLS[2], MeSH[3]), can help improve medical multimedia IR. Two common techniques are *query expansion* [4, 11] and *semantic annotation* of images [16].

3. OBJECTIVES AND CONTRIBUTION

As explained in previous sections, *medical case retrieval* (MCR) is a relevant problem in computer science whose known solutions for large and heterogeneous data sets are too ineffective to be of practical value. This PhD project therefore aims at designing an MCR model that is able to deliver a substantially better retrieval performance on such data sets than known solutions. Moreover, the proposed techniques need to be both efficient and robust to be applicable to large medical data sets of diverse content.

Considering the retrieval methods used for the ImageCLEF MCR challenge in 2013 (see Section 1), the most obvious potential for improvement seems to be in data fusion methods combining different modalities of case representation (text and images) and external knowledge. The focus of this work will therefore be on *multimodal* approaches to MCR. However, in order to achieve successful data fusion with visual modalities, improvement of visual-only retrieval performance is a necessary goal, too.

More precisely, this PhD project will address the following research objectives constituting its scientific contribution: (**O1**) Determine the reasons for the moderate retrieval performance of current multimodal techniques on the ImageCLEF MCR data set. (**O2**) Design a novel MCR model combining different modalities of case representations and information sources (without relevance feedback) to enable a substantial improvement of retrieval performance on the ImageCLEF 2013 MCR data set, achieving at least 30% MAP. (**O3**) Using the system resulting from O2, investigate the potential of further improvement of retrieval performance by long-term learning from medical expert users.

4. APPROACH

As there is no other recent comparative study of multimodal MCR techniques than that of ad-hoc solutions to the ImageCLEF MCR challenge [9], pursuing objective **O1** requires selecting, implementing, evaluating, and analyzing some of the most promising known approaches to MCR. Moreover, to understand the reasons for their retrieval performance, statistical properties of features extracted from the ImageCLEF MCR data set need to be investigated.

Designing a better MCR model according to objective **O2** includes the sub-problems of (1) choosing well-performing text retrieval techniques, (2) improving visual retrieval performance, (3) utilizing medical knowledge for text and visual retrieval, and (4) combining text and visual retrieval by data fusion methods. The semantic gap problem can be addressed by detecting semantically meaningful *concepts* in multimedia documents using pattern recognition techniques. It is hoped that semantic case similarity can be expressed in a simpler and more robust way in terms of concepts than in terms of document features. Meaningful concepts can

[2]`http://www.nlm.nih.gov/research/umls/`
[3]`http://www.nlm.nih.gov/mesh/`

be taken from medical thesauri (e.g. MeSH), ontologies, or medical image categorization systems (e.g. IRMA).

Proper evaluation of a long-term learning system according to **O3** would require a user study with several (e.g. 20) representative medical experts and an appropriate experimental design to derive statistically significant results. Due to the difficulty and costs of enlisting so many medical expert users, evaluation of the system according to **O3** will simulate experts by using part of the relevance judgments (ground truth) provided with the ImageCLEF MCR data set.

5. PREVIOUS AND FURTHER WORK

The PhD proposal has been accepted by AAU in March 2013[4]. We participated in the ImageCLEF 2013 MCR task using a simple text retrieval approach utilizing MeSH terms for query and document expansion [29]. We then extended the approach to include pseudo-relevance feedback, and recently we completed a technical report systematically evaluating more than 500 combinations of these textual MCR methods [30]. The best method combinations achieve state-of-the-art retrieval performance on the ImageCLEF 2013 MCR data set, as depicted in Figure 1.

Previous work established a basis for research objectives **O1** and **O2**, restricted to text retrieval and the utilization of a medical thesaurus (MeSH). The next project phase will extend work on these objectives to visual and concept-based retrieval. The incorporation of data fusion methods should provide results for **O1** and **O2** in fall 2015. The investigation of relevance feedback for long-term learning (**O3**) is planned to be finished in summer 2016, and the PhD thesis should be completed until end of 2016.

6. SUPERVISORS

Laszlo Böszörmenyi, Alpen-Adria-Universität Klagenfurt, Austria.
Oge Marques, Florida Atlantic University, Boca Raton, FL, USA.

7. REFERENCES

[1] S. Abdou and J. Savoy. Searching in Medline: Query expansion and manual indexing evaluation. *Inf. Process. Manage.*, 44(2):781–789, Mar. 2008.

[2] G. Amati and C. J. Van Rijsbergen. Probabilistic models of information retrieval based on measuring the divergence from randomness. *ACM Trans. Inf. Syst.*, 20(4):357–389, Oct. 2002.

[3] S. Begum, M. Ahmed, P. Funk, N. Xiong, and M. Folke. Case-based reasoning systems in the health sciences: A survey of recent trends and developments. *Systems, Man, and Cybernetics, Part C: Applications and Reviews, IEEE Transactions on*, 41(4):421–434, July 2011.

[4] J. Bhogal, A. Macfarlane, and P. Smith. A review of ontology based query expansion. *Inf. Process. Manag.*, 43(4):866–886, July 2007.

[5] C. Carpineto and G. Romano. A survey of automatic query expansion in information retrieval. *ACM Comput. Surv.*, 44(1):1:1–1:50, Jan. 2012.

[4]`https://www-itec.uni-klu.ac.at/~mt/2013/03/phd-proposal/`

[6] O. Chapelle, B. Schölkopf, and A. Zien. *Semi-Supervised Learning*. The MIT Press, 1st edition, 2010.

[7] M. Cord and P. H. Gosselin. Image retrieval using long-term semantic learning. In *Image Processing, 2006 IEEE International Conference on*, pages 2909–2912. IEEE, 2006.

[8] R. Datta, D. Joshi, J. Li, and J. Z. Wang. Image retrieval: Ideas, influences, and trends of the new age. *ACM Comput. Surv.*, 40(2):5:1–5:60, May 2008.

[9] A. G. S. de Herrera, J. Kalpathy-Cramer, D. Demner-Fushman, S. Antani, and H. Müller. Overview of the ImageCLEF 2013 medical tasks. In *Working notes of CLEF 2013*, Valencia, Spain, 2013.

[10] T. Deselaers, D. Keysers, and H. Ney. Features for image retrieval: an experimental comparison. *Inf. Retr.*, 11(2):77–107, Apr. 2008.

[11] M. C. Díaz-Galiano, M. Martín-Valdivia, and L. A. Ureña López. Query expansion with a medical ontology to improve a multimodal information retrieval system. *Comput. Biol. Med.*, 39(4):396–403, Apr. 2009.

[12] H. Eidenberger. Evaluation and analysis of similarity measures for content-based visual information retrieval. *Multimedia Systems*, 12(2):71–87, 2006.

[13] A. García Seco de Herrera and H. Müller. Fusion techniques in biomedical information retrieval. In B. Ionescu, J. Benois-Pineau, T. Piatrik, and G. Quénot, editors, *Fusion in Computer Vision*, Advances in Computer Vision and Pattern Recognition, pages 209–228. Springer International Publishing, 2014.

[14] R. Haux. Medical informatics: Past, present, future. *International Journal of Medical Informatics*, 79(9):599–610, 2010.

[15] K. Kawamoto, C. A. Houlihan, E. A. Balas, and D. F. Lobach. Improving clinical practice using clinical decision support systems: a systematic review of trials to identify features critical to success. *British Medical Journal*, 330(7494):765, 2005.

[16] C. Kurtz, A. Depeursinge, S. Napel, C. F. Beaulieu, and D. L. Rubin. On combining image-based and ontological semantic dissimilarities for medical image retrieval applications. *Medical Image Analysis*, 18(7):1082–1100, 2014.

[17] T. M. Lehmann, H. Schubert, D. Keysers, M. Kohnen, and B. B. Wein. The IRMA code for unique classification of medical images. In *Medical Imaging 2003*, pages 440–451. International Society for Optics and Photonics, 2003.

[18] X. Liu and W. B. Croft. Statistical language modeling for information retrieval. *Annual Review of Information Science and Technology*, 39(1):1–31, 2005.

[19] H. Müller, P. Clough, T. Deselaers, and B. Caputo, editors. *ImageCLEF - Experimental Evaluation in Visual Information Retrieval*, volume 32 of *The Information Retrieval Series*. Springer Berlin Heidelberg, 2010.

[20] H. Müller, N. Michoux, D. Bandon, and A. Geissbuhler. A review of content-based image retrieval systems in medical applications – clinical

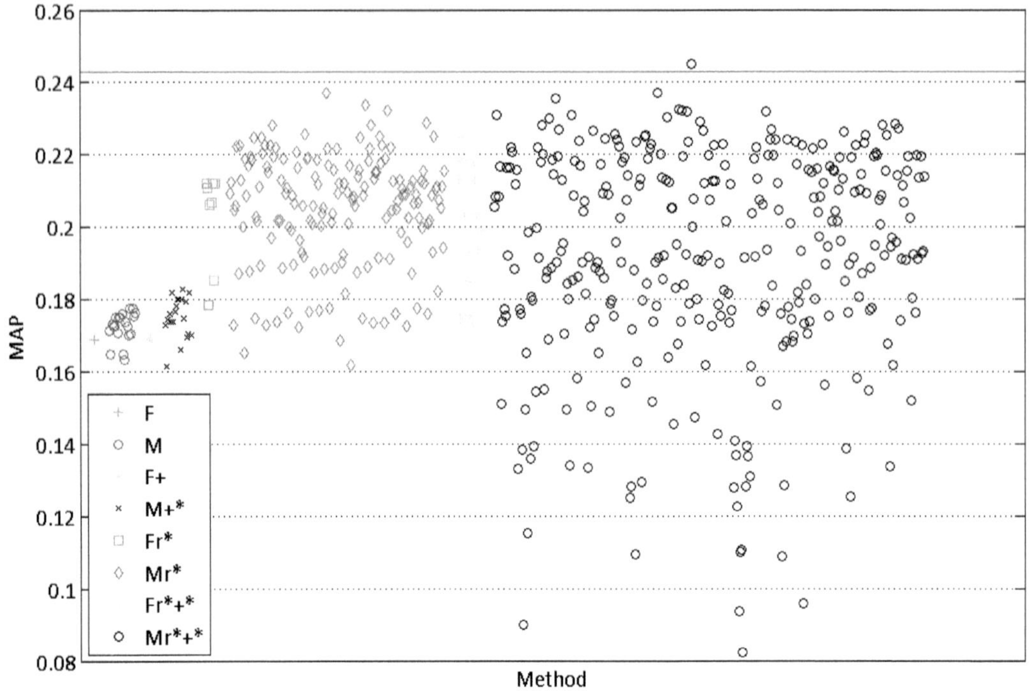

Figure 1: Scatter plot of 546 combinations of query and document expansion methods with parameters optimized on ImageCLEF 2012 dataset and evaluated on ImageCLEF 2013 MCR dataset. Method combinations are grouped according to utilized techniques: fulltext-only (F), MeSH query expansion (M), local feedback (r*), document expansion (+, +*). The horizontal line at MAP 0.2429 corresponds to the best run submitted to ImageCLEF 2013 [9].

benefits and future directions. *International Journal of Medical Informatics*, 73(1):1 – 23, 2004.

[21] M. Rahman, S. Antani, and G. Thoma. A learning-based similarity fusion and filtering approach for biomedical image retrieval using SVM classification and relevance feedback. *IEEE Trans. Inf. Tech. Biomedicine*, 15(4):640–646, July 2011.

[22] M. M. Rahman, D. You, M. S. Simpson, S. K. Antani, D. Demner-Fushman, and G. R. Thoma. Multimodal biomedical image retrieval using hierarchical classification and modality fusion. *International Journal of Multimedia Information Retrieval*, 2(3):159–173, 2013.

[23] S. E. Robertson and K. Sparck Jones. Relevance weighting of search terms. *Journal of the American Society for Information Science*, 27(3):129–146, 1976.

[24] D. L. Rubin, N. H. Shah, and N. F. Noy. Biomedical ontologies: a functional perspective. *Briefings in Bioinformatics*, 9(1):75–90, 2008.

[25] I. Ruthven and M. Lalmas. A survey on the use of relevance feedback for information access systems. *The Knowledge Engineering Review*, 18(02):95–145, 2003.

[26] G. Salton, A. Wong, and C. S. Yang. A vector space model for automatic indexing. *Commun. ACM*, 18(11):613–620, Nov. 1975.

[27] A. W. M. Smeulders, M. Worring, S. Santini, A. Gupta, and R. Jain. Content-based image retrieval at the end of the early years. *IEEE Trans. Pattern Anal. Mach. Intell.*, 22(12):1349–1380, Dec. 2000.

[28] C. G. M. Snoek and M. Worring. Concept-based video retrieval. *Found. Trends Inf. Retr.*, 2(4):215–322, Apr. 2009.

[29] M. Taschwer. Text-based medical case retrieval using MeSH ontology. In P. Forner, R. Navigli, and D. Tufis, editors, *CLEF 2013 Evaluation Labs and Workshop, Online Working Notes*, 2013.

[30] M. Taschwer. Textual methods for medical case retrieval. Technical Report TR/ITEC/14/2.01, Institute of Information Technology (ITEC), Alpen-Adria-Universität Klagenfurt, Austria, May 2014. `http://www-itec.uni-klu.ac.at/bib/files/textual-mcr.pdf`.

[31] L. Valet, G. Mauris, and P. Bolon. A statistical overview of recent literature in information fusion. *IEEE Aerospace and Electronic Systems Magazine*, 16(3):7–14, 2001.

[32] S. Wu. Linear combination of component results in information retrieval. *Data Knowl. Eng.*, 71(1):114–126, Jan. 2012.

[33] X. S. Zhou and T. S. Huang. Relevance feedback in image retrieval: A comprehensive review. *Multimedia systems*, 8(6):536–544, 2003.

[34] X. S. Zhou, S. Zillner, M. Moeller, M. Sintek, Y. Zhan, A. Krishnan, and A. Gupta. Semantics and CBIR: a medical imaging perspective. In *Proceedings of the 2008 International Conference on Content-based Image and Video Retrieval*, CIVR '08, pages 571–580, New York, NY, USA, 2008. ACM.

Mobile Video Broadcasting Services - Combining Video Composition and Network Efficient Transmission

Stefan Wilk
Distributed Multimedia Systems
TU Darmstadt, Germany
swilk@cs.tu-darmstadt.de
Supervisor: Wolfgang Effelsberg

ABSTRACT

Mobile video broadcasting services offer the opportunity to instantly share video from mobile handhelds to a large audience over the Internet. Our research focuses on large-scale events that attract dozens of users to record video in parallel. In such scenarios, our aim is to design a collaborative mobile video broadcasting service that composes video streams from multiple sources to create one video stream with enhanced perceived quality. Our realization of such a service combines high quality video streaming and at the same time reduces the network load.

Categories and Subject Descriptors

C.2.4 [**Computer Systems Organization**]: Computer-Communication Networks - Distributed Systems

Keywords

video composition; mix; cellular; mobile video broadcast

1. INTRODUCTION

Sports or music events motivate dozens in the audience to record video using their smart phones. Many of them would like to instantly share their experience with friends and family staying at home. For the remote viewers, the video stream is often of a limited quality due to the limited recording skills or the bad positioning of users recording the event. Additionally, data caps in cellular network contracts constrain the broadcast duration or quality of such a stream. As in those large-scale events not only one single person but several want to share recordings, different video views could be combined to create high quality video and at the same time reduce the generated up-link traffic, if the devices cooperate to create a single video stream. For this our system calculates the recording quality of each individual video view and broadcasts the best ranked. A mobile video composition algorithm is required that analyzes the specific attributes of user-generated video (UGV), quantifies them near real-time and delivers only the best view at a time over the throughput-limited networks.

MM'14, November 3–7, 2014, Orlando, Florida, USA.

http://dx.doi.org/10.1145/2647868.2654857.

2. RELATED WORK

Scenarios for mobile broadcasting services are studied by the 3GGP [1]. They published a scenario overview on media broadcasting which shows a clear motivation for such services, but does not name any solutions on how such systems are designed or even implemented. A special type of such a service is CoStream [3] which aims at in-situ video streaming. To enhance the experience of people standing in the last rows of an audience friends or strangers share a video stream recorded from a superior position and stream it to their smart device. Research on mobile video broadcasting services focusing on in-situ streaming include the studies of Engstrom on how users collaboratively create videos. In Engstrom's work [4] the scenario of video jocking is described and algorithms discussed on ensuring a suitable video quality of the composed video mix. With Shrestha's virtual director [8] an automatic algorithm based on an objective quality function was realized. It maximizes the utility of the quality function for music video clips integrating the completeness of the composed video, suitable cutting points, length of the individual shots and diversity of views. MoviMash [7] is an advanced approach existing for mobile broadcasting services. The system combines a video quality metric with inspection of video recording degradations. MoviMash integrates an avoidance strategy for recording degradations, such as camera shakes. All prior work concentrates on the usage of video analysis algorithms. CriCri [2] shows a first step towards replacing video analysis with mechanisms, that leverage different sensors in the recording devices to compose the video. The advantage of such an approach lies especially in the significant reduced processing time and load.

Our research focuses in contrast to existing ones on specific qualitative attributes common in user-generated video and wants to use those attributed to compose one high quality video mix from different video sources. At the same time by only using one video stream at a time the required network traffic should be reduced. Such an approach has not yet been discussed in literature.

3. RESEARCH QUESTIONS

Our aim is to enable mobile video broadcasting of one high quality stream composed from different video views to a remote set of viewers near real-time. By near real-time we imply delays common in current IP-based professional live video, e.g. by TV stations. These delays can reach up to one minute. The resulting two research questions are 'RQ1: How to ensure end-to-end quality of experience (QoE) in mobile broadcasting services?' and 'RQ2: How to coordinate mobile broadcasters to reduce network traffic?'.

As the quality of the video stream broadcast depends on the abilities of the recording users, our first research question discusses quality deviations for viewers resulting from the limited abilities of smart phones and non-professional cameramen to record video. The camera sensors and lacking skills of users result in significant quality degradations in comparison to recordings by skilled cameramen with professional equipment. It is necessary to understand what are the reasons and effects of this quality degradations on the perceived quality. In addition, parallel broadcasting from multiple cameras offers the unique opportunity to leverage different views and compose one superior video mix.

In the second research question we investigate how to upload high quality video streams over resource constrained cellular networks. In comparison to the down-link, usually on the up-link of cellular networks the bandwidth is limited. As the same channel is shared for up- and down-link and the number of participants in one cell affect the available throughput, data-intensive upload tasks for a crowd of people are not feasible if they utilize the network at the same time. An efficient algorithm to coordinate the access to the limited upload capacity can reduce the generated network load.

4. EXPECTED CONTRIBUTIONS

We plan four contributions to the field of research. In a first step, the contributions are integration into a consistent software architecture shown in Figure 1. First, the understanding of quality in user-generated video shall be shaped which enables our second contribution to compose video streams recorded from mobile handhelds more efficiently. To achieve video composition highly complex and computational intensive algorithms are necessary. To limit the complexity we will leverage the capabilities of mobile phones to analyze a video stream and as a fourth contribution monitor, manage and adapt to the existing network resources.

4.1 Understanding Quality in UGV

First, we address the issue that not much is known on the specific degradations in UGV. Especially in recordings from a crowd, the video recordings suffer significant from degradations such as camera shaking, harmful occlusions or misalignment of the camera. The resulting quality of a video stream should not only integrate the effects of video compression artifacts and map their impact to a Mean Opinion Score (MOS_{Video}) but adds the impact of recording degradations. First results illustrate that recording degradations have a significant impact on the perceived quality and that the impact differs for different video genres [10]. Identified degradations include camera shakes, occlusions or camera misalignments. Results indicate a strong effect of motion induced by camera shakes or size of an occlusion as illustrated in the following equation for the video genre entertainment. For camera shakes, the amplitude (a_{ampl}), speed (a_{spe}) and duration (a_{dur}), for harmful occlusions the size (b_{size}) as well as the duration (b_{dur}) and regarding camera misalignments the size (c_{size}) and duration (c_{dur}) are evaluated.

Table 1: Quality Model for camera shake, harmful occlusion and camera misalignment (Genre: 'Entertainment').

Camera Shake ($R^2 = 0.83$)		
$MOS_S = a_0 + a_{amp} * x_{amp} + a_{dur} * x_{dur} + a_{spe} * x_{spe}$		
$a_{amp} = -0.67$	$a_{dur} = -0.07$	$a_{spe} = -3.1$
Harmful Occlusion ($R^2 = 0.91$)		
$MOS_O = b_0 + b_{size} * y_{size} + b_{dur} * y_{dur}$		
$b_{size} = -4.96$	$b_{dur} = -0.09$	
Camera Misalignment ($R^2 = 0.73$)		
$MOS_{CM} = c_0 + c_{size} * z_{size} + c_{dur} * z_{dur}$		
$c_{size} = -2.83$	$c_{dur} = -0.12$	

Additionally, crowded audiences offer the possibility to gather video streams from different positions including varying distances and recording angles to the respective event. In our work [11], we evaluated the impact of the recording position on the perceived quality. Especially, the distance to the event has a monotonically increasing, negative impact on the perceived quality. Both parameters are monitored and used to predict a Mean Opinion Score ($MOS_{Position}$).

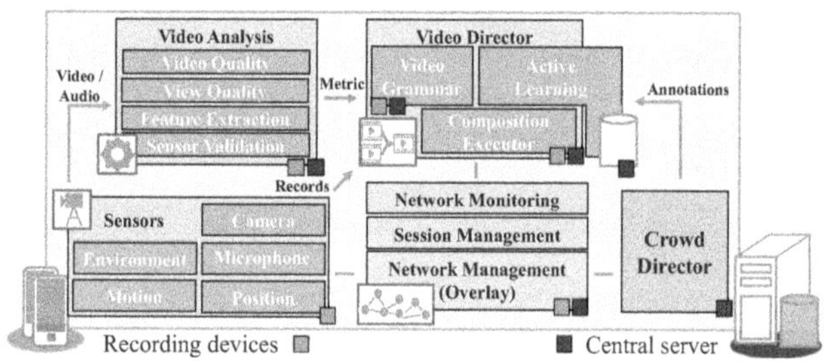

Figure 1: Overview on the system architecture of the planned system

As a result, our architecture overview in Figure 1 shows a sensor framework which will be integrated into a mobile application that reads microphone and camera to record video. Those videos are analyzed by a video analysis component that uses extraction of SIFT features [5] to detect rapid movement as indicator for camera shakes and reduced features as indicator for occurring occlusions. View quality is calculated as a minimum of an expected Mean Opinion Scores (MOS) estimated by algorithms for the video quality, e.g. measured by existing no-reference metric, the impact of the degradations camera shake, misalignment and harmful occlusions as well as the MOS of the distance to an event and the recording angle. Per video segment, e.g. per $i = 0.5s$ a total MOS can be calculated. This relies on perfectly synced video streams, so that similar video content can be compared. Existing approaches for syncing different UGV streams such as NTP (Network Time Protocol)-timestamps and audio fingerprints are used.

$$MOS_{Total,i} = Min(MOS_{Video}, MOS_S, MOS_{CM}, MOS_O, MOS_{Position}); \quad (1)$$

4.2 Sensor-enabled video analysis

Our aim is a live broadcast of a recorded video composition. Classical approaches do solely rely on analysis of individual pixel attributes and can not always achieve calculation of quality in time. This becomes especially critical when those approaches shall run using the resources of the smart phone only. By using internal sensors for location and orientation information for deciding which video view is preferable in comparison to others can be retrieved while recording.

Especially regarding the recording degradations mentioned in Section 4.1 which include e.g. the camera shaking or misalignment of cameras, the additional sensors in smart phones can reliably identify quality reduction without the necessity of highly computational complex video analysis algorithms. In this work, we focus on the camera shaking which can be measured by a 3D - accelerometer and compass available in standard smart phones. Since even small movements and the sensors' proneness to errors could negatively influence the findings, a high-pass filter is applied to all three dimensions of the accelerometer as well as compass readings. A combination of compass and accelerometer readings indicate that a shake is present. Its attributes: the speed, duration and amplitude can be measured on the accelerometer solely. Shakes of different speeds and amplitudes can be identified by creating a sample window of the past n values. Here, n is dynamically chosen on basis of the current, continuous movement. In contrast to camera tilts and pans, shakes can be identified by at least once changing the direction to a significantly differing direction and a relative small number of n. n is reset if no movement occurs anymore. Parameters affecting a camera shake, as illustrated in Table 1 can thus be approximated by:

$$x_{dur} = \frac{n}{\frac{samples}{s}} \tag{2}$$

$$x_{speed} = Normalize(x_{dur} * avg(reading_{accel.})) \tag{3}$$

$$x_{ampl} = Normalize(x_{speed} * x_{dur}) \tag{4}$$

As available sensors can not identify all qualitative aspects without analyzing the recorded video, its analysis is still used. One major reason to not solely base decisions on motion and location sensors is that they are prone to errors, due to magnetic field changes or hardware inferred inaccuracies.

4.3 Video Composition from Different Views

In large-scale events, multiple video recordings of the same scene can be expected. Creating a video composition from the different video views is based on the insights on perceived quality in user-generated video. The video director should thus be enabled to execute different composition strategies. An initial, simple composition approach relies on the findings of Section 4.1 - 4.2 and selects video streams based on $MOS_{Total,i}$, for video segments of 0.5 seconds length. A delay between the live event and the composed video stream of twenty seconds is chosen. Five seconds are used for the technical composition of video, whereas up to fifteen seconds can be used for identifying recording degradations (see Figure 2). The impact of a recording degradation, e.g. camera shake, cannot be calculated based on solely one 0.5 second segment. Thus, the impact of recording degradations is thus estimated on a window including $Min(n, 30)$ segments (representing 15 seconds), whereas the actual video quality is based on the most current segment only. To integrates human perception, we aim at training our system by an active learning approach to compose a multitude of different video streams. The required training data is gathered by using an approach called crowdsourcing. Crowdsourcing delegates micro-tasks, e.g. the decision which view should be broadcast next, to a large amount of anonymous workers. Thus, the video director learns about shot diversity, video and view quality impact on the watching experience by an active learning approach. For each large-scale stream recruited workers compose the initial minutes of a stream and by this train the respective automatic algorithm with data gathered from previous streams and the crowdsourced data. By this a high precision of video composition can be achieved across genres - as every new genre can be newly trained. For the resulting architecture a component called CrowdDirector exists, that allows efficient near-real time, manual composition of a video even for dozens of views. The CrowdDirector is stopped after five minutes of operations and invoked depending on users quitting recording or new ones joining the video stream.

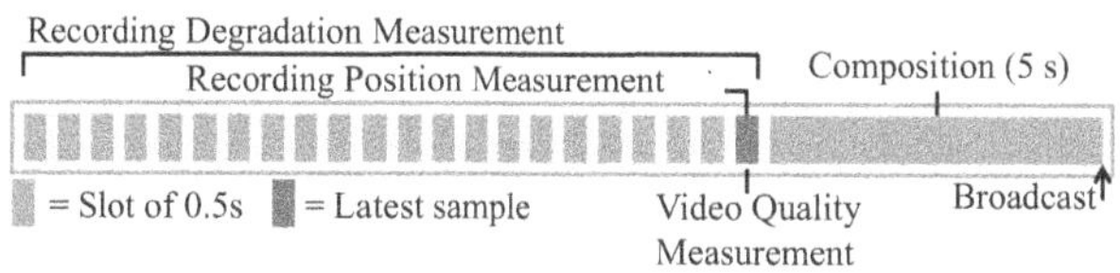

Figure 2: Sample window for calculation of recording degradations, video quality and position quality.

4.4 Network-Supported Video Collection

Our last contribution aims at reducing network load in cellular networks by combining the connectivity of devices and the sensing capabilities to identify recording degradations mentioned in the previous contributions. An overlay is being built that allows to decentrally coordinate the recording devices. Those devices should exchange as much information as necessary to decide which video view should be sent next. For most of the broadcast time the network has to handle only one high quality video stream at a time. All of our components illustrated in Figure 1 are based on the network monitoring and management component. The network component builds an overlay to the physical network and organizes the collection of the video streams and their transmission to a central server. It monitors for each node in the overlay, network related metrics such as delay, throughput and quality-related metrics gathered by the video analysis and sensor framework. Additionally, factors such as the current available data caps in cellular networks or the battery level of a device influence decisions. The session management combines the gathered video and sensor readings with a discrete timestamps and allows synchronization of video from different sources. Especially for the associated audio track, a correct time sync between the video streams is important. We concentrate on the upload of video streams from different sources to a central entity and rely for the remaining transmission path on standardized video dissemination protocols.

4.5 Centralization vs. Decentralization

One central challenge in our research is to find a suitable approach for the upload of video views in different scenarios.

The upload can be achieved by a central coordinating entity or coordinated decentrally. A central server can gather all video streams and make a global decision on which view shall be broadcast. Even though this may sound as a non-network efficient approach it can still reduce load in comparison to parallel upload of all m video streams, if for the decision making reduced quality versions of the video can be uploaded. In contrast to that, every device on its own could decide whether its view is suitable to be uploaded. This can only be done on local information and for methods that can handle local and reduced information. A relaxed version of local decisions is an approach that allows the devices to coordinate and communicate and thus find a suitable decision. This could be beneficial as the regional communication could be routed over one of the many network interfaces of today's smart devices. Therefore, this would not affect the cellular network that builds a significant bottleneck for uploading multimedia. Figure 1 illustrates which components can be run locally and which do only work on a central server enabling a global view. An initial approach for gathering monitoring data in order to make a network efficient decision on which video view shall be broadcast is given by Stohr [9].

5. TOWARDS AN EVALUATION

Assessing the performance of the proposed mobile broadcasting service is planned in prototypical and simulative ways. Basis for the prototypical evaluation are videos recorded from large-scale events. In a first step, small-scale prototypical versions of the system will help to evaluate algorithms for video composition. The assessment of the perceived quality of a video composition is based on subjective quality assessment in a pair-wise comparison of different video composition strategies. Recorded videos fused by other sensor readings are then used to allow simulative evaluation of the systems, especially of the network communication, as a prototypical evaluation alone can not scale as well as ensure reproducible results. To ensure reproducible evaluations the JIKU dataset [6], a public dataset for user-generated video including multiple, parallel recordings of the same scene fused by sensor readings, are used.

Based on the findings in Section 4.1, the quality of three, thirty second long, video recordings fused by sensor readings is estimated. The MOS is calculated for camera shakes only and thus can be calculated based on the metrics discussed earlier. We assume that the original video has a MOS of 5, and that a MOS equal or less than 3.5 is degraded in a way that continuous processing on the server is not necessary. Views with a MOS less than 3.5 are thus not transferred to the server. All videos are encoded with a target bitrate of around 1950 kbit/s Figure 3 shows that evaluating sensor readings on the devices may already significantly reduce the overall network traffic.

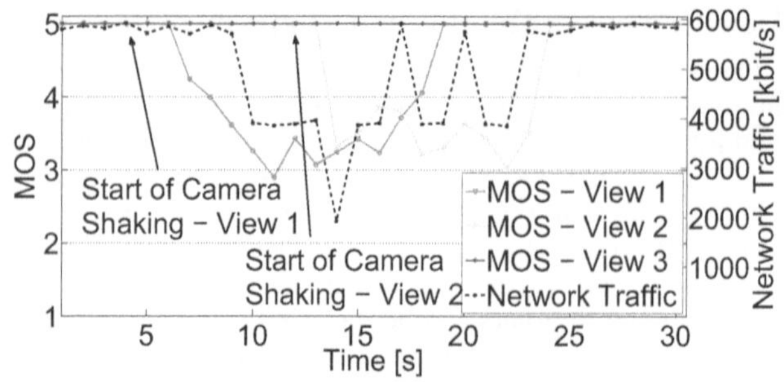

Figure 3: Quality of three views affected by camera shaking and resulting network traffic.

Acknowledgments

This work has been funded by the DFG as part of the CRC 1053 MAKI.

6. REFERENCES

[1] 3GPP. TR 22.947 - Study on Personal Broadcast Service (PBS) (Release 11). Technical report.

[2] F. Cricri, I. Curcio, S. Mate, K. Dabov, and M. Gabbouj. Sensor-based analysis of user generated video for multi-camera video remixing. In *Advances in Multimedia Modeling*, volume 7131 of *Lecture Notes in Computer Science*, pages 255–265. 2012.

[3] N. Dezfuli, J. Huber, S. Olberding, and M. Mühlhäuser. CoStream: In-situ Co-construction of Shared Experiences Through Mobile Video Sharing During Live Events. In *ACM Annual Conference on Human Factors in Computing Systems Extended Abstracts - CHI EA*, pages 2477–2482, 2012.

[4] A. Engström, M. Esbjörnsson, and O. Juhlin. Mobile Collaborative Live Video Mixing. In *International Conference on Human Computer Interaction with Mobile Devices and Services - MobileHCI*, pages 157–166, 2008.

[5] D. G. Lowe. Distinctive image features from scale-invariant keypoints. *International Journal on Computer Vision*, 60(2):91–110, 2004.

[6] M. Saini, S. P. Venkatagiri, W. T. Ooi, and M. C. Chan. The jiku mobile video dataset. In *ACM Multimedia Systems Conference - MMSys*, pages 108–113, 2013.

[7] M. K. Saini, R. Gadde, S. Yan, and W. T. Ooi. MoViMash: Online Mobile Video Mashup. In *ACM International Conference on Multimedia - MM*, pages 139–148, 2012.

[8] P. Shrestha, P. H. de With, H. Weda, M. Barbieri, and E. H. Aarts. Automatic mashup generation from multiple-camera concert recordings. In *ACM International Conference on Multimedia - MM*, pages 541–550, 2010.

[9] D. Stohr, S. Wilk, and W. Effelsberg. Monitoring of user generated video broadcasting services. In *ACM International Workshop on Internet-Scale Multimedia Management - ISMM*, 2014.

[10] S. Wilk and W. Effelsberg. The influence of camera shakes, harmful occlusions and camera misalignment on the perceived quality in user-generated video. In *IEEE International Conference on Multimedia and Expo (ICME)*, 2014.

[11] S. Wilk and W. Effelsberg. Systematic assessment of the video recording position for user-generated event videos. In *ACM International Conference on Multimedia - MM*, 2014.

Music-Information Retrieval in Environments Containing Acoustic Noise

David Grunberg
Department of Electrical and Computer Engineering
Drexel University
3141 Market Street
Philadelphia, Pennsylvania, USA
dgrunberg@drexel.edu

ABSTRACT

In the field of Music-Information Retrieval (Music-IR), algorithms are used to analyze musical signals and estimate high-level features such as tempi and beat locations. These features can then be used in tasks to enhance the experience of listening to music. Most conventional Music-IR algorithms are trained and evaluated on audio that is taken directly from professional recordings with little acoustic noise. However, humans often listen to music in noisy environments, such as dance clubs, crowded bars, and outdoor concert venues. Music-IR algorithms that could function accurately even in these environments would therefore be able to reliably process more of the audio that humans hear. In this paper, I propose methods to perform Music-IR tasks on music that has been contaminated by acoustic noise. These methods incorporate algorithms such as Probabilistic Latent Component Analysis (PLCA) and Harmonic-Percussive Source Separation (HPSS) in order to identify important elements of the noisy musical signal. As an example, a noise-robust beat tracker utilizing these techniques is described.

Categories and Subject Descriptors

H.5.5 [**Information Interfaces and Presentation**]: Sound and Music Computing

General Terms

Design, Experimentation, Performance

Keywords

Music-Information Retrieval, Music, Acoustic Noise

1. INTRODUCTION

Researchers in the field of Music-Information Retrieval, or *Music-IR*, seek to design automated systems to extract high-level features from musical works. Such features, which include beat locations and tempi, can then be used in systems that assist users as they listen to and enjoy music. If a band wishes to incorporate robots or other computer-controlled elements into their performances, for instance, knowledge of beat locations can help ensure that those elements are synchronized with the human musicians. As another example, automatic tempo extraction can help an exerciser choose music with the same speed as their workout, making for a more enjoyable experience. Due in part to its wide utility, this field is now studied by many researchers. The Music Information Retrieval Evaluation eXchange (MIREX), an annual Music-IR competition which has run continuously since 2005, features a vast array of algorithms from all over the world [6].

While this field is advancing rapidly, many of the best Music-IR algorithms and evaluations still focus on noise-free, professional-quality audio. For example, all of the datasets used in the 2013 MIREX beat tracking competition came from clean digital recordings, even the dataset designed to be difficult to track [12]. However, humans listen to much of their music in noisy environments, ranging from crowded bars and dance clubs to outdoor concert venues, and the noise in these environments can contaminate the acoustic signal of the music. As a result, while many Music-IR systems are well adapted to clean, idealized audio, they are not necessarily able to deal with the noise and other distortions present in much of the music humans enjoy.

This work involves the development of noise-robust Music-IR systems. Since the vast majority of existing Music-IR datasets contain only clean audio tracks, methods for collecting datasets of music with various types of acoustic noise are discussed. Subsequently, an algorithm for decomposing an acoustic signal into its component parts is described. Such a system is useful for isolating important elements of noisy musical signals. This algorithm is then used in a noise-robust system for estimating the tempo and the beat locations in a piece of music. This paper finished by exploring some prospective work that could be used to further refine the proposed techniques.

MM'14, November 3–7, 2014, Orlando, FL, USA.

http://dx.doi.org/10.1145/2647868.2654858.

2. RELATED WORK

One method for dealing with noisy audio is to attempt to remove the noise before processing the remaining signal. Methods such as spectral subtraction, in which the noise spectrum is estimated and subtracted from the overall signal, are suboptimal for this purpose because they can create artifacts [1, 2]. As such, techniques were developed that apply gain factors to each spectral bin based on its esti-

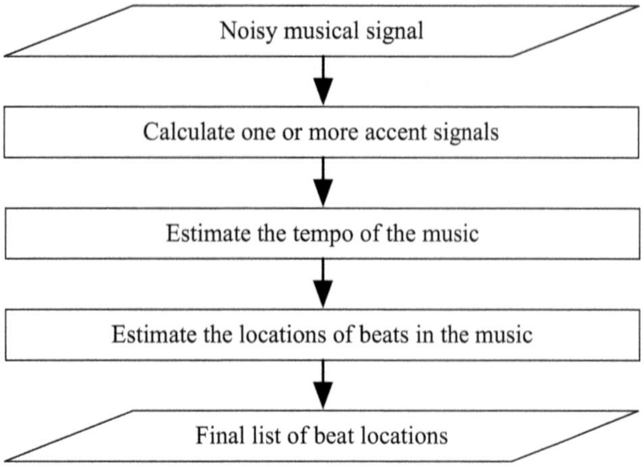

Figure 1: General algorithm for beat tracking.

mated Signal to Noise Ratio (SNR), suppressing only bins that are sufficiently noisy [3]. The result is a cleaner signal with fewer artifacts. However, such noise reduction methods are still imperfect and have difficulty removing all of the noise from a signal. Even with the best systems of this kind, Music-IR algorithms that operate on audio heard in noisy environments will likely have to deal with some noise.

Probabilistic Latent Component Analysis can be used to estimate the content of spectral bins that are obscured by noise [16]. With this method, a set of components that comprise the spectrogram are estimated with an Expectation-Maximization algorithm. Simultaneously, the probability of any particular missing value being formed from a weighted sum of particular components is also estimated. Subjects reported that audio cleaned using this algorithm sounded better than noisy audio not reconstructed with this system.

There are multiple kinds of noise that must be considered when developing a noise-robust algorithm. The noise produced by a moving robot, also called *ego noise*, for instance, is different from that produced by humming lights [13]. Motor noises are nonstationary, as they are based on the position and velocity of the motors, which do not remain constant. This noise may also become somewhat periodic if the robot moves in a repeating pattern, potentially resulting in a situation where the system tracks the robot's noise and not the music. In order to guarantee that a system is noise-robust, particularly in environments incorporating musical robots, Music-IR algorithms designed to be used in noisy environments should be evaluated on audio containing robot noise as well as other noise sources.

In this paper, I give an example algorithm for tempo estimation and beat tracking. This task is generally decomposed into three separate steps (Figure 1) [14]. First, the acoustic waveform of the music is converted into one or more lower-dimensional representations called 'accent signals' which have local extrema at beat locations. Second, the system analyzes the accent signal(s) to estimate the tempo of the music. Finally, the system uses the estimated tempo and accent signal(s) to determine beat locations. While beat tracking systems vary in terms of the individual algorithms and features, most of them utilize these three steps [9].

3. PROPOSED APPROACH

My goal is to design Music-IR algorithms that can perform accurately not just on audio that is taken directly from clean, professionally-produced digital recordings, but also on music recorded from noisy acoustic channels. By obtaining noisy data and building algorithms that can reliably function on that music, I hope to create Music-IR tools that function on more of the music that humans enjoy.

One desired property of my final system is that it be robust to multiple types of noise. This will allow for it to be more flexible than if it were only robust to specific noise sources. I therefore am recording datasets of audio contaminated by a variety of different noise sources. This will allow me to evaluate how my system performs on conventional noise signals such as the humming of lights as well as more difficult noise sources such as the ego noise produced by robots [13]. I am also annotating the music in these datasets with ground-truth values for the high-level features that I am searching for, such as tempo and beat locations, in order to better evaluate the accuracy of my algorithms.

When designing a system that is to process noisy data, there are two general approaches. One is to try to remove as much of the noise as possible from the signal and then process the signal normally, and the other is to try to process the noisy signal in some manner that is robust to noise. The former approach has the disadvantage that noise reduction algorithms are both unlikely to remove all of the noise, and can introduce distortions into the signal [2]. As such, I am building systems that, rather than removing noise, are designed to performed well even if the audio is noisy.

In summary, I am gathering annotated datasets of audio contaminated with multiple types of noise, and then designing noise-robust Music-IR algorithms that will be tested on those datasets. I am using Probabilistic Latent Component Analysis (PLCA) and Harmonic-Percussive Source Separation (HPSS) in order to find important information from the signals even in the presence of noise. I have already designed a beat-tracking algorithm that uses these methods to calculate possible accent signals. Subsequently, my beat tracker uses a periodicity estimator and a dynamic programming algorithms to obtain the tempo and beat estimates.

4. CONTRIBUTIONS

My contributions thus far can be grouped into two areas. First, I collected multiple datasets of musical audio contaminated with various types of noise. Second, I designed a beat tracking algorithm that is robust to the noises in the datasets. Both aspects of my work are important for the continued pursuit of noise-robust Music-IR in general.

4.1 Datasets

My first step was to gather datasets of noisy audio. I collected twenty songs with clearly identifiable beats as my baseline set of 'clean' songs and verified that the songs could be accurately tracked by conventional beat trackers. This helped to ensure that, if my tracker performed poorly on the music after I added noise, the low accuracies would be due to the noise and not the music itself. I then manually marked all of the beats in each song. This provided me with ground-truth data that I could use to evaluate my system.

The next step was to add noise sources to the audio. In order to set up a recording apparatus in a noisy environment, I mounted microphones on and around a Hubo robot (Figure

Figure 2: A Hubo robot.

2). Hubo was used in order to provide additional sources of noise that would not be present in an ordinary empty room. I played the clean music through a speaker and recorded it on the microphones, taking one dataset in which the robot was on but unmoving, and others in which the robot was moving its arms either randomly, in a predetermined pattern, or in synchrony with the music. The first dataset contained noise from the robot's fans and computers, in addition to sounds provided by the room itself such as lighting hums. The other datasets added ego noise as well. Finally, the ground-truth annotations were added to both sets of noisy music tracks.

4.2 Algorithm

My beat tracking algorithm begins by taking five seconds of audio and calculating its magnitude spectrum (Figure 3). An implementation of HPSS is then performed on the spectrum [8]. Beats are often more percussive than harmonic in nature, so HPSS allows the system to discard harmonic data and use only the more meaningful percussive component.

The percussive component is then processed by PLCA, which uses an Expectation-Maximization Algorithm to decompose the audio into 20 components [10, 16]. This method estimates the components and their activation probabilities over time. A component with a periodic beat will likely have large activation values spaced at that period and small values elsewhere. As such, the activations of the components are potential accent signals for estimating beat positions. I determined that activations of individual components would be more likely to provide reliable information in noisy environments than conventional beat tracking features such as spectral contrast or spectral flux, which are evaluated over the entire audio signal (e.g., the mixture of all the components) and so may be distorted by noise [9]. I thus chose to use PLCA, which can accurately identify such components, for the decomposition step.

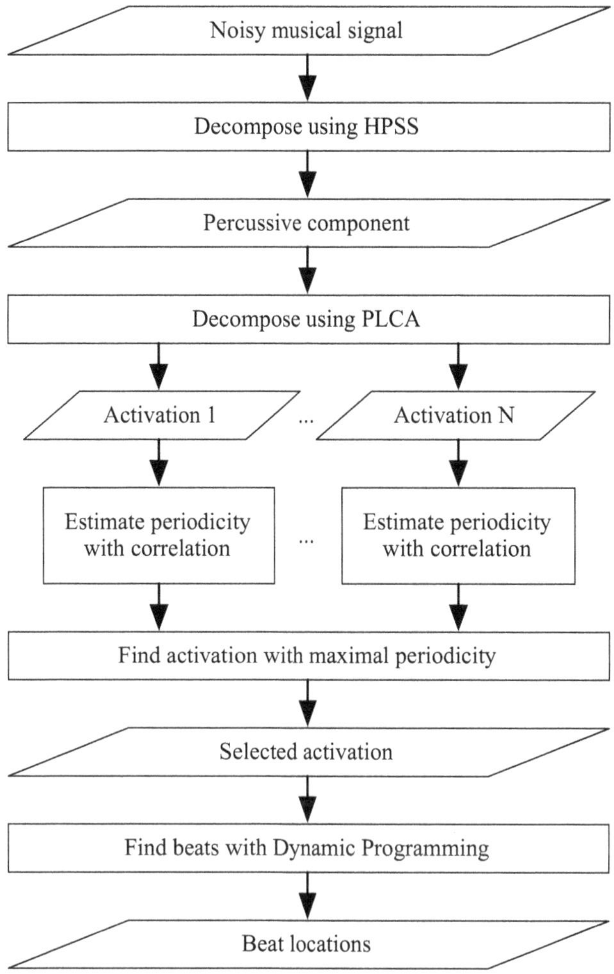

Figure 3: The beat tracking algorithm.

The activations for each component are then correlated with trains of impulses spaced at intervals corresponding to various tempi. The activation signal with the highest correlation is considered to be the most periodic, and thus the best accent signal of the group. The period of the impulse train at that correlation is used to estimate the tempo of the music. From there, dynamic programming is used to find the best sequence of beats spaced according to that tempo and occurring at local maxima of the accent signal.

4.3 Results

In order to determine the negative effects of noise, I evaluated my noisy audio datasets on a beat tracker not designed for noise robustness [11]. As expected, performance dropped sharply. The clean dataset achieved an average F-Measure score of about .98, very close to the maximal value of 1. The dataset taken with a randomly moving robot, however, did no better than .84. Spectral subtraction not only failed to bring accuracy back up to .98, but also required substantial fine-tuning that limited its general utility. This demonstrated how deleterious noise can be on the performance of conventional beat trackers. It also indicated that a noise-removal approach was unlikely to work as well as I wished, so a noise-robust algorithm could be preferable.

Table 1: Average beat tracker accuracy for various metrics on noisy musical audio.

Tracker	Dataset 1 (stationary robot) FMeasure	Dataset 1 (stationary robot) Information Gain	Dataset 1 (stationary robot) CMLc	Dataset 2 (moving robot) FMeasure	Dataset 2 (moving robot) Information Gain	Dataset 2 (moving robot) CMLc
Proposed	**91.4**	**91.6**	**90.1**	**82.5**	**75.4**	**77.8**
Autocorrelation	82.9	78.8	79.5	77.1	65.5	70.5
Tracker 1 [5]	61.1	55.9	56.5	55.7	48.5	41.2
Tracker 2 [7]	77.1	47.1	40.4	76.3	44.7	41.2
Tracker 3 [15]	60.9	48.1	27.7	58.5	44.5	27.0

I also evaluated my beat tracker algorithm on the noisy audio. My tracker was evaluated on two of my audio datasets: one in which the robot did not move (denoted *Dataset 1*) and one taken while Hubo moved its arms periodically (*Dataset 2*). Its performance is compared using three standard beat tracking metrics ([4]) with a similar system that uses autocorrelation instead of correlation for the periodicity step, as well as with three state-of-the-art trackers, in Table 1 [5, 7, 15]. These three trackers were selected for use in a multiple-tracker system that was restricted to only 5 trackers, confirming their utility [12]. Even on the harder dataset, the proposed system still surpassed the other systems. More results are detailed at [10].

5. PLANNED WORK

I plan to advance this work in three main areas. The first is expanding the dataset by using music from a wider variety of artists and genres and by re-recording the audio in environments containing different types of noise. This will help validate the robustness of my algorithm.

I will also enable my algorithm to utilize multiple components from the acoustic signal. These components could be used to help determine multiple rhythmic sources in a single piece of music, and could also help categorize different types of beats. If a piece used a bass drum to play the onbeats and a hi-hat to play the other beats, for example, then by examining the PLCA components any particular beat could be identified as belonging to the appropriate category.

Finally, I will develop a program for the Hubo that uses the beats estimated by my algorithm in order to respond to live music, such as by tapping along. This will be another step towards enabling robots to respond to music. It will also be a suitable demonstration of the utility of my work.

6. ACKNOWLEDGEMENTS

This work was supported by NSF grant #CNS-0960061 MRI-R2: Development of a Common Platform for Unifying Humanoids Research and by a NSF Graduate Research Fellowship.

7. REFERENCES

[1] S. Boll. Suppresion of acoustic noise in speech using spectral subtraction. *IEEE Transactions on Acoustics, Speech, and Signal Processing*, 27(2):113–120, 1979.

[2] O. Cappe. Elimination of the musical noise phenomenon with the ephraim and malah noise suppressor. *IEEE Transactions on Speech and Audio Processing*, 2(2):345–349, April 1994.

[3] I. Cohen. Speech enhancement using a noncausal a priori SNR estimator. *IEEE Signal Processing Letters*, 11(9):725–728, September 2004.

[4] M. Davies, N. Degara, and M. Plumbley. Evaluation methods for musical audio beat tracking algorithms. Technical Report C4DM-TR-09-06, Queen Mary University of London: Center for Digital Music, 2009.

[5] S. Dixon. Evaluation of the audio beat tracking system beatroot. *Journal of New Music Research*, 36(1):39–50, March 2007.

[6] J. S. Downie. The music information retrieval evaluation exchange (2005-2007): A window into music information retrieval research. *Acoustical Science and Technology*, 29(4):247–255, 2008.

[7] D. P. W. Ellis. Beat tracking by dynamic programming. *Journal of New Music Research*, 36(1):51–60, 2007.

[8] D. FitzGerald. Harmonic/percussive separation using median filtering. In *Proceedings of the International Conference on Digital Audio Effects*, 2010.

[9] F. Gouyon, S. Dixon, and G. Widmer. Evaluating low-level features for beat classification and tracking. In *Proceedings of the IEEE International Conference on Acoustics, Speech, and Signal Processing*, volume 4, pages 1309–1312, Honolulu, USA, April 2007.

[10] D. Grunberg and Y. Kim. Rapidly learning musical beats in the presence of environmental and robot ego noise. In *Proceedings of the International Conference on Intelligent Robots and Systems (in press)*, 2014.

[11] D. Grunberg, D. Lofaro, P. Oh, and Y. Kim. Robot audition and beat identification in noisy environments. In *Proceedings of the International Conference on Intelligent Robots and Systems*, pages 2916–2921, 2011.

[12] A. Holzapfel et al. Selective sampling for beat tracking evaluation. *IEEE Transactions on Audio, Speech, and Language Processing*, 20(9):2539–2548, 2012.

[13] G. Ince et al. Robust ego noise suppression of a robot. In *Trends in Applied Intelligent Systems, LNAI 6096, Lecture Notes in Computer Science*, pages 62–71. Springer-Verlag, June 2010.

[14] M.-Y. Kao et al. Tempo and beat tracking for audio signals with music genre classification. *International Journal of Intelligent Information and Database Systems*, 3(3):275–290, August 2009.

[15] J. L. Oliveira et al. IBT: A real-time tempo and beat tracking system. In *Proc. of the 2010 International Society on Music Information Retrieval*, pages 291–296, 2010.

[16] P. Smaragdis, B. Raj, and M. Shashanka. Missing data imputation for spectral audio signals. In *Proceedings of the IEEE International Workshop on Machine Learning for Signal Processing*, 2009.

Automated Multi-Track Mixing and Analysis of Instrument Mixtures

Jeffrey Scott
Music and Entertainment Technology Laboratory (MET-lab)
Electrical and Computer Engineering Department - Drexel University
Philadelphia, USA
jjscott@drexel.edu

ABSTRACT

Access to hardware and software tools for producing music has become commonplace in the digital landscape. While the means to produce music have become widely available, significant time must be invested to attain professional results. Mixing multi-channel audio requires techniques and training far beyond the knowledge of the average music software user. Achieving balance and clarity in a mixture comprising a multitude of instrument layers requires experience in evaluating and modifying the individual elements and their sum. Creating a mix involves many technical concerns (level balancing, dynamic range control, stereo panning, spectral balance) as well as artistic decisions (modulation effects, distortion effects, side-chaining, etc.). This work proposes methods to model the relationships between a set of multi-channel audio tracks based on short-time spectral-temporal characteristics and long term dynamics. The goal is to create a parameterized space based on high level perceptual cues to drive processing decisions in a multi-track audio setting.

Categories and Subject Descriptors

H.5.5 [**Information Interfaces and P resentation**]: Sound and Music Computing

Keywords

timbre; multi-channel audio; automatic mixing; instrument mixtures; clustering

1. INTRODUCTION

The pervasive use of digital tools for creating, recording, producing and editing audio has led to a desire for increased automation and efficiency in said tools used to complete these tasks. Although there are a wide variety of digital audio workstations (DAW) and plug-in suites available, the level of expertise required to operate them proficiently inhibits many newcomers from obtaining reasonable results even with a significant amount of effort. This has led to an exploration in the audio signal processing community for methods of automatically analyzing audio and improving the perceived quality. Several significant difficulties arise when attempting this task. The qualitative difference between the preference of individuals, the wide range of timbre, dynamics as well as instrumentation and the multitude of production techniques available present ample hurdles to overcome.

MM'14, November 3–7, 2014, Orlando, FL, USA.

http://dx.doi.org/10.1145/2647868.2654859.

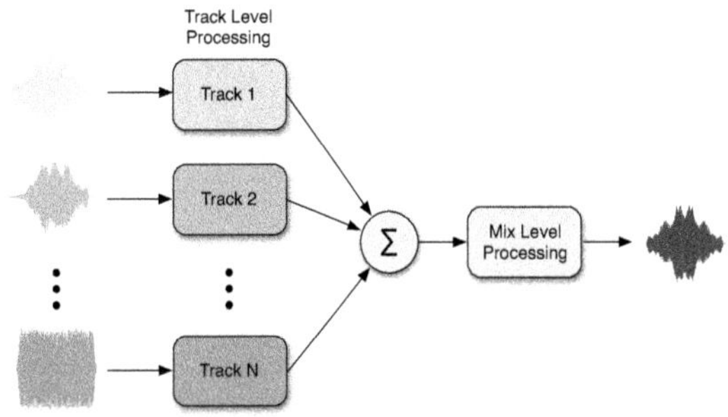

Figure 1: Diagram picturing the basic process of multi-channel audio mixing.

Research in this area is fairly new, yet has been gaining momentum in the past several years. Many disciplines are involved in pursuing an understanding of and processing framework for multi-track analysis and mixing. Signal processing, music cognition, machine learning and human computer interaction are all important aspects in developing approaches to tackle the relevant issues.

This thesis approaches the automated multi-channel mixing problem from several different angles. First we use supervised machine learning to approximate mixing tasks from data. A set of parameters is estimated from a corpus of multi-track sources and modeled using acoustic features extracted directly from the audio. The proposed work attempts to create a feature space that captures the spectro-temporal dynamics of individual instruments in a mixture. Tracks will be clustered in the space and processing will be applied based on a mapping between processing parameters and feature space location.

2. RELATED WORK

This section provides a brief overview of relevant work in the areas of automatic mixing and multi-timbral processing and analysis.

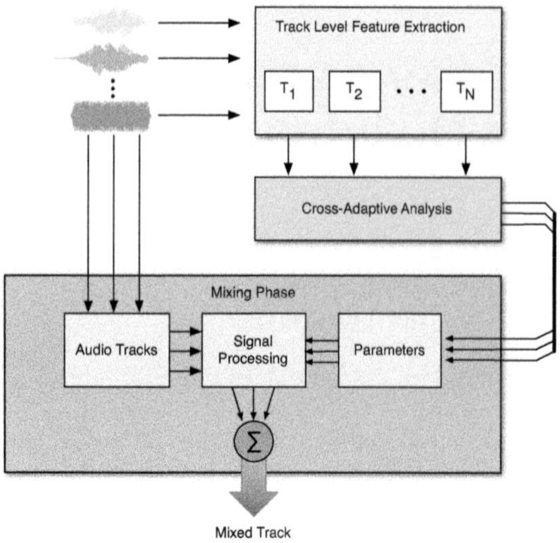

Figure 2: Signal flow and architecture of a cross-adaptive mixing model.

Early work on automatic mixing dealt with live situations primarily focused on speaking engagements with multiple microphones [1]. The goal in this scenario was to selectively deactivate microphones when they were receiving no input, thereby reducing feedback as well as comb filtering effects due to the multi-microphone setup.

More recent work in the live setting focuses on creating a more balanced and artifact free mixture. Methods for adjusting the gains for both the performer monitor mixes as well as the front of house (audience) mix are explored in [6]. These methods rely on an equal loudness assumption that attempts to normalize the perceptual loudness of the sources in the mixture to ensure that all layers can be heard by the listener. A detailed explanation of several methods for automatically modifying panning, equalization, levels and time offset correction can be found in [5].

2.1 Cross-Adaptive Methods

The most essential concept of modern approaches to automating multi-channel instrument mixing is to consider the signal characteristics in terms of how they relate to the other tracks in the ensemble. In a cross-adaptive processing architecture, features such as energy, loudness and spectral content are computed on each input source and compared to both other individual sources and the mixture as a whole.

The basic architecture of a cross-adaptive mixing system is depicted in Figure 2. Each track is analyzed individually, producing a desired feature set that is informative for a target goal. If the goal is to determine gain levels for each track, features such as RMS energy (multiple time scales) and the frequency spectrum will be passed to the cross adaptive analysis block. Here, the features will be compared across tracks using psychoacoustic principles of loudness and masking as well as encoded information about general audio engineering practices.

Reiss *et al.* have done extensive work in developing real-time mixing systems for levels, equalization, dynamic range compression and panning [7]. In addition to developing the cross-adaptive approach in Figure 2, they have conducted structured listening tests to evaluate the performance

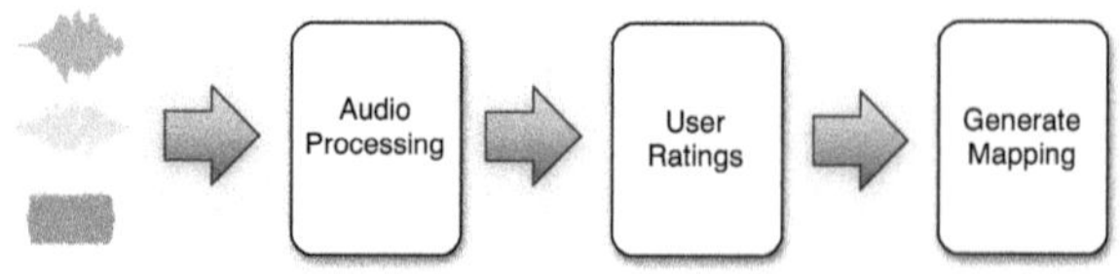

Figure 3: Modeling procedure to relate words that describe sound and timbre to audio signal processing parameters.

of their systems. In comparisons between unmixed audio, manually mixed audio and automatically mixed audio, their methods reliably outperform the unmixed audio and consistently approach or even surpass the mixes created by trained engineers.

2.2 Relating Perceptual Terms to Audio Effects

Mixing engineers and musicians use a wide variety of terms to describe sound and timbre [3]. In the context of a recording or mixing session, the conversation between musicians and the recording/mixing engineer will often involve such semantic descriptors as *bright*, *muddy*, *metallic* and *warm*. Several works attempt to link high level descriptive terms with parameters of audio effects that manipulate the sound [4, 8].

The general framework for developing these systems relies on gathering perceptual ratings of modifications to audio and recording the parameters used for modification. In [8], Sabin *et. al* attempt to find a personalized method for applying equalization curves to input audio. Through applying a variety of equalization curves to audio examples and recording user ratings of semantic audio descriptors in response to the processing they were able to learn which frequency bands effected which terms using regression techniques. From this, a personalized equalizer was developed that allowed a user to increase the brightness based upon their learned preferences. The next section discusses experiments already completed toward the overall thesis goals.

3. COMPLETED WORK

In the Music Information Retrieval (Music-IR) community, large datasets for training and evaluating models are notoriously hard to obtain and share due to the commercial nature of the content. This difficulty is compounded when using multi-track sources due to the relative lack of availability compared to fully mixed and mastered tracks.

Two datasets are employed in the experiments mentioned below. For the first corpus, one song per artist is selected randomly from the RockBand® game, resulting in a total of 48 songs.

The second dataset consists of 135 songs across a variety of genres. The genres include Acoustic, Alternative, Country, Dance, Electronic, Hip-Hop, Indie, Jazz, Rock and Metal. The songs were obtained from three primary sources: Weathervane Music[1], Sound on Sound[2] and a multi-track dataset used for song structure segmentation [2].

[1]http://weathervanemusic.org/

[2]http://www.soundonsound.com/

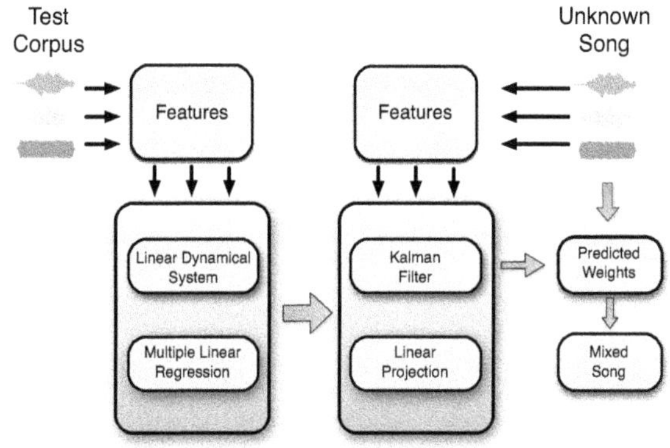

Figure 4: Supervised machine learning of gain coefficients using LDS and MLR.

3.1 Supervised Learning Experiments

The first set of experiments attempts to predict time-varying mixing coefficients directly from audio signals. The framework for these experiments is depicted in Figure 4.

First, we assume that each mixing coefficient vector α is a linear combination of our features $\{y_1, \ldots, y_m\}$

$$\boldsymbol{\alpha} = \mathbf{Y}\boldsymbol{\beta}. \tag{1}$$

Here, Y is an $N \times M$ matrix, M is the number of features per frame, N is the number of frames. The projection matrix β is computed in the least squares sense.

Additionaly, we treat the time-varying mixing coefficients α as the latent states resulting from some noisy process and our features, y as noisy observations of the output of a linear dynamical system (LDS). For a detailed explanation of these experiments see [9, 11]

Training and testing is performed in a typical manner for a supervised machine learning task. Given the relatively small size ($N = 48$) of the dataset we opt to use leave-one-out cross-validation, training on $N - 1$ songs and testing on the remaining song. This process is repeated for all N songs such that each is a test song only once. Figure 5 shows the predicted and actual weights plotted on the same axis for each instrument in the song "Constant Motion" by Dream Theater.

3.2 Instrument Based Processing

In this approach we attempt to codify some common practices and apply them to multi-track drum audio. It is quite difficult to define a set of hard and fast rules for mixing audio yet there do exist some commonalities that many agree upon. We apply some basic techniques to improve the balance and quality of the drums via stereo panning, filtering and level adjustment. The motivation for the processing techniques is derived from mixing engineer interviews as well as authoritative sources on mixing [3, 12].

3.2.1 Listening Evaluation

To evaluate the ability of the model to appropriately mix the drum tracks together, a listening test is performed where participants noted their preference for the individual monaural tracks summed versus the mix generated with the model [10]. The ground truth instrument labels are used for generating the mixes using the model. Ten songs were selected at random from the dataset and a 15 second clip for each song was selected so that as many of the individual drum tracks were active as possible.

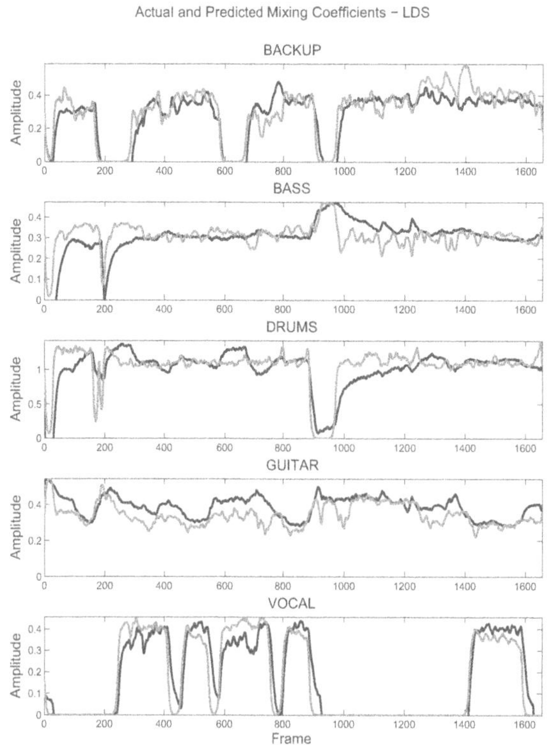

Figure 5: Results for weighting coefficient prediction using LDS. The estimated ground truth weights are shown in gray and the predicted coefficients are depicted in red.

Figure 6 shows the results of the listening test. For six of the ten songs, the model is preferred over the summed mix and listeners prefer two of the ten monaural summed mixes. Songs 7, 8 and 10 contain some drum loops from a library and do not adhere to the 'standard' recording technique of having kick, snare, tom and overhead microphones. The dataset consists of material from various sources and varying quality. Some material is recorded professionally and sounds reasonably balanced through just summing the tracks. The proposed method obtains fair performance on a

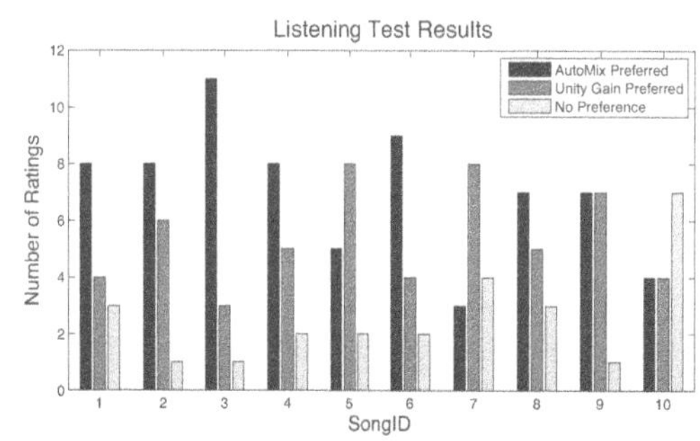

Figure 6: Listening test results showing the number of ratings for each clip pair.

certain class of song in the dataset but is not able to gracefully handle inconsistencies in recording quality present the dataset. The work here demonstrates the possible potential of a hierarchical system that combines both best practices and common techniques of mixing engineers with more sophisticated models of instrument identification, however there is significant room for improvement.

4. PROPOSED WORK

This section describes the goals of the thesis and the methods and models that will be explored. Low level features are computed directly from the audio and are the the input to the system, followed by a mid-level representation that captures the short-time spectro-temporal characteristics and long term dynamics. We then present methods to cluster these mid-level representations into a continuous space that will inform sound similarity based on the salient time and frequency domain features. Figure 7 depicts the modeling process.

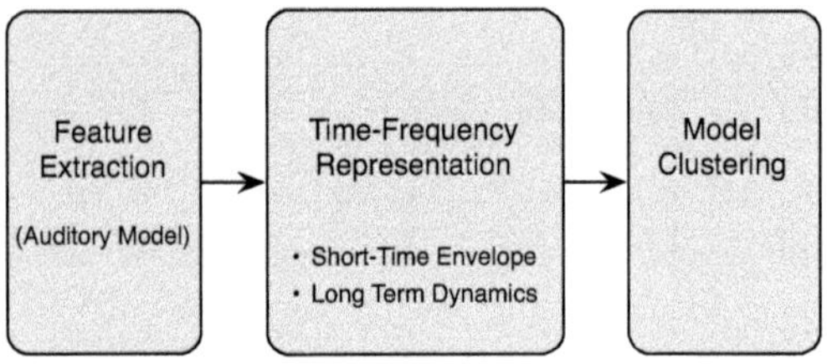

Figure 7: Proposed modeling architecture for developing a continuous dynamic timbre space.

The time-frequency representations are designed to capture two key aspects of each track. First, the short-time spectro-temporal characteristics of the sounds, salient to the perception of timbre, are modeled. To develop this representation, perceptual transforms that model the way humans process sound will be leveraged. The logarithmic scaling of frequency in the auditory system will be modeled using critical bands, Bark or mel scaling. Loudness compensation can be approximated using Fletcher-Munson curves or the more recent International Telecom Union reccommendation for loudness modeling which was developed for complex sounds, not just pure tones (sinusoids). Second, the long term dynamics of the audio source should be encoded in this mid-level representation. For this task, we will investigate Dynamic Texture Models and Dirichlet processes.

After learning a model of the time-frequency characteristics for the sounds in the dataset, we will perform unsupervised clustering in the parameter space of the models used in the mid-level representation stage. The goal of this step is to develop a space where audio tracks are grouped based on their role and contribution to the overall instrument mixture. Ideally instruments sharing the same spectro-temporal characteristics and long term dynamics will be grouped together. The location of an unknown track in the space would be particularly useful for developing algorithms for automatically mixing multi-channel audio.

The space will be evaluated using structured perceptual listening tests to determine the effectiveness of the system. Participants will be asked to rate the similarity of audio clip pairs based on the criteria that we hope to capture in the mid-level representation stage. Statistical correlation between distance in the model parameter space and the perceptual similarity is desired. The rankings can then be used to optimize the space through non-linear transformations based on the perceptual criteria.

The proposed work seeks to validate the organization of the sounds using a hierarchical stochastic approach and infer the similarities captured by the multi-stage modeling procedure. The analysis of the space by listening experiments will be analogous to the perceptual experiments in Section 2.2 that attempted to identify differences in perception of audio production techniques. We will use a ranking based evaluation which is common in the Music-IR community for song similarity and related tasks. The organization of tracks within the space will dictate a mapping of parameters of signal processing blocks to the feature space for automatic processing of multi-channel audio.

5. REFERENCES

[1] D. Dugan. Automatic microphone mixing. *J. Audio Eng. Soc*, 23(6):442–449, 1975.

[2] S. Hargreaves, A. Klapuri, and M. Sandler. Structural Segmentation of Multitrack Audio. *IEEE Transactions on Audio, Speech, and Language Processing*, 20(10):2637–2647, 2012.

[3] R. Izhaki. *Mixing Audio: Concepts, Practices and Tools*. Elsevier Ltd., 1 edition, 2008.

[4] B. Pardo, D. Little, and D. Gergle. Building a personalized audio equalizer interface with transfer learning and active learning. In *Proceedings of the 2nd International ACM Workshop on Music Information Retrieval with User-Centered and Multimodal Strategies*, pages 13–18, New York, USA, 2012. ACM.

[5] E. Perez-Gonzalez. *Advanced Automatic Mixing Tools for Music*. PhD thesis, 2010.

[6] E. Perez-Gonzalez and J. D. Reiss. Automatic gain and fader control for live mixing. In *IEEE Workshop on Applications of Signal Processing to Audio and Acoustics*, 2009.

[7] J. D. Reiss. Intelligent systems for mixing multichannel audio. In *Proceedings of the 17th International Conference on Digital Signal Processing (DSP)*, pages 1–6, July 2011.

[8] A. T. Sabin and B. Pardo. A method for rapid personalization of audio equalization parameters. *Proceedings of ACM Multimedia*, pages 769–772, 2009.

[9] J. Scott and Y. E. Kim. Analysis of acoustic features for automated multi-track mixing. In *International Society for Music Information Retrieval Conference*, Miami, Florida, 2011.

[10] J. Scott and Y. E. Kim. Instrument Identification Informed Multi-Track Mixing. In *International Society for Music Information Retrieval Conference*, Curitiba, Brazil, November 2013.

[11] J. Scott, M. Prockup, E. M. Schmidt, and Y. E. Kim. Automatic multi-track mixing using linear dynamical systems. In *Sound and Music Computing Conference*, Padova, Italy, 2011.

[12] M. Senior. *Mixing Secrets for the Small Studio*. Focal Press, 1 edition, 2011.

Local Selection of Features for Image Search and Annotation

Jichao Sun
New Jersey Institute of Technology
Newark, New Jersey
js87@njit.edu

ABSTRACT

In image applications, direct representations of images typically involve hundreds or thousands of features and not all the features are relevant for any given object. Errors introduced into similarity measurements by irrelevant or noisy features are detrimental to the semantic performance of content-based image retrieval. Feature selection techniques can be used to identify indiscriminative features from the entire image database. However, such global approach neglects the possibility that the feature importance may vary across different images or classes of images. We propose several techniques for the local selection of features for image databases. By checking the local neighborhood of each image, our methods determine the feature importance with respect to the image and select different feature sets for individual images. We also design methods based on the proposed local selection schemes for K-NN graph construction, image search, and graph-based image annotation. We provide experimental results on two image datasets to demonstrate the effectiveness of our methods.

Categories and Subject Descriptors

H.2.4 [**Database Management**]: Systems—*Multimedia Databases*

Keywords

feature selection, local selection of features, semantic quality, subjective feature space, K-nearest neighbor graph, content-based image retrieval, graph-based image annotation

1. INTRODUCTION

Nearest neighbor search is a fundamental component of many established methods for content-based image retrieval (CBIR) and automated image annotation. The semantic quality of the search results, which can be measured as the proportion of images in the query result sharing the same class label as their query images, relies heavily on the representation of images. The existence of irrelevant features in the image representation may overwhelm the contributions of the relevant ones in similarity search. Image feature selection which constructs a reduced feature set from the original feature space is a well-known approach for boosting the effectiveness of semantic image retrieval.

Traditional feature selection approaches are global in the sense that they compute a single set of features across the entire database. In image retrieval, supervised feature selection is widely used when image labels are available. The quality of a candidate feature set can be evaluated using a learning algorithm such as the Bayesian classifier adopted in [8]. Distribution-based approaches are popular in scoring the importance of individual features. For example, the mutual information which measures the degree of mutual dependence between two variables was adopted in [3] to guide feature selection.

Supervised feature selection has its limitations on image databases when the semantic labels are few or missing. An unsupervised feature selection method was proposed in [2] for medical image retrieval. However, the computational cost is high due to the use of a clustering wrapper for feature evaluation. Laplacian Score (LS), an unsupervised method for feature selection of generic data, ranks individual features according to their locality-preserving abilities [4]. Spectral feature selection ($SPEC$) [10] presents a unified framework based on spectral graph theory for both supervised and unsupervised feature selection. The unsupervised discriminative feature selection ($UDFS$) algorithm incorporates discriminative analysis and $L_{2,1}$-norm minimization into a joint framework [9]. Better results were achieved by LS, $SPEC$ and $UDFS$ in clustering and classification tasks, although no evidence was provided to indicate that their direct use in CBIR improves the performance of retrieval tasks.

The methods mentioned above discard noisy features from all data points to reduce the dimensionality of the database. Such global approaches, however neglect the possibility that a feature that is relevant for one image (or one image class) may be irrelevant for another. It is reasonable to find a feature set local to each image in an effort to reduce the negative impact of locally irrelevant features. To this end, we study the following two problems in this work: (1) designing methods for the detection of locally noisy features with respect to individual images; and (2) utilizing the computed (different) feature sets in applications to image search and annotation.

MM'14, November 3–7, 2014, Orlando, FL, USA.

http://dx.doi.org/10.1145/2647868.2654863.

In Section 2, we present three supervised/unsupervised techniques for the local selection of image features. These techniques are then incorporated into different algorithms for K-NN graph construction, image search and graph-based image annotation. We provide experimental results on two image datasets to demonstrate the effectiveness of the proposed methods for different image applications in Section 3. A summary of the proposed methods and a discussion on the ongoing work and other possible research directions are given in Section 4.

2. LOCAL SELECTION OF IMAGE FEATURES AND ITS APPLICATIONS

We propose techniques for the local selection of image features, based on which several methods are developed for the applications to CBIR and image annotation.

2.1 Local Laplacian Score and Feature Sparsif cation for K-NN Graph Construction

K-NN graphs are an essential component of many established methods for CBIR and image annotation. The performance of these methods relies heavily on the semantic quality of the K-NN graphs, which can be evaluated by: *graph correctness* $= (\#correct\ neighbors)/(\#images \times K)$, where a correct neighbor is one whose class label coincides with that of the query image. For example, in image label propagation, each graph edge connecting two unrelated image nodes is a source of error, in that it suggests that these two images should share the same label.

To enhance the semantic quality of the K-NN graph, in [5] we propose the Local Laplacian Score for the detection of locally noisy features, and embed it into an approximate K-NN graph construction framework *NN-Descent* [1].

Given a dataset D consisting of n data points represented by m-dimensional feature vectors, we denote the r-th feature by $\mathbf{f}_r = (f_{r1}, f_{r2}, \ldots, f_{rn})^T$, where $r = 1, \ldots, m$, and f_{ri} ($i = 1, \ldots, n$) is the feature value of $\mathbf{f}_r$ taken from data point $x_i \in D$. Given a nearest neighbor graph G of dataset D, the Laplacian Score [4] of the r-th feature can be computed as:

$$LS(r) = \frac{\sum_{ij}(f_{ri} - f_{rj})^2 S_{ij}}{var(\mathbf{f}_r)}, \tag{1}$$

where $var(\mathbf{f}_r)$ is the estimated variance of the values of feature $\mathbf{f}_r$, and S_{ij} is the RBF kernel on feature vectors x_i and x_j representing the i-th and j-th data points, respectively.

For the identification of noisy features relative to each data point, we define as follows the Local Laplacian Score (LLS) of the r-th feature for item x_i which represents the contribution to the LS in Eq. 1 that can be attributed to x_i:

$$LLS_i(r) = \frac{\sum_{j}(f_{ri} - f_{rj})^2 S_{ij}}{var(\mathbf{f}_r)}. \tag{2}$$

It can be found that, if a feature is noisy for a given class, many data points from this class would tend to agree on its identification as such. A consensus, however, does not in general occur among data points drawn from different classes. We adopt a straightforward method for the detection of noisy features local to node i using LLS, in which the m features are sorted in descending order of $LLS_i(r)$, and returns the first z ($z > 0$) features. We refer to these z features as the *locally noisy features* of x_i, and to the remaining $(m - z)$ features as the *subjective features* of x_i.

Traditional feature selection methods cannot be applied to the reduction of the locally noisy features identified by LLS, as the importance of a feature varies from one data point to another. Instead of discarding a feature from the entire dataset, we modify the noisy feature values for individual data points in an effort to reduce intra-class distances. As a heuristic solution, we propose to change the values of the locally noisy features to 0, which is the the global mean for standardized features. We refer to this process as *sparsification*. The LLS feature ranking and sparsification is then integrated into an iterative K-NN graph construction method *NN-Descent*. The combined method, named *NNF-Descent*, first computes an approximate K-NN graph based on the standardized feature vectors. In each iteration of *NNF-Descent*, a small number of locally noisy features detected by LLS are sparsified for each image. One *NN-Descent*-based iteration is then performed, which essentially involves the re-computation of the distance values from each image to its current neighbors, and the K-NN updating through checking whether two neighbors of a same image could serve as better neighbors in each other's K-NN list. During the sparsification, the centers of the classes can change. However, the data points in each class converge towards their new centers as the sparsification rate increases.

The iterative feature ranking and K-NN updating are mutually beneficial: an updated K-NN graph improves the accuracy of feature ranking, and the sparsification of noisy features improves the semantic quality of the K-NN graph in return. We refer the reader to [5] for a detailed analysis of the complete algorithm.

2.2 Generalized Laplacian Score and Image Ranking in Subjective Feature Spaces

In this section, we propose a method that takes advantage of the different feature sets computed for individual images without modifying the original feature values. First, we define the Generalized Laplacian Score (GLS) of the r-th feature for x_i as a linear combination of $LLS_i(r)$ with the average contribution to $LS(r)$:

$$GLS_i(r) = (1 - \beta) \cdot \frac{LS(r)}{n} + \beta \cdot LLS_i(r), \tag{3}$$

where β is a weighting factor in the range of $[0, 1]$, controlling the contributions of LS and LLS.

The selection of a subset of features for data point i can be accomplished in the same way as in Section 2.1. We can represent the *subjective feature set* of x_i by a mask vector: $F_i = (b_1, b_2, \ldots, b_m) \in \{0, 1\}^m$, where $F_i[r] = b_r$ ($r = 1, \ldots, m$) is a boolean value equal to 1 if and only if the r-th feature is a subjective feature of x_i. F_i also straightforwardly defines an $(m-z)$-dimensional feature space for x_i. We refer to this space as a *subjective feature space* of item x_i, and use F_i to denote both the subjective feature set and the corresponding subjective feature space for x_i.

Let $d(\cdot, \cdot)$ be a distance function over the items of D with respect to the full set of features. Given a subjective feature space F_i for x_i, we denote the distance between x_i and x_j in F_i by $d_{F_i}(x_i, x_j) = d(F_i(x_i), F_i(x_j))$, where $F_i(\cdot)$ is the projection of a feature vector from the full feature space to the subspace F_i.

To utilize the different sets of features computed by GLS in an image search application, we propose a novel querying strategy which ranks the query image in the subjective feature spaces of the candidate images and selects the candidate images which correspond to the subjective feature spaces wherein the query image is ranked highly.

First, a subjective feature space F_i is computed for each item $x_i \in D$. Given a query q, the distance values $d_{F_i}(x_i, q)$ are computed for all $x_i \in D$. A direct comparison of these distance values would have no intuitive meaning, as they are computed from different feature spaces. To make proper use of these distances, we first compute $\overline{d_{F_i}}$, the *mean distance* from x_i to the other items of D with respect space F_i, then normalize $d_{F_i}(x_i, q)$ by $\overline{d_{F_i}}$. The ratio — referred to as the *ranking score* (RS) of q in F_i with respect to x_i — is used as the rank of q in the subjective feature space F_i.

Based on *GLS* and *RS*, we outline an image search prototype (*GLS+RS*) as follows: (1) Compute an approximate K-NN graph for the image database in the full feature space for *GLS*; (2) Compute a subjective feature space for each database image, and the ranking scores of the query image in the computed subjective feature spaces; (3) Return the images corresponding to the subjective features spaces wherein the query image is ranked highly.

2.3 Local Selection of Features for Labeled Images

In typical graph-based image annotation algorithms, a nearest neighbor graph (for example, a K-NN graph) is built based on the similarities between image feature vectors. The image labels are propagated from the labeled images to the unlabeled images along the graph edges according to certain weighting and combination rules. The quality of the edges leading from labeled images to unlabeled images is critical for the success of these algorithms.

To improve the quality of the edges from labeled images, we propose a supervised method for computing reduced feature sets for individual labeled images. The idea is that each feature of a labeled image is used in isolation to rank other labeled images; the features that assign high ranks to related neighboring images are treated as more important. By deleting the least important features, a different feature set is computed for each labeled image, and is used in the ranking of unlabeled images.

This idea is adopted as a preprocessing step in a graph-based image annotation method *SW-KProp+* [6]. When the proportion of correct edges leading from labeled images increases, better annotation performance can be achieved.

3. EXPERIMENTS

3.1 Datasets

We provide experimental results on two image datasets MNIST and Google-23, to show the effectiveness of our local selection schemes on image search and annotation. MNIST has 70,000 images of handwritten digits [7]. The 784 pixel values of each image were treated as its image features. Except for the experiments in Section 2.2, we constructed a reduced subset of MNIST containing 10,000 images, by randomly selecting 1000 images for each digit. Google-23 is described in [6], which consists of 6686 faces extracted from web images of 23 celebrities. The total dimension of each feature vector is 1937.

We also conducted experiments on some other datasets including web images and non-image data; the experimental results are omitted in this abstract due to the space limit.

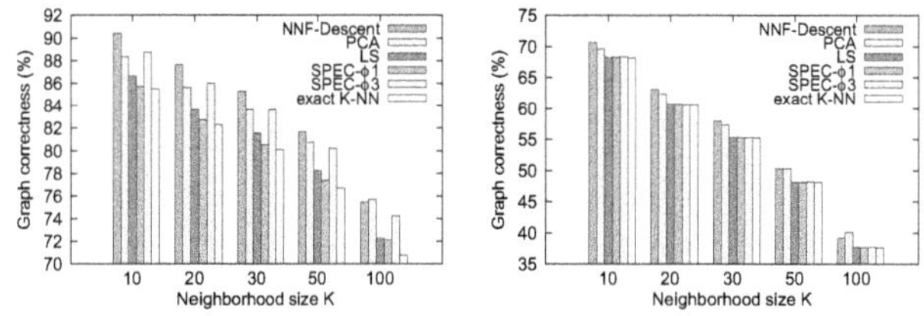

(a) MNIST (b) Google-23

Figure 1: *NNF-Descent* vs. competing methods.

3.2 Similarity Graph Construction

We compared *NNF-Descent* with principle component analysis (*PCA*), *LS*, *SPEC-ϕ1* and *SPEC-ϕ3* with respect to the correctness of produced K-NN graphs.

The neighborhood size for the target graph was set at $10, 20, 30, 50$ and 100. The number of features sparsified in each iteration was 5. For each experimental run of *NNF-Descent*, we computed the best graph correctness score over 50 iterations. The average computed from 5 runs was reported for each dataset. For the other methods, for each data point, 5 least important features were discarded per iteration, and an exact K-NN graph was computed from the resulting set of reduced feature vectors. Over all K-NN graphs produced the best correctness value achieved was reported. The performance of the exact K-NN graph computed from the original feature vectors is plotted as a baseline.

It can be seen from Fig. 1 that for all choices considered for the value of K, *NNF-Descent* achieved graph correctness scores better than those of the exact K-NN graphs. In almost all cases, our method clearly outperformed its competitors. When K is large, *PCA* outperformed the other methods. This outcome can be explained by the semantic quality of the K-NN graphs upon which *NNF-Descent*, *LS* and *SPEC* rank features — when the semantic quality of the K-NN graph degrades, the detection of noisy features becomes less reliable.

3.3 Image Similarity Search

We compared *GLS+RS* with approaches based on *LS*, data variance and random feature selection. In each experimental run, MNIST and Google-23 were firstly split into a query set containing 100 random images and a candidate set containing the rest images. We also collected 100K faces from Wikipedia Commons as noise (referred to as WikiFaces) and appended them to the candidate set of Google-23. Except for *GLS+RS*, the other methods selected features globally — that is, if a feature was identified as a noise feature in the candidate set, it was also discarded from the query image, and the original distance function was used directly on the lower-dimensional feature vectors.

The results reported in Fig. 2 are the averages over 5 test runs. The proportion of features identified as noise was varied from 0 to 50%. As a baseline for comparison, the performance of sequential search in the full feature space was plotted as a dashed line in each figure (labeled as '*Full*').

It is clear from Fig. 2 that *GLS+RS* achieved consistently better results over its competitors which used the original distance function. This improvement can be attributed to two aspects: the image ranking strategy (when $z = 0$), and the *GLS* feature selection (when $z > 0$). On the other hand, traditional methods for filter-based unsupervised feature se-

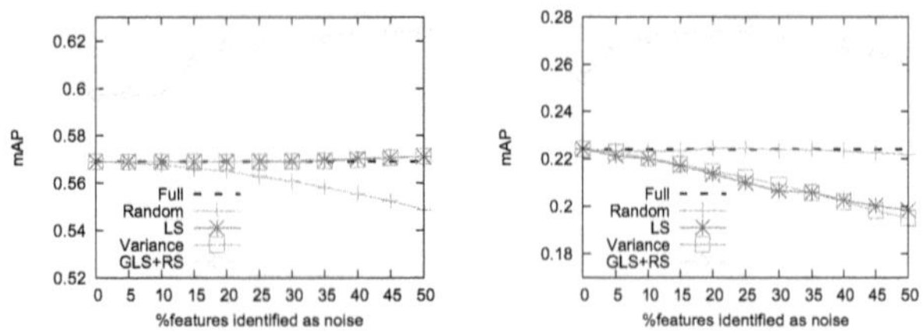

(a) MNIST (b) Google-23+WikiFaces

Figure 2: *GLS+RS* vs. competing methods.

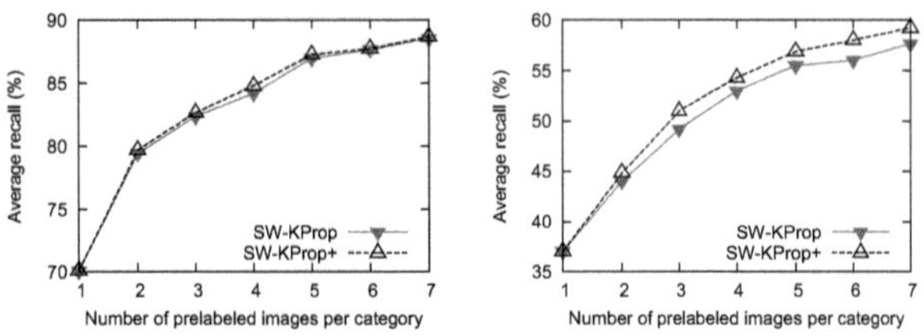

(a) MNIST (b) Google-23

Figure 3: *SW-KProp* vs. *SW-KProp+*.

lection yield little or no improvement in the semantic quality of CBIR results.

3.4 Graph-based Image Annotation

We compared *SW-KProp* with *SW-KProp+* in an image labeling task. Both methods propagate label scores from labeled images to unlabeled images in a similarity graph; *SW-KProp+* extends *SW-KProp* by utilizing the technique described in Section 3.3 in the computation of the similarity graph [6]. The number of prelabeled images ranged from 1 to 7. The overall annotation performance is evaluated, that is: $recall = (\#correctly\ labeled\ test\ items)/(\#test\ items)$.

The results can be found in Fig. 3. On Google-23, *SW-KProp+* outperformed *SW-KProp*, when the number of prelabeled images per category was larger than 1. This implies that with only a few images of the same category, *SW-KProp+* can effectively select a subset of features with better discriminative ability for each prelabeled image, and enhance the quality of the similarity graph by recomputing the neighborhood of prelabeled images.

However on MNIST, the use of the feature selection technique for prelabeled images did not lead to a significant improvement for this dataset. One possible reason is that MNIST is a relatively easy dataset whose original image descriptors are already of sufficient quality. The improvement on the edges from labeled images had little effect on the overall performance of label propagation.

4. DISCUSSION AND FUTURE WORK

In this thesis work, we summarize the methods we proposed for the local selection of image features. We proposed Local Laplacian Score (*LLS*) and Generalized Laplacian Score (*GLS*) as two unsupervised methods to construct a reduced feature set for each database image. *LLS* is embedded into *NN-Descent* for efficient and effective *K*-NN graph computation; a new ranking scheme is applied to the feature sets produced by *GLS* in an image search prototype. For graph-based image annotation, a supervised method is proposed for the computation of a discriminative feature set for each labeled image, by which, semantically related labeled-unlabeled image pairs are more likely to be connected in the similarity graph. Note that we are proposing methods for the identification of important feature dimensions for individual images rather than a new type of image feature.

Our ongoing work is focused on the extension of *GLS+RS*, which suffers from large computational cost as the query image is ranked with respect to all database images. One possible solution is to utilize an index structure to filter similar images of the query image. The query image is then ranked in the subjective feature spaces of the filtered images for query refinement. Other possible research directions include: (1) the applications of the proposed methods to other types of data; (2) a combination of query expansion and *GLS+RS* in CBIR approaches; (3) a study of the local selection methods on sparse feature vectors, such as bag-of-visual-words; and (4) the use of the MapReduce framework in the parallization of the graph construction.

5. REFERENCES

[1] W. Dong, M. Charikar, and K. Li. Efficient *k*-nearest neighbor graph construction for generic similarity measures. In *Proceedings of the 20th International Conference on World Wide Web*, pages 577–586, 2011.

[2] J. G. Dy, C. E. Brodley, A. C. Kak, L. S. Broderick, and A. M. Aisen. Unsupervised feature selection applied to content-based retrieval of lung images. *IEEE Trans. Pattern Anal. Mach. Intell.*, 25(3):373–378, 2003.

[3] E. Guldogan and M. Gabbouj. Feature selection for content-based image retrieval. *Signal, Image and Video Processing*, 2(3):241–250, 2008.

[4] X. He, D. Cai, and P. Niyogi. Laplacian score for feature selection. In *Advances in Neural Information Processing Systems 18*, pages 507–514. MIT Press, 2006.

[5] M. E. Houle, X. Ma, V. Oria, and J. Sun. Improving the quality of K-NN graphs for image databases through vector sparsification. In *Proceedings of the International Conference on Multimedia Retrieval*, pages 89–96, 2014.

[6] M. E. Houle, V. Oria, S. Satoh, and J. Sun. Annotation propagation in image databases using similarity graphs. *TOMCCAP*, 10(1):7, 2013.

[7] Y. LeCun, L. Bottou, Y. Bengio, and P. Haffner. Gradient-based learning applied to document recognition. *Proc. IEEE*, 86(11):2278–2324, 1998.

[8] Y. Sun and B. Bhanu. Image retrieval with feature selection and relevance feedback. In *Proceedings of the 17th IEEE International Conference on Image Processing*, pages 3209–3212, Sept 2010.

[9] Y. Yang, H. T. Shen, Z. Ma, Z. Huang, and X. Zhou. $l_{2,1}$-norm regularized discriminative feature selection for unsupervised learning. In *Proceedings of the International Joint Conferences on Artificial Intelligence*, pages 1589–1594, 2011.

[10] Z. Zhao and H. Liu. Spectral feature selection for supervised and unsupervised learning. In *Proceedings of the 24th International Conference on Machine Learning*, pages 1151–1157, 2007.

Segmentation and Indexing of Endoscopic Videos

Manfred Jürgen Primus
Institute of Information Technology
Universität Klagenfurt, Klagenfurt, Austria
mprimus@itec.aau.at

ABSTRACT

Over the last few years it has become common to archive video recordings of endoscopic surgeries. These videos are of high value for medics, junior doctors, patients and hospital management but currently they are used rarely or not at all. Each day tens to hundreds of hours of new videos are added to archives without metadata that would support content-based search. In order to fully utilize these videos it is necessary to analyze the content of the recordings. Endoscopic videos are in some aspects fundamentally different to other types of videos. Therefore, pre-existing content-based analysis methods must be tested for their ability to operate with this kind of video and, if required, they must be adopted or new methods must be found. Especially, we address video segmentation and indexing in this work. We present our preliminary work and ideas for future work to add content-based information to endoscopic videos.

Categories and Subject Descriptors

H.3.1 [**Information Storage and Retrieval**]: Content Analysis and Indexing

General Terms

Design, Experimentation, Algorithms, Performance

Keywords

Video indexing, Video segmentation, Medical Systems

1. INTRODUCTION

Minimally invasive surgery, also known as "keyhole surgery", is an operation method where small instruments and a camera are inserted in the body through small incisions. This kind of procedures reduces risks and complaints of the patients compared to conventional surgery methods. Not surprisingly, the number of minimally invasive procedures is growing. A main point of minimally invasive surgeries is the transmission of the operation area captured by an endoscopic camera to a number of screens. Naturally, the video data can be recorded and archived, which is even mandatory by law in some countries (e.g., the Netherlands).

The recordings of the operations have high benefit for various medical fields like medical education and training, quality assurance, patient information, patient documentation and planning of operations. That the video data is used in a limited manner only can be attributed to the lack of any metadata except date and time, name of the patient, kind of operation and the name of the surgeon. It is obvious that surgeons will have usually no time to annotate videos after hours of surgical interventions. To make the video data useful for them, the recordings must be analyzed automatically in a first step. This analysis shall be designed to identify objects in the videos like instruments and tissues as well as general and special movement patterns. Furthermore, it shall enable the possibility to find semantically meaningful segments in the videos by linking existing knowledge such as the descriptions of standard procedures (e. g., cholecystectomy, which is the removal of the gallbladder) and metadata from the analysis of the videos.

2. PROBLEM DESCRIPTION

Videos recorded during endoscopic interventions have characteristics that circumvent the direct application of common computer vision and image retrieval algorithms. The first obvious trait is that endoscopic videos are single-shot videos. Second, the temporal color distribution is very unvaried, which means that the predominant color over the whole video is a kind of red with slight variations. Next, the magnification of the video content is immense, which leads to huge changes in scale when objects are moved away and toward the camera or if the camera is moved. Because of this magnification and the closeness of the camera to the objects the covered distances of moved objects between succesive frames is much larger than in usual movies. This frequently leads to an occurence of motion blur. Another spectacularity is that occlusions and coverages of objects – instruments and tissues – happen quite often. Concluding should be mentioned that the instruments are very similar, both in color and in shape.

In Section 3 we summarize publications that focus on the analysis and segmentation of endoscopic videos. Presented segmentation methods rely heavily on specific features of single procedures. E.g., [6, 7, 4] use the appearance of blurry frames to detect segment boundaries in recordings of colon inspections. The appearance of reflections is used to find

MM'14, November 3–November 7, 2014, Orlando, Florida, USA.

http://dx.doi.org/10.1145/2647868.2654861 .

scenes with surgical interactions additional to the inspection of the colon [5]. Both specific features are not applicable for surgical operations, where blurryness is undesirable and scenes without visible instruments are rare. Other works are based on the assumption that standard procedures are similar over time and kind of execution [14, 3].

The aim of our work is the development of a general framework. This framework should segment different types of endoscopic videos into their main phases, find important scenes and frame representations, and identify differences between in-order and out-of-order (abnormal) behavior. It makes use of algorithms for recognition of movement and trajectory patterns, detection and recognition of instruments, tissues and actions. Existing algorithms must be tested, evaluated and adopted and if necessary new algorithms must be developed. Finally, the algorithms are used to index the video files and to find the important scenes and frames, and the boundaries of the specified phases.

To illustrate our idea we outline the following use case. The seven phases of a cholecystectomy are described in an structured textual description (e.g., an XML-file). For each phase the used instruments, actions, visible tissues and parts of the body, sequence of actions or sequence of the usage of instruments, are listed. Additionally, important scenes or excerpts are textually represented by constraints defining time, actions or visible objects. For example, an important part in a cholecystectomy is called *critical-view-of-safety*. The sequence of interactions is the dissection of the anatomic structures of the triangle of the Calot area, which is the separation of the cystic duct and artery. After that the ducts are ligated with a clipping device and cutted with a scissor. These three segments – separation, clipping and cutting of the ducts – can be found when the instruments and the sequence of usage are recognized. Additionally, clipping and cutting have clear motion patterns, which increases the possibility to identify these scenes. An important excerpt shows the result of the cutting, where there is no movement at all and the cut surface with the clips is shown. Finally In this paper, we present our pioneering work in the area of content-based analysis of video recordings of different endoscopic procedures, but also on work in progress. What's more, we would like to evolve possibilities, how expert knowledge can be used to improve the performance of the analysis methods.

3. RELATED WORK

Koprinska et al. point out that the first step in video analysis is the partition of the videos in temporal segements [10]. However, even newer approaches as described in [8, 2] are not applicable as they mainly target color differences. Another technique for temporal segmentation is scene segmentation. An overview about this state-of-the-art techniques can be found in [9]. The authors divide the approaches in three main categories and combinations of these. Two of the main categories — text-based and audio-based — are not applicable to the field of endoscopic videos, because these recordings do usually not contain textual or acoustical content. The remaining category is addressed to visual segmentation methods. Within this category endoscopic videos are identified as single-shot videos. For this kind of videos other reference points must be identified as for shot boundaries in conventional videos.

Cao et al. divide videos from colonoscopy inspections into six segments, where each segment shows one section of the colon. The beginning of each new section is marked by the physician saying a specific keyword [6]. This approach requires an additional effort for the doctor. In [7] the acoustical model is exchanged by a visual one. Each kink in the colon, which also marks the beginning of a section, results in blurry frames, when the endoscope is moved around it. After passing a curve the focus must be set again. This pattern of sharp frames, blurry frames followed by frames with increasing sharpness is used to find segment boundaries. In [4] they use light reflections of the bright wire of some instruments to identify scenes, where therapeutic actions or biopsies are done during the inspection. The results can be improved by enhancing the images and by considering the insertion direction of the instruments [5].

The usage of certain instruments can be a hint to segment endoscopic videos. This serves as the basis for the segmentation method of Padoy et al. [14]. Each time, when a particular instrument is used, a signal is recorded that indicates the use of this instrument. According to the significance of the instrument to the current phase of the operation the appearance of the instrument is weighted. The occurrence of the instruments is synchronized temporally to training data with an adaptive time warping algorithm. A more sophisticated but similar approach is found by Blum et al. [3]. The frames are represented by a global descriptor. Subsequently, the videos are segmented by a canonical correlation analysis based on training data.

Other works use temporal features to recognize segments in endoscopic videos. Stanek et al. use the variance of the mean-red and the mean-red-normalized pixel values per frame within a temporal window to recognize inside-the-patient frames and outside-the-patient frames [17]. This information is used to combine frames to segments belonging to the procedure and frames not belonging to the procedure. Münzer et al. use a global Hue value from the HSV color space to segment the video into out-of-patient segments and relevant segments [13]. Furthermore, they detect very dark frames using an average intensity level and blurry frames using Difference-of-Gaussians. Finally, the dark, the out-of-patient and the blurry frames are composed to irrelevant segments if the frequence of occurrence within a temporal window is above a threshold. Lin et al. use motion features such as guestures, speed, and acceleration to find suturing tasks and segment them into eight elementary guestures [11].

A key task in indexing endoscopic videos is the detection and the recognition of instruments. Speidel et al. segment instruments spatially using a Bayes classifier to calculate the probability if a color from the H-S plane belongs to an instrument-shaft or to a tissue [16]. Subsequently, they use again a Bayes classifier to find the tip of the instrument based on the location of the shaft. Finally, the contour of the instrument is calculated and the instrument is recognized using a parametric eigenspace representation. Allan et al. use scale-invariant feature transform (SIFT), color-based SIFT, and Histogram of Oriented Gradients (HOG) as features for a random forest classifier [1].

4. CONTRIBUTIONS AND PLANNED WORK

Two main limitations can be addressed to all methods shown in Section 3. Some handle algorithms for a unique kind of endoscopic surgery. The others work well with singular images but applied to videos they show problems that are stated below in more detail. However, a key point in the proposed framework is not only the detection of instruments in endoscopic videos, but also the recognition, which instrument(s) is/are currently used in a frame or during a time period. This is important because many parts of interventions can be identified by the instruments that are used. The number of visible instruments alone can be helpful classifying certain scenes. This assumption leads to following experiments implemented by use of the OpenCV framework.

Instruments are artificial objects in a natural area. For humans the edges of the instruments seem to be well distinguishable from their surroundings. This observation let us undertake trials with the canny edge detector. Surprisingly, the results were not useful for instrument detection. The Canny algorithm contains a number of adjustable parameters, which affect the results. The first parameter affects the size of the Gaussian smoothing filter. Two threshold parameters are used for the hysteresis procedure that separates irrelevant from relevant content. If a combination of parameters have been found for one frame, they rarely fit for neighboring frames. Severall reasons have been identified for this behavior. One reason is a smooth transition between background and some parts of the instruments. Sometimes this is induced by the shadow of the instruments, but mainly because the background is reflected slightly by the instruments. Also the textures of the tissues have a negative impact. An improvement by the use of the Hough line detector cannot be achieved.

Another approach to find the edges of the instruments is the calculation of pixel gradients and their orientation. Our assumption is that the orientation of the gradients must be well-aligned along two parallel lines because of the straight edges of the instruments. Tissue and body parts typically do not show two parallel lines. Again, the outcome of this approach was not promising. As additional problems to the before mentioned we identified strong noise and slightly visible block artifacts. Noise reduction and reduction of the block artifacts by the use of Gaussian smoothing does not increase the performance. A further problem is motion blur, which occurs quite often. Endoscopic cameras are very close to the captured objects and magnify the scene to give a good view of the operation area. These factors favor the presence of motion blur.

Currently, a often used procedure for object classification is the use of Bag-of-Visual-Words (BoW) in combination with Support Vector Machines (SVM). To gather baseline data for instrument classification in laparoscopic videos we used this approach with dense sampled ORB features. For the evaluation four different vocabulary sizes and four differently sized grids were chosen. As result we get 16 different combinations of density of the ORB features and vocabulary sizes. The precision and recall values for the instruments that appear in a cholecystectomy do not show a single combination that provides reasonable good results for all of the instruments. Based on this work further hypotheses arised. First, we want to evaluate if the performance of this approach can be improved using the time component of videos. More precisely, we assume that frames, where instruments are falsely recognized are sparsely distributed and frames, where instruments are correctly classified appear in a bigger cluster. Second, we want to show that spatial segmentation of instruments in frames will increase the performance clearly.

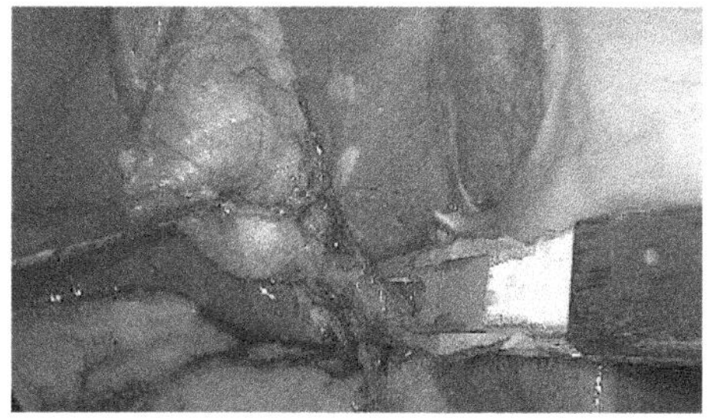

(a) Original image

(b) Segmented instruments

Figure 1: Image from a cholecystectomy (a) and the corresponding spatial segmentation of the instruments (b).

For the spatial segmentation of instruments within frames we analysed different color spaces. Although color differences between consecutive frames in endoscopic videos are usually very small, there are measurable differences between areas showing instruments and areas showing tissues and background. The single channels of the RGB color space do not provide helpful information. Conversely, the S-channel of the HSV color space and the a-channel of the Lab color space show a major potential to separate pixels belonging to an instrument from the rest of the image. The saturation of pixels of instruments is on average significantly lower than the saturation of pixels outside an instrument. The same distinctness also applies to the "a" values in the Lab color space. This value represents the red-green opponent channel and it can be used for spatial segmentation as shown in Figure 1. It is based on the simple fact that the tissue and parts of the body show higher red values and simultaneously lower green values whilst red and green values of instruments are more or less equal. The spatial segmentation of the instruments will also be used to describe trajectories of the instruments, which will be used for classification of actions.

An approach for classification of simple actions like camera movement, insertion and removement of instruments based on temporal segmentation of endoscopic videos has been presented in [15]. The segmentation is related on temporal and spatial differences of motion patterns caused by camera movement and instrument movement. To identify these patterns Kanade-Lucas-Tomasi (KLT) tracking is used. The traces of the tracking points are grouped into nine areas. For each area a singular motion value is calculated. The videos can be segmented by a simple comparison of these values. Camera movement is indicated if the values are similar but high. If all values are low neither the camera is moved nor an instrument. The movement of an instrument shows differently sized values in the areas. We have also shown that this approach can be used to segment different actions performed by the surgeons. A rising edge of the motion curve in an area is an indicator that an instrument has been inserted. A falling edge of the motion curve shows that an instrument has been removed. Additionally, some actions done with instruments show almost identical motion patterns. It is planned to treat these observations in a further work.

As soon as automatic indexing and segmentation of selected endoscopic procedures has feasible results we plan to implement two applications. The purpose of the first application is the use of the segmentation results for keyframe extraction. The second application addresses the utilization for video summarization to improve the results [12] by adding semantics. Important parts of standard procedures are known beforehand and can be used to mark these important positions in the procedure in a description file. We aim that this knowledge can be used to improve keyframe extraction and video summarization significantly.

5. RESEARCH METHODS

The outcome of this work will be improved or new algorithms for (1) temporal video segmentation, (2) indexing the content of the videos, and (3) creation of video summaries and keyframe extraction. Based on traditional research methods the first step after an extensive literature survey are tests with commonly used algorithms. If these algorithms run into problems, difficulties must be identified and lead to the design of improved or new algorithms, as required. Iterative prototypes will be implemented that are used for proof-of-concept, to perform tests and for evaluations in order to compare with existing algorithms. For the evaluation of the performance of the different algorithms ground truth data has to be built. Additionally, user studies with domain experts will be performed to evaluate the benefits of the proposed methods in each field.

Acknowledgment

This work was supported by Lakeside Labs GmbH, Klagenfurt, Austria and funding from the European Regional Development Fund and the Carinthian Economic Promotion Fund (KWF) under grant KWF - 20214 22573 33955.

6. REFERENCES

[1] M. Allan, S. Ourselin, S. Thompson, D. J. Hawkes, J. Kelly, and D. Stoyanov. Toward detection and localization of instruments in minimally invasive surgery. *IEEE Transactions on Biomedical Engineering*, 60(4):1050–1058, Apr. 2013.

[2] A. Amiri and M. Fathy. Video shot boundary detection using generalized eigenvalue decomposition and gaussian transition detection. *Computing and Informatics*, 30(3):595–619, 2012.

[3] T. Blum, H. Feußner, and N. Navab. Modeling and segmentation of surgical workflow from laparoscopic video. In T. Jiang, N. Navab, J. P. W. Pluim, and M. A. Viergever, editors, *MICCAI (3)*, volume 6363 of *LNCS*, pages 400–407. Springer, 2010.

[4] Y. Cao, D. Li, W. Tavanapong, J. Oh, J. Wong, and P. C. de Groen. Parsing and browsing tools for colonoscopy videos. In *Proc. of the 12th ACM Int. Conf. on Multimedia*, MULTIMEDIA '04, pages 844–851, New York, NY, USA, 2004. ACM.

[5] Y. Cao, D. Liu, W. Tavanapong, J. Wong, J. Oh, and P. de Groen. Computer-aided detection of diagnostic and therapeutic operations in colonoscopy videos. *Biomedical Engineering, IEEE Transactions on*, 54(7):1268–1279, July 2007.

[6] Y. Cao, W. Tavanapong, K. Kim, J. Wong, J. Oh, and P. de Groen. A framework for parsing colonoscopy videos for semantic units. In *Multimedia and Expo, 2004. ICME '04. 2004 IEEE International Conference on*, volume 3, pages 1879–1882, June 2004.

[7] Y. Cao, W. Tavanapong, D. Li, J. Oh, P. Groen, and J. Wong. A visual model approach for parsing colonoscopy videos. In P. Enser, Y. Kompatsiaris, N. O'Connor, A. Smeaton, and A. Smeulders, editors, *Image and Video Retrieval*, volume 3115 of *LNCS*, pages 160–169. Springer Berlin Heidelberg, 2004.

[8] O. Chum, J. Philbin, M. Isard, and A. Zisserman. Scalable near identical image and shot detection. In *Proc. of the 6th ACM international conference on Image and video retrieval*, pages 549–556, 2007.

[9] M. Del Fabro and L. Böszörmenyi. State-of-the-art and future challenges in video scene detection: a survey. *Multimedia systems*, 19(5):427–454, 2013.

[10] I. Koprinska and S. Carrato. Temporal video segmentation: A survey. *Signal processing: Image communication*, 16(5):477–500, 2001.

[11] H. C. Lin, I. Shafran, T. E. Murphy, A. M. Okamura, D. D. Yuh, and G. D. Hager. Automatic detection and segmentation of robot-assisted surgical motions. In *MICCAI*, pages 802–810. Springer, 2005.

[12] M. Lux, O. Marques, K. Schoeffmann, L. Böszörmenyi, and G. Lajtai. A novel tool for summarization of arthroscopic videos. *Multimedia Tools and Applications*, 46(2-3):521–544, 2010.

[13] B. Münzer, K. Schoeffmann, and L. Böszörmenyi. Relevance segmentation of laparoscopic videos. In *Proc. of IEEE Int. Symp. on Multimedia (ISM 2013)*, pages 84–91, Anaheim, California, USA, 2013.

[14] N. Padoy, T. Blum, I. Essa, H. Feussner, M.-O. Berger, and N. Navab. A boosted segmentation method for surgical workflow analysis. In N. Ayache, S. Ourselin, and A. Maeder, editors, *MICCAI 2007*, volume 4791 of *LNCS*, pages 102–109. Springer Berlin Heidelberg, 2007.

[15] M. J. Primus, K. Schoeffmann, and L. Böszörmenyi. Segmentation of recorded endoscopic videos by detecting significant motion changes. In *Proc. of the Int. WS on Content-Based Multimedia Indexing (CBMI 2013)*, pages 223–228, 2013.

[16] S. Speidel, J. Benzko, S. Krappe, G. Sudra, P. Azad, B. P. Müller-Stich, C. Gutt, and R. Dillmann. Automatic classification of minimally invasive instruments based on endoscopic image sequences. pages 72610A–72610A–8, Feb. 2009.

[17] S. R. Stanek, W. Tavanapong, J. Wong, J. H. Oh, and P. C. de Groen. Automatic real-time detection of endoscopic procedures using temporal features. *Computer Methods and Programs in Biomedicine*, 108(2):524–535, Nov. 2012.

Learning Recognition of Semantically Relevant Video Segments from Endoscopy Videos Contributed and Edited in a Private Social Network

Desara Xhura
Institute of Information Technology
Alpen-Adria University of Klagenfurt, Austria
desara.xhura@aau.at

ABSTRACT

Besides the great benefit of minimizing intrusions made in body, endoscopic surgery has the advantage of producing abundant documentation regarding the procedure as well. Recordings can be used not only to document the surgery but as a mean for learning and improving experts knowledge too. To minimize time and effort that experts invest in preparing informative endoscopic videos, tools that can automatically identify interesting parts in videos are needed. To achieve this, an annotated data set is required. This paper presents an approach for collecting endoscopic videos and related experts knowledge. For this, a social network with integrated video annotation and presentation tools is used. Experts can upload, annotate and share their videos with other physicians. In the background their interactions with the videos are recorded, interpreted and used to derive predictive models or improve existing ones. Once a prediction model is derived, its results will be displayed to physicians as suggestions, which can be integrated into their video annotations. Physicians choice to either keep these suggestions or discard them will serve as a feedback to the learned model and used to refine the derived knowledge.

Categories and Subject Descriptors

H.5.1 [**Multimedia Information systems**]: Video; H.3.3 [**Information Search and Retrieval**]: Relevance feedback, Information filtering; H.3.5 [**On-line Information Services**]: Data sharing; I.2.10 [**Vision and Scene Understanding**]: Video analysis

Keywords

Social network; endoscopic video; video editing; video annotation; pattern recognition

MM'14, November 03 - 07 2014, Orlando, FL, USA

http://dx.doi.org/10.1145/2647868.2654860.

1. INTRODUCTION

Finding semantically interesting parts in recordings of endoscopic surgeries is a challenging task. Without having a physician to manually annotate or provide extra information we are currently able to only identify some irrelevant parts such as: parts recorded out from the patients body or parts that are blurry [1]. To find which parts are relevant, describe a certain phase in the surgery or carry no relevant information, knowledge derived or provided from physicians is needed. Gathering such knowledge is hard. Physicians tend to be very busy, consequently they have few time to invest in research projects. Therefore the amount of collected data tends to be small, the learned models often are too specialized to a single surgeon or to a very specific procedure. At the other hand physicians often need to annotate their recordings either for documentation, showing them to their patients, colleagues, or using them as a learning material for their students. These annotations can become useful when it comes to improving automatic learning algorithms. Explicit or implicit knowledge can be gathered from physicians by monitoring this annotations and interactions with endoscopic video recordings. This knowledge can be used to build a ground truth data set that can serve as a basis for making automatic annotations. To do so, a tool that facilitates physicians interaction, annotation and sharing of informative videos is needed. In this context a social network specialized for physicians will be used. This social network integrates several video editing techniques and allows different experts to collaboratively edit endoscopic video contents and share them among each other. In the background the interaction with the video editing tool will be monitored and interpreted in such a way that relevant information is derived.

Using a social network has several benefits, foremost is the fact that a social network provides the advantage to reach many specialists. This means that different physicians can contribute. Even if their contribution is not very frequent good learning results can still be achieved. Furthermore, studies [11] show that there is an increasing interest from patients and physicians to contribute to the increasing knowledge and awareness related to medical conditions. In the last decade, more than 20 different health related social networks came to existence [11]. Data contributed in these social networks is making possible analysing different cures, finding different patterns that emerge in medical conditions and improving existing health care systems. Integrating video editing tools in social network adds new ways to better analyse and understand video data. Data from video editing tools can provide knowledge regarding the video content. For example if a physician zooms on a part or extracts images out of it, there is a high chance that this part is relevant.

2. RELATED WORK

Researchers' interest on analysing endoscopic surgeries increased with the increasing amount of endoscopic video recordings. These videos made possible different analysis and the development of new techniques for assisting physicians. Up to now research on automatic analysis of endoscopic surgeries is oriented in five main areas:

1. Automatic key frame extraction.
2. Identification of semantically relevant parts.
3. Identification of workflows (also known as automatic identification of phases in an endoscopic surgery).
4. Automatic recognition of surgical instruments.
5. Automatic recognition of particular issues, anomalies.

Key frame extraction techniques are mostly used to summarize endoscopic surgeries and minimize the time experts spend on searching through endoscopic videos. To accomplish this, research mostly used unsupervised learning techniques. This includes: (1) extraction of global or local features from video frames, (2) clustering of frames based on the similarity of their features, finally (3) building a summary by selecting as key frame at least one frame from each cluster [8, 4].

Identification of semantically relevant parts of videos requires always a training data set, where physicians or people with knowledge in the area annotate video frames based on their relevance. The knowledge from experts can be captured in different forms. Cao et. al [3] for example, used the audio recordings of colonoscopy videos to identify relevant scenes. In their study they used a data set of 35 videos, all captured from the same endoscopist. Their results showed a high precision and recall respectively 95% and 81%. In this case the data set used was quite small and the results might change when videos of another physician are analyzed.

Finding workflows in endoscopic surgeries has different purposes. One is to get a better understanding on how a procedure is performed, point out when there are deviations and give hints to surgeons. Another reason is to facilitate the search and navigation through the video. Padoy et. al [10] present a notable approach for detecting workflows in laparoscopic cholecystectomies (a special kind of endoscopic surgery) videos. For their study they used a data set of 16 videos coming from surgeries performed from four different physicians.

Tracking and identifying surgical instruments can help on improving the recognition of surgery workflows and at the same time indicate the type of surgery. Automatic recognition of particular issues at the other hand can assist surgeons. In both cases the techniques used are similar. They involve the use of an annotated data set of videos for training. Annotations are based on key frames. Color and texture features are extracted and used for learning. An example is the study from Iakovidis et al. [5]. In this study the authors used a set of color and texture based features combined with

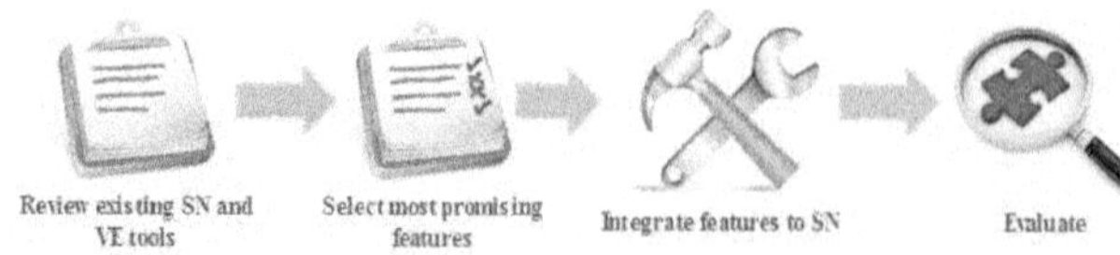

Figure 1: An overview of the social network development approach.

machine learning algorithms to automatically detect adenomas in gastrointestinal videos. For their study the authors used a data set containing 86 videos each of which was histologically evaluated and lasted only 10 seconds long. The authors claim that they have a maximum accuracy of 93.8% for detecting adenomas. Similarly Boufarta et al. [2] presents a color based technique to automatically track instruments in endoscopic videos.

Some other related research goes in the context of: (i) interactive video annotations, (ii) tracking user behaviors, (iii) learning from social media. Video annotating techniques have been mostly researched to improve online, knowledge sharing and teaching systems. In this context often technologies like hypervideo [1] are used. Laiola et al. [6] present a web based annotation tool that facilitates collaborative commenting of video content, video hyperlinking and selective viewing. Lux et. al [9] present an approach for medical experts to manually annotate medical videos by drawing on them and adding audio comments. User behavior has long been studied too. Several systems for tracking user behavior in Web have been developed [7]. These systems mostly focus on tracking mouse clicks and movements. There are some contributions in the context of mining social networks as well. They relate mostly to predicting group dynamics, future links and detecting social events. In this research the focus goes to studies performed with data contributed on health related social networks. Swan [11] presents an extensive summary of existing health related social networks and the way their data is being used in research.

3. APPROACH

It makes no difference if the task is to meaningfully segment videos, extract representative key frames or recognize certain diseases. To be able to automatically analyse endoscopic videos we need expert knowledge. In this context the following question arises:

"What knowledge can be implicitly derived from the way experts use, edit or annotate their videos?".

To be able to answer this question, first we need to understand how physicians edit their videos and what information these actions can provide. Consequently, some techniques to (1) edit video content and (2) collect data are needed. The content of this section is separated into two main parts. The first part gives an overview on the techniques used to gather physicians knowledge. The second part introduces a model for learning from the gathered knowledge.

3.1 Collecting data

[1]Hypervideo is a video stream that contains embedded links to other multimedia. In such videos users can click on components appearing during the video stream to navigate to other multimedia elements.

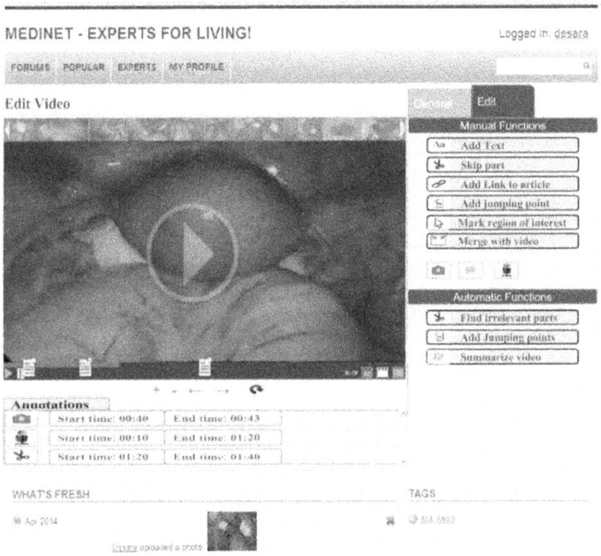

Figure 2: A sample from the video editing interface.

For gathering experts knowledge a private social network will be used. This social network will provide tools for editing endoscopic videos as well as for sharing and viewing edited videos. Four main steps are involved in the development of this platform (see Figure 1). First existing video editing tools and social networks are reviewed and their best practices deployed. Once the platform completes, user studies will be conducted. Users will be asked to evaluate features provided from the platform based on two criterias, usability and intuitiveness. The resulting platform will have common features provided by general social networks and a set of manual and automatic functions for editing video content (see Figure 2.). Manual functions include interactions such as: cutting out video parts, adding navigation points or different annotations. They will serve as a mean for collecting examples of ground truth. Manual functions require physicians to navigate through the video content and add time-based annotations to it. Automatic functions will be used to test and refine the learned patterns. They suggest video sequences to physicians where annotations would be needed or something potentially relevant is happening. Physicians can decide to use the provided suggestions in their final video or ignore them.

3.2 Learning Approach

This part focuses on: (i) interpreting the collected data, (ii) learning patterns from it, (iii) evaluating learned patterns and (iv) refining results (see Figure 3). Knowledge will be collected from physicians in two different levels. First based on the new data coming from physicians. Secondly based on the feedback physicians give by using the automatic functions. It is expected that the way physicians edit their videos can provide information for all the five research areas mentioned in Section 2. This research address three of them: (1) finding relevant video segments, (2) finding representative key frames, (3) and identifying surgery workflows.

As we will have different physicians and they will not be explicitly asked to annotate videos. The following challenges might arise: (i) physician actions might be misinterpreted, resulting in noisy information, (ii) some physicians might find some parts more interesting then others do, resulting in conflicting tags, (iii) physicians' annotations of workflows might differ. The following sections provide a more detailed description for each of the phases involved in the learning part.

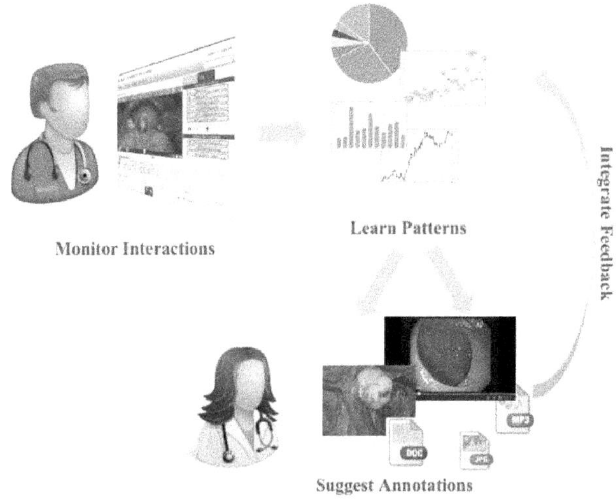

Figure 3: Learning approach.

3.2.1 Interpreting user interactions

The first step in the learning process will be the interpretation of user's actions. For instance, if the physician skipped or deleted a part of the video, we could hypothesize that this part is not relevant. Consequently, use it as training data for learning patterns that indicate presence of irrelevant video frames. Which action will be considered depends on what task is addressed. To find out relevant video parts we will use a weighting algorithm where each annotation will increase the relevance coefficient of the part. In this case an annotation can be titling, an audio comment, drawing, link or article. Actions such as skip or fast-forward will serve to decrease the relevance coefficient of a video part. To find relevant key frames, relevant video parts derived from the first task will be used. Similarly to literature [8], the frames of these parts will be clustered and a key frame per cluster will be chosen. In addition the algorithm will use patterns learned from key frames that previous physicians selected. Actions that provide information related to the workflow, are the added jumping points in the video. For this task, text and audio analysis might be very helpful too but due to the complexity of the task they will be out of scope for this thesis. The result of this part is a data set of labeled video frames

To prove if the implicitly extracted knowledge represents the ground truth, a user study is planned. In this study physicians will be separated in two groups. One group is asked to manually annotate videos for each of the three tasks. The other group will be asked to create descriptive summaries from the same endoscopic videos with the help of the social network. Physicians from both groups will work on the same videos, however their annotations will be hidden from each other. The goal of this study is to see, to what extent we can gather physicians knowledge implicitly and what types of challenges we should expect.

3.2.2 Learning patterns

Learning patterns will involve using a set of algorithms for extracting local and global features out of video frames and applying machine learning algorithms to them. In this part high level features, such as time and previously known aspects (e.g. phases of a surgical workflow), will be considered and added as descriptive dimensions to the training data. For learning, clustering and classification techniques will be combined in such a way that best practices of semi-supervised learning are applied. The result of this part is expected to be a set of different predictive models which combined will serve for identifying relevant video segments.

3.2.3 Evaluation

Evaluation is performed in tow levels. First a *cross validation* algorithm is used. This algorithm: (i) takes as input the interpreted data, (ii) separates it into training and testing data, (iii) uses semi-supervised learning algorithms to derive a model from the training data,(iv) uses the learned model to predict labels for the testing data and (v) measures the *accuracy*, *precision* and *recall* of the learned model. This gets repeated several times and the best learned models are chosen. These models are later used for the functions that make automatic suggestions to physicians. Automatic functions will be used as a second evaluation for the learned patterns. They will suggest actions to the users. Users can decide to either accept, correct or refuse these actions. Their decision will serve as feedback for the learned patterns. An accept-action will reinforce the use of the learned pattern by increasing its accuracy, a correct-action will provide extra information for learning and a deny-action will weaken the learned pattern by decreasing its accuracy.

4. CONCLUSION

There are several aspects which we could learn from endoscopic surgeries and several techniques to address different problems. One of the main problems researchers face is the fact that, for achieving good results constant collaboration between physicians and researchers is needed. To promote this collaboration the use of a combination between video editing techniques and social networks was proposed. With the completion of this work the following contributions are expected:

- A framework that aids the collection of physicians' knowledge by simultaneously avoiding the drawback of being too intrusive to them.
- Discovery of new patterns that indicate semantic relevance in endoscopic surgery.
- A ground truth data set that open doors for further research.

Further contributions might emerge during the development of this project.

5. REFERENCES

[1] K. S. B. Muenzer and L. Boeszoermenyi. Relevance segmentation of laparoscopic videos. *IEEE International Symposium on Multimedia*, pages 84–91, December 2013.

[2] L. Bouarfa, O. Akman, A. Schneider, P. P. Jonker, and J. Dankelman. In-vivo real-time tracking of surgical instruments in endoscopic video. *Minimally Invasive Therapy Allied Technologies*, 21(3):129–134, 2012.

[3] Y. Cao, W. Tavanapong, K. Kim, J. Wong, J. Oh, and P. de Groen. A framework for parsing colonoscopy videos for semantic units. *Multimedia and Expo, 2004. ICME '04. 2004 IEEE International Conference*, 3(2):1879–1882, June 2004.

[4] D. Iakovidis, S. Tsevas, and A. Polydorou. Reduction of capsule endoscopy reading times by unsupervised image mining. *Computerized Medical Imaging and Graphics*, 34(6):471 – 478, September 2010.

[5] D. K. Iakovidis, D. E. Maroulis, and S. A. Karkanis. An intelligent system for automatic detection of gastrointestinal adenomas in video endoscopy. *Computers in Biology and Medicine*, 36(10):1084 – 1103, 2006.

[6] R. Laiola Guimarães, P. Cesar, and D. C. Bulterman. Creating and sharing personalized time-based annotations of videos on the web. *Proceedings of the 10th ACM Symposium on Document Engineering*, 10(10):27 – 36, 2010.

[7] L. A. Leiva and R. Vivo. Web browsing behavior analysis and interactive hypervideo. *ACM Trans. Web 7*, 6(2):492–525, February 2009.

[8] M. Lux, O. Marques, K. Schoeffmann, L. Boeszoermenyi, and G. Lajtai. A novel tool for summarization of arthroscopic videos. *Computers in Biology and Medicine*, 46:521 ï£¡ 544, September 2009.

[9] M. Lux and M. Riegler. Annotation of endoscopic videos on mobile devices: A bottom-up approach. *ACM Multimedia Systems Conference*, 4:141 – 145, January 2009.

[10] N. Padoy, T. Blumb, S. A. Ahmadib, H. Feussnerc, M. O. Bergerd, and N. Navabb. Medical image analysis. *ACM Trans. Program. Lang. Syst.*, 16(3):632 – 641, April 2012.

[11] M. Swan. Emerging patient-driven health care models: an examination of health social networks,consumer personalized medicine and quantified self-tracking. *International journal of environmental research and public health*, 3(2):1879–1882, June 2004.

Multimodal Alignment of Videos

Research Summary for the Doctoral Symposium

Mario Guggenberger
Institute of Information Technology
Alpen-Adria-Universität Klagenfurt
9020 Klagenfurt am Wörthersee, Austria
mg@itec.aau.at

ABSTRACT

Most multimedia synchronization methods developed in the past are unimodal and consider only the audio data or the video data. Just recently, methods started to emerge that embrace multimodality by utilizing both audio and video processing to improve synchronization results. Although promising, their results are still not sufficient for fully automatic synchronization of recordings from heterogeneous sources. Video processing is also often too expensive to be used on large corpora of recordings, e.g. as they are commonly produced by crowds at social events. In my doctoral thesis, I will try to develop synchronization methods further by (a) examining fundamental problems that are usually ignored by lab-developed methods and therefore compromising real-world applications, (b) creating a publicly available synchronization-method benchmarking dataset, and (c) developing a low-level video feature based synchronization method with a computational complexity not higher than current state of the art audio-based methods.

Categories and Subject Descriptors

I.4 [**Image Processing and Computer Vision**]: Miscellaneous; H.5.5 [**Information Interfaces and Presentation**]: Sound and Music Computing—*Signal analysis, synthesis, and processing*

Keywords

Audio, video, features, time drift, synchronization, multimodality, crowd

1. INTRODUCTION

Even though much effort has been put into the domain of multimedia video processing during the last decades, there are still many unsolved or just partially solved problems left to be explored. One of those problems is the automatic synchronization of continuous single-shot videos. I consider videos that have been recorded at the same place (within a restricted and semantically meaningful area, e.g. the area in front of a stage) and the same time (within a restricted time frame, e.g. during the same concert or theatrical performance). Although these videos depict the same visual 3-dimensional scene mapped to a sequence of 2-dimensional image frames, their content often differs in terms of perspective, movement, recording parameters, frame rate, data format, or resolution. These differences result from the usage of different types of cameras, experience of the operators and intended purposes of recording. Synchronizing all those recordings from an event opens up various interesting use cases like detecting key moments by looking at the frequency of concurrent recordings, temporal stitching of clips to get a complete and continuous coverage of a whole event, creating vivid videos by switching between different perspectives or showing different shots side-by-side, improving presentation quality by picking the best audio and video tracks from concurrent recordings, or reconstructing 3D scenes from recordings of different angles. A popular use case for synchronization are musical or theatrical stage performances where usually many people capture video clips with ubiquitous devices like cameras and smartphones, and newly emerging devices like action cameras and video recording glasses might promote this use case even more. Another important use case are coordinated amateur productions involving multiple consumer recording devices. Although the synchronization of temporally and spatially overlapping videos can be done manually, it is a very tedious and time-consuming task waiting to be solved or at least supported by automatic methods. Currently published methods are still very limited and often not prepared for real-world use.

MM'14, November 3–7, 2014, Orlando, FL, USA.

http://dx.doi.org/10.1145/2647868.2654862 .

2. GOALS

The purpose of my dissertation is to improve the current state of the art in synchronization of continuous single-shot videos towards a precision that mitigates all time-offset distractions and other irregularities that spoil the feeling of synchrony, and to proceed from laboratory concepts towards real-world use. I want to investigate and find methods to achieve precise temporal synchronization of videos without explicitly examining their semantics and without complex high-level processing. The ultimate goal is to reach a level at which the synchronization is so accurate, that a human does not notice any unexpected or negative effects when watching synchronized videos side-by-side and hearing a mix of all the videos' audio signals. While this is not a use case itself, it guarantees a level of synchronization quality that other use cases can be built upon. Reaching this level might be a long way, but my work will set the first steps towards this direction and towards problems that have not been considered yet. I will specifically focus on the following:

1. **Time drift.** All recording devices have an inherent error of time, which results from inaccuracies and instabilities in hardware crystal oscillators that coordinate the sampling and frame rates. This drift is individual in each device, and a deviation from the nominal sampling rate leads to changes in the recording speed. This makes recordings from different devices incompatible, because their recordings basically exist on different time bases, making parallel playback impossible. The drift is not always noticeable as it depends on different parameters, e.g. the relative drift between devices used in a recording session, and the lengths of the individual recordings. Professional studios and production companies use specialized equipment fed by a common clock signal to avoid the problem, but such devices are usually too expensive for amateurs, and not an option for crowds. This drift needs to be detected and avoided or removed to get a constant synchronization accuracy over time. Just calculating the offset between two videos [6, 9] is insufficient because it aligns them only at a single point and synchronization is lost with increasing distance to that point.
2. **Benchmarking.** Although many synchronization methods exist in the literature, they cannot be objectively compared because their evaluation is usually carried out on custom datasets, which are sometimes very far from a real-world use case. An accurate ground truth for a big dataset would allow a comparison in terms of computational complexity, spacial complexity, synchronization rate, and synchronization accuracy.
3. **Audio/video offsets.** Offsets between the audio and video track of a recording are either introduced by the system, e.g. the encoding pipeline, or by the difference between the speed of sound and light. Recording a scene from up-front and 300 meters distance yields an audio delay of one second between the two recordings at recording time. Audio-based synchronization of the two recordings therefore leads to an offset of one second between the corresponding video tracks, leading to undesired effects when displaying them side by side or switching between them. This means that a good synchronization result requires additional multimodal processing to remove these offsets.
4. **Pure video synchronization.** Purely video-based synchronization methods usually demand complex high-level processing, e.g. feature trajectories [8], or are tied to special use cases, e.g. still camera flashes [9]. I anticipate a video-based algorithm for general use with lower computational complexity compared to currently published methods.

3. RELATED WORK

The related work on this topic is manifold, spanning from the basics of low and high level audio and video processing, fingerprinting, indexing, feature (series) correlation, over to audio, video and multimodal synchronization methods, up to applications like recording quality assessment, automatic (a.k.a. virtual) directing, summary generation, 3D scene reconstruction, and forensics.

Automatic temporal synchronization methods can generally be divided into three types: audio-based [5], video-based [8], and multimodal [6, 9], which is usually a combination of audio- and video-based methods. They are often built upon fingerprinting algorithms and cross-correlation of low-level features or events (e.g. audio frequency or video motion onsets). The prevalent use of audio data as a synchronization reference is a reasonable choice due to the usually omnidirectional pickup patterns of microphones, compared to the strong directionality of video frames. While many methods have their basic building blocks in common, the actual implementations vary greatly, and their evaluations vary even more – they are usually carried out on custom datasets which makes a comparison in terms of runtime, memory consumption, and particularly the synchronization rate and quality, impossible. If datasets are too small, they might (un)intentionally mask problems of complexity. If clips are too short or taken from homogeneous sources, they might mask drift. If the media quality of clips is too high or recorded in lab settings, they might mask low robustness. There are also methods that impose constraints which I want to avoid, because they cannot be used in the uncontrolled domain of user generated recordings. For example, crowd sourced videos cannot be synchronized if there are hard constraints that demand stationary cameras, or manual configuration of cameras. Soft constraints can be fulfilled by post processing, e.g. identical sampling rates can be achieved by resampling. A recent but not exhaustive overview of multi-camera synchronization methods can be found in [6].

4. APPROACH

Since it is not known which features and methods are suitable for the synchronization task, an iterative prototype-driven development approach will be used. Prototypes will be benchmarked by classic measures like precision and recall, ROC curves and F-score.

The first step in this project is to create a precise synchronization ground truth which my developed methods can be evaluated on. As mentioned in Section 3, there is no published dataset available without heavy downsides, and above all, none supplies a clearly defined synchronization ground truth. As a basis, I selected the publicly available Jiku Mobile Video Dataset [7], that contains hundreds of videos recorded by members of the crowd with mobile devices under various conditions at five different musical events, and which therefore perfectly represents a real-world use case. I have additional access to non-public datasets from other research projects. Using a crowd-sourced dataset limits the benchmarking comparability mainly to the crowd use case, but it is an emerging topic and it is also a good check on robustness, as the performance of synchronization methods will tend to perform even better on higher quality recordings like in the case of an amateur production. Creating a synchronization ground truth on this real-world dataset renders also the examination of time drift necessary.

The second step is to extend the audio-based synchronization method from my Master's thesis [1] with short-time video synchronization. This is the first step towards multimodality. At this stage, synchronization points will already be known from the audio synchronization, but they will not be perfectly precise due to some degree of inaccuracy inherent to the audio method, and the video tracks will not

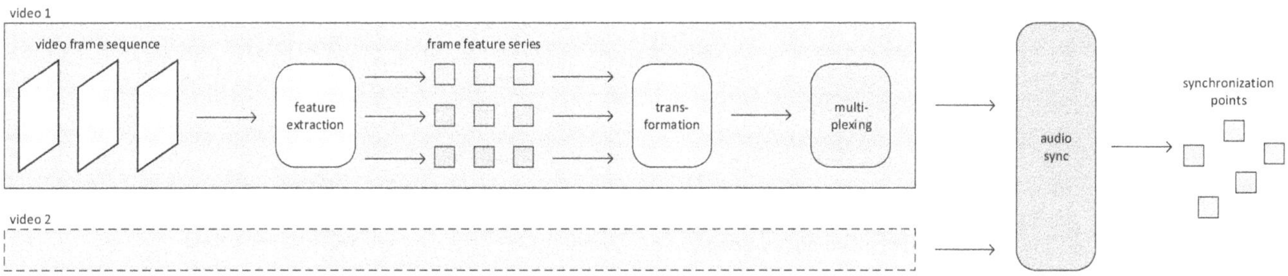

Figure 1: Schematic overview of the anticipated video synchronization system processing two overlapping videos. The final system will be able to process an arbitrary number of videos.

be perfectly in sync due to different speeds of sound and light. Short-time synchronization will try to remove offsets and improve synchronization points, depending on sampling and frame rates, as precise as possible by thoroughly analyzing the multimedia data in a short surrounding interval of a few seconds. The video synchronization extension will be based on local and global low-level features based on color, luminance, or motion, of which possible candidates will be identified and the best fitting ones assessed.

The third step is to develop the video-based synchronization approach into a long-time method, that can process long-running videos in their entirety, with the goal to be usable standalone. Since video frames are usually much less frequent than audio samples, it will not be able to reach an accuracy that is satisfactory enough for related audio tracks, but it will suffice for videos, and it will make the synchronization of videos without audio tracks possible. Section 3 references some already existing video processing synchronization methods, but the novelty of the approach here will be the much higher efficiency through a much lower computational and spacial complexity. I want to introduce a new way of video synchronization by converting the video synchronization problem into an audio synchronization problem through a transformation of multiple time-series of low-level feature values into a single audio-like signal in the audio sample or frequency domain, as sketched in Figure 1. This distantly relates to sonification, where non-audio data gets transformed to audio signals. It will enable the use of the already manifold existing audio synchronization algorithms and audio processing tools and save a lot of time and effort in designing and implementing new video synchronization tools. Focus will be put on the robustness of the method to avoid unnecessary restrictions on applicable use cases. I will conclude with an evaluation of the performance of multimodal synchronization by combining the synchronization results obtained from audio and video.

5. RESULTS

The starting point and foundation of this work is my Master's thesis [1] and the developed synchronization software presented in [2]. In the thesis, I have developed a synchronization method based on audio fingerprinting. Due to its low computational demands, it can be applied to large collections of recordings at once, and I evaluated it on various datasets for real-world applicability. It synchronizes all recordings that belong together (also non-overlapping ones through transitivity), and separates unrelated clusters of overlapping recordings from each other. Besides the automatic synchronization, the software provides a rich graphical interface to the user. It allows precise manual synchronization of recordings and thorough inspection of the automatically calculated synchronization points. It also provides helpful tools for easy manual detection and compensation of drift. Additionally, it includes functions to refine synchronization points through cross-correlation and the detection of non-linear drift through dynamic time warping, which even allows the synchronization of different interpretations (covers) of the same piece of music through non-linear resampling. Summing up, it is a very helpful toolbox for synchronizing and analyzing synchronization results which I have been using for almost all my follow-up research. It is currently limited to audio processing, but designed for extendibility with additional processing methods.

The first contribution of my dissertation research shows that time drift is a major problem that needs to be taken care of. It affects all recordings from non-professional grade devices, particularly mobile devices. The only exception are special cases where the involved devices suffer from comparable amounts of drift, in which case the effect can be ignored. Detailed measurements have shown that the drift can largely differ between different kinds of device makes and models, but its variance is limited inside a production batch of the same make and model. Due to different influences like temperature, age and power supply, the drift is not linear; its main influence is temperature, but the major part of the drift is a constant originating from production. The measured drift of a device at room temperature turned out to be sufficient for removing most of it in post-processing, e.g. by resampling, which turned out to be the most favorable method for drift removal in audio tracks. Drift removal in video tracks remains an open topic and novel methods need to be sought for, since simple methods like resampling or frame dropping/duplicating leads to highly visible quality degradations. This paper is still in submission.

The second contribution is a mobile app that is capable of instant drift measurements of playback and recording devices [3]. A measurement is always conducted between two devices, where one acts as the source of a test tone, and the other as the target that analyzes the tone. By precisely measuring the frequency shift between the two devices, it can quickly calculate the drift and show it to the user on the fly. This tool serves as technical demo to make the community aware of the problem, but also helps to determine devices that go well together for multi-camera recording, or to remove the drift in post-production.

The third contribution is a synchronization ground truth for the Jiku Mobile Video Dataset by using a semi-automatic approach that focuses on the audio tracks. Reviews from two A-conferences attest the dataset great potential, still it has been rejected for being out of scope which makes it also still being in the submission stage. Reviewers acknowledge the need of such a testing ground and benchmarking dataset in the community for video synchronization techniques. The dataset has been cleaned from drift and hundreds of synchronization points that were used to create the ground truth have been adjusted and validated manually. Based on the ground truth, I was able to show that cross-correlation cannot be used to validate or improve the manually defined synchronization points, backing their high accuracy and validity. By evaluating the fingerprinting synchronization method in my Master's thesis, I have shown that this dataset is a precious tool for the assessment of synchronization algorithms, as it allows for very precise measurements of the overall performance and effects of fine-tuning.

An additional contribution worth pointing out is the evaluation of a developed tablet application for the annotation of endoscopic surgery videos [4]. My dissertation research was originally planned to include semantic synchronization of videos recorded at different times or places but containing semantically similar content, e.g. the same surgery carried out on different patients. Since I have shown that non-linear synchronization of different interpretations of pieces of music can work very well, the idea was to synchronize surgery videos to help surgeons find similar sections in videos of similar surgeries. The purpose of the tablet app was to collect metadata that supports the synchronization, but I had to remove this approach from my dissertation research due to time constraints. If time permits, I will still evaluate the possibility of synchronizing such recordings with the developed video synchronization method combined with dynamic time warping to account for the non-linear mapping of the videos.

6. WORK IN PROGRESS

Current work in progress is the preparation for the development of the video-based synchronization method. I am starting with building a framework for the system depicted in Figure 1, selecting feature candidates, building synthetic test sequences, recording basic real-world test videos, and evaluating their possible usefulness through prototyping. Once potential features have been selected, I will build a processing library that transforms video streams into pseudo-audio streams that can be analyzed by audio synchronization methods. The major challenge will probably be the encoding scheme. I expect that the differences between sequential frame features will be more appropriate than the absolute feature values. Scalar feature value series can presumably be directly encoded as time-series signals, or by amplitude (AM) or frequency modulation (FM) on carrier signals. Complex series, e.g from histograms, can probably be encoded by AM or FM on carrier signals of different frequencies, or encoded in the frequency domain and transformed to the time domain by iFFT. I anticipate a scheme to combine multiple features into one output signal by encoding them into different frequency bands. I also anticipate this idea to work since audio synchronization methods heavily rely on energy peaks or sharp local changes in the spectrogram, and changes in the video signal with an appropriate transformation should yield similar patterns. As a simple example, encoding a signal by taking just the luminance of a video as the single feature will yield a signal that can be similarly analyzed like the flash detection in [9], and adding additional features could make the method more robust and versatile for different use cases. If this turns out to be wrong, it should at least be possible to customize the method for different use cases by selecting individual combinations of features based on the visual properties of the videos to be processed.

7. ACKNOWLEDGMENTS

This work was supported by Lakeside Labs GmbH, Klagenfurt, Austria, and funding from the European Regional Development Fund (ERDF) and the Carinthian Economic Promotion Fund (KWF) under grant 20214/22573/33955.

8. REFERENCES

[1] M. Guggenberger. Synchronisation von Multimediadaten auf Basis von Audiospuren. Master's thesis, Alpen-Adria-Universität Klagenfurt, Austria, 2012.

[2] M. Guggenberger, M. Lux, and L. Böszörmenyi. Audioalign - synchronization of A/V-streams based on audio data. In *Multimedia (ISM), 2012 IEEE International Symposium on*, pages 382–383, 2012.

[3] M. Guggenberger, M. Lux, and L. Böszörmenyi. Clockdrift: A mobile application for measuring drift in multimedia devices. In *Proceedings of the 22st ACM International Conference on Multimedia*, MM '14, New York, NY, USA, 2014. ACM. to appear.

[4] M. Guggenberger, M. Riegler, M. Lux, and P. Halvorsen. Event understanding in endoscopic surgery videos. In *Proceedings of the ACM Multimedia 2014 Workshop on Human Centered Event Understanding*, New York, NY, USA, 2014. ACM. to appear.

[5] L. Kennedy and M. Naaman. Less talk, more rock: Automated organization of community-contributed collections of concert videos. In *Proceedings of the 18th International Conference on World Wide Web*, WWW '09, pages 311–320, New York, NY, USA, 2009. ACM.

[6] A. Llagostera Casanovas and A. Cavallaro. Audio-visual events for multi-camera synchronization. *Multimedia Tools and Applications*, pages 1–24, 2014.

[7] M. Saini, S. P. Venkatagiri, W. T. Ooi, and M. C. Chan. The jiku mobile video dataset. In *Proceedings of the 4th ACM Multimedia Systems Conference*, MMSys '13, pages 108–113, New York, NY, USA, 2013. ACM.

[8] S. Shankar, J. Lasenby, and A. Kokaram. Warping trajectories for video synchronization. In *Proceedings of the 4th ACM/IEEE International Workshop on Analysis and Retrieval of Tracked Events and Motion in Imagery Stream*, ARTEMIS '13, pages 41–48, New York, NY, USA, 2013. ACM.

[9] P. Shrestha, M. Barbieri, H. Weda, and D. Sekulovski. Synchronization of multiple camera videos using audio-visual features. *Multimedia, IEEE Transactions on*, 12(1):79–92, 2010.

libLDB: A Library for Extracting Ultrafast and Distinctive Binary Feature Description

Xin Yang[1], Chong Huang[2], Kwang-Ting (Tim) Cheng[1]

[1]Dept. of ECE, University of California, Santa Barbara, CA 93106, USA

[2]School of ICE, Beijing University of Posts and Telecommunications, Beijing, 100876, China

xinyang@umail.ucsb.edu, chonghuang@umail.ucsb.edu, timcheng@ece.ucsb.edu

ABSTRACT

This paper gives an overview of libLDB — a C++ library for extracting an ultrafast and distinctive binary feature LDB (Local Difference Binary) from an image patch. LDB directly computes a binary string using simple intensity and gradient difference tests on pairwise grid cells within the patch. Relying on integral images, the average intensity and gradients of each grid cell can be obtained by only 4~8 add/subtract operations, yielding an ultrafast runtime. A multiple gridding strategy is applied to capture the distinct patterns of the patch at different spatial granularities, leading to a high distinctiveness of LDB. LDB is very suitable for vision apps which require real-time performance, especially for apps running on mobile handheld devices, such as real-time mobile object recognition and tracking, markerless mobile augmented reality, mobile panorama stitching. This software is available under the GNU General Public License (GPL) v3.

Categories and Subject Descriptors

I.4.7 [Image Processing and Computer Vision]: Feature Measurement – *feature representation*; I.5 [Pattern Recognition]: General

Keywords

Binary feature description, distinctiveness, efficiency, mobile handheld devices, mobile augmented reality, mobile object recognition and tracking

1. INTRODUCTION

Feature point descriptors are widely used in many computer vision tasks such as markerless augmented reality (AR), object recognition and tracking, image retrieval, and simultaneous localization and mapping (SLAM). Their broad applications have driven the development of a plethora of descriptors [1-8]. Notable results include SIFT [5] and SURF [6]. Several open source libraries, such as VLFeat [10], OpenSURF [11], have been released for extracting SIFT and SURF.

MM'14, November 3–7, 2014, Orlando, Florida, USA.

http://dx.doi.org/10.1145/2647868.2654888

With the proliferation of mobile devices equipped with low-cost high-quality cameras, there is an increasing demand of running vision apps on mobile handheld devices. However, SIFT and SURF descriptors which require computation of gradients for every image pixel within an image patch are usually too computationally heavy for low-power mobile devices, especially for apps which demand real-time performance. The increasing demand of running vision apps efficiently on mobile devices stimulates the development of lightweight binary descriptors. BRISK [1], FREAK [2], BRIEF [13] and its variant rBRIEF (or ORB descriptor) [3] are some good examples. These descriptors aim primarily at fast runtime by directly generating bit strings by simple binary tests comparing pixel intensities in a smoothed image patch. In addition, they are also very efficient to store and to match (simply computing the Hamming distance between descriptors via XOR and bit count operations). Optimized implementation of these descriptors has been already included in OpenCV library [12]. However, these binary descriptors utilize overly simplified information, i.e. raw intensities of a subset of pixels within an image patch for binary tests, and thus have low discriminative ability. Lack of distinctiveness incurs lots of false matches when matching between two images or against a large database. A large number of operations are usually required for post-verification methods (e.g. PROSAC [14]) to discover and validate matching consensus, increasing the runtime of the entire process.

In this paper, we introduce an open source package — libLDB, for extracting a new binary descriptor called Local Difference Binary (LDB) [7-9]. libLDB provides a distinctive replacement to existing binary features that has similar construction runtime yet generates much fewer false correspondences and in turn reduces the runtime for the entire matching and post-verification process. libLDB is capable for real-time image matching applications running on both standard PCs and low-power mobile handheld devices, e.g. feature-based object detection and recognition, patching tracking, augmented reality, panorama stitching.

The rest of the paper is organized as follows. Sec. 2 presents a framework of LDB extraction followed by detailed description of the principle components of the library. In sec. 3, we evaluate the performance of LDB for mobile object recognition. Sec. 4 concludes the paper.

2. LIBRARY COMPONENTS

We briefly overview the key idea of LDB followed by detailed description of libLDB implementation, an explanation of how to use libLDB and a simple application demonstration.

Given an image patch, LDB divides the patch into $n \times n$ equal-sized grid cells and extract average intensity I_{avg} and gradients, d_x and d_y, from each grid cell. Then, LDB compares I_{avg}, d_x and d_y between pairwise grid cells respectively: if the comparison result is larger than 0, the corresponding bit is set to 1, otherwise it is set to 0. In this way, we can generate a binary bit string for an image patch. To enhance the robustness of LDB descriptors, we employ Gaussian pyramid and dominant orientation estimation to achieve scale invariance and rotation invariance. In addition, a multiple gridding strategy (i.e. partition a patch into different number of grid cells) is also leveraged to encode the structure of at different spatial granularities, enhancing distinctiveness of LDB.

libLDB implementation consists of 5 principle components: Gaussian pyramid construction, dominant orientation estimation, upright/rotated integral image construction, binary tests on pairwise grid cells, and bit selection and concatenation. Fig.1 illustrates the workflow of LDB feature extraction.

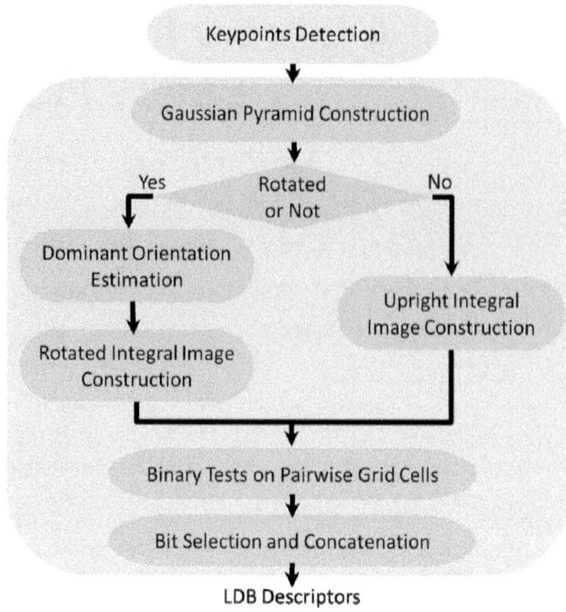

Fig.1: Workflow of LDB feature extraction

2.1 Gaussian Pyramid Construction

In order to achieve scale-invariance for LDB descriptors, we utilize Gaussian pyramid technique and compute LDB descriptors at the corresponding level of the pyramid for detected points. Specifically, given an image $I(x, y)$, we repeatedly smooth the image with Gaussian filters $G(x, y, \sigma_i)$ with increasing sigma values σ_i to construct a Gaussian pyramid Pyr_i ($1 \le i \le L$) (see Eq. 1). In libLDB, the scale factor between consecutive pyramid levels is set to 1.2 and the number of scales is set to 3.

$$Pyr_i = I(x,y) * G(x,y,\sigma_i) = \frac{1}{2\pi\sigma_i} e^{-(x^2+y^2)/2\sigma_i^2}, \quad 1 \le i \le L \tag{1}$$

Once a Gaussian pyramid is constructed, we select a proper level of pyramid to compute LDB descriptors. In particular, for point detectors (e.g. SIFT detector) which provide salient scale of a detected point we crop an $N \times N$ patch centered around the point from the salient scale of the pyramid and then compute a LDB descriptor from the patch. For other detectors (e.g. ORB detector) which do not estimate the salient scales, for each detected point we crop patches at all levels of pyramid and compute LDB descriptors for them.

2.2 Dominant Orientation Estimation

Rotation-invariance is achieved by computing a dominant orientation for every image patch and rotating a patch to its dominant orientation before computing its LDB descriptor. Many dominate orientation estimation methods can be used and libLDB implements the intensity moments-based method for its efficiency and robustness. Specifically, the intensity moment of a patch is defined as:

$$m_{pq} = \sum_{x,y} x^p y^q I(x,y) \tag{2}$$

where $I(x,y)$ is image intensity of location (x, y). With the intensity moments of a patch, the intensity centroid of the patch is defined as:

$$C = (\frac{m_{10}}{m_{00}}, \frac{m_{01}}{m_{00}}) \tag{3}$$

In most scenarios intensity centroid of a patch is offset from its geometric center. According to this fact, we construct a vector $\overrightarrow{OC}$ from the geometric center O to the intensity centroid C. The orientation of the patch then simply is:

$$\theta = \tan^{-1}(m_{01}, m_{10}) = \tan^{-1}\left(\frac{\sum_{x,y} yI(x,y)}{\sum_{x,y} xI(x,y)}\right) \tag{4}$$

2.3 Integral Image Construction

libLDB leverages the integral image technique to efficiently compute average intensity I_{avg} and gradients d_x and d_y within a grid cell. Each value of an *upright integral image* at location (x, y) is calculated by summing up intensities above and to the left of (x, y). Accordingly, I_{avg}, d_x and d_y of a grid cell can be computed using 20 add/sub operations and two divide operations in total.

However, in order to achieve rotation invariance, image patches are rotated to their respective dominant orientations. In this case, the *upright integral image* of an entire image cannot be directly used because the patch axis is not parallel to the integral image axis. For these scenarios, libLDB provides an implementation for computing *rotated integral image* for each rotated patch. The rotated integral image of a patch is calculated by summing up pixels along the dominant orientation instead of the horizontal axis. Based on the *rotated integral image* of the patch, we can efficiently compute I_{avg}, d_x and d_y of any grid cell within the patch.

Two major computations for generating a *rotated integral image* lie in the calculation of rotated coordinates and interpolation for a steered patch. Intuitively, an efficient way to runtime of these two computations is to quantize the orientations and pre-storing the rotated coordinates in a lookup table. However, experimental results show that a fine orientation quantization usually leads to a large lookup table, and in turn, results in long runtime due to slow memory access. Therefore, libLDB computes rotated coordinates and uses nearest neighbor interpolation to generate a steered patch on-the-fly. Experimental result on Thinpad T420 shows that this implementation is faster than performing orientation quantization and using a lookup table.

2.4 Binary Tests on Pairwise Grid Cells

Once an upright integral image or rotated integral images are constructed, libLDB divides each image patch into $n \times n$ equal-sized grids, extract average intensity and gradients from each grid cell and perform binary test τ on a pair of grid cells (i and j) as:

$$\tau(Func(i), Func(j)) := \begin{cases} 1 & if(Func(i), Func(j)) > 0 \ and \ i \neq j, \\ 0 & otherwise \end{cases} \quad (5)$$

where $Func(\cdot) = \{I_{avg}, d_x, d_y\}$.

The choice of the grid size n influences both robustness and distinctiveness of the LDB descriptor. Fine gridding enhances the distinctiveness of LDB while degrades its robustness since corresponding grids of two similar patches could be misaligned even for a small amount of patch shifting. Coarse gridding, on the other hand, results in a more stable but less distinctive descriptor. In libLDB implements a multiple gridding strategy, i.e. each image patch is partitioned in multiple ways (i.e. 2×2, 3×3, 4×4, and 5×5 in libLDB) from each of which a LDB binary string is derived. The strings resulting from all the partitions are then concatenated to form an initial LDB descriptor.

2.5 Bit Selection and Concatenation

Performing binary tests on pairwise grid cells at four gridding levels (i.e. 2×2, 3×3, 4×4 and 5×5) results in a string of 1386 bits. Many of those bits are actually correlated with each other and may not be distinctive enough. We select a subset of salient bits out the entire bit set by a modified AdaBoost method [8]. In libLDB, we provided the 256 selected bit indexes which were trained based on the Library dataset [15]. Finally, libLDB concatenates those selected bits to form a 32-byte binary description.

2.6 How to Use libLDB

libLDB provides two public functions for users to call:

1) **LDB::LDB(int _patchSize):** a constructor in which parameters of LDB are initialize. Users can determine the patch size for computing LDB descriptors. By default, this value is set to 48.
2) **void LDB::compute(const Mat& _image, vector& _keypoints, Mat& _descriptors, bool _flag)**: a function which performs LDB feature extraction for an input grayscale image.
   _image: an input grayscale image

   _keypoints: input keypoints detected by a point detector

   _descriptors: output 32-byte LDB binary descriptors

   _flag: an input Boolean parameter determines whether LDB descriptors are steered or not. If it is set to 1, dominate orientation for every keypoint will be estimated and *rotated integral images* are calculated; otherwise, *upright integral image* of an entire image is calculated.

(a)

(b)

(c)

Fig.2: Matching results of LDB for image pairs with perspective changes (a), rotation changes (b) and scale changes (c), respectively.

We provide a sample code to demonstrate how to use libLDB for LDB extraction and image matching based on LDB. In this demo, we detect keypoints using ORB point detector and compute LDB descriptors. Then, for each keypoint we search its nearest neighbor using a brute-force matching. The putative matches (e.g. the ratio between the shortest and second shortest distance is lower 0.8) are then used in RANSAC-based homography estimation. The demo is developed based on Red Hat Enterprise Linux Server release 5.5 (Tikanga), OpenCV 2.4.0 and GCC 4.7.1.

Users can use the command **"./ldb _image1 _image2 _flag"** to execute the demo. **_image1** and **_image2** indicate the path of two input images respectively and **_flag** is a Boolean parameter determines which LDB is steered or not. Fig. 2 illustrates the outputs of demo, i.e. matching results of LDB for three images pairs with perspective changes, rotation changes and scale changes respectively. Lines indicate corresponding feature points matched based on LDB and green boxes indicate the homograph changes between two images.

3. PERFORMANCE

We evaluated the performance of LDB for mobile object recognition task by implementing a conventional pipeline. Specifically, the pipeline includes the following three steps: 1) ORB keypoint detection and LDB descriptor construction, 2) candidate images selection by matching each query LDB descriptor to all LDB descriptors in the database and returning

Desc.	Detection Rate (%)	Precision (%)	Constr. Time (ms)	Recog. Time (ms)
ORB-32	93.3	98.6	0.146	7.26
LDB-32	96.3	99.0	0.139	2.55
BRISK-64	97.7	99.4	0.034	7.64
FREAK-64	98.3	99.5	0.108	24.65
SURF-64	83.8	92.9	1.488	-

Table 1: Comparing performance of descriptors for recognizing 1140 manually captured images on Google Nexus 4 smartphone.

top-ranked database image with most matches as candidate images, and 3) post verification to select the most relevant image with most number of consistent matches.

The evaluation is performed on a database contains 228 planar objects [16], including 109 document images and 119 natural images. For each database image, we manually captured five pictures as the query images: one was taken with minor geometric changes and the other four were taken with up-scaling, down-scaling, rotation and shifting changes respectively. As a result, there are a total of 1140 query images.

In our experiment, with ORB, BRISK, FREAK and LDB all being binary descriptors, Locality Sensitive Hashing (LSH) is chosen for approximate nearest neighbor (ANN) search instead of brute-forcing matching.

We employ five metrics for performance evaluation:
1) *Detection Rate*: the number of correctly recognized objects over the total number of objects;
2) *Precision*: the number of correctly recognized objects over the total number of recognized objects;
3) *Construction Time*: the average time cost for constructing a descriptor;
4) *Recognition Time*: the average time cost for searching the ANN of a query descriptor from the database;
All the time cost is recorded based on running the code on a single core of Google Nexus 4, operating at 1.5GHz and using Android 4.2 Jelly Bean operating system. The memory cost is read from the task manager of a PC.

Table 1 shows the comparison results. According to the results, LDB-32 achieves similar detection rate and precision as state-of-the-art binary descriptors. Considering the total time cost including runtimes for both descriptor constrcution and matching, LDB-32 is 2.8X faster than ORB, ~3X faster than BRISK and 9.5X faster than FREAK.

4. CONCLUSION

We developed an open source library for extracting ultrafast and highly distinctive binary feature LDB. Despite this project is still in an early development stage (without SSE or NEON acceleration on x86 and ARM processors respectively), it already shows fast runtime and good performance of recognition and tracking on mobile devices. Our plan is to further optimize the code and include hardware acceleration. In addition, we also plan to include Android source code of applying LDB to mobile object recognition and tracking, source code for salient bit selection based on AdaBoost learning.

5. REFERENCES

[1] Leutengger, S., Chli, M., and Siegwart, R.Y., BRISK: Binary Robust Invariant Scalable Keypoints. *In Proc. of International Conference on Computer Vision*, 2011, Barcelona, Spain.

[2] Alahi, A., Ortiz, R., and Vandergheynst, P. FREAK: Fast Retinal Keypoint, *In Proc. of Computer Vision and Pattern Recognition*, 2012.

[3] Rublee, E., Rabaud, V., Konolige, K., and Bradski, G., ORB: An Efficient Alternative to SIFT or SURF. *In Proc. of International Conference on Computer Vision*, 2011, Barcelona, Spain.

[4] Rosten, Edward, and Tom Drummond. Machine learning for high-speed corner detection. *In Proc. of European Conference on Computer Vision*, 2006.

[5] Bay, H., Ess, A., Tuytelaars, T. and Gool, L.V., SURF: Speeded-Up Robust Features. *In Procs. of European Conference on Computer Vision*, 2006.

[6] Lowe, D. G., Distinctive Image Features from Scale-Invariant Keypoints. *In International Journal of Computer Vision*, 60, 2, pp. 91-110, 2004.

[7] Yang, X., and K.-T. Cheng. LDB: An ultra-fast feature for scalable Augmented Reality on mobile devices. *In Proc. of International Symposium on Mixed and Augmented Reality*, 2012.

[8] Yang, X., and K.-T. Cheng. Learning Optimized Local Difference Binaries for Scalable Augmented Reality on Mobile Devices. *IEEE Transaction on Visualization and Computer Graphics*, 2014.

[9] Yang, X., and K.-T. Cheng. Local Difference Binary for Ultra-fast and Distinctive Feature Description. *IEEE Transaction on Pattern Recognition and Machine Intelligence*, vol. 36, no. 1, 2014.

[10] VLFeat: http://www.vlfeat.org/

[11] OpenSURF: http://www.chrisevansdev.com/computer-vision-opensurf.html

[12] OpenCV: http://www.chrisevansdev.com/computer-vision-opensurf.html

[13] Calonder, M., Lepetit, V., Strecha, C., and Fua, P., Brief: Binary Robust Independent Elementary Features. *In Proc. of European Conference on Computer Vision*, 2010.

[14] Chum, O., and Matas, J., Matching with PROSAC — progressive sample consensus. *In Proc. of Computer Vision and Pattern Recognition*, vol 1, p: 220–226, 2005.

[15] Winder, S., Hua, G., and Brown, M., Picking the Best DAISY, *In Proc. of Computer Vision and Pattern Recognition*, 2009.

[16] Yang, X., Liu, Q., Liao, C.Y., and Cheng, K.-T. Large-scale EMM identification Based on Geometry-Constrained Visual Word Correspondence Voting. *In Proc. of ACM International Conference on Multimedia retrieval*, 2011.

Caffe: Convolutional Architecture for Fast Feature Embedding*

Yangqing Jia*, Evan Shelhamer*, Jeff Donahue, Sergey Karayev,
Jonathan Long, Ross Girshick, Sergio Guadarrama, Trevor Darrell
UC Berkeley EECS, Berkeley, CA 94702
{jiayq,shelhamer,jdonahue,sergeyk,jonlong,rbg,sguada,trevor}@eecs.berkeley.edu

ABSTRACT

Caffe provides multimedia scientists and practitioners with a clean and modifiable framework for state-of-the-art deep learning algorithms and a collection of reference models. The framework is a BSD-licensed C++ library with Python and MATLAB bindings for training and deploying general-purpose convolutional neural networks and other deep models efficiently on commodity architectures. Caffe fits industry and internet-scale media needs by CUDA GPU computation, processing over 40 million images a day on a single K40 or Titan GPU ($\approx$ 2.5 ms per image). By separating model representation from actual implementation, Caffe allows experimentation and seamless switching among platforms for ease of development and deployment from prototyping machines to cloud environments.

Caffe is maintained and developed by the Berkeley Vision and Learning Center (BVLC) with the help of an active community of contributors on GitHub. It powers ongoing research projects, large-scale industrial applications, and startup prototypes in vision, speech, and multimedia.

Categories and Subject Descriptors

I.5.1 [**Pattern Recognition**]: [Applications–Computer vision]; D.2.2 [**Software Engineering**]: [Design Tools and Techniques–Software libraries]; I.5.1 [**Pattern Recognition**]: [Models–Neural Nets]

General Terms

Algorithms, Design, Experimentation

Keywords

Open Source; Computer Vision; Neural Networks; Parallel Computation; Machine Learning

*Corresponding Authors. The work was done while Yangqing Jia was a graduate student at Berkeley. He is currently a research scientist at Google, 1600 Amphitheater Pkwy, Mountain View, CA 94043.

MM'14, November 3–7, 2014, Orlando, Florida, USA.

ACM 978-1-4503-3063-3/14/11 ...$15.00.
http://dx.doi.org/10.1145/2647868.2654889.

1. INTRODUCTION

A key problem in multimedia data analysis is discovery of effective representations for sensory inputs—images, soundwaves, haptics, etc. While performance of conventional, handcrafted features has plateaued in recent years, new developments in deep compositional architectures have kept performance levels rising [8]. Deep models have outperformed hand-engineered feature representations in many domains, and made learning possible in domains where engineered features were lacking entirely.

We are particularly motivated by large-scale visual recognition, where a specific type of deep architecture has achieved a commanding lead on the state-of-the-art. These *Convolutional Neural Networks*, or CNNs, are discriminatively trained via back-propagation through layers of convolutional filters and other operations such as rectification and pooling. Following the early success of digit classification in the 90's, these models have recently surpassed all known methods for large-scale visual recognition, and have been adopted by industry heavyweights such as Google, Facebook, and Baidu for image understanding and search.

While deep neural networks have attracted enthusiastic interest within computer vision and beyond, replication of published results can involve months of work by a researcher or engineer. Sometimes researchers deem it worthwhile to release trained models along with the paper advertising their performance. But trained models alone are not sufficient for rapid research progress and emerging commercial applications, and few toolboxes offer truly off-the-shelf deployment of state-of-the-art models—and those that do are often not computationally efficient and thus unsuitable for commercial deployment.

To address such problems, we present Caffe, a fully open-source framework that affords clear access to deep architectures. The code is written in clean, efficient C++, with CUDA used for GPU computation, and nearly complete, well-supported bindings to Python/Numpy and MATLAB. Caffe adheres to software engineering best practices, providing unit tests for correctness and experimental rigor and speed for deployment. It is also well-suited for research use, due to the careful modularity of the code, and the clean separation of network definition (usually the novel part of deep learning research) from actual implementation.

In Caffe, multimedia scientists and practitioners have an orderly and extensible toolkit for state-of-the-art deep learning algorithms, with reference models provided out of the box. Fast CUDA code and GPU computation fit industry needs by achieving processing speeds of more than 40 mil-

Framework	License	Core language	Binding(s)	CPU	GPU	Open source	Training	Pretrained models	Development
Caffe	BSD	C++	Python, MATLAB	✓	✓	✓	✓	✓	distributed
cuda-convnet [7]	unspecified	C++	Python		✓	✓	✓		discontinued
Decaf [2]	BSD	Python		✓		✓	✓	✓	discontinued
OverFeat [9]	unspecified	Lua	C++,Python	✓				✓	centralized
Theano/Pylearn2 [4]	BSD	Python		✓	✓	✓	✓		distributed
Torch7 [1]	BSD	Lua		✓	✓	✓	✓		distributed

Table 1: Comparison of popular deep learning frameworks. *Core language* is the main library language, while *bindings* have an officially supported library interface for feature extraction, training, etc. *CPU* indicates availability of host-only computation, no GPU usage (e.g., for cluster deployment); *GPU* indicates the GPU computation capability essential for training modern CNNs.

lion images per day on a single K40 or Titan GPU. The same models can be run in CPU or GPU mode on a variety of hardware: Caffe separates the representation from the actual implementation, and seamless switching between heterogeneous platforms furthers development and deployment—Caffe can even be run in the cloud.

While Caffe was first designed for vision, it has been adopted and improved by users in speech recognition, robotics, neuroscience, and astronomy. We hope to see this trend continue so that further sciences and industries can take advantage of deep learning.

Caffe is maintained and developed by the BVLC with the active efforts of several graduate students, and welcomes open-source contributions at `http://github.com/BVLC/caffe`. We thank all of our contributors for their work!

2. HIGHLIGHTS OF CAFFE

Caffe provides a complete toolkit for training, testing, finetuning, and deploying models, with well-documented examples for all of these tasks. As such, it's an ideal starting point for researchers and other developers looking to jump into state-of-the-art machine learning. At the same time, it's likely the fastest available implementation of these algorithms, making it immediately useful for industrial deployment.

Modularity. The software is designed from the beginning to be as modular as possible, allowing easy extension to new data formats, network layers, and loss functions. Lots of layers and loss functions are already implemented, and plentiful examples show how these are composed into trainable recognition systems for various tasks.

Separation of representation and implementation. Caffe model definitions are written as config files using the Protocol Buffer language. Caffe supports network architectures in the form of arbitrary directed acyclic graphs. Upon instantiation, Caffe reserves exactly as much memory as needed for the network, and abstracts from its underlying location in host or GPU. Switching between a CPU and GPU implementation is exactly one function call.

Test coverage. Every single module in Caffe has a test, and no new code is accepted into the project without corresponding tests. This allows rapid improvements and refactoring of the codebase, and imparts a welcome feeling of peacefulness to the researchers using the code.

Python and MATLAB bindings. For rapid prototyping and interfacing with existing research code, Caffe provides Python and MATLAB bindings. Both languages may be used to construct networks and classify inputs. The Python bindings also expose the solver module for easy prototyping of new training procedures.

Pre-trained reference models. Caffe provides (for academic and non-commercial use—not BSD license) reference models for visual tasks, including the landmark "AlexNet" ImageNet model [8] with variations and the R-CNN detection model [3]. More are scheduled for release. We are strong proponents of reproducible research: we hope that a common software substrate will foster quick progress in the search over network architectures and applications.

2.1 Comparison to related software

We summarize the landscape of convolutional neural network software used in recent publications in Table 1. While our list is incomplete, we have included the toolkits that are most notable to the best of our knowledge. Caffe differs from other contemporary CNN frameworks in two major ways:

(1) The implementation is completely C++ based, which eases integration into existing C++ systems and interfaces common in industry. The CPU mode removes the barrier of specialized hardware for deployment and experiments once a model is trained.

(2) Reference models are provided off-the-shelf for quick experimentation with state-of-the-art results, without the need for costly re-learning. By finetuning for related tasks, such as those explored by [2], these models provide a warm-start to new research and applications. Crucially, we publish not only the trained models but also the recipes and code to reproduce them.

3. ARCHITECTURE

3.1 Data Storage

Caffe stores and communicates data in 4-dimensional arrays called *blobs*.

Blobs provide a unified memory interface, holding batches of images (or other data), parameters, or parameter updates. Blobs conceal the computational and mental overhead of mixed CPU/GPU operation by synchronizing from the CPU host to the GPU device as needed. In practice, one loads data from the disk to a blob in CPU code, calls a CUDA kernel to do GPU computation, and ferries the blob off to the next layer, ignoring low-level details while maintaining a high level of performance. Memory on the host and device is allocated on demand (lazily) for efficient memory usage.

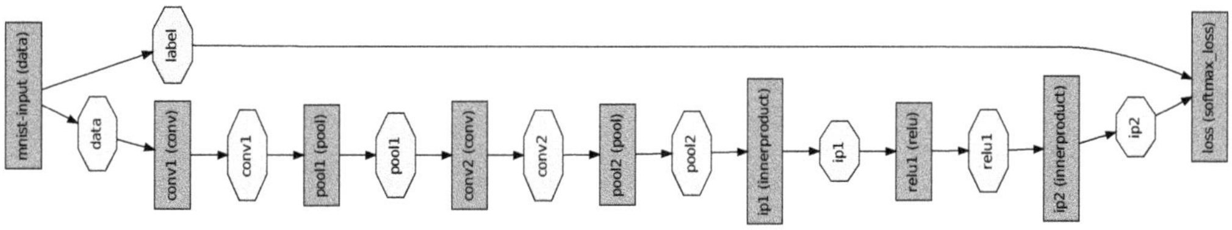

Figure 1: An MNIST digit classification example of a Caffe network, where blue boxes represent layers and yellow octagons represent data blobs produced by or fed into the layers.

Models are saved to disk as Google Protocol Buffers[1], which have several important features: minimal-size binary strings when serialized, efficient serialization, a human-readable text format compatible with the binary version, and efficient interface implementations in multiple languages, most notably C++ and Python.

Large-scale data is stored in LevelDB[2] databases. In our test program, LevelDB and Protocol Buffers provide a throughput of 150MB/s on commodity machines with minimal CPU impact. Thanks to layer-wise design (discussed below) and code modularity, we have recently added support for other data sources, including some contributed by the open source community.

3.2 Layers

A Caffe layer is the essence of a neural network layer: it takes one or more blobs as input, and yields one or more blobs as output. Layers have two key responsibilities for the operation of the network as a whole: a *forward pass* that takes the inputs and produces the outputs, and a *backward pass* that takes the gradient with respect to the output, and computes the gradients with respect to the parameters and to the inputs, which are in turn back-propagated to earlier layers.

Caffe provides a complete set of layer types including: convolution, pooling, inner products, nonlinearities like rectified linear and logistic, local response normalization, elementwise operations, and losses like softmax and hinge. These are all the types needed for state-of-the-art visual tasks. Coding custom layers requires minimal effort due to the compositional construction of networks.

3.3 Networks and Run Mode

Caffe does all the bookkeeping for any directed acyclic graph of layers, ensuring correctness of the forward and backward passes. Caffe models are end-to-end machine learning systems. A typical network begins with a data layer that loads from disk and ends with a loss layer that computes the objective for a task such as classification or reconstruction.

The network is run on CPU or GPU by setting a single switch. Layers come with corresponding CPU and GPU routines that produce identical results (with tests to prove it). The CPU/GPU switch is seamless and independent of the model definition.

3.4 Training A Network

Caffe trains models by the fast and standard stochastic gradient descent algorithm. Figure 1 shows a typical example of a Caffe network (for MNIST digit classification) during training: a data layer fetches the images and labels from disk, passes it through multiple layers such as convolution, pooling and rectified linear transforms, and feeds the final prediction into a classification loss layer that produces the loss and gradients which train the whole network. This example is found in the Caffe source code at `examples/lenet/lenet_train.prototxt`. Data are processed in mini-batches that pass through the network sequentially. Vital to training are learning rate decay schedules, momentum, and snapshots for stopping and resuming, all of which are implemented and documented.

Figure 2: An example of the Caffe object classification demo. Try it out yourself online!

Finetuning, the adaptation of an existing model to new architectures or data, is a standard method in Caffe. From a snapshot of an existing network and a model definition for the new network, Caffe finetunes the old model weights for the new task and initializes new weights as needed. This capability is essential for tasks such as knowledge transfer [2], object detection [3], and object retrieval [5].

4. APPLICATIONS AND EXAMPLES

In its first six months since public release, Caffe has already been used in a large number of research projects at UC Berkeley and other universities, achieving state-of-the-art performance on a number of tasks. Members of Berkeley EECS have also collaborated with several industry partners such as Facebook [11] and Adobe [6], using Caffe or its direct precursor (Decaf) to obtain state-of-the-art results.

Object Classification Caffe has an online demo[3] showing state-of-the-art object classification on images provided by the users, including via mobile phone. The demo takes the image and tries to categorize it into one of the 1,000 ImageNet categories[4]. A typical classification result is shown in Figure 2.

Furthermore, we have successfully trained a model with all 10,000 categories of the full ImageNet dataset by finetuning this network. The resulting network has been applied to open vocabulary object retrieval [5].

[1] `https://code.google.com/p/protobuf/`
[2] `https://code.google.com/p/leveldb/`
[3] `http://demo.caffe.berkeleyvision.org/`
[4] `http://www.image-net.org/challenges/LSVRC/2013/`

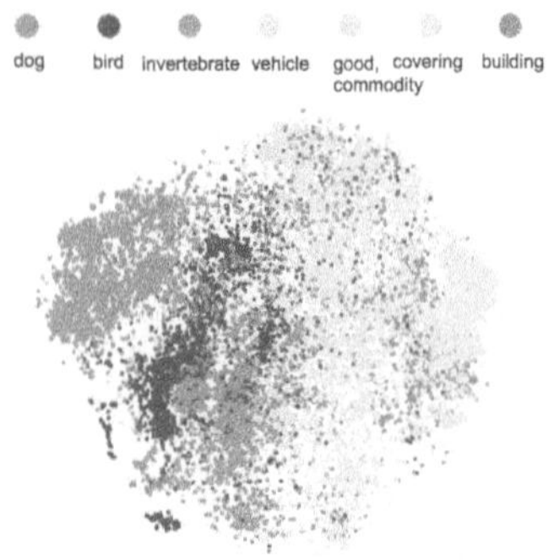

Figure 3: Features extracted from a deep network, visualized in a 2-dimensional space. Note the clear separation between categories, indicative of a successful embedding.

Learning Semantic Features In addition to end-to-end training, Caffe can also be used to extract semantic features from images using a pre-trained network. These features can be used "downstream" in other vision tasks with great success [2]. Figure 3 shows a two-dimensional embedding of all the ImageNet validation images, colored by a coarse category that they come from. The nice separation testifies to a successful semantic embedding.

Intriguingly, this learned feature is useful for a lot more than object categories. For example, Karayev et al. have shown promising results finding images of different styles such as "Vintage" and "Romantic" using Caffe features (Figure 4) [6].

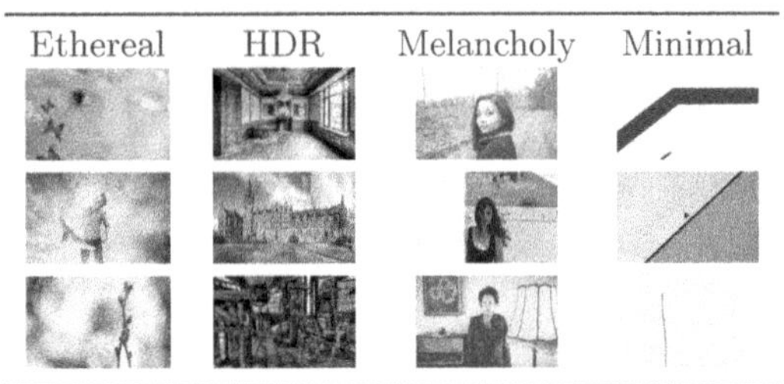

Figure 4: Top three most-confident positive predictions on the Flickr Style dataset, using a Caffe-trained classifier.

Object Detection Most notably, Caffe has enabled us to obtain **by far** the best performance on object detection, evaluated on the hardest academic datasets: the PASCAL VOC 2007-2012 and the ImageNet 2013 Detection challenge [3].

Girshick et al. [3] have combined Caffe together with techniques such as Selective Search [10] to effectively perform simultaneous localization and recognition in natural images. Figure 5 shows a sketch of their approach.

Beginners' Guides To help users get started with installing, using, and modifying Caffe, we have provided instructions and tutorials on the Caffe webpage. The tutorials range from small demos (MNIST digit recognition) to serious deployments (end-to-end learning on ImageNet).

Although these tutorials serve as effective documentation of the functionality of Caffe, the Caffe source code additionally provides detailed inline documentation on all modules.

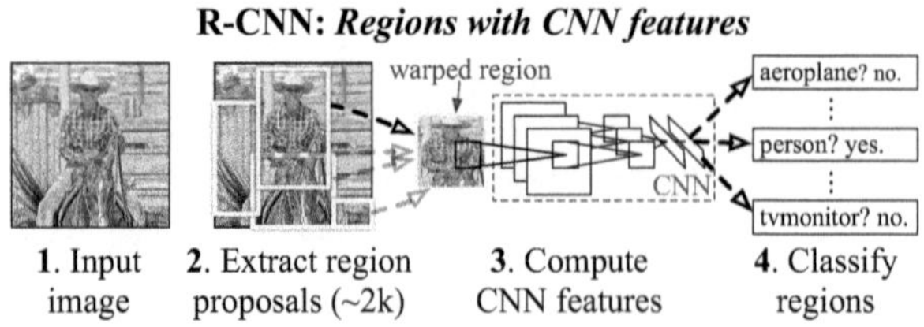

Figure 5: The R-CNN pipeline that uses Caffe for object detection.

This documentation will be exposed in a standalone web interface in the near future.

5. AVAILABILITY

Source code is published BSD-licensed on GitHub.[5] Project details, step-wise tutorials, and pre-trained models are on the homepage.[6] Development is done in Linux and OS X, and users have reported Windows builds. A public Caffe Amazon EC2 instance is coming soon.

6. ACKNOWLEDGEMENTS

We would like to thank NVIDIA for GPU donation, the BVLC sponsors (`http://bvlc.eecs.berkeley.edu/`), and our open source community.

7. REFERENCES

[1] R. Collobert, K. Kavukcuoglu, and C. Farabet. Torch7: A MATLAB-like environment for machine learning. In *BigLearn, NIPS Workshop*, 2011.

[2] J. Donahue, Y. Jia, O. Vinyals, J. Hoffman, N. Zhang, E. Tzeng, and T. Darrell. Decaf: A deep convolutional activation feature for generic visual recognition. In *ICML*, 2014.

[3] R. Girshick, J. Donahue, T. Darrell, and J. Malik. Rich feature hierarchies for accurate object detection and semantic segmentation. In *CVPR*, 2014.

[4] I. Goodfellow, D. Warde-Farley, P. Lamblin, V. Dumoulin, M. Mirza, R. Pascanu, J. Bergstra, F. Bastien, and Y. Bengio. Pylearn2: a machine learning research library. *arXiv preprint 1308.4214*, 2013.

[5] S. Guadarrama, E. Rodner, K. Saenko, N. Zhang, R. Farrell, J. Donahue, and T. Darrell. Open-vocabulary object retrieval. In *RSS*, 2014.

[6] S. Karayev, M. Trentacoste, H. Han, A. Agarwala, T. Darrell, A. Hertzmann, and H. Winnemoeller. Recognizing image style. *arXiv preprint 1311.3715*, 2013.

[7] A. Krizhevsky. cuda-convnet. https://code.google.com/p/cuda-convnet/, 2012.

[8] A. Krizhevsky, I. Sutskever, and G. Hinton. ImageNet classification with deep convolutional neural networks. In *NIPS*, 2012.

[9] P. Sermanet, D. Eigen, X. Zhang, M. Mathieu, R. Fergus, and Y. LeCun. Overfeat: Integrated recognition, localization and detection using convolutional networks. In *ICLR*, 2014.

[10] J. Uijlings, K. van de Sande, T. Gevers, and A. Smeulders. Selective search for object recognition. *IJCV*, 2013.

[11] N. Zhang, M. Paluri, M. Ranzato, T. Darrell, and L. Bourdev. Panda: Pose aligned networks for deep attribute modeling. In *CVPR*, 2014.

[5] `https://github.com/BVLC/caffe/`

[6] `http://caffe.berkeleyvision.org/`

Menpo: A Comprehensive Platform for Parametric Image Alignment and Visual Deformable Models

Joan Alabort-i-Medina*, Epameinondas Antonakos*, James Booth*, Patrick Snape*
and Stefanos Zafeiriou
Department of Computing, Imperial College London
180 Queens Gate, London SW7 2AZ, UK
{ja310, e.antonakos, jab08, p.snape, szafeiri}@imperial.ac.uk

ABSTRACT

The Menpo Project, hosted at `http://www.menpo.io`, is a BSD-licensed software platform providing a complete and comprehensive solution for annotating, building, fitting and evaluating deformable visual models from image data. Menpo is a powerful and flexible cross-platform framework written in Python that works on Linux, OS X and Windows. Menpo has been designed to allow for easy adaptation of Lucas-Kanade (LK) parametric image alignment techniques, and goes a step further in providing all the necessary tools for building and fitting state-of-the-art deformable models such as Active Appearance Models (AAMs), Constrained Local Models (CLMs) and regression-based methods (such as the Supervised Descent Method (SDM)). These methods are extensively used for facial point localisation although they can be applied to many other deformable objects. Menpo makes it easy to understand and evaluate these complex algorithms, providing tools for visualisation, analysis, and performance assessment. A key challenge in building deformable models is data annotation; Menpo expedites this process by providing a simple web-based annotation tool hosted at `http://www.landmarker.io`. The Menpo Project is thoroughly documented and provides extensive examples for all of its features. We believe the project is ideal for researchers, practitioners and students alike.

Categories and Subject Descriptors

I.5.4 [**Pattern Recognition**]: Applications—*computer vision*; D.0 [**Software**]: General

General Terms

Algorithms; Design; Experimentation

*Alphabetical order due to equal contribution

MM '14 November 03 - 07 2014, Orlando, FL, USA

http://dx.doi.org/10.1145/2647868.2654890

Figure 1: The Menpo Project provides all the tools necessary to perform facial point localisation.

Keywords

Active Appearance Models; Constrained Local Models; Supervised Descent Method; Regression; Python

1. INTRODUCTION

Rigid and non-rigid image alignment and the closely related field of visual deformable models (i.e., models of non-rigid visual objects, such as human faces) are all well-studied areas of computer vision, which have created a wealth of scientific research and countless applications. Despite this, there is still a noteworthy lack of high quality open source software in this area. Most existing packages are encrypted, compiled, non-maintained, badly structured or difficult to modify, all characteristics which make them unsuitable for adoption in cutting edge scientific research. Furthermore, the lack of an open source package that implements the most important techniques of the field in a unified manner obstructs the possibility to fairly assess the various methods against one another. We believe that the qualities and characteristics of the Menpo Project make it a suitable candidate to fill this existing gap.

Among the previously mentioned parametric image alignment algorithms, Lucas-Kanade (LK) [1] is arguably the most popular. Active Appearance Models (AAMs) [2] are an extension of LK to the problem of generative deformable model fitting that have recently been shown to achieve state-of-the-art results [3]. Similar performance has been achieved with discriminative part-based model techniques such as Constrained Local Models (CLMs) [4] and the recently proposed Supervised Descent Method (SDM) [5].

Some implementations of the above methods are publicly available. Various implementations of LK are provided in [1] and an implementation of AAM building and fitting is given in [6]. To the best of our knowledge, for the recent state-of-the-art LK [7], AAMs [8,9], CLMs [4] and SDMs [5], only compiled, encrypted, or pre-trained implementations exist (some are provided by our group[1]). In particular, it should be noted that whilst many packages provide fitting algorithms, few provide training code.

Menpo provides robust open source implementations of all the above algorithms and is designed and developed to be flexible and simple to use. One of Menpo's most powerful features is the unification of the algorithms within a single framework, which enables easier investigation of new research areas. Furthermore, it provides implementations of many powerful features and descriptors used in computer vision, such as Local Binary Patterns [10], Histogram of Oriented Gradients (HOGs) [11] and Image Gradient Orientations (IGOs) [7], all of which can be employed in the deformable model algorithms.

2. ARCHITECTURE

Choice of programming language. Menpo is primarily written in Python. The use of Python was motivated by its free availability on all platforms, unlike its major competitor in computer vision, Matlab. We believe this is hugely important for reproducible open science. Python provides a very flexible environment for performing research, and recent innovations such as the IPython notebook [13] have made it incredibly simple to provide documentation via examples. The vast majority of the execution time in Menpo is actually spent in highly efficient numerical libraries and bespoke C++ code, allowing us to achieve sufficient performance for real time facial point tracking whilst not compromising on the huge flexibility that Menpo offers.

Importing assets. Menpo can ingest a large range of 2D and 3D asset and annotation formats, and normalises differences between formats to provide consistent data to users. All major image types are supported, along with a number of common annotation formats used within the computer vision community. Because Menpo has been built with extensibility in mind, adding support for new asset formats is very simple. Since deformable modelling commonly requires pre-annotated data, Menpo will automatically import all annotation formats that have the same name as an importable file. For example, importing an entire facial database of images along with their annotations is as simple as:

```
import menpo.io as mio
images = list(mio.import_images("./trainset/*"))
```

High-level types. At Menpo's core are powerful `Image` and `PointCloud` classes. All types support rich introspection and visualisation, which is of huge benefit when working interactively in an IPython Notebook. The `Transform` subclasses in Menpo provide a simple interface for manipulating data inside container types. All Menpo container types are transformable, and when a transform is applied on a container, all attached data is transformed too. For example, when rotating an image any attached landmarks are also rotated.

Vector representation. Computer vision algorithms are frequently formulated as linear algebra problems in high dimensional spaces, where each image is stripped into a vector form. Unfortunately, it is rare for the complete problem to be formulated in such a manner, as some operations still need to be applied in the image domain (e.g. calculating the gradient). Menpo bridges this gap by supporting bi-directional vectorisation of data through its `Vectorizable` interface. Through this, any type can be safely and efficiently converted to a vector form and back again, allowing for algorithms to be efficiently marshaled into vector and matrix forms.

3. ALGORITHMS

Menpo contains at its core two major families of algorithms: generative LK techniques, including AAMs, and discriminative part-based models, which consist of CLMs and SDMs. For all algorithms training and fitting implementations are provided, something which uniquely differentiates Menpo from other packages.

Lucas-Kanade. The LK family of algorithms seek to minimise the discrepancies between a given input image and either a template image (LK) or an appearance model (AAM). This is achieved in a generative manner, whereby parameters are computed in order to correctly warp one of the images into the reference frame of the other. Optimisation of these parameters is usually achieved via a Gauss-Newton approximation and a number of formulations of the cost function have been proposed. Within Menpo, we have implementations of all major LK algorithms [1] (forward additive/compositional, inverse additive/compositional) and all major AAM algorithms (project-out [1] and alternating [9]). Building and fitting an AAM is extremely simple, requiring only 4 lines of code:

```
from menpo.fitmultilevel.aam import *
aam = AAMBuilder().build(images)  # Build
aam_fit = LucasKanadeAAMFitter(aam)  # Fit
result = aam_fit.fit(test_image, initial_shape)
```

CLMs are part-based deformable models that fit global parametric models of shape to images by maximising the joint probability of their landmarks being correctly aligned. To this end, a set of individual discriminative classifiers that model the probability of each landmark being correctly aligned are learnt from the local appearance region around each landmark. Fitting consists of maximising the joint probability of each classifier whilst ensuring that the final shape is highly plausible under the global parametric shape model. Menpo has an implementation of the well-known Regularized-Landmark Mean-Shift algorithm proposed by Saragih et. al in [4]. The obvious advantage of Menpo's implementation with respect to other existing implementations is the ease with which new appearance representations and different discriminative classifiers can be incorporated in to the existing framework.

Regression-based techniques aim at solving the same type of problem solved by deformable models such as AAMs

[1]We have recorded more than 10K downloads for our implementations of some of the above techniques in the past couple of years.

[2]`http://www.visionopen.com/downloads/open-source-software/vosm/`

Table 1: Comparison of existing implementations. No other package provides implementations of training and fitting for the AAM, CLM and regression-based methods.

Tool	Environment	License	LK Image Alignment	AAM		CLM		Regression	
				Train	Fit	Train	Fit	Train	Fit
Menpo	Python	BSD	+	+	+	+	+	+	+
DeMoLib [6]	C++	Academic	-	+	+	-	-	-	-
Intraface [5]	C++/Matlab	Academic	-	-	-	-	-	-	+
FaceTracker [4]	C++	Academic	-	-	-	-	+	-	-
DRMF [12]	Matlab	Academic	-	-	-	-	+	-	-
VOSM[2]	C++	LGPL	-	+	+	-	-	-	-
[1]	Matlab	-	+	-	-	-	-	-	-

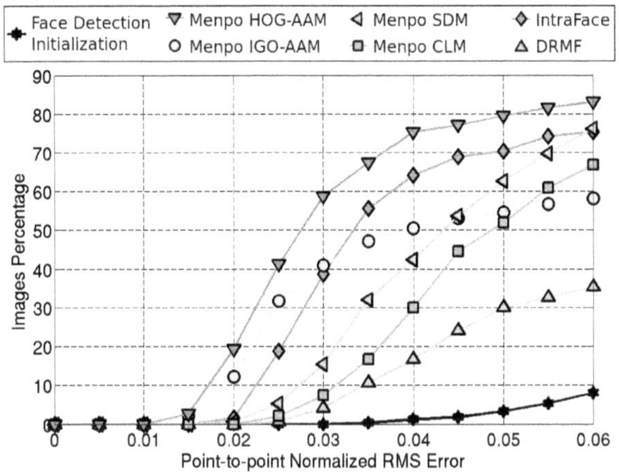

Figure 2: Performance comparison between some of Menpo's basic methods (SDM, CLMs, HOG and IGO AAMs) and two other available packages (Intraface [5] and DRMF with CLMs [12]) on AFW database.

or CLMs; i.e. finding the optimal position of the set of landmarks describing the shape of an object of interest in an image. These techniques attempt to solve the problem by generally learning a cascade of functional mappings (commonly referred to as a cascade of regressors) between the object appearance and the optimal landmark configuration. Due to the availability of high quality annotated data in some areas of computer vision (such as non-rigid face alignment), these techniques have become effective and extremely attractive due to their extremely low computational fitting complexity. Menpo provides a complete framework for developing cascade-regression methods for object landmark localisation. More specifically, Menpo provides a flexible implementation of the popular Supervised Descent Method (SDM) [5], and cascade-regression implementations for fitting Deformable Models that are the direct application of the Supervised Descent approach to CLMs (similar to [12]) and AAMs.

4. FITTING PERFORMANCE

Due to the rich functionality of Menpo, several experiments could be run to assess performance. However, due to lack of space, we restrict the performance evaluation to the problem of non-rigid face alignment "in-the-wild".

The experiment of Figure 2 compares the fitting accuracy of four representative algorithms implemented in Menpo against two publicly available but closed-source implementations of state-of-the-art methods using two popular "in-the-wild" face databases. The four Menpo algorithms under test are as follows: (1) the Alternating Inverse Compositional algorithm for fitting AAMs using IGO features (Menpo IGO-AAMs) [8] and (2) HOG features (Menpo HOG-AAMs) [3], (3) the Regularised Landmark Mean-Shift [4] algorithm for CLMs fitting using HOG features (Menpo CLMs) and (4) the Supervised Descent Method [5] using HOG features (Menpo SDMs). All algorithms were trained using the same 811 annotated training images of the publicly available LFPW database [14] provided by the 300W Challenge[3] [15].

We test against: (1) the DRMF Matlab implementation provided by [12][4] and (2) the SIFT-SDMs Matlab implementation of [5][5]. Due to the closed source nature of these implementations it is impossible to know what data was used to train the models, however through personal communication with the authors we know several thousand images were employed.

Results are reported for the 337 annotated images from the Annotated Faces in the Wild (AFW) database[3] [16]. All methods were initialised using the publicly available bounding box face detections[3]. Note that these initialisations are particularly challenging, and so the experiment emphasises the robustness of the techniques. For each method, the Cumulative Error Distribution (CED) curves over 49 landmark points is reported in Fig. 2. The results indicate that on the whole Menpo is comparable to state-of-the-art, even given the deficiencies in training data used. Menpo HOG-AAM is by far the most accurate technique, although it is admittedly much slower than the SDM family of methods.

It should be noted that due to the fact that the third-party techniques tested do not provide training implementations it is impossible to guarantee a fair test. The aim of the experiment is rather to demonstrate that Menpo's open-source implementations can compete against the state-of-the-art. We choose to train our techniques with a fairly small cohort of publicly available images due to the considerable computational requirements of the training process. It is hoped that this decision ensures that the results reported here are readily reproducible by the interested reader.

One of the aims of Menpo is to promote open, reproducible science. To that end, the full code for reproducing the results reported here will be made available before publication on the Menpo website. Going forwards we intend to maintain a standardised suite of tests based around the experiments performed in this paper for the community to have a single

[3] `http://ibug.doc.ic.ac.uk/resources/300-W/`

[4] `https://sites.google.com/site/akshayasthana/clm-wild-code`

[5] `http://www.humansensing.cs.cmu.edu/intraface/`

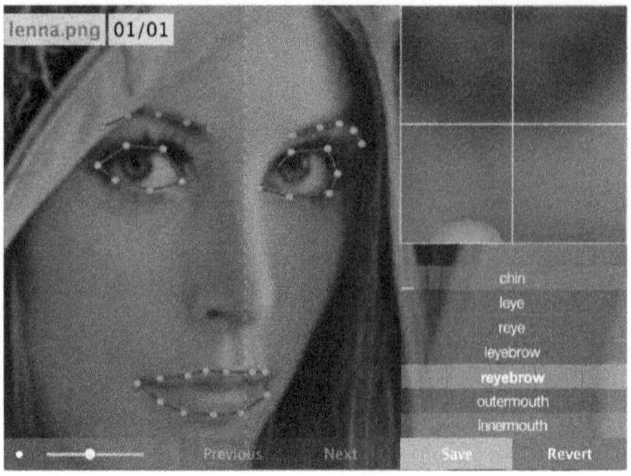

Figure 3: An example screenshot of the web based landmarking software.

point of reference for comparing cutting edge techniques.

5. APPLICATIONS

Building Menpo on top of Python makes it extremely easy to integrate into different applications. Currently the Menpo Project hosts two applications built on top of Menpo.

Web based landmarker `http://www.landmarker.io` is a web application for annotating 2D and 3D data. It has no dependencies beyond a modern web browser such as Google Chrome and is designed to be trivial to use. Most importantly, the decentralisation of the landmarking software means researchers can recruit annotators by simply directing them to the website. The annotations and assets themselves are served to the client from a separate server component which is run by the user. This allows researches to benefit from the web-based nature of the tool without having to compromise privacy or security. The server utilises Menpo to import assets and save out annotations. An example screenshot is given in Figure 3. In the future, the tool will use Menpo to provide initial estimations of the correct points for the images and meshes of interest.

Real-time tracker Menpo-Tracker is an experimental application for detecting and tracking object landmarks in real-time on a standard laptop. It defines a general framework for tracking deformable objects (it is not specifically tailored to faces) using SDM objects built using Menpo. This tracking application is implemented in Python and utilises OpenCV for video acquisition. We have high hopes that due to the accessibility of Python and it's widespread user base, Menpo-Tracker will attract users from communities outside of computer vision. We have plans for Menpo-Tracker to be able to track object landmarks in real-time using GPU-based implementations of AAMs and CLMs built using future iterations of Menpo.

6. CONCLUSION

We present Menpo, the first, to the best of our knowledge, complete platform for parametric image alignment and deformable model construction, fitting and performance evaluation. Menpo is flexible and there are many interesting areas where it can be extended to provide further state-of-the-art implementations. Currently, we are working on implementing construction and fitting of 3D Morphable Models (a lot of work has already been done towards this direction - Menpo includes an off-screen OpenGL rasterizer for the purpose, and all the tools necessary to visualise and work with 3D triangular meshes). Most importantly, we wish for Menpo to become an important set of reference implementations for researchers interested in the parametric image alignment and deformable modelling fields.

7. ACKNOWLEDGMENT

The work of Joan Alabort-i-Medina and Patrick Snape was funded by the Qualcomm Innovation Fellowship and by an EPSRC DTA from Imperial College London. The work of James Booth was funded by an EPSRC DTA from Imperial College London. The work of Epameinondas Antonakos and Stefanos Zafeiriou was partially supported by the EPSRC project EP/J017787/1 (4DFAB).

8. REFERENCES

[1] S. Baker and I. Matthews, "Lucas-kanade 20 years on: A unifying framework," *IJCV*, vol. 56, no. 3, pp. 221–255, 2004.

[2] T. Cootes *et al.*, "Active appearance models," *IEEE T-PAMI*, vol. 23, no. 6, pp. 681–685, 2001.

[3] E. Antonakos *et al.*, "Hog active appearance models," in *ICIP*, 2014.

[4] J. Saragih *et al.*, "Deformable model fitting by regularized landmark mean-shift," *IJCV*, vol. 91, no. 2, pp. 200–215, 2011.

[5] X. Xiong and F. De la Torre, "Supervised descent method and its applications to face alignment," in *CVPR*, pp. 532–539, 2013.

[6] J. Saragih and R. Goecke, "Learning aam fitting through simulation," *Pat. Rec.*, vol. 42, no. 11, pp. 2628–2636, 2009.

[7] G. Tzimiropoulos *et al.*, "Robust and efficient parametric face alignment," in *ICCV*, 2011.

[8] G. Tzimiropoulos *et al.*, "Generic active appearance models revisited," in *ACCV*, pp. 650–663, 2012.

[9] G. Papandreou and P. Maragos, "Adaptive and constrained algorithms for inverse compositional active appearance model fitting," in *CVPR*, pp. 1–8, 2008.

[10] T. Ojala *et al.*, "Multiresolution gray-scale and rotation invariant texture classification with local binary patterns," *IEEE T-PAMI*, vol. 24, no. 7, pp. 971–987, 2002.

[11] N. Dalal and B. Triggs, "Histograms of oriented gradients for human detection," in *CVPR*, pp. 886–893, 2005.

[12] A. Asthana *et al.*, "Robust discriminative response map fitting with constrained local models," in *CVPR*, pp. 3444–3451, 2013.

[13] F. Perez and B. Granger, "IPython: a system for interactive scientific computing," *CiSE*, vol. 9, no. 3, pp. 21–29, 2007.

[14] P. N. Belhumeur *et al.*, "Localizing parts of faces using a consensus of exemplars," in *CVPR*, 2011.

[15] C. Sagonas *et al.*, "300 faces in-the-wild challenge: The first facial landmark localization challenge," in *ICCV-W 2013*, pp. 397–403, 2013.

[16] X. Zhu *et al.*, "Face detection, pose estimation, and landmark localization in the wild," in *CVPR*, 2012.

VideoLat - an Extensible Tool for Multimedia Delay Measurements

Jack Jansen
CWI: Centrum Wiskunde & Informatica
Science park 123
1098 XG Amsterdam, the Netherlands
+31 20 5924300
Jack.Jansen@cwi.nl

ABSTRACT

When using a videoconferencing system there will always be a delay from sender to receiver. Such delays affect human communication, and therefore knowing the delay is a major factor in judging the expected quality of experience of the conferencing system. Additionally, for implementors, tuning the system to reduce delay requires an ability to effectively and easily gather delay metrics on a potentially wide range of settings. In order to support this process, we make available a system called *videoLat*. VideoLat provides an innovative approach to understand glass-to-glass video delays and speaker-to-microphone audio delays. VideoLat can be used as-is to do audio and video roundtrip delays of black box systems, but by making it available as open source we want to enable people to extend and modify it for different scenarios, such as measuring one-way delays or delay of camera switching.

Categories and Subject Descriptors

B.8.2 [**Hardware**]: Performance and Reliability - Performance Analysis and Design Aids; H.4.3 [**Information System Applications**] Communication Applications - Computer conferencing, teleconferencing, and videoconferencing.

General Terms

Measurement, Performance, Experimentation, Human Factors.

Keywords

Delay measurement; video conferencing.

1. INTRODUCTION

Audio and video playout delays are a fact of life for conferencing systems and other multimedia processing systems. These delays are unavoidable: each and every component in a digital conferencing chain will introduce a non-zero delay, and even in an ideal world where all processing was instantaneous and all networks were infinitely fast, there would still be the delays introduced by time-slotted standards (such as frame rates), and by the physical distance between sender and receiver and the fact that the speed of light is finite.

MM '14, November 03 - 07 2014, Orlando, FL, USA.

ACM 978-1-4503-3063-3/14/11...$15.00.
http://dx.doi.org/10.1145/2647868.2654891

Delays in videoconferencing have a large effect on the way people communicate [4][5][6] and are an important factor in the quality of experience of a conferencing system. Therefore, being able to measure this delay is a first step in evaluating the performance of a video conferencing system, and possibly optimizing it. Being able to measure audio and video delays is valuable in a wide range of scenarios and target audiences, such as

- evaluating closed commercial conferencing systems for their applicability to a certain use case (end users),
- determining the effect of the latest codec optimizations implemented (developers),
- comparing network protocol change implications (network operators).

The current standard way to measure user-perceived delay (as opposed to measuring only the network or codec delay, which is only part of the picture) is to presume that audio delay is less - or less important - than video delay and measure only the latter. Video delay is then measured by putting sending and receiving system side by side, capture input and output of the system being measured in a single shot with an extra camera, augmented by a timer. The footage of this extra camera is then examined offline, usually manually, after which the delay is computed. This is potentially a time-consuming and error-prone process. Xu et al [7] improve on this by using OCR for the offline matching, but their system still requires sender and receiver to be physically side by side. The vDelay [1] and AvCloak [3] tools go a step further and can do automatic measurements in realtime of a real conferencing setup, with the latter also measuring audio/video synchronization. However, neither can be used on turnkey systems, because they simulate hardware or require screen scraping to do their job. This method also means these systems do not include all camera and display delays as perceived by the end user.

In this paper we present videoLat, an open source tool that enables glass-to-glass video delay measurements, and sound-to-sound audio delay measurements. VideoLat is open source, and designed to be extensible, making it adaptable to other multimedia delay measurements. For example, measuring stream switching delays, or A/V synchronization requires only a minimal amount of code.

A previous version of videoLat was described in [2] but while the principle of operation is the same, this version is a completely modified code base to enable a better user interface, extensibility, and support for non-visual media (such as audio).

2. DESIGN

VideoLat is intended to be the "digital multimeter" for multimedia delay testing: a tool you pick up to get a quick idea of how a system performs, from an end user point of view, independent of

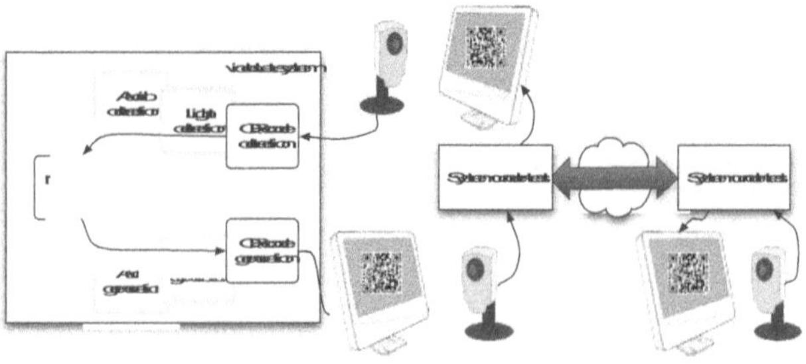

Figure 1 - Black Box Measurement

the system under test, and easy to use. This has led to a number of design principles:

- results reported should be as close as possible to user-perceived delays,
- videoLat itself runs on a dedicated system, not on the system under test,
- setup and operation should not put much of a burden on the operator.

The general design is based on videoLat generating images (or sounds) that are computer-detectable. These are then fed through the system under test, which should reproduce them (after a delay) on their output device, from which the videoLat system will pick them up again. Figure 1 shows how this works for a video delay measurement: the videoLat display shows a QR-code which the conferencing camera picks up and transmits. The remote conferencing camera is pointed at the screen (or at a mirror so it can see the screen) and transmitted back. Here the videoLat camera picks it up again and the QR-code detector will trigger once the previous QR-code transmitted is received. The delay is computed, and the whole procedure repeated with a new QR-code. After a large number of measurements the average delay and standard deviation are computed.

There is one caveat: this delay includes the delay caused by the internal processing of videoLat itself. Therefore, before doing a real measurement, the operator should first do a calibration run with the exact same videoLat system, as shown in figure 2. This self-delay will then be subtracted from the real measurement.

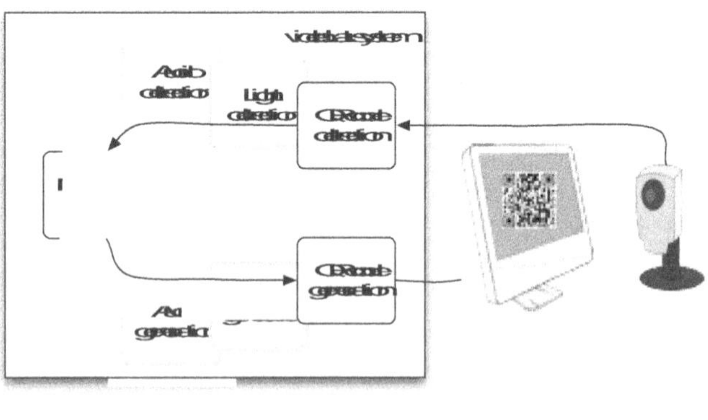

Figure 2 - Calibration Self-measurement

3. EXAMPLE USE CASE

Doing a video delay measurement of Skype (or any other conferencing videoconferencing tool) from scratch requires a MacBook and an external USB webcam, in addition to the machine used for Skype. Technically a desktop Mac or a builtin camera work, but then positioning the hardware becomes difficult. After downloading videoLat via http://www.videolat.org (or building it as explained in section 5) you do a calibration run by selecting the *New Measurement* command and selecting *Video Roundtrip Calibration*. Figure 3 show how this setup works in practice. Builtin help is available on the details. You point the camera at the videoLat screen and run the calibration, which shows the running average and standard deviation. Typically you would do about thousand measurements, but you can watch the average and standard deviation to guide this.

After you press *Stop* you see the results of your calibration as shown in figure 4 and if the distribution looks reasonable you save the calibration. Practically speaking, the calibration run shown in figure 4 is less than optimal: ideally the delays of the calibration run should be close to normally distributed because this will reduce the impact of measurement system idiosyncrasies on your real measurement.

Figure 3 - Calibration setup, picture (a) and screen shot (b)

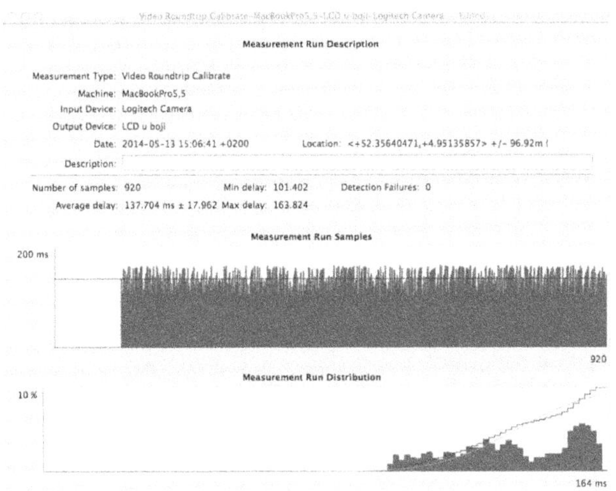

Figure 4 - Calibration Results

You now setup a Skype call, and instruct the remote participant to either point their camera at their screen (if physically possible) or use a mirror so the camera can see the Skype window. Locally, you make sure the Skype camera see the MacBook screen and theMacBook camera sees the Skype screen. You then run videoLat again, this time selecting a *Video Roundtrip* measurement and using the previous calibration measurement as the base. During the preparation phase you position cameras and screens such that the QR codes are best visible, and videoLat will determine whether mirroring is involved and determine an estimated value for the expected delay.

After running the measurement (which will probably take considerably longer than the calibration) you get a results display similar to the one for the calibration. You can also open older measurements, for comparison, and you can save the measurement for future reference. You can also export the results as three CSV files, which can be imported into a spreadsheet or graphing application for further processing.

4. IMPLEMENTATION

VideoLat only runs on MacOSX, with an iOS version expected in the near future. The reason for this is that initial experiments showed that AVFoundation, the Apple media capture framework, was the only framework that was able to produce timestamped video frames where the timestamps showed some semblance to the actual time of grabbing. Because videoLat intends to do user-perceived measurements this is an important feature: discrepancies between the actual capture time and the recorded capture time can skew the results, especially if these discrepancies are not normally distributed or dependent on some hidden variable (such as operating system scheduler policy).

VideoLat is structured around a plugin paradigm. For each measurement type there are four objects that need to be implemented: a measurement controller, a media generator, a media grabber and a detector. The controller handles the user interface of the measurement run (to allow selection of the camera to use, for example) and drives the other three components to do successive measurements.

Aside from the QR-code components mentioned previously there is also a complete set of audio components (generator, recorder, detector) to do audio delay measurements. In addition there are video components to do video delay measurements using simple black or white images (or light/no light conditions) and components that can generate and detect light/no light using dedicated arduino or (commercial) LabJack hardware. The video black/white modules are compatible with the hardware light/no-light modules, so these can be mixed to do a delay measurement of only a camera or only a screen.

Beside the measurement functionality there is code to display and compare measurement results, and to export to CSV-files so the data can be plotted or analyzed in a spreadsheet or another external tool.

The core of videoLat is implemented in Objective C, but the APIs are all available in Python as well, and because Python also has a good interface to Foundation and other OSX toolkits it is possible to create new components either in Objective C or Python. C++ is a third option.

VideoLat uses the open source libraries libzbar [8], libzint [9] and libpng [10] for QR-code generation and detection, and the freely available libLabJack [11] when interfacing to that specific hardware. VideoLat is licensed under the GPL license.

5. BUILDING AND EXTENDING

VideoLat can be built on MacOSX 10.7 or later. To build videoLat from source go to http://sourceforge.net/projects/videolat/ and download either the source tar file or clone the subversion repository. To build without any modifications open a Terminal window and run `scripts/build.sh` which will build videoLat after building the third-party libraries libzbar and libzint, and possibly warning you that you need to build libpng yourself (which is included with some OSX versions but not always). It will tell you where the application can be found after building.

If you want to extend, modify or debug videoLat you open the project file `videoLat.xcodeproj` and build in XCode. The Debug and Release targets are what you would normally use, the Distribution target you use if you want to create a signed copy for distribution (in which case you probably know about all the Apple-enforced rules for this).

The main APIs to use when extending videoLat are defined and documented in `Protocols.h`, and generic base class implementations for those are available. Detailed documentation on extending videoLat can be found on http://www.videolat.org.

6. EXTENSION AREAS

VideoLat is made available as open source because we feel there are many other types of delay measurements that can provide interesting insights into the operation of conferencing systems that cannot be handled by a turnkey measurement system. As an example, if the system under test has an API to switch cameras it is possible to extend VideoLat so that it emits such an API call. Then, by pointing the two cameras at different printed QR-codes videoLat can be used to measure the delay until a human viewer sees the result of a camera switch.

There are also a number of areas in which videoLat could use some improvement that are of general application. For example:

- one-way measurements are not supported as well as round-trip measurements, and some use cases, such as broadcasting, would benefit from one-way measurements,
- a mobile version (iPhone, iPad) would greatly enhance the “digital multimeter” role, especially with one-way measurements,
- audio delay measurements are currently painful because of audio feedback and echo cancellation and suppression,
- audio/video synchronization measurements as in [3] would be a great addition.

The author would be delighted to cooperate with people interested in these areas.

7. ACKNOWLEDGEMENTS

This work was supported in part by funding from the European Community's Seventh Framework Programme (FP7/2007-2013) Vconect project, under grant agreement no. ICT-2011-287760.

8. REFERENCES

[1] Boyaci, O., Forte, A., Baset, S. and Schulzrinne, H.. vDelay: A Tool to Measure Capture-to-Display Latency and Frame Rate. 11th IEEE International Symposium on Multimedia, 2009, pp. 194-200. DOI=10.1109/ISM.2009.46

[2] Jack Jansen and Dick C. A. Bulterman. User-centric video delay measurements. Proceeding of the 23rd ACM Workshop on Network and Operating Systems Support for Digital Audio and Video (NOSSDAV '13). ACM, New York, NY, USA, 37-42. DOI=10.1145/2460782.2460789

[3] Kryczka, A., Arefin, A. and Nahrstedt, K... AvCloak: A Tool for Black Box Latency Measurements in Video Conferencing Applications. IEEE ISM (2013) pp. 271-278. DOI=10.1109/ISM.2013.52

[4] Claire O'Malley, Steve Langton, Anne Anderson, Gwyneth Doherty-Sneddon and Vicky Bruce. Comparison of face-to-face and video-mediated interaction. Interacting with Computers (1996) vol. 8 (2) pp. 177-192. Elsevier, Amsterdam, the Netherlands. DOI=10.1016/0953-5438(96)01027-2

[5] Karen Ruhleder and Brigitte Jordan. Co-constructing non-mutual realities: Delay-generated trouble in distributed interaction. Computer Supported Cooperative Work (CSCW) (2001) vol. 10 (1), pp. 113-138. Springer, Heidelberg, Germany. DOI=10.1023/A:1011243905593

[6] Jennifer Tam, Elizbeth Carter, Sara Kiesler, and Jessica Hodgins. 2012. Video increases the perception of naturalness during remote interactions with latency. In Proceedings of the 2012 ACM annual conference extended abstracts on Human Factors in Computing Systems Extended Abstracts (CHI EA '12). ACM, New York, NY, USA, 2045-2050. DOI=10.1145/2223656.2223750

[7] Yang Xu, Chenguang Yu, Jingjiang Li, and Yong Liu. 2012. Video telephony for end-consumers: measurement study of Google+, iChat, and Skype. In Proceedings of the 2012 ACM conference on Internet measurement conference (IMC '12). ACM, New York, NY, USA, 371-384. DOI=10.1145/2398776.2398816

[8] Zbar bar code reader. URL=http://zbar.sourceforge.net. Downloaded at 2014-05-18.

[9] Zint Barcode Generator. URL=http://zint.github.io. Downloaded at 2014-05-18.

[10] Portable Network Graphics. URL=http://www.libpng.org. Downloaded at 2014-05-18.

[11] LabJack. URL=http://labjack.com/support/software. Downloaded at 2014-05-18.

The Yael Library

Matthijs Douze
Inria
655 av. de l'Europe, Montbonnot 38334
Saint-Ismier, France
matthijs.douze@inria.fr

Hervé Jégou
Inria
Campus de Beaulieu
35042 Rennes, France
herve.jegou@inria.fr

ABSTRACT

This paper introduces YAEL, a library implementing computationally intensive functions used in large scale image retrieval, such as neighbor search, clustering and inverted files. The library offers interfaces for C, Python and Matlab. Along with a brief tutorial, we analyze and discuss some of our implementation choices, and their impact on efficiency.

`http://yael.gforge.inria.fr/`

Categories and Subject Descriptors. D.0. [Software]: General; I.4.7.0 Image processing and computer vision

Keywords: nearest neighbor; indexing; clustering; image search

1. MOTIVATION AND OVERVIEW

The motivation of YAEL is twofold: We aim at providing

- core and optimized instructions and methods commonly used for large-scale multimedia retrieval systems;
- more sophisticated functions associated with state-of-the-art methods, such as the Fisher vector [11, 10], VLAD [8, 10], Hamming Embedding [5, 6] or more generally methods based on inverted file systems, such as selective match kernels [13].

Having these two kinds of functions implemented in the core library, we can rapidly disseminate open source packages reproducing the results of recent papers for image retrieval. YAEL is intended as an API and does not implement a retrieval system in an integrated manner: only a few test programs are available for key tasks such as k-means. Yet this can be done on top of it with a few dozen lines of Matlab or Python code.

For the sake of testing the library, we provide one sample package relying on YAEL, which implements an image retrieval system based on the Fisher vector. Yet we mention that several of such packages are available online, each being associated with a particular task and publisehd method. Section 3 lists a few of these, along with download statistics.

MM '14, November 03–07 2014, Orlando, FL, USA

http://dx.doi.org/10.1145/2647868.2654892.

Design choices. YAEL is designed to handle dense data in float, as it is primarily used for signal processing tasks where the quality of the representation is determined by the number of dimensions rather than the precision of the components. In the Matlab interface, single matrices, and float32 in Python.

YAEL was designed initially to manipulate matrices in C. It was interfaced for Python using SWIG, which gives low-level access to the full library. An additional Numpy layer (ynumpy) is provided for high-level functions. The most important functions of YAEL are wrapped in Mex to be callable from Matlab.

Performance is very important. YAEL has computed k-means with hundreds of thousand centroids and routinely manipulate matrices that occupy more than 1/2 the machine's RAM. This means it has to be lightweight and 64-bit clean.

The design choices of YAEL are governed by efficiency concerns more than by portability. The library is maintained for Linux and MacOS. Although an older version of the library was ported to Windows OS, only a few functions of the Matlab interface work on this platform.

Dependencies. YAEL relies on as few external libraries as possible. The only mandatory ones are BLAS/Lapack (for performance) and the Python/C API. Other libraries (Matlab's mex, Arpack, OpenMP) are optional.

Threading. Functions of significant complexity are parallelized. The level at which threading occurs must be chosen carefully: at the BLAS level, the YAEL function or the calling function. Therefore, YAEL functions often take a nt parameter, the number of threads.

Interface. YAEL contains hundreds of functions at the C level. Only a few are exported in Matlab and Python, as many basic matrix operations are natively available in these environments. In C, the functions are prefixed with the type of data they operate on. For example, fvec_max takes a fvec, or "float vector" array as input. In Matlab, most of the functions are prefixed with yael_. In Python, YAEL is available via the ynumpy module, which provides a sufficient context.

The rest of this paper is organized as follows. Section 2 lists the main functions, and shows on a few representative cases how we have optimized the functions. Section 3 shows the current impact of Yael with respect to various indicators: number of downloads, derived packages and research papers referring to the URL library.

2. MAIN FUNCTIONS

Here we review the implementation of YAEL's main functions, with their names in C. Table 1 gives the Python and Matlab equivalents of these functions.

Matlab function	Python function	Description
yael_kmax		Find the k largest elements of a vector (or set of vectors)
yael_kmin		Find the k smallest elements of a vector (or set of vectors)
yael_cross_distances	cross_distances	Compute all distances between two sets of vectors
yael_hamming		Compute all Hamming distances between two sets of packed bit-vectors
yael_nn	knn	Find the nearest neighbors in a set for various distances
yael_kmeans	kmeans	Learn a k-means quantizer from a set of input vectors
yael_gmm	gmm_learn	Estimate a GMM from an input set of vectors
yael_fisher	fisher	Compute the GMM- Fisher vector associated with a given set
yael_ivf		Handle (construct, query, etc) an inverted file structure

Table 1: Main functions in the Matlab interfaces of YAEL, and corresponding Python functions.

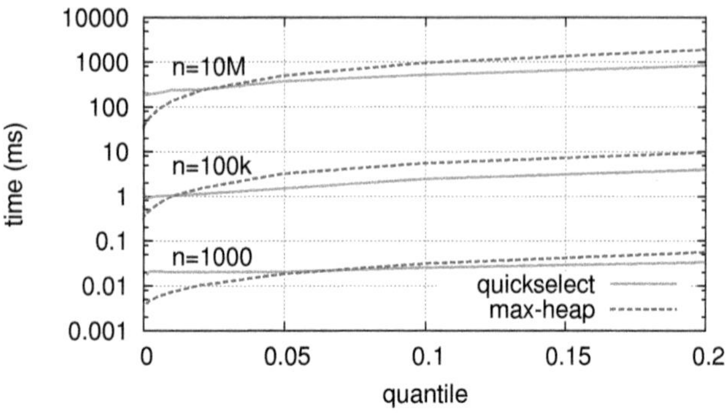

Figure 1: Runtime of the quickselect and max-heap methods to find a quantile in a table of uniformly distributed scalars (one computing core).

2.1 k-smallest values query

YAEL contains two implementations of the algorithm to find the k smallest values of a table of scalars:

- The quick-select algorithm (a.k.a. Hoare method). It amounts to applying a quick-sort on the table, but without handling the fraction of the table that does not contain the quantile limit.
- The max-heap algorithm, that maintains the set of k smallest values seen so far in a max-heap. The max-heap is a binary tree optimized to perform the operations "remove the largest value" and "insert a new value", both of which having complexity $\log(k)$.

Figure 1 shows that for smaller quantiles, the max-heap is faster. The function fvec_k_min automatically switches between the two versions, depending on the parameter k and number of elements.

2.2 Searching neighbors

Image retrieval requires finding similar elements on large scale. YAEL implements exact algorithms to retrieve nearest neighbors. For larger scale, one may resort to indexing structures such as those proposed in the inverted file structure of YAEL (see Subsection 2.6).

Exhaustively searching for nearest neighbors requires to compute the distance matrix $D \in \mathbb{R}^{m\times n}$ from the query vectors $X \in \mathbb{R}^{d\times n}$ to the database vectors $Y \in \mathbb{R}^{d\times m}$ (in the Euclidean case). Then, the smallest value in each column j of D is selected: it corresponds to the the nearest neighbor of query j. Both computations are performed in blocks to improve cache locality and because D may not fit in memory.

Euclidean space. We exploit the equivalence:

$$D = S(X)1_n^\top + 1_m^\top S(Y) - 2X^\top Y \qquad (1)$$

where 1_n is a $n-$vector of ones and $S(X)$ is the vector of squared norms of the columns X. The costly operation is the $X^\top Y$, for which we use the BLAS sgemm. When more than one nearest neighbor is required, we use a max-heap over the columns of D, as discussed in the previous subsection.

Hamming space. To compute Hamming distances, we employ the `xor` and SSE4.2 popcnt instructions: the Hamming distance between two 64-bit integers is computed in two processor cycles. Hamming distances are typically employed to retrieve all vectors within a given distance to the query. Therefore, unlike in the k-NN case, the list of neighbors must be adjusted during the query.

Other distances. The cosine similarity is optimized with matrix multiplication and cache optimization. The ℓ_1 and χ^2 distances are optimized using specific SSE instructions.

2.3 Principal Component Analysis

Dimensionality reduction with PCA is widely used. However, many implementations are not tractable for a large number of high-dimensional vectors,. YAEL provides distinct implementations for Matlab and C. The Matlab function yael_pca automatically switches between the Gram and the covariance methods [2]. Hereafter, we detail the variants implemented in the C interface, which include both these variants and tricks that limits the memory consumption.

Computing the PCA of a set of vectors $X = [x_1 \dots x_n] \in \mathbb{R}^{d\times n}$ proceeds as follows.

- centering the data:

$$\bar{X} = X - \bar{x}1_n^\top \quad \text{with} \quad \bar{x} = \frac{1}{n}\sum_{i=1}^{n} x_i \qquad (2)$$

- computing the SVD decomposition of $\bar{X}$: $\bar{X} = U\Sigma V^\top$ where $U \in \mathbb{R}^{d\times d}$ and $V \in \mathbb{R}^{n\times n}$ are orthogonal matrices and $\Sigma \in \mathbb{R}^{d\times n}$ is positive diagonal, padded with zeros on the right or bottom, with elements $[\sigma_1^2, \dots, \sigma_{\min(d,n)}^2]$.The singular values are sorted: $\sigma_1 \geq \sigma_2 \geq \dots \geq \sigma_{\min(d,n)}$.

Given this decomposition, the PCA reduction of a vector $x \in \mathbb{R}^d$ (not necessarily from the initial $\{x_1 \dots x_n\}$) is $x' = U^\top(x - \bar{x})$. Its main property is that, if vectors are drawn from a multidimensional Gaussian, the subvector x'_k of the k first components of x' is as close as possible to x'. Therefore, the PCA is often used to reduce the dimensionality from $\mathbb{R}^d$ to $\mathbb{R}^k$.

The only data we need to perform dimensionality reduction is $\bar{x}$ and the first k columns of U. Thus, the complete SVD is not necessary. There are two cases:

- Most often, $n > d$, *i.e.*, we have enough training data. In this case only the eigenvalues σ_i^2 and vectors U for the empirical covariance matrix $\bar{X}\bar{X}^\top$ are computed. The cost of computing these eigenvectors is $9d^3$ flops [3, algorithm 8.3.3].

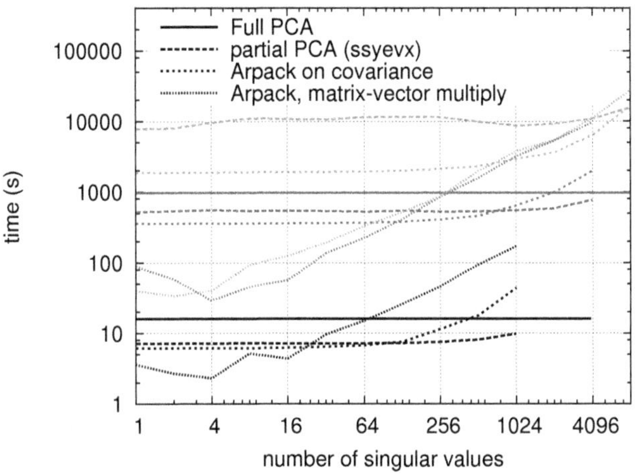

Figure 2: Cost of computing partial PCAs using different methods, on matrices of various sizes (on a 40-core computer): black = 4096×40000, blue = 16384×160000, red = 65536×88000. *Best viewed in color.*

- When $d > n$, it is more efficient [2] to compute the eigenvectors V of the Gram matrix $\bar{X}^\top \bar{X}$. Denoting $(u_i)_{i=1...d}$ and $(v_j)_{i=1...n}$ the columns of U and V respectively, $u_i = 1/\sigma_i^2 X v_i$ for $i = 1 \ldots n$. The remaining columns can be obtained by completing the orthonormal basis.

Finding eigenvalues in YAEL uses the Lapack ssyev function. When the data matrix X is too large to fit in RAM, the mean $\bar{x}$ and covariance $\bar{X}\bar{X}^\top$ are computed in a single pass over the matrix, using YAEL's pca_online_* functions.

Partial PCA. When the number of required dimensions $k \ll d$, it is possible to efficiently compute only part of the eigenvalues and eigenvectors. This can be done either by:

- reducing the matrix to tridiagonal form, then only partially diagonalizing this representation (Lapack function ssyevx).
- using an iterative Lanczos method [3, section 9.1] to compute the required components. The advantage is that the covariance matrix does not need to be computed, because it is used only to perform matrix-vector operations $\bar{X}\bar{X}^\top v$ for a given $v \in \mathbb{R}^d$. YAEL uses the Arpack ssaupd/sseupd functions.

Figure 2 shows the cost of computing a partial PCA. The on-the-fly multiplication is more efficient when k is small because the covariance matrix is not computed. For larger k, Arpack is faster at first, then Lapack's tridiagonalization.

These functions are implemented in YAEL's fmat_new_pca_part and pca_online_complete_part functions.

2.4 k-means Clustering

The cost of the k-means clustering is determined by that of the nearest-neighbor search (see Section 2.2). Despite its simplicity, the performance and stability of k-means depend on some implementation details:

- initialization: YAEL can use a random or the kmeans++-style initialization [1]. We observed, however, that for a large number of centroids, the random initialization is as good, and it is much faster because kmeans++ cannot be parallelized. The user can also provide his own initialization for the centroids.
- vanishing clusters: sometimes no more points are assigned to a cluster. This happens even on "well-behaved" datasets, for example when training product quantization [7] vocabularies on very large vectors that may be sparse. In this case, YAEL randomly chooses another cluster and splits it in two, in a way that avoids a new cluster to vanish at the next iteration. This a done by selecting a big cluster associated with centroid c. Two clusters are obtained from it as $c - \varepsilon$ and $c + \varepsilon$, where ε is a small random perturbation vector.
- restarting: kmeans computes the solution to an optimization problem using an iterative method that converges to a local minimum. The YAEL kmeans can perform this optimization starting from different initial points and select the best one.

Several functions are available for k-means in the C interface of YAEL, depending on the desired output (average error per cluster, assignment, etc) and initialization options. In Matlab, k-means is called with function yael_kmeans, see help yael_kmeans for possible options. For instance, a simple call is done by

```
[C, I] = yael_kmeans (v, k, 'niter', niter);
```

where C is a matrix containing the k clusters, and I indicates to which cluster each input vector v is assigned.

2.5 Fisher vectors

The YAEL Gaussian Mixture Model [2, Section 2.3.9] estimation is initialized from a kmeans vocabulary of the same size, then expectation-maximization steps are performed. A set of vectors can be aggregated to a Fisher vector [11]. This is particularly useful to generate an image representation from local descriptors.

The two functions are implemented in YAEL's gmm_learn and gmm_fisher. A toy Matlab package implementing a baseline based on Fisher is available online, see Section 3. A similar Python package is provided for the open-source competition to illustrate YAEL's capabilities.

2.6 Inverted files

Inverted file systems [14] are a key component of existing large-scale image and video retrieval methods. For image search, they are widely adopted to implement the similarity computation for the methods derived from the seminal Video-Google paper [12], where sparse bag-of-words vectors are to be compared in an efficient way.

Although an inverted file system can be implemented by a sparse matrix-vector multiplication, a devoted implementation can be more efficient. Furthermore, more precise image search systems have been subsequently proposed, such as Hamming Embedding [6], selective match kernel [13] or nearest neighbor search with product quantization [7]. These strategies add some per-descriptor information, given in a form of a short code, *e.g.*, a binary vector.

YAEL implements a generic inverted system capable of storing and exploiting such additional information in the retrieval phase. It can be used with any quantizer, since the quantization is done externally. For instance, in the Matlab interface, one can learn and produce a structure for Hamming Embedding by providing a function handler for the quantizer (exact Euclidean assignment in the example below) when calling the yael_ivf_he function:

```
>> quantizer=@yael_nn;
>> qparams=yael_kmeans(xtrain, k,'niter',20);
>> ivfhe=yael_ivf_he (k,nbits,x,quantizer,qparams);
```

The entry point for all operations is the function yael_ivf: adding new elements, performing queries, saving and loading an inverted file, etc. A full example is given in the subdirectory `test/matlab` of the YAEL package.

3. IMPACT OF YAEL

This section gives a brief overview of the impact of YAEL, both in terms of packages that depend on it, and with respect to usage statistics measured by the number of downloads. In addition, we mention that about 20 papers or reports refer to YAEL, as indicated by the results of the Google scholar query "gforge inria yael".

3.1 Derived software

Several software use YAEL as a core library, in particular online packages that reproduce the results of papers[1]. Hereafter, we briefly describe a few of these packages developed at Inria.

VLAD and Fisher – Image representations. The packages have been released to reproduce the results of the corresponding papers [8, 10]. They are available online on a dedicated webpage[2]. The Fisher implementation reproduces the results of the original authors at Xerox Research Center Europe.

Product quantization [7] is a state-of-the-art method for approximate nearest neighbor search in the compressed domain. A commercial version of this algorithm is proposed by Inria. Alternately, an open-source toy package in Matlab is available online[3], and depends on YAEL. Another package implementing approximate search with short codes implements the **anti-sparse** binarization technique [9] is derived from YAEL[4].

Babaz – Audio similarity search. Babaz [4] is an audio search engine[5] for video copy detection based on the audio track. The library is also usable in applications like Shazaam, however in this context there are faster and as accurate methods specifically devoted to music search. The method implemented has been used for Trecvid'2011, where it obtained the best results for the audio part.

Selective match kernels [13] are a state-of-the-art method for image search, with a focus on best ranking performance. It relies on YAEL's inverted file. A full package reproducing the paper's results is available online in the download section[6] of YAEL.

3.2 Download statistics

YAEL is released on Inria's gforge, a facility similar to that provided by Sourceforge. This offers several facilities like trackers and forums. It also produces usage statistics. For instance, Figure 3 reports the number of downloads per month between April 2010 (first release) and December 2013. The last version v371 and related packages have been downloaded 2200 times in the last five months (between December 2013 and May 2014), 1275 of these downloads corresponding to the core library. The library clearly has an increasing success, presumably because of the increasing number of packages relying on it.

As a final note, several demonstrators, in-house code and commercial software employ YAEL as a core library. YAEL is used in the Inria bigimbaz image search engine since 2008, which indexes over 10 millions images, to perform efficient image queries submitted by the users on the online interface[7]. YAEL was used in the winning submissions to Trecvid Multimedia Event Detection in 2012 and 2013.

[1] http://people.rennes.inria.fr/Herve.Jegou/software.html

[2] http://lear.inrialpes.fr/src/inria_fisher

[3] http://people.rennes.inria.fr/Herve.Jegou/projects/ann.html

[4] https://gforge.inria.fr/projects/antisparse

[5] http://babaz.gforge.inria.fr/

[6] https://gforge.inria.fr/frs/?group_id=2151

[7] http://bigimbaz.inrialpes.fr

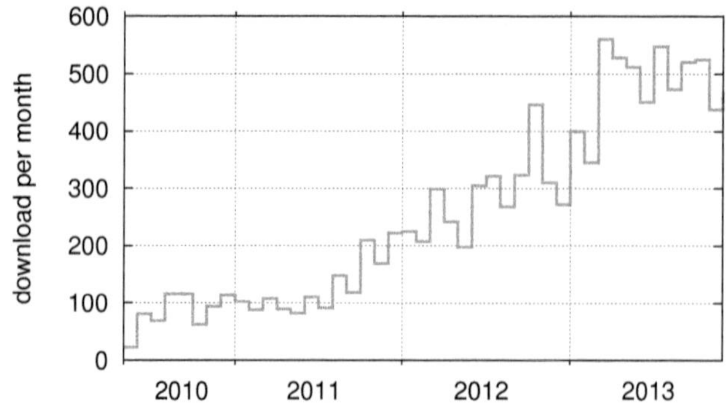

Figure 3: Statistics on YAEL files downloads. These measures include all files (including documentation files and related packages), but not the SVN checkouts or updates by developers and privileged users at Inria.

4. CONCLUSION

YAEL is a library which offers computationally intensive functions that are critical for large scale image search. Its main purpose is to facilitate the reproducibility of results, thanks to release of packages associated with research papers. Yael offers C, python and Matlab interfaces for Linux and MacOS operating systems. The core functions are heavily optimized with SSE operations and calls to Lapack/Blas matrix libraries. The development process follows the motto "release soon, release often".

5. ACKNOWLEDGEMENTS

The library was first developed in the context of the Quaero program. It is currently supported by ERC VIAMASS no. 336054.

6. REFERENCES

[1] D. Arthur and S. Vassilvitskii. k-means++: the advantages of careful seeding. In *ACM-SIAM symposium on Discrete algorithms*, 2007.

[2] C. M. Bishop. *Pattern Recognition and Machine Learning*. Springer, 2007.

[3] G. H. Golub and C. F. V. Loan. *Matrix Computations*. John Hopkins University Press, Baltimore and London, second edition, 1991.

[4] H. Jégou, J. Delhumeau, J. Yuan, G. Gravier, and P. Gros. Babaz: a large scale audio search system for video copy detection. In *ICASSP*, Mar. 2012.

[5] H. Jégou, M. Douze, and C. Schmid. Hamming embedding and weak geometric consistency for large scale image search. In *ECCV*, Oct. 2008.

[6] H. Jégou, M. Douze, and C. Schmid. Improving bag-of-features for large scale image search. *IJCV*, 87(3):316–336, Feb. 2010.

[7] H. Jégou, M. Douze, and C. Schmid. Product quantization for nearest neighbor search. *Trans. PAMI*, 33(1):117–128, Jan. 2011.

[8] H. Jégou, M. Douze, C. Schmid, and P. Pérez. Aggregating local descriptors into a compact image representation. In *CVPR*, 2010.

[9] H. Jégou, T. Furon, and J.-J. Fuchs. Anti-sparse coding for approximate nearest neighbor search. In *ICASSP*, Mar. 2012.

[10] H. Jégou, F. Perronnin, M. Douze, J. Sánchez, P. Pérez, and C. Schmid. Aggregating local descriptors into compact codes. In *Trans. PAMI*, 2012.

[11] F. Perronnin and C. R. Dance. Fisher kernels on visual vocabularies for image categorization. In *CVPR*, 2007.

[12] J. Sivic and A. Zisserman. Video Google: A text retrieval approach to object matching in videos. In *ICCV*, 2003.

[13] G. Tolias, Y. Avrithis, and H. Jégou. To aggregate or not to aggregate: Selective match kernels for image search. In *ICCV*, 2013.

[14] J. Zobel and A. Moffat. Inverted files for text search engines. *ACM Computing Surveys*, 38(2):6, 2006.

Loki+Lire: A Framework to Create Web-Based Multimedia Search Engines

Giuseppe Becchi, Marco Bertini[*],
Lorenzo Cioni, Alberto Del Bimbo,
Andrea Ferracani, Daniele Pezzatini[†]
Università degli Studi di Firenze - MICC
Firenze, Italy
[name.surname]@unifi.it

Mathias Lux
Klagenfurt University - ITEC
Klagenfurt, Austria
mlux@itec.aau.at

ABSTRACT

In this paper we present Loki+Lire, a framework for the creation of web-based interfaces for search, annotation and presentation of multimedia data. The framework provides tools to ingest, transcode, present, annotate and index different types of media such as images, videos, audio files and textual documents. The front-end is compliant with the latest HTML5 standards, while the back-end allows system administrators to create processing pipelines that can be adapted for different tasks and purposes.

The system has been developed in a modular way, aiming at creating loosely coupled components, letting developers to use it as a whole or to select only the parts that are needed to develop their own tools and systems.

Categories and Subject Descriptors

H.3.5 [**Information Storage and Retrieval**]: Online Information Services; H.4 [**Information Systems Applications**]: Miscellaneous

General Terms

Algorithms, Design, Experimentation

Keywords

Semantic multimedia annotation; retrieval; content-based multimedia retrieval; open source software

1. INTRODUCTION

Two important trends of multimedia production and consumption of the latest years are *i)* the fact that anyone, from end users to professionals, have become creators of every type of digital data, producing any type of media documents that may range from textual documents (e.g. presentations) to images, audio and videos; *ii)* the fact that these media are consumed, distributed and presented through the web. Under these circumstances it is necessary to develop systems and components that are capable to handle diverse media, accounting for their different presentation and for how users interact with them. From the point of view of content managers it is required to create different processing, annotating and indexing pipelines that let to provide different types of services, such as keyword-based retrieval or content-based multimedia retrieval. The system presented in this paper caters for all these needs: the media presentation components, tailored for each type of media, allow to browse, search and annotate, while the back-end components let to create processing pipelines that include ingestion, transcoding and indexing.

The framework can be used for different purposes and by different users, such as:

- Researchers who need an interface to demo their own annotation systems, that can be added as processes in the back-end;
- Researchers and practitioners who need to embed just some of the Loki+Lire components in their own interfaces, e.g. to create demo or commercial web services;
- Researchers who need components to create ground truth annotations to create datasets or validate experiments, e.g. using web-based crowd-sourced services such as Amazon Mechanical Turk;
- Content managers or media producers who need to archive and retrieve one or more of the different types of media handled by the framework;
- Lecturers and teachers who need an educative tool for their courses related to multimedia.

2. THE SYSTEM

The system has been designed using a loosely coupled approach for all its components, that have been developed as plugins for well-established frameworks like jQuery or tools like Solr/Lucene. This approach lets users to deploy it as a whole or to select only the components, either from the front-end or the back-end, that are needed. In particular, all the interface components of Loki are fully scriptable and

[*]Corresponding author
[†]Authors listed in alphabetical order

MM'14, November 3–7, 2014, Orlando, Florida USA.
ACM 978-1-4503-3063-3/14/11 ...$15.00.
http://dx.doi.org/10.1145/2647868.2654893.

can be easily embedded in other systems; similarly, the back-end components are web services that can be substituted or reused. The fronted components provide all the widgets required to create a user interface, while the back-end components manage users, resources metadata, media features and annotations, and media processing pipelines. A full cross-media search engine is provided as an example application (Fig. 1 shows an example of the main search interface).

Figure 1: Cross-media search interface built using the Loki+Lire framework.

2.1 The Front-End

The fronted components have been developed fully respecting the HTML5 standard using HTML5 and CSS3 for the presentation and JavaScript for the business logic. Two JavaScript frameworks have been used to create snappier and more interactive widgets: AngularJS and JQuery, comprising some extensions of the latter framework, such as jQuery UI. In particular, using AngularJS it has been possible to develop the interface components using the Model-View-Controller design pattern. In MVC terms, the View corresponds to the HTML code, while the operations on the model, that interact with the presentation and are part of the Controller, are written in JavaScript.

The media components, developed as jQuery plugins – thus allowing their integration in other web-based systems that use jQuery – let to visualize media, annotate them (it is possible to activate this functionality depending on the access level of a user), search within the media that is being shown. These widgets interact with the back-end using SOAP web services. All the components have a large number of properties that let to personalize their functionalities and appearance.

2.1.1 Video

The video player component (Fig. 2) shows videos and their annotations synchronized according to their timecode, allowing also for frame accurate annotations. The plugin offers different levels of functionality and can be adapted from a simple video player to a fully-fledged annotation tool changing a single configuration parameter. Annotations can be either tags/keywords or results of speech transcriptions. When a new annotation is added a keyframe is extracted and indexed for CBIR. The component provides also search capability within the same video, showing previews of the result frames (when hovering over the retrieved results), and can be used for keyframe-based CBIR. Clicking on the similar frames, shown inside an expandable panel of the widget, the player starts the video they belong to at their timecode. Similar frames may come from the same or different videos.

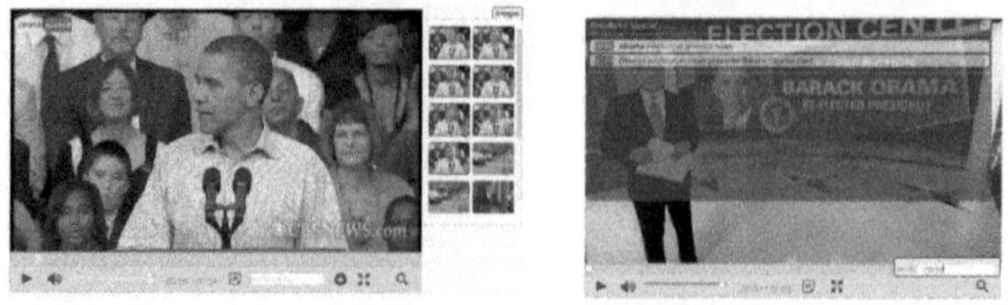

Figure 2: Video component: video with overlaid annotations and frames visually similar to the one currently shown *(left)*; search within the video player: hovering on a result shows the corresponding keyframe in the player.*(right)*.

2.1.2 Audio

The audio component (Fig. 3) is similar to the video component, and has the same properties to activate the functionalities required for the application in which it is embedded. The main difference is that it shows the audio wave form, that can be used as a cue when browsing and annotating the audio file. Since it is not yet possible to compute this wave form in realtime using JavaScript, it is automatically computed during the ingestion and transcoding of the audio files by a back-end service.

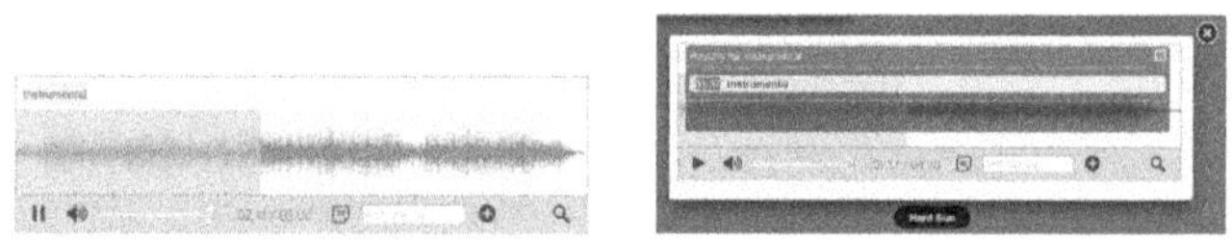

Figure 3: Audio component: audio file with overlaid annotations *(left)*; search within the audio player *(right)*.

2.1.3 Image

The image component (Fig. 4) has some differences w.r.t. audio and video components, in that annotations are not shown as overlays and there is no need to perform searches within the same media. On the other hand it allows to annotate the whole image or just a portion of it. Hovering on localized annotations related bounding boxes are shown.

Figure 4: Image component: image with annotations: clicking on the + sign it is possible to annotate the whole image *(left)*; localized image annotations *(right)*.

2.1.4 Document

The document component (Fig. 5) shows textual documents using SVG for each page and JPEG for the thumbnails that are arranged as a scrollable list on one side of the widget main view and allow document navigation. Thanks to SVG it is possible to easily zoom in and out of the page, or move it while it is zoomed. Page thumbnails are used also when showing the results of the intra-document search, that behaves thus similarly to video search. User annotations can be localized within specific portions of the page, thus behaving similarly to the image component. Furthermore the component allows collaboration. The user can choose to visualise only his or other users' annotations. Each author's annotation is visualised with its own color and shows the nickname of the user by who was added.

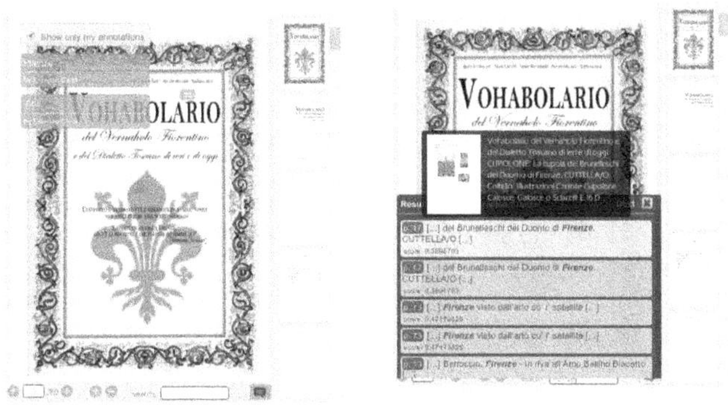

Figure 5: Document component: document with opened and localized annotations *(left)*; searching within the same document, with thumbnail of a result *(right)*.

2.1.5 *Loki: a cross-media search engine*

A full-fledged cross-media search engine (Fig. 1) is provided, so that it can be used as an application itself or as a starting point for developers who want to start to use the framework. This application uses all the components described above and the back-end components and functionalities described in the next section.

The system starts letting users to search with a keyword or uploading a media from their PC (Fig. 6). Users that log in the system can create collections by selecting the search results that are more interesting for them. Results can be filtered using two facets, media type and concepts (Fig. 7), and are clustered based on their similarity to provide a more diverse and compact result set (Fig. 8). Similarity search is activated by dragging and dropping a result item in the search area; if no content-based similarity is possible (e.g. between an image and an audio file) then keyword similarity is used (e.g. using image tags and audio tags).

2.2 The Back-End

The main components of the back-end are: *i)* a relational database to manage media, metadata, semantic annotations (i.e. tags and concepts automatically detected or added by users using the fronted components), media collections and users, e.g. to let users create their own sets of media by uploading them to the system or by starring their preferred results when searching media; *ii)* a Solr server instance to store syntactic annotations (low-level features used for CBIR, obtained using the Lire plugin) and indexing all media data and annotations to perform cross-media searches; *iii)* SOAP web services to perform CRUD operations on the annotations; *iv)* scripts to ingest and transcode media to the formats that can be handled by the HTML5 presentation components that are part of the front-end. These components have been developed in PHP and Java.

Figure 6: Cross-media search interface built using the Loki+Lire framework: starting searches; since the user is logged in the system he can save the best results to create his own personalized collection of media items.

Figure 7: Search facets: concepts *(left)*; media type *(right)*.

Figure 8: Results cluster: visualization of a closed cluster of images/keyframes *(left)*; visualization of the content of the cluster: it is possible to inspect and interact with each element of the cluster *(right)*.

2.2.1 *Lire: a Solr plugin for high performance CBIR*

This component is used to index images and keyframes, providing CBIR functionality to the framework. It is used also to create clusters of images and keyframes that are visually similar, thus improving the diversity of retrieved results both when searching with keywords or by similarity.

While Solr is a well known and well performing text search engine, the Lire plugin extends it by *i)* piggy-backing the content based image features onto indexed text documents, and *ii)* hashing the features in a way, so that the inverted index search can be used for sub-linear retrieval. Basically, the hash values are used to identify a set of $n \gg l$ candidate results, whereas l is the number of desired results. Within these n candidates l results are found with linear search. Most critical points are the linear search within the candidate set, for which the feature vectors have to be loaded and decoded as fast as possible, and the hashing function, which should provide hashes diverse enough to work well with the index, but yet with enough of engineered hash collisions to provide a good candidate set.

Main additions to Solr are the request handler for content based, visual search, a sort and re-rank function for text retrieval results based on visual similarity, and an ingest routine and data model for the visual features [1, 2]. Furthermore, a Solr entity processor takes care of automatic ingest from various data sources including RSS and Atom feeds and data bases. Currently five global image features are supported by the Lire Solr plugin: MPEG-7 ColorLayout and EdgeHistogram [3], JCD [4], PHOG [5] and a color histogram in the opponent color space. This provides a broad range of different types of features with (fuzzy) color and texture, as well as joint histograms. Other features can be added easily. SIFT feature indexing and search has already been contributed by the open source community. While the development of the Lire Solr plugin is an ongoing project, its current form is extremely stable and is for instance applied for trademark search by the World Intellectual Property Organization (WIPO)[1].

2.2.2 Media transcoding

HTML5 has introduced new tags to handle multimedia content: `<video>`, `<audio>` and `<svg>`, that let to embed these media without requiring plugins such as Adobe Flash. However browsers do not support all the same set of media containers (i.e. file formats) and codecs, thus ingested videos have to be converted to MPEG-4 files with H.264 compression, OGV/Theora and Google WebM, while audio files have to be transcoded to MP3 and OGG/Vorbis formats. Images that are not already PNG or JPEG are converted to JPEG. The most complex operation is required for text documents, like Powerpoint or Word: they are converted to SVG (allowing an infinite level of zooming due to the vectorial nature of this format) and to JPEG (to provide thumbnails).

3. INSTALLATION AND LICENSES

The project web page is available at `http://www.micc.unifi.it/vim/opensource/`. Source code, precompiled libraries for a fast installation, and full installation instructions are available on `https://github.com/miccunifi/Loki`. The Loki license is the Apache License 2.0, that allows to use it in commercial products and, in case of private use does not require the release of the code. To install the Loki+Lire framework there is need of a web server (e.g. Apache), a SQL database server (e.g. MySQL) and an application server (e.g. Apache Tomcat) with Solr. Download and install the latest Solr under Tomcat following the official Apache instructions[2]. Copy the whole `web/` folder into the document root of the Loki+Lire installation on the HTTP server. Create a database restoring the SQL schema dump in `install/db/`. Copy the all the JAR libs (among which there is the Lire Solr plugin) from `install/solr/lib` into the Solr installation. Check the Solr configuration files in `install/solr/conf/`, in particular check that the `<lib />` directives in `solr-config.xml` link correctly to the JAR files, and check the definition of the SQL data import handler `data-config.xml` (change DB user and password used to access the SQL server as well as URLs - all marked with `<!- FILL VALUE xxx ->`). Copy the updated files to the Solr configuration folder. Modify the following Loki configuration files with values of Tomcat, Solr and database servers: *i)* `app/js/serviceInclude.js`, *ii)* `service/config/db-default.php`, *iii)* `app/config.php`, *iv)* `app/js/config.js`, .

Lire as well as the Lire Solr plugin are licensed under GNU General Public License (GPL) v2. Lire Solr is provided as is at `https://bitbucket.org/dermotte/liresolr`. To install only the Lire Solr plugin (without the Loki components) in a running Solr instance use the following instructions. After downloading the source code from the repository, a single JAR should be generated using Apache Ant[3] (ant task *dist*). Then, after adding this jar to the classpath so that Solr can find it, the new request handler and the sort function have to be added to the solrconfig.xml file. Finally, the fields for content based retrieval – two for each visual feature – are added to the index schema along with the definition of the custom index field type storing the feature vectors. Detailed installation instructions are given on `https://bitbucket.org/dermotte/liresolr`.

Acknowledgments. Part of the research leading to these results has received funding from the EU 7th FP managed by REA (FP7/2007-2013) under grant agreement no. 262428.

4. REFERENCES

[1] Mathias Lux. LIRE: open source image retrieval in Java. In *Proc. of ACM Multimedia*, pages 843–846, 2013.

[2] Mathias Lux and Glenn Macstravic. The LIRE request handler: A Solr plug-in for large scale content based image retrieval. In Cathal Gurrin, Frank Hopfgartner, Wolfgang Hurst, Havard Johansen, Hyowon Lee, and Noel O'Connor, editors, *Proceedings of the 20th MultiMedia Modeling Conference (MMM 2014)*, volume 8326 of *Lecture Notes in Computer Science*, pages 374–377, Dublin, IE, Jan 2014. Springer International Publishing.

[3] Shih-Fu Chang, Thomas Sikora, and Atul Puri. Overview of the MPEG-7 standard. *IEEE Transactions on Circuits and Systems for Video Technology*, 11(6):688–695, June 2001.

[4] Savvas A. Chatzichristofis, Yiannis S. Boutalis, and Mathias Lux. Selection of the proper compact composite descriptor for improving content based image retrieval. In *The Sixth IASTED International Conference on Signal Processing, Pattern Recognition and Applications SPPRA 2009*, 2009.

[5] Anna Bosch, Andrew Zisserman, and Xavier Munoz. Representing shape with a spatial pyramid kernel. In *Proceedings of the 6th ACM international conference on Image and video retrieval*, CIVR '07, pages 401–408, New York, NY, USA, 2007. ACM.

[1] see the image filter in the WIPO Brand DB at `http://www.wipo.int/branddb/`

[2] `https://wiki.apache.org/solr/SolrTomcat#Installing_Solr_instances_under_Tomcat`

[3] `http://ant.apache.org/`

Audiovisual Resynthesis in an Augmented Reality

Parag Mital
Dartmouth College
Hanover, NH
parag@pkmital.com

ABSTRACT

"Resynthesizing Perception" immserses participants within an audiovisual augmented reality using goggles and headphones while they explore their environment. What they hear and see is a computationally generative synthesis of what they would normally hear and see. By demonstrating the associations and juxtapositions the synthesis creates, the aim is to bring to light questions of the nature of representations supporting perception. Two modes of operation are possible. In the first model, while a participant is immersed, salient auditory events from the surrounding environment are stored and continually aggregated to a database. Similarly, for vision, using a model of exogenous attention, proto-objects of the ongoing dynamic visual scene are continually stored using a camera mounted to goggles on the participant's head. The aggregated salient auditory events and proto-objects form a set of representations which are used to resynthesize the microphone and camera inputs in real-time. In the second model, instead of extracting representations from the real world, an existing database of representations already extracted from scenes such as images of paintings and natural auditory scenes are used for synthesizing the real world. This work was previously exhibited at the Victoria and Albert Museum in London. Of the 1373 people to participate in the installation, 21 participants agreed to be filmed and fill out a questionnaire. We report their feedback and show that "Resynthesizing Perception" is an engaging and thought-provoking experience questioning the nature of perceptual representations.

Categories and Subject Descriptors

H.5.1 [**Multimedia Information Systems**]: Artificial, augmented, and virtual realities

1. INTRODUCTION

Many theories of perception suggest that our perception is derived from internal representations of the sensory information entering our senses but that we are unaware of their details [1, 9, 8]. These representations, denoted by salient auditory events and visual proto-objects, are theorized to be the latest stage of pre-attentive processing and the earliest stage of representation acted upon by attentional machinery. They also do not require semantics or language in order to be represented, but rather provide a basis for understanding objects and events in the world. As we do not have access to them, what are the representations supporting these processes? How are they modeled, what do they look or sound like, what can they explain, and what can they not explain? Rather than attempt to answer these questions through the traditional sciences, we attempt to open a dialogue around them through an arts practice.

This practice is defined by scene synthesis: a computationally generative collage process making use of a computational model of salient auditory events and visual proto-object representations. We place participants within a real-time audiovisual scene synthesis using virtual reality goggles and headphones. Representations of the auditory and visual scenes as measured by a microphone and a head-mounted camera are continually learned while the participant experiences an ongoing scene synthesis process. In one scenario, no explicitly predefined database is used for synthesizing the ongoing scene. Rather, the scene is recreated using sonic and visual representations the software learns over time. By continually associating the incoming input with its aggregated stored representations, we attempt to create syntheses questioning how associations in similar representations may be perceived and re-contextualized.

Ideally, the stored representations will allow for a synthesis indistinguishable from its target. However, what happens when they are entierly unlike the stimuli? For instance, what if we have only learned representations of the sonic world of 'trees' and 'birds'. How would we then synthesize an acoustic scene full of voices? Or in the visual case, what if we had only formed representations composed by paintings of Hieryonomous Bosch, and then had to synthesize the natural visual world as we are used to it? In a second scenario, we allow participants to ask these questions by choosing pre-built models which have been trained on databases of various visual scenes such as those depicted in paintings by Bosch, Van Gogh, and Monet, for the visual synthesis, and scenes such as different musical genres or natural auditory scenes, for the auditory synthesis.

We first contextualize our work within related arts practices. We then briefly motivate our computational models of auditory and visual representations based on literature in auditory streaming and proto-objects, respectively, and

MM'14, November 3–7, 2014, Orlando, Florida, USA.

http://dx.doi.org/10.1145/2647868.2655617.

then describe our methods. We then show a few example syntheses and report feedback from an exhibition in London at the Victoria and Albert Museum in 2012.

2. RELATED PRACTICES

Our synthesis process can be seen as a form of a computationally generative collage. Historically, collage is an arts practice which appropriates fragments of culture for its materials. Depending on its medium, it juxtaposes, often chaotically, fragments such as photographs or clips of sound, removing them from their original context. By doing so, it is capable of communicating new interpretations which the original fragments alone could not have provided.

The juxtaposition of fragments of sound as an arts practice has roots at least as early as musique concrète, a compositional technique assembling various natural found sounds in order to produce a collage of sound. Digital Sampling came in the 1970's allowing sound segments to be triggered using an interface such as a keyboard or pad. More recent techniques have focused on granuar or concatenative synthesis, where a target sound is matched to a stored database of segments or sounds (for a more in-depth review of these practices, see [3]).

Visual collage practices making use of computation are abundant within graphics communities, and have taken various forms from compositing, texture synthesis, example-based synthesis, and various methods for artistic stylization. Indeed our own synthesis engine is a repurposing of a previous artistic stylization framework known as corpus based visual synthesis [5, 3].

3. METHODS

3.1 Augmented Reality

The exhibition in 2012 had participants wear the Vuzix Wrap920AR goggles. These goggles house two small CRT screens (640 x 480 @ 30Hz with 31 degree field of view), with two front-facing cameras. Due to procesing limitations, only one camera feed was synthesized and displayed on both CRT screens. Since then, this work has been migrated for the Oculus Rift with a camera mounted to the front, as this setup offers an increased field of view and a design which masks all light except for the display. The processing occurs on a laptop nearby, meaning participants are only able to explore as far as the length of the cable (2 meters).

Participants were also invited to wear a pair of headphones, a Beyerdyanmic DT 770 Pro. These were chosen as being comfortable to wear, sanitary (i.e. as opposed to in-ear monitors), and having excellent acoustic isolation due to its closed ear design. The processing for audio occurs on an iPhone, as the application is self-contained in the iOS app, "Memory Mosaic", freely available on the app store[1] [3].

3.2 Computational Synthesis Engine

3.2.1 Visual

Our visual model attempts to actively describe a visual scene, simulating the movements of the eye using an exogenous attention model [6], and representing a scene by its

[1]`https://itunes.apple.com/us/app/memory-mosaic/id475759669?mt=8`

(a) Original Image (b) Visual Acuity Filter

Figure 1: 1a: Original frame; 1b: Examples of how the exogenous attention map (inlayed in the image) is used to simulate the point of fixation (drawn as a black/white circle as seen over the man potting).

proto-objects [8, 5, 3]. This model effectively describes the shape and color of finer detailed regions at points of likely fixations, and coarser details in places less likely to be fixated. To do so, we first use a previously motivated model of exogenous attention to define the dynamic visual salience of the scene built using contrasts in a dense optical flow map [6, 3]. The point of highest saliency along with the entire saliency map's entropy is then fed to visual acuity filter simulating the logarithmic drop in spatial resolution outside of the point of fixation. An example in shown in Figure 1. As the entropy is low, the blurring is quite substantial, removing many of the details more likely to be unattended such as the high frequency edges in the bricks, grass, and leaves.

The output of this image is then used for corpus based visual synthesis (CBVS) [5]. The underlying algorithm of CBVS, maximally stable color regions [2], affords us the ability to sort coarse to fine blobs based on their level sets. We can further define the coarse to fine precision using simple parameters such as timesteps and placing a threshold on the minimum region size. For real-time aggregation of content, we only aggregate proto-objects every 300 ms, as this temporal resolution is also the average time of a fixation [6]. Only proto-objects whose description falls beyond a threshold of a metric computing color and shape similarity are stored. As space is limited, we refer the reader to the paper on CBVS for more details, including examples of visual synthesis using corpora of Van Gogh, Monet, Klimt, and others [5, 3].

In Figures 2 and 3, we show two examples of visual scene synthesis. We also show an example of visual scene synthesis using an alternate database of Hieryonymous Bosch, producing the scene in Figure 2d. In the latter example, we also reveal more of the attention map (3b), its effect on the visual acuity map (3c), and how this distributes the spatial scale of proto-objects (3d).

3.2.2 Audio

Our auditory model is inspired by auditory streaming [1] and evidence of event related potentials demonstrating the brains remarkable ability to detect temporally incoherent auditory events even without our attention to the task (e.g. mismatch negativity) [9]. We model event detection, store them, and then use the same events for resynthesizing any newly detected salient auditory events. The saliency of an event is denoted by its temporal incoherence, which is described by the event's ability to explain the current auditory model (described in [4, 3]). This model is represented as

(a) Original video feed (b) Proto-objects

(c) Visual synthesis (d) Visual synthesis using Bosch

Figure 2: An example of the real-time visual synthesis. 2a Original image. 2b Proto-objects. 2c Visual synthesis using an aggregated database of the same scene. 2d Visual synthesis using a database of Hieryonomous Bosch paintings.

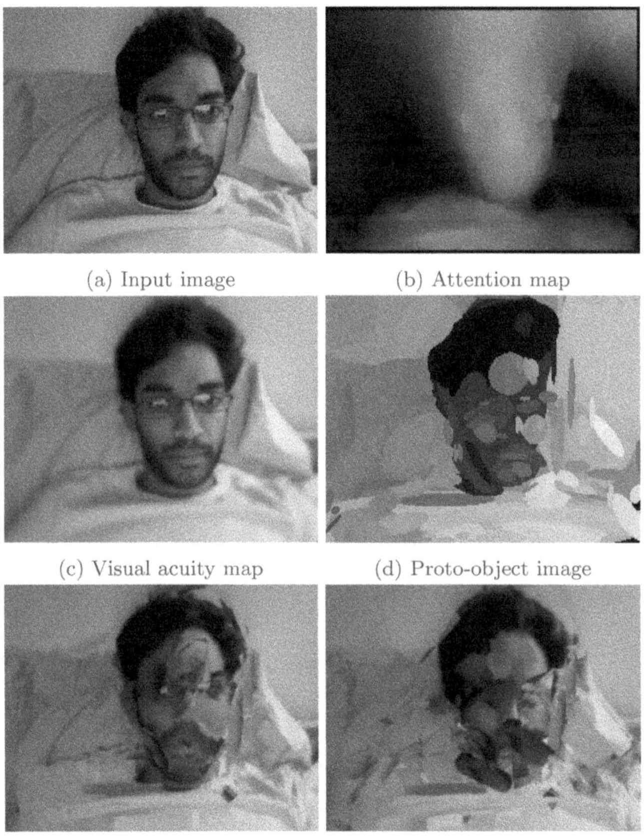

(a) Input image (b) Attention map

(c) Visual acuity map (d) Proto-object image

(e) Synthesized image (f) Another synthesized image

Figure 3: Example processing for producing visual syntheses. The input video 3a is analyzed for the most likely focal point in 3b. This point is used in the synthetic acuity map shown in 3c. This image is used in finding the proto-objects shown in 3d. And finally matched to the existing database to produce the example syntheses in 3e and 3f.

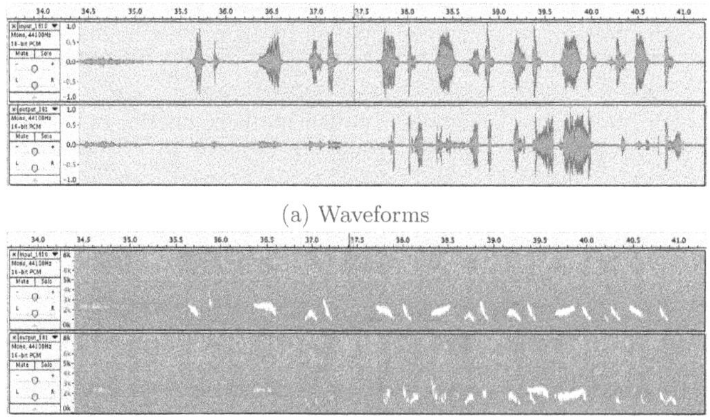

(a) Waveforms

(b) Spectrums

Figure 4: Here we visually represent auditory scene synthesis as its signal and spectrogram. The clip is of David Attenborough documenting the Lyre bird. The original is displayed on top of the synthesis in each case.

a Gaussian Mixture of Mel-Frequency Cepstral Coefficients, their deltas, and their delta deltas. Due to space constraints, we refer the reader to the full implementation details for our event detection model in [4, 3].

Once events have been segmented, their features are concatenated, and matching is done using dynamic time warping. We optimize for real-time performance using recent boundary constraints [7] and for Apple hardware using the Accelerate framework (source code freely available online at `github.com/pkmital`. Finally, synthesis is performed using the Dirac3 LE Time Stretching algorithm[2]. This allows for sequence matches with different lengths to be played back without changing the pitch of the original sample.

In Figure 4, we show an example of audio scene synthesis represented as its original and synthesized waveforms and spectrograms. Notice how the first few large jumps in the original signal's amplitude are matched quite well for their spectra, though not in amplitude. In the later parts of the audio file, the synthesis appears much closer in amplitude, as it has learned more loud sounds, while the spectra is still matched fairly well, though with significant discontinuities.

4. FEEDBACK

Feedback was collected during an exhibition called "Augmented Reality Hallucinations" held at the Victoria and Albert Museum in London in 2012 during the Digital Design Weekend (part of the London Design Festival). The exhibition ran for 2 days from 10 a.m. to 5 p.m. The total number of people attending my exhibit alone as reported by the V&A Museum on Saturday was 445 adults and 128 under 18s and on Sunday, 590 adults and 210 under 18s for a total of 1373 people. Of these, 21 participants agreed to be filmed, photographed, and fill out a questionnaire.

On the feedback form (see [3] for the form and full details of the participant's responses), participants made many qualitative comments regarding the visual aesthetics. For instance, when participants were asked, "Did this experience make you think of anything you had seen or heard before?", three participants made references to their experiences on hallucinogens and two to dreams. Also of note in

[2] `dirac.dspdimension.com`

the qualitative feedback were references to art styles such as, "It reminded me of Francis Bacon's Figurative style" and "The movement was Impressionistic, almost painterly". When asked, "What did you dislike most about the experience?", of note were the responses, "Would have liked more depth in colour", "Not sure what I was seeing at first with the goggles", and "Hard to understand how it works."

Quantitative feedback is summarized in Figure 6. The feedback demonstrates that participants overall rated the visual experience higher than the auditory experience. One possible reason for this may be expressed in the qualititative feedback, with one participant writing, "The granular-like sound is a bit too extreme with headphones." Though another participant also found that "The sound was definitely an enhancement. Not quite the same without."

Participants also made a number of comments regarding perception. When asked what they liked about the experience, participants wrote, "the changing of the perception of reality", "it made me think of how our brain deconstructs and reconstructs elements of perception, particularly in the goggles", "the effect on my perception about the environment and myself as well".

Augmented Reality Hallucinations was also featured in the article, "See Like A Bug On Acid", on the media blog `createdigitalmotion.com`. Editor in-chief Peter Kirn says of the work, "What's great about this project is the way in which it alters reality - with the aid of video input".

Figure 5: A few participants of the installation wearing the AR goggles. Headphones (shown in the top picture to the left) were worn at times, though are not shown being worn here. Photos by the author. Participants gave written consent to be photographed.

5. CONCLUSION

We have described "Resynthesizing Perception", an augmented reality experience employing a computational model of visual and auditory perception to synthesize the world around us. It functions in two possible modes: (1) by aggregating representations learned from the world, and (2), by

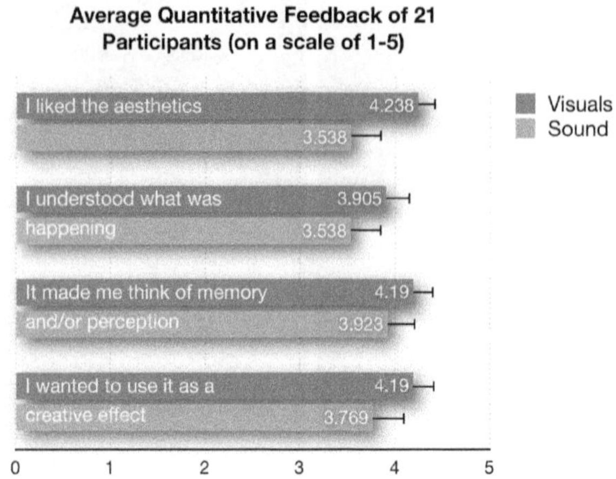

Figure 6: Feedback where 21 participants were asked to rate different aspects of the auditory and visual synthesis. Error bars depict +/- 1 S.E.

using a predefined database of representations learned from different scenes such as those of painters and auditory scenes of nature or different musical recordings. By demonstrating the associations and juxtapositions the synthesis creates, its aim is to bring to light questions of the nature of representations supporting perception. One failing of the model has been that we consider either modality separately. Certainly many multisensory and crossmodal effects have been demonstrated in the literature (e.g. the auditory override of visual perception as demonstrated in the double flash illusion and the visual override of auditory perception as demonstrated in the McGurk effect). It would be interesting to explore such interactions in the future.

6. REFERENCES

[1] A. S. Bregman. *Auditory Scene Analysis: The Perceptual Organization of Sound.* A Bradford Book (September 29, 1994), 1990.

[2] P.-E. Forssén. Maximally stable colour regions for recognition and matching. In *Computer Vision and Pattern Recognition, 2007. CVPR '07. IEEE Conference on*, pages 1–8, Minneapolis, MN, 2007. IEEE.

[3] P. K. Mital. *Audiovisual Scene Synthesis.* Ph.d. dissertation, Goldsmiths, University of London, 2014.

[4] P. K. Mital and M. Grierson. Mining Unlabeled Electronic Music Databases through 3D Interactive Visualization of Latent Component Relationships. In *NIME 2013: New Interfaces for Musical Expression*, Seoul, Korea, 2013.

[5] P. K. Mital, M. Grierson, and T. J. Smith. Corpus-based visual synthesis. In *Proceedings of the ACM Symposium on Applied Perception - SAP '13*, pages 51–58, New York, New York, USA, Aug. 2013. ACM Press.

[6] P. K. Mital, T. J. Smith, R. L. Hill, and J. M. Henderson. Clustering of Gaze During Dynamic Scene Viewing is Predicted by Motion. *Cognitive Computation*, 3(1):5–24, Oct. 2010.

[7] T. Rakthanmanon, B. Campana, A. Mueen, G. Batista, B. Westover, Q. Zhu, J. Zakaria, and E. Keogh. Searching and mining trillions of time series subsequences under dynamic time warping. *Proceedings of the 18th ACM SIGKDD international conference on Knowledge discovery and data mining - KDD '12*, page 262, 2012.

[8] R. a. Rensink. The Dynamic Representation of Scenes. *Visual Cognition*, 7(1-3):17–42, Jan. 2000.

[9] I. Winkler, S. L. Denham, and I. Nelken. Modeling the auditory scene: predictive regularity representations and perceptual objects. *Trends in cognitive sciences*, 13(12):532–40, Dec. 2009.

Sound-Light Giblet

Charles Roberts
AlloSphere Research Group
University of California at Santa Barbara
charlie@charlie-roberts.com

ABSTRACT

We describe an audiovisual live coding performance created using *Gibber*, a creative coding environment that runs in the browser. The performance takes advantage of novel affordances for rapidly creating music, shaders, and mappings that tie together audio and visual modalities.

Categories and Subject Descriptors

D.2.6 [**Programming Environments**]: Interactive Environments; J.5 [**Arts and Humanities**]: Performing Arts

General Terms

Design, Human Factors

Keywords

Multimodal Programming, Live coding, Audio, Graphics, Web, JavaScript, Creative Coding, Live Performance

1. INTRODUCTION

In its modern canonical form, a *live coding* performance consists of a performer connecting their laptop to a projector (and possibly speakers) and generating of work of audiovisual art in realtime by coding it in front of the audience [1, 3]. In a twist meant to address a lack of transparency often found in digital performance practice, the code editor that the performer uses is projected so that the audience can follow along with the code as the performer types it. Through source code text, algorithmic processes are potentially illuminated to audience members. An important characteristic of live coding environments is enabling dynamic evaluation of source code; by injecting new code into a running program algorithms can be changed without requiring breaks in audiovisual output that would typically occur during compilation.

The majority of live coding environments to date have focused on audio programming, but some, such as Fluxus[1], have primarily focused on generative visuals. A narrower subset, including *Impromptu* [9] and *LuaAV* [10], enable both audio and graphics to be coded simultaneously. A recent development in the live coding community is the ability to perform using browser-based technologies [7, 4, 2]. I created the environment used in this performance, *Gibber*[2], which runs in any modern web browser and affords live coding performances consisting of temporally synchronized audiovisual content.

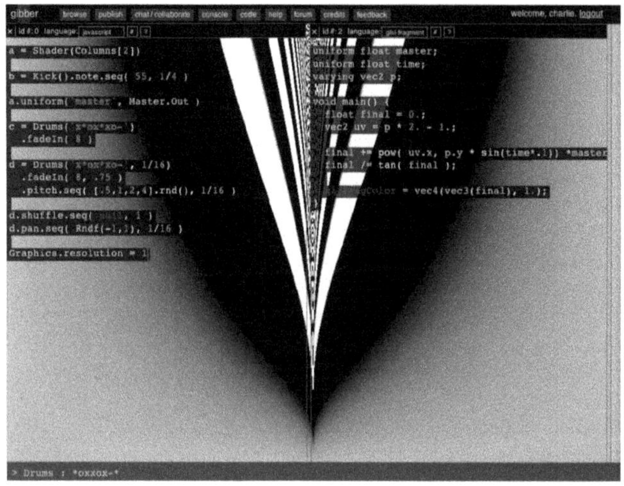

Figure 1: Split-screen coding in Gibber. Generative visuals are presented in the background of source code text. To the left is JavaScript, while on the right is a GLSL fragment shader.

2. PERFORMANCE

In the performance, I generate music and visuals inside of the Chrome web browser using Gibber. The visuals take the form of a generative OpenGL fragment shader, which is continuously iterated and recompiled on-the-fly over the course of the performance. The fragment shader responds to the music I generate via mapping abstractions that enable cross-modal, multi-rate mappings to be expressed with a minimal amount of code. For example, consider the following code mapping the rotation of a cube to a sine oscillator's frequency:

[1]http://www.pawfal.org/fluxus/

[2]http://gibber.mat.ucsb.edu

MM'14, November 03 - 07 2014, Orlando, FL, USA.

ACM 978-1-4503-3063-3/14/11 $15.00.
http://dx.doi.org/10.1145/2647868.2655618

```
a = Cube(); b = Sine();
a.rotation = b.Frequency;
```

In the above example, the actual mapping takes only a single line of code. The capitalization of the `Frequency` property serves as an indicator to Gibber to create a continuous mapping between the properties instead of using the instantaneous frequency value. This minimal notation enables performers to rapidly experiment with a variety of mappings between audio and visual elements during the course of a performance [8].

The audio consists of generative electronic dance music, typical of the Algorave movement[3]. Both the audio and visual content begins minimally, and gradually increase in complexity as code is iterated, expanded, and explored.

3. CONCLUSION

This performance showcases technical capabilities of its authoring environment, Gibber. These abilities include the ability to live code audiovisual performances inside of the browser and to rapidly conduct aesthetic experiments with cross-modal mappings. For scientists and artists interested in programming education, it is important to note the end-user programming language for Gibber is JavaScript; this enables syntax learned while exploring Gibber to easily transfer to other domains. The ability to rapidly realize audiovisual content through dynamic code injection (an implicit requirement for live coding performance, although *slow coding*[4] practices do exist) also benefits programming students by providing more immediate feedback than other creative coding environments used for education such as Scratch [6] or Processing [5].

4. ACKNOWLEDGMENTS

The Robert W. Deutsch Foundation supported this research with generous graduate and post-doctoral fellowships.

5. REFERENCES

[1] N. Collins, A. McLean, J. Rohrhuber, and A. Ward. Live coding in laptop performance. *Organised Sound*, 8(03):321–330, 2003.

[2] D. Della Casa and G. John. LiveCodeLab 2.0 and its language LiveCodeLang. In *Proceedings of the second ACM SIGPLAN workshop on Functional art, music, modeling & design*. ACM, 2014.

[3] T. Magnusson. Herding cats: Observing live coding in the wild. *Computer Music Journal*, 38(1):8–16, 2014.

[4] C. McKinney. Quick live coding collaboration in the web browser. In *Proceedings of the 2014 Conference on New Interfaces for Musical Expression*, pages 379–382, 2014.

[5] C. Reas and B. Fry. Processing: programming for the media arts. *AI & SOCIETY*, 20(4):526–538, 2006.

[6] M. Resnick, J. Maloney, A. Monroy-Hernández, N. Rusk, E. Eastmond, K. Brennan, A. Millner, E. Rosenbaum, J. Silver, B. Silverman, et al. Scratch: programming for all. *Communications of the ACM*, 52(11):60–67, 2009.

[3]http://algorave.com/about

[4]http://www.ludions.com/slowcode/

Figure 2: Live coding in Gibber in fullscreen mode, which hides GUI elements that are not needed in live performance. Keyboard macros allow the performer to quickly switch between editing JavaScript and GLSL.

[7] C. Roberts and J. Kuchera-Morin. Gibber: Live coding audio in the browser. *Proceedings of the International Computer Music Conference*, 2012.

[8] C. Roberts, M. Wright, J. Kuchera-Morin, and T. Höllerer. Rapid creation and publication of digital musical instruments. In *Proceedings of the 2014 Conference on New Interfaces for Musical Expression*, pages 239–242, 2014.

[9] A. Sorensen. Impromptu: An interactive programming environment for composition and performance. In *Proceedings of the Australasian Computer Music Conference*, 2005.

[10] G. Wakefield, W. Smith, and C. Roberts. LuaAV: Extensibility and Heterogeneity for Audiovisual Computing. *Proceedings of Linux Audio Conference*, 2010.

Gone: An Interactive Experience for Two People

Michael Riegler
Simula Research Laboratory AS, NO
michael@simula.no

Mathias Lux
Klagenfurt University, AT
mlux@itec.aau.at

Christian Zellot
Klagenfurt University, AT
czellot@edu.uni-klu.ac.at

Lukas Knoch
Klagenfurt University, AT
lukas.knoch@aau.at

Horst Schnattler
Klangkulisse e.U., Austria
post@klangkulisse.at

Sabrina Napetschnig
Klagenfurt University, AT
s.besteck@gmail.com

ABSTRACT

In this paper we present a multimedia art installation which uses human computer interaction to give the user the possibility to experience how blind people perceive the world and how hard it can be. The installation follows the classical co-operative game pattern, where a group of people – in this case two – have to work together to achieve a goal. With these basic characteristics in mind we consider our submission a *serious game*. With this serious game we show how multimedia can be used for making people more attentive for problems of other people and that multimedia, and in this case serious games, are indeed a useful tool for letting people experience situations they have not been aware of before.

Categories and Subject Descriptors

H.5.m [**Information Interfaces and Presentation**]: Miscellaneous—*Art Games*

Keywords

Interactive; Multimedia; Art; Game

Figure 1: Intro scene of the game.

1. INTRODUCTION

In modern societies people feel often alone with their thoughts, troubles, fears or their specific and unique view of the world. Although they may be amongst others and interconnected by modern media technologies.

We do not often care about others and about their problems. A common indication is the anonymity in public transport. For example if one is travelling with a crowded bus it is more and more recognizable that people are more attracted by their phone than by their surrounding people. One, can very often observe that if a disabled person wants to enter the bus or metro and needs assistance along the way only very few people around are willing to help. While we can consider that many people may not pay attention to their surroundings, we can also hypothesize that people are not able to feel empathy with those in need as they do not recognize the troublesome situation not being able to see through the eyes of the affected persons. Furthermore people sometimes do not want to help because they not know how to interact in the correct way with other people. So before they pretend to do something that can offend other people they prefer to ignore them.

To make a start raising awareness we initiated a project, where many people worked together to create a serious game that allows two people to (i) experience the world through ears of a blind person and (ii) to help a blind person with extremely limited communication possibilities. It can be considered a two player, co-operative serious game. One player directs the other player through a house by turning on and off sources of sound, while the other player has to find the way to a specific spot solely by listening and steering the avatar based on the sound emissions triggered be the other player.

In the remainder of this paper we first describe the story and creation process of the serious game, we then investigate

MM'14, November 03 - 07 2014, Orlando, FL, USA.

http://dx.doi.org/10.1145/2647868.2655619

the technology and installation, and finally discuss the user experience and reception of the installation by testers from a small, exploratory user study.

2. GONE

Gone is a two player serious game where one player steers a blind man, Thomas, through a house, by exclusively using acoustic indications. The other player provides the acoustic indications, playing the ghost of Thomas' late wife, who has come back to help her lone husband. The story is also visually outlined in Figures 1 and 2, which are part of the introduction animation of Gone. The original storyline of the serious game is:

> *As Thomas' wife died in a car crash, he couldn't recover from the pain the accident inflicted. Thomas is blind and cannot manage his everyday live by himself in this situation. To not leave Thomas behind alone, his wife comes back as a ghost and interacts with objects in their house to guide Thomas to objects symbolizing shared memories and, therefore, to provide emotional closure.*

Figure 2: Screen from the introduction.

One player is using a computer screen, beamer or display device and plays the ghost of Thomas' wife. She can interact with objects by turning on sound sources in a ground plan of their house. Those sources can be for instance rattling leaves of potted plants, radios, water tabs, fans, clocks, hair dryers, or telephones. Each of the sound sources has a distinct volume and length. For instance, the potted plant leaves rattle for half a second, while the clock ticks for 10 seconds. Sounds cannot be turned off by the ghost. The other player, playing the role of Thomas, is sitting turned away from the screen with headphones on to hear the sound becoming louder or quieter depending on his position and field of view. He can also hear the direction of the sound and move forward or backward with a game pad. The goal of *Gone* is to guide Thomas to all relevant positions in their house only by sound. When Thomas reaches the spots, he recalls positive as well as negative events from their joined live by hearing music, sounds (e.g. the song of their wedding), or finding objects connected to a memory. These memories and their emotional impact are explained in audio. After recalling four different memories, Thomas achieves emotional closure and can go on with his life and the ghost of his wife finds peace.

The game was initially brainstormed and implemented within the Global Game Jam (GGJ)[1] in January 2014, at a local GGJ event in Graz, Austria. This gave us the unique opportunity to build a highly motivated group of people of different professions, who have not worked together before in such a way. An initial version was created, tested and presented at the GGJ event in Graz and included the actual game with one single memory spot to find. The game was later extended by a menu screen, more sophisticated asset management, and three further memories to find (now four in total) as well as a full screen mode, higher resolution and a new tutorial and credits screen for the submission to the ACM Multimedia Conference 2014 Arts Track and has never been displayed publicly in such an installation before.

3. TECHNOLOGY & INSTALLATION

Game development gained a lot of attention in research recently and is a rising field with a lot of possible applications like gamification or games with a purpose. In the last years though people started considering games as art, including the interaction, the visual and audio design, and the way games are able to convey experiences in an interactive fashion. A lot of games, especially among the so-called *indie games* (short for independent games, which are often considered independent from game publishers or large studios), often aim for more artistic, social aspects or aspects of unique interactive experience rather than pure and simple entertainment value. Games can be seen as an interactive multimedia experience, hence they have the ability to arouse art for the viewer on an individual basis and extended freedom of interpretation.

Artistic games (art games) are connected to serious games in a way that both aim to extend games beyond pure entertainment. The ambition of serious games is to design them in such a way that they, beside providing a way to have fun, also generate useful information, or communicate and teach concepts and information. Serious games used in research are for instance described in [4]. Furthermore, the area of serious games and therefore gamification of certain tasks is a rising field in multimedia research. Examples for such games can be found in [2, 1] and [3]. In the first paper the authors use gamification to boost the accuracy of search results. The second paper uses a serious game approach to get ambiguous feedback for people recognition. In the last paper Pothineni et al. try to mould online behaviour trough an incentive based game design. All these papers show that the idea of games can be used for much broader purposes than just playing.

Art games, however, are often designed and produced with different intentions. Art games may try to trigger certain reactions from the player, like an emotional response or an intellectual response. One great and recent example is

[1] `http://globalgamejam.org/`

the game *Papers, Please*[2], developed by Lucas Pope. The game won numerous awards including from Ars Technica, The New Yorker, Wired, and Forbes. In this game players work for the Ministry of Admission of the fictional country of Arstotzka. They have to check passports and decide for each case upon admission, refusal, or even arrest of the applicant. Sloppy or slow work leads to loss of income, and the player is always short of money for medicine, food, and heating for his family. This game lets players experience a shear hopeless situation, where a single clerk has to work so that his family does not starve, but on the other side has to decide upon the lives of others.

Gone aims into a similar direction. We let players experience (i) the situation of blind people and (ii) those that can only communicate in a very restricted way with their environment.

3.1 Technology and Usage

Gone has been developed in Java, using libGDX[3], a cross-platform, open source, game development framework. It provides an easy way to create 2D interactive programs based on OpenGL on MacOS, Windows, Linux, Android, iOS and for the Web. While it's mainly targeted at desktop platforms, the software part of Gone can easily be adapted to mobile devices and the web.

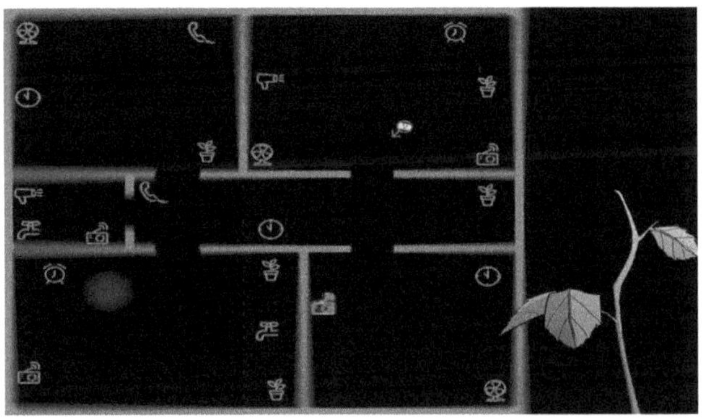

Figure 3: Screenshot of Gone. Thomas is currently in the northeast room, looking southwest. The memory to recall is found in the southwest room. The radio highlighted in the southeast room is currently generating noise. The rose on the right hand side serves as a progress indicator and grows to full bloom when finding all the memories.

Figure 3 shows the general game screen. The icon indicating position and view direction of Thomas is in the northeast room. The rose serves as a progress indicator and grows to full bloom when recalling all the memories (see Figure 4). The player of the ghost clicks on the icons in the house and then they generate noise. As long as they are emitting sound, they are highlighted (see radio icon in Figure 3 in the southeast room). While the ghost has to steer Thomas to the memory (pulsing blue circle, in the southwest room in Figure 3), Thomas of course cannot walk through walls, so he has to be steered through doors. For the player controlling Thomas' icon, the stereo headphones give indications on the (i) direction by changing the volume on the stereo channels, (ii) the distance by change in the overall volume, and (iii) if the noise comes from behind by applying a low-pass filter. The aesthetic of the game, including colors, drawings and audio, are kept in a way that it is able to transfer the dramatic and sad mood of the game's topic to the players over the audio and optical channel.

Figure 4: The rose serves as a progress indicator and grows to full bloom after all four memories have been recalled.

3.2 Installation

Figure 5 shows how the installation is set up. The user who wants to experience the game as Thomas has to enter a cabin. The player inside the cabin gets a wireless game pad (i.e., a Xbox 360 controller) and a wireless headset. Both components are not attached to cables, so the player does not get any hint for direction. This leads to loss of orientation within the cabin and further helps Gone to convey the feeling of blindness, to the player. On the outside a mini projector is mounted which projects the current game for the audience to a display, i.e., a wall. The second player operates a laptop which is positioned outside the cabin. By interacting with objects on the screen simply by clicking on them with the mouse, sound effects are generated to be heard by the player playing the role of Thomas. Due to the simulated blindness navigation is solely based on audio clues from the stereo head phones. The audience can observe the game and the movement of the player. Leaving the cabin opened on the wall opposite to the projection allows the audience to see the reaction of the player who controls Thomas inside the cabin.

Note at that point that the software for the installation is available as open source software project and all the content including audio and visual assets are shared under a creative commons license[4].

4. RECEPTION

To get an idea if (i) the goal of the serious game can be reached in a cooperative way, i.e., one players can steer the other by triggering sounds to a specific point in the game plan, and (ii) if the installation is able to generate an emotional reaction from the players, we undertook an exploratory study with ten participants. Each of the participants had to play the game using both roles, Thomas

[2]http://papersplea.se/

[3]http://libgdx.badlogicgames.com/

[4]https://bitbucket.org/dermotte/gone

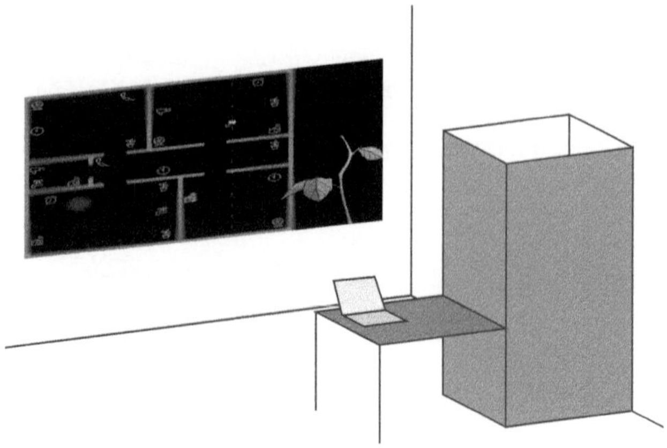

Figure 5: The setup of gone. One player is in the black cabin with the headphones on. The other player steers using the laptop computer and a mouse.

as well as the ghost of his late wife. After the successful completion of the task, i.e., finding all four memories, the participants answered questionnaire with five questions:

- How did you feel while playing the game? (rate from 1 very good to 5 very bad)
- Did Gone help you imagine how it would be to be blind?
- Describe in one word what you did feel while playing the game.
- Do you think that the game triggered an emotional response in you?
- If yes, what kind of emotional response?

From the questionnaire we could infer that only a small part of the participants would rate their overall feeling while playing the game as *good* (3 participants). Most of them (5 participants) described their overall feeling as *neutral*, 2 participants reported an overall *bad feeling*. This is an indication that the serious game and it serious topic is conveyed and considered as such. Even more, nine out of ten players could imagine how it would be to be blind during the time they experienced Gone as Thomas. So it gave them a way to experience the world blind people have to cope with, on an every day basis.

In the questionnaire participants described their feelings at most with negative adjectives: *helpless*, *sad* (2 times), *sympathetic*, *fear*, *unhappy*, *disoriented* and *confusing*. Two study participants described their feelings with *normal* and *nothing*. More than the half of the players said that the game triggered an emotional response. The exploratory study indicates that Gone is able to create the intended reaction within those experiencing the serious game, and, therefore, Gone offers a way to help people raise their individual awareness for blind people and those with limited capabilities of communication.

5. CONCLUSION

The novel art installation presented in this paper combines video games, art, human computer interaction and human to human interaction to a system, which has the potential to make people more aware of their surroundings with the primary goal to simulate the experience blind people have moving through their world. Within an exploratory study Gone has shown potential to make people think about a critical topic, which in this case was the difficulty of disabled persons to master everyday things like navigating in the own house. The use of a game in the art installation again shows how broad and rich the multimedia area is, and that games can be used for more than just enjoyment.

We are aware that Gone can approximate the feeling to be blind only so far, but Gone provides a controlled environment with a low entry barrier. It's easy to set up and has shown it's potential in an exploratory study. We sincerely hope to reach a lot of people through ACM MM. Note that the the software part of this installation is available under open source / creative commons license. Therefore, we assume the installation can be re-produced by interested readers. However, we have to point out that reducing the installation to a minimum reduces the interactive experience and does not serve the experience we want to convey well.

6. ACKNOWLEDGEMENTS

We would like to thank all the testers and contributors to the project. The team was a great mixture of different professions, including audio and visual artists, interaction designers, programmers and critical voices. The local GGJ event in Graz, Austria, provided good grounds for an initial prototype, therefore, thanks to Spraylight GmbH and Johanna Pirker.

This work was supported by Lakeside Labs GmbH, Klagenfurt, Austria and funding from the European Regional Development Fund and the Carinthian Economic Promotion Fund (KWF) under grant KWF-20214/25557/37319 and by the iAD center for Research-based Innovation (project number 174867) funded by the Norwegian Research Council.

7. ADDITIONAL AUTHORS

Additional authors: Julian Kogler (Game Design, Austria, email: `admin@ny24.at`), Claus Degendorfer (CodeFlügel GmbH, Austria, email: `claus.degendorfer@codefluegel.com`), Norbert Spot (CodeFlügel GmbH, Austria, email: `norbert.spot@codefluegel.com`) and Manuel Zoderer (CodeFlügel GmbH, Austria, email: `manuel.zoderer@codefluegel.com`).

8. REFERENCES

[1] M. Brenner, N. Mirza, and E. Izquierdo. People recognition using gamified ambiguous feedback. In *Proceedings of the First International Workshop on Gamification for Information Retrieval*, pages 22–26. ACM, 2014.

[2] M. Lux, M. Guggenberger, and M. Riegler. Picturesort: gamification of image ranking. In *Proceedings of the First International Workshop on Gamification for Information Retrieval*, pages 57–60. ACM, 2014.

[3] D. Pothineni, P. Mishra, A. Rasheed, and D. Sundararajan. Incentive design to mould online behavior: a game mechanics perspective. In *Proceedings of the First International Workshop on Gamification for Information Retrieval*, pages 27–32. ACM, 2014.

[4] L. Von Ahn and L. Dabbish. Designing games with a purpose. *Communications of the ACM*, 51(8):58–67, 2008.

Circles and Sounds

Sarah Linebaugh
790 Huff Road NW, Apt. 5020
Atlanta GA 30318
281-793-0449
slinebaugh9@gmail.com

ABSTRACT

The exploration of real-time, interactive motion graphics in a live environment is a response to the exponential growth of technology in culture and the human desire to engage in meaningful experiences. Interactive installations draw from the concepts of the New Aesthetic and Relational Aesthetics to create art that depends on cutting-edge technology while emphasizing human interaction and connectedness. The use of graphics that respond in real-time are a hallmark of the medium. Immediate responses from the technology allow the user to engage with the artwork instantaneously. By doing so, they can create meanings that are unique to themselves.

My interactive art installation, *Circles and Sounds,* combines art and technology in a way that will allow the user to engage with the technology to create their own real-time graphics and sound experience that is completely unique to them.

Categories and Subject Descriptors

J.5 [**Computer Applications**]: Arts and Humanities - *Arts, fine and performing;* I.4.8 [**Computing Methodologies**]: **Image Processing and Computer Vision, Scene Analysis -*Depth Cues; Tracking; Motion;***

Keywords

Interactive art, Installation, Motion graphics, Real-time, Kinect, Quartz Composer

1. INTRODUCTION

In recent history, society has seen two trends develop. The first is the exponential growth of technology and society's increasing dependence on it and interdependence with it. The second has developed as a result of the first: as society is immersed deeper into technology, the desire to step away from the isolation it can bring has become stronger. This is a push toward two seemingly different directions: the desire for the latest and greatest and a craving for meaningful interactions. Out of these desires, new trends are developing in the art world that combine both of them in explorations that are both cutting edge and innately human. Interactive art in live settings often uses technology in ways that have been previously unseen, and it encourages a pioneering spirit in developing new technologies. At the same time, many of these works are inoperable or meaningless without human engagement and creation.

Interactive art references aesthetics like the New Aesthetic[1] and Relational Aesthetics [2] to create a combination that is both uniquely technical and collaborative. The New Aesthetic draws from the visual language of pixels, bytes and glitches given to us by the machines we use. It is an aesthetic completely unique to the last few generations, yet it has become so prevalent within our culture that it is being cultivated as style, as art, and as language. Relational Art or Relational Aesthetics is an aesthetic that bases itself on the concept of art as a form of social exchange. The artist is seen as the catalyst in relational art, rather than being at the center. The aesthetic creates inter-subjective encounters in which meaning is established collectively, rather than individually.

Another important aspect of interactive art is that it takes place in real-time. Immediate responses from the technology allow the user to engage with the artwork instantaneously. By doing so, they can create meanings that are unique to themselves. Interactive art is often on the cutting edge of the latest technological developments since many of the artworks are based on new ideas that have not been done before. Because of this, interactive art is intimately connected to the electronics, code, and maker/hacker communities, which is completely alien to other forms of art.

The field of motion graphics has found itself merging into interactive art as well. The use of graphics in a live setting has grown exponentially in recent times. Graphics are no longer confined to televisions and computer screens but are found at concerts, in outdoor projection, on walls, in museums, and many other places. Graphics that respond in real-time are often integral parts of interactive artworks, and many companies that previously created motion graphics for television or film are now using graphics in unique ways that engage with a multitude of environments.

Interactive art, and specifically motion graphics in interactive art, is born out of an effort to respond to two seemingly disparate trends in society. Its use of new, cutting edge technology to connect with the core human desire to create meaningful interactions is something that is new to the art world and is only recently beginning to find its feet.[3] As technology continues to evolve, interactive art will be at the forefront of creating meaningful connections for its audiences in ways that correspond with their current cultural landscapes.

MM '14, Nov 03-07, 2014, Orlando, FL, USA
ACM 978-1-4503-3063-3/14/11.
http://dx.doi.org/10.1145/2647868.2655620

2. THE NEW AESTHETIC AND RELATIONAL AESTHETICS

2.1. The New Aesthetic

The New Aesthetic is an aesthetic that has existed within culture for quite a while but has only recently been given a name. In May of 2011, a young English man named James Bridle, armed with a few photos and a Tumblr blog, announced what some are calling the next big art movement: "The New Aesthetic." Bridle showcased imagery of art made with Google Earth photos, low-polygon styles in car and shoe design, and pixel patterns in art, design, fashion, landscaping and architecture – all pointing to the idea that the visual language of the machine has been appropriated by humans, and we are using it to express ourselves and our ideas. Engaging the technical as human beings is something that is relatively new to the past few generations, but it is now an unavoidable part of our culture. The New Aesthetic is just the label assigned to the visible manifestations of this new cultural reality.

2.2 Relational Aesthetics

A second aesthetic that has been discussed in recent times is that of Relational Aesthetics. Spearheaded by French critic Nicolas Bourriaud, Relational Art or Relational Aesthetics is "a set of artistic practices which take as their theoretical and practical point of departure the whole of human relations and their social context, rather than an independent and private space." [2] In his book, *Relational Aesthetics*, Bourriaud focuses on art as a form of social exchange. He draws attention to the artist as someone who could be viewed as the catalyst in relational art, rather than being at the center. The concept seeks to establish inter-subjective encounters in which meaning is established collectively rather than individually. In her article, "Antagonism and Relational Aesthetics," Claire Bishop describes art works fitting within this aesthetic as something that is entirely beholden to the contingencies of its environment and audience rather than a discrete, portable, autonomous work of art:

> This audience is envisaged as a community: rather than a one-to-one relationship between work of art and viewer, relational art sets up situations in which viewers are not just addressed as a collective, social entity, but are actually given the wherewithal to create a community, however temporary or utopian this may be.[4]

The goal of the aesthetic is to emphasize the temporal, the collective experience, and possibly, the creation of a functioning 'microtopia' in the present. This emphasis on togetherness and the creation of a common experience is central to Relational Aesthetics.

So how do these two aesthetics intersect? Since before Bourriaud first put pen to paper in the nineties to comment on the art world's response to the human desire for "face-to-face" interaction in the wake of the virtual relationships of the Internet, this interplay between humans and machines has been at work. We have seen culture both embrace the machine and all of its pixel-ly aesthetics and language, yet also push back with the desire for more human interaction. However, especially in recent years, there has been an initiative to marry them both. Specifically in the art world, there have been numerous installations that combine both the New Aesthetic and the Relational Art, both the high-tech and the interactive.

3. INTERACTIVE ART: TECHNOLOGY AND HUMANITY

3.1. What is interactive art?

One trend that has been seen in the art world in the last twenty years is that of interactivity in installation art. Many artists who engage in producing work in this vein rely on science and technology to work with their aesthetic concept in order to make the artwork a reality. In their article, "Living Laboratories: Making and Curating Interactive Art," Lizzie Muller and Ernest Edmonds define interactive art as "audience and machine...working in dialogue to produce a unique artwork for each audience encounter." [5] They refer to Edmond's earlier work, where he describes interactive art as a matrix of the artist, the audience and the artifact, or the "art system." Each element of the matrix is actively involved in the creation of the artwork, and "meaning occurs through the process of exchange, and interactivity itself is the very medium of the work".

Simon Penny, in his article, "From A to D and Back Again: The Emerging Aesthetics of Interactive Art," defines what interactivity means and how it can be applied to artwork:

> An interactive system is a machine system which reacts in the moment, by virtue of automated reasoning based on data from its sensory apparatus. An Interactive Artwork is such a system which addresses artistic issues. A painting is an instance of representation. A film is a sequence of representations. Interactive artworks are not instances of representation, they are virtual machines which themselves produce instances of representation based on real-time inputs.[6]

He describes interactive art as having two tasks: first, to discover the nuances and modalities of the interactive dynamic and figure out how to apply them to the aesthetic goals. Second, to integrate the aesthetically manipulated interactive dynamic with the other components of the work.The central aspect to these tasks (and to the artwork that is created from them) is time. Penny stresses the concept of real-time as being the most important aspect of interactive art:

> The difference between an interactive application and handwritten correspondence is essentially one of time. There is a time frame which is perceived by humans as 'real-time' response, it is the time frame of physiological reaction. Slower (or faster) than this is not 'real-time'. Switching a light switch produces a real-time response, but it is simplistic. Interactivity allows reactions by a machine in real time which are intellectually and cognitively complex. This defines the medium.[6]

It is this real-time response that makes interactive art extremely engaging and enables it – despite its added trappings of technology – to tap into the distinctly human need for connection and experience. In this aspect, interactive art can be seen as a cousin of Relational Art, an aesthetic that engages with concepts of human relations and environments.

3.2 The maker/hacker movement and open-source technology

Because real-time response is a crucial aspect of the medium, using technology to achieve this has become an integral part of interactive art. Many interactive installations rely on open-source software and technology and often use techniques or resources that correspond with the renegade maker/hacker mentality.[7] These resources are typically developed by interested communities, and developers are usually volunteers. Access to source code is open and free, and licenses are non-restrictive. Because these resources are easy to obtain, the communities surrounding them are often robust and provide valuable information and support in their application. This open-source mentality has led to continued exploration and invention with these technologies, which allows for the spread of unique concepts and unlimited possibilities to create something new. This creative usage of technology has found a natural home within interactive installations, where it is used in unique ways to bring the artist's vision to life.[7]

4. CIRCLES AND SOUNDS INSTALLATION

Using the principles I have found in my research of interactive art and motion graphics, the *Circles and Sounds* installation allows the user to create their own graphics and sound experience. Incorporating the principles of the New Aesthetic and Relational Aesthetics, the installation draws from the language of technology while requiring a human element for creation. Graphics and sounds respond in real-time to positioning and gestures by participants, allowing them to facilitate the creation of the artwork.

Drawing from open-source technology and information from the maker/hacker community, a software program called Quartz Composer is used for creation of the visuals. Motion tracking information is provided through use of a Microsoft Kinect. The graphics consist of circles that overlay each other in a particle system. As the user moves around in front of the installation, the circles follow. The height of the circles will be determined by the height of the user's arms. If the arms are raised, the circles will rise. If the arms are lowered, the circles will lower. The size of the circles will be based on the relative position of the user as well. The closer the user gets to the installation, the smaller the circles become. The farther away the user positions him or herself, the larger the circles become.

Sound also corresponds to the movements of the user. Using the Kinect in conjunction with the audio software program Ableton Live, users are able to manipulate the pitch of the track playing by raising or lowering their arms. Moving closer or farther away will manipulate volume.

The installation will consist of a projector and a blank canvas that the graphics will be projected onto. When a person approaches the canvas, the Kinect picks up on their movements and triggers the applications. Quartz Composer is used to read the joint information sent by the Kinect to control the graphics, and Ableton Live is used to control sound. The graphics are pre-made in After Effects.

Through the building and execution of this installation, I hope to explore many of the principles and techniques previously discussed in this thesis, such as the New Aesthetic, Relational Aesthetics, interactivity in art and real-time responsiveness, the use of graphics in a live setting, projection, and the creation of graphics in real-time.

Figure 1. Mock-ups of the installation in progress. As the figure moves his arms and re-positions his body, the circles follow and respond to his gestures.

Technology has become an entrenched part of our society, often pushing people away from connectedness and social exchange, but through this project I will explore how it can be used to bring people together and facilitate human interaction. I also hope to explore the concept of the "artist" and the creation of art as a collective experience. The project will also examine art as a temporal event. Unlike a sculpture or a painting, this piece will only exist for a certain period of time and will be dependent upon those who chose to participate. In that sense, it differs greatly from "works of art" in the traditional sense, which are made by one particular person and exist indefinitely.

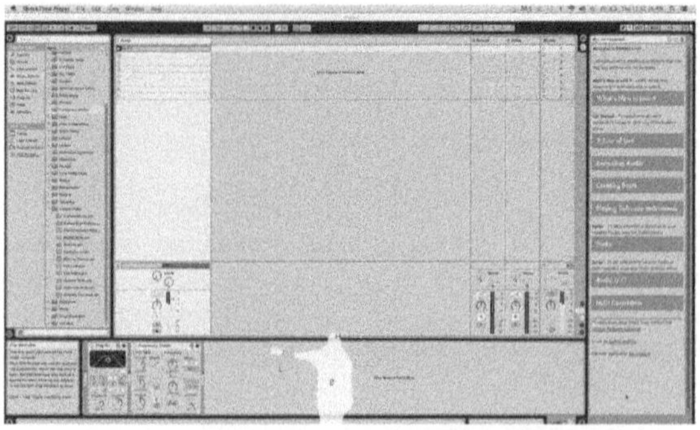

Figure 2. Ableton Live corresponding with data from the Kinect. As the figure moves his arms and re-positions his body, the sounds will react and respond in accordance.

5. CONCLUSION

Real-time, interactive installations are positioned in a unique place. They have feet firmly planted in both the art world and the science world. They have a deep dependency on technology because they require real-time responsiveness, but they also require human input to even be brought into existence. This combination allows for the fusing of the New Aesthetic and Relational Aesthetics to perhaps bring about a completely different aesthetic that has yet to be defined.

Interactive art has also expanded the field of motion graphics. Graphics that respond in real-time are often integral parts of interactive artworks, and motion design has found a home in a variety of live settings, such as projections, concerts, events, museums, and galleries. Interactive art also challenges the concept of the "artist." Many of the pieces require active participation from their admirers rather than passive observation. As such, they are created collectively rather than by a single person. The "artist" can be seen more as a facilitator than the sole creator.

Interactive art, and specifically motion graphics in interactive art, allows technology to connect with the core human desire to create meaningful interactions. Its potential is limited only by the ideas behind the works themselves. As technology continues to evolve, interactive art will continue to be at the forefront of creating significant experiences for its audiences and allow them to use technology in ways that bring them closer together.

6. REFERENCES

1. Sterling, Bruce. "An Essay on the New Aesthetic." Wired. 2 April 1996. Web. 11 March 2013.
2. Bourriaud, Nicolas. *Relational Aesthetics*. Les presses du reel, 2002. Print.
3. Holt-Lunstad, Julianne, Timothy B. Smith, J. Bradley Layton. "Social Relationships and Mortality Risk: A Meta-analytic Review." PLos Medicine, 7.7. July 2010. Web. 11 July 2014.
4. Bishop, Claire. "Antagonism and Relational Aesthetics." George Baker. 110 (2004): 49-50. Web. 5 Feb. 2013.
5. Muller, Lizzie and Ernest Edmonds. "Living Laboratories: Making and Curating Interactive Art." Electronic Art and Animation Catalog. (2006): 147-149. Web. 11 March 2013.
6. Penny, Simon. "From A to D and Back Again: The Emerging Aesthetics of Interactive Art." *Leonardo Electronic Almanac.* April 1996. Web. 11 March 2013.
7. Chayka, Kyle. "How Open Source is Disrupting Visual Art." The Creator's Project. 4 April 2012. Web. 11 July 2014.

Qi Visualizer - An Interactive Pulse Spectrogram Visualization using Mobile Participatory Biometrics

Yuan-Yi Fan
Media Arts and Technology, University of California Santa Barbara
3309 Phelps Hall
Santa Barbara, USA
dannyfan@mat.ucsb.edu

ABSTRACT

Qi is an ancient concept of life energy in various cultures and it represents continuous ineffable dialogues between the human heart with the body. The goal of Qi Visualizer is to translate the ineffable dialogues into a collective data visualization of pulse spectrograms via audience participation using smartphone photoplethysmography. Informed by our earlier studies, we believe spectrogram is the most effective visual language to invoke broader perception of Qi across cultures and disciplines. In our design process, we extend our notion of audience as constituents of a system for collective expression in this novel Qi Visualizer interactive installation. Specifically, we consider audience members as objects and their responses as processes in a system to guide our visualization strategies. Significance of this work is two fold. In terms of data visualization, we streamline data acquisition and visualization processes into an immediate interactive experience in Qi Visualizer installation. In terms of interactive art, the significance may be conceived as a new process shifting tactile-textual translations in a pulse examination to imaging-visual transformations of the pulse spectrograms visualization via audience participation. Similar to voiceprint, a heart rate harmonic signature in the spectrogram is seen as an artistic interpretation of Qi in this installation.

Categories and Subject Descriptors

H.5.m [**Information Interfaces And Presentation**]: Miscellaneous; J.5 [**Computer Applications**]: Arts and Humanity—*fine arts.*

General Terms

Design, Experimentation

Keywords

Interactive multimedia art, pulse spectrogram, data visualization, smartphone photoplethysmography

MM'14, November 3–7, 2014, Orlando, Florida, USA.

ACM 978-1-4503-3063-3/14/11 ...$15.00.
http://dx.doi.org/10.1145/2647868.2655621.

1. INTRODUCTION

Qi is an ancient concept of life energy in various cultures and pulse-examination is one of the techniques used to translate tactile perception of pulsation into poetic descriptions of pulse morphology [7]. In addition to pulse, flow, and wave concepts used to understand energy transmission in human body, summarized in Figure 1, the resonance perspective has recently been introduced to explain that the harmonic spectrum of pulse wave is a result of the heart output and the matching condition of the human body [10, 11, 3]. Inspired by the poetic descriptions of pulse morphology and the elegant harmonics on the pulse spectrum, our Form of Resonance series [1] addresses the link between the harmonics and Qi by translating data into visual, sonic, and spatial studies. In our previous studies, the data was captured and presented through custom synchronous and asynchronous technological systems. Informed by these experiments, we believe that spectrogram is the most effective visual language to invoke broader perception of Qi across cultures and disciplines. As the current project of our Form of Resonance series, Qi-Visualizer amplifies such a translation through visualizing pulse spectrograms collected from the audience with sound. The data is captured using a smartphone's camera as a pulse oximeter. Significance of this project may be conceived as a new process shifting tactile-textual translations in a pulse examination to imaging-visual transformations of the pulse spectrograms visualization via audience participation. Similar to voiceprint, a heart rate harmonic signature in a spectrogram is seen as an artistic interpretation of Qi in this installation.

2. RELATED WORKS

To the best of our knowledge, there have not been closely related works that incorporate an artistic interpretation of Qi via data visualization, pulse spectrogram acquisition using smartphone photoplethysmography, and audience participation in the field of interactive art. However, recent scientific research has shown an emergent interest in mobile biometrics, particularly the smartphone photoplethysmography for heart rate computation [6]. On the other hand, there are numerous artists who use human pulse signal in their works [1, 9].

2.1 Biometrics in Interactive Art

The Pulse Index [9] installation records participants' fingerprints and heart rates at the same time for visualization

[1]http://www.yuanyifan.com/?p=1602

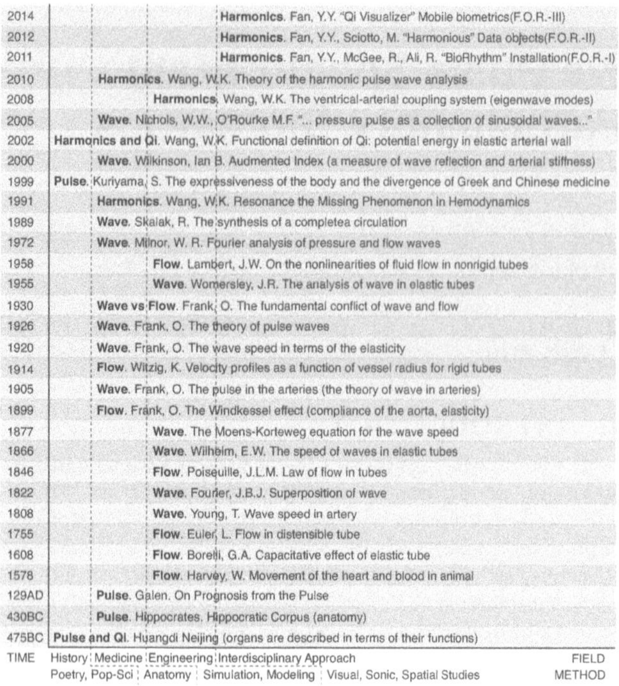

Figure 1: The historical context and our prior works of Form of Resonance series (abbreviated as F.O.R.)

on a large display. An apparatus consisting of a digital microscope and a heart rate sensor is used to capture the desired data. Despite the use of heart rate in most interactive installations, Qi Visualizer is the first known interactive installation that creates forms using heart rate harmonic signature in order to trigger inquiry about the historical context associated with this data, illustrated in Figure 1.

2.2 Audience Participation in Interactive Art

In the 1950s, audience participation was a new artistic interest in creating possible situations that uncontrollable factors of artworks may lead to [8]. These uncontrollable factors of an interactive artwork can be spectators' explicit behaviors or their implicit physiological responses. In our case, we collect implicit physiological responses from an audience. Noise in photoplethysmography signal caused by motion and light is the uncontrollable factors that add artistic artifacts in our data visualization. We also extend the idea of "audience as constituents of a system for collective expression" from our earlier study [4], and consider audience members as objects and their responses as processes in a system to guide our visualization strategies.

2.3 Participatory Sensing

The idea of participatory sensing is that groups of people contribute sensory information to form a body of knowledge [2]. In this paper, we focus on creating an interactive situation where a group of people can easily contribute their pulse spectrograms via our smartphone photoplethysmography application. As an enabler, our interactive situation may allow the audience to relate the collective sensory information visualization to the body of knowledge of Qi.

2.4 Data Visualization

The seven stages of visualizing data include acquire, parse, filter, mine, represent, refine, and interact [5]. In this paper, we try to streamline these stages in our installation to create an interactive situation where our artistic message can be effectively delivered to the audience through participation.

3. DESIGN AND IMPLEMENTATION

3.1 Design Concept

In our design process, we extend this notion of "audience as constituents of a system for collective expression" from our earlier work [4]. Specifically, we consider audience members as objects and their responses as processes to guide our interactive system design and visualization strategies, illustrated in Figure 2.

3.2 Implementation

A system is designed and programmed for our Qi Visualizer interactive installation. The system consists of a server application and at least one client application. The client application is a mobile participatory biometrics application that captures, computes, and uploads a pulse spectrogram from a participant's iPhone. The server application can receive the pulse spectrogram from the participant and then visualize pulse spectrograms collectively in three different modes. These visualization modes include a Cartesian coordinate system, a cylindrical coordinate system, and in a transparent overlay system.

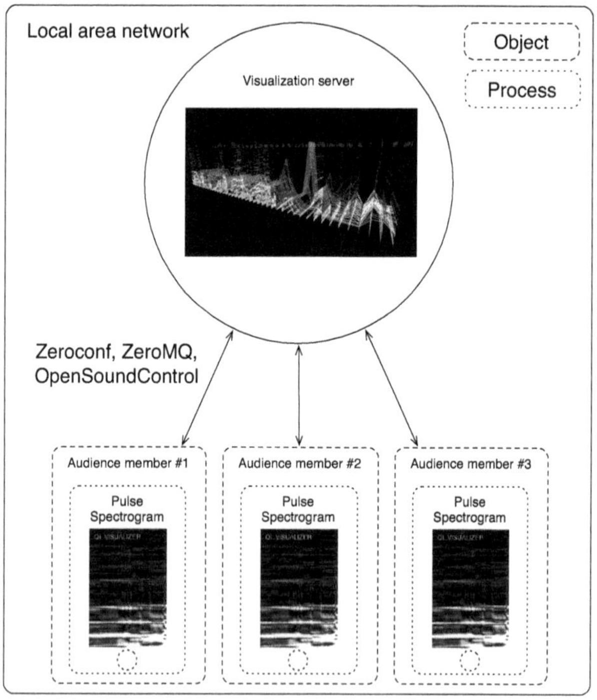

Figure 2: Design concept.

To streamline data collection and facilitate audience participation in our installation, we use four network-related technologies, including Zero Configuration Networking[2], ZeroMQ[3], OpenSoundControl[4], and the iOS app store as a convenient way to distribute mobile participatory biometrics applications.

The client application consists of smartphone photoplethysmography functionality, network functionality, and a simple interface for user instructions. To capture and compute a pulse spectrogram using smartphone photoplethysmography, signal processing and signal conditioning processes in the client application are illustrated in Figure 3. To instruct a user to participate in this installation, the simple user interface is shown in Figure 4. This client application is now available as the Qi Visualizer app and is downloadable from the App Store[5]. A user can participate by tweeting his or her Qi or pulse spectrogram using our app. We use a special version of our client application in the actual interactive installation. The only different is we use ZeroMQ instead of Twitter API in the special version of our client application in the actual installation.

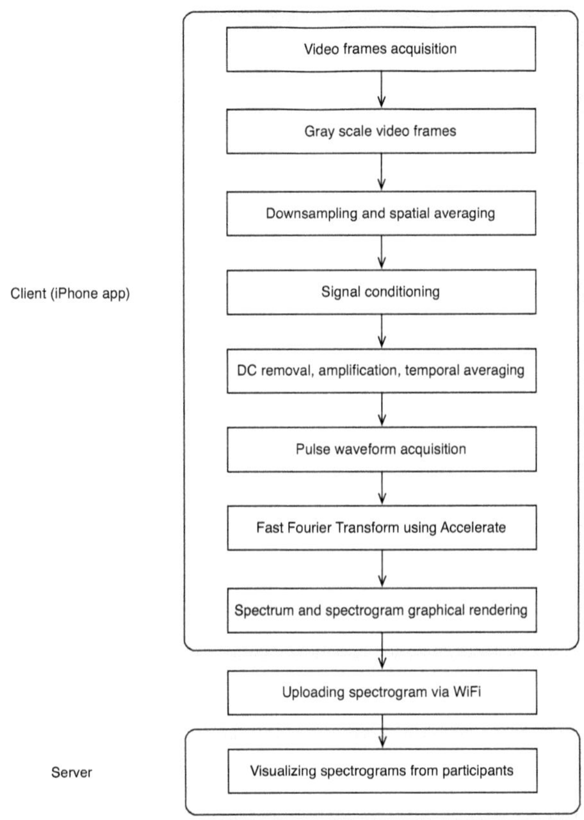

Figure 3: Pulse spectrogram acquisition process in our client application.

In designing our server application, audience members are considered as objects and their responses are considered as processed in this interactive system. With our notion of audience abstraction for interactive system design, we examine different strategies to inspect the collective sensory information from the audience. We start by visualizing this data in a Cartesian coordinate system and in a cylindrical coordinate system. In the Cartesian coordinate system mode, the visualization is static and only adds a slice of spectrogram when a participant uploads his or her spectrogram. The cylindrical coordinate system mode is dynamic as it rotates around its y axis at a fixed rate. The system recomputes the spacing between two slices of spectrograms when there is a new spectrogram uploaded. Two other visualization strategies we implement in this system are varying opacity of spectrograms and creating lines by connecting pixels across all the spectrograms. We connect a pixel that has the maximum value in a column within a spectrogram to the one in the following spectrograms. The purpose of varying opacity is to examine common patterns or clusters of energy distribution across all spectrograms in the Cartesian coordinate system mode. The purpose of creating lines by connecting pixels is to generate artistic forms as well as to seek possible clues for our future works. In these visualizations, each slice of spectrogram represents a participant and the pattern within this spectrogram is a trace that the participant leaves after interacting with our installation. In Figure 5, we demonstrate these visualization modes using data from 40 participants at the Digital Arts Expo in California Institute of the Arts on May 8th, 2014.

In Figure 4, there are five modes in the client application. When a user launches the Qi Visualizer iOS application, the user will be given an instruction in Mode-I on how to participate in this installation. To proceed, the user can do a tap gesture to go to the next mode for pulse signal acquisition in Mode-II. In Mode-II, the user can adjust his or her finger position against the camera lens when the signal detection quality is bad. After successful data collection for eight seconds, the user will be able to see a pulse spectrum in Mode-III. After another eight seconds of data collection, the user will be able to see a pulse spectrogram in Mode-IV, where he or she can do tap gesture again to upload the pulse spectrogram to a remote server. After uploading, the user will automatically enter Mode-V, where individual information, group information, and the difference between them are displayed. To return to mode-I, the user can do a slide gesture to restart.

4. DOCUMENTATION

4.1 Installation components

Components of this installation include a projector, a music stand, a laptop, a WiFi router, an iPhone, an iPad, and headphones or speakers. To collect the pulse spectrogram from a participant, at least one iPhone is required for this installation. To instruct a participant how to interact with this system, the iPad is placed on the music stand playing back a video introduction of this installation. The WiFi router is required for data transmission between the iPhone and the laptop. The focus of this installation is visualization and the sound component of this installation can be rendered either using headphones or speakers.

[2]http://www.zeroconf.org/
[3]http://zeromq.org/
[4]http://opensoundcontrol.org/
[5]https://itunes.apple.com/us/app/qi-visualizer/id807624975?mt=8

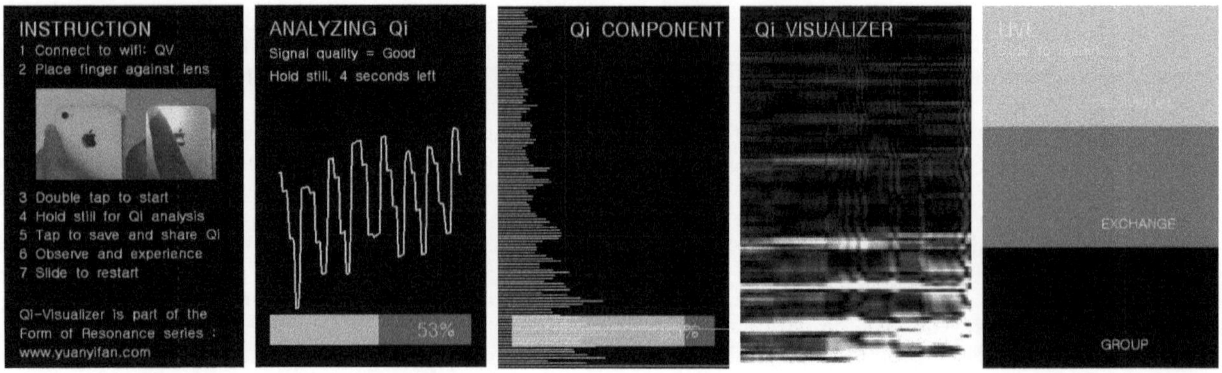

Figure 4: ©2014, Yuan-Yi Fan. User instructions on our client interface. A snapshot of user experience of our client interface is shown in order from left to right.

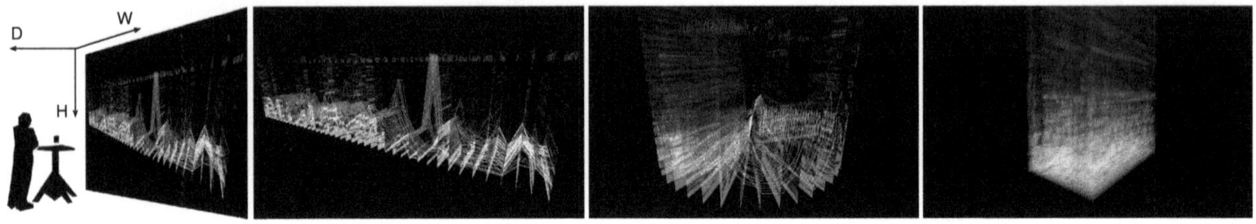

Figure 5: ©2014, Yuan-Yi Fan. The left image shows the minimum space for Qi Visualizer installation (6 by 4 by 3 meter, D*W*H). Data from 40 participants during our first installation is visualized in a Cartesian coordinate system mode, a cylindrical coordinate system mode, and a transparent overlay mode.

4.2 Installations

Qi Visualizer was selected and first installed at the Walt Disney Modular Theater, Digital Arts Expo, California Institute of the Arts, May 8-9th, 2014 [6]. Later, Qi Visualizer was also selected and presented at the first L.A.S.T. (Life Art Science and Technology) Festival[7] at ZERO1 Garage, San Jose, California, June 6-7th, 2014.

5. FUTURE WORKS

Qi Visualizer is an ongoing research that seeks effective strategies of visualization and interaction to trigger an audience's inquiry about both the data and its associated stories. We plan to systematically examine strategies and media to transform the same dataset into more effective messages in intriguing ways.

6. REFERENCES

[1] M. Ballora, B. Pennycook, P. C. Ivanov, L. Glass, and A. L. Goldberger. Heart rate sonification: A new approach to medical diagnosis. *Leonardo*, 37(1):41–46, 2004.

[2] J. A. Burke, D. Estrin, M. Hansen, A. Parker, N. Ramanathan, S. Reddy, and M. B. Srivastava. Participatory sensing. In *In the Proceedings of the International Workshop on World-Sensor-Web (WSW'2006)*. ACM, 2006.

[3] A. de Sá Ferreira and A. J. Lopes. Pulse waveform analysis as a bridge between pulse examination in chinese medicine and cardiology. *Chinese journal of integrative medicine*, 19(4):307–314, 2013.

[4] Y.-Y. Fan, F. M. Sciotto, and J. Kuchera-Morin. Time giver: An installation of collective expression using mobile ppg and eeg in the allosphere. *Proceedings of the IEEE VIS Arts Program (VISAP)*, 2013.

[5] B. Fry. *Visualizing Data: Exploring and Explaining Data with the Processing Environment.* " O'Reilly Media, Inc.", 2007.

[6] E. Jonathan and M. Leahy. Investigating a smartphone imaging unit for photoplethysmography. *Physiological measurement*, 31(11):N79, 2010.

[7] S. Kuriyama. *The expressiveness of the body and the divergence of Greek and Chinese medicine.* Zone Books New York, 1999.

[8] K. Kwastek. *Aesthetics of Interaction in Digital Art.* MIT Press, 2013.

[9] R. Lozano-Hemmer. Pulse Index. `http://www.lozano-hemmer.com/pulse_index.php`, 2010. [Online; accessed 24-June-2014].

[10] Y. Wang, S. Chang, Y. Wu, T. Hsu, and W. Wang. Resonance. the missing phenomenon in hemodynamics. *Circulation research*, 69(1):246–249, 1991.

[11] Y.-Y. L. Wang, T.-L. Hsu, M.-Y. Jan, and W.-K. Wang. Review: theory and applications of the harmonic analysis of arterial pressure pulse waves. *Journal of Medical and Biological Engineering*, 30(3):125–131, 2010.

[6]http://digitalartsexpo.calarts.edu/

[7]http://www.scaruffi.com/last/

Stoicheia: Architecture, Sound and Tesla's Apotheosis

Jean-Michel Crettaz
Media Arts and Technology
University of California, Santa Barbara
3309 Phelps Hall
Santa Barbara, California, 93106
www.slaphq.com
jmc@slaphq.com

F. Myles Sciotto
Media Arts and Technology
University of California, Santa Barbara
3309 Phelps Hall
Santa Barbara, California, 93106
www.soCinematic.com
f.myles@gmail.com

ABSTRACT

Stoicheia, is an immersive installation focusing on the making of a synthetic ecology and informing the process of architecture using sound. After the reception of enigmatic radio signals in 1899, Tesla began work for many years to perfect the receiving and transmitting equipment that was needed to better pick up and translate his aural discoveries. Stoicheia explores similar notions of Telsa's Aether using specific data feeds and scanning techniques to create a dynamic spatial soundscape drawing upon an experience of immediacy, and ephemeral interplay between the agencies that maintain a continuously self-adaptive sonic and physical environment.

Keywords

Synthetic Ecologies; Digital Architecture Processes; World-making; Spatial Sound; Soundscape; 3D Scanning; Robotic Control; New Agencies; Tesla

1. INTRODUCTION

After the reception of enigmatic radio signals in 1899, Tesla began work for many years to perfect the receiving and transmitting equipment that was needed to better pick up and translate his aural discoveries. In 1925 Tesla writes: "The sounds I am listening to every night at first appear to be human voices conversing back and forth in a language I cannot understand. I find it difficult to imagine that I am actually hearing real voices from people not of this planet. There must be a more simple explanation that has so far eluded me." Tesla developed an antithesis to Einstein's Special Theory in The Dynamic Theory of Gravity and The Environmental Energy. In the text "Voices in the Aether"[5], Tesla proposed there is no energy in matter other than energy received from its environment.

Stoicheia, is an dynamic soundscape installation dedicated to Tesla's "Voices in the Aether" postulate: This sound architecture project relies on the both a dynamic merger and progressive modulation of three complementary data sources:

- The robotic and optical scanning of four fossilized objects, embodying the classical states of matter: solid, liquid, gas and plasma.
- The sensing of local electromagnetic fields with EMF sensors.
- Local geologic seismic activity feed via USGS.

The three data sources converge through real-time computing and unfold a spatialized soundscape made of dynamic sound signals transgressing through their origins. The robotic scanning path of the four elements is computationally controlled, self-regulating system that continuously re-evaluates and varies in order to sustain a balanced sound ecology in sonic architecture that engages and encourages engagement [2].

Stoicheia draws an experience of immediacy, and ephemeral interplay between the agencies that maintain a continuously self-adaptive sonic and physical environment. As Tesla hypothesized, Stoicheia absorbs sound energy from its environment and projects it through the movement of the four elementary stages.

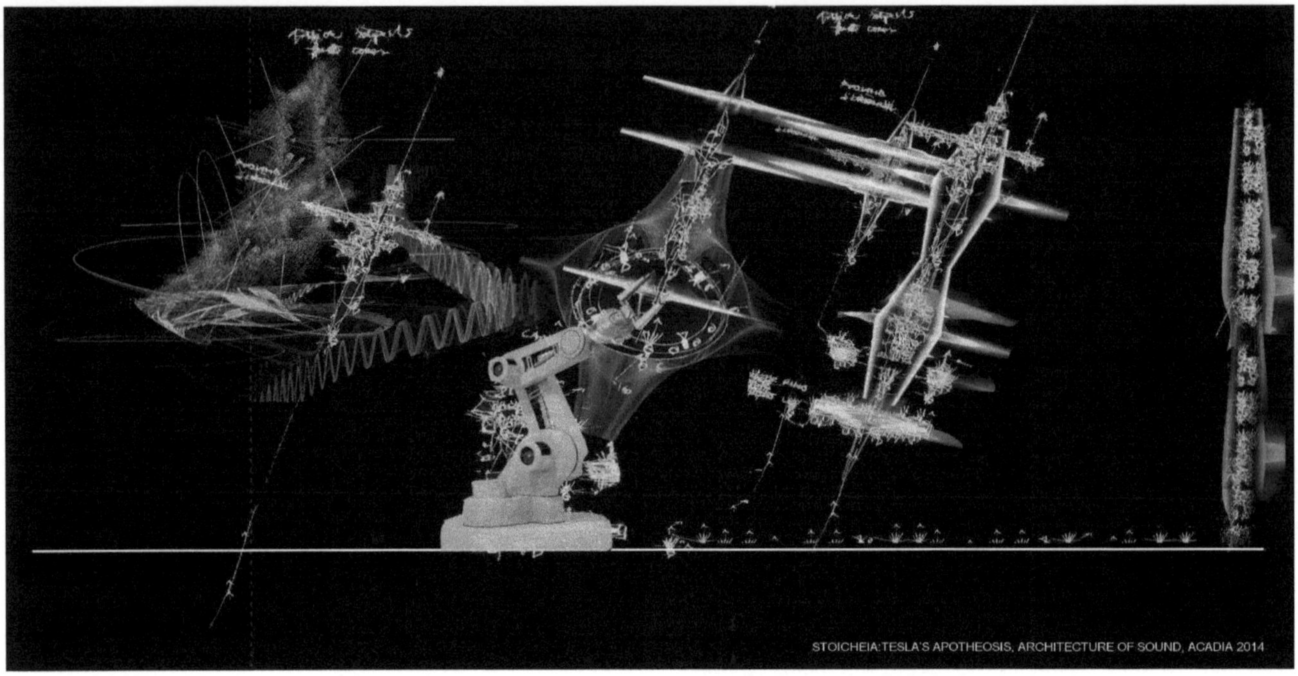

Figure 1: Stoicheia collage illustrating 4 elemental objects being scanned ©Crettaz, Sciotto

2. INSTALLATION EXPERIENCE

The installation takes place within an enclosed space, approx. 30'(w) x 30'(d) x15'(h). A 5-axis robot arm (Figure 3) with a 3D scanner attached moves through 4 suspended multi-material objects that represent the 4 elements. Combined with an array of 4 EMF antennas that monitor local EM modulation and the local seismic activity via xml feed, these scanning sources provide qualitative data about the represented elemental flux. The connected data is analyzed and sonified using 3D, 3rd order ambisonic algorithms that spatialize the audio through 16.4 system (Figure 5) . There are 4 hue-variable spotlights that illuminate the suspended objects creating low ambient pulsing patterns that are composed with the sound. The installation is composed of 4 object and process components:

- Elementary Objects:
  Four (4) fossilized objects, embodying the classical states.
- Scanning Process:
  The robotic scanning of the four elementary objects.
- SoundScape:
  An evolving ambisonic spatial sound ecology.
- Drawings:
  Drawings of the each object: scanned, construction.

Elementary Objects

Four object elements are suspended in the space. Each Elementary model is a different multi-material model, composed of multiple 3D printed materials along with scale model fabricated pieces and connection elements (Figure 7). These are each suspended by electro-luminate wire surrounded and are illuminated by a parametrical controlled low ambient light source and are located within reach of a robotic arm.

Scanning Process

A computer controlled robot arm (Figure 3) sits on a pedestal in the center of the room and scans and analyzes the elemental objects using a Depth sensor (Figure 4) to decipher surface articulations and proportions. This data is is analyzed and translated into the a soundscape along with the other input fees (see Analysis and Design Section).

Soundscape

The Soundscape with be created using a series of physical and virtual components. Consisting of a 16.4 Channel surround (Figure 5) sound system and a virtual sounds generation controlled by software the scanned and collected data will be sonified and spatialized.

- 16 channels are arranged in equidistance along the room periphery (above and below) along with 4 subwoofers located in each room corner.
- Ambisonics: A full-sphere 3D surround sound technique (Figure 2) that triangulates the sound source amongst a spatial sound array [3].
- Spatial Sound Array: Stoicheia will feature two (2) Octophonic sound arrays. An Octophonic system is a form of audio reproduction that presents eight discrete audio channels using eight speakers arranged in a circle within the space with azimuths of -45 and 45 degrees.

Drawings

A series of drawings will be produced using the scanned data, oriented path data, collected intensity data; these are all overlaid and illustrated through time (see Analysis and Design Section) of each element object. These drawings are exhibited next to the elemental construction drawing (Figure 8) .

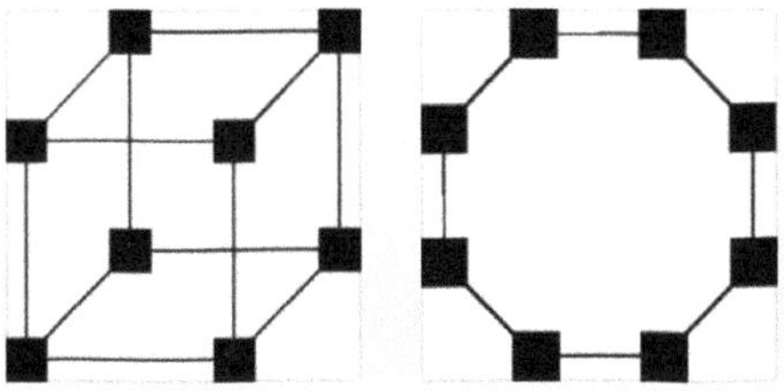

Figure 2: Duel Octophonic speaker layout using Ambisonics

3. ANALYSIS AND GENERATION

Data-Sensing

The project ecology supports three data sources:

- Four (4) local EMF Electro-Magnetic Field sensors that detect the modulated EMF field of the space.
- One (1) robotic operated IR optical 3D scanner head that scans the four elementary objects.
- One (1) real-time data feed from USGS which denotes seismic activity for the surrounding area.

Data Analysis

The analysis is done in real-time, at frame-rate and consists of the following processes:

- The complied sensor data taken from the EMF, Robotic scanner and Seismic data feed is transcribed into a virtual field of forces.
- The virtual field of forces is scanned to determine intensities that are translated into a map of matrixes and analyzed for the following geometric and texture characteristics:
  - Resolution
  - Displacement
  - Mesh Continuity
  - Mesh Contrast
- The resulting matrix is fed-back into the robotic control path parameters and alters the direction and speed that changes the overall visual and sonic and visual resolution.

Data Translation

The resulting data analysis will translate the resolution characteristics into sound and light through 4-scaled structures [6].

- Micro-Structure = Timbre (Grains)
- Mini-Structure = Note (Seconds)
- Meso-Structure = Polyrhythm, Scale (10's Seconds)
- Macro-Structure = Global Evolution (10's Minutes)

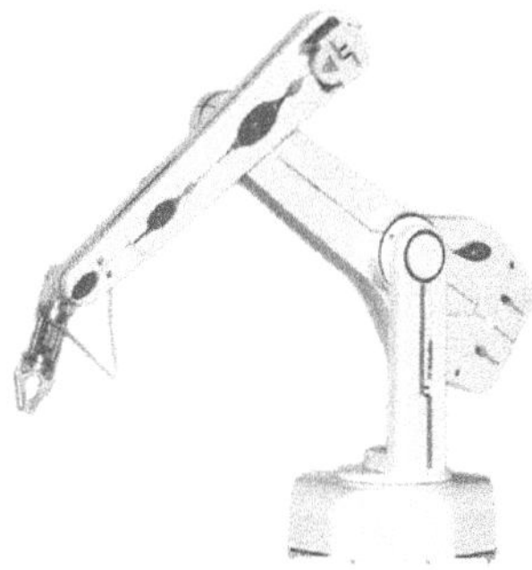

Figure 3: Strobotics r14 5-axis Robot Arm

Figure 4: Microsoft Kinect 360 used for Robotic Scanning

Figure 5: Anthony Gallo Acoustics, 16.4 system

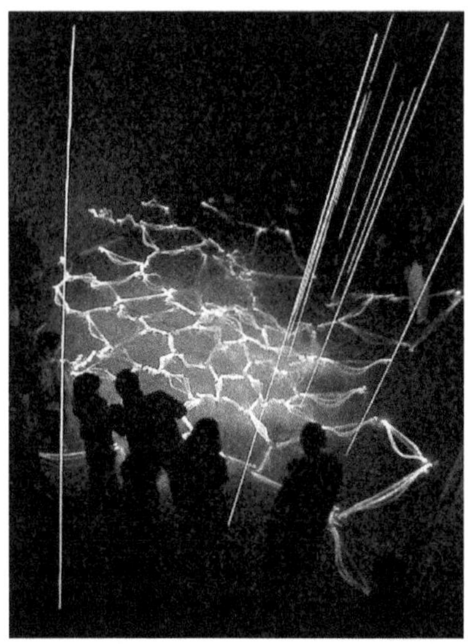

Figure 6: Synthetic Ecology Precedent (Quasar, SCI-Arc, 2008) ©Crettaz

4. SYNTHETIC ECOLOGIES

Naturally occurring ecologies appear near unlimited in the number of agents and potentials for spatial expansion and interaction. On the other hand, manmade ecologies are restricted by the number of pre-conceived communication components and the capacity of complex adaptive mutation. The Stoicheia ensemble attempts to reverse that model by suggesting an ephemeral body initiated by changes and mutations originated in harvested data-streams of external sources i.e. EMF Electromagnetic Fields and seismic activity, and a model made of references extending its tangible physical scale. With energy describing a primary state of matter, Stoicheia ventures a soundscape [4] conceived of energy entities drawn from near intangible to solidified objects.

5. CONCLUSION

This Installation nurtures the idea of making visible the invisible (Figure 6). Attempting to physicalize the experience of such phenomena is known as data representation architecture [1]. Data Representation Architecture is built from an element of reality and constructed into a space (real or virtual) by a digital process, and through many of these acting together and creating an ecological system the subtleties and affects of multimodal experiences can be developed.

The Stoicheia project presents a sound-essay conceived as a sonic work informing a spatial light and sound experience. The work originates and embodies a variety of fascinating energy to matter, and matter to energy relationships. Inspired by Tesla's convictions to listen into deep space reminds us of the necessity to sound far beyond our perceived boundaries and the preparedness to engage with the unknown and barely perceivable.

Acknowledgements

The following persons and institutions have supported this installation and the accompanying research, Marcos Novak (Professor, UCSB), Dr. Curtis Roads (Professor UCSB), Marco Peljhan (Robotics), Antony Gallo Acoustics (Audio), Evolution Audio (Audio), Bentley System (Engineering).

6. REFERENCES

[1] J. Bermudez, J. Agutter, D. Westenskow, S. Foresti, Y. Zhang, D. Gondeck-Becker, N. Syroid, B. Lilly, D. Strayer, and F. Drews. Data representation architecture. visualization design methods, theory and technology applied to anesthesiology. *ACADIA?2000 Proceedings. Washington DC*, pages 91–102, 2000.

[2] O. Eliasson. Your Engagement has Consequences. *Experiment Marathon: Serpentine Gallery*, 2009.

[3] W. G. and S. W. COSM Documentation. *http://www.allosphere.ucsb.edu/cosm/*, 2008.

[4] R. M. Schafer. *The soundscape: Our sonic environment and the tuning of the world.* Inner Traditions/Bear & Co, 1993.

[5] T. Swartz. *The Lost Journals of Nikola Tesla.* Global Communications, 2000.

[6] I. Xenakis. *Formalized music: thought and mathematics in composition.* Number 6. Pendragon Press, 1992.

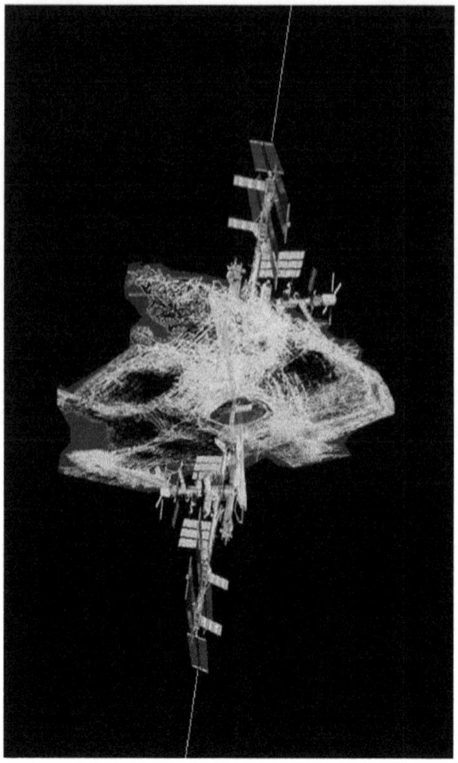

Figure 7: Elemental Object Model Study ©Crettaz, Sciotto

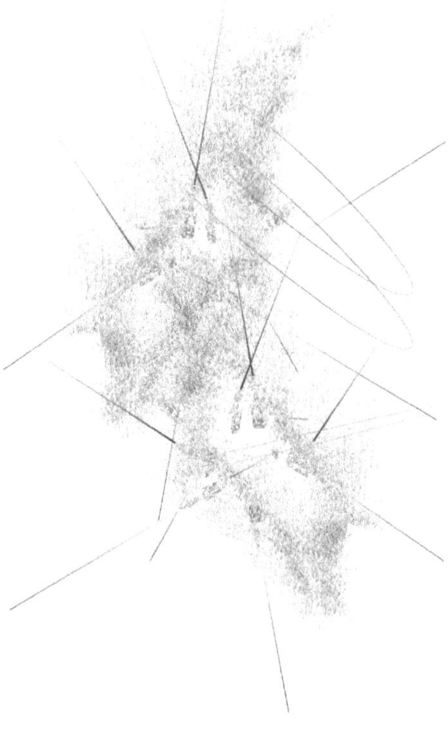

Figure 8: Elemental Object Drawing Study ©Crettaz, Sciotto

States of Diffusion for n+1 Devices

Lonce Wyse
Communications and New Media
National University of Singapore
lonce.wyse@nus.edu.sg

ABSTRACT

States of Diffusion is a participative audio installation artwork that explores patterns of sound transformation that move through space as they evolve spectrally. Six one-minute segments exploring themes of intonation and timing of events across possibly many different audio sources are coordinated via a web server. The spatial diffusion flows through mobile devices held by visitors to the gallery. Visitors also exert a subtle influence over sound through the movement of their device and their movement through the gallery.

Categories and Subject Descriptors

H.5.5 [**Information Systems**]: Information Interfaces and Presentation (HCI) – *sound and music computing.*

General Terms

Design; Human Factors

Keywords

Sonic Art; Interactive Audio; Collaboration; Mobility; Web Audio API.

1. OVERVIEW

States of Diffusion is composed for "n+1 devices", where the "n" (1 to 40) are mobile devices brought in to the space and held by gallery visitors, and the "1" is a multi (2, 4, or 8)-channel sound system installed in a gallery space. As the piece evolves, the source of sound is passed between the gallery speakers and hand-held devices. Sound moves across the space through varying patterns of diffusion from the speakers on the mobile devices.

The piece is organized as six one-minute "movements," each based on a different spectrally evolving sound pattern, each using a different strategy for sound diffusion appropriate for the sonic elements being developed. The sound and the diffusion patters are responsive to the movement of gallery visitors through the sensors on the mobile devices. The audience members also determine the spatial diffusion patterns by walking around the space with their devices from which sound is emitted. In this way, audience members physically co-create the sonic space for and with each other.

MM'14, November 3–7, 2014, Orlando, Florida, USA.

ACM 978-1-4503-3063-3/14/11...$15.00.
http://dx.doi.org/10.1145/2647868.2655623

2. STRUCTURE AND INTERACTION

The platform supporting *States of Diffusion* is a client/server style architecture. Two different websites are served – one for the Gallery sound system, and one for the Visitors. The Gallery and Visitor clients join the piece by pointing their mobile device browsers to the *States of Diffusion* website, and then communicate with each other by exchanging messages via the server using a "chat room" type of architecture.

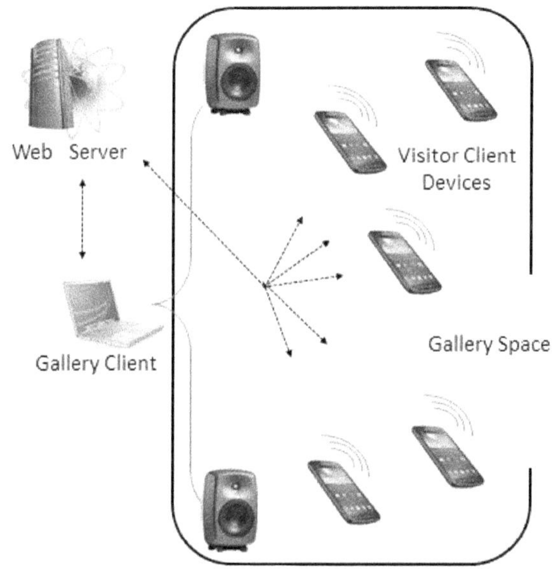

Figure 1. Clients point browsers to the web server to access the *States of Diffusion* website. The Gallery Client determines the progression through 6 movements comprising the work, and sends messages to the Visitor Client mobile devices to coordinate the sound creation and spatial diffusion between the participants.

The Gallery Client is heard through full-range high-fidelity speakers installed in the gallery. The Gallery Client is also responsible for the coordination between all sounding devices, and determines the transition between the six movements of the piece, notifying all other clients as they occur. The Visitor clients all run the same sound-generating program, but each produces different sound at different times (producing the movement of sound through the space) based on an ID each client is assigned when visitors join, messages from the Gallery Client, and the timing within each of the six segments. Variability in the sounds produced on different clients is also a result of input from device sensors and depends on the direction and angle the devices are pointing as visitors move around the space.

3. ARTISTIC OBJECTIVES

States of Diffusion is about people coming together in one space to collectively create sonic environments with each other. Each of the six movements is related to the others, but distinct in sonic focus. For example, one is based on harmonics of a low (60 Hz) fundamental with a rich overtone structure generated by the Gallery Client's speakers. Visitor devices emit sine tones that are slightly mistuned as the devices move to create "beating" which, because the devices are distributed in the space, seem to move around the space as they constructively and destructively interfere with each other. Two other movements explore rich musical chords (one with singing human voices, the other with breathy synthetic tones) where the movement through space is achieved through the coordination of timing across participant devices. Another movement "granularizes"[6] an environmental sound which shifts in and out of recognizability as the length and density of the grains created by different devices change due to central timing coordination in conjunction with the movement of the devices. Transition between the six segments of the piece overlap slightly, and are related by musical key and/or spatial rhythm. All segments are designed to encourage careful listening and slow exploratory activity as people walk around the gallery establishing different spatial relationships amongst themselves.

3.1 Related Artistic Work

There is long tradition in music of moving sound in space across multitudes of speakers. One of the most well-known systems is the Acousmonium constructed by composer François Bayle at the Groupe de Recherches Musicales (GRM) in Paris[4]. It was comprised of some 80 speakers spread over a stage along with several though the audience. Sound was frequently "diffused" live by a composer or engineer, even if the sound was coming from fixed media such as tape or CD.

Moving speakers have also been used for musical purposes. *Speaker Swinging* by Gordon Monahan used oscillators broadcasting tones over 3 loudspeakers that were swung in circles on speakers at the end of a tether. More recently, the *Pocket Gamelan* series of pieces by Greg Schiemer[5] used mobile phones swung in a similar way. These pieces use space and sound source motion as an integral part of the musical work.

Mobile phones provided by audience members were used in the 2001 *Dialtones (A Telesymphony)* by Golan Levin. This piece is performed by live performers dialing phones that have been prepared with ringtones according to audience seating assignments. In this way, both the sound and the spatial dimensions of the piece were "choreographed" [3].

States of Diffusion thus draws on several historical musical threads, while taking advantage of emerging web technologies that are sensitive in real time to the number of participants and their motion through the space in order to synthesize and diffuse the sound. Visitors are free to explore the interactive elements by moving around the gallery space and moving their devices thereby creating a hybrid between an installation piece and a participative performance.

4. THE VISTOR EXPERIENCE

The gallery space is dimly lit and contains speakers in the corners. A poster identifies the piece, and contains a QR code and a website address that visitors use to direct their mobile device browsers to the State of Diffusion website as the enter.

The website for display on the Visitor Clients has a minimalistic graphic design, with a compass-like icon displaying the compass direction and angle (pitch) of their device. The interactive graphics provide visual feedback designed to encourage and reinforce the movements the audience participants make which influence the sound played on their device.

Devices held by different visitors make sounds at different times – sometimes overlapping, sometimes not. When a given device makes sound, its display also brightens with color – each of the six segments of the piece are associated with a different color. This visual component plays an aesthetic role (imagine fireflies in a field at dusk). As sound moves across the space, so does the pattern of illumination. The light also functions as feedback to make it clear to each participant when their own device is making sound, and to heighten the awareness of their own role in the overall structure of the work.

The piece works for anywhere from one to forty simultaneous visitors. The server knows how many visitor devices are participating at any given time, and assigns "roles" to clients accordingly so that the experience is rich enough when there is only a single or several visitors, yet not too dense when there are many. As visitors walk around, they change the spatial configuration of the sound sources in the gallery. Visitors may enter and leave the gallery at their leisure.

5. TECHNICAL INFORMATION

States of Diffusion is built entirely with HTML5 technologies for both networking and sound synthesis. The server is written using node.js [2], along with the Express web applications framework, and the WebSockets library for network communication.

The client code is written in JavaScript and uses the newly-emerging W3C standard Web Audio API [1] for real-time sound synthesis and the jsaSound sound modeling library written by the author [7]. The jsaSound library "wraps" the low-level Web Audio API with high-level sound-model building capabilities for sound developers, and provides a simple API for interactive for web developers[8].

The recent developments in real-time browser-based sound synthesis technology (along with other HTML5, sensor and processing capabilities of mobile devices) make this kind of co-located inter-browser coordinated sound piece possible merely by having participants navigate to a website. The server is located on the Internet, so that no special apparatus and no local network is necessary (although it may also be run on a local area network if necessary). The installation infrastructure has been tested with up to 40 simultaneously engaged clients, and runs on modern major browsers (Chrome, Safari, Opera) on Mac, PC or mobile devices running Android, iOS, and Windows operating systems.

This is the premier installation of *States of Diffusion*, although the infrastructure and sound synthesis software has been developed during the course of several previous projects.

6. ACKNOWLEDGMENTS

Software used to construct this work is open source and available on GitHub and at http://anclab.org/Software. Thanks to Kumar Subramanian and other contributors to the open source Web Audio ecosystem upon whose shoulders the jsaSound library and *States of Diffusion* are built.

7. REFERENCES

1. Adenot, P., Wilson, C., and Rogers, C., eds. Web Audio API. 2013. http://www.w3.org/TR/webaudio/.

2. Dahl, R. Node. js: Evented I/O for V8 JavaScript. 2012. http://node.js.org.

3. Levin, G. A Personal Chronology of Audiovisual Systems Research. *Proceedings of the 2005 International Conference on New interfaces for Musical Expression*, (2005).

4. Moore, A., Moore, D., and Mooney, J. M2 Diffusion – The live diffusion of sound in space. *Proceedings of the International Computer Music Conference*, ICMA (2004).

5. Schiemer, G. and Havryliv, M. Pocket Gamelan: tuneable trajectories for flying sources in Mandala 3 and Mandala 4. *Proceedings of the 2006 International Conference on New Interfaces for Musical Expression*, (2006).

6. Truax, B. Real-Time Granular Synthesis with a Digital Signal Processor. *Computer Music Journal 12*, 2 (1988), 14–26.

7. Wyse, L. and Subramanian, S.K. The Viability of the Web Browser as a Computer Music Platform. *Computer Music Journal 37*, 4 (2013), 10–23.

8. Wyse, L. Interactive Audio Web Development Workflow. *Proceedings of the 22nd ACM International Conference on Multimedia*, (2014).

Fine-grained Visual Faceted Search

Julien Champ
INRA, LIRMM
ARCAD FEDER project
Montpellier, France

Alexis Joly
INRIA, LIRMM
Montpellier, France

Pierre Bonnet
CIRAD, AMAP
ARCAD FEDER project
Montpellier, France

ABSTRACT

This paper presents an interactive information retrieval scheme extending classical faceted search with fine-grained visual facets. Consistent visual words are extracted offline by constructing a matching graph at the region image level and splitting the graph in relevant clusters. Visual and textual facets are then indexed in the same faceted search engine, all of them being dynamically reranked according to their filtering efficiency before being presented to the end-user. To enhance their interpretability, each facet value is illustrated by a representative picture automatically selected from the matching graph in an adaptive way.

Categories and Subject Descriptors: H.3.3 [Information Systems]: Information Search and Retrieval

Keywords: search;visual;facet;image;browsing; fine-grained; plant; species; identification.

1. INTRODUCTION

Faceted search has become the de facto search methodology for content rich web applications, in particular online stores and digital libraries. A faceted search system allows each item in the database to be assigned multiple classifications, enabling the classifications to be ordered in multiple ways, rather than in a single, pre-determined, taxonomic order. Facets are typically derived from pre-existing fields in the item's metadata or manually built from the analysis of the items. Using visual facets complementary to textual ones has already been addressed in a few previous works [2, 1, 9]. The principle is to automatically compute the facets by image clustering techniques and to display image links rather than textual links in the graphical user interface. As discussed in [2], visual faceted search might overcome several limitations of text oriented facets including incompleteness and inaccuracy of the meta-data.

In this paper, we stress another interest of visual faceting in the case of expert data to be searched by any user. We focus in particular on the problem of identifying the species of an observed living organism without any expertise in botany or zoology. This challenge, sometimes known as the *taxonomic gap*, is recognized as a major issue towards setting up effective and sustainable ecological surveillance tools. Determining the scientific name of a plant or an animal is actually still the primary key to index or access related data. But unfortunately, the usage of expert identification tools such as dichotomous keys and online floras requires a deep knowledge of the morphological description language. Even high-level categories such as the main types of fruit (achene, drupe, capsule, nut, etc.), leaves (compound ,bipenates, etc.) are not understood by most users.

In this paper, we introduce two complementary visual faceted search mechanisms in order to widen access to such fine-grained attributes. The first one attempts to visually illustrate pre-existing expert facets in the data whereas the other one attempts to discover new facets from the visual contents. Both rely on the offline construction and clustering of a dense visual matching graph computed at the region level (contrary to previous visual faceted search proposals [2, 1, 9] that relied on image-centric clustering and global visual features).

MM'14, November 3–7, 2014, Orlando, Florida, USA.
ACM 978-1-4503-3063-3/14/11.
http://dx.doi.org/10.1145/2647868.2654875.

2. AUTOMATIC EXTRACTION OF FINE-GRAINED VISUAL FACETS

Visual facets are automatically extracted from each of the sub-collection of pictures used in our application: leaves, flowers, fruits and trunks (containing themselves categories that might be visually and semantically very similar). This is done through the following steps:

Hash-based K-NN search. The approximate K-Nearest Neighbors (K-NN) of each local feature $\mathbf{x}_j$ belonging to an image I of the dataset are computed efficiently thanks to the hash-based multi-probe search method introduced in [5]. Its principle is to train an adaptive search model at indexing time through kernel density estimates computed on exact K-NN samples. This model is used at search time to select the most probable buckets to be visited so as to retrieve on average a fraction α of the real K-NN's (α was set to 0.80 in all our experiments). The advantage of this method compared to other state-of-the-art methods (such as PQ-code [4]) is that it allows controlling accurately the quality of the retrieved K-NN while being applicable to any quantization function and metrics. In our case, the original scheme is transposed to the use of a more effective hash function (RMMH [6]) and to the application of the Hamming Embedding principle [3].

Matching graphs construction. A consistent matching graph is computed efficiently on top of the raw visual NN's using the RANdom Sampling and Search algorithm introduced in [8]. It allows matching efficiently feature sets with local geometric constraints by iteratively and adaptively selecting features and their neighborhood in the whole collection. As plants are not rigid objects, we however relaxed the affine geometric constraints used in the original method and used instead neighborhood constraints with an adaptive radius computed as the distance of the m-the spatial neighbor of the primary searched local feature. A matching graph is computed in this way for each of the used sub-collection of pictures (i.e. leaves, flowers, fruits and trunks).

Matching graphs clustering The matching graphs produced by the previous step are then processed by the MCL algorithm [10] in order to group image regions in relevant clusters. To derive facets potentially useful at different granularities, MCL is run several times on each matching graph but with different inflation values (typically at 3 granularities).

3. FACETED SEARCH ENGINE AND GUI

Automatically extracted visual facets are indexed through Apache Solr faceting module as any structured field (the cluster identifier being used as field value). Plant species are considered as the main index entries (i.e. as *documents* using Solr's terminology). Each species is then associated with a number of multi-valued visual facets, corresponding to the cluster id's of the images of that species in each of the MCL partition (and each organ). Complementary, available text-based facets are also integrated in the faceted search module (in our case <Inflorescence type>, <Infruitescence type>, <Flower colour>, <Leaf type>). Both the automatically extracted visual facets and the text-based facets are displayed to the user using representative images for each facet value (rather than texts like in classical applications). The representative image of each facet value is dynamically computed from the fine-grained matching graph so as to adapt it to the previous user search actions. This is simply done by selecting the most connected node (i.e. image region) among all the nodes belonging to the species that were not filtered before. The images containing the selected nodes are roughly cropped before being displayed on the GUI according to the position and size of the selected image region.

Before being presented to the user, all facets (textual and visual) are dynamically reranked according to their filtering efficiency on the remaining species. This is done by computing the following normalized entropy as relevance score of each facet:

$$S(X) = -\sum_{i=1}^{n} \frac{p(x_i).log_2(p(x_i))}{n}$$

where n is the number of values observed in the search results for facet X and x_i is the i-th observed value (e.g. value *red* for facet *flower color*). Ranking all facets according to that score allows to highlight the most informative while penalizing the ones with too much possible values. The number n of observed values is displayed to the user on the GUI as well as the number of species matching each facet value.

4. DATA AND DEMO

Our fine-grained visual faceting scheme is demonstrated on a set of 500 plant species living in France area correspond-

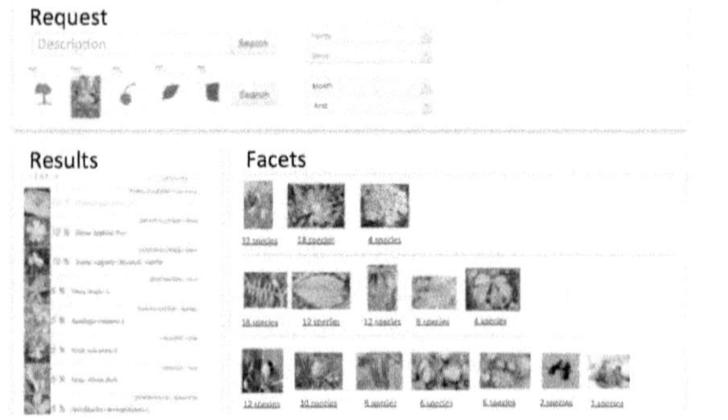

ing to the species included in CLEF plant identification task 2014 (within LifeCLEF *lab* [7]). Textual facets were extracted from TelaBotanica[1] eFlore sheets (leaf, flower and fruit type, flower color, vernacular name). Full text search is performed on the 500 wikipedia articles of the selected species. The demonstration of the system presented at ACM MM 2014 conference will be organized as a user trial, involving a volunteer tester among the audience for each demo session. The volunteer tester will be provided a picture of a plant or a plant organ and will be in charge of determining what it is. The amount of time to succeed and the logs will be analyzed afterwards and contribute to the evaluation of the system.

5. REFERENCES

[1] I. Bartolini and P. Ciaccia. Integrating semantic and visual facets for browsing digital photo collections. In *SEBD*, pages 65–72, 2009.

[2] M. J. Henry, S. Hampton, A. Endert, I. Roberts, and D. Payne. Multifacet: A faceted interface for browsing large multimedia collections. In *Multimedia (ISM), 2013 IEEE International Symposium on*, pages 347–350. IEEE, 2013.

[3] H. Jegou, M. Douze, and C. Schmid. Hamming embedding and weak geometric consistency for large scale image search. In *Computer Vision–ECCV 2008*, pages 304–317. Springer, 2008.

[4] H. Jegou, M. Douze, and C. Schmid. Product quantization for nearest neighbor search. *Pattern Analysis and Machine Intelligence, IEEE Transactions on*, 33(1):117–128, 2011.

[5] A. Joly and O. Buisson. A posteriori multi-probe locality sensitive hashing. In *Proceedings of the 16th ACM international conference on Multimedia*, pages 209–218. ACM, 2008.

[6] A. Joly and O. Buisson. Random maximum margin hashing. In *Computer Vision and Pattern Recognition (CVPR), 2011 IEEE Conference on*, pages 873–880. IEEE, 2011.

[7] A. Joly, H. Müller, H. Goëau, H. Glotin, C. Spampinato, A. Rauber, P. Bonnet, W.-P. Vellinga, and B. Fisher. Lifeclef: Multimedia life species identification. In *ACM Workshop on Environmental Multimedia Retrieval*, 2014.

[8] P. Letessier, O. Buisson, and A. Joly. Consistent visual words mining with adaptive sampling. In *Proceedings of the 1st ACM International Conference on Multimedia Retrieval*, page 49. ACM, 2011.

[9] W. Muller, M. Zech, A. Henrich, and D. Blank. Visualflamenco: Dependable, interactive image browsing based on visual properties. In *Content-Based Multimedia Indexing, 2008. CBMI 2008. International Workshop on*, pages 568–575. IEEE, 2008.

[10] S. Van Dongen. A cluster algorithm for graphs. *Report-Information systems*, (10):1–40, 2000.

[1] http://www.tela-botanica.org/

Real-time Query-by-Image Video Search System

Andre Araujo, David Chen, Peter Vajda and Bernd Girod
Department of Electrical Engineering, Stanford University, Stanford, CA 94305, U.S.A.
{afaraujo, dmchen, pvajda, bgirod}@stanford.edu

ABSTRACT

We demonstrate a novel multimedia system that continuously indexes videos and enables real-time search using images, with a broad range of potential applications. Television shows are recorded and indexed continuously, and iconic images from recent events are discovered automatically. Users can query an uploaded image or an image in the web. When a result is served, the user can play the video clip from the beginning or from the point in time where the retrieved image was found.

Categories and Subject Descriptors

H.3.3 [**Information Storage and Retrieval**]: Information Search and Retrieval

Keywords

query-by-image, trending images, video indexing, video search

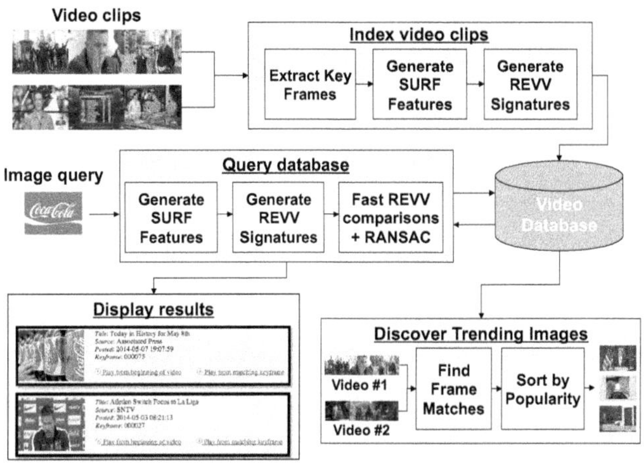

Figure 1: Overview of our query-by-image video search system.

1. INTRODUCTION

Despite the widespread adoption of visual search systems in recent years, a large body of visual content, in the form of videos, cannot be searched using a query image with today's commercial systems. There has been research in this area [1, 6, 7], but no practical system has emerged. We introduce a system that continuously indexes new videos and allows search using images.

This type of technology has a diverse set of potential applications. For advertisement monitoring, users can find all points in time in a video where a particular logo or object was shown. In education, users might use a slide to find the point in time in a lecture video where a certain concept was explained [4]. For content linking, users could use an image in an article to find related video stories. Or they could snap a picture from a display showing a video to get more information about it.

There are, however, several challenges. Videos present an enormous amount of data: the memory usage and search latency for such a system can be significant. To address both of these issues, we use a scheme based on the Residual Enhanced Visual Vector (REVV) [3], a state-of-the-art image retrieval technique. In this technical demo, we present our live, real-time query-by-image video search system that can index a large database of news videos. Please see our demonstration video[1] for additional information and also visit the system's website[2].

MM'14, November 3–7, 2014, Orlando, Florida, USA.
ACM 978-1-4503-3063-3/14/11.
http://dx.doi.org/10.1145/2647868.2654867.

2. SYSTEM ARCHITECTURE

Figure 1 presents a block diagram of our system. The main blocks are described in the following subsections. We use the system front-end developed for the *Eigennews* project [5]. A diverse set of television news programs from 59 channels are recorded, and the videos are analyzed using a multimodal approach [5]. Around 500 video clips are generated per day, and their average duration is 3 minutes.

2.1 Index video clips

For each video clip, we extract keyframes at 1 fps. SURF features [2] are extracted from each keyframe and aggregated into a REVV global signature [3]. The REVV signature enables very memory-efficient indexing and fast retrieval. Each keyframe's REVV signature is stored in memory for fast querying, while the keyframe's SURF descriptors are stored in disk – they will be used in the geometric verification step, which is performed for a small number of keyframes.

Video indexing happens continuously in the background, updating the database with the most current news programs. We use a predefined threshold on the number of keyframes the system can index, in order to limit memory utilization. When a new video is to be included in the database, we check if this threshold is surpassed. If it is, the oldest video in the database is removed before the new video is included. Our memory limitation corresponds to 1 million keyframes, which allows for about 10 days of news videos to be indexed

[1]http://blackhole1.stanford.edu/vidsearch/VideoSearchDemo.mov
[2]http://videosearch.stanford.edu

Figure 2: Examples of trending images detected on May 6, 2014.

in the system. This way, our system always indexes news programs from the most recent 10 days.

After a 30 minute news program is uploaded, the system takes on average 15 minutes to segment it into individual stories (generating one video clip per story), relate the stories to each other and extract metadata [5]. After that, the process from keyframe extraction to including the new REVV signatures in the database takes on average 5 minutes. In our system, each REVV signature utilizes 190 centroids and our system needs to store on average a 512-byte REVV signature per keyframe. With the 1 million keyframe budget, our system needs about 500 MB to index news programs from the past 10 days.

2.2 Query database

Once an image query is submitted, the system immediately extracts SURF features and then generates a query REVV signature. The query's REVV signature can be compared to the database's REVV signatures using bitwise operations [3], which speeds up this step. This process generates a ranked list with the most similar keyframes (according to the REVV comparisons) on top.

After this initial pass over the database, we go over the generated list and match some of the top keyframes to the query image, based on their SURF features. In this process, we first find pairs of query and database features that are sufficiently close, and then try to find an affine transformation between them using RANSAC. We consider a keyframe to be a match if there are at least 8 inliers.

In this process, keyframes that are close in time tend to be ranked closely in the list generated using REVV signatures. During the geometric verification step, we avoid checking keyframes that are within 5 seconds of previously checked keyframes, to avoid redundant computation. The geometric verification step checks 100 keyframes and this near-duplicate removal strategy allows for diverse videos to be compared.

Other system tasks during query time include retrieving the video information in a database, fetching and converting the image if necessary. On average, results are served 7 seconds after a query is initiated, using one core on an Intel Xeon 2.4GHz processor.

2.3 Discover trending images

Once a new video is indexed in the database, we match it against videos that were uploaded in the most recent 24 hours to find trending images. These are iconic images that were broadcast by multiple channels, and usually correspond to important events. Each new video is matched against recent videos only from different channels, in order to find images that were broadcast by different news sources. The matching process uses a similar approach to the one described in the previous subsection, using a combination of REVV and SURF matching, and takes on average 81 seconds per video.

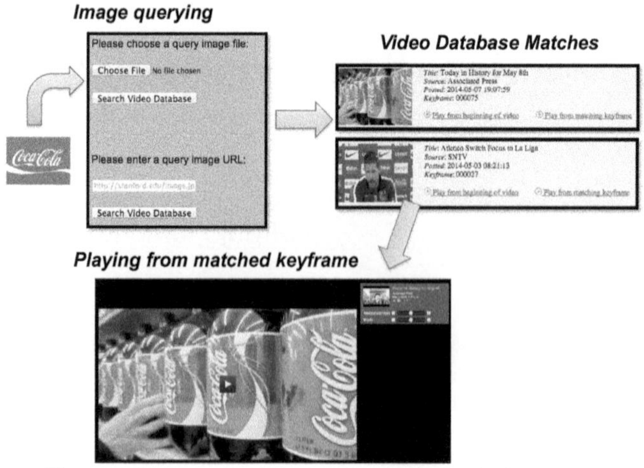

Figure 3: An example of the user interaction with the system.

Figure 2 shows detected trending images from May 6, 2014. They find stories related to the kidnapped Nigerian girls, the World Cup, Ukraine crisis, a tragic accident, climate change and Hillary Clinton's presidential ambitions, all among the top news stories covered in that day.

3. USER INTERFACE

Figure 3 presents a sample of the webpages that the user can access during an interaction with the system. From the system's homepage, an image can be uploaded from the user's computer, or by pasting the URL of an image from the web. Suggested queries and trending images are also presented in the system's webpage. Once the user submits an image query or clicks on a suggested image, the results page is presented. The matched keyframe is displayed for each match, along with detailed information about the program/channel name, clip title, date/time and exact keyframe in the video clip. The interface further allows the user to play the discovered video clip within the *Eigennews* system, either from the beginning or from the exact point in time where the matching keyframe occurred.

4. REFERENCES

[1] A. Araujo, M. Makar, V. Chandrasekhar, D. Chen, S. Tsai, H. Chen, R. Angst, and B. Girod. Efficient video search using image queries. In *Proc. ICIP*, 2014.

[2] H. Bay, A. Ess, T. Tuytelaars, and L. Van Gool. SURF: Speeded Up Robust Features. *CVIU*, 110(3), 2008.

[3] D. Chen, S. Tsai, V. Chandrasekhar, G. Takacs, R. Vedantham, R. Grzeszczuk, and B. Girod. Residual Enhanced Visual Vector as a Compact Signature for Mobile Visual Search. *Signal Processing*, 93(8), 2013.

[4] N.-M. Cheung, D. Chen, V. Chandrasekhar, S. Tsai, G. Takacs, S. Halawa, and B. Girod. Restoration of Out-of-focus Lecture Video by Automatic Slide Matching. In *Proc. ACM Multimedia*, 2010.

[5] M. Daneshi, P. Vajda, D. Chen, S. Tsai, M. Yu, A. Araujo, H. Chen, and B. Girod. EigenNews: Generating and Delivering Personalized News Videos. In *Proc. IEEE BRUREC*, 2013.

[6] P. Over, G. Awad, M. Michel, J. Fiscus, G. Sanders, W. Kraaij, A. F. Smeaton, and G. Quenot. TRECVID 2013 – An Overview of the Goals, Tasks, Data, Evaluation Mechanisms and Metrics. In *Proc. TRECVID*, 2013.

[7] J. Sivic and A. Zisserman. Video Google: Efficient visual search of videos. *Toward Category-Level Object Recognition*, 4170, 2006.

Automatic Real-Time Zooming and Panning on Salient Objects from a Panoramic Video

Vamsidhar Reddy Gaddam, Ragnar Langseth, Håkon Kvale Stensland,
Carsten Griwodz, Pål Halvorsen, Øystein Landsverk

Simula Research Laboratory & University of Oslo, Norway
{vamsidhg, ragnarla, haakonks, griff, paalh, oystesla}@ifi.uio.no

ABSTRACT

The proposed demo shows how our system automatically zooms and pans into tracked objects in panorama videos. At the conference site, we will set up a two-camera version of the system, generating live panorama videos, where the system zooms and pans tracking people using colored hats. Additionally, using a stored soccer game video from a five 2K camera setup at Alfheim stadium in Tromsø from the European league game between Tromsø IL and Tottenham Hotspurs, the system automatically follows the ball.

Categories and Subject Descriptors

H.5.1 [**Multimedia Information Systems**]: Video; I.4.9 [**Applications**]: Video

General Terms

Experimentation; performance

Keywords

Demonstration; panorama video; zoom; panning; real-time; tracking

1. INTRODUCTION

In several fields, especially in surveillance and sports, Pan-Tilt-Zoom (PTZ) cameras have gained popularity with their ability to use the camera sensor efficiently. Yet, one problem that a physically moving system inherently has is that it does not capture and store the data that is not currently in it's field of view. Here, we present a system that generates panorama video in real-time, and we introduce a *virtual* PTZ camera system extracting data from the panorama that is capable of following targets in real-time.

Such a system can be useful when multiple PTZ camera views are demanded for multiple targets. In order to keep the costs low, it is useful to use the same camera setup to create multiple camera views. Several panoramic capture systems have been demonstrated before with different shortcomings like ease of mobility [2], cost [5] and manual input [1].

In this demonstration, we present two versions of our system. The first demonstration is a live, scaled down version of our sport stadium system using two 2K cameras zooming into live recorded video at the conference venue. A few funny colored hats are provided to users that act like targets. Then, the system will be able to track and zoom into the desired target automatically in real-time. The second is a demonstration that uses a recorded five 2K-camera panorama video from Alfheim stadium where our current prototype is installed. The demo will allow users to interact with the virtual camera in both stored and live scenes.

MM'14, November 3–7, 2014, Orlando, Florida, USA.
ACM 978-1-4503-3063-3/14/11.
http://dx.doi.org/10.1145/2647868.2654882

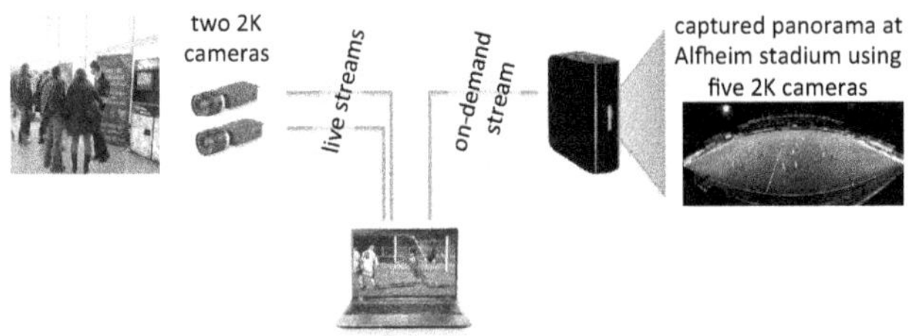

Figure 1: Demonstration setup

2. SYSTEM OVERVIEW

The system presented in this demo is part of a larger system where the current prototype is running at Alfheim stadium in Tromsø. This system has been presented before [4, 3], but without the possibility to automatically zoom and pan into a high-resolution panorama tracking selected objects.

The relevant part of the system in this context is divided into a panorama generation part, the object-tracking part and a video delivery part. The delivery side of the system supports both user-controlled interactive and automatically tracking virtual cameras. A sketch of our system is given in figure 1, and in the subsections below, we give more details of the different components of our system.

2.1 Real-time Panorama Video Capture

To generate a live panorama video, we use two 2K Basler industry vision cameras each of resolution 2046×1086 pixels along with 8 mm lenses. The cameras are shutter synchronized using our custom trigger solution. A recording machine grabs the frames, aligns them and stitches into a cylindrical panorama. The system automatically avoids effects due to parallax by finding dynamic seams that do not pass through moving objects.

Furthermore, to capture the entire soccer field, we use the same Basler cameras. To maximize the panorama resolution, the cameras are rotated by 90°, giving a panorama video of 4450x2000. Moreover, the cameras are mounted in a circular pattern. This means that they are pitched, yawed and rolled to look directly through a point 5 cm in front of the lenses reducing the parallax effects, and the capture system also dynamically determines the required exposure depending on changing light conditions. After the generation of the panorama video, it is encoded and compressed using x264. At the moment, with a focus on video quality, the system still demands a large network bandwidth to the full resolution panorama video. However, there are large potentials for trading of quality for lower bandwidth requirements.

2.2 Live object tracking

In the current setup, the object tracking module is a stand-alone program to support later improvements like distributed processing and multi-sensor fusion. The current tracker is a relatively simple tracking by detection. The major requirement is to be able to track objects introduced or disappeared during the process.

First, an adaptive background subtraction is performed, where the background is updated at regular intervals. Then, color-thresholding followed by object detection leads to a position of objects of different color. Once the positions for a video segment are succesfuly found, the position data is made available to the viewer which is described next. Even though this process currently shares the same resources as the stitching process, tracking is acheived with an average execution time of 7 ms per frame.

2.3 Live Automatic/Manual virtual viewer

Once the panoramic videos are encoded, they are made available to the client program running the virtual camera via HTTP segment streaming along with the position data if available. The client has two modes, an automatic mode and a manual mode. The manual mode allows the user to interact with the virtual camera, where one can pan/tilt/zoom manually into the live stream.

More importantly in this demo, the automatic mode follows a few heuristics to keep the demanded target in the virtual view yet provide a smooth video. The zoom for the on-site demo is set to be fixed because of the unknown 3D structure of the area, whereas in the soccer field the zoom variable also changes depending on the ball position in the field.

In addition to the virtual view, a preview window is presented where the portion of panorama that is being fetched, corrected for a perspective view and displayed is highlighted. This preview window proves to be a rather useful feature when developing the servoing algorithms. In addition, it also demonstrates that the virtual view is not a simple crop from the panorama video.

All the processing except for downloading and decoding the video frame happens on a GPU to utilize the parallel processing power. The client has been tested on both Mac and PC with different capabilities. Nevertheless the average processing time is approximately 12 ms per frame on commodity graphics hardware.

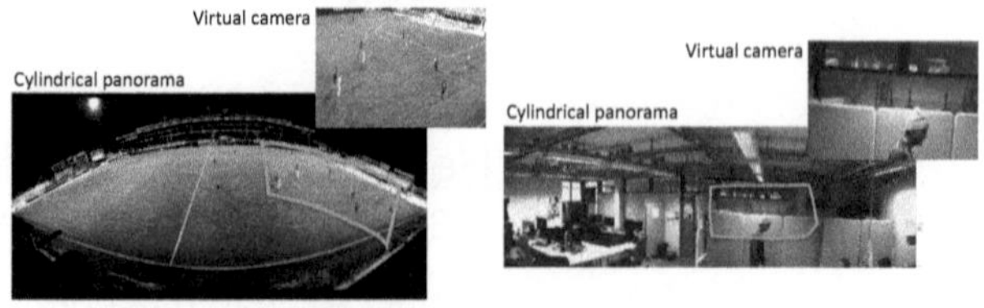

Figure 2: The virtual camera is generated from the region of interest marked in the panorama video. Note that it is not a simple crop from the bigger video.

3. DEMONSTRATION

In this demo, we present a system for real-time interactive zooming and panning of panorama video. The general setup is shown in figure 1. We use two types of panorama input. We use a stored panorama video captured in the Alfheim soccer stadium, i.e., the European League game between Tromsø IL and Tottenham Hotspurs. The video was recorded using five 2K industrial cameras, and processed and stitched in a distributed system. We also use a live system using two 2K cameras on site to generate the panorama video. Both the stored-video and the live-video demos work in real-time where the system zooms and pans into tracked objects, i.e., the ball in the soccer game and people wearing colored hats in the live panorame video[1].

Acknowledgments

This work has been performed in the context of the *iAD* center for Research-based Innovation (project number 174867) funded by the Norwegian Research Council.

4. REFERENCES

[1] P. Carr and R. Hartley. Portable multi-megapixel camera with real-time recording and playback. In *Proc. of DICTA*, pages 74–80, 2009.

[2] P. Carr, M. Mistry, and I. Matthews. Hybrid robotic/virtual pan-tilt-zom cameras for autonomous event recording. In *Proc. of ACM MM*, pages 193–202, 2013.

[3] V. R. Gaddam, R. Langseth, S. Ljødal, P. Gurdjos, V. Charvillat, C. Griwodz, and P. Halvorsen. Interactive zoom and panning from live panoramic video. In *Proc. of ACM NOSSDAV*, Mar. 2014.

[4] P. Halvorsen, S. Sægrov, A. Mortensen, D. K. Kristensen, A. Eichhorn, M. Stenhaug, S. Dahl, H. K. Stensland, V. R. Gaddam, C. Griwodz, and D. Johansen. Bagadus: An integrated system for arena sports analytics – a soccer case study. In *Proc. of ACM MMSys*, pages 48–59, Mar. 2013.

[5] O. Schreer, I. Feldmann, C. Weissig, P. Kauff, and R. Schafer. Ultrahigh-resolution panoramic imaging for format-agnostic video production. *Proceedings of the IEEE*, 101(1):99–114, Jan 2013.

[1] http://home.ifi.uio.no/vamsidhg/acmdemo.mp4

Event Detection in Broadcasting Video for Halfpipe Sports

Hao-Kai Wen, Wei-Che Chang, Chia-Hu Chang, Yin-Tzu Lin, and Ja-Ling Wu
National Taiwan University
{r01922083, r02922031}@csie.ntu.edu.tw,
{chchang, known, wjl}@cmlab.csie.ntu.edu.tw

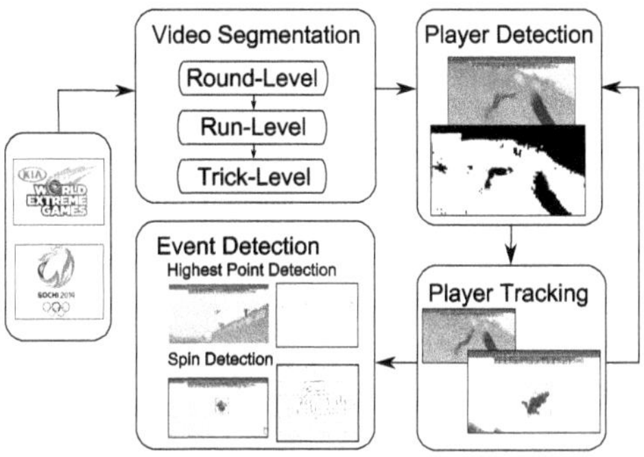

Figure 1: Flowchart of the proposed system.

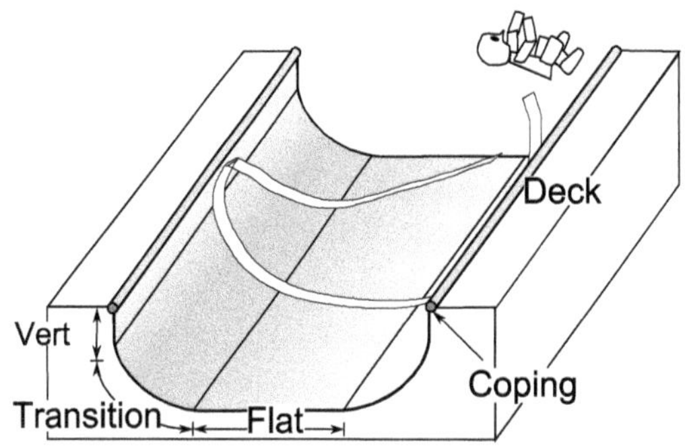

Figure 2: Structure of a halfpipe.

ABSTRACT

In this work, a low-cost and efficient system is proposed to automatically analyze the halfpipe (HP) sports videos. In addition to the court color ratio information, we find the player region by using salient object detection mechanisms to face the challenge of motion blurred scenes in HP videos. Besides, a novel and efficient method for detecting the spin event is proposed on the basis of native motion vectors existing in a compressed video. Experimental results show that the proposed system is effective in recognizing the hard-to-be-detected spin events in HP videos.

Categories and Subject Descriptors

H.3.1 [**Information Storage and Retrieval**]: Content Analysis and Indexing—*Indexing methods*

Keywords

halfpipe; vert ramp; sports video; action recognition

1. INTRODUCTION

A halfpipe (HP) is one of the most popular terrains in gravity sports like snowboarding, skateboarding, skiing, freestyle BMX, and inline skating[1]. For players of HP sports, a common way to improve their skills is to learn by imitation. In order to learn the best tricks in the world, they imitate tricks performed by elite players through watching recorded broadcast videos, such as Sochi 2014 Olympics and KIA World Extreme Games. As shown in the top-left part of Figure 1, a general HP contest can be hierarchically divided into rounds and runs. In each run, all contestants will take their turns to perform tricks. For each player's turn, she or he starts from one side of the HP, i.e., the vert, passes through the flat, reaches to another vert, and goes back and forth several times, as shown in Figure 2. Each time the player flies above the vert, she or he performs one type of tricks, such as spin or grab. We defined a trick segment as a period of time during which the player passes through the flat, reaches to one of the verts, and then goes back to the flat. Finding a particular trick in a video is time-consuming and labor-intensive because certain tricks may be sparse in the video and the timestamps of them are unknown to a video watcher. As a result, finding trick segments and recognizing trick types automatically are highly wanted by and beneficial to HP players.

Recognizing the trick type in HP videos is challenging because (i) there are often more than one shots taken at different locations by shoulder-mount camcorders in a single trick segment, and (ii) the scenes in an HP video are motion blurred since players move fast. As a result, it is difficult to estimate global motion by using either pixel-based method (e.g., optical flow) or feature-based method (e.g., SIFT matching). And thus, segmenting a player's silhouette by background subtraction techniques becomes impractical.

MM'14, November 3–7, 2014, Orlando, Florida, USA.
ACM 978-1-4503-3063-3/14/11.
http://dx.doi.org/10.1145/2647868.2654883 .

[1]https://en.wikipedia.org/wiki/Half-pipe

Most of the existing studies [1] recognized the actions of players with the help of wearable sensors. However, it is hard to apply sensor-based methods to all contestants because of privacy issues. Therefore, in the proposed system, HP contest videos are automatically analyzed with low-cost and efficient methods without sensor information. The flowchart of the proposed system is illustrated in Figure 1. We will address how HP sports videos become readable with the aid of video segmentation, player detection and tracking, and event detection mechanisms, presented in the following sections. Please also refer to our demo video[2] for real illustrations.

2. VIDEO SEGMENTATION

By using the scoreboard information, we segment an input HP broadcasting video into run-level segments. By observation, we found that the percentage of coverage of HP court color in the scene is relatively high when the player is on the flat. So the video could be segmented into trick segments by finding peaks in the ratio curve of the court color coverage along the time line. However, the peaks may happen several times in between the two verts because of shot transitions, which affect the distribution of the peaks in the curve of color coverage ratio. To improve the precision of the segmentation, we apply a moving average filter, of about half a trick long, on the curve of color coverage ratio.

3. PLAYER DETECTION AND TRACKING

When a player moves fast on an HP, the background is blurred but the player is relatively clear because the camera moves along with the player. So we perform multi-scale contrast saliency detection[2] to find player region candidates. Besides, the scenes in these frames are often composed of a player surrounded by the HP court, i.e., the scenes are of high coverage ratio of the court color. As a result, the connected components in the non-court color parts of the scene can be also chosen as player region candidates. Finally, the player region can be detected by combining the salient object region and the non-court color region in the frames with high court color coverage ratio. For other scenes, we apply the algorithm proposed in [3] to track the player. Since several shot changes may occur in one trick segment, we also re-estimate the player region at each detected shot change.

4. EVENT DETECTION

To recognize the event in each trick segment, i.e., the type of tricks , we detect the moment when the player reaches the highest point because the player's moves near to the highest point are representative of performed tricks. Once the player flies above the HP, she or he can be treated as a projectile. And the scene will stop changing when the highest point is reached. Meanwhile, the coverage ratio of court color will remain low for a few frames. As a result, we detected the highest points in trick segments by finding the valleys of the color coverage ratio used in Section 2.

Then, we intend to recognize if there is a spin – one major type of HP tricks. The movements of the native motion vectors, of a compressed video, will behave like a circle , as shown in Figure 3, when a player performs a spin trick. As a result, the following mechanism is suggested to recognize

[2]http://www.cmlab.csie.ntu.edu.tw/~r01922083/halfpipeEvent/

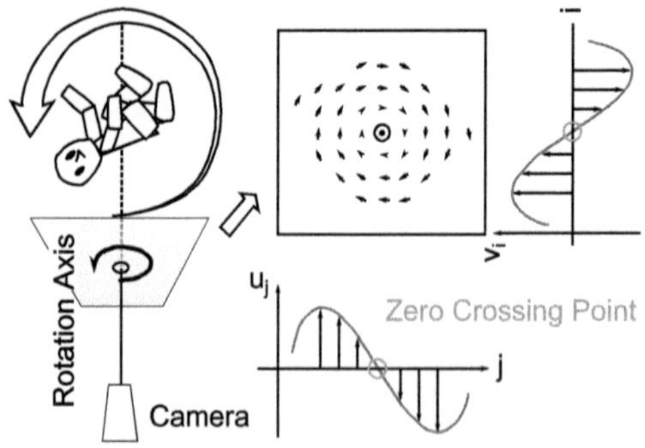

Figure 3: Schematic diagram for detecting spins.

such an event. Let $A \in \mathbb{C}^{M\times N}$ be the matrix representing the motion field of the player region, where $\mathbb{C}$ denotes the complex field. We accumulate the vertical components of A along the horizontal axis, $u_j = \sum_{i=1}^{M} \text{Im}(A_{i,j})$, and likewise the horizontal components along the vertical axis, i.e., $v_i = \sum_{j=1}^{N} \text{Re}(A_{i,j})$. As shown in Figure 3, vectors u and v will across the axes (zero values), once they reach the center of the circle. However, motion vectors may not form a perfect circle because the rotating movements behind the body of the player cannot be captured by the camera when the rotation axis of the player is nearly parallel to the camera view. In such a situation, some part of the circle may be missed, but fortunately, either u or v could still capture the pre-described property. So, we could recognize a spin event by counting the number of zero crossing points in u and v of the detected highest point, and its neighboring frames. The more frames with only one zero crossing point in u or v, the more likely that there is a spin in a trick.

5. RESULTS

To evaluate, we used the video of "KIA World Extreme Games 2013–AIL Vert" from Youtube (in H.264 format). Eito Yasutoko's 2nd run and Nikolaj Najdenov's 1st run were chosen as testing video sequences. Each run in the contest is of 45 seconds long. In Eito Yasutoko's 2nd run, the result of the highest points detection are 9 hits, 0 false alarm, and 1 miss. There is a miss because the player falls in that run. For spin detection, there are 4 hits, 1 false alarm, and 0 miss. In Nikolaj Najdenov's 1st, the result of the highest points detection are 9 hits, 0 false alarm, and 2 misses. For spin detection, there are 3 hits, 0 false alarm, and 2 misses. The miss detections are due to the relatively small detected player region in the scene.

6. REFERENCES

[1] J. Harding, C. Mackintosh, A. Hahn, and D. James. Classification of aerial acrobatics in elite half-pipe snowboarding using body mounted inertial sensors. In *The Eng. of Sport 7*, pages 447–456. Springer Paris, 2008.

[2] T. Liu, Z. Yuan, J. Sun, J. Wang, N. Zheng, X. Tang, and H.-Y. Shum. Learning to detect a salient object. *IEEE trans. PAMI*, 33(2), 2011.

[3] J. Ning, L. Zhang, D. Zhang, and C. Wu. Robust mean-shift tracking with corrected background-weighted histogram. *IET Comput. Vis.*, 6(1):62–69, January 2012.

Wally: A Scalable Distributed Automated Video Surveillance System with Rich Search Functionalities*

Jianquan Liu, Shoji Nishimura, Takuya Araki
Green Platform Research Laboratories, NEC Corporation
1753 Shimonumabe, Nakahara-ku, Kawasaki, Kanagawa 211-8666, Japan
{j-liu@ct, s-nishimura@bk, t-araki@dc}.jp.nec.com

ABSTRACT

In this demo, we present Wally, a scalable distributed automated video surveillance system. Wally provides users with rich search functionalities for surveillance, such as instant and historical search based on face or clothing feature by specifying multiple conditions. Unlike most existing systems that focus on video analysis but do not well consider system scalability and search functionality, Wally takes into account both of them, and is developed as a commercial level system for realistic surveillance. To achieve this, we 1) employ relational database, in-memory cache, key-value store, and indexing techniques to ensure the system scalability when it meets Big Data, and 2) develop user-friendly interfaces to enable users to search key frames by rich functionalities. It is estimated by our extensive evaluations that Wally can complete a search task within 50 minutes from the videos captured one day by 1000 real-time cameras, while human monitoring needs 1000x24 man-hours.

Categories and Subject Descriptors

H.2.4 [**Database Management**]: Systems—*Distributed databases, Multimedia databases*; H.3 [**Information Storage and Retrieval**]

Keywords

Video surveillance; Multimedia database; Distributed system

1. INTRODUCTION

Video surveillance has been studied for over two decades [6]. Most current video surveillance systems need human operators for constant monitoring. However, nowadays surveillance camera has become a ubiquitous aspect of the modern urban landscape, installed in shopping malls, buildings, stations, and other public places. The number of cameras will exceed the capacity of personnel available. To overcome this limitation, a major effort in the computer vision and artificial intelligence community is to develop automated system for the real-time monitoring of people, vehicles, and other objects [7]. However, most existing work mainly focuses on typical tasks of video analysis including object detection, recognition, tracking and behavior analysis. Storing videos for future or immediate utilization, such as search, lacks attention [4]. Thus, surveillance system focusing on search functionality remains a challenge.

On the other hand, it is forecasted that surveillance video will grow to 5.6 zettabytes in 2020, sharing over 42% of Big Data [3]. When video surveillance system meets such Big Data, the distributed aspect remains another research challenge. However, researchers have not paid much attention to the scalability of distributed video surveillance system [5, 6].

*Demo video: `http://jpn.nec.com/rd/crl/spp/wally.wmv`.

MM'14, Nov 03-07 2014, Orlando, FL, USA
ACM 978-1-4503-3063-3/14/11.
http://dx.doi.org/10.1145/2647868.2654872 .

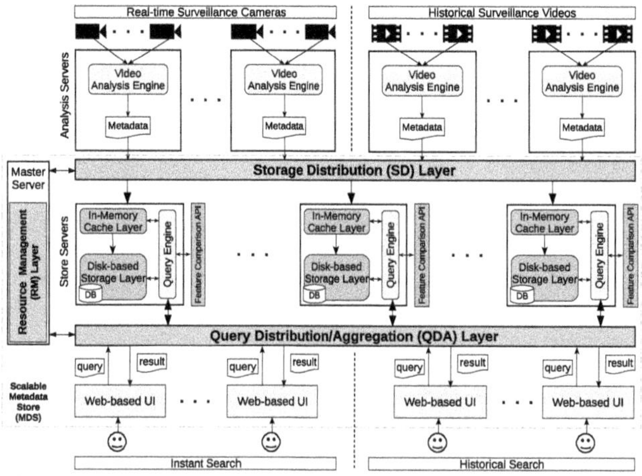

Figure 1: Architecture of Wally. The system consists of analysis servers and a scalable metadata store. The metadata extracted from video analysis engine includes face/clothing feature, gender, and age of detected person. For details, refer to Section 2.

Motivated by both of the aforementioned challenges, we develop Wally, a scalable distributed automated video surveillance system, which takes into account system scalability and search functionality. Wally is a well designed and implemented commercial level system, of which the architecture is shown in Figure 1. To build such a real-world system, the most difficult and significant thing is to guarantee the scalability and usability.

For instance, let us assume such a realistic scenario. There are 1000 cameras installed in a big shopping mall for surveillance. It is reported that a suspicious person, whose name is *Wally*, entered the shopping mall yesterday. Now, the police want to find out "*Where's Wally?*" In this case, playing back yesterday's videos to seek *Wally* becomes a critical problem. As we know, first, the metadata such as face features extracted from these videos are too big, which can reach about 1300GB. Here, we assume that a camera generates video in 15fps, and face features extracted from one frame are about 1KB. If it is needed to track back the videos one month ago, the case will become more terrible. A surveillance system not only for monitoring but also for search is required to be distributed and scalable to store large-scale metadata for immediate or future utilization. Second, the results of content-based video search, such as face-feature-based, should be precise to ensure the usability for surveillance. This requires an excellent video analysis engine to provide high precise feature extraction and comparison.

In this work, we carefully design and implement Wally to meet the above-mentioned guarantees by integrating state-of-the-art techniques as follows. We employ key-value store technique to realize the scalability, and incorporate the commercial products NeoFace® [1] and FieldAnalyst® [1] to ensure the usability. NeoFace® is the world's best face recognition technology [2], which can provide high precision for surveillance as a video analysis engine.

2. ARCHITECTURE & IMPLEMENTATION

Architecture. Figure 1 illustrates the system architecture of Wally. The system consists of 1) analysis servers and 2) a scalable metadata store (abbr. **MDS**). The metadata, here, indicates arbitrary type of data extracted from raw videos, including face and clothing feature, time, gender, and age. As shown in Figure 1, video analysis engines embedded in analysis servers, receive the videos input from real-time cameras or historical archives, then analyze the videos to extract metadata, and finally output the metadata to MDS. Subsequently, inside of MDS, the storage distribution (SD) layer communicates with master server, and requests the resource management (RM) layer to assign proper store servers for storing metadata. When queries are issued from users by web-based UIs, they are first sent to the query distribution/aggregation (QDA) layer. Immediately, the QDA layer communicates with master server, asking the RM layer for assigning proper store servers to execute search tasks. Meanwhile, the QDA layer will progressively aggregate search results output by query engines and respond to users.

In Figure 1, it is worth noting that we design a novel key-value scheme in the RM, SD, and QDA layers to realize the distributed architecture, which lets store servers be scaled out dynamically. Furthermore, we design an in-memory cache layer in a store server to keep latest metadata, which makes metadata searchable immediately so that Wally can provide instant search. In addition, query engines are designed as extendable components, which are pluggable with any feature comparison APIs provided by video analysis engines. This makes Wally very flexible and adaptable in case an external analysis engine is newly appended, modified, or upgraded.

Implementation. In Wally, since we adopt the commercial products NeoFace® and FieldAnalyst® as video analysis engines, their details are not described here. Instead, to guarantee the system scalability and search functionality, we carefully implement the MDS to meet the requirements in two major real-world usecases.

One of the most common tasks for surveillance is to store huge metadata and to generate alerts when a suspicious person or unusual activity is detected. In this case, Wally should have sufficient ability to store real-time video for instant search. It means that Wally should make the recent metadata searchable and provide quick search response. To achieve this, we employ in-memory cache technique integrated with B-tree indexing technique to enhance search efficiency. Furthermore, we apply the First In First Out (FIFO) algorithm as an eviction policy for cache management, which makes the latest metadata reachable for instant search. The evicted data will be flushed onto disk-based MySQL databases. In order to balance the utilization of storage servers, we implement the key-value store by designing key sharding in a round-robin manner.

Another common usecase is that the police often need to play back historical videos to seek the target criminal after a crime occurred. In this scenario, Wally should provide a mechanism to scan all historical videos to find out the key frames as quickly as possible. To achieve this, we implement query engines that can progressively retrieve top-k similar results in parallel, by collaboratively accessing the in-memory cache and on-disk database.

3. INTERFACE OVERVIEW

In this section we briefly introduce the interface of Wally to present its rich search functionalities. As shown in Figure 2, the interface design is simple and web-based yet user-friendly. Wally provides users with rich search functionalities by combinations among 1) search modes, 2) search flows, and 3) search options.

Search modes. Wally has three search modes: 1) *search by outfit*, in which users can execute a search by specifying a clothing feature from an input picture or text keyword. For instance, given a picture containing a person and then dragging the mouse to select

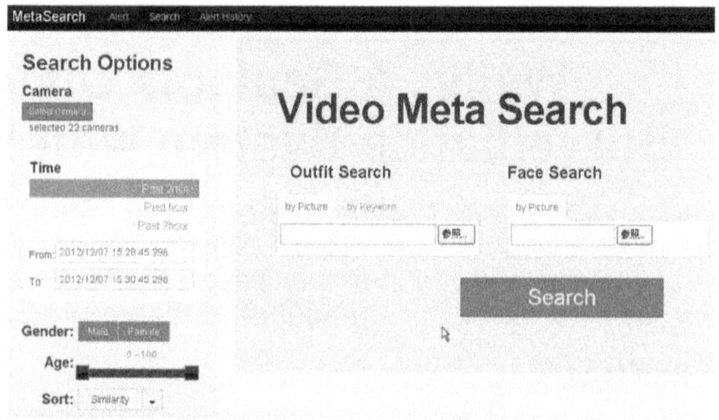

Figure 2: A snapshot of Wally. The screen is divided into three panels: top, left, and right. Top menu panel allows users to switch the system for alert monitoring or for search; Left option panel provides users with multiple search conditions; Right main panel enables users to perform a search by specifying outfit or face.

a region of clothes, or given a text keyword such as "red shirt", the system will automatically generate a proper clothing feature submitted to query engines. 2) *search by face*, in which users can input a face picture to perform a search using face feature that is automatically extracted by the system. 3) *search from alert*, in which users can monitor the detection of suspicious person or unusual activity, and then trigger a search when an alert raises from detection.

Search flows. Wally provides two search flows: 1) *instant search* and 2) *historical search*. As mentioned in Section 2, instant search takes advantage of in-memory cache to perform efficient search when a suspicious person or unusual activity is detected. Historical search exploits the power of parallelism to execute a full search over huge volume historical videos.

Search options. In Wally, the above-mentioned search modes and search flows can be specified with search options as follows. 1) *Camera ID* indicates the video source; 2) *Time range* specifies the time period to be searched; 3) *Gender* and 4) *Age range* specify the possible gender and age range, respectively, which is estimated by the FieldAnalyst® engine; and 5) *Sort type* specifies the type used to sort search results.

4. EVALUATIONS

To evaluate the performance of Wally, we implemented video analysis engines in C++ and the scalable metadata store in Java. We equipped 8 storage servers each with 32G memory for evaluation. We used 27 cameras in our experiments, which gather real surveillance videos from different positions of buildings such as entrance gates, totally about 108 hours. We varied the number of storage servers, the number of cameras, and the length of videos to examine the system scalability and search efficiency. By our extensive evaluations, we confirmed that the scalability and efficiency fits with ideal case nearly as our expectation. It is estimated that if Wally is built by 25 storage servers each equipped with 32G memory, it can complete a historical search task within 50 minutes from the videos captured one day by 1000 real-time cameras, while human monitoring needs 1000x24 man-hours.

5. REFERENCES

[1] NeoFace®, FieldAnalyst®. http://jpn.nec.com/face/.

[2] NIST MBE. http://www.nist.gov/itl/iad/ig/mbe.cfm.

[3] J. Gantz and D. Reinsel. The Digital Universe in 2020: Big Data, Bigger Digital Shadows, and Biggest Growth in the Far East. *IDC Technical Report*, Dec. 2012.

[4] W. Hu, D. Xie, Z. Fu, W. Zeng, and S. J. Maybank. Semantic-based surveillance video retrieval. *IEEE TIP*, 16(4):1168–1181, 2007.

[5] P. Korshunov and W. T. Ooi. Critical video quality for distributed automated video surveillance. In *ACM MM*, pages 151–160, 2005.

[6] T. Räty. Survey on contemporary remote surveillance systems for public safety. *IEEE TSMCC*, 40(5):493–515, 2010.

[7] M. Shah, O. Javed, and K. Shafique. Automated visual surveillance in realistic scenarios. *IEEE MultiMedia*, 14(1):30–39, 2007.

Deep Search with Attribute-aware Deep Network

Junshi Huang*, Wei Xia*, and Shuicheng Yan
National University of Singapore, Singapore
{junshi.huang, weixia, eleyans}@nus.edu.sg

ABSTRACT

In this demo, we present *Deep Search*, an attribute-aware fashion-related retrieval system, based on the convolutional neural network by taking clothes as a concrete example. In this system, the visual appearance and semantic attributes of products can be seamlessly integrated into our model in a "dividing and combining" manner. Rather than modelling one attribute per classifier, we design a holistic tree-structure network for exploiting multiple attributes simultaneously, with each branch of network corresponding to one attribute. Therefore, the high-level feature from the conjunction layer of the network can comprehensively preserve both the visual and semantic information of products. The promising retrieval results indicate the great potential of neural feature for attribute-aware retrieval task. The supplementary slides can be found in `http://goo.gl/zpobN6`.

Categories and Subject Descriptors

H.3.3 [**Information Storage and Retrieval**]: Information Search and Retrieval—*Information filtering*

Keywords

Attribute-aware retrieval system, tree-structure, deep network

1. INTRODUCTION

It is well-known that fashion-related online shopping is becoming increasingly popular in daily life, within which the clothes take a considerable proportion. To search for the products of interest, the customers often exploit very specific visual content (*e.g.* daily photos) and/or semantic tags (*e.g.* attributes) as the queries, which leads to the emergence of content-based and/or text-based retrieval system. However, people are often hampered by the lack of precise description of products during the searching procedure. Meanwhile, few search engines have the ability to capture the visual and semantic information of products simultaneously. Particularly, the semantic information of products known as attribute is usually composed of several different semantic concepts, and thus cannot be simply modelled as a multi-label annotation task. One common way of dealing with such multi-attribute queries is to train one classifier for each attribute independently, and concatenate the predicted attribute values to judge their fitness to the queries. However, the interrelationship between attributes may be ignored for such approaches.

* means the first two authors contribute equally to the paper

MM'14, November 3–7, 2014, Orlando, Florida, USA.
ACM 978-1-4503-3063-3/14/11.
http://dx.doi.org/10.1145/2647868.2654885.

Figure 1: Exemplar results of Deep Search. The first column is the query cropped by human detector. The rest eight images are the top-8 retrieval images.

In this demo, by taking clothes as concrete example, we leverage the advantage of deep convolutional neural network for multi-attribute clothes retrieval. Different from the multi-label image annotation task, we treat the attributes of clothes from the low-level layers of network in an integrative way, and separate them at the high-level layers. The conjunction layer can thus capture the comprehensive information of attributes, which consequently leads to a promising performance in the retrieval task. Moreover, by using the ImageNet database for pre-training, the texture information of clothes can be firmly grasped by our model. The capabilities of visual and semantic representations of our retrieval system can be illustrated by some examples in Figure 1.

2. SYSTEM FRAMEWORK

The framework of Deep Search is illustrated in Figure 2. Given an image, the upper body is cropped by a human detector and resized as the query, which is fed into our neural network to extract the high-level representation feature of clothes. Then, the extracted feature from the conjunction layer is used to conduct a similarity search to seek for the visually and semantically similar clothes from the clothes repository.

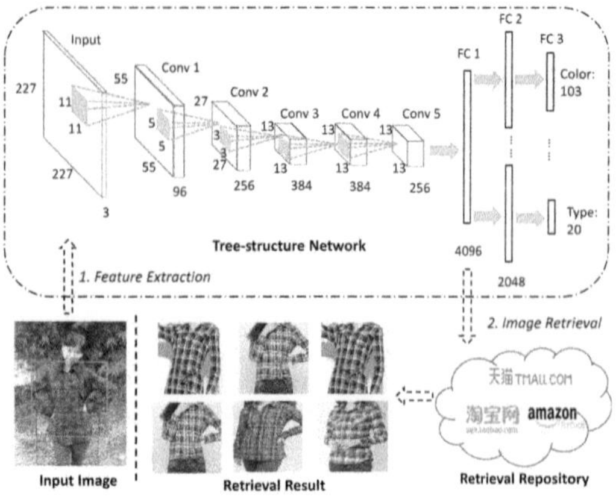

Figure 2: The framework of Deep Search. The red box in the input image is the detected upper-body. The feature of cropped image extracted by the tree-structure network is used to search for the similar clothes.

2.1 Data Collection

Overall, 206,235 clothes images and descriptions are crawled from several online shopping websites, *e.g.* Taobao, Tmall, and Amazon *etc.* With template matching, seven attributes, *i.e.* pattern, sleeve, button panel, collar, style, color, and type, are extracted from the descriptions. After filtering out the images with less than four attributes, 150,117 clothes images are remained for model training and clothes retrieval.

2.2 Upper-body Detection

To overcome cluttered background, a detector is used to extract the clothes from photos. Specifically, we train a grammar model [1] for human detection, and use the middle parts of the model to represent the upper-body.

2.3 Training and Feature Learning

In this section, we present a tree-structure network fine-tuned on a multi-attribute database for feature learning. It is worth noting that the multiple attributes are modelled by a holistic network simultaneously.

Generally, we pre-train the network on ILSVRC-2012 training set with similar configuration to Krizhevsky *et al.*[2], and fine-tune it on the clothes dataset. In specific, we substitute the last two fully connected layers with seven sub-networks. Each sub-network is a branch that models one attribute. The neuron number in the output-layer of each branch equals to the number of corresponding attribute values. In this tree-structure network, the visual features from the low-level layers are shared among attributes; while the semantic features from the high-level layers are learned separately. During training, the weights of the first four convolutional layers are fixed, and the remaining layers are updated with smaller learning rates.

One special layer of the network is the conjunction layer connecting the first fully connected layer with the seven branches. Since the activation and gradients are divided and combined in this layer during the forward and backward procedure respectively, we refer the training strategy of our network as "dividing and combining". Obviously, this conjunction layer acts as a route between low-level layers and high-level layers, which agglomerates the low-level visual feature and the high-level semantic feature simultaneously. Therefore, the activation of this conjunction layer is used as the retrieval feature in Deep Search.

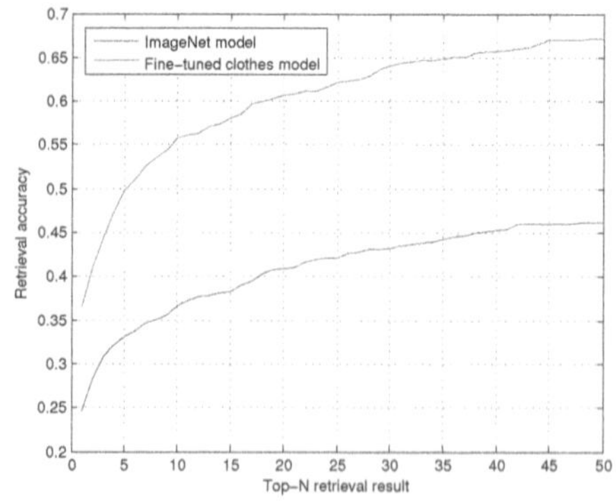

Figure 3: The retrieval performance of baseline and Deep Search.

3. EXPERIMENT

In this experiment, we evaluate the Deep Search on our collected database with 624 query photos uploaded by the customers. The pre-trained convolutional network on ImageNet dataset is used as the baseline. Given a query image, the top-N retrieval result is considered as correct if the corresponding product image is found among them.

The retrieval performance is presented in Figure 3. Generally, the Deep Search achieves an accuracy of 55.83% at top-10 retrieval result, which significantly outperforms the ImageNet model (36.73%). For qualitative evaluation, some results of our model are presented in Figure 1.

For the runtime, it takes about 1.3 second to detect a photo of 500 $\times$ 300 pixels on a machine with 1.8 GHz CPU and 32GB of RAM. With a GTX Titan, it spends about 20 ms on feature extraction. The overall retrieval time of Deep Search on our database is about 1.5 second per query.

In the demonstration, we will present the performance of Deep Search on on-site photos, and exhibit the retrieval result of Deep Search on the collected database. We will also release our retrieval system online for public testing.

4. CONCLUSIONS

In this demo, by taking clothes as example, we present an attribute-aware retrieval system on our collected clothes database with 150,117 images. To integrate the multiple attributes of clothes into one holistic model, we propose a tree-structure convolutional neural network for feature learning. Specifically, the low-level visual features are shared by all attributes, and each branch at the high-level layers of the network models the semantic information of each attribute independently. For initialization, this model is pre-trained on ILSVRC-2012 training set. With the tree-structure model, the "dividing and combining" strategy is used for fine-tuning. The conjunction layer connecting the low-level layers and high-level branches is then used to extract feature for clothes retrieval. The experiment result indicates that the Deep Search achieves superior retrieval performance on our database.

5. REFERENCES

[1] R. Girshick, P. Felzenszwalb, and D. McAllester. Object detection with grammar models. 2011.

[2] A. Krizhevsky, I. Sutskever, and G. Hinton. Imagenet classification with deep convolutional neural networks. 2012.

Virtual Director Adapting Visual Presentation to Conversation Context in Group Videoconferencing – An Interactive Demo

Rene Kaiser and Wolfgang Weiss
Institute for Information and Communication Technologies
JOANNEUM RESEARCH
Graz, Austria
rene.kaiser@joanneum.at,
wolfgang.weiss@joanneum.at

Manolis Falelakis and Marian F. Ursu
Department of Computing
Goldsmiths, University of London
London, UK
m.falelakis@gold.ac.uk,
marian.ursu@york.ac.uk

ABSTRACT

In this technical demonstration, we invite visitors to join a group videoconferencing session with remote participants across Europe, using the Vconect system. This research prototype automatically takes decisions about the presentation of available video streams by processing the audio stream from each participant. It observes patterns in turn-taking behavior and dynamically computes conversation metrics to automatically decide, for each conversation node's screen, how to compose (in layout) and mix (in time) the streams originating from the other nodes. The demo invites to discuss future possibilities in video mediated group communication beyond the currently implemented functionality of the demo system.

Categories and Subject Descriptors

H.4.3 [**Information Systems Applications**]: Communications Applications—*Computer conferencing, teleconferencing, and videoconferencing*

Keywords

videoconferencing, communication orchestration, Virtual Director, video mediated group communication, telepresence

1. MEDIATED GROUP COMMUNICATION

The role of mediated audio-visual communication keeps increasing in our daily lives, mainly driven by the availability of broadband services and mobile devices. Apart from business purposes, the need to support social communication with dedicated technology becomes stronger and stronger in a global world where many friends and families live far apart. Some requirements to such systems have been worked on for years (e.g. telepresence), however, their functionality and intelligence are only at the beginning. Several commercial videoconferencing solutions already support a certain level of intelligent behavior in automatically and dynamically deciding how to present the audio-visual live streams to the users, but many challenges remain in this research area both in understanding user needs and technical realization. Such mediated communication systems need to adapt to the conversation context — people might join and leave communication sessions any time; some might move to side conversations; some conversations might be more animated than others; the network capabilities might vary.

This demo showcases a prototype system from an ongoing research activity that aims to push the current state-of-the-art along several dimensions. The Vconect[1] project investigates novel ways of supporting mediated audio-visual communication for ad-hoc groups. One problem implied by such video communication setups is that for each participant, there are multiple video streams available as options for being currently shown, i.e. when there are n participants and each is equipped with 1 camera, $n - 1$ video streams are candidates for being displayed at each client (no self-view assumed). The question is how to optimally deal with them. A simple solution is to show all video streams side by side on one screen, referred to as *tiled layout*. This would however not scale to larger groups or work on small screens, and would not respect the dynamics of the conversation and the users' inherently changing communication needs at all.

We set out to investigate more sophisticated solutions with the aim of achieving better communication support through intelligent camera selection and presentation. By dynamically calculating conversation metrics that indicate the aspects of the *dynamics* of a conversation (based on speech patterns, cp. work on conversation analysis, e.g. [3]), our system automatically selects a suitable visual layout and assigns to each region a particular video stream. In technical terms, this is realized by a software component which automatically executes a mixing process of different video streams, also known as a *Virtual Director* [1]. In the realm of video communication, we refer to this process as *communication orchestration* [4].

The remaining sections elaborate on the research behind the concept of a Virtual Director, and illustrate what visitors can expect to interactively experience at the demo.

MM'14, November 3–7, 2014, Orlando, Florida, USA.
ACM 978-1-4503-3063-3/14/11.
http://dx.doi.org/10.1145/2647868.2654874.

[1] `http://www.vconect-project.eu/`

2. VIRTUAL DIRECTOR

Virtual Director software components resemble the decision making processes behind compiling live TV broadcast. However, supporting communication processes and the individual needs of each participant is overall a completely different challenge to the narrative functions in broadcast. Communication orchestration can be regarded as a reasoning process which operates in real-time for each participant, screen, or location participating in a communication session. It builds upon audio and video processing infrastructure and executes camera control and audio-visual composition (cp. different setup in [4]). Vconect's Virtual Director is a central server-side software component that automatically decides on camera selections and visual layout changes by reasoning on *cues* from all clients involved. The core of the engine's logic is implemented declaratively using forward-chaining rules that are executed by an event processing engine. Detailed examples working with *full screen layout* only are explained in [2]. The component is implemented as a three step process:

Cue extraction: Real-time audio analysis extracts low-level cues in each client, in this instance "audio-activity on or off". This information in our system is based on simple voice activity detection[2], however, it could easily be extended to other modalities like detection of persons, facial expressions, pitch of voice or gestures.

Fusion and interpretation: Low-level cues are aggregated in the *Semantic Lifting* module of the Virtual Director. Higher-level semantic events that concern the communication as a whole, such as a "turn-shift", are detected while properties of the state of the interaction, such as "active speaker" or "crosstalk", are evaluated continuously. In contrast to low-level cues, these events based on higher-level concepts can directly be evaluated by decision making components. The Semantic Lifting module also calculates conversation metrics such as "turn shifts per active participant" or "active participation duration per participant" based on sliding temporal windows. These conversation metrics allow to robustly infer e.g. monologue situations or the "heatedness" of the discussion.

Decision making: Based on lifted events and conversation metrics, a set of mixing rules are executed that select from pre-defined visual layouts and reason which video stream to present in which region of the layout, based on the conversation context.

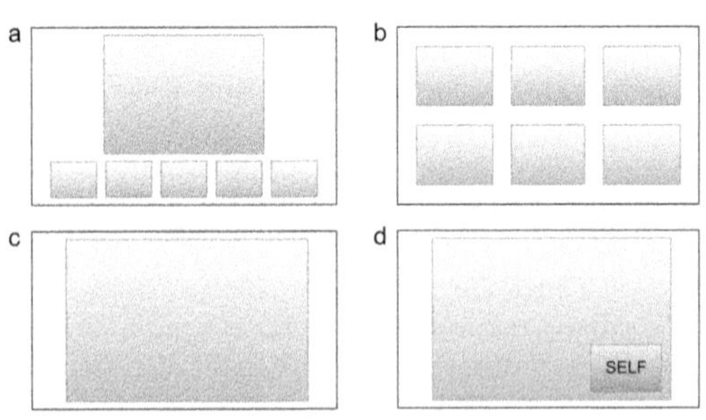

Figure 1: (a) Layout with focus on one person. (b) Tiled view layout. (c) Full screen layout. (d) Full screen layout with self-view.

[2]See: `https://www.itu.int/rec/T-REC-G.720.1/en`

3. THE DEMO

This demo allows to interactively join a video communication session with a group of remote participants. Besides allowing visitors to experience the quality of the Virtual Director's automatic behavior, the demo operators will incite visitors to think about the reasoning principles that the current implementation realizes, and to reflect on future possibilities and limitations of this concept. The system allows disabling the layout switching mechanism in order to manually select a mode. Self-view can be enabled or disabled, inviting to discuss in which situations users would like to see themselves or not. Equipment (proper headset, HD camera) and active remote participants from several European countries will be prepared to ensure an interesting conversation.

This paragraph sketches several simplified examples of Vconect's Virtual Director behavior. Figure 1a illustrates a layout with focus on one person and smaller tiles for all other participants. This is suitable for situations when a single person is currently talking and has the *turn* of the conversation, the screen is big enough to show smaller views, the number of participants does not exceed more then about 10 people, and the conversation is at low or average pace. If the conversation gets more heated/animated, meaning there is a high number of turn shifts among more than two participants within a certain time window, it is assumed to be beneficial for the user to see all participants at the same time. Therefore, the visual layout as illustrated in Figure 1b is selected, but this can only be applied if certain other rules allow a switch at this point. A full screen layout which has only one video stream and an optional self-view (Figures 1c and 1d) might be chosen for participants on the passive end of a monologue.

As these simplified examples suggest, communication orchestration is a large interdisciplinary research area. We have only uncovered the tip of the iceberg so far both in technical features and understanding user needs.

4. ACKNOWLEDGMENTS

The research leading to these results has received funding from the European Community's Seventh Framework Programme (FP7/2007-2013) under grant agreement no. ICT-2011-287760. We thank all partners who contributed to the Vconect system for their support for this demo.

5. REFERENCES

[1] R. Kaiser and W. Weiss. *Media Production, Delivery and Interaction for Platform Independent Systems: Format-Agnostic Media*, chapter Virtual Director. Wiley, 2014.

[2] R. Kaiser, W. Weiss, M. Falelakis, S. Michalakopoulos, and M. Ursu. A rule-based virtual director enhancing group communication. In *ICME'12 Workshops*, pages 187–192, July 2012.

[3] A. J. Sellen. Speech patterns in video-mediated conversations. pages 49–59. ACM, 1992.

[4] M. F. Ursu, M. Groen, M. Falelakis, M. Frantzis, V. Zsombori, and R. Kaiser. Orchestration: Tv-like mixing grammars applied to video-communication for social groups. In *Proceedings of MM'13*, pages 333–342, New York, NY, USA, 2013. ACM.

SmartVisio: Interactive Sketch Recognition with Natural Correction and Editing

Jie Wu[†]*, Changhu Wang[‡], Liqing Zhang[†], Yong Rui[‡]
[†]Key Laboratory of Shanghai Education Commission for Intelligent Interaction and Cognitive Engineering, Department of Computer Science and Engineering, Shanghai Jiao Tong University
[‡]Microsoft Research, Beijing, P. R. China
wujie27@gmail.com, chw@microsoft.com, zhang-lq@cs.sjtu.edu.cn, yongrui@microsoft.com

ABSTRACT

In this work, we introduce the SmartVisio system for interactive hand-drawn shape/diagram recognition. Different from existing work, SmartVisio is a real-time sketch recognition system based on Visio, to recognize hand-drawn flowchart/diagram with flexible interactions. This system enables a user to draw shapes or diagrams on the Visio interface, and then the hand-drawn shapes are automatically converted to formal shapes in real-time. To satisfy the interaction needs from common users, we propose an algorithm to detect a user's correction and editing during drawing, and then recognize in real time. We also propose a novel symbol recognition algorithm to better recognize or differentiate some visually similar shapes. By enabling users' natural correction/editing on various shapes, our system makes flowchart/diagram production much more natural and easier.

Categories and Subject Descriptors

H.3.1 [**Information Storage and Retrieval**]: Content Analysis and Indexing

Keywords

Sketch Recognition; Sketched Diagram Recognition; Correction and Editing; User Interface

1. INTRODUCTION

Sketching provides a natural way for us to create flowcharts and diagrams in the early design process. In the informal environment of sketching, we can use a pen to explore and refine our rough ideas through natural corrections and editing from time to time. It is highly desired if we have a practical system to recognize sketched symbols and then interactively

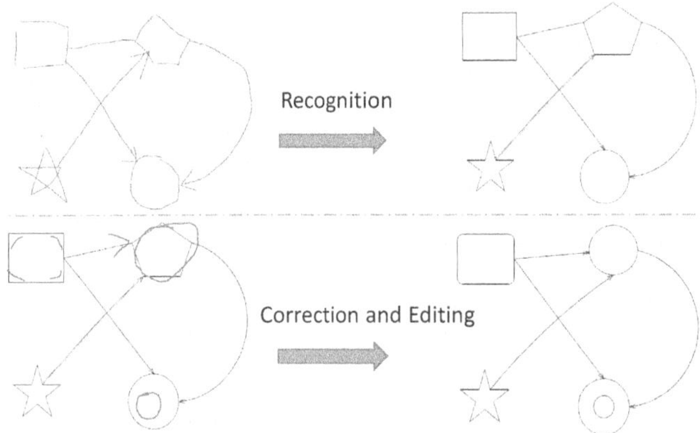

Figure 1: Illustration of the SmartVisio system. Users can draw various shapes and connectors in this system, which can be automatically segmented, recognized, and replaced by formal shapes. Users are also able to add strokes to correct or edit any part of the diagram, which will be refined in real time.

convert to formal shapes. It will make flowchart/diagram production more natural and easier, especially with the increasing popularity of touch-screen devices.

There has been a significant amount of work in recognizing diverse hand-drawn shapes, such as symbols [2], flowcharts, diagrams [3], or general objects [5]. From the view of sketch complexity, it can be classified to two categories, i.e., isolated hand-drawn symbol recognition [2], and full hand-drawn sketch recognition [1, 3, 4]. The former one has the assumption that there is only one shape in the sketch, while the latter one is not based on this assumption and thus needs to segment and recognize the strokes at the same time.

In spite of continuous research efforts, there is still not much technology transfer of sketch recognition in real products, even in the current era of touch screens. For example, the leading software for general flowchart/diagram creation, Visio, still relies on the traditional point-click-drag style of interaction. This gap mainly comes from the following two aspects, **1) the challenges from shape data in real systems.** In Visio, there are about 70 shapes only in stencil 'basic shapes' and 'arrow shapes', and thousands of shapes in total, in which some shapes are quite similar, such as the rectangles with different corner types, the stars with differ-

*Jie Wu performed this work while being an intern at Microsoft Research Asia.

MM'14, August 24–27, 2014, New York, NY, USA.
ACM 978-1-4503-3063-3/14/11.
http://dx.doi.org/10.1145/2647868.2654864.

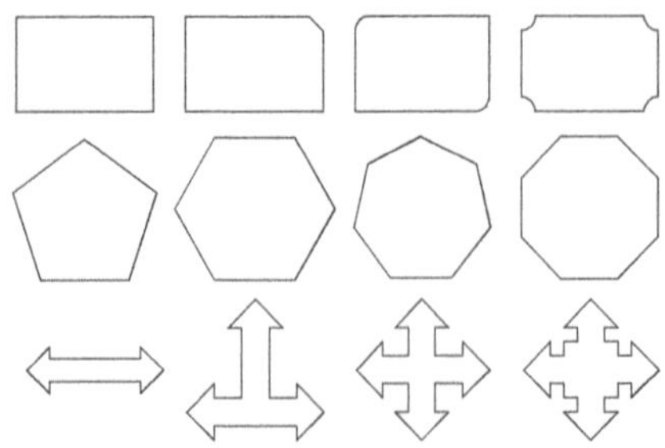

Figure 2: Visually similar shapes in Visio. Top row: similar shapes with local difference. Middle row: globally similar shapes. Bottom row: shapes with inclusion relation.

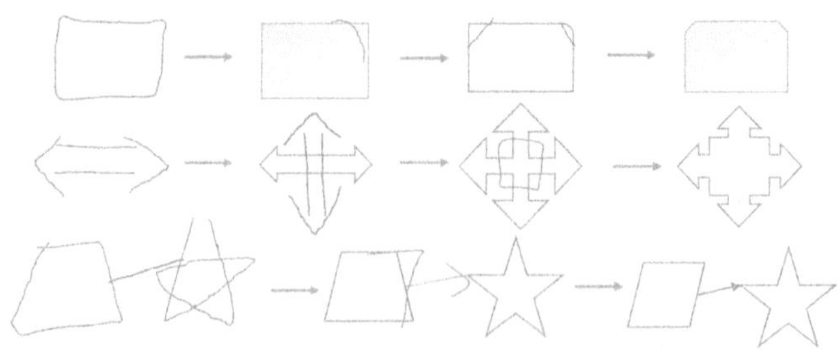

Figure 3: Illustration of the online interactive correction and editing on formal shapes in SmartVisio system.

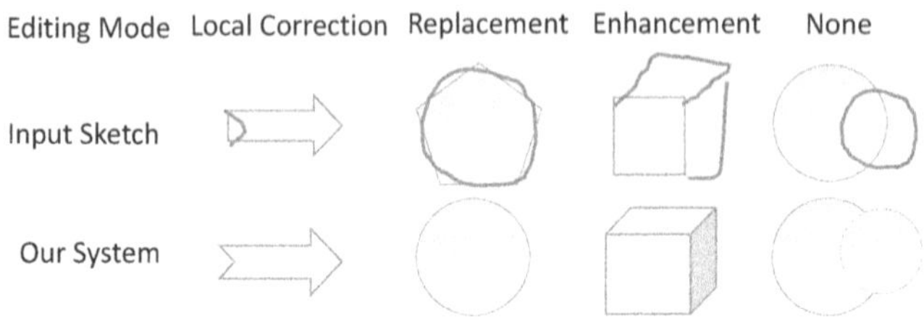

Figure 4: Visual examples of adding correction/editing on formal shapes for each of the four editing modes in SmartVisio system.

ent number of points, as shown in Fig. 2. **2) The interaction needs from common users.** It is observed that users often add strokes to an existing symbol, to correct or edit the original shape [1, 2]. In a real system such as Visio where very similar shapes exists, it will be more natural for a user to change a shape (e.g. pentagon) to a related shape (e.g. circle) in an interactive way, because of a correction or mind changing.

In this work, we present SmartVisio system, which is a real-time sketch recognition system [6] based on Visio, to recognize hand-drawn flowchart/diagram with *flexible interactions*, as shown in Fig. 1. In order to meet the interaction needs from common users, we propose an algorithm [6] to detect users' natural correction and editing on existing shapes, and then recognize the symbols in real time. We also propose a novel symbol recognition algorithm [6], in order to better differentiate and recognize some visually similar shapes. Besides isolated symbol recognition and correction, SmartVisio can also recognize full diagrams/flowchart based on the proposed full diagram recognition framework.

2. SYSTEM OVERVIEW

In this section, we briefly introduce the major functions of SmartVisio step-by-step.

Isolated Sketch Recognition

Draw a shape in the visio interface, as shown in Fig. 3. Then, the sketch will be converted to the recognized formal shape. This mode assumes that the user draws one object each time. The system starts to recognize strokes after the user stops sketching for 700 ms.

Full Sketch Recognition

Besides the isolated sketch recognition, the SmartVisio system can also recognize hand-drawn full diagram. This mode acts like a piece of paper. After a user draws all things and click the 'recognize' button, the full sketch recognition is performed, and formal shapes automatically replace the hand-drawn sketches in real time. Note that the shapes also have connectivity relationships. For example, in Fig. 1, the arrows are connected to the nearby shapes, facilitating diagram production.

Correction and Editing

In our system, user can easily add strokes to existing shapes, to change a shape (e.g. rectangle) to a related shape (e.g. 'single snip corner rectangle'), because of a correction or mind changing. Due to this powerful function, user can perform a series of online correction/editing interactively, which is convenient for diagram production as shown in Fig. 3.

User can perform any of the four editing modes we defined according to visual similarity between shapes: 1) *local correction* for similar shapes with local difference, 2) *replacement* for globally similar shapes, 3) *enhancement* for shapes with inclusion relation, and 4) *None* for shapes that are not similar at all. The example results of adding correction/editing on formal shapes are shown in Fig. 4.

3. ACKNOWLEDGEMENTS

The work of Jie Wu and Liqing Zhang was partially supported by the national natural science foundation of China (Grant Nos 61272251,91120305).

4. REFERENCES

[1] T. Hammond and B. Paulson. Recognizing sketched multistroke primitives. *TIIS*, 1(1):4, 2011.

[2] T. Y. Ouyang and R. Davis. A visual approach to sketched symbol recognition. In *IJCAI*, pages 1463–1468, 2009.

[3] E. J. Peterson, T. F. Stahovich, E. Doi, and C. Alvarado. Grouping strokes into shapes in hand-drawn diagrams. In *AAAI*, pages 974–979, 2010.

[4] Z. Sun, C. Wang, L. Zhang, and L. Zhang. Free hand-drawn sketch segmentation. In *ECCV*, pages 626–639. 2012.

[5] Z. Sun, C. Wang, L. Zhang, and L. Zhang. Query-adaptive shape topic mining for hand-drawn sketch recognition. In *ACM Multimedia*, pages 519–528, 2012.

[6] J. Wu, C. Wang, L. Zhang, and Y. Rui. Sketch recognition with natural correction and editing. In *AAAI*, 2014 (to appear).

Taste+: Digitally Enhancing Taste Sensations of Food and Beverages

Nimesha Ranasinghe
Department of Computer Science
New York University Abu Dhabi, UAE
nimesha82@gmail.com

Kuan-Yi Lee, Gajan Suthokumar
Keio-NUS CUTE Center, National University of Singapore
kuanyi22@gmail.com, gajan004@gmail.com

Ellen Yi-Luen Do
Keio-NUS CUTE Center, National University of Singapore
ellendo@acm.org

ABSTRACT

In recent years, digital media technologies expand horizons into non-traditional sensory modalities, for instance, the sense of taste. This demonstration presents 'taste+,' which digitally improves the taste sensations of food and beverages without additional flavoring ingredients. It primarily utilizes weak and controlled electrical pulses on the human tongue to enhance sourness, saltiness, and bitterness of food or beverages. Taste+ consists of two prototype utensils, a bottle and a spoon. Both utensils have embedded electronic control modules to achieve enhanced taste sensations. These modules apply controlled electrical pulses on the tongue through silver electrodes attached to the mouth pieces. Furthermore, different superimposed colors symbolize distinct taste sensations, lemon green represents sour, ocean blue is salty, red for red wine bitter. The initial experimental results suggested that sourness and saltiness are the main sensations that could be evoked while bitterness has comparatively mild responses. Furthermore, we also observed several mixed sensations such as salty-sour together.

Categories and Subject Descriptors

H.5.m. [**Information Interfaces and Presentation (e.g. HCI)**]: Miscellaneous

General Terms

Design; Measurement; Experimentation

Keywords

Taste media; Digital Taste; Gustation; Virtual reality

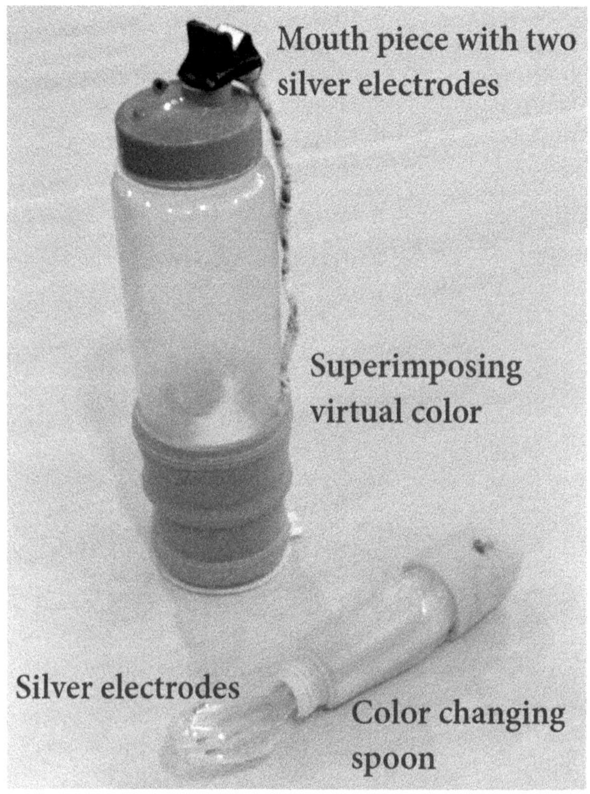

Figure 1: Two prototype utensils of Taste+: bottle and spoon

1. INTRODUCTION

People have been using various spices, salt, lime juice, soy sauce, and similar flavoring ingredients for a long time to make food and beverages more delicious. Recently, artificial flavoring solutions such as Monosodium glutamate (MSG) and artificial soft drinks become widely popular due to the advancements in food and flavor technologies. However, these artificial flavoring solutions have many complications and cause health problems in the world, for example, obesity [3, 1].

At present, flavoring solutions to food and beverages are produced by blending natural or artificial ingredients (mostly chemicals) and there are no definite strategies available to enhance flavors by digital means. Thus, we present taste+[1],

MM'14, November 3–7, 2014, Orlando, Florida, USA.
ACM 978-1-4503-3063-3/14/11.
http://dx.doi.org/10.1145/2647868.2654878.

[1]http://youtu.be/kU66Pe_xcMA

Figure 2: Different settings of taste+ and user interactions

an electronic taste altering bottle and spoon as shown in Figure 1.

The bottle has a rotating mechanical dial interface and three RGB Light-Emitting Diodes (LED) at the bottom to adjust the color and the taste of the drink by twisting the dial according to their preferences. The specially designed straw interface with two silver electrodes controls weak-electrical pulses on the tip of the tongue to simulate sour, salty, and bitter sensations digitally. Moreover, the spoon enables users to enhance sourness and saltiness digitally by pressing two buttons on the spoon. Two silver electrodes at the bottom of the spoon electrically stimulate the user's tongue when he or she places food on top of the tongue.

2. METHOD

In recent studies, virtually superimposing different colors onto a drink as well as electrical stimulation on the tongue have been explored as viable taste simulating methods as described in [4, 7]. In Addition, as disclosed in [2], color of the cutlery is also affecting the taste sensations of food. Consequently, the Taste+ utensils utilize these methods to enhance the taste sensations of food and beverages. Different parameters of electrical stimulation and virtual color settings are finalized based on several preliminary investigations and existing literature [5, 6, 7] and mentioned below:

- **Sour** (magnitude of current: 120μA, frequency: 600Hz), color: **Green**
- **Salty** (magnitude of current: 40μA, frequency: 200Hz), color: **Blue**
- **Bitter** - only for the bottle (magnitude of current: 120μA, frequency: 600Hz - reversed polarity), color: **Red**

3. INITIAL EXPERIMENTS

For initial experiments, we used plain water in the bottle and asked participants to eat porridge using the spoon. 30 participants (22 male and 8 female) were recruited for the experiment aged between 21-28; M = 23; SD = 2.54. The participants were randomly chosen and had no training before being tested. All participants were in good health and reported no taste or smell problems. We let the users change the settings (color and magnitude of the current) of both the utensils and ask them to report the sensations if there are any. The accuracy percentage of each sensation are calculated individually: bottle (sour: 76%, salty: 56%, and bitter: 40%) and spoon (sour: 83% and salty: 63%). Interestingly, they also try to correlate RGB colors with taste sensations: blue with salty, green with sour, and red with bitter. These initial findings together with more complex perceptions such as tingling and spicy sensations deserve thorough investigations in the future.

4. DEMO EXPERIENCE

During the demonstration, users experience different taste sensations such as sour, salty, and bitter through the taste+ utensils. They may drink plain water with altered taste sensations using the water bottle while enjoying porridge or soup (by superimposing digital salty or sour sensations) with the taste+ spoon. Taste+ incorporates controlled-electrical stimuli with the parameters of, magnitude of current: 20μA - 120μA and frequency: 200Hz - 600Hz, to alter the sensations. In addition, due to hygiene issues, before each demonstration, we rinse electrodes using tap water, then sterilize using 70% isopropyl alcohol swabs, followed by deionized water.

5. ACKNOWLEDGMENTS

This research is supported by the Singapore National Research Foundation under its International Research Center Keio-NUS CUTE Center @ Singapore Funding Initiative and administered by the IDM Program Office.

6. REFERENCES

[1] C. M. Apovian. Sugar-sweetened soft drinks, obesity, and type 2 diabetes. *Jama*, 292(8):978–979, 2004.

[2] V. Harrar and C. Spence. The taste of cutlery: how the taste of food is affected by the weight, size, shape, and colour of the cutlery used to eat it. *Flavour*, 2(1):1–13, 2013.

[3] J. James and D. Kerr. Prevention of childhood obesity by reducing soft drinks. *International journal of obesity*, 29:S54–S57, 2005.

[4] T. Narumi, M. Sato, T. Tanikawa, and M. Hirose. Evaluating cross-sensory perception of superimposing virtual color onto real drink: toward realization of pseudo-gustatory displays. In *Proceedings of the 1st Augmented Human International Conference*, page 18. ACM, 2010.

[5] N. Ranasinghe, A. D. Cheok, and R. Nakatsu. Taste/ip: the sensation of taste for digital communication. In *Proceedings of the 14th ACM international conference on Multimodal interaction*, pages 409–416, 2012.

[6] N. Ranasinghe, K. Karunanayaka, and A. D. e. a. Cheok. Digital taste and smell communication. In *Proceedings of the 6th International Conference on Body Area Networks*, pages 78–84, 2011.

[7] N. Ranasinghe, R. Nakatsu, H. Nii, and P. Gopalakrishnakone. Tongue mounted interface for digitally actuating the sense of taste. In *Wearable Computers (ISWC), 2012 16th International Symposium on*, pages 80–87. IEEE, 2012.

Reverbalize: A Crowdsourced Reverberation Controller

Prem Seetharaman
Northwestern University
EECS Department
prem@u.northwestern.edu

Bryan Pardo
Northwestern University
EECS Department
pardo@northwestern.edu

ABSTRACT

One of the most commonly-used audio production tools is the reverberator. Reverberators apply subtle or large echo effects to sound and are typically used in commercial audio recordings. Current reverberator interfaces are often complex and hard-to-understand. In this work, we describe Reverbalize, a novel and easy-to-use interface for a reverberator. Reverbalize uses crowdsourced data to create a 2-dimensional map of adjectives used to describe reverberation (e.g. "underwater'). Adjacent words describe similar reverberation effects. Word size correlates with agreement for the definition of a word. To use Reverbalize, the user simply clicks on the descriptive adjective that best describes the desired effect. The tool modifies the sound accordingly. A text search box also lets the user type in the desired word.

Categories and Subject Descriptors

H.5.2 [**User Interfaces**]: User-centered design; H.5.5 [**Sound and Music Computing**]: Signal analysis, synthesis, and processing

Keywords

Human computation; audio engineering; interfaces

1. INTRODUCTION

In the physical world, reverberation is created by the reflections of sound off of the solid surfaces (e.g. walls) of an enclosed space. These reflections result in a decaying series of echoes that modify the sound's loudness, timbre, and perceived spatial characteristics. In the digital realm, reverberation (reverb) can be simulated using networks of delays and gains to create a decaying series of echoes. The tool that does this is called a reverberator.

The reverberator is one of the most commonly-used audio production tools. Reverberation can make the audio sound as if it were recorded in a different acoustic environment (e.g. change a recording made in a sound booth to sound like one recorded in a cathedral), and are used to increase the pleasantness of the sound.

MM'14, November 3–7, 2014, Orlando, Florida, USA.
ACM 978-1-4503-3063-3/14/11.
http://dx.doi.org/10.1145/2647868.2654876 .

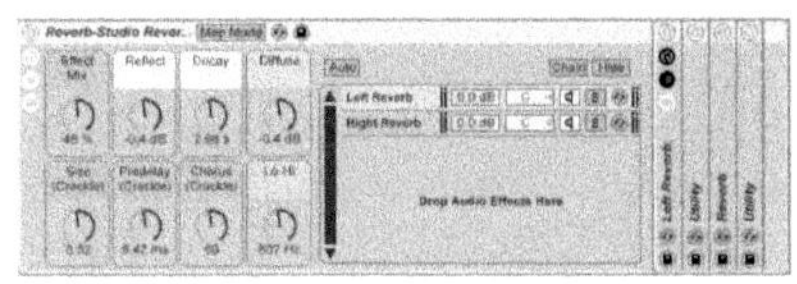

Figure 1: A standard parametric reverberator.

Figure 1 shows the interface of a typical professional quality parametric reverberator. While the "effect mix" and the "decay" dials may make intuitive sense, other dials like "predelay" have no obvious meaning to the average person. This is because the controls are conceptualized in terms of the underlying processes used to create the reverberation effect, as opposed to perceptually relevant terms. Musicians and producers often conceptualize the effect of reverb using words like "deep" or "spacious". Much of audio production involves bridging the gap between artistic goals and the manipulation of the available audio tools.

2. ENGINEERING CONCEPT

Our concept is to make an interface for reverberation based on natural language adjectives a layman would use to describe reverberation. This interface should be easy to navigate and also show the relationship between words (e.g. is "deep" more like "spacious" or "warm"?). The goal is to provide clear affordances that allow natural navigation through the set of options. We do this by building the interface from a crowd-sourced data set of natural language descriptors provided by the SocialReverb project.

Using data from SocialReverb, we create a 2-D map (see Section 5) that visualizes the relationships between descriptive words provided by the crowd. By associating these words with the parameters used to manipulate a reverberator, we create a new kind of reverberation controller, shown in Figure 2. Users explore the space of reverberation options by clicking and dragging around the map, using the words as a guide. When a word is highlighted, the associated reverb is applied to the sound. The slider to the right lets the user filter out words that don't show strong agreement across the population about the effect. If the user would rather quickly jump to a concept, they can type a word in the search box.

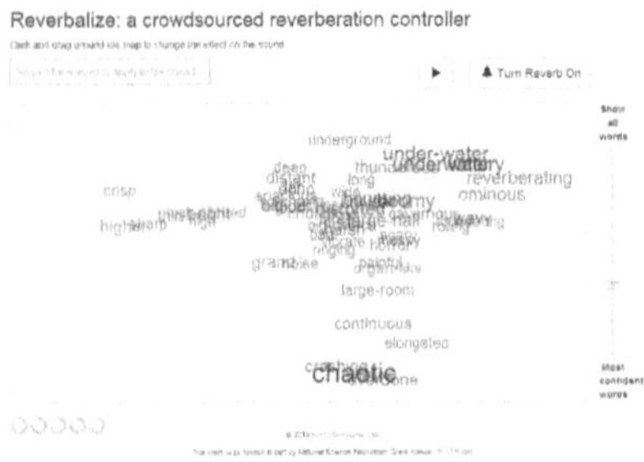

Figure 2: The proposed interface.

3. PROPOSED DEMONSTRATION

The demonstration is implemented using the Web Audio API and runs in a Chrome browser. The demonstration will consist of a laptop computer connected to our web server. All audio processing is implemented locally in the browser, so there are no latency issues. The user will be able to try the concept-map controller shown in Figure 2 and listen to the effect over a pair of provided high-quality headphones. We will also provide a standard interface for comparison.

4. NOVELTY AND RELATED WORK

This is the first controller we are aware of that builds an interface for an audio production tool using a word map built from crowdsourced data as the interaction paradigm.

Commercial reverberation tools attempt to simplify the interface with a list of presets (saved settings given a name like "warm church long"). Preset names are chosen by experts and may not have meaning to laymen. Further, a simple list gives no clue about the relationship between presets. Some commercial tools (e.g. iZotope Ozone) have hundreds of presets, making the preset list nearly as difficult to navigate as the original interface. Our map-based interface using labels learned from the crowd addresses these issues.

Convolution reverberation tools (e.g. Altiverb) provide lists of locations (e.g. "Carnegie Hall") where the impulse response of a space was taken. While users can imagine the effect a location may have on a sound, many words used to describe reverberation (e.g. "warm") are not particular location names. Our map includes these more natural descriptors.

There is some prior work in building audio controllers using verbal descriptors. A 2-dimensional audio equalizer was implemented in [4]. The interface lets users explore different equalizations in a 2-D map. However, it uses only four labels ("bright", "warm", "tinny", "dark") provided by the authors, rather than hundreds of words crowdsourced from a large group of users. Also, the interface is for equalization, rather than reverberation. [2] creates a similar interface and employs more descriptors of higher complexity ("warm hi-cut", "less sizzly"). However, it also implements an equalization tool, rather than a reverberation tool, and the labels are chosen by the authors. Amateur musicians considered some of these terms too technical. Our system circumvents this issue by crowdsourcing terms used by laymen.

5. CROWDSOURCING A CONCEPT MAP

The concept map is built using data collected by the SocialReverb (socialreverb.org) project. To date, the project has collected 3388 descriptive words from 658 users describing 256 different reverberation effects (reverbs). Participants are recruited on Amazon Mechanical Turk. When teaching SocialReverb the participant listens once to an audio sample, and then again to the same sample with some reverb applied. They are then asked to type in words of their own choice that describe the effect of the reverb. They are then shown a list of words provided by other users, and asked to select the words they agree also describe this reverb. Each time a word is used to describe a reverb, we add the reverb to the set of reverbs associated with that word.

Each reverb is represented by a vector of five measurements: reverberation time, echo density, clarity, central time, and spectral centroid ([3]). Once we find all reverbs associated with a word (e.g. "warm"), we use the averages of the five measure as the word definition. This gives a five-dimensional definition that can be used to set a reverberator to modify a sound to make it "warm" (or some other word).

In the data, some words (e.g. "warm") are applied broadly to a wide variety of reverberation effects and others ("boomy") are more specific and are associated with a narrow range of reverbs. We can measure the consistency of a word definition by measuring the variance of the associated reverbs along each of the measured dimensions. If variance is low, the reverbs associated with the word have similar qualities. If the variance is high, many different sorts of reverb are associated with the word.

The map contains only words which have been used to label at least 15 instances of reverberation. For each such word, we calculate a definition and measure its consistency. This places each word in a 5-D space. We project this 5-D space onto two dimensions, using multidimensional scaling [1]. On the resulting 2-D map, word position is the center of the distribution of reverberation settings associated with the word. Each word is scaled using its variance. Larger words indicate greater consistency of definition.

6. VIDEO LINK

A video describing and presenting Reverbalize can be found at `http://prem.seeth.org/static/reverbalize.mp4`.

7. ACKNOWLEDGEMENTS

This work is supported by National Science Foundation Grant 1116384.

References

[1] Ingwer Borg and Patrick JF Groenen. *Modern multidimensional scaling: Theory and applications.* Springer, 2005.

[2] S Mecklenburg and J Loviscach. "subjEQt: Controlling an equalizer through subjective terms". In: *CHI'06 Extended Abstracts on Human Factors in Computing Systems* (2006).

[3] Zafar Rafii and Bryan Pardo. "A Digital Reverberator Controlled through Measures of the Reverberation". In: *Northwestern University, Technical Report* (2009).

[4] AT Sabin and B Pardo. "2DEQ: an intuitive audio equalizer". In: *Proceedings of the 7th ACM conference on Creativity and Cognition* (2009).

SynthAssist: An Audio Synthesizer Programmed with Vocal Imitation

Mark Cartwright
Northwestern University
EECS Department
mcartwright@u.northwestern.edu

Bryan Pardo
Northwestern University
EECS Department
pardo@northwestern.edu

ABSTRACT

While programming an audio synthesizer can be difficult, if a user has a general idea of the sound they are trying to program, they may be able to imitate it with their voice. In this technical demonstration, we demonstrate SynthAssist, a system that allows the user to program an audio synthesizer using vocal imitation and interactive feedback. This system treats synthesizer programming as an audio information retrieval task. To account for the limitations of the human voice, it compares vocal imitations to synthesizer sounds by using both absolute and relative temporal shapes of relevant audio features, and it refines the query and feature weights using relevance feedback.

Categories and Subject Descriptors

H.5.5. [**Sound and Music Computing**]: Systems; H.5.2. [**User Interfaces**]: Interaction styles; H.5.1. [**Multimedia Information Systems**]: Audio input/output

General Terms

Human Factors

Keywords

Audio; music; synthesis; vocal imitation

1. INTRODUCTION

As software-based audio synthesizers have become more advanced, their interfaces have become more complex and therefore harder to use. Many synthesizer interfaces have one hundred or more controls (e.g. Apple's ES2 synthesizer has 125 controls), many of which are difficult to understand without significant synthesis experience. The search space of even simple synthesizers (15 controls) is complex enough that it is difficult for novices to actualize their ideas. Even for experienced users, the tedium of these interfaces takes them out of their creative flow state, hampering productivity. Some manufacturers address this problem by having many, many presets (e.g. Native Instruments Kore Browser). However, searching through a vast number of presets can be a task as daunting as using a complex synthesizer.

In this technical demonstration, we demonstrate SynthAssist [1], a system that interactively helps the user find their desired sound (synthesizer patch) in the space of sounds generated by an audio synthesizer. The goal is to make synthesizers more accessible, letting users focus on high-level goals (e.g. 'sound brassy') instead of low-level controls (e.g. 'What does the LFO1Asym knob do?'). SynthAssist accomplishes this by allowing the user to communicate their desired sound with a vocal imitation of the sound, a method of communication shown to be effective in a recent study [2]. The inspiration for SynthAssist was how one might interact with a professional music producer or sound designer: imitate the desired outcome vocally (e.g. "make a sound that goes like <sound effect made vocally>"), have the producer design a few options based on the example, give them evaluative feedback (e.g "that doesn't sound as good as the previous example.")

MM'14, November 3–7, 2014, Orlando, Florida, USA.
ACM 978-1-4503-3063-3/14/11.
http://dx.doi.org/10.1145/2647868.2654880.

2. SYNTHASSSIST SYSTEM

With SynthAssist, a user can quickly and easily search through thousands of synthesizer sounds to find the desired option. The interaction for a session in SynthAssist is as follows:

1. To communicate their desired audio concept, the user provides one or more input examples by either recording a new sound (e.g. vocalize an example) or choosing a prerecorded sound.
2. The user rates how close each example is to the target sound.
3. Based on the ratings, SynthAssist estimates what the target sound must be like.
4. SynthAssist generates suggestions from the synthesizer that are similar to the estimated target sound.
5. The user rates how close the suggestions are to the desired target sound.
6. If a suggestion is good enough, return the synthesizer parameters. Else, repeat Steps 3 through 6.

Figure 1 shows a screenshot of SynthAssist. Each suggestion is represented by one of the colored circles. When a user clicks or moves a suggestion, the synthesizer sound

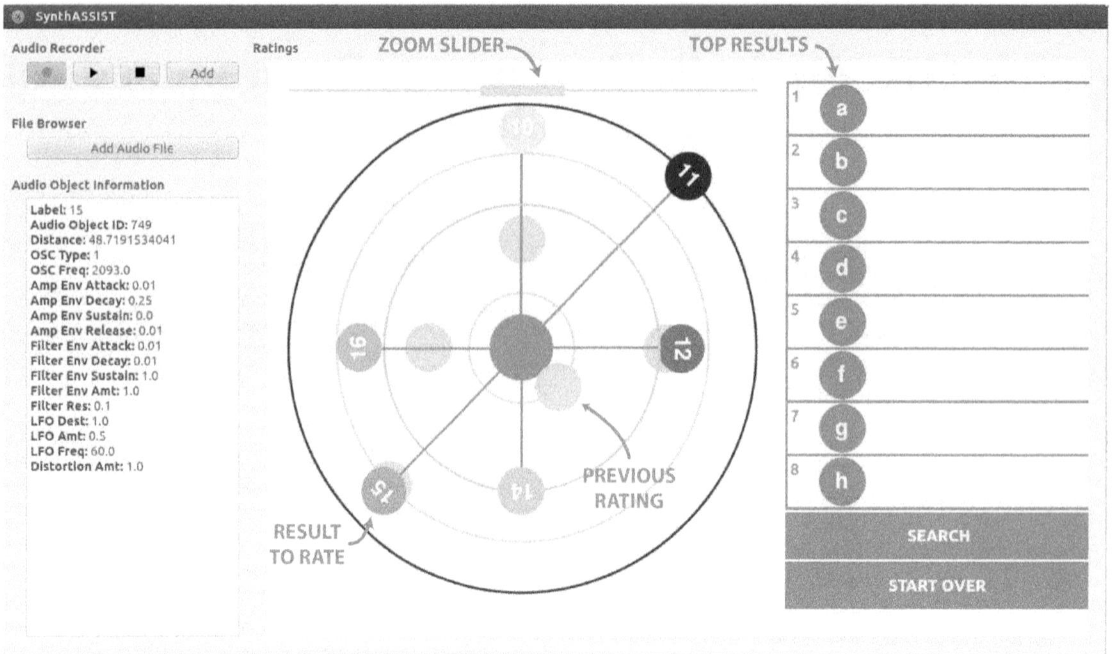

Figure 1: Screenshot of SynthAssist

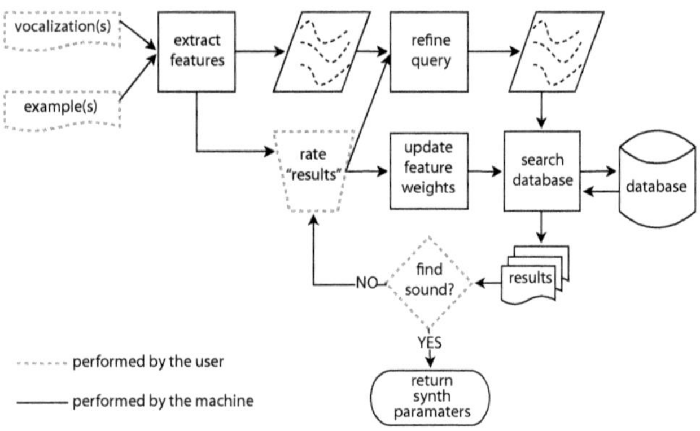

Figure 2: System flow of SynthAssist.

changes. Users rate how similar suggestions are to their target by moving them closer to or farther from the center, "hub", circle. If a suggestion is irrelevant, the user can inform SynthAssist and remove it from the screen by double clicking on it. Dragging a suggestion to the center of the circle indicates indicates this is the desired sound and terminates the interaction. The overall system architecture is shown in Figure 2.

In the SynthAssist system, we want to support vocal imitation queries. Our approach is described in [1]. While the human voice has a limited timbral range, it can very expressive with respect to how it changes in time. For example, your voice may not be able to exactly imitate your favorite Moog bass sound, but you may be able to imitate how the sound changes over the course of a note (e.g. pitch, loudness, brightness, noisiness, etc.). When comparing sounds in SynthAssist, we focus on these changes over the course of a note.

In this demonstration, 10,000 parameter combinations and their resulting sounds have been sampled from an audio synthesizer. Absolute and relative time series of several audio features are extracted from both the query and sampled sounds. The time series of the query are compared to those of the sampled sounds using dynamic time warping. The distance measure and query are refined using a relevance feedback mechanism for time series.

3. THE DEMONSTRATION

In the demonstration of SynthAssist, a computer will be set up running the SynthAssist software. Users will be able to record their vocal imitations and use them as input to the system to interactively program a synthesizer sound. Users can interact with the system either by itself or in a musical context, programming a sound for an existing keyboard line in a song. In both modes, the user can use a piano keyboard to play the synthesizer.

A video of an example search session and an explanation of the system can be found at `http://music.eecs.northwestern.edu/videos/SynthAssist.mov`.

4. ACKNOWLEDGMENTS

This work was supported by NSF Grant Nos. IIS-1116384 and DGE-0824162.

5. REFERENCES

[1] M. Cartwright and B. Pardo. Synthassist: Querying an audio synthesizer by vocal imitation. In *Conference on New Interfaces for Musical Expression*, London, 2014.

[2] G. Lemaitre and D. Rocchesso. On the effectiveness of vocal imitations and verbal descriptions of sounds. *The Journal of the Acoustical Society of America*, 135(2):862–873, 2014.

Eat As Much As You Can: A Kinect-based Facial Rehabilitation Game Based on Mouth and Tongue Movements

Yong-Xiang Wang, Li-Yun Lo and Min-Chun Hu
Department of Computer Science and Information Engineering, National Cheng Kung University, Taiwan
{plunger, liyun.lo, trimy}@mislab.csie.ncku.edu.tw

ABSTRACT

In this demo, we present a Kinect-based interactive game which provides patients of facial palsy with a better and more fun way to perform facial physical therapy. By letting the user get scores when he/she bites or licks the virtual foods falling from the sky, the game goads the user into exercising their facial muscles. A robust bite action detector and an efficient tip-of-tongue locating method are developed to realize this game. Based on the head pose estimated by the depth clue, we classify the face orientation and locate the mouth region in each frame. The movements of lips are measured to detect the bite action, and different strategies are designed to more accurately detect the tip-of-tongue for various face orientations. The experimental results show that our method can be successfully applied to different users.

Categories and Subject Descriptors

H.5.2 [**Information Systems**]: User Interfaces – *interaction styles.* I.3.6 [**Computing Methodologies**]: Methodology and Techniques – *interaction techniques.*

General Terms

Algorithms, Human Factor

Keywords

Tip-of-tongue detection, Kinect, head pose, depth information.

1. INTRODUCTION

This demo presents an innovative way of interactive games – playing by using the mouth and tongue movements with the aid of Kinect. For patients of facial palsy, interactive games commanded by the mouth and tongue can help them exercise their facial muscles and consequently effects facial physical therapy [1, 2, 3]. Conventional Tongue Drive Systems (TDS) use tongue motion to control devices or play games based on an array of magnetic sensors either mounted on a dental retainer and clipped on the outside of the teeth (internal TDS or iTDS) or on a headset (external TDS or eTDS) positioned near the cheeks [4, 5]. Magnetic sensors are wearable but not sharable due to the hygiene issue. Therefore, we employ the Kinect sensor, which can be used by different people, to acquire the mouth and tongue motion information based on computer vision techniques.

MM'14, November 3–7, 2014, Orlando, Florida, USA.
ACM 978-1-4503-3063-3/14/11.
http://dx.doi.org/10.1145/2647868.2654887

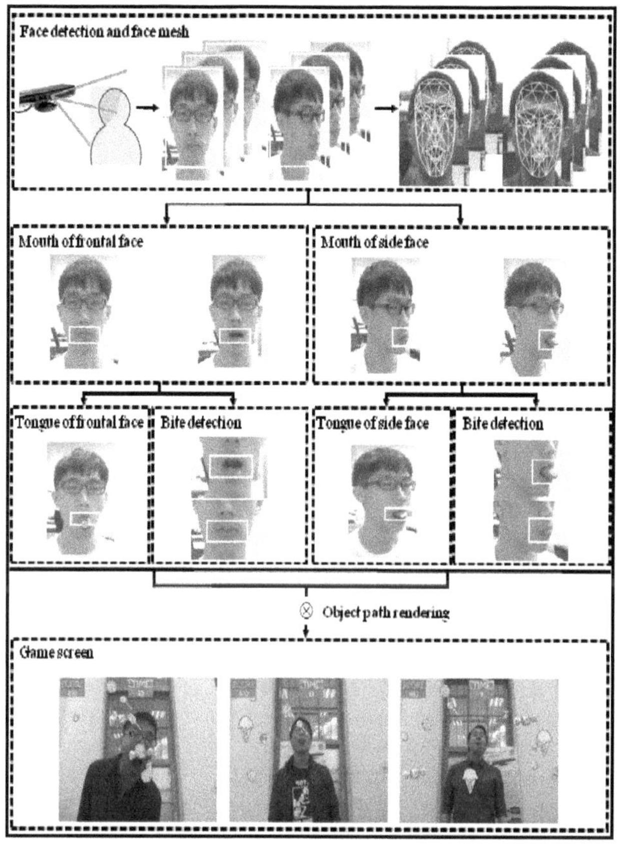

Figure 1. The proposed system framework.

Figure 1 illustrates our system framework. We take the advantage of Microsoft Face Tracking SDK [6] to detect the user's face and extract face features, such as the head pose and the 3D coordinates of the tracked points on the face mesh. The positions of the upper lip and the jaw are used to classify the mouth into close or open, which is an important clue for detecting the bite action. Meanwhile, the depth information inside the mouth region is utilized to locate the tip-of-tongue. Note that the face orientation has great impact on the depth distribution inside the mouth region. Therefore we first identify the face as frontal or side face and apply different strategies to more precisely locate the tip-of-tongue according to the face orientation. An interactive game, named "Eat As Much As You Can," is designed to prove that our idea is workable. In this game, we develop an object path rendering component to generate virtual foods falling from the top of the screen, and the player has to bite or lick specific virtual food to get higher scores. This kind of interactive game not only benefits patients of facial palsy, but also helps general users to keep their cheeks toned, firm their jaw lines, and consequently make them look younger.

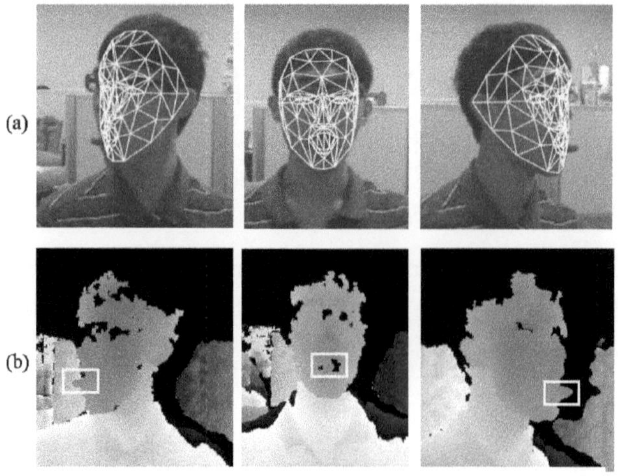

Figure 2. (a) Face meshes of different face orientations. (b) Depth information of different face orientations.

2. Bite and Tip-of-Tongue Detection

After applying Microsoft Face Tracking SDK [6] to each frame, we obtain the face mesh, as shown in Figure 2(a), and the face orientation is identified as frontal or side face according to the yaw angle of the head pose. The Animation Unit (AU) provided by the Face Tracking SDK measures two values, i.e. the "Upper Lip Raiser" and the "Jaw Lowerer," to indicate how the user moves his/her mouth. These two values range from -1 to 1, corresponding to the possibility of mouth closed to mouth open. Therefore, the bite action can be detected by checking if these two values change rapidly from large negative values to large positive values.

To locate the tip-of-tongue efficiently, we first define a rough mouth region as indicated by the yellow rectangles in Figure 2(b), and search for the exact position of the tip-of-tongue. The mouth region is constructed based on four tracked points around the mouth, i.e. OutsideRightCornerMouth, OutsideLeftCornerMouth, MiddleBottomUpperLip, and MiddleTopLowerLip, which are also provided by the Face Tracking SDK. For the frontal face, the tip-of-tongue can be easily detected by finding the pixel with minimum depth value inside the mouth region [7]. To make sure the user exactly sticks out his/her tongue, we further examine if the minimum depth value is much smaller than the depth values of feature points on the user's lip. However, for side faces, this strategy fails since the depth value of the tip-of-tongue is usually not the global minimum inside the mouth region. To tackle this problem, we first find the pixel having the local minimum depth value along each column inside the mouth region, and then compare these local minimums with the depth of their upper and lower neighboring pixels. For the side faces, the tongue is supposed to be stuck out in the same direction of the face orientation, and the upper and lower pixels of the tip-of-tongue should have larger depth values since they are usually the background pixels

3. EXPERIMENTAL RESULTS

To evaluate the accuracy of our bite detection and the tip-of-tongue detection method, we conducted our experiments on 237 images (with resolution of 640x480) sampled from the videos captured while 5 different players interacting with our game, "Eat As Much As You Can". The bite action is 100% detected due to the robustness of the animation unit provided by the Face Tracking SDK. We calculate the Euclidean distance between the position of the detected tip-of-tongue and the ground truth. Table 1 and Table 2 show the mean and standard deviation of the distance for each face orientation, respectively. Note that since our system mainly depends on the accuracy of the Face Tracking SDK, we only take the frames that the face is detected successfully to be evaluated. More results can be seen in our demo video: https://www.youtube.com/user/MISLABMM2014.

Table 1. Mean distance (pixel) with different face orientations.

	Left	Center	Right
Top	13.5305	12.9177	15.7190
Middle	11.5263	9.6028	8.6472
Down	17.3419	8.6511	7.4664

Table 2. Standard deviation with different face orientations.

	Left	Center	Right
Top	6.4902	10.5789	10.2373
Middle	8.2501	5.4451	5.3365
Down	14.2902	4.5012	4.7064

4. CONCLUSIONS

We present a Kinect-based interactive game which provides patients of facial palsy with a better and more fun way to perform facial physical therapy. A robust bite action detector and an efficient tip-of-tongue locating method are developed to realize this game. By letting the user get scores when he/she bites or licks the virtual foods falling from the sky, the game goads the user into exercising their facial muscles. The experimental results show that the proposed bite detection and tip-of-tongue detection methods can be successfully applied to different users.

5. REFERENCES

[1] Nadine, P. C., John A.R., Hao W., Michelle A. J., Laura M., Keith K. 2009. Effect of tongue exercise on protrusive force and muscle fiber area in aging rats. *Journal of Speech, Language, and Hearing Research*. 52 (June 2009), 732-744.

[2] Ren W. H., Ao H. W., Lin Q., Xu Z.G., Zhang B. 2013. Efficacy of mouth opening exercises in treating trismus after maxillectomy. *Chinese Medical Journal*. 126, 14 (Jul. 2013), 2666-2669.

[3] Robbins, J., Kays S.A., Gangnon R.E., Hind J.A., Hewitt A.L., Gentry L.R., Taylor A.J. 2007. The effects of lingual exercise in stroke patients with dysphagia. *Archives of Physical Medicine and Rehabilitation*. 88, 2 (Feb. 2007), 150-158.

[4] Kothari M., Svensson P., Jensen J., Holm T. D., Nielsen M. S., Mosegaard T., Nielsen J. F., Ghovanloo M., Baad-Hansen L. 2014. Tongue-controlled computer game: a new approach for rehabilitation of tongue motor function. *Archives of Physical Medicine and Rehabilitation*. 95, 3 (Mar. 2014), 524-530.

[5] Xueliang H., Ghovanloo M. 2012. Tongue drive: a wireless tongue- operated means for people with severe disabilities to communicate their intentions. *IEEE Communications Magazine*. 50, 10 (Oct. 2012), 128-135.

[6] Windows SDK for Kinect - Face tracking: http://msdn.microsoft.com/en-us/library/jj130970.aspx

[7] Tip-of-tongue detection: http://tangochen.com/blog/?p=450

A Multimedia E-Health Framework Towards An Interactive And Non-Invasive Therapy Monitoring Environment

Ahmad Qamar*, Imad Afyouni*, Delwar Hossain*, Faizan Ur Rehman*, Asad Toonsi§, Md. Abdur Rahman*#, Saleh Basalamah*

*Advanced Media Laboratory, Umm Al-Qura University, Makkah, KSA

§Department of Pediatrics, Maternity and Children Hospital, Makkah, KSA

#Multimedia Communications Research Laboratory, University of Ottawa, Canada

{amqamar,fsrehman,smbasalamah}@uqu.edu.sa, iafyouni@gistic.org, rahman@mcrlab.uottawa.ca, atoonsi@advancedmedialab.com, mdelwar@iict.buet.ac.bd

ABSTRACT

This paper presents a multimedia e-health framework to conduct therapy sessions by collecting live therapeutic data of patients in a non-invasive way. Using our proposed framework, a therapist can model complex gestures by mapping them to a set of primitive actions and generate high-level therapies. Two inexpensive 3D motion tracking sensors, a Kinect and a Leap, are used to collect motion data of a given subject. Data can then be displayed on screen in a live manner or recorded for offline replaying and analysis. The system incorporates an intelligent authoring tool for therapy design, and produces live plots that show the quality of improvement metrics for a given patient.

Categories and Subject Descriptors

H.5.1 [**Multimedia Information Systems**];
I.5.4 [**Computing Methodologies**]: *Computer vision*

General Terms

Design; Human Factors

Keywords

e-Health; Kinect; Leap; Therapy; Authoring Interface

1. INTRODUCTION

Research has shown that proper therapies for disabilities that might affect human body such as hemiplegia[1], can help affected patients to quickly return to normal life. The lack of trained professionals with respect to the growing number of patients has prompted the development of automated e-health systems for physical rehabilitation. Previous studies suggest gathering kinematic therapy data and generating post-therapy analytics reports regarding the situation of the patient [2]. Other solutions require attaching a large number of sensors to the body to make measurements in an invasive manner [3]. On the other hand, robot-based solutions are more accurate but extremely expensive [1].

This paper presents an e-health framework that offers several advantages over traditional systems for therapy design and monitoring. First of all, using the Kinect 3D sensor, the system tracks movements of 25 joints in the body with 30 frames per second (fps). This gives us the ability to record the motion of each joint over time as well as its Range Of Motion (ROM). Secondly, a single Leap Motion device is integrated, which can detect 18 different primitive hand therapies [4]. Thirdly, the system is web-based; hence, users do not need complex and expensive setup on their client machines. Fourthly, the system shows physical world activity as a serious game environment, and provides live view of the body movements and hand joints with angular and rotational data. We have created 3D serious games related to hand-therapy, and developed algorithms to capture raw joint data from different joints of a subject's hand. Fifthly, a novel authoring interface has been developed for therapy design. This authoring interface allows a therapist to define the joints of interest based on a human body anatomy model. The system allows a user to save the therapy session in her own repository and share it only with a community of interest over a dedicated cloud environment. The system also allows replaying any session in 3D environment where a therapist can monitor her patient, and a patient can see the model therapy suggested by the therapist. Finally a therapist, a patient or a caregiver can see the live plots consisting of quality of improvement metrics by analyzing current or past therapy session data.

The remainder of the paper is organized as follows. Section 2 describes the architecture of the developed framework, while Section 3 highlights the demonstration scenario.

2. SYSTEM ARCHITECTURE

Our system has three types of users: (i) a patient; (ii) a therapist; and (iii) a caregiver. The system is based on a knowledge base of primitive movements for different joints of the body. Through a therapy authoring interface built into the system, a therapist or an expert can devise a custom therapy based on these primitive gestures with a very high degree of freedom. These therapies can be stored online in the system repository and can be shared by different

[1]Disability that affects the body and joint movements in one half of the body

MM'14, November 3–7, 2014, Orlando, Florida, USA.
ACM 978-1-4503-3063-3/14/11
http://dx.doi.org/10.1145/2647868.2654877.

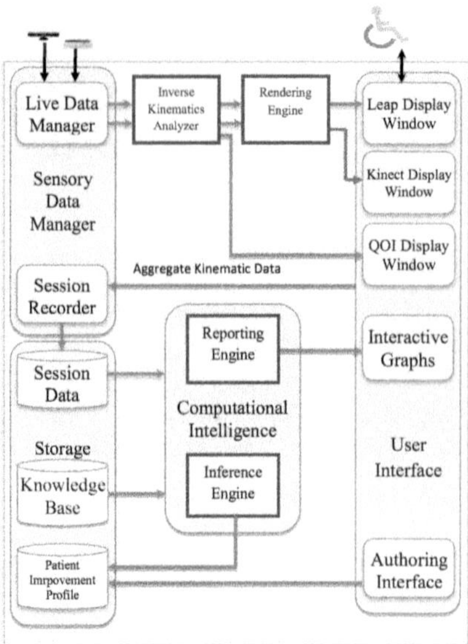

Figure 1: System Architecture

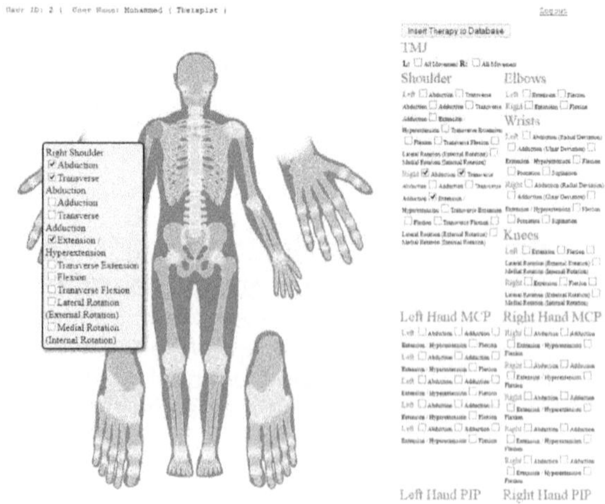

Figure 2: Authoring interface for therapy design

therapists. The therapist associates the exercise to a specific therapy stored earlier in database and uploads data to the cloud storage. This exercise is then assigned to any patient suffering from a related disability. While the patient enjoys an immersive game playing experience, the data captured by the sensors is stored in a predefined format for later playback, processing, and mining. Another important aspect of our system is its ability to extract the status of different joints and display it live on screen. As an example, a user performing the pronation/supination movement of the hand can see on the display window when her hand is in pronation or supination state, as well as the transition between these two states. Following are the details of the different components as illustrated in Figure 1:

The **Sensor Input** includes the Kinect and the Leap Motion Controller that are used to collect joint motion data. The Leap provides high resolution spatial data for the fingers and the thumb. The **Live Data Manager** processes the raw stream coming from the sensors. It saves a copy of the data to the local storage and forwards another copy to the rendering engine. The **Inverse Kinematics Analyzer** reads data streams and infers inverse kinematic variables such as the state of different joints and forwards it to the **Quality of Improvement Display Window**. The **Rendering Engine** is in charge of displaying data on the screen in different formats. The Kinect stream is drawn as a stick figure while the Leap stream is rendered as hands made up of 3D boxes.

The **Session Recorder** component is in charge of recording sensor data to a local disk or in the cloud. The **Computational Intelligence Engine** takes the list of joint-movements from database for a particular therapy and filters the session files based on these movements. Extracted data is processed by the **Inference Engine** to detect rehabilitation patterns and then sent to the **Reporting Engine** to be plotted in a visually attractive manner. The **Knowledge Base** stores the therapies designed by the therapist. The Reporting Engine consults the therapy knowledge base to know which joints need to be tracked and plotted in each therapy session. **Interactive Graphs** are plotted by the system from session data files stored in the cloud. The **Authoring Interface** provides the therapist with an easy to use environment for designing therapies (Figure 2). The interface displays a human body anatomy model, where each of the trackable joints is displayed as a hotspot on the body.

3. DEMONSTRATION SCENARIO

During the demonstration, we will show a quick scenario where a user having a therapist account records a sample session for a given exercise. Some example operations are executed to show the interaction with the motion sensors. After a therapy has been established, a patient user will first replay the corresponding session in 3D environment to understand the model therapy suggested by the therapist. The patient will then record different sessions and see live plots consisting of quality of improvement metrics by analyzing current or past therapy session data.

4. ACKNOWLEDGMENTS

This work was supported by the NSTIP strategic technologies program (11-INF1703-10 and 11-INF1700-10) in the Kingdom of Saudi Arabia.

5. REFERENCES

[1] S. E. Fasoli, H. I. Krebs, J. Stein, W. Frontera, R. Hughes, and N. Hogan. Robotic therapy for chronic motor impairments after stroke: Follow-up results. *Archives of Physical Medicine and Rehabilitation*, 85(7):1106–1111, 2004.

[2] A. Gustus, G. Stillfried, J. Visser, H. Jörntell, and P. van der Smagt. Human hand modelling: kinematics, dynamics, applications. *Biological cybernetics*, 106(11-12):741–755, 2012.

[3] M. Ma and K. Bechkoum. Serious games for movement therapy after stroke. In *Proceedings of the IEEE International Conference on Systems, Man and Cybernetics*, pages 1872–1877. IEEE, 2008.

[4] F. Weichert, D. Bachmann, B. Rudak, and D. Fisseler. Analysis of the accuracy and robustness of the leap motion controller. *Sensors*, 13(5):6380, 2013.

EventEye: Monitoring Evolving Events from Tweet Streams

Hongyun Cai [#], Zhongxian Tang [*], Yang Yang [#†], Zi Huang [#]

[#] The University of Queensland, Australia

[*] Zhejiang University, China

[†] University of Electronic Science and Technology of China, China

h.cai2@uq.edu.au, kohntzx@gmail.com, dlyyang@gmail.com, huang@itee.uq.edu.au

ABSTRACT

With the rapid growth in popularity of social websites, social event detection has become one of the hottest research topics. However, continuously monitoring social events has not been well studied. In this demo, we present a novel system called EventEye to effectively monitor evolving events and visualize their evolving paths, which are discovered from tweet streams. In particular, four event operations are defined for our proposed stream clustering algorithm to capture the evolutions over time and a multi-layer indexing structure is designed to support efficient event search from large-scale event databases. In our system, events are visualized in different views, including evolution graph, timeline, map view, etc. [1]

Categories and Subject Descriptors

H.3.1 [**Information Storage and Retrieval**]: Content Analysis and Indexing

Keywords

Evolving Events Monitoring; Event Indexing; Event Visualization

1. INTRODUCTION

Twitter is one of the most popular online social network service. The dynamically updated tweets provide a wide variety of real-time information which covers a diverse range of real-life events happening all over the world. With the rapid growth of tweets posted everyday, how to efficiently and effectively detect meaningful events and monitor their evolutions to reveal the implicit triggering relationships among events is in high demand.

Event detection in Twitter is usually defined as clustering tweets which share similar textual contents. Although a lot of efforts have been made on social event detection, most of them omit the evolutions of the events. Among them, the single-pass incremental clustering has been widely adopted for event detection in social media [2]. However, it has two limitations. First, it lacks indexing support to the large-scale social data. Second, the evolutions of the events are not monitored. The most similar work to ours is the KeySee system proposed in [3]. KeySee detects events from social stream and tracks the event evolution patterns. They use the sliding time window strategy along with a density-based clustering algorithm to identify events from the data stream. However, the evolution graph is constructed by treating each event snapshot as a node and the trajectory between snapshots as paths. So the evolution of an event is only checked when the time window moves. This may cause losing track of the evolution of highly dynamic events or storing redundant snapshots for steady events.

In this paper, we propose an evolving events monitoring and visualization system, called EventEye, for Twitter. In this system, a Multi-layer Inverted List (MIL) indexing structure is designed to support efficient event manipulation, including event maintaining and event identifying. The traditional single-pass incremental clustering algorithm is extended by taking into account four newly defined event evolution operations to detect events and capture their evolutions over time. The proposed incremental clustering algorithm enables the event detection and monitoring process in real time, which does not require any prior settings such as sliding window size, etc. Users can browse current events or search historical events at any time. To expatiate an event, we adopt different event visualizations including evolution graph, timeline, map view, word cloud, representative tweets and images. Especially, to visualize the evolution of an event, all its relevant events and the associated evolving relationships are illustrated by an evolution graph, where each node represents an event and the edge between any two nodes indicates their evolving relationship.

2. SYSTEM OVERVIEW

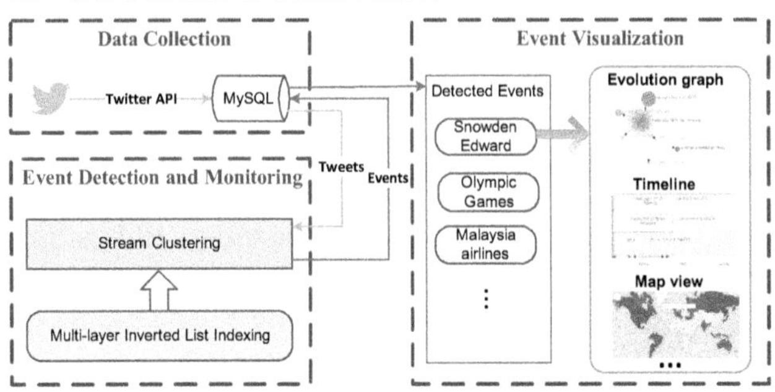

Figure 1: System Architecture

The system architecture is illustrated in Figure 1. Tweets are collected via Twitter API and stored in the database. Our proposed stream clustering algorithm is applied on the collected tweets to detect events and monitor their evolutions. We define four event operations for our clustering algorithm including creation, absorption, split and merge, to capture the evolution patterns. With the aid of these four operations, the evolutions of the events are recorded in real time. Unlike KeySee which only checks the evolution patterns when sliding window moves, the arrival of any new tweet could trigger split or merge in our system. Specifically, for

[1]The supplementary file is available at https://www.dropbox.com/s/n1pnf0otmlk8jsp/EventEye.pptx

MM'14, November 3–7, 2014, Orlando, Florida, USA.
ACM 978-1-4503-3063-3/14/11.
http://dx.doi.org/10.1145/2647868.2654871 .

each newly arrived tweet e, its nearest neighbour E_{NN} (the event that has largest similarity between e among all the existing events) is first found. If the similarity between e and E_{NN} is below a predefined threshold θ, a singleton event containing only e is created, otherwise e is absorbed by E_{NN}. After the absorption, if the radius (the smallest similarity from the tweets in E_{NN} to the cluster center) of E_{NN} is smaller than θ, E_{NN} is split into two new events. Once the split is conducted, the newly split events may be merged with nearby events if the merged event satisfies the radius threshold θ. As for the efficiency consideration, MIL indexing structure is proposed as the first event indexing structure to support large-scale dynamically evolving event maintenance and facilitate efficient event search. MIL is a multi-layer indexing structure, which organizes events in different layers guided by different information-specific levels. It inspects most relevant event lists on the lowest layer to avoid exhaustive accesses to longer event lists on the upper layer. After events are detected, users can browse current events or search the historical events at any time. Five views are used to visualize a specified event, including: timeline, evolution graph, map view, word cloud and representative tweets and images. The first three are the major visualization interfaces in our system and will be introduced in the following subsections one by one.

2.1 Timeline of the Detected Events

Figure 2: Timeline

To browse the detected events in the system, we design a timeline display of events. One essential characteristic of the social events lies in their temporal orders. Listing events chronologically based on the event starting time gives users a clear view of the event sets. By selecting the start time and the end time in the timeline, events happened within the defined time span will be displayed, with their parallel or sequential relationships along the timeline indicated. Users can also zoom in and out the timeline to view events at different time resolutions. In Figure 2, event "Putin attended a conference" is shown, while all detected events that happened nearby are listed in the timeline.

2.2 Evolution Graph for Event Monitoring

Previous work mostly focus on the detection of the event. Some of them have devoted their efforts on event tracking that trails the details of one specified event in real time. For example, in [1], the authors track the representative tweets of an event and mine geographical diffusion trajectory on the map. Instead of tracking one individual event, we monitor the event evolution among relevant events. The relationships between an event and all its relevant events will be recorded in our system and be illustrated as a graph (e.g., the left diagram of Figure 3), where merge and split operations are clearly displayed. The arrows indicate the event triggering or evolving paths. For example, event "Snowden arrives in Moscow" and event "Putin grants asylum to Snowden" trigger event "Obama cancels vladimir Putin meeting". The timeline is also applied to visualize the event evolutions, where all related events are ordered by their emerging time, so that users can easily get the antecedents and descendant of the events at a glance. By clicking an event on the relationship graph, its hotness value will be shown on the right side of the window (e.g., the bar graph in Figure 3).

Figure 3: Evolution Graph

2.3 Map View for Event Popularity Analysis

Tweets keep arriving as a spatio-temporal stream. Besides of the timestamp, location also provides important information. Country information is recorded in the database. We analyse and display different popularities in different countries on the map, based on which users get the distribution of the diverse spatial popularities of an event. This distribution provides the answers of some important questions such as whether an event is a regional event or a global event, which countries are interested in this kind of events most, and so on. In addition to the popularity distribution, users can further check the details of this event (e.g., word cloud, representative tweets and images) in each country. This helps users to have a better understanding of the global events. For instance, people from different countries have different opinions on the event that Snowden leaks NSA documents. Various opinions from different countries can be compared in our map view straightforwardly.

3. EVALUATIONS

To evaluate the performance of our system EventEye, we collected 10,681,232 tweets posted from August 1st, 2013 to November 30th, 2013 using Twitter API. We recommend the top 30 hottest events for each day. The experimental results show that EventEye achieves 69.09% precision which outperforms KeySee (62.13%). Furthermore, on average, EventEye only takes around one third of the time to process daily collected data (nearly 90 thousands tweets), i.e., 103.46 seconds vs 352.77 seconds.

4. CONCLUSIONS

We have demonstrated a social event evolution monitoring and visualization system for Twitter. We proposed a novel stream clustering algorithm along with a multi-layer indexing structure to detect social events against large-scale tweets streaming and monitor their evolutions in real time. The events are further visualized with multiple views vividly.

5. REFERENCES

[1] X. Gao, J. Cao, Z. Jin, X. Li, and J. Li. Gesodeck: a geo-social event detection and tracking system. In *ACM Multimedia*, pages 471–472, 2013.

[2] Y. Jie, L. Andrew, C. Mark, R. Bella, and P. Robert. Using social media to enhance emergency situation awareness. *IEEE Intelligent Systems*, 27(6):52–59, 2012.

[3] P. Lee, L. V. S. Lakshmanan, and E. E. Milios. Keysee: supporting keyword search on evolving events in social streams. In *KDD*, pages 1478–1481, 2013.

3D Immersive Cardiopulmonary Resuscitation (CPR) Trainer

Yuan Tian†, Suraj Raghuraman†, Yin Yang‡, Xiaohu Guo†, Balakrishnan Prabhakaran†

†University of Texas at Dallas
800 W Campbell Road
Richardson, TX 75080 USA
{yxt114020,suraj,xguo,praba}@utdallas.edu

‡University of New Mexico
1 University Blvd NE
Albuquerque, NM 87131 USA
yyang@ece.unm.edu

ABSTRACT

Cardiopulmonary resuscitation (CPR) plays a primary role in first-aid treatment. Instead of the traditional instructor-led training course, we propose a virtual reality system which provides an immersive 3D environment for CPR training with visual and haptic feedback. To simulate a real world CPR experience, our immersive trainer system enables a trainee to perform CPR compressions to a virtual human, inside the virtual world. During the training procedure, the trainee can not only watch his/her 3D image performing CPR, but also feel the force feedback from the chest compressions in real-time. To further enhance the visual fidelity, a haptic-enabled deformable model is applied to show the visual change of chest during compression.

Categories and Subject Descriptors

I.3 [**Computing Methodologies**]: COMPUTER GRAPHICS; I.3.2 [**COMPUTER GRAPHICS**]: Three-Dimensional Graphics and Realism—*Virtual reality*

Keywords

Virtual Reality; CPR training; Haptic Rendering; Visual Occlusion;

1. INTRODUCTION

Cardiopulmonary resuscitation is a primary emergency procedure and instructor-led training courses remain popular. Now multimedia techniques are utilized to develop self-directed learning systems, and CPR feedback/prompt devices to improve CPR performance and evaluate quality. Recent research [4] shows that in self-directed CPR training, performance will improve if the trainee is allowed to watch his/her own motions, since visual feedback will naturally lead to consciousness of wrong motion. Therefore we propose an immersive virtual reality trainer, that enables a trainee to perform CPR training in a 3D virtual world. Our system provides visual and haptic feedback which helps to learn the essentials of the exercise. As shown in Fig. 1, in a real world training environment, the trainee will face a Kinect camera, and compress an Omega.3 haptic device, in real-time to perform chest compressions. At the same time, the trainee will see a virtual world on a screen, which includes a 3D virtual human placed in a supine position, and the trainee's live image captured by the Kinect camera.

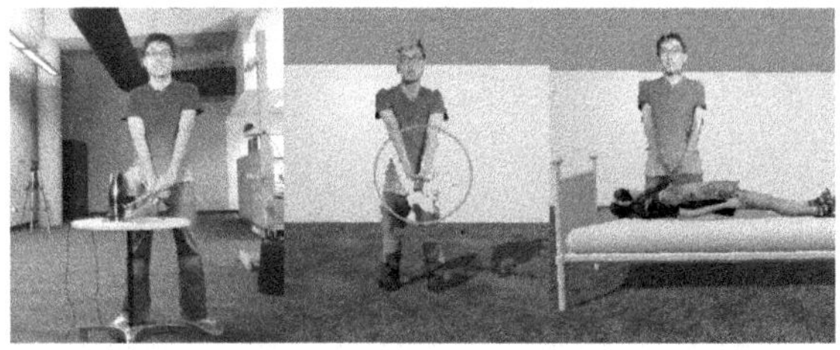

(a) (b) (c)

Figure 1: The immersive CPR trainer. (a) shows the real-world scene, (b) shows the visual occlusion problem,(c) shows the virtual world scene.

2. CHALLENGES

Visual Occlusion The scene captured by the kinect has lots of equipment surrounding the trainee, this causes occlusion. The trainee is always behind the haptic device and the table, due to this the entire body of the trainee cannot be captured and rendered directly, as shown in Fig. 1(b). Since an Omega.3 haptic device is placed in front of the trainee, and the trainee will cross his/her hands in front of his/her body, the captured 3D image will have white holes.

Chest Deformation The second challenge is to show the visual result of the chest compression of the virtual human, which is related to how much the trainee push down on the haptic handle. On the one hand, we need a fast and stable deformable method to simulate the plausible visual compression; on the other hand, a smooth and stable force feedback needs to be provided to the trainee.

Sychronization The haptic device and kinect generate data at different frame rates. Due to its high data rate of 1KHZ the haptic information always leads the kinect data. A very fast deformation algorithm used by the system generates the deformation in real time, resulting in haptic-based deformation not matching the kinect based live model prediction.

MM'14, November 3–7, 2014, Orlando, Florida, USA.
ACM 978-1-4503-3063-3/14/11.
http://dx.doi.org/10.1145/2647868.2654881.

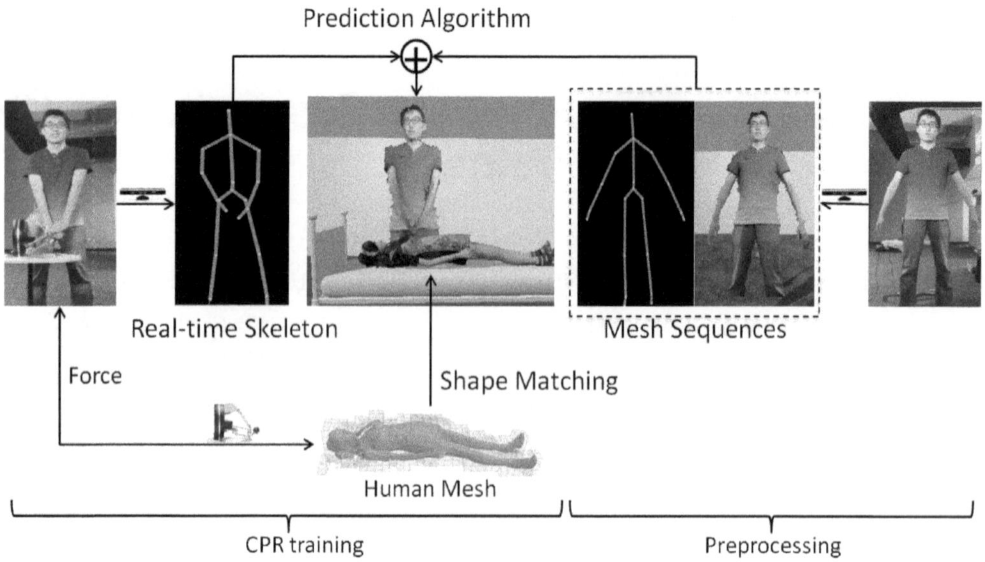

Figure 2: The working procedure of immersive CPR trainer.

3. OUR SOLUTION

The system is setup by positioning the kinect below the display and the haptic device right in front of the display in direct view of the camera. Then the haptic device is positioned at the high and low position to calibrate the camera, haptic and virtual space. Once this calibration is done the system is ready to use. Every time a new trainee steps in a few frames of the complete person are captured. Typically even one frame is sufficient, or multiple can be used as shown in the supplementary video. Then the trainee takes the position behind the haptic device and performs the CPR compressions on the haptic device that are visualized by the system on the display in front. The system provides both visual and audio clues when the activity is not performed correctly, such as bending the elbows, or low compressing frequency.

To address the first challenge of visual occlusion, we utilize a prediction based algorithm [2]: which needs a short preprocessing, and predicts a live mesh, without the visual occlusion based on skeleton. First, we capture a sequence of meshes and skeletons of the trainee without haptic device. When the training procedure begins, the Kinect camera is only utilized to produce trainee's skeletal joint information and the algorithm will regenerate a live mesh model for the trainee based on the prediction algorithm. The procedure of this algorithm is shown in Fig. 2.

The second challenge could be solved by an haptic-enabled deformation model [3], which applies a shape matching [1] method to simulate the deformation stably. We firstly produce a voxel mesh for the triangle mesh of the human model. Except the chest, other parts of the human model will not perform simulation. Constraint particle coupling [3] can provide smooth force feedback at 1KHz frequency while HIP (Haptic Interaction Point) is interacting with the mesh. As shown in Fig.2, when the trainee compresses the haptic handle, collision detection is performed between HIP and the mesh, and then compute the force feedback for the trainee, finally shape matching generates the chest deformation.

To solve the synchronization issue, we use the calibration performed between the haptic space and the Kinect space for the positioning of the trainee in the virtual environment. Since at every millisecond the position of HIP is known and we also know that the trainee is moving the device using both hands, we can reposition the hands of the trainee in the virtual space every millisecond. Since the prediction method is based on the position of the joints of the skeleton. The change in the position of the hand results in the corresponding change on the live model of the trainee.

4. RESULTS

Our virtual reality system provides an immersive 3D environment that enables CPR training. With smooth haptic feedback, the trainee could feel the force corresponding to each chest compression. To enhance the visual performance, a geometric based method is utilized to generate the visual change of the human chest under the compression. Through prediction-based algorithm, we provide a high-fidelity experience where trainee is placed inside a virtual world and performing CPR on a virtual human.

5. ACKNOWLEDGMENTS

This material is based upon work supported by the National Science Foundation under Grant No. 1012975. Any opinions, findings, and conclusions or recommendations expressed in this material are those of the author(s) and do not necessarily reflect the views of the National Science Foundation.

6. REFERENCES

[1] M. Müller, B. Heidelberger, M. Teschner, and M. Gross. Meshless deformations based on shape matching. SIGGRAPH '05, pages 471–478.

[2] S. Raghuraman, K. Venkatraman, Z. Wang, B. Prabhakaran, and X. Guo. A 3d tele-immersion streaming approach using skeleton-based prediction. In *Proceedings of the 21st ACM International Conference on Multimedia*, MM '13, pages 721–724, New York, NY, USA, 2013. ACM.

[3] Y. Tian, Y. Yang, X. Guo, and B. Prabhakaran. Haptic-enabled interactive rendering of deformable objects based on shape matching. In *Haptic Audio Visual Environments and Games (HAVE), 2013 IEEE International Symposium on*, pages 75–80, Oct 2013.

[4] J. Yeung, D. Okamoto, J. Soar, and G. D. Perkins. Aed training and its impact on skill acquisition, retention and performance–a systematic review of alternative training methods. *Resuscitation*, 82(6):657–664, 2011.

Taking Good Selfies on Your Phone

Mei-Chen Yeh   Hsiao-Wei Lin

Department of Computer Science and Information Engineering
National Taiwan Normal University, Taipei, Taiwan

myeh@csie.ntnu.edu.tw, allison1125@hotmail.com

ABSTRACT

Selfies are in vogue because smartphones and social media websites have helped popularize the phenomenon whereby people can easily take and share self-portrait photographs. However, taking good selfies is not always a trivial task for end users. In this demonstration we present a tool for guiding users on which angles to take selfies from. Dissimilar to existing techniques that enhance the aesthetic quality of selfies through a post-processing procedure, the proposed approach focuses on the creation of a good look before the photo is captured. A few distinctive patterns automatically discovered from a collection of online profile pictures are used to score a selfie in angle. The technique should enable new features such as "virtual portraitist" for current consumer cameras and smartphones, providing an interactive approach for capturing selfies.

Categories and Subject Descriptors

I.4.9 [**Image Processing and Computer Vision**]: Applications.

General Terms

Algorithms, Experimentation.

Keywords

Selfie, self-portrait, computational photography

1. INTRODUCTION

Selfies are a new form of self-portraits, typically taken with a camera phone or digital camera held at arm's length. As smartphones become ubiquitous, an increasing number of selfies are taken each day with the intention of being uploaded to and shared on social media websites. In November 2013, Oxford Dictionaries announced the word "selfie" as their international Word of the Year 2013, and revealed that the frequency of the word "selfie" in the English language has increased by 17,000% since this time last year [5].

A selfie can be captured in various ways. Some selfies are extreme close-ups, others show part of an arm held straight outward and a few of the great ones even feature the subject standing in front of a mirror so that they can capture their reflection. But the question remains: How does one take a good selfie — one that constitutes positive feedbacks and increased followers? What qualities may make for an unsuccessful selfie? Although numerous mobile apps such as CreamCam [6] and YouCam Perfect [7] have been recently launched to enhance the aesthetic quality of selfies, those tools remain limited to post-

MM'14, November 3–7, 2014, Orlando, Florida, USA.
ACM 978-1-4503-3063-3/14/11.
http://dx.doi.org/10.1145/2647868.2654865

(a) (b) (c)

Figure 1. (a)-(b) The importance of angles in taking a selfie. (c) An example outcome of the proposed approach. The red bar indicates the estimated aesthetic score based on angle. Each triangle represents a pattern of good selfies discovered from a collection of profile pictures.

processing procedures, such as complexion enhancement and blemish (e.g. acne, dark spots, wrinkles) removal. However, certain flaws may not be fixed by using a post-processing step. For example, Fig. 1 (a)-(b) illustrate the importance of angles in taking a selfie. Adjusting the subject's pose after taking the photograph would be difficult.

In this demonstration, we present a fully automatic approach to estimate the aesthetic quality score of a selfie based on angle. Unlike existing techniques, the proposed approach focuses on the recommendation of a good look *before* the photo is captured. We observed that smartphone selfies have common patterns because several guidelines can be used to take good ones. For example, a straight-on or above angle is widely used to avoid double chins. "MySpace Angle" shots that highlight the face and conceal the body can be taken from an especially flattering angle. Based on the observations, we collected images from "The Beauty of Facebook" [8], from which we discovered frequent and distinct patterns (see Fig. 2). An example outcome of the proposed system is shown in Fig. 1 (c). Each colored triangle represents a good pattern detected on the image. The red bar below indicates the estimated aesthetic score ranging from 0 to 100. The score is computed based on the occurrence of good patterns and estimation of head pose. In the following we describe in detail the proposed approach, including the mining of frequent and distinctive patterns, and the demonstration setup.

2. APPROACH

Given a selfie, the proposed approach aims to estimate an aesthetic score from image content. The approach focuses on the computation of how a smartphone is positioned away from a face and how a subject turns his (or her) face to the smartphone. The

Figure 2. A few discriminant frequent patterns discovered from the Beauty of Facebook [8] and Labeled Faces in the Wild [2].

aesthetic quality evaluation is performed in two aspects: 1) the occurrence of good patterns mined from the Beauty of Facebook [8]; 2) the estimates of head pose. Although other factors—such as facial expression—may affect how we perceive the quality of a selfie, the exploration of those factors is beyond the scope of this paper. A comprehensive evaluation for rating a selfie is desirable, although further research is required.

2.1 Mining frequent and distinctive patterns

This work describes a pattern by using a triangle that connects three facial landmarks on a face. We used a simplified version of the method in [3] to detect 11 facial features, resulting in a total of 165 possible triangles. For each triangle we obtained three features (i.e. three angles of a triangle), and each feature is quantized into 7 bins by using the statistics of the angle distributions computed from the Labeled Faces in the Wild (LFW) images [2]; that is, a triangle is indexed by one of the 343 (7^3) possible combinations.

We used a collection of profile pictures from the Beauty of Facebook [8], from which a transaction database D is built. We considered each triangle as an item; therefore, a transaction (i.e. a profile picture) is a set of 165 items (i.e. triangles). An itemset A is called frequent in D if the support of A is larger than or equal to a threshold. Since frequent itemsets are subject to the monotonicity property, the APriori algorithm [1] was used to find frequent itemsets very quickly.

We observed that some items in the discovered frequent itemset occur frequently in the LFW images [2]; however, those items are not useful for distinguishing good selfies from the others. Therefore, we removed the items if they also appear frequently on the LFW images. Figure 2 shows the automatically discovered patterns, which will be used to rate a selfie.

2.2 Scoring a selfie

Given a selfie under evaluation, we firstly detected the occurrence of those discovered patterns. The score was firstly determined based on the detection of those patterns. Consequently, we inferred the orientation of a person's head relative to the view of a camera. More specifically, we estimated the pitch, roll, and yaw angles by computing the relative distances and angles of certain facial landmarks. The angle vector was then compared to those extracted from the Beauty of Facebook [8], and the score is refined based on the weighted distance of the angle vector to its top 10 neighbors. A larger weight value was used in computing the distance of two pitch angles. We finally normalized the score to a range from 0 and 100. Interested readers can find an experimental evaluation of the approach in [4].

3. DEMONSTRATION SETUP

The demonstration has the form of a smartphone application with a graphical user interface shown in Fig. 1 (c). The system streams and displays the video on the screen when the application is activated; meanwhile, good patterns (i.e. colored triangles) are shown if they are detected. The aesthetic quality score computed based on the detection of good patterns and estimated head pose is displayed beneath the selfie. Participants will be invited to take selfies in this interactive manner.

4. ACKNOWLEDGMENTS

This work was supported in part by Ministry of Science and Technology, Taiwan, under Grant No. NSC 102-2221-E-003-026. The authors would like to thank Ya-Ting Lin for her help in implementing the demo.

5. REFERENCES

[1] R. Agrawal, T. Imielinski, and A. N. Swami, "Mining association rules between sets of items in large databases," in *Proc. of ACM SIGMOD*, 1993.

[2] G. B. Huang, M. Ramesh, T. Berg and E. Learned-Miller, "Labeled faces in the wild: a database for studying face recognition in unconstrained environments," University of Massachusetts, Amherst, Technical Report, 2007.

[3] X. Xiong and F. De la Torre, "Supervised descent method and its application to face alignment," in *Proc. of IEEE CVPR*, 2013.

[4] M. -C. Yeh and H. -W. Lin, "Virtual portraitist: aesthetic evaluation of selfies based on angle," in *Proc. of ACM MM*, 2014.

[5] Oxford Dictionaries Word of the Year 2013. Retrieved 7 May 2014. http://blog.oxforddictionaries.com/press-releases/oxford-dictionaries-word-of-the-year-2013

[6] CreamCam. Retrieved 7 May 2014. http://creamcamapp.com/

[7] YouCam Perfect. Retrieved 7 May 2014. http://www.cyberlink.com/stat/product/CyberLink_app/YouCam_Perfect/enu/YouCam_Perfect.jsp

[8] The Beauty of Facebook. Retrieved 7 May 2014. http://beauty.zones.gamebase.com.tw/wall

WeMash: An Online System for Web Video Mashup

Peng Wang Yang Yang Zi Huang Jiewei Cao Heng Tao Shen
School of Information Technology and Electrical Engineering
The University of Queensland, Australia
{p.wang6,yang.yang,uqzhuang,j.cao3,uqhshen}@uq.edu.au

ABSTRACT

The explosive growth of video content on the Web has been revolutionizing the way people share, exchange and perceive information. At the same time, however, the massive amount of Web video content may degrade user experience in that it is tedious and time-consuming to view relevant videos uploaded by different users and grasp the gist of their content. In this demonstration, we demonstrate a system that takes Web videos related to a query event as the input and automatically generates a short mashup video that can well describe the essence of the query. Specifically, we first identify shot cliques composed of near-duplicate shots and infer their semantic meanings by resorting to relevant Web images. Then a shot clique selection algorithm is performed to select representative content according to the twofold importance of the shot cliques evaluated, namely content importance and semantic importance, with content diversity considered. Finally, the selected shot cliques are organized into a mashup video based on semantic and temporal cues.[1]

Categories and Subject Descriptors

H.3.3 [**Information Search and Retrieval**]: Retrieval

General Terms

Algorithms, Design

Keywords

Web Video, Video Mashup, Shot Clique, Semantic Inference

1. INTRODUCTION

Recent years have witnessed the explosive growth of videos on the Web. While enjoying the rich information, users tend to be overwhelmed by the massive amount of disorganized video content. The Web videos related to a query may vary dramatically from one another in terms of length, quality and/or visual content, which makes digesting video content by no means easy.

To assist users to better understand the essence of Web videos, a system should be able to extract representative content and organize the content in a user-friendly way. The task is, however, challenging. On one hand, different from constrained videos (e.g., surveillance videos, news videos, performance videos [3], etc.), Web videos often lack reliable auxiliary information (e.g., audio signal and/or transcripts) and are in most cases irregularly organized in terms of temporal order. On the other hand, representative content extraction from Web videos is difficult due to complex semantic structure covered by video content and existence of considerable noisy content. Most existing work select important content based on near-duplicate detection [1]. However, using reoccurrence characteristic solely as metric to determine the importance of video content is not reliable. Also, how to effectively organize the selected Web video content in order to help users to better understand the query event is rarely researched.

In this demonstration, we present a novel online system for Web video mashup (called WeMash) to automatically analyze, summarize and organize Web videos related to a query event by jointly using visual content, semantics and temporal cues. To be specific, we devise an effective mechanism to select most representative content by considering both content importance and semantic importance. Then the selected content is organized into semantic clusters and ordered into a temporal sequence to form a mashup video composed of important and comprehensive yet diverse content, which can well describe the essence of the event.

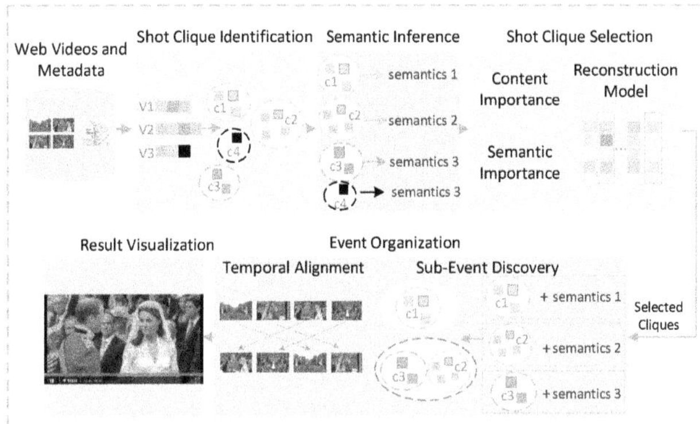

Figure 1: Framework of WeMash.

[1]Supplementary slides can be visited at www.dropbox.com/s/3al9he8mo33ij8g/mm_slides.pptx

MM'14, November 3-7, 2014, Orlando, Fl, USA
ACM 978-1-4503-3063-3/14/11.
http://dx.doi.org/10.1145/2647868.2654868.

2. TECHNOLOGY

Figure 1 shows the framework of our system, WeMash. As can be seen, the system is mainly composed of the following components:

- **Shot Clique Identification:** Web videos related to a query often share partial content overlaps and the repetitively occurred shots often carry important information. Inspired by this assumption, the shots are grouped into shot cliques based on near-duplicate detection [2]. The shot that has most neighbours in a shot clique serves as the representative of the clique.
- **Semantic Inference:** Employment of semantic information can compensate visual content in describing and organizing an event. On one hand, combining both semantic and content reoccurrence information together can make shot clique selection more reliable. One the other hand, semantic cues play an important role in unveiling semantic structure of the event. To infer the semantics of shot cliques, we first mine keywords from the metadata accompanied to Web videos and then estimate the affinity values of the shot cliques to the keywords by resorting to the relevant Web images to the keywords.
- **Representative Shot Clique Selection:** To select representative shot cliques, we first evaluate the twofold importance of shot cliques: content importance and semantic importance. While the former reflects the occurrence frequency of the content, the latter is measured as the relevance between the visual content and the key semantic component of the event. Then shot clique selection is formulated as a weighted dictionary selection problem from which important content are more likely to be selected and diversity of content is taken into consideration as well.
- **Content Organization:** Selected shot cliques are further organized into a unified mashup video towards a better understanding of the event. First, the shot cliques are grouped into various subevents based on the semantics associated with the shot cliques. Then, for each subevent, we conduct temporal alignment on the shot cliques via mining their relative temporal orders within the original videos.

3. SYSTEM AND USER INTERFACE

3.1 Interface

We have developed an online system for WeMash. Using our system, users can obtain a static summary of videos related to a query in the form of storyboard and create a mashup video with content organized into subevents and a temporally-aligned sequence. As shown in Figure 2, the user interface is mainly composed of three panels. When giving a query and clicking "Search", its relevant Web videos will be listed in the left panel all of which can be played using the bottom-right video player. Then the users can either generate the storyboard summary of the videos or directly create the mashup using default settings. The storyboard summary in the upper-right panel displays the selected representative shots and their corresponding textual descriptions inferred

Figure 2: Interface for WeMash.

as semantic meanings. Users can determine whether a shot will be selected to construct the mashup video or not using checkbox. Also, the length of the mashup video can be dynamically controlled via adjusting the trackbar. Based on the selected shots and video length setted, users are able to create a mashup video accompanied with corresponding textual description.

3.2 Performance

We evaluate the performance of our system using a set of hot events with diverse topics including "social", "sports", "entertainment", "political" and "technology". Both quantitative and qualitative experiments are conducted. For the objective evaluation of important content selection, we manually labelled the ground truth. The mean precision rate of content selection is 87.75% and the mean recall rate is 78.88%, both of which are significantly improved compared to near-duplicate detection based method. This proves the effectiveness of our content selection algorithm in selecting representative content. Also, we conduct subjective evaluation to evaluate the practicality of our system. The system is evaluated from three aspects, "information coverage", "conciseness", and "can mashup help to better understand the query event?". Ten users are invited to give scores from 1 to 10 (higher score indicates better performance) to the mashup results based on their judgments. The corresponding mean scores for the above three criteria are 8.59, 7.83, and 7.88 (score for storyboard is 6.75). The evaluation results indicate that our system is practical and can help users to better understand the event in short time.

4. REFERENCES

[1] R. Hong, J. Tang, H.-K. Tan, C.-W. Ngo, S. Yan, and T.-S. Chua. Beyond search: Event driven summarization for web videos. *TOMCCAP*, 2011.

[2] J. Liu, Z. Huang, H. Cai, H. T. Shen, C.-W. Ngo, and W. Wang. Near-duplicate video retrieval: Current research and future trends. *ACM Comput. Surv.*, 45(4), 2013.

[3] M. K. Saini, R. Gadde, S. Yan, and W. T. Ooi. Movimash: Online mobile video mashup. In *ACM Multimedia*, pages 139–148, 2012.

FreeViewer: An Intelligent Director for 3D Tele-Immersion System

Zhenhuan Gao Shannon Chen Klara Nahrstedt
Department of Computer Science
University of Illinois at Urbana-Champaign
{zgao11, cchen116, klara}@illinois.edu

ABSTRACT

This paper proposes FreeViewer, a 3D Tele-Immersion view-control system that allows viewers to see arbitrary side of the performer by intelligently choosing the streams of a subset of cameras and changing the point of view in a 3D virtual space. The view changing is actuated by the change of the sensor data from wearable devices (eg. Google Glass, smartphone) on the performer able to monitor the current orientation.

Categories and Subject Descriptors

J.7 [COMPUTERS IN OTHER SYSTEMS]: Real time

Keywords

3D tele-immersion; multi-modality; free view

1. INTRODUCTION

3D Tele-immersion (3DTI) system enables remote users to view the local scene and even to interact with local users in a virtual 3D space, which has promoted lots of potential applications such as remote therapy [1]. In general, a 3DTI system consists of several sites distributed at different physical locations. All the sites transmit the 3D data captured by multiple 3D cameras over either a dedicated network or a shared network such as Internet. After each site gathers the data from all the other sites, it renders everything in a common virtual space in a real-time manner.

In a traditional 2D live video streaming system, the interactivity of end users, choosing a specified viewpoint, has been crippled by the fact that they can only choose to see the physical scene captured by a physical camera, but not between two physical cameras. However, through depth estimation and interpolation among multiple 3D video streams captured from different angles, the 3DTI system makes it possible rendering a 3D space where the viewers can view physical scene from arbitrary viewpoint as if there existed a virtual camera capturing at that viewpoint with the same view angle.

MM'14, November 3–7, 2014, Orlando, Florida, USA.
ACM 978-1-4503-3063-3/14/11.
http://dx.doi.org/10.1145/2647868.2654873 .

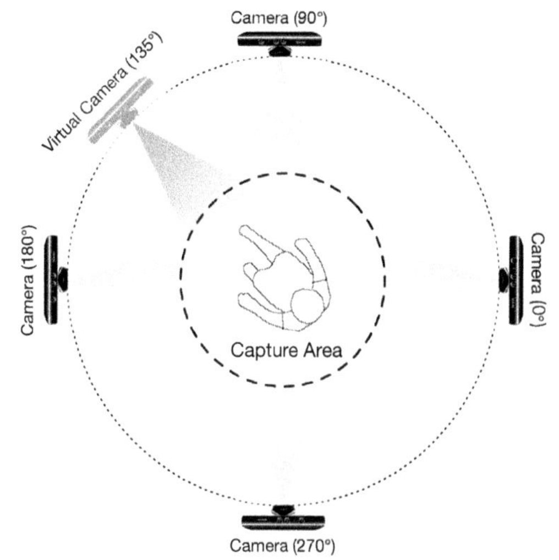

Figure 1: The bird view of FreeViewer deployment

One possible solution to realize free viewpoint (FV) viewing of a physical scene is to create a complete 3D model by aggregating the 3D streams from the cameras all of which can cover 360 degree view. The viewing user is then able to choose arbitrary viewpoint to see any side of this complete 3D model. However, creation and delivery of such a complete 3D object makes bandwidth and computation requirements inevitably high. Hence, we need to look for alternative solutions for FV viewing to decrease the computational and networking requirements. For example, in the 3DTI system, the back side of the model, which is invisible to the viewer, is redundant. The computation related to the data of the back could be avoided to reduce latency.

In this paper, to tackle the FV viewing problem, we propose FreeViewer, a 3DTI view-control system at the physical scene that supports free viewpoint with low requirements on computation power and bandwidth and is suitable to assist the real-time peer-to-peer 3D content distribution among large scale viewers. Figure 1 illustrates an example of the deployment of FreeViewer. There are 4 3D cameras deployed in the area with the same angular difference and the same distance from the center of the capturing area. A performer stays in the capturing area with a varying orientation. The objective of FreeViewer is no matter which direction the performer is facing, it always renders the scene of the performer's front side as if there was a virtual camera facing the performer.

2. SYSTEM OVERVIEW

This section gives an overview of the FreeViewer system architecture (Figure 2) including several important functional services.

2.1 3D View Tracking Service

3D View Tracking is an advanced service that performs cooperation between wearable device and orientation monitoring module to capture user's head direction. Traditional user interaction solutions for 3DTI systems are often naive and simply relying on standard iuput devices(mouse, keyboard) to control visual devices and receive visual feedback. We present a user interaction solution based on wearable devices. That is, we use Google Glass as the input interaction device to enable tracking the rotational movement of the user's head. The tracking service allows users to interact with the system in a natural way without any additional manual operation such as "press some keys" or "drag the mouse". We choose Google Glass because of its portability and easiness to estimate the facing orientation.

The orientation monitoring module also maintains a connection with the Google Glass to receive the sensor data and then feeds them to capturing service and rendering service.

2.2 Capturing Service

As previously stated, in a 3D virtual space at a specified viewpoint, a viewer can only see one side of an object which can be covered by at most two 3D cameras. This means in order to render the scene from any viewpoint at any time, our system only needs the streams from two cameras. Given the orientation returned by the Google Glass, the capturing service decides the streams from which cameras to acquire according to the known physical deployment of the cameras. Then this service synchronizes the color and depth streams from both of the cameras chosen and sends the frames to the processing service to create a partial 3D model.

In fact, it not only reduces the bandwidth consumption of the network resources but also practically relieves the interference effect [2] between different 3D cameras (e.g., Kinect).

2.3 3D Point Cloud Processing Service

The 3D cloud point processing service aims to use the color stream and the depth streams from the 3D cameras to generate two 3D model (Point Clouds [3]) and to merge them in to a complete model so that the intersecting areas between them could overlap perfectly. The problem of such consistent alignment is known as registration.

However, the most famous registration algorithm, the iterative closest point algorithm, is too slow to support realtime processing. Fortunately, in our deployment, we already know the physical positions and orientations of all cameras around the captured physical scene because the cameras are fixed prior to filming and the capturing of actions in front of the cameras. Thus, we adopt the pre-configuration and calibration technique to obtain the coordinates-transformation relationship between a main camera and the other cameras. Then after the system starts to run, the processing service transforms all 3D point clouds from the original cameras' co-

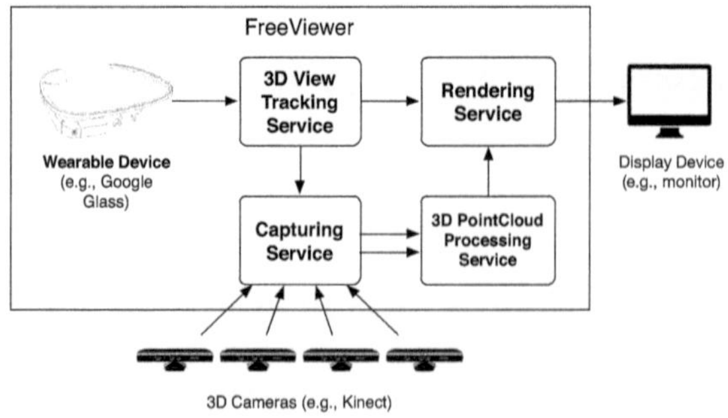

Figure 2: FreeViewer Architecture

ordinate system to the coordinate system of the main camera, which aligns them properly.

Finally, this service delivers the merged point cloud, which is also a partial 3D model, to the rendering service.

2.4 Rendering Service

The rendering service takes two inputs, the performer's current orientation, coming from the 3D view-tracking service, and the correspondent partial 3D model in terms of merged point cloud. Based on the user's orientation and the geometric relationship between the deployed cameras, the rendering service calculates the virtual camera's viewpoint and view angle. Then it uses standard OpenGL API to render the synthesized scene on the display device. Also, in order to provide truly immersive visual feedback, the display device can also be a head-mounted display or even another Google Glass with OpenGL ES support.

3. ACKNOWLEDGEMENTS

This material is based upon work supported by NSF Grant CNS10-12194.

4. CONCLUSIONS

The presented demo shows the attractiveness of the FreeViewer system in terms of view-changing capabilities for a user via her wearable device such as the Google Glass in multi-camera immersive environment. The view-tracking technique is based on the sensor data from wearable devices. Compared to complete 3D model reconstruction, FreeViewer can achieve the same FV viewing and the same 3D video quality with less computation and network bandwidth, which is highly favorable under resource-limited scenarios.

5. REFERENCES

[1] Klara Nahrstedt. 3d teleimmersion for remote injury assessment. In *Proceedings of the 2012 International Workshop on Socially-aware Multimedia*, SAM '12, pages 21–24, New York, NY, USA, 2012. ACM.

[2] D. Alex Butler, Shahram Izadi, Otmar Hilliges, David Molyneaux, Steve Hodges, and David Kim. Shake'n'sense: Reducing interference for overlapping structured light depth cameras. In *Proceedings of the SIGCHI Conference on Human Factors in Computing Systems*, CHI '12, pages 1933–1936, New York, NY, USA, 2012. ACM.

[3] Point cloud library. `http://pointclouds.org/`.

MiSCon: A Hot Plugging Tool for Real-time Motion-based System Control *

Jun Chen, Chaokun Wang, Lei Yang, Qingfu Wen and Xu Wang
School of Software, Tsinghua University, Beijing 100084, China
{chenjun12,yanglei11,wenqf11,xu-wang11}@mails.thu.edu.cn, chaokun@tsinghua.edu.cn

ABSTRACT

In this demonstration, we proposed a hot plugging tool for the real-time motion-based system control, which is more portable and application-independent than the existing commercial motion-based sensing devices such as Kinect, Wii and PlayStation Move. This tool captures and recognizes people's real-time motions through the built-in camera of PCs, mobile phones or tablets, and automatically executes the system events which have been mapped with people's customized body motion, e.g., the head and the fist. The tool relieves people from the conventional ways to play games and use applications, and enables them to customize their preferred ways to control the systems.

Categories and Subject Descriptors

I.4.1 [**Image Processing and Computer Vision**]: Digitization and Image Capture.

Keywords

Hot Plugging; Motion Detection; System Control; MiSCon.

1. INTRODUCTION

Most people's daily works on computers are constrained by the positions and the operational ways of keyboard, mouse and other devices. Though the Bluetooth-based devices relieve people from working at a fixed position, the conventional ways to operate these devices, e.g., typing, clicking and scrolling, still limit the user experience. In recent years, as the motion sensing input devices — Kinect, Wii and PlayStation Move appear, many games and applications are developed based on these devices to facilitate human-computer interactions [1, 2, 3, 4]. However, there are still some limitations of these devices: (1) The games and applications are dependent on the device, and the users have to bring the device wherever they play the games or use the applications; (2) The device is not free, and not all people can afford it; (3) It is difficult to use these devices to control the other games and applications which are not developed based on them. In contrast, camera is much cheaper, more lightweight and portable, and cameras almost exist on every laptop, mobile phone and tablet device. Thus, the camera-based applications have the potential to be of high demands as a low-cost or even free substitute of the aforementioned devices for user entertainment or experience promotion.

Figure 1: Real-time system control with MiSCon.

In this demonstration, we bring forward a hot plugging tool, called **MiSCon**, for the real-time **M**ot**i**on-based **S**ystem **Con**trol. MiSCon captures and recognizes people's motion through the camera, and triggers the corresponding events which have been previously mapped to in the controlled system. This tool enables users to interact with the systems, e.g., PCs, mobile phones and tablets, with the body movement like the head and the fist as illustrated in Fig. 1. Compared with Kinect, Wii and PlayStation Move, MiSCon has the following advantages: (1) MiSCon does not require extra device besides the camera which is basically equipped on most PCs, mobile phones and tablets. Thus, MiSCon is more portable and convenient. (2) The users do not need to spend money since MiSCon can be installed on their existing electronic devices which have a built-in camera. (3) MiSCon is hot plugging and it can control many existing games or applications by mapping people's motion to the events on the system, like the keyboard events, the mouse events and the screen-touching events.

2. SYSTEM OVERVIEW

The workflow of MiSCon is illustrated in Fig. 2. Basically, there are three stages: the detection training stage, the event mapping stage and the working stage.

The detection training stage. MiSCon supports the motion-based system control by many parts of human body, e.g., face, fist and palm, as long as the detection is properly

*Corresponding author: chaokun@tsinghua.edu.cn.

MM'14, Nov 03-07 2014, Orlando, FL, USA.
ACM 978-1-4503-3063-3/14/11.
http://dx.doi.org/10.1145/2647868.2654866 .

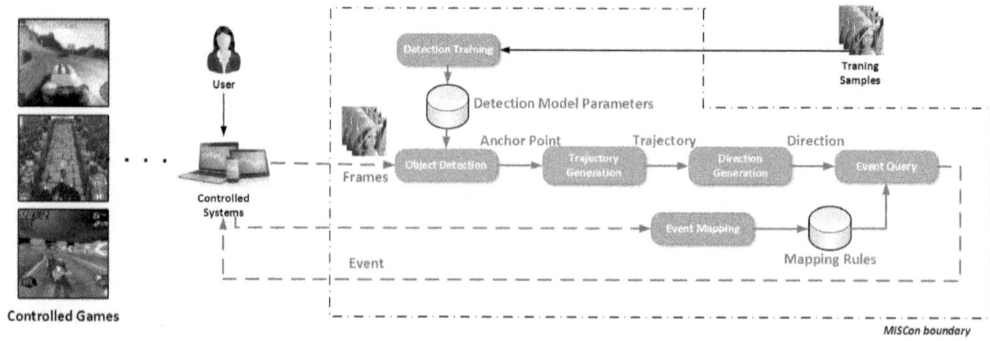

Figure 2: The workflow of MiSCon. The solid arrow-lines represent the workflow inside MiSCon, and the dashed arrow-lines represent the interactions between MiSCon and the controlled system.

Figure 3: The main window of MiSCon.

trained offline. The object detection in MiSCon is conducted using the OpenCV library, and the detected target is determined by the type of the training samples. Thus, users can customize their controlling types according to their preferences. The training parameters of the detection model are stored for later real-time detection in the working stage.

The event mapping stage. MiSCon enables users to map their motions to the available events in the system, like the direction button events on the keyboard, and the left or right click event of the mouse. Users can configure event mapping in the main window of MiSCon as shown in Fig. 3. The mapping is recorded by directly conducting the target event in the focused textbox. For the body motion, MiSCon currently supports the recognition of four moving directions, i.e., upwards, downwards, left and right. It means users can map up to four different events at the same time in the current MiSCon, and more motion supports will be available by extending our current work.

The working stage. People use MiSCon to control their systems in the working stage. Firstly, the camera captures the consecutive frames of people's motions in real time. The object detection component detects the target region of human body in the current scene and records the anchor point of each frame. The anchor point is usually chosen as the geometric center of the detected region. Secondly, the trajectory generation component analyzes the relative position of each anchor point in the consecutive frames and generates the motion trajectory. Thirdly, the direction generation component reduces the noise in the trajectory and computes its major direction. At last, the event query component finds the corresponding event among the pre-defined rules generated in the event mapping stage. The event will be executed once it is recognized. Thus, MiSCon completes the controlling procedure from the body motion to the system events.

3. DEMONSTRATION

MiSCon is developed to enable users to customize their preferred ways to control systems without the limitation of the motion sensing devices, the charges and the applications. As shown in Fig. 3, users can map system event to the motion directions and select the controlling types, e.g., face or fist, on the left panel. The real-time scene and the detected region is shown on the right panel. By clicking on the 'Start' button, MiSCon will be activated and users are allowed to control the system in the way they have configured.

Fig. 1 demonstrates the real-time control of the motorcycle and the car-racing games with the head and the fist using MiSCon. The motorcycle/car will move in the same direction as the player's head/fist moves. Of course, the user can also map the moving direction of the motorcycle/car to the different moving directions of the head/fist, e.g., the opposite directions. Besides these games, MiSCon can also control other games and applications in different ways such as the Temple Run and the Flappy Bird games with the head control, or the slideshow of public speech and the demonstration of system prototype with the fist/palm control. Since only basic moving directions are recognized in the current MiSCon, the real-time performance is fast.

To some extent, MiSCon can be considered as the bridge between the body motion and the system events. As long as the games or applications can be controlled by the input devices such as the keyboard, the mouse and the touchscreen, they can also be controlled by MiSCon. In addition, MiSCon is also lightweight and easy to access. People can use MiSCon on their PCs, mobile phones and tablets without extra charges for the motion sensing devices.

4. ACKNOWLEDGEMENT

This work was supported by the National Natural Science Foundation of China (No. 61373023, No. 61170064) and the National High Technology Research and Development Program of China (No. 2013AA013204).

5. REFERENCES

[1] C.-W. Chen, M.-C. Hu, W.-H. Cheng, C.-H. Chang, J.-H. Lai, and J.-L. Wu. Action tutor: Real-time exemplar-based sequential movement assessment with kinect sensor. In *ACM Multimedia*, pages 1263–1264, 2012.

[2] K. M. Gerling, I. J. Livingston, L. E. Nacke, and R. L. Mandryk. Full-body motion-based game interaction for older adults. In *CHI*, pages 1873–1882, 2012.

[3] K. Isbister. *Motion-Based Game Design: How to Design Quality Movement Games for Wii, Kinect, and Move*. Morgan Kaufmann, San Francisco, CA, USA, first edition, 2013.

[4] D. Wu, F. Zhu, L. Shao, and H. Zhang. One shot learnining gesture recognition with kinect sensor. In *ACM Multimedia*, pages 1303–1304, 2012.

CeleLabel: An Interactive System for Annotating Celebrities in Web Videos

Zhineng Chen[1], Jinfeng Bai[1], Chong-Wah Ngo[2], Bailan Feng[1], Bo Xu[1]
{zhineng.chen, jinfeng.bai}@ia.ac.cn, cscwngo@cityu.edu.hk, {bailan.feng, xubo}@ia.ac.cn

[1] Institute of Automation
Chinese Academy of Sciences
Beijing, China

[2] Department of Computer Science
City University of Hong Kong
Hong Kong, China

ABSTRACT

Manual annotation of celebrities in Web videos is an essential task in many people-related Web services. The task, however, poses a significant challenge even to skillful annotators, mainly due to the large quantity of unfamiliar and greatly varied celebrities, and the lack of a customized system for it. This work develops CeleLabel, an interactive system for manually annotating celebrities in the Web video domain. The peculiarity of CeleLabel is to exploit and display multiple types of information that could assist the annotation, including video content, context surrounding and within a video, celebrity images on the Web, and human factors. Using the system, annotators can interactively switch between two views, i.e., merging similar faces and labeling faces with names, to approach the annotation. User studies show that the CeleLabel leads to a much better labeling efficiency and satisfaction.

Categories and Subject Descriptors

H.5.4 [**Information Interfaces and Presentation**]: Hypertext/Hypermedia

Keywords

Celebrity annotation; Web video; interactive system

1. INTRODUCTION

Manual annotation is a popular mean to create ground truth labels in many visual tasks. This work focuses on building an interactive system for annotating celebrities in the Web video domain, i.e., identifying the celebrities appearing in Web videos and labeling them with their corresponding names. The task becomes increasingly important with the explosion of people-related Web videos and services. However, the annotation of celebrities in Web videos poses a significant challenge even to skillful annotators, mainly due to the following three reasons:

- Web video repositories cover a large number of celebrities with a wide range of nations and professions, in which most celebrities are not familiar to annotators.
- Celebrities maybe with significant variations in visual appearance both within and among videos, such that it might be difficult to correctly distinguish them from others.
- There is no customized system for this problem so far, such that multiple clues for the annotation could not be leveraged.

MM'14, November 3–7, 2014, Orlando, Florida, USA.
ACM 978-1-4503-3063-3/14/11.
http://dx.doi.org/10.1145/2647868.2654879

In the past few years, a number of efforts have been devoted to building databases for challenging visual problems, such as the Trecvid collaborative annotation [1]. These efforts, despite making substantial progress, mainly focus on annotating common concepts or objects which are intuitive for humans. Celebrities, however, are much more special concepts whose inter-class differences are less obvious and not easily described. It would be quite difficult to annotate them if, in the simplest way, only snapshots containing people is presented to annotators. To ease the problem of annotation, it is essential to provide more information about the video and the celebrities to annotators.

Motivated by this observation, we develop a system named CeleLabel for supporting the manual annotation of celebrities in the Web video domain. CeleLabel exploits four types of information to facilitate the annotation: video content, context surrounding and within a video, celebrity images on the Web and human factors. Given a Web video, face tracks and candidate celebrity names are extracted. Based on this, relevant celebrity images are collected from the Web. Parallel, the face tracks are ranked based on several content based factors. At the labeling stage, the annotation task is proceed by either merging two similar faces or labeling the top ranked face track with a candidate celebrity name. Meanwhile, celebrity images most similar to the top ranked track are also displayed for reference. With the labeling continues, the ranking of remaining face tracks are adjusted after every labeling action, by incorporating additional contextual clues and human factors like human perception habits, face track co-occurrence, etc, ensuring that the face track suggested to annotators is always the worthiest. Since multiple clues that could be exploited to facilitate the annotation are leveraged, CeleLabel leads to a much better labeling efficiency and satisfaction as demonstrated in user studies.

2. TECHNOLOGIES

2.1 Preprocessing

Web videos are first preprocessed to extract candidate celebrity names and face tracks. In the implementation, we employ the Wikipedia-based name entity extraction method [2] to extract names from metadata (title and tags) surrounding the given video, and apply the detection-based tracking method [3] to extract face tracks from the video, respectively.

2.2 Merging Similar Faces

It is common that faces of a single person fall into different extracted face tracks. These tracks are visually similar to each other. Compared with determining their respective name correspondence, it is easier to determine whether they refer to the same individual. Therefore, we develop a merging view for annotating face tracks from the angle of merging two similar face tracks rather than separately assigning names to them. The similarity measurement between face track f_i and f_j, denoted as $sim(f_i, f_j)$, is defined as:

$$sim(f_i, f_j) = e^{-\Delta t_{i,j}/t_\theta} \cdot (1 - CO_{i,j}) \cdot vs(f_i, f_j) \quad (1)$$

In the formula, $e^{-\Delta t_{i,j}/t_\theta}$ is a time-decay function, in which $\Delta t_{i,j}$ is the appearing time difference between track f_i and f_j, t_θ is a time slot threshold controlling the influence of time difference. The function favors "nearby" tracks rather than "far away" tracks, thus the time consistency is preserved to some extent. $CO_{i,j}$ is the co-occurrence status of the two tracks. If they are time-overlapped, $CO_{i,j}$ equals to 1, otherwise it is 0. By this way, time-overlapped face tracks would not appear in the merge view even their faces are similar, as two faces co-occurred hardly refer to the same identity. $vs(f_i, f_j)$ is the visual similarity defined as the minimum distance between faces of the two tracks:

$$vs(f_i, f_j) = \min_{f_m^i \in f_i, f_n^j \in f_j, i \neq j} \|f_m^i - f_n^j\| \quad (2)$$

where f_m^i is facial feature of the *m*-th face of track f_i. In the merging view, face track pairs are suggested to annotators according to their $sim(f_i, f_j)$.

2.3 Labeling Faces with Names

Parallel to the merging view, we also develop a labeling view to let annotators directly label faces with names. To determine which face track is the most worthy suggested to annotators, video content, context clues of the video and human factors are jointly investigated. The suggestion score of face track f_i is defined as:

$$Sug_i = (1 - P_i) \cdot (\overline{Sai_i} + \overline{JS_i}) \quad (3)$$

In the formula, P_i is a function representing whether track f_i has been skipped by annotators at the labeling stage. P_i equals to 1 if it is, otherwise it is 0. $\overline{Sai_i}$ and $\overline{JS_i}$ are the normalized salience Sai_i and joint similarity JS_i of face track f_i. The face tracks are ranked and suggested to annotators according to their suggestion scores. The salience Sai_i is computed by:

$$Sai_i = e^{-s_\theta/s_i} + e^{-d_\theta/d_i} \quad (4)$$

In the formula, variable s_i and d_i are the average size and duration of track f_i, respectively. s_θ and d_θ are two thresholds set empirically to control the influence of the two variables. The salience measurement favors to suggest large and long face tracks.

On the other hand, JS_i suggests face tracks by considering both human factors and the similarity in Eq. (1). It is defined as:

$$JS_i = \sum_{j=1}^{K} L_j \cdot sim(f_i, f_j) \quad (5)$$

where K is the number of face tracks in the video, L_j is a function indicating the manual labeling status of track f_j. It equals to 1 if already labeled, and 0 if not labeled yet. JS_i gives higher score to tracks which are similar to previously labeled ones in general.

According to above formulas, the top ranked face tracks trend to have the following properties: salient in the video, visually similar, and nearby but no overlapped to previous annotated tracks. All the properties are basically in accordance with human perception habits. At the labeling stage, annotators can choose either the merging view or the labeling view to conduct the annotation.

2.4 Celebrity Images

Because of unfamiliar with the celebrities, it is common that annotators are unsure about who refers to the presented face track. In such cases, consulting external sources about relevant celebrities seems to be a wise choice. Based on this observation, we collect and present relevant celebrity images as follows.

Firstly, we use extracted celebrity names one-by-one to issue Google Image Search, and crawl the top ranked Web images for every celebrity. Secondly, the celebrities are ranked, according to the average similarity between images of the celebrity and the face track currently displayed in the labeling view, to decide which celebrity should be shown first. Thirdly, images of the shown celebrity are also ranked according to their similarity to the displayed face track, to determine which images to be presented.

2.5 Interface

The interface of CeleLabel consists of three building blocks, i.e., annotating area, reference area, and history. The annotating area provides the two annotation views: the merging view displays two most similar tracks, annotators can click either "same" to merge them, or "next" to load the next two most similar tracks; the labeling view displays a representative faces of the top ranked track and the celebrity names. Annotators can select a celebrity name, "unknown", or "Not Face" to label the track as a celebrity, an unknown person or a false positive track. The reference area presents a celebrity name and six of its images, helping annotators to compare and distinguish who refers to the track. Annotators can click "next" or "prev" to load the next or previous similar celebrity name and its images for reference. The history displays already labeled face tracks and their names, serving as a summary of the current annotation. Content of the three areas are updated dynamically with every labeling action. An illustrative demo of the system is available at www.youtube.com/watch?v=q_jFVIyMHek.

3. USER STUDY

To evaluate the effectiveness of CeleLabel, we recruit 10 assessors to experience the annotation using both the CeleLabel and a baseline system, which shows only face snapshots of a video and its surrounding title and tags. Our objective is to evaluate whether the annotation of celebrities in Web videos could be boosted by using the proposed CeleLabel.

In the study, 20 preprocessed Web videos are given. The assessors are divided into two groups each with 5 people. The first group is asked to annotate the first 10 videos using CeleLabel and the other 10 videos using the baseline system. On the contrary, the other group is asked to annotate the first 10 videos using the baseline and the other 10 videos using CeleLabel. They are asked to manually annotate all extracted face tracks. The time spent on annotation is automatically recorded by both systems. Besides, the scores (1-5) are given by each assessors to evaluate the user experience. The higher score indicates the higher satisfaction. The results show that compared with the baselines (326 seconds and 2.3 on average), CeleLabel achieves much better performance (147 seconds and 4.4 on average). Besides, all assessors agree on that the display of relevant celebrity images is quite helpful. Some assessors also point out that the show of annotation history is useful. The user study clearly shows, by offering more clues about the video and the celebrities to annotators, CeleLabel provides a much better labeling efficiency and satisfaction.

4. ACKNOWLEDGMENTS

The work described in this paper was supported by the National Natural Science Foundation of China (#61303175, #61228205).

5. REFERENCES

[1] P. Over et al. Trecvid 2011: an overview of the goals, tasks, data, evaluation mechanisms and metrics. *TREC Video Retrieval Evaluation*, 2011.

[2] Z. Chen, J. Cao, T. Xia, Y. Song, et al. Web video retagging. *Multimed. Tools Appl.*. 55(1): pp. 53-82, 2011.

[3] M. Everingham, J. Sivic, and A. Zisserman. Taking the bite out of automated naming of characters in TV video. *Image Vision Comput.*. 27(5): pp. 545-559, 2009.

FoodCam-256: A Large-scale Real-time Mobile Food Recognition System employing High-Dimensional Features and Compression of Classifier Weights

Yoshiyuki Kawano Keiji Yanai
Department of Informatics, The University of Electro-Communications
Chofu, Tokyo 182-8585 JAPAN
{kawano-y,yanai}@mm.cs.uec.ac.jp

ABSTRACT

In the demo, we demonstrate a large-scale food recognition system employing high-dimensional Fisher Vector and liner one-vs-rest classifiers. Since all the processes on image recognition perform on a smartphone, the system does not require an external image recognition server, and runs on an ordinary smartphone in a real-time way.

The proposed system can recognize 256 kinds of food by using the UEC-Food256 food image dataset we built by ourselves recently as a training dataset. To implement an image recognition system employing high-dimensional features on mobile devices, we propose linear weight compression method to save memory. In the experiments, we proved that the proposed compression methods make a little performance loss, while we can reduce the amount of weight vectors to 1/8. The proposed system has not only food recognition function but also the functions of estimation of food calorie and nutritious and recording a user's eating habits.

In the experiments with 100 kinds of food categories, we have achieved the 74.4% classification rate for the top 5 category candidates. The prototype system is open to the public as an Android-based smartphone application.

Categories and Subject Descriptors

H.4.0 [**Information Systems Applications**]: General

Keywords

mobile visual recognition; food image classification; mobile application

1. INTRODUCTION

In recent years, food habit recording services for smartphones have become popular. They can awake users' food habit problems such as bad food balance and unhealthy food trend, which is useful for disease prevention and diet. However, most of such services require selecting eaten food items from hierarchical menus by hand, which is too time-consuming and troublesome for most of the people to continue using such services for a long period.

Most of the existing mobile image recognition systems such as Google Goggles need to send images to high-performance servers, which must makes communication delay, requires communication costs, and the availability of which depends on network conditions. On the other hand, image recognition on the client side, that is, on a smartphone is much more promising in terms of availability, communication cost, delay, and server costs. Due to recent rapid progress of smartphones, they have obtained enough computational power for real-time image recognition. Then, by taking advantage of rich computational power of recent smartphones as well as recent advanced object recognition techniques, in this demo, we propose a real-time food recognition system which runs on a common smartphone. To boost accuracy and speed of food image recognition, we adopt high-dimensional Fisher Vector and linear classifiers with compressed weights, and implement a system as a multi-threaded system for using quad CPU cores effectively.

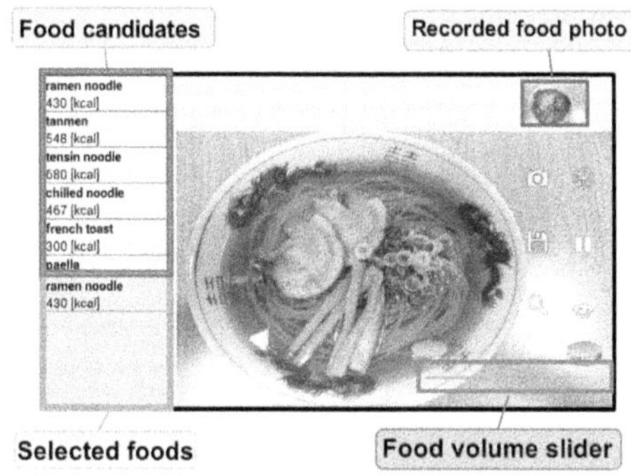

Figure 1: The screenshot of the main screen of the proposed system.

Since the recognition process on the proposed system is performed repeatedly about twice a second, a user can search for good position of a smartphone camera to recognize foods accurately by moving it continuously without pushing a camera shutter button. This is a big advantage of a real-time image recognition system on a mobile device.

We have implemented this system as an Android smartphone application so as to use quad CPU cores effectively for real-time recognition. As a result, the system takes only 0.19 second for one-time food recognition. In the experiments, we have achieved the 74.4% classification rate for the top 5 category candidates which outperformed the classification rate of our previous server-side food image recognition system.

To summarize novelties of the proposed system, it consists of three folds: The novelty of the proposed system is (1) recognizing a large number of food categories, 256 foods (2) adopting the state-of-the-art Fisher Vector with modified HoG (RootHoG) and color patches, and (3) using classifier weight compression which we newly proposed to realize a large-scale recognition with high dimensional features.

MM'14, November 03-07 2014, Orlando, FL, USA.
ACM 978-1-4503-3063-3/14/11.
http://dx.doi.org/10.1145/2647868.2654869.

2. SYSTEM OVERVIEW

The final objective of the proposed system is to support users to record daily foods and check their food eating habits. To do that easily, we embedded a large-scale food image recognition engine on the proposed system.

The processing flow of the proposed system is as follows:

1. A user points a smartphone camera toward food items before eating them. The system is continuously acquiring frame images from the camera device in the background.

2. Food recognition is carried out continuously about twice per second for the captured frame images.

3. We extract RootHoG patches and color patches, and code them into Fisher Vector (FV) representation with level-1 Spatial Pyramid. The total dimension of the FV is 35,840. We apply one-vs-rest linear classifiers with compressed weights to the FV, and obtain top five food candidates. Note that linear classifier weights are trained in advance with the UEC-Food256 data set.

4. After food image recognition, the top five food item candidates are shown on the screen as shown in Figure 1.

5. A user selects food items from the food candidate list by touching on the screen, if found. Before selecting food items, a user can indicate relative rough volume of selected food item by the slider on the right bottom on the screen for calorie estimation. If not, user moves a smartphone slightly and go back to 1.

6. The name, calorie and nutrition of the recognized food items are shown on the screen and are recorded in the system.

3. IMPLEMENTATION AND EVALUATION

In this section, we describe the implementation of the prototype system briefly.

3.1 New Food Dataset: UEC-Food256

UEC-Food256 is a newly-constructed food image dataset, which consists of 256 kinds of foods. Each category has more than 100 images. It has been built by extending UEC-Food100 [1] with transfer learning and crowd-sourcing automatically. The detail is submitted to ECCV2014 as a technical paper.

3.2 RootHoG and Color Patches with Fisher Vectors

We use RootHOG patches and Color patches as local features, and code them into Fisher Vectors (FV) with level-1 Spatial Pyramid after applying PCA. RootHOG is an element-wise square root of the L1 normalized HOG, which is inspired by "RootSIFT" [2]. In fact, in the preliminary experiments, RootHOG leaded to the better performance than original HOG. Finally, we obtain a 35,840-dim feature vector for each image.

3.3 Linear Classifier with Weight Compression

We adopt 1-vs-rest linear classifiers for estimation of food categories. To train linear classifier weights, we use AROW [3].

Since we have 256 food categories, the total amount of required memory to store all the classifier weight vectors in the float representation is 35MB. This is too much for one Android application. Then, we propose a scalar-based compression method for weight vectors of linear classifiers. This method has a good characteristic that we do not need to uncompress the compressed vector when evaluating the corresponding classifier.

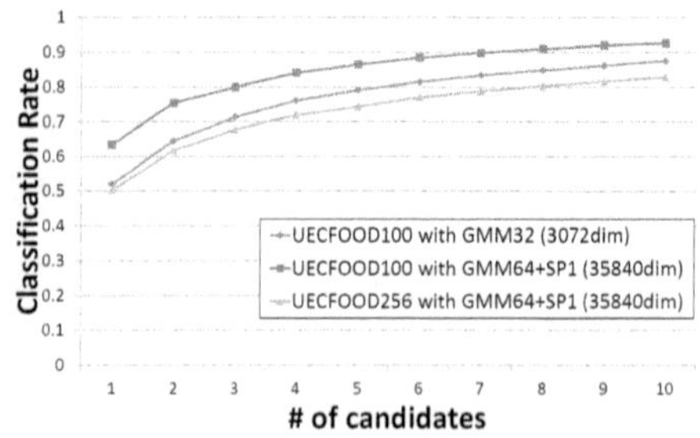

Figure 2: Classification rates by the proposed method and the our previous work [4]

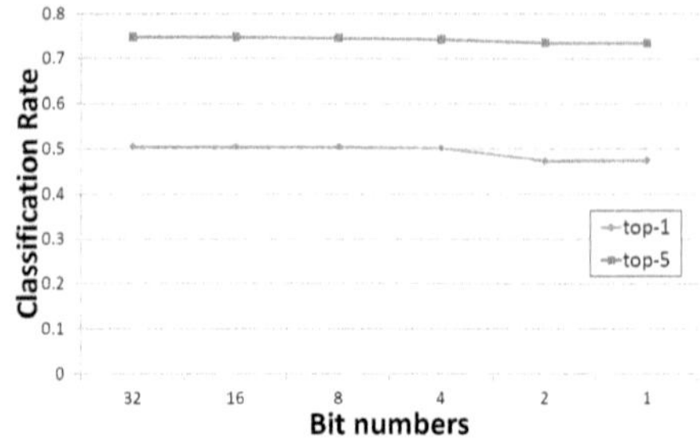

Figure 3: Classification rates with different compression ratio.

3.4 Evaluation

For reference, we show the experimental results on 256 food classification with 5-fold cross validation. The top-1 and top-5 rate were 50.1% and 74.4%, respectively. Figure3 shows the classification rate within the top n candidates. The blue lines corresponds to the previous work [4] where HoG and color patches with Fisher Vector was adopted for 100-class food classification. Because we adopted no weight compression in the previous work, possible dimension of the feature vector was 3072, which was much lower than this work. On the other hand, the proposed method can handle higher dimensional (35,840-dim) feature vectors with weight compression, which brings performance boost as shown in the red line in case of 100 categories. The recognition accuracy of the proposed system for 256 food categories is indicated by the green line, which is slightly below the previous 100 food category system. Introducing higher dimension features prevented large performance drop due to 2.5 times increase of the number of food categories.

Figure 3 shows the performance loss by linear classifier weight compression. When no compression is introduced, the bit number is 32. In the proposed system, we adopted the 4-bit, which brought 1/8 reduction of memory requirement to store weight vectors. The figure shows the 4-bit representation brought almost no perform ace drop.

Finally, we measured the processing time for one-time recognition using Samsung Galaxy NoteII (1.6GHz 4 cores, 4 threads, Android 4.1). We implemented the system so as to use quad-core effectively. As a result, it took only 0.19 seconds.

From these evaluations, we showed the effectiveness of our proposed method employing higher dimensional FV and linear weight compression.

Note that Android application of the proposed mobile food recognition system and the UEC-Food256 dataset can be downloaded from `http://foodcam.mobi/`.

4. REFERENCES

[1] Y. Matsuda, H. Hoashi, and K. Yanai, "Recognition of multiple-food images by detecting candidate regions," in *Proc. of ICME*, 2012.

[2] R Arandjelovic and A Zisserman, "Three things everyone should know to improve object retrieval," in *CVPR*, pp. 2911–2918, 2012.

[3] K Crammer, A Kulesza, and M. Dredze, "Adaptive regularization of weight vectors," *Machine Learning*, vol. 91, no. 2, pp. 155–187, 2013.

[4] Y. Kawano and K. Yanai, "Rapid mobile object recognition using fisher vector," in *Proc. of Asian Conference on Pattern Recognition*, 2013.

HMD Viewing Spherical Video Streaming System

Daisuke Ochi[†]
ochi.daisuke@lab.ntt.co.jp
Yutaka Kunita[†]
Kensaku Fujii[†]
Akira Kojima[†]

Shinnosuke Iwaki[††]
shinnosuke_iwaki@dwango.co.jp
Junichi Hirose[††]

[†]NTT Media Intelligence Laboratories, Nippon Telegraph and Telephone Corporation
1-1, Hikari-no-oka, Yokosuka-Shi, Kanagawa, Japan

[††]DWANGO Co., Ltd.
KABUKIZA TOWER., 4-12-15 Ginza, Chuo-ku, Tokyo, Japan

ABSTRACT

We propose a video streaming system that lets users view their favorite sections through an HMD (head mount display) from a video recorded by a spherical (360-degree) camera. Although spherical video streaming tends to consume a lot of bitrate for its huge image area, our system consumes a reasonable amount of bitrate by assigning higher bitrate only for the user's viewing area, not for the area outside of it. Technical Demos of the system with an Oculus Rift HMD will be performed to demonstrate it enables them to view images at a bitrate of about 2.5 Mbps.

Categories and Subject Descriptors

H.5.1 [Information Interfaces and Presentation]: Multimedia Information Systems—Video; H.5.2 [Information Interfaces and Presentation]: User Interfaces—Evaluation/methodology

General Terms

Design

Keywords

Head mount display; Spherical video; Video streaming; Immersive experience

1. INTRODUCTION

Providing an immersive experience to remote users has been a challenging problem for a number of years. The most recent focus in this regard has been on head mounted displays (HMDs) especially equipped with a sophisticated orientation sensor. The Oculus Rift HMD [1] occupies a leading position among HMDs due to the immersiveness with low image latency it provides after users have made head motions. These features enable users to get a feeling of genuine "presence," especially in computer graphics (CG) games such as those of the first-person shooter genre.

To provide greater reality, a number of services [2, 3] are now offering not CG but actual spherical (360-degree) video recorded by a spherical camera. These services allow users to view their favorite video sections as if they actually were at the remote site, through the use of many types of devices including HMDs. Unfortunately, most services merely offer local applications or ordinary streaming video with insufficient image quality. This is because spherical video tends to have much more area and consume much more bitrate than ordinary streaming video [4] for images of the same high quality.

To address this issue, we propose a spherical video streaming system that not only reduces the bitrate consumed by applying our previously reported approach [5], but also enables users to enjoy immersive experience by viewing a remote site through the HMD. In our approach, instead of assigning and streaming a video that has the same bitrate in all areas uniformly, videos that have different bitrates are streamed simultaneously. A higher bitrate is assigned for the user's viewing area while a lower one is assigned for other areas. To provide an even better viewing experience, the proposed system also implements a text communication style using comments, emoticons, or onomatopoeic words.

2. SYSTEM OVERVIEW

Our system mainly consists of two parts: the spherical video streaming system and the video player. The former's functions include video recording, encoding, and streaming. The latter is an HMD application for a viewing client. Specifics are given in the next two subsections.

2.1 Spherical Video Streaming System

First, a spherical video that is expanded into a rectangular shape is captured by a spherical camera (Fig.1A). Next, applying our approach [5], the system divides the video into many overlapped tile-shaped videos after copying it in low resolution that covers the whole area in one tile-shaped video. We then encode both every divided tile-shaped video in advance at higher bitrate (higher-bitrate video) and the

MM'14, November 3–7, 2014, Orlando, Florida, USA.
ACM 978-1-4503-3063-3/14/11.
http://dx.doi.org/10.1145/2647868.2654870

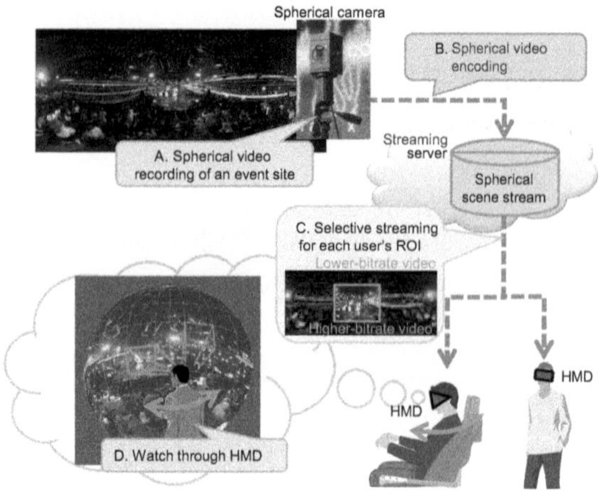

Figure 1: The concept of proposed system.

low resolution video at lower bitrate (lower-bitrate video) of H.264 Annex H (MVC) format (Fig.1B). Finally, one of the higher-bitrate videos requested by the player are sent in the HTTP protocol. Whenever one of them is sent, it is sent with the lower-bitrate video simultaneously (Fig.1C) so that no holes will be shown while the player is requesting another higher-bitrate video.

2.2 Video Player

The HMD worn by the viewing user is equipped with an orientation sensor whose values are used to fetch the higher-bitrate video for the user's gazing direction. After the video is fetched, it is remapped with the lower-bitrate video in the spherical coordinates and rendered (Fig.1D). The player requests another higher-bitrate video when it detects the user's head motion has stopped.

The user can also read comments posted by other users who are beyond the network; these are posted in the same space as that for the spherical video. These comments can help users identify the most exciting moments in the video.

3. DEMONSTRATIONS

We will conduct demonstrations of the system with an Oculus Rift HMD to help us appraise its performance. In the demonstrations, the system showed live performance contents recorded by a Ladybug3 [6] spherical camera. The original size of the captured video is 2560×1280 pixel size and its frame rate is 16 or 30 fps. The higher-bitrate video is sent along with the HMD orientation (Fig. 2(a)). The size of the higher-bitrate video in every 20° is 960×480 pixels, which covers almost all of the user's viewing area in the HMD display. We assign 2 Mbps and 0.5 Mbps bitrates for the higher- and lower-bitrate videos, respectively (Fig.3). These are reasonable values, although they are rather smaller than those for an actual network environment, e.g., the 8 Mbps recommendation for high definition (HD) size videos in YouTube [4]. With the system's current configuration, it takes 2.6 seconds on average to fetch a higher-bitrate video after detecting the user's head motion has stopped (Fig. 2(b) and 2(c)).

4. CONCLUSION

We have proposed a spherical video streaming system that not only reduces the bitrate consumed by applying our pre-

(a) Initial position (higher-bitrate video is in front of user's view).

(b) Right after the timing of (a) when user turns head to left.

(c) About 2.6 seconds later from (b) (the region follows user's head motion).

Figure 2: User's view examples in the HMD (images for left and right eyes).

(a) 0.5Mbps.

(b) 2Mbps.

Figure 3: A cropped examples from lower- and higher-bitrate video.

viously reported approach, but also enables users to enjoy immersive experience by viewing a remote site from an actual video through a head mounted display (HMD).

In future, it will be necessary for us to show our system's validity by conducting user studies regarding such factors as the arrival latency of higher-bitrate video, video quality, and client usability. In terms of the interface, another challenge will be to develop a method fortyping out the comments users make while wearing the HMD.

5. REFERENCES

[1] Oculus VR, Inc., Oculus Software Development Kit Overview, *https://developer.oculusvr.com/*, 2014.

[2] MATIvision, Dream Theater 360, *http://www.mativision.com/*, 2014.

[3] Immersive Video Solutions, im 360, *http://www.immersivevideosolutions.com*, 2013.

[4] YouTube, LLC, Advanced encoding settings, *https://support.google.com/youtube/answer/1722171?hl= en.*

[5] H. Kimata, D. Ochi, A. Kameda, H. Noto, K. Fukazawa, and A. Kojima, Mobile and Multi-device Interactive Panorama Video Distribution System, *2012 IEEE 1st Global Conference on Consumer Electronics* (*GCCE2012*), 574-578, October 2012.

[6] Point Grey Research, Inc., Ladybug3 Product Data Sheet, *http://ww2.ptgrey.com/*.

Jiku Director 2.0: A Mobile Video Mashup System with Zoom and Pan Using Motion Maps

Duong-Trung-Dung Nguyen
National University of Singapore
nguyend1@comp.nus.edu.sg

Axel Carlier
Université de Toulouse
axel.carlier@enseeiht.fr

Wei Tsang Ooi
National University of Singapore
ooiwt@comp.nus.edu.sg

Vincent Charvillat
Université de Toulouse
vincent.charvillat@enseeiht.fr

ABSTRACT

In this demonstration, we show an automated mobile video mashup system that takes a set of videos filming the same scene as input, and generate an output mashup video consisting of temporally coherent clips selected from these input videos. The key difference of our system over the existing state-of-the-art is that it can generate virtual close-up shots and three camera operations: zooming in, zooming out, and panning, automatically. To achieve this, the system first computes the motion maps of the input videos and then determines a set of rectangles that correspond to highly interesting regions (in terms of motion). The choice of which shot types to use is done heuristically, ensuring diversity and coherency in the content presented in the mashup.

Categories and Subject Descriptors: H.5.1 [Multimedia Information Systems]: Video; I.2.10 [Vision and Scene Understanding]: Video Analysis; Motion

Keywords: Mobile Video; Virtual Director; Video Mashup

1. INTRODUCTION

The proliferation of mobile devices equipped with high-quality cameras and video capturing software has led to a new phenomenon – during public events, it is common to have many people filming the scene at the same time. A single video filmed by a user, however, might not capture the scene completely, due to tired arms, depleted battery, limited viewing angle, etc. Furthermore, mobile videos tend to be of low quality, due to shaking hands, occlusion, and overexposure/underexposure. Even if the above problems are avoided, a video filmed from one single viewpoint is monotonous and could be boring to watch.

To address these issues, researchers have proposed algorithms and systems that automatically stitch the videos filmed by multiple users (of the same event) into a mashup video that is temporally coherent, by switching between the videos. The system operates much like a human director that switches between different cameras shooting an event. Two such prominent systems are the *Virtual Director* system proposed by Shrestha et al. [3] and the *Jiku Director* system developed by us [1].

We have extended Jiku Director with the ability to automatically zoom and pan. This extension is the focus of this demonstration and is motivated by the following. The existing systems produce a mashup video that always shows the scenes as filmed by the users. This limitation has two implications. First, the camera motions in these mashups are limited only to the physical movement of the cameras or zoom control operated by the users when they filmed the scene. In contrast, human directors often adopt zooming in, zooming out, and panning, as a way to add dynamics into the camera shots. Second, the field size[1] of the produced mashup is limited by that decided by the users when they filmed the scene (which are mostly long to medium shots). In contrast, human directors use a mixed of shot types, including close-up shots to affect the narrative of the production.

The new version of Jiku Director (2.0) addresses the lack of camera motions and close-up shots in the following way. The system, besides deciding which input video to use in the output mashup video, also decides a region of interest (ROI) in the selected input videos. The ROI can then be cropped to produce a close-up shot. Virtual camera motions can be produced in the mashup (through cropping) to simulate zooming effects in to, or out from, the ROI. The system could also decide to have two ROIs, and virtually pans the camera from one ROI to another.

The next section describes (i) how the system computes the ROIs, (ii) how it decides which ROI to use, and finally (iii) which shot type/camera motions to generate in the output.

2. JIKU DIRECTOR 2.0

2.1 Background

We begin with a brief description of Jiku Director. Readers are referred to [1] for a description of the system, and to [2] for a detailed description of MoViMash, the underlying mashup algorithm.

Jiku Director is a Web-based application for sharing user-generated videos. A screenshot of the system is shown in Figure 1. A user can upload videos of an event which they have filmed and share it with others. The videos are organized based on events. For each event, Jiku Director can generate a "representative" video of the event, by mashing up all the videos (of that event) that have

[1] Field size refers to how much of the subject and the surrounding area is framed in a shot

MM'14, November 3–7, 2014, Orlando, Florida, USA.
ACM 978-1-4503-3063-3/14/11. http://dx.doi.org/10.1145/2647868.2654884.

been uploaded. At each decision time, the mashup algorithm first filters out bad quality videos (shaky, tilted, occluded) through simple content-based analysis. The remaining videos are then selected based on the view angle and distance to the stage of the event. The algorithm imitates a human director (through learning from professionally edited videos) in deciding which angle and distance to choose and what is the length of the clip to use from the chosen video. If there is more than one video with approximately the same angle and distance, the algorithm picks the clip from the best quality video camera that has not been recently picked before.

Figure 1: Screenshot of the Web Interface of Jiku Director

2.2 Computing Candidate ROIs

To support zooming and panning in Jiku Director, we first need to compute the "interesting regions" for each video. A region is defined by a 3D ((x, y) coordinates and time) bounding box, parameterized by its position, width, height, starting and ending frame.

To build the bounding boxes, we start by computing the motion maps at each frame, normalizing the difference between the current frame and the previous frame. The motion map obtained is viewed as a probability distribution, following which we sample 500 points for each frame. We therefore build a set of moving points with three coordinates: two spatial coordinates (in pixels), and one temporal coordinate (frame index).

We use Mean-Shift clustering to cluster the moving points. Mean-Shift converges towards the modes of a distribution, which, in our case, are the spatio-temporal regions with the highest quantity of motion. It also associates each point from the data to one mode to build clusters. We ignore transient clusters that exist less than one second or clusters with too few (< 30) moving points in each frame.

For each remaining cluster, we create one corresponding bounding box. The starting frame (resp. ending frame) of the bounding box is the minimum (resp. maximum) of the third coordinate value from all points in the cluster. To determine the remaining parameters of the bounding box, we use the Levenberg-Marquardt algorithm to compute the smaller bounding box that contains at least 95% of all points in the cluster. We use this threshold to limit the size of the bounding boxes, and allow for larger zooms during the video mashup. Figure 2 shows bounding boxes from two sample frames filmed from two different cameras.

Figure 2: Bounding Boxes

2.3 Deciding the ROI

Each object appearing in each frame is associated with a bounding box and a centroid with a weight indicating the average number of clustering points of the associated cluster per frame.

We rank the bounding box of each object in order of their importance in the scene. In each video clip, each object i has an *importance* value, $I(i, t) = \sum_j v_j(t)w_j(t)$, where $v_j(t)$ is 1 if object j appears in the bounding box i at time t and 0 otherwise; $w_j(t)$ is the average number of clustering points of cluster j per frame at time t. The intuition here is that a bounding box with more clustering points is more important. Note that even though each bounding box is associated with an object, other objects may appear in the bounding box. Naturally, a bounding box that contains multiple important objects becomes important.

2.4 Choosing the Shot Type

The output of our heuristic for selecting the next shot will be a sequence of *shots* (t, j, B, l, m), where t is the beginning time of the shot, j is the camera to choose the shot from, B is the set of regions of interest to use in this shot, l is the length of the shot, and m is the virtual camera movement in this shot.[2]

Jiku Director will decide the best camera j in each shot. Once j is fixed, we determine t, B, l, and m as follows. Let L_{max} be the maximum possible shot length (we use $L_{max} = 7s$). To determine the current shot, we look at the most important bounding boxes and objects at each time instance for the next L_{max} seconds in the video shot by camera j. B is set to the most important bounding boxes that frequently appear in the next L_{max}. To decide l (and therefore, the next t), we stop the current shot at the time when these bounding boxes disappear.

It remains to determine m for the current shot. The choice of m can be either: wide-angle shot, close-up shot, move the camera (zoom in, zoom out, or pan). The heuristic follows the following principles: (i) there should not be frequent camera movement, and (ii) the choice of m should observe continuity editing. It should avoid an abrupt illogical shot transition. To do that, a wide-angle shot is used after each close-up, zoom or pan shot as a re-establishing shot.

3. DEMONSTRATION

During the demonstration, we will show the features of Jiku Director in general, with a focus on generation of a mashup video that consists of zoom and pan camera motion and close up shots.

Acknowledgement. This research is supported by the Singapore National Research Foundation under its International Research Centre @ Singapore Funding Initiative and administered by the IDM Programme Office.

4. REFERENCES

[1] D.-T.-D. Nguyen, M. Saini, V.-T. Nguyen, and W. T. Ooi. Jiku Director: a mobile video mashup system. In *Proceedings of the ACM Multimedia*, MM '13, pages 477–478, Barcelona, Spain, 2013.

[2] M. K. Saini, R. Gadde, S. Yan, and W. T. Ooi. MoViMash: Online mobile video mashup. In *Proceedings of the ACM Multimedia*, MM '12, pages 139–148, Nara, Japan, 2012.

[3] P. Shrestha, H. Weda, M. Barbieri, E. H. Aarts, et al. Automatic mashup generation from multiple-camera concert recordings. In *Proceedings of the ACM Multimedia*, MM '10, pages 541–550, Florence, Italy, 2010.

[2] In contrast, the first version of Jiku Director only decides on (t, j, l).

ClockDrift: A Mobile Application for Measuring Drift in Multimedia Devices

Mario Guggenberger
mg@itec.aau.at

Mathias Lux
mlux@itec.aau.at

Laszlo Böszörmenyi
lb@itec.aau.at

Institute of Information Technology
Alpen-Adria-Universität Klagenfurt
9020 Klagenfurt am Wörthersee, Austria

ABSTRACT

Parallel recordings made at the same event with different devices, e.g. by visitors of a concert, contain semantically the same content but do not run at the same speed when played back in parallel on a computer, which makes their synchronization difficult. This effect, time drift, concerns all current consumer multimedia recording devices and results from their internal clocks not running at the same speed, leading to deviations from their nominal sampling rates. We present a mobile application capable of conducting instant measurements of this time drift, thus helping in determining devices that go well together, or correcting the speed differences in post processing.

Categories and Subject Descriptors

H.5.1 [**Information Interfaces and Presentation**]: Multimedia Information Systems—*Audio input/output*; H.5.5 [**Information Interfaces and Presentation**]: Sound and Music Computing—*Signal analysis, synthesis, and processing*

Keywords

Audio, recording, clock drift, time drift, synchronization

1. INTRODUCTION

Electronic devices like smartphones, tablets, audio recorders and video cameras are usually based on complex electronic circuits, whose actions are coordinated by clock signals. These signals are generated by crystal oscillators, which usually do not exactly run at their specified nominal frequency, but deviate a little bit and are also prone to environmental influences. This means that a clock signal oscillating at 1 Hz nominal frequency will in reality, when measured in UTC time, oscillate at a rate of $1 + \epsilon$ Hz, where the error, called *drift*, is usually very small but measurable. Since the audio codec's sample rate and the video codec's frame rate

MM'14, November 3–7, 2014, Orlando, Florida, USA.
ACM 978-1-4503-3063-3/14/11.
http://dx.doi.org/10.1145/2647868.2654886.

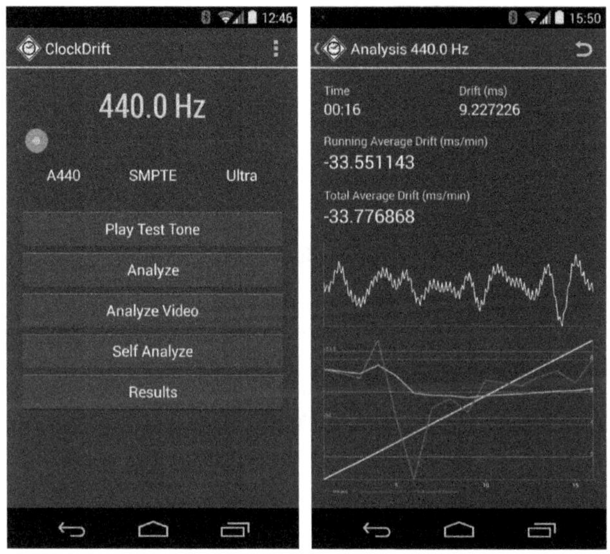

(a) Main menu (b) Analysis screen

Figure 1: The main screens in our app: (a) contains the main functions, (b) shows the drift in ms/min (can be switched to ppm, ms/h, s/h, frequency and percentage by tapping), the zero-crossing distances in green and the measurement progress chart on the bottom.

are derived from this signal, they are also influenced by the drift. This leads to playback and recording processes being carried out slightly off their nominal rates (like e.g. specified in the file header) and results in stretched or reduced nominal run times, whose deviation we call *time drift*. This deviation leads to problems when synchronizing parallel recordings made with different devices at the same event, e.g. at a music concert. When comparing the recordings side by side, one can often notice that their speeds do not match perfectly and they, when synchronized at some point, will drift apart and not stay in sync during their whole length. Depending on the drift rate, it becomes noticeable to humans after some hours in the best case, and after a few minutes in the worst case. This concerns recordings from uncontrolled environments, e.g. crowd sourced videos from music concerts, as well as coordinated productions by amateurs. A very basic example for an amateur production is a recording of a talk or interview with a video camera and a separate audio recording from a high quality voice recorder, and adding a second camera perspective or an additional audio recording of the interviewer or audience only makes the problem worse. Due to cost, many amateurs do not have any alternatives but using unsynchronized consumer/prosumer equipment which is susceptible to the drift problem. In highly professional environments, devices are usually fed by a common master clock signal at recording time to avoid this problem. In the scientific multimedia community, we could only find one recent paper addressing the problem [1] and none proposing a solution. In this demo, we are going to focus on the audio sampling rate drift and present a mobile application specifically made to quickly measure the drift rate in multimedia devices.

2. TIME DRIFT

Clock drift leads to deviations in the audio playback and recording sample rates in devices, which result in pitch shifts in, and bandwidth changes of the transmitted signals, but also impact the run times of played or recorded files. This change of run time is what we call the time drift. While drift in oscillators is commonly specified in parts per million (ppm), we specify it in milliseconds per minute (ms/min) for more intuitive understanding.

To measure the relative drift between two devices A and B, we play back a sine wave with a nominal frequency f_n on device A, and record it with device B. We then measure the frequency f_r in the recorded data and use it to calculate the total drift factor $d_t = f_n/f_r$. In case of drift, f_r is slightly off f_n and therefore the factor slightly off 1. This kind of measurement is sufficient to compensate the drift in recordings made with two or more devices by measuring all devices from one reference playback device and resampling or stretching the recordings according to the calculated drift factor. Measuring the absolute drift of a device off UTC time requires a calibrated measurement device, e.g a high-precision spectrum analyzer. Again, the device to be measured plays back a sine wave at f_n Hz and the playback drift factor $d_p = f_n/f_p$ can be determined through the measured frequency output f_p from the playback device. Since the hardware audio codec of a device C derives the playback sample rate from the same clock signal as the recording sample rate, we can assume that both sample rates are the same, thus both drift factors are equal and therefore $d_p^C \equiv d_r^C$.

Table 1 lists measurements of several different devices. It is important to note that the measured values are not absolute constants since temperature has measurable influence on the drift, and there is a variance between devices of the same model. Exemplary measurements of different devices have shown a variance of ≈ 1 ms/min between $-20\,°C$ and $+50\,°C$ in temperature, and a standard deviation of ≈ 0.1 ms/min between five LG Nexus 5 and eight Asus Nexus 7 devices. These values clearly show that there are huge differences between different devices, which make certain multimedia use cases, e.g. the synchronization of parallel and overlapping recordings of events, a non-trivial task.

3. CLOCKDRIFT APP

Our app is available for free through the Google Play Store[1]. Its two fundamental functions are to (i) act as a playback source by playing out a test signal, and to (ii) act

[1]http://www-itec.aau.at/~maguggen/clockdrift/

Table 1: Measured drifts of various multimedia recording devices in ms/min.

Device	Type	Drift
Acer Iconia A200	Tablet	0.8
Apple iPad 2 Wi-Fi	Tablet	0.8
Apple iPod touch 4G	Media Player	25.0
Asus Nexus 7 2012 Wi-Fi	Tablet	0.2
LG Nexus 4	Smartphone	0.4
Samsung Galaxy Note 10.1	Tablet	1.0
Samsung Galaxy S II	Smartphone	16.4
Samsung Galaxy Spica	Smartphone	-0.9

as a recording target that analyzes the incoming signal on the fly and displays the measured drift to the user. The main screens are shown in Figure 1. A measurement works by playing a sine wave at the source and isolating it at the target from the incoming signal with a narrow band-pass filter centered around the chosen frequency, which can be freely adjusted by the user up into the imperceptible ultrasonic band. The filtered signal then gets further processed by measuring the distances between consecutive zero-crossings of the waveform and averaging them over time, resulting in a precise frequency measurement that can be transformed to a drift reading. The distances are calculated to sub-sample precision by linearly interpolating the zero-crossing points from their neighboring sample values, which almost instantly leads to a precise drift rate determination. The measurement is further improved by determining the strength of the incoming signal and only measuring while its energy is sufficient, else the analysis gets paused and a hint shown to the user. The measurements can be stored locally on the device. This data also contains additional device metadata, which can, together with the measurement data, be submitted to our server with the goal to build a database of device drift indicators. A detailed user guide explaining all the app's functionality is available online[1].

4. CONCLUSION

We presented a method to measure the clock drift or time drift in multimedia devices capable of audio playback or recording, and described our Android app specifically developed for the purpose of quick on-the-go measurements of the drift. We have shown that common, often used devices like smartphones can suffer from enormous drift that makes the synchronization of even short recordings with a few minutes length impossible without further post-processing. In possible future work we will take a look specifically at video recording, which in a minority of devices seems to depend on another clock source and leads to different measurement results compared to audio only recordings.

5. ACKNOWLEDGMENTS

This work was supported by Lakeside Labs GmbH, Klagenfurt, Austria, and funding from the European Regional Development Fund (ERDF) and the Carinthian Economic Promotion Fund (KWF) under grant 20214/22573/33955.

6. REFERENCES

[1] A. L. Casanovas and A. Cavallaro. Audio-visual events for multi-camera synchronization. *Multimedia Tools and Applications*, March 2014.

Scalable Image Search with Reliable Binary Code

Guangxin Ren†, Junjie Cai‡, Shipeng Li§, Nenghai Yu† and Qi Tian‡
†University of Science and Technology of China
‡Univeristy of Texas at San Antonio
§Microsoft Research Asia
gxren@mail.ustc.edu.cn; xmq994@my.utsa.edu; spli@microsoft.com;
ynh@ustc.edu.cn; qitian@cs.utsa.edu

ABSTRACT

In many existing image retrieval algorithms, Bag-of-Words (BoW) model has been widely adopted for image representation. To achieve accurate indexing and efficient retrieval, local features such as the SIFT descriptor are extracted and quantized to visual words. One of the most popular quantization scheme is scalar quantization, which generates binary signature with an empirical threshold value. However, such binarization strategy inevitably suffers from the quantization loss induced by each quantized bit and impairs the effectiveness of search performance. In this paper, we investigate the reliability of each bit in scalar quantization and propose a novel reliable binary SIFT feature. We move one step ahead to incorporate the reliability in both index word expansion and feature similarity. Our proposed approach not only accelerates the search speed by narrowing search space, but also improves the retrieval accuracy by alleviating the impact of unreliable quantized bits. Experimental results demonstrate that the proposed approach achieves significant improvement in retrieval efficiency and accuracy.

Categories and Subject Descriptors

H.3.3 [**Information Search and Retrieval**]: Retrieval Models

General Terms

Information Search and Retrieval

Keywords

Binary code; Image Search

1. INTRODUCTION

This paper considers the task of near duplicate image retrieval in large scale databases. Given a query image, our goal is to find all images sharing similar appearance in real time. As the well-known saying goes, "A picture is worth a thousand words", images generally convey large amount of information. Many state-of-the-art retrieval systems rely on the Bag-of-Words (BoW) representation [,]. In this model, local features such as the SIFT descriptor [ ] are extracted and quantized to *visual words* using a pre-trained *codebook*. Then, an inverted index is leveraged to reduce computational burden and memory requirements, enabling fast on-line retrieval. However, conventional retrieval strategy has several drawbacks: (1) the visual codebook has to be trained in advance and the training process is computationally expensive especially with a large amount of sample features. (2) the effectiveness of codebook construction in feature quantization relies on the collection of image features and codebook generation methods (e.g. Vocabulary Tree [ ], k-means). (3) with many new features collected, updating a large visual codebook requires a wealth of effort and re-clustering features is computationally inefficient. Stepping into the era of big data, the explosive growth of Web images motivates us to restudy this problem in a very large scale.

Instead of being trapped in such dilemmas, researchers have explored a myriad of approaches to improve search performance. Jegou *et al.* [ ] proposed the Vector of Locally Aggregated Descriptors(VLAD) which are derived from local descriptors to replace the Bag-of-Words histogram. But search results of the VLAD pipeline are severely limited to the cluster center of training sets. Any cluster inconsistency can severely impact search performance. In addition, a couple of compact and efficient binary feature descriptors(e.g. ORB [ ], FREAK [ ], BRISK [ ]) have been proposed for visual matching applications. Among them, Zhou *et al.* [ ] proposed a novel binary SIFT with *Scalar Quantization*(SQ), which is free from any kind of training or codebook generation step. Specifically, it directly binarizes each bin of original 128-bin SIFT descriptors based on the intrinsic characteristic (median value). To reduce the quantization loss from binarization, index word expansion strategy has been adopted to improve the search recall. Experimental results reveal that this simple quantization approach outperforms several state-of-art quantization approaches, such as soft assignment approaches [ ]. However, some quantized feature bits are unreliable under the heuristic quantization framework. For the original bins whose magnitudes are closer to the quantizing threshold (median value), they are less likely to generate reliable quantized bits due to the noise and threshold selection. These unreliable quantized bits will degrade the retrieval accuracy.

Motivated by the above observations, we explicitly address the reliability issue for scalar quantization and present an image retrieval framework with reliable binary SIFT descriptor. We investigate and overcome the reliability obstacles in three aspects, which are feature quantization, index word expansion and feature similarity respectively. First, we quantize the original feature bins into binary features and then incorporate reliability information of each bin with its distance to the threshold. Second, expanded index words are generated by flipping the unreliable bits, which greatly narrow the necessary search space and benefit efficiency. At last,

MM'14, November 3–7, 2014, Orlando, Florida, USA.

http://dx.doi.org/10.1145/2647868.2654956.

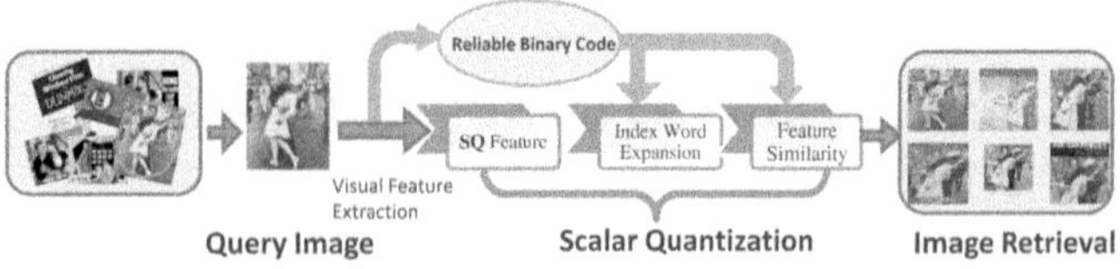

Figure 1: Flowchart of scalable image search with reliable binary code.

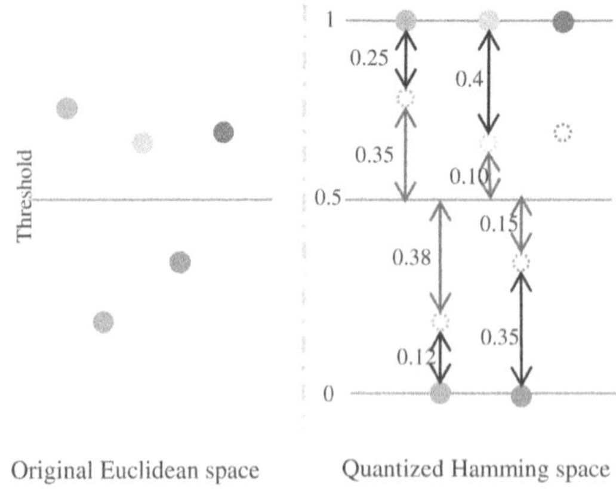

Figure 2: A toy example to visualize unreliable bits problem.

we leverage a weighted Hamming distance to reduce the impact of unreliable bits, so that effective image retrieval can be achieved. Figure 1 illustrates our proposed framework in comparison with the approach of scalar quantization.

The main contribution of this paper can be summarized as follows:

- We investigate and address the reliability problem for scalar quantization with a novel reliable binary SIFT descriptor.
- We evaluate the proposed binary descriptor and demonstrate its efficiency and effectiveness in two public image datasets: DupImage and Holidays.

The rest of this paper is organized as follows. In Section 2, we describe the formulation of our proposed method, including constructing reliable binary code and indexing with inverted file structure. Experimental results on two publicly available datasets are reported in Section 3, followed by the conclusion in Section 4.

2. SEARCH WITH RELIABLE BINARY CODE

In this section, we first explicitly indicate the problem of unreliable bit in SQ. Then, we describe how to extract reliable feature from original feature and explore them in the inverted file structure.

2.1 Revisit Scalar Quantization

Different from traditional codebook-based methods, SQ does not need any training or codebook generation step. The generated descriptor achieves compact representation of the original SIFT descriptor and demonstrates to well keep the discriminative power of SIFT feature. Specifically, given a SIFT descriptor represented as $(f_1, f_2, ...f_{128})^T$, a 256-bit binary feature $\mathbf{b}$ can be produced as follows:

$$(b_i, b_{i+128}) = \begin{cases} (1,1), & \text{if } f_i > \hat{th}_1, \\ (1,0), & \text{if } \hat{th}_2 \le f_i \le \hat{th}_1, \\ (0,0), & \text{if } f_i \le \hat{th}_2 \end{cases} \quad (1)$$

where $b_i (i = 1, 2, \ldots, 256)$ is the ith entry of the resulting binary feature $\mathbf{b}$. Thresholds $\hat{th}_1 = (g_{64} + g_{65})/2$ and $\hat{th}_2 = (g_{32} + g_{22})/2$, where $(g_1, g_2, ..., g_{128})^T$ is the sorted vector of $(f_1, f_2, ...f_{128})^T$ in descending order. Then the top 32 bits of SQ feature is utilized as index word. However, the simple process of feature quantization might miss some candidate features which have some flipping bits(e.g. 0 to 1) on top 32-bit index words caused by noise. As the toy example shown in Figure 2, the quantization threshold is 0.5. If a bin magnitude is larger than threshold, it would be binarized to 1, otherwise, to 0. Compared with green and blue bins, the yellow and red bins are much close to the threshold and the quantized bits of two bins are less reliable since they are generated with large quantization error (red: 0.35, yellow: 0.4). The disadvantages of these unreliable quantized bits are: (1) large quantization error would cause Hamming distance of unreliable quantized bits fail to capture real Euclidean distance of original bins. (2) the quantized result of unreliable bits are much easier to be distributed by noise. For instance, if the noise decreases the original bin by 0.12 that is imposed on yellow bin, then the quantized bit would flip 1 to 0, but it has no impact on quantized bit on blue one. Such unreliable quantized bit problem is non-trival, due to its significant impact on both search speed and retrieval accuracy.

2.2 Construct Reliable Binary Code

Since unreliable quantized bits are harmful, we should indicate which quantized bits are unreliable during scalar quantization and make special treatment on them in retrieval process. In the step of feature quantization, we propose a 256-D reliable binary code $(r_1, r_2, ..., r_{256})^T$ to indicate reliable quantized bit:

$$r_i = \begin{cases} 0, \text{if } d_i < d \\ 1, \text{if } d_i \ge d \end{cases} \quad (2)$$

where d_i is the distance of feature f_i to quantized threshold:

$$d_i = \begin{cases} \left| f_i - \hat{th}_1 \right|, & \text{if } i = 1, ..., 128 \\ \left| f_{i-128} - \hat{th}_2 \right|, & \text{if } i = 129, ..., 256 \end{cases} \quad (3)$$

We simply set the parameter d to be s_n where $(s_1, s_2, ..., s_{256})$ is the sorted order of $(d_1, d_2, ..., d_{256})$ in ascending order, since total number of unreliable bits could be adjusted by n directly.

Inspired by SQ, to find the candidate features which have some flipping bits, an index word expansion step is introduced to enumerate all bit flipping possibilities without discrimination. Due to the limit of time cost, the SQ index word expansion scheme can handle at most 2 flipping bits and produce $529(C_{32}^2 + C_{32}^1 + 1)$ index words [ ]. In Figure 2, we could see that the bit flipping is more likely to happen on unreliable quantized bits. Hence, we propose the index word expansion by only flipping the unreliable bits. In this case, we can deal with more flipping bits with smaller search space. For instance, if we handle 8 flipping bits that are caused by unreliable quantized bits, then we generate $256(2^8)$ index words which is almost half of 529 index words generated by SQ scheme. The toy example of two index word expansion schemes are illustrated in Figure 3.

The distance on unreliable quantized bits has been amplified after quantization which impairs discriminative power of quantized bits in Hamming space. To alleviate such impact induced by unreliable bits, we formulate and adjust the weight on distance calculation:

$$Dist = w_1 \cdot H_r + w_2 \cdot H_u \quad (4)$$

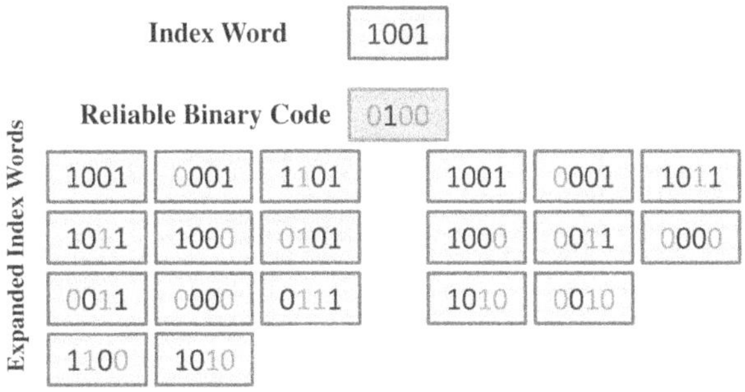

(a) SQ Flipping scheme (b) RBC Flipping Scheme

Figure 3: Toy example of index word expansion in (a) Scalar Quantization(SQ) with 2 flipping bits expansion (b) RSC flipping scheme with 3 flipping bits on unreliable bits expansion.

where H_r is Hamming distance on reliable quantized bits and H_u is the distance on unreliable quantized bits. The parameters w_1 and w_2 are the weights to adjust the combination and are empirically set to 1 and 0.25 in this paper.

2.3 Search with Inverted File Structure

In image search, the problem of feature matching between images can be considered as finding a feature's nearest or approximately nearest neighbors within a certain range. When the feature amount becomes very large, say, over one million, it is too computationally expensive to find the nearest neighbors by linearly comparing all of features' binary vectors. To address this issue, an inverted file structure, which is leveraged from text retrieval, can be used for scalable indexing of a large-scale image dataset.

In traditional inverted-file structure for image search, a group of visual words are pre-trained. Each visual word is followed with an entry list of image features which were quantized to visual word. Each indexed feature in the list records its image ID and some other clues [ ]. In our work, for a descriptor q in a query image, we utilize first 32 bit as the index words and the rest bits of features are recorded in the entry list of the corresponding code word. We formulate the image retrieval as a voting problem. Each verified feature casts a vote to the corresponding target image. We define the similarity between two images by cardinality of matched feature set. Finally, the target images are ranked by their similarity scores and returned to the users as retrieved results.

3. EXPERIMENTS

We conduct experimental comparisons with several state-of-the-art approaches, including Vocabulary Tree(VT) [ ] and Scalar Quantization [ ]. We also evaluate performance using only Indexed Word Expansion and only Hamming Distance calculation, named as IWE and HD, respectively. The evaluation is performed on two publicly available datasets, DupImage [ ] and Holidays [ ]. We implemented the experiments on a server with a 16-core 2.4GHz and 16 GB memory. Similar to [ ][ ], mean Average Precision(mAP) is adopted to evaluate the performance of all methods.

3.1 Evaluation on DupImage Dataset

The DupImage dataset contains 1104 images collected from 33 groups, including "Mona Lisa", "StarBucks Logo" etc. We mix the dataset with one million images crawled from the Web. To evaluate the performance with respect to the size of dataset, we construct three smaller dataset ($50K$,$200K$, and $500K$) by sampling the dataset. For baseline approaches of Vocabulary Tree and

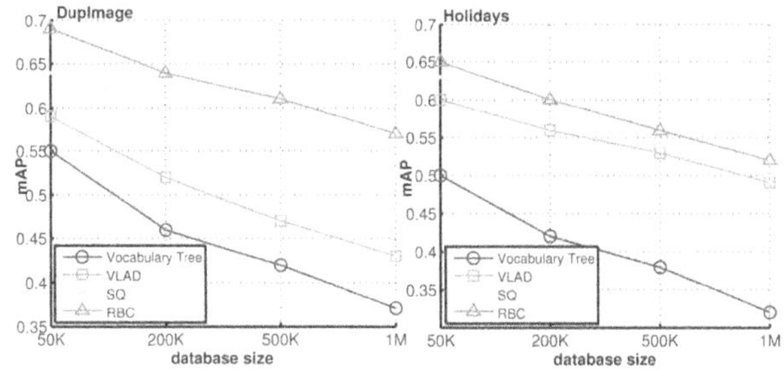

Figure 4: Image retrieval performance comparison of various methods with different database sizes.

Table 1: mAP performance comparison for one million database size.

Methods	VT	VLAD	SQ	IWD	HD	RBC
DupImage	0.37	0.44	0.54	0.55	0.57	**0.58**
Holidays	0.32	0.49	0.50	0.51	0.51	**0.53**

VLAD, the following parameter setting is utilized: we adopt one-million visual codebook (a vocabulary tree with branch factor as 10 and level number as 6). In VLAD, The dictionary size is 64 and the parameter of power-law normalization is 0.5. And for Scalar Quantization, the Hamming distance is set as 24 and 2 bits are flipped to produce 529 expanded index words. As aforementioned, we set the total number of unreliable bits n as 40 and at most 8 flipping bits are handled in index word expansion step. The Hamming distance parameters w_1 and w_2 are empirically selected as 1 and 0.25,respectively. Figure 4 provides the performance comparison of different approaches in terms of mAP. We can see that our scheme based on Reliable Binary Code (RBC) outperforms both VT and SQ approaches. Our approach demonstrates consistent superiority over conventional approaches for all tested dataset sizes.

In addition, we observe from the comparison each variant of RBC-based approach (IWD, HD) can improve the retrieval accuracy, this is mainly due to two reasons. First, the procedure of IWD is constructed to find missed candidates via flipping more unreliable bits. Second, the HD step reduces the weight of unreliable bits such that the modified distance can better reflect Euclidean distance of original feature bins. Moreover, Table 1 illustrates the mAP comparisons when we investigate the variants of our proposed RBC approach. We can see that it achieves the best performance and yields an mAP of 0.54 when the complementary capacity of two steps are fully explored. It shows that search performance significantly improves when we utilize the proposed reliable binary codes.

3.2 Evaluation on Holidays Dataset

To further test the effectiveness of our algorithm, we validate it on the Holidays dataset. This dataset contains personal holiday photos provided by INRIA [ ]. The dataset itself contains 1491 images. A subset of 500 images serves as queries. Each query is compared to the other 1490 images in a leave-one-out fashion. To evaluate the performance on a large scale, a distractor dataset of one million images downloaded from Flickr is also provided.

We use the same parameter setting as selected in the previous subsection. Figure 4 shows the performance comparison results of our approach with baseline approaches. When the size of dataset is 50K, our method achieves a mAP of 0.65 and obtains 28.0% and 8.3% relative improvement compared with VT and SQ, respectively. It can also be observed that our approach shows consistent

Table 2: Comparison on average query time cost of different methods on the one-million image database.

Methods	VT	VLAD	SQ	RBC
Time(seconds)	0.11	0.10	0.47	**0.24**

Table 3: Time cost comparison to index one million features for all approaches.

Methods	VT	VLAD	SQ	RBC
Time(seconds)	53.72	64.83	18.86	**15.23**
Memory(byte)	156M	324	**NA**	**NA**

improvement to SQ when the database size increases to $1M$. It is interesting to to note that, as database size increases, the accuracy improvement of our approach over SQ becomes smaller. This is partially due to the tradeoff between parameters w_1 and w_2. Also, to increase unreliable flipping bits n might also influence the performance. In Figure 5, we show some visualized results on a large scale image dataset for various queries, such as "StarBucks Logo", "Uncle Sam", etc. The images that can not be retrieved by SQ are highlighted by color boxes.

3.3 Efficiency Analysis

We also evaluate our approach from the aspect of efficiency. Table 2 shows the average time cost per query for all retrieval approaches. VLAD is the most efficient method which takes $0.10s$ for each query. SQ takes $0.47s$ per query since involves 529 expanded index words. Compared with SQ, our approach with Reliable Binary Code saves almost half of search time, because it only searches 256 expanded index words. Although our approach costs more time than the baseline approach, it may still meet users' expectation of fast response time (average 0.31 second per query) but with much higher search accuracy.

Besides the efficiency comparison of on-line query, we also investigate the off-line indexing performance. Table 3 shows time cost comparison to index one million features for various retrieval approaches. Benefiting in part from binary features, it can be observed that our approach is very efficient in indexing one million features, which takes 15.23 to index one million reliable binary codes. Our approach with RBC is 3 and 4 times faster than VT and VLAD, respectively. It should be noted that that another distinctiveness of our approach from others is that no visual codebook needs to be trained which could save much computation. In contrast, for the VT method, a large visual codebook has to be trained in a time-consuming way. Moreover, it is still unclear whether such a codebook could capture the sample distribution in high dimensional feature (128-D). For instance, a hierarchical vocabulary tree requires $156M$ memory to be loaded into main memory. And the memory cost of VLAD approach for codebook is 324 bytes. In contrast, our approach based on RSC does not need memory to store a pre-trained codebook.

4. CONCLUSION

In this paper, we explicitly analyze the unreliable quantized bit problem of scalar quantization and introduce a novel reliable binary code. We extend original scalar quantization by embedding reliability information in two aspects: (1) the expanded index words are generated based on unreliable bits, which greatly reduce the search time and accelerate the speed. (2) we embed the reliability information into the Hamming distance formula, that alleviates the impact of unreliability and improve the retrieval accuracy. Experimental results on two public datasets have demonstrated the effectiveness and efficiency of the proposed approach. Our approach can also be combined and enhanced by several post-processing techniques to further improve the image retrieval performance.

Figure 5: Retrieved image results based on multiple tables. The left most images are the queries. Returned images before the first false positive are shown. Images failed to be retrieved by SQ are highlighted by color boxes.

5. ACKNOWLEDGMENT

This work was supported in part to Dr. Tian by ARO grant W911NF-12-1-0057, and Faculty Research Award by NEC Laboratories of America, respectively. This work was supported in part by National Science Foundation of China (NSFC) under contract No. 61128007.

6. REFERENCES

[1] D. G. Lowe. Distinctive image features from scale-invariant keypoints. In *IJCV*, 2007.

[2] H. Jegou, M. Douze and C. Schmid. Hamming embedding and weak geometric consistency for large scale image search. In *ECCV*, 2008.

[3] P. Raghavan, C. D. Manning and H. Schtze. An introduction to information retrieval. Cambridge University Press, 2008.

[4] H. Jegou, F. Perronnin, M. Douze, J. Sanchez and C. Schmid. Aggregating local descriptors into compact codes. In *PAMI*, 2012.

[5] W. Zhou, Y. Lu, H. Li, Y. Song and Q. Tian. Spatial Coding for large scale partial-duplicate web image search. In *MM*, 2010.

[6] H. Jegou, M. Douze and C. Schmid. Improving bag-of-features for large scale image search. In *IJCV*, 2010.

[7] D. Niester and H. Stewenius. Scalable recognition with a vocabulary tree. In *CVPR*, 2006.

[8] J. Cai, Z.-J. Zha, Q. Tian and Z. Wang. Semi-Automatic Flickr Group Suggestion. In *MMM*, 2011.

[9] E. Rublee, V. Rabaud, K. Konolige and G. Bradski. ORB: An efficient alternative to SIFT or SURF. In *ICCV*, 2011.

[10] O. Chum and J. Matas. Fast computation of min-Hash signatures for image collections. In *CVPR*, 2012.

[11] W. Zhou, Y. Lu, H. Li and Q. Tian. Scalar quantization for large scale image search. In *MM*, 2012.

[12] A. Alahi, R. Ortiz and P. Vandergheynst. Freak:fast retina keypoint. In *CVPR*, 2012.

[13] J. Cai, Z.-J. Zha, W. Zhou and Q. Tian. Attribute-assisted Reranking for Web Image Retrieval. In *MM*, 2012.

[14] S. StefanLeutenegger, M. Chli and R. Siegwart. Brisk: binary robust invariant scalable keypoints. In *ICCV*, 2011.

[15] J. Philbin, O. Chum, M. Isard, J. Sivic and A. Zisserman. Lost in quantization: Improving particular object retrieval in large scale image database. In *CVPR*, 2008.

[16] J. Cai, Q. Liu, C. Francine, D. Joshi and Q. Tian,. Scalable Image Search with Multiple Index Tables. In *ICMR*, 2014.

[17] L. Zheng and S. Wang. Visual Phraselet: Refining Spatial Constraints for Large Scale Image Search. In *Signal Processing Letters*, 2013.

Chic or Social: Visual Popularity Analysis in Online Fashion Networks

Kota Yamaguchi
Tohoku University
Sendai, Miyagi, Japan
kyamagu@vision.is.tohoku.ac.jp

Tamara L. Berg
University of North Carolina
Chapel Hill, NC, USA
tlberg@cs.unc.edu

Luis E. Ortiz
Stony Brook University
Stony Brook, NY, USA
leortiz@cs.stonybrook.edu

ABSTRACT

From Flickr to Facebook to Pinterest, pictures are increasingly becoming a core content type in social networks. But, how important is this visual content and how does it influence behavior in the network? In this paper we study the effects of visual, textual, and social factors on popularity in a large real-world network focused on fashion. We make use of state of the art computer vision techniques for clothing representation, as well as network and text information to predict post popularity in both in-network and out-of-network scenarios. Our experiments find significant statistical evidence that social factors dominate the in-network scenario, but that combinations of content and social factors can be helpful for predicting popularity outside of the network. This in depth study of image popularity in social networks suggests that social factors should be carefully considered for research involving social network photos.

Categories and Subject Descriptors

I.2.10 [**Vision and Scene Understanding**]: Perceptual reasoning

General Terms

Experimentation; Human Factors; Measurement

Keywords

Social multimedia; Online fashion networks

1. INTRODUCTION

Nearly every blog or social network utilizes a combination of images, text, and other modalities (e.g. location) to convey information and promote interaction. In many online communities the amount of visual data is quite vast, sometimes representing the main source of content. Despite the active research in social multimedia and social popularity hypothesis [15], it is not well-studied *how much* the content quality and the network is influencing to the resulting visual content popularity. In this paper, we take a big-data approach to quantitatively study social influence in a real-world online social network specialized in fashion.

MM'14, November 03 - 07 2014, Orlando, FL, USA

http://dx.doi.org/10.1145/2647868.2654958.

Figure 1: An example of a Chictopia post.

We purposely choose a fashion-focused online community, Chictopia, for the following reasons: 1) The network is large and real-world, with over 175k users and 600k pictures, 2) Content in this network is mainly visual, consisting of "outfit of the day" pictures uploaded by users, 3) The community is focused on a single topic (fashion), which yields relatively consistent user based popularity in contrast to general photos with diverse categories [7], 4) The relevant data is publicly and readily available online, 5) We can take advantage of state of the art computer vision techniques for recognizing clothing in fashion images [19] to help extract the visual content most relevant to popularity.

In a network focused around fashion and style, one might assume that visual content would be the most influential factor for popularity. However, we find that social factors dominate both visual and textual factors in prediction models, even in a community where outfits are purportedly rated based on their fashion style. Furthermore, studying the effects of content outside of the social network, we find that this social bias does not appear, but rather the social and content information together provide a good predictory for popularity. These insights are useful for multimedia researchers and engineers seeking to exploit human behavior in social network applications.

The following list summarizes our contributions:

- Models to predict popularity of outfit pictures incorporating visual, social, and textual factors.
- A new computer vision feature for representing outfit style based on clothing parsing (semantic segmentation of clothing items)
- A large-scale empirical study of social vs. content influence on popularity in a real-world, uncontrolled fashion network
- A large crowdsourcing effort to simulate the socially isolated condition

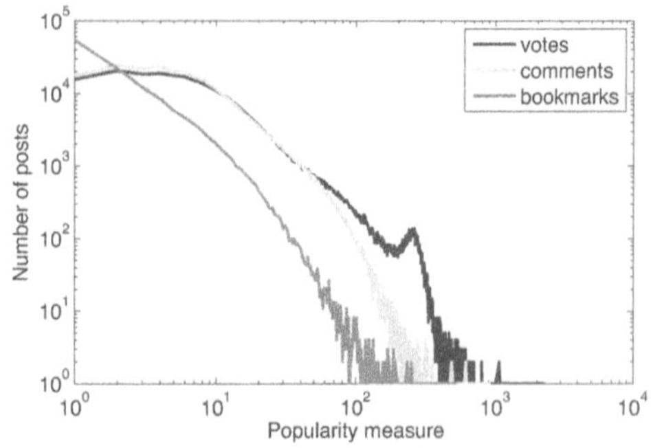

Figure 2: Distribution of voting, commenting, and bookmarked based popularity in Chictopia. The number of votes shows a slight kink perhaps due to front-page highlighting or special promotion by the website.

Type	Name	Modality	Vector	Size
Social	User identity	Network	Sparse	1,000
	Node degrees	Network	Dense	6
	Previous posts	Metadata	Dense	1
Content	Tag TF-IDF	Textual	Sparse	1,000
	Style descriptor	Visual	Dense	441
	Parse descriptor	Visual	Dense	1060
	Color entropy	Visual	Dense	6
	Image composition	Visual	Dense	6
Other	Date bias	Metadata	Sparse	58

Table 1: Summary of the content models.

- Studies of within-network and outside of network scenarios, including empirical findings of asymmetry in content popularity prediction for these scenarios

Related Work: Our work is related to a growing interest in popularity prediction of online content. Work in this direction has mainly looked into early social reaction to content and the prediction of popularity growth in videos [5, 16, 14, 3, 4], news [10, 18], and discussion forums [9]. Some very recent work has looked into visual influence on popularity or behavior [2, 6, 1, 7], or in the reverse direction, to categorize visual contents using social information [8]. Social influence on popularity seen in these studies is also consistent with social browsing behavior on Flickr [11, 17]. We distinguish ourselves from the previous work in that: we focus on a community devoted to fashion, and in particular to rating outfits, our main goal is to evaluate *how* much social influence affects popularity for in and out of network scenarios, we take advantage of recent state-of-the-art computer vision approaches to recognize clothing (rather than general visual features or content), and we take a big-data approach using real-world data from a social networking site focused on a single topic (fashion).

2. DATASET

We collect data from `chictopia.com`, a social fashion network where users post pictures of their daily outfits along with a title, description, and several labels. Figure 1 shows an example of picture and metadata we can observe. We initially collect 617,708 posts from Chictopia. To compare visual features consistently across images, we run a state of the art pose detector to automatically select pictures with a standing person detected. This leaves us with 328,604 pictures, dating from March 2008 to Dec 2012, with 34,327 unique users.

Figure 3: Style descriptor (left) and parse descriptor (right). Style descriptor extracts visual information from patches while parse descriptor extracts information from the predicted clothing parse (semantic assignment of pixels to garment labels).

The observable popularity measures in this data are the number of *votes*, *comments*, and *bookmarks* associated with each post. As is the case with any web content, Chictopia popularity reveals a long-tailed distribution. Figure 2 plots the popularity histogram from all 617K posts. To deal with the difficulty in such distribution, we consider log-votes as the popularity of posts in our experiments.

3. CONTENT REPRESENTATION

We represent a post as a vector of the quantized information sources available for the post. Two major components are modeled for each post: social factors and content factors. Social factors capture information related to the user and their social status within the network, whereas content factors are to capture the quality of the content. In addition to social and content factors, we extract timestamp information to account for the popularity change due to seasons and site growth over time. We use a sparse indicator to represent the month of the post (a 58 dimensional vector in our experiments). Table 1 summarizes all of the terms of our model. All factors are appropriately normalized.

3.1 Social factors

User identity: We represent the identity of users using a sparse indicator vector. To constrain feature dimensionality we restrict this indicator vector to the top-1000 most frequent users. Posts from the same user will all have the same feature vector.

Node degree: We use counts and log-counts of friends, followers, and followees of the user as a six-element feature vector. Posts from the same user will all have the same feature. Note that we empirically tested other network features, but none produced a better prediction than node degree.

User Expertise: We use the number of previous posts from the same user as a scalar feature, related to user expertise.

3.2 Content factors

Tag TF-IDF: In Chictopia, a user can label each individual post with various structured tags indicating general style, occasion, colors, brands, clothing types, in addition to free-form words. We first extract unigrams and bigrams from all the tags and treat them as a document, and compute TF-IDF weights. As in the case of user identity, to constrain the dimensionality of this feature, we only consider the 1000 most frequent n-grams found in the training samples.

Style descriptor: The style descriptor is a state-of-the-art visual clothing representation proposed in [19] for fashion image retrieval, and considered a comprehensive representation of the overall fashion style. The descriptor is based

Factors	In-network				Out-of-network			
	R^2	Spearman	Accuracy 25%	Accuracy 75%	R^2	Spearman	Accuracy 25%	Accuracy 75%
Social	0.491 ±0.005	0.682 ±0.004	**0.847** ±0.002	**0.779** ±0.003	0.423 ±0.011	0.634 ±0.007	0.845 ±0.004	0.787 ±0.005
Content	0.248 ±0.005	0.485 ±0.005	0.778 ±0.003	0.737 ±0.003	0.428 ±0.012	0.647 ±0.008	**0.888** ±0.004	**0.862** ±0.004
Social+Content	**0.493** ±0.005	**0.685** ±0.004	0.845 ±0.002	0.775 ±0.002	**0.473** ±0.014	**0.686** ±0.008	0.884 ±0.004	0.858 ±0.004

Table 2: Regression and top-K% classification on the observed popularity with accompanying 95% bootstrapped confidence intervals on error. For cleaner presentation, the tiny asymmetric difference in confidence intervals are rounded.

on image patches localized on the person's body by pose estimation. At each patch, various features including color, texture, shape, and skin-hair probability are extracted and pooled to produce a high-level description of fashion.

Parse descriptor: In addition to the style descriptor, we develop a new fashion-focused image descriptor based on clothing parsing [19], which we call *parse descriptor*. Clothing parsing is the task of assigning a semantic garment (or skin or background) label to each pixel in the image. The parse descriptor is designed to represent the appearance of individual garment items found in a picture, and we experimentally verified that the parse descriptor in combination with the style descriptor gives a strong prediction. We consider the parse descriptor to be the most important representation in content analysis, because the parse descriptor specifically captures the appearance of a person's garment items. Figure 3 illustrates the style and parse descriptors.

We compute the parse descriptor in the following steps: 1) Compute clothing parse using [19], and obtain 10 masks corresponding to specific garment groups, such as *outer top*, *dress*, or *footware*. Note that we map the original 56 garment categories [19] to 10 garment sets to improve robustness. 2) Extract RGB color, Lab color, Texture response, HOG descriptor, distance from image border, and probability of skin and hair at every pixel. 3) Compute mean-std pooling of the extracted features in each region. 4) Concatenate all pooled features over 10 regions (1060 dimensions).

Color entropy: We compute the entropy of RGB and Lab color from the image. This feature helps distinguish drawings from natural photos.

Image composition: Given a bounding box encompassing the person (estimated by the pose detector), we measure the overall composition of how the person is depicted relative to the image frame as, 1) normalized width, height, and area; 2) normalized x and y displacement from the center of the image; and 3) normalized distance from the image center.

4. IN-NETWORK POPULARITY

Experimental protocol: We first apply a linear regression analysis on the log-votes of the posts using social, content, and a combination of social and content factors. For this analysis, we adopt R^2 and Spearman coefficients as measures of fitness of prediction to the truth. These measures are evaluated on a statistical bootstrapping protocol with our 328K posts; We randomly resample posts, subsample this dataset to 10,000 posts (for computational tractability), and evaluate the above measures with a 90%-10% train-test split. This process is repeated 100 times to derive statistical significance.

We also apply a classification based analysis, in which we predict a binary indicator of being Top K% in popularity. In this experiment, we vary our threshold for 25% and 75% quantiles of the votes in the training samples to see the difference between the most popular and least popular posts. The performance is measured in terms of accuracy.

Results: In-network column of Table 2 shows the results of regression analysis. The regression models fit significantly better when social factors are present, suggesting a user's social connections largely dominates the popularity of their posts over the content itself. However, we should note that social factors may also be highly correlated with content quality – users with many followers may tend to wear highly fashionable outfits. Nevertheless, our results indicate that the influence of content quality is considerably smaller than network influence.

Classification reveals an asymmetry between top 25% and top 75% prediction, indicating the prediction of the most popular posts is easier than predicting the least popular posts. We suspect that this is partly due to the consistently better quality of top-rated pictures and partly due to social bias more strongly affecting popular posts. Also, the slightly smaller difference between the social-only and the content-only model in top 75% prediction suggests that popularity is less affected by social influence in least popular posts.

5. OUT-OF-NETWORK POPULARITY

To examine the effects of social and content factors more deeply, we utilize *crowdsourcing* to emulate a content network without social relationships. We run the popularity voting process in Amazon Mechanical Turk, where no social network exist.

Our task shows the crowd worker 50 random large-resolution images in sequence, and asks them to vote on the picture if they find it *chic*. For quality control, we measure how long it takes each worker to complete this first step and reject a worker's votes if they completed too quickly or didn't display enough variation in their voting procedure. We perform our experiments by randomly selecting 3,000 posts (from our dataset of 328k) and instantiating the above tasks 60 times. We assign 25 workers to each of the 60 resulting tasks. Therefore, any post on each task can obtain up to 25 *chic* votes.

Using the voting data from the crowd, we apply the same analysis. Our main interest here is, however, the influence of the social factors observed in Chictopia on crowd popularity. We use the same bootstrap method from the 3,000 posts to compare the social-only, content-only, and combined models in this experiment. Here, social factors are taken from Chictopia dataset which has no relationship to crowd popularity.

Results: Results are shown in The out-of-network column of Table 2 shows the result. Given our previous results, we initially expected the social factors to lead to much weaker predictors. However, the results suggest that social factors (from Chictopia) still lead to comparable predicators in regression. We conjecture that the solid regression result of the social factors is due to the user and content quality correlation.

Also, the combined model (social + content) is significantly better than any single-factored model in regression. One possible explanation to this result is that the social factors are actually providing complementary information to the content factors in predicting the *unbiased* popularity from the crowd, as opposed to the biased popularity in the network where social influence is by far the stronger predicator of popularity. We observed the asymmetry of prediction also in the out-of-network condition, but to weaker extent perhaps due to no social bias in voting.

Apart from factorizing content and social influence, we can also use our learned models to predict the popularity of photos. Figure 4 shows an example of the most and least popular pictures predicted by one of our models. There is clearly a distinction in visual quality between the most and the least popular pictures. Perhaps it is also possible to build a system that can predict *unbiased* content popularity. Such prediction could be useful for many e-commerce applications, such as automatic outfit quality feedback [12], socially-aware fashion recommendation [13]. Stable popularity prediction can benefit in online ad optimization and traffic balancing. It is our future work to use this insight to build a socially-aware multimedia system.

In summary, the out-of-network popularity analysis yield insights that suggest 1) social factors contain not only network information but also some aspect of content evaluation, 2) content factors capture different aspects of popularity than social, and 3) their combination yields better predictions for content popularity.

(a) Predicted most popular

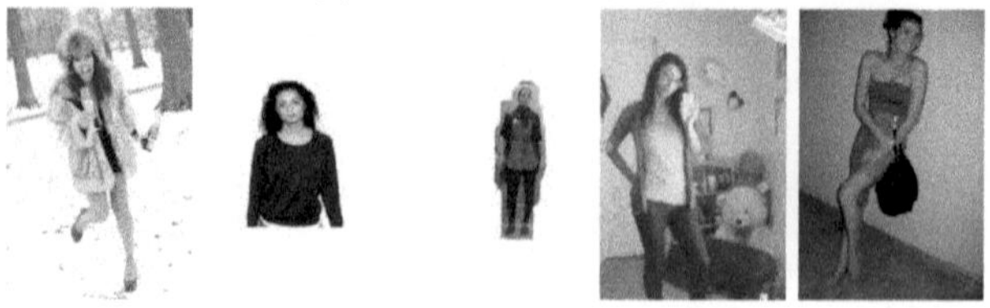

(b) Predicted least popular

Figure 4: Prediction examples from our combined model.

6. CONCLUSIONS

We presented a vision-based approach to quantitatively evaluate the influence of social and content factors on fashion pictures. Our content representation takes advantage of various sources of information from computer vision, natural language processing, and the network itself. Through experiments, we showed statistical evidence of dominant social influence in networked media and the strength of social factors in unbiased content evaluation. One lesson from our experiments is that any attempt to learn subjective measures such as aesthetics from social content should explicitly consider social influence.

7. ACKNOWLEDGEMENTS

Research supported by Google Faculty Award, "Seeing Social: Exploiting Computer Vision in Online Communities," NSF Career Award #1054133 and #1054541.

8. REFERENCES

[1] S. Bakhshi, D. Shamma, and E. Gilbert. Faces engage us: Photos with faces attract more likes and comments on instagram. *CHI*, 2014.

[2] J. Biel and D. Gatica-Perez. The youtube lens: Crowdsourced personality impressions and audiovisual analysis of vlogs. *Multimedia*, 15(1):41–55, 2013.

[3] Y. Borghol, S. Ardono, and N. Carlsson. The untold story of the clones: Content-agnostic factors that impact youtube video popularity. *KDD*, 2012.

[4] A. Brodersen, S. Scellato, and M. Wattenhofer. Youtube around the world: geographic popularity of videos. In *WWW*, pages 241–250. ACM, 2012.

[5] M. Cha, H. Kwak, P. Rodriguez, Y.-Y. Ahn, and S. Moon. I tube, you tube, everybody tubes: analyzing the world's largest user generated content video system. In *IMC*. ACM, 2007.

[6] S. Chang, V. Kumar, E. Gilbert, and L. G. Terveen. Specialization, homophily, and gender in a social curation site: Findings from pinterest. In *CSCW*, pages 674–686. ACM, 2014.

[7] A. Khosla, A. D. Sarma, and R. Hamid. What makes an image popular? *WWW*, 2014.

[8] A. Kimura, K. Ishiguro, M. Yamada, A. Marcos Alvarez, K. Kataoka, and K. Murasaki. Image context discovery from socially curated contents. In *ACM Multimedia*, pages 565–568, 2013.

[9] J. G. Lee, S. Moon, and K. Salamatian. An approach to model and predict the popularity of online contents with explanatory factors. In *WI-IAT*, volume 1, pages 623–630. IEEE, 2010.

[10] K. Lerman and T. Hogg. Using a model of social dynamics to predict popularity of news. In *WWW*, pages 621–630. ACM, 2010.

[11] K. Lerman and L. A. Jones. Social browsing on flickr. *ICWSM*, 2007.

[12] L. Liu, H. Xu, J. Xing, S. Liu, X. Zhou, and S. Yan. Wow! you are so beautiful today! In *ACM Multimedia*, pages 3–12, 2013.

[13] S. Liu, J. Feng, Z. Song, T. Zhang, H. Lu, C. Xu, and S. Yan. Hi, magic closet, tell me what to wear! In *ACM Multimedia*, pages 619–628. ACM, 2012.

[14] L.-P. Morency, R. Mihalcea, and P. Doshi. Towards multimodal sentiment analysis: Harvesting opinions from the web. In *ICMI*, pages 169–176. ACM, 2011.

[15] M. Slaney. Web-scale multimedia analysis: does content matter? *MultiMedia, IEEE*, 18(2):12–15, 2011.

[16] G. Szabo and B. A. Huberman. Predicting the popularity of online content. *Communications of the ACM*, 53(8):80–88, 2010.

[17] M. Trevisiol, L. Chiarandini, L. M. Aiello, and A. Jaimes. Image ranking based on user browsing behavior. In *SIGIR*, pages 445–454. ACM, 2012.

[18] H. M. Ung. Social influence, popularity and interestingness of online contents. In *ICWSM*, 2011.

[19] K. Yamaguchi, M. H. Kiapour, and T. L. Berg. Paper doll parsing: Retrieving similar styles to parse clothing items. *ICCV*, 2013.

n-gram Models for Video Semantic Indexing *

Nakamasa Inoue
Tokyo Institute of Technology, Tokyo, Japan
inoue@ks.cs.titech.ac.jp

Koichi Shinoda
Tokyo Institute of Technology, Tokyo, Japan
shinoda@cs.titech.ac.jp

ABSTRACT

We propose n-gram modeling of shot sequences for video semantic indexing, in which semantic concepts are extracted from a video shot. Most previous studies for this task have assumed that video shots in a video clip are independent from each other. We model the time-dependency between them assuming that n-consecutive video shots are dependent. Our models improve the robustness against occlusion and camera-angle changes by effectively using information from the previous video shots. In our experiments on the TRECVID 2012 Semantic Indexing Benchmark, we applied the proposed models to a system using Gaussian mixture models and support vector machines. Mean average precision was improved from 30.62% to 32.14%, which is the best performance on the TRECVID 2012 Semantic Indexing to the best of our knowledge.

Categories and Subject Descriptors

I.4 [**Computing Methodologies**]: Image Processing and Computer Vision; I.4.9 [**Applications**]: Multimedia Search and Recommendation

Keywords

Semantic Indexing; Video Search; Gaussian Mixture Models; n-gram Models

1. INTRODUCTION

With advances in data-sharing technologies and services, a large amount of video data has made been available on the Internet. To find and recognize specific objects, events, and scenes in video, semantic indexing is a necessary technique in many multimedia applications such as video search, summarization, surveillance, and robot vision. Here, semantic indexing is the process of automatically detecting semantic concepts such as Car, Boat, Singing and Cityscape. It has been a challenging task due to the semantic gap [1], i.e., the lack of correspondence between the high-level semantic concepts and the low-level features representing colors, textures, shapes, and audio features extracted from video.

A recent trend is to develop a statistical method in which a set of examples is used to learn a model for bridging the semantic gap. For example, statistical image representations such as bag-of-visual-words (BoW) [2] and Gaussian mixture models (GMMs) [3, 4, 5] have shown to be effective for video semantic indexing. The BoW represents an image by a histogram of low-level features such as SIFT features. The GMM-supervector representation [4] and the Fisher-vector representation [5], which extend the BoW to a probabilistic framework, have shown the best performance in detecting semantic concepts from Internet archive videos in the recent TREC Video Retrieval (TRECVID) workshops [6, 7, 8].

To detect semantic concepts from video data, a video clip is often divided into video shots, and we often assume that video shots are independent from each other. However, this assumption is not realistic since in one video clip the same object or scene frequently appears in more than one video shots. For example, we observe that the ship appears in three video shots in a video clip in Figure 1. This observation brings us to an idea to improve semantic indexing systems by modeling time-series relationships between video shots.

Some studies have shown that time-series models such as hidden Markov models (HMMs) are effective to represent temporal structures in news videos or sports videos. For example, in baseball videos, scene transitions are effectively represented by HMMs with low-level visual and audio features [9]. Specific human activities, for example actions in a kitchen, are also represented by HMMs [10]. However, since these methods are optimized for well-structured videos, they are not always effective for consumer-generated videos on Internet archives, which do not have pre-defined structures such as scene transitions in sports videos.

We propose n-gram models, which represents time-series relationships between video shots by assuming that n-consecutive video shots are dependent from each other. We extend the well-known n-gram language models for natural language processing or speech recognition to model a video clip for video semantic indexing. While we evaluate proposed models to a semantic indexing system using GMM-supervectors for 6 types of visual and audio features [8], they can be utilized in any semantic indexing systems as post-processing for re-evaluating detection scores.

This paper is organized as follows. Section 2 presents the proposed n-gram models. Section 3 presents our experiments on the TRECVID 2012 Semantic Indexing Benchmark. Section 4 concludes this work and describes our future work.

9*(Produces the permission block, and copyright information). For use with SIG-ALTERNATE.CLS. Supported by ACM.

MM'14, November 3–7, 2014, Orlando, Florida, USA.

http://dx.doi.org/10.1145/2647868.2654961 .

Figure 1: An example of a video clip, which is divided into 7 video shots. The 3rd to 5th video shots are positive examples of "Ship". The ships in the 3rd and the 5th video shots are difficult to detect.

2. N-GRAM MODELS

Let's focus on a video clip divided into N video shots. We assume that a shot-independent detection score s_i for each concept is given for each video shot ($i = 1, 2, \cdots, N$). For example, detection score obtained from a one-versus-rest SVM in BoW [2] and GMM [3, 4, 5] systems can provide the shot-independent detection score. Our n-gram models re-evaluate each score by considering time-series patterns. Let w_i be a random variable that is equal to $+1$ if a targeted semantic concept appears in the i-th video shot and otherwise -1 ($i = 1, 2, \cdots, N$). Here we estimate a conditional probability $p(w_i = +1|s_1, s_2, \cdots, s_N)$ where score distributions are modeled by Gaussian distributions for the given shot-independent scores. In the following subsections, we first present an n-gram model for $n = 2$, which we call a bi-gram model. The bi-gram model assumes the current and previous two video shots are dependent and the others are independent. Second, we extend it to $n > 2$ by increasing the number of dependent video shots from two to n. Finally, we present a full-gram model, which assume all N video shots are dependent.

2.1 Bi-Gram

Assuming that the current i-th and the previous $(i-1)$-th video shots are dependent and the others are independent, we have $p(w_i|s_1, s_2, \cdots, s_N) = p(w_i|s_{i-1}, s_i)$. Thus, the bi-gram model estimates it for each video shot as follows.

Since $p(w_i|s_{i-1}, s_i)$ is a marginal probability, we have

$$p(w_i|s_{i-1}, s_i) = \sum_{w_{i-1}} p(w_{i-1}, w_i|s_{i-1}, s_i) \quad (1)$$

$$= \sum_{w_{i-1}} p(w_{i-1}|s_{i-1})p(w_i|w_{i-1}, s_i). \quad (2)$$

by applying the chain rule. Eq. (2) shows that estimation of two probabilities, i) $p(w_{i-1}|s_{i-1})$ and ii) $p(w_i|w_{i-1}, s_i)$, is needed.

i) Estimation of $p(w_{i-1}|s_{i-1})$

To estimate a probability $p(w_{i-1}|s_{i-1})$, we use Gaussian distributions to represent score distributions as follows. Since we have

$$p(w_{i-1}|s_{i-1}) = \frac{p(s_{i-1}|w_{i-1})p(w_{i-1})}{\sum_{w_{i-1}} p(s_{i-1}|w_{i-1})p(w_{i-1})}. \quad (3)$$

by applying the Bayesian theorem, we estimate $p(s_{i-1}|w_{i-1})$ as

$$\hat{p}(s_{i-1}|w_{i-1} = x) = \mathcal{N}(\mu_x, \sigma_x) \quad (4)$$

where $x \in \{+1, -1\}$ and

$$\mathcal{N}(\mu_x, \sigma_x) = \frac{1}{\sqrt{2\pi}\hat{\sigma}_x} \exp\left(-\frac{1}{2\hat{\sigma}_x^2}(s_{i-1} - \hat{\mu}_x)^2\right) \quad (5)$$

is a pdf of a Gaussian distribution with a mean vector $\hat{\mu}_x$ and a standard deviation $\hat{\sigma}_x$. The maximum likelihood method is used to estimate the mean vector and the standard deviation. Another probability $p(w_{i-1})$ in Eq.(3) is estimated by counting the number of examples in training data as

$$\hat{p}(w_{i-1} = x) = \frac{N_x}{N_{+1} + N_{-1}}, \quad (6)$$

where $x \in \{+1, -1\}$, N_{+1} is the number of positive samples and N_{-1} is the number of negative samples.

ii) Estimation of $p(w_i|w_{i-1}, s_i)$

A probability $p(w_i|w_{i-1}, s_i)$ is estimated in the same way as above, with the exception that w_{i-1} is a given value. Since the Bayesian theorem gives

$$p(w_i|w_{i-1}, s_i) = \frac{p(s_i|w_{i-1}, w_i)p(w_i|w_{i-1})}{\sum_{w_i} p(s_i|w_{i-1}, w_i)p(w_i|w_{i-1})}, \quad (7)$$

we estimate $p(s_i|w_{i-1}, w_i)$ and $p(w_i|w_{i-1})$ as follows:

$$\hat{p}(s_i|w_{i-1} = x, w_i = y) = \mathcal{N}(\hat{\mu}_{x,y}, \hat{\sigma}_{x,y}), \quad (8)$$

$$\hat{p}(w_i = y|w_{i-1} = x) = \frac{N_{x,y}}{N_{-1,y} + N_{+1,y}}, \quad (9)$$

where $x, y \in \{+1, -1\}$, $\mathcal{N}$ is a pdf of Gaussian distribution, $\mu_{x,y}$ is a mean vector, $\sigma_{x,y}$ is a standard deviation, and $N_{x,y}$ is the number of samples matched with a pattern (x, y). Here, we have four patterns: $(+1, +1), (+1, -1), (-1, +1)$ and $(-1, -1)$. For example, $N_{-1,+1}$ is the number of positive samples whose previous sample is negative. Note that the probability estimation in Eq. (6) and Eq. (9) is the same as the standard n-gram models for natural language processing.

2.2 Extension to $n > 2$

Here, we extend the bi-gram model to n-gram models for $n > 2$, which assume n-consecutive video shots are dependent, i.e.,

$$p(w_i|s_1, s_2, \cdots, s_N) = p(w_i|s_{i-n+1}, \cdots, s_{i-1}, s_i). \quad (10)$$

By applying the chain rule, we have

$$p(w_i|s_{i-n+1}, \cdots, s_{i-1}, s_i) =$$

$$\sum_{w_{i-1},\cdots,w_{i-n}} p(w_{i-n+1}|s_{i-n+1}) \prod_{j=1}^{n-1} p(w_{i-j+1}|w_{i-n+1}, \cdots, w_{i-j}, s_{i-j+1}). \quad (11)$$

Probabilities $p(w_{i-n+1}|s_{i-n+1})$ and $p(w_{i-j+1}|w_{i-n+1}, \cdots, w_{i-j}, s_{i-j+1})$ are estimated in the same way as in Sec 2.1 i) and ii), respectively, by using Gaussian distributions and by counting the number of pattern matches. We call n-gram models for $n = 1, 2$, and 3, uni-gram, bi-gram, and tri-gram, respectively. Note that the uni-gram represents original scores with the exception that the scores are mapped in the range of $[0, 1]$.

2.3 Full-Gram

A full-gram model assumes all video shots are dependent. Since parameter estimation becomes difficult as the number of dependent video shots increases, the full-gram model uses the maximum score of shot-independent scores instead of using all scores. We expect that the full-gram model improves the robustness against occlusion and camera-angle changes, since the maximum score is often obtained from the *most relevant* video shot, for example, in which the targeted semantic concept appears in the center of a video frame without occlusion. Information from the most relevant video shot helps to detect objects under occlusion or scenes taken from different angles.

Let $w_m = \max_i w_i$ and $s_m = \max_i s_i$, the full-gram model assumes that

$$p(w_i|s_1, s_2, \cdots, s_N) = p(w_i|s_m, s_i). \quad (12)$$

Since $p(w_i = +1|w_m = -1) = 0$, we have

$$p(w_i|s_m, s_i) = \sum_{w_m} p(w_m|s_m)p(w_i|w_m, s_i) \quad (13)$$

$$= p(w_m = +1|s_m)p(w_i|w_m = +1, s_i). \quad (14)$$

Probabilities $p(w_m = +1|s_m)$ and $p(w_i|w_m = +1, s_i)$ are estimated by using Gaussian distributions and by counting the number of positive and negative samples as in Sec 2.1 i) and ii).

3. EXPERIMENTS

3.1 Experimental Setup

We evaluate our method on the TRECVID 2012 Semantic Indexing Benchmark [11, 12]. The dataset consists of 28,035 Internet video clips with creative commons licenses. Shot boundaries for each video clip are provided with the dataset. The total number of video shots is 547,634, which is divided into 402,000 for training and 145,634 for testing. The task is to detect 50 semantic concepts including objects, actions and scenes, e.g. Airplane, Boat_Ship, Singing, Bicycling, Basketball, and Nighttime, from each video shot. The evaluation measure is Mean Average Precision (Mean AP) over the 50 semantic concepts, which is calculated by using the official toolkit and annotations [13].

To obtain shot-independent scores, we follow the system in [8], which extends the bag-of-visual-word [2] to a probabilistic framework using Gaussian mixture models. First, the following 6 types of low-level descriptors are extracted from each video shot: 1) Har-SIFT: Scale-Invariant Feature Transform (SIFT) features extracted by using the Harris-Affine detector, 2) Hes-SIFT: SIFT features extracted by using the Hessian-Affine detector, 3) Dense-SIFTHue: densely sampled SIFT and Hue histogram features, 4) Dense-HOG: densely sampled Histogram of Oriented Gradients (HOG) features, 5) Dense-LBP: densely sampled Local Binary Pattern (LBP) features, 6) MFCC: audio features. Second, a GMM supervector [4] is extracted for each type of low-level feature. Finally, the average score of support-vector-machine (SVM) scores is obtained for each video shot, which is used for a shot-independent score in our experiments. The parameters of n-gram models are estimated on the training data set.

Method	Mean AP (%)
Baseline (Uni-gram)	30.62
Bi-gram	31.19
Tri-gram	31.21
Full-gram	32.14

Table 1: Mean APs on TRECVID 2012 Semantic Indexing. The baseline is our system using 6 types of visual and audio features. Bi-gram ($n = 2$), Tri-gram ($n = 3$), and Full-gram models are applied to the baseline system.

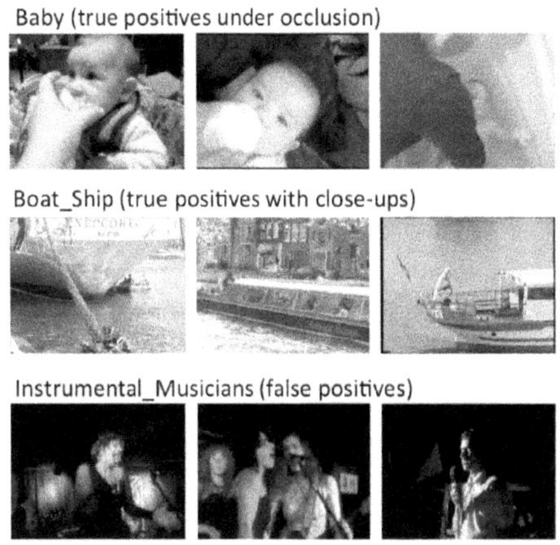

Figure 3: Examples of video shots whose rank was improved by introducing the full-gram model.

3.2 Experimental Results

3.2.1 Results of n-gram models

Table 1 compares Mean AP for our baseline and proposed models. The bi-gram model ($n = 2$) performed better than the baseline, with an improvement of 0.57% in Mean AP. By the tri-gram model ($n = 3$), we had no significant improvement from the bi-gram model. We need a robust method against data insufficiency problems to improve the performance of the tri-gram, since the number of training samples matched with a pattern of length n becomes small and insufficient to estimate parameters as n increases.

The full-gram model in Table 1 performed the best among the proposed models and achieved 32.14% in Mean AP. We observed that APs for Boat_Ship, Baby, Basketball, Oceans are improved by more than 5.0% as shown in Figure 2. Occluded and/or close-up objects and scenes taken from different angles are effectively detected by introducing the full-gram model. For examples, the rank of babies under occlusion and close-up ships were much improved compared with the baseline (Figure 3). The rank of Basketball scenes taken from different angles were also improved. On the other hand, for Instrumental_Musician, some musicians without musical instruments were falsely detected since musical instruments appeared in a past video shot in the same video clip. We

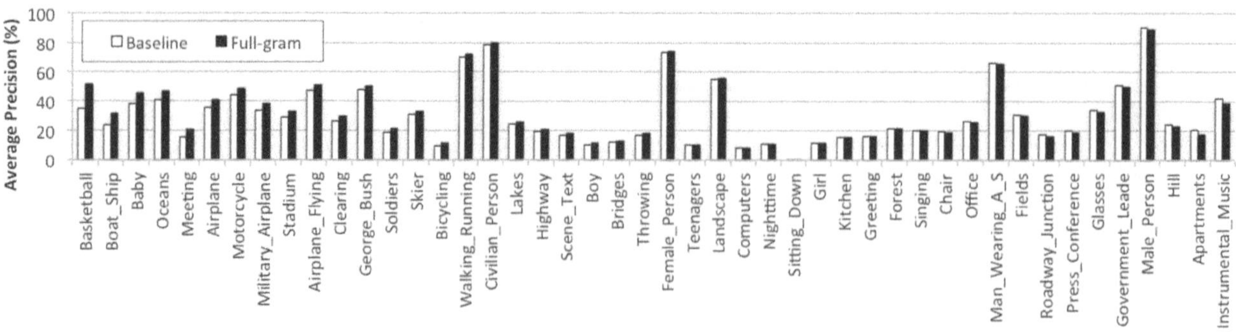

Figure 2: Average Precision (AP) by semantic concepts.

Feature Type	Mean AP (%)	
	Baseline	Full-gram
Har-SIFT	18.27	20.28
Hes-SIFT	17.86	19.73
Dense-SIFT	20.19	21.48
Dense-HOG	23.54	25.35
Dense-LBP	23.60	25.66
MFCC	7.87	8.52

Table 2: Mean Average Precision by Feature Types.

focused on the relationship between video shots in this work, while modeling the visual and audio relationship would be interesting as the next step to solve this problem.

Finally, Table 2 shows the effectiveness of the full-gram model for all types of low-level features used in our experiments. Since Mean AP was improved for all feature types, we conclude that information captured by the full-gram model is complementary to that captured by any type of low-level descriptors.

3.2.2 Comparison with Other Methods

Figure 4 shows performance comparison of our method with the other methods in TRECVID 2012 Semantic Indexing Official Submissions. As can be seen, we achieved better performance than the best of the submissions. Since improved low-level descriptors such as color-SIFT and Dense-trajectories are used in the other methods, we expect that performance will be further improved by introducing our proposed models to these methods.

4. CONCLUSION

In this work, we proposed n-gram models for video semantic indexing, which represent time-series relationships between video shots. Our experiments on the TRECVID 2012 Semantic Indexing Benchmark have shown that our models improve the robustness against occlusion and camera-angle changes. Mean average precision was improved from 30.62% to 32.14% by introducing the full-gram model to a system using GMM supervectors. Our future work focus on modeling visual and audio relationships along with temporal-spatial relationships between objects and events in video. Robust parameter estimation for n-gram models is also an interesting topic for our future work.

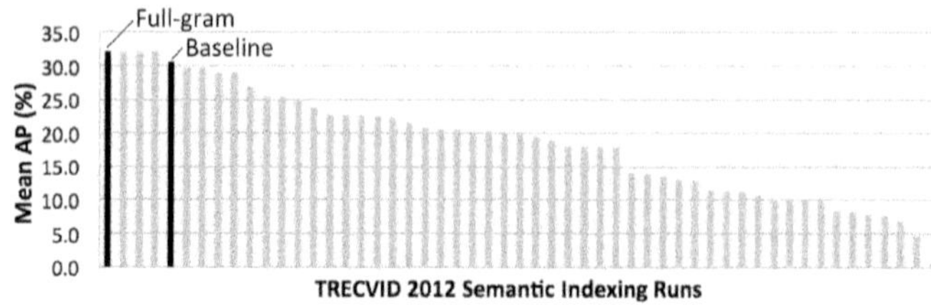

Figure 4: Comparison of our methods with TRECVID 2012 Semantic Indexing Submissions. Mean AP of the best submission was 32.10%.

5. REFERENCES

[1] A.W.M. Smeulders, M. Worring, S. Santini, A. Gupta, R. Jain. Content-based image retrieval at the end of the early years. *In IEEE Trans. on PAMI*, vol.22, no.12, pp.1349–1380, 2000.

[2] G. Csurka, C. Dance, L. Fan, J. Willamowski, and C. Bray. Visual categorization with bags of keypoints. *Proc. ECCV SLCV workshop*, pages 59–74, 2004.

[3] F. Perronnin, C. Dance, G. Csurka, and M. Bressan. Adapted vocabularies for generic visual categorization. *Proc. ECCV*, pages 464–475, 2006.

[4] N. Inoue, and K. Shinoda. A Fast and Accurate Video Semantic-Indexing System Using Fast MAP Adaptation and GMM Supervectors. *In IEEE Trans. on Multimedia*, vol.14, no.4, pages 1196–1205, 2012.

[5] F. Perronnin, S. Jorge, and T. Mensink. Improving the fisher kernel for large-scale image classification. *Proc. ECCV*, pages 143–156, 2010.

[6] P. Over, et al. TRECVID 2013 – An Overview of the Goals, Tasks, Data, Evaluation Mechanisms and Metrics. *Proc. TRECVID workshop*, 2013.

[7] C.G.M. Snoek, et al. The MediaMill TRECVID 2012 Semantic Video Search Engine. *Proc. TRECVID workshop*, 2012.

[8] N. Inoue, et al., Semantic Indexing Using GMM Supervectors and Tree-structured GMMs (TokyoTech+Canon at TRECVID 2011). *Proc. TRECVID workshop*, 2011.

[9] R. Ando, K. Shinoda, S. Furui, and T. Mochizuki. Robust scene Recognition Using Language Models for Scene Contexts. *Proc. ACM MIR workshop*, pp. 99–106, 2004.

[10] H. Kuehne, A. Arslan, and T. Serre, The Language of Actions: Recovering the Syntax and Semantics of Goal-Directed Human Activities *Proc. CVPR*, 2014.

[11] A. F. Smeaton, P. Over, and W. Kraaij. Evaluation campaigns and TRECVid. *Proc. ACM MIR workshop*, pp.321–330, 2006.

[12] A. F. Smeaton, P. Over, and W. Kraaij. High-Level Feature Detection from Video in TRECVid: a 5-Year Retrospective of Achievements. *In Multimedia Content Analysis, Theory and Applications*, Springer Verlag, pp.151–174, 2009.

[13] S. Ayache, and G. Quéenot. Video Corpus Annotation using Active Learning. *Proc. ECIR*, pp.187–198, 2008.

Line-Based Drawing Style Description for Manga Classification

Wei-Ta Chu
National Chung Cheng University
Chiayi, Taiwan
wtchu@cs.ccu.edu.tw

Ying-Chieh Chao
National Chung Cheng University
Chiayi, Taiwan
raff1219@hotmail.com

ABSTRACT

Diversity of drawing styles of mangas can be easily perceived by humans, but are hard to be described in text. We design computational features derived from line segments to describe drawing styles, enabling style classification such as discriminating mangas targeting youth boys and youth girls, and discriminating artworks produced by different artists. With statistical analysis, we found that drawing styles can be effectively characterized by the proposed features such that explicit (e.g., density of line segments) or implicit (e.g., included angles between lines) observations can be made to facilitate various manga style classification.

Categories and Subject Descriptors

I.4.7 [**Image Processing and Computer Vision**]: Feature Measurement—*Feature representation, Size and shape, Texture*; I.5.2 [**Pattern Recognition**]: Design Methodology—*Feature evaluation and selection*

General Terms

Design, Measurement, Performance

Keywords

Line features; statistical analysis; manga style classification

1. INTRODUCTION

As large amounts of artistic images have been digitized and shared online, artwork analysis has attracted increasing attention recently. For example, Li et al. [ ] designed brushstroke features and conducted statistical analysis to distinguish von Gogh's paintings from his contemporaries'. Garneiro et al. [ ] collected a monochromatic artistic image database associated with global semantic annotation, local compositional annotation, and pose annotation. Artistic image annotation and retrieval were formulated as optimization problems, and several features and algorithms were compared to show the computer vision community several interesting challenges. Arora et al. [ ] studied classification methods and features to achieve artistic genre classification, such as Renaissance, Baroque, and Impressionism.

The aforementioned works were mainly proposed for oil or watercolor paintings. However, *comics*, as an another important artistic type, has not been well studied from neither the aspect of feature design nor classification. In addition to text-based metadata, drawing style is an important characteristic for readers to retrieve or manage comic images. Comic style classification is thus an important foundation for users to access comics in a content-based manner. Different from paintings constituted by color regions, characters/objects in comics are mainly concretized by lines. In this paper we specifically focus on monochromatic Japanese comics, or *manga*, which is a major part of Japanese publishing industry and builds a market of 5.5 billion US dollars at least in year 2009. There are no color regions in manga[1], and thus global distributions of conventional visual features are not expected to work well. Human beings can easily recognize different artists' drawing styles, but the mechanism and features for us to do this are not clear. In view of this, we attempt to propose features specifically designed for manga, and investigate how these features benefit manga style analysis. Contributions of this paper are summarized as follows.

- Manga-specific feature design: We design manga-specific features extracted from line segments. Density and magnitude of lines, relationship between nearby lines, and many other line properties constitute an artist's drawing style.
- Feature analysis: We investigate how the proposed features can be used to discriminate different styles by statistical analysis. From this process we reveal implicit characteristics to describe an artist's style or specific topics.
- Applications: With the proposed features and statistical analysis, we enable several applications that have not been developed before. For example, drawing styles and content in youth boy magazines (shonen manga) and in youth girl magazines (shojo manga) are quite different and can be discriminated based on the proposed features. We also investigate how to discriminate different artists' works. These novel applications facilitate large-scale manga browsing and retrieval.

2. PREPROCESSING

Panel segmentation. Given a comic page, we first segment panels in this page so that features can be extracted from individual panels later. The method proposed in [ ] is adopted and modified to build this segmentation module. First, connected components in this page are found and labeled, and a minimum bounding box

[1] In the following, we will use manga and comic interchangeably.

MM'14, November 3–7, 2014, Orlando, Florida, USA.
Copyright 2014 ACM 978-1-4503-3063-3/14/11 ...$15.00.
http://dx.doi.org/10.1145/2647868.2654962.

covering each connected component is then determined. The boxes of sizes smaller than a predefined threshold or are inside other bigger boxes are removed. Finally, overlapped boxed are merged, i.e., a larger minimum bounding box covering all overlapped boxes is determined, and each of the remaining box corresponds to a panel. The top row of Figure 2 shows an example of the process.

Speech balloon detection. Because speech balloons are only slightly relevant to drawing styles, we would like to segment balloon regions and exclude them from the feature extraction process. A speech balloon has the following two characteristics. First, the region around a balloon's boundary is usually blank. Second, words in the balloon are aligned regularly, either in the left-to-right and then top-to-down order (western reading style) or in the top-to-down and then right-to-left order (Chinese and Japanese reading styles). Based on the initial minimum bounding boxes extracted in the beginning of the panel segmentation module, by the first characteristic we detect candidates of balloons by finding the boxes with blank regions nearby box boundaries. For each candidate box, intensity values of pixels inside are respectively projected onto the horizontal and vertical axes, and a horizontal profile and a vertical profile are obtained. We then calculate autocorrelation between profile values in each profile. If the highest five autocorrelation values are all larger than an adaptive threshold, the corresponding bounding box is viewed to contain a speech balloon. In this work the threshold is set as 1.1 times the average profile value. The bottom row of Figure 2 shows examples of speech balloon detection, in the representation of red rectangles.

Character detection. We cannot describe comic styles without character information. However, detecting characters in comics is not trivial, because current face detection methods are mainly developed for real human's face and cannot be directly employed. Therefore, we instead detect eyes first, which is relatively easier in comics because eye regions are nearly round with unique texture, and then extend the eye regions outward to determine a region that covers the character's face and hair. To develop the eye detector, we collect positive and negative eye samples, extract histogram of oriented gradient (HOG) from them, and use the support vector machine (SVM) to build a eye classifier. Given a panel where balloons have been removed, the multi-scale sliding window approach is adopted to detect eyes by the SVM-based eye classifier. Sliding windows of three different sizes, i.e., $0.1W \times 0.1W$, $0.2W \times 0.2W$, and $0.3W \times 0.3W$ (W is width of the panel), are respectively constructed in the detection process. Finally, the region covering a character's head (mainly including face and hair) is determined by extending eye regions outward.

Figure 1: Examples of preprocessing results. Top row, left to right: original comic page, initial connected components, results of panel segmentation. Bottom row: results of speech balloon detection (red rectangles) and character detection (blue rectangles) in two selected panels.

Figure 2: Sample results of line segment detection. Left: source image; middle: edge detection results; right: line segment results, where different line segments are shown in different colors (better seen in color version).

3. LINE FEATURE EXTRACTION

We can easily observe difference of strokes in mangas of different styles or in different topics. Characteristics of strokes may include density, magnitude, length, orientation, and so on. They are all roughly related to *lines* drew to represent characters. Therefore, based on the character region extracted by the character detection module, we design six line features to describe configurations of strokes and edges.

From the character region, the Canny edge detection algorithm is first adopted to calculate edge magnitude of each pixel, and then the edge linking algorithm implemented by Kovesi [ ] is used to detect edges. Because the detected edges would be curved or very long, we further adopt the line segment fitting algorithm, also implemented by Kovesi, to segment edges into straight line segments. The set of straight line segments is the foundation for line feature extraction. Figure 2 shows two sample results of line segment detection, from which we can visually inspect that different drawing styles may yield different line segment characteristics in terms of number of lines, density, and so on. In the following, we describe details of line features.

Included angle between lines (ℓ_1). For any two spatially adjacent lines, we calculate the included angle between them by $\theta = \arccos \frac{\langle \boldsymbol{u}, \boldsymbol{v} \rangle}{\|\boldsymbol{u}\|\|\boldsymbol{v}\|}$. Include angles between line segments in a panel are then equally quantized into twelve ranges, and thus the feature ℓ_1 of a panel can be represented as a 12-dimensional histogram.

Line orientation (ℓ_2). Orientation of a line segment is defined as the included angle between it and the horizontal axis. Orientations of line segments in a panel are also equally quantized into twelve ranges, and thus the feature ℓ_2 can also be represented as a 12-dimensional orientation histogram.

Density of line segments (ℓ_3). Density of line segments is an important factor of drawing style. We first calculate the centroid $\boldsymbol{c} = (x_c, y_c)$ of each line segment by $x_c = \frac{1}{\|\mathcal{L}\|} \sum_{x_i \in \mathcal{L}} x_i$ and $y_c = \frac{1}{\|\mathcal{L}\|} \sum_{y_i \in \mathcal{L}} y_i$, where $\mathcal{L}$ is the set of pixels in the line segment, and (x_i, y_i) is the coordinate of the ith pixel in the segment. A line segment $\mathcal{L}_b$ is said to be in the neighborhood of the line segment $\mathcal{L}_a$ if the distance between their centroids is less than the adaptive threshold $t = \min(W, H) \times 0.04$, where W and H are width and height of the panel, respectively. For each line segment in a panel, we calculate the number of lines in its neighborhood, and the information over all line segments are gathered to form the feature ℓ_3, in the representation a 20-dimensional histogram, i.e., densities of nearby lines are quantized into twenty ranges.

Orientation of nearby lines (ℓ_4). Similar to ℓ_2, orientations of a line segment's nearby lines are calculated, and such information over all line segments in a panel are gathered to form ℓ_4, in the representation of a 12-dimensional orientation histogram (with appropriate normalization).

Number of nearby lines with similar orientation (ℓ_5). To a line segment $\mathcal{L}$, we calculate the number of its nearby lines that have similar orientation to $\mathcal{L}$, i.e., their orientations are quantized into the same range. Such information over all line segments in a panel are again gathered to form a 20-dimensional histogram.

Line strength (ℓ_6). Comics designed for boys and girls usually have different styles in strokes, in the representation of density as well as strength of line segments. To capture variations of line strengths, we embed a design in the framework of Canny edge detection, which includes noise reduction, finding edge gradient, non-maximum suppression, and thresholding. At the thresholding stage, all possible thresholds can be thought to constitute a threshold space. This space is equally divided into twenty subspaces, indicating twenty different settings of the high threshold and the low threshold. Twenty threshold settings are respectively applied to the edge gradients corresponding to a panel, yielding twenty different edge maps $\mathcal{E}_1, \mathcal{E}_2, ..., \mathcal{E}_{21}$, showing all detailed edges ($\mathcal{E}_1$) to strong edges only ($\mathcal{E}_{21}$). Suppose that the sums of gradient for $\mathcal{E}_1, \mathcal{E}_2, ..., \mathcal{E}_{21}$ are $E_1, E_2, ..., E_{21}$, respectively, the feature ℓ_6 is a 20-dimensional vector $(\frac{E_2}{E_1}, \frac{E_3}{E_1}, ..., \frac{E_{21}}{E_1})$.

4. STATISTICAL ANALYSIS

Based on the aforementioned features, we would like to investigate *how the proposed features benefit manga style classification*? In the current work, we focus on two style classification tasks: discriminating mangas in youth boy magazines (shonen manga) and in youth girl magazines (shojo manga), and discriminating artists who produced mangas of the same topic, i.e., baseball games. To examine whether a feature is statistically significant in discriminating mangas of different styles, we set the null hypothesis that two groups have the same average in this feature, and use a two-sided permutation test to compute the p-value [ ]. Smaller p-values indicate stronger evidence against the null hypothesis, i.e., statistics of this feature in two groups are statistically different.

Discriminating between shonen mangas and shojo mangas. We collected shonen mangas from *Shonen Jump*, *Shonen Magazine*, and *Shonen Sunday* (three most popular shonen manga magazines in Japan), and collected shojo mangas from *Bessatsu Margaret*, *Bessatsu Friend*, and *Sho-Comi*. Totally 240 panels were extracted from the collected shonen mangas and shojo mangas, respectively, to conduct the following statistical analysis. To analyze line features, features $\ell_1, \ell_2, ..., \ell_6$ are calculated from each panel, and panels in shonen mangas and shojo mangas are compared by the two-sided permutation test. A feature is said to differ between two groups at significance level α if its corresponding p-value is below a threshold α. In many statistical studies as well as this work, the threshold α is set as 0.05.

Table 1 shows p-values of different features for discriminating shonen mangas and shojo mangas. The features with p-values below 0.05 are especially shown in bold face. We see that include angles (ℓ_1), nearby lines with similar orientations (ℓ_5), and line strength (ℓ_6) are more statistically significant. To get insights from these statistical results, we show sample characters from shonen

Table 1: P-values of different features for discriminating between shonen mangas and shojo mangas.

	ℓ_1	ℓ_2	ℓ_3	ℓ_4	ℓ_5	ℓ_6
p-value	**0.040**	0.415	0.152	0.430	**0.017**	**0.011**

Figure 3: Sample characters from shonen mangas (left three) and shojo mangas (right three).

mangas and shojo mangas in Figure 3, where we can visually see that 1) more lines with similar orientations, especially in hair regions, are in shojo mangas (larger ℓ_5); and 2) more strong strokes, and thus large line strengths, are in shonen mangas (larger ℓ_6). The statistical results match with the visual inspection, and the corresponding features are expected to contribute more in discriminating shonen mangas from shojo mangas.

We respectively randomly selected fifteen panels from shonen mangas and shojo mangas, extracted features, and then calculated the normalized Euclidean distance between features. Figure 4(a) and Figure 4(b) show the distance matrices calculated based on ℓ_5 and ℓ_6, respectively, where the (i, j)th entry denotes the distance between the ith panel and the jth panel; the first fifteen panels come from shonen mangas, and the last fifteen panels come from shojo mangas. We can see that distances between the panels from the same type of mangas are generally small. This trend can be easily seen especially in Figure 4(b).

Discriminating between artists drawing baseball mangas. We further study whether the proposed features are able to discriminate different artists' drawing styles. To eliminate the influence of semantics variations, we limit this study to baseball mangas, which are quite popular in Japan and several famous artists have related artworks. In this work, we respectively collected eighty panels from *Ace of Diamond* by Terajima Yuji (TU), *MIX* by Mitsuru Adachi (MA), and *Big Windup* by Mizushima Tsutomu (MT). Two-sided permutation tests are then conducted to examine statistical significance of features in discriminating three pairs of artists, i.e., TU vs. MA, TU vs. MT, and MA vs. MT.

Table 2 shows p-values of different features in discriminating artists. As drawing styles would differ from different perspectives, we see statistically significant features change when we focus on different artist pairs. For example, TU's and MA's artworks mainly differ in the features of included angles (ℓ_1), density (ℓ_3), similar orientation (ℓ_5), and line strength (ℓ_6), while TU's and MT's artworks differ in the features of line orientation (ℓ_2) and similar orientation (ℓ_5). Sample characters from three artists' works are shown in Figure 5 for visual inspection of effective features. For example, we can clearly see that MA's works have low line density, yielding smaller values in ℓ_3 and ℓ_5. This can also be seen from the line segment results shown in Figure 2, where the top row shows a TU's character and the bottom row shows a MA's character.

We respectively randomly selected ten panels from TU's mangas and MA's mangas and then calculated the normalized Euclidean distance between features. Figure 4(c) and Figure 4(d) show the distance matrices calculated based on ℓ_3 and ℓ_5, respectively, where we can see panels can be clearly categorized into two groups. Distances between panels of the same artist's work are generally low, indicating the consistency of drawing style of an artist.

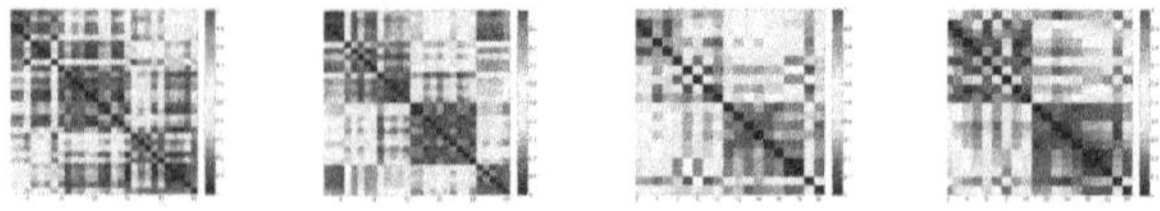

(a) (b) (c) (d)

Figure 4: Distance matrices between panels in different styles. Left two: Distance matrices calculated by comparing shonen mangas and shojo mangas based on ℓ_5 and ℓ_6, respectively. Right two: Distance matrices calculated by comparing TU's mangas and MA's mangas based on ℓ_3 and ℓ_5, respectively.

Table 2: P-values of different features for discriminating between artists.

	ℓ_1	ℓ_2	ℓ_3	ℓ_4	ℓ_5	ℓ_6
TU vs. MA	**0.037**	0.183	**0.000**	0.277	**0.000**	**0.000**
TU vs. MT	0.105	**0.006**	0.075	**0.007**	0.199	0.074
MA vs. MT	0.325	0.091	0.161	0.061	**0.011**	**0.000**

Figure 6 is an interesting illustration showing different artists' drawing styles in terms of line features. We calculate the third order moment (skewness) of features ℓ_1, ℓ_2, ..., ℓ_6. Although the skewness value is just a coarse representation of a high-dimensional histogram, after appropriate shifting and normalization, from Figure 6 we can clearly see difference between artists and demonstrate effectiveness of the proposed features.

5. APPLICATIONS

Discriminating between shonen mangas and shojo mangas. Based on the proposed features, we construct a classifier to discriminate shonen and shojo mangas based on the support vector machine. According to the statistical test results shown in Table 1, we respectively construct SVM classifiers based on ℓ_1 only, ℓ_5 only, ℓ_6 only, and combination of all proposed features. The five-fold cross validation scheme is adopted in training and testing, and classification accuracies based on different features are shown in Table 3. Although shonen (shojo) manga magazines contain various mangas produced by different artists and thus the intra-class variations are large, Table 3 shows that the proposed features yield encouraging classification performance. The best classification accuracy can be achieved when all features are combined.

Discriminating between artists drawing baseball mangas. According to Table 2, effective features discriminating different artist pairs are different. Therefore, we respectively construct SVM classifiers based on individual features, and construct an SVM classifier based on all features as well. The five-fold cross validation scheme is also used in training and testing. Table 4 shows classification accuracies of discriminating different artist pairs based on different feature settings. Because Ma's drawing style is apparently different from others, classification accuracies of the first and third pair are quite high. Because Ma's artworks often have little variation on line strength, the feature ℓ_6 solely can be a strong clue for classification. On the other hand, to discriminate TU from MT, combining all features yield the best classification performance.

Figure 5: Sample characters from *Ace of Diamond* (left two), *MIX* (middle two), and *Big Windup* (right tow).

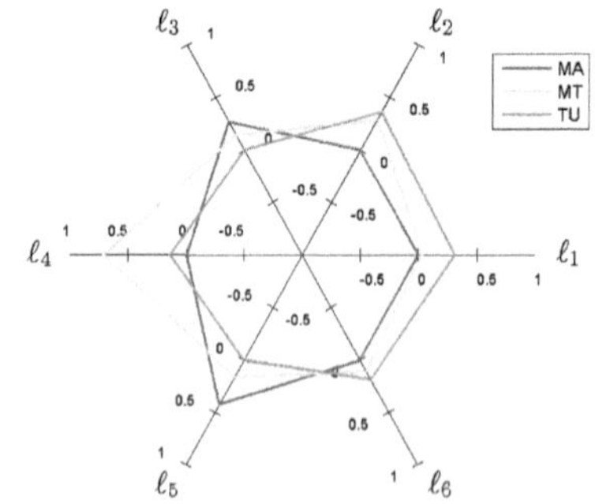

Figure 6: The spider chart showing different artists' drawing styles in terms of line features.

Table 3: Classification accuracy of discriminating between shonen mangas and shojo mangas.

	ℓ_1	ℓ_5	ℓ_6	combine
Accuracy	73.7	70.3	74.5	82.0

6. CONCLUSION

In this paper we propose manga-specific features to describe drawing styles, enabling style classification such as discriminating shonen and shojo mangas, and discriminating artworks produced by different artists. With statistical analysis, features effective to describe various styles are investigated and are used to construct SVM classifiers for style classification. We observe several interesting facts about manga styles, and obtain encouraging classification performance even with simple features. With such study, style-based comics browsing or retrieval would be developed in the future. Furthermore, more elegant features are to be proposed, and manga styles can be discussed in more detail.

Acknowledgement The work was partially supported by the Ministry of Science and Technology in Taiwan under the grants NSC101-2221-E-194-055-MY2 and MOST103-2221-E-194-027-MY3.

7. REFERENCES

[1] K. Arai and T. Herman. Method for automatic e-comic scene frame extraction for reading comic on mobile devices. In *International Conference on Information Technology*, pages 370–375, 2010.

[2] R. Arora and A. Elgammal. Towards automated classification of fine-art painting style: a comparative study. In *ICPR*, pages 3541–3544, 2012.

[3] G. Carneiro, N. de Silva, A. Del Bue, and J. Costeira. Artistic image classification: an analysis on the printart database. In *ECCV*, pages 143–157, 2012.

[4] P. Kovesi. School of computer science and software engineering. http://web.csse.uwa.edu.au/.

[5] J. Li, L. Yeo, E. Hendriks, and J. Wang. Rhythmic brushstrokes distinguish van gogh from his contemporaries: findings via automated brushstroke extraction. *IEEE TPAMI*, 34(6):1159–1176, 2012.

Table 4: Classification accuracies of discriminating between artists.

	ℓ_1	ℓ_2	ℓ_3	ℓ_4	ℓ_5	ℓ_6	combine
TU vs. MA	74.28	64.20	70.00	62.14	77.85	**90.71**	90.00
TU vs. MT	65	72.85	62.85	72.85	50.00	69.28	**76.11**
MA vs. MT	71.42	67.14	64.29	68.57	74.28	**86.42**	86.11

Supervised Hashing with Error Correcting Codes

Fatih Cakir Stan Sclaroff
Department of Computer Science
Boston University
Boston, MA 02215 USA
{fcakir, sclaroff}@cs.bu.edu

ABSTRACT

One widely-used solution to expedite similarity search of multimedia data is to construct hash functions to map the data into a Hamming space where linear search is known to be fast and often sublinear solutions perform well. In this paper, we propose a Boosting based formulation for supervised learning of the hash functions that is based on Error Correcting Codes. This approach allows us to apply established theoretical results for Boosting in our analysis of our hashing solution. Specifically, we show that the training accuracy in Boosting can be considered as a lower bound on the (empirical) Mean Average Precision (mAP) score. In experiments with three image retrieval benchmarks, the proposed formulation yields significant improvement in mAP over state-of-the-art supervised hashing methods, while using fewer bits in the hash codes.

Categories and Subject Descriptors

H.3.3 [**Information Search and Retrieval**]: Retrieval models

Keywords

Hashing; similarity search; error correcting codes

1. INTRODUCTION

Vast amounts of multimedia data are increasingly available on the Internet; photo collection websites, such as Flickr, are reported to contain billions of images [1], while Internet users upload 100 hours of videos to social platforms such as YouTube per minute [13]. This explosive growth brings new challenges to researchers, particularly in storing and supporting efficient and accurate responses to users' queries of these immense data repositories. In this work, we focus on the nearest neighbor retrieval problem, where a ranked set of semantically-similar items are to be efficiently and accurately retrieved to match the user's query to a large image database.

One widely-used solution to expedite similarity search is to construct hash functions to map the data into a Hamming space where linear search is known to be fast and often sublinear solutions perform well. Early work leveraged Locality Sensitive Hashing (LSH) [2], which ensures the retrieval of the nearest neighbor(s) to be within a scale of the true neighbor in sublinear time. Supervised and unsupervised solutions have also been proposed for mapping data instances to binary codes such that semantic or metric-wise similar neighbors have similar codes [10, 12, 4, 11, 7, 6]. With the ability to leverage label information, supervised solutions have shown to outperform unsupervised methods when the task is to retrieve semantically similar neighbors [11, 6, 5].

An ideal hashing method should achieve high retrieval performance in sublinear time with a low memory footprint. We demonstrate that when the goal is to retrieve semantically similar neighbors, a Boosting formulation that is based on Error Correcting Codes (ECCs) [9] outperforms state-of-the-art techniques while satisfying these properties. In addition, this approach allows us to apply established theoretical results for Boosting in our analysis of our hashing solution. Specifically, we show that the training accuracy in Boosting can be considered as a lower bound on the (empirical) Mean Average Precision (mAP) score. Moreover, the proposed Boosting approach has no out-of-sample extension problems, unlike some competing methods, e.g., [12].

Earlier work considered the use of ECCs [14], where the hash functions are learned by ridge regression analysis between the inputs (classes) and the ECCs. This approach requires a user-defined preference for the ECCs, which is usually hard to predetermine. In contrast, our Boosting approach allows us to adaptively generate these ECCs while also leveraging the theoretical guarantees of the Boosting algorithm in attaining direct optimization for the expected mean Average Precision (mAP) retrieval performance.

In experiments with three benchmark image datasets, the proposed approach attains improved mAP vs state-of-the-art supervised hashing techniques.

2. METHODOLOGY

Given a set of data points with label information, the problem is to assign each instance a binary hash code such that semantically similar points are mapped to nearby codes. As already noted above, such codes can enable rapid nearest neighbor search, which is crucial in many multimedia retrieval problems such as image annotation [3], label-based image retrieval [11], etc.

Formally, let $\mathcal{H}$ denote the $B-$dimensional Hamming space. Given a set of instances with label information, $\mathcal{D} = \{(\mathbf{x}_i, y_i)_{i=1,..,N} | \mathbf{x}_i \in \mathcal{X}, y_i \in \mathcal{Y}\}$ where $\mathcal{X}$ and $\mathcal{Y}$ denote the feature and label space[1], respectively, the goal of hashing is to find a mapping (or hashing) $f : \mathcal{X} \rightarrow \mathcal{H}$ such that a particular proximity between the set of inputs is preserved in the Hamming space.

We will consider the Adaboost.OC algorithm [9] which will provide us with two distinct mappings. This method is a well known

[1]We will assume $\mathcal{Y} = \{1, ..., C\}$.

MM'14, November 03 - 07 2014, Orlando, FL, USA.

http://dx.doi.org/10.1145/2647868.2654963.

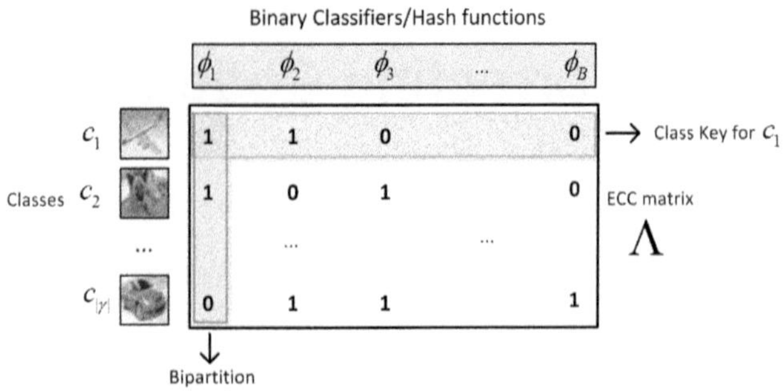

Figure 1: An example ECC matrix. Each column describes the bipartitioning of the data and and each row, dubbed as *class keys*, denotes the target outputs of a particular class in such partitions. A binary classifier for each column is learned.

meta-classifier that can be used in conjunction with many learning algorithms with different loss functions.

The algorithm involves training a set of binary classifiers $\Phi(\mathbf{x}) = \{\phi_1(\mathbf{x}), ..., \phi_B(\mathbf{x})\}$ on randomly bipartitioned data. This partitioning information is embedded in an 'ECC' matrix $\Lambda \in \{0,1\}^{C \times B}$ where each column describes the bipartitioning and each row denotes the target outputs of a particular class in such partitions. The number of rows is equal to the number of classes, thus a unique binary code, dubbed as *class key*, is assigned for each class. Let us denote these class keys (rows of matrix Λ) as $\varphi_1, ..., \varphi_C$. Fig. 1 illustrates an example of a coding matrix.

We will assign two separate binary codes for a point $\mathbf{x}$. The first is obtained from mapping Φ, i.e., it is the vector formed by the outputs of the binary classifiers, $\Phi(\mathbf{x}) = [\phi_1(\mathbf{x}), ..., \phi_B(\mathbf{x})]$. The second binary code is obtained by comparing $\Phi(\mathbf{x})$ with each class key and taking the 'closest' one. This corresponds to a minimum distance decoding scheme, which is robust to hash function errors in mapping queries during retrieval. Formally, it is φ_{i^*} where $i^* = \arg\min_{i \in \{1,...,C\}} D_h(\varphi_i, \Phi(\mathbf{x}))$ and D_h is the Hamming distance.

Notice that there are only C distinct codes of this type (C hash bins), consequently many instances will be hashed to the same code. On the other hand, the cardinality of the range of mapping Φ is 2^B, thus it does not necessarily assign the same binary code to instances with the same label, but it does assign them to nearby codes (cf. Fig. 2). From now on, we simply use $\mathbf{f}(\mathbf{x})_\Phi$ and $\mathbf{f}(\mathbf{x})_\psi$ to denote the two binary codes of $\mathbf{x}$.

Given a query $(\mathbf{x}_q, y_q)$, we would like to retrieve all instances, preferably having the same class data points ranked as highest. Notice that we can do retrieval based on the two different sets of binary codes of the data. Retrieval based on $\mathbf{f}(\cdot)_\psi$ has $\mathcal{O}(1)$ complexity since comparing class keys with $\mathbf{f}(\mathbf{x}_q)_\psi$ is enough to rank all data points. Also, the space complexity of the codes are $\mathcal{O}(1)$ but we do need a data structure that maps instances to these codes. We refer to this as *class key based retrieval.*

Alternatively, we can do retrieval by considering $\mathbf{f}(\cdot)_\Phi$. We consider a linear scan of the data, which has $\mathcal{O}(N)$ complexity. The space complexity is also $\mathcal{O}(N)$ but the binary codes can be stored in a far more compact manner. We refer to this as *instance based retrieval*. Fig. 2 illustrates these two different mappings.

Weiss et al. [12] pose two important properties for a "good" code: (1) the code corresponding to a novel input should be easily computed and (2) compact codes should be adequate enough to represent the data. Adaboost.OC already satisfies the first property as it does not have out-of-sample problems since the binary classifiers are defined on the entire domain of the feature space. The compactness of a code usually depends on the ability to produce uncorrelated and balanced mappings. Boosting handles the correlation problem by altering the probability distribution weights of the instances in each round. This allows the algorithm to focus on the "harder" to classify instances in subsequent iterations. This may not result in balanced mappings but, as demonstrated in the experiments, our method outperforms other techniques that explicity constrain the mappings to be balanced. For Boosting, in early iterations, the mappings are more balanced owing to the fact the the distribution is more uniform; however, in subsequent iterations, hash functions are generated that are focused on instances that previously were incorrectly mapped.

In addition to these properties we provide an analysis for the retrieval performance as the code length increases for this boosting approach. Although this analysis is only based on a class key based retrieval scheme it is important since for example, it ensures the performance increase in a retrieval application with lengthier codes. First let us give Claim 1 which connects the retrieval performance to the accuracy of the Adaboost.OC algorithm.

CLAIM 1. *$1 - \epsilon \leq$ mAP where $\epsilon = \mathbb{E}_D[\![y_i \neq H(x_i)]\!]$ is the empirical error of Adaboost.OC with H being its associated strong classifier having identical weak learner weights and mAP $= \mathbb{E}_D[\![aP(x_i)]\!]$ is the empirical mean of average precision values (aP)* [2].

PROOF. Note that $1 - \epsilon = \mathbb{E}_D[\![y_i = H(x_i)]\!]$. If $y_i = H(x_i)$ then $[\![y_i = H(x_i)]\!] = 1$ and aP(x_i) = 1. If $y_i \neq H(x_i)$ then $[\![y_i = H(x_i)]\!] = 0$ and $0 <$ aP$(x_i) < 1$. Thus $\mathbb{E}_D[\![y_i = H(x_i)]\!] \leq \mathbb{E}_D[\![\text{aP}(x_i)]\!]$.

□

Simple as it is, Claim 1 is important as we immediately observe that as the training error approaches zero, a property that Adaboost satisfies, the empirical mAP value approaches to 1. Thus, the Adaboost.OC algorithm allows us to consider the mAP score indirectly as our objective function to be maximized while also ensuring that as the code length increases the retrieval performance improves. We formally state this in the following corollary.

COROLLARY 1. *As $B \to \infty$ the empirical mAP score of the class key based retrieval scheme approaches to 1.*

PROOF. Immediate from Theorem 1 [9] and Claim 1. □

3. EXPERIMENTS

We have evaluated our approach on three datasets. We employ three different learning algorithms; decision stumps (Stump), decision trees (Tree) and linear SVMs (LSVM), and show performance results for both class key and instance based retrieval (suffixed with *-b* and *-s*, respectively). We compare our approach against six state-of-the-art supervised hashing methods; STH [15], SPLH [11], BRE [4], MLH [7], SHK [6] and TSH-KSH [5]. These methods have shown to outperform earlier supervised and unsupervised techniques such as [10, 8, 12].

For evaluation, the mean average precision (mAP) scores are computed at varying bit lengths. In all these settings a true neighbor of an instance is one that has the same label with it. For all cases we follow a similar protocol as in [11, 6, 15] to construct our training and test set.

[2] D is the uniform distribution.

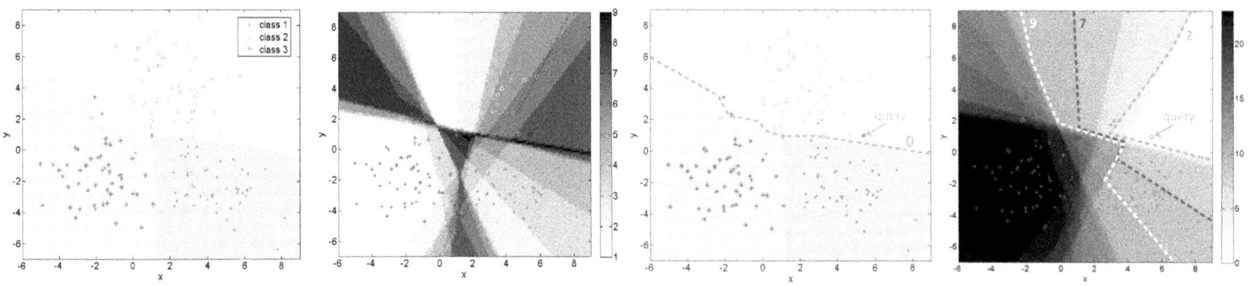

(a) (b) (c) (d)

Figure 2: A toy example in $\mathbb{R}^2$. (a) shows three classes (red, green, blue) generated from three different Gaussian distributions. Associated with each class is a *class key*. Each point is assigned two binary codes; one is generated from mapping Φ ($\mathbf{f}(\cdot)_{\Phi}$) and the second is the corresponding 'closest' class key to Φ ($\mathbf{f}(\cdot)_{\psi}$). As shown, for each class key there is a region in the feature space that is closer to that class key than to any other. (b) further partitions each such region according to the distance between the two mappings. (c) Given a query, class based retrieval considers $\mathbf{f}(\mathbf{x})_{\psi}$, thus it has a Hamming distance 0 with all other points in the green region. Consequently it will return these points first. (d) Instance based retrieval considers binary codes obtained from $\mathbf{f}(\mathbf{x})_{\Phi}$.

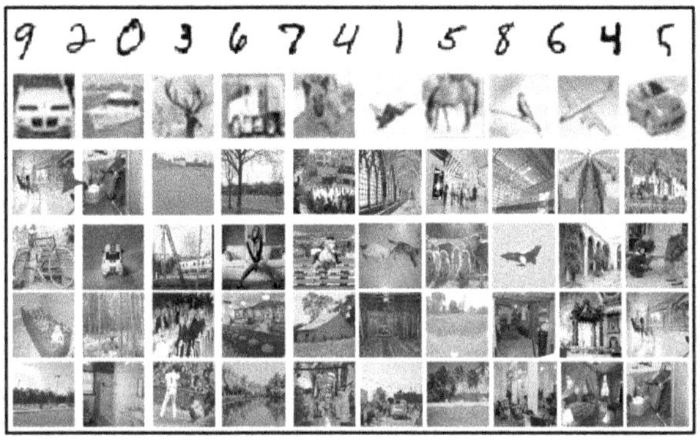

Figure 3: Sample images from MNIST digits, CIFAR-10 and SUN397 datasets.

We use the MATLAB implementations of the aforementioned learning techniques. The experiments were conducted on a workstation with Intel Xeon CPU @ 2.67 GHz and 12 GB of RAM.

3.1 Datasets

The MNIST benchmark contains 70K digit samples where each sample is associated with a label from 0 to 9. The dataset is partitioned into two parts; a training and a test set having 69K and 1K samples, respectively. We additionally sample 2K instances from the training set to learn the hash functions. The rest of the training data is used to populate the hash table.

The CIFAR-10 benchmark contains 60K samples from 10 different categories. We partition this dataset into a training set with 59K samples and a test set with 1K samples. 2K instances are sampled from the training set to learn the hash functions, and the remaining training data is used to populate the hash table.

The SUN397 dataset contains roughly 40K samples from 397 categories. We sample 30 instances from each class to construct our test set. The rest constitutes the training set, where again a subset is sampled (20 instances per class) to learn the hash functions, and the remaining training data is used to populate the hash table.

3.2 Results

Table 1 shows the results for the MNIST digits benchmark. Tree-b and TSH-KSH achieves the highest accuracy with a significant improvement over other state-of-the-art techniques. Note also the rapid increase in performance for certain learning algorithms as the number of bits increases, e.g. Stump-b and Tree-s. TSH yields superior performance when shorter codes are used; this may be due to the easiness of the MNIST dataset and the fact that TSH is formulated to give 'good' codes with fewer bits. However, as discussed shortly, in relatively more difficult benchmarks our method outperforms TSH even when such short codes are used.

Table 2 displays the running times to learn the hash functions for the MNIST benchmark. We observe that using decision stumps as the weak learner results in the fastest training times, excluding STHs. Note that it is considerably slower to learn the hashing parameters for certain methods with lengthier codes, e.g. SPLH.

Table 3 shows the results for the CIFAR-10 benchmark. In this dataset, LSVM-b shows nearly a two-fold improvement in mAP vs the best performing state-of-the-art technique TSH-KSH for all bit lengths. Also, the 12 bit LSVM-b outperforms all competing methods with 512 bits. Note that, while state-of-the-art methods have a slight increase in performance with lengthier bit codes; LSVM-b, Tree-b and Stump-b have a much more rapid increase.

Table 4 shows the results for SUN397 dataset. Due to the large number of categories the retrieval performance is lower when compared to previous benchmarks, especially with fewer bits. We again observe that the 12 bit LSVM-b significantly outperforms all competing methods with 512 bits. For instance-based retrieval, our method with decision stumps shows superior performance, attaining a 0.0123 mAP score at 512 bits. More importantly, the performance increases substantially for LSVM-b, Tree-b and Stump-b, as opposed to modest increases for competing techniques.

Overall, our proposed formulation provides a significant advantage in terms of both space and time complexity (higher or equivalent accuracy, with fewer bits). This could prove to be a crucial advantage over past supervised hashing methods, particularly when indexing larger and larger datasets.

Finally, in comparing our class key vs. instance based retrieval formulations, we observe that the former yields superior performance. This is expected as the minimum distance decoding scheme can compensate for a portion of hash function errors in the retrieval stage. Nevertheless, both retrieval schemes can also be used in conjuction. For instance, once a query is hashed to one of the C bins according to $\mathbf{f}(\cdot)_{\psi}$, the binary codes $\mathbf{f}(\cdot)_{\Phi}$ can be used to rank the instances within that bin. Given the query in Fig. 2 (c) , this corresponds to ranking the points in the green region that normally have

Table 1: Mean Average Precision for the MNIST digits.

Method	Mean Average Precision (Random = 0.1)					
	12 bits	48 bits	64 bits	128 bits	256 bits	512 bits
STHs [15]	0.399	0.382	0.397	0.431	0.448	0.458
SPLH [11]	0.135	0.184	0.185	0.202	0.344	0.374
BRE [4]	0.409	0.585	0.63	0.682	0.691	0.686
MLH [7]	0.302	0.442	0.495	0.538	0.562	0.571
SHK [6]	0.772	0.849	0.855	0.855	0.852	0.877
TSH-KSH [5]	**0.89**	**0.91**	**0.922**	0.928	0.933	0.933
Stump-s	0.292	0.406	0.449	0.462	0.484	0.491
Tree-s	0.538	0.671	0.80	0.84	0.859	0.887
LSVM-s	0.628	0.676	0.725	0.739	0.771	0.759
Stump-b	0.529	0.645	0.71	0.765	0.795	0.826
Tree-b	0.799	0.876	0.915	**0.947**	**0.94**	**0.943**
LSVM-b	0.807	0.843	0.857	0.875	0.874	0.887

Table 2: Runtime results in seconds for MNIST digist dataset.

Method	MNIST	
	12 bits	512 bits
STHs [15]	0.6	24.2
SPLH [11]	99	7480.3
BRE [4]	58	1625.2
MLH [7]	63	3977.7
SHK [6]	132	3136.7
TSH-KSH [5]	59.2	2607.6
Stump	41.2	1643.2
Tree	80	4535.2
LSVM	78.5	5111.4

Table 3: Mean Average Precision for the CIFAR-10.

Method	Mean Average Precision (Random = 0.1)					
	12 bits	48 bits	64 bits	128 bits	256 bits	512 bits
STHs [15]	0.178	0.164	0.164	0.17	0.181	0.187
SPLH [11]	0.122	0.152	0.162	0.193	0.21	0.224
BRE [4]	0.159	0.186	0.195	0.206	0.21	0.217
MLH [7]	0.15	0.179	0.182	0.19	0.194	0.197
SHK [6]	0.25	0.312	0.312	0.338	0.326	0.33
TSH-KSH [5]	0.30	0.355	0.358	0.375	0.385	0.389
Stump-s	0.145	0.159	0.168	0.178	0.189	0.187
Tree-s	0.121	0.15	0.162	0.19	0.221	0.237
LSVM-s	0.225	0.271	0.275	0.294	0.293	0.292
Stump-b	0.336	0.404	0.425	0.473	0.51	0.543
Tree-b	0.335	0.457	0.458	0.521	0.575	0.578
LSVM-b	**0.49**	**0.581**	**0.59**	**0.604**	**0.605**	**0.642**

Table 4: Mean Average Precision for the SUN397.

Method	Mean Average Precision ($\times 10^{-1}$, Random = 0.025)					
	12 bits	48 bits	64 bits	128 bits	256 bits	512 bits
STHs [15]	0.049	0.079	0.087	0.115	0.144	0.157
SPLH [11]	0.058	0.053	0.052	0.05	0.055	0.063
BRE [4]	0.058	0.076	0.087	0.095	0.11	0.119
MLH [7]	0.056	0.057	0.057	0.058	0.063	0.082
SHK [6]	0.085	0.087	0.091	0.094	0.098	0.120
TSH-KSH [5]	0.032	0.037	0.040	0.049	0.060	0.071
Stump-s	0.051	0.071	0.083	0.095	0.11	0.123
Tree-s	0.031	0.032	0.033	0.035	0.04	0.049
LSVM-s	0.068	0.09	0.09	0.095	0.101	0.107
Stump-b	0.107	0.134	0.137	0.146	0.189	0.222
Tree-b	0.105	0.115	0.133	0.153	0.194	0.286
LSVM-b	**0.12**	**0.178**	**0.209**	**0.224**	**0.317**	**0.422**

a zero Hamming distance with the query based on $\mathbf{f}(\cdot)_{\psi}$. Thus, this ECC based Boosting method works best in conjunction with a class key based retrieval scheme, where instances associated with the same label ought to be retrieved in a ranked manner, e.g. for label-based retrieval problems such as automatic image tagging or annotation.

4. CONCLUSION

Our proposed ECC based Boosting method for supervised hashing method yields significant gains in retrieval performance vs. state-of-the-art techniques. Moreover, the proposed formulation provides higher accuracy, with fewer bits to store for the hash codes.

On the other hand, what are the limitations? First, such an approach is suitable for applications where the binary code can be treated as a particular 'label'. Secondly, the training inputs must be associated with label information. Lastly, there is the question of how the method extends to new classes; however, this issue of generalizing to unseen classes is also a problem of existing supervised hashing work. These are fertile topics for future investigation.

Acknowledgments

This work was supported in part through NSF grants 1029430 and 0910908, and by a PhD fellowship from the Turkey's Ministry of National Education.

5. REFERENCES

[1] http://blog.flickr.net/en/2011/08/04/.

[2] A. Gionis, P. Indyk, and R. Motwani. Similarity search in high dimensions via hashing. In *Proc. VLDB*, 1999.

[3] M. Guillaumin, T. Mensink, J. Verbeek, and C. Schmid. Tagprop: Discriminative metric learning in nearest neighbor models for image auto-annotation. In *In Proc. ICCV*, 2009.

[4] B. Kulis and T. Darrell. Learning to hash with binary reconstructive embeddings. In *Proc. NIPS*, 2009.

[5] G. Lin, C. Shen, D. Suter, and A. van den Hengel. A general two-step approach to learning-based hashing. In *Proc. ICCV*, 2013.

[6] J. W. Liu, Wei and, R. Ji, Y.-G. Jiang, and S.-F. Chang. Supervised hashing with kernels. In *Proc. CVPR*, 2012.

[7] M. Norouzi and D. J. Fleet. Minimal loss hashing for compact binary codes. In *Proc. ICML*, 2011.

[8] R. Salakhutdinov and G. Hinton. Semantic hashing. *Int. J. Approx. Reasoning*, 50(7):969–978, 2009.

[9] R. E. Schapire. Using output codes to boost multiclass learning problems. In *Proc. ICML*, 1997.

[10] G. Shakhnarovich, P. Viola, and T. Darrell. Fast pose estimation with parameter sensitive hashing. In *Proc. ICCV*, 2003.

[11] J. Wang, S. Kumar, and S.-F. Chang. Semi-supervised hashing for large-scale search. *IEEE TPAMI*, 34(12):2393–2406, 2012.

[12] Y. Weiss, A. Torralba, and R. Fergus. Spectral hashing. In *Proc. NIPS*, 2008.

[13] http://www.youtube.com/yt/press/.

[14] Z. Yu, D. Cai, and X. He. Error-correcting output hashing in fast similarity search. In *Proc. ICIMCS*, 2010.

[15] D. Zhang, J. Wang, D. Cai, and J. Lu. Self-taught hashing for fast similarity search. In *Proc. ACM SIGIR*, 2010.

Pedestrian Attribute Recognition At Far Distance

Yubin Deng, Ping Luo, Chen Change Loy, Xiaoou Tang
Dept. of Information Engineering
The Chinese University of Hong Kong
danny.s.deng.ds@gmail.com, lp011@ie.cuhk.edu.hk, ccloy@ie.cuhk.edu.hk,
xtang@ie.cuhk.edu.hk

ABSTRACT

The capability of recognizing pedestrian attributes, such as gender and clothing style, at far distance, is of practical interest in far-view surveillance scenarios where face and body close-shots are hardly available. We make two contributions in this paper. First, we release a new pedestrian attribute dataset, which is by far the largest and most diverse of its kind. We show that the large-scale dataset facilitates the learning of robust attribute detectors with good generalization performance. Second, we present the benchmark performance by SVM-based method and propose an alternative approach that exploits context of neighboring pedestrian images for improved attribute inference.

Categories and Subject Descriptors

H.2.8 [**Database Applications**]: Image databases

Keywords

Large-scale database; attribute classification.

1. INTRODUCTION

Visual recognition of pedestrian attributes, such as gender, age, clothing style, is an emerging research topic in computer vision research, due to its high application potential in areas such as video-based business intelligence [ ] and visual surveillance [ ]. In many real-world surveillance scenarios, clear close-shots of face and body regions are not available. Thus, attribute recognition has to be performed at far distance using full body appearance (which can be partially occluded) in the absence of critical face/close-shot body visual information.

There are two fundamental challenges in attribute inference at far distance: 1) *Appearance diversity* - owing to diverse appearances of pedestrian clothing and uncontrollable multi-factor variations such as illumination and camera viewing angle, there exist large intra-class variations among different images for the same attribute. Learning to detect such attributes requires a rich set of training samples. Relying on a single source and small-scale training data would easily lead to an unrealistic model that generalizes poorly to unknown domains due to the inherent data bias. 2) *Appearance ambiguity* - far-view attribute recognition is an exceptionally difficult task due to inherent visual ambiguity and poor quality of visual features obtained from far view field (Fig. 1). In particular, an individual image may only occupy a few tens of imagery pixels whilst only a tiny fraction of them are truly distinctive for attribute classification. Often, parts of the body are occluded, either by obstacles or other pedestrians, which further increases the difficulty of extracting relevant features for inference. For instance, images with the 'carrying backpack' attribute may not necessarily have the full bag visible due to pedestrian posture (Fig. 1).

Figure 1: The new PETA dataset contains far more images and attribute annotations than existing datasets. Positive and negative sample images are indicated by blue and red boxes, respectively.

Existing datasets do not reflect the diversity nature in real-world environment. In view of this shortcoming, we introduce and release a new large-scale PEdesTrian Attribute (PETA) dataset[1]. The dataset is by far the largest of its kind, covering more than 60 attributes on 19000 images. As can be seen from Fig. 1, in comparison with existing datasets, PETA is more diverse and challenging in terms of imagery variations and complexity. More details are presented in Sec. 2. Apart from releasing the new dataset, we also propose an alternative approach for attribute recogni-

[1] http://mmlab.ie.cuhk.edu.hk/projects/PETA.html

MM'14, November 3–7, 2014, Orlando, Florida, USA.

http://dx.doi.org/10.1145/2647868.2654966.

tion with emphasis to mitigating the visual ambiguity of appearance features. Specifically, instead of treating an image independently, we consider inference with the help from neighboring pedestrian images whose appearances look alike. We hypothesize that neighboring samples share natural invariance in their feature space, which could be treated as a form of regularization or context. As such, attribute inference of an image can be locally constrained by its neighbors to obtain a more reliable prediction. To this end, we view multiple pedestrian images as forming a Markov Random Field (MRF) graph. The underlying graph topology is automatically inferred, with node associations weighted by pairwise image similarity. The similarity can be estimated as the conventional Euclidean distance or more elaborated decision forest-based similarity with feature selection [,]. By carrying out inference on the graph, we jointly reason and estimate the attribute probability of all images in the graph.

It is worth noting that MRF inference for smoothing [ ] is commonly applied in image segmentation [ ], but this paper is the first work that explores this approach for pedestrian attribute inference. We summarize our contributions as follows: 1) we introduce the largest pedestrian attribute dataset to date to facilitate future research on attribute classification at far distance; 2) we present the benchmark performance by SVM-based method [ ] and propose an alternative approach that exploits context of neighboring images for improved attribute inference. Thanks to the neighboring context, our model is capable of accurately detecting subtle attributes, which may otherwise be mis-detected from single image.

2. PEDESTRIAN ATTRIBUTE DATASET

Statistics: We carefully chose and organized 10 publicly available small-scale datasets to construct the new PEdesTrian Attribute (PETA) dataset[2,3]. The name, size, and main characteristics of constituent datasets, are summarized in the table in Fig. 2. The PETA dataset thus consists of 19000 images, with resolution ranging from 17 × 39 to 169 × 365 pixels. Organizing these datasets are not straightforward. First, we carefully removed erroneous images or duplicated copies from each datasets. In addition, each image is newly labeled with 61 binary and 4 multi-class attributes. The binary attributes cover an exhaustive set of characteristics of interest, including demographics (e.g. gender and age range), appearance (e.g. hair style), upper and lower body clothing style (e.g. casual or formal), and accessories. The four multi-class attributes encompass 11 basic color namings [ ], respectively, for footwear, hair, upper-body clothing, and lower-body clothing. The distribution of a binary attribute is considered balanced if the ratio of larger to smaller class is no more than 20:1. As such, out of the 61 binary attributes, 31 are balanced. Fig. 2(b) depicts the distribution of a few attributes with sample images[4].

Uniqueness: Compared to existing pedestrian attribute dataset, this new attribute dataset has three notable uniqueness: (1) *Larger size*: the size of the PETA dataset is over 5× and 15× larger than the APiS and VIPeR datasets, respectively. (2) *High diversity*: we deliberately selected smaller-scale datasets collected under different conditions from diverse scenes to enrich the composition of the new attribute dataset. As can be seen from Fig. 1 and summarized in the table in Fig. 2(a), despite that the constituents of PETA are all captured from far view field, they exhibit large differences in terms of lighting condition, camera viewing angles, image resolutions, background complexity, and indoor/outdoor environments. (3) *Rich annotations*: The PETA dataset contains far richer annotations in comparison with existing datasets, such as VIPeR [ ], with only 15 binary attributes, and APiS [ ], with 11 binary and 2 multi-class attributes, It is worth pointing out that the 61 annotated attributes in PETA dataset include the 15 attributes that are suggested by the UK Home Office and UK police to be the most valuable in tracking and criminal identification [ ].

Usage: Visual understanding through semantic attributes is an active research topic in the multimedia research community, e.g. [ ], for the applications such as image retrieval and recommendation systems [, ,]. This dataset can serve as an alternative benchmark. More specifically, the new dataset can be used in visual surveillance research on pedestrian tracking, detection, re-identification, and activity analysis. Furthermore, the visual attributes can potentially be integrated with multi-sources of information, e.g. audio, textual annotation, sensor signals, for multimedia surveillance [,]. In the next section, we present two benchmarking methods for attribute classification, a fundamental task in visual understanding.

3. BASELINE METHODS

Baseline 1. SVM with intersection kernel (ikSVM) [ ][5] reduces both the time and space complexities from $\mathcal{O}(mn)$ of the traditional linear kernel SVM to $\mathcal{O}(n)$. Here, m and n are the number of the support vectors and the dimension of feature vectors. Previous study [ ] has applied this method successfully for pedestrian attribute classification. Cross validation for slack parameter C is performed as in [ ].

Baseline 2. To improve attribute inference, we exploit the context of neighboring images by Markov Random Field (MRF), which is an undirect graph, where each node represents a random variable and each edge represents the relation between two connected nodes. The energy function of MRF over a graph G can be defined as follows

$$E_{MRF}(G) = \sum_{u \in G} C_u(l_u) + \sum_{u \in G} \sum_{v \in N(u)} S_{uv}(l_u, l_v), \quad (1)$$

where $u, v \in G$ are two random variables in the graph and l_u denotes the state of u. C_u and S_{uv} signify the unary cost and pairwise cost functions, respectively. More precisely, they indicate the cost of assigning state l_u to variable u as well as the cost of assigning states to neighboring nodes u, v, which is determined based on the graph structure (e.g., assigning different states to nodes that are similar is penalized). $N(u)$ is a set of variables that are the neighbors of u.

In this work, each random variable corresponds to an image and the relation between two variables corresponds

[2]Images in PETA dataset are all exclusive from those in APiS [ ].

[3]All images in PETA are freely available for academic use except i-LIDS, which requires application to United Kingdom Home Office, https://www.gov.uk/imagery-library-for-intelligent-detection-systems.

[4]Sample images of the datasets and the full distributions of all attributes can found in the supplementary material.

[5]http://www.cs.berkeley.edu/~smaji/projects/fiksvm/

Datasets	#Images	Camera angle	View point	Illumination	Resolution	Scene
3DPeS	1012	high	varying	varying	from 31x100 to 236x178	outdoor
CAVIAR4REID	1220	ground	varying	low	from 17x39 to 72x141	outdoor
CUHK	4563	high	varying	varying	80x160	outdoor
GRID	1275	varying	frontal&back	low	from 29x67 to 169x365	indoor
i-LIDS	477	medium	back	high	from 32x76 to 115x294	indoor
MIT	888	ground	back	high	64x128	outdoor
PRID	1134	high	profile	low	64x128	outdoor
SARC3D	200	medium	varying	varying	from 54x187 to 150x307	outdoor
TownCentre	6967	medium	varying	medium	from 44x109 to 148x332	outdoor
VIPeR	1264	ground	varying	varying	48x128	outdoor
Total = PETA	**19000**	**varying**	**varying**	**varying**	**varying**	**varying**

(a)

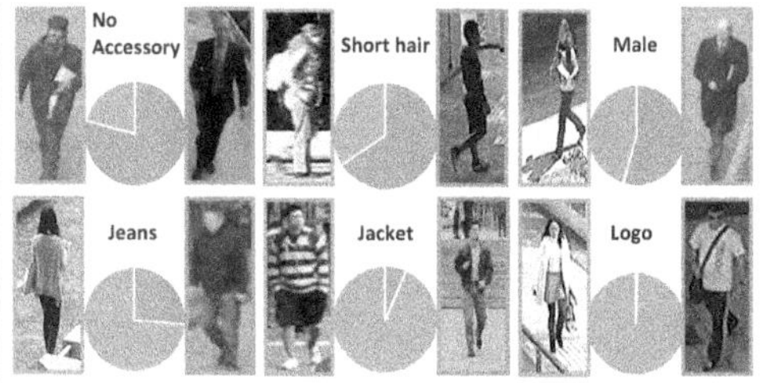

(b)

Figure 2: (a) The composition of PETA dataset. (b) Examples of attributes with their distribution (blue: positive, orange: negative).

to the similarity between images. The states of variable are the values of the image attribute, which is $l_u \in \{0, 1\}$. The unary function is modeled by

$$C_u(l_u) = -\log P(l_u|u), \tag{2}$$

where $P(l_u|u)$ is the probability of predicting the attribute value of image u as l_u. This probability is learned by ikSVM.

Now we consider the definition of the pairwise function. To define affinity between nodes, a simple way widely adopted by existing methods, such as [ ], is the Gaussian kernel, $\exp\{-\frac{\|u-v\|^2}{\sigma^2}\}$, in which u, v indicate the feature vectors of two images and σ is a coefficient that needs to be tuned. The graph built on this kernel function can model the global smoothness among images. However, when large variations are presented, one may consider modeling the local smoothness and discovering the intrinsic manifold of the data. Thus, an alternative is to employ the random forest (RF) [ ] to learn the pairwise function [,]. The RF we adopted is unsupervised, i.e. it takes unlabeled test samples as input. The output is pairwise sample similarity derived from the data partitioning discovered at the leaf nodes of RF. The unsupervised RF can be learned using the pseudo two-class method as in [, ,]. Specifically, we treat the original unlabeled test samples as first class. The pseudo second class is created by sampling at random from the univariate distributions of the unlabeled test samples. With this strategy, the unsupervised RF learning problem becomes a canonical classification problem that can be solved by conventional classification forest training method. Specifically, the information gain of unsupervised RF is identical to that of conventional supervised RF, defined as

$$\Delta\mathcal{I} = \mathcal{I}_p - \frac{n_l}{n_p}\mathcal{I}_l - \frac{n_r}{n_p}\mathcal{I}_r, \tag{3}$$

where p, l, and r refer to a splitting node and its left and right child. The variable n denotes the number of samples at a node, $n_p = n_r + n_l$. $\mathcal{I}$ is the Gini impurity measure at each node [ ].

The pairwise function is expressed as

$$S_{uv}(l_u, l_v)) = \begin{cases} \frac{1}{T}\sum_{t=1}^{T}\exp\{-dist^t(u,v)\} & \text{if } l_u \neq l_v, \\ 0 & \text{otherwise.} \end{cases} \tag{4}$$

Here, $dist^t(u, v) = 0$ if u, v fall into the same leaf node and $dist^t(u, v) = +\infty$ otherwise, where t is the index of tree. Since the graph is dense, the inference of MRF is difficult. Thus, we build a k-NN sparse graph by limiting the number of neighbors for each node. We set $k = 5$ in our experiment. Eq.(1) can be efficiently solved by the min-cut/max-flow algorithm introduced in [ ].

4. EXPERIMENT

We present benchmark results on PETA by evaluating the performance of intersection kernel SVM (ikSVM) [ ], MRF with Gaussian kernel (MRFg), and MRF with random forest (MRFr), as discussed in Sec.3.

We randomly partitioned the dataset images into 9,500 for training, 1,900 for verification and 7,600 for testing. We selected 35 attributes for our study, consisting of the 15 most important attributes in video surveillance proposed by human experts [ ], [ ] and 20 difficult yet interesting attributes chosen by us, covering all body parts of the pedestrian and different prevalence of the attributes. For example, 'sunglasses' and 'v-neck' have a limited number of positive examples. For the attributes with unbalanced positives and negatives samples, we trained ikSVM for each attribute by augmenting the positive training examples to the same size as negative examples with small variations in scale and orientation. This is to avoid bias due to imbalanced data. For MRFg and MRFr, we built the graphs using two different schemes. The first scheme, symbolized by MRFg_1 and MRFr_1, is to construct the graphs with only the testing images. The second one, symbolized by MRFg_2 and MRFr_2, is to include both training and testing samples in the graphs.

Features. Low-level color and texture features have been proven robust in describing pedestrian images [ ], including 8 color channels such as RGB, HSV, and YCbCr, and 21 texture channels obtained by the Gabor and Schmid filters on the luminance channel. The setting of the parameters of the Gabor and Schmid filters are given in [ ]. We horizontally partitioned the image into six strips and then extracted the above feature channels, each of which is described by a bin-size of 16. Finally, a 2784-dimensional feature vector is obtained for each image.

As shown in Table 1, we report attribute detection accuracy as [ ] and have the following observations. First, the MRF-based methods outperform ikSVM on most of the attributes. For instance, MRFr_2 achieves an average of 3.4% improvement over ikSVM for the 'age' attributes shown on the top. This is significant in a dataset with large appearance diversity and ambiguity and it demonstrates that graph regularization can improve attribute inference. Second, the MRF graphs built with the second scheme is superior compared to the first scheme. This is reasonable because using both the training and testing data can better cover the image space. Third, for many important attributes, such as 'hair' and 'gender', random forest works much better than Gaussian kernel. It is worth pointing out that all methods perform poorly on attributes with imbalanced positive-negative distribution, such as 'logo', 'sandals', 'sunglasses', and 'v-neck'.

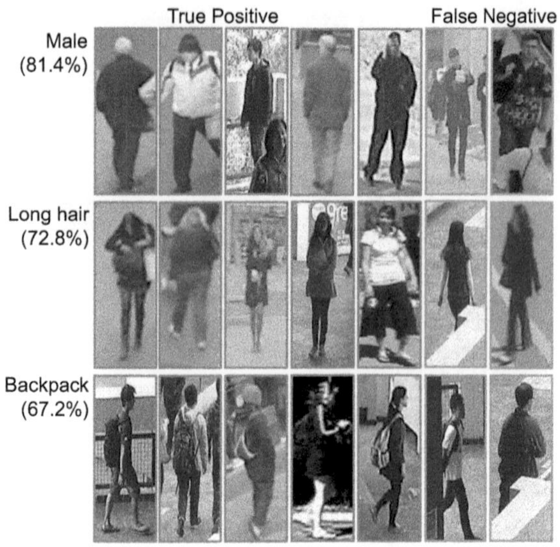

Figure 3: Examples of attribute classification.

Fig. 3 shows some attribute classification results using forest MRF. By exploiting the hidden context information, we obtain good accuracy on gender and hair attributes. False negative samples typically result from occlusion (e.g. backpack), color ambiguity (long hair) and background noise (male).

5. CONCLUSIONS

This paper presents a new large-scale dataset (PETA) sized at 19000 images with 61 annotated attributes. To cope with such large and diverse data in the context of attribute classification, we explored and proposed a novel approach by exploiting the neighborhood information among image samples. We showed that accurate attribute detection can be achieved with the automatically inferred neighborhood graph topology. Future work will involve the evaluation of other popular algorithms in attribute classification using our dataset. We hope that this dataset could serve as a new benchmark for the more realistic training and testing of algorithms.

Table 1: Accuracy on the PETA dataset.

Attribute	ikSVM	MRFg1	MRFg2	MRFr1	MRFr2
Age16-30	80.4	80.9	81.7	80.9	**83.8**
Age31-45	73.6	74.6	76.2	74.0	**78.8**
Age46-60	73.1	74.1	75.2	73.2	**76.4**
AgeAbove61	87.2	87.2	88.2	86.3	**89.0**
Backpack	66.7	67.1	67.1	67.0	**67.2**
CarryingOther	64.6	64.9	66.8	64.6	**68.0**
Casual lower	70.7	70.9	**71.6**	70.4	71.3
Casual upper	70.3	70.4	71.2	69.8	**71.3**
Formal lower	71.0	71.2	71.8	71.2	**71.9**
Formal upper	70.0	70.3	**70.4**	70.3	70.0
Hat	82.3	82.9	84.3	82.3	**86.7**
Jacket	67.7	68.3	**68.4**	68.1	67.9
Jeans	74.9	75.2	**76.1**	75.0	76.0
Leather shoes	78.9	80.1	80.9	79.1	**81.7**
Logo	**51.1**	**51.1**	**51.1**	**51.1**	50.7
Long hair	71.5	71.7	72.6	71.8	**72.8**
Male	79.7	80.3	80.9	80.6	**81.4**
MessengerBag	71.8	72.9	74.3	72.7	**75.5**
Muffler	88.0	88.3	89.5	86.5	**91.3**
No accessory	76.8	77.2	78.6	77.1	**80.0**
No carrying	70.4	70.6	**71.6**	70.6	71.5
Plaid	64.0	64.5	64.5	**65.0**	**65.0**
Plastic bag	74.9	74.9	75.5	73.9	**75.5**
Sandals	**50.3**	**50.3**	**50.3**	**50.3**	**50.3**
Shoes	70.6	71.0	72.5	70.8	**73.6**
Shorts	56.0	**56.5**	**56.5**	**56.5**	**56.5**
ShortSleeve	71.3	71.7	**71.8**	71.7	71.6
Skirt	64.0	64.0	64.0	64.0	**64.3**
Sneaker	67.5	68.1	69.0	68.2	**69.3**
Stripes	51.5	**52.3**	**52.3**	**52.3**	**52.3**
Sunglasses	**52.4**	**52.4**	**52.4**	51.8	51.7
Trousers	74.0	74.5	75.7	75.7	**76.5**
T-shirt	64.3	64.5	**64.6**	63.6	64.2
UpperOther	80.7	80.7	81.8	81.1	**83.9**
V-Neck	**51.1**	**51.1**	**51.1**	**51.1**	**51.1**
AVERAGE	69.5	69.9	70.6	69.7	**71.1**

6. REFERENCES

[1] Y. Boykov and V. Kolmogorov. An experimental comparison of min-cut/max-flow algorithms for energy minimization in vision. *TPAMI*, 2004.

[2] L. Breiman. Random forests. *Machine learning*, 2001.

[3] J. Cai, Z.-J. Zha, W. Zhou, and Q. Tian. Attribute-assisted reranking for web image retrieval. In *MM*, pages 873–876. ACM, 2012.

[4] R. Cucchiara. Multimedia surveillance systems. In *Int. workshop on video surveillance & sensor networks*. ACM, 2005.

[5] S. Gong, M. Cristani, C. C. Loy, and T. Hospedales. The re-identification challenge. In S. Gong, M. Cristani, S. Yan, and C. C. Loy, editors, *Person Re-Identification*. Springer, 2013.

[6] D. Gray, S. Brennan, and H. Tao. Evaluating appearance models for recognition, reacquisition, and tracking. In *IEEE PETS*, 2007.

[7] Y. Han, F. Wu, X. Lu, Q. Tian, Y. Zhuang, and J. Luo. Correlated attribute transfer with multi-task graph-guided fusion. In *MM*. ACM, 2012.

[8] R. Layne, T. M. Hospedales, S. Gong, et al. Person re-identification by attributes. BMVC, 2012.

[9] S. Z. Li. *Markov random field modeling in computer vision*. Springer-Verlag New York, Inc., 1995.

[10] B. Liu, Y. Xia, and P. S. Yu. Clustering through decision tree construction. In *CIKM*. ACM, 2000.

[11] L. Liu, H. Xu, J. Xing, S. Liu, X. Zhou, and S. Yan. Wow! you are so beautiful today! ACM-MM, 2013.

[12] P. Luo, X. Wang, and X. Tang. A deep sum-product architecture for robust facial attributes analysis. ICCV, 2013.

[13] S. Maji, A. C. Berg, and J. Malik. Classification using intersection kernel support vector machines is efficient. CVPR, 2008.

[14] T. Nortcliffe. People analysis cctv investigator handbook. *Home Office Centre of Applied Science and Technology*, 2011.

[15] C. Rother, T. Minka, A. Blake, and V. Kolmogorov. Cosegmentation of image pairs by histogram matching-incorporating a global constraint into MRFs. CVPR, 2006.

[16] C. Shan, F. Porikli, T. Xiang, and S. Gong. *Video Analytics for Business Intelligence*, volume 409. Springer, 2012.

[17] J. Van De Weijer, C. Schmid, J. Verbeek, and D. Larlus. Learning color names for real-world applications. *TIP*, 18(7):1512–1523, 2009.

[18] Z.-J. Zha, X.-S. Hua, T. Mei, J. Wang, G.-J. Qi, and Z. Wang. Joint multi-label multi-instance learning for image classification. CVPR, 2008.

[19] J. Zhu, S. Liao, Z. Lei, D. Yi, and S. Z. Li. Pedestrian attribute classification in surveillance: Database and evaluation. In *ICCV Workshop*, 2013.

[20] X. Zhu, C. C. Loy, and S. Gong. Video synopsis by heterogeneous multi-source correlation. In *ICCV*, 2013.

[21] X. Zhu, C. C. Loy, and S. Gong. Constructing robust affinity graph for spectral clustering. In *CVPR*, 2014.

MSVA: Musical Street View Animator: An Effective and Efficient Way to Enjoy the Street Views of Your Journey

Yin-Tzu Lin, Po-Nien Chen, Chia-Hu Chang, Ja-Ling Wu
National Taiwan University
{known,dudebrotim,chchang,wjl}@cmlab.csie.ntu.edu.tw

ABSTRACT

Google Maps with Street View (GSV) provides ways to explore the world but it lacks efficient ways to present a journey. Hyperlapse provides another ways for quick glimpsing the street-views along the route; however, its viewing experience is also not comfortable and could be tedious when the route is long-distance. In this paper, we provide an efficient and enjoyable way to present street view sequences of long journey. Street view journey video accompanied with locally listened music will be produced by the proposed approach. During the move between locations, we use the speed control techniques for animation production to improve the viewing experience. User evaluation results show that the proposed method increases the satisfaction of users in viewing the street view sequences.

Categories and Subject Descriptors

H.5.1 [**Information Interfaces and Presentation**]: Multimedia Information Systems

General Terms

Design, Human Factors

Keywords

musical video; google street view; animation; musical medley

1. INTRODUCTION

All over the world, there are lots of remarkable places well worth visiting once in our lifetime. Nowadays, making a tour around the world becomes more and more convenient with the increasingly rich travel information and well-developed transportation systems. While traveling abroad, we can see the attractive scenes, the historical buildings, the street-views with different cultures, and hear the music played locally. All of these stimuli of fresh perceptions can relax our body and free our mind from burdens and stresses.

MM'14, November 3–7, 2014, Orlando, Florida, USA.

http://dx.doi.org/10.1145/2647868.2654967 .

Google Maps with Street View (GSV) provides map-based web services to let users explore places on the map and see the 360-degree images of correspondent scenery around most of the world. These spherical panoramas were created by stitching the photos taken from various Google-adapted vehicles. Then, each spherical panorama point was aligned to the correspondent coordinate on the map based on their geo-information. Therefore, users can click arrow in GSV to move toward the image closest to a specifically chosen location. While transiting from current panorama to the nearest place, GSV utilizes a rough 3D model, where the panorama photos are mapped onto, to create an animated perspective change on the crossfaded areas of images. In this way, the transitions between distinct panoramas will be smoothed and produce a walk-through effect as well, although the point-to-point panoramas are sparse. However, if we try to continuously view all the street views along a trip route, it would be tedious because one have to keep clicking the arrow continuously. In addition, all the generated views cannot be easily shared with others. Although users can search for a series of attractions in web-based travel communities and explore the paths between them via GSV, all the planned and/or interested path cannot easily be organized and recorded into the touring videos.

Teehan+Lax Labs's Google Street View Hyperlapse tool [11] provides the time-lapse photography effect in viewing GSV. The images are played with constant and fast speed, but the video becomes long and tedious when long-distance street view sequence is the target, which makes the viewer feel dizzy when the viewing time is long.

The collections of GSV panoramas keep increasing and publicly available. How to well make use of such tremendous but sparse and noisy street view panoramas to generate a pleasant journey video accompanied with the locally played music, for promoting tourism and sharing travel experiences, is an important but challenging issue. In this paper, we provide an efficient and enjoyable way to present street view sequences, as shown in Figure 1. The flow chart of the proposed system is shown in Figure 2. The processes for each step will be detailed in the following sections.

2. INCIDENTAL MUSIC CREATION

There are many ways to match music with visual contents, e.g. low level content-aware matching (color↔chord, motion↔tempo [7]) or high level semantic matching (emotion/mood [1], context [3]). In our application, we would like to provide users the music played locally at certain time. Thus, we take the geo-information as the cue in choosing music to accompany street view sequence. In order to han-

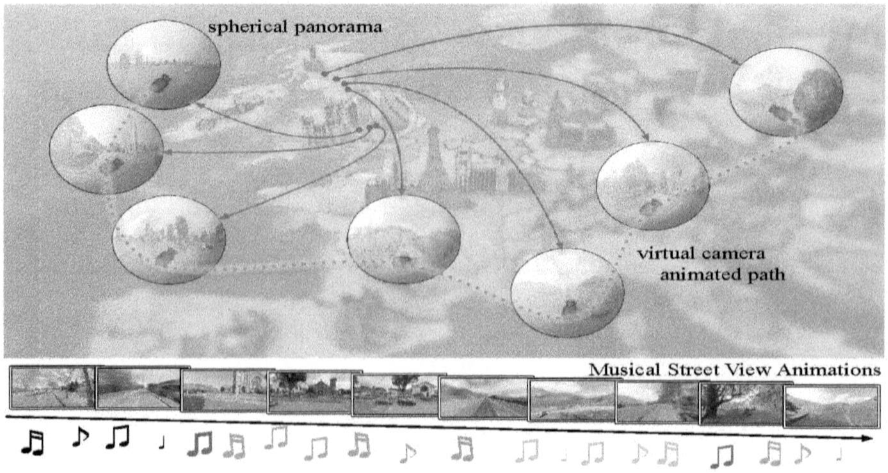

Figure 1: This figure depicts the essential idea of the musical street view animation system. Given a set of attractions' locations and the viewing orientations, our system can dynamically estimate the virtual camera orientations and pacing according to the proposed animated transition schemes, which are inspired by 12 basic principles of Disney's animation [4], for each Google street view panoramas along a navigating path. Then, the street view image sequences including the specified input key frames and the drive-through frames are generated. In addition, the music, which is popularly listened by the people at or near the locations, will be mined from the social media (e.g., Twitter) and be highlighted to create an incidental music. With these, the system automatically generates the musical street view animation to provide an efficient and enjoyable way to dramatically glide through the attractions.

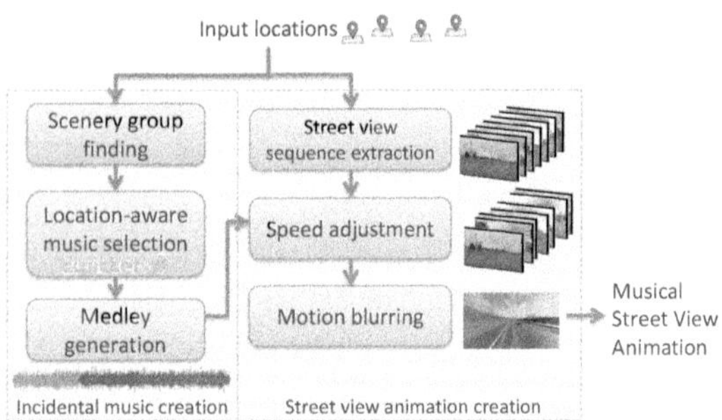

Figure 2: Flowchart of the proposed system

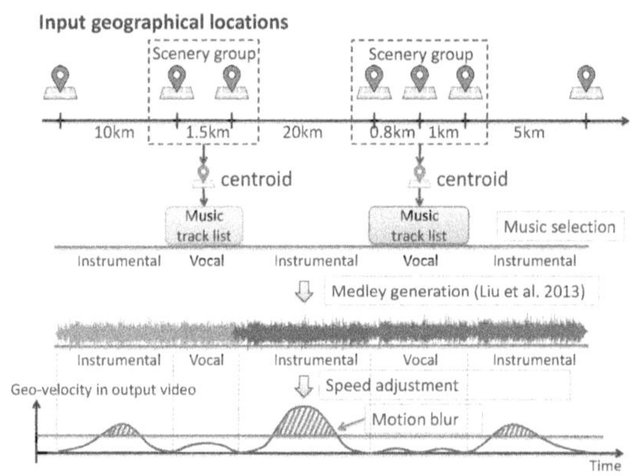

Figure 3: Schematic diagram of our system

dle different music tracks picked by multiple locations while keeping the completeness and smoothness of the incidental music, we use the method proposed in [8] to generate musical medleys as our incidental music. A medley is a kind of music piece that is composed of existing music excerpts. With Liu et al. [8]'s method, it is able to create medleys according to the specified conditions, such as the medley structure or the must-use clips. The pre-described flexibility makes us easy to create incidental music that could match to the conditions in our application. We design an incidental music creation process as shown in Figure 3. First, we group locations with the distances less than a certain value (e.g., 2.5km) as a scenery group. Then, we specify our target medley structure according to the number of the scenery groups. We assign the positions of scenery groups as vocal segments and other parts as instrumental segments. The reason is that vocal parts of a popular song are often thought to be topics of a song and listeners may pay more attention to vocal parts. The scenery group contains neighboring tourist attractions would also grab higher attention from the audience. Take Figure 3 as an example, the medley structure is Instrumental-Vocal-Instrumental-Vocal-Instrumental. After specifying the medley structure, the specified vocal segments should be chosen from the music rank list that is generated according to the centroid of each scenery group. Then, the other parts of the medley will be auto-completed by [8].

2.1 Location-aware Music Selection

In this section, we describe the details of selecting music tracks according to the given GPS coordinates of a scenery group. There are several methods to recommend music according to location cues, for example, choosing traditional music with respect to the input location [9], or as Kaminskas et al. [5] proposed, a place of interest (POI) can be matched to music tracks by their relationships on the ontology graph, or by their overlap ratio of emotional and physical tags. Here we used musicmicro dataset provided by Schedl [10] for its easy accessibility. In the dataset, Schedl collected 594,306 music-related microblogs (e.g., containing hash tags #nowplaying, #itunes, etc.) by 136,866 users in 722 different cities in 180 countries on Twitter from November 2011 to September 2012. Such popular musics from the past can bring audience back in time and evoke their old memories. Each record r in the dataset reports a user was listening to a music track t_r at certain geo-location p_r (by GPS coordinates) at a certain time (month, weekday). We would like to pick music tracks that are listened by users near to the query location and the number of listened times are also high enough (popular around the area). So, we first take the listening records at locations with distances less than a given distance D to the query point as candidates (We could also choose the records in the same city or country of the query location as candidates). For each candidate record r, we define a weight score $w(q,r) = 1 - \frac{gdist(q,p_r)}{D}$, where q is the GPS coordinate of the query point, and $gdist(q,p_r)$ is the geo-distance of q and p_r computed by Haversine formula[1]. Then, we accumulate the weight of each record according to the music track listened. That is, the score of each track t is defined as $score(q,t) = \sum_{r \in R_D(q,t)} w(q,r)$, $R_D(q,t) = \{r | gdist(p_r, q) \leq D \text{ and } t_r = t\}$. Finally, we add another weight to the final score to eliminate the effect of repeatedly choosing widely listened songs. That is, $scoreW(q,t) = \log \frac{|R|}{|R(t)|} \cdot score(q,t)$, where, R is the set of all records, and $R(t) = \{r | t_r = t\}$. This weighting mechanism is similar to the concept of inverse document frequency (IDF) widely adopted in the field of text retrieval.

3. STREET VIEW ANIMATION CREATION

To generate vivid street view animations, we utilize Google's API to estimate a routing path connecting the given points, and then retrieve all the panoramas along the path. After projecting the panorama images onto a spherical model, the street view images can be rendered according to specified viewing angles. Then, the system can create animations by taking the street view images as the source materials to be displayed in a rapid succession. Generally, the time intervals between adjacent, yet distinct, street view images are set as a constant value. However, such kind of constant animation pacing tends to be dull especially for viewing large-scale street views. Inspired by 12 basic principles of Disney' s animation [4], we proposed the following animated transition scheme. When moving toward next attraction far from current location, the transition pacing will be gradually increased at the starting point, reached an extreme in the middle, and then be gradually decreased at the end. With such a slow-in/slow-out effect (SI/SO), the street view animations can direct viewers to carefully watch the remarkable attractions but quickly pass through the distant views between them. As for the attractions that are close to each other, the transition pacing will be kept constant. In this way, the proposed system can create a "scenic car driving" metaphor, which is similar to Smart Player [2], and provide an effective and efficient way to display the street view images.

[1]https://en.wikipedia.org/wiki/Haversine_formula

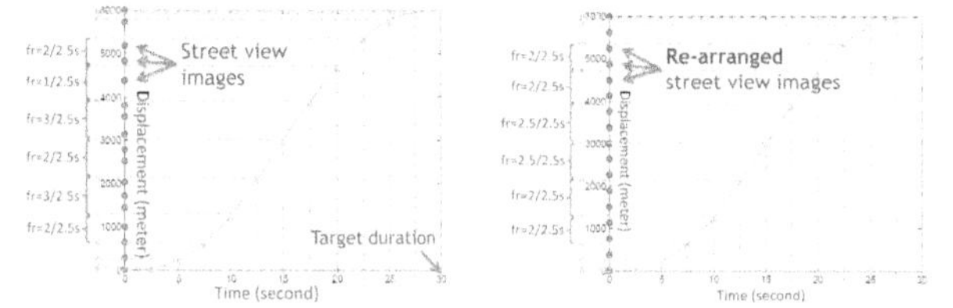

(a) Original (b) Rearranged

Figure 4: Schematic diagram for calculating the frame-rate.

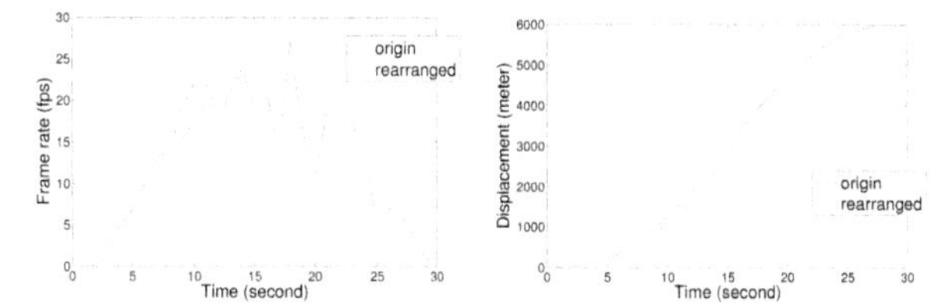

(a) fr-t plot (b) D-t plot

Figure 5: Fr-t and D-t plot of original and rearranged animations.

3.1 Speed Adjustment

By conducting preliminary tests with 9 users, we found that the actual speed perception is not simply frame-rate dependent, but is highly affected by the geo-velocity (calculated via geo-displacement over time interval between street view images). However, frame-rate variation may still cause unsmoothness in visual motion perception. On the basis of these observations, we design the following playing speed adjustment method to reduce the effect of speed variations. A five-order Bézier curve is used to approximate the easing function for simulating SISO effects. The relation of geo-displacement of each street view image over time can be shown in Equation (1), where $\mathbf{s}(t)$ is the geo-displacement of the current street view image (at time t) to the start point, and $\mathbf{P}_2$, $\mathbf{P}_3$ are control points of the chosen Bézier curve[2].

$$\mathbf{s}(t) = 10t^2(1-t)^3\mathbf{P}_2 + 10t^3(1-t)^2\mathbf{P}_3 + 5t^4 - 4t^5. \quad (1)$$

We let $\mathbf{P}_2 = \frac{d_s}{S}$, $\mathbf{P}_3 = 1 - \frac{d_e}{S}$, where S is the geo-distance between the start and the end points, d_s and d_e are the distances of the positions that we wish to start speeding up and slowing down, respectively. Then, a practical method to compute the frame-rate of the street view sequence is illustrated in Figure 4(a). The vertical and the horizontal axes of the generated curve are first scaled to the real geo-displacement and the target duration that we wish the street view animation to play, respectively. The target duration can be set according to the duration of the incidental music created in Section 2. Then, the street view images can be plotted on the vertical axis, as illustrated by the red dots in Figure 4(a). Afterwards, we divide the target duration into equal length intervals, and for each time interval, we calculate the frame-rate of that interval by counting how many street view images lie in the corresponding displacement interval. The resulting frame-rate to time (fr-t) plot and the geo-displacement to time (D-t) plot are shown in Figure 5.

[2]$\mathbf{P}_0 = \mathbf{P}_1 = 0$, $\mathbf{P}_4 = \mathbf{P}_5 = 1$

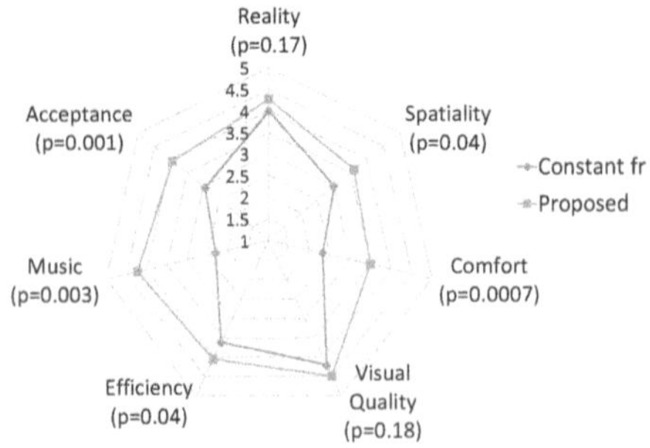

Figure 6: The average score of each performance evaluation dimension.

However, we found that the frame-rate moves up and down along the time because the geo-distance between consecutive street view images varies with the situation encountered while the photos were taken, e.g., the driving speed. This effect causes users to perceive unsmooth motions. Fortunately, the variation of the geo-distance intervals between consecutive street view images is not large. As a result, we rearrange the street view images to make the number of images lay in the time intervals uniformly distributed along the time axis, as shown in Figure 4(b). Then, the resulting fr-t plot (Figure 5(a)) can be smoothed along the time axis while not causing too stiff penalties for the D-t plot (Figure 5(b)).

3.2 Motion Blur

To further reinforce the impression of high speed and enhance the smoothness in visual motion perception, a velocity-based motion blur filter is applied to the street view images when the geo-velocity is higher than a threshold (as shown in the bottom part of Figure 3). While moving forward, the vanish point of each street view, which indicates the motion direction, will be estimated by using the method proposed in [6] and be set as the center of the applied zoom blur effect. The higher the speed is, the more the blur amount is applied. By leveraging the motion blur effect, the viewing experience can be enriched in a less dizzy manner.

4. EVALUATION

In the user evaluation, we compared two street view animation schemes: constant rate [11], and the proposed one. In the constant playing scheme, the street view image sequences are played with a constant frame rate of 30 fps (frame per second) without incidental music. Seven locations around Sutton, London and Buttermere, North West England are selected as inputs to create street view animations[3]. Eighteen users (16 males and 2 females) aged around 20-60 participated in the evaluation. Evaluators were asked to grade from 1 to 7 on both street view animation to show their satisfactions (higher scores for better satisfaction) with respective to each of the following perspectives:

- *Reality*: How do they feel about the reality of "scenic car driving" in the street view animation?
- *Spatiality*: How strong sense of the geographical relation does the street view animation offer?
- *Comfort*: How comfortable while viewing the street view animation? (dizzy feeling means less comfort)
- *Visual Quality*: How smooth is the visual motion perception in the street view animation?
- *Efficiency*: How efficient is the way of previewing scenic spots via viewing the street view animation?
- *Music*: How is the incidental music matched with the street view animation?
- *Acceptance*: How do they feel about the overall system?

The average scores are illustrated in Figure 6. The differences between the proposed and the constant frame-rate methods in terms of reality and visual quality are relatively small while in all the other perspectives, the proposed method statistically significantly outscored the constant rate counterpart. The result indicates that adding animation effect will not affect the reality and visual quality of the street view, but can increase efficiency and comfort. Besides, the evaluators are satisfied with the match of incidental music and the street view animation with the average score higher than four.

5. CONCLUSIONS

In this paper, we provide an efficient and enjoyable way to create street view journey videos, by accompanying with locally listened musics and adding animation effects to it. The user evaluations show that the proposed method is effective in enhancing the feelings of efficiency and comfort. We believe our work can assist people easily create and share attractive journey videos with music according to their own trip path. In addition, more tourism promotion videos can be produced to benefit the travel industry. In the future, we plan to conduct more user tests in deciding a proper compromise between the geo-velocity and the smoothness of frame-rate to further improve the comfort of the video. Besides, other music selection methods are also worthy of exploring to enhance the entire viewing experience.

6. REFERENCES

[1] C.-H. Chen, M.-F. Weng, S.-K. Jeng, and Y.-Y. Chung. Emotion-based music visualization using photos. In *Proc. MMM*, pages 1–11, 2008.

[2] K. Cheng, S. Luo, B. Chen, and H. Chu. SmartPlayer: user-centric video fast-forwarding. In *Proc. SIGCHI*, pages 789–798, 2009.

[3] P. Dunker, P. Popp, and R. Cook. Content-aware Auto-soundtracks for Personal Photo Music Slideshows. In *Proc. ICME*, 2011.

[4] O. Johnston and F. Thomas. *The Illusion of Life: Disney Animation.* 1981.

[5] M. Kaminskas, F. Ricci, and M. Schedl. Location-aware music recommendation using auto-tagging and hybrid matching. *Proc. RecSys*, pages 17–24, 2013.

[6] H. Kong, J.-Y. Audibert, and J. Ponce. General road detection from a single image. *IEEE Trans. IP*, 19(8):2211–20, Aug. 2010.

[7] Y.-T. Lin, T.-H. Tsai, M.-C. Hu, and W.-H. Cheng. Semantic based Background Music Recommendation for Home Videos. In *Proc. MMM*, pages 283–290, 2014.

[8] I.-T. Liu, Y.-T. Lin, and J.-L. Wu. Music Cut and Paste: A Personalized Musical Medley Generating System. In *Proc. ISMIR*, Curitiba, PR, Brazil, 2013.

[9] C. Parker, D. Joshi, P. Lei, and J. Luo. Finding geographically representative music via social media. *Proc. MIRUM*, page 27, 2011.

[10] M. Schedl. Leveraging microblogs for spatiotemporal music information retrieval. In *Proc. ECIR, LNCS 7814*, Moscow, Russia, 2013.

[11] Teehan+LaxLabs. Google Street View Hyperlapse. http://hyperlapse.tllabs.io/.

[3]The generated animations can be found at `http://www.cmlab.csie.ntu.edu.tw/~known/street/results/`

QoE-driven Unsupervised Image Categorization for Optimized Web Delivery

[Short Paper]

Parvez Ahammad, Brian Kennedy, Padmapani Ganti, Hariharan Kolam
Instart Logic Inc., 2307 Leghorn Street, Mountain View, CA, USA.
parvez@ieee.org; {bkennedy, pganti, hkolam}@instartlogic.com.

ABSTRACT

Due to rapid growth in the richness of web applications and the multitude of wireless devices on which web content can be consumed, optimizing the content delivery of dynamic web applications represents an important technical challenge. One of the keys to solving the wireless web performance puzzle is that of efficient image content delivery. Since the critical factor in image delivery is the end-user experience, we propose a simple quantitative metric for characterizing the Quality of Experience (QoE) for any given image that gets sent through a web delivery service (WDS) pipeline. This quantitative signature, termed VoQS (*variation of quality signature*), allows any two arbitrary images to be compared in the context of web delivery performance. We then use VoQS in conjunction with an unsupervised learning algorithm to group similarly performing images into coherent groups for optimized web delivery. Using a large database of images compiled from multiple content providers and diverse device-optimized formats, we demonstrate that our approach allows large image databases to be efficiently parsed into coherent groups in a content-dependent and device-targeted manner for optimized image content delivery. Our approach significantly decreases the average bits per image that need to be delivered across large image databases (by 43% in our experiments) while preserving the perceptual quality across the entire image database. We also discuss how such a categorization approach can be leveraged for real-time web delivery of novel image data.

Categories and Subject Descriptors

H.3.5 [**Online Information Services**]: Web-based services; I.5.3 [**Pattern Recognition**]: Clustering—*algorithms, similarity measures*; I.4.7 [**Image Processing and Computer Vision**]: Feature measurement

Keywords

Web delivery service (WDS); Quality of experience (QoE); Image categorization; Multimedia delivery; Unsupervised clustering

MM'14, November 3–7, 2014, Orlando, Florida, USA.
ACM 978-1-4503-3063-3/14/11.
http://dx.doi.org/10.1145/2647868.2654982 .

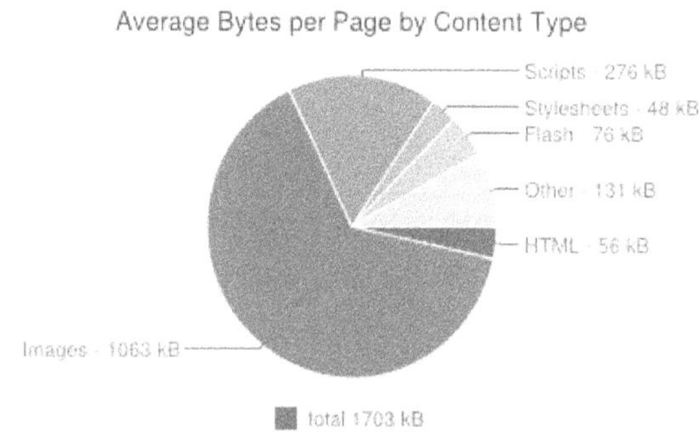

Figure 1: Content types across internet webpages: March 2014. [7].

1. INTRODUCTION

A key feature of present day internet is the ubiquitous presence of highly dynamic web applications and diverse set of mobile devices with sophisticated displays. The average size of the internet webpages has been steadily increasing (with a 50% increase from May 2012 to June 2013) [14] and the average load times of image-rich websites has also been on the rise. Images represent the most significant portion of data content on an average webpage online [7] (see Figure 1). Consider a web delivery service (WDS) that serves millions of images from content providers to a large variety of internet-enabled devices. When a user attempts to access a webpage containing some images on her internet-enabled device, the WDS quickly needs to deliver the images to the user's device in a manner that maximizes the QoE for the user. In this context, there are two potential modes of delivery for the requested images, namely the full-download mode and the partial-download mode. In the full-download mode, the web application (such as browser) downloads the entire image content onto the user's device and then displays the image. In the context of dynamic multimedia-rich content accessed in a mobile environment, this can lead to unacceptable transfer times and low QoE for user. In contrast, in partial-download mode, the web application starts to render the image on the user device as soon as a portion of the image file is buffered [12]. Due to shorter latencies in initiating the display of image content and an efficient prioritization of bandwidth, the partial-download mode promises significant improvement in QoE.

Several critical problems arise for practical image delivery using partial-download mode on a WDS: (a) lack of a universally applicable threshold for determining the deliverable image buffer size, (b) lack of a quantitative definition for QoE for a given image, and (c) challenge of having to decide a relevant threshold for every single image in large-scale WDSs.

1.1 Related work

While there is a significant body of research in computer vision and image processing fields on image categorization [8, 3], very little of that work deals with the context of quality degradation of images as they pass through a web delivery pipeline. Our work draws inspiration from the image quality assessment literature [9, 15] and extends it to a novel problem domain. The existing industrial solutions for lowering the network footprint of image data, termed FEO (front-end optimization) methods, typically achieve lower network footprint by reducing the quality of images in the database by transcoding the images while lowering the compression quality of the images (among other optimization tricks) to adapt to the network constraints [13]. For the remainder of the paper, we will refer to the compression quality adjustment based procedures as FEO-CQ approaches. FEO-CQ approaches do not take into account the diversity of images in a database and can only be optimal when they are applied in a content-aware manner to every single image in the corpus one at a time (thus being very inefficient).

In this paper, we focus on the partial-download mode of image content delivery, and propose a simple quantitative measure for QoE of image delivery on the web, termed VoQS (*variation of quality signature*). Using VoQS, we then demonstrate an unsupervised image categorization solution that can coherently group large datasets of images into clusters of similar QoE, thus enabling an efficient content-aware image delivery solution across large-scale WDS.

2. PROPOSED APPROACH

Our proposed approach has an offline component and an online component (see Figure 2). Offline computation involves computing VoQ signatures for large database of images, using the VoQS based similarity (equation 6) to cluster the database and finding the best exemplars for each cluster. Online computation involves computing VoQS for the incoming image, comparing it to the VoQS of the stored exemplars to find the nearest neighbor and selecting an appropriate transmission buffer size based on the nearest exemplar. In the following sections, we provide further explanation of the formulations used in our pipeline.

2.1 A QoE signature for web delivery

Let us start by observing that the key parameter in the partial-download mode of image-delivery is the threshold (t) selected for initial rendering of the image. For simplicity, we treat it as a percentage of the image size, thus $0 \leq t \leq 100$. Let's denote *variation of quality signature* (VoQS) of a delivered image I as $Q(I)$, and an image rendered at delivery threshold t as I_t. Note that:

$$Q(I) \triangleq [\bar{q}(I_{10}), .., \bar{q}(I_t), ..\bar{q}(I_{100})] \quad (1)$$

such that $\bar{q}(I_{100}) \triangleq 1$ and $\bar{q}(I_0) \triangleq 0$ and t is the discrete delivery cut-off point where $0 \leq t \leq 100$.

Given an original reference image I and its thresholded(noisy) version I_t, one can measure $\bar{q}(I_t)$ in several ways. A key requirement for $\bar{q}(I_t)$ in a WDS framework is that it needs to be efficient to compute while capturing the perceptual similarity between I and I_t.

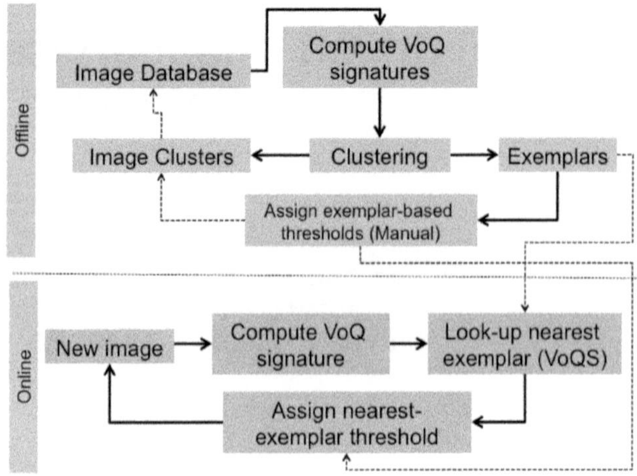

Figure 2: Flow chart of our proposed approach.

Computing the value of $\bar{q}(I_t)$ is closely related to the problem of image quality assessment, which has been a fundamental problem in human visual perception and computer vision literature [5]. While one reasonable way to estimate $\bar{q}(I_t)$ is by soliciting subjective feedback from several users [2], such an approach does not scale up to large image datasets, and can be potentially very time-consuming. Objective measurement of image quality is an active area of research, and many proposals exist without a clear winner so far. In our work, we compute $\bar{q}(I_t)$ through a combination of peak signal-to-noise ratio (PSNR) [9] and structural similarity metric (SSIM) [15]. While PSNR is amenable to efficient computation, SSIM tries to explicitly model the function of human visual system. Let us denote PSNR of a streamed image I_t as $p(I_t)$ and SSIM of the streamed image as $s(I_t)$. Then,

$$e(I, I_t) = \frac{1}{N}\sum_{i=1}^{N}((I^i - I_t^i)^2) \quad (2)$$

$$p(I_t) = 10log_{10}\frac{l^2}{e(I, I_t)} \quad (3)$$

$$s(x,y) = \{\frac{2\mu_x\mu_y + C_1}{\mu_x^2 + \mu_y^2 + C_1} . \frac{2\sigma_x\sigma_y + C_2}{\sigma_x^2 + \sigma_y^2 + C_2} . \frac{\sigma_{xy} + C_3}{\sigma_x\sigma_y + C_3}\} \text{ [15]} \quad (4)$$

$$\bar{q}(I_t) = [p(I_t), s(I_t)] \quad (5)$$

where x and y are corresponding small aggregating moving window regions chosen in I and I_t respectively (see [15] for $s(I_t)$ computation details). In practice, it is important to normalize the components of $Q(I)$ (such as PSNR or SSIM), so we compute z-scores [1] of each component of $Q(I)$ across the entire image database and use them for our computations.

2.2 Offline QoE driven image categorization

The *variation of quality signature* (VoQS) defines a metric space for the large-scale database of images, where the similarity between any two images I' and I'' is defined as:

$$sim(I', I'') = -\sqrt{\sum(Q(I') - Q(I''))^2} \quad (6)$$

This formulation allows a quantitative comparison between any two arbitrary images in the context of web content delivery.

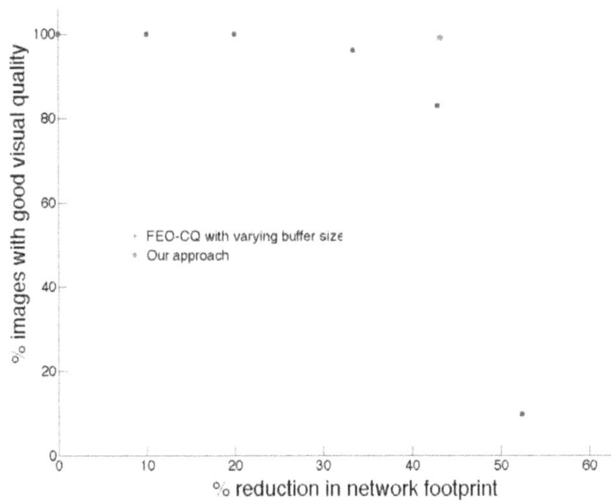

Figure 3: Results: Trade-off between overall % reduction in network footprint vs. % of images with good quality; Blue dots show results for FEO-CQ approach with different buffer size settings and Red dot shows our result.

Figure 4: Results: Examples from an algorithmically discovered image cluster that tolerates buffer size of 40% of the original file size (thus enabling a significantly smaller network footprint) with minimal loss of QoE (dataset available upon request).

We used affinity propagation algorithm [4] in conjunction with the image similarity measure defined above to find QoE-driven image clusters from the database. While other unsupervised techniques such as K-means clustering [6] or EM algorithm [11] can be used for this purpose, affinity propagation has the advantage of not requiring a pre-specification of the number of expected clusters. Affinity propagation's complexity is quadratic in the number of images, thus making it unsuitable for cases where the image database contains several millions of images. In such cases, the practical choice is to use K-means algorithm, which has linear computational complexity. The length of the VoQS vector also linearly impacts the computational complexity of the algorithm (both in the online and offline computations) - so care must be taken in choosing the number of quantized steps t (see equation 1).

2.3 Online buffer estimation for novel images

Categorization via affinity propagation [4] readily provides an exemplar (best representative) image for each derived cluster, which can be used for manually determining the appropriate buffer size for the entire cluster. This simplifies the problem of threshold selection (to decide the buffer size) for large-scale image databases by reducing it to decisions on a few chosen exemplar images. Assuming that an offline categorization step has been computed on a large-scale WDS image database, when a novel image needs to be delivered, one can simply compute its VoQS measure and compare it to the VoQS measures of the offline computed exemplars. The buffer size for the novel image is chosen using efficient nearest-neighbor look-up among the offline computed exemplars.

3. EXPERIMENTAL RESULTS

3.1 QoE driven categorization of image datasets

To test the scalability and general applicability of our proposed method, we collected a dataset of 2238 images sampled from multiple content providers, servers and vendors (see Figure 4). All the images used in our experiments are at least 10KB or above. We evaluated the performance as follows:

1. offline: Compute VoQS for each image and perform unsupervised categorization of the entire dataset.
2. offline: Assign the optimal delivery threshold (buffer size) for each cluster based on the cluster exemplar alone.
3. offline: Check all the thresholded images for every cluster and estimate the images that render poorly at the selected buffer size. Error rate is estimated as the percentage of images that rendered poorly given the assigned buffer size determined via our QoE driven categorization algorithm.

Using our proposed method, we needed to only manually select buffer sizes for about 40 exemplar images in order to assign appropriate buffer sizes for the entire set of 2238 images. We found that the optimal buffer sizes ranged from 50% of the original image size to 80% of the original image size. Over the entire set of 2238 images, we found that 18 images were assigned a buffer value that rendered the thresholded version slightly noticeable in its perceptual degradation compared to the original image. This amounts to 0.8% error for the entire database while allowing a very efficient processing (approximately two orders of magnitude faster). Using the optimal buffer sizes estimated through our approach for the current experimental dataset, the network footprint can be lowered from 90,024 KB to 51,121 KB - thus resulting in 43.2% improvement in bandwidth usage.

Compared to the FEO-CQ approach of selecting one best-guess compression parameter for the entire image dataset, our approach delivered a superior trade-off between overall reduction in network footprint for the number of images delivered with good quality (see the graph in Figure 3). It is worth noting that our approach finds the a near-optimal solution that is well-adapted to the underlying image quality distribution in the given WDS image database.

Using our approach, it is also relatively easy to discover clusters of images that show very little perceptual degra-

Categories	Smartphone	Laptop	Tablet	Desktop
Smartphone	100%	0%	0%	0%
Laptop	0%	100%	0%	0%
Tablet	0%	0%	100%	0%
Desktop	0%	0%	0%	100%

Table 1: Confusion matrix: QoE driven categorization results for device-optimized images (N=28)

dation despite very stringent buffer size allocation. These clusters are of particular interest since they allow maximum savings in bandwidth and time while having no effect on user perception of image quality (see Figure 4 for example).

3.2 Categorization of device-optimized images

The ability to categorize and select images that are appropriately targeted for a particular device display format has significant commercial value in today's mobile web market. In order to evaluate the suitability of our algorithmic pipeline for this application, we collected a small dataset of images [10] that were optimized for viewing on devices with different resolutions (e.g.: smart phone, tablet device, computer monitor etc.).

In our QoE driven categorization experiments using this device-optimized image dataset (N=28), the proposed algorithm perfectly separated the images into the four device-optimized categories, namely: tablet, smartphone, desktop and laptop (see Table 1). Since our approach does not explicitly model the variations in device-types, our results suggest that it is possible to optimize device-targeted image delivery in an automated fashion using our proposed approach. In scenarios where feedback from user-device is available to the WDS, this may enable efficient retargeting of the image content based on the device-type. The proposed framework may also be useful in designing automated solutions for delivering responsive images in dynamic content delivery scenarios.

4. SUMMARY AND FUTURE DIRECTIONS

In this paper, we tackled the issue of reducing the network capacity required to deliver images to a variety of internet-enabled devices. We presented a mechanism that allows unsupervised clustering of images into groups with similar *quality variation* signatures. Assuming progressive image encoding that allows rendering after partial download, our approach can determine when the image download process can be cut off without degrading image quality noticeably. As part of our approach, we proposed a quantitative quality variation measure, VoQS, which allows comparison of QoE between any two arbitrary images in the context of a web delivery service pipeline. Our algorithm would be run over an existing set of images offline to calculate clusters and then new images can be "compared" in real-time to reference images per cluster to determine efficiently to which cluster they belong. Our approach allows automated processing of large image WDS databases in a content-aware manner, and can further improve the existing web delivery optimization methods. Our approach also enables efficient estimation of optimal buffer sizes for large-scale image databases and enables significant bandwidth savings across the overall WDS network.

While VoQS is simple and intuitive, it is composed of components such as SSIM, which themselves can be further improved. In particular, components related to SSIM can be slow to compute and this can be made more efficient in future. Supervised approaches that use some ground-truth information to improve the VoQS definition as well as the similarity computations are another future avenue of research. The overall algorithmic approach proposed in this paper for quality based categorization and web delivery can be easily generalized to alternative choices of quality variation measures in future.

5. REFERENCES

[1] A. Jain, K. N., and Ross, A. Score normalization in multimodal biometric systems. *Pattern recognition 38*, 12 (2005), 2270–2285.

[2] BT.500-11, I.-R. R. *Methodology for the subjective assessment of the quality of television images.* International Telecommunication Union, Geneva, Switzerland, 2002.

[3] Chen, Y., and Wang, J. Image categorization by learning and reasoning with regions. *The Journal of Machine Learning Research 5* (2004), 913–939.

[4] Frey, B., and Dueck, D. Clustering by passing messages between data points. *Science 315* (2007), 972–976.

[5] Gregory, R. Eye and brain: the psychology of seeing. *Oxford University Press* (June 1998).

[6] Hartigan, J. A., and Wong, M. A. Algorithm AS 136: A k-means clustering algorithm. *Applied statistics* (1979), 100–108.

[7] HTTPArchive. *http://httparchive.org/interesting.php?a=All*, 2014.

[8] J. Shotton, M. J., and Cipolla, R. Semantic texton forests for image categorization and segmentation. *Proceedings of IEEE Conf. on Computer Vision and Pattern Recognition (CVPR)* (2008).

[9] Marmolin, H. Subjective MSE measures. *IEEE Trans. on Systems, Man, and Cybernetics 16*, 3 (1986).

[10] MediaQueries. *http://mediaqueri.es/about/*, 2014.

[11] P. Bradley, U. F., and Reina, C. Scaling EM (expectation-maximization) clustering to large databases. *Microsoft Research Technical Report MSR-TR-98-35* (1998).

[12] Rauschenbach, U., and Schumann, H. Adaptive image transmission. *Proceedings of International Conf. in Central Europe on Computer Graphics and Visualization (WSCG)* (1997), 434–443.

[13] S. Chandra, C. E., and Vahdat, A. Differentiated multimedia web services using quality aware transcoding. *Proceedings of Nineteenth Annual Joint Conference of the IEEE Computer and Communications Societies (INFOCOM) 2* (2000), 961–969.

[14] WebPerformanceToday. *http://www.webperformancetoday.com/2013/06/05/web-page-growth-2010-2013/*, 2013.

[15] Z. Wang, A. Bovik, H. S., and Simoncelli, E. Image quality assessment: from error visibility to structural similarity. *IEEE Trans. on Image Processing. 13*, 4 (2004), 600–612.

Speech Emotion Recognition Using CNN

Zhengwei Huang[†], Ming Dong[‡], Qirong Mao[†], Yongzhao Zhan[†]

† School of Computer Science and Communication Engineering
Jiangsu University
Zhenjiang, Jiangsu Province, 212013, China
{mao_qr,yzzhan}@mail.ujs.edu.cn

‡ Department of Computer Science
Wayne State University
Detroit, MI 48202, USA
mdong@cs.wayne.edu
zhengwei.hg@gmail.com

ABSTRACT

Deep learning systems, such as Convolutional Neural Networks (CNNs), can infer a hierarchical representation of input data that facilitates categorization. In this paper, we propose to learn affect-salient features for Speech Emotion Recognition (SER) using semi-CNN. The training of semi-CNN has two stages. In the first stage, unlabeled samples are used to learn candidate features by contractive convolutional neural network with reconstruction penalization. The candidate features, in the second step, are used as the input to semi-CNN to learn affect-salient, discriminative features using a novel objective function that encourages the feature saliency, orthogonality and discrimination. Our experiment results on benchmark datasets show that our approach leads to stable and robust recognition performance in complex scenes (e.g., with speaker and environment distortion), and outperforms several well-established SER features.

Categories and Subject Descriptors

I.5.2 [**Computing Methodologies**]: Pattern Recognition-Design Methodology[Feature evaluation and selection]

Keywords

Speech emotion recognition; Salient feature learning

1. INTRODUCTION

As an essential way of human emotional behavior understanding, in the past decades, Speech Emotion Recognition (SER) has attracted a great deal of attention in human-centered computing. In SER, one of the central research issues is how to extract discriminative, affect-salient features from speech signals. In this direction, a number of speech emotion features have been proposed in the literature, and they can be roughly classified into four categories [1]: 1) acoustic features, 2) linguistic features (words and discourse), 3) hybrid features that use both acoustic and linguistic information, and 4) context information (e.g., subject and gender). However, it is unclear if these hand-tuned feature sets can sufficiently and efficiently characterize the emotional content of speech. Moreover, their performance varies greatly in different scenarios. Finally, automatic extraction of some of these features can be difficult. For example, existing Automatic Speech Recognition (ASR) systems cannot reliably recognize all the verbal content of emotional speech. Extracting semantic discourse information is even more challenging, which, in many cases, has to be performed manually.

Thus, in SER, it is important to explore new strategies that can obtain the optimal feature set that is invariant to nuisance factors while maintaining discriminative with respect to the task of emotion recognition. Recently, in many situations where labeled data is limited or not available, deep learning systems, such as Convolutional Neural Networks (CNNs), are shown to have the capability to infer a hierarchical feature representation that facilitates categorization (e.g., image understanding [2] and ASR [3]). For SER, while many previous works about deep neural network focused on learning discriminative features [4, 5] from input, but did not consider to disentangle factors of variation.

In the paper, we propose to learn affect-salient features for SER using semi-supervised Convolutional Neural Network (semi-CNN), in which simple features are learned in the lower layers, and affect-salient, discriminative features are obtained in the higher layers. We propose a novel objective function to train semi-CNN by encouraging the feature saliency, orthogonality and discrimination. Our experiment results on several benchmark datasets show that our approach leads to stable and robust recognition performance in complex scenes (e.g. with speaker variation and noise), and outperforms several well-established SER features.

The major contribution of this paper is:

1. To our best knowledge, this is the first paper introducing feature learning to SER, in which the optimal feature set can be effectively and automatically learned by semi-CNN with a few labeled samples.

2. By introducing a novel objective function to train semi-CNN, we can extract affect-salient features for SER by disentangling emotions from other factors such as speakers and noise. Specifically, the candidate features from unsupervised learning are divided into two blocks, related to emotion and other remaining factors, respectively. The emotion-related features are discriminative and robust, leading to great performance improvement on SER.

MM'14, November 3–7, 2014, Orlando, FL, USA.

http://dx.doi.org/10.1145/2647868.2654984 .

The rest of the paper is organized as follows. Section 2 presents our semi-CNN-based feature learning algorithm in details. Section 3 describes SER benchmark datasets and reports our experimental results. Conclusion and future direction are discussed in Section 4.

2. LEARNING SALIENT FEATURES FOR SER

The architecture of semi-CNN is shown in Fig. 1, which has an input layer, one convolutional layer, one fully connected layer and a SVM classifier. We use spectrogram of the speech signal as the input of semi-CNN. Following the hierarchy of semi-CNN, the features learned at each layer become increasingly invariant to nuisance factors while maintaining affect-salient with respect to the goal of SER.

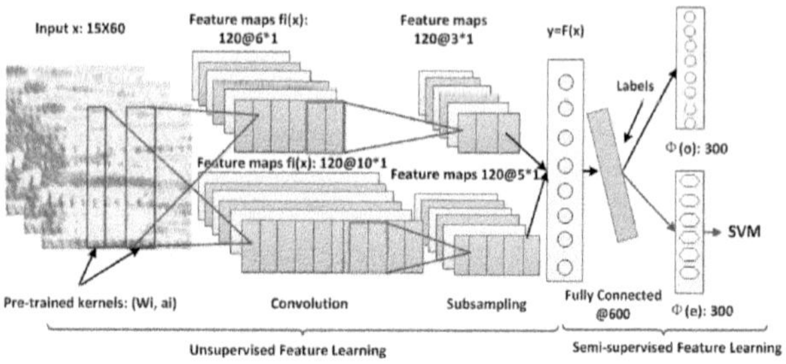

Figure 1: System Pipeline. The input is spectrogram with two different resolutions. Through unsupervised feature learning, our system obtains one long feature vector $y = F(x)$, based on which, the semi-supervised feature learning produces the affect-salient features $\phi^{(e)}$ and the nuisance features $\phi^{(o)}$. Finally, affect-salient features are fed to a linear SVM for SER.

Specifically, the input layer of semi-CNN in our system has 900 neurons to receive normalized spectrogram fragments of size 15×60. The convolutional layer consists of three consecutive operations: convolution with kernels, non-linear activation function, and pooling. The convolutional layer contains 120 kernels with two fixed sizes of 6×60 and 10×60, respectively. The kernel is pre-trained by unsupervised auto-encoder feature learning patch-wise. The size of the feature maps in the convolutional layer is 10×1 and 6×1, respectively.

The feature in our system is given as follows:

$$h(x) = sigmoid(Wx + \alpha), \quad (1)$$

where W is the weight matrix (kernel), $x \in D_x$ is a spectrogram fragment (D_x is the set of the input), and α is the bias. In feature pooling, one of the frequently used functions is down-sampling. We perform down-sampling using mean operation with a window size 2×1. The output layer has 600 fully connected neurons, each neuron corresponding to one feature, which are employed as the input of the fully-connected layer to disentangle factors of variation. Finally, the affect-salient feature block of the final feature vector is passed to a SVM classifier to determine the emotion class of the speech utterance.

2.1 Unsupervised Feature Learning

The auto-encoder has two parts: encoder and decoder [6]. The encoder learns a function h to map an input $x \in D_x$ to a feature vector $h(x) \in D_{x'}$, and the decoder reconstructs the input by minimizing the reconstruction error. Usually, the learning is done by training each layer individually and use the current layer codes to feed the next layer.

To capture the structure of the input spectrogram at different scales, we consider kernels with multiple sizes. Instead of generating kernels randomly, we pre-train kernels by sparse auto-encoder. Sparse auto-encoder is trained with patches extracted randomly at different locations, and the size of which matches that of the convolutional kernels being learned. Assuming that we have n different kernel sizes denoted as l_i-by-h_i, ($i = 1, 2, 3, ..., n$), we can get the kernel (W^i, α^i) after we pre-train independently a sparse auto-encoder for each kernel size. In our system, we employ two kernel sizes: 6×60 and 10×60.

After we get the kernel (W^i, α^i), we compute the corresponding feature maps on the whole spectrogram by applying (W^i, α^i) to each l_i-by-h_i patch of the input spectrogram:

$$f^i(x) = s(conv(W^i, x) + \alpha^i), \quad (2)$$

where $conv()$ denotes the convolution operation. Then, we perform down-sampling using mean operation with window size $m \times n$ and get the feature map $F^i_j = mean_{k \in win_j}(f^i_k(x))$, where win_j denotes the jth window. All the pooled features for kernel i are stacked into one feature vector $F^i(x)$, and then the final output feature vector y of the convolutional layer is given as:

$$y = [(F^1_1(x), ..., F^1_j(x), ..., F^1_N(x)), ..., (F^n_1(x), ..., F^n_j(x), ..., F^n_N(x))] \quad (3)$$

where N is the number of windows. y is used as the input of semi-supervised feature learning to disentangle emotion-salient factors from others.

2.2 Semi-supervised Feature Learning

While the data is encoded into a single feature vector y after unsupervised feature learning, an input is mapped into two distinct blocks of features: one $(\phi^{(e)}(y))$ that encodes affect-salient factors of its input, and one $(\phi^{(o)}(y))$ that encodes all other factors. Both feature blocks are trained to cooperate to reconstruct their common input y with a reconstruction loss function:

$$\hat{y} = g([\phi^{(e)}(y), \phi^{(o)}(y)]) = s(U^T(\phi^{(e)}(y) + \phi^{(o)}(y)) + \delta), \quad (4)$$

where U^T is the weight matrix in the fully-connected network, and δ_i is an offset to capture the mean value of y.

Given (x, z), the labeled training set with input spectrogram fragment x and emotion label z, the $\phi^{(e)}(y)$ block is also trained to predict the emotion label $z(y)$ when the label is available. The class prediction is given by the logistic regression of the discriminative block $\phi^{(e)}(y)$, which is learned by the sigmoid function over an affine transformation of the $\phi^{(e)}(y)$ block:

$$\hat{z}_i = s(A_i \phi^{(e)}(y) + \rho_i), \quad (5)$$

where the weight matrix A_i maps the $\phi^{(e)}(y)$ block to prediction for class i, and ρ_i is the class specific bias. The corresponding discriminant component of the overall loss function is:

$$L_{DISC}(z, \hat{z}) = -\sum_{i=1}^{C} z_i log(\hat{z_i}) + (1 - z_i) log(1 - \hat{z_i}), \quad (6)$$

where C is the number of emotion classes, and z and $\hat{z}$ are the ground truth and the logistic regression output, respectively.

Since a salient feature for SER is usually a sensitive feature for reconstruction error or discrimination error, the features responded strongly to this property tend to be more important. We measure the saliency for each input as the sum of its weight saliency. Specifically, the saliency for input i is defined as,

$$S_i = \sum_{k\in\varphi(i)} Saliency(w_k) = \frac{1}{2}\sum_{k\in\varphi(i)} \frac{\partial^2 MSE}{\partial w_k^2} w_k^2. \quad (7)$$

where $\varphi(i)$ is the set of weights connected input i and w_k is the k-th weight. In Equation 7, MSE denotes the Mean Squared Error. For features in $\phi^{(e)}(y)$, both the reconstruction and discrimination errors are taken into consideration, while for features in $\phi^{(o)}(y)$, only the reconstruction error is considered. The cost function is given as:

$$\mathcal{J}_{SAL} = -\frac{1}{2}\sum \frac{\partial^2 \parallel y-\hat{y} \parallel^2}{\partial w_k^2} w_k^2 - \frac{1}{2}\sum_{k\in\phi^{(e)}(y)} \frac{\partial^2 L_{DISC}(z,\hat{z})}{\partial w_k^2} w_k^2, \quad (8)$$

where the first term encourages salient features in $\phi^{(e)}(y)$ and $\phi^{(o)}(y)$ to reconstruction error, and the second term encourages affect-salient features in $\phi^{(o)}(y)$ to discriminative error. This objective is achieved through weight suppression during training.

To encourages $\phi^{(e)}(y)$ and $\phi^{(o)}(y)$ to present different directions of variation in the input y, we ask each sensitivity vector $\frac{\partial \phi_i^{(e)}(y)}{\partial y}$ of the i-th discriminant feature $\phi_i^{(e)}$ to prefer being orthogonal to every sensitivity vector $\frac{\partial \phi_j^{(o)}(y)}{\partial y}$ associated with the j-th non-discriminant feature $\phi_j^{(o)}$. This penalty component is denoted as $\mathcal{J}_{orth}$:

$$\mathcal{J}_{orth} = \sum_{i,j} \left(\frac{\partial F_i^{(e)}(y)}{\partial y} \cdot \frac{\partial F_j^{(o)}(y)}{\partial y}\right)^2. \quad (9)$$

Putting all the components of the loss function together we get:

$$\mathcal{L}(\theta) = \sum_{y=F(x)} L(y, g(h(y))) + \sum_{(x,z)\in S} L_{DISC}(z,\hat{z}) + \lambda_1 \mathcal{J}_{SAL} + \lambda_2 \mathcal{J}_{orth}. \quad (10)$$

The coefficients λ_1 and λ_2 weigh the contribution of the saliency penalty and the orthogonality penalty to the overall loss function, respectively, and they are empirically set as $\lambda_1 = 1$ and $\lambda_2 = 2$.

3. EXPERIMENTS & RESULTS

3.1 Datasets & Experimental Setup

Our affect-salient feature learning method was evaluated on four public emotional speech databases with different languages: Surrey Audio-Visual Expressed Emotion (SAVEE) Database [7], Berlin Emotional Database (Emo-DB) [8], Danish Emotional Speech database (DES) [9], Mandarin Emotional Speech database (MES) [10].

We first split the data into training dataset and testing dataset. In the unsupervised feature learning stage, we train kernels using one third of randomly selected data in the training dataset of each database. The labels are removed and not used in this stage. Later, we train CNN with the speech utterances in the training dataset. In our experiments, we first convert the time-domain signals into spectrograms. The spectrogram has a 20 ms window size with a 10 ms overlap. The spectrogram was further processed using Principal Component Analysis (PCA) whitening (with 60 components) to reduce its dimensionality.

We evaluate affect-salient features based on the classification accuracy and compare it with several other well-established feature representations: spectrogram representation ("RAW" features), acoustic features, Teager Energy Operator (TEO), and Local Invariant Features (LIF). We also compare features obtained in our system with and without affect-salient penalty (the third term in Equation 10) or orthogonality penalty (the fourth term in Equation 10), denoted as semi-CNN(no_s)) and semi-CNN (no_or) respectively). We determine the parameters C and σ for SVM by grid search. We also evaluate robustness of our method with respect to the common disturbing factors in SER, i.e., the speaker variation and environment distortion.

3.2 Performance Evaluation

3.2.1 *Accuracy On Public Emotional Speech Databases*

In this section, we report the recognition accuracy using 5-fold cross-validation based on features learned in different stages of semi-CNN: single non-convolutional one-layer kernels (K1, K2), LIF, affect-salient features $\phi^{(e)}$, and non-discriminative features $\phi^{(o)}$. In all cases, an SVM classifier is used for the emotion classification. These results in Figure 2 clearly show that each successive layer in semi-CNN helps to disentangle discriminative features, yielding better classification performance. Notice that on all the databases, the accuracy obtained by using affect-salient features is much higher than that obtained by the non-discriminative features, both are obtained in the last layer of semi-CNN.

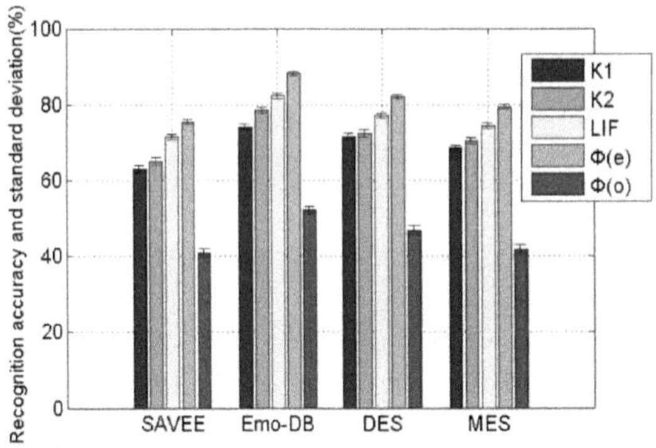

Figure 2: Average recognition accuracy and standard deviation with features learned in different stages of semi-CNN.

3.2.2 *Robustness To Speaker Variation*

In this section, we evaluate the features learned by semi-CNN by comparing it with other well-established feature representations with respect to speaker variance. Table 1 clearly show that all the learned features (i.e., LIF, semi-CNN(no_s), semi-CNN(no_or) and semi-CNN) outperform baseline features (RAW, TEO, and acoustic features), and semi-CNN achieves the highest accuracy in all cases (10% to 15% higher than the popular acoustic features). Notice that in the case of speaker-independent, that is, the speakers in

Table 1: **SER accuracy and standard deviation with speaker variation (single speaker, speaker-dependent/independent).**

speaker	database	RAW	TEO	acoustic	LIF	semi-CNN(no_or)	semi-CNN(no_s)	semi-CNN
single speaker	SAVEE	31.4±1.56	68.3±1.45	72.4±1.23	82.9±0.75	85.0±0.69	88.6±0.67	**89.7**±0.35
	Emo-DB	40.5±1.23	77.2±1.41	85.8±1.09	88.7±0.99	92.7±0.73	90.5±0.82	**93.7**±0.28
	DES	38.9±1.43	69.1±1.35	75.6±1.15	84.3±0.81	90.0±1.84	88.9±0.53	**90.8**±0.26
	MES	39.1±1.36	70.7±1.19	77.1±1.03	84.1±0.75	84.9±1.87	87.1±0.63	**90.2**±0.29
speaker-dep	SAVEE	29.4±1.64	58.8±1.47	65.0±1.21	69.4±0.79	86.7±3.75	73.3±0.66	**75.4**±0.42
	Emo-DB	37.2±1.45	66.4±1.48	72.3±1.15	80.5±0.81	74.7±1.7	86.4±0.63	**88.3**±0.31
	DES	34.6±1.42	65.3±1.41	71.1±1.25	76.8±0.93	78.9±0.57	79.9±0.58	**82.1**±0.45
	MES	35.5±1.53	60.6±1.37	67.8±1.38	72.5±0.98	77.2±2.10	76.3±0.61	**79.3**±0.50
speaker-indep	SAVEE	26.7±1.83	51.3±1.65	59.5±1.25	62.6±0.80	63.3±0.94	67.0±0.71	**73.6**±0.51
	Emo-DB	35.9±1.62	61.2±1.35	69.3±1.12	79.5±0.73	81.4±0.61	82.9±0.69	**85.2**±0.45
	DES	32.6±1.72	59.3±1.58	66.8±1.37	72.5±0.83	74.6±0.85	76.1±0.72	**79.9**±0.53
	MES	30.7±1.77	57.5±1.66	64.5±1.39	71.0±0.86	76.1±1.76	75.9±0.74	**78.3**±0.61

Table 2: **SER accuracy and standard deviation with environmental distortion (noise and channel).**

Environment Distortion	database	RAW	TEO	acoustic	LIF	semi-CNN(no_or)	semi-CNN(no_s)	semi-CNN
noise	SAVEE	16.2±2.02	38.5±1.93	49.5±1.96	53.6±0.88	55.7±0.89	53.8±0.91	**62.2**±0.56
	Emo-DB	28.3±1.98	47.6±1.99	55.6±1.72	68.2±0.83	74.6±0.71	76.8±0.63	**80.1**±0.53
	DES	26.7±1.96	40.6±2.01	53.3±1.68	67.8±0.91	75.1±0.98	73.2±0.80	**77.9**±0.55
	MES	28.6±1.92	43.2±1.65	50.2±1.73	64.1±1.09	69.3±1.06	70.8±0.75	**72.7**±0.70
channel	SAVEE	16.7±1.97	48.7±1.77	56.6±1.89	58.2±0.93	63.2±1.15	58.7±0.68	**69.0**±0.58
	Emo-DB	34.3±1.82	59.9±1.77	68.6±1.65	76.1±0.92	80.5±0.79	82.3±0.81	**84.5**±0.49
	DES	31.2±1.56	57.2±1.63	67.8±1.44	72.7±1.05	75.2±0.94	76.6±0.68	**77.9**±0.57
	MES	32.3±1.62	53.7±1.44	61.7±1.55	67.5±1.01	69.5±1.13	70.2±0.80	**74.8**±0.77

training set are mismatched with those in the testing set, semi-CNN has the smallest standard deviation on all the databases, which indicates that semi-CNN is able to learn a feature representation that is salient to emotion while being robust to speaker variations.

3.2.3 Robustness To Environment Distortion

Next, we report the results obtained with respect to distortions caused by the environment. In Table 2, noise means that the utterances in the test set are corrupted by the Gaussian noise of 20db. Channel means that the sampling frequency of the utterances in the test set is modified as 16 kHz, which is different from that of the samples in the training set. The accuracy of clean speech is the same as those of the second row in Table 1. Clearly, among the five methods semi-CNN achieves the highest and the most stable accuracy (the smallest standard deviation) for all the cases. In addition, feature learning methods all outperform baseline features.

4. CONCLUSION

In this paper we introduce feature learning in SER and propose to learn emotion-salient features using semi-CNN. Semi-CNN is trained in two stages: first unsupervised and then semi-supervised. In semi-supervised training, we propose a novel object function for semi-CNN that encourages the feature saliency, orthogonality, and discrimination for SER. Experiments on four public emotional speech databases show superior performance of our features with respect to speaker variation and environment distortion when compared with several well-established feature representations.

5. ACKNOWLEDGMENTS

This work was partially supported by the National Nature Science Foundation of China (No. 61272211 and No. 61170126), and by the Six Talent Peaks Foundation of Jiangsu Province (No.DZXX-027).

6. REFERENCES

[1] I. Luengo, E. Navas, and I. HernÃąez, "Feature analysis and evaluation for automatic emotion identification in speech," *IEEE Trans. Multimedia*, vol. 12, no. 6, pp. 490–501, 2010.

[2] Z. Han and J. J. et. al., "Face image super-resolution via nearest feature line," in *ACM Multimedia*, Nara, Japan, Oct. 2012, pp. 769–772.

[3] D. Yu, M. L. Seltzer, J. Li, J. T. Huang, and S. Frank, "Feature learning in deep neural networks - studies on speech recognition tasks," in *ICLR*, Scottsdale, Arizona, USA, May 2013.

[4] Y. Kim and H. L. et. al., "Deep learning for robust feature generation in audio-visual emotion recognition," Vancouver, British Columbia, Canada, 2013.

[5] D. Le and E. M. Provost, "Emotion recognition from spontaneous speech using hidden markov models with deep belief networks," Olomouc, Czech Republic, 2013.

[6] J. Lu, J. Hu, X. Zhou, and Y. Shang, "Activity-based person identification using sparse coding and discriminative metric learning," in *ACM Multimedia*, Nara, Japan, Oct. 2012, pp. 1061–1064.

[7] S. Haq, P. Jackson, and J. Edge, "Speaker-dependent audio-visual emotion recognition," in *AVSP*, Norwich, UK, Sept. 2009, pp. 53–58.

[8] F. Burkhardt, A. Paeschke, M. Rolfes, and W. Sendlmeier, "A database of german emotional speech," in *Interspeech*, Lissabon, Portugal, Sept. 2005, pp. 1517–1520.

[9] I. Engberg and A. Hansen. (1996) Documentation of the Danish emotional speech database DES. [Online]. Available: http://cpk.auc.dk/tb/speech/emotions/

[10] L. Fu, X. Mao, and L. Chen, "Speaker independent emotion recognition based on SVM/HMMs fusion system," in *ICALIP*, Shanghai, China, July 2008, pp. 61–65.

Attractive or Not? Beauty Prediction with Attractiveness-Aware Encoders and Robust Late Fusion

Shuyang Wang[1], Ming Shao[1], and Yun Fu[1,2]
[1]Department of Electrical & Computer Engineering,
[2]College of Computer & Information Science,
Northeastern University, Boston, MA, USA
{shuyangwang, mingshao, yunfu}@ece.neu.edu

ABSTRACT

Facial attractiveness is an ever-lasting issue in art and social science. It also draws considerable attention from multimedia community recently. In this paper, we develop a framework highlighting attractiveness-aware feature extracted from a pair of auto-encoders in order to learn human-like assessment of facial beauty. Our work is fully-automatic that does not require any landmark and puts no restrictions on the face pose, expressions, and lighting conditions; therefore, it is applicable on a larger and more diverse dataset. To this end, first, a pair of auto-encoders is built respectively with "beauty" images and "non-beauty" images, which can be used to extract attractiveness-aware features by putting test images into both encoders. Second, we further enhance the performance using an efficient robust low-rank fusion framework to integrate the predicted confidence scores which are obtained based on certain kinds of features. We show that our attractiveness-aware model with multiple layers of auto-encoders produces appealing results and performs better than previous appearance-based approaches.

Categories and Subject Descriptors

I.2.6 [**Learning**]: Knowledge acquisition; H.4.m [**Information Systems Applications**]: Miscellaneous

General Terms

Algorithms, Performance, Experimentation, Verification

Keywords

Facial Attractiveness Assessment; Auto-encoder; Attractiveness-aware Feature; Late Fusion.

1. INTRODUCTION

Facial beauty and its measure has been widely debated for centuries. In psychology community, a lot of research efforts have been spend on finding some biologically based standard that humans from different cultures, genders and ages could share as common preferences. Some good candidates for this kind of standard including the idea of golden ration [7], facial thirds or facial trisection [4], averageness [2] and symmetry [5]. Since that time, researches in this area have shifted over to computer scientists for the need of more complex feature representations. More detailed research survey in human science is provided by Rhodes [11].

It is still in its early stage using machine for attractiveness prediction, and only few works have been published, most of which by now are "geodesic ratio" based methods. Ever since the preliminary feature based facial beauty scoring system proposed by Aarabi, et al. [1], various geometrical features were extracted to determine the attractiveness based on facial symmetry, golden rations, or neoclassical canons. Although these methods produce promising results, they all suffer from (1) heavy duty of landmarks annotation and (2) non-unified criterion for attractiveness. Therefore, a fully automatic paradigm learned by machine is highly preferred.

The first attempt to do appearance-based attractiveness prediction was by Whitehill, et al. [14]. They used eigenface and Gabor filter analysis over 2000 photographs using ε-SVM. Sutic, et al. [12] used eigenfaces with different classification method such as KNN and AdaBoost. Gray et al. [6] built a multiscale model to extract feature to feed into a classical linear regression model for predicting facial beauty. In the recent work of Yan [15], a cost-sensitive ordinal regression was proposed to categorize face in order of beauty.

Motivated by these works, which directly apply off-the-shelf facial descriptors to attractiveness prediction, we pro-

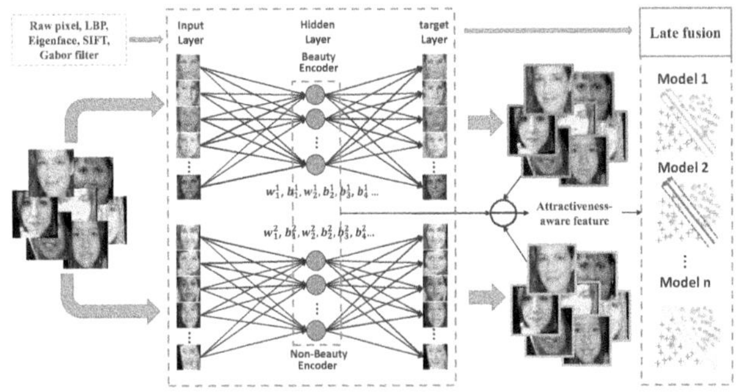

Figure 1: Framework of our system. First, we train a pair of auto-encoders according to the rating of the training images, by which we could get the attractiveness-aware features. Next, the late fusion is introduced in our framework to produce a more robust result.

MM'14, November 3–7, 2014, Orlando, Florida, USA.
Copyright 2014 ACM 978-1-4503-3063-3/14/11 ...$15.00.
http://dx.doi.org/10.1145/2647868.2654986.

pose an attractiveness-aware auto-encoder to search for better representations for facial attractiveness. Our main contributions include the followings: (1) Provide a fully automatic framework with no landmark annotation requirement, which therefore could be extended to the "wild" dataset collected either from social website (e.g., *hotornot*) or customers; (2) Integrate several low-level features for high-level attractiveness-aware descriptors; (3) Introduce a low-rank representation late fusion framework [16] to boost the performance of ranking scores from different features.

2. ATTRACTIVENESS MODELING

There are several ways to model the attractiveness of human beauty based on facial images [9]: (1) Geometry-based method, (2) Appearance-based method, and (3) Hybrid method. To adapt our model to most practical scenarios, we only consider the facial appearance as our subject, and use several popular visual descriptors to extract the low-level features: raw pixel, Eigenface, LBP, SIFT, and Gabor filter.

The above hand-craft visual descriptors have been successfully adopted in face recognition, object recognition/detection, video analysis. However, how to better utilize them for facial attractiveness representation is still an open question. Direct application of these features may only reveal identity information of the subject rather than attractiveness. We, therefore, propose to use auto-encoder to further refine the low-level feature, and seek for attractiveness-aware representations.

2.1 Building Auto-encoders

Suppose we have n_m facial images labeled "more attractive" and n_l images labeled "less attractive". Their low-level feature representation are $[x_1, x_2, \ldots, x_{n_m}]$, $[x_1, x_2, \ldots, x_{n_l}]$, $x \in \mathbb{R}^D$, where D is the dimensionality of the visual descriptor. There are two important non-linear transform functions in the feed-forward process of the auto-encoder. The first one is responsible to "input→hidden units", while the second one for the "hidden units→output". We denote the two transforms as: $T_1 : a_i = \sigma(W_1 x_i + b_1)$, and $T_2 : h(x_i) = \sigma(W_2 a_i + b_2)$, respectively, where $W_1 \in \mathbb{R}^{d \times D}$, $b_1 \in \mathbb{R}^d$, $W_2 \in \mathbb{R}^{D \times d}$, $b_2 \in \mathbb{R}^D$, and σ is the sigmoid function which has the form $\sigma(x) = (1+e^{-x})^{-1}$. Auto-encoder is essentially a single hidden layer neural network, but with identical input and output, meaning the auto-encoder encourages the output to be as similar to the input as possible, namely,

$$\min_{W_1,b_1,W_2,b_2} L(x) = \min_{W_1,b_1,W_2,b_2} \frac{1}{2n} \sum_i \|x_i - h(x_i)\|_2^2, \quad (1)$$

where n is the number of images. In this way, the neurons in the hidden layer can be seen as a good representation for the input, since they are able to reconstruct the data with less elements.

To avoid over-fitting of the auto-encoder, we introduce two extra terms: a regularization term, and a KL divergence term that enables high dimensionality of the hidden layer by avoiding trivial solutions of the identity function. Then the model in Eq. (1) is reformulated as:

$$\min_{W_1,W_2,b_1,b_2} L(x) + \lambda_1(\|W_1\|_2^2 + \|W_2\|_2^2) + \lambda_2 \sum_{i=1}^{d} \mathrm{KL}(\rho \| \hat{\rho}_i),$$

where $\|\cdot\|_2^2$ is the square of the Frobenius norm of a matrix, $\mathrm{KL}(\cdot)$ is the KL divergence, $\hat{\rho}_i$ is the average of the activation of the ith hidden unit ($\hat{\rho}_i = \frac{1}{n}\sum_j a_j^{(i)}$), and ρ is a very small number, say 0.05. The intuition behind of KL divergence is to suppress the values of the activation of the hidden units, and therefore avoid arbitrary large values. In practice, we solve this unconstraint optimization problem using L-BFGS optimizor [10] , which enables to address large-scale data with limited memory.

The above auto-encoder can be formulated in a deep structure by a layer-wise training scheme. That is, we train the first layer auto-encoder and then use its hidden units as the input and output of the second layer auto-encoder. We continue this process until the number of the layers is reached. In our attractiveness modeling, we train two separate deep auto-encoders by the rating of the images, meaning one auto-encoder uses more attractive faces as both inputs and outputs, while another uses less attractive as both inputs and outputs.

2.2 Attractiveness-Aware Representation

Suppose we have learned two auto-encoders AE_1 and AE_2 for more attractive and less attractive faces. We can extract two attractiveness representations for any test. An interesting phenomenon is that attractive faces share common characteristics, while less attractive faces are more diverse, inspiring us that the reconstructions for the test images from AE_1 and AE_2 may render differently. This is because attractive faces are more similar, and the reconstruction of AE_1 beautifies the input face towards the attractive template learned during the training. On the other hand, the diversity of less attractive faces leads to nothing but an identity function, meaning AE_2 always reproduces the input.

The above discussion indicates that the reconstruction of more attractive and less attractive faces from AE_1 and AE_2 are different. Suppose x_i is the visual descriptor for an attractive face, while x_j for a less attractive face. Since we have learned two auto-encoders for both more and less attractive faces, we then use $\hat{x}$ as the output of AE_1, and use $\tilde{x}$ as the output of AE_2. Now, we can explicitly model the above assumption as:

$$\hat{x}_i \approx x_i, \tilde{x}_i \approx x_i, \quad \hat{x}_j \neq x_j, \tilde{x}_j \approx x_j. \quad (2)$$

These relations may feature the attractiveness of the test face, as AE_2 always reproduce the input but the AE_1 will beatify the input by generating an attractive face. In other words, the difference of the outputs between the AE_1 and AE_2 is meaningful if we consider the following relations:

$$\begin{cases} \|\hat{x} - \tilde{x}\| \approx 0, & \text{if } x \text{ represents a more attractive face;} \\ \|\hat{x} - \tilde{x}\| > 0, & \text{if } x \text{ represents a less attractive face.} \end{cases} \quad (3)$$

Therefore, the vector $\hat{x} - \tilde{x}$ has potential to be a good attractiveness-aware representation.

3. LOW-RANK LATE FUSION

The criterion shown in Eq. (3) is a good indicator for attractiveness prediction with any appropriate visual descriptor. However, we may include more than one predictions by different types of visual descriptors: Raw pixel, Eigenface, LBP, SIFT, Gabor filter. In addition, not all the facial partitions are equally critical to the attractiveness decision. The predictions from either different visual descriptors or different partitions feature the different aspects of the attractiveness; but also incur controversy, since the results may disagree with each other. This introduces an interesting problem called late fusion [16] that studies how to fuse prediction results from different models or classifiers.

Suppose we have n test samples, each of them has m scores from m different models. These results constitute an $m \times n$ score matrix Y with each score as an element of the matrix. Since the rows represent the scores of different classifiers, they potentially have consistence, meaning the row space of the matrix is not very large, and the rank of Y is low. Therefore, we propose a novel representation that can better describe the row space of the score matrix, and in turn, reveal the intrinsic structure of Y and prediction results. Since Y has rational to be an low-rank matrix, it can be reconstructed by itself as well as another low-rank co-efficient matrix Z, under a mild condition:

$$\min_{Z} \operatorname{rank}(Z), \text{ s.t. } Y = YZ. \quad (4)$$

However, the above problem is non-convex due to the introduction of rank minimization. Most research works recently use the nuclear norm as the convex surrogate of the original problem, and solve the following convex problem instead:

$$\min_{Z} \|Z\|_* + \lambda\|E\|_{2,1}, \text{ s.t. } Y = YZ + E, \quad (5)$$

where $\|\cdot\|_*$ is matrix nuclear norm, λ is a balancing parameter, $\|E\|_{2,1} = \sum_i \|E_{:,i}\|_2$ and E compensates for the part that deviates from the low-rank structure. The solution of the above is non-trivial and unique if the column space of Y is sufficiently large. For more details refer to [8]

To train a classifier for attractiveness prediction, we also need to transform the training data into the representation similar to the test data. Therefore, we use $Y = [Y_l, Y_u]$ instead in Eq. (5), where Y_l and Y_u represent the score matrix of the labeled and unlabeled data.

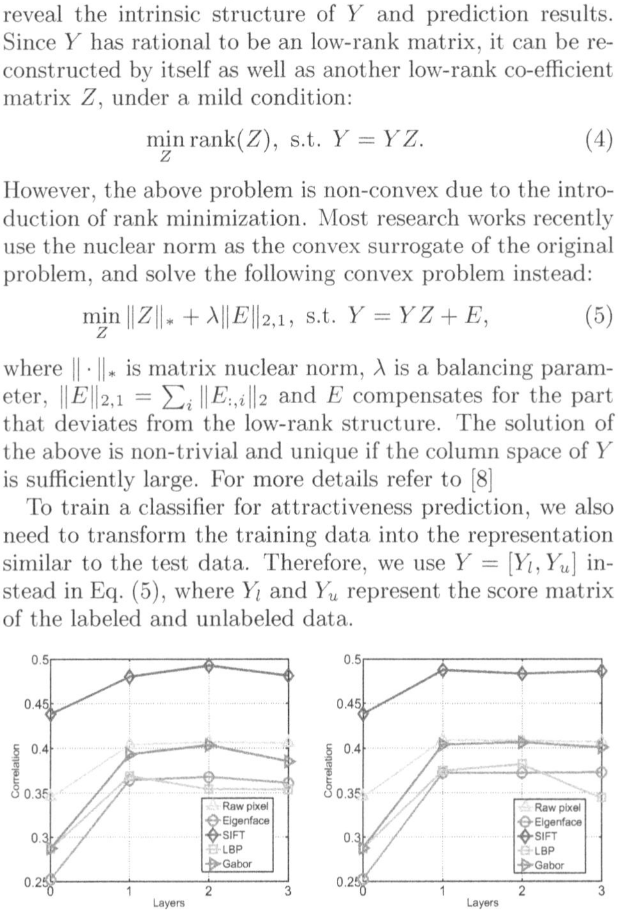

Figure 2: Assessment correlation of our method with different numbers of hidden layers (Layers = 1,2,3). Layers = 0 means we directly use four visual descriptors for the assessment.

4. EXPERIMENTS

In this section, we evaluate our method by conducting attractiveness score assessment experiments, meaning each algorithm gives a human-like score prediction. We use Pearson's correlation to quantitatively measure the predicted scores using human rating scores as the ground truth.

4.1 Dataset and Experimental Setting

We use the same dataset as Davis et al. [3] and Sutic et al. [12] to evaluate our method. The images and corresponding attractiveness scores have been collected from *www.hotornot.com*, and was pre-processed by White et al. [13]. In the pre-processing, automatic face detection was applied on each image, and followed by an alignment procedure that maps face onto canonical locations. The resulting database contains 2253 female images and 1745 male images. Each person in the dataset has an assigned beauty rating, ranging from 1 to 10, which is the average score from at least 50 votes. The rectifies images were downsampled to 86 by 86 pixels.

To generate more/less attractive datasets, a boundary value was used to split the original database into two equal parts. Note that we use 2056 female photos in this paper, and the boundary value is 7.9 (median of all scores). This split leads to 1028 more attractive faces and 1028 less attractive faces. From the two sides, we randomly chose 514 more attractive images and 514 less attractiveness images (1028 in total) as training data and the remaining 1028 images as testing data.

4.2 Results and Analysis

Attractiveness score assessment: We consider several popular visual descriptors to extract the low-level features: Raw pixel, Eigenface, LBP, SIFT, and Gabor filter. Then five pairs of auto-encoders are built by respectively employing the five descriptors as both the model's input and output. For each pair of auto-encoders, we extract two kinds of attractiveness-aware feature. The first feature is a direct application of the auto-encoder that concatenates the hidden units of two auto-encoders as the new representation. The second feature is the proposed attractiveness-aware representation that uses the vector $\hat{x} - \tilde{x}$ as the new representation. Finally, the two representations are fed into ridge-regression to predict test images' attractiveness scores.

Fig. 2 shows the results of two proposed representations with different number of hidden layers. The baseline is shown as "Layer = 0", where the regression model is trained directly by hand-craft descriptors [14, 12, 15]. Note that the left figure shows the results of the concatenation of hidden units, while the right represents using the difference between the two outputs of the auto-encoder pair. Clearly, for all visual descriptors, the two proposed representation achieves better results, which suggests that attractiveness-aware feature obtained from our model gives a better representations for facial beauty.

Low-Rank Late Fusion: Each regression model trained with one specific attractiveness-aware feature yield a ranking score. Then the Low-Rank Late Fusion (LRLF) scheme [16] is designed to fuse the produced m scores by removing the prediction errors from each model.

Table 1: Correlation score of different features on different patches along with the final fused results.

Patch	Raw pixel	Eigenface	SIFT	LBP	Gabor
Whole	0.4068	0.3679	0.4927	0.3691	0.4036
	0.4090	0.3729	0.4876	0.3822	0.4065
Upper	0.3530	0.3152	0.3957	0.3376	0.3880
	0.3426	0.3107	0.4110	0.3703	0.3631
Lower	0.3385	0.3392	0.4364	0.3099	0.3498
	0.3303	0.3140	0.4457	0.2921	0.3402
Right	0.3035	0.3134	0.4444	0.2520	0.3739
	0.2876	0.3241	0.4548	0.2908	0.3677
Left	0.3765	0.3814	0.4262	0.3364	0.4219
	0.3530	0.3695	0.4411	0.3578	0.4359
Fused	**0.5343**				

In our experiments, we have 1028 test samples, and each of them have 10 scores from 5 different descriptors (each visual descriptor produce two attractiveness-aware features and corresponding scores). Furthermore, in addition to using the whole face, we exploit the impact of face patches, i.e., upper, lower, left and right half of face. Therefore, these results constitute an 1028×50 score matrix Y with each score as an element. Then we apply low-rank representation on the matrix, and use the learned low-rank coefficient matrix Z as the new fused feature. Table 1 shows the result of using LRLF on 50 scores. We can conclude that the system performs better with robust late fusion. Note for each patch, we have two rows' results associated with two attractiveness-aware features using $[\hat{a}, \tilde{a}]$ and $\hat{x} - \tilde{x}$, respectively. It can be seen that, the difference between two representations is not large.

We further give an intuitive visualization of our system in Fig. 3, which shows the top ten and bottom ten images from the first dataset, according to the rating from humans and machine based on the final fused prediction results. Other than the above dataset, we also evaluate our method in the dataset provided by Gray et al. [6], which is also downloaded from *www.hotornot.com*, but without alignment. We follow their experiment setting, which uses 1028 training data and 1028 testing data for comparison. The comparison results are shown in Table 2. Note that our auto-encoder framework can also be applied on their Multiscale Model to produce more attractiveness-aware features, thereby, improving the assessment results and that could be our future work.

Table 2: Assessment correlation of two methods

Method	Correlation without alignment
Multiscale Model[6]	0.425
Our	0.437

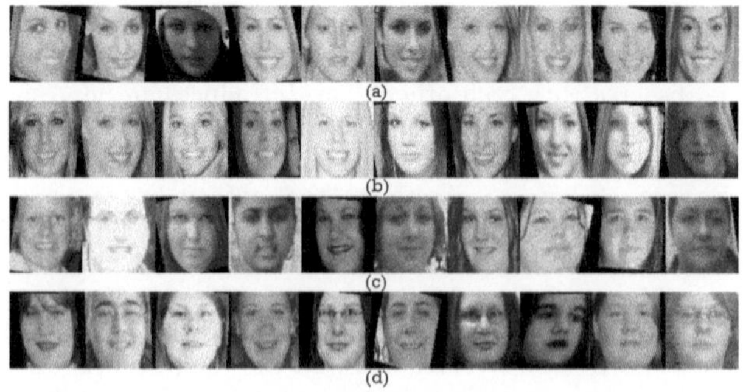

Figure 3: The most (a/b) and least (c/d) ten beauty images rating by humans (a/c) and machine (b/d)

5. CONCLUSIONS

We proposed an auto-encoder-based framework to extract attractiveness-aware features which was used to perform facial beauty assessment. Specifically, we introduced pair of auto-encoders trained by more attractive faces and less attractive faces separately to better represent the attractiveness-aware feature and produce a final attractiveness score by fusing several predictions from different facial patches and visual descriptors. Extensive experiments manifest the effectiveness of the proposed framework, and show significant improvements over the state-of-the-art approaches.

6. ACKNOWLEDGMENTS

This research is supported in part by the ONR Young Investigator Award N00014-14-1-0484, U.S. Army Research Office Young Investigator Award W911NF-14-1-0218, and Air Force Office of Scientific Research Award FA9550-12-1-0201.

7. REFERENCES

[1] P. Aarabi, D. Hughes, K. Mohajer, and M. Emami. The automatic measurement of facial beauty. In *IEEE International Conference on Systems, Man, and Cybernetics*, volume 4, pages 2644–2647. IEEE, 2001.

[2] T. R. Alley and M. R. Cunningham. Averaged faces are attractive, but very attractive faces are not average. 1991.

[3] B. C. Davis and S. Lazebnik. Analysis of human attractiveness using manifold kernel regression. In *ICIP*, pages 109–112. IEEE, 2008.

[4] L. G. Farkas and J. C. Kolar. Anthropometrics and art in the aesthetics of women's faces. *Clinics in Plastic Surgery*, 14(4):599–616, 1987.

[5] K. Grammer and R. Thornhill. Human facial attractiveness and sexual selection: The role of symmetry and averageness. *Journal of Comparative Psychology*, 108(3):233, 1994.

[6] D. Gray, K. Yu, W. Xu, and Y. Gong. Predicting facial beauty without landmarks. In *ECCV*, pages 434–447. Springer, 2010.

[7] Y. Jefferson. Facial beauty-establishing a universal standard. *International Journal of Orthodontics-Milwaukee-*, 15(1):9–26, 2004.

[8] G. Liu, Z. Lin, S. Yan, J. Sun, Y. Yu, and Y. Ma. Robust recovery of subspace structures by low-rank representation. *TPAMI*, 35(1):171–184, 2013.

[9] Y. Mu. Computational facial attractiveness prediction by aesthetics-aware features. *Neurocomputing*, 99:59–64, 2013.

[10] J. Nocedal. Updating quasi-newton matrices with limited storage. *Mathematics of Computation*, 35(151):773–782, 1980.

[11] G. Rhodes. The evolutionary psychology of facial beauty. *Annu. Rev. Psychol.*, 57:199–226, 2006.

[12] D. Sutic, I. Breskovic, R. Huic, and I. Jukic. Automatic evaluation of facial attractiveness. In *International Convention on Information and Communication Technology, Electronics and Microelectronics*, pages 1339–1342. IEEE, 2010.

[13] R. White, A. Eden, and M. Maire. Automatic prediction of human attractiveness. *UC Berkeley CS280A Project*, 1:2, 2004.

[14] J. Whitehill and J. R. Movellan. Personalized facial attractiveness prediction. In *IEEE International Conference on Automatic Face and Gesture Recognition*, pages 1–7. IEEE, 2008.

[15] H. Yan. Cost-sensitive ordinal regression for fully automatic facial beauty assessment. *Neurocomputing*, 129(0):334 – 342, 2014.

[16] G. Ye, D. Liu, I.-H. Jhuo, and S.-F. Chang. Robust late fusion with rank minimization. In *CVPR*, pages 3021–3028. IEEE, 2012.

AWtoolbox: Characterizing Audio Information Using Audio Words

Chin-Chia Michael Yeh, Ping-Keng Jao, and Yi-Hsuan Yang
Research Center for IT Innovation, Academia Sinica, Taiwan
{mcyeh, nafraw, yang}@citi.sinica.edu.tw

ABSTRACT

This paper presents the AWtoolbox, an open-source software designed for extracting the audio word (AW) representation of audio signals. The toolbox comes with a graphical user interface that helps a user design custom AW extraction pipelines and various algorithms for feature encoding, dictionary learning, result rectification, pooling, normalization and others. This paper also reports a benchmark comparing eight AW representations computed by the toolbox against state-of-the-art low-level and mid-level timbre, rhythmic and tonal descriptors of music and sound. The evaluation result shows that sparse coding (SC) based AW representation leads to very competitive performances across the three tested sound and music classification tasks. AWtoolbox is available for download at `http://mac.citi.sinica.edu.tw/awtoolbox`.

Categories and Subject Descriptors

H.5 [**Information Interfaces and Presentation**]: Multimedia Information Systems, Sound and Music Computing

Keywords

Audio feature; audio word; vector quantization; sparse coding; sound classification; music auto-tagging

1. INTRODUCTION

Representing audio information in a symbolic and text-like fashion analogous to the bag-of-words feature prevalent in text classification is not a new topic. The classic vector quantization approach represents a series of audio feature vectors extracted from an audio signal by the occurrence of codewords in a pre-built dictionary (codebook), leading to the so-called audio word (AW) representation for the entire signal [9,12]. Comparing to conventional audio features, an AW representation is characteristic of its ability of symbolizing any local audio event as a codeword, its flexibility of using an arbitrary large number of codewords learned from a corpus of audio data in an unsupervised fashion, and its light dependence on domain knowledge for feature design.

MM'14, November 3–7, 2014, Orlando, Florida, USA.

ACM 978-1-4503-3063-3/14/11 ...$15.00.
http://dx.doi.org/10.1145/2647868.2654989 .

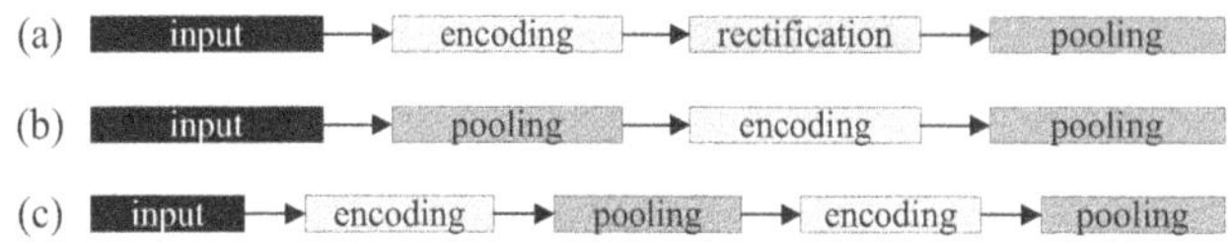

Figure 1: Three examples of AW extraction pipeline.

Therefore, it has been considered an powerful alternative to conventional hand-crafted audio features.

However, due to the advancement of AW encoding and dictionary learning algorithms [2,11,13,17,19], it is not easy to keep track of different proposals of AW extraction algorithms and make comprehensive comparisons. For example, sparse coding (SC) has received considerable attention in recent years and its variants have been used extensively in various audio-related research [4,14,15]. Post-processing methods such as encoding result rectification and normalization [3,7] have also been claimed important. Because of the lack of a standardized implementation of the related algorithms under a unified framework, it is difficult to compare the results reported in different works and gain insights.

In light of this, we present in this paper the AWtoolbox, an open-source graphic user interface application intended to facilitate the implementation and development of various AW extraction pipelines. We also report a benchmark comparing the performance of various AW representations calculated by the toolbox and conventional audio features for three different sound and music classification tasks.

2. AWTOOLBOX OVERVIEW

We define five atomic functional layers of AW extraction: `input`, `encoding`, `rectification`, `pooling` and `other`, whose details are presented later. As Figure 1 illustrates, different AW representations can be obtained by not only using different algorithms for each layer, but also cascading the functional layers in different ways. The same layer can be applied multiple times, using not necessarily the same algorithm each time. It is this versatility of the AW representation that makes it important to allow the users to define the number and order of these layers on their own. In a nutshell, with the proposed toolbox, extracting a custom AW representation can be done with the following steps:

- **Designing**: Users can graphically design the process by creating and arranging various kinds of layers for generating the desired AW representation. For visualization purpose, layers are color coded based on their types. For instance, the `input` layer is colored black and the `pooling` layer is colored light blue.
- **Dictionary learning**: Users can either provide a previous built dictionary or prepare a corpus for con-

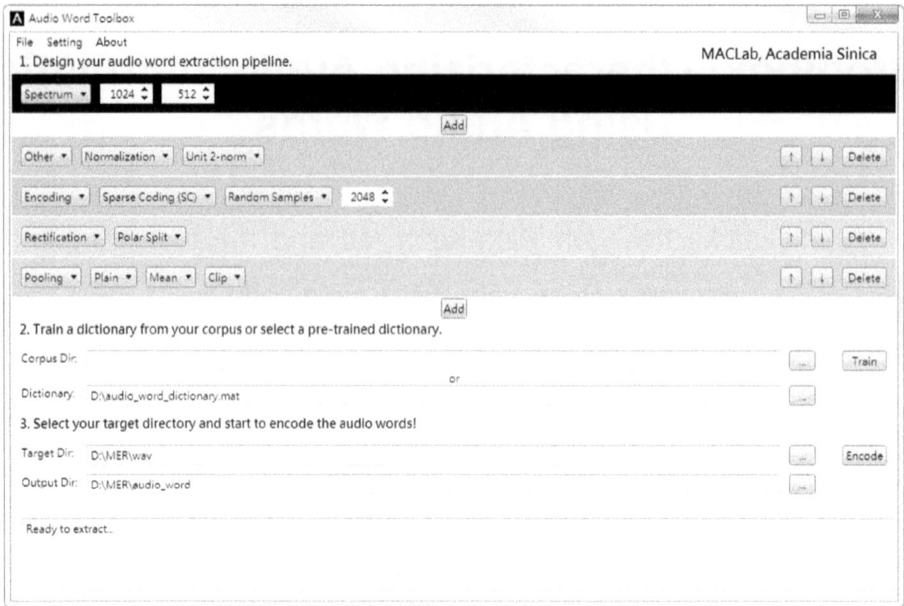

Figure 2: An screenshot of the graphical user interface of AWtoolbox.

structing the dictionary. The dictionary and the corresponding user-specified design can be saved for later use.

- **Audio word encoding**: When the desired dictionary is trained or selected, all the audio clips under the input directory will be encoded to generate the AW representation once the "Encode" button is pressed.

Figure 2 shows the graphical user interface of AWtoolbox. Currently, AWtoolbox is only available for the Windows platform. It is written in C#, with .NET assembly built from MATLAB codes for the underlying algorithms. The C# and MATLAB source codes are distributed under GPLv3 license. Please visit AWtoolbox's website for example workflow on AW extraction.

The `input` layer is the first layer in any AW extraction pipeline, transforming an input audio stream into a series of t frame-level feature vectors that are further processed in subsequent layers. Low-level feature representations applicable here include log power spectrum (SPEC), Mel-frequency cepstral coefficients (MFCC), sonogram, and chromagram, among others, extracted with the frame rate and hop size specified by a user. While MFCC-based AWs have been found effective in both audio and video classification problems [9, 12], it has been reported [15] that sparse coding works better with primitive features (e.g. SPEC) instead of sophisticated features because primitive features preserve more details of the raw signal.

The `encoding` layer converts an input vector (e.g. MFCC) $\mathbf{x} \in \mathbb{R}^m$ into the encoding result $\boldsymbol{\alpha} \in \mathbb{R}^k$ using a dictionary $\mathbf{D} \in \mathbb{R}^{m \times k}$ and an encoding method, where k denotes the number of codewords in $\mathbf{D}$. When there are t input vectors from an audio clip, we encode each vector individually. This involves the specification of an encoding algorithm and a dictionary learning algorithm. If desired, `encoding` can be applied multiple times, as Figure 1(c) depicts, to mimic the structure of deep neural nets [4,13]. Specifically, we consider the following four state-of-the-art encoding algorithms:

- **Vector quantization (VQ)** represents $\mathbf{x}$ by a one-hot binary vector $\boldsymbol{\alpha}$ according to the nearest codeword $\mathbf{d}_j \in \mathbb{R}^m$ in $\mathbf{D}$. Namely, only an α_j is 1 and the rest of $\boldsymbol{\alpha}$ are 0, where $j = \text{argmin}_p\ z_p$ and $z_p = \|\mathbf{x} - \mathbf{d}_p\|_2^2$.
- **Triangle coding (TC)**, a 'soft' variant of VQ [12], obtains a real-valued $\boldsymbol{\alpha}$ by $\alpha_j = \max\{0, \mu(\mathbf{z}) - z_j\}, \forall j$, where $\mu(\mathbf{z}) = \frac{1}{k}\sum_{p=1}^{k} z_p$ is the mean of these distances.
- **Sparse coding (SC)** represents the input signal by a sparse combination of the dictionary codewords by solving the following LASSO problem [2],

$$\boldsymbol{\alpha}^* = \underset{\boldsymbol{\alpha}}{\text{argmin}} \frac{1}{2}\|\mathbf{x} - \mathbf{D}\boldsymbol{\alpha}\|_2^2 + \lambda\|\boldsymbol{\alpha}\|_1 , \tag{1}$$

  where λ controls the balance between the reconstruction error $\|\mathbf{x} - \mathbf{D}\boldsymbol{\alpha}\|_2^2$ and the sparsity $\|\boldsymbol{\alpha}\|_1 = \sum|\alpha_j|$, which is a convex relaxation of the l_0 norm $\|\boldsymbol{\alpha}\|_0 = \sum|\alpha_j|^0$. A recommended value for λ is $1/\sqrt{\min(m,k)}$ [11]. For the case of $k \gg m$, it has been shown that SC outperforms VQ for audio classification problems [15].
- **Modified LASSO screening coding (SCS)** is a variant of SC with much lower computational cost due to a theoretically-justified mechanism to filter out codewords not useful for reconstructing the input signal before solving Eq. 1 [17]. We adopt an algorithm tailored for audio signals proposed in [8] and employ clip-level rather than frame-level screening for better efficiency in time and memory usage. With SCS, we can afford using larger k for the dictionary.

As for dictionary learning, the following three widely-used, unsupervised algorithms are considered:

- ***k*-means** generates a dictionary by using each cluster center as a codeword after applying k-means clustering to the training corpus. This algorithm is usually used for VQ-based representation [9, 12].
- **Online dictionary learning (ODL)** learns a dictionary by optimizing the following equation using stochastic gradient descent [11],

$$\mathbf{D}^* = \underset{\mathbf{D}}{\text{argmin}} \frac{1}{N}\sum_{n=1}^{N}\left(\frac{1}{2}\|\mathbf{x}^{(n)} - \mathbf{D}\boldsymbol{\alpha}^{(n)}\|_2^2 + \lambda\|\boldsymbol{\alpha}^{(n)}\|_1\right), \tag{2}$$

where N denotes the number of low-level feature vectors in the training corpus and n indexes the training instances. Variants of Eq. 2 that consider other cost functions such as non-negativity, group sparisty and structure sparsity have also been proposed [2].

- **Random exemplar extraction (REE)** randomly extracts k examples from the training corpus and directly uses the extracted examples as codewords for the dictionary. Therefore, it bypasses the computational cost involved in clustering or solving Eq. 2. It has been found that using such a random dictionary is effective when the dictionary size k is large [8].

The `rectification` layer applies rectifying non-linearity to the encoding result for improving representation power [3].

- **Absolute value** simply applies the absolute value function to all the elements of the input to this layer.
- **Polarity splitting** splits the positive and negative elements of the input data into separate ones and concatenates them after changing the sign of the negative ones [3]. For example, as Figure 1(a) shows, when the input is the time-varying encoding result $\mathbf{A} \in \mathbb{R}^{k \times t}$, the output of polarity splitting would be $\hat{\mathbf{A}} \in \mathbb{R}^{2k \times t}$, $\hat{\mathbf{A}} = [\max\{0, \mathbf{A}\}^{\mathrm{T}},\ \max\{0, -\mathbf{A}\}^{\mathrm{T}}]^{\mathrm{T}}$.

The `pooling` layer summarizes a time-varying vector sequence by aggregation operators such as taking the mean or maximum or by other advanced multi-scale pooling techniques such as temporal pyramid pooling [7]. Pooling can be done either in the clip-level or in the segment-level (a segment is a subset of a clip consisting of multiple consecutive frames), and after or before the `encoding` layer. For example, in Figure 1(a) the `pooling` layer combines the frame-level encoding results $\mathbf{A} \in \mathbb{R}^{k \times t}$ to form a k-dimensional clip-level feature vector (e.g. $\frac{1}{t}\sum \boldsymbol{\alpha}_i$ for the case of mean pooling) that can be used for classification. Figure 1(b) shows another example that pools the frame-level low-level features into segment-level ones and uses the latter for encoding, which might improve the robustness of the AW representation to small temporal distortion.

The `other` layer is added to accommodate other functions related to AW extraction but do not belong to the other four layers. We consider the following three algorithms:

- **Normalization** is important for AW representations. For instance, it has been shown that taking the square root of $\boldsymbol{\alpha}$ (a.k.a. power normalization or probability product kernel transform) improves the linear discriminability of AW representations [12, 19].
- **Random sampling** exploits the repetitive nature of music signals and randomly samples (with replacement) the frame-level features of an audio clip to reduce the number of frames t to be encoded [19].
- **Consecutive frame concatenation** concatenates multiple vectors to capture temporal information [13]; can be performed after the `input` or `encoding` layer.

3. BENCHMARK

To validate the effectiveness of the AW representations in characterizing audio information, we compare eleven AW and non-AW features for three fairly different audio classification tasks. The features we consider include:

- **SPEC**: log-scale spectrum calculated with 1,024-point and half overlapping frames.
- **MFCC**: 20-D MFCC computed for each frame and aggregated by mean pooling. MFCC is included as the baselines.
- **AW-MFCC-VQ-REE** is extracted by using MFCC at the `input` layer, VQ and REE for encoding and dictionary learning at the `encoding` layer, and mean pooling at the `pooling` layer. The dictionary size is set to $k = 2,048$. A dictionary is constructed (in an unsupervised fashion) from the training and test sets of each of the three datasets, respectively, without assessing the class labels. The other seven AW representations, such as AW-MFCC-SC-REE and AW-SPEC-SCS-REE, are extracted similarly but using different algorithms at the `input` and `encoding` layers. However, an absolute-value `rectification` layer is applied to SC and SCS before pooling, because their encoding results have both positive and negative values. In addition, as SCS is more efficient than SC, we set $k = 16,384$ for SCS to evaluate the benefit of using a larger dictionary.
- **MIR** is a set of 177-D features representing the state-of-the-art "hand-crafted" music/audio features calculated by using the MIRtoolbox [10]. It includes two measures of energy, five descriptors of rhythm (e.g., average tempo, pulse clarity and event density), 148 timbre/spectral descriptors (e.g. MFCC, spectral centroid, flux, roughness, irregularity and zero-crossing rate) and 22 tonal descriptors (e.g. pitch class profile, key clarity and musical mode). It is considered as a strong baseline in that it captures not only timbre but also the rhythmic and harmonic aspects of music signals, whereas the AW representations we consider are based on only spectral features (i.e. MFCC or SPEC).

Prior to feature extraction, all audio clips are converted to 22,050 Hz single channel waveform.

3.1 Audio Classification Tasks

We perform the benchmark using the following three data sets to ensure the result is generalizable.

- **FreeSound** consists of 20,626 audio clips collected from Freesound (`http://www.freesound.org`). Each clip is manually labeled with one of the following five categories: `sound effect`, `soundscape`, `speech`, `instrument sample` and `complex music fragment` [6]. As the clips are annotated with mutually exclusive labels, we formulate the problem as a multi-class classification one and report the average classification accuracy (ACC). We consider the first 30s for overly long clips for feature extraction and use ten-fold cross validation (CV) for evaluation.
- **CAL** is a subset of the dataset collected by Tingle *et al.* [16] for music auto-tagging, which contains the genre and acoustic annotation of music labeled by professional music editors of the music service company Pandora (`http://www.pandora.com`). With the 7digital API (`http://www.7digital.com`) we collect the 30s audio previews of 7,799 songs, spanning 140 genres and sub-genres, such as `classical`, `rock`, `teen pop`, `motown`, `salsa`, `latin` and `deathcore metal`. We consider it as a multi-label problem and evaluate the precision for tag-based retrieval using the training/test splits (akin to five-fold CV) defined by [16]. The performance measures are mean average precision (MAP), precision at rank ten (P@10) and precision at rank R (P@R), R being the number of relevant clips [16].

Table 1: **The results of the benchmark, with the top two results for each performance metric highlighted.**

Feature	Dimension	FreeSound	CAL			MER		
		ACC	MAP	P@10	P@R	MAP	P@10	P@R
MFCC	20	0.365	0.067	0.076	0.069	0.021	0.026	0.031
MIR [10]	177	**0.551**	**0.153**	**0.188**	**0.164**	0.043	0.079	0.065
AW-MFCC-VQ-REE	2,048	0.459	0.076	0.110	0.085	0.075	0.235	0.130
AW-MFCC-TC-REE	2,048	0.479	0.106	0.139	0.120	0.038	0.081	0.060
AW-MFCC-SC-REE	2,048	0.465	0.083	0.113	0.093	0.079	0.258	0.135
AW-MFCC-SCS-REE	16,384	0.450	0.074	0.105	0.082	0.105	**0.314**	0.154
AW-SPEC-VQ-REE	2,048	0.497	0.109	0.149	0.120	0.063	0.179	0.122
AW-SPEC-TC-REE	2,048	0.533	0.138	0.170	0.149	0.044	0.070	0.058
AW-SPEC-SC-REE	2,048	**0.545**	**0.143**	**0.188**	**0.157**	**0.111**	0.300	**0.171**
AW-SPEC-SCS-REE	16,384	0.530	0.120	0.164	0.135	**0.111**	**0.323**	**0.162**

- **MER** contains 31,427 30s audio previews labeled with 190 music emotion tags [18] by the crowd of last.fm users (`http://www.last.fm`). These are the songs considered as most relevant to the emotion tags according to the `Tag.getTopTracks()` function of the last.fm API. We consider the subset of 43 emotion tags which appear in the Affective Norm for English Words [1], such as `sad`, `lazy`, `relaxed`, `happy`, `romantic`, `fun` and `angry`, and evaluate the accuracy for tag-based retrieval using the training/test split specified in [18].

We use the simple l_2-regularized l_2-loss linear support vector machine (SVM) algorithm implemented by LIBLINEAR [5] for classifier training and prediction. The SVM parameter C is tuned by an inner CV on the training set. We use power normalization for AW representations and z-score normalization for the MFCC and MIR features.

3.2 Results

Table 1 shows the results of this benchmark, from which the following observations can be made. First, generally speaking MIR features and SC-based AW features achieve the best results for all the three tasks, outperforming MFCC by a large margin. Moreover, while MIR features perform slightly better for the first two tasks, SC-based AW features lead to significantly better precision than the rivals for the MER task. This validates the effectiveness of an AW representation in representing audio information, even though it is based on only primitive spectral features randomly drawn from an audio collection and is computed without exploiting specific knowledge of the signal (i.e. music theories). The P@10 for MER reaches 0.323, which shows out of the top 10 ranked songs for each tag on average more than 3 of them are relevant. Second, by comparing the AW features, we see that generally better results for the tasks we considered are obtained by using SPEC rather than MFCC for the `input` layer, and SC-based algorithms (i.e. SC and SCS) rather than VQ or TC for the `encoding` layer. This shows the importance for the AWtoolbox to accommodate a variety of AW extraction pipelines to be experimented with by a user. Finally, according to our evaluation it is sufficient to use a dictionary of medium size (i.e. 2,048 for AW-SPEC-SC-REE) instead of a large one. It takes around 17 seconds for computing the AW-SPEC-SC-REE for a 30 seconds music clip.

4. CONCLUSIONS

In this paper, we have presented the AWtoolbox to facilitate the use of various AW features in representing audio information. The toolbox is characteristic of its flexibility in designing new AW extraction pipelines and its expandability in including new algorithms. The effectiveness of the resulting feature representations have been validated through three fairly different audio and music classification tasks. We hope that the AWtoolbox can also be useful for other tasks such as audiovisual video content analysis, audio-based duplicate detection (e.g. cover song identification), similarity estimation, visualization, and reconstruction-related tasks such as source separation and audio synthesis.

5. REFERENCES

[1] [Online] `http://csea.phhp.ufl.edu/media/`.

[2] F. Bach et al. Optimization with sparsity-inducing penalties. *FTML*, 2012.

[3] A. Coates and A. Ng. The importance of encoding versus training with sparse coding and vector quantization. In *ICML*, pages 921–928, 2011.

[4] L. Deng and X. Li. Machine learning paradigms for speech recognition: An overview. *TASLP*, 21(5):1060–1089, 2013.

[5] R.-E. Fan et al. LIBLINEAR: A library for large linear classification. *JMLR*, 2008.

[6] F. Font et al. Audio clip classification using social tags and the effect of tag expansion. In *Semantic Audio*, 2014.

[7] P.-S. Huang et al. Pooling robust shift-invariant sparse representations of acoustic signals. In *Interspeech*, 2012.

[8] P.-K. Jao et al. Modified LASSO screening for audio word-based music classification using large-scale dictionary. In *ICASSP*, 2014.

[9] Y.-G. Jiang. SUPER: Towards real-time event recognition in internet video. In *ICMR*, 2012.

[10] O. Lartillot and P. Toiviainen. A Matlab toolbox for musical feature extraction from audio. In *DAFx*, 2007.

[11] J. Mairal et al. Online dictionary learning for sparse coding. In *ICML*, pages 689–696, 2009.

[12] B. McFee et al. Learning content similarity for music recommendation. *TASLP*, 20(8):2207–2218, 2012.

[13] J. Nam et al. Learning sparse feature representations for music annotation and retrieval. In *ISMIR*, 2012.

[14] E. C. Smith and M. S. Lewicki. Efficient auditory coding. *Nature*, 439(7079):978–982, 2006.

[15] L. Su, C.-C. M. Yeh, J.-Y. Liu, J.-C. Wang, and Y.-H. Yang. A systematic evaluation of the bag-of-frames representation for music information retrieval. *TMM*, 2014.

[16] D. Tingle et al. Exploring automatic music annotation with "acoustically-objective" tags. In *MIR*, 2010.

[17] Z. J. Xiang et al. Learning sparse representations of high dimensional data on large scale dictionaries. In *NIPS*, 2011.

[18] Y.-H. Yang and J.-Y. Liu. Quantitative study of music listening behavior in a social and affective context. *TMM*, 15(6):1304–1315, Oct 2013.

[19] C.-C. M. Yeh et al. Improving music auto-tagging by intra-song instance bagging. In *ICASSP*, 2014.

Screencast in the Wild: Performance and Limitations

Chih-Fan Hsu[1], De-Yu Chen[1], Chun-Ying Huang[2], Cheng-Hsin Hsu[3], and Kuan-Ta Chen[1]
[1]Institute of Information Science, Academia Sinica
[2]Department of Computer Science and Engineering, National Taiwan Ocean University
[3]Department of Computer Science, National Tsing Hua University

ABSTRACT

Displays without associated computing devices are increasingly more popular, and the binding between computing devices and displays is no longer one-to-one but more dynamic and adaptive. *Screencast* technologies enable such dynamic binding over ad hoc one-hop networks or Wi-Fi access points. In this paper, we design and conduct the first detailed measurement study on the performance of state-of-the-art screencast technologies. By varying the user demands and network conditions, we find that Splashtop and Miracast outperform other screencast technologies under typical setups. Our experiments also show that the screencast technologies either: (i) do not dynamically adjust bitrate or (ii) employ a suboptimal adaptation strategy. The developers of future screencast technologies are suggested to pay more attentions on the bitrate adaptation strategy, e.g., by leveraging cross-layer optimization paradigm.

Categories and Subject Descriptors: H.5 [Information Systems Applications]: Multimedia Information Systems

Keywords: Measurement; streaming; wireless networks; experiments

1. INTRODUCTION

Increasingly more, and often larger and less expensive, digital displays have been deployed in homes, offices, schools, shops, and other public/private spaces. For example, several vendors have proposed to make refrigerators and washing machines more intelligent and embed displays in them. On the other hand, the display technology is evolving quickly, and we will soon have elastic displays on newspapers, business cards, or clothes. Such next-generation displays will likely come without associated computing devices, but instead rely on other devices, such as smartphones, for the computation and data hosting. We envision that by that time, the binding between computing devices and displays will be no longer one-to-one but more dynamic and adaptive than what we have today. In fact, a recent study shows that people move across different displays on average 21 times per hour [7], showing the importance of efficient dynamic binding between computing devices and displays.

Such dynamic binding is best realized via *screencast*, which refers to sending the audio/video streams captured on computing devices over wireless channels to one or multiple larger displays in real-time for better viewing experience. Screencast seamlessly addresses the grand challenge of insufficient display real-estate of mobile and wearable devices, and has attracted significant attentions from both the academia and industry. For example, several open-source projects [1, 5] support one-to-one, one-to-many, or many-to-many screencast among smartphones, tablets, laptop/desktop computers. There are also several commercial technologies realizing screencast using dedicated hardware chips and software packages, including AirPlay, Chromecast, Miracast, MirrorOp, and Splashtop. The commercial screencast technologies are more widely deployed, compared to the open-source counterparts. Therefore, the chance for a user to run into a large display compatible with the commercial technologies is way higher. Nonetheless, the performance of the existing screencast technologies has not been studied in the literature, which may be attributed to their closed and proprietary nature.

In this paper, we conduct extensive experiments to quantify the performance of the screencast technologies using a real setup. We control 5 system parameters: frame rate, resolution, bandwidth, network delay, and packet loss rate. We adopt 4 objective performance metrics: video bitrate, graphic quality, end-to-end latency, and frame loss rate. Our in-depth analysis reveals several novel insights and leads to design suggestions to future screencast technologies. To our best knowledge, this paper is the first comprehensive measurement and comparison study on screencast technologies.

2. RELATED WORK

Screencast is one of the real-time remote graphical applications, and the performance of these applications has been studied in the literature. For example, Tolia et al. [8] and Lagar-Cavilla et al. [6] analyze the performance of VNC (Virtual Network Computing), and Claypool et al. [3] and Chen et al. [2] study the performance of cloud games. The quality of commercial screencast technologies has not received attentions in the research community. He et al. [4] conduct a user study on Chromecast with about 20 participants to determine the user tolerance thresholds on video quality (in PSNR), rendering quality (in frame loss rate), freeze time ratio, and rate of freeze events. The user study is done using a Chromecast emulator. Their work is different from ours in several ways: (i) we consider objective perfor-

MM '14, November 03 - 07 2014, Orlando, FL, USA.

http://dx.doi.org/10.1145/2647868.2654991.

Table 1: The Considered Parameters

Parameter		Values		
Content	Frame rate	15 fps	30 fps	**60 fps**
	Resolution	896x504	N/A	**1366x768**
Network	Bandwidth	4 Mbps	6 Mbps	**Unlimited**
	Delay	200 ms	100 ms	**0 ms**
	Packet loss rate	2%	1%	**0%**

mance metrics, (ii) we consider multiple screencast technologies, and (iii) we use real setups in the wild for experiments.

3. METHODOLOGY

3.1 Screencast Technologies

We first introduce the considered screencast technologies.

- **AirPlay** is a proprietary protocol designed by Apple. AirPlay supports streaming audio, video, photos, and meta-data over wireless channels.
- **Chromecast** is a digital media player which is capable of directly streaming audio/video contents via Wi-Fi from the Internet or a local network. For screencast, a user can use Google Cast Chrome extension, which uses WebRTC API to cast content from the web browser or desktop to the Chromecast device.
- **Miracast** is a peer-to-peer wireless standard for screencasting over Wi-Fi Direct. Miracast-compatible devices can serve as Miracast senders and receivers. There are also Miracast adapters capable of rendering the screens through HDMI or USB ports.
- **MirrorOp** and **Splashtop** offer pure software solutions, which require the users to install proprietary applications at both the sender and receiver.

3.2 Content Types

We consider 9 content types in the following 3 categories.

- **Gaming**: including first-person shooter, racing, and turn-based strategy games.
- **Movie/TV**: including dialogue movie scene, car chasing movie scene, and talk show.
- **Interactive applications**: including Google street view browsing, slides editing, and web surfing.

For fair comparisons, we record the screens of different content types into videos. In particular, we extract one minute of representative video for each content type and concatenate them into a single 9-minute long video.

3.3 System Parameters

We consider two groups of parameters: content and network, which we believe impose direct and non-trivial impacts on screencast quality. Content parameters are related to the quality of source videos, including *frame rate* and *resolution*. We change the frame sampling rates to generate multiple videos, and set 60 fps as the default frame rate. We also vary the resolutions at 1366x768 (default[1]) and 896x504. For the latter case, we place the video at the center of the (larger) screen without resizing it. This is because we believe image resizing would cause loss of details and bias our results. Network parameters are related to the wireless network conditions. We use dummynet to control the *bandwidth*, *delay*, and *packet loss rate* (packet loss) of the outgoing channel of sender devices. The default bandwidth is not throttled, delay is 0 ms, and packet loss rate is 0%. In our experiments, a system parameter is set to different values while all other parameters are fixed at their default values. The detailed system parameters values are listed in Table 1, with the default values in boldface.

[1]iOS does not support 1366x768, and we pick the closest resolution, 1440x900, instead.

Table 2: Specifications of Measured Technologies

Technology	AirPlay	Chromecast	Miracast	MirrorOp	Splashtop
Hardware/SW	Hardware	Hardware	Hardware	Software	Software
Connectivity	AP	AP	Wi-Fi Direct	AP/Internet	AP/Internet
Protocol	TCP	UDP	UDP	TCP	TCP
Proprietary	Yes	Yes	No	Yes	Yes

3.4 Experiment Setup

There are several components in the experiment: a sender and a receiver for each screencast technology, and a Wi-Fi AP, which is mandatory for all technologies except Miracast. The specifications of the screencast technologies are summarized in Table 2, and the detailed experiment setups are given below.

- **AirPlay.** The sender is a MacBook Pro running OS X 10.9.2, with a 2.4 GHz Intel Core i5 processor and 8 GB memory, while the receiver is an Apple TV. They are connected to the same Wi-Fi AP before the sender can discover, connect, and stream screens to the receiver.
- **Chromecast.** The sender is a Lenovo ThinkPad X240 notebook running Windows 8.1, with 1.6 GHz Intel Core i5 processor and 8GB memory and the receiver is a Chromecast dongle. The only way for screencasting using Chromecast is by Google Cast Chrome extension. Once the sender is connected to the Wi-Fi AP, it can discover and connect to any available devices on the same Wi-Fi network.
- **Miracast.** We use the Lenovo notebook as the sender. For the receiver, we use a Netgear Push2TV Miracast adapter. Miracast is based on Wi-Fi Direct and supported by Windows 8.1. As long as the receiver is placed within an acceptable range to the sender, Windows 8.1 provides a simple interface for screencasting the desktop to the receiver.
- **MirrorOp** and **Splashtop.** The Lenovo notebook serves as the sender, while a PC running Windows 7, with an Intel Core i7 processor as the receiver. To use these two services, a user needs to create an account, and run the sender and receiver programs on the respective machines. Once both machines are logged in, they can discover and connect to each other.

We note that some screencast technologies have been realized by multiple vendors, and we cannot cover all implementations in this paper. Instead, we pick a popular implementation for each technology, but our measurement methodology can be applied to other implementations.

3.5 Performance Metrics

We measure the following performance metrics.

- **Bitrate.** The average amount of data per unit time transmitted from the sender to receiver.
- **Latency.** The time difference between each video frame is rendered at the sender and at the receiver.
- **Frame loss rate** (frame loss). The fraction of video frames that are not rendered at the receiver.
- **Video quality** (quality). The video quality rendered at the receiver compared to the original video captured by the sender. Both SSIM and PSNR are used.

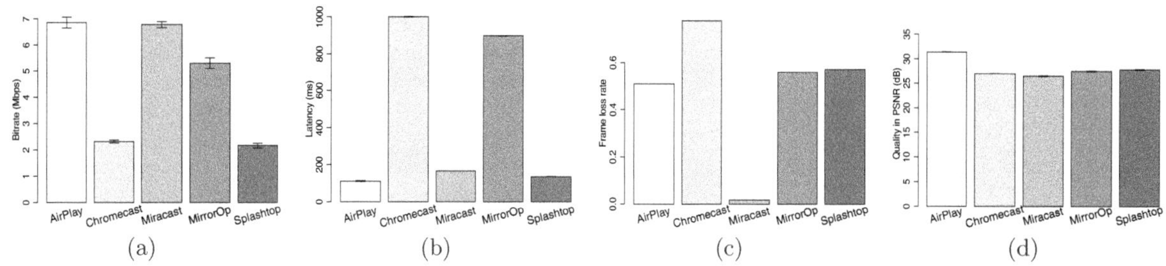

Figure 1: Performance of screencast technologies: (a) bitrate, (b) latency, (c) frame loss, and (d) quality in PSNR. The error bars represent the standard errors.

3.6 Experiment Procedure

For each technology, we first connect the sender and receiver, play the video with diverse content types at the sender, and measure the four performance metrics. We repeat the experiment several times with different system parameters. To facilitate our measurements, we have added a unique color bar on each frame of the source content as their frame id, which can be readily recognized.

To measure the bitrate used by the screencast technologies, we run a packet analyzer at the sender to keep track of the outgoing packets during the experiments. For measuring the graphic quality, we direct the HDMI output of the receiver to a PC, which is referred to as the *recorder*. The Windows 7 PC is equipped with an Avermedia video capture card to record the videos. To measure the quality degradation, each frame of the recorded video is matched to its counterpart in the source video, using the frame id. Last, we calculate the SSIM and PSNR values. The frame loss rate can also be measured by matching the frames.

To measure the user-perceived latency, we direct the rendered videos of both the sender and receiver to two side-by-side monitors via HDMI. We then set up a Canon EOS 600D camera to record the two monitors at the same time. To capture every frame rendered on the monitors, we set the recording frame rate of the camera to 60 fps, which equals the highest frame rate in our parameter settings. The recorded video is then processed to compute the latency of each frame, by comparing the timestamps when the frame is rendered by the sender and receiver.

4. MEASUREMENT RESULTS

4.1 Overall Performance

We report the results under the default system parameters (see Table 1). Each experiment lasts for 9 minutes 18 seconds, with 33480 video frames. For each screencast technology, we first calculate the bitrate, latency, and video quality of individual video frames rendered by the receiver (i.e., lost frames are not considered). We then compute the mean and standard error across all video frames. We also derive the frame loss rate of each experiment. We plot the results in Figure 1, and make several observations. First, AirPlay and Miracast both lead to high bitrate and low latency, while Miracast achieves much lower frame loss rate. Second, although Chromecast incurs very low bitrate, it suffers from high latency and high frame loss rate. Third, Splashtop and MirrorOp achieve similar frame loss rate and video quality, but Splashtop leads to lower bitrate and latency. Last, screencast technologies other than AirPlay lead to roughly the same video quality in PSNR. Based on these observations, we conclude that: (i) Miracast is the best hardware-based screencast technology and (ii) Splashtop is the best software-based screencast technology under the default system parameters. Last, we mention that we omit the figure of quality in SSIM, because it shows almost identical trends as PSNR (Figure 1(d)).

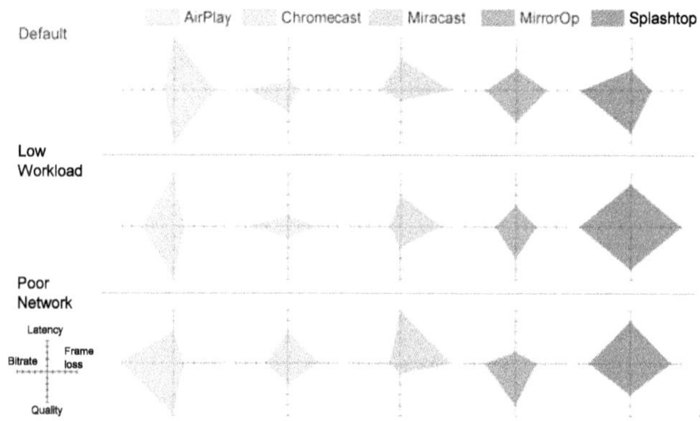

Figure 2: Ranks of different screencast technologies under different conditions. Ticks closer to the origins represent lower ranks (worse performance).

We next study the performance of these screencast technologies under different conditions. In addition to the default condition, we define a *low workload* condition by reducing the frame rate to 15 fps, which may be sufficient for non-multimedia applications, such as email clients and office suites. We also define a *poor network* condition, by incurring 200 ms network delay and 2% packet loss rate, while capping the network bandwidth at 6 Mbps[2]. For these three conditions, we compute the mean performance metrics, and rank the screencast technologies on each metric independently[3]. We then plot the results in Figure 2. This figure reveals that: (i) Splashtop performs the best and balanced in general, and it is never ranked the last in all aspects, (ii) AirPlay and Miracast perform well in some aspects, but poorly in others, and (iii) Chromecast and MirrorOp result in inferior performance than other hardware-based and software-based screencast technologies, respectively. In summary, Miracast outperforms other hardware-based screencast technologies, and AirPlay suffers from high frame loss rate under low

[2]We also cap the network bandwidth at 4 Mbps, but several screencast technologies stop working under that constraint.
[3]We use PSNR as the quality metric, but SSIM leads to nearly identical ranking.

workload and poor network conditions. Splashtop outperforms other software-based screencast technologies.

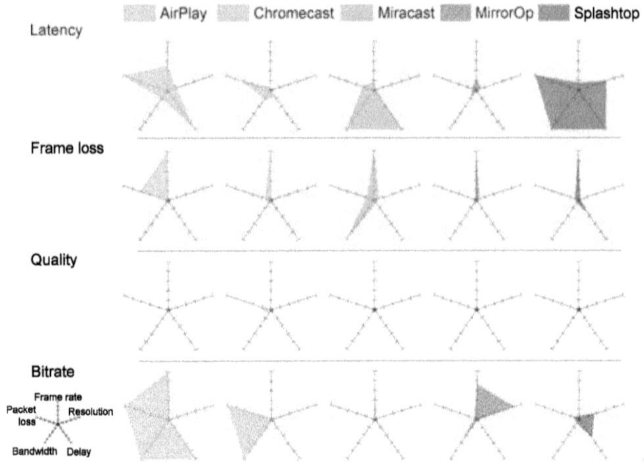

Figure 3: Susceptibility of different screencast technologies under different parameters. Smaller susceptibility (closer to the origins) means less vulnerable to dynamic environments.

4.2 Susceptibility Comparison

We perform susceptibility analysis to quantify how much impact each system parameter incurs on each performance metric with different screencast technologies. For each screencast technology, we vary a system parameter while fixing all other system parameters at their default values. We repeat the experiment multiple times, and compute the mean performance of each experiment. For each metric, we then compute the ratio between the range (i.e., difference between the maximum and minimum) and the minimum, which is referred to as susceptibility. If the resulting susceptibility is larger than 1, we set it to be 1. Smaller susceptibility means more stable performance; larger susceptibility indicates higher dependency on some system parameters.

We report the resulting susceptibility in Figure 3, where ticks closer to the origins indicate smaller susceptibility. We make several observations. First, Splashtop and Miracast have relatively low susceptibility in general, except user-perceived latency. In particular, packet loss, bandwidth, and network delay affect their user-perceived latency the most. Fortunately, since screencast senders and receivers are likely to be collocated, severely poor network conditions are unlikely to happen. Therefore, Splashtop and Miracast still outperform over other screencast technologies. Second, the bitrate of AirPlay is extremely susceptible to network conditions and frame rate. That is, AirPlay aggressively adjusts its bitrate to cope with the dynamics of user demands (frame rate) and network conditions. Intuitively, this should give AirPlay a performance edge over other screencast technologies. It is however surprising to see that AirPlay performs the worst in dynamic network conditions (low workload and poor network in Figure 2), compared to other screencast technologies. A closer analysis on why AirPlay's bitrate adaptation strategy does not work well is one of our future tasks. Last, Chromecast and MirrorOp have relatively low susceptibility. In fact, as illustrated in Figure 1, the largest issues of Chromecast and MirrorOp are high latency and high frame loss rate, which unfortunately are not alleviated by better network conditions and lower resolution. Instead, the only system parameter that could ease these two issues is the frame rate. Therefore, Chromecast and MirrorOp are less suitable to higher frame rates (say, 60 fps).

4.3 Summary

We briefly summarize our main findings in the following.

- Splashtop performs the best and balanced in general with low susceptibility except user-perceived latency. The extreme network conditions are less common in screencast setups, where the senders and receivers are connected by one-hop ad-hoc link or via a Wi-Fi AP.
- Miracast performs the best among all hardware-based screencast technologies. Compared to Splashtop, Miracast's performance is slightly inferior, but Miracast adaptors are less expensive than dedicated receiver computers. Hence, Miracast has a better price/performance ratio than Splashtop.
- AirPlay aggressively adapts its streaming bitrate based on user demand and network conditions. It, however, suffers from high frame loss rate, indicating a suboptimal adaptation strategy.

5. CONCLUSION

In this paper, we have presented detailed measurement methodology and conducted the first comparison study on the state-of-the-art screencast technologies. This is the first measurement study using real screencast setups. Our methodology is also applicable to other screencast technologies, which may be developed in the future. We have found that Splashtop and Miracast perform the best. Our experiments also reveal some common shortcomings: (i) technologies other than AirPlay do not adapt the bitrate under different user demands and network conditions, and (ii) AirPlay's bitrate adaptation strategy however results in bad performance under low workload and poor network conditions. Future screencast developers should carefully design the bitrate adaptation strategy, and maybe leverage the low-level wireless characteristics via cross-layer optimization paradigm.

References

[1] S. Chandra, J. Boreczky, and L. Rowe. High performance many-to-many Intranet screen sharing with DisplayCast. *ACM Transactions on Multimedia Computing, Communications, and Applications*, 10(2), Feb 2014.
[2] K. Chen, Y. Chang, H. Hsu, D. Chen, C. Huang, and C. Hsu. On the quality of service of cloud gaming systems. *IEEE Transactions on Multimedia*, 16(2), Feb 2014.
[3] M. Claypool, D. Finkel, A. Grant, and M. Solano. Thin to win? network performance analysis of the OnLive thin client game system. In *Proc. of ACM Workshop on Network and Systems Support for Games*, Nov 2012.
[4] Y. He, K. Fei, G. Fernandez, and E. Delp. Video quality assessment for Web content mirroring. In *Proc. of Imaging and Multimedia Analytics in a Web and Mobile World*, Mar 2014.
[5] C. Huang, K. Chen, D. Chen, H. Hsu, and C. Hsu. GamingAnywhere: The first open source cloud gaming system. *ACM Transactions on Multimedia Computing, Communications, and Applications*, 10(1), Jan 2014.
[6] H. A. Lagar-Cavilla, N. Tolia, E. de Lara, M. Satyanarayanan, and D. O'Hallaron. Interactive resource-intensive applications made easy. In *Proc. of the ACM/IFIP/USENIX International Conference on Middleware*, Nov 2007.
[7] People swap devices 21 times an hour, says OMD, 2014. `http://www.campaignlive.co.uk/news/1225960/`.
[8] N. Tolia, D. Andersen, and M. Satyanarayanan. Quantifying interactive user experience on thin clients. *Computer*, 39(3), 2006.

One-Pass Video Stabilization on Mobile Devices

Wei Jiang Zhenyu Wu John Wus Heather Yu
Huawei Media Lab
Bridgewater, New Jersey
{wei.jiang, zhenyu.wu, john.wus, heatheryu}@huawei.com

ABSTRACT

We study real-time one-pass video stabilization on mobile devices such as smartphones and tablets. A localized camera path planning framework is proposed, where through maintaining a forward or backward-looking buffer window, the short-term camera trajectory is locally optimized according to cinematographic rules. Also, we propose a hybrid autocorrective path optimization algorithm, where the system automatically switches among different motion models according to the actual video adaptively. Using a multithreading mechanism, the proposed method can be implemented on mobile devices to achieve real-time one-pass video stabilization. Evaluation on a large variety of consumer videos demonstrates the effectiveness of our system.

Categories and Subject Descriptors

I.2.10 [**rti ial ntelligen e**]: Vision and Scene Understanding—*Video analysis*; I.4.m [**mage Pro essing and Compute Vision**]: Miscellaneous

General Terms

Algorithms; Experimentation

Keywords

Video stabilization; mobile; real-time

1. INTRODUCTION

With the widespread prevalence of mobile devices such as smartphones and tablets, mobile video capture has become an inseparable part of our everyday life. For normal users, it is hard to hold a mobile camera steady, and the captured videos usually appear remarkably shaky. Video stabilization has been extensively studied in recent years. One approach is to assume some available prior knowledge about the camera, such as the camera-dependent inter-frame delay [1]; the intrinsic camera matrix [4]; and the calibrated inertial sensors [8]. However, due to the inevitable gyro drift and sensor noises, camera translation computed from the inertial sensors are prone to error, while the assumption of pure camera rotation is unrealistic for most consumer videos shooting non-planer scenes. Moveover, dedicated calibration is usually required to obtain such camera-dependent priors, which makes these methods impractical for general consumers.

Without assumptions of the camera priors, most existing software-based stabilization methods post-process the shaky video through the following three steps. First, the parametric camera motion between consecutive frames is estimated based on the visual appearance. Then, an optimal intended smooth camera trajectory is estimated and the high-frequency fluctuations are removed. After that, a stabilized video is synthesized by warping the original frames based on the estimated smooth trajectory. Early work [13] applied low-pass filters to remove high-frequency motion. Kalman filters and particle filters were also used to remove short-term image fluctuations based on the past data statistics [3, 15]. Some others assumed prior motion models such as polynomial curves [2] or exponential maps over camera trajectory segments [5]. Recently, Grundmann *et al.* [7] used a systematic L_1-norm optimization to generate a camera path that followed cinematography rules. This approach was further extended in [6] by adopting a homography mixture to rectify rolling shutter effects. These techniques have been successfully used by the built-in YouTube stabilizer. To fundamentally solve the parallax problem caused by the non-negligible depth variation in the scene, 3D camera motion was estimated and smoothed [10]. To avoid the fragile 3D reconstruction, robust long feature trajectories were directly smoothed in [11]. Instead of using the dense depth information, a space-time path smoothing approach was proposed in [12], where a homography mesh was used to maintain the spatially-variant camera paths.

Although good stabilization results can be achieved during post-processing, existing methods generally cannot perform satisfactorily for real-time stabilizing general mobile consumer videos. First, in many cases, robust long feature tracks cannot be obtained due to various reasons such as rapid camera motion, occlusions, *etc.* Methods like [11] appear to be fragile in practice. Second, due to the limited memory and computation power on mobile devices, methods requiring high-quality SIFT/SURF feature matching [12, 15], requiring extra motion inpainting [5, 13], or requiring expensive optimization [6] are not suitable for real-time processing of HD videos. Third, previous fast video stabilizers such as [3] are based on motion filtering, and they usually need scene-dependent parameter tuning. For

MM'14, November 3–7, 2014, Orlando, Florida, USA.
Copyright 2014 ACM 978-1-4503-3063-3/14/11 ...$15.00.
http://dx.doi.org/10.1145/2647868.2654995.

example, an aggressive filtering gives a more stabilized camera path but larger out-of-bound areas. Normal users do not have the knowledge or interest in such parameter tuning. Fourth, a practical system should gracefully degenerate, *i.e.*, we should not produce a result worse than the original video. Finally, a real-time mobile stabilizer should use a one-pass (streamable) framework, *i.e.*, we should stabilize videos during capture instead of in post-processes after capture.

In this paper, we study real-time one-pass video stabilization on mobile devices. Figure 1 shows the framework of the overall system. The real-time stabilization ability can be achieved through a multithreading mechanism. The video capture thread A maintains a forward or backward-looking buffer during the normal video capture process, where an L-length (*e.g.*, 1 sec) video sequence is stored in the buffer. The camera path planning thread B estimates the short-term camera trajectory over the buffered video sequence and computes the intended smooth camera trajectory for stabilization. Specifically, a tree-splitting based approach is developed where hybrid motion models are used for improved stabilization according to cinematographic rules. Finally, the frame synthesis thread C computes the target stabilized frames by warping the original frames according to the computed smooth camera trajectory. This system framework supports two types of real-time stabilization strategies: zero-latency streamable stabilization using a pure backward-looking buffer, or streamable stabilization using a forward-looking buffer (or a mixture of forward and backward-looking buffer) with a delay of the buffer length. We evaluate our algorithm over a large variety of consumer videos that are publicly available. Experiments demonstrate robust performance for real-time mobile video stabilization compared to traditional video stabilizers.

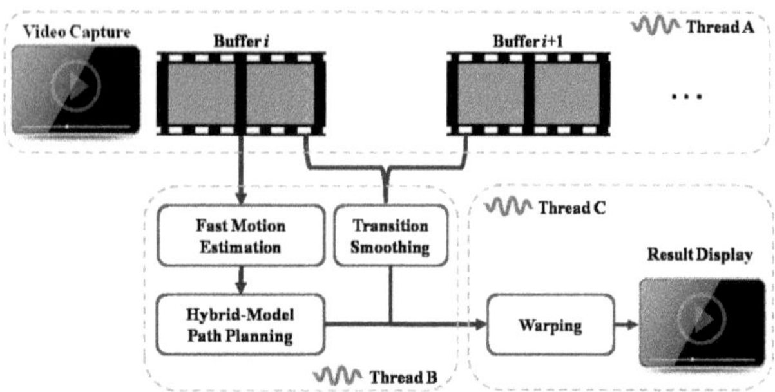

Figure 1: The o erall rame or o our approa h

2. ONE-PASS VIDEO STABILIZATION

Consider a 2D image point $[u_i, v_i]^T$ in one image and $[u_j, v_j]^T$ in another, a 3×3 homography $\mathbf{H}$ is generally used to relate the pixel coordinates as:

$$[u_j, v_j, 1]^T \approx \mathbf{H}[u_i, v_i, 1]^T, \quad (1)$$

where $\approx$ means equal up to a scale, and therefore $\mathbf{H}$ has 8 degrees-of-freedom (DOF). When applied to every pixel, we obtain the image $_j$ as a warped version of the image $_i$. Assuming linear projectivity, the homography $\mathbf{H}$ reduces to a 5-DOF affine transformation $\mathbf{T}$. Assuming single rotation and isotropic scaling, $\mathbf{T}$ further reduces to a 4-DOF similarity transformation :

$$[u_j, v_j, 1]^T \approx \ [u_i, v_i, 1]^T. \quad (2)$$

In general, models with higher DOF are more descriptive and powerful for stabilization. However, higher DOF models are more sensitive to errors in feature tracking and motion estimation, and can generate more severe artifacts when such errors occur. In comparison, lower DOF models are less powerful but are more robust to computation errors.

In this work we use a hybrid approach where both homography and similarity models are used for improved video stabilization. From our observation, when the camera motion can be robustly estimated with well tracked features, the high DOF homography is quite powerful in general with skew and perspective correction compared to low DOF affine or similarity models. However, when motion estimation is inaccurate, homographies can present large skew and perspective artifacts. When such problems occur, the low DOF similarity model is significantly more robust than the other models. Therefore, we choose to use the high DOF homography and low DOF similarity transformation in our system.

2.1 Fast motion estimation

We extract the fast binary ORB (Oriented FAST and Rotation BRIEF) keypoints [14] over each frame, which is approximately 20 times faster than SURF and 400 times faster than SIFT over 1920×1080 HD videos. The ORB descriptors have been previously shown efficient in object detection and tracking [9]. To reduce the number of local points for robust and fast tracking, a grid-based mechanism is further adopted. A 16×16 grid is used to spread the detected feature points into different cells. Only the strongest point having the highest response value is selected for each cell. After that the Kanade-Lucas-Tomasi (KLT) tracker is used to compute feature point correspondences between adjacent image frames. Following the standard procedure, the inter-frame motion transformation matrices (*e.g.*, homography, affine, or similarity transformation matrices) can be estimated by using RANSAC and outlier feature rejection.

2.2 Path planning with hybrid motion models

As discussed in [7], from a cinematographic standpoint, the most pleasant viewing experience is conveyed by the use of either static cameras (*i.e.*, a constant camera path), panning ones mounted on tripods or cameras placed onto a dolly (*i.e.*, a camera path of constant velocity). Without loss of generality, let $\mathbf{W}$ denote a 2D transformation matrix ($\mathbf{W}$ can be homography, affine, or similarity transformation). The above cinematographic characteristics can be described as a camera path with a constant transformation $\mathbf{W}$, where a static camera can be represented by an identity matrix $\mathbf{W}$. We optimize our camera path over the buffered segment to mimic the professional footage. Specifically, from motion estimation described in Section 2.1, we get a set of inter-frame homographies over the buffered L-length segment:

$$_{i+1} = \mathbf{W}^{i,i+1} \ _i, \ i = 1, \ldots, L-1, \quad (3)$$

where $\mathbf{W}$ is an 8-DOF homography. Based on cinematographic rules, we would like to get a target video sequence that is as stable as possible. Also, the target video sequence should provide reasonable viewing window and avoid excessive skew and perspective artifacts. To achieve these goals, we pursue a piece-wise stable camera path over the buffered segment, use a constraint for the out-of-bound area size, and place bounds on the skewness of the warped frame.

Intuitively, over a stable l-length piece of camera path, the optimal constant transformation $\mathbf{W}_c$ can be estimated by minimizing the following cost function:

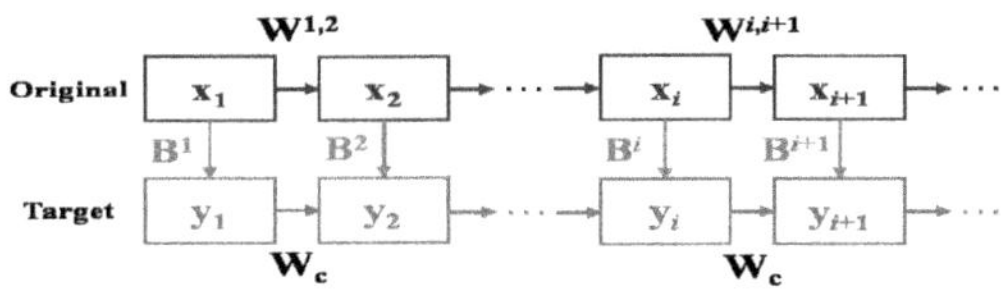

Figure 2: elations o original and target rames

$$\min \sum_{i=1-1}^{l} || \;_{i+1} - \mathbf{W}_c \;_i||^2.$$

In practice, $\mathbf{W}_c$ is obtained by aggregating all the inter-frame feature correspondences from the l frames and then feeding these correspondences into the standard motion estimation method used in Section 2.1.

Let $\;_i$ denote the target warped frame of an original frame $\;_i$, and $\;_i$ should follow the optimized camera path:

$$\;_{i+1} = \mathbf{W}_c \;_i. \quad (4)$$

As shown in Figure 2, a transformation $\mathbf{B}_i$ can be computed to warp the original frame $\;_i$ to generate the target frame $\;_i$, which corrects the original transformation matrix $\mathbf{W}^{i,i+1}$ to the optimized transformation $\mathbf{W}_c$.

Given two pieces of stable camera trajectory, a simple yet effective approach is used to smooth the transition part. The frames around the boundary of each connecting piece are treated as a whole stable subsegment, and feature correspondences of these frames are aggregated to compute another transformation matrix around the transition area, which is used to rectify the transition frames. Note that another possible approach is to apply low-pass filters such as [3] to smooth the transition area. But as illustrated in Figure 3, this method usually generates large misalignment artifacts and out-of-bound areas. In comparison, our approach keeps some level of transition inconsistency as a tradeoff to avoid severe artifacts and provide larger viewing window.

(a) our path planning. (b) low-pass filtering.

Figure : llustration o di erent amera paths

Now our problem turns to how to divide the original camera path into piece-wise stable segments so that we can use the above approach to stabilize each piece and then smooth the inter-piece transitions accordingly. Due to the real-time low-cost optimization requirements, we use a very fast tree splitting method. To avoid severe skew and perspective artifacts, *e.g.*, from feature tracking failures, we place relatively tight bounds on the skewness of the warped frames. We require that the four corners of a warped frame $\;_i$ cannot deviate from the corresponding corners of the previous warped frame $\;_{i-1}$ by more than 5%. Also, we check the size of the accumulated out-of-bound area over a stable piece of camera path, and we require that the compensated frames need to preserve 80% of the original viewing window. When either of these constraints is violated, we split the corresponding piece of camera path in half, and recompute the optimized stable camera path over each half respectively. We recursively half-split the camera path pieces until one of the two stop criterions is met: all pieces of the camera path complies with the two constraints, or there are too few frames (*e.g.*, less than 5) in an unsatisfactory piece to further split it.

When the tree-splitting path optimization process stops, if there still exist unsatisfactory pieces, it indicates that there are large artifacts in the warped frames using homographies. The artifacts may be caused by abrupt large object/camera motion or the lack of robust features. In such a case, we reduce the motion model and use the low DOF similarity transformation instead. That is, we redo the tree-splitting path planning described above using similarity transformation as $\mathbf{W}$. After similarity-based tree-splitting path optimization, if there still exist unsatisfactory pieces, to avoid unpleasant artifacts, we choose not to process the corresponding frames in such places, *i.e.*, we keep original frames and our system gracefully degrades over such frames. The entire workflow is summarized in Figure 4.

It is worth mentioning that the work of [7] also uses both similarity and homography in path optimization. The major differences between our work and that of [7] are: (1) the path optimization in [7] is over the whole camera trajectory, while our localized path planning is over buffered segments for real-time streaming, and (2) the work of [7] uses the similarity model for general stabilization and uses homographies only in transition areas to alleviate misalignments, while we use both homography and similarity transformation for general stabilization where the system automatically switches models according to the actual videos adaptively.

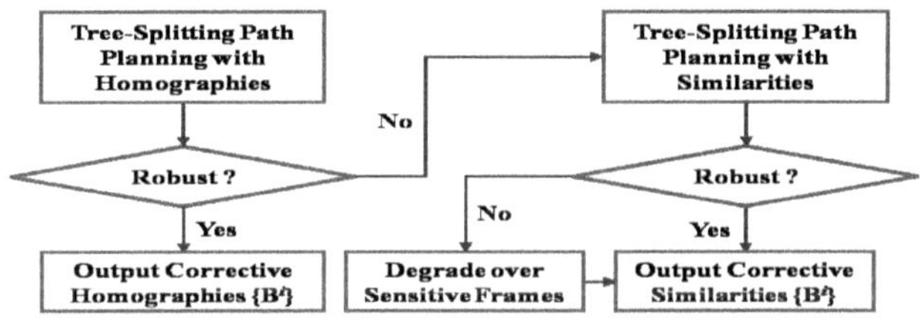

Figure 4: Path planning ith h brid motion models

2.3 Result synthesis and discussion

In the frame synthesis thread C, the set of corrective transformation matrices $\{\mathbf{B}^i\}$ can be directly used to warp the original frames $\{\;_i\}$ into stabilized frames $\{\;_i\}$. The main computation of the whole system lies in feature tracking and frame synthesis. Camera path planning is quite fast, since the computation is only over transformation matrices and point coordinates, which does not involve video frames. Our non-optimized Android implementation can run at 6fps.

In general, employing a forward-looking buffer gives better stabilization performance, with a price of an overall delay of the buffer size. Using a pure backward-looking buffer, we can achieve zero-latency stabilization, with less robust stabilization results. We use a mixed 1.5-sec buffer in our implementation, comprising a 1-sec forward-looking and a 0.5-sec backward-looking buffer.

The underlying assumption for 2D transformation may not hold sometimes, *i.e.*, the captured scene may have large depth variations with non-negligible camera translation, resulting wobbling artifacts. Such artifacts can also be caused by fast moving rolling shutter cameras. With the tight skewness and viewing window constraints, we may generate a camera path with many short pieces, which alleviates the wobble distortions but gives limited stabilization. Also, for videos lacking robustly tracked features, *e.g.*, videos with large textureless regions or excessive blur, our algorithm may choose not to process most parts of such videos.

3. EXPERIMENTS

We evaluate our algorithm over 60 videos that are publicly available. These videos are commonly used by previous pub-

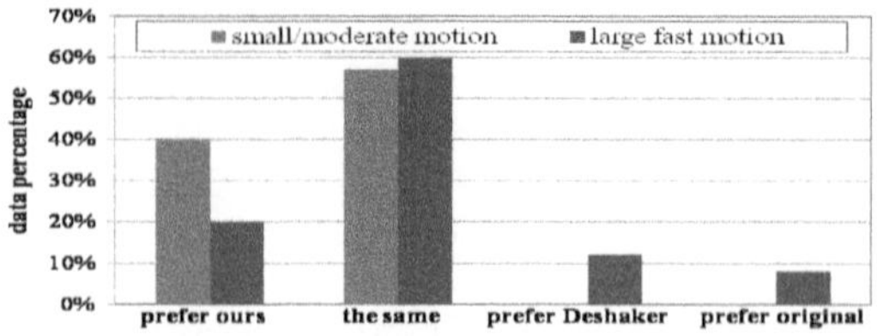

Figure 5: ubje ti e ran ing results

lications and were collected by [12] to cover a large variety of camera motion and scene types, including simple/mild motion, quick rotation, zooming, large parallax, driving, crowd and running. Since there is no publicly available implementation of prior arts for real-time video stabilization, we compare our system with the commercial Deshaker filter for VirtualDub [16], which is a two-pass approach but is relatively fast. It is worth mentioning that we have also tested the low-pass-filtering based methods over these videos and found that such methods did not perform very well in general without careful parameter tuning, due to the complicated camera motion and scene content.

A user study was conducted to subjectively evaluate and compare our method with the Deshaker filter. For each video, we played the original video, our stabilized video, and the Deshaker stabilized video side by side in random order, which was then presented to 5 different users to provide a preference rank. These were amateur cell phone users, 2 females and 3 males, aged between 25 to 50 with professions varying from students to engineers. Figure 5 gives the users' overall ranking results. From the figure we can see that over the 35 videos with mild to moderate camera motion (*e.g.*, relatively slow panning, zooming, walking, *etc.*), our method outperforms the Deshaker filter where 40% of times users prefer our method and 57% times users think our method and the Deshaker filters work similarly. Only over one video, users prefer the Deshaker results rather than our method. Also, both our method and the Deshaker filter can robustly stabilize such videos, *i.e.*, users prefer the stabilized videos 100% to the original ones. Besides the one-pass processing ability, we observe another main advantage of our method. With the tight constraint on output skewness and window size, our method can provide a good viewing window in general. In comparison, the Deshaker filter sometimes over-crops the window when large camera motion occurs, and as a result, generates very large out of bound areas. Figure 6 gives some examples.

When there is large-scale fast camera motion (*e.g.*, fast panning, rotation, zooming, *etc.*), over the remaining 25 videos, the difference between our method and the Deshaker filter becomes less obvious. For such videos, users prefer our method 20% of times while prefer the Deshaker filter 12% times, and 60% times users cannot tell which stabilization method is better. In general, our method is able to remove most of the shakiness and avoid obvious wobbling effect, resulting from the cinematographic rule based motion modeling and the tight constraints. However, when there are a lot of camera trajectory segments, the non-negligible motion inconsistency will affect user experience. In comparison, the Deshaker filter does not have the motion inconsistency problem, but can only remove a certain amount of shakiness. As a result, noticeable shakiness usually remains, and the motion transition areas often present obvious wobbling artifacts. When very large camera shake occurs, such as in the 8% videos captured by a fast running person or on

Figure 6: Comparisons o the output indo size

a driving car, neither our method nor the Deshaker filter can give reliable stabilization. Based on the above phenomena, we can conclude that our method outperforms the Deshaker filter in two aspects. First, our method provides one-pass real-time on-device processing ability, and second, our method gives better stabilization performance over videos with small/moderate camera motion and performs similarly to the Deshaker filter when large fast camera motion occurs.

4. CONCLUSIONS

We proposed one-pass mobile video stabilization with localized camera path planning using hybrid motion models. Through maintaining a forward or backward-looking buffer and performing localized trajectory optimization, we achieved real-time streamable video stabilization. By automatically switching motion models according to the actual video, the appropriate models were adaptively used for improved stabilization. Experiments on a large variety of consumer videos showed the effectiveness of our method.

5. REFERENCES

[1] S. Baker, and et al. Removing rolling shutter wobble. *IEEE CVPR*, pages 2392-2399, 2010.

[2] B. Chen, and et al. Capturing intention-based full-frame video stabilization. *Comp. Grap. Forum*, 27:1805-1814, 2008.

[3] S. Erturk. Real-time digital image stabilization using kalman filters. *Real-Time Imaging*, 8(4):317–328, 2002.

[4] P. Forssen and E. Ringaby. Rectifying rolling shutter video from hand-held devices. *IEEE CVPR*, pages 507-514, 2010.

[5] M. Gleicher and F. Liu. Re-cinematography: Improving the camerawork of casual video. *ACM TOMCCAP*, 5(1), 2008.

[6] M. Grundmann, and et al. Calibration-free rolling shutter removal. *IEEE ICCP*, Seattle, WA, 2012.

[7] M. Grundmann, V. Kwatra, and I. Essa. Auto-directed video stabilization with robust l1 optimal camera paths. *IEEE CVPR*, Colorado Springs, June, 2011.

[8] G. Hanning, and et al. Stabilizing cell phone videos using inertial measurement sensors. *Int'l Wksp Mob. Vis.*, 2011.

[9] J. Heinly, E. Dunn, and J. Frahm. Comparative evaluation of binary features. *ECCV*, pages 759-773, 2012.

[10] F. Liu, and et al. Content-preserving warps for 3d video stabilization. *ACM SIGGRAPH*, 2009.

[11] F. Liu, and et al. Subspace video stabilization. *ACM Trans. Graphics*, 30(1):4:1-4:10, 2011.

[12] S. Liu, and et al. Bundled camera paths for video stabilization. *ACM SIGGRAPH*, 2013.

[13] Y. Matsushita, and et al. Full-frame video stabilization with motion inpainting. *IEEE Trans. PAMI*, 28:1150-1163, 2006.

[14] E. Rublee, and et al. Orb: an efficient alternative to sift and surf. *IEEE ICCV*, pages 2564-2571, 2011.

[15] J. Yang, D. Schonfeld, and M. Mohamed. Video stabilization based on particle filter tracking of projected camera motion. *IEEE Trans. CSVT*, 19(7):945–954, 2009.

[16] VirtualDub Deshaker. *http://guthspot.se/video/deshaker.htm.*

You Talkin' to Me? Recognizing Complex Human Interactions in Unconstrained Videos

Bo Zhang
University of Trento, Italy
bzhang@disi.unitn.it

Yan Yan
University of Trento, Italy
tom.yan.555@gmail.com

Nicola Conci
University of Trento, Italy
conci@disi.unitn.it

Nicu Sebe
University of Trento, Italy
sebe@disi.unitn.it

ABSTRACT

Nowadays, due to the exponential growth of the user generated videos and the prevailing videos sharing communities such as YouTube and Hulu, recognizing complex human activities in the wild becomes increasingly important in the research community. These videos are hard to study due to the frequent changes of camera viewpoint, multiple people moving in the scene, fast body movements, and varied lengths of video clips. In this paper, we propose a novel framework to analyze human interactions in TV shows. Firstly, we exploit the motion interchange pattern (MIP) to detect camera viewpoint changes in a video, and extract the salient motion points in the bounding box that covers the region of interest (ROI) in each frame. Then, we compute the large displacement optical flow for the salient pixels in the bounding box, and build the histogram of oriented optical flow as the motion feature vector for each frame. Finally, the self-similarity matrix (SSM) is adopted to capture the global temporal correlation of frames in a video. After extracting the SSM descriptors, the video feature vector can be constructed through different encoding approaches. The proposed framework works well in practice for unconstrained videos. We validate our approach on the TV human interaction (TVHI) dataset, and the experimental results demonstrate the efficacy of our strategy.

Categories and Subject Descriptors

I.4 [**Image Processing and Computer Vision**]: Applications

Keywords

Activity Recognition; Motion Interchange Pattern; Large Displacement Optical Flow; Self-similarity Matrix

MM'14, November 3–7, 2014, Orlando, Florida, USA.

http://dx.doi.org/10.1145/2647868.2654996 .

1. INTRODUCTION

Recognition of human activities has received increasing research effort in the recent years. In this work, we are interested in classifying complex human activities in unconstrained videos (*e.g.*, movies, sports, and webcams). Particularly, we aim at recognizing two-person interactions in TV shows. We choose the TVHI dataset [10] as our benchmark. This dataset is very challenging due to: (i) frequent changes of camera viewpoint; (ii) multiple people moving in the scene; (iii) fast body movements, and (iv) short video clips that often do not provide sufficient contextual information. For human activity recognition, Laptev [6] proposed a spatio-temporal interest points (STIP) detector to capture significant motion patterns in a video, where HOG and HOF are exploited to describe the motion features in the neighborhood of each STIP. In [2, 11], the dense trajectory was exploited to represent motions in a video, where HOG, HOF, and MBH are used to describe the motion features that surround the trajectory. All these local space-time features are combined with a certain encoding scheme (*e.g.*, *bag-of-words*, *sparse coding*, *Fisher descriptor*), so as to generate the feature vector of each video. More recently, structural learning methods have been widely adopted to model the global space-time structure for activity recognition. In [10, 13], the authors used HOG as the spatial feature for each person, and exploited the structured learning to model the spatial relationships between different people in the scene. In [7], Liang *et al.* modeled human actions through an ensemble of spatio-temporal compositions, and adopted a spatio-temporal AND-OR graph to represent the latent structure of actions. In [3, 9], web images were introduced to recognize human activities in videos.

For our framework, we firstly exploit the motion interchange pattern (MIP) [5] to detect the sudden change of camera viewpoint, so as to filter out the frames that hinder the motion feature extraction. For multiple people moving in the scene, we use the bounding boxes to identify persons who are involved in the activities. In order to deal with fast body movements, we adopt the large displacement optical flow (LDOF) [1] to estimate the motion information for each pixel. Since the traditional tools (*e.g.*, HMM, CRF) are not suited for modeling the temporal structure of human activities in very short videos, we use the self-similarity matrix (SSM) based on the histogram of oriented LDOF to model the whole evolution of human behavior. We mainly focus on the region of interest (ROI), with the purpose of highlighting the role of motion features in the classification task. Examples of the ROI are presented in Figure 1. To obtain the ROI, we exploit the bounding box of human head (provided by [10]), and the region of human torso is computed as 2.5 times the size of the head region. The ROI is estimated by merging all the regions of human torso in each frame.

Figure 1: Examples of ROI. The green bounding boxes indicate human torsos, while the red bounding boxes are the interest regions.

To summarize, the main contributions of this paper are: (i) the adoption of MIP to extract salient motion points in each frame, by simultaneously filtering the feature discontinuity introduced by the shot changes, (ii) the use of histogram of LDOF on the extracted motion points for interaction classification, and (iii) a novel framework for analysing human interactions in the wild, which allows for camera motion, changes of viewpoint in unconstrained environments.

2. FRAMEWORK

The overall procedure of our approach is presented in Figure 2 and the details are further discussed in the following sections.

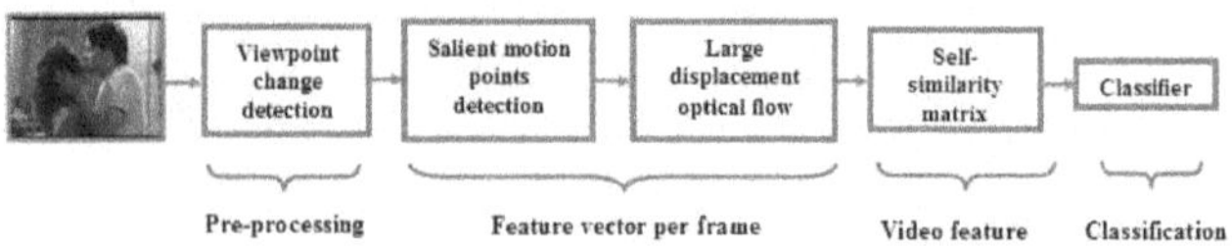

Figure 2: The proposed framework.

2.1 Motion Interchange Pattern

Videos in TV shows always contain frequent shot changes that exert side-effects in the feature extraction procedure (*e.g.*, the computation of optical flow).

In our work, we exploit MIP to detect viewpoint changes in video sequences. For each pixel $p(x, y, t)$ in a video, MIP computes the compatibility of a local 3×3 patch centered at p in the current frame with respect to two different patches (denoted as i and j, respectively) located in the previous and next frames (see [5] for details). The angle between patch i and j is denoted as α=0°, 45°, 90°,..., 315°. When considering all the combinations of i and j, the encoding scheme generates a 64-bit descriptor $S(p)$, where each bit (denoted as $S_{i,j}(p)$) corresponds to a different combination of i and j. The compatibility of two local patches is measured through the sum of squared differences (SSD) score. Each $S_{i,j}(p)$ is computed according to Eq (1), where the threshold θ is set to 1296 according to [5]:

$$S_{i,j}(p) = \begin{cases} +1; & \text{if } SSD_i - SSD_j > -\theta \\ 0; & \text{if } |SSD_j - SSD_i| \leqslant \theta \\ -1; & \text{if } SSD_i - SSD_j < -\theta \end{cases} \quad (1)$$

For the shot boundary detection, we only consider the direction α=0°, thus generating a 8-bit MIP indicator that consists of '-1', '0', and '+1' bits. We compute the number of non-zero bits for each pixel, and then build a 9-dimensional histogram with the range of [0,8] for each frame. Next, we subtract the number of '+1' and '-1' bits for each pixel, and generate a 17-dimensional histogram for each frame, ranging from -8 to 8. The concatenation of these two histograms is used to train the classifier. As presented in Figure 3, the camera shot boundary exhibits distinct visual patterns on the MIP maps. Two one-class SVMs are trained to recognize the last frame in the previous shot and the first frame in the next shot, respectively. The shot boundary can be detected when the distinct patterns (the *blue* and the *red* MIP maps in Figure 3) appear in two successive frames in a video sequence.

Figure 3: Shot boundary detection using MIP.

2.2 Frame-based Motion Feature Vector

Although the ROI identifies the region where the activity is occurring, there still exists pixels within the ROI that are not strictly related to human interactions. To address this, we build a *motion mask* that highlights the salient pixels corresponding to distinct motions automatically. First, we compute the MIP indicator discussed in Section 2.1 for each pixel in the region of interest. Then, we calculate the number of non-zero bits in the MIP indicator. If the number of non-zero bits is larger than a threshold ε, we consider the corresponding pixel to be a salient motion point. On the contrary, when the number of non-zero bits is less than ε, it suggests that the relevant pixel has not been affected by a strong variation. As the non-zero bits in the MIP indicator ranges from 0 to 8, we set ε=4 in our work. After filtering out the camera shot boundaries and extracting the salient motion pixels in the region of interest, we build the feature vector for each frame. As fast motion and gradual camera movements are very common phenomena in TV shows, we adopt the large displacement optical flow [1] to estimate the motion information for the salient pixels.

The large displacement optical flow (LDOF) computes the dense optical flow field within successive frames that contain pixels with large displacements (*e.g.*, fast motion of hand in *handshake* or *highfive*). The LDOF integrates descriptor matching into the coarse-to-fine variational optical flow framework. Given two successive frames I_1 and I_2, the displacement field (denoted as $w = (u, v)$) between the two images can be computed by optimizing the energy functional as in Eq (2):

$$\begin{aligned} E(w) = &\int_\Omega \Psi(|I_2(x + w(x)) - I_1(x)|^2)dx + \\ \gamma &\int_\Omega |\nabla I_2(x + w(x)) - \nabla I_1(x)|^2)dx + \\ \alpha &\int_\Omega \Psi(|\nabla u(x)|^2 + |\nabla v(x)|^2)dx + \\ \beta &\int_\Omega \delta(x)\rho(x)\Psi(|w(x) - w_{desc}(x)|^2)dx \end{aligned} \quad (2)$$

where Ω is the image domain, $\Psi(s^2)=\sqrt{s^2+\epsilon^2}$, ϵ=0.001, ∇ is the derivation operator. The first two terms in Eq (2) are the intensity and the gradient constancy, respectively. The 3rd term is the smooth constraint on the optical flow. In the 4th term, the descriptor match $w_{desc}(x)$ is combined with the variational optical flow framework. $\delta(x)$ is a delta function indicating if a descriptor match is available, and $\rho(x)$ denotes the confidence of the match. More details about the above model and the corresponding optimization solutions can be found in [1]. An example of the *motion mask* and LDOF is presented in Figure 4.

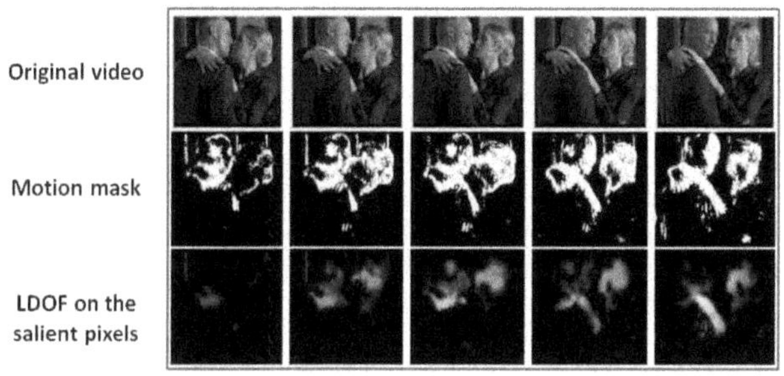

Figure 4: Examples of the *motion mask* and LDOF.

We then build a 30-bin histogram of the oriented LDOF (denoted as HO-LODF) on the basis of the salient pixels, where each bin covers 12 degrees. Each salient pixel is assigned to the bin corresponding to its optical flow orientation, and weighted by the magnitude. The obtained histogram is normalized (in l_2 norm) to generate the feature vector for each frame.

2.3 Modeling Evolution of Human Activities

We exploit the self-similarity matrix (SSM) to model the evolution of human activities. SSM descriptors have proved to be stable features under view changes [4, 12] for the same action. Therefore, it is a good strategy to model the evolution of human activities based on SSM. For a sequence of images $\mathcal{I} = \{I_1, I_2, ..., I_T\}$, a SSM of $\mathcal{I}$ is a square symmetric matrix of size $T \times T$:

$$[e_{ij}]_{i,j=1,2,...,T} = \begin{bmatrix} 0 & e_{12} & e_{13} & \cdots & e_{1T} \\ e_{21} & 0 & e_{23} & \cdots & e_{2T} \\ e_{31} & e_{32} & 0 & \cdots & e_{3T} \\ \vdots & \vdots & \vdots & \ddots & \vdots \\ e_{T1} & e_{T2} & e_{T3} & \cdots & 0 \end{bmatrix} \quad (3)$$

where e_{ij} is the distance between a certain low-level feature extracted in frames I_i and I_j, respectively. The exact structure of this matrix depends on the feature and the distance measure used for computing the entries e_{ij}. In this paper, we use the Euclidean distance and frame-based feature discussed in Section 2.2 to construct the similarity matrix. Once SSMs have been computed, the same strategy described in [4] is adopted for calculating local descriptors at multiple temporal scales. For each SSM diagonal point, three local descriptors are computed corresponding to three different diameters of the log-polar domain (namely, 28, 42 and 56 frames in diameter). Different encoding models can be used to compute a single histogram associated to each video sequence (see Section 3).

An example of SSMs is shown in Figure 5. SSMs computed with different low-level features are different, since each feature captures specific properties of the action. Moreover, SSMs are stable over different people performing the same action.

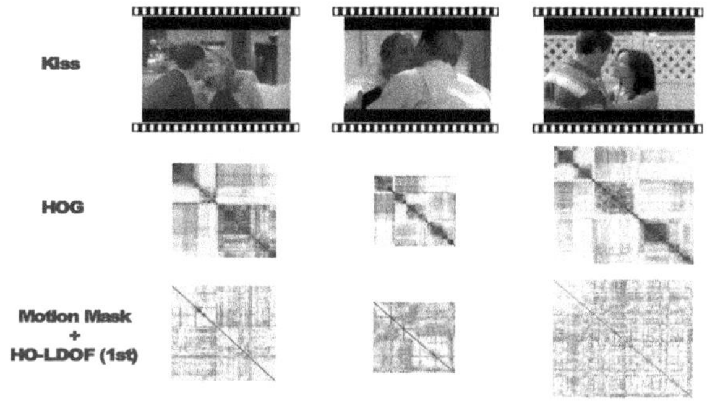

Figure 5: Example of *kiss*: SSMs obtained using the HOG feature (2nd scenes) and the proposed method (3rd row).

3. EXPERIMENTAL RESULTS

3.1 Dataset

TVHI dataset [7] is used to validate our approach. This dataset consists of four different types of two-person interactions, namely, *handshake*, *highfive*, *hug*, and *kiss*, where each category contains 50 sample videos. Negative samples that do not contain any kind of interaction are not considered in the classification task.

3.2 Results

Comparison with different STIP-based models: We follow the standard training/test partitions as suggested in [10], and compare with the recent results presented in [8], which exploits different STIP-based models for interaction recognition. Classification performance is measured in terms of the average precision (AP) rate as listed in Table 1. We present the precision rate for each type of interaction in Table 2. Although we focus on recognition in this work, our method is still comparable with the approach in [10], where the structured SVM is adopted in interaction retrieval task.

Table 1: The comparison of different STIP-based models in [8] and our method for human interaction recognition.

Method	AP
Harris3D STIP + BoW (k-means)	0.3551
Dense STIP + BoW (k-means)	0.3923
Dense STIP + Random Dictionary	0.3859
Dense STIP + Compressed Dictionary	0.3854
Dense STIP + Class-specific Dictionary	0.3689
Our approach	**0.4833**

Table 2: Precision rate for each type of interaction.

	handshake	*highfive*	*hug*	*kiss*	Average
Our Method	**0.5278**	**0.5802**	**0.5091**	**0.4059**	**0.5058**
Structured SVM [10]	0.3935	0.4582	0.4699	0.3760	0.4244

Results on different frame-based features: We compute the self-similarity matrices on the basis of other frame-based features in the region of interest: (i) HOG; (ii) HOF based on the Farneback's optical flow (denoted as 'Dense HOF'); (iii) HO-LDOF in the whole region of interest (denoted as 'Dense HO-LDOF'). Moreover, we compare both the 1st and 2nd order optical flow when computing the HO-LDOF. The 1st order optical flow highlights the variations in a frame, whereas, the 2nd order optical flow emphasizes the motion boundaries. SSM descriptors are encoded using the *bag-of-words* scheme. In order to avoid the bias of the standard partitions in [10], we randomly split the dataset evenly into training and test sets 10 times. Classification is measured using the average accuracy. The results are demonstrated in Figure 6.

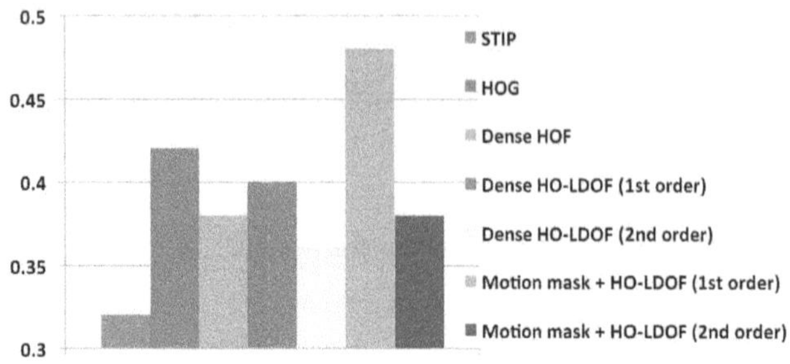

Figure 6: The average classification accuracy using different frame-based features.

From Figure 6, we can conclude: (1) By combining with SSM and the *bag-of-words* approach, both HOG and dense HOF achieve better results compared to the standard STIP method; (2) The performance of dense HOF is worse than HOG and dense HO-LDOF(1st order), as the estimation of optical flow is not accurate in unconstrained videos that contain fast motion and gradual camera movements; (3) The performance of 2nd order HO-LDOF is worse than 1st order HO-LDOF, but still better than the STIP feature; (4) *Motion mask* allows extracting better motion points, and further improves the classification performance.

Table 3: Comparison of encoding strategies.

Encoding Method	Average accuracy
Bag-of-words (BOW)	48.1%
Kernel Codebook (KCB)	49.0%
Fisher Encoding (FK)	50.1%
Locality constrained linear coding (LLC)	49.6%

Results on different encoding schemes: Finally, we combine the SSM descriptor (*motion mask*+1st order LDOF) with different encoding strategies. The classification results are presented in Table 3, where the Fisher encoding scheme achieves the best performance. The corresponding confusion matrix is presented in Figure 7, where *handshake* and *hug* achieve the best classification accuracy. For *highfive*, a large portion (30%) is mis-classified as *handshake*. This is because some patterns of hand movements are shared by these two behaviors. *Kiss* is confused with *hug* to a great extent (37%), which is due to the fact that in many videos, *hug* is only a sub-pattern of *kiss*, thus making it difficult to separate them properly.

4. CONCLUSIONS

In this paper, we exploit MIP to detect camera viewpoint changes in TV human interaction videos, and construct a *motion mask* to extract the salient motion points in each frame. The histogram of LDOF on the salient motion

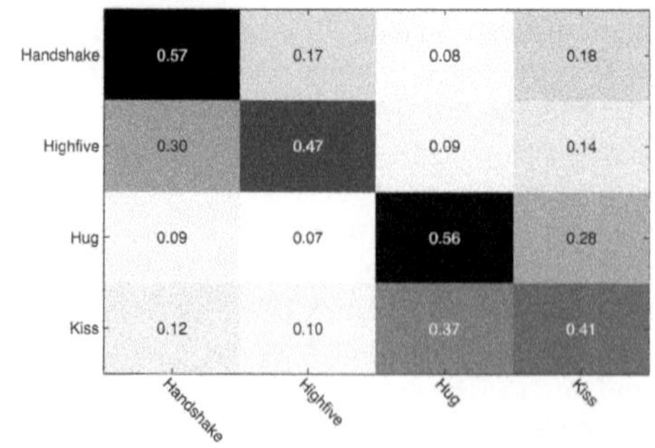

Figure 7: Confusion Matrix on the TVHI dataset.

points is then computed for each frame, to obtain the self-similarity matrix of the entire video. Experimental results show that combined with LDOF, the salient motion points provide more discriminating capabilities in the classification task in unrestricted videos.

5. REFERENCES

[1] T. Brox and J. Malik. Large displacement optical flow: descriptor matching in variational motion estimation. *IEEE TPAMI*, 33(3):500–513, 2011.

[2] Z. Hao, Q. Zhang, E. Ezquierdo, and N. Sang. Human action recognition by fast dense trajectories. In *ACM Multimedia*, 2013.

[3] N. Ikizler-Cinbis and S. Sclaroff. Web-based classifiers for human action recognition. *IEEE TMM*, 14(4):1031–1045, 2012.

[4] I. Junejo, E. Dexter, I. Laptev, and P. Perez. View-independent action recognition from temporal self-similarities. *IEEE TPAMI*, 33(1):172–185, 2011.

[5] O. Kliper-Gross, Y. Gurovich, T. Hassner, and L. Wolf. Motion interchange patterns for action recognition in unconstrained videos. In *ECCV*. 2012.

[6] I. Laptev. On space-time interest points. *IJCV*, 64(2):107–123, 2005.

[7] X. Liang, L. Lin, and L. Cao. Learning latent spatio-temporal compositional model for human action recognition. In *ACM Multimedia*, 2013.

[8] M. Marín-Jiménez, E. Yeguas, and N. P. D. L. Blanca. Exploring stip-based models for recognizing human interactions in tv videos. *Pattern Recognition Letters*, 34(15):1819–1828, 2013.

[9] M. Merler, B. Huang, L. Xie, G. Hua, and A. Natsev. Semantic model vectors for complex video event recognition. *IEEE TMM*, 14(1):88–101, 2012.

[10] A. Patron-Perez, M. Marszalek, I. Reid, and A. Zisserman. Structured learning of human interactions in tv shows. *IEEE TPAMI*, 34(12):2441–2453, 2012.

[11] H. Wang, A. Klaser, C. Schmid, and C. Liu. Action recognition by dense trajectories. In *CVPR*, 2011.

[12] Y. Yan, G. Liu, E. Ricci, and N. Sebe. Multi-task linear discriminant analysis for multi-view action recognition. In *ICIP*, 2013.

[13] Y. Yan, E. Ricci, R. Subramanian, O. Lanz, and N. Sebe. No matter where you are: Flexible graph-guided multi-task learning for multi-view head pose classification under target motion. In *ICCV*, 2013.

Instructional Videos for Unsupervised Harvesting and Learning of Action Examples

Shoou-I Yu
Carnegie Mellon University
5000 Forbes Avenue
Pittsburgh, PA, 15213, USA
iyu@cs.cmu.edu

Lu Jiang
Carnegie Mellon University
5000 Forbes Avenue
Pittsburgh, PA, 15213, USA
lujiang@cs.cmu.edu

Alexander Hauptmann
Carnegie Mellon University
5000 Forbes Avenue
Pittsburgh, PA, 15213, USA
alex@cs.cmu.edu

ABSTRACT

Online instructional videos have become a popular way for people to learn new skills encompassing art, cooking and sports. As watching instructional videos is a natural way for humans to learn, analogously, machines can also gain knowledge from these videos. We propose to utilize the large amount of instructional videos available online to harvest examples of various actions in an *unsupervised* fashion. The key observation is that in instructional videos, the instructor's action is highly correlated with the instructor's narration. By leveraging this correlation, we can exploit the timing of action corresponding terms in the speech transcript to temporally localize actions in the video and harvest action examples. The proposed method is scalable as it requires no human intervention. Experiments show that the examples harvested are of reasonably good quality, and action detectors trained on data collected by our unsupervised method yields comparable performance with detectors trained with manually collected data on the TRECVID Multimedia Event Detection task.

Categories and Subject Descriptors

H.3.1 [**Information Storage and Retrieval**]: Content Analysis and Indexing; H.4 [**Information Systems Applications**]: Miscellaneous

General Terms

Algorithms, Experimentation, Performance

Keywords

Semantic Action Detection; Unsupervised Data Collection; Multimedia Event Detection

1. INTRODUCTION

Online user-generated instructional videos, also known as *How-To* videos, have become a rich resource for people to learn everyday skills encompassing art, cooking and sports. Instructional videos teach viewers how to perform a specific task through clear explanations and demonstrations by the instructor. In the recent substantial growth on media such as YouTube, a considerable number of user-generated instructional videos covering a wide variety of tasks are available online for humans to view and learn.

Figure 1: Positive "drill hole" examples harvested from instructional videos in an unsupervised fashion. Blue words correspond to action signifiers, and the red words correspond to verb-noun pairs found by a dependency parser. Drilling holes in diverse contexts such as in walls and on ice are collected.

Since instructional videos are designed to facilitate learning for humans, analogously, machines should also be able to learn from this rich resource. In this paper, we focus on exploiting instructional videos to harvest examples of different actions in an *unsupervised* fashion. Semantic action and concept detectors trained on video data play an important role in various video content analysis tasks such as multimedia event detection [15, 10, 7, 17, 3, 11]. However, training a semantic detector requires a pool of positive examples, which is tedious to collect manually. Manual labeling of video data is more challenging than image data as the former requires an extra step in temporally localizing the action. For example, the collection of the TRECVID Semantic Indexing data set [12], which is a very large annotated video data set, required many person years of effort from more than 20 companies and universities. The 346 manually annotated concepts in this data set includes 35 action related concepts with a total 17,000 positive examples. The positive exam-

MM'14, November 3–7, 2014, Orlando, Florida, USA.

http://dx.doi.org/10.1145/2647868.2654997.

ples of other existing video data sets such as UCF50 [14] and HMDB51 [8] were also collected manually.

In light of the aforementioned problems, we propose to harvest examples of various actions in an unsupervised fashion by utilizing the large amount of instructional videos online. We exploit the visual-speech correlation in instructional videos for unsupervised action example collection. To teach effectively, instructors in the instructional video will not only *visually* demonstrate what they are doing at each step, but also *verbally* explain the details of each step nearly simultaneously. For example, the instructor will verbally say "I am going to take my drill and drill a hole" while drilling a hole into some wood as shown in Figure 1. This semantic audio-visual correlation residing in instructional videos is the key to our unsupervised action example collection method. When the instructor verbally say phrases such as "going to" or "let us", which signify that some action will occur immediately, we identify the action that will be visible in the video using the speech transcript and Natural Language Processing techniques. The action examples localized in this unsupervised fashion can be used to train semantic action detectors. In sum, our contributions are as follows.

1. We propose to utilize the ever-increasing instructional videos available on the Internet to harvest positive examples for video action detectors in an *unsupervised* fashion. As the examples are obtained without any human intervention, the proposed method is scalable.
2. Experiments show that action examples harvested with our method are of reasonable quality, and detectors trained with the harvested data performs comparably with detectors trained on manually collected data in the TRECVID Multimedia Event Detection task [12].

2. RELATED WORK

The challenge of efficient collection of image or video annotations has been tackled in different ways, but most existing methods still require a human in the loop. The annotations of ImageNet [5] and TRECVID Semantic Indexing [12] were all collected manually. ImageNet utilized the Amazon Mechanical Turk (AMT) platform to acquire annotations. The annotation of Semantic Indexing data required many person years of effort from more than 20 participants including companies and universities around the world. This collaborative annotation process was tedious and time-consuming. To make the annotation task less tedious and more fun, "Gamification" [16, 6] transformed the annotation task to a game so that as humans play the game, more and more annotations are collected. Using this method, the labels are obtained as a by-product of a competitive game, but designing an interesting game which will attract many players is very challenging. A method to collect image training data without a human in the loop is to utilize search engine output [5]. However, existing work mainly focused on *still images*, but our method focuses on temporal localization of actions in *videos*, which is more challenging.

3. UNSUPERVISED DATA COLLECTION

We observe temporal correlation between speech and actions in instructional videos and utilize the correlation to collect examples for actions in an unsupervised fashion. Our pipeline is shown in Figure 2. Given an instructional video, the speech transcript is obtained from either closed-captions or automatic speech recognition output. The next step is to scan the transcript and look for sentences containing *action signifiers* such as "going to" and "let us", which signify that some action will occur in the near future. Having found the action signifier in a sentence, a dependency parser [4] parses the sentence to determine which verb and noun were described by the action signifier. Specifically, we look for *direct object* (*dobj*) relations [4]. The *dobj* relation shows which noun is the accusative object of a verb. For example, in the sentence "You are going to bend your left leg", the verb "bend" and the noun "leg" form a *dobj* relation. We assume that as the instructor verbally say the sentence with the action signifier, the instructor is also performing the verb in the *dobj* relation to the noun in the *dobj* relation. Therefore, under this assumption, the speech timing information of the *dobj* relation is utilized to localize the action. This assumption is substantiated through manual verification in Section 4.1. This process is performed over the whole data set to get a diverse set of *dobj* relations each with many positive examples. Non-visual *dobj* relations such as "ask me" and "take care" can be filtered out with a predefined ontology of visible words such as ImageNet's ontology [5, 19]. The final output is a list of *dobj* relations, each with many positive video examples extracted in an unsupervised fashion from instructional videos.

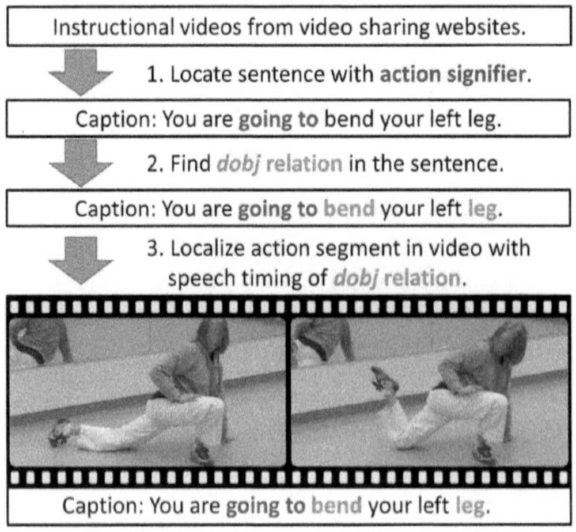

Figure 2: Pipeline for unsupervised harvesting of action examples from instructional videos.

There are three main advantages to our method. First, collection of action examples is completely unsupervised. Therefore, even though the action signifiers may not locate all instances of a given action in the video, we still can collect large amounts of positive examples with no manual labor cost as more instructional videos are uploaded. This is barely possible for data sets collected with manual labor [14, 8, 12]. Second, action examples are associated with context. For example, instead of just learning the action "cut", our method automatically learns objects associated with this action, such as "cut onion", "cut paper" and "cut hair" as shown in Figure 3. Finally, as more data is collected from instructional videos on various tasks, more diverse actions tend to be collected. For example, in Figure 1, we collected diverse positive examples for "drill hole". Holes could either be drilled in wood, in a wall or even in ice.

4. EXPERIMENTS

To evaluate the performance of our unsupervised action example collection, we downloaded around 73,000 videos

Category	Verb and Noun Both Correct	Verb Correct	Noun Correct
Ball Sports	0.256	0.280	0.727
Cooking	0.623	0.692	0.742
Exercise / Yoga	0.866	0.889	0.948
Sewing / Tools	0.727	0.735	0.860
Average	0.618	0.649	0.819

Table 1: Average accuracy of collected action examples for 38 classes from different categories.

from online archives such as Creative Commons, Youku, Tudou and YouTube. For each video, the raw closed-captions are available. We will discuss how to utilize videos without closed-captions in Section 5. The closed-captions were processed using the method detailed in Section 3. The action signifiers used were "going to", "gonna", "let us", "let's" "we'll", and "we will". The Stanford Dependency Parser [4] was used for parsing. The verbs and nouns were stemmed with the Porter Stemmer [13] for all *dobj* relations found to remove morphological differences. All *dobj* relations which occur less than 20 times were removed. As the coverage of the visible verb and noun ontology from [19] was not perfect, we manually filtered out non-visual relations. At the end, 25,835 positive examples were collected for 541 *dobj* relations. To extract video segments for a given *dobj* relation, we segment out a 10 second video which starts 2.5 seconds before the *dobj* relation was spoken and ends 7.5 seconds after. This is based on the observation that the action usually occurs slightly after the instructor mentions the *dobj* relation. The quality of the collected labels is evaluated in two aspects. First, the accuracy of the collected labels was manually assessed. Second, we compared the effectiveness of the action detectors trained from our collected examples to detectors trained on manually annotated data when used as an intermediate representation for another separate task called Multimedia Event Detection (MED).

4.1 Accuracy of Collected Labels

As our unsupervised method is based on the assumption that the actions and the speech in instructional videos are highly correlated, we verified this assumption by manually inspecting 38 representative classes and computing the accuracy of the collected label for each class. Given a collected positive example and its corresponding *dobj* relation, there are different levels of correctness; either both the verb and the noun is correct, or only the verb or noun is correct. A verb or noun is correct if the action or object can be seen in the video, respectively. The results are shown in Table 1. Due to space constraints, the 38 classes were grouped into 4 rough categories. The "Ball Sports" category contains relations such as "catch ball" and "hit ball". The "Cooking" category contains relations such as "cut tomatoes", and "pour milk". The "Exercise / Yoga" category contains relations such as "bend elbows" and "lift heel". The "Sewing / Tools" category contains relations such as "cut paper", "use screwdriver" and "wrap yarn". In general, for categories other than ball sports, the *dobj* relation is completely correct 70% of the time. For "Exercise / Yoga", the performance goes up to 86.6% because the speech and this type of actions are highly correlated. For "Ball Sports", the speech and action are lowly correlated as most instructors will do all the explaining first before performing the action, thus making the accuracy low. However, for the accuracy of the nouns,

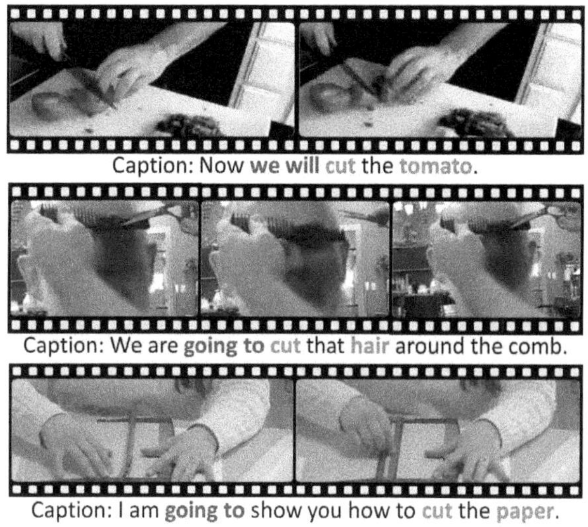

Figure 3: Positive examples for verb "cut" collected from instructional videos. Our method collected the verb "cut" in many different contexts; from cutting with scissors, knives to paper cutters.

our performance is still 72.7% on "Ball Sports". The results substantiate that our assumption on audio-visual correlation holds for most actions.

4.2 Intermediate Representation for MED

We compared the effectiveness of detectors trained on our harvested examples to detectors trained with manually annotated data from UCF50 [14] and HMDB51 [8]. An ideal method for evaluating action detectors from different data sets is to compute cross data set performance for actions the data sets have in common. However, as there are very few shared actions across data sets, we could not perform this experiment. Therefore, the effectiveness and generalizability of the detectors trained from each data set were evaluated by utilizing the output of the detectors as an intermediate representation for MED [9]. To create an intermediate representation for each MED video, each detector was predicted on the feature vector corresponding to the video, thus getting a n dimensional intermediate representation, where n is the number of action detectors. This representation was used to perform event detection with a χ^2 SVM [1]. The TRECVID MED 2011 development set [12] consisting of 9746 videos was used. For the evaluation metric, Mean Average Precision (MAP) was computed on 18 events.

Action detectors were trained using state-of-the-art Improved Trajectories [18] with a Fisher Vector [2] representation. One-against-all linear SVMs were used. Detectors were trained using all the data from HMDB51 and UCF50 to obtain 51 and 50 detectors respectively. From our collected data, 541 action detectors were trained. As a baseline which is labeled as "Clustering" in Table 2 and Figure 4, we ignored the labels of the 25,835 harvested examples and clustered the data into 541 clusters. The cluster assignments of each data point were treated as a pseudo-label and used to train 541 non-semantic detectors. This compares how good our collected labels are compared to pseudo-labels found by clustering. For a fair comparison between data sets with a different number of detectors, we randomly selected $d \in \{10, 25, 50, 100, 250, 541\}$ detectors from each data set. The prediction score of the d selected detectors on a video

Data Set	Number of Intermediate Action Detectors					
	10	25	50	100	250	541
HMDB51 (Manual)	7.9 ± 0.4	16.3 ± 0.4	23.6 ± 0.1	Not applicable. Only has 51 classes		
UCF50 (Manual)	6.8 ± 0.3	12.9 ± 0.3	18.7 ± 0.0	Not applicable. Only has 50 classes		
Clustering (Unsupervised)	5.5 ± 0.3	10.0 ± 0.3	13.6 ± 0.4	17.7 ± 0.4	22.6 ± 0.4	26.7 ± 0.0
Ours (Unsupervised)	5.7 ± 0.3	11.4 ± 0.4	19.2 ± 0.4	25.8 ± 0.4	33.9 ± 0.3	38.3 ± 0.0

Table 2: MAP (x100) on MED w.r.t. the number of intermediate action detectors.

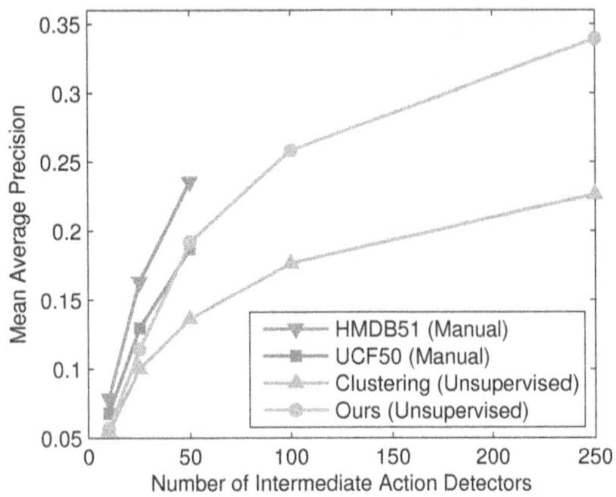

Figure 4: MAP on MED w.r.t. number of intermediate action detectors. More details are in Table 2.

were used as an intermediate representation and evaluated on MED. For each d, random sampling was repeated 30 times for each data set.

The performance is shown in Table 2 and Figure 4. The 95% confidence interval is shown in Table 2. From Figure 4, we see that the detectors trained on labels collected in an unsupervised fashion performs as well as or even better than the detectors trained on manually labeled data. For example, at 50 dimensions, our performance outperforms UCF50 with a statistical significant difference at p-value of 0.0058, according to the paired t-test. Also, by comparing our result with the "Clustering" result, we see that detectors trained with labels collected by utilizing the correlation between speech and actions significantly outperforms detectors trained with pseudo-labels found by clustering. These results suggest that the action examples collected by our proposed method contain more semantic information than the detectors trained simply from clustering. In sum, we hypothesize that the collected labels capture semantic information, thus enabling our detectors to perform as good as the detectors trained from manually collected data.

5. CONCLUSIONS AND FUTURE WORK

Given the positive results of our proposed unsupervised action example harvesting method, our method may represent a new direction to collecting large amounts of examples on a wide variety of actions for semantic action detection in videos. In this paper, as a pilot study, only videos with closed-captions were used. To further improve the scalability by utilizing instructional videos without closed-captions, the transcript can be obtained by the state-of-the-art Automatic Speech Recognition methods. The recognized transcripts are expected to have reasonable accuracy because in instructional videos, the speaker is often close to camera and speaks very clearly. We plan to study this problem in future.

6. ACKNOWLEDGMENTS

This paper was partially supported by the US Department of Defense the U. S. Army Research Office (W911NF-13-1-0277) and partially supported by the National Science Foundation under Grant Number IIS-12511827. Any opinions, findings, and conclusions or recommendations expressed in this material are those of the authors and do not necessarily reflect the views of ARO and NSF.

7. REFERENCES

[1] C.-C. Chang and C.-J. Lin. LIBSVM: A library for support vector machines. In *ACM Transactions on Intelligent Systems and Technology*, 2011.

[2] K. Chatfield, V. Lempitsky, A. Vedaldi, and A. Zisserman. The devil is in the details: an evaluation of recent feature encoding methods. In *BMVC*, 2011.

[3] J. Chen, Y. Cui, G. Ye, D. Liu, and S.-F. Chang. Event-driven semantic concept discovery by exploiting weakly tagged internet images. In *ICMR*, 2014.

[4] M.-C. De Marneffe, B. MacCartney, C. D. Manning, et al. Generating typed dependency parses from phrase structure parses. In *LREC*, 2006.

[5] J. Deng, W. Dong, R. Socher, L.-J. Li, K. Li, and L. Fei-Fei. Imagenet: A large-scale hierarchical image database. In *CVPR*, 2009.

[6] J. Deng, J. Krause, and L. Fei-Fei. Fine-grained crowdsourcing for fine-grained recognition. In *CVPR*, 2013.

[7] L. Jiang, T. Mitamura, S.-I. Yu, and A. G. Hauptmann. Zero-example event search using multimodal pseudo relevance feedback. In *ICMR*, 2014.

[8] H. Kuehne, H. Jhuang, E. Garrote, T. Poggio, and T. Serre. HMDB: a large video database for human motion recognition. In *ICCV*, 2011.

[9] Z.-Z. Lan, L. Jiang, S.-I. Yu, S. Rawat, Y. Cai, C. Gao, S. Xu, H. Shen, X. Li, Y. Wang, et al. CMU-Informedia @ TRECVID 2013 multimedia event detection. In *TREC Video Retrieval Evaluation*, 2013.

[10] M. Mazloom, A. Habibian, and C. G. Snoek. Querying for video events by semantic signatures from few examples. In *ACM MM*, 2013.

[11] P. Natarajan, S. Wu, S. Vitaladevuni, X. Zhuang, S. Tsakalidis, U. Park, and R. Prasad. Multimodal feature fusion for robust event detection in web videos. In *CVPR*, 2012.

[12] P. Over, G. Awad, J. Fiscus, B. Antonishek, M. Michel, A. F. Smeaton, W. Kraaij, G. Quénot, et al. Trecvid 2011-an overview of the goals, tasks, data, evaluation mechanisms and metrics. In *TREC Video Retrieval Evaluation*, 2011.

[13] M. F. Porter. An algorithm for suffix stripping. In *Electronic library and information systems*, 1980.

[14] K. K. Reddy and M. Shah. Recognizing 50 human action categories of web videos. In *Machine Vision and Applications*, 2013.

[15] W. Tong, Y. Yang, L. Jiang, S.-I. Yu, Z. Lan, Z. Ma, W. Sze, E. Younessian, and A. Hauptmann. E-lamp: integration of innovative ideas for multimedia event detection. In *Machine Vision and Applications*, 2014.

[16] L. Von Ahn and L. Dabbish. Labeling images with a computer game. In *CHI*, 2004.

[17] E. F. Can and R. Manmatha. Modeling concept dependencies for event detection. In *ICMR*, 2014.

[18] H. Wang, C. Schmid, et al. Action recognition with improved trajectories. In *ICCV*, 2013.

[19] S. Zinger, C. Millet, B. Mathieu, G. Grefenstette, P. Hède, and P.-A. Moëllic. Extracting an ontology of portrayable objects from wordnet. In *MUSCLE / ImageCLEF workshop on Image and Video retrieval evaluation*, 2005.

Beautifying Fisheye Images using Orientation and Shape Cues

Xiaobo Wang[1], Xiaochun Cao[2,*], Xiaojie Guo[2], Zhanjie Song[1]
[1]School of Science, Tianjin University.
[2]State Key Laboratory of Information Security, IIE, CAS.
{tjuwxb,zhanjiesong}@tju.edu.cn, {caoxiaochun, guoxiaojie}@iie.ac.cn

ABSTRACT

Fisheye images, due to their wide range of vision, become more and more popular in our daily life. However, the fisheye images usually suffer from misalignment that reduces their visual pleasure. In this paper, we develop a computational method for enhancing the aesthetics of such images by exploiting the orientation and shape cues. More specifically, the orientation cue is based on the observation that cameras are often oriented when taking photos, so that their upvectors are parallel to vertical linear structures in the scene. While the shape one refers to that after repositing the fisheye image, the circular shape should be preserved. By employing these two rules as our basic aesthetic guidelines, our method can correct the rotation angle between the camera coordinate and the world coordinate to make the virtual camera oriented, and complete the missing part. Experimental results on a number of challenging indoor and outdoor fisheye images show the effectiveness of our approach, and demonstrate the superior aesthetics of the proposed method compared to the state-of-the-arts.

Categories and Subject Descriptors

I.3 [**Computer Graphics**]: Graphics Utilities; Picture/Image Generation.

Keywords

Computational aesthetics; Fisheye image reposition; Seam carving

1. INTRODUCTION

Aesthetics, in the world of art and photography, refers to the principle of the nature and appreciation of beauty. Judging the aesthetic qualities of photographs, especially for fisheye images, is a highly subjective task and involves the personal sentiment and taste [5]. Hence, there is no unanimously agreed standard for measuring aesthetic values. Despite these challenges, we still believe that certain rules in photographic images could enhance the sense impression.

*Corresponding author

MM'14, November 3–7, 2014, Orlando, Florida, USA.
Copyright 2014 ACM 978-1-4503-3063-3/14/11 ...$15.00.
http://dx.doi.org/10.1145/2647868.2655000.

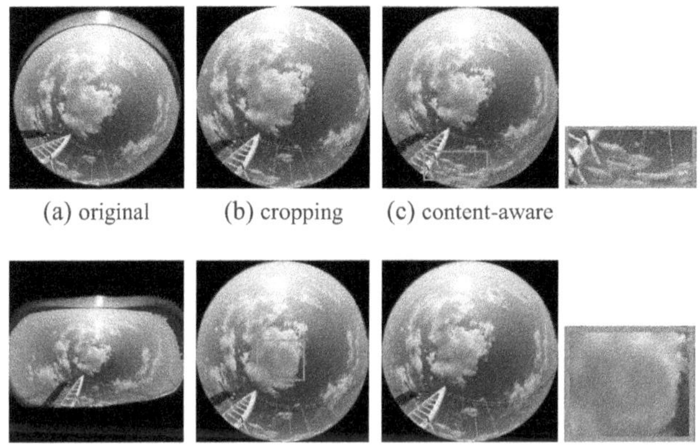

(a) original (b) cropping (c) content-aware

(d) carroll (e) seam carving (f) our method

Figure 1: Visual comparison. (a) Original fisheye image. (b) Cropped result using the largest inner rectangle. (c) Result of "content-aware fill" in Adobe Photoshop CS6. (d) Corrected as much as possible by Carroll's method [2]. (e) Result of the original Seam Carving algorithm [1]. (f) Result of our method. The zoom-in red boxes show the artifacts.

The most popular way to increase the aesthetic appreciation of fisheye images is to correct the distortions. As is known, fisheye cameras are designed to cover the whole hemispherical field in front of the camera by mapping a sphere to a plane. This is difficult as the sphere is not a developable surface. Any mapping from a sphere to a planar surface in fisheye imaging systems will introduce perceptual distortions. To mitigate the effect of distortions, hundreds of projections trading off different types of distortions [2] have been designed in last decades, but none is able to avoid all distortions. Because of this long-realized fact, typical users appear accustomed to and tolerant of these distortions, especially for radially-symmetric circular fisheye images. In addition, millions of circular fisheye images have been shared on the Internet like Flickr. Therefore, instead of correcting the distorted fisheye images like [2, 4], we attempt to find another way to correct such images.

In this work, two priors are harnessed to guide the process of fisheye image content correction. Very often, cameras are oriented when taking images [2]. We call this the *orientation* prior. The other prior, namely the *shape*, is that the circular shape should still be preserved after repositing the original fisheye image. Our method mainly contains two steps as shown in Fig. 2. The first step is to reposit the original fisheye image. Plenty of literature on fisheye camera pose estimation has been published in recent years. Swaminathan and Nayar [8] develop a fisheye camera pose estimating method by enforcing that the straight lines remain straight under

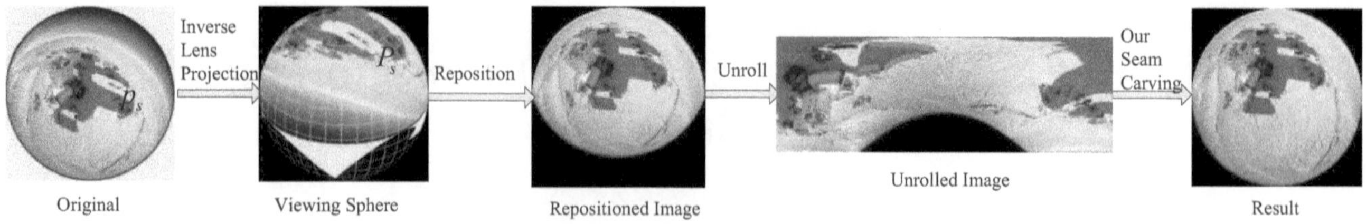

Figure 2: The framework of our proposed fisheye image content correction method.

perspective projection, but the complexity of conic fitting limits its applicability. Li and Hai [4] propose a H-pattern to estimate the fisheye camera pose. By considering the simplicity, we adopt the method [4] by modifying the extraction of H pattern. The second step is to complete the missing pixels. After unrolling the reposited fisheye image, the unrolled version may have some pixels missed. To handle this, a simple solution is to crop the unrolled image with the largest inner rectangle and then scale it into the original size. But simply cropping the image is highly likely to lose much content and reduce the impression of a wide field of view (Fig. 1(b)). Another solution like content-aware fill may fail synthesizing its semantic content, and even the successful synthesis may not be a faithful record of the real scene (Fig. 1(c)). The warping method [3] is complicated and, for our completion, would also lead to severe local distortions because of the very concave boundary. The seam carving method [1] inserts seams along paths of pixels with low energy in a repetitive fashion, and minimizes the loss of important information in an image without severe distortions. The algorithm is simple and efficient, but frequently fails to preserve structural information such as straight lines and regular shapes. To overcome the limitation, some algorithms introduce the forward energy with different functions to reduce the visual artifacts caused by the seam removal [6, 7]. But for our completion, directly using the above seam carving method may lead to severe distortions (Fig. 1(e)).

In this paper, we present an improved seam carving method to preserve regular structures, especially, straight lines and smooth curves. The idea is similar to [3] in the sense that we insert seams into the sub-image to complete the missing part. Contrary to [3], we aim to preserve the line structure, which runs across the sub-image when inserting seams, and avoid choosing the same seam as much as possible when inserting the next seam.

The main contributions of this paper are summarized as follows:

- Identifying two fisheye image aesthetic guidelines, and facilitating a fisheye image editing tool.
- Proposing an improved seam carving method for our completion.

2. OUR METHOD

As shown in Fig. 2, our fisheye image content correction scheme first reads in a fisheye image, and the original visual information on the viewing sphere is readily recovered by an inverse fisheye projection, $\theta = f/r$, the most common equidistance projection model, where r is the distance to the projection point in the image from the optical center, θ is the angle between an incident ray and the optical axis, f is the focal length. We then reposit the information on the viewing sphere to make the virtual fisheye camera oriented, and obtain the reposited image by fisheye projection. Since the reposited fisheye image is radially-symmetric, we obtain the rectangle image by unrolling the reposited fisheye image. Finally, we insert seams by using our modification of seam carving algorithm until the target rectangle is filled up.

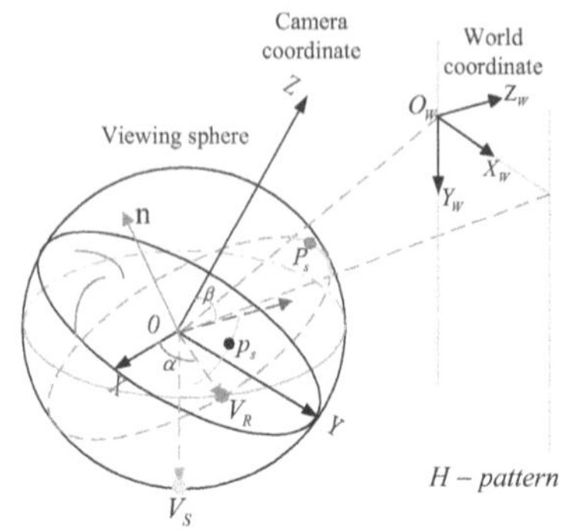

Figure 3: Virtual fisheye camera pose estimation. The rotation angle between the world coordinate and the camera coordinate is (α, β).

2.1 Repositing on viewing sphere

Based on the work [4] on fisheye camera pose estimation, we need to extract two distorted vertical lines and one distorted horizontal line in the fisheye image (marked as yellow in Fig. 2), called H-pattern. In practice, the horizon line and the two vertical lines may be not intersected. Moreover, user-specified lines of H-pattern are often not exactly placed on the straight features, although close to them. And please note that the distorted straight lines in the fisheye image are represented as arcs of great circles on the viewing sphere. By taking into account these two issues, we first sample a line as a set of points (≥ 5) with the sampling density proportional to the arc length on the viewing sphere. These points are then moved within a small neighborhood onto the pixels with the highest gradient values by using the Sobel operator after bilateral filtering. The new points are mapped onto the viewing sphere to obtain the best fitting great circle arc, which satisfies

$$\underset{\mathrm{n}}{argmin} \sum_{s} (\mathrm{P_s} \cdot \mathrm{n})^2, \tag{1}$$

where n is the normal vector to the great circle plane, and $\mathrm{P_s} = (X_s, Y_s, Z_s)$ is the Cartesian coordinate of the sth sample point on the viewing sphere. The refined sample points p_s are then obtained by projecting P_s onto the fitted arc.

After refining the H-pattern, the vanishing point V_S is calculated by the two parallel vertical lines. Then, using the normal vector pointing to V_S from the origin O, we can determine a plane passing through the center of the spherical image (marked in green in Fig. 3). The intersection of the plane and the horizontal line is another vanishing point V_R. Using these two vanishing points V_S and V_R, we can compute the relative orientation matrix R_{WC}, between the camera coordinate and the world coordinate systems, and obtain the rotational angle (α, β), where $\alpha \in [-\pi, \pi]$, $\beta \in [-\frac{\pi}{2}, \frac{\pi}{2}]$. We then correct the rotation angle (α, β) to make the virtual fisheye camera oriented and get the reposited fisheye image by fisheye projection.

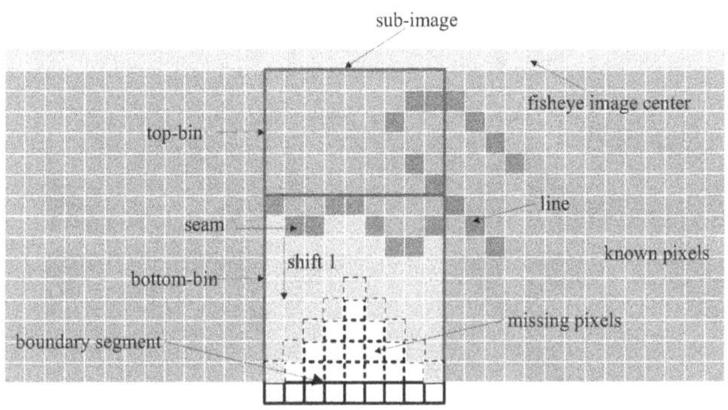

Figure 4: The unrolled fisheye image.

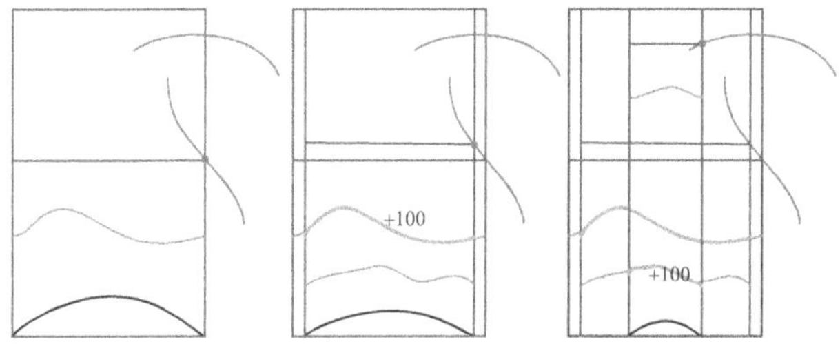

Figure 5: Visualization of the basic idea of our seam inserting algorithm. The optimal seam (red) selected in the bottom-bin of sub-image (the bottom purple box). After inserting the seam, the boundary of image (black) shift one pixel to the bottom, the energy of the seam and its duplicate is increased (green). Then the next seam will not be the same seam selected in the former step.

2.2 Structure-Aware completion

We unroll the reposited fisheye image into rectangle in a certain direction which make sure that the missing pixels are not separated (shown as Fig. 4). Our completion insert seams in part of the image, and preserve the structure information.

The original Seam Carving algorithm [1] inserts horizontal/vertical seams through the image. An improved seam Carving algorithm [7] uses forward energy to reduce the visual artifacts. However, we want a seam to be not through the image, so directly use the seam carving algorithm will not solve our completion. The seam inserting method in [3] defines a boundary segment as a connected sequence of missing pixels on the target rectangular boundary. Each time they select the longest boundary segment and insert one seam in the sub-image (Fig. 4). Our idea is similar to [3] in the sense of inserting seams in sub-image, but our sub-image is from the second row to the last row since the first row is the fisheye image center.

To preserve the structure information, we find the bottom intersection point of the lines and the sub-image (marked as blue in Fig. 5), this will divide the sub-image into two part, the top-bin and the bottom-bin of the sub-image (Fig. 4). Our seam carving algorithm starts by computing an energy value for each pixel in the bottom-bin of the sub-image based on the gradient. For the missing pixels in the sub-image, we assign an infinite cost (10^8) to prevent the seam from passing them. We also use forward energy as proposed by [7], where seam is computed by minimizing the cumulative energy M for all the possible connected seams for each entry (i, j):

$$M(i,j) = e(i,j) + min \begin{cases} M(i-1,j-1) + C_D(i,j) \\ M(i,j-1) + C_R(i,j) \\ M(i+1,j-1) + C_U(i,j) \end{cases}, \quad (2)$$

where

$$C_U(i,j) = |I(i+1,j) - I(i-1,j)| + |I(i,j+1) - I(i-1,j)|$$
$$C_R(i,j) = |I(i+1,j) - I(i-1,j)|$$
$$C_D(i,j) = |I(i+1,j) - I(i-1,j)| + |I(i,j-1) - I(i-1,j)|,$$

I is the unrolled fisheye image, $e(i, j)$ is the gradient energy function in (i, j). For the known pixels in the sub-image, we define an additional energy map e_a and initialize an offset value to each gradient with zero. Thus the energy change into $\hat{e} = e + e_a$. All seams are calculated based on the energy values $\hat{e}$ and the optimal seam is selected. This seam shares the same starting and ending x-coordinates as the selected boundary segment (Fig. 4). We duplicate the pixels of the optimal seam by averaging them with their top and bottom neighbors, and shift all the pixels on the bottom of this seam by one pixel to the bottom. Then the optical seam and its duplicate of the offset energy map are increased by a value of 100 in each pixel. When calculating the next optimal seam, the values of the offset energy map are added to the gradient values. After the modification of the offset energy map, the pixels of the optimal seam are removed and this avoid choosing the same seam in the following iterations. Fig. 5 visualizes the modification of the basic idea. We repeatedly insert seams in this way until the rectangle boundary has no missing pixels.

3. EXPERIMENT RESULTS

We evaluate our seam carving method by showing results on a variety of real cases in Figure 1, 2, 6 and 7. We first compare our method with the correcting distortion method of Carroll, which is a straightforward way to correct fisheye images. As illustrated in Fig. 6(d), for the upward-looking and downward-looking cases, our results are apparently more aesthetic. For the cases of frontward-looking, Carroll's results look more natural. But the shape always change and our results are still comparable.

We then compare our completion method with cropping, content-aware fill, seam carving. As illustrated in Fig. 6, cropping obviously loses too much content (Fig. 6(b)). Content-aware fill fails to synthesize the semantic content, *e.g.*, for the beach in the downward-looking case, the fence in the upward-looking case, and the wall in the frontward-looking case (Fig. 6(c)). Seam carving is unable to preserve the regular structures in images such as smooth curves (Fig. 6(e)). Our method successfully completes the missing part without introducing noticeable artifacts for most of cases (Fig. 6(f)). The distortion is distributed and acceptable.

Finally, we give the subjective aesthetic score by users. Each time six images are randomly shown on one screen: the input, cropping result, content-aware fill result, carroll correction result, seam carving result, and our result. The volunteers need to choose their most preference. Our experiment has 100 participants, including 20 researchers with computer graphics/vision backgrounds and 80 students outside this community. The researchers are mainly from CAS while the students are from Tianjin University. Fig. 8 shows the experiment results and our method is substantially preferred.

4. CONCLUSIONS

In this paper, we have proposed a novel method to correct fisheye images, which exploits two rules, say orientation and shape, as basic aesthetic guidelines. To complete the missing part and put our focus on the distribution of seams and the preservation of structure information, we have improved the original seam carving method. The distribution of the inserted seams preserve the line structure and introduce less distortions. Compared with other methods, our method has achieved significantly better results in most cases. But

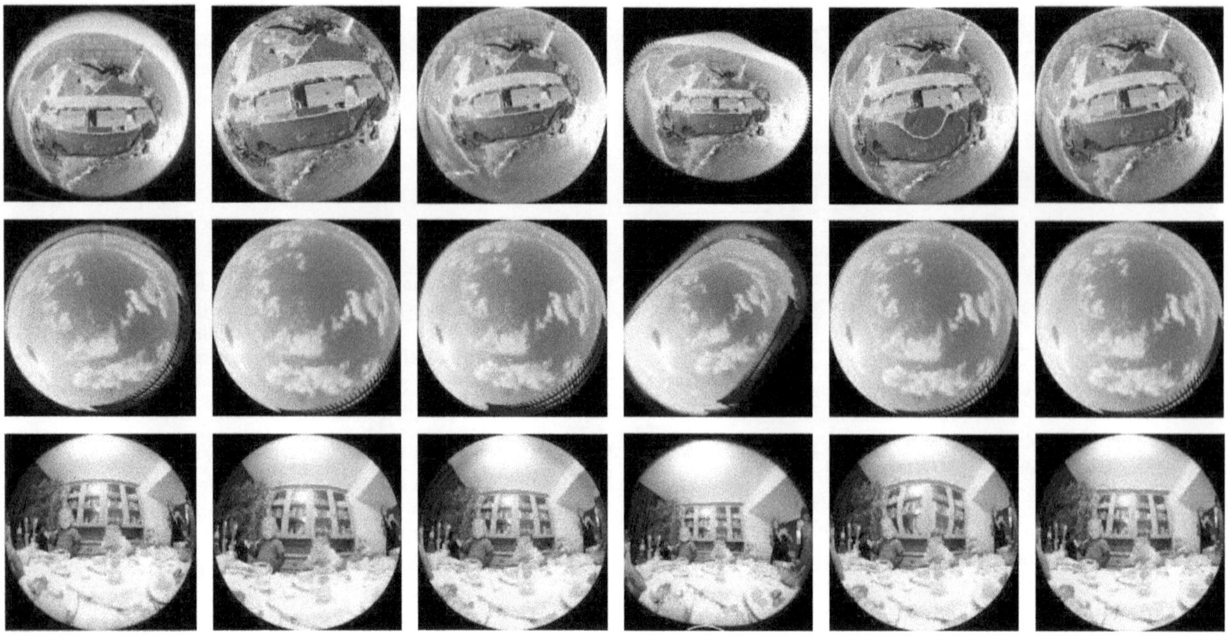

(a) (b) (c) (d) (e) (f)

Figure 6: Comparisons with other methods. The first column to the the last column are original images, cropping results, content-aware fill results, Carroll results, seam carving results and our results. The first row to the last row are downward-looking fisheye image, upward-looking fisheye image, frontward-looking fisheye image. The rotation angle are (7°,18°), (20°,6°), (0°,−13°).

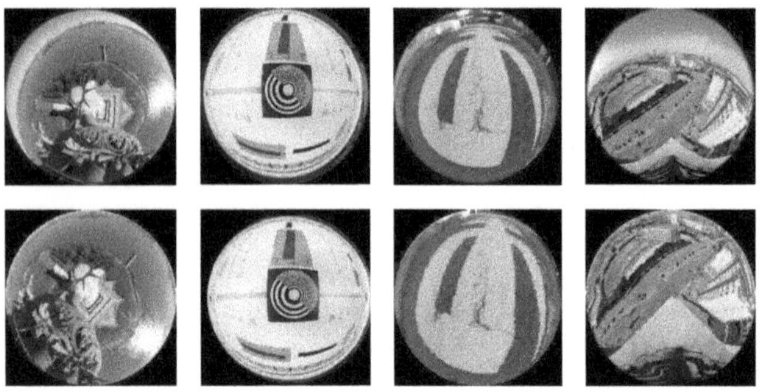

Figure 7: More results of our method. The first row are original fisheye images, the second row are our results. The last column is a failure.

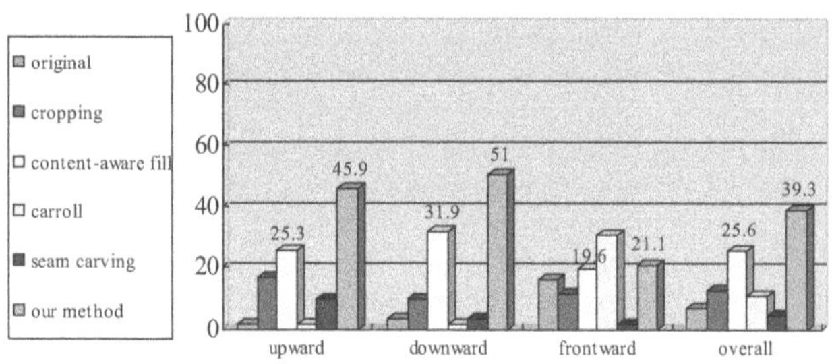

Figure 8: The subjective experiment results. The numbers are shown in percentage and averaged on 100 participants. The preference in each case 30 images.

our method may fail (the last column in Fig. 7) when the missing part is too large, when the lines are located in the bottom of sub-image, which appears to be a common challenge for seam carving methods. We would like to further explore the completion method (*e.g.* warping) in the future.

5. ACKNOWLEDGMENTS

This work was supported by National Natural Science Foundation of China (No. 61332012, 61379014), National High-tech R&D Program of China (2012AA011503), and 100 Talents Programme of The Chinese Academy of Sciences.

6. REFERENCES

[1] S. Avidan and A. Shamir. Seam carving for content-aware image resizing. *ACM Trans. Graph.*, 26(3):10, 2007.

[2] R. Carroll, M. Agrawal, and A. Agarwala. Optimizing content-preserving projections for wide-angle images. *ACM Trans. Graph.*, 28(3):1–9, 2009.

[3] H. Kaiming, C. Huiwen, and S. Jian. Rectangling panoramic images via warping. *ACM Trans. Graph.*, 32(4):1–10, 2013.

[4] S. Li and Y. Hai. Estimating camera pose from h-pattern of parking lot. In *ICRA*, pages 3954–3959, 2010.

[5] L. Ligang, C. Renjie, W. Lior, and C.-O. Daniel. Optimizing photo composition. *Computer Graphic Forum (Proceedings of Eurographics)*, 29(2):469–478, 2010.

[6] H. Noh and B. Han. Seam carving with forward gradient difference maps. In *ACM MM*, pages 709–712, 2012.

[7] M. Rubinstein, A. Shamir, and S. Avidan. Improved seam carving for video retargeting. *ACM Trans. Graph.*, 27(3):1–9, 2008.

[8] R. Swaminathan and S. K. Nayar. Nonmetric calibration of wide-angle lenses and polycameras. *IEEE TPAMI*, 22(10):1172–1178, 2000.

Temporal Fusion Approach Using Segment Weight for Affect Recognition from Body Movements

Jianfeng Xu
ji-xu@kddilabs.jp

Shigeyuki Sakazawa
sakazawa@kddilabs.jp

Media and HTML5 Application Laboratory, KDDI R&D Laboratories, Inc.
2-1-15 Ohara, Fujimino-shi, Saitama, 356-8502 JAPAN

ABSTRACT

In the field of affect recognition, most researchers have focused on using multimodal fusion while temporal fusion techniques have yet to be adequately explored. This paper demonstrates that a powerful temporal fusion approach can significantly improve the performance of affect recognition. As a typical approach in state-of-the-art methods, the segment-based affect recognition technique from body movements is used as a baseline, whereby a body movement is parsed into a sequence of motion clips (called *segments*) and all segments are treated as being the same using a majority voting strategy. Our basic idea is that different types of segments have different influences/weights in recognizing the affective state. To verify this idea, an entropy-based method is proposed to estimate the segment weights in supervised and unsupervised learning. Furthermore, the recognition results from all segments are fused with the segment weights using the sum rule. Our experimental results on a public data set demonstrate that the segment weights can greatly improve the percentage of correctness (accuracy) from the baseline.

Categories and Subject Descriptors

I.5 [**Pattern Recognition**]: Clustering; J.4 [**Computer Applications**]: Social and Behavioural Sciences

Keywords

Affect recognition, Temporal fusion, Entropy

1. INTRODUCTION

Despite the huge efforts made by the academic and industrial communities, affect recognition remains a very challenging issue [7, 9], but one that has a great potential in many applications, for example, human computer interaction [14]. In previous decades, great progress was achieved by fusing multimodal cues such as speech, facial expressions, and body movements [14]. In addition to multimodal fusion, psychological research has shown that the temporal dynamics of body movements, facial expressions and speech play an important role in the interpretation of emotional displays [6, 14]. In this paper, the system input consists of a body movement (motion capture data), which is a time-series of skeletal poses with articulated joints and can be easily captured by commercially available devices such as Kinect^{TM}. The system output is the discrete affective state conveyed by the body movement such as anger, happiness, or sadness. According to the survey paper by Karg et al. [7], in a typical affect recognition approach from body movements, the body movement is parsed into a sequence of motion clips (called *segments*) and the final recognition result is derived from all segments. Therefore, this paper defines the term *temporal fusion* as the integration of multiple segments of body movements in the temporal domain.

Although temporal fusion is just as important as multimodal fusion [6], little research has been conducted that systematically analyzes the temporal fusion approach for affect recognition [7, 9, 14]. In multimodal fusion research [14], there are two main types of fusion strategy, feature-level and decision-level, which can also be used as temporal fusion strategies. However, feature-level fusion has the well-known "curse of dimensionality" problem [14]. Therefore, similar to multimodal fusion, we believe that decision-level fusion is more suitable, where the recognition results of all segments are finally combined together, as shown in Fig. 2. Actually, in the case of body movements, the simple majority voting strategy is used in state-of-the-art techniques [1, 5, 7]. In this paper, we will show that this strategy has a number of shortcomings and propose an improved method. A well-known fact is that body movements like gestures have a temporal structure with multiple phases such as the preparation, stroke, and retraction phases [5, 11]. In the majority of gestures, the affective state is mostly expressed via the stroke phase. Based on this key observation, our basic idea is that different types of segments have different influences/weights in recognizing the affective state.

However, it is very challenging to estimate the segment weight properly due to the semantic gap problem. Basically, the segments are divided using low level features like motion velocity [1]. There is no guarantee that the divided segment has semantic meaning let alone determine which phase a segment is in, which itself is a challenging research issue [5]. In this paper, we propose a practical approach to estimate the segment weights in the space of low level features. After classifying the segments, the segment class with high uncertainty is regarded as having low confidence, and is thus assigned a low weight. Naturally, entropy is employed as a measure of the uncertainty when calculating the

MM'14, November 03–07, 2014, Orlando, FL, USA.

http://dx.doi.org/10.1145/2647868.2655008.

segment weight. Our experimental results demonstrate that decision-level fusion with segment weights can significantly improve the performance of affect recognition. In this paper, the term "phase" is basically a concept in high level while the term "class" is a cluster derived from low level features.

Our technical contributions are summarized as follows.

1. We propose a temporal fusion approach using segment weights for affect recognition from body movements. We argue that temporal fusion strategies are essential in affect recognition, which can be used in conjunction with conventional multimodal fusion strategies.
2. To estimate the segment weights, an entropy-based method is designed for both supervised and unsupervised learning [3]. Our methods only use low level features, which are directly available in conventional methods. Therefore, our methods are compatible with most existing techniques. The experiments demonstrate the effectiveness of our method.

2. BASELINE AND ITS PROBLEMS

Karg et al. [7] summarized a typical flow chart of existing methods for affect recognition from body movements in a recent survey paper, where the four basic steps are as follows.

1. Motion data processing. This step is to obtain signals such as motion trajectories of joints from sensor data.
2. Temporal segmentation. This step is to parse the entire body movement into a sequence of motion clips.
3. Feature extraction. This step is to extract a feature vector from the signals in a motion clip.
4. Affect detection. This step is to detect the affective state conveyed by the body movement, where the detection function is learned in a training stage.

The input data, regardless of whether it is training data or test data, is a body movement. Note that the input data should be a single action such as a knocking motion. We implement the flow chart following Bernhardt et al. [1].

Because our data, which come from the University of Glasgow [12], are recorded in the joint positions, Step 1 can be omitted. In the case where the motion data are in the form of a rotational representation (e.g. Euler angles), the forward kinematics can be used to calculate the joint positions.

In Step 2, the motion velocity is calculated as the average velocity of all joints. Basically, when the motion velocity is greater or less than a threshold, the motion will be segmented. In order to find the best threshold, several trials are performed where the threshold is varied within a reasonable range, and the one that has the maximal number of segments is selected as the best one [1].

In Step 3, the feature vector in a segment includes the average relative position, the average motion velocity, the average motion acceleration, and the average motion jerk for some particular joints such as hand and elbow [1].

In Step 4, a training stage is performed in advance to learn the detection function for the affect detection of a segment. First, the above three steps need to be performed for the training data. Then, the segments in Step 3 are classified by K-means, where the class number is determined manually according to prior knowledge. Finally, in each class, the detection function is learned by the Support Vector Machine (SVM), where the LIBSVM library is used with a scaling operation required by [2]. After the training stage, given a segment in the test motion, it is first classified into a class with K-means. Then, the detection function for the class is used to determine the affective state of the segment. The affective state for the entire motion is determined by a majority voting strategy, which selects the most frequent one.

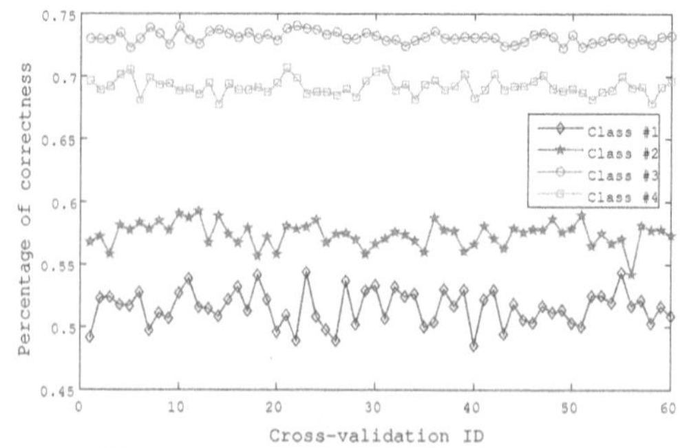

Figure 1: The percentage of correctness for segment classes in the training data of knocking motions, which shows that different types of segments have different ability to detect the affective state.

In Sect. 1, we mentioned that the segments in the stroke phase are more important in expressing the affective state than those in other phases. However, the above conventional method, as the baseline in this paper, treats all segments the same. In this section, we present some experimental results about this problem. As Fig. 1 shows, the various classes differ from each other in terms of the percentage of correctness (e.g. Class #3 is much more effective than Class #1), which means that different types of segments have different ability to detect the affective state. Therefore, we believe that different classes should have different influences in affect recognition.

3. THE PROPOSED METHOD

3.1 System Framework

Basically, we use similar techniques to the baseline (e.g. segmentation by motion velocity, classification by K-means, and affect detection by SVM) in our system but with the addition of temporal fusion, which is shown by the red rectangle in Fig. 2. For temporal fusion, the input is the detection result in each class, which is a histogram of all segments in that class. The output is the detection result from all classes with segment weights. This will be described in Sect. 3.2.

3.2 Temporal Fusion Approach

To verify our idea that different types of segments have different influences in affect recognition, two core research issues need to be addressed. First, given a set of recognition results from all segments, how do we estimate the most influential segments (or the segment weights)? Second, once the segment weights are assigned, how do we best fuse them to improve the affect recognition? Because the second issue was analyzed in other studies such as audio analysis [4] and multimodal fusion [5, 14], we can follow their framework. Kittler et al. [8] reported that the sum rule outperforms other fusion schemes such as the product rule, max rule, min rule or median rule. However, even though it is essential, the first issue has not been fully explored within an affect recognition context. In this paper, our main focus is proposing effective solutions to the first issue.

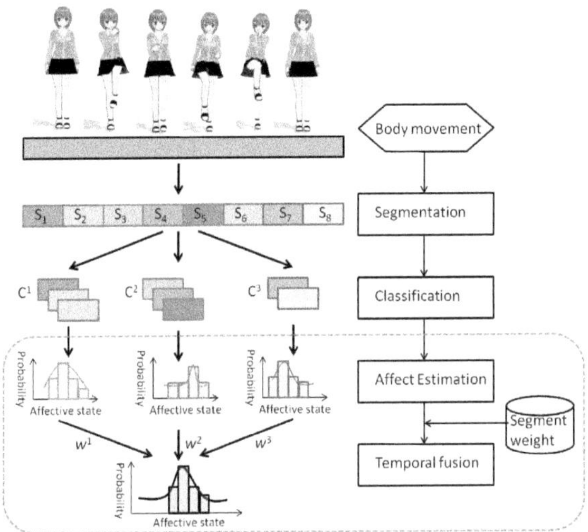

Figure 2: The framework of affect recognition from body movements, where a temporal fusion approach using segment weight is shown by the red rectangle.

Suppose we have M classes for all N segments in a body movement as shown in Fig. 2. For a segment S_i belonging to class C^j, the detection result is denoted as $e(S_i)$, which is an element of a set $E = \{e_1, e_2, \cdots, e_K\}$ of discrete affective states. Therefore, given the above information, our task is (1) to estimate a weight w^j for the class C^j; and (2) to determine the affective state e^{all} of the body movement.

Weight Estimation: Because we do not know which phase class C^j belongs to, we cannot directly estimate the weight by prior knowledge that the stroke phase is more important than the preparation phase and retraction phase in expressing the affective state. The *assumption* is that a segment class C^j with high uncertainty usually has a low level confidence, thus it should be assigned a low weight. Naturally, entropy is employed as a measure of the uncertainty to calculate the segment weight, which is calculated as

$$H^j(E) = -\sum_{e(S_i)\in E} P^j(e(S_i)) \log P^j(e(S_i)) \quad (1)$$

$$w^j = \exp(-H^j(E)) / \sum_{j=1}^{M} \exp(-H^j(E)) \quad (2)$$

where $P^j(e(S_i))$ denotes the detection probability of affective states in class C^j, calculated as the normalized histogram of detected affective states in class C^j. Note that the higher the entropy is, the lower the weight is.

In real applications, we have to consider two cases. In the first case, the training data are available (the so-called supervised learning (SL) case), where we have multiple body movements in multiple affective labels. Only those body movements with the same affective labels can be counted together in the same histogram of detection results in class C^j. For example, we collect all the segments from all body movements with the happy labels in the training data and those collected segments are detected as different affective states $e(S_i)$, forming a histogram as shown in Fig. 3. Note that those segments from different affective labels cannot be counted in the same histogram although they belong to the same class. This is because detection results from different affective labels have different statistical characteristics in their histograms as shown in Fig. 3. Therefore, the histograms are counted for different classes and different affective labels. In total, we obtain $M * K$ histograms as shown in Fig. 3. Finally, we need to average the entropy $H^j(E_k)$ in all the affective labels E_k by $H^j(E) = 1/K \cdot \sum_{k=1}^{K} H^j(E_k)$.

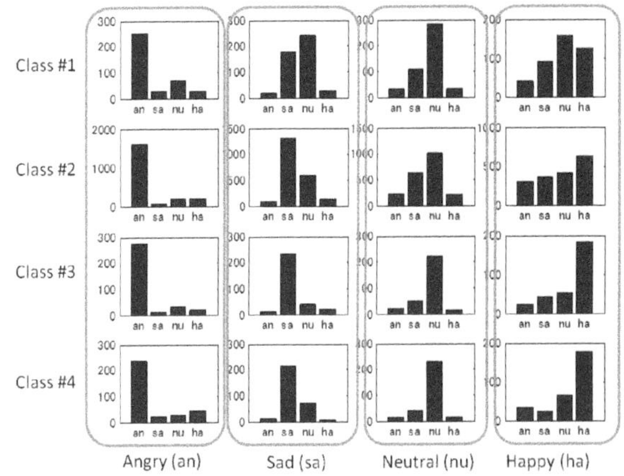

Figure 3: The histograms of detection results for different classes (Y-axis) and different affective labels (X-axis) from the training data of knocking motions.

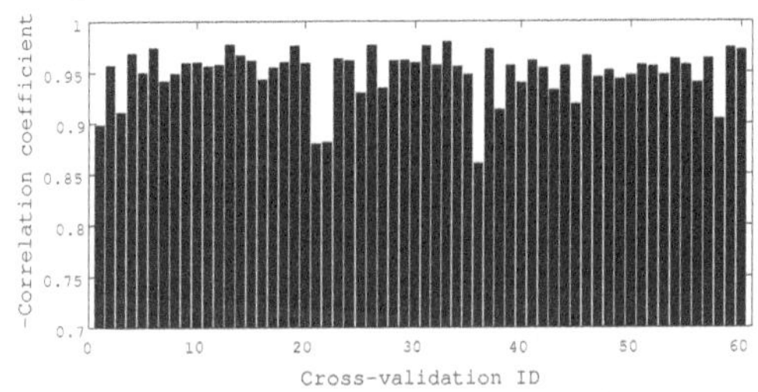

Figure 4: The correlation between the entropy and the percentage of correctness for all classes and all affective labels from the training data of knocking motions.

In the second case, only test data are available (the so-called unsupervised learning (UL) case). In this case, all the segments have the same affective label and the histograms for a class can be directly obtained.

To confirm the *assumption*, we calculate the correlation between the entropy and the percentage of correctness for all classes and all affective labels in the training data. The result in Fig. 4 shows that the correlation is very high and stable with an average value of -0.9489 and standard deviation of 0.0249, which implies that the uncertainty or entropy is highly related to the percentage of correctness (accuracy).

Fusion Strategy: Using the segment weights, we fuse the detection probability by the sum rule, which can be derived by the Bayesian theory [8].

$$P(e(S_i)) = \sum_{j=1}^{M} w^j \cdot P^j(e(S_i)) \quad (3)$$

where $P(e(S_i))$ denotes the fused detection probability of affective states $e(S_i) \in E$.

Finally, the recognition result for the entire body movement is determined by the maximum posterior probability.

4. EXPERIMENTS AND ANALYSIS

In this session, we will evaluate the performance of our algorithm and discuss the results. Similar to Bernhardt et al. [1], we use the knocking motions from the public database [12] to run Leave-One-Subject-Out cross-validation (LOSO-CV) tests. Overall,there are 60 subjects performing 5 trials

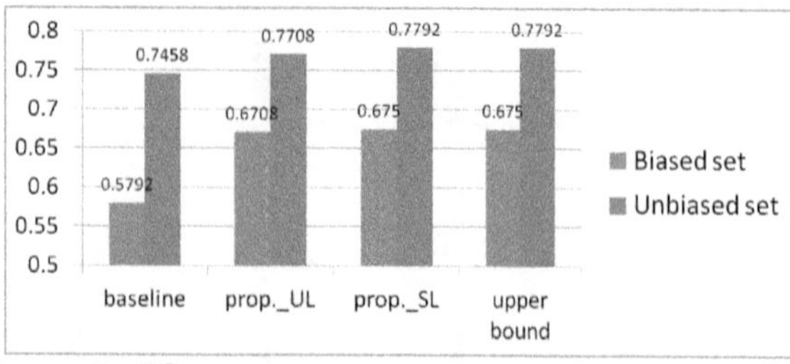

Figure 5: The average percentage of correctness for all 60 iterations of the cross-validation.

in 4 affective states (neutral, happy, angry and sad), resulting in 1,200 samples of body movements. For each iteration of the cross-validation the system was therefore trained on 1180 samples and validated on 20 samples.

We compare four methods including the baseline, the proposed method in the unsupervised learning case, the proposed method in the supervised learning case, and an upper bound in the supervised learning case. The parameter setting follows the baseline [1]. For example, the number of classes for K-means is set as 4. For feature vectors in a segment, we also consider two sets as the baseline [1], which includes one set with personal bias and another set without personal bias. To remove personal bias [1], his/her average of feature vectors in all affective states is subtracted.

We obtained the following results.

(1) Our methods in both the unsupervised learning and supervised learning cases, on average, outperform the baseline for all 60 iterations of the cross-validation as shown in Fig. 5. The average gain for the biased set is 9.16% and 9.58%, respectively. The average gain for the unbiased set is 2.50% and 3.34%, respectively. The fact that the gain is smaller in the unbiased set is understandable. As Bernhardt et al. [1] pointed out, the percentage of correctness for the unbiased set is at a very high level, which is even better than the level that can be attained by a human being. Therefore, it is more difficult to obtain gains.

(2) Basically, the performance for supervised learning should be better than that for unsupervised learning because the data size to estimate the segment weights is rather different. However, in many real applications, the training data are unavailable. Fortunately, the degree of degradation is very small (0.42% for the biased set or 0.84% for the unbiased set) as shown in Fig. 5, which demonstrates that our entropy-based estimation approach is very robust.

(3) Furthermore, in the case of supervised learning, we can estimate the segment weight by the percentage of correctness instead of entropy, which is a kind of upper bound for the current framework. The experimental results in Fig. 5 show that our entropy-based method has performance comparable to the upper bound, which benefits from the high correlation between them.

One interesting observation comes from Fig. 3. Besides the fact that different types of segments have different influences in affect recognition, it is also true that different affective labels have different discrimination ability. Figure 3 makes it clear that a body movement with an angry label is easier to detect than one with a happy label. This seems reasonable because a human being basically changes his/her gestures far more when in an angry state than in a happy one [10]. However, it is a chicken and egg situation where we need the segment weight to detect affective state or the affective state to estimate segment weight.

5. CONCLUSIONS AND FUTURE WORK

This paper focused on the temporal fusion approach in affect recognition from body movements, which has not yet been exploited even though it plays an essential role. Our basic idea on segment weight is inspired by the psychological fact that the segments in the stroke phase are more expressive of the affective state than those in other phases. To estimate the segment weight, based on the correlation between the uncertainty and the percentage of correctness, we propose entropy as a measure in both supervised learning and unsupervised learning.

In the future, we want to extend the evaluation to the more challenging non-acted movements [13]. In addition, although we only evaluated our idea in relation to body movements, we believe that it will work well for other modalities such as facial expressions and speech, which will be the object of our future work. Another area to be dealt with in the future is the chicken and egg situation mentioned in Sect. 4. An expectation-maximization(EM)-like algorithm may be an effective approach to clarify the relationship between affective states and segment weights.

6. REFERENCES

[1] D. Bernhardt and P. Robinson. Detecting affect from non-stylised body motions. In *Affective Computing and Intelligent Interaction*, pages 59–70. 2007.

[2] C.-C. Chang and C.-J. Lin. LIBSVM: A library for support vector machines. *ACM Trans. on Intelligent Systems and Technology*, 2:27:1–27:27, 2011.

[3] P. De Silva, A. Kleinsmith, and N. Bianchi-Berthouze. Towards unsupervised detection of affective body posture nuances. In *Affective Comput. and Intell. Interaction*, pages 32–39. 2005.

[4] C. Dietrich, F. Schwenker, and G. Palm. Classification of time series utilizing temporal and decision fusion. In *Multiple Classifier Systems*, pages 378–387. 2001.

[5] H. Gunes and M. Piccardi. Automatic temporal segment detection and affect recognition from face and body display. *Systems, Man, and Cybernetics, Part B: Cybernetics, IEEE Trans. on*, 39(1):64–84, Feb 2009.

[6] H. Gunes, M. Piccardi, and M. Pantic. *From the Lab to the Real World: Affect Recognition using Multiple Cues and Modalities*, pages 185–218. 2008.

[7] M. Karg, A. Samadani, R. Gorbet, K. Kuhnlenz, J. Hoey, and D. Kulic. Body movements for affective expression: A survey of automatic recognition and generation. *Affective Computing, IEEE Trans. on*, 4(4):341–359, 2013.

[8] J. Kittler, M. Hatef, R. P. W. Duin, and J. Matas. On combining classifiers. *Pattern Analysis and Machine Intelligence, IEEE Trans. on*, 20(3):226–239, 1998.

[9] A. Kleinsmith and N. Bianchi-Berthouze. Affective body expression perception and recognition: A survey. *Affective Computing, IEEE Transactions on*, 4(1):15–33, Jan 2013.

[10] A. Kleinsmith, T. Fushimi, and N. Bianchi-Berthouze. An incremental and interactive affective posture recognition system. In *International Workshop on Adapting the Interaction Style to Affective Factors*, pages 378–387. 2005.

[11] S. Kopp, B. Krenn, S. Marsella, A. Marshall, C. Pelachaud, H. Pirker, K. Thórisson, and H. VilhjÃąlmsson. Towards a common framework for multimodal generation: The behavior markup language. In *Intelligent Virtual Agents*, pages 205–217. 2006.

[12] Y. Ma, H. Paterson, and F. Pollick. A motion capture library for the study of identity, gender, and emotion perception from biological motion. *Behavior Research Methods*, 38(1):134–141, 2006.

[13] N. Savva, A. Scarinzi, and N. Bianchi-Berthouze. Continuous recognition of player's affective body expression as dynamic quality of aesthetic experience. *Computational Intelligence and AI in Games, IEEE Trans. on*, 4(3):199–212, Sept 2012.

[14] Z. Zeng, M. Pantic, G. Roisman, and T. Huang. A survey of affect recognition methods: Audio, visual, and spontaneous expressions. *Pattern Analysis and Machine Intelligence, IEEE Trans. on*, 31(1):39–58, Jan 2009.

sTrack: Secure Tracking in Community Surveillance

Chun-Te Chu, Jaeyeon Jung, Zicheng Liu, Ratul Mahajan
Microsoft
{chch, jjung, zliu, ratul}@microsoft.com

ABSTRACT

We present sTrack, a system that can track objects across multiple cameras without sharing any visual information between two cameras except whether an object was seen by both. To achieve this challenging privacy goal, we leverage recent advances in secure two-party computation and multi-camera tracking. We derive a new distance metric learning technique that is more suited for secure computation. Compared to the existing methods, our technique has lower complexity in secure computation without sacrificing the tracking accuracy. We implement it using a new Boolean circuit for secure tracking. Experiments using real datasets show that the performance overhead of secure tracking is low, adding only a few seconds over non-private tracking.

Categories and Subject Descriptors

I.4.8 [**Scene Analysis**]: Tracking; K.4.1 [**Public Policy Issues**]: Privacy

Keywords

Tracking; Privacy-preserving; Secure Two-Party Computation; Distance Metric Learning; Human Re-identification

1. INTRODUCTION

In conventional surveillance systems (e.g., those deployed in airports, subways, and corporate buildings), multi-camera tracking is extremely useful to fight crime. For example, when an investigator spots a suspicious person entering a building from one of the surveillance videos, she may want to know where he left the building. If the building has multiple entry-exit points, tracking across cameras is needed. Tremendous progress has been made on multi-camera tracking [3][6][13][23], and commercial systems include this ability [10]. As all cameras have the same owner (e.g., a government agency or a company), current techniques do not isolate the information from different cameras.

However, privacy concerns severely limit the applicability of multi-camera tracking to residential community surveillance. Householders in many communities, including those in high-crime neighborhood, are loath to law enforcement deploying surveillance cameras in areas because of privacy issues [2]. Camera feeds contain many aspects of their lives that are unrelated to crime and are potentially embarrassing [11]. The concerns around sharing camera feeds are unfortunate because processing feeds across them would enable community-wide surveillance to detect suspicious activities and objects across cameras (e.g., a person knocking on several doors, a car cruising the neighborhood), which individual cameras cannot detect. One possibility is for each home to send its feed to a central party (e.g., law enforcement or a corporation), and for this party to run one of the existing surveillance algorithms. However, householders are often unwilling to share their camera data with third-parties [2].

We investigate an alternative, peer-to-peer approach in which cameras communicate to each other to determine if they saw the same object. Our goal is to enable cameras to cooperate in order to track suspicious objects (e.g., unknown people or cars) without revealing any information about the objects to other cameras except matching outcomes. We assume that each family only has access to the video feeds from their own cameras. Each time the camera identifies an object of interest, it checks with peer cameras from other families to determine whether they saw the same object. This determination can be made using a distance function over the object features that individual cameras extract. However, private information may be revealed if the cameras share the raw values of the feature vectors (e.g., it is possible to identify the object using color histogram).

To address this privacy risk, we explore if secure two-party computation (2PC) can be used for privately matching objects. 2PC allows two participants to compute any function over their inputs, without revealing anything but the function output (and what may be inferred from it). Much progress [12][14][15][16] has been made recently towards reducing the overhead of 2PC. In this paper, we show that 2PC can enable high-accuracy, low-overhead multi-camera tracking.

This paper makes the following contributions:

1. We present a new metric learning technique that permits an efficient secure two-party computation with significantly lower complexity. It has low overhead because it refactors the problem such that cameras do the complex portions of the computation (e.g., matrix multiplication) locally and the portions that are computed jointly are simple. Experiments with real datasets show the overhead of our technique is 6 to 200 times lower than the prior approaches [8][23] without sacrificing the accuracy.

Like the prior techniques, distance metric learning is used in many domains such as matching hand-written text, face recognition, and matching biometric features. Thus, although we focus on multi-camera tracking, our technique may enable privacy-preserving matching in other domains as well.

2. We implement our technique in a distributed community surveillance system, presenting the first instance of privacy-preserving peer-to-peer multi-camera tracking system. Experiments show that the overhead of secure tracking is low, adding only a few seconds over non-private tracking.

2. BACKGROUND AND RELATED WORK

2.1 Privacy-Preserving Video Surveillance

To our knowledge, our work is the first one focusing on peer-to-peer privacy-preserving tracking over multiple cameras. Much previous effort has focused on privacy concerns with respect to

MM '14, November 03 - 07 2014, Orlando, FL, USA

http://dx.doi.org/10.1145/2647868.2655010

Table 1. Distance computation

	intermediate steps	circuits needed
1	$\mathbf{W}^T\hat{\mathbf{x}}_i$, $\mathbf{W}^T\hat{\mathbf{x}}_j$	(local computation)
2	$\mathbf{W}^T\hat{\mathbf{x}}_i - \mathbf{W}^T\hat{\mathbf{x}}_j$	q subtraction
3	$\Vert \mathbf{W}^T\hat{\mathbf{x}}_i - \mathbf{W}^T\hat{\mathbf{x}}_j \Vert^2$	q multiplication $q-1$ addition

the video surveillance without peer-to-peer multiple cameras collaboration [5][18][20]. Other techniques [1][17] are complementary to our effort and cannot be applied to multi-camera tracking in which cameras do not trust each other.

2.2 Secure Computation

Yao's garbled circuit (GC) approach provides a foundation to securely compute a function represented as a Boolean circuit [21]. References [12][14][15] show how these circuits are constructed efficiently. We implement secure matching using Huang et al.'s library [12] with the optimizations proposed by Kolesnikov et al. [14]. The complexity of each secure operation, i.e., the size of the garbled circuit, increases in the order of $O(n^2)$ for multiplication operation, while it increases linearly ($O(n)$) for other operations.

2.3 Object Matching Across Cameras

Matching function computes the distance between two feature vectors extracted from individual cameras to determine similarity. Recent computer vision algorithms employ machine learning approaches to "learn" a distance metric using training data [6][8][23]. We build on these works to show that 1) secure computation on these methods incurs high overhead, and 2) distance computation can be transformed such that its overhead is significantly lowered while accuracy is not impacted.

3. GARBLED CIRCUIT DISTANCE COMPUTATION (GCDC)

Multi-camera tracking involves matching objects seen by different cameras. Two cameras jointly evaluate a distance function $D(\hat{\mathbf{x}}_i, \hat{\mathbf{x}}_j)$ where $\hat{\mathbf{x}}_i$ and $\hat{\mathbf{x}}_j \in \mathbb{R}^r$ are the feature vectors extracted from the objects. If the distance is smaller than a threshold, the objects are deemed the same. The goal of metric learning is to learn a distance function $D(\cdot,\cdot)$ that can well-discriminate same objects and different objects by learning a projection matrix $\mathbf{W} \in \mathbb{R}^{r\times q}$, $q \le r$, which projects feature vectors onto a new space. Normally, Euclidean distance is computed after projection [6][23]. The computation is shown in Table 1. The complexity of the secure computation is determined only by the joint computation, which in this case involves subtraction, addition and multiplication. To avoid expensive multiplication operation, we propose a new distance metric learning technique, garbled circuit distance computation (GCDC), which uses histogram intersection instead of Euclidean distance to reduce the joint computation. Histogram intersection has been shown to be an effective metric in pattern recognition [22]. It is defined as

$$HI(\mathbf{h}_i, \mathbf{h}_j) = \sum_{k=1}^{q} min(h_i^k, h_j^k), \quad (1)$$

where $\mathbf{h}_i = [h_i^1 \dots h_i^q]^T \in \mathbb{R}_+^q$, $\mathbf{h}_j = [h_j^1 \dots h_j^q]^T \in \mathbb{R}_+^q$ are vectors with nonnegative entries. We define our distance function as:

$$D(\hat{\mathbf{x}}_i, \hat{\mathbf{x}}_j) = -HI(\mathbf{W}^T\hat{\mathbf{x}}_i + T\mathbf{1}, \mathbf{W}^T\hat{\mathbf{x}}_j + T\mathbf{1})$$

$$= -\sum_{k=1}^{q} min(\mathbf{w}_k{}^T\hat{\mathbf{x}}_i + T, \mathbf{w}_k{}^T\hat{\mathbf{x}}_j + T), \quad (2)$$

where $\mathbf{W} = [\mathbf{w}_1 \dots \mathbf{w}_q] \in \mathbb{R}^{r\times q}$, $q \le r$, and $T \ge 0$.

Table 2. Our GCDC computation

	intermediate steps	circuits needed
1	$\mathbf{W}^T\hat{\mathbf{x}}_i + T\mathbf{1}$, $\mathbf{W}^T\hat{\mathbf{x}}_j + T\mathbf{1}$	(local computation)
2	min(.)	q min operation
3	$\sum_{k=1}^{q}$ min(.)	$(q-1)$ addition

T is a predefined parameter that ensures the non-negativity of $\mathbf{w}_k{}^T\hat{\mathbf{x}}_i + T$ for any feature vector $\hat{\mathbf{x}}_i$. Note that although the value of $D(\cdot,\cdot)$ seems to be negative, we can add a positive scalar constant to make it a valid distance metric, without changing the formulation of our metric learning, so we discard the scalar in the following discussion. The complexity of $D(\cdot,\cdot)$ is shown in Table 2. Note that significant computation is local, and joint computation uses only simple operations (minimum and addition).

Just defining $D(\cdot,\cdot)$ is not enough. For it to be a valid approach, we also need an efficient way to learn $\mathbf{W}$. Our learning approach is motivated by [8]. Let $\mathbb{O}^p$ denote the positive training set consisting of matched feature vector pairs, and $\mathbb{O}^n$ denote the negative training set consisting of unmatched feature vector pairs. The goal is to learn a linear projection matrix, such that the pairs in set $\mathbb{O}^p$ have small distances, and the pairs in set $\mathbb{O}^n$ have large distances. Define a conditional distribution over points $i \ne j$ as

$$p^{\mathbf{W}}(j|i) = \frac{e^{-D(\hat{\mathbf{x}}_i, \hat{\mathbf{x}}_j)}}{\sum_{k\ne i} e^{-D(\hat{\mathbf{x}}_i, \hat{\mathbf{x}}_k)}} \qquad i \ne j. \quad (3)$$

Ideally, if all the pairs in set $\mathbb{O}^p$ have small distance, and all the pairs in set $\mathbb{O}^n$ have large distances, the distribution would become "bi-level", that is,

$$p_0(j|i) \propto \begin{cases} 1 & if\ (\hat{\mathbf{x}}_i, \hat{\mathbf{x}}_j) \in \mathbb{O}^p \\ 0 & if\ (\hat{\mathbf{x}}_i, \hat{\mathbf{x}}_j) \in \mathbb{O}^n \end{cases} \quad (4)$$

Therefore, the first cost function $f_1(\mathbf{W})$ same as [8] is defined as

$$f_1(\mathbf{W}) = \sum_i KL[p_0(j|i)|p^{\mathbf{W}}(j|i)]$$

$$= \sum_i \sum_{j\ne i} p_0(j|i) \times log(\frac{p_0(j|i)}{p^{\mathbf{W}}(j|i)}), \quad (5)$$

where $KL[\cdot|\cdot]$ is K-L divergence that measures the distance between two distributions.

We further introduce a regularization term $f_2(\mathbf{W})$ to bound the values of $\mathbf{W}^T\hat{\mathbf{x}}_i$ in such a way that we can always find a nonnegative scalar T to make all the entries in $\mathbf{W}^T\hat{\mathbf{x}}_i + T\mathbf{1}$ nonnegative for all i.

$$f_2(\mathbf{W}) = \sum_{k=1}^{q} \mathbf{w}_k{}^T\mathbf{w}_k = Tr(\mathbf{W}^T\mathbf{W}) \quad (6)$$

Moreover, to satisfy the equality of self-distance, that is,

$$D(\hat{\mathbf{x}}_k, \hat{\mathbf{x}}_k) = D(\hat{\mathbf{x}}_l, \hat{\mathbf{x}}_l) \qquad \forall\ k \ne l \quad (7)$$

an additional term $f_3(\mathbf{W})$ is added,

$$f_3(\mathbf{W}) = \sum_i (\sum_{k=1}^{q} \mathbf{w}_k{}^T\hat{\mathbf{x}}_i)^2 \quad (8)$$

The final objective is the sum of the three terms above:

$$J(\mathbf{W}) = f_1(\mathbf{W}) + f_2(\mathbf{W}) + f_3(\mathbf{W}) \quad (9)$$

The metric learning problem is formulated as finding $\mathbf{W}$ that minimizes the objective function $J(\mathbf{W})$. Gradient descent method is employed to solve the optimization problem. After $\mathbf{W}$ is learned, distance between two objects can be evaluated. There is a match if the value is smaller than a predefined threshold. For more detailed derivation, please refer to [4].

(a) (b)

Figure 1. Examples of the snapshots in the database. (a) the same person under different cameras. (b) the same car under different cameras.

4. sTrack: DESIGN & IMPLEMENTATION

Our system is developed as an application on top of HomeOS [7]. Each site (i.e., camera) in sTrack is configured with information about its peer sites for object matching. This information includes the peer's location relative to the site and how to contact it (IP address and port) for matching requests. Each site independently tracks objects' information within its own view, including location, entry/exit timestamps, and features.

We employ state of the art computer vision algorithms for single camera tracking, including background subtraction, Kalman filtering, and kernel tracking [4]. Each camera performs tracking as above and stores entry and exit time stamps, tracking history, and feature vectors of all the objects in its own local database. This information is used when the camera performs the evaluation of the matching function between a local object and objects captured by other cameras. As in [23], we divide an object into six horizontal regions. In each region, the color histograms of RGB, YCbCr, and HSV color spaces are extracted. Each channel has 16 bins, and the histograms are concatenated into the feature vector in a 864-dimension feature space. One can, if needed, include more features, e.g., texture, edge features or even biometric features like faces, to enhance accuracy, and our proposed metric learning method can be applied without change.

When an object enters the view of Site A, the feature vector is extracted, and the matching process is initialized against all peer sites. (We currently issue match requests for all objects entering the view; in the future, it could be limited to suspicious objects such as those that have never been seen before or those specified by users.) For these processes, we term the initiator of the process (Site A) as the client and other sites as servers. Each server performs a match against each object that appeared in the server's view within a 10 minute window. The window size can be determined based on the user's interest or the prior knowledge about the topology of the cameras.

We implement our secure computation, including distance function and thresholding, using Huang et al.'s library [12]. The details can be found in [4]. The output (obtained by both parties) is a binary value indicating if the client's object matched against any of the server's objects. No other information is leaked between sites. Matching outcomes allow Site A to learn where the object came from. Match requests can also be issued sometime after the object exits the camera's view, to learn where the object goes. We do not implement this currently and instead rely on incoming match requests from peers to learn this information. Based on the results of the match requests, each site can independently infer the activity pattern of suspicious objects.

5. EXPERIMENTAL RESULTS

5.1 GCDC Accuracy

First, we conduct offline testing by using four real datasets to compare GCDC and other metric learning techniques [8][23] in terms of matching accuracy and secure computation overhead. We use two public datasets, VIPeR [9] and i-LIDS [19], and two of our own datasets, which we call *human dataset* and *car dataset*. Fig. 1 shows some example images. For each dataset, in each trial

Table 3. Complexity and accuracy summary table

VIPeR dataset	Non-XOR gates	AUC
PRDC	499,623	0.8515
PRDC_woABS	579	0.7468
MCC	10,298	0.9059
GCDC	1,778	0.9017
iLIDS dataset		
PRDC	499,623	0.8151
PRDC_woABS	579	0.6404
MCC	11,022	0.8697
GCDC	1,902	0.8653
human dataset		
PRDC	379,902	0.8473
PRDC_woABS	2,175	0.7643
MCC	10,009	0.9062
GCDC	1,729	0.9272
car dataset		
PRDC	379,902	0.8877
PRDC_woABS	579	0.8395
MCC	7,831	0.9471
GCDC	1,351	0.9567

we randomly select 80 objects (68 for our car dataset) as the training set to learn the parameters in offline training stage, and randomly select 15 objects as the testing set. The two sets do not overlap. We evaluate the matching functions against 15 objects based on the learned parameters. In real settings, a camera may capture objects at a faster (slower) rate if pointed at a busy (quite) street. We use 15 to represent a moderately busy street. We report the average of ten trials for each dataset.

We use AUC (Area Under Curve) of Receiver Operational Characteristic (ROC) curve as the accuracy evaluation metric. The complexity of the secure computation is determined by the number of non XOR gates in the garbled circuits [14][15]. Table 3 shows the comparison for different matching functions. PRDC_woABS [23] has the minimum number of non XOR gates for three datasets but has very poor accuracy. We thus do not consider it to be a viable method. Both PRDC [23] and MCC [8] provide accurate matching. GCDC has similarly high accuracy and even outperforms PRDC and MCC for two datasets. Non-XOR gates for GCDC is on average 261x and 6x fewer than PRDC and MCC, respectively. In retrospect, this result is not surprising; those previous approaches were not designed with secure computation in mind. Thus, we conclude that GCDC is promising for secure object matching. Readers can refer to [4] where the details of implementation and analysis are provided.

5.2 sTrack Performance

Unlike the offline testing in Section 5.1 where the well-cropped images are used, here we quantify the end-to-end accuracy of our system which includes inaccuracies due to imperfect object extraction/tracking in each camera's view. For this experiment, we use the video clips from our datasets with total length 47 minutes as the input to our system. The system has two sites, and each site is fed the video gathered by one of the cameras in the datasets. As in the actual system, each site performs independently single camera tracking within its own view and store objects' information in its local database. The sites perform object matching using the parameters learned in offline training. Fig. 2 shows the matching accuracy. Compared to offline testing, we see that there is only a slight loss in accuracy due to errors in within-camera tracking.

We now benchmark the performance of secure matching. For this benchmark, we use two relatively cheap and weak computers

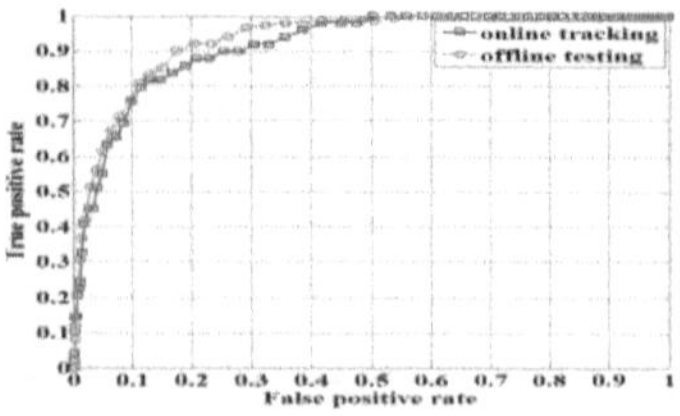

Figure 2. Online tracking accuracy.

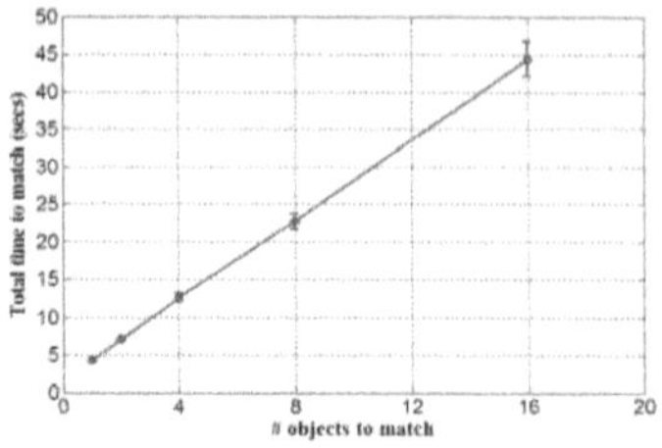

Figure 3. Mean and standard deviation of the time to securely match objects.

on purpose, Windows 8 netbooks with 1 GHz processor and 2 GB memory. We expect that many camera sites will not be equipped with a powerful computer and will instead use small, headless PCs or embedded processors like smart cameras. Using a network emulator, we introduce a round-trip network delay of 100 ms between the netbooks to mimic real-world situations in which sites may not have low-latency network paths between them. We measure the total time from the client issuing the match request to it recovering the results of the match. Thus, this time includes the time for initial handshake in which the client learns about the ports on which the server processes are running and the time to start client and server processes. We conduct ten different trials with each number of objects and plot the mean and standard deviation across those trials. Fig. 3 shows the results as a function of the number of objects against which a match is performed (i.e., the number of objects that the server saw in the specified time window). We see that the time to securely match objects increases linearly with the number of objects. For single-object matches, the time is roughly 4 seconds. For matching 4-16 objects, the total time is roughly 3 seconds per match. Thus, even if as many as 20 objects need to be matched, it will complete in under a minute.

This level of performance, which was obtained on relatively weak computers, can lead to a practical, real-time surveillance system. Consider the following back-of-the-envelope analysis. Let the community be such that one new object enters every X minutes on average, each camera needs to consult N neighbors, and that the time period of interest is Y minutes. In this community, a camera will issue $\frac{N}{X}$ requests per minute for matching, where each request will involve $\frac{Y}{X}$ object matches. Thus, a camera needs to perform $2 \times \frac{Y}{X} \times \frac{N}{X}$ matches per minute. The factor of two is due to the fact that a camera will answer match requests as well. With $X = 5$, $N = 10$, $Y = 10$ in a normal community neighborhood, it results in 8 matches per minute, well within the performance of our system.

6. CONCLUSION

We presented a system, sTrack, that embodies a set of techniques for tracking objects across cameras without leaking any visual information other than the binary matching result. It is based on a new distance metric learning approach that, compared to state-of-art approaches, has 6-200 times lower overhead and similar or better matching accuracy. Experiments show that the performance overhead of private tracking is moderate, taking around 3 seconds even on a netbook. Distance metric learning is a powerful approach for matching in a range of domains (e.g., face recognition, biometric matching, etc); we hope our work will spur privacy-preserving matching in all such domains. For more details about this work, please refer to [4].

7. REFERENCES

[1] S. Avidan and M. Butman, "Blind vision," *ECCV*, May, 2006.

[2] A.J. Brush, J. Jung, R. Mahajan, and F. Martinez, "Digital Neighborhood Watch: Investigating the Sharing of Camera Data amongst Neighbors", *CSCW*, Feb 2013.

[3] C. Chu and J. Hwang, "Fully unsupervised learning of camera link models for tracking humans across nonoverlapping cameras," *IEEE Transactions on Circuits and Systems for Video Technology*, 2014.

[4] C. Chu, J. Jung, Z. Liu and R. Mahajan, "sTrack: Secure Tracking in Community Surveillance," *Microsoft Research, TechReport, MSR-TR-2014-7*, 2014.

[5] Y. Chen, C. Chu, J. Hwang, and J. Yoo, "A privacy-preserving human tracking scheme in centralized cloud based camera network," *IEEE Conf. on Communications*, 2014.

[6] M. Dikmen, E. Akbas, T. S. Huang, and N. Ahuja, "Pedestrian recognition with a learned metric," *ACCV*, 2010.

[7] C. Dixon, R. Mahajan, S. Agarwal, A.J. Brush, B. Lee, S. Saroiu, and P. Bahl, "An operating system for the home," *Proc. NSDI*, 2012.

[8] A. Globerson and R. Roweis, "Metric learning by collapsing classes," *Proc. NIPS*, 2005.

[9] D. Gray, S. Brennan, and H. Tao, "Evaluating Appearance Models for Recognition, Reacquisition, and Tracking," *Proc. IEEE International Workshop on Performance Evaluation for Tracking and Surveillance (PETS)*, October, 2007.

[10] http://www.videosurveillance.com/neighborhoods.asp. Last accessed in Aug 2014.

[11] http://www.sfgate.com/crime/article/Oakland-hills-residents-fight-crime-with-cameras-3687341.php. Last accessed in Aug 2014.

[12] Y. Huang, D. Evans, J. Katz, and L. Malka, "Faster secure two-party computation using garbled circuits," *20th USENIX Security Symposium*, Aug, 2011.

[13] O. Javed, K. Shafique, and M. Shah, "Appearance modeling for tracking in multiple non-overlapping cameras," *CVPR*, 2005.

[14] V. Kolesnikov, A.-R. Sadeghi, and T. Schneider, "Improved Garbled Circuit Building Blocks and Applications to Auctions and Computing Minima", *Proc. CANS* 2009.

[15] V. Kolesnikov and T. Schneider, "Improved garbled circuit: Free XOR gates and applications", *Proc. ICALP*, 2008.

[16] B. Kreuter, a. shelat, and C.-H. Shen, "Billion-Gate Secure Computation with Malicious Adversaries", *Proc. USENIX Security*, 2012.

[17] M. Osadchy, B. Pinkas, A. Jarrous, and B. Moskovich, "SCiFI-A system for secure face identification," *IEEE Symposium on Security and Privacy*, 2010.

[18] A. Senior, S. Pankanti, A. Hampapur, L. Brown, Y.-L. Tian, A. Ekin, J. Connell, C. F. Shu, and M. Lu, "Enabling Video Privacy through Computer Vision", *IEEE Security and Privacy*, 2005.

[19] UK Home Office, "The Image Library for Intelligent Detection Systems (i-LIDS): Multiple Camera Tracking (MCT)," 2008.

[20] M. Upmanyu, A. M. Namboodiri, K. Srinathan, and C.V. Jawahar, "Efficient Privacy Preserving Video Surveillance", *IEEE Proc. Intl. Conf. on Computer Vision (ICCV)*, 2009.

[21] A. C. Yao, "How to Generate and Exchange Secrets", *Proc. Foundations of Computer Science*, 1986.

[22] W. Zhang, S. Shan, W. Gao, X. Chen, and H. Zhang, "Local gabor binary pattern histogram sequence (lgbphs): A novel non-statistical model for face representation and recognition," *Proc. ICCV*, 2005.

[23] W. Zheng, S. Gong, and T. Xiang, "Person re-identification by probabilistic relative distance comparison," *Proc. CVPR*, 2011.

Searching for Recent Celebrity Images in Microblog Platform

Na Zhao[†], Richang Hong[†], Meng Wang[†], Xuegang Hu[†], Tat-Seng Chua[‡]
[†] School of Computer and Information, Hefei University of Technology
[‡] School of Computing, National University of Singapore
zhaona311@gmail.com, hongrc@hfut.edu.cn, eric.mengwang@gmail.com, jsjxhuxg@hfut.edu.cn, chuats@comp.nus.edu.sg

ABSTRACT

With the explosive growth and widespread accessibility of image content in social media, many users are eagerly searching for most recent and relevant images on topics of their interests. However, most current microblog platforms merely make use of textual information, specifically, keywords, for image search which cannot achieve satisfactory results since in most cases image content is inconsistent with textual content. In this paper we tackle this problem under the application of searching for celebrity image. The proposed method is based on the idea of refining the initial text-based search results by utilizing multimedia plus social information. Given a text search query, we first obtain an initial text-based result. Next, we extract a seed tweet set whose images contain faces recognized as celebrities and texts contain the expanded keywords. Third, we extend the seed set based on visual and user information. Lastly, we employ a multi-modal graph based learning method to properly rank the obtained tweets by integrating social and visual information. Extensive experiments on data collected from Tencent Weibo demonstrate that our proposed method could approximately achieve 3-fold improvement in results as compared to the text baseline, typically used in microblog search service.

Categories and Subject Descriptors

H.3.3 [**Information Search and Retrieval**]: Search process

Keywords

Microblog Image Search; Social Content; Visual Content; Graph Learning

1. INTRODUCTION

In recent years, social media has undergone a rapid development. Among the social media, microblog platforms have attracted the most attention, and have been used as daily tools to acquire prevailing information. As a result, information search especially image search in microblog plays a more and more important role due to the availability of large amount of images uploaded by users every day.

Generally, users pay more attention to fresh information. Hence current microblog platforms, like Twitter and Tencent Weibo, provide a "most recent" image search service by ordering the resultant images in chronological order. However, there are two key problems with the current services. One is that they just perform retrieval based on text content which is frequently inconsistent with its associated image. According to statistic in [4], only 30% of tweets have the consistency between textual and image information. As a result, a large number of resultant images are irrelevant. Take Tecent Weibo as an example, if we input "Kai-Fu Lee"[1] as a query for image search, among the top 5 returned results sorted in time sequence, only one image tweet is really relevant, as shown by the red box in Figure 1(a). The other problem is that when ranking the returned images, they just take time factor into account while ignoring the relevance of images. But for users, they care both recency and relevance. From the above, we can see that currently available text based image search service in microblog is far from satisfactory. In addition, by performing analysis of large-scale query logs and supplemental qualitative data, Teevan et al. [6] demonstrated that people are more interested with queries of celebrity names in microblog search. Therefore, in this paper we tackle these two problems in most recent microblog image search with celebrity queries.

There have been many works devoted to conducting image search. Image search engines like Google Image Search offer the service based on the textual information in web page instead of the real visual content. In recent years, content based image retrieval has become popular and it supports the use of image as the query like in [5] but the obtained results are only similar to the exact input image and the appearance variation is not accounted for. More recently, multimedia information has been utilized for image search by combining ink, textual, and visual information for image search result clustering and found to be helpful in [2]. Different from web image search, text in microblog is always noisy and the textual content is frequently inconsistent with visual content [4]. On the other hand, we can take advantage of some specific features like *Mention* and *Hashtag* for better performance. To search for images related to celebrities, face recognition is intuitively the most effective method.

MM'14, August 24–27, 2014, New York, NY, USA.

http://dx.doi.org/10.1145/2647868.2655011.

[1]It corresponds to "李开复" in simplified Chinese.

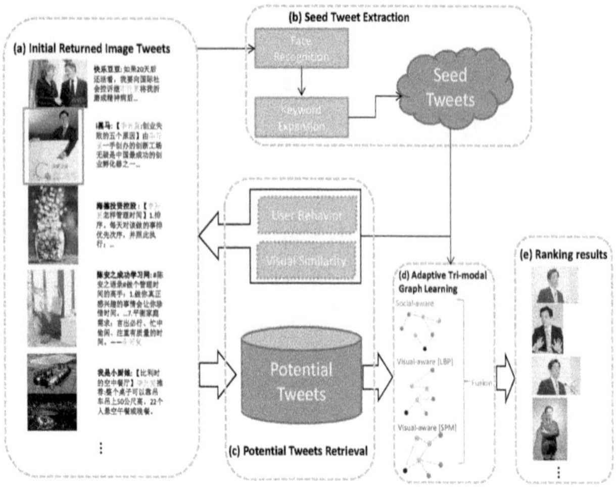

Figure 1: The framework of our proposed method.

However, although the most recent face recognition work can achieve a high accuracy [3], it will fail frequently when used on images in microblog as those images are usually fuzzy, in low resolution and with small faces or side-view faces. Besides, there are many images where no face shows up but the back of celebrity can be clearly identified. For such images, face recognition cannot work.

In this work we propose a novel approach to search for recent celebrity images in microblog. To our knowledge, there is no existing work that deal with this problem. Taking recency and relevance into account, we incorporate textual, social and visual information into the proposed approach. Based on the initial text based search results, face recognition is first conducted. To complement the limited accuracy of face recognition, we extract extended keywords to generate more highly relevant tweets called *seed tweets*. Then we extend seed tweet set to gather more potential tweets by utilizing user behavior and visual similarity. To rank all the obtained seed and potential tweets, we adopt a tri-modal graph-based learning algorithm to adaptively integrate social and visual information which are expressed in three modalities: social-aware and two visual-aware modalities with two different visual features. Finally, we evaluate the proposed method on a real-world dataset containing 0.1 million microblogs of 100 different person names crawled from Tencent Weibo. To ensure efficiency, we limit the computation in the initial text-based results. Experimental results demonstrate that we could approximately achieve three-fold improvement as compared to the text-based results.

2. THE PROPOSED METHOD

2.1 Seed Tweet Extraction

In order to search for the most recent and relevant images of celebrities in microblog, our first step is to extract a set of seed tweets whose images are regarded as highly related to this celebrity. Given a text query with the name of the celebrity using the "most recent" ranking option, microblog platform returns search results in chronological order. We denote the results as $T_o = \{T_1, ..., T_n\}$ where each T_i is a tweet. As we can see in Figure 1(a), a high proportion of returned images are irrelevant as the search criteria is text based. To obtain a set of seed tweets where the results are mostly relevant, we adopt a two step scheme consisting of face recognition and keyword expansion.

During offline training process of face recognition, we collected images containing celebrity faces by Google Image Search. To crop the face from images as positive samples, we employ face detection as proposed in [1]. Subsequently we implement the Eigenfaces algorithm [8] for training the face recognition model. Thus, given a tweet image, face recognition is run to verify whether it is the celebrity. Then the tweet images likely to contain the celebrity faces are kept as part of seed set, denoted as T_f. How T_f is related to the celebrity depends on the face recognition performance. However, in our work, the average precision of face recognition has just reached 75.8% and the average recall is only 46.52% which are not good enough to identify all the highly relevant tweets in T_o.

Therefore we need to do filtering on T_f in order to remove those false positives. Here we propose a text based method based on keyword expansion technique. To generate expanding keywords, we compute the frequency of each word in T_f. The top N frequent words which are not in stop word set are chosen as the expanded keywords. The tweets among T_f containing the expanded keywords are set as the seed tweets which we denote as T_s. According to experiments, the average accuracy of T_s is 85.6%. T_s contains highly relevant images but it covers only a small fraction of images related to the celebrity because many relevant images are not searchable by current set of keywords; and face recognition often fails to detect faces or recognize the detected face correctly.

2.2 Potential Tweets Retrieval

In this section, we extend the seed tweets to include more possibly relevant tweets. To efficiently obtain more relevant tweets, we analyze the seed tweets from two aspects. First, we identify the behavior pattern of users. The users who posted more than k number of seed tweets are selected as active users. Here we set k to 2 as the set T_s is small. We set all the tweets posted by active users, denoted as T_u, as one part of potential tweet set. Meanwhile, the visual information is also taken into account. We respectively calculate visual distance between every seed image and images in T_o and add the top K similar images, denoted as T_v, to the potential tweet set. Here we employ Euclidean distance on image features which will be detailed at Section 2.4. Finally, we obtain the final potential tweet set, denoted as $T_p(T_p = T_u \bigcup T_v)$.

2.3 Adaptive Tri-modal Graph Learning Algorithm

Having obtained the seed set T_s and the expanded potential set T_p, the next step is to rank these tweets according to the relevance to the celebrity. Here we propose a tri-modal graph learning algorithm to adaptively integrate visual and social information.

First, we assume that there are m tweets in $\mathcal{T}(T_s \bigcup T_p)$, $\mathcal{T} = \{t_1, t_2, \ldots, t_m\}$, and the relevance score vector of $\mathcal{T}$ is $\mathbf{r} = [r_1, r_2, \ldots, r_m]^{\mathrm{T}}$. Next a graph-based ranking framework is used to predict whether the tweets in $\mathcal{T}$ are relevant to the input celebrity. This problem is formulated as minimizing the following cost function [7]

$$\mathcal{Q}(\mathbf{r}) = \mathcal{R}_{NLap}(\mathbf{r}, \mathcal{T}) + \sigma \times \mathcal{D}(\mathbf{r}, \bar{\mathbf{r}}). \quad (1)$$

The two terms on the right side of equation (1) respectively represent the regularization term that maintains visual consistency and the distance term that measures the difference between ranking score list and original ranking list. Here σ is a scaling parameter for modulating the effect of distance. $\bar{\mathbf{r}} = [\bar{r}_1, \bar{r}_2, \dots, \bar{r}_m]^{\mathrm{T}}$ is the initial ranking score list.

There are usually two forms for regularization term: graph Laplacian regularizer and normalized graph Laplacian regularizer. Here we utilize the latter as Tian et al. [7] verified its effectiveness over graph Laplacian:

$$\mathcal{R}_{NLap}(\mathbf{r}, \mathcal{T}) = \sum_{i,j=1}^{n} W_{ij} \parallel \frac{r_i}{d_{ii}} - \frac{r_j}{d_{jj}} \parallel^2 = \mathbf{r}^T L_n \mathbf{r}, \qquad (2)$$

where $L_n = \mathbf{D}^{-1/2}(\mathbf{D}-\mathbf{W})\mathbf{D}^{-1/2}$ is the normalized Laplacian matrix. Here $\mathbf{W}$ is a similarity matrix in which W_{ij} indicates the similarity of t_i and t_j, and $\mathbf{D}$ is a diagonal matrix with $d_{ii} = \sum_j W_{ij}$.

We estimate the similarity between the i-th and j-th tweets with a Mahalanobis distance metric which takes into account the correlations of the data set and can be learned by an optimization framework:

$$W_{ij} = \exp(-(t_i - t_j)^{\mathrm{T}}\mathbf{S}(t_i - t_j)) = \exp(-||\mathbf{M}(t_i - t_j)||^2), \quad (3)$$

where $\mathbf{S}$ is a symmtric positive semi-definite real matrix, which can be decomposed as $\mathbf{S} = \mathbf{M}^{\mathrm{T}}\mathbf{M}$. Here we denote $\mathbf{M}$ as a d-by-d diagonal matrix. Then equation (3) is equivalent to transforming each tweet t_i to $\mathbf{M}t_i$.

In order to integrate visual and social information into this graph learning framework, we regard each feature description of the tweet, such as visual or social feature, as a modality. Hence, according to extracted feature described in Section 2.4, there are three different modalities: two kinds of visual aware modalities and one social aware modality. Then we consider integrating different modalities to model adaptive multiple graph learning. In this work, we linearly combine the normalized graph Laplacian regularizers of the three modalities:

$$\begin{aligned}\mathcal{R}_{NLap}(\mathbf{r}, \mathcal{T}, \lambda) = &\sum_{i,j} \lambda_1 W_{ij}^s \parallel \frac{r_i}{d_{ii}^s} - \frac{r_j}{d_{jj}^s} \parallel^2 + \sum_{i,j} \lambda_2 W_{ij}^l \parallel \frac{r_i}{d_{ii}^l} - \frac{r_j}{d_{jj}^l} \parallel^2 \\ &+ \sum_{i,j} \lambda_3 W_{ij}^v \parallel \frac{r_i}{d_{ii}^v} - \frac{r_j}{d_{jj}^v} \parallel^2 + \varphi \parallel \lambda \parallel^2,\end{aligned} \qquad (4)$$

where $W_{ij}^k = \exp(-||\mathbf{M}^k(t_i^k - t_j^k)||^2)$. Here the first term of right side of equation (4) is the social aware modality while the second (LBP) and third (SPM) are the visual aware modalities. The last term is used to adaptively modulate the impacts of these three modalities. λ_k is the weight for each modality, it satisfies $0 \leq \lambda_k \leq 1$ and $\sum_{k=1}^{3} \lambda_k = 1$. φ is a coefficient to learn the weights.

As for distance term in the cost function, we choose squared loss term as it can easily solve the optimization framework. Accordingly, the cost function can be formulated as the following form:

$$\begin{aligned}\mathcal{Q}(\mathbf{r}, \lambda) = &\sum_{i,j} \lambda_1 W_{ij}^s \parallel \frac{r_i}{d_{ii}^s} - \frac{r_j}{d_{jj}^s} \parallel^2 + \sum_{i,j} \lambda_2 W_{ij}^l \parallel \frac{r_i}{d_{ii}^l} - \frac{r_j}{d_{jj}^l} \parallel^2 \\ &+ \sum_{i,j} \lambda_3 W_{ij}^v \parallel \frac{r_i}{d_{ii}^v} - \frac{r_j}{d_{jj}^v} \parallel^2 + \sigma \parallel \mathbf{r} - \bar{\mathbf{r}} \parallel^2 + \varphi \parallel \lambda \parallel^2 .\end{aligned} \qquad (5)$$

For equation (5), we adopt an alternating optimization method to solve it, which is analogous to the solution in [9].

2.4 Tweet Features

For each image tweet, we extract the following two sets of features:

1) Social features.
- 6-dimensional social features. The features include 3-dimensional relationship features (whether the tweet poster is a followee, follower or friend of the target person), the related mention feature (indicated by a "@" symbol to explicitly address the target person in the tweets), the related hashtag feature (tags surrounded with # symbol to indicate discussed topics about the target person), and the URLs presence feature.

2) Visual features.
- 11,564-dimensional LBP features. We first resize each image into 64×64 pixels. Then we extract local binary pattern (LBP) histograms from it and concatenated them into a single, spatially enhanced feature histogram efficiently representing the whole image.
- 21,504-dimensional SPM features. The SIFT features are extracted from densely located patches centered at every 6 pixels on each image and the size of the patches is fixed as 16×16 pixels. We construct a visual word dictionary containing 1024 words from the training samples via K-means clustering. Each SIFT feature vector is encoded into a 1024-dimensional code vector via vector quantization. Then the code vector from each image are pooled into a 21,504-dimensional feature vector in a spatial pyramid manner.

3. EXPERIMENTS

3.1 Experimental Settings

In this work, we demonstrate the performance of the proposed method by using Tencent Weibo, China's leading microblogging service. As we focus on celebrity image search, we selected Top 100 names based on Celebrity Popularity List which ranked by number of followers. These celebrities include actors, musicians, politicians, athletes and so on. We then used image search function of Tencent using the celebrity names as queries with "most recent" ranking option to collect the image tweets as well as their associated user relationship information for the period from 1th March to 30th June 2012. Due to the insufficiency of returned results for some queries, we discarded these queries. Finally, we obtained a dataset consisting of 80 names, 125,900 image tweets and 23,481,896 user relationship pairs. As there is no ground truth for our dataset, each image is annotated by three volunteers with a three level of relevance, using the scores of 0,1,2 to respectively denote very relevant, relevant, and irrelevant images.

In our method, there are two parameters, i.e., φ and σ (equation(5)). To study the effect of the two parameters, we set up a tuning dataset by randomly selecting a subset from the dataset. The tuning set contains 8 names. As there should be no overlap between tuning set and testing set, we define the tweets from the remaining names as testing set.

To construct face model of face recognition, for each query we respectively crawled 800 images as the positive samples and 1000 images as negative samples from Google. These images were all preprocessed by face detection to produce face images. Since the average precision of face detection method is about 71.04%, we artificially removed those false detected results so as to build superior face models.

In order to measure the performance of our method, we adopted Mean Average Precision (MAP) which is a standard evaluation criterion in information retrieval.

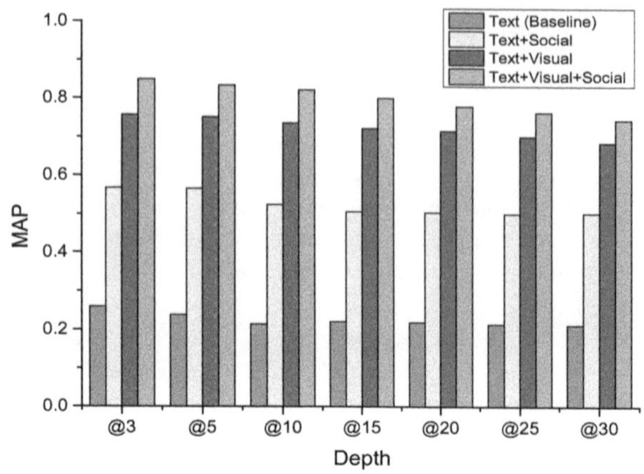

Figure 2: Comparison of the MAP@N measurement for results obtained by different methods.

3.2 Experimental results

In this section, we compare our proposed approach that integrates visual and social information into initial text-based results with the methods that only leverage one kind of information. We consider the text-based search result as the baseline, denoted as "Text"; and we use "Text+Visual" to denote the method that leverages visual information containing two kinds of visual features described in Section 2.4. Similarly, "Text+Social" is used to denote the method that leverages social information. Finally, "Text+Visual+Social" represents our proposed method.

We first compare the MAP measures with different depth of these methods. Figure 2 illustrates the MAP@3, MAP@5, MAP@10, MAP@15, MAP@20, MAP@25, MAP@30 measurements obtained by these methods in testing set. From the figure we can see that all the methods achieve encouraging improvements as compared to the baseline. Moreover, the "Text+Visual+Social" approach consistently and substantially achieves better performance than "Text+Social" and "Text+Visual" methods. From these results, we can conclude that visual and social information are both helpful for searching the most recent and relevant images. Furthermore, we observe that our proposed method is able to improve the MAP metric twice or thrice as compared to the baseline.

Next we compare the most recent results obtained by different methods. The top 5 results for an example query "An Yixuan" are demonstrated in Figure 3. The first row shows the most recent images in the initial text-based ranking list, where most of them are irrelevant. From the second and third rows, we can observe that the obtained results by "Text+Social", "Text+Visual" methods have been improved to different degrees. However, they still contain at least one irrelevant image in the top 5 results. The last row ranked by our proposed method obtains the best performance in which the most recent top 5 images are all relevant.

Figure 3: Top 5 results obtained by Baseline and different methods for the example query "An Yixuan". The relevant images are labeled by red rectangle box.

4. CONCLUSIONS

In this work, we proposed an effective framework to tackle the problem of recent celebrity image search in microblog. Face recognition and expanded keywords matching were employed to generate a seed tweet set based on which more potential tweets were gathered by using user behavior and visual similarity. To rank these tweets, a tri-modal graph learning method was used. In this way, our method successfully integrated textual, visual and social information. Experimental results on a real life dataset from Tencent Weibo demonstrated the effectiveness of our proposed approach.

Acknowledge

This work was partially supported by the State Key Development Program of the Basic Research Program of China (grant 2013CB336500) and NUS-Tsinghua Extreme Search (NExT) project (grant R-252-300-001-490).

5. REFERENCES

[1] Y. Abramson, B. Steux, and H. Ghorayeb. Yet even faster (yef) real-time object detection. *IJISTA*, 2(2):102–112, 2007.

[2] D. Cai, X. He, Z. Li, W.-Y. Ma, and J.-R. Wen. Hierarchical clustering of www image search results using visual, textual and link information. In *Proceedings of MM*, pages 952–959. ACM, 2004.

[3] H. Fan, Z. Cao, Y. Jiang, Q. Yin, and C. Doudou. Learning deep face representation. *arXiv*, 2014.

[4] Y. Gao, F. Wang, H. Luan, and T.-S. Chua. Brand data gathering from social media streams. In *Proceedings of ICMR*. ACM, 2014.

[5] J. Sivic and A. Zisserman. Video google: A text retrieval approach to object matching in videos. In *Proceedings of ICCV*, volume 2, pages 1470–1477, 2003.

[6] J. Teevan, D. Ramage, and M. R. Morris. # twittersearch: a comparison of microblog search and web search. In *WSDM*, pages 35–44. ACM, 2011.

[7] X. Tian, L. Yang, J. Wang, Y. Yang, X. Wu, and X.-S. Hua. Bayesian video search reranking. In *Proceedings of MM*, pages 131–140. ACM, 2008.

[8] M. A. Turk and A. P. Pentland. Face recognition using eigenfaces. In *CVPR*, pages 586–591. IEEE, 1991.

[9] M. Wang, H. Li, D. Tao, K. Lu, and X. Wu. Multimodal graph-based reranking for web image search. *TIP*, 21(11):4649–4661, 2012.

Organizing Video Search Results to Adapted Semantic Hierarchies for Topic-based Browsing

Jiajun Wang[1], Yu-Gang Jiang[1], Qiang Wang[1], Kuiyuan Yang[2], Chong-Wah Ngo[3]
[1]School of Computer Science, Shanghai Key Laboratory of Intelligent Information Processing, Fudan University, Shanghai, China
[2]Microsoft Research Asia, Beijing, China
[3]Department of Computer Science, City University of Hong Kong, Hong Kong, China
{jiajunwang13, ygj, qiangwang}@fudan.edu.cn,
kuyang@microsoft.com, cscwngo@cityu.edu.hk

ABSTRACT

Organizing video search results into semantically structured hierarchies can greatly improve the efficiency of browsing complex query topics. Traditional hierarchical clustering techniques are inadequate since they lack the ability to generate semantically interpretable structures. In this paper, we introduce an approach to organize video search results to an adapted semantic hierarchy. As many hot search topics such as celebrities and famous cities have Wikipedia pages where hierarchical topic structures are available, we start from the Wikipedia hierarchies and adjust the structures according to the characteristics of the returned videos from a search engine. Ordinary clustering based on textual information of the videos is performed to discover the hidden topic structures in the video search results, which are used to adapt the hierarchy extracted from Wikipedia. After that, a simple optimization problem is formulated to assign the videos to each node of the hierarchy considering three important criteria. Experiments conducted on a Youtube video dataset verify the effectiveness of our approach.

Categories and Subject Descriptors

H.3.3 [**Information Storage and Retrieval**]: Information Search and Retrieval

Keywords

Search result organization, video search, hierarchical structure, hierarchy adaptation.

1. INTRODUCTION

Existing Web video search engines, such as the YouTube, return video ranking list given a specific query, which is acceptable if the users only want to find a single video like a movie trailer or an MTV. But when the query is a complex topic with hidden structures, finding or understanding different aspects of the topic based on a long list of videos is time-consuming, and often is impossible with a single search. For example, when a user searches for "Steven Spielberg", he/she may want to know the career of the director, his personal life, his achievements and so on. In this case, a hierarchical organization of the videos with nodes covering the aforementioned facets is a much better choice.

In the domain of *reorganizing* search results, a popular method is to cluster the results into several units or groups [14, 7, 3]. Although clustering is a good way to capture the hidden facets of a complex topic, a major drawback is that, without an overall semantic structure, even a set of well-extracted clusters may appear messy to the users, let alone clusters without proper human-readable labels.

Hierarchical clustering is slightly better than the traditional *flat* clustering, and has been adopted to build a hierarchical structure [1, 2]. However, no matter agglomerative or divisive, hierarchical clustering lacks the ability to create a semantically cohesive topic structure due to the noise in Web contents. Prototype-based hierarchical clustering (PHC) [9] is a method proposed to overcome this disadvantage. By clustering on the basis of a predefined prototype hierarchy, PHC can ensure the semantic cohesiveness of the hierarchy, but the prototype hierarchy need to be adapted to better befit the video domain.

Near-duplicate video search has also been widely applied to group visually similar videos, which is weakly related to this work. In [13, 5, 12], the authors focused on mining topic structures with near-duplicate search in news videos, since there could be a large amount of near-duplicates on the Internet when a breaking news event happens. However, when the search topic extends beyond news events, near-duplicate search becomes not so useful, but still can serve as a tool to remove content redundancy in the search results.

In this paper, we propose an approach to organize the ranking lists from video search to a semantic hierarchy for efficient browsing, which combines the advantages of both the traditional clustering techniques and the PHC. The entire process is illustrated in Figure 1. First, we cluster textual information of the retrieved videos of a query topic to discover the hidden topic structures, called salient phrases. Second, the salient phrases are assigned to the leaf nodes of a prototype hierarchy extracted from corresponding Wikipedia pages, and the nodes with no video clusters are pruned from the hierarchy. In this way, the prototype hierarchy is

MM'14, November 03–07, 2014, Orlando, FL, USA.
Copyright 2014 ACM 978-1-4503-3063-3/14/11 ...$15.00.
http://dx.doi.org/10.1145/2647868.2655012.

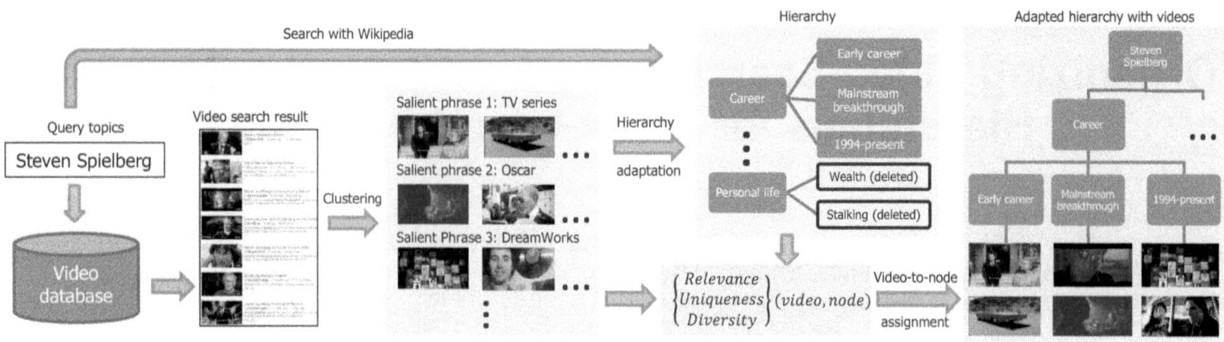

Figure 1: Illustration of our approach. Given a hot query topic, we first retrieve relevant videos using online video search engines and also download a hierarchy for the topic from Wikipedia. The hierarchy is then adapted by analyzing the retrieved videos. Finally, videos are selected and assigned to the nodes of the adapted hierarchy for efficient browsing, by considering three criteria. See texts for more explanations.

adapted to better reflect the topic structure of video search results. After that, we formulate an optimization problem in which videos are assigned to each node of the adapted hierarchy by considering multimodal information. This work is similar to [11] which also assigns videos to hierarchies for visualization. However, our approach has the capability of adapting the prototype hierarchies, which is more suitable for organizing the video search results.

2. OUR APPROACH

In this section, we will first propose the method for prototype hierarchy adaptation, and then describe a simple optimization-based video assignment process to put the videos on the modified hierarchy.

2.1 Prototype Hierarchy Adaptation

Since the prototype hierarchy extracted from the Wikipedia was constructed for textual descriptions of the topic, some nodes are not suitable for videos and should be removed. To discover the hidden facets in the search results for prototype hierarchy adaptation, we use the clustering algorithm in [14], which formulates the clustering process into a salient phrase ranking problem. Given a set of candidate phrases, it calculates several textual properties to model the probability of each phrase as a topic cluster. The calculated textual properties include tf-idf, phrase length, intra-cluster similarity, cluster entropy and phrase contextual entropy. Then a regression model is trained to combine the five properties to a final salient score. The top-ranked phrases are considered as salient phrases, and the video cluster corresponding to each salient phrase contains the videos with that phrase in textual descriptions. Finally, video cluster pairs with an overlapping rate (i.e., the percentage of shared videos between the pair) over 50% are deemed as similar salient phrases and are merged together.

The candidate phrases used above are prepared by the following procedure. We first extract all the n-grams ($n \leq 3$) from the title of each video as candidate phrases. Then, the mutual information (MI) [4] between phrases and video texts is used to quantify how informative each phrase is to all videos. The MI value of a phrase t is defined as:

$$MI(t) = \sum_{v} p(v,t) \log \frac{p(v,t)}{p(v)p(t)},$$

where v denotes a video, and the probability terms in the above equation can be derived from phrase co-occurrence statistics in the video contexts. With uninformative phrases discarded, the final set of candidate phrases is created.

The mined video clusters is used to adapt the prototype hierarchy by assigning the video clusters to the leaf nodes of the hierarchy. We use the method proposed in [11] to define the video-to-node similarity. All the texts are represented by the vector space model with tf-idf weighting, and the terms with hyper-links in the Wikipedia page are defined as important terms and assigned with empirically enlarged weights. The video-to-node similarity is then calculated as the Cosine similarity between the vector representations of the video texts and the texts under the node from the Wikipedia page. After that, the similarity between a video cluster C and a node n is defined as follows:

$$Sim_t(C,n) = \frac{1}{|C|} \sum_{v \in C} Sim_t(v,n),$$

where $Sim_t(v,n)$ is the video-to-node similarity and the subscript t indicates that the similarity is based on texts. Finally, a video cluster is assigned to the leaf node with the highest similarity value. After assigning all the video clusters to the nodes, leaf nodes with no assigned video clusters are pruned from the hierarchy.

2.2 Video-to-Node Assignment

In the browsing of a video hierarchy, there are three problems to be addressed to improve user experiences: 1) videos under each node should be semantically related to the node; 2) videos related to only one node rather than to several nodes are preferred (i.e., highly focused contents); and 3) near-duplicate videos should be avoided. The algorithm in [11] solves the three problems by using three criteria: relevance, uniqueness, diversity, which are integrated into an optimization problem. We adopt a similar method but use a different definition of uniqueness, which was found to be better. The criteria are defined as follows:

$$Rel(v,n) = Sim_t(v,n),$$

$$Uniq(v,n) = \frac{Sim_t(v,n)}{\sum_{n_j \in Leaf} Sim_t(v,n_j)},$$

$$Div(v,n) = \max_{v_j \in n} (Sim_v(v,v_j)),$$

where uniqueness is only defined on videos under the leaf nodes since videos relevant to a child node is surely related to the parent nodes. The subscript v in Sim_v indicates that similarity is calculated by near-duplicate visual search. To compute the visual similarity, we apply a state-of-the-art solution of near-duplicate search with the SIFT feature [8], Hamming embedding based fast matching [6], and temporal frame alignment [10]. Given a video pair, their visual similarity is defined as the percentage of the shared near-duplicate keyframes.

With the three criteria, the objective function for video-to-node assignment is defined as follows:

$$\mathcal{F} = \sum_{v,n} \beta \cdot Rel(v,n) * Uniq(v,n) - (1-\beta) \cdot Div(v,n).$$

By maximizing the objective function, the most suitable videos can be added to each node. For the sake of efficiency, we employ a greedy algorithm to solve the optimization, which inserts one video to a node at each step. To speed up the process, the videos are only selected from the corresponding video clusters (related to the salient phrases) assigned to the node in the hierarchy adaptation process. Note that using the salient phrase clustering outcomes also helps improve the precision of the selected videos, compared with the brute-force selection from the entire collection. The video assignment terminates after all the nodes are added with sufficient videos.

3. EXPERIMENTS

3.1 Dataset

We pick two very popular topic categories, celebrities and cities, to validate the effectiveness of our proposed approach. In collecting the dataset, for each topic, its respective Wikipedia page was first downloaded, from which the hierarchy, the texts under each node, and the terms with hyper-links (i.e., the more important terms) were extracted. We then searched the topic name in YouTube to download videos and their surrounding contexts. Table 1 summarizes the dataset.

Table 1: Statistics of the collected dataset. The first five topics are celebrities, and the last five are cities. Numbers in the parenthesis are the amount of leaf nodes in the corresponding Wikipedia hierarchies.

ID	Topic	# Videos	# Nodes (leaf)
1	Barack Obama	1887	31 (22)
2	Steven Spielberg	1618	23 (20)
3	Michael Jackson	1404	25 (22)
4	Michael Schumacher	1371	26 (19)
5	Steve Jobs	1870	31 (24)
6	London	2144	41 (33)
7	Chicago	2020	36 (28)
8	Los Angeles	2020	27 (20)
9	New York City	1834	31 (23)
10	Paris	1936	45 (35)

3.2 Evaluation Plan

We split the evaluations into three parts. The first part is to evaluate the salient phrases produced from video clustering. We manually labeled the correct salient phrases and calculated the percentage of the correctly assigned phrases.

The second part is to inspect the video-to-node assignment results using the three criteria. The metrics used for evaluating the three criteria are listed below:

Relevance: Precision is used to measure the relevance criterion. Videos are manually labeled to their relevant nodes to compute precision.

Uniqueness: The average of uniqueness value of the videos, i.e., the mean value of $Uniq(v,n)$, in the leaf nodes are computed.

Diversity: Diversity is measured by the percentage of the selected videos that are redundant. If the visual similarity between two videos is over 0.5, one of them is redundant.

In the assignment procedure, at most 5 videos are selected for each parent (non-leaf) node. Since all the leaf nodes have a number of assigned salient phrases during the hierarchy adaptation process, we assigned at most $2\times\#SalientPhrases$ videos to each leaf node. The number of assigned videos is dependent on the number of salient phrases of each leaf node, which is good as a leaf node is semantically more diversified if it has more salient phrases and thus should be assigned more videos to fully capture the diversity. For the sake of comparison, we also assigned videos to the original hierarchy without adaptation.

The third part of the evaluation is a user study. We evaluated three systems:

List: Videos are organized to a rank list (from YouTube search engine).

H: Videos are organized to the original hierarchy.

AH: Videos are organized to the adapted hierarchy by our approach.

Ten human subjects were involved in the user study, who were asked to compare the results for each topic and to rate the three systems from four aspects:

Presentation: Is the organization of the videos useful in quickly locating needed information?

Precision: Are the videos generally relevant to the topic?

Conciseness: Is there significant redundant information?

Satisfaction: Overall satisfaction of the results.

3.3 Results and Discussions

The results of first two evaluations are summarized in Table 2. We first discuss the first part which aims to evaluate the precision of the assigned salient phrases. From the results, we can see that the performance varies across topics. This measure highly depends on the relevance of the retrieved videos from YouTube to the query topics. If the retrieved videos are not very relevant, the precision of the salient phrases will be low. Therefore this number has close connections to the relevance criterion in the second part of the evaluation. Overall, with a mean precision of 63%, the procedure of salient phrase discovery is rather effective.

Then we move to the next part which evaluates the three criteria in video-to-node assignment (columns 3-8 in Table 2). Compared with the baseline ("H"), results of all the three criteria are significantly improved. The relevance value has a dramatic increase of 20% due to the hierarchy adaptation function of our approach. For instance, in the hierarchy of topic "London", unsuitable nodes with no related videos like "Toponymy", "Prehistory and antiquity" are deleted, and useful nodes like "Accent" and "Leisure and entertainment" are preserved. After the adaptation, the hierarchy originally to organize texts becomes more suitable for videos, and thus the relevance of the assigned videos can

Table 2: **Results of the first two evaluations. For the salient phrase clustering (indicated by "Clustering" in the table), P stands for the precision of the salient phrases. In video-to-node assignment, R, U and D are relevance, uniqueness, and diversity respectively. See Section 3.2 for the metric definitions. Note that for diversity, lower value is better.**

ID	Clustering	Video-to-Node Assignment					
	P (%)	R (%)		U (%)		D (%)	
		H	AH	H	AH	H	AH
1	78	41	70	41	47	5.8	1.0
2	55	39	59	36	42	8.7	1.7
3	50	31	51	27	31	10.4	1.6
4	46	15	42	32	44	7.7	0.7
5	61	21	45	29	41	6.5	0.0
6	67	33	58	35	56	5.4	0.0
7	78	44	53	39	45	4.4	0.0
8	82	43	61	53	65	1.5	0.0
9	70	39	51	36	40	2.0	0.6
10	43	26	35	29	34	0.9	1.1
Mean	63	33	53	36	45	5.3	0.7

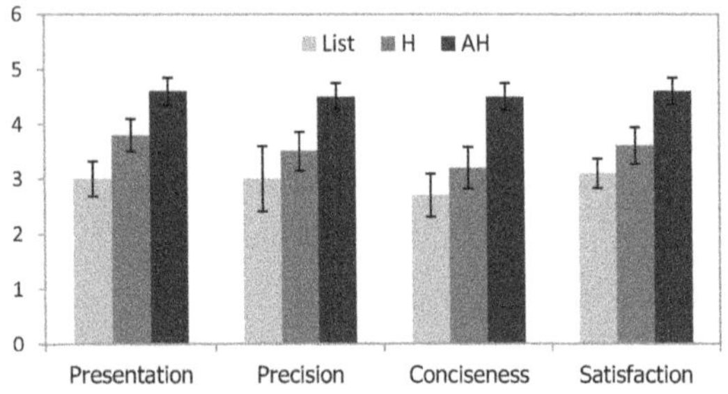

Figure 2: Subjective evaluation scores of the List, H and AH approaches, ranging from 1 (worst) to 5 (best). Our AH achieves the highest scores.

be largely enhanced. In addition, although our definition of uniqueness is straightforward, it is very effective (9% higher than the baseline). Finally, we see that for four topics, the diversity value is reduced to zero, and all the other topics have values lower than 2%, which is fairly satisfying.

Results of the user study are shown in Figure 2. The traditional list-based system has the lowest score mainly because mixing videos of all the facets creates difficulties in fully understanding the topic. Our approach AH achieves the highest scores in all the criteria. For presentation and precision, because the adaptation of the hierarchy makes it more focused for video organization, while in the meantime also can improve the precision of the assigned videos (see Table 2), it is easy to understand that the users are more satisfied in both criteria. The conciseness of AH is higher because of the near-duplicate removal function. With the good performance in presentation, precision and conciseness, the highest rating of satisfaction is rather natural.

4. CONCLUSIONS

We have introduced an approach to organize video search results to an adapted semantic hierarchy for efficient browsing. Given a topic, we started from the hierarchy extracted from its corresponding Wikipedia page, and adapted the hierarchy by analyzing the video search results. The retrieved videos were then assigned to the nodes of the adapted hierarchy according to three criteria. Results on a well-defined dataset have verified the effectiveness of our approach. One promising future work is to further enhance the adaptation method in our approach, by not only removing irrelevant nodes but also adding useful nodes. Adding nodes automatically is dangerous as many found clusters are semantically uninterpretable. Therefore, an interaction process may be designed with users in the loop to reach this goal. After all, the hierarchical organization of video search results does not need to be fully online, an efficient offline approach with minimal user interactions to pre-generate the hierarchical results for hot search topics would be a big surplus to the current video search engines.

5. ACKNOWLEDGEMENTS

This work was supported in part by the National Natural Science Foundation of China (#61228205, #61201387), a National 863 Program (#2014AA015101), a Key Technologies Research and Development Program (#2013BAH09F01), and three grants from the Science and Technology Commission of Shanghai Municipality (#13PJ1400400, #13511504503, #12511501602).

6. REFERENCES

[1] D. Cai, X. He, Z. Li, W.-Y. Ma, and J.-R. Wen. Hierarchical clustering of www image search results using visual, textual and link information. In *ACM MM*, 2004.
[2] P. Ferragina and A. Gulli. A personalized search engine based on web-snippet hierarchical clustering. *Software: Practice and Experience*, 38(2):189–225, 2008.
[3] J. Goldberger, S. Gordon, and H. Greenspan. Unsupervised image-set clustering using an information theoretic framework. *IEEE TIP*, 15(2):449–458, 2006.
[4] W. H. Hsu and S.-F. Chang. Topic tracking across broadcast news videos with visual duplicates and semantic concepts. In *IEEE ICIP*, 2006.
[5] I. Ide, T. Kinoshita, T. Takahashi, H. Mo, N. Katayama, S. Satoh, and H. Murase. Exploiting the chronological semantic structure in a large-scale broadcast news video archive for its efficient exploration. In *APSIPA ASC*, 2010.
[6] H. Jegou, M. Douze, and C. Schmid. Hamming embedding and weak geometric consistency for large scale image search. In *ECCV*. 2008.
[7] F. Jing, C. Wang, Y. Yao, K. Deng, L. Zhang, and W.-Y. Ma. iGroup: web image search results clustering. In *ACM MM*, 2006.
[8] D. G. Lowe. Distinctive image features from scale-invariant keypoints. *IJCV*, 60(2):91–110, 2004.
[9] Z.-Y. Ming, K. Wang, and T.-S. Chua. Prototype hierarchy based clustering for the categorization and navigation of web collections. In *ACM SIGIR*, 2010.
[10] H.-K. Tan, C.-W. Ngo, R. Hong, and T.-S. Chua. Scalable detection of partial near-duplicate videos by visual-temporal consistency. In *ACM MM*, 2009.
[11] S. Tan, Y.-G. Jiang, and C.-W. Ngo. Placing videos on a semantic hierarchy for search result navigation. *ACM TOMCCAP*, 2014.
[12] X. Wu, Y.-J. Lu, Q. Peng, and C.-W. Ngo. Mining event structures from web videos. *IEEE MM*, 2011.
[13] X. Wu, C.-W. Ngo, and Q. Li. Threading and autodocumenting news videos: a promising solution to rapidly browse news topics. *IEEE SPM*, 23(2):59–68, 2006.
[14] H.-J. Zeng, Q.-C. He, Z. Chen, W.-Y. Ma, and J. Ma. Learning to cluster web search results. In *ACM SIGIR*, 2004.

Real-Time Summarization of User-Generated Videos Based on Semantic Recognition

Xi Wang[1], Yu-Gang Jiang[1], Zhenhua Chai[2], Zichen Gu[2], Xinyu Du[2], Dong Wang[2]
[1]School of Computer Science, Shanghai Key Laboratory of Intelligent Information Processing,
Fudan University, Shanghai, China
[2]Huawei Technologies, Beijing, China
{xwang10, ygj}@fudan.edu.cn
{chaizhenhua, guzichen, duxinyu, dave.wangdong}@huawei.com

ABSTRACT

User-generated contents play an important role in the Internet video-sharing activities. Techniques for summarizing the user-generated videos (UGVs) into short representative clips are useful in many applications. This paper introduces an approach for UGV summarization based on semantic recognition. Different from other types of videos like movies or broadcasting news, where the semantic contents may vary greatly across different shots, most UGVs have only a single long shot with relatively consistent high-level semantics. Therefore, a few semantically representative segments are generally sufficient for a UGV summary, which can be selected based on the distribution of semantic recognition scores. In addition, due to the poor shooting quality of many UGVs, factors such as camera shaking and lighting condition are also considered to achieve more pleasant summaries. Experiments on over 100 UGVs with both subjective and objective evaluations show that our approach clearly outperforms several alternative methods and is highly efficient. Using a regular laptop, it can produce a summary for a 2-minute video in just 10 seconds.

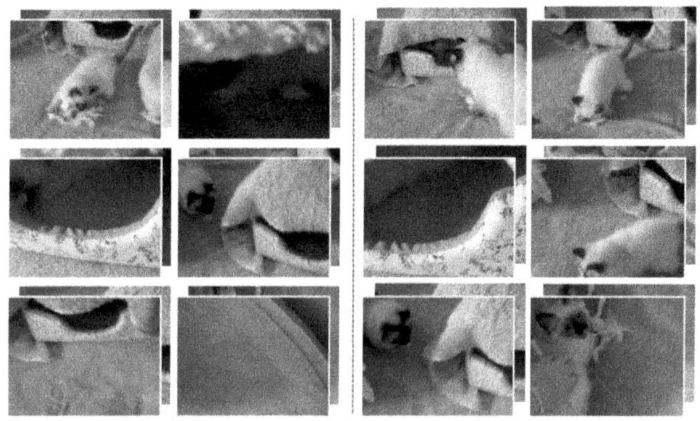

Figure 1: Sampled frames from (left) an original UGV at 1/24 fps, and (right) the summary generated by our approach at 1/2 fps. The frames are ordered from left to right and top to bottom. Key contents related to the major semantics in this video (cat playing) are well preserved in the summary.

Categories and Subject Descriptors

I.2.10 [**Artificial Intelligence**]: Vision and Scene Understanding - Video analysis

Keywords

Video Summarization, Semantic Recognition, User-Generated Videos

1. INTRODUCTION

As the amount of user-generated videos (UGVs) grows rapidly on the Internet, techniques for efficiently managing them are becoming increasingly important. For example, summarizing a UGV into a short clip is needed in many applications. One straightforward use-case is efficient content browsing. By viewing the summaries, people can understand the major contents of the UGVs very quickly.

Typically, there are two categories of video summarization approaches, divided based on the formats of the outputs. The first one is key-frame based summarization, also known as static storyboard summarization, which extracts a collection of static key-frames to form a summary [4, 11]. In contrast, the second category, dynamic skimming summary, produces a short clip consisting of several video segments selected from the original video [8]. In this paper, we propose a semantics-driven UGV summarization approach, which belongs to the latter category.

The major contribution of this work is an approach that harnesses semantic recognition results to select representative segments. Starting from efficiently recognizing video semantics, we define a simple scheme to pick the segments that have relatively more reliable recognition results, which are also consistent with the dominate semantics of the entire video. In addition, because the UGVs are mostly captured by amateur users with handheld devices, the quality of the videos vary and camera shaking may happen frequently. Therefore, our approach also integrates simple factors that judge the quality of the segments. On a set of over 100 UGVs downloaded from YouTube, we conduct both subjective and

MM'14, November 03 - 07 2014, Orlando, FL, USA

http://dx.doi.org/10.1145/2647868.2655013.

objective evaluations to validate the effectiveness of our approach, and compare with a few recent alternative methods.

In the literature, research on video summarization was mostly done on professionally produced videos, which are very long and consist of multiple shots. Many works relied on low-level information like frame differences [11] or motion cues [8], which can hardly generate satisfying results on the UGVs, partly due to the poor shooting quality of these videos. A few recent studies started to use high-level features such as important objects [5], object tracks [4] or tag localization [9] to address this problem. In [5], Lu and Grauman modeled the influence between sub-events of egocentric videos and designed a method to find a chain of video segments that conveys a fluid story. Wang et al. [9] integrated video tag localization into event-driven video summarization, and Mei et al. [7] proposed a method to compress long videos while maintaining the maximum amount of information. Very recently, Khosla et al. [3] focused on summarizing the UGVs by selecting key-shots visually similar to Web images, which are considered to contain rich and representative information as people often pick the best moment to take pictures. The key difference of our approach is that we use semantic recognition instead of matching to the auxiliary Web image collections. As will be discussed in the experiments, our approach is very efficient and outperforms the image matching based pipeline with clear margins.

In the following, we first describe a user survey to discover important clues for selecting representative segments in UGV summarization. After that we elaborate the proposed approach and discuss experimental results.

2. A SURVEY

We conducted a user survey to determine what kinds of video segments should be included in a UGV summary. Observations from this study motivated the approach presented in this paper.

We randomly selected 200 UGVs from Youtube with durations ranging from 2 to 10 minutes. Ten human subjects with different backgrounds and gender were selected. After viewing each video, the subjects were asked to mark a few short segments that *are representative and should be included in a summary.* A short justification was also needed to explain why each segment was selected.

After carefully inspecting all the results, we had the following major observations:

- The chosen segments should have strong connection to the dominate semantics (story) of the original video.
- All the selected segments from a video should, collectively, provide the needed information for users to understand the original story with little redundancy.
- Quality is important. Low quality segments should be avoided in the summary.

Besides, we also found that the audio clue was important for a number of segment selections. For example, some selected segments are a part of a longer sub-clip that contains beautiful music. However, the desirable length of the UGV summarization is short. Chopping the soundtracks into segments of a few seconds and then merging some selected discontinuous ones will not be understandable by the users. This is the main reason that audio was not considered in most video summarization approaches, including ours.

3. OUR APPROACH

According to the survey, we design an approach integrating both semantic recognition and quality estimation for UGV summarization. First, the videos need to be partitioned into short segments, among which representative ones will be selected to form the summaries. As most UGVs contain only a single shot, shot boundary detection used in the traditional summarization approaches cannot be deployed here. Therefore we use simple uniform segmentation to partition each video into multiple segments (2 seconds each). Semantic recognition is then performed on each segment, using the fast algorithm proposed in [1]. We use the algorithm because it can recognize tens of categories with high accuracy within only a few seconds.

More formally, a UGV is represented as a collection of N segments $\{s_1, s_2, \ldots, s_N\}$, where a segment s_j is described by a K-dimensional semantic distribution vector e_j, containing prediction scores of K semantic classes. k-means clustering is performed to group these segments into L clusters $C = \{C_1, C_2, \ldots, C_L\}$. The similarity of the segments is measured by the χ^2 distance, which was found to be better than the traditional Euclidean distance. Segments within the same cluster are semantically similar, but may represent different stage of a story if they are temporally far way from each other. To ensure that we may select temporally discontinuous segments but not the temporally adjacent ones within the same cluster, we further split the clusters into a set of segment groups $G = \{G_1, G_2, \ldots, G_T\}$, where $T \geq L$ and each group only contains a set of continuous segments from the same cluster. A group may contain only a single segment if the segment does not have temporal neighbors within the corresponding cluster.

Next, we define a criterion that helps us pick at most one segment from each group. The first factor to be considered is representativeness based on the semantic recognition results. As indicated from the survey, a good summary should highlight the major semantics in the original video. To this end, we define a semantic score of a segment s_i as:

$$\mathcal{E}(s_i) = e_i^T \cdot \mu \times \sqrt{\frac{1}{K}\sum_{j=1}^{K}(e_{i,j} - \bar{e_i})^2}, \qquad (1)$$

where e_i^T is the transpose of the semantic vector e_i of s_i, $\mu = \frac{1}{N}\sum_i^N e_i$ is the semantic distribution of the entire video, and $\bar{e_i}$ denotes the average value of all the dimensions of e_i. The first part of this equation, i.e., $e_i^T \cdot \mu$, ensures a high score of a segment if it is semantically consistent with the overall video. The remaining part prefers semantic prediction scores with a larger variance, which indicates that the classifiers are more confident as the scores are either very high or very low (far from the decision boundary).

The second factor considered in our approach is video quality, which is defined as follows:

$$\mathcal{Q}(s_i) = exp(-P_{s_i}/P) + exp(-\Delta L_{s_i}/L_{max}). \qquad (2)$$

The first part evaluates motion stability, based on P batches of frames extracted from a segment s_i, each of which contains three successive frames. P_{s_i} is the number of batches containing severe motion, determined by the angle between the global motion vectors of nearby frames [6]. Since most UGVs are in the H.264/MPEG-4 format, we can directly use the MPEG motion vector. For those not in this format, we may either convert the format first, or use alternative

Figure 2: Visual comparison of our summary with three methods. The original video is sampled at 1/12 fps and the summaries are sampled at 1 fps. Our approach has a clear focus on the major semantics of the video ("playing baseball"), while the others contain several "noisy" scenes.

methods such as [10] to estimate global motion. The second part of Equation 2 evaluates lighting imbalance, where ΔL_{s_i} measures the range of average brightness of the frames in the segment s_i, and L_{max} is the maximum brightness value of the original video [10].

Integrating the discussions above, the overall score of a segment is defined as:

$$\mathcal{O}(s_i) = \mathcal{E}(s_i) + \lambda \cdot \mathcal{Q}(s_i), \quad (3)$$

where λ balances the influences of the semantic score and the quality score. Based on this measure, the top-t segments from different segment groups in G are selected to form the summary.

4. EXPERIMENTS

In this section, we evaluate our proposed approach and compare with alternative methods. We randomly select 150 UGVs from the Columbia Consumer Video database [2], which also provides annotations of 20 semantic categories, covering several popular events frequently seen in UGVs (e.g., "playing baseball"). Following [1], 20 efficient classifiers are trained using dense SURF (Speeded Up Robust Features) and MFCC (Mel-Frequency Cepstral Coefficients) features, and we use the prediction scores of these classifiers to form the semantic distribution vector e for each segment (i.e., $K = 20$). A part of the Columbia Consumer Video database [2] is adopted in this training process. For the balance parameter λ, we empirically set it to 0.5. We set both the number of clusters L and the number of selected segments t to 6, leading to a summary of fixed length (12 seconds), which was observed to be suitable in applications like fast video browsing on mobile platforms.

4.1 Compared Approaches

Three approaches are adopted for comparison:

- k-means: This method simply clusters the segments and selects those closing to each cluster centroid. The bag-of-words representation based on the SIFT features is used to represent each segment.
- Story-driven summarization [5]. Three measures called story, importance and diversity scores were defined to summarize very long egocentric videos. A few minor modifications were made in our implementation to control the length of the summary.
- Image-based summarization: We also implemented a system using a similar idea from [3], which, as mentioned in Section 1, assumes that images contain rich and important information, and segments visually similar to a dominate group of images should be selected. For each of the 20 semantic categories, we retrieved 800 images from Google image search. Then the χ^2 distance is used to measure the feature similarity between the images and the video frames.

The video summaries generated by these approaches range from 8 to 16 seconds, which are similar to that generated by our approach.

Table 1: Subjective evaluation results. The *overall* row shows average scores of the three criteria. Our approach outperforms all the compared methods.

Approach	k-means	Story-driven	Image-based	Ours
Accuracy	3.868	3.960	4.061	**4.308**
Coverage	3.556	3.627	3.773	**3.946**
Quality	3.595	3.596	3.703	**3.911**
Overall	*3.673*	*3.728*	*3.846*	***4.055***

4.2 Results and Discussions

4.2.1 *Subjective Evaluation*

Like most previous works on video summarization, we first adopt subjective evaluation to measure the quality of the video summaries. 10 subjects were involved in this study, whose ages range from 22–50 and have different backgrounds. For each video in our dataset, we show the entire original video to the subjects first, followed by the four summaries (one by our approach and three from the compared approaches). To ensure a fair evaluation, the summaries are shown in random order with no indications of the methods used. After viewing these summaries, the subjects were asked to provide scores (integer values from 1 to 5) according to three criteria: (1) Accuracy: most segments of the summary have strong connections to the dominate high-level semantics of the original video; (2) Coverage: the summary contain sufficient information to understand the original story with little content redundancy; and (3) Quality: the quality of most segments in the summary is good.

The results are summarized in Table 1. As shown in the table, our approach significantly outperforms all the three compared methods. Due to the use of the semantic recognition, our approach achieves very good scores particularly in terms of the "accuracy" criterion. The k-means based method is the worst as it does not consider any semantic information like the other three methods. The story-driven and the image-based approaches, however, focus on different levels of semantics (i.e., objects) and different sources of semantics (i.e., from Web images), respectively. The results

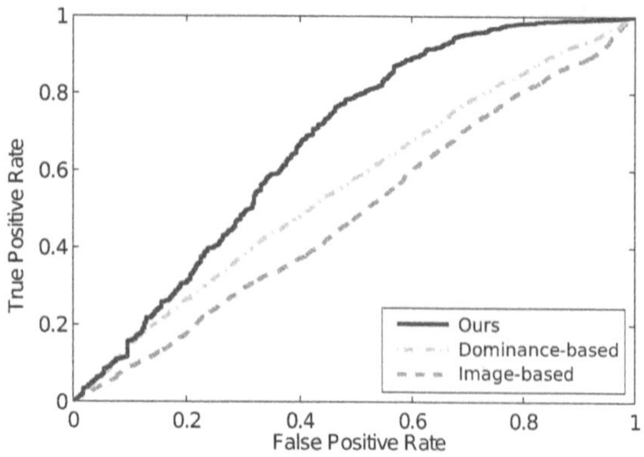

Figure 3: Comparison on the capability of selecting semantically representative segments.

clearly suggest that, for UGV summarization, higher level semantics related to the overall story of the videos are more important. In addition, the scores of the "quality" criterion indicate that the simple method defined in Equation 2 works fairly well. The compared approaches do not have the function of evaluating visual quality and thus received lower scores. Finally, due to the partitioning of the videos into different segment groups and the limitation of selecting maximally only one segment from each group, the semantic coverage of our approach is also better than all the other methods.

4.2.2 Picking Semantically Representative Segments

In this subsection, we adopt objective evaluation to measure the power of our approach in selecting semantically representative segments. We randomly selected 50 videos from the test set, determined the dominant semantics (story) of each video, and manually annotated whether a segment is related to the dominant semantics. Equation 1 is then used to measure the scores of the segments, which are ranked and ROC curves are plotted in Figure 3, in comparison with two methods. One of them is the image-based summarization method, which uses Web images of similar high-level semantic categories to locate representative segments. As shown in the figure, this method generates almost random results, which is due to the fact that a significant data domain gap exists between the Web images and the UGVs. The other compared method is based on the dominant visual appearances of a segment, determined by its similarities to all the other segments. In other words, a segment is more representative and important if it is visually similar to a large number of segments in the video. As can be seen from the figure, it outperforms the image-based method but is much worse than our approach. The story-driven summarization method is not compared here because it only exploits lower level object semantics.

4.2.3 Speed Efficiency

We conclude this section by discussing the speed efficiency of our approach. The semantic recognition module is based on the work in [1], which only needs around 8 seconds to process of 2-minute video, including both feature extraction and classification. Notice that the classification part in this recognition process is very efficient (a few milliseconds per sample), therefore adding more semantic classes does not significantly increase the computational cost. The quality measure is based on the motion vectors from MPEG-4, which are extremely fast to compute. Therefore, our approach is very efficient. On average, it only requires 10 seconds to summarize a 2-minute UGV, using a regular laptop.

5. CONCLUSIONS

We have introduced an efficient approach for UGV summarization based on semantic recognition. High-level semantics were firstly recognized on segment-level, and a simple criterion was defined to utilize the recognition outputs for selecting semantically representative segments. The quality of the video segments was also considered to avoid selecting segments containing severe camera motion, which widely exists in the UGVs captured by handheld devices.

We conducted both subjective evaluations of the summaries and objective evaluations on the power of selecting semantically representative segments. The results have clearly validated the effectiveness of our approach, and have corroborated a fact that high-level semantics are important in UGV summarization.

Acknowledgement

This work was supported in part by Huawei Technologies, a National 863 Program (#2014AA015101), a Key Technologies Research and Development Program (#2013BAH-09F01), and three grants from the Science and Technology Commission of Shanghai Municipality (#13PJ1400400, #13511504503, #12511501602).

6. REFERENCES

[1] Y.-G. Jiang. SUPER: towards real-time event recognition in internet videos. In *Proceedings of ICMR*, 2012.

[2] Y.-G. Jiang, G. Ye, S.-F. Chang, D. Ellis, and A. C. Loui. Consumer video understanding: A benchmark database and an evaluation of human and machine performance. In *Proceedings of ICMR*, 2011.

[3] A. Khosla, R. Hamid, C.-J. Lin, and N. Sundaresan. Large-scale video summarization using web-image priors. In *Proceedings of CVPR*, 2013.

[4] D. Liu, G. Hua, and T. Chen. A hierarchical visual model for video object summarization. *IEEE TPAMI*, 32(12):2178–2190, 2010.

[5] Z. Lu and K. Grauman. Story-driven summarization for egocentric video. In *Proceedings of CVPR*, 2013.

[6] Y. Luo and X. Tang. Photo and video quality evaluation: Focusing on the subject. In *Proceedings of ECCV*. 2008.

[7] T. Mei, L.-X. Tang, J. Tang, and X.-S. Hua. Near-lossless semantic video summarization and its applications to video analysis. *ACM TOMCCAP*, 9(3):1–23, 2013.

[8] C.-W. Ngo, Y.-F. Ma, and H.-J. Zhang. Video summarization and scene detection by graph modeling. *IEEE TCSVT*, 15(2):296–305, 2005.

[9] M. Wang, R. Hong, G. Li, Z.-J. Zha, S. Yan, and T.-S. Chua. Event driven web video summarization by tag localization and key-shot identification. *IEEE TMM*, 14(4):975–985, 2012.

[10] W.-Q. Yan and M. S. Kankanhalli. Detection and removal of lighting & shaking artifacts in home videos. In *Proceedings of ACM Multimedia*, 2002.

[11] H. J. Zhang, J. Wu, D. Zhong, and S. W. Smoliar. An integrated system for content-based video retrieval and browsing. *Pattern Recognition*, 30(4):643–658, 1997.

Hacking Chinese Touclick CAPTCHA by Multi-Scale Corner Structure Model with Fast Pattern Matching

Yunhang Shen, Rongrong Ji, Donglin Cao, and Min Wang
Department of Cognitive Science, School of Information Science and Engineering
Xiamen University, Xiamen, Fujian, P. R. China, 361005
{rrji,another}@xmu.edu.cn, {yhshen, wangmin}@stu.xmu.edu.cn

ABSTRACT

In this paper, we tackle the challenge of hacking CAPTCHA (Completely Automated Public Turing test to tell Computers and Humans Apart), which is widely used to identify machine and human in webpage registration and authorization [17]. More specially, we target at touclick Chinese CAPTCHA that is recently popular in mobile application scenario. Hacking such CAPTCHA is much more challenging and left unexploited in the literature. Our main idea is a multi-scale Corner based Structure Model, termed CSM, with a very efficient pattern matching scheme. CSM can accurately capture the intrinsic statistics of touclick Chinese CAPTCHA against background clutters. We demonstrate the efficiency and effectiveness of the proposed approach by extensive experiments on a Chinese touclick CAPTCHA dataset collected from Internet forums. We report encouraging results with an overall success rate of almost 100% and an averaged detection speed of 170 millisecond. Upon our work, we also provide suggestions on improving the current CAPTCHA-based human-machine identification systems.

Categories and Subject Descriptors

D.4.6 [**OPERATING SYSTEMS**]: Security and Protection—*Verification*

General Terms

Security, Human Factors, Verification

Keywords

CAPTCHA; Touclick; Multimedia Security

1. INTRODUCTION

Coming with the explosive growth of Chinese forums and Mobile Internet, Chinese character based touclick CAPTCHA has now widely used in online verification to identify human from machine, with application to registration, comment, and personal identification. Here, the word touclick means touching and clicking the CAPTCHA, which is easy for human but hard for machine to pass. Touclick CAPTCHA is different from the traditional one, especially in its interaction that is very suitable for mobile input. The traditional CAPTCHA requires human to recognize and input the context shown in the image. Then, the algorithm identifies human from machine by comparing the true answer with the input. On the contrary, as illustrated in Fig.1, the touclick CAPTCHA draws some characters on an image with background clutters. At the bottom of the image, a text hint requires the user to sequentially click the special characters (the red characters in Fig.1) on the image. The test will identify human if the characters clicked exactly correspond to the red characters shown at the bottom of Fig.1. To pass this type of CAPTCHA, the click operation should be on the right positions with the right order. As the user input is simplified, this type of CAPTCHA is very suitable for mobile usage.

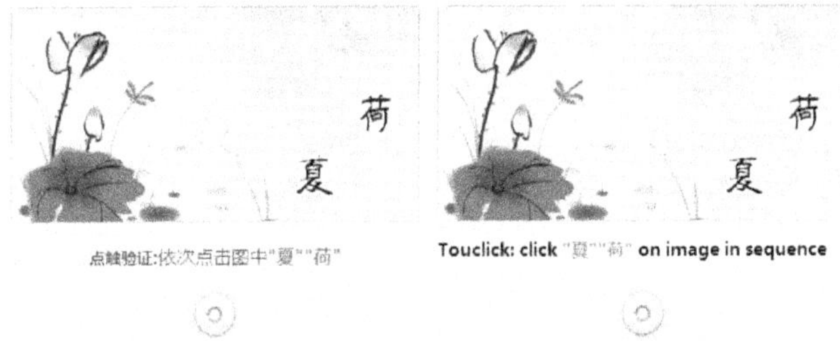

Figure 1: Left is original CAPTCHA. Right is CAPTCHA with hint text translated into English.

Such type of CAPTCHA have introduced higher challenges: Comparing to English based CAPTCHA (with at most 26 uppercase letters, 26 lowercase letters, and 10 Numbers), there are far more Chinese characters to be identified, e.g., several thousands of characters together with a dozen of fonts. This results in a huge burden in manual labeling of training sets, especially for the case of using recognition based approaches [12, 13, 18, 19, 4, 6]. Moreover, the recognition of individual Chinese characters is far more challenging comparing to that of English ones. For instance, two characters similar in shape can be totally different in meaning, e.g. "大" and "太"; while in another instance they are different in the stroke length e.g. "土" and "士".

In this paper, we tackle the challenge of hacking the touclick Chinese CAPTCHA by designing an efficient yet accurate

MM'14, November 03 - 07 2014, Orlando, FL, USA

http://dx.doi.org/10.1145/2647868.2655017.

Figure 2: Left are images drew hint characters. Right are original images.

Figure 3: Preprocessed images.

recognition algorithm. Our solution is a multi-scale Corner based Structure Model, termed CSM, in combination with a fast character pattern matching algorithm to avoid the time-consuming procedure of classifier training. The pattern matching approach is inspired by [5] to locate the character area in the CAPTCHA image. Our matching is also very accurate that avoids the time-consuming spatial verifications. This enables us to achieve a success rate of almost 100% on the touclick Chinese CAPTCHA. We demonstrate our excellent performance with comparisons to several alternatives on a collected Chinese touclick CAPTCHA dataset.

The rest of this paper is organized as follows: Section 2 discusses related work. Section 3 gives details of the CSM algorithm. The experiments are given in Section 4, and Section 5 concludes this paper and discusses our future work.

2. RELATED WORK

Hacking English character based CAPTCHA has been studied previously. For example, Mori and Malik [12] had developed an efficient method based on shape context matching that could identify the word in an EZ-Gimpy image with a success rate of 92%, and the requisite 3 words in a Gimpy image with a 33% success rate. In 2004, Moy et al [13] used two distortion estimation techniques for object that solve EZ-Gimpy and Gimpy-r, two of the visual CAPTCHA with high degrees of success. In 2007, Yan [18] broken a number of CAPTCHA (including those hosted at Captchaservice.org, a web service for CAPTCHA generation) with almost 100% success rate by simply counting the number of pixels of each segmented character. It is worth to note that aforementioned schemes were all resistant to the best commercial OCR software at that time. In 2008, work in [19] has achieved a success rate of higher than 90% against a text-based CAPTCHA designed by Microsoft. Chellapilla and Samar [4] attacked a number of visual CAPTCHA taken from the web with machine learning algorithms, achieving a success rate from 4.89% to 66.2%. In general, most previous CAPTCHA recognition systems contains three steps: 1. A preprocessing step to remove noise and binarize the image. 2. An image segmentation to identify the single character regions. 3. An OCR or classifier based Characters recognition component. The classifier is trained via models like artificial neural network. In the work of [4], it is demonstrated that the segmentation step is much more difficult than the recognition step, which is especially true given the proliferation of cutting-edge machine learning techniques. Yet, image segmentation is still widely regarded as an open problem in the computer vision community. In 2011, work in [1] applied a specialized variant of shape contexts to match entire words at once, and was capable of solving at least 5% of the challenges generated by three versions of reCAPTCHA. In 2013, Google reported a 99.8% accuracy on the hardest category of reCAPTCHA using deep convolutional neural networks by skipping the segmentation step [6]. However, it is computational burdensome that requires extensive computing resources.

3. MULTI-SCALE CSM

In this section, we depict the technical details of the proposed multi-scale Corner based Structure Model.

3.1 Preprocessing

Two images are needed to accomplish one matching, i.e. one is the CAPTCHA image, and the other is generated by our procedure with characters required in the bottom hint on it. As illustrated in Fig 2, we draw the characters required in the hint on a new image in order to match with the characters on CAPTCHA image. We preprocess image to remove noise, and then convert image from RGB color space to gray, as shown in Fig 3.

3.2 Chinese Character Model

Most modern Chinese characters are consisted of five basic strokes, i.e., "一", "丨", "丿", "丶", and "乛". As a result, it is imaginable that features extracted by blob detections or affine invariant feature detections would be quite similar and unable to distinguish different Chinese characters. In addition, Chinese character is square, in which the basic strokes cross to each other and produce a lot of corners. As the intersection of two edges, a corner represents a point in which the directions of these two edges change. Different characters contain different structure of corner features, which acts as a major hint in distinguishing one character from the other. It requires us to pay more attention to the structure and relative position of strokes in describing Chinese character.

To detect corner, one important characteristic is to measure the gradient of the corner region, which should have high variation in more than one directions. We follow this principle and use the Shi-Tomasi corner detector [15], which is the improvement of Harris corner detector [7]. To this end, we denote P as a set of corner features detected in a Chinese character.

$$P = \{kp_1, kp_2, \cdots, kp_n\}$$

Value n denotes the number of corner features in a Chinese character and value kp_i denotes a corner key point that contains information such as coordinates of the key point, diameter of the meaningful key point neighborhood, orientation of the key point, and octave. We extract descriptor of the key point by function $f()$:

$$c_i = f(kp_i)$$

Value c_i is a vector that denotes descriptor of the ith corner feature kp_i. Subsequently, a Chinese character can be described as a set of corner descriptors as follows:

$$w = \{c_1, c_2, \cdots, c_n\}$$

In the formula above, value w denotes the overall features of a Chinese character. It is noted that we make an assumption that each feature is independent, and therefore we do not consider the relation among features.

As the characters in the images are not inherently scaled, we further detect points over multiple levels of a Gaussian pyramid on the image, which ensures us to handle the scale variation.

3.3 Character Pattern Matching

We calculate the similarity between two corner features using the Euclidean distance. We set vector p as a descriptor of a Chinese character and q as a descriptor of another Chinese character, i.e.,

$$p = (p_i, p_2, \cdots, p_n),\ q = (q_i, q_2, \cdots, q_n)$$

The Euclidean distance between descriptor p and q is:

$$d(p,q) = \sqrt{(p_1 - q_1)^2 + (p_2 - q_2)^2 + \cdots + (p_n - q_n)^2}$$

A Brute-force matching is adopted to find similar descriptors. For each descriptor in the first set, we find the closest descriptor in the second set by trying each one. The following formula denotes that descriptor c in the first descriptor set w match to descriptor $\pi(c)$ in another descriptor set w'.

$$\pi(c) = \arg\min_{c' \epsilon w'} d(c, c')\ c \epsilon w$$

where w denotes the first descriptor set, w' denotes the set of unmatched descriptor in the second descriptor set.

As the hint images were drawn by our program and are clear without any noise, all the features detected on the hint images are useful. Hence, the features set of hint images should be the first set and features set of the CAPTCHA images should be the second set in Brute-force matching.

To find the areas where the characters may lie on, first we found out the set u which contains the descriptor in the second image that matched from descriptor of first image. For each descriptor in set u, we count the number of descriptor in set u which around it with a radius value r. Value r is a threshold value defined by us according to the size of characters. We arrange the numbers from max to min. And the positions of top n descriptors are the centers where characters lie on.

4. EXPERIMENT

We collected 500 CAPTCHA samples with 179 pixels height and 356 pixels width from some Chinese websites from 2013 October to 2014 March.

4.1 Experiment setup

We implemented the procedure in Java and tested it on laptop with a 2.4GHz Intel Core i3 CPU and 6GB RAM on Windows 7 operating system.

As an alternative solution, we implemented other feature detectors, i.e., SIFT [9], FAST [14], BRISK [8], Hessian affine region [11], SURF [2], and MSER [10], to compare with our Shi-Tomasi corner detector.

We also used Tesseract [16], which is probably the most accurate open source OCR engine available, to detect Chinese characters in CAPTCHA images. We offered the preprocessed image to Tesseract to recognize the Chinese characters and watched whether the result was right or wrong. We use accuracy to evaluate the performance.

4.2 Result

For Chinese characters, first it has several thousands of Chinese characters and more than a dozen of character fonts in common use. It is a huge project to collect and label all Chinese character samples. Second, classification and recognition of Chinese characters are far greater difficult than those of English letters and Numbers.Classifier was not good for Chinese character recognition.

Table 1: Comparison of Different Types of Features

Method	Accuracy	Time(ms)	Feature Number
CSM	100%	170(125-1078)	43(28-84)
FAST based	88.6%	270(159-1206)	56(40-95)
SIFT based	48%	219(160-1395)	17(9-41)
BRISK based	43%	750(585-2400)	15(10-26)
Hessian affine	42.6%	424(408-1691)	17(10-37)
SURF based	40.4%	794(386-1742)	31(20-72)
MSER based	11.2%	157(111-1130)	5(2-12)

Table 2: Comparison of Different Method of Finding the Areas where the Characters Lie on in CSM

Method	Accuracy
Counting Features Number	100%
RANSAC based	97.6%

As shown in Tab. 1, a significant improvement can be seen when corner feature detection are used to provide the characters feature detection, resulting in an error as low as 0.0% compared to 52% for SIFT algorithm for 500 testing CAPTCHA. FAST based method achieves a good performance but no as well as CSM, because FAST detection is not a pure corner detection. This result reveals that corner features can describe more detail structure information of Chinese character than other types of features.

We ran the procedure 10 times on the test sets on our platform and on average our procedure took 170 milliseconds to recognize a CAPTCHA images. The Tab. 1 shows that our recognition is very efficient: at most, it takes no more than 1078 milliseconds to finish recognition of a CAPTCHA image.

As shown in Tab 2, it can be seen when the method of simply counting the number of features is used to find the areas where the characters may lie on, resulting in an error as low as 0.0% compared to 2.4% for RANSAC-based algorithm for 500 testing CAPTCHA in CSM. This result reveals that the above assumption of the independence of Chinese corner features is significant.

Another experiment was recognizing Chinese characters with ORC engine. Most results of the Tesseract were messy codes or empty content, only several Chinese characters were recognized in all 500 CAPTCHA. In fact, detect and recognize Chinese characters are far more challenge than English letters and Numbers with OCR engine. Besides it is CAPTCHA with different fonts and disturbed background.

4.3 Case Study

In Fig. 4 and Fig. 5, we shows the detected features based on CSM and SIFT on two samples. We found CSM have largest amount of average features number for a Chinese character in Tab. 1. It indicates that Chinese character has more corner structure features than blob features.

Fig 6 and Fig 7 display the matching of the two samples. In CSM most features in first image had matched to the features in second images correctly. However matching of

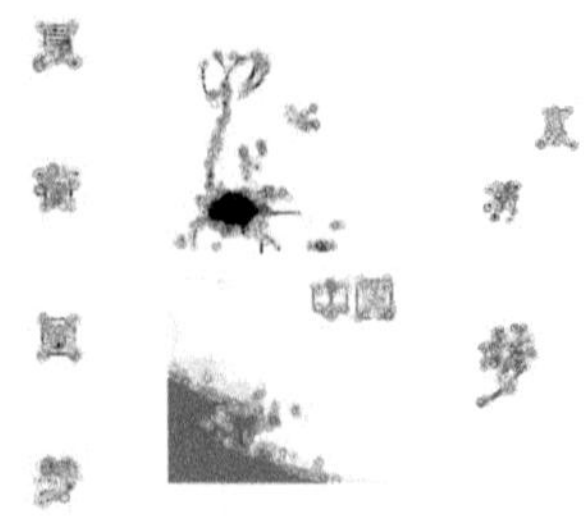

Figure 4: CSM features

Figure 5: SIFT features

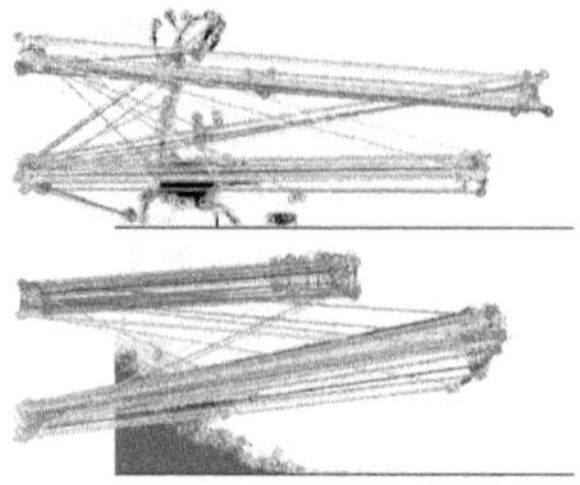

Figure 6: CSM features matching

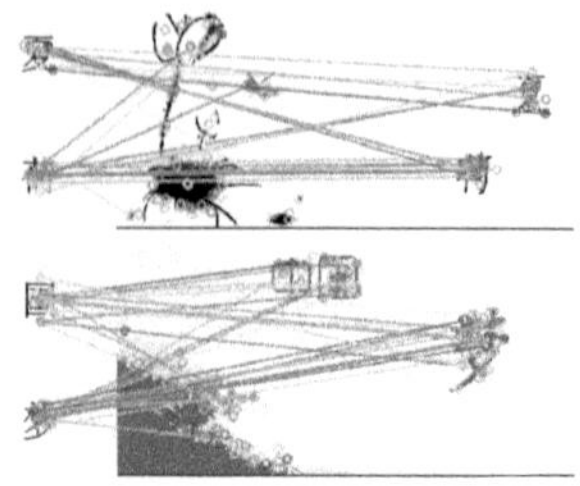

Figure 7: SIFT features matching

Figure 8: Result of CSM recognition

Figure 9: Result of SIFT recognition

SIFT is unsatisfactory. Fig 8 and Fig 9 show the final result of recognitions for CSM and SIFT.

5. CONCLUSIONS

In this paper, we study the challenge of hacking Chinese character based, touclick CAPTCHA. Our main idea is a multi-scale Corner based Structure Model, which can robustly capture the intrinsic structure of Chinese characters, as well as making extremely fast pattern matching to align identified characters. We have reported significant performance over alternative approaches including many other types of features matching and OCR based recognition. In our future work, we will further extend our work to include richer features such as shape context [3], as well as more accurate binarization schemes to filter out background noise, which has shown negative effects against our matching accuracy.

6. ACKNOWLEDGEMENTS

This work is supported by the Nature Science Foundation of China (No. 61373076), the Fundamental Research Funds for the Central Universities (No.2013121026), and the 985 Project of Xiamen University.

7. REFERENCES

[1] P. Baecher, N. Büscher, M. Fischlin, and B. Milde. Breaking recaptcha: a holistic approach via shape recognition. In *Future Challenges in Security and Privacy for Academia and Industry*, pages 56–67. Springer, 2011.

[2] H. Bay, T. Tuytelaars, and L. Van Gool. Surf: Speeded up robust features. In *Computer Vision–ECCV 2006*, pages 404–417. Springer, 2006.

[3] S. Belongie, G. Mori, and J. Malik. Matching with shape contexts. In *Statistics and Analysis of Shapes*, pages 81–105. Springer, 2006.

[4] K. Chellapilla and P. Y. Simard. Using machine learning to break visual human interaction proofs (hips). In *NIPS*, 2004.

[5] J. F. Gimpel. A theory of discrete patterns and their implementation in snobol4. *Communications of the ACM*, 16(2):91–100, 1973.

[6] I. J. Goodfellow, Y. Bulatov, J. Ibarz, S. Arnoud, and V. Shet. Multi-digit number recognition from street view imagery using deep convolutional neural networks. *arXiv preprint arXiv:1312.6082*, 2013.

[7] C. Harris and M. Stephens. A combined corner and edge detector. In *Alvey vision conference*, volume 15, page 50. Manchester, UK, 1988.

[8] S. Leutenegger, M. Chli, and R. Y. Siegwart. Brisk: Binary robust invariant scalable keypoints. In *Computer Vision (ICCV), 2011 IEEE International Conference on*, pages 2548–2555. IEEE, 2011.

[9] D. G. Lowe. Object recognition from local scale-invariant features. In *Computer vision, 1999. The proceedings of the seventh IEEE international conference on*, volume 2, pages 1150–1157. Ieee, 1999.

[10] J. Matas, O. Chum, M. Urban, and T. Pajdla. Robust wide-baseline stereo from maximally stable extremal regions. *Image and vision computing*, 22(10):761–767, 2004.

[11] K. Mikolajczyk and C. Schmid. An affine invariant interest point detector. In *Computer Vision–ECCV 2002*, pages 128–142. Springer, 2002.

[12] G. Mori and J. Malik. Recognizing objects in adversarial clutter: Breaking a visual captcha. In *Computer Vision and Pattern Recognition, 2003. Proceedings. 2003 IEEE Computer Society Conference on*, volume 1, pages I–134. IEEE, 2003.

[13] G. Moy, N. Jones, C. Harkless, and R. Potter. Distortion estimation techniques in solving visual captchas. In *Computer Vision and Pattern Recognition, 2004. CVPR 2004. Proceedings of the 2004 IEEE Computer Society Conference on*, volume 2, pages II–23. IEEE, 2004.

[14] E. Rosten and T. Drummond. Machine learning for high-speed corner detection. In *Computer Vision–ECCV 2006*, pages 430–443. Springer, 2006.

[15] J. Shi and C. Tomasi. Good features to track. In *Computer Vision and Pattern Recognition, 1994. Proceedings CVPR'94., 1994 IEEE Computer Society Conference on*, pages 593–600. IEEE, 1994.

[16] R. Smith. An overview of the tesseract ocr engine. In *ICDAR*, volume 7, pages 629–633, 2007.

[17] L. Von Ahn, M. Blum, and J. Langford. Telling humans and computers apart automatically. *Communications of the ACM*, 47(2):56–60, 2004.

[18] J. Yan and A. S. El Ahmad. Breaking visual captchas with naive pattern recognition algorithms. In *Computer Security Applications Conference, 2007. ACSAC 2007. Twenty-Third Annual*, pages 279–291. IEEE, 2007.

[19] J. Yan and A. S. El Ahmad. A low-cost attack on a microsoft captcha. In *Proceedings of the 15th ACM conference on Computer and communications security*, pages 543–554. ACM, 2008.

Orthogonal Gaussian Process for Automatic Age Estimation

Kai Zhu[1,2], Dihong Gong[1], Zhifeng Li[1], and Xiaoou Tang[1,2]

[1]Shenzhen Key Lab of Computer Vision and Pattern Recognition
Shenzhen Institutes of Advanced Technology, Chinese Academy of Sciences, China
[2]Department of Information Engineering, The Chinese University of Hong Kong, China
{dh.gong, zhifeng.li}@siat.ac.cn, {zk013, xtang}@ie.cuhk.edu.hk

ABSTRACT
Age Estimation from facial images has been receiving increasing interest due to its important applications. Among the existing age estimation algorithms, the personalized approaches have been shown to be the most effective ones. However, most of the person-specific approaches (e.g. MTWGP [1], AGES [2], WAS [3]) rely heavily on the availability of training images across different ages for a single subject, which is very difficult to satisfy in practical applications. In order to overcome this problem, we propose a new approach to age estimation, called Orthogonal Gaussian Process (OGP). Compared to standard Gaussian Process, OGP is much more efficient while maintaining the discriminatory power of the standard Gaussian Process. Based on OGP, we further propose an improvement of OGP called anisotropic OGP (A-OGP) to enhance the age estimation performance. Extensive experiments are conducted to demonstrate the state-of-the-art estimation accuracy of our new algorithm on several public-domain face aging datasets: FG-NET face dataset with 82 different subjects, Morph Album 1 dataset with more than 600 subjects, and Morph Album 2 with about 20,000 different subjects.

Categories and Subject Descriptors
I.4.9 [**IMAGE PROCESSING AND COMPUTER VISION**]: Applications; I.5.4 [**PATTERN RECOGNITION**]: Applications

Keywords
Age Estimation; Face Image; Gaussian Process

1. INTRODUCTION
Automatic age estimation refers to estimating human age based on an input face image, which has a lot of potential applications in real world, such as human computer interaction and multimedia communication. However, it remains a challenging problem due to the following reasons: 1) human faces have large variability (e.g. expressions or poses) that is irrelevant to age; 2) living habits and working conditions can have significant effect on the age of human face; and 3) age-related discriminative information is usually more difficult to obtain since it has slightly weaker influence on people's appearance compared with the other factors. Recently, lots of works [1-4, 12-22] have been made to address this problem.

Regression vs. Classification. The age estimation problem can be either treated as multiclass *classification problem* when each age is taken as a class label or *regression problem* where each age is used as a regression value. In the set of classification approaches, individual models are learned for different classes, and the estimation process involves finding the best matching model that can fit the testing samples. For example, Geng et al. [2] in 2007 proposed AGES algorithm to model the aging pattern, which is defined as the sequence of a particular individual's face images sorted in time order, by constructing a representative subspace. Two years later, Geng et al. [4] proposed another classification based algorithm, the MSA, to learn aging patterning through a series of multilinear subspace analysis operating on three-dimensional tensors for age prediction. In both of the works, the age estimation for testing person is based on model comparison: the age of the testing person is predicted as the corresponding age of the model which fits the testing person the best.

The regression based methods, unlike the classification based approaches, treat ages as regression values and in the testing process age will be predicted as the output of regression models learned from training data. The regression approaches have been shown to be generally more effective for age estimation than the classification ones, as the former approaches can preserve the intrinsic ordering of ages.

Global vs. Person-specific. Another perspective of viewing the existing approaches is by whether the learned age estimator is specific to subjects or not. The person-specific approaches learn one model for each specific person, and at the testing stage the identity information of the testing person is used to select model matching the testing person for either classification or regression. The rationale behind this kind of treatment is based on the observation that the aging process of human beings is quite person-specific, which means different persons have different aging patterns which are associated with the person's genes or living habits. The representative work based on person-specific models include the AGES algorithm [2] that learns one aging subspace for each person, and then at the testing stage the age of the testing person is predicted by a model whose corresponding training person best matches the testing person. Another representative work is [1] proposed by Zhang et al. in 2010, which is based on Multi-Task Warped Gaussian Process (MTWGP) for regression. The MTWGP algorithm assigns the same noise level of Gaussian process for samples from the person while different

MM'14, November 3–7, 2014, Orlando, Florida, USA.

http://dx.doi.org/10.1145/2647868.2655020

noise levels for samples from different subjects. Interestingly, although it is also a person-specific approach, unlike the AGES, at the testing stage it does not require the identity information for the testing person. There are two major limitations for person-specific approaches. The first is that it relies heavily on the availability of training faces for a single person of different age levels. Practically, it is usually difficult to collect face images with different ages for the same person. The second limitation lies in the fact that their model complexity will increase significantly as the number of training samples increase, which may limit the application of these methods.

Compared with the person-specific approaches, the global estimation algorithms can overcome the aforementioned limitations to some extent. The global estimation algorithms treat all the training samples equally, and thus they don't need to introduce new model or model parameters to accommodate the newly available training samples. For example, in [16] Guo et al. introduced the age manifold learning scheme for extracting face aging features and designed a locally adjusted robust regressor for learning and prediction of human ages. In [17], Xiao et al. proposed the mkNN algorithm for age prediction which learns the distance metric to preserve the local neighborhoods of training samples and at the same time maximize the distances between data that are not in the same neighborhood in a semantic space based on a specially designed distance.

In this paper, we propose a new algorithm, called Orthogonal Gaussian Process (OGP), to address the automatic age estimation problem. The OGP approach is based on the Gaussian Process for regression, but the optimization of OGP is over an orthogonal space, which is much more efficient than the standard GP, as supported by our experimental results. Based on OGP, we further propose an anisotropic OGP (A-OGP) algorithm to improve the age estimation accuracy. Extensive experiments are conducted on several public-domain face aging databases to demonstrate the effectiveness of our algorithms.

The major contributions of this paper are summarized as follows: 1) Propose an OGP algorithm that is more computationally efficient than the standard GP, which enables large-scale automatic age estimation from face images. 2) Based on OGP, propose an anisotropic noise level learning algorithm called A-OGP, which has been shown to be beneficial to improving age estimation accuracy. 3) Demonstrate the state-of-the-art performance on both the FG-NET and Morph Album face aging databases.

2. Orthogonal Gaussian Process

2.1 Warped Gaussian Process Revisited.

The Warped Gaussian Process (WGP) [5] is a generalization to the standard Gaussian Process (GP) for regression, where the regression targets are warped into a latent space by a nonlinear monotonic function so that the transformed data can be well-modelled by a GP.

Suppose we are given a dataset D, consisting of N pairs of input vectors $X_N = \{\vec{x}_n\}_{n=1}^N$ and real-valued targets $Y_N = \{y_n\}_{n=1}^N$ which are transformed into latent space $G_N = \{g_\theta(y_n)\}_{n=1}^N$ with a monotonic function $g_\theta: \mathbb{R} \to \mathbb{R}$ parameterized by θ. Then our training aim is to learn a set of model parameters (α, β, θ) where $\alpha, \beta > 0$ such that the following negative log-likelihood function can be minimized:

$$l = \frac{1}{2}[\vec{g}^T(\alpha K + \beta I_N)^{-1}\vec{g} + \ln|\alpha K + \beta I_N|] - \sum_{i=1}^N \ln g'_\theta(y_n), \quad (1)$$

where $\vec{g} = (g_\theta(y_1), \ldots, g_\theta(y_n))^T$, $K_{mn} = exp^{-\frac{\|\vec{x}_m - \vec{x}_n\|^2}{2\sigma^2}}$, and I_N is the $N \times N$ identity matrix. Based on the successful application of WGP in [1], we set the transformation function as:

$$g_\theta(y) = a\ln(by + c) + d,$$

where $a, b > 0$ to ensure the function is monotonically increasing. The derivatives with regards to model parameters are given by:

$$\frac{\partial l}{\partial \alpha} = \frac{1}{2}\mathrm{tr}([\widetilde{K}^{-1} - \widetilde{K}^{-1}\vec{g}\vec{g}^T\widetilde{K}^{-1}]K)$$

$$\frac{\partial l}{\partial \beta} = \frac{1}{2}\mathrm{tr}([\widetilde{K}^{-1} - \widetilde{K}^{-1}\vec{g}\vec{g}^T\widetilde{K}^{-1}])$$

$$\frac{\partial l}{\partial \theta} = \vec{g}^T\widetilde{K}^{-1}\frac{\partial \vec{g}}{\partial \theta} - \sum_{i=1}^N \frac{\partial \ln g'_\theta(y_n)}{\partial \theta},$$

where $\widetilde{K} = \alpha K + \beta I_N$. Then the probelm can be solved by gradient-based optimization algorithms such as conjugate methods.

At the testing stage, suppose we are given a testing feature $\vec{t}$, then the prediction value is given by: $m = \vec{k}_t^T\widetilde{K}^{-1}\vec{g}$,

where $\vec{k}_t = \left[\alpha exp^{-\frac{\|\vec{x}_1 - \vec{t}\|^2}{2\sigma^2}}, \ldots, \alpha exp^{-\frac{\|\vec{x}_N - \vec{t}\|^2}{2\sigma^2}}\right]^T$. In our experiments, we found that it gives the best performance when $\sigma^2 = \frac{1}{N^2}\sum_{i=1}^N\sum_{j=1}^N\|\vec{x}_i - \vec{x}_j\|^2$.

2.2 Orthogonal Gaussian Process

The major computational cost of WGP in each iteration step involves an inversion of matrix $\widetilde{K}$ which is of size $N \times N$, where N is the number of training samples. In large scale applications where N is very large, the computational cost can be rather expensive. In this part, we introduce a mathematically equivalent algorithm, called Orthogonal Gaussian Process (OGP), which optimizes the model parameters in a transformed space where efficient computation is enabled.

We begin by decomposing K in (1) into three matrices using Singular Value Decomposition (SVD) such that:

$$K = USU^T, \quad (2)$$

where U is an orthogonal matrix such that $UU^T = I$. $S = diag(\lambda_1, \ldots, \lambda_N)$ is diagonal matrix whose diagonal elements are real-valued positive eigenvalues as K is symmetric positive definite. Substitute (2) into (1), we immediately obtain

$$l = \frac{1}{2}\sum_{n=1}^N\left(\frac{h_n^2}{\alpha\lambda_n + \beta} + \ln(\alpha\lambda_n + \beta)\right) - \sum_{i=1}^N \ln g'_\theta(y_n), \quad (3)$$

where $h_n = \vec{u}_n^T\vec{g}$, and $\vec{u}_n$ is the *n-th* column vector of U. With this transformed representation, we can easily obtain the derivatives as:

$$\frac{\partial l}{\partial \alpha} = \frac{1}{2}\sum_{n=1}^N \frac{(\alpha\lambda_n + \beta - h_n^2)\lambda_n}{(\alpha\lambda_n + \beta)^2},$$

$$\frac{\partial l}{\partial \beta} = \frac{1}{2}\sum_{n=1}^N \frac{(\alpha\lambda_n + \beta - h_n^2)}{(\alpha\lambda_n + \beta)^2},$$

$$\frac{\partial l}{\partial \theta} = \sum_{n=1}^N \frac{g_n}{\alpha\lambda_n + \beta}\frac{\partial g_n}{\partial \theta} - \sum_{i=1}^N \frac{\partial \ln g'_\theta(y_n)}{\partial \theta},$$

where g_n is the *n-th* element of $\vec{g}$.

We can see that our algorithm only requires to compute some scalar multiplications at each iteration step, which is rather fast and efficient. The major computational cost of the OGP comes from the SVD for matrix K of size $N \times N$, which needs to be made for only once. Compared with the standard WGP which requires to compute the inversion of $N \times N$ matrix for each iteration step, our approach has a much better computational efficiency in practice. In addition, as each iteration of WGP is very costive, practically we have to stop before the convergence, which usually gives solution of slightly lower accuracy.

2.3 Anisotropic OGP (A-OGP)

Based on the proposed OGP, we further propose an anisotropic OGP (A-OGP) algorithm to improve the age estimation performance, described as follows.

From (3) we can see l can be minimized w.r.t. α and β when $\alpha\lambda_n + \beta = h_n^2$ for $n = 1, \ldots, N$, which can be written in a vector form:

$$\vec{h}_2 = \alpha\vec{\lambda} + \beta\vec{1}, \quad (4)$$

where $\vec{h}_2 = (h_1^2, \ldots, h_N^2)^T$ and $\vec{\lambda} = (\lambda_1, \ldots, \lambda_N)^T$. Generally this equation doesn't hold since $\vec{h}_2$ is of dimension N and cannot be represented by $span(\vec{\lambda}, \vec{1})$ when $N > 2$. In an ARD anisotropic GP model, the positive scalar β is replaced by a vector whose elements are all positive, which gives

$$\vec{h}_2 = \alpha\vec{\lambda} + \vec{\beta}. \quad (5)$$

This kind of treatment, however, has to introduce an extra of $(N - 1)$ free parameters, which usually over-fits to the training data (in our experiments, we found that model (5) yields much worse performance than (4)).

The idea of our anisotropic model, is to introduce limited amount of free parameters such that l can be effectively reduced while at the same time avoid introducing too much model complexity. Suppose we want to introduce M ($M \ll N$) free parameters, then based on the current estimate of α, we can easily see that the smaller the angle between $\vec{\beta}$ and $\vec{h}_2 - \alpha\vec{\lambda}$, the better we can approximate $\vec{h}_2$ with $\alpha\vec{\lambda} + \vec{\beta}$. Based on this observation, we first cluster the elements of $\vec{h}_2 - \alpha\vec{\lambda}$ vector into M groups, and then for elements belonging to the same group, we assign the same value for $\vec{\beta}$, which gives a $\vec{\beta}$ of M distinct values. For example, if $M = 3$ and $\vec{h}_2 - \alpha\vec{\lambda} = [1\ 2\ 4\ 9\ 5\ 8]$, we can form three groups: {1,2}, {4,5}, and {8,9}. The corresponding $\vec{\beta}$ is $[\beta_1\ \beta_1\ \beta_2\ \beta_3\ \beta_2\ \beta_3\ ]$. Here $\vec{\beta}$ has only $M = 3$ free parameters, and optimally $\vec{\beta} = [1.5, 1.5, 4.5, 8.5, 4.5, 8.5\ ]$ gives the best approximation to $\vec{h}_2$ with $\alpha\vec{\lambda} + \vec{\beta}$.

Our anisotropic model relates to both ARD anisotropic model and algorithms proposed in [1]. The ARD anisotropic model, however, has high risk of over-fitting due to unavoidable high model complexity. In [1], the authors also introduced limited amount of freedom for $\vec{\beta}$, based on the assumption that "*samples from the same subject should share the same noise level*". According to this assumption, samples from the same subject will be assigned the same value. This kind of treatment has to introduce extra priors over $\vec{\beta}$ in order to avoid over-fitting occurred in the ARD anisotropic model. At the same time the number of free parameters in [1] for $\vec{\beta}$ grows linearly with the number of subjects for training. Another advantage of our anisotropic model over [1] lies in the fact that our anisotropic model is based on OGP, thus our model doesn't rely on any assumption and has a clearer mathematic explanation.

3. Automatic Face Preprocessing Pipeline

In this section, we introduce the detailed techniques for face preprocessing including face normalization and feature extraction. At the beginning of the pipeline, we use a commercial facial landmarks detector [6] to locate position of landmarks. Based on these landmarks, we normalize the face by piecewise triangle-based affine warping [7], where the example normalized faces are shown in Figure 1. Then, we extract two types of facial features, the Dense Scale Invariant Feature Transform (DSIFT) [8] and Multi-scales Local Binary Patterns (MLBP) [9], which are then fused by concatenation into a single long feature. In the final step, we reduce the dimension of facial features and suppress the noise by applying Principle Component Analysis (PCA) on long features (we retain 99% energy in the PCA).

4. Experiments

4.1 Databases

There are two well-known public domain aging databases: FG-NET [10] and Morph [11]. The FG-NET dataset consists of 82 different individuals, with each one having multiple images taken at different age levels. The Morph database has two separate datasets: Album 1 and Album 2. The Morph Album 1 only contains 1690 face images from 625 different subjects. The Morph Album 2 is the largest face aging dataset available in the public domain. It consists of about 78,000 face images from about 20,000 people. Figure 1 shows some example face images for FG-NET and Morph as well as the corresponding faces normalized with techniques introduced in section 3.1.

Figure 1. The first row shows the original example faces for FG-NET dataset (left) and Morph Album 2 (right) dataset. The second row shows the corresponding normalized faces.

For the FG-NET and Morph Album 1 datasets, we use the Leave One Person Out (LOPO) testing strategy that is a common practice in this field. While for the Morph Album 2 dataset, we randomly select 1,000 subjects as testing, and the rest subjects as training (note that there is no overlap for subjects between training and testing sets). All the results in this paper are reported as the Mean Age Error (MAE).

4.2 Comparison for computational efficiency.

We first compare the computational efficiency of our algorithm (OGP and A-OGP) with the WGP algorithm. For fair comparison, the running time is reported as average training time on the same machine over 5 random split of the Morph Album 1 dataset. The size of training samples varies from 100 subjects to 600 subjects with increment step of 100. The results are shown in Table 1, from which we can observe there is a significant improvement of our approach over WGP in computational efficiency.

Table 1. Comparison of training time (in seconds).

	100	200	300	400	500	600
WGP	0.223	0.462	0.920	2.171	2.533	4.802
OGP	0.054	0.071	0.109	0.210	0.287	0.594
AOGP	0.063	0.084	0.121	0.231	0.314	0.613

4.3 Evaluation of our algorithm under different settings.

In order to explore the effectiveness for different components of our algorithm, we compare their MAE performances under different configurations. The results are shown in Table 2 for FG-NET dataset and Table 3 for Morph Album 1 dataset, from which we have three observations: 1) compared with the WGP, our baseline algorithm OGP has a slightly better performance which we believe comes from the fact optimization over an orthogonal space can obtain a better local optima solution; 2) The Anisotropic OGP (A-OGP) has a clear performance improvement over both the OGP and WGP, which reveals the effectiveness of the our anisotropic algorithm; 3) The combination of local feature descriptors can also help to improve the age estimation accuracy.

Table 2. MAE on FG-NET dataset

	DSIFT	MLBP	DSIFT+MLBP
WGP	5.24	5.38	5.13
OGP	5.12	5.30	4.98
A-OGP	4.87	5.02	**4.76**

Table 3. MAE on Morph Album 1 dataset

	DSIFT	MLBP	DSIFT+MLBP
WGP	5.08	5.42	4.88
OGP	5.02	5.16	4.76
A-OGP	4.34	4.57	**4.12**

4.4 Benchmark comparison on FG-NET database.

In Table 4, we compare our algorithm with the existing state-of-the-art algorithms on the FG-NET dataset. Note that all the algorithms are using the same LOPO testing strategy. From these results, we can see that our algorithm has achieved the state-of-the-art accuracy over all the existing approaches. There are several points that we want to highlight: 1) our result is based on fully automatic program including the face detection and normalization (which may unavoidably produce some misalignments), while in [1] and [2] the authors are using manually labeled landmarks for face alignment; 2) compared with the MTWGP algorithm, our algorithm is more efficient in computation because the MTWGP is theoretically slower than the WGP in Table 2; 3) compared with MTWGP, our algorithm does not require large enough amount (i.e. more than 10) of training faces for a single person, which makes our algorithm more applicable to practical applications.

Table 4. Benchmark comparison on FG-NET dataset

AAS [12]	WAS [3]	AGES [2]	KAGES [13]	RUN1 [14]	MSA [4]
14.83	8.06	6.77	6.18	5.78	5.36
RUN2 [15]	LARR [16]	mkNN [17]	MTWGP [1]	TSR [19]	**Proposed**
5.33	5.07	4.93	4.83	5.90	**4.76**

4.5 Benchmark comparison on Morph Database.

In Table 5, we compare our algorithm against the existing state-of-the-art algorithms on the Morph Album 1 dataset. Note that being unable to learn models on MORPH Album 1 dataset where each person has approximately 2 images, all the listed algorithms except for ours are trained with FG-NET face dataset. For our algorithm, we present MAE results for both training with FG-NET data and Morph Album 1 data (LOPO). From these results, we have two observations: First, on the same testing configuration (where age estimators are trained from FG-NET dataset), our algorithm has a significant improvement over the existing state-of-the methods; Second, our algorithm can achieve another major boost in accuracy when trained with face images from Album 1 using LOPO strategy.

Finally, we compare our approach against the previously published results on the MORPH Album 2 dataset, as reported in Table 6. Compared to the FGNET and MORPH Album 1 datasets, very few related works have been done on this dataset. It is very clear that our approach also outperforms the others in this dataset.

Table 5. Benchmark comparison on Morph Album 1 dataset.

AAS [12]	WAS [3]	AGES [2]	RUN1 [14]	LARR [16]
20.93	9.32	8.83	8.34	7.94
mkNN [17]	MTWGP [1]	The method in [20]	**Proposed (FG-NET training)**	**Proposed (LOPO)**
10.31	6.71	5.41	**5.25**	**4.12**

Table 6. Benchmark comparison on Morph Album 2 dataset.

Algorithms	OHRank [21]	KPLS [22]	**Proposed**
MAE	6.1	4.2	**3.92**

5. CONCLUSIONS

In this paper, we have proposed a new approach called Orthogonal Gaussian Process for automatic age estimation. Extensive experiments are conducted on several public-domain face aging databases to demonstrate the effectiveness of our approach over the state-of-the-art.

6. ACKNOWLEDGMENTS

This work was supported by grants from Natural Science Foundation of China (61103164), Guangdong Innovative Research Team Program (No. 201001D0104648280), and Strategic Priority Research Program of the Chinese Academy of S ciences (Grant No. XDA06010500).

7. REFERENCES

[1] Y. Zhang, D. Y. Yeung, "Multi-task warped gaussian process for personalized age estimation," In *CVPR*, 2010.

[2] X. Geng, Z. Zhou, and K. Smith-Miles, "Automatic age estimation based on facial aging patterns" *TPAMI*, 2007.

[3] A. Lanitis, C.J. Taylor, and T. Cootes, "Toward Automatic Simulation of Aging Effects on Face Images," *TPAMI*, 2002.

[4] X. Geng and K. Smith-Miles, "Facial age estimation by multilinear subspace analysis". In *ICASSP*, 2009.

[5] E. Snelson, C.E. Rasmussen, Z. Ghahramani, "Warped Gaussian Processes", In *NIPS*, 2003.

[6] https://www.luxand.com/

[7] I. Matthews, S. Baker, "Active Appearance Models Revisited", *IJCV*, 2004.

[8] D. G. Lowe, "Object recognition from local scale-invariant features". In *ICCV*, 1999.

[9] T. Mäenpää, M. Pietikäinen, "Multi-scale binary patterns for texture analysis", In Image Analysis, 2003.

[10] FG-NET Aging Database, http://www.fgnet.rsunit.com/.

[11] K. R. Jr. and T. Tesafaye, "Morph: A longitudinal image database of normal adult age-progression", In *FG*, 2006.

[12] A. Lanitis, C. Draganova, and C. Christodoulou, "Comparing Different Classifiers for Automatic Age Estimation," *IEEE Trans. Systems, Man, and Cybernetics B*, 2004.

[13] X. Geng, K. Smith-Miles, and Z. Zhou. "Facial age estimation by nonlinear aging pattern subspace", In *ACM MM*, 2008.

[14] S. Yan, H. Wang, T. S. Huang, Q. Yang, and X. Tang. "Ranking with uncertain labels", In *ICME*, 2007.

[15] S. Yan, X. Zhou, M. Liu, M. Hasegawa-Johnson, and T. S. Huang. "Regression from patch-kernel", In *CVPR*, 2008.

[16] G. Guo, Y. Fu, C. R. Dyer, and T. S. Huang. "Image-based human age estimation by manifold learning and locally adjusted robust regression", *IEEE Trans. on Image Processing*, 2008.

[17] B. Xiao, X. Yang, Y. Xu, and H. Zha. "Learning distance metric for regression by semi-definite programming with application to human age estimation", In *ACM MM*, 2009.

[18] P. Thukral, K. Mitra, and R. Chellappa, "A hierarchical approach for human age estimation", in *Proc. IEEE ICASSP*, 2012.

[19] T. Wu, P. Turaga, and R. Chellappa, "Age estimation and face verification across aging using landmarks," *IEEE Trans. Information Forensics and Security*, Dec. 2012.

[20] Y. Chen and C. Hsu, "Subspace Learning for Facial Age Estimation Via Pairwise Age Ranking," *IEEE Transactions on Information Forensics and Security*, Dec. 2013.

[21] K. Chang, C. Chen, and Y. Hung, "Ordinal hyperplanes ranker with cost sensitivities for age estimation," *CVPR* 2011.

[22] G. Guo and G. Mu, "Simultaneous dimensionality reduction and human age estimation via kernel partial least squares regression," in *Proc. CVPR*, 2012.

Points of Interest Detection from Multiple Sensor-Rich Videos in Geo-Space

Ying Zhang*, Roger Zimmermann*, Luming Zhang*, David A. Shamma†
*School of Computing, National University of Singapore, Singapore 117417
†Yahoo Labs, San Francisco, CA, USA, 94103
{yingz118,rogerz,zhanglm}@comp.nus.edu.sg, aymans@acm.org

ABSTRACT

Recently, the popularity of user generated videos has highlighted efficient video indexing and browsing as an urgent problem. Points of interest (POI) detection is a technique to address this issue by establishing the implicit relationship among different media resources. The majority of existing studies detect POI by visual similarity, leveraging computer vision techniques. However, these methods suffer from high computational complexity when processing large-scale video sets and are challenging due to the sparse visual correlation among different consumer videos. The advent of geo-referenced videos provides an opportunity to detect POIs in an efficient manner. In this work, we first propose a probability model to formulate the capture intention distribution for video frames. Second, we detect the POIs by considering the contributions from multiple videos. Evaluations demonstrate that our algorithm successfully detects POIs with a reduced error distance from several dozens to a few meters.

Categories and Subject Descriptors

H.3.5 [**Information Storage and Retrieval**]: Online Information Services

Keywords

Location based service; geo-tagging; sensor data mining

1. INTRODUCTION

The volume of user generated videos is growing at a rapid rate owing to the advanced camera technologies and the popularity of mobile devices [9]. When modeled correctly, there exists the opportunity to capture the group work, the collective intent of users, in these systems for recommendation, analysis and organization. To efficiently manage and index voluminous sets of consumer videos, methods for points of interest (POI) detection have been developed to extract objects on which people are more interested to focus. The majority of existing studies detect POIs from visual similarity, leveraging computer vision techniques [11, 5]. However, due to the overwhelming amount of video material and the computational complexity, it is not always realistic to exhaustively process all input videos in a similar manner. Furthermore, there usually exist only sparse visual connections among different consumer recordings [8], which creates additional challenges for existing solutions.

The advent of sensor-rich videos has opened up new opportunities to understand video semantics [10]. Attached to these videos is rich sensor metadata and we are interested in the *geo-referenced videos* whose sensor data is closely tied to geo-properties. Such data can be used to detect POIs efficiently. A POI in geo-space is the scene location where multiple camera views are captured together [4]. Only a few prior studies have leveraged similar contextual information for POI detection. Thomee [7] proposed an approach to locate POIs from geo-referenced photos. However, it works better for well-known landmarks because input photos are collected by landmark names, followed by a manual inspection on if these photos contain clear landmark views. This approach can hardly be applied to videos as such manually labeling is laboursome. Hao *et al.* [4] introduced a method for POI detection from geo-referenced videos by assuming POIs are solely located along the central camera viewing direction with equal distance probability. However, POIs are often located within the whole visible area of a video frame with various probabilities. Additionally, this approach uses all frames for POI detection, which unjustly favors the longer videos implicitly. In order to overcome these drawbacks, we propose a probabilistic model to locate POIs from videos' geographic metadata without any prior information.

MM'14, November 3–7, 2014, Orlando, Florida, USA.
Copyright 2014 ACM 978-1-4503-3063-3/14/11 ...$15.00.
http://dx.doi.org/10.1145/2647868.2655027.

2. PROBABILISTIC MODEL FOR POI DETECTION FROM MULTIPLE VIDEOS

Geo-referenced videos are captured by continuously collecting locations and camera viewing directions together with the videos. This is easily achievable today as smartphones contain all necessary sensors. What follows introduces how sensor data is used to model the coverage area for a video frame as spatial objects. A camera positioned at a given point $\mathcal{L}$ in geo-space captures a scene whose covered area is represented by a *field-of-view* (FOV)). In this work, we adopt a 2D FOV model [1] using four parameters: $FOV \equiv \langle \mathcal{L}, \theta, \alpha, R \rangle$: (1) The camera position $\mathcal{L}$ is read from GPS. (2) Camera direction θ is obtained from digital compass with the north as zero. (3) The angle α is obtained based on the camera and lens properties for the current zoom level. R is the maximum visible distance at which an object can be recognized. Each video frame is associated with a FOV.

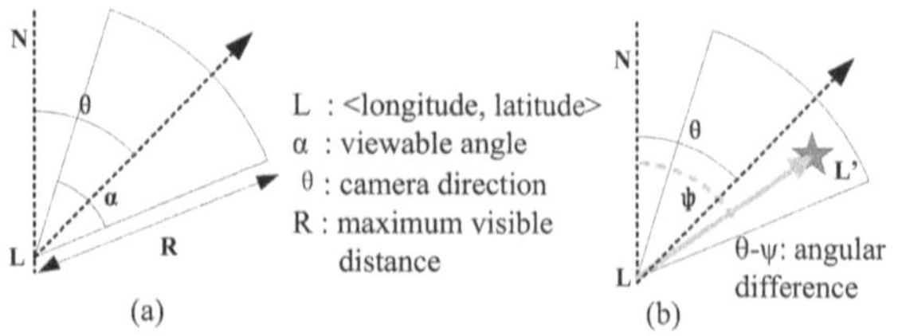

Figure 1: Illustration of (a) FOV in 2D space and (b) angular difference.

Conceptually, a POI is the scene location where multiple camera views are captured together. Similar to the PageRank idea, the more videos capture a location, the more likely this location is a POI. This motivates us to propose a probabilistic model to describe the POI distribution within a queried region. We divide the target space (denoted as $\mathbb{R}$) into $W \times H$ equally-spaced grids-cells $G = \{g_i^j\}, i = 1 \sim W, j = 1 \sim H$. We define a map POI as a $W \times H$ matrix. Each entry gains a value, say $POI(i,j)$, to indicate the probability its corresponding space grid cell g_i^j is a POI. Given a set of video frames F, $POI(i,j)$ is computed by the following equation:

$$POI(i,j) = \frac{c(g_i^j, F)}{\sum_{g \in G} c(g, F)} \quad (1)$$

where $c(g, F)$ is a counter indicating how likely this grid reflects the common capture intention from all videos and it is computed by the following equation:

$$c(g, F) = \sum_{m=1}^{|V|} \sum_{n=1}^{|v_m|} \mathbf{CI}(\mathcal{L}_g, FOV_m^n) \quad (2)$$

In this equation, $\mathcal{L}_g$ denotes the centroid of a grid cell g and $\mathbf{CI}(\mathcal{L}_g, FOV_m^n)$ is a value indicating the probability grid cell g being the capture intention within the frame f_m^n (denoted by its FOV). The following introduces how to formulate the capture intention distribution for video frames.

2.1 Capture Intention Distribution for Video Frames

Generally, a photographer is more likely to capture their intentions at the center of an image, *i.e.*, along the camera viewing direction. However, it is common for the main object (intention) to be off-center during a continuous camera motion. As an illustration in Fig. 1 (b), the main object (marked as a star) located with an angular difference $|\varphi - \theta|$ from the camera viewing direction. For example, a target is captured from its left to right for completeness and the angular difference is gradually changing accordingly. Inspired by this, we formulate such intention (angular) distribution for a video frame ($FOV \equiv \langle \mathcal{L}, \theta, \alpha, R \rangle$) by the following equation:

$$\mathbf{CI}_a(\mathcal{L}', FOV) = \begin{cases} \frac{e^{-\frac{(\theta - \varphi(\mathcal{L}', \mathcal{L}))^2}{2\sigma_a^2}}}{\sqrt{2\pi}\sigma_a} & : \ |\theta - \varphi(\mathcal{L}, \mathcal{L}')| \le \frac{\alpha}{2} \\ 0 : & \ otherwise. \end{cases},$$

where $\mathcal{L}'$ is any location in a target space, φ is the direction from $\mathcal{L}$ to $\mathcal{L}'$ and σ is a parameter to control the Gaussian distribution.

From the distance perspective, users intend to capture objects nearby the camera location for better visibility except when the distant object is big in size. So a location $\mathcal{L}'$, under a single FOV, gains a capture intention probability from its distance to the camera location:

$$\mathbf{CI}_d(\mathcal{L}', FOV) = \begin{cases} \frac{1}{\sqrt{2\pi}\sigma_d} e^{-\frac{||\mathcal{L}', \mathcal{L}||^2}{2\sigma_d^2}} & : \ ||\mathcal{L}', \mathcal{L}|| \le R \\ 0 : & \ otherwise. \end{cases},$$

where $||\cdot, \cdot||$ is a distance measurement for which we use the Euclidean distance in this paper. So for a single video frame its capture intention distribution is formulated in the following equation for $\forall \mathcal{L}' \in \mathbb{R}$:

$$\mathbf{CI}(\mathcal{L}', FOV \equiv \langle \mathcal{L}, \theta, \alpha, R \rangle) = \mathbf{CI}_a(\mathcal{L}', FOV) \cdot \mathbf{CI}_d(\mathcal{L}', FOV)$$

2.2 POI Detection from Multiple Videos

By substituting the above equation to Eqn. 2, we can obtain the counter for each grid and hence can compute the POI probability using Eqn. 1. However, this formulation implicitly favors the videos with longer duration. So we introduce an auxiliary variable ρ for each frame, indicating its contribution to the POI detection as in Eqn. 3.

$$c(g, F) = \sum_{m=1}^{|V|} \sum_{n=1}^{|v_m|} \rho_m^n \mathbf{CI}(\mathcal{L}_g, FOV_m^n) \quad (3)$$

In this work, we only import frames with sufficient spatial informativeness for POI detection, which can additionally reduce the overall computation workload:

$$\rho_i = \begin{cases} 1 : & I_i > Th \\ 0 : & \text{otherwise} \end{cases},$$

where I_i is an informativeness measurement indicating how well a frame y_i preserves the complete information among all video frames. Each frame is presented as a $N = W \times H$ dimentional vector by unrolling the grid-counters from its own POI map. Assume for each frame, its informativeness is computed as $y = g(f) = w^T f + \epsilon$, where ϵ is a noise factor. The loss function is defined as the average square error: $loss(y) = E(y - \hat{y})^2$ where $\hat{y}$ is reconstructed from a set of informative frames. These informative pieces are selected to satisfy a minimization the loss between its true value and the predicted value among all video frames:

$$\min \frac{1}{n} \sum_{i=1}^{n} E(loss(y_i))$$

This problem can be solved by the active learning techniques in machine learning field and the above minimization equation is converted to an convex relaxation version for optimization results [2]:

$$\min_{\beta, \kappa} \sum_{i=1}^{n} ||f_i - F^T \kappa_i||^2 + \sum_{j=1}^{n} \frac{\kappa_{i,j}^2}{\beta_j} + \gamma ||\beta||_1$$

β, κ are two regulation variables and can be computed by for example an existing solution [3] which uses the kernel trick to map the original data into a reproducing kernel Hilbert Space for results improvement. Value β is also an indicator of informativeness level so that the frames with β over than a threshold are added to the candidate set for POI detection. The overall workflow for multi-video POI detection is summarized in Alg. 1.

Algorithm 1 POI Map Generation from Multiple Videos.

```
Require: V: videos; Th: an informativeness threshold
Initialize an empty candidate set K for POI detection.
for each video v_i ∈ V do
    Calculate the β value for each video frame.
    Add the frames with β > Th to candidate set K.
end for
Initialize an empty POI map P.
for each frame f_i ∈ K do
    Calculate the frame POI Map ℙ_i.
    Update the POI map : P = merge(P, P_i).
end for
Return POI.
```

3. EXPERIMENTS

3.1 Data Setup

We conducted experiments on a real data set GeoVid (geovid.org). These videos were recorded among three years on smartphones running Android 2.2 with fixed resolutions at 720×480 pixels and frame rate at 24 or 30 frame/second. The minimum sampling rate for the location and orientation information is around 5 sample/second. We retrieved videos in four areas in Singapore downtown where dense videos had been collected with data statistics in Table 1, and detected POIs from each of them.

Table 1: Data statistics.

	# Videos	Duration (s)	Covered space (m^2)
Set(1)	25	3760	5847.325
Set(2)	28	1025	992.627
Set(3)	49	1290	1451.978
Set(4)	32	2730	387.047

3.2 POI Detection

We generated the POI maps for each test example and plotted their contours in Fig. 2. The probability values were scalded between 0 and 1 by dividing by their maxima and were labeled on each contour level for a clear explanation. The figures intuitively show that POIs do not equally distributed in the space but with probability variations smoothly spreading over the whole target space.

To evaluate the performance of our approach, we compared our algorithm (denoted as *Keyframe Pool*) with two other methods. The first method [4] (denoted as *Baseline*) also leverages the geo-referenced videos for POI detection but it assumes POIs are solely located along the central camera view direction with equal distance probabilities. The second (denoted as *Single Pool*) follows our *Keyframe Pool* approach but without any frame filtering. Using each of the above three methods, we generated the POI maps for all test examples. Due to page constraints, we visualized their contour plots for the first two test examples in Fig 3. The contours were plotted on top of a map for intuition.

In Fig. 3, the first three subfigures in each row correspond to the POI contours using the above three approaches. By checking the original video sensor data and looking into the popular regions among these ROI plots (areas with higher values, in red color), we found that the baseline method detected more popular regions that are nearer to the camera locations but the other two methods detected more popular areas distant from the camera locations. A plausible

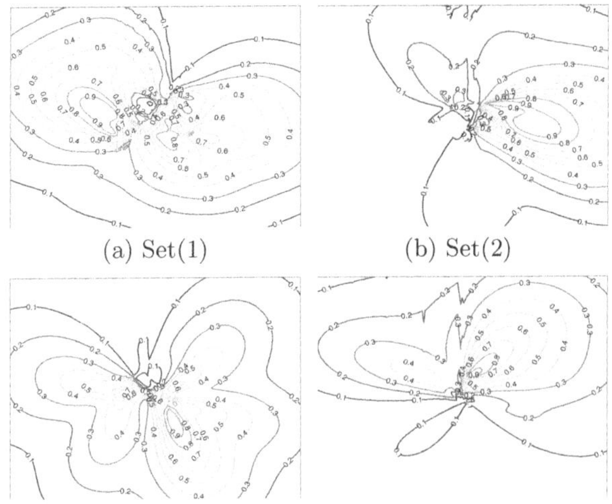

(a) Set(1) (b) Set(2)

(c) Set(3) (d) Set(4)

Figure 2: The contour plots of the scaled POI maps for four test cases.

explanation is that video frames that sharing similar camera locations and viewing directions are prone to have similar coverage. However, if assuming POIs are located only along the central camera view directions, the distant grids within the visible regions among these frames are less likely to be overlapped to each other than the nearby grids. *Single Pool* and *Keyframe Pool* produced POIs in a similar way and hence generated similar distributions. A key difference is that *Keyframe Pool* emphasizes a location more if it is shared among multi-*video* while the *Single Pool* emphasizes a location shared among multi-*frame*. This is because *Keyframe Pool* filters frames with low informativeness and hence a video with much longer duration will not overwhelmingly suppress the contribution from other shorter videos to the POI probabilities. We extracted in total 9 and 8 local maximal regions in the two POI maps generated using Keyframe Pool method and labeled them in Figs. 3(d) and 3(h). Each centroid was assigned a name by searching its nearest semantic objects (or watching the videos if the POIs are event places) with a sample image shown in Fig. 3.2. Most of these POIs are popular places that can also be referred from external tourism databases.

Table 2: Distance to the ground truth under three algorithms (unit: meters).

	Average			Standard Deviation		
	Baseline	Single	Key	Baseline	Single	Key
Set(1)	19.158	0.465	0.182	37.420	0.855	0.542
Set(2)	10.912	0.169	0.108	7.370	0.275	0.129
Set(3)	5.376	0.375	0.347	8.218	0.673	0.547
Set(4)	9.587	0.144	0.119	6.204	0.258	0.229

As a further validation, we extracted a list of tags in the same space from each video set [6]. Each tag corresponds to an object with a ranking indicating how well the object is visible in these videos. Highly ranked objects are expected to be assigned as POIs with higher probability as well, *i.e.*, detected POIs are close to these visible objects. So we generated the top 10-50 visible objects, extracted their locations as ground-truth. Meanwhile for each POI centroid, we computed the distance to the nearest object in ground-truth and summed them together with results in Table 2. Compared with the Baseline, the distance are reduced from a

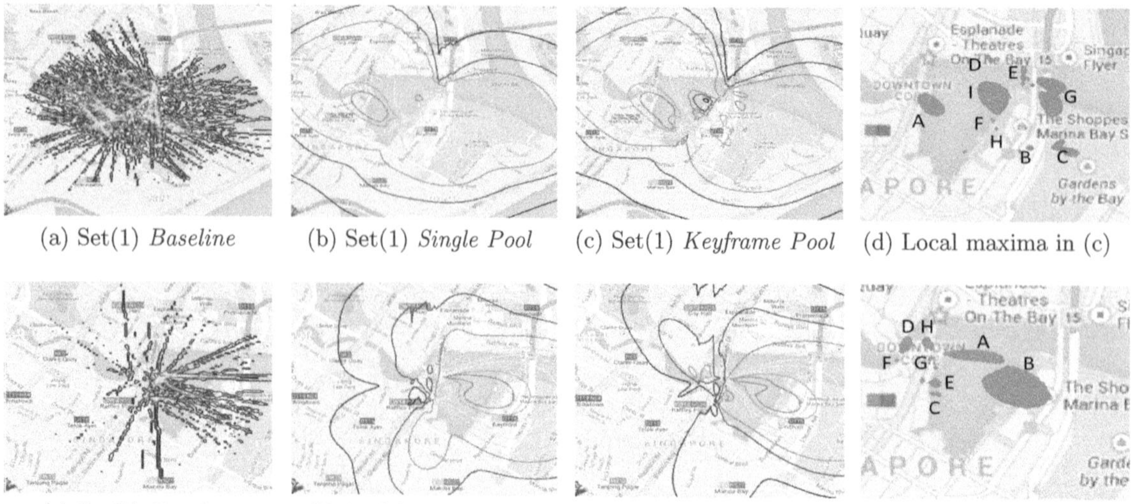

(a) Set(1) *Baseline* (b) Set(1) *Single Pool* (c) Set(1) *Keyframe Pool* (d) Local maxima in (c)

(e) Set(2) *Baseline* (f) Set(2) *Single Pool* (g) Set(2) *Keyframe Pool* (h) Local maxima in (g)

Figure 3: Comparison among three methods for Set(1) and Set(2).

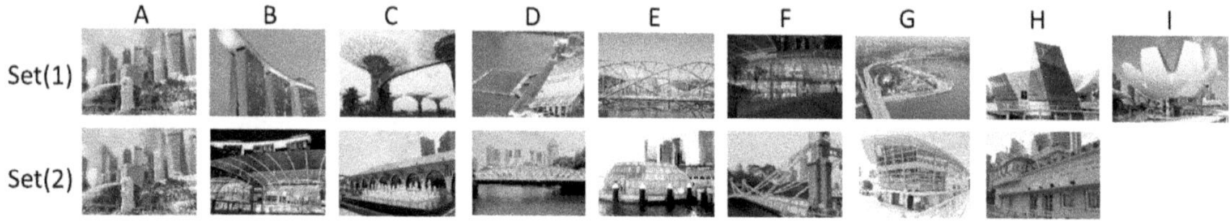

Figure 4: Sample images of POIs in Set(1) – A: One Fullerton/Merlion, B: Marina Bay Sands Tower, C: Gardens by the Bay South, D: The Float, E: Double Helix Bridge, F: Shoppes at Marina Bay Sands, G: East Coast Parkway (Part), H: Crystal Pavilion North, I: Art Science Museum. Set(2) – A: Merlion/Boating, B: Shoppes at Marina Bay Sands, C: Clifford Pier, D: Anderson Bridge, E: The Fullerton Pavilion, F: Cavenagh Bridge, G: One Fullterton, H: The Fullerton Waterboat House.

few dozens to several meters, indicating our algorithm can produce reasonable results that well map to the real world.

4. CONCLUSIONS

In this work, we propose a probability model to formulate the capture intention distribution for video frames and design an algorithm for POI detection by considering the contributions from multiple videos. Experiment results demonstrate that our algorithm detects POIs with distance error reduced from several dozens to a few meters.

Acknowledgements

This research has been supported by the Singapore National Research Foundation under its International Research Centre @ Singapore Funding Initiative and administered by the IDM Programme Office through the Centre of Social Media Innovations for Communities (COSMIC).

5. REFERENCES

[1] S. Arslan Ay, R. Zimmermann, and S. H. Kim. Viewable Scene Modeling for Geospatial Video Search. In 16th *ACM International Conference on Multimedia*, pages 309–318, October 2008.

[2] M. Belkin, P. Niyogi, and V. Sindhwani. Manifold Regularization: A Geometric Framework for Learning from Labeled and Unlabeled Examples. *The Journal of Machine Learning Research*, 7:2399–2434, 2006.

[3] D. Cai and X. He. Manifold Adaptive Experimental Design for Text Categorization. *IEEE Transactions on Knowledge and Data Engineering (TKDE)*, 24(4):707–719, 2012.

[4] J. Hao, G. Wang, B. Seo, and R. Zimmermann. Keyframe Presentation for Browsing of User-generated Videos on Map Interfaces. In 19th *ACM International Conference on Multimedia*, pages 1013–1016, November 2011.

[5] B. Platel, E. Balmachnova, L. M. J. Florack, and B. M. ter Haar Romeny. Top-Points as Interest Points for Image Matching. In *European Conference on Computer Vision*, pages 418–429. May 2006.

[6] Z. Shen, S. Arslan Ay, S. H. Kim, and R. Zimmermann. Automatic Tag Generation and Ranking for Sensor-rich Outdoor Videos. In 19th *ACM International Conference on Multimedia*, pages 93–102, November 2011.

[7] B. Thomee. Localization of Points of Interest from Georeferenced and Oriented Photographs. In *ACM International Workshop on Geotagging and Its Applications in Multimedia*, pages 19–24, October 2013.

[8] J. Yang, J. Luo, J. Yu, and T. Huang. Photo Stream Alignment and Summarization for Collaborative Photo Collection and Sharing. *IEEE Transactions on Multimedia (TMM)*, 14(6):1642–1651, 2012.

[9] Y. Yang, Y. Yang, and H. T. Shen. Effective Transfer Tagging from Image to Video. *ACM Transactions on Multimedia Computing, Communications and Applications (TOMCCAP)*, 9(2):14:1–14:20, 2013.

[10] Y.-T. Zheng, Z.-J. Zha, and T.-S. Chua. Research and Applications on Georeferenced Multimedia: a Survey. *Multimedia Tools and Applications (MTAP)*, 51(1):77–98, 2011.

[11] Q.-Y. Zhou and V. Koltun. Dense Scene Reconstruction with Points of Interest. *ACM Transactions on Graphics*, 32(4):112:1–112:8, 2013.

Recognizing Human Activities from Smartphone Sensor Signals

Arindam Ghosh
DISI
University of Trento
Trento, Italy
aghosh@disi.unitn.it

Giuseppe Riccardi
DISI
University of Trento
Trento, Italy
riccardi@disi.unitn.it

ABSTRACT

In context-aware computing, Human Activity Recognition (HAR) aims to understand the current activity of users from their connected sensors. Smartphones with their various sensors are opening a new frontier in building human-centered applications for understanding users' personal and world contexts. While in-lab and controlled activity recognition systems have yielded very good results, they do not perform well under in-the-wild scenarios. The objective of this paper is to 1) Investigate how audio signal can complement and improve other on-board sensors (accelerometer and gyroscope) for activity recognition; 2) Design and evaluate the fusion of such multiple signal streams to optimize performance and sampling rate. We show that fusion of these signal streams, including audio, achieves high performance even at very low sampling rates; 3) Evaluate the performance of the multi-stream human activity recognition under different real end-user activity conditions.

Categories and Subject Descriptors

I.5.4 [**Pattern Recognition**]: Applications—*Signal processing*; H.1.2 [**Information Systems**]: User/Machine Systems—*Human factors*

Keywords

Human Activity Recognition; Signal Fusion; Smartphone Sensing

1. INTRODUCTION

In context-aware computing, Human Activity Recognition (HAR) aims to understand the current activity of users from their connected sensors. Portable sensors platforms are either wearable or smartphone-based. In the first case, wearable computers are designed to deliver target signals such as Heart Rate, Skin Temperature, Galvanic Skin Response. In the second case smartphone platforms are usually designed to support sensors such as gyroscope, accelerometer, microphone. These sensors can be used for understanding the user's activity which can provide us with contextual information about the user's present state. Knowing whether a user is sitting or walking or commuting can significantly affect human-computer interaction. Activity Recognition has been used in various fields from monitoring the elderly [13] to providing contextual recommendations [2].

Activity recognition systems can be classified as vision based, sensor based, or a fusion of the two. While vision based systems use external cameras [16] to monitor the users and hence are limited in their application scenario, sensor based systems are usually wearable and can monitor users in more unconstrained environments. Till recent years in most sensor-based approaches, users had to attach multiple dedicated motion sensors [11] to various parts of the body such as legs, arms, and waist. While such systems have been able to achieve high recognition performances, they require elaborate set up and can be uncomfortable to wear and hence are not very suitable for long-term monitoring.

The recent proliferation of smartphones with their plethora of sensors have opened up a new frontier in context aware human computer interaction. Most modern smartphones have embedded sensors such as microphone, camera, accelerometer and gyroscope. Accelerometer and gyroscope sensors have been successfully used to detect human activity [1], understand human mobility patterns [4], and monitor Activities of Daily Living [17]. Scientists have also exploited the microphone on smartphones for daily activity recognition. The SoundSense [10] project used the microphone on a smartphone for detecting and modeling sound events in everyday life. Bieber et al [3] combined the accelerometer and microphone sensors for detecting everyday activities. Schuller et al in [15] used the microphone of a smartphone for acoustic geo-sensing to automatically determine a cyclists route.

However, smartphone sensors are not robust, and performance of a single-sensor based classification systems leads to sub-optimal and non-robust performances. The quality and response of on-board accelerometer and gyroscope sensors vary across manufacturers and devices. Certain smartphones do not have dedicated gyroscope hardware, and implement it in software propagating errors from accelerometer into gyroscope readings. The accelerometer performance for activity recognition task degrades rapidly when the user is playing a game on the smartphone or using an application. Similarly, as reported in [10] audio data cannot be the sole source of information when the phone is in a backpack or the

MM'14, November 3–7, 2014, Orlando, Florida, USA.

http://dx.doi.org/10.1145/2647868.2655034.

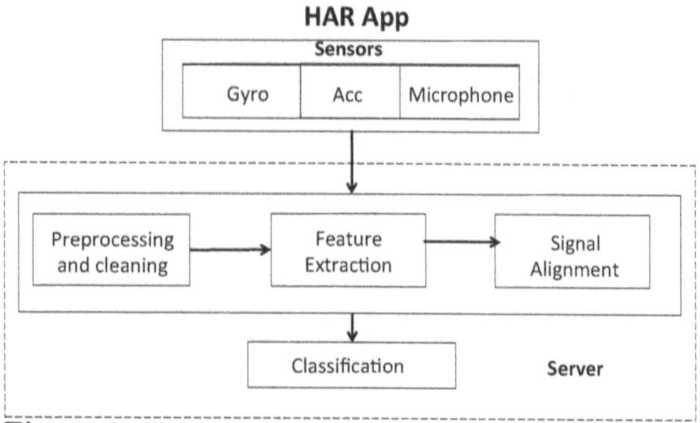

Figure 1: The process diagram. The embedded smartphone sensors record data and stream them to the server where pre-processing, feature-extraction and alignment, and classification steps are performed.

user is on a call. The solution is to use multiple weak signals and combine them to improve the recognition of a user's activity state. Combining multiple sensors can also lead to opportunistic sensing, thus improving the energy consumption of the phone by smart decisions on turning on/off sensors at appropriate times.

Proper evaluation of an activity recognition system is another challenge. Although activity recognition using smartphone data is a popular research field, very few publicly available corpora have raw data available. Even then, most of the corpora were created under controlled environments with static phone placements, or scripted activities where the user does not otherwise use the smartphone during the data collection. Therefore we carried out our own data collection on the Android and iOS platforms in a naturalistic settings. We also collected a smaller "stress-test" corpus where the data was collected while the participants were actively using the phone [1].

2. DATA COLLECTION

Two sets of data collection were performed to the hypotheses. Each experiment involved 15 (9 male and 6 female) participants. Participants varied in age between 25 and 40. The devices used were smartphones running android [2] (10 participants) and iOS[3] (5 participants) operating systems. Participants were located in various cities in Italy, Spain, and India, thus providing our data a wide variability. While a separate application was developed for each platform, both applications had the same functionality and recorded data from the same set of sensors. The applications sampled the *tri-axial accelerometer sensor, gyroscope sensor, location sensor, and microphone* during the data collection phase. The tri-axial accelerometer and gyroscope data was recorded at the rate of 40 Hz, and audio was recorded with a 8 KHz sampling rate. Location data was collected at the rate of 1 sample per 5 minutes, and was used only for validation and was not a part of the activity recognition process. Also, the participants often turned off location service on their phone to decrease power consumption.

The first data collection was a controlled scenario where the participant did not interact with the phone during the length of the experiment. Data was collected for six activities. They are: *Walking, Standing, Sitting, Driving, Travelling by bus, and Travelling by train.* The data collection protocol involved the participant launching the application before starting an activity, marking the activity start point on the application, and going on with the activity, finally marking the end when the activity was over. Participants were free to carry the phone as they wanted, but had to annotate the phone placement (pocket, purse, in hand, etc) at the start of the activity using a multiple choice drop-down in the application. The participants were asked to upload the data to our servers at the end of the day. From our data we observe that in majority of the cases, the phone was carried on the body (front or back trouser/jacket pocket), with 3 instances of the phone being placed in the purse. We ignored two instances where the participant was sitting and the phone was kept on the table.

The participants were free to delete sessions in case there was any undesired characteristic to the data. This could include personal data (audio,location) which the participants did not wish to share.

We collected approximately 31.6 hours of data (See Table 1), with each individual activity session ranging from 5 minutes (mostly walking) to 1 hour (commuting).

Walking	Standing	Sitting	Driving	By Bus	Train
4.12	8.31	8.23	3.13	2.19	5.12

Table 1: Activity Distribution in hours for normal activities. The participants placed the phones in pre-defined positions and did not interact with the phone during the experiment. Reported numbers are in hours.

Walking	Standing	Sitting	By car	By Bus	Train
0.32	1.21	3.23	2.19	2.47	1.3

Table 2: Activity Distribution for noisy activities. The participants were actively using their phones(playing games,texting or typing emails) during this experiment.Reported numbers are in hours.

For the second data collection, our goal was to collect data while the participants were actively using the phone. Most activity recognition experiments have low performance in real scenarios because they ignore the fact that people interact with their smartphones. During this data collection, the participants were asked to play games or type email or text messages for the duration of the data collection. We replaced the driving scenario with *Travelling by car* during this experiment. Approximately 10 hours of data (See Table 2) was collected for this scenario.

3. EXPERIMENTS AND RESULTS

3.1 Feature Extraction

To remove unwanted noise from the beginning and end of each activity session, we remove the first and last N seconds of the data. N was taken at T/10 seconds with a max value of N=30 seconds where T was the duration of the activity session. We only consider sessions which lasted at least 5 minutes for our experiments.

We divide each(Acc, and Gyro) signal channel into a 3 second sliding window with 50% overlap which has been shown to be effective [1, 14] window size for best performance in activity recognition using smartphones.

[1]The data is available for research purpose only. Please contact http://sisl.disi.unitn.it/
[2]version 4.0 and higher
[3]iOS 6 and higher

3.1.1 Accelerometer and Gyroscope

Accelerometer and Gyroscope each have 3 axes x,y,z. We first compute the acceleration magnitude, given by:

$$A_{norm} = \sqrt{{A_x}^2 + {A_y}^2 + {A_z}^2}$$

Now for each of the x, y, z, axes and norm of the accelerometer and gyroscope data we extract standard features for each 3-second window. We calculate the mean, standard deviation, min, max, number of peaks, number of zero crossings, inter-peak distances, etc for each of the accelerometer and gyroscope axes.

3.1.2 Audio

We use the same window size for processing and extracting features from the audio signal. While extracting features, we segment the audio stream into small uniform frames. Standard frame-sizes for audio processing lie between 25-46 milliseconds. In our case we use a 23 milliseconds half-overlapping subframes of audio as used by McKinney et al [12].

For the audio signal, we use Opensmile [7] to extract features. The following are the main features for each window:

1. Zero crossing rate - ZCR is defined as the number of time-domain zero-crossings within a frame.
2. RMS Energy - We use the Simple Moving Average of the mean, standard deviation, skewness, max, min, and range of the RMS energy of each window.
3. MFCCs which are very commonly used in Speech and Speaker recognition, have been recently used for recognition of environmental Sound [5]. We use the Simple Moving Average of the mean, standard deviation, skewness, max, min and range of 12 MFCCs for each window.

Durrent et al. [6] defines sensor fusion configuration as complementary if the sensors do not directly depend on each other. While older smartphones use a software gyroscope, modern smartphones (which were used for our experiments) have a dedicated gyroscope chip. So in our experiment we treat the sensor channels as complimentary and use the absolute time for each sensor event (recorded during our data collection) to align the data. We perform a feature-level fusion (early fusion) of the different streams by concatenating the time-aligned feature sets before the learning stage. For each classification experiment we perform feature-vector normalization before training. For each window, all feature-vectors form a $m \times n$ matrix where m is the *window size* $\times$ *sampling rate* for that window and n is the *length of each feature vector*. For each feature f_{ij} in the feature vector where i=1 ... n is the number of the feature ,and j is the jth row we normalize the feature using:

$$f_{ij} = \frac{f_{ij} - Min(f_{ij})}{Max(f_{ij}) - Min(f_{ij})}, i = 1 \ldots n; j = 1 \ldots m$$

3.2 Classification and Results

We used the WEKA machine learning toolkit [8] to test different classifiers using the above normalized features. First we used the data from the first experiment with the highest sampling rate to choose a classifier. We tested three different classifiers : Support Vector Machines, J48 decision trees, and random forests. Random forests provided us with the best F-measures (see Table 3), hence further classification was done with random forest for the different sets of experiments. For all classification experiments results were obtained by 15-fold (leave-one-subject-out) cross validation where each fold corresponds to the data for one subject. We used the full feature set with data sampled at 40 samples/second.

Signal	**Acc**	**Gyro**	**Audio**	Acc Gyro	Acc Gyro Audio
SVM	0.85	0.79	0.79	0.87	0.91
Decision Trees	0.85	0.82	0.83	0.85	0.90
Random Forest	**0.91**	**0.84**	**0.85**	**0.93**	**0.98**

Table 3: Average F-measure of 15-fold (one-fold-per-user) cross validation for the classification algorithms tested with the full feature set with data sampled at 40 samples/second and a 3-second sliding window

A major problem with using sensors is that polling them continuously can lead to power drain. One of the goals of our experiment was to determine how gracefully the recognition quality decreases when the sampling rate is decreased.

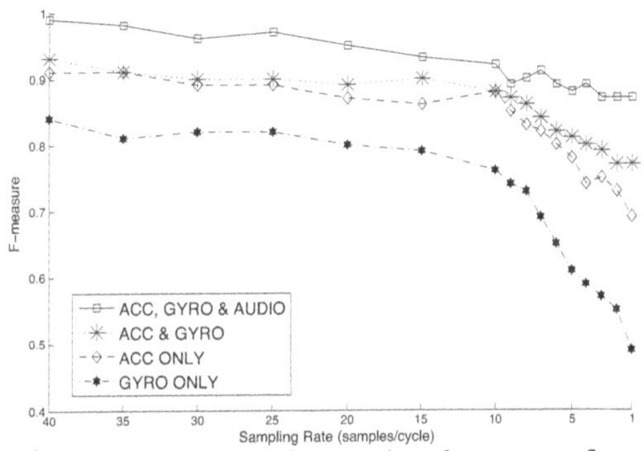

Figure 2: Effect of stepwise decrease of sampling rate (from 40 to 1 samples/sec) on F-measure. We see that adding audio leads to better accuracy at lower sampling of acc and gyro sensors.

We carried out LOSO cross-validation classification experiments using random forests. We experimented with different window sizes and a 3-second window was confirmed to be the best. Krause et. al in [9] showed that sampling rate of sensors has a direct effect on the battery life of a wearable device and decreasing sampling rate lowers power consumption. We performed stepwise downsampling of the accelerometer and gyroscope signals from 40 sample/sec to 1 sample/sec. From Figure 2 we see that accelerometer performance(F-measure) drops from 0.91 to 0.69 when the sampling rate is decreased from 40 to 1 sample/sec. Gyroscope performance (F-measure) drops more steeply from 0.84 to 0.49 in this range. A combination of Accelerometer and Gyroscope fairs comparatively better, degrading from 0.93 to 0.77. Adding audio signals from the microphone not only helps to provide better results at higher sampling rate (0.98 at 40 samples/sec), but also helps to balance the drop to only 0.89 at the lower end. However, we did not experiment with different sampling rates of the audio because of the limitation of the audio format for recording. AAC audio coding, which is the standard audio codec on both iOS and android does not support compression below 8 kHz. So all experiments with audio were carried out at this sampling rate.

From Table 4 we see that under controlled experimental conditions, accelerometer performance can be a good measure for understanding a participant's current motion pro-

Signal	Avg precision	Avg Recall	Avg F-measure
Acc	0.90±0.02	0.91±0.03	0.91±0.03
Gyro	0.83±0.08	0.84±0.07	0.84±0.08
Audio	0.85±0.06	0.86±0.07	0.85±0.07
Acc Gyro	0.93±0.06	0.92±0.06	0.93±0.06
Acc Gyro Audio	**0.98**±0.05	**0.97**±0.05	**0.98±0.05**

Table 4: Average Precision, Recall and F-measure using random forests. For this experiment the participants were requested to place the phones at pre-defined location and not use it during the experiment

Signal	Avg precision	Avg Recall	Avg F-measure
Acc	0.75±0.13	0.77±0.10	0.76±0.11
Gyro	0.70±0.17	0.74±0.16	0.72±0.16
Audio	0.85±0.08	0.85±0.09	0.85±0.08
Acc Gyro	0.79±0.13	0.80±0.12	0.80±0.13
Acc Gyro Audio	**0.86±0.11**	**0.88±0.11**	**0.87±0.12**

Table 5: Average Precision, Recall and F-measure of sensor channels using random forests. For this experiment the participants were actively using the phone during data collection

file. In this experiment the participants were expected not to interact with the phone for the duration of the experiment. While post-processing we ensured that we removed all instances where the screen of the phone was unlocked for durations longer than 10 seconds during a data collection session since it indicated that the participant was using the phone. However, since the participants were free to carry the phones as they wanted, this data collection is less controlled than other controlled data collection [1, 4] for activity recognition.

Table 5 shows the recognition results when the participants were actively using the device phone while performing an activity. Average precision for single sensor channels is lower than in the controlled experiments reported in Table 4 . The accelerometer and gyroscope individually perform lower (F-measures 0.76 and 0.72 respectively) than in the controlled scenario (F-measures 0.91 and 0.84 respectively). While combining the two sensor streams improves the recognition rates (F-mseasure 0.80), combining the motion sensor channels with audio achieves the best results (F-measure 0.87) under this scenario.

4. CONCLUSIONS

In this paper we have explored the use and combination of multiple weak smartphone sensors. We show that while smartphone sensor quality drops heavily during real-world usage, combining multiple signal streams can lead to better recognition results. We also exploit the less-used microphone sensor on a smartphone. We show that by leveraging audio features we can achieve high results. By combining audio features with other weak sensor features we can come up with a robust activity recognition scheme.

5. REFERENCES

[1] D. Anguita, A. Ghio, L. Oneto, X. Parra, and J. L. Reyes-Ortiz. Human activity recognition on smartphones using a multiclass hardware-friendly support vector machine. In *Ambient Assisted Living and Home Care*, pages 216–223. Springer, 2012.

[2] V. Bellotti, B. Begole, E. H. Chi, N. Ducheneaut, J. Fang, E. Isaacs, T. King, M. W. Newman, K. Partridge, B. Price, et al. Activity-based serendipitous recommendations with the magitti mobile leisure guide. In *Proceedings of the SIGCHI Conference on Human Factors in Computing Systems*, pages 1157–1166. ACM, 2008.

[3] G. Bieber, A. Luthardt, C. Peter, and B. Urban. The hearing trousers pocket: activity recognition by alternative sensors. In *Proceedings of the 4th International Conference on PErvasive Technologies Related to Assistive Environments*, page 44. ACM, 2011.

[4] Y. Chon, E. Talipov, H. Shin, and H. Cha. Mobility prediction-based smartphone energy optimization for everyday location monitoring. In *Proceedings of the 9th ACM conference on embedded networked sensor systems*, pages 82–95. ACM, 2011.

[5] S. Chu, S. Narayanan, and C.-C. Kuo. Environmental sound recognition with time–frequency audio features. *Audio, Speech, and Language Processing, IEEE Transactions on*, 17(6):1142–1158, 2009.

[6] H. F. Durrant-Whyte. Sensor models and multisensor integration. *The International Journal of Robotics Research*, 7(6):97–113, 1988.

[7] F. Eyben, M. Wöllmer, and B. Schuller. Opensmile: the munich versatile and fast open-source audio feature extractor. In *Proceedings of the international conference on Multimedia*, pages 1459–1462. ACM, 2010.

[8] M. Hall, E. Frank, G. Holmes, B. Pfahringer, P. Reutemann, and I. H. Witten. The weka data mining software: an update. *ACM SIGKDD explorations newsletter*, 11(1):10–18, 2009.

[9] A. Krause, M. Ihmig, E. Rankin, D. Leong, S. Gupta, D. Siewiorek, A. Smailagic, M. Deisher, and U. Sengupta. Trading off prediction accuracy and power consumption for context-aware wearable computing. In *Wearable Computers, 2005. Proceedings. Ninth IEEE International Symposium on*, pages 20–26. IEEE, 2005.

[10] H. Lu, W. Pan, N. D. Lane, T. Choudhury, and A. T. Campbell. Soundsense: scalable sound sensing for people-centric applications on mobile phones. In *Proceedings of the 7th international conference on Mobile systems, applications, and services*, pages 165–178. ACM, 2009.

[11] U. Maurer, A. Smailagic, D. P. Siewiorek, and M. Deisher. Activity recognition and monitoring using multiple sensors on different body positions. In *Wearable and Implantable Body Sensor Networks, 2006. BSN 2006. International Workshop on*, pages 4–pp. IEEE, 2006.

[12] M. F. McKinney and J. Breebaart. Features for audio and music classification. In *ISMIR*, volume 3, pages 151–158, 2003.

[13] G. Perolle, P. Fraisse, M. Mavros, and I. Etxeberria. Automatic fall detection and activity monitoring for elderly. *Proceedings of MEDETEL*, 2006.

[14] A. Reiss, G. Hendeby, and D. Stricker. A competitive approach for human activity recognition on smartphones. In *ESANN 2013*, pages 455–460. ESANN, 2013.

[15] B. Schuller, F. Pokorny, S. Ladstatter, M. Fellner, F. Graf, and L. Paletta. Acoustic geo-sensing: Recognising cyclists' route, route direction, and route progress from cell-phone audio. In *Acoustics, Speech and Signal Processing (ICASSP), 2013 IEEE International Conference on*, pages 453–457. IEEE, 2013.

[16] D. Weinland, R. Ronfard, and E. Boyer. A survey of vision-based methods for action representation, segmentation and recognition. *Computer Vision and Image Understanding*, 115(2):224–241, 2011.

[17] C. Zhu and W. Sheng. Human daily activity recognition in robot-assisted living using multi-sensor fusion. In *Robotics and Automation, 2009. ICRA'09. IEEE International Conference on*, pages 2154–2159. IEEE, 2009.

Twitter-driven YouTube Views: Beyond Individual Influencers

Honglin Yu, Lexing Xie, Scott Sanner
The Australian National University and NICTA, Canberra, Australia
honglin.yu@anu.edu.au, lexing.xie@anu.edu.au, ssanner@nicta.com.au

ABSTRACT

This paper proposes a novel method to predict increases in YouTube viewcount driven from the Twitter social network. Specifically, we aim to predict two types of viewcount increases: a sudden increase in viewcount (named as JUMP), and the viewcount shortly after the upload of a new video (named as EARLY). Experiments on hundreds of thousands of videos and millions of tweets show that Twitter-derived features alone can predict whether a video will be in the top 5% for EARLY popularity with 0.7 Precision@100. Furthermore, our results reveal that while individual influence is indeed important for predicting how Twitter drives YouTube views, it is a diversity of interest from the most active to the least active Twitter users mentioning a video (measured by the variation in their total activity) that is *most* informative for both JUMP and EARLY prediction. In summary, by going beyond features that quantify individual influence and additionally leveraging collective features of activity variation, we are able to obtain an effective cross-network predictor of Twitter-driven YouTube views.

Category and Subject Descriptors H.2.8 DATABASE MANAGEMENT Database Applications — data mining

Keywords Popularity prediction; social media; YouTube; Twitter

1. INTRODUCTION

Predicting item popularity in social media is a well-recognized open problem. Take YouTube videos, for example, where particular interesting and challenging questions include "will an obscure video suddenly become very popular, and when?", "which videos will be the top 5% popular ones in 1, 2, or 3 months?", and "when will the attention on a very popular video fade out, if ever?" Questions like these are inherently difficult, because determining popular items in social media not only relates to the attention dynamics of online videos, it is also affected by many complex factors from virality to news events to seasonality that make it difficult to quantify the interplay of such phenomena. Despite the mounting challenge, such prediction tasks are important both in their value for understanding collective online behavior, and in a wide range of applications from content discovery and recommendation to video distribution infrastructure to online advertisement.

MM'14, November 3–7, 2014, Orlando, Florida, USA.

ACM http://dx.doi.org/10.1145/2647868.2655037.

This work is related to several areas in online video and social media popularity. Early studies included large-scale profiling of content [5] and their social networks [7]. Subsequent measurements provided statistics on video popularity [6] and its geographic distribution [4]. A number of recent works focused on forecasting popularity: YouTube video views are found to be predictable from recent viewcount history [13, 15], aggregate video sharing behavior is found to be related to geographical, social and temporal sharing trends [16], and the lifecycle of trending topics in the news are found to generalize from historically similar topics across multiple information platforms [2]. More recently, researchers started to examine video sharing behavior on microblogs. Abisheva *et al* [1] performed a large-scale profiling of the YouTube video audience by analyzing Twitter and Roy *et al* [14] used tweets to improve YouTube video recommendation. In video popularity prediction, viewcount-based methods tend to fit smooth trends well, but are inherently unable to predict sudden changes in popularity that may be driven by external sources such as Twitter. Cross-platform social media content has seen recent success for predicting individual consumption [19]. In this paper, we investigate whether Twitter feeds can also help predict YouTube video popularity.

This work investigates two particular challenging scenarios for YouTube video popularity prediction. The first is a sudden increase in viewcount, called "jumps", which are often triggered by external events and referrals. Fig 1(a) shows a short video having an abrupt increase of 1.5 million views after receiving little attention in the first 4 months after its upload – interestingly, we also note a few hundred tweets linking to this video right around the jump. The second scenario is predicting the popularity of newly uploaded videos, when no or very little viewcount history is available; this task can also be helped by information from external networks – as shown in Fig 1(b), a wave of tweets about this video started right around its upload, and viewcount continued to rise even after the tweet volume faded out. Our insight for tackling these two challenging scenarios is the effective use of content and user information from Twitter. Going beyond the conventional wisdom of social influencers [8], we design features to capture the volume of tweets, the network position and connectivity of users, and the dynamic interactions among tweets and users. We train SVM classifiers using these features for two prediction tasks, called JUMP and EARLY.

Our results demonstrate that Twitter information can be effectively used to predict YouTube viewcount, with a prediction system built from tens of thousands of videos mentioned by millions of tweets during a 3-month period in 2009. We observe that for viewcount JUMP, leveraging Twitter features nearly quadruples the performance from viewcount history, with a 0.46 Precision@100, compared to 0.12 using viewcount alone. When viewcount history is not available (EARLY), we can predict the top 5% popular videos

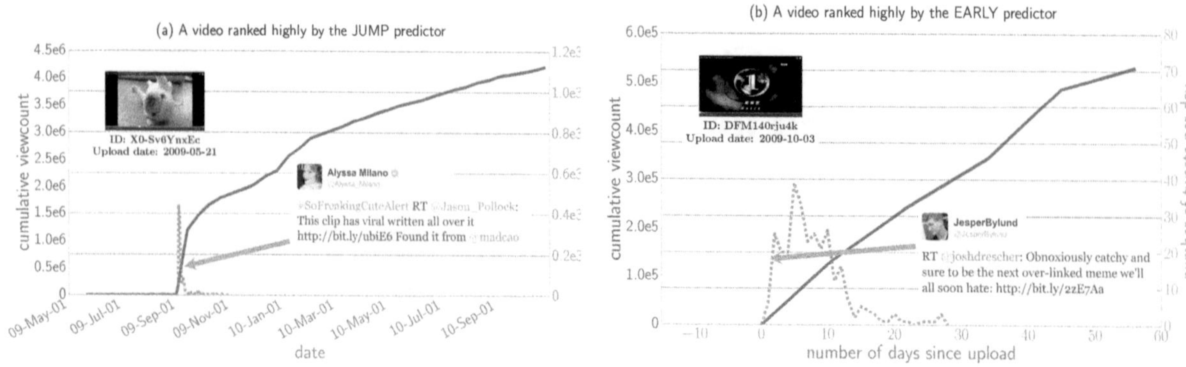

Figure 1: Examples of top predictions for JUMP and EARLY. (a) A video having less than 9000 views in its first 3 months, and then gaining 1.2 million views within 15 days (date format of x-axis: yy-mmm-dd). The insert shows a tweet linking to this video by celebrity user Alyssa Milano[2]. (b) A video with a few dozen Twitter mentions and nearly 2×10^5 views in its first 15 days. Note that the video popularity continues to rise even after the tweet volume has tapered off, illustrating the prediction power of "early tweets".

over their first 90 days with a 0.70 Precision@100, using only Twitter information from the first 15 days. Among many critical insights, we note that Twitter features describing user interactions are more predictive than features describing their social network derived influence; furthermore, aggregating these user interaction levels by standard deviation is most predictive of a video's popularity in both EARLY and JUMP, indicating that a diverse range of interactions is more important than average or total interactions.

2. DATA PROCESSING

We used three data sources: the YouTube video history providing total viewcounts received over time, a subset of tweets over a three-month period, and the Twitter user graph from the same period.

We obtain **YouTube viewcount history** from a video's webpage, when it's made available by the video owner. This history contains the number of views a video has received since its upload, in 100 evenly spaced time intervals, with daily viewcount obtained by temporal interpolation[3]. We use a collection of 467-million tweets of from 2009 [17]; this sample is estimated to contain about 20-30% of all posts published on Twitter during the 6-month period, and was authored by about 20 million users. Each tweet is represented as three fields: *author*, e.g., http://twitter.com/annieng ; *timestamp*, e.g., 2009-06-07 02:07:42; *tweet content*, e.g. "in LA now". We use a snapshot of the **Twitter user graph** from 2009 [11], with each user as a node, and each following relationship as a directed edge from a user to one of his/her followers.

We extracted URLs from all tweets and resolved shortened URLs, retaining references to YouTube videos. We found $1,624,274$ Twitter users tweeted YouTube video links at least once and that there are $2,350,881$ unique videos, of which $1,549,532$ (65.9%) are still online as of Oct 2013. Within this subset, $1,067,895$ (68.9%), have their viewcount history publicly available. We call the subset of tweets containing videos with available history *video tweets*. We match the tweets and the Twitter user graph dataset in order to extract the user graph information of the observed video tweets. About 80% of the users can be identified by matching the username directly, for 20% of the users we did not find a match. A tweet is dropped from the collection if its author cannot be identified.

We process tweets to extract tags and user interactions. We rely on text processing for this since our historical tweets collection does not contain the full Twitter API feed (where many interactions are already encoded). We extract **hashtags** and **mentions** by finding words prefixed with # and @ symbols. We also extract non-broadcasting tweets (**nbcTweet**) – when a tweet starts by mentioning a user, it is treated as a targeted interaction between the author the user being mentioned, and the followers of the author will not see this tweet in their timeline. We extract variations of retweet (**RT**). Symbols for retweeting have evolved since the early days of Twitter [10], and there are still a diverse set of symbols in use in the 2009 data. We extract ten major variants, i.e., *RT, R/T, via, HT, H/T, OH, retweet, ret*, plus two variants of the "recycle" symbol (♲).

[2] http://en.wikipedia.org/wiki/Alyssa_Milano

[3] The temporal granularity of viewcount history is about 12 days (with 1,100+ days between August 1, 2009 and data collection in Oct 2012) and varies depending on the video upload date.

3. PREDICTING VIDEO VIEWS

We begin describing the features and prediction tasks by defining units of data over time. We take a sliding time window of length τ as a unit for feature extraction and viewcount prediction. We define time index $t \in \{0, 1, \ldots, T\}$ with increments of τ. With slight overload of notation, index 0 may represent the real-world interval $[0, \tau)$, or time point $t = 0$, the interpretation should be clear from context. For a YouTube video v, denote its total viewcount (i.e. number of views received since upload) on time t as $c_v(t)$, and the viewcount increment between t and $t+1$ as $\Delta c_v(t)$. We use $U_v(t)$ to denote the set of Twitter users who tweeted video v in time interval t. In this work, the prediction targets are videos tweeted between August and November 2009 with $T = 93\ days$, and $\tau = 15\ days$ due to viewcount data granularity. Tweets published before August are used to compute features.

3.1 Features from YouTube and Twitter

We extract one set of YouTube features and four sets of Twitter features for prediction. There are two general types of aggregated Twitter features we investigate: those directly involving TWEETs on the video and those involving the users who have tweeted on a video. Among the latter type, we further make distinctions among ACTIVE, PASSIVE, and social GRAPH features of those users.

YT-VIEWS is the number views a video v receives in two time intervals before time t on which we are making a prediction, i.e. $[\Delta c_v(t-2), \Delta c_v(t-1)]$. Historical viewcount is shown to highly correlate with future viewcounts [15], and using more than one historical interval is shown to further improve prediction [13]. We chose two intervals via cross-validation. This feature is comparable to those used in prior work [15, 13], and used as the baseline for predicting JUMP .

TWEET includes five counting metrics that describe the properties of video tweets about video v in interval t: $T.tweet(v,t)$ is the number of video tweets; $T.hashtag(v,t)$ is the number of times a hashtag is used; $T.mention(v,t)$ and $T.nbcTweet(v,t)$ are the numbers of broadcasting and non-broadcasting mentions, respec-

Table 1: Six summary statistics for user features. u: a Twitter user; U: a set of Twitter users; $f(u)$: a user feature.

Name	Description
sum-log	$\sum_{u\in U}\log(f(u)+1)$
log-sum	$\log(\sum_{u\in U}(f(u))+1)$
mean-log	$\frac{1}{\lvert U\rvert}(\sum_{u\in U}\log(f(u)+1))$
log-mean	$\log((\frac{1}{\lvert U\rvert}(\sum_{u\in U}f(u))+1))$
std-log	$std(\{\log(f(u)+1)\}_{u\in U})$
log-std	$\log(std(\{f(u)\}_{u\in U})+1)$

tively; $T.RT(v,t)$ is the number of retweets for each of the 10 variants. Intuitively, videos are likely to obtain more views when they are tweeted or are part of twitter interactions (via hashtags, mentions, or retweets).

GRAPH consists of three features computed from the Twitter user graph. For a Twitter user u, $G.outdegree(u)$ is the number of followers he/she has. $G.pagerank(u)$ contains the pagerank score of a user, robust measure of a user's influence for hashtag adoption [18]. $G.hubauthority(u)$ contain a pair of hub and authority scores [9]. A Twitter user has high hub score if her followees have high authority scores; she has high authority scores if her followers have high hub scores.

ACTIVE consists of five types of behavior features for Twitter user u up to time $t-1$. They are denoted as $A.tweet(u)$, $A.hashtag(u)$, $A.mention(u)$, $A.nbcTweet(u)$, $A.RT(u)$ to capture the users' tweet volume, use of hashtags, sending of broadcasting and non-broadcasting mentions and retweet behaviors, respectively. Moreover, each feature type is represented with a number of metric variants. $A.tweet(u)$ includes four variants: the total and per-day average of all and unique tweets. Each interaction feature (hashtag, nbcTweet, mention, RT) includes four variants: the total number of interactions, its average per day; the number of unique user-to-user interactions, and its average per day.

PASSIVE consists of three behavior features that Twitter user u receives from other users up to time $t-1$. Denoted as $P.nbcTweet(u)$, $P.mention(u)$ and $P.RT(u)$, they represent interactions where user u is mentioned in broadcasting or non-broadcasting tweets, and retweeted, respectively. Each of these interactions features has the same metric variants as those for ACTIVE features.

Both active and passive features have been recognized as capturing user influence within Twitter [18], here we use them to infer YouTube popularity. Note that features from tweets are computed from dataset inception, i.e. 2009-05-31 [17]. Furthermore, we aggregate the GRAPH, ACTIVE and PASSIVE features from the set of users tweeting about the same video into six summary statistics. These statistics incorporate three kinds of aggregation – sum, mean, standard deviation (std); over two scaling variants – log-aggregate or aggregate-log. The method to compute them can be found in Table 1. This is to account for the variable number of users tweeting each video, and being able to generalize across users. An overview of all features is in Table 2. Note that the feature dimensionality includes summary statistics for all user features and all metric variants, e.g., A.RT (and P.RT) has 10 RT literals $\times$ 4 metric variants $\times$ 6 summary statistics, totaling 240 dimensions.

3.2 Two Prediction Tasks

JUMP captures cases when a video gains a large number of views in a relatively short period of time. For video v, denote the total viewcount gained between time 0 and T as $\Delta c_v(0,T)$; we compute the *normalized* gain during interval t as $r_v(t)=\Delta c_v(t)/\Delta c_v(0,T)$. For a video v, a *jump* is deemed to have occurred in time t if $\Delta c_v(t)$ has more than 50 views; $\Delta c_v(t-1)$ is not more than $\Delta c_v(0,T)/T$, the average gain over interval $[0,T)$; and $r_v(t)\geq\alpha$ with pre-defined threshold α. Defining jumps using such normalized increments allows us to compare videos that undergo popularity changes at very different levels, e.g., from hundreds to millions of views.

Table 2: Youtube and Twitter feature summary (Sec 3.1)

Feature group	Feature name	# of dimensions
YT-VIEWS	viewcount	2
TWEET	T.tweet	1
	T.hashtag	1
	T.mention	1
	T.nbcTweet	1
	T.RT	10
GRAPH	G.outdegree	6
	G.pagerank	6
	G.hubauthority	12
ACTIVE	A.tweet	24
	A.hashtag	24
	A.mention	24
	A.nbcTweet	24
	A.RT	240
PASSIVE	P.mention	24
	P.nbcTweet	24
	P.RT	240

EARLY captures cases when a video receives a significant number of views just after being uploaded. We take the most popular videos as prediction targets, i.e., those having the most viewcount in their first $\hat{\tau}$ days, denoted as $\Delta c_v(0,\hat{\tau})>\beta$, with a pre-defined threshold β. Prior approaches that rely on historical viewcount [13, 15] cannot be used to analyze such phenomenon.

Binary classifiers are trained with linear support vector machines for each task. We use $\alpha=0.5$, and $\beta=10^4$, high thresholds that yield popular videos which are likely to be mentioned in tweets. The empirical YouTube viewcount distributions are long-tailed, and do not show a clear separation around these (or any other) values. To this end, thresholds separating the top few percent videos are equally valid conceptually. Fig 1 (a) and (b) contain example videos in the respective JUMP and EARLY classes, which are ranked highly by our algorithm.

4. EXPERIMENTS

We evaluate JUMP and EARLY prediction with the following settings. For JUMP, each time interval t with at least one tweet about video v becomes an instance, there are 6,156 positive JUMP instances with a random guess prior of 1.2%. The five feature groups are specified in Section 3, and ALL is a result of concatenating features from all available groups. For EARLY, each video (in its first $\hat{\tau}$ days) becomes an instance. Results are reported on 29,998 videos, out of which about 5.3%, or 1,591 are positive examples. We report average precision (AP) [12] and Precision@100, with the average and the 95% confidence interval over 5-fold cross-validation with stratified sampling (preserving the random guess probability).

Table 3 summarizes the performance of different features for JUMP . We can see that among the four types of Twitter features, each improves upon results using viewcount history only. The best predictor doubles the AP and nearly quadruples the Precision@100 vs. viewcounts, and with Precision@100 at 0.46, almost half of the top-ranked videos actually contain a JUMP . In addition, differentiating users and taking into account user history (with GRAPH, ACTIVE and PASSIVE) perform significantly better than viewcounts or tweet properties.

Table 4 summarizes the prediction performance of EARLY , with the same feature groups as JUMP except that YT-VIEWS is unavailable for newly uploaded videos. The prediction is done for the first 15 days, and then $\hat{\tau}=30,60$ and 90 days. Longer term predictions are done with ACTIVE features, because (1) it is best-performing feature group – only 0.05 away from ALL in prec@100; (2) these features only need user history for the video tweets, and do not

Table 3: Performance for JUMP prediction. See Sec 4.

Features	Avg Prec	Prec@100
Random	0.012	0.012
YT-VIEWS	0.056 ± 0.006	0.125 ± 0.028
YT-VIEWS+TWEET	0.058 ± 0.002	0.204 ± 0.041
YT-VIEWS+GRAPH	0.097 ± 0.007	0.406 ± 0.023
YT-VIEWS+ACTIVE	0.105 ± 0.003	0.432 ± 0.057
YT-VIEWS+PASSIVE	0.104 ± 0.005	0.444 ± 0.044
ALL	0.113 ± 0.008	0.460 ± 0.053

Table 4: Performance for EARLY prediction. See Sec 4.

$\hat{\tau}$	Feature	Avg Prec	Prec@100
all	Random	0.053	0.053
15-d	TWEET	0.248 ± 0.142	0.450 ± 0.229
15-d	GRAPH	0.382 ± 0.030	0.646 ± 0.044
15-d	ACTIVE	0.441 ± 0.027	0.702 ± 0.058
15-d	PASSIVE	0.375 ± 0.055	0.656 ± 0.088
15-d	ALL	0.463 ± 0.029	0.750 ± 0.045
30-d	ACTIVE	0.421 ± 0.023	0.686 ± 0.060
60-d	ACTIVE	0.435 ± 0.024	0.722 ± 0.018
90-d	ACTIVE	0.424 ± 0.026	0.720 ± 0.043

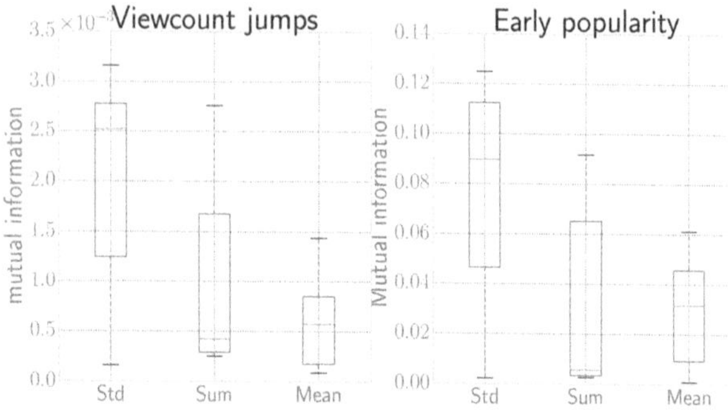

Figure 2: Box plots of mutual information grouped by feature aggregates. The most informative features are generated by std aggregation for both JUMP and EARLY .

need Twitter GRAPH or PASSIVE interactions, which are expensive to obtain. It is encouraging to see that the top 5% most popular videos can be predicted with an AP of more than 0.40, and there are 70+ correct entries in the top 100. Moreover, this accuracy is maintained from 15 to 90 days.

We perform an analysis on the informativeness of individual feature dimensions described in Sec 3. We compute the mutual information between the target class $Y \in 0, 1$ and each feature X, as $I(X;Y) = \sum_x \sum_y p(x,y) \log \frac{p(x,y)}{p(x)p(y)}$. The larger the mutual information, the more informative a feature is towards predicting the target. Fig 2 contains box plots of such mutual information on user features (GRAPH, ACTIVE and PASSIVE) grouped by the three feature aggregation methods: std, sum, and mean. We can see that the majority of most informative features (e.g. top 1/6 above the median for std) are std-features, with sum features moderately informative and mean features the least informative. A high standard deviation for a feature implies that there is broad interest across a spectrum of users with a range of activity and interaction levels. This concurs with a recent observation on hyperlinks in Twitter [3] – that having a diverse set of users (std) mentioning an item is helpful for improving its popularity.

5. CONCLUSION

In this work, we showed user and content information from Twitter can be effectively used to predict content popularity on YouTube, as shown in two challenging tasks – predicting viewcount JUMP and EARLY popularity – both with significant and quantifiable performance gains. These results are encouraging in that they show viewcounts are predictable from one external source alone, without taking into account the influence from many other social and traditional media sources (Reddit, Tumblr, Pinterest, Facebook, ...). Furthermore, the results show the predictive power of different features and aggregation methods and reveal that having a diverse range of users and associated tweeting activities is more informative than the total or average volume of activity of these users and also more informative than other features – including those based on social network derived measures of influence. This work raises many interesting avenues of future work, such as leveraging diffusion patterns on Twitter to further improve popularity prediction and quantifying the roles of "influencers" vs. "grassroots" users.

Acknowledgments NICTA is funded by the Australian Government as represented by the Department of Broadband, Communications and the Digital Economy and the Australian Research Council through the ICT Centre of Excellence program.This work was supported in part by the US Air Force Research Laboratory, under agreement number FA2386-12-1-4041 and Australian Research Council under project DP140102185.

6. REFERENCES

[1] A. Abisheva, V. R. K. Garimella, D. Garcia, and I. Weber. Who watches (and shares) what on youtube? and when?: using twitter to understand youtube viewership. In *WSDM*, pages 593–602, 2014.

[2] T. Althoff, D. Borth, J. Hees, and A. Dengel. Analysis and forecasting of trending topics in online media streams. In *ACM Multimedia*, 2013.

[3] E. Bakshy, J. M. Hofman, W. A. Mason, and D. J. Watts. Everyone's an influencer: quantifying influence on twitter. WSDM '11, pages 65–74, 2011.

[4] A. Brodersen, S. Scellato, and M. Wattenhofer. Youtube around the world: geographic popularity of videos. WWW '12.

[5] M. Cha, H. Kwak, P. Rodriguez, Y.-Y. Ahn, and S. Moon. I tube, you tube, everybody tubes: analyzing the world's largest user generated content video system. IMC '07, pages 1–14, 2007.

[6] G. Chatzopoulou, C. Sheng, and M. Faloutsos. A first step towards understanding popularity in youtube. In *INFOCOM Workshops*, pages 1–6, 2010.

[7] X. Cheng, C. Dale, and J. Liu. Statistics and social network of youtube videos. In *Quality of Service, 2008. IWQoS 2008. 16th International Workshop on*, pages 229–238, 2008.

[8] M. Gladwell. *The tipping point: How little things can make a big difference*. Hachette Digital, Inc., 2006.

[9] J. M. Kleinberg. Authoritative sources in a hyperlinked environment. *Journal of the ACM (JACM)*, 46(5):604–632, 1999.

[10] F. Kooti, H. Yang, M. Cha, K. Gummadi, and W. A. Mason. The emergence of conventions in online social networks. In *AAAI ICWSM*, 2012.

[11] H. Kwak, C. Lee, H. Park, and S. Moon. What is twitter, a social network or a news media? In *WWW*, pages 591–600. ACM, 2010.

[12] C. D. Manning, P. Raghavan, and H. Schütze. chapter Evaluation in information retrieval. Cambridge University Press, 2008.

[13] H. Pinto, J. M. Almeida, and M. A. Gonçalves. Using early view patterns to predict the popularity of youtube videos. WSDM '13.

[14] S. D. Roy, T. Mei, W. Zeng, and S. Li. Socialtransfer: cross-domain transfer learning from social streams for media applications. In *ACM Multimedia*, pages 649–658. ACM, 2012.

[15] G. Szabo and B. A. Huberman. Predicting the popularity of online content. *Commun. ACM*, 53(8):80–88, Aug. 2010.

[16] Z. Wang, L. Sun, X. Chen, W. Zhu, J. Liu, M. Chen, and S. Yang. Propagation-based social-aware replication for social video contents. MM '12, pages 29–38, 2012.

[17] J. Yang and J. Leskovec. Patterns of temporal variation in online media. WSDM, pages 177–186, 2011.

[18] L. Yang, T. Sun, M. Zhang, and Q. Mei. We know what @you #tag: does the dual role affect hashtag adoption? WWW '12, pages 261–270, 2012.

[19] Y. Zhang and M. Pennacchiotti. Predicting purchase behaviors from social media. In *WWW '13*, pages 1521–1532, 2013.

Decoding Auditory Saliency from FMRI Brain Imaging

Shijie Zhao[1, 2*], Xi Jiang[2*], Junwei Han[1**], Xintao Hu[1], Dajiang Zhu[2], Jinglei Lv[1, 2], Tuo Zhang[1, 2], Lei Guo[1], Tianming Liu[2**]

[1]School of Automation, Northwestern Polytechnical University, Xi'an, Shaanxi 710072, China; [2]Cortical Architecture Imaging and Discovery Lab, Department of Computer Science and Bioimaging Research Center, The University of Georgia, Athens, GA 30602, USA

{shijiezhao666, superjx2318, junweihan2010, xintao.hu, dajiang.zhu, lvjinglei, zhangtuo.npu}@gmail.com; lguo@nwpu.edu.cn; tliu@uga.edu *Co-first authors; **Co-corresponding authors

ABSTRACT

Given the growing number of available audio streams through a variety of sources and distribution channels, effective and advanced computational audio analysis has received increasing interest in the multimedia field. However, the effectiveness of current audio analysis strategies might be hampered due to the lack of effective representation of high-level semantics perceived by the human and the lack of effective approaches to bridging the gaps between most low-level acoustic features and high-level semantic features. This semantic gap has become the 'bottleneck' problem in audio analysis. In this paper, we propose a computational framework to decode biologically-plausible auditory saliency using high-level features derived from functional magnetic resonance imaging (fMRI) which monitors the human brain's response under the natural stimulus of audio listening. Specifically, we identify meaningful intrinsic brain networks which are involved in audio listening via effective online dictionary learning and sparse representation of whole-brain fMRI signals, reconstruct auditory saliency features using those identified brain network components, and perform group-wise analysis to identify consistent 'brain decoders' of the saliency features across different excerpts and participants. Experimental results demonstrate that the auditory saliency features are effectively decoded via our methods, which potentially provide opportunities for various applications in the multimedia field.

Categories and Subject Descriptors

H.1.2 [**User/Machine Systems**]: Human information processing; H.5.1 [**Multimedia Information Systems**]: Audio/Video.

General Terms

Algorithms, Design, Experimentation, Human Factors.

Keywords

Auditory saliency; Semantic gap; Decoding model; Functional magnetic resonance imaging

MM '14, November 3 – 7, 2014, Orlando, FL, USA.

http://dx.doi.org/10.1145/2647868.2655039

1. INTRODUCTION

Given the growing number of available audio streams through a variety of sources and distribution channels, effective and advanced computational audio analysis has received increasing interest in the multimedia field to advance content-based audio studies such as data representation, classification and retrieval. For previous audio analyses, three major categories of approaches have been largely adopted, including learning from users' interactions and feedback [1], constructing biologically-plausible acoustic features [2], and associating low-level acoustic features with the audio data semantics description [3], and remarkable successes have been achieved. However, the effectiveness of those strategies might be hampered due to the lack of effective representation of high-level semantics perceived by the human and the lack of effective approaches to bridging the gaps between most low-level acoustic features and high-level semantic features. This semantic gap has become the 'bottleneck' problem in audio analysis.

Interestingly, there is increasing effort from both multimedia and brain science researchers to integrate neuroscience knowledge and neuroimaging techniques (e.g., EEG [4, 5] and fMRI [6-9]) with audio analysis to bridge the semantic gaps. One of the milestone work reported that acoustic speech perceived by the human can be effectively decoded by fMRI signals [6]. In [6], the authors applied a data-mining algorithm to fMRI data and retrieved what and to whom a volunteer was listening from fMRI-derived neural fingerprints which were spatially distributed and insensitive to acoustic variations of the input as demonstrated in [6], thus permitting the fMRI-based recognition of learned voices from previously unheard utterances and of learned speech from other unknown speakers. In another milestone work [7], the authors proposed an iterative machine-learning algorithm which modeled spatially distributed fMRI-derived brain response patterns. It demonstrated that sound category information which was not identified via conventional contrast-based analysis was successfully detected via multi-voxel pattern analyses [7].

Moreover, there have been efforts in studying the neural basis of audio perception and understanding [10, 11]. As reported in [10,11], music perception and understanding involve widely distributed human brain areas and functional interactions among large scale brain networks, which provide the theoretical foundation for deriving whole brain semantic features to perform low-level feature decoding. Note that fMRI-derived semantic features have successfully served as 'brain decoders' of visual stimuli [12]. However, the extraction of high-level features as well as whether those features effectively decode low-/middle-level acoustic features for audio are still virtually unexplored.

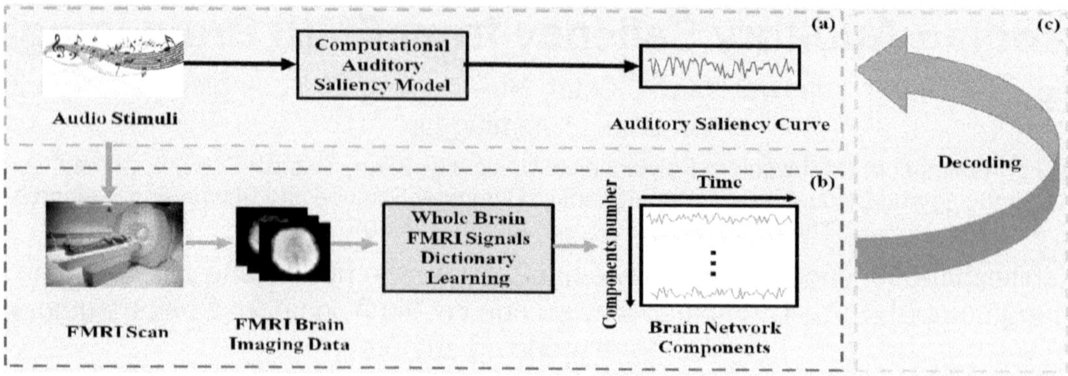

Figure 1. Overview of the proposed computational framework. The three major steps ((a)-(c)) are separated by dashed boxes.

In this paper, we propose a computational framework to decode biologically-plausible auditory saliency features using high-level features derived from fMRI brain signals under the natural stimulus of audio listening. There are three major steps as shown in Figs.1a-1c. First, for each audio excerpt, we extract its auditory saliency curve via a biological-plausible computational auditory saliency model [13]. Second, for the whole-brain fMRI signals under the natural stimulus of the specific audio excerpt listening, we identify meaningful intrinsic brain networks which are involved in audio listening via effective online dictionary learning and sparse representation approach [14]. Those identified brain networks are the high-level semantic features involved in the audio listening. Third, for each audio excerpt, we reconstruct the auditory saliency curve using those identified brain network components in second step, and perform group-wise analysis to identify consistent 'brain decoders' of the saliency feature across different excerpts and participants. Experimental results demonstrated the effectiveness of the high-level semantic features extracted in step 2 and provided us a new sight of the neural basis of audio perception.

2. DATA ACQUISITION

Three categories of audio streams (classical music, pop music, and speech in English) were used in our experiments. For each of the three categories, seven representative excerpts were selected. The excerpts were taken from legal copies of MP3 compressed audio files and further checked to ensure the recording qualities [11]. Each excerpt was about 90s long, resulting in 3 × 7 × 90 s = 31.5 minutes of audio data. Seven healthy university students were recruited and scanned in a GE 3T Signa MRI system (GE Healthcare, Milwaukee, WI) using an 8-channel head coil. All listeners were familiar with pop/classic music and proficient in English, and didn't know the excerpts to be played before hand. For each participant, their whole-brain fMRI signals under the natural stimulus of each of the 21 excerpts were recorded respectively. Note that the 21 excerpts were randomly ordered to avoid the influence of the internal structure of audio data on the human brain's perception. The TR (repetition time) of fMRI scan is 1.5s thus generating 60 brain fMRI volumes (time points) for each excerpt. Other parameters were as follows: 64x64 matrix, 4mm slice thickness, 220mm FOV, 30 slices, TE=25ms, ASSET=2. The pre-processing of fMRI data is referred to [11].

3. THE PROPOSED APPROACH

3.1 Auditory saliency feature extraction

Saliency describes what is more likely to attract our attention, which is one of the most successful biologically-plausible computational models for naturalistic audio analysis [13]. We calculated the saliency features for each audio excerpt by using the widely accepted and unified method proposed in [13]. Specifically, first, the specific audio excerpt was spitted into audio segments (each with TR duration) and preprocessed using Fourier analysis [13]. In this way, each audio segment was represented as a time-by-frequency image. Second, for each image, five features including intensity, frequency, contrast, temporal contrast and orientation which mimic the neural response were extracted (more details are in [13]), and 'activation maps' were built based on those local features and a single master saliency map was generated through normalizing and combing these activation maps [13]. Third, for the specific audio excerpt, we constructed the original auditory saliency curve by concatenating the maximum value for each master saliency map [13]. Finally, the original auditory saliency curve was convolved with the canonical hemodynamic response function to form the final auditory saliency curve [13] using Statistical Parametric Mapping (SPM) toolbox (http://www.fil.ion.ucl.ac.uk/spm/). Note that the auditory saliency curve has the same length as the fMRI scan time points, as well as the brain network components, which will be detailed in Section 3.2.

3.2 High-level brain features extraction

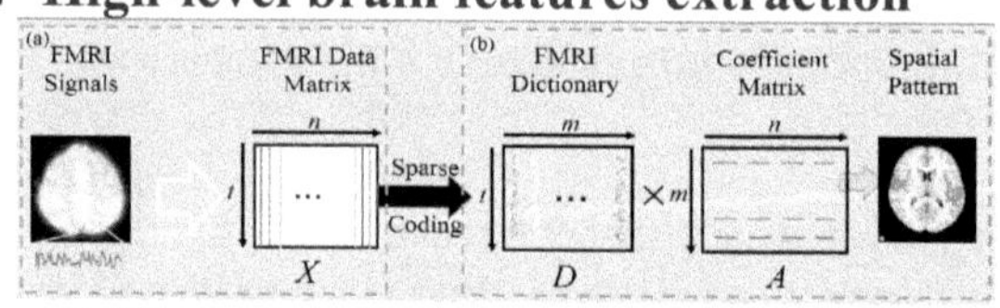

Figure 2. Illustration of sparse representation of fMRI signals using an effective online dictionary learning approach.

In this section, we identified meaningful intrinsic brain networks which were involved in audio listening via effective online dictionary learning and sparse representation approach [14] as illustrated in Fig 2. First, we extracted whole brain fMRI signals under the natural stimulus of the specific audio excerpt listening, and aggregated them into a big signal matrix $X \in \mathbb{R}^{t \times n}$, where t is the number of time points and n is the number of voxels of whole brain. Second, by using the effective online dictionary learning and sparse coding method [14], each fMRI signal vector x_i in X was modeled as a linear combination of atoms of a learned meaningful and over-complete dictionary $D = [d_1, d_2, ..., d_m]$, i.e., $x_i = D \times A_i$ and $X = D \times A$, where A is the coefficient weight matrix for sparse representation and each row A_i is the corresponding coefficient vector for dictionary atom d_i. Note that each dictionary atom represents a specific meaningful brain network whose temporal feature is represented by d_i (Fig. 2), and whose spatial pattern is represented by projecting corresponding A_i in coefficient matrix back into the fMRI image space (Fig. 2).

We defined m as the number of atoms in the dictionary. Learning an effective over-complete dictionary $D \in \mathbb{R}^{t \times m}$ should satisfy that $m>t$ and $m<<n$ [14]. In this paper, we experimentally set m = 200 which is bigger than t = 60 (time points of fMRI data) and much smaller than number of whole brain voxels n=16K. The cost function of the fMRI signal matrix X is formulated in Eq. (1) by considering the average loss of regression of n signals.

$$\ell(x_i, D) \triangleq \min_{A_i \in \mathbb{R}^m} \frac{1}{2}\|x_i - DA_i\|_2^2 + \lambda \|A_i\|_1 \quad (1)$$

where ℓ_1 regularization is used to yield a sparse solution of A_i, and λ is a regularization parameter to trade-off the regression residual and sparsity level. The columns $d_1, d_2, ..., d_m$ are constrained by Eq. (2) to prevent D from arbitrarily large values.

$$C \triangleq \{D \in \mathbb{R}^{t \times m} \ s.t. \ \forall j = 1, \ldots m, d_j^T d_j \leq 1\} \quad (2)$$

$$\min_{D \in C, A \in \mathbb{R}^{m \times n}} \frac{1}{2}\|X - DA\|_F^2 + \lambda \|A\|_{1,1} \quad (3)$$

The problem of minimizing Eq. (1) is then rewritten as a matrix factorization problem in Eq. (3) and solved as an ℓ_1-regularized linear least-squares problem to learn an optimized A [14]. We experimentally set the value of λ in this paper.

Once we identified brain networks (dictionary atoms) for each excerpt of each participant, we characterized and clustered all brain networks based on ten well-known and meaningful intrinsic brain network templates [15] as detailed in Section 4.1. In brief, the spatial pattern overlap rate (defined as the percentage of the voxels simultaneously recruited in both two spatial patterns) between the given atom and each of the ten intrinsic brain network templates were calculated respectively, and the atom was clustered into the specific brain network with the highest spatial overlap rate.

3.3 Brain decoding and group analysis

Once we obtained temporal features of those identified brain network components merely based on fMRI signals in section 3.2, we decoded the auditory saliency curve for each audio excerpt (Section 3.1) using those features, and performed group analysis to identify consistent 'brain decoders' of the saliency feature across different excerpts and participants. Specifically, for each audio excerpt, we adopted temporal features of all brain network components identified merely based on fMRI signals to reconstruct the auditory saliency curve using the same sparse representation scheme which was solved as an ℓ_1-regularized linear least-squares problem [14]. Our premise is that sparsity constrains during reconstruction can significantly increase the interpretability of the results and decrease the complexity of the decoding models [16]. After sparse reconstruction, only a small number of atoms with nonzero coefficient vectors were retained, which are considered to have significant contribution to the auditory saliency curve reconstruction and thus are named as significant atoms. We finally analyzed the distribution of those significant atoms in the ten brain networks across different excerpts/subjects, assessed the group-wise distribution of significant atoms, and identified group-wise consistent 'brain decoders' of auditory saliency curve decoding.

4. EXPERIMENT RESULTS

4.1 Brain networks characterization

Fig. 3 shows the ten characterized meaningful and intrinsic brain networks [15] which are identified in audio listening. These brain networks are consistent across all participants and excerpts, including medial, occipital pole, and lateral visual areas (#1-#3, respectively), default mode network (#4), cerebellum (#5), motor network (#6), auditory network (#7), executive control network (#8), middle frontal and orbital and superior parietal areas (#9-#10). More details of these networks are referred to [15]. We can see that the characterized brain networks are similar with the corresponding brain network templates, indicating the effectiveness of our sparse representation approach to identify meaningful intrinsic networks involved in audio listening.

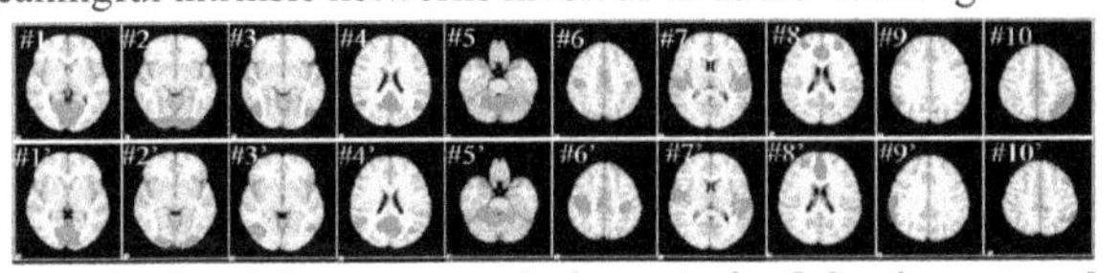

Figure 3. Spatial patterns of characterized brain networks. The first row shows ten meaningful brain network templates [15]. The second row shows the ten corresponding characterized brain networks in our fMRI data.

4.2 Sparse reconstruction of saliency curve

Fig. 4 shows the examples of decoded auditory saliency curves via the sparse reconstruction approach detailed in Section 3.3. Quantitatively, the mean Pearson correlation coefficient between the reconstructed auditory saliency curve and the original auditory saliency curve across all excerpts and participants is 0.95, indicating the effectiveness of our sparse reconstruction approach in Section 3.3.

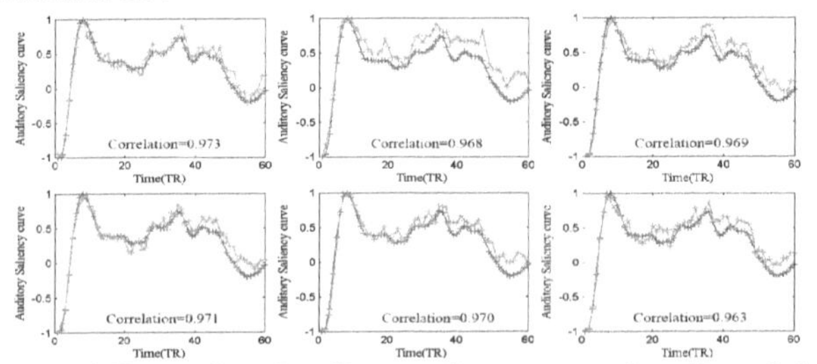

Figure 4. Examples of auditory saliency curve decoding of the same audio excerpt in six participants. In each sub figure, the blue curve is the original auditory saliency curve and the red one is the decoded auditory saliency curve.

4.3 Group-wise consistent decoding patterns

We performed group-wise distribution of significant atoms analysis in Section 3.3 to identify consistent 'brain decoders' of auditory saliency curve. Figs.5a-5g show the distribution of the significant atoms in the ten brain networks for all audio excerpts of each participant, respectively. We can see that the distribution of the significant atoms is reasonably consistent across different participants. That is, brain networks #7 and #5 have more significant atoms than the other networks in most of the participants. Our explanations from brain neuroscience are: as illustrated in Section 4.1, brain network #7 is the auditory network including the primary and association auditory cortices and most strongly corresponding to action-execution-speech, perception-audition and cognition-language-speech tasks [15]. Brain network #5 covers the cerebellum area and corresponds strongly to action-execution and perception activities [15]. It is therefore reasonable that these two brain networks play more

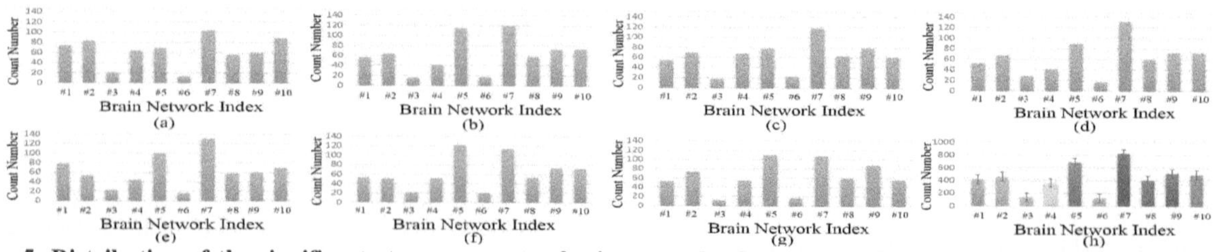

Figure 5: Distribution of the significant atoms across ten brain networks. In each sub figure, the horizontal axis is the brain network index and the vertical axis is the counted number of signifiant atoms. (a)-(g): distribution of significant atoms of each of seven participants, respectively. (h): group averaged distribution of significant atoms across all participants and excerpts.

important roles in the decoding of auditory saliency curve. Fig.5h shows the group averaged distribution of the significant atoms across all participants and excerpts, which serves as the consistent 'brain decoders' of auditory saliency.

5. CONCLUSION AND FUTURE WORK

In this paper, we have proposed a novel computational framework to decode biologically-plausible auditory saliency curves using high-level brain network features derived from natural stimulus fMRI brain imaging via effective online dictionary leaning and sparse coding approach. Experimental results have demonstrated that the auditory saliency curves can be successfully and effectively decoded via our methods, which potentially provide opportunities for bridging the semantic gap and advancing various applications in the multimedia field. In the future, we will apply the proposed method to decode more biologically-plausible and semantic features of music/speech, analyze those features for each type of music/speech separately, and leverage those 'brain decoders' for audio classification or retrieval.

6. ACKNOWLEDGMENTS

J. Han was supported by the National Science Foundation of China under Grant 91120005, NPU-FFR-JC20120237, and Doctoral Fund of Ministry of Education of China under grant 20136102110037. X. Hu was supported by the National Science Foundation of China under Grant 61103061 and Program for New Century Excellent Talents in University under grant NCET-13-0472. T. Liu was supported by the NIH Career Award (NIH EB006878), NIH R01 DA033393, NSF CAREER Award IIS-1149260, NIH R01 AG-042599, NSF BME-1302089, and The University of Georgia start-up funding. Shijie Zhao was supported by the Chinese scholarship council.

7. REFERENCES

[1] Rui, Y., Huang, T. S., Ortega, M., and Mehrotra, S. 1998. Relevance feedback: a power tool for interactive content-based image retrieval. *IEEE. T. CIRC. SYST. VID*, 8, 5(Sep. 1998), 644-655.

[2] Lu, L., Hanjalic, A. 2008. Audio keywords discovery for text-like audio content analysis and retrieval. *IEEE. T. MULTIMEDIA*, 10, 1(Jan. 2008), 74-85.

[3] Dai, W., Chen, Y., Xue, G. R., Yang, Q., and Yu, Y. 2008. Translated Learning: Transfer Learning across Different Feature Spaces. *In Proceedings of the 22nd Annual Conference on Neural Information Processing Systems*. NIPS, Vancouver, Canada, 353-360.

[4] Hadjidimitriou, S. K., and Hadjileontiadis, L. J. 2012. Toward an EEG-based recognition of music liking using time-frequency analysis. *IEEE. T. BIO.-MED. ENG*, 59, 12(Sep. 2012), 3498-3510.

[5] Cummings, A., Čeponienė, R., Koyama, A., Saygin, A. P., Townsend, J., and Dick, F. 2006. Auditory semantic networks for words and natural sounds. *BRAIN. RES*, 115, 1(Oct. 2006), 92-107.

[6] Formisano, E., De Martino, F., Bonte, M., and Goebel, R. 2008. "Who" Is Saying" What"? Brain-Based Decoding of Human Voice and Speech. *SCIENCE*, 322, 5903 (Nov. 2008), 970-973.

[7] Koelsch, S. 2011. Toward a neural basis of music perception–a review and updated model. *FRONT. PSYCHOL*, 2, 110 (Apr. 2011).

[8] Koelsch, S. 2011. Towards a neural basis of processing musical semantics. *PHYS. LIFE. REV*, 8, 2 (June. 2011), 89-105.

[9] Han, J., Ji, X., Hu, X., Jiang, X., and Liu, T. 2013. Representing and retrieving video shots in human-centric brain imaging space. *IEEE. T. IMAGE. PROCESS*, 22, 7 (July.2013), 2723-2736.

[10] Staeren, N., Renvall, H., De Martino, F., Goebel, R., and Formisano, E. 2009. Sound categories are represented as distributed patterns in the human auditory cortex. *CURR. BIOL*, 19, 6 (Mar. 2009), 498-502.

[11] Jiang, X., Zhang, T., Hu, X., Lu, L., Han, J., Guo, L., and Liu, T. 2012. Music/speech classification using high-level features derived from fMRI brain imaging. *In Proceedings of the 20th ACM international conference on Multimedia*. ACM, New York, NY, 825-828.

[12] Kay, K. N., & Gallant, J. L. 2009. I can see what you see. *NAT. NEUROSCI*, 12, 245(Dec. 2009), 245-245.

[13] Bordier, C., Puja, F., and Macaluso, E. 2013. Sensory processing during viewing of cinematographic material: Computational modeling and functional neuroimaging. *NEUROIMAGE*, 67, 15 (Feb. 2013), 213-226.

[14] Mairal, J., Bach, F., Ponce, J., and Sapiro, G. 2010. Online learning for matrix factorization and sparse coding. *J. MACH. LEARN. RES*, 11 (Mar. 2010), 19-60.

[15] Smith, S. M., Fox, P. T., Miller, K. L., Glahn, D. C., Fox, P. M., Mackay, C. E., and Beckmann, C. F. 2009. Correspondence of the brain's functional architecture during activation and rest. Proceedings of the National Academy of Sciences, 106, 31 (Aug. 2009), 13040-13045.

[16] Ryali, S., Supekar, K., Abrams, D. A., and Menon, V. 2010. Sparse logistic regression for whole-brain classification of fMRI data. *NEUROIMAGE*, 51, 2 (June. 2010), 752-7.

Crowd Counting via Head Detection and Motion Flow Estimation

Huiyuan Fu, Huadong Ma, Hongtian Xiao
Beijing Key Laboratory of Intelligent Telecommunications Software and Multimedia
Beijing University of Posts and Telecommunications
Beijing, China
fhy@bupt.edu.cn,mhd@bupt.edu.cn,buptxht@gmail.com

ABSTRACT

Crowd counting with heavy occlusions is highly desired for public security. However, few works have been studied towards this goal. Most previous systems only count passing people robustly without heavy occlusions, else they have to estimate the crowds to a certain extent. To solve this difficult problem, this paper proposes an effective algorithm by combining head detection and motion flow estimation together. First, we detect each head in the crowd by using our proposed scene-adaptive scheme on depth data. Then, we estimate the motion flow based on the interest points in each head region on color data. We can ultimately achieve multi-direction crowd counting results with the loop of above steps. Based on this approach, we have built a practical system for reliable crowd counting. Extensive experimental results show that our system is effective.

Categories and Subject Descriptors

I.4.8 [**Image Processing and computer vision**]: Scene Analysis—*object recognition*; I.4.9 [**Image Processing and computer vision**]: Applications; I.5.4 [**Pattern recognition**]: Applications—*computer vision, signal processing*

General Terms

Algorithms, Design, Experimentation

Keywords

Public security; head detection; motion flow estimation; crowd counting

1. INTRODUCTION

Robust crowd counting with heavy occlusions is highly desired for public security. For example, knowing the crowd density in public places can help managers identify unsafe situations. As another example, the public museum managers can obtain the current number of crowd entering by the real-time people flow information. It is so important, however, reliable crowd counting in complex environments is still far from being completely solved.

Recently, a large number of methods have been proposed for crowd counting or people counting [1, 2, 4, 7, 8, 9, 11]. Because of the limited space, we only list some literatures above. The authors of [11] proposed a method for estimating the crowd, but they can not accurately count the number of current flow. The authors of [1, 2, 4, 7] can count passing people well in the relatively simple environments. However, they will inevitably be affected by the complicated environments with heavy occlusions. In our previous works, we have studied the problem of crowd counting based on RGB-D information. With a squint view depth camera, we proposed a real-time template matching based approach for crowd counting [8]. The result is convincing. With a top view depth camera, we proposed a scene-adaptive head detection based approach for crowd counting [9]. However, we can not obtain multi-direction crowd counting result synchronously via these methods.

In this paper, we propose a new scheme for multi-direction crowd counting with very heavy occlusions. We combine the depth data based head detection and motion flow estimation together. To our knowledge, we are the first to use this scheme for this task in so complicated scenes with a top view camera. First, we can detect each head in the crowd by using our proposed scene-adaptive scheme on depth data. Second, motion flow estimation is based on the interest points in each detected head region on color data. This will promote the matching accuracy of flow vectors. Moreover, we can generate the semantic trajectory point for the final multi-direction crowd counting. Based on this approach, we have built a practical system for multi-direction crowd counting.

The rest of this paper is organized as follows: Section 2 introduces our proposed method. Experimental results and analysis are described in Section 3. Finally, Section 4 concludes the work.

2. OUR APPROACH

As seen in Fig. 1, the original RGB and depth images are Fig. 1(a) and Fig. 1(b), respectively. We use our proposed scene-adaptive scheme (as seen in Algorithm 1) for head detection, and the details can be seen in our previous work [9]. Fig. 1(d) shows the final head detection result.

When we get each detected head (see Fig. 2(a)) using above approach, we will use the motion flow estimation algorithm in the following. First, we use the typical harris corner detector [5] to extract the interest key points (with

MM'14, November 3–7, 2014, Orlando, Florida, USA.

http://dx.doi.org/10.1145/2647868.2655040 .

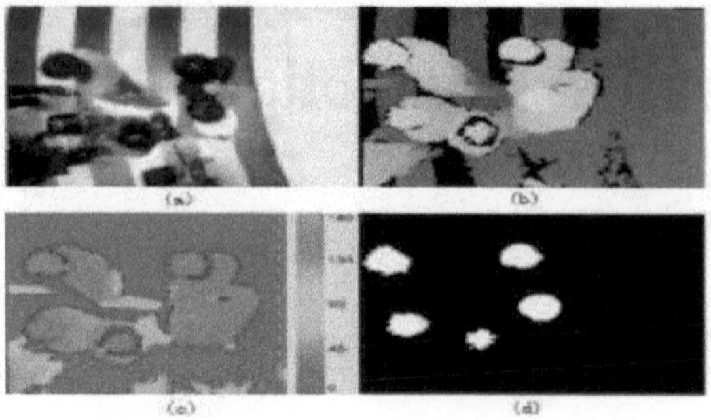

Figure 1: Scene-adaptive head detection in complicated scenes. (a) raw RGB data; (b) raw depth data; (c) our constructed depth map in color format; (d) final head detection result.

Algorithm 1 Scene-adaptive head detection

Require: Fig. 1(a) and Fig. 1(b)
Ensure: Fig. 1(d)

1: Capture each pixel's depth value in the specific area at current frame, and add it to an array D_{xy}.
2: Get the median value of the specific area's pixel corresponding array D_{xy}.
3: Update this median value $\overline{D}_{xy}$.
4: Goto step 1, until the end of median value $\overline{D}_{xy}$'s convergence.
5: Take $\overline{D}_{xy}$ as our final floor depth D_{floor}.
6: Use the threshold Th to distinguish persons and floor roughly in current scene.
7: **if** $Th < D_{floor}$ **then**
8:     Remove the adjacent region between the persons and the floor. The result can be seen in Fig. 1(c).
9: **end if**
10: Use $T = H.\frac{P}{D}$ to obtain a threshold to find the border of head region.
11: Get the extreme high point in Fig. 1(c), set it to m_0.
12: Add the value m_0 to the coordinate array M.
13: Traverse each coordinate in the array M.
14: Calculate the head region by $[m_0 - T, m_0]$.
15: Fill the obtained head from each point m_0 in color.

---

the salient features). We use the dimensional matrix for feature point detection as follows:

$$H(p) = \begin{bmatrix} \frac{\partial^2 I}{\partial x^2} & \frac{\partial^2 I}{\partial x \partial y} \\ \frac{\partial^2 I}{\partial x \partial y} & \frac{\partial^2 I}{\partial y^2} \end{bmatrix} \quad (1)$$

where $H(p)$ means the corner features. Moreover, we will use the self-correlation matrix around each point for Harris corner point. The matrix can be defined as follows:

$$F(x,y) = \begin{bmatrix} \sum\limits_{-K \leq i,j \leq K} \phi_1(x) & \sum\limits_{-K \leq i,j \leq K} \phi_2(x,y) \\ \sum\limits_{-K \leq i,j \leq K} \phi_2(x,y) & \sum\limits_{-K \leq i,j \leq K} \phi_1(y) \end{bmatrix} \quad (2)$$

where $\phi_1(x)$, $\phi_1(y)$, and $\phi_2(x,y)$ can be defined as follows: $\phi_1(x) = w_{i,j} {I_x}^2(x+i, y+j)$, $\phi_2(x,y) = w_{i,j} I_x(x+i, y+j) I_y(x+i, y+j)$, and $\phi_1(y) = w_{i,j} {I_y}^2(x+i, y+j)$ respectively. $w_{i,j}$ means the normalization weight ratio.

When we get the corners, we will adopt the motion flow estimation method to match them. In our method, we use the classical optical flow objective function in its spatially discrete form as follows:

$$\begin{aligned} E(u,v) = \sum_{i,j} \{ & \rho_D(I_1(i,j) - I_2(i + u_{i,j}, j + v_{i,j})) \\ & + \lambda[\rho_S(u_{i,j} - u_{i+1,j}) + \rho_S(u_{i,j} - u_{i,j+1}) \\ & + \rho_S(v_{i,j} - v_{i+1,j}) + \rho_S(v_{i,j} - v_{i,j+1})]\} \end{aligned} \quad (3)$$

As seen in Fig. 2(b), we can get the motion flow of each head. The reason why our process is based on each head is that this will effectively reduce the detection error. In Fig. 2(c), we amplify the flow estimation process in each head. The green point represents the corner point, and the red lines mean the motion flow (the corner point with green color is the initial point of the motion flow). In order to make sure each head has feature points for the final matching, we will add a man-made feature point (blue color) in the head region (see Fig. 2(c)).

When we obtain corners in the previous frame, and then get another corners in the following frame. The traditional method will use the motion flow estimation to match and find the flow. In this paper, we do not use this strategy. Instead, we combine flow estimation with previous depth based head detection. First, we try to find out the corners in the head region. Then, we cluster these corners to only one clustering point in one head region. The point in the previous frame can be defined as follows:

$$F = \frac{\sum_{i=1}^{n} p_i(x,y)}{n} \quad (4)$$

where F means the previous frame, and $p_i(x,y), i = 1, 2, ..., n$ means the corner points in this frame (n means the sum of corners in the head region). As the same reason, the point in the following frame can be defined as follows:

$$F' = \frac{\sum_{i=1}^{n} p_i'(x,y)}{n} \quad (5)$$

where F' means the following frame, and $p_i'(x,y), i = 1, 2, ..., n$ means the corner points in this frame (n means the sum of corners in the head region). In this way, we can construct the motion flows from $p_i(x,y)$ to $p_i'(x,y)$ in these two frames F and F' of each matched head.

Finally, our flow estimation scheme can get the semantic trajectories by combing the points together.

3. EXPERIMENTAL RESULTS

As seen in Fig. 3, we testify our system with the Microsoft kinect camera which can provide depth and color

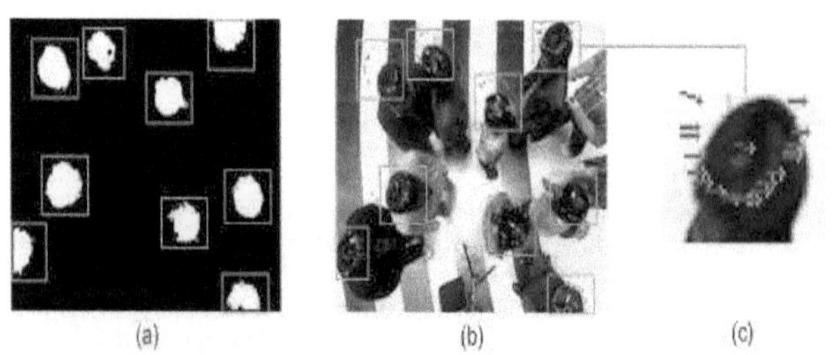

Figure 2: Motion flow estimation. (a) head detection result; (b) motion flow estimation result combined with head detection; (c) amplifying motion flow estimation result in one head.

information simultaneously. Fig. 1 (a) is an example captured scene of our camera. Some typical scenes in this paper are the same as in our previous work [9]. We compare with other approaches in extensive different fields: the depth only method and flow only method, the depth joint blob tracking methods, the typical kinect(depth) based state-of-art algorithms, and the multi-directional crowd counting performance. All tested methods were implemented in C++ on a standard PC with Inter Core I5 CPU with 2 G memory, and the frame size is 320 × 240.

First, we compare our algorithm combines depth based head detection and color based motion flow estimation (called depth + flow) with two typical methods: depth based motion flow estimation (called depth only) and common color based motion flow estimation [10] (called flow only). As seen in Fig. 4, the horizontal axis represents for classifying the flow vector's length to 4 regions, and the vertical axis represents for counting the flow numbers of each region. The flow vector's length is mainly related to video's frame rate. In all of our experiments, we set the FPS (frames per second) to 25. Under this setup, correct flow vector's length should be within 5 basis. Fig. 4 shows that depth only method has the lowest statistical results in the correct region. Flow only method is much better than the depth only method because of its error flows are scare. Comparing to these two methods, our method is the best. Fig. 5 shows the visual results of these three methods. We can find that our approach can obtain right result, but depth only method and flow only method have the incorrect results. Because depth only method extracts features based on depth image whose features are not very rich, it will result in matching error easily. Flow only method has the lower error flow vectors, however, the flow estimation [10] based method can not distinguish each moving person well.

Second, we compare the algorithm with traditional tracking based method [6] using a kinect. As seen in Fig. 2, after detecting each head, we adopt motion flow estimation method for final crowd counting. In fact, all of the experiments are based on that. Traditional tracking based method will track the blobs based on the head detection results of Fig. 1(d), it is an effective method overall. In our experiment, we testify our method (depth + flow) and traditional method (depth + blob tracking) in two instances: mid and heavy crowded, respectively. As seen in Fig. 6 and Fig. 7, our method can achieve more better result under the heavy crowded instances.

Then, we compare our method with current typical depth camera (kinect) based algorithms [3, 9]. We try to implement the method of [3] for comparison. The general result is listed in Table 1. We can find that our previous method [9] and our current method both have high accuracy, speed and availability. However, the previous method can only do bidirectional crowd counting task. In this paper, our method can count the crowd with arbitrary multi-directional simultaneously. Because our method is based on motion flow, it is relatively flexible. The method of [3] is not very suitable for the complex situations due to the poor segmentation result in the crowded blobs. Then, we evaluate our method in four typical scenes: building, entrance, corridor and export. We count the number of the crowd with a long time period. Table 2 shows we can obtain an accurate counting result in real time.

Finally, we testify our method for multi-direction crowd counting. We try to count the crowd with bidirectional, four-directional and eight-directional, respectively. Fig. 8 gives out the statistical results. In Fig. 9, we show the statistical crowd trajectory results of our method. These obtained trajectories can be used for semantic scene understanding.

Figure 3: Experimental setup. Some of typical scenes in our experiment.

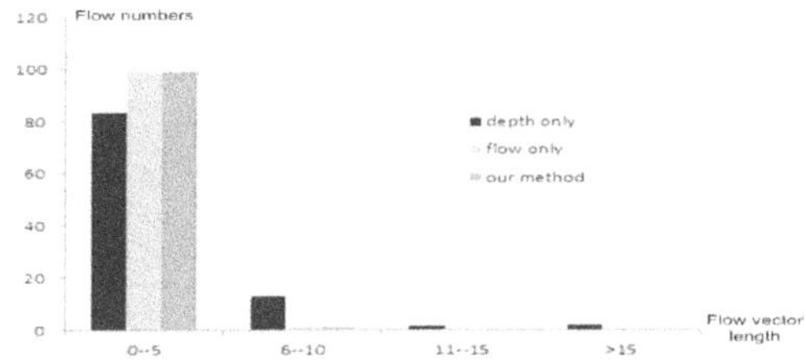

Figure 4: Comparison with two typical algorithms on flow statistical results.

Figure 5: Comparison with two typical algorithms on practical visual results. (a) depth only method; (b) flow only method; (c) our method combined depth and flow together.

4. ACKNOWLEDGMENT

The research is supported by the National High Technology Research and Development Program of China under Grant No.2014AA015101; the Natural Natural Science Foundation of China under Grant No. 61402048; the Funds for Creative Research Groups of China under Grant No. 61121001; the National Internet of Things Special Fund.

Algorithms / Functions	Hsieh [3]	Fu [9]	ours
High accuracy	N	Y	Y
High speed	N	Y	Y
Count with multi-directional	N	N	Y
Count in density traffic	N	Y	Y

Table 1: Comparison with current typical depth (kinect) based algorithms for crowd counting.

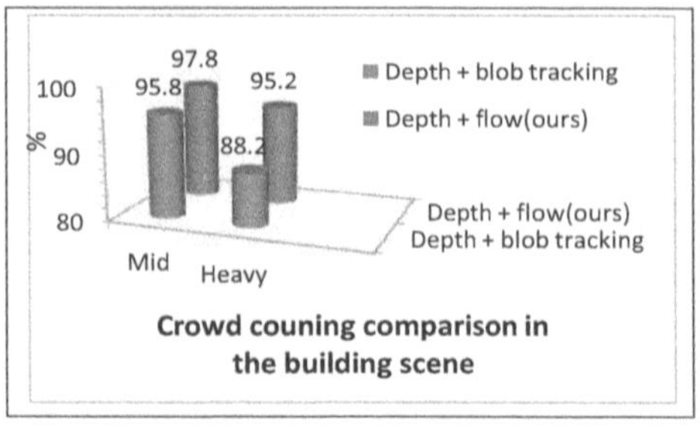

Figure 6: Comparison on crowd counting precision estimation with depth + blob tracking method in building scene.

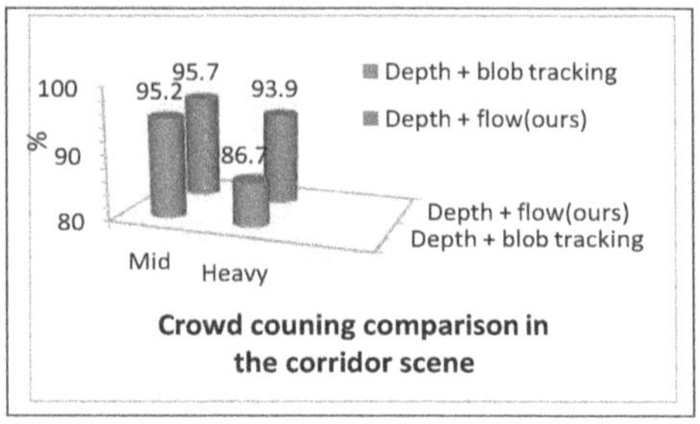

Figure 7: Comparison on crowd counting precision estimation with depth + blob tracking method in corridor scene.

5. CONCLUSION

In this paper, we propose a new scheme for crowd counting in complicated scenes with heavy occlusions. Our contribution is mainly on combining the depth data based head detection and color data based motion flow estimation together. We evaluate our algorithm in many fields, and the experimental results demonstrate this new scheme can achieve significant improvement. Based on this approach, we have built a practical system for crowd counting facing the complicated scenes. The obtained results show that the system is effective. In the future, we will use our current obtained crowd trajectories for semantic information mining and scene understanding.

		In	Out		Speed
Building	Truth	420	316	Detect	28.7FPS
	Result	396	295	Total	20.5FPS
	Accuracy	94.3%	93.4%		
Entrance	Truth	825	783	Detect	26.5FPS
	Result	769	805	Total	18.2FPS
	Accuracy	93.2%	97.3%		
Corridor	Truth	523	680	Detect	35.1FPS
	Result	551	632	Total	24.9FPS
	Accuracy	94.9%	92.9%		
Export	Truth	636	671	Detect	26.7FPS
	Result	588	629	total	19.2FPS
	Accuracy	92.5%	93.7%		

Table 2: Test for accuracy and speed of our method for crowd counting.

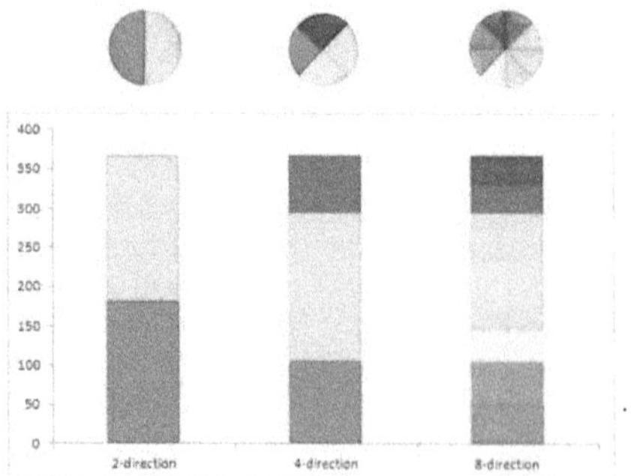

Figure 8: Statistical crowd counting results. (colors represent different directions)

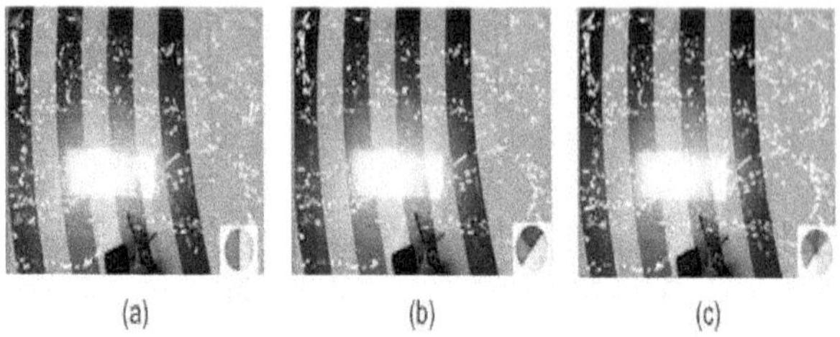

Figure 9: Statistical crowd trajectory results. (colors represent different directions)

6. REFERENCES

[1] L. Snidaro and C. Micheloni and C. Chiavedale, Video security for ambient intelligence, IEEE Transactions on Systems, Man and Cybernetics, Part A, 133-144, 2005.

[2] B. Antic and D. Letic and D. Culibrk and V. Crnojevic, K-MEANS based segmentation for real-time zenithal people counting, ICIP, 2565-2568, 2009.

[3] C. Hsieh et al, A Kinect-Based People-flow Counting System, IEEE International Symposium on Intelligent Signal Processing and Communication Systems, 2012.

[4] Y. Cong and H. F. Gong and S. C. Zhu and Y. D. Tang, Flow mosaicking: real-time pedestrian counting without scene-specific learning, CVPR, 1093-1100, 2009.

[5] J. Shi and c. Tomasi, Good features to track, CVPR, 593-600, 1994.

[6] R. T. Collins, Mean-shift blob tracking through scale space, CVPR, 2003.

[7] H. D. Ma and C. B. Zeng and C. X. Ling, A reliable people counting system via multiple cameras, ACM Transactions on Intelligent Systems and Technology, 1-22, 2012.

[8] H. Y. Fu and H. D. Ma and T. H. Xiao, Real-time accurate crowd counting based on RGB-D information, IEEE International Conference on Image Processing, 2685-2688, 2012.

[9] H. Y. Fu and H. D. Ma and T. H. Xiao, Scene-adaptive accurate and fast vertical crowd counting via joint using depth and color information, Multimedia Tools and Applications, online, 2013.

[10] J. Y. Bouguet, Pyramidal implementation of the affine lucas kanade feature tracker description of the algorithm, Intel Corporation, 2001.

[11] P. Kilambi et al, Estimating pedestrian counts in groups, Computer Vision and Image Understanding, 43-59, 2008.

Semantic Feature Projection for Continuous Emotion Analysis

Prasanth Lade, Troy McDaniel, Sethuraman Panchanathan
Center for Cognitive Ubiquitous Computing
Arizona State University
prasanthl@asu.edu, troy.mcdaniel@asu.edu, panch@asu.edu

ABSTRACT

Affective computing researchers have recently been focusing on continuous emotion dimensions like arousal and valence. This dual coordinate affect space can explain many of the discrete emotions like sadness, anger, joy, etc. In the area of continuous emotion recognition, Principal Component Analysis (PCA) models are generally used to enhance the performance of various image and audio features by projecting them to a new space where the new features are less correlated. We instead, propose that quantizing and projecting the features to a latent topic space performs better than PCA. Specifically we extract these topic features using Latent Dirichlet Allocation (LDA) models. We show that topic models project the original features to a latent feature space that is more coherent and useful for continuous emotion recognition than PCA. Unlike PCA where no semantics can be attributed to the new features, topic features can have a visual and semantic interpretation which can be used in personalized HCI applications and Assistive technologies. Our hypothesis in this work has been validated using the AVEC 2012 continuous emotion challenge dataset.

Categories and Subject Descriptors

I.4 [**Image Processing and Computer Vision**]: Feature Measurement—*Feature Representation*

Keywords

Topic models , Continuous Affect Recognition, Feature Comparison

1. INTRODUCTION

Medical diagnosis of patients, federal investigations, human-computer interactions and many other applications need an understanding of human emotions. This research work addresses the application of social interaction assistance for people who are blind. When an individual who is blind interacts with a person, it is necessary to perceive his or her counterpart's emotions so that there is a positive influence and feedback during the conversation. This application requires a two layered approach where in the lower layer the blind user is provided with actual facial movements that are correlated to the person's facial emotions and the upper layer provides the continuous or discrete emotions to the user. This needs pattern recognition algorithms that can extract discernible features from image and audio data, learn their relationship with emotions, predict the appropriate emotional state and deliver the prediction to the visually impaired. Happy, sad, disgust, surprise, contempt and anger are most widely accepted states and will be called discrete emotions throughout this document. In recent years new dimensions of emotions are gaining popularity viz. arousal (energy) and valence (positivity). Unlike discrete emotions, each of these dimensions can be assigned a real number within a given range and thus are called continuous dimensions and arousal and valence can be used to define most of the discrete emotions.

To address these problems, algorithms that can extract meaningful features and can learn an association between features and emotions are needed. In recent years, probabilistic topic models have made significant contribution to both feature learning as well as supervised learning. Features extracted from video and audio frames are projected to a new latent topic space and these topics are used to predict emotions. This latent topic space is richer than the original feature space as it considers correlations and co-occurrences within features. In this work we show that these topic features are semantically richer and perform better than the most popularly used lower dimension projection techniques such as Principal Component Analysis (PCA).

MM '14 November 03 - 07 2014, Orlando, FL, USA

http://dx.doi.org/10.1145/2647868.2655042.

2. RELATED WORK

Feature extraction and analysis is a primary area of research in emotion recognition. Facial landmarks extracted using active shape models (ASM) and active appearance models (AAM) are used as geometric features to predict emotions in [3]. Mean appearance models, linear binary patterns (LBP) [5], local phase quantizations (LPQs), histogram of gradients (HOG), scale invariant feature transform (SIFT) and Gabor features are few examples of appearance features used for emotion recognition. Once features are extracted, their dimensionality is reduced using either Principal Component Analysis [4] or Independent Component Analysis [8].

In general, the image and audio feature space is projected to a lower dimensional space which is then mapped to the

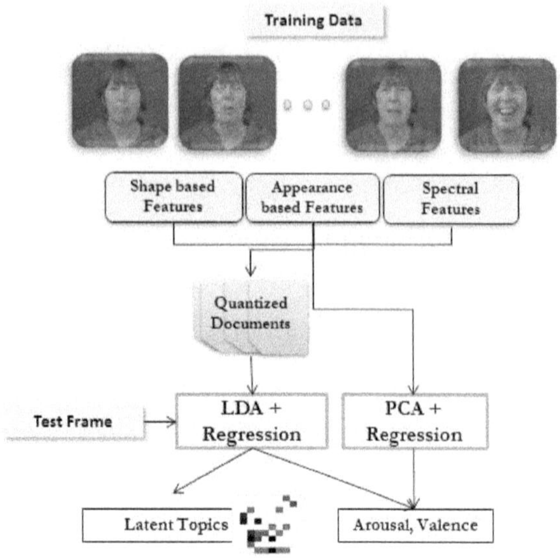

Figure 1: Experimental Methodology used in this work

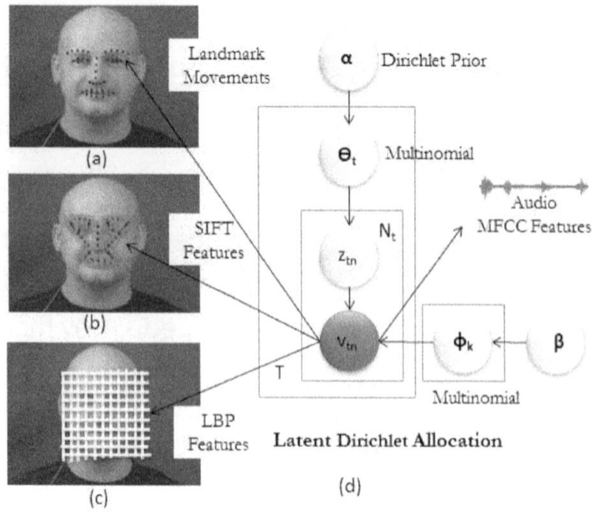

Figure 2: The LDA graphical model and the four features used in this work

emotion space. Existing dimension reduction techniques try to reduce the correlation between features but lose semantic information in the process. In text mining, probabilistic topic models are used to project the word features to a latent topic simplex and the new features are used in unsupervised and supervised settings. Blei et al [1] have proposed the Latent Dirichlet Allocation (LDA) model which is a more generalized topic model with explicit modeling of all the variables using multinomial-dirichlet conjugate distributions. In recent years topic models have been gaining popularity in image and video analysis and few works like [6], [7] and [2] have used LDA on audio and images for affect analysis. In this work we propose the use of topic models to project geometric, appearance and audio features from videos onto the topic space, analyze their interpretation and performance on continuous emotion recognition and compare its performance with PCA.

3. PROPOSED METHODOLOGY

The experimental methodology used in this work is shown in Figure 1, where a set of video frames are used to train the models. Video frames are converted to *video documents* by quantizing various image and audio features. These training documents are supplied to Latent Dirichlet Allocation Model to learn the latent topic space. The new topic features generated using LDA are used to train the regression algorithms with arousal and valence emotions as the dependent variables. The features of an unseen test frame are projected to the new topic space and the new features are used to predict emotions. PCA can only be used to predict emotions whereas it can be seen that LDA outputs extra topic projections that can be visualized or provided to users through Haptic interfaces. Topic models propose that every document contains latent concepts called topics. Probabilistic topic models are mixture models that model each document as a multinomial mixture of topics and each topic as a multinomial distribution over words. In the context of facial video processing, we can consider either an entire video or an individual video frame as a document. There is a lot of activity within each facial video or facial image document which can be possibly explained using latent topics. We hypothesize that the affective state of a person can be explained by identifying these latent topics. Similar to the definition of a textual topic which is a group of related words, video topics are defined as collections of co-occurring image/video features. This co-occurrence can be either spatial (in the case of an individual frame) or temporal (in the case of a video) and can be exploited to recognize different emotional states.

3.1 Topic Extraction from Base Features

Figure 2(d) shows the Latent Dirichlet Allocation graphical model, where the outer plate represents a document and the inner plate corresponds to a word. $\boldsymbol{\theta_t}$ is a multinomial distribution of topics in a document t and $\boldsymbol{\phi_k}$ is a multinomial distribution of words in a topic k. Given a set of K topics, each word v_{tn} in a document t is generated by assigning a topic z_{tn} from the distribution $\boldsymbol{\theta_t}$ and then generating a word from the topic distribution $\boldsymbol{\phi_{z_{tn}}}$. In LDA model the only observed variable is $\boldsymbol{v}$ and all other variables are latent variables. Now, given a set of documents, distributions $\boldsymbol{\theta_t}$ and $\boldsymbol{\phi_k}$ are inferred using Gibbs Sampling or Variational EM. In this work, we have used the variational Bayes approach to estimate the topics and the two parameters α and β have been selected using cross validation.

In order to use the LDA model the features have to be quantized to words and the details follow. As shown in Figure 2, four different *base* features viz. facial landmark movements (LM), SIFT features, Linear binary patterns from image frames and MFCC spectral features from audio frames have been considered. We have used the API provided by Xuehan et al. [9] to track 49 landmarks from facial videos. The landmarks from all videos are rotated, scaled and aligned with respect to the neutral frame (used the one shown in Figure 2) and the changes in the movements are quantized to $R-\theta$ space with four orientations for θ and 20 bins for the R. The 49 tracked landmarks are interpolated to 71 points as shown in Figure 2 (b) and SIFT features have been extracted at a scale of $S = 2$ and the features at the

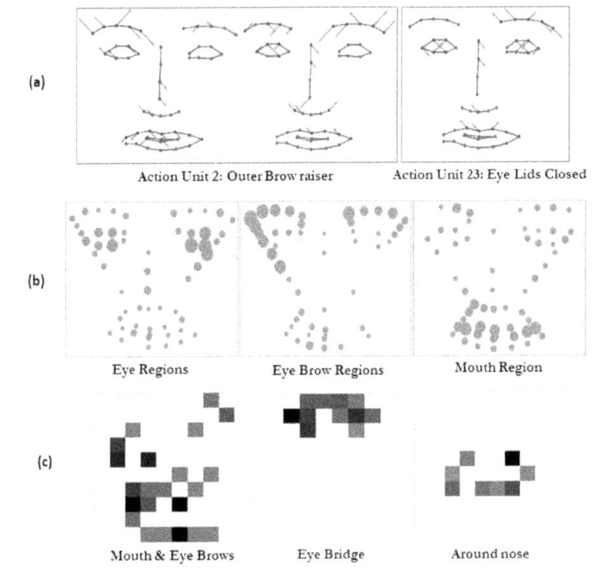

Figure 3: Plots of topics extracted from (a) Landmark (b) SIFT and (c) LBP features

optimal orientations have been considered. KMeans with cosine, KL-divergence and euclidean distances have been used to quantize SIFT features at each landmark. Figure2 (c) shows LBP features extracted from 100 image blocks and KMeans has been used to vector quantize these features. The final set of features are the spectral coefficients (1242) from audio at each frame. Each feature vector is quantized using Kmeans and the nearest centroid is assigned. The total vocabulary sizes of quantized words used for LDA are 196, 3550, 5900 and 62100 for LM, SIFT, LBP and Audio features respectively.

4. VISUAL INTERPRETATION

We hypothesize that latent topic features have a semantic interpretation and thus can be used to convey lower level information about changes in facial texture to a visually impaired person. We have used videos provided for the AVEC2012 challenge [5] to extract topics and perform our analysis. We have used LDA model with the optimal parameters (see Section 5 for details) to extract topics from different features. The topics extracted using geometric features, correspond to patterns of movements on the human face and the appearance features based topics provide information about changes in textures of the face. Facial plots of various topics can be seen in Figure 3, where the topics extracted from landmark, SIFT and LBP features are displayed in (a), (b) and (c) respectively. The angle and length of arrows in Figure 3(a) correspond to the direction and amount of landmark movements. It can be observed that sets of topics in fact have a correspondence with Facial Action units. The sizes of blobs plotted in Figure 3(b) correspond to the amount of influence (probability) the SIFT features at that landmark have on that topic. We find that each topic is modeling spatially correlated landmarks (that belong to a region) as they have similar textures e.g. the topics plotted model eyes, eyebrows and mouth regions respectively. The topics from LBP are plotted in 10 x 10 blocks as each word corresponds to a block. Figure 3(c) shows three

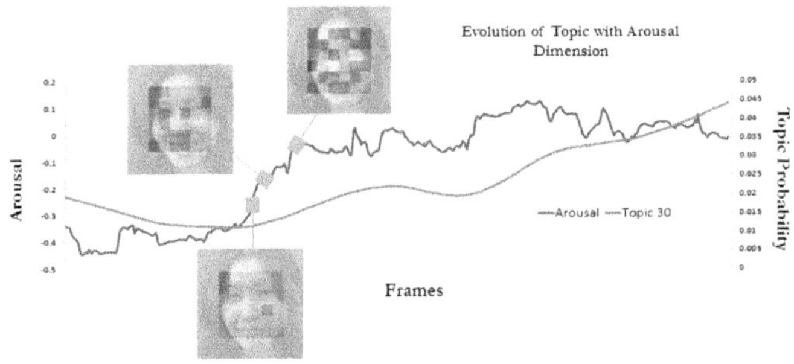

Figure 4: Evolution of LBP based topics with Arousal dimensions.

such topics active in the mouth-eyebrow, nose/eye bridge and around nose-cheek regions. We observe that each of the features produce different topics whose influence is felt in different ways and regions.

Along with a semantic connotation associated with topics, our experiments have also shown that these topics can be displayed in real time on a human face. The best topics corresponding to a region or a landmark can be delivered through haptic or visual interfaces which provide overall changes in face textures and movements. Another interesting observation is that topics are correlated with arousal and valence emotions. Figure 4 shows a sample plot of a video where the changes in arousal have been plotted along with the probability of Topic 30 extracted from block wise LBP features. There is a direct correlation between the topic probability and the emotion and the topic plots at different points of time are overlaid on the plot.

5. PERFORMANCE EVALUATION

To test the performance of projected features on continuous emotion recognition, we used 31 training videos (7 subjects) from AVEC2102 dataset and used the 32 development videos (8 subjects) for testing. We evaluated the mean cross correlations between the actual and predicted response labels averaged across all development videos. The parameters corresponding to the LDA model are the α, β and the number of topics K. We used a grid search approach to select the best parameters using cross validation on training videos. Video frames have been sampled at 30 ams and audio frames that do not have audio have been filtered. We have used 50 K-Means clusters for quantizing Audio and SIFT features. The optimal number topics for LM was 50 whereas 30 topics were selected for Audio, LBP and SIFT features. We used topic distributions extracted from four features viz. landmarks (LM), SIFT, LBP and Audio features which we address as Base features, as new LDA features. Once the dimensionality of the base features is reduced using PCA and LDA we have used Support Vector Regressors with to RBF kernels to predict arousal and valence separately. The results of arousal and valence prediction using different features are shown in Table 1. The mean cross correlations between predicted and actual emotions over all development videos using each of the features are shown on the left side. Since the size (number of frames) of each development video is different, we also calculated the weighted cross correlation weighted by the video size so that longer videos get more weightage. This is useful

	Arousal						Valence					
	Mean			Weighted Mean			Mean			Weighted Mean		
	Base	PCA	LDA	Base	PCA	LDA	Base	PCA	LDA	Base	PCA	LDA
LM	0.037	0.023	0.177	0.009	0.003	0.196	0.011	0.011	0.127	0.010	0.010	0.190
LBP	0.190	0.090	0.191	0.150	0.138	0.195	0.207	0.240	0.264	0.280	0.310	0.308
SIFT	0.190	0.242	0.207	0.170	0.230	0.190	0.07	0.022	0.128	0.050	0.030	0.078
Audio	0.0609	0.069	0.277	0.032	0.023	0.294	0.001	0.001	0.113	0.013	0.130	0.195

Table 1: Cross-correlation values on AVEC development videos

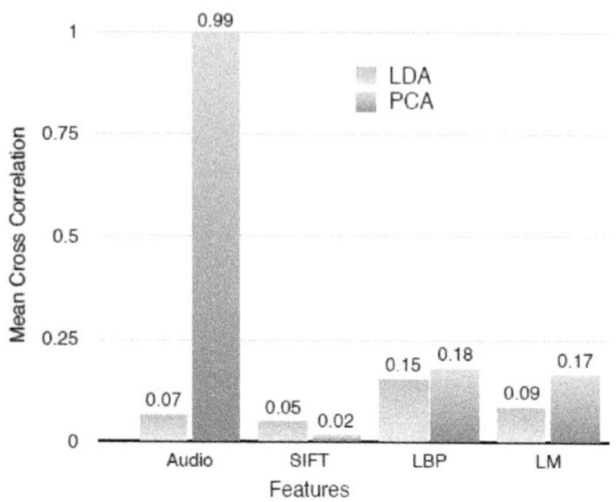

Figure 5: Mean cross correlations between features extracted using LDA and PCA (the lower the better)

because longer videos have more changes in emotions and better performance on longer videos implies the algorithm is able to model these changes. The Base algorithm uses the base features without any projection and dimensionality reduction. We have compared the results from two dimensionality reduction techniques, PCA and LDA. We can observe from the results that almost across all features on board, LDA features have performed better than the Base and PCA features. SIFT features are an exception to this and the probable reason could be that the quantization technique may not be sufficiently capturing all the histograms due to high dimensionality (128 dimensions).

Table 1 also gives useful insights about the effect of each feature on arousal and valence. Audio based topic features have performed better in arousal prediction than valence. Landmark features in contrast performed equally well in predicting both arousal and valence. LBP and SIFT features counter interact in modeling valence and arousal respectively. In order to show the contrast between PCA and LDA we also calculated correlations within LDA and PCA based features. Figure 5 shows the mean cross correlations within features extracted using PCA and LDA. It can be seen that LDA features are less correlated to each other in comparison to PCA except for the SIFT features which may explain the lower performance of LDA.

6. CONCLUSIONS AND FUTURE WORK

In this paper we have used Latent Dirichilet Allocation models to project image and audio features to a latent topic space. These topic features have meaning and can be used to provide lower level facial information to individuals who are blind. We also showed that this projection technique is comparable to PCA and evaluated its performance on arousal and valence prediction. Also the LDA features are less correlated than the PCA based projections. During our analysis we observed that certain topics that are highly correlated to arousal or valence are given low probability which effects the prediction capability of features. To handle this, in future, we want to use supervised LDA models where the emotions can influence the topics that are extracted. We also plan to use continuous topic models where the features need not be quantized and a continuous Gaussian distribution will be used instead of a discrete multinomial distribution.

7. ACKNOWLEDGMENTS

This material is based upon work supported by the National Science Foundation (NSF) under Grant No. 1116360. Any opinions, findings, and conclusions or recommendations expressed in this material are those of the author(s) and do not necessarily reflect the views of the National Science Foundation.

8. REFERENCES

[1] D. M. Blei, A. Y. Ng, and M. I. Jordan. Latent dirichlet allocation. *J. M. L. R.*, Mar. 2003.

[2] P. Lade, V. Balasubramanian, H. Venkateswara, and S. Panchanathan. Detection of changes in human affect dimensions using an adaptive temporal topic model. In *IEEE ICME*, 2013.

[3] P. Lucey, J. Cohn, T. Kanade, J. Saragih, Z. Ambadar, and I. Matthews. The extended cohn-kanade dataset (ck+): A complete dataset for action unit and emotion-specified expression. In *CVPRW*, 2010.

[4] J. Nicolle, V. Rapp, K. Bailly, L. Prevost, and M. Chetouani. Robust continuous prediction of human emotions using multiscale dynamic cues. In *ACM ICMI*, 2012.

[5] B. Schuller, M. Valstar, R. Cowie, and M. Pantic. Avec 2012: The continuous audio/visual emotion challenge - an introduction. In *ACM ICMI*, 2012.

[6] M. Shah, L. Miao, C. Chakrabarti, and A. Spanias. A speech emotion recognition framework based on latent dirichlet allocation: Algorithm and fpga implementation. In *ICASSP*, 2013.

[7] L. Shang and K.-P. Chan. A temporal latent topic model for facial expression recognition. In *ACCV*, 2010.

[8] Y.-s. Shin. Recognizing facial expressions with pca and ica onto dimension of the emotion. pages 916–922. Springer Berlin Heidelberg, 2006.

[9] Xuehan-Xiong and F. De la Torre. Supervised descent method and its application to face alignment. In *IEEE CVPR*, 2013.

Real-time Crowd Detection Based on Gradient Magnitude Entropy Model

Huiyuan Fu, Huadong Ma
Beijing Key Laboratory of Intelligent Telecommunications Software and Multimedia
Beijing University of Posts and Telecommunications
Beijing, China
fhy@bupt.edu.cn,mhd@bupt.edu.cn

ABSTRACT

Reliable and real-time crowd detection is one of the most important tasks in intelligent video surveillance system. Previous works focus on counting the number of pedestrians in the crowd directly or use holistic features of crowd scenes for crowd detection. However, the former methods will be invalid in complex crowded scenes, and the latter methods will be confused for feature selection. In this paper, we propose a simple but effective model - Gradient Magnitude Entropy (GME) model for crowd detection. Our model is based on a key observation - the value of GME in a region which will increase as the number of pedestrians grows. Thus, we can estimate the degree of crowd when the value of GME is larger than some threshold, without counting the number of pedestrians. Extensive experiments show that our GME model outperforms state-of-the-art techniques on several challenging datasets. Furthermore, our method can process in real time for practical surveillance applications.

Categories and Subject Descriptors

I.4.8 [**Image Processing and computer vision**]: Scene Analysis—*object recognition*

General Terms

Algorithms, Experimentation, Performance

Keywords

real time crowd detection; gradient magnitude entropy

1. INTRODUCTION

The problem of real-time crowd monitoring is crucial for human life and safety. Over crowded pedestrians can cause delays and potential hazard in public places, such as underground passage, shopping center and street. The control of people flow in crowded areas is an important task for safety monitors. Because human observers might miss some information when facing a large number of video cameras, automated techniques for monitoring crowds are necessary.

However, automated crowd detection is a challenging problem. An intuitive way is to count the number of people in the surveillance place. Although a lot of algorithms about human detection [1, 2, 3] have been proposed, they will fail badly to count the number of pedestrians in a heavy crowd environment. This is because there are many heavy occlusions and lack of visibility between pedestrians in crowded scenes, which make it very hard to detect pedestrians accurately even using multiple cameras [4, 5]. Some approaches [6, 7, 8, 9] were proposed to utilize the holistic features of crowd scenes to detect crowd. These features include SIFT descriptor, discrete orthogonal moment features, and texture features. However the features of these works are relatively general, and can not eminently reflect the crowd variation in real time.

In this paper, we consider to use the variational information of scene to detect pedestrian crowd in video sequences. We find that as the number of pedestrians grows, the number of pixels with large value of gradient magnitude will increase simultaneously even there are many heavy occlusions between pedestrians (Fig.1). To quantitatively describe the variational information, we compute the entropy on the histogram of gradient magnitude for each frame. If the value of entropy is greater than some threshold, we can conclude the region is crowded without counting the number of pedestrians. In this way, we propose a simple but effective measure for crowd called Gradient Magnitude Entropy (GME). GME model is inspired by the HOG detector [1], which is a well known human detector. Similar to HOG, we compute the gradient magnitude for each pixel. But we compute the histogram in the whole image, without dividing the image

Figure 1: Visualization of gradient magnitude in non-crowded and crowded scenes.

MM'14, November 3–7, 2014, Orlando, Florida, USA.
Copyright 2014 ACM 978-1-4503-3063-3/14/11 ...$15.00.
http://dx.doi.org/10.1145/2647868.2655043.

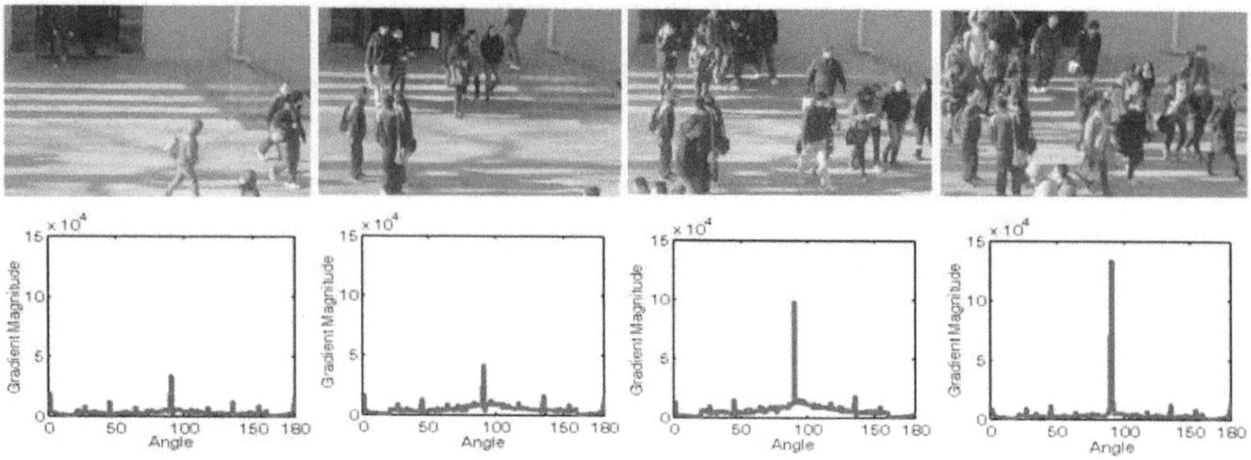

Figure 2: The gradient magnitude around 90° grows significantly with the increase of crowd density.

into grids. We will show that our method is more suitable to describe the crowd than HOG and other state-of-the-art human detectors. We will also show that our method is superior to the state-of-the-art crowd detection approaches.

In the rest of the paper, we give a detailed description of our algorithm and experimental results.

2. GME MODEL

Crowd can be defined as a group of spatially proximate objects of a certain class [6]. In this paper we are specially focusing pedestrian crowd. Our GME model can be separated into three computational steps: gradient magnitude, histogram of gradient magnitude, and gradient magnitude entropy. We will introduce these three computational steps in the following sections.

2.1 Gradient Magnitude

The input RGB image is first gamma corrected to compensate the deviation of intensity value between the camera display and the real scene.

Then, we calculate the gradient magnitude of the corrected image. We use 1-D [-1 0 1] masks to each color channel, and take the largest one as the pixel's gradient magnitude. Fig. 1 gives a visualization of gradient magnitude in non-crowded and crowded scenes. We can see that when some regions are occupied by pedestrians, the corresponding pixels' gradient magnitude will increase.

As the number of pedestrians grow, the number of pixels with large value of gradient magnitude will increase simultaneously even there are many heavy occlusions between pedestrians. This phenomenon can be interpreted by the histogram of gradient magnitude, which is described in the next section.

2.2 Histogram of Gradient Magnitude

We use the histogram of gradient magnitude to analyze the variation of gradient magnitude for a crowded scene. For the calculation of HOG detector, the image will be divided into cells. Each cell has a histogram of oriented gradient, and the concatenation of all cells' histograms constitute the final HOG detector.

Unlike the HOG detector, we do not divide the image into cells. We first compute the gradient orientation for each pixel. The range of gradient orientation is 0° - 180°. Then, the gradient magnitude of each pixel in the whole image is voted into 180 bins according to the orientation of the pixelą́s gradient. We also try to apply 360 bins to the histogram, but the performance will be degraded slightly.

Thus, we can compute the histogram of gradient magnitude for different density scenes. We define four types of densities: very low, low, moderate, and high. The first row of Fig. 2 shows sample image of crowds at different density. For the 50 frames of each density scene, we compute their corresponding histogram of gradient magnitude respectively. Then we can obtain the histogram of average gradient magnitude for each density scene (Fig.2(second row)). From the illustration of Fig. 2, we can see that the gradient magnitude around 90° grow significantly with the increase of crowd density.

Furthermore, we notice that the variation of histograms is only around 90°. Little changes take place in other bins of the histogram. This result illustrates that the mask of gradient magnitude is more sensitive to the upstanding objects. This is an important result which can be used in the next section.

2.3 Gradient Magnitude Entropy

After obtaining the histogram of gradient magnitude, we can compute the gradient magnitude entropy (GME) of an image. Let h_i denote the value of gradient magnitude for the i-th bin of histogram. We define the GME as follows:

$$\text{GME} = -\sum_{i=0}^{180} p_i \log p_i \qquad (1)$$

where p_i is the probability of gradient magnitude for the i-th bin of histogram, which can be defined as

$$p_i = h_i \Big/ \sum_{i=0}^{180} h_i \qquad (2)$$

We find that as the number of pedestrians grows, the value of GME of the region will increase simultaneously. This is because in statistical mechanics, entropy is essentially a measure of the number of ways in which a system may be arranged, often taken to be a measure of disorder. Therefore, GME can quantitatively measure the density variation of a crowded scene.

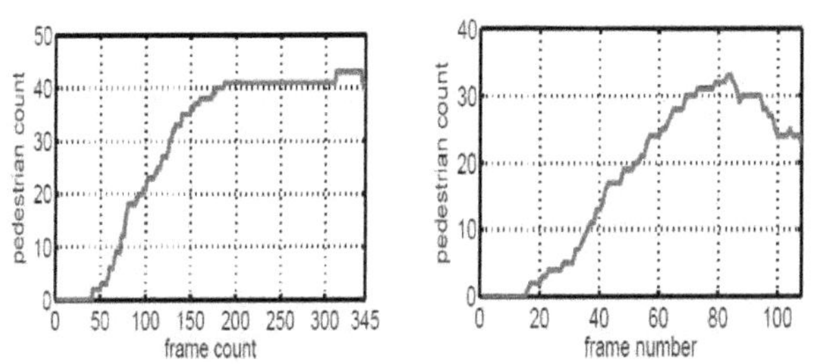

Figure 3: Ground-truth pedestrian count over time on sequence S1.L3.14-33 (a) and S3.14-37 (b) of PETS dataset.

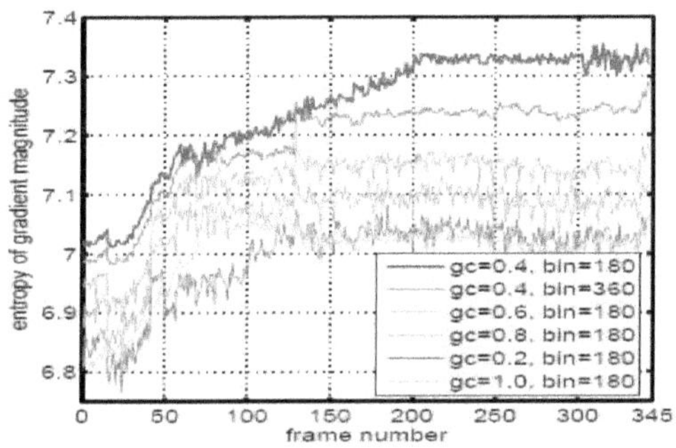

Figure 4: Verification for GME model on sequence S1.L3.14-33 of PETS dataset.

At the first of surveillance, we can always find a frame f_0 with no pedestrians (or a very few pedestrians). We denote the GME value f_0 as GME_0, and denote the GME value of the j-th frame as GME_j. Let D_e denote the difference between GME_j and GME_0, i.e.

$$De = GME_j - GME_0 \tag{3}$$

If D_e greater than some threshold τ, we can conclude the region is crowded while without counting the number of pedestrians.

We also try to use the energy and homogeneity to measure the crowd, which are also used in [8]. Let GM_p denote the value of gradient magnitude of pixel p in an image. The energy E_g of an image can be defined as

$$Eg = \sum_p GM_p \tag{4}$$

The homogeneity H of an image can be defined as

$$H = \sum_{i=0}^{180} \frac{h_i}{1+i^2} \tag{5}$$

We find that E_g and H can also grow as the number of pedestrians increases in a surveillance region.

To reduce the influence of the local variation in illumination and foreground-background contrast, the L2-Hys normalization [1] is applied to the feature vector.

3. EXPERIMENTS

In this section, we first evaluate various settings of parameters for the GME model. Then, we compare the performance of GME model with other crowd measures. Finally, we evaluate the performance of GME model and state-of-the-art approaches.

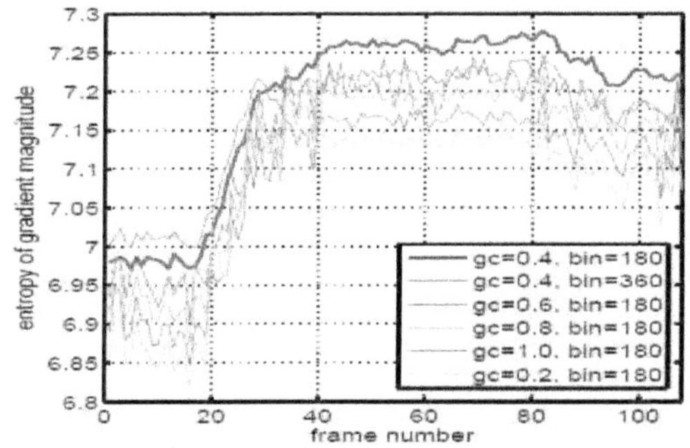

Figure 5: Verification for GME model on sequence S3.14-37 of PETS dataset.

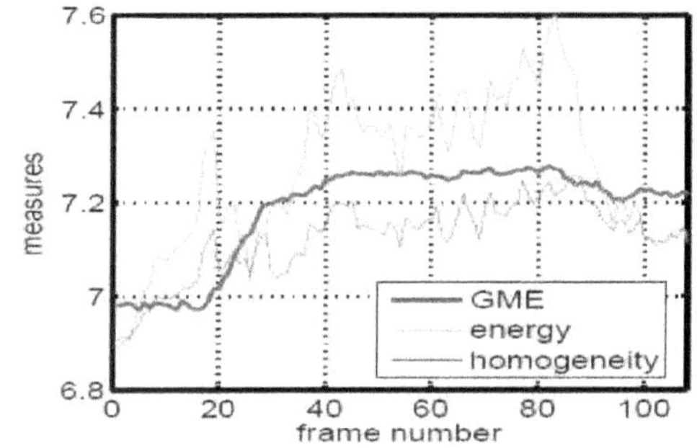

Figure 6: Performance comparison with other crowd measures on sequence S3.14-37 of the PETS dataset.

We use the PETS dataset [10] as our test set. This dataset presents videos recorded at White Knights Campus, University of Reading, UK. This dataset contains different crowd activities and up to approximately forty actors. We choose sequences S1.L3.14-33 and S3.14-37 on the PETS dataset as our test sequences. Fig. 3 shows the variation of the the number of pedestrians for these two regions. The parameters we evaluate for the GME model include the gamma coefficient gc, bin's number of the histogram, and the threshold τ. The value of gc we test for the GME model are 0.2, 0.4, 0.6, 0.8, and 1. Fig. 4 and Fig. 5 show the GME model can track the variation of pedestrians' amount best when the value of gc is 0.4. Fig. 4 and Fig. 5 also show that the GME model performs worst when the value of gc is 1. We also see that the 180 bins of histogram makes the GME model perform better than the 360 bins of histogram. Ac-

	S1.L3.14-33		S3.14-37	
	Non-crowd	Crowd	Non-crowd	Crowd
Our GME	98%	92%	97%	93%
sift SVM	85%	81%	85%	86%
TIOCM	86%	80%	82%	81%
GLDM	81%	79%	80%	78%
HOG	90%	0%	89%	0%
DPM	92%	0%	95%	0%
Poselet	93%	0%	96%	0%
HGM-SVM	60%	62%	61%	59%

Table 1: Comparison with state-of-the-art methods for detection accuracy on PETS dataset.

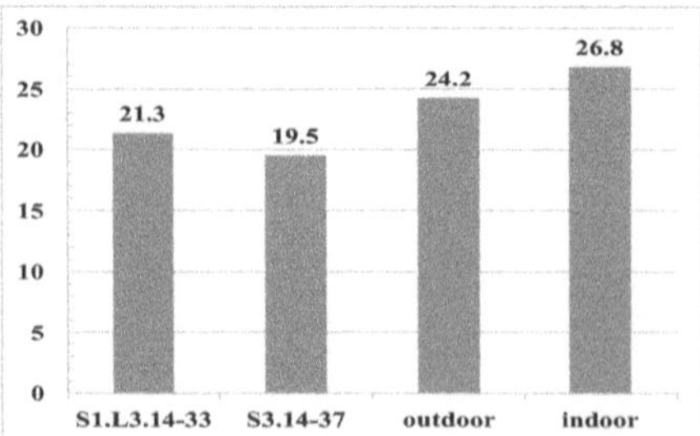

Figure 7: Test the processing speed (fps: frame per second) of our approach in different scenes.

cording to the experimental result, we choose 0.4 (gc) and 180 (bin's number) as our final parameters for the GME model. As described in Section 2.3, we try to use the energy Eg and homogeneity H to measure the crowd. For the convenience of comparison, we reduce the value Eg and H, i.e., $E_g = E_g/10^6 + 3.8$, and $H = H/10^4 + 4.5$. This is reasonable because we only concern the variational trend of Eg and H. From the illustration of Fig. 6, we can see that Eg and H can also grow as the number of pedestrians increases in a surveillance region. But the GME model can track the variation of pedestrians' amount much better than both of these two measures. This is probably because that entropy is more suitable to describe the disorder of crowded scenes than energy and homogeneity.

To evaluate the detection accuracy of the GME model, we manually label the crowded frames and non-crowded frames according to our definition of crowd for both of these two sequences. We compare our method with state-of-the-art approaches for crowd detection, including sift-SVM [6], TIOCM [7], and GLDM [8]. Table 1 shows that our method outperforms these approaches for both non-crowded and crowded frames on sequence S1.L3.14-33 and S3.14-37 respectively.

To further evaluate the performance of the GME model, we record two crowded video sequences in our campus for around 1 hour at 25 frames per second. The first video is recorded at an outdoor scene with 640×480 pixels per frame and good lighting. The size of surveillance area is about 10×15 meters, and can contain no more than 50 pedestrians. Thus, we define crowd for this scene as the number of pedestrians is more than 35. The second video is recorded at an indoor scene with 320×240 pixels per frame and inadequate lighting. The size of surveillance area is about 6×15meters, and can contain no more than 20 pedestrians. Thus, we define crowd for this scene as the number of pedestrians is more than 15. The first frames of these two sequences contain no pedestrian. Thus the value of GME_0 in Eq. 3 can be obtained by computing the value of GME of the first frame. Table 2 shows that our method achieves 92% and 87% detection accuracy on the outdoor sequences and the indoor sequences respectively. These results show that our method can perform well on various scenes, camera settings, and lighting.

	Outdoor scene	Indoor scene
Our GME	92%	87%
sift SVM	82%	70%
TIOCM	81%	62%
GLDM	78%	61%

Table 2: Comparison with state-of-the-art methods for detection accuracy on our dataset.

Based on the proposed algorithm, we have implemented the crowd detection system using C++ programming language. we do many experiments in our system to evaluate the processing speed of our method. As seen in Fig. 7, the speed in sequence S1.L3.14-33 and S3.14-37 of the PETS dataset, and our own captured outdoor and indoor datasets is real time(with 2.5 GHz dual core CPU and 2GB RAM).

4. ACKNOWLEDGMENT

The research is supported by the National High Technology Research and Development Program of China under Grant No.2014AA015101; the Natural Natural Science Foundation of China under Grant No. 61402048; the Funds for Creative Research Groups of China under Grant No. 61121001; the National Internet of Things Special Fund.

5. CONCLUSION

In this paper, we have proposed a simple but powerful crowd detection approach, called Gradient Magnitude Entropy (GME). Our GME model can reflect the variation of the crowd even there are many heavy occlusions between pedestrians. Thus, we can detect crowds when the value of GME is larger than some threshold, without counting the number of pedestrians. Our method outperforms state-of-the-art techniques on various scenes, camera settings, and lighting. Furthermore, our method can process frames in real time on an ordinary computer.

6. REFERENCES

[1] N. Dalal and B. Triggs, Histograms of oriented gradients for human detection, CVPR, 2005.
[2] P. Felzenszwalb and R. Girshick and D. McAllester and D. Ramanan, Object Detection with Discriminatively Trained Part-Based Models, IEEE trans. PAMI, 2010.
[3] X. Ren and D. Ramanan, Histograms of Sparse Codes for Object Detection, CVPR, 2013.
[4] S. Khan and M. Shah, Tracking multiple occluding people by localizing on multiple scene planes, ECCV, 2010.
[5] W. Ge and R. Collins, Crowd Detection with a Multiview Sampler, IEEE trans. PAMI, 2008.
[6] O. Arandjelovic, Crowd detection from still images, BMVC, 2008.
[7] H. Rahmalan and M. Nixon and J. Carter, On crowd density estimation for surveillance, Institution of Engineering and Technology Conference on Crime and Security, 2007.
[8] A. Marana and S. Velastin and L. Costa and R. Lotufo, Estimation of crowd density using image processing, IEE Colloquium on Image Processing for Security Applications, 2002.
[9] D. Kim and Y. Lee and B. Ku and H. Ko, Crowd Density Estimation Using Multi-class Adaboost, IEEE International Conference on Advanced Video and Signal-Based Surveillance, 2012.
[10] J. Ferryman and A. Shahrokni, PETS2009: Dataset and challenge, IEEE International Workshop on Performance Evaluation of Tracking and Surveillance (PETS-Winter), 2009.

Face Recognition from Multiple Images per Subject

Yang Mu
University of Massachusetts Boston
100 Morrissey Boulevard
Boston, MA, US 02125
yangmu@cs.umb.edu

Henry Z Lo
University of Massachusetts Boston
100 Morrissey Boulevard
Boston, MA, US 02125
henryzlo@cs.umb.edu

Wei Ding*
University of Massachusetts Boston
100 Morrissey Boulevard
Boston, MA, US 02125
ding@cs.umb.edu

Dacheng Tao
University of Technology Sydney
235 Jones Street
Ultimo, NSW 2007, Australia
dacheng.tao@uts.edu.au

ABSTRACT

For face recognition, we show that knowing that each subject corresponds to multiple face images can improve classification performance. For domains such as video surveillance, it is easy to deduce which group of images belong to the same subject; in domains such as family album identification, we lose group membership information but there is still a group of images for each subject. We define these two types of problems as *multiple faces per subject*. In this paper, we propose a Bipart framework to take advantage of this group information in the testing set as well as in the training set. From these two sources of information, two models are learned independently and combined to form a unified discriminative distance space. Furthermore, this framework is generalized to allow both subspace learning and distance metric learning methods to take advantage of this group information. Bipart is evaluated on the multiple faces per subject problem using several benchmark datasets, including video and static image data, subjects of various ages, various lighting conditions, and many facial expressions. Comparisons against state-of-the-art distance and subspace learning methods demonstrate much better performance when utilizing group information with the Bipart framework.

Categories and Subject Descriptors

G.4.9 [**Image Precessing and Computer Vision**]: Applications; I.2.6 [**Learning**]: Parameter learning

Keywords

Face recognition, Set classification, Set distance metric learning

*Corresponding author

MM'14, November 3–7, 2014, Orlando, Florida, USA.

http://dx.doi.org/10.1145/2647868.2655054 .

1. INTRODUCTION

When recognizing a face present in many images, these images can be thought of as forming a group. Intuitively, using this group information, i.e. knowing what other images have the same face, should improve recognition performance. In this paper, we consider this information in two scenarios.

In the first, what images have the same face is known in the test set. This information is trivially present in the training set. This scenario applies to face recognition in videos, in which object tracking can recognize the same face across frames, but cannot deduce the identity of that face. We call this the *multiple faces with group identity* problem.

In the second scenario, only the existence of face groups is known. For example, in face recognition in a family album, each person corresponds to a group of face images, but we do not know which images constitute this group. We call this *multiple faces with unknown groups*. We show that just knowing that image groups exist can provide valuable information through unsupervised learning.

In both scenarios, we show that by using group information, which is available in both training and test data, facial recognition accuracy can be improved.

Our proposed *Bipart framework* takes advantage of this information. The approach independently learns distance metrics from the training and test sets, then combines them into one distance metric. This framework differs from semi-supervised discriminant analysis (SDA) [2], which does not consider group identity information, and from set classification methods [3, 9], which only work when group identity information is known. The Bipart framework can be applied to both cases [6].

We demonstrate the Bipart framework by using two locally-learned distance metrics. In addition to using our own distance metrics, Bipart can also combine any two projection matrices, including those formed by subspace learning techniques [5, 13], or distance metric learning methods [12, 10]. Furthermore, these matrices can be learned via supervised methods [10] or unsupervised methods [5].

In its supervised form, Bipart can utilize group identity information in the test set to form constraints. In its semi-supervised form, Bipart can deal with situations where this information is not available; instead of utilizing known group identities, these groups are inferred in an unsupervised way.

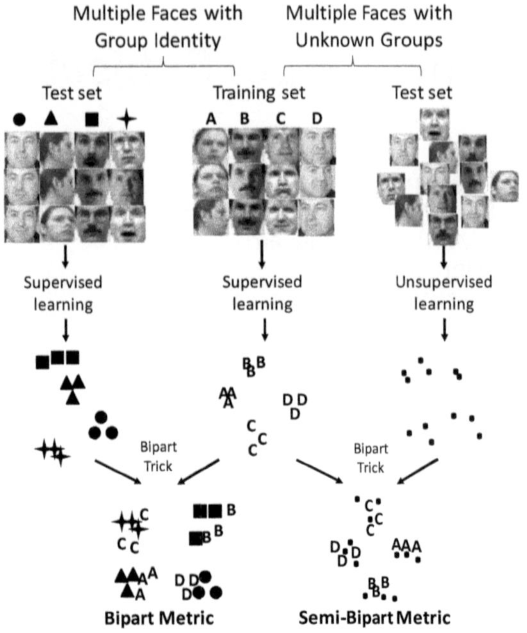

Figure 1: The Bipart framework in its supervised and semi-supervised forms. Both learn two distance metrics from the training and test sets. When the test set has group identity information, its metric can be learned with labeled groups, resulting in supervised Bipart. When this information is not available, the test metric must be learned unsupervised, resulting in semi-supervised Bipart.

It is assumed that group identity information is always available in the training set; see Figure 1 for a visual description.

2. BIPART DISTANCE LEARNING

We propose the Bipart method, which uses two distance metrics: one learned from the training set, and the other from the test set.

2.1 Bipart Trick

With any two images $\mathbf{x}_i$ and $\mathbf{x}_j$ in the data set, the distance metric $\mathbf{A}$ is in the form of

$$d_{\mathbf{A}}(\mathbf{x}_i, \mathbf{x}_j) = \|\mathbf{x}_i - \mathbf{x}_j\|_{\mathbf{A}} = \sqrt{(\mathbf{x}_i - \mathbf{x}_j)^T \mathbf{A} (\mathbf{x}_i - \mathbf{x}_j)}, \quad (1)$$

where $\mathbf{A}$ is positive semi-definite, and parameterizes a family of Mahalanobis distances. Replacing $\mathbf{A}$ with $\mathbf{W}^T\mathbf{W}$ in Equation (1) using Cholesky decomposition, we get:

$$\begin{aligned} d_{\mathbf{A}}(\mathbf{x}_i, \mathbf{x}_j) &= \sqrt{(\mathbf{x}_i - \mathbf{x}_j)^T \mathbf{W}\mathbf{W}^T (\mathbf{x}_i - \mathbf{x}_j)} \\ &= \left\| \mathbf{W}^T (\mathbf{x}_i - \mathbf{x}_j) \right\|. \end{aligned} \quad (2)$$

The Bipart trick fuses two distance metrics by replacing $\mathbf{W}$ with $\mathbf{W}_1\mathbf{W}_2$. Therefore, the Bipart distance metric is:

$$d_{\mathbf{A}}(\mathbf{x}_i, \mathbf{x}_j) = \left\| \mathbf{W}_2^T \mathbf{W}_1^T (\mathbf{x}_i - \mathbf{x}_j) \right\|, \quad (3)$$

where $\mathbf{W}_1$ and $\mathbf{W}_2$ correspond to the distance metrics learned from test and training data respectively. Note the similarity between Equations (2) and (3).

Equation (3) is equivalent to projecting the original face images to $\mathbb{R}^{d_1}$ space using $\mathbf{W}_1$, then to $\mathbb{R}^{d_2}$ space using $\mathbf{W}_2$. $\mathbf{W}_2$ plays a more important role, as it preserves the previously projected information. Which set (testing or training) we use to learn which matrix is discussed in Section 3.

2.2 Bipart Distance Metric Objective

To demonstrate how $\mathbf{W}_1$ and $\mathbf{W}_2$ in Equation (3) are learned, we show $\mathbf{W}_1$. $\mathbf{W}_2$ follows the same procedure.

For each image $\mathbf{x}_i$, we minimize the distance from the other images in the block $\mathbf{B}_i^s$ containing $\mathbf{x}_i$, where $\mathbf{B}_i^s$ is the group of face images corresponding to the same subject:

$$\arg\min_{\mathbf{A}_1} \sum_{i=1}^{n_1} \sum_{p=1}^{k_i^s} d^2_{\mathbf{A}_1}(\mathbf{x}_i, \mathbf{x}_p^{\mathbf{B}_i^s}), \quad (4)$$

Likewise, $\mathbf{B}_i^d$, which contains images similar to $\mathbf{x}_i$ but corresponds to different subject with $\mathbf{x}_i$, form the dissimilarity constraints:

$$\arg\max_{\mathbf{A}_1} \sum_{i=1}^{n_1} \sum_{q=1}^{k_i^d} d^2_{\mathbf{A}_1}(\mathbf{x}_i, \mathbf{x}_q^{\mathbf{B}_i^d}), \quad (5)$$

where $A_1 = \mathbf{W}_1^T\mathbf{W}_1$ is the distance metric learned; n_1, k_i^s and k_i^d are the numbers of examples in the test set blocks $\mathbf{B}_i^s$ and $\mathbf{B}_i^d$ respectively; $\mathbf{x}_p^{\mathbf{B}_i^s}$ and $\mathbf{x}_q^{\mathbf{B}_i^d}$ are the pth and q^{th} images in $\mathbf{B}_i^s$ and $\mathbf{B}_i^d$.

Equations (4) and (5) combine to form the objective function:

$$\arg\min_{\mathbf{A}_1} \sum_{i=1}^{n_1} \left(\sum_{p=1}^{k_i^s} d^2_{\mathbf{A}_1}(\mathbf{x}_i, \mathbf{x}_p^{\mathbf{B}_i^s}) - \beta \sum_{q=1}^{k_i^d} d^2_{\mathbf{A}_1}(\mathbf{x}_i, \mathbf{x}_q^{\mathbf{B}_i^d}) \right), \quad (6)$$

where β quantifies the relative importance of the two types of constraints.

The distance metric $\mathbf{A}_1$ as well as $\mathbf{W}_1$ can be solved from Equation (6). Under $\mathbf{A}_1$, the distance between any two examples is equivalent to the Euclidean distance projected using the projection matrix $\mathbf{W}_1$ [7]. $\mathbf{W}_2$ is learned from the training set. With $\mathbf{W}_1$ and $\mathbf{W}_2$, we can obtain the final distance metric $\mathbf{A}$ by Equation (3).

3. BIPART FRAMEWORK

Bipart bridges subspace learning and distance metric learning. In Equation (3), we can use a projection matrix $\mathbf{W}$, as done in subspace learning; conversely, we can use Equation (4), replacing $\mathbf{A}_1$ with any metric $\mathbf{A}$ used in distance learning.

The objectives of linearized subspace learning algorithms can be transformed into the following form:

$$\arg\min_{\mathbf{W}} \operatorname{tr}(\mathbf{W}^T\mathbf{X}\mathbf{L}\mathbf{X}^T\mathbf{W}). \quad (7)$$

For example, LPP [5] adds the constraint $\mathbf{W}^T\mathbf{X}\mathbf{X}^T\mathbf{W} = \mathbf{I}_d$, and PCA, LDA, ONPP add the constraint $\mathbf{W}^T\mathbf{W} = \mathbf{I}_d$ on Equation (7). The differences in constructing the matrix $\mathbf{L}$ embody the various motivations of spectral analysis based subspace learning methods.

On the other hand, distance metric approaches can be formulated as follows:

$$\begin{aligned} &\arg\min_{\mathbf{A}} \textstyle\sum_{(\mathbf{x}_i,\mathbf{x}_j)\in S} d^2_{\mathbf{A}}(\mathbf{x}_i, \mathbf{x}_j), \\ &s.t. \textstyle\sum_{(\mathbf{x}_i,\mathbf{x}_j)\in D} d^2_{\mathbf{A}}(\mathbf{x}_i, \mathbf{x}_j) \geq \theta \end{aligned} \quad (8)$$

where S contains sample pairs with the same class label, while D contains sample pairs from different classes. Almost all distance metric approaches minimize the similarity constraint as their main objective. The differences lie in optimizing the dissimilarity constraints. For example, Xing's method [12] sets $\theta = 1$, while LMNN[10] defines $\theta = 1 + \sum_{(\mathbf{x}_i,\mathbf{x}_j)\in S} d^2_{\mathbf{A}}(\mathbf{x}_i, \mathbf{x}_j)$ in Equation (8). Our Bipart method simply maximizes θ when optimizing the similarity objective function, which is defined in Equations (4) and (5).

To incorporate and improve subspace learning and distance metric learning methods, Bipart can be used as either a part of a supervised or semi-supervised framework.

Supervised Form: Supervised Bipart can be used to deal with multiple faces with known groups. In this form, group identity in the test set is known and used to train a distance metric. Though $\mathbf{W}_1$ and $\mathbf{W}_2$ can learned from either the test or training set, $\mathbf{W}_1$ should be learned from the set with more information. In our case, we learn $\mathbf{W}_1$ from the test set, since there are more testing images.

After learning $\mathbf{W}_1$ and $\mathbf{W}_2$, we combine the two distance metrics using the Bipart trick. This sequential projection results in a single projection which contains information from both the training and test sets.

A similar method for combining two matrices is LFDA [8], which combines and optimizes both LPP and LDA into one objective function. However, unlike LFDA which only uses training set information, Bipart sequentially combines data from both the training set and test set. In addition, Bipart does not require Laplacian matrices, and thus is applicable to any method which can be formulated as either Equation (7) or (8) [12, 10].

Performance for the Bipart metric $\mathbf{W}_1\mathbf{W}_2$ will be no worse than the performance either $\mathbf{W}_1$ or $\mathbf{W}_2$. When $\mathbf{W}_2$ is full rank, the performance of $\mathbf{W}_1\mathbf{W}_2$ will always be the same as $\mathbf{W}_1$, since there is no dimensionality reduction from $\mathbf{W}_2$. If $\mathbf{W}_2$ does not contribute to the overall performance, it can be set as an identity matrix.

Though we use the distance matrices described in the previous section, Bipart can be generalized to a supervised framework by replacing $\mathbf{W}_1$ and $\mathbf{W}_2$ with any projection matrix learned using supervised subspace learning or distance metric learning methods, as mentioned in Equations (7) and (8).

Semi-Supervised Form: Semi-supervised Bipart (semi-Bipart) can be used for face recognition problems with unknown groups. In this case, $\mathbf{W}_1$ is learned from the training set, and $\mathbf{W}_2$ from the test set. Without known group information, the test set must be learned without supervision, using only the objective function in Equation (4), with $\mathbf{B}_i^s$ being formed via k-nearest-neighbors. Many unsupervised dimensionality reduction methods are ready to be plugged into the semi-Bipart framework, e.g. locally linear embedding (LLE) [7] and many variants of spectral clustering. Unlike the semi-supervised methods discussed in [2] which use a linear tuning parameter to balance the weights between supervised and unsupervised parts, Bipart smoothly combines both parts without needing a tuning parameter.

4. EXPERIMENTS

4.1 Data

We used four face recognition datasets: 11 face images each from 15 individuals in the Yale face database, with various facial expressions; 564 total face images from 20 individuals in the UMIST face database, with various poses; 560 total face images from 80 subjects in the ChokePoint surveillance video dataset [11], with variations in illumination, pose, sharpness, and alignment; 11 images each from 66 individuals in FG-NET dataset [1], where subject age is ranges from newborn to 69. Figure 2 shows some sample images from these datasets.

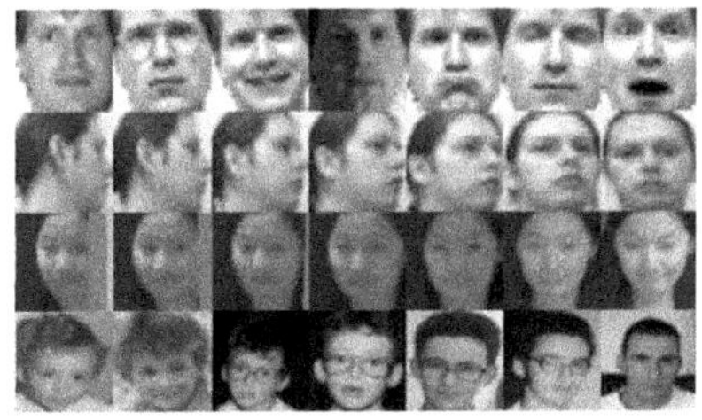

Figure 2: Images from our data sets. From the top row to the bottom: YALE, UMIST, ChokePoint, and FG-NET.

YALE, UMIST, and ChokePoint images were aligned and cropped according to eyes, scaled to 40×40, and normalized to have gray scale values between 0 and 255. In FG-NET, each image contains 68 labeled points describing shape features; Active Appearance Model (AAM) features [4] were extracted from these points. In order to capture 98% of the variance of the whole data, 458 model parameters were extracted according to the AAM to represent each individual.

4.2 Methods

We compared Bipart with the standard subspace learning methods LDA (or Fisherface) and LPP (or Laplacianface) [5]; a semi-supervised method, semi-supervised discriminant analysis (SDA) [2]; a popular set classification method, linear affine hull based image set distance (L-AHISD) [3]; and a state-of-the-art distance learning method, large margin nearest-neighbor (LMNN) [10].

Default parameter settings for all methods were used, and only the dimension of the resulting subspaces were tuned. We set $k_i^d = t + 1$ for Bipart, $k_i^d = 0$ for semi-Bipart, and $k_i^s = t - 1$ for both, where t is the number of training samples. β was set to 0.4 for all the experiments. The dimension d_1 was automatically determined by using k-nearest-neighbors on the training set. The final dimension d_2 was chosen to be the best performing value. After projection, nearest neighbor was used to classify faces.

4.3 Experimental Design

In these experiments, one group of face images is provided for each subject. In the training set, subject labels were given for these groups, while in the test set, they were not. The goal was to correctly identify the subject of the group.

This group identity information was used directly in the supervised Bipart framework and L-AHISD; in the other methods, voting was applied between the images in the group to determine the identity of the group.

Unknown group experiments. As in the group identity experiments, each subject was assumed to have multiple images. However, the image to subject groupings were not given for the test set. We used semi-Bipart for this problem, and constructed group information in the test set using k-nearest-neighbors. L-AHISD was not applicable in this

Multiple Faces with Unknown Groups

Dataset	t	Semi-Bipart	LMNN	L-AHISD	LDA	SDA	LPP
YALE	2	$59.78 \pm 4.04(20)$	$55.33 \pm 5.04(119)$	n/a	$54.15 \pm 5.44(14)$	$52.52 \pm 4.06(14)$	$56.67 \pm 3.72(18)$
	4	$76.38 \pm 4.04(30)$	$74.29 \pm 3.08(42)$	n/a	$73.81 \pm 4.07(14)$	$68.48 \pm 4.15(14)$	$74.48 \pm 3.26(21)$
UMIST	2	$83.01 \pm 3.81(12)$	$78.45 \pm 4.42(125)$	n/a	$66.58 \pm 3.02(18)$	$68.86 \pm 3.52(18)$	$66.84 \pm 3.67(26)$
	4	$92.97 \pm 2.55(16)$	$92.10 \pm 2.53(15)$	n/a	$81.37 \pm 4.04(19)$	$84.61 \pm 3.82(19)$	$76.53 \pm 20.53(48)$
ChokePoint	2	$57.77 \pm 2.23(109)$	$62.38 \pm 1.91(35)$	n/a	$54.75 \pm 2.31(74)$	$51.40 \pm 2.36(79)$	$56.17 \pm 2.31(105)$
	4	$77.37 \pm 2.62(53)$	$77.50 \pm 2.14(58)$	n/a	$68.63 \pm 2.99(69)$	$64.00 \pm 3.48(80)$	$69.04 \pm 2.75(144)$
FG-NET	2	$46.57 \pm 2.04(91)$	$41.62 \pm 2.37(304)$	n/a	$26.52 \pm 1.48(63)$	$32.96 \pm 2.12(65)$	$19.36 \pm 1.95(85)$
	4	$64.29 \pm 1.22(186)$	$58.79 \pm 1.60(413)$	n/a	$53.90 \pm 1.47(60)$	$53.03 \pm 1.85(58)$	$21.04 \pm 1.56(79)$

Multiple Faces with Group Identity

Dataset	t	Bipart	LMNN	L-AHISD	LDA	SDA	LPP
YALE	2	$97.33 \pm 4.66(14)$	$82.67 \pm 6.44(119)$	80.00 ± 12.57	$86.67 \pm 8.31(14)$	$80.67 \pm 9.66(14)$	$87.33 \pm 5.84(18)$
	4	$99.33 \pm 2.11(41)$	$94.00 \pm 3.78(42)$	95.33 ± 6.32	$96.00 \pm 4.66(14)$	$92.00 \pm 8.78(14)$	$96.67 \pm 5.67(21)$
UMIST	2	$97.72 \pm 3.40(12)$	$93.94 \pm 5.32(125)$	100.00 ± 0.00	$93.61 \pm 4.92(18)$	$88.43 \pm 7.16(18)$	$93.91 \pm 5.92(26)$
	4	$99.70 \pm 0.96(14)$	$98.48 \pm 2.60(15)$	100.00 ± 0.00	$96.79 \pm 4.34(19)$	$95.41 \pm 3.97(19)$	$92.79 \pm 13.78(48)$
ChokePoint	2	$84.75 \pm 3.48(54)$	$75.38 \pm 4.08(35)$	84.12 ± 3.59	$67.13 \pm 5.68(74)$	$61.88 \pm 5.31(79)$	$71.00 \pm 4.03(105)$
	4	$93.88 \pm 1.61(47)$	$85.00 \pm 2.50(58)$	90.50 ± 2.65	$76.62 \pm 5.47(69)$	$71.50 \pm 4.16(80)$	$77.62 \pm 4.43(144)$
FG-NET	2	$85.30 \pm 3.57(248)$	$73.79 \pm 3.35(304)$	62.88 ± 4.36	$52.73 \pm 6.69(63)$	$56.52 \pm 5.25(65)$	$39.55 \pm 4.76(85)$
	4	$91.97 \pm 2.48(360)$	$90.00 \pm 2.04(413)$	79.85 ± 3.71	$87.12 \pm 3.99(60)$	$85.30 \pm 4.58(58)$	$41.82 \pm 5.16(79)$

Table 1: Averaged accuracy and standard deviations for various methods and datasets over ten-fold cross-validation. t is the number of training samples per subject. Numbers in the parentheses are the dimensions of the final projection space.

setting. SDA and semi-Bipart used both the training and the test set; all other methods only learned from the training set.

We used $t = 2, 4$ samples per person for training; all remaining samples are used for testing. For each t, test and training sets were generated using random splits 10 times.

4.4 Results

Averaged accuracies and standard deviations are shown in table 1. In the unknown group experiments, semi-Bipart performed the best, followed by LMNN, which as shown in Equation 8 has a similar objective function. However, semi-Bipart has stronger constraints on dissimilar faces, and exploits discriminative information in the test set. LDA, SDA and LPP found lower-dimensional subspaces, but were not as accurate.

In the group identity experiments, supervised Bipart and L-AHISD achieve better performance than other methods which only use group identity information for voting. Bipart, by using information in both training and test sets, outperforms L-AHISD on most datasets.

Performance for all methods improved with more training data (higher t in table 1). However, more training data in our experimental design means less testing data. Since Bipart uses test data to augment the learned projection when training data is scarce, the performance gap between Bipart and other methods is expected to shrink with higher t.

5. ACKNOWLEDGEMENTS

The work was partially funded by the University of Massachusetts Boston Proposal Development Grant 2014 and the Australian Research Council Projects FT-130101457 and DP-140102164.

6. REFERENCES

[1] Fg-net database: http://www.fgnet.rsunit.com.

[2] D. Cai, X. He, and J. Han. Semi-supervised discriminant analysis. *ICCV*, pages 1–7, 2007.

[3] H. Cevikalp and B. Triggs. Face recognition based on image sets. In *CVPR*, pages 2567–2573. IEEE, 2010.

[4] T. F. Cootes, G. J. Edwards, and C. J. Taylor. Active appearance models. *IEEE TPAMI*, 23:681–685, 2001.

[5] X. He and P. Niyogi. Locality preserving projections. In *NIPS*, 2003.

[6] Y. Mu, H. Lo, W. Ding, K. Amaral, and S. Crouter. Bipart: Learning block structure for activity detection. *IEEE Transactions on Knowledge and Data Engineering*, 99:1, 2014.

[7] S. T. Roweis and L. K. Saul. Nonlinear dimensionality reduction by locally linear embedding. *Science*, 290(5500):2323–2326, 2000.

[8] M. Sugiyama. Dimensionality reduction of multimodal labeled data by local fisher discriminant analysis. *JMLR*, 8:1027–1061, 2007.

[9] R. Wang, S. Shan, X. Chen, Q. Dai, and W. Gao. Manifold-manifold distance and its application to face recognition with image sets. *IEEE Transactions on Image Processing*, 21(10):4466–4479, 2012.

[10] K. Weinberger and L. Saul. Distance metric learning for large margin nearest neighbor classification. *JMLR*, 10:207–244, June 2009.

[11] Y. Wong and S. C. et al. Patch-based probabilistic image quality assessment for face selection and improved video-based face recognition. In *CVPRW*, 2011.

[12] E. Xing and A. N. et al. Distance metric learning, with application to clustering with side-information. In *NIPS*, pages 505–512, 2002.

[13] T. Zhang, D. Tao, and J. Yang. Discriminative locality alignment. In *ECCV*, pages 725–738, 2008.

Admission Control for Wireless Adaptive HTTP Streaming: An Evidence Theory Based Approach

Zhisheng Yan
The State University of New York at Buffalo

Chang Wen Chen
The State University of New York at Buffalo

Bin Liu
University of Science and Technology of China

ABSTRACT

In this research, we propose an evidence theory based admission control scheme for wireless cellular adaptive HTTP streaming systems. This novel scheme allows us to effectively address the uncertainty and inaccuracy in QoE management and network estimation, and seamlessly grant or deny the access requests. Specifically, based on recent work of QoE continuum model and QoE continuum driven adaptation algorithm, we utilize Dempster-Shafer evidence theory to assign proper degree of belief to admission, rejection and an uncertainty decision for each user's evidence. We then can strategically combine the weighted evidence of multiple users and make the final decision. The evaluation results show that the proposed scheme can provide satisfactory QoE for both existing and new users while still achieving comparable bandwidth efficiency.

Categories and Subject Descriptors

H.5.1 [**Multimedia Information Systems**]: Video

General Terms

Algorithms; Human Factors

Keywords

Adaptive streaming; admission control; QoE continuum; evidence theory

1. INTRODUCTION

In the past few years, video streaming over wireless Internet has been rapidly booming, thanks to the development of high-performance smart phones, tablets, and laptops, as well as the growing demand of watching videos anywhere and anytime. In an effort to improve the bandwidth efficiency of HTTP streaming in wireless environment, adaptive HTTP streaming has recently been standardized [1]. The source video is encoded in several quality versions and is split into small segments. At each switching point, the client requests the most appropriate segment based on the network conditions. That way, the user can enjoy the video with highest possible quality while still efficiently utilizing the bandwidth.

Many rate adaptation schemes have been proposed to enhance the Quality of Experience (QoE) of users [2–5]. They all assume that the number of users in the system is fixed and the available bandwidth of a client is always larger than the lowest video bit-rate. However, the number of users changes dynamically in reality. When the number of streaming flows is so large that the total bandwidth requirement is beyond the system capacity, users would experience QoE degradation. To overcome such challenges, proper network regulation policy is critically needed to grant or deny the service requests from new users.

One challenge of designing such an effective admission control scheme is to appropriately assess users' QoE in order to make a QoE-driven decision. Although reasonable QoE modeling improves system design, such objective QoE assessment cannot adequately reflect subjective human feeling. This is especially true when mobile users are watching video under time-varying environment. Another crucial challenge is how to handle the system uncertainty introduced in network estimation and admit/reject the new user accordingly. Due to the time-varying fading and path loss, estimating network status of wireless networks is generally of uncertainty and dynamics. The probability of different network status is also not known accurately. Thereby, both uncertainty and inaccuracy need to be effectively captured during the admission control.

Admission control in wireless networks was originally studied for cellular networks with general data services. A comprehensive survey on admission control in wireless networks was presented in [6]. Admission control schemes for wireless video services have been recently proposed. They usually formulate admission constraints by considering available bandwidth [7, 8], objective QoE metric [9] or QoE distribution [5], and multiple QoS parameters using cross-layer notion [10]. However, most of the existing works are not targeted at adaptive HTTP streaming, where both the initial request of the new user and the current service of existing users can be adjusted in order to accommodate the new user. More importantly, all of them adopt an on-off decision-making logic, as illustrated in Fig. 1. The admission probability would be 1.0 as long as certain decision scores are larger than the thresholds and vice versa. Considering the various types of system uncertainty, such deterministic logic lacks flexibility and could cause inaccurate decisions when the estimated decision score (e.g., 0.21) is close to the thresh-

MM'14, November 3–7, 2014, Orlando, Florida, USA.

http://dx.doi.org/10.1145/2647868.2655056.

old (e.g., $\theta = 0.2$). Besides, the decision score in existing work is usually obtained by averaging the individual score of each user. Such simple combination logic fails to recognize the different contribution of each individual user.

The major contribution of this research is in the development of an admission control scheme for adaptive HTTP streaming within one wireless cell. It can guarantee the QoE of both new and existing users, and minimize the negative effects of system uncertainty while efficiently utilizing the bandwidth. Specifically, we first adopt a *QoE continuum* driven rate adaptation algorithm to effectively improve the playback quality and smoothness of users. By exploiting *Dempster-Shafer evidence theory*, we recognize the adaptation results as the evidence for the usual admission and rejection decision, as well as an additional "uncertainty" decision in order to address the inflexibility in on-off decision logic. We then derive the overall belief for each decision from multiple user evidences by using differential trust weighting. This way, the proposed scheme is able to handle system uncertainty and most efficiently regulate the network access.

2. SYSTEM MODELS

2.1 System Architecture

In the proposed streaming system, the source video is split into segments with the same length T. Each segment is encoded into multiple levels of quality. Since modern internet videos are usually variable-bit-rate video, a single-value representation using average bit-rate may not accurately reflect the actual size of each individual segment to be downloaded. Hence, we propose to adopt fine-grained video representations and characterize the video segment by a tuple represented by quantization parameter and file size, i.e., $(\mathbf{QP}, \mathbf{FS})$, in order to capture video characteristics in a segment scale and execute more efficient adaptation.

In this research, we consider a wireless adaptive HTTP streaming system under cellular environments. The proposed admission control scheme targets at one cell, where $\mathcal{U}$ is the set of users and each user is indexed by $i, i = 1, 2 \cdots N$. For simplicity of discussion, we assume that one user can only establish one streaming flow with the server.

Under the wireless shared bandwidth, individual adaptation and admission control using local information by each client could lead to unfair and inefficient performance. For instance, even though two clients have the same channel condition and priority, the client with an initial request for higher quality tends to continuously request a high-quality video and vice versa for the client with low-quality initial request. This is because the two clients remain a high and low local throughput measurement, respectively. In fact, if the second client knows the condition and priority of the first client, it could have requested a better video such that two users achieve a relatively fair experience, e.g., a medium-quality video. Therefore, we propose to move the intelligence of adaptation and admission control to base station (BS) while not intervening the standard adaptive HTTP streaming architecture. Thus we can explore the collective knowledge and constraints of multiple streams. The proposed system works as follows. The video server initially sends out the Media Presentation Description so that video representation information is available to the users and BS. At each adaptation period whose length equals to the segment length, a user requests a segment based on throughput calculation that needs very low complexity. This request can be recognized as a *naive suggestion* and thereby no corresponding local client's operating system or hardware optimization is operated, which indicates there would be no conflict if the client request is modified. Instead of relaying the request directly, BS in the proposed system will intercept the request and may revise the client request based on the cell-wide adaptation strategy. Notice that information feedback from the clients is used for the BS adaptation. This is feasible under current adaptive HTTP streaming framework because 3GPP has standardized the quality metrics reporting process for clients [1]. If there is a new user request before the current switching point, BS would proceed to the admission control, wherein the current QoE and estimated QoE are regarded as the evidence for the decision-making process to ensure the QoE provision for both existing users and new user. This way, all users are able to enjoy the video with optimized QoE while neither the user nor the video server is aware of the adaptation and admission control done by BS.

2.2 QoE Continuum Driven Adaptation

QoE at a certain moment should be assessed in a temporally continuous manner by considering both the previously displayed frames and currently displayed frame. Hence, we adopt a QoE continuum model [11], which has been extensively validated by using various types of tests and videos. The QoE continuum experience E at frame j can be derived as the weighted sum of instantaneous experience over all displaying moments until the measuring moment, i.e.,

$$E_j = \lambda E_{j-1} + (1 - \lambda) e_j \tag{1}$$

where E_{j-1} is the QoE continuum experience at the previous frame, λ is the memory constant that characterizes the importance of previous viewing experience, and e_j is the instantaneous experience at frame j. E_j, $|e_j|$ and λ all belong to $(0,1]$. Details on how to calculate e_j that is decided by QP can be found in [11].

To guarantee the QoE continuum among multiple clients, we adopt the same adaptation algorithm in [4]. BS can find the optimal level of video segment, indicated by (QP, FS), for each user i at time t by solving an optimization problem, where the objective is to maximize the average QoE continuum of all possible users at next switching point $t + T$, subjective to the cellular resource constraint, i.e.,

$$\begin{array}{ll} \max_{(\mathbf{QP},\mathbf{FS})} & \frac{1}{N} \sum_{i \in \mathcal{U}} E_{i,t+T} \\ \text{s. t.} & \sum_{i \in \mathcal{U}} \frac{FS_i}{TB_{i,max}} \leq 1 \end{array} \tag{2}$$

where $B_{i,max}$ is the maximum bandwidth of user i that can be mapped from channel quality indicator using 3GPP standard table. Based on the current buffer status feedback from the users and a given quality level, $E_{i,t+T}$ can be calculated using (1). The adaptation wisdom behind (2) is to assign higher quality level to those users who are experiencing lower QoE continuum and a better channel status. The optimization problem can be efficiently solved by using a greedy algorithm [4].

3. PROPOSED ADMISSION CONTROL

3.1 Applying Evidence Theory

Recall that the criterion for admission control is whether or not admitting the new request would undermine the QoE continuum of existing users or the new user in the near future. How to make a system-level decision based on estimated QoE of multiple users is non-trivial due to the system

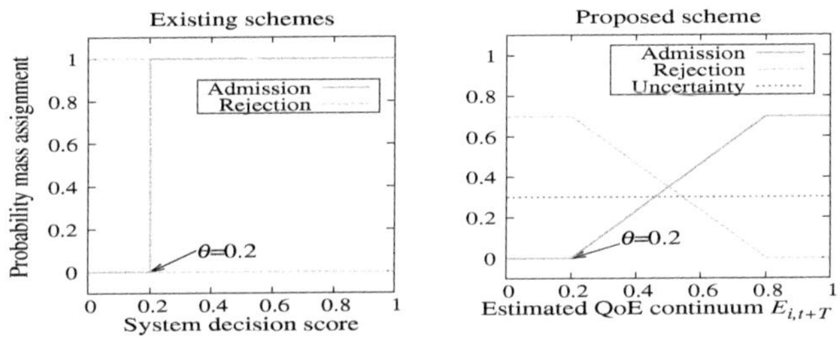

Figure 1: Probability mass assignment in existing schemes and the proposed scheme ($\theta = 0.2$).

uncertainty. Here we propose to exploit Dempster-Shafer evidence theory (DST) [12], wherein the degree of belief for different decisions can be obtained from the evidence of estimated QoE. We prefer DST because it allows for assigning support to not only single hypothesis but also to union of hypotheses. Here we introduce an uncertainty decision U, which means either admitting (AD) or rejecting (RJ) the new user is acceptable. In other words, we can assign degree of belief to U if certain part of evidence provides no support to either AD or RJ. This is especially more plausible than on-off decision logic, where only the definitive decisions (i.e., AD and RJ) are supported. Moreover, unlike existing schemes that acquire the system decision score by averaging individual user scores, we propose a DST-based weighting method to combine the estimated QoE of multiple users.

3.2 Making Admission Decision

The admission control scheme starts by estimating user i's QoE continuum, $E_{i,t+T}$, at the next switching point. This is accomplished by running the adaptation algorithm with the assumption that the new user is admitted using (2). In DST, the probability mass assignment m_i is a value in [0,1] indicating how much support that user i provides to a certain decision and the total m_i of all possible decisions is 1.0. Here we use the simple yet effective piecewise linear assignment [12]. Furthermore, we apply a weight factor for each user using differential trust scheme [12] in order to account for their different level of uncertainty and trustiness. The m_i for AD, RJ, and U decision can be expressed as

$$m_i(AD) = \begin{cases} 0 & E_{i,t+T} \le \theta \\ \omega_i(\frac{1}{1-2\theta}E_{i,t+T} - \frac{\theta}{1-2\theta}) & \theta < E_{i,t+T} < 1-\theta \\ \omega_i & E_{i,t+T} \ge 1-\theta \end{cases} \quad (3)$$

$$m_i(RJ) = \omega_i - m_i(AD) \quad (4)$$

$$m_i(U) = 1 - m_i(AD) - m_i(RJ) = 1 - \omega_i \quad (5)$$

where ω_i is the weight factor of user i and $\omega_i \in [0, 1]$. The illustration of the probability mass assignment is shown in Fig. 1. The rationale behind such assignment is that although $E_{i,t+T}$ going over and under certain thresholds ($1-\theta$ and θ) leads us towards a quite certain decision, our beliefs should be treated with an increased support in between. Furthermore, by applying the differential trust scheme, the probability mass assigned to the uncertainty decision of the relatively untrusted users is effectively raised. That way, we can take into account the trustiness of each user and accordingly enhance the accuracy of the assignment.

The weight factor is dictated by the user evidence's historical impact to the system decision. Provided that the new user is eventually admitted, user i's evidence is considered as

Table 1: Encoding Parameters of Source Video

	l_1	l_2	l_3	l_4	l_5
Seg 1 (bytes)	11924	23399	46128	92394	124772
Seg 2 (bytes)	11098	22067	42383	84770	115719
Seg 3 (bytes)	9300	20041	40242	82783	113240
Seg 4 (bytes)	11715	23217	44488	89569	121986
Seg 5 (bytes)	15619	30158	56136	106233	140522

positive if user i provides more support to AD than RJ and all users can indeed enjoy satisfactory watching experience during the next period. However, if user i supports more to RJ or any user experiences unacceptable video, the evidence is regarded as negative. If the new user is ultimately rejected, the rationale is similar. Hence, the weight factor is given by

$$\omega_i(t) = (1-\rho)\sum_{g=1}^{\infty} c_i(t - gT)\rho^g \quad (6)$$

where ρ is the remnant factor that indicates how rapidly the past performance would be disregarded, $c_i(t) = 1$ when the user evidence at t is positive and $c_i(t) = 0$ otherwise.

By using the Dempster's rule of combination, we can then infer the system decision in a collaborative fashion based on individual support from the users. The combined probability mass assignment of user i and j for AD is given by

$$m_{i,j}(AD) = \frac{1}{1-K} \sum_{H_i \cap H_j = AD \neq \varnothing} m_i(H_i)m_j(H_j) \quad (7)$$

where $K = \sum_{H_i \cap H_j = \varnothing} m_i(H_i)m_j(H_j)$. H_i and H_j is the hypothesis of user i and j, respectively (i.e., AD, RJ or U). Since the Dempster's rule of combination is associative, we can combine the individual support from more than two users accordingly. Finally, the belief and plausibility of AD can be expressed as follow.

$$bel(AD) = \sum_{H \subseteq AD} m_{combo}(H) \quad (8)$$

$$pl(AD) = \sum_{H \cap AD \neq \varnothing} m_{combo}(H) \quad (9)$$

Similarly, the belief and plausibility of rejection and uncertainty decision can be calculated and then the final decision can be made by comparing the belief and plausibility of AD and RJ decision. The decision with larger belief or larger plausibility (when beliefs for two decisions are equal) is considered as the final system decision.

4. PERFORMANCE EVALUATIONS

In this section, we compare the performance of streaming systems with different admission control schemes using ns-2. We implement two reference schemes (referred as *Inst* and *Avr*) that use instantaneous quality and average quality as the decision metric, respectively. Both reference schemes combine the scores from multiple users by averaging and make the decision using on-off logic. Here we focus on a 3G High-Speed Downlink Packet Access (HSDPA) network as the underlying cellular network using the simulation model in [13] with typical network settings. We encode the "Stefan" test sequence into 5 levels H.264/AVC video with $QP \in \{47, 42, 37, 32, 30\}$ using JM 18.4 encoder. The segment length T is 2 seconds and the frame rate is 25 fps. The test sequence has 250 frames and these 5 segments are repeatedly streamed. The file size FS of each segment for each level l is shown in Table 1. We set λ to be 0.71 [11] and ρ to be 0.5. The initial $E_{i,t}$ and ω_i are both 1. Initially, two

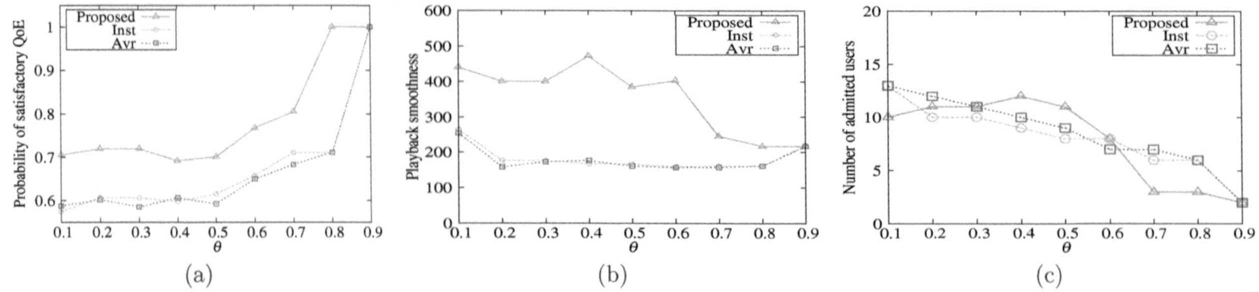

Figure 2: Evaluations results: a) Probability of satisfied QoE versus θ; b) Expected length of one playback round without level change versus θ; c) Number of admitted users after the evaluations versus θ.

users are enjoying the video services. The service request rate is one user per ten seconds. Note that we assume users will not end services during the evaluations.

We compare the performance of different systems under various θ, whose significance was introduced in Fig. 1. We disregard the cases where no admission ($\theta = 1$) or no rejection ($\theta = 0$) is allowed. We show the probability of satisfactory QoE (i.e., $E_{i,t} > 0.5$, which corresponds to $MOS > 3$) in Fig. 2a. We observe that a user is more likely to be satisfied with the video by using the proposed system since new request is admitted only if the QoE continuum of both the new and existing users can be ensured. When θ increases to 0.9, all new requests turn out to be rejected in three systems, which brings the equal 1.0 probability of QoE satisfaction. Note that the satisfaction is not accomplished at the expense of bandwidth utilization, which we will discuss later.

To evaluate the video consistency, we employ the playback smoothness metric in [3]. The metric is defined as the expected length of one playback round without level change, i.e., $\sqrt{\sum_{p=1}^{P}(n_p^2)/P}$. Here the continuous playback of one level is defined as one round and it consists of n_p frames. There are P rounds in total. As shown in Fig. 2b, the proposed scheme attains a significant better playback smoothness, which in turn contributes to its higher QoE continuum.

We also show the number of admitted users after the evaluation ends to evaluate the bandwidth utilization. Such user number can be treated as stable since we found that the evaluation time (200 seconds) is long enough and all systems keep a constant user number after 165th second. In Fig. 2c, we observe that the proposed system achieves a comparable bandwidth utilization as the reference systems.

5. CONCLUSION

In this paper, we propose an evidence theory based admission control scheme to address the issues caused by inaccurate QoE and network measurement in cellular adaptive HTTP streaming. By assigning degree of belief to the uncertain decision and combining the weighted individual user support, we can derive a system decision that guarantees QoE continuum and bandwidth utilization. Future work shall be focused on extending the linear user request model to more general cases. Besides, the termination of services needs to be dynamically considered in developing future admission control schemes.

6. ACKNOWLEDGMENTS

This research is supported by NSF Grant 1405594 and NSF Grant 0915842.

7. REFERENCES

[1] Progressive download and dynamic adaptive streaming over http. 3GPP TS 26.247 v12.1.0, 2013, Available: http://goo.gl/4EJbvd.

[2] T. Wirth, Y. Sánchez, B. Holfeld, and T. Schierl. Advanced downlink lte radio resource management for http-streaming. In *ACM MM*, pages 1037–1040, Nara, Japen, October 2012.

[3] S. Xiang, L. Cai, and J. Pan. Adaptive scalable video streaming in wireless networks. In *ACM MMSys*, pages 167–172, Chapel Hill, USA, February 2012.

[4] Z. Yan, J. Xue, and C. W. Chen. Qoe continuum driven http adaptive streaming over multi-client wireless networks. In *IEEE International Conference on Multimedia and Expo (ICME)* , Chengdu, China, July 2014.

[5] C. Chen, X. Zhu, G. de Veciana, A. C. Bovik, and Jr. R. W. Heath. Rate adaptation and admission control for video transmission with subjective quality constraints. *IEEE Journal of Selected Topics in Signal Processing*, 2014, early access.

[6] M. H. Ahmed. Call admission control in wireless networks: A comprehensive survey. *IEEE Communications Surveys and Tutorials*, 7(1):50–69, 2005.

[7] P. Koutsakis. Using traffic prediction and estimation of provider revenue for a joint geo satellite mac/cac scheme. *Wireless Networks*, 17(3):797–815, April 2011.

[8] M. Halldórsson and P. Mitra. Wireless capacity and admission control in cognitive radio. In *IEEE INFOCOM*, pages 855–863, Orlando, March 2012.

[9] K. Piamrat, A. Ksentini, C. Viho, and J. Bonnin. Qoe-aware admission control for multimedia applications in ieee 802.11 wireless networks. In *IEEE VTC-Fall*, pages 1–5, Orlando, USA, September 2008.

[10] R. Balakrishnan and B. Canberk. Traffic-aware qos provisioning and admission control in ofdma hybrid small cells. *IEEE Transactions on Vehicular Technology*, 63(2):802–810, February 2014.

[11] J. Xue, D.-Q. Zhang, H. Yu and C. W. Chen. Assessing quality of experience for adaptive http video streaming. In *IEEE ICME Workshop on Emerging Multimedia Systems and Applications*, 2014.

[12] H. Wu. *Sensor Data Fusion for Context-aware Computing Using Dempster-Shafer Theory*. PhD thesis, Carnegie Mellon University, 2003.

[13] A. M. Mutairi and U. A. Baroudi. Ns-2 enhancements for detailed hsdpa simulations. In *Proc. of 3rd VALUETOOLS*, Brussels, Belgium, October 2008.

Matrix Completion for Cross-view Pairwise Constraint Propagation

Zheng Yang, Yao Hu, Haifeng Liu*, Huajun Chen, Zhaohui Wu
College of Computer Science, Zhejiang University
Hangzhou, Zhejiang, China
{yzzju,yaoohu,haifengliu,huajunsir,wzh}@zju.edu.cn

ABSTRACT

As pairwise constraints are usually easier to access than label information, pairwise constraint propagation attracts more and more attention in semi-supervised learning. Most existing pairwise constraint propagation methods are based on canonical graph propagation model, which heavily depends on the edge weights in the graph and cannot preserve local and global consistency simultaneously. In order to address this drawback, we cast cross-view pairwise constraint propagation into a problem of low rank matrix completion and propose a Matrix Completion method for cross-view Pairwise Constraint Propagation(MCPCP). With low rank requirement and graph regularization, our MCPCP can preserve local and global consistency simultaneously. We develop an algorithm based on alternating direction method of multipliers(ADMM) to solve the optimization problem. Finally, the effectiveness of MCPCP is demonstrated in cross-view multimedia retrieval.

Categories and Subject Descriptors

H.3.3 [**n ormation torage and etrie al**]: Information Search and Retrieval

General Terms

Algorithms

Keywords

pairwise constraint propagation; matrix completion; multimedia retrieval

1. INTRODUCTION

Pairwise constraints, which specify whether two objects belong to the same class or not, are easier to access than label information and have been widely used for many machine learning tasks, like constrained clustering, multimedia retrieval[8], semi-supervised classification and so on. Pairwise constraint propagation is an effective algorithm to solve these tasks. It aims to fully utilize the available constraints through constraint propagation. LGC[10] and GFH[11] are two canonical label propagation methods, which propagate labels through a graph. Most pairwise constraint propagation methods are based on this kind of graph model. Given a dataset $\mathcal{X}$ with n points, the first p of them are labeled with c labels and the remaining points are unlabeled. LGC regularization framework has the following form:

$$\min_F \frac{1}{2}\left(\sum_{i,j=1}^{n} W_{ij} \left\| \frac{1}{\sqrt{D_{ii}}} F_i - \frac{1}{\sqrt{D_{jj}}} F_j \right\|^2 + \mu \sum_{i=1}^{n} \|F_i - Y_i\|^2 \right), \tag{1}$$

where $W \in \mathcal{R}^{n\times n}$ is a weight matrix of the dataset, D is a diagonal matrix with $D_{ii} = \sum W_{ij}$ and $\mu > 0$ is a regularization parameter. F and Y are $n \times c$ indicator response matrices. Y is the initial one with $Y_{ij} = 1$ if x_i is labeled as $y_i = j$ and $Y_{ij} = 0$ otherwise. And F is to be learned which labels each point x_i as a label $y_i = \arg\max_{1\leq j \leq c} F_{ij}$. F_i, F_j and Y_i are all row vectors which represent the label assignments.

As we know, the key to the success of semi-supervised learning is the cluster assumption[11], which indicates nearby objects are likely to have the same label and objects on the same structure are likely to have the same label. The first assumption is local consistency and the second one is global consistency. The two terms in problem (1) aim at these assumptions, respectively. However, the second term cannot preserve global consistency well when the number of labeled samples is not big enough to reveal global structure. Hence, the graph becomes more important as both local and global consistency depend on it. In the past years, many researchers have devoted to constructing better graph[12, 4]. Besides, the second term requires that the final classifying functions should not change too much from the initial label assignments. It is reasonable for the labeled samples but may be ill for unlabeled samples.

In this paper, we focus our attention on cross-view pairwise constraint propagation. Different from canonical methods, we cast it into a matrix completion problem: we use a **relation matri** to represent the pairwise constraint between objects from different media views. Each entry in the relation matrix is a real number that represents the relevance of two corresponding objects. Some of the entries are available in advance. To complete the relation matrix, we propose a Matrix Complete algorithm for cross-view Pairwise Constraint Propagation(MCPCP). MCPCP

*The corresponding author.

MM'14, November 03 - 07 2014, Orlando, Florida, USA.
Copyright 2014 ACM 978-1-4503-3063-3/14/11 ...$15.00.
http://dx.doi.org/10.1145/2647868.2655057 .

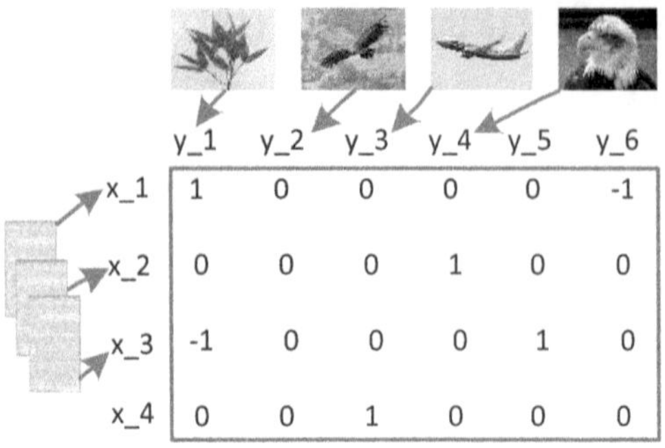

Figure 1: E ample o relation matri Y

requires that the relation matrix should be low rank and fixes the values at observed entries. It has been proved that the low-rank representation can capture the global structure(such as multiple clusters and subspaces)[6]. These two are fundamental requirements for matrix completion. Besides, MCPCP introduces graph regularization to preserve local consistency. So our MCPCP can preserve local and global consistency simultaneously.

2. CROSS-VIEW PAIRWISE CONSTRAINT PROPAGATION ALGORITHM

In this section, we define cross-view Pairwise Constraint Propagation problem and introduce our Matrix Complete algorithm for cross-view Pairwise Constraint Propagation.

Since cross-view problem can be readily decomposed into a series of two-view subproblems. For the convenience of interpretation, we just focus on two-view problem in this paper. Let $\{\mathcal{X}, \mathcal{Y}\}$ be a two-view dataset, where $\mathcal{X} = \{x_1, x_2, \ldots, x_m\}$ and $\mathcal{Y} = \{y_1, y_2, \ldots, y_n\}$. Pairwise constraints on the two-view dataset consist of must-link constrain set $\mathcal{M} = \{(x_i, y_j) : l(x_i) = l(y_j)\}$ and cannot-link constrain set $\mathcal{C} = \{(x_i, y_j) : l(x_i) \neq l(y_j)\}$. We denote relation matrix $F \in \mathcal{R}^{m \times n}$ to represent the real relevance of objects from different views. Note that, positive f_{ij} correspond to a must-link constraint and negative f_{ij} correspond to a cannot-link. The absolute value of f_{ij} denotes confidence score. With this definition, we denote initial(or observed) relation matrix over the dataset with matrix $Y \in \mathcal{R}^{m \times n}$, where $Y_{ij} = 1$ if $(x_i, y_j) \in \mathcal{M}$, $Y_{ij} = -1$ if $(x_i, y_j) \in \mathcal{C}$, $Y_{ij} = 0$ otherwise. Initial relation matrix Y is illustrated in Figure 1. We achieve pairwise constraint propagation by completing the entries in Y whose values are 0 in the beginning.

Canonical methods achieve this goal by letting every point iteratively spread its constraint information to its neighbors until a global stable state is achieved. Actually, initial relation matrix Y can be viewed as an incomplete matrix if we consider the entries corresponding with $\mathcal{M}$ and $\mathcal{C}$ as observed entries and the others as unknown entries, respectively. Cross-view Pairwise Constraint Propagation aims to learn the complete matrix which can reveal all the relations. Note that, the complete relation matrix F^* is a low-rank matrix. Considering row/column relation vectors as feature vectors of row/column objects, we know that both row objects and column objects can be always clustered into some clusters. It is reasonable to expect that each cluster corresponds to a linear intrinsic subspace, which means there exist a small number of underlying intrinsic relation vectors in F^* such that all the relation vectors are derived from a linear combination of these intrinsic relation vectors. This is called low rank assumption. Therefore, Pairwise Constraint Propagation is a low-rank matrix completion problem.

Now, we consider low-rank Matrix Completion for cross-view Pairwise Constraint Propagation(MCPCP). Liu et al.[7] have demonstrated low-rank representation can capture the global structure(such as multiple clusters and subspaces) of the whole data. A good semi-supervised algorithm should preserve global and local consistency simultaneously. To preserve local consistency, we introduce graph regularization. Given graph $\mathcal{G}_x = (\mathcal{X}, W_x)$ and $\mathcal{G}_y = (\mathcal{Y}, W_y)$ constructed over the dataset $\mathcal{X}$ and $\mathcal{Y}$, we achieve cross-view Pairwise Constraint Propagation by solving the following optimization problem:

$$
\begin{aligned}
&\min_F \mathcal{L}(F) \\
&= rank\|F\| + \beta_x \sum_{i,j=1}^{m} W_{xij} \left\| \frac{1}{\sqrt{D_{xii}}} F_{i:} - \frac{1}{\sqrt{D_{xjj}}} F_{j:} \right\|^2 \\
&+ \beta_y \sum_{i,j=1}^{n} W_{yij} \left\| \frac{1}{\sqrt{D_{yii}}} F_{:i} - \frac{1}{\sqrt{D_{yjj}}} F_{:j} \right\|^2 \\
&s.t. \quad P_\Omega(F) = Y
\end{aligned} \tag{2}
$$

where

$$
[P_\Omega(F)]_{ij} = \begin{cases} F_{ij} & \text{if } (i,j) \in \Omega \\ & \text{if } (i,j) \notin \Omega \end{cases}, \tag{3}
$$

D_x and D_y are diagonal matrix with $D_{xii} = \sum_j W_{xij}$ and $D_{yii} = \sum_j W_{yij}$. $\beta_x, \beta_y > 0$ are trade-off parameters between local smoothness and low rankness. And Ω represents the observed(nonzero) entries in Y.

3. OPTIMIZATION

Because of rank minimization term, solving problem (2) is NP-hard. Fortunately, it has been proved that minimization of the rank function can be achieved using the minimizer obtained with the Nuclear Norm under broad conditions[3]. So we relax problem (2) by solving the following function:

$$
\begin{aligned}
\min_F \mathcal{L}(F) = &\|F\|_* + \beta_x Tr(F^T L_x F) + \beta_y Tr(F L_y F^T) \\
&s.t. \quad P_\Omega(F) = Y
\end{aligned} \tag{4}
$$

where $L_x = I - S_x$ and $L_y = I - S_y$ with $S_x = D_x^{-1/2} W_x D_x^{-1/2}$ and $S_y = D_y^{-1/2} W_y D_y^{-1/2}$. $\|F\|_* = \sum_{i=1}^{min(m,n)} \sigma_i(F)$ is the Nuclear Norm and $\sigma_i(F)$ is the ith largest singular value of F.

Next, we use ADMM method[1] to solve problem (4). In order to make the objective function separable, we first introduce two auxiliary variables H and Q:

$$
\begin{aligned}
\min_F \mathcal{L}(F) = &\|F\|_* + \beta_x Tr(H^T L_x H) + \beta_y Tr(Q L_y Q^T) \\
&s.t. \quad H = F, P_\Omega(H) = Y \\
&\qquad Q = F, P_\Omega(Q) = Y
\end{aligned} \tag{5}
$$

The augmented lagrange function of (5) is

$$\begin{aligned}&\mathcal{L}(F,H,Q,Z1,Z2,\mu)\\=&\|F\|_*+\beta_x Tr(H^TL_xH)+\beta_y Tr(QL_yQ^T)\\&+Tr(Z1^T(H-F))+Tr(Z2^T(Q-F))\\&+\frac{\mu}{2}[\|H-F\|^2+\|Q-F\|^2]\end{aligned} \tag{6}$$

where $\mu > 0$ is the penalty parameter. Given the initial setting $F_1 = Y$, $H_1 = Y$, $Q_1 = Y$, $Z1_1 = Y$ and $Z2_1 = Y$, the optimization problem (5) can be solved via the following subproblems:

ubproblem F:

$$\begin{aligned}F_{k+1}=&\arg\min_F \mathcal{L}(F,H_k,Q_k,Z1_k,Z2_k,\mu)\\=&\arg\min_F \|F\|_*+Tr(Z1_k^T(H_k-F))\\&+Tr(Z2_k^T(Q_k-F))+\frac{\mu}{2}[\|H_k-F\|^2+\|Q_k-F\|^2]\end{aligned} \tag{7}$$

Ignoring constant terms and with some algebra, this can be rewritten as

$$F_{k+1}=\arg\min_F \|F\|_*+\mu\|F-\frac{1}{2}(H_k+Q_k+\frac{Z1_k+Z2_k}{\mu})\|^2 \tag{8}$$

So the closed form solution of problem (7) is

$$F_{k+1}=\mathcal{D}_{\frac{1}{2\mu}}\big(\frac{1}{2}(H_k+Q_k+\frac{1}{\mu}(Z1_k+Z2_k)\big) \tag{9}$$

where $\mathcal{D}$ is singular value thresholding operator[3].

ubproblem H:

$$\begin{aligned}H_{k+1}=&\arg\min_H \beta_x Tr(H^TL_xH)+Tr(Z1_k^T(H-F_{k+1}))\\&+\frac{\mu}{2}\|H-F_{k+1}\|^2.\\s.t.\quad&P_\Omega(H)=Y\end{aligned} \tag{10}$$

Let the partial derivatives with respect to H vanish. With some algebra, we can get the following equation:

$$(2\beta_xL_x+\mu I)H=\mu F_{k+1}-Z1_k. \tag{11}$$

Since $2\beta_xL_x+\mu I$ is positive definite, we have:

$$H_{k+1}=(2\beta_xL_x+\mu I)^{-1}(\mu F_{k+1}-Z1_k). \tag{12}$$

Actually, the matrix inverse $(2\beta_xL_x+\mu I)^{-1}$ can be calculate in advance and only need to be calculated once. Then, we fix the observed values and obtain

$$H_{k+1}=Y+P_{\Omega^c}(H_{k+1}). \tag{13}$$

Algorithm 1: MCPCP

nput: Y, W_x, W_y, β_x, β_y, ϵ and μ

nitialize: $F_1 = Y$, $H_1 = Y$, $Q_1 = Y$, $Z1_1 = Y$ and $Z2_1 = Y$

Output: F.

1) Calculate L_x by $L_x = I - S_x$, where $S_x = D^{-1/2}W_xD^{-1/2}$ and D is a diagonal matrix with its $D_{ii}=\sum_j W_{xij}$.
2) Calculate L_y by $L_y = I - S_y$, where $S_y = D^{-1/2}W_yD^{-1/2}$ and D is a diagonal matrix with its $D_{ii}=\sum_j W_{yij}$.
3) $A=(2\beta_xL_x+\mu I)^{-1}$.
4) $B=(2\beta_yL_y+\mu I)^{-1}$.
5) **repeat:**
6) Update F_{k+1} by Eq. (9).
7) Update H_{k+1} by $H_{k+1}=A(\mu F_{k+1}-Z1_k)$. Fix values at observed entries $H_{k+1}=P_\Omega(Y)+P_{\Omega^c}(H_{k+1})$.
8) Update Q_{k+1} by $Q_{k+1}=(\mu F_{k+1}-Z2_k)B$. Fix values at observed entries $Q_{k+1}=P_\Omega(Y)+P_{\Omega^c}(Q_{k+1})$.
9) $Z1_{k+1}=Z1_k+\mu(H_{k+1}-F_{k+1})$.
10) $Z2_{k+1}=Z2_k+\mu(Q_{k+1}-H_{k+1})$.
11) **until** $\|F_{k+1}-F_k\|^2\le\epsilon$.

ubproblem :

$$\begin{aligned}Q_{k+1}=&\arg\min_Q \beta_y Tr(QL_yQ^T)+Tr(Z2_k^T(Q-F_{k+1}))\\&+\frac{\mu}{2}\|Q-F_{k+1}\|^2\\s.t.\quad&P_\Omega(Q)=Y\end{aligned} \tag{14}$$

Similar with *Subproblem H*, we have

$$Q_{k+1}=(\mu F_{k+1}-Z2_k)(2\beta_yL_y+\mu I)^{-1} \tag{15}$$

and

$$Q_{k+1}=Y+P_{\Omega^c}(Q_{k+1}). \tag{16}$$

ubproblem Z1 and Z2:

$Z1$ and $Z2$ can be calculated as follows:

$$Z1_{k+1}=Z1_k+\mu(H_{k+1}-F_{k+1}); \tag{17}$$

$$Z2_{k+1}=Z2_k+\mu(Q_{k+1}-H_{k+1}). \tag{18}$$

We summarize the whole procedure of our solution for problem (5), which is called MCPCP, in Algorithm 1. It is apparent that the main computational cost in each iteration is the computation of SVD in singular value thresholding operator. However, computing the full SVD for MCPCP is unnecessary. So PROPACK[5] can be used to accelerate the computation and make our algorithm more efficient for large-size problems. What is more, we use k-NN graph, which means L_x and L_y are sparse matrixes and the inversion calculation can be solved very efficiently as Cai *.et al* did in GNMF[2]. The convergence of Algorithm 1 is guaranteed by the ADMM[1].

Table 1: The retrie al results on Wi i data set b the M P s ores The bold numbers are the best results

Algorithm	Image Query	Text Query	Average
CM	0.2706	0.2294	0.250
Inter-CP	0.552	0.546	0.549
MCPCP	**576**	**556**	**566**

4. EXPERIMENTAL RESULTS

In this section, we evaluate our MCPCP on real world application. As the obtained relation matrix F^* represents the relevance between objects from different views. Naturally, our MCPCP can be used in cross-view retrieval by sorting the relevant relation vectors. The most straightforward way for cross-view retrieval is similarity comparison. We compare our method with two representative methods, Correlation matching(CM) and Inter-CP[8]. The first is a similarity comparison method and the second is a pairwise constraint propagation method.

Dataset: We use Wiki text-image dataset[9] in our experiment. The Wiki dataset consists of 2866 text-image pairs from 10 different classes. Among them, texts are represented by 10 dimensional latent Dirichlet allocation model and each image has a 128 dimensional SIFT histogram feature.

ettings: Different from [8] which divided the data points into training and testing part and obtained all the pairwise constraints of training data from the label information, we adopted another way. We do not divide the data and use less pairwise constraints. The initial pairwise constraints contain must-link constraints obtained from paired points(text-image) and the same number of cannot-link constraints. That is to say, we use 5732 pairwise constraints in our experiment and only half of them should be given manually. These cannot-link constraints are chosen randomly. For graph regularization, we use the normalized correlation as the similarity measure and construct two k-NN graphs on image and text sets, respectively. In our algorithm, there are four parameters. We set $k = 40$ for Inter-CP and our MCPCP, experimentally. All the other parameters are obtained by cross-validation. Specifically, we set $\beta_x = 1$, $\beta_y = 1$, $\mu = 100$ and $k = 40$ for MCPCP. For Inter-CP and our MCPCP, we achieve retrieval by sorting the relevant learned relation vector.

esults: Two tasks of cross-view retrieval are considered: text retrieval using an Image Query and image retrieval using a Text Query. The retrieval results are measured with mean average precision(MAP), a widely used method in the retrieval literature. The results are listed in Table 1. From the results, we can find the performance of MCPCP and Inter-CP is better than that of CM. This is because these two methods not only utilize pairwise constraints but local structure of each view. Considering global and local structure, our MCPCP achieves the best result which has 1.7% improvement in MAP averagely compared with that of Inter-CP.

5. CONCLUSION

In this paper, we proposed a novel method for pairwise constraint propagation by casting it into a problem of low-rank matrix completion. We analyzed this method and pointed out this model can capture global structure of the whole data. In order to preserve local consistency at the same time, we introduced graph regularization. The experimental results in cross-view retrieval demonstrated the effectiveness of our pairwise constraint propagation method. This method can be used in tag-completion, multi-label learning and other semi-supervised learning problems.

6. ACKNOWLEDGEMENTS

This work was supported in part by the National Basic Research Program of China (973 Program) under Grant 2013CB336500, in part by the National Natural Science Foundation of China under Grant 61379071 and Grant 91120302, and in part by the National High-tech R&D Program of China (863 Program) under Grant 2012AA02A601.

7. REFERENCES

[1] S. Boyd, N. Parikh, E. Chu, B. Peleato, and J. Eckstein. Distributed optimization and statistical learning via the alternating direction method of multipliers. *Foundations and Trends® in Machine Learning*, 3(1):1–122, 2011.

[2] D. Cai, X. He, J. Han, and T. S. Huang. Graph regularized nonnegative matrix factorization for data representation. *IEEE Transactions on PAMI*, 33(8):1548–1560, 2011.

[3] J.-F. Cai, E. J. Candès, and Z. Shen. A singular value thresholding algorithm for matrix completion. *SIAM Journal on Optimization*, 20(4):1956–1982, 2010.

[4] M. Karasuyama and H. Mamitsuka. Manifold-based similarity adaptation for label propagation. In *NIPS*, pages 1547–1555, 2013.

[5] R. M. Larsen. Lanczos bidiagonalization with partial reorthogonalization. *DAIMI Report Series*, 27(537), 1998.

[6] G. Liu, Z. Lin, S. Yan, J. Sun, Y. Yu, and Y. Ma. Robust recovery of subspace structures by low-rank representation. *IEEE Transactions on PAMI*, 35(1):171–184, 2013.

[7] G. Liu, Z. Lin, and Y. Yu. Robust subspace segmentation by low-rank representation. In *ICML*, pages 663–670, 2010.

[8] Z. Lu and Y. Peng. Unified constraint propagation on multi-view data. In *AAAI*, 2013.

[9] N. Rasiwasia, J. Costa Pereira, E. Coviello, G. Doyle, G. R. Lanckriet, R. Levy, and N. Vasconcelos. A new approach to cross-modal multimedia retrieval. In *ACM MM*, pages 251–260. ACM, 2010.

[10] D. Zhou, O. Bousquet, T. N. Lal, J. Weston, and B. Schölkopf. Learning with local and global consistency. In *NIPS*, volume 16, pages 321–328, 2003.

[11] X. Zhu, Z. Ghahramani, J. Lafferty, et al. Semi-supervised learning using gaussian fields and harmonic functions. In *ICML*, volume 3, pages 912–919, 2003.

[12] L. Zhuang, H. Gao, Z. Lin, Y. Ma, X. Zhang, and N. Yu. Non-negative low rank and sparse graph for semi-supervised learning. In *CVPR*, pages 2328–2335. IEEE, 2012.

Cross-Media Hashing with Neural Networks

Yueting Zhuang[†], Zhou Yu[†], Wei Wang[‡], Fei Wu[†], Siliang Tang[†], Jian Shao[†]
[†]College of Computer Science, Zhejiang University, China
[‡]School of Computing, National University of Singapore, Singapore
[†]{yzhuang, yuz, wufei, jshao}@zju.edu.cn, [†]siliang.tang@gmail.com,
[‡]wangwei@comp.nus.edu.sg

ABSTRACT

Cross-media hashing, which conducts cross-media retrieval by embedding data from different modalities into a common low-dimensional hamming space, has attracted intensive attention in recent years. This is motivated by the facts a) the multi-modal data is widespread, e.g., the web images on Flickr are associated with tags, and b) hashing is an effective technique towards large-scale high-dimensional data processing, which is exactly the situation of cross-media retrieval. Inspired by recent advances in deep learning, we propose a cross-media hashing approach based on multi-modal neural networks. By restricting in the learning objective a) the hash codes for relevant cross-media data being similar, and b) the hash codes being discriminative for predicting the class labels, the learned Hamming space is expected to well capture the cross-media semantic relationships and to be semantically discriminative. The experiments on two real-world data sets show that our approach achieves superior cross-media retrieval performance compared with the state-of-the-art methods.

Categories and Subject Descriptors

H.3.3 [**Information Search and Retrieval**]: Information Search and Retrieval

Keywords

Cross-media hashing; Neural networks

1. INTRODUCTION

With the rapid development of Internet and social networks, huge amount of multi-modal data (e.g., images and texts) is being generated at every moment. For example, one uploaded image on the Flickr web site is usually tagged with some related descriptions or labels. It is desirable to support cross-media retrieval across different modalities. In terms of the large-scale property of the multi-modal web data, hashing techniques that have been intensively investigated for the large-scale retrieval applications, become the natural choice. Consequently, cross-media hashing which incorporates hashing techniques into cross-media retrieval, is a hot research focus recently.

Many cross-media hashing approaches have been proposed in recent years [2, 3, 9, 8]. The first one was proposed by Bronstein *et al.* in CMSSH [2]. Specifically, given two modalities of data sets, CMSSH learns two groups of hash functions to ensure that if two data points (with different modalities) are relevant, their corresponding hash codes are similar and otherwise dissimilar. However, CMSSH only preserves the inter-modal correlation but ignores the intra-modal similarity. Kumar *et al.* extended Spectral Hashing [7] from the traditional uni-modal setting to the multi-modal scenario and proposed CVH [3]. CVH attempts to generate the hash codes by minimizing the distance of hash codes for the similar data and maximizing the distance for the dissimilar data, which preserves the inter-modal and intra-modal similarities at the same time. MLBE employs a generative probabilistic model to encode the intra-similarity and inter-similarity of data across multiple modalities according to the estimation of maximum a posteriori [9].

Most of the existing cross-media hashing approaches exploit the symbiosis of multi-modal data when learning hash functions. However, they do not consider the discriminative capability of the learned hash codes, which is significantly important for cross-media retrieval. Yu *et al.* propose D-CDH which incorporate discriminative capability into cross-media hashing for the first time and achieve significant improvement over the existing cross-media hashing approaches [8]. However, DCDH has a limitation that it requires each data point in the training set to be discriminative to a unique class label thus can not handle the multi-class scenario, which weakens its applicability to the real-world data sets.

In this paper, we propose to learn the hash functions with the data symbiosis and discriminative capability into consideration. Specifically, we minimize two loss functions in our learning objective: a) the distance of hash codes for symbiosis data to make semantic relevant data have similar hash codes; b) the inconsistency of hash codes and class labels to make the hash codes discriminative. Motivated by the recent remarkable advances of deep learning for multi-modal data [5, 4], we exploit the NN to learn the hash functions, referred as Cross-Media Neural Network Hashing (CMNNH). Due to the flexibility of designing the NN, we can easily apply the above two loss functions on different layers of NN and optimize them through back propagation.

MM'14, November 3–7, 2014, Orlando, Florida, USA.

http://dx.doi.org/10.1145/2647868.2655059.

2. THE FRAMEWORK OF CMNNH

2.1 Notations

To simplify our presentation, we assume that the data points come from two modalities (e.g., images and texts): $X = [x_1, ..., x_{n_x}] \in \mathbb{R}^{d_x \times n_x}$, $Y = [y_1, ..., y_{n_y}] \in \mathbb{R}^{d_y \times n_y}$, where X and Y are the matrix representation of the data points, d_x and d_y denote the dimensionality of the data points from the two modalities, respectively (usually, $d_x \neq d_y$), n_x and n_y denote the number of the data points in the data sets X and Y, respectively. In our scenario, the data from different modality has pairwise relationship, i.e., each data point x_i is associated with a data point y_i, which means $n_x = n_y = n$. Therefore, we use n instead of n_x and n_y in the following sections. Besides, $T = [t_1, ..., t_n] \in \mathbb{R}^{c \times n}$ is the class label matrix for the training set, where each $t_i \in \mathbb{R}^c$ is the ground-truth class label vector for the i-th training pair, and c is the total number of labels. $t_{ij} = 1$ means the i-th training pair is labeled with the j-th label and 0 otherwise. Each class label vector t_i is normalized by $t_i = t_i/\|t_i\|_1$.

The objective of CMNNH is to learn two hash functions H^x and H^y to project the data points from different modalities into a shared Hamming space: $H^x : \mathbb{R}^{d_x} \rightarrow \{-1, 1\}^k$ and $H^y : \mathbb{R}^{d_y} \rightarrow \{-1, 1\}^k$, where k is the dimensionality of the shared space (i.e., the length of hash codes).

2.2 The Network Structure of CMNNH

The network structure of CMNNH can be seen as a combination of two modality-specific NNs as shown in Figure 1. Each NN consists of L layers: one layer for the input data, one layer for the hash codes, one layer for the output (class label) predictions, and the rest $L-2$ layers for the hash functions, respectively. For simplification, we assume all the NNs have the same number of layers in this paper. In practice, the number of hash function layers for each NN can be different.

Denote the two NNs corresponding to X and Y as NN^x and NN^y, respectively. For each $x \in X$ ($y \in Y$ in a similar way), we forward x layer-by-layer through NN^x to generate the representation of each layer, i.e., $x^{(1)}, ..., x^{(L)}$ (for simplification, we directly use x to represent $x^{(1)}$). The lth layer takes $x^{(l)}$ as the input and uses a projection function to transform it to $x^{(l+1)}$ in the next layer:

$$x^{(l+1)} = f^{(l)}(W^{(l)} x^{(l)}) \tag{1}$$

where $x^{(l)}$ and $x^{(l+1)}$ are the feature representation in the lth and $l+1^{th}$ layer, respectively; W^l is the projection matrix. $f^{(l)}(\cdot)$ is the activation function, which is usually the *sigmoid* or *tanh* function for $l = 1$ to $L-2$, and is the *softmax* function for $l = L-1$.

From the perspective of the hash function H^x, it takes x as input, forwards x to the hash code layer (the $L-1^{th}$ layer), and outputs the k-dimensional binary hash codes:

$$H^x(x) = sign(x^{(L-1)}) \tag{2}$$

where $x^{(L-1)} \in \mathbb{R}^k$ is a k-dimensional real-value vector, and we use the *sign* function to convert $x^{(L-1)}$ to a binary hash code. The hash function H^y is formulated by analogy.

Nevertheless, the *sign* function is not differentiable, and thus is hard to optimize directly. We simply remove the *sign* function at the hash function learning stage and add it at the testing stage similar with most of other hashing approaches [7, 2, 3].

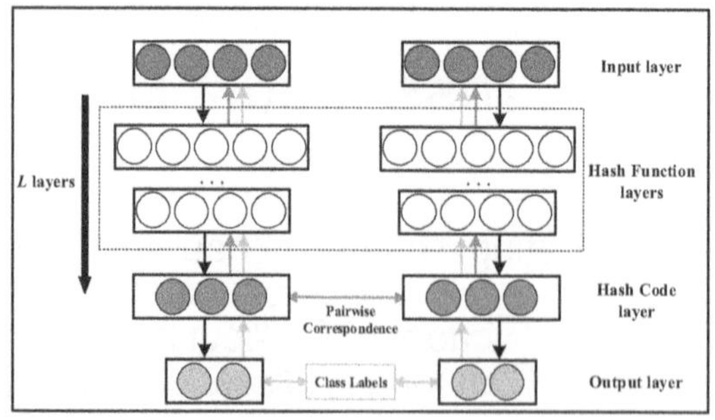

Figure 1: The illustration of hashing with multi-modal data (e.g., the pairs of images and texts) by a deep model in CMNNH, which not only disentangles the intrinsical structures of uni-modal data, but also faithfully preserves modality-specific correlation and discriminative cues (best viewed in color).

So far, the two networks NN^x and NN^y are still independent, which does not exploit any prior symbiosis of the data from different modalities. To associate NN^x with NN^y, we add two constraints:

- **Inter-modal pairwise correspondence:** the hash code layer should preserve the prior inter-modal correspondence. For each paired x_i and y_i, their hash codes $x_i^{(L-1)}$ and $y_i^{(L-1)}$ should be equal or similar.
- **Intra-modal discriminative capability:** the feature representation for x on the output layer, i.e., x^L, should be consistent with its ground-truth class labels.

The first constraint aims at preserving the inter-modal similarity which is of crucial importance in cross-media retrieval. However, merely preserving the inter-modal correlation often results in poor performance since the shared embedding space is not semantically discriminative. Therefore, we introduce additional supervised information, i.e., the class label side information, to make hash codes discriminative for predicting the class labels. The flowchart of CMNNH is given in Figure 1.

2.3 Learning Algorithm of CMNNH

The learning of CMNNH consists of two stages, namely pre-training and fine-tuning.

Pre-training is a commonly used technique for providing a good parameters initialization and preventing the learned neural network from being trapped in a bad local optimum. In CMNNH, we choose the stacked autoencoder (SAE) to pre-train each layer of the NN^x and NN^y sequentially [1].

After NN^x and NN^y are well initialized, we fine-tune the parameters by optimizing an loss function according to the two constraints. First, to preserve inter-modal pairwise correspondence, we define a loss function based on the least square error of pairwise inter-modal correspondence:

$$\ell_1(x, y) = \frac{1}{2}\|x^{(L-1)} - y^{(L-1)}\|_F^2 \tag{3}$$

Second, to preserve the intra-modal discriminative capability, we use the commonly used *softmax* regression function as the loss function on the output layer as follows.

$$\ell_2(x, y, t) = \text{KL}(x^{(L)}, t) + \text{KL}(y^{(L)}, t) \tag{4}$$

where t is the class label for x and y, KL($\cdot$) is the KL-divergence function. The loss of the output layer will be back propagated to its former layers, so the hash code layer is discriminative. Finally, we integrate the two loss functions for all the data points in X and Y and minimize the overall loss function as follows:

$$\mathcal{J} = \sum_{i=1}^{n} \ell_1(x_i, y_i) + \lambda \sum_{i=1}^{n} \ell_2(x_i, y_i, t_i) \quad (5)$$

where λ is a hyper-parameter to balance the two losses.

With the collaborative effect of the two loss functions, the learned hash functions H^x and H^y are expected to embed the data sets X and Y into the same space with the hash codes: a) preserving the inter-modal correlation; b) semantically discriminative.

The training of CMNNH is conducted by the classical back-propagation method. After NN^x and NN^y are trained, we obtain the hash functions H^x and H^y using Eq.(2). The overall procedures of CMNNH is given in Algorithm 1.

Algorithm 1 CMNNH

Input: data sets X,Y,T,λ
Output: The hash functions H^x, H^y
1: $\text{NN}^x \leftarrow \text{SAE}(X)$
2: $\text{NN}^y \leftarrow \text{SAE}(Y)$
3: **repeat**
4: Pick a random pair (x_i, y_i) and their corresponding label vector t_i
5: Make a gradient step for $\lambda\ell_2(x_i, y_i, t_i)$
6: Update NN^x and NN^y, respectively
7: Make a gradient step for $\ell_1(x_i, y_i)$
8: Update NN^x and NN^y, respectively
9: **until** stopping criteria is met

3. EXPERIMENTS

3.1 Experimental Setup

We use two real-world data sets Wikipedia feature articles (abbreviated as Wiki) [1] and NUS-WIDE[2]. Both data sets are bi-modal containing images and texts.

The Wiki data set consists of 2,866 Wikipedia documents. Each document contains one text-image pair and is labeled by one of 10 semantic categories. For the image modality, we extract 1,000-D Bag-of-Visual-Words (BoVW) for each image. For the text modality, we calculate the frequency of all words and select the most representative words to quantize all texts into 5,000-D Bag-of-Words (BoW).

The NUS-WIDE data set contains 269,648 images and is manually annotated with 81 categories. Each image with its annotated tags can be taken as a pair of image-text data. We select those pairs that belong to one of the 10 largest categories. For the image modality, 500-D BoVW are extracted for each image. For the text modality, the corresponding tags of each image are represented by a 1,000-D BoW.

For both data sets, we setup the NNs with the the number of layers $L = 3$, i.e., the input layer is directly connected to the hash code layer. The parameters between the input layer and hash code layer are initialized by modality-specific SAE. The reason for this setting is to give a fair comparison since all the compared methods adopt shadow models. Besides, even using the 3-layers structure, we achieve good results.

[1] `http://www.svcl.ucsd.edu/projects/crossmodal/`
[2] `http://lms.comp.nus.edu.sg/research/NUS-WIDE.htm`

Table 1: The details of the data sets used in the experiments

Data Set	Wiki	NUS-Wide
Image NN structure	(1,000-k-10)	(500-k-10)
Text NN structure	(5,000-k-10)	(1,000-k-10)
Data set size	2,866	186,577
Training set size	1,000	10,000
Validation set size*	866/866	5,000/20,000
Testing set size*	866/1,000	5,000/146,577

* *k in the NN structure indicates the hash code length. Partitions are ordered by query/database set respectively, and the query set are randomly sampled from the database set.*

The hyper-parameter λ is set to 10, which achieves the optimal results on the validation set and the activation function for each layer (except the output layer) is set to the sigmoid function.

We conduct two retrieval schemes in the experiments : 1) Image query vs. Text database ($\mathbf{I} \rightarrow \mathbf{T}$): use image queries to retrieve relevant texts. 2) Text query vs. Image Database ($\mathbf{T} \rightarrow \mathbf{I}$): use text queries to retrieve relevant images. For the two retrieval schemes, we compare CMNNH with the state-of-the-art cross-media hashing methods: CMSSH [2], CVH [3], MLBE [9] and LCMH [10]. However MLBE fails to learn the hash function on the NUS-Wide data set due to its high complexity on both training and testing stages.

The details of the data sets are summarized in Table 1. To evaluate the performance of the cross-media retrieval results, we adopt the Mean Average Precision (MAP) criterion.

3.2 Performance Comparison

We evaluate the cross-media retrieval performance with code length varying from 16 to 48 and report results in terms of MAP in Table 2 and 3.

It can be noted that CMNNH significantly outperforms the counterparts over different code lengths. The is because that none of the compared methods consider the discriminative capability, while the hash codes generated by CMNNH are discriminative and well represent the semantic information. Besides, with the increasing of the code length, the performance of all the counterparts have a setback. A possible reason for this observation is that the learned hash functions is farther from the optimal solutions when the code length gets larger. In contrast, CMNNH does not suffer from the it which reveals the fact that incorporating discriminative capability facilitate the performance of cross-media retrieval.

3.3 Discussion of Discriminative Capability

To show the discriminative capability of the hash codes, we investigate the embedding Hamming space. We use the text modality on the Wiki data set since it has rich textual information and is convenient for illustrations.

First, we use the t-SNE method [6] to map the hash codes of the texts into 2-dimensional space as shown in Figure 2. From Figure 2, we can see that the hash codes of CMNNH are grouped according to their class labels, and explicit margins are observed among different classes. By contrast, the hash codes distribution of the other approaches do not have similar discriminative effect.

Second, we can also demonstrate the topic words by using the weight matrix $W^{(1)} \in \mathbb{R}^{k \times d_y}$ from the textual NN. For each row in $W^{(1)}$, the row weights indicate the contribution

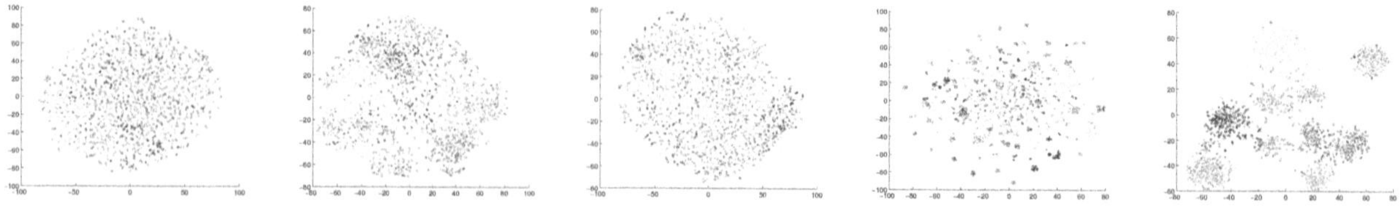

(a) CVH (b) CMSSH (c) MLBE (d) LCMH (e) CMNNH

Figure 2: 2D t-SNE feature visualization of the hash codes on the textual modality of the Wiki data set. The same color indicates the hash codes have the same class label (best viewed in color).

Table 2: The MAP performance comparison on the Wiki data set.

Task	Methods	Hash code length		
		$k = 16$	$k = 32$	$k = 48$
I → T	CVH	0.1436	0.1382	0.1363
	CMSSH	0.1446	0.1384	0.1396
	MLBE	0.1393	0.1371	0.1358
	LCMH	0.1256	0.1269	0.1287
	CMNNH	**0.1917**	**0.2172**	**0.2186**
T → I	CVH	0.1380	0.1340	0.1331
	CMSSH	0.1391	0.1340	0.1353
	MLBE	0.1351	0.1367	0.1322
	LCMH	0.1242	0.1238	0.1245
	CMNNH	**0.1523**	**0.1672**	**0.1658**

Table 3: The MAP performance comparison on the NUS-Wide data set.

Task	Methods	Hash code length		
		$k = 16$	$k = 32$	$k = 48$
I → T	CVH	0.3626	0.3552	0.3522
	CMSSH	0.3608	0.3603	0.3602
	MLBE	-	-	-
	LCMH	0.3417	0.3420	0.3426
	CMNNH	**0.4071**	**0.4266**	**0.4271**
T → I	CVH	0.3621	0.3546	0.3516
	CMSSH	0.3566	0.3657	0.3426
	MLBE	-	-	-
	LCMH	0.3404	0.3407	0.3414
	CMNNH	**0.3958**	**0.4094**	**0.4171**

of all words to the corresponding "topic" in the Hamming space. The larger the weight value $W_{ij}^{(1)}$ is, the more positive correlation between i-th topic and j-th word. The top 5 words for four topics are given in Table 4, and we manually assign the most probable class labels for the four topics. From Table 4, we can find that the topic words in each line reflect a certain topic (i.e., class label).

4. CONCLUSIONS

In this paper, we propose a cross-media hashing approach based on neural networks named CMNNH, which learns the hash functions taking both the data symbiosis and discriminative capability into consideration. The hash functions are pre-trained using SAE and fine-tuned using the traditional back-propagation algorithm. The experimental results on the two data sets demonstrate the effectiveness of CMNNH.

Table 4: The representative topic words and its most probable class labels.

Class Labels	Representative Topic Words
History	Lords Rome Reign Augustus Crown
Sport	Champion Player Football Coach Stadium
Geography	Creek Park Ridge Valley Forest
Art	Theater Fiction Actress Film Poem

5. ACKNOWLEDGEMENT

This work is supported in part by National Basic Research Program of China (2012CB316400), NSFC (No.61105074), 863 program (2012AA012505), the Fundamental Research Funds for the Central Universities and Chinese Knowledge Center of Engineering Science and Technology (CKCEST) and Program for New Century Excellent Talents in University, Zhejiang Provincial Natural Science Foundation of China (No.LQ14F010004, No.LY14F020027)

6. REFERENCES

[1] Y. Bengio. Learning deep architectures for ai. *Foundations and trends in Machine Learning*, 2(1):1–127, 2009.

[2] M. Bronstein, A. Bronstein, F. Michel, and N. Paragios. Data fusion through cross-modality metric learning using similarity-sensitive hashing. In *CVPR*, pages 3594–3601, 2010.

[3] S. Kumar and R. Udupa. Learning hash functions for cross-view similarity search. In *IJCAI*, pages 1360–1365, 2011.

[4] J. Ngiam, A. Khosla, M. Kim, J. Nam, H. Lee, and A. Y. Ng. Multimodal deep learning. In *ICML*, pages 689–696, 2011.

[5] N. Srivastava and R. Salakhutdinov. Multimodal learning with deep boltzmann machines. In *NIPS*, pages 2222–2230, 2012.

[6] L. Van der Maaten and G. Hinton. Visualizing data using t-sne. *JMLR*, 9(11), 2008.

[7] Y. Weiss, A. Torralba, and R. Fergus. Spectral hashing. In *NIPS*, 2008.

[8] Z. Yu, F. Wu, Y. Yang, Q. Tian, J. Luo, and Y. Zhuang. Discriminative coupled dictionary hashing for fast cross-media retrieval. In *SIGIR*, pages 395–404, 2014.

[9] Y. Zhen and D. Yeung. A probabilistic model for multimodal hash function learning. In *SIGKDD*, 2012.

[10] X. Zhu, Z. Huang, H. T. Shen, and X. Zhao. Linear cross-modal hashing for efficient multimedia search. In *ACM MM*, pages 143–152, 2013.

How Your Portrait Impresses People? Inferring Personality Impressions from Portrait Contents

Jie Nie, Peng Cui
Department of Computer Science and Technology,
Tsinghua University, Beijing, China
{niejie,cuip}@tsinghua.edu.cn

Yan Yan, Lei Huang, Zhen Li, Zhiqiang Wei
Department of Computer Science and Technology,
Ocean University of China, Qingdao, China
{yanyan.azj, ithuanglei, lizhen0130}@gmail.com,
weizhiqiang@ouc.edu.cn

ABSTRACT

Whenever looking at a stranger's portrait, besides observable appearance, we always build a personality impression implicitly in our subconscious. It is quite interesting to ask how a portrait impresses people. This paper presents a novel method to infer personality impression from portrait. Firstly, a questionnaire is applied to demonstrate the consistence of people's impression. And then personality-related features are explored through the statistical analysis method. Finally, features are trained using Support Vector Machine. Experimental results demonstrate our method could achieve a precision of 52.14% and a recall of 52.78% on inferring 4 personalities from 2,463 randomly selected portraits of people downloaded from "Google images". Improvements of 44.04% and 37.91% are reported compared to a baseline method. And features contribution analysis deeply unveils the correspondence between portrait contents and personality impressions. Demonstrations with respect to visual patterns in portrait collages of different personalities further prove the effectiveness of the proposed method. Furthermore, we apply our method to analyze portraits of Hillary Clinton and obtain an interesting multifaceted figure of this famous politics, which is another proof of both our concept and method.

Categories and Subject Descriptors

H.3.0 [**Information Storage and Retrieval**]: General; J.4 [**Social and Behavioral Sciences**]: Sociology

General Terms

Algorithms, Performance

Keywords

Portrait; Personality impression; Feature extraction; Cognitive process;

1. INTRODUCTION

Whenever immersed in irritable mood, president De Gaulle must drove to the Louvre where Leonardo Da Vinci's masterpiece "Mona Lisa" is exhibited. This great painting vanished all his troubles and sorrow, and brought him fresh melodies. It is not the fancy face that helps Mona Lisa conquers the world, but the perfect humanity hidden in her figure. Although we have no idea of Mona Lisa's actual personality traits, however, undoubtedly, this portrait leaves a gentle, kindness and wisdom figure in the mind of the whole humanity. This reflects a common phenomenon in our daily life: when we are looking at a stranger's portrait photo, besides certain visual attributes, e.g. facial expression, garment, age, gender, the implicit cognitive process has built a personality figure in our subconscious, like "she seems very ambitious", "he looks like a trustworthy person" or "he is energetic" and so on. Thus, the question is: before we know a person, how his/her portrait photo impresses people? Answering this question could not only help us to configure a satisfied first impression, but also could improve the performance of computer when interacting with human.

Inferring affections from multimedia, such as video, audio and visual contents has attracted more and more attentions of scientists. Machajdik et al. [4] exploit theoretical and empirical concepts from psychology and art theory to extract and combine low-level features that represent the emotional content of an image. Jia et al. [2] detect author's affection from both fundamental features in image and information from social networks. However, All these works have stayed at emotional level. But Multimedia as a form of communication among humanity, impress people in more abstract ways, like belief, intention and personality. So far, only two groups of researchers [1, 3] extend potential information embedded in multimedia to excavate out human personality. However, compared to this paper, there are two fundamental differences: 1) Cristani et al. [1] infer one's personality traits from photo corpus amount of 300 posts as his/her favorite on Flickr. While Fitzgerald's work [3] studies the perception of profile pictures and all the elements that can appear in a profile on social media. Our work focuses on single portrait photo (avatar), and inferring personality of the one in the photo. Images in both previous works are of sufficient flexibility, which could be animals, plants, landscape or abstract, and are far away from this work. 2) Both previous works attention on the agreement between the actual personality traits and traits attributed by others based on these images, however this paper never concerns one's actual traits but attentions on the agreement of traits attributed by different people. In other words, we study how the observable portrait contents figure one's personality impression? To answer this question, one has to further deal with the following problems:

1) Is there a universal principle to follow when people attribute personality traits to a stranger according to his portrait photo? If no, it is impossible to infer personality traits from portrait images.

2) If yes, it means people will achieve agreement on the same image in their cognitive process. Thus it is significant to find out the principle how portrait contents impress people's impression.

MM '14, November 03 - 07 2014, Orlando, FL, USA
Copyright 2014 ACM 978-1-4503-3063-3/14/11©$15.00.
http://dx.doi.org/10.1145/2647868.2655062

In this paper, we systematically studied the problem of inferring personality impression traits from portrait images. Firstly, we answered the first question by a questionnaire targeted to demonstrate the existence of the universal principle guiding people's impression. And then, image contents closely related to personality traits were screened out by statistics, which lead us a reasonable way to extract and combine low-level features that impact on personality impression. Finally, we trained features using Support Vector Machine (SVM) and inferred personalities of 2,463 portraits of people downloaded from "Google images" to demonstrate our idea. This paper shows not only there are visual patterns correlated to the personality traits from portrait images, but also possible to infer personality impression from a portrait picture.

2. QUESTIONNAIRE

The questionnaire aims to test the agreement of people's first impression when looking at a stranger's portrait. 400 portraits of 400 ordinary people are randomly selected from Google manually. The questionnaire includes 400 questions, and each question contains one portrait of an ordinary people and four options that refer to four personality types as "Artisan", "Guardian", "Idealist" and "Rational". This "four temperaments" may have origins in ancient Egypt or Mesopotamia and given name by Plato. Keirsey expanded on the ancient study and create "Keirsey Temperament Sorter" theory [5], which is one of the most popular configurations to assess personality traits. A brief description of each temperament is as follows:

- Artisan—Bold, Creative, Unconventional;
- Guardian—Trustworthy, Modest, Cautious;
- Idealist—Romantic, Compassionate, Trusting;
- Rational—Pragmatic, Ambitious, Dominate;

100 people are investigated in the questionnaire. Each person is asked to attribute a personality tag to a portrait in accordance with his/her first impression. In order to demonstrate the existence of a universal principle leading people's impression, we set a null hypothesis stating that the personality impressions are random, which means for every photo, the four personalities are equally likely to occur. Then, chi-squared test is adopted to determine whether people's selection obeys "discrete uniform distribution."

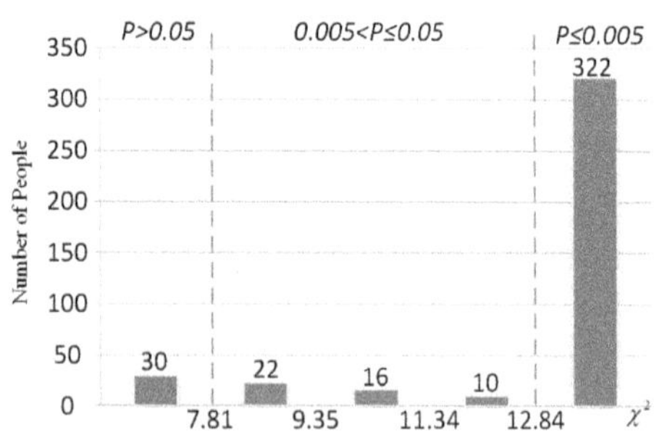

Figure 1: Histogram of Chi-Square Values.

To test the hypothesis for 400 questions, 400 χ^2 values are calculated. Figure1 shows these statistics. Consultation of chi-squared distribution for 3 degree of freedom (we have four personalities here) shows that probability of observing χ^2 value higher than 7.81 if four personalities are equally distributed is approximately lower than 0.05(P<0.05). The observation that this probability for 370(92.5%) samples is lower than 0.05, including 322(80.5%) samples lower than 0.005(P<0.005), definitely rejects the null hypothesis and further proves of the consistence of people's first impression, which just answers the first question.

3. METHODS

3.1 Portrait Contents and Personality Traits

Above questionnaire demonstrated that portrait impress people in certain universal ways when figuring one's personality. Continually, we discuss what factors make efforts when human subconscious starts processing a portrait photo to build an impression. We considered all observable contents (defined as "visual parameters") in a portrait photo (in Table 1) and facial

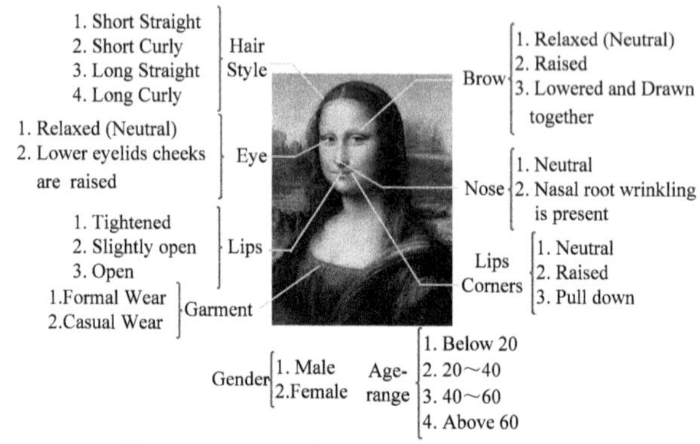

Figure 2: Portrait Content Descriptions.

actions. (See Figure 2.) Descriptions infer from [6].

To unveiling the relationship between visual parameters and personality types, 400 test portraits are tagged with visual parameters manually. Then we use Multinomial logistic regression model to fit the data. Definitely, we are more concern about what parameters affect people's judgment. Here we simply represent the model as $M\_L(E,P)$, where $E=\{e_i\}, 1\le i\le 10$, e_i is visual parameters descripted in Table 1, and P is a set including four personalities. We use likelihood ratio test to compare the contribution of different parameters in the model,

$$\begin{aligned} Sig.(e_i) &= Probability(LRT(e_i)) \\ &= Probability(-2\ln(\frac{Likelihood(M\_L(E-\{e_i\},P))}{Likelihood(M\_L(E,P))})) \end{aligned} \quad (1)$$

where $LRT(e_i) \sim \chi^2$. Inferring from experience, we set a threshold as 0.05. If $Sig.(e_i) < 0.05$, the correspondence parameter e_i has effect to the data. Further if $Sig.(e_i) < 0.01$, the correspondence parameter e_i has significant effect to the data.

Table 1: Likelihood ratio test

Visual Parameters	$LRT(e_i)$	$Sig.(e_i)$	Visual Parameters	$LRT(e_i)$	$Sig.(e_i)$
e_1 : Brow	13.789	.032	e_6 : Hair style	20.894	.013
e_2 : Eye	1.068	.785	e_7 : Garment	32.022	.000
e_3 : Nose	2.149	.542	e_8 : Hue	2.874	.411
e_4 : Lips	20.730	.002	e_9 : Gender	57.110	.000
e_5 : Lip corners	38.279	.000	e_{10} : Age range	42.637	.000

Table 2: Features and descriptions.

Category	No.	Name	Length	Short Description
Facial Content	1	Brow	76	Histogram of Gradient (HOG) and local Binary Pattern (LBP) Descriptors
	2	Lips	78	HOG and LBP Descriptors
	3	Lip corners	39	HOG and LBP Descriptors
Appearance	4	Hair style	13	MPEG-7 Texture Browsing Descriptor; Ratio of hair length and face length;
	5	Garment	6	Vision based garment descriptor in Reference [8]
Social Attributes	6	Gender	16	Geometrical Features in Reference [7]
	7	Age -range	18	Proportion of facial features in Reference [9] and wrinkle descriptor using MPEG-7 Texture Descriptor

Table 1 shows the result of likelihood ratio test of different visual parameters. According to the results, Lip corners, Garment, Gender, and Age range have most intense effect on personality impression, followed by Lips, Hairstyle and Brow, while the others have little impact.

3.2 Features

How to accurately describe personality with features is a totally novel issue. From above statistics, we adopted a wide though not exhaustive, but personality-related, spectrum of features, here grouped into three families, See Table 2, and then trained by LibSVM[10].

Active Appearance Model [11] is applied to every portrait to locate and mark facial regions as a pre-procession and features No. 1, 2, 3 are extracted from corresponding regions.

4. EXPERIMENTS

4.1 Experiment Setup

To evaluate our method objectively, we build a portrait dataset containing 3,000 portraits randomly downloaded from "Google images", and 20 volunteers are asked to attribute a personality trait to each piece. For each image, if the agreement of traits attributed by different people achieves 50%, the image is tagged by the personality word occurs with maximum frequency. 537 portraits are filtered out since these images are indecisive to any personality types. Remaining 2,463 images assigned with personality tags are our ground truth including 589 "Artisans", 733 "Guardians", 482 "Idealist" and 659 "Rationals". We randomly choose 150 portraits from each personality as training samples.

4.2 Results and Analysis

4.2.1 Performance comparison

Table 3 shows the performance of personality prediction with different feature combinations. Here we set features in reference [1] as baseline, and compared our method with it. Our Features include all features descripted in Table 2 in section 3.2, which achieves a precision of 52.14% and a recall of 52.78% on inferring people's personality into four categories, and improves baseline by a 44.04% and a 37.91%. Baseline method gets poor performance since its features are toward general image; however, our further proved features are impact on personality. The Non-facial Features including features No. 4, 5, 6 and 7, particularly remove facial contents. It is interesting to see that it has poor performance with "Guardian". Since "Guardian" represents trustworthy, this result unveils that the perception of trustworthiness may be directly affected by face.

4.2.2 Features contribution analysis

We now analyze how different features can help inferring personalities by training each feature to predict personality types. From Table 4, we can see that all the features have contributions to infer personalities. Furthermore, lips corners are most useful in term of F1-mearsure, which achieves 33.14%, while brow and garment features are most useful in term of precision and recall respectively. This result shows not only the contribution of different features in inferring personalities but also tells us principles from psychology perspective. For example, people's first impression is mostly affect by smile.

Table 4: Features contribution analysis (%).

No.	Feature	Precision	Recall	F1-Mearsure
1	Brow	34.32	33.33	32.46
2	Lips	13.71	27.78	16.33
3	Lips corners	32.99	36.11	33.14
4	Hairstyle	6.25	25.00	10.00
5	Garment	20.11	40.22	26.78
6	Gender	20.29	36.11	25.74
7	Age-range	28.10	29.17	19.45

4.2.3 Personality collages

Figure 3 shows a randomly selection of portrait images labeled with "Artisans", "Guardians", "Idealists" and "Rationals" respectively by our classifiers. It is interesting to see that few females appear in "Guardians" and "Rationals" collage (1.63%, 14.93% respectively) and few males (4.17%) appear in "Idealist" collage. And, people in collage "Artisans" are always young (78.35%) with big smile (68.04%) and casual wear (64.95%), while in collage " Rationals" are middle aged (54.74%), no smile (88.06%) and formal wear (86.57%). In "Guardians", Senior People (62.90%) with slightly smile (62.90%) take up more positions, which strongly proves the effectiveness of features.

4.2.4 Multi-faceted Hillary Clinton

Portrait images of Hillary Clinton are downloaded from Google's image. Here we applied our methods to predict personalities of each portrait. Figure 4 shows the result of the classification. It

Table 3: Performance of personality prediction with different feature combinations (%).

Personality	Precision			Recall			F1-Mearsure		
	Baseline	**Our Method**	Non-facial Features	Baseline	**Our Method**	Non-facial Features	Baseline	**Our Method**	Non-facial Features
Artisan	10.37	**60.00**	46.67	15.44	**16.67**	38.89	12.41	**26.08**	42.42
Guardian	6.40	**37.50**	6.45	3.67	**16.67**	5.23	4.67	**23.07**	5.78
Idealist	9.14	**64.00**	66.67	28.37	**88.88**	88.89	13.83	**74.41**	76.19
Rational	6.50	**47.06**	45.45	12.00	**88.88**	83.33	8.43	**61.63**	58.82
Average	8.10	**52.14**	39.70	14.87	**52.78**	52.78	9.84	**46.30**	45.80

shows different portraits will leave different impressions even for the same person.

Figure 3: Portrait collages of 4 personalities: (a) Artisans Collage; (b) Guardians Collage; (c) Idealists Collage; (d) Rationals Collage.

Figure 4: A multi-faceted Hillary Clinton: (a) Artisan Hillary; (b) Guardian Hillary; (c) Idealist Hillary; (d) Rational Hillary.

5. CONCLUSIONS

In this paper, we introduce an interesting problem on how to infer personality impression from portrait images. To address this issue, we firstly demonstrated the agreement of people's impression on personality and proposed that it is the portrait content that applied to people's cognitive process and figured one's personality traits in first impression. Then upon statistical analysis, personality-oriented features are explored, grouped and trained. Comprehensive experiments strongly demonstrate the effectiveness of our method. Future work will concentrate on features refining and design, and more personality-oriented features will be proposed for further improving the prediction accuracy.

6. ACKNOWLEDGMENTS

This research was supported by National Natural Science Foundation of China, No. 61370022 and No. 61210008; International Science and Technology Cooperation Program of China No. 2013DFG12870; Fundamental Research Funds for the Central Universities, No. 201413021.

7. REFERENCES

[1] M. Cristani, A. Vinciarelli, C. Segalin, and A. Perina. "Unveiling the multimedia unconscious: implicit cognitive processes and multimedia content analysis". In Proceedings of the ACM international conference on Multimedia, pp. 213-222, 2013.

[2] J. Jia, S. Wu, X. Wang, P. Hu, L. Cai, and J. Tang. "Can we understand van gogh's mood?: learning to infer affects from images in social networks". In Proceedings of the ACM International Conference on Multimedia, pp. 857-860, 2012.

[3] S. Fitzgerald, D.C. Evans, and R.K. Green. "Is your profile picture worth 1000 words? Photo characteristics associated with personality impression agreement". In Proceedings of the AAAI International Conference on Weblogs and Social Media, 2009.

[4] J. Machajdik, and A. Hanbury. "Affective image classification using features inspired by psychology and art theory". In Proceedings of the ACM International Conference on Multimedia, pp. 83-92, 2010.

[5] Keirsey.com, http://www.keirsey.com.

[6] P. Ekman and W.V. Friesen, "Facial Action Coding System", Consulting Psychologist Press, Palo Alto, CA, 1978.

[7] R. Brunelli and T. Poggio. "HyperBF networks for gender classification". In Proceedings of the DARPA Image Understanding Workshop, pages 311-314, 1992.

[8] L. Huang, T. Xia, Y. Zhang and S. Lin. "Finding suits in images of people". In Proceedings of the International Conference on Multimedia Modeling, pages 485-494, 2012.

[9] Y. Kwon, N. Lobo. "Automatic feature detection and age classification of human faces in digital images", U.S. Patent 5781650. 1998.07.

[10] C. Chang and C. Lin, "LIBSVM : a library for support vector machines". ACM Transactions on Intelligent Systems and Technology, 2(27), pages 1-27, 2011.

[11] T. F. Cootes, G. J. Edwards, and C. J. Taylor. "Active appearance models". IEEE Transactions on pattern analysis and machine intelligence, 23(6), pages 681-685, 2001.

Who's Time Is It Anyway?

Investigating the Accuracy of Camera Timestamps

Bart Thomee
Yahoo Labs
San Francisco, CA, USA
bthomee@yahoo-inc.com

Jose G. Moreno
Normandie University
Caen, France
jose.moreno@unicaen.fr

David A. Shamma
Yahoo Labs
San Francisco, CA, USA
aymans@acm.org

ABSTRACT

People take photos all over the world at all times of day; each photo depicting a place and a moment worth capturing. In the context of multimedia analysis and social computing, accurate location and time information about where and when these photos were taken is of importance for understanding event semantics, image content and many other purposes. While location information associated with photos is known to be relatively accurate, time is not. From a sample of 10 million public Flickr photos, we observe that 37% of the photos differ more than an hour between their camera timestamps and GPS timestamps with respect to local time at the locations where the photos were taken. Erroneous time information may adversely influence the correctness of any kind of temporal analysis that relies on camera timestamps, as well as research and real-world applications that require accurate knowledge of when and where photos were captured. In light of our observations we propose a simple yet effective metadata-only technique for improving the accuracy of camera timestamps.

Categories and Subject Descriptors

H.3.1 [**Information Storage and Retrieval**]: Content Analysis and Indexing

Keywords

Georeferenced photos; GPS information; time accuracy

1. INTRODUCTION

Spatial and temporal metadata of photos is frequently used in the research community to analyze the behavior of how people act and move in the world [3, 7, 10]. In the absence of GPS information, such techniques rely on the location that is manually supplied by the user and on the timestamp of the internal clock of the camera, which at the moment of capture gets written as EXIF metadata alongside the photo. The implicit assumption in these scenarios is that people are generally able to retrospectively place their photos at the location where they were taken and that they are able to keep the clock of their camera up to date. This assumption is particularly important when location and time form the vital ingredients of a proposed technique, for example when recommending time-dependent travel itineraries for tourists visiting a city for the first time [2]. Some online photo sharing services also include or rely on a non-representative photo uploaded time instead.

The alternative to camera time is to focus on GPS data, which is designed to provide highly accurate location and time information. Many portable devices have integrated GPS receivers, such as modern photo cameras and smartphones which are the most popular cameras on many websites like Flickr[1]. These devices have a limited battery life and need to trade off spending energy against refreshing the data [5]. At the moment a photo is taken the GPS measurements may thus be several minutes or even hours old. The GPS receiver may additionally continue to broadcast its last known location and time, even when it is not able to obtain updated information at all, for instance when the cameraphone is indoors. While GPS is claimed to currently have a root mean square error of just 4 meters [9], the actual accuracy obtained can vary depending on manufacturing quality of the receiver, structural interference, atmospheric conditions and signal reception. For example, GPS devices have been shown to provide inaccurate positioning with maximum errors exceeding 300m across a wide range of urban areas, where even with good visibility the maximum error could be greater than 100m [6], while a study on mobile Foursquare check-ins revealed a median error of 70m and a mean error of 551m [8]. A recent ethnographic study has also shown reported cameraphone GPS positioning to deviate off target [1] during navigation tasks.

To the best of our knowledge, no one has yet investigated whether camera timestamps and GPS timestamps correspond with local time at the locations where the photos were taken. Intuitively, it is particularly easy to forget to change the clock of the camera when time shifts between summer and winter time, or when one travels between different time zones. The internal clock may further automatically reset itself when the batteries of the camera run out. Even though smartphones, which are increasingly used as cameras, are capable of obtaining local time information directly from the cell towers they are connected with, this functionality is overridden when the clock is manually set. In the case of the Apple iPhone, if it is set in 'Airplane mode'

MM'14, November 3–7, 2014, Orlando, FL, USA.

http://dx.doi.org/10.1145/2647868.2655066.

[1]`https://www.flickr.com/cameras/` Accessed 4/2014.

the last cached GPS information is stamped on every photo taken. Erroneous time information may adversely influence the correctness of any kind of temporal analysis based on photo timestamps. Gaining an understanding of the error range is therefore important, and in this paper we therefore set out to assess the extent of which camera timestamps, GPS timestamps, and local time differ from each other. To reduce the timestamp error we further propose a simple yet effective metadata-only technique that can correct the camera timestamps of all photos in a session when at least one of the photos is also associated with a GPS timestamp.

2. TIMESTAMP ANALYSIS

The correctness of the camera timestamp depends entirely on the user keeping the internal clock of the camera up to date. While we assume the camera timestamps refer to local time at the location of capture, the GPS timestamps, according to the EXIF specifications, refer to Coordinated Universal Time (UTC) instead and as such need to be converted to local time first. We used the `tz_world`[2] collection of shape files that capture the boundaries of the IANA time zones[3] across the world to assign the GPS location associated with a photo to its designated time zone. Each time zone is associated with a time offset with respect to the UTC time zone, where the offset may vary between summer time or winter time. The GPS location and timestamp together thus allow us to determine the correct offset in seconds to apply to the GPS timestamp to convert it to local time. From this point forward we will refer to the GPS timestamp converted to local time as the GPS_L timestamp.

If one forgets to adjust the camera clock when traveling to a different time zone then the camera timestamps will be ahead or behind local time by at most 24 hours (e.g. flying from Kiritimati to Hawaii). Furthermore, the transitions from summer time to winter time and vice versa also change the time of day, so that if the camera clock is not adjusted accordingly then its timestamps will differ from local time by half an hour (Lord Howe Island, Australia) or one hour (rest of the world, if daylight savings is observed). In addition, if the GPS device was not able to refresh its data at the moment of capture (e.g. the user is indoors), the GPS_L timestamps will be behind local time with an amount that depends on the previous instant it managed to perform a refresh, which may be minutes, hours or even months.

In the next section we first analyze the discrepancies between the camera and GPS_L timestamps, which we follow up with an investigation into the extent of which both timestamps differ from local time given a set of reference photos.

2.1 Differences

We queried the Flickr API for photos that contained a camera timestamp, a GPS timestamp and a GPS location in their EXIF metadata, yielding a total of 10 million photos. For each photo we computed the differences between its camera and GPS_L timestamps, as shown in Figure 1. Our results indicate that 60% of the camera and GPS_L timestamps differ less than 10 minutes from each other, 63% less than 1 hour, 90% less than 24 hours and 93% less than 48 hours. In 19% of the cases the camera and GPS_L timestamps are exactly the same. We further observed an interesting hourly pattern, suggesting that changes in time zone and daylight savings do affect whether the camera and GPS_L timestamps correspond with each other, while two other high peaks occur at a difference of 24 hours, suggesting a mistake made by the user in setting the date of the camera clock one day forward or backward compared to the actual date. Overall, we see that in 28% of the cases the camera timestamps are behind the GPS_L timestamps in time, clearly indicating that these camera timestamps are incorrect, since GPS_L timestamps either exactly reflect local time or are already a certain amount of time behind local time due to staleness. The other 53% of the time that the camera timestamps are ahead of the GPS_L timestamps does not allow us to draw any conclusions yet, since this hinges on the correctness of both timestamps with respect to local time.

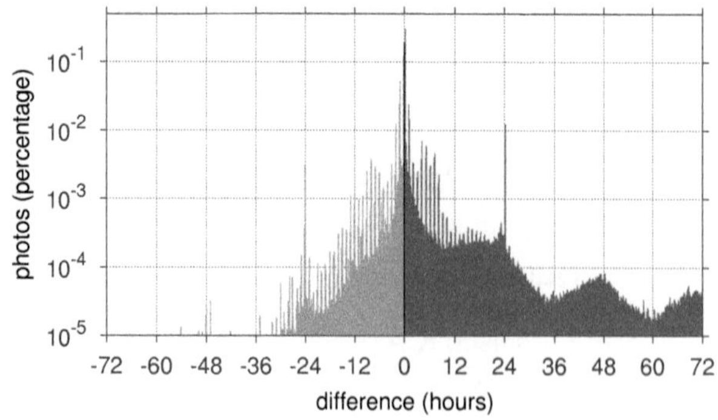

Figure 1: Histogram showing the differences between camera timestamps and GPS_L timestamps based on a sample of 10 million public Flickr photos. The negative (red) values refer to camera timestamps that are behind the GPS_L timestamps in time, whereas the reverse is the case for the positive (blue) values. The plot is shown on a logarithmic scale to emphasize the hourly peaks. Each bar represents a 10 minute window.

2.2 Accuracy

We now set out to investigate whether the camera and GPS_L timestamps actually reflect the local time at the locations where the photos were taken. To do so, we require a ground truth dataset of photos captured at known moments in time. To this end, we filtered our earlier dataset for photos that were associated with the tag `clock` or with the name of a famous landmark that contains a clock, such as the Big Ben in London and the Steam Clock in Vancouver. To avoid a bias towards particular users, cameras and time zones, we retained at most one photo per user+camera+time zone combination. We then visually inspected the remaining photos to see whether they showed a clock and, if so, from the clock face manually coded the actual time of day when each photo was taken. We discarded photos of clocks that could be ambiguously interpreted or when they appeared to be broken, see Figure 2, unless the photo's title, description, tags or comments suggested otherwise. After performing the three aforementioned filtering steps we ultimately ended up with 750 photos of clocks in our ground truth collection.

We show the results of the comparison between camera timestamps, GPS_L timestamps and local time in Table 1. As can be seen, while both timestamps can be very accurate, they can also produce errors in the order of hours. Even though the GPS_L timestamps are slightly more ac-

[2]`http://efele.net/maps/tz/world/` Accessed 4/2014.
[3]`http://www.iana.org/time-zones` Accessed 4/2014.

Taken by `J` Taken by `North Charleston` Taken by `coba` Taken by `Dauvit Alexander`

Figure 2: Examples of photos inspected for inclusion in the ground truth collection. The time of day of the clock in the first photo can be accurately estimated at 17:00, whereas in the second photo it is not clear whether the time expressed is 7:47 or 19:47. The third clock is shown at an angle that makes it difficult to accurately estimate the time of day, while the last clock seems to be broken. Of these four photos we would only have retained the first one.

Table 1: Difference in minutes between the perceived local time of the clocks in our ground truth collection and the camera and GPS_L timestamps.

	Camera	GPS_L
Minimum	0	0
1st Quartile	1	1
2nd Quartile	3	2
3rd Quartile	61	59
Maximum	668	672
Average	76	65

curate than the camera timestamps, the difference between them is small. Note that due to clocks typically only showing the time but not the date, our current evaluation is limited to assessing the correctness of the timestamps with respect to time of day only, and therefore the differences between the actual and the reported times may in reality amount to several days, weeks, or even months.

3. TIMESTAMP CORRECTION

Our results indicate that the camera and GPS_L timestamps can yield good approximations of the actual local time, but the errors can also be large. Thus, for reliable application in real-world scenarios the accuracy of the timestamps needs to be further improved. Based on a manual inspection of sessions produced by different users and cameras, we often observed cases in which the GPS_L timestamp correctly reflected local time when the camera timestamp did not, and vice versa. We will exploit this observation to automatically generate a corrected timestamp that is able to reduce the error with respect to local time even further. However, we remain with the issue that only a relatively small percentage of photos has GPS metadata. To address this, we exploit the notion that users will typically not just take a single photo, but are likely to take many more within a short timespan of each other—we call such a sequence of photos a *session*. We hypothesize, when considering all sessions that include at least one photo with a GPS_L timestamp, that we can reduce the error of all camera timestamps in a session with respect to local time by propagating the most accurate GPS_L timestamp to all photos; this way we mitigate the effects of any stale GPS_L timestamps by focusing on only the photo that has the most recently updated GPS information.

3.1 Sessions

To form sessions, we first queried the Flickr API for all available photos taken by the same users and their cameras that provided the photos of the clocks in our ground truth dataset. Per user+camera combination we then aggregated all photos that were captured less than τ seconds apart according to their camera timestamp. While the camera timestamps may or may not accurately represent local time, we assume they do correspond with the order in which the photos were taken and correctly reflect the period of time that passed between two consecutively taken photos. We only focus on sessions containing at least one photo with GPS information, since otherwise we have no point of reference we can exploit for correction. When a session spans multiple time zones—the odds of which increase as τ increases—we split the session into as many sessions as it has time zones and place photos without GPS information in the same session to which its time-wise closest photo with GPS information was assigned.

3.2 Correction offset

When a session contains more than one photo with GPS metadata, we address the potential staleness of this metadata by first determining which photo has the most recently refreshed GPS information. We do so by picking the photo where the difference obtained by subtracting the camera timestamp from the GPS_L timestamp is maximal (i.e. least negative or most positive). Namely, the more recently the GPS information was refreshed the smaller its difference with the camera timestamp, and vice versa; this holds irrespective of whether the camera timestamp correctly reflects the actual time or not. We then use this difference as the correction offset that we will apply to the camera timestamps of all photos in a session. While the most recently updated GPS_L timestamp may still not correctly reflect the time at which the photo was actually captured, it nonetheless provides the optimal time estimate given the circumstances. Our earlier manual inspection of sessions produced by different users and cameras yielded the following features that we will also exploit for producing improved timestamps.

Staleness. When the most recently updated GPS_L timestamp refers to a moment in time that is more than 24 hours behind the camera timestamp, we found that it was more likely for the GPS_L timestamp to be stale than for the user to have accidentally set the camera clock more than one day ahead of the actual time. In such situations we do not apply a correction offset to the photos in the session and simply use the original camera timestamps instead.

Reorder. As part of pre-share photo organization [4], we noticed that users occasionally reordered their photos by manually changing the camera timestamps before uploading

Table 2: Difference in minutes between the perceived local time of the clocks in our ground truth collection and the camera and GPS_L timestamps, as well as our technique using different values of τ to create the sessions.

	Camera	GPS_L	$\tau = -$	$\tau = 1h$	$\tau = 2h$	$\tau = 3h$	$\tau = 4h$	$\tau = 6h$	$\tau = 12h$	$\tau = 24h$	$\tau = 48h$
Minimum	0	0	0	0	0	0	0	0	0	0	0
1st Quartile	1	1	1	1	1	1	1	1	1	1	1
2nd Quartile	3	2	2	2	2	2	2	2	2	2	2
3rd Quartile	61	59	55	50	51	51	51	52	52	58	59
Maximum	668	672	671	665	665	665	665	665	665	665	665
Average	76	65	55	54	55	55	55	56	56	57	57

them to Flickr. Since a manual reordering of photos can lead to an incorrect correction offset, we detect such sessions by ordering all photos in a session by increasing camera timestamps and verifying that the GPS_L timestamps also monotonically increase. When we identify a reordered session, we do not apply a correction offset to the photos.

Shift. We observed that occasionally the GPS timestamps seem to already refer to local time rather than to UTC time. To address this, when the difference between the GPS_L timestamp of a photo and its corresponding camera timestamp is approximately identical to the time zone offset, we subtract the time zone offset from the correction offset.

3.3 Evaluation

We created sessions using different values of τ between 1 and 48 hours to assess the effect of session length on the accuracy of the timestamps that were corrected by our technique. The advantage of sessions created with a large τ is that these will generally contain more photos, such that the timestamps of a larger number of photos can be corrected than is the case for sessions created with a smaller τ. Furthermore, with more photos available, it is more likely that at least one of them will have a very accurate GPS_L timestamp that can be propagated to all photos. Yet, if an inaccurate timestamp is propagated to all photos in a long session, then all of them will end up incorrectly reflecting local time. We also evaluate the accuracy of the corrected timestamps when each photo is assigned to its own session ($\tau = -$), which effectively only applies the **staleness** and **shift** features of our technique.

For each of the sessions containing one of the ground truth clock photos, we compare our manually annotated local time with the camera timestamp, the GPS_L timestamp and the corrected timestamp produced by our technique. We show the results in Table 2. We can see that our technique is able to reduce the errors of the corrected timestamps with respect to local time, on average by approximately 20 minutes compared to the camera timestamps and 10 minutes to the GPS_L timestamps. When each photo forms its own session ($\tau = -$) it already reduces the error observed at the 3rd quartile and the average error, but not the maximum error. A τ of 1 hour yields the lowest errors, whereas an increase of τ yields an increase in error, albeit still lower than those obtained when using the camera or GPS_L timestamps. Yet, the average session length with $\tau = 1h$ was 15 photos, whereas with $\tau = 48h$ the average session length increased to 66 photos, which means that for a given application scenario the optimal τ should be selected based on the trade-off between the desired accuracy of the timestamps and the quantity of timestamps of which the error can be reduced.

4. CONCLUSIONS

We presented an analysis into the accuracy of the camera and GPS timestamps with respect to local time. We observed that 37% of the photos differ more than an hour between their camera and GPS timestamps with respect to local time at the locations where the photos were taken. We further showed that, while the majority of the timestamps closely approximated local time, they on average exhibiting errors of more than an hour. In light of our observations we proposed a simple technique that reduced the errors by on average 20 minutes compared to camera timestamps and 10 minutes compared to GPS timestamps. While we acknowledge our improvements are modest, we achieved the error reductions solely by applying a fully automatic metadata-only technique to a session of photos. In future work we aim to involve textual analysis, visual analysis, and daily sunrise/sunset time tables to further reduce the errors. We additionally intend to obtain photos that have been taken at a known date, time, and location, in order to fully assess the accuracy of camera and GPS timestamps, and how GPS staleness affects capture location accuracy.

5. REFERENCES

[1] B. Brown, M. McGregor, and E. Laurier. iPhone in vivo: video analysis of mobile device use. In *CHI*, pages 1031–1040, 2013.

[2] M. D. Choudhury, M. Feldman, S. Amer-Yahia, N. Golbandi, R. Lempel, and C. Yu. Automatic Construction of Travel Itineraries using Social Breadcrumbs. In *HT*, pages 35–44, 2010.

[3] L. S. Kennedy, M. Naaman, S. Ahern, R. Nair, and T. Rattenbury. How Flickr helps us make sense of the world: context and content in community-contributed media collections. In *MM*, pages 631–640, 2007.

[4] D. Kirk, A. Sellen, C. Rother, and K. Wood. Understanding photowork. In *CHI*, pages 761–770, 2006.

[5] M. B. Kjærgaard, J. Langdal, G. Torben, and T. Toftkjær. EnTracked: energy-efficient robust position tracking for mobile devices. In *MobiSys*, pages 221–234, 2009.

[6] J. Paek, J. Kim, and R. Govindan. Energy-efficient rate-adaptive GPS-based positioning for smartphones. In *MobiSys*, pages 299–314, 2010.

[7] T. Rattenbury, N. Good, and M. Naaman. Towards automatic extraction of event and place semantics from Flickr tags. In *SIGIR*, pages 103–110, 2007.

[8] B. Shaw, J. Shea, S. Sinha, and A. Hogue. Learning to rank for spatiotemporal search. In *WSDM*, pages 717–726, 2013.

[9] United States Department of Defense. *Global positioning system standard positioning service performance standard.* 4th edition, 2008.

[10] Y. Zheng, L. Zhang, X. Xie, and W.-Y. Ma. Mining interesting locations and travel sequences from GPS trajectories. In *WWW*, pages 1–10, 2009.

Jointly Discovering Fine-grained and Coarse-grained Sentiments via Topic Modeling

Hanqi Wang, Fei Wu, Xi Li, Siliang Tang, Jian Shao, Yueting Zhuang
College of Computer Science, Zhejiang University
Hangzhou, Zhejiang, China
{hanqiw, wufei, xilizju, siliang, jshao, yzhuang}@zju.edu.cn

ABSTRACT

The ever-increasing user-generated contents in social media and other web services make it highly desirable to discover opinions of users on all kinds of topics. Motivated by the assumption that individual word and paragraph in documents will deliver *fine-grained* (e.g., "laudatory", "annoyed" or "boring") and *coarse-grained* (e.g., positive, negative or neutral) sentiments about certain topics respectively, this paper focuses on a deeper thematic level to jointly disentangle fine-grained and coarse-grained opinions towards topics in terms of sentiment analysis, named as *LDA with multi-grained sentiments* (MgS-LDA). As a result, the proposed MgS-LDA not only discovers the topics in social media, but also identifies opinions about a given topic in terms of fine-grained and coarse-grained sentiment. Results of several experiments show that our proposed MgS-LDA achieves better performance on both sentimental classification and topic modeling than related methods.

Categories and Subject Descriptors

I.5.2 [**Design Methodology**]: Classifier design and evaluation

Keywords

Topic Modeling; Sentiment Analysis; Fine-grained Sentiments

1. INTRODUCTION

More and more users in social media now publish online dairies and comments to express their opinions about various topics. For example, there are plenty of positive opinions regarding the style of a movie or negative ones on the service of a product on the Internet. The wide coverage of topics and abundance of opinions in social media make it extremely valuable to a wide range of applications, such as opinion search for ordinary users, opinion tracking for business intelligence, and user behavior prediction for potential advertising. Meanwhile, recent work in this field has begun to concentrate on opinion analysis towards multimedia data like tweets with images posted along with them [3].

Most of previous approaches conduct sentiment classification to discover the overall polarity of opinions expressed in social media. However, sentiments are highly related to topics. For instance, a positive sentiment towards a restaurant may simultaneously contains a positive opinion on its food and a negative one regarding its facility, or vice versa. Several approaches therefore have been proposed to discover both topics in social media and opinions about them in a collaborative manner, most of which adopt similar technique applied in cross-domain topic modeling [4]. For example, Mei et al. [7] propose an approach to model the mixture of topics and sentiments in weblogs, named as topic-sentiment mixture (TSM). Multi-aspect sentiment model (MAS) [9] is proposed later aiming to extract and aggregate specific sentimental words related to different topics. The joint sentiment-topic model (JST) and its re-parameterized version (reversed JST) [6] are designed to explicitly identify the sentimental polarities expressed by words in documents, which have better performance in sentiment classification than the other aforementioned methods.

We argue that different levels of literal units (e.g., words or paragraphs) of social media may have different intrinsic power to deliver multi-grained sentiments. That is to say, paragraphs tend to deliver sentimental polarities (i.e., positive, negative or neutral) as an overall attitude, which are referred to as *coarse-grained* sentiments in this paper. On the contrary, each word could likely remark one *fine-grained* sentiment (e.g., "laudatory", "annoyed" or "boring") instead to express the exact feeling of the user. For example, the word "cry" appearing in one comment about a tragic drama favors the fine-grained sentiment "sad", while identifying it to be either positive or negative would be a bit perplexing.

As a result, it is attractive to clarify both the fine-grained and coarse-grained sentiments about different topics during topic modeling. In this paper, we propose a novel approach based on latent Dirichlet allocation (LDA) [2], aiming to detect topics as well as their fine-grained and coarse-grained opinions. This approach, which is named as *LDA with multi-grained sentiments* (MgS-LDA), attempts to identify fine-grained sentiments for words and coarse-grained sentiments for paragraphs respectively. Compared to those work that have the fine-grained sentiments out of consideration, our proposed MgS-LDA has a more appropriate representation of sentiments, which boosts the performance of both topic modeling and sentiment classification.

MM'14, August 24–27, 2014, New York, NY, USA.

http://dx.doi.org/10.1145/2647868.2655067.

Table 1: The notations used in MgS-LDA

Notation	Description
α, $\boldsymbol{\beta}$, γ	hyper parameter of topic proportions $\boldsymbol{\theta}$, topics $\boldsymbol{\phi}$ and fine-grained sentiment proportions $\boldsymbol{\mu}$
η, σ, λ	coefficients, variance and penalty factor of ridge regression
$w_{d,p,i}$	the i-th word in the p-th paragraph of the d-th document
$t_{d,p,i}$	part-of-speech of $w_{d,p,i}$
$z_{d,p,i}$	topic assignment of $w_{d,p,i}$
$s_{d,p,i}$	fine-grained sentiment assignment of $w_{d,p,i}$
$y_{d,p}$	coarse-grained sentiment of the p-th paragraph in the d-th document

2. THE PROPOSED MGS-LDA MODEL

2.1 Formulation

The part-of-speech of individual word accurately reflects its innate characteristic [8]. Hence, our proposed MgS-LDA assumes that the fine-grained sentiment of each word is determined by both the topic assigned to the word and the part-of-speech of the word itself. Meanwhile, the coarse-grained sentiments are represented as the response of regression, where the ridge regression is used instead in order to train a more robust classification model.

Table 1 gives out the notations used in our paper. We assume that there are K topics and S fine-grained sentiments throughout the corpus. MgS-LDA extends every topic ϕ_k to several variants $\phi_{s,k}$ (the s-th fine-grained sentiment in the k-th topic, where $s \in \{1, 2, ..., S\}$ and $k \in \{1, 2, ..., K\}$). Each fine-grained sentiment has a proportion $\mu_{t,k}$ corresponding to the t-th part-of-speech and the k-th topic, where $t \in \{1, 2, ..., T\}$. Denoting Dirichlet and multinomial distributions as "Dir" and "Mult" respectively, the whole generative process of our proposed MgS-LDA is as follows:

1. For each part-of-speech t and each topic k, draw fine-grained sentiment proportions $\mu_{t,k} \sim \text{Dir}(\gamma_t)$
2. For each fine-grained sentiment s and each topic k, draw word proportions $\phi_{s,k} \sim \text{Dir}(\beta_s)$
3. For each document d:
   1) Draw topic proportions $\theta_d \sim \text{Dir}(\alpha)$
   2) For each paragraph p in the document d:
      a) Sample each topic assignment $z_{d,p,i} \sim \text{Mult}(\theta_d)$
      b) Sample each fine-grained sentiment assignment $s_{d,p,i} \sim \text{Mult}(\mu_{t_{d,p,i},z_{d,p,i}})$
      c) Sample each word $w_{d,p,i} \sim \text{Mult}(\phi_{s_{d,p,i},z_{d,p,i}})$
      d) Draw coarse-grained sentiment y_{dp}

Figure 1 is the graphical representation of MgS-LDA. Central plates from outer to inner represent the documents, the paragraphs in each document, and the words in each paragraph respectively. The shaded nodes indicate observations, while others represent latent variables. The black dots are the hyper parameters.

2.2 Training Process

An EM strategy is utilized to accomplish the training process of our proposed MgS-LDA, which contains posterior inference and parameter estimation. The posterior inference is to compute the conditional distribution of latent variables $\{\boldsymbol{\theta}, \boldsymbol{\phi}, \boldsymbol{\mu}, \boldsymbol{z}, \boldsymbol{s}\}$ given observations $\{\boldsymbol{w}, \boldsymbol{t}\}$, which is an intractable problem same as in other topic models. Therefore, some approximate methods are commonly conducted as substitutes, among which variational inference [2] and Gibbs sampling [5] are the two mainstream ones. We utilize collapsed Gibbs sampling in the E-step of our algorithm, in

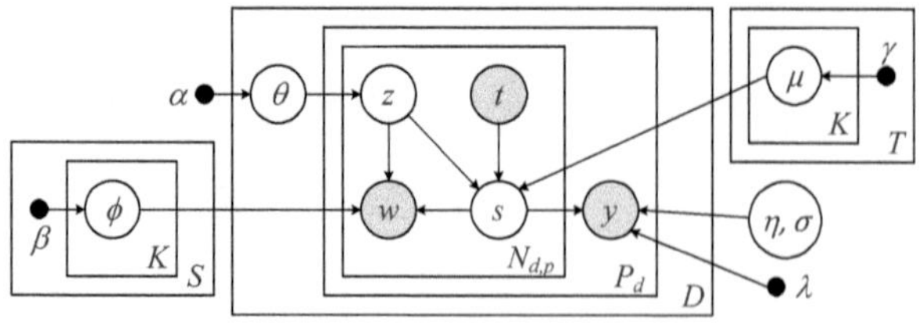

Figure 1: Graphical representation of MgS-LDA.

which $\boldsymbol{\theta}$, $\boldsymbol{\phi}$ and $\boldsymbol{\mu}$ are integrated out. Denoting $\{\boldsymbol{w}, \boldsymbol{z}, \boldsymbol{s}, \boldsymbol{t}, \boldsymbol{y}\}$ and $\{\alpha, \boldsymbol{\beta}, \gamma, \eta, \sigma, \lambda\}$ as $\boldsymbol{\Phi}$ and $\boldsymbol{\Psi}$ respectively, the joint distribution of MgS-LDA can be written as

$$\begin{aligned} p(\boldsymbol{\Phi}|\boldsymbol{\Psi}) = \; & p(\boldsymbol{t})p(\boldsymbol{z}, \boldsymbol{\theta}, \alpha)p(\boldsymbol{s}|\boldsymbol{z}, \boldsymbol{\mu}, \gamma) \\ \times \; & p(\boldsymbol{y}|\boldsymbol{s}, \eta, \sigma, \lambda)p(\boldsymbol{w}|\boldsymbol{z}, \boldsymbol{s}, \boldsymbol{\phi}, \beta) \end{aligned} \tag{1}$$

where

$$\begin{aligned} p(\boldsymbol{z}|\boldsymbol{\theta}, \alpha) &= \prod_{d=1}^{D} \frac{\Gamma(\sum_{k=1}^{K} \alpha_k)}{\prod_{k=1}^{K} \Gamma(\alpha_k)} \frac{\prod_{k=1}^{K} \Gamma(\alpha_k + n_{d,k})}{\Gamma(\sum_{k=1}^{K} \alpha_k + n_{d,k})} \\ p(\boldsymbol{s}|\boldsymbol{z}, \boldsymbol{\mu}, \gamma) &= \prod_{t=1}^{T} \prod_{k=1}^{K} \frac{\Gamma(\sum_{s=1}^{S} \gamma_{t,s})}{\prod_{s=1}^{S} \Gamma(\gamma_{t,s})} \frac{\prod_{s=1}^{S} \Gamma(\gamma_{t,s} + n_{t,k,s})}{\Gamma(\sum_{s=1}^{S} \gamma_{t,s} + n_{t,k,s})} \\ p(\boldsymbol{y}|\boldsymbol{s}, \eta, \sigma, \lambda) &= \frac{1}{\sqrt{2\pi\sigma^2}} \exp\{\frac{\|y_{d,p} - \eta^T \bar{\boldsymbol{s}}_{d,p}\|_2^2 + \frac{\lambda}{2}\|\eta\|_2^2}{-2\sigma^2}\} \\ p(\boldsymbol{w}|\boldsymbol{z}, \boldsymbol{s}, \boldsymbol{\phi}, \beta) &= \prod_{s=1}^{S} \prod_{k=1}^{K} \frac{\Gamma(\sum_{v=1}^{V} \beta_{s,v})}{\prod_{v=1}^{V} \Gamma(\beta_{s,v})} \frac{\prod_{v=1}^{V} \Gamma(\beta_{s,v} + n_{s,k,v})}{\Gamma(\sum_{v=1}^{V} \beta_{s,v} + n_{s,k,v})} \end{aligned} \tag{2}$$

and $n_{d,k}$ denotes the number of words in the d-th document expressing the k-th topic, while $n_{s,k,v}$ is the number of the distinct word v that is assigned to the k-th topic and the s-th fine-grained sentiment. We denote $n_{t,k,s}$ as the number of words having part-of-speech t, topic assignment k and fine-grained sentiment s. $\bar{\boldsymbol{s}}_{d,p}$ denotes the empirical proportions of fine-grained sentiments in the p-th paragraph of the d-th document. $\Gamma(\cdot)$ is the Gamma function.

Then we are able to derive the rule for updating Markov chain. To sample topic $z_{d,p,i}$ and fine-grained sentiment $s_{d,p,i}$ for their corresponding word $w_{d,p,i}$, we have

$$\begin{aligned} & p(z_{d,p,i} = k, s_{d,p,i} = s|\boldsymbol{\Phi}_{-\{z_{d,p,i}, s_{d,p,i}\}}, \boldsymbol{\Psi}) \\ \propto \; & (\alpha_k + n_{d,k}) \frac{\gamma_{t,s} + n_{t,k,s}}{\sum_{s=1}^{S} \gamma_{t,s} + n_{t,k,s}} \frac{\beta_{s,v} + n_{s,k,v}}{\sum_{v=1}^{V} \beta_{s,v} + n_{s,k,v}} \\ \times \; & \exp\{\frac{1}{\sigma^2} \frac{\eta_s}{n_{d,p}} (y_{d,p} - \frac{n_{d,p,s}}{n_{d,p}} - \frac{\eta_s}{2n_{d,p}})\} \end{aligned} \tag{3}$$

where $n_{d,p,s}$ denotes the number of words assigned to the s-th fine-grained sentiment in the p-th paragraph of the d-th document, $\sum_{s=1}^{S} n_{d,p,s} = n_{d,p}$. We can iteratively sample the assignments of latent variables $\boldsymbol{z}$ and $\boldsymbol{s}$, and estimate multinomial distributions $\boldsymbol{\phi}$ and $\boldsymbol{\mu}$ when it converges.

In M-step, we estimate regression parameters η and σ by maximizing the joint likelihood of the model given other variables and parameters fixed, which is equivalent to $\max_{\eta,\sigma} \log p(\boldsymbol{y}|\bar{\boldsymbol{s}}, \eta, \sigma, \lambda)$, and the solution is obtained by

$$\begin{aligned} \bar{\eta} &= (\bar{\boldsymbol{s}}\bar{\boldsymbol{s}}^T + \lambda)^{-1}\bar{\boldsymbol{s}}\boldsymbol{y}, \\ \bar{\sigma}^2 &= \frac{1}{\sum_{d=1}^{D} P_d}(\boldsymbol{y}\boldsymbol{y}^T - \boldsymbol{y}^T\bar{\boldsymbol{s}}^T\bar{\eta}) \end{aligned} \tag{4}$$

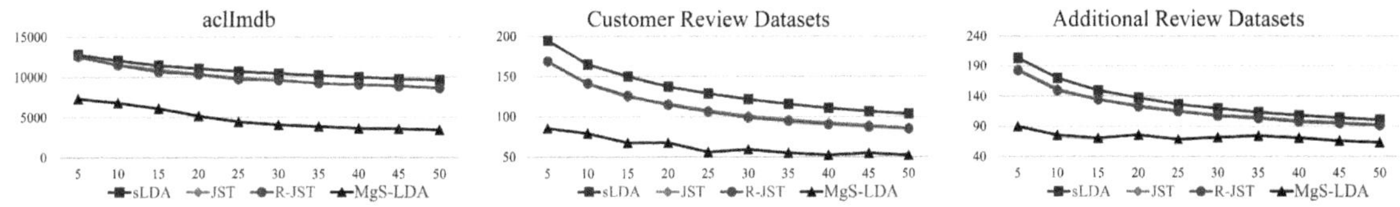

Figure 2: The comparisons of perplexity on different corpora (curves of JST and reversed JST are extremely similar). The vertical axis is the perplexity and the horizontal axis is the number of topics.

Table 2: The statistics of datasets

	documents	paragraphs	words	vocabulary size
aclImdb				
Train	25,000	25,000	4,380,036	28,180
Test	25,000	25,000	4,279,066	
Customer Review Datasets				
Train	157	881	18,563	713
Test	157	849	18,878	
Additional Review Datasets				
Train	163	1,027	18,220	776
Test	163	1,106	23,037	

Table 3: The performance of sentiment classification

Metrics	sLDA	JST	reversed JST	MgS-LDA
aclImdb				
macro F1	0.6867	0.6838	0.6957	**0.7014**
micro F1	0.6901	0.6911	0.7047	**0.7113**
Customer Review Datasets				
macro F1	0.6051	0.6673	0.6602	**0.6726**
micro F1	0.7185	0.6820	0.6938	**0.7233**
Additional Review Datasets				
macro F1	0.5842	**0.6395**	0.6272	0.6063
micro F1	0.7464	0.7439	0.7410	**0.7542**

2.3 Prediction

After posterior inference and parameter estimation are accomplished, our approach is able to predict the coarse-grained sentiments of paragraphs in documents that are unseen before, with topics and fine-grained sentiment proportions fixed. This problem amounts to take the expectation of response $\boldsymbol{y}$ given $\boldsymbol{\phi}$, $\boldsymbol{\mu}$ and regression parameters. We perform the process of collapsed Gibbs sampling on the new documents, and then calculate the expectation of $\boldsymbol{y}$ that $\mathrm{E}[\boldsymbol{y}|\boldsymbol{\Phi}_{-\boldsymbol{y}}, \boldsymbol{\Psi}, \boldsymbol{\phi}, \boldsymbol{\mu}] = \bar{\boldsymbol{s}}^T \eta$.

3. EXPERIMENTS

3.1 Datasets

Three benchmark datasets are utilized in our experiments. The first one is Large Movie Review Dataset (aclImdb) [1] in which every review has only one paragraph, each paragraph is therefore regarded as a document in our proposed MgS-LDA. In order to verify the effectiveness of introducing the paragraph layer, two other corpora, namely Customer Review Datasets and Additional Review Datasets [2] are also employed in the experiments. These two datasets contain customer reviews of electronic products, while the comment on each distinct aspect of a product is taken as individual paragraph in the document and is elaborately annotated with a coarse-grained sentiment. Stop words and words occurring less than 10 times are removed. Some statistics of the datasets after pre-processing can be found in Table 2.

3.2 Quantitative Evaluation

The performance of sentimental polarity classification is evaluated by comparing the estimated coarse-grained sentiment of each paragraph to the ground truth in test data. We compare our proposed MgS-LDA with sLDA [1], JST and reversed JST [6]. It should be clarified that though JST and reversed JST are formulated in an unsupervised manner, the topic-word distributions $\boldsymbol{\phi}$ in their models are designed to be pre-trained by a group of prior knowledge [6].

For all the four models, we set $\alpha = 0.01$, $\beta = 0.01$, and for models that can detect sentiments in given data, the hyper parameter of sentiment proportion γ is set to be 0.01. In sLDA and MgS-LDA, η are randomly generated from $\{-1, 1\}$, σ^2 is set to be 1 initially, and λ is fixed to $1e^{-4}$. According to the observed results in model selection, we set the number of topics K to be 20, 5, and 7 in experiments on aclImdb, Customer Review Datasets and Additional Review Datasets respectively, and fix the number of fine-grained sentiments S to 6. The experiment of each method is repeated 10 times, and the average results are reported in terms of two metrics, namely macro F1 and micro F1.

Table 3 presents the performance of sentimental polarity classification obtained by all the above-mentioned methods on different corpora, in which results shown in boldface are the best ones. It is observed that our proposed MgS-LDA has the best performance in most comparisons due to its aptitude to the discovery of the latent topics and their both coarse-grained and fine-grained sentiments. A possible reason why JST achieves higher macro F1 than MgS-LDA in Additional Review Datasets is that, this dataset is small and unbalanced (e.g., too many positive paragraphs in training data), causing classification by regression (i.e., sLDA and MgS-LDA) to produce unsatisfied results.

Another metric that measuring the generalization ability of topic models is the *perplexity* of test data, that lower perplexity indicates better generalization performance [2]. The perplexity of different approaches over three corpora are shown in Figure 2. It is observed that MgS-LDA gains the lowest perplexity under different number of topics.

3.3 Qualitative Performance

The topics obtained by topic models are commonly represented by words having the highest probability in the corresponding distribution of each topic, and can be manually labeled according to the most representative words and the ground truth in data. Samples of topics in different sentiments as well as their topical words obtained on various

[1] http://ai.stanford.edu/~amaas/data/sentiment

[2] http://www.cs.uic.edu/~liub/FBS/sentiment-analysis.html

Table 4: Two topics as well as their topical words with *coarse-grained* or *fine-grained* sentiments obtained by MgS-LDA or comparing methods. The probability of each word belonging to its topic is shown in italic.

one topic in aclImdb: *Thriller and Suspense Films*							
JST		reversed JST		MgS-LDA			
positive	negative	positive	negative	laudatory	boring	funny	objective
good (*0.035*) budget (*0.031*) movie (*0.026*) suspense (*0.023*) plot (*0.018*)	dumb (*0.035*) you (*0.032*) tell (*0.021*) plot (*0.021*) predictable (*0.019*)	film (*0.039*) story (*0.035*) good (*0.026*) some (*0.018*) suspense (*0.018*)	movie (*0.036*) dumb (*0.034*) you (*0.026*) club (*0.023*) watch (*0.019*)	good (*0.114*) great (*0.036*) special (*0.034*) first (*0.026*) wonderful (*0.019*)	you (*0.098*) watch (*0.058*) dumb (*0.039*) unfortunately (*0.035*) acting (*0.026*)	laughing (*0.067*) time (*0.019*) story (*0.018*) ridiculous (*0.017*) funny (*0.017*)	people (*0.154*) movie (*0.064*) film (*0.036*) characters (*0.027*) scene (*0.025*)
one topic in Customer Review Datasets: *Canon G3 Camera*							
JST		reversed JST		MgS-LDA			
positive	negative	positive	negative	awesome	annoyed	expensive	objective
camera (*0.039*)	camera (*0.043*)	camera (*0.036*)	camera (*0.035*)	great (*0.063*)	had (*0.094*)	purchased (*0.085*)	camera (*0.207*)
you (*0.037*)	time (*0.023*)	you (*0.028*)	you (*0.031*)	good (*0.050*)	bad (*0.072*)	you (*0.074*)	canon (*0.072*)
easy (*0.033*)	canon (*0.023*)	use (*0.024*)	bad (*0.027*)	easy (*0.042*)	more (*0.046*)	expensive (*0.066*)	you (*0.047*)
flash (*0.028*)	buy (*0.022*)	digital (*0.024*)	canon (*0.027*)	features (*0.036*)	complaint (*0.024*)	cannon (*0.066*)	digital (*0.037*)
get (*0.022*)	you (*0.021*)	canon (*0.020*)	cost (*0.021*)	other (*0.024*)	bought (*0.024*)	price (*0.023*)	online (*0.037*)

Table 5: The proportions of part-of-speech words delivering subjective or objective information.

part-of-speech	subjective emotions	objective statements
nouns	38.6%	61.4%
personal Pronouns	52.1%	47.9%
adjectives	91.2%	8.8%
verbs	32.7%	67.3%
adverbs	87.7%	12.3%

corpora are shown in Table 4 (sLDA is excluded in this experiment since it cannot discover sentiments in word-level). These two topics are manually labeled as *Thriller and Suspense Films* and *Canon G3 Camera*. It can be observed that many of topical-words found by MgS-LDA are very vivid and emotional to deliver their fine-grained sentiments, while those delivering sentimental polarities in JST and reversed JST are a bit apathetic. Our proposed MgS-LDA is also capable of identifying the "objective" fine-grained sentiment, though words like "you" are so common that they are found in various kinds of opinions.

In Table 5, we illustrate the proportions of words having different part-of-speech to express subjective or objective information respectively, where adjectives and adverbs seems to be more likely to deliver subjective sentiments than other words such as nouns and verbs. It confirms the assumption in MgS-LDA that the part-of-speech of individual word strongly affects its tendency to express its innate emotion.

4. CONCLUSION

In this paper, an approach called MgS-LDA is proposed to discover the latent topics in social media as well as their corresponding fine-grained and coarse-grained sentiments. Other than traditional methods, the proposed MgS-LDA has a more appropriate representation of sentiments. Experimental results show that MgS-LDA achieves better performance on both sentimental polarity classification and topic modeling than other methods.

5. ACKNOWLEDGMENTS

This work is supported in part by National Basic Research Program of China (2012CB316400), NSFC (61105074), 863 program (2012AA012505), the Fundamental Research Funds for the Central Universities, Chinese Knowledge Center of Engineering Science and Technology (CKCEST), Program for New Century Excellent Talents in University and Zhejiang Provincial Natural Science Foundation of China (No. LQ14F010004, LY14F020027).

6. REFERENCES

[1] D. M. Blei and J. D. Mcauliffe. Supervised topic models. In *Advances in Neural Information Processing Systems*, pages 121–128, 2007.

[2] D. M. Blei, A. Y. Ng, and M. I. Jordan. Latent dirichlet allocation. *Journal of Machine Learning Research*, 3:993–1022, 2003.

[3] D. Borth, R. Ji, T. Chen, T. Breuel, and S.-F. Chang. Large-scale visual sentiment ontology and detectors using adjective noun pairs. In *Proceedings of the 21st ACM International Conference on Multimedia*, pages 223–232, 2013.

[4] H. Gao, S. Tang, Y. Zhang, D. Jiang, F. Wu, and Y. Zhuang. Supervised cross-collection topic modeling. In *Proceedings of the 20th ACM International Conference on Multimedia*, pages 957–960, 2012.

[5] T. L. Griffiths and M. Steyvers. Finding scientific topics. In *Proceedings of the National Academy of Sciences*, volume 101, pages 5228–5235, 2004.

[6] C. Lin, Y. He, R. Everson, and S. Ruger. Weakly supervised joint sentiment-topic detection from text. *IEEE Transactions on Knowledge and Data Engineering*, 24(6):1134–1145, 2012.

[7] Q. Mei, X. Ling, M. Wondra, H. Su, and C. Zhai. Topic sentiment mixture: modeling facets and opinions in weblogs. In *Proceedings of the 16th International Conference on World Wide Web*, pages 171–180, 2007.

[8] S. Tang, H. Wang, J. Shao, F. Wu, M. Chen, and Y. Zhuang. πLDA: document clustering with selective structural constraints. In *Proceedings of the 21st ACM International Conference on Multimedia*, pages 753–756, 2013.

[9] I. Titov and R. McDonald. A joint model of text and aspect ratings for sentiment summarization. In *Proceedings of the 46th Annual Meeting of the Association for Computational Linguistics: Human Language Technology*, pages 308–316, 2008.

A Real-Time Smart Assistant for Video Surveillance Through Handheld Devices

Hao Kuang[1], Benjamin Guthier[1], Mukesh Saini[1], Dwarikanath Mahapatra[2], Abdulmotaleb El Saddik[1]
[1]MCRLab, University of Ottawa, Canada
[1]{hkuan041, bguthier, msain2, elsaddik}@uottawa.ca
[2]Department of Computer Science, ETH Zurich, Switzerland
[2]dwarikanath.mahapatra@inf.ethz.ch

ABSTRACT

In a remote surveillance system, a high resolution surveillance camera streams its video to a user's handheld device. Such devices are unable to make use of the high resolution video due to their limited display size and bandwidth. In this paper, we propose a method to assist the mobile operator of the surveillance camera in focusing on sensitive regions of the video. Our system automatically identifies relevant regions. We introduce a pan and zoom strategy to ensure that the operator is able to see fine details in these areas while maintaining contextual knowledge. Regions of interest are identified using foreground detection as well as face and body detection. The efficacy of the proposed method is demonstrated through a user study. Our proposed method was reported to be more useful than two comparable approaches for getting an understanding of the activities in a surveillance scene while maintaining context.

Categories and Subject Descriptors

I.4.9 [**Image Processing and Computer Vision**]: Applications

General Terms

Algorithms

1. INTRODUCTION

Remote video surveillance systems use high resolution cameras to monitor security-critical areas like a parking lot or the entrance to a home. The captured video is streamed to a remote place where an operator can view it using a handheld device. In such scenarios, it may be undesirable to transmit the full resolution video to a bandwidth-limited handheld device. The screen of the device may also be too small to distinguish important details in the full view of the scene. Zooming into certain regions on the other hand comes with the risk of missing critical events in non-visible parts of the video and context from the surrounding may be lost. The user of a remote surveillance system thus needs to make a compromise between zooming in on detail and obtaining contextual information. This form of manually controlling the zooming and panning is tedious.

We propose a system to assist a user in remote surveillance with a handheld device. If no explicit control input is given by the user, the system automatically selects a region of interest (ROI) to zoom into and periodically displays the complete view to provide the necessary context. This selection is performed on the surveillance site to save bandwidth for transmission. Throughout this paper, we use the term *sensitivity* to denote the relevance of a certain part of the scene to the surveillance task. Sensitive regions are identified in real-time by employing a foreground detection method and by detecting faces and human bodies. In addition to the computed sensitivity, we allow user-defined static sensitivity. A user may for example find an entrance to a building relevant even if there are currently no people walking by. User-defined sensitivity also allows to avoid non-security critical areas with large amounts of motion, like trees moving in the wind. Our assistant selects the ROI that currently has the highest combined sensitivity and zooms into it. After a certain amount of time, it zooms out again to provide context. It then continues with the next sensitive region. The sensitivity of a region that has already been viewed is penalized to avoid selecting the same region twice. This penalty is lessened over time to allow the ROI to be selected again.

A field of research that is related to our work is *video retargeting*. Techniques in this field adapt high resolution videos to devices with a small display size like smartphones. The general goal is to fit as much of the "important" content as possible into the retargeted video. Importance may be measured from low level features such as saliency, contrast and gradients, or from higher level processing like face detection. Kopf et al. [4] give an overview of the vast number of existing approaches. Due to space limitations, we can only focus on the most prominent ones here.

The method presented in [5] crops and scales the frames of a video based on the importance of the pixels. This is done in a way that balances the loss of detail that occurs when downscaling with the loss of content when cropping. The currently shown area can be moved over the input video to create artificial pans and cuts whenever appropriate.

Techniques based on *Seam Carving* (see for example [3]) detect partially contiguous seams of less important pixels inside a frame and remove them. The size of the video is

MM'14, November 3–7, 2014, Orlando, Florida, USA.

ACM 978-1-4503-3063-3/14/11 ...$15.00.
http://dx.doi.org/10.1145/2647868.2655070.

thus reduced by removing unstructured areas between the important objects. Similarly, approaches based on *Warping* (see [9]) subdivide video frames into a rectangular mesh grid and transform each cell non-uniformly. Cells containing high importance remain mostly unchanged while unimportant cells may be warped. The advantage of Warping and Seam Carving over cropping is that content may be removed from the inside of a frame as opposed to only from the border. However, they also change the content of the frame, which makes them unsuitable for surveillance. The distance between objects may change which may have a severe impact on the context.

In general, video retargeting techniques have a different focus and are thus not applicable to a surveillance scenario. This is due to the following reasons. Low-level visual importance is generally not a good indicator for sensitivity in surveillance. A highly structured but static background may be interesting to a casual viewer but may have little relevance for security purposes. Also, video retargeting may discard certain areas of a video entirely as long as the result is aesthetically pleasing. In surveillance, discarding content is unacceptable. However, preservation of content can be achieved at the expense of aesthetics, e.g., by introducing artificial zooms. Furthermore, the common assumption of availability of the entire video beforehand is not valid in a real-time surveillance scenario.

An approach that is specific to retargeting of real-time surveillance videos was presented in [2]. After detecting sensitive areas from the difference of two consecutive frames, the video is cropped and zoomed to the target size using a moving ROI. Artificial cuts may be introduced if necessary. The work is based on a scenario where the retargeted video is shown in a small area on a big screen, where an overview of the entire scene is also available. This is not the case when showing the video on a mobile device. Furthermore, the simple form of sensitivity map that is being used without considering user preferences may lead to a bias towards moving high-contrast objects, even when they are not relevant to security (e.g., a flag waving in the background).

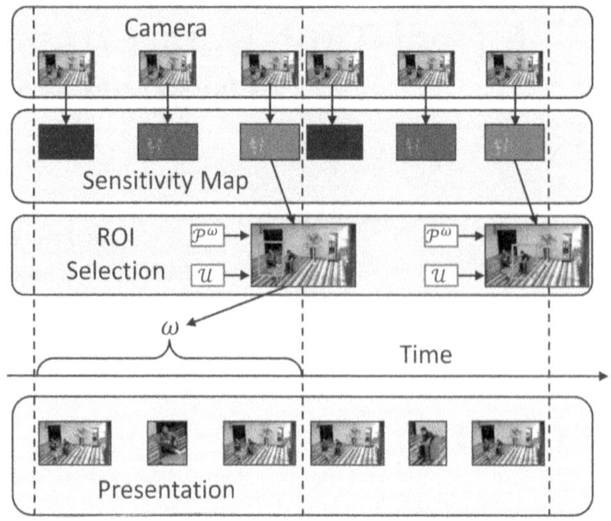

Figure 1: Overview of our proposed remote video surveillance assistant. A sensitivity map is calculated for every frame. It is accumulated over ω frames and then passed to the ROI selection. The sensitivity, penalty and user input maps are combined to select a ROI. The presentation component operates with a delay of ω frames. It zooms into the ROI over the course of ω frames.

2. VIDEO SURVEILLANCE ASSISTANT

Our assistant for video surveillance on handheld devices consists of three components that work together: Sensitivity map computation, ROI selection, and presentation. It uses a buffer of ω frames which allows it to look into the future when selecting an ROI. This introduces a latency of ω frames, which is in the order of five to ten seconds. In a remote surveillance system, where the user is typically far away from the site under surveillance, such a latency is uncritical. Note that the buffer is located at the surveillance site; no buffer is required on the mobile device.

The sensitivity map component obtains the latest frame from the camera and calculates a sensitivity map $\mathcal{S}$ for the frame. Over the course of ω frames, the $\mathcal{S}$ are summed up to an accumulated sensitivity map $\mathcal{S}^\omega$ which is then passed on to the ROI selection component. We use the ω superscript to denote maps that are used only once every ω frames. The ROI selection component combines $\mathcal{S}^\omega$ with the static user input $\mathcal{U}$ and the penalty map $\mathcal{P}^\omega$. The result is a decision map $\mathcal{D}^\omega$ from which the ROI to be displayed is calculated. This ROI is passed on to the presentation component, which now processes the end of the video buffer. Over the duration of ω frames, the presenter smoothly zooms into the selected ROI and zooms out again. The resulting resized frames are sent over the network to the handheld device. See Figure 1 for an overview of the system.

The sensitivity map component and the presenter operate in sync with each other and the frame rate of the camera, but with ω frames delay between camera and presentation. ROI selection is triggered each time ω frames have been accumulated. Details on the three components is given in the following sections.

2.1 Sensitivity Map

In a surveillance scenario, humans are generally the main focus of attention. In order to recognize humans in a video, further attention must be paid to their faces. In addition to that, objects moving relatively to the static background, i.e. foreground objects, are also interesting. Our sensitivity map is thus computed from the results of face detection, human body detection and foreground object detection.

We begin by obtaining the latest frame from the camera and storing it in the buffer for later use by the presentation component. The approaches [8] and [1] are then used on the frame to detect faces and human bodies, respectively. Faces and bodies are represented by bounding boxes containing them. From these, we create two binary images I_f and I_b that are 1 in areas where faces and bodies were detected and 0 otherwise. Moving foreground objects are detected using the Gaussian mixture model presented in [7]. The result is a binary image I_o with pixels belonging to a moving foreground object being 1. The sensitivity map $\mathcal{S}$ for the frame is then calculated as $\mathcal{S} = I_f + I_b + I_o$. Calculating $\mathcal{S}$ like this automatically prioritizes faces over human bodies

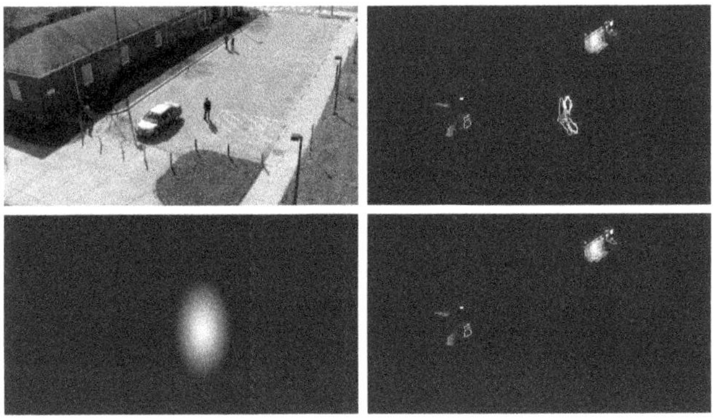

Figure 2: The top left image shows a frame from a surveillance video. The top right frame shows the accumulated sensitivity map $\mathcal{S}^\omega$. The person in the center gets chosen as the next ROI. As a result of the chosen ROI, the penalty map on the bottom left gets updated. After ω frames, the previously chosen region gets penalized in the sensitivity map and will not be chosen again (bottom right).

(because $I_f \subseteq I_b$) and moving bodies over moving objects (when $I_b \subseteq I_o$). The face of a person walking through the scene for example would be included in $\mathcal{S}$ three times.

Our system needs to detect the area of the video with the highest sensitivity over the course of ω frames. For this reason, the sensitivity maps for each frame in this timespan are summed up into an accumulated sensitivity map $\mathcal{S}^\omega$. Accumulating the sensitivity also eliminates spuriously detected faces and human bodies and reduces the impact of noise in I_o. Once $\mathcal{S}^\omega$ has been accumulated over ω frames, it is passed on to the ROI selection component.

2.2 ROI Selection

The sensitivity map $\mathcal{S}^\omega$ as defined above cannot always identify the most important aspects of the scene. Importance also depends on context, which is difficult to assess algorithmically. In a hallway for example, the entrance area is more important to focus on than the walls. A surveillance video of a parking lot might also include parts of the adjacent road which could be outside of the scope of surveillance. It is thus important to include user input into the decision making process. We model the user input as a map $\mathcal{U}$ of the same size as $\mathcal{S}^\omega$ which gives an offset to the sensitivity. Since this information is mostly static, it needs to be defined only once when the system is set up.

In order to not display the same region over and over, we give a penalty to the sensitivity of a region that has been presented to the operator before. Our penalty map $\mathcal{P}^\omega$ has values between zero and one with higher values meaning a higher penalty. After having selected an ROI to display, we calculate a 2D Gaussian function for the chosen ROI. Its mean is the center of the ROI, and the variances are chosen relative to the width and height of the ROI. This Gaussian function is added to $\mathcal{P}^\omega$. The process of penalizing a previously chosen ROI is illustrated in Figure 2. Every ω frames when a new ROI is selected, the penalty map is multiplied by a factor $\alpha \in [0, 1]$ to decrease the penalty over time. The sensitivity of a selected ROI is thus reduced at first, and its sensitivity then slowly increases back to its original value.

When a new $\mathcal{S}^\omega$ is available – once every ω frames – it is combined with the user input and the penalty map to form a final decision map. The decision map $\mathcal{D}^\omega$ is defined as

$$\mathcal{D}^\omega = (1 - \mathcal{P}^\omega) \cdot (\mathcal{S}^\omega + \mathcal{U}). \quad (1)$$

All operators used here process the maps pixel-wise.

For the purpose of ROI detection, $\mathcal{D}^\omega$ is converted into a binary image by applying a low threshold. Morphological operations are then used to reduce noise. Next, the system extracts contours from white areas in the binary image and merges adjacent contours if necessary. The bounding boxes of the connected contours are the potential regions of interest to zoom into. For each potential ROI, we compute a decision value. It is calculated by summing up all values inside the ROI in the original unthresholded $\mathcal{D}^\omega$. This allows ranking of the potential ROIs according to the amount of sensitivity they contain. The ROI with the highest decision value is selected and sent to the presentation component.

2.3 Presentation

The presentation component creates the output frames that are sent to the remote operator. At the beginning of each block of ω frames, it is given an ROI for the entire block. The frames of the block are contained in the buffer. Note that the ROI selection may give rectangular areas with an arbitrary aspect ratio. The aspect ratio $\phi = w/h$ of the ROI is generally not identical to the target aspect ratio ϕ_t. $\phi < \phi_t$ means that the chosen ROI is too high. We thus increase the width of the ROI as $w = \phi_t h$, so that the aspect ratios match again. The case $\phi > \phi_t$ is handled analogously. This guarantees that the selected region is fully contained in the created view.

The presentation of a block of frames always starts and ends with a fully zoomed out overview. Within the block, it zooms into the ROI, stays zoomed in for a certain amount of time and then zooms out again. Zooming is implemented as an interpolation between the parameters of the full frame and the chosen ROI. We use cubic spine interpolation for smooth zooming. Like this, an interpolated ROI for the current frame is calculated. The presenter takes the oldest frame from the buffer and crops it according to the interpolated ROI. The cropped frame is then scaled to the target resolution and sent over the network.

3. EXPERIMENTAL RESULTS

The main goal of our approach is to resize the video from a surveillance camera so that it can be used for remote monitoring on a mobile device with a small screen size. We evaluated our approach in a user study with 22 male and 7 female non-expert subjects. The average age was 25 with a standard deviation of 4. Four surveillance videos with a resolution of 1920×1080 and a length of one minute were used. They were taken from the VIRAT database, which was designed for performance assessment of activity detection algorithms [6]. Representative frames from the four scenarios are shown in Figure 3.

As the target resolution, we chose 384×216, which is $1/5$ of the original resolution. Three different videos of the target resolution were created for each scenario: A scaled

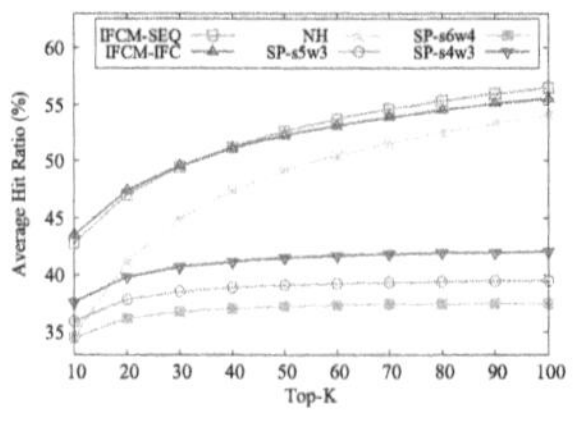

Figure 1: The comparison on accuracy with the baselines ($\alpha = 0.5$).

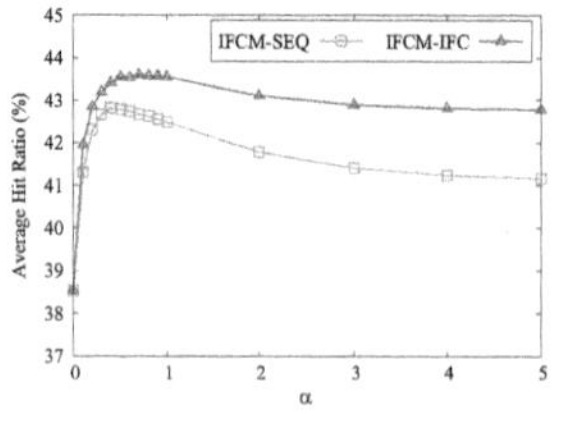

Figure 2: The impact of α on the accuracy performance (Top-10).

on the average hit ratio compared with the baselines, especially when only a small number of songs are recommended each time. Usually, recommender systems are not expected to give a large number of recommendations for a user each time, which will jeopardize the user friendliness. IFCM-IFC dominates IFCM-SEQ in accuracy when Top-K$\leq$40. This proves that IFCM-IFC stresses more of interest loss in computing transition probabilities and therefore promotes the rankings of related songs. As we have pointed out, the higher accuracy the method has when only a small number of songs are recommended each time, the higher practical value the method will be of. Thus, we consider IFCM-IFC as a little optimization based on IFCM-SEQ. In average, our methods (IFCM-SEQ and IFCM-IFC) have about 5% absolute improvement in average hit ratios compared with NH, and even larger compared with SP.

Fig. 2 illustrates the influence of α on the average hit ratio of Top-10 results. The larger the value of α is, the faster the interest is forgetting and the more significant recency effect the model assumes. However, the decline of curves in Fig. 2 after $\alpha > 1$ elucidates that over-assumption on the recency effect could also fail the IFC model. The optimal setting of α is around 0.5 which is also the value obtained using our learning method. We can see the influence of α is smooth when $\alpha \geq 0.2$, especially for IFCM-IFC. Thus, the proposed method based on IFC model is considered to be robust.

We also evaluated the accuracy performance of our method given different lengths of input playlists (Fig. 3). The distribution of the length of playlists in the training set and the test set is illustrated in Fig. 3(a). Generally, there are more short playlists than the long ones since the number of playlists drops as the playlist length increases. This observation fits the real situation that most people usually listen to a small number of distinct songs during one session. Fig. 3(b) shows the average hit ratio of our method within the different-length groups of playlists. Interestingly, we observed higher average hit ratio in the group of playlists whose length is between 10 and 14. Beyond or below this range, it leads to lower average hit ratios, and worst in the >= 30 group (playlists with no less than 30 distinct songs). We may conclude that the effect of human retention of interest has upper and lower boundaries, and inside the range, IFC model has the best performance, while outside the range, IFC model may suffer from random effects (below the lower bound) or noises (beyond the upper bound).

In sum, the experimental results show that IFC model can significantly improve the accuracy performance in music recommendations.

5. CONCLUSIONS

In this paper, we proposed a novel music recommendation method based on the IFC model to predict a user's

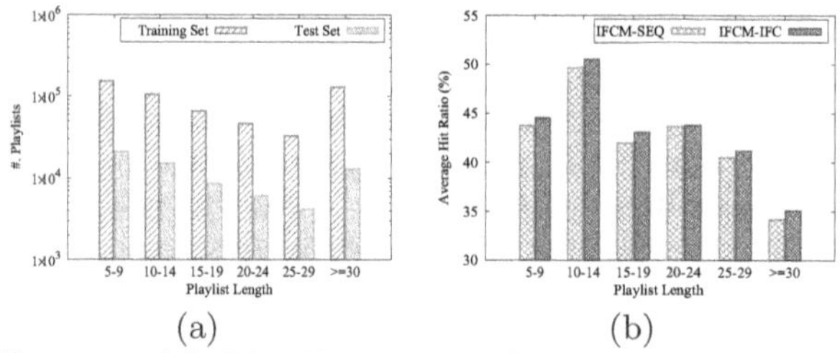

Figure 3: (a) Distribution of playlists with different length in both the training set and the test set. (b) Accuracy performance in different length groups of playlists (Top-10).

next choice considering the recency effects in people's listening to music. We presented the recommendation framework with two open ends — the computation of transition probabilities and prior probabilities. We brought forward the sequence-based and the IFC-based solutions to our problem. The experimental results showed a significant improvement in the accuracy of our music recommendation method compared with the baselines. In the future, we will consider to improve the IFC model by considering more other existing forgetting curve models.

6. ACKNOWLEDGEMENT

This work was supported by the National Natural Science Foundation of China (No. 61373023, No. 61170064) and the National High Technology Research and Development Program of China (No. 2013AA013204).

7. REFERENCES

[1] A. Anderson, R. Kumar, A. Tomkins, and S. Vassilvitskii. The dynamics of repeat consumption. In *WWW*, pages 419–430, 2014.

[2] L. Averell and A. Heathcote. The form of the forgetting curve and the fate of memories. *Journal of Mathematical Psychology*, 55:25–35, 2011.

[3] G. Bonnin and D. Jannach. A comparison of playlist generation strategies for music recommendation and a new baseline scheme. In *Workshops at the AAAI Conference on Artificial Intelligence*, pages 16–23, 2013.

[4] J. Bu, S. Tan, C. Chen, C. Wang, H. Wu, L. Zhang, and X. He. Music recommendation by unified hypergraph: combining social media information and music content. In *ACM Multimedia*, pages 391–400, 2010.

[5] C.-M. Chen, M.-F. Tsai, J.-Y. Liu, and Y.-H. Yang. Using emotional context from article for contextual music recommendation. In *ACM Multimedia*, pages 649–652, 2013.

[6] H. Ebbinghaus. *Memory; A Contribution to Experimental Psychology*. New York by Teachers College, Columbia University, 1885.

[7] R. Greene and A. Samuel. Recency and suffix effects in serial recall of musical stimuli. *J Exp Psychol Learn Mem Cogn*, 12(4):517–524, 1986.

[8] N. Hariri, B. Mobasher, and R. Burke. Context-aware music recommendation based on latent topic sequential patterns. In *RecSys*, pages 131–138, 2012.

[9] N. Koenigstein, G. Dror, and Y. Koren. Yahoo! music recommendations: modeling music ratings with temporal dynamics and item taxonomy. In *RecSys*, pages 165–172, 2011.

[10] N. Natarajan, D. Shin, and I. S. Dhillon. Which app will you use next? collaborative filtering with interactional context. In *RecSys*, pages 201–208, 2013.

[11] J. Pei, J. Han, B. Mortazavi-Asl, H. Pinto, Q. Chen, U. Dayal, and M.-C. Hsu. Prefixspan: mining sequential patterns effectively by prefix-projected pattern growth. In *ICDE*, pages 215–224, 2001.

[12] X. Wang, D. Rosenblum, and Y. Wang. Context-aware mobile music recommendation for daily activities. In *ACM Multimedia*, pages 99–108, 2012.

[13] Y.-H. Yang and J.-Y. Liu. Quantitative study of music listening behavior in a social and affective context. *IEEE Transactions on Multimedia*, 15(6):1304–1315, 2013.

Figure 2: The top left image shows a frame from a surveillance video. The top right frame shows the accumulated sensitivity map $\mathcal{S}^\omega$. The person in the center gets chosen as the next ROI. As a result of the chosen ROI, the penalty map on the bottom left gets updated. After ω frames, the previously chosen region gets penalized in the sensitivity map and will not be chosen again (bottom right).

(because $I_f \subseteq I_b$) and moving bodies over moving objects (when $I_b \subseteq I_o$). The face of a person walking through the scene for example would be included in $\mathcal{S}$ three times.

Our system needs to detect the area of the video with the highest sensitivity over the course of ω frames. For this reason, the sensitivity maps for each frame in this timespan are summed up into an accumulated sensitivity map $\mathcal{S}^\omega$. Accumulating the sensitivity also eliminates spuriously detected faces and human bodies and reduces the impact of noise in I_o. Once $\mathcal{S}^\omega$ has been accumulated over ω frames, it is passed on to the ROI selection component.

2.2 ROI Selection

The sensitivity map $\mathcal{S}^\omega$ as defined above cannot always identify the most important aspects of the scene. Importance also depends on context, which is difficult to assess algorithmically. In a hallway for example, the entrance area is more important to focus on than the walls. A surveillance video of a parking lot might also include parts of the adjacent road which could be outside of the scope of surveillance. It is thus important to include user input into the decision making process. We model the user input as a map $\mathcal{U}$ of the same size as $\mathcal{S}^\omega$ which gives an offset to the sensitivity. Since this information is mostly static, it needs to be defined only once when the system is set up.

In order to not display the same region over and over, we give a penalty to the sensitivity of a region that has been presented to the operator before. Our penalty map $\mathcal{P}^\omega$ has values between zero and one with higher values meaning a higher penalty. After having selected an ROI to display, we calculate a 2D Gaussian function for the chosen ROI. Its mean is the center of the ROI, and the variances are chosen relative to the width and height of the ROI. This Gaussian function is added to $\mathcal{P}^\omega$. The process of penalizing a previously chosen ROI is illustrated in Figure 2. Every ω frames when a new ROI is selected, the penalty map is multiplied by a factor $\alpha \in [0, 1]$ to decrease the penalty over time. The sensitivity of a selected ROI is thus reduced at first, and its sensitivity then slowly increases back to its original value.

When a new $\mathcal{S}^\omega$ is available – once every ω frames – it is combined with the user input and the penalty map to form a final decision map. The decision map $\mathcal{D}^\omega$ is defined as

$$\mathcal{D}^\omega = (1 - \mathcal{P}^\omega) \cdot (\mathcal{S}^\omega + \mathcal{U}). \quad (1)$$

All operators used here process the maps pixel-wise.

For the purpose of ROI detection, $\mathcal{D}^\omega$ is converted into a binary image by applying a low threshold. Morphological operations are then used to reduce noise. Next, the system extracts contours from white areas in the binary image and merges adjacent contours if necessary. The bounding boxes of the connected contours are the potential regions of interest to zoom into. For each potential ROI, we compute a decision value. It is calculated by summing up all values inside the ROI in the original unthresholded $\mathcal{D}^\omega$. This allows ranking of the potential ROIs according to the amount of sensitivity they contain. The ROI with the highest decision value is selected and sent to the presentation component.

2.3 Presentation

The presentation component creates the output frames that are sent to the remote operator. At the beginning of each block of ω frames, it is given an ROI for the entire block. The frames of the block are contained in the buffer. Note that the ROI selection may give rectangular areas with an arbitrary aspect ratio. The aspect ratio $\phi = w/h$ of the ROI is generally not identical to the target aspect ratio ϕ_t. $\phi < \phi_t$ means that the chosen ROI is too high. We thus increase the width of the ROI as $w = \phi_t h$, so that the aspect ratios match again. The case $\phi > \phi_t$ is handled analogously. This guarantees that the selected region is fully contained in the created view.

The presentation of a block of frames always starts and ends with a fully zoomed out overview. Within the block, it zooms into the ROI, stays zoomed in for a certain amount of time and then zooms out again. Zooming is implemented as an interpolation between the parameters of the full frame and the chosen ROI. We use cubic spine interpolation for smooth zooming. Like this, an interpolated ROI for the current frame is calculated. The presenter takes the oldest frame from the buffer and crops it according to the interpolated ROI. The cropped frame is then scaled to the target resolution and sent over the network.

3. EXPERIMENTAL RESULTS

The main goal of our approach is to resize the video from a surveillance camera so that it can be used for remote monitoring on a mobile device with a small screen size. We evaluated our approach in a user study with 22 male and 7 female non-expert subjects. The average age was 25 with a standard deviation of 4. Four surveillance videos with a resolution of 1920×1080 and a length of one minute were used. They were taken from the VIRAT database, which was designed for performance assessment of activity detection algorithms [6]. Representative frames from the four scenarios are shown in Figure 3.

As the target resolution, we chose 384×216, which is $1/5$ of the original resolution. Three different videos of the target resolution were created for each scenario: A scaled

Statement	Scaled	Pan Only	Proposed
1	3.1 (1.4)	3.3 (1.0)	4.5 (0.9)
2	2.6 (1.2)	3.3 (0.8)	4.3 (1.0)
3	2.6 (1.2)	3.2 (1.0)	4.5 (0.8)
4	3.7 (1.0)	3.1 (1.0)	2.1 (1.2)
5	2.7 (1.3)	3.3 (1.0)	4.4 (0.8)

Table 1: Agreement scores for the five statements and the three approaches. The values are averaged over the four scenes and all participants, with the standard deviation given in parentheses.

down version of the original video which served as a baseline for the evaluation ("scaled"), the video created by the proposed method ("proposed"), and a video that uses the proposed ROI selection, but only pans between the ROIs without zooming out to the full overview in between ("pan only").

The users were given a brief introduction. Their task was to assume the role of a security operator who monitors the area and detects abnormal activities. All three versions of the scenario were shown next to each other simultaneously. After watching the videos, the users were given five statements about each version. They had to rate each statement on a scale from 1 (strongly disagree) to 5 (strongly agree). The statements were:

1. the video provides full coverage of the site,
2. the video provides all details of the site,
3. the camera motion was helpful in monitoring the area,
4. the video is boring, and
5. it is easy to understand the activities in the video.

The website we used for the study can be found at [1].

Table 1 shows the results of our study. Since the users' ratings were similar across all four scenarios, we only show the averaged values here. From the table, it can be seen that our approach achieves better results than the two compared methods in all five considered categories. Note that for statement 4 (the video is boring), a lower value is better. Out of the two other approaches (scaled and pan only), the video that pans between the ROIs seems to be more useful. This is due to the small output resolution. The scaled version was too small to be useful for monitoring. In statements 1 to 3 and 5, our approach obtains an average score between 4.3 and 4.5. This indicates that the participants of the study generally found our retargeting approach to provide videos that were helpful in the given surveillance task.

4. CONCLUSIONS

We proposed a smart assistant for remote video surveillance on a handheld device. A high-resolution surveillance video was retargeted to a smaller resolution to be displayable on a small screen and save bandwidth. This was done by first identifying regions of interest in the video and then zooming into these regions one after another. An overview of

[1]https://sites.google.com/site/acm2014ssa/

Figure 3: Example frames from the four scenes used in the study. All are outdoor surveillance scenes and the camera is static. The fourth scene (bottom right) is a parking lot. Here, the adjacent road was out of the scope of surveillance. By specifying user input, the motion outside the parking lot is ignored when selecting an ROI.

the entire sceen is given periodically to provide the necessary context to the operator. The results of our user study show, that the proposed method provides full coverage of the scene while also showing the detail that is necessary for understanding the activities therein. The users generally reported that the smart assistant system was helpful in remote monitoring a scene under surveillance.

5. REFERENCES

[1] N. Dalal and B. Triggs. Histograms of oriented gradients for human detection. In *Proc. of the Computer Vision and Pattern Recognition*, volume 1, pages 886–893. IEEE, 2005.

[2] H. El-Alfy, D. Jacobs, and L. Davis. Multi-scale video cropping. In *Proc. of the 15th int. conf. on Multimedia*, pages 97–106. ACM, 2007.

[3] M. Grundmann, V. Kwatra, M. Han, and I. Essa. Discontinuous seam-carving for video retargeting. In *Proc. of the CVPR*, pages 569–576. IEEE, 2010.

[4] S. Kopf, T. Haenselmann, J. Kiess, B. Guthier, and W. Effelsberg. Algorithms for video retargeting. *MTAP*, 51(2):819–861, 2011.

[5] F. Liu and M. Gleicher. Video retargeting: automating pan and scan. In *Proc. of the 14th int. conf. on Multimedia*, pages 241–250. ACM, 2006.

[6] S. Oh, A. Hoogs, A. Perera, N. Cuntoor, C.-C. Chen, J. T. Lee, S. Mukherjee, et al. A large-scale benchmark dataset for event recognition in surveillance video. In *Proc. of the CVPR*, pages 3153–3160. IEEE, 2011.

[7] C. Stauffer and W. E. L. Grimson. Adaptive background mixture models for real-time tracking. In *Proc. of the CVPR*, volume 2. IEEE, 1999.

[8] P. Viola and M. Jones. Rapid object detection using a boosted cascade of simple features. In *Proc. of the Computer Vision and Pattern Recognition*, volume 1, pages I–511 – I–518. IEEE, 2001.

[9] Y.-S. Wang, J.-H. Hsiao, O. Sorkine, and T.-Y. Lee. Scalable and coherent video resizing with per-frame optimization. In *ToG*, volume 30, page 88. ACM, 2011.

Modeling the Interest-Forgetting Curve for Music Recommendation *

Jun Chen Chaokun Wang Jianmin Wang
School of Software, Tsinghua University, Beijing 100084, China
chenjun12@mails.thu.edu.cn, chaokun@tsinghua.edu.cn, jimwang@tsinghua.edu.cn

ABSTRACT

Music recommendation plays a key role in our daily lives as well as in the multimedia industry. This paper adapts the memory forgetting curve to model the human *interest-forgetting curve* for music recommendations based on the observation of recency effects in people's listening to music. Two music recommendation methods are proposed using this model with respect to the sequence-based and the IFC-based transition probabilities, respectively. We also bring forward a learning method to approximate the global optimal or personalized interest-forgetting speed(s). The experimental results show that our methods can significantly improve the accuracy in music recommendations. Meanwhile, the IFC-based method outperforms the sequence-based method when recommendation list is short at each time.

Categories and Subject Descriptors

H.3.3 [**Information Storage and Retrieval**]: Information Search and Retrieval—*Information filtering*.

Keywords

Music Recommendation; Interest-Forgetting Curve; Recency Effect.

1. INTRODUCTION

In time domain, people's consumption of music can be grouped by playlists (equivalently sessions, in this work) which consist of user preferred songs in an order. The analysis on these music playlists gives us insights on how listening behaviors could reveal people's emotional states, user contexts and short-term preferences [13]. Music recommendations [4, 9], especially the context-aware branches [5, 8, 10, 12], directly benefit from the analysis of user's playlists. The work in [8] first infers latent topics from the frequently used tags for each song, and mines sequential patterns of latent topics for recommendations. The research in [10] clusters users into groups and separately computes song-to-song transition probabilities within each group, based on which the recommendations are conducted using random walks. The performance of these methods heavily depends on user contexts which can be inferred from mobile sensor data [12], user articles [5], or user interactions with systems [10].

Besides, *recency effects* have also been observed in people's listening to music [1, 7], where people have a tendency to recall the recently heard songs other than those heard long ago. A straightforward intuition is that songs consumed more recently contribute more to the understanding of current user context, which leads to non-increasing weights as the consumption timestamps get farther from now. Thus, we believe it is reasonable and appropriate to use the forgetting curve [2, 6] to model this feature.

Given a user's current music playlist, we would like to explore the impacts of the heard songs upon the user's next listening choice. However, since the short-term music preference of users usually changes rapidly, it is nontrivial to predict what (s)he likes next, especially when the playlist contains dissimilar songs of different genres, from different artists and periods. Many existing works uniformly or randomly initialize the impacts of the heard songs in recommendations [3, 8, 10]. But it could lead to information loss compared with weighted initializations considering the recency effects in people's listening to music. This paper attempts to model how recently heard music pieces affect people's next listening choices by incorporating the concept of *interest-forgetting curve* which is inspired by human's memory forgetting curve. Our method models the interest losing rate of users, and assigns descending initial weights to the heard songs in playlists in determining the next listening choice.

The main contributions of this paper include:

- We brought forward a novel *interest-forgetting curve model* with two music recommendation methods, which could more accurately characterize how recently heard songs affect people's next listening choices.
- We also proposed a learning method to approximate the global optimal or personalized *interest-forgetting speed(s)*.
- The experimental results showed that our methods outperformed two widely used baselines in music recommendations.

2. INTEREST-FORGETTING CURVE

The memory forgetting curve was first introduced by Ebbinghaus [6] as expressed by an exponential formula (Eq. 1). The

*Corresponding author: Chaokun Wang.

MM'14, November 03 - 07 2014, Orlando, FL, USA.

http://dx.doi.org/10.1145/2647868.2654954.

retention, R, of memory on a certain event decreases while time elapses (i.e., t increases) from the happening of that event. The strength of memory, S, controls how fast we forget about events. The forgetting curve has been studied to help people obtain lasting memories. For example, S can be strengthened through people's over-learning on events, which leads to a shallower forgetting curve.

$$R = e^{-\frac{t}{S}}. \tag{1}$$

There are also some variants of forgetting curve models such as the power-law curve and the S-shaped curve [2]. We'd like to adapt these aforementioned forgetting curves to model the recency effects in people's listening to music to improve the recommendation accuracy. Therefore, we bring forward the concept of *Interest-Forgetting Curve* (abbr. IFC) which is expressed as,

$$R = e^{-\alpha t}, \quad \alpha \in \mathbb{R}_{\geq 0}, \tag{2}$$

where t is the time interval from the happening of an event till now, and α is a non-negative real parameter to control the interest-forgetting speed. The larger the value of α is, the faster the interest loses as time elapses. Particularly, if $\alpha = 0$, then IFC is degenerated to the uniform weighted model, i.e., no interest on the past events is lost. IFC characterizes how much interest of a happened event is retained by now. The more interest the heard song has retained, the more likely it will affect people's next listening choice according to the recency effects. For example, if current time is t_c and we heard song s_i and s_j at time t_{s_i} and t_{s_j} ($t_{s_j}<t_{s_i}<t_c$), respectively, then their retentions by now are $R_{s_i} = e^{-\alpha(t_c - t_{s_i})}$ and $R_{s_j} = e^{-\alpha(t_c - t_{s_j})}$, respectively, and s_i is considered more likely to have an effect upon the next listening choice compared with s_j since $R_{s_i} \geq R_{s_j}$. Besides, if we compute individual interest-forgetting speed α_u for each user u, we'll get a personalized IFC model.

The exponential representation of IFC in Eq. 2 can be extended to other forgetting curve models to compute the interest retention of the heard songs. We used this basic and widely accepted exponential form in this work.

3. MUSIC RECOMMENDATION WITH IFC MODEL

3.1 Problem Formulation

Let $\mathcal{S} = \{s_1, s_2, ..., s_{|\mathcal{S}|}\}$ denote the set of songs, and $\mathcal{U} = \{u_1, u_2, ..., u_{|\mathcal{U}|}\}$ be the set of users in the data set. Songs are consumed one after another in a playlist by a user. The directed transition probabilities between songs are represented by an $|\mathcal{S}| \times |\mathcal{S}|$ row-normalized asymmetric matrix M where entry $M(s_i, s_j) \geq 0$ is the probability of listening song s_j right after listening s_i. Each user u has a set of music playlists, $\mathcal{P}^u = \{p_1^u, p_2^u, ..., p_{l_u}^u\}$, while each playlist contains a sequence of ordered songs, $p_i^u \in \mathcal{S}^*$[1].

Our music recommendation problem can be formulated as: Given u's current playlist $\hat{p^u}$ (current session has not expired yet), past playlists set $\mathcal{P}^u$ of u, and the transition probability matrix M, we recommend the Top-K most probable songs for u to listen in the next considering u's oblivion of interest on past songs. The recommended songs are selected by their observing probabilities (Eq. 3). To avoid the trivial repetition of a same song, we only recommend songs which have not yet been observed in the current playlist.

[1] $\mathcal{S}^*$ is the Kleene closure of the song set $\mathcal{S}$.

$$s_{rec} = \operatorname*{argmax}_{s_i \in \mathcal{S}} \Pr(s_i | \hat{p^u}, \mathcal{P}^u, M). \tag{3}$$

3.2 Recommendation Framework

We define the probability of recommending song s_i as the sum of probabilities to visit s_i via any song s_j appeared in the current playlist (Eq. 4).

$$\Pr(s_i | \hat{p^u}, \mathcal{P}^u, M) = \sum_{s_j \in \hat{p^u}} \Pr(s_j | \hat{p^u}) M(s_j, s_i). \tag{4}$$

Since we do not recommend the observed songs in the current playlist as described in Section 3.1, the above computation should be limited on a small set of candidates as,

$$\mathcal{C}_{\hat{p^u}} = \{s_x | \exists s_j \in \hat{p^u} \wedge M(s_j, s_x) > 0 \wedge s_x \notin \hat{p^u}\}. \tag{5}$$

$\mathcal{C}_{\hat{p^u}}$ contains the unobserved songs in the neighborhood of $\hat{p^u}$. Thus, $M(s_j, s_i)$ in Eq. 4 should be replaced by its neighborhood-normalized value $M_{\mathcal{C}_{\hat{p^u}}}(s_j, s_i)$ (Eq. 6).

$$M_{\mathcal{C}_{\hat{p^u}}}(s_j, s_i) = \frac{M(s_j, s_i)}{\sum_{s_x \in \mathcal{C}_{\hat{p^u}}} M(s_j, s_x)}. \tag{6}$$

We can make our recommendations based on the probabilities of songs to be observed using the aforementioned equations. The factor of *interest-forgetting* is implanted into the definitions of $M(s_j, s_i)$ and $\Pr(s_j | \hat{p^u})$, which will be discussed in detail by modeling IFC next.

3.3 Modeling IFC in Recommendation

3.3.1 Computing Transition Probabilities

The transition probability $M(s_i, s_j)$ is very important to represent directed weighted pairwise relations between songs. We proposed two definitions of $M(s_i, s_j)$ with respect to our two recommendation methods.

Sequence-based transition probabilities. Let $\{\cdot\}_{seq}$ be the representation of a sequence. We say $\{s_i, s_j\}_{seq} \subseteq p$ *iff* $\{s_i, s_j\}_{seq}$ is a subsequence of playlist p. Then, we present the sequence-based $M(s_i, s_j)$ as,

$$M_{SEQ}(s_i, s_j) = \frac{\sum_{u \in \mathcal{U}} \sum_{p \in \mathcal{P}^u} \mathbb{1}_{\{s_i, s_j\}_{seq} \subseteq p}}{\sum_{u \in \mathcal{U}} \sum_{p \in \mathcal{P}^u} \mathbb{1}_{\{s_i\}_{seq} \subseteq p}}, \tag{7}$$

where $\mathbb{1}_{cond}$ is the indicator function which returns 1 when *cond* is satisfied and otherwise returns 0. This definition captures the percentage of sequential co-occurrences of songs.

IFC-based transition probabilities. By considering the oblivion of interest on past songs, we bring forward the IFC-based $M(s_i, s_j)$ as,

$$M_{IFC}(s_i, s_j) = \frac{\sum_{u \in \mathcal{U}} \sum_{p \in \mathcal{P}^u} e^{-\alpha(p(s_j) - p(s_i))} \cdot \mathbb{1}_{\{s_i, s_j\}_{seq} \subseteq p}}{\sum_{s_x} \sum_{u \in \mathcal{U}} \sum_{p \in \mathcal{P}^u} e^{-\alpha(p(s_x) - p(s_i))} \cdot \mathbb{1}_{\{s_i, s_x\}_{seq} \subseteq p}}, \tag{8}$$

where $p(s_i)$ represents the position index of s_i in p, and α is the interest-forgetting speed. Without loss of generality, the position index starts with 1 from the first heard song in the playlist and increases by 1 when jumping to the next song each time. This IFC-based definition takes the relative listening time steps into accounts when computing the relations between songs in line with Eq. 2. Compared with $M_{SEQ}(s_i, s_j)$, $M_{IFC}(s_i, s_j)$ could be more accurate to describe the pairwise relations between songs, but its performance is apt to be affected by the setting of α. The effectiveness of these two methods and the influence of α will be evaluated in later experiments.

3.3.2 Computing Prior Probabilities

Based on the properties of IFC, the more recently the songs are heard, the more important they are supposed to be to affect people's next listening choice, and the higher prior probabilities they should have. According to Eq. 2, we proposed our definition of prior probabilities,

$$\Pr(s_j|\hat{p^u}) = \frac{e^{-\alpha(|\hat{p^u}|-\hat{p^u}(s_j))}}{\sum_{s_x\in\hat{p^u}} e^{-\alpha(|\hat{p^u}|-\hat{p^u}(s_x))}}, \quad (9)$$

where $|\hat{p^u}|$ is the number of songs in $\hat{p^u}$ while $\hat{p^u}(s_j)$ is the position index of s_j in $\hat{p^u}$. This definition gives descending prior probabilities to the heard songs in current session as their listening timestamps get farther from now, which is in line with the properties of IFC in Section 2.

3.3.3 Learning Interest-Forgetting Speed

Throughout the modeling of $M(s_i, s_j)$ and $\Pr(s_j|\hat{p^u})$ based on the exponential form of forgetting curve in Eq. 2, α is the only parameter remaining unknown. Though Eq. 2 can be replaced by more complex forgetting curve models [2], we simplify the problem here and leave the extensions in our future work. If α is properly set, the IFC model will be more accurate to represent the weighted importance of the heard songs in determining people's next listening choice. Here we proposed a learning method to compute the near-optimal value of α. Given a set of training playlists, our intuitive goal is to maximize the average probability of correctly recommending the last song in each playlist p while using the rest $|p|-1$ songs as input. The objective function is shown in Eq. 10, where $\mathcal{P}_{train}$ is the set of training playlists, $\hat{s^p}$ is the last song in playlist p, $\setminus$ is the set minus operator, and $M_{\mathcal{C}_p}$ is the neighborhood-normalized transition probability matrix (Eq. 6).

$$\begin{aligned} G(\alpha) &= \max_{\alpha\in\Re_{\geq 0}} \frac{1}{|\mathcal{P}_{train}|} \sum_{p\in\mathcal{P}_{train}} \Pr(\hat{s^p}|p\setminus\{\hat{s^p}\}, \mathcal{P}_{train}, M_{\mathcal{C}_p}) \quad (10) \\ &= \max_{\alpha\in\Re_{\geq 0}} \frac{1}{|\mathcal{P}_{train}|} \sum_{p\in\mathcal{P}_{train}} \sum_{s_j\in p\setminus\{\hat{s^p}\}} \Pr(s_j|p\setminus\{\hat{s^p}\}) M_{\mathcal{C}_p}(s_j, \hat{s^p}). \end{aligned}$$

Since the transition probability matrix M is considered to be fixed for a given data set, we therefore only need to learn a proper α for $\Pr(s_j|p)$. Thus, when using $M_{IFC}(s_i, s_j)$ as the representation of transition probabilities, we first compute $M_{IFC}(s_i, s_j)$ with a pre-defined α_{pre} (e.g., $\alpha_{pre} = 1.0$), and then we conduct the learning method to get a near-optimal α for $\Pr(s_j|p)$. Since $\Pr(s_j|p)$ (Eq. 9) is derivable on α, $G(\alpha)$ is therefore also derivable on α. However, it is difficult to compute the optimal α given $\frac{\partial G(\alpha)}{\partial \alpha} = 0$, because the partial derivative is the sum of many different α-related exponential components. But we can use a gradient method to get a near-optimal α value by iteratively increasing or decreasing α according to the sign of the partial derivative.

Moreover, the proposed learning method can be extended to compute personalized interest-forgetting speed α_u. If we replace $\mathcal{P}_{train}$ with $\mathcal{P}^u$ in Eq. 10, we will get personalized α_u for each individual user u with the minimum effort. The personalized IFC model is more suitable than IFC model if the data set is considered to be personalized.

4. EXPERIMENTS

Now that we have developed our music recommendation methods based on the IFC model, we turn to conduct experiments to evaluate the performance of our method compared with the baselines. We begin by introducing the experimental settings, and then analyze the evaluation results.

4.1 Experimental Settings

We conducted the experiments on the Last.fm data set [2] which contains users' history of binary music consumption with timestamps. This data set consists of 10,244,067 music listening records collected from 992 users on 964,463 songs. We partitioned each user's listening history into playlists with a timeout bound as 30 minutes which is an empirical setting — neither too long nor too short. If the idle time between two adjacent listening records is beyond 30 minutes, these two listening records are partitioned into the former and the latter playlists, respectively. Inside a playlist, if the idle period between any two adjacent listening records is less than 30 seconds, we assumed the user disliked the former song, and we removed the former listening record from the playlist. If one song appeared more than once in a same playlist, we only preserved its first occurrence and removed the rest repetitions. Furthermore, to minimize the inaccuracy caused by very short playlists, we only considered those playlists with at least 5 distinct songs. For playlists containing more than 30 distinct songs, we only preserve their first 30 distinct songs as playlists. There are totally 599,353 playlists generated from the data set. We randomly sampled 67,911 playlists as the test set which covers all users. The training set consists of the rest 531,442 playlists. Apparently, the larger the training set is, the more accurate the IFC will be to model people's listening preferences.

Since we do not predict ratings on songs like [9] and no other information besides binary listening records is available in this data set, we compared our method with two widely used baselines — the Neighborhood method (abbr. NH) [3] and the Sequential Pattern method (abbr. SP) [8]. NH and SP are similar to our work and only use binary listening records as input. NH computes Top-N neighbors for the input playlist using cosine similarity, e.g., $N = 100$. It recommends songs with the highest frequencies among the Top-N neighbors. SP firstly mines the sequential patterns using PrefixSpan method [11], and then recommends songs with the largest confidence by appending the candidate songs to the tail of the input sequence. For the SP method, we conducted experiments with different supports of frequencies and window sizes, e.g., SP-s5w3 represents the SP method with support as 5 and window size as 3.

4.2 Evaluations

We first evaluated the accuracy performance of our method compared with the baselines. The training set was used to construct the transition probability matrix M, and to learn the near-optimal forgetting speed α. The evaluation was performed on the test set. We evaluated the methods using the average hit ratio which is the average ratio of correctly predicting the last heard song in each playlist p while using its rest $|p|-1$ listening records as input. Two implementations of M defined in Section 3.3.1 were both evaluated. The method using $M_{SEQ}(s_i, s_j)$ and $\Pr(s_j|\hat{p^u})$ is denoted as IFCM-SEQ, while the one using $M_{IFM}(s_i, s_j)$ and $\Pr(s_j|\hat{p^u})$ is denoted as IFCM-IFC.

Fig. 1 shows the comparison on accuracy performance. It is evident that our methods have significant improvement

[2]http://www.dtic.upf.edu/~ocelma/MusicRecommendation-Dataset/lastfm-1K.html

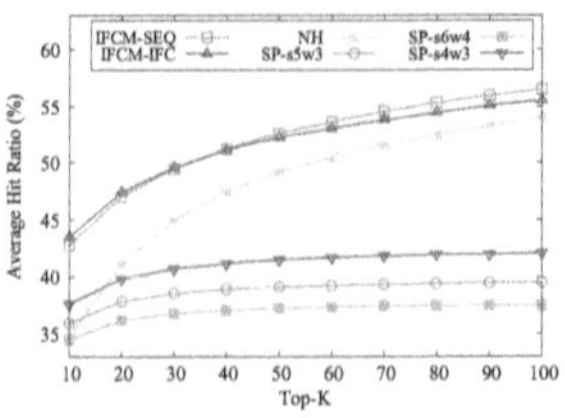

Figure 1: The comparison on accuracy with the baselines ($\alpha = 0.5$).

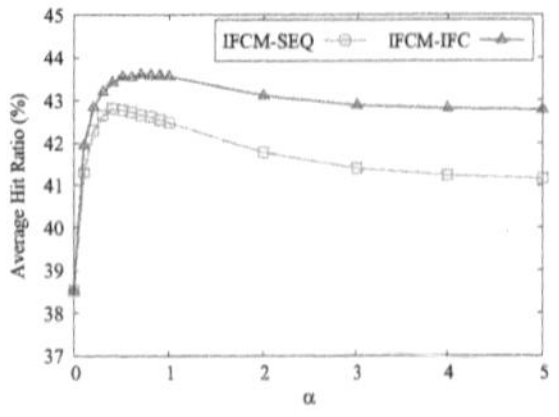

Figure 2: The impact of α on the accuracy performance (Top-10).

on the average hit ratio compared with the baselines, especially when only a small number of songs are recommended each time. Usually, recommender systems are not expected to give a large number of recommendations for a user each time, which will jeopardize the user friendliness. IFCM-IFC dominates IFCM-SEQ in accuracy when Top-K≤40. This proves that IFCM-IFC stresses more of interest loss in computing transition probabilities and therefore promotes the rankings of related songs. As we have pointed out, the higher accuracy the method has when only a small number of songs are recommended each time, the higher practical value the method will be of. Thus, we consider IFCM-IFC as a little optimization based on IFCM-SEQ. In average, our methods (IFCM-SEQ and IFCM-IFC) have about 5% absolute improvement in average hit ratios compared with NH, and even larger compared with SP.

Fig. 2 illustrates the influence of α on the average hit ratio of Top-10 results. The larger the value of α is, the faster the interest is forgetting and the more significant recency effect the model assumes. However, the decline of curves in Fig. 2 after $\alpha > 1$ elucidates that over-assumption on the recency effect could also fail the IFC model. The optimal setting of α is around 0.5 which is also the value obtained using our learning method. We can see the influence of α is smooth when $\alpha \geq 0.2$, especially for IFCM-IFC. Thus, the proposed method based on IFC model is considered to be robust.

We also evaluated the accuracy performance of our method given different lengths of input playlists (Fig. 3). The distribution of the length of playlists in the training set and the test set is illustrated in Fig. 3(a). Generally, there are more short playlists than the long ones since the number of playlists drops as the playlist length increases. This observation fits the real situation that most people usually listen to a small number of distinct songs during one session. Fig. 3(b) shows the average hit ratio of our method within the different-length groups of playlists. Interestingly, we observed higher average hit ratio in the group of playlists whose length is between 10 and 14. Beyond or below this range, it leads to lower average hit ratios, and worst in the >= 30 group (playlists with no less than 30 distinct songs). We may conclude that the effect of human retention of interest has upper and lower boundaries, and inside the range, IFC model has the best performance, while outside the range, IFC model may suffer from random effects (below the lower bound) or noises (beyond the upper bound).

In sum, the experimental results show that IFC model can significantly improve the accuracy performance in music recommendations.

5. CONCLUSIONS

In this paper, we proposed a novel music recommendation method based on the IFC model to predict a user's

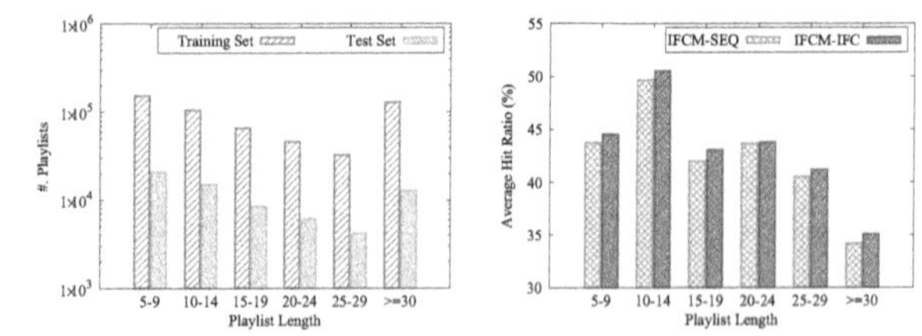

(a) (b)

Figure 3: (a) Distribution of playlists with different length in both the training set and the test set. (b) Accuracy performance in different length groups of playlists (Top-10).

next choice considering the recency effects in people's listening to music. We presented the recommendation framework with two open ends — the computation of transition probabilities and prior probabilities. We brought forward the sequence-based and the IFC-based solutions to our problem. The experimental results showed a significant improvement in the accuracy of our music recommendation method compared with the baselines. In the future, we will consider to improve the IFC model by considering more other existing forgetting curve models.

6. ACKNOWLEDGEMENT

This work was supported by the National Natural Science Foundation of China (No. 61373023, No. 61170064) and the National High Technology Research and Development Program of China (No. 2013AA013204).

7. REFERENCES

[1] A. Anderson, R. Kumar, A. Tomkins, and S. Vassilvitskii. The dynamics of repeat consumption. In *WWW*, pages 419–430, 2014.

[2] L. Averell and A. Heathcote. The form of the forgetting curve and the fate of memories. *Journal of Mathematical Psychology*, 55:25–35, 2011.

[3] G. Bonnin and D. Jannach. A comparison of playlist generation strategies for music recommendation and a new baseline scheme. In *Workshops at the AAAI Conference on Artificial Intelligence*, pages 16–23, 2013.

[4] J. Bu, S. Tan, C. Chen, C. Wang, H. Wu, L. Zhang, and X. He. Music recommendation by unified hypergraph: combining social media information and music content. In *ACM Multimedia*, pages 391–400, 2010.

[5] C.-M. Chen, M.-F. Tsai, J.-Y. Liu, and Y.-H. Yang. Using emotional context from article for contextual music recommendation. In *ACM Multimedia*, pages 649–652, 2013.

[6] H. Ebbinghaus. *Memory; A Contribution to Experimental Psychology*. New York by Teachers College, Columbia University, 1885.

[7] R. Greene and A. Samuel. Recency and suffix effects in serial recall of musical stimuli. *J Exp Psychol Learn Mem Cogn*, 12(4):517–524, 1986.

[8] N. Hariri, B. Mobasher, and R. Burke. Context-aware music recommendation based on latent topic sequential patterns. In *RecSys*, pages 131–138, 2012.

[9] N. Koenigstein, G. Dror, and Y. Koren. Yahoo! music recommendations: modeling music ratings with temporal dynamics and item taxonomy. In *RecSys*, pages 165–172, 2011.

[10] N. Natarajan, D. Shin, and I. S. Dhillon. Which app will you use next? collaborative filtering with interactional context. In *RecSys*, pages 201–208, 2013.

[11] J. Pei, J. Han, B. Mortazavi-Asl, H. Pinto, Q. Chen, U. Dayal, and M.-C. Hsu. Prefixspan: mining sequential patterns effectively by prefix-projected pattern growth. In *ICDE*, pages 215–224, 2001.

[12] X. Wang, D. Rosenblum, and Y. Wang. Context-aware mobile music recommendation for daily activities. In *ACM Multimedia*, pages 99–108, 2012.

[13] Y.-H. Yang and J.-Y. Liu. Quantitative study of music listening behavior in a social and affective context. *IEEE Transactions on Multimedia*, 15(6):1304–1315, 2013.

Learning to Assess Image Retargeting

Bahetiyaer Bare, Ke Li, Weiyi Wang, Bo Yan
School of Computer Science
Shanghai Key Laboratory of Intelligent Information Processing
Fudan University, Shanghai, China
byan@fudan.edu.cn

ABSTRACT

Content-aware image retargeting enables images to fit different devices with various aspect ratios while preserving salient contents. Meanwhile, assessing the quality of image retargeting and unifying both subjective and objective evaluation have become a prominent challenge. In this paper, we propose an image quality assessment based on Radial Basis Function (RBF) neural network. We propose a new feature of image retargeting evaluation, which adapts structural similarity (SSIM) and saliency. By also including other existing features, we build a neural network to assess the quality of the retargeted image. The neural network is trained to combine the above-mentioned features. The accuracy of our proposed assessment is verified by simulations and it possesses huge practical significance.

Categories and Subject Descriptors

I.3.3 [**Computer Graphics**]: Picture/Image Generation—*Display algorithms*

General Terms

Algorithms

Keywords

Image retargeting; Machine learning; RBF neural network; SSIM; SIFT.

1. INTRODUCTION

As the diversity of display device such as mobile phones and tablets escalates, the importance of image retargeting has become more and more significant. Image retargeting is a technique to adjust original images into user-defined size and simultaneously preserve the important regions or shapes. Based on the idea of expanding or shrinking the image by the regions which are not so important according to the computed energy map, retargeting method enables the viewers perceive as few changes in the retargeted image as possible. While image retargeting has become more and more common in our daily life, people requires higher quality of retargeted images or videos. The developed methods, such as seam carving [1], try to preserve the salient shape and content of the original image. Later on, multi-operator operation is proposed to obtain better results by combining multiple methods than those using only a single method [2]. By applying a sequence of operators including seam carving, scaling and cropping dynamically, every step of the process are promised to be the best one.

If the perceptual quality of images is high in value, the retargeted image is obtained with good quality. Thus evaluation of image retargeting is needed to aid image retargeting. Human subjective judgment of the images is the most reliable value for the assessment. Gathering a large number of judgers, subjective evaluation asks the judgers to give their judgment and opinions. Human assessment is ideal for the problem but it is time and money consuming and difficult to implement. There is no possibility to ask human to supervise the retargeting process. Thus object image assessment is desirable.

In [3], objective distance metrics such as color layout descriptor, bidirectional warping and edge histogram are used on assessing the quality of images. In [4] SSIM is proposed based on the assumption that HVS is highly adapted for extracting statistic structural information. And SSIM is one of the most successful metrics for image quality assessment according to the experimental result. But the methods mentioned above requires the distorted images to have the same size as the original image. Obviously, these methods can not be implemented directly to assess retargeted images.

Until now, much less has been done to evaluate the quality of retargeted images quality. To the best of our knowledge, only a few studies has been conducted to apply to retargeting case. In [5], global geometric structures and local pixel correspondence are established to evaluate the visual quality of the retargeted image. An objective metric simulating the human vision system is presented in the paper. The method uses a top-down manner that organize the features from global to local viewpoints which is a new objective assessment metric.

In this paper we intend to approximate the human assessment of retargeted image using machine learning method, and propose an image retargeting assessment method based on Radial Basis Function (RBF) neural network. We select a bag of features including a new feature of saliency weighted SSIM and several existing assessment features. Experi-

MM'14, November 03 - 07 2014, Orlando, FL, USA

http://dx.doi.org/10.1145/2647868.2654957 .

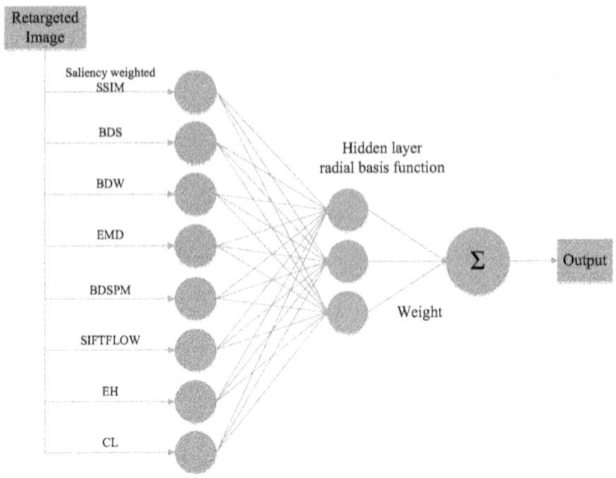

Figure 1: Framework of our approach.

mental results show that the assessment computed by our proposed method closely matches the subjective scores e-valuated by human, indicating that our method unifies the human perception.

The rest of the paper is organized as follows. Firstly, we briefly introduce the radial basis function neural network in Section 2. Then in Section 3, 8 features will be introduced. Among these features, we will highlight the SIFT weighted SSIM. Following it, we will present the training process of RBF neural network in Section 4. In Section 5 we will present the process of our experiment. The training and testing data will be presented and the results of our method will be demonstrated. In addition, our method will be compared with the existed retargeting assessment approach. Finally, we draw our conclusions in Section 6.

2. RBF NEURAL NETWORK

Subject assessment is time-consuming and expensive thus it is not practical to assess quality by human. But we can consider the obtained subjective score as the ground truth of the image perceptual quality. Using machine learning method, we can train specific models to accomplish the retargeting assessment. In this paper, we choose RBF neural network to learn the pattern of subjective assessment. While considering the ground truth (subjective score) as the output of the network, we regard objective assessment together with the saliency weighted SSIM as the input of the neural network. We adapt the SSIM to the retargeting assessment case to achieve better results.

Fig. 1 shows the framework of our approach. In this paper we make following contributions:

- We adapt the RBF neural network to learn the model of retargeting assessment.
- We propose a saliency weighted SSIM as a new feature of the neural network.

In the field of mathematical modeling, a radial basis function network is an artificial neural network that uses radial basis functions as activation functions. By training the neural network, we can obtain the output as a linear combination of radial basis function of the inputs and neuron parameters. A function is radial basis (RBF) if its output depends on (is a non-increasing function of) the distance of the input from a given stored vector.

There are three layers in a RBF network: an input layer, a hidden layer with a non-linear RBF activation function and a linear output layer. The input is modeled as a vector of real numbers and the output is then a scalar function of the input vector and is given by

$$\varphi(x) = \sum_{i=1}^{N} a_i \rho(\|x - c_i\|) \tag{1}$$

where N is the number of neurons in the hidden layer; c_i is the center vector for neuron i; and a_i is the weight of neuron i in the linear output neuron. The norm is typically taken to be the Euclidean distance and the radial basis function is commonly taken to be Gaussian.

$$\rho(\|x - c_i\|) = \exp\left[-\beta\|x - c_i\|^2\right] \tag{2}$$

For Gaussian RBF this sensitivity may be tuned by adjusting the spread σ, where a larger spread implies less sensitivity. An RBF network with enough hidden neurons can approximate any continuous function with arbitrary precision.

3. INPUT FEATURES

In this section we present the input features of the neural network. The features are the proposed saliency weighted SSIM and other seven existing assessment methods. After the learning process which will be presented in later section, we will get a combination of these features to build an assessment model to evaluate retargeted images.

We propose a new assessment feature called Saliency Weighted SSIM in this paper. SSIM is a method to measure the similarity between two images. It's a improvement to traditional methods like PSNR and MSE. SSIM consider image degradation as perceived change in structural information. Thus it has better performance than the methods that estimate perceived errors. But SSIM requires the distorted image having the same size as the original image. Thus S-SIM cannot be implemented directly to image retargeting assessment. To handle this problem, we use scale invariant feature transform (SIFT) [6] to aid the SSIM algorithm to assess the images of different sizes.

Given an original image and a distorted image, two scale spaces $SP(I_{original})$ and $SP(I_{retarget})$ are constructed. Using the local extrema detection method mentioned in [6] we can detect key points in the images. The image is convolved with Gaussian filters at different scales, and then the difference of successive Gaussian-blurred images are taken. Key points are then taken as $maxima/minima$ of the difference of Gaussians that occur at multiple scales. The low contrast key points or hose are poorly localized along a edge are rejected. After that, each key point is assigned one or more orientations based on local image gradient directions. Thus the key point descriptor can be achieved.

We match the key points in original image and retargeted image. An example of the matching is illustrated in the Fig. 2. Assuming there are $nPair$ matched pairs of key points, we propose a simplified, non-weighted similarity metric:

$$Sim_{non-w}(I_{ori}, I_{ret}) = \frac{1}{nPair} \sum_{i=1}^{nPair} SSIM\left(p_i, p_i^{'}\right) \tag{3}$$

Figure 2: An example of key point matching.

where p_i is a key point in original image and p'_i is corresponding key point in the retargeted image. $SSIM()$ is the SSIM metric using a local 9×9 square window. The more similar two images are, the more correspondences between two images are.

Considering the human vision system is more sensitive to salient regions and is likely to focus on the salient objects, not all the matched pixels have the same importance. Thus we use saliency to improve the similarity algorithm proposed above. As mentioned, the SSIM uses the local 9×9 square window to compute the similarity, we calculate the average saliency in that 9×9 window and weigh the similarity with the average saliency. Thus the weight of each window is set to be

$$\omega_i = \frac{1}{n} \sum_{p_j \in window_i} saliency(p_j) \tag{4}$$

where n is the number of all pixels in the window. In this case, the window is 9×9, thus n is set to 81. Thus the saliency weighted SSIM is

$$Sim_w(I_{ori}, I_{ret}) = \frac{1}{nPair} \sum_{i=1}^{nPair} \omega_i \times SSIM\left(p_i, p_i^{'}\right) \tag{5}$$

Other 7 features used in RetargetMe dataset [7] include: Bidirectional Similarity(BDS)[8], Bidirectional Warping(BDW) [2], SIFT Flow(SIFTflow) [9], Earth Moverąŕs Distance(EMD), Color Layout Descriptor Patch Match(BDSPM)[10], Edge Histogram(EH) [11], and Color Layout Descriptor(CL) [12].

4. TRAINING THE NEURAL NETWORK

In the training process, the following parameters are determined:

- The number of neurons in the hidden layer
- The center vectors in the hidden layer
- The radius of each RBF function in each dimension
- The weights applied to the RBF function.

To train the RBF network we need to follow a two-step algorithm. In the first step we choose the center vectors in the hidden layer. The centers can be randomly sampled from some sets of examples. And a third back-propagation step is applied to tune all the parameters.

The second step a linear model with coefficients ω_i to the hidden layer's outputs with respect to some objective function such as the least squares function. By choosing optimal weights, minimization of the least squares objective function optimizes accuracy of fit. Our object is to obtain the linear combination of the features above. The goal of learning is to estimate the linear weights of these features.

In this process, the input X is the above-mentioned eight features of the retargeted images processed by different retargeting methods, the output is the order of subjective votes of these images. After the training process, we can obtain the linear combination of the features and the model to assess retargeted images.

5. EVALUATION

5.1 Dataset

We conducted the following experiment to examine the validity of our proposed method. In this experiment we use the images and content on RetargetMe [7]. We choose the 37 analysis images which have users' voting analysis. For each image, eight different retargeting methods are applied thus every image has eight retargeted images generated by distinct methods. These eight retargeting methods include:

The dataset uses eight retargeting methods, including: Scaling(SCL), Cropping(CR), Seam Carving(SC) [1], Shiftmaps(SM) [13], Nonhomogeneous warping(WARP) [14], Streaming Video(SV) [15]. The complexity of computation of retargeting varies. But in our case the complexity is not taken into consideration.

Eight retargeting methods are ranked by the number of votes received. Thus for each original image we have a rank for the eight different retargeting methods. We regard the users' vote as the ground truth of the image perceptual quality. We will use these rankings to train our neural network as well as examine our proposed method.

5.2 Training and Testing

We apply the eight assessment method to each of the retargeted image in the database and obtaining 37×8 assessment results. We use 30 sets of images and assessment results to train the RBF network and the other 7 sets are used for testing.

In the training process, the RBF network takes the eight assessment results of a retargeted image as the input and the rank of the image. In this case:

$$X_i = result_i \tag{6}$$

$$Y \in \{1, 2, 3, 4, 5, 6, 7, 8\} \tag{7}$$

where $result_i$ is the evaluation of ith assessment method and Y is the rank of the image. After learning the 30×8 sets of data, we obtain the model of our assessment model.

According to the properties of RBF neural network, the model we obtained is a combination of these features. Thus when we assess the retargeted images using the model we learned, we can make a optimal choice on deciding the importance of each assessment methods and how we take the values computed with these methods.

In the testing process, we choose the remaining seven sets of data to test our algorithm. We evaluate each of the eight retargeted images using different approaches. These evaluations form the X vector which indicate the assessment of each approach waiting to be analyzed. And the RBF neural network takes these evaluation as inputs and gives a number of each of these eight images by using the model we have learned from the former 30 sets of data. In this process the

	SRCC			KRCC		
Metrics	Mean	STD	p-value	Mean	STD	p-value
BDS	0.0238	0.3701	0.8705	0.0306	0.2668	0.7717
BDW	0.068	0.3906	0.6612	0.0816	0.2718	0.4571
EMD	0.1667	0.5777	0.4742	0.1327	0.4507	0.4657
BDSPM	0.1122	0.4445	0.5289	0.0816	0.351	0.5609
SIFT FLOW	0.0782	0.437	0.6525	0.051	0.3394	0.7046
EH	-0.105	0.3693	0.4786	-0.061	0.284	0.5891
CL	-0.15	0.3091	0.2475	-0.112	0.2137	0.214
SSIM	0.0034	0.4236	0.9837	-0.041	0.3026	0.7334
Ours	0.4762	0.3686	0.0142	0.3571	0.3221	0.0262

Table 1: Comparison results. The first 30 set of images are training sets and the latter 7 sets are testing sets.

values are weighted and transformed in a non-linear manner and the output Y is determined by the processed values. After computing the output of the eight images, a ranking of eight methods is obtained.

5.3 Results and Comparison

For each of the seven original image, both subjective and objective rankings of the retargeted image is obtained to be compared. Kendall's rank-order correlation coefficient (KRCC) [16] and Spearman's rank-order correlation coefficient (SRCC) [17] are computed to measure the level of agreement between the subjective rankings and objective rankings obtained using different kinds of assessment method including the proposed one. In both case, higher correlation coefficient indicated higher agreement, and both measures ranges form -1 to 1. If the rank order is completely the same, the correlation coefficient will be 1.

For every assessment method, we compute the mean and standard deviation of the KRCC and SRCC values across all the seven test sets. Comparitions are made between our proposed method and other assessment approaches. The result is shown in Table 1. From this table, we can observe that our method outperforms all other objective assessment measures significantly. We can also observe that the average result of SRCC is around 0.4762, which means there are still much variations from subjective judgement.

6. CONCLUSION

In this paper we propose a new retargeting assessment method using radial basis function network and other assessment methods. We propose a saliency weighted SSIM to adapt SSIM to retargeting case. We also combine existing assessment methods to form the input vector of our radial basis function network. We use the images and rankings in RetargetMe dataset to train and test our method. Machine learning is implemented in retargeting case and achieves a good performance. Promising quality prediction is achieved in testing the trained neural network. However, more work needs to be done in areas such as other feature selection and other machine learning methods to better establish this method.

7. ACKNOWLEDGMENTS

This work is supported by NSFC (Grant No.: 61370158).

8. REFERENCES

[1] M. Rubinstein, A. Shamir, and S. Avidan. Improved seam carving for video retargeting. In *ACM Transactions on Graphics (TOG)*, volume 27, page 16, 2008.

[2] M. Rubinstein, A. Shamir, and S. Avidan. Multi-operator media retargeting. *ACM Transactions on Graphics (TOG)*, 28(3):1–11, 2009.

[3] Michael Rubinstein, Diego Gutierrez, Olga Sorkine, and Ariel Shamir. A comparative study of image retargeting. *ACM Transactions on Graphics (Proc. SIGGRAPH Asia)*, 29(5):160:1–160:10, 2010.

[4] Zhou Wang, Alan C Bovik, Hamid R Sheikh, and Eero P Simoncelli. Image quality assessment: From error visibility to structural similarity. *IEEE Transactions on Image Processing*, 13(4):600–612, 2004.

[5] Y.J. Liu, X. Luo, Y.M. Xuan, W.F. Chen, and X.L. Fu. Image retargeting quality assessment. In *Computer Graphics Forum*, volume 30, pages 583–592. Wiley Online Library, 2011.

[6] David G Lowe. Distinctive image features from scale-invariant keypoints. *International journal of computer vision*, 60(2):91–110, 2004.

[7] Michael Rubinstein, Diego Gutierrez, Olga Sorkine, and Ariel Shamir. A comparative study of image retargeting. *ACM Transactions on Graphics (Proc. SIGGRAPH Asia)*, 29(5):160:1–160:10, 2010.

[8] Denis Simakov, Yaron Caspi, Eli Shechtman, and Michal Irani. Summarizing visual data using bidirectional similarity. In *IEEE Conference on Computer Vision and Pattern Recognition (CVPR 2008)*, pages 1–8, 2008.

[9] Ce Liu, Jenny Yuen, Antonio Torralba, Josef Sivic, and William T Freeman. Sift flow: dense correspondence across different scenes. In *European Conference on Computer Vision (ECCV 2008)*, pages 28–42, 2008.

[10] Connelly Barnes, Eli Shechtman, Adam Finkelstein, and Dan Goldman. Patchmatch: a randomized correspondence algorithm for structural image editing. *ACM Transactions on Graphics-TOG*, 28(3):24, 2009.

[11] Bangalore S Manjunath, J-R Ohm, Vinod V. Vasudevan, and Akio Yamada. Color and texture descriptors. *IEEE Transactions on Circuits and Systems for Video Technology,*, 11(6):703–715, 2001.

[12] Eiji Kasutani and Akio Yamada. The MPEG-7 color layout descriptor: a compact image feature description for high-speed image/video segment retrieval. In *International Conference on Image Processing (ICIP'2001)*, volume 1, pages 674–677. IEEE, 2001.

[13] Y. Pritch, E. Kav-Venaki, and S. Peleg. Shift-map image editing. In *2009 IEEE 12th International Conference on Computer Vision*, pages 151–158, 2009.

[14] L. Wolf, M. Guttmann, and D. Cohen-Or. Non-homogeneous content-driven video-retargeting. In *IEEE 11th International Conference on Computer Vision, 2007. ICCV 2007.*, pages 1 -6, oct. 2007.

[15] Philipp Krähenbühl, Manuel Lang, Alexander Hornung, and Markus Gross. A system for retargeting of streaming video. In *ACM Transactions on Graphics (TOG)*, volume 28, page 126. ACM, 2009.

[16] Maurice G Kendall. A new measure of rank correlation. *Biometrika*, 30(1/2):81–93, 1938.

[17] Jerome L Myers, Arnold D Well, and Robert Frederick Lorch. *Research design and statistical analysis.* Routledge, 2010.

Efficient Image Retargeting via Adaptive Pixel Fusion

Bo Yan, Xiaochu Yang, Ke Li
School of Computer Science
Shanghai Key Laboratory of Intelligent Information Processing
Fudan University, Shanghai, China
byan@fudan.edu.cn

ABSTRACT

This paper presents a new image retargeting method, which is able to provide both high efficiency and quality. Firstly, our method calculates the image resizing factors in both horizontal and vertical directions. Then, it resizes the image in these both directions sequentially in order to achieve the target aspect ratio with the help of our proposed mapping functions. Finally, the reconstructed image can be uniformly scaled to the target resolution. Experimental results show that our method is not only cost effective in terms of computational resource, but also provides visually pleasing resized images.

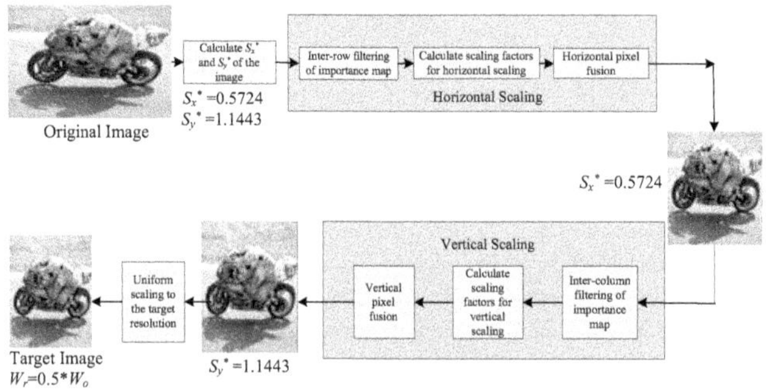

Figure 1: Procedure of our proposed method.

Categories and Subject Descriptors

I.3.3 [**Computer Graphics**]: Picture/Image Generation—*Display algorithms*

General Terms

Algorithms

Keywords

image retargeting; scaling factor; pixel fusion.

1. INTRODUCTION

Recently due to the escalating diversity of display devices, image retargeting plays a more and more significant role to support image display with varying formats, resolutions, sizes, and aspect ratios. However, current industry solutions to this requirement are basic and not very effective.

Recent image retargeting approaches aim at converting the image to a new target resolution or aspect ratio while preserving the salient content. They can be classified into three main branches in terms of the essential ideas: removing pixels from an image (discrete methods) [1], merging pixels of an image (continuous methods)[2] and combining these methods together (hybrid methods) [3]. Although the increasingly sophisticated retargeting methods can provide higher quality and accuracy to some extent, the relatively high computational complexity hinders these algorithms from industrial applications.

In this paper, we present an efficient image retargeting method based on non-uniform scaling. Firstly, our method calculates the image resizing factors in both horizontal and vertical (x and y) directions in order to achieve the target aspect ratio. Then based on the scaling factors derived from our proposed mapping functions, the image will be non-uniformly scaled in both x and y directions sequentially. Finally, the reconstructed image can be uniformly scaled to the target resolution. Experimental results prove that our method not only costs very little in time, memory and computational resources, but also provides visually comfortable resized images.

MM'14, November 03 - 07 2014, Orlando, FL, USA

http://dx.doi.org/10.1145/2647868.2654959 .

2. REFERRED WORK

Different from traditional image retargeting methods, Wang *et al.*[4] propose to resize image $I_o(x, y)$ with size $W_o \times H_o$ to a new image $I_r(x, y)$ with size $W_r \times H_r$ by retargeting the image aspect ratio, which is able to well preserve the image structure. Specifically, it first estimates the compressibility rates in both x and y directions, denoted by r_x and r_y respectively.

Let S_x and S_y denote the resizing factors in x and y directions respectively, and

$$\beta = (\mathrm{W_r} \cdot H_o)/(W_o \cdot H_r), S_x = \beta \cdot S_y \tag{1}$$

The optimized S_x and S_y are derived by minimizing the energy E as [4]:

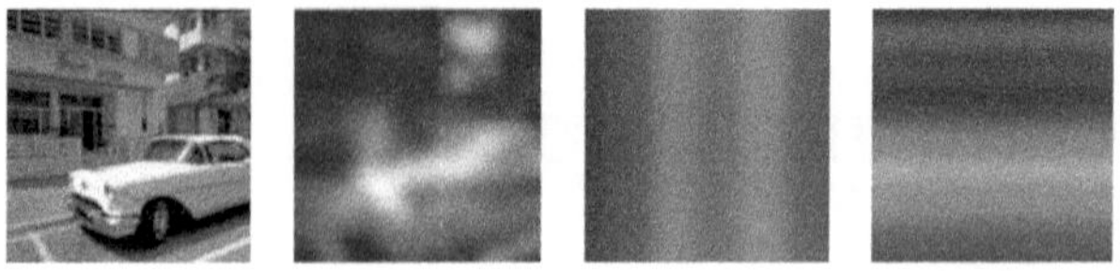

Figure 2: (a) Original input image; (b) importance map; (c) inter-row filtering; (d) inter-column filtering. Bright areas are important areas.

$$E = (s_x - 1)^2 + (s_y - 1)^2 + \omega \cdot \left((1 - r_x - s_x)^2 + (1 + r_y - s_y)^2\right) \quad (2)$$

where the weighting ω can be obtained according to the image gradient [4].

Finally, based upon a warping based approach [2], the original $W_o \times H_o$ image can be resized to size $(S_x^* W_o \times S_y^* H_o)$. The aspect ratio of this new image is same as that of the target image. Therefore this image can be uniformly scaled to the target resolution $(W_r \times H_r)$ [4].

This method is very effective to preserve structures but quite time-consuming. In order to improve the efficiency, we will propose a new efficient image retargeting method.

3. OUR PROPOSED METHOD

In this paper, we only consider resizing the image on horizontal direction. Fig. 1 shows the procedure of our algorithms. As shown in this figure, firstly the optimized resizing factors in x and y directions S_x^* and S_y^* are calculated. Then, with our proposed mapping functions, the image will be scaled in both x and y directions sequentially based on S_x^* and S_y^* respectively, in order to resize the image to the target aspect ratio. Finally, the obtained image can be uniformly scaled from $(S_x^* W_o \times S_y^* H_o)$ to the target resolution $(W_r \times H_r)$.

3.1 Calculation of Image Resizing Factor

Let $R_o = \frac{W_o}{H_o}$ and $R_r = \frac{W_r}{H_r}$ denote the aspect ratios of the original image and target image respectively. Thus, we can obtain the following linear relationship between R_r and R_o as:

$$R_r = R_o \frac{S_x}{S_y} \quad (3)$$

As defined in (1), β denotes the ratio of the aspect ratios of the target image and original image. Thus, the safe line for (S_x, S_y) defined in [4] can be represented as:

$$(1 + sgn(\beta - 1) \cdot r_x, 1 - sgn(\beta - 1) \cdot r_y) \quad (4)$$

where $sgn(x)$ function returns the sign of x. The safe line presents a measurement of the bottom line of the compressibility rate [4].

In this way, the energy function defined in (2) can be rewritten as:

$$E' = (S_x - 1)^2 + \omega \cdot (1 + sgn(\beta - 1) \cdot r_x - S_x)^2 + (S_y - 1)^2 + \omega \cdot (1 - sgn(\beta - 1) \cdot r_y - S_y)^2 \quad (5)$$

The optimal S_x^* and S_y^* can be obtained by minimizing E' in (5).

3.2 Horizontal scaling for images with S_x^*

In our method, importance map is represented by the saliency of every pixel, which is computed by Itti's algorithm [5]. Fig.2 (a) and Fig.2 (b) show the original test image and its importance map. The bright regions are important regions. Based on the importance map, the pixel horizontal scaling factors can be obtained. Before scaling, inter-row importance coherence filtering needs to be performed to retain coherence after the scaling of each row. The filtering formula is given as [6]:

$$IM'(x, y) = \frac{\sum_{k=1}^{H_o} IM(x, k)}{H_o} \quad (6)$$

where $IM(x, y)$ denotes the importance value on the xth column and the yth row. The filtered $IM'(x, y)$ is the average importance value in each column. An example of a vertically filtered importance map is shown in Fig.2 (c).

Let's use $S(x, y)$ indicate the scaling factor for pixel (x, y). If $S_x^* < 1$, $S(x, y) > 1$ is not allowed, which will deform the image significantly. In order to avoid this problem, we propose to calculate $S(x, y)$ with (7). Let's use N_{col} to denote the number of columns which satisfy $S(x, y) \geq 1$. We will initially set N_{col} to be 0 and set $S(x, y)$ to be S_x^*. After calculating $S(x, y)$ with (7), we will search the columns which satisfy $S(x, y) \geq 1$ to update N_{col}. These columns' scaling factors will be set as 1. Then the scaling factors of the remaining columns will be re-calculated as:

$$S(x, y) = \frac{(W_i - N_{col}) \cdot IM'(x, y)}{\sum_{k=1, S(k,y)<1}^{W_o} IM'(k, y)}, \quad W_i \leq W_o \quad (7)$$

where W_i is obtained as:

$$W_i = W_o \times S_x^* \quad (8)$$

This process will be repeated until all the columns' scaling factors satisfy $S(x, y) \leq 1$. The result can be observed from Fig. 2 (c).

Similarly, for the case of $(S_x^* > 1)$, $S(x, y) < 1$ is not allowed. Similar steps will be performed. Different from (7), let's use N_{col} to denote the number of columns which satisfy $S(x, y) \leq 1$. Then the scaling factors of the remaining columns will be re-calculated as:

$$S(x, y) = \frac{(W_i - N_{col}) / IM'(x, y)}{\sum_{k=1, S(k,y)>1}^{W_o} 1/IM'(k, y)}, \quad W_i > W_o \quad (9)$$

After obtaining the scaling map $S(x, y)$, the resized intermediate image $I_i(x, y)$ is generated with pixel fusion proposed by [7]. This method works as follows. Assuming the image is resized horizontally, the width of each pixel will be scaled from unity to a fractional number according to the scaling factor of the pixel. Then the linear combination of pixels, weighted by their widths, composes the resized pixels, whose widths are one unit.

3.3 Vertical scaling for images with S_y^*

Firstly the saliency map of the resized intermediate image $I_i(x, y)$, which is denoted by $IM_i(x, y)$, is calculated by resizing the saliency map with the scaling map $S(x, y)$ in (7). Then the inter-column importance coherence filtering is performed to retain coherence after the scaling of each column as:

$$IM'_i(x,y) = \frac{\sum_{k=1}^{W_i} IM_i(k,y)}{W_i} \tag{10}$$

Then similarly if $S^*_y < 1$, the scaling factors of the each row is calculated as:

$$S(x,y) = \frac{(H_i - N_{row}) \cdot IM'_i(x,y)}{\sum_{k=1,S(x,k)<1}^{H_o} IM'_i(x,k)}, \quad H_i \le H_o \tag{11}$$

where H_i is obtained as:

$$H_i = H_o \times S^*_y \tag{12}$$

The filtered $IM'_i(x,y)$ is the average importance value in each row derived from (6). Same as (7), N_{row} denotes the number of rows which satisfy $S(x,y) \ge 1$ and it is initially set to be 0.

If $(S^*_y > 1)$, $S(x,y) < 1$ is not allowed. Similar steps will be performed. Different from (11), let's use N_{row} to denote the number of rows which satisfy $S(x,y) \le 1$. Then the scaling factors of the remaining rows will be re-calculated as:

$$S(x,y) = \frac{(H_i - N_{row})/IM'_i(x,y)}{\sum_{k=1,S(x,k)>1}^{H_o} 1/IM'_i(x,k)}, \quad H_i > H_o \tag{13}$$

Fig. 2 (d) shows an example of vertical scaling for images.

With the help of pixel fusion, the new image with the resolution of $(S^*_x W_o \times S^*_y H_o)$ can be reconstructed. The aspect ratio of this new image is the same as that of the target image (R_r). Therefore, this image can be uniformly scaled to the target resolution $(W_r \times H_r)$.

4. EXPERIMENT RESULTS AND DISCUSSIONS

In order to evaluate the performance of our proposed method, we test it on the *RetargetMe* image retargeting benchmark provided by [10]. All images are resized to half the original width. The results of several other state-of-the-art techniques are shown as comparison to our method, including uniform scaling (US), seam-carving (SC) [1], Wang *et al.*'s CA [4], Ding *et al.*'s importance filtering method (IF) [8], and Panozzo *et al.*'s As-Similar-As-Possible (ASAP) [9]. The processing environment has an Intel® Xeon® CPU with 3.1 GHz operational frequency and 2G bytes RAM size under Windows® Server 2003 operating system. All the algorithms are implemented by MATLAB.

4.1 Performance Comparison

We theoretically compare the computational complexity of our method with that of ASAP [9], which is a state-of-the-art technique for fast image retargeting. For both ASAP and our method, the most important work is how to obtain the scaling factors of each pixel. The computational complexity of assigning scaling factors in ASAP is $O(W_o + H_o)$. In contrast, ours is only $O(W_o)$, which is much less than that of ASAP. We verified the theoretical analysis result by simulations, which consider the computational efficiency as a major criterion in evaluating the performance of the proposed algorithm. Therefore, we record the processing time of the methods and compare them in Table 1. In this table, "Reduction Rate (RR)" denotes the processing time reduction percentage of our proposed method compared with [9]. As Table 1 shows, the processing time of our algorithm is much less than those of SC [1], CA [4] and IF [8]. Even more remarkably, the efficiency of our proposed method is higher than that of ASAP [9] (by up to 90.65% processing time reduction), which is a state-of-the-art technique for fast image retargeting. The simulation result has well demonstrated the consistency with the theoretical analysis result.

Table 1: Processing time comparisons with uniform scaling, CA[4], seam-carving[1], importance filtering [8], ASAP [9] and our method.

Image	Size	Time (s)						RR
		US	CA	SC	IF	ASAP	Ours	
artroom	1024x813	0.014	29.55	1048.72	8.85	0.37	0.19	48.65%
battleship	1014x749	0.013	26.60	888.28	7.37	0.33	0.15	54.55%
bedroom	1024x683	0.011	25.17	801.58	6.52	0.33	0.14	57.58%
bike	460x300	0.0034	5.16	50.78	0.71	0.31	0.030	90.65%
blueman	1024x681	0.011	23.51	797.92	6.42	0.32	0.15	53.13%
boat	819x541	0.0082	16.03	365.22	3.42	0.32	0.090	70.94%
bottle	1024x697	0.012	28.08	826.50	6.66	0.33	0.15	54.55%
b.house	1024x683	0.012	25.96	802.00	6.40	0.34	0.14	58.82%
butterfly	615x422	0.012	28.05	831.47	6.76	0.33	0.15	54.55%
C.house	1022x755	0.014	30.05	931.14	7.69	0.34	0.16	52.94%
car	1014x747	0.013	26.85	884.14	7.31	0.36	0.15	58.33%
car1	384x385	0.0020	5.35	49.75	0.89	0.29	0.030	88.97%
car2	500x375	0.0041	6.72	80.97	1.10	0.30	0.040	87.67%
cat	1024x683	0.012	25.04	802.46	6.39	0.34	0.14	58.82%
child	1024x680	0.012	26.83	796.46	6.44	0.33	0.15	54.55%
Deck	1023x623	0.011	23.95	698.02	5.42	0.33	0.14	57.58%
D.girl	1024x673	0.012	25.35	782.82	6.27	0.34	0.14	58.82%
eagle	600x402	0.0051	8.34	128.47	1.50	0.30	0.050	82.67%
face	392x300	0.0030	4.03	36.83	0.60	0.27	0.030	90.37%
moto	615x409	0.0053	8.22	138.54	1.56	0.30	0.050	82.00%
painting2	1024x683	0.012	24.61	801.12	6.40	0.34	0.14	58.82%
pencils	615x410	0.0053	9.75	138.98	1.58	0.30	0.050	83.33%
ski	1003x661	0.011	24.25	732.08	5.93	0.33	0.14	57.58%
soccer	500x356	0.0040	6.58	75.11	1.02	0.29	0.040	86.90%
Stuck	749x963	0.0046	28.17	716.21	8.60	0.32	0.15	53.13%
tower	1024x683	0.012	26.83	801.61	6.40	0.33	0.14	57.58%
twobirds	600x450	0.0056	10.91	150.44	1.82	0.31	0.050	82.58%

In addition to efficiency, the quality of our resized images is as good as, or even better than, other methods. A set of comparative results are shown in Fig.3. From these figures, we may observe that US will lead to notorious distortion of important details. SC [1] may distort the structure due to removing too many seams. Warping-based CA [4] can directly cut some important regions of images. ASAP [9] may result in the unnatural scales. IF [8] will cut the image's right edge due to its limitation. In contrast, our proposed method tends to minimize all these flaws when resizing the image.

4.2 User Study

Because there is no widely-accepted objective metric to compare different retargeting methods so far, we perform a psycho-visual testing of these methods in a concise setting, evaluate our method by conducting a user study with 21 participants from diverse backgrounds and ages. In our psycho-visual tests, participants were presented with an original image and two retargeting images side by side, and they were asked to answer which retargeting result they preferred. The users were kept naive about the purpose of the experiment and were not provided with any special technical instructions [11].

We used 10 images in the experiment and resized each image to 50% width using ASAP [9], CA [4], SC [1], IF [8], US and our method. Therefore, for each image there were 15 pairwise comparisons, and each participant was asked

Figure 3: Example : comparison with the existing methods. From left to right: Original image, uniform scaling, seam-carving[1], Ding *et al.*'s IF method[8], Wang *et al.*'s CA [4], Panozzo *et al.*'s ASAP [9], and our proposed method. All images are resized to half width ($W'/W = 0.5$).

Table 2: Pairwise comparison results between our method, CA [4], SC [1], IF [8], ASAP [9] and US.

outperforms	Ours	CA	IF	SC	US	ASAP	Total	Prefer%
Ours	-	153	142	167	166	151	779	74.19%
CA	57	-	106	143	107	92	505	48.10%
IF	68	104	-	121	140	109	542	51.62%
SC	43	67	89	-	75	42	316	30.10%
US	44	103	70	135	-	69	421	40.10%
ASAP	59	118	101	168	141	-	587	55.90%

to make $15 \times 10 = 150$ comparisons. The questions were presented in random order to avoid bias. We obtained a total of $150 \times 21 = 3150$ answers, and each method was compared $5 \times 10 \times 21 = 1050$ times.

Table 2 shows the summary of the obtained results. Entry a_{ij} in the middle of the table means method i was preferred a_{ij} times over method j. Overall, our method was preferred in 74.19% (779/1050) of the times it was compared. In contrast, CA was favored only in 48.10% (505/1050), IF in 51.62% (542/1050), SC in 30.10% (316/1050), US in 40.10% (421/1050), ASAP in 55.90% (587/1050). It should be noted that the results of our visual-psycho tests are indicative due to the conciseness of the chosen setting.

4.3 Analysis and Discussion of Contribution and Limitation

Pixel fusion in image retargeting is based on the assignment of scaling factors. Our proposed method is able to efficiently and effectively assign the scaling factors: closer to 1 for important pixels and farther from 1 for less important ones. With our proposed method the important region in the original image will keep almost the same size in the resized image, which has been verified by lots of comparative results.

It should be noted that our method proposes to use the same scale for pixels at same column/row in horizontal/vertical scaling. It excludes the localized rotations of images and has less freedom than general variational warping. As a result, some special structures such as straight lines in an image cannot be preserved if they are not strictly horizontally or vertically aligned, which is similar as that of ASAP in [9].

However, our proposed method is able to preserve most structures as demonstrated in the results, with much less computational complexity than other state-of-the-art techniques (up to 90.65% processing time reduction as shown in Table 1). Therefore, our method possesses huge potential of practical applications.

5. CONCLUSIONS

In this paper, we presented a new image retargeting method by retargeting the aspect ratio, which is able to provide both efficiency and quality. It proposes to resize the image in both x and y directions sequentially in order to achieve the target aspect ratio based on our proposed mapping functions, and then directly uniformly scale the reconstructed image to achieve the target resolution. The most remarkable features of our method are low complexity and high quality.

6. ACKNOWLEDGMENTS

This work is supported by NSFC (Grant No.: 61370158).

7. REFERENCES

[1] S. Avidan and A. Shamir. Seam carving for content-aware image resizing. In *ACM Transactions on Graphics (TOG)*, volume 26, page 10, 2007.

[2] L. Wolf, M. Guttmann, and D. Cohen-Or. Non-homogeneous content-driven video-retargeting. In *IEEE 11th International Conference on Computer Vision (ICCV 2007)*, pages 1–6, 2007.

[3] M. Rubinstein, A. Shamir, and S. Avidan. Multi-operator media retargeting. In *ACM Transactions on Graphics (TOG)*, volume 28, page 23, 2009.

[4] Shu-Fan Wang and Shang-Hong Lai. Compressibility-aware media retargeting with structure preserving. *IEEE Transactions on Image Processing*, 20(3):855 –865, Mar. 2011.

[5] L. Itti, C. Koch, and E. Niebur. A model of saliency-based visual attention for rapid scene analysis. *IEEE Transactions on Pattern Analysis and Machine Intelligence*, 20(11):1254 –1259, nov 1998.

[6] K. Sun, B. Yan, and Y. Gao. Lowcomplexity content-aware image retargeting. In *2012 19th IEEE International Conference on Image Processing (ICIP)*, pages 2105–2108, Sept 2012.

[7] Tzu-Chieh Yen, Chia-Ming Tsai, and Chia-Wen Lin. Maintaining temporal coherence in video retargeting using mosaic-guided scaling. *IEEE Transactions on Image Processing*, 20(8):2339 –2351, aug. 2011.

[8] Y. Ding, J. Xiao, and J. Yu. Importance filtering for image retargeting. In *2011 IEEE Conference on Computer Vision and Pattern Recognition (CVPR)*, pages 89–96, 2011.

[9] D. Panozzo, O. Weber, and O. Sorkine. Robust image retargeting via axis-aligned deformation. In *Computer Graphics Forum*, volume 31, pages 229–236, 2012.

[10] Michael Rubinstein, Diego Gutierrez, Olga Sorkine, and Ariel Shamir. A comparative study of image retargeting. *ACM Transactions on Graphics (Proc. SIGGRAPH Asia)*, 29(5):160:1–160:10, 2010.

[11] B. Yan, K. Sun, and L. Liu. Matching-area-based seam carving for video retargeting. *IEEE Transactions on Circuits and Systems for Video Technology*, 23(2):302–310, 2013.

Learning Compact Face Representation: Packing a Face into an int32

Haoqiang Fan[* †]
Tsinghua University
fhq13@mails.tsinghua.edu.cn

Mu Yang[†]
Tsinghua University
m-yang11@mails.tsinghua.edu.cn

Zhimin Cao
Megvii Inc.
czm@megvii.com

Yuning Jiang
Megvii Inc.
jyn@megvii.com

Qi Yin
Megvii Inc.
yq@megvii.com

ABSTRACT

This paper addresses the problem of producing very compact representation of a face image for large-scale face search and analysis tasks. In tradition, the compactness of face representation is achieved by a dimension reduction step after representation extraction. However, the dimension reduction usually degrades the discriminative ability of the original representation drastically. In this paper, we present a deep learning framework which optimizes the compactness and discriminative ability jointly. The learnt representation can be as compact as 32 bit (same as the int32) and still produce highly discriminative performance (91.4% on LFW benchmark). Based on the extreme compactness, we show that traditional face analysis tasks (e.g. gender analysis) can be effectively solved by a Look-Up-Table approach given a large-scale face data set.

Categories and Subject Descriptors

I.4 [**Image Processing And Computer Vision**]: Image Representation; H.3 [**Information Storage And Retrieval**]: Content Analysis and Indexing

Keywords

face recognition; face search; deep learning

1. INTRODUCTION

Numerous vision tasks benefit from a compact representation of the image data. In face search/analysis tasks, the vector representation of a face image is typically of very high dimension [2] to preserve sufficient discriminative ability.

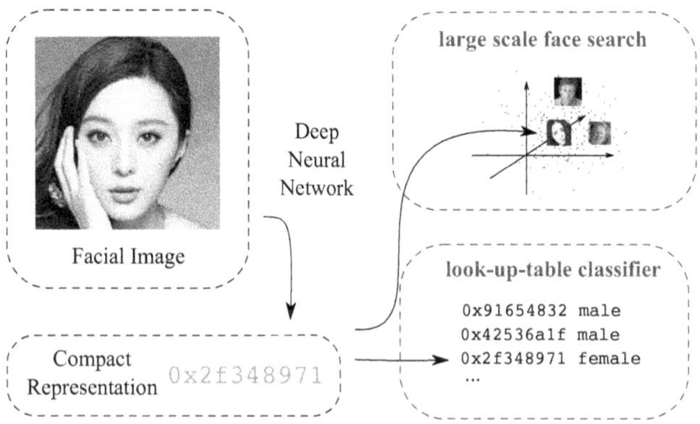

Figure 1: Compact face representation. Our system exploits deep neural networks to produce extremely compact face representation that can fit into a 32-bit integer. The short and low-dimensional representation facilitates efficient large scale face search. In addition, it enables very simple classifiers for face attribute analysis given large scale data set.

In tradition, a face representation of thousands of dimensions has already been considered as "compact" in the community of face recognition. Some dimension reduction or quantization methods may be adopted to compress the representation dimension for the applications of large-scale face systems. However, the discriminative ability is usually decreased due to the compactness requirement. As a result, existing methods make different tradeoffs between compactness and discriminative ability.

To pursue a compact and discriminative representation of a face image, our key observation is that the compactness and discriminative ability should be optimized together. The compactness of the representation is decided by the feature dimension and discreteness strategy. For the feature dimension part, a dimension reduction step is usually adopted after representation extracted. Discreteness is another key issue in the representation learning. Storing quantized or categorical information requires less bits than storing a real-value variable. For example, an int32 data structure can store a single bin of 32-bit feature or four independent bins of 8-bit. Since existing dimension reduction and discreteness [4, 11, 5, 1] methods are all post-processing. The dis-

*This work was done when Haoqiang Fan was a visiting student at Megvii Inc..
†Ordered lexicographically. Equal contribution.

MM'14, August 24–27, 2014, New York, NY, USA.

ACM 978-1-4503-3063-3/14/11 ...$15.00.
http://dx.doi.org/10.1145/2647868.2654960.

criminative ability will degrade drastically during these two steps.

In this paper, we present a new deep learning framework called Deep Compactness Learning, which can tackle the aforementioned problems in a unified framework. Our contributions are summarized as follows:

1. We propose a deep learning framework which can optimize the compactness and discriminative ability of face representation jointly.

2. We conduct extensive experiments to show our representation learning framework achieves good tradeoff between compactness and discriminative ability (91.4% accuracy on LFW benchmark with 32-bit length).

3. We demonstrate the advantage of our extreme compact representation in the applications of face search and analysis tasks.

2. DEEP COMPACTNESS LEARNING

In this section, we describe the details of our deep representation learning framework. The compactness and discriminative ability of the representation is jointly optimized in a unified CNN framework.

2.1 Joint Optimization Framework

In order to make the representation compact, we have to incorporate the low-dimension and discreteness constraint into our framework. The representation is formulated as a function from image data to a feature space:

$$f : M_{h\times w}(\mathbb{R}) \to \mathbb{R}^n. \tag{1}$$

A loss function is used to learn the function map according to certain criteria. We adopt a pair-based loss function which encourages the identity-preserving property of the learned representation:

$$\mathcal{L} = \sum_{x_1,x_2} L\left(\alpha\left|f(x_1) - f(x_2)\right| - \beta, \delta(x_1,x_2)\right), \tag{2}$$

where $\delta(\cdot,\cdot)$ indicates whether the two images belong to the same person (-1 for same, 1 for different), and

$$L(y,l) = \log\left(1 + e^{-ly}\right). \tag{3}$$

The loss function encourages small distance between the matched (same identity) face pairs and large distance between unmatched pairs. In this way, the feature preserves the discriminative information about the face.

The low-dimension constraint is enforced by setting the model's output dimension n to a small enough number. To produce a 32-bit representation, we can set $n = 32$ and the representation becomes a binary representation. We also allow even smaller n so that more bits can be assigned to each dimension (e.g. 4 bits for each of the 8 dimensions). Using more than one bit has the advantage of forming a hierarchical structure in the feature space so that the data points can be indexed at different levels of granularity. However, some applications explicitly demand binary representation, so we treat the binary and non-binary cases separately.

Another constraint is discreteness, which means each dimension of the model's output has to be rounded:

$$f(x) = \left\lfloor 2^Q f_{\text{model}}(x) \right\rfloor, \tag{4}$$

where Q corresponds to the number of bits available for encoding one dimension, and $f_{\text{model}}(x) \in [0,1)^n$.

However, the non-differentiable rounding operator posses problem to gradient-based learning algorithms. To overcome this obstacle, we propose three different techniques. The first technique called "rounding error term" is the most straight forward. A "noise" term $\tilde{f}(x)$ is introduced to model the error brought by rounding:

$$f(x) = 2^Q f_{\text{model}}(x) + \tilde{f}(x), \tag{5}$$

where $\tilde{f}(x)$ corresponds to the residual. When computing the gradient of the loss function with respect to model parameters, this term is treated as a constant.

The technique works well for non-binary cases. However, its performance is suboptimal when Q becomes as low as 1. Therefore, we propose two different specialized techniques to handle the binary case.

The first technique associates the model's real valued output with a random n-bit variable. The i-th bit of $f(x)$ has a probability of $f_{\text{model}}(x)_i$ to be 1 and $1 - f_{\text{model}}(x)_i$ probability to be 0. The bits are independent. Then we take the expectation of the loss function:

$$\mathcal{L}' = \sum_{x_1,x_2} \mathrm{E}\left[L(\alpha\left|f(x_1) - f(x_2)\right| - \beta, \delta(x_1,x_2))\right], \tag{6}$$

where the expectation is taken over the random choices of $f(x_1)$ and $f(x_2)$. It is easy to verify that $\mathcal{L}'$ is differentiable with respect to the model's output. Computing the expectation directly is intractable. However, it can be efficiently computed by dynamic programming. For x_1 and x_2, let $D_{i,j}$ be the probability that $f(x_1)$ and $f(x_2)$ differs at j bits in their first i bits. We have

$$\begin{aligned} D_{i,j} = \; & (1 - p_1 - p_2 + 2p_1p_2)D_{i-1,j} \\ & + (p_1 + p_2 - 2p_1p_2)D_{i-1,j-1}, \end{aligned} \tag{7}$$

where $p_1 = f(x_1)_i, p_2 = f(x_2)_i$. The boundary conditions are $D_{0,0} = 1$ and $D_{i,-1} = 0$.

Another technique aims at minimizing the error introduced by rounding. The idea is to encourage the model to output binarized value by adding a standard deviation term:

$$\mathcal{L}' = \mathcal{L} + \omega \sum_i \mathrm{Std}(f(x)_i), \tag{8}$$

where $\mathrm{Std}(\cdot)$ denotes the standard deviation across the training set.

Our framework is jointly optimized in the sense that both the requirements of compactness and discriminative power are tightly incorporated into the framework. This is in contrast to other methods which use hashing or dimensionality reduction algorithms as a post-processing step.

2.2 Deep Learning Model

We formulate the function family using CNN (Convolutional Neural Network). The CNN is a composition of multiple linear and non-linear operators.

$$f_{\text{cnn}}(x) = f_n\left(f_{n-1}\left(\cdots f_1\left(x\right)\cdots\right)\right). \tag{9}$$

The first type of the operators is the convolution which filters the multi-channel image signal:

$$C_W(x)_{i,j,k} = \sum_{u,v,w} W_{u,v,k,w} x_{i-u,j-v,w} + B_k. \tag{10}$$

Another operator is max-pooling which reduces the size of the image:

$$M_s(x)_{i,j,k} = \max_{0 \le u,v < s} x_{is-u,js-v,k}. \quad (11)$$

Non-linearity is introduced to the network by using element-wise non-linear operators:

$$g(x) = \text{abs}(\tanh(x)). \quad (12)$$

This activation function is inspired by [7] which reveals its advantage in the object recognition task.

The structure of a typical CNN is illustrated in Figure 2.

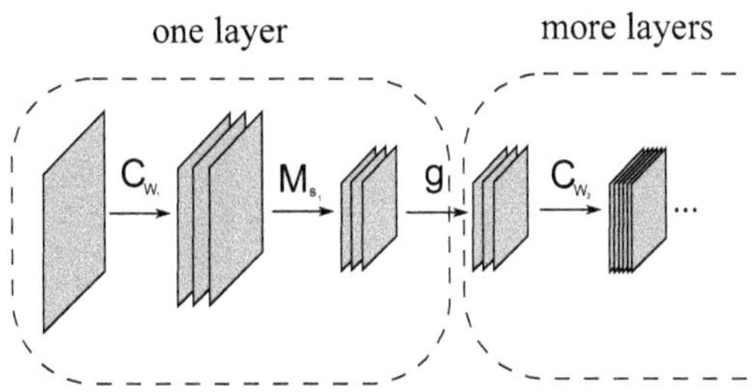

Figure 2: Typical structure of convolutional neural network. Convolution, max-pooling and non-linear operators are three key modules to form a multi-layer convolutional neural network.

3. EXPERIMENT

3.1 Effects of Representation Learning

Firstly we evaluate the proposed framework on face verification task to validate the effectiveness of our method. Our experiment is conducted on the Labelled Faces in the Wild (LFW) [6] data set. We use an outside training set (around 630 thousand faces crawled from the web) which has little overlap with LFW (less than 0.6% pictures in LFW appear as near duplicate in our training set). A 6-layer neural network containing 9 million parameters is employed in our system (inspired by [3]). The parameters in the neural networks are optimized by Stochastic Gradient Descent, and standard deep learning techniques including greedy pre-training are adopted to further accelerate training process.

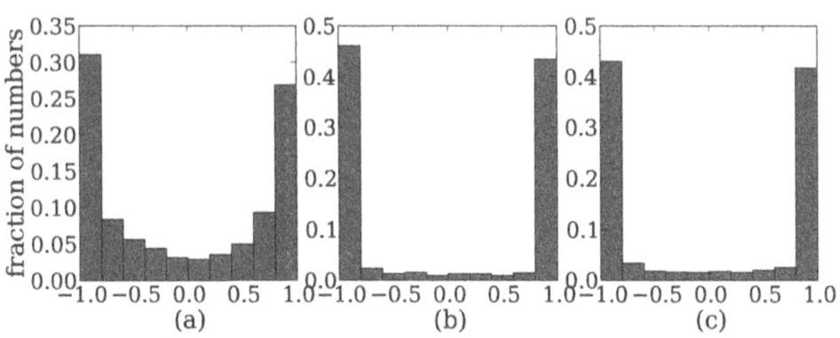

Figure 3: Demonstration of binarized activation value. All the three techniques (a. rounding error term; b. dynamic programming; c. standard deviation) encourage the neurons' output to saturate.

We study two categories of 32-bit representations. The first category is the binary representation in which each bit corresponds to one binarized dimension. The three techniques described in Section 2.1 are implemented and compared. It is observed in the experiment that all these techniques effectively encourage the activation function to saturate (Figure 3). As shown in Table 1, with the dynamic programming technique or the standard deviation technique, our representation achieves 88.5% verification accuracy on LFW. As a comparison, we evaluated a baseline method based on high dimensional LBP and PCA [2]. Though it achieves an accuracy of 96% when more than 1000 dimensions are used, the performance drastically degrades to 81% when the dimension is reduced to 32.

Table 1: Face verification accuracy on the LFW benchmark with the binary representation. The table lists accuracy achieved by different techniques to handle the binarization constraint.

Length	Method	Accuracy
32 bits	rounding error term	87.7%
32 bits	dynamic programming	88.4%
32 bits	standard deviation	88.5%

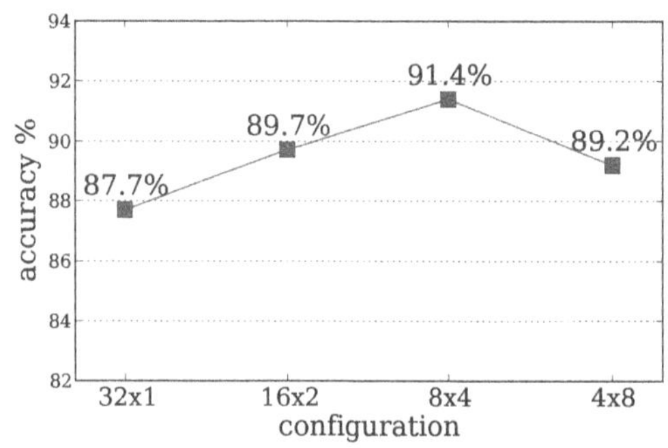

Figure 4: Face verification accuracy obtained by different configurations of the 32 bits. Rounding error term is used to produce quantized features of 32, 16, 8 and 4 dimensions. The best result is achieved by using 4 bits for each of the 8 dimensions.

Conversely, in the second category, each dimension is no longer limited to 1 bit, while the total length of each feature is still 32 bits. We test 4 configurations, from 32×1 to 4×8 bits. The the rounding error term is used to produce discrete features of different dimensions. As shown in Figure 4, the best result is obtained by using 4 bits for each of the 8 dimensions. It achieves an accuracy of 91.4% which is better than the binary representations. It validates the benefits of the flexibility introduced by using multiple bits for one dimension. It is worth mentioning that the 32-bit representation already beats many more complicated and higher-dimensional features [8, 9, 10]. The 8×4 configuration is used throughout remaining face search and classification experiments.

3.2 Applications to Face Search and Analysis

In this subsection we explore the application of the compact representation in face search and analysis.

In large-scale face search, the compact representation is used to build an index for fast nearest neighbour searching. Candidates are quickly generated based on the index, and finer-grained search and re-ranking steps follow. The 32-bit representation divides the feature space into bins. Each bin contains faces with the same 32-bit representation. We focus on evaluating the recall value when only a small fraction of bins are visited during searching. The bins are visited in ascending order of the distance to the query vector. For fair comparison, the evaluation was also conducted on LFW dataset. We choose persons with more than two pictures in the data set and use their faces as queries to search for matched images. The recall rate when different number of bins are visited is recorded in Figure 5. The figure shows that high recall rate can be obtained by visiting less than one thousandth of the total bins, which greatly accelerates the searching.

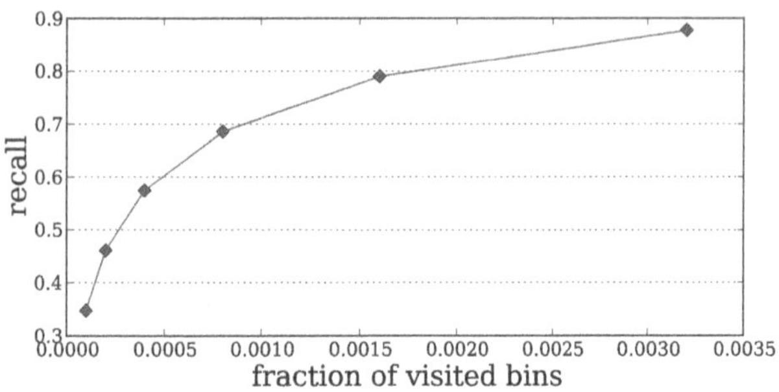

Figure 5: Performance of learnt representation in face search application. This figure shows the recall rate obtained by visiting a small number of bins.

Then we apply the deep face representation in face classification task. The usual way of building classifiers is to learn statistical models based on the feature vectors. As the number of training samples increases, the learning-based methods always suffer from the expensive training cost. Large-scale social network normally maintains a huge image gallery from billions of people, with hundreds of millions of photos uploaded every day. Despite current efforts in online learning and incremental algorithms, it is still difficult to guarantee that the learning process scales well as the training samples continuously come.

When the feature representation is short enough, a scalable and straight forward method of analysis is enabled. The method uses the representation as an entrance and builds a Look Up Table (LUT) for classification. Due to the id-preserving property of the representation, we can hopefully expect the photos belonging to the same bin share common attributes (Figure 6). When the number of training samples is large enough, the accuracy of the classifier approaches the Bayesian error rate. Training and classifying becomes as simple as a table look-up.

Due to limited space, here we construct a prototype system from small-scale data set to illustrate our idea. The task is to predict the gender of the person in a facial image. We gather a training set of 80,000 pictures from existing data sets, and evaluate the performance on the LFW benchmark. As the number of training samples is not large enough, we retrieve data points from nearby bins when doing prediction. We achieve a classification accuracy of 96.8%. We believe as the scale of the data set becomes larger, the performance will be further promoted.

Figure 6: Face samples in different face bins. Based on the representation, the feature space is divided into bins (2^{16} bins in this figure). Clearly, the faces falling in the same bin share a strong correlation with the high-level facial attributes (e.g, gender). This validates our representation bin to be a proper cue for facial attribute analysis.

4. CONCLUSION

We present a new face representation learning approach based on deep learning framework. Our method can jointly optimize the compactness and discriminative ability of the representation in a unified framework. With our extreme compact representation, the face search task can be greatly accelerated and the traditional face analysis task can be effectively solved by large-scale data-driven approach. Extensive experiments justify the effectiveness of our method.

5. REFERENCES

[1] Y. Bengio. Learning deep architectures for ai. *FTML*, 2(1):1–127, 2009.

[2] D. Chen, X. Cao, F. Wen, and J. Sun. Blessing of dimensionality: High-dimensional feature and its efficient compression for face verification. In *CVPR*, pages 3025–3032. IEEE, 2013.

[3] H. Fan, Z. Cao, Y. Jiang, Q. Yin, and C. Doudou. Learning deep face representation. Technical report, Megvii. Inc, Beijing, March 2014.

[4] Y. Gong and S. Lazebnik. Iterative quantization: A procrustean approach to learning binary codes. In *CVPR*, pages 817–824. IEEE, 2011.

[5] G. E. Hinton and R. R. Salakhutdinov. Reducing the dimensionality of data with neural networks. *Science*, 313(5786):504–507, 2006.

[6] G. B. Huang, M. Ramesh, T. Berg, and E. Learned-Miller. Labeled faces in the wild: A database for studying face recognition in unconstrained environments. Technical Report 07-49, University of Massachusetts, Amherst, October 2007.

[7] K. Jarrett, K. Kavukcuoglu, M. Ranzato, and Y. LeCun. What is the best multi-stage architecture for object recognition? In *ICCV*, pages 2146–2153. IEEE, 2009.

[8] N. Kumar, A. C. Berg, P. N. Belhumeur, and S. K. Nayar. Attribute and simile classifiers for face verification. In *ICCV*, pages 365–372. IEEE, 2009.

[9] Y. Taigman and L. Wolf. Leveraging billions of faces to overcome performance barriers in unconstrained face recognition. *arXiv preprint arXiv:1108.1122*, 2011.

[10] Q. Yin, X. Tang, and J. Sun. An associate-predict model for face recognition. In *CVPR*, pages 497–504. IEEE, 2011.

[11] L. Zhang, Y. Zhang, J. Tang, X. Gu, J. Li, and Q. Tian. Topology preserving hashing for similarity search. In *ACMM*, pages 123–132. ACM, 2013.

Person Search in a Scene by Jointly Modeling People Commonness and Person Uniqueness

Yuanlu Xu
Sun Yat-Sen University
eng.yuanlu.xu@ieee.org

Bingpeng Ma
Univ. of China Academy Sci.
bpma@ucas.ac.cn

Rui Huang*
Huazhong Univ. of Sci.&Tech.
ruihuang@hust.edu.cn

Liang Lin
Sun Yat-Sen University
linliang@ieee.org

ABSTRACT

This paper presents a novel framework for a multimedia search task: searching a person in a scene using human body appearance. Existing works mostly focus on two independent problems related to this task, i.e., people detection and person re-identification. However, a sequential combination of these two components does not solve the person search problem seamlessly for two reasons: 1) the errors in people detection are carried into person re-identification unavoidably; 2) the setting of person re-identification is different from that of person search which is essentially a verification problem. To bridge this gap, we propose a unified framework which jointly models the commonness of people (for detection) and the uniqueness of a person (for identification). We demonstrate superior performance of our approach on public benchmarks compared with the sequential combination of the state-of-the-art detection and identification algorithms.

Categories and Subject Descriptors

I.4 [**Image Processing and Computer Vision**]: Miscellaneous

General Terms

Theory; Algorithm; Experimentation

Keywords

person search; generative model; GMM; Fisher vector

1. INTRODUCTION

Over the past few decades, mature and low-cost vision acquisition equipments substantially boosted academic studies and industrial applications in vision related multimedia. One of the fastest growing areas is intelligent surveillance. From the perspective of public security, searching suspects and missing people in surveillance footage is an effective procedure to help solve cases. Hereby, we investigate this particular multimedia search problem, i.e., **person search**, aiming at locating a specific person in a scene given a query image using visual clues.

The most-researched clue for this task is face. Both face detection and recognition have achieved impressive performance through decades of research. However, due to the low resolution and pose variation of individuals in typical surveillance footage, faces are often deemed of limited usefulness. Going beyond faces, human body appearance is another important clue for searching a person in a scene. Nevertheless, there is a gap between the current research trends and the actual task we are facing.

Person search can be viewed as a special case of image search, or content-based image retrieval [10, 7], which has long been studied in the multimedia field. Traditional image search does not make use of the prior knowledge about

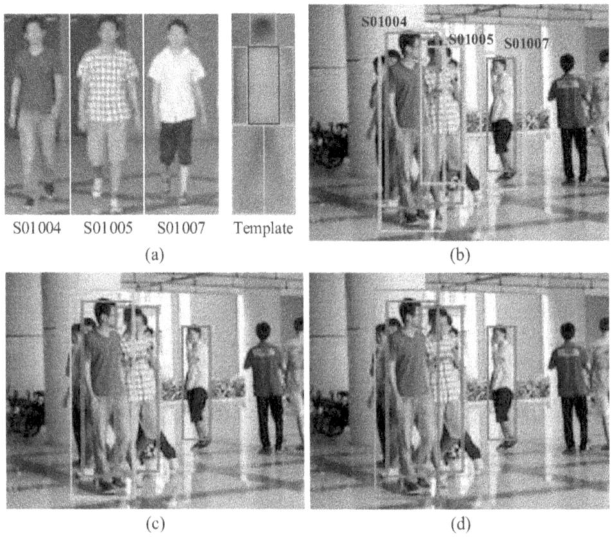

Figure 1: An illustration of searching a person in a scene. (a) Query images and template. (b) The results of our search approach. Blue rectangles are the groundtruth and green ones the correctly identified persons. (c) The people detection results from HOG-based detector. (d) The person re-identification fails to identify the correct person based on the detection results.

*Corresponding author. This work was supported in part by NSFC 61105014, 61332016, Hi-Tech R&D Program of China (no.2013AA013801), Special Project on Integration of Industry, Education and Research of Guangdong (no.2012B091100148), and Fundamental Research Funds for the Central Universities (no.13lgjc26).

MM'14, November 3–7, 2014, Orlando, Florida, USA.

ACM 978-1-4503-3063-3/14/11 ...$15.00.
http://dx.doi.org/10.1145/2647868.2654965.

the object category that the queried object belongs to, while in person search we know that the query image contains a person. The benefit is that we can now use this knowledge to facilitate our searching procedure, e.g., by incorporating the common characteristics of human body obtained from a training set besides the query image itself. Another difference is that person search is instance-level search that calls for a higher degree of accuracy for practical use than general image search.

Besides image search, extensive studies have been conducted on two other problems related to person search, i.e., people detection and person re-identification. People detection tries to find all the people in a scene, which is different from our mission of seeking a specific person given a query image. One of the most influential people detection methods employs the Histograms of Oriented Gradients (HOG) features and a linear SVM classifier [1]. The state-of-the-art general object detection methods such as Deformable Part Models (DPM) [4] can also be used for people detection. We refer the readers to a detailed review [2]. From the object detection point of view, person search is an extreme case of fine-grained object detection, i.e., instance-level detection.

To achieve the goal of person search, a further identification step is required to follow people detection, that is, a mode to match images of people using the whole body appearance, which is usually called person re-identification. Previous works on person re-identification can be roughly divided into the following two categories. *Learning-based* methods tend to learn the discriminative features [6], distance metric [14] or transformations [8] across views and cameras of the same person. Despite acknowledged success, learning-based methods suffer from model over-fitting and currently are unsuitable for large-scale data. *Matching-based* approaches, on the other hand, aim at localizing and comparing the corresponding image patches [9, 13], image segments [3] or body parts [12] in images.

However, there are two drawbacks in solving the person search task by sequentially combining people detection and person re-identification. First, person re-identification focuses on measuring the similarity of two windows (manually cropped or obtained by detection) containing the roughly aligned human subjects. Thus, the overall performance of identifying a specific person in a scene heavily relies on the performance of the people detector. Although good progress has been made on people detection, the results are not as promising when there are occluded people, as illustrated in Fig. 1. Obviously, a false positive or false negative reported by the people detector will unavoidably generate a corresponding false positive or false negative in the subsequent person re-identification results.

Second, the setting of person re-identification is different from the setting of person search. In current person re-identification research, for each window to be identified, a gallery set is commonly given so that the identity of the window can be classified or ranked according to the gallery. While in the person search task, for each candidate window, there is only one query image to be verified against. Therefore, many current person re-identification methods [6, 14] do not work in this setting.

These observations inspire us to treat the person search problem in a unified way rather than solving it in a sequential fashion. We hereby propose a framework to jointly optimize the detection of people and the identification of the queried person. The philosophy behind our proposal is that people detection algorithms use the most common features (**commonness**) shared by all human bodies to distinguish them from other objects, while the person re-identification algorithms need the most distinctive features (**uniqueness**) that are unique to a certain person to discriminate him/her against other people. Recent studies have shown that even small salient regions in appearance play an important role in identification [13]. However, in the sequential framework, the salient regions may easily be ignored by the people detector, especially if they belong to an occluded person, which results in false negatives in detection and consequently in the final results of search. On the other hand, if we only focus on the uniqueness of the queried person, we may be able to pick up the salient regions, but will probably pick up many false positives from the background as well.

In particular, our algorithm finds the queried person by testing a binary classifier in sliding windows throughout the image spatially and across scale levels, followed by non-maximum suppression to remove multiple responses of the classifier on the same individual at slightly shifted spatial locations and neighboring scales. This binary classifier is trained to verify whether the queried person is present in the current window or not and consists of two components: 1) a generative model representing the commonness of people using the average probabilistic distribution of the training data; 2) a Fisher vector feature [11] representing the uniqueness of a person, using the learned generative model as the kernel. The final verification is based on fusion of the commonness of the human body (to reduce false positives) and the uniqueness of the queried person (to reduce false negatives).

The main contributions are: 1) we argue that the simple combination of current solutions to the related problems (e.g., people detection and person re-identification) does not straightforwardly solve the new person search problem; 2) we propose a unified framework for person search by jointly modeling people commonness and person uniqueness, and show its superiority with experiments.

2. PROPOSED FRAMEWORK

In this section, we introduce a unified framework for person search. Given a query image I_q and a scene I_s, we want to find the possible location L the queried person stayed at. Since we know we are looking for a person, which belongs to the category of people, we can also make use of an additional set of images of people, T. The problem can be solved by maximizing a posterior

$$\begin{aligned} P(L|I_q, I_s, T) &\propto P(L|I_s, T)\, P(L|I_q, I_s) \\ &\propto e^{-D_{com}(L, I_s, T)} \cdot e^{-D_{uni}(L, I_q, I_s)}, \end{aligned} \quad (1)$$

because T is independent to I_q, and assuming a uniform prior for L. $D_{com}(\cdot)$ and $D_{uni}(\cdot)$ are two distance functions measuring respective commonness (Sec. 2.2) and uniqueness (Sec. 2.3), based on appearance computed locally (Sec. 2.1).

2.1 Local Descriptor

To take advantage of the common spatial configuration of human bodies (e.g., mostly standing upright, often appearing symmetric) without using sophisticated part matching algorithms, we describe the entire window with six smaller rectangles roughly corresponding to the six human body parts (i.e., head, torso, left and right arms, left and right legs), as shown in Fig. 1(a). The template is empirically derived from the average image of the training set. Feature extraction and model training are performed in each part separately. For clarity, we limit the following discussion in one part. The complete feature or model is a concatenation of the part features or models.

In order to capture the structure, color, gradient and orientation information, we use a very concise 7-dimensional low-level descriptor for each pixel [9]:

$$f(x,y) = [\tilde{x}, \tilde{y}, I(x,y), \frac{\partial I}{\partial x}, \frac{\partial I}{\partial y}, \frac{\partial^2 I}{\partial x^2}, \frac{\partial^2 I}{\partial y^2}], \quad (2)$$

where $\tilde{x}$ and $\tilde{y}$ are the pixel relative coordinates within the part, $I(x,y)$ is the pixel intensity at position (x,y), $\frac{\partial I}{\partial x}$ and $\frac{\partial I}{\partial y}$ are the first-order derivatives of image I with respect to the horizontal and vertical directions, while $\frac{\partial^2 I}{\partial x^2}$ and $\frac{\partial^2 I}{\partial y^2}$ are the second-order derivatives. The descriptors are further whitened in each part. For color images, we convert the color space to HSV and extract such descriptors in each color channel separately.

2.2 GMM Encoded Commonness

We use a generative model, in particular, a Gaussian Mixture Model (GMM) to capture the commonness of shape and appearance of human bodies. Given the training images, we learn a GMM for each part using the extracted local descriptors. The learned model is denoted by $\Theta = \{(\mu_k, \sigma_k, \pi_k) : k = 1, \ldots, K\}$, where μ_k, σ_k and π_k are the mean, covariance and prior probability of the k-th Gaussian component, respectively. In our implementation, K is empirically set to 16 for each body part and σ_k is diagonal [9].

Since we train the GMM with various images of different people, we consider the trained GMM a representation of people commonness. In essence, these learned Gaussian components can be regarded as the building blocks of the shape and appearance of human bodies while the prior distribution $\Pi = [\pi_1, \ldots, \pi_K]^\top$ describes how the common human body is constructed by these building blocks. We can compute the posterior probability w_{ik} of a local descriptor f_i being generated by the kth Gaussian component

$$w_{ik} = p(k|f_i; \mu_k, \sigma_k) = \frac{\pi_k \mathcal{N}(f_i; \mu_k, \sigma_k)}{\sum_{j=1}^{K} \pi_k \mathcal{N}(f_i; \mu_k, \sigma_k)}. \quad (3)$$

The distance function $D_{com}(\cdot)$ is then defined as

$$D_{com}(L, I_s, T) = \| \sum_{i \in idx(I_s(L))} ([w_{i1}, \ldots, w_{iK}]^\top - \Pi) \|_2, \quad (4)$$

where $idx(I_s(L))$ is the set of indices within the window $I_s(L)$. Intuitively, if the posterior of different Gaussian components deviates far from the prior mixture weights, the contents of the window are less likely to resemble a human body. We use this measure to eliminate false positives that do not contain or well localize a human body.

2.3 Fisher Vector Encoded Uniqueness

The Fisher vector [11] is an image representation which is usually used in visual classification and has seen success in person re-identification. Hereby, we incorporate it with the learned GMM model to describe the uniqueness of a specific person's appearance. For a given window W, we compute the mean and covariance deviation vectors u_k and v_k for each of the K components in the Gaussian mixture models, and the Fisher vector is the concatenation of the deviation vectors u_k and v_k, i.e., $\Phi(W) = [u_1, v_1, \ldots, u_K, v_K]^\top$, where

$$\begin{aligned} u_k &= \frac{1}{|W|\sqrt{\pi_k}} \sum_{i \in idx(W)} w_{ik} \frac{f_i - \mu_k}{\sigma_k}, \\ v_k &= \frac{1}{|W|\sqrt{2\pi_k}} \sum_{i \in idx(W)} w_{ik} \left[\left(\frac{f_i - \mu_k}{\sigma_k} \right)^2 - 1 \right]. \end{aligned} \quad (5)$$

The distance function $D_{uni}(\cdot)$ is then defined as

$$D_{uni}(L, I_q, I_s) = \| \Phi(I_s(L)) - \Phi(I_q) \|_2 . \quad (6)$$

The final decision of whether a candidate window contains the queried person is made by jointly measuring the commonness and uniqueness (Eqn. 1) with a proper threshold learned from the training data.

2.4 Searching Strategy

The entire framework follows the sliding window strategy. For each candidate window, a binary decision of whether it includes the queried person is made. We further perform multi-scale scanning against scale variations and non-maximum suppression to remove redundant responses. One different strategy employed in our framework is that the redundant responses are pruned using additional identity information, that is, if two overlapped windows are identified as two different subjects, they will not be merged; while in the original protocol for detection, responses of all people are put together for pruning and hence occluded people can be incorrectly merged with the person in the front. This way we can effectively reduce false negatives.

3. EXPERIMENTS

In this section, we show our experimental results and comparisons to other approaches on public benchmarks.

3.1 Datasets and Settings

We validate our method on two public datasets: CAMPUS-Human [12] and EPFL [5], as shown in Tab. 1. The ground truth ID and bounding box of each target person are provided in these two datasets. Other public Re-ID datasets are unsuitable for our task without scene images.

Table 1: Dataset information

Dataset	ID	Query	Scene	Target	Scene Res.
CAMPUS	74	370	214	1519	640×360
EPFL	30	70	80	294	360×288

To better evaluate our method, we separate the CAMPUS-Human dataset into two different scenarios, one crowded scenario S1 with more than 10 people in one shot and one sparse scenario S2 with less than 10 people. For both datasets, we use all query images belonging to the same person for search, and scanning every scene shot to locate the queried person. All the parameters are fixed in the experiments, including scanning scale factor 1.1, window size 60×180, window stride 8 (on both horizontal and vertical directions).

3.2 Experimental Results

To objectively evaluate our approach, we setup two baselines for comparison: 1) sequentially applying HOG-based people detection [1] and person re-identification using Fisher vectors [9] (*Detect+ID Seq*); 2) combining these two techniques more tightly by fusing the detection score and the identification difference (*Detect+ID Jnt*), the fusion weight is found by cross validation and set as 0.25(4−DetectScore)+ IDDifference. Besides, we analyze the component effectiveness of the proposed method with two settings: 1) using only uniqueness as in the general image search task (*Our Uniq*); 2) using both commonness and uniqueness (*Our Full*).

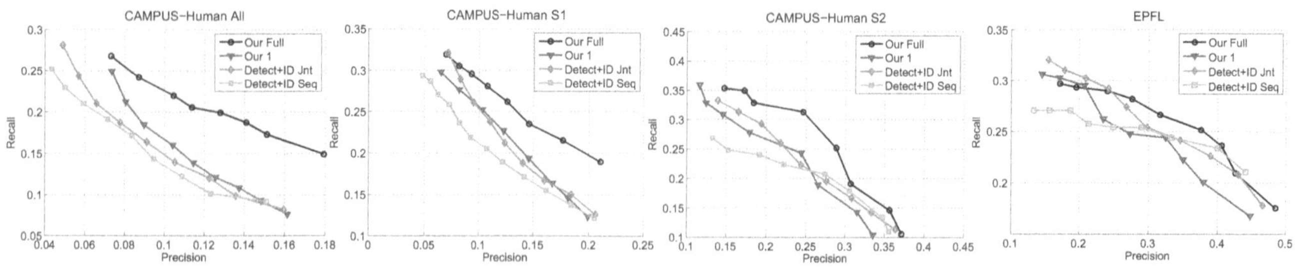

Figure 2: Performance comparisons using PR curves on CAMPUS-Human All, CAMPUS-Human S1, CAMPUS-Human S2 and EPFL datasets.

Figure 3: Person search results generated by our method. Given query persons, green and red rectangles in scene images are respective correct and false locations, compared with the groundtruth with blue ones.

Table 2: Quantitative results on two public datasets.

Method	CAMPUS-Human All	CAMPUS-Human S1	CAMPUS-Human S2	EPFL
Our Full	**16.28%**	**19.96%**	**27.55%**	**30.15%**
Our Uniq	13.59%	17.65%	24.47%	27.87%
Detect+ID Jnt	12.15%	16.54%	24.12%	29.72%
Detect+ID Seq	11.51%	15.82%	23.96%	29.54%

We adopt the PASCAL Challenge criterion to evaluate the localization results: a match is counted as the correct match only if the intersection-over-union ratio (**IoU**) with the groundtruth bounding box is greater than 50%. We utilize the F-score as the benchmark metric, which measures the accuracy of person search by considering both recall and precision. The F-scores and PR curves of all experiments on both datasets are quantitatively reported in Table. 2 and Fig. 2, and qualitatively shown in Fig. 3, respectively.

From the results, we conclude that our unified framework outperforms the other searching strategies in general. *Detect+ID Jnt* works better than *Detect+ID Seq*, supporting our advocation for joint modeling of detection and identification. However, because the detection score and identification score are two naturally different metrics, the direct combination of such scores does not work as well as our fundamentally coupled framework (*Our Full*). The improvements of *Our Full* over the baselines are smaller on the EPFL dataset because this dataset is relatively easy for the detectors.

4. CONCLUSIONS

In this paper, we propose a unified framework for person search, a practical multimedia search problem, by jointly modeling the commonness of people and the uniqueness of the queried person. The efficiency is still a concern due to the high computational cost in each sliding window. We are exploring the state-of-the-art region proposal methods to replace the sliding window protocol, as well as more efficient approaches to model commonness and uniqueness.

5. REFERENCES

[1] N. Dalal and B. Triggs. Histograms of oriented gradients for human detection. *CVPR*, 2005.

[2] P. Dollár, C. Wojek, B. Schiele, and P. Perona. Pedestrian detection: An evaluation of the state of the art. *TPAMI*, 2012.

[3] M. Farenzena, L. Bazzani, A. Perina, V. Murino, and M. Cristani. Person re-identification by symmetry-driven accumulation of local features. *CVPR*, 2010.

[4] P. F. Felzenszwalb, R. B. Girshick, D. McAllester, and D. Ramanan. Object detection with discriminatively trained part based models. *TPAMI*, 2010.

[5] F. Fleuret, E. Turetken, and P. Fua. Multiple object tracking using k-shortest paths optimization. *TPAMI*, 2011.

[6] D. Gray and H. Tao. Viewpoint invariant pedestrian recognition with an ensemble of localized features. *ECCV*, 2008.

[7] P. Jain, B. Kulis, and K. Grauman. Fast image search for learned metrics. *CVPR*, 2008.

[8] W. Li and X. Wang. Locally aligned feature transforms across views. *CVPR*, 2013.

[9] B. Ma, Y. Su, and F. Jurie. Local descriptors encoded by fisher vectors for person re-identification. *ECCV Workshops*, 2012.

[10] Y. Rui, T. S. Huang, and S.-F. Chang. Image retrieval: Current techniques, promising directions, and open issues. *J. Vis. Commun. Image Represent.*, 10(1):39–62, 1999.

[11] J. Sanchez, F. Perronnin, T. Mensink, and J. Verbeek. Image classification with the fisher vector: Theory and practice. *IJCV*, 2013.

[12] Y. Xu, L. Lin, W. Zheng, and X. Liu. Human re-identification by matching compositional template with cluster sampling. *ICCV*, 2013.

[13] R. Zhao, W. Ouyang, and X. Wang. Unsupervised salience learning for person re-identification. *CVPR*, 2013.

[14] W. Zheng, S. Gong, and T. Xiang. Re-identification by relative distance comparison. *TPAMI*, 2013.

Object Tracking using Reformative Transductive Learning with Sample Variational Correspondence

Tao Zhuo, Peng Zhang and Yanning Zhang
School of Computer Science
Northwestern Polytechnical University, China
zhuotao@mail.nwpu.edu.cn
zh0036ng@nwpu.edu.cn
ynzhang@nwpu.edu.cn

Wei Huang
School of Information Engineering
Nanchang University, China
huangwei@ncu.edu.cn

Hichem Sahli
Dept. of Electronics and Informatics(ETRO)
Vrije Universiteit Brussel, Belgium
Interuniversity Microelectronics Center, Leuven, Belgium
hsahli@vub.ac.be

ABSTRACT

Tracking-by-learning strategies have effectively solved many challenging problems for visual tracking. When labeled samples are limited, the learning performance can be improved by exploiting unlabeled ones. Thus, a key issue for semi-supervised learning is the label assignment of the unlabeled samples, which is the principal focus of transductive learning. Unfortunately, the optimization scheme employed by the transductive learning is hard to be applied to online tracking because of its large amount of computation for sample labeling. In this paper, a reformative transductive learning was proposed with the variational correspondence between the learning samples, which are utilized to build an effective matching cost function for more efficient label assignment during the learning of representative separators. By using a weighted accumulative average to update the coefficients via a fixed budget of support vectors, the proposed tracking has been demonstrated to outperform most of the state-of-art trackers.

Categories and Subject Descriptors

I.4.8 [**Image Processing and Computer Vision**]: Scene Analysis—*Tracking*

Keywords

Tracking; transductive learning; variational correspondence

1. INTRODUCTION

Arbitrary object tracking is a popular yet challenging problem because of large and unpredictable variance of objects' appearance. Some conventional trackers assumed that the target objects to be known in advance, and designed appearance models for offline learning based on diverse prior knowledge [7]. Unfortunately, tracking failure usually happens for those pre-trained trackers, as most of the realistic scenarios require objects to be specified at runtime. Therefore, semi-supervised online tracking strategies have been brought out more and more frequently in recently proposed tracking studies [13, 8, 9].

The most popular way of conducting online tracking is to update the appearance model and make it suitable for distinguishing the object from background on-the-fly. Due to the deficiency knowledge to the learner before learning starts, the cursory constraints among training data leads to performance degradation when updating classifiers. Hence, in order to introduce more rational paradigms between labeled/unlabeled data for classifier updates, Kalal *et al.* proposed a P-N learning scheme and applied it to the problem of online tracking-by-learning [13]. P-N learning establishes the structure of the training samples by exploiting the positive and negative constraints, which restricts the labeling operation. This framework also helps to guide the design of more sophisticated structural constraints that can fulfill the stability requirements of the learning. However, its limitation reside in its usage of inaccurate output decision strategy. In many cases, tracking failure is still hard to be avoided because of the inaccurate estimation between unreliable frames. Following the ideas of data selection in self-learning [14] and label assignment in transductive learning [21], Steven *et al.* proposed a self-paced learning approach SPLTT to select trustworthy frames using additional training data. By retrospectively editing and selecting previous frames for learning, SPLTT tracker is able to handle challenging situations in tracking, including occlusion/absence and large scale changes of object during long-term tracking. However, handling historical information without budget mechanism still makes SPLTT tracker suffering from the accumulated noise information.

Recently, learning via sample structural constraints has demonstrated promising performance for whole object tracking as relative geometry relationship inside and between objects can be effectively represented and incorporated for classifiers learning. Zhang *et al.* proposed structure-preserving tracker (SPOT) [24] within a pictorial-structures framework [6]. The SPOT tracker not only substantially improve the tracking performance in multi-objects scenarios, but also ameliorate single object tracking by including additional de-

MM'14, November 3–7, 2014, Orlando, Florida, USA.
Copyright 2014 ACM 978-1-4503-3063-3/14/11 ...$15.00.
http://dx.doi.org/10.1145/2647868.2654968

tectors for object parts in the tracker. Without depending on a heuristic intermediate step for producing labeled binary samples during classifier update, Hare *et al.* [8] proposed a structured output tracking (Struck) strategy with learning. Their method is able to avoid the need of intermediate classification step by explicitly allowing the output space to express different trackers' needs. With kernelized structured online SVM learning, Struck is able to achieve state-of-art tracking performance in many challenge scenarios [22].

Based on the above introduced state-of-art trackers, it can be summarized that, a good tracking design needs to consider the following indispensable factors: (1) unlabeled data plays an essential role in self-learning strategies; (2)structural constraint of samples heavily influences the tracking performance through semi-supervised learning; (3) reasonable budget scheme of historical learning results should be able to benefit classifier updating.

In this study, inspired by the large-margin theory of semi-supervised learning with representative samples in [17], a practical and robust tracking by ameliorating the online learning process with above discussed factors is introduced for the first time. The proposed learning strategy utilizes the variational correspondence in pixel-wise and descriptor-wise between data samples for label assignment. Compared with the sample labeling by intrinsical clustering convergence during online learning, using the matching costs constraints has demonstrated its efficiency and reliability. With a scheme of weighted accumulative average to update coefficients of a fixed budget of support vectors, the proposed tracking shows more robust in many challenging scenes including rotation, intrinsic compression/stretching, aspect ratio changes, etc.

The organization of the paper is as follows: Section 2 introduces the proposed learning strategy and section 3 briefly presents our online learning tracking framework. Section 4 shows experiment results and discussion and section 5 gives the conclusion of this paper.

2. LARGE MARGIN LEARNING WITH SAMPLE MATCHING COSTS

According to the large margin framework and low-density assumption in [4] about favoring the decision boundary across the low-density regions, there are labeled data pairs $(\mathbf{x}, y) \in \mathcal{L}$, where $\mathcal{L} = \{(\mathbf{x}_1, y_1), ..., (\mathbf{x}_l, y_l), \mathbf{x} \in \mathbb{R}^n, y \in \{1, -1\}\}$ and sufficient unlabeled ones $\tilde{\mathcal{L}} = \{x_{l+1}, ..., x_{l+\tilde{l}}\}$, where l and $\tilde{l}$ are the number of labeled and unlabeled instances. By extending the semi-supervised learning support vector machine [4] to learn the optimal hyperplane and the labels for unlabeled instances simultaneously, the task of SVMs classification is to find an objective function $f = \mathbf{w} \cdot \Phi(\mathbf{x}) + b$, which can realize the optimization as:

$$\min_{\mathbf{w}} \left\{ \frac{1}{2} \|\mathbf{w}\|^2 + C_1 \sum_{i=1}^{l} h(y_i, f(\mathbf{x}_i)) + C_2 \sum_{j=1}^{\tilde{l}} \tilde{h}(|f(\mathbf{x}_j)|) \right\} \quad (1)$$

Where $\Phi(\mathbf{x})$ is a feature mapping induced by the kernel trick K [21]. C_1 and C_2 are the regularization parameters that balance the computational cost and the empirical error on labeled as well as unlabeled data. The $h(\cdot)$ and $\tilde{h}(|\cdot|)$ denote the hinge loss for labeled data and symmetric hinge loss for unlabeled data respectively [12], the $(\cdot)$ is defined as $h(y_i, f(\mathbf{x}_i)) = \max\{0, yf(\mathbf{x}) - 1\}$.

It has been verified by [4] that some large margin low-density separators should exist and coincide well with the labeled data. Therefore, Eq.(1) enforces the decision boundary to lie in low-density regions. To avoid the optimization process of Eq.(1) being stuck into a local minimum, an effective approach by integrating a global simulated annealing search and efficient sampling strategy named s4vm [17] was introduced by Li *et al.* to find those crucial diverse large-margin low density separators. The s4vm utilizes a clustering algorithm to identify the representative separators when finding those large-margin low density candidates, but its deficiency of the data constraints make the interactive self-learning convergence of s4vm hard to guarantee the optimality of the final output. Inspired by this point, a learning strategy bases on Eq.(1) with sample structural constraints is proposed as:

$$\min_{\mathbf{w}_k} \left\{ \sum_{k=1}^{\kappa} \left(\frac{1}{2} \|\mathbf{w}_k\|^2 + C_1 \sum_{i=1}^{l} h_i + C_2 \sum_{j=1}^{\tilde{l}} \tilde{h}_j \right) + \eta \cdot \sum_{1 \le k \ne k' \le \kappa} \mathbf{I}(\mathbb{E}_\Psi + \mathbb{E}_\Phi \ge 1 - \epsilon) \right\} \quad (2)$$

Where, κ is the number of low density separators and η is a constant parameter. The identity function $\mathbf{I}$ calculates the penalty quantity of these diversity separators in a pairwise manner, which also denotes the structural constraints for online training data labeling by using sum of matching cost functions $\mathbb{E}_\Psi$ and $\mathbb{E}_\Phi$ in point-wise and descriptor-wise.

Let $\mathbf{t}$ be the translation between different data samples which is regarded as the variational correspondence between different data $\mathbf{x}_i$ and $\mathbf{x}_j$ [3], the pixel-wise matching cost $\mathbb{E}_\Psi$ can be defined as a variational model [11]:

$$\mathbb{E}_\Psi(\mathbf{t}) = E_{int}^\Psi + \alpha E_{grad}^\Psi + \beta E_{smooth}^\Psi \quad (3)$$

The first term E_{int}^Ψ denotes the deviations penalty between the corresponding points which have the same gray intensity value. Meanwhile, considering the influence of the illumination changes , the E_{int}^Ψ may not be always stable, therefore, a gradient based supplementary factor E_{grad}^Ψ is introduced to achieve the brightness invariance. However, only optimizing the sum of $E_{int}^\Psi + E_{grad}^\Psi$ might result in some ambiguous solutions, a regularity term E_{smooth}^Ψ is then enforced to avoid the inconsistent of realistic correspondences by penalizing the large discrepancies in the matching locations of neighboring points.

$$E_{int}^\Psi(\mathbf{p}, \mathbf{t}) = \int_\Omega \Psi(|\mathbf{x}_j(\mathbf{p} + \mathbf{t}(\mathbf{p})) - \mathbf{x}_i(\mathbf{p})|^2) dt$$
$$E_{grad}^\Psi(\mathbf{p}, \mathbf{t}) = \int_\Omega \Psi(|\nabla \mathbf{x}_j(\mathbf{p} + \mathbf{t}(\mathbf{p})) - \nabla \mathbf{x}_j(\mathbf{p})|^2) dt$$
$$E_{smooth}^\Psi(\mathbf{p}, \mathbf{t}) = \int_\Omega \Psi(|\nabla u(\mathbf{p})|^2 + |\nabla v(\mathbf{p})|^2) d\mathbf{p} \quad (4)$$

Another matching cost function $\mathbb{E}_\Phi$ is defined for grid cell correspondence between data samples, which is a multi-scale extension of descriptor-wise matching with a pyramid graph model [10]. Let $d(\mathbf{p})$ be the feature descriptor extracted at location $\mathbf{p}$ and n be the total number of the descriptors, the matching cost function across all the pyramid levels $\lambda \in \Lambda$ can be represented as:

$$E_\Phi(\mathbf{t}, \mathbf{s}) = \sum_\Lambda \Phi(\mathbf{t}_\lambda, \mathbf{s}_\lambda) + \gamma \sum \|\mathbf{s}_\lambda - \mathbf{s}_{\lambda'}\|_1 \quad (5)$$

where

$$\Phi(\mathbf{t}, \mathbf{s}) = \frac{1}{n} \sum_\Omega \min(\|d_i(\mathbf{p}) - d_j(\mathbf{s}(\mathbf{p} + \mathbf{t}))\|_1, \theta) \quad (6)$$

For robustness to outliers, a truncated L1 norm is utilized for descriptor distance with a threshold θ. A scale variable $\mathbf{s}$ is introduced by a scale smoothness term with an associated weight constant γ.

3. TRACKING FRAMEWORK

The proposed tracking is constructed within a tracking-by-detection framework, the online tracking consists of an appearance model and a motion model. When initial states of an object are specified, the motion model is used to generate the feature consistent (*e.g.*, brightness, SIFT or SURF) of a pixel or patch between consecutive frames, which is the variational correspondence among the learning samples. During tracking process, the online transductive learning will be applied to update the appearance model. For a comprehensive consideration, we design an optional strategy which takes the advantage of both tracking and detection output to obtain more accurate target state. During model updates, a budget maintenance scheme is introduced to utilize the historical learning results for more robust tracking performance.

Initialization: in the initialization stage, the object is represented by HoG Features generated from a normalized image patch (normally using 32×32 bounding box) based on the manually ground truth. When tracking starts, the samples region are generated within a given radius and the sampling number m is also specified ($m \geq 60$), which guarantees sufficient learning data. The initial data labels are assigned according to the bounding box overlap, which is defined as $VOR = \frac{Area(B_{gt} \cap B_t)}{Area(B_{gt} \cup B_t)}$, where B_t and B_{gt} are the sampled bounding box and target bounding box repectively. During online classification, to speed up the process, we used an adaptive step search instead of pixel-wise sampling to obtain the candidate samples with a radius areas. The adaptive step ratio was set to $\rho = 0.1$ in both horizontal and vertical directions.

Optional Strategy: to achieve a robust tracking with online learning, we introduced a motion model based on median flow [13] to compensate the possible tracking drift. Instead of using the weighted mean to combine the output from appearance model *bbox1* and motion model *bbox2*, we propose an optional strategy to obtain more robust and accurate result *bbox*.

$$bbox = \begin{cases} bbox2, if\ \delta > \theta_{vor} \wedge y_t^* > 0 \\ bbox1, otherwise \end{cases} \tag{7}$$

where δ denotes the VOR between *bbox1* and *bbox2*, y_t^* represents the highest score from the appearance model and θ_{vor} is a pre-defined threshold. With this strategy, the inaccuracy happened with appearance model can be effectively calibrated by motion and finally alleviating the error accumulation caused by model update.

For the issue of scale change, suppose s_b^{k-1} is the size of the bounding box in previous frame, p_{1i}^{k-1} and p_{2i}^{k-1} are the selected point pairs within the bounding box, n is the number of the chosen point pairs. If p_{1i}^k and p_{2i}^k are the corresponding point pairs of p_{1i}^{k-1} and p_{2i}^{k-1} in current frame, the scale of target can be obtained by using the distance ratio of a set of corresponding points between two consecutive frames as:

$$s_b^k = s_b^{k-1} \frac{1}{n} \sum_{i=1}^{n} \frac{||p_{1i}^k - p_{2i}^k||}{||p_{1i}^{k-1} - p_{2i}^{k-1}||}, p_{1i}^{k-1} \neq p_{2i}^{k-1} \tag{8}$$

Budget Issue: the appearance model learning is carried out within each frame independently. Due to the recurrent variation of the object's appearance as tracking goes, a budget maintenance for historical training results need to be employed. It is assumed that more recently obtained support vectors would provide more contributions compared to the prior ones for sample evaluation, therefore, we incorporate a set of weights into the trained support vectors buffer $\{\mathbf{w}, C_1, C_2\}$ and used the weighted mean $\{\bar{\mathbf{w}}^t, \bar{C}_1^t, \bar{C}_2^t\}$ for evaluation in *t-th* frame as:

$$\bar{\mathbf{w}}^t = \frac{1}{\tau} \sum_{t=1}^{\tau} \pi^{\tau - t} \mathbf{w}^t, \bar{C}_{1,2}^t = \frac{1}{\tau} \sum_{t=1}^{\tau} \pi^{\tau - t} C_{1,2}^t \tag{9}$$

Where τ is the size of $\mathbf{w}$, $\{\mathbf{w}^t, C_1^t, C_2^t\}$ denotes the *t-th* added support vectors. $\pi \in (0, 1]$ is a forget factor which denotes the belief of optimum output of each frame. In order to make sure that the number of support vectors does not exceed specific limitations, a mechanism of 'the bottom out system' is employed to incorporate a budget into the proposed tracking study. Its main idea is to remove the support vector which has the smallest measurement $\|\Delta \mathbf{w}\|^2$ to the weight vector $\mathbf{w}$. After that, corresponding coefficients of the remaining support vectors need to be updated in order to compensate changes caused by the removal of support vectors. Given a fixed budget T, if $\tau > T$, we remove the earliest support vectors $\{\mathbf{w}^1, C_1^1, C_2^1\}$ from the buffer and add the new one. Then the corresponding coefficients of the current support vectors are specified with π, as shown in Eq.(9).

4. EXPERIMENT

We evaluate the proposed tracking with 20 video sequences coming from the benchmark datasets [22], which contains various tracking targets (*e.g.*, face, pedestrian, sporter, car, toy) and different challenging scenarios, such as scale and illumination change, occlusion, fast movement, out of plane rotation and background clutters. To demonstrate the tracking performance of the proposed tracking, we compared it with 11 representative state-of-the-art tracking approaches: CT [23], CSK [5], LOT [18], DFT [19], VTS [16], Struck [8], LSK [1], CXT [20], VTD [15], TLD [13] and MIL [2].

For quantitative evaluation of the tracking performance, we used the average VOR (Pascal VOC overlap ratio) and average CLE (center location error) [22] as the measurements, the results are shown in Table.1 and Table.2 respectively. The overall satisfactory performance has confirmed that the proposed method can achieve more robust tracking in a variety of challenging scenarios including illumination and scale variation, fast movement, deformation, background clutters, heavy occlusion and out of plane rotation, and so on. In addition, the success plot and precision plot (shown in Figure.1) [22] are also used to demonstrate the general performance of all the tracking approaches. In our experiment, the thresholds of success plot are specified from 0 to 0.9 by step 0.1. For same threshold, the higher the plot, more robust of the tracking. The thresholds of precision plot are specified from 10 to 50 by step 10, the higher the accurate.

Since the proposed tracking is based on the tracking-by-detection framework, drift may happen when similar objects occlusion happens for some time span. In addition, the computational cost of our work mainly concentrates on the process of feature extraction. The tracking framework is im-

Table 1: The average VORs of the 12 trackers on 20 video sequences

Sequence	Ours	CT	CSK	LOT	DFT	VTS	Struck	LSK	CXT	VTD	TLD	MIL
Boy	**0.73**	0.42	0.72	0.47	0.72	0.42	0.70	0.66	0.35	0.67	0.66	0.65
Car4	**0.77**	0.14	0.32	0.15	0.19	0.36	0.39	0.28	0.16	0.36	0.19	0.21
CarScale	**0.73**	0.48	0.52	0.26	0.48	0.48	0.50	0.52	0.45	0.47	0.47	0.52
Couple	**0.65**	0.05	0.31	0.49	0.08	0.35	0.55	0.07	0.06	0.08	0.32	0.52
Crossing	**0.64**	0.57	0.56	0.28	0.45	0.34	0.28	0.33	0.44	0.34	0.45	0.62
David	**0.78**	0.31	0.39	0.31	0.43	0.47	0.43	0.59	0.57	0.46	0.64	0.30
David3	**0.75**	0.23	0.48	0.50	0.59	0.25	0.71	0.46	0.09	0.18	0.05	0.29
Deer	**0.70**	0.03	0.59	0.17	0.58	0.05	0.61	0.35	0.39	0.06	0.47	0.45
Dog1	**0.82**	0.65	0.65	0.41	0.57	0.62	0.66	0.65	0.69	0.60	0.54	0.59
Faceocc2	**0.81**	0.57	0.63	0.52	0.62	0.74	0.63	0.56	0.71	0.74	0.62	0.56
Fish	**0.86**	0.68	0.77	0.37	0.74	0.64	0.56	0.54	0.69	0.60	0.68	0.54
Football	**0.64**	0.46	0.49	0.47	0.54	0.60	0.45	0.51	0.50	0.61	0.44	0.49
Mhyang	**0.86**	0.48	0.80	0.45	0.34	0.84	0.79	0.70	0.81	0.80	0.82	0.64
MountainBike	**0.80**	0.12	0.78	0.54	0.78	0.36	0.69	0.10	0.10	0.51	0.12	0.15
Singer1	**0.75**	0.31	0.31	0.13	0.04	0.43	0.31	0.08	0.56	0.43	0.57	0.21
Singer2	**0.63**	0.14	0.05	0.08	0.26	0.04	0.05	0.04	0.06	0.04	0.03	0.05
Subway	**0.78**	0.03	0.16	0.19	0.35	0.17	0.68	0.44	0.15	0.16	0.65	0.15
Sylvester	0.58	0.53	0.62	0.33	0.18	0.57	**0.66**	0.15	0.64	0.57	0.49	0.55
Trellis	**0.57**	0.35	0.29	0.33	0.29	0.41	0.48	0.22	0.56	0.45	0.52	0.35
Woman	0.58	0.14	0.18	0.10	0.57	0.06	**0.72**	0.14	0.11	0.06	0.32	0.14
Average	**0.72**	0.33	0.48	0.33	0.44	0.41	0.54	0.37	0.41	0.41	0.45	0.40

Table 2: The average CLEs of the 12 trackers on 20 video sequences

Sequence	Ours	CT	CSK	LOT	DFT	VTS	Struck	LSK	CXT	VTD	TLD	MIL
Boy	5.7	34.1	3.2	49.5	2.4	46.4	3.5	**2.2**	28.1	7.8	3.6	6.3
Car4	**6.0**	92.0	41.1	114.9	108.4	37.4	11.8	42.5	72.4	33.2	84.4	59.5
CarScale	22.1	73.8	27.8	97.4	74.3	37.9	37.0	12.2	34.8	34.3	14.2	*11.5*
Couple	**10.4**	101.7	73.3	39.3	112.4	42.7	32.3	112.2	102.0	104.0	35.6	37.0
Crossing	**4.4**	7.3	8.9	91.5	23.8	42.5	72.3	45.8	18.7	42.9	22.4	7.0
David	6.0	31.5	16.9	30.8	14.3	16.0	7.3	5.5	**4.2**	15.9	12.5	39.8
David3	10.7	85.5	58.9	**8.7**	56.4	103.7	8.8	72.3	224.7	180.6	208.8	102.3
Deer	10.6	233.9	6.8	80.9	9.7	222.9	**7.7**	90.9	25.3	219.2	20.3	30.3
Dog1	6.3	8.4	3.6	36.2	19.9	16.6	4.9	6.7	**2.8**	17.5	4.7	11.8
Faceocc2	7.5	20.4	7.5	19.5	10.3	7.5	**6.3**	15.8	7.3	7.5	18.2	21.9
Fish	**6.2**	15.2	8.4	38.6	6.4	12.5	22.2	20.1	8.8	15.7	12.7	19.9
Football	11.1	15.7	15.5	12.2	9.0	5.9	19.5	14.3	12.5	**4.7**	12.6	11.8
Mhyang	3.1	27.2	3.4	36.2	46.9	3.5	**2.8**	9.6	2.9	4.1	5.8	14.3
MountainBike	**6.1**	215.7	6.8	29.1	6.5	115.8	10.2	221.7	209.6	42.0	128.9	201.7
Singer1	**6.8**	14.3	23.5	164.3	212.6	12.8	11.0	114.7	26.9	9.1	26.6	44.1
Singer2	**26.2**	116.7	170.1	155.7	75.9	178.7	173.4	173.9	194.8	178.7	189.1	161.9
Subway	**3.8**	151.1	172.9	147.6	58.9	143.5	5.1	28.0	141.3	143.9	6.5	149.8
Sylvester	17.6	14.9	8.4	29.2	87.4	19.0	**5.5**	78.4	13.4	19.2	15.5	15.8
Trellis	21.7	40.1	65.6	41.6	43.5	35.0	**12.4**	72.6	20.2	31.5	15.2	38.7
Woman	17.7	121.1	215.4	141.7	7.8	152.6	**2.2**	85	131.0	116.5	150.0	121.7
Average	**10.5**	71.0	46.9	68.2	49.3	62.6	22.84	63.52	63.4	63.08	44.30	55.35

plemented by MATLAB on a workstation with Intel Core i7 3.4GHz. The average running speed is 5pfs without any code optimization. If using C++/OpenCV with CUDA parallel programming, the proposed tracking would be able to fulfil the real-time requirement.

5. CONCLUSION

In this paper, we proposed a robust online tracking framework for unknown object tracking. After a thorough investigation of the transductive learning strategy, we incorporated a sample variational correspondence into the online learning of appearance model. With the proposed optional strategy to balance the result between tracking and detection, robust and accurate tracking can be achieved by the proposed work. Compared with other recently proposed state-of-art trackers on challenging sequences on benchmark datasets, we demonstrated that our tracking strategy shows more satisfactory performance in different challenging scenarios.

6. ACKNOWLEDGMENTS

This research is supported by Research Fund for the Doctoral Program of Higher Education of China 20126102120055, National Natural Science Foundation of China 61301194 & 61231016 & 61363046, foundation grant from NWPU 3102014JSJ0014 and Jiangxi Provincial department of Science and Technology 20142BBE50023, 20142BAB217033.

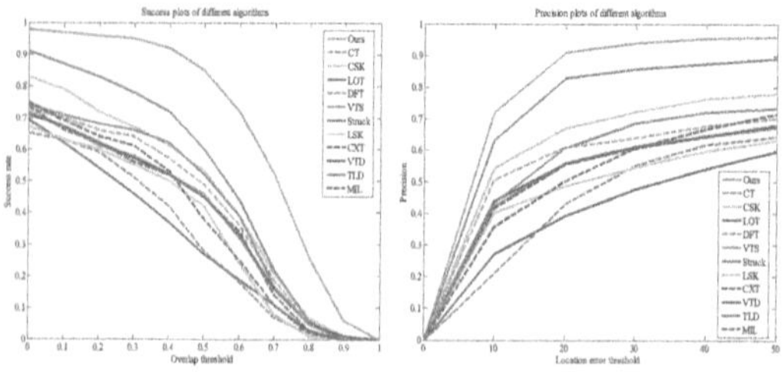

(a) (b)

Figure 1: The success plots (a) and precision plots (b) with different thresholds.

7. REFERENCES

[1] L. Y. B. Liu, J. Huang and C. Kulikowsk. Robust tracking using local sparse appearance model and k-selection. *CVPR*, 2011.

[2] B. Babenko, M.-H. Yang, and S. Belongie. Visual tracking with online multiple instance learning. *CVPR*, pages 983–990, 2009.

[3] T. Brox and J. Malik. Large dispacement optical flow: Descriptor matching in variational motion estimation. *TPAMI*, 33:500–513, 2010.

[4] R. Collobert, F. Sinz, J. Weston, and L. Bottou. Large scale transductive svms. *JMLR*, pages 1687–1712, 2006.

[5] P. M. F. Henriques, R. Caseiro and J. Batista. Exploiting the circulant structure of tracking-by-detection with kernels. *ECCV*, 2012.

[6] P. Felzenszwalb, R. Girshick, D. McAllester, and D. Ramanan. Object detection with discriminatively trained part based models. *TPAMI*, 32(9):1627–1645, 2010.

[7] S. Gu, Y. Zheng, and C. Tomasi. Linear time offline tracking and lower envelope algorithms. *ICCV*, pages 1840–1846, 2011.

[8] S. Hare, A. Saffari, and P. H. S. Torr. Struck: Structured output tracking with kernels. *ICCV*, pages 263 – 270, 2011.

[9] J. S. III and D. Ramanan. Self-paced learning for long-term tracking. *CVPR*, pages 2379–2386, 2013.

[10] F. S. J. Kim, C. Liu and K. Grauman. Deformatble spatial pyramid matching for fast dense correspondence. *CVPR*, 2013.

[11] R. D. J.B. Zin and A. Bartoli. A general dense image matching framework combining direct and feature-based costs. *ICCV*, 2013.

[12] T. Joachims. Transductive inference for text classification using support vector machines. *ICML*, 1999.

[13] Z. Kalal, K. Mikolajczyk, and J. Matas. Tracking-learning-detection. *TPAMI*, 6(1):1409–1422, 2010.

[14] M. Kumar, B. Packer, and D. Koller. Self-paced learning for latent variable models. *NIPS*, 2010.

[15] J. Kwon and K. M. Lee. Visual tracking decomposition. *CVPR*, 2010.

[16] J. Kwon and K. M. Lee. Tracking by sampling trackers. *ICCV*, 2011.

[17] Y. Li and Z. Zhou. Towards making unlabeled data never hurt. *ICML*, 2011.

[18] D. L. S. Oron, A. Bar-Hillel and S. Avidan. Locally orderless tracking. *CVPR*, 2012.

[19] L. Sevilla-Lara and E. Learned-Miller. Distribution fields for tracking. *CVPR*, 2012.

[20] N. V. T. B. Dinh and G. Medioni. Context tracker: Exploring supporters and distracters in unconstrained environments. *CVPR*, 2011.

[21] V. Vapnik. *The Nature of Statistical Learning Theory*, 1995.

[22] Y. Wu, J. Lim, and M.-H. Yang. Online object tracking: A benchmark. *CVPR*, pages 2411–2418, 2013.

[23] K. Zhang, L. Zhang, and M.-H. Yang. Real-time compressive tracking. *ECCV*, pages 864–877, 2012.

[24] L. Zhang and L. Maaten. Structure preserving object tracker. *CVPR*, pages 1838–1845, 2013.

Multimodal Dynamic Networks for Gesture Recognition

Di Wu, Ling Shao
Department of Electronic and Electrical Engineering
The University of Sheffield, Sheffield S1 3JD, UK.
{elp10dw,ling.shao}@sheffield.ac.uk

ABSTRACT

Multimodal input is a real-world situation in gesture recognition applications such as sign language recognition. In this paper, we propose a novel bi-modal (audio and skeleton joints) dynamic network for gesture recognition. First, state-of-the-art dynamic Deep Belief Networks are deployed to extract high level audio and skeletal joints representations. Then, instead of traditional late fusion, we adopt another layer of perceptron for cross modality learning taking the input from each individual net's penultimate layer. Finally, to account for temporal dynamics, the learned shared representations are used for estimating the emission probability to infer action sequences. In particular, we demonstrate that multimodal feature learning will extract semantically meaningful shared representations, outperforming individual modalities, and the early fusion scheme's efficacy against the traditional method of late fusion.

Categories and Subject Descriptors

H.1.2 [**User/Machine Systems**]: Human information processing; I.2.14 [**Artificial Intelligence**]: [video analysis, motion]

General Terms

Algorithm, Experimentation

Keywords

Gesture Recognition; Human-Computer Interaction; Multimodal Fusion; Deep Belief Networks

1. INTRODUCTION

Gesture recognition has been a popular research field in recent years due to its promising application prospects in human-computer interaction. In the early days of gesture recognition research, most approaches were controller-based, in which users had to wear or hold certain hardware for motion data capturing. In vision-based approaches, usersŠ motion data are captured by cameras and numerous computer vision methods have been successfully adopted into this area for further data analysis and understanding. Over the last few years, with the immense popularity of the Kinect, there has been renewed interest in developing methods for human gesture and action recognition from both 3D skeletal data and audio data captured synchronously by the device.

Deep learning is an emerging field of machine learning focusing on learning representations of data and has recently found success in a variety of domains, from computer vision to speech recognition, natural language processing, web search ranking, and even online advertising. The ability of deep learning methods to capture the semantics of data is, however, limited by both the complexity of the models and the intrinsic richness of the input to the system. In particular, current methods only consider a single modality leading to an impoverished model of the world. Sensory data are inherently multimodal instead: images are often associated with text; videos contain both visual and audio signals; text is often related to social content from public media; etc. It is expected that the cross-modality structure may yield a big leap forward in machine understanding of the world.

Multimodal learning involves relating information from multiple sources. For example, images and depth scans are correlated at first-order as depth discontinuities often manifest as strong edges in images. Conversely, audio and visual data for gesture recognition have correlations at a "mid-level", as phonemes and joints motions; it can be difficult to relate joint spatio-temporal information to audio waveforms or spectrograms. Learning from multimodal inputs is technically challenging because different modalities have different statistics and different kinds of representations. For instance, text is discrete and often represented by very large and sparse vectors, while images are represented by dense tensors that exhibit strong local correlations. Traditional multi-agent systems tend to adopt the late fusion scheme by normalizing the confident values from an individual modality for final prediction, ignoring the subtle intrinsic properties within different modalities. Fortunately, deep learning has the promise to learn adaptive representations from the input, potentially bridging the gap between these different modalities.

In this paper, a novel framework of bimodal dynamic networks is proposed for continuous gesture recognition given 3D joint positions and the audio utterance of the gesture to-

MM'14, November 3–7, 2014, Orlando, Florida, USA.
Copyright 2014 ACM 978-1-4503-3063-3/14/11 ...$15.00.
http://dx.doi.org/10.1145/2647868.2654969.

kens.We focus on data driven analysis of acyclic audio-video sequence labeling problems.

Problem formulation: Given a multimodal input sequence $\mathbf{X^m} = \{\mathbf{x_1^m}, \mathbf{x_2^m}, \dots, \mathbf{x_t^m}\}$, where $\mathbf{m}$ is the modal index (in our experimentm=**2** because we only use audio and skeleton inputs), instead of finding the global label $\mathbf{Y}$ directly, we dissect the problem into finding the individual $\{\hat{\mathbf{y_1}}, \hat{\mathbf{y_2}}, \dots, \hat{\mathbf{y_t}}\}$ and reasoning with a higher level Markov field to obtain the most likely label $\hat{\mathbf{Y}}$.

Contributions:

i) Relying on a pure learning approach, all the knowledge in the model comes from the data without sophisticated preprocessing or dimensionality reduction via manifold learning methods. The proposed feed forward neural networks offer several potential advantages as a better estimator for emission probabilities of the Markov field over the traditional paradigms (*e.g.* Gaussian mixture models) because its estimation of the posteriori probabilities does not require detailed assumptions about the data distribution. An advantage of a fully-automatic learning-based method is that it incorporates the feature learning and classification procedures in a unified framework by minimizing the energy (*i.e.* optimizing the object function). Therefore, the proposed framework is more adaptable to different object functions or different input sensory modalities.

ii) Instead of brutally flattening a sequence as in [7] where a fixed number of input frames is required, we employ a dynamic time programming scheme, dissecting the problem into modeling frame-based emission probability. The system is scalable to various time length sequences and is easily adapted for simultaneously segmenting and recognizing video sequences, discovering anchor points.

iii) The multimodal framework learns the shared representation from multiple high level feature representations. Experimental results show the gains over late fusion methods and it opens the door for an early fusion fashion of generative time series modeling.

The model has been designed with bi-modal gesture recognition in mind, but should lend itself well to other multimodal high-dimensional time series.

2. ARCHITECTURE

The overall architecture of our proposed model is shown in Figure 1. The individual emission probability estimators are based on the state-of-the-art architectures as in [5, 12]. Specifically, a Deep Belief Network is deployed for each modality to estimate the output emission probability. Because both feature modalities $\mathbf{X^m}$ are continuous instead of binomial features, the first visible layer is a Gaussian Restricted Boltzmann Machine to model the energy term:

$$E(v,h;\theta) = -\sum_{i=1}^{D}\frac{(v_i-b_i)^2}{2\sigma_i^2} - \sum_{i=1}^{D}\sum_{j=1}^{F}W_{ij}h_j\frac{v_i}{\sigma_i} - \sum_{j=1}^{F}a_jh_j \quad (1)$$

where model parameters $\theta = \{W, b, a, \sigma\}$ with W_{ij} representing the symmetric interaction term between visible unit i and hidden unit j while b_i and a_j are their bias terms with visible unit variance σ. D and F are the numbers of visible and hidden units.

The outputs of the neural net are the hidden states learned by force alignment during the supervised training process. Once each individual modality is trained, the penultimate

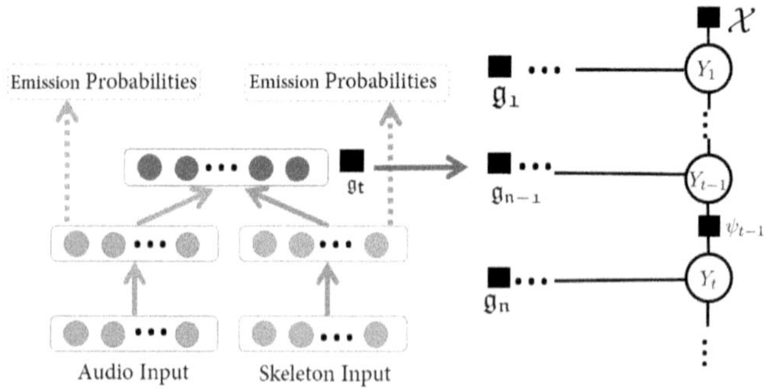

Figure 1: Architecture of the multimodal dynamic networks: each modality (audio or skeleton input) is first pre-trained by a Deep Belief Network, and their penultimate layers are fused together to generate a shared representation for dual modalities. The outputs are the emission probabilities $\mathfrak{g}_t$ for temporal dynamic modeling. In our experiments, we assume each of the conditional distributions per frame is independent of all previous observations except the most recent, hence the higher level is specified as a Hidden Markov Model.

layer is extracted and fused for the shared representation. Then, the standard backpropagation can be adopted for adjusting the weight W^m for each modality m:

$$W^m = W^m - \alpha\frac{\partial}{\partial W^m}J(W) \quad (2)$$

where α is the annealed learning rate and $J(W)$ is the cost function (cross-entropy) of the last layer perceptron by feed forwarding the fused penultimate layers from mutli-modalities. The output of the network is $p(X_t|Y_t)$ denoting the fused emission probability and is denoted by $\mathfrak{g}_t$ in Figure 1.

Assuming each of the conditional distributions is independent of all previous observations except for the most recent, the full probability model is now specified as HMM:

$$p(Y_{1:T}, X_{1:T}) = p(Y_1)p(X_1|Y_1)\prod_{t=2}^{T}p(X_t|Y_t)p(Y_t|Y_{t-1}), \quad (3)$$

where $p(Y_1)$ is the prior on the first hidden state and in all our experiments, we have a uniform prior, and $p(H_t|H_{t-1})$ is the transition dynamic model. We can infer the action presence in a new sequence by Viterbi decoding as:

$$V_{t,\mathcal{Y}} = P(Y_t|X_t) + \log(\max_{\mathcal{Y}\in\mathcal{Y}_a}(V_{t-1,\mathcal{Y}})) \quad (4)$$

where initial state $V_{1,\mathcal{Y}} = \log(P(Y_1|X_1))$. From the inference results, we define the probability of an action $a \in \mathcal{A}$ as $p(y_t = a|x_{1:t}) = V_{T,\mathcal{Y}}$.

Related Work

The proposed framework is mostly related to the works of [7, 10] in that, instead of the traditional late fusion, all resort to an early fusion scheme. In [7], the input sequences are treated as a holistic entity, hence, the method is not adaptable to various time length input. A multimodal Deep Boltzmann Machine is introduced in [10] to learn a good generative model of the joint space of image and text inputs for information retrieval.

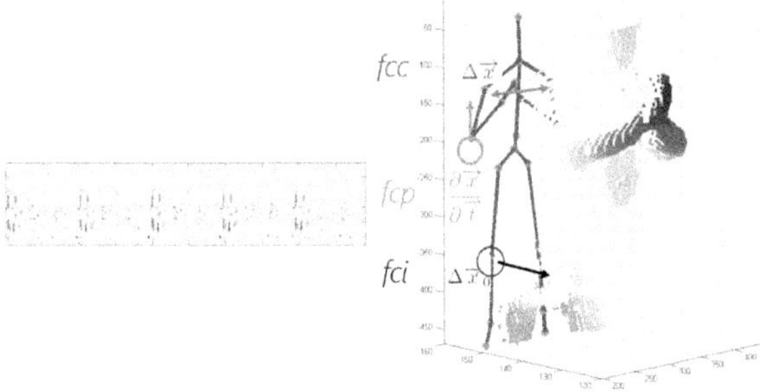

Figure 2: Input modules: left–audio input in the form of MFCC, and in order to conform to the 20 fps, 5 frames are concatenated together (10-ms fixed frame rate); right–skeleton 3D positional features.

Modality and Method	Classification rate
Audio Only, DBN+HMM [5]	0.554
Skeleton Only, DBN+HMM [12]	0.586
Audio + Skeleton, Model averaging	0.668
Multimodal DBN+HMM	***0.701***

Table 1: Recognition accuracy compared to the individual modal method and the multimodal confident score averaging scheme (late fusion).

In order to model the time series data, the unimodal of our architecture is built upon the framework of [5, 12] which deploy Deep Belief Networks in the place of Gaussian Mixture Models to model the emission probabilities for Hidden Markov Models. However, our proposed framework is the first work to learn the shared representation for modeling multimodal dynamic time series inputs.

3. EXPERIMENTS

ChaLearn Italian Gesture Recognition

This dataset is on "multiple instance, user independent learning" [2] of gestures. We focus on the skeletal modality and audio modality. There are 20 Italian cultural/anthropological signs, *i.e.,vattene, vieniqui, perfetto, furbo, cheduepalle, chevuoi, daccordo, seipazzo, combinato, freganiente , ok, cosatifarei, basta, prendere, noncenepiu, fame, tantotempo, buonissimo, messidaccordo, sonostufo.* We use the subset where the label data are provided during our evaluation process. The set contains 393 labeled sequences with a total of 7754 gestures. We used 350 sequences for training and the rest 43 sequences for testing, where each sequence contains 20 unique gestures. In the training set, there are in total 339,700 frames (20 fps). Note that a large number of frames is advantageous in our model settings over other nonparametric models for estimating skeletal human poses.

Audio Features

The speech was analyzed using a 25-ms Hamming window with a 10-ms fixed frame rate. We represented the speech using 12th-order Mel frequency cepstral coefficients (MFCCs) and energy, along with their first and second temporal derivatives. In order to conform to the 20 fps, 5 frames are concatenated together (10-ms fixed frame rate). Hence one audio frame will be of dimensionality $39*5 = 195$. The data were normalized so that, averaged over the training cases, each coefficient or first derivative or second derivative had zero mean and unit variance.

Skeleton Features

Only upper body joints are relevant to our discriminative gesture recognition tasks. Therefor, we consider only the 9 upper body joints for our task (full body joints have been compared, but as expected, led to inferior results compared to upper body 9 joints). The 9 upper body joints used are *"ShoulderCenter, ShoulderLeft, ElbowLeft, WristLeft, HandLeft, ShoulderRight, ElbowRight, WristRight, HandRight"*.

The 3D coordinates of N joints of current frame c are given as: $X_c = \{x_1^c, x_2^c, \ldots, x_N^c\}$. We deploy 3D positional pairwise differences of joints [13] for observation domain $\mathcal{X}$. They capture posture features, motion features and offset features by direction concatenation: $\mathcal{X} = [f_{cc}, f_{cp}, f_{ci}]$ as demonstrated in Figure 2.

$$f_{cc} = \{x_i^c - x_j^c | i, j = 1, 2, \ldots, N; i \neq j\}$$
$$f_{cp} = \{x_i^c - x_j^p | x_i^c \in X_c; x_j^p \in X_p\}$$
$$f_{ci} = \{x_i^c - x_j^I | x_i^c \in X_c; x_j^I \in X_I\}$$

This results in a raw dimension of $N_{\mathcal{X}} = N_{joints} * (N_{joints} - 1)/2 + N_{joints}^2 + N_{joints}^2) * 3$ where N_{joints} is the number of joints used. Hence, in our experiment, $N_{joints} = 9, N_{\mathcal{X}} = 594$. Note that before extracting any features, all the 3D joint coordinates are transformed from the world coordinate system to a person centric coordinate system by placing the HipCenter (or ShoulderCenter if applied) at the origin. By including temporal differences f_{cp}, f_{ci} partially overcomes the very strong conditional independence assumption of HMMs, *i.e.*, successive frames are independent given the hidden states of the HMM.

Admittedly, we do not completely neglect human prior knowledge about information extraction for relevant static postures, velocity and offset overall dynamics of motion data. Nevertheless, the aforementioned three attributes are all very crude pairwise features without any tweak into the dataset or handpicking the most relevant pairwise, triple wise, *etc.* , designed features [1, 6, 8, 9]. A similar data driven approach has been adopted in [3] where random forest classifiers were adapted to the problem of recognizing gestures using a bundle of 35 frames. These sets of feature extraction processes resemble the *Mel Frequency Cepstral Coefficients (MFCCs)* for the speech recognition community [5].

Dynamic Networks Setup

All DBNs were pre-trained with a fixed recipe using stochastic gradient decent with a mini-batch size of 128 training cases. For Gaussian-binary RBMs, we ran 225 epochs with a fixed learning rate of 0.002 while for binary-binary RBMs we used 75 epochs with a learning rate of 0.02 and with a mini-batch size of 100 training cases. Unsupervised initializations tend to avoid local minima and increase the network's performance stability. For fine-tuning, the learning rate starts at 0.1 with 0.998 scaling after each epoch. To prevent complex co-adaptations in which a feature detector is only helpful in the context of several other specific feature detectors, we dropout [4] half of the feature detectors.

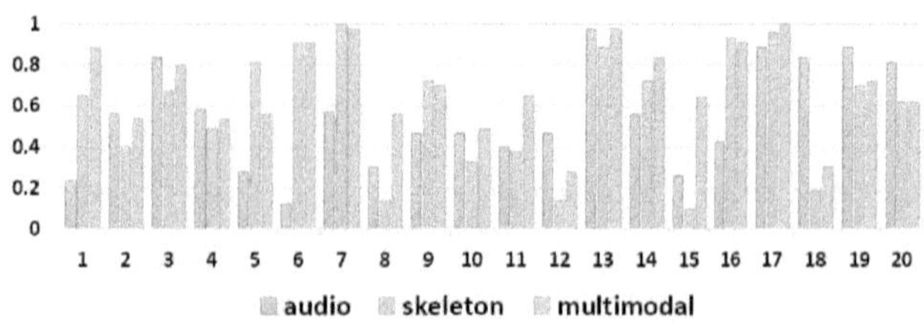

Figure 3: Comparison of individual gesture class classification rates among different modalities.

For high level feature extraction, we fix the network architecture as $[N_{\mathcal{X}}, N_2, 1000, 1000, 1000, 1000, N_{\mathcal{TC}}]$ where $N_{\mathcal{X}}$ is the observation domain dimension and N_2 is the number of hidden nodes in *GRBM*. For audio modality, $N_{\mathcal{X}} = 195, N_2 = 1000$ and for skeletal modality, $N_{\mathcal{X}} = 594, N_2 = 2000$; $N_{\mathcal{TC}}$ is the output target class. And, in all our experiments, the number of states associated with an individual action $N_{\mathcal{H}_a}$ is chosen as 10 for modeling the states of an action class.

Once each individual modality's Deep Belief Network finishes fine tuning, we combine the multi-DBNs and extract their penultimate layers and further run 200 epochs to slightly adjust the weights for each individual modal DBN. Though we believe further carefully fine-tuned parameters would lead to more competitive results, in order to avoid "creeping overfitting", as algorithms over time become too adapted to the dataset, essentially memorizing all its idiosyncrasies and losing the ability to generalize [11], we would like to treat the model as the aforementioned more generic approach.

Results & Computational Complexity Analysis

We compare our model with the state-of-the-art methods using individual input modals and the baseline multimodal method by averaging the individual modal output confident scores in Table 1. It can be seen that both multimodal recognition rates are considerably higher than a single modal input. And the proposed framework of early fusion outperforms the confident score averaging scheme. We further plot the classification rate for each gesture class among different modalities in Figure 3. The bar plot shows the complementary information between two modalities: even when one modality achieves low recognition rate, the multimodal fusion achieves on par with another modality, *e.g.*, gesture 6; when both modalities generate noisy output, the shared multimodal scheme could learn the complementary representation and achieve a superior result, *e.g.*, gesture 15.

With a low inference cost, our framework can perform real-time gesture recognition. Specifically, a single feed forward neural network incurs trivial computation time, linearly in $\mathcal{O}(mT)$ and the complexity of Viterbi algorithm is $\mathcal{O}(T * |S|^2)$ with the number of modalities m, the number of frames T and the state number S.

4. CONCLUSION

Hand-engineered, task-specific features are often less adaptive and time-consuming to design. This difficulty is more pronounced with multimodal data as the features have to relate multiple data sources. In this paper, we presented a framework that utilizes Deep Belief Networks for modeling emission probabilities at frame-level, and introduced the shared representation for learning multimodal sensory inputs. The framework can be used to extract a unified representation that fuses various modalities together for modeling time series data. Our experimental results on bi-modal time series data, *i.e.*, audio and skeletal joints data, show that the multimodal DBN+HMM framework can learn a good model of the joint space of multiple sensory inputs, and is consistently as good as/better than the unimodal input. The proposed model also outperforms the traditional late fusion scheme, opening the door for exploring the complementary representation among multimodal inputs. It also suggests that learning features directly from data is a very important research direction and the learning-based methods are not only more generalizable to many domains, but also are powerful in combining with other well-studied probabilistic graphical models for modeling and reasoning dynamic sequences.

5. REFERENCES

[1] R. Chaudhry, F. Ofli, G. Kurillo, R. Bajcsy, and R. Vidal. Bio-inspired dynamic 3d discriminative skeletal features for human action recognition. In *IEEE Conference on Computer Vision and Pattern Recognition Workshops*, 2013.

[2] S. Escalera, J. Gonzàlez, X. Baró, M. Reyes, O. Lopés, I. Guyon, V. Athitsos, and H. J. Escalante. Multi-modal gesture recognition challenge 2013: Dataset and results. In *ChaLearn Multi-Modal Gesture Recognition Grand Challenge and Workshop*. ACM, 2013.

[3] S. Fothergill, H. M. Mentis, P. Kohli, and S. Nowozin. Instructing people for training gestural interactive systems. In *CHI*. ACM, 2012.

[4] G. E. Hinton, N. Srivastava, A. Krizhevsky, I. Sutskever, and R. R. Salakhutdinov. Improving neural networks by preventing co-adaptation of feature detectors. *arXiv preprint arXiv:1207.0580*, 2012.

[5] A. Mohamed, G. E. Dahl, and G. Hinton. Acoustic modeling using deep belief networks. *Audio, Speech, and Language Processing, IEEE Transactions on*, 2012.

[6] M. Müller and T. Röder. Motion templates for automatic classification and retrieval of motion capture data. In *SIGGRAPH/Eurographics symposium on Computer animation*. Eurographics Association, 2006.

[7] J. Ngiam, A. Khosla, M. Kim, J. Nam, H. Lee, and A. Y. Ng. Multimodal deep learning. In *International Conference on Machine Learning*. IEEE, 2011.

[8] S. Nowozin and J. Shotton. Action points: A representation for low-latency online human action recognition. Technical report, Technical report, 2012.

[9] F. Ofli, R. Chaudhry, G. Kurillo, R. Vidal, and R. Bajcsy. Sequence of the most informative joints (smij): A new representation for human skeletal action recognition. *Journal of Visual Communication and Image Representation*, 2013.

[10] N. Srivastava and R. Salakhutdinov. Multimodal learning with deep boltzmann machines. In *Neural Information Processing Systems*, 2012.

[11] A. Torralba and A. A. Efros. Unbiased look at dataset bias. In *IEEE Conference on Computer Vision and Pattern Recognition*, 2011.

[12] D. Wu and L. Shao. Leveraging hierarchical parametric networks for skeletal joints based action segmentation and recognition. In *IEEE Conference on Computer Vision and Pattern Recognition*, 2014.

[13] X. Yang and Y. Tian. Eigenjoints-based action recognition using naive-bayes-nearest-neighbor. In *IEEE Conference on Computer Vision and Pattern Recognition Workshops*, 2012.

Event Detection based on Twitter Enthusiasm Degree for Generating a Sports Highlight Video

Keisuke Doman
School of Eng.,
Chukyo University, Japan
kdoman@sist.chukyo-u.ac.jp

Taishi Tomita*
School of Eng.,
Nagoya University, Japan

Ichiro Ide
Graduate School of Info. Sci.,
Nagoya University, Japan
ide@is.nagoya-u.ac.jp

Daisuke Deguchi
Info. and Communications Headquarters,
Nagoya University, Japan
ddeguchi@nagoya-u.jp

Hiroshi Murase
Graduate School of Info. Sci.,
Nagoya University, Japan
murase@nagoya-u.jp

ABSTRACT

This paper presents a Twitter-based event detection method based on "Twitter Enthusiasm Degrees (TED)" toward generating a highlight video of a sports game. Existing methods not only depend on both languages and sports types but also often falsely detect non-target events. In contrast, the proposed method detects sports events using TEDs calculated from several kinds of string features independent of languages and sports. We applied the proposed method to actual sports games, and compared the detected events with the events present in broadcasted highlight videos, and confirmed the effectiveness and the language and sports type independencies of the proposed method.

Categories and Subject Descriptors

H.4 [**Information Systems Applications**]: Miscellaneous

Keywords

Social media; sports video; highlight; event detection

1. INTRODUCTION

The techniques for automatic summarization of broadcast videos are becoming more important in recent years. Among various kinds of broadcast videos, summarizing sports game videos is more important because some sports games last for a long duration [1]. When summarizing a sports game video, we should take into account the viewpoint of the viewers so as to let them understand not only the game flow but also the atmosphere of the game such as the excitement at each event of the game. We here call such a summarized video a "highlight video". The viewers are excited by events such as a goal, a play that assists a goal and a goal-scoring opportunity, because they are closely related to the winning or the losing of a game. In this paper, we focus on automatic detection of such kinds of events from a sports game in order to generate its highlight video.

Table 1: Examples of tweets on the London Olympic women's soccer final: Japan vs. USA.

Posted time	Tweets
19:55:07 UTC−6	GOOOOOOOOOOOOOOOOAA AAAAAAAAALLLLLLLLLLLL!!!
19:55:08 UTC−8	Go #TeamUSA!
19:55:10 UTC+2	US. leads Japan 1-0 at halftime in gold medal women's soccer match.
19:55:12 UTC+9	うああああああああああああ 切り替えの遅さが目立つなぁ
19:55:15 UTC−5	GOAL #TEAMUSA !!!!!!!!!!!! Up 2:0 in the 55th Minutes!!!

As an information source for detecting such events from a sports game, we make use of Twitter that is currently the most popular micro-blogging service. The number of active Twitter users was more than 140 million by March, 2012 and is increasing afterwards [2]. The biggest advantage of using Twitter for our research purpose is that it provides instantaneous information. That is, Twitter users who are watching a sports game can post their messages called "tweets" in real-time as shown in Table 1. Viewers from various countries tweet their feelings (excitement or disappointment) at each event in various languages within 140 characters. Twitter also has functions for interactions with others. For example, the function "retweet" enables Twitter users to easily repost someone else's tweet. In addition, "hashtags" indicated by keywords or phrases prefixed with the symbol "#" can be added in a tweet in order to categorize the message. This function helps users to easily search tweets on a specific topic, to find users who have common interests, and so on. Furthermore, Twitter Inc. provides the Twitter Streaming

*Currently at Japan Broadcasting Corporation.

MM'14, November 3–7, 2014, Orlando, Florida, USA.

ACM 978-1-4503-3063-3/14/11 ...$15.00.
http://dx.doi.org/10.1145/2647868.2654973.

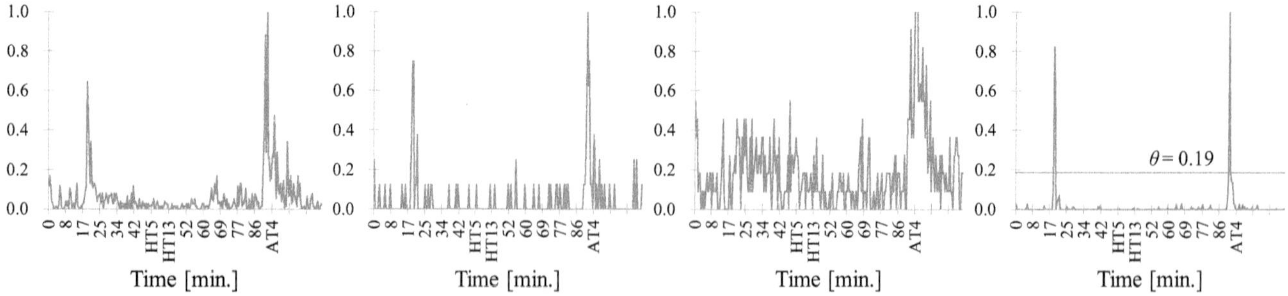

(a) Feature value: E (b) Feature value: L (c) Feature value: R (d) TED

Figure 1: Example of the feature values (E, L and R) and the TED calculated by the proposed method for the UEFA EURO2012 quarterfinal: Spain vs. France (Spain scored in the 19th minute of the first half, and added a goal by a penalty kick in the 1st minute of the second-half additional time (AT1)).

API. We can collect tweets posted during the target game by using these functions and APIs.

Focusing on the relationship between Twitter and sports, some Twitter-based methods for summarizing a sports video have been proposed [3, 4]. These methods can accurately recognize events in a sports video by analyzing the phrases in Twitter tweets. This approach, however, not only requires a list of phrases specific to the target sports but also highly depends on the language of the tweets. In addition, although these methods detect events based on the increase or the decrease of the number of tweets, it increases not only at the occurrence of an event but also at the end of an event [5]. Thus, these methods cannot simply be applied to our task to prevent false detection of events where the viewers are not excited.

This paper proposes a method that detects sports events based on a feature named "Twitter Enthusiasm Degree" (TED) which is derived from certain string patterns in tweets. The TED here is calculated by integrating three kinds of features: two kinds of features that express the users' excitement in addition to a feature that represents the end of an event. By this way, without any complex audio and/or video analysis, we expect to generate a highlight video that includes events where the viewers are excited.

Compared with the previous work [3, 4], the contribution of the proposed method is that 1) it does not require a list of phrases according to the target sports and 2) it does not depend on the language of the tweets. As for the scope of application of the proposed method, we target two different types of sports: soccer and baseball. These two sports are different in both the process of scoring and the structure of a game. In addition, many tweets regarding the events in these two types of games should be posted due to their world-wide popularity. Therefore, we confirm both the former and the latter contributions by applying the proposed method to the games of these two sports.

2. PROPOSED METHOD

The proposed method detects events that should be included in a highlight video of a target sports game by calculating and thresholding the Twitter Enthusiasm Degree (TED). A highlight video can be automatically generated by collecting the scenes at all the detected events in the game.

The TED here is defined as follows:

$$\mathrm{TED} \equiv E \times L \times (1 - R), \tag{1}$$

where E is the frequency of exclamation marks, L is the number of tweets including a repeated expression and R is the number of retweets. Here, both E and L are for evaluating the excitement of users, whereas R is for evaluating the end of an event. The TED becomes higher when E and L are higher and R is lower. We assume that events with higher TEDs as those that should be included in a highlight video. Note that each feature value is calculated for a time window of $w = 30$ [sec.] and normalized in the range of [0,1]. As a result, we obtain TEDs in the range of [0,1] for every w [sec.].

We explain below the details of each feature and the threshold for the TED with actually-posted tweets on the UEFA EURO2012 quarterfinal: Spain vs. France (Fig. 1).

2.1 Features for calculating the TED

The features used in the proposed method are as follows.

Frequency of exclamations: E.

The excitements or disappointments of Twitter users watching a sports game appear in their tweets particularly at goal-related events. Thus, we focused on the exclamation mark "!" which is a symbol to express excitement. We assumed that the number of exclamation marks in a tweet reflects the degree of excitement of the user. That is, many exclamation marks in an user's tweet means that he/she is very excited (cf. the last row in Table 1). Such tendency actually can be seen around the goal-scoring events in Fig. 1(a).

Number of tweets using repeated expressions: L.

Characters are often repeated like "GOOOOOOAAAAAL-LLL!!!" as a way of expressing an user's excitement (cf. the first row in Table 1). The proposed method extracts and counts tweets where a character is repeated multiple times (more than five times in the following experiments). Similarly to the feature value E, the feature value increases around the goal-scoring events in Fig. 1(b).

Number of retweets: R.

As mentioned earlier, the number of tweets increases not only at an event but also just after each event [5]. Since

Table 2: Experimental data.

Game	Date	Match	# of scoring events	Duration	# of tweets
S1 (Soccer)	July 1, 2012	UEFA EURO2012: Final	4	165 min.	410,363
S2 (Soccer)	Dec. 16, 2012	2012 FIFA CWC: Final	1	120 min.	22,075
B1 (Baseball)	Oct. 30, 2012	NPB Japan Series: Third match	10	270 min.	28,979
B2 (Baseball)	Oct. 31 2012	NPB Japan Series: Fourth match	1	270 min.	35,359

Table 3: Experimental results: Comparison of events broadcasted by broadcast stations A, B and C with events detected by the proposed method ("–" indicates that no highlight video was broadcasted).

(a) Numbers of events in Game S1

Event	Broadcast station			Proposed method	
	A	B	C	$\alpha = 2$	$\alpha = 1$
Goal	4	–	–	4	4
Start/End	0	–	–	0	2
Others	0	–	–	0	0

(b) Numbers of events in Game S2

Event	Broadcast station			Proposed method	
	A	B	C	$\alpha = 2$	$\alpha = 1$
Goal	1	–	–	1	1
Start/End	0	–	–	1	1
Others	2	–	–	0	3

(c) Numbers of events in Game B1

Event	Broadcast station			Proposed method	
	A	B	C	$\alpha = 2$	$\alpha = 1$
Score	4	7	8	7	10
Start/End	1	1	1	1	1
Others	0	6	7	1	6

(d) Numbers of events in Game B2

Event	Broadcast station			Proposed method	
	A	B	C	$\alpha = 2$	$\alpha = 1$
Score	1	1	1	1	1
Start/End	1	1	1	1	1
Others	10	2	5	6	12

video sections just after each event should be excluded from a highlight video of a sports game, we try to reduce its effect. Here, we focused on the characteristics of retweets; In order to retweet, a user needs to find a tweet, insert the prefix "RT" into the original tweet, and sometimes add his/her own comment. It is difficult to follow these steps on the exact moment of a goal-scoring event. As a result, retweets are delayed, and consequently posted at or after the end of the event. This means that the end of an event could be detected by using the number of retweets. The number of retweets actually increases just after a goal-scoring event and at the end of the game in Fig. 1(c).

2.2 Threshold for detecting highlights

A threshold θ for TED is determined as follows:

$$\theta = \mu + \alpha \times \sigma, \tag{2}$$

where μ and σ are the mean and the standard deviation of TEDs in a game, respectively, and α is the parameter for adjusting the threshold θ. Events with higher TEDs than the threshold θ are detected for generating the highlight video of the game. By controlling α, we expect to detect not only goal-scoring events but also exciting events such as a scarce goal-miss or a play that assists a goal. Accordingly, the proposed method can flexibly generate a highlight video of a sports game depending on our needs.

For the game in Fig. 1, the threshold is $\theta = 0.19$ with $\alpha = 2$ as shown in Fig. 1(d). In this case, the TED is over the threshold in the 19th minute of the first half and in the 1st minute of the second-half additional time. These exactly matched with the actual goal-scoring events in the game.

3. EXPERIMENTS

We investigated the effectiveness of the proposed method through the following experiments.

3.1 Method

We evaluated the performance of the proposed method by comparing two sets of events: one was detected by the proposed method, and the other was included in the actually-broadcasted highlight video. The experimental data is shown in Table 2. The tweets here were collected by filtering all the tweets posted to Twitter with hashtags: "#euro2012" for Game S1, "#CWD" for Game S2, "#kyojin" and "#lovefighters" for both Games B1 and B2. We used the parameter $\alpha = 2$ or $\alpha = 1$ in Eq. (2) in order to further analize the characteristics of the proposed method in depth.

3.2 Results

Experimental results are shown in Table 3. Each table shows the number of events detected by the proposed method as well as the number of events included in the highlight videos broadcasted by broadcast stations A, B and C. Note that a highlight video was broadcasted only by broadcast station A for Games S1 and S2 as indicated by "–". For reference, Fig. 2 shows examples of the TEDs calculated by the proposed method for Games S1 and B1. As we can see from these results, the proposed method could detect all of the broadcast highlights when $\alpha = 1$. Scoring events are the most important for a sports game and exciting for the viewers of the game. The proposed method also detected other events such as a hit and a fine play. This was because TEDs reflected the viewers' excitement by consecutive hits, viewers' excitement in excaping from a pinch through a fantastic play, and so on. Detecting such events are also important in order to generate a highlight video considering the viewpoint of the viewers. From these results, we confirmed that the proposed method is effective for event detection toward generating a highlight sports video.

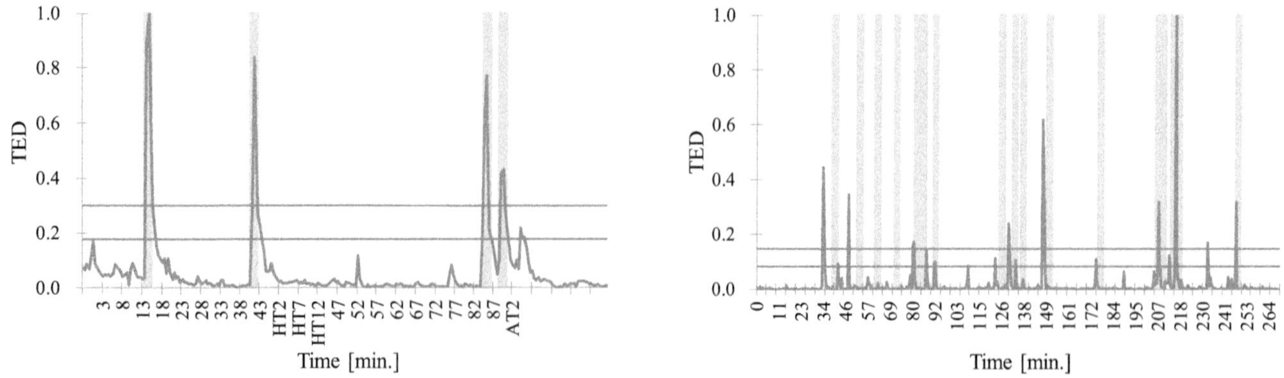

(a) Game S1 ("HT" and "AT" represent the half and the additional time, respectively)

(b) Game B1

Figure 2: Example of the calculated TEDs (The colored bars in the background of each graph area indicate the sections included in more than one broadcast highlight videos).

3.3 Discussions

We here discuss the characteristics and the effectiveness of the proposed method based on the experimental results.

Independency to languages and sports types.

We evaluated the performance of the proposed method with multilingual tweets on different types of sports games. The tweets were written in various languages such as English, Japanese, Spanish, and Italian. The proposed method could effectively detect events using such tweets, which shows the language independency of the proposed method. Also, the proposed method could detect events in different types of sports games that are important for generating a highlight video without any modification of its framework. This shows the sports-type independency of the proposed method.

Adequacy in respect of the viewers' viewpoint.

Some events could not be detected by the proposed method, although they were included in the broadcasted highlight videos. One was a less exciting scoring event in the top half of the fifth inning in Game B1 (Fig. 2(b)). That is, runners stood at first and second bases with no out, and then the offensive team got a score via a double play. As a result, the viewers were not excited so much, although it was a scoring event. It would be difficult to detect such an event using the proposed method based on the viewers' enthusiasm. Although such scoring events are important in respect of understanding the game flow, we consider that it was an adequate result in respect of considering the viewers' viewpoint.

Criteria for including events in a highlight video.

The event at the end of Game B1 (Fig. 2(b)) was detected falsely by the proposed method even when $\alpha = 2$, which was not expected. This was because the TED increased by viewers' excitement from the winning / losing. It can be regarded as false detection since the current purpose of this research is to detect events during the game. This result, however, indicates that viewers are excited when the winning or losing is decided. In some cases, it may be better to include such a feverish event into the end of the highlight video of the game. This should be considered as one of our future work.

4. CONCLUSION

This paper presented an event detection method based on a Twitter Enthusiasm Degree (TED) towards generating a highlight video of a sports game. The proposed method calculates TEDs by integrating two features for evaluating the excitement of users and one feature for evaluating the end of an event. Experimental results showed not only the effectiveness of event detection for generating a highlight video but also the independency of the proposed method to languages and sports types. One of the future work is to consider viewers' viewpoint in more depth by analyzing the criteria for including events in a highlight video.

5. REFERENCES

[1] L. Xie, P. Xu, S.-F. Chang, A. Divakaran, and H. Sun. Structure analysis of soccer video with domain knowledge and hidden Markov models. *Pattern Recognition Letters*, 25(7):767–775, May 2008.

[2] Twitter Blog. Twitter turns six. `http://blog.twitter.com/2012/03/twitter-turns-six`. (Feb. 7, 2013).

[3] J. Lanagan and A.F. Smeaton. Using twitter to detect and tag important events in live sports. In *5th AAAI Int'l Conf. on Weblogs and Social Media*, pages 542–545, July 2011.

[4] S. Zhao, L. Zhong, J. Wickramasuriya, and V. Vasudevan. Human as real-time sensors of social and physical events: A case study of twitter and sports games. Technical Report TR0620–2011, Rice University and Motorola Labs, June 2011.

[5] D.A. Shamma, L. Kennedy, and E.F. Churchill. Tweet the debates: Understanding community annotation of uncollected sources. In *1st ACM SIGMM Workshop on Social Media*, pages 3–10, October 2009.

Boosting Cross-media Retrieval via Visual-Auditory Feature Analysis and Relevance Feedback

Hong Zhang[1,2,3], Junsong Yuan[3], Xingyu Gao[4,5], Zhenyu Chen[4]
[1]College of Computer Science & Technology, Wuhan University of Science and Technology, China
[2]Hubei Province Key Laboratory of Intelligent Information Processing & Real-time Industrial System, China
[3]School of EEE, Nanyang Technological University, Singapore
[4]Institute of Computing Technology, Chinese Academy of Sciences, Beijing, China
[5]School of Computer Engineering, Nanyang Technological University, Singapore
zhanghong_wust@163.com, jsyuan@ntu.edu.sg

ABSTRACT

Different types of multimedia data express high-level semantics from different aspects. How to learn comprehensive high-level semantics from different types of data and enable efficient cross-media retrieval becomes an emerging hot issue. There are abundant correlations among heterogeneous low-level media content, which makes it challenging to query cross-media data effectively. In this paper, we propose a new cross-media retrieval method based on short-term and long-term relevance feedback. Our method mainly focuses on two typical types of media data, i.e. image and audio. First, we build multimodal representation via statistical canonical correlation between image and audio feature matrices, and define cross-media distance metric for similarity measure; then we propose optimization strategy based on relevance feedback, which fuses short-term learning results and long-term accumulated knowledge into the objective function. Experiments on image-audio dataset have demonstrated the superiority of our method over several existing algorithms.

Categories and Subject Descriptors

H.3.3 [**Information Search and Retrieval**]: Retrieval Models

General Terms

Algorithms, Design.

Keywords

Cross-media retrieval; feature analysis; relevance feedback

1. INTRODUCTION

Cross-media retrieval is emerging as a new search paradigm that enables seamless information processing from different types of data. Plenty of work has been done on cross-media retrieval [1][5][7][14], and these methods do provide effective ways to better manage multimodal data. However, there are two issues mostly remain uncovered.

MM'14, November 3–7, 2014, Orlando, Florida, USA.

http://dx.doi.org/10.1145/2647868.2654975

The first issue is: most of the existing works focused on web images and their tagging texts, while the analysis of images and other types of multimedia data was mostly ignored. For example, [2] proposed supervised coupled dictionary learning with group structures for Wiki Text-Image data; [3] proposed effective multimodal stacked auto-encoders for retrieval among web images and associated tags. Very limited research efforts were devoted to content-based cross-media retrieval among other types of media data, such as image-audio database [9][14]. In fact, audio is an important kind of sensory information, which affects a lot on human perception [4]. It is interesting and challenging to learn cross-media semantics for retrieval from image and audio data simultaneously.

The other issue is that most related works do not pay enough attention to long-term optimization of cross-media retrieval results. Generally, these works share a similar two-step processing strategy [3][5]. First, they learn a set of mapping functions to project high-dimensional features into a common low-dimensional latent space. Second, a multi-dimensional index in the metric space is built for applications like efficient retrieval [3][9], classification [7], event detection [8], etc. User interactions in relevance feedback provide useful prior knowledge that could be used to narrow the semantic gap [1]. However, it turns out to be a great challenge to mine accumulated prior knowledge with long-term relevance feedback because there are abundant correlations among heterogeneous media data.

Regarding above two issues, we propose a new cross-media retrieval and optimization method for image and audio data based on relevance feedback. For example, users can query images of an animal by submitting either its images or a sound of its roaring. Specifically, we first analyze underlying statistical correlation between visual feature matrix of images and auditory feature matrix of audios, find a correlation-preserved mapping to a low-dimension isomorphic space where the cross-media distance is define for similarity retrieval. Furthermore, we propose short-term learning within a single query session and long-term learning over the course of many query sessions for performance optimization. For long-term learning, we classify positive and negative feedbacks into pair-wise constraints, based on which two discriminative functions are defined. The short-term optimizing results are fused into the objective function together with the long-term learning results to improve multimodal data representation. Our approach not only explores global statistical cross-media correlation between image and audio data, but also optimizes data representation via relevance feedback.

2. MULTIMODAL REPRESENTATION

In this section, we analyze statistical correlation between image features and audio features to construct multimodal representation and estimate cross-media distance, based on which cross-media retrieval is generated.

Since different types of multimedia data are heterogeneous in low-level features, cross-media distance in feature level is not directly measurable. Therefore, we first analyze canonical correlation between image feature vectors and audio feature vectors to generate a correlation-based unified multimodal representation for all training samples. Formally, let I denote image feature matrix, A denote audio feature matrix. Motivated by CCA (Canonical Correlation Analysis) which has been used in many data mining applications[12][14], we calculate basis vectors for image and audio samples such that the correlation between the projections of the two sets of samples onto the basis vectors are mutually maximized, that is:

$$\max_{W_1,W_2} corr(IW_1, AW_2) = \max_{W_1,W_2} \frac{(IW_1, AW_2)}{\|IW_1\|\|AW_2\|} = \max_{W_1,W_2} \frac{W_1' C_{IA} W_2}{\sqrt{W_1' C_{II} W_1 W_2' C_{AA} W_2}} \quad (1)$$

where C is covariance matrix, W_1 and W_2 are the transformation matrices. Since the solution of equation (1) is not affected by re-scaling W_1 or W_2 either together or independently, the optimization of (1) is equivalent to maximizing the numerator subject to $W_1'C_{II}W_1=1$ and $W_2'C_{AA}W_2=1$. Then with Lagrange multiplier method we can find solutions for W_1 and W_2 by $C_{IA}C_{AA}^{-1}C_{AI}W_1=\lambda^2 C_{II}W_1$, which is a generalized Eigenproblem. By choosing the same number of eigenvectors, we not only maximize canonical correlation between image and audio feature matrices, but also transfer them into the same dimensions.

Let $X=\{x_1,x_2,...,x_n\}' \in \mathrm{R}^{n\times d}$ denote the isomorphic multimodal representation of image and audio data with the total number of n where d is the dimension after CCA process. We calculate the Euclidean distance between any two samples $x_i, x_j, (i,j \in [1,n], i \neq j)$, and obtain the corresponding distance matrix $\mathrm{H} \in \mathrm{R}^{n\times n}$.

We further analyze multimodal geometrical structure of all samples based on the matrix $\mathrm{H} \in \mathrm{R}^{n\times n}$. Specifically, we construct a multimodal adjacency graph $G(V,E)$: for any sample x_i, there is a corresponding vertex $v_i \in V$ and for any two vertices $v_i, v_j \in V$, we put an edge between them with distance c_{ij} which is defined as follows:

$$c_{ij} = \begin{cases} \mathrm{H}_{ij}, & if\ \mathrm{H}_{ij} < \varepsilon \\ \infty, & otherwise \end{cases} \quad (2)$$

where ε is a distance reflecting the measurement of locality. To model the global geometrical structure, we define the length of a path as the sum of all pair-wise distances along the path, and replace the value of c_{ij} with the length of the shortest path between v_i, v_j. So far, cross-media retrieval can be generated based on the geodesic distance on the multimodal graph.

3. RELEVANCE FEEDBACK

Although in recent years, relevance feedback has been studied from the perspective of machine learning, most of which are used for application of content-based image retrieval [13]. However, in cross-media retrieval that we target at, relevance feedback covers not only images but also audios. Besides, most learning methods only take into account current query session and the knowledge obtained from the past user interactions with the system is forgotten. Therefore, in this section, we propose both short-term and long-term strategies to further explore prior knowledge over the course of many query sessions so as to improve cross-media retrieval performance.

3.1 Short-term Refinement

Here we present a simple way to update distance c_{ij} gradually. Intuitively, the samples marked by the user as positive examples in a query session share some common semantics. Therefore, in short-term relevance feedback, we shorten the distance between them. Similarly, we can lengthen the distances between the positive examples and negative examples, as follows:

$$c_{ij} = c_{ij}/\alpha \ (if\ x_i, x_j \in \mathrm{K}^+) \quad (3)$$

$$c_{ij} = c_{ij} \cdot \beta \ (if\ x_i \in \mathrm{K}^+ \ \&\ x_j \in \mathrm{K}^-) \quad (4)$$

where $\alpha > 1$ and $\beta > 1$. K^+ and K^- represent positive feedbacks and negative feedbacks respectively. Then we define the weight of edges on the multimodal graph as below:

$$w_{ij} = \begin{cases} \exp(-c_{ij}/t), & if\ c_{ij} < \rho \\ 0, & otherwise \end{cases} \quad (5)$$

where t, ρ are suitable constants.

Let $Y=\{y_1,y_2,...,y_n\}' \in \mathrm{R}^{n\times k}$ denote the optimized multimodal representation. Then the objective of the whole relevance feedback strategy is to learn a mapping from $X=\{x_1,x_2,...,x_n\}'$ to $Y=\{y_1,y_2,...,y_n\}'$. That is, for any $x_i \in X (1 \le i \le n)$ we have:

$$y_i = M^T x_i \quad (6)$$

where $M \in \mathrm{R}^{d\times k}$ is the projection matrix.

It is reasonable that a "good" mapping should minimize the objective function $\sum (y_i - y_j)^2 w_{ij}$, which incurs a heavy penalty if neighboring data i and j are mapped far apart. Then we have:

$$\sum_{i,j} (y_i - y_j)^2 w_{ij} = 2\sum_i M^T x_i D_{ii} x_i^T M - 2\sum_{i,j} M^T x_i w_{ij} x_i^T M = 2M^T \mathrm{X}(\mathrm{D}-W) X^T M \quad (7)$$

where $W=[w_{ij}]$, $L=D-W$ is a Laplacian matrix and D is a diagonal matrix defined as $D_{ii}=\sum_j w_{ji}$. Thus the minimization problem is:

$$\min_{M^T M = I} tr(M^T X L X^T M) \quad (8)$$

3.2 Long-term Relevance Feedback

Formally, we define two sets of data pairs P_t and N_t based on the positive and negative sample sets the user labels in the t-th round of relevance feedback. In P_t each pair of data is of the same labels, and in N_t each pair of data is of different labels. For long-term relevance feedback we define:

$$P = \bigcup_t P_t, \quad N = \bigcup_t N_t \quad (9)$$

In this way, data pairs in P are semantically similar to each other and those in N are semantically dissimilar to each other, which can be used as pairwise constraints. The sum of squared distances of data pairs $(x_i, x_j) \in P$ can be calculated as follows:

$$\sum_{(x_i,x_j)\in P} (M^T x_i - M^T x_j)^T (M^T x_i - M^T x_j) = \sum_{(x_i,x_j)\in P} \mathrm{tr}[M^T (x_i - x_j)(x_i - x_j)^T M] = tr(M^T S_w M) \quad (10)$$

where $S_w = \sum_{(x_i,x_j)\in P} (x_i - x_j)(x_i - x_j)^T$ and tr is the trace operator. The distances among data pairs $(x_i, x_j) \in P$ should be as small as possible. Thus we have the following function:

$$\min_{M^T M = I} tr(M^T S_w M) \tag{11}$$

in which the constraint $M^T M = I$ is imposed to prevent arbitrary scaling of the projection. Similarly, the distances between data pairs from N should be as large as possible. Thus we have:

$$\max_{M^T M = I} tr(M^T S_b M) \tag{12}$$

where $S_b = \sum_{(x_i,x_j)\in N} (x_i - x_j)(x_i - x_j)^T$.

3.3 Combining Short- & Long-term Learning

So far, the relevance feedback strategy should satisfy not only (8) but also (11)(12) in order to preserve refined locality structure and benefit from accumulated pairwise constraints. Motivated by [6] which proposed an image classification method via cluster distance optimization, we merge (8)(11)(12) into an overall discriminative objective function as below:

$$\max_{M^T M = I} tr[M^T S_b M (M^T S_t M + \delta M^T X L X^T M)^{-1}] \tag{13}$$

where $S_t = S_b + S_w$ denotes the total scatter matrix and the coefficient δ balances the model complexity and the empirical loss. Then the solution of the optimal matrix M is given by the maximum eigenvalues to the generalized eigenvalue problem in form of $XLX^T M = \lambda X(I + \delta L)X^T M$. Based on above discussions, the optimization process is listed below.

Algorithm 1. Relevance feedback algorithm

Input: distance matrix $C = [c_{ij}]$;

similar set P and dissimilar set N;

Output: optimized multimodal representation Y.

1. Calculate the weight matrix $W = [w_{ij}]$ in (5), and obtain the Laplacian matrix L in (8);
2. Calculate data sets P and N in Eq.(9) based on long-term relevance feedback;
3. Calculate pairwise constraint matrices S_t, S_b;
4. Compute $M = [m_1, m_2, ..., m_c]$, in which $m_1, m_2, ..., m_c$ are the eigenvectors corresponding to the c largest non-zero eigenvalues of (13), and map x_i to the optimized multimodal subspace with $y_i = M^T x_i \ (1 \le i \le n)$.

4. EXPERIMENTS

We test our proposed algorithm for cross-media retrieval between image and audio data, and provide an extensive performance study of our algorithm in comparison with the state-of-the-art methods. Precision is defined as the percentage of correctly retrieved samples in the top-k-returned results.

4.1 Datasets

The image-audio dataset is collected from Corel image gallery, Webpages, etc. There are 4800 image and audio samples in total, which are grouped into 12 categories, such as zither, dog, dolphin, bird, elephant, tiger, explosion, car, train etc. In our experiments, if a returned result and the query example are in the same category, it is regarded as a correct result. Two types of visual features are extracted and normalized, including color correlogram in Hue Saturation Value color space and Tamura Texture. Auditory features include Mel-frequency Cepstral Coefficients (MFCC), Centroid, Rolloff and Spectral Flux. Since audio is a kind of time series data, we employ Fuzzy Clustering method [10] on original auditory features to get isomorphic indexes.

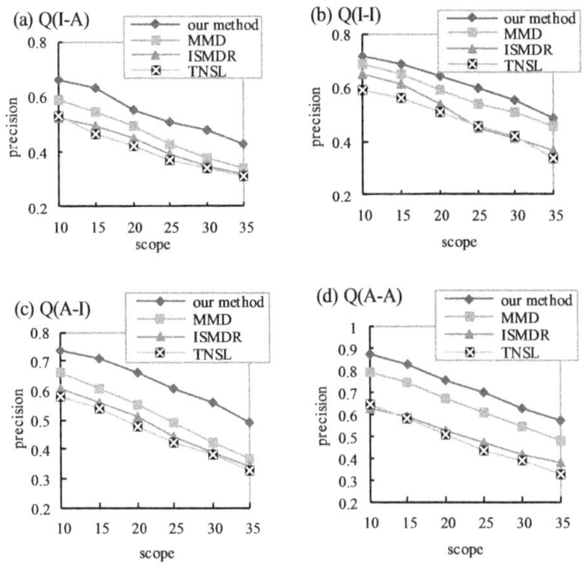

Figure 1(a)(b)(c)(d). Retrieval performance comparison of different algorithms in different retrieval scenarios

4.2 Performance Comparison

We compare our method with three content-based cross-media retrieval and relevance feedback methods: the Multimedia Document (MMD) method in [9], the Isomorphic and Sparse Multimodal Data Representation (ISMDR) method in [14] and Tagging-based Nonnegative Subspace Learning (TNSL) method in [11]. We randomly choose 20% of images and audios in each category as query examples to perform cross-media retrieval, and for each query, we select at most 3 positive and 3 negative multimedia objects, which could be images or audios, from returned results. The user's relevance feedbacks are used for both sort-term and long-term learning.

Since query examples and retrieval results could be images or audios, we generate four types of queries to give detailed comparisons, namely *Q(I-A)*, *Q(I-I)*, *Q(A-I)*, *Q(A-A)*. For instance, *Q(I-A)* searches relevant audio samples given an image example. Figure 1 shows the average *precision-scope* curves of different algorithms after relevance feedback. We have the following observations from Figure 1: our method outperforms the other three methods in four retrieval scenarios. For example, in Figure 2(c) Q(A-I), when the number of returned images is 15 the precision is 0.712 with our method, while the MMD, ISMDR and TNSL methods achieve precision of 0.611, 0.564 and 0.543 respectively. The performance gain of our method is probably attributed to the following reasons:

(1) ISMDR, TNSL and MMD methods optimize cross-media similarity with the help of surrounding texts or strictly selected auxiliary tags which express semantic information more directly than audios do; (2) our algorithm utilizes feature-level image-audio statistical correlation and optimizes multimodal data representation in relevance feedback, which are ignored in the other three methods; (3) the MMD method takes a global view on

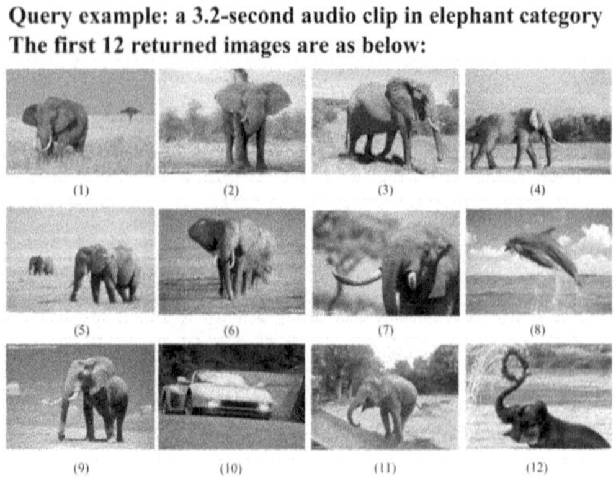

Figure. 2 An example of *Q(A-I)*

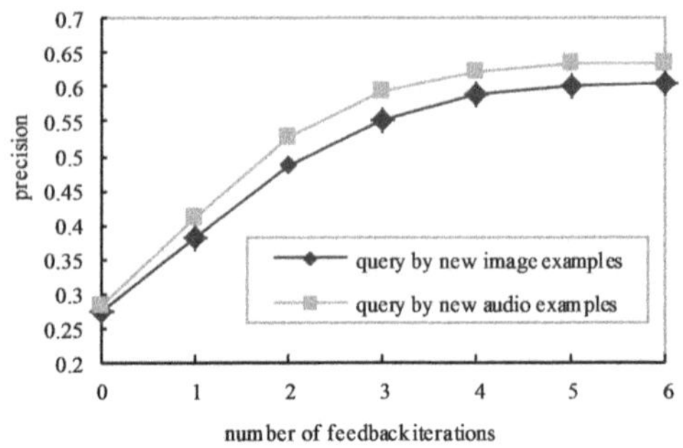

Figure. 3. Average results of querying by new examples

different objects in the multimedia documents, thus it is more flexible and capable to different retrieval scenarios compared to ISMDR and TNSL methods.

Figure 2 gives an example of Q(A-I). We submit an example of a 3.2-second audio clip selected from elephant category, and the first 12 returned images are shown in Figure 2. It can be seen that 10 images are corrected returned.

4.3 Query Example outside the Database

Above results are obtained when the query examples are in the database. If a query example is out of the database, we call it a new sample. We perform retrieval with new samples to evaluate the generalization capability of our algorithm. 360 images and 360 audios are used as queries outside the training database for testing. Although the testing set have no optimized multimodal representations, we can use the transformation matrices learned in equation (1) for initial feature mapping, and then calculate the Euclidean distances between testing set and training set, based on which cross-media retrieval could be generated. Further, we make use of relevance feedback to narrow the semantic gap. We classify cross-media retrieval into querying by new audio examples and querying by new image examples.

Figure 3 shows precision performance by looking at the top 20 returns. It can be seen that the performances of querying by new examples are good overall. Although when no relevance feedback is involved, some new images and audios are well recognized, the precision performances climb to 0.592 and 0.553 for querying with new audios and querying with new images respectively at the third round of relevance feedback. As users interact with the system, querying with new images and new audios can be further optimized with our long-term learning model.

5. CONCLUSIONS

In this paper, we propose a new cross-media retrieval method based short-term and long-term relevance feedback. Our approach first learns a multimodal representation via statistical correlation analysis between image and audio features, and generates flexible cross-media retrieval; more importantly, by fusing both accumulated discriminative knowledge and local data structure into the objective function of relevance feedback, we improve multimodal representation for retrieval performance optimization. Experiment results of cross medial retrieval on image-audio dataset confirm the improvements of our method over previous works in search accuracy.

ACKNOWLEDGEMENT

This work is supported by National Natural Science Foundation of China (No.61373109, No.61003127), State Key Laboratory of Software Engineering (SKLSE2012-09-31).

REFERENCES

[1] Yang Y., Nie F.P., Xu D., et al. 2012. A Multimedia Retrieval Framework based on Semi-Supervised Ranking and Relevance Feedback. *IEEE Transactions on Pattern Analysis and Machine Intelligence.* 34(4):723-742.

[2] Zhuang Y.T., Wang Y.F., Wu F., et al. 2013. Supervised Coupled Dictionary Learning with Group Structures for Multi-modal Retrieval. *Proceeding of the 27th Conference on Artificial Intelligence.* 1070-1076.

[3] Wang W., Ooi B.C., Yang X.Y., et al. 2014. Effective multi-modal retrieval based on stacked auto-encoders. *International Conference on Very Large Data Bases.*

[4] McGurk H., MacDonald J. 1976. Hearing Lips and Seeing Voices. *Nature*, 264: 746-748.

[5] Yang Y., Ma Z.G., Hauptmann A., et al. 2013. Feature Selection for Multimedia Analysis by Sharing Information among Multiple Tasks. *IEEE Transactions on Multimedia.* 15(3):661-669.

[6] Cai D., He X.F., Han J.W. 2007. Semi-supervised Discriminant Analysis. *International Conference on Computer Vision.* 1-7.

[7] Srivastava N., Salakhutdinov R. 2012. Multimodal Learning with Deep Boltzmann Machines. *In Neural Information Processing Systems.* 2231-2239.

[8] Yuan J.S., Luo J.B. and Wu Y.. 2010. Mining Compositional Features from GPS and Visual Cues for Event Recognition in Photo Collections, *IEEE Trans. on Multimedia*, 12(7):705-716.

[9] Yang Y., Zhuang Y.T. and Wang W.H. 2008. Heterogeneous multimedia data semantics mining using content and location context. *ACM Multimedia Conference.* 655-658.

[10] Zhang H., Liu J. and Ma Z.G. 2013. Fusing inherent and external knowledge with nonlinear learning for cross-media retrieval. *Neurocomputing* vol.119, 10-16.

[11] Gupta S.K., Phung D., Adams B. et al. 2010. Nonnegative shared subspace learning and its application to social media retrieval. *ACM International Conference on Knowledge Discovery and Data Mining.* 1169-1178.

[12] Sun T., Chen S. 2007. Locality preserving CCA with applications to data visualization and pose estimation. *Image and Vision Computing.* Vol.25, 531-543.

[13] Yu J., and Tian Q. 2006. Learning Image Manifolds by Semantic Subspace Projection. *ACM Multimedia Conference.* 297-306.

[14] Zhang H., Chen L. 2013. Isomorphic and Sparse Multimodal Data Representation based on Correlation Analysis. *International Conference on Image Processing.* 3959-3962.

Transfer in Photography Composition

Hui-Tang Chang
Graduate Institute of Electrical Engineering, National Taiwan University, Taipei, Taiwan
r02921089@ntu.edu.tw

Yu-Chiang Frank Wang
Research Center for IT Innovation, Academia Sinica, Taipei, Taiwan
ycwang@citi.sinica.edu.tw

Ming-Syan Chen
Research Center for IT Innovation, Academia Sinica, Taipei, Taiwan
mschen@iis.sinica.edu.tw

ABSTRACT

In this paper, we propose novel photography recomposition method, which aims at transferring the photography composition of a reference image to an input image automatically. Without any user interaction, our approach first identifies the salient foreground objects or image regions of interest, and the recomposition is performed by solving a graph-matching based optimization task. With additional post-processing step to preserve the locality and boundary information of the recomposed visual components, we can solve the task of photography recomposition without the uses of any prior knowledge on photography or predetermined image aesthetics rules. Experiments on a variety of images, including transferring the photography composition from real photos, sketches or even paintings, would confirm the effectiveness of our proposed method.

Figure 1: Example of photography recomposition.

Categories and Subject Descriptors

I.4.3 [**Image Processing & computer vision**]: Enhancement; I.4.9 [**Image Processing & computer vision**]: Applications; I.5.4 [**Pattern Recognition**]: Applications - Computer Vision

General Terms

Algorithms, Experimentation

Keywords

Photography Composition; Graph Matching; Image Aesthetics; Computational Photography

1. INTRODUCTION

Digital cameras and smart phones nowadays are equipped with high-end lenses, sensors, or processors, which allow users to capture high-quality photos easily. When it comes to assess or adjust the corresponding image aesthetics, parameters such as exposure, focus, and color balance are typically the factors to be considered. For example, high dynamic range (HDR) techniques provide precise exposure information, tone mapping or color transfer algorithms can be applied to alter the color information based on reference images, and the light-field camera can be applied to refocus the output image as a post-processing procedure.

Nevertheless, proper exposure, focus, or color settings cannot guarantee satisfactory photo quality. The geometric structure of visual components in an image, also known as *photography composition*, also plays an important role in image aesthetics [1, 5]. Generally, photography composition is determined when the user presses the shutter button, and it cannot be easily adjusted by explicit camera parameters. In recent years, researchers started to advance predefined photographic composition rules, and applied image processing algorithms to improve the aesthetics of the images [12, 11, 2, 6, 8]. However, in practice, photos in different scenarios typically have distinct photographic rules to consider. Moreover, artistic photos do not necessarily follow such photographic rules. In other words, if particular photo styles of artistic photos or masterpieces are of interest, taking photos with pre-defined rules will not result in desirable outputs. Since existing works on image aesthetics did not attempt to learn the visual composition from reference photos (e.g., high-quality and relevant photos of interest), their robustness and flexibility in generalizing composition rules to photos taken in different scenarios or styles will be limited.

More specifically, existing image recomposition techniques typically aim at cropping (or re-targeting) the input image for image aesthetics enhancement. For example, Nishiyama et al. [8] proposed sensation-based cropping for learning im-

MM'14, November 3–7, 2014, Orlando, Florida, USA.

http://dx.doi.org/10.1145/2647868.2654976.

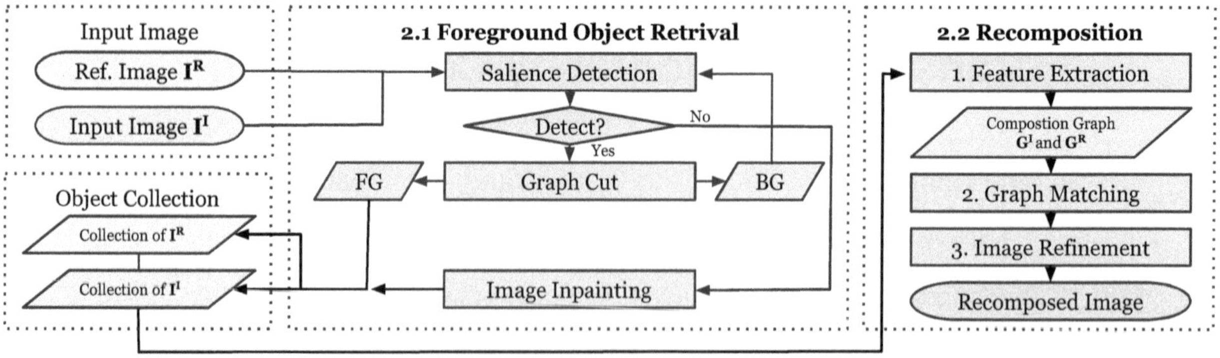

Figure 2: Our proposed framework for photography recomposition.

age aesthetics models. On the other hand, Santella et al. [10] and Liu et al. [6] used eye-tracking data and pre-defined photography composition for image cropping, respectively. While Bhattacharya et al. [2] trained their aesthetics models from pre-collected labeled (scored) image data for recomposition, Zhang et al. [12] further took the relation between image visual components into consideration, so that those components can be moved to proper locations. In [11], the authors proposed to adjust image foreground/background saliency for improving image aesthetics. However, the above methods still require pre-determined rules or pre-collected training data for performing photography recomposition.

The goal of our work is to improve image aesthetics by transferring photography composition from a reference to an input image, as depicted in Figure 1. Given such an image pair, we propose a novel transfer learning algorithm for addressing the resulting *photography composition transfer* problem (i.e., *cross-image* photography recomposition). With the image regions of interest in both images automatically identified, we perform a graph-matching based algorithm for determining the optimal photography composition for the input image based on that of the reference image. It is worth noting that, our work is *not* to produce *higher* image aesthetic scores by adjusting camera parameters. Instead, our focus is to transfer the photography composition from a reference image to the input image, without any pre-defined rules for image composition or aesthetics.

2. OUR PROPOSED FRAMEWORK

To transfer photography composition from one image to another, our proposed framework consists of two major components. First, the salient foreground objects from both input and reference images need to be extracted. Next, the matching and transferring of such regions across images will be performed for recomposition purposes. The flowchart of our proposed framework is shown in Figure 2, and we detail the two components in the following subsections.

2.1 Foreground Object Retrieval

In order to perform photography recomposition for the input and reference image pair automatically, we first identify foreground or salient image regions from each image for later recomposition processes. As suggested by [12], we advance saliency-based information for detect the aforementioned image regions.

To be more precise, given an image I and an empty object set $\mathbf{O}$, we apply the saliency detection approach of [3] for deriving the saliency map $S(I)$ for I. For the image region with the highest $S(I)$ and above a predetermined threshold, it will be viewed as the salient region. We then utilize GrabCut [9] for segmenting this region into the collection $\mathbf{O}$, and this salient region will be removed from I. As depicted in Figure 3, this process will be iteratively performed, until all salient regions are identified and collected in $\mathbf{O}$.

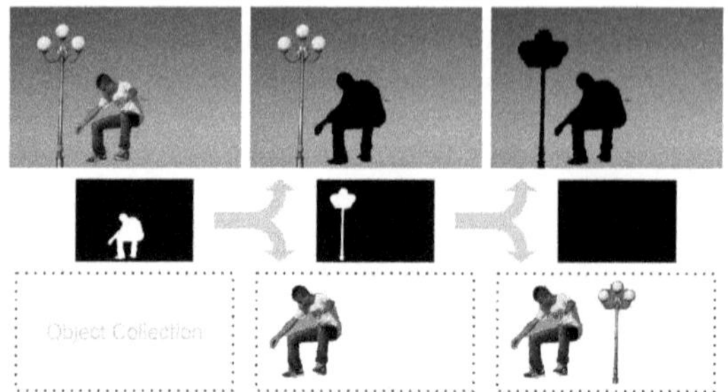

Figure 3: Illustration of our saliency-based foreground object retrieval which iteratively identifies foreground image regions from an image.

With salient foreground regions successfully segmented from both input and reference images, we then recover the corresponding backgrounds (before performing photography recomposition). In our work, we apply and extend image inpainting techniques of [7] for addressing this task, so that both input and reference images with background only can be properly reconstructed (see the image at the top-right corner in Figure 3 for example).

2.2 Cross-Image Photography Recomposition

2.2.1 *Image Representation via Composition Graphs*

As discussed in Section 2.1, salient foreground image regions will be first retrieved from both input and reference images. In order to perform photography recomposition across these two images, we choose to describe the extracted image regions of each image in terms of their shape and scale information via graph-based representations.

In our work, we define a *composition graph* $G = (V, E, A)$ for describing an image and its salient foreground regions, in which V denote the vertices representing the extracted salient regions, E are the edges connecting between the vertices, and A indicate the attributes for each vertex and edge. For each salient image region in an image, we consider its geometric shape and size for describing the shape and scale in-

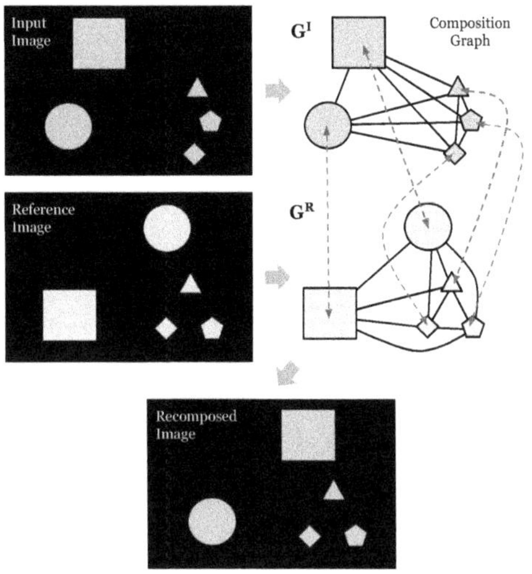

Figure 4: Illustration of graph matching for photography recomposition. The dotted lines denote the matching between the vertices of the associated composition graphs.

formation, respectively. That is, each vertex $v_x \in V$ has two associated attributes, shape $\mathbf{a}_p(x) \in A$ and scale $\mathbf{a}_s(x) \in A$. The former is represented by downscaling each image region to a 8×8 grayscale matrix, and the latter is measured by the area of that region. As for the edges, we take the Euclidean distance between each vertex pair in V for representing the relative-location attribute for E. In other words, each edge $e_{xy} \in E$ has an attribute $\mathbf{a}_l(x, y) \in A$.

2.2.2 Recomposition via Graph Matching

Given G^I and G^R as the composition graphs of the input and reference images, respectively, performing cross-image photography recomposition requires one to determine the affinity (i.e., similarity) between these two graphs. Let us denote the affinity function as $f(G^I, G^R)$. For the affinity of vertices $v_x^I \in V^I$ and $v_m^R \in V^R$, we have the similarity of the corresponding shape attributes as $f_p(v_x^I, v_m^R)$, and that of scale attributes as $f_s(v_x^I, v_m^R)$. In other words, the affinity of vertex is calculated as follows:

$$f(v_x^I, v_m^R) = \alpha f_p(v_x^I, v_m^R) + (1 - \alpha) f_s(v_x^I, v_m^R), \quad (1)$$

where we set $\alpha = 0.5$ for simplicity. Both f_p and f_s are calculated as the inverse of the Euclidean distance between the vertex attributes as the resulting similarity values.

For the affinity of edges $e_{xy}^I \in E^I$ and $e_{mn}^R \in E^R$, the associated affinity function output is calcualted by:

$$f(e_{xy}^I, e_{mn}^R) = 1/\|\mathbf{a}_l^I(x, y) - \mathbf{a}_l^R(m, n)\|. \quad (2)$$

With the above definitions of the affinity functions, we construct the affinity matrix $\mathbf{W}$ of dimension $|V^I||V^R| \times |V^I||V^R|$. We note that, each diagonal term in $\mathbf{W}$ is $w_{xm;xm} = f(v_x^I, v_m^R)$, which denotes the similarity between vertices v_x^I and v_m^R, while the off-diagonal terms $w_{xm;yn} = f(e_{xy}^I, e_{mn}^R)$ represent those between edges e_{xy}^I and e_{mn}^R for matching.

As noted earlier, our photography recomposition is performed via solving a graph-matching based optimization problem. With the affinity $\mathbf{W}$ between the two graphs G^I and G^R obtained, our goal turns into the determination of a indicator matrix $\mathbf{Z} \in \{0, 1\}^{|V^I| \times |V^R|}$, in which $z_{xm} = 1$ indicates a successful matching between V_x^I and V_m^R. For computa-

Figure 5: Example of recomposition refinement. Images from left to right: outputs without and with refinement.

tion purposes, we convert $\mathbf{Z}$ into vector $\mathbf{z} \in \{0, 1\}^{|V^I||V^R|}$, and we solve the following optimization problem instead:

$$\max \left(\mathbf{z}^T \mathbf{W} \mathbf{z}\right), \text{s.t.} \sum_{k=1}^{|V^R|} z_{xk} \leq 1, \ \sum_{k=1}^{|V^I|} z_{km} \leq 1, \ \forall x, m. \quad (3)$$

We note that, the constraints in (3) guarantees the one-to-one matching between G^I to G^R, while (3) itself is an Integer Quadratic Program (IQP) problem, which known to be NP-hard. In our work, we apply the method proposed in [4] for solving (3). Figure 4 illustrates our proposed algorithm and procedure for performing photography recomposition between input and reference images, in which the salient foreground regions are replaced by geometric shapes for simplicity. From this figure, we see that the green rectangle and the orange circle are matched based on their relative location information, instead of shape or scale. This explains why we can achieve satisfactory matching for practical recomposition scenarios.

2.2.3 Recomposition Refinement

As shown in Figure 5, it is possible that the graph matching output would result in recomposed visual components which are not properly positioned in the input image. In order to address this potential problem, we consider a local search range for the recomposed visual components (i.e., foreground image regions), so that the refined output will be consistent with the background in the original input image.

To perform this post-processing step for refinement, for each recomposed image region, we calculate the difference between the pixel values along its boundaries and those along the background regions (to be located). We perform such operations to search for the optimal location (within R pixels, typically within 15% of the width or height of the image, and penalized by the observed location shift), and the one corresponding to the minimum difference value would determine the final recomposition result.

3. EXPERIMENTS

In our experiments, we perform photography recomposition on multiple types of input and reference images, including transferring the composition from images of photos, sketches, and paintings. All the image data are obtained from prior related works or websites[1] . It is worth noting

[1] Input (i) and reference (r) images obtained from:
Fig.6(d)/i and Fig.7(a)/r are taken or painted by auther.
Fig.6(b)/i,(c)/i,(e)/i and Fig.7(a)/i cited from [12].
Fig.6(a)/i,(b)/r cited from [11] Fig.6(a)/r free to use for non-commercial http://goo.gl/m61C2q
Fig.6(d)/r photo and caption by Niko Saunio, National Geographics
Fig.6(f)/i CC BY-SA 3.0 by Nikunj vasoya http://goo.gl/SXiKqa
Fig.6(f)/r public domain http://goo.gl/9Q44pP
Fig.7(b)/r "Wave Runners Two kids on the beach." by Kay Crain

Figure 6: Photography recomposition using real-world photos as references.

Figure 7: Transferring from sketches or paintings.

that, we aim at verifying our framework rather than pursuing high aesthetic score. Figures 6 and 7 present our empirical results. In Figure 6, both input and reference images are photos taken in real-world scenarios. From this figure, we see that our method is able to handle images with single or multiple salient foreground regions (i.e., 1 in Figure 6(a), 2 in Figures 6(b) to (d), 3 in Figure 6(e), and a larger number of foreground objects in Figure 6(f)). We note that, for simplicity, we only consider the cases where the numbers of foreground objects in the input and reference images are the same. From the above results, we see that we not only transferred the photography composition from reference to input images, locations and boundaries of the recomposed regions were also properly aligned/presented in the final outputs. This is due to the uses of our image inpainting and post-processing techniques for image refinement.

In Figure 7, we show additional experiments using sketches or paintings as the reference images. This would be preferable for scenarios when one prefers to draw an image draft as particular user-specific composition rules, or when one aims at taking photos by mimicking famous paintings. From the above experiments, the effectiveness and robustness of our proposed method for automatic photography recomposition can be successfully verified.

4. CONCLUSION

We presented a novel graph matching based algorithm for photography recomposition. Different from prior works which required predefined aesthetics rules or user interaction, our method is able to identify salient foreground regions, followed by the matching across images for transferring the composition automatically. Our experiments on multiple types of images verified the effectiveness and robustness of our proposed method. Future research extensions include the study and transfer of photography composition from particular image styles or themes, or the retrieval of similar composition from online image or video data.

5. REFERENCE

[1] R. Arnheim. *Art and Visual Perception: a Psychology of the Creative Eye.* Univ. of California, 1969.

[2] S. Bhattacharya, R. Sukthankar, and M. Shah. A framework for photo-quality assessment and enhancement based on visual aesthetics. In *ACM Multimedia*, 2010.

[3] M.-M. Cheng, G.-X. Zhang, N. Mitra, X. Huang, and S.-M. Hu. Global contrast based salient region detection. In *IEEE CVPR*, 2011.

[4] T. Cour, P. Srinivasan, and J. Shi. Balanced graph matching. In *NIPS*. 2007.

[5] M. Freeman. *The Photographer's Eye: Composition and Design for Better Digital Photos.* Focal Press, 2007.

[6] L. Liu, R. Chen, L. Wolf, and D. Cohen-Or. Optimizing photo composition. *Computer Graphics Forum*, 2010.

[7] A. Mansfield, M. Prasad, C. Rother, T. Sharp, P. Kohli, and L. V. Gool. Transforming image completion. In *BMVC*, 2011.

[8] M. Nishiyama, T. Okabe, Y. Sato, and I. Sato. Sensation-based photo cropping. In *ACM Multimedia*, 2009.

[9] C. Rother, V. Kolmogorov, and A. Blake. "grabcut": Interactive foreground extraction using iterated graph cuts. In *ACM SIGGRAPH*, 2004.

[10] A. Santella, M. Agrawala, D. DeCarlo, D. Salesin, and M. Cohen. Gaze-based interaction for semi-automatic photo cropping. In *SIGCHI*, 2006.

[11] L.-K. Wong and K.-L. Wong. Enhancing visual dominance by semantics-preserving image recomposition. In *ACM Multimedia*, 2012.

[12] F.-L. Zhang, M. Wang, and S.-M. Hu. Aesthetic image enhancement by dependence-aware object recomposition. *IEEE Trans. Multimedia*, 2013.

Eyes Whisper Depression

A CCA based Multimodal Approach

Heysem Kaya*
Department of Computer Engineering
Boğaziçi University
34342, İstanbul, Turkey
heysem@boun.edu.tr

Albert Ali Salah
Department of Computer Engineering
Boğaziçi University
34342, İstanbul, Turkey
salah@boun.edu.tr

ABSTRACT

This paper presents our work on ACM MM Audio Visual Emotion Corpus 2013 (AVEC 2013) depression recognition sub-challenge using the baseline features in accordance with the challenge protocol. We use Canonical Correlation Analysis for audio-visual fusion as well as covariate extraction for the target task. The video baseline provides histograms of local phase quantization features extracted from 4x4=16 regions of the detected face. We summarize the video features over segments of length 20 seconds using mode and range functionals. We observe that features of range functional that measure the variance tendency provides statistically significantly higher canonical correlation than mode functional features that measure the mean tendency. Moreover, when audio-visual features are used with varying number of covariates per region, the regions that were consistently found the best are the ones corresponding to two eyes and the right part of the mouth. We reach 9.44 Root Mean Square Error on the challenge test set using audio-visual decision fusion, improving the video baseline 30% relative.

Categories and Subject Descriptors

G.3 [**Mathematics of Computing**]: Probability and Statistics–Correlation and regression analysis; I.4.7 [**Image Processing and Computer Vision**]: Feature Measurement; I.5.4 [**Computing Methodologies**]: Pattern Recognition-Signal processing

General Terms

Human-Computer Interaction

Keywords

canonical correlation analysis; audio-visual emotion corpus; audio-visual fusion; feature extraction; depression recognition

*Corresponding author

MM'14, November 3–7, 2014, Orlando, Florida, USA.

http://dx.doi.org/10.1145/2647868.2654978.

1. INTRODUCTION

A fundamental aspect of human communication is nonverbal. In order for computing machinery to advance, not only the commands but also the traits (e.g. cultural background, personality) and the states (e.g. sleepiness, emotions) of the interacting individual should be taken into account. Moreover, the computer based systems can also be employed to detect and monitor the level of a long term illness, such as Alzheimer's disease or depression. This way, it will be possible for the patients to self-monitor their progress anytime, anywhere. The study on the field can help reduce the economic cost of diagnosis at a global scale and allow the patients/medical doctors to get timely feedback.

ACM MM Audio-Visual Emotion Corpus and Challenge 2013 (AVEC 2013) focused on prediction of self-reported level of depression [13]. Depression can be defined as a state of low mood and aversion to activity that can affect a person's thoughts, feelings, behaviors, and sense of well-being. The participating individuals are recorded via a web cam while they are guided by a presentation to do various tasks such as singing, reading and counting. The level of depression is measured by Beck-Depression Index II (BDI-II), a 21 item multiple-choice inventory [2]. The organizers provided baseline video and acoustic features along with the video clips partitioned into training, developments and test sets.

In this paper, we focus on extracting covariates of the target variable as highly informative features. We employ Canonical Correlation Analysis (CCA) for this purpose. We also use CCA for audio-visual feature level fusion. CCA is a statistical method that aims find linear projections for two views/representations of a semantic object that maximizes the mutual correlation [7, 6]. It is shown that when two representations of the same object (no matter whether they are from the same modality or not) are fused using CCA, the resulting features are more robust than the individual views [10]. CCA has a variety of applications in pattern recognition, ranging from multi-modal fusion [6, 10] to feature selection [8].

A recent study on AVEC 2013 corpus benefits from CCA as an acoustic feature selector, where the authors utilize the projection vector to rank the features [8]. Here instead, we use CCA for feature extraction in video and audio-visual modalities. We fuse the regional video features with the selected acoustic features from [8]. To focus on the discriminative power of the extracted covariate, we use 1-Nearest Neighbor (1-NN) as a smoother, and then average the predictions over the clip to get a final score. When individual regression performances of fused features are compared, the best results are consistently observed with regions corresponding to right eye, left eye and right half of the mouth. The stillness of the eyes, measured with the low variance of features from these regions, is found to be correlated with depression. Therefore, the preliminary studies show that eyes indicate depressive mood.

The remainder of this paper is organized as follows. In the next section we provide background on CCA. Then in Section 3 we briefly introduce the corpus and baseline feature sets. In Section 4 we give experimental results, and in Section 5 conclude.

2. BACKGROUND: CANONICAL CORRELATION ANALYSIS

Proposed early in 1936 by Hotelling [7], CCA seeks to maximize the mutual correlation between two sets of variables by finding linear projections for each set. Mathematically, CCA seeks to maximize the mutual correlation between two representations of the same semantic phenomenon (e. g. audio and video of a speech) denoted $X \in \mathbb{R}^{n \times d}$ and $Y \in \mathbb{R}^{n \times p}$, where n denote the number of paired samples, via:

$$\rho(X, Y) = \sup_{w,v} corr(Xw, Yv), \quad (1)$$

where "corr" corresponds to Pearson's correlation, w and v correspond to the projection vectors of X and Y, respectively. Let C_{XY} denote the cross-set covariance between the sets X and Y, and similarly let C_{XX} denote within set covariance for X. The problem given in eq. (1) can be reformulated as:

$$\rho(X, Y) = \sup_{w,v} \frac{w^T C_{XY} v}{\sqrt{w^T C_{XX} w \cdot v^T C_{YY} v}}. \quad (2)$$

The formulation in Eq. (2) can be converted into a generalized eigenproblem for both projections (i. e. w and v), the solution can be shown [6] to have the form of:

$$C_{XX}^{-1} C_{XY} C_{YY}^{-1} C_{YX} w = \lambda w, \quad (3)$$

where the correlation appears to be the square root of eigenvalue:

$$\rho(X, Y) = \sqrt{\lambda}. \quad (4)$$

To attain maximal correlation, the eigenvector corresponding to the largest eigenvalue in Eq. (3) should be selected. Similarly, by restricting the new vectors to be uncorrelated with the previous ones, it can be shown that the projection matrices for each set are spanned by the k eigenvectors corresponding to the k largest eigenvalues. Non-linearity can be incorporated into CCA using the *kernel trick* [6] or deep neural networks (DNN) [1]. Non-linear feature reduction using CCA can be benefited in classification exploiting non-linear feature interactions such as SVM.

We next introduce the AVEC 2013 data used for experimental validation.

3. THE CORPUS AND FEATURES

AVEC 2013 [13] uses a subset of the audio-visual depressive language corpus (AVDLC), which includes 340 video clips of subjects performing a Human-Computer Interaction task while being recorded by a webcam and a microphone. In AVDLC, the total number of subjects is 292 and only one person appears per clip, i. e. some subjects feature in more than one clip. The clip duration ranges from 20 to 50 minutes, with a total duration of 240 hours. The age of subjects ranges from 25 to 63. The target variable (BDI-II score) range is 0-45. Recorded behavior includes speaking out loud while solving a task, counting from 1 to 10, reading excerpts of a novel and a fable, singing, free talk: telling the best event and a sad event from childhood. The depression levels were labeled per clip using Beck Depression Inventory-II (BDI-II) [2], a subjective self-reported 21 item multiple-choice inventory.

For the AVEC 2013 challenge, the recordings were split into three partitions: training, development, and test sets of 50 recordings each, respectively.

3.1 Baseline Feature Sets

The AVEC 2013 audio baseline feature set, which provides an extended set of features with respect to AVEC 2012 [12], consists of 2 268 features extracted using TUM's open source feature extractor openSMILE [5]. Due to space limitations, the reader is referred to the challenge paper [13] for the details of the Low Level Descriptors (LLDs - e. g. F0, MFCC bands 0-12) and functionals (e. g. mean, std). The audio features are obtained using functionals operating over LLD contours in four segmentations: short (3 sec. with 2 sec. shifts), long (20 sec. with 2 sec. shifts) Voice Activity Detected segmentation (VAD-Seg) and per clip. Since the challenge paper reports best results on Depression Sub-Challenge (DSC) with long segmented acoustic feature set, we focus on this segmentation and synchronize the video features accordingly. The distribution of instances is given in Table 1.

Table 1: Instance distribution per segmentation

#	Train	Dev	Test
Per Clip	50	50	50
VAD Seg	6015	5763	5946
Short Seg	23863	23513	23824
Long Seg	23439	23087	23399

The baseline video features consist of geometric features (e. g. head pose and coordinates) and Local Phase Quantization features (LPQ). The geometric features (Geo) are 8 dimensional. The LPQ features are computed by taking 2-D Discrete Fourier Transform (DFT) of M-by-M neighborhood of each pixel in the gray scale image. The 2D-DFT is computed at four frequencies $\{[a,0]^T, [0,a]^T, [a,a]^T, [a,-a]^T\}$, $a = 1/M$, which correspond to 4 of 8 neighboring frequency bins centered at the pixel of interest. The real and imaginary parts of resulting four complex numbers are separately quantized using a threshold of 0, that gives an 8 bit string. The 8 bit string is then converted into an integer value in the range 0-255. The pixel based values are finally converted into a histogram of 256 bins. Since this histogram representation does not keep the structural information of facial features, the face is divided into $4 \times 4 = 16$ regions and an LPQ histogram is computed per region. On the overall, the baseline LPQ feature set provides $16 \times 256 = 4096$ features for each face detected frame. Before we proceed with the experiments, we provide canonical correlation analysis of long segmented baseline features in the next section.

3.2 Analysis of Features

As mentioned earlier, the video features are synchronized with the long segmented audio features. For this purpose, the frame-wise video features are summarized over windows of 20 seconds with a shift of 2 seconds. Two summarizing functionals are used. We use mode functional as a robust alternative measuring the mean tendency and range functional as a robust alternative for variance. The reason we prefer these alternatives is that data contains 0 values when face is undetected. For mode computation, all the features are independently discretized into histograms of 1000 bins in min-max feature value range. Then after mode computation, they were transformed back using the mean value of the corresponding bin. The summary of Canonical Correlation (ρ) of synchronized video features against the depression labels are given in Table 2.

Table 2: Canonical correlations of video features vs. depression labels in the training set

Set	Dim	ρ
All	8208	0.959
Mode (LPQ+Geo)	4104	0.893
Range (LPQ+Geo)	4104	0.952
LPQ	8192	0.948
Geo	16	0.301

It is important to note that the long segmented audio features provide a canonical correlation of 0.794 against the labels. From the table we observe that features using range functional give more information about the target variable than the mode features. To investigate this effect in statistical manner, we computed the ρ of video features against the target variable in 16 regions, separately. The mean±std ρ statistics computed over regions are 0.77 ± 0.03, 0.80 ± 0.02, and 0.87 ± 0.01 for mode features, range features and combination of them, respectively. Administering a paired two tailed t-test on the canonical correlation of regional features, we found that range functional provides statistically higher canonical correlation ($p < 0.001$) than mode features. Moreover, the combined set provides much better performance compared to range only features ($p < 10^{-12}$). The reason for high canonical correlation of mode features and better performance of range functional can be accounted by the tendency of mean features to encode the identity of the individual rather than the depression level.

4. EXPERIMENTAL RESULTS

In our experiments we adhere to the challenge protocol. We use the training set and optimize our model hyper parameters on the development set. When a viable method and hyper parameter set is obtained, we re-train a model using training plus development set to predict the independent test set, the labels of which are unknown. Our aim is to surpass the challenge test set baselines provided in the paper. The sub-challenge measure for depression is Root Mean Squared Error (RMSE), while to ease the comparison Mean Absolute Error(MAE) is also provided. The test set baseline RMSE scores for DSC are 14.12 and 13.61 for audio and video modalities, respectively.

The best test set RMSE results reported on AVEC 2013 Corpus/DSC are listed in Table 3. We see that the best two scores are obtained using audio only modality. In this paper, we are interested in utilizing the visual cues and the robustness of audio-visual fusion.

Table 3: Best test set results reported on AVEC 2013/DSC

Work	Modality	RMSE
Kaya et al. [8]	Audio	9.78
Cummins et al. [4]	Audio	10.17
Meng et al. [9]	Audio-visual	10.96
Cummins et al. [3]	Audio	11.37

4.1 Experiments with Video Features

In the previous section ρ of regional features were given. Here we utilize the canonical covariates obtained from regional video features. For this, we remove the training set mean of each regional LPQ features (mode plus range) and apply the projection to development set. We then apply 1-NN regressor on the resulting 16-dimensional covariate space and obtain 6.90 MAE, 8.61 RMSE on the development set. If we combine the decisions of regional regressors instead, we get 7.61 MAE, 9.16 RMSE. When only the best 6 regional regressors are combined, the performance barely reaches the feature level combination: 7.07 MAE, 8.56 RMSE.

4.2 Audio-Visual Fusion

Here we repeat the feature selection experiments on a recent CCA based study on the same corpus and challenge [8]. We fuse the selected 387 acoustic features with each of regional visual features using CCA. Since CCA provides projections from either views, i. e. video and audio features, we utilize the video projections. The number of covariates in CCA is limited to the minimum of matrix ranks of two views. Since the selected audio features are smaller in number (387 as opposed to 512 video features) and they are linearly independent, the maximum number of covariates is 387. We apply a second level CCA between $p = \{50, 100, 150, 200, 250\}$ covariates from each region and the target labels to obtain a final single covariate for regression. The RMSE performance of regional regressors with varying number of covariates are given in Fig. 1. We observe that the best three regional regressors are always number 6, 7 and 10, which correspond to left eye, right eye and the right part of the mouth, respectively. This is intuitive as the most potent parts of the face for action recognition are eyes and mouth area. This preliminary result helps reduce the computations to one quarter by focusing on the inner 2-by-2 square in the 4-by-4 partitioning of facial image. Moreover, the RMSE is observed to decrease up to 200 covariates but does not improve further. We finally concatenate all the local audio-visual covariates into a feature vector and apply CCA against the target labels to obtain a single depression covariate. The best RMSE results were obtained when 100 regional audio-visual covariates are combined (i.e. 1600 features) for second stage CCA in a similar fashion to Ensemble CCA [11]. An interesting finding is that the development set correlation of audio-visual covariates is higher than the training set. With 100 local covariates, the training set ρ is found as 0.930 and development set ρ is 0.952. For video modality ρ reduces from 0.948 to 0.636, whereas in audio modality the decrease is more dramatic (from 0.794 to 0.306).

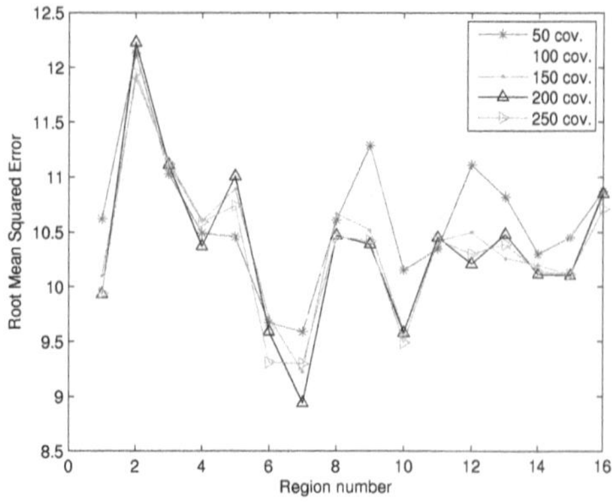

Figure 1: Canonical correlations of regional video features vs. depression labels in the training set

For the test set we retrain training and development sets for the video-only model with 16 regional covariates (M1), video-only model using only 3 best performing regions (M2), audio-visual fusion with 150 covariates (M3), and decision fusion of M2 with audio-only model proposed in [8](M4). The results given in Table 4 indicate that audio-visual feature level fusion does not improve over video only features, while audio-visual decision fusion provides the best result. Note that all results are better than the challenge baselines.

Table 4: Challenge test set results

Model	Modality	MAE	RMSE
M1	Video	7.97	9.94
M2	Video	7.86	9.72
M3	Audio-visual (feature level)	8.79	10.81
M4	Audio-visual (decision fusion)	7.68	9.44

Considering scores given in Table 3, our best test set score obtained using depression covariates as features and 1-NN regressor ranks the second after the state-of-the-art. The regressor and its hyper parameter were not optimized in this study, in order to sharpen the effect of the feature transformation. The study can be improved by employing more potent visual descriptors and more sophisticated regressors.

5. CONCLUSIONS AND OUTLOOK

In this study we utilize Canonical Correlation Analysis to extract depression covariates in visual and audio-visual modalities. We see facial regions that correspond to eyes and mouth area provide the best regression scores. Moreover, when a functional over the frame level features is used, range functional measuring the variance tendency is observed to be significantly better than the mode functional for mean tendency. We also observe that multi-modal fusion yields more robust covariates in the development set, which may be important for affect recognition. The challenge test set scores indicate the efficacy of our simple approach. The best test set results are obtained with audio-visual decision fusion. In our future work, we will extend the study to affect recognition and focus more on inner facial regions.

6. REFERENCES

[1] G. Andrew, R. Arora, J. Bilmes, and K. Livescu. Deep canonical correlation analysis. In *Proc. of the 30th Intl. Conference on Machine Learning*, pages 1247–1255, Atlanta ,Georgia, USA, 2013.

[2] A. Beck, R. Steer, R. Ball, and W. Ranieri. Comparison of beck depression inventories -ia and -ii in psychiatric outpatients. *Journal of Personality Assessment*, 67(3):588–597, 1996.

[3] N. Cummins, J. Epps, V. Sethu, and J. Krajewski. Variability compensation in small data: Oversampled extraction of i-vectors for the classification of depressed speech. In *Acoustics, Speech and Signal Processing (ICASSP), 2014 IEEE International Conference on*, pages 970–974, May 2014.

[4] N. Cummins, J. Joshi, A. Dhall, V. Sethu, R. Goecke, and J. Epps. Diagnosis of depression by behavioural signals: a multimodal approach. In *Proc. of the 3rd ACM Intl. Workshop on Audio/Visual Emotion Challenge*, AVEC '13, pages 11–20, 2013.

[5] F. Eyben, M. Wöllmer, and B. Schuller. Opensmile: the munich versatile and fast open-source audio feature extractor. In *Proc. of the intl. conf. on Multimedia*, pages 1459–1462. ACM, 2010.

[6] D. R. Hardoon, S. Szedmak, and J. Shawe-Taylor. Canonical correlation analysis: An overview with application to learning methods. *Neural Computation*, 16(12):2639–2664, 2004.

[7] H. Hotelling. Relations between two sets of variates. *Biometrika*, 28(3/4):321–377, 1936.

[8] H. Kaya, F. Eyben, A. A. Salah, and B. W. Schuller. CCA Based Feature Selection with Application to Continuous Depression Recognition from Acoustic Speech Features. In *Proc. IEEE Intl. Conference on Acoustics, Speech, and Signal Processing (ICASSP 2014)*, pages 3757–3761, 2014.

[9] H. Meng, D. Huang, H. Wang, H. Yang, M. AI-Shuraifi, and Y. Wang. Depression recognition based on dynamic facial and vocal expression features using partial least square regression. In *Proc. of the 3rd ACM Intl. Workshop on Audio/Visual Emotion Challenge*, AVEC '13, pages 21–30, 2013.

[10] C. O. Sakar. *Multi-View Feature Extraction based on Canonical Correlation Analysis*. PhD thesis, Institute for Graduate Studies in Science and Engineering, Boğaziçi University, Jan 2014.

[11] C. O. Sakar, O. Kursun, and S. F. Gurgen. Ensemble canonical correlation analysis. *Applied intelligence*, 40(2):291–304, 2014.

[12] B. Schuller, M. Valstar, F. Eyben, R. Cowie, and M. Pantic. AVEC 2012 – The Continuous Audio/Visual Emotion Challenge. In L.-P. Morency, D. Bohus, H. K. Aghajan, J. Cassell, A. Nijholt, and J. Epps, editors, *Proc. of the 14th ACM Intl. Conference on Multimodal Interaction, ICMI*, pages 449–456, Santa Monica, CA, October 2012. ACM.

[13] M. Valstar, B. Schuller, K. Smith, F. Eyben, B. Jiang, S. Bilakhia, S. Schnieder, R. Cowie, and M. Pantic. AVEC 2013–The Continuous Audio/Visual Emotion and Depression Recognition Challenge. In *Proc. of the 3rd ACM Intl. Workshop on Audio/Visual Emotion Challenge*, AVEC '13, pages 3–10, 2013.

Just Browsing?
Understanding User Journeys in Online TV

Yehia Elkhatib•, Rebecca Killick◇, Mu Mu•, and Nicholas Race•
•School of Computing and Communications, ◇Department of Mathematics and Statistics
Lancaster University, UK
{i.lastname}@lancaster.ac.uk

ABSTRACT

Understanding the dynamics of user interactions and the behaviour of users as they browse for content is vital for advancements in content discovery, service personalisation, and recommendation engines which ultimately improve quality of user experience. In this paper, we analyse how more than 1,100 users browse an online TV service over a period of six months. Through the use of model-based clustering, we identify distinctive groups of users with discernible browsing patterns that vary during the course of the day.

Categories and Subject Descriptors

H.5.1 [**Multimedia Information Systems**]: Evaluation/methodology; H.5.2 [**User Interfaces**]: Interaction styles

Keywords

Online TV; User behaviour; Modelling

1. INTRODUCTION

Consumers are exhibiting an increasing appetite for accessing TV content over the Internet, either as live or catchup /on-demand (VoD) streaming services. In 2013, over a third (36%) of UK internet users claimed to use such services every week [9]. Previous studies have investigated user behaviour in a course-grained fashion in terms of item popularity, channel switching, and consumption rate. However, little effort has been spent to understand the contextual information related to user browsing activities; and in particular the behaviour that occurs before a user starts consuming an item of content. This initial 'journey' has a significant effect on user experience, resulting in them either finding something to watch or ultimately signing off from the service. Learning from these journeys could lead to significant advances in service personalisation and performance, such as dynamically optimising the user interface and strategically caching content based on user and time. Several online media services have become conscious to the fact that monitoring and understanding user interactions are essential methods to improve efficiency of content distribution, advertisement revenues and quality of user experience. This is achieved through an analysis of mouse click sequences and content consumption characteristics.

In this study we provide an insight into such browsing habits. We analyse the browsing behaviour (including time of day) of 1,100+ users over the course of six months from a university campus online TV service that offers both live and VoD content to students and staff. Aiming at providing useful metrics to enhance recommenders and personalisation of media services, the paper applies clustering methods to generalise the findings in modelling user activities. We arrive at different ways in which users look for content and how behaviour patterns change over the 24 hours of the day.

The paper proceeds as follows. Section 2 provides background and discusses related work, Section 3 introduces the Vision online TV system and the dataset analysed in this paper, Section 4 studies the temporal dynamics of user browsing behaviour through the clustering of user interactions, and Section 5 concludes and relates future work.

2. BACKGROUND AND RELATED WORK

The primary motivation of many studies (e.g. [1, 8]) has been to understand the impact of video requests on the network, driven by the impetus to improve performance through intelligent pre-fetching and content caching. Few studies have considered temporal dynamics: Yu et al. identified periodic changes in video requests (as a reflection of user interest) over different scales [14]. Cha et al. studied user behaviour in terms of channel switching and its relationship to content genre, time of day, and region [2]. Qiu et al. and Kim et al. incorporated diurnal patterns into modelling channel/genre popularity, and differentiated users into groups based on channel/genre interest [10, 6]. Sanchez et al. modelled user interests in an IPTV service based on content consumption [11]. Keller et al. also studied user interactions related to search to improve post-search navigation [5]. Wang et al. employed sequence- and time-based clickstreams to detect malicious users through clustering [13].

Current work on activity in multimedia systems is mostly based on one or two deterministic metrics such as playback requests and user ratings. While these metrics are effective in studying the one-mode user-content relationship for user-based recommenders, there is significant value in studying the contextual information capturing a user's stream of browsing activities prior to the consumption of content. An example of this is the effect of how system features are pre-

MM '14, November 03 – 07 2014, Orlando, FL, USA

http://dx.doi.org/10.1145/2647868.2654980.

sented on content discovery and consumption (cf. [12]) as well as user experience.

The modelling of web page browsing activities is generally based on the frequency and order of clicks or page loads. For a media service, the amount of time spent on web pages of specific functions also provides crucial context indicating user's content navigation preference such as relaxed browsing without specific intention or quick keyword search to locate a piece of content in mind.

This paper focuses on mapping user browsing journeys in an online TV service through defining and modelling the contextual information related to how the users find content.

3. VISION SERVICE AND USER DATA

3.1 IPTV system overview

Vision is an online TV service that is free for students and staff of Lancaster University. It provides a Living Lab environment with real users and workload for research and development work related to content retrieval, media distribution and quality of user experience. Between service launch in October 2013 and March 2014, Vision drew 1,100+ registered users with ≈34,710 sessions. In accordance with the university's ethical guidelines, Vision does *not* collect any personal user information such as age, gender, etc.

A total of 30 national TV and 20 radio channels are made available as live streams using a number of transcoding and media servers. The TV channels are continuously recorded and automatically partitioned into programmes, based on EPG data. These programmes are added to the VoD repository which holds over 30 days worth of catch-up content.

User facing functionalities are manifested in 7 web pages, each distinguishable by a unique ID: *Dashboard*, *What's On*, *On Demand*, *Programme Guide*, *My Library*, *My History*, *Search Results*, and *Playback*. The Dashboard (Fig. 1(a)) incorporates a recommender (based on highly customised collaborative filtering), watch list (a shortened list of saved items), and social trending features (trending content within the user community). Playback page (Fig. 1(b)) encapsulates a media player, programme information, and social features. What's On offers currently airing and upcoming programmes of each live TV channel. Users can browse the entire VoD repository via the On Demand page by name, genre, length, etc. Programme Guide provides a grid view of the TV schedule. Vision users may also add items to a personal library (via My Library). Users can access their viewing record on My History and resume playing a programme from where they left off on any device.

3.2 User and service statistics

As a research platform, Vision focuses on gathering user feedback through periodic survey and finely grained quantitative user activity data. A dedicated *statistics service* captures user interactions for comprehensive social and user behaviour analysis. A *report engine* resides in user devices (in JavaScript) to i) catch time-coded events such as playback requests, periodic heartbeats of media player, keyword searches or page loads, ii) pre-process the data, and iii) post the statistics to the *stats ingest service* to be stored for data analysis. An aggregation of faceted usage statistics reveals page navigation and content viewing experience in Vision. For instance, the system is able to tell that from 18:05:01, user 3 spent 2 minutes going through live programmes on What's On, then spent 14 minutes browsing On Demand, and finally resumed an episode of *Flog It* from My History.

(a) Dashboard (b) Playback page

Figure 1: Vision web interface

3.3 Journey of user interaction

We extract all recorded user activities of 1109 users (excluding admin and test accounts) for the period 02/10/13–17/03/14. A user session is identified when the user activity stream becomes idle for 30 minutes, the standard notion of a visit in Web analytics [7]. Each session may contain one or more playback requests. Every playback request is seen as the termination of a user's journey of seeking content to watch. Therefore we define each playback request along with the relevant user interactions prior to the request as a *journey*. The journey gives an insight into how each user, at a particular time of the day, navigates between service pages before playback commences. A total of 67,089 journeys are recognised for the experimentation period. One specific element of user journey is the proportion of browsing time spent on each service page pt_n (where n is the page id). pt_n captures the characteristics of each user playback journey, hence is exploited as a metric to study the user similarities with respect to content navigation and to investigate whether browsing preference changes over time.

4. TEMPORAL DYNAMICS AND CLUSTERING OF BROWSING ACTIVITIES

4.1 Initial observations

Related work (such as [2, 1, 8]) has already shed light on how user playback requests change over different time scales (day, week, month, etc.) In this work, however, we investigate whether a similar time dependency applies to users' browsing activities and their interactions with the service.

Our periodic user surveys and interviews suggested that most of our user population start using our TV service from the late afternoon after lectures. Many users also claimed that they have developed the habit of watching a few TV programmes before they go to sleep around midnight.

First, we examine feature use over the hours of the day. We find no strong deduction when using such co-variate time information. We conjecture that this is due to variance in user-days; e.g. two users could be using Vision while having breakfast, but that means 7am for one and 10am for the other. We then consider dividing the day into a number of time slots wherein user activity seems to conform to a strong trend. In Fig. 3, we plot the average number of all user journeys over the 24 hours. In order to achieve a

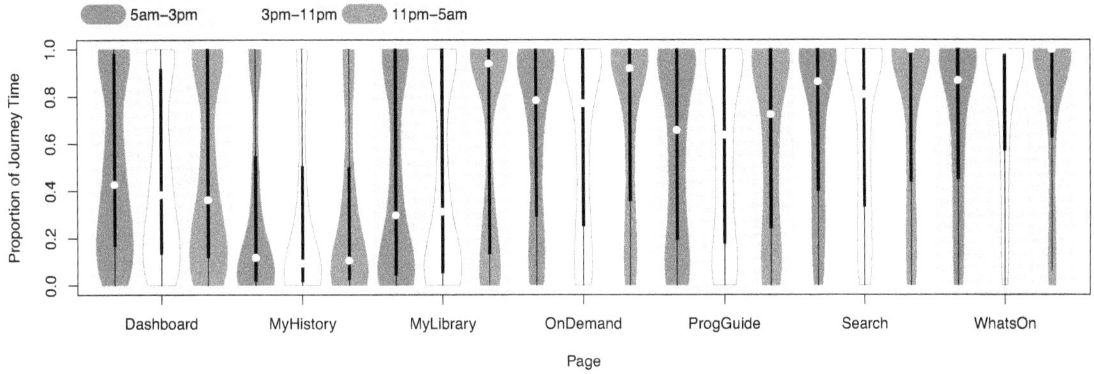

Figure 2: Violin plot of the average proportion of journey time spent on each page in each time segment.

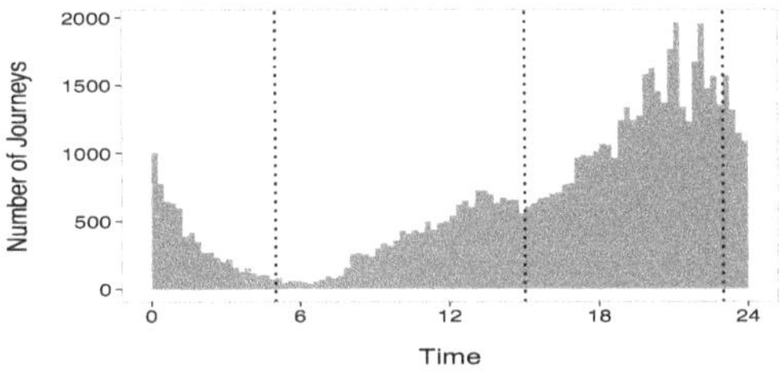

Figure 3: Density of journeys per 1/4 hour.

meaningful classification, we bin user activities into three main time segments: 5am-3pm, 3pm-11pm, and 11pm-5am.

Based on this, we inspect the journeys in each segment to investigate whether we can generalise the patterns of user behaviour in groups within each time segment and how the patterns change over time. Fig. 2 characterises our findings in a violin plot. For each of the seven Vision service pages per time segment, the figure offers a box plot to illustrate the median proportion of time spent on the page relative to the journey duration. The box plot also presents the first and third quartiles, signified by thin lines at the extremes. Additionally, the figure depicts the overall distribution as a density function plotted in colour around the box plot.

We learn some interesting findings from this figure, the first and most crucial of which is that the vast majority of users have journeys that belong to several clusters. Furthermore, there is a discernible difference in the role some of the pages play in user journeys across the time segments. For instance, My Library and Search are far more prevalent in the third time segment. This confirms the first of our suspicions that users utilise the system features in a different manner across various times in a day. However, the 'hourglass' like shapes of the densities suggest different features within as well as between time segments. Inspired by such findings, we launch a deeper analysis of the affinity user journeys have with the pages during the different time segments.

4.2 Analysis of browsing behaviour

We employ clustering to identify different types of users, expecting to see significant overlap between the different types of content browsing behaviour. Traditional nonparametric clustering methods such as K-means may struggle to identify any clusters [4]. Thus, we use model-based clustering in order to identify clusters and assume Gaussian distributions for each cluster. Whilst the original page time pt_n data are proportions (restricted to [0,1]) we rescale these to the real line to make the Gaussian assumption more appropriate. All the calculations to fit the clusters were performed using the `EMCluster` [3] package in `R`.

The clustering of the journey data resulted in 4, 5, 5 clusters for the 5am-3pm, 3pm-11pm and 11pm-5am time segments, respectively, with the highest significance. The average proportion of time spent per page within each cluster is depicted in Fig. 4.

For the time period 5am-3pm we observe key differences between the 4 clusters. Out of the seven pages to seek content: cluster 1 browses in six pages with no usage of the My History; cluster 2 browses in two pages with 40% of the time spent on Dashboard and the remaining 60% spent browsing live channels on What's On; cluster 3 browses in two pages with the majority of the time (86%) on Search; cluster 4 browses in all pages with 50% of time spent on My Library. In this time segment it is clear that we have two types of users who are easily satisfied, namely those in clusters 2 or 3 who either identify content through the Dashboard (which is the default landing page of the service) and through What's On or Search, respectively. The remaining two groups, 1 and 4, are less easily satisfied and are willing to spend more time interacting with the entire system looking around all pages before deciding on content. These journeys also appear to be from users without a predetermined consumption intent, eventually finding content through one of the live channels or perhaps resorting to something from their profile (My Library/My History) when other means do not succeed.

For the 5 clusters of journeys in the time period 3pm-11pm we have the following key differences: Out of the seven pages to find content, cluster 1 uses two pages with most of the time (87%) spent on What's On; cluster 2 uses three pages with 88% on Dashboard; cluster 3 uses all pages almost equally; cluster 4 uses four pages with 70% attention to On Demand; cluster 5 uses three pages with nearly all browsing activities (99%) on Search. Here, the majority of journeys (58.8%, cluster 1) favour live content. These are users who tune in at a specific time to watch primetime programmes. In contrast, users in cluster 5 identify content through keyword search. Interestingly, cluster 4 is the only cluster across the three time periods where browsing for On Demand content takes up the majority of their journey time.

For the 11pm-5am segment: cluster 1 uses four pages with 65% of time on What's On; cluster 2 use five pages with 44%

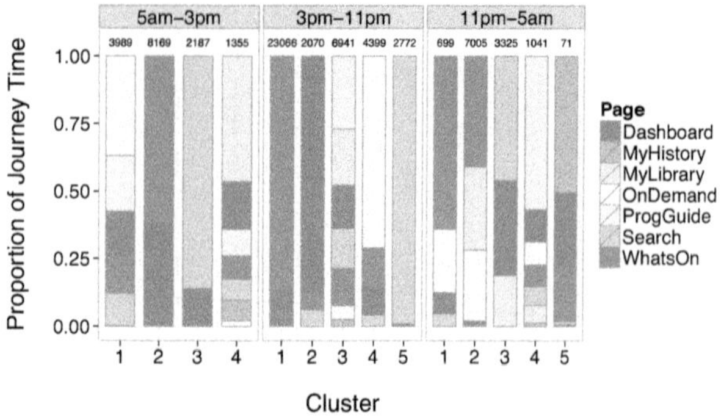

Figure 4: The proportions of time spent on each page between clusters and across time segments.

on What's On, 33% on My Library, 28% on On Demand; cluster 3 uses four pages with 47% Search and 36% Dashboard; cluster 4 uses all pages with 59% of time browsing Programme Guide; cluster 5 also uses all pages but with half of the time on My History. Unsurprisingly, browsing at this time of the day involves less time spent on What's On as the quality of live content declines, and much more towards the different VoD channels. Most users find items from My Library or the On Demand catalogue. The next group is perhaps more specific and rely heavily on Search. The third group is more reliant on the Programme Guide as a means of catching up on programmes missed earlier in the day.

These results show clear differences between the time segments especially with access to VoD content (via On Demand, My Library, etc.) being common to several clusters in the 11pm-5am segment compared to belonging to 1 cluster in the other time segments. Similarly, the 11pm-5am segment is the only time when the Programme Guide is used as the primary content portal for a cluster. In contrast, the use of My Library is only prevalent in the 5am-3pm segment.

In summary, the results provide insight into the different habits of users browsing an online TV service. In particular, through the use of clustering we have identified distinctive groups of users with consistent browsing behaviour exhibited during different periods of the day.

5. CONCLUSIONS

We used model-based clustering to distinguish groups of similar user browsing habits in an online TV Living Lab environment. We identified a number of statistically significant clusters each of which capture thousands of user browsing journeys with distinct behavioural patterns. This could easily be leveraged by service features to personalise user experience in finding content (e.g. adapting the user interface, seeding personalised recommenders) or to increase revenue (e.g. promoting content).

Although our dataset relates to one online TV service, the followed methodology and derived conclusions can be adopted by similar online media services. The outcomes from this case study present an initial step towards understanding user behaviour and content discovery in relation to different contextual factors. We plan future efforts to enhance the analysis with further contextual information. A metric we plan to include is the proportion of content watched beyond the end of a journey, which we hope will provide insight into the relationship between user engagement and journey characteristics.

6. ACKNOWLEDGMENTS

This work was supported in part by European Commission FP7 grants 318343 (STEER) and 603662 (FI-Content2).

7. REFERENCES

[1] H. Abrahamsson and M. Nordmark. Program popularity and viewer behaviour in a large TV-on-demand system. In *Proc. IMC*, pages 199–210. ACM, 2012.

[2] M. Cha, P. Rodriguez, J. Crowcroft, S. Moon, and X. Amatriain. Watching television over an IP network. In *Proc. IMC*, pages 71–84. ACM, 2008.

[3] W.-C. Chen, R. Maitra, and V. Melnykov. *EMCluster: EM Algorithm for Model-Based Clustering of Finite Mixture Gaussian Distribution.* R package v0.2-4.

[4] K. A. Heller and Z. Ghahramani. A nonparametric bayesian approach to modeling overlapping clusters. In *Proc. Conference on Artificial Intelligence and Statistics*, pages 187–194, 2007.

[5] M. Keller, P. Mühlschlegel, and H. Hartenstein. Search result presentation: Supporting post-search navigation by integration of taxonomy data. In *Proc. WWW Companion Conference*, pages 1269–1274, 2013.

[6] J. Kim, C. Hwang, E. Paik, and Y. Lee. Analysis of IPTV user behaviors with MapReduce. In *Proc. Conference on Advanced Communication Technology*, pages 1199–1204, 2012.

[7] R. Krishnan, S.S.and Sitaraman. Video stream quality impacts viewer behavior: Inferring causality using quasi-experimental designs. *IEEE/ACM Trans. Networking*, 21:2001–2014, 2013.

[8] G. Nencioni, N. Sastry, J. Chandaria, and J. Crowcroft. Understanding and decreasing the network footprint of over-the-top on-demand delivery of TV content. In *Proc. WWW*, pages 965–976, 2013.

[9] Ofcom. The communications market. `http://stakeholders.ofcom.org.uk/market-data-research/market-data/communications-market-reports/cmr13`, Aug 2013.

[10] T. Qiu, Z. Ge, S. Lee, J. Wang, Q. Zhao, and J. Xu. Modeling channel popularity dynamics in a large IPTV system. In *Proc. SIGMETRICS*, pages 275–286. ACM, 2009.

[11] F. Sanchez, M. Barrilero, F. Alvarez, and G. Cisneros. User interest modeling for social TV-recommender systems based on audiovisual consumption. *Multimedia Systems*, 19:493–507, 2013.

[12] G. Tyson, Y. Elkhatib, N. Sastry, and S. Uhlig. Demystifying porn 2.0: A look into a major adult video streaming website. In *Proc. IMC*, pages 417–426. ACM, 2013.

[13] G. Wang, T. Konolige, C. Wilson, X. Wang, H. Zheng, and B. Y. Zhao. You are how you click: Clickstream analysis for sybil detection. In *Proc. USENIX Security Symposium*, pages 241–256, 2013.

[14] H. Yu, D. Zheng, B. Y. Zhao, and W. Zheng. Understanding user behavior in large-scale video-on-demand systems. *SIGOPS Operating System Review*, 40(4):333–344, 2006.

Inductive Transfer Deep Hashing for Image Retrieval

Xinyu Ou
Huazhong University of Science and Technology
1037 Luoyu Rd., Wuhan 430074, China
Yunnan Open University
113 Xuefu Rd., Kunming 650223, China
ouxinyu@hust.edu.cn

Lingyu Yan, Hefei Ling*, Cong Liu, Maolin Liu
Huazhong University of Science and Technology
1037 Luoyu Rd., Wuhan 430074, China
{yanranyaya, lhefei}@hust.edu.cn,
liucongwust@gmail.com,
u201014564@hust.edu.cn

ABSTRACT

With the explosive increase of online images, fast similarity search is increasingly critical for large scale image retrieval. Several hashing methods have been proposed to accelerate image retrieval, a promising way is semantic hashing which designs compact binary codes for a large number of images so that semantically similar images are mapped to similar codes. Supervised methods can handle such semantic similarity but they are prone to overfitting when the labeled data is few or noisy. In this paper, we concentrate on this issue and propose a novel Inductive Transfer Deep Hashing (ITDH) approach for semantic hashing based image retrieval. A transfer deep learning algorithm has been employed to learn the robust image representation, and the neighborhood-structure preserved method has been used to mapped the image into discriminative hash codes in hamming space. The combination of the two techniques ensures that we obtain a good feature representation and a fast query speed without depending on large amounts of labeled data. Experimental results demonstrate that the proposed approach is superior to some state-of-the-art methods.

Categories and Subject Descriptors

H.3.3 [**Information Search and Retrieval**]: Retrieval models, Search process

Keywords

Inductive Transfer Leaning; Deep Learning; Image Retrieval; Neighborhood-Structure Preserved; Semantic Hashing

1. INTRODUCTION

Due to the exponential growth of online images, it is necessary to consider searching among large number of images, which is very time-consuming and unscalable. To tackle the problem of large scale image applications, machine learning is introduced into the field of image representation to discover the hidden semantic patterns among images.

Based on feature extraction, many hashing methods are proposed to generate compact and discriminative image representation. Tang et al.[11] develop a global method using nonnegative matrix factorization (NMF), which first convert image into a fixed-sized pixel array and then generate secondary image by rearranging pixels and applying NMF to produce a feature-bearing hash code, after that, the fingerprint is coarsely quantized into binary string and scrambled to generate the image fingerprint. Wang et al.[12] have proposed a semi-supervised hashing method (SSH) that incorporates pairwise semantic similarity and dissimilarity constraints from labeled data, which minimized the empirical error on the labeled data while maximizing entropy of the generated hash bits over the unlabeled data. Similarity Sensitive Coding (SSC)[9] adopts boosting approach, they first train AdaBoost classifiers with similar pairs of items as positive examples (and also non-similar pairs of items as negative examples in SCC), and then take the output of all (decision stump) weak learners on a given document as its binary code. Self-taught hashing (STH)[14] is proposed and considered as one of the state-of-the-art works[6]. However, it suffers overfitting problem since the operations of generating hash codes for traing data and hash function for test data are independently handled, which will lead to poor generalization ability. Minimal loss hashing (MLH)[7] that have shown higher search accuracy than unsupervised hashing approaches, but they all impose difficult optimization and slow training mechanisms. Spectral hashing (SpH)[13] uses a separable Laplacian eigenfunction formulation that ends up assigning more bits to directions along which the data has a greater range. However, this approach is somewhat heuristic and relies on an unrealistic assumption that the data is uniformly distributed in a high-dimensional rectangle.

With no regard of feature extraction, many research works have shown that the deep learning based approaches [5, 10] can provide a good performance in many image related tasks. Those methods normally need to use the autoencoders to pre-train a multiple-layer neural network, and then the pre-trained network in deep learning can be regarded as a representation function for new images, and the output vectors of those neural nodes can be viewed as a representation of the new images. Some deep learning method are proposed

*Hefei Ling is the corresponding author.

MM '14 November 03 - 07 2014, Orlando, FL, USA

http://dx.doi.org/10.1145/2647868.2654987.

to implement image [4] or text[2, 8] retrieval task, these technique pushes the retrieval field significantly forward.

Motivated by recent progresses in deep neural network and manifold learning, we will focus on the image representation learning, which is composed of a novel autoencoders based learning and a transfer learning based generation for image hashing and representation. We first construct an objective function for autoencoders to learn the hash function for training images, which not only consider the reconstruction error during encoding but also consider the neighborhood-structure of data. Then we minimize corresponding objective function in every layer of our multi-layer autoencoders. After that, we apply transfer learning to learn the hash code of new images for image representation.The rest of this paper is organized as follows: In section 2, we illustrate our new auto-encoder for image representation learning. In section 3, we detail the transfer learning based generation. Extensive experimental results are presented in Section 4. Finally, we provide a conclusion in Section 5.

2. NEIGHBORHOOD-STRUCTURE PRESERVED AUTOENCODERS

To discover the latent structure of the original data, the neighborhood structure of the data should be preserved to guarantee its discrimination, which means that perceptually similar image should be mapped into similar hash code in hamming space and vice verse.

Given training image data $X = [x_1, x_2, \ldots, x_n] \in \mathbb{R}^{p \times n}$, we want to get hash codes denoted by $H = [h_1, h_2, \ldots, h_n]^T \in \{0,1\}^{n \times c}$ (c is the length of the hash codes). To exploit the local neighborhood structure of a data, we construct a $n \times n$ similarity matrix S as

$$S_{ij} = \begin{cases} 1 & ,\text{if} \quad x_i \in N_k(x_j) \quad or \quad x_j \in N_k(x_i) \\ 0 & ,\text{otherwise} \end{cases} \quad . \tag{1}$$

where $N_k(x)$ represents the set of k-nearest-neighbors of feature vector x.

The Hamming distance between two binary codes h_i and h_j (corresponding to data x_i and x_j) is given by the number of bits that are different between them. To preserve the neighborhood structure, we seek to minimize the weighted average Hamming distance which represents the neighborhood-structure

$$\sum_{i=1}^{n}\sum_{j=1}^{n} S_{ij} \|h_i - h_j\|^2 = 2tr(H^T(N-S)H) \quad . \tag{2}$$

where $N_{ii} = \sum_{j=1}^{n} S_{ij}$ and other elements are zero.

Combine the neighborhood-structure preservation and reconstruction error, we get an unified objective function for our auto-encoder

$$\arg\min \|X - Q\|^2 + \lambda tr(H^T(N-S)H) \quad . \tag{3}$$

where λ is a coefficient and

$$\begin{aligned} H &= sigmoid(W_H X + b_H) \\ Q &= sigmoid(W_Q H + b_Q) \end{aligned} \quad . \tag{4}$$

By applying Broyden-Fletcher-Goldfarb-Shanno (BFGS) training algorithm, we get the learning parameter W_H and b_H for further hashing.

3. TRANSFERRING IMAGE REPRESENTATION

We present an approach that begins to learn a slight feature representation by using the unlabeled data X_u. By applying this learned representation to the labeled data X_l, we obtain a higher level representation of the labeled data, and an easier supervised learning task. To adapt our modified version of the sparse autoencoders algorithm to the new task and the new domain, we continue training the parameters by using a labeled dataset. Inductive transfer learning method is employed, different weight are assigned to the loss function of the target task to make sure that better performance in target domain can be achieved. The proposed method assumed that the parameters set $\boldsymbol{W}$ and $\boldsymbol{b}$ in an l-layer neural networks for target task can be divided into two parts. One is a share parameters set derived from the source task and the other is a special parameters set added in the target task.

$$\boldsymbol{W}_T = \begin{cases} \boldsymbol{W}_S & ,2 < l < k-1 \\ \boldsymbol{W}_{T'} & ,k < l < n_l \end{cases} \tag{5}$$

$$\boldsymbol{b}_T = \begin{cases} \boldsymbol{b}_S & ,2 < l < k-1 \\ \boldsymbol{b}_{T'} & ,k < l < n_l \end{cases} \tag{6}$$

where $\boldsymbol{W}_S$ and $\boldsymbol{W}_T$ are parameters set of the neural networks for the source task and the target learning task, respectively. $\boldsymbol{W}_{T'}$ is specific parameters set for the target task. By assuming $h_{\boldsymbol{W},\boldsymbol{b}}(\boldsymbol{x}) = f(\boldsymbol{W}^T\boldsymbol{x} + \boldsymbol{b})$ to be the activation function for source task S and target task T, an extension of sparse autoencoders to target transfer learning case can be written as the following:

$$\begin{aligned} J(\boldsymbol{W},\boldsymbol{b}) = & \frac{1}{m}\left(\sum_{i=1}^{m}\left(\frac{1}{2}\|h_{(\boldsymbol{W},\boldsymbol{b})}(x^{(i)}) - y^{(i)}\|^2\right)\right) \\ & + \frac{\psi}{2}\left(\sum_{l=1}^{k-1}(\boldsymbol{W}_S^{(l)})^2 + \sum_{l=k}^{n_l}(\boldsymbol{W}_{T'}^{(l)})^2\right) \\ & + \beta\sum_{j=1}^{s} KL(\rho\|\hat{\rho}_j) \end{aligned} \tag{7}$$

$$s.t.\, \boldsymbol{W} = \boldsymbol{W}_T, \boldsymbol{b} = \boldsymbol{b}_T, \boldsymbol{W}_S^{(l)} \in \{S,T\}, \boldsymbol{W}_{T'}^{(l)} \in \{T\}$$

The first term in the definition of $J(\boldsymbol{W},\boldsymbol{b})$ is an average sum-of-squares error term, the second term is a regularization term that tends to decrease the magnitude of the weights, and helps prevent overfitting, the third term is sparsity penalty term. ψ is the weight decay parameter which controls the relative importance of the terms, ρ is a sparsity parameter (typically a small value close to zero), $\hat{\rho}$ is the average activation of hidden unit j, s is the number of neurons in the hidden layer, the index j is summing over the hidden units in neural network, β controls the weight of the sparsity penalty term. $\boldsymbol{W}_S$ and $\boldsymbol{b}_S$ are unchanged from the source task, by solving the optimization problem above, we can learn the parameter $\boldsymbol{W}_{T'}$ and $\boldsymbol{b}_{T'}$ simultaneously.

In order to achieve the transfer, in the target network, we remove the output layer of the source network and add several adaptation layers formed by fully connected layers that use the $\boldsymbol{W}_{T'}$ and $\boldsymbol{b}_{T'}$ as network parameters. Now, we can compute the parameters as follows:

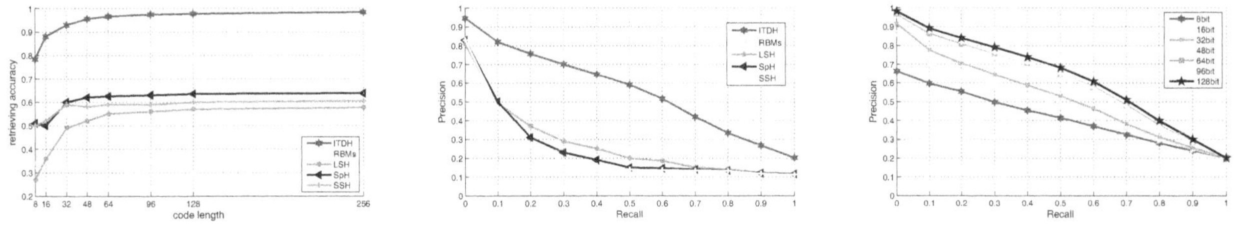

(a) (b) (c)

Figure 1: (a) Retrieving accuracy and (b) Precision-Recall curve of the different algorithm on MNIST. (c) Precision-Recall curve of the ITDH under various code length on MNIST.

1. Perform a feedforward pass, computing the activations for each layers respectively, using the equations defining the forward propagation steps.

2. For the output layer n_l, set: $\delta^{(n_l)} = -(y - a^{(n_l)}) \bullet f'(z^{(n_l)})$.

3. For layer $l = n_l - 1, n_l - 2, ..., k$, set:

$$\delta^{(l)} = (\boldsymbol{W}_{T'}^{(l)} \delta^{(l+1)}) \bullet f'(z^{n_l}) \quad (8)$$

4. For layer $l = k-1, k-2, ..., 2$, keep $\boldsymbol{W}_S^{(l)}$ of target task equals the $\boldsymbol{W}_S^{(l)}$ of source task, and set:

$$\delta^{(l)} = ((\boldsymbol{W}_S^{(l)}) \delta^{(l+1)}) \bullet f'(z^{n_l}) \quad (9)$$

5. For layer $l = k-1, k-2, ..., 2$, keep $\boldsymbol{W}_S^{(l)}$ and $\boldsymbol{b}_S^{(l)}$ not change. For layer $l = n_l - 1, n_l - 2, ..., k$, implement parameter iteration of batch gradient descent, set:

$$\Delta \boldsymbol{W}_{T'}^{(l)} := \boldsymbol{W}_{T'}^{(l)} + \delta^{(l+1)} (a^{(l)})^T \quad (10)$$

$$\Delta \boldsymbol{b}_{T'}^{(l)} := \boldsymbol{b}_{T'}^{(l)} + \delta^{(l+1)} \quad (11)$$

By update the parameters, we can repeatedly take steps of gradient descent to reduce our target cost function $J(\boldsymbol{W}, \boldsymbol{b})$ to train our neural network.

4. EXPERIMENTS

To validate that our approach Inductive Transfer Deep Hashing (ITDH) achieves better retrieving performance, we compare it with Locality Sensitive Hashing (LSH)[1], Semi-Supervised Hashing (SSH)[12], Spectral Hashing (SH)[13] and Restricted Boltzmann Machines (RBMs)[3] on the M-NIST digit dataset and STL-10 dataset in this section. We first using the transfer deep learning algorithm to extract image feature, then transform it into hash codes, and through the hamming-distance between the query sample and all training samples to measure the similarity, then according to the similarity sorting the query results, finally, we using precision-recall curve to measure the performance of the algorithms.

4.1 MNIST Digits

The MNIST dataset consists of a total of 70000 handwritten digit sample, each of size 28×28 pixels. Each sample is associated with a label from 0 to 9. Our goal is to distinguish between the digits from 0 to 4. We use the digits 5 to 9 as our "unlabeled" dataset with which to train the source neural network, then use a labeled dataset which consists 15298 digits from 0 to 4 to train the target neural network. The rest of the remaining 15298 digits from 0 to 4 are used to test the efficiency of our algorithm. RBMs train neural networks using the unlabeled data for training and using the labeled pairs for fine-tuning. Our network is designed to be very simple, the source architecture consists of two stack autoencoders layers, one full-connection layer and one output layer(for extract hash codes), such as 200-200-400F-output. The target architecture similar to source architecture, just added a full-connection before the output layer. Given a dataset, we use each sample in the test set as a query to retrieve samples in the training set within a specific Hamming distance(which is fixed at 0 in our experiment), and then compute standard retrieval performance measure: Precision-Recall curve and retrieving accuracy. To determine whether a retrieved object is relevant to the given query, we adopted the evaluation methodology that retrieving same category samples which are considered as ground-truth relevant samples.

Figure 1a shows the retrieving accuracy of the proposed approach(ITDH) compared to SSH, SH, LSH and RBMs algorithm. In order to show the influences of code length on the retrieval performance, we vary the code length from 8 to 256 bits. We first find all the relevant objects whose Hamming distance to the query equals 0, then consider the most frequently appearing label responding to the relevant objects as the label of the query. Finally accuracy is computed by the ratio that the retrieval label equals the original one. Compared with other algorithms, the retrieval accuracy of our approach is 1.5 times as other methods. In addition, the Precision-Recall curve for 48-bit codes is shown in Figure 1b, which clearly demonstrates proposed approach achieve the best performance over the entire Hamming ranking space.

Figure 1c shows the Precision-Recall curve of difference code Length. With the increase of the code length, the image retrieval performance increases. It is chiefly because that the more hidden layer neurons can learn the rich feature which improve the ability of image recognition in deep network. Since the number of the neurons of the last hidden layer is the code length of image, the length of code directly impact on the final image retrieval performance. On the MNIST dataset, when increasing the number of the neurons of the last hidden layer from 8-bit codes to 48-bit codes, algorithm performance is tending towards stability.

We provides the training and testing time (including feature learning and retrieval) for different methods. Clearly, RBMs and ITDH is most expensive to train, RBMs needs at least 3.5 orders of magnitude more time than other algo-

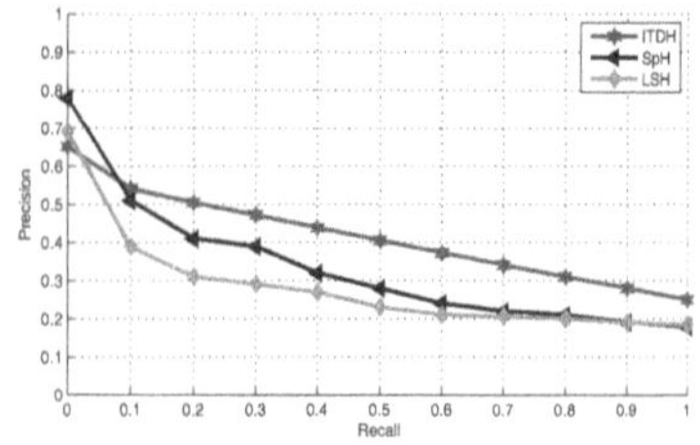

Figure 2: Precision-Recall curve on STL-10

rithms, while ITDH needs at least 2.5 orders of magnitude more time. LSH needs negligible training time since the projections are randomly generated, instead of being learned. SSH and SH take need a bit more time to training than LSH. Summarize, the code generation time can be ranked as: RBMs $\gg$ ITDH $\gg$ SH $\approx$ SSH >LSH. In terms of test time, RBMs is still most expensive because it computes the binary codes for a query using multi-layer neural network. ITDH is a neural network, but due to the simple structure, it take similar test time of others. LSH are the fastest techniques. SH and SSH require a little more time than LSH due to the computation of nonlinear sinusoidal functions to generate each bit. So, the test time can be ranked as: RBMs $\gg$ ITDH $\approx$ SH $\approx$ SSH >LSH.

4.2 STL-10 dataset

The STL-10 dataset is an image recognition dataset for developing unsupervised learning algorithms. It has 10 classes, 5000 training images (500 images per class), 8000 test images (800 images per class) and 100000 unlabeled images. We use the unlabeled images set for source task to learn image features and apply the representations for target task to train train set and test set. Figure 2 shows the quantitative evaluation of different methods. The proposed approach outperform the other methods in most of the cases performing significantly better than all the compared methods for higher bits as expected.

5. CONCLUSIONS

The main contribution of this paper is a novel Inductive Transfer Deep Hashing (ITDH) approach for semantic hashing based fast similarity search. The proposed method combines the neighborhood-structure of data with a transfer learning algorithm to learn the hash function for training images, which is formulated as minimizing empirical error while maximizing variance and independence of hash bits over the labeled and unlabeled data. By solving the problem of finding small codes for large data into two stages: unsupervised learning and supervised learning, we achieve a flexibility algorithm architecture. Due to neural net can be viewed as a way for learning feature expression, each neuron can be regarded as a cell of image sample. Through the learning by a large number of unlabeled data, can make the cells of images more ordinary, while by learning labeled data, neural net can better combine with these cells to express the target image. The experiments on two image datasets show that the proposed approach outperforms several existing state-of-the-art techniques. In the future, we shall apply this technique to other complex benchmark dataset and achieve even higher effectiveness and efficiency by employ more powerful unsupervised or supervised learning algorithms. It would also be interesting to combine semantic hashing with GPU computing(or distributed computing) to further improve the speed and scalability of similarity search.

6. ACKNOWLEDGMENTS

This work is supported by the NSF of China under Grant No.61272409, the applied basic research of youth-project of Yunnan Provincial Science and Technology Department under Grant No.2012FD0034.

7. REFERENCES

[1] A. Gionis, P. Indyk, R. Motwani, et al. Similarity search in high dimensions via hashing. In *VLDB*, volume 99, pages 518–529, 1999.

[2] G. Hinton and R. Salakhutdinov. Discovering binary codes for documents by learning deep generative models. *Topics in Cognitive Science*, 3(1):74–91, 2011.

[3] G. E. Hinton and R. R. Salakhutdinov. Reducing the dimensionality of data with neural networks. *Science*, 313(5786):504–507, 2006.

[4] A. Krizhevsky and G. E. Hinton. Using very deep autoencoders for content-based image retrieval. In *ESANN*. Citeseer, 2011.

[5] A. Krizhevsky, I. Sutskever, and G. E. Hinton. Imagenet classification with deep convolutional neural networks. In *NIPS*, volume 1, page 4, 2012.

[6] P. Li, M. Wang, J. Cheng, C. Xu, and H. Lu. Spectral hashing with semantically consistent graph for image indexing. *Multimedia, IEEE Transactions on*, 15(1):141–152, 2013.

[7] M. Norouzi and D. M. Blei. Minimal loss hashing for compact binary codes. In *Proceedings of the 28th International Conference on Machine Learning (ICML-11)*, pages 353–360, 2011.

[8] R. Salakhutdinov and G. Hinton. Semantic hashing. *International Journal of Approximate Reasoning*, 50(7):969–978, 2009.

[9] G. Shakhnarovich, P. Viola, and T. Darrell. Fast pose estimation with parameter-sensitive hashing. In *Computer Vision, 2003. Proceedings. Ninth IEEE International Conference on*, pages 750–757. IEEE, 2003.

[10] R. Socher, B. Huval, B. P. Bath, C. D. Manning, and A. Y. Ng. Convolutional-recursive deep learning for 3d object classification. In *NIPS*, pages 665–673, 2012.

[11] Z. Tang, S. Wang, X. Zhang, W. Wei, and S. Su. Robust image hashing for tamper detection using non-negative matrix factorization. *Journal of Ubiquitous Convergence Technology*, 2(1):pp–18, 2008.

[12] J. Wang, S. Kumar, and S.-F. Chang. Semi-supervised hashing for scalable image retrieval. In *Computer Vision and Pattern Recognition (CVPR), 2010 IEEE Conference on*, pages 3424–3431. IEEE, 2010.

[13] Y. Weiss, A. Torralba, and R. Fergus. Spectral hashing. In *NIPS*, volume 9, page 6, 2008.

[14] D. Zhang, J. Wang, D. Cai, and J. Lu. Self-taught hashing for fast similarity search. In *Proceedings of the 33rd international ACM SIGIR conference on Research and development in information retrieval*, pages 18–25. ACM, 2010.

What Can We Learn about Motion Videos from Still Images?

Jianguang Zhang [1], Yahong Han [1,3], Jinhui Tang [2], Qinghua Hu [1,3], Jianmin Jiang [4]
1. School of Computer Science and Technology, Tianjin University, China
2. School of Computer Science and Technology, Nanjing University of Science and Technology, China
3. Tianjin Key Laboratory of Cognitive Computing and Application
4. School of Computer Science & Software Engineering, Shenzhen University, China
lynxzjg@tju.edu.cn, yahong@tju.edu.cn, tangjh1981@gmail.com, huqinghua@tju.edu.cn, jianmin.jiang@szu.edu.cn

ABSTRACT

Human action recognition from motion videos plays an important role in multimedia analysis. Different from the temporal cues of action series in motion videos, the motion tendency can also be revealed from the still images or key frames. Thus, if the action knowledge in related still images can be well adapted to the target motion videos, we would have a great chance to improve the performance of video action recognition. In this paper, we propose a framework of Still-to-Motion Adaptation (SMA) for human action recognition. Common visual features are extracted both from the related images and target videos' key frames, by which the gap between still images and videos are bridged. Meanwhile, to utilize the un-labeled training videos in target domain, we incorporate a semi-supervised process into our framework. By minimizing the difference of action prediction from still features and motion features, we formulate the still-to-motion adaptation into a joint optimization process. Experiments successfully demonstrate the effectiveness of the proposed framework and show the better performance of action recognition compared with the state-of-the-art methods. We also analyze the impact on the recognition results of target videos by knowledge adaptation from still images.

Categories and Subject Descriptors

I.5.2 [**Pattern Recognition**]: Design Methodology—*Classifier design and evaluation*; I.2.10 [**Artificial Intelligence**]: Vision and Scene Understanding—*Motion, Video analysis*

Keywords

Domain Adaptation; Action Recognition; Images; Videos

1. INTRODUCTION

Human action recognition in motion videos has many potential applications in multimedia event detection and surveillance, etc. One straightforward solution for this problem is to use the local space-time features (e.g. STIP, MoSIFT) to represent the characteristic shapes and motions of the videos. However, these methods do not explore the semantically meaningful components of an action, such as related objects, human appearance, posture, and so on. Recently, many works have been done to explore the interaction between objects and human pose. However these methods suffer from the problems caused by false object detections or inaccurate pose estimations. Besides the action recognition from motion videos, human action tendency can also be conveyed from still images [3][12]. For example, Gupta *et al.* [3] utilized the contextual information for action recognition from still images. Just like the human pose 'riding' of still images in Figure 1, due to the different objects 'horse' and 'bike', the still images from top row is inferred to be 'Biking' and the still images from bottom row to be 'Horse Riding'. This method has been proved to improve the performance of human action recognition in still images when object context is considered. Yao *et al.* [12] used action bases in still images for human action recognition. In Figure 1, the action bases of still images include 'riding', 'bike', 'road', 'horse', 'grass', and so on. To obtain the semantically meaningful interpretation of the still images, the still images are represented by the sparse set of these action bases. This method shows that we can extract many meaningful action bases from still images.

As shown in Figure 1, semantically related still images may have the same pose, objects, and appearance as motion videos. If these information are taken into account, we can further obtain the coherent semantic of human action in motion videos and achieve better recognition accuracy. Recent

Figure 1: An illustration of still images and motion videos on the topics of 'Biking' and 'Horse Riding'

MM'14, November 03 - 07, 2014, Orlando, FL, USA.

http://dx.doi.org/10.1145/2647868.2654992.

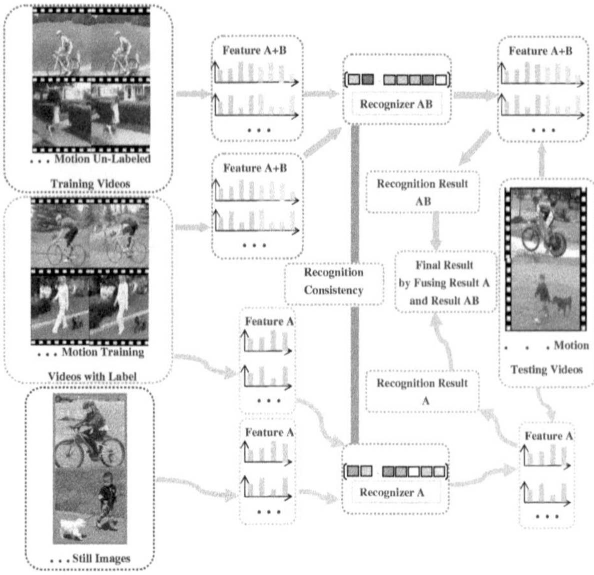

Figure 2: The flowchart of SMA. We first extract common feature A and heterogenous feature B. The yellow and blue lines are the semi-supervised learning and domain adaptation processes respectively. The recognizer A is optimized by knowledge adaptation from still images. Another recognizer AB is trained based on both feature A and B. We integrate two recognizers into a joint optimization process.

studies of adaptation from images to videos have shown better performance in applications of cross-media tagging [10] and retrieval [8]. Thus taking a motion video set as the target domain and an related image set to be adapted as auxiliary domain, the adapted knowledge can help improving the performance of action recognition of motion videos. In this paper, we propose a framework of Still-to-Motion Adaptation (SMA) for human action recognition. In our method, we extract the common visual features from both still images and the key frames of motion videos. And then the knowledge can be adapted based on such shared space of the common features. Meanwhile, the heterogeneous visual features are extracted from the video domain and are combined with the common visual features. In order to make use of unlabeled motion videos, a semi-supervised recognizer is trained based on the combined visual features in videos domain. The flowchart of SMA is shown in Figure 2. The final recognition results of testing motion videos are refined by fusing the results of aforementioned two Recognizers.

2. ADAPTATION FROM STILL IMAGES TO MOTION VIDEOS

As shown in Figure 2, the common visual feature A is extracted from auxiliary images and video key frames. Let $X_i = [X_i^1, X_i^2, ..., X_i^{n_i}] \in R^{d_i \times n_i}$, denote the representations of n_i still images using feature A, d_i is the dimension of feature A. For each individual video, it can be represented as a sequence of key frames. We also extract feature A from key frames of target videos for adapting relevant knowledge. Denote the representations of n_v labeled videos as $X_v = [X_v^1, X_v^2, ..., X_v^{n_v}] \in R^{d_i \times n_v}$. Let $y_v = [y_v^1, y_v^2, ..., y_v^{n_v}]^T \in \{0,1\}^{n_v \times 1}$ imply the labels for videos. $y_v^j = 1$ if the jth video is a positive sample whereas $y_v^j = 0$ otherwise.

In order to minimize the gap between the feature A representations and semantic labels of videos, we use the $\ell_{2,1}$-norm to define the objective function because it is robust to outliers [5]. The objective function can be written as:

$$\min_{W_v, b_v} \left\| X_v^T W_v + 1_v b_v - y_v \right\|_{2,1} \tag{1}$$

where $W_v = [w_v^1, .., w_v^{d_i}]^T \in R^{d_i \times 1}$ is the action recognizer of target videos. $b_v \in R^1$ is a bias term and $1_v \in R^{n_v \times 1}$ denotes a column vector with all ones. For exploring the related knowledge from auxiliary images, we denote the label matrix $Y_i = [y_i^1, y_i^2, ..., y_i^{n_i}]^T \in \{0,1\}^{n_i \times n_c}$ where n_c indicates the number of action classes. $Y_i^{jk} = 1$ is X_i^j belongs to the kth class, while $Y_i^{jk} = 0$ otherwise. Similarly to Eq.(1), we realize that by the following objective function:

$$\min_{W_i, b_i} \left\| X_i^T W_i + 1_i b_i - Y_i \right\|_{2,1} \tag{2}$$

where $W_i = [w_i^1, .., w_i^{d_i}]^T \in R^{d_i \times n_c}$ is the recognizer of auxiliary images. $b_i \in R^{1 \times n_c}$ is a bias term and $1_i \in R^{n_i \times 1}$ denotes a column vector with all ones. When the target domain and auxiliary domain have many relevant knowledge, we can learn some shared component. Taking the action 'walking with dog' as an example, we may learn shared components about object 'dog', human pose 'walking', and human appearance from both target videos and auxiliary images. In [9], sparse model is used to eliminate redundancy and noise. In this way, we can propose $\|W\|_{2,p}^p$ to uncover the common information shared by W_v and W_i, where $W = [W_v, W_i]$ and $\|.\|_{2,p}$ denotes the $\ell_{2,p}$−norm $(0 < p < 2)$. The objective function can be written as:

$$\begin{aligned} \min_{W_v, b_v, W_i, b_i} & \left\| X_v^T W_v + 1_v b_v - y_v \right\|_{2,1} \\ & + \left\| X_i^T W_i + 1_i b_i - Y_i \right\|_{2,1} + \lambda \|W\|_{2,p}^p \end{aligned} \tag{3}$$

where λ is regularization parameter. By minimizing the objective function, we optimize the recognizer of target videos by using the knowledge adapted from auxiliary images.

As shown in Figure 2, we extract the heterogeneous visual feature B from target video domain. The concatenation of A and B features is feature A+B whose dimension is d_j.

The semi-supervised leaning can leverage the unlabeled data to infer a more accurate recognizer. To fully utilize labeled and unlabeled videos, We add the semi-supervised process [10] of target video domain into Eq.(3). Suppose there are n training videos $U_v = [U_v^1, ..., U_v^{n_v}, U_v^{n_v+1}, ..., U_v^n] \in R^{d_j \times n}$ represented by feature A+B, in which the first n_v videos are labeled samples. We denote $y = [y^1, y^2, ..., y^n]^T \in \{0,1\}^{n \times 1}$ as the label information. Given a labeled video U_v^j, if it is a positive sample, $y^j = 1$, otherwise $y^j = 0$. If U_v^j is not a labeled video, $y^j = 0$. $f = [f^1, f^2, ..., f^n]^T \in \{0,1\}^{n \times 1}$ is the predicted label [10]. We propose the the objective function of semi-supervised process as:

$$\begin{aligned} \min_{f, W_u, b_u} & \; Tr(f^T L f) + Tr((f - y)^T S (f - y)) \\ & + \left\| U_v^T W_u + 1_u b_u - f \right\|_{2,1} \end{aligned} \tag{4}$$

where $W_u \in R^{d_j \times 1}$ is action recognizer which correlates U_v with their labels y, $1_u \in R^{n \times 1}$ is column vector with all ones and $b_u \in R^1$ is a bias term. L is the graph Laplacian matrix and S is a diagonal matrix whose diagonal element $S_{jj} = \infty$ if U_v^j is labeled and $S_{jj} = 1$ otherwise [10].

As shown in Figure 2, in order to obtain the clear interpretation of human actions in videos, two recognizer W_v and W_u are jointly augmented for action recognition. We achieve this by minimizing the Frobenius norm $\left\|X_v^T W_v - U_v^T W_u\right\|_F^2$. We propose the objective function of SMA as following:

$$\begin{aligned} \min_{f,W_u,W_v,W_i,b_u,b_i} \; & Tr(f^T L f) + Tr((f-y)^T S(f-y)) \\ & + \left\|U_v^T W_u + 1_u b_u - f\right\|_{2,1} + \left\|X_v^T W_v - U_v^T W_u\right\|_F^2 + \beta \left\|W_v\right\|_F^2 \\ & + \left\|X_i^T W_i + 1_i b_i - Y_i\right\|_{2,1} + \beta \left\|W_i\right\|_F^2 + \lambda \left\|W\right\|_{2,p}^p \end{aligned} \quad (5)$$

where β is the regularization parameters. The optimization problems can be solved by using the alternating optimization method [5]. Once the W_u and W_v for n_c classes are obtained, we can easily get n_c groups of recognition parameters $\{W_u^r, W_v^r\}|_{r=1}^{n_c}$. Then we apply them to the testing videos for action recognition. For each class, the decision values of them are normalized and their sum are the final decision values of the testing videos.

3. EXPERIMENTS

In this section, we conduct experiments to compare SMA with two transfer learning methods HFA [2] and HF-SAR [5], semi-supervised transfer learning methods IAA [4], and a baseline method SVM. The average accuracy over all action categories is chosen as the evaluation metric.

3.1 Datasets and Extracted Features

There are not completely overlapping categories in these available image and video databases. To evaluate the proposed method of knowledge adaption, we manually construct two couples of related auxiliary image and target video domains. (1) Stanford40 [12] and UCF101 [6]: The Stanford40 consists of 40 diverse action images. The UCF101 is a dataset of realistic action videos, having 101 categories. We choose ten overlapping categories from Stanford40 and UCF101 as auxiliary image set and target video set respectively. (2) 'Actions from Still Databases' and UCF101: To further evaluate whether still images coming from various sources may contribute differently to the motion videos recognition, we select ten overlapping classes between UCF101 and an extended image dataset, which includes three open benchmark datasets (i.e. Still DB [3], PPMI [11], and Willow-Actions[1]). In the following, we denote the extended dataset as 'Actions from Still Databases' (ASD). In Table 1, we summarize the chosen categories, where '→' denotes the direction of adaptation from auxiliary domain to target domain.

Table 1: The chosen overlapping categories

Datasets	Stanford40→UCF101	ASD→UCF101
The overlapping categories	Archery	Biking
	Biking	Cricket Bowling
	Brushing Teeth	Cricket Shot
	Cutting In Kitchen	Horse Riding
	Frisbee Catch	Playing Cello
	Horse Riding	Playing Flute
	Playing Guitar	Playing Guitar
	Playing Violin	Playing Violin
	Rowing	Tennis Swing
	Walking with Dog	Volleyball Spiking

We select 50 images from each overlapping categories for knowledge adaption and sample 50% videos for training and take the remaining videos as testing data. We conduct more experiments to study the performance variance when the ratios of labeled video data are set to 10%, 20%, and 30%.

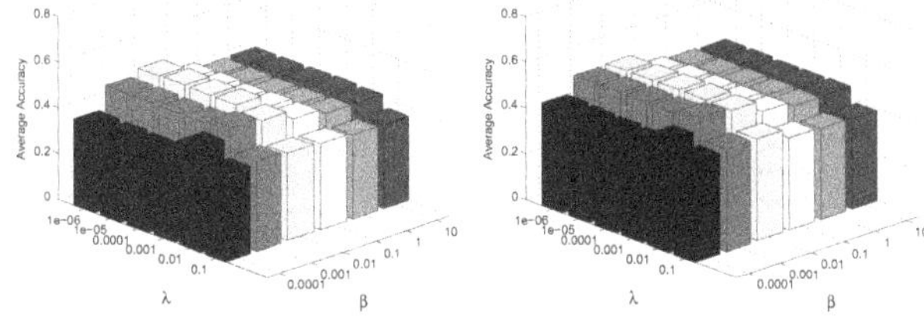

(a) Stanford40→UCF101 (b) ASD→UCF101

Figure 3: Parameter λ and β tuning of the experiments.

We extract SIFT features from key frames of target videos and images. The STIP features [7] are extracted from video domain. We perform the Bag-of-Words mapping for SIFT and STIP features to form the common visual feature A and the heterogeneous feature B. We set the number of visual words of feature A and B to 400 and 600 respectively.

3.2 Parameters Setting

In the experiment, we fix the parameter $k = 10$, which is used in the k-nearest neighbors of Laplacian matrix L. The parameter p in Eq.(5) is set to $p = 1.5$. Figure 3 shows the parameter tuning results of Stanford40→UCF101 and ASD→UCF1-01. The best performance is obtained when $\lambda = 1e^{-5}$, $\beta = 0.01$ and $\lambda = 0.01$, $\beta = 0.001$ respectively.

Table 2: Comparison results on Stanford40→UCF101

Ratio	SVM	HF-SAR [5]	HFA [2]	IAA [4]	SMA
10%	0.3864	0.4467	0.4413	0.4874	**0.5087**
20%	0.4838	0.5532	0.5640	0.5593	**0.5939**
30%	0.5078	0.5643	0.5857	0.5915	**0.6298**

Table 3: Comparison results on ASD→UCF101

Ratio	SVM	HF-SAR [5]	HFA [2]	IAA [4]	SMA
10%	0.3927	0.4557	0.4824	0.5042	**0.5367**
20%	0.4938	0.5396	0.5169	0.5317	**0.5625**
30%	0.5254	0.5869	0.5905	0.5916	**0.6281**

3.3 Comparison Results

We compare SMA with different methods on Stanford40→UCF101 and ASD→UCF101. As shown in Table 2 and 3, we report the results when the ratio of labeled training videos is 10%, 20%, and 30%, respectively. From the results we observe: (1) In both experiments, SMA achieves the best performances. SMA gains performance improvement of 4%, 5%, 6%, and 6%, 4%, 6% over these algorithms for each ratio of labeled training videos respectively. (2) Since SVM do not involve an adaptation process and cannot borrow the knowledge from the still images, the performance of action recognition is lower than HF-SAR, HFA, IAA, and SMA. (3) Because our method involves a semi-supervised learning process to utilize both labeled and unlabeled training videos in target domain. SMA outperforms other adaptation methods for different ratios of labeled training videos.

3.4 Impacts of Still-to-Motion Adaptation

In this section, we investigate the different impacts when the auxiliary images are different. We construct two new auxiliary domains. (1) The 'Walking with Dog' images of

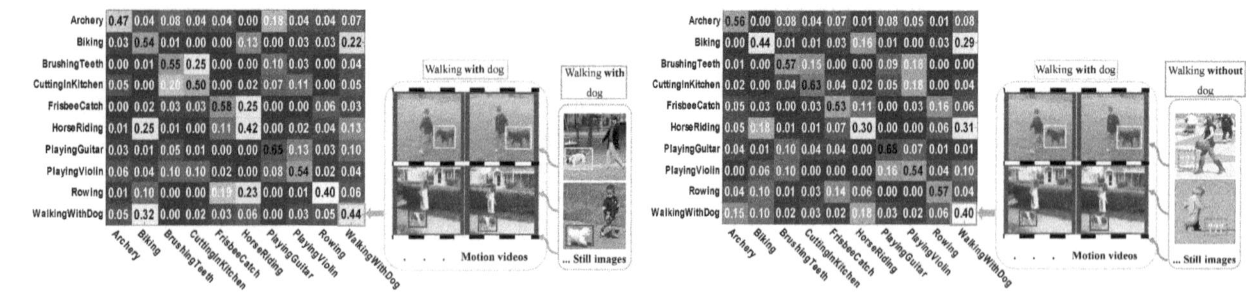

(a) Stanford40→UCF101 (b) NS→UCF101

Figure 4: Where is my dog? The action recognition results of experiments by adapting different knowledge on the topic of 'walking with dog'.

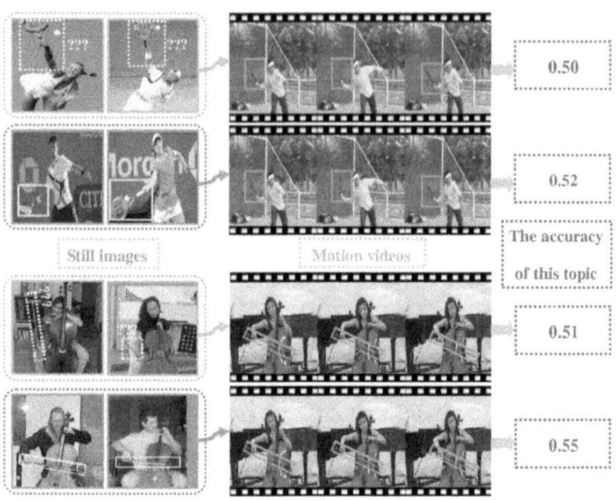

Figure 5: Recognition results of two actions 'Tennis Swing' and 'Playing Cello' by different knowledge adaptation. First and third Rows are the results of NID→UCF101 respectively. Second and fourth Rows are the corresponding results of ASD→UCF101.

Stanford40→UCF101 are replaced by 'Walking Without Dog' images of Willow-Actions. (2) The 'Playing Cello' and 'Tennis Forehand' images of ASD→UCF101 are replaced by 'With Cello' and 'Tennis Serve' images of PPMI and Still DB. We denote two new auxiliary domains as 'New Stanford40' (NS) and 'New Image Databases' (NID) respectively. In order to distinguish the different actions, as shown in Figure 4 and 5, the key parts of actions are marked with bounding box.

Firstly, considering whether the object 'dog' appear in auxiliary images or not, we show the comparison results between Stanford40→UCF101 and NS→UCF101 in Figure 4. (1) It can be seen that using still images with the object 'dog' has clear advantage over not using it for recognition accuracy of the action 'walking with dog', since there is not the feature of 'dog' in auxiliary domain, which makes recognizer consider 'dog' as the irrelevant information in motion videos and disturb recognition accuracy of this topic. (2) The recognition accuracy of NS→UCF101 is 0.5217, which is higher than that of Stanford40→UCF101. This phenomenon shows that still images coming from various sources may provide more relevant information for total recognition accuracy.

Secondly, to further study the impact of different auxiliary images, we show the performance comparison between ASD→UCF101 and NID→UCF101 in Figure 5. We observe from Figure 5 that the better results are obtained when the human poses between target videos and auxiliary images are more similar. The reason is that more related knowledge is adapted from auxiliary images to target videos and thus improve the performance of action recognition.

4. CONCLUSION

In this paper, we propose an recognizer of Still-to-Motion Adaptation, which borrows the knowledge adapted from auxiliary images. Meanwhile, it utilizes un-labeled target videos. The experiments show that the knowledge adapted from images can influence the recognition results of videos, and our method achieves a better performance for action recognition.

5. ACKNOWLEDGMENTS

This work is supported by the National Program on Key Basic Research Project under Grant (2013CB329304), National Natural Science Foundation of China under Grants (61202166, 61222210) and Doctoral Fund of Ministry of Education of China under Grant (20120032120042).

6. REFERENCES

[1] V. Delaitre, I. Laptev, and J. Sivic. Recognizing human actions in still images: a study of bag-of-features and part-based representations. In *BMVC (2010)*.

[2] L. Duan, D. Xu, and I. Tsang. Learning with augmented features for heterogeneous domain adaptation. In *ICML (2012)*.

[3] A. Gupta, A. Kembhavi, and L. S. Davis. Observing human-object interactions: Using spatial and functional compatibility for recognition. *IEEE Transactions on PAMI*, 2009.

[4] Y. Han, Y. Yang, Z. Ma, H. Shen, N. Sebe, and X. Zhou. Image attribute adaptation. *IEEE Transactions on Multimedia*, 2014.

[5] Z. Ma, Y. Yang, N. Sebe, and A. G. Hauptmann. Knowledge adaptation with partially shared features for event detection using few exemplars. *IEEE Transactions on PAMI*, 2014.

[6] K. Soomro, A. R. Zamir, and M. Shah. Ucf101: A dataset of 101 human actions classes from videos in the wild. *CRCV-TR-12-01*, November 2012.

[7] H. Wang, M. M. Ullah, A. Klaser, I. Laptev, C. Schmid, et al. Evaluation of local spatio-temporal features for action recognition. In *BMVC(2009)*.

[8] F. Wu, X. Lu, Z. Zhang, S. Yan, Y. Rui, and Y. Zhuang. Cross-media semantic representation via bi-directional learning to rank. In *ACM MM (2013)*.

[9] Y. Yang, Z. Ma, A. G. Hauptmann, and N. Sebe. Feature selection for multimedia analysis by sharing information among multiple tasks. *IEEE Transactions on Multimedia*, 2013.

[10] Y. Yang, Y. Yang, Z. Huang, and H. T. Shen. Transfer tagging from image to video. In *ACM MM (2011)*.

[11] B. Yao and L. Fei-Fei. Grouplet: A structured image representation for recognizing human and object interactions. In *CVPR (2010)*.

[12] B. Yao, X. Jiang, A. Khosla, A. L. Lin, L. Guibas, and L. Fei-Fei. Human action recognition by learning bases of action attributes and parts. In *ICCV (2011)*.

Modeling Attributes from Category-Attribute Proportions

Felix X. Yu[1] Liangliang Cao[2] Michele Merler[2]
Noel Codella[2] Tao Chen[1] John R. Smith[2] Shih-Fu Chang[1]
[1]Columbia University [2]IBM Research
{yuxinnan, taochen, sfchang}@ee.columbia.edu
{liangliang.cao, mimerler, nccodell, jsmith}@us.ibm.com

ABSTRACT

Attribute-based representation has been widely used in visual recognition and retrieval due to its interpretability and cross-category generalization properties. However, classic attribute learning requires manually labeling attributes on the images, which is very expensive, and not scalable. In this paper, we propose to model attributes from category-attribute proportions. The proposed framework can model attributes without attribute labels on the images. Specifically, given a multi-class image datasets with N categories, we model an attribute, based on an N-dimensional category-attribute proportion vector, where each element of the vector characterizes the proportion of images in the corresponding category having the attribute. The attribute learning can be formulated as a learning from label proportion (LLP) problem. Our method is based on a newly proposed machine learning algorithm called $\propto$SVM. Finding the category-attribute proportions is much easier than manually labeling images, but it is still not a trivial task. We further propose to estimate the proportions from multiple modalities such as human commonsense knowledge, NLP tools, and other domain knowledge. The value of the proposed approach is demonstrated by various applications including modeling animal attributes, visual sentiment attributes, and scene attributes.

Categories and Subject Descriptors

I.5.4 [**Applications**]: Computer Vision

Keywords

visual attribute; visual recognition; learning from label proportions

1. INTRODUCTION

Attributes often refer to human nameable properties that are shared across categories. Some examples are animal attributes (furry, striped, black), scene attributes (open, natural, indoor), visual sentiment attributes (happy, sad, lovely), and human attributes (long hair, round face, blue eye). Due to the interpretability and cross-category generalization properties, attributes have been used in various applications including face verification [4], image retrieval [11, 14], action recognition [7], and recognition with few or zero examples [6, 13]. Attributes are sometimes referred as "concepts" in multimedia [12].

MM'14, November 3–7, 2014, Orlando, Florida, USA.
Copyright 2014 ACM 978-1-4503-3063-3/14/11 ...$15.00.
http://dx.doi.org/10.1145/2647868.2654993.

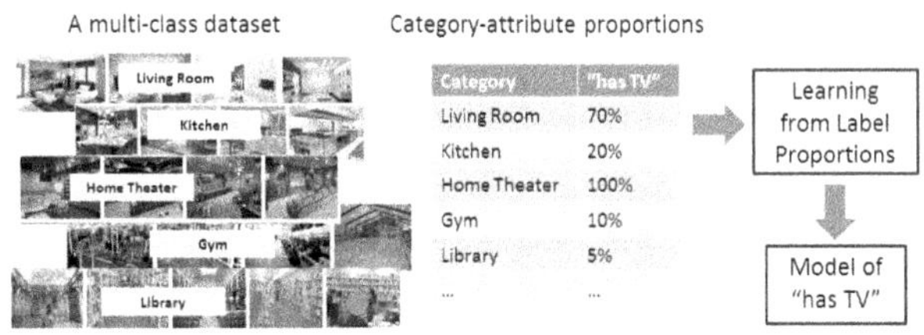

Figure 1: Illustration of the proposed framework for modeling the attribute "has TV". The input includes a multi-class dataset, and a category-attribute proportion vector. The output is an attribute model to predict "has TV" for new images.

Unfortunately, conventional attribute modeling requires expensive human efforts to label the attributes on a set of images. In this paper, we propose *attribute modeling based on category-attribute proportions*, an efficient attribute modeling framework, which requires no attribute labeling on the images. Figure 1 illustrates our framework by a conceptual example of modeling the attribute "has TV". The input includes two parts:

- A multi-class image datasets of N categories, i.e. a set of images, each with a category label. Such datasets are widely available in various visual domains, such as objects, scenes, animals, human faces etc.
- An N-dimensional category-attribute proportion vector, where the i-th dimension of the vector characterizes the *proportion* of positive images of the attribute in the i-th category.

Given the above input, the attribute learning problem naturally fits the machine learning framework called *learning from label proportions* (LLP) [10, 16]. We can then use the existing LLP techniques to train an attribute classifier, whose output can be used to predict whether the attribute is present in a new image. The above framework requires no attribute labels on the images for training. Intuitively, it is more efficient to collect the category-attribute label proportions than image-level attribute labels. For example, based on statistics, or commonsense, "80% bears are black", "90% Asians are with black hair", and "70% living rooms have a TV".

Our work makes the following contributions. We propose a framework to model attributes based on category-attribute proportions, in which no image-level attribute labels are needed (Section 1). Finding the category-attribute proportions is still not a trivial task. To this end, we propose methods for efficiently estimating the category-attribute proportions from different modalities, such as automatic NLP tools, and manual efforts with minimal human interactions (Section 3). The effectiveness of the proportion method is verified by various applications including modeling animal attribute, sentiment attributes, and scene attributes (Section 4).

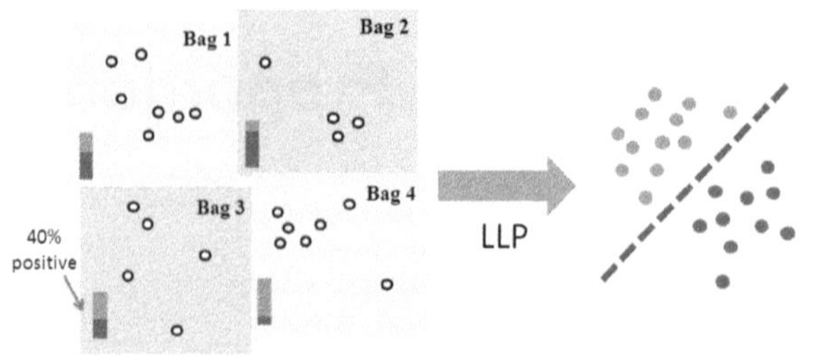

Figure 2: Illustration of learning from label proportions (LLP). In this examples, the training data is provided in 4 bags, each with its label proportion. The learned model is a separating hyperplane to classify the individual instances.

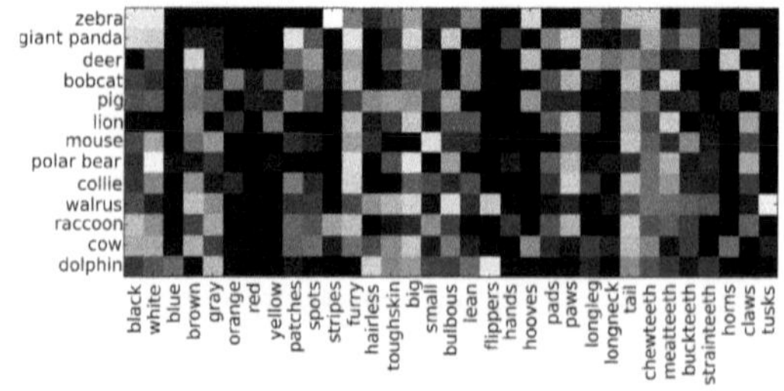

Figure 3: Manually defined category-attribute similarity matrix copied from [6]: the rows are the categories, and the columns are the attributes. This matrix is obtained from human judgments on the "relative strength of association" between attributes and animal categories.

2. LEARNING FROM LABEL PROPORTIONS

The learning setting. Key to the proposed approach is a machine learning setting called learning from label proportions (LLP). LLP is a binary learning setting, where the training data is provided in "groups" or "bags", and for each bag, only the proportion of positive instances is given. The task is to learn a model to predict the labels of the individual instances. Figure 2 illustrates a toy example of LLP. Compared to supervised learning, where the exact labels of all the training instances are known, only the label proportions for the bags are given in LLP. Therefore, LLP is a very challenging problem. Recently there have been several LLP algorithms proposed with encouraging results [10, 16]. The feasibility of this learning setting has also been verified from a theoretical perspective [15]. LLP has broad applications in political science, marketing, and healthcare. Very recently, in the multimedia and computer vision communities, LLP has been successfully applied in video event detection [5].

Applying LLP to attribute modeling. As introduced in Section 1, our problem can be viewed as a learning with label proportion setting. Here the bags are defined by the N categories, each containing some corresponding images (instances). The proportions are represented by a category-attribute proportion vector. The task is to model the attribute based on such information. In the case of modeling k attributes, we will need an $N \times k$ category-attribute proportion matrix, where the i-th column characterizes the proportion for the i-th attribute, $i = 1, \cdots, k$. For simplicity, the k attributes are modeled independently in this work.

The $\propto$SVM algorithms. Among the LLP algorithms, a recently proposed method called $\propto$SVM has been shown to outperform the alternatives [16]. We therefore use this algorithm in our work. $\propto$SVM is based on a generalization of SVM. Compared to SVM, $\propto$SVM models the unknown instance labels as latent variables. It also includes one additional loss function of the label proportions. The algorithm jointly optimizes both the model parameters and the latent labels in a large-margin framework. In other words, $\propto$SVM tries to find a large-margin classifier which is compatible with the given label proportions, with the help of latent labels. Our implementation of $\propto$SVM is based on the alter-$\propto$SVM algorithm[1], with liblinear as the underlying QP solver.

3. COLLECTING CATEGORY-ATTRIBUTE PROPORTIONS

Collecting the *exact* category-attribute proportion is still a challenging problem. In this section, we propose several ways of efficiently estimating the proportions.

[1]`https://github.com/felixyu/pSVM`

3.1 Human knowledge based

Perhaps the most straightforward method is to estimate the proportions based on human commonsense. For example, it is easy to know things like "80% bears are black", "100% home theater have TVs". To alleviate the bias of individual user, one can estimate the proportion based on averaged value of multiple persons. In addition, to make the human interaction task easier, one can also discrete the proportion values, for example, into 0, 1/3, 2/3, 1.

Similar method has been used in modeling the category-level attributes in [6]. Figure 3 shows a subset of the category-attribute similarity matrix on the AwA dataset. [6] treats this matrix as a "visual similarity" matrix. When training the attributes, they binarize the matrix, and treat the images of all positive categories as positive for the corresponding attribute. Unfortunately, the binarization will lead to huge information loss. Different from the above work, we treat this matrix as a proportion matrix. Based on the animal dataset provided in [6]. we will show by experiments (based on user study) that LLP provides better results than the binarization approach.

3.2 NLP tools based

To make the above commonsense based approach more efficient and scalable, we can also use NLP tools to automatically build such a category-attribute proportion matrix. For example, the ConceptNet[2] can be used to construct a category-attribute similarity matrix. The ConceptNet is a hypergraph that links a large amount of concepts (words) by the knowledge discovered from Wikipedia and WordNet, or provided by community contributors. The concept similarity can be computed by searching the shortest path in this graph. We apply the association function of the Web API of ConceptNet 5 to get the semantic similarity between the categories and attributes. After getting this semantic similarity matrix, we use the normalized similarity as the estimation of the proportions. We demonstrate this NLP tool based approach in the experiment section by modeling visual sentiment attributes.

3.3 Transferring domain knowledge and domain statistics

The proportions can also be borrowed from knowledge of other domains. For example, we can get the "black hair" proportion of different ethnic groups of people based on genetic research. And by combining such statistics with a multi-ethnic group human face dataset, we can model the attribute "black hair". In addition, the proportions can be borrowed from another dataset whose proportion is available. We will show one application of this approach, modeling scene attributes, in the experiment section.

[2]`http://conceptnet5.media.mit.edu/`

Categories	Attributes	Source of Proportions	Evaluation Method
Animals	Animal visual properties	Commonsense by human	User study
Sentiment attributes	Sentiment attributes	Commonsense by ConceptNet	Test on a labeled set
Scenes	Scene properties	Borrowed from another dataset	Application-based (event detection)

Table 1: Summary of the three applications explored in our experiments.

3.4 Discussion

The proposed attribute modeling technique provides an efficient alternative to the classic approaches. However there are some limitations. First, the estimated category-attribute proportion has to be close to the *exact* proportion of the dataset. This may not be true if the multi-class dataset is very biased, or if the number of images in each category is very small. Second, enough number of categories are needed. For example, the method is not going to work in the worst case scenario where only a single category and a single category-attribute proportion value is available.

4. EXPERIMENTS

We demonstrate the power of the proposed framework in three different applications: modeling animal attributes, modeling sentiment attributes, and modeling scene attributes. The three applications are summarized in Table 3.1. The parameters of the LLP algorithm are tuned based on cross-validation in terms of the proportion loss. The algorithm we use has the same computational complexity of linear SVM (it scales linearly to the number of images). In practice, the LLP algorithm is several times slower than linear SVM due to the alternating minimization process [16].

4.1 Modeling Attributes of Animals

Setting. Our first experiment consists in modeling animal attributes on the AwA dataset [6], which contains 30,475 images of 50 animal categories. Each image is uniquely labeled as one of the 50 categories. Associated with the dataset, there is a category-attribute similarity matrix of 85 attributes based on manual efforts mentioned in Section 3.1. A subset of the category-attribute matrix is shown in Figure 3. We use the same set of low-level features provided in [6]. In order to model the attributes, [6] first thresholds the matrix to a 0/1 matrix. They then train 85 attribute classifiers, where for each attribute, all the images belonging to the positive categories are treated as positive, and all images belonging to negative categories are treated as negative. The binarization step obviously leads to a big information loss.

Method. In this work, we treat the similarity matrix as a category-attribute proportion matrix, and train the attribute models with $\propto$SVM. We use 50% images for training and 50% for testing.

Evaluation. As there is no labeled images for the 85 attributes, it is hard to directly compare our method with the baselines quantitatively. For evaluation, we perform a preliminary user study. For each attribute, 20 images are randomly selected from the top-100 ranked images for each method. Human subjects are then asked to determine which method produces better attribute modeling results. The subjects are 5 graduate students majoring in engineering and business, who are not aware of the underlying learning framework. In this experiment, the users prefer our results over the baseline ones 74% of the time. This clearly demonstrates the plausibility of the newly proposed framework.

4.2 Modeling Sentiment Attributes

Setting. We consider the task of modeling object-based sentiment attributes such as "happy dog", and "crazy car". Such attributes are defined in [1, 3]. In this work we consider three nouns: dog, car, face and the sentiment attributes associated with them. This results in 77 sentiment attributes (or adjective-noun pairs, ANPs)

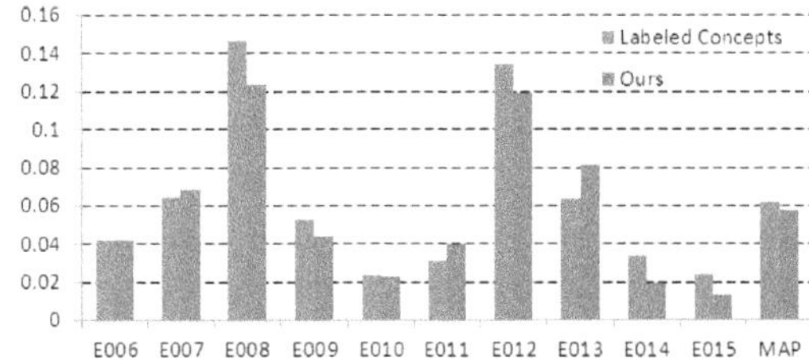

Figure 6: Event detection APs based on our attribute models, and the manual concept models. The modeled attributes (without manual labeling process) provides very competitive results compared to the concepts (with manual labeling process).

to be modeled. Such ANPs appear widely in social media. We use the data and features provided by [1]: for each ANP, there is a set of images collected by querying that ANP on Flickr. [1] uses such labels to train one-vs-all linear SVMs to model the ANPs. One critical problem for this approach is that many sentiment attributes are intrinsically ambiguous. For example, a "cute dog" can also be a "lovely dog". Therefore, when modeling "lovely dog", some images belonging to "cute dog" should also be positive.

Method. To solve the above problem, we first use the method of Section 3.2 to collect the semantic similarity between every pairs of ANPs. We then use our framework to model the ANPs. Different from other applications, both the categories and the attributes are ANPs. The proposed framework is used to improve the modeling of existing attributes, rather than learning new ones.

Evaluation. To evaluate the ANP modeling performance, for each ANP, we manually label 40 positive images, and 100 negative images from a separate set. Multiple people are involved in the labeling process, and images with inconsistent labels are discarded. Figure 4 compares our ANP modeling performance with [1]. Our approach dramatically outperforms the baseline for most of the sentiment attributes. Our method provides a relative performance gain of 30% in terms of the Mean Average Precision.

4.3 Modeling Scene Attributes

Setting. Concept classifiers have been successfully used in video event detection [2, 8]. In such systems, concept classifiers (about scenes, objects, activities etc.) are trained based on a set of labeled images visually related to the event detection task. The trained classifiers are used as feature extractors to obtain mid-level semantic representations of video frames for event detection. Key to the above event detection paradigm is a set of comprehensive concepts. In order to model one additional concept, traditional approaches require an expensive manual labeling process to label the concepts on the images. The objective of this experiment is to model the 102 scene attributes defined by [9] with the IMARS images [2, 8], without the requirement of manual labeling. Some examples of the scene attributes are "cold", "dry", and "rusty". Existing IMARS concepts do not cover the 102 attributes.

Method. We first compute the empirical category-attribute proportions based on a separate multi-class scene datasets with 717 categories ("SUN attribute dataset") [9], in which each image comes with the attribute labels. Such proportions are then used on the IMARS set to model the attributes. For each of the 717 categories, we can find the corresponding set of images on IMARS based on

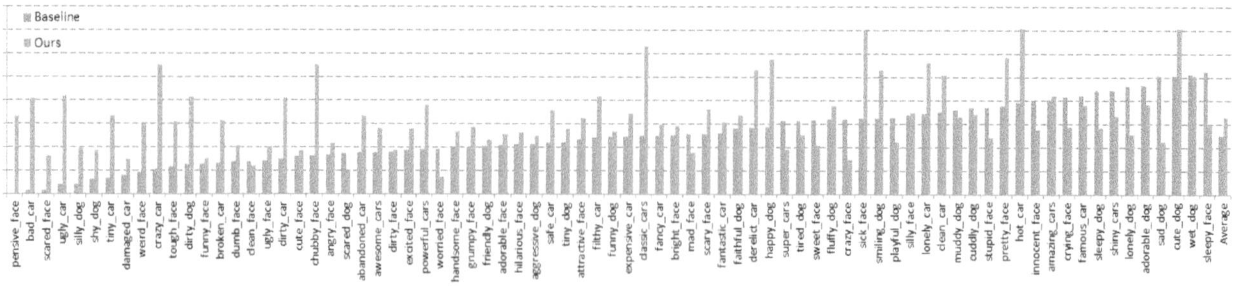

Figure 4: Experiment result of sentiment attribute modeling. The figure shows AP@20 of our method and the baseline (binary SVM). The AP is computed based on a labeled evaluation set.

(a) bathing (b) cold (c) dry (d) reading (e) rusty

Figure 5: Top ranked images of the learned scene attributes classifiers on IMARS.

the concept labels[3]. The supervised information is a 717×102 dimensional category-attribute proportion matrix. We then train 102 $\propto$SVM classifiers to model the attributes.

Evaluation. Figure 5 visualizes a few modeled attributes by the top ranked images of IMARS. We can qualitatively see that the attribute classifiers can successfully capture the corresponding visual properties. We further apply the learned attribute models in the event detection task. The evaluation is based the TRECVID MED 2011 events with the evaluation set and pipeline described in [2, 8]. The baseline method is the concepts trained by manual labels. The attributes modeled by category-attribute proportions are very competitive compared to the manually labeled concepts in terms of the average precision on the event detection task. For certain events, e.g., E007, E013, the performance of the attributes even outperforms the manual concepts. In summary, the proposed technique provides an efficient way of expanding IMARS concept classifiers for event detection.

5. CONCLUSION

We proposed a novel framework of modeling attributes based on category-attribute proportions. The framework is based on a machine learning setting called learning from label proportions (LLP). We showed that the category-attribute proportion can be efficiently estimated by various methods. The effectiveness of the proposed scheme has been demonstrated by various applications including modeling animal attributes, sentiment attributes, and scene attributes.

Acknowledgement This work was supported by the Intelligence Advanced Research Projects Activity (IARPA) via Department of Interior National Business Center contract number D11PC20070. The U.S. Government is authorized to reproduce and distribute reprints for Governmental purposes notwithstanding any copyright annotation thereon. Disclaimer: The views and conclusions contained herein are those of the authors and should not be interpreted as necessarily representing the official policies or endorsements, either express or implied, of IARPA, DoI/NBC, or the U.S. Government. We thank Quoc-Bao Nguyen and Matthew Hill for their help. Felix Yu is partly supported by the IBM PhD Fellowship.

[3]Note that one could train the attribute models based on SUN attribute dataset directly. But such attribute models do not lead to satisfactory result on IMARS due to cross-domain issues. Instead, the proportions of the two datasets are empirically very similar.

6. REFERENCES

[1] D. Borth, R. Ji, T. Chen, T. Breuel, and S.-F. Chang. Large-scale visual sentiment ontology and detectors using adjective noun pairs. In *ACM Multimedia*, 2013.

[2] L. Brown et al. IBM Research and Columbia University TRECVID-2013 Multimedia Event Detection (MED), Multimedia Event Recounting (MER), and Semantic Indexing (SIN) Systems. In *NIST TRECVID Workshop*, 2013.

[3] T. Chen, F.X. Yu, J. Chen, Y. Cui, Y.-Y. Chen, and S.-F. Chang. Object-based visual sentiment concept analysis and application. In *ACM Multimedia*, 2014.

[4] N. Kumar, A.C. Berg, P.N. Belhumeur, and S.K. Nayar. Attribute and simile classifiers for face verification. In *CVPR*, 2009.

[5] K.-T. Lai, F.X. Yu, M.-S. Chen, and S.-F. Chang. Video event detection by inferring temporal instance labels. In *CVPR*, 2014.

[6] C.H. Lampert, H. Nickisch, and S. Harmeling. Learning to detect unseen object classes by between-class attribute transfer. In *CVPR*, 2009.

[7] J. Liu, B. Kuipers, and S. Savarese. Recognizing human actions by attributes. In *CVPR*, 2011.

[8] M. Merler, B. Huang, L. Xie, G. Hua, and A. Natsev. Semantic model vectors for complex video event recognition. *IEEE Transactions on Multimedia*, 14(1):88–101, 2012.

[9] G. Patterson and J. Hays. Sun attribute database: Discovering, annotating, and recognizing scene attributes. In *CVPR*, 2012.

[10] N. Quadrianto, A.J. Smola, T.S. Caetano, and Q.V. Le. Estimating labels from label proportions. In *ICML*, 2008.

[11] B. Siddiquie, R.S. Feris, and L.S. Davis. Image ranking and retrieval based on multi-attribute queries. In *CVPR*, 2011.

[12] J.R. Smith, M. Naphade, and A. Natsev. Multimedia semantic indexing using model vectors. In *ICME*, 2003.

[13] F.X. Yu, L. Cao, R.S Feris, J.R. Smith, and S.-F. Chang. Designing category-level attributes for discriminative visual recognition. In *CVPR*, 2013.

[14] F.X. Yu, R. Ji, M.-H. Tsai, G. Ye, and S.-F. Chang. Weak attributes for large-scale image retrieval. In *CVPR*, 2012.

[15] F.X. Yu, S. Kumar, T. Jebara, and S.-F. Chang. On learning with label proportions. *arXiv preprint arXiv:1402.5902*, 2014.

[16] F.X. Yu, D. Liu, Sanjiv K., T. Jebara, and S.-F. Chang. $\propto$SVM for learning with label proportions. In *ICML*, 2013.

Exploiting Correlation Consensus: Towards Subspace Clustering for Multi-modal Data

Yang Wang[†‡], Xuemin Lin[†], Lin Wu[†], Wenjie Zhang[†] and Qing Zhang[‡†]
[†]The University of New South Wales, Sydney, Australia
[‡]Australia E-Health Research Centre
{wangy,lxue,linw,zhangw}@cse.unsw.edu.au, qing.zhang@csiro.au

ABSTRACT

Often, a data object described by many features can be decomposed as multi-modalities, which always provide complementary information to each other. In this paper, we study subspace clustering for multi-modal data by effectively exploiting data correlation consensus across modalities, while keeping individual modalities well encapsulated. Our technique can yield a more ideal data similarity matrix, which encodes strong data correlations for the cross-modal data objects in the same subspace.

To these ends, we propose a novel angular based regularizer coupled with our objective function, which is aided by trace lasso and minimized to yield sparse representation vectors encoding data correlations in multiple modalities. As a result, the sparse code vectors of the same cross-modal data have small angular difference so as to achieve the data correlation consensus simultaneously. This can generate a compatible data similarity matrix for multi-modal data. The final subspace clustering result is obtained by applying spectral clustering on such data similarity matrix.

Categories and Subject Descriptors

I.5.3 [**Clustering**]: Similarity measures

Keywords

Correlation Consensus; Angular based Regularizer; Multi-modal Data

1. INTRODUCTION

The nature of visual data, in practice, is multi-modality, *e.g.*, an image can be described by a color modality or a shape modality. These multiple modalities often encode compatible and complementary information, which naturally motivates one to leverage them to obtain better performance than the result yielded by single modality, or simply concatenating all modalities into a monolithic one.

MM'14, November 03–07 2014, Orlando, FL, USA.

ACM 978-1-4503-3063-3/14/11 ...$15.00.
http://dx.doi.org/10.1145/2647868.2654999.

Among the studies of leveraging complementary information from multi-modal data, unsupervised clustering on multi-modal data is the most practical, due to the largely available unlabeled multi-modal data in real life. As shown in [6, 14, 13], data objects with high dimensions are always drawn from a union of subspaces, motivating numerous approaches of subspace clustering for multi-modal data.

Kumar *et al.* [10] presented a co-training [4, 16] based method to achieve a compatible multi-view similarity matrix in eigen-subspaces spanned by Laplacian matrix, such that the similarity matrix in one view is affected by that from another view. However, they simply calculate similarity matrix in a K-nearest neighbors manner, which degrades the performance when data points are nearby the intersection of two distinction subspaces. That is, the neighborhoods of a data point may cover the data points from different subspaces. The same problem holds in [11] as well. Chaudhuri *et al.* [5] proposed to project the multi-modal data into one common subspace, then apply the clustering algorithm, *e.g.*, K-means, to yield the subspace clustering results. Such method, however, is sensitive to data initialization. Specifically, it requires the data initialization strictly follow the Gaussian distribution while keeping different groups of data objects separated. Besides, the number of dimension for the projected subspace needs to be known in advance. Matrix factorization is also utilized to perform subspace clustering for multi-modal data, such as [1, 9], where the essential idea is to first concatenate the features of heterogeneous modalities into a single-long feature representation, then non-negative matrix factorization is applied to get subspace clustering results. One limitation of such one-combo-fits-all strategy is that the data correlation information in each original view-specific feature space is not well exploited. To combat this limitation, Liu *et al.* [12] proposed a joint non-negative matrix factorization paradigm on each individual modality to compute distinct coefficient matrices, which are then regularized towards a common consensus that represents the clustering structure shared by all modalities. This method, however, suffers from the drawback that the dimension number of latent reduced subspace needs to be manually parameterized, rather than automatically.

In light of above raised limitations, we propose a novel technique to address these limitations. The basic idea is we learn a data similarity matrix by aggregating data correlations from multiple modalities, and these correlations are consensus to each other whilst their individualities are well-encapsulated. Then the spectral clustering is applied to this data similarity matrix to obtain the subspace clustering results. Specifically, we propose a novel angular based regularizer to regularize our objective function, which is facilitated by trace lasso through its fantastic grouping effect in subspaces [13]. The objective function is minimized to sort out data correlations, encoded as the sparse representation vectors for data points under each modality. Meanwhile, sparse code vectors towards the same data object across modalities exhibit a small-angled difference.

The intuition of minimizing the angular based regularizer comes from the fact that if two distinct sparse code vectors encode the similar data correlations, then there will be a small angle between them. Now a natural question arises: whether the two distinct sparse codes of the same data object across modalities are similar? The answer is "yes". A common assumption holds in most multi-view based clustering methods, *e.g.,* [12], is that the same data set under different modalities should characterize the similar cluster structure, and clustering is largely determined by the data correlations representing similarities under various modalities. This observation has been validated by extensive experiments on real-world image datasets.

Our major contributions are summarized as follows.

- To the best of our knowledge, we are the first to consider the application of trace lasso on subspace clustering (See Section 2.2) for multi-modal data.
- To exploit the data correlation consensus across modalities, we propose a novel angular based regularizer over the data sparse codes in multi-modalities (See Section 2.3). The objective function is minimized and regularized by the new regularizer to achieve the goal.
- An efficient optimizing process is designed to optimize the proposed objective function (See Section 3). Experiments on real-world image datasets are conducted to demonstrate the effectiveness of our algorithm.

2. PROPOSED TECHNIQUE

2.1 Problem Definition

Let $X = \{x_k\}_{k=1}^n$ be data point set with n data points. Suppose each data object has V modalities, without loss of generality, for i^{th} modality, $X^i = \{x_k^i\}_{k=1}^n$, $(i = 1, \dots, V)$, x_k^i is the representation of x_k under i^{th} modality, and s_k^i is the sparse representation vector of x_k^i based on X^i. The trace lasso [8] is defined as $\|X^i Diag(s_k^i)\|_*$, where $Diag(s_k^i)$ represents diagonal matrix with all diagonal elements corresponding to the entries of s_k^i, $\|A\|_*$ denotes the nuclear norm (the sum of all the singular value) of a matrix A. The norms of $\|a\|_1$ and $\|a\|_2$ denote the ℓ_1-norm and ℓ_2-norm of a vector a.

With the above notations defined, we aim to learn the sparse representations s_k^i of each x_k^i based on X^i $(i = 1, \dots, V)$. These sparse codes are then used to construct a compatible similarity matrix W for multi-modal data. Finally, the spectral clustering is applied upon W to perform subspace clustering for multi-modal data.

2.2 Modeling data correlations in single modality

We propose to deploy trace lasso to model data correlations. That is, high correlations hold for the data points from the same subspace, no (weak) correlations for those from distinct subspaces. As shown in [13], trace lasso is more adaptive than ℓ_1 or ℓ_2 norms, and it is equal to ℓ_1-norm or ℓ_2-norm if data points are uncorrelated (orthogonal) or highly correlated. Thereby, we have $\|s_k^i\|_2 \leqslant \|X^i Diag(s_k^i)\|_* \leqslant \|s_k^i\|_1$.The sparse representation s_k^i of x_k^i can well reflects the correlations between x_k^i and other data points under i^{th} modality. Thus, we formulate the problem of learning sparse code vectors of each data point in i^{th} modality as:

$$\min_{s_k^i} \frac{1}{2}\|x_k^i - X_k^i s_k^i\|_2^2 + \lambda \|X_k^i Diag(s_k^i)\|_*, \tag{1}$$

where X_k^i represents the data set with x_k^i excluded. The parameter λ controls the effect from trace lasso term. Through trace lasso, s_k^i is composed of approximately the equal coefficients yet large weights on a few data points, implying their strong correlations with x_k^i. Meanwhile, the coefficients of data having no (weak) correlation with x_k^i are set to be 0. The claims also apply on $j^{th} (j \neq i)$ modality.

Eq. (1) is made on single modality. How to extend it to the context of multi-modalities? The answer, however, is nontrivial partially due to the fact that many multi-view learning methods, *e.g.,* [15], are aided by common label spaces across modalities. Hence, without label information, it becomes more challenging to exploit their consensus property shared by modalities. To this end, below, we propose to exploit correlation consensus across modalities.

2.3 Exploiting correlation consensus in multiple modalities

Inspired by multi-view clustering [12]: the true underlying clustering would assign corresponding data objects across modalities into the same cluster, we propose to exploit the data correlation consensus w.r.t. modalities, which critically determines the subspace clustering on multi-modal data.

Basic idea: Why angular based similarity? We are expected to effectively exploit the correlations across modalities but keep their individuality well-encapsulated. The question is how to quantify the similarity between the data correlations from different modalities? One may directly use a distance metric, *e.g.,* Euclidean distance, to measure data objects across modalities. It is, however, infeasible because data points in different views might not be comparable in the same scale. Fortunately, the sparse code of one point, *e.g.,* s_k^i for x_k^i, can well reflect the correlations between x_k^i and other data points under i^{th} modality. Another nice property is that sparse codes for different modalities have the same dimension. These properties drive us to quantify the **angular based similarity** over sparse codes of multi-modal data. This is equivalent to quantifying the data correlations in X under different modalities. This enables us to propose a novel regularizer term, $\pi(s_k)$, to encode the cosine similarity among s_k^i regarding x_k^i for multi-modality.

Mathematically, $\pi(s_k)$ can be defined as

$$\pi(s_k) = -\sum_{i,j \neq i}^{V} \frac{(s_k^i)^T \cdot s_k^j}{\|s_k^i\|_2 \|s_k^j\|_2}. \tag{2}$$

The objective function in Eq. (3) needs to be minimized, thus, we add minus sign "−" in Eq. (2).

Combining Eq. (1) with Eq. (2), we confirm our objective function as

$$\min_{s_k^i} \sum_i^V \beta_i \left(\frac{1}{2} \|x_k^i - X_k^i s_k^i\|_2^2 + \lambda \|X_k^i Diag(s_k^i)\|_* \right) + \gamma \pi(s_k), \tag{3}$$

where the parameter β_i controls the contribution from i^{th} modality and $\sum_{i=1}^V \beta_i = 1$. γ is a weight parameter on $\pi(s_k)$, which is able to correlate modalities by essentially regulating the structural consensus over dictionaries. In summary, we aim to learn sparse codes s_k^i of x_k^i for each modality i by optimizing Eq. (3), which will be discussed in Section 3.

3. OPTIMIZATION STRATEGY

The difficulty of optimizing Eq. (3) lies in its non-joint-convex for M_k^i and s_k^i, along with non-smoothness for trace lasso. We alternatively optimize each variable by fixing others. We initialize each s_k^i by optimizing the Eq. (1) via Alternating Direction Method (ADM) in [13], by setting λ to be 0.15. We derive an equivalent variational formulation of the trace norm [2]. Assume $M \in \mathbb{R}^{n \times m}$, then the trace norm of M is equal to

$$\|M\|_* = \frac{1}{2} \inf_{S \succeq 0} tr(M^T S^{-1} M) + tr(S), \tag{4}$$

where the infimum is achieved when $S = (MM^T)^{1/2}$, then we recast Eq. (3) to be

$$\begin{aligned} \min_{s_k^i} \inf_{M_k^i \succeq 0} & \sum_i^V \frac{\beta_i}{2} \|x_k^i - X_k^i s_k^i\|_2^2 \\ & + \frac{\lambda \beta_i}{2} \left(tr\left((S_k^i)^2 (X_k^i)^T (M_k^i)^{-1} X_k^i \right) + tr(M_k^i) \right) + \gamma \pi(s_k), \end{aligned} \tag{5}$$

where $S_k^i = Diag(s_k^i)$.

Updating M_k^i with fixed s_k^i. The optimization problem in Eq. (5) is convex in M_k^i. We conduct coordinate descent procedure to optimize M_k^i for each x_k^i. Given s_k^i, we have the closed form solution of M_k^i as

$$M_k^i = (X_k^i (S_k^i)^2 (X_k^i)^T)^{1/2} \tag{6}$$

Updating s_k^i with fixed M_k^i. We propose to adopt GIST [7] algorithm to optimize s_k^i, due to its effectiveness in addressing non-convex and non-smoothness optimization problems, and this strategy is **well converged** as proved by [7]. Denote by $F(s_k^i)$ the objective function over s_k^i, that is,

$$\begin{aligned} F(s_k^i) = & \frac{\beta_i}{2} \|x_k^i - X_k^i s_k^i\|_2^2 + \frac{\lambda \beta_i}{2} tr\left((S_k^i)^2 (X_k^i)^T (M_k^i)^{-1} X_k^i \right) \\ & - \gamma \sum_{l \neq i}^V \frac{(s_k^l)^T \cdot s_k^j}{\|s_k^l\|_2 \|s_k^j\|_2}. \end{aligned}$$

Let $s_k^i(j)$ be the jth entry of $s_k^i \in \mathbb{R}^m$, and $s_k^i \geq 0$ (each entry is large or equal to 0). It is common to set $\|s_k^i\|_2 = 1$ for any i, then the subgradient of $F(s_k^i)$ at $s_k^i(j)$ is

$$\begin{aligned} \eta_j = \frac{\partial F(s_k^i)}{\partial s_k^i(j)} = & \beta_i X_k^i(\cdot, j)^T (x_k^i - \sum_{l \neq j} X_k^i(\cdot, l) s_k^i(l) - X_k^i(\cdot, j) s_k^i(j)) \\ & + \lambda \beta_i s_k^i(j) K_i(j, j) - \gamma \sum_{l \neq i}^V s_k^l(j), \end{aligned}$$

where $K_i = (X_k^i)^T (M_k^i)^{-1} X_k^i$, $X_k^i(\cdot, j)$ denotes the jth column of X_k^i. We assume the sub-gradient of $F(s_k^i)$ at point s_k^i can be computed as $g = (\eta_1, \ldots, \eta_m)$. Consider a series of updated sparse codes $s_k^i[t]$ and the associated subgradients $g[t]$ $(1 \leq t \leq p)$ at time stamp t, then we have

$$F(s_k^i[t]) \geq F_p(s_k^i[t]) = \max_{1 \leq t \leq p} \{F(s_k^i[t-1]) + (s_k^i[t] - s_k^i[t-1]) g[t-1]\}. \tag{7}$$

Given the previous prox-center point $s_k^i[t-1]$, it seeks the next potential candidate point by minimizing the piecewise linear lower bound:

$$s_k^i[t] = \underset{\|s_k^i\|=1, s_k^i \geq 0}{\operatorname{argmin}} \; F_p(s_k^i) + \frac{\omega_p}{2} \|s_k^i[t] - s_k^i[t-1]\|^2. \tag{8}$$

We stop the iteration and report the optimal s_k^i if the approximation error residual for s_k^i, measured by $F(s_k^i[t]) - F(s_k^i[t-1])$, is less than a predefined threshold ϵ (In our experiments, ϵ is set to be 10^{-2}). Otherwise, we conduct a line search between $s_k^i[t-1]$ and $s_k^i[t]$ to reproduce a new candidate and repeat the above process until convergence. We follow [3] to initialize and update the step size ω_p.

Remark. The convergence for optimizing Eq. (3) is determined by optimizing s_k^i, as M_k^i enjoys a closed form at each step. It is convergent for updating s_k^i due to the convergence property of GIST algorithm [7]. We calculate the similarity between k^{th} and l^{th} data objects under i^{th} modality, such as $W_i(k, l) = \frac{s_k^i(l) + s_l^i(k)}{2}$. The final affinity matrix regarding all modalities is calculated as $W = \sum_i^V W_i$, which is further utilized for subspace clustering.

4. EXPERIMENTAL RESULTS

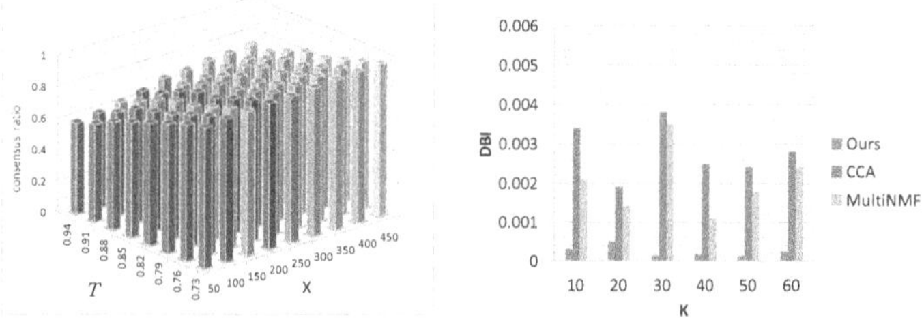

(a) (b)

Figure 1: (a) The values of consensus ratios versus number of training data and thresholds for our method. (b) The evaluation on cluster qualities of different methods.

4.1 Datasets and Competitors

Datasets. Three real world image datasets are used in our experiment.

- **UCI Handwritten Digit Dataset** [1]: This handwritten digits (0-9) dataset consists of 2,000 examples. We construct two modalities, with first modality being the 76 Fourier coefficients and second modality being the 240 pixel averages in 2×3 windows.
- **CMU PIE Face Database** [2]: This dataset contains 68 subjects with 41,368 face images. Each image is 32×32, and we use four kinds of features as four modalities: LBP (256-dim), HOG (100-dim), and grey levels (128-dim).
- **PASCAL VOC 2010 Database**: This dataset contains 10,103 images from 20 classes. We adopt four types of

[1] http://archive.ics.uci.edu/ml/datasets.html
[2] http://www.ri.cmu.edu/projects/project_418.html

Method	Accuracy(%)			Normalized Mutual Information(%)		
	UCI	CMU-PIE	PASCAL	UCI	CMU-PIE	PASCAL
BSV-SSC	69.028±0.010	70.255±0.013	62.381±0.009	52.622±0.010	51.457±0.009	56.403±0.009
ConcatSSC	70.832±0.007	65.735±0.011	60.228±0.006	54.055±0.011	48.829±0.008	51.520±0.009
CCA	76.114±0.004	77.482±0.006	70.010±0.006	61.671±0.007	60.227±0.006	58.731±0.008
Co-train-SC	84.642±0.002	83.070±0.007	76.125±0.004	77.011±0.005	71.420±0.004	66.592±0.006
MultiNMF	88.014±0.003	86.807±0.004	80.227±0.007	80.257±0.010	77.561±0.011	69.882±0.011
Ours	**93.149±0.001**	**90.006±0.003**	**87.540±0.004**	**86.553±0.009**	**82.716±0.010**	**74.660±0.010**

Table 1: Clustering performance on three real image datasets.

features corresponding four modalities: color moments (255-dim), color histogram (64-dim), edge distribution (73-dim), and wavelet texture (128-dim).

We consider five algorithms as competitors in our experiments: (1) The best single view on Sparse Subspace Clustering (**BSV-SSC**), (2) Concatenating the features of each view on Sparse Subspace Clustering (**ConcatSSC**), (3) multi-view clustering via Canonical Correlation Analysis (**CCA**) [5], (4) Co-training based multi-view Spectral Clustering (**Co-train-SC**) [10], (5) Multi-view NMF (**MultiNMF**) [12]. Please refer to the section 1 for the discussions on [5], [10] and [12]. We omit the details here due to limited spaces. The clustering results are evaluated by validating the obtained label of each data point with the label provided by the dataset. Two widely adopted metrics, the accuracy (AC) and normalized mutual information (NMI) are used to measure the clustering performance. Please refer to [10] for detailed definitions. The sparsity parameter λ is set 0.15 in all experiments by cross-validation, β_i for each modality equally to be $\frac{1}{V}$. Parameter γ, in Eq. (3), controlling angular based regularization is set by grid search on $\{0.1, \ldots, 0.9\}$.

4.2 Clustering results

Table 1 shows the clustering performances of different algorithms on the three datasets. We can observe that our algorithm outperforms the second best counterpart **MultiNMF** by a margin of 5.8%(7.8%) on UCI, 3.7%(6.6%) on CMU-PIE, 9.1%(6.8%) on PASCAL, in terms of accuracy(NMI). One reason is that our method can automatically learn a good similarity matrix by aggregating consensus data correlations across modalities instead of manually setting the dimension number of reduced subspaces. Moreover, the improvement gain is significantly higher between our method and other alternatives, which are **CCA**, **Co-train-SC**, **ConcatSSC**, and **BSV-SSC**.

We demonstrate the stableness and robustness by comparing with **CCA**, and **MultiNMF**. Both need to manually set the dimension number of reduced subspaces, *i.e.*, number of clusters. To evaluate the quality of clusters $\{U_l\}_{l=1}^K$, we use Davies-Bouldin Index (DBI) to measure the uniqueness of clusters w.r.t. the unified similarity measure.

$$DBI(\{U_l\}_{l=1}^K) = \frac{1}{K}\sum_{i=1}^{K} \max_{j \neq i} \frac{d(c_i, c_j)}{\sigma_i + \sigma_j}, \quad (9)$$

where c_x is the centroid of U_x, $d(c_i, c_j)$ is the similarity between c_i and c_j, σ_x is the average similarity of vertices in U_x to c_x. Fig.1 (b) shows the DBI comparison on CMU-PIE with various K values. Our method has the lowest DBI, while other methods have higher DBIs. This indicates that our parameter-free algorithm can discover true clusterings more robustly through adaptively correlating data consensus across modalities. As a comparison, manually set up the values of K makes **CCA** and **MultiNMF** sensitive to parameters and less effective in clustering quality.

4.3 Consensus study

To show the correlation consensus propertied by angular term $\pi(s_k)$, we conduct another experiment on PASCAL VOC 2010 wherein a training set X is composed of randomly selected images numbering from 50 to 450. The rest are taken as test samples. The consensus threshold is T, whose value is discretely set from 0.73 to 0.94. We employ the consensus ratio as the evaluation metric, defined as calculating the number of test samples whose values of Eq. (2) are larger or equal to T. The results are shown in Fig.1 (a). It can be seen that as more training samples get involved, we can have larger values of consensus ratio, implying learned sparse codes are more consensus. However, the consensus ratios naturally decrease when cosine values become higher, implying a more restrict consensus. Overall, our method shows a good performance even with a relatively small training set and large values of T.

5. CONCLUSIONS

In this paper, we propose a novel approach towards subspace clustering on multi-modal data. Unlike existing methods, our proposed method can well achieve the consensus of data correlations across modalities, encoded by learned sparse code vectors w.r.t. each modality. This method is able to automatically uncover true underlying clusters. Experimental results validate the effectiveness of our method.

6. REFERENCES

[1] Z. Akata, C. Thurau, and C. Bauckhage. Non-negative matrix factorization in multimodality data for segmentation and label prediction. In *ICCV Winter-workshop*, 2011.

[2] A. Argyriou, T.Evgeniou, and M. Pontil. Multi-task feature learning. In *NIPS*, 2007.

[3] J. R. BIRGE, L. Qi, and Z. Wei. Convergence analysis of some methods for minimizing a nonsmooth convex function. *Journal of optimization theory and applications*, 97:105–122, 1990.

[4] A. Blum and T. Mitchell. Combining labeled and unlabeled data with co-training. In *COLT*, 1998.

[5] K. Chaudhuri, S. Kakade, K. Livescu, and K. Sridharan. Multi-view clustering via canonical correlation analysis. In *ICML*, 2009.

[6] E. Elhamifar and R. Vidal. Sparse subspace clustering. In *CVPR*, 2009.

[7] P. Gong, C. Zhang, Z. Lu, jianhua Z. Huang, and J. Ye. A general iterative shrinkage and thresholding algorithm for non-convex regularized optimization problems. In *ICML*, 2013.

[8] E. Grave, G. Obozinski, and F. Bach. Trace lasso: a trace norm regularization for correlated designs. In *NIPS*, 2011.

[9] D. Greene and P. Cunningham. A matrix factorization approach for integrating multiple data views. In *ECML/PKDD*, 2009.

[10] A. Kumar and H. D. III. A co-training approach for multi-view spectral clustering. In *ICML*, 2011.

[11] A. Kumar, P. Rai, and H. D. III. Co-regularized multi-view spectral clustering. In *NIPS*, 2011.

[12] J. Liu, C. Wang, J. Gao, and J. Han. Multi-view clustering via joint nonnegative matrix factorization. In *SDM*, 2013.

[13] C.-Y. Lu, J. Feng, Z. Lin, and S. Yan. Correlation adaptive subspace segmentation by trace lasso. In *ICCV*, 2013.

[14] Y. Pang, Z. Ji, P. Jing, and X. Li. Ranking graph embedding for learning to rerank. *IEEE Trans. Neural Netw. Learning Syst*, 24(8):1292–1303, 2013.

[15] H. Wang, F. Nie, H. Huang, and C. Ding. Heterogeneous visual feature fusion via sparse multimodal machine. In *CVPR*, 2013.

[16] Y. Wang, X. Lin, and Q. Zhang. Towards metric fusion on multi-view data: a cross-view based graph random walk approach. In *CIKM*, 2013.

Learning Multimodal Neural Network with Ranking Examples

Xinyan Lu, Fei Wu, Xi Li, Yin Zhang, Weiming Lu, Donghui Wang, Yueting Zhuang
College of Computer Science
Zhejiang University, China
{xinyanlu,wufei,xilizju,zhangyin98,luwm,dhwang,yzhuang}@zju.edu.cn

ABSTRACT

To support cross-modal information retrieval, cross-modal *learning to rank* approaches utilize ranking examples (e.g., an example may be a text query and its corresponding ranked images) to learn appropriate ranking (similarity) function. However, the fact that each modality is represented with intrinsically different low-level features hinders these approaches from better reducing the heterogeneity-gap between the modalities and thus giving satisfactory retrieval results. In this paper, we consider learning with neural networks, from the perspective of optimizing the listwise ranking loss of the cross-modal ranking examples. The proposed model, named Cross-Modal Ranking Neural Network (CMRNN), benefits from the advance of both neural networks on learning high-level semantics and *learning to rank* techniques on learning ranking function, such that the learned cross-modal ranking function is implicitly embedded in the learned high-level representation for data objects with different modalities (e.g., text and imagery) to perform cross-modal retrieval directly. We compare CMRNN to existing state-of-the-art cross-modal ranking methods on two datasets and show that it achieves a better performance.

Categories and Subject Descriptors

H.3.3 [**Information Search and Retrieval**]: Retrieval Models

Keywords

Cross-modal Ranking; Learning to rank; Representation Learning

INTRODUCTION

With the rapid development of multimedia technology, today many real-world applications involve multimodal data. For conducting cross-modal retrieval, one category of approaches are based on the rankings of the data related to the queries (e.g., an example may be a text query and its corresponding ranked images) to learn ranking functions which optimize for certain ranking loss, such as PAMIR [5], SSI [1] and LSCMR [6].

It is obvious that the intra-modality feature representation plays an important role in learning cross-modal ranking functions for these approaches: imagine how much easier when dealing with multimodal data that are all with high-level semantic features. However, each modality usually has a different kind of low-level representation and intrinsic structure. For example, text is usually represented as discrete sparse word-count vectors, whereas an image is represented using pixel intensities or low-level visual feature vectors. This makes it hard for these approaches to discover the relationships across modalities.

On the other hand, deep neural networks (DNNs) that learn a transformation of a low-level representation to a high-level representation have shown their powerful ability to the tasks of learning multimodal representation. One straightforward consideration is that train individual neural network separately for different modality and then apply existing approaches based on the features previously learned by the DNNs, which will be used as baselines in the experiments. However in this scheme, the final ranking performance is limited since it is hard for the ranking loss to be back-propagated to the pre-trained neural network which can boost the discriminative representation for cross-modal ranking.

In this work, we seek to bridge the gap between neural networks and cross-modal ranking. By adapting techniques of *learning to rank*, we propose a new multimodal neural network named Cross-Modal Ranking Neural Networks (CMRNN) to support cross-modal ranking. Specifically, CMRNN outputs the relevance scores of the retrieved documents given a query in another modality, and then the documents are ranked by their relevance scores (see Figure 1).

It is worthwhile to highlight the main contribution of the proposed model. Not only the model learns high-level feature representation for data objects with different modalities, but more importantly the ranking loss is back-propagated to train the modality-specific neural networks and thus the learned cross-modal ranking function is implicitly embedded in the learned high-level feature representation that are optimized for cross-modal retrieval performance (in other words, the learned high-level features have the discriminative power for cross-modal ranking). Therefore, the proposed model benefits from both the most recent advances in neural networks and learning to rank techniques.

Related work The authors of [8] propose a multimodal Deep Boltzmann Machine for learning a generative model of data that consists of multiple input modalities. The model works by learning a joint representation over the space of multimodal inputs, which is useful for cross-modal retrieval. Note that the multimodal DBM is trained with paired multimodal training data, and it is not optimized directly for the final retrieval performance. Methods like [7] based on autoencoders and [4] based on CCA have similar incentive.

A model termed DeViSE, proposed in [3], leverages textual data to learn semantic relationships between labels and explicitly maps images into a rich semantic embedding space via a linear transfor-

MM'14, November 3–7, 2014, Orlando, Florida, USA.
Copyright 2014 ACM 978-1-4503-3063-3/14/11 ...$15.00.
http://dx.doi.org/10.1145/2647868.2655001.

mation. The model is trained to produce a high dot-product similarity between the transformed visual output and the vector representation of the correct label. Given an image, pairwise ranking loss is first calculated between the correct label and the other labels, and then back-propagated into the core visual model to fine-tune the visual representation. In the proposed model, the explicit linear transformation alignment is absorbed into the process of learning the high-level representation; Moreover, listwise ranking strategy is used in the proposed model.

THE CMRNN MODEL

For an explicit articulation in the rest of this section, the model is only described in the case of text-query-image retrieval. We report the experiments in both scenarios of image-query-text retrieval and text-query-image retrieval.

Notation

Given a training set of N samples, each contains a text query $q^{(i)}$ ($i = 1, \ldots, N$) as well as a list of corresponding retrieved images $D^{(i)} = (d_1^{(i)}, d_2^{(i)}, \ldots, d_{n^{(i)}}^{(i)})$, where $n^{(i)}$ denotes the size of $D^{(i)}$. Furthermore, each list of retrieved images $D^{(i)}$ is associated with their true judgments (ranking scores) $Y^{(i)} = (y_1^{(i)}, y_2^{(i)}, \ldots, y_{n^{(i)}}^{(i)})$ where $y_j^{(i)}$ denotes the judgment on image $d_j^{(i)}$ with respect to text query $q^{(i)}$. The judgment $y_j^{(i)}$ represents the relevance degree of $d_j^{(i)}$ to $q^{(i)}$, and can be a score explicitly or implicitly given by humans. For example, $y_j^{(i)}$ can be the number of clicks on $d_j^{(i)}$ given query $q^{(i)}$, or an expert judgment on the relevance level of $d_j^{(i)}$ to query $q^{(i)}$. The higher $y_j^{(i)}$, the stronger relevance.

The ranking function

A ranking function $f(q, d)$ between a text query q and an image d is to be learned according to a pre-defined ranking loss. The learned function f maps each text-image pair to a ranking score based on their semantic relevance. Given a text query q and an image d, we tend to learn the scoring function as a dot product of two vectors $f_u(q)$ and $f_v(d)$ in the K-dimensional latent space:

$$f(q, d) = f_u(q)^T f_v(d) \tag{1}$$

where $f_u(q) \in \mathbb{R}^K$ and $f_v(d) \in \mathbb{R}^K$.

To better discover modality-intrinsic structure, neural networks are used to represent the text queries and images in this work: $f_u(q)$ refers to map the query text q from its original text space to the K-dimensional latent space by a neural network, and $f_v(d)$ refers to map the retrieved image d from its original image space to the K-dimensional latent space by another neural network. Therefore, the text query and the retrieved image are mapped to a common K-dimensional latent space, and then their similarity is measured by a dot product of the two vectors in the K-dimensional space, which is commonly used to measure the matching between textual vectors.

Given a text query $q^{(i)}$, for each image $d_j^{(i)}$ in $D^{(i)}$, the ranking function outputs a relevance score $z_j^{(i)} = f(q^{(i)}, d_j^{(i)})$. For the list of images $D^{(i)}$, a list of scores $Z^{(i)} = (z_1^{(i)}, z_2^{(i)}, \ldots, z_{n^{(i)}}^{(i)})$ is obtained. The objective of learning is formalized as minimizing the empirical ranking loss with respect to the training data:

$$E = \sum_{i=1}^{N} L(Y^{(i)}, Z^{(i)}),$$

where L is a listwise loss function that we will define shortly.

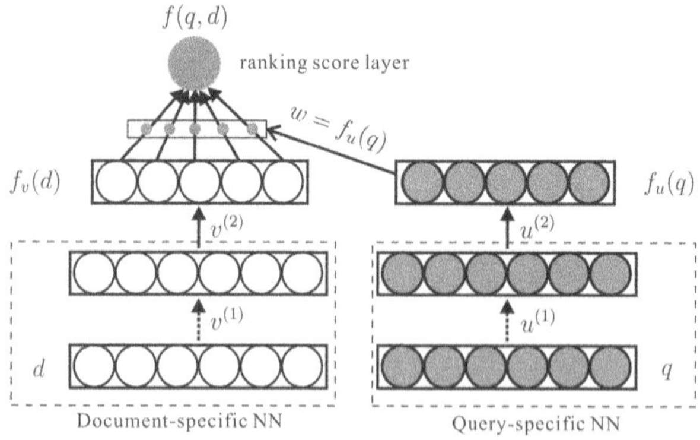

Figure 1: The architecture of the proposed cross-modal ranking neural network. If the output layers of the two modality-specific NN have unequal number of units, one can extend both the architectures by one *deeper* layer with an equal number of output units.

The architecture of the proposed cross-modal ranking neural network is depicted in Figure 1. Consider modeling each data modality (i.e., text or imagery) using separate neural networks where the text and images are represented as the outputs of the modality-specific NN, respectively. Then the document-specific NN (i.e., the image-specific NN) is extended by an additional ranking score layer with only one output unit, where the weights that connect the scoring unit are specified by the outputs of the query-specific NN (i.e., the text-specific NN). In this way, the outputs of the query-specific NN act as part of parameters of the ranking function which ranks the retrieved images by their relevance to the query text. It is shown that the output of the scoring unit is exactly $f(q, d)$ in Eq. (1) when we set the activation function of the unit to be linear, and then the learned multimodal representation is stored as the outputs of the modality-specific NN.

For conducting text-query-image retrieval, the neural network is first fed by the text query and the output of the text-specific NN is taken as the weights that connect the score unit. The images are then fed into the neural network to output their ranking scores. Finally, we rank the images in descending order of their scores.

Motivated by [2], the top one probability of an image being ranked on the top for a given text query, given the scores of all the target retrieved images, is defined as

$$P_s(d_j^{(i)}) = \frac{\exp(s_j^{(i)})}{\sum_{k=1}^{n^{(i)}} \exp(s_k^{(i)})}[1] \tag{2}$$

where $s_j^{(i)}$ is the ranking score of image d_j with respect to query $q^{(i)}$. With the use of top one probability, given two lists of scores we use Cross Entropy as metric (note that $\sum_{j=1}^{n^{(i)}} P_s(d_j^{(i)}) = 1$), the listwise loss function becomes

$$L(Y^{(i)}, Z^{(i)}) = -\sum_{j=1}^{n^{(i)}} P_{y^{(i)}}(d_j^{(i)}) \log P_{z^{(i)}}(d_j^{(i)}) \tag{3}$$

Learning method

Denote the ranking function based on the neural network model as f, the query-specific neural network as f_u (parameterized by

[1]More precisely, $P_s(d_j^{(i)})$ should be $P_s(d_j^{(i)}, q^{(i)})$ where we have omitted the query for simplicity.

u) and the document-specific neural network as f_v (parameterized by v). The weights that connecting to the ranking score unit are denoted as w (i.e., $w = f_u(q)$). The rest is to learn the parameters u and v. Note that for simplicity we have omitted the superscript i denoting the i-th training example.

Given the parameters of the neural networks, a forward propagation is first performed for one or a mini-batch of ranking example(s), then the errors propagate backwards from the output nodes to the input nodes regarding the network's modifiable weights and finally the weights are updated by a gradient descent step. Taking derivatives of $L(Y, Z)$ with respect to w, we have

$$\nabla w = \frac{\partial L(Y,Z)}{\partial w} = -\sum_{j=1}^{n} P_y(d_j)\frac{\partial \log(P_z(d_j))}{\partial w}$$

Note that

$$\log P_z(d_j) = f(q,d_j) - \log\sum_{i=1}^{n}\exp(f(q,d_i))$$

$$\frac{\partial \log P_z(d_j)}{\partial w} = \frac{\partial f(q,d_j)}{\partial w} - \sum_{i=1}^{n} P_z(d_i)\frac{\partial f(q,d_i)}{\partial w}$$

and with some derivation we get

$$\nabla w = \sum_{j=1}^{n}(P_z(d_j) - P_y(d_j))f_v(d_j) \tag{4}$$

The derivatives of $L(Y, Z)$ with respect to u and v are deduced in a similar manner as follows:

$$\begin{aligned}\nabla u &= \sum_{j=1}^{n}(P_z(d_j) - P_y(d_j))f_v^T(d_j)\frac{\partial f_u(q)}{\partial u} \\ &= (\nabla w)^T\frac{\partial f_u(q)}{\partial u} \qquad (5)\\ \nabla v &= \sum_{j=1}^{n}(P_z(d_j) - P_y(d_j))f_u^T(q)\frac{\partial f_v(d_j)}{\partial v} \\ &= w^T\left(\sum_{j=1}^{n}(P_z(d_j) - P_y(d_j))\frac{\partial f_v(d_j)}{\partial v}\right) \qquad (6)\end{aligned}$$

Note that we can deduce $\partial f_u(q)/\partial u$ and $\partial f_v(d_j)/\partial v$ via classical back-propagation algorithm which depend on the structure of the query-specific NN and the document-specific NN, respectively. Therefore, we can evaluate the required derivatives ∇u and ∇v, and apply the gradient descent step.

EXPERIMENTS AND RESULTS

Datesets Two public real-world datasets are used in the comparative experiments. Both the datasets are bi-modal with the image and the associated text modalities. The statistics of the two datasets are summarized in Table 1.

The Wikipedia feature articles[2] dataset consists of 2,866 images, each with a short paragraph describing the image. The images are labeled with exactly one of the 10 different semantic classes, such as art and geography. For text, we extract 5,000D bag-of-words feature vectors with the TF-IDF weighting scheme. For images, 1,000D bag-of-visual-words feature vectors are extracted by clustering SIFT points with k-means. A target document is relevant to a query if they belong to the same semantic class. The NUS-WIDE[3] dataset contains 133,208 images with 1,000 tags and 81 concepts, which are pruned from the NUS dataset by keeping the images that have at least one tag and one concept. For the feature representation, we use the publicly available 1,000D text feature vector (namely tags) and 500D image feature vector based on SIFT BoVW kindly provided by the authors. A target document is relevant if it shares at least one concept with the query. However, we also note that the relevant judgement can be obtained from the abundance of users' clickthrough data with little overhead.

[2]http://www.svcl.ucsd.edu/projects/crossmodal/

[3]http://lms.comp.nus.edu.sg/research/NUS-WIDE.htm

Table 1: The statistics of the datasets used.

	Wikipedia	NUS-WIDE
Avg. # of words/image	117.5	7.73
# of neurons in Image NN	1000-50	500-50
# of neurons in Text NN	5000-50	1000-50
Documents Partition[a]	1,500/500 866	13,320/23,977 95,911
Queries Partition[a]	1,500/500 866	13,320/2,000 2,000

[a] Partitions are ordered by training/validation/testing.

Experimental setup The training examples are generated as follows: for each text (image) query, we randomly selected 40 images (text documents) in the other modality in the training set as candidates and then the selected target documents are automatically labeled as relevant or irrelevant. We observed little difference when different sampling strategies were applied. While for validation and testing, we randomly select text (image) queries and all the images (text documents) in the other modality in the validation/test set are regarded as retrieval candidates.

The structures of modality-specific neural networks are listed in Table 1. The proposed model is trained with sigmoid activation, momentum of 0.3 and weight decay of 0.0001. We adjust the learning rate manually from 0.01 to 0.0001. The size of each mini-batch is set to 100. Autoencoder with one hidden layer (50 units) is used to pre-train the modality-specific neural networks. The learned features by autoencoders are also served as the input features to all the comparative methods.

Evaluation metric The standard ranking performance metric *Mean Average Precision* (MAP) is used for comparison. Let $p^* = \text{rank}(y)$ (true ranking with two rank value $+1$ and -1) and $p = \text{rank}(z)$ (predicted ranking with a total order). Given a query and a set of R retrieved target documents, the *Average Precision* (AP) is defined as

$$\text{AP}(p^*, p) = \frac{1}{M}\sum_{j=1}^{R} Prec(j)\cdot Rel(j) \tag{7}$$

where M is the number of the relevant documents in the retrieved set, $Prec(j)$ the percentage of the relevant documents in the top j documents in predicted ranking p and $Rel(j)$ an indicator function equaling 1 if the item at rank j in predicted ranking p is a relevant document, zero otherwise. We then average the AP values from all the queries in the query set to obtain the MAP score. In the experiments, R is the number of the retrieved documents to be examined, where we set $R = 50$ or $R = all$ for all the retrieved documents.

Performance comparison We compare CMRNN with other state-of-the-art models. All the comparative models (PAMIR[5], SSI[1] and LSCMR[6]) are elaborately chosen to be trained with ranking examples for fair comparison.

Table 2 reports the performance of CMRNN and the other comparative models on the test set of the Wiki dataset, showing that CMRNN outperforms all the comparing methods on both direc-

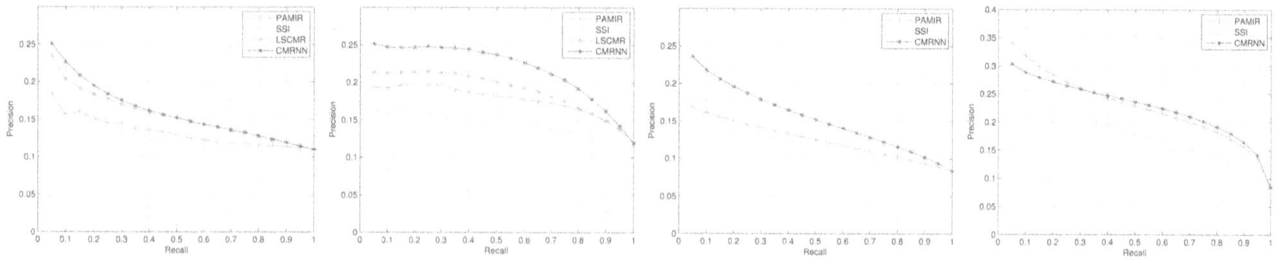

(a) Wiki Text Query (b) Wiki Image Query (c) NUS Text Query (d) NUS Image Query

Figure 2: Precision-Recall curves on the two datasets.

Table 2: The performance comparison in terms of MAP@R scores on the Wiki dataset.

	Text Query		Image Query	
	$R = 50$	$R = all$	$R = 50$	$R = all$
PAMIR	0.2344	0.1361	0.1763	0.1786
SSI	0.2058	0.1309	0.1834	0.1470
LSCMR	0.2520	0.1597	0.2010	0.1919
CMRNN	**0.2712**	**0.1649**	**0.2563**	**0.2216**

Table 3: The performance comparison in terms of MAP@R scores on the NUS dataset.

	Text Query		Image Query	
	$R = 50$	$R = all$	$R = 50$	$R = all$
PAMIR	0.2026	0.1265	**0.4682**	**0.2331**
SSI	0.2163	0.1200	0.4259	0.1830
LSCMR	-	-	-	-
CMRNN	**0.3193**	**0.1569**	0.4402	0.2319

tions of the retrieval. The Precision-Recall curves on both directions are reported in Figure 2(a) and 2(b).

The improvement of CMRNN on the NUS dataset is not as significant as that on the Wiki dataset. The MAP scores of all the methods over NUS dataset are shown in Table 3 and the Precision-Recall curves are reported in Figure 2(c) and 2(d). For text-query-image retrieval, CMRNN outperforms the other comparative methods again, while for the other direction, PAMIR have a slightly better overall performance than CMRNN. The reason why PAMIR even beat CMRNN in the case of image-query-text retrieval may be as follows. As shown in Table 1, the average number of words per image in the NUS dataset is much smaller than that in the Wiki dataset. The short text doesn't provide sufficient word occurrences and thus is fuzzy. Given an image query, fine-tuning the modality-specific NN by the ranking loss with respect to fuzzy short text may play a counteractive effect and degrade the performance.

It is observed that LSCMR performs most closely to CMRNN on the Wiki dataset, however LSCMR fails to train a ranking model on the NUS dataset. For NUS dataset, we sample 10% of the documents to form the training set, and thus for each direction of retrieval about 13k queries (with 530k corresponding documents) are used for training. Note that the weight updating step of LSCMR requires the full batch of training examples, which makes it hard for LSCMR to deal with such large set of ranking examples. By contrast, the weight updating step of the other three comparative methods (PAMIR, SSI and CMRNN) requires only a mini-batch of ranking examples, and consequently the three methods (including the proposed CMRNN) can benefit from the large amount of ranking examples.

CONCLUSION

In this paper, a new multimodal model is presented to solving the problem of cross-modal ranking. Benefiting from both neural networks and learning to rank techniques, the proposed model can learn high-level feature representation which has the discriminative power for cross-modal ranking and the learning procedure is shown efficient for practice. We have also demonstrated the effectiveness of the proposed method CMRNN and have shown significant improvements over the comparative methods on two real-world datasets.

ACKNOWLEDGEMENTS

This work is supported in part by National Basic Research Program of China (2010CB327900), NSFC (61103099), 863 program (2012AA012505), the Fundamental Research Funds for the Central Universities, Chinese Knowledge Center of Engineering Science and Technology (CKCEST), Program for New Century Excellent Talents in University, and Zhejiang Provincial Natural Science Foundation of China (LQ13F020001, LQ14F010004).

REFERENCES

[1] B. Bai, J. Weston, D. Grangier, R. Collobert, K. Sadamasa, Y. Qi, O. Chapelle, and K. Weinberger. Learning to rank with (a lot of) word features. *Information Retrieval*, 13(3):291–314, 2010.

[2] Z. Cao, T. Qin, T.-Y. Liu, M.-F. Tsai, and H. Li. Learning to rank: from pairwise approach to listwise approach. In *Proceedings of the 24th international conference on Machine learning*, pages 129–136. ACM, 2007.

[3] A. Frome, G. S. Corrado, J. Shlens, S. Bengio, J. Dean, T. Mikolov, et al. Devise: A deep visual-semantic embedding model. In *Advances in Neural Information Processing Systems*, pages 2121–2129, 2013.

[4] A. Galen, A. Raman, B. Jeff, and L. Karen. Deep canonical correlation analysis. In *International Conference on Machine Learning*, pages 1247–1255, 2013.

[5] D. Grangier and S. Bengio. A discriminative kernel-based approach to rank images from text queries. *IEEE Transactions on Pattern Analysis and Machine Intelligence*, 30(8):1371–1384, 2008.

[6] X. Lu, F. Wu, S. Tang, Z. Zhang, X. He, and Y. Zhuang. A low rank structural large margin method for cross-modal ranking. In *Proceedings of the 36th international ACM SIGIR conference on Research and development in information retrieval*, pages 433–442. ACM, 2013.

[7] J. Ngiam, A. Khosla, M. Kim, J. Nam, H. Lee, and A. Ng. Multimodal deep learning. In *Proceedings of the 28th International Conference on Machine Learning*, pages 689–696, 2011.

[8] N. Srivastava and R. Salakhutdinov. Multimodal learning with deep boltzmann machines. In *Advances in Neural Information Processing Systems 25*, pages 2231–2239, 2012.

Supervised Discriminative Hashing for Compact Binary Codes *

Viet Anh Nguyen[1], Jiwen Lu[1], Minh N. Do[2]
[1]Advanced Digital Sciences Center, Singapore
[2]University of Illinois at Urbana-Champaign, IL, USA
{vanguyen,jiwen.lu}@adsc.com.sg, minhdo@illinois.edu

ABSTRACT

Binary hashing has been increasingly popular for efficient similarity search in large-scale vision problems. This paper presents a novel Supervised Discriminative Hashing (SDH) method by jointly modeling the global and local manifold structures. Specifically, a family of discriminative hash functions is designed to map data points of the original high-dimensional space into nearby compact binary codes while preserving the geometrical similarity and discriminant properties in both global and local neighborhoods. Furthermore, the quantization loss between the original data and the binary codes together with the even binary code distribution are also taken into account in the optimization to generate more efficient and compact binary codes. Experimental results have demonstrated the proposed method outperforms the state-of-the-art.

Categories and Subject Descriptors

H.3.3 [**Information Storage and Retrieval**]: Information Search and Retrieval

Keywords

Hashing; approximate nearest neighbor search; binary codes; supervised hashing

1. INTRODUCTION

Recent years have witnessed the increasing popularity of hashing to support approximate nearest neighbor (ANN) search in large-scale vision problems (e.g., image retrieval, object recognition, pose estimation, etc.). The principle behind hashing is to construct a set of similarity preserving hash functions to map similar data points of the original high-dimensional space into nearby compact binary codes. As a result, similarity search can be efficiently computed on the basis of the Hamming distance with millions of distances per second and result in a substantial search time reduction even in an exhaustive search manner. In addition, compact binary codes also enable storage efficiency for the explosive growth of large-scale databases containing millions or even billions of data points.

Hashing methods can be broadly divided into two main categories: *data-independent* and *data-dependent* methods. The most popular data-independent hashing techniques are the Locality Sensitive Hashing (LSH) family [1] and its extension Shift-Invariant Kernels Hashing (SIKH) [6], which generate random projection bases from a Gaussian distribution as a set of hash functions to approximate the cosine similarity. Being data-independent, LSH and its extension require multiple hash tables with long binary codes to achieve an acceptable performance that may not scale well with the growth of data. To generate more compact binary codes, many data-dependent methods have been proposed to learn the hash functions using the training data. Most popular methods are Spectral Hashing (SH) [10], PCA-Hash (PCAH) [8], and Iterative Quantization (ITQ) [2]. To capture the semantic neighbors and improve the search performance, a number of supervised data-dependent methods have also been proposed by leveraging on the labeled data. The most representative methods include Binary Reconstruction Embedding (BRE) [4], Minimal Loss Hashing (MLH) [5], Semi-Supervised Hashing (SSH) [9], and LDA-Hash [7].

In general, the major shortcoming of the aforementioned methods is to consider only the global data structure in the design while ignoring the underlying local manifold structure, especially in real-world data. Without sufficient samples, the intrinsic global structure may be difficult to estimate and prone to overfitting. To capture meaningful neighbors in such a case, few methods have been proposed to discover the sub-manifold characteristics of the original data space [3, 12]. Dimensional-reduction based method in [3] is computationally intensive and not well suited for ANN search. Meanwhile, the method proposed in [12] has relied only on the local similarity structure to learn the robust hash functions. Whereas it may be effective for a certain dataset, such an approach may suffer from a locally optimal binary code solution due to the lack of the global data structure information.

In this paper, we propose a novel Supervised Discriminative Hashing (SDH) method by jointly considering the global and local manifold structures. In particular, a set of hash functions is designed to preserve the geometrical similarity and discriminant properties in both global and local neighborhoods. Sharing the spirit of Linear Discriminative Analysis (LDA), the key idea here is to minimize the Hamming distances of the binary codes from the same classes while simultaneously maximizing those from the different classes. Unlike the LDA approach, we formulate the objective function to discover the intrinsic local manifold as well. To generate more efficient and compact binary codes, the quantization loss between the original data points and the binary codes together with the even

*This study is supported by the research grant for the Human Sixth Sense Programme at the Advanced Digital Sciences Center from Singapore's Agency for Science, Technology and Research (A*STAR).

MM'14, November 3–7, 2014, Orlando, Florida, USA.
Copyright 2014 ACM 978-1-4503-3063-3/14/11 ...$15.00.
http://dx.doi.org/10.1145/2647868.2655003.

distribution of the binary codes will also be considered. Extensive experimental results have shown the superior performance of the proposed hashing method compared to the state-of-the-art.

2. PROPOSED METHOD

2.1 Notations and Definitions

Given a dataset of N data points $\mathcal{X} = \{\mathbf{x}_n\}_{n=1}^{N} \in \mathbb{R}^D$ that forms the data matrix $\mathbf{X} \in \mathbb{R}^{D \times N}$, where each column is a data point. The principle of binary hashing is to use a set of hash functions $\mathbf{H} = \{h_k : \mathbb{R}^D \rightarrow \mathbb{H}\}_{k=1}^{K}$ to map each $\mathbf{x}_n$ to $\mathbf{H}(\mathbf{x}_n) \in \mathbb{H}^K$ that is the K-dimensional Hamming space $\mathbb{H}^K \in \{-1, 1\}^K$. The binary code of $\mathbf{x}_n$ is denoted as $\mathbf{y}_n = \mathbf{H}(\mathbf{x}_n)$ that forms the n-th column of the binary code matrix $\mathbf{Y} \in \{-1, 1\}^{K \times N}$. In this work, we use the affine embedding as a hash function. Specifically, given a projection vector $\mathbf{w}_k \in \mathbb{R}^D$, the k-th hash function is defined as

$$h_k(\mathbf{x}_n) = \text{sgn}(\mathbf{w}_k^T \mathbf{x}_n + b_k) \tag{1}$$

where

$$\text{sgn}(v) = \begin{cases} 1 & \text{if } v \geq 0 \\ -1 & \text{otherwise} \end{cases} \tag{2}$$

and b_k is the mean of the projected data. Without loss of generality, we could assume the data are zero-centered and simply set b_k to 0. Let $\mathbf{W} = [\mathbf{w}_1, ..., \mathbf{w}_K] \in \mathbb{R}^{D \times K}$, we can write $\mathbf{y}_n = \text{sgn}(\mathbf{W}^T \mathbf{x}_n)$. Thus, the entire binary coding process can be represented in matrix form as $\mathbf{Y} = \text{sgn}(\mathbf{W}^T \mathbf{X})$, where $\text{sgn}(\mathbf{W}^T \mathbf{X})$ is the matrix of signs of individual elements.

2.2 Formulation

To generate discriminative representations, we exploit both the global and local manifolds of the data. Inspired by LDA that jointly minimizes the in-class covariance and maximizes the covariance across classes, we introduce the empirical term in the objective function in order to favor the data points in the same class to be close to each other while simultaneously maximizing the distances between different classes. Suppose a set of N data points $\mathbf{x}_1, \mathbf{x}_2, ..., \mathbf{x}_N \in \mathbb{R}^D$, belong to C classes. The empirical term for discovering the global data structure can be defined as

$$J_{\text{e,global}}(\mathbf{W}) = \sum_c \sum_k \sum_{\mathbf{x}_n \in \mathcal{X}_c} ||h_k(\mathbf{x}_n) - \mu_k^c||^2 - \alpha_{\text{global}} \sum_c \sum_k N_c ||\mu_k^c - \mu_k||^2 \tag{3}$$

where $\mathcal{X}_c$ is the set of data points that belong to class c, N_c is the number of data points in class c, μ_k^c is the mean of the k-th binary code bit of the data points in class c, μ is the total sample mean of the k-th binary code bit, and α_{global} is the regularization parameter. Using vector form, the global empirical term can be rearranged as

$$J_{\text{e,global}}(\mathbf{W}) = \mathbf{tr}\left\{\sum_c \sum_{\mathbf{y}_n \in \mathcal{Y}_c} (\mathbf{y}_n - \boldsymbol{\mu}_c)(\mathbf{y}_n - \boldsymbol{\mu}_c)^T - \alpha_{\text{global}} \sum_c N_c (\boldsymbol{\mu}_c - \boldsymbol{\mu})(\boldsymbol{\mu}_c - \boldsymbol{\mu})^T\right\} \tag{4}$$

where $\mathcal{Y}_c$ denotes the set of binary codes of the data points in class c. Note that the first term of $J_{\text{e,global}}(\mathbf{W})$ resembles the variance within the classes while the second term represents the variance between the classes of the training data that is incorporated as a penalty term. With the assumption of zero-mean data samples, i.e. $\boldsymbol{\mu} = \mathbf{0}$, the second term becomes $\sum_c N_c \boldsymbol{\mu}_c \boldsymbol{\mu}_c^T$. Using simple expansion and arrangement, it is easy to show that

$$J_{\text{e,global}}(\mathbf{W}) = \mathbf{tr}\left\{\sum_c \sum_{\mathbf{y}_n \in \mathcal{Y}_c} \mathbf{y}_n \mathbf{y}_n^T - (1 + \alpha_{\text{global}}) \sum_c N_c \boldsymbol{\mu}_c \boldsymbol{\mu}_C^T\right\} \tag{5}$$

Furthermore, to discover the intrinsic local manifold structure we construct a intra-class local neighborhood for each $\mathbf{x}_n$ denoted as $\mathcal{X}_{\text{intra}}^n \subset \mathcal{X}$ that contains its L_{intra} most similar data points of the same class as $\mathbf{x}_n$ measured by the Euclidean distance in the original space. Similarly, a inter-class local neighborhood $\mathcal{X}_{\text{inter}}^n \subset \mathcal{X}$ comprises of the L_{inter} most nearest data points that belong to different classes from $\mathbf{x}_n$. Intuitively, we want to learn a $\mathbf{W}$ that gives the same bits for $\mathbf{x}_n$ and $\mathbf{x}_l \in \mathcal{X}_{\text{intra}}^n$ and different bits for $\mathbf{x}_n$ and $\mathbf{x}_l \in \mathcal{X}_{\text{inter}}^n$. A local empirical term for discovering the intrinsic local manifold structure is defined as

$$J_{\text{e,local}}(\mathbf{W}) = \sum_n \sum_k \left\{ \sum_{\mathbf{x}_l \in \mathcal{X}_{\text{intra}}^n} ||h_k(\mathbf{x}_n) - h_k(\mathbf{x}_l)||^2 - \alpha_{\text{local}} \sum_{\mathbf{x}_l \in \mathcal{X}_{\text{inter}}^n} ||h_k(\mathbf{x}_n) - h_k(\mathbf{x}_l)||^2 \right\} \tag{6}$$

where α_{local} is the regularization parameter. Denote $\mathcal{Y}_{\text{intra}}^n$ and $\mathcal{Y}_{\text{inter}}^n$ be the sets of the binary codes for data points in $\mathcal{X}_{\text{intra}}^n$ and $\mathcal{X}_{\text{inter}}^n$, respectively. Using vector form, the local empirical objective term can be rearranged as

$$J_{\text{e,local}}(\mathbf{W}) = \mathbf{tr}\left\{\sum_n \sum_{\mathbf{y}_l \in \mathcal{Y}_{\text{intra}}^n} (\mathbf{y}_n - \mathbf{y}_l)(\mathbf{y}_n - \mathbf{y}_l)^T - \alpha_{\text{local}} \sum_n \sum_{\mathbf{y}_l \in \mathcal{Y}_{\text{inter}}^n} (\mathbf{y}_n - \mathbf{y}_l)(\mathbf{y}_n - \mathbf{y}_l)^T\right\} \tag{7}$$

Thus, the empirical objective function to learn the optimal projection matrix $\mathbf{W}$ can be written as

$$J_{\text{e}}(\mathbf{W}) = J_{\text{e,global}}(\mathbf{W}) + \alpha J_{\text{e,local}}(\mathbf{W}) \tag{8}$$

where α is the regularization parameter tuning the influence of the local empirical term. Since $J_{\text{e}}(\mathbf{W})$ is non-differentiable due to the non-linear $\text{sgn}(\cdot)$, minimizing such an objective function is an NP-hard problem. Similar to the spectral hashing method [10], we adopt the spectral relaxation by relaxing the sign of projection with its signed magnitude. With simple simplification, we can rewrite the empirical terms as follows

$$J_{\text{e,global}}(\mathbf{W}) = \mathbf{tr}\left\{\mathbf{W}^T \mathbf{X} \mathbf{X}^T \mathbf{W} - (1 + \alpha_{\text{global}}) \sum_c N_c \mathbf{W}^T \mathbf{u}_c \mathbf{u}_c^T \mathbf{W}\right\} \tag{9}$$

$$= \mathbf{tr}\{\mathbf{W}^T \mathbf{P}_{\text{global}} \mathbf{W}\} \tag{10}$$

where

$$\mathbf{P}_{\text{global}} = \mathbf{X}\mathbf{X}^T - (1 + \alpha_{\text{global}}) \sum_c N_c \mathbf{u}_c \mathbf{u}_c^T \tag{11}$$

and $\mathbf{u}_c$ is the mean vector of data points in the c-th class. Similarly, we have

$$J_{\text{e,local}}(\mathbf{W}) = \mathbf{tr}\left\{\sum_n \sum_{\mathbf{x}_l \in \mathcal{X}_{\text{intra}}^n} \mathbf{W}^T (\mathbf{x}_n - \mathbf{x}_l)(\mathbf{x}_n - \mathbf{x}_l)^T \mathbf{W} - \alpha_{\text{local}} \sum_n \sum_{\mathbf{x}_l \in \mathcal{X}_{\text{inter}}^n} \mathbf{W}^T (\mathbf{x}_n - \mathbf{x}_l)(\mathbf{x}_n - \mathbf{x}_l)^T \mathbf{W}\right\}$$

$$= \mathbf{tr}\{\mathbf{W}^T \mathbf{P}_{\text{local}} \mathbf{W}\} \tag{12}$$

where

$$\mathbf{P}_{\text{local}} = \sum_n \sum_{\mathbf{x}_l \in \mathcal{X}^n_{\text{intra}}} (\mathbf{x}_n - \mathbf{x}_l)(\mathbf{x}_n - \mathbf{x}_l)^T$$
$$-\alpha_{\text{local}} \sum_n \sum_{\mathbf{x}_l \in \mathcal{X}^n_{\text{inter}}} (\mathbf{x}_n - \mathbf{x}_l)(\mathbf{x}_n - \mathbf{x}_l)^T \quad (13)$$

By combining Eq. (10) and Eq. (12), we can rewrite the overall empirical term as

$$\mathbf{J}_e(\mathbf{W}) = \mathbf{tr}\{\mathbf{W}^T(\mathbf{P}_{\text{global}} + \alpha\mathbf{P}_{\text{local}})\mathbf{W}\} \quad (14)$$

With the constraint $\mathbf{W}^T\mathbf{W} = \mathbf{I}$ to ensure the bits uncorrelated, for a K bit code, the projection matrix $\mathbf{W}$ can be obtained by taking the K eigenvectors of the readjusted matrix $\mathbf{P} = \mathbf{P}_{\text{global}} + \alpha\mathbf{P}_{\text{local}}$ corresponding to the K smallest eigenvalues. In our implementation, we use such a projection matrix construction to initialize $\mathbf{W}$.

Meanwhile, to avoid overfitting and retain generalization, we use several regularizers that reflect the desirable properties of hash codes. One of the key conditions is to minimize the quantization loss in the training set, which can be defined by a loss function

$$J_q(\mathbf{W}) = \sum_n ||\mathbf{y}_n - \mathbf{W}^T\mathbf{x}_n||^2 = ||\mathbf{Y} - \mathbf{W}^T\mathbf{X}||_F^2 \quad (15)$$

To obtain a compact hash code, it requires each bit to fire 50% of the time, which can be represented by $\sum_n \mathbf{y}_n = \mathbf{0}$. We enforce this constraint by adding the bit balancing regularizer

$$J_b(\mathbf{W}) = ||\sum_n \mathbf{y}_n||^2 = ||\mathbf{Y1}|_F^2 \quad (16)$$

where $\mathbf{1} \in \mathbb{R}^N$ is the column vector of all 1 elements. Combining the empirical and regularization terms, the overall objective function is given as

$$J(\mathbf{W}) = J_e(\mathbf{W}) + \lambda J_q(\mathbf{W}) + \beta J_b(\mathbf{W}) \quad (17)$$

where λ and β are the regularization parameters. Similar to the empirical terms, the bit balancing constraint regularizer can also be relaxed as

$$J_b(\mathbf{W}) = \mathbf{tr}\{\mathbf{Y11}^T\mathbf{Y}^T\} \cong \mathbf{tr}\{\mathbf{W}^T\mathbf{XQX}^T\mathbf{W}\} \quad (18)$$

where $\mathbf{Q} = \mathbf{11}^T \in \mathbb{R}^{N\times N}$ contains all 1 elements. With the above relaxation, we can rewrite the objective function in (17) as

$$J(\mathbf{W}) = \mathbf{tr}\{\mathbf{W}^T\mathbf{PW}\} + \lambda||\mathbf{Y} - \mathbf{W}^T\mathbf{X}||_F^2 + \beta\mathbf{tr}\{\mathbf{W}^T\mathbf{XQX}^T\mathbf{W}\}$$
$$\text{s.t.} \quad \mathbf{W}^T\mathbf{W} = \mathbf{I} \quad (19)$$

2.3 Optimization Solution

While the final objective function in (19) is not convex for $\mathbf{W}$ and $\mathbf{Y}$ simultaneously, it is convex to one of them when the other is fixed. Thus, we will optimize the objective function in an iterative manner. Particularly, $\mathbf{W}$ and $\mathbf{Y}$ are alternatively updated to minimize the objective function when the other variable is fixed. These two alternating steps in each iteration are as follows.

Fix W and update Y. With a fixed $\mathbf{W}$, minimizing $J(\mathbf{W})$ is equivalent to minimizing the following term

$$||\mathbf{Y} - \mathbf{W}^T\mathbf{X}||_F^2 = ||\mathbf{Y}||_F^2 + ||\mathbf{W}^T\mathbf{X}||_F^2 - 2\mathbf{tr}\{\mathbf{YX}^T\mathbf{W}\} = NK + ||\mathbf{W}^T\mathbf{X}||_F^2 - 2\mathbf{tr}\{\mathbf{YX}^T\mathbf{W}\} \quad (20)$$

It has been shown in [2] that the solution of the binary code matrix $\mathbf{Y}$ for minimizing Eq. (20) can be given by

$$\mathbf{Y} = \text{sgn}(\mathbf{W}^T\mathbf{X}) \quad (21)$$

As a result, we use such an assignment to update $\mathbf{Y}$ in our paper.

Fix Y and update W. Since the binary code matrix $\mathbf{Y}$ and the training data $\mathbf{X}$ are fixed, minimizing the objective function in (19) is equivalent to minimizing the following function

$$J(\mathbf{W}) = \mathbf{tr}\{\mathbf{W}^T\mathbf{PW}\} + \lambda\mathbf{tr}\{\mathbf{W}^T\mathbf{XX}^T\mathbf{W}\} - 2\lambda\mathbf{tr}\{\mathbf{YX}^T\mathbf{W}\} + \beta\mathbf{tr}\{\mathbf{W}^T\mathbf{XQX}^T\mathbf{W}\}$$
$$\text{s.t.} \quad \mathbf{W}^T\mathbf{W} = \mathbf{I} \quad (22)$$

It is rather challenging to find a close form solution for the above function. In our work, we adopt the gradient descent approach with the curvilinear search algorithm in [11] to solve $\mathbf{W}$. Algorithm 1 below summarizes the detailed procedure of the proposed supervised discriminative hashing method.

Algorithm 1: Supervised Discriminative Hashing

INPUT: Training set $\mathcal{X} = \{\mathbf{x}_n\}_{n=1}^N$, parameters α, λ, β, iteration number T, and binary code length K

OUTPUT: Projection matrix $\mathbf{W}$

Step 1: Initialization

1.1 Construct $\mathcal{X}^n_{\text{intra}}$ and $\mathcal{X}^n_{\text{inter}}$ for each $\mathbf{x}_n$ using k-NN search

1.2 Initialize $\mathbf{W}$ by selecting the K eigenvectors of $\mathbf{P}$ corresponding the K smallest eigenvalues.

Step 2: Optimization

FOR $t = 1, 2, ..., T$. **REPEAT**

2.1 Fix $\mathbf{W}$ and update $\mathbf{Y}$ using Eq. (21)

2.2 Fix $\mathbf{Y}$ and update $\mathbf{W}$ by minimizing Eq. (22)

2.3 IF $|\mathbf{W}^t - \mathbf{W}^{t-1}| < \epsilon$, **GOTO Step 3**

Step 3: Output

Output the projection matrix $\mathbf{W}$

---

3. EXPERIMENTAL RESULTS

We evaluated the proposed hashing method in image retrieval by comparing with a few state-of-the-art methods in both unsupervised and supervised categories. They include LSH [1], SH [10], SIKH [6], PCAH [8], ITQ [2], supervised BRE [4], LDAH [7], and SSH [9]. For implementation, we used the source codes provided by the authors and followed their instructions to tune the parameters. For supervised methods, we extracted a small set of labeled samples in each dataset for training purpose and used for all supervised methods. We evaluated two versions of SDH: 1) without using local empirical term (SDH-0), 2) with using both global and local empirical terms (SDH-1). The regularization parameters were roughly tuned using the cross validation technique.

3.1 Dataset and protocols

The experiments were conducted using two benchmark datasets: CIFAR10[1] and Caltech256[2]. The CIFAR10 dataset consists of 60,000 images of size 32×32 pixels labeled in 10 classes. We used 512-dimensional GIST descriptors to represent the images. For evaluation, we randomly sampled 1,000 images as queries, 2,000 images (200 images per class) for the supervised training purpose, and the remaining images for the database construction. The Caltech256 dataset contains a total of 30,607 images grouped in 256 object categories with more than 80 images per category. We randomly sampled 1,280 images as queries (5 images per class), a set

[1] http://www.cs.toronto.edu/ kriz/cifar.html
[2] http://authors.library.caltech.edu/7694/

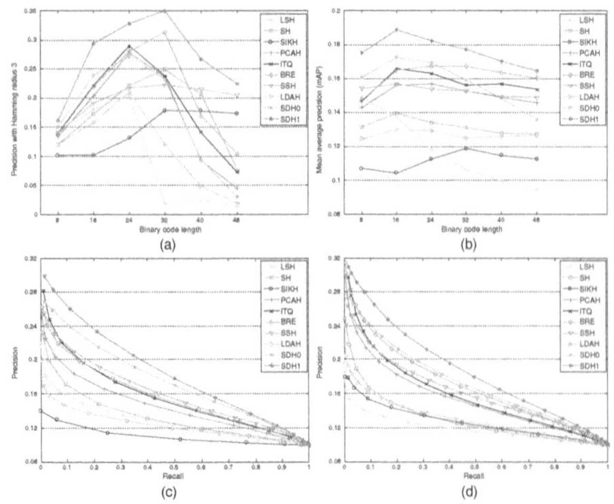

Figure 1: Comparative evaluation on the CIFAR dataset. (a) Precision within Hamming radius 3 using hash lookup, (b) Mean average precision (mAP) using hash lookup, (c) Recall-precision curve of hash lookup with 16 bits, (d) Recall-precision curve of hash lookup with 32 bits.

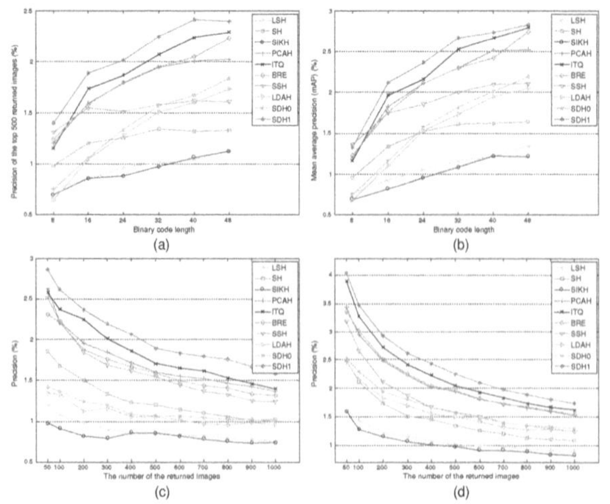

Figure 2: Comparative evaluation on the Caltech256 dataset. (a) Precision of the top 500 returned image using Hamming ranking, (b) Mean average precision (mAP) using Hamming ranking, (c) Mean precision curve of Hamming ranking with 16 bits, (d) Mean precision curve of Hamming ranking with 32 bits.

of 5,120 random images (20 images per class) as the training data, and the remaining images for the database. Similar to CIFAR10, 512-dimensional GIST image descriptors were used.

We used the class labels as ground truth to evaluate the returned images. Two search protocols were used: 1) Hash lookup within a Hamming radius 3, 2) Hamming ranking of the top 500 returned images. We reported the widely used measures including the average precision, recall-precision curve, and the mean average precision (mAP) using 8 to 48 hash bits.

3.2 Results

The performance curves for CIFAR10 and Caltech256 datasets are shown in Figs. 1 and 2, respectively. The precision and mAP curves obtained by using hash lookup (CIFAR10) and Hamming ranking (Caltech256) show the proposed method outperformed the existing methods, indicating more accurate performance of the returned results. Not surprisingly, unsupervised methods such as LSH and SIKH could not provide the good performance due to the lack of discrimination compared to the other supervised methods including the proposed SDH. Considering only the global structure, SDH-0 shares some similarity with LDAH while providing a better performance. This is because the quantization loss is jointly optimized in the binary code learning. However, these methods are not always better than the state-of-the-art. By modeling both global and local manifolds, SDH-1 could significantly improve the search performance compared to SDH-0. Note that the average precisions by hash lookup of the most methods drop at longer code lengths. This can be explained as many queries were failed to return any neighbor within a targeted Hamming radius. However, it can be seen that the proposed SDH-1 resulted in less precision reduction at longer code lengths compared to the other methods.

For further evaluation, Figs. 1(c,d) shows the recall-precision curves of hash lookup while Figs. 2(c,d) show the average precision curves of Hamming ranking by varying the number of the returned images. The results also confirm the trends observed in Figs. 1(a,b) and Figs. 2(a,b) for the two benchmark datasets, indicating the superior performance of the proposed method.

4. CONCLUSIONS

We have presented in this paper a novel Supervised Discriminative Hashing (SDH) method by jointly modeling the global and local manifold structures. Specifically, a family of discriminative hash functions has been designed to map data points of the original high-dimensional space into nearby compact binary codes so that the Hamming distances of the binary codes from the same classes are minimized while simultaneously maximizing those from the different classes in both global and local neighborhoods. In addition, the quantization loss between the original data and the binary codes together with the even binary code distribution have also been taken into account in the binary code learning in order to generate more efficient and compact codes. Experimental results have shown the proposed method outperforms the state-of-the-art.

5. REFERENCES

[1] A. Gionis *et al.* Similarity search in high dimensions via hashing. In *Proc. VLDB*, 1999.

[2] Y. Gong *et al.* Iterative quantization: a procrustean approach to learning binary codes for large-scale image retrieval. *TPAMI*, 2012.

[3] X. He. Incremental semi-supervised subspace learning for image retrieval. In *Proc. ACM MM*, 2004.

[4] B. Kulis and T. Darrell. Learning to hash with binary reconstructive embeddings. In *Proc. NIPS*, 2009.

[5] M. Norouzi and D. Fleet. Minimal loss hashing for compact binary codes. In *Proc. Int. Conf. Mach. Learn.*, 2011.

[6] M. Raginsky and S. Lazebnik. Locality sensitive binary codes from shift-invariant kernels. In *Proc. NIPS*, 2009.

[7] C. Strecha *et al.* Ldahash: Improved matching with smaller descriptors. *TPAMI*, 2012.

[8] J. Wang *et al.* Sequential projection learning for hashing with compact codes. In *Proc. ICML*, 2010.

[9] J. Wang *et al.* Semi-supervised hashing for large scale search. *TPAMI*, 2012.

[10] Y. Weiss *et al.* Spectral hashing. In *Proc. NIPS*, 2008.

[11] Z. Wen and Y. Yin. A feasible method for optimization with orthogonality constraints. *Mathematical Programming*, 2013.

[12] D. Zhang *et al.* Self-taught hashing for fast similarity search. In *Proc. Annual ACM SIGIR Conf.*, 2010.

Personalized Visual Vocabulary Adaption for Social Image Retrieval

Zhenxing Niu[1], Shiliang Zhang[2], Xinbo Gao[1], Qi Tian[2]
[1]Xidian University. [2]University of Texas at San Antonio
zhenxingniu@gmail.com xbgao@ieee.org slzhang.jdl@gmail.com qitian@cs.utsa.edu

ABSTRACT

With the popularity of mobile devices and social networks, users can easily build their personalized image sets. Thus, personalized image analysis, indexing, and retrieval have become important topics in social media analysis. Because of users' diverse preferences, their personalized image sets are usually related to specif c topics and show large feature distribution bias from general Internet images. Therefore, the visual vocabulary trained on general Internet images may could not f t across users' personalized image sets very well. To improve the image retrieval performance on personalized image sets, we propose the personalized visual vocabulary adaption which removes non-discriminative visual words and replaces them with more exact and discriminative ones, *i.e.*, adapt a general vocabulary toward a specif c user's image set. The proposed algorithm updates the visual vocabulary during off-line feature quantization, and operates on a limited number of visual words, hence shows satisfying eff ciency. Extensive experiments of image search on public datasets demonstrate the eff ciency and superior performance of our approach.

Categories and Subject Descriptors

I.2.10 [**Vision and Scene Understanding**]: VISIONS

Keywords

Visual Vocabulary; Large-Scale Visual Search; Social Media

1. INTRODUCTION

With the popularity of mobile devices and social networks, users can easily generate, download, and build their personalized image sets. Furthermore, the scale of users' personalized image sets also grows rapidly. This trend makes personalized image analysis, indexing, and retrieval become important research topics in social media analysis [,].

In large-scale image retrieval, a general visual vocabulary is commonly trained by clustering a large number of SIFT [ ] descriptors which are extracted from general Internet images. After generating a visual vocabulary, we will build indexes for a target image sets.

MM'14, November 3–7, 2014, Orlando, Florida, USA.
Copyright 2014 ACM 978-1-4503-3063-3/14/11 ...$15.00.
http://dx.doi.org/10.1145/2647868.2655006.

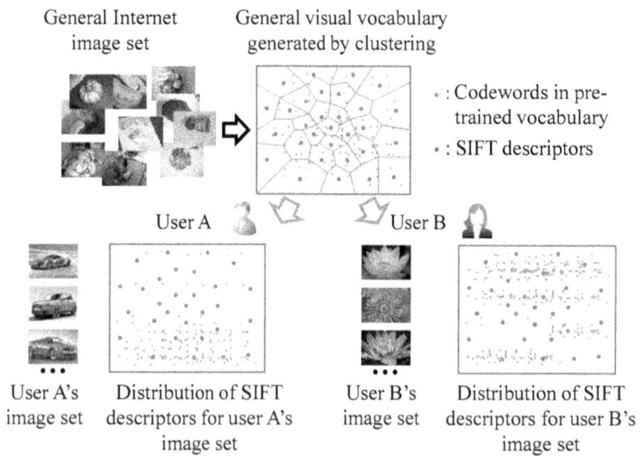

Figure 1: The visual vocabulary trained on an general Internet images is not optimal for users' image sets, since there is a large distribution bias on feature distribution between them.

In particular, for each image in the target image sets, it is indexed by extracting and quantizing its local descriptors like SIFT [ ] with their nearest codewords [ ]. Therefore, a good visual vocabulary should make less quantization error, and it is crucial for the performance of image retrieval system.

Tremendous progresses has been achieved in recent years to improve the discriminative power of visual vocabulary. In [ ], the authors introduce distance metric learning to decrease the quantization error. More related vocabulary learning algorithms will be discussed in Sec.2. However, most of existing vocabulary learning algorithms are based on a hypothesis, *i.e.*, the distribution of SIFT descriptors from training images should algin with the distribution on testing images.

On the other hand, a personalized image set may ref ect a user's preference and show specif c focuses and topics. For example in Fig.1, one user may like autos and collect lots of auto pictures in his image set, while another user may collect lots of f ower pictures. Therefore, there may exist a large bias on the feature distribution between the users' images and the general Internet images. Consequently, as illustrated in Fig.1, it will make relative large quantization error to represent personalized images with a general visual vocabulary, since it is trained and optimized on general Internet images.

Although new vocabularies could be trained on users' image sets, this is expensive to conduct, especially for a large number of users. These properties in personalized image sets motivate us to design new vocabulary learning algorithms to not only make use of general vocabulary but also reduce quantization errors.

In this paper, we propose to dynamically adapt the per-trained general visual vocabulary to f t the user's personalized image set to chase a reasonably trade-off between efficiency and accuracy. The basic idea of our vocabulary adaption algorithm is straightforward and effective. An ideal visual vocabulary should minimize the quantization error on a user's image set [ ]. According to this criteria, given a pre-trained vocabulary we first represent the user's images with it, *i.e.*, quantizing each local descriptor with its nearest codeword. During this process, the quantization errors could be estimated for each codeword. Then, the codewords with large quantization errors–which is regarded as non-discriminative codewords–are replaced with a set of new codewords, which produce smaller quantization error.

Moreover, this algorithm also can be applied to update the vocabulary when the user's image set is changed by adding or deleting images. In addition, because the vocabulary adaption happens during off-line feature quantization and only operates on a limited number of codewords, it shows high efficiency.

To validate our algorithms, we use *UKbench* [ ] and *Oxford5K* [ ] to simulate two personalized image sets from two users, because they focus on human made objects and landmark images, respectively. Given a general vocabulary trained on an independent Internet image set, we adapt it to *UKbench* and *Oxford5K* respectively. Experimental results on image search show that our algorithm dramatically improves the retrieval performance. The contributions of this paper can be summarized as follows:

- To our best knowledge, this work is an original effort on studying user-centric image retrieval in social media analysis by personalized visual vocabulary adaption.
- We only amend the vocabulary adaption. Our framework can be easily plugged into existing image retrieval advances working on feature quantization [ ], local context analysis [ ], and retrieval fusion [ ] to achieve better performance.

2. RELATED WORK

Representing bag of local invariant features [,] by visual vocabulary has demonstrated an exceptional scalability for large-scale image search [ ]. By representing SIFT descriptors with their nearest visual words, images hence could be represented as Bag-of-visual Words (BoWs) models [ ]. With information retrieval approaches like inverted file indexes, BoWs model is well-suited to large-scale image search task [ ].

However, as discussed in may works [, , , ,], traditional visual vocabulary shows limited discriminative power because it loses the spatial clues in images and results in quantization error in BoWs model. To conquer these issues, lots of efforts have been made by embedding extra Hamming code to decrease the quantization error [ ], and encoding spatial configurations of local features [, ,], *etc.* Although significant progress has been made, most of these works all based on the potential hypothesis that the distribution of training data should algin with the distribution of testing data. Hence there are little works focus on visual vocabulary adaption.

Recently, there is a work related to vocabulary adaption [ ]. A method of cluster center adaption is proposed in [ ]. However, it only adjust the position of some visual words without removing or adding new visual words. In contrast, our method could remove some non-discriminative visual words and replace them with some more exact and discriminative visual words.

3. PROPOSED METHOD

As aforementioned, we have a general vocabulary which is trained on an *independent* Internet image set. For a specific user, we want

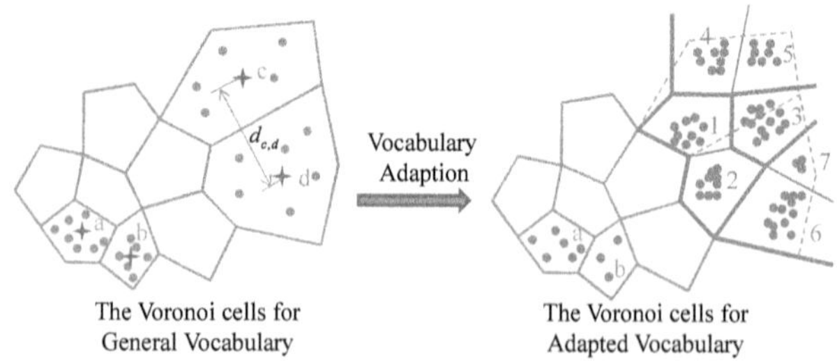

Figure 2: Illustrations of visual vocabulary adaption. The left and right figures denote the general vocabulary C and the adapted vocabulary $\tilde{C}$, respectively. The blue and red points indicates SIFT descriptors extracted from *independent* and *target* image sets, respectively. After adaption, the discriminative codewords a and b are remained, and the non-discriminative codewords c and d are replaced with new codewords $1, 2, ..., 7$.

to update this vocabulary for his personalized image set, which is called *target* image set in this paper. In the followings, we present how we adapt the general vocabulary toward the target image set.

3.1 Problem Formulation

Let $X = \{x_1, ..., x_N\}$ be a set of SIFT descriptors extracted from the target image set. And a general vocabulary C is known, *i.e.*, $C = \{c_1, ..., c_M\}$. Let the adapted vocabulary be $\tilde{C} = \tilde{C}_{com} \cup \tilde{C}_{new}$, where the $\tilde{C}_{com}$ with size of $|\tilde{C}_{com}| = W$ is the common subset of codewords shared between C and $\tilde{C}$, and the $\tilde{C}_{new}$ with size of $|\tilde{C}_{new}| = L$ are the new codewords generated after vocabulary adaption. Given the adapted vocabulary $\tilde{C}$, one SIFT descriptor x_n can be quantized into a corresponding visual word $\boldsymbol{v}_n$, where the hard assignment strategy is employed, *i.e.*, only one element of $\boldsymbol{v}_n$ is nonzero.

Thus, with the constraint on the size of $\tilde{C}_{com}$ and $\tilde{C}_{new}$, the problem of vocabulary adaption can be formulated as finding the optimal adapted vocabulary $\tilde{C}$ and visual words $V = \{\boldsymbol{v}_n\}$ by minimizing the quantization error between visual words and SIFT descriptors in X, *i.e.*,

$$\min_{\tilde{C},V} \sum_{n=1}^{N} ||x_n - \boldsymbol{v}_n\tilde{C}||^2 \quad (1)$$
$$\text{subject to } |\tilde{C}_{com}| = W, |\tilde{C}_{new}| = L.$$

Since both vocabulary $\tilde{C}$ and visual words V should be optimized, an iterative algorithm is usually employed to solve such problem, *i.e.*, the step for optimizing V with fixed $\tilde{C}$ and the step for optimizing $\tilde{C}$ with fixed V are iteratively conduct. The step for optimizing V is similar to traditional hard assignment issues which can be solved easily.

Regards to the optimization of $\tilde{C}$, we follow the method of Hierarchical K-means (HKM) [ ]. Differently, we avoid to re-train a new vocabulary since it is time-consuming. Instead, we make efficient use of the pre-trained vocabulary and only adjust some visual words.

The underlaying reason that the pre-trained vocabulary C is not the optimal vocabulary for target set X is: the C is trained on an independent image set G. Therefore, C is optimal for G rather than X. As shown in Fig.2, one vocabulary can be illustrated as some Voronoi cells and corresponding codewords (*i.e.*, the centers of Voronoi cells). For example, the pre-trained vocabulary C is illustrated at the left in the Fig.2, where SIFT descriptors extracted from the independent image set are denoted as the blue points.

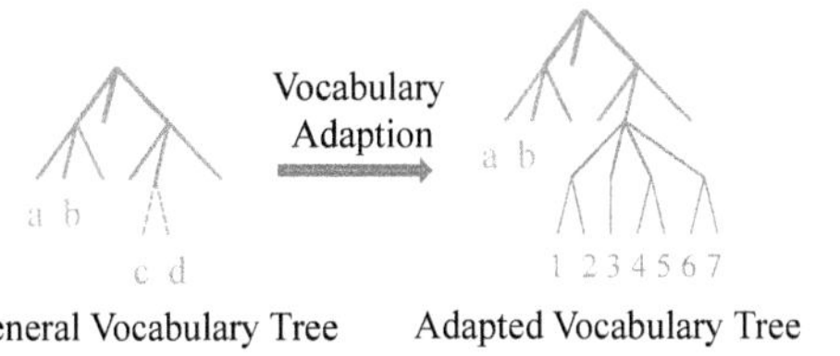

Figure 3: Illustrations of visual vocabulary adaption. The left and right f gures are the general vocabulary and the adapted vocabulary, respectively. The non-discriminative codewords c and d are replaced with new codewords $1, 2, ..., 7$.

Obviously in Fig.2, the Voronoi cells a and b are relatively small, while cells c and d are relatively large. K-Means clustering generates such results because densely distributed data needs f ner quantization to decrease the quantization error. However, for SIFT descriptors from target image set (denoted as the red points at the right in Fig.2), they may fall into the large Voronoi cells c and d, even they are densely distributed. This obviously produces large quantization error. Therefore, the C is not the optimal vocabulary for target image set X.

3.2 Vocabulary Adaption

In the followings, we present how to adapt C as $\tilde{C}$ for the target image set. Brief y, we f rst identify some non-discriminative codewords, then replace them with some new codewords.

According to Eq.1, those codewords can be regard as non- discriminative codewords if: (1) their Voronoi cells contain densely distributed target SIFT descriptors; *and* (2) the sizes of their Voronoi cells are relative large (*e.g.*, like cells c and d); *and* (3) the variance of target SIFT descriptors in a Voronoi cell is relatively large.

To measure the size of a Voronoi cell, we average the distances between it and its neighbor cells. Specif cally, let c_i be the codeword for Voronoi cell i, and let $d_{ik} = ||c_i - c_k||^2$ be the distance between codewords c_i and c_k. For each cell i, we f nd its K-nearest neighbor cells according the distance $\{d_{ik}, k = 1, ..., K\}$. Thus, the size s_i of cell i can be measured as

$$s_i = \frac{1}{K}\sum_{k=1}^{K} d_{ik} = \frac{1}{K}\sum_{k=1}^{K} ||c_i - c_k||^2 \quad (2)$$

For the variance v_i related to each codeword c_i, we collect the target SIFT descriptors $x_t, t = 1, ..., T$ assigned to codeword c_i, and compute v_i as

$$v_i = \frac{1}{T}\sum_{t=1}^{T} ||x_t - c_i||^2 \quad (3)$$

As aforementioned, we can identify non-discriminative codewords in the C as follows: Firstly, we count the number of target SIFT descriptors assigned to each codeword, and keep top 60% codewords with large SIFT number as candidates. Secondly, we calculate the size and variance for each candidate according to Eq.2 and 3, respectively. Finally, the candidate codewords which size and variance larger than given thresholds are f nally regarded as non-discriminative codewords.

After acquiring the non-discriminative codewords, we collect all target SIFT descriptors assigned to them, and use these SIFT descriptors to train new codewords with HKM. A new adapted vocabulary $\tilde{C}$ is f nally generated by replacing the non-discriminative codewords with new generated codewords, as shown in Fig.3.

4. EXPERIMENTS

4.1 Experimental Setup

To evaluate the proposed method, we crawl 1 million Flickr images as the *independent* image set, which is used to train the general visual vocabulary. In addition, we use *UKbench* [ ] and *Oxford5K* [ ] to simulate two personalized image sets from two users, because they focus on human made objects and landmark images respectively. Specif cally, *UKbench* dataset contains $2,550$ objects under 4 different viewpoints. *Oxford5K* contains $5,062$ landmark images downloaded from Flickr.

The retrieval method based on vocabulary tree [ ] is used as the baseline in our experiments. In particular, we extract SIFT descriptors from interest points detected by Difference of Gaussian (DoG) [ ]. During clustering, we employ HKM for generating vocabulary tree. And hard assignment strategy is used for feature quantization. It is also noticed that our method is not restricted to the type of local descriptor.

We adopt the metrics in the original papers of the 2 datasets to evaluate the retrieval performance: the recall rate for the top-4 candidates (referred as the N-S score) for the *UKbench*, and the mAP (mean average precision) for *Oxford5K*.

4.2 The vocabulary adaption

The vocabulary tree C is constructed by hierarchically clustering of 100 million SIFT descriptors extracted from the independent image set (*i.e.*, 1 million Flickr images). We evaluate our algorithm on two general vocabularies with size of $|C| = 100k$ and $|C| = 537k$ respectively. The f rst one is a vocabulary tree with $B = 10$ and $L = 6$ (about $100k$ leaf nodes), and the second one is a vocabulary tree with $B = 14$ and $L = 5$ (about $537k$ leaf nodes).

Firstly, we consider how the retrieval performance is inf uenced by the quantity of adapted codewords. To this end, we evaluate our algorithm by varying the quantity of adapted codewords. In particular, we will remove the non-discriminative codewords of the general vocabulary C in different percentage P_r, and replace them with new generated codewords in equal amounts. Take the general vocabulary of size $|C| = 100k$ as an example, if we remove $P_r = 20\%$, *e.g.*, $|C| \times 20\% = 20k$ non-discriminative codewords in the general vocabulary C, and then we will replace them with $20k$ new generated codewords. In the end, the size of the adapted vocabulary is equal to the size of the general vocabulary, *i.e.*, $|\tilde{C}| = |C| = 100k$.

From Figure 4, it is obviously that the retrieval performance will be improved by enlarging the quantity of adapted codewords.

Secondly, we will evaluate the performance of the proposed vocabulary adaption method. The key for visual vocabulary adaption is how to identify those non-discriminative codewords and replace them with discriminative codewords. As aforementioned, we give 3 criterions to identify and select those non-discriminative codewords, *i.e.*, the number of SIFT descriptors assigned to a codeword, the size and variance related to such codeword.

For comparison, we evaluate another strategy for selecting non-discriminative codewords, *i.e.*, random selection, which selects codewords randomly from the general vocabulary C, and regard them as non-discriminative codewords. Then, we replace them with new codewords in the same way.

From Figure 4, it is obvious that the proposed selection strategy outperforms the random selection strategy. This result justif es that our 3 criterions are helpful to identify non-discriminative codewords.

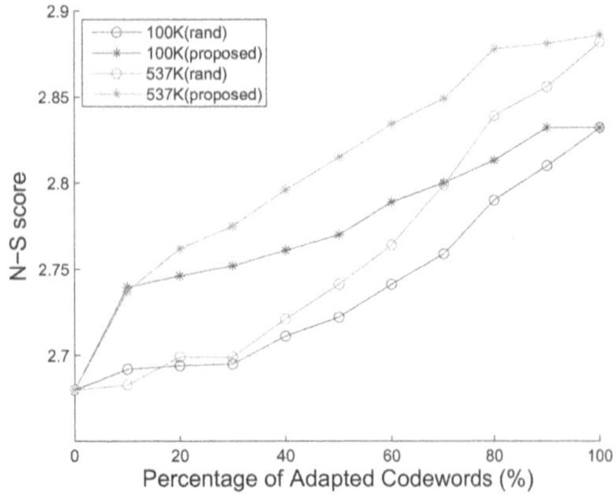

Figure 4: Comparisons of two adaption strategies w.r.t the percentage of adapted codewords.

4.3 Discussion

Usually, the vocabulary adaption is regarded as a tread-off between accuracy and eff ciency. If more computing resource is available, lots of codewords can be selected and adapted, and then we will achieve a better accuracy at the cost of computing time. On the contrary, we should select and replace some non-discriminative codewords to keep the eff ciency of the vocabulary adaption.

Moreover, if the vocabulary are totally replaced, *e.g.*, $P_r = 100\%$, it should achieve the best accuracy of retrieval. In addition, it is also supposed as same as that a total new vocabulary is totally trained on the target dataset, and they are supposed to achieve the same retrieval accuracy.

Surprisedly, we found that the method of $P_r = 100\%$ vocabulary adaption can achieved better retrieval accuracy than the method of training a total new vocabulary on the target dataset. As shown in Table 1, for the size of $|C| = 100k$, the method of $P_r = 100\%$ vocabulary adaption (denoted as *Adapted vocabulary*) achieves retrieval accuracy 2.832, and the method of training a total new vocabulary on the target dataset (denoted as *Target vocabulary*) achieves retrieval accuracy 2.830. The difference between them are more large when the size of vocabulary increases, *e.g.*, for $|C| = 537k$.

We found the reason of this phenomenon is that the method of *Target vocabulary* initializes the K-means clustering with some randomly selected codewords. On the contrast, the method of *Adapted vocabulary* initializes the K-means clustering with more non- discriminative codewords (*e.g.*, the number of SIFT descriptors assigned to such codeword are relatively large). As a result, such initialization of *Adapted vocabulary* can improved the performance of K-means clustering and vocabulary generation.

5. CONCLUSIONS

In this paper, we proposed a method of vocabulary adaption for personalized visual search. Based on a general visual vocabulary trained on an independent image set, we obtain an adapted vocabulary for a specif c target image set by replacing some non-discriminative visual words with better ones. In such way, without re-training a new vocabulary, we effectively solves the issue that the pre-trained visual vocabulary may couldn't f t the user's image set very well. The proposed algorithms update the visual vocabulary during off-line feature quantization, and operate on a limited number of visual words, hence show satisfying eff ciency. Extensive experiments of image search on public datasets demonstrate the eff ciency and superior performance of our approach.

Table 1: Performance comparisons among three vocabularies on *UKbench* dataset: on general vocabulary (*i.e.,* without adaption), on target vocabulary (which is totally trained with the target dataset), and on the adapted vocabulary (*i.e.,* the proposed method with $P_r = 100\%$ adaption).

Methods	$\|C\| = 100k$	$\|C\| = 537k$
General vocabulary [ ]	2.696	2.663
Target vocabulary	2.830	2.816
Adapted vocabulary	**2.832**	**2.886**

6. ACKNOWLEDGMENTS

This research was supported partly by the NSFC (Grant Nos. 61125204, 61172146), the Fundamental Research Funds for the Central Universities (Grant Nos. K5051202048, BDZ021403 and JB149901), Microsoft Research Asia Project based Funding (Grant No. FY13-RES-OPP-034), the Program for Changjiang Scholars and Innovative Research Team in University of China (No.IRT13088) and the Shaanxi Innovative Research Team for Key Science and Technology (No.2012KCT-02). Dr. Qi Tian is partly supported by ARO grant W911NF-12-1-0057, Faculty Research Awards by NEC Labs American, and NSFC Grant 61128007 respectively.

7. REFERENCES

[1] R. Arandjelovi and A. Zisserman. All about vlad. In *CVPR*, 2013.

[2] J. Cai, Q. Liu, C. Francine, D. Joshi, and Q. Tian. Scalable image search with multiple index tables. In *ICMR*, 2014.

[3] P. Cui, S. Liu, W. Zhu, H. Luan, T.-S. Chua, and S. Yang. Social-sensed image search. In *ACM Transactions on Information System*, 2014.

[4] H. Jégou, M. Douze, and C. Schmid. Hamming embedding and weak geometric consistency for large scale image search. In *ECCV*, 2008.

[5] D. G. Lowe. Distinctive image features from scale invariant keypoints. *IJCV*, 60(2):91–110, 2004.

[6] D. Nistér and H. Stewénius. Scalable recognition with a vocabulary tree. In *CVPR*, 2006.

[7] Z. Niu, G. Hua, X. Gao, and Q. Tian. Context aware topic model for scene recognition. In *CVPR*, 2012.

[8] Z. Niu, G. Hua, X. Gao, and Q. Tian. Semi-supervised relational topic model for weakly annotated image recognition in social media. In *CVPR*, 2014.

[9] J. Philbin, O. Chum, M. Isard, J. Sivic, and A. Zisserman. Object retrieval with large vocabularies and fast spatial matching. In *CVPR*, 2007.

[10] X. Shen, Z. Lin, J. Brandt, S. Avidan, and Y. Wu. Object retrieval and localization with spatially-constrained similarity measure and k-NN reranking. In *CVPR*, 2012.

[11] J. Sivic and A. Zisserman. Video google: A text retrieval approach to object matching in videos. In *ICCV*, 2003.

[12] X. Wang, M. Yang, T. Cour, S. Zhu, K. Yu, and T. X. Han. Contextual weighting for vocabulary tree based image retrieval. In *ICCV*, 2011.

[13] S. Zhang, Q. Huang, G. Hua, S. Jiang, W. Gao, and Q. Tian. Building contextual visual vocabulary for large-scale image applications. In *ACM Multimedia*, 2010.

[14] S. Zhang, Q. Tian, G. Hua, Q. Huang, and W. Gao. Descriptive visual words and visual phrases for image applications. In *ACM Multimedia*, 2009.

[15] S. Zhang, M. Yang, T. Cour, K. Yu, and D. N. Metaxas. Query specif c fusion for image retrieval. In *ECCV*, volume 2, pages 660–673, 2012.

[16] S. Zhang, M. Yang, X. Wang, Y. Lin, and Q. Tian. Semantic-aware co-indexing for image retrieval. In *ICCV*, 2013.

[17] L. Zheng and S. Wang. Visual phraselet: Ref ning spatial constraints for large scale image search. In *Signal Processing Letters*, 2013.

Co-saliency Detection via Base Reconstruction

Xiaochun Cao [1,2], Yupeng Cheng [1,*], Zhiqiang Tao [1], Huazhu Fu [3]

[1] School of Computer Science and Technology, Tianjin University
[2] State Key Laboratory of Information Security, Chinese Academy of Sciences
[3] School of Computer Engineering, Nanyang Technological University
chengyupeng2008@hotmail.com

ABSTRACT

Co-saliency aims at detecting common saliency in a series of images, which is useful for a variety of multimedia applications. In this paper, we address the co-saliency detection to a reconstruction problem: the foreground could be well reconstructed by using the reconstruction bases, which are extracted from each image and have the similar appearances in the feature space. We f rstly obtain a candidate set by measuring the saliency prior of each image. Relevance information among the multiple images is utilized to remove the inaccuracy reconstruction bases. Finally, with the updated reconstruction bases, we rebuild the images and provide the reconstruction error regarded as a negative correlational value in co-saliency measurement. The satisfactory quantitative and qualitative experimental results on two benchmark datasets demonstrate the efficiency and effectiveness of our method.

Categories and Subject Descriptors

I.4.6 [**Image Processing And Computer Vision**]: Segmentation—*Region growing, partitioning*

Keywords

Co-saliency detection; base selection; reconstruction

1. INTRODUCTION

In recent years, increasing researches and technical reports focus on measuring the image saliency, which further proves a signif cant effect of saliency in computer vision [6]. Jacobs *et al.* [7] f rstly propose 'co-saliency' detection searching the unique object in a series of similar images. Extending the concept of saliency to 'multiple' images is a great signif cance, while the requirement of 'common' image narrows the range of its applications. To broaden the usage of co-saliency, later article [5] completes the task in a relaxed def nition, which aims to extracted common salient object from multiple images with no subject to 'similar'. [5] proposes a state-of-the-art cluster-based co-saliency method with three visual attention cues are devised to effectively measure the cluster saliency. Since it learns the global correspondence between a series of images during the clustering process, multiple images co-saliency task can be well completed. However, this method is too sensitive to the clustering result.

*Corresponding author

MM'14, November 3–7, 2014, Orlando, Florida, USA.

http://dx.doi.org/10.1145/2647868.2655007 .

Figure 1: **Examples of co-saliency detection results. The f rst row is the input images. The second row is saliency map generated by the existing methods [9], and the last row is our co-saliency results.**

Recently, a saliency detection method named DSR is provided by [9]. This method makes full use of the visual information of each individual image. It achieves single saliency detection by modelling the simple center bias as a reconstruction problem, where the incompletion of background templates can be well managed. However, DSR [9] is designed for single saliency detection. The center prior is invalid for co-saliency detection from multiple images. And the background template is also invalid in detecting co-saliency from the multiple images which contains the different backgrounds. Moreover, the saliency outliers, which are treated as the single saliency in a few of images, can not be depressed. In this paper, we improve the background templates by using a novel reconstruction bases extracted by the saliency prior and handle the outliers via a selection step.

Fig. 1 shows the comparison between DSR [9] and our method. DSR [9] measures single saliency by background templates obtained from the edge of image. It is weakened in the 'no center prior' cases which frequently exist in co-saliency detection (*e.g.* the person in red at the second image is wrongly depressed). Although the dense reconstruction of DSR [9] can resist this problem by Principal Component Analysis (PCA) to some extend, it also suffers from the situation that large part of foreground exists in the edge of image. As shown in the second row, DSR [9] provides perfect results in the f rst and third images since they are correspond to the center bias. However, when the co-salient foreground appears

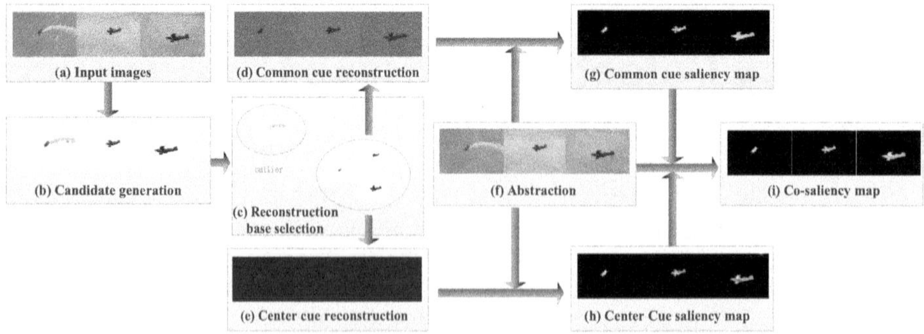

Figure 2: The framework of our reconstruction based co-saliency detection method.

at the edge (the second example) or outlier exists at the center (the last one), the detection result is undesirable as co-saliency. In contrast, our method uses reconstruction base of foreground in place of background templates and utilizes the reconstruction to complement the inaccuracy of single saliency to achieve the co-saliency task. The second and fourth examples illustrate the robustness of our method on complex images.

2. PROPOSED METHOD

Our method is based on the observation that the similarity of co-saliency regions makes them well reconstructed by each other, which is helpful in distinguishing the co-saliency and the background. Based on the def nition of co-saliency, we have the following two roles:

1. The co-saliency is a subset of the single saliency. In other words, the result of single saliency detection method contains the co-saliency region and single saliency appearing in only a part of the image set.

2. Co-salient foregrounds are similar and have close locations in the feature space. This case results in low reconstruction errors with reconstructing the co-salient foregrounds base on each other.

Based on the above roles, we propose a co-saliency detection method via reconstruction error of each image. Fig. 2 shows the framework of our approach. Given a set of images (a), our method generates a candidate set (b), where each image is segmented into a group of superpixels and estimated by various saliency algorithms. We select the reconstruction base (c) by evaluating the occurrence rate on all images. Clusters with low occurrence rate are regarded as outliers and removed from the candidate set (b). Afterwards, we reconstruct each image (d-e) by using common/center cues and compute the reconstruction error comparing with the abstraction of the original image (f), which results in a pair of saliency maps (g-h). Finally, our f nal co-saliency map (i) is generated by gathering the two saliency maps (g-h).

2.1 Candidate generation

We propose the candidate generation step aiming at extracting a rough reconstruction bases via the single saliency detection. Given N input images $\mathcal{I} = \{I^i\}_{i=1}^N$, M saliency detection methods are employed to generate $N \times M$ saliency maps $\{S_j^i\}_{j=1}^M$. To better evaluate the structural information, we f rstly obtain a set of superpixels $\mathcal{X}^i = \{x_p^i\}_{p=1}^{n^i}$ by using method [1] on each image I^i, where n^i denotes the number of superpixels in image I^i. A binary map b_j^i is then computed to represent the voting superpixels by saliency map S_j^i:

$$b_j^i(x_p^i) = \begin{cases} 1, & f_{mean}(S_j^i, x_p^i) \geq \alpha_1 \cdot f_{max}(S_j^i, \mathcal{X}^i) \\ 0, & otherwise \end{cases}, \quad (1)$$

where $f_{mean}(S_j^i, x_p^i)$ computes the mean value of all pixels in superpixel x_p^i by saliency map S_j^i, and $f_{max}(S_j^i, \mathcal{X}^i)$ denotes the max value of all the mean saliency score of $\mathcal{X}^i$. α_1 is a threshold and we set $\alpha_1 = 0.5$ in our experiment. A voting map B^i considering all the saliency map $\{S_j^i\}_{j=1}^M$ is then generated by:

$$B^i = \frac{1}{M}\sum_{j=1}^{M} b_j^i. \quad (2)$$

where B^i has the same size with image I^i and each elements corresponding to a pixel. As all pixels are gathered into a group of superpixels, this map B^i can be explained as how likely a superpixel should be extracted as a candidate. Therefore, a local candidate set f^i of image I^i is def ned as:

$$f^i = d(B^i - \alpha_2 \cdot \mathbf{E}) \cdot I^i, \quad (3)$$

where $\mathbf{E}$ whose all elements are 1 has the same dimension with B^i and α_2 is also a threshold and we set $\alpha_2 = 0.5$ in the experiment. $d(\cdot)$ binaries the input matrix (or value), assign 1 for positive elements, and 0 otherwise. Gathering all local candidate sets of each image, we f nally obtain a candidate set $\mathcal{F} = \{f^i\}_{i=1}^N$ for the input image set $\mathcal{I}$.

2.2 Reconstruction Base selection

Since co-saliency is def ned on the common saliency in all images, the co-saliency bases must be repeated emerge in the candidate set and acquire the advantage of the quantity. Based on this, we then select the reconstruction bases. Given the global reconstruction bases set $\mathcal{F}$, we employ kmeans to cluster all the superpixels into K clusters $C = \{C_k\}_{k=1}^K$. Then a K-bin histogram $\mathbf{z} = \{z_k\}_{k=1}^K$ is created to describe the occurrence rate of all the clusters C in the N input images:

$$z_k = \frac{1}{N}\sum_{i=1}^{N} f(C_k, I^i), \quad k = 1...K \quad (4)$$

where $f()$ is a binary function, which represents whether the cluster C_k appears in image I^i. If C_k appears in image I^i, $f = 1$, otherwise $f = 0$. At last, the reconstruction base set $\mathcal{G} = \{G_k\}_{k=1}^{n^k}$ is generated by:

$$G_k = \begin{cases} C_k, & z_k \geq \alpha_3 \\ 0, & z_k < \alpha_3 \end{cases}, \quad k = 1...K \quad (5)$$

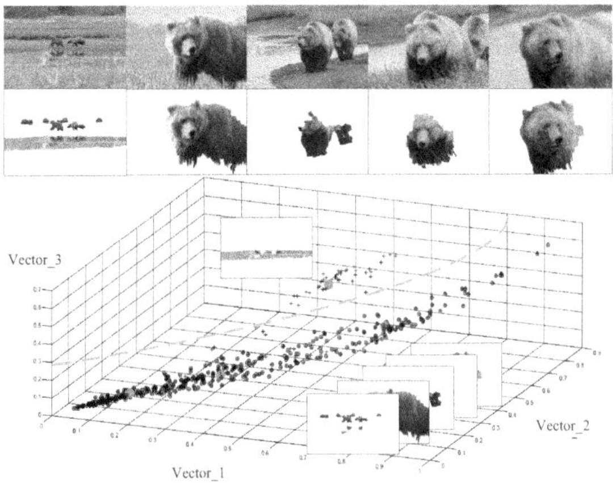

Figure 3: An general view of clustering and f ltrating. The f rst row contains the input images. The second row shows the initial candidate set. The map at bottom is a visual feature space of the f rst three dimensions (*i.e.* RGB color space). Each superpixel in the candidate set is represented by a black cross '+'. Red circles point the clustering center (in this case, clustering number $K = 4$). We mark the selected reconstruction base by $\oplus$. Finally, the selected (up) and unselected (down) superpixels are separated by a blue line.

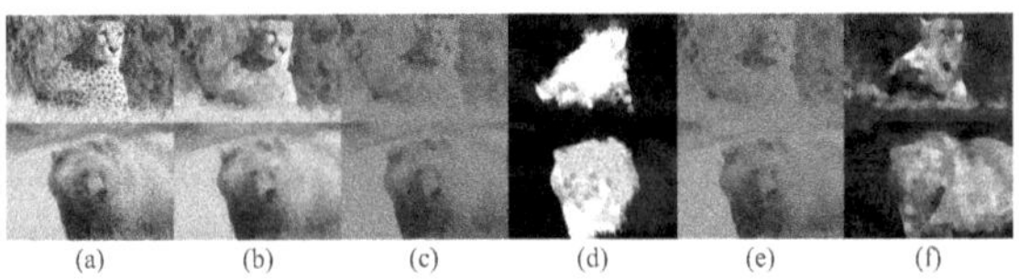

Figure 4: The samples of reconstruction, where the images come from the different co-saliency task. (a) Input images. (b) Abstraction of each image. (c) Common cue reconstruction result. (d) Saliency map based on Common cue. (e) Center cue reconstruction result. (f) Saliency map based on Center cue.

where α_3 is a threshold and we set $\alpha_3 = 0.7$ in our work. Fig. 3 shows an example of base selection in feature space. Depending on the candidate set in second row, the cluster result is shown in a feature space. It is easy to see that the river is wrongly obtained by candidate generation. While, as the river has a different location with the foreground in the feature space, it can be accurately removed from the candidate set.

2.3 Reconstruction error

After obtaining the reconstruction base set $\mathcal{G}$, we map the bases and images I to an 8-dimension feature space (RGB (3D) and Lab (3D) color, intensity (1D) and the variance of the above 7-dimension in a superpixel) and measure the co-saliency by image construction error following the assumption that there must be a difference between the foreground and background. Each image I^i is then represented as $\mathbf{X}^i = [\mathbf{x}^i_1, \mathbf{x}^i_2, ..., \mathbf{x}^i_{n^i}] \in \mathbb{R}^{8 \times N^i}$. We employ two cues to reconstruct the saliency map, common cue and center cue. The outliers is handling by the candidate selection. The missing foreground is covered via center cue. And Common cue is designed for depressing the background.

2.3.1 *Common cue reconstruction*

Implementing the image reconstruction directly by the reconstruction base set $\mathcal{G}$ is a naive but useful way in measuring the co-saliency. As there are a group of superpixels named reconstruction bases belong to $\mathcal{G}$, we reorder them as $\{\mathbf{l}_h\}^H_{h=1} = \mathcal{G}$ once again for facilitating the description. ($\mathbf{l}_h \in \mathbb{R}^{1 \times H}$ and $\mathcal{G} = [\mathbf{l}_1, \mathbf{l}_2, ..., \mathbf{l}_H] \in \mathbb{R}^{D \times H}$). To better suppress the background, we employ the reconstruction bases for sparse representation, and encode the image superpixel $\mathbf{x}^i_p$ by:

$$\hat{\beta}^i_p = \underset{\beta^i_p}{argmin} \|\mathbf{x}^i_p - \mathcal{G}\beta^i_p\| + \lambda \|\beta^i_p\|_1, \tag{6}$$

and the reconstruction error of the common cue is:

$$\varepsilon^i_p = \|\mathbf{x}^i_p - \mathcal{G}\hat{\beta}^i_p\|. \tag{7}$$

With the reconstruction error, we could obtain the common cue saliency map (Sec 2.3.3). Fig. 4(c-d) show an example of common cue reconstruction result and saliency map. Since all the reconstruction bases are used in sparse encoding, wood (the f rst row) and river (the second row) in the background are well depressed. However, this approach seriously suffers from the foreground missing of saliency prior. The second row is an obvious example. Body of bear is lost when this part does not exist in reconstruction bases, which results in a high reconstruction error comparing with the head.

2.3.2 *Center cue reconstruction*

To recover the missing foreground, which is removed by saliency prior, we model the foreground by a group of centers in $\mathcal{G}$. Note that, the centers generated from the f ltrating is an optional choice. However, we can not guarantee that the number of remaining clusters is enough for modelling. Therefore, we extract J center bases $\{\mathbf{U}_j\}^J_{j=1} = \mathcal{U}$ from the reconstruction bases set $\mathcal{G}$ by k-means.

In this way, the foreground is represented by J center base vectors, and each part of foreground is estimated equally no matter whether it constitutes the reconstruction bases $\mathcal{G}$ or not. With the center bases $\mathcal{U}$, we compute the coefficient of superpixel $\mathbf{x}^i_p$ by:

$$\hat{\gamma}^i_p = \underset{\gamma^i_p}{argmin} \|\mathbf{x}^i_p - \mathcal{U}\gamma^i_p\|, \tag{8}$$

where no regularity term is used, since the number of centers is much less than the original reconstruction bases, which can not apply the sparse representation. And the center reconstruction errors is:

$$\eta^i_p = \|\mathbf{x}^i_p - \mathcal{U}\hat{\gamma}^i_p\|. \tag{9}$$

Similar with the common cue, we could generate the center cue saliency map (Sec 2.3.3) via the reconstruction error. Fig. 4(e-f) is center reconstruction result and saliency map. Although the body part is lost in common cue reconstruction, saliency map based on center cue reconstruction cover the foreground by the similarity. Nevertheless, when the background is complex and resemble the foreground (such as the f rst row in Fig. 4(f)), the performance of center cue may be weakened.

In summary, common reconstruction performs well in depressing the awkward background, but sensitive to the saliency prior. Center reconstruction integrates the incomplete foreground while suffers from the complicated background. Hence, the two kinds of reconstruction is complementary to each other and the fusion can achieve a relatively good performance.

2.3.3 *Saliency map*

We then follow Lu [9] accomplishing the multi-scale to ref ned the error of common/center cues and compute the error of each

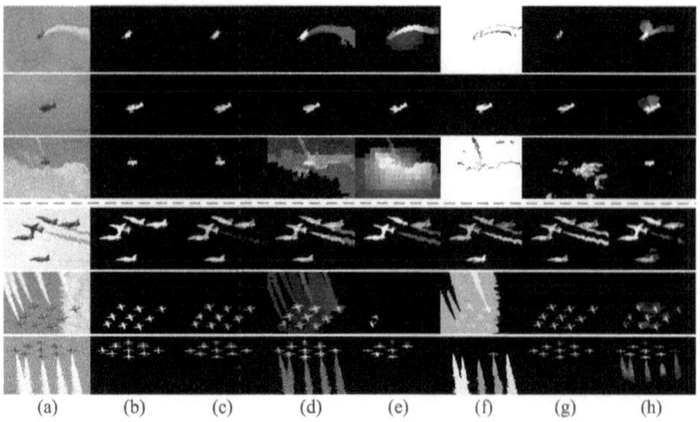

Figure 5: Two examples of saliency detection results. (a) Input images. (b) Ground truth. The example shows a comparison of our algorithm (c) with other saliency methods including (d) RC [4], (e) MR [11], (f) HS [10], (g) FU [5], (h) DSR [9].

pixel z by:

$$E(z) = \frac{\sum_{s=1}^{N_s} \omega_{zn}(s)v_n(s)}{\sum_{s=1}^{N_s} \omega_{zn}}, \omega_{zn}(s) = \frac{1}{\|f_z - \mathbf{x}_{n(s)}\|_2}, \tag{10}$$

where N_s is the number of scale, and $v_n(s)$ is the error $\hat{\gamma}_p^i$ or $\hat{\beta}_p^i$ in scale n_s. f_z is the feature vector of pixel z, and $n(s)$ denotes the label of superpixel including pixel z in scale s. $\omega_{zn}(s)$ regards the similarity of pixel z with its corresponding superpixel as the weight to average the reconstruction errors in multi-scale. Finally, since the error is negative correlational value in co-saliency measurement the saliency of pixel z is computed by:

$$S(z) = -log(E(z)). \tag{11}$$

Each reconstruction error (common cue or center cue) produce a saliency result (Fig. 2(g-h)). Gathering both of them, we acquire the f nal saliency map (Fig. 2(i)).

3. EXPERIMENT

We evaluate our algorithm on two benchmark data sets, and compare our method with seven state-of-the-art saliency detection methods, RC [4], MR [11], HS [10], DSR [9], LI [8] and co-saliency detection methods FU [5] and CAO [3]. (Note that, in this paper, we employ f ve single saliency methods including MR [11], HS [10], RC [4], DSR [9], and the spatial cue on single saliency in FU [5] to be saliency prior in candidate generation.)

The f rst experiment tests on the Icoseg dataset [2]. LI [8] is not included since it can only handle a pair of images. Fig. 6(a) shows the Precision-Recall curves of our method and other saliency methods. Our method outperforms all the saliency approaches. The second dataset is Image pair [8]. Fig. 6(b) shows the results and our method overcomes all the other methods on f-measure (**F** beside each method is the f-measure). Nevertheless, because of the simpleness of this data set, each method has a kind of improvement and this situation f nally results in a reducing superiority of our approach for the coming of performance ceiling.

Fig. 5 shows some visual saliency detection results. RC [4] fails in low contrast between foreground and outliers. MR [11] and HS [10] achieve high accuracy in some example (second row), but the instability weakens their performance in the overall comparison. DSR [9] still suffers from the center outliers. Although FU [5] well performs in most images, it struggles from the red smog in the forth row. Our method outperforms in the competition and well depress the smog, which is awkward to most algorithms.

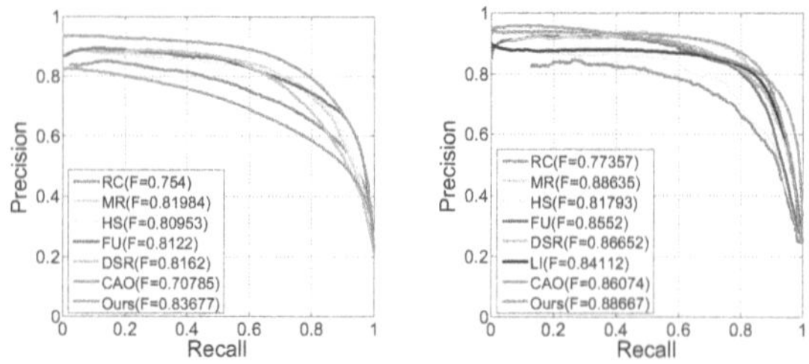

(a) co-saliency on Icoseg (b) co-saliency on Image pair

Figure 6: The PR curves of saliency detection on two dataset.

4. CONCLUSIONS

In this paper, we propose a co-saliency detection method based on reconstruction error. The reconstruction base is obtained by the global correspondence selection. With the common and center cues, our method depress the background and handle the missing foreground. The experiments demonstrate our method outperform the state-of-the-art co-saliency methods.

5. ACKNOWLEDGEMENT

This work was supported by National Natural Science Foundation of China (No. 61332012), National High-tech R&D Program of China (2014BAK11B03), and 100 Talents Programme of The Chinese Academy of Sciences.

6. REFERENCES

[1] R. Achanta, A. Shaji, K. Smith, A. Lucchi, P. Fua, and S. Susstrunk. Slic superpixels compared to state-of-the-art superpixel methods. *TPAMI*, 34(11):2274–2282, 2012.

[2] D. Batra, A. Kowdle, D. Parikh, J. Luo, and T. Chen. Interactively co-segmentating topically related images with intelligent scribble guidance. *Int. J. Comput. Vision*, 93(3):273–292, 2011.

[3] X. Cao, Z. Tao, B. Zhang, H. Fu, and X. Li. Saliency map fusion based on rank-one constraint. In *International Conference on Multimedia and Expo*, pages 1–6, 2013.

[4] M. Cheng, G. Zhang, N. J. Mitra, X. Huang, and S. Hu. Global contrast based salient region detection. In *CVPR*, pages 409–416, 2011.

[5] H. Fu, X. Cao, and Z. Tu. Cluster-based co-saliency detection. *TIP*, 22(10):3766–3778, 2013.

[6] L. Itti, C. Koch, and E. Niebur. A model of saliency-based visual attention for rapid scene analysis. *TPAMI*, 20(11):1254–1259, 1998.

[7] D. E. Jacobs, D. B. Goldman, and E. Shechtman. Cosaliency: Where people look when comparing images. In *Proc. UIST*, pages 219–228, 2010.

[8] H. Li and K. N. Ngan. A co-saliency model of image pairs. *TIP*, 20(12):3365–3375, 2011.

[9] X. Li, H. Lu, L. Zhang, X. Ruan, and M.-H. Yang. Saliency detection via dense and sparse reconstruction. In *ICCV*, pages 2976–2983, 2013.

[10] Q. Yan, L. Xu, J. Shi, and J. Jia. Hierarchical saliency detection. In *CVPR*, pages 1155–1162, 2013.

[11] C. Yang, L. Zhang, H. Lu, X. Ruan, and M.-H. Yang. Saliency detection via graph-based manifold ranking. In *CVPR*, pages 3166–3173, 2013.

Automatic Facial Image Annotation and Retrieval by Integrating Voice Label and Visual Appearance

Hong-Wun Jheng, Bor-Chun Chen, Yan-Ying Chen, Winston Hsu
National Taiwan University, Taipei, Taiwan
{jhenghw, sirius42, yanying}@cmlab.csie.ntu.edu.tw, winston@csie.ntu.edu.tw

ABSTRACT

Annotation is important for managing and retrieving a large amount of photos, but it is generally labor-intensive and time-consuming. However, speaking while taking photos is straightforward and effortless, and using voice for annotation is faster than typing words. To best reduce the manual cost of annotating photos, we propose a novel framework which utilizes the scarce spoken annotations recorded while capturing as voice labels and automatically label every facial image in the photo collection. To accomplish this goal, we employ a probabilistic graphical model which integrates voice labels and visual appearances for inference. Combined with group prior estimation and gender attribute association, we can achieve an outstanding performance on the proposed synthesized group photo collections.

Categories and Subject Descriptors

H.3.3 [**INFORMATION STORAGE AND RETRIEVAL**]: Information Search and Retrieval

Keywords

Face Annotation; Spoken Annotation; Image Retrieval

1 Introduction

It is easier than ever to use digital cameras to capture every beautiful moments in life, which are usually accompanied with friends and family. Effective methods are highly demanded to help us managing and searching in the fast-growing personal or group photos. For the purpose of recognizing people in the photos, a traditional approach is to train a classifier using a certain amount of samples as training set, which needs us to manually attach identity labels to facial images. But this process may be so tedious that few people would put their efforts into annotation after taking the photos [13]. On the other hand, using voice for annotation is much easier because speaking while capturing photos is straightforward. Many researches have employed speech recognition techniques for photo annotation and retrieval [4, 8, 10], however, most of these works do not take visual appearance into account. Instead of recognizing the speech or individually annotating each photo, we proposed a novel framework which utilizes a few spoken annotations as identity labels to automatically label every facial image in the photo collection. Figure 1 shows an example that the photographer can

MM'14, November 03 - 07 2014, Orlando, FL, USA.

http://dx.doi.org/10.1145/2647868.2655015 .

Figure 1: Some of the photos in the collection contain scarce spoken annotations which are recorded while capturing, and a probabilistic graphical model is employed to propagate these scarce annotations and utilize them to label every facial image in the collection.

arbitrarily say some names of the people he/she is capturing, and the voices are recorded at the same time. Then these voices will be utilized as identity labels to annotate each facial image in photos automatically.

In order to propagate scarce amount of labels in the personal photo collections, Brenner et al. [2] propose a probabilistic graphical model among faces in collections, which depends on the observed training samples with known labels. Gallagher et al. [6] identify people in group photos using group prior by training a classifier with a set of candidate names labeled on photos. However, these works still require users to manually annotate photos with explicit text labels. In this paper, we propose to jointly use voice label and visual appearance to solve the image annotation problem.

There are two main challenges in using voice label for annotation. First, the association between spoken annotations and faces in a photo is ambiguous. Second, the explicit text labels for each person are not available. In order to solve these problems, we first find latent identities by clustering those spoken annotations. We then construct a probabilistic graphical model to infer identities of the faces in the photos. To further increase the accuracy of the model, we incorporate group prior estimation and gender attribute association. Using the proposed method, each face can be automatically assigned to a voice identity label, and we can easily use these voice identity labels for facial image retrieval.

To sum up, our contribution includes, 1) we propose a novel way to reduce the effort for human to annotate and retrieve photos; 2) we set up a graphical model combining facial images and spoken annotations to infer the identity of each facial image; 3) we propose an effective group prior estimation and leverage the gender attribute association between appearances and identities as cues for inference.

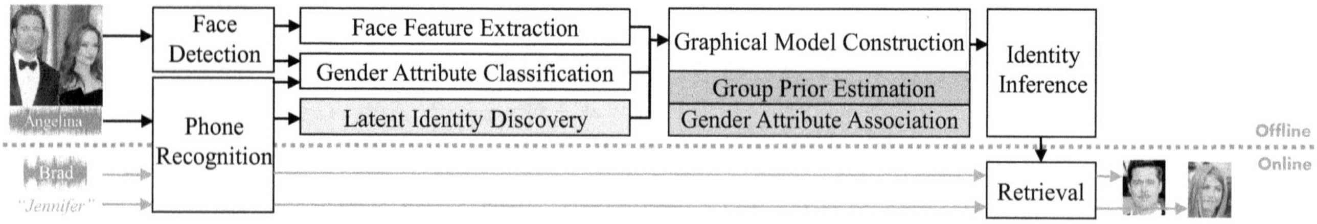

Figure 2: An overview of our proposed system.

2 Proposed Method

2.1 System Overview

First, we preprocess the spoken annotations[1] embedded on photos. Instead of recognizing the speech or using acoustic features (e.g., MFCCs) directly, we convert each spoken annotation into phone sequence which can be either recognized from audio signal with acoustic model [12] or looked up from pronouncing dictionary using text as query [14]. For every photo, we apply face detection algorithm to find the locations of the faces in the photo. For each face, we follow the work [3] to extract high-dimensional local binary pattern as face features, which can achieve near-human performance for face verification on the LFW [9] dataset. Then, we find latent identities by clustering spoken annotations, we then employ a joint probabilistic graphical model to automatically label every facial image in the collection with the voice labels. Finally, facial images of a specific person (hereafter referred to as *subject*) can be retrieved by either calling the subject again easily or typing his name as query. The overview of the proposed framework can be found in Figure 2.

2.2 Latent Identity Discovery

What we call a person usually denotes an identity of him/her, and it may include nicknames, family titles, etc. For example, someone with name "Elizabeth" might be called "Liza", and we usually call our mother "Mom" instead of her real name. Therefore, even if we have the name list of all the subjects in the collection as a phonetic dictionary, we are not able to use automatic speech recognition to find the identities of the spoken annotations. However, when the amount of the spoken annotations recorded in a photo collection are sufficient, clustering algorithm such as affinity propagation [5] can be applied to cluster these annotations according to the distance[2] between pairs of phone sequences. Each cluster can be considered as a latent identity, and the instance of this kind of identity can be represented by a cluster center data point, *exemplar.* Exemplar here is both a voice and a label, thus we term it *voice-label* in this paper. Although affinity propagation algorithm automatically determines the number of clusters K based on the input preference λ, it might be very different from the actual number of distinct subjects. We will discuss the impact of clustering to our approaches in Section 3.2.

2.3 Graphical Model Construction

In our approach, there is no observed training samples with known identity labels, but we have another special labels stand for the identities of subjects, voice-label. Although it does not indicate which facial image is associated with which voice-label, we can construct a pairwise Markov Network by connecting faces (nodes) among all photos with undirected edges and modeling the pairwise potentials between connected nodes to infer the joint statistics $\hat{y} = \{y_i\}$ of voice-labels over all nodes i in the graph. The probability distributions over these variables have the following form, where u is the unary and p the pairwise potentials, and Z is the normalization constant which ensures that the model defines a valid probability distribution:

$$P(y_1, y_2, \ldots, y_N) = \frac{1}{Z} \prod_i u_i(y_i) \prod_{(i,j), i \neq j} p_{i,j}(y_i, y_j). \quad (1)$$

The maximum a posterior (MAP) solution can reflect the most likely configuration $\hat{y}^*$, and it can be expressed as:

$$\hat{y}^* = \arg\max_{\hat{y}} P(\hat{y}). \quad (2)$$

Unary potentials express the probabilities of nodes assigned to individual voice-labels. A naive potential can be formulated according to the observation that faces in a photo g have higher potentials to those voice-labels annotated on g. Thus the unary potentials of these nodes can then be defined as follows, where K is the total number of distinct voice-labels in the photo collections, $g^{(f)}$ is the set of faces appearing in photo g, and $g^{(v)}$ is the set of voice-labels annotated for g:

$$u_i(y_i) = \begin{cases} \frac{1}{|g^{(f)}|} & \text{, if } y_i \in g^{(v)} \\ \frac{1 - \frac{|g^{(v)}|}{|g^{(f)}|}}{K - |g^{(v)}|} & \text{, otherwise.} \end{cases} \quad (3)$$

For example, given a photo contains 5 subjects, and the photographer annotated 2 of them by speaking their names while capturing. After applying the process mentioned in Section 2.2, we have 2 voice-labels in this photo. Any subjects in this photo might correspond to the annotated names. Thus each of them has the probabilities 1/5 to take on these 2 voice-labels respectively, and remaining 3/5 are evenly distributed to other K-2 voice-labels.

Pairwise potentials describe the relationships between connected nodes. Faces that have high similarity in visual feature space should be encouraged to have the same identity. In addition, *unique object constraint* states that any faces from a single photo must be different identities. Instead of constructing fully connected graph, for each node, we connect it with M nearest neighbors to form *similarity edges*, and connect those in the same photo with *dissimilarity edges.* Hence, pairwise potential can be defined as follows, where τ is a parameter larger than 1:

$$p_{i,j}(y_i, y_j) = \begin{cases} \tau & \text{, if } y_i = y_j \wedge edge(i,j) \text{ is similarity edge} \\ 0 & \text{, if } y_i = y_j \wedge edge(i,j) \text{ is dissimilarity edge} \\ 1 & \text{, otherwise.} \end{cases} \quad (4)$$

2.3.1 *Group Prior Estimation*

To decrease the entropy of unary potentials of all subjects in an annotated photo containing group of subjects, we estimate which face might have the higher potential for the specific voice-label. If there is a bunch of photos containing voice-label "T-AA-M" respectively, it is expected that each of them contains a subject whose name is "Tom." In other words, when the spoken annotations with similar

[1] Here we assume the spoken annotations are the recorded utterances which contain only the names of the subjects.

[2] Here we use Levenshtein distance as our distance measure, which takes into account phone hits, substitutions, deletions and insertions.

semantics are clustered together, we believe that the most frequent subject appearing among those associated photos is the one who has that identity. Based on the assumption, we estimate the prior probabilities for any faces in an annotated group photo in the following form:

$$\Psi_i(y) = \frac{\mathcal{K}(y,i)}{\sum_{p \in g^{(f)}} \mathcal{K}(y,p)}, \tag{5}$$

$$\text{where } \mathcal{K}(y,i) = \frac{1}{|G_y|} \sum_{p \in G_y} Sim(p,i). \tag{6}$$

G_y is the set of faces appearing in those photos containing voice-label y, and $Sim(p,i)$ denotes the similarity between faces p and i in feature space. To make prior a valid probability distribution, we normalize (5) for each node i. In addition, we add a smoothness term ϵ before normalization to make sure that the probabilities of a node being assigned any other voice-labels would not be zero:

$$u_i^{(GPE)}(y) = \frac{\Psi_i(y) + \epsilon}{\sum_y \Psi_i(y)}. \tag{7}$$

2.3.2 Gender Attribute Association

Gender attribute is another helpful cue for inference. For example, since we have the knowledge that "Angelina" is a female name, it is reasonable to infer that it should be attached on the facial image looks like a female in the photo. Gallagher et al. [7] have shown that the appearance of a person is not independent of the name. Inspired by their work, we train a simple 3-gram model for phonetic gender attribute classification with Support Vector Machines (SVMs), and the training data is collected from the U.S. Social Security baby name database [1]. In our application, the spoken annotations could be family titles and nicknames, we also collected some samples from the Internet for training. Note that all of these texts for training are converted to phone sequences according to the CMU Pronouncing Dictionary [14]. We then incorporate this phonetic gender attribute classification model with the facial attributes classification model proposed by Kumar et al. [11] to weight the unary potential u as:

$$\Omega_i(y) = \begin{cases} \omega \cdot u(y) & \text{, if } Attr(i) = Attr(y) \\ u(y) & \text{, otherwise,} \end{cases} \tag{8}$$

where $Attr(y)$ is the gender attribute recognized given with either a facial image or a phone sequence as input, and ω is a weight parameter larger than 1. Similar to Section 2.3.1, we make it a valid probability distribution by normalization:

$$u_i^{(GAA)}(y) = \frac{\Omega_i(y)}{\sum_y \Omega_i(y)}. \tag{9}$$

2.4 Retrieval

The recorded spoken annotations are what subjects are called by others in our application. After automatically labeling every facial image in the collection with voice-labels using method proposed in Section 2.3, these labeled facial images can be retrieved by comparing the similarity of phone sequences between query and voice-labels. Thus the query can be either the recorded utterances which will be recognized to phone sequences with acoustic model, or the text which will be mapped to phone sequences by following the format used for speech recognition and synthesis [14].

3 Experimental Results

Primarily, we introduce the datasets used in our experiments. To fully evaluate the proposed methods, we need the group photo collections including explicit ground truth like names of every facial image in any photos. We also need other datasets which contain more subjects in a single photo, so that we can evaluate the effect of the group prior estimation proposed in Section 2.3.1. Such datasets with sufficient size are usually not easy to collect, so we propose a synthesized collection which can suit our requirements. Label Face in the Wild (LFW) [9] contains face images of celebrities collected from the Internet with full names as metadata, and 51 of all subjects have more than 20 images. Although there is only one subject in a single image, we can make it a simulation group photo collection by randomly combining those images to form group subjects in single photos, and keep the constraint that a subject can only appear once in a photo.

Table 1: Distribution of face number in each photo on different datasets. Each of these 3 datasets contains 2,398 facial images but different amount of photos.

	1	2	3	4	5	6	7+	No. photos
Type-A	812	436	164	40	10	2	0	1500
Type-B	249	250	220	133	61	16	17	1000
Type-C	33	46	62	92	78	87	102	500

Table 2: Accuray of methods on different datasets.

	Type-A	Type-B	Type-C
(1)Baseline	56.4%	39.2%	27.5%
(2)Basic Graphical Model	79.8%	70.9%	65.6%
(3) 2 + "GPE"	81.4%	76.1%	72.8%
(4) 2 + "GAA"	81.6%	73.6%	67.7%
(5) 2 + "GPE"+ "GAA"	**81.9%**	**77.2%**	**73.1%**

We select at most 200 images for each of these 51 subjects and get 2,398 images in total. By varying the maximum amount of photos, we get different types of datasets, as shown in Table 1. Type-A simulates the collection that subjects were usually captured alone (e.g., selfies), Type-C shows the phenomenon that people in this collection prefer to take group photos. Type-B is in between.

We also simulate the annotated and query utterances by generating phone sequences with accuracy rate of 80%, using the 39 phone set proposed in [12], and the reference utterances are first names of subjects. We test various amounts of spoken annotations on these three datasets with the proposed methods, and also make sure that each subject in the datasets is at least annotated once. Since the result of the clustering and the chosen faces to be annotated impact the follow-up inference works, we repeat all the experiments twenty times and randomly annotate subjects in the collection with given size each time and then average the final results.

We present a baseline for comparison which is a modification of the traditional face recognition approach. We consider those annotated photos as a training set even though we do not know which facial images should be assigned to which annotations. Considering every facial image in the collection as a query, we retrieve similarity faces from training set. Then we vote the most frequent voice-label among these photos which the similar faces are depicted, because the subject might have high probability to be annotated in these photos. Note that if every photo in the training set contains only one facial image, this approach is just a traditional k-nearest neighbors classification algorithm.

Following are some detail statistics in our implementation. The performance of the employed face feature, the high dimensional version of LBP [3], achieves rank one recognition rate of 81% using leave-one-out cross-validation on all 2,398 faces in the dataset. The accuracy of gender attribute classified with [11] and our phonetic model are around 81.22% and 70% respectively.

3.1 Performance on Different Datasets

In the first experiment, we evaluate the performance of the proposed approaches on the three datasets. We restrict the amount of annotations to 10% of all the facial images in datasets. For the proposed graphical models, we empirically determine the potential parameter τ to 1.2, the gender association weight ω to 1.8, the number of similar neighbors M to 6, and we set the preference λ of affinity propagation to median similarity in this experiment. For the baseline, we adopt the best results with k ranging from three to ten for comparison. Each voice-label is originally a spoken annotation for a subject, and it makes a hit if the labeled facial image is the specific subject. So the accuracy can be defined as the hit rate among all the faces in the collection. As shown in Table 2, the proposed approach outperforms the baseline among the three datasets. Taking Type-A dataset as an example, the basic graphical model is at least 23.4% higher than the baseline. When the experiment is carried out on Type-C, the baseline suffers from a significant accuracy drop from 56.4% to 27.5%, but the basic graphical model drops no more than 15%. It is notable that the proposed group prior estimation version "GPE" have a significant 7.2% improvement on Type-C than 1.6% on Type-A dataset, which proves the effectiveness of the proposed group prior estimation method. Besides, another proposed enhanced version using gender attribute association "GAA" can also bring 1% $\sim$ 2% gain among these datasets, though there are only 9 females in the 51 subjects.

3.2 Performance with Partial Annotations

In this experiment, we first evaluate the performance of baseline and "GPE+GAA" enhanced graphical model with various amounts of spoken annotations ranging from 5% to 40% on Type-B dataset. If not otherwise mentioned, we use the same parameters as in Section 3.1. This time we also record the number of clusters after affinity propagation at each amount.

Figure 3(a) shows the proposed graphical model achieves an outstanding 90% when the amount of spoken annotations is 20%, and the baseline also shows steady improvement as the amount increases. However, we can see that the number of clusters also increases as the amount of annotations increases. Since we have only 51 distinct subjects in dataset totally, the number of the clusters are obviously much more than 51 when the amount of annotations increases from 5%. Although more annotations can bring better accuracy, the improvement is not satisfying.

We then investigate relationship between the accuracy and the number of clusters by varying the value of preference λ, and fix the amount of annotations to 40%. As shown in Figure 3(b), when the number of clusters K gets close to 51, both approaches have the best results and both approaches suffer from a significant accuracy drop when K is less than 51. On the other hand, when K increases from 51 to 271, the accuracy of the proposed graphical model drops 7% only, while the accuracy drop of baseline is 20%, which means that the proposed graphical model outperforms the baseline when K is larger than the real number of subjects.

3.3 Facial Image Retrieval

Finally, we evaluate the performance of facial image retrieval of both baseline and "GPE+GAA" enhanced graphical model based on the results in Section 3.1 on Type-B dataset. When all the facial images are labeled with voice-labels (phone sequences), we retrieve the specific target subject from the collection by generating phone sequences with 80% accuracy rate as queries, and rank the retrieved facial images according to the similarity of phone sequences. For each subject we test 30 queries, and compute the mean average precision of all 51 $\times$ 30 queries for each approach. The mean average precision of baseline is 0.21 while using the proposed approach we can achieve 0.37. This not only shows the better result of "GPE+GAA" graphical model compared to the baseline, but also supports the effectiveness of the proposed framework.

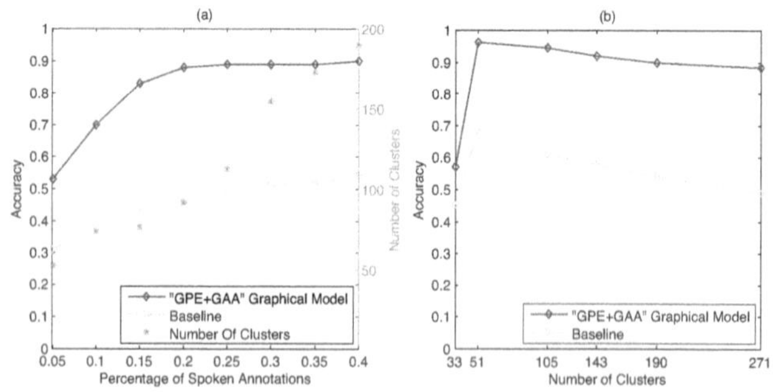

Figure 3: (a) Accuracy and number of clusters depending on different amount of spoken annotations while fixing the preference. (b) Accuracy depending on different number of clusters by varying the preference while fixing the amount of spoken annotations to 40%.

4 Conclusion

We propose a novel and effective way to manage and retrieve the large consumer photos which usually contain groups of people in a single photo by annotating their names with voices. A graph-based approach is proposed to effectively propagate scarce spoken annotations to every facial image in the collections. We also leverage the associations between visual appearances and phonetic identities of subjects to improve the inference. Determining the optimal parameters is still an issue when there is no training set prepared. However, maximizing the likelihood of the joint probabilistic distribution might be an alternative for automatic parameter selection. In the future work, we will exploit more context cues (e.g., time, geo-locations, etc.) and other content-based techniques for the proposed system.

5 References

[1] U. S. S. Administration. Baby name database. *URL: http://www.socialsecurity.gov/OACT/babynames/.*

[2] M. Brenner and E. Izquierdo. Graph-based recognition in photo collections using social semantics. In *Proceedings of the 2011 ACM workshop on Social and behavioural networked media access*, pages 47–52. ACM, 2011.

[3] D. Chen, X. Cao, F. Wen, and J. Sun. Blessing of dimensionality: High-dimensional feature and its efficient compression for face verification. In *Computer Vision and Pattern Recognition (CVPR), 2013 IEEE Conference on*, pages 3025–3032. IEEE, 2013.

[4] J. Chen, T. Tan, and P. Mulhem. A method for photograph indexing using speech annotation. In *Advances in Multimedia Information Processing–PCM 2001*, pages 867–872. Springer, 2001.

[5] B. J. Frey and D. Dueck. Clustering by passing messages between data points. *science*, 315(5814):972–976, 2007.

[6] A. C. Gallagher and T. Chen. Using group prior to identify people in consumer images. In *Computer Vision and Pattern Recognition, 2007. CVPR'07. IEEE Conference on*, pages 1–8. IEEE, 2007.

[7] A. C. Gallagher and T. Chen. Estimating age, gender, and identity using first name priors. In *Computer Vision and Pattern Recognition, 2008. CVPR 2008. IEEE Conference on*, pages 1–8. IEEE, 2008.

[8] T. J. Hazen, B. Sherry, and M. Adler. Speech-based annotation and retrieval of digital photographs. In *INTERSPEECH*, volume 7, pages 2165–2168, 2007.

[9] G. B. Huang, M. Ramesh, T. Berg, and E. Learned-Miller. Labeled faces in the wild: A database for studying face recognition in unconstrained environments. Technical Report 07-49, University of Massachusetts, Amherst, October 2007.

[10] D. V. Kalashnikov, S. Mehrotra, J. Xu, and N. Venkatasubramanian. A semantics-based approach for speech annotation of images. *Knowledge and Data Engineering, IEEE Transactions on*, 23(9):1373–1387, 2011.

[11] N. Kumar, A. C. Berg, P. N. Belhumeur, and S. K. Nayar. Attribute and simile classifiers for face verification. In *Computer Vision, 2009 IEEE 12th International Conference on*, pages 365–372. IEEE, 2009.

[12] K.-F. Lee and H.-W. Hon. Speaker-independent phone recognition using hidden markov models. *Acoustics, Speech and Signal Processing, IEEE Transactions on*, 37(11):1641–1648, 1989.

[13] K. Rodden and K. R. Wood. How do people manage their digital photographs? In *Proceedings of the SIGCHI conference on Human factors in computing systems*, pages 409–416. ACM, 2003.

[14] R. L. Weide. The cmu pronouncing dictionary. *URL: http://www.speech.cs.cmu.edu/cgi-bin/cmudict*, 1998.

Query-Adaptive Hash Code Ranking for Fast Nearest Neighbor Search

Tianxu Ji† Xianglong Liu†* Cheng Deng‡ Lei Huang† Bo Lang†
†State Key Lab of Software Development Environment, Beihang University, Beijing, China
‡School of Electronic Engineering, Xidian University, Xi'an, China
{jitianxu, xlliu, huanglei, langbo}@nlsde.buaa.edu.cn chdeng.xd@gmail.com

ABSTRACT

Recently hash-based nearest neighbor search has become attractive in many applications due to its compressed storage and fast query speed. However, the quantization in the hashing process usually degenerates its discriminative power when using Hamming distance ranking. To enable fine-grained ranking, hash bit weighting has been proved as a promising solution. Though achieving satisfying performance improvement, state-of-the-art weighting methods usually heavily rely on the projection's distribution assumption, and thus can hardly be directly applied to more general types of hashing algorithms. In this paper, we propose a new ranking method named QRank with query-adaptive bitwise weights by exploiting both the discriminative power of each hash function and their complement for nearest neighbor search. QRank is a general weighting method for all kinds of hashing algorithms without any strict assumptions. Experimental results on two well-known benchmarks MNIST and NUS-WIDE show that the proposed method can achieve up to 17.11% performance gains over state-of-the-art methods.

Categories and Subject Descriptors

H.3.1 [**Information Storage and Retrieval**]: Content Analysis and Indexing; H.3.3 [**Information Storage and Retrieval**]: Information Search and Retrieval; I.2.6 [**Artificial Intelligence**]: Learning

Keywords

Hash Bit Weighting; Hash Code Ranking; Weighted Hamming Distance; Locality Sensitive Hashing

*corresponding author

MM'14, November 03–07, 2014, Orlando, FL, USA.

http://dx.doi.org/10.1145/2647868.2655018 .

1. INTRODUCTION

Hash based nearest neighbor search has attracted great attentions in many areas, such as large-scale visual search, data mining, pattern recognition and machine learning [4]. As the most well-known method, Locality-Sensitive Hashing (LSH) pioneered the hashing paradigm [1]. It projects and quantizes high-dimensional data to the binary hash code, and gains efficiency in terms of storage cost and query speed by computing the Hamming distance. Its theoretical analysis meanwhile ensures that nearest neighbors of each point are mapped to the same hash code with a high probability.

Due to the random generation of hash projections, LSH usually needs a quite large budget of hash functions to achieve desired discriminative power, which certainly brings large memory and time consumption. Many following work devote to pursuing compact hash codes in unsupervised [10,15] and supervised manner [5, 12]. Besides, there are a variety of powerful techniques to improve the compactness of hash codes like nonlinear hashing [6,9], multiple features [12, 13], multiple bits [10] and bit selection [11].

The Hamming distance ranking helps achieve compressed storage and fast computation in hash-based nearest neighbor search. However, the quantization in hashing loses the exact ranking information among the samples, and thus degenerates the discriminative power of the Hamming distance measurement. For instance, in practice there exist more than one buckets that share the same Hamming distance to the query, and subsequently samples falling in these buckets will be ranked equally using Hamming distance. To improve the ranking accuracy using Hamming distance, it is necessary to enable fine-grained ranking by alleviating the quantization loss. One of the most powerful and successful techniques is hash bit weighting, which assesses the quality of each hash bit to improve the discriminative power of the hash code. Similar to traditional visual reranking [2], such process can be efficiently performed only on the top ranked results within certain Hamming radius.

Along this direction, [8] proposed a query-adaptive Hamming distance ranking method using the learned bitwise weights for a diverse set of predefined semantic concept classes. [17] studied a query-sensitive hash code ranking algorithm (QsRank) for PCA-based hashing algorithms without compressing query points to discrete hash codes. [16] also presented a state-of-the-art weighted Hamming distance ranking algorithm (WhRank) based on the data-adaptive and query-sensitive bitwise weight. Though achieving promising performance improvement, methods like WhRank heavily rely on the assumption of data distribution (eg., Laplace dis-

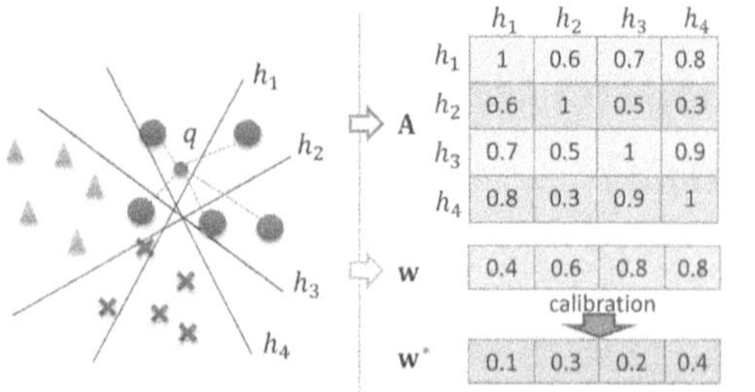

Figure 1: Demonstration of the proposed method.

tribution for spectral hashing [15]). Moreover, these methods are usually designed for projection based hashing algorithms. Therefore, they can hardly be directly applied for nonlinear hashing algorithms like spherical hashing [7] and K-means hashing [6].

In this paper, we propose a new ranking method with weighted hamming distance. By exploiting the similarity between the query and database samples, we learn a set of query-adaptive bitwise weights that characterize both the discriminative power of each hash function and their complement for nearest neighbor search. Assigning different weights to individual hash bit will distinguish the results sharing the same hamming distance, and obtain a more fine-grained and accurate ranking order. Compared to existing methods, our method is more general for different types of hashing algorithms, without strict assumptions on the data distribution. Meanwhile, it can faithfully enhance the overall discriminative power of the weighted Hamming distance.

The rest of the paper is organized as follows: The details of our approach are present in Section 2. Section 3 describes settings of our experiments and discusses the experimental results. Finally, we conclude in Section 4.

2. THE PROPOSED APPROACH

In this section, we propose the query-adaptive ranking method (named QRank) using weighted hamming distance. It utilizes the similarity relationship between the query point and its neighbors in the database to measure the overall discriminative power of the hash code, simultaneously considering both the quality of hash functions and their correlations.

2.1 Query-Adaptive Weight

Given a set of n training samples $\{x_i \in \mathbb{R}^d, i = 1, \dots, n\}$ and a set of m hash functions $H(\cdot) = \{h_1(\cdot), \dots, h_m(\cdot)\}$, each training sample x_i is encoded into hash bit $y_{ik} = h_k(x_i) \in \{-1, 1\}$ by the k-th hash function. With the hash functions and corresponding weights w, the weighted Hamming distance between any two points x_i and x_j are usually defined as $d_h(x_i, x_j) = \sum_{k=1}^{m} w_k(y_{ik} \otimes y_{jk})$.

To improve the ranking precision of the weighted distance d_h, a data-dependent and query-adaptive w_k should be learnt to characterize the overall quality of the k-th hash function in H. Intuitively, for a query point q, a hash function well preserving q's nearest neighbors NN(q) (eg., h_3 and h_4 in Figure 1) should play a more important role in the weighted Hamming distance, and thus a larger weight should be assigned to it.

Formally, for a high-quality hash function h_k, if $p \in \text{NN}(q)$, then the higher its similarity $s(p, q)$ to q, the larger the probability that $h_k(q) = h_k(p)$. Therefore, based on the neighbor preservation of each hash function, we define its weight using the spectral embedding loss [11, 15]:

$$\begin{aligned} w_k &= -\frac{1}{2} \sum_{p \in \text{NN}(q)} s(q,p) \| h_k(q) - h_k(p) \|^2 \\ &= \sum_{p \in \text{NN}(q)} s(q,p) h_k(q) h_k(p) + const. \end{aligned} \tag{1}$$

where we constrain $\sum_{p \in NN(q)} s(q,p) = 1$. Note that in the above definition the similarity can be adaptively tailored for different scenarios.

To make the weight positive and sensitive to the capability of neighbor preservation, in practice we use the following form with $\gamma > 0$:

$$w_k = \exp\left[\gamma \sum_{p \in \text{NN}(q)} s(q,p) h_k(q) h_k(p)\right]. \tag{2}$$

In the above definition, one important question is how to efficiently find the query's nearest neighbors NN(q) at the online query stage. It is infeasible to find the exact ones among the whole database. One way to speedup the computation is choosing $n_l \ll n$ landmarks to represent the database using various techniques like K-means, where the approximated nearest neighbors can be quickly discovered by linear scan. We adopt the simple way by randomly sampling n_l points as the landmarks at the offline training stage.

2.2 Weight Calibration

As Figure 1 demonstrates that hash function h_3 and h_4 shows satisfying capability of neighbor preservation for query q, but the large correlation between them indicates undesired redundancy between them. Instead, though function h_2 performs worse than h_3 and h_4, but it serves as a complement to h_4, with which they together can well preserve all neighbor relations of q. This observation motivates us to further calibrate the query-adaptive weights, taking the correlations among all hash functions into consideration.

Given any pair of hash functions h_i and h_j from H, if they behave similarly on a certain set of data points (i.e., the hash bits encoded by them are quite similar), then we can regard that the two hash functions are strongly correlated. In practice, to improve the overall discriminative power of the hash codes, uncorrelated (or independent) and high-quality hash functions should be given higher priority.

Since computing higher-order independence among hash functions is quite expensive, we approximately evaluate the independence based on the pair-wise correlations between them. Specifically, we introduce the mutual independence between hash functions based on the mutual information MI(y_i, y_j)) between the bit variables y_i and y_j generated by hash function h_i and h_j:

$$a_{ij} = \exp\left[-\lambda \text{MI}(y_i, y_j)\right], \tag{3}$$

where $\lambda > 0$ and $a_{ij} = a_{ji}$, forming a symmetrical independence matrix $A = (a_{ij})$.

Then we calibrate the query-adaptive weights w_k by reweighing it using a positive variable π_k. Namely, the new bitwise query-adaptive weight is given by

$$w_k^* = w_k \pi_k, \tag{4}$$

which should overall maximize both the neighbor preservation and the independence between hash functions. We formulate it as the following quadratic programming problem:

$$\max_{\pi} \quad \sum_{ij} w_i^* w_j^* a_{ij} \qquad (5)$$
$$s.t. \quad \mathbf{1}^T \pi = 1, \ \pi \succeq 0.$$

The above problem can be efficiently solved by a number of powerful techniques like replicator dynamics [11].

2.3 Data-Dependent Similarity

As aforementioned, the similarity between the query and database samples plays an important role in pursuing query-adaptive weights in Sec. 2.1. Since in practice data points are usually distributed on certain manifold, the standard Euclidean metric cannot strictly capture their global similarities. To obtain similarity measurement adaptive to different datasets, we adopt the anchor graph to represent any sample x by $z(x)$ based on their local neighbor relations to anchors points $\mathcal{U} = \{u_k \in \mathbb{R}^d\}_{k=1}^r$, which can be generated efficiently by clustering or sampling [10]:

$$[z(x)]_j = \begin{cases} \frac{\mathcal{K}(x,u_j)}{\sum_{u'_j \in \mathrm{NN}(x)} \mathcal{K}(x,u_{j'})}, & \text{if } u_j \in \mathrm{NN}(x) \\ 0, & \text{otherwise} \end{cases} \qquad (6)$$

where $\mathrm{NN}(x)$ denotes x's nearest anchors in $\mathcal{U}$ according to the predefined kernel function $\mathcal{K}(x, u_j)$ (e.g., Gaussian kernel). The highly sparse $z(x)$ serves as a nonlinear and discriminative feature representation, and can be used to efficiently approximate the data-dependent similarities between samples. Specifically, for query q and any point p, their similarity can be computed by

$$s(p, q) = \exp(-\|z(p) - z(q)\|^2/\sigma^2), \qquad (7)$$

where σ is set to the largest distance between $z(p)$ and $z(q)$.

2.4 Online Query

At the offline stage, both n_l sampled landmarks and r anchors can be obtained efficiently, and the landmarks can be represented using anchors in $O(n_l r)$. At the online stage, first the query feature is transformed into anchor representation and used to compute its similarities to the landmarks in $O(r+n_l)$, second the query-adaptive weights can be obtained by quadratic programming (5) in polynomial time, and finally the results are fast ranked according to the weighted hamming distances.

3. EXPERIMENTS

To evaluate the proposed query-adaptive hash code ranking method (QRank), we conduct extensive experiments on the real-world image datasets MNIST and NUS-WIDE:

MNIST: it includes 70K 784 dimensional images, each of which is associated with a digit label from '0' to '9'.

NUS-WIDE: it is one of largest real-world labeled image datasets, consisting of 270K images with 81 ground truth concept tags, and we consider 25 most frequent tags.

We compare QRank with the state-of-the-art binary codes ranking method WhRank [16] over a variety of baseline hashing algorithms including Locality Sensitive Hashing (LSH) [1], Spectral Hashing (SH) [15], Kernelized Locality-Sensitive Hashing (KLSH) [9], PCA-Hashing (PCAH) [14], Iterative Quantization (ITQ) [3], Spherical Hashing (SPH) [7], K-means Hashing (KMH) [6]. Since WhRank outperformed

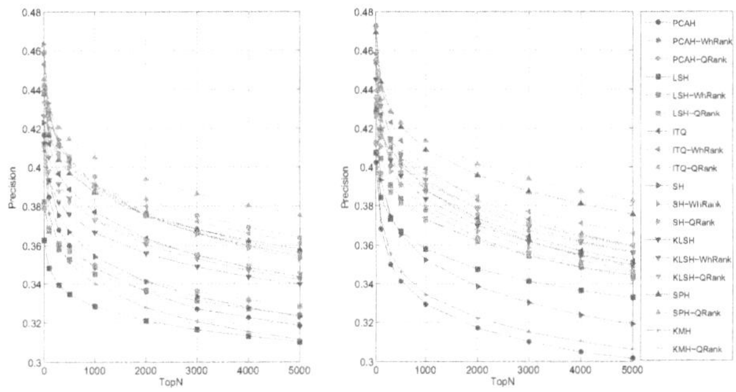

(a) Precision @ 48 bits (b) Precision @ 96 bits

Figure 3: Performances comparison on NUS-WIDE.

QsRank [17] significantly as reported in [16], we omit the direct comparison between our QRank and QsRank.

We adopt the popular performance metric including precision, recall and mean average precision (MAP) in our experiments. All results are averaged over 10 independent runs to suppress the randomness. For each run, we randomly sample 5,000 images as the training data, 3,000 as the landmarks and 1,000 as query images. The true nearest neighbors are defined as the images sharing at least one common tag.

3.1 Results and Discussions

Figure 2 shows the precision and recall curves respectively using 48 and 96 bits on MINST. We can easily find out that both hash bit weighting methods (WhRank and QRank) achieved better performances than the baseline hashing algorithms. The observation indicates that the hash code ranking based on weighted Hamming distance hopefully serves as a promising solution to boosting the performance of hash-based retrieval. In all cases, our proposed QRank consistently achieves the superior performances to WhRank over different hashing algorithms. Figure 4(a) depicts the overall performance evaluation using MAP with 96 hash bits, where we get a similar observation that QRank outperforms WhRank significantly, e.g., compared to WhRank, QRank obtains 17.11%, 11.36%, 14.06% and 11.39% performance gains respectively over LSH, ITQ, SH and KLSH.

Besides MNIST, Figure 3 and 4(b) present the precision curves and MAP on the NUS-WIDE dataset when using 48 and 96 bits. By comparing the performance of QRank with that of WhRank and baseline hashing algorithms, we get a similar conclusion as on MNIST that both QRank and WhRank can enhance the discriminative power of hash functions by weighting them elegantly, and meanwhile in all cases QRank clearly outperforms WhRank owing to its comprehensive capability of distinguishing high-quality functions.

It is worth noting that since WhRank depends on the distribution of the projected samples, it cannot be directly applied to hashing algorithms like SPH and KMH. Instead, the proposed method derives the bitwise weight only relying on the data-dependent similarity. Therefore, it can not only capture the neighbor relations of the query, but also possess universality suiting for all hashing algorithms. Figure 2-4 show that QRank obtains significant performance gains over SPH and KMH in all cases.

We investigate the effect of different parts of QRank in Table 1 by comparing the performance of QRank with or without the weight calibration (named QRank$^-$). The results are reported over LSH, SH, PCAH and ITQ respectively using 96 bits on MNIST. It is obvious that QRank$^-$

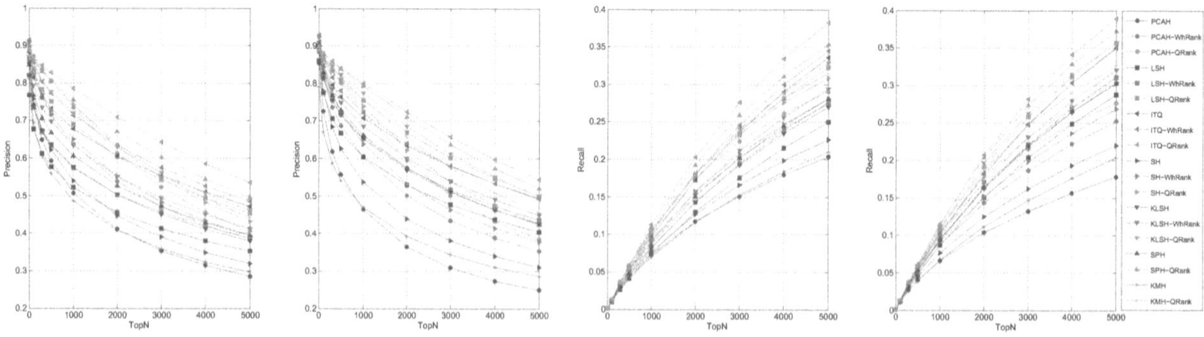

(a) Precision @ 48 bits (b) Precision @ 96 bits (c) Recall @ 48 bits (d) Recall @ 96 bits

Figure 2: Performances comparison on MNIST.

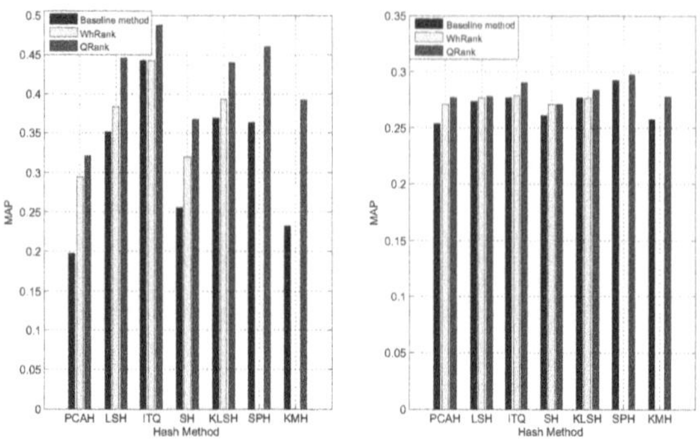

(a) MNIST @ 96 bits (b) NUS-WIDE @ 96 bits

Figure 4: MAP (%) on MNIST and NUS-WIDE.

Table 1: MAP (%) of different parts of QRank on MNIST

Ranking Method	LSH	SH	PCAH	ITQ
Baseline	35.53	25.91	19.87	44.14
QRank$^-$	40.71	31.39	22.07	46.87
QRank	**44.77**	**37.02**	**32.32**	**49.15**

only using query-adaptive weights without considering the redundance among hash functions is able to boost the hashing performance, but QRank appended with the weight calibration can further bring significant (up to 46.44%) performance gains. This indicates that both the individual quality of each hash function and their complement are critical for fine-grained neighbor ranking.

Finally, we present the time cost of different methods in Table 2. We can see that though our QRank spends more time than WhRank on learning query-adaptive weight (50.19 ms), on the whole this part is relatively small and the online query is quite efficient in practice.

4. CONCLUSIONS

As described in this paper, we proposed a new hash code ranking method named QRank, which learns a query-adaptive bitwise weights by simultaneously considering both the individual quality of each hash function and their complement for nearest neighbor search. Compared to state-of-the-art weighting methods, QRank serves as a general solution to enabling fine-grained ranking over all kinds of hashing algorithms. Due to both the data-dependent similarity and query-adaptive weights, QRank significantly and efficiently boosts the ranking performance in practice.

Table 2: Time cost (ms) of different methods on MNIST

	Baseline Hash	WhRank	QRank
weight computing	0	1.27	50.19
distance ranking	39.18	141.15	141.15
Total time	39.18	142.42	191.34

5. ACKNOWLEDGMENTS

This work is supported in part by NSFC 61370125 and 61101250, YWF-14-JSJXY-010, NCET-12-0917, SKLSDE 2013ZX-05 and 2014ZX-07.

6. REFERENCES

[1] M. Datar, N. Immorlica, P. Indyk, and V. S. Mirrokni. Locality-sensitive hashing scheme based on p-stable distributions. In *SCG*, 2004.

[2] C. Deng, R. Ji, W. Liu, D. Tao, and X. Gao. Visual reranking through weakly supervised multi-graph learning. In *IEEE ICCV*, 2013.

[3] Y. Gong and S. Lazebnik. Iterative quantization: A procrustean approach to learning binary codes. In *IEEE CVPR*, pages 817 –824, june 2011.

[4] J. He, J. Feng, X. Liu, T. Cheng, T.-H. Lin, H. Chung, and S.-F. Chang. Mobile product search with bag of hash bits and boundary reranking. In *IEEE CVPR*, 2012.

[5] J. He, W. Liu, and S.-F. Chang. Scalable similarity search with optimized kernel hashing. In *ACM SIGKDD*, 2010.

[6] K. He, F. Wen, and J. Sun. K-means hashing: An affinity-preserving quantization method for learning binary compact codes. In *CVPR*, 2013.

[7] J. Heo, Y. Lee, J. He, S.-F. Chang, and S. Yoon. Spherical hashing. In *CVPR*, 2012.

[8] Y.-G. Jiang, J. Wang, and C. Shih-Fu. Lost in binarization: query-adaptive ranking for similar image search with compact codes. In *ACM ICMR*, 2011.

[9] B. Kulis and K. Grauman. Kernelized locality-sensitive hashing for scalable image search. In *IEEE ICCV*, 2009.

[10] W. Liu, J. Wang, S. Kumar, and S.-F. Chang. Hashing with graphs. In *ICML*, 2011.

[11] X. Liu, J. He, B. Lang, and S.-F. Chang. Hash bit selection: a unified solution for selection problems in hashing. In *IEEE CVPR*, 2013.

[12] X. Liu, J. He, D. Liu, and B. Lang. Compact kernel hashing with multiple features. In *ACM MM*, 2012.

[13] J. Song, Y. Yang, Z. Huang, H. T. Shen, and R. Hong. Multiple feature hashing for real-time large scale near-duplicate video retrieval. In *ACM MM*, 2011.

[14] J. Wang, S. Kumar, and S.-F. Chang. Semi-supervised hashing for scalable image retrieval. In *IEEE CVPR*, 2010.

[15] Y. Weiss, A. Torralba, and R. Fergus. Spectral hashing. In *NIPS*, 2008.

[16] L. Zhang, Y. Zhang, J. Tang, K. Lu, and Q. Tian. Binary code ranking with weighted hamming distance. In *CVPR*, 2013.

[17] X. Zhang, L. Zhang, and S. Heung-Yeung. Qsrank: Query-sensitive hash code ranking for efficient ϵ-neighbor search. In *CVPR*, 2012.

Systematic Assessment of the Video Recording Position for User-generated Event Videos

Stefan Wilk
Distributed Multimedia Systems
TU Darmstadt, Germany
stefan.wilk@cs.tu-darmstadt.de

Wolfgang Effelsberg
Distributed Multimedia Systems
TU Darmstadt, Germany
effelsberg@cs.tu-darmstadt.de

ABSTRACT

The increasing capabilities of mobile handhelds to record high definition videos enable us to share moments with friends and the public. In large-scale events such as concerts, the manifold of potential views recorded by the audience allows to watch an event from different perspectives. In this work, we elaborate on the effects of different recording positions on quality and show that especially with retail smart phone camera sensors the quality differs as the position changes. This is a first systematic approach to describe why user-generated video sequences differ in terms of quality depending on changing recording positions. To achieve a sound understanding, we conduct a large-scale systematic subjective study using crowdsourcing, inspecting the effect of distance and orientation of a recorder in relation to the event taking place. Our results indicate an effect of the recording position on the perceived quality of a video.

Categories and Subject Descriptors

H.5.1 [**Multimedia Information Systems**]: Evaluation/Methodology

Keywords

User-generated Video; Crowdsourcing; perspective; distance; orientation; smart phone; Video quality; QoE

1. INTRODUCTION

Sport events or music festivals motivate hundreds in the audience to save precious moments as digital video. Video sharing sites, such as YouTube, profit from the fact that those clips are uploaded and shared with the public. Many of the recorded video clips show the same scene but recorded from different positions. The question thus arises in what ways the recording position affects the perceived quality for a potential watcher. The knowledge about its relation to the quality can help to tune recommender systems of video sharing sites. In addition, video mashup systems, which allow to automatically direct a video mix from different recording cameras, and the recording users could benefit from this knowledge.

This work elaborates on different positions and angles for recording an event. To conduct an in-depth empirical analysis on the effect of the position on the perceived quality, we had to record several sequences in the genres sports, entertainment and scenery from different positions at the same time. We have conducted experiments on a crowdsourcing mediating platform and validated results in a lab setting. The sequences were evaluated by 451 assessors.

Video quality can be determined using objective video quality metrics. Especially full-reference methods such as VQM by Pinson [3] result in values with high correlation to the subjectively perceived quality. But at the same time they require high processing times. No-reference methods exist that enable real-time computation, e.g. Yang's approach [4], but with reduced precision. However, none of these metrics so far can estimate the effect of different positions in the recording phase of a video creation process as they were designed to identify compression and network artifacts. Crowdsourcing is a new technique in multimedia research that allows us to perform a large-scale, subjective user study at low cost. Crowdsourcing is based on the design of small and well-defined tasks that can be completed in minutes. These tasks are provisioned to an anonymous group of people using a mediating platform. In contrast to regular subjective lab tests the evaluation can be easily distributed to a less biased and at the same time larger group of users. This advantage comes with the drawback of anonymous assessors conducting the tests in a remote location with reduced control of the test settings. Properties and best practices for conducting video quality assessments using the crowd are well described in the work of Hossfeld [1].

The contribution of this work is the systematic evaluation of recording positions on the perceived quality in different live performances. Our work illustrates a significant negative impact of a increasing distance to the recorded live performance, whereas differing recording angles show no significant differences.

2. APPROACH

This section discusses the setup of our crowdsourced video quality assessment to evaluate the effects of different positions while recording a scene in video. In a first step, different video sequences had to be recorded in order to create

MM'14, November 3–7, 2014, Orlando, Florida, USA.
Copyright 2014 ACM 978-1-4503-3063-3/14/11 ...$15.00.
http://dx.doi.org/10.1145/2647868.2655022.

a dataset that contains enough material to be evaluated on large-scale. The qualitative assessment is based on crowdsourcing using a web-based evaluation system. Our crowdsourcing experiment asks different unknown users, in the following called assessors, to watch multiple video sequences of the same event. The task of the assessor is to judge on the perceived video quality of each sequence using the Single Stimulus Continuous Quality Scale (SSCQS) recommended by the ITU [2]. Tasks are clustered in so called campaigns. Each campaign represents a distinct set of video sequences from one of the genres: 'sports', 'entertainment' or 'scenery'. Each scene is recorded from different distances and angles which resulted in 8 evaluated events in 79 sequences. The sequence order has been chosen randomly for each assessor which in combination with the large number of assessors reduces the effect of biasing the subjective ratings by a fixed viewing order. In total 451 assessors assessed the sequences which resulted in 3160 ratings. The video clips are evaluated in regard of the distance to the event and the angle. Zero degree represents a frontal view to e.g. the stage as depicted in Figure 1. Only valid angles and distances were chosen

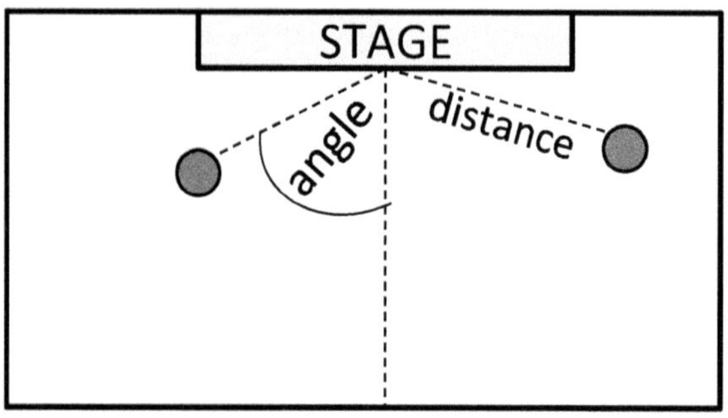

Figure 1: Illustration on measured attributes of a position: distance and angle

depending on the genre of the recorded event. This means e.g. for recording a concert far beyond one hundred meters will not result in a sensible recording quality using standard smart phones. These clips have been discarded. Another example is a 'scenery' sequence such as the Eiffel tower in Paris for which distances of several hundred meters will result in good video quality. Those sequences are included in the dataset. Thus, we cluster the distance into: close-up, medium, medium-long and long shot. In addition, we list for each scenario the distances that are associated with the different category levels. The angles of the orientations are measured in 10 degree steps from the origin with 0 to 90 degrees. The assumption is that beyond the 90 degrees angle no sensible recording can be created. In those cases, harmful occlusions occur due to the setup of a classical, proscenium show stage. For central staging, e.g. in a stadium an rectangular stage was assumed and each side is evaluated on its own.

The videos that were basis for this evaluation were recorded during sports events (a soccer game and motor sports) different entertainment events such as concerts or shows, and points of interest in different cities ('scenery'). Entertainment and sports videos have been recorded during live performances in Darmstadt and Frankfurt, Germany. Entertainment videos include a circus comedy event (Entertainment 1), an artistic performance including rapid movements due to jumps (Entertainment 2) and a music concert with a crowded audience. Sports events recorded include a soccer game (Sport 2) and a motorbike competition including jumps. All recordings show the same region of interest, but with different level of detail. Scenery sequences have been taken in Paris, France showing the Eiffel tower in different views (Scenery 1) and in Darmstadt, Germany of a historic building (Scenery 2) and representative statues (Scenery 3). Table 1 lists the recorded events and the preferred recording distances.

All video sequences have a duration between 9 and 12 seconds. The audio tracks are removed from the videos. The video sequences are lossy compressed during recording and have a resolution of 4CIF. The camera has been set up to ensure low quantization rates during encoding. Lossy encoded videos are used as those are predominantly used in UGV. For the crowdsourcing as well as the lab tests we ensure that the video clips could be played continuously without stalling. Examples of the videos are shown in Figure 2.

The lab experiment was conducted with 15 test subjects based on the recommendations of the ITU [2]. This included a random selection of test subjects, a test for viewing impairments of the subjects, proper lighting conditions, room and technical settings. A training session in the lab setting and a qualification test in the crowdsourcing group have been held but no data from the training session or qualification test is used in our final results. Subjective quality assessments but especially crowdsourced evaluations suffer from the lack of reliability of the assessors. A data cleaning step based on the recommendation of the ITU [2] has been conducted. In addition, the valid ratings received from the assessors may show very biased results as many assessors tend to rate in the lower regions of our 5-point SSCQS scale, whereas others will more likely give high scores. To compensate this issue we normalized the gathered ratings. Normalization of the ratings calculates the value r'_{ij} of a assessor i and video j from the original rating r_{ij} corrected by an adjustment of the mean rating of an assessor $\overline{r_i}$ by the mean of the campaign $\overline{r}$, where each campaign represents one recorded event with several sequences.

$$r'_{ij} = r_{ij} - (\overline{r_i} - \overline{r}) \quad (1)$$

All ratings are aggregated to the Mean Opinion Score (MOS) by:

$$MOS_j = r_j = \frac{\sum_{i=1}^{N} r'_{ij}}{N} \quad (2)$$

3. RESULTS

The results describe the distance to a recorded event as well as the angle under which it was recorded.

3.1 Impact of the Distance

The impact of distance to the observed event may be one of the major factors for decreased visibility and thus reduced quality. Figure 3 shows the distribution of the perceived quality for varying distances using the same orientation. It shows that the distance has an observable effect for different recordings.

For the 'entertainment' genre, in this case a concert, our results indicate that the close-ups are seen as a preferable shot type for short music recordings. In this case close-up means, that a limited part of the stage is shown, and the fo-

Sports 2 Entertainment 3 Entertainment 1

Figure 2: Impressions of our video dataset used to evaluate the perceived quality based on the recording position.

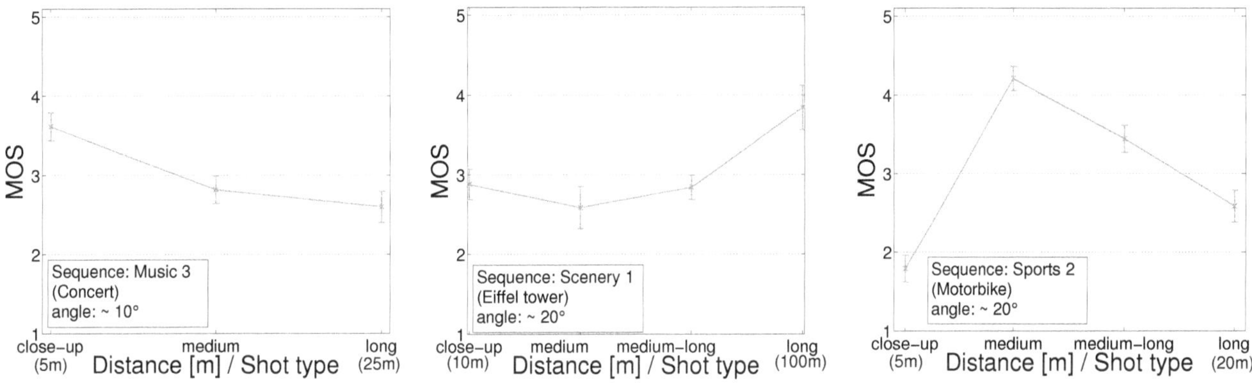

(1) Entertainment 3 - Concert (2) Scenery 1 - Eiffel tower (3) Sport 2 - Motorbike

Figure 3: Perceived quality of recordings from different distances with the same orientation for (left) Entertainment 1, (center) Scenery 1 and (right) Sports 2.

cus lies on the main performer, omitting the assisting band. The video was recorded only some meters away from the stage, not using any internal software-assisted zoom functionality of the camera. From the close-up to more distant shot types only a minor quality degradation can be observed (see Figure 3 - left). Distances from 5 up to 30 meters are preferred in stage performances. For the entertainment genre it can be observed that close-ups and medium shots or in general: close distances to the stage - result in best qualities. Distances beyond 30 meters lead to a significant drop in perceived quality due to the evaluated frame size of the videos and the technical limitations of smart phone camera sensors.

In addition, the assessors were asked to annotate the Region of Interest (RoI). Although the annotated RoI in most cases showed a significantly larger region of the scene, the sub-region building the close-up was preferred in the concert clips. A more significant drop of the perceived quality was observed for the sequences in the genres 'Scenery' as well as 'Sports'. In case of the 'Scenery' sequences, e.g. sequence 'Scenery 1' (see Figure 3 - center) the perceived quality increases with the distance at least until the point when the whole RoI can be seen in the sequence. It seems that scenery recordings include a wider border region around the RoI in comparison to the entertainment sequences, which indicates that the viewers are more interested in the surroundings of the point of interest. For the sports recordings the medium shots show the main actor, e.g., the soccer player leading the ball or the motorbike rider performing stunts. This distance is preferred in comparison to close-ups or far distant overview shots. This indicates that a preferred shot type for our user-generated sport clips is recorded in a medium shot distance, allowing a combination of overview as well as close connection to the central actions in the game. The figure as well as the evaluations of the other sequences (see Table 1) allow us to conclude that a sweet spot for a distance can be determined depending on the genre of the video. Within the genres, the specific event recorded shows only small deviations for the preferred shot type.

Table 1: Description of the different events evaluated in the experiments.

Event	Content	Preferred shot
Entertainment 1	Circus show	medium (15 m)
Entertainment 2	Artistic show	medium (15 m)
Entertainment 3	Concert	close (5 m)
Scenery 1	Eiffel tower	long (100 m)
Scenery 2	Historic building	long (60 m)
Scenery 3	Statue	medium (17 m)
Sports 1	Soccer	medium (15 m)
Sports 2	Motorbike	medium (11 m)

3.2 Impact of Recording Angle

The orientation, i.e., from which angle a scene is recorded, builds the second factor we evaluated in this work. The perceived quality represents similar quality levels in all genres for angles between 0 and 70 degrees. Significant differences in the perceived quality may result from some little differences

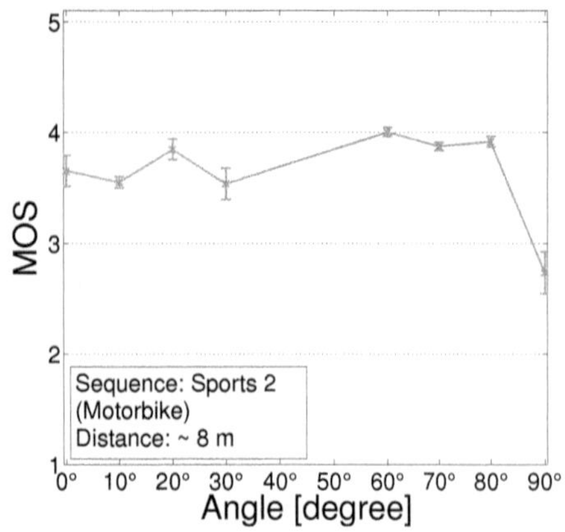

Figure 4: Perceived quality in different orientations for the observed scene 'Sports 1'

Table 2: Correlation of the MOS between crowdsourcing and lab experiments.

Genre	Pearson	Spearman
Music	0.7137	0.7692
Show	0.9854	1
Scenery	0.9375	0.8571

in the recordings that cannot be avoided in non-synthetical data. In extreme cases, especially with 80 to 90 degrees or more, it can be observed that the quality drops significantly (see Figure 4). We conclude that approaches for identification of the orientation of a recording in relation to the observed event should limit their effort on the identification of extreme angles as they may limit the perceived quality. In contrast to that, our results indicate that videos recorded at angles common in events with clear separation of stage and audience areas can result in good to excellent quality. Similar results were found in other genres which indicate that the orientation, at least in non-professional recordings is not as important as other factors. In future work, we will elaborate on the effect of orientations of different recordings in long-running sequences of several minutes. Our expectation is that the importance of diversity in long-running videos will boost the effect of different orientations.

4. CORRELATION

Although the reliability of our workers is ensured in our crowdsourced evaluation applying the methods mentioned in Section 2, we still had to ensure that the ratings retrieved in a remote, uncontrolled setting correlate with controlled lab settings. A lab test based on ITU-R BT.500-13 [2] with 15 test subjects was conducted for the sequences in the three genres. For the purpose of demonstrating a correlation the Pearson's R coefficient as well as the Spearman Rank was chosen. The Pearson's coefficient calculates how much the points scatter around a linear trend, whereas the Spearman Rank shows whether a monotonic function can describe the relationship of the crowd and the lab datasets. In Table 2 the Pearson's coefficient as well as the Spearman Rank for the different video groups can be retrieved.

Especially for the genres 'Sports' and 'Scenery' a high correlation between the perceived quality in the remote crowdsourced experiments can be observed. The 'Entertainment' sequences show slightly differing results especially for the reduced quality for increasing distances. In comparison to the crowdsourced tests increasing distances are perceived degrading the quality significantly more. Due to the low number of lab participants, we believe the crowdsourced results to be more reliable.

5. CONCLUSION

Mobile handhelds capable of recording video allow all of us to share experiences during events such as concerts or sport games with the world. On video sharing sites, multiple videos of the same event are uploaded. Visitors of such sites do not know the quality of the recordings. Many different attributes affect the quality of such a video clip. One of them is the recording position. This work describes the impact of video recording positions on the perceived quality in UGV. It is the first systematic crowdsourced, subjective analysis of the impact of different positions on the perceived quality in user-generated video. The results indicate a strong influence of the distance on the perceived quality. In contrast to this, the orientation seems to have a limited impact on sequences recorded by non-professionals. Additionally, we show that the preferred view differs depending on the recorded scene and event. By using the results of this work, recommender systems for video sharing sites can be designed in a more efficient way - ranking the results of a search depending on the recording position. Our next step includes the investigation whether these findings in combination with position data gathered from smart phone sensors can be used to perform optimal view selection for video summary and video mashup algorithms.

Acknowledgments

This work has been funded by the German Research Foundation (DFG) in the Collaborative Research Center (SFB) 1053 'MAKI: Multi-Mechanism-Adaptation for the Future Internet'.

6. REFERENCES

[1] T. Hossfeld, C. Keimel, M. Hirth, B. Gardlo, J. Habigt, K. Diepold, and P. Tran-Gia. Best practices for QoE Crowdtesting: QoE assessment with Crowdsourcing. *IEEE Transactions on Multimedia*, 16:541–558, 2014.

[2] ITU-R. BT.500: Methodology for the subjective assessment of the quality of television pictures (ITU-R BT.500-13). Technical report, International Telcommunications Union, 2012.

[3] M. Pinson and S. Wolf. A new standardized method for objectively measuring video quality. *IEEE Transactions on Broadcasting*, 50(3):312–322, 2004.

[4] F. Yang, S. Wan, Y. Chang, and H. Wu. A novel objective no-reference metric for digital video quality assessment. *IEEE Signal Processing Letters*, 12(10):685–688, 2005.

BAP: Bimodal Attribute Prediction for Zero-Shot Image Categorization

Hanhui Li Donghui Li Xiaonan Luo

National Engineering Research Center of Digital Life, State-Province Joint Laboratory of Digital Home Interactive Applications, School of Information Science & Technology, Sun Yat-sen University, China

Research Institute of Sun Yat-sen University in Shenzhen, China

lnslxn@mail.sysu.edu.cn

ABSTRACT

Recent advances in attribute-based methods provide the zero-shot learning problem with practical solutions. In attribute-based methods, visual attributes are introduced to fill the gap between low-level image features and high-level semantic information. This paper proposes a novel bimodal attribute prediction model called BAP, which can better predict visual attributes in images. BAP fuses advantages of the conventional direct attribute prediction (DAP) and indirect attribute prediction (IAP) on the level of attribute prediction. It contains an attribute-classifier pooling process that generates a large amount of base classifiers and a combination strategy that integrates these classifiers. We explore and propose four BAP models with different combination strategies in this paper, and experimentally show that our BAP outperforms the conventional models both in offline and online zero-shot image categorization.

Categories and Subject Descriptors

H.3 [**INFORMATION STORAGE AND RETRIEVAL**]: [Content Analysis and Indexing]

General Terms

Algorithms, Experimentation

Keywords

Zero-shot Learning; Attribute Prediction; Image Categorization

1. INTRODUCTION

Describing images by visual attributes draws much attention recently, since attributes can act as a bridge between low-level image features and high-level object classes [1]. Attribute-based methods offer a practical solution to the so called zero-shot learning problem [2], which is trying to classify images into categories with no training examples of these categories offered. The original attribute-based solutions proposed by Lampert et al.[5] can be divided into two classes, the direct attribute prediction (DAP) model and the indirect attribute prediction (IAP) model. Each of these models has its own advantages and disadvantages: DAP is dependent on attribute, and has higher accuracy [5, 2], but is lack of flexibility while IAP is just the opposite. Although there is extensive research on attribute-based methods, we notice that most of the existing research pursues its improvement *within* the framework of either the DAP or IAP. However, *how to fuse the advantages of both models to get an accurate and flexible model* is still a challenging problem, and we believe that this problem is worth studying for the following reasons:

Effectiveness. Each of the two models has its own set of attributes that it has a better performance on. Hence, it's reasonable that combining these two models together in a proper way will give us a better result.

Efficiency. Considering the problem of online incremental zero-shot learning that the number of categories increases incrementally, the retraining time cost of DAP can be huge because it needs much more attributes to distinguish classes while that of IAP is small because we just need to train classifiers for the new categories. But remember that the accuracy of DAP is higher than that of IAP, it is quite practical if we can combine some classifiers trained from DAP with the IAP model to reduce the retraining time cost while maintaining the same accuracy as DAP.

A lot of research has been carried out since the attribute-based method was proposed. Wang et al.[8] introduced a discriminative latent model that applied the latent SVM framework. They treated visual attributes as the latent variables, which is similar to DAP but not applicable for zero-shot learning. Li et al.[6] applied this model into recommendation system and built up a novel occasion-oriented clothing recommendation system called "Magic Closet". Kovashka et al.[3] proposed a relative attribute ranking method to search images. Yahong et al.[1] constructed a graph structure that allowed learning correlations between attributes via a structured multi-task regression optimization. Pichai et al.[2] used an self-organizing and incremental network, which can be considered as a clustering method, to reduce the training time of both two models remarkably. Naman et al.[7] explored the dominance of attributes, which is a measure of how likely an attribute stands out when we look at an image. All these advanced methods or applications are still in the framework of either DAP or IAP, hence our problem is unsolved yet.

We propose our bimodal attribute prediction (BAP) for zero-shot learning in this paper. Our BAP is composed of

MM'14, November 3–7, 2014, Orlando, Florida, USA.

http://dx.doi.org/10.1145/2647868.2655023.

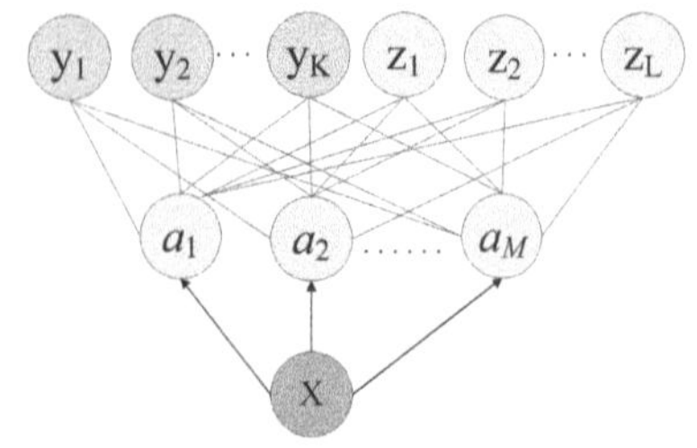

(a) DAP

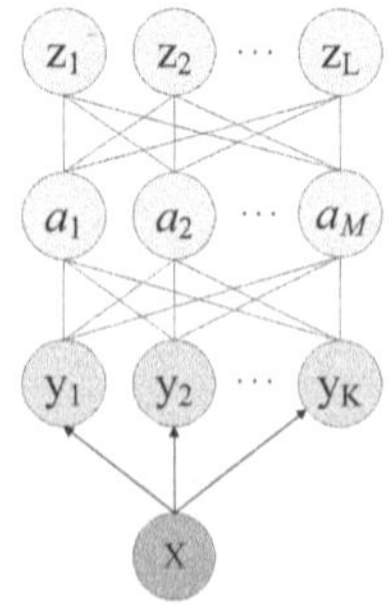

(b) IAP

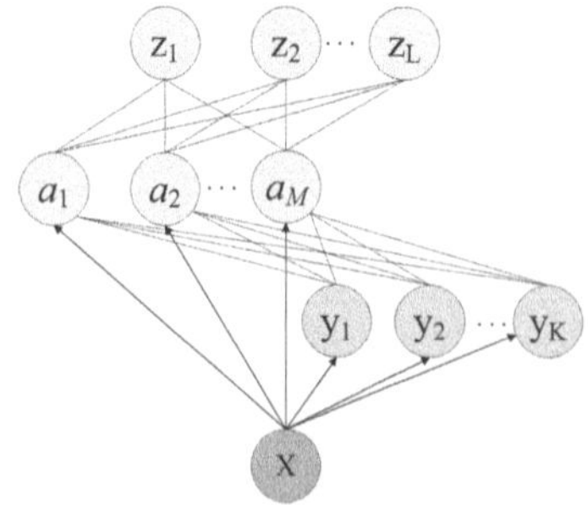

(c) BAP

Figure 1: Graphical representations of the DAP, IAP and our BAP model. The DAP and IAP are combined on the attribute prediction level in our BAP model.

a pooling of attribute classifiers and a corresponding combination strategy. The main contributions of this paper are threefold. Firstly, Our BAP combines DAP and IAP on an attribute prediction level, allowing adding various attribute prediction models without much modification. Secondly, we propose four combination strategies and experimental evaluation shows that each combined model outperforms DAP or IAP. Lastly, our BAP model is suitable for zero-shot learning in either online mode or offline mode, and maintains better performances than those of conventional models.

2. PRELIMINARY

In this section we briefly review the zero-shot object categorization problem and the attribute-based solution introduced by Lampert et al.[5].

Zero-shot object categorization: Let X be an arbitrary feature space of images, $Y = y_1, ...y_K$ be a set of K classes, $Z = z_1, ...z_L$ be a set of L classes and $Y \cap Z = \emptyset$. The task is to train a classifier $f : X \to Z$, from N given training examples $(x_1, l_1), ..., (x_N, l_N) \subset X \times Y$.

Attribute-based solution: The key idea of attribute-based solution to this problem is to introduce attributes as an intermediate layer between images and classes. In more detail, the attribute-based solution first represents all the classes with M binary attributes, i.e., for a training class y, we denote it as $y = a^y = (a_1^y, ...a_M^y)$, for any $m \in 1...M, a_m^y = 1$ if class y has the m-th attribute and it is 0 otherwise. Then the posterior probability of a given image x belonging to test class z is calculated in the following way:

$$p(z|x) = \sum_{a \in \{0,1\}^M} p(z|a)p(a|x) = \frac{p(z)}{p(a^z)} \prod_{m=1}^{M} p(a_m^z|x) \quad (1)$$

$p(z)$ is the test class prior probability and $p(a^z)$ is the attribute prior probability, both of them are independent from the specific input images, so we just need to focus on $p(a_m^z|x)$, which is the probability that the truth value of m-th attribute inferred from x is equal to that of class z. As mentioned before, methods estimating $p(a_m^z|x)$ can be divided into two models: DAP and IAP. The DAP model learns a classifier for each attribute then uses it directly to estimate $p(a_m^z|x)$. The IAP model first learns a classifier for each class in the training set to obtain $p(y_k|x), k = 1, ..., K$, which is the probability of x belonging to class y_k, then $p(a_m^z|x)$ is calculated by $p(a_m^z|x) = \sum_{k=1}^{K} p(a_m^z|y_k)p(y_k|x)$, where $p(a_m^z|y_k) = [[a_m^z == a_m^y]]$ and $[[]]$ is the Iverson bracket. Figure 1(a) and 1(b) show the models of DAP and IAP respectively.

3. BIMODAL ATTRIBUTE PREDICTION

Since the effects of attribute-based methods depend on $p(a_m^z|x)$, and both of DAP and IAP are trying to estimate it precisely, problem that how to get a better model may be solved via combining the estimations. What's more, combination on this level allows applying new basic models into our framework without too much modification. Hence, we consider it as a multiple classifiers ensemble problem in machine learning and propose our BAP model. Our model is composed of two parts: attribute-classifier pooling and combination strategies. The attribute-classifier pooling part will generate thousands of base classifiers, and then the output of these base classifiers will be integrated by adopting one of the combination strategies. We propose four different combination strategies here, including soft voting, decision template, top-k stacking and dynamic classifier selection. The graphical representation of our BAP model is showed in Figure 1(c).

3.1 Attribute-Classifier Pooling

The purpose of attribute-classifier pooling is to generate enough base classifiers for combination. Instead of training only one classifier for each attribute (class) like the DAP (IAP) model, we train N_c classifiers by adopting the idea of bagging [9]: for each attribute (class), we collect N_c training subsets by sampling from the original training set with replacement. Each training subset contains N_s positive and negative samples and N_s is set to a much smaller value than the number of instances in the original training set. Then we learn a Support Vector Machine (SVM) for each training subset, therefore we get a total of $N_c \times (K + M)$ classifiers. And remember that in the IAP model, we use the output of K class classifiers to predict the presence of an attribute, so for each attribute we can get $2 \cdot N_c$ estimations. For convenience sake, we do not consider the estimations come from DAP or IAP, so we refer N_c as $2 \cdot N_c$ throughout the rest of this paper. Our attribute-classifier pooling has advantages in two main aspects: On the one hand, pooling helps to increase the diversity of base classifiers, since they are learnt on different subsets. On the other hand, for stable classifiers like SVM, their accuracy will not change much if there are enough training samples, so selecting a small but adequate subset will help to reduce time cost and the time cost can be further reduced by parallel computing. We also sample N_v instances from the original training set to generate a validation set. This validation set will be used to measure the accuracy of base classifiers. Also, for the purpose of avoiding the risk of overfitting [9], this validation set will be used as a training set for some combination strategies, i.e., combination via meta-learning.

3.2 Combination strategies

Let $p_{ij}(x), i = 1, ..., M, j = 1, ..., N_c$ be the j-th estimation of probability that the i-th attribute appears in image x and

$H_i(x)$ be the combined prediction of the i-th attribute. Here we introduce four combination strategies to calculate $H_i(x)$.

3.2.1 Soft Voting

Soft voting is an intuitional choice for combination due to its concise implementation, and is the only combination strategy that can be used without extra learning process among our four combination strategies. It is a variation of majority voting and its combined output is,

$$H_i(x) = \sum_{j=1}^{N_c} w_{ij} p_{ij}(x), \qquad w_{ij}(x) = \frac{acc_{ij}}{\sum_{j=1}^{N_c} acc_{ij}} \tag{2}$$

where $w_{ij}(x)$ is the weight of the j-th estimation of i-th attribute. This combination strategy will give higher weight to the strong classifiers.

3.2.2 Decision Template

We extend the decision template method proposed in [4] by incorporating nearest neigbours algorithm. Firstly, a decision profile is built for each attribute as the following matrix by using the validation set:

$$DT_i = \begin{bmatrix} p_{i1}(x_1), p_{i2}(x_1), \ldots, p_{iN_c}(x_1) \\ p_{i1}(x_2), p_{i2}(x_2), \ldots, p_{iN_c}(x_2) \\ \vdots \\ p_{i1}(x_{N_v}), p_{i2}(x_{N_v}), \ldots, p_{iN_c}(x_{N_v}) \end{bmatrix} = \begin{bmatrix} a_i(x_1) \\ a_i(x_2) \\ \vdots \\ a_i(x_{N_v}) \end{bmatrix} \tag{3}$$

where $i = 1,\ldots,M$ and $a_i(x_j), j = 1, \ldots, N_v$ is called the crisp decision, which is a binary variable that is equal to 1 if the i-th attribute presents in the j-th validation sample and it is 0 otherwise. Then we define two center decision templates, the 1-center and the 0-center, by finding center of instances whose crisp decisions are equal to 1 and 0 respectively. And at the testing stage, for every instance in the test set, we convert it into a profile representation, that is $x = (p_{i1}(x), p_{i2}(x), \ldots, p_{iN_c}(x))$, then instead of setting its crisp decision as that of the nearest center in [4], we use the k-nearest neighbors (kNN) algorithm to find out its k_{DT} nearest neighbors in the decision profile. And for each neighbor, we set its crisp decision as its own nearest center. Finally, the output of $H_i(x)$ can be calculated by using a majority voting of these neighbors' crisp decisions.

3.2.3 Top-k Stacking

Stacking is a meta-learning method that uses the output of base classifiers as features to train a new classifier. However, in our experiment, we find that if we just combine weak base classifiers simply in this way, the experiment results are worse than those of the DAP model and IAP model. So we propose our Top-k stacking method, which is a stacking method with feature selection. In more detail, for each attribute, we sort classifiers in the attribute-classifier pool by accuracy and select the top k_{TS} classifiers as the candidate base classifiers. Then we define our combined prediction as

$$H_i(x) = \sum_{j=1}^{k_{TS}} w_{ij} p_{ij}(x) + b_i \tag{4}$$

where w_{ij} is the weight and b_i is the bias term. We calculate these parameters via solving the following optimization problem:

$$\min \sum_{v=1}^{N_v} \left(\sum_{j=1}^{k_{TS}} w_{ij} p_{ij}(x_v) + b_i - a_i(x_v)\right)^2 \tag{5}$$

In our experiment, we solve (5) by the support vector regression. Finally, we perform a non-maximal suppression to further improve the accuracy. That is, we evaluate our combined model on the validation set, if the accuracy of the combined prediction is lower than that of the DAP model or the IAP model, we will select models with the highest accuracy, and calculate the mean of these models' estimation values as the output of our combined model.

3.2.4 Dynamic Classifier Selection

Unlike the above three combination strategies, the dynamic classifier selection method aims to select the best classifier for each instance in the test set. Here we also propose a dynamic grouping classifiers selection method which tries to find a group of classifiers instead of just the best one. Our method splits classifiers in the attribute-classifier pool into several groups based on their accuracy and estimation values of each instance, that is, given an instance x, we define the distance $d(c_j, c_{j'}, x)$ between two classifier c_j and $c_{j'}$ as

$$d(c_j, c_{j'}, x) = \lambda(p_{ij}(x) - p_{ij'}(x))^2 + (1-\lambda)(acc_{ij} - acc_{ij'})^2 \tag{6}$$

where $j = 1, \ldots, N_c, j' = 1, \ldots, N_c$ and λ is an empirical constant. The first term in (6) measures difference between the estimations of the two classifiers, while the second term measures difference of their accuracy on the validation set. Under this definition, classifiers that have similar performances will be grouped together. Based on our defined distance, we then perform the k-means clustering algorithm to assign all the classifiers into k_{DCS} groups and select the group with the highest mean accuracy. Finally, we perform soft voting among the selected group to get the estimation.

4. EXPERIMENTAL EVALUATION

We evaluate our BAP model on the Animals with Attributes dataset collected by Lampert et al.[3], which contains 50 animal classes, 85 attributes and 30475 images. We use the default train/test split that selects 40 classes as the training set and the rest 10 classes as the test set. And the pre-extracted features are used to guarantee a fair comparison. Our experiment contains the offline and online parts. For the offline part, we train the proposed BAP model with all the attribute classifiers of DAP and IAP. Because the set of attribute is fixed, so we don't have to consider the retraining time cost of DAP or IAP. For the online part, we simulate the process of incremental zero-shot learning by randomly selecting several attribute classifiers of DAP and combine them with all classifiers of IAP. Reason for doing so is that we want to reuse classifiers of DAP as many as possible, instead of retraining the whole of them to get a DAP model. And training new classifiers to update IAP is necessary because it is a guarantee of covering the attributes domain.

For each attribute, we train $N_c = 100$ classifiers and each classifier is trained on $N_s = 100$ instances. Using this scale, time for training a single classifier on a laptop (CPU: 3.4 GHz) is less than 10 seconds. We also select a validation set with $N_v = 3000$ instances from the training set. Other parameters in BAP are set as $K_{DT} = 24$, $K_{TS} = 77$, $\lambda = 0.5$, $K_{DCS} = 10$.

Most of the models we evaluated here use the maximum a posteriori probability (MAP) estimation to infer the category of a given image except the BAP model with decision template, whose output is binary. In this case, we will use the Hamming distance to calculate the similarity between a given image's attribute-based representation and that of a test class. We also implement DAP and IAP with Hamming distance and consider them as the baselines.

Table 1. shows the mean offline accuracy of the DAP, IAP and our BAP model, including soft voting (SV), deci-

	DAP-H	IAP-H	DAP	IAP	SV	DT	TS	DCS
Accuracy	27.58%	28.99%	31.61%	30.88%	33.15%	**29.01%**	34.69%	33.23%

Table 1: Performance evaluation of the proposed BAP model against DAP and IAP in offline mode. Accuracy is measured by precision here.

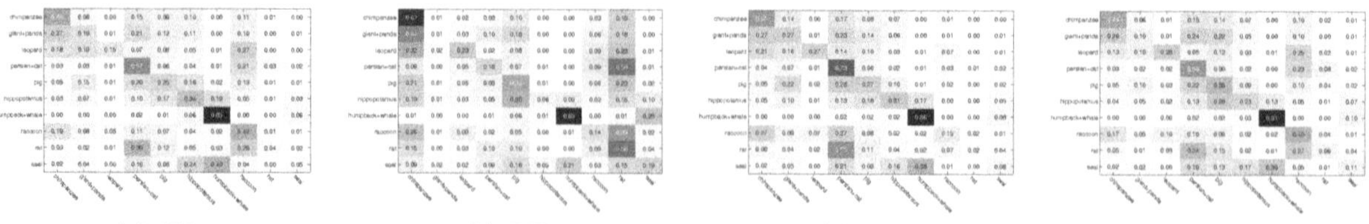

(a) SV (b) DT (c) TS (d) DCS

Figure 2: Confusion matrices between 10 test classes predicted by offline BAP.

sion template (DT), top-k stacking (TS) and dynamic classifier selection (DCS). And the accuracy can be calculated by the mean of diagonal of the confusion matrices showed in Figure 2. It is easy to see that all the combined methods outperform the conventional methods except DT. Although DT is worse than the conventional methods using maximal posterior probability, it is better than those with Hamming distance. This is mainly because of information lost during the transformation from probability value to binary value in attribute prediction. However, since the goal of our BAP is to generate a new model which is better than all the base models (DAP-H and IAP-H), we can still consider DT as a successful combination strategy.

As to the online zero-shot problem, we also evaluate our BAP model by adding attribute classifiers of DAP incrementally into the attribute-classifier pool. The experiment results are showed in Figure 3. Note that though all the BAP models have better performances than that of the I-AP model, their stabilities are quite different. SV and DCS maintain stable performances while the performance of DT is proportional to the number of classifiers added into the pool. And TS is the most unstable model that a certain oscillation appears on the accuracy curve. This phenomenon can be explained by using the idea of attribute dominance [7]. That is, remember that the attributes we added are selected randomly, then we do not know whether it is easy to distinguish them or not. Hence, the performance of TS will be lowered if we introduce some extra "hard" attributes.

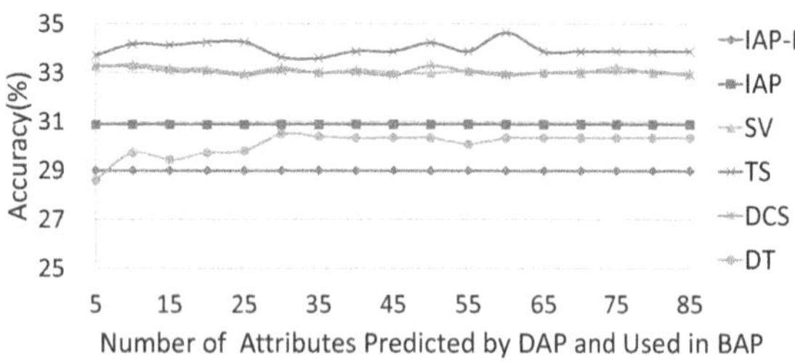

Figure 3: Accuracy of BAP in online mode. The horizontal axis represents the number of attributes that predicted by DAP and then used in BAP.

5. CONCLUSIONS

In this paper we try to fuse the advantages of the conventional DAP and IAP model to generate a better prediction of presence of attributes. A two steps bimodal method called BAP is proposed. And we propose four combination strategies used in BAP, including soft voting, decision template, top-k stacking and dynamic classifier selection to combine predictions from different models. It is demonstrated that the proposed BAP can boost the performances of attribute-based methods for zero-shot image classification, both in offline and online situations.

6. ACKNOWLEDGEMENTS

This research is supported by the National Natural Science Foundation of China (61320106008), NSFC-Guangdong Joint Fund (No. U1135003), Science and Technology Planning Project of Guangdong Province (2012B050300013), and Projects for International Cooperation of Guangzhou (No. 2013J4500004). Xiaonan Luo is the corresponding author.

7. REFERENCES

[1] Y. Han, F. Wu, X. Lu, Q. Tian, Y. Zhuang, and J. Luo. Correlated attribute transfer with multi-task graph-guided fusion. In *Proceedings of the 20th ACM international conference on Multimedia*, pages 529–538. ACM, 2012.

[2] P. Kankuekul, A. Kawewong, S. Tangruamsub, and O. Hasegawa. Online incremental attribute-based zero-shot learning. In *Computer Vision and Pattern Recognition (CVPR), 2012 IEEE Conference on*, pages 3657–3664. IEEE, 2012.

[3] A. Kovashka, D. Parikh, and K. Grauman. Whittlesearch: Image search with relative attribute feedback. In *Computer Vision and Pattern Recognition (CVPR), 2012 IEEE Conference on*, pages 2973–2980. IEEE, 2012.

[4] L. I. Kuncheva, J. C. Bezdek, and R. P. Duin. Decision templates for multiple classifier fusion: an experimental comparison. *Pattern Recognition*, 34(2):299–314, 2001.

[5] C. H. Lampert, H. Nickisch, and S. Harmeling. Learning to detect unseen object classes by between-class attribute transfer. In *Computer Vision and Pattern Recognition, 2009. CVPR 2009. IEEE Conference on*, pages 951–958. IEEE, 2009.

[6] S. Liu, J. Feng, Z. Song, T. Zhang, H. Lu, C. Xu, and S. Yan. Hi, magic closet, tell me what to wear! In *Proceedings of the 20th ACM international conference on Multimedia*, pages 619–628. ACM, 2012.

[7] N. Turakhia and D. Parikh. Attribute dominance: What pops out. ICCV, 2013.

[8] Y. Wang and G. Mori. A discriminative latent model of object classes and attributes. In *Computer Vision–ECCV 2010*, pages 155–168. Springer, 2010.

[9] Z.-H. Zhou. *Ensemble methods: foundations and algorithms*. CRC Press, 2012.

Building a Self-Learning Eye Gaze Model from User Interaction Data

Michael Xuelin Huang, Tiffany C.K. Kwok, Grace Ngai, Hong Va Leong, Stephen C.F. Chan
Department of Computing
Hong Kong Polytechnic University
Hong Kong, China
{csxhuang,csgngai,cshleong,csschan}@comp.polyu.edu.hk, tiffany.ck.kwok@gmail.com

ABSTRACT

Most eye gaze estimation systems rely on explicit calibration, which is inconvenient to the user, limits the amount of possible training data and consequently the performance. Since there is likely a strong correlation between gaze and interaction cues, such as cursor and caret locations, a supervised learning algorithm can learn the complex mapping between gaze features and the gaze point by training on incremental data collected implicitly from normal computer interactions. We develop a set of robust geometric gaze features and a corresponding data validation mechanism that identifies good training data from noisy interaction-informed data collected in real-use scenarios. Based on a study of gaze movement patterns, we apply behavior-informed validation to extract gaze features that correspond with the interaction cue, and data-driven validation provides another level of crosschecking using previous good data. Experimental evaluation shows that the proposed method achieves an average error of 4.06°, and demonstrates the effectiveness of the proposed gaze estimation method and corresponding validation mechanism.

Categories and Subject Descriptors

H.1.2 [**Models and Principles**]: User/Machine Systems—*Human factors*; I.5.m [**Pattern Recognition**]: Miscellaneous.

General Terms

Experimentation; Human Factors.

Keywords

Gaze estimation; supervised learning; implicit modeling; data validation

1. INTRODUCTION

Gaze information, as a reflection of human attention, cognition and even desire and emotion, has great potential applications in a large number of domains, including interaction and diagnostics [7]. As a result, eye gaze research has been continuously popular for more than 30 years [8].

In general, gaze estimation methods can be categorized as feature-based or appearance-based [8]. Feature-based methods extract eye features such as eye contour, corners, pupil center and glint(s) (under active light sources), and are able to achieve relatively high accuracy. However, accurate and robust feature extraction requires specialized equipment such as infrared (IR) light source(s) or head mounted devices. Appearance-based approaches use the image itself as input and map it to screen coordinates. These approaches implicitly estimate the relevant gaze features, such as eye geometric features, camera calibration parameters and personal variance. They are more versatile for general use as they do not require any special devices, and they can be interesting for multimedia domains, like quality assessment and gaming using gaze information. However, they are sensitive to noise caused by variance of lighting condition, head pose, and individuality.

There have been some efforts into the use of low-cost off-the-shelf equipment for gaze estimation. Such approaches clearly require the use of gaze features that are robust to visual variances, and an accurate method of obtaining calibration data. Some researchers have proposed to use visual salient information for implicit gaze calibration [1][9], but the computed saliency model is not always consistent with the point of regard (PoR), or the true location of the gaze point on the screen [9]. Lu et al. [12] investigate regression on sparse data and introduce a synthesis framework [11] to produce training samples for unseen head poses. These approaches require explicit calibration and are sensitive to lighting variance. Sugano et al. proposed an alternate model, which collects mouse click data as the ground truth to incrementally update the gaze model [15]. Their approach assumes that users are looking at the point that they click on. However, in unconstrained real-use situations, this may not always be an accurate assumption.

This paper proposes to utilize the numerous interaction-informed gaze points that are generated during regular, daily human computer interaction to train an eye gaze model. These gaze points correspond to interactions with the mouse and keyboard, and can be obtained automatically from the interaction events. Unlike previous work, we take into consideration the *characteristics* of the eye movement patterns during the interaction event to inform our model and identify reliable instances for training. By taking into account both gaze and head pose features, it may be possible to achieve head pose invariance even with standard low-cost equipment. Our objective is to unobtrusively collect reliable training data to build a reliable model for off-the-shelf equipment that fits the individual gaze attributes, such as inter-ocular distance, eye and face contour, etc.

To the best of our knowledge, there is no prior work that investigates automated data validation techniques for gaze model learning from daily, noisy interaction cues. The contributions of this paper are thus as follows: we propose (1) an interaction-informed method for practical collection of data for gaze modeling, (2) a set of robust features for gaze estimation, and (3) the corresponding data processing and validation mechanism to identify good interaction-informed data for training.

MM'14, November 3-7, 2014, Orlando, FL, USA.

http://dx.doi.org/10.1145/2647868.2655031

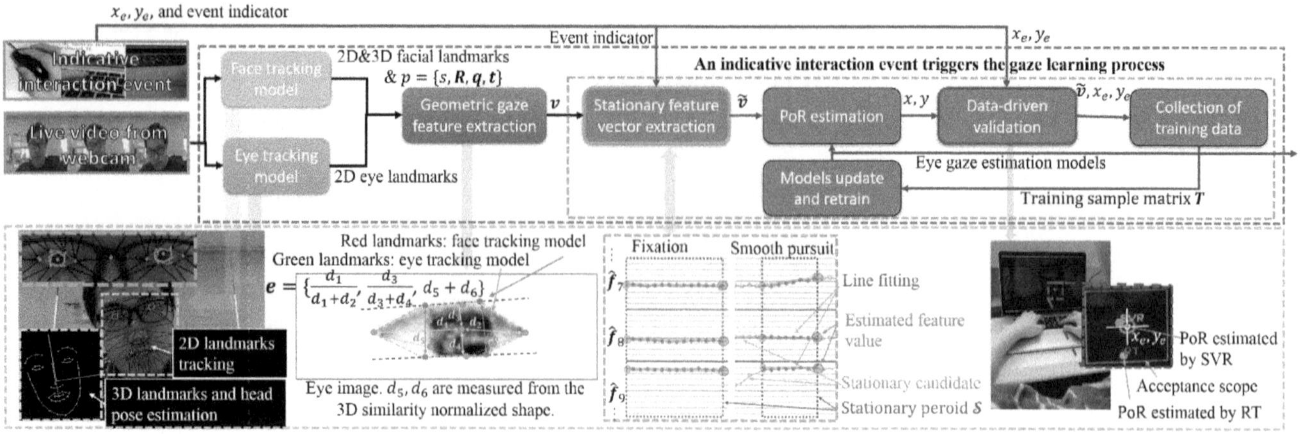

Figure 1. System Schematic

2. METHODOLOGY

Figure 1 shows our system schematic. A standard webcam streams a live video of the user's head and shoulders while his mouse movements and keystrokes are tracked by the system. Two independent tracking models are applied to the video stream to extract face and eye landmarks and the corresponding parameters, based on which the gaze feature vector $\tilde{\boldsymbol{v}}$ is extracted and processed from the eye image.

We start by collecting 100 instances for our initial model. Each instance is collected upon an interaction event; we use the video frame immediately preceding the interaction event to generate our feature vector for training and the location of the mouse click or the caret (for keyboard events) is taken as the PoR of the user. Two machine-learning algorithms, support vector regression (SVR) [6] and regression tree (RT) [10], are used to build PoR estimation models from these initial instances.

Upon the arrival of new interaction events, the estimated PoRs (x, y) from the models are compared with the interaction-informed PoR (x_e, y_e) from the mouse and keyboard data. If the PoRs match, the gaze feature vector $\tilde{\boldsymbol{v}}$ and the interaction-informed PoR (x_e, y_e) will be retained and used to adapt and retrain the gaze regression model for the user.

2.1 Extracting Gaze Features from Video

2.1.1 Head Pose Estimation

To obtain accurate locations of the facial landmarks and head pose information, we apply Saragih's Constrained Local Model (CLM) [14]. CLMs generate parametric models for face alignment based on the point distribution model (PDM) [5] and the localized patch model, which reflect the interdependency and the local appearance of the landmarks, respectively.

We use a 3D CLM model in our experiments. The 3D vertices of the facial landmarks can be represented by $\boldsymbol{x} = (\boldsymbol{x}_1, \ldots, \boldsymbol{x}_M)^T$, where $\boldsymbol{x}_i = (x_i, y_i, z_i)$ denotes the coordinate of the ith landmark in the camera coordinate and M(=66) is the number of facial landmarks (see notation[1]). Procrustes alignment [4] is used to normalize the rigid transformation and Principal Component Analysis (PCA) is applied to approximate the non-rigid deformation of the given samples. Therefore, the face images and corresponding annotated landmarks can be represented by $\boldsymbol{x}_i(p) = s\boldsymbol{R}(\bar{\boldsymbol{x}}_i + \boldsymbol{\Phi}_i\boldsymbol{q}) + \boldsymbol{t}, i \in [1, M]$, where $\boldsymbol{x}_i(p)$ and $\bar{\boldsymbol{x}}_i$ represent the 3D and mean coordinates of the ith landmark, respectively; $\boldsymbol{\Phi}_i$ the sub-matrix of the basis of variation of the ith landmark; and $\boldsymbol{p} = \{s, \boldsymbol{R}, \boldsymbol{q}, \boldsymbol{t}\}$ the PDM parameters: a head scaling s, a three-axis orientation $\boldsymbol{R}$, a global head translation $\boldsymbol{t}$ and a non-rigid transformation vector $\boldsymbol{q}$.

Generally, the objective of CLM fitting is, given an image $\mathcal{I}$, to determine the PDM parameter $\boldsymbol{p}$ so as to minimize the misalignment of the landmark with the cost function $f(\boldsymbol{p}) = \mathcal{R}(\boldsymbol{p}) + \sum_{i=1}^{M} \mathcal{L}_i(\boldsymbol{x}_i; \mathcal{I})$. This can also be viewed as maximizing the likelihood of both the global geometric shape deformation $\mathcal{R}(\boldsymbol{p})$ and the local patch textural information of the landmarks, $\sum_{i=1}^{M} \mathcal{L}_i(\boldsymbol{x}_i; \mathcal{I})$. However, due to the nature of the training image data and the influence of local maxima in optimization, CLM tracking tends to fail under poor lighting condition and certain kinds of expressions, e.g. mouth corner depression. To improve localization accuracy of the landmarks and to facilitate head pose estimation, we use the Supervised Descent Method (SDM) to optimize 48 facial landmarks [16]. Unlike CLM, SDM learns the sequence of descent directions for individual landmarks from training data, by minimizing the following function over the descent direction $\Delta\boldsymbol{x}$, $f(\boldsymbol{x}_c + \Delta\boldsymbol{x}) = \|\mathcal{A}(\boldsymbol{x}_c + \Delta\boldsymbol{x}) - \mathcal{A}_*\|_2^2$, where $\boldsymbol{x}_c$ denotes the initial configuration of the landmarks, $\mathcal{A}$ represents the appearance feature extraction and $\mathcal{A}_*$ the appearance feature near the manually annotated landmarks. During tracking, SDM optimizes the landmark localization with the learnt descent directions.

Our approach uses SDM for fast and robust face tracking. For each frame, we use the SDM fitting results as the initial state for CLM fitting. This improves the localization accuracy and reduces the time needed for convergence. CLM optimization then provides us with the 2D and 3D facial landmarks and the parameters $\boldsymbol{p}$. By removing the rigid geometric variation ($s, \boldsymbol{R}$ and $\boldsymbol{t}$), the similarity-normalized shape, i.e. the aligned 3D landmarks, can be obtained.

2.1.2 Pupil Center Estimation

An accurate estimation of gaze direction requires knowing the location of pupil center. However, in unconstrained situations, the appearance information of the eye region usually fails to provide a clear cue for the pupil center. Additionally, we observe that quite often in real-use scenarios, low video resolution and reflections on glasses and cornea may make the region of the pupil and its periphery unobservable.

---

[1] Bold capital letter denotes a matrix $\boldsymbol{F}$, bold lower-case letters a column vector $\boldsymbol{f}$. $\boldsymbol{f}_j$ represents the j-th column of the matrix $\boldsymbol{F}$. f_{ij} denotes the scalar in the row i and column j of the matrix $\boldsymbol{F}$.

To address issues caused by the unconstrained environment and noisy images with low resolution, we use eye geometric features to estimate the pupil center. The general idea is to track landmarks with good salient features on the iris contour and eye lid corners, and deduce the pupil center locations based on their geometric interdependency. We therefore apply eye CLMs to track the eye landmarks, including the pupil center (Figure 1). To validate the eye tracking state, we apply a robust but rough tracking model using the integral image [13] to approximate the pupil center from the eye image, with the assumption that the darkest rectangular area is the iris. If the CLM estimation is too distant from the integral image approximation, we assume that the CLM tracking has failed and we redetect the eye for tracking.

Based on the landmarks identified from the face and the eye trackers, we extract n (=12) gaze features and construct a gaze feature vector $\boldsymbol{v} = [s, \boldsymbol{R}, \boldsymbol{t}, \boldsymbol{e}_r, \boldsymbol{e}_l]^T$, $\boldsymbol{v} \in \Re^{n\times 1}$, where $s, \boldsymbol{R}, \boldsymbol{t}$ are the head pose features obtained from CLM, while $\boldsymbol{e}_r, \boldsymbol{e}_l$ denote the eye features from both eyes. Figure 1 shows the eye features, which include eye rotations (yaw and roll) and eyelid openness.

2.2 A Two-Layer Mechanism for Validating Collected Data

The most frequent gaze patterns occurring during human computer interaction are fixations, smooth pursuits, saccades and blinks. Fixation indicates a stationary gaze. Smooth pursuit denotes relatively slow gaze movements, while saccades refer to eye movements that rapidly direct towards a stationary target. Sugano et al. [15] collected data from mouseclicks based on the assumption that people tend to fixate on what they click. Our observations, however, suggest that in normal human-computer interactions, this assumption that the position of the mouseclick is the PoR at that time instance may not be valid. By the time the click occurs, the gaze may have already moved, or the gaze may be on a large image link. In addition, mouse interactions represent only a small percentage of human interactions with the computer.

We generalize Sugano et al's assumption to other interaction activities, and we postulate that people's gaze patterns are highly consistent with particular interaction events. Table 1 shows some examples. In addition, we focus on identifying periods of fixation and smooth pursuit as time periods where the PoR of the user is most likely to correlate with the location of the interaction event.

2.2.1 Behavior-Informed Validation – Extracting a Stationary Feature Vector

We refer to the gaze feature during fixation and smooth pursuit as "stationary" or "stationary with small trend" for simplicity. Since the raw gaze feature vector is extracted based on the identified landmarks from the statistical tracking models, it contains high frequency noise caused by temporal jitter from landmark localization. For each feature, we therefore perform a linear interpolation to resample the feature signal (sample rate: 15Hz) over the previous 1-second window prior to the interaction event. When an event is captured, we use the feature vectors in the previous m(=15) frames prior to the event to construct the gaze feature matrix $\boldsymbol{F} \in \Re^{m\times n}$. In addition, low-pass filtering in the frequency domain is applied to remove the high frequency temporal jitter from the signal while maintaining the main component without overmuch distortion. The filtered signal is calculated as $\hat{\boldsymbol{f}}_j = \mathcal{F}^{-1}[\mathcal{F}(\boldsymbol{f}_j) * \mathcal{H}(\omega)]$, where $\mathcal{F}$ and $\mathcal{F}^{-1}$ indicate the one-dimensional forward and inverse Discrete Fourier transform, respectively, and the filter $\mathcal{H}(\omega) = \begin{cases} 1, & \omega \le \omega_h \\ 0, & \text{otherwise} \end{cases}$, where ω_h (=2.5Hz in our work) is the cutoff frequency.

Table 1. Examples of Interaction-Informed Gaze Patterns

Interaction event	Human intention	Potential gaze pattern and informed PoR
Mouse left button click	Link or button selection	Fixation/smooth pursuit on the mouse cursor
Mouse left button double-click	Word selection in document editing	Fixation on the mouse cursor
Keyboard button down	Word typing	Fixation/smooth pursuit on the typing caret

We then determine when the signals are in a stationary state. We apply a threshold $\boldsymbol{\varepsilon} \in \Re^{n\times 1}$ to evaluate the temporal variations of the features. $\boldsymbol{\varepsilon}$ is calculated as $\boldsymbol{\varepsilon} = 0.05\boldsymbol{r}$, where $\boldsymbol{r} \in \Re^{n\times 1}$ is the range of the feature values. The frame whose corresponding feature vector satisfies the following condition is considered to potentially be within the stationary period,

$$\prod_{j=1}^{n} H(\varepsilon_j^2 - \dot{\hat{f}}_{ij}^2) = 1 \tag{1}$$

where $H(x) = (1 + \text{sgn}(x))/2$ is the Heaviside step function and $\dot{\hat{f}}_{ij}$ is the value of the ith frame of the 1st order signal of $\hat{\boldsymbol{f}}_j$. After all m frames in the feature matrix $\boldsymbol{F}$ have been tested, a backward search is performed to locate the stationary period that is closest to the interaction event and has a duration longer than 0.3 second (3 times the minimum fixation duration [8]). This resulting period, represented as a sequence of frames $\mathcal{S}$, is considered the corresponding stationary state to the interaction event.

Since features in the stationary state are relatively stable, we apply linear regression to approximate the final gaze feature vector $\tilde{\boldsymbol{v}}$. M-estimator is used to iteratively fit the line using the weighted least-squares algorithm to minimize $\sum_{i\in\mathcal{S}} \rho(d_{ij})$, where $\rho(d) = 2(\sqrt{1 + d^2/2} - 1)$ is the distance function and d_{ij} denotes the difference between $\hat{f}_{ij}$ and its fitted value $\tilde{f}_{ij}$. Setting k as the last frame of $\mathcal{S}$, the resulting value for the jth gaze feature should be $\tilde{f}_{kj}$. This generates a final input feature vector for the classifier, $\tilde{\boldsymbol{v}} = [\tilde{f}_{k1}, \dots, \tilde{f}_{kn}]^T$.

2.2.2 Data-Driven Validation

The behavior-informed validation looks for the stationary period corresponding to the received interaction event. However, it is possible that for some interactions, the user's PoR may not be anywhere near the location of the interaction event – for example, when the user is watching a movie with the mouse pointer poised over the "pause" button. The data-driven validation uses the previous collected data as an additional point of validation to determine the goodness of the feature vector $\tilde{\boldsymbol{v}}$ and the corresponding assumed interaction PoR (x_e, y_e).

Passing $\tilde{\boldsymbol{v}}$ through the trained SVR/RT models generates estimated PoRs (x_{SVR}, y_{SVR}) and (x_{RT}, y_{RT}). Comparing the estimated PoRs with the location of the interaction event, (x_e, y_e) gives us estimation errors e_{SVR} and e_{RT}. The feature vector $\tilde{\boldsymbol{v}}$ and the corresponding interaction-informed PoR (x_e, y_e) is retained if $\boldsymbol{min}(e_{SVR}, e_{RT}) \le \lambda$, where λ is a threshold that is set to 1/10 of the screen diagonal in our work. The validated gaze vector and its interaction-informed PoR (x_e, y_e) is stored into the training sample matrices ($\boldsymbol{T} \in \Re^{14\times 100w}$, w is the number of matrices), of which the ith column $\boldsymbol{t}_i = [\tilde{\boldsymbol{v}}_i^T, x_{ei}, y_{ei}]^T$. $\boldsymbol{T}$ is used to retrain and update the SVR/RT after every 100 new instances collected.

Our approach therefore uses a dual-level validation. First of all, by requiring the gaze features to be stationary, the behavior-informed

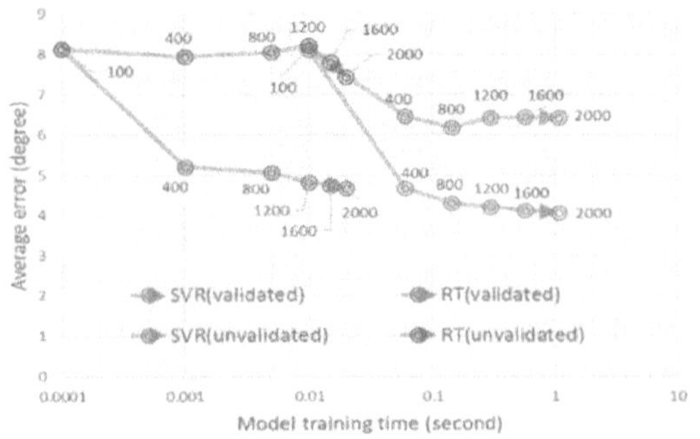

Figure 2. Performance and training time comparison between SVR and RT with/without the data validation mechanism

validation ensures the interaction-informed correspondence through the gaze movement patterns. Secondly, the data-driven validation uses the current gaze estimation model, trained on previously-collected data, and the location of the interaction event, to filter out potentially noisy input data.

3. EXPERIMENTAL EVALUATION

To demonstrate the effectiveness of the proposed method for gaze estimation and the corresponding data validation mechanism, we recruited 5 subjects (3 female, aged 20-30). They were free to adjust head pose, body posture and chair height for their comfort during the experiments. All the experiments were run on a standard 15-inch MacBook Pro, with the screen resolution set to 1920x1200, and the built-in webcam used for data collection. Approximated by the CLM results, the head to screen distance in the training data ranges from 305~634mm (mean: 533mm; sd: 59mm) and the head pitch from -6°~24° (mean: 12.6°; sd: 5.5°).

Subjects were instructed to work on tasks that involved interactions, such as writing and browsing. (This being the end of the semester, most subjects chose to work on their term reports.) The experiment finished once sufficient keyboard and mouse events (2,000 instances) were collected, approximately 3 hours on average. This is longer than the 10-minute data collection process from previous work [15], but it should be noted that (1) our data collection is implicit rather than explicit, and (2) the previous work does not address the issue of inconsistency between PoR and interaction event location.

For testing, we followed Cerrolaza et al's protocol [3] to capture gaze on 8x8 grids at different distances (450, 500, 550 mm in our case). Two state-of-the-art regression models are evaluated (SVR and RT) in the experiments. Radial basis function kernel is applied for SVR as suggested by Bennett et al. [2].

Figure 2 shows the relation between the model training time and the performance of the gaze estimation models. The performance is measured by the average error [15] over all calibration points and subjects. For comparison, we present the performance on both validated and unvalidated data. The red and blue markers indicate the results of models trained with validated data, while the purple and green represent models that use all interaction-informed data. Different markers denote the performance of increasing amounts of training data, at 100, 400, 800, 1200, 1600 and 2000 instances. The models trained on validated data achieve average error of 4.06° for SVR and 4.68° for RT (i.e. mean absolute error: 37 and 43 mm respectively). This is comparable to state of the art work [11][12][15] with similar head motions.

More importantly, by increasing the amount of training data, the error of the validated models decreases smoothly. However, the error of the unvalidated models fluctuate. Moreover, with just 400 training instances, the validated models significantly outperform the best performances achieved on unvalidated data (4.66° vs. 7.44° for SVR; 5.20° vs. 6.16° for RT). This is because additional data in real-use situations contains much noise, which hurts performance. It corroborates our hypothesis that validation is necessary when working with interaction-informed data collected from real-use situations. This indicates both the effectiveness and importance of our proposed validation mechanism.

4. CONCLUSIONS

This paper proposes a novel approach to extract robust gaze features and the corresponding data validation mechanism to facilitate the use of interaction-informed data for gaze estimation. Experimental evaluations demonstrate that the proposed method can effectively apply daily interaction cues to train an eye gaze model without an explicit calibration phase, achieving performance comparable to that of state-of-the-art methods, but using low-cost off-the-shelf devices. In our future work, we plan to further investigate the impact of data skew and significant head pose variance in long-term experiments.

This work was partially supported by grants PolyU 5248/10E and PolyU 5222/13E from the Hong Kong Polytechnic University and the Hong Kong Research Grants Council, respectively.

5. REFERENCES

[1] Alnajar, F., Gevers, T., Valenti, R. and Ghebreab, S. Calibration-Free Gaze Estimation Using Human Gaze Patterns. In *IEEE ICCV*, 2013, 137-144.

[2] Bennett, K.P. Nonlinear Eye Gaze Mapping Function Estimation via Support Vector Regression. In *ICPR,* 2006, 1132-1135.

[3] Cerrolaza, J.J., Villanueva, A. and Cabeza, R. Study of Polynomial Mapping Functions in Video-Oculography Eye Trackers. *ACM Trans. on Computer-Human Interaction*. 19, 2, 2012, 1-25.

[4] Cootes, T.F., Edwards, G.J. and Taylor, C.J. Active appearance models. *IEEE Trans on Pattern Analysis and Machine Intelligence*. 23, 6, 2001, 681-685.

[5] Cootes, T.F. and Taylor, C.J. Active Shape Models - "Smart Snakes." *BMVC,*1992, 266-275.

[6] Drucker, H., Burges, C.J.C., Kaufman, L., Smola, A. and Vapnik, V. Support vector regression machines. In *NIPS,* 1997, 155-161.

[7] Duchowski, A.T. *Eye Tracking Methodology: Theory and Practice*. Springer London. 2003.

[8] Hansen, D.W. and Ji, Q. In the eye of the beholder: a survey of models for eyes and gaze. *IEEE Trans on Pattern Analysis and Machine Intelligence*. 32, 3, 2010, 478-500.

[9] Judd, T., Ehinger, K., Durand, F. and Torralba, A. Learning to predict where humans look. *IEEE ICCV,* 2009, 2106-2113.

[10] Leo Breiman 2001. Random Forests. *Machine Learning*. 45, 1. 2001, 5-32.

[11] Lu, F., Okabe, T., Sugano, Y. and Sato, Y. Learning gaze biases with head motion for head pose-free gaze estimation. *Image and Vision Computing*. 32, 3, 2014, 169-179.

[12] Lu, F., Sugano, Y., Okabe, T. and Sato, Y. Inferring Human Gaze from Appearance via Adaptive Linear Regression. *IEEE Trans on Pattern Analysis and Machine Intelligence*. 2014, 1-1.

[13] Paul Viola, M.J. Robust Real-time Object Detection. *Int. J. Computer Vision*. 2001.

[14] Saragih, J.M., Lucey, S. and Cohn, J.F. Face alignment through subspace constrained mean-shifts. *ICCV*. 2009, 1034-1041.

[15] Sugano, Y., Matsushita, Y., Sato, Y. and Koike, H. An Incremental Learning Method for Unconstrained Gaze Estimation. In *ECCV,* 2008, 656–667.

[16] Xiong, X. and De la Torre, F. Supervised Descent Method and Its Applications to Face Alignment. *CVPR,* 2013, 532–539.

Toward an Estimation of User Tagging Credibility for Social Image Retrieval

Alexandru Lucian Ginsca[1,4], Adrian Popescu[1], Bogdan Ionescu[2] , Anil Armagan[3], Ioannis Kanellos[4]
[1]CEA, LIST, Vision and Content Engineering Laboratory, 91191 Gif-sur-Yvette, France
[2]LAPI, University "Politehnica" of Bucharest, 061071, Romania
[3]Bilkent University, Ankara, Turkey
[4]TELECOM Bretagne, France
{alexandru.ginsca, adrian.popescu}@cea.fr, bionescu@alpha.imag.pub.ro, anil.armagan@bilkent.edu.tr, ioannis.kanellos@telecom-bretagne.eu

ABSTRACT

Existing image retrieval systems exploit textual or/and visual information to return results. Retrieval is mostly focused on data themselves and disregards the data sources. In Web 2.0 platforms, the quality of annotations provided by different users can vary strongly. To account for this variability, we complement existing methods by introducing user tagging credibility in the retrieval process. Tagging credibility is automatically estimated by leveraging a large set of visual concept classifiers learned with Overfeat, a convolutional neural network (CNN) feature. A good image retrieval system should return results that are both relevant and diversified and here we tackle both challenges. Classically, we diversify results by using a k-Means algorithm and increase relevance by favoring images uploaded by users with good credibility estimates. Evaluation is performed on DIV400, a publicly available social image retrieval dataset and shows that our method is competitive with existing approaches.

1. INTRODUCTION

Existing works have identified relevance and diversity as two core properties of efficient image retrieval systems. Given that these two characteristics are antinomic, different methods have been proposed to find a good compromise between them. Classically, relevance was primarily estimated by using textual weighting schemes. However, with the improvement of low-level image descriptors, multimedia fusion schemes also gained traction. Diversity is usually improved by applying clustering algorithms which rely on textual or/and visual cues [14]. In addition, the usefulness of social cues was also explored for Web 2.0 platforms [9] but this aspect remains secondary.

Our work is focused on the estimation and exploitation of user credibility, a cue which was not previously exploited in multimedia retrieval and is complementary to those cited above. We investigate user tagging credibility in the context of social multimedia mining and address the following research questions: Q_1 - is it possible to automatically estimate user tagging credibility for Web 2.0 multimedia data? Q_2 - how should credibility be integrated in existing multimedia retrieval systems? Q_3 - what is the additional complexity of credibility estimation?

We propose an image retrieval technique that ensures a good balance of results diversity and relevance. Evaluation is performed on the DIV400 dataset, a retrieval dataset created in the context of the MediaEval 2013 Diverse Social Images Task [6]. Retrieval results are diversified using a k-Means algorithm with user-based cluster ranking. The novelty comes from relevance improvement obtained by integrating user tagging credibility. In an initial step, credibility scores are computed by probing user tag-image pairs against a large array of visual concept models learned from ImageNet [3] and by aggregating classification scores at user level. At retrieval time, images are reranked based on the credibility scores of the users who uploaded them. In addition, face and blur detection are applied to discard potentially irrelevant images. Our technique is compared to state of the art systems that were submitted to Diverse Social Images Task [6] and interesting performances are obtained for both diversification and relevance.

2. RELATED WORK

Web credibility was studied under three main aspects: informing about, analyzing and estimating credibility. The first two directions fall outside the immediate scope of our work. Automatic credibility estimation is a recent trend in Web content analysis; it is mostly applied to textual documents, such as tweets [1] or Web pages [12]. Also related is the automatic assessment of crowdsourcer credibility, which is investigated in [7]. However, none of these works is focused on multimedia content and literature regarding multimedia credibility is limited. Xu et al. [15] aim to help users filter multimedia news by targeting credible content. They propose methods to evaluate multimedia news by comparing visual descriptions and textual descriptions respectively, as well as their combination. Yamamoto and Tanaka [16] have built ImageAlert, a system that focuses on text-image credibility. While interesting, existing work on multimedia content credibility estimation is preliminary and deserves further investigation. The estimation of individual tag rel-

MM'14, November 3–7, 2014, Orlando, Florida, USA.

http://dx.doi.org/10.1145/2647868.2655033.

evance is related to our work. Li et al. [10] have proposed a neighbor voting framework which exploits neighbor voting to assess tag quality. More recently, Gao et al. [5] introduce a hypergraph framework to jointly model visual and textual cues of social media images. Their approach compares favorably to other existing methods but has a high computational cost at query time. We estimate credibility independently of a given topic and thus drastically reduce processing complexity at query time. [10, 5] do not aggregate relevance at user level and focus on individual tags. Both works need a large amount of data annotated with targeted tags and their efficiency on less common tags is questionable.

Due to its large size and availability, Flickr is an interesting playground for different multimedia mining tasks. Techniques that rely on social media data in order to improve image retrieval are also related to our objectives. Van Leuken et al. [14] focus on the usage of visual features to diversify image search results. Their contribution is twofold: proposition of lightweight clustering techniques and dynamic weighting of visual features. However, they do not study the use of social cues. Kennedy and Naaman [9] exploit temporal and spatial metadata, as well as user counts, for location clustering. This approach is interesting but social cues are processed at an image level and there is no aggregation at the user level, such as the one proposed here.

The usefulness of user tagging credibility estimation for image retrieval was not evaluated in previous works. To perform evaluation, we need a dataset with identified contributors. The DIV400 dataset [6] fits our needs. It sets up a domain retrieval scenario, i.e. tourism, and the primary focus of the evaluation exercise is to improve retrieval diversity. The dataset includes images of 396 tourist points of interest (POIs) and is further described in Section 6. The most efficient approaches tried on DIV400 are described in [8] and [2]. Jain et al. [8] use re-ranking with proximity search to improve precision and a Greedy Min-Max diversifier based on temporal user information. Corney et al. [2] report their best results with a Greedy optimization of a VLAD representation of SURFs.

3. VISUAL CONTENT PROCESSING

Our diversification approach is mainly based on visual content mining. To keep abreast with the latest advances in the field, we use Overfeat [13], a powerful CNN-based feature, to model credibility and to process the DIV400 dataset. In addition, we remove faces and blurred images, which are potentially irrelevant for a part of the topics.

ImageNet Concept Learning

ImageNet [3] is a manually labeled dataset which includes over 14 million images of nearly $22,000$ concepts. This dataset is well suited here insofar as we want to model a diversified range of tag-image pairs. The basic brick in modeling user tagging credibility is a verification of tag-image content relation. For instance, if an image is tagged with *dog*, it is then compared to *dog* models from ImageNet. We select the $17,462$ ImageNet concepts which are represented by at least 100 images and build binary classifiers to model them. Image content is represented using the default configuration of Overfeat [13], followed by a L2-normalization of the features.

Let $\{I_i, y_i\}_{i=1..N}$ be the training set associated with the c-th concept of ImageNet. I_i is a training image and $y_i \in \{-1, 1\}$ its corresponding binary label. To learn models quickly, for a concept with N positive examples, we select the first N negative examples from a unique negative set, built from concepts which are not modeled. We capture the visual appearance of the c-th concept, using a linear model $\mathbf{W}^c \in \mathbb{R}^{S_f+1}$. S_f is the image feature size. The last dimension, $(\mathbf{W}^c)_{S_f+1}$, corresponds to the model bias. $\mathbf{W}^c$ is learned by minimizing the L2-regularized logistic loss:

$$\mathbf{W}^c = \arg\min_{\bar{\mathbf{W}}^c} \frac{1}{2}\|\bar{\mathbf{W}}^{\mathbf{c}}\|_2^2 + C\sum_{i=1}^{N} \log(1 + e^{-y_i \bar{\mathbf{W}}^{cT}\mathbf{f}_i}). \quad (1)$$

Here, $\mathbf{f}_i = f(I_i) \in \mathbf{R}^{S_f+1}$ is an image feature capturing I_i content information. It should be noted that $(\mathbf{f}_i)_{S_f+1} = 1\, \forall i$ since it correlates with the model bias. $C \geq 0$ is a penalty parameter. A Quasi-Newton descent [11] is used to solve (1)[1]. Classification scores are normalized between 0 and 1 using a logistic function.

Dataset Processing

Overfeat features are also extracted for DIV400 images. PCA is applied to these features to obtain a more compact representation of images and thus accelerate retrieval. Preliminary tests have already shown that results obtained with the first 256 PCA dimensions are equivalent to those obtained with the default Overfeat configuration (4096 dimensions). Inspired by [8], face and blur detection is applied to the dataset. Face detection is implemented with the standard OpenCV algorithm[2]. Another set of tests has shown that direct removal of images containing faces does not improve results. Consequently, given a set of POI images and the associated user set t_u, face removal is performed based on p_u, the proportion of users from the set t_u which upload face images. Face images are retained for p_u values lower than a threshold ($th(p_u)$) and discarded otherwise. In order for p_u to be meaningful, we impose face removal only on the POIs with at least $th(t_u)$ contributors. p_u exploits social consensus about usefulness of face images and is optimized on the devset of DIV400. Blur detection is performed using thresholded gradient. Similar to face retrieval, a threshold $th(b)$ for blur removal is learned on the devset of DIV400.

4. USER CREDIBILITY ESTIMATION

User tagging credibility is estimated by exploiting ImageNet visual models (Section 3). For each user, we download at most 300 images whose textual annotations match at least one ImageNet concept. Flickr annotations are selected either from tags or from the image title and are all referred as tags hereafter. We perform multiword detection in order to match multiwords from ImageNet. Tags are tested against corresponding ImageNet concepts to obtain individual relevance scores. User tagging credibility estimation (*cred(U)*) is obtained by averaging scores from individual tag-image pairs.

Visual models are built on top of ImageNet concepts, which are often ambiguous, and tested for Flickr annotations. For instance, if an unknown image annotated with *dog* is tested, which of the three senses of *dog* from Figure 1 should be used? An inspection of Flickr results shows that most images annotated with *dog* depict *animals* but there are some of them which depict *dog* as *food* and *dog*

[1] We rely on the liblinear implementation from [4].
[2] http://opencv.org/

Figure 1: Different senses of *dog* in ImageNet.

as *support*. Our credibility estimator should be able to automatically select the right sense of *dog* for the content of the tested image. A simple way to process ambiguity is to compare the tag-image pair to all models available for the tag and retain only the maximum classification score. Preliminary tests showed that this procedure has good behavior and it is thus used in the experiments. Beyond ambiguity, another problem is the coverage of ImageNet, with some important senses of words not being included. For instance, *berlin* is represented as *car* but not as *city*. These problems represent limitations of our method and their tackling would probably improve credibility estimations.

5. IMAGE RETRIEVAL METHOD

We propose a retrieval method which diversifies images using k-Means and improves relevance with credibility estimations. Let $\mathbf{L_F} = \{(I_1, U_1), (I_2, U_2), (I_3, U_1), ..., (I_N, U_M)\}$ be the ranked list of Flickr images which should be reranked. Here (I_i, U_j) denote image-user pairs. Our retrieval method can be broken down into three steps: initial filtering, cluster ranking and image ranking.

Image Filtering In this step, we remove from $\mathbf{L_F}$ all pairs (I_i, U_j) for which I_i qualifies for face or blur removal.

Cluster Ranking After image filtering, we perform k-Means clustering to diversify the topic representation. Let $\mathbf{C_F} = \{C_1, C_2, ..., C_k\}$ be the clustered version of $\mathbf{L_F}$. Inspired by [9], we rank clusters based on *#Users*, the number of distinct users which contribute to each cluster. Ranking based on *#Users* gives priority to clusters which show social consensus. When ties appear with *#Users*, they are broken by using the top Flickr rank among the images of the user with the highest credibility score *cred(U)* from each cluster. As a result, we obtain $\mathbf{C_F^R} = \{C_3, C_k, C_2, ..., C_1\}$, a list of clusters ranked using social cues. For comparison, we also rank clusters based on their raw image count (*#Images*).

Image Sorting We exploit credibility estimation to sort images within clusters. Let $C_c = \{(I_1, U_1), (I_3, U_5), (I_8, U_1)\}$ be a cluster with its images ranked by Flickr. Assuming that $cred(U_5) > cred(U_1)$, the sorted representation of the cluster will be $C_c^R = \{(I_3, U_5), (I_1, U_1), (I_8, U_1)\}$. In C_c^R, priority is given to images uploaded by users with higher credibility score.

The final image ranking $\mathbf{L_F^R}$ is obtained by iterating over $\mathbf{C_F^R}$, the ranked list of clusters, and by selecting each time the first unseen image from C_c^R, the sorted images of C_c.

6. EVALUATION

Dataset Description We evaluate our retrieval method with the DIV400 dataset, which is thoroughly described in [6]. It consists of a development dataset (50 tourist POIs, 5,118 photos) and a testing dataset (346 POIs, 38,300 photos). Each POI is represented with up to 150 photos and associated metadata retrieved with Flickr's default "relevance" algorithm. Relevance and diversity annotations are available for each photo. Photos are considered relevant if they depict a common photo representation of the POI. A set of photos is considered to be diverse if it depicts complementary visual characteristics of the target POI. Clusters are manually built from relevant images of each POI. The main objective of the evaluation from [6] is diversity, which is captured with cluster recall at N (CR@N). However, since a good retrieval method should find a good compromise between relevance and diversity, we also report precision (P@N) and their combination, F1@N.

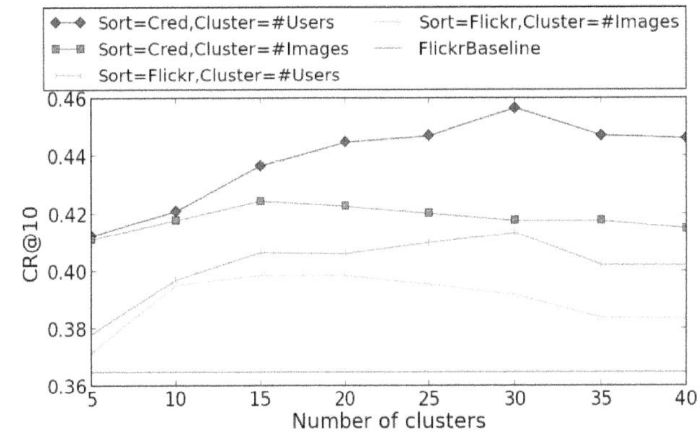

Figure 2: CR@10 performances with different clustering methods and different numbers of clusters on the testset of DIV400. *Sort* denotes the type of image sorting used within clusters. *Cred* is a sorting based on user credibility and *Flickr* is the original Flickr ordering. "Cluster" denotes the cluster ranking method. *#Users* and *#Images* represent the user and image counts of a cluster.

Clustering Analysis In Figure 2, we illustrate the impact of the number of clusters on clustering performances. Within each cluster, *Cred*, the credibility based image sorting outperforms the use of the initial Flickr sorting in all settings. Intuitively, the best overall results are obtained when *#Users* and *Cred* are combined for inter- and intra-cluster ranking. With 30 clusters, *Flickr + #Users* brings a 2 CR@10 points improvement of results compared to *Flickr + Images*. This result confirms the conclusions of [9], namely that the use of social cues for cluster ranking is beneficial. More importantly, the introduction of credibility estimation (*Cred + #Users*) further improves CR@10 by 4 points. We present results on the testset here because they are obtained by averaging a larger number of topics. However, similar results are obtained on the devset and *Cred + #Users* with 30 clusters is used for further experiments.

Global performances In table 1, we present the results obtained with the best credibility based retrieval method, described in Section 5. It combines clustering and user credibility estimates and produces a reranked list of images $\mathbf{L_F^R}$. For comparison, we also present results obtained by the two most efficient existing methods tested on DIV400 [6].

Method	metrics	@10	@20	@30
SOTON-WAIS [8]	P	**0.8158**	**0.7788**	0.7414
	CR	0.4398	0.6197	0.7216
	F1	0.5455	**0.6607**	0.7019
SocSens [2]	P	0.733	0.7487	**0.7603**
	CR	0.4291	0.6314	0.7228
	F1	0.5209	0.6595	**0.7087**
$\mathbf{L_F^R}$	P	0.7822	0.7154	0.6927
	CR	**0.4567**	**0.6582**	**0.7801**
	F1	**0.5526**	0.659	0.7073

Table 1: Comparison of retrieval results obtained with different methods on DIV400 and CR@N, P@N and F1@N metrics. SOTON-WAIS [8] and SocSens [2] are the two most efficient retrieval methods proposed at MediaEval Diverse Images 2013. $\mathbf{L_F^R}$ corresponds to a setting with *Cred+#Users* and 30 clusters (figure 2).

To understand the impact of face and blur removal, we briefly present results obtained when we skip one of these steps. When no prefiltering is used CR@10 is 0.4437. The use of blur removal or of face removal augments the score to 0.4476 and to 0.4536 respectively. While image filtering is beneficial, the main contribution comes from the use of credibility and of user centered clustering.

A comparison of our method to [8] and [2] shows that cluster recall is improved at all cut-off points. For CR@10, the official metric associated to DIV400, the improvement is close to 2 and 3 points. Confirming other results obtained on DIV400, which show that clustering hurts precision, the P@10 obtained with $\mathbf{L_F^R}$ is lower than those obtained in [8]. However, the F1@10 score of our method is slightly better. This comparison shows that our approach is competitive. It also departs from existing retrieval methods by the central role given to social cues and particularly to credibility.

7. CONCLUSIONS

This paper proposes an exploration of the introduction of user tagging credibility estimation in image retrieval systems. Evaluation results show that credibility is a good complement to direct text and/or visual content analysis.

Preliminary answers are provided to the research questions listed in the introduction. A credibility model based on text-image pairs assessment was proposed in response to Q_1. The main limitations of our method come from: the mismatch between the background visual resource and the datasets used for retrieval, the limited amount of modeled tags available for some users, the imperfection of visual models and the exclusive use of tag-image content relations. Credibility scores were obtained by comparing user tags to ImageNet concepts with no adaptation whatsoever to the evaluation dataset, which is made of tourist POIs. The fact that credibility estimations are effective even in this difficult setting accounts for their usefulness. In the future, we will extend the background visual resource in order to narrow the gap between it and retrieval datasets. New concepts can be learned from noisy Web datasets and their availability would contribute to the reduction of the number of users for which reliable credibility scores cannot be obtained. Visual models creation was focused on scalability but, since these models are learned offline, they will be improved by using larger and adapted negative sets. Following work in the textual domain [1], credibility estimation can be cast as a machine learning problem, with the addition of other cues than tag-image pairs.

In response to Q_2, credibility estimations were integrated with a classical clustering algorithm. The performance gains obtained through the use of credibility account for its usefulness in retrieval. The use of credibility in more sophisticated retrieval schemes ([8], [2]) will be investigated. Finally, additional complexity is added to the retrieval framework (Q_3) but affects retrieval steps which are performed offline. These steps, including feature extraction, visual model learning and credibility estimations, can be repeated periodically to follow the dataset evolution. At query time, only a reranking of images which accounts for credibility is required and this procedure has negligible effects compared to clustering.

8. ACKNOWLEDGMENT

This research was supported by the MUCKE project funded within the FP7 CHIST-ERA scheme.

9. REFERENCES

[1] C. Castillo and al. Information credibility on twitter. In *Proc. of WWW 2011*, pages 675–684.

[2] D. Corney and al. Socialsensor: Finding diverse images at mediaeval 2013. In *Proc. of MediaEval Wksp. 2013.*

[3] J. Deng and al. ImageNet: A Large-Scale Hierarchical Image Database. In *Proc. of CVPR 2009.*

[4] R.-E. Fan and al. Liblinear: A library for large linear classification. *JMLR*, 2008.

[5] Y. Gao and al. Visual-textual joint relevance learning for tag-based social image search. *IEEE TIP*, 22(1), 2013.

[6] B. Ionescu and al. Div400: A social image retrieval result diversification dataset. *ACM MMSys 2014.*

[7] P. G. Ipeirotis and al. Quality management on amazon mechanical turk. In *HCOMP 2010.*

[8] N. Jain and al. Experiments in diversifying flickr result sets. In *Proc. of MediaEval Wksp. 2013.*

[9] L. S. Kennedy and M. Naaman. Generating diverse and representative image search results for landmarks. In *Proc. of WWW 2008*, pages 297–306.

[10] X. Li and al. Learning tag relevance by neighbor voting for social image retrieval. In *ACM MIR 2008.*

[11] C.-J. Lin and al. Trust region newton method for logistic regression. *JMLR*, 2008.

[12] A. Olteanu and al. Web credibility: Features exploration and credibility prediction. *ECIR 2013.*

[13] P. Sermanet and al. Overfeat: Integrated recognition, localization and detection using convolutional networks. *CoRR*, 2013.

[14] R. H. van Leuken and al. Visual diversification of image search results. In *Proc. of WWW 2009.*

[15] L. Xu and al. Credibility-oriented ranking of multimedia news based on a material-opinion model. *Web-Age Inf. Mgmt.*, pages 290–301, 2011.

[16] Y. Yamamoto and K. Tanaka. Imagealert: credibility analysis of text-image pairs on the web. *SAC 2011.*

Affective Image Retrieval via Multi-Graph Learning

Sicheng Zhao†, Hongxun Yao†, You Yang‡, Yanhao Zhang†

†School of Computer Science and Technology, Harbin Institute of Technology, China.
‡Department of Electronics and Information Engineering, Huazhong University of Science and Technology, China.
{zsc, h.yao, yhzhang}@hit.edu.cn; yangyou@hust.edu.cn

ABSTRACT

Images can convey rich emotions to viewers. Recent research on image emotion analysis mainly focused on affective image classification, trying to find features that can classify emotions better. We concentrate on affective image retrieval and investigate the performance of different features on different kinds of images in a multi-graph learning framework. Firstly, we extract commonly used features of different levels for each image. Generic features and features derived from elements-of-art are extracted as low-level features. Attributes and interpretable principles-of-art based features are viewed as mid-level features, while semantic concepts described by adjective noun pairs and facial expressions are extracted as high-level features. Secondly, we construct single graph for each kind of feature to test the retrieval performance. Finally, we combine the multiple graphs together in a regularization framework to learn the optimized weights of each graph to efficiently explore the complementation of different features. Extensive experiments are conducted on five datasets and the results demonstrate the effectiveness of the proposed method.

(a) Fear (b) Excitement

(c) Sadness (d) Contentment

Figure 1: The emotions of different kinds of images are dominated by different features: (a) Aesthetic features (low saturation, cool color, low contrast of hue); (b) Attributes (snow, skiing); (c) Semantic concepts described by adjective noun pairs (broken car); (d) Facial expressions (happiness).

Categories and Subject Descriptors

H.3.3 [**Information storage and retrieval**]: Information Search and Retrieval; I.4.7 [**Image processing and computer vision**]: Feature Measurement

General Terms

Algorithms, Experimentation, Performance

Keywords

Affective Image Retrieval; Image Emotion; Multi-Graph Learning

1. INTRODUCTION

With the rapid development of social networks, such as Twitter and Weibo, people tend to express and share their opinions and emotions online using text and images. Understanding the emotions implied in the increasing repository of data is of vital importance to behavior sciences [12] and enables wide applications, such as human decision making and brand monitoring [1].

While sentiment analysis in text is relative mature [12], emotion analysis in images is still in its infancy, due to the subjective evaluation and the "affective gap" [4]. Recent research mainly focused on affective image classification, trying to find features that can classify emotions better. Lu *et al.* [8] investigated the computability of emotion through *shape* features. Inspired from psychology and art theory, Machajdik *et al.* [10] extracted features of different levels, including *color* and *texture* as low-level features, *composition* as mid-level features, and *human faces* and *skin* as high-level features. Zhao *et al.* [21] proposed to extract principles-of-art based emotion features, which are more interpretable by humans and have stronger link to emotions than the elements-of-art based ones. Mid-level scene attributes are used for binary sentiment classification [19]. A large scale visual sentiment ontology and detectors are proposed to detect 1,200 high-level adjective noun pairs [1]. Besides, social correlation features are extracted for social network images [6].

Meanwhile, low-level visual features, such as SIFT, are widely used for content based image retrieval. However, they cannot perform well for image retrieval on the affective level [16].

In this paper, we concentrate on affective image retrieval and investigate the performance of different features on different kinds of images, as emotions can be conveyed by various features, as shown in Figure 1. For example, principles-of-art features, such as balance and contrast, mainly contribute to emotions of artistic and abstract images [21]. Facial expressions may determine the emotion of the images containing faces, while semantic concepts

MM '14, November 03 - 07 2014, Orlando, FL, USA.
Copyright 2014 ACM 978-1-4503-3063-3/14/11...$15.00.
http://dx.doi.org/10.1145/2647868.2655035.

Table 1: Summary of the extracted features of different levels. '#' indicates the dimension of each feature.

Levels	Generality	Short Description	#
Low	*Generic*	GIST, HOG2x2, self-similarity and geometric context color histogram features [17] [13]	512+6300+6300+3920
	Special	Color: Mean saturation, brightness and hue, PAD, colorfulness and color names [10]	1+1+4+3+1+11
		Texture: Tamura, Wavelet and GLCM [10]	3+12+12
Mid	*Generic*	Attributes [13] [19]	102
	Special	Principles-of-art: balance, emphasis, harmony, variety, gradation, movement [21]	60+18+2+60+9+16
High	*Generic*	Semantic concepts based on adjective noun pairs [1]	1200
	Special	Facial expressions [18]	8

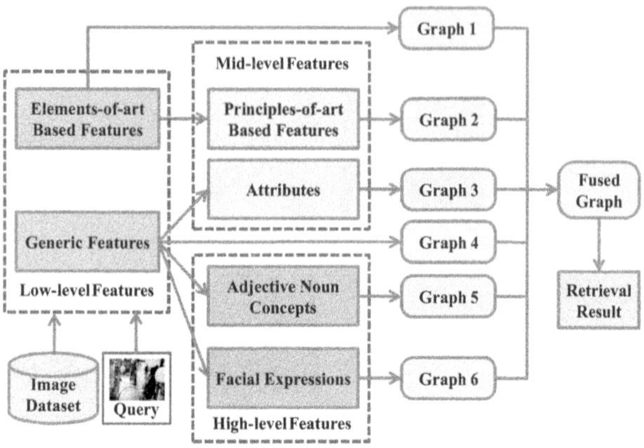

Figure 2: The framework of proposed affective image retrieval.

described by adjective noun pairs, such as beautiful flower, play an important role in expressing emotions of many natural images. Features of three different levels and two different generalities are extracted for each image based on related research on multimedia and computer vision. We then combine these features in a multi-graph learning framework [15] for affective image retrieval task. The framework of the proposed method is illustrated in Figure 2.

2. METHOD

In this section, we introduce the proposed method, including the extracted emotion features and the multi-graph learning model.

2.1 Emotion Features

2.1.1 Low-level Features

Low-level features suffer from the difficulty of easy interpretation by humans. For **generic** features, we choose HOG2x2, self-similarity, GIST and geometric context color histogram features as in [17] [13], because they are each individually powerful and can describe distinct visual phenomena in a scene perspective.

We also extract **special** features derived from elements of art, including color and texture [10]. Low-level color features include mean saturation and brightness, vector based mean hue, emotional coordinates (pleasure, arousal and dominance) based on brightness and saturation, colorfulness and color names. Low-level texture features include Tamura texture, Wavelet textures and gray-level co-occurrence matrix (GLCM) based texture [10].

2.1.2 Mid-level Features

Mid-level features are more semantic, more interpretable by humans and have stronger link to emotions than low-level features [21]. For **generic** features, we choose five types of attributes people tend to describe scenes: (1) materials (mental), (2) surface properties (dirty), (3) functions or affordances (reading), (4) spatial envelop attributes (cluttered) and (5) object presence (flowers). Based on the criteria of descent detection accuracy, potentially correlation to one emotion and easy understanding, we choose 102 attributes as in [13]. All the four generic low-level features are used to train attribute classifiers based on 14,340 images in SUN database [17]. The consensus labels (2 or 3 votes) are selected as positive and otherwise negative. SVM implemented in Liblinear toolbox[1] is used as classifiers for time saving. Finally, we can get a 102 dimensional binary vector of attribute features.

Features inspired from principles of art, including balance, contrast, harmony, variety, gradation, and movement are extracted as **special** features [21]. Please refer to [21] for details.

2.1.3 High-level Features

High-level features are the semantic contents contained in images. People can easily understand the emotions conveyed in images by recognizing the semantics. We choose concepts described by 1,200 adjective noun pairs (ANPs) [1] as **generic** features. The ANPs are detected by a large detector library SentiBank [1], which is trained using GIST, a 3×256 dimension color histogram, a 53 dimensional LBP descriptor, a Bag-of-Words quantized descriptor using a 1,000 word dictionary with a 2-layer spatial pyramid and max pooling, and a 2,000 dimensional attribute on about 500k images downloaded from Flickr. Liblinear SVM is used as classifiers and early fusion is adopted. The advantages of ANP are that it turns a neutral noun into an ANP with strong emotions and makes the concepts more detectable, as compared to nouns and adjectives, respectively. A 1,200 dimensional binary vector is obtained.

Meanwhile, we extract 8 kinds of facial expressions (*anger*, *contempt*, *disgust*, *fear*, *happiness*, *sadness*, *surprise*, *neutral*) [9] as **special** high-level features. Compositional features of local Haar appearance features are built by a minimum error based optimization strategy, which are embedded into an improved AdaBoost algorithm [18] [20]. Trained on CK+ database [9], the method performs well even on low intensity expressions [18]. As some images do not contain faces, we conduct face detection first using the Viola-Jones algorithm [14] implemented in OpenCV. The expressions of images detected without faces are set as *neutral*. Finally, we can get a 8 dimensional vector, each element of which indicates the number of related facial expressions in the image.

2.2 Multi-Graph Learning

Multi-graph learning [15] is the extension of single-graph learning and is widely used for reranking in various domains. In each graph, the vertices represent images and the edges reflect the similarities between image pairs.

Suppose we have N graphs $\mathbf{G}_1, \mathbf{G}_2, \cdots, \mathbf{G}_N$, each $\mathbf{G}_n$ is an

[1] http://www.csie.ntu.edu.tw/~cjlin/liblinear/

affinity matrix, where $\mathbf{G}_{n,ij}$ is the similarity between the ith and jth images in the nth graph. Given the labels Y and similarity matrix, we aim to get the relevance scores r. The N graphs can be integrated into a regularization framework [15],

$$\mathcal{Q}(r) = \sum_{n=1}^{N} \alpha_n \left(\sum_{i,j} \mathbf{G}_{n,ij} \left| \frac{r_i}{\sqrt{\mathbf{\Lambda}_{n,ij}}} - \frac{r_j}{\sqrt{\mathbf{\Lambda}_{n,ij}}} \right|^2 + \mu_n \sum_i |r_i - Y_i|^2 \right), \quad r = \arg\min_r \mathcal{Q}(r), \tag{1}$$

where $\alpha = [\alpha_1, ..., \alpha_N]$ is a weight vector, $\alpha_n > 0$, $\sum_{n=1}^{N} \alpha_n = 1$, and $\mathbf{\Lambda}_n$ is a diagonal matrix with $\mathbf{\Lambda}_{n,ii} = \sum_j \mathbf{G}_{n,ij}$. The closed-form solution of Equ. (1) is

$$r = \left(\mathbf{I} + \frac{\sum_{n=1}^{N} \alpha_n \mathbf{L}_n}{\sum_{n=1}^{N} \alpha_n \mu_n} \right)^{-1} Y, \tag{2}$$

where $\mathbf{L}_n = \mathbf{\Lambda}_n^{-1/2}(\mathbf{\Lambda}_n - \mathbf{G}_n)\mathbf{\Lambda}_n^{-1/2}$ is the normalized graph Laplacian. For computational efficiency, α is regarded as variables and Equ. (1) should be optimized with respect to both r and α [15]. To avoid that only extreme points are selected, a relaxation is made as follows [15],

$$\mathcal{Q}(r, \alpha) = \sum_{n=1}^{N} \alpha_n^{\lambda} \left(\sum_{i,j} \mathbf{G}_{n,ij} \left| \frac{r_i}{\sqrt{\mathbf{\Lambda}_{n,ij}}} - \frac{r_j}{\sqrt{\mathbf{\Lambda}_{n,ij}}} \right|^2 + \mu_n \sum_i |r_i - Y_i|^2 \right), \quad [r, \alpha] = \arg\min_{r,\alpha} \mathcal{Q}(r, \alpha). \tag{3}$$

Based on the fact that $\mathcal{Q}$ is convex with respect to both r and α [15], we can iteratively update r and α to minimize $\mathcal{Q}(f, \alpha)$. The detailed iterative solution algorithm and its corresponding convergence proof can be referred in [15]. The optimal choice of λ ($\lambda > 1$) depends on the complementation of the features. In practice, λ is decided by corss-validation.

When dealing with single kind of features, the multi-graph learning becomes single-graph learning. It means that $N = 1, \alpha = 1$, thus there is no need to optimize α. We can directly use the closed-form solution of f in Equ. (2) with $\alpha = 1$.

As our goal in this paper is to retrieve emotionally similar images to the query image, namely a retrieval task, we set Y_i as

$$Y_i = \begin{cases} 1, & \text{if image } i \text{ is the query image,} \\ 0, & \text{otherwise.} \end{cases} \tag{4}$$

As described in Section 2.1, we adopt 6 kinds of features, so we can construct 6 single graphs (see Figure 2). As each kind of feature (e.g. low-level special) is composed of different components (e.g. color, texture), we use the average similarity as the overall similarity. For the mth component ($m = 1, \ldots, M_n$) of the nth kind of features ($n = 1, \ldots, 6$), the sub-graph is generated by

$$G_{n,ij}^m = \begin{cases} exp\left(-\frac{d(x_{in}^m, x_{jn}^m)}{\sigma_n^m}\right), & \text{if } i \neq j, \\ 0, & \text{otherwise,} \end{cases} \tag{5}$$

where $d(.,.)$ is a specified distance function, x_{in}^m is the related feature vector of the mth component of the nth kind of features for image i, and σ_n^m is set as the average distance of the distance matrix of this component. Here the Euclidean distance is used for $d(.,.)$ and the final $n$the graph is $G_n = \frac{1}{M_n} \sum_{m=1}^{M_n} G_n^m$.

3. EXPERIMENTS

To evaluate the effectiveness of the proposed affective image retrieval method, we carry out experiments on several datasets.

3.1 Datasets

Subset A of IAPS dataset (**IAPSa**) includes 395 images [11], selected from a standard emotion evoking image set in psychology, named International Affective Picture System (IAPS) [7].

Artistic dataset (**ArtPhoto**) consists of 806 artistic photographs from a photo sharing site searched by emotion categories [10].

Abstract dataset (**Abstract**) includes 228 peer rated abstract paintings without contextual content [10].

The images in these three datasets (**IAPSa**, **ArtPhoto**, **Abstract**) are categorized into eight discreet categories [11]: *Anger*, *Disgust*, *Fear*, *Sad*, *Amusement*, *Awe*, *Contentment*, and *Excitement*.

The Geneva affective picture database (**GAPED**) consists of 520 negative images, 121 positive images and 89 neutral images [2].

Tweet dataset (**Tweet**) includes 470 positive tweets and 133 negative tweets [1] crawled from PeopleBrowsr with 21 hashtags.

3.2 Evaluation Criteria

We employ several widely used measurements as in [3].

(1) **Nearest neighbor rate** (**NN**) is defined as the percentage that the first returned image and the query image express the same emotions, indicating the performance as a nearest neighbor classifier.

(2) **First tier** (**FT**) and **second tier** (**ST**) are defined as the recall of the top N retrieval results. For the class with m relevant images in the whole dataset, $N = m$ for FT and $N = 2m$ for ST. That is, $FT = n_m/m$, $ST = n_{2m}/m$, where n_m and n_{2m} are the number of relevant images in the top m and $2m$ retrieval results.

(3) **Precision-recall curve**. Precision and recall are defined as $Pre = n/q$, $Rec = n/m$, where n is the number of relevant images among the first q retrieval results.

(4) F_1 **score** (F_1). F_1 is a measure of accuracy based Precision-Recall value, defined as $F_1 = 2 \cdot Pre \cdot Rec/(Pre + Rec)$. Here we consider the top 20 retrieval results.

(5) **Discounted cumulative gain** (**DCG**) [5] measures the importance of different positions of relevant results, assuming that users consider the frontal results more.

(6) **Average normalized modified retrieval rank** (**ANMRR**) [3] is a rank based metric, which takes into account the ranking sequence of relevant images within the retrieved images.

All the six measurements range from 0 to 1. Higher value represents better performance for the first five measurements and lower value indicates better performance for ANMRR.

3.3 Results and Discussion

Each image in the dataset is selected as query image and the average performance is computed. The precision-recall curves of different methods are shown in Figure 4, where 'LowGen', 'LowArt', 'MidAtt', 'MidArt', 'HighANP' and 'HighExp' represent single-graph learning methods based on low generic, low special, mid generic, mid special, high generic and high special features, respectively, while 'Fusion' is the proposed multi-graph learning mehtod. The performance comparison of other evaluation measurements are illustrated in Figure 3. Some detailed retrieval results of the proposed method are shown in Figure 5.

From these results, we can conclude that: (1) Different features perform differently on different kinds of images. Though performing well for traditional CBIR, the low-level generic features are not a good choice for affective image retrieval. (2) Generally, the fusion of different kinds of features outperforms single feature based method, because multi-graph learning can explore the complementation of different features. (3) For **Abstract** images, features inspired from art theory outperform others, as few attributes, concepts or faces are detected. (4) The emotions in **IAPS**, **GAPED** and **Tweet** datasets are often evoked by the presence of a certain object

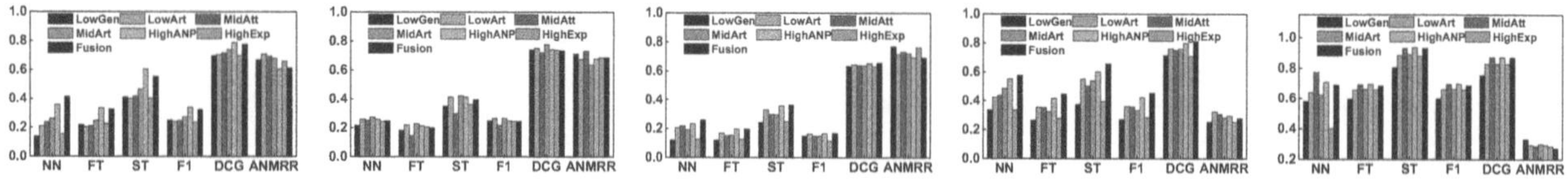

(a) IAPSa (b) Abstract (c) ArtPhoto (d) GAPED (e) Tweet

Figure 3: Average performance comparison of different methods for several measurements on different datasets.

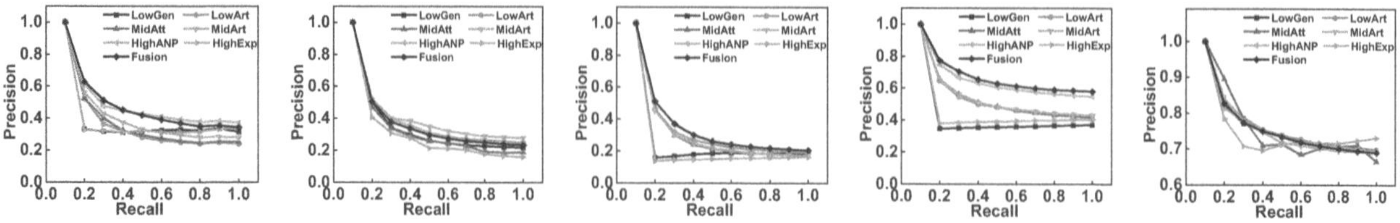

(a) IAPSa (b) Abstract (c) ArtPhoto (d) GAPED (e) Tweet

Figure 4: Average precision-recall curve comparison of different methods on different datasets.

(a) Amusement (b) Sadness

(c) Contentment (d) Fear

Figure 5: Some retrieval results of the proposed method. The first image of each group is the query image. Correct retrieval results are surrounded by green and thick frames while incorrect ones by red and dashed frames.

or special semantics. Therefore, the high level features, especially semantic concepts described by ANPs, perform well. (5) The overall performance of all methods is still not satisfying. To accurately understand the image emotions and retrieve emotionally similar images, there is still a long way to go.

4. CONCLUSION

In this paper, we proposed to use multi-graph learning for affective image retrieval based on features of different levels and different generalities that may contribute to express image emotions. We tested the performances of different features and combine them by multi-graph learning. The experiments conducted on five datasets demonstrated that the proposed method is effective to retrieve emotionally similar images. It should be noted that this method can be easily extended to more kinds of features and learning methods. We will try to firstly classify the images into different types and then select the best features for affective image retrieval. Comparison with state-of-the-art will be added in an extended version.

5. ACKNOWLEDGEMENTS

This work was supported by National Natural Science Foundation of China (No. 61071180) and Key Program (No. 61133003). Sicheng Zhao was also supported by the Ph.D. Short-Term Overseas Visiting Scholar Program of Harbin Institute of Technology.

6. REFERENCES

[1] D. Borth et al. Large-scale visual sentiment ontology and detectors using adjective noun pairs. In *MM*, 2013.

[2] E. S. Dan-Glauser and K. R. Scherer. The geneva affective picture database (gaped): a new 730-picture database focusing on valence and normative significance. *Behavior research methods*, 43(2):468–477, 2011.

[3] Y. Gao et al. 3-d object retrieval and recognition with hypergraph analysis. *IEEE TIP*, 21(9):4290–4303, 2012.

[4] A. Hanjalic. Extracting moods from pictures and sounds: Towards truly personalized tv. *IEEE Signal Processing Magazine*, 23(2):90–100, 2006.

[5] K. Järvelin and J. Kekäläinen. Cumulated gain-based evaluation of ir techniques. *ACM TOIS*, 20(4):422–446, 2002.

[6] J. Jia et al. Can we understand van gogh's mood? learning to infer affects from images in social networks. In *MM*, 2012.

[7] P. Lang et al. *International affective picture system (IAPS): Affective ratings of pictures and instruction manual*. NIMH, Center for the Study of Emotion & Attention, 2005.

[8] X. Lu et al. On shape and the computability of emotions. In *MM*, 2012.

[9] P. Lucey et al. The extended cohn-kanade dataset (ck+): A complete dataset for action unit and emotion-specified expression. In *CVPR Workshops*, 2010.

[10] J. Machajdik and A. Hanbury. Affective image classification using features inspired by psychology and art theory. In *MM*, 2010.

[11] J. Mikels et al. Emotional category data on images from the international affective picture system. *Behavior research methods*, 37(4):626–630, 2005.

[12] B. Pang and L. Lee. Opinion mining and sentiment analysis. *Information Retrieval*, 2(1-2):1–135, 2008.

[13] G. Patterson and J. Hays. Sun attribute database: Discovering, annotating, and recognizing scene attributes. In *CVPR*, 2012.

[14] P. Viola et al. Robust real-time face detection. *IJCV*, 57(2):137–154, 2004.

[15] M. Wang et al. Unified video annotation via multigraph learning. *IEEE TCSVT*, 19(5):733–746, 2009.

[16] W. Wang et al. A survey on emotional semantic image retrieval. In *ICIP*, 2008.

[17] J. Xiao et al. Sun database: Large-scale scene recognition from abbey to zoo. In *CVPR*, 2010.

[18] P. Yang et al. Exploring facial expressions with compositional features. In *CVPR*, 2010.

[19] J. Yuan et al. Sentribute: image sentiment analysis from a mid-level perspective. In *WISDOM*, 2013.

[20] S. Zhao et al. Video indexing and recommendation based on affective analysis of viewers. In *ACM MM*, 2011.

[21] S. Zhao et al. Exploring principles-of-art features for image emotion recognition. In *ACM MM*, 2014.

Recognizing Thousands of Legal Entities through Instance-based Visual Classification

Valentin Leveau
INA / INRIA Zenith, France
valentin.leveau@ina.fr

Alexis Joly
INRIA Zenith, France
alexis.joly@inria.fr

Olivier Buisson
INA, France
olivier.buisson@ina.fr

Pierre Letessier
INA, France

Patrick Valduriez
INRIA Zenith, France

ABSTRACT

This paper considers the problem of recognizing legal entities in visual contents in a similar way to named-entity recognizers for text documents. Whereas previous works were restricted to the recognition of a few tens of logotypes, we generalize the problem to the recognition of thousands of legal persons, each being modeled by a rich corporate identity automatically built from web images. We introduce a new geometrically-consistent instance-based classification method that is shown to outperform state-of-the-art techniques on several challenging datasets while being much more scalable. Further experiments performed on an automatic web crawl of 5,824 legal entities demonstrates the scalability of the approach.

1. INTRODUCTION

Legal entities (such as firms, government bodies, political parties, societies, associations, etc.) are entities other than natural persons (human being) created by law and recognized as having duties and rights. It does not exist any estimation of the number of such legal entities but they are omnipresent in our all day life as well as in all media contents. Beyond their legal identity, most of them also have a corporate visual identity, that is a set of graphical rules and elements providing an organisation with visibility and recognizability (graphic charter, logotype, insignia, colors, polices, fonts, etc.). As for natural persons, it is therefore possible to recognize them automatically in visual contents in order to provide automatic annotations. This is of high interest for many applications involving huge amounts of weakly annotated image or video contents (YouTube, social media, TV archives, etc.).

Whereas legal entity recognition is considered as an important challenge in the text community (e.g. the freebase repository contains 741K organisations, 160K educational institutions or 31K sport teams), the problem has received little attention in the multimedia community. Existing works and techniques (see section 2) are limited to the recognition of few tens of classes (37 logos in BelgaLogos dataset[1], 32 logos in FlickrLogos dataset [18]), each targeted entity being modeled by a single logotype. In this paper, we generalize the problem to the recognition of thousands of legal persons, each being modeled by a rich visual identity automatically built from web images. The proposed method relies on a geometrically-consistent instance classification technique that is described in section 3 and evaluated in section 4.

MM '14, November 03 - 07 2014, Orlando, FL, USA
Copyright 2014 ACM 978-1-4503-3063-3/14/11 ...$15.00.
http://dx.doi.org/10.1145/2647868.2655038 ...$15.00.

2. RELATED WORKS

As the number of legal entities to be recognized is very large, the problem is primarily related to large-scale image classification. Existing methods and techniques for this problem are typically based on local descriptors pooling techniques (BoW [19], Fisher vectors [13], SPM [10]) and the use of efficient classifiers in the high-dimensional embedded space such as linear support vector machines [14]. An alternative is *deep convolutional neural networks* that have been recently proved to achieve similar results on large-scale image datasets such as ImageNet [9]. The problem we are targeting is however slightly different. Because the visual identity of a legal entity is actually aimed at guarantying its recognizability, it relies on visual objects with small intra-class variations (such as logos, landmarks, insignias, etc.) but in highly cluttered contexts (very small objects & weak image-level annotations). This problem has been referred as *instance classification* in a recent paper of Krapac et al. [8] and is at the crossroad between *object recognition* and *instance-level image retrieval*. The method they propose is based on a feature-wise prototype selection approach: local descriptors are all kept in their original form (without quantization) and a distance-adaptive prototype is trained for each of them in a supervised way. They report some consistent performance improvements over several state-of-the-art classification methods (including Fisher Vectors [14]).

The other family of techniques related to our work is *instance-based image retrieval* techniques [2] and in particular the ones focused on logo retrieval [18, 6]. These techniques are primarily aimed at retrieving instances of a given query object in an unsupervised way but any of them can be used for classification purposes when the search is performed on

[1]http://www-rocq.inria.fr/imedia/belga-logo.html

a labelled set of pictures (typically by voting on the top-K retrieved images or through any other instance-based classifier). They usually rely on local descriptors quantization methods (such as hamming embedding [1], data-dependent hashing [7] or product quantizer [4]) and scalable indexing structures (such as inverted lists or hash tables). This allows matching all local descriptors one by one in the full index and favors a more precise matching of small objects in highly cluttered pictures. Using geometry in addition to this raw scheme has been proved to achieve further performance gains, either by the inclusion of weak geometry constraints in the matching phase [3] or by post-checking the geometry consistency of the matches, typically by using a RANSAC algorithm [6]. The method proposed in this paper improves such techniques in order to construct precise class-specific saliency maps and build a strong image classifier highly robust to noise and clutter.

3. PROPOSED METHOD

We consider a training set S of $|S|$ pictures weakly annotated with one or several labels among $|C|$ classes (corresponding to one or several legal entities presumably recognizable in the picture). Each picture is described by a set of local descriptors (SIFT [11] in our experiments) forming a reference dataset of N local features $\mathbf{x}_i$. Our instance-based geometrically-consistent classification scheme can be summarized as follows: local descriptors are extracted from the query image I_q and searched independently in the reference set using an efficient K-NN search scheme. A local geometry consistency checking is then performed at every potential region of interest using a newly introduced sliding RANSAC procedure. The resulting lists of checked patches are then back-propagated in the query image and merged in order to produce pixel-wise saliency maps for each of the retrieved label. A strong classifier is finally derived from the class-specific saliency maps through a max-pooling strategy.

Hash-based K-NN search. The approximate K-Nearest Neighbors (K-NN) of each local feature $\mathbf{x}_j^Q$ belonging to a query image I_Q are computed efficiently thanks to the hash-based multi-probe search method introduced in [5]. Its principle is to train an adaptive search model at indexing time through kernel density estimates computed on exact K-NN samples. This model is used at search time to select the most probable buckets to be visited so as to retrieve on average a fraction α of the real K-NN's (α was set to 0.80 in all our experiments). The advantage of this method compared to other state-of-the-art methods (such as PQ-code [4] or Soft-Assignment [16]) is that it allows controlling accurately the quality of the retrieved K-NN while being applicable to any quantization function and metrics.

In our case, the original scheme is transposed to the use of a more effective hash function and to the application of the Hamming Embedding principle [1]. More precisely, we used RMMH [7], a recent data-dependent hash function family, in order to embed the original feature vectors in compact binary hash codes of 128 bits (the parameter M of RMMH was fixed to $M = 32$). The $k = log_2(N)$ first bits of the hash codes are used as keys of a hash map containing the N 128-bits hash codes divided into the 2^k buckets. Still at indexing time, the search model is estimated based on the exact K-NN's in the 128-bits Hamming space rather than in the original space. It has actually be shown in [7] that RMMH somehow works as an unsupervised metric learning technique and can provide better matches in the embedded space than in the original one. At search time, the query feature $\mathbf{x}_j^Q$ is also embedded via RMMH and the resulting 128-bits hash code $\mathbf{h}_j^Q$ is passed to the probabilistic multi-probe algorithm (see [5] for more details). Once the most probable buckets have been selected, the top-K matches are computed as the K nearest hash codes according to the Hamming distance between the query hash code $\mathbf{h}_j^Q$ and the hash codes belonging to the selected buckets.

Sliding RANSAC. Post-checking the geometric consistency of the raw visual matches is an efficient strategy to filter false positives and consolidate good matches. The RANSAC algorithm has notably been successful in rigid objects retrieval [15] in particular logos [6]. Some recent variants such as MAC-RANSAC [17] provide even better results in the context of multiple localized objects by either constraining the distance of the randomized candidate pairs or by iteratively removing validated matches from the pool of candidates. But even with such improvements, a global RANSAC algorithm applied at the image-level is not adapted to the detection of very small objects in highly cluttered images for which the percentage of inlier pairs of matches can be typically lower than 0.1% of the whole set of possible pairs. Furthermore, as it is computed on the retrieved images one by one, it does not allow consolidating locally the matches from different training images.

To address these issues, we introduce a *sliding* RANSAC strategy aimed at checking the geometric consistency locally for each of the N_Q query features of the query image I_Q. More precisely, for a given local feature $\mathbf{x}_j^Q \in I_Q$, its m spatial nearest neighbors are computed so as to define a candidate region of interest to be geometrically checked in all the retrieved pictures (i.e. in the ones having some visual matches within the $m+1$ lists of K-NN's). For a given candidate region of interest and a given retrieved image, the RANSAC algorithm then works in a standard fashion (in our experiments, we used a scale-rotation-translation model and 100 iterations per local run). Note that the support of both the *random sampling* and the *consensus* phases is bounded by the set of local features belonging to the current region of interest. This allows improving the recall and the precision of the inliers compared to classical global RANSAC algorithm. The parameter m controls the locality constraint of the geometry consistency analysis. Ideally, it should fit the size of the targeted objects of interest. Too large values of m would lead to the same problem than a global RANSAC. Too small values of m would degrade the dynamic of the number of inliers and possibly miss some consistent matches. In our experiments, m was trained by cross-validation.

Class-specific geometry consistency maps. The output of the sliding RANSAC algorithm is a set of N_Q lists of consolidated results (i.e. one list per query feature $\mathbf{x}_j^Q$). Each consolidated result $R_{j,t}^Q$ is itself defined as a set of individual matches of the form $(\mathbf{x}_{j'}^Q, \mathbf{x}_{t'})$ where the $\mathbf{x}_{j'}^Q$ belong to the m spatial neighbors of $\mathbf{x}_j^Q$ and the $\mathbf{x}_{t'}$ belong to an image I_t of the training set. In order to construct saliency maps, we first associate each consolidated result $R_{j,t}^Q$ with an individual geometry consistency score $f_{j,t}^Q$ and a bounding box

(a) Raw query image

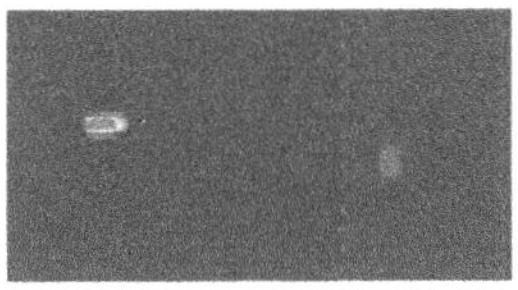

(b) Class *Base*

(c) Class *Quick*

Figure 1: Class-specific geometry consistency maps.

$B^Q_{j,t}$ in the query image. Rather than simply counting the number of inlier matches, the score $f^Q_{j,t}$ is computed as the sum of the inverse rank of the matched features $\mathbf{x}_{t'}$ (rank in the K-NN's of $\mathbf{x}^Q_{j'}$). This allows giving more importance to the most confident visual matches. The bounding box $B^Q_{j,t}$ is defined as the minimum bounding rectangle containing all the individually matched features $\mathbf{x}^Q_{j'} \in R^Q_{j,t}$.
The pixel-wise consistency score $g^Q_c(w,h)$ of a pixel (w,h) according to class label c is then computed by (i) selecting the consolidated results $R^Q_{j,t}$ whose bounding box $B^Q_{j,t}$ intercepts (w,h) (ii) grouping them according to the provenance image I_t and averaging the scores $f^Q_{j,t}$ for each group (iii) summing the averaged scores of the groups whose provenance images I_t are labeled with c. This allows voting on the number of pictures retrieved for label c and weighting each vote by an average geometry consistency in each image. Figure 1 displays two saliency maps $g^Q_c(w,h)$ computed for two distinct class labels in a single query image.

Multi-label Scoring. As illustrated by Figure 1, the saliency maps produced by the previous step could be easily used for a precise localization of the visual patterns recognized for each of the retrieved legal entity. The scope of the present paper is however only on classification so that we only use the maps to build a strong classifier at the image level. This is done by simply taking the value of the most salient pixel in each map (i.e for each returned label):

$$s^Q(c) = \max_{(\mathbf{w},\mathbf{h})} g^Q_c(w,h) \tag{1}$$

where $s^Q(c)$ is the detection score of the label c.
As shown in Figure 1, this last step also acts as a disambiguation procedure where different classes can co-occur in different images and bring geometry consistency in other class-specific saliency maps.

To decide whether a given legal entity is detected or not, a threshold τ_s is applied on the $s^Q(c)$ scores (several annotations can thus be produced for each image). To better model the density distribution over the classes, a normalization is then applied according to:

$$p^Q(c) = \frac{s^Q(c)}{\sum_{c'} s^Q(c')} \tag{2}$$

where $p^Q(c)$ is the probability estimation of the presence of the label c.

Discussion. The main line of this paper is to use online geometry consistency checking to disambiguate instance-based matches rather than training discriminative models offline. This is justified in several ways. First, our training phase is reduced to a simple indexing process with a linear time and space complexity $O(N)$. The prototype selection technique of [8] requires computing the $20,000$-NN's of each of the N features of the training set, leading to a much more important training time (over-linear in N). Concerning the memory storage, their method requires at least 8 times more RAM to store the original SIFT features. Besides, the complexity of other state-of-the-art methods making use of pooling and SVM's is typically $O(N + |C|.|S|^2)$ so that they are less scalable in both the number of classes and the number of images. Beyond scalability, our method has several other advantages including the easy management of multi-labeled images, the fine grained localisation of the recognized patterns making them highly interpretable and the possibility of dynamically inserting additional training images in an incremental way.

4. EXPERIMENTS

Evaluation metric and datasets. Classification effectiveness is measured by the Mean Average Precision (mAP), which is commonly defined as the mean of the per-class average precisions. The evaluation is performed on 3 datasets of the literature and one newly introduced dataset dedicated to the large-scale recognition of legal entities:
FlickrLogos32 [18] - 8,240 images composed of 2,240 images labelled with 32 logo classes and 6000 distractors considered as a no-logo class. Evaluation protocol is the same than [8].
BelgaLogoII [6] - 10,000 images containing 2695 instances of 37 different logos. The main difference with FlickrLogos32 is that images are multi-labeled and that that the average size of the logos is much lower. Evaluation is completed by leave-one-out queries.
Vehicles29 [8] - 10,622 images labelled with 29 car models of 7 brands (divided into 5,266 training and 5,356 test images). Evaluation protocol is the same than [8].
LegalEntities5K - 371,924 images noisy labelled with 5,824 legal entities. This dataset was automatically created by querying Google Image search engine with the entities names. The list of the entities is the union of several thesaurus found on the web and contains world-wide companies, associations, organizations and sport teams. To try limiting noise, we kept only the top-20 to top-1000 results as a function of the popularity of the tag (number of pages returned by Google). A test set was built by taking the $2,500$ of the most popular tags of the dataset. A second test set was created by intersecting the whole Flickr32 dataset with the labels of LegalEntities5K (540 test images belonging to 18 classes).

Method	FlickrL32	Vehicles29
Fisher Vectors (128x4,096)	0.866	0.497
Prototype voting [8]	0.914	0.557
Our method (S-Ransac)	**0.928**	**0.597**

Table 1: Classification performances.

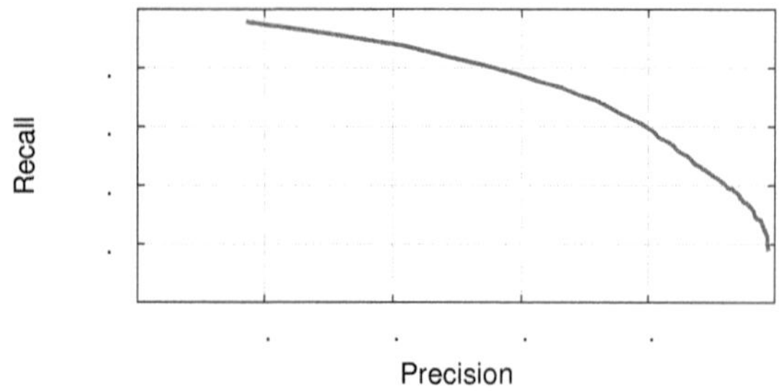

Figure 2: Recall-precision curve of our method on the multi-labeled dataset BelgaLogos.

Features and parameters setting. Local features are SIFT features [11] extracted around interest points detected by the rotation-invariant Harris-Hessian-Laplace detector [12]. The two main parameters of our method, i.e. the spatial neighborhood size m and the detection threshold τ_s were trained by cross-validation on the training sets of *FlickrLogos32* and *Vehicles29*. m was set to 5% of the number of descriptors for each query image ans τ_s was set to 5.

Comparative study. Table 1 reproduces the results of [8] and reports our own results using the same evaluation protocol. It can be seen that our method outperforms the previous baseline of [8] (and de facto the other state-of-the-art classification methods) on the two experimented datasets, whereas the training stage of our method is much more scalable. It took respectively 13 minutes and 22 minutes to index and to compute the a posteriori multi-probe search model of the 51,054,054 descriptors of the Vehicles29 training set and the 91,800,540 descriptors of the FlickerLogos32 training set (including distractors images). The good results achieved by our method on the *Vehicles29* dataset shows that it is well suited for such fine-grained image classification tasks even if it is not the primary goal of this paper.

Multiple labels. To evaluate our method in the context of multi-labeled images, we used the challenging BelgaLogos dataset. For this experiment, we randomly chose 1,000 images of the dataset that contain at least one labeled logo. Our method achieves a mAP of 82.30 which is quite impressive knowing that this dataset involves very small objects in highly cluttered contexts. To better illustrate the relevance of the produced labels for each played queries, Figure 2 displays the precision-recall curve of our method when varying the detection threshold τ_s. It shows that very high precision or recall values might be obtained depending on the applicative constraints.

Large-scale experiment on thousands of legal entities. It took 1 hour and 55 minutes to index the 500,957,407 SIFT features of the *LegalEntities5K* dataset and to compute the a posteriori multi-probe search model. Table 2 reports the results achieved on the two test tests in terms of mAP and search time. It shows that that the effectiveness of our method is still very satisfactory considering that (i) the number of classes in the training set is two orders of magnitude higher (ii) the training set was built automatically without any human validation and therefore contains a high level of noise.

Benchmark	mAP	Avg Search time
2.5K images / LegalEntities5K	**0.686**	7.4 sec
FlickrLogos / LegalEntities5K	**0.648**	6.3 sec

Table 2: Classification results and computation time on the *LegalEntities5K* dataset (Intel(R) Xeon(R) E5-2650 CPU 2.00GHz).

5. CONCLUSION

The work reported in this paper was a first attempt towards deploying real-world visual-based entity recognizers at the web scale. It did show the importance of using fine-grained geometry in this regard and demonstrated the advantage of instance-based classification methods in terms of scalability. Future works will focus on collecting and denoising training data in a more elaborated way than the proof of concept presented in this paper.

6. REFERENCES

[1] A. Andoni and P. Indyk. Near-optimal hashing algorithms for approximate nearest neighbor in high dimensions. In *FOCS*, 2006.

[2] R. Arandjelovic and A. Zisserman. Three things everyone should know to improve object retrieval. In *CVPR*, 2012.

[3] H. Jegou, M. Douze, and C. Schmid. Hamming embedding and weak geometric consistency for large scale image search. In *ECCV*, 2008.

[4] H. Jegou, M. Douze, and C. Schmid. Product quantization for nearest neighbor search. *PAMI*, 2011.

[5] A. Joly and O. Buisson. A posteriori multi-probe locality sensitive hashing. In *ACM MM*, 2008.

[6] A. Joly and O. Buisson. Logo retrieval with a contrario visual query expansion. In *ACM MM*, 2009.

[7] A. Joly and O. Buisson. Random maximum margin hashing. In *CVPR*, 2011.

[8] J. Krapac, F. Perronnin, T. Furon, and H. Jégou. Instance classification with prototype selection. In *ICMR*, 2014.

[9] A. Krizhevsky, I. Sutskever, and G. E. Hinton. Imagenet classification with deep convolutional neural networks. In *NIPS*, 2012.

[10] S. Lazebnik, C. Schmid, and J. Ponce. Beyond bags of features: Spatial pyramid matching for recognizing natural scene categories. In *CVPR*, 2006.

[11] D. Lowe. Object recognition from local scale-invariant features. In *ICCV*, 1999.

[12] K. Mikolajczyk and C. Schmid. An affine invariant interest point detector. *ECCV*, 2002.

[13] F. Perronnin and C. Dance. Fisher kernels on visual vocabularies for image categorization. In *CVPR*, 2007.

[14] F. Perronnin, J. Sánchez, and T. Mensik. Improving the fisher kernel for large-scale image classification. In *ECCV*, 2010.

[15] J. Philbin. *Scalable Object Retrieval in Very Large Image Collections.* PhD thesis, University of Oxford, 2010.

[16] J. Philbin, O. Chum, M. Isard, J. Sivic, and A. Zisserman. Lost in quantization: Improving particular object retrieval in large scale image databases. In *CVPR*, 2008.

[17] J. Rabin, J. Delon, Y. Gousseau, and L. Moisan. Mac-ransac: a robust algorithm for the recognition of multiple objects. In *3DPTV*, 2010.

[18] S. Romberg, L. G. Pueyo, R. Lienhart, and R. van Zwol. Scalable logo recognition in real-world images. In *ICMR*, 2011.

[19] J. Sivic and A. Zisserman. Video google: A text retrieval approach to object matching in videos. In *CVPR*, 2003.

Automatic Fine-grained Hyperlinking of Videos within a Closed Collection using Scene Segmentation

Evlampios Apostolidis
CERTH-ITI
Thessaloniki, Greece
apostolid@iti.gr

Vasileios Mezaris
CERTH-ITI
Thessaloniki, Greece
bmezaris@iti.gr

Mathilde Sahuguet
EURECOM
Sophia Antipolis, France
sahuguet@eurecom.fr

Benoit Huet
EURECOM
Sophia Antipolis, France
huet@eurecom.fr

Barbora Červenková
University of Economics
Prague, Czech Republic
cervenkovab@gmail.com

Daniel Stein
Fraunhofer IAIS
Sankt Augustin, Germany
daniel.stein@iais.fraunhofer.de

ABSTRACT

This paper introduces a framework for establishing links between related media fragments within a collection of videos. A set of analysis techniques is applied for extracting information from different types of data. Visual-based shot and scene segmentation is performed for defining media fragments at different granularity levels, while visual cues are detected from keyframes of the video via concept detection and optical character recognition (OCR). Keyword extraction is applied on textual data such as the output of OCR, subtitles and metadata. This set of results is used for the automatic identification and linking of related media fragments. The proposed framework exhibited competitive performance in the Video Hyperlinking sub-task of MediaEval 2013, indicating that video scene segmentation can provide more meaningful segments, compared to other decomposition methods, for hyperlinking purposes.

Categories and Subject Descriptors: H.3.3 [Information Search and Retrieval]: Retrieval models; H.3.1 [Information Storage and Retrieval]: Content Analysis and Indexing

Keywords: Video hyperlinking; scene segmentation; concept detection; keyword extraction; data indexing

1. INTRODUCTION

Nowadays there is a constantly increasing volume of media on the web, available either on video-sharing web-sites such as YouTube and Vimeo, or within multimedia collections of content providers such as web-based broadcasters and news organizations. A very natural paradigm of exploring this content includes a user that watches a video and then needs to follow up on an interesting fragment of it (denoted "anchor" or "context" in sequel), by easily navigating to other videos or video fragments on the same topic, featuring the same persons, places or objects. The goal of video hyperlinking is to provide links to the user for accessing related content, thus supporting and facilitating the navigation within a multimedia collection. This is by no means a trivial task, particularly at a fine-granularity level (fragment-level). Text-based search and retrieval strategies can be used only when textual information has already been assigned to the videos by human annotators, and even so, such annotations most often briefly describe each entire video rather than specifically the relevant segments of it. This highlights two main weaknesses of the current approaches for establishing such links between multimedia content items: the definition of semantically meaningful and coherent parts of the content using simple temporal segmentation strategies that rely either on low-level visual or textual data is not sufficient, while due to the known semantic gap, automatic hyperlinking based on text features only fails to exploit the rich multi-modal content of videos.

Aiming to address these problems, we propose a framework that creates story-telling multimedia fragments from videos, and exploits the high-level semantics of the visual stream for assessing the relevance between media fragments and for establishing links whenever is appropriate. Using the created links a viewer can efficiently navigate, when seeking relevant content within a multimedia collection, according to the vision of video hyperlinking.

MM'14, November 3–7, 2014, Orlando, Florida, USA.
Copyright 2014 ACM 978-1-4503-3063-3/14/11 ...$15.00.
http://dx.doi.org/10.1145/2647868.2655041.

2. RELATED WORK

Several approaches for video hyperlinking have been proposed and evaluated in the last couple of years, mainly in the scope of the Hyperlinking sub-task of the MediaEval benchmarking activity. The relevant literature includes methods that either rely only on textual or visual information, or combine these different modalities using various fusion and re-ranking schemes, for linking related media fragments.

A unimodal text-based method that combines fixed-length segmented transcripts (created by automatic speech recognition (ASR)), enriched with extracted entities, and an unsupervised similarity metric for identifying relevant media fragments, was introduced in [8]. A similar approach that evaluates similarity on the video-level and a more detailed segment-level using partitioned ASR transcripts and extracted entities was presented in [5], while another method that defines fragments by performing a term-based speech segmentation was introduced in [11]. The algorithm of [7] creates a short-list of semantically related videos based on ASR transcripts, and then defines the appropriate fragments by constructing word similarity graphs, or by evaluating the lexical cohesion. Another unimodal approach based exclusively on visual information was proposed in [16], where the visual similarity between shots is assessed by representing the keyframes of the corresponding shots using a Bag-of-Words model built from local descriptors.

Alternatively, multimodal hyperlinking methods that combine text- and visual-based analysis were also proposed. In [10], similar media fragments are defined by building a graph based on keywords extracted from ASR transcripts, while visual similarity is assessed with the help of local descriptors. In [4], the video is initially segmented into topics based on ASR transcripts and subtitles, and a list with the most relevant segments to a given "anchor" is defined via cosine similarity. Visual similarity between these segments and the "anchor" is then assessed using visual concepts, and the re-ranked list of segments is the final output of the algorithm. A similar approach was introduced in [3], where the textual similarity is computed based on matching terms and named entities, and the visual similarity is estimated by extracting local descriptors from each 5-th frame of the video segments.

Textual information extracted from subtitles, ASR transcripts or metadata, can be a good indicator about the relevance between entire videos. However, the definition of appropriate media fragments within videos that are closely related to the human information needs is a key goal of video hyperlinking. Text-only approaches for specifying these segments lack the information included in the visual stream, often over-segmenting the media items, while visual shot segments are too fine-grained for describing an entire story telling part of the video. Aiming to address this problem, differently from any other work on this topic, we propose a video hyperlinking framework where the elementary temporal segments are automatically formed by a method for the segmentation of video in scenes, which are subsequently annotated by using a rich set of audio-visual analysis techniques.

3. PROPOSED APPROACH

This section describes the overall architecture of the proposed system, focusing further on the scene segmentation analysis module which defines media fragments that are used as starting and ending points of the hyperlinking procedure.

3.1 Overall hyperlinking framework

As shown in Fig. 1, the proposed framework consists of two main components. The analysis component includes all the utilized analysis modules, and can be further divided in a group of visual-based techniques and a method that processes textual information. The storage component contains the data storage and indexing structures that facilitate the retrieval and linking of related media fragments.

The off-line processing of the multimedia collection starts by decomposing the videos into shots (e.g., using [2]) and extracting, for each shot, a number of representative keyframes that will be used as input in subsequent visual analysis techniques. Then, the scene segmentation technique of [13] groups the detected shot segments into bigger story-telling units (scenes), aiming to define a more meaningful fragmentation of the video. Using the keyframes, visual cues are extracted by performing OCR and visual concept detection. OCR is based on the tesseract engine[1] and the text localization algorithm presented in [14]. Visual concepts are detected from each keyframe by applying the concept detection algorithm of [12], which uses a sub-set of 10 base detectors per concept and a set of 151 semantic concepts selected from the list of concepts defined in the TRECVID 2012 SIN task [9]. OCR results and any other available textual resources (e.g., the videos' subtitles and metadata) are fed to the utilized keyword extraction algorithm, which is the one presented in [15]. The output of this analysis is a number of keywords and visual concepts which are assigned to different video fragments.

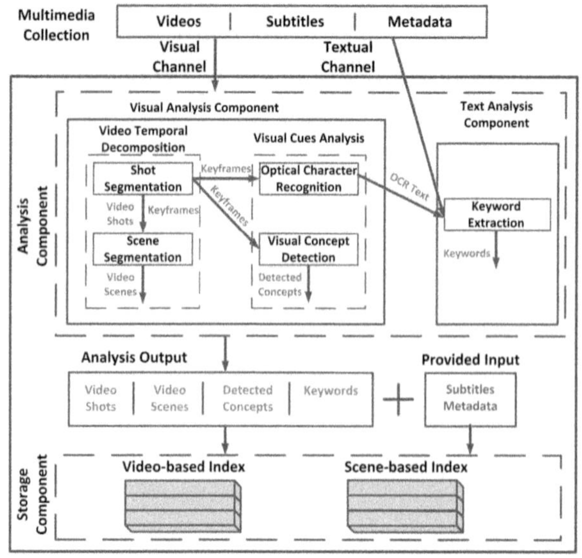

Figure 1: The proposed framework for multi-modal analysis and indexing, that supports the retrieval and hyperlinking of media fragments.

The produced analysis results, along with the subtitles and metadata of the videos, are indexed using the storage component of the framework. This is based on the Solr/Lucene platform and creates indexes that contain data at two granularities: the video level and the scene level.

3.2 Temporal video segmentation into scenes

As already mentioned, starting from a decomposition of each video of the multimedia collection into shots, the proposed framework defines a more meaningful video segmentation into story-telling parts. For this, the scene segmentation algorithm of [13] is utilized. This method groups shots into sets that correspond to individual scenes of the video, based on content similarity and temporal consistency among shots. Content similarity in our experiments means visual similarity, and the latter was assessed by computing and comparing the HSV histograms of the keyframes of different shots. Visual similarity and temporal consistency are jointly considered during the grouping of the shots into scenes, with the help of two extensions of the well known Scene Transition Graph (STG) algorithm [17]. The first extension reduces the computational cost of STG-based shot grouping by consid-

[1]http://code.google.com/p/tesseract-ocr/

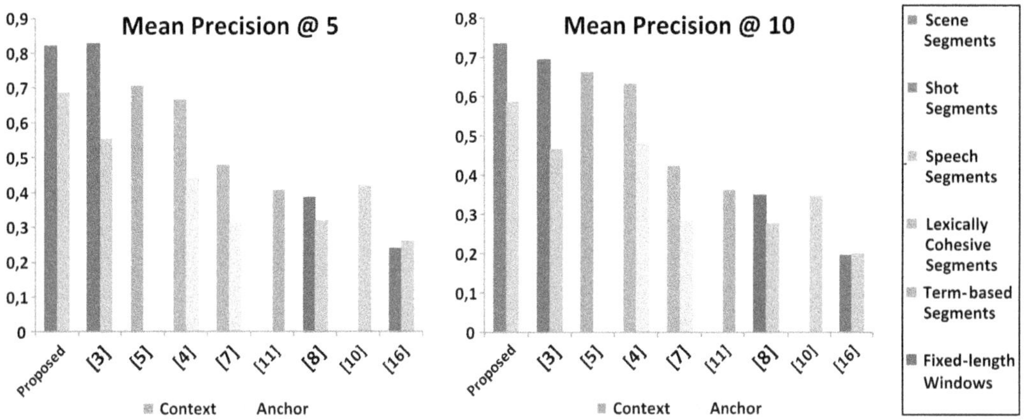

Figure 2: The best mean performance of each participating approach in the Hyperlinking sub-task of MediaEval 2013, also in relation to the segmentation unit employed by each team (see legend on the right).

ering shot linking transitivity and the fact that scenes are by definition convex sets of shots. The second one builds on the former to construct a probabilistic framework that alleviates the need for manual STG parameter selection. Based on these extensions, and as reported in [13], the applied technique is capable of identifying automatically the scene-level structure of videos belonging to different genres (e.g., documentaries, movies), providing results that match well the human expectations, while the needed processing time is only a very small fraction ($< 1\%$) of the overall analysis.

4. EXPERIMENTAL RESULTS

The performance of the proposed framework was evaluated on the Hyperlinking sub-task of the MediaEval 2013 benchmarking activity [6]. The used dataset is made of 1667 hours of video (2323 videos from BBC) of various content, such as news shows, talk shows, sitcoms and documentaries. For each video the organizers provided also manually transcribed subtitles, ASR transcripts, textual metadata and automatically detected shot boundaries and keyframes.

The goal of the Hyperlinking sub-task is to search a multimedia collection for content related to a given media fragment. Specifically, the task organizers defined a set of 30 "anchors" (media fragments described by the video's name and their start and end times; thus, no further temporal segmentation of them is necessary), which are used as the basis for seeking related content within the provided collection. For each "anchor", a broader yet related temporal segment with contextual information about the "anchor", called "context", was also defined. For evaluating the hyperlinking performance, Precision @ k (which counts the number of relevant fragments within the top k of the ranked list of hyperlinks, with k being 5 and 10) was used. Moreover, three slightly different functions were defined for measuring the relevance of a retrieved segment; the "overlap relevance", which considers the temporal overlap between a retrieved segment and the actual one; the "binned relevance", which assigns segments into bins; and the "tolerance to irrelevance", which takes into account only the start times of the retrieved segments [1].

Given a pair of "anchor" and "context" fragments the proposed framework initially creates automatically two queries, one using only the "anchor" information and another one using both "anchor" and "context" information, which are going to be applied on the created indexes (Section 3.1). These queries are defined by extracting keywords from the subtitles of the "anchor"/"context" fragments, and by applying visual concept detection. The latter is performed on the keyframes of all shots of the corresponding media fragment and its results are combined using max pooling (i.e., keeping for each concept the highest confidence score). Our framework then applies these queries on the video-level index; this step filters the entire collection of videos, resulting in a much smaller set of potentially relevant videos. Using the new limited set of videos, the same queries are applied on the scene-level index, and a ranked list with the scenes that were identified as the most relevant ones is returned, forming the output of the proposed system.

Figure 2 illustrates the best mean performance of each participating team in MediaEval 2013 (in terms of Precision @ k using the "overlap relevance" metric) when only the "anchor" or the "anchor" and "context" information is exploited, also indicating (by color) which were the segmentation units utilized by each approach. As shown, when only the "anchor" is known, our proposed approach exhibits the highest performance for k equal to 5 or 10, while it is among the top-2 highest performers when "context" information is also included. Specifically, the k-th first items (hyperlinks) proposed by our system to the user are very likely to include the needed media fragment (over 80% for the top-5 and over 70% for the top-10). Moreover, the comparison of the different video decomposition approaches shows that the visual-based segmentation techniques (scene or shot segmentation) are more effective than other speech-based, text-based or fixed-window segmentation methods.

The competitiveness of the developed hyperlinking approach is also highlighted in Table 1. This table contains the best scores of each participating team for the Mean Precision @ 5 and @ 10 measures, according to the different defined relevance functions (highest scores are in bold font; a dash means that no run was submitted to MediaEval 2013). As shown, the proposed framework achieves the best performance in 11 out of 12 cases.

We also ran an experiment with a variation of our approach that used a simple temporal window (defined by

Table 1: The best Mean Precision @ 5 and @ 10 scores (for the different relevance measures) for the teams participating to the Hyperlinking sub-task of MediaEval 2013, using "anchor" and "context" information.

	Mean Precision @ 5						Mean Precision @ 10					
	Overlap Relevance		Binned Relevance		Toll. to Irrelevance		Overlap Relevance		Binned Relevance		Toll. to Irrelevance	
	Context	Anchor	Context	Anchor	Context	Anchor	Context	Anchor	Context	Anchor	Context	Anchor
Proposed	0,8200	**0,6867**	**0,7200**	**0,6600**	**0,6933**	**0,6133**	**0,7333**	**0,5867**	**0,6333**	**0,5467**	**0,6367**	**0,5133**
[3]	**0,8267**	0,5533	0,5400	0,5333	0,5933	0,5133	0,6933	0,4667	0,3867	0,4333	0,4433	0,4200
[5]	0,7067	-	0,6000	-	0,5333	-	0,6633	-	0,5667	-	0,4667	-
[4]	0,6667	0,4400	0,6333	0,5000	0,4600	0,3867	0,6333	0,4833	0,5167	0,4867	0,4433	0,4033
[7]	0,4800	0,3133	0,4600	0,3400	0,4667	0,3133	0,4233	0,2833	0,4100	0,3000	0,4100	0,2733
[11]	-	0,4067	-	0,3933	-	0,3600	-	0,3633	-	0,3500	-	0,3267
[8]	0,3867	0,3200	0,3867	0,3267	0,3667	0,3067	0,3500	0,2767	0,3500	0,2800	0,3233	0,2600
[10]	-	0,4200	-	0,4000	-	0,3400	-	0,3467	-	0,3267	-	0,2900
[16]	0,2400	0,2600	0,2400	0,2600	0,2333	0,2467	0,1967	0,2000	0,1967	0,1900	0,1933	0,1900
Windowing	0,5733	0,4467	0,6067	0,5000	0,4600	0,3467	0,4833	0,3200	0,5333	0,3733	0,4000	0,2533

grouping shots that are no more than 10 sec. apart) for determining the temporal segments used for hyperlinking, instead of the outcome of scene segmentation (last row of Table 1). The comparison again indicates that automatically detected scenes are more meaningful video fragments for hyperlinking, compared to simpler temporal segmentations (e.g., windowing).

5. CONCLUSIONS

In this paper we presented an approach for analysing multimedia collections aiming to define meaningful media fragments and create links between related content. The proposed framework consists of a set of multi-modal analysis techniques, which include methods for video segmentation and for the identification of visual cues, as well as an algorithm for extracting keywords from textual data. Our participation in the Hyperlinking sub-task of MediaEval 2013 and related experiments showed that the proposed framework performs very well, and highlighted the importance of video scenes in video hyperlinking tasks.

6. ACKNOWLEDGMENTS

This work was supported by the European Commission under contract FP7-287911 LinkedTV.

7. ADDITIONAL AUTHORS

Additional authors: Stefan Eickeler (Fraunhofer IAIS, email: stefan.eickeler@iais.fraunhofer.de), José Luis Redondo García (Eurecom, email: redondo@eurecom.fr), Raphaël Troncy (Eurecom, email: troncy@eurecom.fr) and Lukás Pikora (University of Economics Prague, email: lukas.pikora@vse.cz).

8. REFERENCES

[1] R. Aly, M. Eskevich, R. Ordelman, et al. Adapting binary information retrieval evaluation metrics for segment-based retrieval tasks. Technical report, ArXiv e-prints, 2013.

[2] E. Apostolidis and V. Mezaris. Fast shot segmentation combining global and local visual descriptors. In *Proc. IEEE ICASSP*, Florence, Italy, May 2014.

[3] W. Bailer, M. Lokaj, and H. Stiegler. Context in video search: Is close-by good enough when using linking? In *ACM ICMR*, Glasgow, UK, April 1-4 2014.

[4] C. A. Bhatt, N. Pappas, M. Habibi, et al. Multimodal reranking of content-based recommendations for hyperlinking video snippets. In *ACM ICMR*, Glasgow, UK, April 1-4 2014.

[5] S. Chen, G. J. F. Jones, and N. E. O'Connor. DCU linking runs at MediaEval 2013: Search and Hyperlinking task. In *MediaEval*, 2013.

[6] M. Eskevich, R. Aly, R. Ordelman, et al. The Search and Hyperlinking task at MediaEval 2013. In *MediaEval*, 2013.

[7] C. Guinaudeau, A.-R. Simon, G. Gravier, et al. HITS and IRISA at MediaEval 2013: Search and Hyperlinking task. In *MediaEval*, 2013.

[8] T. D. Nies, W. D. Neve, E. Mannens, et al. Ghent University-iMinds at MediaEval 2013: An unsupervised named entity-based similarity measure for search and hyperlinking. In *MediaEval*, 2013.

[9] P. Over, G. Awad, M. Michel, et al. TRECVID 2012 – An overview of the goals, tasks, data, evaluation mechanisms and metrics. In *Proc. of TRECVID 2012*. NIST, USA, 2012.

[10] J. Preston, J. S. Hare, S. Samangooei, et al. A unified, modular and multimodal approach to search and hyperlinking video. In *MediaEval*, 2013.

[11] K. Schouten, R. Aly, and R. Ordelman. Searching and Hyperlinking using word importance segment boundaries in MediaEval 2013. In *MediaEval*, 2013.

[12] P. Sidiropoulos, V. Mezaris, and I. Kompatsiaris. Enhancing video concept detection with the use of tomographs. In *Proc. IEEE ICIP*, 2013.

[13] P. Sidiropoulos, V. Mezaris, I. Kompatsiaris, et al. Temporal video segmentation to scenes using high-level audiovisual features. *IEEE Trans. on CSVT*, 21(8):1163–1177, Aug. 2011.

[14] D. Stein, S. Eickeler, R. Bardeli, et al. Think before you link – Meeting content constraints when linking television to the web. In *NEM Summit 2013, 28-30 October 2013, Nantes, France*.

[15] S. Tschöpel and D. Schneider. A lightweight keyword and tag-cloud retrieval algorithm for automatic speech recognition transcripts. In *Proc. 11th Annual Conf. of the Int. Speech Communication Association*, 2010.

[16] C. Ventura, M. Tella-Amo, and X. G. i Nieto. UPC at MediaEval 2013 Hyperlinking task. In *MediaEval*, 2013.

[17] M. Yeung, B.-L. Yeo, and B. Liu. Segmentation of video by clustering and graph analysis. *Comp. Vision and Image Underst.*, 71(1):94–109, July 1998.

Automatic Maya Hieroglyph Retrieval Using Shape and Context Information

Rui Hu
Idiap Research Institute
Switzerland
rhu@idiap.ch

Carlos Pallán Gayol
University of Bonn
Germany
pallan.carlos@gmail.com

Guido Krempel
University of Bonn
Germany
tilalhix@gmail.com

Jean-Marc Odobez
Idiap Research Institute,
EPFL
Switzerland
odobez@idiap.ch

Daniel Gatica-Perez
Idiap Research Institute,
EPFL
Switzerland
gatica@idiap.ch

ABSTRACT

We propose an automatic Maya hieroglyph retrieval method integrating shape and glyph context information. Two recent local shape descriptors, Gradient Field Histogram of Orientation Gradient (GF-HOG) and Histogram of Orientation Shape Context (HOOSC), are evaluated. To encode the context information, we propose to convert each Maya glyph block into a first-order Markov chain and apply the co-occurrence of neighbouring glyphs. The retrieval results obtained based on visual matching are therefore re-ranked. Experimental results show that our method can significantly improve the glyph retrieval accuracy even with a basic co-occurrence model. Furthermore, two unique glyph datasets are contributed which can be used as novel shape benchmarks in future research.

Categories and Subject Descriptors

H.3 [**Information Storage and Retrieval**]: Information Search and Retrieval; I.4 [**Image Processing and Computer Vision**]: Feature Measurement—*Feature representation*

Keywords

Maya hieroglyph; image retrieval; shape descriptors; glyph co-occurrence; Markov model

1. INTRODUCTION

The Maya civilization is one of the major cultural developments in ancient Mesoamerica. It began to flourish during the Pre-Classic period (2000 BC to AD 250), reached the peak of development during the Classic period (AD 250-900), and continued throughout the Post-Classic period.

MM'14, November 3–7, 2014, Orlando, Florida, USA.

ACM 978-1-4503-3063-3/14/11 ...$15.00.
http://dx.doi.org/10.1145/2647868.2655044.

Figure 1: Codex Dresden. Main hieroglyphic text on page 65a. Green arrows indicate reading order of the glyph blocks.

Most Maya texts were written during the Classic period on ceramic vessels and stone monuments to record historical events. There are also Maya texts written on personal items such as wooden lintels, mural paintings, bones, etc. A special type of Maya textual sources are the so called Codices, which are stuccoed and painted bark paper books, folded in laparello format. Such books usually contain both textual and iconographic information, survived from the Post-Classic period. Fig.1 illustrates one exemplified main text from page 65a of the Dresden Codex (high resolution images of this codex are available at the SLUB website [2]).

Maya texts are usually composed of glyph blocks arranged in double-columns. The usual reading order is from left to right and from top to bottom by means of double columns (Fig.1). Due to the flexibility in artistic freedom of Maya writing, diverse forms and different glyph-variants were in used. Thus the graphic conventions within a glyph block can vary greatly. One glyph block could contain one or multiple glyphs; and it could correlate with a morpheme, an individual word, or even an entire sentence. The choice could be due to economic, religious or aesthetic reasons. Individual glyph recognition is crucial to Maya script decoding.

Maya decipherment has about 200 years of scholarly tradition. Over 1000 signs have been discovered. While about 80% of signs can be read phonetically, the meaning of some 40% logograms remain unknown [8]. Epigraphers often spend a tremendous amount of time looking at traditional printed catalogs to identify unknown glyphs. Therefore, the aim of this work is to facilitate these tasks by automatic recognition of Maya glyphs using shape and context information.

Related work. Computer vision algorithms have shown the potential of providing new insights in automatic visual

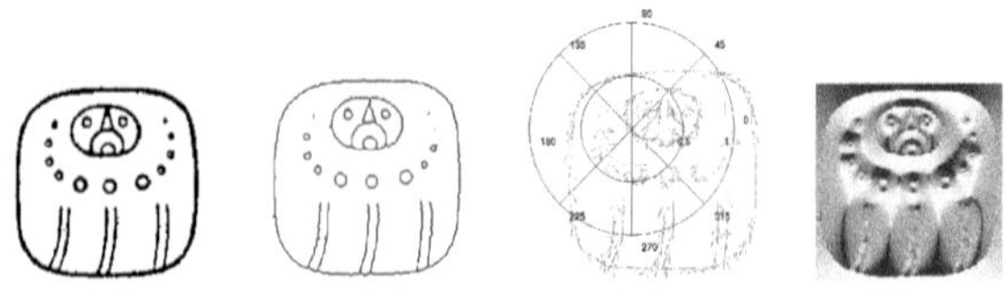

(a) (b) (c) (d)

Figure 2: (a) Original glyph (taken from [12]); (b) thinning; (c) HOOSC spatial quantization of a given pivot; (d) gradient field for GF-HOG computation.

analysis of cultural heritage, which can significantly facilitate the daily work of related scholars. Previous works address Maya glyph retrieval as a shape matching problem.

Shape based retrieval systems include curve fitting [4], point-to-point matching [3], grid based matching [5], etc. These works either do not scale well over large datasets, or only offer limited flexibility over affine transformation. Recently, local shape descriptors [6, 7, 10] have been proposed and used in a Bag-of-Visual-Words (BoVW) framework for shape based retrieval. Such method can be scaled sub-linearly with appropriate search structures, and also offers certain degrees of freedom of affine invariance. Our work follows this approach.

One of the first attempts of automatic Maya glyph retrieval is [9], where shape context is used to represent and match between single glyphs. A shape descriptor (HOOSC) is proposed in [10], and used in the BoVW system for Maya glyph retrieval. The retrieval performance is improved in [11] by using only the intermediate spatial scope, as well as carefully pre-processing glyphs into thinned edges, and evenly pick pivot points. In another direction, GF-HOG [7] was recently developed in the context of sketch based retrieval to overcome the limitation of HOG-like local shape descriptors when applied to shapes rather than images.

These previous Maya glyph retrieval works have framed the glyph retrieval problem without considering any specific structure of Maya writing as a language. In contrast, language modelling has been widely used in machine translation and speech recognition. Glyph context information has recently been applied in [6] for Egyptian hieroglyph analysis with limited performance improvement. To the best of our knowledge, Maya glyph co-occurrence that captures context information in language has never been considered in automatic Maya glyph analysis systems.

Contribution. In this paper we investigate the following questions. First, given the promising results GF-HOG has achieved for sketch-based image retrieval, how would it perform on glyph data? Second, would glyph co-occurrence information help improve the shape based glyph retrieval accuracy? As exemplified by [6], co-occurrence appears not consistent enough for the task of Egyptian hieroglyph retrieval. Another contribution of this paper regards two glyph datasets collected and produced from multiple sources (see section 4.1). Both datasets can be used as shape benchmarks, and one of them can also be used to further study the Maya language model. Expert epigraphers in our team contribute tremendous effort in creating these two datasets.

2. SHAPE BASED GLYPH RETRIEVAL

Each glyph is represented by a set of local shape descriptors. The BoVW approach is then applied.

T0501	T0502	T0668	T0757	T0102	T0103

/b'a/	/ma/	/cha/	/b'a/	/ki/	/ta/

Table 1: Thompson numbers, visual examples, and the syllabic values of glyph pairs. Each pair contains two different signs of similar visual features. All images are taken from [12]

2.1 Shape representation

We use the local shape descriptors HOOSC and GF-HOG for our glyph retrieval tasks. Since they achieves the current state-of-the-art performance on shape based Maya hieroglyph retrieval and sketch based image retrieval separately.

HOOSC. Since Maya glyphs often present stroke lines with different degrees of thickness, we first apply a thinning algorithm [11] to get a thinned version of the glyph, see Fig.2 (b) for example. A uniformly sampled subset of points along the contour is then selected as the pivot set. For each pivot point, we calculate the HOOSC descriptor by computing the histogram of orientation within each spatial bin of a local grid centred at the pivot's location, as illustrated in Fig.2 (c). We consider 8 orientations and 2 rings. The outer ring covers the average pairwise distance between each pair of points along the contour; the inner ring covers half of this distance. The final descriptor of a given point is the concatenation of histograms of 16 grids. We use a 8 bin histogram for each grid, which forms a 128-dimensional feature vector.

GF-HOG. Compared with natural images, shapes like glyphs provide only sparse spatial information. Thus, instead of computing HOG on the sparse gradient field along the contour, GF-HOG aims to encode a richer structure information within each local window. This is achieved by interpolating a dense gradient field from the sparse orientation field using a Laplacian constraint. It can be solved using a Possion equation with Dirichlet boundary condition. See [7] for detail. In our work, the gradient field is generated from the thinned glyph (Fig.2 (b)). Fig.2 (d) shows an example of the extracted gradient field. HOG descriptors are then extracted from the dense gradient field around each pivot point using a 4×4 grid. A 8-bin orientation histogram is computed within each grid. This results in a 128-dimensional feature vector. Following [7], we compute HOG descriptor over three window sizes to improve the scale invariance.

2.2 BoVW based retrieval system

BoVW approach is applied to quantify local features and represent the full shape with a histogram. Specifically, given the local descriptors extracted from each glyph, k-means clustering is applied to generate a set of k clusters. Each cluster is referred to as a 'visual word' and the set of k clusters defines the vocabulary of the system. A frequency histogram which represents the count of the visual words extracted from an image is then used as a global descriptor.

Given a query G and a database glyph D represented by their histograms H^G and H^D, we compute the Cityblock distance to measure the dissimilarity between G and D:

$$d(G, D) = \sum_{1 \leq i \leq k} |H^G(i) - H^D(i)| \quad (1)$$

where each histogram is normalized so that $\sum_{1 \leq i \leq k} H(i) = 1$.

glyph block	glyph string

Table 2: Generating glyph strings from blocks.

3. GLYPH CO-OCCURRENCE

Using shape alone to represent and distinguish between glyphs is often ambiguous for many reasons. First, different signs often share similar visual features, see for example Table 1. Furthermore, glyphs of the same sign category vary with time, location, as well as with individual styles, calligraphies and renderings of different artists. For example, the first block in table 2 and the third block in Fig.3 are both *cha-ki* (the name of the rain god). Finally, the surviving historical Maya scripts often lose their visual quality over time; as such, it is often the case that noise is introduced and data is partially missing. Therefore, we propose to use glyph co-occurrence to complement the visual information and help improve the retrieval accuracy.

3.1 Glyph co-occurrence in Maya writing

In Maya hieroglyphic writing, glyph blocks were frequently composed of combinations, conflations and mergings of individual signs. Glyph co-occurrence within single glyph blocks could encode valuable information. The reading order within a block usually follows the basic rule of left-to-right and top-to-bottom. We propose to convert each glyph block into a linear string of glyphs, according to this reading order, as shown in Table 2. Given a glyph string, we consider the 1st-order co-occurrence of neighbouring glyphs.

Co-occurrence model. We extract glyph co-occurrence information from the classic Thompson hieroglyphic catalog [12]. Despite its outmoded taxonomy, it remains one of the most comprehensive and widely used list of Maya glyphs. It covers 892 signs extracted from both codices and monuments. Thompson categorises signs into affixes, main signs and portraits (note that this categorisation method is no longer used in recent research of Maya writing). Affixes often co-occur with main signs, portraits as well as affixes to form blocks. In his book, Thompson provides two glyph co-occurrence tables, listing co-occurring signs discovered at that time for each affix, distinguishing whether it is used as prefix or postfix. However, no frequency information is given in these tables, and co-occurrence between main signs and portraits is not listed. We extract a co-occurrence matrix C from these tables:

$$C(S_i, S_j) = \begin{cases} 1 & \text{sign } S_i \text{ appears before sign } S_j, \\ \alpha & \text{otherwise.} \end{cases} \quad (2)$$

where α is a smoothing factor that accounts for missing co-occurring glyph pairs in the two co-occurrence tables. Here we set $\alpha = 0.01$. Note that $C(S_i, S_j) \neq C(S_j, S_i)$.

Co-occurrence for glyph labelling. Denote by $G_{1:n} = [G_1, \ldots, G_i, \ldots, G_n]$ the observed glyph string, and by $S_{1:n}$ the sequence of recognized states, where S_i indicates the Thompson number annotated with glyph G_i. Considering the glyph string $G_{1:n}$ as a 1st-order Markov chain, the probability of labelling it to a sequence of states $S_{1:n}$ is:

$$P(S_{1:n}|G_{1:n}) \propto P(G_1|S_1) \prod_{2 \leq i \leq n} (P(G_i|S_i)P(S_i|S_{i-1})), \quad (3)$$

Figure 3: Example glyph blocks of the MC dataset.

where $P(S_i|S_{i-1})$ denotes the transition probability from the previous state S_{i-1} to the current state S_i. Here we use $C(S_{i-1}, S_i)$ to approximate this probability. $P(G_i|S_i)$ refers to the likelihood of glyph G_i being labelled as sign S_i. To encode this term we use the visual similarity between G_i and the glyph example of S_i in the database, and define $P(G_i|S_i) \propto e^{-d(G_i,S_i)/\lambda}$, where $d(G_i, S_i)$ is computed using Eq.(1), λ is a scale factor set to the average distance of the top 50 ranked results for all queries.

3.2 Retrieval system

We solve glyph recognition through retrieval, i.e. by ranking the database glyphs D (signs in Thompson catalog [12]) based on their similarity with the query. When only shape information is considered, the score of a query glyph G_i being labelled by sign D, is computed by their shape likelihood:

$$Score^{shape}(S_i = D) \propto P(G_i|S_i = D). \quad (4)$$

In our model, we propose to rank the glyphs according to

$$Score^{shape+context}(S_i = D) = \max_{S_{1:i-1;i+1:n}} P(S_{1:n}|G_{1:n}) \quad (5)$$

which means, given $S_i = D$ finding the sequence of Thompson labels $S_{1:n}$ that provides the maximum probability to label $G_{1:n}$, under the model in Eq.(3). This can be efficiently computed using the Viterbi algorithm. In other words, the score of the glyph G_i being recognized as $S_i = D$ now takes into account all observed glyphs in the string, with the effect that a glyph D that normally co-occurs with glyphs that are visually likely at neighbouring positions will receive a higher weights.

4. EXPERIMENTS

Two sets of experiments are conducted. In the first case, we compare the two local shape descriptors GF-HOG and HOOSC for shape based single-glyph retrieval. In the second case, we incorporate context information within single blocks to improve the glyph retrieval accuracy.

4.1 Datasets

Two glyph datasets are contributed, both requiring dedicated expertise of expert epigraphers to collect and compile.

Maya Syllabic dataset (MS). MS is an adapted version of the Syllabic Maya dataset used in [11], which contains manually segmented glyphs from various resources by experts. With the support of experts in our team, we refined the dataset by correcting a few glyph categories and removing uncertain glyphs. Note that the grouping of glyphs is based on the Thompson catalog of Mayan glyph signs, not on shape. The resulting dataset contains 1044 glyphs of 25 sign categories. We randomly selected 20% glyphs from each category to form the query set, resulting in a total of 207 glyphs. All remaining glyphs formed the test set.

Maya Codex dataset (MC)[1]. MC is a new high-quality Maya hieroglyph dataset developed by experts in our team. Currently, it contains 176 glyphs from 72 blocks segmented from two Maya codices (Dresden and Madrid), along with

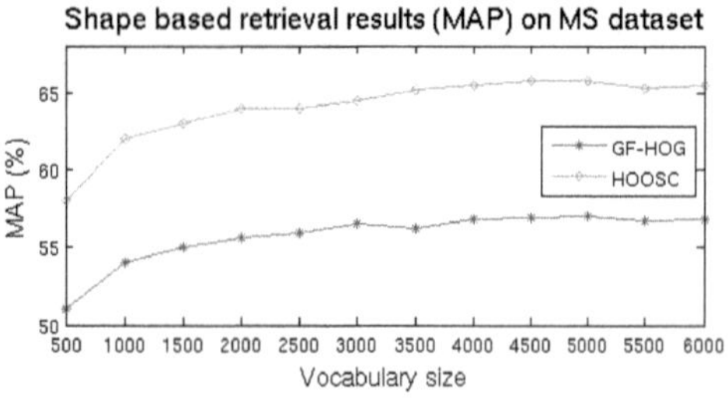

Figure 4: Shape based retrieval results (MAP) with varying vocabulary size on the MS dataset.

their segmented individual glyphs and corresponding annotations. See table 2 and Fig.3 for examples. Our work has defined consistent conventions to generate high-quality vectorial representations of the three existant Maya codices (Dresden, Madrid, Paris) using Adobe Illustrator. Note that these three codices are named after the places where they are currently exhibited. Given that individual signs are structured within blocks, this dataset can also be used to study the Maya language model. Currently, we only have a limited amount of examples available, since epigraphers require about 30 minutes to render a high quality glyph-block depending on complexity and preservation factors. We are constantly enlarging and improving this dataset. To automatically label glyphs from the MC dataset, we use them as queries to match with the 892 signs of the Thompson catalog [12], which we have scanned and manually segmented.

4.2 Results

Fig.4 shows the Mean Average Precision (MAP) of using GF-HOG and HOOSC on the MS dataset. From the curves we can see that HOOSC outperforms GF-HOG for around 8% on average with varying vocabulary sizes.

Glyph retrieval on the MC dataset is a more challenging task. Indeed, in spite of the large visual variability of single glyph categories, most signs of the catalog [12] are represented by only one instance. Furthermore, catalog signs of different categories often share similar visual feature. Finally, query glyphs are often noisy due to degradations, and partially missing due to occlusion by other glyphs from the same block. We conduct two retrieval experiments (without or with block context, see Eq.(4) and Eq.(5)) on this dataset. For each experimental condition, Fig.5 displays the results as the average over all queries of the ranking of the correct match over 892 different sign categories. The results confirms that HOOSC achieves slightly better results than GF-HOG. It also demonstrate that incorporating context through glyph co-occurrence improves the ranking significantly (around 40 on average) for both descriptors. This shows that our approach based on glyph co-occurrence is highly beneficial even if the applied co-occurrence model is rather approximate.

5. DISCUSSION AND FUTURE WORK

This paper presented a new Maya hieroglyph retrieval method using shape and glyph context information, by means of which two glyph datasets were also contributed.

We evaluated two local shape descriptors using the BoVW approach. Experimental results showed that HOOSC achieves higher retrieval accuracy than GF-HOG on both datasets. Future work evaluating these two descriptors will take larger shape datasets of more diverse resources into consideration.

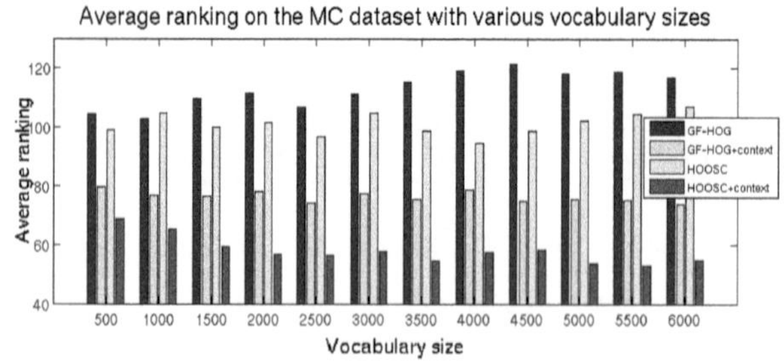

Figure 5: Average ranking using two shape descriptors and context information on the MC dataset.

Although the co-occurrence information we applied here is at an incipient stage, the results suggest that the context within Maya glyph blocks indeed encodes valuable information. In the future, more complete glyph context information will be extracted, which can be used in various Maya hieroglyph analysis tasks, such as assisting the decipherment of signs whose semantic meaning remain problematic, by analysing their context from various resources.

Our ongoing work also includes automatic Maya text detection, block segmentation, as well as glyph detection and segmentation within blocks. This would help both epigraphers and public users for research and education purposes.

6. ACKNOWLEDGMENTS

We thank the Swiss National Science Foundation (SNSF) and the German Research Foundation (DFG) for their support. All images in Fig.1, Table 2 and Fig.3 were produced by C. Pallan and G. Krempel as part of the MAAYA project.

7. REFERENCES

[1] MC dataset. `www.idiap.ch/dataset/maya-codex`.

[2] SLUB library. `http://digital.slub-dresden.de/werkansicht/dlf/2967/1/`.

[3] S. Belongie, J. Malik, and J. Puzicha. Shape matching and object recognition using shape contexts. *PAMI*, pages 509–522, 2002.

[4] A. Del Bimbo and P. Pala. Visual image retrieval by elastic matching of user sketches. *PAMI*, pages 121–132, 1997.

[5] M. Eitz, K. Hildebrand, T. Boubekeur, and M. Alexa. A descriptor for large scale image retrieval based on sketched feature lines. In *SBM*, pages 29–36, 2009.

[6] M. Franken and J. van Gemert. Automatic egyptian hieroglyph recognition by retrieving images as texts. In *ACM Multimedia*, pages 765–768, 2013.

[7] R. Hu and J. P. Collomosse. A performance evaluation of gradient field hog descriptor for sketch based image retrieval. *CVIU*, pages 790–806, 2013.

[8] H. Kettunen and C. Helmke. *Introduction to Maya Hieroglyphs - XVII European Maya Conference.* University of Helsinki, 2012.

[9] E. Roman-Rangel, C. Pallan-Gayol, J.-M. Odobez, and D. Gatica-Perez. Retrieving ancient maya glyphs with shape context. In *ICCV workshop on eHeritage and Digital Art Preservation*, pages 988–995, 2009.

[10] E. Roman-Rangel, C. Pallan-Gayol, J.-M. Odobez, and D. Gatica-Perez. Analyzing ancient maya glyph collections with contextual shape descriptors. *IJCV*, pages 101–117, 2011.

[11] E. Roman-Rangel, C. Pallan-Gayol, J.-M. Odobez, and D. Gatica-Perez. Searching the past: an improved shape descriptor to retrieve maya hieroglyphs. In *ACM Multimedia*, pages 163–172, 2011.

[12] J. E. S. Thompson. *A catalog of Maya Hieroglyphs.* University of Oklahoma Press, 1962.

A Dataset and Taxonomy for Urban Sound Research

Justin Salamon[1,2], Christopher Jacoby[1], Juan Pablo Bello[1]
[1]Music and Audio Research Laboratory, New York University
[2]Center for Urban Science and Progress, New York University
{justin.salamon, cbj238, jpbello}@nyu.edu

ABSTRACT

Automatic urban sound classification is a growing area of research with applications in multimedia retrieval and urban informatics. In this paper we identify two main barriers to research in this area – the lack of a common taxonomy and the scarceness of large, real-world, annotated data. To address these issues we present a taxonomy of urban sounds and a new dataset, *UrbanSound*, containing 27 hours of audio with 18.5 hours of annotated sound event occurrences across 10 sound classes. The challenges presented by the new dataset are studied through a series of experiments using a baseline classification system.

Categories and Subject Descriptors

H.3.1 [**Information Systems**]: Content Analysis and Indexing; H.5.5 [**Information Systems**]: Sound and Music Computing

Keywords

Urban sound; dataset; taxonomy; classification

1. INTRODUCTION

The automatic classification of environmental sound is a growing research field with multiple applications to large-scale, content-based multimedia indexing and retrieval (e.g. [13, 16, 10]). In particular, the sonic analysis of *urban* environments is the subject of increased interest, partly enabled by multimedia sensor networks [15], as well as by large quantities of online multimedia content depicting urban scenes. However, while there is a large body of research in related areas such as speech, music and bioacoustics, work on the analysis of urban acoustics environments is relatively scarce. Furthermore, when existent, it mostly focuses on the classification of auditory scene type, e.g. street, park, as opposed to the identification of sound sources in those scenes, e.g. car horn, engine idling, bird tweet. See [5] for an example.

MM'14, November 3–7, 2014, Orlando, Florida, USA.

ACM 978-1-4503-3063-3/14/11 ...$15.00.
http://dx.doi.org/10.1145/2647868.2655045.

One of the main challenges and hindrances to urban sound research is the lack of labeled audio data. Previous work has focused on audio from carefully produced movies or television tracks [3]; from specific environments such as elevators or office spaces [13, 8]; and on commercial or proprietary datasets [11, 4]. The large effort involved in manually annotating real-world data means datasets based on field recordings tend to be relatively small (e.g. the event detection dataset of the IEEE AASP Challenge [8] consists of 24 recordings per each of 17 classes). A second challenge faced by the research community is the lack of a common vocabulary when working with urban sounds. This means the classification of sounds into semantic groups may vary from study to study, making it hard to compare results.

The goal of this paper is to address the two aforementioned challenges. In Section 2 we propose a taxonomy for urban sound sources to facilitate a common framework for research. Then, in Section 3 we present *UrbanSound*, a dataset of 27 hours of field recordings containing thousands of labeled sound source occurrences. To the best of the authors' knowledge this is the largest free dataset of labelled urban sound events available for research. To understand the complexity and challenges presented by this new dataset, we run a series of baseline sound classification experiments, described in Section 4. The paper concludes with a summary in Section 5.

2. URBAN SOUND TAXONOMY

The taxonomical categorization of environmental sounds, a common first step in sound classification, has been extensively studied in the context of perceptual soundscape research [14]. Specific efforts to describe urban sounds have often been limited to subsets of broader taxonomies of acoustic environments [2], and thus only partially address the needs of systematic urban sound analysis. For an exhaustive review of previous work the reader is referred to [12].

In our view, an urban sound taxonomy should satisfy the following three requirements: (1) it should factor in previous research and proposed taxonomies, (2) it should aim to be as detailed as possible, going down to low-level sound sources such as "car horn" (versus "transportation") and "jackhammer" (versus "construction"), (3) it should, in its first iteration, focus on sounds that are of specific relevance to urban sound research, such as sounds that contribute to urban noise pollution. To address (1), we decided to base our taxonomy on the subset of [2] dedicated to the urban acoustic environment. We define 4 top level groups: human, nature, mechanical and music, which are common to most previ-

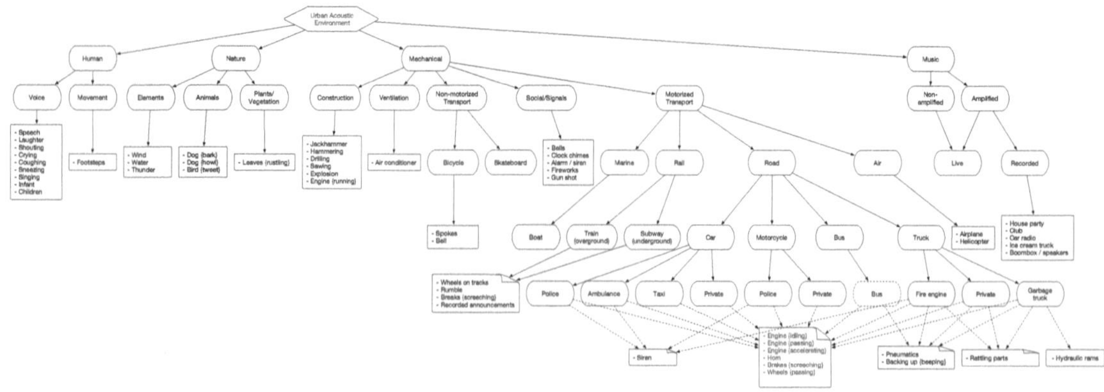

Figure 1: Urban Sound Taxonomy.

ously proposed taxonomies [12]. To address (2), we specify that the leaves of the taxonomy should be sufficiently low-level to be unambiguous – e.g. car "brakes", "engine" or "horn", instead of simply "car". Finally to address (3), we examined all the noise complaints filed through New York City's 311 service from 2010 to date[1] (over 370,000), and built the taxonomy around the most frequently complained about sound categories and sources – construction (e.g. jackhammer), traffic noise (car and truck horns, idling engines), loud music, air conditioners and dog barks to name a few.

The resulting taxonomy is provided in Figure 1. Further information about the principles and process behind the construction of the taxonomy, as well as a scalable digital version, are available online[2]. Rounded rectangles represent high-level semantic classes (e.g. mechanical sounds). The leaves of the taxonomy (rectangles with sharp edges) correspond to classes of concrete sound sources (e.g. siren, footsteps). For conciseness, leaves can be shared by several high-level classes (indicated by an earmark). Since the number of possible sound sources in an urban setting is very large (potentially infinite), we consider the taxonomy to be a constant work in progress rather than fixed. We plan to continue expanding and reformulating the taxonomy as we increase the scope of sounds covered by our research, by engaging the international research community and promoting a collaborative effort via (for instance) dedicated workshops.

3. THE URBANSOUND DATASET

In addition, we have collected a dataset of annotated urban sounds including 10 low-level classes from the taxonomy: air conditioner, car horn, children playing, dog bark, drilling, engine idling, gun shot, jackhammer, siren and street music. With the exception of "children playing" and "gun shot" which were added for variety, all other classes were selected due to the high frequency in which they appear in urban noise complaints, as noted in the previous section. The dataset is called *UrbanSound*. Due to the manual annotation effort required (see below) we limited the number of classes to 10, which we consider a good starting point. We intend to extend it to more classes in future iterations. For a review of existing datasets and related literature cf. footnote 2.

Before compiling the dataset, we set three main goals: (1) it should contain sounds that occur in an urban environment, (2) all recordings must be real field-recordings, (3) the dataset should be sufficiently large and varied in terms of sounds and recording conditions such that it will be useful for training scalable algorithms capable of analyzing real data from sensor networks or multimedia repositories. To accomplish these goals, we turned to Freesound[3], an online sound repository containing over 160,000 user-uploaded recordings under a creative commons license. Freesound contains a large amount of field recordings, many of which are in urban settings. Using the Freesound API we were able to search and download a subset of the repository, and exploit the user-provided metadata (title, description and tags) to significantly speed up the annotation process.

For each class, we started by downloading all sounds returned by the Freesound search engine when using the class name as a query (e.g. "jackhammer"), resulting in over 3000 recordings summing to just over 60 hours of audio. We then manually checked every recording by listening to it and inspecting the user-provided metadata, only keeping those that were actual field recordings where the sound class of interest was present somewhere in the recording. After this first filtering stage we were left with 1314 recordings summing to just over 27 hours of audio. Next, given all the recordings for a specific sound class, we used Audacity[4] to label the start and end times of every occurrence of the sound in each recording, with an additional *salience* description indicating whether the occurrence was subjectively perceived to be in the foreground or background of the recording. This resulted in a total of 3075 labeled occurrences amounting to 18.5 hours of labeled audio. The distribution of total occurrence duration per class and per salience is in Fig. 2(a).

The resulting collection of 1314 full length recordings with corresponding sound occurrence and salience annotations, *UrbanSound*, is freely available online (cf. footnote 2) for research purposes. The audio is provided in the same format in which it was originally uploaded to Freesound. Note that the duration of source occurrences in the set can vary from 1-2 s (e.g. gun shot sounds) to over 30 s (continuous sounds such as jackhammers or idling engines).

For research on sound source identification, we created an additional subset of short audio snippets which we call the *UrbanSound8K* subset, also available online. In [5] the authors conducted a listening test and found that 4 seconds were sufficient for subjects to identify environmental sounds with 82% accuracy, and consequently use a 4 s clip duration in their experiments with automatic classification. Following

[1] `https://nycopendata.socrata.com/data`
[2] `http://serv.cusp.nyu.edu/projects/urbansounddataset/`
[3] `http://www.freesound.org`
[4] `http://audacity.sourceforge.net/`

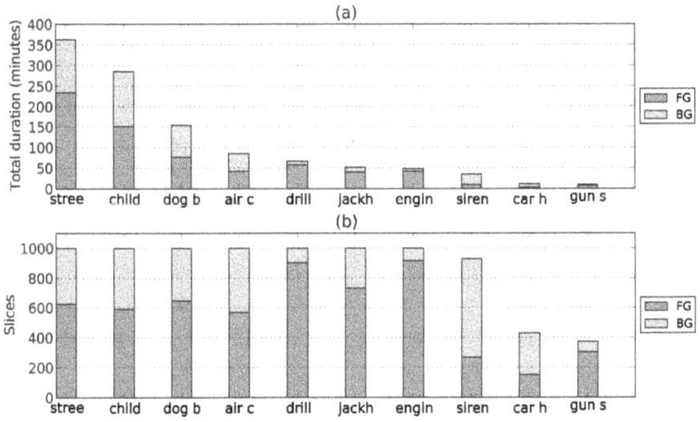

Figure 2: (a) Total occurrence duration per class in UrbanSound. (b) Slices per class in UrbanSound8K. Breakdown by foreground (FG) / background (BG).

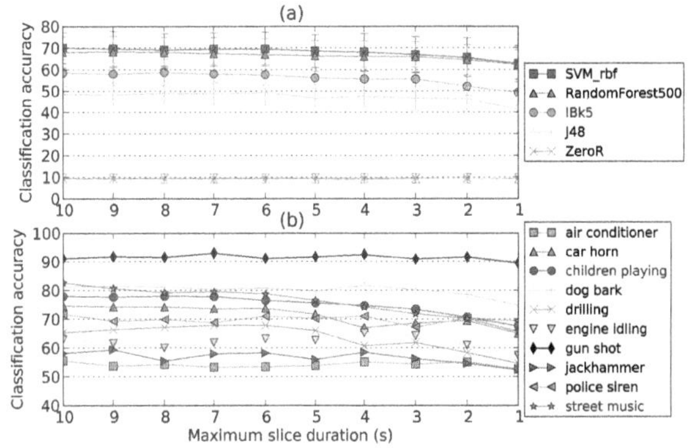

Figure 3: Classification accuracy vs maximum slice duration: (a) by classifier, (b) by class for SVM.

their findings, we set a maximum occurrence duration limit of 4 seconds, and segment longer occurrences into 4 s slices using a sliding window with a hop size of 2 s. To avoid large differences in the class distribution, we set a limit of 1000 slices per class, resulting in a total of 8732 labeled slices (8.75 hours). The distribution of slices per class in UrbanSound8K with a breakdown into salience is provided in Figure 2(b).

4. SOUND CLASSIFICATION

In order to learn about the characteristics and challenges presented by this new dataset, we run a set of classification experiments using a baseline approach. Note that we are not searching for an optimal combination of feature/classifier parameters to maximize accuracy, but rather are interested in learning about the characteristics of the dataset itself.

4.1 Feature extraction

In all of the following experiments, we extract Mel-Frequency Cepstral Coefficients (MFCC) from the audio slices using the Essentia audio analysis library [1]. MFCCs are commonly used in environmental sound analysis (including recent work [4]) and frequently used as a competitive baseline to benchmark novel techniques [7]. In all experiments we extract the features on a per-frame basis using a window size of 23.2 ms and 50% frame overlap. We compute 40 Mel bands between 0 and 22050 Hz and keep the first 25 MFCC coefficients (we do not apply any pre-emphasis nor liftering). The per-frame values for each coefficient are summarized across time using the following summary statistics: minimum, maximum, median, mean, variance, skewness, kurtosis and the mean and variance of the first and second derivatives, resulting in a feature vector of dimension 225 per slice.

4.2 Experimental setup

To experiment with different classification algorithms we use the Weka data mining software [9]. Every experiment is run using 10-fold cross validation. Within each fold we perform correlation-based attribute selection to avoid overfitting the training data. As it is not our goal to find an optimal parametrization, all classification algorithms are used with their default parameter settings. For each experiment we report the average accuracy across all 10 folds.

Important care must be taken when creating the folds – since there are multiple slices coming from the same original recording, if we generate the folds completely randomly, we may end up with slices from the same recording used both for training and testing, which can lead to artificially high classification accuracies. To avoid this, we designed a random allocation process of slices into folds such that all slices originating from the same Freesound recording go into the same fold, whilst trying to balance the number of slices-per fold for each sound class. The UrbanSound8K subset available online provides the audio slices grouped into 10 folds generated using this methodology. In this way, researchers interested in comparing their results to our baseline are guaranteed unbiased and comparable results.

4.3 Results

In Section 3 we motivated our choice of 4 s as the maximum slice duration for UrbanSound8K. In this first experiment we examine how the choice of this threshold affects the performance of the baseline approach. To this end, we generated 10 copies of UrbanSound8K, each time varying the maximum slice duration from 10 s down to 1 s. To ensure the observed changes in accuracy are not an artifact of a specific classification algorithm, we compare 5 different algorithms: decision tree (J48), k-NN ($k = 5$), random forest (500 trees), support vector machine (radial basis function kernel), and a baseline majority vote classifier (ZeroR).

The results are presented in Figure 3(a). The difference in performance between all classifiers is statistically significant (paired t-test with $p < 0.001$) except for the top two (SVM and random forest). More importantly, we observe consistent behavior across all classifiers – performance remains stable from 10 to 6 s, after which it starts decreasing gradually. However, if we consider the top performing classifier (SVM), there is no statistically significant difference between performance using 6s slices and 4s slices (whereas below 4s the difference becomes significant), in accordance with [5] and supporting the choice of 4 s slices for UrbanSound8K. Further insight can be gained by observing the per-class accuracies for the SVM, provided in Figure 3(b). We see that different sound classes are affected differently by the slice duration: classes such as gun shot and siren have fast events that are clearly identifiable at short temporal scales and are thus mostly unaffected by duration; while classes such as street music and children playing drop almost monotonically, showing the importance of analyzing them at longer temporal scales and suggesting multi-scale analysis could be a relevant path for urban sound research.

To understand the relative difference in performance between classes, we examined the confusion matrix for the SVM classifier on UrbanSound8K. We found that the clas-

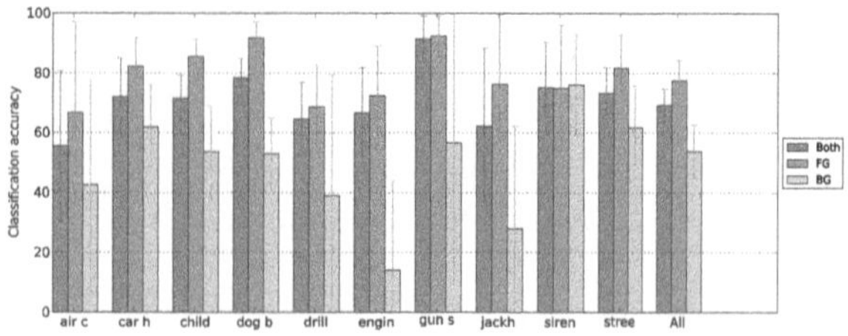

Figure 4: Accuracy as a function of salience.

sifier mostly confuses three pairs of classes: air conditioners and idling engines, jackhammers and drills, children and street music. This makes sense, as the timbre of each pair is quite similar (for the last pair the presence of complex harmonic tones is a possible cause). We see that the baseline bag-of-frames approach based on MFCCs fails especially on wide-band noise-like continuous sounds, and we intend to investigate approaches that better model the temporal dynamics of energy and timbre as part of future work.

However, the relative similarity between sound classes is only part of the story. As explained in Section 3, every sound occurrence in the dataset is also labeled with a (subjective) salience label – foreground (FG) and background (BG, also used to label occurrences where there are other equally-salient sources). Intuitively, one would expect the baseline algorithm to do better on slices where there is less background interference, especially since MFCCs are known to be sensitive to noise [6]. In this final experiment, we compare the performance of the SVM classifier for each class as a function of salience, displayed in Figure 4. As expected, we see a considerable difference in performance between sounds labeled FG and BG, the exception being sirens, possibly because their frequency content does not overlap with most other sources (by design). Whilst we cannot quantify the effect of interference from this experiment due to the subjectivity of the labeling, the results point to an important challenge presented by the dataset – identifying sound sources in the presence of (real) background noise. This problem is an active area of research (e.g. [6]), and we believe this real-world dataset will further empower the research community in coming up with novel solutions to this problem.

5. SUMMARY

Automatic urban sound classification can benefit a variety of multimedia applications. In this paper we identified two main barriers to research in this area – the lack of a common taxonomy and the scarceness of large, real-world, annotated data. To address the first issue we presented the Urban Sound Taxonomy, based on previous soundscape research with a focus on sound classes from real noise-complaint data. To address the second issue we presented UrbanSound, a dataset containing 27 hours of audio with 18.5 hours of manually labelled sound occurrences. We also presented UrbanSound8K, a subset of the dataset designed for training sound classification algorithms. Through a series of classification experiments we studied the challenges presented by the dataset, and identified avenues for future research: sensitivity to temporal scale in the analysis, confusion due to timbre similarity (especially for noise-like continuous sounds), and sensitivity to background interference. We believe the dataset will open the path to new an exciting research in sound and multimedia applications with a focus on urban environments and urban informatics.

6. ACKNOWLEDGMENTS

This work was supported by a seed grant from New York University's Center for Urban Science and Progress (CUSP).

7. REFERENCES

[1] D. Bogdanov, N. Wack, E. Gómez, S. Gulati, P. Herrera, O. Mayor, G. Roma, J. Salamon, J. Zapata, and X. Serra. ESSENTIA: an open-source library for sound and music analysis. In *21st ACM Int. Conf. on Multimedia*, pages 855–858, 2013.

[2] A. L. Brown, J. Kang, and T. Gjestland. Towards standardization in soundscape preference assessment. *Applied Acoustics*, 72(6):387–392, 2011.

[3] L.-H. Cai, L. Lu, A. Hanjalic, H.-J. Zhang, and L.-H. Cai. A flexible framework for key audio effects detection and auditory context inference. *IEEE TASLP*, 14(3):1026–1039, 2006.

[4] S. Chaudhuri and B. Raj. Unsupervised hierarchical structure induction for deeper semantic analysis of audio. In *IEEE ICASSP*, pages 833–837, 2013.

[5] S. Chu, S. Narayanan, and C.-C. Kuo. Environmental sound recognition with time-frequency audio features. *IEEE TASLP*, 17(6):1142–1158, 2009.

[6] C. V. Cotton and D. P. W. Ellis. Spectral vs. spectro-temporal features for acoustic event detection. In *IEEE WASPAA'11*, pages 69–72, 2011.

[7] D. P. W. Ellis, X. Zeng, and J. H. McDermott. Classifying soundtracks with audio texture features. In *IEEE ICASSP*, pages 5880–5883, 2011.

[8] D. Giannoulis, D. Stowell, E. Benetos, M. Rossignol, M. Lagrange, and M. D. Plumbley. A database and challenge for acoustic scene classification and event detection. In *21st EUSIPCO*, 2013.

[9] M. Hall, E. Frank, G. Holmes, B. Pfahringer, P. Reutemann, and I. H. Witten. The WEKA data mining software: an update. *SIGKDD Explorations Newsletter*, 11(1):10–18, 2009.

[10] T. Heittola, A. Mesaros, A. Eronen, and T. Virtanen. Audio context recognition using audio event histograms. In *18th EUSIPCO*, pages 1272–1276, 2010.

[11] T. Heittola, A. Mesaros, A. Eronen, and T. Virtanen. Context-dependent sound event detection. *EURASIP JASMP*, 2013(1), 2013.

[12] S. R. Payne, W. J. Davies, and M. D. Adams. Research into the practical and policy applications of soundscape concepts and techniques in urban areas. DEFRA, HMSO, London, UK, 2009.

[13] R. Radhakrishnan, A. Divakaran, and P. Smaragdis. Audio analysis for surveillance applications. In *IEEE WASPAA'05*, pages 158–161, 2005.

[14] R. M. Schafer. *The Soundscape: Our Sonic Environment and the Tuning of the World.* Destiny Books, 1993.

[15] D. Steele, J. D. Krijnders, and C. Guastavino. The sensor city initiative: cognitive sensors for soundscape transformations. In *GIS Ostrava*, pages 1–8, 2013.

[16] M. Xu, C. Xu, L. Duan, J. S. Jin, and S. Luo. Audio keywords generation for sports video analysis. *ACM TOMCCAP*, 4(2):1–23, 2008.

Instructive Video Retrieval Based on Hybrid Ranking and Attribute Learning

A Case Study on Surgical Skill Training

Lin Chen, Peng Zhang, Baoxin Li
Computer Science and Engineering
Arizona State University, Tempe, AZ, 85281
{lchen109, pzhang41, baoxin.li}@asu.edu

ABSTRACT

Video-based systems have been increasingly used in various training tasks in applications like sports, dancing, and surgery. One key task to add automation to such systems is to automatically select reference videos for a given training video of a trainee. In this paper, we formulate a new problem of instructive video retrieval and propose a solution using both attribute learning and learning to rank. The method first evaluates a user's skill attributes by relative attribute learning. Then, the most critical skill attribute in need of improvement is selected and reported to the user. Finally, a hybrid ranking learning to rank method is employed to retrieve instructive videos from a dataset, which serve as reference for the user. Two main technical problems are solved in this method. First, we combine both skill and visual feature to characterize skill superiority and context similarity. Second, we propose a hybrid ranking approach that works with both pair-wise and point-wise labels of the data. The benefit of the proposed method over other heuristic methods is demonstrated by both objective and subjective experiments, using surgical training videos as a case study.

Categories and Subject Descriptors

I.4 [**Image Processing and Computer Vision**]: Application

Keywords

Video Retrieval; Attribute Learning; Learning to Rank

1. INTRODUCTION

Video-based training systems have found many applications in sports, dancing, and surgery, etc., where cameras are used to record and/or monitor performance of the trainees. Wherever expert supervision is scarce/expensive, a system that can provide automatic feedback based on a trainee's performance would be desired for a trainee's self-improvement. One important type of feedback is to provide verbal instructions based on analysis of the trainee's performance *and* illustrative videos of other higher-skilled performers. We term this as instructive video retrieval.

MM'14, November 03–07, 2014, Orlando, FL, USA.
Copyright 2014 ACM 978-1-4503-3063-3/14/11 ...$15.00.
http://dx.doi.org/10.1145/2647868.2655050.

Instructive video retrieval is a new problem that is different from traditional video retrieval tasks such as nearly-duplicated video retrieval and concept retrieval.In this new problem, we need to focus on whether the retrieved video is helpful for skill improvement. To our knowledge, this is a new research effort with little prior art. One challenge of such task lies in the inherent vagueness and subjectivity of the term "instructive", which makes it difficult to formulate a retrieval cost function. In this work, the instructiveness of a video is defined by considering three criteria: specificity, superiority and similarity. Specificity requires that the illustrative video should be selected w.r.t. a trainee's skill weakness and a corresponding verbal instruction would be provided telling why this video is recommended. Superiority refers to that the illustrative video should represent a better skill on the weakness aspect (attribute) of the trainee. Similarity means that the illustrative video should have a similar operation context (e.g., performing similar actions) to the trainee's video so that it is easy for the trainee to figure out how to imitate and improve skills.

Considering these criteria, in this paper, we design an instructive video retrieval method based on attribute learning and learning to rank, using surgical training as a case study. Our hybrid ranking approach combines both pair-wise (relative) and point-wise (binary) data, making it flexible in handling variable levels of availability of labeled training data in a practical application. The major contribution of this paper is three-fold. First, we formulate the new problem of instructive video retrieval and propose a learning-based solution. Second, in the chosen case study, both skill attributes and operation context features are designed to implement the general approach for delivering good performance. Last, we present a hybrid ranking SVM to take advantage of both pair-wise and point-wise labels for more effective ranking under sparse and noisy labels.

2. RELATED WORK

Human skill assessment is a research topic with a long history originated from psychology where skill is defined as the relation between task difficulties and the resources paid for and quality gained from the task[3]. There are generally two ways for automatic skill evaluation. One is to build a model for different skill levels, and use the model distance from the user's performance for skill assessment, e.g., [2]. This method provides an overall skill assessment but it is not specific enough to tell trainees how to improve. The other is to provide performance metrics based on motion feature statistics, e.g., [1]. But these mere metric are difficult to use for coaching. Our attribute learning method adopted skill attributes from domain knowledge[2]. Therefore, it can not only evaluate different skill aspects, but also generate instructions understandable to trainees. Moreover, we can retrieve an illustrative video via attribute analysis, which is one big step further than only skill evaluation.

Attribute learning maps low-level image feature to intermediate visual attributes, e.g. fur, color, and stripe, rather than high-level category labels, e.g. zebra. The introduction of semantic attributes greatly improves human-computer-interaction capability and boosts many learning applications with human involved [6]. Our work is related to multi-attribute image retrieval, since we will consider all skill attributes for instructive video selection. The multi-attribute fusion function can either be designed from heuristics, e.g., L1 norm of matching score on each attribute[8], or be learned from model assumption, and the model can be either generative graphical model, e.g., Bayesian network[9], or discriminative function, e.g., SVM[10]. We formulate our problem in a discriminative function since generative models requires more training samples while heuristic fusion is difficult due to the vagueness of instructiveness.

Learning to rank [4] is different from traditional heuristic method where ranking metrics is learned from labels. There are generally three types of labels for LR problem: point-wise, pair-wise and list-wise. However, there are new challenges in the instruction video retrieval problem. First, due to the high cost of labeling real training videos by expert surgeons, the training labels are typically very sparse. Second, the labels may be noisy because of the vagueness in instructiveness concept and the subjective nature of the problem. To this end, we present a hybrid-ranking SVM method to take advantage of both point-wise and pair-wise labels. There are other hybrid methods. For example, [5] uses isotonic regression to optimize pair-wise margin among samples of different relevance levels where point-wise relevance constraint can be further incorporated. In [7], pair-wise margin between different relevance levels are formulated in list-wise NDCG cost function and the function can be solved by unconstraint optimization. These methods only use point-wise label and their hybrid only appears in cost function. In contrast, our method makes use of both point-wise and pair-wise labels and we can thus even differentiate pairs on the same relevance level.

3. SURGICAL TRAINING TASK

The Fundamentals of Laparoscopic Surgery (FLS) training box has been widely used in minimally-invasive surgery training. The system is a box simulating the human body and a trainee uses tools going into the box through two small holes to perform surgical actions. The trainees (Fig. 1 Left) can only watch the inside of the box through a monitor, which is captured by an on-board camera (Fig. 1 Right).

In this training procedure, a trainee is required to lift one of the six objects with a grasper in one hand, transfer the object to another hand, and then place it on a peg on the other side of the board. Once all six objects have been transferred, the process is reversed from one side to the other. The peg transfer operation consists of 3 primitive actions in Tab. 1. Ideally, we should perform each primitive action once to finish one peg transfer cycle. For six objects being transferred from left to right and backward, there are totally 12 cycles in one training session.

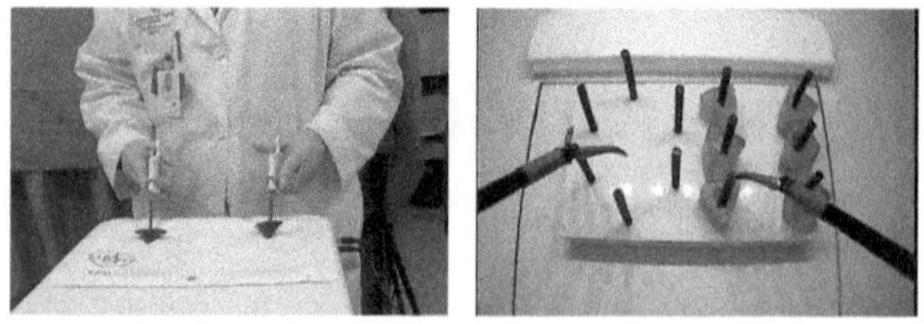

Figure 1: Illustrating the FLS system.

Table 1: Primitive Actions of Peg Transfer

Name	Description
Lift	Move grasper to a peg with object and raise the object off
Transfer	Move the two graspers together and pass the object from one grasper to another
Place	Move grasper to an empty peg and release the object

Surgical skill can be evaluated by a set of attributes. Following the popular Global Rating Index for Technical Skills[2], we adopt several important skill attributes most relevant to the peg transfer task for skill evaluation and instructive video retrieval. These attributes are listed in Tab. 2.

4. METHODOLOGY

Given a clip of trainee's operation, our task is retrieving and recommending an instructive video clip for skill improvement. We propose to solve this task in three steps as elaborated below.

4.1 Critical Skill Attributes Selection

To retrieve instructive videos for a trainee's skill improvement, we must first figure out the operation weakness. A lowest attribute value does not always mean the most urgent attribute in need of improvement. The weakest attribute should be the one that the trainee did poorly while most other people are significantly better.

We first perform normalization across different attributes so that the values of the skill attributes would reflect their respective urgency to be improved, shown in Eq (1):

$$a'_{k,i} = P_k(a \geq a_{k,i} + S_k), (1 \leq k \leq K) \quad (1)$$

where $a_{k,i}$ is the attribute value of the k-th skill attribute $A_k (1 \leq k \leq K)$ for the i-th video V_i. $P_k(.)$ is the probability distribution of attribute A_k on a pre-defined video database and the S_k is the significance threshold of A_k. In fact, Eq (1) is an "inverse" normalization into attribute importance, because higher skill attribute value represents less urgent attribute to improve and will leads to lower normalization value. The success of (1) lies in a well-constructed database with video clips from people of different skill levels.

Table 2: Skill Attributes for Surgical Skill

Attribute	Define
Time and motion	Unnecessary moves and time cost
Flow of operation	Moves smoothly without stop
Bimanual dexterity	Cooperation between hands
Instrument handling	Tentative operations and errors

The second processing step is attribute comparison. Given a user's performance video V_i, and a retrieved video V_j, we measure how much V_j can help V_i on the attribute A_k. This is called the utility of V_j to V_i on A_k, and is measured by the difference between the normalized attribute values in (1) as

$$u_{k,i,j} = (a'_{k,j} - a'_{k,i})/(a'_{k,i}), (1 \le k \le K) \quad (2)$$

4.2 Skill and Operation Context Features

Let $\boldsymbol{f}_{q,d}$ be the ranking feature derived from the pair of a trainee's video V_q and a reference video V_d. $f_{q,d}$ should consist of both skill context and operation context to embody the specificity, superiority, and similarity.

Specificity is determined by the normalized attribute importance in (1). Superiority principle can be described by the difference between the normalized attribute value of V_q and V_i in (2). So we define the skill context feature as:

$$\boldsymbol{f}^{(s)}_{q,d} = [\boldsymbol{a}_q, \boldsymbol{a}_d, \boldsymbol{u}_{q,d}] \quad (3)$$

where $\boldsymbol{a}_q/\boldsymbol{a}_d$ are the normalized attributes value vector of V_q/V_d as $\boldsymbol{a}_q = [a'_{k,q}]$ and $\boldsymbol{u}_{q,d}$ is the utility vector of V_d to V_q as $\boldsymbol{u}_{q,d} = [u_{k,q,d}]$, where $k = 1, \cdots, K$.

Similarity principle means V_d should have a similar operation context as V_q, e.g., using the same hand and with similar surroundings. To measure this, first we divide the operation context of an image I into blocks $B_n, n = 1, \ldots, N$. Each B_n is described by a block context vector $\boldsymbol{b}_n = [c_1, \ldots, c_M]$ where c_m is the area portion of the m-th region category, e.g., object and peg, in block B_n. Since FLS box is a controlled environment with significant color difference among region categories, the area portion c_m can be obtained by color segmentation and tracking. Second, we describe the similarity between a frame I in V_q and its peer frame I' in V_d based on block similarity. Each block may have different importance for the similarity by its relative position to the grasper. To address this, we take the block containing the grasper tip of I as the reference center, and order all blocks by the distance and angle to the center. Suppose $B_n, n = 1, \ldots, N$ are already ordered by the above rule, so the first block B_1 contains the reference center. The blocks B'_n of frame I' will follow the same order so that B'_n and B_n are of the same location. The block context vector $\boldsymbol{b_n}$ already conveys block context, since it is derived from object segmentation. So the block similarity can be directly defined as the inner product of block context vectors, and the similarity between I and I' is defined as:

$$s(I; I') = [\langle b_1, b'_1 \rangle, \ldots, \langle b_N, b'_N \rangle]. \quad (4)$$

Then the operation context feature of video pair (V_q, V_d) can be represented as

$$\boldsymbol{f}^{(v)}_{q,i} = [\boldsymbol{s}(I_0; I'_0), \boldsymbol{s}(I_1; I'_1)], \quad (5)$$

where $I_0/I_1(I'_0/I'_1)$ is the start/end frame of $V_q(V_d)$.

The final ranking feature of video pair (V_q, V_d) is:

$$f_{q,d} = [f^{(s)}_{q,d}, f^{(v)}_{q,i}] \quad (6)$$

which will guarantee specificity, superiority, and similarity principles for the following learning to rank.

4.3 Hybrid Ranking SVM

With the selected attribute and extracted ranking features, we now propose to employ hybrid ranking SVM to take advantage of both point-wise and pair-wise labels. Pair-wise ranking SVM, also called ranking SVM[6], tries to find a projection vector w to satisfy the pair label under maximal margin assumption. Point-wise ranking SVM tries to find a projection vector and a set of intersections related to different relevance level in maximal margin spirit, e.g. CO SVM[4]. The pair-wise and point-wise methods have their advantages and disadvantages. The pair-wise label is very expensive, but it can provide precise order between two samples. The point-wise label is less expensive, but it can't rank samples of the same relevance level. Since video labeling is very expensive, the labeling can be very sparse. It is better to combine the two label types for more effective ranking. For example, we can include the pair-wise label between relevant samples to augment the point-wise label.

The direct combination the cost function and constraints in [6] and [4] is not desirable, because it fix the margin thresh of point-wise and pair-wise sample to equal value, i.e. 1. Our idea is to introduce an extra variable K as the margin thresh, and reformulate SVM as below:

$$\begin{aligned} \min_{\boldsymbol{w},\varepsilon,w_0,\gamma,K} & \frac{1}{2}\|\boldsymbol{w}\|_2^2 + C_1\sum\nolimits_{i=1}^{m} \varepsilon_i + C_2\sum\nolimits_{i=1}^{m} \gamma_i \\ s.t. \ & y_i \cdot \langle w, \boldsymbol{x}_i^{(1)} - \boldsymbol{x}_i^{(2)} \rangle \ge 1 - \varepsilon_i \\ & z_i \cdot (\langle \boldsymbol{w}, x_i \rangle + w_0) \ge K - \gamma_i \\ & \gamma_i \ge 0, \varepsilon_i \ge 0. \end{aligned} \quad (7)$$

where $\boldsymbol{w}$ is the ranking model; $y_i = 1(-1)$ means $\boldsymbol{x}_i^{(1)}$ is superior (inferior) to $\boldsymbol{x}_i^{(2)}$; $z_i = 1(-1)$ means x_i is instructive/non-instructive; ε and γ are slack variables. This problem can be solved by quadratic programming.

Table 3: The ranking result of pair-wised, point-wised and hybrid ranking SVM in simulated data.

Noise	Cosine			Kendall		
	Pair	Point	Hybrid	Pair	Point	Hybrid
1%	0.39	0.47	0.49	0.25	0.32	0.33
10%	0.28	0.40	0.42	0.18	0.26	0.28
30%	0.15	0.19	0.24	0.09	0.12	0.15

Table 4: The classification and ranking accuracy (%) on surgical video data of three primitive actions.

	Lift	Transfer	Drop
Point/Hybrid	78.1/80.7	83.7/84.4	83.4/88.4
Pair/Hybrid	75.7/76.3	90.0/89.8	89.3/90.4

5. EXPERIMENTS

We first show the efficiency of hybrid-ranking SVM by both simulation and real surgical video data. Then we show the effectiveness of our instructive video retrieval system. For each of the three primitive actions, our surgical video dataset consist of 240 video clips on different skill levels, i.e. from novice to expert. So there are totally 720 video clips.

5.1 Simulation Experiment

We first compared our Hybrid-based SVM approach (7) with two baseline approaches of pair-wise method[6] and point-wise method[4]. The simulated dataset are uniformly generated with 150 point-wise samples and 150 pairs-wise samples, whose labels are decided by a randomly generated projection vector w. Additionally, noise is added into the label for robustness test. Tab. 3 shows the experiment result of the three approaches when noise are added by 1%, 10% and 30%. Two measures are adopted to compare the performance. The first measure is the direction cosine similarity between the projection vector of trained model and the originally generated one; the other measure is the Kendall rank correlation coefficient of the projection result. Result in Tab. 3 shows that the point-wise label is much more efficient than pair-wised label in learning the true projection angle. However, the hybrid-ranking SVM can still improve the ranking accuracy by combining both point-wise and pair-wise labels. And the improvement is more significant with the increase of noise level.

5.2 Surgical Data Classification and Ranking

The training data were labeled in the following procedure. Given a random action clip as query, we randomly pick another two clips from the clips with significant higher attribute values. Then the expert surgeon would evaluate if the returned clips is instructive or not instructive. If both of the two clips are instructive, the expert would further provide a pair-wise label indicating which clip is more instructive. The labeling process follows the three criterions discussed above. For each of the 3 primitive actions, we generated 30 queries and 8 pairs of clips for each query.

Similarly, we illustrate the benefit of hybrid ranking SVM by comparison with both point-wise and pair-wise SVM. We train hybrid ranking SVM with both the point and pair labels acquired in the above process, while the point-wise and pair-wise SVM are trained with their corresponding labels. Tab. 4 shows the classification and the ranking accuracies of the hybrid-ranking SVM based on the combination of both point and pairwise labels, compared with the purely point-wise and pair-wise based approaches. Each entry shows the accuracy in lift/transfer/drop action. The results show that our hybrid approach provides better accuracy than the two baseline methods.

5.3 Instructive Video Selection

Finally we compare our video with a baseline method that randomly selects one expert video clip of the primitive action. The subjective comparison protocol is as follows. We recruited 6 subjects who had no prior knowledge on the dataset. For each subject, 10 clips for each primitive action are given as query. For each query, both our hybrid ranking SVM and the baseline method will return an instructive clip. So there are totally 60 queries for each of the 3 primitive actions. For each returned video pairs, the subjects need to evaluate whether the video is instructive in improving the operation in the query video, and which one is more instructive. The comparative result in Tab. 5 shows that our hybrid ranking SVM performs much better than the baseline method in selecting instructive videos. The first row shows the percentage of instructive coaching videos returned by our hybrid/baseline approaches. The second row shows the percentage that the returned video of our approach is more/equal/less instructive than the baseline approach. Result shows that, the returned videos by our approach are almost all instructive, apparently higher than the baseline approach. Even in the case that both returned videos from two approaches are instructive, our approach would recommend more instructive videos than the baseline approach by large majority.

Table 5: Subjective evaluation results (%) of instructive video selection.

	Lift	Transfer	Drop
Instructive	98.1/74.8	98.3/83.1	99.2/73.4
Superiority	61.1/21.3/17.6	73.2/15.5/11.3	68.1/16.1/15.8

6. CONCLUSIONS

We formulated a new problem of instructive video retrieval and developed a solution in the case study of surgical training video. In defining the problem based on three criteria, we allow the otherwise abstract and subjective task to be attacked by relative attribute learning. To facilitate a realistic solution, considering the poor availability of labeled data, we proposed a new hybrid ranking method to approximate instructive score from both attribute skill and visual operation context features which are designed to embody the three criterions, taking advantage of both point-wise and pair-wise labels. Stimulation and real data experiments demonstrated the approach is effective and thus can be a promising solution to the instructive video retrieval problem.

7. ACKNOWLEDGMENTS

The work was supported in part by National Science Foundation (NSF) (Grant 0904778). The views expressed in this material are those of the author(s) and do not necessarily reflect the views of NSF.

8. REFERENCES

[1] D. S. Alexiadis, P. Kelly, P. Daras, N. E. O'Connor, T. Boubekeur, and M. B. Moussa. Evaluating a dancer's performance using kinect-based skeleton tracking. In *ACM MM*, 2011.

[2] J. D. Doyle, E. M. Webber, and R. S. Sidhu. A universal global rating scale for the evaluation of technical skills in the operating room. *The American Journal of Surgery*, 2007.

[3] P. M. Fitts and J. R. Peterson. Information Capacity of Discrete Motor Responses. *J Exp Psychol*, Feb. 1964.

[4] T.-Y. Liu. Learning to rank for information retrieval. *Found. Trends Inf. Retr.*, Mar. 2009.

[5] T. Moon, A. Smola, Y. Chang, and Z. Zheng. Intervalrank: Isotonic regression with listwise and pairwise constraints. In *WSDM*, 2010.

[6] D. Parikh and K. Grauman. Relative attributes. In *ICCV*, Nov 2011.

[7] C. Renjifo and C. Carmen. The discounted cumulative margin penalty: Rank-learning with a list-wise loss and pair-wise margins. In *MLSP*, Sept 2012.

[8] W. Scheirer, N. Kumar, P. N. Belhumeur, and T. E. Boult. Multi-attribute spaces: Calibration for attribute fusion and similarity search. In *CVPR*, June 2012.

[9] W. Scheirer, N. Kumar, K. Ricanek, P. Belhumeur, and T. Boult. Fusing with context: A bayesian approach to combining descriptive attributes. In *IJCB*, Oct 2011.

[10] B. Siddiquie, R. Feris, and L. Davis. Image ranking and retrieval based on multi-attribute queries. In *CVPR*, 2011.

A Real-Time Smart Display Detection System

Shu Shi*
Ricoh Innovations Corp.
2882 Sand Hill Rd, Ste 115
Menlo Park, CA, United States
pkuslick@gmail.com

John Barrus
Ricoh Innovations Corp.
2882 Sand Hill Rd, Ste 115
Menlo Park, CA, United States
barrus@ric.ricoh.com

ABSTRACT

A smart display detection system is proposed that allows users to connect with displays using mobile cameras. The smart displays dynamically update a server with information about the current screen content and the system matches captured images from mobile devices with the screen information. A synchronized timestamped matching strategy is employed to achieve high performance in detecting screens playing motion intensive video and an aggressive feature selection method is used to minimize bandwidth requirements.

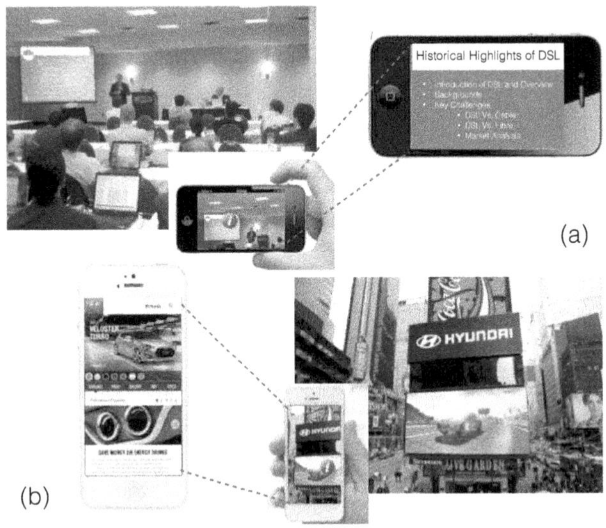

Figure 1: Smart display detection applications

Categories and Subject Descriptors

H.5.1 [**Multimedia Information Systems**]: Video

General Terms

Design, Performance

Keywords

Display detection; synchronized matching; feature compression; bandwidth

1. INTRODUCTION

The mobile cameras included with modern smartphones are increasingly used to access information. Many smartphone apps use mobile cameras as barcode and QR code scanners. Several visual search systems, such as Google Goggles™ [1], Ricoh Ocutag™ [2], etc., have been developed for landmark recognition and product recognition using mobile devices. In this paper, we propose a smart display detection system that can automatically identify the screens of smart displays within images so that a connection between a mobile device and a smart display can be established automatically.

We define a smart display as a display that can provide additional information to a connected mobile device. Here are two examples showing why smart display detection is useful. Figure 1(a) shows a conference presentation scenario. It is difficult for audience members to discern small text details appearing on the projector screen. Moreover, the audience may not finish reading the current slide before the speaker moves on to the next page. If the projector is a smart display, the user can use the proposed smart display detection app to snap a photo of the screen and connect to the projector to access all current and recent slide images in high resolution. In Figure 1(b), a user is attracted to a commercial playing on a large display and wants to know more about the product, such as product name, model, website URL and so on. In order to do so, the user may have to wait until the information is shown on the screen and take one or multiple photos of it. If the video screen is a smart display and can be detected through our proposed system, the user can simply point the mobile camera at the screen. With a press of the shutter, the display detection system can find the screen and redirect the mobile device to the full version of the commercial video or to the web page of the advertised product.

*Dr. Shi is now with AT&T Research Labs. This work was completed when he was working at Ricoh Innovations Corp.
[1]http://www.google.com/mobile/goggles/
[2]http://www.ocutag.com/

MM'14, November 3–7, 2014, Orlando, Florida, USA.

http://dx.doi.org/10.1145/2647868.2655052 .

There have been several related systems proposed in the literature. VR Code [12] displays patterned information on a screen that is invisible to human eyes but visible to digital cameras so that the mobile device can recognize which screen it is pointed at. The presentation retrieval system discussed in [5] allows a user to retrieve presentation slides using captured images. TvTak[3] is a mobile app that can recognize which TV program is shown by snapping a photo of the TV screen. The TV screen within the captured image can be recognized based on the screen position and aspect ratio information. The image/video fingerprints are extracted to match the TV program database [1]. Another mobile video retrieval system [3] also supports video search using a photo of the video screen but the video database must be preprocessed before the search can be performed.

The proposed smart display detection system takes a content based approach. It compares the local features of the captured image and the screen images that are dynamically updated by smart displays to find the best match. In particular, we use synchronized timestamped matching to enhance the detection accuracy for the screens playing motion intensive video and reduce the display bandwidth usage by uploading only the selected feature points. Compared to the aforementioned related work, our system (a) does not require special display or camera devices (vs. VR Code); (b) can detect a screen playing live video content (vs. [5] and video retrieval systems); (c) can detect multiple screens within one camera image and work even if only a partial screen is captured (vs. TvTak).

For the rest of the paper, we will introduce the system design and architecture in Section 2. In Section 3, we will discuss two major challenges: how to detect video screens accurately and how to reduce upload bandwidth for smart displays. We have implemented a prototype system and some experimental results are shown in Section 4. Section 5 concludes with a discussion of some limitations of our system.

2. SYSTEM DESIGN

The proposed system is comprised of three components: an image registration server, one or more smart displays, and one or more mobile clients. Figure 2 shows an illustration of the system framework. A smart display registers with the server in order to be detected by mobile users. The registration process requires the display to specify the display information (including the geographic location of the smart display), the properties of content shown on the screen (e.g., the screen resolution, whether the content is played repeatedly, whether the content is live or pre-recorded, etc.) and the service information that the display can provide to mobile users (like a URL for high resolution versions of the content). After registration, the smart display continuously monitors the display frame buffer and sends updates to the image registration server.

The mobile client is a camera based app. When the user tries to detect whether there are smart displays in the current camera view, the app sends a geo-tagged image (or a small video clip) to the server as a query. The image registration server organizes the screen updates from all registered smart displays in a database. Upon receiving a mobile query, it tries to find the smart displays appearing in the query image by performing image matching between the query image and the dynamically constructed search database. We take the conventional BoW (Bag of Words) approach to match the query image with the screen images stored in the database. The SIFT features [9] are extracted for matching and the RANSAC algorithm [6] is used to find enough consistent matches for homographic matrix estimation.

[3]http://www.tvtak.com

Figure 2: System Framework

The most important difference between the proposed system and other mobile visual search systems surveyed in [8] is that the search database needs to be dynamically updated based on the latest screen updates from smart displays. Depending on the content displayed on the screens, there can be multiple screen updates every second, which makes time consuming indexing methods (e.g., vocabulary tree and inverted index) not applicable to our system. Instead, we take a multiple randomized kd-trees [11] approach similar to [4]. Upon receiving a mobile query, the server builds a randomized kd-tree for every screen image within the search range. Since the mobile query is geo-tagged and all smart displays are managed based on the location information provided during registration, the server can search only the displays geographically close to the mobile user, which significantly reduces the total number of kd-trees to search. Moreover, the constructed kd-trees are saved for future queries but will be discarded if the screen is updated. After feature matching, geometric verification is performed for all screen candidates with sufficient inliers. Acceptance rules for verification results specific to our system consider size, aspect ratio and orientation.

Unlike TvTak [1], such an feature matching method does not require the whole smart display screen to be placed in the center of the image for recognition. The smart display screen can appear anywhere in the image or even partially occluded as long as there are enough matching features extracted. It also works for the scenario when more than one smart displays appear within the same image. Our system searches the whole database and finds all successful matches.

On the mobile client, once the query response is received, the detected smart display screens are marked. User can touch or use gestures to switch from the camera view to the smart display service view. For most smart displays, the service may just be a link to a web page or mobile app. In

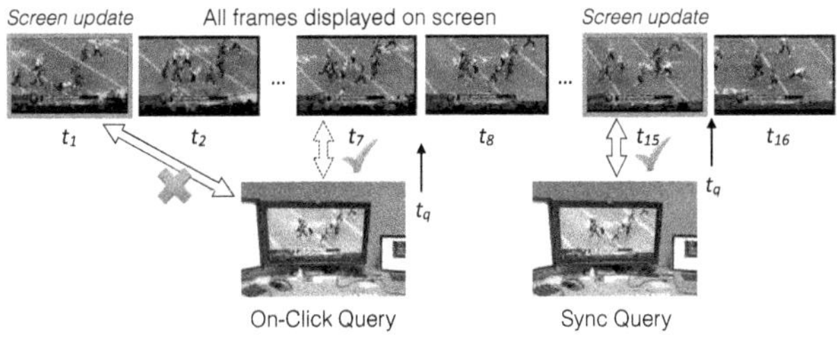

Figure 3: Query problem with low sampling rate

order to enhance the user experience of using display detection, we also propose two smart display services, which can be easily hosted by the image registration server without any extra effort from smart displays: video browsing and recent screen browsing (screen history).

Video browsing is for the smart display that is playing a pre-recorded video repeatedly (e.g., commercial video screen in Figure 1(b)). If the smart display uploads the pre-recorded video to the image registration server at the registration phase, the server can provide the mobile user a streaming link to the original video when the smart display is detected. Recent screen browsing is only for the smart display showing static screens (e.g., PowerPoint presentation in Figure 1(a)). In this case, the server should save all screen updates so that the mobile user can browse all recent screen images.

3. TECHNICAL CHALLENGES

In implementing the prototype system, we discovered several technical challenges. In this section, we discuss two of the major challenges.

3.1 Video Matching

We only discuss the case of matching non-preprocessed video content in this paper. For the case where video content is available for preprocessing, please refer to other video retrieval systems [3]. In our system, we take a timestamped matching approach. The smart display assigns a timestamp t_i to every screen image S_i immediately **after** it is copied from the frame buffer. The timestamp is stored with the corresponding screen update and transmitted to the server. The mobile client also assigns a timestamp t_q with every query Q right **before** the camera captures the image. We use SNTP [10] protocol to synchronize the time of all devices at the initialization phase. Such a timestamp strategy makes sure that for any query image with t_q and the screen image with t_i, if the screen appears in the query image and $t_q > t_i$, then either S_i or its subsequent frames appears in Q. Therefore, on the server side, when the query image Q arrives, the screen image with the timestamp $\max\{t_i \mid t_i < t_q\}$ should be selected to match with Q. This timestamped matching approach does not require pre-processing but finds the most appropriate frame to match. It can also correctly handle the case where multiple screens are playing the same video content but where the video is not synchronized.

The performance of this timestamped matching approach is primarily affected by the sampling rate of screen updates and how query images are captured. Ideally, if the smart display sends an update of every frame shown on the screen to the server (i.e., the sampling rate equals to the video frame rate), the query image captured at any time can be matched with the correct screen source using the aforementioned timestamped matching method. However, processing every frame would require an excessive amount of computation and significant network bandwidth. In practice, due to bandwidth and computational limitations, the smart displays can only sample the screen buffer at a much lower rate than the original video frame rate. In this case, the method of query image capture directly affects the detection accuracy. For example in Figure 3, the video frame rate is 30 fps while the maximum sampling rate is only 2 fps. Thus, only 2 screen frames (t_1 and t_{15}) are sent to the server. If the query image is captured immediately after the user initiates the request, which we call "on-click" capture, it will have a timestamp t_q close to t_7. Since the server only has the screen update at t_1, the matching may fail because the frame at t_1 is significantly different from the frame at t_7 due to large viewpoint changes, object motion or scene changes.

To address this problem, we synchronized display sampling and mobile queries as follows: smart displays are triggered to process screen images only at the 1/4 second marks, 1/2 second marks, or 1 second marks, depending on the sampling rate. Meanwhile, when the mobile client generates a trigger, it captures up to three images, at the nearest 1/4 second, 1/2 second and 1 second marks. All images are bundled together as a query and sent to the server for matching. By taking multiple images, the query can accommodate smart displays with different sampling rates and increase the chance of finding successful matches. For example, in Figure 3, the "sync" query image has a t_q close to t_{15} so that it can be appropriately matched with the available screen update.

3.2 Bandwidth Reduction

Algorithm 1 Pseudo code of selecting repeated features

```
while true do
    S = copy_screen();
    curr_feat = feat_detect(S);
    good_match = feat_match(prev_feat, curr_feat);
    for i = 1 → good_match.size() do
        if prev_upload.contains(good_match[i]) then
            curr_upload.add_repeat_feat(good_match[i]);
        else
            prev_upload.add_feat(good_match[i]);
            curr_upload.add_repeat_feat(good_match[i]);
        end if
    end for
    upload_to_server(prev_upload);
    prev_feat = curr_feat;
    prev_upload = curr_upload;
end while
```

Minimizing the upload bandwidth allows a server to support more smart displays. The bandwidth reduction techniques we have implemented include: downscaling the screen image for processing (e.g., to no more than 640×480), using advanced coding tools to compress screen images (e.g., x264 [7]), and uploading only the features with low bit rate descriptors (e.g., CHoG [2]). Moreover, we propose a new method of uploading the selected features. The display does not upload all features to the server, but only the features repeated in time-adjacent screen frames. The main idea is not to waste bandwidth on isolated features appearing only in a single frame. The pseudo code of the proposed selec-

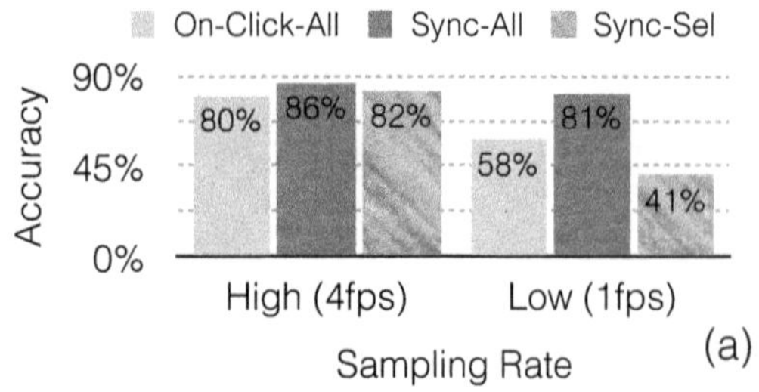

Format	Average Size (bits) per Frame		
All Features	702 feat	702K (SIFT)	42K (CHoG)
Repeated Features	95 feat	95K (SIFT)	6K (CHoG)
JPEG		380K	
x264, no B frame		50K	

(b)

Figure 4: Accuracy and bandwidth

tion method is shown in Algorithm 1. The drawback of this method is that it needs to buffer one additional sampled frame to check for repeated features, and a delay the length of one sampling interval is added to the server response time to mobile client.

4. EXPERIMENTS

Though our prototype system supports real-time display detection, for evaluation purposes we recorded the display content and a set of captured images from a mobile phone as a test data set. All experiments are tested with the same data set. We have selected popular TV commercials on YouTube[4] to play on the display screen. We captured three test data sets by taking 100 query photos (around 2000 screen updates) per set. The detection accuracy results are shown in Figure 4(a). "On-click-All" means to use "On-Click" query capturing strategy with all feature points. "Sync-All" means synchronized sampling and querying with all feature points. "Sync-Sel" means synchronized sampling and query with selected repeated features. The proposed "Sync" strategy outperforms "On-Click", especially when the sampling rate is low. When using the selected features, "Sync-Sel" is only slightly worse than "Sync-All" when the sampling rate is high but, as expected, the performance drops significantly when the sampling rate is low. Fewer features repeat in adjacent frames when the sampling rate is 1 second. Figure 4(b) compares the bandwidth usage of four different methods, including the proposed feature selection. By sending only the repeated features to the server, the number of features to upload is reduced from 702 to 95 per frame. If we adopt a low bit rate descriptor CHoG [2] for encoding features, we can further reduce the bandwidth requirement. Note that the repeated features require extra bits to refer to previously uploaded features. Therefore the actual bandwidth requirement will be slightly higher than the number shown in Figure 4(b).

5. CONCLUSION

We have introduced a smart display detection system that can accurately find display screens playing either static or dynamic content within an image captured on a mobile device. Our system requires no pre-processing and little network bandwidth but achieves a relatively high accuracy in detecting even motion intensive video screens. However, our system still has several limitations. For example, the system cannot detect a screen containing an image with few features. Additional characterization of the system is needed in a realistic setting, including situations with difficult lighting and a variety of mobile devices and video sources.

[4]http://goo.gl/4ZgQwD

6. REFERENCES

[1] D. Amselem, Y. Hava, A. Shavit, and D. Shavit. Devices, systems, methods, and media for detecting, indexing, and comparing video signals from a video display in a background scene using a camera-enabled device, Jan. 16 2014. US Patent App. 13/821,983.

[2] V. Chandrasekhar, G. Takacs, D. Chen, S. Tsai, R. Grzeszczuk, and B. Girod. Chog: Compressed histogram of gradients a low bit-rate feature descriptor. In *Computer Vision and Pattern Recognition, 2009. CVPR 2009. IEEE Conference on*, pages 2504–2511. IEEE, 2009.

[3] D. Chen, N.-M. Cheung, S. Tsai, V. Chandrasekhar, G. Takacs, R. Vedantham, R. Grzeszczuk, and B. Girod. Dynamic selection of a feature-rich query frame for mobile video retrieval. In *Image Processing (ICIP), 2010 17th IEEE International Conference on*, pages 1017–1020. IEEE, 2010.

[4] X. Chen and M. Koskela. Mobile visual search from dynamic image databases. In *Image Analysis*, pages 196–205. Springer, 2011.

[5] B. Erol, D.-S. Lee, and J. J. Hull. Retrieval of presentation recordings with digital camera images. In *IEEE Conference on Computer Vision and Pattern Recognition, Jun.* Citeseer.

[6] M. A. Fischler and R. C. Bolles. Random sample consensus: a paradigm for model fitting with applications to image analysis and automated cartography. *Communications of the ACM*, 24(6):381–395, 1981.

[7] J. Garrett-Glaser. x264: The best low-latency video streaming platform in the world, January 2010. `http://x264dev.multimedia.cx/archives/249`.

[8] B. Girod, V. Chandrasekhar, D. M. Chen, N.-M. Cheung, R. Grzeszczuk, Y. Reznik, G. Takacs, S. S. Tsai, and R. Vedantham. Mobile visual search. *Signal Processing Magazine, IEEE*, 28(4):61–76, 2011.

[9] D. G. Lowe. Distinctive image features from scale-invariant keypoints. *International journal of computer vision*, 60(2):91–110, 2004.

[10] D. L. Mills. Simple network time protocol (sntp) version 4 for ipv4, ipv6 and osi. 2006.

[11] C. Silpa-Anan and R. Hartley. Optimised kd-trees for fast image descriptor matching. In *Computer Vision and Pattern Recognition, 2008. CVPR 2008. IEEE Conference on*, pages 1–8. IEEE, 2008.

[12] G. Woo, A. Lippman, and R. Raskar. Vrcodes: Unobtrusive and active visual codes for interaction by exploiting rolling shutter. In *Mixed and Augmented Reality (ISMAR), 2012 IEEE International Symposium on*, pages 59–64. IEEE, 2012.

Pose Maker: A Pose Recommendation System for Person in the Landscape Photographing

Shuang Ma[†‡], Yangyu Fan[†], Chang Wen Chen[‡]
[†] Northwestern Polytechnical Universty, Xi'an, P. R. China
[‡] State University of New York at Buffalo, Buffalo, NY, USA

ABSTRACT

To pose like a fashion model and to take professional grade photo are always two challenging tasks, especially for novice users. *Pose Maker*, an innovative system for pose and photo composition recommendation and synthesis, is developed in this work. Given a user-provided clothing color and gender, this system shall not only offer some suitable poses, but also assist users to take high visual quality photos by generating the visual effect of person in the landscape pictures. To recommend poses, we first propose a view specific professional learning model to help users select several compatible poses for a given image. Based on selection results, a hierarchical pose image synthesis module is designed to synthesize the selected poses along with the scene to be captured in the most suitable position and size taking into consideration several important factors in picture composition, including aesthetic photography principles, color harmony and focal length parameters. Extensive experimental evaluations and analysis on test images of various conditions demonstrate the effectiveness of the proposed system.

Categories and Subject Descriptors

I.4 [**Image Processing and Computer Vision**]: Applications

General Terms

Algorithm, Experimentation, Performance

Keywords

Pose Recommendation; Professional Learning; Synthesis Module

1. INTRODUCTION

Everybody wants to be captured like a fashion model and to make their portrait photo looks like professional ones. However, it usually requires years of practice and experience to take professional grade photos. To assist users with professional suggestions, a photographing recommendation system has been developed to assist smartphone users to take professional grade photos by learning photography rules and through social context [1, 2]. Similarly, a system that generates suggestion by mining the underlying knowledge of professional photographers from massively crawled professional photos has been proposed in [3]. In order to guide users taking appealing photos, some aesthetic principles and photo quality assessment attributes need to be investigated. Towards this goal, a scene-dependent aesthetic model which jointly leveraging the geo-context and visual content to assess photo quality is presented in [3]. Some describable image attributes that human might use to evaluate an image have also been investigated in [5]. A semantics-preserving wrap that can be used to enhance the visual dominance is studied in [6]. However, these existing research attempts are predominantly focusing on how to find a good view enclosure and are mostly restricted to landscape photos. For portrait photo recommendation, a framework for recommending position and poses by searching for some similar reference photos based on attention composition features is presented in [7]. However, this work just simply copy the pose in the reference photo without considering whether the position and size are appropriate for the specific view or not. Furthermore, the suggested pose is represented by boxes, which made it impracticable and obscure for users.

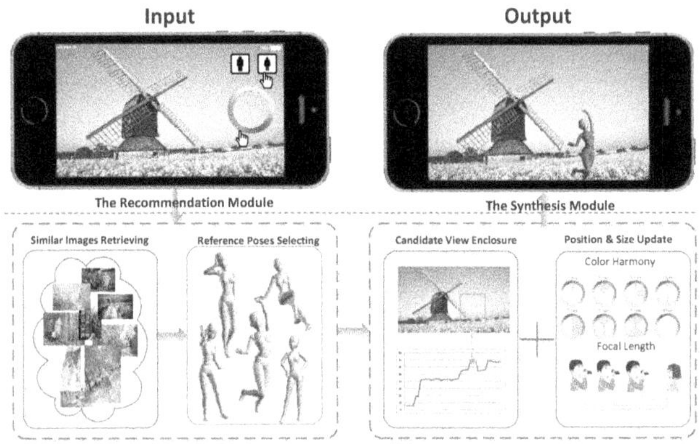

Figure 1: Overview of the proposed *Pose Maker* System.

The proposed system is different from previous works in that this system attempts to help users to select poses according to specific view with visually appealing synthesized pictorial effects by formulating the pose recommendation process as a constrained energy minimization problem. An overview of the proposed system is shown in Figure 1. To the best of our knowledge, this paper represents the first attempt at interactive pose recommendation. Instead of recommending poses blindly, a view specific professional learning approach has been developed to recommend to the mobile device users the most suitable poses mimicking the reasoning process of a professional photographer. Moreover, this system will generate several possible visual effect images by synthesize the recommended poses with the certain scene, which lead to much better user experience. Finally, we develop a hierarchical optimization procedure to improve the effectiveness of the proposed *Pose Maker*.

MM'14, November 3–7, 2014, Orlando, Florida, USA.

http://dx.doi.org/10.1145/2647868.2655053.

2. PROBLEM FORMULATION

To accomplish the objective of pose recommendation, we first collect professional on-line sharing photos to from a reference dataset via crawling. This dataset contains over 3000 professional portrait photos with a variety of poses, which are manually annotated by *Pose Studio* for each photo.

In our previous work [8], we have developed a novel scheme to determine the location and size of a rectangular enclosure for placing human in the landscape photographing. The location and size of such enclosure have been obtained by investigating a set of aesthetic composition rules and visual perception principles so as to construct an aesthetic score prediction model. This model can compute a position score η_j to measure visual quality in terms of overall photo composition. Then we shall conduct a study on professional photos to define a proper initial size $\vec{z}_o\,(h_o, w_o)$ for the enclosure of human into the picture of a given scene. Finally, we utilize an efficient hierarchical search to obtain a set of candidate enclosures $\vec{\Phi} = \vec{e}_1, \vec{e}_2, \cdots, \vec{e}_{N_e}$ for placing human in the scene. Such series of steps is shown in Figure 2.

Now, the input to the proposed system includes the query landscape image I_o, a set of candidate enclosures $\vec{\Phi} = \vec{e}_1, \vec{e}_2, \cdots, \vec{e}_{N_e}$, each enclosure's position score η_j and the initial size $\vec{z}_o(h_o, w_o)$. $\vec{e}_j = (x_j, y_j)$ is the center coordinates of j_{th} enclosure of the input query photo I_o. HSV color vector $\vec{c}$ and g are provided by the user, which represent the user's clothing color and gender, respectively. The dataset we built is represented by $\vec{\mathbb{R}} = (\vec{R}_1, \vec{R}_2, \cdots \vec{R}_{N_{pro}})$ in which $\vec{R}_i = (I_i, p_i)$, I_i is i_{th} reference photo and p_i is i_{th} pose for I_i. Let $\vec{z}_i(h_i, w_i)$ be the size of p_i. The objective of this research is (1) to find a set of reference poses $\Gamma' = \mathrm{p}_1', p_2', \cdots, p_{N_{ref}}'$ by searching for some images similar to I_o in terms of background composition, and (2) to optimize the position and size considering $\vec{c}$, g and focal length parameters by minimizing the energy $E(S)$ to be defined later. $S = S(i), i \in [1, N_{pro}]$ completely specifies the pose selection and synthesis problem. $S(i) = (a_i, (x_i, y_i), \vec{z}_i, \vec{c}, g)$ indicates the center coordinate (x_i, y_i) and size $\vec{z}_i$ of the pose p_i, color $\vec{c}$ and gender g. $a_i = \mathbf{1}(p_i \in \vec{\mathbb{R}}')$ is the indicator variable. The energy of S consists of two terms as defined below:

$$E\,(S) = \omega_r E_r\,(S) + \omega_s E_s\,(S) \tag{1}$$

The recommendation term E_r evaluates the consistency of the reference poses while the synthesis term E_s measures how well the generated visual effect following the aesthetic rules. ω_r and ω_s are the weighting of the energy terms E_r and E_s, respectively. Each of the energy terms will be described in the following in more detail.

3. THE RECOMMENDATION MODULE

The recommendation module is developed to select reference poses for the query photo. To accomplish this, relevant images containing similar background composition are retrieved. In order to obtain the most relevant images from the database, we jointly consider the spatial distribution of content and the saliency which represent the underlying principles of professional photographers.

Spatial Distribution of Content. To obtain the reference photos, we propose to adopt graph-based method as in [9] for image segmentation. We also use the HoG (histogram of gradient) [10] texture feature and the three dimensional compositional feature [7] to represent these patches. For the HoG feature, we divide each patch into 4×4 grids, and the accumulated local histogram of 8 gradient directions over pixels are calculated for each grid. Thus, 131 ($4 \times 4 \times 8{+}3$) dimension descriptors are generated for each patch. Finally, we use feature distance $D_{con}(I_i) = f\,(I_o, I_i)$ between the query photo and each photo to rank the nearest neighbors.

Spatial Distribution of Saliency. In addition, the distribution

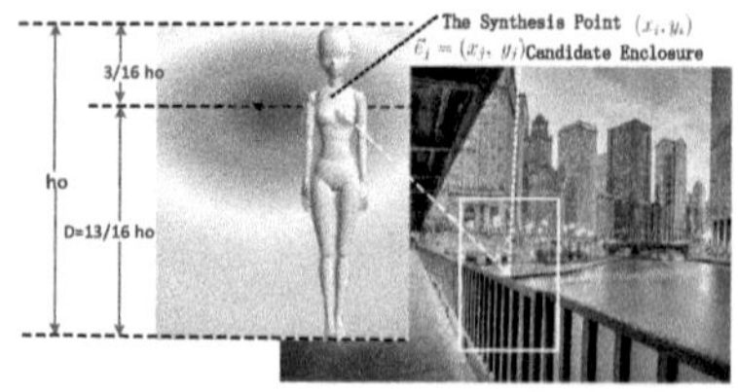

Figure 2: The synthesis point located at the enclosure center.

visual attention represented by saliencies also affect the overall composition of background. Therefore, the spatial distribution of saliency will also be utilized to capture the overall composition. However, the placement of a person in the landscape will substantially alter the overall saliency distribution. In order to correctly represent scene structure without stressing the person subject, we modified the decaying exponential function in [7] by properly weakening the saliency of subject area Sub:

$$M^*(x,y) = \begin{cases} M(x,y) & otherwise \\ M(x,y) \cdot e^{-\xi M(x,y)} & M\,(x,y) \in Sub \end{cases} \tag{2}$$

where M refers to the initial saliency map which is obtained by [11]. M^* is the decay saliency map, Sub is the subject region in I_i which is defined by [10]. We divide M^* into 5×5 grids and the average saliency value in each grid is calculated to form a vector to represent the saliency spatial distribution. We obtain the nearest results according to $D_{sal}(I_i) = f(I_o, I_i)$. Thus the reference set $\vec{\mathbb{R}}'$ can be organized by the following optimization:

$$\vec{\mathbb{R}}' = \mathop{\arg\min}_{i \in \vec{\mathbb{R}}} \left(D_{con}\,(i) + D_{sal}\,(i)\right) \tag{3}$$

On top of the content and saliency attributes, we also consider that the views and favours of the photo represent its likeability by users. Hence, the recommendation term E_r is defined as follows:

$$E_r\,(S) = -\sum_{i=1}^{N_{pro}} a_i l_i \tag{4}$$

$$l_{\mathrm{i}} = 1 - \exp\{-(\alpha \cdot views\mathrm{v}I_i + \beta \cdot favorsI_i)\} \tag{5}$$

where l_{i} is the likeability value of image I_i, which is defined by [1]. The energy term E_r is a function of all indicator variables $a_1, \ldots a_{N_{pro}}$. It will favor the most popular poses and also encourage the use of as many poses as possible.

4. THE SYNTHESIS MODULE

Once the reference poses are selected, we propose to carefully synthesize each pose into appealing and attractive visual effect images for users. This is accomplished by (1) generating an initial position considering color harmonic schemes and hue count based on the input enclosures, as shown in Figure 3, (2) updating the initial position and size based on photography constrains, such as focal length parameters, as shown in Figure 4, (3) iteratively optimizing the position and size.

4.1 Initial Position Generation

Color Harmony. Eight color schemes have been discovered to quantify color harmony [12]. In order to pop out the subject from local surrounding, we adopt the *Complementary* color scheme, i.e. the types of L, I, Y and X. In this paper, $T_{m,\alpha}$ represents a m-type template under a certain rotating angle α, where $m \in \{L, I, Y, X\}$, $\alpha \in [0, 2\pi)$. We follow the scheme reported in [13] to define the matching function $\rho\,(\theta_{i,j}, T_{m,\alpha})$ between the local surrounding $\theta_{i,j}$ and the harmonic scheme $T_{m,\alpha}$ as follows:

$$\rho(\cdot) = \frac{\left(\sum_t H^H_{\theta_{i,j}}(t) \cdot T_{m,\alpha}(t)\right)^2}{\max(H^H_{\theta_{i,j}}) \cdot \sum_t T_{m,\alpha}(t)},\; 0 \le t \le BIN \tag{6}$$

Figure 3: Different positions with respect to user specified colors. Right column shows the hue wheel of local surroudings.

where $H^H_{\theta_{i,j}}$ is the histogram of the H channel of $\theta_{i,j}$. BIN and $\max(H^H_{\theta_{i,j}})$ are the number of bins and maximum value of the histogram, respectively. $T_{m,\alpha}(t) = \mathbf{1}(t \in \mathbb{Q})$ is the t_{th} bin value of the harmonic scheme, $\mathbb{Q}$ is the gray sector. $\theta_{i,j}$ is the local surrounding as shown in Figure 3, i.e. the region that contain the subject, which is defined as follow:

$$\theta_{i,j} = \left\{ \hat{I}_{i,j}(x,y) \,|\, |x - x_j| = \mu h_i,\ |y - y_j| = \nu w_i \right\} \quad (7)$$

where μ and ν are parameters that control the size of $\theta_{i,j}$. $\hat{I}_{i,j}$ is the synthesized image using I with p_i into the j_{th} enclosure.

Hue Count. It has been shown that the number of unique hues in most professional photos is actually less than the snapshots [14]. Therefore we calculate the hue count $q^h_{\theta_{i,j}}$ of $\theta_{i,j}$ defined by [14] to measure its simplicity.

Considering the fusion of the three factors we discussed earlier, i.e. the initial enclosure score η_j, which is illustrated in section 2, measurement of the color harmony $\rho(\theta_{i,j}, T_{m,\alpha})$ and the hue count $q^h_{\theta_{i,j}}$. A function measuring the fitness of subject placement $F(\cdot)$ can be defined as follows:

$$F(\cdot) = \eta_j + (1 - \exp\{-(\omega_\rho \rho(\theta_{i,j},\ T_{m^*,\alpha^*}) + \omega_q(-q^h_{\theta_{i,j}}))\}) \quad (8)$$

Therefore, the initial position $(x_o,\ y_o)$ can be achieved by:

$$(x_o, y_o) = \arg\max_{i \in \vec{\mathbb{R}}',\ j \in \vec{\Phi}} F(\eta_j, \rho(\theta_{i,j},\ T_{m^*,\alpha^*}), q^h_{\theta_{i,j}}) \quad (9)$$

$$(m^*,\ \alpha^*) = \underset{\substack{m \in \{L,I,Y,X\} \\ \alpha \in [0,2\pi) \\ i \in \vec{\mathbb{R}}',\ j \in \vec{\Phi}}}{\operatorname{argmax}} \rho(\theta_{i,j},\ T_{m,\alpha}) \quad (10)$$

4.2 Position and Size Update

It is well known that, a human's body is 8 heads high [15], which means $h_o = 8heads$. As indicated in [16], people's attention focuses on the head area of the subject. Inspired by this study, we shall use the point located at $\frac{3}{16}h_o$ from top to down, as the center of the pose synthesis as shown in Figure 2. Therefore, the composition type σ_N can be decided based on the initial position $(x_o,\ y_o)$ and the initial size $\vec{z}_o\,(h_o, w_o)$:

$$\begin{cases} N = 1 & (whole\ body) & D \geq 0.81h_o \\ N = 2 & (upper\ knees) & 0.56h_o \leq D < 0.81h_o \\ N = 3 & (upper\ body) & 0.35h_o \leq D < 0.56h_o \\ N = 4 & (upper\ breast) & 0.13h_o \leq D < 0.35h_o \end{cases} \quad (11)$$

where $D = I_H - x_o$, I_H is the height of I_o. As to the left-right bounds of D in (11), e.g. If $D \geq (h_o - \frac{3}{16}h_o)$, $N = 1$. The other bounds can be obtained via similar procedure. According to the Canon's study [17], we can further obtain the capturing distance u based on type σ_N and the focal length f of I_o. Then, an approximate height $\hat{h}$, which can be displayed on I_o according to the certain f, u and the subject's actual height H, can be computed:

Figure 4: Size varies from different positions. The dashed rectangles represent the energy minimization procedure.

$$\hat{h} = Hf/(u - f) \quad (12)$$

We decide H according to the gender information g, i.e. female is 1650mm and male is 1850mm. Then, the pose height zoom parameter τ can be computed. Next, we can update the size to $\vec{z}\,(h_i, w_i)$, where $h_i = \tau h_o$, and $w_i = \tau w_o$. The position will also be updated to $\vec{e}_{opt}\,(x_{opt}, y_{opt})$, where $x_{opt} = H_I\,(1 - \tau) + \tau x_o$. Finally, the synthesis term E_s can be obtained by:

$$E_s(S) = -\sum_{i=1}^{N_{pro}} a_i \cdot F\left(\eta_{opt}, \rho(\theta_{i,o},\ T_{m^*,\alpha^*}), q^h_{\theta_{i,j}}\right) \quad (13)$$

where η_{opt} is the score computed by enclosure $\vec{e}_{opt}(x_{opt}, y_{opt})$, $\theta_{i,o}$ is the local region computed by center (x_{opt}, y_{opt}) and size $\vec{z}(h_i, w_i)$. Hence, E_s is a function of all variables of S with $S(i) = (a_i,\ (x_i,\ y_i),\ \vec{z}_i,\ \vec{c},\ g), \forall i \in [1, N_{pro}]$.

4.3 Energy Minimization

To obtain optimal position and size, we carry out an iterative process. The initial point is set as: $\vec{e}_{opt}(x_{opt}, y_{opt})$. We update the position as: $\vec{e}_t(x,y) \leftarrow \vec{e}_{t-1} + \vec{\mu}$, where $\vec{\mu}$ is obtained by:

$$\vec{\mu}^* = \underset{\vec{\mu}' \in \{\vec{\mu}^{(n)}\} \cup \{0\}}{\operatorname{argmin}} E_s(a_t, (\tilde{e}_{t-1} + \vec{\mu}'), \vec{z}_t, \vec{c}, g) \quad (14)$$

$\{\vec{\mu}^{(n)}\}^N_{n=1}$ is N $(N = 10)$ randomly generated vectors from a two-dimensional Gaussian distribution.

5. EXPERIMENTS

To show the effectiveness of finding position by considering color, we set a pair of complementary color as input, the results are shown in Figure 3. The images from left to right in each row are visual effect picture, local surrounding and the hue wheel corresponding to it. We can see that, the suggested position varied with different input color. The hue wheels are subjected to L type of the color harmony scheme, which can highlight the subject. In addition, we show that different position will consequently lead to different size as shown in Figure 4. We can see that, the position varies when color changes. Then, the size also changes for different position of placement. Top 3 visual effect images for one query photo as well as their reference photos (on the left of each visual effect images) are shown in the first row of Figure 5, which proves that we not only can suggest one optimal pose for users, but also can offer them multiple suggestions to choose from. The second row of Figure 5 lists 3 instances for female and male respectively. We can see that, the proposed *Pose Maker* can provide suggestions corresponding to different genders, even for the same scene. Some top final results and their reference photos are shown in Figure 6.

To validate the proposed *Pose Maker* system, we also conducted subjective evaluations. 15 females and 12 males with age ranging from 20 to over 30 are invited to rate the recommendation results and the corresponding query photos for comparison. Among them, 2 subjects are experts, 10 subjects have more than five years

Figure 5: Top 3 fianl visual effect images for a query photo (first row) and 3 results instances for female and male (second row).

Figure 6: Some final visual effect images with their reference photos. Bottom right is the result of subjecs evaluation.

of photography experiences with single lens reflex cameras. The subjects are asked to rate each photo according to position, pose and overall respects. As shown in Figure 6, the satisfaction rate from overall respect for both female and male reaches over 85%, while the unsatisfactory rate is only under 5%. In summary, the proposed *Pose Maker* provides a visually appealing recommendation system for mobile users, which shall lead to an enhanced user experiences. This system is indeed able to find satisfactory poses for most scenery pictures to synthesize the pose with scene, which is particularly useful for novice photographers.

6. CONCLUSION

In this paper, we have presented a *Pose Maker* system for interactive pose recommendation and synthesis. To the best of our knowledge, this is the first attempt to investigate into a fully practical and visually pleasant system that simultaneously deals with pose and photo composition recommendation and synthesis. Based on the proposed scene specific professional learning model, the proposed system can select several suitable poses. Based on these reference poses, a synthesis model can generate the final visual effect images incorporating aesthetic photography principles with natural and appealing results. Extensive experiments and user studies have been carried out to show that the proposed *Pose Maker* system is indeed appropriate and appealing for novice mobile users.

7. REFERENCES

[1] W. Y. Yin, T. Mei, C. W. Chen, and S. Li. Socialized mobile photography: learning to photograph with social context via mobile devices. *IEEE Trans. Multimedia*, 16(1):184-200, 2014.

[2] W. Y. Yin, T. Mei, and C. W. Chen. Crowdsourced learning to photograph via mobile devices. In *Proc.* of *ICME*, pages 812-817, 2012.

[3] B. Cheng, B. Ni, S. Yan, and Q. Tian. Learning to photograph. In *Proc.* of *ACM MM*, pages 291-300, 2010.

[4] W. Y. Yin, T. Mei, C. W. Chen. Assessing photo quality with geo-context and crowdsourced photos. In *Proc.* of *VCIP*, pages 27-30, 2012.

[5] S. Dhar, V. Ordonez, and T. L. Berg. High level describable attributes for predicting aesthetics and interestingness. in *Proc.* of *CVPR*, pages 1657-1664, 2011.

[6] L. K. Wong and K. L. Wong. Enhancing visual dominance by semantics-preserving image recomposition. In *Proc.* of *ACM MM*, pages 845-848, 2012.

[7] Y. H. Zhang, X. S. Sun, H. X. Yao, L. Qin and Q. M. Huang. Aesthetic composition represetation for portrait photographing recommendation. In *Proc.* of *ICIP*, pages 2753-2756, 2012.

[8] S. Ma, Y. Y. Fan and C. W. Chen. Finding your spot: a photography suggestion system for placing human in the scene. In *Proc.* of *ICIP*, 2014.

[9] P. Felzenszwalb and D. Huttenlocher. Efficient graph-based image segmentation. *Int. J. Computer Vision*, 59(2): 167-181, 2004.

[10] N. Dalal, B. Triggs. Histograms of oriented gradients for human detection. In *Proc.* of *CVPR*, pages 886-893, 2005.

[11] C. Yang; L. H. Zhang; H. C. Lu, X. Ruan and M. H. Yang. Saliency detection via graph-based manifold ranking. In *Proc.* of *CVPR*, pages 3166-3173, 2013.

[12] D. Cohen-Or, O. Sorkine, R. Gal, T. Leyvand and Y. Q. Xu. Color harmonization. *ACM Trans. Graph.*, 25(3):624-630, 2006.

[13] Z. Tang, Z. J. Miao, Y. L. Wan. Image composition with color harmonization. In *Proc.* of *Int. Conf. IVCNZ*, pages 1-8, 2010.

[14] Y. Ke, X. Tang, and F. Jing. The design of high-level features for photo quality assessment. In *Proc.* of *CVPR*, pages 419-426, 2006.

[15] http: //en.wikipedia.org/wiki/Body_ proportions

[16] K. W. Yun; Y. F. Peng; D. Samaras, G. J. Zelinsky, T. L. Berg. Studying relationships between human gaze, description and computer vision. In *Proc.* of *CVPR*, pages 739-746, 2013.

[17] http: //www.canon.com.cn/specialsite/canon_ portrait

Representing Musical Patterns via the Rhythmic Style Histogram Feature

Matthew Prockup
MET-Lab
Drexel University, ECE Dept
3141 Chestnut St.
Philadelphia, PA 19104
mprockup@drexel.edu

Jeffrey Scott
MET-Lab
Drexel University, ECE Dept
3141 Chestnut St.
Philadelphia, PA 19104
jjscott@drexel.edu

Youngmoo E. Kim
MET-Lab
Drexel University, ECE Dept
3141 Chestnut St.
Philadelphia, PA 19104
ykim@drexel.edu

ABSTRACT

When listening to music, humans often focus on melodic and rhythmic elements to identify specific songs or genres. While these representations may be quite simple, they still capture and differentiate higher level aspects of music such as expressive intent and musical style. In this work we seek to extract and represent rhythmic patterns from a polyphonic corpus of audio encompassing a number of styles. A compact feature is designed that probabilistically models rhythmic activations within musical beat divisions through histograms of Inter-Onset-Intervals (IOI). Onset detection functions are calculated from multiple frequency bands of a perceptually motivated filter bank. This allows for patterns of lower pitched and higher pitched onsets to be described separately. Through a set of supervised and unsupervised experiments, we show that this feature is well suited for a variety of tasks in which quantifying rhythmic style is necessary.

Categories and Subject Descriptors

H.5.5 [**Information Interfaces and Presentation**]: Sound and Music Computing; I.5 [**Computing Methodologies**]: Pattern Recognition

General Terms

Design; Experimentation; Evaluation

Keywords

Music Information Retrieval; Rhythmic Style; Expression

1. INTRODUCTION

Humans identify with the two basic components of melody and rhythm in order to describe and differentiate songs. With these simple components, one can usually recognize higher level concepts such as the style and other expressive components of a piece of music. Previous work has studied both style and expression of a song as a whole, but few efforts focus on deconstructing and quantifying these individual components to discover the specific roles that each of them play. In the context of this paper, we explore methods to represent rhythmic elements and provide analyses for their ability to distinguish rhythmic style.

There is a large body of previous work on beat-tracking [3, 11], but in extracting only beats, much of the rhythmic subtlety is discarded. There are, however, several systems that use rhythmic information in order to better inform beat tracking algorithms. One such system in [1] uses domain knowledge to improve onset detection, one of the key components in a beat tracking system. The system then trims spurious onsets by finding only those that make sense rhythmically based on a set of synthesized templates.

In [6] the authors introduce the beat spectrum. This is a compact feature that represents periodicities in the self-alignment of an audio signal. Capturing a similar, yet more compact feature, is a primary motivation of this work.

Recent efforts have expanded beyond beat tracking to capture elements of rhythm, style and expression [4, 10, 13]. In [13], source separation of harmonic and percussive components is applied then used to derive multiple sets of rhythmic pattern templates and bassline templates. A compact set of rhythm and bass line features are calculated based on a song's alignment to the learned templates.

We propose a representation that probabilistically models Inter-Onset-Intervals (IOI) at the tatum positions between beat locations. The Rhythmic Style Histogram Feature (RSHF) is designed to be tempo invariant and capture rhythmic subtleties across different frequency ranges. The following section describes the feature computation in detail.

2. RHYTHMIC FEATURE DESIGN

In order to represent rhythmic style, the RSHF is designed to probabilistically model inter-onset-intervals across multiple frequency bands. The signal flow of the RSHF calculation is shown in Figure 1.

2.1 Deriving the RSHF

The percussive component of Harmonic Percussive Source Separation (Figure 1a) is computed [5] and fed into a beat tracker to extract beat locations. The beat tracker employed is based on dynamic programming. This algorithm is further explained in [3] and publicly available via LibROSA[1]. The

[1]https://github.com/bmcfee/librosa

MM'14, November 3–7, 2014, Orlando, Florida, USA.
Copyright 2014 ACM 978-1-4503-3063-3/14/11 ...$15.00.
http://dx.doi.org/10.1145/2647868.2655058.

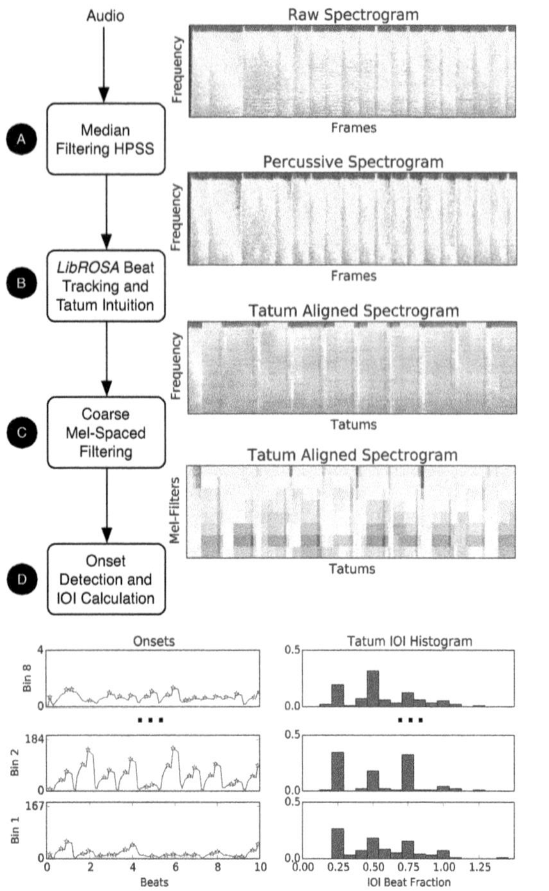

Figure 1: RSHF design and calculation.

percussive power spectrum is quantized into twelve equally spaced bins between successive beat locations (Figure 1b). Twelve frames per beat is chosen to allow for rhythms with both duple and triple feels to accurately quantize to a tatum position.

The tatum aligned spectrum is processed using a coarse Mel-spaced filter bank. The output of each Mel-filter becomes an independent onset signal $X_f[t]$, where f is the filter channel and t is the tatum position (Figure 1c). The onset detection signals are then modified by subtracting the output of a moving average filter with a window length w and a tail multiplier m, yielding

$$Y_f[t] = X_f[t] - \frac{\sum_{k=t-mw}^{t+w} X_f[k]}{mw + w}. \quad (1)$$

This process emphasizes large changes in the signal and the asymmetric window prevents false detection of offsets as onsets. Onsets are defined as the local maxima of the filtered signals $Y_f[t]$ within a window of length w. The calculation of the onset positions is similar to the method described in [1].

Using the tatum-aligned onset positions, the IOIs for each Mel-frequency band are calculated (Figure 1d). The raw RSHF feature becomes a stacked set of histograms denoting the empirical probability of the IOI values for each Mel-Frequency band. An example of this feature is shown in Figure 2. In the lower frequency range, there is more probability mass in tatums that are at 1/4 and 3/4 of the beat. This shows that both 16th note and dotted 8th notes are common. In this example, it is representative of repetitive swing-like pattern in the bass drum composed of a dotted 8th note followed by a 16th note. In the higher frequency components there is high probability for IOI equal to 1/2 of a beat. This means that there is likely a steady 8th note pattern, played possibly by a hi-hat or ride cymbal.

It is important to note that the RSHF is sensitive to the quality of the onset detection function and the beat tracker employed as part of the front-end system. Errors in the beat tracking may lead to improper binning in the metrical divisions defining the tatum-aligned spectrogram in Figure 1C.

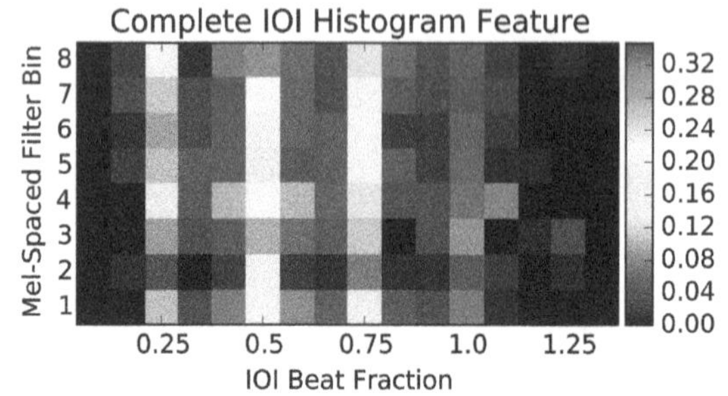

Figure 2: Rhythmic Style Histogram Feature.

2.2 Meaningful Dimensionality Reduction

While RSHF is an intuitive representation of repetitive rhythmic style, its dimensionality can become quite large depending on the number of tatum divisions and Mel-filters desired. This can become prohibitive when applying certain machine learning techniques.

In order to accommodate these more complex methods, a reduced dimensionality is required. However, in reducing the RSHF, we seek to still maintain its intuitive meaning. This is done through Non-Negative Matrix Factorization (NMF). The basic goal of NMF is to factorize a matrix V into two matrices ($V = W \times H$). The rows of H are a set of learned basis components over all examples and the columns of W are the activations of those components [9]. Performing NMF on the RSHF yields a rhythmic tatum basis across all examples. This effectively reduces the dimensionality in a manner that is still representative of the original rhythmic structure.

3. FEATURE SALIENCE EXPERIMENTS

In order to test the salience of the RSHF, a set of both supervised and unsupervised machine learning experiments are performed. These experiments show that the feature has the potential to predict previously known intuitions about rhythm and style as well as reveal meaningful correlations learned directly from data that are sometimes difficult to quantify. It is important to note that while the following results are not state of the art in this stand-alone context, the RSHF is definitely salient, and has the potential to improve and inform other systems and tasks [13].

A set of classification tasks using the popular Ballroom Dataset [7] are performed. The dataset's audio examples are 30 seconds in length, and are labeled with a specific ballroom dance style. This dataset is chosen because its labels apply directly to terms that reference quantifiable attributes of the music, and not to cultural popularity (e.g. genre).

3.1 Supervised Experiments

The goal of the first supervised experiment is to classify the Ballroom Dataset with respect to the given ballroom style label. This is performed using an SVM classifier with a Radial Basis Function (RBF) kernel. The dataset is split into 30% test and 70% train and the parameters of the model are fit using 10-fold cross validation. The experiment is repeated with the raw RSHF, NMF and PCA features. Results for style classification are presented in Table 1. This task has been performed by many others previously in [2, 12, 8] with classification results surpassing 90%. The goal of this work is not to solve this task specifically, but to show its salience in this domain. It was also shown that tempo alone is a good descriptor of styles on the Ballroom Dataset [12]. The beat-tracking algorithm inherently includes an estimate of tempo. By including that estimate along with the RSHF, classification is improved.

Feature	Dim.	RSHF Alone	Dim.	RSHF & Tempo
RAW	96	0.562 ± 0.035	96	0.755 ± 0.017
PCA	10	0.574 ± 0.044	26	0.777 ± 0.018
NMF	10	0.568 ± 0.019	17	0.761 ± 0.017

Table 1: Accuracies in the style task for the raw RSHF and the best performing reductions.

In the second experiment we classify whether a given piece has duple or triple feel using the same experimental setup. In the case of NMF and PCA, the result for the number of components with the highest classification accuracy is shown. In both cases the raw style feature performs well. By adding tempo, classification accuracy is improved once again. These results are shown in Table 2. Additionally, both classification experiments show that by reducing the dimensionality in a meaningful way, such as using activations of learned NMF bases, classification performance is maintained.

Feature	Dim.	RSHF Alone	Dim.	RSHF & Tempo
RAW	96	0.831 ± 0.017	96	0.937 ± 0.033
PCA	2	0.854 ± 0.023	3	0.954 ± 0.018
NMF	13	0.851 ± 0.044	3	0.937 ± 0.014

Table 2: Accuracies in the duple vs. triple task for the raw RSHF and the best performing reductions.

3.2 Unsupervised Experiments

In certain analysis tasks of expression and style, hard labels are not sufficient to describe a certain musical phenomena. It may be necessary for expression and style components to sit in a continuous space and employ unsupervised methods to find meaningful correlations and relationships in the data. In order to test the RSHF's effectiveness in this unsupervised domain, we performed a set of simple k-means clustering experiments ($k = 2$ and $k = 4$).

In order to explore the cluster space, the RSHF feature is shown along with the annotated ground truth labels for style and feel in Figure 3. The 96 dimensional feature is shown using t-distributed Stochastic Neighbor Embedding. t-SNE is a tool for visualizing high dimensional data by preserving the distance between points in a lower dimensional space. More on t-SNE can be found in [14]. Notice that while the different classes of style-labeled and feel-labeled data overlap, each occupies a unique area throughout the space.

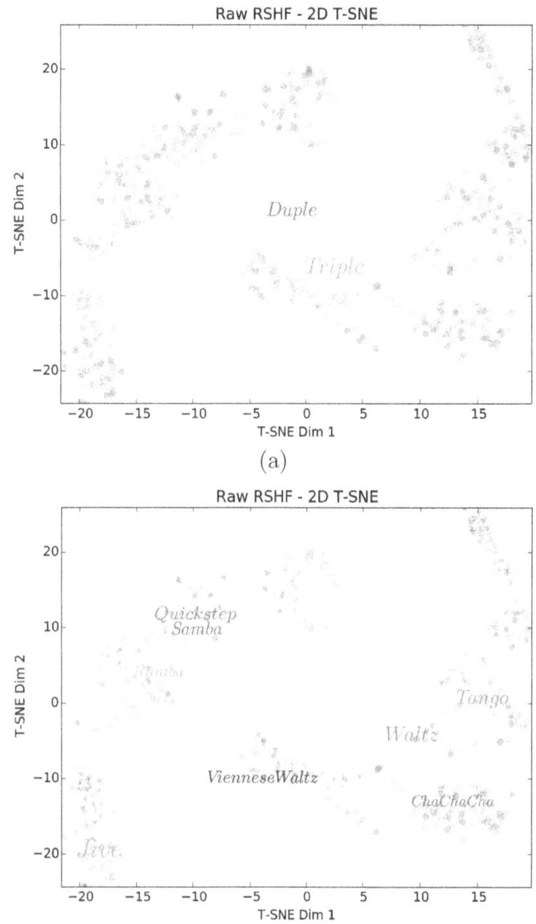

(a) (b)

Figure 3: The projections of the raw RSHF feature into 2 dimensions for (a) duple/triple designation and (b) individual style classifications.

In Figure 3, Quickstep, Samba, and Rumba group together. All of these styles are syncopated in nature, meaning the rhythmic emphasis does not always lie on the down beat. Additionally, these styles tend to be rhythmically dense, which is another reason for their similarity in the RSHF space. In contrast, Waltz, Viennese Waltz, and ChaChaCha are very straight-forward styles with a heavy downbeat emphasis. Waltz rhythms are also composed with 3 beats per measure, unlike the rest of the styles which have 4. In their grouping together, this notion of triple feel is captured as well. The Viennese Waltz is quicker and more rhythmically dense the the traditional Waltz. Jive employs a compound duple meter, in that there are four beats per measure, but the eighth notes are usually swung, giving it a fast triple feel as well. Because of this, Jive and Viennese Waltz form their own grouping. Within this groping, it is also shown that the duple and triple meter are still somewhat separated.

In order to capture these empirical observations organically, k-means clustering is performed on the RSHF. The results of the unsupervised clustering is shown in Figure 4. The percentages of the original style labels contained within a specific cluster are shown for all clusters. In the $k = 2$ clustering, the somewhat obvious separation of the convex and concave arc structures in the data occurs. The complex and more dense styles cluster apart from the simpler straight-forward styles. As the number of clusters increases to $k = 4$, each of the styles start to separate. Jive and Viennese Waltz separate from the other dense rhythms, which can be attributed to the triple and compound meters of Waltz and Jive versus the simple meters of Quickstep, Rumba, and Samba. The more straight-forward rhythmic styles also start to split. Tango and ChaChaCha still group tightly due to the fact that their rhythms are composed of very similar structures with a heavy emphasis on the beat. Both Waltz styles also start to separate into multiple groups. Some of the Viennese Waltz and Waltz rhythms group together in their own cluster, while others tend to group with other more similarly dense and less dense styles.

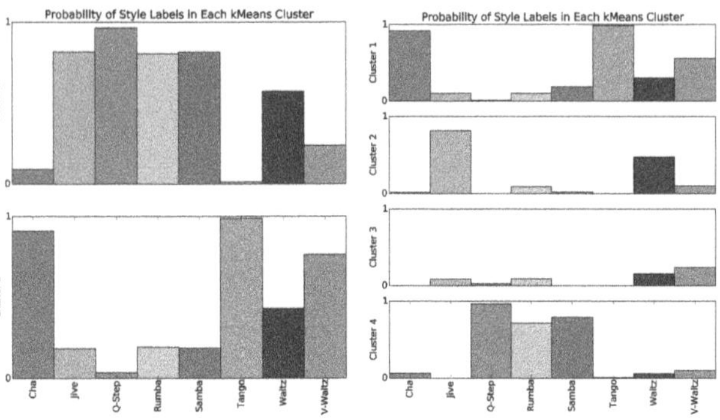

(a) (b)

Figure 4: The percentage of each style label in each k-means cluster for (a) $k = 2$ and (b) $k = 4$.

4. CONCLUSIONS AND FUTURE WORK

The Rhythmic Style Histogram Feature captures musically informative patterns in a compact form, leveraging tatum-aligned IOI interval histograms over multiple Mel-spaced frequency bands. Through a set of supervised and unsupervised machine learning experiments, we showed that the RSHF is informative for the task of rhythmic style classification and analysis. Additionally, forms of dimensionality reduction such as NMF further reduce the representation of the RSHF and maintain the underlying musical meaning.

In future work, the RSHF can be improved by adding additional components that relate to rhythmic style. In its current state, the feature's IOI histograms are based solely on raw counts. It could be more informative to scale the IOIs summed in the histogram by the magnitude of the respective peaks in the onset detection function. This would make higher onset peaks more meaningful. Additionally we can incorporate some notion of phase. In the current representation, tatums on the downbeat and tatums on the upbeat are treated the same if their IOI's are the same. The incorporation would allow for systems to distinguish this phenomenon.

The RSHF has many future implications in the domain of rhythmic style analysis as a whole as well. One possible use is the learning of musically informed transition probabilities for an HMM to detect onsets (similar to [1]). Because the RSHF feature is a probabilistic model, and intuitively maintains rhythmic components, it can be informative in the generation of rhythmic styles as well. This generation is also tunable among different frequency bands, allowing it to capture and synthesize rhythms that have contrasting low pitched and high pitched components, such as a kick drum vs a snare drum.

All in all, one of the best attributes of the RSHF is its ability to adapt to many different applications. It through this adaptability that the RSHF can aid in a wide variety of tasks within domains that require an analysis of rhythmic style.

5. REFERENCES

[1] N. Degara, M. E. P. Davies, A. Pena, and M. D. Plumbley. Onset event decoding exploiting the rhythmic structure of polyphonic music. *J. Sel. Topics Signal Processing*, 5(6):1228–1239, 2011.

[2] S. Dixon, F. Gouyon, and G. Widmer. Towards characterisation of music via rhythmic patterns. *ISMIR*, 2004.

[3] D. Ellis. Beat tracking by dynamic programming. *Journal of New Music Research*, 36(1):51–60, 2007.

[4] T. V. et al. Automatic genre classification of latin american music using characteristic rhythmic patterns. In *Audio Mostly Conference*, page 16, 2010.

[5] D. FitzGerald. Harmonic/percussive separation using median filtering. *DAFx*, 2010.

[6] J. Foote and S. Uchihashi. The beat spectrum: a new approach to rhythm analysis. *ICME*, 2001.

[7] F. Gouyon, A. Klapuri, S. Dixon, M. Alonso, G. Tzanetakis, C. Uhle, and P. Cano. An experimental comparison of audio tempo induction algorithms. *IEEE Tran. Audio, Speech, and Language Processing*, 14(5):1832–1844, Sept 2006.

[8] A. Holzapfel and Y. Stylianou. Scale transform in rhythmic similarity of music. *IEEE Tran. Audio, Speech, and Language Processing*, 19(1):176–185, January 2011.

[9] D. D. Lee and H. S. Seung. Learning the parts of objects by non-negative matrix factorization. *Nature*, 401(6755):788–791, 1999.

[10] M. Leimeister, D. Gaertner, and C. Dittmar. Rhythmic classification of electronic dance music. *AES Semantic Audio*, Jan 2014.

[11] J. L. Oliveira et al. IBT: A real-time tempo and beat tracking system. *ISMIR*, 2010.

[12] B. Schuller, F. Eyben, and G. Rigoll. Fast and robust meter and tempo recognition for the automatic discrimination of ballroom dance styles. *ICASSP*, April 2007.

[13] E. Tsunoo, G. Tzanetakis, N. Ono, and S. Sagayama. Beyond timbral statistics: Improving music classification using percussive patterns and bass lines. *IEEE Tran. Audio, Speech, and Language Processing*, 19(4):1003–1014, May 2011.

[14] L. Van der Maaten and G. Hinton. Visualizing data using t-sne. *Journal of Machine Learning Research*, 9(11), 2008.

Mobile Photo Album Management with Multiscale Timeline*

Kolbeinn Karlsson†
Huawei Media Lab
Bridgewater, New Jersey
kk752@cornell.edu

Wei Jiang
Huawei Media Lab
Bridgewater, New Jersey
wei.jiang@huawei.com

Dong-Qing Zhang
Huawei Media Lab
Bridgewater, New Jersey
dongqing.zhang@huawei.com

ABSTRACT

Traditional photo browsing systems developed for PCs are inefficient for browsing and searching of large photo albums on mobile devices due to the small screen size and limited mobile processing power. We propose a new concept in this paper, the multiscale timeline, where photos are grouped into clusters and displayed sequentially on a scaled timeline with user controllable time scales, enabling multiscale overview of the photo album for efficient browsing and searching. To address the slow speed of re-clustering when new photos are added, a new incremental spectral clustering algorithm is further developed, which is an order of magnitude faster than the traditional spectral clustering algorithm and its conventional incremental version. Our implementation of the system on mobile devices shows a better user experience and browsing efficiency based on the experiments over large real-world photo collections.

Categories and Subject Descriptors

H3.3 [**Information Storage and Retrieval**]: Information Search and Retrieval; H.5.1 [**Information Interfaces and Presentation**]: Multimedia Information Systems

General Terms

Algorithms, Experimentation

Keywords

Multiscale timeline; mobile album; incremental clustering

1. INTRODUCTION

With the prevalence of high-quality mobile cameras with large storage, we have witnessed an explosive amount of mobile photos. It is more and more popular that a large number of such photos are stored on the mobile device, and effective on-device photo management has become increasingly important. Traditional mobile photo browsers, *e.g.*, on iOS and Android systems, follow the file browsers in PCs, where photos in a folder are presented in a flat grid-based view, as shown in Fig. 1 (a). Such browsers can be very inefficient in dealing with large-scale albums. First, mobile devices normally have small screens, and it can be very hard for users to browse through the album or to locate individual photos. Moreover, users often take multiple near-duplicate photos of the same scene, *e.g.*, in burst mode. A flat display of all these photos on the small screen further reduces the efficiency of on-device photo browsing. Second, it is important to convey the photos' time order in a browsing system, but simply laying out a large number of photos in a flat timeline (as shown in Fig. 1 (b)) may not be efficient. It is even harder than in the grid-based view to swipe through the large album to locate photos of interest. Finally, in addition to the capture time, the photos' visual content is also useful for effective browsing and search. For instance, in cases where a lot of photos are captured close in time but with highly different content, *e.g.*, during a vacation, the visual content can help organize such photos more efficiently.

Large-scale photo album management has been extensively studied on conventional PCs, where large screens and strong computational powers are available. For example, systems like Time Quilt [4] and Photoland [12] organize photos based on visual features and metadata, and systems like PhotoMesa [2] and PhotoFinder [5] focus on screen layout and/or user queries. Commercial solutions like Apple's *iPhoto* and Google's *Picasa* rely heavily on user tags and manual sorting. None of these systems, however, can easily be used for on-device mobile photo management, due to the limited screen size and processing power on mobile systems.

To facilitate photo browsing on mobile devices, some on-device presentation systems have been developed to arrange photos on non-uniform grids [11] or on three-dimensional structures [1, 15]. However, the underlying photo organization remains unchanged. Some other work aims at both photo organization and presentation [6, 7, 8] by clustering photos based on time, faces, and background features. However, the clustering result is still presented in an inflexible grid-based view or a simple flat timeline.

Addressing the characteristics of on-device mobile photo browsing, we propose a ***multiscale timeline*** framework to effectively organize and browse photos based on both time and visual content. Fig. 1 (c) illustrates the concept of the multiscale timeline. Each time scale corresponds to a certain

*Figures 1 and 3 modified from original submission due to copyright restrictions.

†Currently with Cornell University.

MM'14, November 3–7, 2014, Orlando, Florida, USA.
Copyright 2014 ACM 978-1-4503-3063-3/14/11 ...$15.00.
http://dx.doi.org/10.1145/2647868.2655060.

(a) grid-based view

(b) single flat timeline

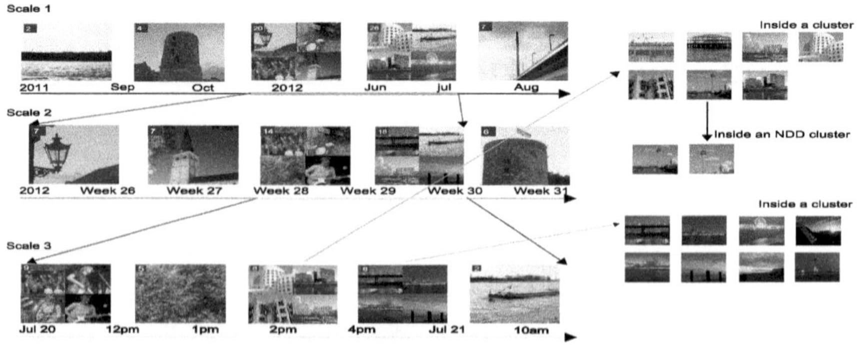

(c) multiscale timeline

Figure 1: Comparison of different browsing schemes.

level of granularity to partition the album, where photos are clustered at that level for users to browse. The multiscale timeline provides multiple granularities to organize photos, where users can quickly switch among different time scales to examine different levels of details of the album. For efficient browsing, each cluster is presented as a thumbnail consisting of a set of automatically selected representative images from the cluster. To accommodate the limited processing power in mobile devices, a multiscale one-step incremental spectral clustering algorithm is also proposed to quickly cluster photos at multiple time scales with a complexity approaching $O(n)$. To further improve browsing efficiency, near-duplicate photos are automatically detected based on both time and visual features, and are collapsed to a single representation to save space on small screens. We implement our system on an Android tablet. Evaluation over two large consumer albums from Flickr demonstrates the effectiveness of our multiscale timeline system.

2. MULTISCALE TIMELINE ALBUMING

Many previous photo clustering algorithms attempt to cluster photos by events in order to categorize the photos in a way that the user would do. A major problem, however, is that events are inherently multiscale. For instance, an event could be a group of people posing in front of a camera, a day spent at a theme park, or a week-long vacation. It is not only difficult to predict which scale the user would want to use to sort the album, but the scale might also change depending on what the user is looking for at the moment. Therefore we cluster the photo album on multiple scales and allow the user to browse all of them. To efficiently browse the clustering results we introduce the concept of multiscale timeline clusters, which is illustrated in Fig. 2. On each scale, the clusters (*i.e.* their representative thumbnails) are placed sequentially on a timeline that the user can browse using the pan and flick gestures. The user can also quickly change the time scale using the pinch gestures, as though to "zoom" between scales. The user can inspect the contents of a cluster by tapping its thumbnail. The contents of the inspected cluster is presented as either a traditional grid-based view or as another multiscale timeline depending on whether or not the photo number in the cluster exceeds a predetermined threshold. The multiscale time line clusters are created by extracting time and content-based features from the photos and performing an efficient one-step incremental clustering algorithm on the extracted feature sets.

Figure 2: Multiscale clustering of photos (scales S1-S4), which supports multiscale timeline browsing.

2.1 Features and Near-Duplicate Detection

Both time and visual features are used for clustering and browsing the photo album, which effectively complement each other to improve the system performance. The timestamp of each photo is extracted from the metadata, and three types of visual features are extracted from each image: A bag-of-words representation using SURF local descriptors (SURF BoW), a 64-bin uniform *Lab* color histogram, and the global grid-based color moment (GBCM) also in *Lab* color space. The SURF BoW uses a codebook of size 500, built by K-means clustering of randomly sampled SURF descriptors over the album. The 225-dimensional GBCM feature consists of the first three color moments computed over 5x5 image grids.

For fast near-duplicate detection, we use a cascade of binary classifiers similar to [13], based on both time and visual features. First, by comparing timestamps of image pairs, we quickly rule out most pairs that could not possibly be near-duplicates. Then a relatively fast binary classifier using GBCM is used to further rule out non-near-duplicates. The remaining pairs are finally classified by a binary classifier using the SURF BoW features. All these classifiers are trained offline using a set of ground-truth near-duplicate images and are tuned towards a low rate of false positives, so that the chance of collapsing non-near-duplicate images is kept very low. Each group of near-duplicate images is treated as one image for clustering and browsing, whose features are the average timestamp and visual features of the entire group.

2.2 Incremental Multiscale Clustering

Assuming that we have N different scales, the initial multiscale clustering is conducted over each scale individually based on the spectral clustering algorithm [9]. After that, when a new image is added, a fast one-step incremental spectral clustering algorithm is performed.

2.2.1 Overall spectral clustering

On each scale, a sparse similarity matrix $\mathbf{S}$ of the entire photo album is constructed based on an aggregated similarity measure that is the convex combination of the K similarity functions defined on time and visual features:

$$S(y_i, y_j) = \sum_{k=1}^{K} \alpha_k S_k(y_i, y_j) \quad (1)$$

where $\alpha_k \geq 0$ for $k = 1, \ldots, K$ and $\sum_{k=1}^{K} \alpha_k = 1$. Each entry $S_k(y_i, y_j)$ in $\mathbf{S}$ is the similarity between point y_i and point y_j for each feature, based on the Gaussian kernel:

$$S_k(y_i, y_j) = \exp\left(-a_k d_k(y_i, y_j)^2 / \sigma_k^2\right) \quad (2)$$

where $d_k(\cdot,\cdot)$ is the appropriate distance metric of feature k. Both the constants a_k and the scaling factors α_k are varied across different scales in such a way that, for larger scales, the time difference dominates, since photos taken far away from each other normally do not share similar contents and should not be clustered together. As the scale becomes smaller, the weights of the content features increase. All similarity values below a sparsity threshold are set to zero.

Following the recipe of [9], the initial spectral clustering is performed by solving the generalized eigenvalue system:

$$Lx = \lambda Dx \quad (3)$$

where L is the graph Laplacian computed as $L = D - A$; A is a similarity matrix whose entries are $A_{ij} = S(y_i, y_j)$ if $i \neq j$ and $A_{ii} = 0$; and the degree matrix D is diagonal with $D_{ii} = \sum_j A_{ij}$. L and D are both symmetric. The number of clusters is automatically determined from the eigengap [14].

2.2.2 *One-step incremental clustering*

Even for a sparse L, efficient algorithms such as the Lanczos method can still require $O(n^{1.5})$ complexity to solve Equation (3). For mobile users, reclustering the entire album everytime a new image is added can be unbearable, especially for large n. To avoid frequent reclustering, we propose an incremental spectral clustering algorithm based on a well-known result from perturbation theory [10]. Let ΔL and ΔD denote the perturbations (change) to L and D, respectively. Then the first-order perturbation of the eigenvalue, $\Delta\lambda$, is given by:

$$\Delta\lambda = \frac{x^T(\Delta L - \lambda \Delta D)x}{x^T D x} \quad (4)$$

It is shown in [10] that the perturbation of the eigenvector, Δx, can be obtained by solving the following linear system:

$$\phi \Delta x = h \quad (5)$$

where $\phi = L - \lambda D$ and $h = (\Delta\lambda D + \lambda \Delta D - \Delta L)x$. Let's assume that at a certain stage, n points have been clustered already. When a new data point y_{n+1} is added, the perturbation ΔL is the difference between the new Laplacian, L_{n+1}, and a zero-padded L_n:

$$\Delta L = L_{n+1} - \begin{bmatrix} L_n & 0 \\ 0 & 0 \end{bmatrix} = \begin{bmatrix} B & -b \\ -b^T & b^T \mathbf{1} \end{bmatrix} \quad (6)$$

where $B = \text{diag}(b)$, $\mathbf{1}$ is a vector of all ones, and b is the n-dimensional vector whose i-th entry is the similarity between point y_{n+1} and y_i. Likewise, the perturbation of the degree matrix can be decomposed the same way:

$$\Delta D = D_{n+1} - \begin{bmatrix} D_n & 0 \\ 0 & 0 \end{bmatrix} = \begin{bmatrix} B & 0 \\ 0 & b^T \mathbf{1} \end{bmatrix} \quad (7)$$

By putting Equations (6) and (7) into Equation (4), we get:

$$\Delta\lambda = (1 - \lambda)\frac{x^T B x}{x^T D x} \quad (8)$$

As both B and D are diagonal, Equation (8) can be efficiently computed in $O(n)$. The perturbation method is only a first-order approximation, so error will build up over time. Therefore, the full clustering algorithm will be performed again after M updates, where M is determined empirically.

We name the above proposed method the one-step incremental clustering algorithm since only one step is required to update each eigenvector. This is in comparison with the original incremental spectral clustering method in [10], where the effect of adding each image is decomposed into a series of similarity changes in $\mathbf{S}$, each change corresponding to solving a sparse linear system for each eigenvector. As a result, our one-step incremental clustering is dozens of times faster than the method of [10] on average, based on our implementation.

2.3 Selecting Representative Images

When the user browses the photo album, each cluster will be presented by a thumbnail consisting of one or more automatically selected representative images. The thumbnail is constructed differently depending on the size of the cluster. For cluster sizes below a predetermined threshold T, the image with the highest degree centrality is selected as the representative image as suggested in [3]. If the clusters are larger than T, four images are selected to create a collage thumbnail by first dividing the cluster into four subclusters using spectral clustering, then finding the image with the highest degree centrality in each of the subclusters.

3. EXPERIMENTS

The proposed multiscale timeline albuming system is implemented in a Samsung Galaxy Tablet, a screen capture shown in Fig. 3. Users can use the pinch gesture or buttons on the screen to zoom in/out the time scales, and tap the cluster thumbnails to inspect images in a particular cluster. In our implementation, we cluster the data on four different scales (*i.e.* $N = 4$). The top scale is over the whole collection. For smaller scales, the image collection is divided up into chunks spanning a single month, week, or day, and each chunk is then clustered separately. An added benefit of such division is the further computation speedup, since spectral clustering has superlinear complexity.

Due to the privacy concern of using private mobile photos, we decided to create the test data sets using the images under Creative Commons License from Flickr, where the characteristics of many albums are very similar to those of personal albums on mobile devices. The selection criteria included time span, which should be several years and evenly distributed; and content, which should not include a lot of post-processed images. At last, two Flickr users satisfying the above requirements were selected among 25 candidates. Dataset 1 has 2092 photos taken over a period of 40 months, and dataset 2 has 3442 photos taken over a period of 13 months.

The performance of the incremental clustering algorithm is evaluated by comparing the clustering quality and speed with the regular spectral clustering algorithm when a new image is added. The quality is evaluated using normalized mutual information (NMI) compared with batch spectral clustering. That is, we use batch spectral clustering of the entire dataset as the ground truth and compare the incrementally clustered dataset at different stages to the ground truth using NMI. Fig. 4 (a) shows the comparison results. The NMI measures how similar the incremental result is to the batch result of the entire dataset. As we see in the figure, the incremental clustering becomes more unlike the ground

Figure 3: The screenshot of the implemented system

truth after each step due to the approximation of first order perturbation. This is remedied by rerunning batch clustering periodically to limit the error accumulation. The number of updates to run before rerunning the batch version is chosen to balance the trade-off between performance and speed. We see that the algorithm performs considerably better on dataset 2 than 1. The difference reflects the higher sparsity of dataset 1, since the system in eqn. 5 becomes more ill-conditioned as the Laplacian becomes sparser. Fig. 4 (b) shows the speed comparison of incremental clustering and batch clustering when one photo is added. The figure shows that while the time lapse per increment clearly increases with every increment for the batch version, the incremental version stays nearly constant.

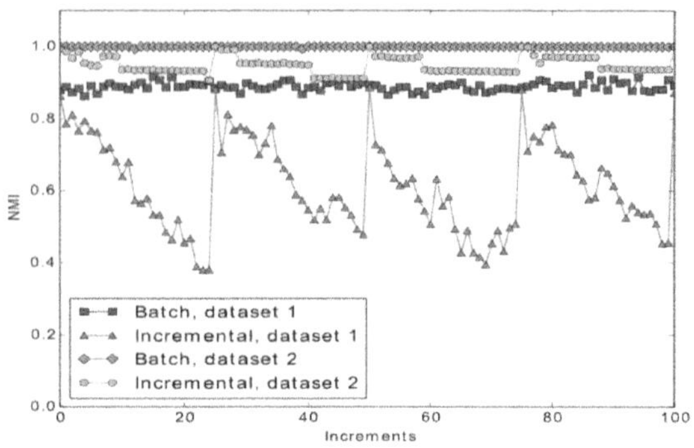

(a) quality of clustering

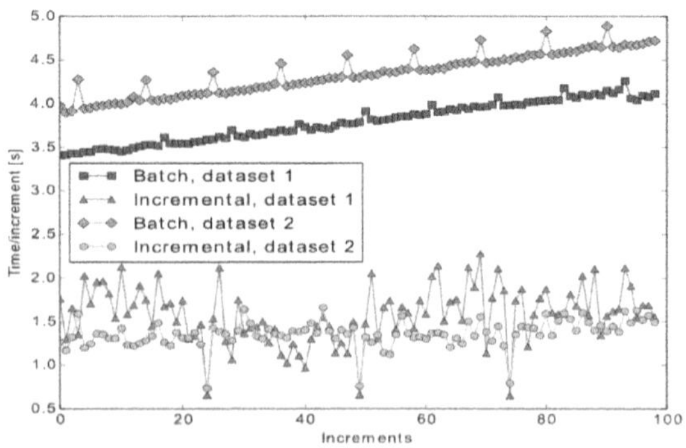

(b) time per increment

Figure 4: Incremental spectral clustering versus batch clustering

4. CONCLUSION

A new album system is proposed for photo browsing on mobile devices, which typically have limited screen size and processing power. The multiscale timeline design is introduced to address the problem of limited screen size and for more efficient photo browsing. And a new incremental spectral clustering algorithm is developed to speed up the spectral clustering algorithm when new photos are added to the album. The implemented mobile application using the multiscale timeline concept results in a more efficient browsing experience, and the new incremental clustering algorithm significantly accelerates the speed of album reorganization when new photos are added on large photo albums. Future work may include refining the system for continuous time scale change, and further improving clustering accuracy.

5. REFERENCES

[1] D. Ahlström, and et al. A user study on image browsing on touchscreens. In *ACM Multimedia*, pages 925–928, 2012.

[2] B.B. Bederson. Photomesa: a zoomable image browser using quantum treemaps and bubblemaps. In *ACM UIST*, pages 71–80, 2001.

[3] W.T. Chu and C.H. Lin. Automatic summarization of travel photos using near-duplication detection and feature filtering. In *ACM Multimedia*, pages 1129–1130, 2009.

[4] D.F. Huynh, and et al. Time quilt: scaling up zoomable photo browsers for large, unstructured photo collections. In *ACM CHI EA*, pages 1937–1940, 2005.

[5] H. Kang and B. Shneiderman. Visualization methods for personal photo collections: Browsing and searching in the photofinder. In *IEEE ICME*, 2000.

[6] J. Kim, and et al. Photo cube: An automatic management and search for photos using mobile smartphones. In *IEEE DASC*, pages 1228–1234, 2011.

[7] K. Kim, S. Kim, and H.-G. Cho. A compact photo browser for smartphone imaging system with content-sensitive overlapping layout. In *ACM ICUIMC*, 2012.

[8] M. La Cascia, M. Morana, and S. Sorce. Mobile interface for content-based image management. In *IEEE CISIS*, pages 718–723, 2010.

[9] A. Y. Ng, M. I. Jordan, and Y. Weiss. On spectral clustering1 analysis and an algorithm. *NIPS*, 14:849–856, 2001.

[10] H. Ning, and et al. Incremental spectral clustering by efficiently updating the eigen-system. *Pattern Recognition*, 43(1):113–127, 2010.

[11] K. Ren and J. Calic. Freeeye: interactive intuitive interface for large-scale image browsing. In *ACM Multimedia*, pages 757–760, 2009.

[12] D. Ryu, and et al., Photoland: a new image layout system using spatio-temporal information in digital photos. In *ACM SAC*, pages 1884–1891, 2010.

[13] F. Tang and Y. Gao. Fast near duplicate detection for personal image collections. In *ACM Multimedia*, pages 701–704, 2009.

[14] U. Von Luxburg. A tutorial on spectral clustering. *Statistics and computing*, 17(4):395–416, 2007.

[15] S. Yousefi. 3d photo browsing for future mobile devices. In *ACM Multimedia*, pages 1401–1404, 2012.

Interactive Audio Web Development Workflow

Lonce Wyse
Communications and New Media
National University of Singapore
lonce.wyse@nus.edu.sg

ABSTRACT
New low-level sound synthesis capabilities have recently become available in Web browsers. However, there is a considerable gap between the enabling technology for interactive audio and its wide-spread adoption in Web media content. We identify several areas where technologies are necessary to support the various stages of development and deployment, describe systems we have developed to address those needs, and show how they work together within a specific Web content development scenario.

Categories and Subject Descriptors
H.5.5 [**Information Systems**]: Information Interfaces and Presentation (HCI) – *sound and music computing.*

General Terms
Design; Human Factors

Keywords
Interactive Audio; W3C Web Audio API; Development tools; Web development workflow.

1. INTRODUCTION
Interactive sound has recently been gaining attention in large part due to new standards established by the World Wide Web Consortium (W3C) and implemented on most major browsers running on personal computers and mobile devices. The Web Audio API is comprised of a set of low-level audio "nodes" that can be connected to form signal flow audio graphs for real-time synthesis and processing. The API also defines parameters for influencing the behavior of the algorithms as they are executing so that synthesis can be responsive in real-time to data generated from sources such as graphical or user behavior.

In this paper, we describe three key components of a software ecosystem that we view as critical to the workflow of developers in order for the new interactive audio capabilities to work their way in to the everyday experience of Web media for the masses. The first is a library that supports the construction of audio graphs with rich and complex sonic behaviors which is designed for a specialist developer community that have a professional level of both audio and programming skills. The second is a standard API for interactive sound "models" that provides a simple and powerful means for controlling sounds from applications designed to be used by Web developers who are not audio specialists. The third is a way of organizing and accessing sound models in a database served from "the cloud" which minimizes complexity for Web developers and provides broad and efficient distribution for sound model developers. We describe strategies and implementations for each of these three components, and then demonstrate their utility in the context of a typical Web development workflow.

MM'14, November 3–7, 2014, Orlando, Florida, USA.

ACM 978-1-4503-3063-3/14/11…$15.00.
http://dx.doi.org/10.1145/2647868.2655064

2. SOUND MODELS
We use the term "sound model" (or simply "model") to refer to parameterized algorithms for generating a class of sounds that run in real time. They can be as trivial as a single oscillator or as rich as an algorithmic piece of music, but typically they represent objects (doors, car engines, bells, birds, musical instruments), events (rolling, scraping, bouncing), musical processes (beat patterns, melody generators), or abstract sound-generating algorithms and equations (chaotic dynamical systems)[13]. In popular graphical programming languages for interactive sound such as Max/MSP [14] or PD[9], sound models are known as "patches" in reference to the pre-digital technique of constructing sounds by patching analogue sound generating and processing modules together with cables. We use the term "sound" to refer to a specific instance of an acoustic wave generated naturally or synthetically that might be recorded and stored as a digital audio signal file. Thus a sound model generates a class of sounds that change depending on the parameter values that influence the synthesis algorithm.

The recent Web Audio API[1] breaks new ground for sound synthesis in W3C standards-compliant browsers. Previous to the implementation of the new standard, audio elements (e.g. recorded samples stored in files) could only be triggered, or else could be synthesized in real-time only with browser plug-ins presenting installation obstacles to users, security risks, and non-native performance.

With the Web Audio API, developers use JavaScript to connect audioNodes together into signal flow graphs that are managed by an audioContext to generate sound in real time. There are very few audioNodes available compared to the number of objects in Max/MSP [14] which has in the neighborhood of one thousand objects without counting those available from the community of users. Nonetheless, some rich synthesis models can be constructed, controlled with sample accuracy, and manipulated in real time with the limited set of audioNodes already supported in the Web Audio API. There are also audioNodes that perform convolution and compute power spectra. Since all of the audioNodes are built in to the browser, they are precompiled and run at native speeds. They are also given their own thread, separate from the browser UI thread, so that audio can reliably deliver its stream of audio samples without glitches due to blocking from user and graphical activity in the browser (See [11] for more details about the capabilities and limitations of the current Web Audio API).

The developers who will be able to make use of the full potential of the Web Audio API are skilled programmers with audio knowledge, not typical Web developers. Even for audio specialists, the Web Audio API is fairly "low level." For this reason, we have developed the jsaSound library. jsaSound is a JavaScript library designed to support common sound model-building operations such as generating rhythmic patterns and event loops, encapsulating models so that they behave like audioNodes to be combined in more complex graphs[10], and for hiding complexity when managing resources such as microphone input or audio files. WAAX[4] is another example of a library designed for simplifying sound model development with the Web Audio API.

A key feature of the jsaSound library is support for creating and exposing a consistent interface for users of sound models.

3. A SOUND MODEL API

Sound model parameters can vary greatly in terms of how they affect a model, their natural units, and their names which ideally reflect their function. For example, a "car engine" might expose parameters for RPM, torque, and horsepower, while a "footsteps" model might expose parameters for kilometers per hour, and gait (running or walking)[5]. Similar to the Java plug-in synthesis system ASound[12], jsaSound standardizes the parameter interface by using the parameter name or index as an argument and providing just two "setters", setParam(id, value) and setParamNorm(id, value). The former uses the natural units of the parameter, and the latter takes values in [0,1] and maps them to range defined for the natural units.. setParam (id, value) is also used for string parameters such as file names. Thus the interface for controlling interactive sounds is simply comprised of:

- play()
- release()
- setParam()
- setParamNorm()

Three additional methods are available for getting information about the sound model:

- getParam(id, ["name", "type", "val", "normval", "min", "max"])
- getNumParams() – the number of parameters a sound exposes,
- getAboutText() –developer-supplied text descriptions

The simplicity of the scheme makes real-time interactive control of sounds only incrementally more involved than playing static sound files. The interface allows a Web developer to control sounds "generically" (without needing specific knowledge about individual sound models). It also enables for example, the automatically-generated slider-box graphical interface "player" provided with jsaSound (Figure 1). It facilitates sound model reuse and sharing otherwise impractical with raw heterogeneous Web-Audio API audio graphs stored as JavaScript objects or files.

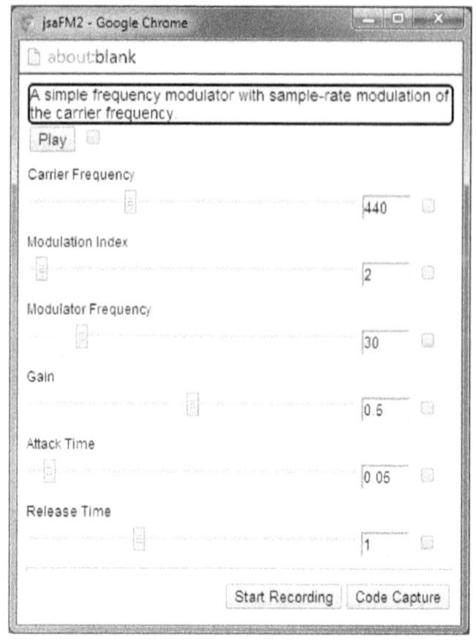

Figure 1. Automatically-generated user interface using the jsaSound model API. The Recording button is used to save user-generated sounds; the Code Capture button generates the JavaScript code for using the model interactively within Web applications (see section 4. A Workflow Example)

4. ORGANIZING MODELS FOR ACCESS

Collections of sounds and music are typically licensed and accessed from databases using textual descriptions for indexing. Sometimes they are distributed as specialized collections, but more often they are searched and "auditioned" on-line and then downloaded individually. There is no such standard way of distributing algorithmic sound models, because there has been no standard system for creating and incorporating them in media content. MIDI-controlled soundbanks and their variants are file systems for instruments and sounds, but the sound sets all use a single "general purpose" synthesizer. There are also several aggregate collections of Max/MSP objects on the Web[1], but most of the sharing of algorithmic audio objects is done in an ad hoc way directly between designers and users of common systems. The standardization of the Web Audio API is likely to generate a demand for a process of distribution for interactive sound models analogous to those currently in place for static sound files.

To understand how sound models might usefully be organized, accessed, and used in media production, it is interesting to consider how large a useful collection of sound models might be. For example, the Freesound collection[6] contains over 160,000 user-contributed sounds, and the Web-based commercial SoundDogs collection numbers over 650,000. A sound model can generate an uncountable number of sounds because it is parameterized and furthermore, parameters can change over time. This might suggest that a database of sound models would be smaller than a corresponding sound file database of similar breadth. However, there are many different ways to synthesize a given sound, and the range of sounds that different models can make may intersect even as each model provides quite distinct behaviors under parametric variation. It is thus reasonable to think of the size of a collection of models as being on the same

[1] See for example, http://cnmat.berkeley.edu/downloads or maxobjects.com.

order as that of an analogous collection of sounds, and therefor that some kind of database scheme would be necessary for management.

There are some interesting opportunities and challenges that arise with databases of sound models due to the characteristics that differentiate them from fixed media elements such as sounds. One opportunity that distinguishes sound model databases arises because they are structured code rather than a "flat" string of data. Model structure can be an important aspect of what a database user is looking for, especially when designing a new model – it is much easier to find useful chunks of code than to write them from scratch. This has been explored extensively by Funkhauser and colleagues in the domain of 3D models. For example, associating high-level semantic feature descriptions with model structure facilitates novice model design creation[3]. Similarity metrics based on model structure can assist database navigation[8], and model building can be accomplished in part by example[7]. A second opportunity for model databases comes from the semantic "meta data" that comes with the names of the parameters that a sound model exposes. Possibilities include musical "pitch" for a bell, "rate" (for footsteps), or "roughness" for s scraping action. All could be usefully exploited for finding and associating sound models. The challenge in constructing and indexing databases of sound models is also in part due to the abstract nature of code. How does one index a model that represents many sounds which might be entirely unrelated perceptually, or that generates many of its useful sounds only under real-time manipulation of its parameters?

Indexing static sound files is more straightforward. The Freesound database of sounds uses two different methods of providing metadata for indexing. One is the sound name and additional descriptive text provided by the sound file contributor. The other is generated automatically by extracting audio features based on a suite of signal processing routines[2] designed for this purpose. Features such as spectral centroid, pitch, and roughness are saved with the sounds and can be used to discover relationships between sounds in the database that can be exploited in, for example, "sounds like" searches.

Our first-pass approach to organizing and searching collections of sound models is to do so indirectly through the sounds that they generate. Model developers use the GUI player (Figure 1) to generate as many different sounds as they feel is necessary to represent the range of possibilities for the model, and then upload the sound(s) to the Freesound database along with a text description used for searches. Each sound in the Freesound database has its own Web page with facilities for visualizing and playing the sound, and for examining the textual data provided by the contributor. Freesound supports HTML descriptions so that the sound model developer can create a graphical button that directly opens the player for the sound model responsible for generating the sound the user found in the database. With the sound model open in the player, users now have access not only to the specific sound they found in the database, but the entire class of sounds and behaviors that the model is capable of generating through interaction.

4.1 Serving from the Cloud

"Serving sound models from the cloud" means having them available on an Internet-connected server which can be accessed as an extension to a file system. For the developer, having code components stored at a location accessed the same way from wherever software is being developed or deployed is convenient and storage-efficient. Also, like other libraries that are often served this way (e.g. Google code libraries[2]), the developer is relieved of the responsibility for updates and bug fixes. One drawback is that Internet access is always necessary, though for Web applications this is generally assumed anyway. Another drawback is a dependency on others for keeping the servers available, as well as a loss of control over access (e.g. a malicious provider could unilaterally change their access policy).

For the sound model supplier, cloud serving supports a variety of licensing and distribution models, as well as the ability to understand how and when sound models are being used by both developers and by end users. This usage data can be valuable in the same way it is for any other cloud-based service provider that monitors and takes advantage of knowledge gleaned from usage patterns to improve services. An overview of how the various components work together can be seen in Figure 2.

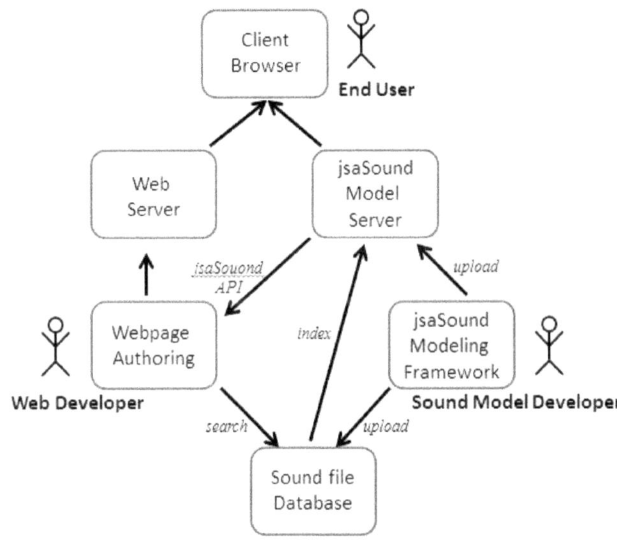

Figure 2. System Overview

jsaSounds are served this way using the light-weight JavaScript server stack based on node.js, express, and socket.io technologies. The require.js library provides functionality that C-programmers are familiar with as "#include." The Web developer-oriented simplicity of interactive sound API can be seen in Figure 3.

5. A WORKFLOW EXAMPLE

The value of the complete ecosystem described above can be appreciated by considering a workflow example.

A Web developer wants to animate an arrow shooting across the screen with a speed dependent on where a user clicks. She decides that the arrow needs a "swish" sound to accompany its flight that must change according to how fast the arrow moves. That is, the sound needs to be interactive with behavior tied to the motion of the graphics.

She navigates her browser to the Freesound.org database, types "swish" as a search term and auditions several of the 248 swish sounds her search returned and chooses the one that has the sonic

[2] https://developers.google.com/speed/libraries/

characteristics she was looking for. Of course, the recorded sound is not flexible in duration nor in the way it changes over time. However, she notices the presence of a button announcing the availability of the synthesis model that generated the swish, and clicks it to bring up the model in the slider-box user interface. She explores the model by moving the swish at various rates. She could record any one of her swish gestures if she needed a static sound different from the one the database search turned up, but for her arrow application, she needs to use the model "live" in her code to maintain its interactivity. She clicks the "generate code" button (Figure 1) which opens a window with the JavaScript text she needs to copy in to her program to load the sound from the server, and to set the default values to those she chose in the slider box. Her one remaining task is to start and stop the sound, and insert a setParameter call wherever she updates the moving arrow graphic, supplying that method with the arrow position. Now, for both her during development, and for the end users who visit her Web page, the sound will be retrieved from the server when the Web page is loaded, and the sonic evolution of the swish will be bound to the position and speed of the arrow.

```
require.config({
  paths: {"jsaSound": "http://animatedsoundworks.com"}
});
require(
  ["jsaSound/jsaModels/jsaFM"], // classic FM
  function (sndFactory) {

    var snd = sndFactory();

    window.onmousedown=function(e){
          snd.play();
    };

    window.onmouseup=function(e){
          snd.release();
    };

    window.onmousemove=function(e){
      //[0,1] normalized x/y mouse positions
          var normX = e.clientX/window.innerWidth;
          var normY = e.clientY/window.innerHeight;

      // setting "Modulation Index" by parameter name
          snd.setParamNorm("Modulation Index", normY);
      // setting "Carrier Frequency" by parameter index
          snd.setParamNorm(1, normX );
    };
  });
```

Figure 3. A complete JavaScript browser application that obtains a sound model from a server and provides real-time user-interaction. Two different forms of the jsaSound parameter setting API are also shown.

6. CONCLUSION

The new Web Audio API enables interactive sound synthesis with native performance on any device with a browser. However, there are different developer communities with different needs that must still be addressed before the technology can be adopted on a massive scale. The jsaSound library provides tools supporting audio specialists in the development of sound models, as well as a standard API for all models that make them reusable, sharable, and straightforward to use for Web developers. Cloud service makes them easy to integrate with the community-supported Freesound.org database indexed by the sounds they are capable of generating, as well as convenient to deploy in Web applications. Remaining future work is just the development of hundreds of thousands of sound models.

7. ACKNOWLEDGMENTS

Thanks to the Freesound.org team at the Universitat Pompeu Fabra Music Technology Group, particularly Frederic Font and Dmitry Bogdanov, for their insights on the inner workings of Freesound. Thanks to Kumar Subramanian for his contributions to jsaSound and to the many other contributors to open source Web audio projects. Thanks to the Sonoport team for seeing the potential of this work in the commercial world. Thank you to the anonymous reviewers for helping to strengthen this presentation.

All software presented in this paper is open source and available at animatedsoundworks.com:8001.

8. REFERENCES

1. Adenot, P., Wilson, C., and Rogers, C. Web Audio API. 2013. http://www.w3.org/TR/webaudio/.
2. Bogdanov, D., Wack, N., Gómez, E., et al. Essentia: An audio analysis library for music information retrieval. *Proceedings of ISMIR*, (2013).
3. Chaudhuri, S., Kalogerakis, E., Giguere, S., and Funkhouser, T. Attribit: content creation with semantic attributes. *Proceedings of the 26th annual ACM symposium on User interface software and technology*, ACM (2013), 193–202.
4. Choi, H. and Berger, J. WAAX: Web Audio API eXtension. *Proceedings of New Interfaces for Musical Expression*, (2013).
5. Cook, P. Modeling Bill's gait: Analysis and parametric synthesis of walking sounds. Audio Engineering Society (2002).
6. Font, F., Roma, G., and Serra, X. Freesound technical demo. ACM (2013).
7. Funkhouser, T. Modeling by example. *ACM Transactions on Graphics 23*, 3 (2004).
8. Kim, V.G., Li, W., Mitra, N.J., Chaudhuri, S., DiVerdi, S., and Funkhouser, T. Learning part-based templates from large collections of 3D shapes. *ACM Transactions on Graphics 32*, 4 (2013), 70.
9. Puckette, M.S. Pure Data: another integrated computer music environment. *Proceedings of the International Computer Music Conference*, ICMA (1996).
10. Subramanian, S.K. Taming the ScriptProcessorNode - Codaholic. http://sriku.org/blog/2013/01/30/taming-the-scriptprocessornode/.
11. Wyse, L. and Subramanian, S.K. The Viability of the Web Browser as a Computer Music Platform. *Computer Music Journal 37*, 4 (2013), 10–23.
12. Wyse, L. A Sound Modeling and Synthesis System Designed for Maximum Usability. *Proceedings of the 2003 International Computer Music Conference: 29th September-4th October 2003, Singapore*, (2003), 447.
13. Wyse, L. Generative Sound Models. *Multimedia Modelling Conference, 2005. MMM 2005. Proceedings of the 11th International*, (2005), 370–377.
14. Zicarelli, D. Cycling '74. 2014. http://cycling74.com/.

What Strikes the Strings of Your Heart? - Multi-Label Dimensionality Reduction for Music Emotion Analysis

Yang Liu[1], Yan Liu[1], Yu Zhao[1], Kien A. Hua[2]
[1]Department of Computing, The Hong Kong Polytechnic University, Hong Kong, P. R. China
[2]Department of Electrical Engineering and Computer Science, University of Central Florida, Orlando, FL, USA
{csygliu, csyliu, csyuzhao}@comp.polyu.edu.hk, kienhua@cs.ucf.edu

ABSTRACT
Music can convey and evoke powerful emotions. This amazing ability has fascinated the general public and also attracted the researchers from different fields to discover the relationship between music and emotion. Psychologists have indicated that some specific characters of rhythm, harmony, melody, and also their combinations can evoke certain kinds of emotions. Their hypotheses are based on real life experience and proved by psychological paradigms on human beings. Aiming at the same target, this paper intends to design a systematic and quantitative framework, and answer three widely interested questions: 1) what are the intrinsic features embedded in music signal that essentially evoke human emotions; 2) to what extent these features influence human emotions; and 3) whether the findings from computational models are consistent with the existing research results from psychological experiments. We formulate the problem as a multi-label dimensionality reduction problem and provide the optimal solution. The proposed multi-emotion similarity preserving embedding technique not only shows better performance in two standard music emotion datasets but also demonstrates some interesting observations for further research in this interdisciplinary topic.

Categories and Subject Descriptors
H.5.5 [**Information Interfaces and Presentation**]: Sound and Music Computing – *modeling*; I.5.2 [**Pattern Recognition**]: Design Methodology – *pattern analysis.*

General Terms
Algorithms, Experimentation, Human Factors

Keywords
Music emotion analysis, multi-label dimensionality reduction, multi-emotion similarity preserving embedding

MM '14, November 3 - 7, 2014, Orlando, FL, USA

http://dx.doi.org/10.1145/2647868.2655068

Figure 1. Note, rhythm, harmony, and melody in music.

1. INTRODUCTION
Music exists in every culture and plays a prominent role in our everyday lives. Besides the purpose of entertainment, the ability to arouse powerful emotions might be a more important reason behind most people's engagement with music [1]. Passionate songs can heat up our hearts while the sad mood can be evoked when listening to sorrowful songs. As the Russian writer Leo Tolstoy said: "Music is the shorthand of emotion". Such an amazing ability of music has fascinated not only the general public but also researchers from different fields throughout the ages [2].

As defined in Drever's psychology dictionary [3], emotion is "a mental state of excitement or perturbation marked by a strong feeling, and usually an impulse towards a definite form of behavior". Ekman presented a classical model of emotions based on the human facial expressions, which divides emotion into six basic classes: anger, happiness, surprise, disgust, sadness, and fear [4]. Following this pioneering work, other emotion models have been proposed specifically for musical emotion representation [1][5][6].

Some psychologists indicated that various elements in music such as rhythm, harmony, and melody play an important role in evoking certain kinds of emotions [7]. Figure 1 illustrates the most basic musical event, note, as well as higher level music structures, rhythm, harmony, and melody. Note is the atom of music described by three main characteristics: duration, pitch and amplitude. Rhythm, one of the most important factors affecting emotional expression [8], generates a regular, repeated pattern of sounds or movements by combining notes of different durations and amplitudes. Harmony, another element related to emotion expression in music, involves the vertical aspect of pitch and how various sounds go together to create pleasing and interesting combinations [9]. Melody is the horizontal unfolding of pitch over time and creates shapes that we identify as songs [9]. Its ascent and descent may be associated with different emotions [7]. However, some researchers argued that even listening to the same melody, people with different cultural backgrounds might have different emotional responses [10]. Besides above components, other factors such as mode [11] and articulation [12] may also contribute to conveying emotions.

Although tremendous strides have already been made in analyzing the relationship between music and emotions, the intrinsic element of music which arouses a specific emotion response in the listener is still far from well-understood [13]. In this paper, we aim to address this issue by employing computational methodology. We formulate the problem as a multi-label dimensionality reduction (MLDR) problem according to following considerations. Dimensionality reduction (DR) aims to find the intrinsic structure embedded in the original space of the raw data for the given goal. To discover the relationship between music and emotion, the raw data are the music and the original feature space can be defined as the music signal representation, which often has thousands of dimensions. The given goal can be defined as linking the human emotion response to some music. Since a song may evoke more than one emotion, the natural way is to annotate an instance with multiple labels [5]. To find out the optimal mapping between the original feature space and the emotion space, a method called multi-emotion similarity preserving embedding (ME-SPE) is proposed in this paper.

2. RELATED WORK

With the rapid development of computer resources, computational modeling has assumed increasing importance in the field of music emotion analysis [13]. In order to uncover the relationship between the music feature space and the emotion space, some researchers formulated it as a machine learning problem [14]-[16]. In music emotion analysis, a song sometimes conveys or evokes more than one emotion [5][15]. So the multi-label learning methods, which allow each data point to be associated with multiple labels [17][18], becomes a suitable tool to analyze the music emotions. Furthermore, the music signals often have a huge number of features, which may contain a large amount of redundant information and thus cause the high computational cost and poor performance of the analysis task. Therefore, MLDR is our first choice for the task of music emotion analysis.

As an active research area in machine learning, MLDR has received much attention in recent years. Yu et al. proposed a method called multi-label informed latent semantic indexing to capture the correlations between multiple labels [19]. Zhang and Zhou introduced an MLDR algorithm by maximizing the dependence between data and corresponding labels [20]. Sun et al. proposed the hypergraph spectral learning [21], which generalize the graph Laplacian to the hypergraph Laplacian for multi-label applications. Other well-known linear DR algorithms such as linear discriminant analysis and canonical correlation analysis have also been extended for multi-label classification [22][23]. Because of its capacity for generating meaningful representations with a reduced dimensionality, MLDR has been widely utilized in many real-world applications such as image annotation [24] and music tagging [25], where the high-dimensional data are naturally associated with more than one label.

3. PROPOSED FRAMEWORK

In order to discover the intrinsic factors in music signals that convey or evoke emotions, in this section, we propose a novel MLDR algorithm dubbed multi-emotion similarity preserving embedding (ME-SPE) to map the original high-dimensional representations into a low-dimensional subspace, in which we hope that a clearer linkage between features and emotions could be discovered.

The idea behind the proposed method is simple: if two pieces of music convey similar emotions, they should possess some hidden features in common. The target of ME-SPE is to find such hidden features. Let $\mathcal{X} = \mathrm{R}^D$ be the high-dimensional feature space of music data, and there is an emotion set $\mathcal{E}$ including m emotion labels. The emotions associated with a piece of music $\mathbf{x}$ constitute a subset of $\mathcal{E}$, which can be represented as an m-dimensional binary vector $\mathbf{y}$, with 1 indicating that the music is able to convey the corresponding emotion and 0 otherwise. All possible outputs constitute the output space $\mathcal{Y} = \{0, 1\}^m$. Given the training set $\{(\mathbf{x}_1,\mathbf{y}_1), ..., (\mathbf{x}_n,\mathbf{y}_n)\}$, ME-SPE aims to learn a transformation matrix $\mathbf{U} = [\mathbf{u}_1, \mathbf{u}_2, ..., \mathbf{u}_d] \in \mathrm{R}^{D\times d}$ to project the original D-dimensional data to a low-dimensional subspace $\mathcal{Z} = \mathrm{R}^d$, with the following objective function:

$$\arg\min_{\mathbf{U}} \sum_{i=1}^{n}\sum_{j=1}^{n} \| \mathbf{U}^T\mathbf{x}_i - \mathbf{U}^T\mathbf{x}_j \|^2 \cdot S_{ij}, \tag{1}$$

where $\mathbf{U}^T\mathbf{x}_i = \mathbf{z}_i \in \mathcal{Z}$ denotes the low-dimensional representation of the i-th piece of music, and S_{ij} denotes the emotional similarity between $\mathbf{z}_i$ and $\mathbf{z}_j$. There are many different ways to define the similarity function S. In our formulation, we choose the form of inner product since it is able to capture the information of correlations between different emotions. Let $S_{ij}=\langle \mathbf{y}_i, \mathbf{y}_j \rangle$, where $\langle\cdot,\cdot\rangle$ denotes the inner product operation, then the similarity matrix $\mathbf{S} = [S_{ij}]_{n\times n} = \mathbf{Y}^T\mathbf{Y}$, where $\mathbf{Y} = [\mathbf{y}_1, \mathbf{y}_2, ..., \mathbf{y}_n] \in \mathrm{R}^{m\times n}$ is the label matrix. Let $\mathbf{y}_{(i)} \in \mathrm{R}^n$ $(i = 1, ..., m)$ be the label indication vector for the i-th emotion. In fact, the transpose of $\mathbf{y}_{(i)}$ is the i-th row of $\mathbf{Y}$. Obviously, the matrix $\mathbf{S}^E = \mathbf{Y}\mathbf{Y}^T$ is an $m\times m$ matrix in which the (i,j)-th component $S_{ij}^E=\langle \mathbf{y}_{(i)}, \mathbf{y}_{(j)} \rangle$ indicates the similarity between the i-th emotion and the j-th emotion. Actually, the matrix $\mathbf{S}$ and $\mathbf{S}^E$ are closely related since they have the same non-zero eigenvalues. Suppose λ is a non-zero eigenvalue of $\mathbf{S}^E$, then we have

$$\mathbf{S}^E\mathbf{a} = \mathbf{Y}\mathbf{Y}^T\mathbf{a} = \lambda\mathbf{a}, \tag{2}$$

where $\mathbf{a}$ is the eigenvector of $\mathbf{S}^E$ corresponding to λ. Left multiply above equation by $\mathbf{Y}^T$, we obtain

$$\mathbf{S}\mathbf{Y}^T\mathbf{a} = \mathbf{Y}^T\mathbf{Y}\mathbf{Y}^T\mathbf{a} = \lambda\mathbf{Y}^T\mathbf{a}, \tag{3}$$

which means that λ is also the eigenvalue of $\mathbf{S}$, with the corresponding eigenvector $\mathbf{Y}^T\mathbf{a}$. Therefore, by formulating the data similarity matrix $\mathbf{S}$, the correlation between different emotions characterized in $\mathbf{S}^E$ is well captured.

To normalize S_{ij}, we define the normalized similarity matrix $\hat{\mathbf{S}}$: $\hat{S}_{ij} = \langle \mathbf{y}_i / \| \mathbf{y}_i \|, \mathbf{y}_j / \| \mathbf{y}_j \| \rangle$, then Eq. (1) becomes

$$\arg\min_{\mathbf{U}} \sum_{i=1}^{n}\sum_{j=1}^{n} \| \mathbf{U}^T\mathbf{x}_i - \mathbf{U}^T\mathbf{x}_j \|^2 \cdot \hat{S}_{ij}. \tag{4}$$

Following some standard derivations in linear algebra, above problem could be reduced to a trace minimization problem:

$$\arg\min_{\mathbf{U}} tr(\mathbf{U}^T\mathbf{X}\mathbf{L}\mathbf{X}^T\mathbf{U}) \tag{5}$$

where $\mathbf{X} = [\mathbf{x}_1, \mathbf{x}_2, ..., \mathbf{x}_n] \in \mathrm{R}^{D\times n}$ is the data matrix, $\mathbf{L} = \mathbf{D} - \hat{\mathbf{S}}$ is the $n\times n$ Laplacian matrix [26], and $\mathbf{D}$ is a diagonal matrix defined as $D_{ii} = \sum_{j=1}^{n} \hat{S}_{ij}$ $(i = 1, ..., n)$. Obviously, $\mathbf{L}$ is positive semi-definite and $\mathbf{D}$ is positive definite. Additionally, we introduce the constraint $\mathbf{U}^T\mathbf{X}\mathbf{D}\mathbf{X}^T\mathbf{U} = \mathbf{I}_d$ to remove the scaling factor in the learning process, where $\mathbf{I}_d$ denotes the d-dimensional identity matrix. For the first projection vector $\mathbf{u}_1$, the problem becomes

Table 1. Performance evaluations of six compared methods by 10-fold cross validations on EMOTIONS dataset

			Original 72-D	PCA	LPP	HSL	ML-LDA	ML-OPLS	ME-SPE
k-NN	Macro average	Precision	0.515±0.027	0.555±0.047	0.574±0.057	0.655±0.038	0.671±0.098	0.665±0.046	**0.708±0.044**
		F1 Score	0.451±0.023	0.461±0.053	0.472±0.035	0.608±0.032	0.540±0.051	0.611±0.041	**0.650±0.047**
	Micro average	Precision	0.520±0.032	0.584±0.052	0.613±0.064	0.659±0.041	0.705±0.058	0.661±0.051	**0.724±0.047**
		F1 Score	0.487±0.029	0.501±0.049	0.523±0.048	0.625±0.034	0.604±0.041	0.622±0.046	**0.678±0.050**
Multi-label k-NN	Average precision		0.699±0.015	0.712±0.004	0.721±0.005	0.790±0.007	0.715±0.006	0.784±0.006	**0.814±0.003**
	One-error		0.401±0.023	0.385±0.009	0.373±0.009	0.296±0.015	0.384±0.014	0.301±0.013	**0.257±0.010**
	Coverage		2.352±0.163	2.270±0.023	2.212±0.029	1.826±0.025	2.250±0.028	1.861±0.004	**1.700±0.019**
	Ranking loss		0.275±0.024	0.260±0.003	0.248±0.005	0.174±0.005	0.256±0.005	0.180±0.007	**0.149±0.003**

$$\arg\min_{\mathbf{u}_1} \mathbf{u}_1^T\mathbf{XLX}^T\mathbf{u}_1 \quad s.t.\ \mathbf{u}_1^T\mathbf{XDX}^T\mathbf{u}_1 = 1 \tag{6}$$

Then we obtain the Lagrangian equation of Eq. (6)

$$L(\mathbf{u}_1,\lambda) = \mathbf{u}_1^T\mathbf{XLX}^T\mathbf{u}_1 - \lambda(\mathbf{u}_1^T\mathbf{XDX}^T\mathbf{u}_1 - 1). \tag{7}$$

Letting $\partial L(\mathbf{u}_1,\lambda)/\partial\mathbf{u}_1 = 0$, then the optimal $\mathbf{u}_1$ of Eq. (6) is the eigenvector corresponding to the smallest non-zero eigenvalues of the generalized eigen-decomposition problem

$$\mathbf{XLX}^T\mathbf{u} = \lambda\mathbf{XDX}^T\mathbf{u}. \tag{8}$$

Similarly, $\mathbf{u}_2$, ..., $\mathbf{u}_d$ are the eigenvectors corresponding to the 2nd, …, dth smallest non-zero eigenvalues of Eq. (8), respectively.

4. EXPERIMENTAL RESULTS

4.1 Experiments on EMOTIONS Dataset

The EMOTIONS dataset [5] includes 593 songs with 6 emotions, and each song is represented by a 72-dimensional vector, in which the first 64 dimensions are the spectral features while the last 8 dimensions are rhythm features.

We demonstrate the effectiveness of ME-SPE by comparing it with five representative DR and MLDR algorithms, including principal component analysis (PCA) [27], locality preserving projections (LPP) [26], hyper-graph spectral learning (HSL) [21], multi-label linear discriminant analysis (ML-LDA) [22], and multi-label orthonormalized partial least squares (ML-OPLS) [23]. We also include the performance on the original 72-dimensional feature space as the baseline.

Two groups of criteria are used to evaluate the performance. In the first group, we use the standard label-based metrics, i.e., the precision and F1 score, as the evaluation criteria [22]. Since precision and F1 score are originally designed for binary classification, we use macro average and micro average to evaluate the overall performance across multiple labels [18]. The k-nearest neighbor (k-NN) classifier is used for final classification after DR. For all these four criteria, the larger the metric value the better the performance. In the second group, we use four standard example-based metrics, i.e., average precision, one-error, coverage, and ranking loss, as the evaluation criteria [18]. The multi-label k-nearest neighbor (ML k-NN) classifier [28] is used for final classification after DR. For average precision, the larger the metric value the better the performance. For one-error, coverage, and ranking loss, the smaller the metric value the better the performance. Here we use k-NN and ML k-NN since they have demonstrated good performance in multi-class classification tasks. For both groups, we perform the 10-fold cross validation and set the number of nearest neighbor k = 10 and reduced dimension $d = m - 1 = 5$, where m is the number of emotion labels. Table 1 reports the average performance of all the algorithms with respect to different evaluation criteria. The results on the 5-dimensional reduced space are better than those on the original 72-dimensional space, which shows the necessity of DR. Moreover, the proposed ME-SPE outperforms other DR algorithms on all criteria.

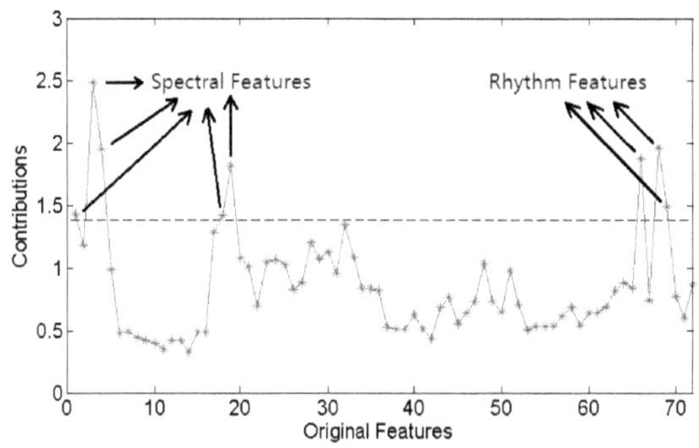

Figure 2. Contributions of all 72 dimensions.

After validated the effectiveness of ME-SPE, we aim to find the most contributing features. For the i-th dimension (i = 1, ..., 72) in the original feature space, we define its contribution as follows:

$$Contribution\_i = \sum_j (1-\lambda_j)|u_{ij}|, \tag{9}$$

where λ_j is the j-th smallest eigenvalue of the generalized eigen problem in Eq. (8), u_{ij} is the i-th element of the j-th eigenvector $\mathbf{u}_j$, and $|\cdot|$ denotes the absolute value operator. Figure 2 shows the contribution of all dimensions of the original feature space.

In order to evaluate the proposed scheme of contribution calculation, we select 8 most contributing features, i.e., the 1st, 3rd, 4th, 18th, 19th, 66th, 68th, and 69th dimensions (as shown in Figure 2), and compare it with the 8 rhythm features. In 8 most contributing features, the 1st, 3rd, 4th, 18th, and 19th dimensions are mean of spectral centroid, mean of spectral flux, mean of the first MFCC coefficient, standard deviation of spectral rolloff, and standard deviation of spectral flux, over all frames, respectively [5]. All these features are belonging to the spectral shape features [29]. The 66th, 68th, and 69th dimensions are rhythm features, which supports the claim in psychology that rhythm contributes to evoking emotions. Table 2 reports the performance (including average precision, one-error, coverage, and ranking loss using multi-label k-NN) of the selected 8 most contributing features as well as that of 8 rhythm features. Obviously, the selected features perform much better than rhythm features, which indicates that the spectral shape features play an irreplaceable role in emotion

Table 2. Performance evaluations of rhythm features and most contributing features by 10-fold cross validations on EMOTIONS dataset

	Rhythm (8-D)	Most contributing (8-D)
Average precision	0.640±0.043	**0.723±0.028**
One-error	0.494±0.074	**0.394±0.056**
Coverage	2.660±0.210	**2.143±0.176**
Ranking loss	0.341±0.050	**0.239±0.026**

Table 3. Performance evaluations of three compared features by 10-fold cross validations on CAL500 dataset

	Original (390,000-D)	Harmony (1594-D)	Ours (8-D)
Average precision	0.414±0.037	0.457±0.032	**0.488±0.010**
One-error	0.667±0.064	0.609±0.086	**0.493±0.041**
Coverage	11.056±0.568	10.117±0.642	**9.040±0.733**
Ranking loss	0.434±0.031	0.365±0.025	**0.307±0.016**

analysis. Furthermore, by comparing the last column of Table 2 with the first column of Table 1, we find that the performance on a small set of contributing features is better than that on the full feature set, which indicates that not all the features in the original space contribute to the emotion analysis task.

4.2 Experiments on CAL500 Dataset

To further demonstrate the effectiveness of features selected by the proposed ME-SPE, we use the CAL500 dataset [6], which is a very high-dimensional dataset, for evaluation. The CAL500 dataset includes 502 songs with 18 emotion labels, and each song is represented by a 390,000-dimensional vector.

We use the same 8 most contributing features selected in the previous experiment. For each of the 502 songs, we generate these 8 features using the original music signals. In order to show the effectiveness of the generated feature vector, we compare it with the original 390,000-D feature vector from the CAL500 dataset as well as the 1594-D harmony feature vector extracted using the MIRToolbox [30]. As shown in Table 3, the performance on harmony features is better than that on original features, which supports the claim in psychology that harmony plays an important role in evoking emotions. More importantly, the performance on our 8-D features is better than that on 1594-D harmony features as well as 390,000-D original features. The reason might be that the original feature space contains a lot of redundant even noisy information, which could affect the performance seriously. Our 8 features are selected according to the proposed objective function, which emphasizes the relationship between emotions and features, and thus outperform a large number of original features.

5. CONCLUSION AND FUTURE WORK

This paper demonstrates that some spectral shape features and rhythm features essentially influence human's emotion by a novel multi-label dimensionality reduction technology. We also provide the quantitative analysis of the contributions from these features to emotion responses.

Our future work will focus on melody, another element that has the influence to emotions. However, to the same melody, the feeling differences among people from different cultures make the mapping between melody and emotions more complex [10]. How to design computational models for melody is a challenging task that we are interested in. Moreover, how would genre of the music impact the selection of emotion features is another interesting direction that we are going to investigate in the future.

6. ACKNOWLEDGMENTS

The authors would like to thank all the anonymous reviewers, whose comments were of great value. This work was supported by 4.61.xx.681C Cognitive Computing Laboratory.

7. REFERENCES

[1] Zentner, M., Grandjean, D., and Scherer K. R. 2008. Emotions evoked by the sound of music: characterization, classification, and measurement. *Emotion*, 8(4), 494-521.

[2] Eerola, T., and Vuoskoski, J. K. 2011. A comparison of the discrete and dimensional models of emotion in music. *Psychol. Music*, 39(1), 18-49.

[3] Drever, J. 1952. *A Dictionary of Psychology*. Baltimore: Penguin Books Ltd.

[4] Ekman, P. 1984. Expression and the nature of emotion. In K. Scherer & P. Ekman (Eds.), *Approaches to emotion*, Hillsdale, NJ: Erlbaum, 319-343.

[5] Trohidis, K., Tsoumakas, G., Kalliris, G., and Vlahavas. I. 2008. Multilabel classification of music into emotions. In *ISMIR*, 325-330.

[6] Turnbull, D., Barrington, L., Torres, D., and Lanckriet, G. 2008. Semantic annotation and retrieval of music and sound effects. *IEEE TASLP*, 16(2), 467-476.

[7] Hevner, K. 1936. Experimental studies of the elements of expression in music. *Am. J. Psychol.*, 48(2), 246-268.

[8] Juslin, P. N. and Sloboda, J. A. 2001. *Music and Emotion: Theory and Research*. New York: Oxford University Press.

[9] Duckworth, W. 2009. *A Creative Approach to Music Fundamentals*. Boston: Schirmer Cengage Learning.

[10] Gregory, A. H., and Varney, N. 1996. Cross-cultural comparisons in the affective response to music. *Psychol. Music*, 24, 47-52.

[11] Laurier, C., Lartillot, O., Eerola, T., and Toiviainen P. 2009. Exploring relationships between audio features and emotion in music. In *Proc. 7th ESCOM*, 260-264.

[12] Eerola, T., Friberg, A., and Bresin, R. 2013. Emotional expression in music: contribution, linearity, and additivity of primary musical cues. *Frontiers in Psychology*, 4, 487:1-12.

[13] Yang, Y.-H, and Chen, H.-H. 2012. Machine recognition of music emotion: A review. *ACM TIST*, 3(3), 40: 1-30.

[14] Wang, J.-C., Yang, Y.-H., Wang, H.-M., and Jeng, S.-K. 2012. The acoustic emotion Gaussians model for emotion-based music annotation and retrieval. In *Proc. the 20th ACM Multimedia*, 89-98.

[15] Li, T. and Ogihara, M. 2003. Detecting emotion in music. In *ISMIR*, 239-240.

[16] Coutinho, E. and Cangelosi, A. 2009. The use of spatio-temporal connectionist models in psychological studies of musical emotions. *Music Perception*, 27(1), 1-15.

[17] Qi, G.-J., Hua, X.-S., Rui, Y., Tang, J., Mei, T., and Zhang, H.-J. 2007. Correlative multi-label video annotation. In *Proc. 15th ACM Multimedia*, 17-26.

[18] Zhang, M.-L., and Zhou, Z.-H. 2014. A review on multi-label learning algorithms. *IEEE TKDE*, 26(8), 1819-1837.

[19] Yu, K., Yu, S., and Tresp, V. 2005. Multi-label informed latent semantic indexing. In *Proc. 28th SIGIR*, 258-265.

[20] Zhang, Y., and Zhou, Z.-H. 2008. Multi-label dimensionality reduction via dependence maximization. In *Proc. 23rd AAAI*, 1503-1505.

[21] Sun, L., Ji, S., and Ye, J. 2008. Hypergraph spectral learning for multi-label classification. In *Proc. 14th ACM SIGKDD*, 668-676.

[22] Wang, H., Ding, C., and Huang, H. 2010. Multi-label linear discriminant analysis. In *Proc. 11th ECCV*, 126-139.

[23] Sun, L., Ji, S., and Ye, J. 2013. *Multi-Label Dimensionality Reduction*. Chapman & Hall/CRC.

[24] Wang, C., Yan, S., Zhang, L., and Zhang, H.-J. 2009. Multi-label sparse coding for automatic image annotation. In *CVPR*, 1643-1650.

[25] Panagakis, Y., Kotropoulos, C., and Arce, G. R. 2010. Sparse multi-label linear embedding nonnegative tensor factorization for automatic music tagging. In *Proc. EUSIPCO 2010*, 492-496.

[26] He, X., and Niyogi, P. 2004. Locality preserving projections. In *NIPS 16*.

[27] Hotelling, H. 1933. Analysis of a complex of statistical variables into principal components, *J. Edu. Psychol.*, 24, 417-441, 498-520.

[28] Zhang, M.-L., and Zhou, Z.-H. 2007. ML-kNN: A lazy learning approach to multi-label learning. *Pattern Recogn.*, 40(7), 2038-2048.

[29] Lerch, A. 2012. *An Introduction to Audio Content Analysis: Applications in Signal Processing and Music Informatics*. Wiley-IEEE.

[30] Lartillot, O., and Toiviainen, P. 2007. MIR in matlab (II): A toolbox for musical feature extraction from audio. In *ISMIR*, 127-130.

Fusing Music and Video Modalities Using Multi-timescale Shared Representations

Bing Xu
Department of Information Engineering
The Chinese University of Hong Kong
xb012@ie.cuhk.edu.hk

Xiaogang Wang
Department of Electronic Engineering
The Chinese University of Hong Kong
xgwang@ee.cuhk.edu.hk

Xiaoou Tang
Department of Information Engineering
The Chinese University of Hong Kong
xtang@ie.cuhk.edu.hk

ABSTRACT

We propose a deep learning architecture to solve the problem of multimodal fusion of multi-timescale temporal data, using music and video parts extracted from Music Videos (MVs) in particular. We capture the correlations between music and video at multiple levels by learning shared feature representations with Deep Belief Networks (DBN). The shared representations combine information from multiple modalities for decision making tasks, and are used to evaluate matching degrees between modalities and to retrieve matched modalities using single or multiple modalities as input. Moreover, we propose a novel deep architecture to handle temporal data at multiple timescales. When processing long sequences with varying length, we propose to extract hierarchical shared representations by concatenating deep representations at different levels, and to perform decision fusion with a feed forward neural network, which takes input from predictions of local and global classifiers trained with shared representations at each level. The effectiveness of our method is demonstrated through MV classification and retrieval.

Categories and Subject Descriptors

H.3.3 [**Information Storage and Retrieval**]: Information Search and Retrieval—*Retrieval models*

Keywords

deep learning; multimodal fusion; music video matching

1. INTRODUCTION

Music and videos, as two popular types of media, cause different human perceptions with music in auditory and video in vision. However, psychology and cognition studies have shown that the information processing procedures of audio and visual signals by human brains are closely related and integrated [2]. In music videos (MVs), music and videos appear in parallel and complement each other. MV expresses the song by using stories and rhythmic dances to complement music. In this work, we try to explore the correlations between musical and visual parts of MVs, and use deep learning to capture such correlations with extracted shared representation across two modalities.

One of the commonly recognized matches in MV is music semantics with video content. For example, sad music is paired with sad faces or girls weeping in videos, and exciting party music is paired with dancing scenes and flashing lights. There is existing work on semantically matching music and images with content [10]. The authors built a database with a large number of music-image pairs extracted from MVs, and used Canonical Correlation Analysis (CCA) to capture the relationship between music and image features. However they did not consider any temporal information of music or videos. Since music and images have complex and

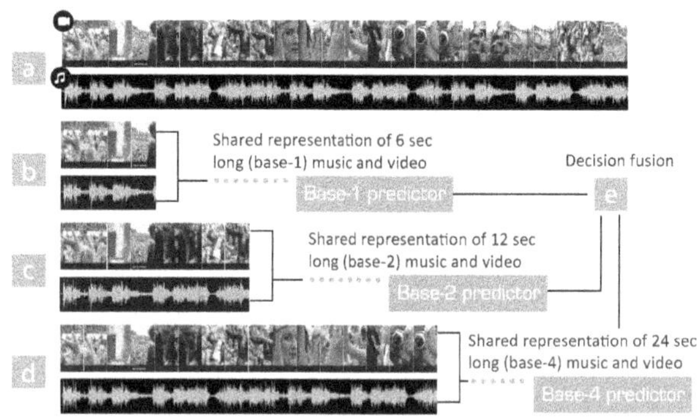

Figure 1: Deep learning multi-timescale shared representations. (a) Raw data of a MV segment. (b) 6 sec long base-1 segments. Deep representations for music and video are extracted separately. Shared representations are extracted by concatenating deep representations and input them to another layer. (c) Concatenation of 2 base-1 segments gives 1 base-2 segment. (d) Concatenation of 4 base-1 segments gives 1 base-4 segment. (e) To make a prediction on a 24 sec long time interval, we fuse predictions from 4 adjacent base-1 predictors, 2 adjacent base-2 predictors and 1 base-4 predictor.

MM'14, November 3–7, 2014, Orlando, Florida, USA.
Copyright 2014 ACM 978-1-4503-3063-3/14/11 ...$15.00.
http://dx.doi.org/10.1145/2647868.2655069.

distinct structures, they simplified the problem by grouping music-image pairs into five clusters and projected them to the music-attribute space.

In our work, deep learning is used to directly model relationships across modalities instead of simplifying the problem through clustering data pairs as in [10]. And we treat music and videos as temporal data and characterize their dynamic temporal and spacial features. In multimodal data analysis, there have been advances using deep learning approaches [9] [8] [11] [6]. Various kinds of modalities have already been covered by these literatures, including text, audio, music, and image. However, none of the existing work focus on fusing temporal multi-modality data. Temporal data are data that represent states in time, such as music and video. Multimodal problems on temporal data usually concern alignment or synchronization among modalities along time axis, and need to deal with multi-timescale problem, i.e., data sequence may have varying length. Our work provides novel solutions to these issues, demonstrating successful fusion of music and video on multiple level.

Our work makes two key contributions. First, we propose a deep learning framework taking well-crafted inter-frame and intra-frame music and video features as input and fuse them at both semantic and temporal level. This essentially makes sure the model captures semantic matches and takes care of data alignment problem. Second, we propose a novel multi-timescale temporal data fusion approach to deal with variable time length, such that our model can fuse modalities both locally and globally on the time axis. The effectiveness of the proposal multi-modality deep learning fusion approach is demonstrated through two experiments, MV retrieval and classification.

2. DATASET AND FEATURE DESIGN

2.1 Dataset preparation

We obtained 2,000 MVs from YouTube with top rated view counts and acquired 40,000 music-video pairs from them. Most of these MVs were published in 2010 to 2014. The MVs are of diversified styles and were performed by more than 600 singers from different countries.

To speed up feature extraction, all the MVs' video parts are down-sampled to a frame rate of 12fps and resolution is scaled to 320×240 pixels. Audio is downgraded to one channel with a sample rate of 44 kHz.

2.2 Video and music features

We cut music and videos in parallel into small segments of 6 seconds without overlapping or skipping, and extract both local and global features for each segment.

We extract image features within each frame as intra-frame features for videos. They include Histograms of Oriented Gradient (HOG), color histograms, and Local Binary Patterns (LBP). We also design inter-frame features that can capture temporal variation of frames, including histograms of Oriented Optical Flow, distances of HOG, color histograms, and LBP for adjacent frames. We calculate statistics of individual feature sets over all the frames in a segment, namely mean and standard deviation, to capture global characteristics for an entire segment. The final feature dimension for a video segment is 7443.

We use a rich set of mid-level musical features [5], including tempo, attack time, attack slope, spectral characteristics (such as brightness, spread, and roughness), timbre features (such as zero crossing, spectral flux), and tonal features (such as chromagram, key clarity). A pooling step is performed on the raw feature vector with a sliding window along the time axis to average the signal. It computes the mean, median, maximum, and minimum within the window to replace the raw features. Similar as in videos, we calculate statistical values for individual types of musical features over the entire segment, including the mean, standard deviation, slope, period frequency, period amplitude, and period entropy. The final feature dimension for an audio segment is 1052.

3. MULTIMODAL FUSION

3.1 Deep model on single modality

Given a single modality data x with its initial feature representation v_x, we build a multilayer generative deep belief network [4]. A Gaussian-Bernoulli Restricted Boltzmann Machine (RBM) [3] with one layer of latent variables h_x^1 is trained using real-valued v_x as input. Then we treat the activations of h_x^1 as input to train another RBM on top of it, obtaining latent variables h_x^2. More layers of RBM can be further trained in this manner to make the model deep. The whole network can be fine tuned after pre-training steps. Such configuration gives a Deep Belief Network model taking v_x as input and giving deep representation h_x^n as output, where n is the number of hidden layers. Deep representations are less modality-specific than raw data representations, and modeling correlations among deep representations of different modalities is much easier [9] [8]. In our experiments we use two layers of stacked RBMs. And input v_x are normalized to have 0 mean and standard deviation of 1.

3.2 Shared representation for multi-modality

Suppose there are m modalities for data fusion. After obtaining deep representations $h_{x_1}^{n_1}$, $h_{x_2}^{n_2}$, ..., $h_{x_m}^{n_m}$ for each modality x_1, x_2, ..., x_m respectively, where n_i is the depth of DBN for modality x_i, all the deep representations are concatenated into one single vector. Using the merged representation as input, we build another RBM on top of it, which gives hidden layer h as our final shared representation. This is equivalent to learning a joint distribution of all the modalities, and representations of different modalities are fused to one. An graphical illustration of this architecture is shown in Figure 2.

3.2.1 Multi-modality decision making

The process of extracting shared representation for multiple modalities can be treated as preprocessing step. Shared representations capture information from all modalities. Using shared representations in decision making problems such as classification, regression gives better result than directly using single modality data or concatenated multimodality initial feature. Any existing classifiers or regressors can be applied on top of them. We will show the application and experimental result in Section 4.

3.2.2 Multi-modality retrieval

All the layers in our model are undirected. Therefore it is possible to use one or more modalities to reconstruct other modalities. Given only v_p as query, we can search for matched v_q from a database. The hidden representation

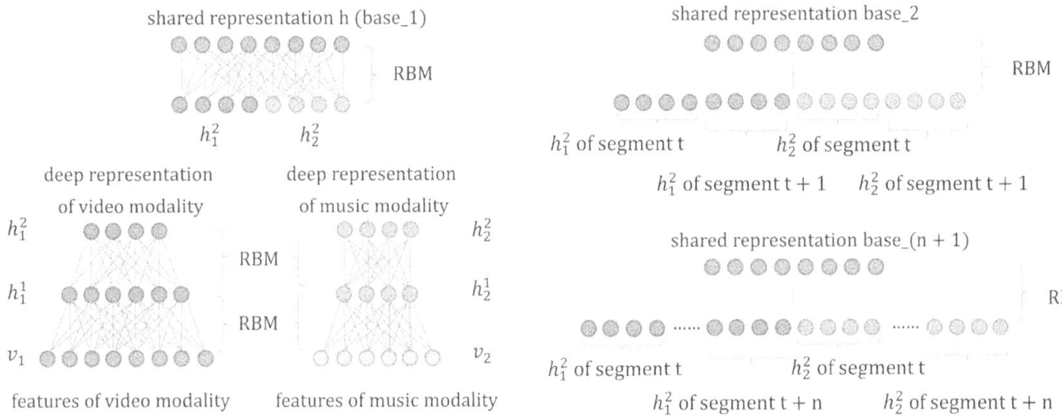

Figure 2: General architecture for extracting multi-timescale shared representation

h_p is first computed from v_p. In the shared RBM, we perform Gibbs sampling by using the conditional distribution $P(h|h_p, h_q)$ to obtain h, and then sample $P(h_q|h)$ to obtain h_q iteratively. Once convergence is reached, h_q can be estimated and easily be backpropagated through its DBN to get $v_q(recon)$. We evaluate the distances between $v_q(recon)$ and all the v_q in the database, and return those with smallest distances as retrieved results.

3.3 Multi-timescale fusion

Decision level fusion is a common strategy in multimodal fusion problems. To deal with long time-scale temporal data, the traditional approach is to fuse modalities on local short segments and average predictions over all short segments in the time interval [1] [7]. However this approach ignores valuable global information that may provide better matching.

Our multi-timescale fusion strategy works in the following way: merging adjacent deep representations within each modality to form hierarchical deep representations (Figure 2), and learning shared representations at different level of hierarchy. It aims at fusing modalities at varying time scales and is much easier to construct than building scale-varying models from bottom up. This approach has several advantages. First, the same set of initial features on the shortest time interval can be reused at different time scales. Therefore, the deep representations for each modality only need to be computed once and the computation is efficient. Second, shared representations at different levels of the hierarchy captures different ranges of cross-modality correlations ranging from local to global, which are complementary to one another. Some long-range characteristics can only be captured by shared representations at higher hierarchy levels.

In a long range matching scenario, one classifier is trained for the shared representation at each hierarchy level . Classifiers from different levels will give decisions on different range (local to global). A final step of decision fusion is performed by using a simple Feed-forward Neural Network (FFNN) to combine the predictions of classifiers at multiple levels.

An exemplar illustration and the architecture of learning multi-timescale shared representations are shown in Figure 1 and 2.

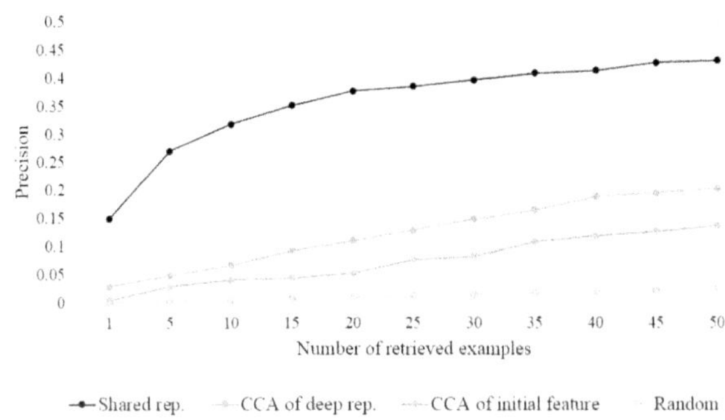

Figure 3: Retrieval precisions using sampling shared rep., CCA with deep rep., CCA with initial features, and random pairing

4. EXPERIMENTS

4.1 Multi-modal retrieval

We construct a video dataset with 2000 video segments, and use 500 audio segments as queries to evaluate the performance of retrieval. Note that the MVs containing these segments are not used in training deep models. We also implement a classic CCA method to evaluate similarity in the same way as [10]. Both CCA and our deep models are trained with 38,000 music-video segment pairs. Figure 3 shows the performance of retrieval using our method and C-CA. We treat the retrieval as successful as long as the top N retrieved examples contains the true match. The precisions of top-N ranks are reported. CCA of deep rep. uses deep representations of videos and audio, and outperforms CCA using initial features as input, which proves deep representations are easier to fuse than initial features. Retrieval with shared representation achieves big improvement over CCA on deep representations or initial features.

4.2 Korean MV classification

A number of YouTube hot clicks are Korean MVs of girl groups and boy bands. Modern Korean MVs are quite distinctive in style. Their music parts have fast tempo and repeated patterns. Their video parts are filled with singers' singing and dancing scenes. In this experiment, we try to learn a classifier to identity Korean MVs. We train an SVM classifier with concatenated initial music and video features

Data input	AP
Video initial feature	0.3123
Video deep rep.	0.5012
Music initial feature	0.2656
Music deep rep.	0.2975
Video and music initial feature (SVM)	0.4542
Shared rep. base-1	0.5585
Shared rep. base-2 (12 sec)	0.5841
Shared rep. base-5 (30 sec)	0.6479
Shared rep. base-10 (60 sec)	0.6025

Table 1: Average precisions of classifiers trained with different data input

as input for comparison. We also demonstrate the effect of multi-timescale fusion of temporal data.

Among 2,000 MVs in our dataset, around 10% are Korean MVs. We cut each MV into segments of 60 seconds, leading to 4,000 segments in total with around 400 Korean MV segments. We randomly obtain 2,000 MV segments containing 200 Korean MV segments as training data, leaving the rest as testing data.

In order to build a multi-timescale fusion model, we cut data into segments of 6 seconds as our base level, denoted by base-1 (40,000 segments in total). Deep representations are extracted for all the base-1 segments. To form a multi-timescale hierarchy, we concatenate the hidden representations of adjacent base-1 segments belonging to the same original 60-second-long segment. We concatenate two adjacent base-1 segments to form 1 base-2 segment (12 seconds long, 20,000 segments in total), concatenate 5 adjacent base-1 segments to form 1 base-5 segment (30 seconds long, 8,000 segments in total), and concatenate 10 adjacent base-1 segments to form 1 base-10 segment (60 seconds long, i.e. the original segments, 4,000 segments in total). One shared RBM is trained on each hierarchy level using base-1, base-2, base-5, and base-10 segments respectively. Then one FFNN classifier is trained with each level's shared RBM individually. We evaluate each classifier's performance using testing data belong to its concatenation level.

With base-1 segments, we also train FFNN classifiers using unimodal input, namely video/music initial features, and video/music deep representations individually. In another comparison, an SVM classifier is trained using concatenated initial music feature and video feature as input. Classifiers' performances are listed in Table 1. Classifiers using shared representations performs much better than those using unimodal representations. Both shared rep. base-1 and SVM use multi-modal input, however, it outperforms SVM by 10%. It shows that the shared representations obtained by deep learning are more effective than the initial features. Noted that AP of shared rep. base-2, base-5 and base-10 are provided for reference only and we do not compare them with others since they use smaller number of data segments (longer length) during training and testing.

In order to deal with long sequences of 60 seconds, we extract predictions from all classifiers and concatenate them into a vector. For each original segment of 60 seconds long, its prediction vector includes 10 local predictions by the base-1 classifier, 5 predictions by the base-2 classifier, 2 predictions by the base-5 classifier, 1 prediction by base-10 classifier. We train a FFNN with prediction vectors and evaluate

Method	AP
Multi-timescale	0.7900
Averaging shared rep. base-1	0.6750
Averaging SVM	0.6130

Table 2: Comparison of multi-timescale representation and averaging on local predictions.

our multi-timescale fusion model performance. As shown in Table 2, our final classifier (Multi-timescale) gives 0.79 average precision, outperforming the strategy of averaging 10 local predictions using either shared representation or SVM.

5. CONCLUSIONS

We propose deep models to explore correlations of music and video in MVs. Shared representations for music and videos are learned with DBNs. A retrieval experiment is conducted to demonstrate the power of the shared representations on matched music and videos. We also show that shared representations combines information of music and video and perform better than unimodal representations in the classification task. A novel method is proposed to handle temporal sequences with varying length, by constructing multi-timescale shared representations. It significantly outperforms averaging predictions on local intervals.

6. REFERENCES

[1] P. K. Atrey, M. A. Hossain, A. E. Saddik, and M. S. Kankanhalli. Multimodal fusion for multimedia analysis: a survey. *Multimedia Systems*, 2010.

[2] R. Cytowic. Synesthesia: A union of the senses. *The MIT Press*, 2002.

[3] G. Hinton. A practical guide to training restricted boltzmann machines. 2010.

[4] G. E. Hinton, S. Osindero, and Y. W. Teh. A fast learning algorithm for deep belief nets. *Neural Computation*, 2006.

[5] O. Lartillot and P. Toiviainen. Mir in matlab (ii): A toolbox for musical feature extraction from audio.

[6] J. Ngiam, A. Khosla, M. Kim, J. Nam, H. Lee, and A. Y. Ng. Multimodal deep learning. *International Conference on Machine Learning (ICML)*, 2011.

[7] A. Oord, S. Dieleman, and B. Schrauwen. Deep content-based music recommendation. *Advances in Neural Information Processing Systems (NIPS)*, 2013.

[8] N. Srivastava and R. Salakhutdinov. Learning representations for multimodal data with deep belief nets. *International Conference on Machine Learning (ICML)*, 2012.

[9] N. Srivastava and R. Salakhutdinov. Multimodal learning with deep boltzmann machines. *Advances in Neural Information Processing Systems (NIPS)*, 2012.

[10] X. Wu, Y. Qiao, X. Wang, and X. Tang. Bridging music and image: A preliminary study with multiple ranking cca learning. *Proceedings of ACM Multimedia*, 2012.

[11] Z. Yuan, J. Sang, Y. Liu2, and C. Xu. Latent feature learning in social media network. *Proceedings of ACM Multimedia*, 2013.

Representing and Recognizing Motion Trajectories: A Tube and Droplet Approach

Yang Zhou[1], Weiyao Lin[1*], Hang Su[1], Jianxin Wu[2], Jinjun Wang[3], Yu Zhou[4]

[1] Dept. of Electronic Engineering, Shanghai Jiao Tong University, China (*Corresponding Author)

[2] National Key Laboratory for Novel Software Technology, Nanjing University, China

[3] Institute of Artificial Intelligence and Robotics, Xi'an Jiao Tong University, China

[4] Institute of Information Engineering, Chinese Academy of Sciences, China

ABSTRACT

This paper addresses the problem of representing and recognizing motion trajectories. We first propose to derive scene-related equipotential lines for points in a motion trajectory and concatenate them to construct a 3D tube for representing the trajectory. Based on this 3D tube, a droplet-based method is further proposed which derives a "water droplet" from the 3D tube and recognizes trajectory activities accordingly. Our proposed 3D tube can effectively embed both motion and scene-related information of a motion trajectory while the proposed droplet-based method can suitably catch the characteristics of the 3D tube for activity recognition. Experimental results demonstrate the effectiveness of our approach.

Categories and Subject Descriptors

I.2.10 [**Vision and Scene Understanding**]: Video analysis

Keywords

Motion trajectory representation; Activity recognition; Droplet

1. INTRODUCTION

Motion trajectories are essential in describing object movement patterns over time. Visual analysis and recognition of motion trajectories are of considerable importance in many applications including video surveillance and video retrieval [1-6]. In this paper, we focus on the effective representation and recognition of motion trajectories.

First, properly representing motion trajectories is crucial in trajectory recognition. Many algorithms [4] directly utilized object locations at different time to represent object motion trajectories. However, this representation method is easily affected by the large variation of motion trajectories. To address this problem, Nascimento et al. [1] proposed low-level dynamic models to decompose trajectories into basic displacements. Chu et al. [2] created heat maps from trajectories to include temporal information while reducing the variances among trajectories. However, most of the existing methods only focus on modeling the absolute movements of objects while the scene-related information (e.g., whether the object is located in an unusual place in a scene) is not embedded. Thus, they will have limitations when recognizing scene-related abnormal activities such as entering an unusual place. Although some methods [3] utilized Gaussian process flows to model the location and velocity probability for each point in a trajectory, these flows are only used to measure the likelihood of a trajectory belonging to a specific trajectory type. Thus, they still do not actually embed information about the scene.

Second, accurately recognizing motion trajectories is another important issue. Some methods applied alignment or dynamic time warping to reduce trajectory variances and performed recognition by finding the most similar trajectory type [2, 4]. However, due to the large uncertainty of object motions, they still cannot completely avoid recognition errors from trajectory variances. Other methods constructed trajectory probability densities or graphical models for different activity patterns and recognized activities accordingly [1, 3, 10, 11]. However, these methods also have disadvantages in: (a) requiring large numbers of training data to achieve reliable probability models, and (b) have limitations in differentiating abnormal activities which only deviate slightly from normal ones [3]. Besides, Lin et al. [6] proposed to calculate transmission energies from trajectories for abnormality detection. Although this method can effectively detect abnormal activities, it still has limitations in differentiating normal activity patterns.

In this paper, we propose a new tube and droplet approach to represent and recognize motion trajectories. The contributions of our approach can be summarized in the following:

(1) We propose to derive scene-related equipotential lines for points in a motion trajectory and concatenate them together to construct a 3D tube for representing the trajectory. The proposed 3D tube can effectively embed both motion and scene-related information of a motion trajectory.

(2) We propose a droplet-based method which derives "water droplets" from 3D tubes and recognizes trajectory activities accordingly. The proposed droplet-based method can i) suitably catch the characteristics of 3D tubes, ii) effectively differentiate subtle normal/abnormal activities, iii) perform recognition with small number of training data.

The remainder of this paper is organized as follows. Section 2 describes the basic ideas of our approach. Section 3 presents the details of our 3D tube and droplet construction steps. Experimental results are shown in Section 4. Section 5 concludes the paper.

2. BASIC IDEAS

As mentioned, in order to properly handle scene-related activities, it is desirable to embed both object motion and scene-related information in trajectory representations. Thus, we propose to utilize 3D tubes to represent trajectories. As shown in Figure 1, (a) is an object motion trajectory, (b) is the equipotential lines for different points in the trajectory in (a), and (c) is a 3D tube representing the trajectory in (a). From Figure 1, we can see that a 3D tube is composed of equipotential lines where each equipotential line describes a point in a trajectory. More specifically, each equipotential line is located at its corresponding trajectory point while its shape is decided by the neighborhood

MM '14, November 03 - 07 2014, Orlando, FL, USA

http://dx.doi.org/10.1145/2647868.2654955

scene around the trajectory point (e.g., a trajectory point located in an unusual region will make its equipotential line shrink, as in Figure 1 and will be described in detail later). In this way, we can effectively embed both motion and scene-related information in a 3D tube with the route of the tube representing object motions and the shape of the tube representing information of the neighborhood scene.

Since 3D tubes include rich and high-dimensional information, the problem then comes to the selection of a suitable method for performing recognition based on these tube features. In this paper, we further propose a droplet-based method for activity recognition. In this method, we first "inject" water in one end of a 3D tube and then achieve a water droplet flowed out from the other end, as in Figure 1 (c). Since different activities are represented by 3D tubes with different shapes, by suitably modeling the water flow process, the flowed droplets can precisely catch the characteristics of 3D tubes. Thus, accurate recognition results can be achieved by parsing the shape of these droplets.

With the basic ideas of 3D tubes and water droplets, we can propose our motion trajectory representation and recognition approach. It is described in detail in the following section.

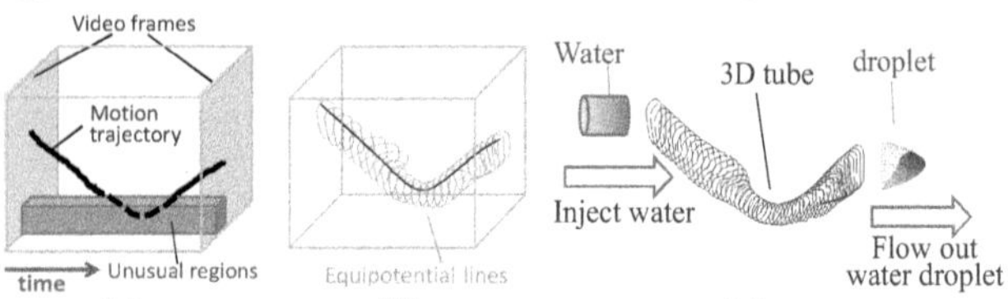

(a) (b) (c)

Figure 1. (a) Object trajectory; (b) Equipotential lines for different points in the trajectory in (a); (c) The final 3D tube representation and the process of droplet-based method.

3. THE APPROACH

The framework of our approach can be described in the following. First, equipotential lines are achieved for all points in the input trajectory. These equipotential lines are derived according to a pre-trained network which encodes the correlations among patches in the scene. Then, equipotential lines for different points are concatenated chronologically to construct a 3D tube for representing the input trajectory. After deriving a water drop by flowing water through the 3D tube, the activity of the input trajectory can be recognized by comparing this water drop with the trained drop shape patterns for different activities. In the following, we will describe details of the proposed approach.

3.1 3D Tube Construction

3.1.1 Network construction

In order to embed scene-related information into 3D tubes, we first need to construct a directed network to describe a scene. In this paper, we divide a scene into non-overlapping patches such that each patch can be viewed as a node in a network while the directed links between neighboring patches can be viewed as the directed edges in a network, as in Figure 2. With this network model, a trajectory moving in a scene can be modeled as a package transmitting through different nodes in its corresponding network. Thus, by properly constructing the edge weights in this network, the information of the scene can be effectively modeled.

In this paper, the directed edge weights between neighboring patches are calculated by:

$$W_{i\to j} = \sum_{k=1}^{N} R_{k,i\to j} \tag{1}$$

where $W_{i\to j}$ is the weight for the directed edge from patch P_i to

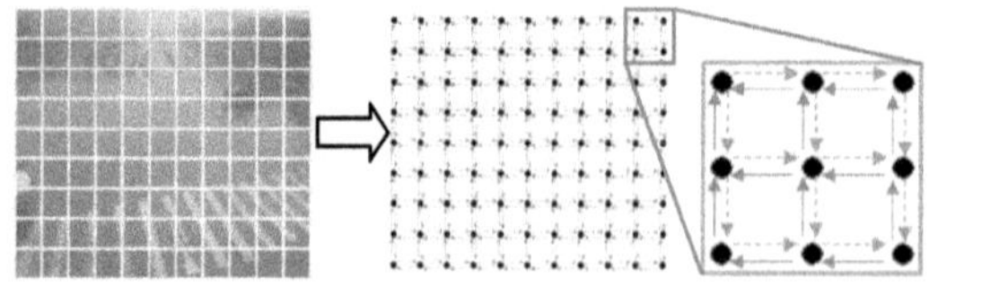

Figure 2. Separate a scene into patches and construct a directed network accordingly.

patch P_j. N is the total number of trajectories in the training set. $R_{k,i\to j}$ is the impact of the k-th training trajectory to edge $P_i \to P_j$. $R_{k,i\to j}$ can be calculated by:

$$R_{k,i\to j} = \sum_{r=1}^{L_k} \max\big(v_{k,r}(i\to j), 0\big)\cdot e^{-\|P_r - P_i\|^2} \tag{2}$$

where L_k is the total number of points in trajectory k. $v_{k,r}(i\to j)$ is the displacement of the r-th point in trajectory k in the direction of $P_i \to P_j$, as in Figure 3. P_r is the patch where point r is located. $\|P_r - P_i\|^2$ is the distance between patches P_i and P_r.

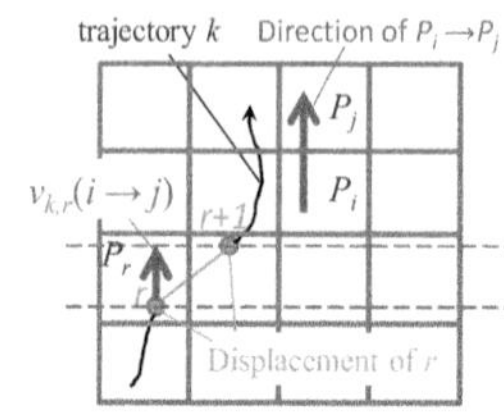

Figure 3. The way to calculate $v_{k,r}(i\to j)$.

From Eqs (1) and (2), we can see that the weight for a directed edge $P_i \to P_j$ is proportional to the total displacement strength of all training trajectory points in the direction of $P_i \to P_j$. Besides, a distance term $\|P_r - P_i\|^2$ is also included such that trajectory points closer to the directed edge will have more impact to the weight $W_{i\to j}$. In this way, if there are large numbers of training trajectories passing through P_i and following the direction of $P_i \to P_j$, a large weight will be assigned to $W_{i\to j}$ meaning that moving from P_i to P_j is normal. On the contrary, a small $W_{i\to j}$ will be assigned to indicate that following $P_i \to P_j$ is abnormal.

3.1.2 Achieving equipotential lines

With the constructed network, we can derive an equipotential line for each point in an input testing trajectory. More specifically, we first achieve an energy map for a trajectory point based on the constructed network, and then derive a constant-energy line from this energy map as the resulting equipotential line.

The energy map for a trajectory point r can be achieved by iteratively propagating energies outwards from the patch of r (i.e. P_r) to other patches in the scene. The trajectory point patch P_r is first allocated with an initial energy E_0=100 before propagation. And during each iteration, the energy propagated from a patch P_i to its outside neighboring patch P_j can be calculated by:

$$E_{i\to j} = E_i \cdot e^{-\frac{\gamma}{W_{i\to j}}} \tag{3}$$

where $E_{i\to j}$ is the energy transmitted from P_i to P_j. E_i is the energy in patch P_i. $W_{i\to j}$ is the weight for the directed edge $P_i \to P_j$ achieved by Eq. (1). And γ is a constant. From Eq. (3), it is clear that fewer energies will be propagated if the motion from P_i to P_j is abnormal (i.e., small $W_{i\to j}$).

Figure 4 (b) and (d) show the energy maps of two points r_a and r_b in a trajectory in (a). In (b), since moving rightward from r_a is normal (because there are lots of dashed blue training trajectories moving rightward around r_a), more energies can be propagated to this direction, thus leading to a long rightward tail in r_a's energy map. Comparatively, in (d), since r_b is located in an unusual/abnormal region (because there is no training trajectories moving around r_b), few energies can be propagated out, thus making r_b's energy map decay quickly around r_b.

With the energy map, the equipotential line can be easily achieved by finding a constant-energy line in the map. In this paper, we find the line whose energy is half of the peak energy E_0, as in Figure 4.

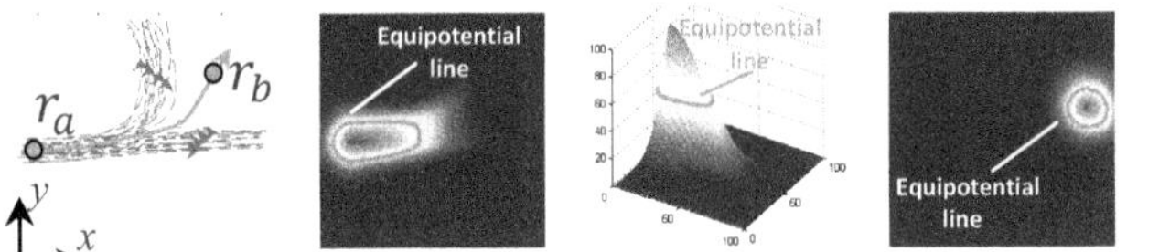

Figure 4. (a) The input trajectory (solid red line) and training trajectories (dashed black lines); (b) and (d): The energy maps and equipotential lines for trajectory points r_a and r_b in (a); (c): The energy map surfaces of (b) in 3D.

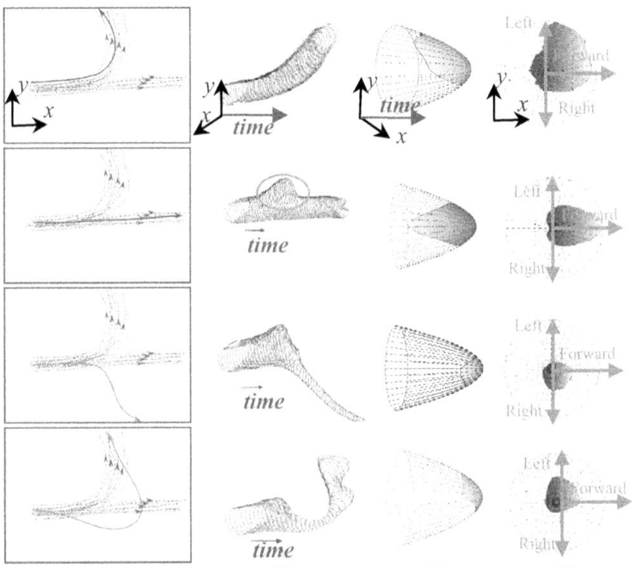

Figure 5. (a) Input trajectories (red/blue solid lines) and training trajectories (black dashed lines); (b) 3D tubes for the input trajectories in (a); (c) Droplets derived from the 3D tubes in (b); (d) Viewing the droplets in (c) from the left side.

3.1.3 Constructing 3D tubes

After deriving equipotential lines for each point in an input trajectory, a 3D tube can be constructed to represent this trajectory by concatenating all equipotential lines according to their temporal order in the trajectory. Figure 5 (b) shows the 3D tubes of the trajectories in (a). From Figure 5, we can see that:

(1) Our proposed 3D tubes include rich information about both trajectories' motion and their relationships with the surrounding scene. For example, the routes of 3D tubes represent actual motions of trajectories. The thicknesses of 3D tubes indicate whether trajectories are normal/abnormal (e.g., tubes will become narrow for abnormal trajectories). Moreover, the shapes of equipotential lines inside 3D tubes also indicate possible normal motion directions (e.g., the convex part in the pink circle in (b) indicates that moving upward (i.e., turn left) is another possible normal motion direction). Therefore, various trajectory activities can be effectively recognized with our 3D tubes.

(2) Compared with the 2D trajectory representation in (a), our 3D tube representation includes an additional time dimension. And this also has the advantage of properly displaying the object's motion speed information such as "stop" and "speed up".

Note that we also normalize 3D tubes to have the same length in order to avoid the influence of different trajectory lengths.

3.2 The Water-Droplet Method

After constructing 3D tubes for input trajectories, we need to find suitable methods to effectively utilize these high-dimensional tube features. In this paper, we propose to inject water into 3D tubes and derive "water droplets" to detect activities, as Figure 1.

Basically, a droplet can be described by a center point r and a set of boundary points h_m, as in Figure 6 (a). We define r as the point which follows the route of the input trajectory when passing through a 3D tube. And h_m is the point following the route constructed by the points on the m-th direction of r on all equipotential lines, as in Figure 6 (b). Assuming that r passes a 3D tube with a constant velocity while the velocity of h_m is changed according to the thickness and shape of the 3D tube, by calculating the relative distances between h_m and r at the tube output, the features of the 3D tube can be effectively captured.

In this paper, we define two distances at a tube output: H_m which is the distance between h_m and r in the time dimension, and D_m which is the distance between h_m and r in the x-y plane, as in Figure 6 (a). In order to simplify calculation, we further assume $D_m = H_m$ such that a 3D droplet can be simply described by H_m in a 2D plane, as in Figure 5 (d). According to the fluid viscosity theory [7], H_m can be calculated by:

$$H_m = \frac{1}{L}\sum_{t=1}^{L} v_{m-r,t} = \frac{1}{L}\sum_{t=1}^{L} \frac{d_{m,t}^2}{\mu(d_{m,t}, \theta_{m,t})} \tag{4}$$

where L is the length of a 3D tube. $d_{m,t}$ is the distance between r_t and $h_{m,t}$, and $\theta_{m,t}$ is the angle between lines $r_t \rightarrow h_{m,t}$ and $r_t \rightarrow r_{t+1}$, as in Figure 6 (b) and (c). Note that $h_{m,t}$ and r_t are the locations of h_m and r at time t when going through a 3D tube (i.e., r_t is the t-th point in a trajectory and h_m is the m-th point on the equipotential line of r_t). $v_{m-r,t} = \frac{d_{m,t}^2}{\mu(d_{m,t}, \theta_{m,t})}$ is the relative time-dimensional velocity between h_m and r at time t. $\mu(d_{m,t}, \theta_{m,t})$ is the viscosity coefficient of the tube calculated by:

$$\mu(d_{m,t}, \theta_{m,t}) = \frac{\beta}{d_{m,t} \cdot (\cos(\theta_{m,t}) + \lambda)} \tag{5}$$

where λ and β are constant values.

From Eqs (4) and (5), we can see that the time-dimensional distance H_m is calculated by accumulating the time-dimensional velocity difference between h_m and r when passing through a 3D tube. The velocity difference $v_{m-r,t}$ is decided by the thickness and shape variations in a 3D tube. When a tube becomes thick (i.e., large $d_{m,t}$ and correspond to normal motions), $v_{m-r,t}$ will be enlarged and create large H_m. Besides, when h_m is located along the motion direction of a trajectory (i.e., the angle between $r_t \rightarrow h_{m,t}$ and $r_t \rightarrow r_{t+1}$ is small), the viscosity from a tube will be small, leading to large H_m.

Figure 5 (c) and (d) show the resulting droplets of the 3D tubes in (b). From Figure 5 (c) and (d), we can observe the effectiveness of our water-droplet method. For example, the droplets of normal tubes (the first and second rows in Figure 5) have large sizes than the droplets of abnormal tubes (the last two rows). Also, the droplets have large sectors in the trajectories' major motion directions. Thus, we can effectively use these droplet features to recognize both normal/abnormal activities and activities of different motion patterns. In our experiments, we construct feature vectors from droplets by concatenating H_m and utilize linear SVMs [8] to recognize activities.

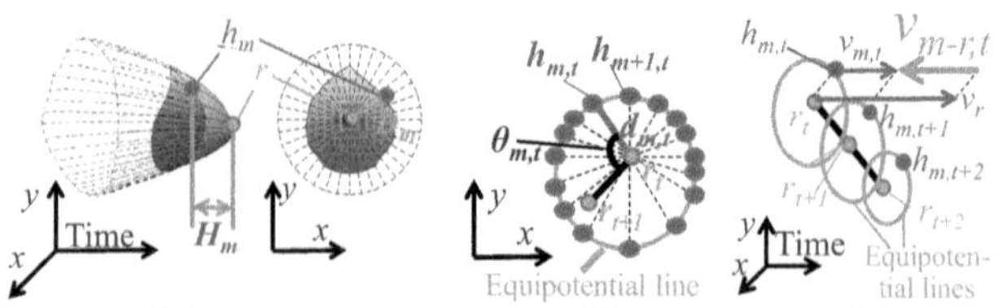

(a) (b) (c)

Figure 6. (a) Center point r, boundary point h_m, and their distances; (b) Illustration of $d_{m,t}$ and $\theta_{m,t}$ at time t; (c) $h_{m,t}$ and r_t at different t and relative velocity $v_{m-r,t}$.

4. EXPERIMENTAL RESULTS

In this section, we show experimental results for our proposed tube and droplet approach. In our experiments, the patch size is set to be 10×10, and γ, λ, and β in Eqs (3) and (5) are set to be 1, 5, and 1, respectively. We first perform experiments on a road dataset that we constructed. The dataset includes 300 trajectories obtained by a tracking method [9] where 200 trajectories are for normal activities and the other 100 trajectories are abnormal ones. The normal trajectories includes seven classes (with about 30 trajectories for each class), as in Figure 7 (a). Besides, some example abnormal trajectories are also displayed in Figure 7 (a). Note that this is a challenging dataset in that: (1) the total number of trajectories in the dataset is small; (2) The motion trajectories within the same class have large variance; (3) Many trajectories from different class are confusing and are difficult to differentiate.

We compare our approach with three methods: the GPRF method [3], the DTW method [4], and the heat-map (HM) method [2]. We split the dataset into 75% training-25% testing parts and perform recognition on the testing part [6]. Four independent experiments are performed where the training and testing sets are randomly selected in each experiment. And the results are averaged. Figure 7 (b) compares the ROC curves for different methods in recognizing normal/abnormal activities. Besides, Table 1 further compares the Miss, False Alarm (FA), and Total Error Rates (TERs) [6] for different methods in differentiating the seven normal activity patterns and the abnormal activity pattern.

From Table 1 and Figure 7 (b), we can see that the compared methods, which mainly perform recognition according to the similarity among trajectories' motion patterns, have low effectiveness when recognizing activities such as "L", "RU", and "RD" since their trajectories are easily confused with other similar activities such as "UL", "U", "R". Comparatively, our proposed approach can achieve obviously better results where the confusing activities are properly differentiated. This is because: (1) our 3D tube representation embeds scene-related information by using narrow tube sections to represent local abnormal displacements. Thus, abnormal activities can be precisely differentiated even if their overall trajectory shapes are similar to normal activities; (2) Our droplet features can catch the subtle motion direction by accumulating velocity differences between boundary and center points in 3D tubes. Thus, the confusing activities such that "R" and "RD" can also be effectively differentiated by our approach.

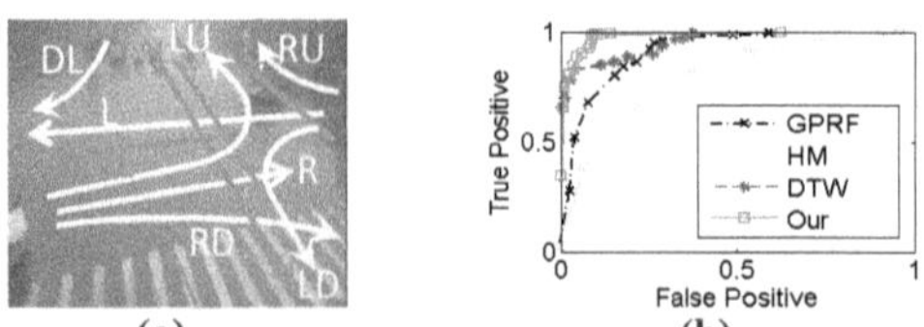

(a) (b)

Figure 7. (a) Examples of normal activities (yellow) and abnormal activities (red); (b) ROC curves of different methods in abnormality detection.

Table 1 Miss, FA, and TER rates in recognizing different normal patterns together with the abnormal activity pattern

		Our	GPRF [3]	DTW [4]	HM [2]
R	Miss	**4.2%**	9.7%	15.3%	8.2%
	FA	**0.5%**	1.4%	1.7%	0.7%
L	Miss	**3.8%**	7.1%	9.3%	11.2%
	FA	**0.2%**	0.5%	1.0%	1.8%
RD	Miss	**3.5%**	10.2%	18.5%	12.4%
	FA	**0.3%**	0.7%	1.4%	1.0%
LU	Miss	**2.6%**	0.3%	0.5%	2.6%
	FA	**0.5%**	0.2%	0.0%	0.4%
LD	Miss	**1.2%**	3.3%	14.1%	8.0%
	FA	**0.2%**	0.2%	0.6%	0.2%
RU	Miss	**2.4%**	14.7%	13.1%	17.9%
	FA	**0.5%**	1.8%	1.5%	2.1%
DL	Miss	**1.3%**	2.5%	1.4%	2.4%
	FA	**0.0%**	0.2%	0.0%	0.4%
Abnormal	Miss	**8.8%**	17.4%	24.3%	23.1%
	FA	**7.9%**	17.0%	26.7%	21.2%
TER		**5.3%**	10.7%	15.4%	14.1%

5. CONCLUSION AND FUTURE WORKS

In this paper, we propose to construct a 3D tube for representing a motion trajectory and then derive a "water droplet" from the 3D tube to recognize the trajectory. Experimental results demonstrate the effectiveness of our approach. Future work includes more experiment on public datasets and comparison with other graphical model-based methods [10, 11].

6. ACKNOWLEDGMENTS

This paper is supported in part by grants: Shanghai Pujiang Program (12PJ1404300), National Science Foundation of China (61471235, 61001146, 61025005, 61303170), Chinese national 973 grants (2010CB7314016), and SMC scholarship of SJTU.

REFERENCES

[1] J. Nascimento, M. Figueiredo, and J. Marques, "Trajectory classification using switched dynamical hidden Markov models," *IEEE Trans. Image Proc.*, pp. 1338-1348, 2010.

[2] H. Chu, W. Lin, J. Wu, X. Zhou, Y. Chen, and H. Li, "A new heat-map-based algorithm for human group activity recognition," *ACM Multimedia (MM)*, pp. 1069-1072, 2012.

[3] K. Kim, D. Lee, and I. Essa, "Gaussian process regression flow for analysis of motion trajectories," *ICCV*, 2011.

[4] C. Rao, A. Yilmaz, and M. Shah, "View-invariant representation and recognition of actions," *IJCV*, 2002.

[5] D. Ellis, E. Sommerlade, and I. Reid, "Modelling pedestrian trajectory patterns with gaussian processes," *Int. Conf. Computer Vision Workshops*, pp. 1229-1234, 2009.

[6] W. Lin, Y. Chen, J. Wu, H. Wang, B. Sheng, and H. Li, "A new network-based algorithm for human activity recognition in videos," *IEEE Trans. CSVT*, 24(5), pp. 826-841, 2014.

[7] V. Streeter, E. Wylie, and K. Bedford, "Fluid Mechanics," *McGraw-Hill press*, 1987.

[8] C. Chang and C. Lin. "LIBSVM: a library for support vector machines," *ACM Trans. Intell. Syst. Tech.*, pp. 1-27, 2011.

[9] R. Hess and A. Fern, "Discriminatively trained particle filters for complex multi-object tracking," *CVPR*, 2009.

[10] X. Wang, K. T. Ma, G. Ng, and E. Grimson, "Trajectory analysis and semantic region modeling using nonparametric hierarchical bayesian models, " *IJCV*, 2011.

[11] B. Morris and M. Trivedi, "Trajectory learning for activity understanding: unsupervised, multilevel, and long-term adaptive approach," *IEEE Trans. PAMI*, 2011.

Multi-modal Language Models for Lecture Video Retrieval

Huizhong Chen[†], Matthew Cooper[‡], Dhiraj Joshi[‡], Bernd Girod[†]

[†]Stanford University
Stanford, CA USA
{hchen2, bgirod}@stanford.edu

[‡]FX Palo Alto Laboratory
Palo Alto, CA USA
{cooper, dhiraj}@fxpal.com

ABSTRACT

We propose Multi-modal Language Models (MLMs), which adapt latent variable techniques for document analysis to exploring co-occurrence relationships in multi-modal data. In this paper, we focus on the application of MLMs to indexing text from slides and speech in lecture videos, and subsequently employ a multi-modal probabilistic ranking function for lecture video retrieval. The MLM achieves highly competitive results against well established retrieval methods such as the Vector Space Model and Probabilistic Latent Semantic Analysis. When noise is present in the data, retrieval performance with MLMs is shown to improve with the quality of the spoken text extracted from the video.

Categories and Subject Descriptors

H.3.1 [**Information Storage and Retrieval**]: Content Analysis and Indexing; H.3.3 [**Information Storage and Retrieval**]: Information Search and Retrieval

General Terms

Algorithms

Keywords

Multi-modal retrieval, latent variable modeling, multi-modal probabilistic ranking

1. INTRODUCTION

The continued growth in user generated video on the internet has exacerbated the need for content search and management tools. A quickly growing sector of internet-distributed content is *expository* or "how-to" video, a genre which includes lecture videos from online courses, presentations from conferences and seminars, and more general demonstration and tutorial videos.

Slide-based lecture videos are amenable to content-based indexing due to the temporal and topical structure the slides provide. Systems can exploit the slide text to enable search functionality inside the videos [1, 6, 14].

Retrieval systems have also extracted text from the spoken audio in lecture videos using automatic speech recognition (ASR) [8]. ASR errors are commonplace due to poor audio recording quality or acoustic mismatch and diminish the spoken text's utility for video retrieval. In some cases, "clean" spoken text is available as manually created closed captions (CC). While slides typically contain sparse and discriminative text, speech is relatively voluminous, improvised, and comprised largely of generic terms.

We propose a model for the co-occurrence of the words in videos' spoken audio and detected slides. Latent variable modeling captures prominent correlations between terms in these modalities while suppressing anomalous coincidences. The resulting model emphasizes semantically meaningful relationships between terms, while reducing dimensionality. We exploit the model's probabilistic framework for improved lecture video retrieval. Our contributions are:

- We propose Multi-modal Language Models (MLMs) to represent co-occurrences of multi-modal data using latent variable modeling.
- We propose a multi-modal probabilistic ranking function for use with the MLMs for lecture video retrieval.
- We introduce the Google I/O Dataset, a new dataset for studying multi-modal lecture video retrieval.

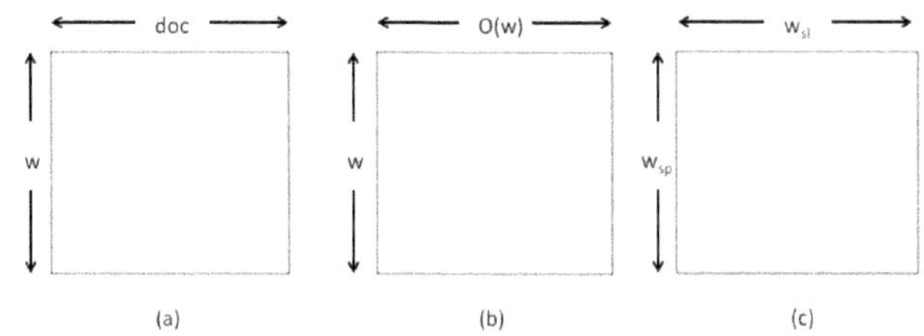

Figure 1: The left panel shows the traditional word-document matrix that is modeled using PLSA and LDA. The middle panel shows the matrix processed in word-topic modeling [5], where the co-occurrence of a word w and its neighborhood words $O(w)$ is modeled. The right panel shows the multi-modal variant we propose in which the co-occurrence of slide words and spoken words are modeled.

MM '14 November 03–07, 2014, Orlando, Florida USA
ACM 978-1-4503-3063-3/14/11:. $15.00.
http://dx.doi.org/10.1145/2647868.2654964 .

2. RELATED WORK

The Vector Space Model (VSM) for information retrieval treats documents as "bags" of words [10] and drives high performance text search systems including Lucene[1]. VSM was applied to lecture video retrieval in [11]. VSM leads naturally to representing the document corpus in a matrix. Figure 1(a) depicts such a matrix in which the rows and columns are indexed by the words and documents respectively. Both Probabilistic Latent Semantic Analysis (PLSA) [7] and Latent Dirichlet Allocation (LDA) [4] model documents using a distribution over latent variables to capture relations between co-occurring words. In [5], Chen proposed Word Topic Models (WTMs) which model the word-word matrix of Figure 1(b). The WTMs implement latent variable models on a finer sub-document level, demonstrating improved performance over conventional PLSA. While [5] constructs latent variable models for (unimodal) text documents, our MLMs are learned from multi-modal text as in Figure 1(c) and detailed in Section 3.

Researchers have applied latent variable models to explore the relation between images' visual features and their text annotations using variants of LDA and PLSA. Barnard et al. [2] developed multi-modal LDA to jointly model a common underlying topic distribution on image region descriptors and annotation words (i.e., tags). Correspondence LDA (Corr-LDA) [3] models a process that first generates region descriptors followed by generation of words (each word is linked to one of the image regions). [12] developed a less constricted multi-modal LDA model allowing for different latent variable distributions in each modality and using regression to more flexibly capture inter-modality relationships.

Multi-layer PLSA [9] models visual features and tags by introducing two layers of latent variables (one being common to the two modalities) into the joint model, and does not require that tags associated with images necessarily describe the visual content. Rasiwasia et al. [13] used canonical correlation analysis (CCA) to model multi-modal data by jointly performing dimension reduction across the two modalities of words and pictures.

In this paper, we build generative models for individual spoken words and slide words, which we call Multi-modal Language Models (MLMs). The MLMs are also learned using Expectation Maximization (EM). In contrast to conventional latent variable models of a unimodal document corpus, MLMs model fine grained multi-modal word-word co-occurrences. This more direct formulation inherits the benefits of reduced dimensionality and noise suppression of prior probabilistic co-occurrence models, but with greatly simplified model training and retrieval.

3. MULTI-MODAL LANGUAGE MODELS

Multi-modal Language Models (MLMs) are latent variable models learned from the *multi-modal* data matrix of Figure 1(c). The matrix entries indicate the number of times a spoken word and a slide word co-occur in the same video. A set of latent variables is introduced to model the essential relationships between slide words and spoken words. Following the graphical model in Figure 2, the joint probability of a slide word w_{sl} and a spoken word w_{sp} is given by:

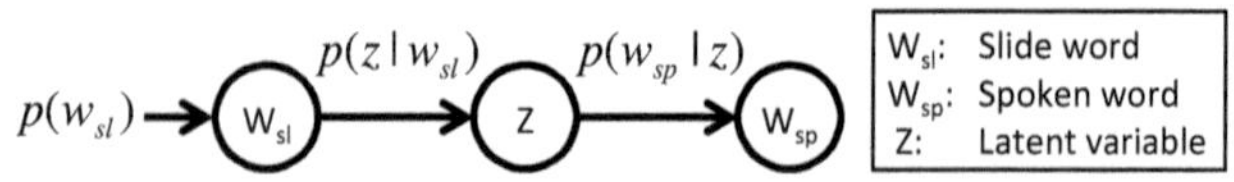

Figure 2: The graphical model of our proposed MLM. The relation between each slide word and spoken word is described by a set of latent variables. The model parameters $p(z|w_{sl})$ and $p(w_{sp}|z)$ can be estimated by the EM algorithm, while the prior of $p(w_{sl})$ is directly obtained from the corpus.

$$p(w_{sp}, w_{sl}) = \sum_z p(w_{sp}|z)p(z|w_{sl})p(w_{sl}) \ . \quad (1)$$

We maximize the likelihood of the data co-occurrence matrix in Figure 1(c) using EM. Throughout, we process the raw word count data using Laplace smoothing [10]. Following the derivations in [7], the EM iterations are:

E-Step: Update

$$p(z|w_{sp}, w_{sl}) = \frac{p(w_{sp}|z)p(z|w_{sl})}{\sum_z p(w_{sp}|z)p(z|w_{sl})} \ , \quad (2)$$

M-Step: Update

$$p(w_{sp}|z) = \frac{\sum_{w_{sl}} \#(w_{sl}, w_{sp})p(z|w_{sl}, w_{sp})}{\sum_{w_{sl}, w_{sp}} \#(w_{sl}, w_{sp})p(z|w_{sl}, w_{sp})} \ , \quad (3)$$

$$p(z|w_{sl}) = \frac{\sum_{w_{sp}} \#(w_{sl}, w_{sp})p(z|w_{sl}, w_{sp})}{\#(w_{sl})} \ . \quad (4)$$

The result of EM training is the MLM for the slide and spoken words in the corpus following (1).

4. RETRIEVAL RANKING FUNCTION

We propose a probabilistic multi-modal ranking score for lecture video retrieval. Each video in the corpus is represented by its associated slide text transcript T_{sl} and spoken text transcript T_{sp}. We utilize $p(z|w_{sp}, w_{sl})$ from (2) to compute the video specific latent variable distribution,

$$p(z|(T_{sl}, T_{sp})) = \sum_{(w_{sl}, w_{sp}) \in (T_{sl}, T_{sp})} \alpha((w_{sl}, w_{sp}), (T_{sl}, T_{sp})) \cdot p(z|w_{sl}, w_{sp}) \ , \quad (5)$$

where $\alpha((w_{sl}, w_{sp}), (T_{sl}, T_{sp}))$ represents the co-occurrence frequency of the word pair (w_{sl}, w_{sp}) observed in the specific video's transcripts (T_{sl}, T_{sp}).

Denote the user query text as T_q. We estimate the query-video relevance by the conditional probability of T_q given (T_{sl}, T_{sp}) from the video:

$$p(T_q|(T_{sl}, T_{sp})) = \prod_{w_q \in T_q} \sum_z p(w_q|z)p(z|(T_{sl}, T_{sp})) \ . \quad (6)$$

Here, $p(z|(T_{sl}, T_{sp}))$ is calculated as in (5), but users' query language model $p(w_q|z)$ is unknown. It is reasonable to assume that the query words obey a similar distribution to the slide words or spoken words in the video corpus. Therefore,

[1]http://lucene.apache.org

(6) can be rewritten by replacing $p(w_q|z)$ with $p(w_{sl}|z)$ and $p(w_{sp}|z)$ respectively:

$$p_{sl}(T_q|(T_{sl},T_{sp})) = \prod_{w_{sl}\in T_q}\sum_z p(w_{sl}|z)p(z|(T_{sl},T_{sp})) , \quad (7)$$

$$p_{sp}(T_q|(T_{sl},T_{sp})) = \prod_{w_{sp}\in T_q}\sum_z p(w_{sp}|z)p(z|(T_{sl},T_{sp})) . \quad (8)$$

We multiply $p_{sl}(T_q|(T_{sl},T_{sp}))$ and $p_{sp}(T_q|(T_{sl},T_{sp}))$ to define the final video ranking score for the query T_q:

$$\hat{p}(T_q|(T_{sl},T_{sp})) = p_{sl}(T_q|(T_{sl},T_{sp}))\cdot p_{sp}(T_q|(T_{sl},T_{sp})) . \quad (9)$$

A notable implementation detail is that the conditional probability $p(z|(T_{sl},T_{sp}))$ in (7) and (8) is query-independent. Therefore, it is pre-computed once per video and stored to accelerate processing at query time.

5. EXPERIMENTS

5.1 The Google I/O Dataset [2]

To validate our video retrieval scheme, we assembled a dataset of 209 presentation videos from Google I/O conferences in the years 2010-2012. The lengths of the videos range from 40 to 60 minutes. By crawling the conference web sites, we collected the following data for each presentation video:

- Slide text from PPT, PDF, HTML5, etc. (PPT)
- Closed-caption speech transcripts (CC)
- OCR extracted slide text from video frames (OCR)
- ASR speech transcripts from YouTube (ASR)

For automatic slide text extraction (OCR), we first automatically detect slide keyframes from the videos using the system in [1]. We then use Microsoft Office document OCR to extract slide text from the resulting video keyframes. The ASR transcript is downloaded from YouTube.

The automatically extracted OCR and ASR data are noisy versions of the actual slide and spoken text. To filter recognition errors, we discard OCR and ASR transcript words that appear only once in the corpus and are not in the english dictionary. We empirically verified that this filtering procedure does not hurt performance, while significantly reducing computation time. After filtering the noisy text, we retain 29,279 and 36,118 unique words for the ASR and OCR lexicons, respectively. In comparison, the lexicon of the error-free text contains 22,786 unique words from CC and 17,013 words from PPT.

Based on the talks' descriptions on the conference web sites, 275 queries were manually generated to simulate user queries. The queries are technical terms such as "listview android widget" and "NFC reader/writer API". Manual ground truth relevance judgments were compiled for all 275 queries across all 209 videos. We use mean average precision (mAP) [10] as the evaluation metric.

[2]The Google I/O dataset is available for download at http://purl.stanford.edu/gc512qf7480

5.2 Baseline methods

We compare MLMs with two well established retrieval methods: VSM and PLSA. The Lucene documentation[3] and [10] describe VSM retrieval. For retrieval using PLSA, we used the following ranking score which is similar to (6):

$$p(T_q|D) = \prod_{w_q\in T_q}\sum_z p(w_q|z)p(z|D) , \quad (10)$$

where D denotes a video. This ranking performed better than the folded-in latent space retrieval proposed in [7]. For each text modality, we used 200 latent variables in the PLSA model.

For multi-modal retrieval, we evaluate both early and late fusion strategies for both VSM and PLSA. For early fusion, the available slide and spoken text are concatenated to represent each video prior to indexing. For late fusion, retrieval scores are first computed independently for slide and spoken data, and then fused in a weighted sum:

$$S_{\text{late fusion}} = \lambda S_{sl} + (1-\lambda)S_{sp} . \quad (11)$$

S_{sl} and S_{sp} represent the retrieval scores of slide and spoken text respectively, and $\lambda \in [0,1]$ is optimized via two-fold cross validation.

5.3 Retrieval with error-free text data

The first set of retrieval experiments uses CC spoken text and PPT slide text, i.e., model training and video retrieval use error-free slide and spoken text transcripts. Table 1 shows the mAP for the MLM trained with 200 latent variables, compared to the early and late fusion results from VSM and PLSA. The MLMs approach significantly outperforms the second best performing method of VSM late fusion, with statistical significance at 99% confidence interval according to the paired t-test.

Table 1: Multi-modal retrieval performance using PPT and CC text on the Google I/O corpus.

	mAP@N		
	N=5	N=10	N=209
VSM early fusion	0.863	0.829	0.777
VSM late fusion	0.869	0.845	0.790
PLSA early fusion	0.858	0.830	0.767
PLSA late fusion	0.806	0.793	0.732
MLM (ours)	**0.902**	**0.875**	**0.830**

5.4 Retrieval with noisy text data

We repeat the experiments using the automatically extracted text from OCR and ASR to represent each video. Here, noisy OCR and ASR text data are employed to train the MLMs and the retrieval mAPs are tabulated in Table 2. While there is no performance gain as in the noise-free case (PDF and CC), the MLMs achieve statistically indistinguishable performance to the competitive VSM late fusion baseline (paired t-test: t = 0.672, p = 0.502).

[3]`http://lucene.apache.org/core/4_0_0/core/org/apache/lucene/search/similarities/TFIDFSimilarity.html`

Table 2: Multi-modal retrieval performance using OCR and ASR text on the Google I/O corpus.

	mAP@N		
	N=5	N=10	N=209
VSM early fusion	0.807	0.780	0.723
VSM late fusion	**0.829**	**0.811**	**0.747**
PLSA early fusion	0.807	0.785	0.708
PLSA late fusion	0.751	0.731	0.647
MLM (ours)	0.822	0.805	0.734

5.5 ASR quality and MLM performance

The results show that the use of noisy slide and spoken text can diminish the effectiveness of MLMs for lecture video retrieval. To analyze the degradation of retrieval performance due to noise in each data modality, we performed experiments using VSM on unimodal data (recall that we have 4 types of unimodal data: PPT, CC, OCR, ASR). The full unimodal VSM results are omitted here for brevity, but retrieval using OCR text performs on par with retrieval using PPT text (mAP@5 for OCR retrieval is only 0.01 lower than PPT), whereas retrieval using ASR text is significantly worse than using CC text (mAP@5 for ASR retrieval is 0.206 lower than CC). We thus hypothesize that poor quality ASR degrades retrieval performance of MLMs trained using OCR-ASR word pairs.

To assess this hypothesis, we divide the 275 queries into two sets, according to whether the query's retrieval Average Precision at the top-5 candidates (AP@5, using noisy text data $T_{sl} = T_{OCR}$ and $T_{sp} = T_{ASR}$) for MLMs outperform that of the VSM late fusion baseline. Set 1 consists of those queries for which the MLMs outperform VSM late fusion, while set 2 contains queries for which the MLMs underperform VSM late fusion. We next examine *unimodal* VSM retrieval performance in terms of mAP@5 on the two query sets, using CC and using ASR. On set 1 queries, the mAP@5 for VSM using CC is 0.149 higher than VSM using ASR. However, on set 2 queries, the mAP@5 difference between VSM using CC and using ASR is 0.227. This substantial difference suggests that the retrieval utility of the ASR text is relatively low for the set 2 queries for which MLM retrieval performance is worse. At the same time, the analogous mAP@5 difference for PPT compared to OCR is 0.044 and -0.005 for set 1 and set 2, respectively. We thus observe a substantial performance gap between the two query sets using spoken text alone and a negligible gap using slide text alone. Therefore, when the quality of automatically extracted ASR text is better, we anticipate the MLMs in turn add greater value for retrieval.

6. CONCLUSIONS

We have proposed Multi-modal Language Models and a probabilistic ranking function for multi-modal video retrieval. We introduce a new dataset, the Google I/O dataset, that contains multi-modal lecture videos and text queries with ground truth relevance judgments. When using error-free PPT and CC transcripts for multi-modal retrieval, MLM significantly outperforms the well established retrieval methods VSM and PLSA. When only the automatically extracted OCR and ASR noisy text are available, our model performs similarly to the best benchmark method. Error analysis suggests that as the quality of the available text from ASR improves, MLMs can achieve additional gains in retrieval performance that surpass the benchmarks.

7. REFERENCES

[1] J. Adcock, M. Cooper, L. Denoue, H. Pirsiavash, and L. A. Rowe. Talkminer: A lecture webcast search engine. In *Proceedings of the International Conference on Multimedia*, MM '10, pages 241–250, 2010.

[2] K. Barnard, P. Duygulu, D. Forsyth, N. de Freitas, D. M. Blei, and M. I. Jordan. Matching words and pictures. *The Journal of Machine Learning Research*, 3:1107–1135, March 2003.

[3] D. M. Blei and M. I. Jordan. Modeling annotated data. In *Proceedings of the 26th Annual International ACM SIGIR Conference on Research and Development in Informaion Retrieval*, SIGIR '03, pages 127–134, 2003.

[4] D. M. Blei, A. Y. Ng, and M. I. Jordan. Latent dirichlet allocation. *The Journal of Machine Learning Research*, 3:993–1022, March 2003.

[5] B. Chen. Word topic models for spoken document retrieval and transcription. *ACM Transactions on Asian Language Information Processing*, 8(1):2:1–2:27, March 2009.

[6] Q. Fan, K. Barnard, A. Amir, and A. Efrat. Robust spatiotemporal matching of electronic slides to presentation videos. *IEEE Transactions on Image Processing*, 20:2315–2328, 2011.

[7] T. Hofmann. Unsupervised learning by probabilistic latent semantic analysis. *Machine Learning*, 42(1/2):177–196, January 2001.

[8] T. Kawahara, Y. Nemoto, and Y. Akita. Automatic lecture transcription by exploiting presentation slide information for language model adaptation. In *IEEE ICASSP*, 2008.

[9] R. Lienhart, S. Romberg, and E. Hörster. Multilayer plsa for multimodal image retrieval. In *Proceedings of the ACM International Conference on Image and Video Retrieval*, CIVR '09, pages 9:1–9:8, 2009.

[10] C. D. Manning, P. Raghavan, and H. Schütze. *Introduction to information retrieval.* Cambridge University Press, 2008.

[11] N. V. Nguyen, J.-M. Ogier, and F. Charneau. Bag of subjects: Lecture videos multimodal indexing. In *Proceedings of the 2013 ACM Symposium on Document Engineering*, pages 225–6, 2013.

[12] D. Putthividhya, H.T. Attias, and S.S. Nagarajan. Topic-regression multi-modal latent dirichlet allocation for image and video annotation. In *IEEE Computer Vision and Pattern Recognition*, 2010.

[13] N. Rasiwasia, J. C. Pereira, E. Coviello, G. Doyle, G. R. G. Lanckriet, R. Levy, and N. Vasconcelos. A new approach to cross-modal multimedia retrieval. In *Proceedings of the International Conference on Multimedia*, MM '10, pages 251–260. ACM, 2010.

[14] A. Vinciarelli and J. Odobez. Application of information retrieval technologies to presentation slides. *IEEE Transactions on Multimedia*, 8(5):981–995, 2006.

Food Detection and Recognition Using Convolutional Neural Network

Hokuto Kagaya
Graduate School of Interdisciplinary Information Studies
The University of Tokyo
kagaya@hal.t.u-tokyo.ac.jp

Kiyoharu Aizawa
Dept. Information and Communication Eng.
The University of Tokyo
aizawa@hal.t.u-tokyo.ac.jp

Makoto Ogawa
foo.log Inc.
ogawa@foo-log.co.jp

ABSTRACT

In this paper, we apply a convolutional neural network (CNN) to the tasks of detecting and recognizing food images. Because of the wide diversity of types of food, image recognition of food items is generally very difficult. However, deep learning has been shown recently to be a very powerful image recognition technique, and CNN is a state-of-the-art approach to deep learning. We applied CNN to the tasks of food detection and recognition through parameter optimization. We constructed a dataset of the most frequent food items in a publicly available food-logging system, and used it to evaluate recognition performance. CNN showed significantly higher accuracy than did traditional support-vector-machine-based methods with handcrafted features. In addition, we found that the convolution kernels show that color dominates the feature extraction process. For food image detection, CNN also showed significantly higher accuracy than a conventional method did.

Categories and Subject Descriptors

I.5.4 [**Computing Methodologies**]: Pattern recognition—*Computer Vision*; I.2.6 [**Artificial Intelligence**]: Learning—*Connectionism and neural nets*

General Terms

Experimentation

Keywords

deep learning; food recognition; food detection; convolutional neural network

1. INTRODUCTION

Diet is very important in human life. Obtaining adequate nutrition from everyday meals is essential for our health. To know what we eat, we often make a record of everyday meals. Such food recording is usually a manual exercise using textual description, but manual recording is tedious and time consuming. To overcome this difficulty, there have been attempts to assist food recording by using information technology. Image recognition of food items would be a good solution to food recording. Taking a picture would then be a sufficient record. However, we know that there is a wide diversity of types of food. Even within the same food category, there is considerable diversity. Therefore, despite the attempts at food item recognition, recognition performance is not yet satisfactory.

Regarding food image recognition, Zhu et al. [12] described food recognition using a small dataset, which was intended to be used in a smartphone-based food-logging system as part of their Technology Assisted Dietary Assessment project. Hoashi et al. [5] examined 85 food items, achieving 62.5% accuracy for the recognition of Japanese food images collected from the Web. They used multiple kernel learning for feature fusion as their machine learning method. The Pittsburgh Fast-Food Image Dataset [4] is a dataset of American fast-food images, which was used to evaluate a food-recognition method in [11, 6]. Food balance, an aspect of nutritional content, was estimated by image processing [2]. Image retrieval was applied to food recording [1].

Deep learning has recently been used in image recognition [8]. Deep learning is a collective term for algorithms having a deep architecture that solves complex problems. The most distinctive characteristic is that better image features for recognition are automatically extracted via training. The convolutional neural network (CNN) [9] is one of the methods that satisfy the requirements of the deep learning approach. CNN is now a state-of-the-art technique for image recognition challenges such as the Large Scale Visual Recognition Challenge [7].

In this paper, we apply CNN to the recognition and detection of food images and evaluate its performance. Our contributions are as follows: (1) we built a dataset for food recognition experiments by using food-domain images obtained from a food logging system available for public use; (2) we optimized CNN's hyper parameters, showing that CNN significantly improved the food recognition accuracy compared with a conventional method using a support vector machine (SVM) with hand-crafted features; (3) through observation of our trained CNN, we found that color features dominate the food recognition process; (4) we showed that CNN has significantly better performance for the task

MM'14, November 3–7, 2014, Orlando, Florida, USA.

http://dx.doi.org/10.1145/2647868.2654970.

of food detection when compared with a baseline method [2].

2. CONVOLUTIONAL NEURAL NETWORKS

The CNN [9] offers a state-of-the-art technique for image recognition. It is a multilayer neural network, whose neurons take small patches of the previous layer as input. It is robust against small shifts and rotations. A CNN system comprises a convolution layer and a pooling (or subsampling) layer.

In the convolution layer, unlike for general fully connected neural networks, weights can be considered as $n \times n$ ($n <$ input size) filters. Each input convolves these filters. Each layer has many filters that generate different outputs. For the image recognition task, the different features are extracted by these filters. The filters are often called (convolution) kernels.

The pooling layer produces the outputs by activation over rectangular regions. There are several activation methods, such as maximum activation and average activation. This makes the CNN's outputs more invariant with respect to position.

A typical CNN comprises multiple convolution and pooling layers, with a fully connected layer to produce the final result of the task. In image classification, each unit of the final layer indicates the class probability.

A CNN has hyper parameters that include the number of middle layers, the size of the convolution kernels, and the active functions. In this paper, we compare the optimization of some of these parameters. In our research, we use cuda-convnet[1], which is a GPU implementation of a CNN in C++ and Python, for the CNN library.

3. BUILDING A DATASET OF ORDINARY FOOD IMAGES

A number of images of ordinary meals are required for the evaluation of food item recognition. A meal image typically involves several food items. In the evaluation of food item recognition, each food item region of the image need to be identified and isolated for the dataset. Food-logging apps available for smartphones can produce very good data for this purpose: we made use of the data produced by FoodLog (FL) [1]. The general public can use FL for their own food recording using both photos and text. The user takes a photo of a meal, and specifies each region involving a food item via the touch panel display of the smartphone by inputting the name of the food item. The food item name is usually chosen from a standard food database. As a result, very clean data about image regions of named food items are produced. In our experiments with food recognition, the domains that users specified were slightly enlarged because users tend to specify undersized regions for the food items. FL is a publicly available app, and, with the number of users growing, the food item dataset is increasing. We collected approximately two months of recorded data from FL, following its launch in 2013. We used approximately 170,000 images. This data is from everyday meals logged by general public FL users. The diversity of the types of food was large and there was heavy bias towards some items. We chose the 10 most frequent food items from this data, as shown in Figure 1 and Table 1. From the table, note that there are more than 10,000 references to the most-frequent item, but only 900 to the least-frequent item. Training a CNN needs a number of data items, and we used these top 10 items for this purpose.

[1]`http://code.google.com/p/cuda-convnet/`

Figure 1: Examples of images used in the dataset.

Table 1: The 10 most-frequent food items on FL for two months.

Item	Quantity
Rice	11560
Miso soup	5786
Green salad	3603
Natto	2338
Yogurt	1724
Cold tofu	1434
Ramen	1070
Curry and rice	979
Grilled salmon	951
Deep-fried chicken	910

4. FOOD RECOGNITION

As mentioned in Section 2, CNN has hyper parameters related to the number of layers, training, preprocessing, and initialization. In this section, we describe the calibration of the number of layers and the number and size of kernels in each layer. In accordance with Krizhevsky's CNN [7], we use local response normalization (LRN) for the normalization after pooling layers. There are two types of LRN, involving either one map or across the maps.

We scaled the dataset images to 80×80. When training and testing, cuda-convnet's python module randomly cropped them to 64×64. We divided the dataset into six sets: four sets were used for training, one for validation, and one for testing. We conducted a 6-fold cross validation. For a comparison between CNN and existing techniques, we prepared three methods using SVM-based recognition using handcrafted features: (1) spatial pyramid matching (SPM) using a color histogram + SVM; (2) GIST features + SVM; (3) The ScSPM package [10], which is a SIFT–BoW-based method.

Table 2 shows the experimental results. The top line shows the average of the 10 trials with the same dataset and hyper parameters. The existing techniques used as baseline methods had about 50–60% accuracy, whereas the CNNs achieved more than 70%. The two-layer CNN performed better than did the three-layer and four-layer CNNs. With respect to kernel size, 5×5 was the best. Use of the two LRN types (same map or across maps) made almost no difference for this dataset. Figure 3 shows confusion matrices. Comparing color features, the accuracy with CNNs was im-

Table 2: **Accuracy of CNNs for various hyper-parameter values compared with three existing techniques.**

Layers	Number of kernels	Size of kernels	Normalization (LRN)	Dataset	Avg.	SD
2	32-32	9-7	1 time	Same dataset and parameters	72.39%	1.48%
*2	32-32	9x9, 7x7	1 time	6-fold cross validation	71.17%	0.83%
2	32-64	9x9, 7x7	1 time	6-fold cross validation	72.94%	0.68%
2	64-64	9x9, 7x7	1 time	6-fold cross validation	70.07%	2.98%
3	32-32-64	5x5, 5x5, 5x5	2 times	6-fold cross validation	69.82%	0.73%
4	32-32-32-64	7x7, 7x7, 5x5, 2x2	3 times	6-fold cross validation	66.57%	0.91%
2	32-32	7x7, 5x5	1 time	6-fold cross validation	72.86%	1.35%
2	32-32	5x5, 3x33	1 time	6-fold cross validation	72.88%	1.68%
2	32-32	5x5, 5x5	1 time	6-fold cross validation	73.69%	1.28%
2	32-32	5x5, 5x5	1 time	6-fold cross validation	**73.70%**	0.81%
SPM + Color + SVM				6-fold cross validation	54.63%	N.A.
GIST + SVM				6-fold cross validation	52.53%	N.A.
ScSPM				6-fold cross validation	60.47%	N.A.

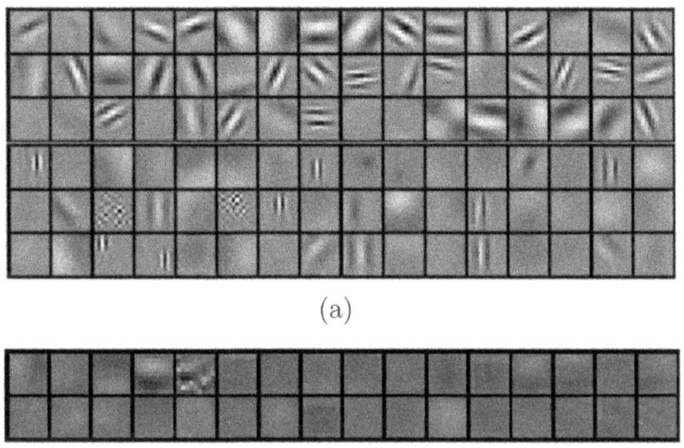

(a)

(b)

Figure 2: Convolution kernels trained using general images: (a) ImageNet [7]) and (b) food images.

	Natto	Yogurt	Green Salad	Deep-fried chicken	Rice	Ramen	Miso soup	Grilled salmon	Cold tofu	Curry and rice
Natto	60.11%	8.33%	2.44%	5.78%	3.33%	4.00%	2.89%	2.00%	6.11%	5.00%
Yogurt	4.89%	65.89%	4.44%	2.11%	7.89%	1.44%	2.67%	1.78%	8.56%	0.33%
Green salad	1.89%	3.11%	72.11%	2.78%	2.22%	7.22%	3.33%	2.67%	3.89%	0.78%
Deep-fried chicken	4.11%	1.67%	2.56%	70.00%	0.89%	3.22%	4.56%	6.22%	3.56%	3.22%
Rice	3.89%	5.33%	2.56%	1.33%	72.78%	2.22%	2.67%	1.33%	6.56%	1.33%
Ramen	3.33%	2.44%	8.00%	3.56%	2.11%	68.22%	3.67%	2.33%	3.56%	2.78%
Miso soup	1.33%	2.22%	3.22%	2.11%	1.56%	4.00%	78.22%	0.78%	4.00%	2.56%
Grilled salmon	2.44%	3.56%	2.44%	9.11%	2.33%	3.33%	1.89%	70.22%	3.78%	0.89%
Cold tofu	5.22%	8.22%	6.00%	4.22%	7.22%	3.89%	5.56%	1.44%	54.67%	3.56%
Curry and rice	2.89%	1.00%	1.44%	4.67%	2.78%	3.44%	2.67%	0.67%	2.00%	78.44%

(a) CNN

	Natto	Yogurt	Green Salad	Deep-fried chicken	Rice	Ramen	Miso soup	Grilled salmon	Cold tofu	Curry and rice
Natto	46.34%	10.00%	1.89%	6.77%	4.56%	4.67%	4.11%	4.22%	9.67%	7.78%
Yogurt	6.34%	61.77%	3.45%	1.89%	8.22%	1.56%	2.56%	4.00%	7.67%	2.56%
Green salad	1.67%	5.11%	56.98%	3.67%	3.33%	9.78%	5.44%	3.67%	8.56%	1.78%
Deep-fried chicken	7.56%	2.33%	2.22%	47.66%	0.78%	6.00%	6.00%	6.67%	5.11%	15.66%
Rice	4.78%	9.44%	2.22%	1.44%	61.23%	2.67%	3.78%	2.22%	10.00%	2.22%
Ramen	4.12%	2.45%	8.23%	5.78%	2.45%	57.62%	6.23%	4.12%	5.67%	3.34%
Miso soup	3.22%	3.11%	4.78%	6.45%	2.11%	5.00%	60.21%	2.22%	5.78%	7.11%
Grilled salmon	6.00%	5.44%	3.89%	7.89%	2.00%	4.22%	2.78%	57.42%	8.11%	2.22%
Cold tofu	6.34%	8.00%	8.56%	6.22%	14.89%	7.67%	5.33%	4.89%	35.01%	3.11%
Curry and rice	5.33%	2.22%	1.56%	12.34%	1.67%	2.78%	5.33%	1.22%	2.78%	64.79%

(b) Color SPM + SVM

Figure 3: Confusion matrices for CNN and one of the traditional techniques. Red cells show the class of high probability. Blue cells show confusion probabilities exceeds 10%.

proved for all items. The blue cells in the results for Color SPM + SVM show high confusion for some combinations of food items of similar colors such as "curry and rice" and "deep-fried chicken." For CNN, the confusion of these items is much reduced.

We obtained additional insights from these results. Figure 2 shows examples of the convolution kernels after the training. The convolution kernels for CNN show the features that are extracted. In the kernels for general images such as ImageNet's images [7], we find edge-specific kernels. However, for food images, almost all the kernels are color-specific. This observation suggests that color features are dominant in food image recognition. This is in agreement with Bosch's report [3], where color features were the best of the handcrafted features for food recognition.

5. FOOD DETECTION

In this section, we consider the food detection task. This is different from food item recognition in that food detection is a binary classification of food and non-food images. Given a whole image that may contain food and background, food detection classifies the image as food or non-food. We conducted an experiment to evaluate CNN's performance.

For this detection task, we used a different dataset because of having to include non-food images. We used 1,234 general food images and 1,980 non-food images, including human faces and landscapes, as the experimental dataset. They were collected from social media. The input images were scaled down to 80 × 80 and cropped to 64 × 64 pixels randomly by the cuda-convnet python module. For comparison, the baseline was the food detection system used by FL [2]. This method uses an SVM as the classifier and employs color features, circular boundary features, and SIFT–BoW features as image features. In our experiment using CNN, we divided all food and non-food images in the dataset into 10 groups. Eight groups were used for training, one for validation and one for testing. Training ended when the validation error ceased to evolve. We used the hyper parameters marked with "*" in Table 2. We conducted 10-fold cross

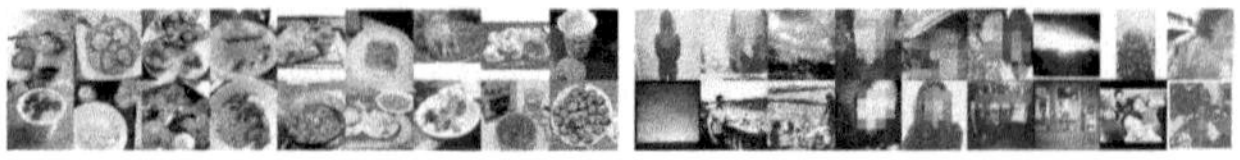

(a) (b)

Figure 4: Examples of images for the detection task: (a) food images and (b) non-food images.

Table 3: Comparison between CNN and the baseline method for the detection task.

Method	Accuracy
Baseline	$89.7 \pm 0.73\%$
CNN	$\mathbf{93.8 \pm 1.39\%}$

validation. For the experiment using the baseline method, we randomly selected the same number (1,200) of food images and non-food images, with 1,000 being used for training the SVM and the remaining 200 being used for testing. We computed the average result over 15 trials.

Table 3 compares the accuracy of the baseline method and CNN, with CNN achieving 93.8% accuracy, which is significantly higher than that for the baseline method. Figure 5 shows some examples of images incorrectly detected by CNN. These images would seem to be hard to detect, even by human observation.

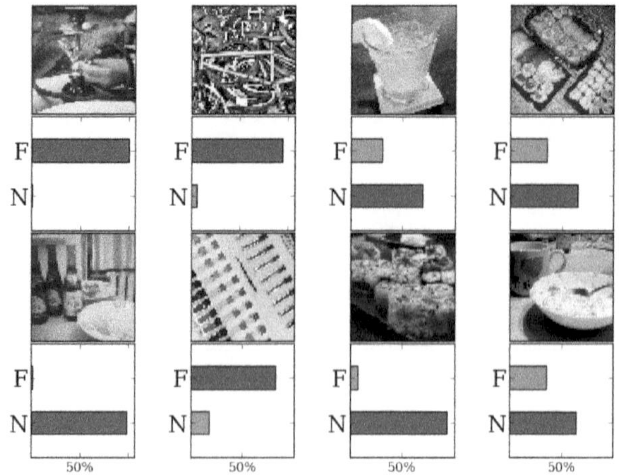

Figure 5: Examples of detection errors. Bar graphs show the class probability, with "F" meaning food, and "N" meaning non-food. Red bars indicate correct class probability, and blue bars indicate predicted (mistaken) class probability.

6. CONCLUSIONS

In this paper, we have addressed the effectiveness of CNNs for food image recognition and detection. First, we built a food image dataset from images uploaded by a large number of real users. Second, we applied CNN to the recognition of 10 food items and evaluated its performance. We found that CNN performed much better than did traditional methods using handcrafted features. Third, through observation of trained convolution kernels, we confirmed that color features are essential to food image recognition. Fourth, we applied CNN to food detection, finding that CNN significantly outperformed a baseline method.

7. ACKNOWLEDGMENTS

This work was partially supported by JST CREST and JSPS Grant-in-Aid for Scientific Research (B).

8. REFERENCES

[1] K. Aizawa, K. Maeda, M. Ogawa, Y. Sato, M. Kasamatsu, K. Waki, and H. Takimoto. Comparative study of the routine daily usability of foodlog: A smartphone-based food recording tool assisted by image retrieval. *Journal of Diabetes Science and Technology*, 8(2):203–208, 2014.

[2] K. Aizawa, Y. Maruyama, H. Li, and G. de Silva. Food balance estimation by using personal dietary tendencies in a multimedia food log. *IEEE Trans. Multimedia*, 15(8):2176–2185, 2013.

[3] M. Bosch, F. Zhu, N. Khanna, C. J. Boushey, and E. J. Delp. Combining global and local features for food identification in dietary assessment. In *IEEE ICIP*, pages 1789–1792, 2011.

[4] M. Chen, K. Dhingra, W. Wu, L. Yang, R. Sukthankar, and J. Yang. Pfid: Pittsburgh fast-food image dataset. In *IEEE ICIP*, 2009.

[5] H. Hoashi, T. Joutou, and K. Yanai. Image recognition of 85 food categories by feature fusion. In *IEEE ISM*, pages 296–301, 2010.

[6] F. Kong and J. Tan. Dietcam: Regular shape food recognition with a camera phone. In *IEEE BSN*, pages 127–132, 2011.

[7] A. Krizhevsky, I. Sutskever, and G. Hinton. Imagenet classification with deep convolutional neural networks. In *NIPS*, pages 1106–1114, 2012.

[8] Q. Le, M. Ranzato, R. Monga, M. Devin, K. Chen, G. Corrado, J. Dean, and A. Ng. Building high-level features using large scale unsupervised learning. In *ICML*, 2012.

[9] Y. LeCun, L. Bottou, Y. Bengio, and P. Haffner. Gradient-based learning applied to document recognition. *Proceedings of the IEEE*, 86(11):2278–2324, 1998.

[10] J. Yang, K. Yu, Y. Gong, and T. Huang. Linear spatial pyramid matching using sparse coding for image classification. In *IEEE CVPR*, pages 1794–1801. IEEE, 2009.

[11] S. Yang, M. Chen, D. Pomerleau, and R. Sukthankar. Food recognition using statistics of pairwise local features. In *IEEE CVPR*, pages 2249–2256, 2010.

[12] F. Zhu, M. Bosch, I. Woo, S. Kim, C. J. Boushey, D. S. Ebert, and E. J. Delp. The use of mobile devices in aiding dietary assessment and evaluation. *IEEE Journal of Selected Topics in Signal Processing*, 4(4):756–766, 2010.

Locality Preserving Discriminative Hashing

Kang Zhao, Hongtao Lu*, Yangcheng He, Shaokun Feng
Key Laboratory of Shanghai Education Commission for Intelligent Interaction and Cognitive Engineering
Department of Computer Science and Engineering, Shanghai Jiao Tong University, P.R.China
{sjtuzk, htlu, clustering, superkkking}@sjtu.edu.cn

ABSTRACT

Hashing for large scale similarity search has become more and more popular because of its improvement in computational speed and storage reduction. Semi-supervised Hashing (SSH) has been proven effective since it integrates both labeled and unlabeled data to leverage semantic similarity while keeping robust to overfitting. However, it ignores the global label information and the local structure of the feature space. In this paper, we concentrate on these two issues and propose a novel semi-supervised hashing method called *Locality Preserving Discriminative Hashing* which combines two classical dimensionality reduction approaches, Linear Discriminant Analysis (LDA) and Locality Preserving Projection (LPP). The proposed method presents a rigorous formulation in which the supervised term tries to maintain the global information of the labeled data while the unsupervised term provides effective regularization to model local relationships of the unlabeled data. We apply an efficient sequential procedure to learn the hashing functions. Experimental comparisons with other state-of-the-art methods on three large scale datasets demonstrate the effectiveness and efficiency of our method.

Categories and Subject Descriptors

H.3 [**Information Storage and Retrieval**]: Content Analysis and Indexing, Information Search and Retrieval; I.2.6 [**Artificial Intelligence**]: Learning

Keywords

Similarity Search; Semi-Supervised Learning; Linear Discriminant Analysis; Locality Preserving Projection

1. INTRODUCTION

The explosive growth of the vision data on the internet has posed a great challenge to many applications in terms of fast similarity search. To handle this problem, hashing based approximate nearest neighbor (ANN) search techniques have recently become more and more popular because of their improvements in computational speed and storage reduction. One of the most popular methods is Locality Sensitive Hashing (LSH) [4]. It makes use of random projections to computer the binary codes of data such that similar codes will be mapped to the same bucket with high probability.

Following LSH, many hashing methods based on unsupervised or supervised learning have been proposed over the last decade. Binary Reconstructive Embedding (BRE) [8] learns the hash functions by minimizing a cost function that measures the difference between the metric and reconstructive distance in Hamming space. LDAHash (LDAH) [10] is proposed to make the Hamming distance minimized between positive pairs and maximized between negative pairs. Another well-designed method is Semi-supervised Hashing (SSH) [11] which minimizes the empirical error on the labeled pairs and maximizes the information theoretic regularization on all data. Unlike the above methods, SSH integrates both label and unlabel information, so it can not only leverage semantic similarity but also keep robust to overfitting. Although SSH is able to generate high-quality hash codes, it just considers pair-wise relations between labeled instances, ignoring the global label information. Further, the maximum variance constraints on all data can not well preserve the neighborhood structure of the feature space.

In this paper, we concentrate on these two issues and propose a novel semi-supervised hashing algorithm named Locality Preserving Discriminative Hashing (LPDH) which combines two classical techniques, Linear Discriminant Analysis (LDA) and Locality Preserving Projection (LPP), to preserve the global and local structures simultaneously. More specifically, we present a rigorous formulation in which the supervised term tries to maintain the global information of the labeled data while the unsupervised term provides effective regularization to model local relationships of the unlabeled data. With an efficient sequential solution to the proposed problem, our method has achieved promising performance on three huge datasets.

Similar to our work, Locally Linear Hashing (LLH) [6] also tries to capture the manifold structure of datasets. But it focuses on the unlabel information of data, *i.e.*, it is unsupervised, differing from our semi-supervised method.

2. RELATED WORK

In this section, we introduce two dimensionality reduction methods, which are closely related to our approach.

*Corresponding author.

MM'14, November 03-07, 2014, Orlando, FL, USA.

http://dx.doi.org/10.1145/2647868.2654971.

2.1 Linear Discriminant Analysis

Linear Discriminant Analysis (LDA) [2, 3] is a popular supervised dimensionality reduction approach. It can efficiently capture the global geometric structure of data. Given a dataset with n samples $\{\mathbf{x}_i, \mathbf{l}_i\}_{i=1}^{n}$ and c classes, where $\mathbf{x}_i \in \mathbb{R}^d$ and $\mathbf{l}_i \in \{0,1\}^c$. Let $l_i(k)$ be the k-th element of $\mathbf{l}_i$. $l_i(k) = 1$, if $\mathbf{x}_i$ is a member of the k-th class; $l_i(k) = 0$, otherwise. By maximizing the following objective function, LDA aims to find a projection matrix $\mathbf{W} = [\mathbf{w}_1, ..., \mathbf{w}_r] \in \mathbb{R}^{d\times r}$ that makes the data points from the same class are close while those from different classes are far away:

$$\mathbf{W}^* = \arg\max_{\mathbf{W}} \frac{tr\{\mathbf{W}^\top \mathbf{S}_b \mathbf{W}\}}{tr\{\mathbf{W}^\top \mathbf{S}_w \mathbf{W}\}}, \tag{1}$$

where $tr\{\cdot\}$ is the trace of a matrix, the matrices $\mathbf{S}_b$ and $\mathbf{S}_w$ that are usually referred to as between-class scatter matrix and within-class scatter matrix are given below:

$$\mathbf{S}_b = \sum_{k=1}^{c} n_k (\mathbf{x}^{(k)} - \mathbf{x})(\mathbf{x}^{(k)} - \mathbf{x})^\top,$$
$$\mathbf{S}_w = \sum_{k=1}^{c}\sum_{i=1}^{n_k} (\mathbf{x}_i^{(k)} - \mathbf{x}^{(k)})(\mathbf{x}_i^{(k)} - \mathbf{x}^{(k)})^\top, \tag{2}$$

where $\mathbf{x}^{(k)}$ is the k-th class mean vector, $\mathbf{x}$ is the centroid of all samples, $\mathbf{x}_i^{(k)}$ is the i-th sample in the k-th class and n_k denotes the number of samples in the k-th class.

2.2 Locality Preserving Projection

Locality Preserving Projection (LPP) [5] is proposed to capture the linear local structure of a dataset. Assume the dataset $\mathbf{X} = [\mathbf{x}_1, \mathbf{x}_2, \cdots, \mathbf{x}_n]^\top \in \mathbb{R}^{n\times d}$ has n data points. LPP first constructs an affinity matrix $\mathbf{A}$, whose entry A_{ij}, representing the similarity of data $\mathbf{x}_i$ and $\mathbf{x}_j$, is defined as follows:

$$A_{ij} = \begin{cases} \exp(\frac{\|\mathbf{x}_i - \mathbf{x}_j\|^2}{\sigma}), & \mathbf{x}_i \in \mathcal{N}_k(\mathbf{x}_j) \ or \ \mathbf{x}_j \in \mathcal{N}_k(\mathbf{x}_i), \\ 0, & otherwise, \end{cases} \tag{3}$$

where $\mathcal{N}_k(\mathbf{x})$ denotes the k-nearest neighbors of $\mathbf{x}$. Let $\mathbf{P} = [\mathbf{p}_1, \cdots, \mathbf{p}_n]^\top \in \mathbb{R}^{n\times r}$ be the projection of all data, i.e., $\mathbf{p}_i = \mathbf{W}^\top \mathbf{x}_i$. Then LPP minimizes the following objective function:

$$\sum_{ij} A_{ij} \|\mathbf{p}_i - \mathbf{p}_j\|^2. \tag{4}$$

Empirically, if $\mathbf{x}_i$ and $\mathbf{x}_j$ are close then $\mathbf{p}_i$ and $\mathbf{p}_j$ will be close as well [5]. It is easy to show that

$$\frac{1}{2}\sum_{ij} A_{ij} \|\mathbf{p}_i - \mathbf{p}_j\|^2 = tr\{\mathbf{P}^\top \mathbf{L} \mathbf{P}\}, \tag{5}$$

where $\mathbf{L} = \mathbf{D} - \mathbf{A}$ is the Laplacian matrix and $\mathbf{D} = diag(\mathbf{A1})$.

3. THE PROPOSED APPROACH

To facilitate our discussion, some notations are given first. Assume we have a dataset $\mathbf{X} \in \mathbb{R}^{n\times d}$, in which a fraction of samples $\mathbf{X}_m = [\mathbf{x}_1, \mathbf{x}_2, \cdots, \mathbf{x}_m]^\top \in \mathbb{R}^{m\times d}$ $(n \gg m)$ are associated with label information $\{\mathbf{l}_i\}_{i=1}^{m}$. Considering the consistency of global and local structures, we use $\mathbf{X}_m$ as training set for both label and unlabel information. Let $\mathbf{Y}_m = [\mathbf{y}_1, \mathbf{y}_2, \cdots, \mathbf{y}_m]^\top \in \mathbb{R}^{m\times r}$ be the r-bit Hamming embedding of $\mathbf{X}_m$. The hash code of the sample $\mathbf{x}_i$ is obtained by a linear transformation followed by a sign function:

$$\mathbf{y}_i = sgn(\mathbf{W}^\top \mathbf{x}_i + \mathbf{b}), \tag{6}$$

where $\mathbf{b} \in \mathbb{R}^r$ is a bias and $\mathbf{W} \in \mathbb{R}^{d\times r}$ is the projection matrix we are going to learn. Without loss of generality, we assume $\mathbf{X}_m$ is zero centered, i.e., $\sum_{i=1}^{m} \mathbf{x}_i = \mathbf{0}$, then $\mathbf{b} = -\frac{1}{m}\sum_{i=1}^{m} \mathbf{W}^\top \mathbf{x}_i = \mathbf{0}$ is ignored in our work. $\mathbf{L}_m, \mathbf{A}_m$ and $\mathbf{D}_m \in \mathbb{R}^{m\times m}$ denote the corresponding Laplacian, affinity and degree matrices of $\mathbf{X}_m$ as defined in prior sections.

3.1 Objective Function

Modeling the local geometrical structure as a regularization term and adding it into the classical LDA framework, we maximize the following function:

$$H(\mathbf{Y}_m, \mathbf{W}) = \frac{tr\{\mathbf{W}^\top \mathbf{S}_b \mathbf{W}\}}{tr\{\mathbf{W}^\top \mathbf{S}_w \mathbf{W} + \rho \mathbf{Y}_m^\top \mathbf{L}_m \mathbf{Y}_m\}}, \tag{7}$$

where ρ is a tradeoff parameter. Such formulation forces the learned hash functions to maximize the between-class distance while minimizing both the within-class distance and the average projection distance between similar neighbors. Consequently, it preserves the global and local structures simultaneously. Note that LDAH only preserves the local structure on the labeled data with pair-wise distance that is quite different from our method.

Motivated by Spectral Hashing (SH) [12], we would like the hash bits to be balanced and uncorrelated with each other, so we have the following problem:

$$\max_{\mathbf{Y}_m, \mathbf{W}} \ H(\mathbf{Y}_m, \mathbf{W}) \tag{8}$$
$$s.t. \ \mathbf{Y}_m \in \{-1,1\}^{m\times r}, \mathbf{Y}_m^\top \mathbf{1} = \mathbf{0}, \mathbf{Y}_m^\top \mathbf{Y}_m = m\mathbf{I}_{r\times r}.$$

3.2 Solving Algorithm

Similar to SSH, we relax the binary constraints $\mathbf{Y}_m \in \{-1,1\}^{m\times r}$ as $\mathbf{Y}_m = \mathbf{X}_m\mathbf{W}$. Then, it is easy to show that the constraints $\mathbf{Y}_m^\top \mathbf{1} = (\mathbf{X}_m\mathbf{W})^\top \mathbf{1} = \mathbf{0}$ will always hold since $\mathbf{X}_m$ is zero centered. We now rewrite our hashing formulation as:

$$\max_{\mathbf{W}} \frac{tr\{\mathbf{W}^\top \mathbf{S}_b \mathbf{W}\}}{tr\{\mathbf{W}^\top \mathbf{S}_t \mathbf{W}\}} \ s.t. \ \mathbf{W}^\top \mathbf{X}_m^\top \mathbf{X}_m \mathbf{W} = m\mathbf{I}_{r\times r}, \tag{9}$$

where $\mathbf{S}_t = \mathbf{S}_w + \rho \mathbf{X}_m^\top \mathbf{L}_m \mathbf{X}_m$.

If we neglect the relaxed decorrelation constraints $\mathbf{W}^\top \mathbf{X}_m^\top \mathbf{X}_m \mathbf{W} = m\mathbf{I}_{r\times r}$, the above optimization problem can be solved by applying an generalized eigen-decomposition on the matrix $\mathbf{S}_t^{-1}\mathbf{S}_b$. However, the performance may be deteriorated without guarantee of low correlation between each projection direction. Besides, the matrix $\mathbf{S}_t^{-1}\mathbf{S}_b$ has at most $c-1$ eigenvectors corresponding to nonzero eigenvalues [3], resulting in the number of hash bits r being bounded by $c-1$, which is infeasible in hashing algorithm. For our approach, we keep the constraints and adopt a sequential procedure to learn the hash functions inspired by [7].

The decorrelation constraints $\mathbf{Y}_m^\top \mathbf{Y}_m = m\mathbf{I}_{r\times r}$ are always satisfied in the diagonal elements, since $sgn(\mathbf{w}_j^\top \mathbf{x}_i) sgn(\mathbf{w}_j^\top \mathbf{x}_i) = 1$ $(1 \le i \le m, 1 \le j \le r)$. Thus we only consider the off-diagonal elements in the constraints $\mathbf{W}^\top \mathbf{X}_m^\top \mathbf{X}_m \mathbf{W} = m\mathbf{I}_{r\times r}$ as in [7], which require

$$\mathbf{w}_i^\top \mathbf{X}_m^\top \mathbf{X}_m \mathbf{w}_j = 0, \ i = 2, ..., r \ and \ j = 1, ..., i-1. \tag{10}$$

The idea of sequential learning is very intuitive. At each iteration, it only involves learning one projection $\mathbf{w}_i$ by forc-

Algorithm 1 Locality Preserving Discriminative Hashing (LPDH)

Input: data $\mathbf{X}_m = [\mathbf{x}_1, \mathbf{x}_2, \cdots, \mathbf{x}_m]^\top$ and label $\{\mathbf{l}_i\}_{i=1}^m$; parameters ρ, α and γ; number of hash bits r.

Output: projection matrix $\mathbf{W}$.

1: Constructing two scatter matrices $\mathbf{S}_b$ and $\mathbf{S}_w$ by (2).

2: Constructing the Laplacian matrix $\mathbf{L}_m$ by $\mathbf{L}_m = \mathbf{D}_m - \mathbf{A}_m$, where $\mathbf{A}_m$ is given by (3) and $\mathbf{D}_m = diag(\mathbf{A}_m\mathbf{1})$.

3: $\mathbf{w}_1 \leftarrow$ the largest eigenvector of $(\mathbf{S}_w + \rho\mathbf{X}_m^\top\mathbf{L}_m\mathbf{X}_m)^{-1}\mathbf{S}_b$.

4: **for** $i = 2, ..., r$ **do**

5: $\quad\mathbf{w}_i \leftarrow$ the largest eigenvector of matrix $(\mathbf{S}_w + \rho\mathbf{X}_m^\top\mathbf{L}_m\mathbf{X}_m + \alpha\sum_{j=1}^{i-1}\gamma^{i-j}\mathbf{X}_m^\top\mathbf{X}_m\mathbf{w}_j\mathbf{w}_j^\top\mathbf{X}_m^\top\mathbf{X}_m)^{-1}\mathbf{S}_b$.

6: **end for**

ing it to satisfy the constraints (10) globally with the previously learned projections $\mathbf{w}_1, ..., \mathbf{w}_{i-1}$. And in order to avoid the "hard orthogonality constraints" stated in SSH, a weight parameter is introduced to de-emphasizes the decorrelation requirements between $\mathbf{w}_i$ and earlier-computed projection vectors. More specifically, we convert (10) into a penalty term added to the objective function in (9) and determine $\mathbf{w}_i$ by solving

$$\max_{\mathbf{w}_i} \frac{\mathbf{w}_i^\top\mathbf{S}_b\mathbf{w}_i}{\mathbf{w}_i^\top\mathbf{S}_t\mathbf{w}_i + \alpha\sum_{j=1}^{i-1}\gamma^{i-j}(\mathbf{w}_i^\top\mathbf{X}_m^\top\mathbf{X}_m\mathbf{w}_j)^2} \quad (11)$$
$$s.t.\ \ \mathbf{w}_i^\top\mathbf{w}_i = 1,$$

where α is a tuning parameter and $\gamma \in (0, 1)$ is the weight parameter mentioned above. Then the sequential objective function in (11) can be rewritten as

$$\frac{\mathbf{w}_i^\top\mathbf{S}_b\mathbf{w}_i}{\mathbf{w}_i^\top\mathbf{S}_t\mathbf{w}_i + \alpha\sum_{j=1}^{i-1}\gamma^{i-j}(\mathbf{w}_i^\top\mathbf{X}_m^\top\mathbf{X}_m\mathbf{w}_j)^2} \quad (12)$$
$$=\frac{\mathbf{w}_i^\top\mathbf{S}_b\mathbf{w}_i}{\mathbf{w}_i^\top(\mathbf{S}_t + \alpha\sum_{j=1}^{i-1}\gamma^{i-j}\mathbf{X}_m^\top\mathbf{X}_m\mathbf{w}_j\mathbf{w}_j^\top\mathbf{X}_m^\top\mathbf{X}_m)\mathbf{w}_i} \quad (13)$$
$$=\frac{\mathbf{w}_i^\top\mathbf{S}_b\mathbf{w}_i}{\mathbf{w}_i^\top\mathbf{S}_t^{(i)}\mathbf{w}_i}, \quad (14)$$

where $\mathbf{S}_t^{(i)} = \mathbf{S}_t + \alpha\sum_{j=1}^{i-1}\gamma^{i-j}\mathbf{X}_m^\top\mathbf{X}_m\mathbf{w}_j\mathbf{w}_j^\top\mathbf{X}_m^\top\mathbf{X}_m$.

One can get the solution by computing the eigenvector of $(\mathbf{S}_t^{(i)})^{-1}\mathbf{S}_b$ with the largest eigenvalue. It is noted that the inverse operation requires matrix $\mathbf{S}_t^{(i)}$ to be nonsingular, which does not hold when the dimensions of data are larger than the number of samples [1]. In practice, for an application in need of large scale similarity search, its data size will far exceed their dimensions. Furthermore, one can use pesudo-inverse instead, if the experimental dataset is quite small.

The proposed sequential learning procedure can efficiently solve the upper bound of eigenvectors problem aforementioned, because at each eigen-decomposition, we just need to compute the largest eigenvector of the target matrix. The whole procedure of LPDH is summarized in Algorithm 1.

3.3 Complexity Analysis

The computational cost for LPDH mainly consists of two parts, matrices calculations and the learning procedure. The matrices calculations are for deriving matrices $\mathbf{S}_b$, $\mathbf{S}_w$ and $\mathbf{L}_m$, which require computations in the order of $O(cd^2)$, $O(md^2)$ and $O(m^2d)$. In the sequential learning procedure, matrix inversion and eigenvalue decomposition both cost $O(d^3)$, $\mathbf{X}_m^\top\mathbf{L}_m\mathbf{X}_m$ and $\mathbf{X}_m^\top\mathbf{X}_m$ can be computed in advance, thus, the time complexity is $O(r(d^3 + rd^2))$. In summary, the total time complexity for training LPDH is bounded by $O(cd^2 + md^2 + m^2d + r(d^3 + rd^2))(m \ll n)$. Experimental results prove our algorithm is scalable.

4. EXPERIMENTS

Our LPDH is essentially semi-supervised, for fair comparison, we mainly compare our method with SSH (we implement the orthogonal (*Orth*), non-orthogonal (*Nonorth*) and sequential (*Sqlh*) algorithms, respectively) and some baselines: Binary Reconstructive Embedding (BRE), LDAHash (LDAH). For LPDH, (10) is converted to a quadratic term leading α to be sensitive to the datasets. So, we normalize the training data before making them zero centered and choose α from $\{10^{-2}, 10^{-1}, 1, 10, 10^2\}$ which yields the best performance by 5-fold cross-validation. Other parameters are given as $\rho = 1$ and $\gamma = 0.9$.

4.1 Datasets and Evaluation Protocols

We have conducted experiments on three well known datasets, **Yale**, **MNIST** and **CIFAR-10**. Yale includes 2432 grayscale face images of 38 people under 64 different angles.[1] We resize each image to 24×21 and use their gray-scale intensity values as features ($d = 504$). MNIST contains 70K 28×28 handwritten digit samples from digit 0 to 9.[2] For each image, we also use the intensity values as features ($d = 784$). CIFAR-10 consists of 60K 32×32 color images in 10 classes, with 6K images per class.[3] We convert each image to a 512D GIST feature [9]. For all datasets, a small number of images are used as query test (200 for Yale, 1K for MNIST and CIFAR-10) and the rest are for training. In addition, we randomly select some images with labels ($m = 200$ for Yale, $m = 2000$ for MNIST and CIFAR-10) from the training set and assign pair-wise semantic information for BRE, LDAH, SSH, and class-wise semantic information for our LPDH based on the image labels.

The true neighbors are defined as when the returned image and the query image share the same semantic labels. We use *Hamming ranking* for quantitative performance measurement as in [11], and then compute the precision and recall curves.

4.2 Results and Discussions

For all three datasets, we present the Precision-Recall curves for 32-bit codes and the precision of returned samples with different length of hash bits in Figures 1, 2 and 3, respectively. From these figures, we find *Orth* performs better on Yale, but nearly has the worst performance on MNIST and CIFAR-10, *i.e.*, it is very sensitive to the datasets. In contrast, our LPDH method outperforms all other state-of-the-art methods on each dataset and each code size, proving its efficiency and stability. *Sqlh* performs almost the second best (except in Yale), since it adopts a similar but different sequential learning procedure just like our LPDH, which can quantify the relationships between each hash function to make them global optimal. As the experimental results illus-

[1] http://vision.ucsd.edu/~leekc/ExtYaleDatabase/ExtYaleB.html

[2] http://yann.lecun.com/exdb/mnist/

[3] http://www.cs.toronto.edu/~kriz/cifar.html

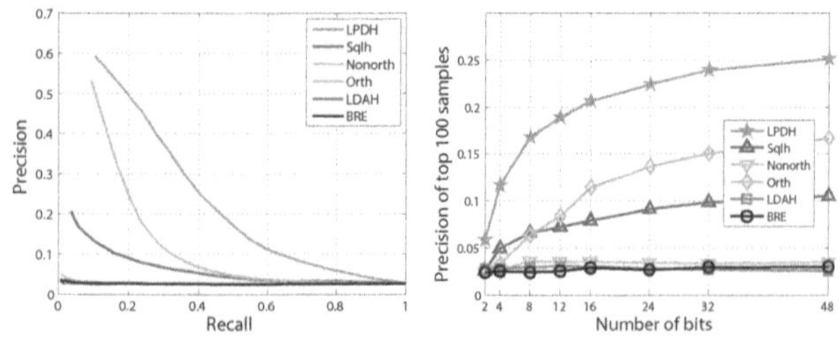

(a) (b)

Figure 1: Results on Yale; (a) Pre-Rec curves; (b) Precision of top 100 samples vs. number of bits.

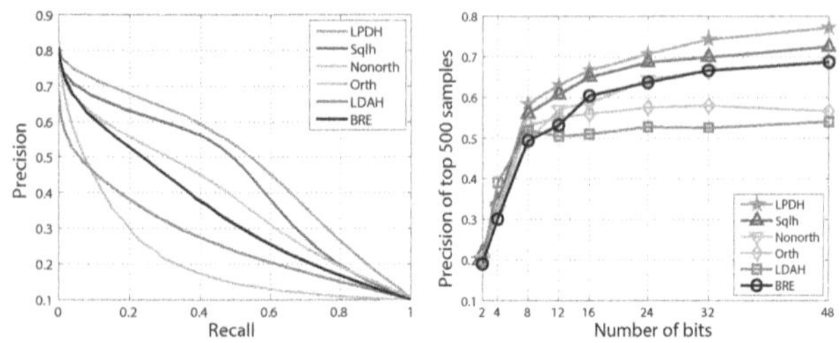

(a) (b)

Figure 2: Results on MNIST; (a) Pre-Rec curves; (b) Precision of top 500 samples vs. number of bits.

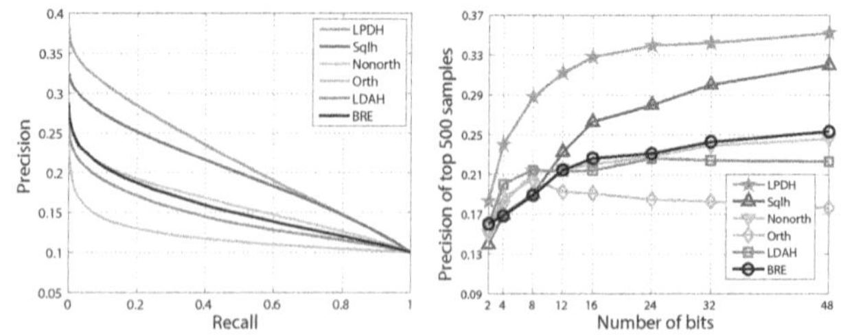

(a) (b)

Figure 3: Results on CIFAR-10; (a) Pre-Rec curves; (b) Precision of top 500 samples vs. number of bits.

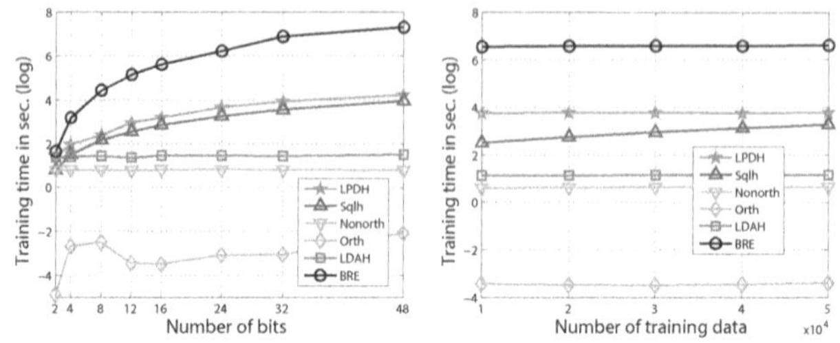

(a) (b)

Figure 4: Training time on CIFAR-10; (a) Time vs. number of bits; (b) Time vs. number of data.

trate, our semi-supervised strategy that preserves the global and local structures simultaneously is more reasonable.

Finally, we record the training time on CIFAR-10. Due to the sequential learning procedure for better performance, LPDH and *Sqlh* need more time than the most hashing methods, but they are still faster than BRE. Considering the large scale similarity search and the learning process running totally off-line, the time of all above methods is acceptable. We skip the test time comparisons, since their query processes are similar and efficient.

5. CONCLUSIONS

In this paper, we have presented a novel semi-supervised hashing method named Locality Preserving Discriminative Hashing which combines two classical dimensionality reduction approaches, LDA and LPP, to preserve the global and local structures simultaneously. Then we apply a sequential procedure to learn the hash functions by successive maximizing local variances subject to decorrelation constraints. Experimental results on three huge datasets demonstrate the effectiveness and efficiency of our method.

6. ACKNOWLEDGMENTS

This work is supported by NSFC (No.61272247 and 6087 3133), the Science and Technology Commission of Shanghai Municipality (Grant No.13511500200), 863 (No.2008AA02Z3 10) in China and the European Union Seventh Frame work Programme (Grant No.247619).

7. REFERENCES

[1] C. M. Bishop et al. *Pattern recognition and machine learning*, volume 1. springer New York, 2006.

[2] R. O. Duda, P. E. Hart, and D. G. Stork. *Pattern classification*. John Wiley & Sons, 2012.

[3] K. Fukunaga. *Introduction to statistical pattern recognition*. Academic press, 1990.

[4] A. Gionis, P. Indyk, R. Motwani, et al. Similarity search in high dimensions via hashing. In *VLDB*, pages 518–529, 1999.

[5] X. He and P. Niyogi. Locality preserving projections. In *NIPS*, 2003.

[6] G. Irie, Z. Li, X.-M. Wu, and S.-F. Chang. Locally linear hashing for extracting non-linear manifolds. In *CVPR*, 2014.

[7] S. Kim, Y. Kang, and S. Choi. Sequential spectral learning to hash with multiple representations. In *ECCV*, pages 538–551. Springer-Verlag, 2012.

[8] B. Kulis and T. Darrell. Learning to hash with binary reconstructive embeddings. In *NIPS*, volume 22, pages 1042–1050, 2009.

[9] A. Oliva and A. Torralba. Modeling the shape of the scene: A holistic representation of the spatial envelope. *International journal of computer vision*, 42(3):145–175, 2001.

[10] C. Strecha, A. M. Bronstein, M. M. Bronstein, and P. Fua. Ldahash: Improved matching with smaller descriptors. *IEEE Transactions on Pattern Analysis and Machine Intelligence*, 34(1):66–78, 2012.

[11] J. Wang, S. Kumar, and S.-F. Chang. Semi-supervised hashing for large-scale search. *IEEE Trans. on Pattern Analysis and Machine Intelligence*, 34(12):2393–2406, 2012.

[12] Y. Weiss, A. Torralba, and R. Fergus. Spectral hashing. In *NIPS*, pages 1753–1760, 2008.

Augmented Image Retrieval using Multi-Order Object Layout with Attributes

Xiaochun Cao[1,2], Xingxing Wei[1,*], Xiaojie Guo[2], Yahong Han[1], Jinhui Tang[3]
[1]School of Computer Science and Technology, Tianjin University.
[2]State Key Laboratory of Information Security, IIE, CAS.
[3]School of Computer Science and Engineering, Nanjing University of Science and Technology.
{caoxiaochun, guoxiaojie}@iie.ac.cn, {xwei, yahong}@tju.edu.cn, jinhuitang@mail.njust.edu.cn

ABSTRACT

In image retrieval, users' search intention is usually specified by textual queries, exemplar images, concept maps, and even sketches, which can only express the search intention partially. These query strategies lack the abilities to indicate the Regions Of Interests (ROIs) and represent the spatial or semantic correlations among the ROIs, which results in the so-called semantic gap between users' search intention and images' low-level visual content. In this paper, we propose a novel image search method, which allows the users to indicate any number of Regions Of Interest (ROIs) within the query as well as utilize various semantic concepts and spatial relations to search images. Specifically, we firstly propose a structured descriptor to jointly represent the categories, attributes, and spatial relations among objects. Then, based on the defined descriptor, our method ranks the images in the database according to the matching scores *w.r.t.* the category, attribute, and spatial relations. We conduct the experiments on the aPascal and aYahoo datasets, and experimental results show the advantage of the proposed method compared to the state of the arts.

Categories and Subject Descriptors

H.3 [**Information Storage and Retrieval**]: Content Analysis and Indexing; Information Search and Retrieval.

Keywords

Image retrieval; Attribute; Region of interest; Object layout

1. INTRODUCTION

Image retrieval plays an important role in enabling people to easily access to the desired images. A variety of retrieval methods have been developed. The input is of various forms such as text [11], image [5], and sketch [1, 2], to represent the query. However, these query strategies can only express the users' search intention partially. For instance, given the query image in Figure 1, users may be interested in the regions of "car", "tree", and "building" (highlighted with the rectangular boxes). These regions attract users' attention because the "car" is above the "building" and "tree" in the vertical direction, which is not coincident with the usual scenario. This abnormalism may appear in many images in the internet, such as photos of the violent conflict, pictures in the stricken area, etc. In these situations, users need to search more such images. Furthermore, in real world, each object has its own attribute informations (such as "red car", "green tree", and "white building", etc). Thus, in order to express the exact search intentions, it would be better to also specify the semantic attributes of each object, such as the color attributes, size attributes, and material attributes, etc. However, all these mentioned semantic cues cannot be appropriately incorporated into the textual queries, exemplar images, color or concept maps [12, 8], and even the sketches. To bridge the "semantic gap" between users' search intention and the low-level visual features [10], we should augment the image search strategies to enable users to indicate their Regions Of Interest (ROIs) within the query image, and can handle these high-level semantic concepts as well as the spatial relations. What's more, because the number of ROIs within an image may be more than two, the framework also should deal with the high-order case. i.e., has the ability to retrieval multiple ROIs within an image.

In this paper, we propose a novel strategy to improve users' search experience. The interface we provide to users only requires users to indicate the ROIs in a selected exemplar query image. The users' search intention is automatically refined and specified by our proposed method. In particular, after obtaining the ROIs, the system will infer their categories, attributes, and spatial relationships. With the inference, we consequently constitute a high-order semantic structure to represent the query and then retrieve the similar images from the database. The flowchart is illustrated in Figure 2.

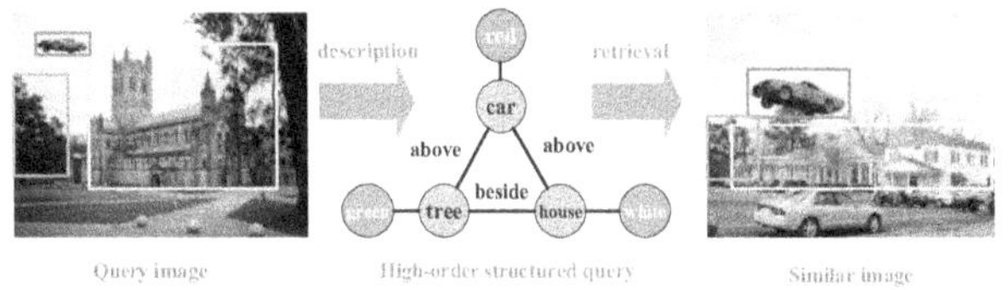

Figure 1: Given the query image, users may be interested in the object layout highlighted with the rectangle boxes. The object layout can be depicted by using categories of objects (car, tree, house), their attributes (red, green, white), and spatial interactions between them (above, beside). This paper aims at retrieving the images having the same layout, including the same categories, attributes, and spatial interactions.

*Corresponding author

MM'14, November 03 - 07 2014, Orlando, FL, USA

http://dx.doi.org/10.1145/2647868.2654972.

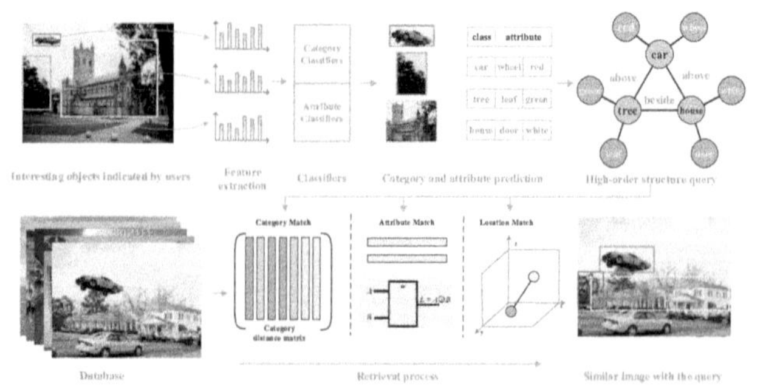

Figure 2: Illustration of our framework. Note that our method is an unsupervised framework, which is different from the work in [7]. In their work, the CRF is used to construct a similar triple with ours. Moreover, ours aims at image retrieval, while [7] aims to generate sentences to describe images.

In summary, the contribution of this paper is two-fold: 1) We present a novel image search strategy that not only allows users to indicate their ROIs, but also can properly handle various high-level semantic queries and spatial relations. 2) We propose a structured descriptor to jointly represent the categories, attributes, and spatial relationships among objects, and design a ranking method to accomplish the image retrieval. The rest of this paper is organized as follows. In Section 2, we detail the proposed framework. Section 3 reports the experimental results, and Section 4 gives the conclusion.

2. PROPOSED FRAMEWORK

2.1 Structured Description for Images

To represent the images, we first train the classifiers in terms of category and attribute using SVM. When users indicate their ROIs, the low-level features of the corresponding bounding boxes are extracted. These features are input to the SVM classifiers to infer the category and attribute labels of the ROIs.

To encode the spatial interactions between two instances, we propose a matrix-based representation method. Suppose there are F instances within an image labeled by R different category labels ($R \leq F$), each instance is assigned a category label ranging from 1 to Q and the attribute label ranging from 1 to M. Thus, a $F \times F$ matrix is established. We then compute the location prior between each category pair via statistically analyzing the training set. For example, the prior may be "sky" should be above "building". Based on this prior, we next compare the location of two instances. If they satisfy the prior, the corresponding location in the matrix is set 1, otherwise, the value is set to -1. If two instances have the same category labels, the value is 0. The matrix is corresponding to a fixed location relationship. If users want to add a new location relationship (for example, the horizontal relationship), they need to compute the corresponding prior in horizontal direction, and then use another matrix to represent it.

We select arbitrary three instances that have different category labels to construct a triangle. In the triangle, each vertex point is associated with an instance ($\mathbf{x}_i, \mathbf{x}_j, \mathbf{x}_q$), and the corresponding value indicates its category label (i, j, q, and $i \neq j \neq q$). As a result, it will produce totally $\binom{R}{3}$ different triangles to vary with the values in vertex ($R \geq 3$). If $R < 3$, we add 0 to the corresponding vertex, and still use a triangle to represent it. Note because a category label may be assigned to multiple instances, the number of triangles within an image will be above $\binom{R}{3}$. In addition, we assign a M dimensional binary vector to each vertex to represent the attributes of the corresponding instance, where 1 denotes the instance has this attribute, and 0 denotes the instance does not have this attribute. If the value of vertex is 0, we assign M zeros to it.

2.2 Image Ranking Based on Triangles

We use the above triangle to represent each image in the dataset. In this way, the image retrieval problem is converted into a triangle matching problem. In order to solve this problem, we first define a category distance matrix to represent the semantic correlation between each two categories. Specifically, we use Eq.1 to compute the correlation strength between two categories:

$$\theta_{ij} = \log \frac{P_{00}P_{11}}{P_{10}P_{01}}, \tag{1}$$

where P_{ij} denotes the probability when i=$\{0,1\}$, and j=$\{0,1\}$.

By using the above formula, we obtain a $Q \times Q$ matrix. If two categories are relevant, the corresponding value in the matrix will be large (In the diagonal, the value is largest, because the category is the most relevant with itself). Based on the proposed category distance matrix, we could search the most relevant category according to a given category. In this way, the objects between two triangles will be assigned. We use the category matched score S_t to represent the matched degree between the query triangle and the t-th triangle in dataset. S_t is defined by the number of objects that are exactly correctly matched with the query triangle.

After the above steps, we assign the objects of query triangle with the objects of the triangles in dataset. Next, we compute the attribute matched score R_t between the corresponding objects. Suppose $\mathbf{y}_i$, $\mathbf{y}_j$ and $\mathbf{y}_q$ are the attribute vectors of the query objects, and $\mathbf{y}'_i$, $\mathbf{y}'_j$ and $\mathbf{y}'_q$ are the attribute vectors for the assigned objects.

$$R_t = \sum([\mathbf{y}_i, \mathbf{y}_j, \mathbf{y}_q]^T \odot [\mathbf{y}'_i, \mathbf{y}'_j, \mathbf{y}'_q]^T), \tag{2}$$

where $[\mathbf{y}_i, \mathbf{y}_j, \mathbf{y}_q]$ denotes concentrating the $\mathbf{y}_i, \mathbf{y}_j, \mathbf{y}_q$ into a long vector. $\odot$ denotes the xnor operator. Eq.2 computes the similarity of the attributes between query triangle and triangles in the dataset.

Consequently, we compute the spatial matched score. Suppose the spatial vector of query triangle is $\mathbf{z}_p$, and the spatial vector of the t-th triangle is $\mathbf{z}_t$. $\mathbf{z}_p$ and $\mathbf{z}_t$ both compose of 1 and -1. We use the following formula to compute the spatial matched score: $Q_t = \|\mathbf{z}_i - \mathbf{z}_j\|$. In order to incorporate S_t, R_t, and Q_t to represent the match degree of images, we normalize S_t, R_t, and Q_t. The final matched score of the t-th triangle is:

$$F_t = \sum_{j=1}^{n} \theta_j \psi_j(I, q), \tag{3}$$

where ψ_j is one metric between the image in the database and the query image. In this work, we only explore the S_t, R_t, and Q_t introduced above. $\theta_i, i = 1, ..., n$ are weight parameters. According to F_t, we can rank the triangles in the dataset, and search the most similar images with the query image.

3. EXPERIMENTS

3.1 Dataset

Two benchmark datasets: aPascal dataset [3] and aYahoo dataset [3] are used in our experiments. aPascal is built based on the Pascal VOC 2008 dataset by assigning the *attribute* labels to each image within it. There are totally 4340 images in the dataset, which are split around 50% train/val and 50% test. In our experiment, we use the 4340 images as our search database, and random select some

(a) (b) (c) (d)

Figure 3: Four example triangles are illustrated. In each triangle, if the number of different categories is less than 3, we use "NULL" to replace the corresponding nodes (as shown in (a) and (c). If there are multiple identical instances, we use multiple triangles to represent them (as shown in (b)).

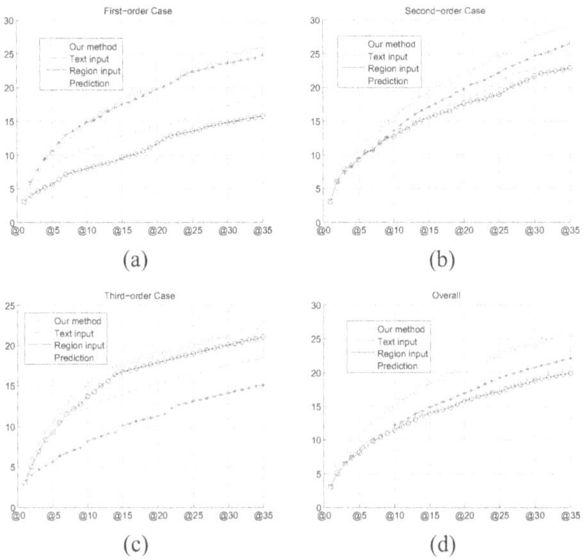

Figure 4: Performance curves. (a), (b), (c) list the comparisons between different methods under the first-order, second-order, and third-order cases, respectively. The average score under all cases is illustrated in (d). "Prediction" denotes the output using inferred category and attribute labels by our method.

images as the queries to accomplish our task. The aPascal dataset contains 20 categories and 64 attributes, covering 10,363 annotated objects. As for aYahoo dataset, there are totally 2237 images downloaded from the internet by using Yahoo search engine. 12 categories and 64 attributes are used to label the 2267 objects. The detailed names of corresponding categories and attributes can be found in [3]. To fairly compare the different retrieval methods, in our experiment, we assume the ground truth bounding box of each object have been detected perfectly in both the aPascal and aYahoo dataseets, and conduct our experiments on this assumption.

We use the same low-level features as in Farhadi *et al* [3]. The base features in [3] contain four types: color, texture, visual words and edges. They use a bag of words style feature for each feature type, which results in a 9751 dimensional feature vector.

3.2 Evaluation Metric

To perform the quantitative evaluation, some volunteers are recruited to label the ground truth. Given a specified query, the image retrieval system ranks the images in the database. For each image, we assign a relevance score to it according to how well the image accords with the search intention of the task. In our experiment, the relevance score is defined in three levels from level 1 to level 3.

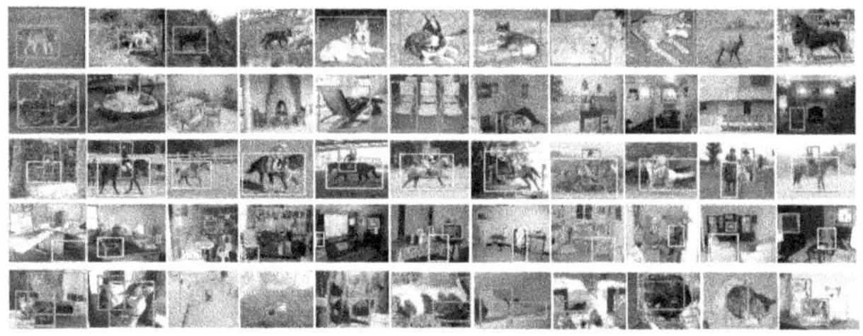

Figure 5: Five examples output by our method. The first row lists the query image, where the indicated ROIs are highlighted with the colorful bounding boxes (one color corresponds to one kind of object). The following ten rows denote the top ten images ranked by our method.

Figure 6: Five examples output by text-input method in terms of the same query used in Figure 5.

Level 3 corresponds to the most relevant (all indicated categories appear, and the object layout is right), and level 1 denotes the least relevant (some categories are missed or the layout of objects is quite different from the query). Level 2 is similar with Level 1, but some attributes are missed. With the ground truth, the Discounted Cumulative Gain (DCG) is used to measure the performance:

$$DCG@p = rel_1 + \sum_{i=2}^{p} \frac{rel_i}{log_2 i}, \quad (4)$$

where rel_i is the relevance score of the image ranked at the i-th place. p is the depth of DCG, and DCG@p represents the DCG score when we select the top p ranked images.

3.3 Experimental Results

Some examples of the structured description are given in Figure 3. We compare two state-of-the-art methods: text-input image search engine and Region-Based Image Retrieval (RBIR) engine [9]. For text-input image search engine, we use the ground-truth category and attribute labels of the ROIs as the input keywords to search the images. The input of region-based image search engine is the same as our method, i.e., the ROIs indicated by users. For the methods above, we both use the ground-truth category and attribute labels. To fairly compare the performance of different image retrieval algorithms, we first use the ground-truth category and attribute labels to accomplish the retrieval task (as done in the text-input and region-based methods), and then give the performance using the inferred category and attribute labels. 20 image search tasks are designed to evaluate the proposed system. In these tasks, 10 tasks involve only one object (first-order case), 6 tasks involve two objects (second-order case), and 4 tasks involve three objects (third-order case). The second-order and third-order cases contain the attribute information and the spatial relationship between objects, while the first-order case only contains the attribute information. The quantitative experimental results are given in Figure 4.

Figure 7: Five examples output by region-based method in terms of the same query used in Figure 5.

Figure 8: Five examples output by our method. The difference from Figure 5 is that the inferred category and attribute labels are used here.

The comparisons between different methods under first-order case, second-order case and third-order case are listed in (a), (b) and (c), respectively. The overall comparison under all cases is given in (d). From the Figure, we see our method achieves the similar performance with the text-input method under the first-order case. This is not difficult to explain, since our model degenerates into the text-input model under this case (i.e., searching images only according to the category and attribute labels). In the second-order and third-order case, with adding the spatial relationship, the performance of text-input method drops, and our method gradually outperforms it. This demonstrates the fact that text-input methods can not handle the tasks with spatial relationship. In addition, we see the region-based method works poorly under the first-order and second-order case, this is because RBIR ranks the images according to the similarity between the low-level features. Therefore, it can not handle the high-level semantic information (such as attributes), resulting in a poor performance. From (d), we see our method achieves the best performance. The performance of our method using the inferred category and attribute labels (both for query and database) is also given in the green curve. We see the performance falls somewhere between the text-input model and region-based method.

For the qualitative comparison, we show the ranked results output by our method, text-input image search engine, and region-baed image search engine in Figure 5, Figure 6, and Figure 7, respectively. In each figure, the first row lists the query image, where the indicated ROIs are highlighted with the colorful bounding boxes (one color corresponds to one kind of object). The following ten rows denote the top ten images ranked by the different methods. The task in the first column is conducted on the aYahoo dataset, and the tasks in the following four columns are conducted on the aPascal dataset. From top to bottom are two first-order cases, one second-order case, one third-order case, and one case that has two same objects within an image. We see our method can retain the spatial relationship between objects. For example, for the task in the third column, the ROIs can be depicted using "person" is above "horse". We see the all the searched images contain the ROIs that "person" is above "horse". For the task in the forth column, the ROIs is depicted using "monitor" is above "bottle", and "bottle" is above "chair". Similarly, the images having the same layout are also searched by our method. In contrast, the text-input and region-based methods can not retain the spatial relationship. We show the qualitative results based on the inferred category and attribute labels in Figure 8. From the figure, we see the categories of some objects are wrong, limiting the performance of our method. Finding out more accurate annotation algorithm will promote our method.

4. CONCLUSIONS

In this paper, we have presented the image retrieval problem that specified Regions Of Interest (ROIs). In the ROIs, various high-level semantic concepts like categories of objects, their attributes, and the spatial relationship between them were jointly considered to accomplish the search. Experiments conducted on two benchmark datasets showed that our method achieved the best performance compared with the state of the arts. Our method can also be used in the large scale image retrieval, where the object bounding boxes can be automatically detected using [4], and the categories and attributes of these boxes can be jointly predicted by our another work [6]. In this way, the categories, attributes and spatial relations of objects in large scale database can be easily obtained.

5. ACKNOWLEDGMENTS

This work was supported by National Natural Science Foundation of China (No. 61332012), 100 Talents Programme of The Chinese Academy of Sciences, and the Opening Project of State Key Laboratory of Digital Publishing Technology. X. Guo was supported by Excellent Young Talent of the Institute of Information Engineering, Chinese Academy of Sciences.

6. REFERENCES

[1] T. Chen, M.-M. Cheng, P. Tan, A. Shamir, and S.-M. Hu. Sketch2photo: internet image montage. *TOG*, 28(5):124, 2009.

[2] M. Eitz, K. Hildebrand, T. Boubekeur, and M. Alexa. Sketch-based image retrieval: Benchmark and bag-of-features descriptors. *TVCG*, 17(11):1624–1636, 2011.

[3] A. Farhadi, I. Endres, D. Hoiem, and D. Forsyth. Describing objects by their attributes. In *CVPR*, pages 1–8, 2009.

[4] P. F. Felzenszwalb, R. B. Girshick, D. McAllester, and D. Ramanan. Object detection with discriminatively trained part-based models. *TPAMI*, 32(9):1627–1645, 2010.

[5] A. Gordoa, J. A. Rodríguez-Serrano, F. Perronnin, and E. Valveny. Leveraging category-level labels for instance-level image retrieval. In *CVPR*, pages 3045–3052, 2012.

[6] Y. Han, X. Wei, X. Cao, Y. Yang, and X. Zhou. Augmenting image descriptions using structured prediction output. *TMM, doi:10.1109/TMM.2014.2321530.*

[7] G. Kulkarni, V. Premraj, S. Dhar, S. Li, Y. Choi, A. C. Berg, and T. L. Berg. Baby talk: Understanding and generating simple image descriptions. In *CVPR*, pages 1601–1608, 2011.

[8] T. Lan, W. Yang, Y. Wang, and G. Mori. Image retrieval with structured object queries using latent ranking svm. In *ECCV*, pages 129–142. 2012.

[9] Y. Liu, D. Zhang, and G. Lu. Region-based image retrieval with high-level semantics using decision tree learning. *Pattern Recognition*, 41(8):2554–2570, 2008.

[10] Y. Liu, D. Zhang, G. Lu, and W.-Y. Ma. A survey of content-based image retrieval with high-level semantics. *Pattern Recognition*, 40(1):262–282, 2007.

[11] J. Sivic and A. Zisserman. Video google: A text retrieval approach to object matching in videos. In *ICCV*, pages 1470–1477, 2003.

[12] H. Xu, J. Wang, X.-S. Hua, and S. Li. Image search by concept map. In *SIGIR*, pages 1–8, 2010.

The Stack-of-Rings Interface for Large-Scale Image Browsing on Mobile Touch Devices

Klaus Schoeffmann
Institute of Information Technology (ITEC)
Klagenfurt University, Austria
ks@itec.aau.at

ABSTRACT

We propose a new interface for browsing large image collections on touch-enabled devices, which allows for faster visual search than a common grid interface. The proposed interface consists of 3D rings arranged in a vertical stack. Each ring can be rotated independently with a horizontal wipe gesture and the whole stack can be moved up and down with vertical wipe gestures. We present results from a user study with 16 participants, where we compared the performance of the proposed interface to the one provided by the default image browsing interface on tablets. The evaluation results show that the proposed interface performs significantly faster than the default interface on the tablet and achieves a significantly better rating by the users.

Categories and Subject Descriptors

H.3.3 [**Information Storage and Retrieval**]: Information Search and Retrieval

General Terms

Design, Experimentation, Algorithms, Performance

Keywords

Image browsing and search, Small screens, Mobile devices

1. INTRODUCTION

Over the last few years we could observe the very quick adoption of tablets as the versatile computing device in several domains. However, while the screen resolution and touch functionality has been dramatically improved over the years, the interfaces for browsing images on tablets remained the same. For example, with a state-of-the-art tablet device, the default photo browsing application can show only about 35 image thumbnails at one screen, in a two-dimensional grid arrangement that is similar to the one on PCs (see Figure 1). It is obvious that this "standard photo browsing interface" is not very well suited to browse large archives of photos because of high interaction effort (i.e., many flick or wipe gestures would be needed to browse through a list of thousands of images). While such an interface is already inconvenient for *undirected search* (i.e., exploring the image collection), it becomes worse for *directed search*, where users want to interactively find a particular image.

In our recent previous work we could show that interfaces with 3D arrangements of image thumbnails can significantly outperform a 2D grid interface in terms of visual search time as well as user experience [1, 12]. However, the interfaces proposed in these works are quite limited in the number of image thumbnails they can show at a convenient size. Therefore, in this paper we propose an interface that builds on the idea of [12] but extends it to large-scale image browsing. More precisely, our interface combines the benefits of the ring interface proposed in [12] with the advantages of a common grid interface, in order to allow browsing of large image collections. We have implemented the proposed interface for a tablet device and evaluated it in direct comparison to the grid interface with a user study with 16 participants. The users of this study had to perform image search tasks in a collection of nearly 1,000 images with both interfaces. Our results show that the proposed interface performs significantly better in terms of search time and is the preferred interface for the majority of the tested users.

MM'14, November 3–7, 2014, Orlando, Florida, USA.

http://dx.doi.org/10.1145/2647868.2654974.

2. RELATED WORK

Several publications can be found in the literature that focus on image browsing interfaces with 3D layouts. Chun et al. [4] propose to use a fish-eye visualization to present more images at a glance (similarly, Divakaran et al. [5] did also propose a fish-eye layout earlier). Schaefer [10] proposes to use the Globe metaphor for visualizing large image collections with hierarchical refinement, where images are arranged according to their median color. Gomi and Itoh [6] use a 3D visualization to present image retrieval results on a mobile device, where thumbnails are arranged along the Z axis according to their context-dependent priority. A similar idea was proposed by Bruneau et al. [3] for visualization of a cluster graph of images. The Photo Explorer proposed by Snavely et al. [13] arranges photos in a 3D layout according to geographic coordinates. Jacucci et al. investigated spherical 3D surrogates for browsing of images [8]. Finally, Nakazato and Huang [9] utilize a CAVE systems to present resulting images of a query according to their similarity in a 3D environment.

It is remarkable that although much effort has been invested in the design and creation of novel 3D visualizations, little effort has been spent on providing empirical evidence that demonstrates their intended advantages. However, there are a few recent works that report on significant improvements of 3D interfaces. For example, Ahlströhm et al. [1] have shown that a globe interface provides significantly better visual search performance than a common 2D interface on a tablet. In another work [12] we could also show that a 3D ring interface can significantly outperform a common 2D interface in both terms of visual search time and user preference. These interfaces, however, were rather developed for smaller set of images (e.g., a few hundreds).

3. PROPOSED INTERFACE

The interface proposed in this paper is an extension of our previous work [2, 11, 12]. However, instead of a single ring of thumbnails, which can be rotated, we propose a stack of rotatable rings that can be scrolled vertically. As shown in Figure 1, this allows to conveniently browse a large collection of images, similarly to the grid interface. Each ring can be rotated with a horizontal wipe gesture and the whole stack can be moved upwards or downwards with a vertical wipe gesture. When the user taps an image thumbnail, the interface switches to full-screen view of the corresponding image. As the interface does not provide clear view to the back of the rings, we use a pinch gesture to open the stack between the rings in order to see the images at the back side of the rings (see Figure 2). Moreover, a wipe gestures with two fingers rotates the whole stack of rings at once.

Figure 1: Left: Screenshot of the *Grid* interface, which is the default interface for image browsing on tablets. The whole list can be dragged up and down by a vertical wipe gesture. Right: Screenshot of the proposed *Stack-of-Rings* interface with the following interaction features: (i) each ring can be rotated separately with a wipe gesture, (ii) rings can be moved apart with a pinch-out gestures, (iii) the entire stack can be rotated (two-finger horizontal wipe) and dragged up and down (vertical wipe).

This *Stack-of-Rings* interface is designed for touch-enabled devices like tablets or smartphones. It can be flexibly optimized to the actual screen size of the device, by changing (1) the radius of the rings and (2) the the view-point (the "perspective of the camera" in the 3D scene), and (3) the number of thumbnails per ring, such that the thumbnails are shown at a convenient size. Moreover, it can handle an arbitrarily large number of thumbnails, similarly to a common grid interface, and hence is more flexible than the interface proposed in [12].

Figure 2: With a pinch gesture users can move rings apart in order to see images in the back.

4. EXPERIMENTAL SETUP

For the evaluation of the proposed interface we performed a user study with 16 users (10 male, 6 female; average age 31.75, s.d. 10.29), where we compared the stack-of-rings interface to the default grid interface on a tablet device (Apple iPad 4 with a 9.7-inch screen; see Figure 1).

For both interfaces the same data set with 990 images was used, which contained diverse photos manually collected from Flickr. In both interfaces the presented image collection was sorted by dominant color with the algorithm described in [12]. In the 3D interface the 990 images were grouped into 30 rings, each containing 33 image thumbnails.

A test session started with a short introduction and a few test trials, before the user had to perform 20 search trials with the first interface and 20 different search trials with the second interface. The order of the two interfaces varied among the users (latin-square) and both interfaces were tested with a short break in between. The trials followed the "known-item-search" (KIS) scenario, where the user knows of an image and knows that it is contained in the collection but does not know where to look for it. This scenario was simulated by first presenting the target image in full-screen mode on the screen as long as needed by the user to memorize it. As soon as the user tapped the screen, the search process was initiated by hiding the target image and presenting the search interface, allowing to search through thumbnails of the whole data set. Thumbnails could be inspected with a single tap interaction. We requested the users to find the target image as fast as possible and logged the search time for every trial. During the search task the target image was not visible on the screen to avoid simple image matching strategies, where only two visible thumbnails on the screen need to be matched quickly. The users were given a maximum time of two minutes to find the corresponding image, otherwise the search task was logged as unsuccessful. The reason for setting a rather strict time limit is that we wanted to force people to find the desired images as fast as possible.

In addition to the time measurement of the search trials, participants were also asked for their subjective impressions of the tested interfaces. More particularly, in a questionnaire to be filled out after a user completed the study, we asked him/her to rate the perceived workload (physical demand, temporal demand, mental demand, required effort, frustration, and perceived own performance) on a 10-point Likert-scale. The questionnaire was designed according to the workload dimensions suggested by the NASA-TLX (Task Load Index) approach [7], which is widely used in the field of Human-Computer-Interaction. Furthermore, we also asked all users to vote for their preferred interface.

5. RESULTS AND DISCUSSION

In the following subsections we discuss the performance of both interfaces in our study in terms of achieved search time and user ratings. From a total of 640 search trials (320 trials with each interface), 177 could not be found within the required time limit of two minutes. 79 of these unsuccessful trials (12.3%) were performed with the grid interface and 98 (15.3%) with the stack-of-rings interface. The analysis of the search time is based on successful search tasks only.

5.1 Search Time of Successful Trials

The median search time over all successful tasks of all users is 43.03 seconds for the grid interface and 29.04 seconds for the stack-of-rings interface, which is a statistically significant result according to a dependent paired-samples t-test ($t(15) = 3.336, p < 0.01$). However, we were also interested on where the significant difference comes from. Therefore, we divided all search tasks into three clusters, where each cluster contains 330 images. Therefore, the clusters simple represent the first, second, and third part of the whole list. For the grid interface, which can only display 35 images at one page, users had to scroll a little bit more than 9 pages for target images in the first cluster and twice or triple as much for the second and third. Similarly, for the stack-of-rings interface (compare Figure 1) this means that target images located in the first cluster were contained in the first 9 rings, which are all on the first page (although only a part of them is visible without interaction), while users had to scroll a full page down for target images in the second cluster and two full pages down for target images in the third cluster.

Figure 3 shows the median search time in seconds for the three different clusters for both interfaces. As apparent in the figure, the search time strongly increases for the grid interface with each cluster, from 17.4s in cluster-1, to 49.64s in cluster-2, and finally to 71.6s in cluster-3. The reason for this significant increase (search time for target images in the last cluster is about 412% higher) is the higher need for scrolling interaction when target images are located in the lower part of the list. This is not the case for the proposed stack-of-rings interface, which groups images into rotatable rings for more convenient browsing (33 images per ring in our setting). This is also reflected by the analysis of the median search time, which is only about 44% higher for target images in the last cluster than for target images in the first cluster (20.4s, 36.5s, 29.5s). The statistical analysis of the data with a two-way repeated-measures ANOVA (analysis of variance) with Greenhouse-Geisser correction showed significant differences for *interface* ($F_{1,15} = 16.172, p < 0.005$) and *cluster* ($F_{1.917,28.756} = 20.793, p < 0.0001$). The difference in search time between the clusters, as apparent in Figure 3, has to be seen in combination with a significant *interface* × *cluster* interaction, indicating that the magnitude of the difference depends on the cluster number ($F_{1.691,25.364} = 10.261, p < 0.005$).

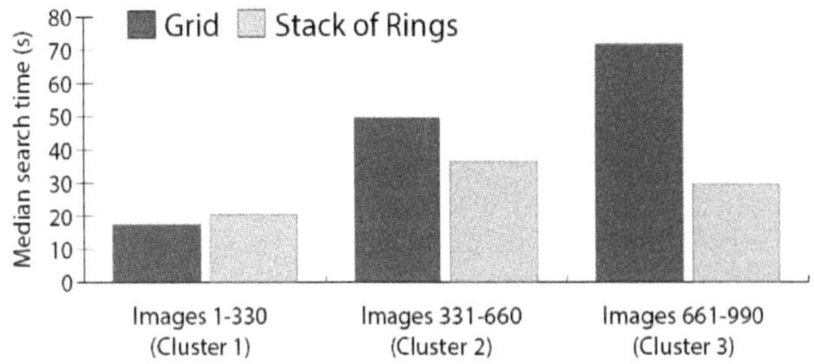

Figure 3: Median search time in seconds for target images located in different areas of the collection.

5.2 User Ratings

Figure 4 shows the average ratings of the users in the NASA-TLX questionnaires for both interfaces. It can be seen that both interfaces perform similarly in terms of mental demand, temporal demand, effort, and frustration. In the figure we can see a difference for physical demand and performance. However, a statistical analysis of the data with Wilcoxon signed rank tests showed that in the ratings of both interface there was only a statistically significant difference for 'performance' ($Z = -2.419, p < 0.05$). This means that for in terms of subjective aspects the stack-of-rings interfaces performs equally good as the grid interface but provides a significantly better support to solve visual image search tasks.

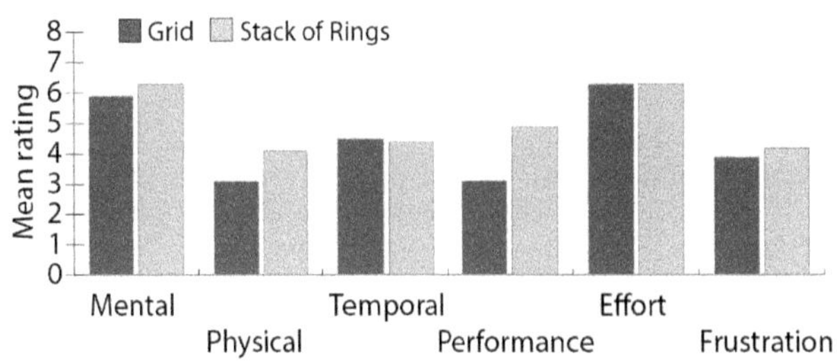

Figure 4: Average rating of the different aspects of the interfaces according to the NASA Task-Load-Index (TLX) [7] on a 10-point Likert scale. Lower ratings are better but for Performance.

In the second part of the questionnaire we asked the participants to answer specific questions for the stack-of-rings interface with a 5-point Likert-scale rating. As evident in Figure 5, the users were quite optimistic about the proposed interface. They strongly agreed that they like the new interface (4.19, s.d. 0.75), that using it was fun (4.38, s.d. 0.81), and they could imagine using it frequently (4.13, s.d. 0.89). They also agreed that the color-based sorting of images was helpful for their search tasks (4.13, s.d. 0.96). Rather neutral – although with positive tendency – are the answers to Q3 and Q4, where we asked if using the new interface was less exhausting than using the grid interface (3.19, s.d. 1.33) and if they felt relaxed when using the interface (3.63, s.d. 1.15). This result can be explained by the fact that the stack-of-ring requires more interaction (for rotating the rings) in order to scroll through all images in the collection.

We also asked the participants of our study about their preferred interface, after they had performed all tests with both interfaces. From all 16 tested users, only 6 preferred the common grid interface (37.5%) and 10 voted for the stack-of-rings interface (62.5%).

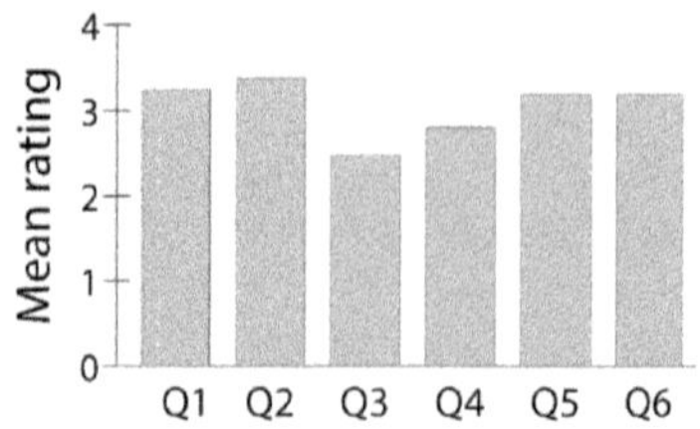

Figure 5: Average rating of specific questions to the stack-of-rings interface on a 5-point Likert scale. Q1: "*I like the new interface.*", Q2: "*Using the interface was fun.*", Q3: "*The search with the proposed interface was less exhausting than with the grid interface.*', Q4: "*I felt relaxed while using the interface.*', Q5: "*I can imagine using this interface frequently.*", Q6: "*The sorting of thumbnails by color was helpful.*'

6. CONCLUSIONS

In this work we proposed a new interface for browsing large collections of images on touch-enabled devices. The proposed interface groups consecutive images into rings that can be rotated independently but also scrolled together with the entire collection (i.e., as stack of rings). This allows to present significantly more images at one screen and easier navigation through the whole collection. The evaluation results of our user study show that this new interface allows significantly faster search for a desired image in the collection (by about 48%), when compared to the commonly used grid interface. It can be expected that the benefit in terms of search time would be even greater when the image collection size increases. The evaluations of the user ratings revealed that the participants consider the interface equal in terms of mental, physical, and temporal demand, as well as in effort and frustration, but found that it better supports visual search. Additionally, they like this new interface, would use it frequently, and experience fun when using it. The majority of tested users (62.5%) consider the proposed interface as better than the grid.

Acknowledgment

The author would like to thank Johannes Zlattinger, who implemented a prototype of the described interface in course of his master thesis and performed the corresponding user study. This work was funded by the Federal Ministry for Transport, Innovation and Technology (bmvit) and the Austrian Science Fund (FWF): TRP 273-N15 and the European Regional Development Fund and the Carinthian Economic Promotion Fund (KWF), supported by Lakeside Labs GmbH, Klagenfurt, Austria.

7. REFERENCES

[1] D. Ahlström, M. A. Hudelist, K. Schoeffmann, and G. Schaefer. A user study on image browsing on touchscreens. In *Proceedings of the 20th ACM International Conference on Multimedia*, MM '12, pages 925–928, New York, NY, USA, 2012. ACM.

[2] C. Beecks, T. Skopal, K. Schoeffmann, and T. Seidl. Towards large-scale multimedia exploration. In *Proceedings of the 5th International Workshop on Ranking in Databases (DBRank 2011)*, pages 31–33, Seattle, WA, USA, August 2011.

[3] P. Bruneau, F. Picarougne, and M. Gelgon. Interactive unsupervised classification and visualization for browsing an image collection. *Pattern Recognition*, 43(2):485 – 493, 2010. Interactive Imaging and Vision.

[4] J. Chun, S. H. Han, H. Im, and Y. S. Park. A method for searching photos on a mobile phone by using the fisheye view technique. *Int. Journal of Industrial Ergonomics*, 41(3):280 – 288, 2011.

[5] A. Divakaran, C. Forlines, T. Lanning, S. Shipman, and K. Wittenburg. Augmenting fast-forward and rewind for personal digital video recorders. In *Consumer Electronics, 2005. ICCE, Int. Conf. on*, pages 43–44, Jan 2005.

[6] A. Gomi and T. Itoh. Mini: A 3d mobile image browser with multi-dimensional datasets. In *Proceedings of the 27th Annual ACM Symposium on Applied Computing*, SAC '12, pages 989–996, New York, NY, USA, 2012. ACM.

[7] S. Hart and L. Staveland. Development of NASA-TLX (Task Load Index): Results of empirical and theoretical research. In *Human mental workload*, pages 139–183. P.A. Hancock and N. Meshkati (Eds.), Amsterdam: Elsevier, 1988.

[8] G. Jacucci, A. Morrison, G. T. Richard, J. Kleimola, P. Peltonen, L. Parisi, and T. Laitinen. Worlds of information: Designing for engagement at a public multi-touch display. In *Proc. of the SIGCHI Conf. on Human Factors in Computing Systems*, CHI '10, pages 2267–2276, New York, NY, USA, 2010. ACM.

[9] M. Nakazato and T. Huang. 3d mars: immersive virtual reality for content-based image retrieval. In *Multimedia and Expo, 2001. ICME 2001. IEEE International Conference on*, pages 44–47, 2001.

[10] G. Schaefer. A next generation browsing environment for large image repositories. *Multimedia Tools and Appl.*, 47:105–120, 2010.

[11] K. Schoeffmann and D. Ahlström. An evaluation of color sorting for image browsing. *International Journal of Multimedia Data Engineering and Management*, 3(1):49–62, mar 2012.

[12] K. Schoeffmann and D. Ahlström. Using a 3d cylindrical interface for image browsing to improve visual search performance. In *Image Analysis for Multimedia Interactive Services (WIAMIS), 2012 13th Int. Workshop on*, pages 1 –4, May 2012.

[13] N. Snavely, S. M. Seitz, and R. Szeliski. Photo tourism: Exploring photo collections in 3d. *ACM Trans. Graph.*, 25(3):835–846, July 2006.

Automatic Personality and Interaction Style Recognition from Facebook Profile Pictures

Fabio Celli
University of Trento
via sommarive 5
Trento, Italy
fabio.celli@unitn.it

Elia Bruni
University of Bozen-Bolzano
Dominikanerplatz 3
Bozen-Bolzano, Italy
elia.bruni@unibz.it

Bruno Lepri
FBK
via sommarive 18
Trento, Italy
lepri@fbk.eu

ABSTRACT

In this paper, we address the issue of personality and interaction style recognition from profile pictures in Facebook. We recruited volunteers among Facebook users and collected a dataset of profile pictures, labeled with gold standard self-assessed personality and interaction style labels. Then, we exploited a bag-of-visual-words technique to extract features from pictures. Finally, different machine learning approaches were used to test the effectiveness of these features in predicting personality and interaction style traits. Our good results show that this task is very promising, because profile pictures convey a lot of information about a user and are directly connected to impression formation and identity management.

Categories and Subject Descriptors

5.5 [**Emotional and Social Signals in Multimedia**]: Novel methods for the classification and representation of interactive social and/or emotional signals

General Terms

Facebook profiling personality pictures algorithms

Keywords

personality recognition, Facebook, data mining, machine learning, feature extraction

1. INTRODUCTION

People spend a considerable amount of effort in order to form and to manage impressions, especially in the initial stage of social interactions [10]. Nowadays, this fundamental process has been modified by the usage of new communication technologies. Social networking technologies, such as Facebook, offer new ways for self-presentations. Several studies reported that Facebook users engage in actively creating, maintaining and modifying an image of selves by adjusting their profiles, including descriptions and pictures, joining groups and displaying their likes and dislikes [12]. Hence, the Facebook profile page can be considered as a mediated representation of the Facebook user. Although users may be tempted to enhance their self-presentations, friends who are both offline and online keep Facebook users' self-presentations in check. Indeed, misrepresentation on profile pages can have serious offline consequences. Therefore, the online profile usually reflect the offline profile, although slightly enhanced [33]. Moreover, social psychology research has also highlighted that personality plays an important role in the way people manage the images they convey in self-presentations [17]. For this reason, some recent studies reported that users can make accurate personality impressions from the information displayed in social network user profiles [33], and have investigated the specific features from user profiles and photos that are more useful to create personality impressions [8]. For example, the results obtained by Hall *et al.* [13] indicate that observers could accurately estimate extraversion, agreeableness and conscientiousness of unknown profile owners. Interestingly, profile pictures were useful for estimating extraversion and agreeableness. Again, Utz [31] associated user extraversion with photo expressiveness. Finally, Van deer Heide *et al.* [32] have shown that in the context of Facebook, photos may have more impact on judgments of extraversion than textual self-disclosures. Based on these previous findings, we propose to automatically predict personality traits and interaction styles from Facebook profile images. Regarding personality, we resort to the big five model [7], a multifactorial approach which owes its name to the five traits it takes as constitutive of people's personality: extraversion, emotional stability/neuroticism, agreeableness, conscientiousness, and openness to experience. Moreover, we also target the prediction of people's interaction traits. To this end, we exploited the interpersonal circumplex, a model for organizing and assessing interpersonal traits [19]. Specifically, the interpersonal circumplex is defined by two orthogonal axes, a vertical axis of dominance or agency and a horizontal axis of affect or warmth. The main contributions of the paper are as follows: 1) We collect a dataset of profile images from 100 Facebook users and we annotate them with gold standard self-assessed personality and interaction style labels; 2) we exploit a bag-of-visual-word representation of images in order to extract relevant visual features; 3) we propose and validate a supervised learning approach, based on Support Vector Machines and logistic regression, to the automatic recognition of personality and interaction style traits from visual features extracted from profile pictures. The rest of the paper is structured as follows: Section 2 describes the relevant previous work on personality recognition, with a particular focus on personality recognition from social media data; Section 3 describes the data collected and used for our experiments; while the definition of the research task and the detailed information on the methodology (feature extraction, feature selection and classification) is provided in Section 4. In Section 5 we present the results and in Section 6 we draw our conclusions.

ACMMM 2014, Orlando, Florida

http://dx.doi.org/10.1145/2647868.2654977.

2. RELATED WORK

Pioneering work addressing automatic recognition of personality was done, among others, by Mairesse *et al.* [21], who investigated systematically the usefulness of different sets of acoustic and textual features, extracted from self-reports and observed data. They reported that the best prediction performance, using text as feature, is on openness to experience. In more recent years, the interest in personality recognition has grown and several studies have started exploring the wealth of behavioral data made available by cameras, microphones [26, 2, 24, 18, 1], wearable sensors [25, 15], and mobile phones [30, 6, 9]. Again, researchers have also focused on personality prediction from small corpora of social network data, like Twitter and Facebook, exploiting either linguistic features in status updates, social features such as friends count, and daily activity [11, 27, 5]. Our paper also uses data from a social network; however it adopts a novel approach using visual features extracted from Facebook profile pictures in order to classify subjects' traits. Interestingly, two recent works addressed the automatic recognition of Big Five traits from self-presentation videos registered in a lab setting [2] and from Youtube conversational vlogs [3]. However, they used different data compared with ones proposed in the current paper. Another novelty introduced in our paper is the classification of interaction style traits and as defined by the interpersonal circumplex [23]. To the best of our knowledge, no previous works in computational domain have targeted the task of interaction style classification from pictures using the interpersonal circumplex.

3. DATA COLLECTION

As we mentioned in section 1, in our study we resorted to the big five factor model, a very popular and widely used model for personality assessments [7], and to the interpersonal circumplex, a model for the assessment of interpersonal behavior that has been used in psychology and psychopathology to identify interpersonal problems and interpersonal values [14, 19]. While the big five factor model measures the individual tendencies, the interpersonal circumplex measures the attitude towards others. The big five factor

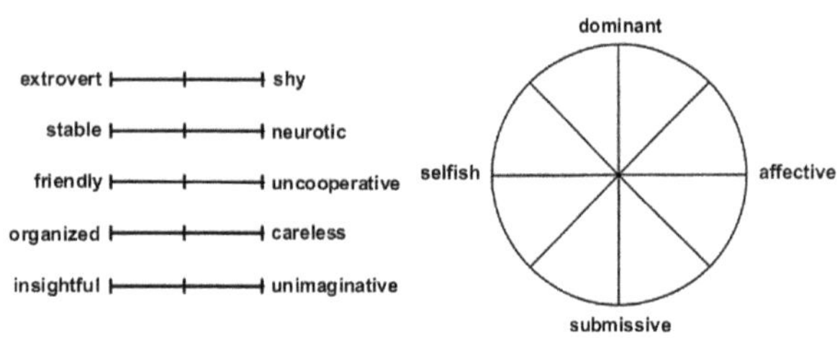

Figure 1: big 5 and interpersonal circumplex

model defines personality along 5 bipolar scales that can be turned into binary classes: extroversion (sociable *vs* shy); emotional stability (secure *vs* neurotic); agreeableness (friendly *vs* ugly); conscientiousness (organized *vs* careless); openness to experience (insightful *vs* unimaginative). The interpersonal circumplex instead defines two orthogonal axes, dominance and affect, as represented in figure 1. We recruited 112 volunteers among Facebook users, most of them among friends and friends-of-friends, in order to have a better control over the data. Using Facebook graph APIs, we collected a dataset of their profile images. Then, we asked to the participants to fill two surveys about individual traits, in order to have gold standard self-assessed personality and interaction style labels. The two surveys are: 1) the big five personality test (BFI-10) [28] and 2) the interpersonal circumplex (IPIP-IPC-32) for interaction styles [23]. We collected the assessments online and removed the data of users with incomplete tests. In the end, we collected the personality and interaction styles of about 100 Facebook users. Both tests are designed to be used when time is limited and take about 5 minutes in total. This allows us to have the full attention of the users.

4. METHODOLOGY

The goal of the paper is to automatically recognize personality traits and interaction styles from Facebook profile images. In the following subsections we will describe the feature extraction and the classification tasks.

4.1 Feature Extraction

In order to extract features from profile images we exploited a Bag-of-Visual-Word (BoVW) representation of images, a popular technique for object recognition inspired by the traditional bag-of-words technique in NLP [29]. Bag-of-Words is a dictionary-based

Figure 2: SIFT features on a profile image

method to represent a document in terms of a cluster of words which are entries of the dictionary. BoVW transfers this idea to images, describing them as a collection of discrete regions called **visual words**. BoVW downplays word arrangement (i.e. the spatial information in the image) and describes the image as a histogram of the frequency of visual words. The set of visual words forms a visual vocabulary, which is constructed by clustering a large corpus of low-level features. The low-level features are handcrafted attributes designed to find local image structures in a repeatable fashion and to encode them in ways that are robust to image transformations such as translation, rotation and affine deformation. There is a large variety of low-level features to use in the BoVW pipeline. In our case, we use the Scale Invariant Feature Transform (SIFT), one of the most popular and effective feature extraction technique used for object recognition [20]. SIFT is invariant to several image transformations such as image scale, orientation, noise and it is also partially invariant to changes in illumination. A SIFT descriptor, as depicted in figure 2 is obtained by concatenating the contents of 4×4 sampling subregions which are explored around each pixel-wise step across the image. For each of the 16 samples, 8 gradient orientations are calculated to obtain a 128-dimensional feature vector. Our resulting BoVW feature vectors have 4096 dimensions which were subsequently reduced in dimensionality to about 90 dimensions by using Singular Value Decomposition [22]. To perform the entire visual pipeline we use VSEM, an open library for visual semantics [4]. VSEM contains a large variety of off-the-shelf low level features, but it does not allow to backtrack to feature types.

Since this is a pilot experiment, we used the largest possible number of features, keeping the number of instances very limited in order to run a manual qualitative analysis (see section 5) of the profile pictures. In the future we will repeat the experiment with a very large dataset.

4.2 Classification and Evaluation

First of all we ran a t-test to compare personality trait scores of our small set to the scores of a set of about 100000 Facebook users randomly sampled from myPersonality [16]. It resulted that the probability of having differences in scores due to chance in a small and large dataset is $p < 0.001$ for all traits. Details are reported in table 1. We could not run a t-test for dominance and affect

trait	t	df	p-value
ext.	11.4	99.1	< 0.001
stab.	-5.1	99.1	< 0.001
agree.	12.6	99.1	< 0.001
consc.	12.1	99.1	< 0.001
open.	8.2	99	< 0.001

Table 1: Detailed results of t-test for the 5 personality traits.

since there are not such dimensions in myPersonality. We formulated the automatic recognition of personality traits and interaction styles from profile pictures as 7 binary classification tasks, one per each trait of personality and interaction style. To this purpose, we balanced the classes of each personality trait with a median split, turning scores into classes and reducing each task to a binary classification. We have few instances of unconscientious and unimaginative people, due to a bias in the participation of Facebook users. Because of the novelty of the task, we experimented with different classification algorithms: naïve bayes (nb), support vectors (svm), decision trees (dt), logistic regression(lr), nearest neighbors (nn), rule learner (rip). We ran a 60% training and 40% test split evaluation (f1-s) and provide f1-scores. We computed two baselines for the calssification tasks: the majority baseline (maj) and the averaged majority baseline (avg maj). The majority baseline is close to 0.5, because we balanced the two classes for each task. The averaged majority baseline is the average of the performance obtained classifying all the instances before in one class and then in the other. Both the baselines were computed using f1-score. We argue that averaged majority is the meaningful baseline for these classification tasks, given the bipolar nature of each personality and interaction style dimension.

task	alg	inst	maj	a-maj	f1-s	acc
ext.	nb	33	.51	.35	**.615**	61.5%
stab.	rip	57	.508	.343	**.609**	60.8%
agree.	svm	30	.5	.333	**.667**	66.6%
consc.	svm	9	.55	.397	**.733**	75%
open.	nn	11	.545	.385	**.732**	74.5%
dom.	lr	51	.509	.344	**.615**	65%
aff.	lr	21	.509	.344	**.619**	62.5%

Table 2: results of classification. alg=algorithm, inst=number of instances, maj=majority, a-maj=averaged majority, f1-s=f1-score with 60% training and 40% test split evaluation, acc=accuracy.

5. DISCUSSION

Results, reported in table 2, show that the information encoded in profile pictures can be successfully exploited for classification of personality and interaction style traits of users in Facebook. Nevertheless there are differences between traits: apart from openness and conscientiousness, that have few instances and require more experiments on a larger scale, agreeableness and extraversion achieve the best performances among personality traits, while dominance and affect achieve performances slightly above f1=.6. Emotional stability is the most difficult trait to predict. This is consistent with the findings that extroversion and agreeableness are accurately estimated by human raters [13] and that extroversion is related to photo expressiveness [31]. More experiments are required to test the finding that observers could accurately estimate conscientiousness from pictures. Unfortunately, the Bag-of-Visual-Words

Figure 3: Examples of profile pictures per trait.

method adopted for the extraction of features from images is not suitable for the interpretation of the pictures' attributes. Nevertheless, we performed clustering on the classified data, using a simple k-means algorithm to automatically retrieve the more similar pictures that were correctly classified, and we checked their similarities manually. This revealed that extrovert and stable people tend to have pictures where they are smiling and they appear with other people. Introverts tend to appear alone, neurotics tend to have images without humans and close-up faces. Not agreeable persons tend to use profile pictures with few colors. Profile pictures of people that is not open to experience tend to have strong spots of light and sometimes darkened figures. Affective people tend to smile in profile pictures. Dominant people tend to have very bright, visible or attractive pictures. Conscientiousness seems to be predictable by eye gazing direction. We included some examples the pictures in the paper, anonymized with out-of-focus spots, see figure 3.

6. CONCLUSION AND FUTURE WORK

In this paper, we successfully exploited a Bag-of-Visual-Words technique to automatically predict personality and interaction styles from profile pictures in Facebook. This is a new and promising task, because profile pictures convey a lot of information about a user and are directly connected to her/his identity. The good, although preliminary, results of the computational classification are in line with the previous findings in the literature about impression formation and personality and with alternative approaches to personality classification. In the future, we would like to test the proposed approach on a larger dataset of Facebook profile pictures.

7. REFERENCES

[1] O. Aran and D. Gatica-Perez. Cross-domain personality prediction: from video blogs to small group meetings. In *Proceedings of the 15th ACM on International conference on multimodal interaction*, pages 127–130. ACM, 2013.

[2] L. M. Batrinca, N. Mana, B. Lepri, F. Pianesi, and N. Sebe. Please, tell me about yourself: automatic personality assessment using short self-presentations. In *Proceedings of the 13th international conference on multimodal interfaces*, pages 255–262. ACM, 2011.

[3] J. Biel and D. Gatica-Perez. The youtube lens: Crowdsourced personality impressions and audiovisual analysis of vlogs. *Multimedia, IEEE Transactions on*, 15(1):41–55, 2013.

[4] E. Bruni, U. Bordignon, A. Liska, J. Uijlings, and I. Sergienya. Vsem: An open library for visual semantics representation. In *Proceedings of ACL*, Sofia, Bulgaria, 2013.

[5] F. Celli and L. Polonio. Relationships between personality and interactions in facebook. In *Social Networking: Recent Trends, Emerging Issues and Future Outlook*, pages 41–54. Nova Science Publishers, Inc., 2013.

[6] G. Chittaranjan, J. Blom, and D. Gatica-Perez. Mining large-scale smartphone data for personality studies. *Personal and Ubiquitous Computing*, 17(3):433–450, 2013.

[7] P. T. Costa and R. R. McCrae. The revised neo personality inventory (neo-pi-r). *The SAGE handbook of personality theory and assessment*, 2:179–198, 2008.

[8] S. Counts and K. B. Stecher. Self-presentation of personality during online profile creation. In *ICWSM*, 2009.

[9] Y.-A. de Montjoye, J. Quoidbach, F. Robic, and A. S. Pentland. Predicting personality using novel mobile phone-based metrics. In *Social Computing, Behavioral-Cultural Modeling and Prediction*, pages 48–55. Springer, 2013.

[10] E. Goffman. *The presentation of self in everyday life*. Garden City, NY Double Day, 1959.

[11] J. Golbeck, C. Robles, and K. Turner. Predicting personality with social media. In *CHI'11 Extended Abstracts on Human Factors in Computing Systems*, pages 253–262. ACM, 2011.

[12] A. L. Gonzales and J. T. Hancock. Identity shift in computer-mediated environments. *Media Psychology*, 11(2):167–185, 2008.

[13] J. A. Hall, N. Pennington, and A. Lueders. Impression management and formation on facebook: A lens model approach. *New Media & Society*, page 1461444813495166, 2013.

[14] L. M. Horowitz. *Interpersonal foundations of psychopathology.* American Psychological Association, 2004.

[15] K. Kalimeri, B. Lepri, and F. Pianesi. Going beyond traits: Multimodal classification of personality states in the wild. In *Proceedings of the 15th ACM on International Conference on Multimodal Interaction*, ICMI '13, pages 27–34, New York, NY, USA, 2013. ACM.

[16] M. Kosinski, Y. Bachrach, P. Kohli, D. Stillwell, and T. Graepel. Manifestations of user personality in website choice and behaviour on online social networks. *Machine Learning*, pages 1–24, 2013.

[17] N. C. Krämer and S. Winter. Impression management 2.0: The relationship of self-esteem, extraversion, self-efficacy, and self-presentation within social networking sites. *Journal of Media Psychology*, 20(3):106, 2008.

[18] B. Lepri, R. Subramanian, K. Kalimeri, J. Staiano, F. Pianesi, and N. Sebe. Connecting meeting behavior with extraversion: A systematic study. *Affective Computing, IEEE Transactions on*, 3(4):443–455, 2012.

[19] K. D. Locke. Circumplex scales of interpersonal values: Reliability, validity, and applicability to interpersonal problems and personality disorders. *Journal of Personality Assessment*, 75(2):249–267, 2000.

[20] D. Lowe. Distinctive image features from scale-invariant keypoints. *International Journal of Computer Vision*, 60(2), 2004.

[21] F. Mairesse, M. A. Walker, M. R. Mehl, and R. K. Moore. Using linguistic cues for the automatic recognition of personality in conversation and text. *Journal of Artificial Intelligence Research*, 30(1):457–500, 2007.

[22] C. Manning, P. Raghavan, and H. Schütze. *Introduction to Information Retrieval*. Cambridge University Press, Cambridge, UK, 2008.

[23] P. M. Markey and C. N. Markey. A brief assessment of the interpersonal circumplex the ipip-ipc. *Assessment*, 16(4):352–361, 2009.

[24] G. Mohammadi and A. Vinciarelli. Automatic personality perception: Prediction of trait attribution based on prosodic features. *Affective Computing, IEEE Transactions on*, 3(3):273–284, 2012.

[25] D. O. Olguın, P. A. Gloor, and A. S. Pentland. Capturing individual and group behavior with wearable sensors. In *Proceedings of the 2009 aaai spring symposium on human behavior modeling, SSS*, volume 9, 2009.

[26] F. Pianesi, N. Mana, A. Cappelletti, B. Lepri, and M. Zancanaro. Multimodal recognition of personality traits in social interactions. In *Proceedings of the 10th international conference on Multimodal interfaces*, pages 53–60. ACM, 2008.

[27] D. Quercia, R. Lambiotte, D. Stillwell, M. Kosinski, and J. Crowcroft. The personality of popular facebook users. In *Proceedings of the ACM 2012 conference on Computer Supported Cooperative Work*, pages 955–964. ACM, 2012.

[28] B. Rammstedt and O. P. John. Measuring personality in one minute or less: A 10-item short version of the big five inventory in english and german. *Journal of Research in Personality*, 41(1):203–212, 2007.

[29] J. Sivic and A. Zisserman. Video Google: A text retrieval approach to object matching in videos. In *Proceedings of ICCV*, pages 1470–1477, Nice, France, 2003.

[30] J. Staiano, B. Lepri, N. Aharony, F. Pianesi, N. Sebe, and A. Pentland. Friends don't lie: inferring personality traits from social network structure. In *Proceedings of the 2012 ACM Conference on Ubiquitous Computing*, pages 321–330. ACM, 2012.

[31] S. Utz. Show me your friends and i will tell you what type of person you are: How one's profile, number of friends, and type of friends influence impression formation on social network sites. *Journal of Computer-Mediated Communication*, 15(2):314–335, 2010.

[32] B. Van Der Heide, J. D. DŠAngelo, and E. M. Schumaker. The effects of verbal versus photographic self-presentation on impression formation in facebook. *Journal of Communication*, 62(1):98–116, 2012.

[33] S. Vazire and S. D. Gosling. e-perceptions: personality impressions based on personal websites. *Journal of personality and social psychology*, 87(1):123, 2004.

Automatic Image Cropping using Visual Composition, Boundary Simplicity and Content Preservation Models

Chen Fang [1], Zhe Lin [2], Radomír Měch [2], Xiaohui Shen [2]
[1] Computer Science Department, Dartmouth College, Hanover, NH, USA
[2] Adobe Research, San Jose, CA, USA
chenfang@cs.dartmouth.edu; {zlin, rmech, xshen}@adobe.com

ABSTRACT

Cropping is one of the most common tasks in image editing for improving the aesthetic quality of a photograph. In this paper, we propose a new, aesthetic photo cropping system which combines three models: *visual composition*, *boundary simplicity*, and *content preservation*. The visual composition model measures the quality of composition for a given crop. Instead of manually defining rules or score functions for composition, we learn the model from a large set of well-composed images via discriminative classifier training. The boundary simplicity model measures the clearness of the crop boundary to avoid object cutting-through. The content preservation model computes the amount of salient information kept in the crop to avoid excluding important content. By assigning a hard lower bound constraint on the content preservation and linearly combining the scores from the visual composition and boundary simplicity models, the resulting system achieves significant improvement over recent cropping methods in both quantitative and qualitative evaluation.

Categories and Subject Descriptors

I.4.3 [**Image processing and computer vision**]: Enhancement—*Geometric correction*

Keywords

image cropping; visual composition; image aesthetic

1. INTRODUCTION

Cropping is an important task in image editing, which is used to improve the aesthetic quality of a photograph. The main goal is to improve photo compositions, e.g. by emphasizing an object of interest, removing undesired regions, and obtaining a better color balance. In photography, many rules such as the rule of thirds, visual balance, or diagonal dominance, are explicitly defined for creating photos with good composition.

MM'14, November 3–7, 2014, Orlando, Florida, USA.
Copyright 2014 ACM 978-1-4503-3063-3/14/11 ...$15.00.
http://dx.doi.org/10.1145/2647868.2654979.

Automatic photo cropping can help novice photographers and professionals by suggesting aesthetically pleasing crops. Although there have been various approaches proposed in the literature including rule-based [2, 6] and learning-based methods [4, 5, 1], it remains a challenging problem due to the complexity of rules and variability of images. Rule-based methods typically encode the rules in score functions to evaluate the composition quality of a crop. These methods do not require a training dataset, but it is difficult to encode all the rules precisely. Learning-based methods try to automatically learn composition rules or score functions from a training set. These methods avoid manual design of composition rules but may suffer from the lack of training data. In general, previous work mainly focused on composition rules and score functions while ignoring the importance of other cues, such as the preservation of important content, and the avoidance of object cutting-through.

The contribution of our work is a novel, learning-based system for automatic cropping of photographs, utilizing a set of cues that are important for improving the aesthetic quality of cropped images. By analyzing a large image dataset of professional crops, we empirically observe that the following three cues are very important: *visual composition*, *boundary simplicity* and *content preservation*. Our quantitative and qualitative experiments also demonstrate that ignoring any of those cues may yield bad croppings. This is in contrast to previous methods, which over-emphasized the composition quality in determining optimal crops.

Visual composition Visual composition refers to the placement or arrangement of visual elements in a photo. The human-centric nature of cropping and the dependency of rules on specific image content suggests that cropping guidelines should be learned from data, instead of being manually encoded [2][6], as it is difficult to cover all guidelines, and capture the variation of personal preference. We build our visual composition model based on a large set of well-composed photos from the Internet[1]. In contrast to [4] which learns composition via generative models such as GMM, we learn a more powerful discriminative model by synthesizing negative examples from well-composed images so that the composition scoring is more accurate with limited training data.

Boundary simplicity When cropping a photo, it is often undesirable to cut through an object, because it may not only ruins the balance, but also create unnecessary distraction. We propose a simple concept, the simplicity or

[1]The dataset is reviewed by professionals to remove ill-composed images.

clearness of the crop boundary to address this problem. We assume that a crop boundary, which goes through visually simpler regions, is less likely to cut through objects. We model the boundary simplicity using the normalized rank of the smoothened gradient along the crop boundaries.

Content preservation Another important constraint for cropping is preserving the important content. Without this constraint, we may obtain crops with good composition and clean boundaries that miss salient elements, e.g. people. Thus, this constraint acts as a regularizer to prevent the photo from being overly cropped. The model used in this paper only relies on saliency information. Incorporating other cues such as face detection or human detection may further improve the performance.

Given the three models, we assign a hard lower-bound constraint on the content preservation and linearly combine the visual composition and boundary simplicity models to score any candidate crops. The resulting system achieves significant improvement over the recent cropping methods both quantitatively and qualitatively.

2. APPROACH DETAILS

In this section, we first introduce the three models used in our cropping framework: visual composition, boundary simplicity and content preservation. Then we describe how these models are used in our cropping algorithm.

2.1 Visual Composition

To build a visual composition model, the following three aspects need to be addressed: (1) an effective feature to encode composition information, (2) a powerful model to learn the knowledge of composition quality, and (3) a dataset of photographs suitable for model learning.

Composition feature When looking at a photo, people are often more easily attracted by certain regions. The spatial configuration of these salient regions plays an important role in determining the composition quality of a photo. We use the method in [3] to generate a saliency map of the original image, which is further used to build a three-level spatial pyramid to encode the spatial configuration. We name it as Spatial Pyramid of Saliency Map (**SPSM**). Compared to [4], our SPSM captures richer and more accurate composition information by considering the multi-level spatial distributions of salient regions.

Model learning Support Vector Regression (SVR) is used to learn a mapping from feature space to composition score. Training examples are encoded using SPSM feature and the label is binary (1 for positive and 0 for negative). The output of SVR given a crop C is denoted as $S_{compos}(C)$.

Training data Positive and negative samples are needed for discriminative training. While the positive samples (i.e., well-composed images) are easy to obtain from professional photography websites, it is rather difficult to get a large number of ill-composed images from online resources. We propose to only collect well-composed photos, and then use random crops of these photos as negative samples. Those random crops are very likely to produce badly composed images, e.g. by cutting through salient objects, by breaking the visual balance or other composition rules.

2.2 Boundary Simplicity

The idea behind the *boundary simplicity* cue is to encourage crop boundaries to pass through visually simpler regions, in order to reduce the chance of cutting through objects. We resort to image gradient, as when crop edge crosses object boundaries, gradient is usually large. Given a crop, we use the average gradient values along the four boundaries with a flipped sign to measure the simplicity and cleaness. We further make it more robust by filtering the original image with a Gaussian filter to remove high frequency textures, e.g. waves on a water surface, which do not form object boundaries. Experimental results show that *boundary simplicity* helps improving cropping results. See Fig.1 for a comparison between cropping results of running our system with and without enabling *boundary simplicity*.

Figure 1: A comparison between crops with and without boundary simplicity. (a) The original image. (b) The gradient magnitude map of the blurred input image. (c) A crop with the boundary simplicity cue. (d) A crop without the boundary simplicity cue.

2.3 Content Preservation

In order to prevent the system from cropping out important regions, we propose using *content preservation* cue. We use visual saliency in this component. Salient objects are those that capture more attention of a human observer. Therefore, a certain amount of salient regions should be kept. The *content preservation* score $S_{content}(C)$ is the ratio of saliency energy that is contained by a crop C to the total saliency energy of the input image. We give an example of a crop with this cue in Fig.2, where by enforcing to keep a certain amount of salient regions we avoid cropping out the person.

2.4 Cropping Algorithm

In this section we present the pipline of our cropping algorithm.

Step 1 - Image analysis
Analyze the input image by extracting the saliency map and image gradient.

Step 2 - Crop candidates
Propose initial crops. Densely sample on a grid over the input image. At each grid location, crops of different sizes and common aspect ratios are generated. With 10,000 initial cropping windows, the entire pipeline (without saliency extraction) takes 0.2 second per image.

Step 3 - Scoring candidates
Feed the crop candidates from step 2 to the three models described above to measure the corresponding scores.

Step 4 - Candidate screen
Remove overly cropped candidates that may miss main salient

Figure 2: A comparison between crops with and without content preservation. (a) The original image. (b) The saliency map of original image, with high saliency intensities around the person. (c) Content preservation forces the crop to include the person, while maintaining good aesthetic quality. (d) A crop without the content preservation cue.

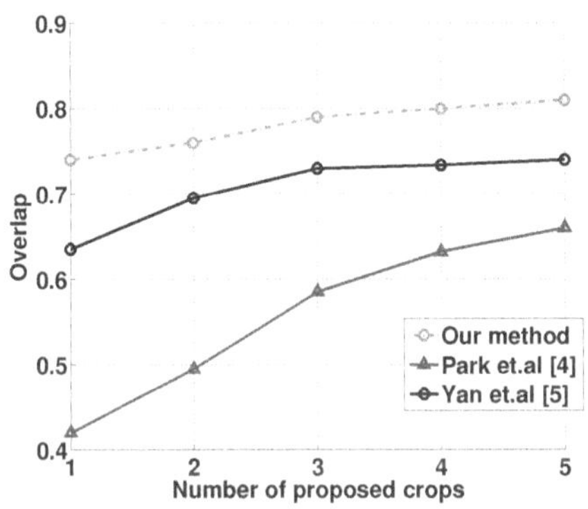

Figure 3: Quantitative comparison between our system and other competing systems.

regions by enforcing a threshold τ on content preservation. We empirically set the τ to 0.4.

Step 5 - Score calibration and combination
Linearly combine *visual composition* and *boundary simplicity*. S_{compos} and $S_{boundary}$ need to be calibrated first. Instead of using the raw score, we use the normalized rank of a candidate crop with respect to each cue. The normalized rank of composition of crop C on image I, which is denoted as $R_{compos}(C, I)$, is simply the percentage of candidates that have higher composition score than C. ($R_{boundary}(C, I)$ is defined similarly.) The final score is a weighted linear combination of R_{compos} and $R_{boundary}$, which is defined as:

$$S_{final}(C, I) = w_1 R_{compos}(C, I) + w_2 R_{boundary}(C, I) \quad (1)$$

where w_1 and w_2 are the weights controling the relative importance of the two terms. In our experiments, the weights (w_1, w_2) are set by validation on a grid of different parameter values. We found that setting w_1 and w_2 to 5 and 1 gives the best performance. However, the weights can also be learned from a human-cropped dataset, e.g. user's crops. The fewer number of parameters not only mitigates overfitting, but also makes it possible to learn only from few human crop examples.

Step 6 - Non-maximum suppression
Due to the large number of candidate crops, we remove redundancy using non-maximum suppression, so that the results are more diverse.

3. EXPERIMENTS

Due to lack of publicly available datasets, we collect our own labelled dataset and compare our method quatitatively and qualitatively to two most recent learning based methods from [4] and [5], representing data-driven and learning-based methods. Furthermore, we also conduct a qualitative comparison to the state of the art rule-based method [2]. As we do not have groudtruth crops of [2], we run our method on their test images and do a visual comparison.

3.1 Dataset

Two datasets are used in our experiments: a training dataset with a large number of well-composed images, and a dataset containing ill-composed[2] images with manual crops provided by qualified experts. As described in Section 2.1, our *visual composition* model is trained on carefully selected, well-composed photographs. Specifically, we download images from Photo.net, remove low-quality images, and collected 3000 high-quality, good composition photos for training. On the other hand, we collect 500 ill-composed photographs, which are then cropped by 10 expert users on Amazon Mechanical Turk who passed a strict qualification test. We call this labelled dataset as human crop dataset. We use all the 3000 images to train both our system and [4]. To train the models of [5] which require both before and after-crop images, the training split of human crop dataset is used. All the evaluation are carried out on the test split of the human crop dataset.

3.2 Quantitative Evaluation

In this section we compare the performance of our system to those in [4] and [5] using the human crop dataset. Specifically, we measure the maximum overlap between the proposed crop candidates and the ground truth, i.e., manual crops by the expert users. The maximum overlap is defined as follows:

$$MaxOverlap(B, G) = \max_{i,j} Overlap(B_i, G_j) \quad (2)$$

where B is the set of proposed crops and G is the ground truth set. We choose the size of B to be equal or less than 5, since most users will not need more than 5 crop suggestions. The function *Overlap*() can be calculated as:

$$Overlap(B_i, G_j) = \frac{B_i \cap G_j}{B_i \cup G_j} \quad (3)$$

As shown in Fig.3, our system consistently outperforms [5] and [4] by a large margin in all top 5 cases. Especially when only considering the top candidate, our system achieves nearly 10% improvement over [5]. This can significantly improve the user satisfaction in practice. As mentioned above, our system and [4] are trained on well-composed photos, while [5] is trained on the human crop dataset, which is expensive and time-comsuming to collect.

3.3 Qualitative Results

Because of the humancentric nature of cropping, qualitative results, such as visual comparison and human evaluation, is as important as quantitative results.

User study We conducted a user study to judge the quality of crop suggestions from our system and competing methods, including [4] and [5]. The test images and their top-3

[2]By 'ill-composed' we mean the images with imperfect composition.

Figure 5: More cropping results of our system. The first row contains original images, and the second row contains top-1 cropping suggestions of our system.

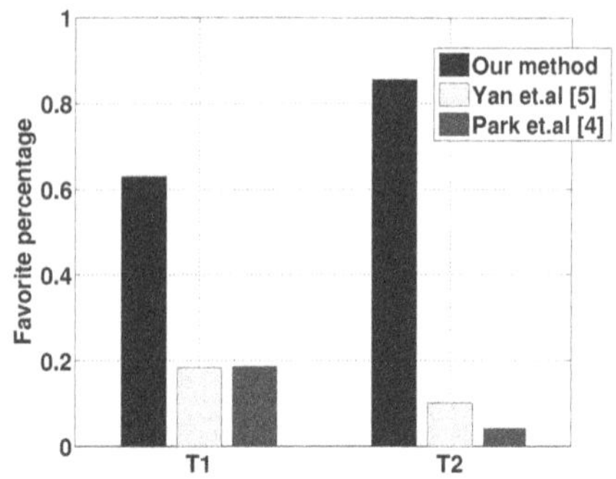

Figure 4: Qualitative results from our user study.

crop suggestions from different methods are passed to three hired professional photographers. We challenge them with two tasks: (T1) which method gives the best crop among all displayed candidates and report the corresponding method. (T2) Which method gives suggestions of the best overall quality, thus experts need to consider their overall fondness of top-3 suggestions. We report the percentage of each method being selected for each task in Fig.4, which is the average result over all experts. It is clear that our method significantly outperforms the other two in both tasks.

Visual comparison To compare with [2], we run our method on their data, which we obtained from the authors. Since we do not have their implementation, we compare our results to theirs showed in their paper and supplementary material. As shown in Fig.6, our results are aesthetically more pleasing than those of [2] (Due to page limit, three representative examples are given in Fig.6.) We conjecture that the difference is due to the fact that our visual composition model is learned from data, which can adaptively adjust to the relative importance of cropping guidelines, whereas [2] strictly follows guidlines encoded in their algorithm.

More results We show more results of our method in Fig.5. Due to space limit, only six examples are listed. More results are included in *supplementary material*.

4. CONCLUSION AND FUTURE WORK

In this paper we propose a simple but effective method for automatic image cropping. It is efficient and easy to implement. Instead of hard coding the cropping rules, we choose to let the system learn those rules from a set of well-composed photos from online resources. In addition to the

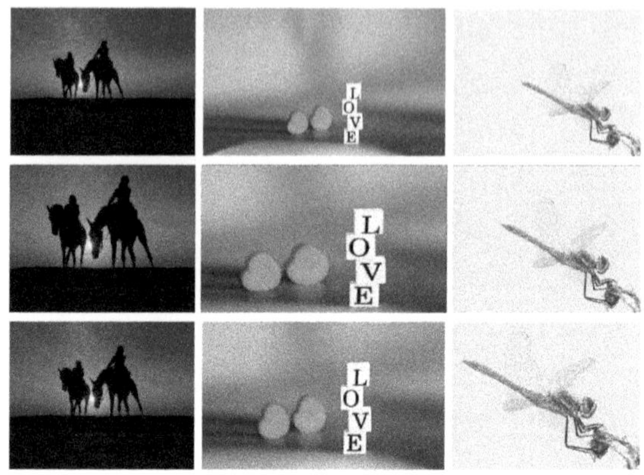

Figure 6: Qualitative comparison between our method and [2]. The original images are in the first row. The second row contains the top-1 cropping results of [2]. The third row contains the top-1 results of our method.

composition cue, we also propose two other cues, *content preservation* and *boundary simplicity*, which preserve the main subjects of the input image and avoid cutting through, respectively. Compared with state-of-the-art systems, our method demonstrates a much better cropping performance in both quantitative and qualitative evaluations. Future work includes exploring other cues, e.g. content semantics. Please contact the authors for dataset details.

5. REFERENCES

[1] B. Cheng, B. Ni, S. Yan, and Q. Tian. Learning to photograph. In *ACM International Conference on Multimedia*, 2010.

[2] L. Liu, R. Chen, L. Wolf, and D. Cohen-Or. Optimizing photo composition. *Eurographics*, 2010.

[3] R. Margolin, A. Tal, and L. Zelnik-Manor. What makes a patch distinct? In *IEEE CVPR*, 2013.

[4] J. Park, J.-Y. Lee, Y.-W. Tai, and I. S. Kweon. Modeling photo composition and its application to photo re-arrangement. In *IEEE ICIP*, 2012.

[5] J. Yan, S. Lin, S. B. Kang, and X. Tang. Learning the change for automatic image cropping. In *IEEE CVPR*, 2013.

[6] M. Zhang, L. Zhang, Y. Sun, L. Feng, and W. Ma. Auto cropping for digital photographs. In *IEEE ICME*, 2005.

Mask Assisted Object Coding with Deep Learning for Object Retrieval in Surveillance Videos

Kezhen Teng[1], Jinqiao Wang[1], Min Xu[2], and Hanqing Lu[1]
[1]National Laboratory of Pattern Recognition, Institute of Automation
Chinese Academy of Sciences, Beijing, China, 100190
[2]iNEXT, School of Computing and Communications, University of Technology, Sydney, Australia
{kezhen.teng,jqwang,luhq}@nlpr.ia.ac.cn, min.xu25@gmail.com

ABSTRACT

Retrieving visual object from a large-scale video dataset is one of multimedia research focuses but a challenging task due to imprecise object extraction and partial occlusion. This paper presents a novel approach to efficiently encode and retrieve visual objects, which addresses some practical complications in surveillance videos. Specifically, we take advantage of the mask information to assist object representation, and develop an encoding method by utilizing highly nonlinear mapping with a deep neural network. Furthermore, we add some occluded noise into the learning process to enhance the robustness of dealing with background noise and partial occlusions. A real-life surveillance video data containing over 10 million objects are built to evaluate the proposed approach. Experimental results show our approach significantly outperforms state-of-the-art solutions for object retrieval in large-scale video dataset.

Categories and Subject Descriptors

I.4.10 [**Image Representation**]: Multidimensional; I.5.4 [**Applications**]: Signal processing

General Terms

Algorithms, Experimentation, Theory

Keywords

Object retrieval, Video search, Autoencoder

1. INTRODUCTION

The increasing number of cameras produce a huge amount of video data. It is an urgent need to develop intelligent techniques for object indexing and retrieval in a large-scale video data. Content-based object retrieval is an advanced multimedia application, which is benefitted from efficient representation [8] and indexation [13, 7] approaches. Although this problem attracts increasing research interests [14, 4, 10, 1, 7] in recent years, developing an efficient object retrieval solution, especially for surveillance videos, is still a challenging task, primarily due to three issues. First, such a solution involves a series of processing, such as background modelling, object extraction and representation, which are all crucial but challenge tasks. Second, the appearance of the same object is inconsistent under different cameras, which add the difficult with the combination of view and pose change. Finally, complex conditions such as low resolution, illumination, noise, shadows, and partial occlusions embodied with surveillance environment, make the objects inherently subtle and even vague for human to recognize, thus considerable computations are required to discern them.

As analysis above, in this paper a content-based object retrieval approach is proposed based on deep learning, which is to encode object together with mask information efficiently. A multi-model deep learning strategy is proposed to restructure the training set and improve retrieval performance when the background is very noisy and with partial occlusions. Moreover, we collect a real-life dataset contains more than 10 million objects for evaluation. Our method outperforms other hash methods 10% on object retrieval in surveillance video.

MM'14, November 3–7, 2014, Orlando, Florida, USA.

http://dx.doi.org/10.1145/2647868.2654981 .

2. RELATED WORK

Object retrieval in surveillance mainly focuses on the objects, such as persons and vehicles [5, 18, 15]. Calderara *et al.* [2] proposed the architecture for person retrieval in multi-camera surveillance with the non-overlapping views, and estimated the color probability distribution with a mixture of Gaussians. Feris *et al.* [5] extracted a set of fine-grained attributes for moving vehicles such as time, direction, dominant color, dimensions and speed, etc. Then they automatically ingested the attribute metadata into a backend database system through a web-based service-oriented architecture. Thornton *et al.* [15] focused on attributes of gender, hair/hat color, clothing color, and bag (if any) position and color. A generative model was proposed to build the corresponding descriptors for person search. Yang and Yu [18] combined color histograms and three different texture descriptors to real-time recognize eight kinds of clothes in surveillance videos.

Recent researches indicate that the generic descriptors extracted from the deep neural networks are very powerful. Hinton [9] applied a 19 layers very deep autoencoder to encode natural images into binary codes and achieve satisfactory results. However, it focused on the whole image, not the object we are interested in. Inspired by [9], in this pa-

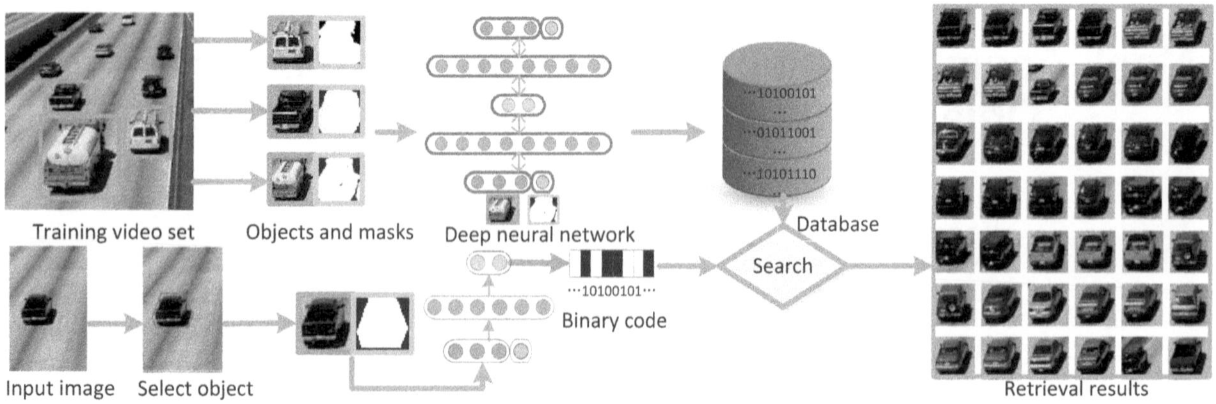

Figure 1: Overall framework.

per through mapping the object and mask information extracted from surveillance videos to short binary codes with deep learning, a very deep representation is learned to ensure similar objects have similar binary codes.

3. OVERVIEW

The framework of the proposed approach is illustrated in Fig. 1. In the training phase, background subtraction and multi-object tracking [19] is performed for surveillance videos to extract active objects such as a person and a car. Two sub-images are extracted for each object: the color image of the object block and the corresponding mask image. Then a multimodel deep neural network is trained to encode the object and mask image into a 128 bit binary vector. In the retrieval phase, user can select an interesting object from the query image through an interactive operation. Afterwards the selected object is encoded with the learned deep neural network. Then the generated 128 bit code is used to retrieve similar objects in the database with hamming distance.

4. DEEP OBJECT REPRESENTATION

Autoencoder (AE) was firstly proposed by Hinton in 2002. As a deep neural network (DNN), it is composed with stacks of restricted Boltzmann machine (RBM) and is used to transfer input vectors into relative short codes with a highly nonlinear mapping function. With the progress of DNN theory and GPU technique, it becomes practical to train AE with acceptable computation ability. The training process is divided into two phases: unsupervised pre-train and supervised fine tune. To initialize the deep neural network, the encode part is trained generatively layer by layer. Then the weights and off-set vectors are unrolled to initialize the decode part. Afterwards, the whole neural network is fine-tuned with back propagation.

4.1 Mask assisted object coding

While in surveillance videos, the same object may appear in different scenes, or the same location in a frame but at different time. Thus they are surrounded with different background noise. Sometimes, e.g. in the case of traffic jam, an object is surrounded by many other objects. The denoised autoencoder (DAE) [16] is designed to increase robustness when dealing with global noise. It is trained to reconstruct a clean "repaired" input from its noisy version. Formally, the input v's noised version $\tilde{v}$ is construct through a stochastic mapping. The noisy version $\tilde{v}$ will be then mapped through AE to reconstruct a clean version of $\tilde{v}$ by $\hat{v}$. Note that the reconstruction error is $L = \sum_{i=1}^{N} |v_i - \hat{v}_i|^2$.

However, DAE is not proper for our object retrieval problem in surveillance videos due to two reasons. First, the encoding phase of DAE is encouraged to be robust for noise in the whole image, not the background area of image. Second, the distribution of foreground object is related to background area. If noise is only added to the background area, the training process will be confused. Details are shown as follows.

Suppose the foreground and background part of input image v are represented by f and b respectively. The appearance of foreground and background are represented by α and β respectively. And objective factors such as lighting, color deviation and stochastic noise are governed by θ. Then the distribution of v is formulated as,

$$p(v|f,b,\alpha,\beta,\theta) \propto p(v|f,b)p(f|\alpha,\theta)p(b|\beta,\theta) \quad (1)$$

Eq. 1 demonstrates that foreground and background are both related to θ. If the noise is added to the background area of image, the right part of Eq. 1 will be changed to $p(v|f,b)p(f|\alpha,\theta)p(b|\beta,\tilde{\theta})$, this will confuse the learning process.

Since moving objects are usually extracted with background subtraction, it is natural to incorporate the mask information to enhance object representation. Inspired by [11, 12], to learn a feature representation robust to different background images, we adopt a mask assisted multimodal deep neural network to learn discriminative object codes.

The mask image is represented by m, which is as the object context information. Then the object encoding solution α can be solved with autoencoder as,

$$\begin{aligned} arg\max_{\alpha} \quad & p(\hat{v},\hat{m}|v,m) \\ \propto \quad & p(\hat{v},\hat{m}|b,f)p(b,f|v,m) \\ \propto \quad & p(\hat{v},\hat{m}|b,f)p(f|\alpha,\theta)p(b|\beta,\theta)p(\alpha,\beta,\theta|v,m) \end{aligned} \quad (2)$$

In fact the optimization problem is often recast as,

$$arg\min_{\alpha} \quad L = |v-\hat{v}|^2 + |m-\hat{m}|^2 \quad (3)$$

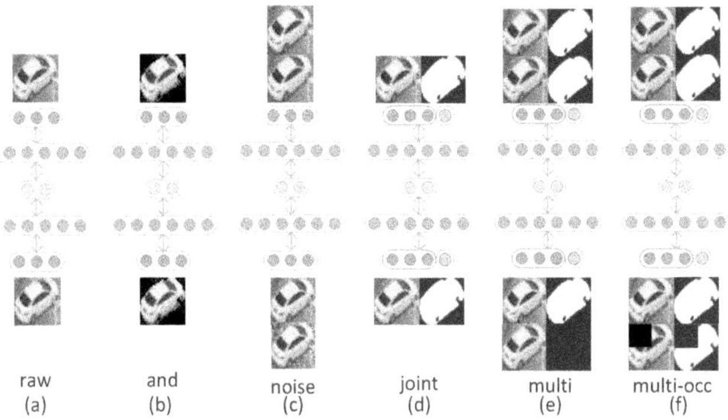

Figure 2: Different coding designs with DNN.

Table 1: Retrieval results of different approaches with 128 bit codes (MAP %).

	original	noise	occlude(0.25)	occlude(0.5)
ITQ(32bit)	39.09	38.28	15.45	4.93
raw(32bit)	46.93	37.92	18.80	5.21
ITQ	52.43	50.20	39.11	6.08
LSH	49.41	46.45	35.81	6.75
SH	48.22	44.98	30.64	8.19
raw	50.02	46.81	23.57	5.90
and	52.98	52.98	40.26	11.39
noise	53.85	50.10	22.64	11.85
joint	62.11	60.91	39.71	12.33
multi	64.91	65.46	40.38	12.56
multi-occ	65.02	60.25	41.27	18.61

By introducing mask information, the multimodel autoencoder could learn the context appearance of object by minimizing the reconstruction error.

To illustrate our multimodel learning structure, different coding designs of deep neural networks are given in Fig. 2. (a) is to directly learn the feature codes with autoencoder. (b) is to learn with the object region only. (c) is to learn with denoising autoencoder. (d), (e) and (f) are our multimodel solutions. (d) is to jointly learn with object images and mask images together. (e) is to multimodel learn with object images and mask images. For multimodel neural network, the training set is copied and divided into two totally equal parts. The first part includes input object images and mask images. In the second part, mask images are all transformed to pure black images. In the pre-training phase, the two parts are both used. while in the fine-tuning phase, both parts are tuned by the first part. Thus even for the user input without effective mask image, this multimodel autoencoder is expected to reconstruct object image with complete mask image. In this way, the deep neural network is supposed not only to encode the object itself, but also to segment it from different background.

4.2 Occlusion processing

Another challenge confronted by surveillance videos is the partial occlusion problem, especially in crowed scene such as shopping mall and residential quarters. To address this challenge, we further add some occlusion noise into the multimodel autoencoder, as shown in Fig. 2(f). The training set is designed to comprise occlusion noise. Specifically, we insert some random patches into the object image, and for each patch the pixels are set to zero. Then these noised images and un-noised images compose the whole training set. In the pre-training phase, the noised images and the un-noised images are both used. While in the fine-tuning phase, those noised patch is fine-tuned with the un-noised patch. In this way, the learned object codes could reconstruct the missing regions for partial occluded object.

5. EXPERIMENTS

5.1 Dataset and setting

Since there no available large scale surveillance dataset that provides the object and mask images, to evaluate the performance of the proposed approaches we collect surveillance videos with HD cameras mounted at residential entrances inside university. We utilize background subtraction and object tracking to extract object images and corresponding mask images, and build a dataset about 10 million objects. The object dataset covers different weather conditions, different lighting effects, and different periods of time.

The color object blocks are resized to 32×32 with three channels and the binary mask images are resized to 32×32 with only one channel. Then a 4096 dimension vector is built to represent the object. To obtain more training instances, all images are flipped left to right to double the training set.

We train on 10 million images that have been preprocessed by subtracting from each pixel to its mean value over all images and then dividing by the standard deviation of each pixels over all images. The first RBM in the stack has 8192 binary hidden units and 4096 linear visible units with unit variance Gaussian noise. All the remaining RBM's have N binary hidden units and $4N$ binary visible units until it reaches the designed size. Details of training process is similar to [9]. The entire training procedure for each multimodel autoencoder takes about 1 day on a Nvidia Tesla M2075.

5.2 Retrieval results

Total 43 queries are used to evaluate the proposed approach. Mean Average Precision (MAP) is used to quantitatively measure the performance. To compare the robustness for background noise and partial occlusion, four groups of queries images were carried out for each approach. The first group includes clean object images and mask images. In the second group, Gaussian noise was added to query images. In the third group, 0.25% of object region in queries is random occluded. The same setting was used for the fourth group queries with occluded block size of 50% of query objects. In addition to the original autoencoder, some classic hashing approaches LSH (locality sensitive hashing) [3], SH (spectral hashing) [17], ITQ (iterative quantization) [6] are also compared, and retrieval results of different approaches with 128 bit codes are shown in Tab. 1.

From Tab. 1, "raw" that directly learns with autoencoder [9] achieves satisfactory results even for short codes (32 bit). But it seems that those linear hash methods achieve better robustness in partial occlusion conditions for 128 bit codes. When mask image is introduced, the retrieval performance is effectively boost even for one modality learning. With 128 bit codes, the MAP is increased 12.09% for "joint" with simple object images and mask images than "raw". For the multi-modality learning "multi", as our expect, the MAP

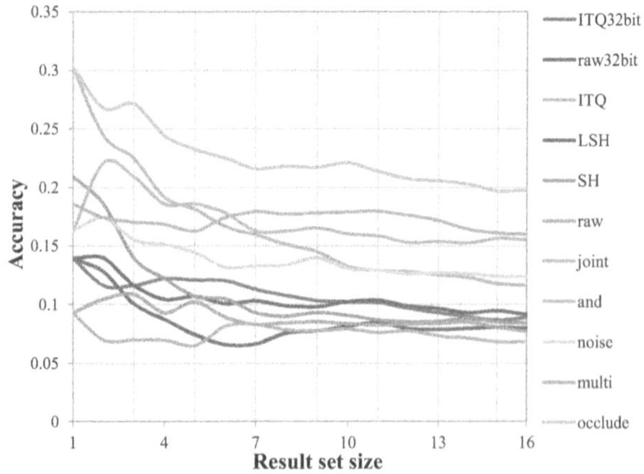

Figure 3: Retrieval accuracy of different approaches.

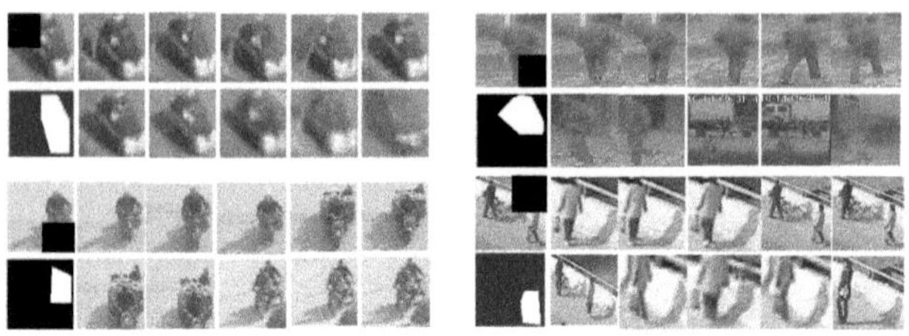

Figure 4: Retrieval results with occlusion.

raised 4.55% in noised conditions. And for the occluded learning "multi-occ", the MAP increased 6.28% for half occlusions than "multi", 10.42% than SH [17].

Fig. 3 shows the accuracy with different result set size in the experiment with 50% occlusion. The mask assisted object coding approaches "joint', "multi" and "multi-occ" outperform hash methods such as LSH [3], SH [17] and ITQ [6]. And the "multi-occ" reaches the best result, which shows the effective of our multimodel DNN for robustness of occlusion. Fig. 4 gives some examples in occlusion conditions.

6. CONCLUSION

In this paper, a mask assisted object encoding approach is presented to boost retrieval performance in surveillance videos. The object image and mask image are used to learn multimodel deep neural network that map similar objects to similar binary codes. Additionally, occlusion noise is added into the training set for reconstructing the whole object to handle partial occlusion. Experiments and comparisons demonstrate the efficiency of the proposed approach.

7. ACKNOWLEDGEMENT

This work was supported by 973 Program (2010CB327905), 863 Program (2014AA015104 and 2014AA015105), and National Natural Science Foundation of China (61273034, and 61332016).

8. REFERENCES

[1] R. Arandjelovic and A. Zisserman. Three things everyone should know to improve object retrieval. In *Computer Vision and Pattern Recognition (CVPR), 2012 IEEE Conference on*, pages 2911–2918, 2012.

[2] S. Calderara, R. Cucchiara, and A. Prati. Multimedia surveillance: content-based retrieval with multicamera people tracking. In *ACM International Workshop on VSSN*, pages 95–100, 2006.

[3] M. Charikar. Similarity estimation techniques from rounding algorithm. In *ACM symposium on Theory of computing*, pages 380–388, 2002.

[4] R. Datta, J. Li, and J. Z. Wang. Content-based image retrieval: approaches and trends of the new age. In *Proceedings of the 7th ACM SIGMM international workshop on Multimedia information retrieval*, pages 253–262, 2005.

[5] R. Feris, B. Siddiquie, Y. Zhai, J. Petterson, L. Brown, and S. Pankanti. Attribute-based vehicle search in crowded surveillance videos. In *Proceedings of the 1st ACM International Conference on Multimedia Retrieval*, page 18, 2011.

[6] Y. Gong and S. Lazebnik. Iterative quantization: a procrustean approach to learning binary codes. In *IEEE Conference on Computer Vision and Pattern Recognition (CVPR)*, 2011.

[7] Y. Gong, S. Lazebnik, A. Gordo, and F. Perronnin. Iterative quantization: A procrustean approach to learning binary codes for large-scale image retrieval. *Pattern Analysis and Machine Intelligence, IEEE Transactions on*, 35(12):2916–2929, 2013.

[8] H. Jégou, M. Douze, C. Schmid, and P. Pérez. Aggregating local descriptors into a compact image representation. In *Computer Vision and Pattern Recognition (CVPR), 2010 IEEE Conference on*, pages 3304–3311, 2010.

[9] A. Krizhevsky and G. E. Hinton. Using very deep autoencoders for content-based image retrieval. In *European Symposium on Artificial Neural Networks*, 2011.

[10] S. Lazebnik, C. Schmid, and J. Ponce. Beyond bags of features: Spatial pyramid matching for recognizing natural scene categories. In *Computer Vision and Pattern Recognition, 2006 IEEE Computer Society Conference on*, volume 2, pages 2169–2178, 2006.

[11] P. Luo, X. Wang, and X. Tang. Hierarchical face parsing via deep learning. In *IEEE Conference on Computer Vision and Pattern Recognition (CVPR)*, pages 2480–2487, 2012.

[12] J. Ngiam, A. Khosla, M. Kim, J. Nam, H. Lee, and A. Y. Ng. Multimodal deep learning. In *Proceedings of the 28th International Conference on Machine Learning (ICML)*, pages 689–696, 2011.

[13] D. Nister and H. Stewenius. Scalable recognition with a vocabulary tree. In *Computer Vision and Pattern Recognition, 2006 IEEE Computer Society Conference on*, volume 2, pages 2161–2168, 2006.

[14] J. Sivic and A. Zisserman. Video google: A text retrieval approach to object matching in videos. In *Computer Vision, 2003. Proceedings. Ninth IEEE International Conference on*, pages 1470–1477, 2003.

[15] J. Thornton, J. Baran-Gale, D. Butler, M. Chan, and H. Zwahlen. Person attribute search for large-area video surveillance. In *IEEE Int. Conf. on Technologies for Homeland Security (HST)*, pages 55–61, 2011.

[16] P. Vincent, H. Larochelle, Y. Bengio, and P.-A. Manzagol. Extracting and composing robust features with denoising autoencoders. In *Proceedings of the 25th international conference on Machine learning*, pages 1096–1103, 2008.

[17] Y. Weiss., A. Torrlaba, and R. Fergus. Spectral hashing. In *Advances in Neural Information Processing System (NIPS)*, 2008.

[18] M. Yang and K. Yu. Real-time clothing recognition in surveillance videos. In *18th IEEE International Conference on Image Processing (ICIP)*, pages 2937–2940, 2011.

[19] Y. Zhang, J. Wang, W. Fu, H. Lu, and H. Xu. Specific vehicle detection and tracking in road environment. In *ICIMCS*, pages 182–186, 2011.

Estimate Gaze Density by Incorporating Emotion

Huiying Liu[1], Min Xu[2], Xiangjian He[2], and Jinqiao Wang[3]
[1]Institute for Infocomm Research, A*STAR, Singapore
[2]University of Technology, Sydney, Australia
[3]National Laboratory of Pattern Recognition, Institute of Automation, CAS, Beijing, China
liuhy@i2r.a-star.edu.sg, min.xu25@gmail.com, xiangjian.he@uts.edu.au, jqwang@nlpr.ia.ac.cn

ABSTRACT

Gaze density estimation has attracted many research efforts in the past years. The factors considered in the existing methods include low level feature saliency, spatial position, and objects. Emotion, as an important factor driving attention, has not been taken into account. In this paper, we are the first to estimate gaze density through incorporating emotion. To estimate the emotion intensity of each position in an image, we consider three aspects, generic emotional content, facial expression intensity, and emotional objects. Generic emotional content is estimated by using Multiple instance learning, which is employed to train an emotion detector from weakly labeled images. Facial expression intensity is estimated by using a ranking method. Emotional objects are detected, by taking blood/injury and worm/snake as examples. Finally, emotion intensity, low level feature saliency, and spatial position, are fused, through a linear support vector machine, to estimate gaze density. The performance is tested on public eye tracking dataset. Experimental results indicate that incorporating emotion does improve the performance of gaze density estimation.

Categories and Subject Descriptors

I.2.10 [**Artificial Intelligence**]: Vision and Scene Understanding

General Terms

Algorithms

Keywords

Visual saliency; visual attention; emotion

1. INTRODUCTION

In the past years, gaze density estimation, as an aspect of visual attention analysis, has attracted many research efforts for its wide applications. Attention is driven by both stimulus and task. Stimulus driven attention is also called bottom-up attention. The representative works include Itti's saliency based method [5], Wang's Site Entropy Rate method [14], attention based on Information Maximization (AIM) method [1], the Saliency Using Natural (SUN) images method [15]. Task driven attention is also known as top-down attention. The representative works include [6] and others. In most of the existing works, the "task" usually refers to object detection, object recognition, scene analysis, and so on. Playing a significant role, emotion drives attention (examples are shown in Fig. 1) but has not been considered for gaze density estimation.

This paper is the first attempt to explore the influence of emotion on gaze. There are many psychology studies that suggest emotion plays an important role in guiding attention [9][12]. The major difficulty of this work is to estimate the emotion intensity of each position of an image. Our solution proposes a learning based emotion detector as major component. The detector is trained through Multiple Instance Learning (MIL), from a weakly labeled dataset, i.e., the images are labeled with emotion type but not the boundary of the emotional content. In addition to the emotion detector, we adopt two types of specific detectors/estimators as

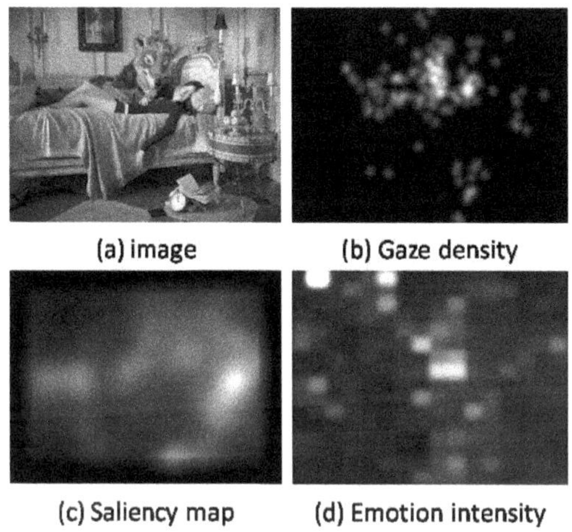

Figure 1: An examples of attention driven by emotion. As shown in the image (a) and the saliency map (c)[14], from the point of view of low level features, the beast is not the most salient part. But as shown in the gaze density map (b), it does attract much attention. The reason is that it evokes emotion, emotion of fear. The emotion intensity is shown in (d).

MM'14, November 3–7, 2014, Orlando, Florida, USA.
Copyright 2014 ACM 978-1-4503-3063-3/14/11 ...$15.00.
http://dx.doi.org/10.1145/2647868.2654983.

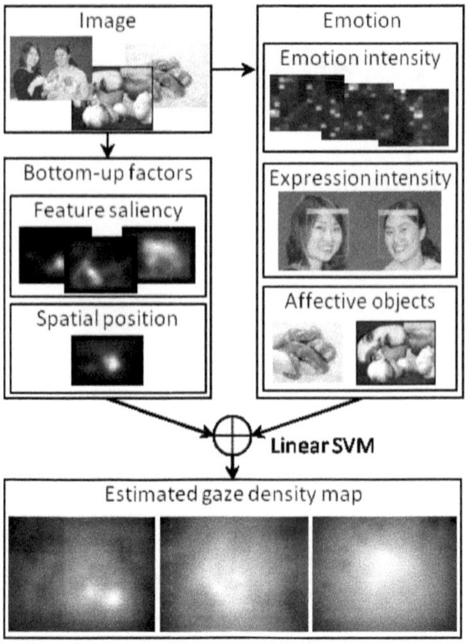

Figure 2: The overview of the method.

complement. One is an expression intensity estimator and the other contains two object detectors, e.g., worm/snake detector and injury detector. After obtaining the emotion intensity, linear Support Vector Machine is applied to fuse emotion with low level feature saliency and spatial position for gaze density estimation.

The major contribution of this paper is that, emotion factor is for the first time considered, as a complementation with the traditional factors, for gaze density estimation. Another contribution is that we propose an emotion intensity estimation method, by using multiple instance learning. As far as we know, this is also the first attempt. Experiments performed on images with rich emotions show that the incorporation of emotion does improve the performance of the baseline methods.

2. INCORPORATING EMOTION INTO GAZE DENSITY ESTIMATION

In this paper, three factors, including spatial position, feature saliency, and emotion are considered for gaze density estimation. For the factor of spatial position, the distance from a pixel to the image center is used as feature. For feature saliency, we adopt the existing methods as baseline, including Itti's method [5], AIM [1], SUN [15], and the SER method [14]. After calculating all the three factors, we fuse them through linear support vector machine to estimate the final gaze density map. Fig. 2 illustrates the overview of our method. In the following sections of the paper, we will focus on the emotion part since this is the most important contribution of our work.

We consider two types of affective images. One type includes the ones representing emotion, e.g., facial expression and body gesture. The other one consists of the images evoking emotion. For example, images of flowers usually evoke the emotion of joyfulness and the ones of snakes often evoke fear. To evaluate the emotion intensity of each position of an image, we consider three aspects. 1) Multiple instance learning is employed to train generic emotion detectors from emotional images. 2) Rank learning is adopted to estimate the intensity of facial expression. 3) We detect several emotional objects, e.g., injury, worm/snake. These three aspects will be detailed in the following subsections.

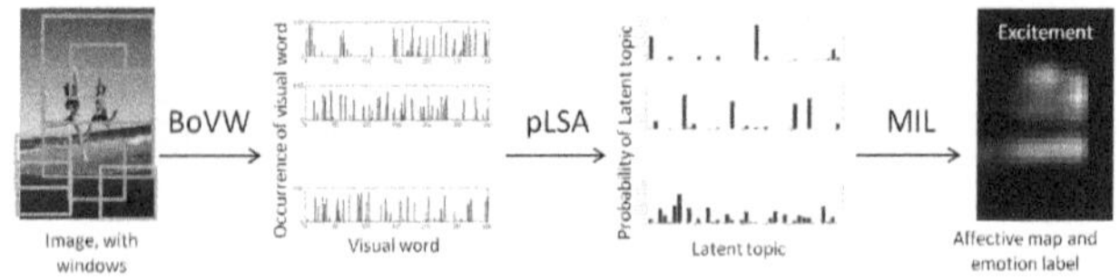

Figure 3: The flowchart of the emotion intensity estimation method.

2.1 Emotion intensity estimation using MIL

To estimate the emotion intensity of each position of an image, we face two major difficulties. The first one is that emotion is so complex that an emotion can be represented by diverse contents. For instance, an image of a beach with sunshine evokes happiness, blooming flowers evokes happiness, a smiling face represents happiness, and jumping is also able to represent happiness. The second difficulty is that it is difficult to collect a training dataset with the emotional content of each image exactly marked out. For the first difficulty, we appeal to probabilistic Latent Semantic Analysis (pLSA) [4] to learn a set of latent topics from affective images. For the second one, we employ multiple instance learning [8] to weaken the need for exact labeling. The profit of using MIL is that it doesn't need exact region label but can learn from weak labels.

The problem of emotion intensity estimation is defined as: given a set of training images, each of them labeled with an emotion type, such as happy, sad, and angry, our target is to train a set of emotion detectors that can be used to estimate the emotion intensity of each position of an arbitrary image. The flowchart of the proposed method is shown in Fig. 3. For a training image, image windows are extracted at multiple scales and multiple positions thus at least one of them covers the emotional content. All the windows extracted from an image compose a bag. The Bag-of-Visual-Words (BoVW) method [3] is adopted to represent image windows. Then probabilistic Latent Semantic Analysis is adopted to represent a window with latent topics. Finally, MIL is used to train from the data an emotion detector. For a given image, we estimate the emotion state of each window using the trained model.

2.1.1 BoVW description and pLSA representation

The emotional state of an image is determined by both the global atmosphere and local contents. In our work, our purpose is to estimate the emotion intensity of each position of an image, e.g., the local content. Therefore local features are more suitable. The feature used by [7], which are delicately designed from the perspective of art and psychology, are mostly global features suitable for classification rather than for intensity estimation. SIFT descriptor is applied as basic feature in our work. Bag-of-Visual-Words is adopted to represent the image windows. Let $W = \{w_1, w_2, ..., w_M\}$ be a vocabulary, with M as the total number of visual words, each image window is represented as $\mathbf{x} = [x_1, x_2, ..., x_M]'$, with x_i indicating the occurrence of word w_i.

For each image window, we further extract latent topics using pLSA, which is verified to be effective for image scene classification [3]. pLSA model associates an unobserved class variable $\mathbf{z} = (z_1, z_2, ..., z_K)$ with each observation (I_i, w_j). K is the number of topics. With this latent variable, the probability of an observation pair (I_i, w_j), which is the occurrence of the visual word w_j in a particular image window I_i, is

$$P(I_i, w_j) = P(I_i) P(w_j|I_i) = P(I_i) \sum_{k=1}^{K} P(w_j|z_k) P(z_k|I_i) \tag{1}$$

$P(w_j|z_k)$ and $P(z_k|I_i)$ are estimated by using Expectation-Maximization (EM) algorithm.

Given an sample, the log probability of a topic is

$$\log P(z_k|I_i) = \sum_{j=1}^{M} \frac{x_{ij}}{\|\mathbf{x}_i\|_1} P(z_k|I_i, w_j) \tag{2}$$

here $P(z_k|I_i, w_j)$ is calculated as

$$P(z_k|I_i, w_j) = \frac{P(w_j|z_k) P(z_k|I_i)}{\sum_{k=1}^{K} P(w_j|z_k) P(z_k|I_i)} \tag{3}$$

Using Eq. (2) and Eq. (3), we estimate the topic distribution of each image window.

2.1.2 MIL estimation

In many cases, the emotion conveyed by an image is mainly contained in an local patch instead of the whole image. For example, for the leftmost image in Fig. 3, it is far-fetched to say that the patches with green borderlines are exciting ones. But the available labeling information is only for the whole image not for each image window. Multiple instance learning is a powerful method to learn from this kind of weakly labeled data[8]. For MIL, each bag of samples can share one label. If there is at least one positive sample in a bag, then the whole bag is labeled as positive. If a bag is labeled as negative, all the samples in the bag are negative.

We adopt an iterative method to train the detectors. At the initializing stage, the image window at the original level is adopted as positive sample to train the detectors. At the following step, the probability of each window to cover the emotional region is estimated, by using the trained detector. The one with the highest probability in a bag is taken as positive to train a new detector. This process is repeated until no change happens when choosing the positive samples.

By using the trained detectors, each image window obtained in section 2.1.1 is assigned a probability of belonging to a particular emotion category. Using the result, we calculate the probability of a pixel belonging to an emotion category. For each pixel in an image, the probability of belonging to a particular emotion category is the average of all the windows covering it.

$$P(i, j, c) = \sum_{(i,j) \in \mathbf{x}_k} P(\mathbf{x}_k, c) \tag{4}$$

here (i, j) is a pixel and c is an emotion category, $\mathbf{x}_k$ is a window.

The probability of a pixel to belong to the emotional region is the summation over all the emotion categories.

$$P(i, j) = \sum_{c} \sum_{(i,j) \in \mathbf{x}_k} P(\mathbf{x}_k, c) P(c) \tag{5}$$

Figure 4: Examples of relative expression and emotional object detection.

here $P(c) = \max_k P(\mathbf{x}_k, c)$ is the probability of the image to belong to category c. Fig. 1 (d) shows an example of emotion intensity estimation result.

2.2 Facial expression intensity estimation

Human faces attract much human attention. This factor has been considered in many works[6] but what is not considered is that facial expression attracts more attention than the faces without expression. Generally speaking, the more intense the expression is, the more attention it attracts. This factor is particularly important for the images with multiple faces.

We borrow the idea of relative attribute to estimate expression intensity [11]. GIST is adopted as feature and rank SVM is employed to train the estimator[10]. The expressions considered are the six ones thought to be recognized universally. They are happy, anger, disgust, fear, surprise, and sad [2]. Fig. 4 (a) shows an example of relative expression. For each detected face, expression intensity is estimated for the six kinds of expression. Then the max of them is applied for gaze density estimation.

2.3 Other emotional object detection

Many objects can evoke emotion. For instance, flowers usually evoke the emotion of happiness, worms evoke disgust and fear, snakes evoke fear, etc. These objects are referred to as emotional objects in this paper. It is hardly to collect a full list of emotional objects so we choose two examples as representative. As shown in [9], fear drives attention more than other emotions. Therefore we choose two objects evoking fear as examples. They are worm/snake and blood/injury. Worm and snake look alike and they evoke the similar emotion, fear. Therefore we train one detector for them. We adopt GIST as feature and employ SVM to train a worm/snake and an blood/injury detector [10]. A sliding window is used to detect the target objects in the images. Finally, we obtain the probability of each pixel to belong to the object. Fig. 4 (b) and (c) show examples of snake detection and blood detection results.

3. EXPERIMENTS

We test our method on the NUSEF eye gaze dataset [13] for the affluent emotion contained in the images. The 446 images publicly available are used in experiment. The emotion intensity estimator are trained on the dataset published in [7].

The size of the vocabulary of BoVW is set as 100, the number of latent topic of pLSA is set as 20. For the lin-

Table 1: Test result of the components.

	ITTI	+MIL	+EXP	+FACE	+EMO
AUC	0.5744	0.5984	0.5893	0.5717	0.7498
t-test		<0.01	<0.01	<0.01*	<0.01

*The t-test result is between +FACE and +EXP.

Table 2: The result of comparison between our method and the baseline methods.

	ITTI	AIM	SUN	SER
baseline	0.5744	0.6727	0.6159	0.7425
with emotion	0.7122	0.7163	0.7020	0.7541
t-test	<0.01	<0.01	<0.01	0.04

ear SVM to fuse all the components, we choose from each training image 20 positive samples randomly from the top 5 percent, and 20 negative samples randomly from the bottom 30 percent. Cross validation is adopted with 50 samples are chosen as test data and the others (about 400 ones) are left for training data.

3.1 Test of the separate components

We first test the effectiveness of the separate components, the MIL based emotion intensity method and the relative expression intensity. For this test, the classic saliency method [5] is adopted as baseline. In our method, we evaluate relative expression intensity for gaze density estimation. Then the question is, is it better than using face directly, since there are many methods use face as a feature for gaze density estimation? To answer this question, we compare the performance of using face and the one using expression. Five sets of results are compared. 1) The baseline saliency method (ITTI). 2) The baseline method with the emotion intensity estimated using MIL (ITTI+MIL). 3) The baseline method with the expression intensity (ITTI+EXP). 4) The baseline method with human face. This is to test if the expression intensity have contributions compared with face (ITTI+FACE). 5) The baseline method with all the components, i.e., the spatial position, MIL emotion intensity, expression intensity, and emotional object detection (ITTI+EMO). The area under the ROC curve and the t-test results are shown in Table 1. The results show that the components are effective and the t-test results show the significance of the improvement.

3.2 Test of the performance

The major contribution of this paper is to incorporate emotion into gaze density estimation. Thus we test the performance of our work on the basis of existing saliency methods. The methods chosen as baseline are 1) Itti's method[5], 2) the AIM method [1], 3) the SUN method SUN [15], and 4) the SER method [14]. Table 2 shows the area under the curves and the t-test result. From the results, we can see that emotion does improve the performance of the saliency methods significantly. Fig. 5 shows two examples. We can see that our method well compliments with saliency and emphasizes the emotional content.

4. CONCLUSION

In this paper, we are the first to incorporate emotion into attention analysis, especially gaze density estimation. Experimental results on eye gaze dataset containing emotion rich images demonstrate the effectiveness of the proposed method. This is the very first attempt to incorporate emotion into attention analysis. Experiments verified the effectiveness of the proposed method.

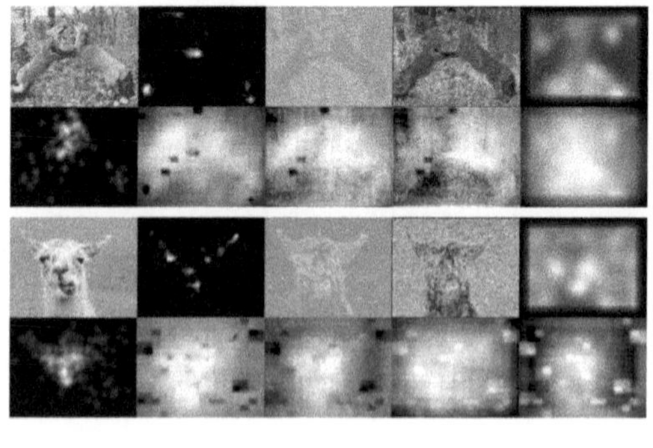

Figure 5: Two examples of gaze density estimation results, compared with the baseline methods. The first columns shows the image (top) and the user gaze density (bottom). The other four columns show the baseline methods (top) and our results (bottom). From left to right, the baseline method are itti's method [5], AIM [1], SUN [15], and SER [14].

5. ACKNOWLEDGMENT

This work was supported by 973 Program (2010CB327905) and National Natural Science Foundation of China (61273034, 61332016).

6. REFERENCES

[1] N. Bruce and J. Tsotsos. Saliency based on information maximization. In *NIPS*, 2006.

[2] P. Ekman. Facial expression and emotion. *American psychologist*, 48(4):384, 1993.

[3] L. Fei-Fei and P. Perona. *A Bayesian hierarchical model for learning natural scene categories.* CVPR, 2005.

[4] T. Hofmann. *Unsupervised learning by probabilistic latent semantic analysis.* Machine Learning, vol. 42, no. 1-2, pp. 177-196, 2001.

[5] L. Itti, C. Koch, and E. Niebur. *A model of saliency-based visual attention for rapid scene analysis.* T-PAMI, vol. 20, no. 11. pp. 1254-1259, 1998.

[6] T. Judd, K. Ehinger, F. Durand, and A. Torralba. *Learning to predict where humans look.* ICCV, pp. 2106-2113, 2009.

[7] J. Machajdik and A. Hanbury. Affective image classification using features inspired by psychology and art theory. In *ACM Multimedia*, pages 83–92, 2010.

[8] O. Maron and A. L. Ratan. Multiple-instance learning for natural scene classification. In *International Conference on Machine Learning*, pages 341–349, 1998.

[9] A. Ohman, A. Flykt, and F. Esteves. Emotion drives attention: Detecting the snake in the grass. *Journal of Experimental Psychoogy: General*, 130(3):466–478, 2001.

[10] A. Oliva and A. Torralba. Building the gist of a scene: The role of global image features in recognition. *Progress in brain research*, 155:23–29, 2006.

[11] D. Parikh and K. Grauman. Relative attributes. In *ICCV*, pages 503–510, 2011.

[12] H. T. Schupp, J. Stockburger, M. Codispoti, M. Junghofer, A. I. Weike, and A. O. Hamm. Selective visual attention to emotion. *Journal of neuroscience*, 27(5):1082–1089, 2007.

[13] R. Subramanian, H. Katti, N. Sebe, M. Kankanhalli, and T.-S. Chua. *An eye fixation database for saliency detection in images.* ECCV, 2010.

[14] W. Wang, Y. Wang, Q. Huang, , and W. Gao. Measuring visual saliency by site entropy rate. In *CVPR*, 2010.

[15] L. Zhang, M. H. Tong, T. K. Marks, H. Shan, , and G. W. Cottrell. *SUN: A Bayesian framework for salience using natural statistics.* Journal of Vision, 8(7):32, 1-20, 2008.

Trajectory Based Jump Pattern Recognition in Broadcast Volleyball Videos

Chun-Chieh Hsu[1], Hua-Tsung Chen[2], Chien-Li Chou[1], Chien-Peng Ho[3], Suh-Yin Lee[1]

[1] Department of Computer Science, National Chiao Tung University, Hsinchu, Taiwan

[2] Information & Communications Technology Lab, National Chiao Tung University, Hsinchu, Taiwan

[3] ICL/Industrial Technology Research Institute, Hsinchu, Taiwan

{hsucch, huatsung, fallwind, sylee}@cs.nctu.edu.tw, cpho@itri.org.tw

ABSTRACT

Jump actions are typically accompanied by spiking and imply significant events in volleyball matches. In this paper, we propose an effective system capable of jump pattern recognition in player moving trajectories from long broadcast volleyball videos. First, the entire video is segmented into clips of rallies by shot segmentation and whistle detection. Then, camera calibration is adopted to find the correspondence between coordinates in the video frames and real-world coordinates. With the homographic transformation matrix computed, real-world player moving trajectories can be derived by a sequence of tracked player locations in video frames. Jump patterns are recognized from the player moving trajectory by using a sliding window scheme with physics-based validation and context constraint. Finally, the jump locations can be estimated and jump tracks can be separated from the planar moving tracks. The experiments conducted on broadcast volleyball videos show promising results.

Categories and Subject Descriptors

I.4.9 [**IMAGE PROCESSING AND COMPUTER VISION**]: Applications

General Terms

Experimentation

Keywords

Sport video analysis; pattern recognition; camera calibration; object localization; trajectory analysis

1. INTRODUCTION

Sports analytics plays a major role in sports industry and sports science due to its commercial benefits and practical applications. Rapid development of sports video analysis tools leads to the proliferation of sports-related statistical data. From the perspective of the professional coaches and players, sports analytics can further investigate the performance of individual or the whole team. Sports analytics can also give the audience an in-depth exploration of the matches. However, typically the sports-related statistical data are manually labeled and analyzed by the sports analyst. Especially in sports broadcasting, it is labor-intensive and time-consuming to collect hand-labeled data since the broadcast videos contain not only the process of matches, but also periods of time-outs or commercials. Therefore, establishing automatic systems for sports analytics is an important issue in the research fields of broadcast sports video analysis.

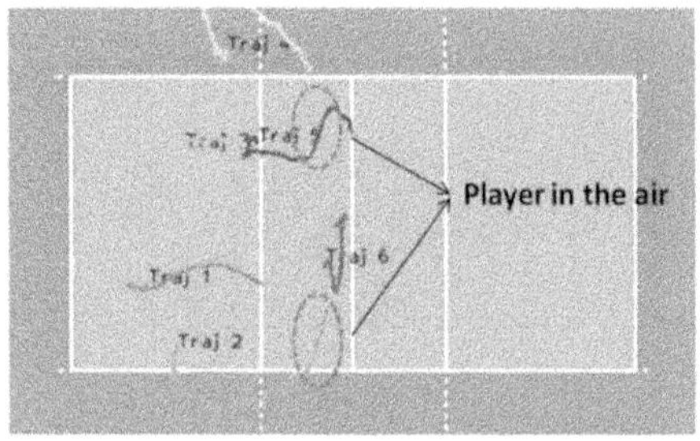

Figure 1. Unforeseen tracks of player moving trajectories.

In volleyball matches, spiking is the most direct and principal way to get points and executing spiking tactics requires interaction between players. Jump actions are typically accompanied by spiking and imply significant events. Hence, the tasks of automatically recognizing jump patterns in player moving trajectories and separating jump tracks from planar moving tracks are of vital importance in volleyball videos analysis.

2. RELATED WORK

Sports analytics generally ranges between two types of processes: *Event Detection* and *Tactic Analysis*. Event detection allows viewers to easily obtain the brief overview of entire matches and acquire the splendid and informative parts of the matches, such as the "goal" in soccer and the "spiking" in volleyball. Most existing researches on event detection aim at extracting the highlights of the matches [1, 14]. Besides, significant events usually result from ball-player and/or player-player interaction. Much effort has been made to develop ball and player tracking techniques [3, 9].

On the other hand, tactic analysis is a further investigation after event detection, and provides not only what happened in the matches, but also where and how the events happened. Tactic analysis can be generally classified into two categories [12]: non-trajectory driven methods and trajectory driven ones. Non-trajectory driven tactic analysis infers tactics from significant events [5, 8]. Trajectory driven tactic analysis bridges the semantic gap between low-level features and high-level events [10, 11, 12]. However, in the aforementioned works, little attention has been paid to the situation of player jumping. A jump action normally brings on an abrupt displacement in a player moving trajectory, since the player unexpectedly leaves the original moving plane. As shown in Figure 1, the unforeseen tracks caused

MM '14, November 3–7, 2014, Orlando, FL, USA

Copyright 2014 ACM 978-1-4503-3063-3/14/11 $15.00.

http://dx.doi.org/10.1145/2647868.2654985

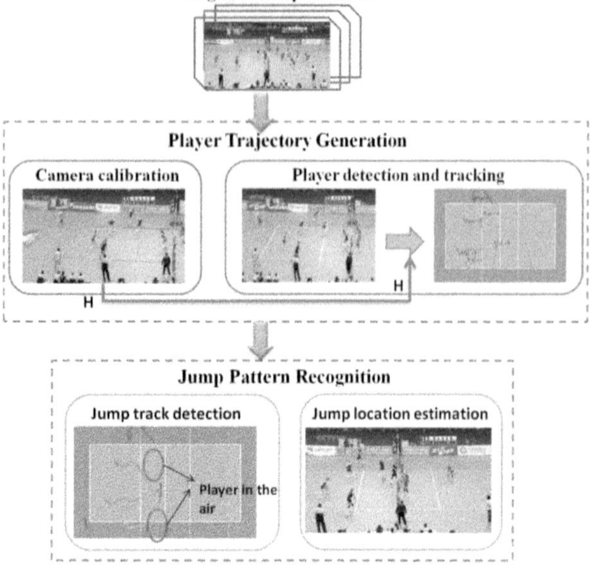

Figure 2. Schematic flowchart of the proposed system.

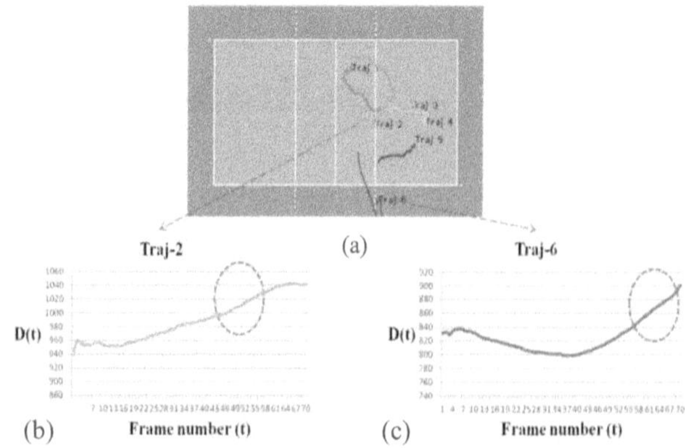

Figure 3. Examples of jump patterns. (a) Generated real-world player trajectories. (b) D(*t*) of player moving upward without a jump action. (c) D(*t*) of a jump action.

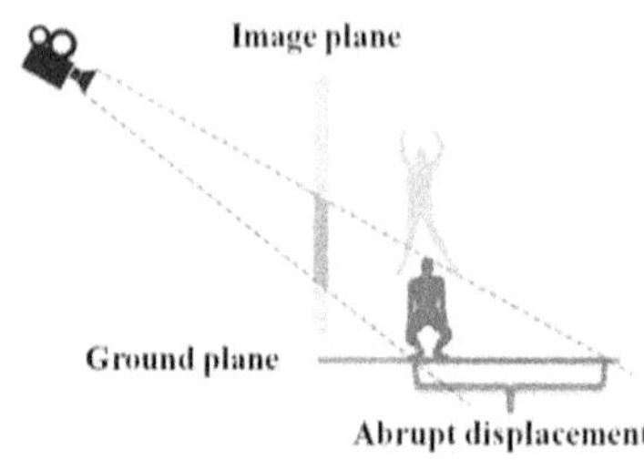

Figure 4. The characteristics of the jump action.

by jump actions (marked by red circles) in the trajectories have a profound impact on investigating the moving strategies executed by players. As a result, it is important to separate jump tracks from player moving trajectories. Our approach is inspired by Chen et al. [2] who propose a physics-based validation approach to recognize jump patterns in 2-on-2 volleyball games with one fixed camera. Although the jump location and the jump height can be estimated, the work should be under the assumption that player heights and 3D transformation between the court in the video and real world court are known in advance. However, for broadcast volleyball videos, the player height information and 3D homographic mapping cannot be easily obtained from a pan-tilt-zoom camera. In this paper, we propose an effective system capable of jump pattern recognition in player trajectories extracted from long broadcast volleyball videos.

3. PROPOSED SYSTEM

The schematic flowchart of the proposed system is illustrated in Figure 2. To begin with, we perform shot segmentation [7] and whistle detection [4] to segment original videos into clips of rallies. Camera calibration is adopted to obtain the correspondence between image coordinates and real-world coordinates. With the homographic transformation matrix computed, real-world player moving trajectories can be derived by a sequence of tracked player locations in video frames. Then we utilize a sliding window scheme to recognize jump patterns in player moving trajectories by adopting physics-based validation and context constraint. Finally, jump locations can be estimated and the planar moving tracks separated from the extracted jump tracks can be exploited for further tactics analysis.

3.1 Player Trajectory Generation

Player trajectories in the real-world court are semantically important because the movement and location of a player tell much about the current player action. For semantic/tactics analysis, it is required to obtain the player trajectories in the real-world court. Camera calibration converts the coordinates in video frames to real-world coordinates. In addition, player detection and tracking are significant and indispensable steps for our proposed system.

3.1.1 Camera Calibration

With the homogeneous coordinates $\boldsymbol{p} = (x, y, 1)$ in image coordinate and $\boldsymbol{p}' = (u, v, 1)$ in the court model coordinate, the transformation $\boldsymbol{Hp} = \boldsymbol{p}'$ defines the mapping between coordinates in video frames and real-world coordinates [6], where $\boldsymbol{H}$ is the homographic transformation matrix.

To solve this eight-parameter perspective transformation, at least four point-correspondences between the positions in image coordinates and on the real-world coordinates are required. In each type of court model, the respective four points are selected for deriving the homographic transformation matrix $\boldsymbol{H}$. (For more details, please refer to [6]).

3.1.2 Player Detection and Tracking

We locate players in broadcast volleyball videos by applying a cascade of boosted classifiers with Histogram of Oriented Gradients [15], which has been widely used in pedestrian detection. Kalman filter [13] is adopted as our tracking mechanism since it provides optimal estimates of system parameters using a series of measurements (locations of player candidates) observed over time. With the homographic transformation matrix $\boldsymbol{H}$, the moving trajectories of the player can be obtained by mapping the foot locations of the tracked player over successive frames onto the real-world court model, as shown in Figure 3(a).

3.2 Jump Pattern Recognition

As shown in Figure 4, when a player is jumping off the original plane, the player appears to form an abrupt displacement in the planar trajectory. Most problems of trajectory driven tactic analysis are caused by the unforeseen tracks of player moving

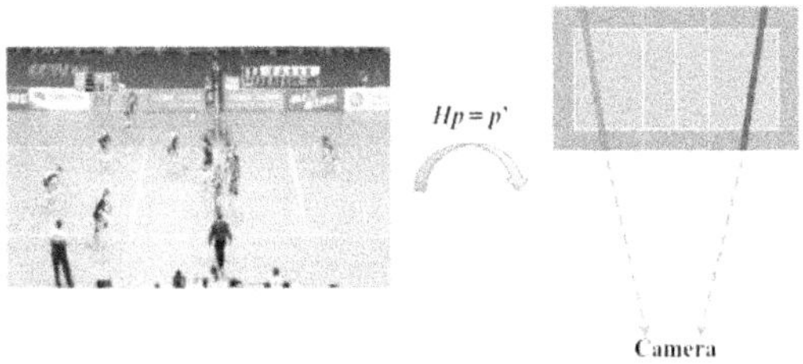

Figure 5. Estimation of the camera location by homographic transformation.

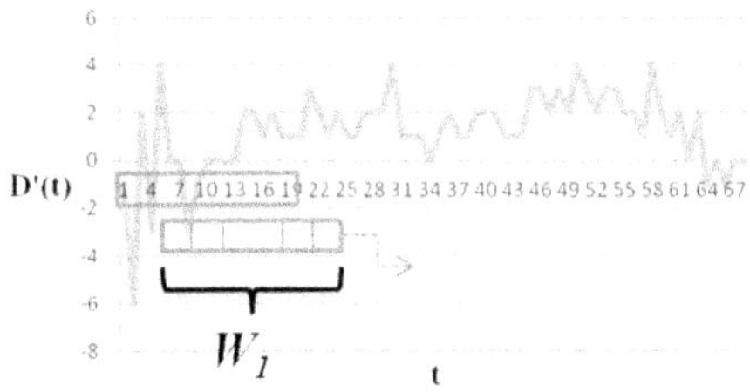

Figure 6. Examples of D'(t) of Figure 3(b) and sliding window scheme.

trajectories. Hence, to separate jump tracks from planar moving tracks is a principal work for further tactic analysis.

3.2.1 Jump Track and Location Extraction

Inspired by Chen et al. [2], we select the distance between the camera location and each tracked player location as our feature for jump track detection. Distinct from [2], with the homographic transformation matrix computed ***H***, the camera location is calculated by converting the viewpoint of camera in image coordinate to the real world court, as shown in Figure 5. As the elapse of time, we can compute the distance D(t) for each tracked player location L(t), as shown in Figure 3(b) and (c).

In [2], a possible jump is located by finding peaks in D(t) since the player will rise and fall in a jump. However, in broadcast volleyball videos, since the camera always focuses on the ball during a rally, it is difficult to retain the entire track of a jump. The falling track of the jump is usually missed or deficient and only the rising track of the jump can be obtained, as presented in Figure 3(a). In fact, the variation of D(t) will be considerably increased when a player is on the rising track of the jump. Hence, we adopt a sliding widow scheme for jump track detection.

As illustrated in Figure 6, the observation window of W_1 frames slides by one frame in each iteration and we accumulate D'(t), the variation of D(t), for each window. If the maximum accumulated D'(t) within the observation window of W_1 frames is greater than a threshold T_{Jump}, the track within the time duration is regarded as a jump track candidate. The process of jump track detection can be formulated as Eq. (1):

$$\mathrm{J}(N) = \begin{cases} 1, \ if \ \max\limits_{1 \le i \le L} \sum_{t=i}^{i+W_1} \mathrm{D}'(t) > T_{Jump} \\ 0, otherwise \end{cases} \quad (1)$$

where J(N) indicates whether the Nth trajectory is a jump track candidate, N is the trajectory index, L is the length of the Nth trajectory, and i is the start frame index of a sliding window.

After detecting the jump track, the start frame of an observation window will be regarded as the jump moment and the jump location can be estimated from the player trajectory. With the estimated jump locations, jump tracks can be distinguished from player moving tracks and the planar moving tracks can be separated.

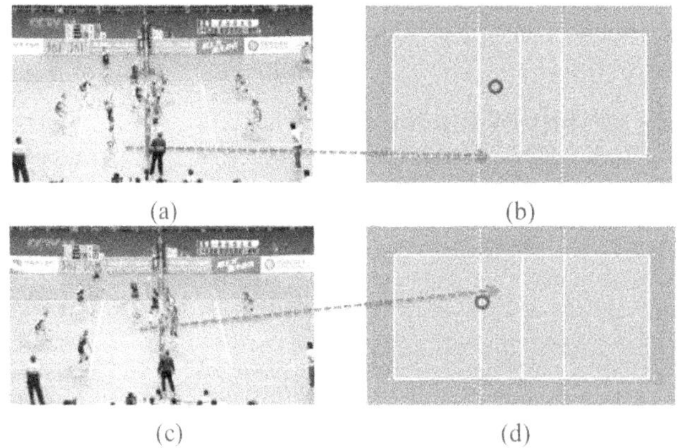

Figure 7. Context constraint. (a)(c) Detected jump location. (b)(d) Separated jump track. Center of team formation is marked by blue circles.

3.2.2 Physics-based and Context-constraint Validation

The sliding widow scheme detects jump tracks by identifying the ascending patterns in the player trajectory. However, similar pattern like player moving distant away from the camera location is also mistaken as jump actions. For example, the ascending pattern in trajectory of a player moving upward, as shown in Figure 3(b), is similar to a real jump track in Figure 3(c). Therefore, a physics-based validation approach is proposed to eliminate false detections of jump track candidates.

When a player is jumping in the air, the jump duration can be derived by Newtonian physics: $\Delta t = \sqrt{2h/g}$, where h is the jump height and g is the gravity. We set the minimum jump height h_{min} = 20 cm to discard the player who does not leave the ground high, and set a tolerant maximum jump height h_{max} = 150 cm due to the fact that the highest jump of a professional volleyball player is about 120 cm. Then, we can infer that the period of ascending patterns in the player trajectory should be within the range of 6 to 20 frames. Hence, we set the observation window size W_1 = 6 to retrieve jump track candidate. For jump pattern validation, we adopt another observation window with size W_2 = 20 to accumulate D'(t) from the start frame of each jump track candidate. A jump candidate is discarded if the accumulated D'(t) within W_2 is greater than the accumulated D'(t) of jump track candidate, which means the player is still rising after W_2 frames.

Besides, the spatial distribution of players is an important context of the matches for tactic inference. In general, spiking events occur at front part of team formation. To exploit the complex context of the matches, we also select the center of team formation as our feature to filter out false detections of jump track candidates, as shown in Figure 7. A jump candidate is discarded if the estimated jump location is behind the midpoint of the team formation. After physics-based and context-constraint validation, false detections of jump track candidates can be eliminated and the proposed jump pattern recognition scheme can be effectively improved.

4. EXPERIMENTS

To demonstrate the effectiveness of the proposed jump pattern recognition approach, we conduct the experiments on the broadcast volleyball videos of 2010 Asian Games. Totally, we have 20 video clips of women's volleyball matches recorded from live broadcast television program with the resolution of 1280 × 720 (29.97 fps).

4.1 Results of Player Detection

To evaluate the performance of player detection based on HOG, we use 4 video clips for training and the remaining 16 video clips for testing. The training dataset contains 1200 player images manually segmented from videos frames and 2400 non-players images automatically segmented from background frames. The number of cascade stage of boosted classifiers with HOG is 15. From the 16 testing video clips, 6741 players are manually labeled as ground truth. Table 1 shows the statistics of player detection. The effectiveness of player detection facilitates the subsequent player tracking scheme.

4.2 Results of Jump Pattern Recognition

We compare three schemes of jump pattern recognition: sliding window scheme (SLW), sliding window scheme adopting physics-based validation (PHY), and sliding window scheme adopting both physics-based and context-constraint validation (PHY+CON), as elaborated in Table 2. Most of the false detections in the PHY scheme occur when there are players moving distant away from the camera and the trajectory segments are within the range of 6 to 20 frames. To reduce the false detections of jump track candidates, we also adopt context constraint in addition to physics-based validation. The recall rate of jump pattern recognition adopting PHY+CON is the same as the PHY, but the precision rate achieves up to 13% improvement after adopting context-constraint validation. Hence, we can effectively recognize jump pattern by applying both physics-based and context-constraint validation to a sliding window scheme.

Table 1. Results of player detection.

Feature	HOG
# Players in all frames	6741
# Correctly located players	5862
# False alarm	504
Precision (%)	92.08
Recall (%)	86.96

Table 2. Results of jump pattern recognition.

	SLW	PHY	PHY+CON
# of retrieved jumps	41	37	31
# Correctly detected jumps	22	26	26
# False alarm	19	11	5
Precision (%)	53.66	70.27	83.87
Recall (%)	78.57	92.86	92.86

5. CONCLUSION

In this paper, we propose an effective system for recognizing jump patterns in player trajectories extracted from long broadcast volleyball videos. A sliding window scheme with physics-based and context-constraint validation is adopted for extracting the jump track. Physics-based validation combines the multimedia contents and physics knowledge for eliminating unrealistic jump patterns. Context-constraint validation provides a chance for domain knowledge of volleyball to involve in the judgment. The detected jump action can assist in discovering the significant events and the separated jump tracks can reduce errors in trajectory driven tactic analysis The experiments conducted on broadcast volleyball videos show promising results of the above two validations in terms of precision and recall rates.

6. ACKNOWLEDGMENTS

This research is supported by projects MOST-103-2221-E-009-154, ICTL-103-Q528, ATU-103-W958, and 101-E-2221-009-087-MY3.

7. REFERENCES

[1] Cheng, C. C. and Hsu, C. T. Fusion of Audio and Motion Information on HMM-Based Highlight Extraction for Baseball Games. *IEEE Trans. on Mul.*, vol. 8, no. 3, pp. 585-599, 2006.

[2] Chen, H. T., Ma, K. L., Chuang, J. H., and Lin, H. H. Recognizing Jump Patterns with Physics-based Validation in Human Moving Trajectory. *J. Vis. Com. and Ima. Rep.*, 2013.

[3] Chen, H. T., Tien, M. C., Chen Y. W., Tsai, W. J., and Lee, S. Y. Physics-based ball tracking and 3D trajectory reconstruction with applications to shooting location estimation in basketball video. *J. Vis. Com. and Ima. Rep.*, vol. 20, no. 3, pp. 204-216, 2009.

[4] Chen, H. T., Tsai, W. J., Lee, S. Y., and Yu, J. Y. Ball tracking and 3D trajectory approximation with applications to tactics analysis from single-camera volleyball sequences. *Mul. Too. and App.*, pp. 1-27, 2011.

[5] Chang, M. H., Tien, M. C., and Wu, J. L. WOW: Wild-open warning for broadcast basketball video based on player trajectory. In *Proceedings of the 17th ACM International Conference on Multimedia*, pp. 821-824, 2009.

[6] Farin, D., Krabbe, S., With, P. H. N. de, and Effelsberg, W. Robust camera calibration for sport videos using court models. *SPIE Sto. and Ret. Met. and App. for Mul.*, vol.5307, pp. 80-91, 2004.

[7] Hanjalic, A. Shot-boundary detection: Unraveled and resolved? *IEEE Trans. Cir. Sys. and Vid. Tec.*, vol. 12, no. 2, pp. 90-105, 2002.

[8] Hsu, C. C., Chen, H. T., Chou, C. L. and Lee, S. Y. Spiking and Blocking Events Detection and Analysis in Volleyball Videos. In *Proceedings of IEEE International Conference on Multimedia & Expo*, pp. 19-24, 2012.

[9] Liu, J., Carr, P., Collins, R. T. and Liu, Y. Tracking Sports Players with Context-Conditioned Motion Models. In *Proceedings of IEEE Conference on Computer Vision and Pattern Recognition*, 2013.

[10] Lucey, P., Oliver, D., Carr, P., Roth, J., and Matthews, I. Assessing team strategy using spatiotemporal data. In *Proceedings of 19th ACM SIGKDD Conference on Knowledge Discovery and Data Mining*, 2013.

[11] Niu, Z., Gao, X. and Tian, Q. Tactic Analysis Based on Real-World Ball Trajectory in Soccer Video. *Pat. Rec.*, vol. 45, no. 5, pp. 1937-1947, 2012.

[12] Perse, M., Kristan, M., Kovacic, S., Vuckovic, G., and Pers, J. A trajectory-based analysis of coordinated team activity in a basketball game. *Com. Vis. and Ima. Und*, 2009.

[13] Welch, G. and Bishop, G. An Introduction to the Kalman Filter. Technical Report, University of North Carolina at Chapel Hill, 2002.

[14] Xiong, Z., Radhakrishnan, R., Divakaran, A. and Huang, T. S. Highlights Extraction from Sports Video Based on an Audio-Visual Marker Detection Framework. In *Proceedings of IEEE International Conference on Multimedia & Expo*, 2005.

[15] Zhu, Q., Avidan, S., Yeh, M. and Cheng, K. Fast Human Detection Using a Cascade of Histograms of Oriented Gradients. *IEEE Conference on Computer Vision and Pattern Recognition*, 2006.

Fast Instance Search Based on Approximate Bichromatic Reverse Nearest Neighbor Search

Masakazu Iwamura, Nobuaki Matozaki, Koichi Kise
Graduate School of Engineering, Osaka Prefecture University
1-1 Gakuencho, Naka, Sakai, Osaka 599-8531, Japan
{masa,kise}@cs.osakafu-u.ac.jp

ABSTRACT

In the TRECVID Instance Search (INS) task, it is known that use of BM25, which is an improvement of the TFIDF, greatly improves retrieval performance. Its calculation, however, requires tremendous amount of computational cost and this fact makes its use intractable. In this paper, we present its efficient computational method. Since the BM25 is obtained by solving the bichromatic reverse nearest neighbor (BRNN) search problem, we propose an approximate method for the problem based on the state-of-the-art approximate nearest neighbor search method, bucket distance hashing (BDH). An experiment using the TRECVID INS 2012 dataset showed that the proposed method reduced computational cost to less than 1/3500 of the brute-force search with keeping the accuracy.

Categories and Subject Descriptors

H.3.3 [Information Search and Retrieval]: Search process

General Terms

Algorithms

Keywords

Bichromatic reverse nearest neighbor search; Approximate algorithm; Video retrieval; BM25; TFIDF

1. INTRODUCTION

Finding a specific thing such as person, object and place from a large-scale video by a computer is a challenge. It is tackled in the Instance Search (INS) task of the TREC Video Retrieval Evaluation (TRECVID)[1].

The most critical problem is how to realize high accuracy. Distinguishing a target from others inherently requires human-like intelligence. For a computer that does not have it, methods that compensate for lack of it are required. A feasible way is based on keypoint matching. That is, the method extracts keypoints from both reference and query video images and casts votes for likely topics based on matching results of keypoints. Recently, it is shown that introducing BM25 ranking function [13] and its improvement, called exponential BM25, as weights of votes into the keypoint matching is quite effective in the INS task [10, 11]. In particular, a method using the exponential BM25 was ranked at the second place in the TRECVID INS 2013 [11].

This fact, however, leads to another critical problem, which is the high computational cost. In order to calculate the TFIDF, BM25 and exponential BM25, all reference keypoints whose nearest neighbors are a given query keypoint have to be found. This is known as the bichromatic reverse nearest neighbor (BRNN) search problem [5]. With the naive method, i.e., the brute-force search, the distances of all combinations of reference and query keypoint pairs have to be calculated. This tremendous amount of computational cost makes their use intractable. Some methods that more efficiently solve the problem than the naive method (e.g., [7, 15, 4]) are known. They, however, do not scale because they are designed to solve the problem *without error*. In the nearest neighbor search problem, which is a related but different problem, it is well-known that approximate methods require much less computational cost by allowing small error (i.e., with slight reduction of retrieval accuracy), compared with the non-approximate methods.

In this paper, we propose an approximate BRNN search method based on the state-of-the-art approximate nearest neighbor search (ANNS) method, bucket distance hashing (BDH) [2]. An experiment using the TRECVID INS 2012 dataset showed that the proposed method reduced computational cost to less than 1/3500 of the brute-force search with keeping the accuracy.

2. RECOGNITION METHOD

2.1 Overview

Figure 1 illustrates a keypoint matching based recognition method that we use in the paper. In (1), keypoints such as SIFT [8], Color SIFT [9] and OpponentSIFT [16] can be used from masked query images of a topic. In (2), for pairing keypoints from reference and query images, fast keypoint matching based on ANNS can be used. However, if the weights of votes such as the TFIDF [3], BM25 [13] and other methods are considered in the succeeding process, it

[1]http://www-nlpir.nist.gov/projects/trecvid/

MM'14, November 3–7, 2014, Orlando, Florida, USA.
Copyright 2014 ACM 978-1-4503-3063-3/14/11 ...$15.00.
http://dx.doi.org/10.1145/2647868.2654988.

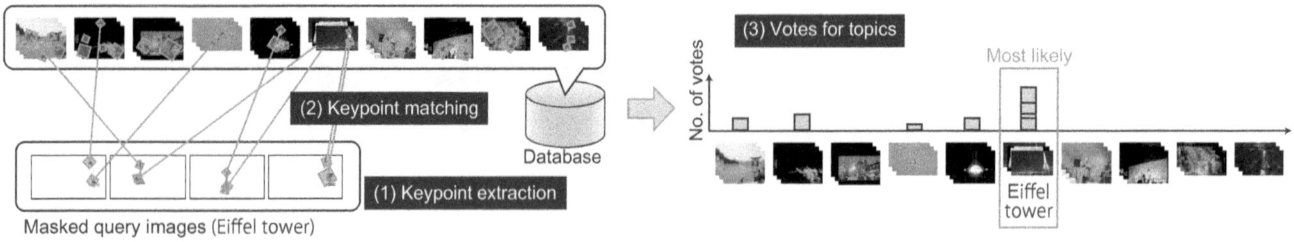

Figure 1: Keypoint matching based recognition method. (1) keypoints are extracted from masked query images of a topic, (2) keypoints from reference and query images are paired, (3) votes for topics are cast based on the keypoint matching result.

is not the case. In (3), votes for topics are cast based on the matching result in (2).

2.2 BM25

The BM25 [13] is an improvement of the TFIDF [3] in terms of taking into account the length of documents. They are originally developed for the document retrieval task. To apply them to the instance search task from videos, a document and a word are regarded as a video (a set of images) and a keypoint, respectively.

For the preparation of defining the weight of BM25 for the instance search task, the Term Frequency (TF) and the Inverse Document Frequency (IDF) are introduced. The TF describes a video v by a query keypoint q_i. The TF $\mathrm{TF}(q_i, v)$ is defined by the number of occurrence of the query keypoint q_i in the video v. The IDF represents the importance of the keypoint q_i. The IDF is given by

$$\mathrm{IDF}(q_i) = \log\left(\frac{N - n_i + 0.5}{n_i + 0.5}\right), \tag{1}$$

where N and n_i are the total number of videos, and the number of videos that contain the query keypoint q_i, respectively. In [12], instead of Eq. (1),

$$\mathrm{IDF2}(q_i) = \log\left(\frac{N - n_i^2 + 0.5}{n_i^2 + 0.5}\right) \tag{2}$$

was used. If the argument of log in Eq. (2) is less than one, $\mathrm{IDF2}(q_i) = 0$, while it is expected to rarely happen. IDF2 is intended to increase the discrimination power of keypoints and shown to be more effective than IDF in [12]. We follow this.

Finally, the weight of the BM25 for a video v and a set of query keypoints $Q = (q_1, \ldots, q_n)$ is given as

$$w(Q, v) = \sum_{q_i \in Q} \frac{\mathrm{IDF2}(q_i) \cdot \mathrm{TF}(q_i, v) \cdot (k+1)}{\mathrm{TF}(q_i, v) + k(1 - b + b\frac{|v|}{\mathrm{avdl}})}, \tag{3}$$

where avdl and $|v|$ are the average number of keypoints per video, and the number of keypoints in the video v, respectively. k and b are parameters. Following [11], $k = 2$ and $b = 0.75$ were used in the paper.

In order to use $\mathrm{TF}(q_i, v)$, how many times the query keypoint q_i appears in the video v has to be calculated. Similarly, in order to use n_i, how many videos contain the query keypoint q_i has to be calculated. They are solved by finding the closest query keypoint(s) to keypoints in videos. This is known as the Bichromatic Reverse Nearest Neighbor (BRNN) search problem. In the next section, we present an approximation algorithm for solving the problem.

3. APPROXIMATE BRNN SEARCH

3.1 Reverse Nearest Neighbor Search

Reverse nearest neighbor (RNN) search problem is to find the nearest neighbor (query) to a datum [5]. This is closely related to the well-known nearest neighbor (NN) search problem, which finds the nearest neighbor (datum) to a given query. The NN search can be formulated as

$$\mathrm{NN}(\boldsymbol{q}) = \{\boldsymbol{r} \in S | \forall \boldsymbol{p} \in S : d(\boldsymbol{q}, \boldsymbol{r}) \le d(\boldsymbol{q}, \boldsymbol{p})\}, \tag{4}$$

where $d(\boldsymbol{a}, \boldsymbol{b})$ is the distance between $\boldsymbol{a}$ and $\boldsymbol{b}$, and S is the set of data. On the other hand, the RNN search can be formulated as

$$\mathrm{RNN}(\boldsymbol{q}) = \{\boldsymbol{r} \in S | \forall \boldsymbol{p} \in S : d(\boldsymbol{r}, \boldsymbol{q}) \le d(\boldsymbol{r}, \boldsymbol{p})\}. \tag{5}$$

The RNN search problem is divided into monochromatic reverse nearest neighbor (MRNN) search (e.g., [17, 6, 14]) that does not distinguish data and queries, and bichromatic reverse nearest neighbor (BRNN) search (e.g., [7, 15, 4]) that does. Since the problem of our interest is the latter, we focus on that below.

3.2 Bucket Distance Hashing

Before presenting the proposed method for the BRNN search problem, let us present the BDH [2] where the proposed method is based on. The BDH is the state-of-the-art ANNS method. It consists of indexing and retrieval processes, which are performed before and after a query is given. Figure 2 illustrates the processes. In the indexing process in Fig. 2(a), data are clustered for efficient retrieval. For clustering, the k-means algorithm is employed. Obtained clusters are called buckets. The retrieval process in Fig. 2(b) are divided into two steps, as most of ANNS methods are. In the first step, nearest neighbor candidates (NNCs) are selected. They are used for distance calculation in the brute-force search in the second step. Since there is no room to improve in the second step, only the first step, i.e., selection of NNCs, is the key to improve the performance of the ANNS method. The BDH employs the branch and bound algorithm for the selection; NNCs are efficiently selected based on their bucket distances where the distances between the query and the centers of the buckets that the data belong. In [2], it is shown that the BDH reduced computation times by one-third compared with the previous state-of-the-art on an experiment using 100 million SIFT features.

The parameters of the BDH are summarized in Table 1. For clustering of the indexing, the k-means algorithm is applied to each subspace of the feature space. The dimensionality p of the subspaces is a parameter. The data are

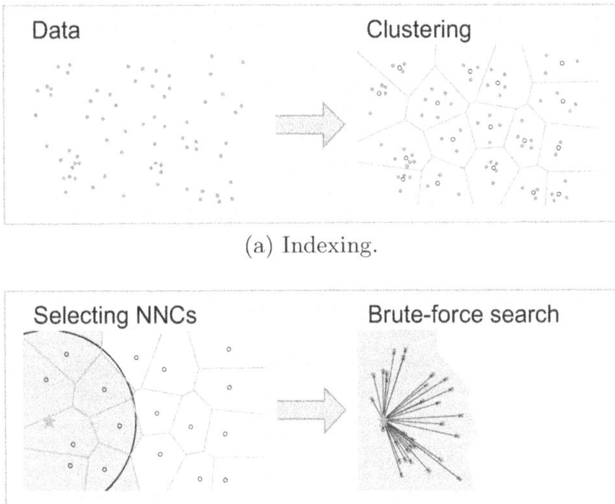

(a) Indexing.

(b) Retrieval.

Figure 2: The indexing and retrieval processes of the bucket distance hashing (BDH). NNC represents nearest neighbor candidate that are used for distance calculation in the brute-force search.

Table 1: Parameters of BDH.

p	The dimensionality of the subspaces for indexing
H_{size}	The size of the hash table
C	The minimum number of NNCs

stored in a hash table. Its size is determined by a parameter H_{size}. There is a parameter C that determines the minimum number of NNCs.

3.3 Proposed Method

The key of the proposed method to solve the BRNN search problem is to borrow the first step of the retrieval process of the BDH. The question arisen is whether it is possible to apply a method designed for the NN search problem to the RNN search problem.

As described in Eqs. (4) and (5), both the NN and RNN search problems are to find the datum (or query) that has the minimum distance. However, the minimum distance in what sense is different. The NN search problem finds *the closest datum from the query*, and the RNN search problem finds *the closest query from the datum*. Since the operation of "finding the one that achieved the minimum distance" should be applied to different thing (either datum or query), the second step (the brute-force search) of the retrieval process of the BDH is not directly applicable. On the other hand, the first step can be directly applicable. This is because it just selects NNCs based on their bucket distances. It is also derived in [1] that an RNN search problem can be reduced to an NN search problem. As long as we use a symmetric distance such as Euclidean distance, the calculated distances are symmetry (i.e., $d(\boldsymbol{a}, \boldsymbol{b}) = d(\boldsymbol{b}, \boldsymbol{a})$). This indicates that an ANNS method with better performance is expected to achieve better performance also in the RNN search problem.

Table 2: Parameters of the proposed method.

p	The dimensionality of the subspaces for indexing
H_{size}	The size of the hash table
R	The search radius of NNCs

Table 3: Parameters of the proposed method used in the experiment.

Parameters	Values
p	2, 3, 4
H_{size}	2^{29}, 2^{30}, 2^{31}
R	0.45, 0.50, 0.5, 0.525, 0.55

Most of the parameters of the BDH are shared with the proposed method, as summarized in Table 2. One exception is that the parameter C that determines the minimum number of NNCs. Instead, a new parameter R that determines the search radius of NNCs is introduced.

4. EXPERIMENT

We used the TRECVID INS 2012 dataset which consists of 76751 Internet videos as references and images of 21 topics as queries. As for the reference images, the videos were sampled at two frames per second, and keypoints of the OpponentSIFT [16] were extracted from the sampled images. Since the feature vectors of the OpponentSIFT were 384 dimensions and too high, 60 dimensions that have the largest variances were extracted using the principal component analysis. At the 60th dimension, the cumulative percentage contribution reached 80%. Then, all feature vectors were normalized so that their norms became one. As for the query images, keypoints were extracted and processed as well as the reference images. In average, a query topic consists of five images.

For the accuracy measure, the mean average precision (MAP) was used. We employed servers where 4 CPUs (AMD Opteron 6328, 2.6GHz, 12 cores) and 512GB memory were installed. All data were stored on memory. Computational times were converted to the ones in the case programs were executed as a single thread on a single core.

We used the brute-force search as the baseline method. In the method, the minimum cosine measure was set to 0.9 because this achieved the best in the preliminary experiment. This means that queries whose cosine measures were less than 0.9 were discarded. While 0.95 was used as the best value in [11], difference in experimental conditions such as different keypoint and different frame rate may lead to a different conclusion from ours. As for the proposed method, the parameters of the proposed approximate BRNN search were changed. The used parameters are summarized in Table 3. In the brute-force search of the proposed method, queries whose cosine measures were less than 0.9 were discarded. Figure 3 shows the relationship between computational time and accuracy. The baseline method took 46 days to achieve a MAP of 0.205. The computational time and accuracy of the proposed method were in the trade-off relationship. It achieved almost same accuracy with less than 20 min. More precisely, a MAP of 0.203 was achieved in 16.2 min. and that of 0.206 was achieved in 18.8 min. Their com-

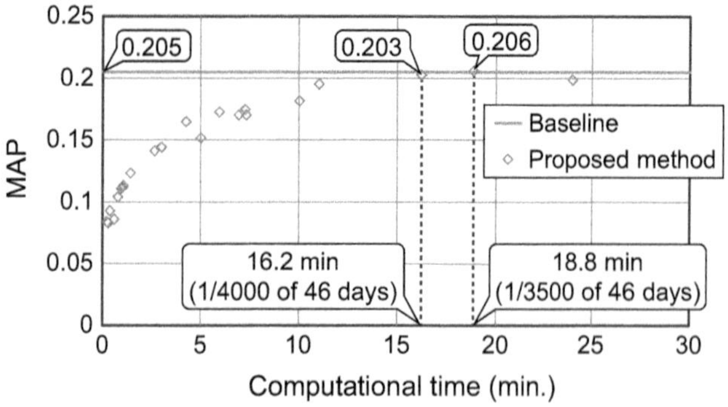

Figure 3: Relationship between computational time (min.) and accuracy (MAP). The computational time of the baseline method was 46 days.

putational times corresponds to about 1/4000 and 1/3500 of 46 days, respectively.

5. CONCLUSION

In this paper, we reduced the computational cost required for achieving high accuracy in the TRECVID Instance Search (INS) task. It is known that use of BM25 and its improvement greatly improve retrieval performance. Their calculation, however, requires tremendous amount of computational cost and this fact makes their use intractable. The BM25 is obtained by solving the bichromatic reverse nearest neighbor (BRNN) search problem.

In this paper, as a scalable solution for the problem, we proposed an approximate bichromatic reverse nearest neighbor (BRNN) search algorithm based on the state-of-the-art approximate nearest neighbor search (ANNS) method, bucket distance hashing (BDH). The idea comes from the inference that an ANNS method with better performance is expected to achieve better performance also in the BRNN search problem. An experiment using the TRECVID INS 2012 dataset showed that the proposed method makes the calculation of BM25 tractable; it reduced computational cost to less than 1/3500 of the brute-force search with keeping the accuracy.

Future work includes experimental comparison with existing approximate BRNN search methods such as [1], whereas the base ANNS method of [1], locality-sensitive hashing (LSH), is far slower than the BDH. Future work also includes application of the proposed method to other tasks than calculation of the BM25 and its variants.

6. ACKNOWLEDGMENTS

This work was supported by JST CREST project, and JSPS KAKENHI #25240028.

7. REFERENCES

[1] D. Arthur and S. Y. Oudot. Reverse nearest neighbors search in high dimensions using locality-sensitive hashing. arXiv.org, Nov. 2010. v1.

[2] M. Iwamura, T. Sato, and K. Kise. What is the most efficient way to select nearest neighbor candidates for fast approximate nearest neighbor search? In Proc. ICCV, Dec. 2013.

[3] K. S. Jones. A statistical interpretation of term specificity and its application in retrieval. Journal of Documentation, 28(5):11–21, 1972.

[4] J. M. Kang, M. F. Mokbel, S. Shekhar, T. Xia, and D. Zhang. Continuous evaluation of monochromatic and bichromatic reverse nearest neighbors. In Proc. IEEE 23rd Int'l Conf. on Data Engineering (ICDE 2007), pages 806–815, 2007.

[5] F. Korn and S. Muthukrishnan. Influence sets based on reverse nearest neighbor queries. In Proc. ACM SIGMOD Int'l Conf. Management of Data, pages 201–212, May 2000.

[6] K.-I. Lin, M. Nolen, and C. Yang. Applying bulk insertion techniques for dynamic reverse nearest neighbor problems. In Proc. 7th Int'l Database Engineering and Applications Symposium, pages 290–297, 2003.

[7] Y. Liu, R. C.-W. Wong, K. Wang, Z. Li, C. Chen, and Z. Chen. A new approach for maximizing bichromatic reverse nearest neighbor search. Knowledge and Information Systems, 36(1):23–58, 2013.

[8] D. G. Lowe. Distinctive image features from scale-invariant keypoints. Int'l Journal of Computer Vision, 60(2):91–110, Nov. 2004.

[9] K. Mikolajczyk and C. Schmid. Scale & affine invariant interest point detectors. Int'l Journal of Computer Vision, 60(1):63–86, 2004.

[10] M. Murata, T. Izumitani, H. Nagano, R. Mukai, K. Kashino, and S. Satoh. Ntt communication science laboratories and national institute of informatics at trecvid 2012 instance search and multimedia event detection tasks. In Proc. TRECVID 2012 Workshop, 2012.

[11] M. Murata, H. Nagano, K. Kunio, and S. Satoh. Ntt communication science laboratories and national institute of informatics at trecvid2013 instance search task. In Proc. TRECVID 2013 Workshop, 2013.

[12] M. Murata, H. Nagano, R. Mukai, K. Kashino, and S. Satoh. Instance video search by images as a query. In IEICE Technical Report, PRMU, volume 112, pages 215–219, Feb. 2013. In Japanese.

[13] S. Robertson and H. Zaragoza. The probabilistic relevance framework: BM25 and beyond. Foundations and Trends in Information Retrieval, 3(4):333–389, 2009.

[14] I. Stanoi, D. Agrawal, and A. E. Abbadi. Reverse nearest neighbor queries for dynamic databases. In Proc. ACM SIGMOD Workshop on Research Issues in Data Mining and Knowledge Discovery, pages 44–53, 2000.

[15] Q. T. Tran, D. Taniar, and M. Safar. Bichromatic reverse nearest-neighbor search in mobile systems. IEEE Systems Journal, 4(2):230–242, 2010.

[16] K. E. A. van de Sande, T. Gevers, and C. G. M. Snoek. Color descriptors for object category recognition. In Proc. 4th European Conference on Color in Graphics, Imaging and Vision (CGIV2008), volume 4, pages 378–381, June 2008.

[17] C. Yang and K.-I. Lin. An index structure for efficient reverse nearest neighbor queries. In Proc. 17th Int'l Conf. on Data Engineering, pages 485–492, 2001.

A Robust Panel Extraction Method for Manga

Xufang Pang, Ying Cao, Rynson W.H. Lau, and Antoni B. Chan
Department of Computer Science, City University of Kong Kong
{pangxufang,caoying59}@gmail.com, {rynson.lau,abchan}@cityu.edu.hk

ABSTRACT

Automatically extracting frames/panels from digital comic pages is crucial for techniques that facilitate comic reading on mobile devices with limited display areas. However, automatic panel extraction for manga, i.e., Japanese comics, can be especially challenging, largely because of its complex panel layout design mixed with various visual symbols throughout the page. In this paper, we propose a robust method for automatically extracting panels from digital manga pages. Our method first extracts the panel block by closing open panels and identifying a page background mask. It then performs a recursive binary splitting to partition the panel block into a set of sub-blocks, where an optimal splitting line at each recursive level is determined adaptively. Finally, it recovers accurate panel shapes from the computed sub-blocks. Our experiments show that the proposed method can robustly segment panels on the manga pages with various styles.

Categories and Subject Descriptors

I.4 [**Computing Methodologies**]: Image Processing and Computer Vision

Keywords

Comics processing, computational manga, panel extraction, adaptive page partitioning

1. INTRODUCTION

Comics is one of most successful storytelling mediums. With rapid development of smartphones and tablets, reading digital comics on mobile devices is becoming increasingly popular. To improve the mobile comic reading experience, one fundamental technical challenge is to automatically partition each comic page into a set of panels, which are then displayed in correct order on the small screen of a mobile device [1]. Recently, manga, as a type of comics, has gained massive popularity and is consumed by a huge audience across the world. Manga is mainly characterized by its unique style in panel composition and layout (such as irregular and borderless panels) [2], as well as extensive use of complex visual symbols (such as sound verbs and background texture). Figure 1 illustrates the stylistic effects common in manga layouts, including: (a) irregular panels (i.e., non-rectangular panel shape), (b) fourth wall break effect (i.e., some part of the foreground object lying outside of the panel boundary), (c) joined panels (i.e., two panels connected by some foreground objects, balloons or other visual effects), (d) unclosed panels (i.e., missing part of the panel boundary), and (e) borderless panels (i.e., no explicit panel boundary). While being able to effectively enhance the expressiveness of manga, these stylistic effects pose unique challenges to the task of automatically extracting panels from manga pages.

Figure 1: Some stylistic effects used in manga.

There are several works for automatic extraction of panels from comic pages, but none of them is capable of dealing with all the aforementioned stylistic effects. Some of the methods detect division lines between adjacent panels using recursive X-Y cut [4], exhaustive search [3] or density gradient [8]. However, the method based on X-Y cut [4] cannot robustly segment irregular panels, and none of these methods can handle unclosed and borderless panels. The method based on the connected component labeling (CCL) algorithm [1] can identify irregular panels as individual components, but fails to separate panels joined by some elements such as sound verbs or balloons. To handle joined panels, a sequence of N erosions followed by N dilations [5] are performed on the CCL mask to cut the connecting elements. However, the results of their algorithm are very sensitive to the value of N. The CCL mask for an unclosed panel may includes a group of fragmented borders as individual components,

ACM MM '14 November 3-7, Orlando, Florida, USA

http://dx.doi.org/10.1145/2647868.2654990.

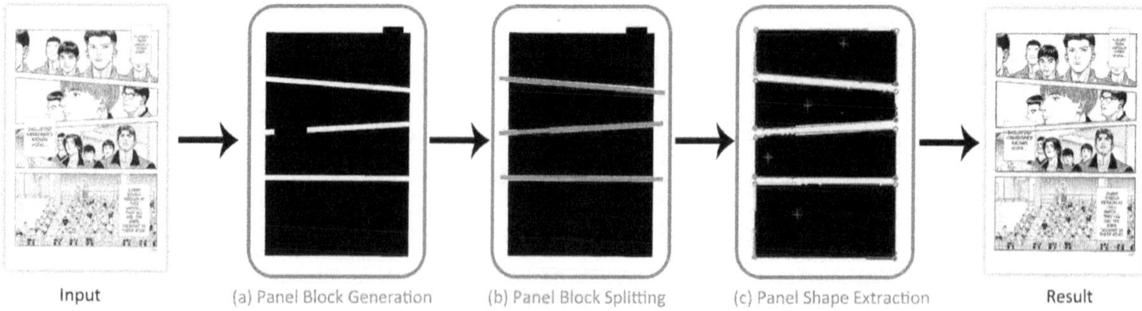

Figure 2: The pipeline of our method.

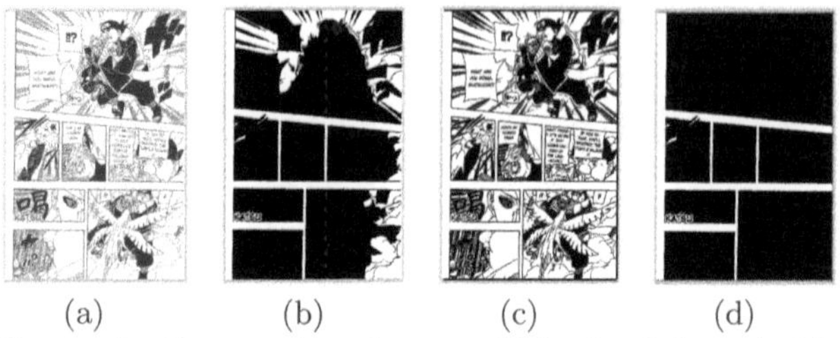

Figure 3: Generating the panel block without/with repairing unclosed panels. (a) Input manga page, and (b) its panel block. (c) Repaired manga page where the open boundaries of the unclosed panels are closed, and (d) its panel block.

making it impossible to obtain a complete panel shape from the erosion process. Although clustering the bounding boxes of the connected components [6] or fitting rectangles to the detected potential border lines and corners [7] may recover the shape of unclosed panels, they are only applicable to regular panels.

In this paper, we propose a robust method to extract panels from manga pages. Our method is composed of three steps: *panel block generation*, *panel block splitting* and *panel shape extraction*. Taking a digital manga page as input, our method first generates a panel block (Fig. 2(a)) by closing open panels and applying the CCL algorithm on the page background. It then adaptively places splitting lines in a recursive manner, which divides the panel block into a list of sub-blocks, each representing a single panel region (Fig. 2(b)). Finally, it recovers accurate panel shapes from the panel regions obtained (Fig. 2(c)).

2. PANEL EXTRACTION METHOD

2.1 Panel Block Generation

Given a manga page, we aim at extracting a panel block, representing a set of candidate panel regions. For this purpose, a common approach is to detect the connected components of black pixels on the foreground characters using the CCL method [1], and group them as panel regions. However, these methods may fail to preserve the panel shape, and could generate a labeling mask with many fragmented pieces. By inspecting manga pages, we observe that a panel may be composed of many disconnected components, but the pixels of the page background are often connected as a whole. Thus, we apply CCL on the page background (i.e., white pixels) to identify connected components as the background mask, and treat the remaining regions in the page as the panel block (Fig. 2(a)).

Handling unclosed panels. Our background mask obtained above may leak into the inside of the unclosed panels with open boundaries, leading to noises inside the panel block (see Fig. 3(b)). To avoid this issue, before computing the background mask, we repair the unclosed panels by adding boundaries to them to close the panels. We observe that the unclosed panels typically appear at the boundaries of a page. Therefore, we insert the missing boundaries by analyzing the intensity values of the pixels along the page boundaries. We first binarize the input manga page by setting the pixels with intensity values lower than 235 to 0, and 1 otherwise. Then, we find the page boundary that contains missing panel boundaries and replace it with a black line. When panel boundaries are missing, the visual contents flow outside the panels, resulting in greater intensity variation along the page boundary. Let $\varphi(x)$ be an intensity function of the binarized image, where x is the position of the pixel along the page boundaries. For each of the four page boundaries, a missing panel boundary is detected if the following conditions are satisfied: $\max(\varphi(x) * x) - \min(\varphi(x) * x) > 0.7 * L_e$ and $\sum_{x=1}^{L_e} \varphi'(x) > 10$, where $\varphi'(x) = \varphi(x) - \varphi(x-1)$ is the intensity gradient between neighboring pixels and L_e is the length of the boundary. A repaired image is shown in Fig. 3(c).

Open panel boundaries can also be caused by the fourth wall break effect, where characters or text break the panel boundaries and leaves part of the boundaries open. This can introduce holes formed by disjoint components inside the panel blocks. To fill the holes, we perform a grouping on the obtained connected components. Specifically, if more than half of a component's convex hull overlaps with another component's, the two components are considered to belong to the same panel, and therefore are merged together.

2.2 Panel Block Splitting

The aim of this step is to split the panel block from the previous step into a list of sub-blocks, each representing an individual panel region. This step is necessary since multiple panel regions may be joined together in the panel block, due to the existence of joined panels or fourth wall break effect (see the second and third panels in Fig. 2(a)). Since the comic layout structure can be formed by recursive partitioning [2], we separate joined regions by recursively applying a binary splitting procedure (see Fig. 2(b)). At each recursion level, we determine an optimal splitting line, which divides the current panel block into two sub-blocks. For example, starting with the whole panel block as the current block,

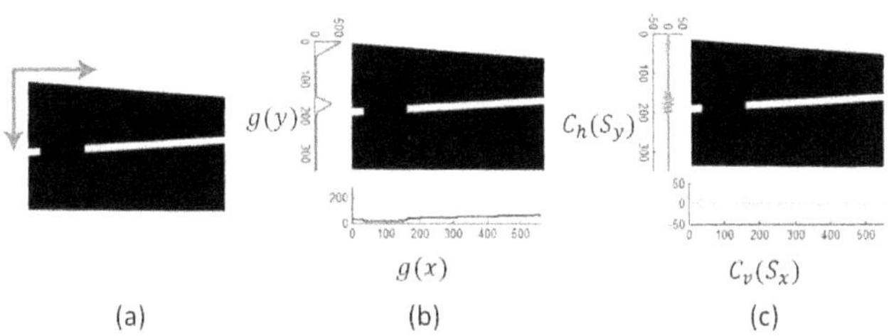

Figure 4: Computing splitting line. (a) current block to be split. (b) accumulated pixel values along horizontal and vertical directions. (c) the cost functions of placing a splitting line along horizontal and vertical directions.

we first split the current block into two sub-blocks using a horizontal or vertical splitting line. Then, each sub-block is regarded as the current block, which is further partitioned in the same binary manner. This process is performed recursively until the current block cannot be divided further.

To determine the locations of splitting lines, previous methods search for black boundaries of panels [7, 8, 1, 4] or white division stripes between the panels [3] on the original comic page, which is time-consuming and susceptible to noise caused by panel contents. Operating on the panel block, we first detect a set of candidate splitting lines (both horizontal and vertical) by evaluating a cost function of inserting a splitting line at a certain place. Then, an optimal splitting line, either horizontal or vertical, is adaptively determined by measuring the confidence values of the candidate splitting lines. For brevity, we focus our discussion on computing horizontal splitting lines. The vertical splitting lines can be computed in a similar way.

Computing candidate splitting lines. We determine the locations of candidate splitting lines based on the prior knowledge of the comic layout: two adjacent panels are often separated by white spacing between them. Thus, a horizontal splitting line should be placed close to the boundary between the panel and white spacing of the current block. To incorporate such knowledge in our approach, we define a *preference function* of placing a splitting line. The current block is first embedded in a 2D Cartesian coordinate system, with row and column corresponding to y-axis and x-axis, respectively (see Fig. 4(a)). Let $I(\mathbf{p})$ be the intensity function of the current block, where $\mathbf{p} = (\mathbf{p}_x, \mathbf{p}_y)$ is the pixel location. The preference function for placing a horizontal splitting line $S_y = \{\mathbf{p}|\mathbf{p}_y = y\}$ is then formulated as

$$C_h(S_y) = 2 * g(y) - g(y+1) - g(y-1), \qquad (1)$$

where $g(y)$ is the accumulated pixel values along S_y, i.e., $g(y) = \sum_{\mathbf{p}\in S_y} I(\mathbf{p})$. $C_h(S_y)$ has larger value at places where the horizontal splitting line is near to the boundary between the panel and white spacing. The horizontal splitting lines with $C_h(S_y) > 0.1 * W$ (W is the width of the current block) are referred to as candidate splitting lines. However, evaluating $C_h(S_y)$ alone cannot effectively detect diagonal white spacing, where $g(\cdot)$ may vary smoothly in a local neighborhood (as shown in Fig. 4(b)). As a result, we also include the horizontal splitting lines with $g(y) > 0.1 * W$, given the fact the splitting lines passing through the diagonal white spacing should include many white pixels. Since multiple horizontal splitting lines may be detected for one white spacing because of the white spacing's thickness, the splitting lines are finally grouped to form splitting stripes, and center lines within the groups are used as the final candidate splitting lines. We group the horizontal splitting lines if their distance is smaller that 30 pixels, and group the diagonal splitting lines if their distance is smaller than 50 pixels.

Eliminating false detection. In the resulting splitting stripes, some horizontal and diagonal stripes may overlap with each other, leading to false detection. We identify a diagonal splitting stripe as a false detection if it overlaps with any other horizontal splitting stripes. In addition, white holes on the current block, which are caused by open boundaries of the unclosed panels, can also give rise to false detection. To address this problem, for horizontal splitting stripes, we remove them if the distance between its leftmost and rightmost black pixels (if any) is larger than $0.7 * W$, i.e., the splitting stripes cut the black panel region on the current block. For each diagonal division stripe, we apply CCL to its local region on the current block. If the region contains more than 5 disjointed components, the stripe is discarded. Otherwise, we fit an ellipse to the component with longest major axis. If the ellipse approximates a long stripe (ratio of the ellipse's minor axis to major axis is smaller than 0.2), we consider the stripe to be a diagonal stripe, and fit a line to it as follows. We denote the stripe's local region as $R(x, y)$. For each column line of $R(x, y)$, we first compute a centroid point that divides the continuous white pixels into equal halves, i.e., $\mathbf{c}_x = \frac{\sum_{y=1}^{h} y * R(x,y)}{\sum_{y=1}^{h} R(x,y)}$. Then, a straight line is fitted to the centroid points, and used as a diagonal splitting line.

Determining an optimal splitting line. To perform binary partitioning adequately at each recursive level, we need to select an optimal splitting line from the computed candidate splitting lines. Take the results in Fig. 5 as an example. Properly partitioning panels in the fourth example should start by splitting the whole page *horizontally* into rows rather than vertically into columns. To this end, after the candidate splitting lines have been computed along both horizontal and vertical directions for the current panel block, we first assign each splitting line a confidence value, which is calculated as the ratio of the number of white pixels to its length. The splitting line that travels across the whole page without cutting the panel block has the highest confidence value of 1. Then, the optimal splitting line is selected as the one with the highest confidence value.

2.3 Panel Shape Extraction

Given a set of panel regions obtained in the previous step, this step aims at recovering accurate panel shape by detecting the four corners of each panel. We begin by computing a convex hull for each panel region and the centroid of the convex hull's vertices C (red crosses in Fig. 2(c)). Then, a 2D Cartesian coordinate system, centered at C, is constructed, thereby separating all the vertices of the convex hull into four quadrants. In each quadrant, we select a vertex that is furthest away from C as the initial corner point. Finally, we optimize the four corner points by performing a local search around each initial corner point so that the area of quadrilateral formed by the four points are maximized. Our implementation uses a circle of 10 pixels in radius as the local search region. This leads to the final panel shape as shown in Fig. 2(c).

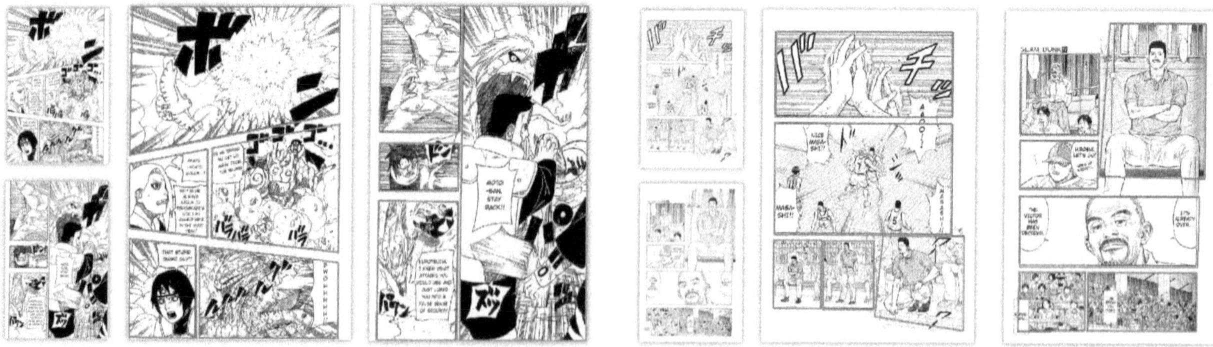

Figure 5: Panel extraction results on four manga pages with different stylistic effects. The left two pages are from "Naruto", and contain the fourth wall break effect, irregular panels and unclosed panels. The right two pages are from "Slum Dunk", and have borderless and joined panels.

3. EXPERIMENTS AND ANALYSIS

To evaluate the effectiveness of the proposed method, we have tested it on numerous manga pages. As shown in Fig. 5, the proposed method can accurately segment out the panels on the manga pages with various stylistic effects.

We have also compared our method with [5], which segments joined panels by performing an erosion-dilatation operation on the labeling mask generated from CCL. We apply both methods to a database of 104 manga pages from "Slum Dunk" and "Naruto". For each page in the database, we manually annotate panels as the ground truth. To evaluate the performance of the panel extraction methods, we calculate segmentation accuracy by computing the overlap ratio (Jaccard index) between the segmented panel and the ground truth. Let $G(x, y)$ and $S(x, y)$ be the masks of the annotated panel and the segmented panel. The overlap ratio ρ is computed as

$$\rho = \frac{|G \cap S|}{|G \cup S|}, \tag{2}$$

where $|M|$ is the number of non-zero pixels in the mask M. If ρ is larger than 90%, the panel is deemed to be successfully segmented. If all panels in a manga page are correctly segmented, it is defined as a successfully segmented page. The results are presented in Table 1. Our method achieves higher rates of successfully segmented panels and pages, and our average overlap ratio for correct segmentation is also higher than [5]. This is largely because [5] cannot properly deal with unclosed panels.

	Page rate %	Panel rate %	Average Overlap Ratio
Our approach	**87.9**	**91.3**	**0.97**
[5]	73.9	74.1	0.94

Table 1: Comparison of our method and [5]. The successful segmentation rates for both pages and panels, and the overlap ratio for successfully segmented panels are given.

Our method may fail to detect the panel shape correctly when a large visual symbol cuts across the panel and breaks the panel boundary. In this case, our panel block generation cannot merge the two disjoint parts caused by the visual symbol, resulting in an incomplete panel shape (as shown in the figure on the right).

4. CONCLUSION

In this paper, we have proposed a robust method for automatically extracting panels from manga pages, which are characterized by various stylistic effects. Our method starts by extracting a panel block, i.e., a set of panel regions. It then employs a recursive binary splitting strategy to partition the panel block into disjoint panel regions, where we dynamically determine the location of an optimal splitting line at each recursion level. Accurate panel shapes are finally obtained from the panel regions. Our results show that our method is insusceptible to various stylistic effects and complex layout style of manga, achieving a higher successful segmentation rate, as compared with previous work. We are interested in further exploring applications that can benefit from our method, such as converting scanned comic pages into a format that is readable on mobile devices, and an automatic comic annotation system for comic analysis.

5. REFERENCES

[1] K. Arai and T. Herman. Method for automatic e-comic scene frame extraction for reading comic on mobile devices. In *Proc. ITNG*, pages 370–375, 2010.

[2] Y. Cao, A. Chan, and R. Lau. Automatic stylistic manga layout. *ACM Trans. on Graphics*, 31(6), 2012.

[3] C. Chan, H. Leung, and T. Komura. Automatic panel extraction of color comic images. In *Proc. PCM*, pages 775–784, 2007.

[4] E. Han, K. Kim, H. Yang, and K. Jung. Frame segmentation used mlp-based x-y recursive for mobile cartoon content. In *LNCS: Human-Computer Interaction*, volume 4552, pages 872–881, 2007.

[5] A. Ho, J. Burie, and J. Ogier. Comics page structure analysis based on automatic panel extraction. In *Proc. IAPR GREC*, 2011.

[6] C. Rigaud, N. Tsopze, J. Burie, and J. Ogier. Robust frame and text extraction from comic books. In *Proc. IAPR GREC*, pages 129–138, 2013.

[7] M. Stommel, L. Merhej, and M. Müller. Segmentation-free detection of comic panels. In *LNCS: Computer Vision and Graphics*, volume 7594, pages 633–640. 2012.

[8] T. Tanaka, K. Shoji, F. Toyama, and J. Miyamichi. Layout analysis of tree-structured scene frames in comic images. In *Proc. IJCAI*, pages 2885–2890, 2007.

RIFF: Retina-inspired Invariant Fast Feature Descriptor

Song Wu Michael S. Lew
LIACS Media Lab, Leiden University
Niels Bohrweg 1, 2333 CA Leiden, The Netherlands
{s.wu, m.s.lew}@liacs.leidenuniv.nl

ABSTRACT
We present the Retina-inspired Invariant Fast Feature, RIFF, which was designed for invariance to scale, rotation, and affine image deformations. The feature descriptor is based on pair-wise comparisons over a sampling pattern loosely based on the human retina and introduces a method for improving accuracy by maximizing the discriminatory power of the point set. A performance evaluation with regard to bag of words based image retrieval on several well-known international datasets demonstrates that the RIFF descriptor has competitive performance to the state-of-the-art descriptors (*e.g.* SIFT, SURF, BRISK, and FREAK).

Categories and Subject Descriptors
Computing methodologies, computer vision

General Terms
Algorithms, Performance, Experimentation

Keywords
Salient point descriptor; bag of words; image copy detection

1. INTRODUCTION
Efficiently establishing the correspondences between images is very useful for numerous applications of computer vision and content-based retrieval, such as content-based image retrieval, image classification, object tracking, and panorama stitching. Salient point methods are a leading approach which has been proven to be effective in many real world applications.

In using salient points, one typically needs a detector and a descriptor. Detectors find the locations (i.e. blob, region, and point) in images which typically are in some way informative. The descriptor gives a model or representation of the local image region. Prior research of salient points has focused on high repeatability detector and robustness to scale and rotation [1].

The SIFT descriptor [2] is the most popular salient point approach. It computes the Difference-of-Gaussian (DoG) operator in the Gaussian scale space, and assigns orientation and descriptor to each salient point based on local gradient histogram. The SURF [3] salient points detector makes use of a box-filter to achieve efficient extrema detection in scale space and it performs well with respect to the criteria of repeatability. The SURF descriptor of each detected salient point is calculated through summing Haar-wavelet responses in the defined region after orientation alignment. Recent binary string descriptors such as BRIEF, ORB, BRISK, and FREAK were proposed with specific advantages such as low memory requirements as well as efficiently matching via hamming distance (bitwise XOR followed by a bit count). BRIEF [4] first uses Gaussian smoothing on the selected image patch, and creates a binary string descriptor via the intensity comparison of randomly sampled pixel-pairs around the patch center. ORB [5] employs the most efficient FAST [6] detector to determine the salient points in different layers of an image pyramid, creates an orientation for each point by the intensity centroid algorithm. It forms the binary string descriptor based on BRIEF and effectively improves the sensitivity to image rotation and scale. BRISK [7] applies FAST score as a measure to determine the extreme points in the image scale pyramid, and generates the descriptor by comparing pair-wise intensities over a decreasing density circular sampling pattern. FREAK [8] also selects pairs of pixels over a decreasing density circular sampling pattern loosely inspired by the retina and then compares their intensities to form a binary vector. Both BRISK and FREAK use the sum of local gradients of selected pairs to estimate the orientation.

The recent wave of salient point detectors each have specific strengths. Some are best for scale changes; others for speed; others for memory requirements. Our goal was to design a detector which was optimized for affine transformations including rotation and scaling. In this paper, we propose a novel discriminate salient point real value descriptor named "RIFF" because the sampling pattern is inspired by the distribution of cones (color vision) in the human eye. The main contributions of this paper are as follows: first, we describe a salient point descriptor which outperforms current methods regarding affine transformations. Moreover, we proposed a measure to rank the generated salient point descriptors so that unstable points will be rejected and the discriminatory power of the set of descriptors will be improved. This is useful for speeding up the process of indexing and matching among large scale descriptors and increasing accuracy.

The rest of the paper is organized as follows: In Section 2, we present the generation of our RIFF local feature descriptor. In Section 3, we describe the datasets and evaluation criterion in the experiment. The performance result of the proposed descriptor compared with current state-of-the-art descriptors are shown in Section 4, and conclusions are given in Section 5.

2. DISCRIMINATE RIFF SALIENT POINT DESCRIPTOR METHOD

2.1 Retina Sampling Pattern Review
The retina sampling pattern is based on topology of human retina from the neuroscience research, which reveals that the spatial

MM '14, November 3–7 2014, Orlando, FL, USA
Copyright 2014 ACM 978-1-4503-3063-3/14/11…$15.00.
http://dx.doi.org/10.1145/2647868.2654994

distribution density of cone cells in the retina decreases exponentially with the distance measure to the center of fovea. Moreover, it is believed that the signal of image passes through from cone cells to ganglion cells and the receptive field of each ganglion cell using Difference of Gaussians (DoG) model with various sizes and encodes such differences into action potentials. Our approach employed the similar retina sampling pattern, which place different size of blocks at the defined location in the pattern. The illustration of the cones density can be seen in Figure 1.

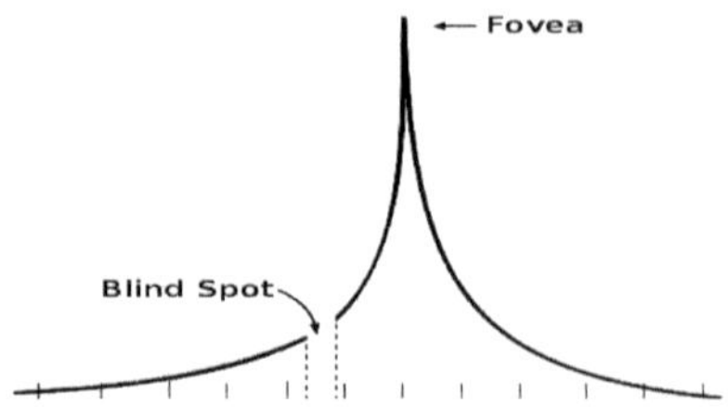

Figure 1. Illustration of the density distribution of cones in the human retina

Inspired by recent work with decreasing circular polar densities in diverse applications from stereo matching to object recognition [7, 8, 9], the sampling pattern for RIFF in 2D decreases exponentially as shown in Figure 2 (a).

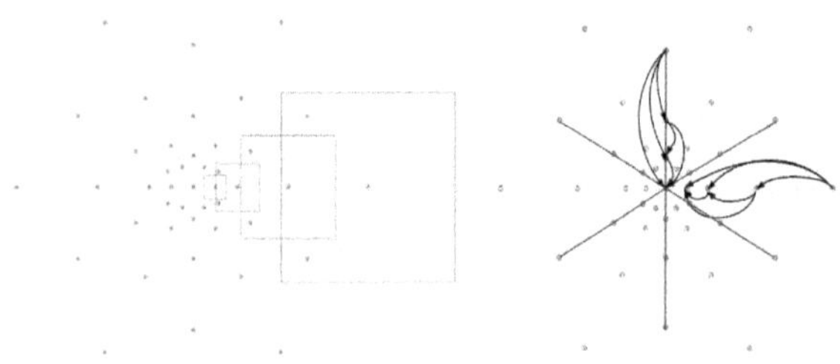

(a) (b)

Figure 2. (a) The 2D decreasing exponential polar sampling pattern for RIFF with N=43 points: the red point denotes the sampling point location, the blue rectangle represents a receptive field, and the size of rectangle corresponds to its Gaussian kernel which used to smooth the intensity values at the sampling points. (b) The pre-defined pair-wise point comparisons on RIFF for 2 of the 12 axes.

2.2 Descriptor Generation

2.2.1 Orientation estimation

Given a set of salient points in an image (detected by the salient point detector), we first position and scale the retina sampling pattern according to the location and scale information (this is computed by the detector) for each specified point, and then calculate an orientation for them.

The popular approach for estimating the orientation angle comes from basic geometry which is to estimate the orientation using local gradients: Δy and Δx and then determine the angle from the arctangent of (Δy/Δx) (for details see FREAK [8]). We also estimate the local gradients by pair-wise differences between equidistant points from the center.

2.2.2 Descriptor building

The procedure of RIFF descriptor generation is different from previous salient point approaches such as BRIEF, ORB, BRISK and FREAK which compare the pixel-pairs intensity in the sampling pattern to generate a binary string feature. Our approach first constructs a structure in the retina sampling pattern rotated by the estimated orientation θ. Let $V = [v_1, \dots v_i, \dots v_d]$ represent a feature vector of a salient point, v_i is a float value obtained by calculating the difference of Gaussian smoothed image intensities of pre-defined pairs over the structure. We defined 6 pair-wise comparisons on each of the 12 axes from the center which resulted in the dimension of the descriptor d as 72. For clarity, we displayed in Figure 2(b) 1 of 6 pair-wise comparisons on the blue axes and 1 of 6 on the yellow axes where each black curve denotes one pair comparison. Since we place a block at each sampling point, the integral image (summed area tables) was used for computational efficiency. Compared with the binary string features, it was not necessary for RIFF to compare the intensity of all possible $N^*(N-1)/2$ sampling pairs, moreover, the dimension of RIFF is smaller than SIFT, which can improve the speed of indexing and matching.

2.2.3 Discriminatory Strategy

Even though location, scale and orientation have been estimated, current salient point detectors have difficulty with affine viewpoint changes such as in Figure 3. We conducted a small internal study which revealed that local ambiguities (nearby salient points with similar feature descriptors) are often the cause of those matching errors.

Figure 3. Matches (blue lines) from using SIFT (OpenCV) salient point approach.

Thus, our goal was to reduce local ambiguity or increase local distinctiveness by eliminating salient points which have similar salient points nearby. We implemented this process by using a ranking scheme to identify stable local features as described next. Consider a set of salient point descriptors $\{f_i, i=1,2,\dots,M\}$, a salient point p in the image I and its feature is f_p. The discriminatory score of the feature is defined according to the measure of similarity when compared to its K nearest neighbors in the image.

$$D_p(p \in I) = \sum_{j=1}^{K} \left\| f_p - f_j \right\|_2 \quad (1)$$

$\|\cdot\|$ denotes the Euclidean distance. Intuitively, the higher discriminatory score demonstrates that the feature of point p is more distinctive than other points. The parameter K is set to 2 in the experiment. Furthermore, we use an exponential function in order to emphasize the discriminate score:

$$D_p^{'}(p \in I) = \exp(-\lambda \cdot |D_p|) \quad (2)$$

$|\cdot|$ denotes the normalization of D_p (in the range [0, 1]), λ is a weight of discriminate score and it is set to 6 in the experiment. We note that after the above process, the smaller D'_p score correlates to more distinctive feature points, so we can sort these scores and define a threshold to filter those unstable salient points. The final set is a smaller number of discriminative features which have are more robust to various image transformations, while

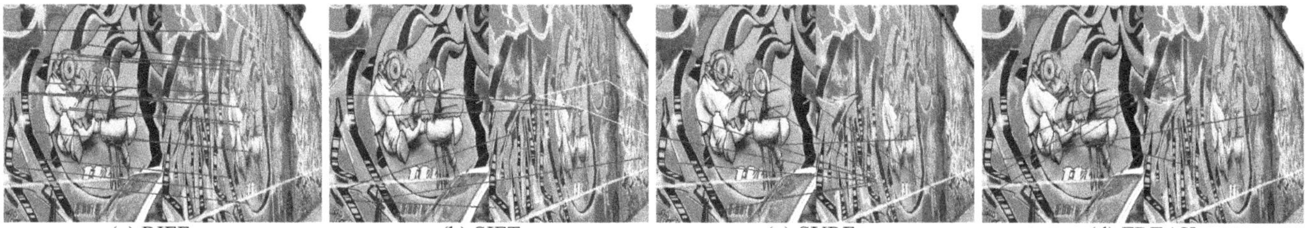

(a) RIFF (b) SIFT (c) SURF (d) FREAK

Figure 5. Illustration of descriptors matching, RIFF as compared to SIFT, SURF, and FREAK on challenge affine object detection (graffiti 1-5 proposed by Mikolajczyk and Schmid[1]).

reducing required subsequent processing, *e.g.,* descriptor indexing as well as dictionary learning in large scale image applications.

3. DATASETS AND EVALUATION CRITERIA

We evaluated our proposed RIFF descriptor with state-of-art local descriptors on three well known benchmark datasets in terms of bag of words based image retrieval. The Nearest Neighbor Distance Ratio (NNDR) is used as the matching strategy to define the similar descriptors between two images. PASCAL VOC 2012 dataset [10], Caltech 256 [11], as well as MIRFLICKER 1M consisting of one million images [12] were used to evaluate the performance on large scale similar (distorted/transformed duplicate) image detection. Additional experiments (stability, recall and precision, etc.) which did not fit space limitations can be found here: http://press.liacs.nl/researchdownloads/. The two descriptors are viewed as a correspondence if $||D_A\text{-}D_B||/||D_A\text{-}D_C||<$*threshold*, where D_B is the first and D_C is the second nearest neighbor of D_A.

We used mAP (mean Average Precision) as a criterion for the evaluation of detection accuracy. The transformed duplicates categories generated for the test mainly include: cropping, content noise, image blur, image compression: JPEG compression 5%-95%, rotation: 30-360 deg., scale: 20-200% and affine transformation: rotation + scale + 60 deg. 3D perspective distortion (Figure 4). 1000 images in each dataset were chosen as queries, and each query image corresponds to 80 duplicates in the evaluation.

Figure 4. Types of image transforms: original (left), rotation and scale (middle), affine - 3D pan rotation (right).

4. EXPERIMENTS AND RESULTS

In the performance evaluation of our proposed RIFF descriptor, we used the SURF salient point detector for locating salient points due to its high repeatability [7]. RIFF was programmed in C++ and the descriptor and datasets can be downloaded from http://press.liacs.nl/researchdownloads/.

4.1 Descriptors Matching

In this part, we set the value of *threshold* in the NNDR 0.75, and the homography between two compared images is estimated by the RANSAC algorithm. In preliminary tests, RIFF exhibited competitive performance in the cases of affine image transformations in comparison to the popular SIFT, SURF, and recent FREAK descriptors as shown in Figure 5.

Time cost and memory space requirement were also evaluated in this part. As summarized in Table 1, binary string features (BRIEF, ORB, BRISK and FREAK) were more computationally efficient and space effective (using an Intel Core i7 Processor (2.67GHz), 12GB of RAM)

Table 1. Comparison of descriptors in terms of extraction time and memory space requirement (5000 descriptors)

Methods	Time cost	memory requirement
SURF+SIFT	5.5 Seconds	2.44M
SURF+SURF	0.3 Seconds	1.22M
SURF+BRIEF	0.044 Seconds	0.15M
SURF+ORB	0.045 Seconds	0.15M
SURF+BRISK	0.058 Seconds	0.3M
SURF+FREAK	0.1 Seconds	0.3M
SURF+RIFF	0.38 Seconds	1.37M

4.2 Image Retrieval Experiments

In this section, we evaluated the proposed RIFF feature descriptor in the area of large scale similar image detection. The bag of visual words model was used. The visual vocabulary was first trained based on the extracted descriptors from PASCAL VOC

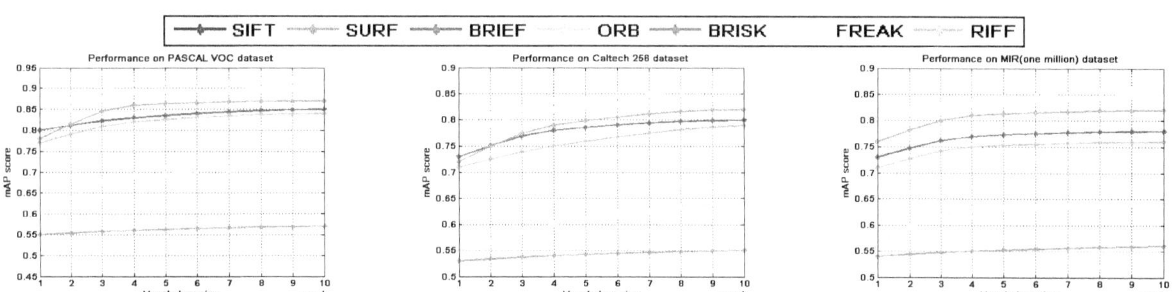

Figure 6. Detection accuracy on three datasets (PASCAL VOC, Caltech 256 and MIRFLICKER).

dataset (with dimensions from 10K to 100K). We used the ANN search to speed up the vocabulary generation. Due to the different properties of real value descriptors and binary string descriptors, the ANN search was based on KD-tree index and multi-probe LSH index respectively [13]. Once the visual vocabulary was generated, descriptors of the images were encoded into a histogram according to the occurrence frequency of each visual word together with the *tf-idf* weighting scheme [14]. The cosine distance measure was adopted to estimate similarity of two images represented by visual words. The compared visual vocabularies were generated by different types of descriptors and the detection accuracy was measured by the mAP score on three datasets. In the following step, we analyzed the final rank and distribution of each category's transformed duplicates on the MIRFLICKER one million dataset.

Overall, RIFF outperformed the other descriptors on the PASCAL VOC, Caltech 256 and MIRFLICKR-1M datasets as shown in Figure 6. Regarding specific transformations as shown in Figure 7, RIFF had the best performance on the distortions related to scale, rotation, and affine transformations. It had average performance on blurring and had competitive performance on the rest of the transformations.

RIFF was roughly 14 times faster than SIFT which makes it amenable to real-time applications. It is slower (and requires

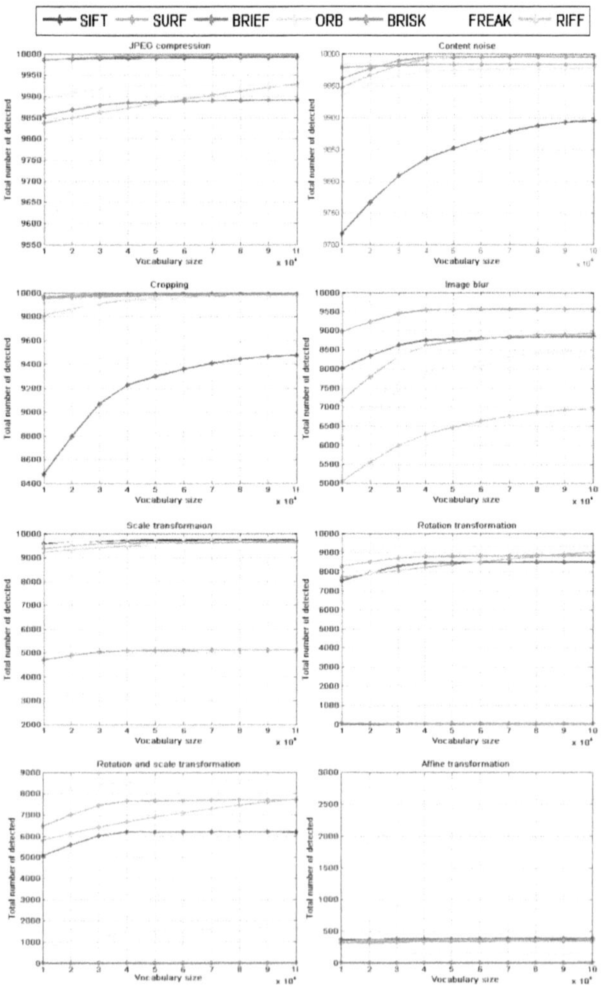

Figure 7. Number of detected duplicates in each transformation category.

more memory) than FREAK, however, it has shown significantly higher accuracy regarding affine transformations as displayed in Figure 5 and Figure 7.

5. CONCLUSIONS

We have proposed a novel salient point descriptor named RIFF which was inspired by the sampling pattern from the human eye (We make no claims of biological relevance). The main contribution of the RIFF descriptor is in constructing the descriptor so that the discriminatory power is optimized by ranking and deleting points with low distinctiveness. From our bag of words image retrieval tests on three well known datasets, RIFF outperformed the other feature descriptors with respect to scale, rotation, and affine transformations.

6. REFERENCES

[1] Mikolajczyk, K., & Schmid, C. 2005. A performance evaluation of local descriptors. *IEEE Transactions on Pattern Analysis and Machine Intelligence*(PAMI), 27(10), 1615–1630.

[2] Lowe, D G. 2004. Distinctive Image Features from Scale-Invariant Keypoints. *Inernational Journal of Computer Vision,* 60(2), 91-110.

[3] Bay, H., Ess, A., Tuytelaars, T., and Van Gool, L. 2008. Speeded-up robust features (SURF). *Computer Vision and Image Understanding*, 110(3), 346-359.

[4] Calonder, M., Lepetit, V., Strecha, C., and Fua, P. 2010. BRIEF: Binary Robust Independent Elementary Features. *European Conference on Computer vision*, 778–792.

[5] Rublee, E., Rabaud, V., Konolige, K., and Bradski, G. 2011. ORB: An Efficient Alternative to SIFT or SURF. *International Conference on Computer Vision*, 2564-2571.

[6] Rosten, E., and Drummond, T. 2006. Machine learning for high-speed corner detection. *European Conference on Computer Vision*, 430-443.

[7] Leutenegger, S., Chli, M., and Siegwart, R. 2011. BRISK: Binary robust invariant scalable keypoints. *International Conference on Computer Vision*, 2548-2555.

[8] Alahi, A., Ortiz, R., and Vandergheynst, P. 2012. FREAK: Fast Retina Keypoint. *IEEE Conference on Computer Vision and Pattern Recognition.*

[9] Tola, E., Lepetit, V., and Fua, P. 2010. Daisy: an Efficient Dense Descriptor Applied to Wide Baseline Stereo. *IEEE Transactions on Pattern Analysis and Machine Intelligence* (PAMI), 32(5):815–830, 2010.

[10] Everingham, M., Van Gool, L., Williams, C.K.I., Winn, J., and Zisserman, A. 2010. The PASCAL Visual Object Classes Challenge 2008 (VOC2008) Results, http://www.pascal-network.org/ challenges/VOC/voc2008

[11] Griffin, G., Holub, A., and Perona, P. 2007. The Caltech 256. California Institute of Technology, Technical Report.

[12] Huiskes, M.J., Thomee, B., and Lew, M.S. 2010. New Trends and Ideas in Visual Concept Detection. *ACM International Conference on MIR*, 527-536.

[13] O'Hara, S., and Draper, B. A. 2013. Are you using the right approximate nearest neighbor algorithm?. *IEEE Workshop on Applications of Computer Vision (WACV)*, 9-14.

[14] Salton G., and McGill, M.J. 1986. Introduction to Modern Information Retrieval. McGraw-Hill.

Stevens' Power Law in 3D Tele-immersion

Towards Subjective Modeling of Multimodal Cyber Interaction

Sabrina Schulte
RWTH Aachen University
sabrina.schulte@rwth-aachen.de

Shannon Chen and Klara Nahrstedt
University of Illinois at Urbana-Champaign
{cchen116, klara}@illinois.edu

ABSTRACT

In this paper we verify the insufficiency of Stevens' power law to describe the relationship between QoS and QoE factors. User studies that target different types of application scenarios of 3D Tele-immersion (3DTI) are conducted and the results show no significant power trend in the relationship between packet loss and perceptual quality metrics. We further verify that activity characteristics, activity objectives, and users' roles in the 3DTI session also have profound effects on the service quality aside to the QoS level. Thus, simple one-factor psychophysical laws are inadequate of serving as a QoS-QoE mapping model.

Categories and Subject Descriptors

H.1.2 [**Information Systems**]: Models and Principles – *human factors*

General Terms

Experimentation, Human Factors, Measurement

Keywords

3D Tele-Immersion; QoE; Stevens' Power Law

1. INTRODUCTION

Quality assessment of distributed interactive multimedia services has shifted from traditional quality of service (QoS) to quality of experience (QoE). However, the time and human effort for compiling user feedbacks under controlled environment makes QoE-based system adaptation infeasible for it cannot keep up with the network dynamics. Thus, mapping models that connect real-time measureable QoS metrics with QoE are essential for efficient utilization of networking resources.

Since more than a decade ago, the thriving of VoIP services (e.g., Skype [2]) urges the investigation of such mapping models to aid the adaptation of bandwidth usage. Power based [3] and log based [6] perceptual models for VoIP scenarios are proved to be practical foundations for network adaptation modules. While elegant closed-form models well describe simple one-dimensional VoIP services, we would like to ask, with the complication of multimodality and application level semantic: *does the elegant psychophysical model still hold in complex multimedia applications such as 3D Tele-immersion?*

The potential of 3D Tele-immersive (3DTI) services has gained its attention from both academia and industry. The development of

MM '14, November 3 – 7, 2014, Orlando, FL, USA

ACM 978-1-4503-3063-3/14/11...$15.00.
http://dx.doi.org/10.1145/2647868.2654998

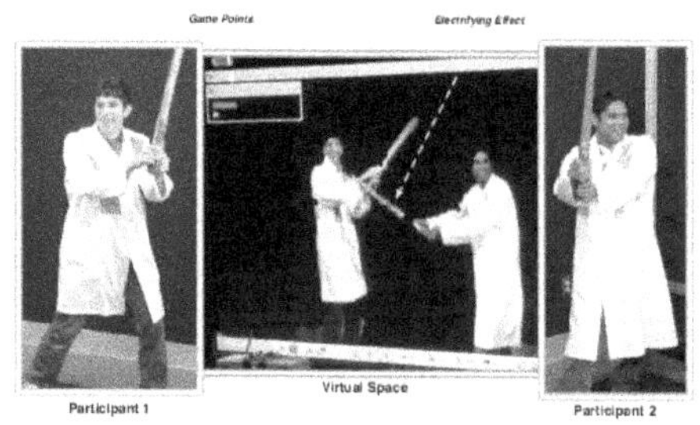

(a) 3DTI activity

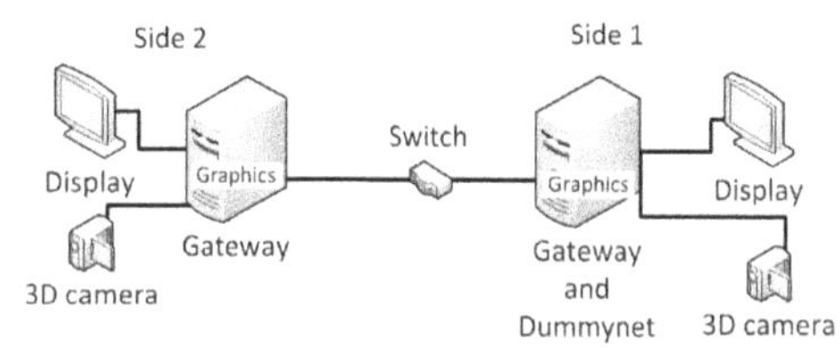

(b) System model

Figure 1. 3DTI system

3DTI systems is currently aiming towards multi-purpose, multi-sites, and multi-modal [7, 9] platforms in order to enable a variety of user activities. In its system view, an efficient adaptation module is essential for the inevitably high bandwidth demand to support its interactive characteristic and complex 3D rendering [8]. Thus, mapping model of QoS-QoE again plays an important role. This paper answers a crucial question on the journey of model building: can (or to what extent can) psychophysical law help us?

Psychophysical laws are results of quantitative psychology [5], a study with long history that well serves the purpose of bridging interdisciplinary studies. The idea is to construct mathematical formula that addresses the relationship between physical stimulus (Φ) and quantified perception (Ψ). Some well-verified laws include the Weber-Fechner Logarithmic Law [5] and the Stevens' Power Law [5]. However, these formula merely focus on simple one-factor stimuli and single human sensory system. For example, the relationship between voltage of the electric shock and level of pain, or weight of an object and the stress perceived when lifting it.

In this paper, we are interested in much more complicated stimulus-perception pair: the packet loss rate versus the perceptual quality of different 3DTI activity sessions. We set the stage with two 3DTI sites with two sets of experiment that target two different application level scenarios. The first one targets fast activities, where users play against each other in a virtual sword fight; while the second experiment targets slow activity, where users play the roles of doctor and patient in a remote physiotherapy session.

We manipulate the condition of the network that connects the two sites and recruit real human users to participate and evaluate the quality of the experiment sessions. Comprehensive user feedbacks including general service quality, sense of control, interactive-ness, win/loss ratio (for gaming activity), sense of achievement, and sense of time are compiled during the experiment. Analysis shows that the oversimplified psychophysical laws do not describe the relationship of multimodal, interactive services as we experience in 3DTI. With the semantic and sensory complication of the application, we need more sophisticated model building framework to capture the intrinsic relationship of QoS-QoE that involves environmental and social confound factors [10].

The rest of the paper is organized as follows. In Section 2 and 3 we introduce the system model and the psychological model under verification. In Section 4 we describe the targeted 3DTI activities and the experiment flow. In Section 5 we present and analyze the experiment results. Finally, in Section 6 we conclude.

2. SYSTEM MODEL

The purpose of 3DTI system is to allow two physically dispersed parties to interact with each other in a virtual space. As shown in Figure 1 the system includes two sites, each consists of a 3D Kinect camera, a gateway with a graphic engine, and a display.

The camera records the user in front of it. This data stream is sent to the local gateway and passed on to the other gateway through the network. Streams received from the local camera and the remote gateway are merged in the graphics engine in the local gateway to render an in-synced virtual space. Artificial elements can also be added into the virtual space via the graphics engine.

In our experiment setting, the two gateways are connected via a LAN switch so that we have full control of the network conditions using *dummynet* [1]. The network allows a maximum packet size of 1500 bytes and has a bandwidth of 100 Mbps.

The image of user in a site will be captured by the camera and presented as point cloud in its stream. The final virtual space is shown on the displays with resolution of 480 x 640 with frame rate around 20 fps.

3. PSYCHOPHYSICAL MODEL

In this section we discuss the psychological background for this paper. We are going to introduce two different psychophysical laws called Weber-Fechner Law [5] and Stevens' Power Law [5]. Both laws describe the relation between a physical stimulus and the sensational magnitude.

The Weber-Fechner Law describes the correlation between a physical stimulus and the sensation magnitude as a logarithmic function. Given a stimulus Φ and its responding quantified perception Ψ, the relationship between Φ and Ψ is described as

$$d\Psi = \mathrm{k} \times \frac{d\Phi}{\Phi}$$

where $d\Psi$ and $d\Phi$ are the difference of stimulus and the difference of perception, respectively, and k is a constant scalar. By integrating both sides of the equation

$$\Psi = \mathrm{k} \times \ln \Phi + c$$

where c is the constant introduced by integration. Hence, the Weber-Fechner law claims that the relationship between a relative stimulus-perception pair is logarithmic, which is proved to be true for most cases including loudness, brightness, sense of touch and heat, and even temporal, spatial, and numerical cognitions [5].

(a) Fast activity (b) Slow activity

Figure 3. Experiment activities

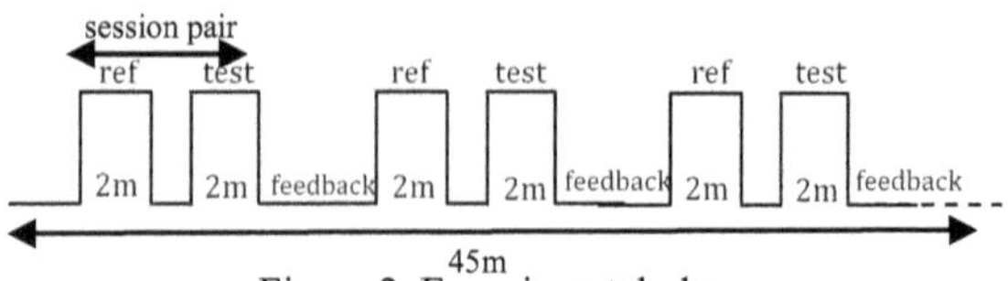

Figure 2. Experimental phase

Later, Stevens' Power Law is developed because Weber-Fechner Law only covers sub-linear relationships between stimulus and perception. Stimuli like electric shock and low temperature have exponential effects on sense of pain and cold [5].

Thus, to cover super-linear, linear and sub-linear relationships, Stevens' Power Law is defined as

$$\Psi = k\Phi^{\Theta}$$

where Θ is a power exponent that determines the relationship. When $\Theta > 1$ the relationship becomes exponential, and when $\Theta < 1$ the relationship is sub-linear. In view of the wider coverage of Stevens' Law, in the rest of the paper we focus on investigating the feasibility of using Stevens' Law to describe the QoS-QoE relationship of 3DTI activities.

4. 3DTI USER STUDY

4.1 Experimental Setup

We recruit eighteen users to participate in our user study. Four of them are female and fourteen are male. All users are affiliate to the *anonymous institute*. We use two separated 3DTI sites to simulate a distributed environment. Both sites are in the same lab but connected via *dummynet* and separated by a visual cover.

All users participate pairwise. At the beginning of each experiment we ask the user to read the description of the experiment and fill out the user information form. After that follows a training phase, which helps the user to get familiar with the activity and the system. We do not limit the time for the training phase, since it is important that the user understands how to interact through the system.

The experimental phase lasts 45 minutes and consists of four session pairs (Figure 2). Each session lasts two minutes. The first session of a pair is the reference session and the second session is the test session. After each session pair, users are asked to fill out a questionnaire. At the end of the whole experiment we ask them to fill out a final questionnaire which refers to the overall experience.

During the reference session we set the *dummynet* to simulate QoS of 4.5% packet loss rate in the link that connects the two sites. During the test session, 0%, 3%, 6%, and 9% packet loss rate are simulated in random order in the four session pairs.

4.2 3DTI User Activities

Based on the activity objectives and characteristics, users' tolerance towards quality degradation can be very different [7]. One

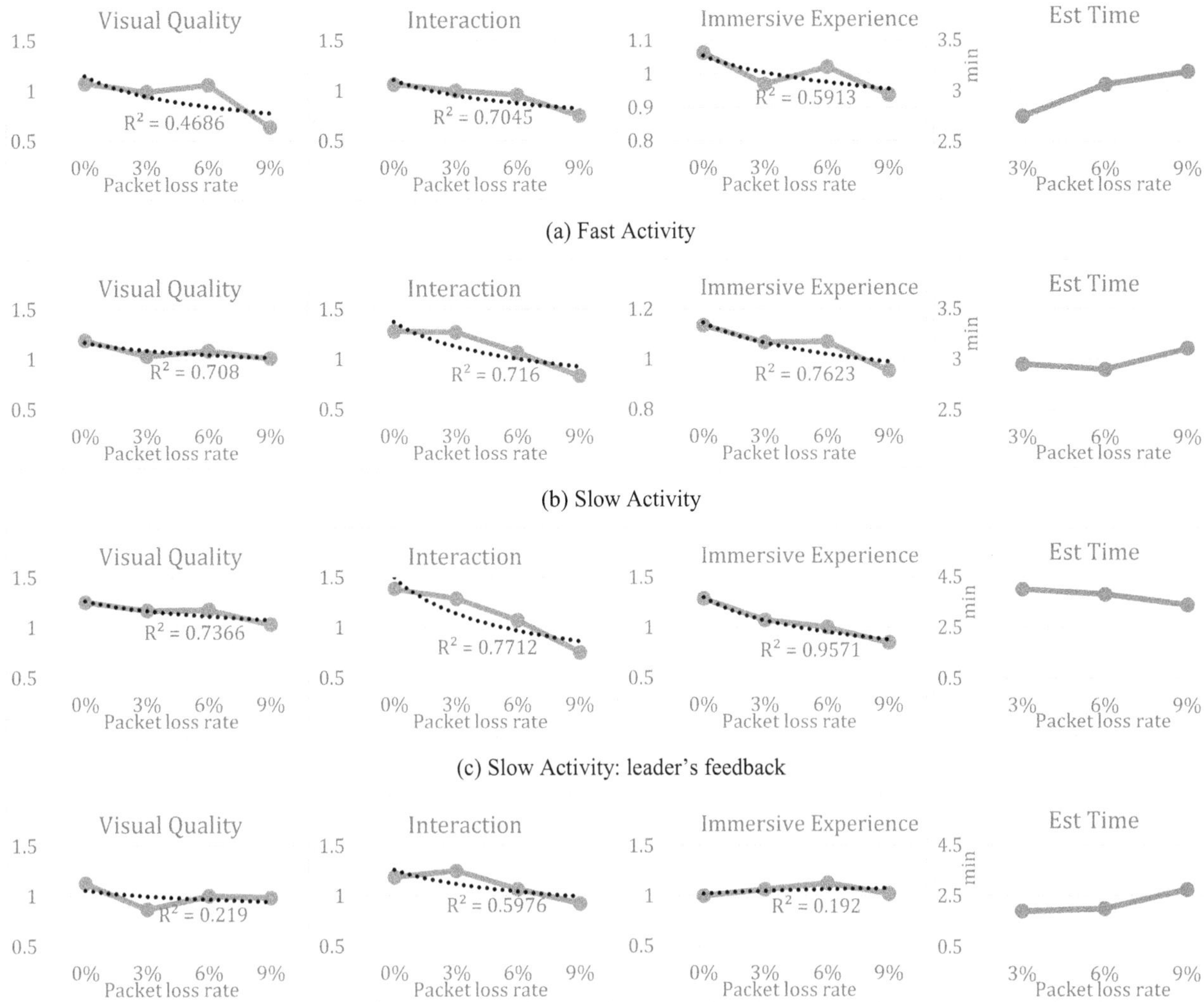

(a) Fast Activity

(b) Slow Activity

(c) Slow Activity: leader's feedback

(d) Slow Activity: follower's feedback

Figure 4. Experiment results

important characteristic of the activities that significantly affects the QoS-QoE relationship is the speed of movement and user interaction. Thus, we study two signature user activities in 3DTI scenarios: the virtual sword fight game, which represents fast activity; and the remote physiotherapy, which represents slow activity.

4.2.1 *Fast Activity*

In the fast activity we simulate a sword fight (Figure 3a). When the users come into the site and raise their right hand they see a sword attached to it in the virtual world. The sword follows the movement of their hands. In the top corners of the display there are the "life points" of the users - one for the user herself and one for her opponent. Each experiment session consists of multiple rounds with the users fighting against each other.

4.2.2 *Slow Activity*

For slow activity we design an application for remote physiotherapy session, in which one user plays the role of a leader (trainer) and the other plays the role of a follower (patient). When the leader comes into the site and raises his right hand in front of the camera, there will be a circle attached to his hand (Figure 3b). The leader's task is to move the circle to a certain position and then instruct the follower to touch the circle in the virtual world with a specified body part. As soon as the follower touches the circle, its color changes to signify a successful touch. The leader then moves it to a new position.

5. RESULTS AND ANALYSIS

In this section we show the results of the experiments and further show that Stevens' Power Law alone is insufficient to cover the QoS-QoE relationship in 3DTI. In the following discussions, we use the normalized MOS (Mean Opinion Score) value to represent the perceptual quality. For each experiment session, the users evaluate the quality by 5-point MOS scale [11]. The normalized MOS is obtained by normalizing the score of a test session by the score of the reference session. Thus, a normalized score greater than 1 indicates an improved quality from the reference while a less than 1 score indicates a degraded quality. Reflecting to Stevens' power law, the stimulus (Φ) is the packet loss rate and the quantified perception (Ψ) is the normalized MOS.

For fast and slow activities, we ask three subjective questions about the visual quality, the interaction, and the overall immersive experience. In addition, we ask the users to estimate the time lapse of an experiment session. This estimated time serves as an indicator of the user's *psychological flow* [4]. The flow measures "the holistic sensation that people feel when they act with total involvement", which is the main intrinsic motivation for people to perform activities that provide no discernible extrinsic rewards [4]. Losing track of time is one explicit trait of flow. We argue that a shorter-than-actual estimated time indicates full concentration supported by an acceptable service quality, while a longer estimated time indicates boredom and reluctance, which can be incurred by the unacceptable service.

5.1 General Analysis

In Figure 4 we show the normalized MOS given by users (y-axis) plotted against the packet loss rate (x-axis). Not surprisingly there is a positive correlation between QoS and QoE degradations, which incurs monotonically decreasing plots in the graphs. However, none of them show a significant trend that complies with the power law. Along with the normalized MOS (solid line) we also show the fitted power-based regression curve (dotted line) on each graph with its goodness-of-fit index (R-square value). As we can see, the small R-square values indicate that the Stevens' power law poorly describes the relationships between the degradation of packet loss (QoS) and the three QoE metrics (visual quality, interaction, immersion) we target in the experiment questions.

Comparing the effect of packet loss to different QoE metrics (columns 1, 2, 3 of Figure 4), we see that interaction metric is the most affected. Packet loss during content transmission results in screen freezes and decrease of frame rate. Therefore, for fast paced interaction (fast activity) and closely collaborative tasks (slow activity), the effect of packet loss is highly aware and causes interruption of the flow of both activities.

On the other hand, the effect of packet loss on the immersive experience is less predictable (column 3 of Figure 4). Comparing to the other two metrics, the immersive experience is a compound result of various variables that reflects many confound factors [10]. Thus, a simplified one-factor QoS-QoE psychological mapping like Stevens' law does not serve the purpose. While frameworks of identifying confound factors in delivery of internet video [10] and VoIP [6] services has been proposed, for intrinsic multimodal service as 3DTI, a comprehensive mapping that covers wide range of human, environmental, and social factors is yet to be seen to our best knowledge.

5.2 Activity Pace: Fast vs. Slow

In this section we focus on analyzing the difference between the two activities (Figure 4a and 4b). The results of ANOVA test shows significant differences regarding different aspects of service quality ($p<0.05$ for interaction and immersive experience). From previous studies of QoS, it is well expected that a visual content with higher level of motion would require a higher frame rate. Packet loss has direct effect on the frame rate perceived at the 3DTI site, thus causing the visual content not being able to keep up with the fast changing movement during the sword fight activity. Users report irritation of not being able to see the movement clearly and motion blur effect during the session, which cause the degradation of MOS feedbacks.

5.3 User Role: Leader vs. Follower

In this section we focus on the slow activity (Figure 4c and 4d). We group the feedbacks by the role a user played in the session to see the effect of activity objectives. From ANOVA of the plots, we see that the leader's QoE is more impacted by packet loss than the follower ($p<0.1$ for visual quality). This is due to the fact that the leader is in charge of the progress of a session. A leader has to give instructions and wait for the follower to react. Thus, QoE of the session depends heavily on whether a leader can accomplish her task smoothly. Frame freeze caused by packet loss confuses the leader about whether her instruction is correctly received or whether the follower has already accomplished the task. The confusion incur lower scores to the interaction and the overall immersive experience at the leader's site.

Comparing the session time lapse estimated by the leaders and the followers (column 4 of Figure 4c and 4d), we find that generally the leader has a longer feeling of time lapse (about double of the time lapse estimated by the followers). From the qualitative feedbacks of the leaders, we find frustration and loss of confidence due to loss of control. The effect of packet loss makes the leading of the session become a difficult and unpleasant task. On the contrary, the task of a follower is merely to receive instruction from the leader and to react accordingly. From the qualitative feedbacks, followers do not even notice the frame freeze sometimes because they think the pauses of the flow are caused by actual pauses of the leader. Thus, there are no specific negative comments towards the interactive-ness at the follower's site.

6. CONCLUSION AND FUTURE WORKS

In this work we verify the insufficiency of Stevens' power law to describe the relationship between QoS and QoE factors. Subjective user studies that target different types of application scenarios of 3DTI are conducted and the results show no significant power trend in the relationship between packet loss and perceptual quality metrics. We further verify that activity characteristics, activity objectives, and users' roles in the 3DTI session also have profound effect on the service quality aside to the QoS level.

To address these confound factors, a comprehensive framework of 3DTI that takes in environmental, social, and psychological factors should be considered. While communities of internet video streaming and VoIP have long involved in the development of similar frameworks, a comparative framework is not seen in 3DTI. The logical next step of 3DTI is to investigate in such direction to aid the delivery of multimodal, interactive multimedia services.

7. REFERENCES

[1] Dummynet. info.iet.unipi.it/~luigi/dummynet/

[2] Skype. www.skype.com

[3] K. Chen, C. Huang, P. Huang et al., "Quantifying Skype User Satisfaction," ACM SIGCOMM, 2006.

[4] M. Csikszentmihalyi. "Finding Flow: The Psychology of Optimal Experience". Basic Books, 1997.

[5] E. B. Goldstein, "Sensation and Perception," 8/e, Wadsworth, 2010.

[6] C. Chen, C. Chu, S. Yeh et al., "Measuring the Perceptual Quality of SKYPE Sources," ACM SIGCOMM CCR, 2012.

[7] S. Chen, P. Xia, and K. Nahrstedt. "Activity-Aware Adaptive Compression: A Morphing-Based Frame Synthesis Application in 3DTI," ACM MM, 2013.

[8] S. Chen, K. Nahrstedt, and I. Gupta, "3DTI Amphitheater: A Manageable 3DTI Environment with Hierarchical Stream Prioritization," ACM MMSys, 2014.

[9] Z. Tang, A. Patel, X. Guoet al., "A Multimodal Virtual Environment for Interacting with 3D Deformable Models," ACM MM, 2010.

[10] A. Balachandran, S. Seshan, V. Sekar et al., "Developing a Predictive Model of Quality of Experience for Internet Video," ACM SIGCOMM, 2013.

[11] ITU-T Recommendation P.800, Methods for Subjective Determination of Transmission Quality, 1996.

Multi-view Multi-task Feature Extraction for Web Image Classification

Zhiqiang Zuo[†], Yong Luo[†], Dacheng Tao[‡], and Chao Xu[†]
[†]Key Laboratory of Machine Perception (Ministry of Education), Peking University, Beijing, China
[‡]Faculty of Engineering and Information Technology, University of Technology, Sydney, Sydney, Australia
zzq12321@gmail.com, yluo180@gmail.com, Dacheng.Tao@uts.edu.au, xuchao@cis.pku.edu.cn

ABSTRACT

The features used in many multimedia analysis-based applications are frequently of very high dimension. Feature extraction offers several advantages in highly dimensional cases, and many recent studies have used multi-task feature extraction approaches, which often outperform single-task feature extraction approaches. However, most of these methods are limited in that they only consider data represented by a single type of feature, even though features usually represent images from multiple views. We therefore propose a novel multi-view multi-task feature extraction (MVMTFE) framework for handling multi-view features for image classification. In particular, MVMTFE simultaneously learns the feature extraction matrix for each view and the view combination coefficients. In this way, MVMTFE not only handles correlated and noisy features, but also utilizes the complementarity of different views to further help reduce feature redundancy in each view. An alternating algorithm is developed for problem optimization and each sub-problem can be efficiently solved. Experiments on an real-world web image dataset demonstrate the effectiveness and superiority of the proposed method.

Categories and Subject Descriptors

I.5.2 [**Pattern Recognition**]: Design Methodology—*Pattern analysis; Feature evaluation and selection*

General Terms

Algorithm, Experimentation, Theory

Keywords

Feature extraction; image classification; multi-task; multi-view

1. INTRODUCTION

Image classification [8, 17] lies at the heart of many multimedia analysis-based applications, such as web image annotation and browsing. In these applications, very high-dimensional feature vectors are usually used to represent the images. For example, some widely-used global (such as GIST [12]) and local (such as SIFT [7]) descriptors can have dimensionality of up to several hundred or thousand when used for image and video classification [16].

Feature extraction [4] is therefore a useful tool for removing irrelevant or redundant information and reducing feature dimensionality. It makes the learning process more efficient, reduces the chance of over-fitting, and improves the generalizability of the model [10, 6]. Feature transformation and feature selection are the two main approaches used for feature extraction, and the latter is often the preferred method [15]. Although traditional feature selection methods usually select features from a single task [4], more recently there has been a focus on joint feature selection across multiple related tasks [11, 10, 6, 14, 16]. This is because joint feature selection can exploit task correlations in order to establish the importance of features, and this approach has been empirically demonstrated to be superior to feature selection on each task separately [11]. Since all of the joint selection methods aim to learn feature selection matrices, which can also be used for feature transformation, we regard these as feature extraction methods in this paper.

Although multi-task feature extraction can effectively handle correlated and noisy features, it is not suitable for image classification problems that contain images represented by multi-view features [9, 18]. Although all the features can be concatenated into a long vector, such a strategy ignores diversity between different features and may lead to a severe "curse of dimensionality". One recent work considers unsupervised multi-view feature extraction [14] based on spectral analysis, but this method is unsuitable for multi-task feature extraction in the supervised scenario considered in this paper.

To overcome the limitations in existing methods, this paper presents a novel supervised multi-view multi-task feature extraction (MVMTFE) algorithm that effectively explores the complementary nature of different views obtained from multiple tasks. In particular, for each view, MVMTFE learns a projection matrix that transforms the data from the feature space to the label space. In the label space, a weighted combination of all the transformed results is then used to approximate the ground-truth labels of the training data. The $l_{2,1}$-norm constraints on the projection matrices make them suitable for both feature selection and feature transformation. Both the projection matrices of different views and the combination weights are learned as a single optimization problem. This approach exploits both the task relationship and also the complementary nature of different views for effective feature extraction.

We thoroughly evaluate the proposed MVMTFE algorithm on the NUS-WIDE-OBJECT web image dataset [2] and compare it to other supervised multi-task feature extraction methods (MTFS [11] and RFS [10]), as well as some popular single-task feature

MM'14, November 3–7, 2014, Orlando, Florida, USA.

ACM 978-1-4503-3063-3/14/11 ...$15.00.
http://dx.doi.org/10.1145/2647868.2655002 .

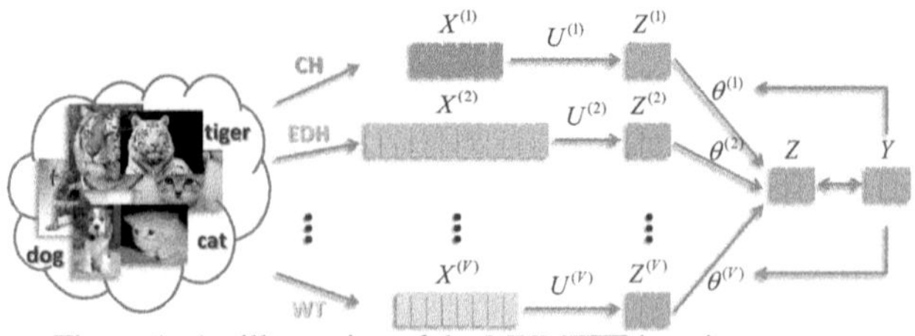

Figure 1: An illustration of the MVMTFE learning process.

extraction algorithms (RELIEF [5] and mRMR [13]) with feature concatenation in order to demonstrate the effectiveness of the proposed algorithm.

2. MVMTFE: MULTI-VIEW MULTI-TASK FEATURE EXTRACTION

First, we briefly introduce the multi-task feature selection (MTFS) framework [11] and its efficient and robust version [10], both of which can be regarded as feature extraction methods. Let the training set be denoted as $D = \{x_n^p, y_n^p\}, n = 1, \ldots, N_p, p = 1, \ldots, P$, where P is the number of tasks, and N_p is the number of training samples of the p'th task. Here, the p'th task is to decide whether or not a sample belongs to the p'th category; the sample feature $x_n^p \in \mathbb{R}^d$ and the corresponding label $y_n^p = 1$ if the p'th class label is manually assigned to it, and 0 otherwise. The general formulation of MTFS is given by

$$\underset{U}{\operatorname{argmin}} \sum_{p=1}^{P} \frac{1}{N_p} \sum_{n=1}^{N_p} L(u_p, x_n^p, y_n^p) + \gamma \sum_{m=1}^{d} \|u^m\|_2, \quad (1)$$

where $U \in \mathbb{R}^{d \times P}$ is a matrix with the model variable u_p for the p'th task in a column. The row u^m represents the variables across tasks associated with the m'th feature. The regularization is actually the $l_{2,1}$-norm $\|U\|_{2,1}$ which encourages sparsity in rows, and thus the importance of an individual feature is evaluated by simultaneously considering multiple tasks. In this way, different tasks help each other to select features assumed to be shared across tasks. Since the input features for different tasks are commonly the same and only the labels change, the x_n^p in (1) can be replaced with x_n. Following on from this work, Nie et al. [10] present a robust formulation by adopting the popular least squares loss for L and utilizing the $l_{2,1}$-norm for both the loss function and regularization.

To handle multi-view image classification, we generalize MTFS and present MVMTFE. Figure 1 illustrates the main procedure of MVMTFE. The feature extraction matrix $U^{(v)}$ is learned for each view by using it to predict the labels of the training data represented by the features $X^{(v)}$.The predicted results $Z^{(v)}, v = 1, \ldots, V$ are then combined as $Z = \Sigma_{v=1}^{V} \theta_v Z^{(v)}$. Using an alternating algorithm, the extraction matrices $U^{(v)}$ and combination weights θ_v are learned by minimizing the error between Z and the ground-truth label Y. Finally, $\{\theta_v U^{(v)}\}$ are used to transform or select features for further classification; the technical details are given below.

The proposed framework can be regarded as a two-layer neural network, only that in the second layer, we constrain the weights to be the same in the same view. The input of the network is a concatenation of $x_n^1, x_n^2, \ldots, x_n^{(v)}$, the middle layer representation is a concatenation of $z_n^1, z_n^2, \ldots, z_n^{(v)}$, and the output is z_n. In the first layer, we individually weight each dimension d of each view v. We then weight each view v in the second layer. Compared to the simple feature concatenation, which has only one weighting layer, we have the following advantageous: 1) According to deep learning theory, using more layers is usually beneficial if abundant training data is available; 2) The view weights in the second layer can be used to weight the selected features for final classification; 3) If the weights of the second layer are set the same, our framework degenerates to the simple concatenation, and thus is more general.

2.1 Problem Formulation

It is common to linearly combine the outputs or decision functions when handling multiple types of features [3], and this motivates us to develop MVMTFE. Let V be the number of views and v be the view index, the general formulation of MVMTFE is

$$\begin{aligned} &\underset{\{U^{(v)},\theta\}}{\operatorname{argmin}} \sum_{p=1}^{P} \frac{1}{N} \sum_{n=1}^{N} L(\hbar_p(x_n), y_n^p) \\ &\quad + \gamma_B \Sigma_{v=1}^{V} \|U^{(v)}\|_{2,1} + \gamma_C \|\theta\|_2^2, \\ &\text{s.t. } \Sigma_{v=1}^{V} \theta_v = 1, \theta_v \geq 0, v = 1, \ldots, V, \end{aligned} \quad (2)$$

where $\hbar_p(x_n) = \Sigma_v \langle \theta_v u_p^{(v)}, x_n^{(v)} \rangle$ is a combination of the outputs from different views, $U^{(v)}$ is the feature extraction matrix of the v'th view, and $\theta = [\theta_1, \ldots, \theta_V]^T$. Both γ_B and γ_C are positive trade-off parameters. By using the least squares loss, we obtain the following compact form:

$$\begin{aligned} &\underset{\{U^{(v)},\theta\}}{\operatorname{argmin}} \frac{1}{N} \|\Sigma_{v=1}^{V} \theta_v (X^{(v)})^T U^{(v)} - Y\|_F^2 \\ &\quad + \gamma_B \Sigma_{v=1}^{V} \|U^{(v)}\|_{2,1} + \gamma_C \|\theta\|_2^2, \\ &\text{s.t. } \Sigma_{v=1}^{V} \theta_v = 1, \theta_v \geq 0, v = 1, \ldots, V, \end{aligned} \quad (3)$$

Here, each $X^{(v)} = [x_1^{(v)}, \ldots, x_N^{(v)}] \in \mathbb{R}^{d_v \times N}$ is the feature matrix of the v'th view and assumed to have been normalized, $Y = [y_1, \ldots, y_N]^T \in \mathbb{R}^{N \times P}$ is the corresponding label matrix.

2.2 Optimization

Two sets of variables, $\{U^{(v)}\}$ and $\{\theta_v\}$, need to be optimized in (3); here we use an alternating strategy. The details of optimizing $\{U^{(v)}\}$ and $\{\theta_v\}$ are as follows:

- **Update for $\{U^{(v)}\}$.** By initializing $\theta_v = \frac{1}{V}$ and for fixed $U^{(v')}, v' = 1, \ldots, V, v' \neq v$, we have the following problem for optimizing $U^{(v)}$,

$$\underset{\{U^{(v)}\}}{\operatorname{argmin}} \, g(U^{(v)}) + \gamma_B \|U^{(v)}\|_{2,1}, \quad (4)$$

where

$$\begin{aligned} g(U^{(v)}) = &\operatorname{tr}((U^{(v)})^T H_{vv} U^{(v)} + 2\Sigma_{v' \neq v} (U^{(v)})^T H_{vv'} U^{(v')}) \\ &- 2\operatorname{tr}((U^{(v)})^T \theta_v X^{(v)} Y), \end{aligned}$$

with each $H_{ij} = \theta_i \theta_j X^{(i)} (X^{(j)})^T$. Taking the derivative of (2) w.r.t. $U^{(v)}$ and setting it to zero, we obtain,

$$U^{(v)} = (H_{vv} + \gamma_B D^{(v)})^{-1} A^{(v)} \quad (5)$$

where $A^{(v)} = (\theta_v X^{(v)} Y - \Sigma_{v' \neq v} H_{vv'} U^{(v')})$, which is irrelevant with $U^{(v)}$, $D^{(v)}$ is a diagonal matrix with the entry $D_{ii}^{(v)} = \frac{1}{2\|u^{(v)i}\|_2}, i = 1, \ldots, d_v$, and $u^{(v)i}$ is the i'th row of $U^{(v)}$. Here, d_v is the feature dimension of the v'th view. This means that $D^{(v)}$ is dependent on $U^{(v)}$. Fortunately, the solution can be obtained efficiently by repeating the following two steps until convergence,

(a) $U_{\tau+1}^{(v)} = (H_{vv} + \gamma_B D_{\tau}^{(v)})^{-1} A^{(v)}$;

(b) update the diagonal matrix $D^{(v)}$ using $U^{(v)}_{\tau+1}$.

Following [10], we can prove the convergence of this iteration algorithm.

• **Update for $\{\boldsymbol{\theta}_v\}$** With the obtained $U^{(v)}, v = 1, \ldots, V$, we can update $\{\theta_v\}$ by solving the following problem,

$$\begin{aligned} &\underset{\theta}{\operatorname{argmin}} \sum_p \| \sum_v \theta_v (X^{(v)})^T u_p^{(v)} - y_p \|_2^2 + \gamma_C \|\theta\|_2^2 \\ &\text{s.t. } \Sigma_{v=1}^V \theta_v = 1, \theta_v \geq 0, \end{aligned} \tag{6}$$

where $u_p^{(v)}$ and y_p is the p'th column of $U^{(v)}$ and Y respectively. The above problem can be rewritten as,

$$\begin{aligned} &\underset{\theta}{\operatorname{argmin}}\ \theta^T H \theta - 2\theta^T h + \gamma_C \|\theta\|_2^2 \\ &\text{s.t. } \Sigma_{v=1}^V \theta_v = 1, \theta_v \geq 0, \end{aligned} \tag{7}$$

where $H = \Sigma_p H_p$ and $h = \Sigma_p h_p$. Here, H_p is a symmetric matrix with the entry $H_p^{(ij)} = (u_p^{(i)})^T X^{(i)} (X^{(j)})^T u_p^{(j)}$ and h_p is a column vector with $h_p^{(i)} = (u_p^{(i)})^T X^{(i)} y_p$. We adopt the coordinate descent algorithm to solve problem (7), in which only two elements θ_i and θ_j are selected to be updated in each iteration, while the others are fixed. By using the Lagrangian of problem (7) we obtain the following update rules for θ_i and θ_j,

$$\begin{cases} \theta_i^* = \dfrac{\gamma_B(\theta_i + \theta_j) + (h_i - h_j) + \varepsilon_{ij}}{H_{ii} - H_{ij} - H_{ji} + H_{jj} + 2\gamma_C} \\ \theta_j^* = \theta_i + \theta_j - \theta_i^*, \end{cases} \tag{8}$$

where $\varepsilon_{ij} = (H_{ii} - H_{ij} - H_{ji} + H_{jj})\theta_i - \Sigma_k (H_{ik} - H_{jk})\theta_k$. To satisfy the constraint $\theta_v \geq 0$, we set $\theta_i^* = 0$ if $\gamma_B(\theta_i + \theta_j) + (h_i - h_j) + \varepsilon_{ij} \leq 0$ and similarly for θ_j^*.

The stopping criterion is the difference between objective values on two consecutive steps. The complexity of MVMTFE is $O(NV^2\tilde{d}P + k_1 k_2 (V\tilde{d}^2 P + V\tilde{d}^3))$ approximately, where $\tilde{d}$ is the largest feature dimension of different views, and k_1, k_2 are the number of iterations of the alternating procedure and calculation of $U^{(v)}$ respectively. Once the solutions $\{U^{(v)}\}$ and $\{\theta_v\}$ have been obtained, we can use them in various ways: 1) directly use $\Sigma_{v=1}^V \theta_v (X^{(v)})^T U^{(v)}$ as the classification results; 2) feature transformation, i.e., use $\Sigma_{v=1}^V \theta_v (X^{(v)})^T U^{(v)}$ as the projected features in the low-dimensional space and then train additional classifiers on these low-dimensional features; or 3) feature selection, i.e., sort the features according to $\|\theta_v u^{(v)i}\|_2, i = 1, \ldots, d_v$ in descending order for the v'th view and then train additional classifiers on top-ranking features. These three strategies are investigated in the following experiments.

3. EXPERIMENTS

We evaluated the effectiveness of MVMTFE on the image classification problem by applying it to the NUS-WIDE-OBJECT dataset [2]. NUS-WIDE-OBJECT is a multi-view real-world web image dataset consisting of 31 classes and 30,000 images in total. Five different features, namely 64-D color histogram, 144-D color autocorrelogram, 73-D edge direction histogram, 128-D wavelet texture, and 225-D block-wise color moments are used to represent each image.

In our experiments, 2,000 images were randomly sampled to construct the training set; 6,000 images were used as the test set; and 2,000 images were used for validation, with the parameters performing best on the validation set used for testing. The training set, test set and validation set were independent. This above procedure was performed five times and the mean accuracies with standard deviations are reported.

3.1 A comparison of the feature transformation and feature selection strategies

As noted, the obtained solutions $\{U^{(v)}\}$ and $\{\theta_v\}$ can be used either for feature transformation or selection. We therefore first compare these strategies and the experimental setup is given as follows,

• **Allfea+linSVM:** concatenate the normalized features of all views without feature extraction, and then train a linear support vector machine (SVM) on these concatenated features.

• **Allfea+kerSVM:** a nonlinear SVM is trained on the concatenated features.

• **MVMTFT:** the matrix $Z = \Sigma_{v=1}^V \theta_v (X_t^{(v)})^T U^{(v)} \in \mathbb{R}^{N_t \times P}$ is directly utilized as the classification results. Here, N_t is the number of test samples and $X_t^{(v)}$ is the test feature matrix of the v'th view.

• **MVMTFT+linSVM:** train a linear SVM on Z by regarding Z as the transformed features in the low-dimensional space.

• **MVMTFS+linSVM:** sort all the features of different views in descending order according to the value $\|\theta_v u^{(v)i}\|_2, v = 1, \ldots, V, i = 1, \ldots, d_v$ and then select the k top-ranked values as the input of a linear SVM classifier.

• **MVMTFS+kerSVM:** train a nonlinear SVM on the features selected by MVMTFS.

We do not apply a nonlinear SVM to the MVMTFT results since almost no improvement is observed compared to the linear case (data not shown). The parameters γ_B and γ_C of the proposed feature extraction method are tuned on the set $\{10^{-5}, 10^{-4}, \ldots, 10^5\}$. For SVM training, we use the libSVM [1] toolbox and tune the penalty factor C on the set $\{10^{-5}, 10^{-4}, \ldots, 10^5\}$ in linear SVM. We use the RBF kernels with the bandwidth parameter γ optimized over the set $\{2^{-8}, 2^{-7}, \ldots, 2^4\}$ for nonlinear SVM. Finally, the number of selected features k in MVMTFS is chosen from the set $\{100, 200, 300, 400, 500\}$.

The experimental results are shown in Figure 2(a). It can be seen that: 1) AllFea and MVMTFS used with the RBF kernel SVM (kerSVM) are superior to when they are used with linear SVM; 2) in general, the performance of MVMTFS improves with an increasing number of selected features, both with RBF kernel SVM and linear SVM. The accuracy of our method does not converge to the baseline like most other feature selection methods, mainly due to the learned weights $\{\theta_v\}$, which helps soft feature selection. When all features are selected our method degenerates to a weighted feature combination; 3) although the performance of MVMTFT without an additional classifier is poorer than the feature selection strategy, it is superior to AllFea with both linear and nonlinear SVM. This indicates that the transformed result is acceptable and that an additional classifier does not always need to be trained for the sake of improving efficiency; and 4) by training a linear SVM on MVMTFT we obtain comparable results to MVMTFS with the RBF kernel, both of which are significantly better than the AllFea baseline. This demonstrates the effectiveness of both the transformed and selected features. In the following experiments, we only report the nonlinear SVM results for the feature selection strategy, since these have been shown to be consistently superior to the linear case.

3.2 A comparison of different feature extraction algorithms

To the best of our knowledge there is still no other supervised multi-view feature selection algorithm. Therefore, in this set of experiments, we compare the proposed multi-view method with several competitive supervised feature extraction algorithms with feature concatenation. The main focus of this paper is to develop an effective feature extraction method and not to build the best image

Table 1: Performance comparison of different feature transformation algorithms.

Methods	Allfea+linSVM	Allfea+kerSVM	MTFT+linSVM	RFT+linSVM	MVMTFT+linSVM
Accuracy	32.35±0.47	34.12±0.61	34.22±0.33	34.72±0.30	**36.68±0.44**

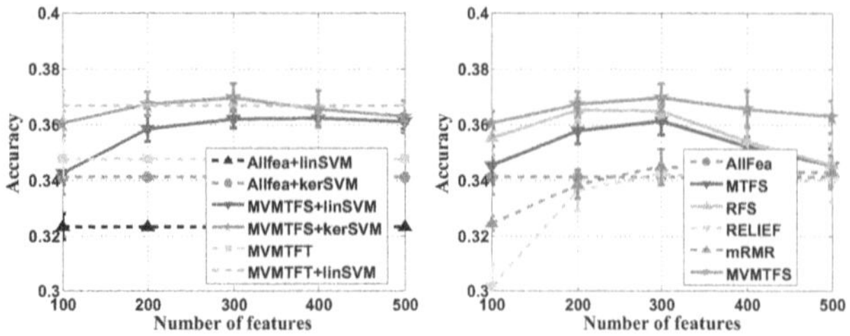

(a) (b)

Figure 2: (a) Performance comparison of the feature transformation and selection strategies; (b) Performance comparison of different feature selection algorithms.

classification system. To make the performance evaluation fair, we do not exploit other known image classification tricks. Specifically, MVMTFE is compared to the following approaches:

• **AllFea**: the baseline in which all features are normalized and concatenated.

• **MTFS [11]**: a supervised multi-task feature selection algorithm. The trade-off parameter γ is set in the range $\{10^{-5}, 10^{-4}, \dots, 10^{5}\}$.

• **RFS [10]**: an efficient and robust supervised multi-task feature selection algorithm that utilizes the $l_{2,1}$-norm for both the least squares loss and the regularization term. The trade-off parameter γ is chosen from the set $\{10^{-5}, 10^{-4}, \dots, 10^{5}\}$.

RELIEF [5] and **mRMR [13]** are two traditional feature selection methods. Both MTFS and RFS are utilized in the same way as MVMTFT for feature transformation, and we call them MTFT and RFT. The feature selection results are shown in Figure 2(b). It can be seen that: 1) the multi-task feature selection is better than the traditional feature selection methods; 2) the performance of RFS and MTFS improves at first but then decreases as the number of selected features k increases. This is because although a larger number of useful features are selected at first, noise features are subsequently introduced. In contrast, the performance of the proposed method retains its advantage due to the reasons presented above for the first set of experiments; and 3) RFS is superior to MTFS, and the improvement decreases when k is larger, since the overlap of the selected features is larger. The proposed MVMTFS outperforms them consistently, especially when k is large, owing to the learned $\{\theta_v\}$.

The feature transformation results are reported in Table 1. We can see that MTFT and RFT are superior to the AllFea baseline with a linear SVM but comparable to the kernel case. The proposed MVMTFT algorithm significantly outperforms all the other methods.

4. CONCLUSION

This paper presents a supervised multi-view multi-task feature extraction (MVMTFE) framework. The framework can simultaneously utilize the information shared between tasks and the complementarity of different views to extract useful information for image classification. Specifically, the framework can be either used for feature transformation (MVMTFT) or as a feature selection method (MVMTFS). We investigated these two strategies and experimentally compared them with other feature extraction methods. We can conclude that: 1) the transformed features are of sufficient quality to be directly used as the classification results; 2) the transformed features are comparable to the selected features when they are used as the input of an additional classifier; and 3) the learned view combination coefficients are significant. When all features are selected MVMTFS becomes a weighted view combination, while traditional feature selection methods degenerate to simply a feature concatenation.

5. ACKONOWLEDGEMENT

This paper is partially supported by NBRPC 2011CB302400, NSFC 61121002, 61375026, JCYJ 20120614152136201, and Australian Research Council Projects FT-130101457, DP-140102164.

6. REFERENCES

[1] C.-C. Chang and C.-J. Lin. Libsvm: a library for support vector machines. *ACM TIST*, 2(3):1–27, 2011.

[2] T.-S. Chua, J. Tang, R. Hong, H. Li, Z. Luo, and Y. Zheng. Nus-wide: a real-world web image database from national university of singapore. In *CIVR*, 2009.

[3] G. Fumera and F. Roli. A theoretical and experimental analysis of linear combiners for multiple classifier systems. *TPAMI*, 27(6):942–956, 2005.

[4] I. Guyon, S. Gunn, M. Nikravesh, and L. Zadeh. *Feature extraction: foundations and applications*. Springer, 2006.

[5] K. Kira and L. A. Rendell. A practical approach to feature selection. In *ML Workshop*, pages 249–256, 1992.

[6] Z. Li, Y. Yang, J. Liu, X. Zhou, and H. Lu. Unsupervised feature selection using nonnegative spectral analysis. In *AAAI*, 2012.

[7] D. Lowe. Distinctive image features from scale-invariant keypoints. *IJCV*, 60(2):91–110, 2004.

[8] Y. Luo, T. Liu, D. Tao, and C. Xu. Decomposition based transfer distance metric learning for image classification. *IEEE TIP*, 23(9):3789–3801, 2014.

[9] Y. Luo, D. Tao, C. X. andChao Xu, H. Liu, and Y. Wen. Multi-view vector-valued manifold regularization for multi-label image classification. *IEEE TNNLS*, 24(5):709–722, 2013.

[10] F. Nie, H. Huang, X. Cai, and C. H. Ding. Efficient and robust feature selection via joint $l_{2,1}$-norms minimization. In *NIPS*, pages 1813–1821, 2010.

[11] G. Obozinski, B. Taskar, and M. Jordan. Multi-task feature selection. In *ICML workshop*, 2006.

[12] A. Oliva and A. Torralba. Modeling the shape of the scene: A holistic representation of the spatial envelope. *IJCV*, 42(3):145–175, 2001.

[13] H. Peng, F. Long, and C. Ding. Feature selection based on mutual information: criteria of max-dependency, max-relevance, and min-redundancy. *TPAMI*, 27:1226–1238, 2005.

[14] J. Tang, X. Hu, H. Gao, and H. Liu. Unsupervised feature selection for multi-view data in social media. In *SDM*, pages 270–278, 2013.

[15] G. Tolias, Y. Kalantidis, and Y. Avrithis. Symcity: feature selection by symmetry for large scale image retrieval. In *ACM MM*, pages 189–198, 2012.

[16] Y. Yan, Z. Xu, G. Liu, Z. Ma, and N. Sebe. Glocal structural feature selection with sparsity for multimedia data understanding. In *ACM MM*, pages 537–540, 2013.

[17] Z.-J. Zha, X.-S. Hua, T. Mei, J. Wang, G.-J. Qi, and Z. Wang. Joint multi-label multi-instance learning for image classification. In *CVPR*, 2008.

[18] Z.-J. Zha, H. Zhang, M. Wang, H.-B. Luan, and T.-S. Chua. Detecting group activities with multi-camera context. *TCSVT*, 23(5):856–869, 2013.

Image Re-ranking with an Alternating Optimization

Shanmin Pang[1], Jianru Xue[1], Zhanning Gao[1], Qi Tian[2]
Institute of Artificial Intelligence and Robotics, Xi'an Jiaotong University[1]
Dept. of Computer Science, University of Texas at San Antonio, Texas, TX 78249[2]
pangshanminn@sina.com, jrxue@xjtu.edu.cn, zhanninggao@gmail.com, wywqtian@gmail.com

ABSTRACT

In this work, we propose an efficient image re-ranking method, without additional memory cost compared with the baseline method [8], to re-rank all retrieved images. The motivation of the proposed method is that, there are usually many visual words in the query image that only give votes to irrelevant images. With this observation, we propose to only use visual words which can help to find relevant images to re-rank the retrieved images. To achieve the goal, we first find some similar images to the query by maximizing a quadratic function when given an initial ranking of the retrieved images. Then we select query visual words with an alternating optimization strategy: (1) at each iteration, select words based on the similar images that we have found and (2) in turn, update the similar images with the selected words. These two steps are repeated until convergence. Experimental results on standard benchmark datasets show that the proposed method outperforms spatial based re-ranking methods.

Categories and Subject Descriptors

H.3.3 [**Information Storage and Retrieval**]: Information Search and Retrieval—*Selection process*

Keywords

Visual Word Selection; Image Re-ranking; Alternating Optimization

1. INTRODUCTION

Increasing attention has been attracted to Content Based Image Retrieval (CBIR) in recent years. Most state-of-the-art CBIR technologies [1, 5, 8, 9] are based on the Bag-of-Word (BoW) model, in which each image is represented as a histogram of visual words. Image querying is typically accomplished in two steps: *searching* and *post-processing*. With an inverted file system, only those images sharing common visual words with the query image are checked in the *searching* step and therefore an initial ranking of the retrieved images can be efficiently generated. After the *searching* step, the *post-processing* step is used to obtain a more precise ranking of the retrieved images.

In the literature, two kinds of *post-processing* techniques often used are spatial verification [6, 8, 10] and query expansion [2, 3]. Spatial verification based methods use the feature layout to spatially verify the consistency of the retrieved images with the query image. Ideally, all retrieved images should be spatially verified. However, due to time consuming, spatial verification is usually performed only on a shortlist of top ranked images. Thus, only the shortlist is subsequently re-ranked based on the number of spatially verified matches. Query expansion strategies use images in the shortlist that are spatially verified to generate new queries. Some relevant features in the new queries, which are not present in the original query, can be used to enrich the original query to further improve the retrieval accuracy.

In this paper, we focus on *post-processing*, and introduce a new re-ranking method which is similar to spatial re-ranking methods as we all use a subset of features in the query to score the retrieved images. As we know, given the query image and a retrieved image, the output of spatial verification procedures is the spatially verified matches, and consequently the spatial re-ranking methods score the image only with a specific subset of words (the spatially verified words) in the query. This means for different retrieved images, spatial re-ranking methods use different subsets of words in the query to score them. Being different with spatial re-ranking methods, the proposed method used a fixed subset of words in the query to score all retrieved images. Compared with spatial re-ranking methods, the proposed method has two major advantages: (1) it is much efficient, and can re-rank all retrieved images; (2) it consumes less memory as it does not need to store region information (such as location and shape) of each indexed feature.

The remainder of this paper is organized as follows. The proposed method is described and evaluated in Section 2 and in Section 3, respectively. We conclude the proposed method in Section 4.

2. THE PROPOSED METHOD

2.1 Motivation

Given a query image q, BoW based image search can be interpreted as a voting scheme [4]: each visual word w_j in q votes images in the database that contain word w_j. This is reasonable if all local features that are quantized to w_j

MM '14 November 03 - 07 2014, Orlando, FL, USA

ACM 978-1-4503-3063-3/14/11 ...$15.00.
http://dx.doi.org/10.1145/2647868.2655004.

Figure 1: Illustration the motivation of the proposed method. Left: a query image with plotted features (the total number is 3233) in the *Oxford* 5K dataset [8]. Right: with a 1M vocabulary, we find about two thirds of features (the number is 2131) only vote irrelevant images to the query.

are indeed similar, i.e., the corresponding local image regions represented by those local features are visually similar. However, due to the limited distinctiveness of descriptors and quantization error, features quantized to w_j may represent irrelevant local image regions. Thus, w_j may only vote images that are irrelevant to q, and consequently it has negative effects on image ranking. In practice, we notice that there are usually many such words in the query. Figure 1 shows an example of this observation.

The goal of this paper is try to alleviate the weakness of the scoring strategy that are discussed above with a re-ranking step. That is, at re-ranking stage, we only use words that can help to find relevant images to vote images, and other words are discarded. In the following subsection, we will describe how to identify the words that can help to find relevant images.

2.2 The algorithm

Our solution to the problem of visual word selection in the query for scoring is inspired by an alternating optimization. Alternating optimization is one of widely used heuristics where optimization over two sets of variables is difficult, but optimization with respect to one while keeping the other fixed is much easier. Many popular methods use this approach, such as K-means, Expectation-Maximization.

The input to our algorithm is the whole set of visual words $\mathcal{W} = \{w_1, \cdots, w_n\}$ in q, and the corresponding retrieved image set $\mathcal{I} = \{I_1, \cdots, I_m\}$ that has been returned by the *searching* step. We use s_i to record the similarity score between q and I_i, and we let $\boldsymbol{s} = (s_1, \cdots, s_m)^T$. Furthermore, without loss of generality, we assume the similarity score between q and I_i is sorted in descending order, that is $s_i \geq s_j$ if $i < j$.

Selecting a subset of $\mathcal{W}$ for scoring can be thought of as a chicken-and-egg problem between (1) finding similar images to q in $\mathcal{I}$ and (2) determining whether w_j is useful or not to help find relevant images. If similar images are given, determining the usefulness of w_j is trivial (w_j should not be used if it dose not appear in any similar image). Conversely, if the usefulness of each visual word is clearly annotated beforehand, the problem of finding the similar images becomes a conventional ranking problem which can be easily solved.

Algorithm 1 Initialize similar images to q

Input: The visual word set $\mathcal{W} = \{w_1, \cdots, w_n\}$ in q, and the top k ranked images $I_1, \cdots, I_k$
1: Build the weighted adjacency matrix $\boldsymbol{A}$ with Eq.(1)
2: **for** $i = 1 : k$ **do**
3: Build the set $\mathcal{T} = \{j | \boldsymbol{A}(i,j) > \tau\} \bigcup \{i\}$, where τ is half of the maximum value of $\boldsymbol{A}$
4: Initialize $\boldsymbol{x}(1)$: $x_j(1) = 1/|\mathcal{T}|$, if $j \in \mathcal{T}$; otherwise $x_j(1) = 0$
5: Obtain the local maximizer $\boldsymbol{x}^*$ with Eq.(3)
6: **end for**
7: Select the local maximizer $\boldsymbol{x}^*$ with the largest number of nonzero elements

Output: The similar image set $\mathcal{I}_s$ corresponding to indexes of nonzero elements of $\boldsymbol{x}^*$

2.2.1 *Initialization*

Given an initial ranking of the retrieved images, we first design a strategy to find some images that are really relevant to q with the top k ranked images. The reason for only using the top k ranked images to initialize similar images is that: (1) computation efficiency; (2) the top k ranked images tend to be more similar to q than other retrieved images; (3) there is no need to recover all similar images at the initialization stage. As we know, in the BoW model, I_i is represented by a vector $\boldsymbol{v}_i$ with length N, where N is the total number of words in a vocabulary. For our purpose, we extract n components of $\boldsymbol{v}_i$ corresponding to $w_1, \cdots, w_n$ to formulate a new vector $\hat{\boldsymbol{v}}_i$. After obtaining $\hat{\boldsymbol{v}}_i$ $(i = 1, \cdots, k)$, we build a graph $\mathcal{G}$ with k vertices, where the i-th vertex represents I_i. The weighted adjacency matrix of $\mathcal{G}$, denoted by $\boldsymbol{A}$, is defined as

$$A(i,j) = \begin{cases} 0, & i = j; \\ \hat{\boldsymbol{v}}_i^T \hat{\boldsymbol{v}}_j, & i \neq j. \end{cases} \tag{1}$$

Obviously, $\boldsymbol{A}$ is symmetric and nonnegative.

The proposed method initializes similar images to q based on the following insight: if both I_i and I_j are similar to q, the similarity between I_i and I_j, measured by $A(i,j)$, should also be large. Thus, according to [7], the problem of finding similar images equals to calculating a maximal clique in $\mathcal{G}$, and each maximal clique can be obtained as a local maximizer of the following quadratic function:

$$\begin{aligned} &maximize\ f(\boldsymbol{x}) = \boldsymbol{x}^T \boldsymbol{A} \boldsymbol{x} \\ &subject\ to \quad \boldsymbol{x} \in \triangle, \end{aligned} \tag{2}$$

where $\triangle = \{\boldsymbol{x} = (x_1, \cdots, x_k)^T \in \mathbb{R}^k | \boldsymbol{x} \geq 0 \ and\ \boldsymbol{1}^T \boldsymbol{x} = 1\}$, and $\boldsymbol{x}$ is an indicator vector over the vertices of $\mathcal{G}$. Given an initialization $\boldsymbol{x}(1)$, Eq.(2) can be efficiently maximized with *replicator equation* [11]:

$$x_j(t+1) = x_j(t) \frac{(\boldsymbol{A}\boldsymbol{x}(t))_j}{\boldsymbol{x}(t)^T \boldsymbol{A} \boldsymbol{x}(t)}, \ j = 1, \cdots, k. \tag{3}$$

After Eq.(3) is converged to $\boldsymbol{x}^*$, we initialize the similar image set $\mathcal{I}_s$ corresponding to indexes of nonzero elements of $\boldsymbol{x}^*$.

In practice, to avoid incorrect results from noises and outliers, a local maximizer with the largest number of similar images is preferred. To achieve this, we give k initializations of $\boldsymbol{x}(1)$. Specifically, for each vertex i, we first build set $\mathcal{T} = \{j | \boldsymbol{A}(i,j) > \tau\} \bigcup \{i\}$, where τ is a threshold and we

Algorithm 2 Query visual word selection for scoring

Input: The visual word set $\mathcal{W} = \{w_1, \cdots, w_n\}$ in q, and the retrieved image set $\mathcal{I} = \{I_1, \cdots, I_m\}$

```
Initialize the similar image set I_s with Algorithm 1, and
  initialize the selected visual word set W_s = ∅
while true do
  for j = 1 : n do
    Compute the probability P(w_j|I_s) that w_j appears
      in I_s
    If Eq.(4) holds, then W_s = W_s ∪ {w_j}      ▷ update W_s
  end for
  Let I_s^old = I_s and I_s = ∅
  for i = 1 : m do
    Score I_i with W_s and get a new score s_i^new
    If Eq.(5) holds, then I_s = I_s ∪ {I_i}      ▷ update I_s
  end for
  if I_s^old ≠ I_s then
    W_s = ∅                                       ▷ not convergence
  else
    Recompute W_s, and w_j is included in W_s if
      P(w_j|I_s) > 0, j = 1, ..., n               ▷ convergence
    Break
  end if
end while
```

Output: The selected visual word subset $\mathcal{W}_s$ that used for scoring

choose τ as half of the maximum value of $\boldsymbol{A}$. Then we set $x_j(1) = 1/|\mathcal{T}|$, if $j \in \mathcal{T}$; otherwise $x_j(1) = 0$. For clarity, we outline the whole initialization process in Algorithm 1.

2.2.2 *Optimize to convergence*

Once we have obtained an initial similar image set $\mathcal{I}_s$ with Algorithm 1, we select a visual subset $\mathcal{W}_s \subseteq \mathcal{W}$ to re-rank the retrieved image set $\mathcal{I}$ with an alternating optimization strategy. Formally, given $\mathcal{I}_s$, w_j is selected if it appears more frequently in $\mathcal{I}$ than in the database:

$$P(w_j|\mathcal{I}_s) > \epsilon P(w_j), \tag{4}$$

where $\epsilon > 1$ is a selection threshold. We find $\epsilon = 3$ works well in practice, so $\epsilon = 3$ is used in the experiments.

In turn, a better similar image set $\mathcal{I}_s$ is expected when $\mathcal{W}_s$ is updated. Specifically, a new similarity score s_i^{new} between I_i and q is computed using words in $\mathcal{W}_s$, and I_i is considered as relevant to q if

$$\frac{s_i^{new}}{s_i} \geq (\frac{|\mathcal{W}_s|}{n})^p, \; i = 1, \cdots, m, \tag{5}$$

where $0 < p < 1$ is a scalar parameter. Intuitively, Eq.(5) uses p to control what degree that I_i agrees with the current $\mathcal{W}_s$. Best results are achieved with $p = 0.5$ and we keep this value throughout all experiments. Naturally, the proposed algorithm optimizes $\mathcal{I}_s$ and $\mathcal{W}_s$ alternatively until convergence, and we summarize it in Algorithm 2.

2.2.3 *Implementation details*

From experimental results, we find when the number of relevant images in the database is small, the *initialization* step may output less than three images, and furthermore, they are often irrelevant to the query. To avoid false results, when the *initialization* step outputs less than three images, we heuristically select words w_j which appear more frequently in the top k ranked images than in the database:

$$\mathcal{W}_s = \{w_j | P(w_j|I_1, \cdots, I_k) > \epsilon P(w_j)\}. \tag{6}$$

For each word w_j in q, we classically use its tf-idf weight to generate an initial ranking of the retrieved images. However, after Algorithm 2 converges, we reweigh $w_j \in \mathcal{W}_s$ by using its occurrence times n_j in $\mathcal{I}_s$. Intuitively, n_j/l_j (l_j is the number of occurrences of w_j in the database) can reflect the importance of w_j: the larger n_j/l_j, the more important w_j and vice versa. To use this property, w_j is weighted by n_j/l_j multiplied by its tf-idf weight for re-ranking.

Table 1: mAP and average re-ranking time cost per query with different k values on the *Oxford 5K* dataset. The mAP of the baseline method [8] is 0.647.

k	10	20	30	50	100
mAP	0.709	0.713	0.714	0.712	0.711
time	0.157 s	0.162 s	0.164 s	0.163 s	0.164 s

3. EXPERIMENTS AND RESULTS

Datasets We apply the proposed method to perform re-ranking in an image retrieval engine, and test it on the *Oxford* 5K dataset [8] and *Oxford* 105K dataset. *Oxford* 5K dataset contains 5062 images and 55 queries with their ground truth retrieval results. *Oxford* 105K is used to test large-scale image retrieval, which consists of *Oxford* 5K and 100K Flickr images. In each image, we detect Hessian Affine regions and use SIFT descriptors to represent these regions.
Evaluation. To demonstrate the contribution of the proposed re-ranking method, we consider the searching with a BoW method [8] as our baseline. We evaluate the proposed method in terms of retrieval accuracy, memory usage and efficiency. As in [1, 3, 2, 4], we measure accuracy using the mean average precision (mAP), where the mean is taken over all queries.
Vocabulary training. With the RootSIFT transformation [1], we first transform SIFT vectors to RootSIFT vectors. After transformation, approximate k-means (AKM) [8] is used to train vocabularies of different sizes on the *Oxford* 5K dataset. In AKM, we use a forest of 8 randomized k-d trees and the default maximum number of iterations is 30.
Impact of k. The k value determines the number of images used for *initialization*. We study its effect to Algorithm 2 with a 500K vocabulary on the *Oxford* 5K dataset. From Table 1, one can find that the proposed algorithm is insensitive to k in both terms of efficiency and accuracy. $k = 30$ gives a little higher mAP than other values and is used throughout the experiments.

3.1 Compare with the baseline

Table 2 compares the retrieval accuracy (mAP) of our method with the baseline method [8] with different vocabulary sizes on the *Oxford* 5K and *Oxford* 105K datasets. From Table 2, one can easily find that the proposed re-ranking method consistently improves the retrieval accuracy of the BoW method [8]. On the *Oxford* 5K dataset, the improvements are over 5% under all vocabulary sizes, and the improvements are up to 7% with vocabulary sizes of 50K and 500K. As our method and other two state-of-the-art re-ranking methods FSM and LPV (see Section 3.2 and Table

Table 2: Retrieval performance (mAP) of the baseline method [8] and the proposed method on the *Oxford* 5K and and 105K datasets.

Dataset	Vocabulary size	BoW [8]	Ours
	50K	0.538	0.608
	100K	0.594	0.654
Oxford 5K	250K	0.641	0.696
	500K	0.647	0.714
	1M	0.651	0.702
Oxford 105K	500K	0.566	0.615

3 for detail) have performance peak at 500K vocabulary on the *Oxford* 5K dataset, we test all methods on the *Oxford* 105K dataset using 500K visual words. On this dataset, our method also gains an 5% improvement compared with the baseline.

The *Oxford* 5K and 105K datasets contain around 15.6MB and 280.5MB features, respectively. For each feature, the baseline method needs 4 bytes to store image ID and another 4 bytes to store the tf-idf weight. Compared with the baseline, the re-ranking step introduced by our method has no additional memory cost. This means both our method and the baseline consume about 124.8MB and 2.2GB memory on the *Oxford* 5K and 105K datasets, respectively.

Since re-ranking, our method is less efficient than the baseline. As listed in Table 1, the increased average runtime per query of our re-ranking method is about 0.16 s.

3.2 Compare with state-of-the-art

In this section, we compare our method with two spatial based re-ranking methods: Fast Spatial Matching (FSM) [8] and Locality Preserving Verification (LPV) [6]. FSM is a RANSAC based mismatch removing method, which generates hypotheses from single correspondences exploiting local feature shape. LPV finds consistent matches by using local linear geometrical structure among a feature point and its neighbors. Since both FSM and LPV are linear in the number of images to match, they perform re-ranking only up to a few top hundred initial results. In the experiments, we find both FSM and LPV take more than 2 ms on average on matching an image pair, thus we set the number of re-ranked images for FSM and LPV to 200. Even so, they both take more than 0.4 s per query, more than twice the time of our method.

In addition to store image ID and the tf-idf weight, LPV needs 4 bytes to store the location of each indexed feature, and therefore the corresponding sizes of the inverted files are 187.2MB and 3.3GB on the *Oxford* 5K and 105K datasets, respectively. Compared with LPV, FSM needs 12 bytes to store the shape of each feature. Thus, FSM consumes 374.4MB and 6.6GB memory on the *Oxford* 5K and 105K datasets, respectively. This means our method can save significant memory compared with FSM and LPV.

We show comparison results (mAP) of FSM, LPV and our method in Table 3. From this table, one can find that FSM performs a little better than LPV on small vocabularies (50K and 100K). While in contrast, the performances of FSM are inferior to those of LPV on large vocabularies (250K, 500K and 1M). On the whole, FSM and LPV have similar performances. Benefiting from more re-ranked images and a new weighting scheme, our method outperforms FSM and LPV consistently on all vocabularies, and the improvements are

Table 3: Comparison results (mAP) of FSM, LPV and our method on the *Oxford* 5K and and 105K datasets.

Dataset	Vocabulary size	FSM	LPV	Ours
	50K	0.578	0.561	0.608
	100K	0.621	0.617	0.654
Oxford 5K	250K	0.659	0.663	0.696
	500K	0.663	0.675	0.714
	1M	0.661	0.672	0.702
Oxford 105K	500K	0.584	0.589	0.615

around 3%. It should be noted that our method is faster and consumes much less memory than FSM and LPV.

4. CONCLUSION

In this paper, a novel efficient re-ranking method without additional memory cost compared with the baseline is proposed for image retrieval. The proposed re-ranking method uses the fact that only a few words in the query are useful to find relevant images. To find these useful words, we first find some relevant images by solving a quadratic optimization problem based on votes from "good" words in the query are coincident in relevant images. Then word selection is achieved with an alternating optimization strategy. The experiment results show that our re-ranking method outperforms spatial based re-ranking methods.

5. ACKNOWLEDGMENTS

This work was supported by National Basic Research Program of China (973 Program) Project 2012CB316400, and the National Natural Science Foundation of China (NSFC) Projects 61273252, 91320301 and 61128007. This work was supported in part to Dr. Qi Tian by ARO grant W911NF-12-1-0057, and Faculty Research Award by NEC Laboratories of America, respectively.

6. REFERENCES

[1] R. Arandjelovic and A. Zisserman. Three things everyone should know to improve object retrieval. In *CVPR*, pages 2911–2918, 2012.

[2] O. Chum, A. Mikulik, M. Perdoch, and J. Matas. Total recall ii: Query expansion revisited. In *CVPR*, pages 889–896, 2011.

[3] O. Chum, J. Philbin, J. Sivic, M. Isard, and A. Zisserman. Total recall: Automatic query expansion with a generative feature model for object retrieval. In *ICCV*, pages 1–8, 2007.

[4] H. Jégou, M. Douze, and C. Schmid. Improving bag-of-features for large scale image search. *IJCV*, 87(3):316–336, 2010.

[5] D. Nister and H. Stewenius. Scalable recognition with a vocabulary tree. In *CVPR*, pages 2161–2168, 2006.

[6] S. Pang, J. Xue, N. Zheng, and Q. Tian. Locality preserving verification for image search. In *ACM Multimedia*, pages 529–532, 2013.

[7] M. Pavan and M. Pelillo. Dominant sets and pairwise clustering. *TPAMI*, 29(1):167–172, 2007.

[8] J. Philbin, O. Chum, M. Isard, J. Sivic, and A. Zisserman. Object retrieval with large vocabularies and fast spatial matching. In *CVPR*, pages 1–8, 2007.

[9] J. Sivic and A. Zisserman. Video google: A text retrieval approach to object matching in videos. In *ICCV*, pages 1470–1477, 2003.

[10] G. Tolias and Y. Avrithis. Speeded-up, relaxed spatial matching. In *ICCV*, pages 1653–1660, 2011.

[11] J. W. Weibull. *Evolutionary game theory.* MIT press, 1997.

Automatic Removal of Visual Stop-Words

Edgar Roman-Rangel
CVMLab - University of Geneva, Switzerland
edgar.romanrangel@unige.ch

Stephane Marchand-Maillet
CVMLab - University of Geneva, Switzerland
stephane.marchand-maillet@unige.ch

ABSTRACT

This paper presents a new methodology for the automatic estimation of the optimal amount of visual words that can be removed from a visual dictionary, such that no harm is induced in the discriminative potential of the resulting bag-of-visual-words representations. The proposed approach relies on a special definition of the entropy of each visual word when considered as a random variable, and a new definition of the overlap of class models computed with a normalized Bhattacharyya coefficient. We combined our proposed methodology with a recent approach that labels visual words as stop-words showing that this combination is beneficial to reduce the dimensionality of bag representations, while obtaining good results in terms of classification accuracy and retrieval performance.

Categories and Subject Descriptors

H.3.3 [**Information Storage and Retrieval**]: Information Search and Retrieval—*Information filtering*; I.5.2 [**Pattern Recognition**]: Design Methodology—*Feature evaluation and selection*

General Terms

Algorithms, Theory

Keywords

Bag-of-visual-words; stop-words; entropy; Bhattacharyya coefficient; content-based image retrieval; image classification

1. INTRODUCTION

The exponential growth of multimedia content that we have witnessed during recent years, demands the development of robust methods for the efficient access to repositories with purposes of image retrieval, classifications, identification, recommendation, etc. Dimensionality reduction is one of such methods that has been actively investigated in the pursuit to optimize the access to repositories [3, 7, 8, 9].

MM'14, November 3–7, 2014, Orlando, Florida, USA.

http://dx.doi.org/10.1145/2647868.2655005.

Recently, a new method was developed to reduce the dimensonality of bag-of-visual-words representations [5]. This method consists on detecting and removing visual stop-words, which are defined as those words that have no important contribution to the image representation, i.e., those words with low discriminative potential to differentiate instances from different visual classes. Mathematically, this method defines a visual stop-word as a feature with high entropy when computed across all classes in a datatset [5]. Although this method has proven to be better than previous works that rely on simply removing words of high or low frequency [7] and PCA-based methods [4] to detect visual stop-words [5], it relies on an empirical estimation of the amount of words to be removed.

In this work, we propose a new method that helps obtaining a more formal estimation of the amount of words to be removed. More precisely, we propose a method that can be trained off-line for a later use on a retrieval or classification setup. The intuition behind our method consists in optimizing a function that combines: (1) the entropy that visual words have when considered as random variables, and whose probability depends on the different visual classes in the dataset; and (2) the overlap that the class models have after the visual words are removed from the dictionary.

We evaluated our method using HOOSC descriptors [6] on two datasets of binary images that exhibit complex shape instances. This evaluation was performed in terms of classification and retrieval performance. Our results show that our proposed method is a good accompaniment for the method in [5], as their combination automatically removes visual stop-words and provides with shorter bag representations that lead to slight improvements in classification and retrieval performance.

The rest of this paper is organized as follows. Section 2 explains the baseline method we selected to detect visual stop-words, and revisits its notation. Section 3 introduces our proposed methodology for the automatic removal of visual stop-words. Section 4 explains the two datasets and the experimental protocol we used to test the proposed method. Section 5 discusses the results of our evaluations. Finally, section 6 presents our conclusions.

2. STOP-WORDS DETECTION

This section briefly reviews a method recently proposed to detect (i.e., label) visual stop-words [5], which we use as baseline for our proposed approach. This method is designed after the intuition that a visual word whose contribution is roughly the same across all the classes has low discriminative power, and therefore, it must be considered as a visual stop-word [5]. Namely, for each visual word in a vocabulary, this method computes its entropy using a probability density function (*pdf*), which is estimated marginalizing its frequency across all visual classes in the image collection [5].

More precisely, for a given visual vocabulary, each of its n words is associated to a random variable W^i that takes values $\{w_1^i, w_2^i, \ldots, w_m^i\}$, and whose *pdf* is defines as,

$$p(w_j) = \frac{f(W^i|C_j)}{\sum_j f(W^i|C_j)}, \quad (1)$$

where, C_j denotes each of the m visual classes within the dataset, and $f(W^i|C_j)$ is the frequency of the visual word associated to W^i in the j-th class.

Therefore, the entropy of the random variable W^i, i.e., the entropy of the i-th visual word, can be computed as,

$$H\left(W^i\right) = -\sum_{j=1}^{m} p(w_j) \cdot \log p(w_j), \quad (2)$$

where the summation operates over all the m visual classes in the dataset. According to this definition of word entropy, the M visual words with the highest entropy are considered as stop-words [5], and therefore removed from the dictionary, i.e., neglected from the bag representation.

However, the value of M needs to be estimated empirically to maximize the performance of specific tasks, e.g., retrieval precision [5]. In section 3, we introduce our method for the automatic estimation of M.

3. AUTOMATIC DETECTION

The method revised through section 2 succeeds in labeling stop-words to reduce the dimensionality of the image representation [5]. However, it is necessary to empirically decide on the amount of words to be removed from the image representation (i.e., to decide on an entropy threshold). In this section, we propose an iterative method for automatic removal of stop-words.

After using Eq. (2) to compute the entropy of all visual word in the dictionary, we remove those words with the highest entropy, one at a time, until a function that evaluates the *goodness* of the remaining dictionary is maximized.

Specifically, we use the intuition that the "optimal" dictionary D^*: (1) is a subset of the initial dictionary; and (2) generates bag representations (or any other type of representation) that are as different as possible for instances of different visual classes. To find such an optimal dictionary, we search for the subset of visual words that minimizes a cost function Z of the overlap of the class models and the entropy of the remaining set of words.

Namely, the automatic detection of stop-words is achieved by considering the initial dictionary D_0 with n initial words. Then, at each iteration t we remove the word with the highest entropy, such that the remaining dictionary D_t only contains $N_t = n - t$ words.

3.1 Overlap between classes

To compute the overlap between classes, first we need to define their respective class models. To this end, we associate each class in the dataset to a random variable C^j that takes values $\{c_1^j, c_2^j, \ldots, c_n^j\}$, whose *pdf* is computed by,

$$p(c_i) = \frac{f(W^i|C^j)}{\sum_i f(W^i|C^j)}, \quad (3)$$

where, similar to Eq. (1), $f(W^i|C^j)$ is the frequency of the visual word associated to W^i in the j-th class. However, the normalizing summation of the denominator is computed over the words instead of the classes. Given the iterative nature of our proposed method, these class models must be recomputed for each remaining dictionary, i.e., each time a visual word is removed from the dictionary.

After the class models of the remaining dictionary are computed, their respective overlap O is computed by,

$$O = \sum_{j=1}^{m} \sum_{k=j+1}^{m} B\left(C^j, C^k\right), \quad (4)$$

where the summation accumulates over each pair of all visual classes, and $B\left(C^a, C^b\right)$ is a normalized Bhattacharyya coefficient [2] between the classes associated to the a-th and b-th random variables respectively, and is computed as,

$$B\left(C^a, C^b\right) = \frac{\sum_{i=1}^{N_t} \sqrt{p(c_i^a) \cdot p(c_i^b)}}{N_t}, \quad (5)$$

where $p(c_i)$ denotes the *pdf* of C as defined in Eq. (3), and N_t is the number of the words in the remaining dictionary.

3.2 Cost function

Using the definition of entropy from Eq. (2) and the definition of overlap from Eq. (4), we iterate removing the word with the highest entropy until the function Z is minimized, where Z is defines as,

$$Z = H(D_t) + k \cdot O, \quad (6)$$

where k is a parameter that controls the contribution of the overlap to the function, and can be estimated during a training phase, and $H(D_t)$ denotes the entropy of the remaining dictionary and is computed by,

$$H(D_t) = \sum_{i=1}^{N_t} H\left(W^i\right), \quad (7)$$

where $H\left(W^i\right)$ is the entropy of each word as defined in Eq. (2), and the summation goes over the subset of words in the remaining dictionary.

The two terms in the cost function in Eq. (6) have the behavior shown in Fig. 1. Namely,

- $H(D_t)$. The entropy of the remaining dictionary will decrease as more visual words are removed from the dictionary.
- O. The overlap of the class models of the remaining dictionary will increase as more visual words are removed.

Finding the optimal dictionary D^* is, in practice, achieved by the optimization of the following function,

$$D^* = arg\min_{D_t}\{Z\}. \quad (8)$$

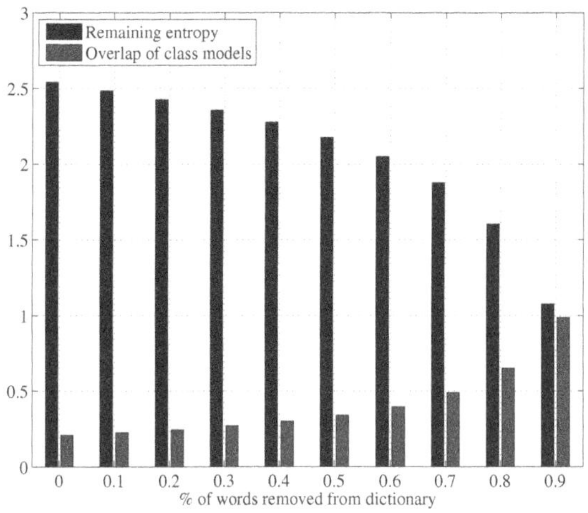

Figure 1: General behavior of the two terms: remaining entropy (H) and overlap (O) of the cost function Z in Eq. (6).

4. EXPERIMENTS

This section briefly introduces the two datasets we used to test our proposed approach, and details the experimental protocol we followed.

4.1 Datasets

To evaluate the proposed method, we used 2 different datasets. Namely, we used:

- A dataset of Maya hieroglyphs [5], which consists of 24 visual classes of syllabic instances of the ancient Maya writing system. Where, each class contains 260 instances in binary format.
- The MPEG-7 Core Experiment CE-Shape-1 Test Set [1], which consists of 70 visual classes of diverse objects, each category having 20 images.

Following [5], we relied on the use of HOOSC descriptors [6] and bag-of-visual-words representations. Namely, we use a visual dictionary of 1000 words, independently estimated for each dataset using the kmeans clustering algorithm. Other dictionary sizes can be evaluated, however, it has been shown that 1000 visual words works well for HOOSC descriptors [5].

4.2 Experimental setup

We validated our proposed methodology independently en each of the datasets. Namely, for a given dataset, we randomly selected 80% of its instances as training set and used them to estimate both the visual dictionary and the optimal value of k (see Eq. (6)). Then, we used the remaining 20% as test set for final validation of the proposed approach.

In practice, we conducted our evaluations in terms of:

- The classification performance using the k nearest neighbors approach (kNN) with k=1; and
- The retrieval precision reported as the mean average precision computed for the first 20 retrieved instances (mAP@20).

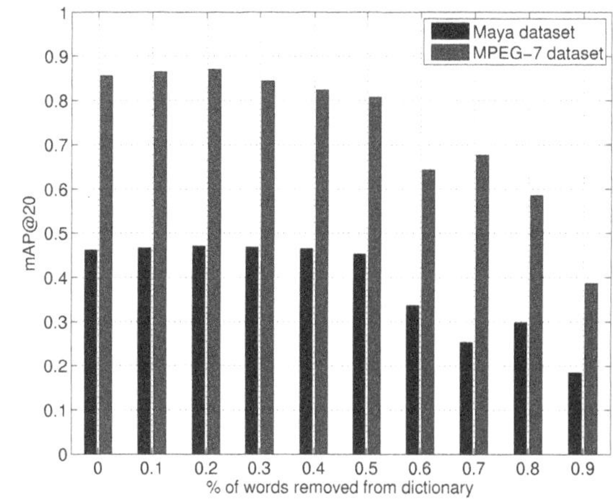

Figure 2: Retrieval precision achieved as visual words are removed from the dictionary using the entropy-based approach from [5] on the training set.

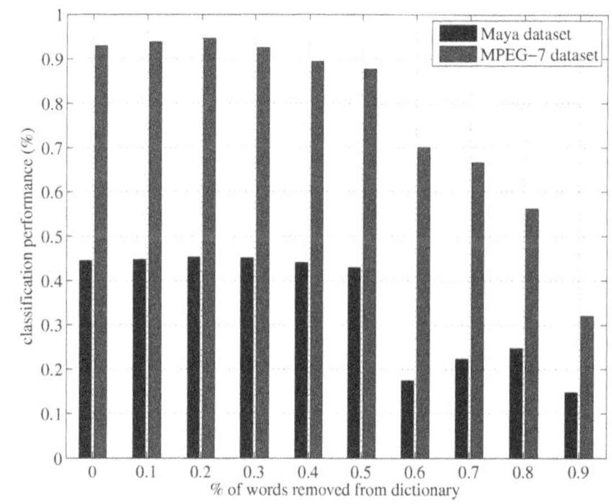

Figure 3: Classification accuracy achieved as visual words are removed from the dictionary using the entropy-based approach from [5] on the training set.

5. RESULTS

5.1 Training

Using the training set and a leave-one-out full cross validation approach, we started by evaluating the impact of gradually removing stop-words relying on the baseline method [5]. Fig. 2 shows the mAP@20 for the two datasets as more words are removed from the dictionary.

Note that the bars in Fig. 2 show a slight improvement when 20% of the visual words are removed from the dictionary of 1000 words, with a subsequent slow decline until 50% where a drastic drop off is visible. This results are consistent across the two datasets and congruent with the results in [5]. As shown in Fig. 3, the classification performance follows similar trends as the words in the dictionary are removed.

After knowing the optimal amount of words to be removed from the dictionary, we searched for the optimal values of the parameter k on the two datasets, also using their respective training sets. Namely, we searched for the value of k that maximizes the cost function Z when 20% of the visual words

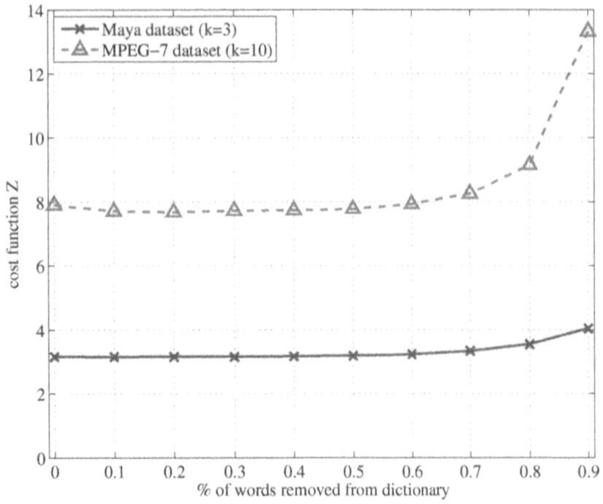

Figure 4: Behavior of the cost function Z (Eq. (6)) as more visual words are removed from the dictionary. These curves are computed using their respective optimal value of the parameter k: $k = 3$ for the Maya dataset, and $k = 10$ for the MPEG dataset.

Table 1: mAP@20 for the two test datasets.

words removed	Maya	MPEG-7
0%	0.462 ± 0.38	0.855 ± 0.20
20%	0.470 ± 0.38	0.870 ± 0.21

are removed, as suggested by Fig. 2 and Fig. 3. We found that $k = 3$ works well for the Maya dataset, whereas $k = 10$ is best for the MPEG-7 dataset. Fig. 4 shows the behavior of the cost function Z, as defined in Eq. (6).

5.2 Testing

After the previously mentioned training phase, we evaluated the retrieval precision and the classification accuracy on the test set using the optimal values of k. Table 1 shows the retrieval precision achieved after removing 20% of the visual words in the dictionary, as suggested by the previous analysis on the training set. These results are consistent with the results from the training set, namely, a slight improvement on the retrieval precision with the advantage of having a shorter representation.

The classification accuracy also followed similar trends during the test phase, as shown in the results in Table 2.

Note that it has been shown that the baseline approach works better that other methods that remove stop-words, such as highest frequency, lowest frequency, or PCA [5]. Therefore, we do not repeated those experiments, as the contribution of this paper focuses on proposing a complementary approach for the automatic estimation of the optimal amount of words to be removed, and not on a method for the actual detection of the such stop-words.

Table 2: Classification accuracy (%) for the two test datasets.

words removed	Maya	MPEG-7
0%	0.445 ± 0.42	0.929 ± 0.23
20%	0.453 ± 0.41	0.946 ± 0.26

6. CONCLUSIONS

We proposed a new methodology to remove visual stop-words and generate short bag representations without harming their discriminative potential. More precisely, an iterative search and removal methodology that replaces the empirical component of a recent approach that detects visual stop-words [5].

The proposed method can be trained off-line for its later application on online systems. Therefore, we expect that it will provide with higher benefits for larger datasets. Also, since this method optimizes a function of the overlap of the class models, it helps generating bag representations of equal, or increased, discriminative power, thus leading to slight improvements in retrieval precision and classification accuracy of binary images.

Acknowledgments

This work was partially supported by the Swiss NSF through the NCCR IM2, and by the Swiss NSF Tepalcatl project P2ELP2_152166.

7. REFERENCES

[1] X. Bai, X. Yang, L. J. Latecki, W. Liu, and Z. Tu. Learning Context-Sensitive Shape Similarity by Graph Transduction. *IEEE Transactions on Pattern Analysis and Machine Intelligence*, 32(5):861–874, 2010.

[2] A. Bhattacharyya. On a measure of divergence between two statistical populations defined by their probability distribution. *Bulletin of the Calcutta Mathematical Society*, 35:99–110, 1943.

[3] J.-H. Hsiao, C.-S. Chen, and M.-S. Chen. A Novel Language-Model-Based Approach for Image Object Mining and ReRanking. In *Proceedings of the IEEE International Conference on Data Mining*, 2008.

[4] H. Jégou and O. Chum. Negative Evidences and Co-occurences in Image Retrieval: The Benefit of PCA and Whitening. In *Proceedings of the European Conference on Computer Vision*, 2012.

[5] E. Roman-Rangel and S. Marchand-Maillet. Stopwords Detection in Bag-of-Visual-Words: The Case of Retrieving Maya Hieroglyphs. In *Proceedings of the International Workshop on Multimedia for Cultural Heritage (MM4CH), at International Conference on Image Analysis and Processing*, 2013.

[6] E. Roman-Rangel, C. Pallan, J.-M. Odobez, and D. Gatica-Perez. Analyzing Ancient Maya Glyph Collections with Contextual Shape Descriptors. *International Journal of Computer Vision*, 94(1):101–117, 2011.

[7] J. Sivic and A. Zisserman. Video google: A text retrieval approach to object matching in videos. In *Proceedings of the IEEE International Conference on Computer Vision*, 2003.

[8] R. van Zwol and L. G. Pueyo. Spatially-aware Indexing for Image Object Retrieval. In *Proceedings of the ACM International Conference on Web Search and Data Mining*, 2012.

[9] L. Zheng and I. Cox. Entropy-Based Static Index Pruning. In *Proceedings of the European Conference on IR Research on Advances in Information Retrieval*, 2009.

Automatic Image Synthesis from Keywords Using Scene Context

Sho Inaba
Grad. School of Information Science and Technology
The University of Tokyo
inaba@mi.t.u-tokyo.ac.jp

Asako Kanezaki
Grad. School of Information Science and Technology
The University of Tokyo
kanezaki@mi.t.u-tokyo.ac.jp

Tatsuya Harada
Grad. School of Information Science and Technology
The University of Tokyo
harada@mi.t.u-tokyo.ac.jp

ABSTRACT

Text is one of the simplest way to express one's idea, and an image is one of the most impactive way to do so. Therefore, if a system can synthesize an image from text without direct user manipulation, novel image synthesis applications will be opened to users without artistic skills. In such a system, which objects to synthesize will be declared in texts. However, information about positional relations and scale of objects is not much provided and must be estimated using common sense. As described in this paper, we develop a system that can automatically synthesize objects to an image, given the background image and class name of the target synthesizing object. With the inputs as the background image and keywords, images for synthesizing objects are searched automatically. Although some previously developed systems that can synthesize an image from sketches and paintings, this is the first system that can estimate the position, scale, and appearance of objects and automatically synthesize them to images without direct user input. We propose a scene context, which indicates the position, scale, and appearance of synthesizing objects. The contribution of this paper is twofold: (1) the scene context extraction method for automatic image synthesis and (2) application of automatic image synthesis using the scene context.

Categories and Subject Descriptors

I.3.3 [**COMPUTER GRAPHICS**]: Picture/Image Generation

General Terms

Algorithms; Performance

Keywords

Spatial Context; Scale Context; Object Appearance; Similar Image Search

1. INTRODUCTION

Numerous camera applications and image processing software has been spreading increasing opportunities for image synthesis. This enhances various studies of automatic image synthesis such as those to synthesize photographic images from paintings or sketches [9, 1] and those to synthesize a single image by collecting parts from a set of photos [12, 6, 8].

Most of the works described above require manual input. For instance, Chen et al. [1] proposed an automatic image synthesis system that retrieves parts for synthesis by user sketches. Here, the size and location of each part are determined according to the sketches given by users. Although a couple of works are able to arrange image parts automatically by placing them as densely as possible [6] or by gathering them to create a collage of another image [8], they do not specifically examine synthesizing natural or photographic images.

However, such systems require users' skills of drawing/arranging objects. Therefore, the system can fail to recognize the input of untrained users. On the other hand, if a system can synthesize a natural image automatically from words and sentences, novel applications of image synthesis will be opened to people without skills of sketches and drawings.

To realize such a system, it is expected to be possible not only to retrieve objects to be synthesized but also to determine their size and location. Zitnick et al. [13] learned the relation between visual scenes containing objects' motions and their relative positions and the sentences which describe the scenes, to synthesize clip art images automatically from texts. However, this work does not deal with natural images. Therefore it synthesizes a fixed background and a handful of objects with simple appearances. Context information of natural images are more frequently used in object detection tasks to increase the accuracy [5]. Here, the "context" means the information of an image's content, such as the tendency for an object to appear (or disappear) and its possible size and location.

We propose a novel method to extract "scene context" which describes the likelihood of size, location and appearance of objects, which requires a source image and labels of objects (e.g. "car") to be synthesized, as the user's input. Our definition of the term "scene context" consists of the following three contexts: "spatial context", which represents the probabilistic distribution of synthesized objects' location, "scale context", which represents the probabilistic distribution of synthesized objects' scale, and "appearance context", which represents the feature of synthesized objects' shape and aspect. We show that our system synthesizes objects in natural images with proper scale, location, shape and aspect.

The main contributions of our manuscript are as follows.

1. We propose a method to extract the probabilistic distribution of synthesized objects' location and scale as spatial context and scale context.
2. We propose a method to train the appearance context used to retrieve synthesized objects with proper shape and aspect.

WOODSTOCK '97 El Paso, Texas USA

http://dx.doi.org/10.1145/2647868.2655009.

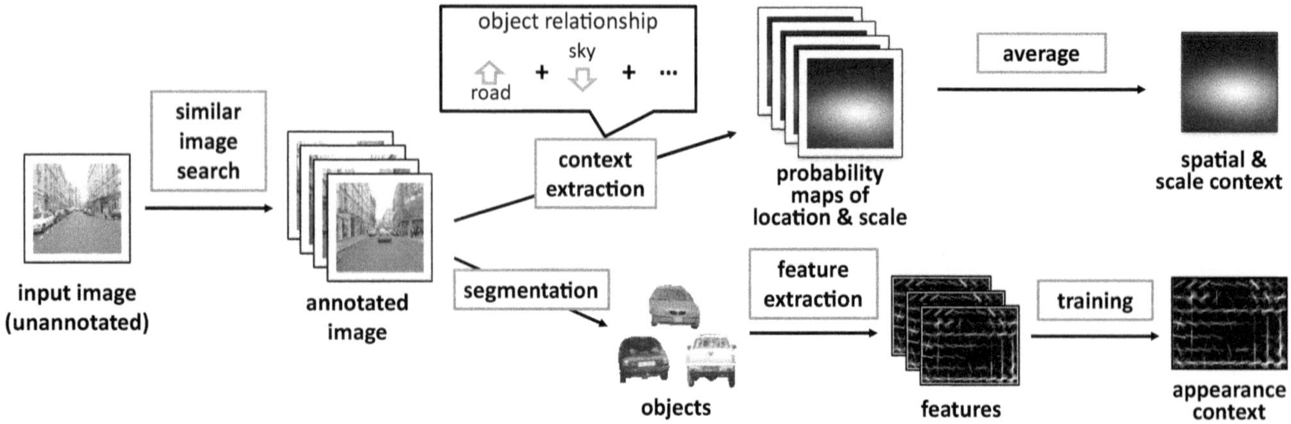

Figure 1: Overview of our system.

3. We demonstrate the effectiveness of our method using scene context (i.e. spatial context, scale context and appearance context) for automatic image synthesis.

2. METHOD

An overview of our system is shown in Fig.1. We search similar images to the input image from the dataset of annotated images. We use the annotation information of the images to extract the scene context. Annotated images are associated with dense object labels for image regions that are created manually. We use bounding boxes of annotated image regions for simplification.

To synthesize an image, our system first retrieves object instances which fit the input image by appearance context. Then it determines their locations by spatial context. Finally, it determines the scale of each object which fits its location by scale context. The procedures of scene context extraction are described as follows.

1. Search similar images to the input image from the dataset of annotated images.
2. Extract spatial context and scale context of each target object class using relative positions and scales of objects in similar images.
3. Average the spatial contexts and scale contexts of all similar images.
4. Extract the features of the instances of each target object class in similar images.
5. Learn the classifier (appearance context) of each target object class with the features of the object instances as positive samples and those of randomly selected regions as negative samples.

We use a GIST descriptor [11] for the similar image search. Although GIST was proposed originally for image classification, it is also used effectively to retrieve images with roughly similar layout [7]. We perform nearest-neighbor search using L1 distance of GIST descriptors to retrieve similar images.

2.1 spatial context and scale context

Context related to object location and scale is represented as the probability $p(x, y, w, h|I, c)$. Here x and y denote the coordinates of the object centroid, w and h respectively denote the width and the height of the object, I denotes the input image, and c denotes the object class. We omit I for the sake of shorthand. The object width w is calculable if the height h and the aspect ratio of the object are known. Therefore we leave out the probability of w. Then we redefine the context of object location and scale as $p(x, y, h|c)$. Presuming no correlation between x and h, it becomes $p(x, y, h|c) = p(x, y|c)p(h|y, c)$, which is the simple multiplication of spatial context $p(x, y|c)$ and scale context $p(h|y, c)$.

We extract spatial and scale contexts using the positional and scale relations between the objects. For example, the position for synthesizing cars should be above the road and under the sky, which can be determined by aggregating the relative positions to surrounding objects. In this manner, the spatial context for target object class c is calculated as follows:

$$p(x, y|c) = \frac{1}{\lambda}\sum_{n=1}^{N} a_{c_n \to c}\, p_{c_n \to c}\left(\frac{x - x_n}{w_n}, \frac{y - y_n}{h_n}\right). \qquad (1)$$

Here N denotes the number of objects in an image, n denotes the object id, c_n denotes the n-th object class, $p_{c_n \to c}(\frac{x-x_n}{w_n}, \frac{y-y_n}{h_n})$ denotes the probability distribution of the relative position between two object classes c_n and c, $a_{c_n \to c}$ denotes the coefficient which represents the weight of the probability distribution, and λ denotes the coefficient which normalizes the summation of $p(x, y|c)$ over an entire image to one. Furthermore, x_n, y_n denote the coordinates of the centroid of the n-th object, whereas w_n and h_n denote the object width and the height.

The scale context is computed as $p(h|y, c) = p(y, h|c)/p(y|c)$, of which the numerator is calculated using the following equation:

$$p(y, h|c) = \frac{1}{\lambda'}\sum_{n=1}^{N} b_{c_n \to c}\, p_{c_n \to c}\left(\frac{y - y_n}{h_n}, \frac{h}{h_n}\right). \qquad (2)$$

Here $p_{c_n \to c}(\frac{y-y_n}{h_n}, \frac{h}{h_n})$ shows the probability distribution of the relative scale of object class c to object class c_n, $b_{c_n \to c}$ denotes the coefficient which represents the weight of the probability distribution, and λ' denotes the coefficient which normalizes the summation of $p(y, h|c)$ over an entire image to one. The denominator $p(y|c)$ is calculated by integrating $p(y, h|c)$ with respect to h.

To compute the probability distributions $p_{c_n \to c}(\frac{x-x_n}{w_n}, \frac{y-y_n}{h_n})$ and $p_{c_n \to c}(\frac{y-y_n}{h_n}, \frac{h}{h_n})$, we fit them to mixture Gaussian distribution using a dataset of annotated images. The coefficients $a_{c_n \to c}$ and $b_{c_n \to c}$ are optimized to maximize the probability p by cross validation of training samples. The scene context of an unannotated image is then computed by averaging the scene contexts of its similar images retrieved from the dataset of annotated images.

2.2 appearance context

Objects look different depending on the surrounding scenery. For example, the orientation of cars that fits to images of a road in the left–right direction and anterior–posterior direction differ. We presume that objects of the same class in similar images look similar. Then we obtain the appearance context from the appearance of objects in images similar to the input image.

Before learning of the appearance context, we select object instances according to their aspect ratios. This step is inspired by an approach to detect objects (e.g. cars and bicycles) that separates training samples of different orientations according to the aspect ratios of the bounding boxes [4]. First, we collect instances of target object class c to a fixed number from top-ranked similar images. Next, we sort the instances by the aspect ratios of their bounding boxes and discard outliers: a certain number of samples with the smallest and largest aspect ratios. The discarded samples are not used for the learning appearance context but are restored for use as materials of image synthesis. Then we learn a classifier of target object class c with the features of the selected instances as positive samples and those of randomly selected regions of other images as negative samples. We use the learned classifier as the appearance context. In contrast to a classifier learned for object detection, which basically scores the likelihood of an instance belonging to a target object class, our classifier scores the likelihood of an instance fitting to the scenery of the input image. The higher the score of the classifier is, the more likely the appearance of an object instance is observed in the input image. This approach is motivated by the fact that a classifier learned with a few positive samples and numerous negative samples tends to detect objects of the same type and orientation [10].

We use a HOG descriptor [3] to describe the object's appearance and to train a linear SVM for a classifier. To eliminate the bias that the number of negative samples as greater than the number of positive samples, we set the weight for positive samples C_1 greater than the weight for negative samples C_2.

3. EXPERIMENT

We conducted an experiment using our method on the SUN09 dataset [2], which was originally used for context based recognition such as object detection. This dataset includes 4,367 images for training and 4,317 images for testing, which are annotated with 111 object labels. Here we used training images as the dataset for a similar image search and also for preliminary training probabilistic distributions of object scales and locations. We used testing images, excluding their annotation data as input images.

Exemplary results of automatic image synthesis are presented in Fig.2. Here we input an image and the label of a target object class ("car" for the left two examples in the top row and "person" for the other examples); then the system synthesized one object instance for each input image. The location and scale of synthesized objects are determined to maximize scores of spatial context and scale context respectively. The image of the synthesized object is selected from similar images with the highest appearance context score from the classifier. These results show that our method computes a plausible scene context and synthesizes an object with proper location, scale and appearance. Furthermore, our method is able to calculate the scene context of an object that does not exist in an input image. There are yet some cases that fail to locate a distant object in the foreground (see the upper right result in Fig.2). Figure 3 presents an illustration of the extracted spatial context of several objects. Here the brightness of an image of spatial context shows the magnitude of the probability that the target object exists.

Figure 3: Example of spatial context extraction.

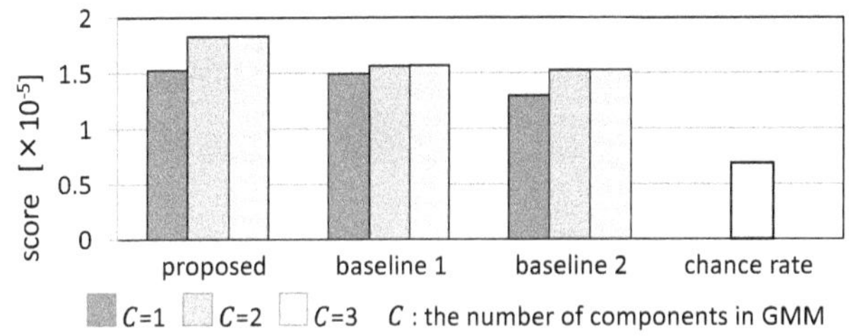

Figure 4: Average context score on test images.

Next, we evaluate the accuracy of predicting objects using the spatial context and scale context. We computed the scores for which the location and scale of predicted objects match those of the actual objects in test images. We compared our method to two baselines: (1) calculate spatial context using the absolute position in entire images instead of relative positions of two objects, and (2) calculate the scale context as $p(h|y, c) = p(h|c)$, which ignores the relation between h and y. Here we divide the 3D space with x, y and h axes into $64 \times 64 \times 64$ grids, so that the chance rate becomes $1/64^3 \approx 3.815 \times 10^{-6}$. The result is shown in Fig.4. We applied one, two, and three as the numbers of components in mixture Gaussian distribution fitting to the probability distribution of two objects' relative position $p_{c_n \to c}(\frac{x-x_n}{w_n}, \frac{y-y_n}{h_n})$. It showed that our method outperformed the two baselines in all cases.

Finally, we use our system to synthesize multiple objects in an input image. We select object instances with the highest scores of appearance context and locate them randomly according to spatial context $p(x, y|c)$. We eliminate regions with $p(x, y|c)$ lower than a certain threshold. We select h for each object with the highest scale context $p(h|y, c)$ according to its location. Then we draw objects in the order of increasing h to locate closer objects in the foreground. An example result of synthesizing multiple objects is shown in Fig.5. We input into the system a single (leftmost) image and the quantities of target objects: two for "car" class and sixteen for the "person" class. As this figure shows, our system can synthesize a natural image with scenery of multiple cars and persons.

4. CONCLUSION

We described a method to extract the scene context which represents the likelihood of the location, scale and appearance of objects to be synthesized in an image. In contrast to previous works that calculate the context as the likelihood of objects which exist in an input image, our method to calculate the spatial context and scale context is applicable to images that do not include objects to be

Figure 2: Example results of synthesizing “car” class and “person” class using scene context.

Figure 5: Example result of synthesizing multiple objects (2 cars and 16 people) using the scene context.

synthesized. Moreover, we developed a method to calculate the appearance context, which evaluates the likelihood of an object’s shape and orientation that fits the target image. However, since anteroposterior relationships between objects in an original image and synthesized objects is not considered (see the upper right result in Fig.2), our future direction is the detection of objects and depth estimation of input images, which can be used to improve the scene context and the synthesized images.

5. REFERENCES

[1] T. Chen, M.-M. Cheng, P. Tan, A. Shamir, and S.-M. Hu. Sketch2Photo: internet image montage. *ACM Transactions on Graphics (SIGGRAPH Asia)*, 28(5):124:1–124:10, 2009.

[2] M. J. Choi, J. J. Lim, A. Torralba, and A. S. Willsky. Exploiting hierarchical context on a large database of object categories. In *Proc. of CVPR*, pages 129–136, 2010.

[3] N. Dalal and B. Triggs. Histograms of oriented gradients for human detection. In *Proc. of CVPR*, pages 886–893, 2005.

[4] P. F. Felzenszwalb, R. B. Girshick, and D. Ramanan. Object detection with discriminatively trained part based models. *IEEE Transaction on Pattern Analysis and Machine Intelligence*, 32(9):1627–1645, 2010.

[5] C. Galleguillous and S. Belongie. Context based object categorization: A critical survey. *Computer Vision and Image Understanding*, 114(6):712–722, 2010.

[6] S. Goferman, A. Tal, and L. Zelnik-Manor. Puzzle-like collage. *Computer Graphics Forum (EuroGraphics)*, 29(2):459–468, 2010.

[7] J. Hays and A. A. Efros. Scene completion using millions of photographs. *ACM Transactions on Graphics (SIGGRAPH)*, 26(3):4, 2007.

[8] H. Huang, L. Zhang, and H.-C. Zhang. Arcimboldo-like collage using internet images. *ACM Transactions on Graphics (SIGGRAPH Asia)*, 30(6):155:1–155:8, 2011.

[9] M. Johnson, G. J. Brostow, J. Shotton, O. Arandjelović, V. Kwatra, and R. Cipolla. Semantic photo synthesis. *Computer Graphics Forum (EuroGraphics)*, 25(3):407–413, 2006.

[10] T. Malisiewicz, A. Gupta, and A. A. Efros. Ensemble of exemplar-svms for object detection and beyond. In *Proc. of ICCV*, pages 89–96, 2011.

[11] A. Oliva and A. Torralba. Modeling the shape of the scene: a holistic representation of the spatial envelope. *Internationali Journal of Computer Vision*, 42(3):145–175, 2001.

[12] C. Rother, L. Bordeaux, Y. Hamadi, and A. Blake. AutoCollage. *ACM Transactions on Graphics (SIGGRAPH)*, 25(3):847–852, 2006.

[13] C. L. Zitnick, D. Parikh, and L. Vanderwende. Learning the visual interpretation of sentences. In *Proc. of ICCV*, pages 1681–1688, 2013.

Face-Based Automatic Personality Perception

Noura Al Moubayed, Yolanda Vazquez-Alvarez, Alex McKay, Alessandro Vinciarelli
University of Glasgow (School of Computing Science) - Sir A.Williams Building, G128QQ Glasgow (UK)
firstname.lastname@glasgow.ac.uk

ABSTRACT

Automatic Personality Perception is the task of automatically predicting the personality traits people attribute to others. This work presents experiments where such a task is performed by mapping facial appearance into the Big-Five personality traits, namely Openness, Conscientiousness, Extraversion, Agreeableness and Neuroticism. The experiments are performed over the pictures of the FERET corpus, originally collected for biometrics purposes, for a total of 829 individuals. The results show that it is possible to automatically predict whether a person is perceived to be above or below median with an accuracy close to 70 percent (depending on the trait).

Categories and Subject Descriptors: J.4 [Computer Applications]: social and behavioral sciences; H.4.3 [Information Systems Applications]: Communications Applications. **General Terms:** Human Factors; Experimentation. **Keywords:** Automatic Personality Perception; Eigenfaces; Big-Five.

1. INTRODUCTION

The social cognition literature shows that people attribute personality traits to others in less than one second after the first contact [11]. The main interest of attributed traits is that they are predicitve of how others behave towards a certain person and, furthermore, they explain better than self-assessed traits the social characteristics of an individual [14]. Trait attribution was shown to take place not only during face-to-face encounters, but also during the consumption of multimedia material (e.g. when people see someone on television), an effect known as *Media Equation* [6]. Therefore, a large body of previous research work has aimed at automatically predicting the traits people attribute to unacquainted others they observe in multimedia material [12].

So far, research on Automatic Personality Perception (APP) has focused mainly on nonverbal behavior (paralanguage, fidgeting, gaze, etc.) and online activities (tagging images as *"favorite"* on Flickr, Facebook profiles, etc.) [12]. In parallel, research on face analysis has targeted the recognition of facial expressions [2], emotions and the inference of attractiveness [3]. The problem of automatically mapping facial appearance into personality traits has been largely neglected in the computing literature (see [12] for the few works that consider the problem). This work aims at filling, at least partially, such a gap and proposes experiments aimed at predicting whether people perceive an individual portrayed in a picture to be above or below median with respect to each of the Big-Five Traits [5].

The experiments have been performed over the frontal face images of the Color FERET database, a corpus originally collected for biometrics purposes (see Section 2). The most challenging aspect of such a corpus is the wide variety in terms of ethnicity, clothes, haircut and any other characteristics that contribute to facial appearance. From this point of view, this work is an advancement with respect to previous experiments that have focused on synthetic faces [7]. In particular, the experiments of this work can be considered more realistic and representative of everyday situations where people observe the portraits of unknwon individuals (e.g., profile pictures on social media, testimonials in advertisements, etc.).

The experiments involve a large sample of 829 individual faces. The largest corpus for face-based APP presented so far in the literature includes only 300 different faces generated artificially [7]. The main advantage in increasing the number of facial images is not only that the statistical reliability of the results improves, but also that it is possible to observe weaker effects (e.g., correlation between features and traits) that might not reach statistical significance with a smaller number of facial images.

The rest of the paper is organized as follows: Section 2 describes the data collection process, Section 3 presents the proposed approach, Section 4 reports on experiments and results, and the final Section 5 draws some conclusions.

2. THE DATA: FACE AND PERSONALITY

The corpus used for the experiments is a selection of 829 images of real faces (a total of 829 different individuals) from the Color FERET database[1], a benchmark for face recognition technologies collected between December 1993 and August 1996. All the selected images are in color and portray individuals of different gender (478 males and 351 females) and ethnic background (63.9% White, 15.3% Asian/Pacific

[1] `http://www.nist.gov/itl/iad/ig/colorferet.cfm`

MM'14, November 03–07, 2014, Orlando, FL, USA.

http://dx.doi.org/10.1145/2647868.2655014.

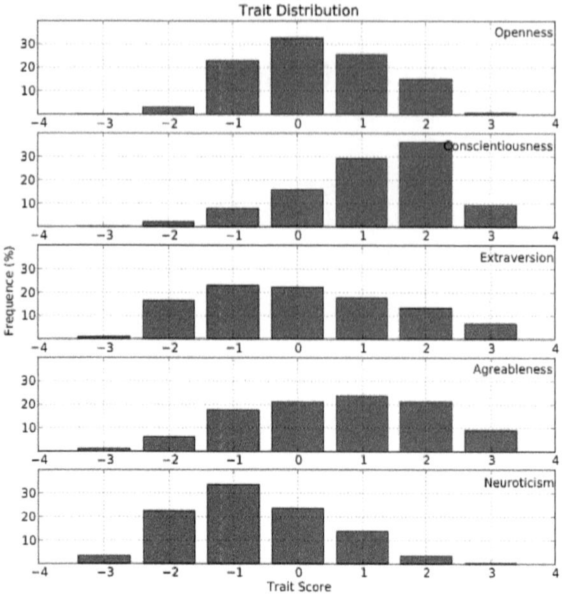

Figure 1: Score distribution for the Big-Five traits.

Islands, 7.6% African, 7.4% Indo-Aryan, 4.6% Hispanic/Latino, 1.1% Arab and 0.1% Native American). The personality assessments were provided by 11 independent judges (5 females, 6 males, aged 20 to 39 years) of White British ethnic background, with normal vision and no hearing problems. They were all paid for their participation. The reason behind the use of several assessors is that the goal of APP is to predict what is common across the traits attributed by different observers [12] and not to predict how one person in particular perceives others. On the other hand, all assessors have the same cultural background in order to avoid noise due to cultural effects.

Each judge filled in the *Big Five Inventory 10* (BFI-10) [5] questionnaire for all 829 images in the database. The BFI-10 includes 10 items (e.g., "*I see this person as someone who is lazy*", "*I see this person as someone who tends to find faults with others*", etc.) and every item of the questionnaire can be rated on a scale from 1:5 (ranging from "Disagree Strongly" to "Agree Strongly"). By summing the answers given to the various items, it is possible to obtain five scores that account for how high a facial image is perceived to be along each of the Big-Five personality dimensions, namely *Openness* (tendency to be curious, creative, artistic, etc.), *Conscientiousness* (tendency to be trustworthy, reliable, efficient, etc.), *Extraversion* (tendency to be sociable, active, etc.), *Agreeableness* (tendency to be kind, generous, etc.) and *Neuroticism* (tendency to be anxious, tense, etc.). Figure 1 shows the observed distribution of scores for the various traits.

The assessments were collected through an online system allowing the judges to see sequentially the 829 pictures and, for each of them, to fill the BFI-10 questionnaire. A judge was allowed to move from one picture to the next only when all BFI-10 items had been answered. The face images were presented in a different randomised order to each judge. After an initial face-to-face introductory session with the experimenters, the judges were asked to fill out the online questionnaires in no more than four weeks. This allowed the judges to complete the assessments in separate sessions (they were asked to work no more than 30 minutes per session in order to avoid tiredness effects), in their own time, without any contact with the other judges and/or the experimenters.

At the end of the assessment collection, there were 11 filled questionnaires per picture (one per judge). The scores resulting from each of them were averaged to provide the final personality assessment. The consistency between the judges was measured in terms of *effective reliability* ρ [8]:

$$\rho = \frac{Nr}{1 + (N-1)r}, \tag{1}$$

where r is the average inter-judge correlation and N is the total number of judges. The ρ value was 0.80 for Openness, 0.86 for Conscientiousness, 0.90 for Extraversion, 0.89 for Agreeableness and 0.79 for Neuroticism. The values are sufficient to achieve accuracies above chance level in the APP task presented in this work (see Section 4).

3. THE APPROACH

The approach proposed in this work includes three main steps, namely face preprocessing, feature extraction and trait prediction. During the first step, the images are converted into grey scale and undergo histogram equalization to normalize the brightness and increase the contrast. The Viola-Jones detector [13] is applied to the resulting images to locate a rectangular region around the face. The rectangle is then extended by 20% on the bottom and 10% on both left and right sides to include neck and ears. The extended rectangles are extracted from the original images and scaled to 65×50 pixels. The goal is to ensure that all samples have the same shape and size while reducing the computational cost of the following steps.

This approach adopts appearance features (see below) that are sensitive to variations in the positions of salient points such as eyes, nostrils, chin tip, lip corners, etc. For this reason, the samples are mapped onto a reference image that corresponds to the average of the corpus. This task is performed using the non-rigid registration approach[2] proposed in [9].

The second step adopts the eigenfaces method [10], one of the face representation techniques most commonly adopted in literature. The eigenfaces are the Principal Components extracted from a set of training images and they constitute a basis in a space where every point corresponds to a different face image. The eigenfaces are ordered according to the amount of variance they account for in the original data. In the experiments presented in this paper, the first 103 eigenfaces correspond to 90% of the variance. A test face is represented with its projections onto the eigenfaces and the exact number of eigenfaces to be retained is set through crossvalidation (see Section 4).

The trait prediction step is performed using Support Vector Machines (SVMs) with both polynomial and Gaussian Radial Basis Function (RBF) kernel [1]. The SVMs were trained with the Sequential Minimal Optimization approach and the hyperparameters were set through crossvalidation (see Section 4).

[2]`www.sas.el.utwente.nl/open/research/ medical_imaging/registration`

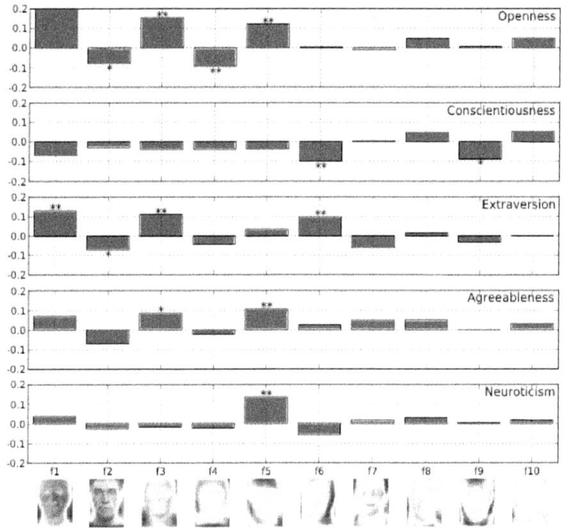

Figure 2: The charts show the Spearman correlation coefficients between the projections onto the first 10 eigenfaces (at the bottom of the figure) and the Big-Five Traits. Overall, the first 10 eigenfaces account for 60% of the variance. The asterisks indicate whether the coefficient is statistically significant at 5% (single asterisk) or 1% (double asterisk) confidence level.

4. EXPERIMENTS AND RESULTS

The experiments were performed over 785 images because the face detection approach did not work correctly for 44 samples (5.5% of the total). The tests followed a K-fold experimental protocol ($K = 20$). The data was first split into K subsets of roughly the same size, then $K - 1$ subsets were used for training while the remaining one was left-out for testing. The process was iterated K times and, at each repetition, a different subset was used for testing. The main advantage of this protocol is that it allows one to use all the data at disposition to test an approach while still ensuring a rigorous separation between training and test set.

The hyperparameters were set through crossvalidation, the values leading to the highest accuracy over the training set were used for the test. The hyperparameters include the number d of eigenfaces to be retained, the order n of the polynomial kernel and the scaling factor γ for the RBF kernel. The values of d, n and γ were searched in the range $[10, 100]$, $[1, 5]$ and $[1, 10^5]$, respectively.

Figure 2 shows the Spearman correlation coefficients between the Big-Five Traits and the projections of the face images onto the first 10 eigenfaces. These latter account for 60% of the data variance and appear at the bottom of the figure. On average, the performance of automatic prediction approaches tends to be higher when the features (or at least a sufficient number of them) covariate to a statistically significant extent with the traits. Furthermore, the correlational analysis can provide indications on the features most likely to influence the outcome of the prediction approaches.

Overall, the Spearman coefficients tend to be weak (the maximum value was observed for Openness and it is 0.3). However, the p-value is lower than 5% for 22% of the projections for Openness, 10% for Conscientiousness, 28% for Extraversion, 26% for Agreeableness and 15% for Neuroticism. This seems to suggest that the covariation between projections and traits is not just the effect of chance (in this case no more than 5% of the features would have p-value lower than 5%), but the result of a consistent relationship between face appearance and personality traits.

The experiments presented in this paper address two tasks: the first is to predict whether an individual is perceived to be *high* (above or equal to the median) or *low* (below median) along each of the Big-Five Traits, the second is to predict whether an individual is in the *top* or *bottom* quartile for each of the Big-Five Traits. The first task is performed using the entire corpus of images at disposition, the second using only half of the data (the images falling in the central quartiles of each trait are discarded). In both cases, the performance is measured in terms of *accuracy*, i.e. percentage of times the approach assigns a face image to the right class.

The results for the first task are reported in the upper plot of Figure 3 using both polynomial and Radial Basis Function (RBF) kernels for the Support Vector Machines. The error bars correspond to the standard deviation of the accuracy across the K folds. According to a two-tailed binomial test, the accuracy difference is statistically significant ($p < 0.01$) with respect to chance (a baseline system that predicts always the class with the highest a-priori probability). The only exception is the performance of the SVMs with polynomial kernel in the case of Conscientiousness. The RBF kernel systematically increases the performance with respect to the polynomial one, but not to a statistically significant extent (according to a two-tailed t-test). The best results are achieved for Openness, Neuroticism and Extraversion. This latter tends to be the best predicted trait in most of the APP experiments presented in the literature [12]. The probable reason is that such trait has been shown to be the one people tend to attribute more easily in zero acquaintance scenarios like the one considered in this work [4]. In this respect, the results seem to confirm the indications of personality psychology.

Experiments similar to those presented in this paper were proposed in [7] over synthetic faces. However, the experiments of such work take into account only samples for which the traits are in the top and bottom quartile of the observed personality scores. Therefore, for the sake of comparison, the first experiment above was repeated with this setup. The main reason for retaining only the judgments at the extremes of the distribution is that these result from higher consensus among the assessors. Hence, the relationship between facial appearance and attributed traits should be more consistent for the samples in the top and bottom quartiles.

The results are reported in the lower plot of Figure 3. The accuracy increases for all traits and for both types of kernel adopted in the SVM. However, the improvement does not appear to be statistically significant (according to a two-tailed t-test). This seems to suggest that the scores belonging to the central quartiles do not result from the averaging over different scores (e.g., the rating 3 can be obtained because all assessors assign 3, but also because some assign 2 and others assign 4), but from substantial agreement across

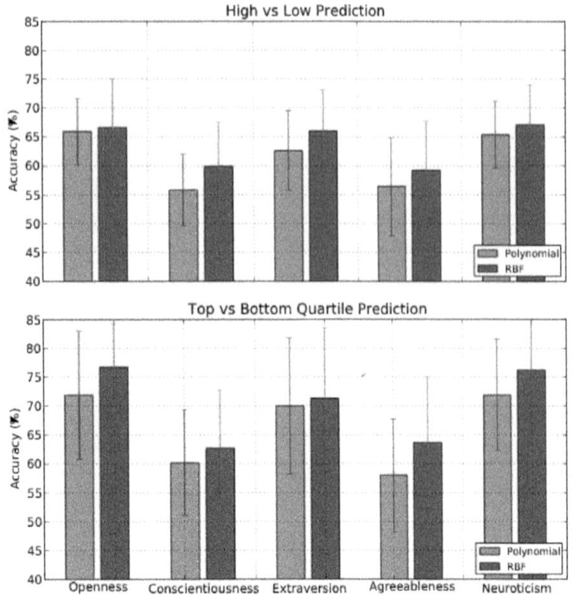

Figure 3: The chart shows the accuracies achieved using Support Vector Machines with polynomial and RBF kernel.

the judges. Such a hypothesis is further corroborated by the reliability values measured in Section 2.

A rigorous comparison between the results of this work and those presented in [7] is not possible because data and trait set are different. However, some orientative indications can still be obtained by taking into account three traits adopted in [7] that can be reasonably matched with one of the Big-Five traits, namely *Extroverted* (corresponding to Extraversion), *Competent* (corresponding to Conscientiousness) and *Likable* (corresponding to Agreeableness). For these three traits, the accuracies are similar to those obtained in this work (when using the same approach as the one adopted here). While not being fully rigorous, the comparison still seems to suggest that the trait attribution process does not change significantly when passing from synthetic to natural images.

5. CONCLUSIONS

This paper has presented experiments on face-based Automatic Personality Perception, i.e. the prediction of the traits people attribute to unacquainted others based on facial appearance. To the best of our knowledge, this is one of the first works dedicated to this problem, previous research on faces having targeted mainly facial expressions [2], emotions and attractiveness [3]. The results show that it is possible to predict with accuracy of around 65% whether an individual portrayed in a picture is perceived to be *high* (above or equal to the median) or *low* (below the median) along Openness, Extraversion and Neuroticism. The accuracy is lower, but significantly above chance, for the other two traits (Conscientiousness and Agreeableness).

Future work will adopt face analysis approaches more sophisticated than the one adopted here, especially when it comes to structural properties such as the distribution of salient facial points (eyes, nostrils, lip corners, etc.). Moreover, the corpus collected for this work gives the possibility of exploring the effect of clothes, hair color, ethnic background and other factors that so far have been largely neglected in the literature.

6. REFERENCES

[1] C. Cortes and V. Vapnik. Support vector machine. *Machine learning*, 20(3):273–297, 1995.

[2] B. Fasel and J. Luettin. Automatic facial expression analysis: a survey. *Pattern Recognition*, 36(1):259–275, 2003.

[3] H. Gunes. A survey of perception and computation of human beauty. In *Proceedings of the Workshop on Human Gesture and Behavior Understanding*, pages 19–24, 2011.

[4] C. Judd, L. James-Hawkins, V. Yzerbyt, and Y. Kashima. Fundamental dimensions of social judgment: Unrdestanding the relations bteween judgments of competence and warmth. *Journal of Personality and Social Psychology*, 89(6):899–913, 2005.

[5] B. Rammstedt and O. John. Measuring personality in one minute or less: A 10-item short version of the Big Five Inventory in English and German. *Journal of Research in Personality*, 41(1):203–212, 2007.

[6] B. Reeves and C. Nass. *The media equation.* Cambridge University Press, 1996.

[7] M. Rojas, D. Masip, A. Todorov, and J. Vitria. Automatic prediction of facial trait judgments: Appearance vs. structural models. *PLoS One*, 6(8):e23323, 2011.

[8] R. Rosenthal. Conducting judgment studies: Some methodological issues. In J. Harrigan, R. Rosenthal, and K. Scherer, editors, *The new handbook of methods in nonverbal behavior research*, pages 199–234. Oxford University Press, 2005.

[9] D. Rueckert, P. Aljabar, R. A. Heckemann, J. V. Hajnal, and A. Hammers. Diffeomorphic registration using B-splines. In *Medical Image Computing and Computer-Assisted Intervention*, volume LNCS 4191, pages 702–709. Springer, 2006.

[10] M. Turk and A. Pentland. Eigenfaces for recognition. *Journal of cognitive neuroscience*, 3(1):71–86, 1991.

[11] J. S. Uleman, S. A. Saribay, and C. M. Gonzalez. Spontaneous inferences, implicit impressions, and implicit theories. *Annual Reviews of Psychology*, 59:329–360, 2008.

[12] A. Vinciarelli and G. Mohammadi. A survey of personality computing. *IEEE Transactions on Affective Computing (to appear)*, 2014.

[13] P. Viola and M. J. Jones. Robust real-time face detection. *International Journal of Computer Vision*, 57(2):137–154, 2004.

[14] A. Wright. Current directions in personality science and the potential for advances through computing. *IEEE Transactions on Affective Computing (to appear)*, 2014.

Facial Attribute Space Compression by Latent Human Topic Discovery

Chia-Hung Lin, Yan-Ying Chen, Bor-Chun Chen, Yu-Lin Hou, Winston Hsu

National Taiwan University, Taipei, Taiwan

{hank.linchiahung, yanying}@gmail.com, {sirius42, houyulin}@cmlab.csie.ntu.edu.tw, winston@csie.ntu.edu.tw

ABSTRACT

Facial attribute is important information for a variety of machine vision tasks including recognition, classification, and retrieval. There arises a strong need for detecting various facial attributes such as gender, age and more which consume more computation and storage resources. Therefore, we propose a compression framework to find fewer significant Latent Human Topics (LHT) to approximate more facial attributes. LHT is a combination of attribute correlation by transferring facial attribute space to compressional space with Singular Value Decomposition (SVD). Using the proposed scheme, we can easily detect the facial attributes from a face image via fast reconstructing the compressed labels automatically detected by a few LHT classifiers. Experimental results show that our system can achieve similar performance with substantially fewer dimensions compared to the original number of facial attributes, and it even shows slight improvements because LHT carry informative attribute correlations learned from data.

Categories and Subject Descriptors

I.4.2 [**IMAGE PROCESSING AND COMPUTER VISION**]: Compression (Coding)-Approximate methods

Keywords

Facial Attribute Detection; Compression; Attribute Correlation

1. INTRODUCTION

With the prosperity of social media and the success of many photo-sharing platforms, like Flickr and Picasa, the volume of community-contributed photos has increased dramatically. To deal with the huge collections of personal photos, facial attribute detection is becoming more important for a variety of machine vision tasks including recognition, annotation, and retrieval.

Facial attribute detection is a multi-label classification problem, i.e. each photo may belong to multiple labels. Most existing studies address this problem with Binary Relevance (BR) approach, which reduces it to multiple independent binary classification problems by detecting each attribute regardless of others and ignores the correlation among facial attributes. Seeing this problem, some works [7, 8] find the correlations between facial attributes to help improve their performance in retrieval and recognition. Scheirer

MM'14, November 3–7 2014, Orlando, Florida, USA

http://dx.doi.org/10.1145/2647868.2655016 .

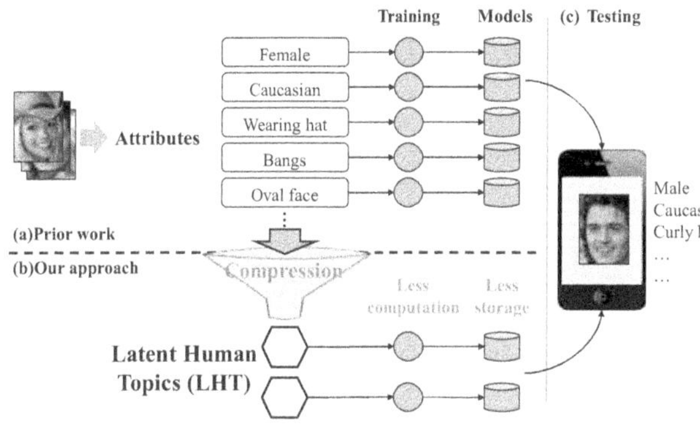

Figure 1: (a) Most previous studies focus on training each facial attribute, gender, age, etc., as a single model. (b) Differently, we aim to find fewer significant Latent Human Topics to approximate the original facial attributes by using label space compression. (c) In the device with limited resource, the fewer amount of LHTs require less computation and less storage but achieve similar attribute detection performance compared to using the original amount of attribute models.

et al. [7] proposed a novel calibration method that improves the combination of independent facial attribute detectors. Siddiquie et al. [8] modelled the natural correlation between facial attributes to improve search results. For instance, a face with beard is most likely to be a face of male. These studies show that exploiting the attribute correlations is a promising direction for improving their recognition.

In this work, We aim to find the Latent Human Topic (LHT) in facial attributes by constructing any potential attribute correlations from data without being limited in pairwise cases. As shown in Figure 1 (a), most previous works [4, 5, 7, 8] train a classifier for each attribute. Differently, we compress attributes to a few LHTs by using SVD and train a classifier for each LHT (cf. Figure 1 (b)). The number of LHTs is smaller than the number of facial attributes, so we can reduce the computational effort of prediction and the storage of models, especially for devices with limited resource (cf. Figure 1 (c)).

To compress facial attributes to LHTs, we use a LSA based method [9] which focuses on compression in the label space rather than the feature space. To the best of our knowledge, this is the first work to use label space compression for inferring the facial attribute correlations and we comprehensively analyze the physical meaning of attribute correlations in latent (human) topic space.

We evaluate our approach on LFW-attributes dataset comprising 2,500 different face images annotated with 38 facial attributes in LFW dataset and show that our method can reduce the computational effort, storage of the models, and

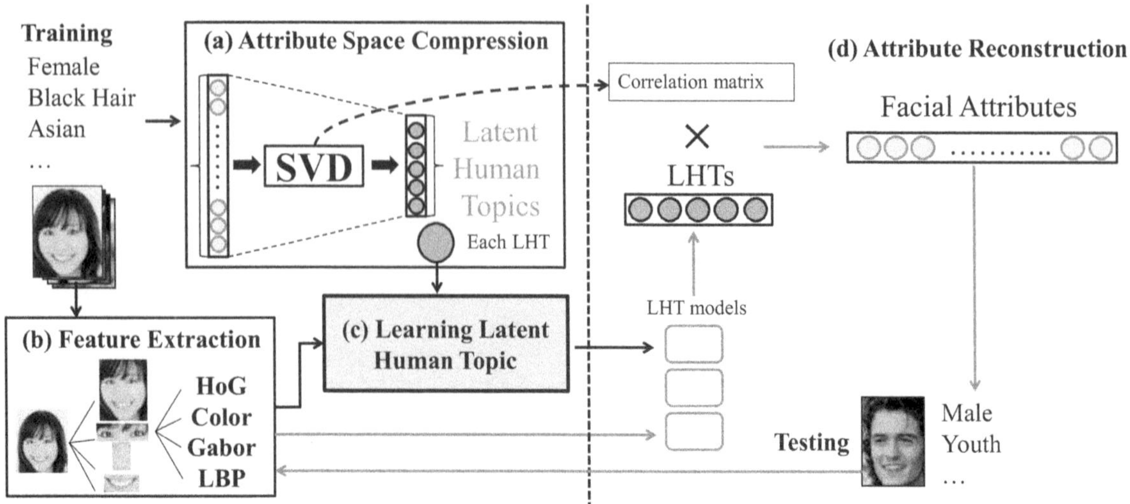

Figure 2: System overview. (a) In training stage, we compress the original facial attribute labels to LHT by using SVD. The correlation matrix constructed by SVD represents the correlation between LHTs and each facial attribute. (b) We extract visual features from each training image, and (c) we use the energy of each LHT for this image as a label to learn LHT detectors. (d) In testing stage, given a test image with extracted visual features, the LHT energy can be predicted by using the LHT detectors and the original attribute labels can be reconstructed through correlation matrix.

achieve similar performance with substantially less dimensions compared to the original facial attribute detection.

2. SYSTEM FRAMEWORK

We propose a compression framework to find fewer significant Latent Human Topics (LHT) to approximate more facial attributes. Figure 2 shows the architecture of our system, which is divided into four main parts. In training stage (black arrows), we compress the original facial attributes to LHTs by using SVD (cf. Figure 2 (a)). The unitary matrix decomposed by SVD represents the correlation between LHTs and each facial attribute, referred as *correlation matrix* in this paper. We then first extract mid-level features which represent different discriminating abilities across facial attributes (cf. Figure 2 (b)). We use Support Vector Regression (SVR) to learn LHT-specific mid-level features and assemble the best combination of mid-level features as a LHT detector (cf. Figure 2 (c)). For each testing image (blue arrows), we apply the same method in train stage to extract the mid-level features and predict the energy of each LHT by our detectors. At last, we can use the correlation matrix to transfer LHT in compressional space to original attribute space (cf. Figure 2 (d)).

2.1 Facial Attribute Space Compression

As shown in Figure 2 (a), we aim at transferring facial attribute space to compressional space to find Latent Human Topics (LHT) based on PLST [9] before training. PLST can accomplish the projection by seeking important correlations between labels through SVD. So we apply this method to the compression of facial attributes which have high correlation. Given a training set $\boldsymbol{S}$ that contains $\boldsymbol{N}$ face images, every image is represented as a $\boldsymbol{K}$-dimensional label vector $y_n \in \{0,1\}^K$, each indicating the presence of a facial attribute in the face. The binary vectors of N training faces form a $\boldsymbol{K} \times \boldsymbol{N}$ attribute matrix $\boldsymbol{Y}$. Then, To define projection matrix $\boldsymbol{U}$, we perform SVD on the $\boldsymbol{K} \times \boldsymbol{N}$ dimensional matrix $\boldsymbol{Y}$ to obtain three matrices [1]:

$$\boldsymbol{Y} = U\Sigma V' \tag{1}$$

From the properties of SVD, (1) can be rewritten as

$$\boldsymbol{H} = U'\boldsymbol{Y} = \Sigma V' \tag{2}$$

where $\boldsymbol{U} \in \mathbb{R}^{\boldsymbol{K}\times\boldsymbol{K}}$ is a projection matrix, each column representing the distribution over $\boldsymbol{K}$ attributes in a LHT. $\boldsymbol{U}$ acts as a correlation matrix between LHTs (compressed labels) and facial attributes (original labels). A column in $\boldsymbol{H}$ indicates the energy of each LHT for a training face. In the next section, we will train LHT detectors to predict the energy for each designated LHT in a given face image.

2.2 Latent Human Topic Detection

Instead of learning facial attributes, we propose to learn LHT because the top $\boldsymbol{M}$ LHTs (ranked by singular value) can approximate the K facial attributes where $\boldsymbol{M}$ we called compression level. When $\boldsymbol{M} << \boldsymbol{K}$, the required classifiers and classification time for LHTs will become much smaller than those required for facial attributes. In this section, we introduce the feature extraction (cf. Figure 2 (b)) and learning method to train LHT detectors (cf. Figure 2 (c)).

2.2.1 Feature Extraction

To construct a training dataset, we create a dataset with 2,500 images which have 38 facial attributes for each face from LFW dataset [3]. Then, we crop the face region extracted from the whole image and locate important facial parts such as eyes, nose and mouth by face detection. We use mid-level features to represent a face.

Mid-level features are the combinations of low-level features (e.g. edge, color, texture) extracted from different facial parts which represent different discriminating abilities across facial attributes (cf. Figure 2(b)). In our implementation, we exploit four types of low-level features (i.e., Log Gabor filter, Pyramid Histogram of Oriented Gradi-

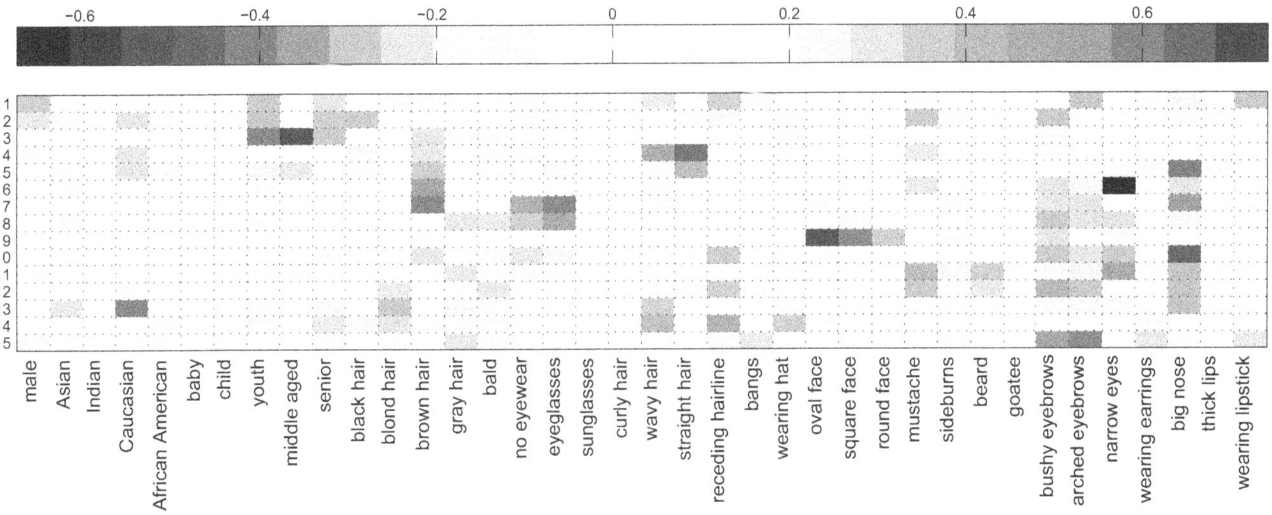

Figure 3: Visualization of correlation matrix. It shows the correlations between LHTs and the original facial attributes. The LHTs are ranked by its corresponding singular values from SVD.

ents (PHoG), grid color moment, Local Binary Pattern) extracted from different facial parts (i.e., eyes, nose, mouth, whole face, whole face with hair). Compared to using low-level features, mid-level features have better semantic meanings [4] for describing facial attributes through multiple modalities. We use Support Vector Regression (SVR) [2] to learn LHT-specific mid-level features because the label of a LHT for a face is a real value indicating the energy of this LHT in the given face.

2.2.2 Ensemble learning

For each LHT, we choose the best combination of mid-level features by using Gradient Boosting [6]. The combination of mid-level features for a designated LHT is adaptively weighted through the boosting scheme and assembled as a LHT detector. Furthermore, the framework have high scalability which is not only generic for various facial attributes but also adapted for LHT which is the combination of attribute correlation in our experiment.

2.3 Facial Attribute Reconstruction

For each testing image, we apply the framework in section 2.2 to extract the features combined by mid-level features and predict the energy of each LHT by our detectors. The predicted LHT energy forms a vector h. Then, we approximate the original attributes by transferring LHT in compressional space to original attribute space (cf. Figure 2 (d)). For a given compression level $\boldsymbol{M}$, $\boldsymbol{M}$ vectors in $\boldsymbol{U}$ with the highest singular value are selected to form the correlation matrix $\boldsymbol{U}_M$. $\boldsymbol{U}_M$ can be used to project the LHT vectors h to the original attributes vector by $\boldsymbol{U}_M h$ resulted in $\mathbb{R}^K$. Because the original attribute space is of binary value, we use the sample rounding to quantize the reconstructed real values to binary case in L1-distance to approximate the original attribute labels.

3. EXPERIMENTS

3.1 Dataset

We build the LFW-attribute dataset consisting of a subset of LFW dataset [3] which totally contains 13,233 face images among 5,749 people. Then, we randomly choose 2,500 different people from LFW dataset, and annotate 38 attributes manually. Figure 3 shows our attribute list. Throughout the experiments, we use the original facial attributes detection without compression [4] as the baseline to evaluate the effect from different compression level of LHTs. We also analyze the correlations among attributes in each LHT and show how it can improve the attribute detection.

3.2 Attribute Correlation Matrix

Attribute correlation matrix means the correlations between LHTs and their distribution over attributes, i.e., the projection matrix $\boldsymbol{U}$ in Eq. 2. Each vector in attribute correlation matrix shows the physical meaning of a LHT, that is, what attributes this typical human genre should have. To analyze each LHT, we visualize the correlation matrix in Figure 3, which comprises the vectors corresponding to the top 15 LHTs in $\boldsymbol{U}$ with the highest singular value. From the property of principle directions, these vectors are the majority of human genres in the given dataset. By the correlation matrix, we can discover the positive and negative correlated attributes to a specific LHT as well as some inter correlations among attributes.

3.2.1 Correlations between LHTs and Attributes

LHT can help us to easily find the natural attribute correlations for a specific human genre. Taking Figure 3 row 1 as an example, male, senior, gray hair, bread, eyeglasses, straight hair, receding hairline, mustache, narrow eyes and big nose are likely to appear with such human genre (the attributes with response > 0). These attributes depict the visual appearance of a typical human genre in our dataset, perhaps senior professionals like politicians or supervisors in LFW celebrity data. Meanwhile, for this typical human genre, they are unlikely to have the attributes like youth, black hair, blond hair, no eyewear, wavy hair, bangs, arched eyebrows, wearing earrings and wearing lipstick.

3.2.2 Correlations among Attributes

Correlations among attributes could be either positive or negative. Positive correlation means certain attributes are

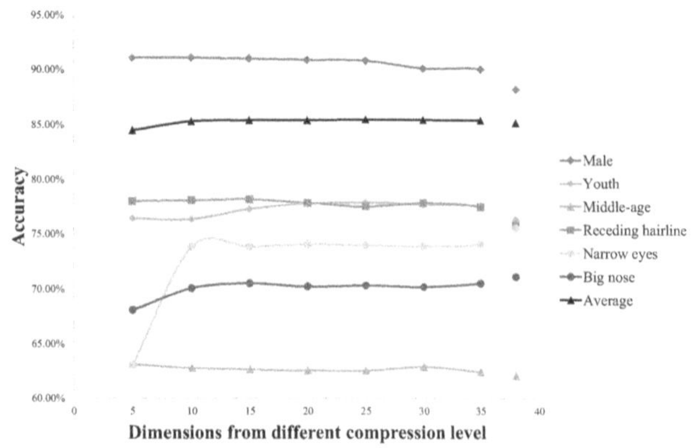

Figure 4: The detection accuracy of sampled attributes in different compression levels (that is, the number of LHTs). It shows that our approach can achieve similar accuracy compared to the original attribute detectors (the rightmost colored marks) by only using 5 to 10 LHT detectors.

likely to appear together; for example, "Asian" and "black hair" in the row 4 and 13 in Figure 3. On the other hand, negative correlation suggests they are less frequently shown in the same person, e.g., "male" and "wearing lipstick" in the row 1 and 15. Likewise, "Caucasian" and "black hair" in the row 2, 4 and 5. Exclusive attributes in the same attribute type are also negatively correlated; for example, youth, middle aged and senior. Most of these phenomena approximate our understanding for conventional human genres.

3.3 Latent Human Topic Detection in Different Compression Level

In this experiment, we aim to compare the accuracy of the LHT detectors in different compression level (cf. $\boldsymbol{M}$ in Section 2.2). We set 7 levels from 5 to 35 (that is, 5 to 35 top LHT vectors) and compare its reconstructed attribute labels with results of the original attribute detectors [4]. To evaluate the accuracy, we average the accuracy with five-fold cross validation in LFW-attributes dataset. In Figure 4, we sample 6 different attributes which have more balance number of positive and negative images in our dataset, and we also calculate the average accuracy (black line) for all attributes in different compression levels. Based on the results shown in Figure 4, we found that,

- The accuracy is similar in different compression level in most attributes except narrow eyes. It suggests even a few of LHTs combined with different attribute correlations they are sufficient to approximate most of the original attributes. Furthermore, because the dimensions of LHT vector are certainly less than original attributes, it can reduce the required storage for detectors and computational effort in prediction, especially in the device with limited resource, like mobile phones or wearable sensors.

- The accuracy of narrow eyes increases dramatically at second level (10 dimensions). As shown in Figure 3, "narrow eyes" has strong negative response in the 6_{th} LHT. It means the 6_{th} LHT is important to narrow eyes, but the detector of "narrow eyes" lacks the information of the 6_{th} LHT at the first compression level (5 top LHT vectors). It then increases dramatically at the 6_{th} level. This observation shows that once the attributes are covered in more LHTs, the reconstruction accuracy will be enhanced accordingly.

- Except "big nose" and "narrow eyes", most attributes are slightly improved by using LHT detectors and facial attribute reconstruction. The improvements are probably ascribed to additional information from the correlations between LHTs and attributes as well as the correlations among attributes.

4. CONCLUSIONS AND FUTURE WORKS

We propose a compression system which can find a few significant Latent Human Topics (LHT) to approximate more facial attributes. The latent topic analysis helps for discovering the attribute combinations frequently shown in a face; meanwhile, it is informative to find the positive and negative correlations among these attributes. In the experiment, we show that the discovered LHTs and attribute correlations match our conventional understanding for conventional human genres. Furthermore, our system can reduce the computational effort and storage while achieving similar performance compared to the original facial attribute space in facial attribute detection. In the future, we will evaluate more other compression methods; for example, we can combine the information of feature space in our compression to improve the correlation and performance. On the other hand, trying to map human-related keywords to the discovered latent human topics. Besides, we can try to find the most significant LHTs by consumer photos collected from different photo-sharing platforms, like Flickr and Instagram, to analysis the human composition of an activity or area.

5. REFERENCES

[1] B. Datta. *Numerical Linear Algebra and Applications.* Brooks/Cole Pub., 1995.

[2] R.-E. Fan, K.-W. Chang, C.-J. Hsieh, X.-R. Wang, and C.-J. Lin. Liblinear: A library for large linear classification. *J. Mach. Learn. Res.*, 9:1871–1874, 2008.

[3] M. R. Gary B. Huang et al. Labeled faces in the wild: A database for studying face recognition in unconstrained environments. Technical Report 07-49, University of Massachusetts, Amherst, 2007.

[4] N. Kumar, P. N. Belhumeur, and S. K. Nayar. FaceTracer: A Search Engine for Large Collections of Images with Faces. In *ECCV*, 2008.

[5] N. Kumar, A. C. Berg, P. N. Belhumeur, and S. K. Nayar. Attribute and Simile Classifiers for Face Verification. In *ICCV*, 2009.

[6] F. Pedregosa, G. Varoquaux, A. Gramfort, and others. Scikit-learn: Machine learning in Python. *Journal of Machine Learning Research*, 12:2825–2830, 2011.

[7] W. Scheirer, N. Kumar, P. N. Belhumeur, and T. E. Boult. Multi-attribute spaces: Calibration for attribute fusion and similarity search. In *CVPR*, 2012.

[8] B. Siddiquie, R. S. Feris, and L. S. Davis. Image ranking and retrieval based on multi-attribute queries. In *CVPR*, 2011.

[9] F. Tai and H.-T. Lin. Multilabel classification with principal label space transformation. *Neural Computation*, 24(9):2508–2542, 2012.

Emotional Analysis of Music: A Comparison of Methods*

Mohammad Soleymani
University of Geneva
Carouge (GE), Switzerland
mohammad.soleymani@unige.ch

Anna Aljanaki
Utrecht University
Utrecht, the Netherlands
a.aljanaki@uu.nl

Yi-Hsuan Yang
Academia Sinica
Taipei, Taiwan
yang@citi.sinica.edu.tw

ABSTRACT

Music as a form of art is intentionally composed to be emotionally expressive. The emotional features of music are invaluable for music indexing and recommendation. In this paper we present a cross-comparison of automatic emotional analysis of music. We created a public dataset of Creative Commons licensed songs. Using valence and arousal model, the songs were annotated both in terms of the emotions that were expressed by the whole excerpt and dynamically with 1 Hz temporal resolution. Each song received 10 annotations on Amazon Mechanical Turk and the annotations were averaged to form a ground truth. Four different systems from three teams and the organizers were employed to tackle this problem in an open challenge. We compare their performances and discuss the best practices. While the effect of a larger feature set was not very apparent in the static emotion estimation, the combination of a comprehensive feature set and a recurrent neural network that models temporal dependencies has largely outperformed the other proposed methods for dynamic music emotion estimation.

Categories and Subject Descriptors

H5.5 [**Information storage and retrieval**]: Content Analysis and Indexing

Keywords

Music; emotion; crowdsourcing; audio features; music emotion recognition; performance evaluation

1. INTRODUCTION

Music as an art is inherently emotionally expressive. The emotional characteristics of music are invaluable for music indexing and recommendation. There are however a number of challenges in identifying the emotion expressed by music. As such, a considerable amount of work has been dedicated to the development of automatic music emotion recognition (MER) systems [2, 10]. This paper presents a cross-comparison of the four different systems proposed to perform this task. The valence-arousal (V-A) model of emotion is used in this work. This is a dimensional model of emotion, in which valence ranges from unpleasant to pleasant emotions, and arousal indicates emotional intensity from passive to activated.

The *Emotion in Music* task was presented in the open challenge[1] MediaEval 2013 benchmarking initiative for multimedia evaluation. The only other evaluation task for MER is the audio mood classification (AMC) task of the annual music information retrieval evaluation exchange (MIREX),[2] which offers the possibility of analyzing the annotated audio files (totaling 600 excerpts) on their own restricted access server. However, AMC describes emotions using five discrete emotion clusters instead of affect dimensions, which do not have origins in psychological research, and some have noted semantic or acoustic overlap between clusters [4]. Furthermore, the dataset only applies a singular static rating per audio excerpt, which belies the time-varying nature of music.

Our new benchmarking corpus employs music licensed under Creative Commons (CC),[3] enabling us to redistribute the content, from the Free Music Archive (FMA),[4] an online library of high-quality music. A 45 seconds excerpt was extracted from a random point of each song to reduce the annotation load and make a uniform dataset. To collect annotations, we have turned to crowdsourcing using Amazon Mechanical Turk (MTurk),[5] which was successfully used by others to label large libraries [7]. We have developed a two-stage procedure for filtering out poor quality workers, where workers must first pass a test demonstrating a thorough understanding of the task, and an ability to produce good quality work. Each excerpt is annotated by a minimum of 10 workers, which is substantially larger than any existing music dataset with dynamic annotations of emotion.

2. DATASET AND TASK DESCRIPTION

The task, presented at MediaEval 2013, was composed of two subtasks. In the first task, the dynamic emotion characterization task, arousal and valence were estimated for the given song dynamically in time, with temporal resolu-

*The work of Aljanaki, Veltkamp and Wiering is supported by the FES project "COMMIT/". See the last section for the rest of the authors.

MM'14, November 03 - 07 2014, Orlando, FL, USA.

ACM 978-1-4503-3063-3/14/11 ...$15.00.
http://dx.doi.org/10.1145/2647868.2655019.

[1]http://www.multimediaeval.org
[2]http://www.music-ir.org/mirex/wiki
[3]http://www.creativecommons.org
[4]http://www.freemusicarchive.org
[5]http://www.mturk.com

tion being one second. The second task, the static emotion characterization task, required participants to deploy multimodal features to automatically detect the overall valence and arousal for each song. We initially developed a dataset of 1,000 songs. However, a set of duplicates were later discovered and removed, which reduced the size of the dataset to 744 songs. The dataset was split between the development set (619 songs) and the evaluation set (125 songs).

The dynamic annotations were collected using a web-interface on a scale from −1 to 1, where the Mechanical Turk workers could dynamically annotate the songs on valence and arousal dimensions separately while the song was being played. The static annotations were made on nine-point scale on valence and arousal for the whole 45 seconds excerpts after the dynamic annotations. We also collected data on other factors that may affect annotations. To estimate annotator's current mood, we use an implicit mood assessment method [5], asking a worker to choose to which extent an artificial noword, e.g., "smon", "twus", or "bimp", expresses a mood. The mood words were "energetic," "aggressive," "helpless," "nervous," "passive," "pleased" and "relaxed," with the four possible answers ranging from "not at all" to "to a great extent." In addition, we automatically collected the time of day in order to study its effect on emotional annotation. For a detailed description of the crowdsourcing techniques employed and dataset statistics we refer the reader to [6]. The database is freely available on the internet[6].

2.1 Data analysis

In order to measure the inter-annotation agreement, we calculated Krippendorff's alpha on an ordinal scale for the static annotations. The Krippendorff's alpha for the static annotations on the whole excerpts were 0.54 for valence and 0.55 for arousal, which are in the range of moderate agreement. For the dynamic annotations, we used Kendall's coefficient of concordance (Kendall's W) with corrected tied ranks to measure inter-annotation agreement. Kendall's W is a non-parametric rank based measure and is a good indicator of the agreement between the shapes of the time series generated by dynamic annotations, which is more important than the worker related constant bias. Kendall's W was calculated for each song separately after discarding the annotations of the first 5 seconds. The average W is 0.17 ± 0.18 for arousal and 0.21 ± 0.22 for valence. The observed agreement was statistically significant (p-value<0.05) for arousal in 70.4% of songs and for valence in 75.5% of songs. Kendall's W showed that agreement among arousal annotations compared to the valence annotations is almost equal for the static annotations and lower for the dynamic annotations. This shows that the workers were more consistent in following the valence trends dynamically.

We have discarded the first 5 samples of dynamic annotations, taking into account the reaction time of the raters. However, this number was chosen arbitrarily, based on our own experience. In order to investigate how long it takes for the raters to get a stable understanding of songs' emotional expressions, we calculated the Krippendorff's alpha on interval scale for all the songs and for all the time samples for both valence and arousal. The results are shown in Figure 1, which shows that valence inter-annotator agreement stabilizes around 10 seconds whereas the arousal dynamic annotations take longer to stabilize. This might be one of the reasons for higher inter-annotator agreement for dynamic valence annotations. We hence conclude that we should have discarded the first 10 to 20 seconds to have more reliable dynamic labels.

[6]http://cvml.unige.ch/databases/emoMusic/

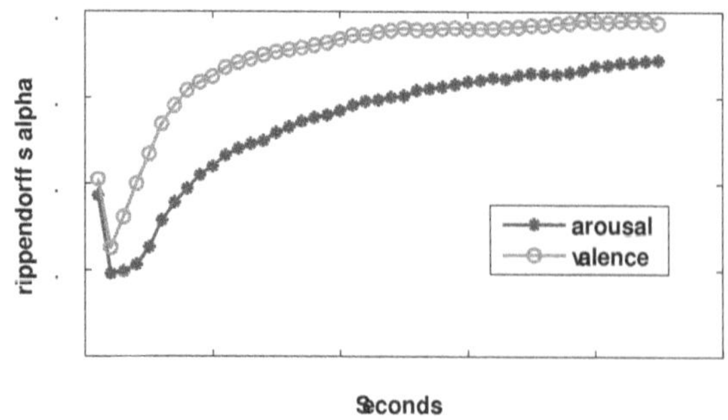

Figure 1: Krippendorff's alpha of dynamic annotations averaged over all dynamic samples.

A mixed linear model was utilized to study the effect of different independent variables on the annotations, once for the static arousal scores and once for the static valence scores. In this model, the independent variables were considered as fixed effect. The independent variables were time of the day, as a nominal variable in hours, and mood scores, as an ordinal variable on four-point scale, assigned to nonwords, e.g., aggressive and energetic. The effect of songs and workers were considered as random effects in the model. We only considered the intercepts to change by the random effects and not the slopes. An analysis of variance (ANOVA) test on the coefficients found some of them to be significantly different from zero and therefore have significant effect on arousal, namely, time of day ($F(23) = 2.35$, $p < 3 \times 10^{-4}$), and energetic ($F(3) = 3.31$, $p < 0.02$) mood score. Mood and time of day did not have any effect on valence.

The averaged dynamic annotations were strongly correlated with the static scores ($\rho_{arousal} = 0.95$ and $\rho_{valence} = 0.94$). Given that the dynamic annotations were done before the static ones this shows that the overall impression of the annotators stayed stable throughout the annotation session.

3. METHODS

The ground truth for the first dynamic task consists of 40 values corresponding to the last 40 seconds of the excerpts, that were averaged across workers. For the static task, we averaged ratings given by the workers to the whole excerpts on both valence and arousal.

To evaluate the estimation models from content features the R^2 statistics and root-mean-square error (RMSE) are reported for static estimation and averaged correlation ($\bar{\rho}$) and RMSE are reported for dynamic estimation. Averaged correlation is a measure of the similarity of the trends and waveforms, whereas the RMSE provides an estimate of how far off the estimations were. The reported measures on dynamic annotated data are averaged for all the excerpts. Random level results are calculated by setting the target to the average score in the development set.

3.1 Baseline method

A simple baseline system was developed by the task organizers to provide a baseline to the participants to beat and compare how well their models are performing. In the following, in conjunction with acoustic feature selection, multivariate linear regression (MLR) was used as the baseline algorithm because of its relatively low computational complexity and its effectiveness. The MLR was trained on the development set and evaluated on the evaluation set.

For the Baseline system we extracted the following features from the audio signals: Mel-frequency cepstrum coefficients, chromagram, octave-based spectral contrast and statistical spectrum descriptors, such as spectral centroid, flux, rolloff and flatness. The Echonest[7] API was used to generate additional timbre, pitch and loudness features.

3.2 TUM system

Technische Universität München (TUM) team's approach is based on supra-segmental features calculated by applying statistical functionals to the contours of frame-wise low-level descriptors (LLDs) over either one-second segments or whole songs. It has been shown in [9] that this set of affective features provides robust cross-domain assessment of emotion (continuous valence and arousal) in speech, music and acoustic events. Despite its rather 'brute-force' nature, it outperformed a hand-crafted set of musically motivated features for MER [9].

The set contains 6,373 features. LLDs include auditory weighted frequency bands, their sum (corresponding to loudness), spectral measures such as centroid, skewness and sharpness. Furthermore, voicing related LLDs such as fundamental frequency (corresponding to 'main melody') and harmonics-to-noise ratio (corresponding to 'percussiveness') are added. Delta regression coefficients are added to capture time dynamics. Statistical functionals include for example mean, moments, quartiles, as well as contour related measurements such as rise and fall times, amplitudes of local maxima, and linear and quadratic regression coefficients. An exhaustive list and a detailed analysis of feature relevance for MER can be found in [9].

TUM used support vector regression (SVR) for song-level regression and bidirectional long short-term memory recurrent neural networks (BLSTM-RNNs) for dynamic regression. In addition, to improve modeling of the dynamic emotion profile, TUM investigated adding delta regression coefficients of the valence and arousal targets as additional regression tasks. The complexity constant for SVR training was varied from 10^{-4} to 10^{-1}. BLSTM-RNNs with two hidden layers (128 LSTM units per layer and direction) were used. Therefore, the first layer performs information reduction to a 128-dimensional feature set. The segments of each song were processed in order, forming sequences. Gradient descent with 25 sequences per weight update was used for training. An early stopping strategy was used, using a held out validation set in each fold. To alleviate over-fitting to the high dimensional input feature set, Gaussian noise with zero mean and standard deviation 0.6 was added to the input activations, and sequences were presented in random order during training. Ten BLSTM-RNN were trained on the ten training folds of the development set; segment level predictions were averaged across networks.

3.3 UAizu system

University of Aizu team (UAizu) proposed the following approach. Features were extracted from excerpts downsampled to 22,050 kHz. UAizu tried various standard features such as MFCC, line spectral pairs, chromagram, timbre features such as spectral centroid, flux and zero crossing rate), spectral crest factor and spectral flatness measure. All feature vectors were calculated using the Marsyas toolbox [8] with 512-sample frames with no overlap. For the dynamic emotion estimation task, first order statistics (mean and standard deviation) of the feature vectors were calculated for a window of about 1 second giving 45 vectors per excerpt. For the static emotion estimation, the same statistics for these 45 vectors were calculated, resulting in a single high dimensional feature vector per song.

Valence and arousal were modeled by separate Gaussian process regression (GPR). UAizu used standard Gaussian likelihood function which allows exact inference to be performed. The GP mean was set to zero and the type of covariance kernel was set a composite function including the sum of squared exponential (SE) and rational quadratic (RQ) function defined as follows:

- `SE`: $k(\mathbf{x},\mathbf{x}') = \sigma^2 \exp(-(\mathbf{x}-\mathbf{x}')^T(\mathbf{x}-\mathbf{x}')/2l^2)$
- `RQ`: $k(\mathbf{x},\mathbf{x}') = \sigma^2(1+(\mathbf{x}-\mathbf{x}')^T(\mathbf{x}-\mathbf{x}')/2\alpha l^2)^{-\alpha}$

where σ and l are parameters learned from the training data.

3.4 UU system

Utrecht University (UU) team used two MATLAB toolboxes, the MIRtoolbox [3] and the PsySound [1], to extract 42 audio features. The features include low-level spectral features, as well as some high level harmonic and rhythmic features such as harmonic change detection function (HCDF) [3], and dynamic loudness (using the model of Chalupper and Fastl [1]). For the dynamic task, the features were extracted from every second of the audio with no overlap; for the static task, the averaged features and their standard deviation was used.

UU discovered some outliers in the data, containing speech, noise and clapping. The most influential ones were removed by calculating Cook's distance for each data point for both valence and arousal regressive models. The outlier points with Cook's $d > 0.05$ both for valence and arousal (4 files) were removed, which increased prediction accuracy.

UU used M5 algorithm to select features. M5 removes the weakest features until no improvement is observed in the estimate of the error given by the Akaike information criterion. For valence, 24 features were selected; for arousal, 27 features out of 42. Among the most important features were loudness (accounted for 44% of variance in case of arousal and 9% of variance in case of valence), spectral centroid, entropy, spectral spread and HCDF.

The dynamic valence and arousal were estimated using SVR with the RBF kernel using WEKA[8], where parameters were optimized manually.

4. RESULTS AND DISCUSSION

All the static and dynamic annotations and subsequently the predictions were scaled between $[-0.5, 0.5]$. A summary of the results is given in Table 1. Both in the static and dynamic task, the arousal estimations are far better than valence estimations. All the RMSE for dynamic estimations of valence and arousal for the three submissions are significantly lower (one-sided Wilcoxon test p-value<0.01) than the random level (averaged training targets) and than the Baseline. The simple Baseline system was able to perform better than random for arousal but fell short of performing

[7] `http://www.echonest.com/`

[8] `http://www.cs.waikato.ac.nz/ml/weka/`

Table 1: To evaluate the estimation models from content features the R^2 statistics and root-mean-square error (RMSE) are reported for static estimation and averaged correlation ($\bar{\rho}$) and RMSE for dynamic estimation. $\bar{\tau}$ is the normalized ranking distance of the retrieved songs using emotions. For RMSE and $\bar{\tau}$, smaller is better and for R^2 and $\bar{\rho}$ larger is better, where RMSE,R^2,$\bar{\tau} \in [0,1]$,$\bar{\rho} \in [-1,1]$. Acronyms: RND: random level, BSL: Baseline

(a) Static

Run	Arousal		Valence		Ranking Dist.
	RMSE	R^2	RMSE	R^2	$\bar{\tau}$
RND	0.16	0	0.15	0	0.43
BSL	0.12	0.48	0.15	0	0.40
TUM	0.10	0.59	0.11	0.42	0.34
UAizu	0.10	0.63	0.12	0.35	0.35
UU	0.10	0.59	0.12	0.31	0.35

(b) Dynamic

Run	Arousal		Valence	
	RMSE	$\bar{\rho}$	RMSE	$\bar{\rho}$
RND	0.25 ± 0.13	0.10 ± 0.33	0.23 ± 0.11	0.05 ± 0.31
BSL	0.25 ± 0.11	0.16 ± 0.36	0.23 ± 0.10	0.06 ± 0.30
TUM	0.08 ± 0.05	0.31 ± 0.37	0.08 ± 0.04	0.19 ± 0.43
UAizu	0.10 ± 0.05	0.11 ± 0.36	0.09 ± 0.05	0.06 ± 0.28
UU	0.10 ± 0.06	0.14 ± 0.28	0.12 ± 0.07	-0.01 ± 0.27

better than random for valence estimation for both static and dynamic subtasks. However, their correlations vary by submissions and emotion dimensions. For the static subtask, all submissions outperformed the provided Baseline. The dynamic subtask appeared to be more challenging and only TUM could consistently beat the baseline performance. The BLSMT-RNN takes advantage of temporal dependencies, which is not supported by MLR, SVR or GPR that was used in the Baseline, UAizu and UU systems.

Although the inter-annotator agreement of valence is higher for the dynamic task, the accuracy of arousal prediction is still higher than that of valence in both static and dynamic tasks, which is consistent with results reported in the literature [2]. The more comprehensive set of features in TUM could outperform the other systems in the static estimation of valence but not arousal. The combination of a large feature set and a recurrent neural network has largely outperformed the other proposed methods for dynamic music emotion estimation. Although it is important to have a model that is intuitive, in practice it is still advantageous to extract a large number of audio features and feed them into a sophisticated machine learning model. UU team also showed that outlier removal and feature selection can improve the performance.

In order to test whether the R^2 and RMSE metrics are representative for real use cases of music information retrieval, we calculated the averaged Kendall Tau $\bar{\tau}$ normalized ranking distance (the smaller the better) of a hypothetical retrieval system as follows. Any given song in the evaluation set was taken as a query by example given to a system that indexes songs based on valence and arousal scores. We then calculated the ranked retrieved results based on their similarity defined by the Euclidean distance of the songs to each other with static valence and arousal scores as features. The ground truth ranking to which the ranking distance was calculated was created based on the ground truth annotations whereas the second ranking was based on the estimated valence and arousal scores by regression models. The results are shown in the last column of Table 1(a). The averaged ranking distances ($\bar{\tau}$) are consistent with the regression evaluation metrics we employed.

From the experience of collecting this dataset we found it important to carefully listen to the audio files to remove outliers and duplicates. Moreover, in order to get a more stable dynamic annotation, we should discard the first few seconds of the annotations; we regret that we only experimented with the case of dropping the first 5 seconds albeit our analysis shows dropping 10 to 20 seconds might be better. Our current study only identifies a few user factors that have some influence on the behavior/preference of the annotators in emotion annotation. In future work, we will explore more factors such as the credential of an MTurk worker, personality traits, gender, age, musical expertise, active musicianship, broadness of taste and familiarity with music.

5. SUMMARY

In this paper, we have presented a comparative study of four systems for automatic music emotion recognition, which employ different feature sets and training schemes. The study is conducted on a novel dataset of substantial size of music dynamically annotated with emotion, with a detailed discussion of the implications of the results. We hope this study can contribute to the advancement of affective analysis in music and other art forms.

6. ADDITIONAL AUTHORS

Michael N. Caro, Drexel University, USA, Florian Eyben, Technische Universität München (TUM), Germany, Konstantin Markov, University of Aizu, Japan, Björn Schuller, TUM/Imperial College London, Germany/UK, Remco Veltkamp, Utrecht University, Netherlands, Felix Weninger, TUM, Germany and Frans Wiering, Utrecht University, Netherlands.

7. REFERENCES

[1] D. Cabrera. PsySound: A computer program for psychoacoustical analysis. *Proc. Australian Acoustical Society Conf.*, pages 47–54, 1999.

[2] Y. E. Kim et al. Music emotion recognition: A state of the art review. In *ISMIR*, 2010.

[3] T. P. Lartillot, O. A Matlab toolbox for musical feature extraction from audio. *Conf. Digital Audio Effects*, 2007.

[4] C. Laurier and P. Herrera. Audio music mood classification using support vector machine. In *MIREX task on Audio Mood Classification*, 2007.

[5] M. Quirin, M. Kazén, and J. Kuhl. When Nonsense Sounds Happy or Helpless: The Implicit Positive and Negative Affect Test (IPANAT). *J. Pers. Soc. Psych.*, 97(3):500–516, 2009.

[6] M. Soleymani et al. 1000 Songs for Emotional Analysis of Music. In *ACM MM*, CrowdMM '13, pages 1–6, 2013.

[7] J. A. Speck et al. A comparative study of collaborative vs. traditional musical mood annotation. In *ISMIR*, 2011.

[8] G. Tzanetakis and P. Cook. Musical genre classification of audio signals. *IEEE Trans. Speech & Audio Processing*, 10(5):293–302, 2002.

[9] F. Weninger et al. On the acoustics of emotion in audio: What speech, music and sound have in common. *Frontiers in Emotion Science*, 4(Article ID 292):1–12, 2013.

[10] Y.-H. Yang and H.-H. Chen. Machine recognition of music emotion: A review. *ACM Trans. Intel. Systems & Technology*, 3(4), 2012.

Clothing Retrieval Based on Local Similarity with Multiple Images

Masaru Mizuochi
The University of Tokyo
mizuochi@mi.t.u-tokyo.ac.jp

Asako Kanezaki
The University of Tokyo
kanezaki@mi.t.u-tokyo.ac.jp

Tatsuya Harada
The University of Tokyo
harada@mi.t.u-tokyo.ac.jp

ABSTRACT

Recently, the online shopping market has been expanded, which has advanced studies of clothing retrieval via image search. For this study, we develop a novel clothing retrieval system considering local similarity, where users can retrieve their desired clothes which are globally similar to an image and partially similar to another image. We propose a method of coding global features by merging local descriptors extracted from multiple images. Furthermore, we design a system that re-evaluates output of similar image search by the similarity of local regions. We demonstrated that our method increased the probability of users finding their desired clothes from 39.7%–55.1%, compared to a standard similar image search system with global features of a single image. Statistical significance is proven using t-tests.

Categories and Subject Descriptors

H.3.3 [**INFORMATION STORAGE AND RETRIEVAL**]: Information Search and Retrieval; I.4.9 [**IMAGE PROCESSING AND COMPUTER VISION**]: Applications

General Terms

Algorithms, Performance

Keywords

garment image search; feature vector coding; local descriptors; user interaction; system design

1. INTRODUCTION

Recently, studies of clothing retrieval via image search have been advanced by expansion of the online shopping market. When users look for their desired garments, it is convenient for them to make a request for improving some part of some selected product. In a store, for instance, users tend to say to a store staff person, "I want a jacket like this one but with a collar like that one", or "I do not like the pocket of this shirt". Nevertheless, it is impossible to retrieve products in such a manner on a conventional online shopping system using global feature-based image search.

MM '14, November 03 - 07 2014, Orlando, FL, USA
Copyright 2014 ACM 978-1-4503-3063-3/14/11 ...$15.00.
http://dx.doi.org/10.1145/2647868.2655021.

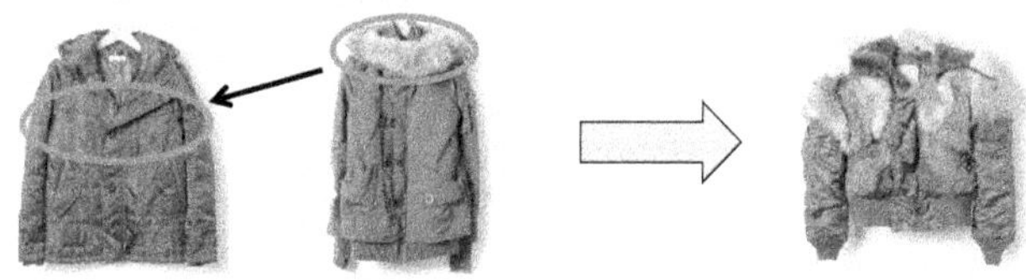

Figure 1: Result of our clothing retrieval system. The retrieved image (right) is globally similar to an input image (left) and partially similar to another image (center). Users can swap different regions of two input images: chest and neck in this example result.

Our objective is to develop a system that retrieves clothing images from a large dataset by considering local similarity of multiple images. To produce this system, we propose a method of coding global features by merging local descriptors extracted from multiple images. Additionally, we design a system which re-evaluates the output of similar image search by similarity of local regions. Our system enables automatic clothing retrieval with multiple images on an online shop, which used to be done manually by store staff. In contrast to a previous work, which replaces a region of an image with the corresponding region of another image [1], our system is able to swap different regions of two input images (see **Figure 1**). The main contributions of our work are the following.

- We develop a novel clothing retrieval system that considers local similarity of multiple images.
- We demonstrate that our method outperformed a global feature based similar image search with statistical significance.

2. RELATED WORK

Previous works have specifically examined unique difficulties of clothing retrieval, which are only slightly considered in general image recognition tasks. Ferrari and Zisserman [2] represents clothes by combinations of attributes that describe various characteristics of clothing images. Chen et al. [3] extracts features of body parts by posing estimation to address significant shape variation caused by a human pose. Background subtraction is also an important problem to recognize snapshots of clothes. Yamaguchi et al. [4] uses similar image retrieval to increase the accuracy of clothing segmentation. With the progress of pose estimation and background subtraction, several works on clothing retrieval from catalogs have appeared. Liu et al. [1] represents clothes in snapshots by several patches segmented via pose estimation. Fu et al. [5] represents clothes as tree structures consisting of body parts and their relative positions. However, these works require indexing of patches

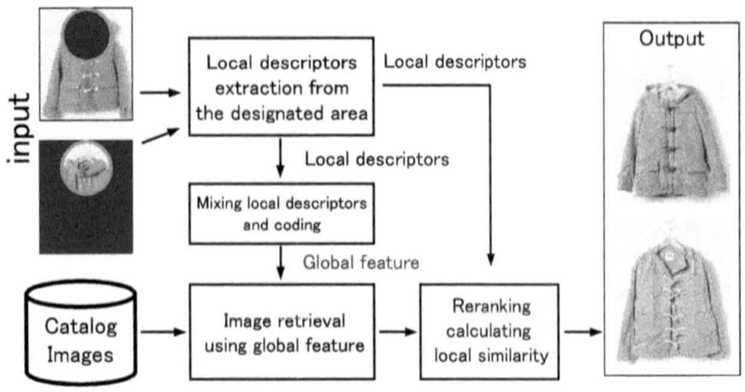

Figure 2: System chart.

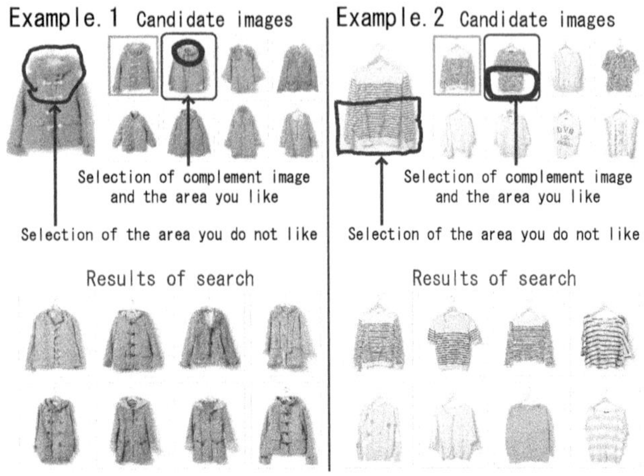

Figure 3: Input and output example.

and region segmentation as a preprocessing. Therefore, they are incapable of dealing with arbitrary user input which strides across multiple patches. Moreover, although Liu et al. [1] enables clothing retrieval which considers local similarity of multiple images, it can only swap a region from an image for the corresponding region from another image.

3. METHOD

In this section, proposed method is described with the **Figure 2**. In the proposed search method, it is assumed that multiple images and the space that is asked as a search result in each image be given as input. First, to perform a search using the global feature, coding to one feature vector is performed by collecting only local descriptors contained in the area specified in each image. At this time, to handle the location information of the features of the garment that is freely deformed correctly, it is proposed to perform the conversion position of the feature points using the skeleton coordinates. Next, the result found by the global feature is re-evaluated using the partial similarity based on the area entered.

The input and output of the proposed system is shown in **Figure 3**. In the each example, the image on the left portrays the input image and the part which the user does not like in the image. The selected region in the right image is an area which the user wants to close the search result. In the left example of output, it is possible to find clothes of a different part of the collar while maintaining the type of coat. Moreover, clothes with short sleeves of the same pattern are made to appear to result in the example on the right.

In the section below, the position conversion to a skeletal coordinate system of local descriptors is shown in 3.1. Coding features using multiple images is shown in 3.2. Re-evaluation of the search result considering the similarity of the local region is described in 3.3.

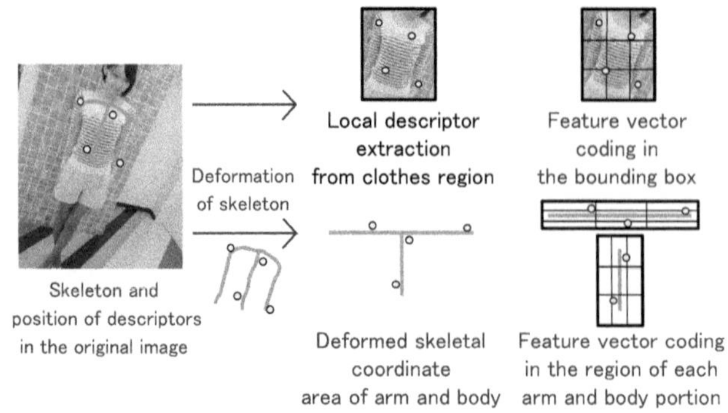

Figure 4: Conversion to a skeletal coordinate system.

3.1 Conversion to skeletal coordinates

Figure 4 represents two kinds of conversions of the position of local descriptors in the proposed skeletal coordinate system and general bounding box. Position conversion into skeletal coordinate system is performed as follows. First, a bone that transforms freely is divided into node n_k, and l_i is the distance of n_i and n_{i-1}. $\boldsymbol{x}$ is the position of local descriptors in the standard coordinate system. In a coordinate system rooted at n_0, position of $\boldsymbol{x}'$ in skeletal coordinate system is represented by the following formula. At this time, $\boldsymbol{x_i}$ and $\boldsymbol{y_i}$ are unit vectors of the coordinate system that is stretched out $\boldsymbol{x_i}$ in the direction of n_{i+1} from n_i. $\boldsymbol{n_i}$ shows the position of n_i in the original coordinate system. At this time, in a coordinate system rooted at n_0, the position in skeletal coordinates $\boldsymbol{x}'$ is represented by the following formula.

$$\boldsymbol{x}' = \Big((\boldsymbol{x} - \boldsymbol{n_t}) \cdot \boldsymbol{x_t} + \sum_{k=1}^{t} l_k\Big)\boldsymbol{x_0} + \Big((\boldsymbol{x} - \boldsymbol{n_t}) \cdot \boldsymbol{y_t}\Big)\boldsymbol{y_0} \quad (1)$$

$$\text{s.t.} \quad t = \arg\min_k \Big(|\boldsymbol{x} - \boldsymbol{n_k}| + |\boldsymbol{x} - \boldsymbol{n_{k+1}}|\Big) \quad (2)$$

3.2 Feature vector coding with multiple images

As the coding technique to the global characteristics of the descriptor for which the position was converted to skeletal coordinate system, Locality-constrained Linear Coding (LLC)[6] is used. In LLC, local descriptors $\boldsymbol{p_i}$ in the image are represented as a combination of neighboring visual words. The respective positions of the local descriptors included in the specified area of the two input image are $\boldsymbol{x_1}, \ldots, \boldsymbol{x_a}, \boldsymbol{x_{a+1}}, \ldots, \boldsymbol{x_{a+b}}$. $\boldsymbol{x}'_1, \ldots, \boldsymbol{x}'_a, \boldsymbol{x}'_{a+1}, \ldots, \boldsymbol{x}'_{a+b}$ are those converted based on skeleton coordinates. a and b are the numbers of descriptors that are included in the respective areas. Feature extraction is conducted using these. Visual words are the centroids obtained by clustering local descriptors of the entire dataset using the k-means. N is the number of visual words. Then they are $\mu_1, \ldots, \mu_N$. When $B = [\mu_{\sigma_1}, \ldots, \mu_{\sigma_K}]$, which includes the K visual words obtained using k Nearest Neighbor (kNN) search is given, coefficient vector $\boldsymbol{\alpha}$ satisfying $\boldsymbol{p_i} \approx B\boldsymbol{\alpha}$ is calculated. For this reason, it is said that LLC is Linear Coding. Descriptor $\boldsymbol{p_i}$ is represented by the following formula using $\boldsymbol{\alpha}$.

$$[\boldsymbol{p_i}]_j = \begin{cases} \boldsymbol{\alpha}_{\delta_j} & (1 \le \delta_j \le K) \\ 0 & (otherwise) \end{cases} \quad (3)$$

δ_j indicates the ranking of the closeness with the j th descriptor $\boldsymbol{p_i}$. Using descriptors obtained $\boldsymbol{p_1}, \ldots, \boldsymbol{p_{a+b}}$, a global feature repre-

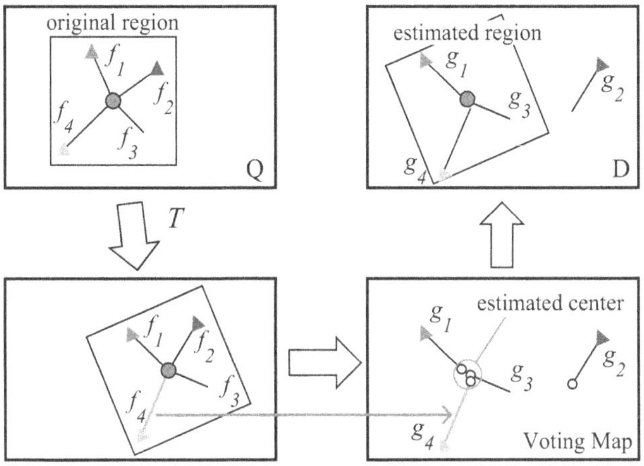

Figure 5: Spatially constrained similarity measure [7].

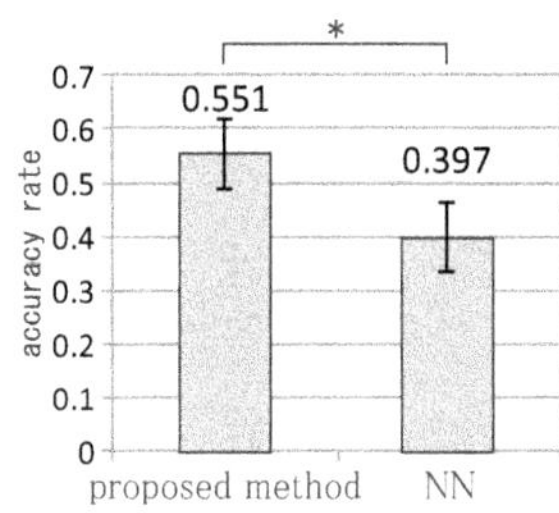

Figure 6: Percentage of correct answers valued by users.

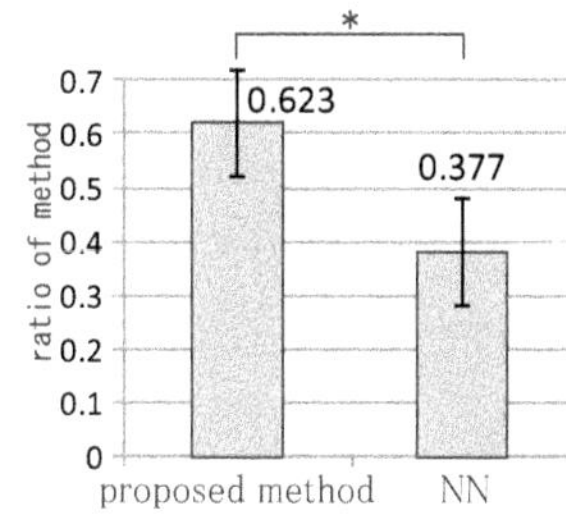

Figure 7: Percentage of each method in correct answers.

senting the entire area is obtained by performing the following max pooling.

$$[\boldsymbol{p}]_j = \max_{i=1,\dots,a+b} [\boldsymbol{p_i}]_j \tag{4}$$

To reduce the search time of the calculation amount, regarding the images in the dataset, it is possible to calculate the feature vector using codebook for each local descriptor. The feature vector is obtained using a combination of descriptors through the process above. The descriptors are obtained from the respective regions in the two images. The search is performed using the feature vector.

3.3 Re-evaluation of the search results

In this section, re-evaluation of the search result by global features using a similarity between each region of the images the user has input is described. As the method to calculate local similarity, a technique called Spatially Constrained Similarity Measure (SCSM) used by Shen et al. [7] is used. An important figure in SCSM was presented in an earlier report **Figure 5**. SCSM explores the place using the grid voting space, called a Voting Map, based on the positional relation of the local descriptors, which have the same code word and which calculates the degree of similarity simultaneously.

The method of calculating the similarity and estimation of similar regions in SCSM is described as follows. In **Figure 5**, when the feature points obtained from the image Q are $f_1, f_2, \dots, f_m$, and the feature points in D are $g_1, g_2, \dots, g_n$, using T obtained degree of similarity D and Q is calculated as follows.

$$S(Q, D|\boldsymbol{T}) = \sum_{k=1}^{N} \sum_{(f_i, g_i) \in X} \frac{idf^2(k)}{tf_Q(k) \cdot tf_D(k)} \tag{5}$$

$$X = \Big((f_i, g_i) | \begin{array}{c} f_i \in Q, g_i \in D \\ \omega(f_i) = \omega(g_i) = k, \\ ||\boldsymbol{T}(L(f_i)) - L(g_i)|| < \varepsilon \end{array} \Big) \tag{6}$$

k represents a visual word in the codebook. N is the codebook size. $\omega(f_i) = \omega(g_i) = k$ denotes that the f_i and g_i are assigned to the same visual word k. $L(f_i)$ and $L(g_i)$ represent the coordinates of f_i and g_i, respectively. In actual calculations, the vote is superimposed on the map divided into a grid for all combinations of feature points that have the same visual word in the two images. The voted position is a point of which the value of a position is the same as the movement vector between the two feature points. Finally, the region which has the highest voting points within the mass represents the projection. At this time, vote points built up in the mass represent the similarity of the two images. When the size of the grid squares is d, and the values of the coordinates of f_i are f_{xi}, f_{yi} respectively, then M as a voting field is found by the following equation if the rotation is not considered.

$$M(x,y) = M(x,y) + 1\Big(x = [\frac{f_{xi} - g_{xj}}{d}], y = [\frac{f_{yi} - g_{yj}}{d}]\Big) \tag{7}$$

4. EXPERIMENT

To evaluate the proposed method considering the local similarity of multiple images, a retrieval system using an image catalog is constructed. The dataset includes about 40,000 images of old top garments displayed in zozotown, a large fashion site[1].

This experiment demonstrates the superiority of the proposed retrieval method by the coding of local descriptors from multiple images. Using two input images (image selected from the candidate image and the original image), the system presents results by mixing the results obtained using the proposed method and the existing method. The user evaluation is conducted by recording which images more closely resemble the target image. In this experiment, the image that is viewed is not fixed. The user performs input freely.

First, subjects selected a single image from a catalog given and specified area they do not like on the image. Moreover, another image and the area in it that they want the result to resemble were selected. At the same time, using a questionnaire, subjects answered what they wanted to do in the search in the description equation. Results of the search using two images as input are displayed with results from two kinds of method mixed randomly. The one method uses the top 10 results obtained using the proposed method. The other one uses the top 10 results obtained by summing the similarity score for the two input images simply. Subjects select zero or more images that are correct as a search result that they asked. Evaluation is performed by specifically addressing how many correct data the results of each method include.

Then 13 subjects repeated each search 6 times using the system. As a local descriptor, three kinds of descriptor were used: RGB-histogram, LBP, and SIFT. Coding to the global features was performed using skeleton coordinate system coding in which backbone sections were divided into the arm portion and a body portion. The pyramid number of Spatial Pyramid Matching (SPM) was $[1 \times 1, 3 \times 1]$. The number of codewords was 1024, and the dimension of each feature became $1024 \times 4 \times 2 = 8192$. Re-evaluation of the search order where the partial similarity was incorporated was performed for the image of the top 10 search results. Therefore, Re-evaluation does not affect the comparison of the two approaches.

Trials were done 78 times. Percentages for images judged by subjects as correct results containing the results of each technique

[1]http://zozotown.com/

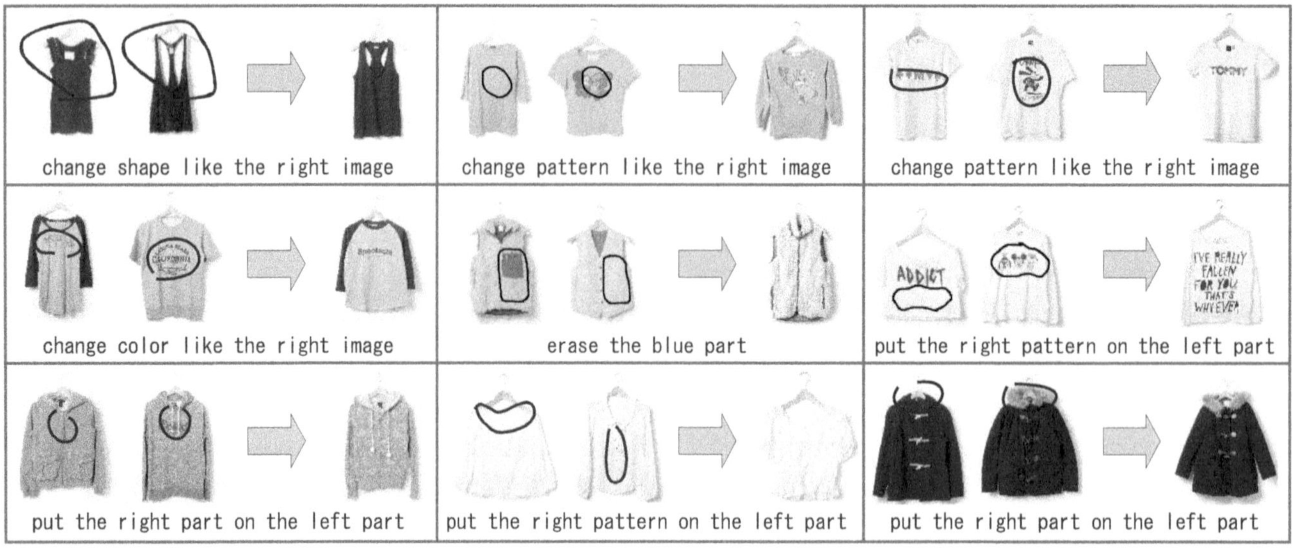

Figure 8: Examples of output. In each example, the left image is a user's input with a disliked region, the middle is a user's input with a liked region, and the right image is an output image that did not appear in the results of the NN, but searched in the top 10 in the proposed method. The sentence under each example is a user's questionnaire about what the user wanted to search.

were 0.551 average in the proposed method and 0.397 in the method using the neighbor searching of the two images (**Figure 6**). This percentage indicates the probability that an image seeking is obtained using the system. Furthermore, the ratios of technique in the image that was selected were 0.623 and 0.377 average (**Figure 7**). About these results, a t-test was performed, then p-values were, respectively, $P = 0.028$, $P = 0.021$. Results show a significant difference between the methods at the 5% level. Finally, the superiority of the proposed method was demonstrated.

Table 1: Reranking by partial similarity.

Rank of the correct data without reranking	5.02
Rank of the correct data with reranking	4.56

In **Table 1**, how the search order was changed by re-evaluation in the proposed method considering partial similarity is shown. The fact that the order of image user has determined the correct answer is raised using a re-evaluation of the similarity of the specified region was confirmed. Examples of results are presented in **Figure 8**. In the figure, an image on the left is an input of the original image. The specified area is the area that the user does not like. Images in the second column are the complement image. What the user evaluated in the final results are images of the third column. They did not appear when using the simple NN. When too small area such as a single button is selected, the search fails, but this method is efficient for the search on the shape and pattern. It is also believed that description by questionnaire survey (in the figure below) conducted before the result comes out matches with the actual results.

5. CONCLUSION

This study proposed a method to perform search coding combining local descriptors by specifying the portion that users do not like in the image and reranking the results calculating the local similarity. We developed a retrieval system incorporating this, and confirmed its usefulness. Through this study, for the search in which there are some areas you want to close locally to multiple images, coding by summation of the local descriptor was confirmed as effective. Additionally, we proposed conversion of the location of descriptors to a skeletal coordinate.

Future issues include calculation of the similarity of clothes image with larger wrinkles and deformation. Furthermore, there is room for improvement in the method selecting the candidate images when choosing the second image in the proposed system. In this experiment, we used results of search using the first image as candidate images. However, to impart diversity to input, it is possible to generate candidate images completely randomly. To provide greater diversity for the designated region, it is possible to perform clustering of the image dataset using the feature extracted only from the region and to present images of the class centers.

6. REFERENCES

[1] Liu, Si and Song, Zheng and Liu, Guangcan and Xu, Changsheng and Lu, Hanqing and Yan, Shuicheng. Street-to-shop: Cross-scenario clothing retrieval via parts alignment and auxiliary set. In Proc. of CVPR. 2012.

[2] Ferrari, Vittorio and Zisserman, Andrew. Learning visual attributes. In Proc. of NIPS. 2008.

[3] Chen, Huizhong and Gallagher, Andrew and Girod, Bernd. Describing clothing by semantic attributes. In Proc. of ECCV. 2012.

[4] Yamaguchi, Kota and Kiapour, M Hadi and Berg, Tamara L. Paper Doll Parsing: Retrieving Similar Styles to Parse Clothing Items. In Proc. of ICCV. 2013.

[5] Fu, Jianlong and Wang, Jinqiao and Li, Zechao and Xu, Min and Lu, Hanqing. Efficient clothing retrieval with semantic-preserving visual phrases. In Proc. of ACCV. 2013.

[6] Wang, Jinjun and Yang, Jianchao and Yu, Kai and Lv, Fengjun and Huang, Thomas and Gong, Yihong. Locality-constrained linear coding for image classification. In Proc. of CVPR. 2010.

[7] Shen, Xiaohui and Lin, Zhe and Brandt, Jonathan and Avidan, Shai and Wu, Ying. Object retrieval and localization with spatially-constrained similarity measure and k-NN re-ranking. In Proc. of CVPR. 2012.

Convolutional Network Features for Scene Recognition

Markus Koskela and Jorma Laaksonen
Department of Information and Computer Science
Aalto University School of Science
PO Box 15400, FI-00076 AALTO, Finland
firstname.lastname@aalto.fi

ABSTRACT

Convolutional neural networks have recently been used to obtain record-breaking results in many vision benchmarks. In addition, the intermediate layer activations of a trained network when exposed to new data sources have been shown to perform very well as generic image features, even when there are substantial differences between the original training data of the network and the new domain. In this paper, we focus on scene recognition and show that convolutional networks trained on mostly object recognition data can successfully be used for feature extraction in this task as well. We train a total of four networks with different training data and architectures, and show that the proposed method combining multiple scales and multiple features obtains state-of-the-art performance on four standard scene datasets.

Categories and Subject Descriptors

H.3.1 [**Information Storage and Retrieval**]: Content Analysis and Indexing; I.4.8 [**Image Processing and Computer Vision**]: Scene Analysis

Keywords

scene recognition; convolutional networks; spatial pyramid; linear classifiers; explicit kernel maps

1. INTRODUCTION

Scene recognition is an important problem in many application areas of image and video processing. A standard approach during the recent years has been to extract several sets of local patch descriptors, encode them into high-dimensional vectors, pool them into an image-level signatures, employ some standard classification algorithm, and possibly use late fusion to combine the results of multiple features. Widely-used encodings have included SIFT bag-of-words with spatial pyramids [11], sparse coding [6, 14], and Fisher vectors [17, 9].

MM'14, November 3–7, 2014, Orlando, Florida, USA.

ACM 978-1-4503-3063-3/14/11 ...$15.00.
http://dx.doi.org/10.1145/2647868.2655024.

Part-based approaches have recently shown high performance in scene recognition [20, 9, 2]. These methods require only weak supervision, that is, no annotations at the parts-level, but only at the class-level. The part-based methods can be considered as extensions of low-level SIFT-type descriptors towards mid-level features that capture more informative visual elements. Another way to see the part-based methods is to view them as extensions of the deformable parts model [5], which has been very succesful in object detection, but where the parts are assumed to have fixed locations, to a more general image classification task.

Another recent development in image classification has been the use of deep convolutional neural networks (CNNs), with excellent results [10, 23, 18, 7]. Still, one drawback with CNNs is that they require huge amounts of training data and delicate tuning of the training parameters. It has, however, been observed that CNNs trained with one visual dataset can function as highly discriminative features even for considerably different data domains and tasks [3, 16, 7].

In this work, CNNs trained with external data and with two different architectures are used as feature extractors in a standard linear-SVM-based multi-feature visual recognition framework for scene recognition. We consider scene recognition to be a particularly interesting task to study using CNNs, as the higher-layer convolutional filters are visually very similar to image parts in part-based methods [23]. We apply our recognition framework to four standard datasets for scene recognition and obtain competitive recognition accuracies, exceeding the current state-of-the-art results, to the best of our knowledge, for all four datasets.

2. RELATED WORK

There has been lots of work done on scene recognition, but we limit the discussion to only the most relevant recent contributions in this section. The Fisher vector encoding can arguably be considered as the current state-of-the-art in local feature based image classification [17, 9]. By measuring the deviation of a sample from a GMM-based generative model in the SIFT descriptor space, one ends up, however, with very high-dimensional image signatures. Comparable results on standard benchmarks have also been obtained using sparse coding [6, 14] and superpixel segmentation [1].

Several part-based methods have recently been proposed as extensions to the methods based on local feature encoding. The part-based methods can be based on training data containing bounding boxes [24] or image-level class annotations [20, 9, 2]. To further increase the classification accuracy, the part-based methods can be combined with local feature encodings, e.g. with Fisher vectors [9, 2].

In particular, the very recent ImageNet classification challenges have been dominated by CNN-based methods [10, 23]. The convolutional networks based on the structure of Krizhevsky et al [10] typically contain five convolutional layers, followed by two fully-connected layers of size 4096 neurons, and the output layer. Existing CNNs, often trained with ImageNet data, have also been used for generic image feature extraction. Several tools exist for this purpose, including OverFeat [18], DeCAF [3], and Caffe [8].

The most similar recent publications to our work are [3, 16, 7]. In [3], a CNN trained with ImageNet 2012 data is applied to object recognition, subcategory recognition, and scene recognition. Our work has been inspired by the scene recognition experiments in [3], as we feel that their baseline classification setup does not fully illustrate the potential of CNN features in this task. The publicly available OverFeat CNN [18], trained with ImageNet 2013 data, is used for several image classification and recognition tasks in [16]. In [7], average, max, and VLAD pooling and multi-scale spatial pyramids are proposed for CNN features, and state-of-the-art results are obtained with several datasets. In this work, we focus on scene recognition. We train several CNNs with different input data and apply a multi-feature recognition framework with hard negative mining [13] and linear SVMs with approximative kernel maps [19], which has been previously succesfully used especially with local features. We compare our features to previous methods based on CNNs, to part-based approaches, and to local feature encodings.

3. SCENE RECOGNITION FRAMEWORK

We extracted four different CNN features from the images. The used CNNs were trained on ImageNet 2010 and 2012 training datasets (about 1.3M images each) using Caffe [8], following as closely as possible the network structure parameters of Krizhevsky et al [10] ("201x-distort" in our notation) and Zeiler & Fergus [23] ("201x-aratio"). Due to different software tools used, our networks are not exact reimplementations. For example, we did not use the convolutional layer RMS renormalization of [23]. The input images for the CNNs were resized to 256×256 pixels, by distorting the aspect ratio for 201x-distort and by cropping the center square for 201x-aratio. A random crop of 227×227 pixels (with a 0.5 probability of horizonal flip) was extracted from input images, and the training data was processed for 90 epochs in mini-batches of 256 (201x-distort) or 128 images (201x-aratio). Due to space constraints, we omit the details of the networks here and point interested readers to [10, 23, 8]. On a 6 GB NVidia GTX Titan GPU card, the training lasted about 7 and 13 days per CNN for 201x-distort and 201x-aratio, respectively.

We use the activations of the first fully-connected layers of each network as our features, as they have been observed to provide the best results (our experiments, and [3, 16]), which results in 4096-dimensional feature vectors. The test images are resized similarly as the training data, and then the center crops of 227×227 pixels are forward-passed through the networks to extract the features. Furthermore, we use the "reverse" spatial pyramid pooling proposed in [7] with two scale levels. Our first level corresponds to the full image, and the second level consists of nine regions of 128×128 pixels with a stride of 64 pixels. The CNN activations of the regions are then pooled using average pooling, and the activations of the different scales are concatenated. The resulting spatial pyramid features are therefore 8192-dimensional.

Table 1: Classification accuracies (and standard deviations) for the scenes-15 dataset

Method	Accuracy	
Lazebnik et al (2006) [11]	0.814 (0.005)	
Sun & Ponce (2013) [20]	0.860 (0.008)	
Zheng et al (2012) [24]	0.863	
Paris et al (2012) [14]	0.870 (0.005)	
Bu et al (2013) [1]	0.894 (0.007)	
Gao et al (2010) [6]	0.898 (0.005)	
	full image	spatial pyr.
2010-aratio	0.887 (0.003)	0.915 (0.003)
2010-distort	0.881 (0.006)	0.908 (0.003)
2012-aratio	0.887 (0.005)	0.913 (0.005)
2012-distort	0.884 (0.006)	0.907 (0.005)
fusion	0.907 (0.003)	**0.921** (0.004)

Table 2: Classification accuracies (and standard deviations) for the uiuc-sports dataset

Method	Accuracy	
Li & Fei-Fei (2007) [12]	0.734	
Gao et al (2010) [6]	0.853 (0.005)	
Sun & Ponce (2013) [20]	0.864 (0.009)	
Zheng et al (2012) [24]	0.872	
Paris et al (2012) [14]	0.877 (0.011)	
	full image	spatial pyr.
2010-aratio	0.935 (0.009)	0.941 (0.007)
2010-distort	0.942 (0.010)	0.944 (0.008)
2012-aratio	0.938 (0.008)	0.946 (0.010)
2012-distort	0.938 (0.011)	0.941 (0.006)
fusion	0.947 (0.010)	**0.948** (0.009)

A one-vs-all linear classifier is trained for each scene category in all experiments, and the scene category with the maximum confidence score is used as the result of the multi-class classification. We apply the homogeneous kernel map approximations of the intersection kernel [21], and use the LIBLINEAR [4] library with the L_2-regularized logistic regression solver. In the fusion experiments, the four features are always late-fused using geometric mean.

4. EXPERIMENTS

We present scene recognition results on four widely used datasets. The Fifteen Scene Categories (*scenes-15*) dataset [11] contains 4485 greyscale images assigned to 15 categories, with 200 to 400 images belonging to each category. We use 100 images per class for training and the rest for testing. The UIUC sports (*uiuc-sports*) dataset [12] contains 8 sports event categories with 137 to 250 images per sports event and a total of 1579 images. We use 70 randomly selected images for training and 60 for testing. For both these datasets, we always use all available negative samples.

The MIT indoor database (*indoor-67*) contains 67 indoor scene categories and a total of 15620 images [15]. On average, 80 images of each class are used for training and 20 for testing. The *sun397* scene benchmark contains 397 scene

Table 3: Averages of per-class classification accuracies for the indoor-67 dataset

Method	Accuracy	
Zheng et al (2012) [24]	0.472	
Bu et al (2013) [1]	0.483	
Sun & Ponce (2013) [20]	0.514	
Razavian et al (2014) [16]	0.584	
Juneja et al (2013) [9] (BoP)	0.461	
(FV)	0.608	
(BoP+FV)	0.631	
Doersch el al (2013) [2] (MLE)	0.640	
(MLE+FV)	0.669	
Gong et al (2014) [7] (full image)	0.537	
(avg pool)	0.656	
(VLAD)	0.689	
	full	s. pyr.
2010-aratio	0.624	0.674
2010-distort	0.601	0.657
2012-aratio	0.627	0.669
2012-distort	0.617	0.657
fusion	0.689	**0.701**

Table 4: Classification accuracies (and standard deviations) for the sun397 dataset

Method	Accuracy	
Xiao et al (2010) [22]	0.380	
Donahue et al (2014) [3]	0.409 (0.003)	
Sánchez et al (SIFT)	0.433 (0.002)	
(2013) [17] (SIFT+LCS)	0.472 (0.002)	
Gong et al (full image)	0.396	
(2014) [7] (avg pool)	0.475	
(VLAD)	0.520	
	full image	spatial pyr.
2010-aratio	0.456 (0.002)	0.503 (0.001)
2010-distort	0.456 (0.004)	0.504 (0.002)
2012-aratio	0.460 (0.002)	0.506 (0.002)
2012-distort	0.454 (0.003)	0.506 (0.003)
fusion	0.519 (0.003)	**0.547** (0.002)

categories and a total 108 756 images [22]. 50 images per category are used for training and for testing. For these datasets, we include two rounds of hard negative mining [13] and sample 1000 negative examples on each round.

For the first two datasets, we use 10 random splits into training and test sets, with *indoor-67* we use the partitions of [15], and with *sun397* we use the same 10 partitions as in [22]. For *indoor-67*, we use average of per-class accuracies (mean of diagonal values of the confusion matrix) as the performance metric. For other datasets, the mean and standard deviation of average multiclass accuracies are calculated.

The results of the experiments are shown in Tables 1–4. For *scenes-15* and *uiuc-sports*, the confusion matrices of the runs achieving the highest accuracies are shown in Figs. 1–2. For *indoor-67* and *sun397*, the detailed results of our experiments can be found at *http://research.ics.aalto.fi/cbir/*.

For all datasets, our results are reported with the four used CNNs and with the full image and spatial pyramid features. In the literature, full image CNN feature results have been reported for *indoor-67* and *sun397* [16, 3, 7]. Our best single features outperform the previously reported results: 0.627 vs. 0.584 [16] for *indoor-67* and 0.460 vs. 0.409 [3] for *sun397*. Using the two-scale pyramid, which doubles the feature dimensionality and requires one to forward-pass several (in our case, ten) image regions through the CNN, further brings a notable performance increase. Overall, the four used CNNs achieve rather similar results, without any clear differences based on either the used architecture or data. Feature fusion systematically improves the results, although the improvement is not as large with the spatial pyramid features. Remarkably, our results with spatial pyramids and feature fusion considerably improve on the best reported results, according to our knowledge, on all datasets.

The SIFT-like local feature encodings can in some sense be considered to form a baseline for any higher-level approaches. On *scenes-15* and *uiuc-sports*, the highest published accuracies, known to us, have been obtained with sparse coding [6, 14]. On *indoor-67* and *sun397*, the best reported accuracies with local features, 0.608 for *indoor-67* [9], and 0.433 for *sun397* (single feature) [17], have been obtained with Fisher vectors. However, these methods result in signature dimensionalities in the order of $O(10^5)$.

The part-based approaches, such as bag-of-parts [9] or [20, 24], have been shown to produce promising results, but often not quite reaching the top-performing local features, except for the mid-level elements [2] in *indoor-67*. Part-based methods can, however, be easily applied as complementary features to local feature encodings to improve the overall recognition accuracy [9, 2] (see Table 3).

The CNN activation features have recently been used to obtain the best known results on the *indoor-67* and *sun397* datasets. The accuracy of the activation features as such (our full image results and [16, 3, 7]) is rather close to the Fisher vectors (whose dimensionality can be almost two orders of magnitude higher). By using multiple scales and concatenating the activations, one can, however, further improve the CNN features. One possibility is to use average pooling, as in our spatial pyramid results and in [7]. It should be noted that we use two scales whereas [7] has three scale levels and a stride of 32, which requires considerably more forward-passes of image regions on a single CNN than our method even with the four CNNs used here. Using a more sophisticated pooling strategy, as the VLAD pooling, including pre- and post-PCA steps to reduce the dimensionality, proposed also in [7], can also improve the results.

5. CONCLUSIONS

The CNN activation features have a great promise as universal representation for various image classification and retrieval tasks. Compared to many existing image signatures, CNN activations are fast to extract, even when applying some kind of a spatial pyramid structure, as the pipeline consist only of image transformations, forward-passes through the CNN, and possible pooling. At the same time, the feature dimensionalities remain modest, especially when compared to e.g. the Fisher vector encoding which in practice requires a separate quantization scheme.

In recent works, part and object based approaches have emerged as a way to construct higher-order models than with SIFT-like local feature encodings. CNN activation features extracted on multiple scales, with the current state-

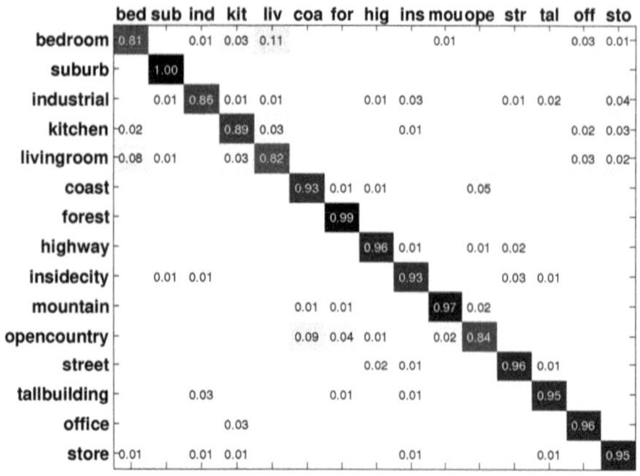

Figure 1: Confusion matrix for the spatial pyramid feature fusion experiment on the scenes-15 dataset

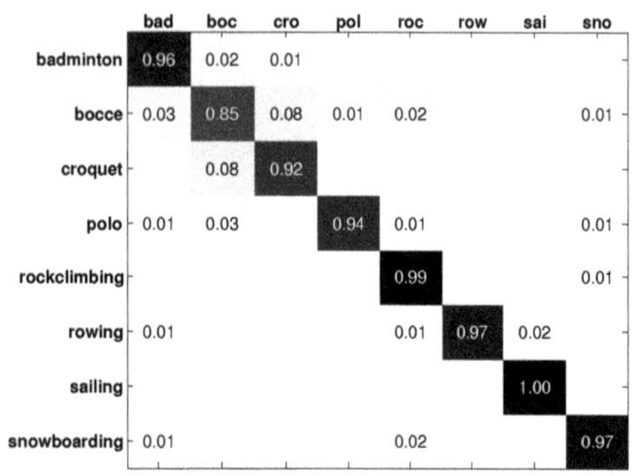

Figure 2: Confusion matrix for the spatial pyramid feature fusion experiment on the uiuc-sports dataset

of-the-art performance reported on several datasets, can be considered as an alternative approach for this purpose.

On the other hand, combining several CNNs can also result in a performance gain as was demonstrated in the experiments of this paper. This has also been observed e.g. in the ImageNet challenges, even when using several networks of identical architecture and trained with the same input data [10, 23]. Even better results can be expected if the variety of the used CNNs would be larger.

6. ACKNOWLEDGMENTS

This work has been funded by the grants 255745 and 251170 of the Academy of Finland, SSP-14183 of EIT ICT Labs, and the D2I SHOK project. The calculations were performed using computer resources within the Aalto University School of Science "Science-IT" project.

7. REFERENCES

[1] S. Bu, Z. Liu, J. Han, and J. Wu. Superpixel segmentation based structural scene recognition. In *ACM Multimedia*, MM '13, 2013.

[2] C. Doersch, A. Gupta, and A. A. Efros. Mid-level visual element discovery as discriminative mode seeking. In *NIPS*, 2013.

[3] J. Donahue, Y. Jia, O. Vinyals, J. Hoffman, N. Zhang, E. Tzeng, and T. Darrell. DeCAF: A deep convolutional activation feature for generic visual recognition. In *ICML*, 2014.

[4] R. Fan, K. Chang, C. Hsieh, X. Wang, and C. Lin. LIBLINEAR: A library for large linear classification. *JMLR*, 9:1871–1874, 2008.

[5] P. Felzenszwalb, R. Girshick, D. McAllester, and D. Ramanan. Object detection with discriminatively trained part-based models. *PAMI*, 32(9), 2010.

[6] S. Gao, I. Tsang, L.-T. Chia, and P. Zhao. Local features are not lonely – Laplacian sparse coding for image classification. In *CVPR*, 2010.

[7] Y. Gong, L. Wang, R. Guo, and S. Lazebnik. Multi-scale orderless pooling of deep convolutional activation features. arXiv.org:1403.1840, March 2014.

[8] Y. Jia. Caffe: An open source convolutional architecture for fast feature embedding. `http://caffe.berkeleyvision.org/`, 2013.

[9] M. Juneja, A. Vedaldi, C. V. Jawahar, and A. Zisserman. Blocks that shout: Distinctive parts for scene classification. In *CVPR*, 2013.

[10] A. Krizhevsky, I. Sutskever, and G. Hinton. ImageNet classification with deep convolutional neural networks. In *NIPS*, 2012.

[11] S. Lazebnik, C. Schmid, and J. Ponce. Beyond bags of features: Spatial pyramid matching for recognizing natural scene categories. In *CVPR*, 2006.

[12] L.-J. Li and L. Fei-Fei. What, where and who? Classifying events by scene and object recognition. In *ICCV*, 2007.

[13] X. Li, C. Snoek, M. Worring, D. Koelma, and A. Smeulders. Bootstrapping visual categorization with relevant negatives. In *IEEE-TMM*, 15(4), 2013.

[14] S. Paris, X. Halkias, and H. Glotin. Sparse coding for histograms of local binary patterns applied for image categorization: Toward a bag-of-scenes analysis. In *ICPR*, 2012.

[15] A. Quattoni and A. Torralba. Recognizing indoor scenes. In *CVPR*, 2009.

[16] A. S. Razavian, H. Azizpour, J. Sullivan, and S. Carlsson. CNN features off-the-shelf: an astounding baseline for recognition. arXiv:1403.6382, March 2014.

[17] J. Sánchez, F. Perronnin, T. Mensink, and J. Verbeek. Image classification with the Fisher Vector: Theory and practice. *IJCV*, 105(3):222–245, 2013.

[18] P. Sermanet, D. Eigen, X. Zhang, M. Mathieu, R. Fergus, and Y. LeCun. OverFeat: Integrated recognition, localization and detection using convolutional networks. In *ICLR*, April 2014.

[19] M. Sjöberg, M. Koskela, S. Ishikawa, and J. Laaksonen. Large-scale visual concept detection with explicit kernel maps and power mean SVM. In *ICMR*, April 2013.

[20] J. Sun and J. Ponce. Learning discriminative part detectors for image classification and cosegmentation. In *ICCV*, 2013.

[21] A. Vedaldi and A. Zisserman. Efficient additive kernels via explicit feature maps. In *CVPR*, 2010.

[22] J. Xiao, J. Hays, K. Ehinger, A. Oliva, and A. Torralba. SUN database: Large-scale scene recognition from abbey to zoo. In *CVPR*, 2010.

[23] M. Zeiler and R. Fergus. Visualizing and understanding convolutional networks. arXiv:1311.2901, November 2013.

[24] Y. Zheng, Y.-G. Jiang, and X. Xue. Learning hybrid part filters for scene recognition. In *ECCV*, 2012.

Perceived Audio Quality for Streaming Stereo Music

Andrew Hines[†*]
andrew.hines@tcd.ie

Eoin Gillen[†]
ogiollae@tcd.ie

Damien Kelly[‡]
damien.kelly@google.com

Jan Skoglund[‡]
jks@google.com

Anil Kokaram[‡]
anil.kokaram@google.com

Naomi Harte[†]
nharte@tcd.ie

[†]Sigmedia, Dept. Electronic and Electrical Engineering, Trinity College Dublin, Ireland
[‡]Google, Inc., Mountain View, California 94043, USA

ABSTRACT

Users of audio-visual streaming services expect an ever increasing quality of experience. Channel bandwidth remains a bottleneck commonly addressed with lossy compression schemes for both the video and audio streams. Anecdotal evidence suggests a strongly perceived link between bit rate and quality. This paper presents three audio quality listening experiments using the ITU MUSHRA methodology to assess a number of audio codecs typically used by streaming services. They were assessed for a range of bit rates using three presentation modes: consumer and studio quality headphones and loudspeakers. Our results indicate that with consumer quality headphones, listeners were not differentiating between codecs with bit rates greater than 48 kb/s ($p>=0.228$). For studio quality headphones and loudspeakers aac-lc at 128 kb/s and higher was differentiated over other codecs ($p<=0.001$). The results provide insights into quality of experience that will guide future development of objective audio quality metrics.

Categories and Subject Descriptors

H.5.5 [**Information Interfaces and Presentation**]: Sound and music Computing

Keywords

Audio Quality; MUSHRA; YouTube; Audio Codec

1. INTRODUCTION

With the rise of YouTube, Netflix, Hulu, Spotify, Pandora and others, it is clear that media streaming has become an established industry. One constant challenge is to deliver an acceptable quality of experience (QoE) [2] across the diverse range of devices on which content is consumed (e.g. mobile, desktop, home theatre) under variable network bandwidth constraints. To accommodate these diverse environments both the video and audio content are transmitted in compressed form using lossy compression schemes. Suitable objective metrics could help automate the evaluation of changes in QoE as a result of this transcoding process. As is well known, the development of these metrics must start with the collection of ground truth quality information. This paper considers two questions in the context of stereo music: i) can the listener perceive differences in the audio quality for the codecs tested and ii) how does presentation mode influence the results, i.e. is the listening hardware a dominant factor over the codec and bit rate? Anecdotal opinions on these issues are pervasive across many internet forums. Headphone listening quality [9], audibility of codec degradations in rooms [14], and codec audio quality [3] have been reported but limited laboratory testing has been published on the interaction between codec and presentation mode for a range of codecs. This paper reports on experiments that provide this ground truth information. A range of codecs and bit rates ("treatments") are examined: aac-he and aac-lc [8] codecs at four bit rates and examples of MP3 and OPUS [16] codecs.

*Supported by Google, Inc. and Enterprise Ireland, Innovation Partnership Project IP-2013 0232.

MM'14, November 3–7, 2014, Orlando, Florida, USA.

ACM 978-1-4503-3063-3/14/11...$15.00.
http://dx.doi.org/10.1145/2647868.2655025.

2. MUSHRA AUDIO QUALITY TESTING

The MUSHRA standard test methodology is defined by ITU-R recommendation BS.1534.1 [13]. During a MUSHRA test, listeners are presented with a labeled reference and a number of unlabelled test samples (stimuli). The listener assigns ratings to the unlabelled samples using a numerical continuous scale ranging from 0 to 100 in five descriptive intervals: bad (0-20); poor (20-40); fair (40-60); good (60-80); and excellent (80-100). An unaltered version of the reference and one or more anchor samples are hidden amongst the treatments under test. The anchors are low-pass filtered versions of the reference. The methodology has been used in a variety of tests showing a good ability to rank low bit rate codecs [10, 7]. Other audio quality test methodologies exist, but for low bit rate codec testing, MUSHRA is a good compromise between an absolute category rating test (e.g. ITU-R BS.1284-1) and a test for almost undetectable impairments (e.g. ITU-R BS.1116-1). Biases in MUSRHA tests have been reported due to stimulus spacing and range equalising effects [18]. A HTML5 user interface for conducting MUSHRA tests via a tablet computer was developed fol-

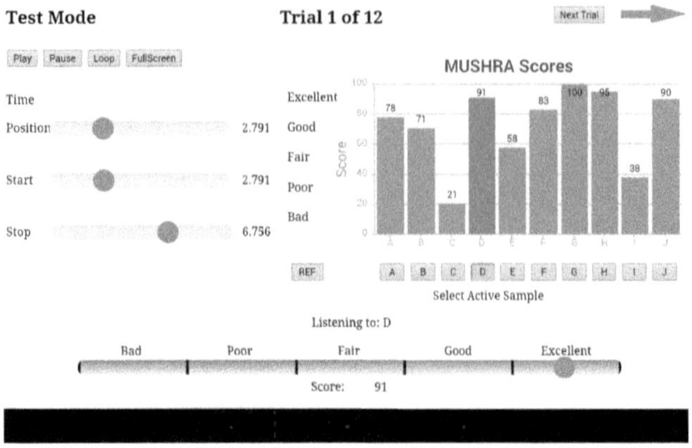

Figure 1: Example of MUSHRA UI screen captured on Nexus 7 tablet

lowing the guidelines set down in the recommendation [13] and is shared for use in research[1]. The layout was adapted to fit within a 7-inch tablet display and to allow touchscreen sliders. The design was altered to replace multiple sliders with a chart which keeps track of the scores assigned in the current trial. A single horizontal score slider below the chart adjusts the score of the currently-active treatment. Treatments are selected using alphabetized buttons below the chart. An example screen is shown in Figure 1. The user interface handles randomisation of the stimuli for presentation during testing. The samples are served from a local web server running on the tablet to remove latency in buffering the samples.

3. METHODS

Experiments were carried out using the MUSHRA test methodology for three presentation modes: loudspeakers and two types of headphones. Stereo music samples of 7 – 15 seconds duration were used covering a variety of musical sounds. Details of the samples can be found in Table 1. The files were all originally sampled at either 48 kHz or 44.1 kHz, 16 bit stereo (so for 44.1 kHz 2-channel audio, the bit rate is 1411.2 kb/s). Reference PCM WAV files were created at 48 kHz for all files. These were then transcoded and resampled using ffmpeg with Fraunhofer aac encoder for aac, libmp3lame for MP3 and libopus for Opus 1.1 to produce a range of treatments that were then formatted as WAV PCM files for presentation. The treatments used are presented in Table 1. There was no perceived level difference between the reference samples and the transcoded treatments. Stereo music clips were used, originating from CDs and the EBU music database [1]. All clips had a sampling frequency of 48 kHz. The first test used 10 samples which matched those used by Hoene et al.[7] in MUSHRA tests to evaluate the OPUS codec. The type of music in each sample is listed in Table 1. The second test kept six of the samples from the first test but replaced 4 samples with 6 alternative samples taken from the EBU database. The substituted samples were replaced with alternatives that are more sensitive to bit-rate reduction and frequency response as indicated in [1]. As in [7], two hidden anchors were used, one lowpass-filtered at 3.5 kHz and one lowpass-filtered at 7.0 kHz. Along with the hidden reference and two anchors, 7

[1]Download available at http://www.sigmedia.tv/tools

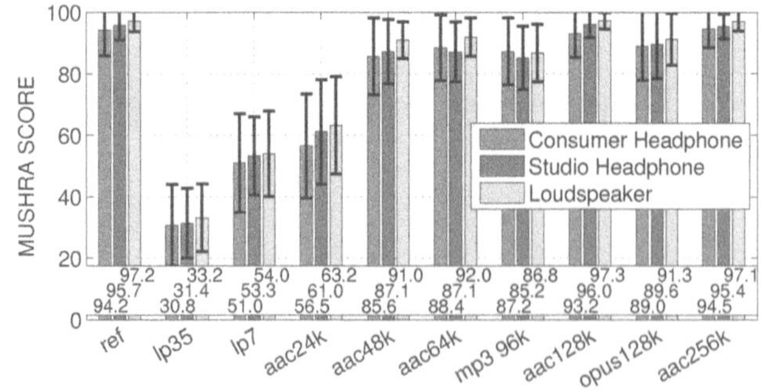

Figure 2: Results by treatment and presentation mode (experiments 1–3) for 6 music samples common to all experiments. Mean values with 95% confidence intervals shown

Table 1: Music Samples

Label	Music Type	Source	Exp.
Boz	Rock/R&B (Boz Scaggs)	CD	1,2,3
Steely	Soft Rock (Steely Dan)	CD	1,2,3
Champs	Rock (Queen)	CD	1
Harry	Jazz (Harry James)	CD	1
Purcell	Classical (Purcell)	CD	1
Electro	Electronica (Matmos)	CD	1
Castanets	Castanets	EBU	1,2,3
Moonlight	Piano (Moonlight Sonata)	CD	1,2,3
Vega	Vocals (Suzanne Vega)	CD	1,2,3
Glock	Glockenspiel	EBU	1,2,3
Bassoon	Arpeggio / Melodious Phrase	EBU	2,3
Harpsichord	Arpeggio / Melodious Phrase	EBU	2,3
Soprano	Soprano singer	EBU	2,3
Guitar	Larry Coryell	EBU	2,3
Ravel	Tzigane	EBU	2,3
Strauss	R. Strauss (Orchestra)	EBU	2,3

treatments were tested, transcoded with a variety of codecs and bit rates. The treatments are listed in Table 2.

Ten expert listeners participated in the tests, which were conducted with one month intervals between experiments. The first experiment was carried out using a laptop in a sound-proofed recording studio. Listeners completed the test individually with a laptop and Superlux HD-668B, over the ear, semi-open back headphones which would be considered to be "consumer quality" (hereafter referred to as consumer). The laptop produced fan noise, raising the ambient noise in the studio from 30 to 39dBA. However, the fan noise was not reported as an issue by participants, possibly due to the partial noise shielding from the headphones. The second test repeated the MUSHRA test using the same 10 listeners listening to the same treatments but with some samples changed (as per Table 1) and using different hardware. The laptop was replaced with a Nexus 7 (2013 edition) tablet and the headphones were replaced with Sennheiser HD558, high-

Table 2: Treatments

Type	Bandwidth	Bit rate (kb/s)
reference	22 kHz/Raw-PCM	1536
anchor 1	3.5 kHz Narrowband	256
anchor 2	7 kHz Wideband	512
mp3	16kHz (SWB)	96 (CBR)
aac-he	20kHz (Fullband)	24
aac-he	20kHz (Fullband)	48
aac-he	20kHz (Fullband)	64
aac-lc	20kHz (Fullband)	128
opus	20kHz (Fullband)	128
aac-lc	20kHz (Fullband)	265

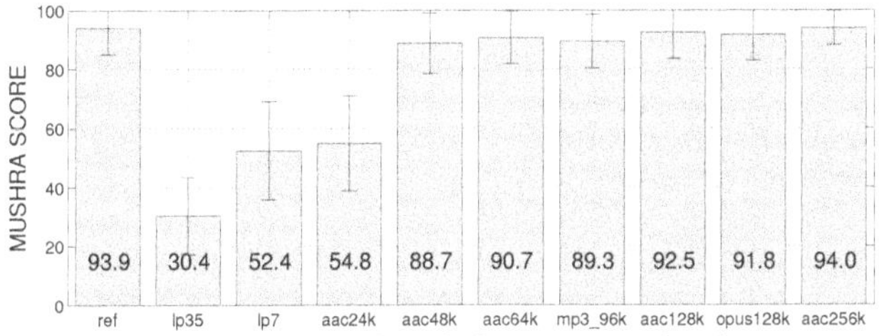

Figure 3: Consumer headphones results by treatment (for 12 music samples and 10 listeners)

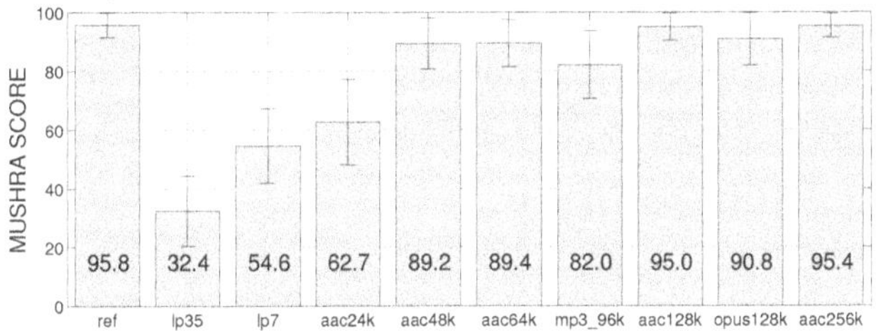

Figure 4: Studio headphones results by treatment (for 12 music samples and 10 listeners)

quality open-backed headphones which would be considered "studio quality" (hereafter referred to as studio). The use of the Nexus tablet eliminated the issue of fan noise which could have posed a problem with open-backed headphones.

A third experiment was conducted using the same materials and listeners as used in the second, but presenting the samples over loudspeakers in a recording studio (hereafter referred to as loudspeaker). The test was conducted using the Nexus 7 tablet MUSHRA test UI connected to a Mackie ONYX 1620 FireWire mixer and presented over Genelec 1031A loudspeakers. The listening point was 1.2m from the loudspeakers and the angle between the loudspeakers was 60 degrees (-30°left; +30°right). Room background noise was measured at 30 dBA and reverberation time was 0.18s at 1kHz, spatially averaged.

4. RESULTS AND DISCUSSION

Figure 2 shows the results for the six music samples that were common to all three presentation modes. The bar charts plot the treatments on the x-axis against the mean MUSHRA scores on the y-axis with 95% confidence intervals.

At first inspection, there is a trend for a modest quality improvement between presentation modes for most treatments with consumer quality headphones having the lowest quality for a given treatment and the loudspeakers having the best quality. There is also a good consistency between experiments for most treatments.

A statistical analysis was carried out using the same technique applied in audio listener tests carried out by the HydrogrenAudio forum [4], i.e. a pairwise resampling-based free step-down analysis using the max(T) algorithm [17, 11]. The consumer headphones showed no statistically significant difference between treatments for aac-he at 48 kb/s and any of the higher bit rate encodings ($p>0.099$ in all cases). For studio headphones and loudspeakers, the aac-lc 128 and 256 kb/s treatments, were still not separable from each other ($p=0.638$ and $p=0.484$ respectively) but have widened the gap over all the other treatments ($p<=0.002$ and $p<=0.033$ respectively). These results reinforce the expectation that the presentation mode is important and lower quality hard-

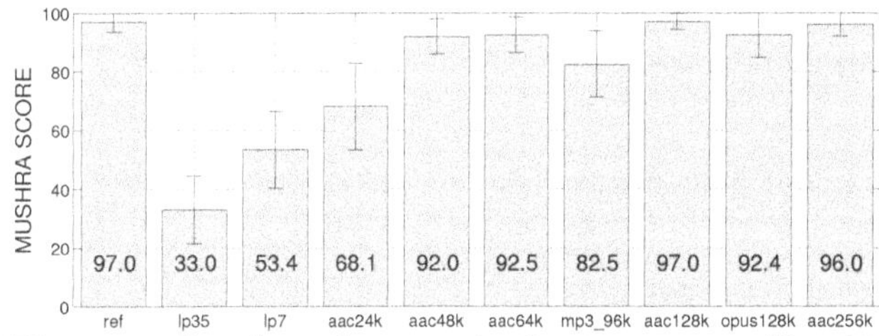

Figure 5: Loudspeaker results by treatment (for 12 music samples and 10 listeners)

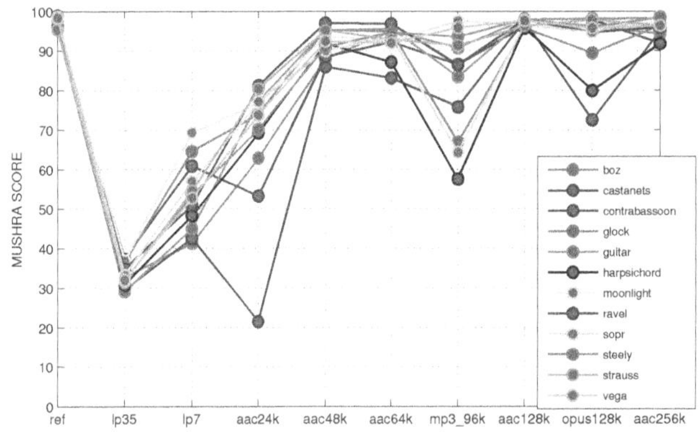

Figure 6: Loudspeaker results breakdown by music sample

ware can mask otherwise perceivable differences between treatment audio quality. However, it should be stressed that the test only compares 3 specific presentation modes labelled with indicative categories (consumer, studio, loudspeaker) and that the quality and frequency response will vary across hardware.

Figure 3 shows result for the consumer headphones, where treatments at bit rates of 48 kb/s and above were not differentiated. Thus this experiment can be excluded for further comparison of treatment quality. Looking at the two other experiments, the results for the studio headphones follow very similar trends to those for the loudspeaker. This can be seen by comparing Figures 4 and 5. Consequently, only the results of the loudspeaker experiment will be used for a detailed analysis of treatments.

The results for the loudspeakers tested with 12 music samples are presented in Figure 5. The treatments can be broken down into a number of sub-groups. Scores for aac-he 24 kb/s were only marginally better than the 7 kHz low-pass anchor, which is not particularly surprising, given the low bit rate was not intended for music presentation. However, a better separation was evident for the higher bit rate codecs. With loudspeakers, listeners' quality perception between aac-he

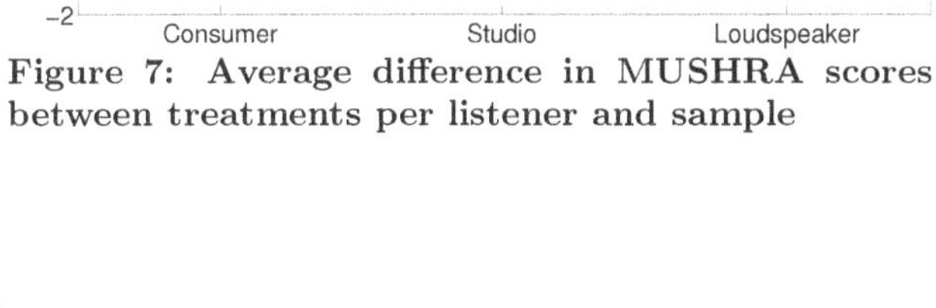

Figure 7: Average difference in MUSHRA scores between treatments per listener and sample

64 kb/s and aac-lc 128 kb/s is evident ($p<0.001$). There was no perceived quality difference for aac-he 64 kb/s over aac-he 48 kb/s ($p=0.965$) and likewise comparing the scores for aac-lc 128 kb/s to aac-lc 256 kb/s ($p=0.484$).

Figure 6 shows a breakdown of the results by sample. The trends remain largely consistent across samples. However, castanets can be seen to be an outlier for acc-he at 24 kb/s as well as MP3 and Opus. A small number of other samples exhibit the same drop in quality for MP3 and Opus as experienced with the castanets sample. This sample is a particularly difficult one for compression algorithms to deal with due to the sharp onset and rolloff times associated with the sound bursts. However, a comparison with the results from [7] showed that Opus performance for the glockenspiel was lower relative to the other samples but not for castanets. An analysis of the parameters used for the Opus transcoding highlighted that the discrepancy was due to a 5ms frame size used by Hoene et al.[7] compared to the ffmpeg default of 20ms used in these tests. Other differences in transcoding parameters were a compression level set to 0 for these tests and a constrained variable bit rate (CVBR) that was not used here. However, this change had a discernible difference in the castanets sample quality when a cursory check was carried out by the authors. The Opus developers have reported the opposite for Opus at 64 kb/s where the quality with 5 ms frames was lower than 20 ms. [15]. This highlights the importance of the codec parameters for some sample types. Conversely, many music samples are robust to a variety of codec parameters. This does call into question the magnitude of the quality difference between aac-lc 128/256 kb/s and Opus 128 kb/s as Opus can potentially be tuned to perform better with other parameters.

To assess the potential of bias due to stimulus spacing and range equalising effects [18], the results were re-analysed to investigate the mean differences between MUSHRA scores for a given treatment. This should show if there is a consistent trend in ranking one treatment higher than the other even if range equalising has occurred for individual listeners. It should also address the problem of tightly bunched stimulus spacing, i.e. having many of the treatments being much closer in quality to the reference than to the anchors. Figure 7 shows the difference between paired treatments for each experiment. The differences are small for all treatments with consumer headphones in experiment 1 and the only trend that changed in experiments 2 and 3 was the difference between aac-he 64 kb/s and aac-lc 128 kb/s.

Initial investigations show that objective measurements need to be treated with caution for low bit rate codec evaluation. Using PEAQ [12] (advanced version, Opticom gmbh), aac-he 24 and 48 kb/s are ranked equally (-3.4 ODG) but aac-lc 128 kb/s is ranked as significantly lower quality than aac-lc 256 kb/s (-2.9 and -2.2 ODG respectively).

5. CONCLUSIONS

The results for consumer headphones showed that the presentation mode can be the dominant factor over treatment type. With low quality headphones there is little difference between the codecs tested above 48 kb/s. The results were bimodal for some codecs and sample types, highlighting that the type of music can be an important factor in whether there is a perceptible quality drop for a given treatment. The parameters used in configuring the codec also matter (i.e. Opus frame size), although the conflicting results point to further investigation being required here. These results indicate that significant bandwidth savings can be achieved given knowledge of listening equipment at the decoder. Practically, if headphones provided a hardware ID-tag input to the playback device and measured the ambient background noise level, the streaming audio codec and bit rate could be adjusted according to the environment. In summary, the choice of codecs and bit rate do matter, but only if the listening equipment is above a quality threshold. These results provide useful insights into the influence of presentation mode, audio sample content, specific codec parameters and bit rates which will inform ongoing work on objective audio metric development, specifically the adaptation of ViSQOL [5, 6] for audio quality estimation.

6. REFERENCES

[1] EBU Tech. 3253-E,Sound quality assessment material. *SQUAM CD (Handbook). EBU Technical Centre Brussels*, 1988.

[2] European Network on Quality of Experience in Multimedia Systems and Services (COST Action IC 1003). Qualinet White Paper on Definitions of Quality of Experience, 2012.

[3] B. Feiten, J. Kroll, A. Raake, M. Wältermann, and U. Wüstenhagen. Evaluation of super-wideband speech and audio codecs. In *Audio Engineering Society Convention 129*, Nov 2010.

[4] H. A. W. Forum. http://hydrogenaudio.org.

[5] A. Hines, J. Skoglund, A. Kokaram, and N. Harte. VISQOL: The Virtual Speech Quality Objective Listener. In *IWAENC*, 2012.

[6] A. Hines, J. Skoglund, A. Kokaram, and N. Harte. Robustness of speech quality metrics to background noise and network degradations: Comparing ViSQOL, PESQ and POLQA. In *Acoustics, Speech and Signal Processing (ICASSP), 2013 IEEE International Conference on*, 2013.

[7] C. Hoene, J.-M. Valin, K. Vos, and J. Skoglund. Summary of opus listening test results – internet-draft. *http://tools.ietf.org/html/draft-ietf-codec-results*, 2012.

[8] ISO/IEC 13818-7:2006. Information technology – Generic coding of moving pictures and associated audio information – Part 7: Advanced Audio Coding (AAC), 2006.

[9] G. Lorho. *Perceived quality evaluation: an application to sound reproduction over headphones.* PhD Thesis, Aalto University, Finland, 2010.

[10] D. Marston and A. Mason. Cascaded audio coding. *EBU Technical Review*, 2005.

[11] G.-C. Pascutto. Bootstrap. www.sjeng.org/bootstrap.html, 2011.

[12] Rec. ITU-R. BS.1387. Perceptual Evaluation of Audio Quality (PEAQ). *International Telecommunication Union*, 1998.

[13] Rec. ITU-R. BS. 1534-1. Method for the Subjective Assessment of Intermediate Sound Quality (MUSHRA). *International Telecommunication Union*, 2003.

[14] D. Schobben and S. van de Par. The effect of room acoustics on mp3 audio quality evaluation. In *Audio Engineering Society Convention 117*, Oct 2004.

[15] J.-M. Valin, G. Maxwell, T. B. Terriberry, and K. Vos. High-quality, low-delay music coding in the opus codec. In *Audio Engineering Society Convention 135*, 2013.

[16] J.-M. Valin, K. Vos, and T. Terriberry. Definition of the Opus Audio Codec. *IETF*, September, 2012.

[17] P. H. Westfall and S. S. Young. *Resampling-Based Multiple Testing: Examples and Methods for p-Value Adjustment. Wiley Series in Probability and Statistics.* John Wiley and Sons, New York, January 1993.

[18] S. Zielinski, P. Hardisty, C. Hummersone, and F. Rumsey. Potential biases in mushra listening tests. In *Audio Engineering Society Convention 123*, 2007.

Discriminating Native from Non-Native Speech Using Fusion of Visual Cues

Christos Georgakis
Dept. of Computing
Imperial College London
cg2212@imperial.ac.uk

Stavros Petridis
Dept. of Computing
Imperial College London
sp104@imperial.ac.uk

Maja Pantic
Dept. of Computing / EEMCS
Imperial College London /
Univ. Twente
London, UK / Enschede, NL
m.pantic@imperial.ac.uk

ABSTRACT

The task of classifying accent, as belonging to a native language speaker or a foreign language speaker, has been so far addressed by means of the audio modality only. However, features extracted from the visual modality have been successfully used to extend or substitute audio-only approaches developed for speech or language recognition. This paper presents a fully automated approach to discriminating native from non-native speech in English, based exclusively on visual appearance features from speech. Long Short-Term Memory Neural Networks (LSTMs) are employed to model accent-related speech dynamics and yield accent-class predictions. Subject-independent experiments are conducted on speech episodes captured by mobile phones from the challenging MOBIO Database. We establish a text-dependent scenario, using only those recordings in which all subjects read the same paragraph. Our results show that decision-level fusion of networks trained with complementary appearance descriptors consistently leads to performance improvement over single-feature systems, with the highest gain in accuracy reaching 7.3%. The best feature combinations achieve classification accuracy of 75%, rendering the proposed method a useful accent classification tool in cases of missing or noisy audio stream.

Categories and Subject Descriptors

I.5.4 [**Computing Methodologies**]: Pattern Recognition—*Applications*; J.m [**Computer Applications**]: Miscellaneous

General Terms

Algorithms, Experimentation

Keywords

Non-Native Speech; Visual-only Accent Classification; Foreign Accent Detection; Visual Speech Processing.

MM'14, November 3–7, 2014, Orlando, Florida, USA.
Copyright 2014 ACM 978-1-4503-3063-3/14/11 ...$15.00.
http://dx.doi.org/10.1145/2647868.2655026.

1. INTRODUCTION

Accent can be identified through a set of pronunciation, articulation, intonation, lexical stress and rhythmic patterns that are common in the speaking style of individuals belonging to a particular language group. Identifying accented speech has emerged as a need to overcome limitations posed by mispronunciations on the efficacy of speech recognisers [4]. Beyond serving as a pre-processing step for speech recognition, accent analysis is essential for applications such as computer-assisted second language learning [14].

Most related work has viewed accent identification as a multiclass classification problem that aims to classify a speech sample to either the native accent of the target language or to one of separately modelled foreign accents. Those approaches mainly use Hidden Markov Models trained on acoustic features, such as prosodic and cepstral features [1]. More recent works [13, 10] have borrowed inspiration from language and speaker recognition to target binary discrimination between native and non-native speech. Shriberg *et al.* [13] employ maximum likelihood regression and phone N-gram features. Omar and Pelecanos [10] use a novel universal background model with Support Vector Machines to detect non-native speakers and their native language.

All the above research on accent classification has ignored features derived from the visual stream. However, the beneficial role of visual information to speech comprehension has been well documented and experimentally validated [12]. Specifically, automated visual-only approaches have been developed for language identification [8]. Another study shows that visual identification of accent is feasible for human observers [5]. These findings indicate that there are visual accent-sensitive cues that can be used to distinguish between native and non-native speakers.

In this paper, subject-independent accent classification experiments are conducted on continuous reading speech samples from the MOBIO Database [7], all captured by mobile phones. Static appearance descriptors are extracted and fed into Long Short-Term Memory Neural Networks (LSTMs) [3] for classification. Our results show that accuracy increases significantly, when accent predictions rely on majority voting from networks that have been separately trained with different appearance features.

2. OVERVIEW OF OUR METHOD

We present a fully-automated solution for discrimination between native and non-native speech in English, using decision-level fusion of visual features. The proposed system is graph-

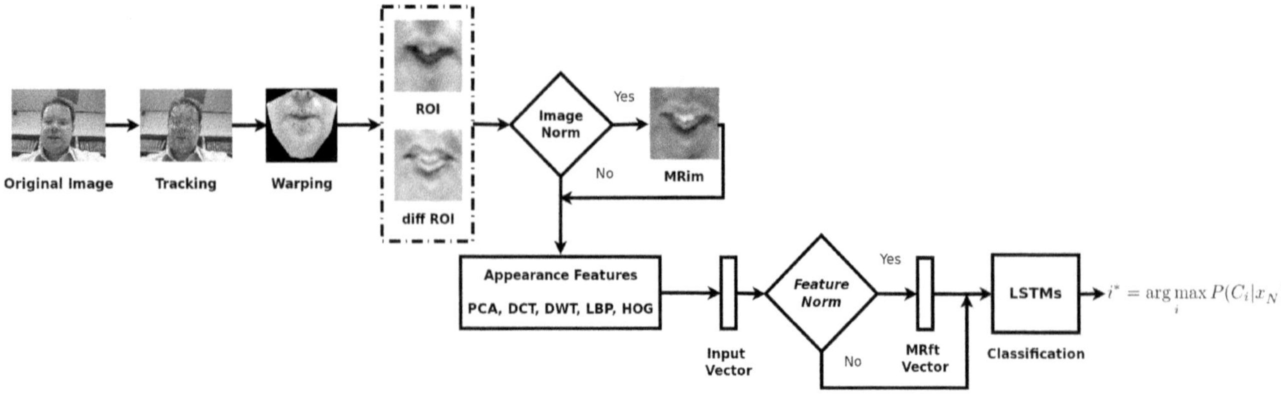

Figure 1: Illustration of the proposed framework for visual-only discrimination between native and non-native speech. The dash-dot line denotes a stage that involves variants, i.e., original or *difference* ROIs.

ically illustrated in Fig. 1. First, a texture warping process yields frontal face images, and the pixel intensities around the lips are used as mouth *Region of Interest* (henceforth termed mouth ROI). In the next stage, we use the mouth ROIs to extract five different appearance features. Different feature normalisation variants are also examined for the appearance descriptors. Finally, static features are forwarded to LSTMs, which assign a single accent label to each sample.

3. DATABASE

The proposed framework is evaluated on speech episodes in English from the MOBIO Database [7], by means of subject-independent experiments. This bimodal database was recorded at six sites in two phases, each comprised of six sessions. For each of the 150 participants, there are totally 192 recordings in English, almost exclusively captured on mobile phones. The visual stream is characterised by high variability in pose and illumination across frames, due to the acquisition device being handheld, while the appearance of subjects and background vary across sessions.

In the current study, we choose to include only the visual speech samples from Phase I in which all subjects read the same text, thus establishing a text-dependent experimental scenario. The data used are balanced over the two classes, with 135 samples belonging to 28 native English speakers and 137 to 28 non-native English speakers. The mean and standard deviation of duration over all samples is 22.5 and 3.4 seconds, respectively. Each video, encoded in variable framerate of mean value 15 fps, is converted in a sequence of still frames. All 272 samples used correspond to utterances of the following paragraph: *"I have signed the MOBIO consent form and I understand that my biometric data is being captured for a database that might be made publicly available for research purposes. I understand that I am solely responsible for the content of my states and my behaviour. I will ensure that when answering a question I do not provide any personal information in response to any question."*

4. STATIC FEATURE EXTRACTION

We initially track 113 characteristic facial points, using the Appearance-Based Tracker [11]. These are manually annotated in the first frame and tracked for the remaining frames. We only use 34 points that correspond to the lower face region, specifically their 2D spatial coordinates (Fig. 2a), along with the coordinates of their pose-free version (Fig. 2b), all provided as a part of the tracker's output. All 34 pose-free points are globally registered according to the location of six base points (see blue points in Fig. 2b), which are relatively invariant to facial deformations.

Next, texture warping is performed to acquire lower face images in frontal view. First, for each frame, two 2D meshes (one for actually tracked points and one for aligned pose-free points), are triangulated. A piecewise affine warp is defined between the corresponding triangles. This warp is then used to map the texture of the mesh in the input image (Fig. 2c), onto the pose-free mesh (Fig. 2d). Each warped lower face is re-sampled to dimension 200×200, and the mouth ROI is extracted as a 94×114 bounding box containing the pixel intensities around the mouth (Fig. 2e). Finally, all mouth ROIs are downsampled to dimension 64×64 (Fig. 2f).

Five different appearance descriptors, all calculated on pixel intensities of the mouth ROIs, are examined; Principal Component Analysis [12], 2D Discrete Cosine Transform [12], Discrete Wavelet Transform [12], Local Binary Patterns [9], and Histograms of Oriented Gradients [2]. For *PCA*, we use those principal components accounting for the 95% of the total intensity variance. For *DCT*, the 2D cosine transform is applied to 8 non-overlapping 32×16 blocks of the ROI. Only four coefficients corresponding to the lowest frequencies are retained for each block and concatenated into a 32-dimensional vector. For *DWT*, ROIs are first rescaled to dimension 16×16, and a Daubechies-4 filter, with 3 levels of decomposition, is used. Our 64-dimensional vector consists of the approximation coefficients of the 3rd level and all the detailed coefficients of the 2nd and 3rd level. For *LBP*, we use the $LBP^{u2}_{(8,1)}$ scheme, which acts in a neighbourhood of 8 pixels on a circle of 1-pixel radius [9]. A 59-bin histogram, encoding the frequency of occurence of the $u2$-"uniform" LBP patterns over the entire ROI, forms our local texture descriptor. For the computation of *HOG*, four orientation bins are used and each ROI is divided into four 32×32 cells, so that dimensionality is comparable to that of the other features (64-element vector).

In order to capture the dynamics of the recorded visual articulations (i.e. changes in the skin appearance around the mouth), even prior to the classification stage, and remove redundant speaker-specific information, we also use *difference ROIs* [6]. These are computed for all frames as the difference in pixel intensities between the current ROI and the

Figure 2: Instances of the ROI extraction process, illustrated on a speech frame from a non-native speaker of MOBIO Database. (a) Actually tracked points, (b) Pose-free points (the 6 base points used for alignment are shown in blue), (c) Triangulated mesh on the lower face image, (d) Triangulated mesh of the aligned pose-free points, (e) Warped frontal lower face and mouth bounding box, (f) Final rescaled mouth ROI.

Table 1: Distribution of Native and Non-Native subjects/samples over the three sets.

	Native	Non-Native	All
Training	14/71	14/65	28/136
Validation	8/32	7/36	15/68
Test	6/32	7/36	13/68
All	**28/135**	**28/137**	**56/272**

ROI at the previous frame. Mean normalisation [12] is also evaluated. The mean feature vector over all speech frames is subtracted from the feature vector of each frame. We call this scheme *mean removal at the feature level (MRft)*. We also examine the alternative of *mean removal at the image level (MRim)* [6], where the mean intensity over the entire utterance is removed from each ROI. Therefore, four different variants for each appearance feature are examined (*MRft, MRim, diffMRft, diffMRim*), with *diff* denoting the use of *difference ROIs*.

5. CLASSIFICATION WITH LSTMS

Long Short-Term Memory Neural Networks (LSTMs) [3] are in principle a variant of traditional recurrent neural networks. They have shown increased ability in capturing contextual statistical regularities in speech, even when those manifest themselves in longer time lags. Their hidden layers contain memory blocks, which are in turn composed of memory cells and three multiplicative gates that perform the operations of write, read and reset.

In the experiments reported in this paper, LSTMs are trained using the RNNLIB Toolbox [3]. The input layer has the size of the input feature vectors, which are corrupted with Gaussian noise of standard deviation 0.6 to improve generalisation. The sigmoid function σ is used for the activation α of the output layer unit, essentially transforming it into the posterior probability $P(C_1|x_n) = \sigma(\alpha)$ for the first accent class (native), where x_n is the feature vector at the n-th frame. Each speech example is classified as either native or non-native according to the value of this score for the vector of the last frame.

In particular, we use networks with one hidden layer. Weights are randomly initialised three times in the range $[-0.1, 0.1]$, and training is done with online gradient descent, with learning rate 10^{-4} and momentum 0.9. The number of blocks in the hidden layer is optimised on the Validation Set in the interval $\{40, 50, \ldots, 180\}$, separately for each feature-normalisation combination. The optimal number of blocks is set to the value yielding the lowest average classification error over the three trials on the Validation Set.

6. EXPERIMENTS

We evaluate the proposed framework by means of subject-independent experiments on visual speech data from MOBIO Database (see section 3). We use exactly 50% of the samples for training. The remaining episodes are equally divided into the Validation Set and the Test Set. All three sets are balanced, in terms of both accent class and gender of the subjects. The distribution of subjects and samples for each class across sets is shown in Table 1.

First, the Validation Set is used to find the optimal LSTM configuration, i.e., the number of blocks in the hidden layer, for each feature-normalisation combination and, subsequently, to reveal the best-performing normalisation for each feature. Results on the Validation Set, in terms of classification accuracy, are presented in Table 2. It is worth noting that more complex networks are needed to model feature vectors that vary less smoothly over time, such as the LBP and HOG local descriptors calculated on the *difference* ROIs (the optimal number of blocks for both $\text{LBP}_{diffMRft}$ and $\text{HOG}_{diffMRft}$ is 180). Furthermore, the *MRim* scheme seems to be more beneficial for features that are more susceptible to registration artefacts and misalignments, such as LBP and PCA. Instead, HOG is not assisted by further image-level processing of the ROIs, since its computation has already catered for intra-ROI illumination normalisation.

The normalisations that account for the highest accuracy percentages (shown in boldface in Table 2), are used for the corresponding features for the Test Set. Results on the Test Set, as yielded by networks trained on a single feature as well as all three- and five-element decision-level combinations, are reported in Table 3. Note that the F1 measure takes similar values for the two classes, indicating that the trained networks are not biased towards one of the classes. LSTMs trained either with DCT or with HOG achieve the highest accuracy of 67.7% amongst the single-feature systems. DCT is well-known for its ability to efficiently encode visual speech dynamics [12]. On the other hand, HOG proves also highly discriminative, presumably thanks to accent-related edge information being captured, such as tale-telling transient features (e.g., bulges and wrinkles). PCA accounts for the lowest accuracy of 60.3%, probably due to its higher susceptibility to registration errors.

The fusion results are obtained by means of majority voting, that is, each test example is assigned to the accent-label predicted by the majority of the three or five networks. As can be seen in Table 3, fusion consistently results in higher accuracy, compared to the single-feature systems. The only exception is the PCA+DCT+DWT combination, which still stays at the same accuracy as that obtained by

Table 2: Results in terms of classification accuracy (%) on the Validation Set of MOBIO speech samples, for the different features and normalisations examined. The accuracy reported for each combination corresponds to the network with the optimal number of memory blocks in the hidden layer, which is shown in the subscript. The best score for each feature among all four normalisations is shown in boldface.

Features/ Normalisations	*MRft*	*MRim*	*diffMRft*	*diffMRim*
PCA	$64.2_{(100)}$	$\mathbf{68.1}_{(70)}$	$65.2_{(100)}$	$66.2_{(70)}$
DCT	$\mathbf{65.2}_{(40)}$	$65.2_{(120)}$	$56.9_{(50)}$	$56.9_{(80)}$
DWT	$67.2_{(70)}$	$67.2_{(130)}$	$\mathbf{71.6}_{(100)}$	$71.6_{(140)}$
LBP	$59.8_{(60)}$	$\mathbf{64.7}_{(60)}$	$61.7_{(180)}$	$60.3_{(60)}$
HOG	$\mathbf{71.6}_{(120)}$	$56.9_{(70)}$	$60.3_{(180)}$	$59.3_{(60)}$

the best-scoring out of the three networks (67.7% by DCT). Fusion leads to higher performance in terms of the other metrics as well (class-wise F1 measures and UAR), in almost all cases. The largest performance boost, in terms of accuracy, over the single-feature schemes, amounts to 7.3%, and is furnished by both the PCA+DCT+LBP and PCA+DCT+HOG combinations. This highlights that those features capture complementary accent-sensitive information in the visual stream. Thus, a projection onto prominent modes of intensity variance (PCA), a block-based frequency decomposition (DCT), and a local descriptor unveiling local texture (LBP) or edge orientation information (HOG), train LSTMs that act efficiently in synergy for the target problem. The five-network combination does not provide additional gain, probably due to redundant information being carried by the couples (DCT, DWT) and (LBP, HOG).

7. CONCLUSION

In this paper, we presented a visual-only approach to discriminating native from non-native speech in English, based on fusion of neural networks trained on visual features. Overall, our results on fixed-content speech episodes provide evidence that accent in speech can be accurately identified when sequential classifiers, trained on complementary appearance descriptors, are combined to yield predictions. We intend to examine how our visual-only framework compares to an identical audio counterpart and experiment with multimodal fusion schemes. We also plan to investigate alternative ways of sequential modelling.

8. ACKNOWLEDGMENTS

This work has been funded by the European Community 7th Framework Programme [FP7/2007-2013] under grant agreement no. 611153 (TERESA). The work of S. Petridis is also supported in part by EPSRC grant EP/H016988/1: Pain rehabilitation: E/Motion-based automated coaching.

9. REFERENCES

[1] L. M. Arslan and J. H. Hansen. Language accent classification in American English. *Speech Com.*, 1996.

[2] N. Dalal and B. Triggs. Histograms of oriented gradients for human detection. In *IEEE CVPR*, 2005.

[3] A. Graves. RNNLIB: A recurrent neural network library for sequence learning problems. http://sourceforge.net/projects/rnnl/.

Table 3: Results on the Test Set of MOBIO speech samples, reported as percentages: Class-wise F1 measure (F1-N for Native, F1-NN for Non-Native), Unweighted Average Recall (UAR), and Classification Accuracy (Acc.), for the various single-feature LSTMs as well as fusion of three and five of them. The highest value achieved for each metric is shown in boldface.

Features	F1-N	F1-NN	UAR	Acc.
PCA	69.7	42.6	62.3	60.3
DCT	67.7	67.7	67.9	67.7
DWT	62.3	69.3	65.8	66.2
LBP	62.3	69.3	65.8	66.2
HOG	65.6	69.4	67.5	67.7
PCA + DCT + DWT	70.3	64.5	68.4	67.7
PCA + DCT + LBP	77.3	72.1	75.9	**75.0**
PCA + DCT + HOG	**77.9**	71.2	**76.0**	**75.0**
PCA + DWT + LBP	70.3	64.5	68.4	67.7
PCA + DWT + HOG	71.2	66.7	69.8	69.1
PCA + LBP + HOG	72.5	71.6	72.4	72.1
DCT + DWT + LBP	70.8	73.2	72.1	72.1
DCT + DWT + HOG	71.0	**75.7**	73.3	73.5
DCT + LBP + HOG	71.6	72.5	72.2	72.1
DWT + LBP + HOG	67.7	73.0	70.3	70.6
All	76.1	73.9	75.5	**75.0**

[4] V. Gupta and P. Mermelstein. Effects of speaker accent on the performance of a speaker-independent, isolated-word recognizer. *J. Acoust. Soc. Am.*, 1982.

[5] A. Irwin, S. Thomas, and M. Pilling. Identification of language and accent through visual speech. In *Speech Prosody*, 2007.

[6] P. J. Lucey. *Lipreading across multiple views*. PhD thesis, 2007.

[7] C. McCool et al. Bi-modal person recognition on a mobile phone: using mobile phone data. In *IEEE ICMEW*, 2012.

[8] J. L. Newman and S. J. Cox. Language Identification Using Visual Features. *IEEE Trans. on Audio, Speech, and Language Processing,*, 20(7):1936–1947, 2012.

[9] T. Ojala, M. Pietikainen, and T. Maenpaa. Multiresolution gray-scale and rotation invariant texture classification with local binary patterns. *IEEE Trans. on PAMI*, 2002.

[10] M. K. Omar and J. Pelecanos. A novel approach to detecting non-native speakers and their native language. In *IEEE ICASSP*, 2010.

[11] J. Orozco, O. Rudovic, J. Gonzàlez, and M. Pantic. Hierarchical On-line Appearance-Based Tracking for 3D Head Pose, Eyebrows, Lips, Eyelids and Irises. *Image and Vision Computing*, February 2013.

[12] G. Potamianos, H. P. Graf, and E. Cosatto. An image transform approach for HMM based automatic lipreading. In *IEEE ICIP*, 1998.

[13] E. Shriberg, L. Ferrer, S. Kajarekar, N. Scheffer, A. Stolcke, and M. Akbacak. Detecting nonnative speech using speaker recognition approaches. In *Proc. IEEE Odyssey Speaker and Language Recognition Workshop*, 2008.

[14] F. William, A. Sangwan, and J. H. L. Hansen. Automatic Accent Assessment Using Phonetic Mismatch and Human Perception. *IEEE Trans. on Audio, Speech & Lang. Proc.*, 2013.

A Framework of Mobile Visual Search Based on the Weighted Matching of Dominant Descriptor

Guoyu Lan, Heng Qi, Keqiu Li, Kai Lin
School of Computer Science and Technology
Dalian University of Technology
Dalian, China

Wenyu Qu, Zhiyang Li
School of Information Science and Technology
Dalian Maritime University
Dalian, China

ABSTRACT

As a kind of interesting mobile application, Mobile Visual Search (MVS) has attracted extensive research efforts from both academy and industry. Most of the MVS systems adopt the client-server framework, in which transmission latency caused by the limited bandwidth in wireless network is a big problem. To address this problem, the state-of-the-art work focuses on designing low bit-rate descriptors for MVS. However, few work focuses on reducing the number of descriptors. To further reduce the latency, we propose a novel framework of MVS based on the weighted matching of dominant descriptor. Firstly, we present an affinity propagation based algorithm for dominant descriptor selection. Secondly, we propose a weighted feature matching method to consider the differences of dominant descriptors in feature matching. By the proposed framework, we not only reduce the network latency in MVS, but also avoid transmitting useless descriptors to improve the retrieval accuracy of MVS. The experimental results on Stanford MVS data set show that when using CHoG descriptors, the proposed framework outperforms the existing framework by reducing more than 40% of the amount of data transmission and increasing 5% of the average retrieval accuracy.

Categories and Subject Descriptors

H.3.3 [**Information Storage and Retrieval**]: Information Search and Retrieval

Keywords

Dominant descriptor; Weighted matching; Mobile visual search

1. INTRODUCTION

Nowadays, Mobile Visual Search (MVS) has been a very popular mobile application [6]. With MVS applications, we can take pictures by the mobile devices as the queries to search similar images or related information. Therefore, we can use such applications for the landmark identification [4], the interested object recognition [11], the product comparison [7], and so on. Generally, MVS applications adopt the client-server framework in which the real-time response subjects to the processing time on the client, the transmission time over the network, and the processing time on the server. Existing work shows that compared to the processing on the client and on the server, the network transmission is usually the bottleneck in MVS [11][10]. Thus the state-of-the-art work of MVS focuses on designing low bit-rate descriptors to reduce the amount of transmission data achieving low network latency [9].

We classify the existing methods for designing low bit-rate descriptors into two kinds. The first kind of methods is to compress raw descriptors by dimensionality reduction [8] or hash coding [7]. The second kind of methods is to design low bit-rate descriptors directly with compression in mind [3]. Although these low bit-rate descriptors ensure the low network latency, there are still two problems as follows:

- When there are a large number of descriptors extracted from the query image, the amount of transmission data is still large. For example, there are 433 SURF descriptors (SURF is one kind of popular low bit-rate descriptor for MVS [1]) extracted from the image shown in Fig 1(a). Because one SURF descriptor is 64 bytes, the total amount of transmission data is almost 27 KB. How to further reduce the amount of transmission data is a problem.

- For a given query image, different descriptors make different contributes for searching. For example, the SURF descriptors extracted from the book in the image shown in Fig 1(a) are critical for searching. The descriptors extracted from the background are useless, even they are noise affecting the retrieval accuracy. How to avoid transmitting useless descriptors should be studied.

To address the above problems, we propose a novel framework of MVS based on the weighted matching of dominant descriptor. When using the proposed framework, we only transmit some dominant descriptors selected from all descriptors of the query image, thereby we can reduce the amount of transmission data and the number of useless descriptors. For example, as shown in Fig 1(b), there are 115 dominant SURF descriptors selected from 433 SURF descriptors. The amount of transmission data is reduced by more than 70%. Moreover, we can see that many useless descriptors extracted from the background are removed.

MM'14, November 03 - 07 2014, Orlando, FL, USA

http://dx.doi.org/10.1145/2647868.2655028.

(a) Original SURF descriptors (b) Dominant SURF descriptors

Figure 1: Examples of original SURF descriptors and the dominant SURF descriptors (This figure is best viewed in color vision).

The proposed framework consists of two parts. The first part is dominant descriptor selection (DDS). We design the DDS algorithm based on Affinity Propagation (AP) [5], in which dominant descriptors can be selected by exchanging similarity values between descriptors. The second part is weighted feature matching. We compute the weighted values of dominant descriptors to represent their differences in feature matching. In this paper, we conduct extensive experiments on the "Stanford Mobile Visual Data Set". The experimental results show that when using CHoG descriptor, the proposed framework outperforms the existing framework by reducing more than 40% of the amount of data transmission and increasing almost 5% of the average retrieval accuracy.

The rest of this paper is organized as follows: we first propose the framework of MVS based on the weighted matching of dominant descriptor in Section 2. Then, we evaluate the proposed framework by experiments on public image data set in Section 3. Finally, we draw conclusions in Section 4.

2. THE PROPOSED FRAMEWORK OF MVS

As shown in Fig 2, the proposed framework consists of the client and the server. On the client side, we firstly extract local feature descriptors from the query image. Then, we perform dominant descriptor selection algorithm to select dominant descriptors. Finally, the client transmits the dominant descriptors to the sever over a wireless network. On the sever side, when receiving the dominant descriptors from the client, we can compute the similarities between the query and the images in the database by feature matching. Based on the similarities ranking, the final retrieval results can be got. The server returns the final retrieval results to the client.

Generally, the feature matching is to find the nearest neighbor of each query descriptor among all descriptors extracted from images in database. The similarity between the query and arbitrary image in the database dependents on the number of the nearest neighbors. For example, if k nearest neighbors of query descriptors are found in the image I, the value of similarity between the query and the image I is k. In the proposed framework, the dominant descriptors are used for searching. Because different dominant descriptors represent different number of other descriptors, we should consider the differences of dominant descriptors in feature matching. In this paper, we propose weighted feature matching for dominant descriptors. We compute weight values to represent the importance of dominant descriptors, thereby we can refine the results of feature matching.

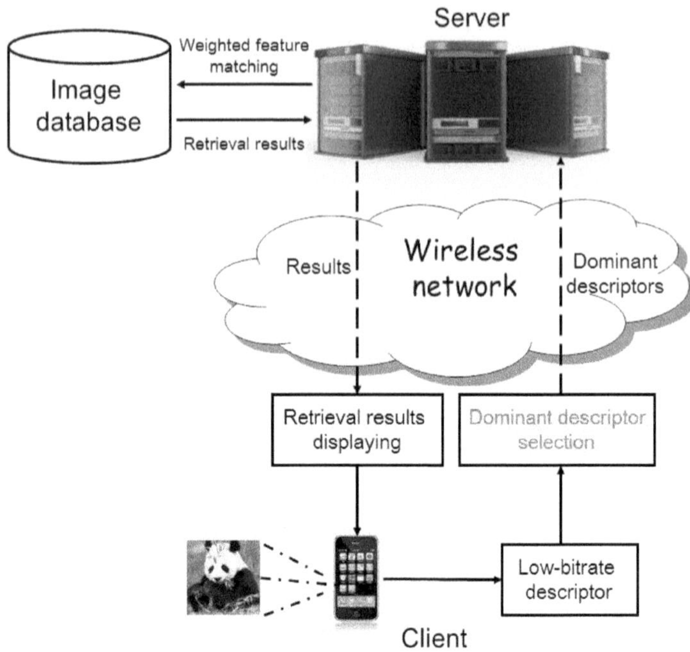

Figure 2: The framework of MVS based on weighted matching of dominant descriptor.

2.1 Dominant Descriptor Selection Algorithm

To select dominant descriptors from a set of descriptors, we proposed an effective algorithm based on the Affinity Propagation (AP) [5]. As shown in Alg. 1, the DDS algorithm is an iteration process. Firstly, we compute the similarities between any pairs of descriptors in the given set by Eq. 1.

$$s(i,j) = - \parallel d_i - d_j \parallel^2, \tag{1}$$

in which d_i and d_j denote two descriptors, and $s(i,j)$ denotes the similarity between d_i and d_j. Secondly, we compute two kinds of messages for exchanging between descriptors. One is "responsibility" denoted by $R(i,j)$, which is sent from the descriptor d_i to descriptor d_j. $R(i,j)$ indicates how well-suited descriptor d_j is to become the dominant descriptor from the view of descriptor d_i. Another is "availability" denoted by $A(i,j)$, which is sent from the descriptor d_j to descriptor d_i. $A(i,j)$ indicates how appropriate it would be for descriptor d_i to select descriptor d_j as the dominant descriptor, taking into account of the support from other descriptors that select d_j as the dominant descriptor. These two kinds of messages are exchanged between descriptors until a high-quality set of dominant descriptors and corresponding clusters gradually emerges or the maximum number of iteration is reached. Finally, we can get a set of dominant descriptors after iteration.

Algorithm 1: The dominant descriptors selection algorithm

Input : $S = \{d_i, 1 \leq i \leq n\}$: a set of local feature descriptors;
m: the maximum number of iteration.
Output: S_d: a set of dominant descriptors.

Computing the similarity matrix S in which $s(i,j)$ is the similarity between d_i and d_j;
Initialization of "responsibility" and "availability" messages: $R(i,j) = 0$ and $A(i,j) = 0$;
for $1 \leq$iter$\leq m$ **do**
  for $1 \leq$i$\leq n$ **do**
    for $1 \leq$j$\leq n$ **do**
      $R(i,j) = s(i,j) - \max_{j' s.t. j' \neq j}\{A(i,j') + s(i,j')\}$;
      if $i \neq j$ **then**
        $A(i,j) = \min\{0, R(j,j) + \sum_{i' s.t. i' \notin \{i,j\}} \max\{0, R(i',j)\}\}$;
      else
        $A(j,j) = \sum_{i' s.t. i' \neq j} \max\{0, R(i',j)\}$;
      $A(i,j) = s(i,j) - \max_{j' s.t. j' \neq j}\{A(i,j') + s(i,j')\}$;
  for $1 \leq$i$\leq n$ **do**
    Solving the problem of $\max_{k s.t. 1 \leq k \leq n}\{R(i,k) + A(i,k)\}$.;
    Putting d_k into the S_d.;
  if $|S_d|_{iter} == |S_d|_{iter-1}$ **then**
    Break;

2.2 The Weighted Feature Matching

Because different dominant descriptors represent different number of other descriptors, we should consider the differences of dominant descriptors in feature matching. Motivated by this, we propose a weighted feature matching method, in which we consider both the importance of dominant descriptor and the distance between dominant descriptor and its nearest neighbor for the exact feature matching. The proposed method consists of five steps as follows:

1. When one descriptor d_i is represented by the dominant descriptor d_k, we define the representation degree of d_k for d_i. Based on the "responsibility" and "availability" messages in DDS algorithm, we can compute the representation degree $P_{i,k}$ as follows:

$$P_{i,k} = \frac{R(i,k) + A(i,k)}{R(k,k) + A(k,k)}. \tag{2}$$

If $i == k$ it means d_k represents itself, thus the representation degree equals 1. If $i \neq k$, $0 \leq P_{i,k} \leq 1$.

2. When each descriptor d_i in one descriptor set C_k is represented by the dominant descriptor d_k, we define the importance of d_k as the summation of all representation degrees $P_{i,k}$. We can compute the importance of d_k denoted by P_k as follows:

$$P_k = \sum_{d_i \in C_k} P_{i,k}. \tag{3}$$

3. In feature matching, we can find the nearest neighbor of d_k. Supposed that d'_k is the nearest neighbor of d_k, the distance between them denoted by D_k can be computed by Euclidean distance.

4. To realize feature matching exactly, we compute a weight value of d_k based on P_k and D_k. The weight value is: $W_k = \frac{P_k}{D_k}$. Then we need to normalize the weight value as follows:

$$W_{k^*} = \frac{W_k}{\sum_{k=1}^{N_d} W_k}, \tag{4}$$

in which N_d denotes the total number of dominant descriptors.

5. Given one query image q, N_d^q denotes the number of dominant descriptors in q, and $W_{k^*}^q$ denotes the normalized weight value of dominant descriptor d_k in q. The final similarity between q and an arbitrary image I in the database is computed as follows:

$$S = \sum_{k=1}^{N_d^q} s_k, \tag{5}$$

in which if the nearest neighbor of d_k is found in the image I, $s_k = W_{k^*}^q$, else $s_k = 0$. According to similarities ranking, we can get the final results.

3. EXPERIMENTS AND PERFORMANCE EVALUATION

In experiments, we select Stanford Mobile Visual Search (SMVS) data set [2] which is popular in existing work of MVS [12]. Compared to other state-of-the-art data sets in computer vision, SMVS data set is built for MVS experiments specially. It consists of the reference images and the query images. The reference images are high quality JPEG compressed color images. The query images are captured by different mobile devices, such as IPhone 4, Palm, Nokia phone, Canon camera, and so on. For image representation, we use Speed Up Robust Features (SURF) [1] and Compressed Histogram of Gradients (CHoG) [3] in experiments, which are the state-of-the-art low bit-rate descriptors in MVS.

Firstly, we compare the amount of data transmission in the proposed framework and the framework without DDS. The amount of data transmission is measured by the average query size, which is the product of the size of one descriptor and the average number of the descriptors in the query. Fig.3 shows the average query size of differen categories in the data set. We can see that the average query size is smaller when transmitting dominant descriptors, especially for SURF descriptors.

Then, we measure the average retrieval accuracy (Accuracy) and the average query size (Size) of all images in SMVS data set. The results are shown in Tab.1. We can see that the proposed framework is better than the framework without DDS. When using SURF descriptor, the proposed framework outperforms the framework without DDS by reducing 85% of the amount of data transmission and increasing almost 1% of the average retrieval accuracy. When using CHoG descriptor, the proposed framework outperforms the framework without DDS by reducing more than 40% of the amount of data transmission and increasing almost 5% of the average retrieval accuracy. We can see that the transmission rate and the accuracy are improved simultaneously without transmitting some useless descriptors.

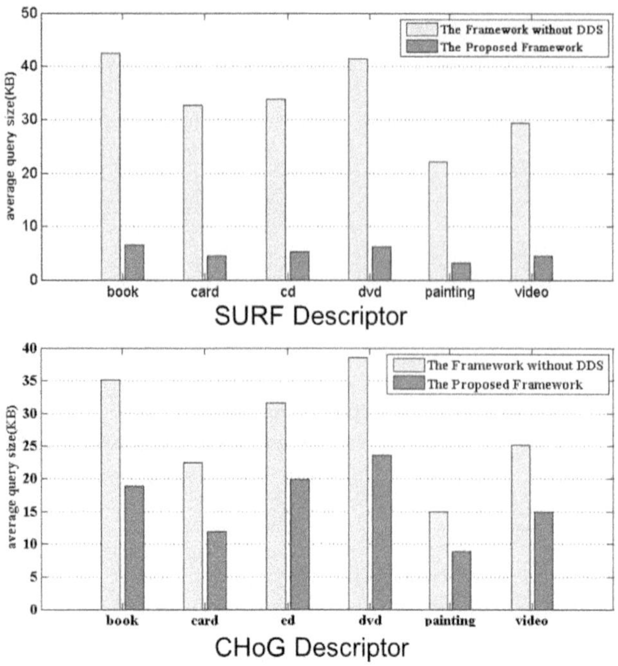

Figure 3: The average query size when using SURF and CHoG descriptors.

Table 1: Comparison of the proposed framework and the existing framework (without DDS)

	SURF		CHoG	
	Accuracy	Size	Accuracy	Size
Existing Framework	86.7%	34.5 KB	80.8%	28.2 KB
Proposed Framework	87.6%	5.2 KB	85.7%	16.5 KB

4. CONCLUSIONS

In this paper, we propose a framework of Mobile Visual Search (MVS) based on the weighted matching of dominant descriptor. The framework consists of dominant descriptor selection and weighted feature matching. By the dominant descriptor selection, we can not only reduce the amount of transmission data to achieve the low network latency, but also eliminate the useless descriptors for searching to improve the retrieval accuracy. By the weighted feature matching, we can incorporate the differences and the importance of dominant descriptors in feature matching. Experiment results on Stanford MVS data set show that the proposed framework achieves significant improvements over the existing framework. In the future work, we will combine the proposed framework and the bag of visual words model to realize large scale MVS.

5. ACKNOWLEDGMENTS

This work is supported by the National Science Foundation for Distinguished Young Scholars of China (Grant 61225010); NSFC Grants 61173161, 61173162, 61173165, 61300187, 61300189, and 61370199; China Postdoctoral Science Foundation funded projects 2013M530916 and 2014T70248; the Fundamental Research Funds for the Central Universities DUT13ZD101 and DUT13JS04.

6. REFERENCES

[1] H. Bay, T. Tuytelaars, and L. V. Gool. Speeded-up robust features (surf). *Computer Vision and Image Understanding (CVIU)*, 110:346–359, 2008.

[2] V. Chandrasekhar, D. M. Chen, S. S. Tsai, N. M. Cheung, H. Chen, G. Takacs, Y. Reznik, R. Vedantham, R. Grzeszczuk, J. Bach, and B. Girod. The stanford mobile visual search data set. *In Proceedings of the 2nd ACM Conference on Multimedia Systems (MMSys)*, pages 117–122, 2011.

[3] V. Chandrasekhar, G. Takacs, D. M. Chen, S. S. Tsai, Y. Reznik, R. Grzeszczuk, and B. Girod. Compressed histogram of gradients: A low-bitrate descriptor. *International Journal of Computer Vision (IJCV)*, 96:384–399, 2012.

[4] D. M. Chen, G. Baatz, K. Koser, and et.al. City-scale landmark identification on mobile devices. *In Proceedings of the 2011 IEEE Computer Society Conference on Computer Vision and Pattern Recognition (CVPR)*, pages 737–744, 2011.

[5] B. J. Frey and D. Dueck. Clustering by passing messages between data points. *Science*, 315:972–976, 2007.

[6] B. Girod, V. Chandrasekhar, D. M. Chen, N. M. Cheung, R. Grzeszczuk, Y. Reznik, G. Takacs, S. S. Tsai, and R. Vedantham. Mobile visual search. *IEEE Signal Processing Magazine*, 28:61–76, 2011.

[7] J. He, J. Feng, X. Liu, T. Cheng, T. H. Lin, H. Chung, and S. F. Chang. Mobile product search with bag of hash bits and boundary reranking. *In Proceedings of the 2012 IEEE Computer Society Conference on Computer Vision and Pattern Recognition (CVPR)*, pages 1–8, 2012.

[8] Y. Ke and R. Sukthankar. Pca-sift: A more distinctive representation for local image descriptors. *In Proceedings of the 2004 IEEE Computer Society Conference on Computer Vision and Pattern Recognition (CVPR)*, pages 526–513, 2004.

[9] Y. C. Su, T. H. Chiu, Y. Y. Chen, C. Y. Yeh, and W. H. Hsu. Enabling low bitrate mobile visual recognition: a performance versus bandwidth evaluation. *In Proceedings of the 21st ACM International Conference on Multimedia (MM)*, pages 73–82, 2013.

[10] S. S. Tsai, D. M. Chen, V. Chandrasekhar, G. Takacs, N. M. Cheung, B. Girod, R. Vedantham, and R. Grzeszczuk. Mobile product recognition. *In Proceedings of the 18th ACM International Conference on Multimedia (MM)*, pages 1587–1590, 2010.

[11] S. S. Tsai, D. M. Chen, J. Singh, and B. Girod. Rate-efficient, real-time cd cover recognition on a camera-phone. *In Proceedings of the 16th ACM International Conference on Multimedia (MM)*, pages 1023–1024, 2008.

[12] J. Xia, K. Gao, D. Zhang, and Z. Mao. Geometric context-preserving progressive transmission in mobile visual search. *In Proceedings of the 20th ACM International Conference on Multimedia (MM)*, pages 953–956, 2012.

Efficient Cross-Domain Image Retrieval by Multi-Level Matching and Spatial Verification for Structural Similarity

Che-Chun Lee[†‡*], Yin-Hsi Kuo[†], Winston H. Hsu[†], Shin'ichi Satoh[‡], Sebastian Agethen[†]
[†]National Taiwan University, Taipei, Taiwan and [‡]National Institute of Informatics, Tokyo, Japan

ABSTRACT

Content-based image retrieval (CBIR) technique is important for browsing the rapidly growing Web images. However, traditional CBIR methods usually fail when the query and database images are in different domains. Instead of focusing on a specific domain, we propose a method to solve the general cross-domain image retrieval problem. This method focuses on the structure of image content but not the detail at pixel level, so it is particularly useful for matching the images across different visual domains e.g., paintings, hand-drawn sketches or photographs. To provide an efficient and effective solution, we analyze the bag-of-words (BoW) matching procedure to find out what causing it to fail in the cross-domain setting. We observe that it is necessary to apply different matching constraints for cross-domain image retrieval; therefore, we propose a multi-level matching process which dynamically selects the most suitable matching constraint for feature matching and adopt a fast spatial verification to describe the structure similarity. Finally, our method is much faster than the state-of-the-art solution and achieves better performance in the experiments.

Categories and Subject Descriptors

H.3.3 [**Information Storage and Retrieval**]: Information Search and Retrieval—*Retrieval models*

Keywords

cross-domain; image retrieval; spatial verification; multi-level matching

1. INTRODUCTION

Efficiently retrieving similar images from vast Web images is essential but very difficult. In the past few years, the bag-of-words (BoW) model [15] has shown promising results for content-based image retrieval. Meanwhile, recent work further proposes more robust image retrieval results by designing better matching criteria [7][9], spatial verification methods [13][16], or feature representations [1][5][6][12].

*Part of the work was conducted during Che-Chun Lee's internship supported by NII International Internship Program.

MM'14, November 3–7, 2014, Orlando, Florida, USA.

http://dx.doi.org/10.1145/2647868.2655032 .

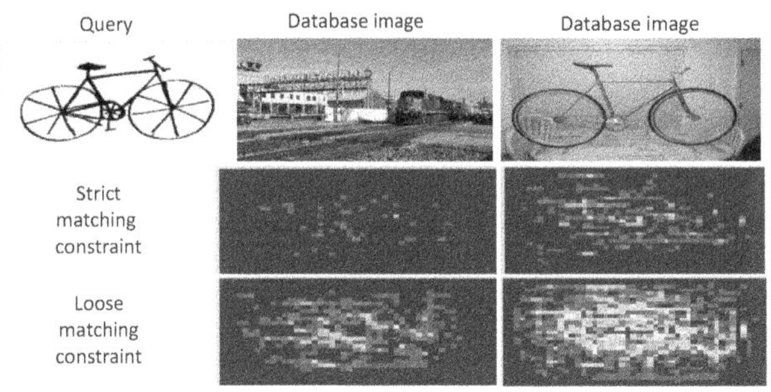

Figure 1: For cross-domain image retrieval, it is hard to retrieve target images (right) by adopting the state-of-the-art approach (strict matching constraint, i.e., more fine codewords) because their details are different. However, we observe that the spatial consistency is more obvious in the offset space (Section 3.3) if we relax the matching constraint (i.e., more coarse codewords).

However, most of them might fail when the query image and database images are in different domains. A domain means a method to represent an object such as painting, sketch or photograph (cf. Figure 1). The most challenging part in cross-domain image retrieval problem is the same target may be different in pixel level such as the two bicycle images in Figure 1. For cross-domain image retrieval, recent work mainly focuses on two particular domains. For example, using paintings to find the photographs [11] or using sketches to find photographs [2]. Nevertheless, these methods are very domain-specific. They are designed to fit a particular domain and difficult to generalize for others. However, Web images are always coming from different domains and it is necessary to propose a general solution for retrieving diverse (across domains) image retrieval results.

The state-of-the-art approach proposes a data-driven solution [14] which learns different weights on patches of a query image. This method focuses on finding the important parts in the query image. They attempt to define the visual similarity function for each query by "data-driven uniqueness." This function (classifier) is trained by one query (positive data) and lots of background images (negative data). The most discriminative parts (patches) from all background images will be paid most attention in the function (i.e., higher similarity scores). It improves the performance notably; however, the online training process is too slow for interactive applications.

To tackle the challenge, we propose an effective and efficient general framework for cross-domain image retrieval. The key idea is the structure of the target object should be spatially consistent even if their visual appearance is quite different. As shown in Figure 1, matched local features between the query and target image are more consistent in all (strict and loose) matching constraints. If we relax the

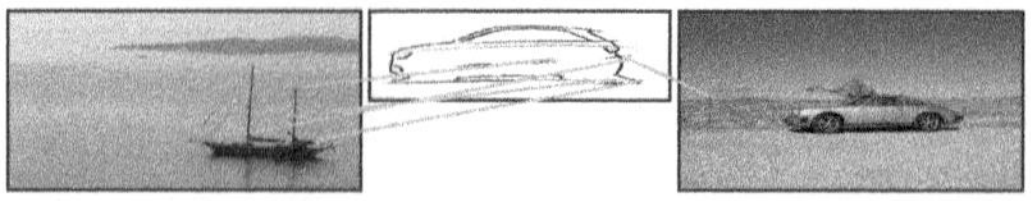

Figure 2: A real example of cross-domain image matching (orange lines mean the matched pairs). A too strict matching constraint (BoW model with 1 million codewords) cannot match the corresponding local features in cross-domain setting.

constraint properly (i.e., adopting more coarse codewords), the consistency will be more obvious. That is to say, the matching constraint (e.g., the granularities of codewords) should be dynamically adjusted to different domains for better image retrieval results. According to this observation, we propose a multi-level matching process which dynamically selects a matching constraint (codeword granularity) to put all different domains on an equal footing and solve the cross-domain problem by comparing their spatial consistency. Finally, we achieve competitive performance as the state-of-the-art data-driven method while the proposed method retains much higher efficiency.

This paper is organized as follows: we describe our observation for cross-domain image retrieval in Section 2. Then, the proposed method is introduced in detail in Section 3. Section 4 shows the performance comparison of our method and the state-of-the-art approaches. Finally, Section 5 concludes our work.

2. OBSERVATIONS

To design an efficient and effective general framework for cross-domain image retrieval, we analyze the problems in the state-of-the-art retrieval method. In the BoW model, each image is described by some local features first. Next, each local feature is quantized to a visual word (VW) by assigning it to the nearest centroid in the codebook. If two local features (one in the query and another in the database image) are quantized to the same visual word, they are considered as a matched pair. After this matching step, they rank database images by the quantity of matched pairs weighted by inverted document frequency. Finally, they further rank the top list by the spatial verification (e.g., RANSAC [4]).

BoW model has shown promising retrieval performance; however, we find that the matching step might fail when we apply to two different domains. As shown in Figure 2, there are only few matched pairs under the cross-domain setting. The problem is that the matching constraint is too strict to match the corresponding local features in different domains. The matching constraint means the distance threshold to decide whether two features are matched. It is decided by the size of codebook. In practice, this codebook is generated by clustering lots of local features to one million groups (codewords). This matching constraint provides enough discriminative power to find the target image in the traditional setting, but it is too strict in the cross-domain setting. However, we cannot find a best and constant constraint in general cross-domain setting because the distance between corresponding local features depends on which domains they are in.

For solving this problem, we relax the strict matching constraint to get the same quantity of matched pairs in all database images. In this step, we use different constraints (i.e., adaptive and hierarchical codeword numbers) to put different domains on an equal footing (cf. Figure 1). Then, all images are ranked by the spatial consistency of matched

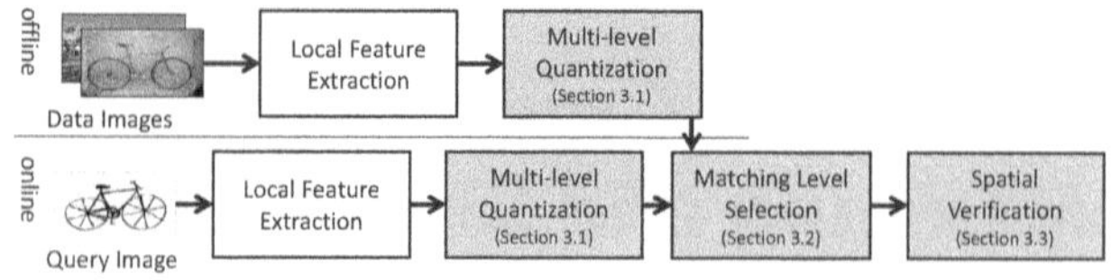

Figure 3: The system flow of our method. Comparing with BoW model, there are three different parts (marked in gray): (1) Multi-level Quantization, (2) Matching Level Selection, and (3) Spatial Verification.

pairs. It is worth mentioning this spatial information is totally lost in the BoW model because the corresponding local features are not matched in the previous step. In contrast, we reserve more possible (low confident) matched pairs first and then verify them by spatial information.

There are three problems we will face when we implement this idea. The first is "how to match local features in many different constraints fast?" The second is "how to choose the matching constraint?" The third is "how to rapidly estimate the spatial consistency of many low confident matched pairs?" We will introduce our solution in details in next sections.

3. PROPOSED METHOD

Instead of designing better feature representations [1][6], we attempt to improve the traditional BoW approach for cross-domain image retrieval. Therefore, our framework is extended from the BoW model, and it can further combine with other existing work. As shown in Figure 3, there are three different parts in our framework to solve the problems we mentioned in the last section.

3.1 Multi-level Quantization and Matching

As aforementioned section, to obtain enough matched pairs for cross-domain images, a direct but slow method to get N matched pairs in all database images is computing distance of all local feature pairs and then choosing the top K pairs in each database image. However, this method is too slow to fit the needs of retrieval task. Instead of that, we use hierarchical k-means (HKM) [10] to build our codebook and use the quantization result in different levels to approximate different matching constraints. HKM is an approximate method of K-means. It is usually used for speeding up the codebook construction and assignment. Comparing with K-means, HKM splits all data into B clusters first and then splits data in the same cluster recursively. After L iterations, we can obtain B^L clusters from all data. If we not only use leaf clusters but also the whole tree, it is just like we build L different codebooks (with different granularities) with size $B^1, \ldots, B^L$.

To efficiently evaluate whether two features are matched in the same level, we encode each leaf cluster by following depth-first order. If any two features are matched, the upper digit will be the same when we represent the cluster number in base-B numeral system. For example, 2 and 7 are 002_3 and 021_3 in base-3 numeral system respectively. Only the first digit is the same so these features are matched at level one. We can use boolean expression $\lfloor \frac{VW_1}{B^n} \rfloor = \lfloor \frac{VW_2}{B^n} \rfloor$ to examine whether they are matched. If it is true, VW_1 and VW_2 are matched at $L - n$ level where L is total levels in the HKM. Moreover, this examination can be accelerated by shift operation when the B is 2.

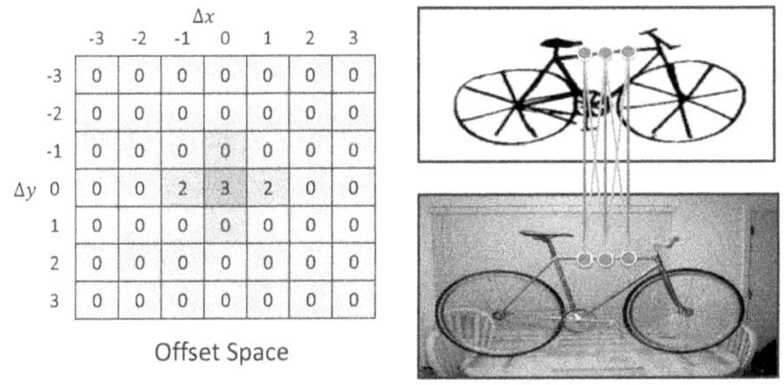

Figure 4: Offset space helps us to find spatially consistent matched pairs efficiently. Although using box filter directly might cause over counting problem (Section 3.3), we can solve it by calculating the matched ratio in the query.

3.2 Matching Level Selection

After encoding each local feature with multi-level quantization step, we apply the dynamic matching level selection process to all images. For putting all images on an equal footing and reserving enough matched pairs (cf. Figure 1), we attempt to get the same quantity of matched pairs in all database images. However, we cannot guarantee they are absolutely the same, because we use an approximate method in the matching step. Based on the multi-level quantization, we examine each level from loose to strict (the first level to the last level). That is to say, when we use coarse level gradually, the number of matched pairs will decrease gradually too. We select the level whose matched pairs are just less than the target quantity. The target quantity (C) is chosen by experiment. We test it from 1 to 13 times of query feature (with dense SIFT (D-SIFT) and 2^{20} HKM). Finally, the best performance is achieved when the quantity is 10 times.

3.3 Spatial Verification for Structural Similarity

After the matching step, we rank all images by their spatial consistency. RANSAC [4] (using in BoW model) is a very general spatial verification method. It can estimate many types of transform, but it becomes very time-consuming when the inlier ratio is low. To obtain enough matched pairs between images in different domains, we relax the matching constraint in the previous step and reserve many low confident matched pairs. Therefore, the traditional RANSAC algorithm might not be suitable for our proposed method. Motivated by the prior work [13][16][17], we utilize the offset space to verify the spatial consistency and further refine the scoring method for better retrieval accuracy.

Offset Space: As shown in the Figure 4, the offset space is the matched pairs' distribution by their difference of feature position (x, y). For example, a matched pair is composed of a query local feature at position $(10, 6)$ and a database local feature at position $(5, 2)$. Then, this pair will be counted in cell $(5, 4)$ in the offset space because $\Delta x = x - x\prime = 10 - 5 = 5, \Delta y = y - y\prime = 6 - 2 = 4$. In other words, each cell in the histogram means a hypothesis of translation transform. The value in cell $(\Delta x, \Delta y)$ means the number of local features in a query image can be matched when we move them $(\Delta x, \Delta y)$, so the ceil with maximum value is the hypothesis that most matched pairs agree on. Finally, for a query image, the maximum value in the offset space indicates the degree of spatial consistency for each database image.

Box Filter: We can utilize the offset space to efficiently calculate the most possible hypothesis; however, only choosing one cell in the offset space may be too strict. There are some corresponding local features shifted a little and can be matched within one step. Hence, we attempt to refine the original scoring method by considering its neighbor cells (i.e., top, bottom, left and right cells as shown in the orange regions in Figure 4) at the same time. We apply a box filter to the original offset space and choose the maximum value as the final score. However, we observe that the performance might become worse because the repeated patterns will be counted multiple times. As the right figure in Figure 4, there are only three corresponding features (the red lines) should be counted in, whereas there are four mismatched pairs (blue lines) besides the correct pairs and the maximum value will becomes 7. Meanwhile, when similar local features appear continually, this problem will become more serious. Therefore, we further propose a matched query ratio in the next paragraph to mitigate this problem and retain the property of box filter that slightly tolerates deformation in the offset space.

Matched Query Ratio: To solve the prior problem, we rigorously constrain each query feature can only be counted once for the final score. In other words, we project the matched pairs in a box filter (i.e., five cells) back into the query space and constrain each location should only contribute one in the final score. To fit this constraint, any value larger than one will be set to one. Finally, we sum up the whole query space to obtain one score for one translation hypothesis and choose the maximum value as the spatial consistency score.

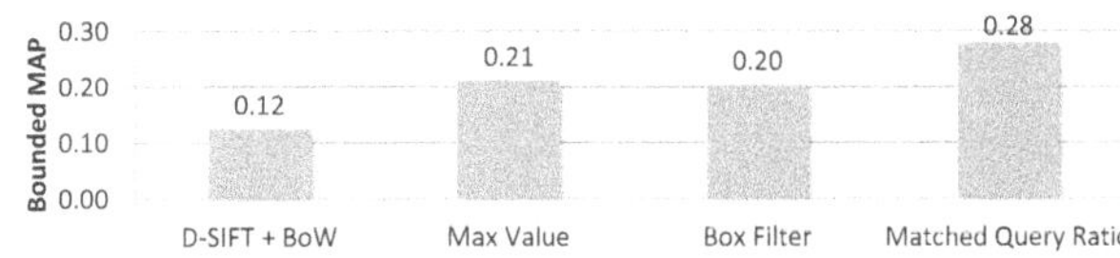

Figure 5: Comparison of different spatial verification approaches (Section 3.3). We achieve 125% relative improvement when using the refined fast spatial verification (Matched Query Ratio).

4. EXPERIMENTS AND DISCUSSIONS

We follow the experimental setting of [14] for comparing with their result. The queries are composed of 38 sketches of car and bicycle. It contains freehand sketches and amateur sketches (cf. Figure 7). Then, we use them to query the PASCAL VOC2007 dataset [3]. The evaluation metric is also the same as [14]. We use the bounded MAP $\frac{\sum_{n=1}^{N} P@n}{N}$ and set N to 150. $P@n$ means precision at n.

Spatial Verification: We adopt the state-of-the-art BoW model with 1 million codebook as the baseline method and compare it with our proposed method ($C = 10$). As shown in Figure 5, we can achieve 69% relative improvement (0.12 to 0.21) when using the maximum value in the original offset space. However, the performance deteriorates when we use the box filter. The reason we have discussed in Section 3.3 is the same visual word appears continually. After solving this problem by matched query ratio method, we can achieve 0.28 bounded MAP. Comparing with the baseline, we achieve 125% relative improvement.

Performance: We compare the performance with the data-driven method (learnt D-SIFT) [14] and BoW model with Hessian-affine detector and SIFT descriptor (HASIFT + BoW). As shown in Figure 6(a), our proposed method

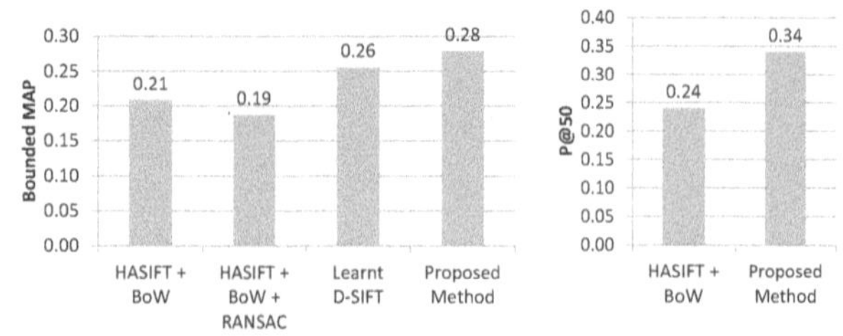

(a) VOC2007 (b) Caltech101

Figure 6: Performance comparison on different datasets. It shows that our proposed method achieves the best retrieval accuracy comparing with other state-of-the-art methods.

achieves the best performance in all baseline methods. We also show two retrieval results in Figure 7. If we apply spatial verification after the BoW matching (HASIFT + BoW + RANSAC), the performance decreases from 0.21 to 0.19. We think the reason is that matched corresponding features are not enough to do the spatial verification. We can achieve competitive performance as the learning-based approach (learnt D-SIFT); moreover, the retrieval time of our proposed method is much shorter than that.

Speed: We show the speed comparison in Table 1. In the data-driven method (learnt D-SIFT), a query image is required for training the classifier, so the retrieval time (All) will take the online training and testing into account. However, training the classifier is very time-consuming and it takes about 6 hours when using one core of Intel Xeon X7460 2.66GHz. For testing, it takes 1 second to examine all possible sliding windows for each database image and total 10,000 seconds for the whole dataset. Hence, it takes about 31,600 seconds for one query task in data-driven approach and it only takes 80 seconds in our proposed method. This is because our proposed method can efficiently and dynamically selects the most suitable matching constraint (Section 3).

Performance in Caltech101: For more complete experiments, we also evaluate our method in Caltech101 dataset [8]. This dataset contains many images from different domains for each category, so we use it to simulate the general cross-domain image retrieval task. We average the precision at 50 (P@50) of all categories and show the result in Figure 6(b). We can see that our method still outperforms the BoW method 42% relatively.

5. CONCLUSIONS AND FUTURE WORK

We propose an effective and efficient general framework for cross-domain image retrieval which focuses on the structure of image content rather than the visual appearance; hence, the proposed method is robust in retrieving images in different domains. In the traditional retrieval methods, they just focus on the details of images, but these strategies do not work well in general cross-domain setting. To focus on the structure, we relax the strict matching constraint in BoW model to derive enough quantity of matched pairs. Utilizing this step, we put different domains on an equal footing. After we obtain enough matched pairs, a fast and improved spatial verification in offset space is applied to all database images to find the most spatially consistent one. Finally, our method achieves better performance and is much faster than the state-of-the-art cross-domain method [14]. In the future, we think this method is easy to extend by using different local features and considering the rotation and scale transformation in spatial verification.

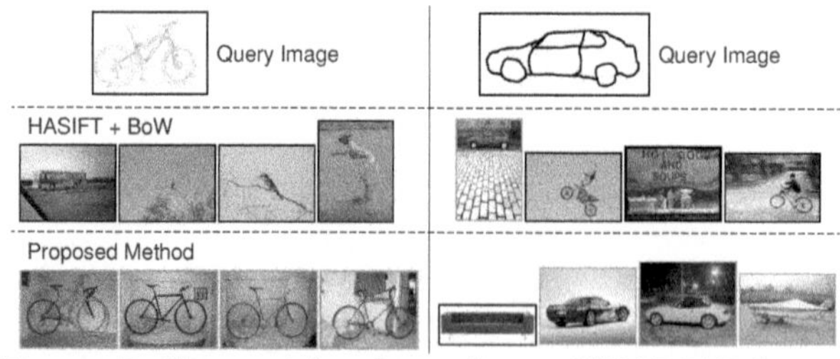

Figure 7: Two retrieval results on VOC2007 dataset for sketch queries. The red rectangle represents the correct results.

Table 1: Speed comparison with learnt D-SIFT and our proposed method (with one query) in VOC2007.

Method (online)	Training	Testing	All
learnt D-SIFT [14]	21,600s	1s	31,600s
Our proposed method	0s	0.008s	80s

6. REFERENCES

[1] M. Bansal et al. Joint spectral correspondence for disparate image matching. In *CVPR*, 2013.

[2] Y. Cao et al. Edgel index for large-scale sketch-based image search. In *CVPR*, 2011.

[3] M. Everingham et al. The PASCAL Visual Object Classes Challenge 2007 (VOC2007) Results. http://www.pascal-network.org/challenges/VOC/voc2007/workshop/index.html.

[4] M. A. Fischler and R. C. Bolles. Random sample consensus: A paradigm for model fitting with applications to image analysis and automated cartography. *CACM*, 24(6):381–395, June 1981.

[5] Y. Gao et al. Visual-textual joint relevance learning for tag-based social image search. *IEEE TIP*, 22(1):363–376, 2013.

[6] D. C. Hauagge and N. Snavely. Image matching using local symmetry features. In *CVPR*, 2012.

[7] H. Jégou et al. Improving bag-of-features for large scale image search. *IJCV*, 87(3):316–336, May 2010.

[8] F.-F. Li et al. One-shot learning of object categories. *IEEE TPAMI*, 28(4):594–611, 2006.

[9] A. Mikulik et al. Learning vocabularies over a fine quantization. *IJCV*, pages 1–13, 2012.

[10] D. Nistér and H. Stewénius. Scalable recognition with a vocabulary tree. In *CVPR*, 2006.

[11] B. C. Russell et al. Automatic alignment of paintings and photographs depicting a 3d scene. In *ICCV Workshops*, 2011.

[12] E. Shechtman et al. Matching local self-similarities across images and videos. In *CVPR*, 2007.

[13] X. Shen et al. Object retrieval and localization with spatially-constrained similarity measure and k-nn re-ranking. In *CVPR*, 2012.

[14] A. Shrivastava et al. Data-driven visual similarity for cross-domain image matching. *ACM TOG*, 30(6):154:1–154:10, Dec. 2011.

[15] J. Sivic et al. Video google: A text retrieval approach to object matching in videos. In *ICCV*, 2003.

[16] G. Tolias and Y. Avrithis. Speeded-up, relaxed spatial matching. In *ICCV*, 2011.

[17] Y. Zhang et al. Image retrieval with geometry-preserving visual phrases. In *CVPR*, 2011.

Learning Like a Toddler: Watching Television Series to Learn Vocabulary from Images and Audio

Emre Yılmaz
ESAT-PSI
KU Leuven, Belgium
eyilmaz@esat.kuleuven.be

Konstantinos Rematas
ESAT-PSI, iMinds
KU Leuven, Belgium
krematas@esat.kuleuven.be

Tinne Tuytelaars
ESAT-PSI, iMinds
KU Leuven, Belgium
tinne.tuytelaars@esat.kuleuven.be

Hugo Van hamme
ESAT-PSI
KU Leuven, Belgium
hugo.vanhamme@esat.kuleuven.be

ABSTRACT

This paper presents the initial findings of our efforts to build an unsupervised multimodal vocabulary learning scheme in a realistic scenario. For this purpose, a new multimodal dataset, called Musti3D, has been created. The Musti3D database contains episodes from an animation series for toddlers. Annotated with audiovisual information, this database is used for the investigation of a non-negative matrix factorization (NMF)-based audiovisual learning technique. The performance of the technique, i.e. correctly matching the audio and visual representations of the objects, has been evaluated by gradually reducing the level of supervision starting from the ground truth transcriptions. Moreover, we have performed experiments using different visual representations and time spans for combining the audiovisual information. The preliminary results show the feasibility of the proposed audiovisual learning framework.

Categories and Subject Descriptors: I.2.6 [Artificial Intelligence]: Learning-*knowledge acquisition, language acquisition*; I.2.m [Artificial Intelligence]: Miscellaneous

General Terms: Algorithms, Languages, Experimentation

Keywords: Audiovisual learning, non-negative matrix factorization, multimodal dataset, discriminative patches, histogram of acoustic co-occurrences

1. INTRODUCTION

In their first few years of life, children learn to name the objects they are confronted with in their environment. To mimic that process with a machine requires learning from at least two modalities, in this case the auditory and the visual, to create a crossmodal model that links the learned object representations in both domains and so establishes the grounding process.

In this work, the task of learning the relation between visual and auditory description of words is formulated as an *unsupervised* learning problem. Unsupervised learning is an important technique to build truly artificially intelligent systems: systems that learn from observing their environment.

While there is a body of work that investigates the unsupervised multimodal analysis of images and text [2, 3, 7, 16], the combination of continuous speech and tags [13] or images and continuous speech [4, 11] are far less studied. In earlier work, visual objects are presented in isolation or on a clean background and the audio is often recorded on purpose for the specific task of teaching a robot the semantics of the visual objects [5, 10, 15].

Both in vision as well as in speech processing, it has been shown that adding a limited amount of weak supervision significantly improves the pattern discovery capabilities. We investigate whether the same benefits of weak supervision can be obtained in an unsupervised setting, replacing the tags by multimodal information, using a non-negative matrix factorization approach for learning from multiple asynchronous input streams [14]. The key assumption is that co-occurrences over different modalities provide a strong cue for semantics or relevance. In particular, we relate properties of objects in images and audio. The described learning task is shown in Figure 1.

Our main contributions can then be summarized as follows: i) we have created and annotated a new multimodal dataset. Our main research question investigates whether it is possible to learn visual and audio representations for objects from watching a television series for toddlers, where the audio describes the visual scene, but at the same time exhibits a large degree of complementarity. ii) we gradually reduce the level of supervision, starting from ground truth transcriptions for both domains to only using segmentation info (bounding boxes and audio word delineations) without grounding. iii) we compare two different visual representations in this context: bag-of-visual-words, which capture relatively low-level image characteristics, and discriminative patches, which can be seen as an example of more mid-level features.

The remainder of this paper is organized as follows. Section 2 details the audio and video features used in the proposed learning scheme. The NMF-based audiovisual learning framework is discussed in Section 3. The experimental setup is explained and the results are presented in Section 4. Section 5 discusses the results and Section 6 concludes the paper.

MM'14, November 3–7, 2014, Orlando, Florida, USA.

http://dx.doi.org/10.1145/2647868.2655036.

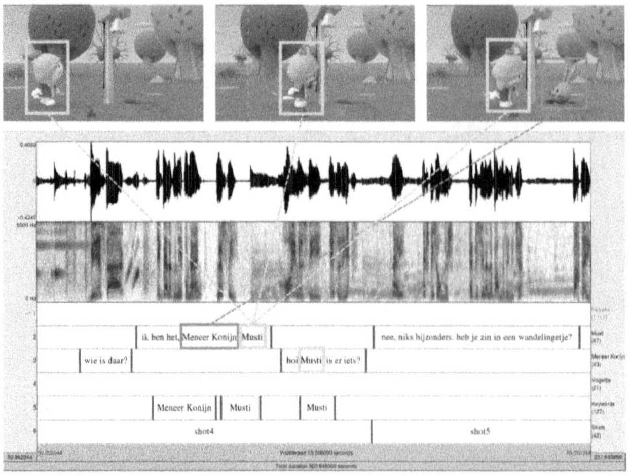

Figure 1: An audiovisual learning example - linking the audio keywords with the visual counterparts.

2. AUDIOVISUAL REPRESENTATIONS

The NMF-based learning framework described in Section 3 can learn object representations from multiple information streams, here the auditory and visual modality and possibly supervisory tags. It requires each *learning example* to be represented as a vector of non-negative values, feature occurrence counts, of a fixed dimension. A learning example accumulates feature counts over a time span in which one expects there would be a relation between the different information streams. In this work, we investigate two choices: the utterance level and the shot level accumulation. A shot is the basic component of a video and commonly defined as an uninterrupted sequence of frames.

2.1 Audio features

The audio information is represented as weighted phone lattice transition probabilities yielding a fixed-length representation of any speech segment with possibly different duration [12]. These features are obtained by labeling the acoustic content of a speech segment with the help of an automatic speech recognizer and accumulating the co-occurrences of each acoustic unit in a histogram.

Using a conventional HMM-based speech recognizer, the network of most probable phone strings (henceforth the phone lattice) is determined. The phone lattice is an acyclic directed graph where the arcs correspond to phones and the nodes mark their start and end times. Every arc is also associated with the acoustic score of the corresponding phone.

The audio features are extracted by transforming this acoustic score into a posterior probability and accumulating the probability of every two consecutive phones ϕ and ψ over the complete phone lattice

$$c(\phi,\psi) = \sum_{\{\alpha:\, h(\alpha)=\phi\}} \; \sum_{\{\beta:\, h(\beta)=\psi\}} p(\alpha)\, p(\beta)\, \Delta_{\alpha\beta} \qquad (1)$$

in which $h(\alpha)$ and $h(\beta)$ return the phone identity, and $p(\alpha)$ and $p(\beta)$ the posterior probability of the arcs α and β, respectively. If the start node of β is equal to the end node of α, then $\Delta_{\alpha\beta}$ is the inverse of the probability of the common node, otherwise it is equal to zero. This node probability is given by the sum of the posterior probabilities of the incoming (or outgoing) arcs of the corresponding node.

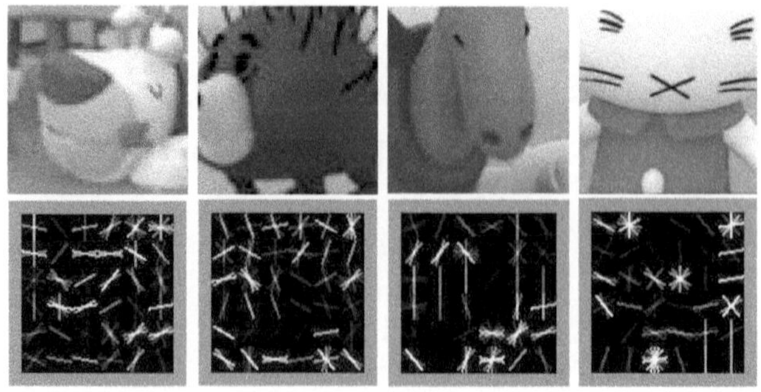

Figure 2: Examples of DPs, together with their (positive) learned weights. Note how the learning focuses on gradients that discriminate the object.

The $c(\phi,\psi)$ values for each speech segment are vectorized and stacked in the columns $\mathbf{V}_a$ of size PxT, in which P is equal to the square of the number of available phones in the alphabet and T is the number of utterances in the database.

2.2 Visual features

2.2.1 *Visual words*

One of the standard approaches to represent images is the Bag of Visual Words (BOW). First, we extract SIFT features from a set of images and we cluster them using k-means; the centers of the resulting clusters are considered as the visual words of a visual vocabulary V_{vis} of size k, with k the predefined number of clusters. Next, for every image we extract dense SIFT and we assign each SIFT descriptor to its closest visual word. By applying sum pooling we generate a histogram representation for the image. Images containing the same object are expected to have overlap in their BOW histograms (similar visual word distribution).

2.2.2 *Discriminative patches*

We additionally consider discriminative patches (DP), a method where each patch captures an aspect of the appearance of specific objects. Following the approach of [1] we want an object specific patch p to be highly activated when the object is present and have low score when other objects or background appears. Therefore we consider a detection task where we train a model w_p for every DP and we use it as a linear classifier to the patches x of a test image:

$$f_p(x) = h(w_p^T x), \qquad (2)$$

with $h(y) = y$ if $y > 0$ and 0 otherwise. Both patches p and x are represented as Histograms of Oriented Gradients (HOG). The weights w_p are learned as an exemplar classifier [9] but instead of a Support Vector Machine we use Linear Discriminant Analysis (LDA) [6]. Assuming that the positive and the negative data come from Gaussian distributions with means μ_p and μ_n and same covariance matrix Σ, the model weights for a patch p are learned:

$$w_p = \Sigma^{-1}(p - \mu_n). \qquad (3)$$

As positive we consider only the HOG features of the patch p, while for estimating μ_n and Σ we use background patches.

The above approach results in one classifier for every sampled patch. However, not all of the patches are suitable for separating the different objects. We select the most discriminative by considering the Mahalanobis distance of a patch to the negative distribution. During testing we scan the image or the bounding box in a sliding window fashion for all

DPs and we keep the score of the maximum activation for each of them (max pooling).

3. NMF-BASED AUDIOVISUAL LEARNING

The links between the audio keywords and video objects are learned by applying non-negative matrix factorization (NMF). The NMF algorithm approximates a non-negative data matrix $\mathbf{V}$ of size MxN as a multiplication of two non-negative matrices $\mathbf{W}$ and $\mathbf{H}$ of dimensionality MxR and RxN respectively. Here, R is chosen so that $R << M$ and $R << N$ in order to obtain a low-rank approximation, i.e. $\mathbf{V}$ is expressed as an approximate linear combination of basis audiovisual vectors (columns of $\mathbf{W}$) scaled by the weights stored in $\mathbf{H}$.

The factorization is achieved by minimizing the generalized Kullback-Leibler divergence (KLD) between $\mathbf{V}$ and its approximation $\mathbf{WH}$ through multiplicative updates [8]. In the proposed framework, the data matrix $\mathbf{V}$ is comprised of two submatrices $\mathbf{V}_a$ representing the audio features and $\mathbf{V}_v$ representing the video features.

$$\begin{bmatrix} \mathbf{V}_a \\ \mathbf{V}_v \end{bmatrix} \approx \begin{bmatrix} \mathbf{W}_a \\ \mathbf{W}_v \end{bmatrix} \mathbf{H} \tag{4}$$

Defining the audio grounding matrix $\mathbf{V}_{ag}$ as

$$V_{ag}^{ij} = \begin{cases} 1 & \text{if an audio keyword } i \text{ is in utterance } j \\ 0 & \text{otherwise,} \end{cases} \tag{5}$$

the unimodal associations are learned by performing the factorization

$$\begin{bmatrix} \mathbf{V}_{ag} \\ \mathbf{V}_a \end{bmatrix} \approx \begin{bmatrix} \mathbf{W}_{ag} \\ \mathbf{W}_a \end{bmatrix} \mathbf{H} \tag{6}$$

where the $\mathbf{W}_{ag}$ is initialized as $\mathbf{W}_{ag} = [\mathbf{I}_K | \mathbf{W}_{gbg}]$. $\mathbf{I}_K$ is a KxK identity matrix where K is the number of audio keywords. $\mathbf{W}_{gbg}$ is a Kx$(R-K)$ matrix with random positive values much smaller than 1.

This setup leads to solutions where each of the K audio keywords is assigned to a single column in $\mathbf{W}_a$. The remaining $(R-K)$ columns, $\mathbf{W}_{gbg}$, are called the *garbage columns* which model other factors like non-keywords or background music. Similarly, the crossmodal associations can be learned by concatenating the audio grounding matrix $\mathbf{V}_{ag}$ with the video features $\mathbf{V}_v$ and following the same procedure as above.

4. EXPERIMENTS

4.1 Dataset

For the audiovisual learning experiments, we have created a new realistic multimodal dataset, called Musti3D, a television series for toddlers with 30 episodes each lasting 5 minutes. We have annotated 22 episodes with various audio and video information such as the orthographic transcription of the utterances, the occurrences of various audio keywords, video objects and the shot boundaries.

We have chosen 12 characters from the series appearing with different frequencies and perform the learning experiments aiming to learn the audiovisual features belonging to these characters. In practice, we have defined 12 video objects and 13 audio keywords (one of the video objects is associated with two audio keywords).

We pick 5 episodes as oracle for evaluation purposes considering the balanced occurrences of the target objects and keywords in the training and test data. The training episodes are used for extracting the reference representations of the target objects and keywords. These reference representations are used to classify the learned audio and visual representations. Due to the unbalanced number of occurrences, we randomly select 10 reference BOW and DP representations for each object and 5 reference HAC representations for each keyword.

4.2 Implementation details

The audio representations are extracted using the annotated keyword boundaries extended with an offset of 0.1 seconds. No additional precaution is taken against the background music. For the HAC feature extraction, phone lattices are generated using a conventional HMM-based automatic speech recognizer. A phonetic set consisting of 40 Dutch phones is used.

For the BOW features, we used dense SIFT at multiple scales and a vocabulary of size 300. To obtain DPs, we sampled approximately 15 patches per bounding box from the training data at multiple scales and we extract features from 6x6 HOG cells. We consider the top 20 DPs per object based on their distance from the negative distribution. For the final image representation, we extract BOW or DP features for each bounding box separately and sum the result.

The final recognition accuracies are obtained after averaging the results of 10 independent trails of 100 NMF iterations. In the experiments using grounding matrices, 3 garbage columns are used resulting in $R_{vg} = 15$ and $R_{ag} = 16$. The learned representations are classified according to the label of the closest reference representation with respect to the generalized KLD.

In the experiments without grounding information, each column of the basis matrices $\mathbf{W}_a$ and $\mathbf{W}_v$ are classified as the label of the closest reference representation. The $\mathbf{W}$ and $\mathbf{H}$ matrices are initialized either in a supervised or unsupervised manner. In the supervised initialization setting, the initial $\mathbf{W}$ and $\mathbf{H}$ are obtained after a single NMF iteration using the visual grounding information. On the other hand, in the unsupervised case, $\mathbf{W}$ and $\mathbf{H}$ are randomly initialized and R is set to 50. The recognition accuracy is obtained as the ratio of the number of unique correct matches to the number of video objects.

4.3 Results

We present the recognition accuracy results in Table 1 listing the experiments that are performed using the video grounding matrix and audio grounding matrix in the upper and middle panel respectively and the experiments without using the grounding information in the lower panel. Firstly, we will focus on the experiments with grounding. The ground truth experiments which are given in the first rows of the upper and middle panels yield that the proposed method is able to find the correct crossmodal match of each video object (audio keyword) with a recognition accuracy of 74% (66%) at utterance-level and 81% (77%) at shot-level.

In the second block of the upper and middle panel, the unimodal learning accuracy of both sources are evaluated. The learned visual representation for shot-level DP features match the reference DP features for 84% of the video objects. Only 24% of the shot-level BOW features match correctly with the reference BOW features. Using utterance-level features slightly improves the accuracy of BOW features to 35%, while it reduces the performance of DP features to

55%. For HAC features, the recognition accuracy is around 71% and 76% for both levels.

In the third blocks, the results of a less supervised crossmodal learning setting, i.e. using the grounding matrices with the crossmodal features (rather than the ground truth crossmodal features), are presented. For visual grounding, both shot- and utterance-level features provide a similar recognition accuracies of 59% and 56% respectively. For audio grounding, the shot-level DP features provide considerably higher performance with 69% compared to the 26% of shot-level BOW features.

The lower panel summarizes the recognition results of the learning experiments without using the grounding information. The upper block shows the results where the basis matrix **W** is initialized in a supervised manner. The shot-level DP features provides 40% recognition accuracy compared to the 29% of the shot-level BOW features. The utterance-level features provide inferior performance for both DP and BOW features. The results in the lower block are obtained with unsupervised initialization of **W**. All features provide around 30 % of recognition accuracy.

Visual grounding	utt.-level	shot-level
+GTvideo-GTaudio	74	81
+GTvideo-BOW feat.	35	24
+GTvideo-DP feat.	55	84
+GTvideo-HAC feat.	56	59
Audio grounding	utt.-level	shot-level
+GTaudio-GTvideo	66	77
+GTaudio-HAC feat.	76	71
+GTaudio-BOW feat.	19	26
+GTaudio-DP feat.	35	69
Learning w/o grounding	utt.-level	shot-level
+BOW feat.-HAC feat. (sup.)	17	29
+DP feat.-HAC feat. (sup.)	10	40
+BOW feat.-HAC feat. (unsup.)	31	25
+DP feat.-HAC feat. (unsup.)	28	30

Table 1: Recognition accuracy results in percentages

5. DISCUSSION

First, based on a set of experiments using ground truth transcripts, we have shown that even though audio and video show a high degree of complementarity, co-occurrence information can guide non-negative matrix factorization to a meaningful solution. The appropriate temporal unit for capturing such co-occurrences seems to be the shot-level.

While not yet fully unsupervised, our experiments are encouraging as they show that data from a TV series for toddlers shows sufficient temporal overlap between object names in audio and occurrences of the corresponding objects in the visual stream to learn object semantics in an unsupervised way. This is a leap forward compared to earlier work, where objects are often shown in isolation or on a clean background and the audio is often recorded on purpose for the specific task of teaching a robot the semantics of objects.

We have also compared two different visual representations: bag-of-visual-words, which capture relatively low-level image characteristics, and DPs, which can be seen as an example of mid-level features. While in the current version the DPs are selected based on some supervision, the superior results obtained with these features clearly illustrate that more powerful mid-level representations are critical for learning in an unsupervised manner.

6. CONCLUSION

In this work, an NMF-based audiovisual learning technique has been described and applied to a realistic multimodal dataset containing episodes from a toddler TV series. At several supervision levels, the performance of the technique has been investigated using different video features and time spans for fusing the audio and visual information. From the results, it can be concluded that the learning approach provided promising results on the task of learning the relation between visual and auditory description of words. Future work includes performing feature extraction in an unsupervised manner rather than using the annotated information and deeper investigation of the impact of background music.

7. ACKNOWLEDGMENTS

This work has been supported by the KU Leuven research grant OT/09/028 (VASI).

8. REFERENCES

[1] M. Aubry, B. C. Russell, and J. Sivic. Painting-to-3D model alignment via discriminative visual elements. *ACM Trans. Graph.*, 33(2):1–14, 2014.

[2] K. Barnard, P. Duygulu, D. Forsyth, N. de Freitas, D. M. Blei, and M. I. Jordan. Matching words and pictures. *J. Mach. Learn. Res.*, 3:1107–1135, Mar. 2003.

[3] D. M. Blei and M. I. Jordan. Modeling annotated data. In *Proc. ACM SIGIR*, pages 127–134, 2003.

[4] J. W. Fisher III, T. Darrell, W. T. F., and P. A. V. Learning joint statistical models for audio-visual fusion and segregation. In *Advances in Neural Information Processing Systems 13*, pages 772–778. 2001.

[5] K. Gold, M. Doniec, C. Crick, and B. Scassellati. Robotic vocabulary building using extension inference and implicit contrast. *Artificial Intelligence*, 173(1):145 – 166, 2009.

[6] B. Hariharan, J. Malik, and D. Ramanan. Discriminative decorrelation for clustering and classification. In *Proc. ECCV*, pages 459–472, 2012.

[7] Y. Jia, M. Salzmann, and T. Darrell. Learning cross-modality similarity for multinomial data. In *Proc. ICCV*, pages 2407–2414, Nov 2011.

[8] D. D. Lee and H. S. Seung. Algorithms for non-negative matrix factorization. In *NIPS*, pages 556–562, 2000.

[9] T. Malisiewicz, A. Gupta, and A. A. Efros. Ensemble of exemplar-SVMs for object detection and beyond. In *Proc. ICCV*, pages 89–96, 2011.

[10] T. Nakamura, T. Nagai, and N. Iwahashi. Grounding of word meanings in multimodal concepts using LDA. In *Proc. IROS*, pages 3943–3948, Oct 2009.

[11] D. K. Roy and A. P. Pentland. Learning words from sights and sounds: a computational model. *Cognitive Science*, 26(1):113–146, 2002.

[12] V. Stouten, K. Demuynck, and H. Van Hamme. Discovering phone patterns in spoken utterances by non-negative matrix factorization. *IEEE Signal Processing Letters*, 15:131–134, 2008.

[13] L. ten Bosch, L. Boves, H. Van hamme, and R. K. Moore. A computational model of language acquisition: The emergence of words. *Fundam. Inf.*, 90(3):229–249, Aug. 2009.

[14] H. Van hamme. Integration of asynchronous knowledge sources in a novel speech recognition framework. In *Proc. ISCA ITRW*, June 2008.

[15] C. Yu and D. H. Ballard. A multimodal learning interface for grounding spoken language in sensory perceptions. *ACM Trans. Appl. Percept.*, 1(1):57–80, 2004.

[16] Y. Zhuang, Y. F. Wang, F. Wu, Y. Zhang, and W. Lu. Supervised coupled dictionary learning with group structures for multi-modal retrieval. In *AAAI*, pages 1070–1076, 2013.

Cuteness Recognition and Localization in the Photos of Animals

Yu Bao
School of Software
Dalian University of Technology
baoyu_dlut@foxmail.com

Jing Yang
College of Arts
Chongqing University
yangjing19900530@163.com

Liangliang Cao
IBM Watson Research Center
liangliang.cao@us.ibm.com

Haojie Li
School of Software
Dalian University of Technology
hjli@dlut.edu.cn

Jinhui Tang
School of Computer Science
Nanjing University of Science and Technology
tangjh1981@acm.org

ABSTRACT

Among the flourishing amount of photos in the social media websites, "cute" images of animals are particularly attractive to the Internet users. This paper considers building an automatic model which can distinguish cute images from non-cute ones. To make the recognition results more interpretable, a lot of efforts are made to find which part of the animal appears attractive to the human users. To validate the success of our proposed method, we collect three new datasets of different animals, i.e., cats, dogs, and rabbits with both cute and non-cute images. Our model obtains promising performance in distinguishing cute images from non-cute ones. Moreover, it outperforms the classical models with not only better recognition accuracy, but also more intuitive localization of the cuteness in the images. The contribution of this paper is three-fold: (1) We collect new datasets for cuteness recognition, (2) We extend the powerful Fisher Vector representation to localize cute part in the animal recognition, and (3) Extensive experimental results show that our proposed method can recognize cute animals of cats, dogs, and rabbits.

Categories and Subject Descriptors

I.5.4 [**Applications**]: Computer Vision; H.4 [**Information Systems Applications**]: Miscellaneous

Keywords

cute images; recognition; localization; cats; dogs; rabbits

1. INTRODUCTION

Dogs, cats, and rabbits are close friends of human being and their photos are very popular in social media. They are among the most popular subjects in social media websites. People are especially interested in "cute" photos of these animals. For example, *Maru*, a cat from Japan has resulted in more than 165 million views on its Youtube channel [1]. Cute photos stimulate positive feeling and intensive emotion and there are many studies in psychology on the "cuteness" of images. Some recent research work [11, 15] showed the power of cuteness and suggested that viewing cute images can promote focused attention and happy emotions.

Figure 1: Some examples of our new dataset of cuteness recognition.

In this paper, we attempt to take a computational approach to understand the cuteness of animal photos. To this end, we downloaded photos from Flickr[2] and asked users to judge whether a photo is cute or not. We selected images according to users' consensus and obtained a dataset with 3,600 photos of dogs, cats and rabbits. The ratio of cute and non-cute photos in this dataset is about 1 : 2. Figure 1 shows some example photos from our dataset.

To learn a statistical model of cuteness from this dataset, we looked into extensive literature on general object recognition. In prevailing object recognition systems, there are two steps to train a classifier: (1) Image description, which extracts features of image and then encode the features to image level representation. (2) Statistical learning, which employs machine learning approaches to train a classifier based on image representation. In the popularly-used effective Bag-of-Visual-Words (BoVW) model [1], the image de-

[1]http://techland.time.com/2012/06/27/a-brief-historyof-cats-on-youtube/
[2]https://www.flickr.com/

MM'14, November 03 - 07 2014, Orlando, FL, USA.
Copyright 2014 ACM 978-1-4503-3063-3/14/11...$15.00.
http://dx.doi.org/10.1145/2647868.2655046.

scription is the histogram of Scale Invariant Feature Transform (SIFT) [10] features, and the statistical model usually uses Support Vector Machine (SVM) to train nonlinear classifiers from high dimensional patterns.

Bag-of-visual-words model has many advantages in solving general object recognition. However, it cannot satisfy the requirement of our cuteness detection problem. We prefer a new model with the following capabilities:

- The model is able to take spatial context into account, and use the neighborhood information to infer whether the subject is cute or not.
- The model could not only determine whether an image is cute or not, but also find which part of the animal is important for inferring .

Traditional bag-of-words model could not satisfy these requirements since it overlooks the spatial information from images. Thus, a reliable and efficient solution needs be developed instead.

Our proposed solution is based on Fisher vector (FV) [14], which employs Gaussian Mixture Model (GMM) to build a parametric generative model for local features. However, classical FV model could only give image-level estimation but is not able to find the cute parts. We extend the previous work on FV and obtain promising results on our dataset. We will explain our method in this paper and report the performance of our method.

To the best of our knowledge, there is no previous work on the cuteness recognition of images. However, there are still a number of previous studies on animal images which are helpful to this study. Many research studies have been carried out on object recognition and detection from cluttered background [2, 3, 7, 12, 20]. A recent research focus is to model highly deformable of animals [8, 13, 17], and another focus is to discriminate different breeds of animals and to identify fine-grained categories [4].

This paper is organized as follows. Section 2 explains the proposed cuteness model in details. Section 3 evaluates the performance of the proposed method on cuteness recognition and localization. We conclude this paper in Section 4.

2. THE PROPOSED METHOD

The cuteness of animal images involves the subtle description of the image. Following previous work, we employ dense SIFT [10] to represent the local features of the animal. We dense sample patches with a stride of step pixel and compute the SIFT features for each patch. The process is repeated at five scales, with a scaling factor. Each SIFT feature is a 128 dimensional descriptor. The next step is how to encode dense features into image level representation.

Traditional bag-of-words model suggests to convert a SIFT vector to an index number which corresponds to an existing visual word in the vocabulary. Though lots of successes have been demonstrated in image retrieval [9], image recognition [16], etc, this method generates a sparse representation and thus lots of information of local descriptor is lost. To keep more information, we follow the Fisher Vector [14] for image representation to reduce the loss of information in BoVW.

Fisher Vector is a method that summarizes a varying number of local feature descriptors (e.g. SIFT). It first fits the Gaussian Mixture Model (GMM) which is a parametric generative model to the set of local features, and then represents the image with the derivatives of the log-likelihood of the model by encoding them with respect to the model parameters [5]. Following [14] ,we train a GMM using the extracted SIFT features and get the parameters $\Theta = (\mu_k,\sigma_k,\pi_k$:k=1,2,...,K). μ_k,σ_k,π_k is mean, covariance and the mixture weight of the GMM. K is the number of Gaussians in the GMM. Let I=(x_1,...,x_N) be a set of d dimensional SIFT features extracted from an image. The GMM associates each vector x_i to a mode k in the mixture with a strength given by the posterior probability:

$$q_{ik} = \frac{exp[-\frac{1}{2}(x_i-\mu_k)^{\mathrm{T}}\sigma_k^{-1}(x_i-\mu_k)]}{\sum_{t=1}^{K} exp[-\frac{1}{2}](x_i-\mu_t)^{\mathrm{T}}\sigma_t^{-1}(x_i-\mu_t)]}$$

For each mode k, consider the mean and covariance deviation vectors:

$$u_{jk} = \frac{1}{N\sqrt{\pi_k}}\sum_{i=1}^{K} q_{ik}\frac{x_{ji}-\mu_{jk}}{\sigma_{jk}}$$

$$v_{jk} = \frac{1}{N\sqrt{\pi_k}}\sum_{i=1}^{K} q_{ik}[(\frac{x_{ji}-\mu_{jk}}{\sigma_{jk}})^2-1]$$

where $j = 1, 2, ..., d$ spans the vector dimensions. The FV of image I is the stacking of the vectors u_k and then of the vectors v_k for each of the K modes in the Gaussian mixtures:

$$\Phi(I) = [...u_k...v_k...]$$

Thus, the FV dimensionality is $2Kd$, where K is the number of Gaussians in the GMM, and d is the dimensionality of the feature vector.

Previous studies employ linear SVM to model Fisher Vectors. Suppose w is the weight vector and b is the bias of SVM, the score of an input x is

$$s = w'x + b$$

Here x represents image feature and s denotes whether this image is cute or not.

We make two moderate extensions on the base of Fisher vectors:

1. We use the spatial information of local descriptor to find the cute part and model a cute part as the neighborhood of ellipse shape.
2. Instead of using SVM directly, we use an ensemble method to select the most useful components for cute animals.

For the first extension, we follow the work in [14] by appending the feature coordinates to the visual features. Thus our dense features have a form like $[SIFT_{xy}, \frac{x}{W}-\frac{1}{2}, \frac{y}{H}-\frac{1}{2}]$, where $SIFT_{xy}$ is the SIFT descriptor at (x,y), and W and H are the width and height of the image. After training a GMM we get the parameters $\Theta = (\mu_k,\sigma_k,\pi_k$:k=1,2,...,K). μ_k and σ_k are the mean and diagonal covariance for k-th Gaussian Model. By looking at the last two dimensions from each Gaussian component, we are able to model the spatial information of the subject. We can interpret the mean vector as the center of an ellipse and use the diagonal covariance to show the skewness of the ellipse. Note that the position of the ellipse is different from image to images. The Fisher vector representation will pool local patches for every image and compute the location adaptively.

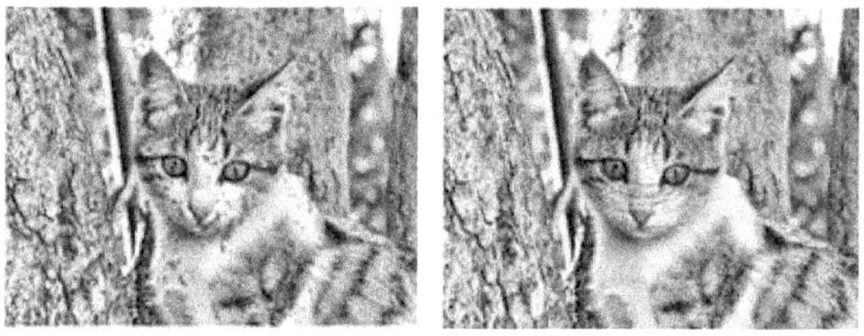

Figure 2: Localize cuteness using the ellipse detection. Left: local patches ranked by classical FV model. Right: ellipses detected by our ensemble model. The blue points indicate SIFT features belonging to the top local patches with high weights. The ellipses correspond to selected "weak" classifiers in Adaboost.

A challenging task along with image-level cuteness recognition is to localize which part of the animal is cute, *i.e.*, to find out which component of GMM corresponds to the cute animal. We makes it possible to evaluate how important certain Gaussians is by using the Adaboost algorithm. The Adaboost [6] is an algorithm for constructing a "strong" classifier as linear combination of "weak" classifiers. Suppose the FV dimensionality is $2Kd$, where K is the number of mixtures in the GMM, and d is the dimensionality of local patch features plus two dimensional coordinates. The weak classifier is a linear SVM model trained on $2d$ features for every component in the FV.

Let $h_t(x)$ be the weak classifier, D_t be the weight of train image and y be the label of train image. Then we start a loop for computing the important Gaussians. First, the weight of every train image is same and we consider selecting a weak classifier with the smallest weighted error,

$$h_t = arg \min_{h_j \in H} \epsilon_j = \sum_{i=1}^{m} D_t(i)[y_i \neq h_j(x_i)]$$

where m is the number of training images and H is the set of weak classifiers.

Second, we compute α to update D_t

$$\alpha_t = \frac{1}{2} log(\frac{1+r_t}{1-r_t}),$$

where

$$r_t = \sum_{i=1}^{m} D_t(i) h_t(x_i) y_i$$

Note that α_t is the weight of the weak classifier which is proportional to r_t, the accuracy of the classifier. Then we update D_t using α_t.

$$D_{t+1}(i) = \frac{D_t(i) exp(-\alpha_t y_i h_t(x_i))}{Z_t},$$

here Z_t is a normalization factor to make D_{t+1} is a distribution. To select more components, we iterate the above procedure and find more h_t. The final strong classifier is

$$H_x = sign(\sum_{t=1}^{T} \alpha_t h_t(x))$$

By combining multiple "weak" classifiers, we can select the GMM components corresponding to the cute animals. Figure 2 shows an example of cuteness localization. It is easy to see the difference between our method and the traditional FV. Traditional FV yields a unified SVM using all the components with the max margin criteria. The resulted SVM optimizes the image level estimation, but fires on too many local patches. In contrast, our ensemble method only picks the top components as the localization of the cute parts.

3. EXPERIMENTS

Table 1: Accuracy of recognizing cute images using our method and traditional bag-of-words model.

	cat	dog	rabbit
BOW+SVM	87.23%	75.81 %	75.95 %
Our method	89.36%	79.78 %	77.04 %

Novel Cuteness Datasets. We collected new datasets with three categories: cat, dog, and rabbit. Each image is labeled with either "cute" or "non-cute". The cat category contains 1826 images with 1298 non-cute and 528 cute images. The dog category contains 1477 images with 987 non-cute image and 490 cute images. The rabbit category contains 1143 images with 761 non-cute image and 372 cute images. For the cat dataset we randomly selected 1100 non-cute images and 428 cute images as training set and the remaining images were used for testing. In the dog dataset, 800 non-cute images and 400 cute images were selected as training set and the remaining images were used as testing set. In rabbit dataset we selected 650 non-cute images and 500 cute images as training set and the remaining images were used as test set.

Experimental Settings and Results. The experiments were carried out by testing three methods on the three categories. We used the following settings: the number of visual word is 512; the number of Gaussian components is 512. We also applied the PCA to SIFT, reducing its dimensionality from 128 to 80. After encoding spatial information, the feature dimension becomes $d = 82$. We trained three cuteness classifiers for the three categories respectively.

To detect the cute parts of interests, we trained an ensemble model with 20 weak classifiers. Each classifier corresponds with a component in the Fisher vector. According to the last two dimensions in each component, we can identify a ellipse region in the image. We plotted these regions if the weak classifier gives positive score. Figure 3 illustrates the detection results. It is easy to see that our model could reliably locate the cute parts of the animal images.

We compared the performance of our cuteness recognition method with the classical bag-of-words (SIFT + SVM) model in Table 1. We can see that our method consistently outperforms the BOW model in all the three datasets. Moreover, the satisfying accuracies (77%-89%) suggest that we can obtain a reliable model for cuteness recognition.

Table 2: Comparing our method and classical Fisher vector.

	mean Acc	number of components
Our method	82.06%	20
Fisher Vector [14]	84.31%	512

Since our model can be viewed as an extension of Fisher vector [14], it is worth comparing the performance of our

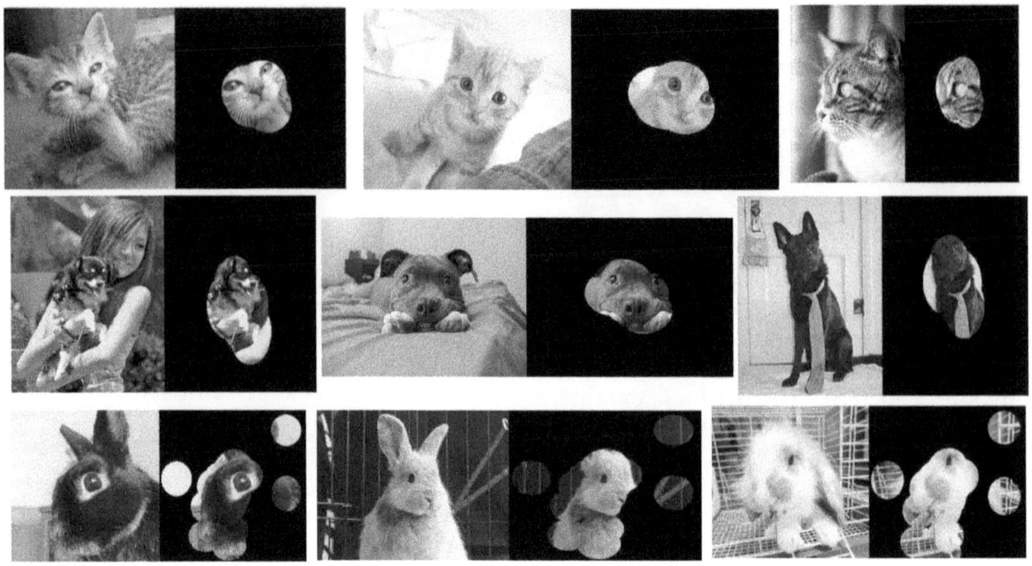

Figure 3: Cuteness localization by our method.

method and FV. As Table 2 shows, our method uses only 20 components, while FV uses 512 components. However, we obtain a comparable accuracy even with a much smaller number of components. The benefits of using less components are validated by Figures 2 and 3, where our model can localize cute parts which can be interpreted by human.

4. CONCLUSIONS

This paper proposes to recognize cute one from non-cute animals, including cats, dogs, and rabbits. We extend the classical Fisher vector method so that our new method can not only determine whether an image is cute or not, but also detect the cute parts in the images. Compared with previous work, the proposed model works reliably and generates clear localization results. In the future, we will apply our method to large scale cuteness detection. Another research interest is to investigate the attribute approach [19, 18] in cuteness recognition.

5. ACKNOWLEDGEMENTS

This work was partially supported by the Natural Science Foundation of China (61173104), National Basic Research Program of China (2014CB347600), and Open Projects Program of National Laboratory of Pattern Recognition.

6. REFERENCES

[1] G. Csurka, C. Dance, L. Fan, J. Willamowski, and C. Bray. Visual categorization with bags of keypoints. In *Workshop on statistical learning in computer vision, ECCV*, 2004.

[2] F. Fleuret and D. Geman. Stationary features and cat detection. *Journal of Machine Learning Research*, 9(11), 2008.

[3] S. Gould, R. Fulton, and D. Koller. Decomposing a scene into geometric and semantically consistent regions. In *ICCV*, 2009.

[4] ImageNet. Fine-grained classification of dogs. http://www.image-net.org/challenges/LSVRC/2012/, 2012.

[5] T. Jaakkola, D. Haussler, et al. Exploiting generative models in discriminative classifiers. In *NIPS*, 1999.

[6] J. M. Jan Ŝochman. Adaboost. *Centre for Machine Perception, Czech Technical University, Prague.*

[7] L. Ladický, P. Sturgess, K. Alahari, C. Russell, and P. H. Torr. What, where and how many? combining object detectors and crfs. In *ECCV*, 2010.

[8] C. H. Lampert, H. Nickisch, and S. Harmeling. Learning to detect unseen object classes by between-class attribute transfer. In *CVPR* , 2009.

[9] H. Li, X. Wang, J. Tang, and C. Zhao. Combining global and local matching of multiple features for precise item image retrieval. *Multimedia systems*, 19(1):37–49, 2013.

[10] D. G. Lowe. Distinctive image features from scale-invariant keypoints. *International journal of computer vision*, 60(2):91–110, 2004.

[11] H. Nittono, M. Fukushima, A. Yano, and H. Moriya. The power of kawaii: Viewing cute images promotes a careful behavior and narrows attentional focus. *PloS one*, 7(9):e46362, 2012.

[12] O. M. Parkhi, A. Vedaldi, C. Jawahar, and A. Zisserman. The truth about cats and dogs. In *ICCV*, 2011.

[13] O. M. Parkhi, A. Vedaldi, A. Zisserman, and C. Jawahar. Cats and dogs. In *CVPR*, 2012.

[14] F. Perronnin, J. Sánchez, and T. Mensink. Improving the fisher kernel for large-scale image classification. In *ECCV*, 2010.

[15] R. Sprengelmeyer, D. Perrett, E. Fagan, et al. The cutest little baby face a hormonal link to sensitivity to cuteness in infant faces. *Psychological Science*, 20(2):149–154, 2009.

[16] S. Tang, Y.-T. Zheng, Y. Wang, and T.-S. Chua. Sparse ensemble learning for concept detection. *Multimedia, IEEE Transactions on*, 14(1):43–54, 2012.

[17] P. Welinder, S. Branson, T. Mita, Cet al. Caltech-ucsd birds 200, 2010

[18] F. X. Yu, L. Cao, R. S. Feris, et al. Designing category-level attributes for discriminative visual recognition. In *CVPR*, 2013.

[19] H. Zhang, Z.-J. Zha, Y. Yang, S. Yan, Y. Gao, and T.-S. Chua. Attribute-augmented semantic hierarchy: towards bridging semantic gap and intention gap in image retrieval. In *ACM Multimedia*, 2013.

[20] W. Zhang, J. Sun, and X. Tang. Cat head detection-how to effectively exploit shape and texture features. In *ECCV*, 2008.

A 3D Fingertips Detecting and Tracking Algorithm based on the Sliding Window

Jun Wu, Wenjing Qiao, Cailiang Kuang
School of Electronics and Information
Northwestern Polytechnical University
You Yi Xi Lu 127, Xi'an, P.R.China
junwu@nwpu.edu.cn

Zhenbao Liu, Shuhui Bu
School of Aeronautics
Northwestern Polytechnical University
You Yi Xi Lu 127, Xi'an, P.R.China
{Liuzhenbao, bushuhui}@nwpu.edu.cn

Junwei Han
School of Automation
Northwestern Polytechnical University
You Yi Xi Lu 127, Xi'an, P.R.China
junweihan2010@gmail.com

ABSTRACT
In this paper, we propose a 3D finger detecting and tracking algorithm (3dFDT) based on a sliding window for RGB-D sequences. Microsoft Kinect is utilized as a 3D depth camera, which provides RGB images and depth data simultaneously. However the depth data have large noises when the background is white. We are focusing on tracking the up or down movements of the fingertips in order to apply in some applications such as playing the piano on the table or "in the air". First, the skin statistical ellipse model is applied to detect the hand skin region, and the pseudo-contours are removed to get the interested hand region. Then, the region center is considered as the center of the palm. Next, the fingertips are located precisely using the convex defect detection based on the refined hand contours. Furthermore, the depth information is aligned to the fingertips in the RGB channels. Finally, the sliding window strategy is employed to stabilize the depth information due to large noises from the depth space especially when dealing with the white surface as backgrounds. The experimental results show that our proposed method is effective, and it can be applied in the real-time applications for non-contact interactions.

Categories and Subject Descriptors
H.5.2 [**Information Interfaces and Presentation**]: User Interfaces - *Input devices and strategies*; I.4.8 [**Image Processing and Computer Vision**]: Scene Analysis - *Depth cues, Tracking;* H.1.2 [**Models and Principles**]: User/Machine Systems - *Human information processing*;

General Terms
Algorithms; Performance; Design; Experimentation.

Keywords
Fingertips Tracking; RGB-D images; Sliding Window; Kinect.

MM '14, November 3 – 7, 2014, Orlando, FL, USA
Copyright 2014 ACM 978-1-4503-3063-3/14/11…$15.00.
http://dx.doi.org/10.1145/2647868.2655047

1. INTRODUCTION
With the rapid development of the HCI interaction and virtual reality, the people prefer to the natural and friendly interaction technologies, such as speech recognition [1] and gesture recognition [2] to control the computers, rather than the traditional keyboard and mouse It gives us perfect experiences to talk or communicate with computers. For the gesture recognition, the multi-touch technique is successful and popular in portable devices [3], and extracts much attentions. While, it need to touch within a 2D plane. In some applications, we need non-contact gesture interaction in a 3D space..

In the early stage, binocular vision system is widely used to get the depth information [4]. While the calibration is necessary before computing. In June 2010, Microsoft released a RGB-D depth camera called Kinect XBOX360. With this type of depth camera, we can easily capture the 3D information for body parts such as the hands. But for tiny object tracking, such as finger tracking, the noises in depth space make it not trivial.

Gesture recognition based on RGB-D image sequences mainly use the depth information to detect the hand and the fingers. Maisto and Panella [5] first build a matrix with depth information; then, for every pixel of the image, its distance from the hand-point along the three axes is checked: if it is less than a threshold, the point will be identified as belonging to the hand. Raheja et al [6] find the palm using the image circular filter, obtain the depth image of the fingers, and locate the fingertips through searching the minimal depth of each fingertips. Liang [7] locates the palm based on distance transform to the hand contour, and performs the palm tracking with a Kalman filter and the fingertip tracking with particle filters. Frati [8] tracks the hand and fingertips in depth space only based on 2D hand contour processing, followed by a Kalman filtering. This way makes the results unstable and sensitive to the depth ranges, and it is prone to fail with the closer (especially white-like) backgrounds.

For tracking fingertips from the RGB-D image sequence, in this paper we need to simplify the scenario based on some basic assumptions: 1) the hand is closer to the camera compared to the other parts of human body. 2) the absolute errors within the regions of the forearm and hand is less than a pre-define threshold. 3) a palm is the biggest region for a hand, and sometimes the palm region is considered as a circle approximately. For most of the existing methods, the general scenario is that the palm is facing to the camera. But in our scenario, the back of the palm is facing to the camera, for example, playing the piano.

In this paper, we propose a fingertip up/down movements tracking algorithm (3dFDT), and use these information as inputs for a human-computer interface. First, the ellipse model is applied to detect the hand skin regions. Then, the center region is considered as the center of the palm. Next, the fingertips are positioned using the convex defect detection from the hand contours. Furthermore, the depth information is aligned to the fingertips in the RGB color spaces. Finally, the sliding window strategy is employed to stabilize the depth information due to the noisy depth information.

2. THE PROPOSED METHOD: 3dFDT

In order to track the finger accurately from a RGB-D camera, we integrate the RGB color space and the Depth space. First, the color data is mainly utilized to segment the hand region and further localize the fingers as well as the fingertips, and then the fingertips are automatically labeled as its real name. Next, the fingertips are tracked in the RGB-and-Depth joint space. At the same time, the sliding window strategy is employed to stabilize the finger depth information. The framework of the 3dFDT algorithm is shown in Fig. 1. The detailed steps are as follows.

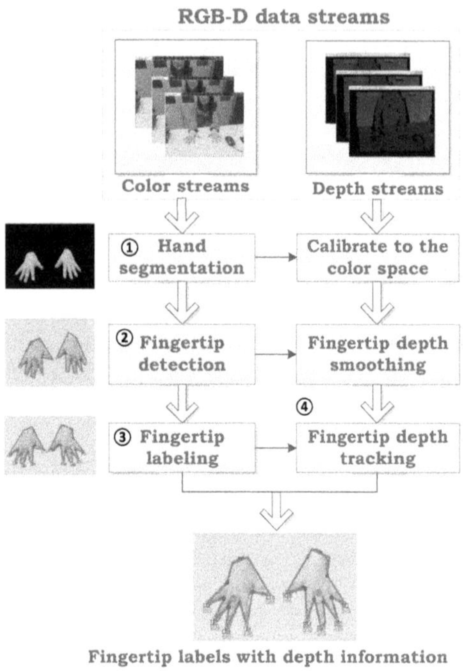

Fig 1. The Flowchart of the Proposed Method (3dFDT).

2.1 Hand Segmentation

In this context, we utilize the skin color model to detect the hands for finger tracking. Since the background and shapes of hand are diverse, it is difficult to differentiate hands from the complicated environments. Thus it is not effective to use the template matching [9] or geometric methods [10]. As the human skin has the unique characteristic in special color space, we make use of the ellipse color model [11] to detect the hands in the YC_rC_b color space.

To learn the statistical ellipse color model for hands, the RGB image is first transferred to YC_rC_b color space. However, the value of Y affects the distribution estimation based on the subspace of C_r and C_b. In this paper, we utilize the nonlinear Karhunen-Loeve transform to project the color data to a new plane, and the statistical elliptical models are:

$$\frac{(x-ec_x)}{a^2}+\frac{(y-ec_y)}{b^2}=1, \quad (1)$$

$$\begin{bmatrix} x \\ y \end{bmatrix}=\begin{bmatrix} \cos\theta & \sin\theta \\ -\sin\theta & \cos\theta \end{bmatrix}\begin{bmatrix} C_b'-c_x \\ C_r'-c_y \end{bmatrix}, \quad (2)$$

where, (x,y) is an arbitrary point in the ellipse, e is the eccentricity, a and b are the semimajor and semiminor axis respectively, (c_x,c_y) is the ellipse center, θ is the angle, and, C_r' with C_b' are the corresponding points in the color space (C_r, C_b). We use an binary image to store the ellipse at the oval. Therefore, when we determine the other pixel, we convert it into coordinates in the (C_r , C_b) color sub-space, and then find the corresponding values of the coordinates in the above ellipse. If non-zero, it is the skin; and vice versa.

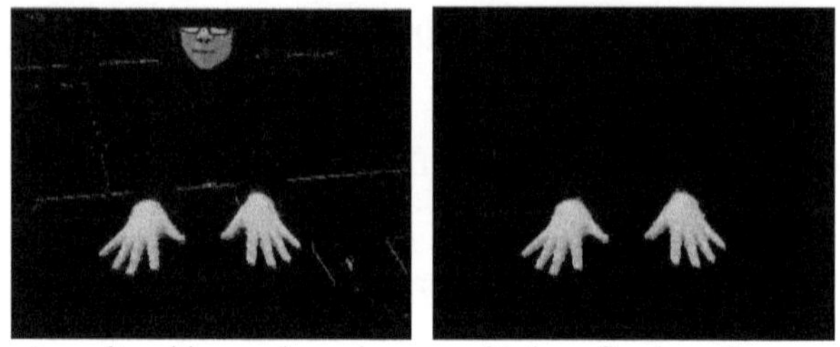

a) results with pseudo-regions b) the refined results

Fig 2. Examples for hand segmentation.

However, some candidate regions detected by the ellipse color model are false because the image might have regions with similar color as the skin. Moreover, other body parts might be active in the results, such as the face and arms, as in Fig.2 (a). They should be removed from the candidate skin regions. Here, we further use the empirical strategies to remove these false candidate regions. Firstly, the true hand regions are supposed to locate in the center, and 20% area around the image is ignored for further processing. Secondly, the small areas (less than 1% area of an image) are filtered out to eliminate noisy regions). As a result, the final hand regions are detected as shown in Fig. 2 (b).

2.2 Fingertip Detection

Based on the hand regions from the hand segmentation, the convex defects as well as the convex hulls are integrated to locate the fingertips. Based on the Graham's scanning algorithm [12], the candidate convex hulls and defects are discovered, which are shown in Fig. 3 (a). The blue bubbles represent the convex defects and the yellow ones denote the convex hulls.

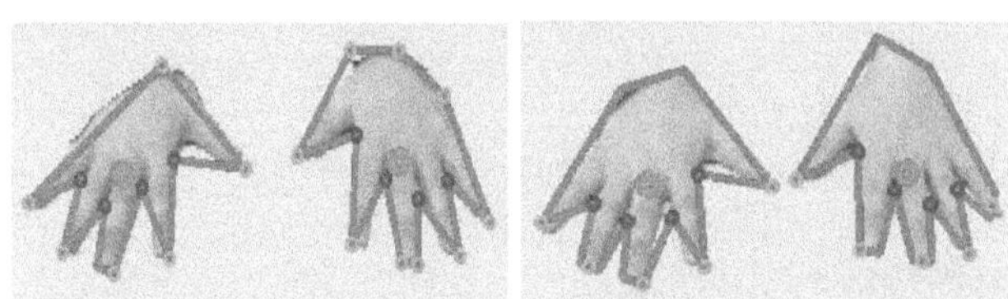

(a) convex hulls/defects candidates (b) refined results of fingertips

Fig 3. Examples for refining fingertip detection.

For these convex candidates as in Fig.3 (a), the empirical rules are further taken into consideration to remove the false candidates: (a) the fingertip candidates should be in the contour of hands. (b) the curvature radius of convex defects would be greater than the threshold μ. (c) the distance and angle between the convex hulls and the center of hands regions should satisfy the following rules,

$$d(P_n(x_i,y_i),C_n(x_c,y_c))=\sqrt{(x_i-x_c)^2+(y_i-y_c)^2}>\gamma, \quad (3)$$

$$|\beta(P_n(x_i,y_i),C_n(x_c,y_c))-\beta(P_n(x_j,y_j),C_n(x_c,y_c))|<\varepsilon, \quad (4)$$

$$\beta(P_n(x_i,y_i),C_n(x_c,y_c)) = \arcsin\frac{|x_i - x_c|}{d(P_n(x_i,y_i),C_n(x_c,y_c))} \quad ,(5)$$

where, $P_n(x_i,y_i)$ is the i-th convex hull with coordinate (x_i,y_i), $C_n(x_c,y_c)$ is the center of one hand regions with coordinate (x_c,y_c). $d(P_n(x_i,y_i),C_n(x_c,y_c))$ is the distance between $P_n(x_i,y_i)$ and $C_n(x_c,y_c)$, and $\beta(P_n(x_i,y_i),C_n(x_c,y_c))$ is the angle of convex hull $P_n(x_i,y_i)$ to the palm center.

That is, 1) if the distance between the convex hull and the center of hands regions is greater than the threshold γ, the candidate should be discarded. 2) two candidates would be merged into one if the difference of their angels to the center is lower than the threshold ε, as in Equation (4). Following these strategies, the convex hulls and defects actually representing the ten fingertips from two hands are kept, as shown in Fig. 3(b).

2.3 Fingertip Labeling

Based on the results for the fingertips detection, we further assign each fingertip a label or a name. Using the distances and angles between the convex hulls and the center of hand region, we are also able to distinguish the fingers. In general, the thumb finger has the largest angle and the little finger has the second largest angle. Then, other fingers would be labeled according to their spatial locations.

As we know, one hand has five different fingers: Thumb (Th), Index (Id), Middle (Mi), Ring (Ri), Little (Li). To distinguish the left (L) and right (R) hand, we add a prefix L- or R- before each label to get ten different labels: "LTh", "LId", "LMi", "LRi", "LLi", "RTh", "RId", "RMi", "RRi", and "RLi".

2.4 Fingertip Depth Tracking

After each fingertip is labeled, we can obtain its depth value. Before using the depth stream, we first align the depth channel with the RGB channel. The convex contour is detected, and the outboard points are marked as the positions of fingertips. According to the morphology of the hands, the real position of the fingertips are within the line across the outboard point and the center of palm, and it is close to the outboard point. When computing the fingertip depth, the neighbor pixels are considered.

When the depth information of each fingertip is determined, we can track it in the depth space. Due to the noisy data from the depth channel, we utilize the sliding window strategy to smooth the depth stream. The difference of depth image within three adjacent frames is calculated. For the *i-th* convex hull (the fingertip), the depth information is calculated as follows:

$$D(i,t) = \begin{cases} D(i,t), & |D(i,t) - \tilde{D}(i,t)| < \tau \\ \tilde{D}(i,t), & otherwises \end{cases} \quad (6)$$

where $D(i,t)$ is the depth of the fingertip with the label i at the time t, and $\tilde{D}(i,t) = \alpha_1 D(i,t-2) + \alpha_2 D(i,t-1)$ is the linear combination of the historical depth information. The parameters α_1 and α_2 are the weights, and $\alpha_1 + \alpha_2 = 1$. The parameter τ is the threshold for the sliding window.

Thus, the fingertip depth is tracked with the help of the sliding windowing, leading to more smooth results.

3. EXPERIMENTS

To evaluate the effectiveness of our proposed method, we first show some examples as intermediate results, such as hand segmentation, fingertip detection and labeling. Then we quantatively evaluate the accuracy of fingertips 3D locating, and then investigate how the sliding window strategy affects the performance. Finally, we evaluate finger labeling and tracking, comparing to the state-of-the-art methods.

3.1 Experimental Setup

We use Kinect XBOX360 as the 3D depth camera to capture the RGB-D image sequences. The initial camera angle is set as -16 degree, and the height of camera is around 51cm above the table.

The main algorithm is implemented in C++, combining the third party libraries as OpenNI2 and OpenCV 2.4.6. Microsoft Visual Studio 2010 is used as the IDE for the development.

In total, 20 volunteers (with different skin colors, different sizes of hands, different clothes as the backgrounds) are invited to participate in the experiments and evaluation. For our 3dFDT algorithm, the main parameters in Equation (3) and (4) are set as: μ=0.9, γ=10, ε=0.3.

3.2 Hand Segmentation, Fingertip Detection

We provide some examples for the results of hand region segmentation, fingertips detection, and fingertips labeling in the RGB-D image sequences, as shown in Fig. 4.

Conditions	Our method: 3dFDT	Method in [8]
close to the white table	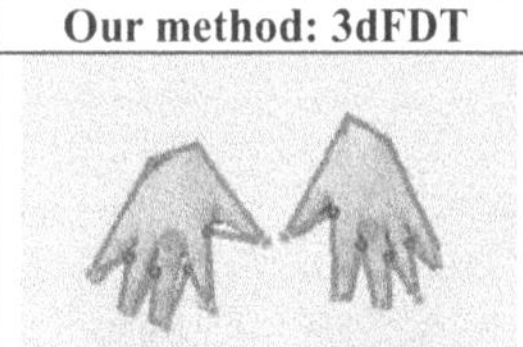	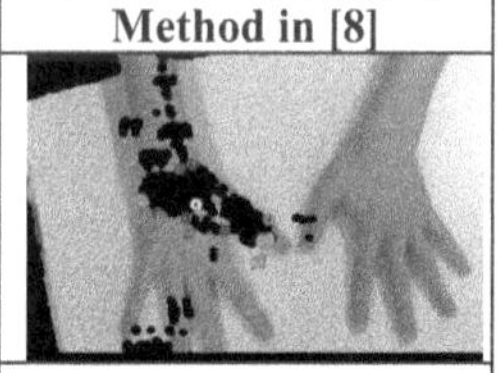
hang in the air; d is in the optimal range-10cm	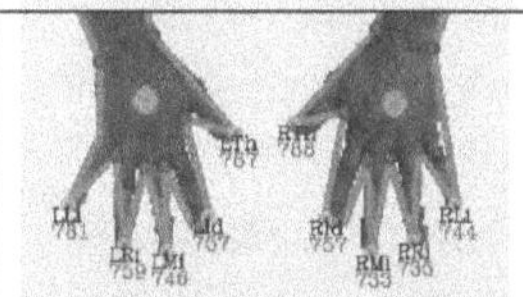 d=0.75m	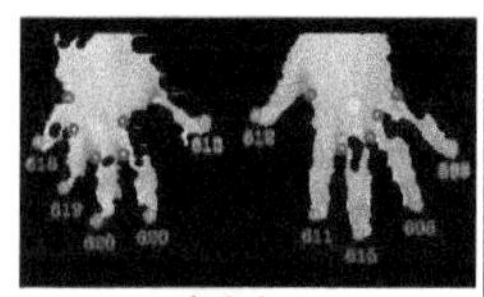 d=0.6m
hang in the air; d is in the optimal range	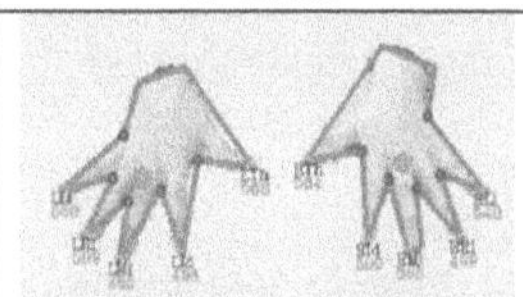 **d=0.85m (optimal)**	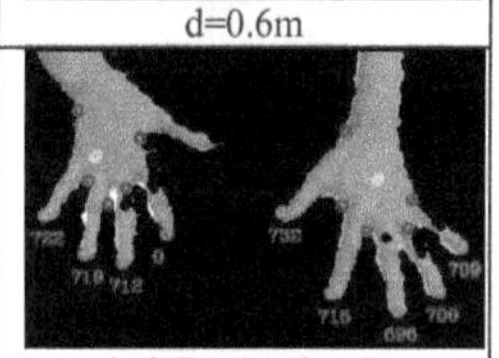 **d=0.7m (optimal)**
hang in the air; d is in the optimal range+10cm	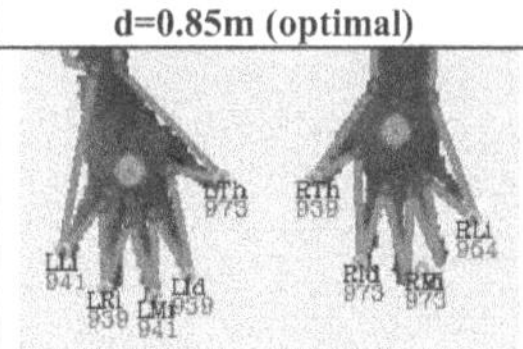 d=0.95m	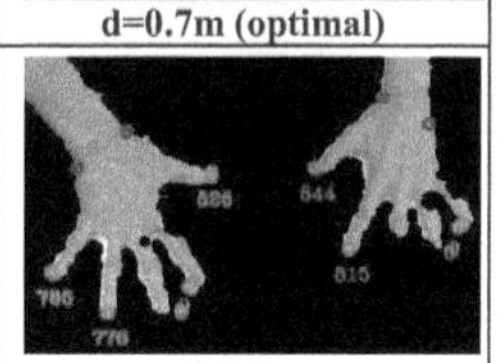 d=0.8m

Fig 4. Results of the finger detection and tracking algorithm.

From this comparison, we can conclude that our proposed method is more effective and robust than the method in [8]. The performance of our method is relatively robust to the depth variances (to the camera). When the optimal reference distance changes +/- 10cm, the method in [8] decrease significantly. Furthermore, when close to the white table, our method is still valid, as in the first row in Fig.4, but that in [8] fails.

3.3 Fingertips Detection Evaluation

We compute the average error depth distance for the fingertip detection in the depth space, as in Table 1. Six short video clips are utilized in this evaluation.

Table 1. Average error distance for fingertips detection.

Methods	Average Error Distance(cm)				
	Thumb	Index	Middle	Ring	Pinky
Our method	**1.63**	**0.93**	**0.78**	**0.74**	**0.69**
method in [7]	1.71	1.04	0.96	0.83	0.77
method in [8]	1.82	1.89	2.07	2.52	2.46

From this table, we can find that our method has the best performance compared to the methods in [7] and [8]. One reason is that we combine the RGB channel and the depth channel, while in [8] only the depth channel is utilized.

3.4 The Depth Sliding Window Evaluation

For tracking with the sliding windowing, we compare the depth variances with different linear combination strategies for the sliding windows (the parameter τ in Equation (6) is set as 10), as illustrated in Fig. 5. From this figure, we can conclude that the sliding window strategy works well for different depth distances, and it is not so sensitive for the linear combination parameters.

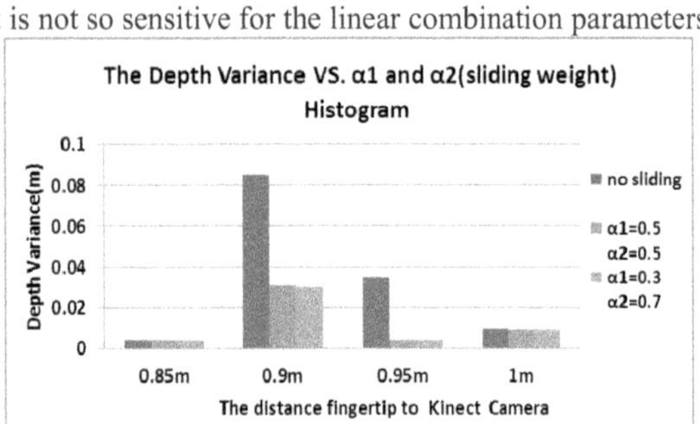

Fig 5. Results of the depth variances vs. the different linear combinations for the sliding window strategy.

3.5 Fingertip Labeling/Tracking Evaluation

The accuracy of the fingertip labeling is listed in the second column in Table 2. The video frames are the same as the data in section 3.3. We set the average distance between the camera and the fingers from 0.7m to 1.2m. The average fingertip depth tracking accuracy of our method and that in [7] are listed in the third and fourth columns in Table 2.

Table 2. The Results of the fingertips labeling/tracking.

Reference Depth to Kinect (m)	Fingertips labeling accuracy (%) -3dFDT	Fingertips depth tracking accuracy (%) -3dFDT	Fingertips depth tracking accuracy (%) in [7]
0.70	88.3	99.3	**96.2**
0.75	96.6	93.7	90.4
0.80	94.4	95.6	86.4
0.85	95.2	**97.4**	83.3
0.90	**96.2**	96.6	72.8
0.95	95.6	91.8	70.6
1.00	88.1	87.2	62.9
1.10	87.8	87.8	60.6
1.20	62.8	72.3	60.4

From this table, we can conclude that the optimal distance setting for our method is around 0.85m (0.7m for [8]). When the distance is less or greater than 0.85m, the performances decrease significantly. When the distance is around 1.2m, only 6 out of 10 fingers can be detected out. The method in [7] is more sensitive than our method in terms of changing of reference distance.

Furthermore, the accuracy of tracking the fingertips up/down movements is listed in Table 3. From this table, we can find that our tracking algorithm 3dFDT works well in the reference distance around 0.80m to 0.85m. And the performance decreases slightly for optimal distances nearby.

Table 3. The accuracy of detecting the fingertips movements. Each accuracy data pair is for the up/down movement.

Ref. distance (m)	0.75	0.80	0.85	0.9
Accuracy (%)	90.0/91.4	93.4/94.2	94.2/94.4	87.8/86.2

4. CONCLUSIONS

In this paper, we propose a 3D finger tracking algorithm (3dFDT) based on a sliding window for 3D depth images. First, the skin ellipse model is applied to detect the hand skin region, and the fingertips are located using the convex defect detection based on the hand contours. Then, the depth information is aligned to the RGB color channel to get the fingertip positions. Finally, the sliding window strategy is employed to stabilize the depth information of the fingertips. The experimental results show that our proposed method is effective, and it overperforms the existing methods. The optimal working depth distance is around 0.85m, and the performance is not so sensitive to the changing of depth range. The sliding window strategy is able to stabilize the depth information for tracking fingertips.

5. ACKNOWLEDGEMENTS

This work is supported by the National Natural Science Foundation of China (No.61103062), the Research Fund for the Doctoral Program of Higher Education (No.20116102120031), the NPU Foundation for Fundamental Research (No.JC201249), the Graduate Starting Seed Fund for NPU (No.Z2014124), and Scientific Research Foundation for Returned Scholars, Ministry of Education of China (2013).

6. REFERENCES

[1] Dahl G. E. et al. Context-dependent pre-trained deep neural networks for large-vocabulary speech recognition[J]. Audio, Speech, and Language Processing, IEEE Transactions on, 2012, 20(1): 30-42.

[2] Chaudhary A. et al. Intelligent approaches to interact with machines using hand gesture recognition in natural way: a survey[J]. IJCSES, 2011, 2(1): 122-133.

[3] Fuccella V. et al. Gestures and widgets: performance in text editing on multi-touch capable mobile devices[C]. ACM SIGCHI'2013, p.p.2785-2794.

[4] Blake R. et al. Binocular vision[J]. Vision research, 2011, 51(7): 754-770.

[5] Maisto M. et al. An accurate algorithm for the identification of fingertips using an RGB-D Camera[J]. Emerging and Selected Topics in Circuits and Systems, IEEE Journal on, 2013, 3(2): 272 - 283.

[6] Raheja, Jagdish L. Et al. Tracking of fingertips and centers of palm using Kinect[C]. IEEE CIMSiM, 2011, p.p. 248-252.

[7] Hui Liang, et al. 3D fingertip and palm tracking in depth image sequences [C]. ACM Multimedia (MM), 2012, p.p.785-788.

[8] Frati, V. et al. Using Kinect for hand tracking and rendering in wearable haptics [C]. IEEE WHC, 2011, p.p.317-321.

[9] Lin Z, Davis L S. Shape-based human detection and segmentation via hierarchical part-template matching[J]. PAMI, IEEE Transactions on, 2010, 32(4): 604-618.

[10] Collumeau J. F. et al. Hand gesture recognition using a dedicated geometric descriptor[C]. IEEE IPTA, 2012, p.p.287-292.

[11] Tan W. et al. Gesture segmentation based on YCb'Cr' color space ellipse fitting skin color modeling[C]. IEEE CCDC, 2012, p.p.1905-1908.

[12] S.G. Akl, Godfried Toussaint, Efficient Convex Hull Algorithms for Pattern Recognition Applications [C], JCPR 1978, p.p.483-487.

Temporal Dropout of Changes Approach to Convolutional Learning of Spatio-Temporal Features

Dubravko Culibrk
University of Trento
Italy
dubravko.culibrk@unitn.it

Nicu Sebe
University of Trento
Italy
sebe@disi.unitn.it

ABSTRACT

The paper addresses the problem of learning features that can account for temporal dynamics present in videos. Although deep convolutional learning methods revolutionized several areas of multimedia and computer vision, there have been relatively few proposals dealing with ways in which these methods can be enabled to make use of motion information, critical to the extraction of useful information from video. We propose a temporal dropout of changes approach for this, which allows us to consider temporal information over a series of frames without increasing the number of training parameters of the network.

To illustrate the potential of the proposed methodology, we focus on the problem of dynamic texture classification. Dynamic textures represent an important form of dynamics present in video data, so far not considered within the framework of deep learning.

Initial results presented in the paper show that the proposed approach, based on a well-known deep convolutional neural network, can achieve state-of-the-art performance on two well-known and challenging dynamic texture classification data sets (DynTex++ and UCLA dynamic texture).

Categories and Subject Descriptors

I.5.4 [**Pattern Recognition**]: Applications—*computer vision*

Keywords

Deep Learning; convolutional neural networks; spatio-temporal features; dynamic texture; temporal dropout

1. INTRODUCTION

The dominant methodology for visual recognition from images and video until recently relied on hand-crafted features [17][7]. Today, we are witnessing a paradigm shift and a growing interest in methods that learn features in both unsupervised and supervised settings.

Current research on deep learning suggests that there is significant potential in using large-scale Neural Networks (NNs) to address machine learning and, in particular, computer vision problems. The Google Brain project showed how an unsupervised AutoEncoder NN with 1 billion connections was able to learn to recognize common objects just by looking at a week's worth of YouTube videos [12]. In 2012, Krizhevsky *et al.* [11] showed how a Convolutional NN (CNN) with 650,000 neurons can be used to classify 1.2M images in the ImageNet Large Scale Visual Recognition data set into 1,000 classes [3], significantly advancing the state of the art. Their approach has recently been successfully extended to object detection achieving beyond-state-of-the-art results on the PASCAL VOC challenge data [7]. Deep learning has also seen several successful applications in the domain of image classification [23][21] and content-based retrieval [19].

When it comes to learning from video data, using deep (convolutional) NNs, few approaches exist [17][12]. However, arguably the most prominent, 3D CNN [9], achieved the best performance in three human action recognition tasks of the TRECVID 2009 Evaluation for Surveillance Event Detection challenge [16], showing the significant potential for such approaches, when large amount of labeled data is available.

Dynamic Textures (DT) represent a set of phenomena occurring in nature, where the perceived changes in the appearance of a system of large number elements are consistent, although the individual elements undergo stochastic changes in theirs. Typically the changes are due to motion (e.g. turbulent water, smoke, vegetation in the wind, insect swarms), but may be the result of the changing intensity of light emitted (e.g. fire). Zhao and Pietikäinen consider such phenomena extensions of the static texture to the temporal domain [22], since the effect is that of a textured object undergoing transformations. Derpanis and Wildes [4], however, point out that the term can apply equally well to simpler phenomena when analyzed in terms of aggregate regional properties (e.g., orderly pedestrian crowds and vehicular traffic).

The ability to recognize DTs based on visual processing is of significance to a number of applications, including, video indexing/retrieval, surveillance and environmental monitoring where they can serve as keys, isolate background clutter (e.g., fluttering vegetation) from activities of interest and detect various critical conditions (e.g., fires), respectively. It comes as no surprise that a significant amount of research effort has been directed toward solving this problem [2][22][13][4][5][20][6]. So far, to the best of our knowledge, no one has attempted to solve the problem of learning high-level features and recognizing DTs using deep NN architectures. Although, as a stochastic spatio-temporal phenomenon, DTs represent a basic domain for testing and evaluating spatio-temporal features.

In this paper we make several contributions: Dynamic texture classification using CNNs is considered for the first time. The proposed methodology exploits changes due to motion to extract

MM'14, November 3–7, 2014, Orlando, Florida, USA.

ACM 978-1-4503-3063-3/14/11 ...$15.00.
http://dx.doi.org/10.1145/2647868.2655048.

dynamic-texture related temporal features and introduces a novel approach to taking into account sequences of frames, without increasing the number of training parameters. We evaluated the proposed methodology on two public, widely used and challenging data sets: DynTex++ [6] and UCLA [5] dynamic texture datasets. The results presented show that we can achieve state of the art classification results.

The rest of the paper is organized as follows: Section 2 deals with the relevant published work. Section 3 describes the proposed methodology. Section 4 discusses experiments performed and results achieved. Section 5 is dedicated to our conclusions.

2. RELATED WORK

2.1 Dynamic Texture Classification

The research into the classification and recognition of dynamic textures continues unabated [4][22][20][6]. A large number of approaches have been proposed over the last ten years. In their 2005 survey Chetverikov and Péteri [2] divided the existing approaches into five classes: methods based on optical flow, methods computing geometric properties in the spatio-temporal domain, methods based on local spatio-temporal filtering, methods using global spatio-temporal transforms and model-based methods that use estimated model parameters as features. Regardless of the type of the approach, they attempt to extract features descriptive of the dynamic texture and classify them by either defining a suitable distance measure and creating a simple distance-based algorithm for comparison or training a machine learning algorithm to achieve the task.

Volume local binary patterns (VLBP) have been proposed by Zhao and Pietikäinen as features to describe dynamic textures [22]. The VLBPs are an extension of the LBP operator widely used in ordinary texture analysis, that combine motion and appearance. They tested their approach using videos generated by extracting parts of the sequences in the DynTex database [13], creating a data set that had 10 examples of a certain class derived from single DynTex sequences. Their classifier is a simple nearest neighbor classifier, based on the log-likelihood statistic that allows them to compare VLBPs, and they used leave-one-group-out (i.e. n/m fold cross-validation [18]) to measure performance, where m corresponds to the number of examples extracted for a single dynamic texture and n is the total number of examples. Various classification rates were achieved depending of whether or not the features used were shift-invariant and how long the feature vector was. Their best result is an accurate classification rate of 95.71%, achieved for a shift-invariant VLBP and a fairly large feature vector $(4, 176$ bins$)$.

Chan and Vasconcelos [1] model the dynamic texture as a linear dynamic system (LDS) and achieve good classification using the Martin distance to compare the models. They evaluated both nearest neighbor and support vector machine (SVM) classifiers and showed that the use of a machine learning algorithm such as SVM can improve the classification significantly. Through the use of the SVM classifier they achieved accurate classification rate of 97.5% on the UCLA database [15]. More recently (2009) their work has been extended by Ravichandran *et al.* [14] to use bags of LDSs to achieve improved view-invariant texture classification, when eight classes of textures are concerned.

Derpanis and Wildes [4] proposed new features based on spatio-temporal oriented energy filters to describe dynamic textures and classify them. They identified 7 semantic categories in the UCLA database (flames, fountain, smoke, turbulence, waves, waterfall, vegetation) and achieved a comparatively low classification rate of 92.3%, on sequences derived from this database. However, they specifically considered shift-invariant recognition, and report improved performance under these conditions.

Recently, an approach based on Dynamic Fractal Spectrum (DFS) of temporal gradient (changes) and intensity, derived from a sequence of DT images, has been proposed [20]. Once the features are extracted, an SVM classifier is used to perform DT classification. To the best of our knowledge, the DFS approach achieves state-of-the-art results on the UCLA and DynTex++ public databases, achieving 100% accuracy on the UCLA for 50-class problem and 89.9% for DynTex++.

As far as we are aware no one has considered the problem of using deep neural networks to learn high-level features and use them as basis for dynamic texture classification/recognition.

2.2 Spatio-Temporal Features for Deep Learning

Several approaches have been prosed that attempt to learn the spatio-temporal features using deep CNNs. The focus of these approaches has been mainly on human action recognition.

The approach proposed by Taylor *et al.* [17] can be viewed as a convolutional extension of the Gated Restricted Boltzmann Machine. The authors showed that the architecture proposed is able to learn correspondences between pairs of images. Based on such features they build a multistage neural network classifier that achieved performance comparable to the state of the art in the domain of human action recognition.

More recently, Le *et al.* [12] proposed another approach that uses unsupervised learning of basic features using independent subspace analysis. They stacked Independent Subspace Analysis networks as subunits to form the final convolutional network. Replacing hand-crafted features with the learned ones yielded state-of-the-art performance on human action recognition. The training is done on 3D blocks of (10) (16×16 pixel) patches from consecutive frames fed as input to the net. They trained on 200,000 video blocks. It is interesting to note that the performance of their approach drops by 10% when only two frames were considered instead of 10.

The 3D CNN [9] is a supervised approach. In contrast with the two previously discussed approaches, the input to the network are not just raw frames. Instead, the input is comprised of greyscale frames, the gradient and optical flow in x and y directions. Buffers of 7 frames centered on the current frame are used as input to 3D convolution kernels. The authors state that blocks of 5-7 frames have empirically been shown to yield the same performance as taking into account the whole sequence. The size of the patches used for the TRECVID data set was 60×40.

In the proposed approach we also consider the grayscale raw information of the frames, the temporal gradient instead of optical flow, but represent the block of frames of interest with a single randomly selected frame. In contrast to other approaches, our approach does not suffer from the increase in the number of training parameters with the expansion of the block (time-interval) considered.

3. TEMPORAL DROPOUT OF CHANGES APPROACH

The proposed approach, shown in Fig. 1 is simple. Similar to the DFS [20] we use greyscale images and temporal gradient (change) information. However, rather than considering only the temporal gradient between the current and previous frame, we would like to consider longer-term motion across a larger block of frames (Group of Pictures - GOP), as typically done in other deep learning approaches [9]. To do so without increasing the number of train-

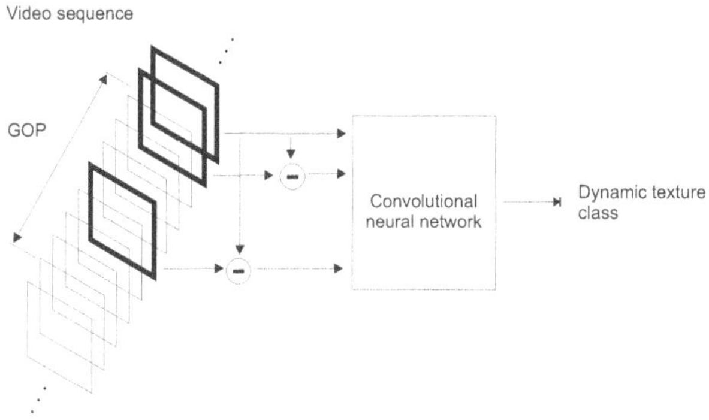

Figure 1: Proposed change detection and temporal dropout approach: The input to the convolutional network is comprised of the greyscale frame, temporal gradient and the gradient between the current frame and a frame randomly selected from a preceding block of frames - Group of Pictures (GOP).

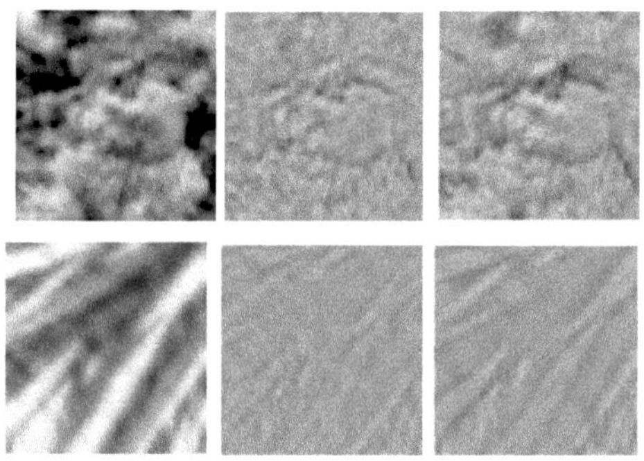

Figure 2: Features from sample frames: Left to right - greyscale, gradient previous frame, gradient random frame. Top - DynTex++ cloth class, bottom - UCLA plant-t-near class.

able parameters, which is a limiting factor in the other proposed appoaches, we use a temporal dropout strategy, whereby a single frame is selected at random from the GOP and a gradient is computed between that frame and the current one.

Our approach is motivated by the dropout mechanism used to reduce overfitting in deep NNs [8], by preventing co-adaptation. In our experiments we used GOP size of 25 frames, as it is represents a second of a 25 fps sequence. This enables us to handle 2.5 times larger sequence of frames than the largest previously considered, without increasing the size of the network.

Fig. 2 shows features extracted for sample frames from the DynTex++ and UCLA data sets. The gradients were scaled to the [0,255] range.

While the proposed approach can be used with any convolutional network architecture, the convolutional neural network used in our experiments is the Krizhevsky *et al.* 650,000 neurons architecture [11], as adapted in [7]. The network contains eight layers, five are convolutional and the remaining three are fully connected. The output of the network is a 128 class softmax, allowing us to use the same architecture to produce the distribution over the classes from both DynTex++ and UCLA datasets (total of 86). The rest is unused, but kept as it does not effect the computational efficiency. The input to the network was reduced by 2 pixels when compared to the original size of the sequences in the databases considered. This allows us to to follow the standard training procedure where

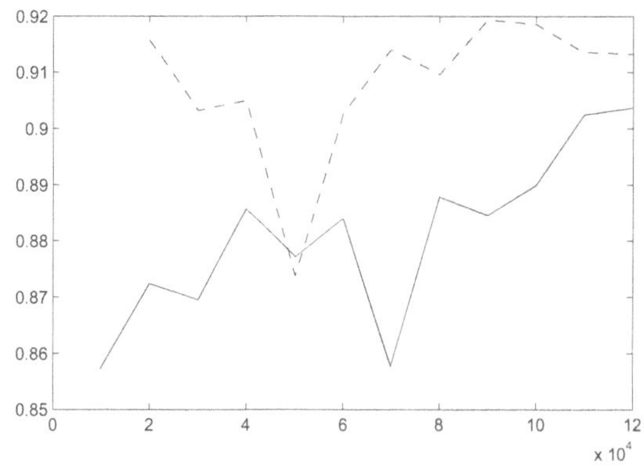

Figure 3: Accuracy during training over iterations: for UCLA data set - dashed line and DynTex++ data set - solid line.

10 patches are created for each input frame. The size of the input was therefore 48×48 pixels in the DynTex++ case and 46×46 in the UCLA. We train our network on a NVIDIA Tesla K40 GPU.

4. EXPERIMENTS AND RESULTS

Three main public DT datasets exist that have been widely used for DT analysis: the UCLA dataset [5], the DynTex dataset [13] and the DynTex++ dataset [6]. Since the DynTex++ dataset is derived from DynTex and seems to be the more challenging dataset of the two, we test the proposed approach on DynTex++ and UCLA datasets and compare with the state-of-the-art results for the DFS method reported in [20].

The UCLA dynamic texture dataset consists of 50 DT classes, each with four grayscale video sequences captured from different viewpoints. Each sequence contains 75, 48×48 pixel frames. In our experiments we used 25% of the data for testing, while the rest was used for training. The split corresponds to the first fold as provided with the dataset.

The DynTex++ dataset contains 36 classes of dynamic texture, each of which contains 100 sequences of a fixed size $50 \times 50 \times 50$. In our experiments we use a random selection of 20% of the sequences as a test set, while the rest form our training set.

We use a GOP of 25 frames and generate a single data instance for each frame after the initial 25 frames. Thus, each sequence of the DyntTex++ was represented with 25 instances per sequence and each UCLA sequence with 50. Each instance is classified separately by the NN and the final classification for a sequence is done by majority voting.

The initial training is done for 20,000 iterations on the larger DynTex++ data set. We than continue training the network either on DynTex++ or UCLA data for a subsequent 100,000 iterations. The training procedure is the same as that used in [7]. The training for our approach takes 24 hours. The classifier accuracy over the training iterations for both datasets is shown in Fig. 3. In all the experiments we used the Caffe implementation of convolutional neural networks [10].

We report two types of accuracy. The per-frame accuracy considers all the frames of the sequence separately and assumes that the decision about the type of the dynamic texture can be made based on a single frame. The sequence-level refers to the accuracy achieved by taking the mode of the per-frame labels as the label of the whole sequence.

The sequence-level accuracy our approach achieved on the UCLA dataset is 98% (a single sequence was misclassified). The top per-

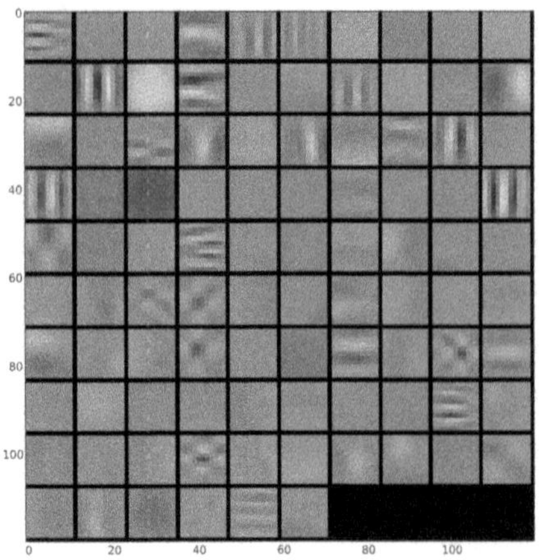

Figure 4: Some of the first convolutional layer filters learned by the network.

frame accuracy achieved over 100,000 iterations was 91.94%. The proposed method's sequence-level classification result is second only to DFS features combined with an SVM classifier. Both the per frame and sequence-level accuracy are above all other methods reported in the literature.

The top per-frame accuracy achieved for the DynTex++ data set is 90.37%, which, even though done at the level of single frames, surpasses the state of the art reported in [20] for sequence-level.

The network is clearly able to learn the features that enable efficient classification of the different DT classes. This can also be seen in Fig. 4, which shows some of the filters from the first layer of the network. The colored information in the figure corresponds to the temporal features learned, while the greyscale represents static features.

5. CONCLUSION

Although the deep learning methods revolutionizes several areas of computer vision, they have not, up to now, been considered for the task of dynamic texture classification. In this paper we show that a deep convolutional neural network can be efficiently used to achieve state-of-the-art DT classification results.

Our approach to learning features relies on temporal gradients and a novel temporal dropout technique, which allows us to consider larger time intervals without increasing the number of learning parameters.

6. ACKNOWLEDGMENTS

This project has received funding from the European Union's Seventh Framework Programme under xLiMe and QoSTREAM, Grant numbers 611346 and 295220.

We gratefully acknowledge the support of NVIDIA Corporation with the donation of the Tesla K40 GPU used for this research.

7. REFERENCES

[1] A. Chan and N. Vasconcelos. Classifying video with kernel dynamic textures. In *CVPR*, pages 1–6. IEEE, 2007.

[2] D. Chetverikov and R. Péteri. A brief survey of dynamic texture description and recognition. *Computer Recognition Systems*, pages 17–26, 2005.

[3] J. Deng, W. Dong, R. Socher, L.-J. Li, K. Li, and L. Fei-Fei. Imagenet: A large-scale hierarchical image database. In *CVPR*, pages 248–255. IEEE, 2009.

[4] K. Derpanis and R. Wildes. Dynamic texture recognition based on distributions of spacetime oriented structure. In *CVPR*, pages 191–198. IEEE, 2010.

[5] G. Doretto, A. Chiuso, Y. N. Wu, and S. Soatto. Dynamic textures. *International Journal of Computer Vision*, 51(2):91–109, 2003.

[6] B. Ghanem and N. Ahuja. Maximum margin distance learning for dynamic texture recognition. In *ECCV*, pages 223–236. Springer, 2010.

[7] R. Girshick, J. Donahue, T. Darrell, and J. Malik. Rich feature hierarchies for accurate object detection and semantic segmentation. *arXiv preprint arXiv:1311.2524*, 2013.

[8] G. E. Hinton, N. Srivastava, A. Krizhevsky, I. Sutskever, and R. R. Salakhutdinov. Improving neural networks by preventing co-adaptation of feature detectors. *arXiv preprint arXiv:1207.0580*, 2012.

[9] S. Ji, W. Xu, M. Yang, and K. Yu. 3d convolutional neural networks for human action recognition. *PAMI*, 35(1):221–231, 2013.

[10] Y. Jia. Caffe: An open source convolutional architecture for fast feature embedding. `http://caffe.berkeleyvision.org/`, 2013.

[11] A. Krizhevsky, I. Sutskever, and G. E. Hinton. Imagenet classification with deep convolutional neural networks. In *NIPS*, volume 1, pages 4–9, 2012.

[12] Q. V. Le, W. Y. Zou, S. Y. Yeung, and A. Y. Ng. Learning hierarchical invariant spatio-temporal features for action recognition with independent subspace analysis. In *CVPR*, pages 3361–3368. IEEE, 2011.

[13] R. Péteri, S. Fazekas, and M. Huiskes. DynTex: A comprehensive database of Dynamic Textures. *Pattern Recognition Letters*, 31(12):1627–1632, 2010.

[14] A. Ravichandran, R. Chaudhry, and R. Vidal. View-invariant dynamic texture recognition using a bag of dynamical systems. In *CVPR*, pages 1651–1657. IEEE, 2009.

[15] P. Saisan, G. Doretto, Y. Wu, and S. Soatto. Dynamic texture recognition. In *CVPR*, pages II–58–II–63. IEEE, 2001.

[16] A. F. Smeaton, P. Over, and W. Kraaij. Evaluation campaigns and trecvid. In *MIR '06: Proceedings of the 8th ACM International Workshop on Multimedia Information Retrieval*, pages 321–330. ACM Press, 2006.

[17] G. W. Taylor, R. Fergus, Y. LeCun, and C. Bregler. Convolutional learning of spatio-temporal features. In *ECCV*, pages 140–153. Springer, 2010.

[18] I. H. Witten and E. Frank. *Data Mining: Practical machine learning tools and techniques, 2nd Edition*. Morgan Kaufmann, San Francisco, 2005.

[19] P. Wu, S. Hoi, H. Xia, P. Zhao, D. Wan, and C. Miao. Online multimodal deep similarity learning with application to image retrieval. In *ACM MM*, pages 153–162, 2013.

[20] Y. Xu, Y. Quan, H. Ling, and H. Ji. Dynamic texture classification using dynamic fractal analysis. In *ICCV*, pages 1219–1226. IEEE, 2011.

[21] Z. Yuan, J. Sang, and C. Xu. Tag-aware image classification via nested deep belief nets. In *ICME*, pages 1–6, 2013.

[22] G. Zhao and M. Pietikainen. Dynamic texture recognition using local binary patterns with an application to facial expressions. *PAMI*, (28):915–928, 2007.

[23] S.-h. Zhong, Y. Liu, and Y. Liu. Bilinear deep learning for image classification. In *ACM MM*, pages 343–352, 2011.

Real-Time HDR Panorama Video

Lorenz Kellerer[1], Vamsidhar Reddy Gaddam[2], Ragnar Langseth[2], Haakon Stensland[2], Carsten Griwodz[2], Dag Johansen[3], Paal Halvorsen[2]

[1]Technical University Graz, Austria
[2]Simula Research Laboratory & University of Oslo, Norway
[3]University of Tromsø, Norway

[1]lkellerer-pirklbauer@student.tugraz.at [3]dag@cs.uit.no
[2]{vamsidhg, ragnarla, haakonks, griff, paalh}@ifi.uio.no

ABSTRACT

The interest for wide field of view panorama video is increasing. In this respect, we have an application that uses an array of cameras that overlook a soccer stadium. The input of these cameras are stitched together to provide a panoramic view of the stadium. One of the challenges we face is that large parts of the field are obscured by shadows on sunny days. Such circumstances cause unsatisfying video quality. We have therefore implemented and evaluated multiple algorithms related to high dynamic range (HDR) video. The evaluation shows that a combination of several approaches gives the most useful results in our scenario.

Categories and Subject Descriptors

H.5.1 [**Multimedia Information Systems**]: Video

General Terms

Experimentation; Measurement; Performance

Keywords

High dynamic range (HDR); Panorama video; Real-time

1. INTRODUCTION

Systems providing panorama videos have gained an increased interest as they can deliver both a higher resolution and a wider field-of-view compared to a single camera. Some of the application scenarios include surveillance, navigation, scenic views, educational exhibits and sports. In our research, we use such panoramas in an arena sport scenario [6], and we are currently able to generate a panorama video of a whole soccer stadium in real time.[12]

However, a major challenge is managing variations in lighting conditions. Our current setup works very well in most weather conditions. However, situations with low and/or bright sun give, as seen in figure 1(a), large challenges over the field. There is a large difference between the amount of light available from areas in the sun and in the shadows, i.e., in a clear day, we only have the choice of having a good dynamic range in one region. When there are intensely bright and dark areas in the image (figure 1(a)), most cameras also have problems creating a representative image. Particularly, in our stadium case study, the sun is significantly lower in the sky than most of the habitable world giving challenges as shown in the figure. In such a case, aiming for a good quality in the sunny areas leads to loss of details in shadows. It should also be noted that professional broadcasters also experience these problems. However, to address this problem, they have people manning cameras (and thus also the exposure settings) as well as a someone controlling the live broadcast performing manual adjustments (figures 1(c) and 1(b)), i.e., they manually select the area of interest probably depending on where the ball is located.

(a) Automatic camera (b) Broadcaster 1 (c) Broadcaster 2

Figure 1: Lighting challenges at our case study stadium. Comparison with two professional broadcasters. (NOTE: images from the same game but different situations)

Due to our aim of a fully automated system, our system needs to handle this without human interaction and in real-time. The problem is related to sub-optimal auto exposure and insufficient dynamic range on the camera sensors. Improvements can be achieved in several ways. In this respect, one could solve common auto exposure problems as proposed in [8] , and use real-time assembling of high-dynamic-range (HDR) video by using low-dynamic-range images [2, 5, 4]. Another important detail in our work is that a panorama texture usually contains a lot of pixels, i.e., 2040 × 5400 in our case, unlike the related works where the maximum resolution handled is Full HD (1920 × 1080). Even though the algorithms do not get affected, this introduces several practical challenges under a real-time constraint. In this paper, we present a panorama pipeline with an HDR module that can handle difficult lighting conditions. This module is a two-step process, first step creates the high dynamic

MM'14, November 3–7, 2014, Orlando, Florida, USA.

ACM 978-1-4503-3063-3/14/11 ...$15.00.
http://dx.doi.org/10.1145/2647868.2655049.

range image and second performs visually pleasing reduction of the dynamic range to normal screens. We have tested 3 different approaches for each step thus giving 9 possible combinations. Our experimental results show that the visual quality is generally improved over the LDR in all the combinations. Moreover some combinations also process 50 fps input to 25 fps HDR panorama video in real-time in our GPU accelerated implementations.

2. HDR ALTERNATIVES

An HDR image can be created by a process called radiance mapping, where multiple LDR images of the same scene are fused together. The fused image as such cannot be displayed using the conventional devices, so a compression of the dynamic range is performed where we preserve details in all regions and maintain a local contrast, i.e., giving a visually pleasing result. This process is called tone mapping. For the rest of the paper, we refer to the final output of tone mapping as the HDR image. We explored three approaches for radiance mapping, and three for tone mapping. We chose radiance mappers based on the criterion that they must merge multiple exposures. For the tone mappers, we picked a representative subset: one very simple to serve as easy comparison to others, one global and one local tone mapper. After extensive material research, we picked algorithms that subjectively provided the most pleasing results.

2.1 Radiance mappers

Debevec. One of the most cited approaches is presented by Debevec *et al.* [3], where the authors try to recover HDR radiance maps from photographs. It performs an estimation of camera response function and then a weighted selection process where the information is extracted from mid-tone regions of different exposures. We made a GPU implementation for the second step alone, since the first step needs to be performed once in a lifetime for a camera.

Robertson. Similar to *Debevec*, Robertson *et al.* [11] proposed a two step mapping with similar modules. But, they introduced a more extensive approach for recovering the camera response function. Thus, the radical changes are only to the offline step of the algorithm.

Tocci. As opposed to the previous approaches, Tocci *et al.* [13] propose a solution that consists of a single online step. The main assumption is that unless close to saturation in intensity, the preferred output pixels are those from the high exposures. Therefore, they introduce an approach that takes saturated pixels from the neighbourhood into consideration. Since this approach requires fetching the same pixels by different threads, we use the GPU's texture memory to exploit the spatial caching feature.

2.2 Tone mappers

Ward. Ward *et al.* [14] proposed an approach where a global scale factor is applied to each pixel, which is dependent on, among other parameters, the average brightness of the input image. A parallel reduction approach [7] for calculating the average over an entire image is implemented as part of our GPU implementation.

Larson. This algorithm proposed by Larson *et al.* [9] performs tonal compression by creating a look-up table per frame to represent a desired histogram. Unlike a simple histogram equalization, the target histogram is computed taking human contrast sensitivity into account.

Reinhard. Reinhard *et al.* [10] try to emulate a technique called "dodging & burning" [1]. This approach relies on the information from local neighbourhood for tonal compression. Adaptive Gaussian kernels are employed along different dimensions to average the exposure value, the adaptive nature is from the fact that the size of these kernels depends on the local contrast changes.

3. EXPERIMENTAL RESULTS

The computer used for the experiments uses a six-core Intel Core i7-3930K at 3.2 GHz with 32 GB quad-channel DDR3 memory and an Nvidia GeForce GTX 680 graphics processing unit with 3GB memory based on the Kepler architecture.

Figure 2: Pipeline modules

We capture the panorama video using five cameras, each with a resolution 2040 × 1080. Since our challenge is mostly due to the large difference in the amount of light available from two different regions (sun-light and shadow), we make two different exposures where one captures the details in shadow region and the other in hightlights. Hence, to generate one high resolution panorama frame, we have 10 images as input to the HDR module.

As seen in Figure 2, our pipeline consists of multiple consecutive steps. First, the captured frames are transferred to the GPU by the *Uploader* module running on the host. Then, the frames are converted to RGB from the recorded bayer pattern by the *Bayer converter* module which are then fed into the *HDR* module. The processed frames are then transferred back to host memory by the *Downloader* module. It must be noted that this is pipelined architecture which implies that when one frame is being processed by the *HDR* module, the next frame could be under processing in the *Bayer* module, and so on.

3.1 Visual Quality

In the following section, we will provide a subjective assessment of the different configurations of our implemented radiance and tone mappers. The input images displayed in figure 3 show a small part of our panorama frames to highlight details. Then, the output of all possible combinations can be seen in figure 5. The visual quality of the resulting image is based on multiple factors [15].

We performed a limited user study to assess the quality of the different configurations of algorithms. Here we asked 12 participants to rate videos obtained by combining the different algorithms. Several emerging patterns can be observed from the results shown in Figure 4. The first concerns the choice of tone-mappers. Here the average score

(a) Low exposure (b) High exposure

Figure 3: Input images for the HDR processing

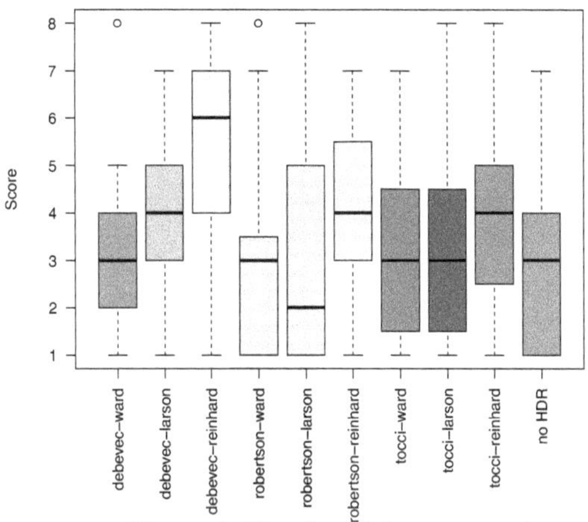

Figure 4: Results of the user study

achieved by *Robertson's* is higher than for the other tone-mappers in every combination with radiance-mappers. A second, less clear trend can be observed for the radiance-mappers. Here *Debevec's* always scores similar or higher than the other proposed radiance-mappers when combined with different tone-mappers

3.2 Execution Time

Real time performance is a major concern for our project. We accomplished this goal on all algorithms except with *Reinhard's* tone mapper. The multiple FFTs for applying the gaussian kernels in this algorithm are performed per frame. Although we use the highly optimized CUFFT library provided by Nvidia, the multiple FFTs still turned out to be a bottleneck. Furthermore, *Reinhard* is consuming a lot of memory. For each stored gauss-kernel, approximately 126 MB have to be allocated.

Furthermore, the combination *Tocci - Larson* is slightly above the real-time threshold, but we believe that with the optimizations mentioned in section 4, we can achieve real time here too.

A detailed listing of execution times can be found in Figure 6. We also executed only the HDR modules without interference from other modules. Those execution times can be seen in Figure 7.

Each of the modules contains several kernels. The scheduling of these kernels on the GPU is managed by CUDA. So, it must be noted that the execution times include the overheads created by scheduling. It can be seen that the execution times of other modules fluctuate when different HDR algorithms are employed. This is from the fact that CUDA schedules the kernels from these modules in different ways depending on the requirements of different modules. The GPU used in our experiments are capable of executing up to 16 kernels concurrently.

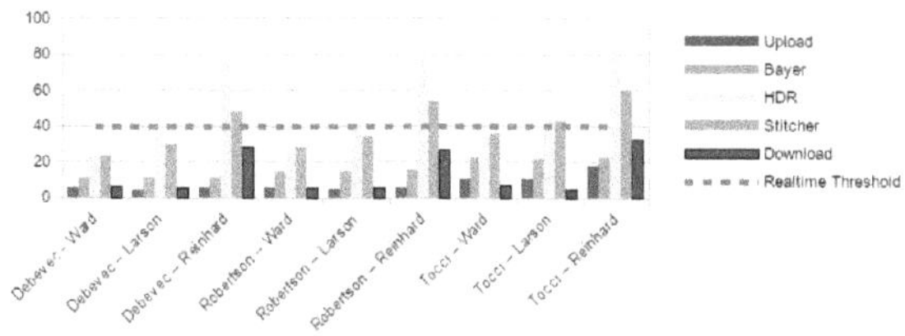

Figure 6: Execution times (ms) of the various modules in different configurations

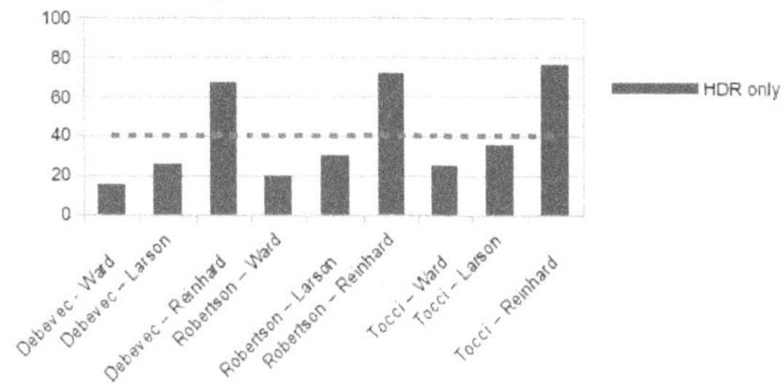

Figure 7: Execution times (ms) of the HDR module in different configurations

3.3 Summary

After taking both visual quality and the execution times into account, we came to a conclusion about the most optimal combination. We believe that using *Debevec's* radiance mapper paired with *Larson's* tone mapper is the best approach. Although *Reinhard's* tone mapper shows promising results, we could not make it pass the real-time requirements, and it also consumed too much memory. Ward's tone mapper produced useless results with our input. *Tocci's* radiance mapper proved to be too complex to efficiently be implemented in CUDA. Also, in our case, it produced undesirable artifacts. Lastly, *Robertson's* radiance mapper also proved to be very good, but the higher dynamic range it produced caused worse results when tone mapped.

4. DISCUSSION

We experimented with the placement of the HDR module within the pipeline. This step can either be performed before or after stitching the individual images together into a panorama. In the end, we decided to do it before because of three reasons:

1. The input to the HDR module is smaller since the stitcher removes overlap. But, this reduction was not enough to have a large impact on the performance.
2. The stitcher struggled with the high exposure input. Since large areas in this input are pure white, the performance of the stitcher suffered.
3. The HDR module also modifies the frame rate from 50fps to 25 fps. Thus, reducing the number of frames to be stitched by half.

We want to further improve the performance of the implementations we deemed worth pursuing. Therefore, we are looking into ways to parallelize Larson's histogram adjustment. Furthermore, we are exploring possibilities to distribute the HDR module on multiple machines. Since the capturing of the raw video is performed on two computers, it would seem advisable to perform HDR in a distributed

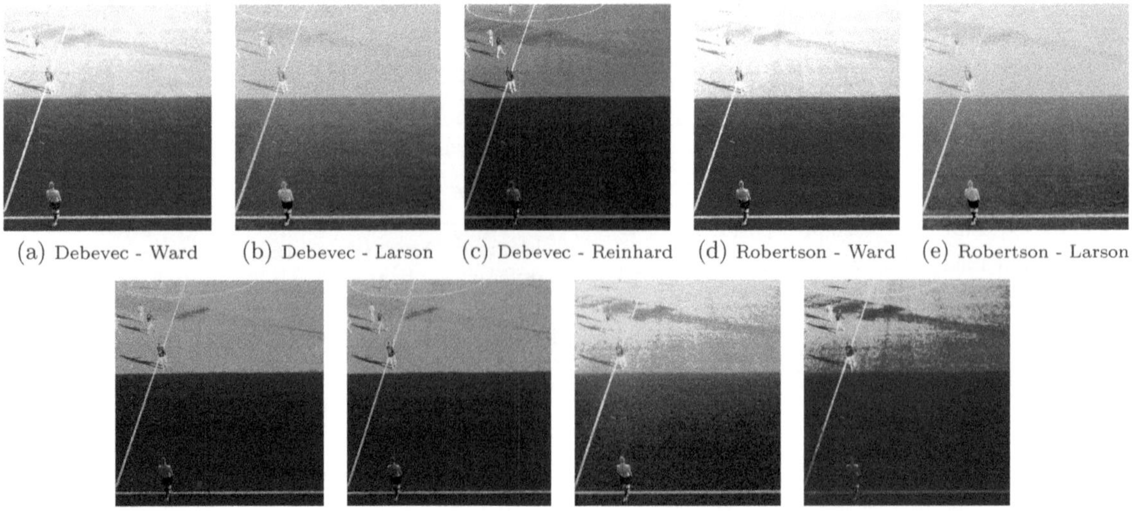

(a) Debevec - Ward (b) Debevec - Larson (c) Debevec - Reinhard (d) Robertson - Ward (e) Robertson - Larson (f) Robertson - Reinhard (g) Tocci - Ward (h) Tocci - Larson (i) Tocci - Reinhard

Figure 5: Visual quality after HDR for the different algorithms using the input images in figure 3

fashion. Lastly, the output of the tone mappers is scaled to a scene brigthness key value. This determines which value is mapped to middle brightness. In the current setup, this value is not changed even if the lighting conditions change. We want to explore ways to dynamically and intelligently change this key value.

5. CONCLUSION

By integrating HDR into our image processing pipeline, we managed to solve the problem of real-time HDR at large resolutions. We implemented various HDR algorithms and evaluated their performance ending up with a favourable combination. Our pipeline can now handle diverse lighting conditions. We can now display the entire soccer field at once despite the high variation in luminance due parts of it being in dark shadows and other in bright sun light. As opposed to the previous approaches [5], we can perform real-time HDR at a far greater resolutions up to 2040×5400.

6. REFERENCES

[1] A. Adams and R. Baker. *The print.* Little, Brown, 1983.

[2] M. A. Ali and S. Mann. Comparametric image compositing: Computationally efficient high dynamic range imaging. In *Proc. of IEEE ICASSP*, pages 913–916, 2012.

[3] P. E. Debevec and J. Malik. Recovering high dynamic range radiance maps from photographs. In *ACM SIGGRAPH 2008 classes*, page 31. ACM, 2008.

[4] B. Guthier, S. Kopf, and W. Effelsberg. Optimal shutter speed sequences for real-time hdr video. In *Proc. of IEEE IST*, pages 303–308, 2012.

[5] B. Guthier, S. Kopf, and W. Effelsberg. A real-time system for capturing hdr videos. In *Proce. of ACM MM*, pages 1473–1476, 2012.

[6] P. Halvorsen, S. Sægrov, A. Mortensen, D. K. Kristensen, A. Eichhorn, M. Stenhaug, S. Dahl, H. K. Stensland, V. R. Gaddam, C. Griwodz, and D. Johansen. Bagadus: An integrated system for arena sports analytics – a soccer case study. In *Proc. of ACM MMSys*, pages 48–59, Mar. 2013.

[7] M. Harris et al. Optimizing parallel reduction in cuda. *NVIDIA Developer Technology*, 2:45, 2007.

[8] W. C. Kao, L. W. Cheng, C. Y. Chien, and W. K. Lin. Robust brightness measurement and exposure control in real-ime video recording. *IEEE Trans. on Instrumentation and Measurement*, 60(4):1206–1216, 2011.

[9] G. W. Larson, H. Rushmeier, and C. Piatko. A visibility matching tone reproduction operator for high dynamic range scenes. *IEEE Trans. on Visualization and Computer Graphics*, 3(4):291–306, 1997.

[10] E. Reinhard, M. Stark, P. Shirley, and J. Ferwerda. Photographic tone reproduction for digital images. *ACM Trans. on Graphics*, 21(3):267–276, 2002.

[11] M. A. Robertson, S. Borman, and R. L. Stevenson. Estimation-theoretic approach to dynamic range enhancement using multiple exposures. *Journal of Electronic Imaging*, 12(2):219–228, 2003.

[12] H. K. Stensland, V. R. Gaddam, M. Tennøe, E. Helgedagsrud, M. Næss, H. K. Alstad, A. Mortensen, R. Langseth, S. Ljødal, O. Landsverk, C. Griwodz, P. Halvorsen, M. Stenhaug, and D. Johansen. Bagadus: An integrated real-time system for soccer analytics. *ACM Trans. Multimedia Comput. Commun. Appl. (TOMCCAP)*, 10(1s):14:1–14:21, Jan. 2014.

[13] M. D. Tocci, C. Kiser, N. Tocci, and P. Sen. A versatile hdr video production system. 30(4):41, 2011.

[14] G. Ward. A contrast-based scalefactor for luminance display. *Graphics gems IV*, pages 415–421, 1994.

[15] M. Čadík, M. Wimmer, L. Neumann, and A. Artusi. Image attributes and quality for evaluation of tone mapping operators. In *National Taiwan University*, pages 35–44. Press, 2006.

Dynamic Resource Management in Cloud-based Distributed Virtual Environments

Yunhua Deng†, Siqi Shen‡, Zhe Huang†, Alexandru Iosup‡, Rynson Lau†
†City University of Hong Kong, China ‡Delft University of Technology, Netherlands
yunhua.deng@my.cityu.edu.hk, s.shen@tudelft.nl, igamenovoer@gmail.com
a.iosup@tudelft.nl, rynson.lau@cityu.edu.hk

ABSTRACT

As an elastic hosting platform, cloud computing has been attracting many attentions for transferring compute-intensive applications from static self-hosting to flexible cloud-based hosting. Distributed virtual environments (DVEs) which typically involve massive users interacting at the same time and feature significant workload dynamics either in spatial due to in-game user mobility or in temporal due to the fluctuating user population, potentially are suitable applications with cloud-based hosting because of the need of resource elasticity. We explore the dynamic resource management for cloud-based DVEs by taking into account their multi-level workload dynamics which differ them from other applications. Simulation results demonstrates the advantages of our developed methods over existing ones.

Categories and Subject Descriptors

Information systems [**Information systems applications**]: Multimedia information systems; Computer systems organization [**Distributed architectures**]: Cloud computing

Keywords

Distributed Virtual Environments; Virtual Worlds; Resource Management; Load Balancing; Cloud Computing; Elasticity

1. INTRODUCTION

Distributed (or networked) virtual environments (DVEs or NVEs) are systems in which users interact with each other and with virtual objects in a shared digital space in real-time through Internet. DVEs are increasingly popular and currently represent a range of applications, such as massively multiplayer online games (MMOGs) which have a specific purpose for gaming (e.g., World of Warcraft) and virtual worlds which have general purposes like collaborative learning, training and socializing (e.g., Second Life). DVEs are designed to create very high degree of immersion with realistic 3D graphics [7] and stereo sound [10] and to support massive users to co-exist in a single and consistent virtual space with scalable server architectures. Most existing MMOGs commonly use the sharding approach by creating multiple copies of the game world each of which can be handled by a server and forcing users to choose to play in one of those independent copies. As users are only allowed to play and interact with others within the same copy hosted by the same server, the scalability problem can be avoided by explicitly limiting the number of users in each copy. Limitations for this sharding approach include not being able to interact with every user and most severely the loss of shared experiences perceived by users. As pointed out by [4], this sharding approach makes the current MMOGs different from general seamless DVEs, as that must maintain a single, persistent and consistent state.

Many research have been made to improve DVE scalability to support larger numbers of users, and most of them are based on distributed-server architectures. On one hand, some efforts focus on reducing the inter-server communication traffic induced by the consistency maintenance using their proposed message filtering techniques. On the other hand, some efforts focus on dynamically adjusting the workload-to-server assignment to adapt to changes in workload distribution among servers to avoid server overloading based on their proposed dynamic load balancing techniques.

Like many Internet-based applications, DVEs tend to feature significant workload fluctuations in different time scales (e.g., hourly, diurnally, weekly, or monthly). This poses another issue apart from the scalability issue and we call it *elasticity issue* which represents the need to adjust server resources dynamically to adapt to global workload changes for achieving high resource efficiency. Previous approaches assume the total load of the system is static; this assumption is not true due to the fluctuation in the number of online players. Their approaches need to provision the servers according to the peak load which leads to waste of resources. Their dynamic load balancing techniques can prevent individual servers from being overloaded only when the global workload remains unchanged or becomes less. If the global workload surpasses the total capacity provided by the currently deployed servers, individual server overloading cannot be avoided anyway. On the other hand, if the global workload reduces significantly, it is not efficient to keep the same amount of capacity as in the peak periods.

Bewaring of the global workload fluctuation nature in MMOGs, a few recent work have been proposed to bring cloud computing paradigm for efficiently hosting MMOGs. For instance, Nae et al. [8] develop a predictor based on neural networks to forecast the global workload and request properly sufficient resources from external data centers (cloud providers) where MMOGs are hosted. Their study is based on a MMOG called RuneScape that uses sharding (i.e., users cannot move across different servers). Hence, as long as pre-

MM'14, November 3-7, Orlando, Florida, USA.

ACM 978-1-4503-3063-3/14/11 ...$15.00.
http://dx.doi.org/10.1145/2647868.2655051.

diction for each server's workload is accurate, there will be no servers getting overloaded. However, in general DVEs that do not use sharding, prediction of the workload in each server is much more difficult as users can move freely instead of keeping staying in the copy hosted by a specific server. For another example, Lee and Chan [6] propose to apply server consolidation technique to adaptively change the number of servers according to the workload changes via periodically consolidating regions of the game world into nearly fewest number of servers based on a bin packing heuristic (first-fit-decreasing). As long as the workload distributed among each region remains relatively constant which is basically true for sharded MMOGs (i.e., users are not moving across different regions handled by different servers) between two consecutive consolidation processes, their approach can work appropriately without causing server overloading. However, the works discussed above are targeted to sharded MMOGs and may not be appropriate for contiguous DVEs [4].

In this work, we focus on the dynamic resource management problem for seamless DVEs. Specifically, we consider both global workload changes induced by user population fluctuations and local workload changes induced by user mobility. Our proposed approach not only improves resource efficiency as compared to those which overlook global workload dynamics (e.g., [3]), but also reduces service interruption induced by resource reallocation as compared to those which overlook local workload dynamics (e.g., [6]). We present the proposed approach and simulation results in Sections 2 and 3, respectively.

2. PROPOSED APPROACH

To support a large number of users co-existing in a shared virtual world, we adopt multi-server DVE architecture with each server handling a partition of the virtual world (and users therein) and together all servers maintaining a single and shared virtual world. For the ease of management and extension, usually the virtual world is designed to be composed of a set of regular-shaped regions (e.g., Second Life consists of over 7,000 regions which form a contiguous map), and each server is assigned a subset of them. Each server maintains the responsiveness and consistency perceived by users residing in the regions within its management.

2.1 Problem Statement

There are two issues induced by user mobility across different regions. The first issue is handover, which happens when a user travels from its current region to a new one (normally it is adjacent but sometimes can be remote if teleporting). An inter-server handover is caused if the new region is hosted by another server which apparently should be more difficult to be handled transparently compared to the intra-server handover (i.e., the new region is hosted by the same server as the old one). Hence, one should consider assigning adjacent regions to the same servers as much as possible. The second issue is that the user distribution across regions is not fixed but dynamic. Hence, the originally load balanced region-to-server assignment may become imbalanced and occasionally some servers may get heavily loaded such that they cannot service more coming users (i.e., *locally under-provisioned*). As long as the total server capacity is enough to host all the users, we can reduce the workload assigned to those under-provisioned servers by transferring some regions from them to those which still have enough capacity.

However, if the total number of users grows significantly such that the total capacity of all servers becomes insufficient (i.e., *globally under-provisioned*), any load balancing process is useless and inevitably we must either add new servers or increase the capacity of existing servers.. The former strategy is generally referred to as *scaling out* while the latter one is *scaling-up*. On the other hand, it should be beneficial if we can reduce the capacity provision during low load periods (i.e., *globally over-provisioned*) to achieve resource efficiency. Strategies related to decreasing the number of servers and existing servers' capacities are referred to as *scaling in* and *scaling down*, respectively. Note that in cloud computing commonly the scaling out or in process is called *horizontal scaling*, while the scaling up or down process is called *vertical scaling*. Figure 1 depicts the framework of our dynamic resource management approach.

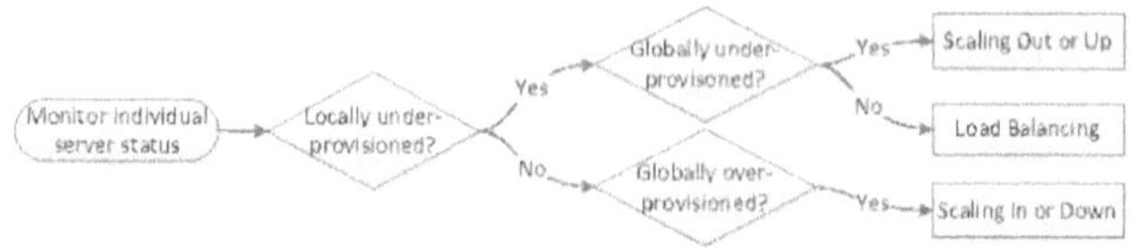

Figure 1: DVE dynamic resource management.

Let's denote $\{s_1, s_2, ..., s_n\}$ as the set of n servers, with $\{l_1, l_2, ..., l_n\}$ and $\{c_1, c_2, ..., c_n\}$ representing their corresponding loads and capacities, respectively. $l^{ttl} = \sum_1^n l_i$ and $c^{ttl} = \sum_1^n c_i$ are the total capacity and total load respectively. As shown by the framework in Figure 1, the resource management process will encounter one of these circumstances: locally under-provisioned if there is any s_i has $c_i \leq l_i * (1+\sigma)$, with σ denoting the minimum required resource redundancy of each server; globally under-provisioned if $c^{ttl} \leq l^{ttl} * (1+\theta)$, with θ denoting the desired global resource redundancy of all servers ($\theta > \sigma$); globally over-provisioned if $c^{ttl} \geq l^{ttl} * (1+\delta)$, with δ denoting the maximum allowed resource redundancy of all servers ($\delta > \theta$).

2.2 Horizontal Scaling

Once detecting $c_i \leq l_i * (1+\sigma)$ and $c^{ttl} \leq l^{ttl} * (1+\theta)$, we trigger *scaling out* algorithm described as follows:

1. add a new server (i.e., request a new instance from the cloud provider), namely s_{n+1}, and transfer regions from the most loaded server, namely s_k, to s_{n+1} until $c_k \geq l_k * (1+\theta)$ or $c_{n+1} \leq l_{n+1} * (1+\theta)$;

2. if either $c_i \leq l_i * (1+\sigma)$ or $c^{ttl} \leq l^{ttl} * (1+\theta)$, go to step 1; otherwise, terminate.

After termination of the above procedure, each server s_i finally has its capacity $c_i \geq l_i*(1+\theta)$ such that achieving the desired global resource redundancy, i.e., $c^{ttl} \geq l^{ttl} * (1+\theta)$.

Once detecting that none of the servers is locally under-provisioned and $c^{ttl} \geq l^{ttl} * (1+\delta)$, we trigger *scaling in* algorithm described as follows:

1. merge s_i with its neighbor s_j (two servers are considered as neighboring if they host adjacent regions) if $c_j \geq (l_i + l_j) * (1+\theta)$ and $(c^{ttl} - c_i) \geq l^{ttl} * (1+\theta)$ by transferring all regions from s_i to s_j and release s_i;

2. repeat step 1 until having gone through all its neighbors; terminate if having gone through all servers.

Note that δ should be set significantly larger than θ in order to avoid unnecessary oscillations between scaling in and out.

The major advantage of horizontal scaling is that one can adjust the capacity to adapt to any workload changes. However, the major drawback is the inevitable inter-server region migrations induced by scaling out or in actions which may affect user experiences and may be worse than the similar migration issue encountered by load balancing among servers because of launching new server instances could take some time when scaling out. Hence, we consider another way for dynamic resource management.

2.3 Vertical Scaling

Normally vertical scaling is done through replacing the old servers by new ones having different capacities [9]. Indeed, the replacement process itself could also affect user experiences as the horizontal scaling does. Recently, there are some advances in both academia (e.g., [2, 5]) and IT industry (e.g., ProfitBricks) making live vertical scaling viable, that is, adjusting servers' sizes in an on-the-fly manner. We make such an assumption for our vertical scaling algorithms.

With the same triggering condition as scaling out algorithm, *scaling up* algorithm can be described as follows:

1. enlarge the capacity of s_i which has $c_i \leq l_i * (1 + \sigma)$ until $c_i \geq l_i * (1 + \theta)$ or $c_i = c^{max}$ (i.e., the maximum allowed size of a server); if $c^{ttl} \geq l^{ttl} * (1+\theta)$, terminate; otherwise, go to next step;
2. enlarge the smallest server s_k (i.e., having the lowest capacity) until $c^{ttl} \geq l^{ttl} * (1+\theta)$ or $c_k = c^{max}$; if $c^{ttl} < l^{ttl} * (1 + \theta)$, repeat this step; otherwise, terminate.

Having the same triggering condition as scaling in algorithm, *scaling down* algorithm can be described as follows:

1. decrease the largest server s_k (i.e., having the highest capacity) until $c_k \leq l_k * (1 + \theta)$, $c_k = c^{min}$ (i.e., the minimum allowed size of a server), or $c^{ttl} \leq l^{ttl} * (1+\theta)$;
2. repeat step 1 until having gone through all servers.

Note that after vertical scaling, servers that are homogeneous originally may become heterogeneous, i.e., having different capacities. This should be taken into account in load balancing, that is, the workload assigned to each server should be proportional to its capacity. However, most existing DVE dynamic load balancing techniques (such as [3] and references therein) do assume that servers are homogeneous. Hence, we extend the method proposed by [3] to handle the server heterogeneity when doing load balancing, i.e., the time when locally under-provisioned event arises but globally under-provisioned event doesn't as illustrated in Figure 1. So far, we have presented our proposed resource management approach and the associated algorithms. Next we present experiments for performance evaluation.

3. EXPERIMENTAL RESULTS

3.1 Simulation Settings

We simulate a virtual world consisting of 10,000 regions each of which has an area of $256m \times 256m$ (comparable to Second Life). We describe the simulation for user mobility as follows. Each user stays in his current region for a period of time randomly sampled from the range of $[T_{min}, T_{max}]$. Upon spending up the chosen time period, he will move to a new region randomly chosen from the adjacent regions of his current region or a random remote region (in case for teleporting). The remote region one of the popular regions, called hotspots, which drives uneven user distributions and we set 20% of regions as hotspots (similar to [3]). Generally, users are moving faster and more frequently for exploration or questing than social interaction. Hence, we simulate two scenarios: *slow-paced mobility*, with $T_{min} = 10$ minutes and $T_{max} = 30$ minutes; *fast-pace mobility*, with $T_{min} = 1$ minute and $T_{max} = 10$ minutes. For user population fluctuations, we adopt the trace used in [6] and magnify it to 100,000 users at the peak period. The simulated period is 1 day with 1 minute per timestep.

Without loss of generality, we assume the maximum number of users can be supported by a server is proportional to its CPU cores. If using instances in Amazon EC2, we can have servers with sizes ranging from 2 to 32 CPU cores (note that the number is the powers of 2). One core can handle up to 50 concurrent users in to Second Life, meaning that one server can support up to 1,600 users. Except for virtual scaling, we assume all servers have the maximum allowed capacity by default.

We compare these methods: *BP*, representing the bin packing based consolidation method [6]; *NS*, representing the method of dynamic load balancing with no scaling [3]; *HS*, representing our horizontal scaling based method; *VS*, representing our vertical scaling based method.

We have the following metrics: *resource allocation*, measured by the number of CPU cores allocated by all servers; *service interruption count*, measured by the number of non-serviced users as they enter the regions managed by fully loaded servers which cannot service any new coming users; *handover count*, measured by the number of inter-server user handovers; *migration count*, measured by the number of users inside those regions being migrated.

The parameters defined in Section 2.1, i.e., σ, θ, and δ are set as follows. $\sigma = 10\%$, meaning that the locally under-provisioned event will be issued if any server s_i has $c_i \leq (100 + 10)\% * l_i$. $\delta = 200\%$, meaning that the globally over-provisioned event will be issued if $c^{ttl} \geq (100 + 200)\% * l^{ttl}$. For θ, we have three options: 25%, 50%, and 100%. Higher θ reduces the chance of server overloading but increases the resource allocation, and vice versa.

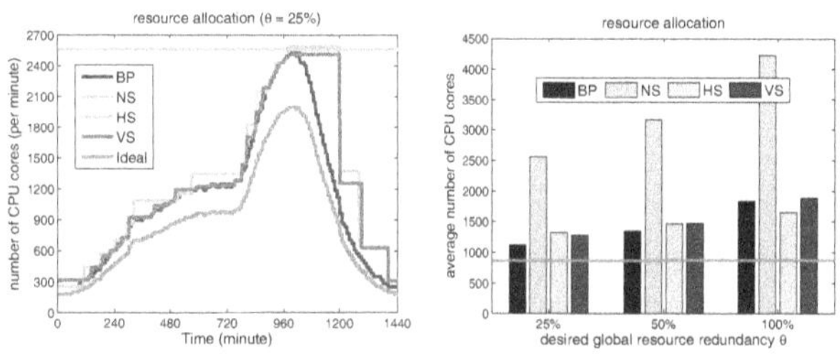

Figure 2: Comparison on instantaneous (left) and average (right) resource allocation.

3.2 Results and Analysis

As results taken with both mobility scenarios are similar, we present only those with fast-paced scenario. Figure 2 (left) shows the resource allocation by each method. We can see that *BP*, *HS* and *VS* adaptively adjusts the resource according to the actual demand (referring to the pink curve), while *NS* statically allocates the amount of resource for preparing the peak load period (around the $1000th$ minute). The average values are shown in Figure 2 (right), and we can see that the allocated resource increases with θ for each method. For example, when $\theta = 100\%$, *BP*, *HS* and *VS* allocate nearly twice as the actual demanded resource on average. Overall, our *HS* and *VS* methods improve the resource efficiency compared to *NS*. Next we explore the advantages of our methods over *BP*.

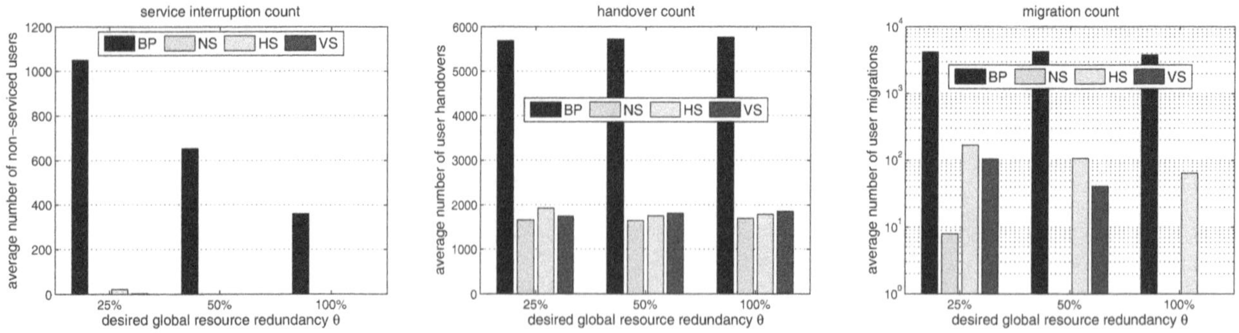

Figure 3: Comparison on interruption count (left), handover count (middle), and migration count (right).

Figure 3 (left) shows that *BP* causes lots of non-serviced users and increasing θ will decrease the service interruption. In contrast, our *HS* and *VS* roughly produces no service interruption as *NS* does even for a small θ, which implicitly indicates that *HS* and *VS* can achieve better resource efficiency than *BP* by using small θ while still maintaining the service but *BP* cannot.

Figure 3 (middle) shows the average amount of user handovers per minute. *BP* has nearly two times of users handovers more than others. This is primarily because *BP* method overlooks the adjacency of regions when assigning them to servers. Apparently there will be more users moving across servers if the adjacent regions of their currently regions are not in the same servers, resulting more frequent changes of workload distribution among servers and then increasing the chance for a originally normally loaded server to quickly become fully loaded.

In Figure 3 (right), we can see that *BP* causes much higher migration count than others. The reason are two-fold. On one hand, as servers are frequently to get fully loaded, *BP* method triggers the resource adjustment process frequently by partitioning the regions into more servers and apparently this will induce many user migrations. On the other hand, repartitioning regions to servers, it does not take the current region-to-server mapping into account, such that regions are likely to be assigned to servers different from their original ones. When comparing between *HS* and *VS*, the latter evidently causes less user migrations, confirming that vertical scaling is potentially a more efficient way than horizontal scaling for cloud-based DVEs. Overall, our methods *HS* and *VS* outperform *BP* by having much smaller impact on system performance while maintaining resource efficiency.

4. CONCLUSION

In this paper, we explore dynamic resource management for seamless DVEs with the objective of improving resource efficiency while not affecting system performance. In specific, we develop horizontal and vertical scaling methods with the incorporation of our recently developed DVE load balancing approach. Simulation results show that our methods significantly outperform existing ones in general.

As an initial work in this field, this paper has several unanswered questions. For instance, we need to compare the horizontal scaling and vertical scaling for DVE dynamic resource management by taking into account all system overheads. Also, we need to conduct the evaluation using real-world deployment and realistic workload traces. Most importantly, we need to evaluate whether the latency perceived by users when we host DVEs in the cloud with dynamic resource management can still be acceptable compared to the time when we host DVEs with dedicated and static server allocation (similar to the study by Barker and Shenoy [1]).

5. ACKNOWLEDGMENTS

This work was partially supported by a GRF grant from RGC of Hong Kong (Project No.: CityU 115112), by the National Basic Research Program of China (2011CB302603 and 2014CB340303), and by the STW/NOW veni grant 11881.

6. REFERENCES

[1] S. Barker and P. Shenoy. Empirical evaluation of latency-sensitive application performance in the cloud. In *Proc. ACM Multimedia Systems*, pages 35–46, 2010.

[2] O. Ben-Yehuda, M. Ben-Yehuda, A. Schuster, and D. Tsafrir. The resource-as-a-service (raas) cloud. In *Proc. USENIX HotCloud*, 2012.

[3] Y. Deng and R. Lau. Dynamic load balancing in distributed virtual environments using heat diffusion. *ACM TOMCCAP*, 10(2), 2014.

[4] J. Dionisio, W. Burns, and R. Gilbert. 3d virtual worlds and the metaverse: Current status and future possibilities. *ACM Computing Surveys*, 45(3), 2013.

[5] R. Han, L. Guo, M. Ghanem, and Y. Guo. Lightweight resource scaling for cloud applications. In *Proc. IEEE/ACM CCGrid*, pages 644–651, 2012.

[6] Y. Lee and K. Chen. Is server consolidation beneficial to mmorpg? a case study of world of warcraft. In *IEEE CLOUD*, pages 435–442, 2010.

[7] S. Mondet, W. Cheng, G. Morin, R. Grigoras, F. Boudon, and W. Ooi. Streaming of plants in distributed virtual environments. In *Proc. ACM Multimedia*, 2008.

[8] V. Nae, A. Iosup, and R. Prodan. Dynamic resource provisioning in massively multiplayer online games. *IEEE TPDS*, 22(3):380–395, 2011.

[9] L. Vaquero, L. Rodero-Merino, and R. Buyya. Dynamically scaling applications in the cloud. *ACM Computer Communication Review*, 41(1):45–52, 2011.

[10] R. Zimmermann and K. Liang. Spatialized audio streaming for networked virtual environments. In *Proc. ACM Multimedia*, pages 299–308, 2008.

Interactive 3D Animation Creation and Viewing System based on Motion Graph and Pose Estimation Method

Masayuki Furukawa,
Hiroshi Kawasaki
Kagoshima University
1-21-24 Korimoto
Kagoshima, Japan
sc108044,
kawasaki@ibe.kagoshima-u.ac.jp

Yasuhiro Akagi
Tokyo University of Agriculture and Technology
2-24-16 Higashi-cho, Koganei
Tokyo, Japan
akagi-y@cc.tuat.ac.jp

Yukiko Kawai
Kyoto Sangyo University
Kamikamomotoyama, Kitaku
Kyoto, Japan
kawai@cc.kyoto-su.ac.jp

ABSTRACT

This paper proposes an interactive 3D animation system specifically aiming efficient control of human motion. However there are various commercial products for creating movies and game contents, those are still difficult to deal with for non-professional users. To ease the creation process and encourage to utilize 3D animation for the general users, e.g., in the field of such as education, medicine and so on, we propose a system using Kinect. The data of skeleton models of human motion estimated by Kinect is processed to generate Motion Graph and finally restructure the data automatically for 3D character models. We also propose an efficient 3D animation viewing system based on touch interface for tablet device, which enables intuitive control of multiple motions of the human activity. To evaluate the effectiveness of the method, we implemented a prototype system and created several 3D animations.

Categories and Subject Descriptors

H.5.1 [Multimedia Information Systems]: Animations; H.5.2 [User Interfaces]: Interaction styles; K.3.1 [Computer Uses in Education]: Computer-assisted instruction

General Terms

Human Factors

Keywords

3D animation; Motion Graph; Realtime 3D scan;

1. INTRODUCTION

Nowadays, 3D computer graphics (3DCG) characters of human, animals and other moving objects can be seen everywhere in the movies, games and etc.

MM'14, November 3–7, 2014, Orlando, Florida, USA.
Copyright 2014 ACM 978-1-4503-3063-3/14/11 ...$15.00.
http://dx.doi.org/10.1145/2647868.2655055.

Those become one of the important categories of multimedia contents.

We call such animated 3DCG characters "3D animations" in the paper. To efficiently make 3D animations, a motion capturing system is commonly used to obtain the motion of the human skeleton. Since such a motion capturing system is basically for professional users and special skills are required to use the 3DCG softwares, it is difficult for non-professional users to create 3D animations. However, small-scale demands (content creation from non-professional users) are rapidly increasing for educational and/or medical purposes for small entities. To realize non-professional users to create a 3D animation without the motion capturing system and special skills on 3DCG, we propose a 3D animation creation system using Kinect [6]. Since a Kinect based system does not require any special devices and additional knowledge, non-professional users can create 3D animation easily without trainings.

The proposed system consists of three parts. The first one is a skeletal motion estimation part using a series of dense 3D point cloud which is captured by Kinect. The second one is an automatic Motion Graph [3] construction part. The third one is a shape interpolation part which realizes smooth transition between two motions. To implement the system, there are two critical issues which must be solved. The first one is low accuracy of skeletal motion estimation by Kinect. The other is a realization of smooth transition between different frames. For the first issue, we propose an exemplar based technique to re-estimate the motion; the technique is based on the assumption that similar motions frequently occur during human activity. For the second issue, we propose a new similarity calculation method for 3D point cloud which uses not only the target frame, but also neighboring frames. We also propose an efficient viewing system of animations using tablet devices, which shows the next candidates of the animation with superimposed information on the tablet devices. To evaluate the effectiveness of the system, we implement a prototype system, create several 3D animations and test the created contents with several users.

2. RELATED WORK

Although human movements seem complex, most of then are actually a repetition or combination of basic movements

(1) Capture (2) Structurization and editing (3) Interactive control of 3D animation

(a) Overview of the system.

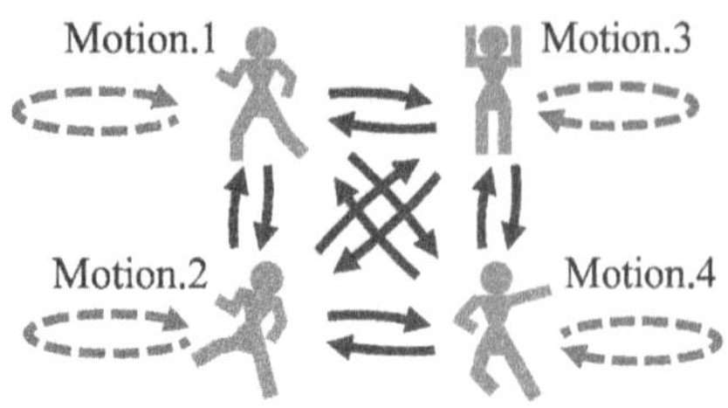

(b) Motion Graph of 3D animation. The solid lines show the transition-edge(s) and the dotted lines show the self-loop(s).

Figure 1: System overview and Motion Graph.

(e.g. walking, hand waving). We call such basic movements "motion primitive" or simply "primitive" in the paper. To create 3D animations, a state transition graph, which is named Motion Graph [3], is commonly used. Motion Graph represents self-loops and transitions between multiple motions. By using the Motion Graph, an editor can efficiently control the motion of a character to create animations. Sine the Motion Graph is useful to control animations interactively, methods which automatically construct Motion Graph by analyzing the captured motions have been proposed [8, 5]. Zhao et al. proposed a method which minimizes the size of Motion Graph [8]. This method is useful to create a digest animation from a long-term motion data. Apostolakis et al. proposed a software to create human animations [2]. This tool can control a human type character by using a rigging technique based on a skeleton structure. Another research defines the similarity of each skeletal motion based on the joint points of the skeleton model [4]. Since those methods are based on accurate skeletal motions captured by the motion capturing systems for professional use, the creation of Motion Graph from the sequential dense 3D point could which has large errors in motion have not been considered yet.

3. 3D ANIMATION CREATION SYSTEM BASED ON MOTION GRAPH

The overview of our content creation system is shown in Figure 1. The 3D animation is created by first capturing the moving human by Kinect (Figure 1(a)-(1)), then analyzing the motion to construct Motion Graph [3] that is a key technique to allow users to easily control 3D character (Figure 1(a)-(2)). In the paper, skeletal motions of the human body are represented by Motion Graph which consists of motion primitives of self-loop as the node and that of transition-edge between the nodes as the edge (Figure 1(b)). Finally, 3D characters are interactively controlled and animated by our viewing system (Figure 1(a)-(3)).

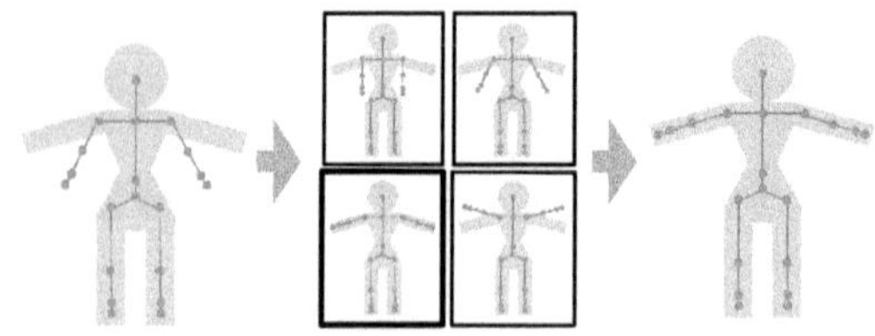

(a) Input frame (b) Exemplar (c) Re-estimation

Figure 2: Exemplar based skeleton re-estimation.

As the detailed steps of our proposed system, firstly we re-estimate the skeleton model which is estimated by Kinect, since the accuracy of the skeleton of Kinect is low (Sec. 3.1). Secondly, a method to create the Motion Graph is described in Sec.3.2. In the section, a similarity calculation method based on the series of the skeleton model is proposed. Finally, an interpolation method to realize the smooth transition of the 3D point cloud as well as the skeletal motion is explained in Sec. 3.3.

3.1 Re-estimation of skeleton by exemplar

Skeletal motions, which used to create Motion Graph, are estimated from the point cloud captured by Kinect. It is known that there are gaps between the skeletons and the point cloud due to inaccuracy of Kinect (Figure 2 (b)). If these frames are selected to be used for a self-loop or a transition-edge, an inconsistent transition will be generated. Therefore, to re-estimate the skeleton we propose a method as follows: (1) Detect frames with low accuracy on skeletal estimation by Kinect. (2) Apply an exemplar based skeleton re-estimation method for the detected low accuracy frames. (3) Reject frames which have lower accuracy than the threshold after step (2).

Frames with low accuracy after the re-estimation step will be excluded for further process to prevent inconsistent transition between motions. In order to detect frames with low accuracy on the skeleton estimation in the step (1), we first calculate the average distance between 3D points of point cloud and their nearest joint of the skeleton, and then, verify that it is below the threshold (Figure 2 (a)). If we leave frames which have the average distance less than 0.1m, only 10% of the total frames remained in the experiments. Based on the assumption that the skeleton includes many repetitions, remained skeletons are considered to be exemplar for the next step (Figure 2 (b)). In the step (2), the skeleton with the minimum average distance from the target 3D point cloud is searched as the correct skeleton (Figure 2 (c)). If the distance is above $0.1m$ after step (2), the frame is excluded from the further process. Valid skeletons increased to 50% of the total frames in the experiments.

3.2 Automatic Motion Graph creation

Motion Graph is created by self-loop and transition edge. Figure 3 shows the examples of detected self-loop and transition-edge on captured sequences. The actual detection process is as follows. First, all the distances for all two-frame pairs (p, q) within the skeletal motion are calculated. Then, frame sets which have the distance below the threshold are selected as candidates for self-loop. Since we consider the shorter loop is better for self-loop, we recalculate the distance by

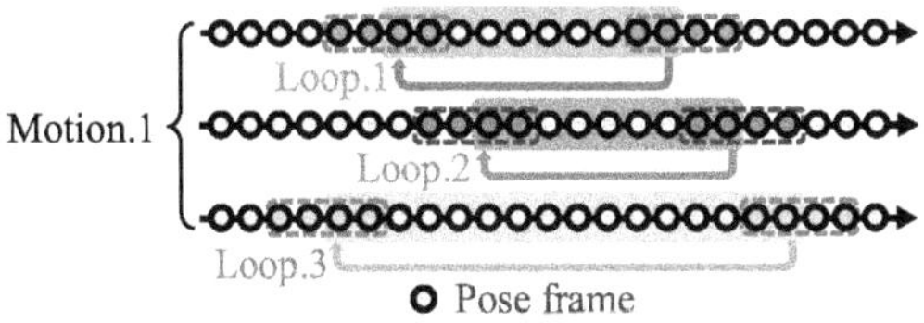

(a) Example of multiple detection of self-loops.

(b) Example of transition-edges between motions.

Figure 3: Definition of self-loop and transition-edge.

taking advantage of the following weight function.

$$W(i,j) = \left| \frac{i-j}{FrameSize} \right|^2, \quad (1)$$

where $FrameSize$ represents the input number of frames of skeletal motion. Finally, we decide the pair of two frames (p, q) with minimum value of $W(p,q) * DistMotion(p,q)$ to define the self-loop motions (Figure 3).

After self-loop motions are detected, transition-edges are detected by calculating all the distances between all combinations of skeletal motions of two motions. Then, the set of two frames of the smallest distance which is below threshold is defined as the transition-edge. To calculate the distance between two skeletal motions, we use the equation proposed by Krüger et al. [4] as follows:

$$DistPose(i,j) = \sum_{k=1}^{n} ||\mathcal{F}_{E,j}^{k} - \mathcal{F}_{E,i}^{k}||, \quad (2)$$

where $\mathcal{F}_E^{n \times d}$ represents feature points of human body (hand, head, etc.), n is a number of feature points, d is a number of dimensions of the feature point, i and j are the time (number of frames) for two motions. When using equation (2) by itself, in some motion cases such as walking, two connections are created at the same pose, but opposite direction and one of them is wrong. To overcome this problem, we use the distance between multi-frame poses as follows:

$$DistMotion(p,q) = \sum_{i=1-N}^{N} \frac{DistPose(p+i, q+i)}{2N}, \quad (3)$$

where N is the window size. By using the equation (3), we can detect the distance between frames in consideration of the direction of the motion.

3.3 Interpolation of skeletal motion for smooth transition between frames

To make the motion primitives of self-loops and transition-edges, the most similar poses are detected to connect the motions as explained in the previous sections; however, they can not be the exact same poses. Therefore, the final 3D animation becomes unnatural, if two frames are simply connected without interpolation. To solve the problem, we replace the original n skeletal motions before/after connecting frames with the interpolated ones. To interpolate the motions, spline function is applied to five successive frames. Effectiveness of the method is evaluated in Sec. 4.3.

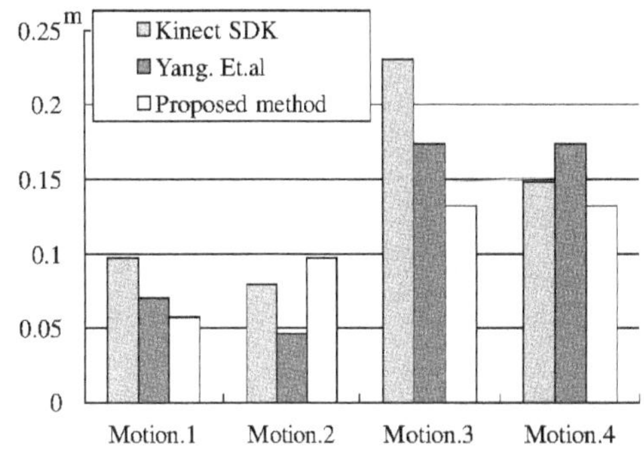

Figure 4: Comparison of the temporal smoothness of skeletal motions estimated by three methods.

4. EXPERIMENT AND EVALUATION

To evaluate our approach, we create 3D animations for experiments based on actual human motion captured by Kinect. We captured four types of gymnastic exercises as: "Stretching arms" (motion 1), "Spreading arms with knees-bent" (motion 2), "Swinging arms" (motion 3) and "Deep breathing" (motion 4).

In the experiments, we evaluate our re-estimation method in Section 4.1, and we also evaluate the effectiveness of the interpolation method for self-loops and transition-edges in Section 4.3. Finally, 3D interactive animations for our viewing system are shown, which can be easily operated by touch interface on tablet devices [1].

4.1 Evaluation of the exemplar based skeleton estimation method.

Since an actual skeletal motion of a human is usually smooth, if a skeletal motion is estimated correctly, the average of the difference of two skeletons between consecutive frames ($\sum_{t=0}^{N-1} DistMotion(t, t+1)/N$, see Eq.3) should have small value. Based on the assumption, we compare the proposed method to other two methods [6, 7]. Figure 4 shows the results. The results of the "Motion 1", "Motion 3" and "Motion 4" show that the proposed method is best among three. However, in the result of "Motion 2", the proposed method is worst. This is because "Motion 2" includes occluded regions and failed to track the movement of arms and legs by Kinect, and thus, enough exemplar data sets are not created for re-estimation. Therefore, the evaluation values of the previous methods are better than the proposed method.

4.2 Evaluation of Automatic Motion Graph creation

We evaluate the quality (the smoothness of the changing frame of motions) of animations which are created by the proposed Motion Graph creation method and those which are created by a human (manually). We ask 16 viewers which animation has smoother transitions than another between motions. In this evaluation, we use four types of self-loop motions (L1, L2, L3, L4) and one transition-edge (T) which consist of Motion 1-4. The results are shown in Fig-

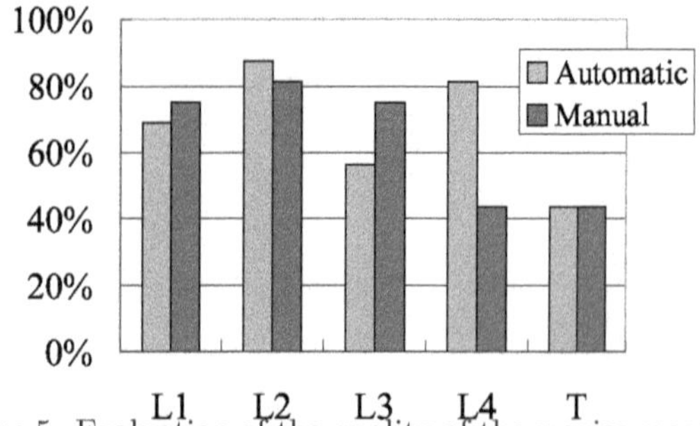

Figure 5: Evaluation of the quality of the movies created by manual process and our automatic Motion Graph construction method.

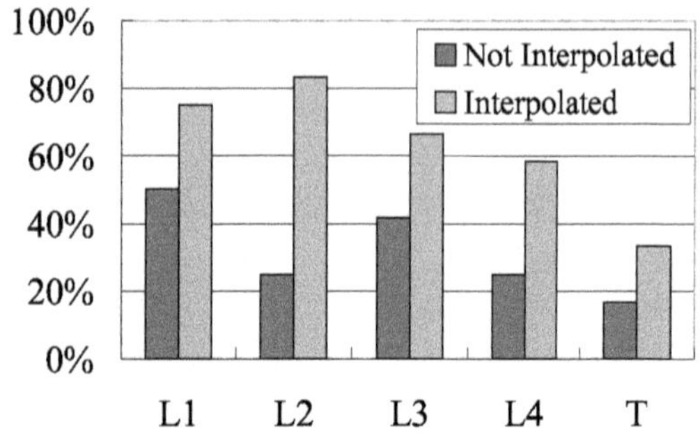

Figure 6: Evaluation of the quality of movie with/without interpolation method.

ure 5. The vertical axis of Figure 5 is the percentage of the viewers who answer the transitions are smooth. These results shows that the Motion Graph is successfully created with smooth motion transitions.

4.3 Evaluation of the interpolation method

We evaluate the effectiveness of the interpolation method which is described in the section 3.3. For this evaluation, we use the same animation in the previous section. Then, 15 viewers are asked which movie is more natural (smoothly change the motions) than the others. The results are shown in Figure 6. The results show that the proposed interpolation method successfully improves the quality on the smooth transitions of the 3D animations for all data.

4.4 Interactive control of 3D animation with tablet devices

Finally, our interactive 3D animation viewing system is evaluated by using our interactive viewing system with the tablet devices where 3D animations are efficiently controlled. 12 viewers are asked five questions after playing the 3D animations with the tablet device. The evaluation results are shown in Table 1. This results show that viewers felt that the contents were more interesting with 3D animation than an ordinary 2D video. It is also confirmed that novelty and user-friendliness of the system are higher than the 2D video. Furthermore, the result regarding the level of comprehension and usability were satisfactory.

5. CONCLUSION

In this paper, we propose an interactive 3D animation system which consists of an automatic 3D animation creation system and an interactive viewing system for tablet devices. For the automatic 3D animation creation system, the automatic Motion Graph creation method and the efficient interpolation technique of 3D point cloud are proposed. To realize automatic creation of Motion Graph, the distance calculation between the series of skeletal motions are proposed. For 3D point cloud interpolation, since the accuracy of estimated motions are generally low with Kinect, the exemplar based re-estimation method of skeletal motions is proposed. The advantages of the method are evaluated by creating the sample 3D animations. As the result, it is confirmed that the system can automatically create the Motion Graph with smooth transitions. More effective re-estimation of the skeleton model is our future research.

Table 1: Evaluation of the viewing system: (Q1) Attractiveness on contents, (Q2) Comprehension on contents, (Q3) Controllability of the contents, (Q4) Novelty of the system and (Q5) Intuitiveness the system interface.

	Percentages of the evaluation				
	Poor	Fair	Average	Good	Excellent
Q1	0.0	8.3	8.3	50.0	33.3
Q2	0.0	0.0	58.3	33.3	8.3
Q3	8.3	16.7	33.3	41.7	0.0
Q4	0.0	8.3	8.3	50.0	33.3
Q5	0.0	25.0	25.0	41.7	8.3

6. REFERENCES

[1] Y. Akagi, M. Furukawa, S. Fukumoto, and H. K. Y. Kawai. Interactive 3d animation system based on touch interface and efficient creation tools. In The 2013 IEEE International Conference on Multimedia and Expo (ICME) 2013 in "Multimedia for Humanity" theme track, 318, pages 1–7, 2013.

[2] K. Apostolakis and P. Daras. Raat - the reverie avatar authoring tool. In Digital Signal Processing (DSP), 2013 18th International Conference on, pages 1–6, July 2013.

[3] L. Kovar, M. Gleicher, and F. Pighin. Motion graphs. In Proceedings of the 29th Annual Conference on Computer Graphics and Interactive Techniques, SIGGRAPH '02, pages 473–482, New York, NY, USA, 2002. ACM.

[4] B. Krüger, J. Tautges, A. Weber, and A. Zinke. Fast local and global similarity searches in large motion capture databases. In Proceedings of the 2010 ACM SIGGRAPH/Eurographics Symposium on Computer Animation, SCA '10, pages 1–10, Aire-la-Ville, Switzerland, Switzerland, 2010. Eurographics Association.

[5] S. Levine, Y. Lee, V. Koltun, and Z. Popović. Space-time planning with parameterized locomotion controllers. ACM Trans. Graph., 30(3):23:1–23:11, may 2011.

[6] Microsoft. Xbox 360 Kinect, 2010. http://www.xbox.com/en-US/kinect.

[7] Y. Yang and D. Ramanan. Articulated pose estimation with flexible mixtures-of-parts. In Proceedings of the 2011 IEEE Conference on Computer Vision and Pattern Recognition, CVPR '11, pages 1385–1392, 2011.

[8] L. Zhao, A. Normoyle, S. Khanna, and A. Safonova. Automatic construction of a minimum size motion graph. In Proceedings of the 2009 ACM SIGGRAPH/Eurographics Symposium on Computer Animation, SCA '09, pages 27–35, New York, NY, USA, 2009. ACM.

Color Transfer based on Spatial Structure for Telepresence

Kentaro Yamada Hiroshi Sankoh Sei Naito
KDDI R&D Laboratories, Inc.
2-1-15 Ohara, Fujimino, Saitama 356-0003, Japan
kr-yamada@kddilabs.jp sankoh@kddilabs.jp sei@kddilabs.jp

ABSTRACT
In this paper, we propose a novel color transfer method based on spatial structure. This work considers an immersive telepresence system, in which distant users can feel as if they are present at a place other than their true location. In preceding studies, the region of an attendee in a remote room is extracted and synthesized on the display of a local room with a preset background image that is similar to the local room. However, the difference between the structure of preset background image and remote room image often degrades the quality of image in the synthesized video. For example, when a part of the human region is occluded by an object that does not exist in the preset background image, the deficient human region is shown despite the inexistence of the occluding object. To solve this problem, instead of using a preset background image, we propose a method that applies a color transfer technique to images of the remote room. Our proposed method can offer users an experience that allows them to feel as if they are in the same room as the other participant of telepresence by changing the colors of the remote room to match the colors of the local room. Furthermore, we have improved the similarity between the rooms based on spatial structure that was overlooked by the conventional color transfer methods. The experimental results show that the proposed method can provide the same-room experience for users in the telepresence system through color similarity of the remote and local room.

Categories and Subject Descriptors
I.4.8 [Image processing and Computer vision]: Scene Analysis – *Range data*; H.4.3 [INFORMATION SYSTEMS APPLICATIONS]: Communications Applications – *Computer conferencing, teleconferencing, and videoconferencing.*

General Terms
Algorithms, Experimentation

Keywords
Telepresence; videoconference; color transfer; RGB-D camera.

1. INTRODUCTION
A telepresence system [1] can reproduce a remote participant with the advanced audio-visual technologies that allow him/her to feel as if he/she is in the same room. It allows global companies to reduce the transportation cost for the purpose of face-to-face meetings. To achieve such an immersive experience at a distance, the current telepresence system such as in [1] requires reconstruction of a physically identical conference room; that is, the remote room needs to construct the room with completely identical furnishings such as the conference table, the chairs and the wallpaper. Such configurations require considerable cost. While there is a demand to reproduce the same-room experience even at such cost, it could discourage users from utilizing the system.

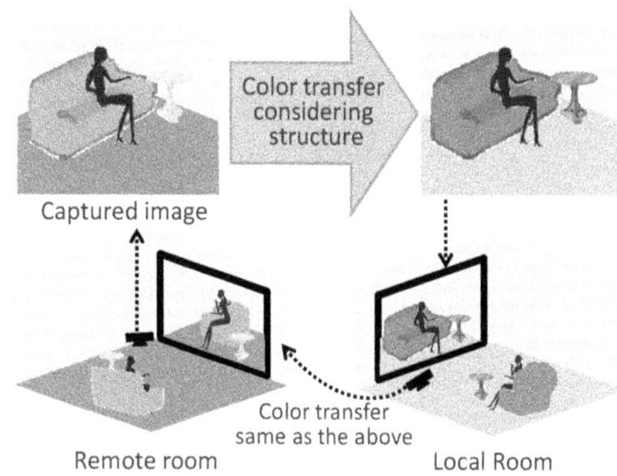

Fig. 1. Concept of color transfer for telepresence

Our motivation for this study is to create a telepresence system for ordinary homes using only an RGB-D camera without the aforementioned identical furnishings. Similarly to our study, telepresence systems based on RGB-D image processing have been proposed. These methods extract the region of a remote participant and synthesize the region in the local display with a preset background image similar to the local room. However, unnatural synthesized texture such as deficient human texture often occurs due to the different structure between the remote room and preset background image. This problem is likely to occur in home telepresence where the participant moves more freely than in a formal conference room. To avoid this problem, our proposed method generates an image based on the image of the actual remote room instead of a preset background image. Color characteristics of the local room are transferred into that of the remote room. Figure 1 shows the concept of color transfer for telepresence. Consistency of the color characteristics allows users to feel as if they are present in the same place. In this paper, we improved similarity between the rooms by considering the spatial structure for color transfer. In addition the processing of each frame is designed to work fast since real-time processing is required for the telepresence system.

MM '14, November 03 - 07 2014, Orlando, FL, USA
Copyright 2014 ACM 978-1-4503-3063-3/14/11…$15.00.
http://dx.doi.org/10.1145/2647868.2655061

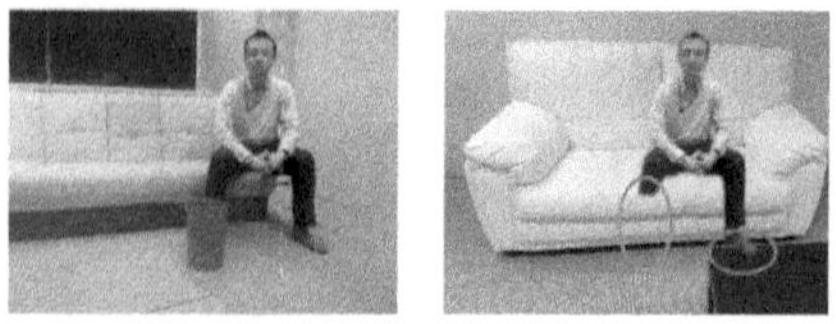

(a) Actual remote room (b) Synthesized image

Fig. 2. An example of degradation in the conventional telepresence methods using the preset background image.

The remainder of this paper is organized as follows. Section 2 overviews related works, Section 3 describes in detail our proposed method, Section 4 presents the experimental results, and finally the paper is concluded in Section 5.

2. RELATED WORK

In order to achieve an immersive experience at a distant location, some telepresence methods based on image processing are proposed [2], [3]. These methods extract the human region from a video of a remote room and synthesize it on the display of the local room with a preset background image of a virtual conference room [2] or an image of the local room [3]. The methods can offer users an experience that allows them to feel as if they are in the same room because the preset background image is more similar to the local environment than the actual background. However, the difference between the structure of the preset background image and the actual remote background often degrades the image quality in the synthesized video. For example, when a part of the human region is occluded by an object, a deficient human region is often synthesized despite the inexistence of an occluding object. In addition, when an object exists in a certain region of the preset background image though no object exists in the corresponding region of the actual remote background, the human region sometimes overlaps the object in the preset background image unnaturally. Figure 2 shows an example of such degradation. The human region was extracted from a remote room as shown in Figure 2 (a) and synthesized in a preset background image as Figure 2 (b). In Figure 2 (b), the red circle shows an example of degradation of a deficient human region and the blue circle shows an example of unnatural overlapping of the human region and an object. The above problem can be rephrased as a problem of arranging the space that has the same structure as the remote room and that is similar to the local room. However, it is impossible to prepare the generic preset background image that satisfies the above conditions of the space, since there are numerous variations of the structures of the remote rooms. Furthermore, using the preset background image limits the variation of the local room. Therefore, the above problem cannot be solved by the method using the preset background image, and the space should be provided dynamically depending on the remote and the local room. We therefore approach the problem from another direction: Our proposed method transforms the actual remote room into a space similar to the local room instead of replacing the background of the remote room with a preset background image. More specifically, color characteristics of the local room are imposed on that of the remote room.

In order to impose an image's color characteristics on another image, some color transfer methods are proposed [4-6]. These conventional approaches applied the reference image's color appearance to the original image by using statistical information, such as mean, standard deviation, and histogram. Considering the application of these techniques for our purpose, consistency of spatial structure is important for offering users a same-room experience. However, since the conventional color transfer methods do not consider the spatial structure of the image, inconsistency in terms of spatial structure often occurs even if the color pattern of the entire image is successfully transferred. For example, the floor's colors of the local and remote room are often different in the result of the conventional methods, and it degrades the same-room experience when they are applied to telepresence.

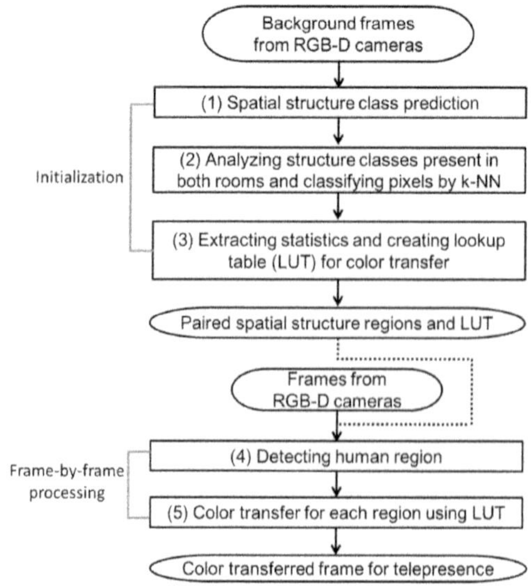

Fig. 3. Flowchart of the proposed method

3. PROPOSED METHOD

In order to overcome the problems mentioned in the previous section, we propose a novel color transfer method based on spatial structure for telepresence. The proposed method does not use the preset background image for the remote user's space but dynamically generates the space that has the same structure as the remote room and that is similar to the local room. By transferring color characteristics of the local room's image to the target image, our proposed method can arrange the space to be similar to the local room. Also, by using the remote room's image as the target image for color transfer, our proposed method achieves the space that has the same structure as the remote room. In addition, in order to solve the problem of color's inconsistency in terms of spatial structure, the proposed method predicts and analyzes the structure of the rooms. The algorithm of analyzing the structures between the local and remote rooms is one of the novel points of the proposed method. Furthermore, we preliminarily create color lookup tables (LUT) for real-time processing.

The proposed method has a series of procedures as shown in Figure 3. The procedures roughly consist of two stages. The first stage (Step 1-3) is the initialization stage to acquire paired regions and LUT for color transfer. The second stage (Step 4, 5) is the frame-by-frame processing stage for a real-time telepresence system. In our system, the input signals are color (RGB) and depth (D) images captured from an RGB-D camera in each room, and the color transferred image that is originally captured from an RGB-D camera in the remote room is obtained as the final output of each frame. The details of each step are discussed in the following subsections.

3.1 Initialization stage

In Step (1), spatial structure class is predicted [7] by using color and depth features. The features include SIFT features, histograms of surface normal, 2D and 3D bounding box dimensions, color histograms and relative depth. A logistic

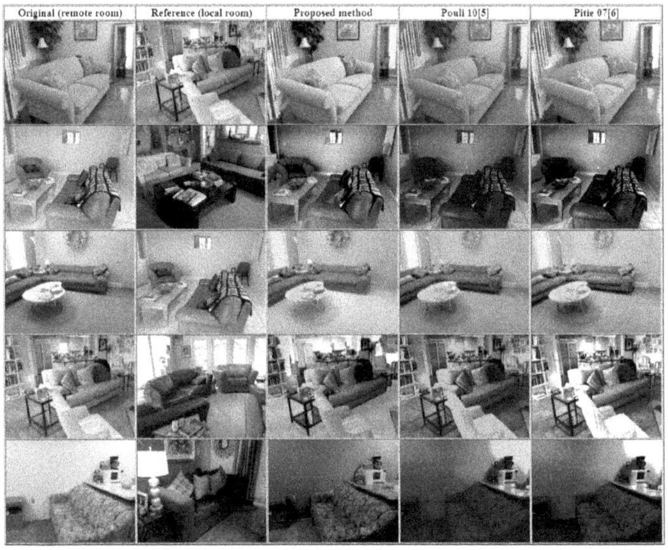

Fig. 4. Experimental results of color transfer on NYU-Depth V2 dataset [7]

regression classifier is preliminarily trained using indoor RGB-D data with dense per-pixel labels annotated by humans. The classifier classify each pixel of images into 4 structure classes defined in [7]: the first class is "ground" for the floor, the second class is "permanent structures" such as walls, ceilings, and columns, the third class is "furniture" such as tables, dressers, and counters, and the fourth class is "props" that are portable objects.

In Step (2), structure classes presenting both rooms are analyzed. Firstly, the number of pixels belonging to each structure class is counted in the captured image for each room. Secondly, structure classes satisfying both of the following conditional inequalities are listed as set ***C***.

$$N_{local}(c) > Th \quad (1)$$

$$N_{remote}(c) > Th \quad (2)$$

The $N_{local}(c)$ and $N_{remote}(c)$ represent the numbers of pixels belonging to structure class c in the local room image and remote room image, respectively, and Th is a threshold. Finally, pixels belonging to the structure classes that do not satisfy the above condition are classified into one of the classes in set ***C***. We used the k-Nearest Neighbors algorithm (k-NN) [8] for the classification where the 5-dimensional vector composed of color values of the pixel in CIELAB color space and (x, y) coordinates of the pixel are used as a feature vector. This k-NN classification is necessary to associate all pixels between the rooms. We employed CIELAB color space since it is based on the characteristics of human visual perception and therefore more suitable for our method compared to RGB color space.

In Step (3), color statistics are extracted from each structure class in set ***C***, and a color lookup table for color transfer is created for each structure class in set ***C***. Mean and standard deviation in CIELAB color space are calculated with respect to each room and each structure class in set ***C***. We create an RGB color lookup table (LUT) for each structure class in set ***C***. The LUT is an array that contains pre-computed results of transformation between each input RGB color and output RGB color. An RGB color (r, g, b) is transformed to another RGB color (r', g', b') as follows. Firstly, (r, g, b) is transformed to a color (L, a, b) in the CIELAB color space. Secondly, the CIELAB transferred color (L', a', b') is calculated using the mean and the standard deviations of each channel of the color space by the following equations

$$L' = (L - \bar{L}^{remote})\frac{\sigma_L{}^{remote}}{\sigma_L{}^{local}} + \bar{L}^{local} \quad (3)$$

$$a' = (a - \bar{a}^{remote})\frac{\sigma_a{}^{remote}}{\sigma_a{}^{local}} + \bar{a}^{local} \quad (4)$$

$$b' = (b - \bar{b}^{remote})\frac{\sigma_b{}^{remote}}{\sigma_b{}^{local}} + \bar{b}^{local} \quad (5)$$

Finally, (r', g', b') is obtained by transforming (L', a', b') into RGB color space.

3.2 Frame-by-frame processing stage

In Step (4), the human region is detected by depth based human detection [10]. Since the color of the human region is sensitive to human visual recognition, the colors of the region are not transferred in our method.

In Step (5), the colors of pixels except the human region are transferred for each structure class using LUT created in Step (3). Specifically, the result of transferred color can be obtained from the LUT by simple array indexing operation. By using pre-computed information, processing cost can be saved and the proposed method can be applied for the real-time telepresence system.

4. EXPERIMENTAL RESULTS

In order to evaluate the effectiveness of the proposed method, we conducted two experiments. In the first experiment, our proposed method was applied to RGB-D data captured from living rooms, which are extracted from the NYU-Depth V2 dataset [7]. Then, the color transfer results were compared with two conventional color transfer methods Pouli and Reinhard [5], Pitie and Kokaram [6]. Results of the conventional methods are generated by using the program provided by the authors of each paper. In the second experiment, in order to confirm the experience of telepresence with our proposed method, we implemented the color transfer method in a PC-based prototype telepresence system. Threshold Th in inequalities (1) and (2) is experimentally set as 10% of the number of pixels in the image.

4.1 Experiment 1: color transfer

The experimental results of color transfer on the NYU-Depth V2 dataset are shown in Figure 4. Color characteristics of the original image, which we call the "remote room", are transferred into other color characteristics of the reference image, which we call the "local room", by three color transfer methods. In the results of conventional methods, color mix up is often observed because all regions in the image are used as a reference. For example, a sofa in the first row's result of Pitie and Kokaram's method [6] in Figure 4 looks reddish since the color of the floor in the local room is mixed into the sofa. In contrast, since our proposed method only considers consistent structure between two images, there are few such artifacts in our results. Additionally, by comparing the local room's image and the color transferred image between regions corresponding to each other in terms of structure class, the colors of such region are often different between the images in the results of conventional methods. For instance, the color of the floor in the fourth row's result of Pouli and Reinhard's method [5] in Figure 4 looks different from the color

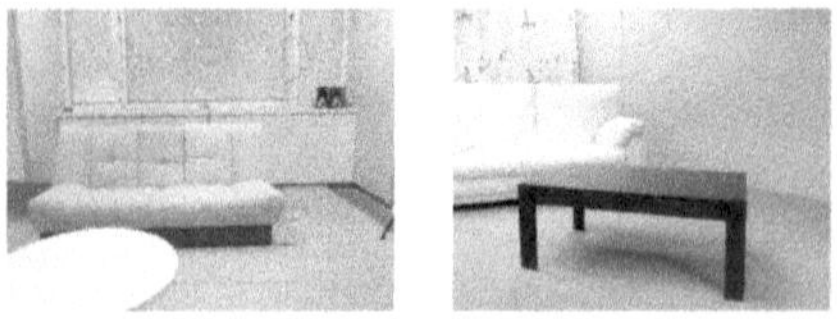

(a) Background of remote room (b) Background of local room

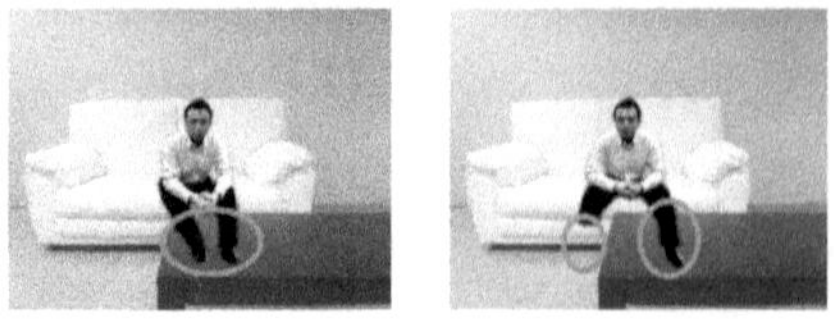

(c) Results of conventional method [3]

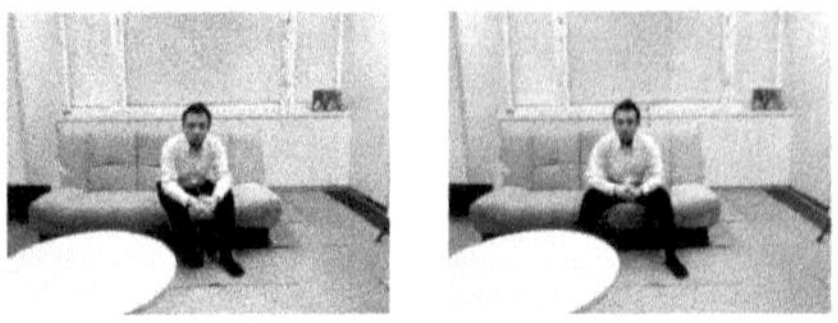

(d) Results of proposed method

(e) Telepresence by using proposed method

Fig. 5. Experimental results of proposed method in telepresence

of the floor in the local room. By contrast, the colors of such structures in our results are more similar to the colors of local room images compared to the conventional method.

4.2 Experiment 2: telepresence

The experimental results of the prototype telepresence system using our proposed method are shown in Figure 5. To confirm that our proposed method solved the problem of the preset background image based telepresence system described in Section 2, we compared it with the preset background image based telepresence system [3]. Note that we employed depth based human region detection [9], although the original work employs multi-view camera based human region segmentation. The difference in methods for acquiring the human region does not cause an essential difference in the results of this comparison. As shown in Figure 5 (c), a degradation of deficient human region is shown in the red circle and unnatural overlapping of the human region and an object is shown in the blue circles in the results of the conventional method. These problems are caused by the difference between the structure of the preset background image and the actual remote room as described in Section 2. In contrast, there is no such inconsistency in the results of our proposed method, since it achieves a space that has the same structure as the remote room by using the actual remote room's image as the target image. Furthermore, we displayed our results in the local room as shown in Figure 5 (e). It was confirmed that our telepresence system offers same-room experience by transforming the remote room image into an image similar to the local room in terms of color characteristics. In our current system, frame-by-frame processing stage takes about only 3 msec/frame when resolutions of color and depth frame are both 640×480.

5. CONCLUSION

In this paper, we propose a novel color transfer method for telepresence. We improved the similarity between the local room and the remote room based on spatial structure that the conventional color transfer methods did not consider. The experimental results revealed that the proposed method can change the colors of indoor-room images better than conventional color transfer methods in terms of application for telepresence. In addition, our method has limitation in the change of structure with time that can be improved by estimating structure change based on feature point tracking, which is our future work.

6. ACKNOWLEDGEMENT

This research was conducted under the research project "R&D on Ultra-Realistic Communication Technology with Innovative 3D Video technology," organized by the National Institute of Information and Communications Technology, Japan.

7. REFERENCES

[1] T. Szigeti, K. McMenamy and R. Saville. 2009. Cisco TelePresence Fundamentals. Cisco Press.

[2] V.A. Nguyen, T. D. Vu, H. Yang, J. Lu, and M. N. Do. 2012. ITEM: Immersive Telepresence for Entertainment and Meeting with Commodity Setup. ACM Multimedia 2012. 1021-1024.

[3] H. Sankoh, M. Sugano and S. Naito. 2013. Robust foreground segmentation from sparsely arranged multi-view cameras. MMSP 2013, 19-24.

[4] E. Reinhard, M. Ashikhmin, B. Gooch, and P. Shirley. 2001. Color transfer between images. IEEE CG&A, 21:34–41.

[5] T. Pouli, E. Reinhard. Progressive histogram reshaping for creative color transfer and tone reproduction. NPAR 2010. 81-90.

[6] F. Pitie´, A. Kokaram, 2007. The linear Monge–Kantorovitch linear colour mapping for example-based colour transfer. CVMP 2007. 1–9.

[7] N. Silberman, D. Hoiem, P. Kohli, and R. Fergus. 2012. Indoor segmentation and support inference from RGBD images. ECCV 2012. 746-760.

[8] N. S. Altman, 1992. An introduction to kernel and nearest-neighbor nonparametric regression. The American Statistician 46 (3). 175–185.

[9] D. Catuhe, 2012. Programming with the Kinect™ for Windows® Software Development Kit. Microsoft Press.

Human Computer Interface for Quadriplegic People Based on Face Position/gesture Detection

Zhen-Peng Bian†‡, Junhui Hou†‡, Lap-Pui Chau†, and Nadia Magnenat-Thalmann‡
†School of Electrical & Electronic Engineering,Nanyang Technological University,Singapore 639798
‡Institute for Media Innovation, Nanyang Technological University, Singapore 639798
Email: {zbian1, houj0001, elpchau, nadiathalmann}@ntu.edu.sg

ABSTRACT

This paper proposes a human computer interface using a single depth camera for quadriplegic people. The nose position is employed to control the cursor along with the commands provided by mouth's status. The detection of nose position and mouth's status is based on randomized decision tree algorithm. The experimental results show that the proposed interface is comfortable, easy to use, robust, and outperforms the existing assistive technology.

Categories and Subject Descriptors

H.5 [INFORMATION INTERFACES AND PRESENTATION]: User Interfaces

General Terms

Applications

Keywords

Assistive technology; quadriplegic; computer access; human-computer interaction (HCI); hand-free interface; vision-based; severe disabilities.

1. INTRODUCTION

Quadriplegic people have great difficulties to use standard input devices of personal computers, such as mouse. Some assistive technologies (ATs) have been developed to help them to control computers. According to [,], ATs for quadriplegic people can be roughly categorized as four groups: (1)Physiological signals based, such as electroencephalogram, electromyogram, and electrooculogram; (2)Voice commands based, such as speech recognition and non-verbal vocalization software; (3)Mechanical motion based, such as sip-and-puff or mouth stick ; (4)Tracking movement of body parts and/or landmarks based, such as head and eye trackers.

To attain the goal of non-contact, ATs based on cameras are alternative interfaces without wearing accessory. In [ ], CameraMouse tracked user-selected and automatically updating template in a RGB video. However, it required another person to start tracking and re-tracking. In [ ], the authors employed the colour of skin to extract the nose and face for tracking, which was vulnerable to regions with similarly colour and illumination of lights. For the same application, the authors in [ ] tracked a face based on a 3D model fitting to 2D features under a cost function of error. However, that tracking required initialization and was vulnerable to illumination of lights.

MM'14, November 3–7, 2014, Orlando, Florida, USA.

http://dx.doi.org/10.1145/2647868.2655063.

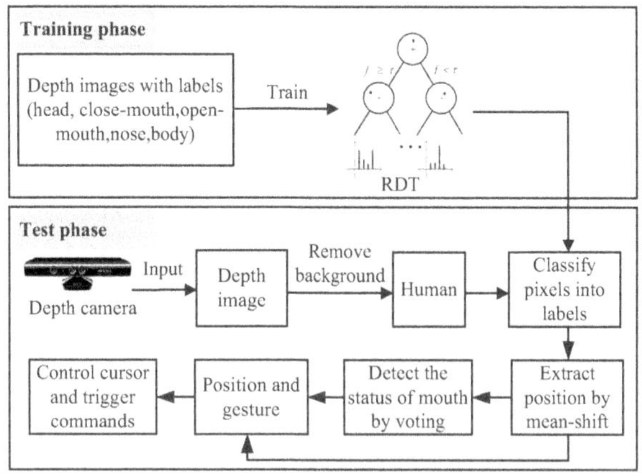

Figure 1: Flow chart of the proposed approach.

The proposed user interface (namely FM) is based on the face position and gesture using a single commercial depth camera. Fig. 1 is the flow chart of our proposed approach. The depth camera is independent of illumination of lights compared with the rivals, i.e., RGB cameras. The detection of face position and gesture is based on fast and robust randomized decision tree (RDT) using a single image, without initialization or re-initialization. The operation of the proposed interface combines the advantages of head motion and the mouth gesture. The proposed system's strengths are comfortable (no body attachment), easy to use (no initialization, no calibration, no guardian) and robust (insensitive to colour or illumination of lights). It can enrich people with severe mobility impaired in their rehabilitation or daily life activities.

2. DETECTION ALGORITHM OF POSITION AND GESTURE

The nose position is employed to control the cursor along

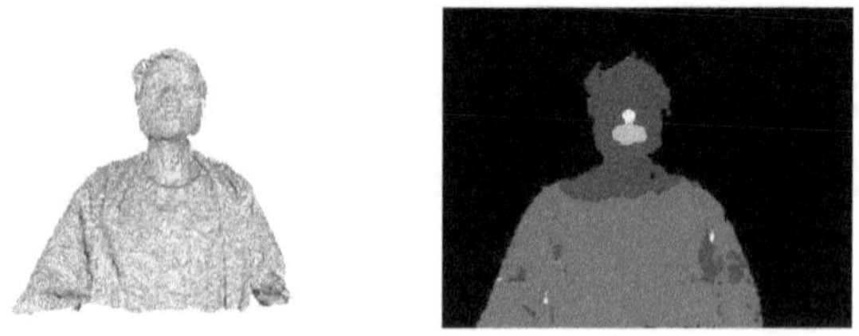

(a) (b)

Figure 2: The result of RDT. (a) Input depth image after removing far distance pixels, shown as mesh; (b) Highest probability labels after RDT classifying, each colour stands for one label.

with the commands provided by mouth's status. Both position and gesture are extracted using a single depth image based on the same framework, i.e., RDT, and do not need any facial model, initialization and re-initialization. The proposed detection algorithm is low computational complexity and robust. The following will present three key points of the detection algorithm, i.e., the training data of RDT, the feature of RDT and the decision approach after RDT classifying. More detail about RDT can be found in [,].

2.1 Training data

The authors in [ ] used RDT algorithm to extract the joint position. We further develop the RDT algorithm to extract positions and gestures together. In [ ], each vertex in the model for training was predefined to a fixed label. In our algorithm, the label of mouth is relative to the mouth status. Before labelling, the mouth status should be known. Then, pixels relative to the mouth are labelled responding to the mouth status. In total, there are five labels, i.e., head, close-mouth, open-mouth, nose and body.

2.2 Feature of RDT

The feature of RDT is the difference of depth values of the test pixel and a neighbour [ ]. The feature can be formulated as

$$f((x_0,y_0)|(\Delta x,\Delta y)) = z(x_0,y_0) - z((x_0,y_0) + \frac{(\Delta x,\Delta y)}{z(x_0,y_0)}) \quad (1)$$

where (x_0, y_0) is the test pixel, $(\Delta x, \Delta y)$ is the offset related to the test pixel (x_0, y_0), $z(x, y)$ is the depth value of the pixel (x, y). $1/z(x, y)$ is used to normalize the offset value. This feature is a special case of the feature in [ ], but this feature is more efficient. In each split node of RDT, one feature is calculated during test phase.

2.3 Decision approach of position and gesture

The results of the classifier of RDT are probabilities of labels for each test pixel, as shown in Fig.2. We propose an approach for the decision of nose position and mouth status based on the per-pixel classification results of RDT.

For the position of nose, a mean-shift algorithm with a weighted Gaussian kernel is employed based on the probabilities of nose. The density estimator for nose position is defined as

$$P_l \propto \sum_{i=1}^{M} w_{il} \exp(-\|\frac{L-L_i}{b_l}\|^2) \quad (2)$$

where P_l is the position of label l, M is the number of total test pixels in the test image I, w_{il} is the pixel weighting, L is a 3D location, L_i is the 3D location of the test pixel (x_i, y_i). b_l is the bandwidth for label l. w_{il} includes two factors: (1) The world surface area related to the depth value z; (2) The probability P from the classifier of RDT. w_{il} is formulated as

$$w_{il} = P(l|(x_i,y_i),I)z(x_i,y_i)^2 \quad (3)$$

For the mouth status, a voting algorithm is employed. The voting metric is formulated as

$$S_m^* = \arg\max_{S_m}(w_{S_m}\max_{L}(\sum_{i=1}^{M} w_{iS_m}\exp(-\|\frac{L-L_i}{b_{S_m}}\|^2))) \quad (4)$$

S_m^* is the final status of mouth, S_m is the status of mouth and w_{S_m} is the weighting of the status of mouth. The mouth status with larger voting value is decided as the result. This detection approach of mouth status avoids the difficult extraction problem of landmarks of the deformation mouth based on a single high noise commercial depth camera. Even after extracting the landmarks of the deformation mouth, the mouth status detection is still a challenge.

3. CONTROL CURSOR AND TRIGGER COMMANDS

This section presents the operation function of proposed interface.

The mouse control mode is based on location, which is the 3D position of nose, since the experimental results in [ ] showed that this mode had the best performance among three mouse modes: direct mode, joystick mode and location mode. The behaviour of location mode is similar with that of the standard mouse. It can provide users with the freedom of controlling the cursor motion, speed, and acceleration in any direction. In this mode, users can also move more efficiently, such as the movement path and command timing. The mapping function is defined as

$$d_x = g_x(x_n - x_0) \quad (5)$$

$$d_y = g_y(y_n - y_0) \quad (6)$$

where d_x (d_y) is the distance between the current cursor location and the reference cursor location of the x (y) coordinate axis, g_x (g_y) is the mapping gain, and x_n (y_n) and x_0 (y_0) are the current and reference nose locations of the x (y) coordinate axis.

The resolution of depth image is a bottleneck for interface based on small amplitude head motion. If the maximum amplitude of nose movement is 140 mm and the resolution in xy plane of depth image is 2 mm, the range of nose movement in the depth image is only 70 pixels. However, the resolution of computer displayer is much higher than 70x70 pixels. Thus, the gain of mapping the nose movement to the cursor movement is large. The range and gain of cursor movement become a trade-off problem. We propose using the mouth gesture to solve this problem. The close status of mouth is employed to enable the movement of cursor and the open status of mouth is employed to disable the movement of cursor. Thus, the user can adjust the head to a comfortable pose when the user open the mouth to disable the movement of cursor. If the pointing target is very far, the user can open mouth and return the head back, and then

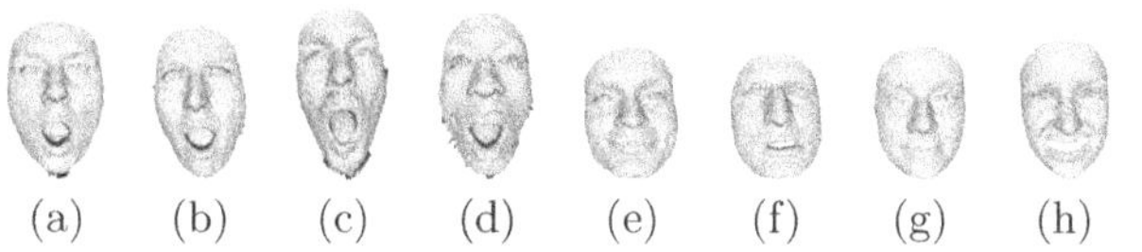

Figure 3: Some examples of Bosphorus 3D face database. (a)-(d) Positive; (e)-(h)Negative.

Table 1: Errors of detection algorithms.

Error	Porposed	SVM1	SVM2	SVM3	SVM4
Positive	2	6	4	**1**	35
Negative	**5**	6	12	17	9
Total errors	**7**	12	16	18	44
Error rate(%)	**0.35**	0.61	0.81	0.91	2.22

continue to move the cursor to the target. Furthermore, this function can quickly stop and fix the cursor to avoid overshooting or jitter to improve the accuracy of pointing when the cursor is pointing at the target.

Combined with the temporal information, a set of interaction commands, e.g., single click and double clicks, can be defined based on the status of mouth. The mouse event of single click is triggered by mouth status sequence of open-close-open during a short time while the mouse event of double clicks is triggered by open-close-open-close.

4. EXPERIMENTS

In this section, the evaluation of our approach is described.

4.1 Evaluation of detection method

To test the robustness of our detection algorithm, the Bosphorus 3D face database [ ] is used, which includes 105 subjects with ground truth mouth poses. 20 challenging poses, i.e., the pose type: LFAU, are used. The mouth stretch LFAU_27 is assigned as positive label(total 105) and the rests are assigned as negative label(total 1876). Fig. 3 shows some examples. We add some Gaussian noise into depth component to the depth images.

The experiments are performed using 10-fold subject cross-validation on the entire dataset, i.e., in each fold subjects for test are never used for training.

Table 1 shows the error result of 10-fold subject cross-validation. For comparison, SVM classifier is used to detect the same mouth status based on the ground truth landmarks of mouth. The detected result of SVM is shown in Table 1. In Table 1, SVM1, SVM2, SVM3 and SVM4 are used quadratic, polynomial, linear and rbf kernel functions, respectively. From Table 1, we can note that there are 7 errors of proposed method while the best result of SVM is 12 errors. The classification result of proposed method is even better than that of SVM with ground truth landmarks.

The nose mean error of proposed method is 4.5 mm in 3D. There is no missed sample for nose detection, and the maximum distance to the ground truth nose position is 11 mm.

A video demonstration of face position/gesture detection based on proposed algorithm is available in the website [1].

[1] http://www.ntu.edu.sg/home/elpchau/Interface2014.wmv

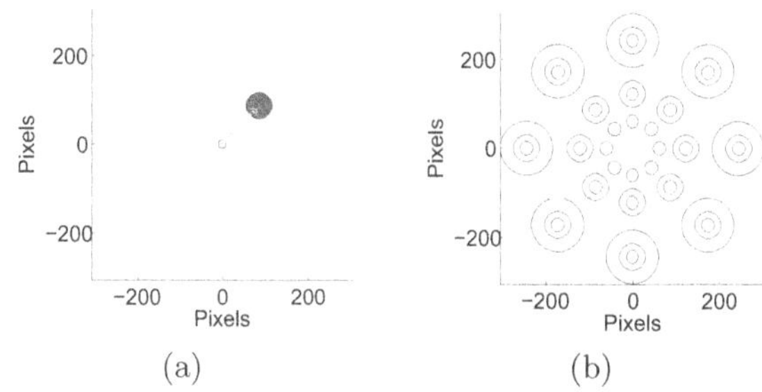

Figure 4: GUI screen for center-out tapping. (a)One randomly appear target. (b)48 possible targets.

Table 2: D-W pair conditions.

D(pixels)	61	122	122	244	244	244
W(pixels)	30	30	61	30	61	122
ID(bits)	1.60	2.34	1.59	3.19	2.32	1.59

In the demo, the face position/gesture detection program was run on a single core of Intel CPU (i5 650, 4 GB of RAM). The detection took 7 ms per frame, which classified all foreground pixels. It shows that the detection algorithm is robust and fast.

4.2 Evaluation of interface operation

4.2.1 Task

The center-out tapping task was used to evaluate the performance of interface operation. The procedure of the task is to move the cursor from the center position to the circular target indicated in blue and select the target, as shown in Fig. 4(a). Each trial begins with the cursor at the center and one target is appeared randomly. Using the proposed interface and CameraMouse, subjects are required to dwell on the target for 500 ms, as suggested in [ ], to select a target. Using the mouse, they are asked to click on the target.

There are 48 different targets per round, as shown in Fig. 4(b). The designed values are the same as that in [ ]. Circular targets with three different diameters W and three different distances D from the center create six D-W pair conditions, as shown in Table 2. Each condition has eight directions (every 45°). Subjects were instructed to move the cursor as fast and as precisely to the center of the targets as possible.

4.2.2 Interfaces

The GUI was developed by openCV and presented to the subjects sitting 80 cm away from a 17.3" LCD monitor with 1600x900 pixels resolution. The task window was a white 610x610 pixels square. To show performance of mouth status using for FM, we measured the performance of three selecting ways of FM, i.e., freeze the nose (dwell time 500 ms), open the mouth (dwell time 500 ms) and click by mouth action (open-close-open). These three ways named as FMf, FMo and FMc. For each subject, the interface order (FMf, FMo, FMc, CameraMouse and mouse) was randomized.

Each interface was used thirty rounds per subject. Table 3 shows the whole test trials. The total trials are 36000. Five able-bodied participants (4 male, 1 female, all were graduate students) took the tests. All of them used computers more

Table 3: Test trials.

Trials	Rounds	Interfaces	Participants	Total trials
48	30	5	5	36000

than six hours per day, but had no prior experience with face interface.

4.2.3 *Performance Measures*

The throughput (TP) and task completion time (TCT) performance measures were considered for the quantitative assessment of the FM performance and its comparison with CameraMouse. Mouse was used as baseline.

Throughput: TP indicates that subjects deliver the amount of information to the computer through an interface, which is defined as

$$TP = \frac{ID}{MT}, \tag{7}$$

where ID is the index of difficulty of the target, measured in bits, and is defined by Shannon's formula as

$$ID = \log_2(\frac{D}{W} + 1). \tag{8}$$

Table 2 shows ID values in our experiments. MT is the movement time from the center to the target, and MT does not include the initiation delay time before the subject moves the cursor and the dwelling or selection time for target selection [ ]. Higher TP is better.

Task Completion Time: TCT indicates the overall subjects' control over the cursor movements. TCT is the total time to complete each round. The counting time is from the first target appearance to the end of the last target. Lower TCT is better.

4.2.4 *Results*

Table 4 shows results of the experiment of interface operation. In Table 4, TPn (TCTn) is defined as that TP (TCT) is normalized by CameraMouse TP (TCT). The mouse throughput is 4.4 bit/s, which is agree with many researches [ ] and indicates that our methodology, GUI functionality, and data analysis are adequate. From Table 4, we can note that FMf, FMo and FMc outperform CameraMouse. TP of FMf is 21% better than that of CameraMouse, and TCT is 9% better. Furthermore, during the test, CameraMouse lost tracking the selected point a few times and needed to re-select the tracking point, which were caused by fast movement. The proposed method avoided the losing problem. They show that the proposed method based on a depth camera and RDT detection is better than CameraMouse based on a RGB camera. There are two major reasons contributed to the improvement: (1)The proposed method allows the user to conveniently adjust the head; (2)The proposed extraction algorithm can extract the position and gesture using a single image avoiding the 'feature drift' problem of CameraMouse during tracking. TPs of FMo and FMc are 55% better than that of CameraMouse and are better than that of FMf. TCTs show the same trend. They show that the mouth action can improve the performance. The difference between the performances of FMo and FMc is small. The click command of mouth took 460 ms per time averaged the whole experiment.

Table 4: Results of interface operation.

	FMf	FMo	FMc	CameraMouse	Mouse
TP(bit/s)	1.8	2.3	2.3	1.5	4.4
TPn(%)	121	155	155	100	293
TCT(min)	5.1	4.6	4.2	5.6	2.3
TCTn(%)	91	82	75	100	41

5. CONCLUSION

This paper has presented a human computer interface using a single depth camera for disabilities. The proposed RDT-based detection algorithm can extract the position of nose and gesture of mouth accurately and fast using a single depth image. Thus, the interface operation achieves superior performance to the existing face tracking interface using a RGB camera. Furthermore, our depth camera based interface is independent of illumination of lights, which improves the robustness, compared to the RGB camera based method. The performance of the interface operation shows that the proposed interface outperforms the existing face tracking interface using a RGB camera.

Acknowledgment

The authors would like to acknowledge the Ph.D. grant from the Institute for Media Innovation, Nanyang Technological University, Singapore.

6. REFERENCES

[1] M. Betke, J. Gips, and P. Fleming. The camera mouse: visual tracking of body features to provide computer access for people with severe disabilities. *IEEE T NEUR SYS REH*, 10(1):1–10, March 2002.

[2] Z. Bian, J. Hou, L. Chau, and N. Magnenat-Thalmann. Fall detection based on body part tracking using a depth camera. *IEEE J BHI*, 2014.

[3] M. Jose and R. Lopes. Human-computer interface controlled by the lip. *IEEE J BHI*, 2014.

[4] T. Morris and V. Chauhan. Facial feature tracking for cursor control. *J NETW COMPUT APPL*, 29(1):62 – 80, 2006.

[5] J. Music, M. Cecic, and B. M. Testing inertial sensor performance as hands-free humancomputer interface. *WSEAS Trans. Comput.*, 8:715–724, Apr. 2009.

[6] A. Savran, B. Sankur, and M. Taha Bilge. Comparative evaluation of 3d vs. 2d modality for automatic detection of facial action units. *Pattern Recogn.*, 45(2):767–782, Feb 2012.

[7] J. Shotton, A. Fitzgibbon, M. Cook, T. Sharp, M. Finocchio, R. Moore, A. Kipman, and A. Blake. Real-time human pose recognition in parts from single depth images. In *CVPR*, pages 1297 –1304, june 2011.

[8] J. Tu, H. Tao, and T. Huang. Face as mouse through visual face tracking. *Comput. Vis. Image Underst.*, 108(1-2):35–40, Oct. 2007.

[9] B. Yousefi, X. Huo, E. Veledar, and M. Ghovanloo. Quantitative and comparative assessment of learning in a tongue-operated computer input device. *IEEE T INF TECHNOL B.*, 15(5):747–757, Sept 2011.

A Multi-Touch DJ Interface with Remote Audience Feedback

Lasse Farnung Laursen[1], Masataka Goto[2], Takeo Igarashi[1]
[1]The University of Tokyo, 7-3-1 Bunkyo-ku, Hongo, Tokyo, Japan
[2]National Institute of Advanced Industrial Science and Technology (AIST), 1-1-1 Umezono, Tsukuba, Japan
gazoo@42.dk, m.goto@aist.go.jp, takeo@acm.org

ABSTRACT

Current DJ interfaces lack direct support for typical digital communication common in social media. We present a novel DJ interface for live internet broadcast performances with remote audience feedback integration. Our multi-touch interface is designed for a table top display, featuring a time-line based visualization. Two studies are presented involving seven DJs, culminating in four live broadcasts gathering and analyzing data to better understand both the DJ and audience perspective. This study is one of the first to look closer at DJs and remote audiences. We present useful insight for future interaction design between DJs and remote audiences, and interface integrated audience feedback.

Categories and Subject Descriptors

H.5.2 [**User Interfaces**]: Graphical user interfaces (GUI); H.5.5 [**Sound and Music Computing**]: Systems

Keywords

Touch Interface; Music Interface; Crowd-based Interaction;

1. INTRODUCTION

Live broadcasting of video and audio streams via services such as YouTube Live, Ustream, and Twitch.tv, has become easy and popular. This type of self-broadcasting is an attractive and natural way for disc-jockeys (DJs)[1] to remotely reach a bigger audience. Traditionally, DJs inhabit a local performance space together with their audience, often involving a significant amount of direct and indirect communication in-between them. This includes subtle visual cues, such as head nodding, smiling, dancing and even occasional verbal communication [4]. However, in the online performance space, new methods of interactions have established themselves. DJs have access to chat rooms where they can directly communicate with the audience, and in some cases even receive a video stream from individual listeners [9].

We propose a novel DJ multimedia interface that integrates state-of-the-art multi-touch table-top DJ controls with communication functions, inspired by modern social media platforms. The interface utilizes a time-line based visualization, supporting intuitive drag and drop element interaction for easy audio cueing. Time-line elements are shown in detail or aggregated, as the user zooms in or out, respectively. This allows for both an overview or in-depth look as needed. Our system supports both a planning style visualization mode, where audio elements remain static during playback, or a more dynamic visualization mode, where audio scrolls by during playback. Both modes can be switched between in real-time to suit the DJ's current mood and needs.

The supported audience feedback includes a discrete positive 'like' which signifies a fondness for a particular occurrence in the performance, detailed comments from individual audience members, and an audience size histogram. All incoming feedback is displayed along audio elements, in the DJ interface in real-time. We explore the new potential offered by fusing feedback delivered by an unseen audience directly into the multimedia interface of the DJ, shedding light on the interaction both from the perspective of the DJ and the audience.

A pilot study was conducted with volunteer DJs testing an early version of the interface, and participating in qualitative interviews. The positive response lead us to conduct four live two-hour remote broadcasts with four DJs and a volunteer remote audience providing real-time feedback via our system. We gathered quantitative feedback from the audience and conducted qualitative interviews with the DJs. Every show featured a minor, yet engaged audience, submitting feedback directly into our DJ multimedia interface. All DJs showed a strong interest in receiving this feedback during their remote performance, and some offered ideas as to how it might improve their local performances, as well.

2. RELATED WORK

Nielsen ratings form the foundation of audience feedback collection, covered by Beville [2]. However, Nielsen ratings and most of the traditional systems described by Beville are passive in nature. Feedback is evaluated posthumously and not in the context of a live performance. A more recent live audience feedback system is 'The Cinematrix Interactive Entertainment System' [3] presented at SIGGRAPH in 1991, and further expanded upon by Maynes-Aminzade et al. [7]. Although audience feedback is handled in a live context, there is no active performer involved other than the audience itself. In this regard, our work more closely resembles that of Barkhuus and Jørgensen [1]. They present the 'Cheering-Meter' used in free-style rap competitions with live performers. However, contrary to our work, Barkhuus and Jørgensen do not consider interaction with a remote audience.

[1]In this paper we refer to radio/club DJs who play and blend multiple musical compositions sequentially, rather than a hip-hop DJ who uses turntables in a more instrumental way, via percussive scratching sounds.

MM'14, November 03–07 2014, Orlando, FL, USA.

ACM 978-1-4503-3063-3/14/11 ...$15.00.
http://dx.doi.org/10.1145/2647868.2655065 .

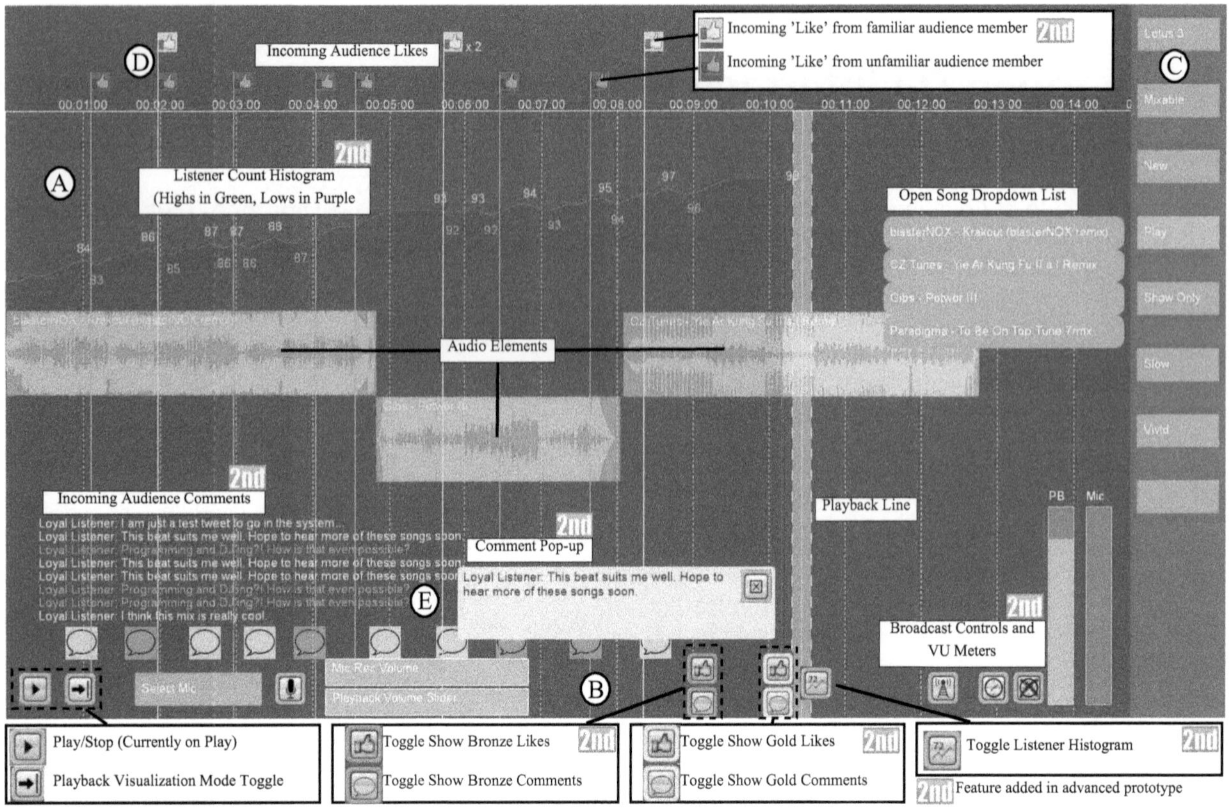

Figure 1: The advanced prototype DJ Interface. Significant additions from the early prototype interface are highlighted by the [2nd] marker.

Contemporary DJ instruments indirectly support remote audience feedback via existing online broadcasting portals. However, this feedback is presented out of context, in a separate interface, dividing the DJ's attention. Shamma et al. [9] investigate remote DJ performances on such a portal, the now defunct Yahoo! Live website. They focus on the community and social aspects of a shared online presence, rather than concrete interactions during live performances.

Gates et al. [4] analyze how DJs gain audience awareness during local performances and present a set of principals for how technology should support this activity. Their principals have influenced our design, despite the fact that their findings are based exclusively on local DJ performances.

Hook investigates interaction design for live performances [5], and provides a comprehensive look of many related live performance interfaces. However, performer-audience interaction is left as future work.

Sgouros [8] presents an interaction framework, enabling multiple users to take part in a performance either as a player or spectator and influence the outcome in real-time. This work shares conceptual similarities with ours, but focuses more on the technical aspects of the system rather than an evaluation of their users experience thereof.

Karnik et al. [6] present an ethnographic study of how DJs use social media as part of their work. In contrast to our work, their focus is exclusively on the use of social media outside of a live performance context.

A vast number of audience response systems also exist in the educational sector. It is important to note that although our work shares similarities with these types of systems, the context for our work is fundamentally different, e.g. a higher focus on cognitive workload and presentation is essential for our interface.

3. INTERFACE DESIGN

Over the course of this work, our interface was tested at two significant stages of its iterative development. Here we describe general features of the interface. Differences between the early- and advanced prototype versions are detailed further below. The advanced prototype interface is depicted in Fig. 1, with significant additions - from the early prototype - highlighted.

The interface consists of a common audio time-line visualization (referred to as the mixmap) marked Ⓐ, general playback and visualization controls at the bottom marked Ⓑ, and a set of drop-down menus for loading audio marked Ⓒ. The entire mixmap supports pinch gesture zooming for an ease of overview and/or detail. All loaded audio elements support intuitive drag-and-drop style interaction. Two modes of visualized playback are supported; static mixmap with a moving playback line, or moving mixmap with a static playback line. The former is ideal for planning ahead and setting up audio elements in advance. The latter mode of visualization is a more dynamic 'on-the-fly' style interaction mode. Switching between the two modes is possible at any time to suit the DJ's current mood and needs.

Differences between the early- and advanced prototype versions are detailed here. Changes were made to better accommodate live internet broadcasting, improve integrated audience feedback, and reflect the DJ's feedback on the early interface. In the early prototype, integrated user feedback consisted of four types of discrete feedback, which would

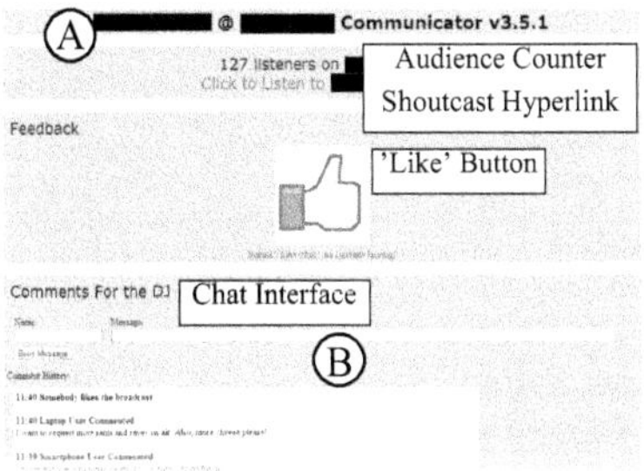

Figure 2: The web-based audience interface.

appear in the area marked Ⓓ. Audience members could send the DJ a 'like', 'dislike', 'volume up', and 'volume down' message. The advanced prototype interface simplified this feedback, retaining only the 'like' feedback, as the DJs mostly commented on its particular usefulness and were wary of overwhelming negative feedback. In accordance with the feedback obtained during the pilot study, the advanced prototype supports categorized listener feedback. Feedback from unfamiliar and familiar listeners are now distinctly displayed in bronze and gold, respectively.

To more faithfully replicate existing online self-broadcasting portals, we also chose to implement support for user comments (similar to Soundcloud) in the advanced interface, marked Ⓔ. The mixmap was also enhanced to include an integrated listener count histogram visualizing local minima and maxima. This provides the DJ a clear overview of the highs and lows of their performance, based on the size of the audience.

The advanced interface also supports feedback filtering as our pilot study indicated a strong preference for this. Audience histogram, bronze and gold 'likes' and comments can each be turned on and off as needed in real-time. The drop-down menus were also improved to enable drag-and-drop interaction, allowing users to easily drag unloaded audio on to the mixmap. Zooming was improved to aggregate discrete 'like' feedback into larger chunks, to ease the DJ's overview, as shown in Fig. 1 (where two gold likes are aggregated). Finally, the advanced interface also adds support for microphones allowing the DJs to respond to any audience feedback and further interact during a performance.

For the live broadcasts, a web-based interface was implemented to enable audience participation, shown in Fig.2. Submitting a 'Like' or a comment produces a drop-down message at the top of the page (marked Ⓐ) informing the user whether or not it was delivered successfully. Comments are submitted anonymously if the user refrains from entering a username in the interface, marked Ⓑ. During a pilot study, audience members expressed interest in viewing fellow listeners comments, which we added support for.

4. EARLY PROTOTYPE PILOT STUDY

Previous work [4, 5, 6] indicates that DJs have an innate desire to please audience members through their performance, and as a result gather both indirect and direct feedback by observing them. Although some forms of more direct feedback (e.g. song requests) are generally frowned upon. During a remote performance, however, the DJ and the audience no longer inhabit that same performance space, and almost all feedback becomes direct as a result.

To further investigate this and related issues, we conducted an in-lab local pilot study of an early prototype version of our interface with five DJs, between the ages of 26-37; four veterans each with 5 to 15 years of experience DJing live in clubs, and one newcomer.

Qualitative feedback was gathered via think-aloud usage sessions, where the DJs were encouraged to freely explore the interface. Given that the performance was not broadcast, audience feedback was simulated by an on-site researcher. Each DJ was interviewed to get insight into their perception of receiving feedback in general, and how local/remote performances differ in terms of wants/needs.

We define *local feedback*, as being traditional types of audience feedback present during a local performance (e.g. dancing, smiling, head nodding, verbal communication, etc.). *Remote feedback* is defined as digital audience feedback commonly found in modern social media (e.g. text messages, likes/dislikes, other discrete expressions of opinion).

All DJs professed a strong interest in receiving *remote feedback* during a remote performance, and merely tentatively interested in receiving it during a local performance. This is not surprising, given the lack of traditional means of feedback gathering when performing remotely. One DJ noted that he had a high interest in knowing where the feedback originated from and consequently how credible it was (random listeners vs. friends/other DJs), corroborated by Karnik et al [6]. All DJs preferred more vague *remote feedback* during a local performance (i.e. like/dislike), as opposed to precise ratings (i.e. 3/5), partially due to the already high number of distractions in a nightclub setting.

As to whether the DJs were likely to change a local performance based on *remote feedback*, some DJs stated they were likely to disregard it completely. Others valued any and all information they were given. Surprisingly, a few DJs stated they were even less likely to react to *remote feedback* during a remote performance.

Phillip Huey: *"I wouldn't do a live [remote] mix, and then get some negative feedback, and [...] just switch genres. I might do that at a [local] club."*

The DJs' opinions also varied in regards to how useful *remote feedback* was, compared to traditional *local feedback*.

Matthew Gammon: *"A like/dislike is very binary and too simple. Seeing someone dancing [...], there are so many non-verbal and verbal cues we can read off of individuals, [...]. Having a lot more to draw from, makes the interpretation easier to go through. [...] With [(likes/dislikes)] you don't know how much they like it or how much they don't like it."*

DJ Modality: *"The feedback was helpful. Particularly if I was doing an online set, that would be really useful. [The feedback] is more direct. If we use a dance floor analogy; People will leave the dance floor [due to fatigue or to get a drink,] not cause they don't like the music [...]. [...] So in that way, dancing is kind of an imprecise metric."*

Despite the fact that previous research paints a very dim view from DJs regarding direct song requests from the audience, some of our volunteers still expressed an interest in receiving them via *remote feedback*.

5. LIVE BROADCAST STUDY

We conducted a live broadcast study with four male DJs, two returning participants, between the ages of 28-33; each with 2 to 11 years of experience DJing live in clubs. Each DJ participated in a live 2 hour internet broadcast show (airing 20:00 local time) broadcast from our lab, and acting as the proverbial host, being in control of the interface for the duration of the performance. An on-site researcher was present to aid the DJ in any issues that might arise unexpectedly, as well as setup and shutdown the broadcast. No other people were in direct attendance and the stations 'regular' audience tuned into the broadcast via the internet. Audience interaction was encouraged vocally as part of the broadcast, and access to the web-based interface was provided via general link on the internet radio homepage. Friends of the DJ were individually directed to a unique link, distinguishing them from other listeners. Interviews were conducted with each DJ both before and after the live broadcast to collect qualitative data. Audience members were asked to fill out an online survey after the conclusion of the broadcast.

We observed the DJs having a preference for the more dynamic visualization mode, as only one of them used the alternative static mode for the majority of their broadcast. Our interfaces were well received by both the audience and the DJs. Both parties frequently engaged one another for the duration of the broadcasts.

Every DJ specifically commented on the usefulness of receiving direct feedback (i.e. likes/comments), as well as indirect feedback (Nr. of listeners) during the shows.

> Mark Jackson: *"It gives you inspiration and energy. [...] It works. I was surprised."*

The DJs generally preferred comments to 'likes', noting it showed more of an effort on behalf of the audience members, and leading to more informed performance improvements.

None of the feedback was toggled off during the live broadcasts. Our observations and quantitative data, shown in Table 1, indicate that the feedback never became overwhelming, and thus required filtering. Its persistent use during broadcasts is an indicator that the DJs found it to be neither intrusive, nor annoying. Some DJs also professed an interest in receiving *remote feedback* during a local performance, although one provided a more hesitant response.

> Matthew Gammon: *"It's interesting to see how people react and what they do. Will it heavily influence what I do? I don't think so."*

One of the DJs saw a strong potential in data mining the collected *remote feedback* to learn more about the audience, even after a local performance. Karnik et al. [6] corroborate this point.

> Dj Vivid: *"It would help me understand my audience better, know what they want to hear, which could lead to better parties or sets. That's important. [...] I can see a lot of uses for that."*

Another DJ hypothesized that some audience members who would normally not provide direct *local feedback*, would be more inclined to provide *remote feedback*.

Our expectation that DJs value feedback differently depending on the origin (random listeners vs. friends/other DJs), was not strongly confirmed. Only one DJ professed an interest in distinguishing the origin.

During the shows we observed an engaged minor portion of the audience, as indicated by the gathered quantitative data in Table 1. This is consistent with social media platforms such as YouTube and Soundcloud, where the more passive views/listens far outranks the NR. of likes/comments. Contrary to these sites, however, our audiences delivered far more comments than likes. Just like the DJs, the audience survey answers indicate comments being preferred to 'likes'. Apart from a single listener, all who participated in the surveys expressed an interest in providing the DJ with feedback. Their interest in providing a local live DJ with similar feedback was present, but less strong.

Day of_Show	Min	Max	Avrg	Likes (B/G)	Com. (B/G)	ALS
Sunday	96	111	104	38/4	96/28	14
Tuesday	121	152	134	13/4	84/8	7
Thursday	131	157	145	29/1	85/21	12
Sunday	94	122	104	14/15	58/52	13

Table 1: Quantitative audience data showing the day of each show, Min/Max/Average number of listeners, Nr. of likes and comments (bronze/gold respectively), and Nr. of answered listener surveys (ALS).

6. CONCLUSION

We performed two qualitative studies, presenting a novel multimedia DJ interface, and a closer look at how DJs perceived *local* and *remote feedback*. Our work builds upon previous research and shows a more nuanced landscape in terms of the DJs wishes/needs for this evolving technology. Every DJ showed a clear interest in receiving integrated feedback during *remote* performances. Some DJs also expressed an interest in receiving this feedback in a *local* context. We believe *local* feedback integration is most useful in situations where direct interaction with individuals is limited, such as larger concerts or festivals. Similar to Barkhuus and Jørgensen [1], we posit that the area of audience-performance interaction is ripe for further exploration.

7. ACKNOWLEDGMENTS

We thank all seven DJs who participated in our user study, Slayradio.org, the associated staff for their assistance, and all our listeners. This work was supported by JSPS KAKENHI Grant Number 24-02734.

8. REFERENCES

[1] L. Barkhuus and T. Jørgensen. Engaging the crowd. In *Proc. ACM CHI '08*, pages 2925–2930, 2008.

[2] H. M. Beville. *Audience ratings: Radio, television and cable.* Routledge, 1988.

[3] L. Carpenter and R. Carpenter. Cinematrix interactive entertainment system, 2001. http://www.cinematrix.com.

[4] C. Gates, S. Subramanian, and C. Gutwin. DJ's Perspectives on Interaction and Awareness in Nightclubs. In *Proc. ACM DIS '06*, pages 70–79, 2006.

[5] J. D. Hook. *Interaction Design for Live Performance.* PhD thesis, Newcastle Univ. School of Comp. Sci., 2013.

[6] M. Karnik, I. Oakley, and V. Nisi. Performing online and offline: How DJs use social networks. In *Human-Computer Interaction–INTERACT 2013*, pages 63–80. Springer, 2013.

[7] D. Maynes-Aminzade, R. Pausch, and S. Seitz. Techniques for interactive audience participation. In *Proc. IEEE ICMI '02*, page 15, 2002.

[8] N. M. Sgouros. Detection, analysis and rendering of audience reactions in distributed multimedia performance. In *Proc. ACM MULTIMEDIA '00*, pages 195–200, 2000.

[9] D. A. Shamma, E. F. Churchill, N. Bobb, and M. Fukuda. Spinning online: A Case Study of Internet Broadcasting by DJs. In *Proc. ACM C&T '09*, pages 175–184, 2009.

Immersive 3D Communication

Wanmin Wu
Ricoh Innovations Corp.
2882 Sand Hill Rd, Suite 115
Menlo Park, CA 94025
1-650-496-5700
wwu@ric.ricoh.com

Cha Zhang
Microsoft Research
One Microsoft Way
Redmond, WA 98052
1-425-706-5751
chazhang@microsoft.com

ABSTRACT
The last few decades have witnessed tremendous advances in telecommunication, with the invention of technologies such as radio, telephone, voice-over-IP, and video conferencing. While all these communication tools are useful and valuable, the ultimate goal of telecommunication is to enable fully immersive remote interaction in a way that simulates or even surpasses the face-to-face experience. Immersive 3D communication technologies are developed aiming at that goal. The objective of this tutorial is to present an overview of the recent advances in immersive 3D communication. Topics include the basics of human 3D perception, new systems and algorithms in real-time 3D scene capture and reconstruction, 3D data compression and dissemination, 3D displays, etc. We intend to provide insights into the latest immersive 3D communication technologies, and highlight some open research challenges for the future.

Categories and Subject Descriptors
H.4.3 [**Communications Applications**]: Computer conferencing, teleconferencing, and videoconferencing;
H.5.3 [**Group and Organization Surfaces**]: Collaborative computing; Computer-supported cooperative work;

Keywords
Immersive 3D communication; real-time multimedia systems; 3D video; 3D audio; avatars; telepresence; haptics.

1. INTRODUCTION
Communication is a basic human need. Its importance in human society has been well recognized for thousands of years [1]. When people are co-located, face-to-face communication flows naturally. However, for people spread at disperse geographical locations, telecommunication systems are essential for effective interaction and collaboration. In the past century, technologies have advanced dramatically to improve remote communication experiences, such as telephone, mobile phone, video-conferencing, etc. While these technologies are widely adopted today, the experiences they provide are still far from that of natural face-to-face communication.

Science-fiction movies and books have depicted visions of the "Holy Grail" of remote communication. Well-known examples include Princess Leia's 3D holographic meeting with Obi-Wan in Star Wars (1977) and the holodeck concept in Star Trek (1974). In reality, significant advances have been made towards these dreams [2]. For example, researchers at HP Labs recently presented a 3D holographic display technology that forms 3D images by projecting different 2D images into different regions of space [3]; University of North Carolina at Chapel Hill demonstrated a telepresence system using head-mounted optical see-through display and occlusion-controlling lighting [4].

This tutorial intends to present a survey of immersive 3D communication technologies and their applications, ranging from the basics of human 3D perception to new systems and algorithms. We explain different modalities of human sensory experiences in remote communication, and discuss how technologies can be used to stimulate such experiences, in particular for the auditory and visual sensory channels.

We will describe materials with a mix of technical breadth and depth, covering not only basic concepts and standard techniques, but also details of state-of-the-art technologies. In addition, we will give examples of real-world systems, prototypes and applications that have been developed in academia and industry. Finally, we will identify a few open research questions for the future work of immersive 3D communication.

2. TUTORIAL DESCRIPTION
2.1 Objective and Intended Audience
The main objective of our tutorial is to give a broad, sound, nonetheless easy-to-understand introduction to the field of immersive 3D communication. Technologies presented here promise experiences that are steps beyond what can be provided by conventional voice-over-IP and/or 2D video conferencing technologies.

The tutorial is customized for intermediate-level students and researchers who are interested in learning about the field. Some background knowledge about general multimedia communication systems is useful for following the tutorial, but not mandatory.

The materials used for this tutorial mostly consist of contemporary books and research articles from multimedia conferences and journals such as ACM Multimedia and IEEE ICME. We plan to distribute slides of the presentation to all participants.

2.2 Structure and Length
The total length of the tutorial is six hours. The tutorial consists of the following parts:

1. **Motivation**. We start the tutorial with an introduction to the brief history of immersive 3D communication, the values of 3D information, key features and objectives

MM '14, Nov 03-07, 2014, Orlando, FL, USA.
ACM 978-1-4503-3063-3/14/11.
http://dx.doi.org/10.1145/2647868.2654848

for 3D communication, and possible applications of immersive 3D communication. (20 minutes)

2. **Basics**. We then proceed to explain some basic background information, including (1) basics of human 3D perception, and (2) basic components of 3D communication systems. The first part discusses fundamentals of human's visual 3D perception (e.g., motion parallax, stereo parallax), auditory 3D/surround perception, and other sensory perception (e.g., touch/haptics). The second part describes basic components of a 3D communication system, such as sensory signal capture, processing, transmission/dissemination, and rendering. Components for different sensory modalities are discussed including video, audio, haptic, etc. (30 minutes)

3. **Technologies**. We then spend the bulk of the time describing 3D immersive communication technologies. This consists of six main parts: (1) audio communication, (2) video communication, (3) avatar and virtual 3D immersion, (4) haptics and other sensory channels, (5) data communication, and (6) human factors/quality-of-experience.

   - *Audio communication (40 minutes)*: We discuss how 3D audio data are used to support immersive 3D communication, including 3D audio capture and rendering techniques. Topics in 3D audio capture include sound source localization and beam forming, multi-channel echo cancellation. The 3D audio rendering part describes aspects such as spatial sound rendering with headphones, 3D audio rendering with speaker arrays, and parametric speakers. Audio synchronization with multi-view video data is also discussed.
   - *Break. (10 minutes)*
   - *Video communication (1 hour)*: We explain how 3D video data can enable immersive 3D communication. This section includes (1) camera array techniques and issues such as synchronization, geometry and color calibration, (2) depth sensors, (3) real-time 3D reconstruction, including depth from camera arrays and depth fusion from multiple sensors, (4) head pose tracking for motion parallax, and (5) 3D displays, including projection-based 3D displays, 3D flat panel displays, and 3D head-mounted displays.
   - *Avatar and virtual 3D immersion (30 minutes)*: We then explain how graphical 3D avatar representations can be used for immersive 3D communication.
   - *Break (10 minutes)*
   - *Haptics and other sensory modalities (30 minutes):* We also describe how haptics and other sensory data are captured, processed, and rendered to provide a rich experience in immersive 3D communication.
   - *Data Communication (1 hour):* The previous parts on audio and video communication focus on the acquisition and presentation aspects of 3D audio and video data. In this part, we discuss techniques for 3D data compression and networking/distribution. The topics in compression include multi-view video compression, video + depth compression, point cloud compression, 3D audio compression, and haptic data compression. Similarly, networking/distribution will be discussed for different media modalities, including real-time 3D video streaming, real-time 3D audio streaming, and real-time haptics data streaming, etc. Further, we describe general data streaming architectures and multi-party/site dissemination issues and techniques.
   - *Break. (10 minutes)*
   - *Human factors/quality-of-experience (20 minutes)*: Human-centric evaluation is important to ultimately assess the effectiveness and usefulness of 3D immersive communication systems. We describe methodologies and challenges for quality-of-experience modeling and measurement of immersive 3D communication systems.

4. **Examples**. There have been many notable systems and demonstrated applications that were developed in academia and industry, such as University of North Carolina at Chapel Hill [4], University of Illinois at Urbana-Champaign with University of California at Berkeley [5], and Microsoft Research [6]. The tutorial shows these systems and applications with images and videos as vivid examples of the current state-of-the-art. (30 minutes)

We end the tutorial with a brief summary and a few open research questions and challenges for future works (10 minutes).

3. SUMMARY

This tutorial aims at introducing the rising and challenging field of immersive 3D remote communication. From the basics of human 3D perception to the various applications, we hope this tutorial provides a comprehensive overview of this exciting field.

4. REFERENCES

[1] D. Stacks & M. Salwen (2009). An Integrated Approach to Communication Theory and Research. New York: Routledge.

[2] J.G. Apostolopoulos, P.A. Chou, W.B. Culbertson, T. Kalker, M.D. Trott & S. Wee, The Road to Immersive Communication. In *Proceedings of the IEEE*, 974-990 2012.

[3] D. Fattal, Z. Peng, T. Tran, S. Vo, M. Fiorentino, J. Brug & R. G. Beausoleil, A multi-directional backlight for a wide-angle, glasses-free three-dimensional display, *Nature 495, 348–351*, 2013.

[4] A. Maimone, X. Yang, N. Dierk, A. State, M. Dou & H. Fuchs, General-Purpose Telepresence with Head-Worn Optical See-Through Displays and Projector-Based Lighting, *IEEE Virtual Reality 2013*.

[5] W. Wu, A. Arefin, G. Kurillo, P. Agarwal, K. Nahrstedt & R. Bajcsy, Color-plus-Depth Level-of-Detail in 3D Tele-immersive Video: A Psychophysical Approach, in *Proc. of ACM Multimedia*, 2011.

[6] C. Zhang, Q. Cai, P. Chou, Z. Zhang & R. Martin-Brualla, Viewport: A Fully Distributed Immersive Teleconferencing System with Infrared Dot Pattern, *IEEE Multimedia Magazine, pp. 17-27, Vol. 20, No. 1*, 2013.

Over-the-Top Content Delivery: State of the Art and Challenges Ahead

Christian Timmerer
Alpen-Adria-Universität Klagenfurt
Universitätsstraße 65-67
A-9020 Klagenfurt, Austria
+43 463 2700 3621
christian.timmerer@itec.aau.at

Ali C. Begen
CISCO
181 Bay St. Suite 3400
Toronto, ON M5J 2T3 Canada
+1 408 525 7308
abegen@cisco.com

ABSTRACT
In this tutorial we present state of the art and challenges ahead in over-the-top content delivery. It particular, the goal of this tutorial is to provide an overview of adaptive media delivery, specifically in the context of HTTP adaptive streaming (HAS) including the recently ratified MPEG-DASH standard. The main focus of the tutorial will be on the common problems in HAS deployments such as client design, QoE optimization, multi-screen and hybrid delivery scenarios, and synchronization issues. For each problem, we will examine proposed solutions along with their pros and cons. In the last part of the tutorial, we will look into the open issues and review the work-in-progress and future research directions.

Categories and Subject Descriptors
H.5.1 [**Information Interfaces and Presentation**]: Multimedia Information Systems – *Video.*

General Terms: Algorithms, Design, Experimentation, Measurement, Performance, Standardization.

Keywords: Adaptive Media Streaming, Dynamic Adaptive Streaming over HTTP, MPEG-DASH, Over-the-top Video.

1. INTRODUCTION
Recently, traditional TV services, Internet TV and mobile streaming services have started converging, which means a particular piece of content can be reached over different types of network. Additionally, new multimedia services such as hybrid-broadcast-broadband and multi-screen are emerging. It is expected that this convergence trend will continue until consumers can get a seamless experience across different platforms for a variety of multimedia services. The massive heterogeneity in terms of consumer devices, network capabilities, and user expectations requires efficient solutions for the transport of modern media in an interoperable and universal fashion. In particular, in recent years, the Internet has become an important channel for the delivery of multimedia. The Hypertext Transfer Protocol (HTTP) is widely adopted on the Internet and it has also become a primary protocol for the delivery of multimedia content.

Standards developing organizations (SDOs) such as MPEG have developed various technologies for multimedia transport and encapsulation, e.g., MPEG-2 Transport Stream and ISO Base Media File Format. These technologies have been widely adopted and deployed for different applications and services, such as digital broadcasting, audio and video transport over the Internet and streaming to mobile phones. At the same time, many other SDOs such as the IETF, IEEE, and 3GPP have provided various protocols to deliver multimedia content packetized or packaged by such MPEG transport technologies.

In practice, however, these multimedia services are typically deployed over best-effort networks using existing infrastructure without any timely delivery guarantees. Thus, the quality as perceived by a consumer – referred to as Quality of Experience (QoE) – becomes critical for the success of these services and their providers. Insufficient network resources may lead to an increased initial delay before service startup or interruptions during the media playout. The resulting waiting and stalling times have a major impact on the QoE. For online video streaming, both live and on-demand, there are several possibilities to adapt the video quality based on the actual network conditions to avoid outages by adaptively managing the playout buffer and/or adaptively changing the bitrate, resolution, and/or frame rate.

The goal of this tutorial is to provide an overview of adaptive media delivery, specifically in the context of HTTP adaptive streaming (HAS) including the recently ratified MPEG standard "Dynamic Adaptive Streaming over HTTP (DASH)" [1][2]. One of the essential differences between HAS and earlier streaming solutions is that the client is in charge of adaptation, thus, directly influences the QoE. This client behavior is not standardized and differentiates players in the market today. In large-scale deployments, client design becomes extremely important for success.

In this tutorial, we will present essential components for an end-to-end HAS system including means for the content creation, distribution, and consumption. The main focus of the tutorial will be on the common problems in HAS deployments such as client design, QoE optimization, multi-screen and hybrid delivery scenarios, and synchronization issues. For each problem, we will examine proposed solutions along with their pros and cons. In the last part of the tutorial, we will look into the open issues and review the work-in-progress and future research directions.

MM '14, Nov 03-07, 2014, Orlando, FL, USA.
ACM 978-1-4503-3063-3/14/11.
http://dx.doi.org/10.1145/2647868.2654849

2. TUTORIAL OUTLINE AND OVERVIEW

The tutorial outline is as follows:

- Introduction to adaptive media delivery and specifically HTTP adaptive streaming (HAS).
- End-to-end HAS workflows: From content creation to consumption.
- Common problems in HAS: QoE optimization, multi-screen and hybrid delivery, synchronization issues.
- Open issues and future research directions in HAS.

Adaptive media streaming is generally referred to as media delivery where the overall system adapts itself to varying conditions both prior to and during the streaming session. In the past decade we observed a transition from push-based streaming (utilizing the RTSP/RTP protocol family) to pull-based streaming (adopting HTTP infrastructure). While the former allows for tailor-made solutions, it requires dedicated infrastructure support whereas the latter is built on top of the existing Internet without explicit support from the underlying networking infrastructure. The advantage of HTTP adaptive streaming is based on its client-centric design, efficient media codecs, and best-effort support from the networking infrastructure. Standards like MPEG-DASH enable interoperability among different implementations.

The end-to-end HAS workflow comprises the generation, provisioning, delivery, and consumption of multiple, time-aligned, segmented versions of the same content which are referred to as representations. Segments of each representation are uniquely identifiable using HTTP uniform resource locators (URLs). The actual provisioning of the content involves standard HTTP servers and its delivery includes also standard HTTP infrastructure such as caches, proxies, and content distribution networks (CDNs). Finally, the consumption requires a client implementation which issues timely HTTP requests for segments of a given representation based on its context environment such as device, codec, bandwidth, resolution, language, subtitles, views, etc.

The client module, which is responsible for issuing the HTTP requests, is commonly referred to as adaptation logic and typically not defined within standards like MPEG-DASH and, thus, is subject to academic research and industry competition. The adaptation logic is also responsible for delivering a seamless user experience including QoE optimizations. New use cases like multi-screen and hybrid (broadband-broadcast) introduce new challenges to HAS clients. For example, social TV requires inter-destination media synchronization where the media playout of geographically distributed users needs to be synchronized in the presence of a real-time communication channel [3].

Finally, open issues and future research directions in HAS include but are not limited to: multi-path/-source delivery, transport (TCP) and application (HTTP) layer optimizations, QoE modeling and quality-based streaming.

3. ACKNOWLEDGMENTS

This work was supported in part by the EC in the context of the ALICANTE (FP7-ICT-248652) and SocialSensor (FP7-ICT-287975) projects and partly performed in the Lakeside Labs research cluster at AAU.

4. BIOGRAPHY OF PRESENTERS

Christian Timmerer is an Associate Professor at the Institute of Information Technology (ITEC), Multimedia Communication Group (MMC), Alpen-Adria-Universität Klagenfurt, Austria. His research interests include immersive multimedia communication, streaming, adaptation, and Quality of Experience (QoE). He was the general chair of QoMEX'13, WIAMIS'08, AVSTP2P'10 (co-located with ACMMM'10), WoMAN'11 (co-located with ICME'11), and TPC co-chair of QoMEX'12. He has participated in several EC-funded projects, notably DANAE, ENTHRONE, P2P-Next, ALICANTE, SocialSensor, and ICoSOLE. He is an Associate Editor for IEEE Computer Science Computing Now, Area Editor for Elsevier Signal Processing: Image Communication, Review Board Member of IEEE MMTC, editor of ACM SIGMM Records, and member of ACM SIGMM Open Source Software Committee. He also participated in ISO/MPEG work for several years, notably in the area of MPEG-21, MPEG-M, MPEG-V, and DASH (incl. DASH Industry Forum). He received his PhD in 2006 from the Klagenfurt University. Follow him on http://www.twitter.com/timse7 and subscribe to his blog http://blog.timmerer.com.

Ali C. Begen is with the Video and Content Platforms Research and Advanced Development Group at Cisco. His interests include networked entertainment, Internet multimedia, transport protocols and content delivery. Ali is currently working on architectures and protocols for next-generation video transport and distribution over IP networks. He is an active contributor in the IETF and MPEG, and has given a number of keynotes, tutorials and guest lectures in these areas.

Ali holds a Ph.D. degree in electrical and computer engineering from Georgia Tech. He received the Best Student-paper Award at IEEE ICIP 2003, the Most-cited Paper Award from Elsevier Signal Processing: Image Communication in 2008, and the Best-paper Award at Packet Video Workshop 2012. Ali has been an editor for the Consumer Communications and Networking series in the IEEE Communications Magazine since 2011 and an associate editor for the IEEE Transactions on Multimedia since 2013. He served as a general co-chair for ACM Multimedia Systems 2011 and Packet Video Workshop 2013. He is a senior member of the IEEE and a senior member of the ACM. Further information on Ali's projects, publications, presentations and professional activities can be found at http://ali.begen.net.

5. REFERENCES

[1] ISO/IEC 23009-1:2014. Information technology — Dynamic adaptive streaming over HTTP (DASH) — Part 1: Media presentation description and segment formats.

[2] Sodagar, I. 2011. The MPEG-DASH Standard for Multimedia Streaming Over the Internet. *IEEE MultiMedia* 18, 4 (October 2011), 62-67.

[3] Timmerer, C., Rainer, B. 2014. The Social Media Experience. IEEE Computer 47, 3 (March 2014), 67-69.

Emerging Topics on Personalized and Localized Multimedia Information Systems

Yi Yu[1], Kiyoharu Aizawa[2], Toshihiko Yamasaki[2], Roger Zimmermann[1]
[1]School of Computing, National University of Singapore, Singapore
[2]Department of Information and Communication Engineering, The University of Tokyo, Japan
{yuy,rogerz}@comp.nus.edu.sg, {aizawa, yamasaki}@hal.t.u-tokyo.ac.jp

ABSTRACT

We are experiencing an era with a rapid increase of data relevant to different aspects of users' daily life. On the one hand, such data contains personal information of each individual user. On the other hand, it also reflects user behaviors related to the society as data of more users is aggregated. These data could not only be very beneficial for studying various lifestyle patterns, but also be used to generate more descriptive and explanatory analysis across the landscape of diverse multimedia data. Using personal mobile devices and web services to systematically explore interesting aspects of people world has attracted much attention recently.

This is a full-day tutorial that addresses emerging topics on personalized and localized multimedia technologies and applications and emphasizes knowledge sensing and discovery in multimedia landscape. This tutorial aims to deliver an overall introduction to multimedia landscapes with multimedia processing, contextual data acquisition, people activity logs, data analytics, geographic-aware multimedia sharing and delivery, and serves as an important lecture on fundamental and advanced research areas of personalized and localized multimedia information systems.

Categories and Subject Descriptors

H.4 [**Information Systems Applications**]: Miscellaneous; I.4.8 [**Image Processing and Computer Vision**]: Scene Analysis—*Sensor Fusion*; G.3 [**Mathematics of Computing**]: Probability and Statistics

Keywords

Personalization, life-logging, check-ins, location-aware applications and services, geographic popularity, multimedia information systems

1. BACKGROUND

Innovations in mobile technology have made it possible for users to interact with various online communities anytime and anywhere. Everyday people create and consume huge amounts of multimedia information and data over the Internet, e.g., fostered by technology innovation and user engagement, more than 100 hours of video are uploaded to YouTube every minute, 700 YouTube video links are shared on Twitter every minute, more than 3.5 million images are uploaded to Flickr daily. This way, every day an immense volume of various user-generated multimedia data is shared on the Internet. Such user-generated data could be a repository that contains different aspects of user's daily life, e.g., a photo on Flickr showing a crane truck working in a construction site could imply "the photographer loves tough trucks", a check-in at Bottega Louie in Downtown Los Angeles could imply "the visitor loves Italian food".

Personal data collected from users could be helpful to mine individual behavioral pattern and provide personalized recommendation and more intelligent services [1][2]. In addition, location as an extra contextual information from individual users is playing an important part in complementing retrieval and recommendation [3]. In particular, trajectories of users are associated with their preferences and can be used for personalized location recommendations. Check-in information at business venues can be used to analyze the geospatial distribution of users [4] and leveraged for geo-fencing services [2] (e.g., mobile advertising), business analytics, and geographic locality of interest [5]. The geospatial distribution of users and social connections between users can be further leveraged to optimize the distributed caching of multimedia data in content delivery networks. In this way, the vast volumes of multimedia data aggregated over time can be used to mine valuable knowledge about user activities in an individual level or a community level.

2. MOTIVATION

The increase of various sharing websites and online social networks has encouraged users to share contents, such as blogs, tweets, images, songs and videos. Not surprisingly, we are able to learn various patterns and user behaviors according to these data, which are likely to have important implications of personal preferences [1] and geographic interests [5] and are useful for a variety of multimedia systems and applications [4]. We have witnessed a paradigm shift towards multimedia data technologies and applications that are able to creatively accommodate or be compatible with e.g., multimedia processing and analysis, retrieval and recommendation optimization, online sharing, and physical activities. This shift inspires us to generate more descriptive and explanatory analysis across the multimedia landscape, to better highlight interesting things hidden behind various multimedia datasets, e.g., user relationships, attractiveness, patterns, and to support the critical intelligence

MM'14, Nov 03-07 2014, Orlando, FL, USA
ACM 978-1-4503-3063-3/14/11.
http://dx.doi.org/10.1145/2647868.2654850.

for end users' decision-making. We aim at addressing personalized and localized multimedia knowledge sensing and discovery, e.g, how to collectively form multimedia knowledge based on heterogenous information from users.

3. OBJECTIVES

This tutorial aims to introduce to the participants the following topics: i) applications and services on the Internet that have been developed to facilitate users' daily needs by utilizing personal preferences, ii) various geotagged multimedia data which help better understand local interest and popularity of multimedia content, iii) multimedia analysis by leveraging geo-social data, iv) the state-of-the-art approaches for location-aware multimedia content discovery and diffusion on the Internet, v) some comparative studies of existing geo-social multimedia systems, and vi) viewpoints, conclusions and trends of geo-tagged multimedia data.

4. TUTORIAL OUTLINE

The tutorial is structured into four main modules. First, we report image and video processing technologies and applications, particularly focusing on analyzing and mining image and video data. Second, we discuss how to discover and recommend personalized events and topics. Third, we give an overview of the latest topics and methods related to socially aware multimedia sharing and diffusion. Finally, we introduce location-aware research trends with various applications and systems in multimedia landscape with demonstration examples.

Module One (90 minutes) provides a comprehensive discussion of various challenges in videos and images processing technologies and applications. We have witnessed a surge of mobile device penetration with affordable prices. This leads more and more location-based social applications which try to locate, reach and interact with users on-the-go and provide various services tailored to the needs of specific users. Leveraging personal data with heterogenous data sources to analyze users' lifestyle and habits, however, is a non-trivial task. Heterogenous multimedia data from the users implies different aspects of user activities and interests. In addition, participants will be provided with an extensive overview of multimedia techniques and they will learn how to combine visual events with user's preferences. Moreover, we report various multimedia examples related to recent development on FoodLog, e.g., multimedia tools for dietary assessment, image processing approaches to analyzing user behavioural logs.

Module Two (90 minutes) explains why and how we may make use of location-aware media information to infer multimedia landscapes, and why and how we may take into account personalized aspect of user activity logs to find most important events and topics from multimedia scenes that satisfy a particular user's needs. Personalization has been a trend of web searching. A method to personalized search is to exploit the location information. As we know, there is a geographic locality in user's interest and culture. These days, search engines can return most relevant local results to users according to the location information in user profiles, while filtering out irrelevant information. Together with some interesting examples of using large-scale user-generated data, we also discuss fundamental components related to user activities. We review intra/inter-city travel recommendation algorithms and systems and we also introduce some interesting topics related to personalized retrieval and recommendations.

Module Three (90 minutes) covers topics and approaches related to geo-social activities, correlating user-centric preference activities, sensing and discovering location-aware knowledge, and geographic-aware multimedia sharing and diffusion. User-generated geo-social data contains user behaviors in the physical world and denotes whereabouts of their social activities. The data of geo-social behaviors also indicates geographic reach and interest of a geo-category context or a multimedia content across the globe. We share some latest studies with participants. Particularly, we explain geo-fencing, which is a promising technique for user-centric mobile location-based services. We introduce map generalization, which is used in many geographic information system and business mapping applications for creating maps at different scales. We also show some examples related to modeling location-based social impact on business attractiveness, geographic distribution of user activities touching upon geographic locality of interest in video views, and the spreading of geo-social multimedia contents on location-based social networks.

Module Four (90 minutes) addresses challenging issues involving the integration of user-centric mobile location-based services and multimedia content sharing platforms on the Internet. We report to the participants various resources covering software tools, public datasets, and crowdsourcing methods applied to the research areas of multimedia, location-based services, and content sharing websites. Every day users create and consume massive amounts of multimedia information and data by recording and transmitting images and videos with mobile devices. We introduce the participants to some developments related to the rapid increase of multimedia data and research on the capacity to store, process, analyze, and understand patterns from multimedia data. We introduce various sensor-rich multimedia technologies, e.g., scene modeling and acquisition, query processing, POI (point of interest) detection and visual distance estimation, and result ranking and presentation. We report various multimedia examples related to recent progress in sensors and integration, e.g., the latest development of GeoVid geo-referenced video smartphone apps and their applications.

5. REFERENCES

[1] K. Aizawa,Y. Maruyama, and H. Li, and C. Morikawa. Food Balance Estimation by Using Personal Dietary Tendencies in Multimedia Food Log. In IEEE Trans. on Multimedia, Vol.15, No.8, pages 2176-2185, 2013.

[2] Y. Yu, S. Tang, and R. Zimmermann. Edge-Based Locality Sensitive Hashing for Efficient Geo-Fencing Application. In ACM SIGSPATIAL GIS, pages 586-589, 2013.

[3] T. Yamasaki, A. Gallagher, and T. Chen. Personalized Intra- and Inter-City Recommendation Using Large-Scale Geotags. In GeoMM Workshop of ACM Multimedia, pages 25-30, 2013.

[4] R. Zimmermann, Y. Yu. Social Interactions over Geographic-Aware Multimedia Systems, A tutorial in Proc. of ACM MM13, pp. 1115-1116, 2013.

[5] A. Brodersen, S. Scellato, and M. Wattenhofer. YouTube Around the World: Geographic Popularity of Videos. In WWW, pages 241-250, 2012.

Learning Knowledge Bases for Text and Multimedia

Lexing Xie
Australian National University, NICTA
Canberra, Australia
lexing.xie@anu.edu.au

Haixun Wang
Google Research
Mountain View, CA, USA
haixun@google.com

ABSTRACT

Knowledge acquisition, representation, and reasoning has been one of the long-standing challenges in artificial intelligence and related application areas. Only in the past few years, massive amounts of structured and semi-structured data that directly or indirectly encode human knowledge became widely available, turning the knowledge representation problems into a computational grand challenge with feasible solutions in sight. The research and development on knowledge bases is becoming a lively fusion area among web information extraction, machine learning, databases and information retrieval, with knowledge over images and multimedia emerging as another new frontier of representation and acquisition. This tutorial aims to present a gentle overview of knowledge bases on text and multimedia, including representation, acquisition, and inference. The content of this tutorial are intended for surveying the field, as well as for educating practitioners and aspiring researchers.

Category and Subject Descriptors I.2.6 ARTIFICIAL INTELLIGENCE Learning — Knowledge acquisition

Keywords knowledge graph, multimedia, learning.

1. A MOTIVATING EXAMPLE

On Mar 24, 2014, families were notified by Malaysia Airline that Flight 370 crashed in the southern India ocean, and all lives onboard were lost. The New York Times ran a headline about the tragedy, but unfortunately, the story was juxtaposed with an iPad Air ad, which ends in an underwater scene. The Times pulled the ad after it was notified by a number of readers.

Glitches like this occurr frequently in computational advertising. To prevent it, machines need to understand not just the text but also the image, and then associate the semantics therein to sentiment analysis. It is clear that knowledge is needed in order to process noisy, ambiguous, and scarce input of heterogenous types. The challenges lie in every aspect of knowledge acquisition, representation, and inferencing. Although we are not yet at a stage of com-

Figure 1: A snapshot of the New York Time homepage, with an iPad Air ad juxtaposed with news about flight MH370.

pletely solving problems such as the one in computational advertisement mentioned above, much recent progress has been made on knowledge intensive text and multimedia processing. This tutorial will survey recent advances on this topic, and discuss fundamental problems, techniques as well as open issues in this vibrant area.

2. TUTORIAL OVERVIEW

This tutorial is structured in three main parts. The first part introduces the background and foundations of knowledge bases, the second part focuses on knowledge acquisition from text and hyper-text data, the third part discusses acquiring and applying knowledge for image and multimedia collections.

Introduction and foundations

- Beyond search: the age of structure-rich knowledge bases. We will introduce the challenge of learning knowledge bases, and its various applications, in order to motivate and inspire the audience of this problem area. This section will also provide a quick overview for the rest of the tutorial.
- A brief history of knowledge bases. We will present a brief historic note contracting knowledge bases from the mid-1980s, from Cyc [8], Wordnet [11], to other manually curated sources such as ConceptNet [10].
- Introduction to knowledge representation. We will discuss the basic representation of knowledge as multi-relational graphs, and compare-and-contrast example

MM'14, November 3–7, 2014, Orlando, Florida, USA.
ACM 978-1-4503-3063-3/14/11.
http://dx.doi.org/10.1145/2647868.2654851 .

contemporary knowledge bases that possess rich node structure, rich edge information, and their different uses.
- The cognitive science of knowledge structure and representation. This part will present relevant literature in cognitive science about the foundation of knowledge structure. We will discuss Rosch's theory of categorization, as well as work in the macroscopic structure of semantic networks [2], and predicting human memory search [6].

Knowledge acquisition, representation and inference for text

Language is the primary medium for encoding and disseminating knowledge. The representation of real-world knowledge in multimedia is tightly connected to, and often grounded in textual representations. This section covers fundamental and frontier techniques web-scale knowledge bases, and paves the way for discussing research challenges on multimedia knowledge.

- Information extraction from web-scale text. We will introduce systems such as YAGO [14], NELL [3], ReVerb [5], Probase [15] that focus on acquiring knowledge from text. We will also discuss core challenges such as bias from syntactic patterns, and how to evaluate the quality of acquired knowledge.
- Building a data driven semantic network. We will discuss how to score the data using measures such as typicality, basic level of categorization, similarity.
- The conceptualization mechanism. We will discuss how inferencing using the semantic network benefits semantic text processing.
- Applications of knowledge graphs.

Knowledge acquisition and applications for multimedia

- Knowledge and relations in computer vision and image understanding. We will discuss a set of diverse set of approaches to represent and acquire knowledge in computer vision, including Visipedia [12], attribute-based visual recognition, and image understanding with knowledge from WordNet.
- Learning knowledge graphs for multimedia. We will discuss a set of diverse set of approaches for constructing knowledge graphs from images and multimedia, from learning relationships within the visual modality [4], to grounding a textual databases to image instances, to learning knowledge graphs from parallel corpora of media and text.
- Embedding and recommendation models for relationship learning. We take a closer look at several mathematical models for learning knowledge relations from rich media, from relation learning as recommendation [13], to inverse random walk approaches [16].
- Application of multimedia knowledge. We will discuss classical and emerging applications, such as search [1] natural language generation[7], video question-answering [9], and others.

We conclude the tutorial with a view to the open research and application challenges. Tutorial materials and an annotated bibliography will be released online. The audience of this tutorial will take away in-depth knowledge on the construction and application of knowledge graphs, acquire a crucial understanding in the technical challenges in designing and using a knowledge graph, and develop an appreciation to state-of-the-art tools and techniques at the frontiers of this area.

Acknowledgments NICTA is funded by the Australian Government as represented by the Department of Broadband, Communications and the Digital Economy and the Australian Research Council through the ICT Centre of Excellence program. This work was supported in part by the Australian Research Council under project DP140102185.

3. REFERENCES

[1] A. B. Benitez and S.-F. Chang. Image classification using multimedia knowledge networks. In *ICIP 2003*, volume 3, pages III–613. IEEE, 2003.

[2] J. Borge-Holthoefer and A. Arenas. Semantic networks: Structure and dynamics. *Entropy*, 12(5):1264–1302, 2010.

[3] A. Carlson, J. Betteridge, B. Kisiel, B. Settles, E. R. Hruschka Jr, and T. M. Mitchell. Toward an architecture for never-ending language learning. In *AAAI*, 2010.

[4] X. Chen, A. Shrivastava, and A. Gupta. Neil: Extracting visual knowledge from web data. ICCV, 2013.

[5] O. Etzioni, M. Banko, S. Soderland, and D. S. Weld. Open information extraction from the web. *Communications of the ACM*, 51(12):68–74, 2008.

[6] T. L. Griffiths, M. Steyvers, and A. Firl. Google and the mind: Predicting fluency with pagerank. *Psychological Science*, 18(12):1069–1076, 2007.

[7] G. Kulkarni, V. Premraj, S. Dhar, S. Li, Y. Choi, A. C. Berg, and T. L. Berg. Baby talk: Understanding and generating simple image descriptions. In *CVPR*, pages 1601–1608. IEEE, 2011.

[8] D. B. Lenat. Cyc: A large-scale investment in knowledge infrastructure. *Communications of the ACM*, 38(11):33–38, 1995.

[9] G. Li, Z. Ming, H. Li, and T.-S. Chua. Video reference: question answering on youtube. MM '09, pages 773–776, 2009.

[10] H. Liu and P. Singh. ConceptNet – a practical commonsense reasoning tool-kit. *BT technology journal*, 22(4):211–226, 2004.

[11] G. Miller. WordNet: a lexical database for English. *Communications of the ACM*, 38(11):39–41, 1995.

[12] P. Perona. Vision of a visipedia. *Proceedings of the IEEE*, 98(8):1526–1534, 2010.

[13] S. Riedel, L. Yao, A. Mccallum, and B. M. Marlin. Relation Extraction with Matrix Factorization and Universal Schemas. In *HLT-NAACL '13*, 2013.

[14] F. M. Suchanek, G. Kasneci, and G. Weikum. Yago: A Core of Semantic Knowledge. In *WWW '07*, 2007.

[15] W. Wu, H. Li, H. Wang, and K. Q. Zhu. Probase: a probabilistic taxonomy for text understanding. SIGMOD, 2012.

[16] L. Xie and X. He. Picture tags and world knowledge: Learning tag relations from visual semantic sources. In *ACM Multimedia*, October 2013.

Social Multimedia Computing

Peng Cui[1], Lexing Xie[2], Jitao Sang[3], Changsheng Xu[3]

[1] Tsinghua University
[2] Australian National University
[3] Institute of Automation, Chinese Academy of Sciences
cuip@tsinghua.edu.cn, lexing.xie@anu.edu.au, {jtsang, csxu}@nlpr.ia.ac.cn

ABSTRACT

This article summarizes the corresponding full-day tutorial at ACM Multimedia 2014. This tutorial reviews recent progresses in social multimedia computing from two perspectives: social-sensed multimedia computing (3 hours) and user-centric social multimedia computing (3 hours).

Categories and Subject Descriptors

H.4.m [**Information Systems Applications**]: Miscellaneous

General Terms

Algorithms, Experimentation, Performance

Keywords

Social Media; Social Multimedia Computing

1. INTRODUCTION

Social media has revolutionized the way people share and access information, from work, daily life, to entertainment. With the ubiquitous presence of capturing devices, multimedia has become the major sharing and interacting medium for information access and communication in various social media networks. There is a clear trend in social media information services for adopting multimedia content. For example, Twitter increases its support on pictures and videos, by releasing its 6-second video sharing app, Vine. Tencent's audio chatting tool, WeChat, has attracted more than 300 million users in less than two years, which is said to replace traditional SMS.

On the other hand, the prominence of social media has also witnessed the social trend in multimedia data generation and consumption. For example, Facebook reportedly sees 350 millions photos uploaded each day as of November 2013; 100 hours of video are uploaded to YouTube every minute, resulting in a total of more than 2 billion videos by the end of 2013. According to Alexa statistics, three out of the four fastest-growing social media websites around 2012-2013 focus on multimedia sharing. Moreover, social media gives birth to many new types of multimedia, e.g., image tweet, audio picture, geo-tagged video, etc. This significantly extends the scope and application areas of multimedia.

The multimedia data generated and consumed under social media circumstances is referred to as social multimedia. Three elements are identified, i.e., multimedia content, user, and interactions (between both user-user and user-content). Impacted by the participatory nature of WEB 2.0, users actively participate in the generation as well as consumption processes. As the hybrid of multimedia and social media, social multimedia enjoys advantages of both direct rich sensory simulation and efficient information access and propagation, thus having great potentials in analysis and utilization.

The emergence of social multimedia has brought challenges as well as opportunities to computing. On one hand, most social multimedia services are user-oriented, making it important to understand user demands from their interactions with the multimedia content. On the other hand, while multimedia content analysis still remains open, the participatory property of social multimedia offers a new solution perspective. Social multimedia computing, a multidisciplinary research and application field, has been developed to understand social multimedia content and connect the social multimedia content with users by exploiting the various social interactions. The potential applications range from information service, communication, entertainment, to healthcare, security, etc.

Thanks to the wide prevalence of social multimedia data and the increasing demands for social multimedia services, there has been a growing number of research on social multimedia computing, evidenced by the volume of papers produced, and many related tracks and special issues in prestigious multimedia conferences and journals. In this tutorial, we review the recent progresses in social multimedia computing from two perspectives.

2. PART I: SOCIAL-SENSED MULTIMEDIA COMPUTING

The ultimate goal of multimedia computing is to deliver multimedia content to users according to their information needs (intentions). Multimedia computing can be decomposed into various stages: multimedia compression (for storage), multimedia communication (for delivery), and multimedia content analysis (for intelligence). Among these, multimedia analysis has become mainstream in the multi-

MM'14, November 3–7, 2014, Orlando, Florida, USA.
ACM 978-1-4503-3063-3/14/11.
http://dx.doi.org/10.1145/2647868.2654852.

media community, and related technologies have advanced significantly since the end of the last century. However, in addition to the notorious Semantic Gap, how to bridge the multimedia content with end users, the lastmile technology for multimedia services, is rarely researched. This lack of understanding directly causes an obvious Intention Gap between multimedia data and the real information needs of users, which has become a bottle-neck in advancing intelligent multimedia computing technologies for use in real applications.

Users' (both crowds' and individuals') intention-related information (including long-term interests, instantaneous intentions, and emotions, etc), their behavior patterns, and ultimately, the common principles of user-multimedia interactions under different contexts can all be sensed from social media, which are summarized by social knowledge on user-multimedia interactions. It is these social knowledge that reflects user needs and establishes a bridge for multimedia data and user needs. How to organically integrate multimedia data, user needs and social knowledge into multimedia computing technology is a critical issue. Here, we propose a new multimedia computing paradigm, social-sensed multimedia computing, to integrate all the recent works that bring social media, a valuable source of sensing user needs and social knowledge, into the loop of multimedia computing. It opens a brand new arena for the multimedia research community with a potentially big impact in both academia and industry.

3. PART II: USER-CENTRIC SOCIAL MULTIMEDIA COMPUTING

Social multimedia computing is very different from traditional and web multimedia computing. Web multimedia computing is heavily related to the WEB1.0 environment, which is dominated by broadcast media developed by professional designers for passive users. In traditional multimedia computing, the analysis focus is the multimedia content, and the goal is content understanding and application, e.g., media content analysis, semantic classification and annotation, structured media authoring. On the contrary, social multimedia computing has an obvious user-centric characteristic: (1) User is the basic data collection unit. Viewing each user as a data sensor, social multimedia is constituted by what users see, listen, think, feel and speak. Moreover, user bridges multimedia network and social network, contributing to most of the social interactions in social multimedia. (2) User is the ultimate information service target. As discussed above, social multimedia services are user-oriented and have a customized trend. Understanding the personalized demands is critical to most social multimedia computing problems.

We present the user-centric research paradigm for social multimedia computing, and organize the related work into three basic tasks of "From users, On users, and For users": (1) From users: user-perceptive multimedia content analysis. Users' social interactions capture what they perceive the multimedia content and can be exploited towards multimedia content analysis. For example, user-contributed picture tags indicate user-perceived visual semantics, user browsing behaviors, such as pause, fast-forward, indicate video structure information. (2) On users: social multimedia activity-based user modeling. Online activities reveals important clues of user background information and are utilized for user modeling of demographic facts, personal interests, social network status, mobility patterns, consuming patters, emotional orientation, etc. (3) For users: customized multimedia services. Given results from user-perceptive multimedia content analysis and user modeling, customized multimedia services are developed to satisfy personalized needs.

4. TUTORIAL OUTLINE

The tutorial will start with a brief joint background section. The following introduces the detailed topics addressed in the two parts, respectively.

Part I: Social-sensed Multimedia Computing

1. Introduction
   a). Current status of multimedia computing
   b). The paradigm of social-sensed multimedia computing
   c). Basic problems and key challenges
2. Sensing user models and behavior patterns from social media
   a). User profiling from social media
   b). User behavioral analysis and modeling
   c). Social graph mining
3. Integrating social knowledge with multimedia computing
   a). Social factor assisted multimedia content understanding
   b). Social-sensed multimedia search and recommendation
   c). Multimedia affective computing
4. Discussions and future directions

Part II: User-centric Social Multimedia Computing

1. Introduction to user-centric social multimedia computing
2. User-perceptive multimedia content analysis (MCA)
   a). MCA based on user-generated metadata
   b). MCA based on user-multimedia interaction
   c). MCA based on user-user interaction
3. Social multimedia activity-based user modeling
   a). User interest modeling
   b). User demographics inference
   c). User social relation analysis
4. Customized multimedia services
   a). Customized multimedia services: challenges
   b). Customized multimedia services: applications
5. User-centric cross-network multimedia computing
   a). Cross-network knowledge association mining
   b). Cross-network user behavior analysis
   c). Cross-network collaborated applications
   d). Discussions and future directions

Video Hyperlinking

Vasileios Mezaris
CERTH-ITI
6th Km. Charilaou-Thermi Road, P.O. Box 60361
Thermi 57001, Greece
bmezaris@iti.gr

Benoit Huet
Eurecom
Campus SophiaTech, 450 Route des Chappes,
06410 Biot Sophia Antipolis, France
benoit.huet@eurecom.fr

ABSTRACT

This is the abstract for the "Video Hyperlinking" tutorial, presented as part of the 2014 ACM Multimedia Conference. Video hyperlinking is the introduction of links that originate from pieces of video material and point to other relevant content, be it video or any other form of digital content. The tutorial presents the state of the art in video hyperlinking approaches and in relevant enabling technologies, such as video analysis and multimedia indexing and retrieval. Several alternative strategies, based on text, visual and/or audio information are introduced, evaluated and discussed, providing the audience with details on what works and what doesn't on real broadcast material.

Categories and Subject Descriptors

H.4 [**Information Systems Applications**]: Miscellaneous

Keywords

Video analysis, video hyperlinks, non-linear video, hypervideo, linked television

1. INTRODUCTION

The tremendous and continuously accelerated growth in the amount of images and videos on the cloud, together with the widespread availability of a wide range of non-PC end-user connected devices (ranging from smartphones and tablets to internet-enabled TV sets), is changing the ways in which people consume visual content. In this environment, the traditional PC-era visual- or text-based search paradigms do not fully meet the expectations of the users, who find it increasingly difficult to navigate in a sea of disassociated video content and discover scattered content items of various origin that may be able to serve their specific information needs, e.g. more information on a story that was briefly presented earlier in the news, or further footage of an object of desire that they just saw in a video. Inspired by the ubiquitous text-based hyperlinks and the way that text hyperlinking has transformed how people navigate through textual and other information, its analogous for video content, i.e. video hyperlinking, is emerging as a promising approach to making video more easily accessible and consumable [1][2]. This tutorial provides a thorough overview of the state of the art in video hyperlinking approaches.

MM'14, Nov. 3–7, 2014, Orlando, FL, USA.
ACM 978-1-4503-3063-3/14/11.
http://dx.doi.org/10.1145/2647868.2654853.

2. VIDEO HYPERLINKING AND CHALLENGES

Video hyperlinking is the introduction of links that originate from meaningful fragments of video content (e.g. a video shot) and point to other relevant content (which may be visual content, e.g. another video or a segment of it, or any other form of content, e.g. an audio recording or a relevant Wikipedia article) - just like traditional hyperlinks originate from meaningful parts of a text (e.g. a key-phrase or a name) and point to other related resources. However, the manual insertion of such links in newly-created videos is a form of content curation that very few content creators would be willing to perform and maintain over time, because of being an undeniably tedious process. What is needed for making hypervideo feasible is the development of methods for the automatic or semi-automatic identification of related content and the generation of the corresponding links, transforming the present day's disassociated videos in the cloud into a connected and easy to navigate hypervideo collection. This brings new challenges in automatically processing the visual content and understanding the information it conveys at different granularities, in processing associated audio and textual information, and in intelligently exploiting all these analysis results for creating meaningful video hyperlinks [4]. It also raises important questions concerning the granularities that are most appropriate for decomposing and linking the video content [3].

3. TUTORIAL CONTENT AND STRUCTURE

This tutorial introduces the vision of hypervideo, and then focuses on two equally important directions: the video (and associated information) analysis that is needed for supporting video hyperlinking; and, the ways for making use of these imperfect analysis results so as to effectively discover and establish meaningful video links at suitable granularity levels. The presentation of the material is structured in three main parts.

The introductory part (Part A), Video Hyperlinking Motivation and Vision, briefly introduces what video hyperlinking is, highlights the functionalities we want to achieve with video hyperlinking, and explains why this is a both important and challenging task.

The motivation and vision discussion is followed by the first of the two more technical parts of the tutorial (Part B), Video fragment creation and annotation for hyperlinking. This starts by establishing an analogy between text hyperlinking and video hyperlinking, in order to explain which video analysis technologies we need for realizing the vision of automatic video hyperlinking and what exact purpose each of them serves. It then goes on to present the state of the art and discuss in more depth a few selected video analysis techniques. These include techniques for:

- Video temporal segmentation to shots
- Video temporal segmentation to scenes
- Visual concept detection
- Event detection

Other potentially relevant technologies, such as duplicate or near-duplicate image detection or object re-detection in video will also be mentioned and briefly commented. The presentation of each of the analysis techniques is not limited to a theoretical study, but includes the presentation of indicative experimental results and demos that clearly illustrate what results these techniques can deliver and how these results contribute to the objective of video hyperlinking. Additional reading for the presented technologies is also listed at the end of each section of the presentation.

In the third part of the tutorial (Part C), having outlined the state of the art in individual video analysis tasks, we discuss how to effectively use and combine their results towards discovering and establishing meaningful video links at suitable granularity levels. Indeed, the granularity at which the various multimodal information is available depends on the modality itself; video frames are displayed 24, 25 or 30 per second while subtitle (or transcript) items, OCR text and other metadata span over many frames, and in some cases (i.e. video title) over the entire video. As part of the process of linking related video content, we provide insight on various approaches using text, audio and visual content analysis results, highlighting what does and what doesn't work. The outcome of related video hyperlinking experiments on real data [5] are shown, evaluated on a public dataset and discussed.

We also identify future directions for better addressing the video hyperlinking problem, and conclude by briefly sketching a few hypervideo usage scenarios and applications.

4. ACKNOWLEDGMENTS

This work was supported by the European Commission under contract FP7-287911 LinkedTV.

5. REFERENCES

[1] Linkedtv: Television linked to the web. http://www.linkedtv.eu/.

[2] Mediaeval benchmarking initiative for multimedia evaluation: Search and hyperlinking task. http://www.multimediaeval.org/mediaeval2014/hyper2014/.

[3] E. Apostolidis, V. Mezaris, M. Sahuguet, B. Huet, B. Cervenkova, D. Stein, S. Eickeler, J. L. R. Garcia, R. Troncy, and L. Pikora. Automatic fine-grained hyperlinking of videos within a closed collection using scene segmentation. In *Proc. ACM Multimedia 2014*, Orlando, FL, USA, November 2014.

[4] L. Nixon, V. Mezaris, and J. Thomsen. Seamlessly interlinking tv and web content to enable linked television. In *ACM Int. Conf. on Interactive Experiences for Television and Online Video (TVX 2014), Adjunct Proceedings*, Newcastle Upon Tyne, UK, June 2014.

[5] M. Sahuguet, B. Huet, B. Cervenkova, E. Apostolidis, V. Mezaris, D. Stein, S. Eickeler, J. L. Redondo Garcia, R. Troncy, and L. Pikora. LinkedTV at MediaEval 2013 search and hyperlinking task. In *MEDIAEVAL 2013, Multimedia Benchmark Workshop, October 18-19, 2013, Barcelona, Spain*, Barcelona, SPAIN, 10 2013.

An Introduction to Arts and Digital Culture Inside Multimedia

David A. Shamma
Yahoo Labs
110 5th Street
San Francisco, CA 94103 USA
aymans@acm.org

Daragh Byrne
School of Design
Carnegie Mellon University
Pittsburgh, PA 15213 USA
daraghb@andrew.cmu.edu

ABSTRACT

The Arts and Digital Culture program has offered a high quality forum for the presentation of interactive and arts-based multimedia applications at the annual ACM Multimedia conference for over a decade. This tutorial will explore the evolution of this program as a guide to new authors considering future participation in this program. By surveying both past technical and past exhibited contributions, this tutorial will offer guidance to artists, researchers and practitioners on success at this multifaceted, interdisciplinary forum at ACM Multimedia.

Categories and Subject Descriptors

J.5 [**Computer Applications**]: Arts and Humanities—*Fine arts, performing arts*; H.5.2 [**Information Systems**]: Information Interfaces and Presentation: User Interfaces—*Theory and methods*

General Terms

Theory, Methods

Keywords

Tutorial, art, culture, multimedia

1. INTRODUCTION

In 2004, ACM Multimedia began its Interactive Arts program as a joint technical track and associated gallery track. The goal was to offer a high quality publication venue for interactive and artistic multimedia systems as well as bring greater socio-cultural awareness into the conference. In 2011, the Arts papers became part of the official Technical Program for Multimedia and in 2012 the best student paper was an Arts submission in Nara Japan. As the area and track grows, we aim for the how and why of the Arts program to reach to new community members as well as begin interoperation with other ACM Special Interest Groups. The purpose of this tutorial is to serve as an introduction to the Interactive Arts and Digital Culture track at ACM MM for both those actively engaged in the Arts as well as those with no previous technical arts engagement.

MM'14, November 3–7, 2014, Orlando, Florida, USA.
ACM 978-1-4503-3063-3/14/11.
http://dx.doi.org/10.1145/2647868.2654854.

2. MOTIVATIONS IN ART AND MM

The ACM SIG Multimedia Arts and Digital Culture Track aims to demonstrate new research opportunities for the multimedia community at large by highlighting innovative artistic or cultural applications of multimedia tools and applications. Over the past ten years, 234 contributions from 577 individuals have been featured in this forum. This includes 70 exhibited works, 58 full paper and 80 short paper contributions along with 8 demonstrations, 17 poster and 1 video submission. 49 authors have presented more than 2 technical (full or short paper) contributions and 8 of which have presented more than 3 technical contributions. Growing from 7 initial contributions in 2004 to a peak of 32 papers in 2007 programmed within the technical track, it has added an average of 15.33 new multidisciplinary and applied reflections on multimedia systems to the discourse featured at ACM Multimedia each year. Complimented by an exhibit, the program has become a strong venue where the role of the aesthetic, humanistic and reflexive perspectives offered by the arts in enriching multimedia systems research.

Jaimes et al. posit art as "one of the most exciting application areas" for human centered multimedia noting the wide variety of ways in which tools and applications for computer vision, content analysis, media representation and beyond may be leveraged in these contexts [1]. As growing track within the Multimedia conference, the Arts and Digital Culture program most clearly articulates this agenda by providing a venue to highlight "innovative use of digital technology in the creation, analysis or critique of cultural artifacts, environments and processes." In so doing it offers a needed forum where practitioners, researchers and artists may intermingle to discuss use of multimedia technology in practice, *in the wild* and in applied arts or cultural contexts. This provides a place to chart not only the reach of multimedia beyond technical or scholarly research but new and emerging areas for multimedia exploration.

While the arts are recognized a key field of applied exploration for multimedia as it often "pushes multimedia software and hardware to limits and in unexpected ways" [2, 1], the integration of multiple cohorts, perspectives and systems scenarios into this applied, interdisciplinary track presents some challenges. The Arts program aims to engage multidisciplinary cohorts, some of which are not versed in research reporting or methodologies in presenting technical contributions of broad relevance to the multimedia community. Moreover, there can exist a two-culture paradigm that can create perceived tensions between the role of arts and the sciences in advancing multimedia systems and in expressing the value of practice-oriented aesthetic or reflexive contributions within the context of scholarly multimedia discourse [3]. This motivates the need for clearer articulation of the value of incorporating multidisciplinary knowledge and arts insights into computational frameworks. Additionally, the program is designed to craft a porous space for interdisciplinary exchange where art, design, and culture intersect with traditional engineering and computer science explorations. Encompassing qualitative and quantitative evaluations, applied explorations, systems, methodologies, case studies and reflections, it produces a complex multifaceted space that can be difficult for a novice author to navigate or enter successfully, especially for those uninitiated individuals with no previous technical arts engagement. This tutorial intends to directly address these challenges by offering guidance to existing and prospective authors in preparing new high quality contributions and in interrogating the lineage of Arts at ACM Multimedia.

Such a tutorial is particularly timely given the increasing interest in integrative explorations that bridge interactive systems with aesthetic and design and arts perspectives. We see a growing body of practitioners, researchers, and artists are working within multidisciplinary contexts including performance, installation artworks, digital narrative, media composition and game design [4]—creating solutions to large scale or 'grand challenges' and in delivering innovative outcomes that can have considerable impact.

The Arts program plays an integral role in consolidating the knowledge produced for multimedia research. Reflecting on a decade of the Digital Arts and Culture program at ACM Multimedia, this tutorial will serve multiple needs both for the program and for potential future contributors to it. First, it hopes to foster support for the Arts program by developing a deepened understanding of the value, role and relationship of arts in multimedia systems exploration among participants. By exploring significant contributions to the program, we hope to encourage multimedia researchers, artists and practitioners to consider and communicate the broader cultural, societal or global significance and impact of their work. The intention is to disambiguate the approaches for presenting high-quality outcomes that reflect research and emerging areas of practice. This hopes to develop participants' knowledge and expertise in reporting on multidisciplinary outcomes.

3. TUTORIAL OUTLINE

The tutorial will provide a tour of the past ten years of the Arts and Digital Culture program as a learning opportunity for those interested in future participation.

1. *Introduction to the Arts program (30 mins):* The workshop will begin with an introduction to the purpose, goals and intent of the Arts program. To achieve this, the past decade of organization, history and contributions to the program will be briefly surveyed. This introduction will emphasize the nature and range of contributions that the program seeks to solicit and their relationship to the broader goals of ACM Multimedia.
2. *Selected works explained (1 hr):* A handful of Arts pieces will be highlighted to explore the variety of successful approaches to presenting high-impact art integrative multimedia work as technical track content at ACM Multimedia. Additionally, they will be used to explore and discuss the relationship between these contributions and the state-of-the-art.
3. *The gallery explained (30 mins):* Beyond providing a night's entertainment at the conference, the gallery is coordinated with the technical program. In this module we will discuss its role within the Arts program and feature successful examples of past exhibitions.
4. *Writing a successful arts program paper (45 mins):* Here we will decompose what makes a great Arts technical paper (and what makes a bad one). This module will aim to demystify the process of writing and Arts paper and provide insight into what program chairs look for, what reviewers examine contributions on and what they often strike against.
5. *Open Discussion:* While we will open the floor for discussion at the end of each module, we will also set aside time at the end of the tutorial for people to dive into their own work and questions as they relate to the Arts and Digital Culture section at SIGMM.

4. MATERIALS

The half-day tutorial will present a series of selected readings that provides an overview of the past 10 years of the Arts and Digital Culture program in addition to selected review of works through available online content[1] and multimedia collateral. These will be assembled and accessible to participants as a website prepared by the tutorial leads. This site will also offer an overview of the tutorial objectives and auxiliary materials. Materials will be cross-listed and posted in the Arts and Digital Culture section of the ACM SIGMM website. Along with an annotated slide-deck and other materials, it is expected that outcomes of the tutorial, discussion points and other participant feedback will be also captured within this site to serve as a resource for the community and in particular those interested in learning more about or participating in the Arts and Digital Culture program in the future.

5. REFERENCES

[1] A. Jaimes, N. Sebe, and D. Gatica-Perez. Human-centered computing: A multimedia perspective. In *Proceedings of the 14th Annual ACM International Conference on Multimedia*, MULTIMEDIA '06, pages 855–864, New York, NY, USA, 2006. ACM.

[2] A. Jaimes, A. Senior, and W. Muench. Acm multimedia interactive art program: An introduction to the presence/absence exhibition. In *Proceedings of the 13th Annual ACM International Conference on Multimedia*, MULTIMEDIA '05, pages 1051–1052, New York, NY, USA, 2005. ACM.

[3] F. J. Lapoint. A sead network analysis of white papers, sead network white papers. `http://seadnetwork.wordpress.com`, 2012.

[4] S. Wilson. *Art+ Science Now.* Thames & Hudson, 2010.

[1]See: `http://bit.ly/artsmmtutorial`

AVEC 2014: the 4th International Audio/Visual Emotion Challenge and Workshop

Michel Valstar
University of Nottingham
Mixed Reality Lab
Nottingham, United Kingdom

Björn Schuller*
Imperial College London
Machine Learning Group
London, United Kingdom

Jarek Krajewski
University of Wuppertal
Schumpeter School of
Business and Economics
Wuppertal, Germany

Roddy Cowie
Queen's University
School of Psychology
Belfast, United Kingdom

Maja Pantic†
Imperial College London
Intelligent Behaviour
Understanding Group
London, United Kingdom

ABSTRACT

The fourth Audio-Visual Emotion Challenge and workshop AVEC 2014 was held in conjunction ACM Multimedia'14. Like the 2013 edition of AVEC, the workshop/challenge addresses the interpretation of social signals represented in both audio and video in terms of high-level continuous dimensions from a large number of clinically depressed patients and controls, with a sub-challenge in self-reported severity of depression estimation. In this summary, we mainly describe participation and its conditions.

Categories and Subject Descriptors

I [**Pattern Recognition**]: Applications

Keywords

Affective Computing; Social Signal Processing; Depression

1. INTRODUCTION

This year's Audio-Visual Emotion Challenge and workshop (AVEC 2014) has been organised in conjunction with the 22nd ACM International Conference on Multimedia, held in Orland, Florida, 3 – 7 November 2014 (ACM-MM'14).

The AVEC 2014's theme is '3D Dimensional Affect and Depression' and it is the fourth competition event aimed at comparison of multimedia processing and machine learning methods for automatic audio, visual and audio-visual emotion analysis, with all participants competing under strictly the same conditions in this first of its kind series [3, 2, 4]. However, further similar endeavours are to be noted in the meanwhile, e. g., [1].

The AVEC 2014 edition features besides emotion recognition the serious and important automatic estimation of levels of depression. Adding objective measures to what is otherwise an entirely subjective process of diagnosing and monitoring depression promises to be an invaluable support to the mental health profession besides the usage in media retrieval systems.

As before, the goal of the Challenge is to provide a common benchmark test set for individual multimodal information processing and to bring together the audio and video emotion recognition communities, to compare the relative merits of the two approaches to emotion recognition under well-defined and strictly comparable conditions and establish to what extent fusion of the approaches is possible and beneficial. A second motivation is the need to advance emotion recognition for multimedia retrieval to a level where behaviomedical systems are able to deal with large volumes of non-prototypical naturalistic behaviour in reaction to known stimuli, as this is exactly the type of data that diagnostic tools and other applications would have to face in the real world.

We were calling for participation in two Sub-Challenges: fully-continuous emotion detection from audio, from video, or from audio-visual information, and estimation of one depression level indicator. As benchmarking database an enhanced subset of the AVEC 2013 audio-visual depression corpus of task-specific human-computer interactions was used. Emotion needed to be recognized in terms of continuous time, *and* continuous valued dimensional affect in three dimensions: valence, arousal and dominance. Depression needed to be estimated in terms of a widely accepted clinical self-report questionnaire, the Beck Depression Inventory II.

Besides participation in the Challenge we were calling for papers addressing the overall topics of this workshop, in particular works that address the differences between audio and video processing of emotive data, and the issues concerning combined audio-visual emotion recognition.

In the following sections, we will describe the participation in this year and outline the conditions for participation in

*The author is further affiliated with Technische Universität München, MISP, Munich, Germany.

†The author is further affiliated with Twente University, EEMCS, Twente, The Netherlands.

MM '14, Nov 03-07 2014, Orlando, FL, USA

ACM ACM 978-1-4503-3063-3/14/11
http://dx.doi.org/10.1145/2647868.2647869 .

particular in the competitive challenge event. We further acknowledge those that helped turn AVEC 2014 into reality.

2. PARTICIPATION

The call for participation and papers attracted registrations of 42 teams (15 more than last year) and 142 team members from all over the world. 6 teams submitted results for the Affect recognition Sub-Challenge (ASC), 12 teams submitted results for the Depression recognition Sub-Challenge (DSC) — overall, at the moment of writing over 60 submissions of results to both Sub-Challenges combined were received (one third of these for the ASC). Finally, 21 paper submissions were received. AVEC 2014 reviewing was double blind, and acceptance was based on relevance to the workshop, novelty, and technical quality. The programme committee accepted 8 papers in addition to the baseline paper as oral presentation (the oral acceptance rate thus equalling 43 %), and further 4 as posters, which were assigned three reviewers, each, and reviewed independently. Again, we hope that these proceedings will serve as a valuable reference for researchers and developers in the area of audio-visual emotion recognition and depression analysis.

3. CHALLENGE CONDITIONS

A baseline paper explaining the dataset, the challenge evaluation procedure, baseline features and baseline results was made available during the ongoing challenge [5]. Due to the sensitive nature of the data, a strict registration for access to the challenge data policy was followed. As in 2013, a web-based database was used, however, we required to sign a new end user license agreement and AVEC 2014 data was encrypted with a new password. After downloading the data participants could directly start their own experiments with the train and development sets. Once they found their best method they should write a paper for the Workshop. At the same time they could compute their results per instance of the test set. Participants' results needed to be sent as a single packed file per Sub-Challenge to the organisers by email and scores were returned within 24 hours during typical working days. As indicated, there were two goals of AVEC 2014: the recognition of the three continuous affect labels (ASC) and the estimation of the self-reported depression indicator BDI-II (BSC).

Each participant had up to five submission attempts per Sub-Challenge. Badly formatted results were not counted towards one of these five submissions. Further, the top-two performers of both Sub-Challenges were asked to submit their program to the organisers at University of Nottingham to verify the results, both on the original test set and extra hold-out data. Delivery was as an executable or, e. g., encrypted Matlab or similar code, and they were asked to work with the organisers in validating their results. The organisers provided for each dimension Pearson's correlation coefficient or the RMS error (for the ASC/DSC, respectively), which is used to rank participants. For the ASC the RMS error was provided as well, which could be used by the authors to further discuss their results in the paper accompanying their submission. Participants could download the Matlab evaluation code for the two Sub-Challenges. This code was not supposed to 'run' on one's machine (more files and the test labels would be needed for that); it is rather just a detailed description of how we calculate the scores.

4. PROGRAM AND COMMITTEE

The workshop is a full-day event held on 7 November 2014 starting with a keynote speech, followed by an introduction to the challenge, a series of paper presentations (oral and posters), a panel discussion, and finally an overview of the challenge results and an announcement of the winners of the two Sub-Challenges.

The organisers — the authors of this summary — would like to thank all participants and in particular also the highly dedicated program committee of this year:
Anton Batliner, FAU, Germany, *Felix Burkhardt*, Deutsche Telekom, Germany, *Rama Chellappa*, University of Maryland, USA, *Mohamed Chetouani*, ISIR, France, *Julien Epps*, UNSW, Australia, *Roland Göcke*, University of Canberra, Australia, *Hatice Gunes*, QMUL, UK, *Marc Méhu*, University of Geneva, Switzerland, *Louis-Philippe Morency*, USC, USA, *Richard Morriss*, University of Nottingham, UK, *Stefan Scherer*, USC, USA, *Stefan Steidl*, FAU, Germany and *Fernando de la Torre*, CMU, USA.

Acknowledgments

The work of Michel Valstar is partly funded by the NIHR-HTC 'MindTech' and Horizon Digital Economy Research, RCUK grant EP/G065802/1. The work of Jarek Krajewski is partly funded by the German Research Foundation (KR3698/4-1).

The challenge in general has been generously supported by the Association for the Advancement of Affective Computing (AAAC, former HUMAINE association) and the EU network of excellence on Social Signal Processing SSPNet (EC's 7th Framework Programme [FP7/20072013] under grant agreement no. 231287).

The authors further acknowledge funding from the EC and ERC (grants nos. 289021, ASC-Inclusion and 338164, iHEARu).

5. REFERENCES

[1] A. Dhall, R. Goecke, J. Joshi, M. Wagner, and T. Gedeon. Emotion Recognition In The Wild Challenge 2013. In *Proceedings ICMI*, pages 509–516, Sydney, Australia, December 2013. ACM.

[2] B. Schuller, M. Valstar, F. Eyben, R. Cowie, and M. Pantic. AVEC 2012 – The Continuous Audio/Visual Emotion Challenge. In *Proceedings ICMI*, pages 449–456, Santa Monica, CA, October 2012. ACM.

[3] B. Schuller, M. Valstar, F. Eyben, G. McKeown, R. Cowie, and M. Pantic. AVEC 2011 - The First International Audio/Visual Emotion Challenge. In *Proceedings ACII*, volume II, pages 415–424. Springer, Memphis, TN, October 2011.

[4] M. Valstar, B. Schuller, J. Krajewski, R. Cowie, and M. Pantic. Workshop summary for the 3rd international audio/visual emotion challenge and workshop (AVEC'13). In *Proceedings MM*, pages 1085–1086, Barcelona, Spain, October 2013. ACM.

[5] M. Valstar, B. Schuller, K. Smith, T. Almaev, F. Eyben, J. Krajewski, R. Cowie, and M. Pantic. AVEC 2014 – The Three Dimensional Affect and Depression Challenge. In *Proceedings of the 4th ACM international workshop on Audio/Visual Emotion Challenge*, Orlando, FL, November 2014. ACM.

The Workshop on Computational Personality Recognition 2014

Fabio Celli
University of Trento,
Trento, Italy
fabio.celli@unitn.it

Bruno Lepri
FBK,
Trento, Italy
lepri@fbk.eu

Joan-Isaac Biel
IDIAP research institute, EPFL
Martigny, Switzerland
jibiel@idiap.ch

Daniel Gatica-Perez
IDIAP research institute,
Martigny, Switzerland
gatica@idiap.ch

Giuseppe Riccardi
University of Trento,
Trento, Italy
riccardi@disi.unitn.it

Fabio Pianesi
FBK,
Trento, Italy
pianesi@fbk.eu

ABSTRACT

The Workshop on Computational Personality Recognition aims to define the state-of-the-art in the field and to provide tools for future standard evaluations in personality recognition tasks. In the WCPR14 we released two different datasets: one of Youtube Vlogs and one of Mobile Phone interactions. We structured the workshop in two tracks: an open shared task, where participants can do any kind of experiment, and a competition. We also distinguished two tasks: A) personality recognition from multimedia data, and B) personality recognition from text only. In this paper we discuss the results of the workshop.

Categories and Subject Descriptors

5.5 [**Emotional and Social Signals in Multimedia**]: Novel methods for the classification and representation of interactive social and/or emotional signals

Keywords

personality recognition; WCPR; multimedia; youtube; evaluation

1. INTRODUCTION

Personality Recognition is an emerging research field that consists in the automatic classification of users' personality traits from various sources, including text [8] and multimedia, [2], [4]. Gold standard labels for an objective evaluation can be obtained by means of the Big5 personality tests [5], which are well-known and widely accepted in psychology and other research fields. The Big5 factor model defines personality along 5 bipolar scales: extraversion (sociable vs. shy); emotional stability (secure vs. neurotic); agreeableness (friendly vs. ugly); conscientiousness (organized vs. careless); openness to experience (insightful vs. unimaginative).

The *Workshop on Computational Personality Recognition*[1] aims to allow participants to compare the performance and quality of different approaches in personality recognition tasks, as well as defining the state-of-the-art. To do that, we stuctured the workshop in two tracks. One track is an open shared task, to test or compare resources, techniques and approaches to the automatic prediction of personality. The other one is a competition, to define a state-of-the-art in the field. We also distinguished two tasks. In **task A** participants aree allowed to use text and multimedia data, while in **task B** they are allowed to use only text. We provided two gold-standard labelled datasets: **Transcriptions of Youtube Video Blogs** (Youtube dataset) [1] and **Mobile Phones interactions** (Mobile dataset) [9]. The Youtube dataset contains 404 users/videos, with transcriptions and observed personality labels. We provided text (246.5k tokens) and feature vectors extracted from videos (including values like pitch, eye gaze direction, camera proximity, energy, time speaking, voice rate etc. See [1] for details), For the Mobile dataset, collected inside the Friends and Family longitudinal study by MIT Human Dynamics group, we provided a sample of 50 users, labeled with self-assessed personality traits, and data about users' proximity, couples, sms and calls. For both datasets we provided training/test splits, official baselines, personality scores and binary personality labels. We also provided instructions for the format of the prediction files and the official personality scorer. Participants to the competition had to deliver the prediction files to test the validity of their experiments.

2. CONTRIBUTIONS AND RESULTS

Participants had about three months to develop their own systems for personality recognition and evaluate the results on the datasets released. We released training and test sets at the same time, because we included the shared task in the workshop. We had 6 papers accepted, all of them ran experiments on the Youtube dataset. Among these, 3 teams participated to the competition, 2 to the shared task and 1 to both.

Farnadi *et al.* tested 6 different regression models (3 variants of Target Stacking, 2 of Ensamble Regressor Chains and one Random Forest) to predict the personality of YouTube video bloggers. They use a feature vector that contains gender, audio/visual and linguistic features, extracted from text by means of psychologic (LIWC, MRC, SPLICE), sentiment and emotions (NRC, SentiStrength) lexical resources. Sarkar *et al.* presented an analysis of audio-visual, sentiment, word statistics and gender features to predict personality traits. they report results with a variety of feature combinations. Verhoeven *et al.* tried to classify personality traits for Youtube

[1]Website: https://sites.google.com/site/wcprst/home/wcpr14

MM'14 Nov 03-07 2014, Orlando, FL, USA
Copyright 2014 ACM 978-1-4503-3063-3/14/11 ...$15.00
http://dx.doi.org/10.1145/2647868.2647870.

text transcriptions using features for gender identification. In the shared task track they ran 10-fold cross validation on the training set to detect which personality traits are predicted best. In the competition they obtained an f1-score of 0.54, averaged over the five personality traits, using gender, liwc and words as features for the prediction of personality from text. Alam & Riccardi exploited a

	set	alg.	task	feat.	avg-f1	avg-rmse
baseline	yt	maj	A/B	-	0.39	0.84
Farnadi	yt	st	A	e,l,s,av	-	**0.76**
Verhoeven	yt	svm	B	n,l,g	0.54	-
Sarkar	yt	lr	A	n,e,s,g,av	0.57	-
Alam	yt	svm	A	s,l,p,e,av	**0.67**	-

Table 1: Results of the competition track. Tasks: A=personality prediction from text and multimedia data; B=personality predictions only from text. Algorithms: st=target stacking, svm=support vector machines, lr=logistic regression, svmr=support vector machine regression. Features: e=emotions/sentiment, l=liwc g=gender, s=statistics on word usage, av=audio/video, n=ngrams/raw text, p=part-of-speech.

large feature space including psycholinguistic, emotional and part-of-speech features, in addition to the audio-visual features provided with the dataset. They obtained very high results automatically combining the best models for each trait. Results of the competition are reported in table 1.

In the shared task, Nowson & Gill trained a model of personality in the Youtube dataset and tested it into the EAR corpus [7], that contains trascriptions of dialogues annotated with personality traits by external observers. They obtain an accuracy of 62% over a baseline of 55% using Naïve Bayes as algoritm and LIWC features. They also report the features that are effective in the different domains. Gievska *et al.* correlated Ekman's 6 emotions [6] with

	set	alg.	task	feat.	result	base
Verhoeven	yt	svm	B	n,l,g	f1=0.555	f1=0.546
Gievska	yt	svm	A	av,g,e,s	f1=0.661	f1=0.508
Nowson	yt+ear	nb	B	l	acc=62%	acc=55%

Table 2: Results of the shared task track. Tasks: A=personality prediction from text and multimedia data; B=personality predictions only from text. Algorithms: nb=naïve bayes, svm=support vector machines, Features: e=emotions, l=liwc g=gender, s=statistics on word usage, av=audio/video, n=ngrams, p=part-of-speech.

the Big Five personality traits, and used those features to augment audio-visual and gender for personality trait classification. They report an F1-score of 0.661 over a baseline of 0.508. Results of the shared task are reported in table 2.

3. DISCUSSION AND CONCLUSION

The results of the WCPR14 confirm once again that personality recognition is a very hard task. The scores achieved by the participants in this edition of the workshop reveal that the state-of-the-art in computational personality recognition from multimedia is around f1=0.67 for the prediction of classes and rmse=0.76 for the prediction of z-scores (normalized between 0 and 1). In task B (personality recognition from text) the state-of-the-art is even lower, but more work is required to test this. Comparing this edition of the shared task to the previous one [3], we see that participants successfully exploited emotions and gender for the prediction of personality traits. The variability of performances among traits is the main problem for the classification, averaged over the five traits. Alam & Riccardi succesfully addressed this problem by voting automatically the best model for each personality trait to obtain a combined model.

In this edition of the Workshop on Computational Personality Recognition, we made available corpora and tools for future evaluations of personality recognition systems. In addition, participants to the workshop have tested many different techniques, feature sets and algoritms for future reference in this and related research fields.

4. ACKNOWLEDGEMENTS

We wish to thank the WCPR14 Programme Committee members: Michal Kosinski (Psychometrics Centre, University of Cambridge); Evgeny A Stepanov (University of Trento); Marco Guerini (FBK); Bruno Lepri (FBK); Matteo Magnani (Uppsala University); Paolo Rosso (University of Valencia); Alastair Gill (King's College, London); Albert Ali Salah (Bogazici University); Scott Nowson (Xerox Research Center); Oya Aran (Idiap Research Institute); Yves-Alexandre de Montojye (MIT Media Lab); Walter Daelemans (University of Antwerp); Francisco Iacobelli (Northwestern University); Scott Nowson (Xerox research Center); Ben Verhoeven (University of Antwerp).

The WCPR14 has received funding from the European Union - Seventh Framework Programme (FP7/2007-2013) under grant agreement 610916: SENSEI.

5. REFERENCES

[1] J. Biel and D. Gatica-Perez. The youtube lens: Crowdsourced personality impressions and audiovisual analysis of vlogs. *Multimedia, IEEE Transactions on*, 15(1):41–55, 2013.

[2] J.-I. Biel, O. Aran, and D. Gatica-Perez. You are known by how you vlog: Personality impressions and nonverbal behavior in youtube. In *ICWSM*, 2011.

[3] F. Celli, F. Pianesi, D. Stillwell, and M. Kosinski. Workshop on computational personality recognition: Shared task. In *WCPR in conjuction to ICWSM 2013*, 2013.

[4] G. Chittaranjan, J. Blom, and D. Gatica-Perez. Who's who with big-five: analyzing and classifying personality traits with smartphones. In *Wearable Computers (ISWC), 2011 15th Annual International Symposium on*, pages 29–36. IEEE, 2011.

[5] P. T. Costa and R. R. McCrae. The revised neo personality inventory (neo-pi-r). *The SAGE handbook of personality theory and assessment*, 2:179–198, 2008.

[6] P. E. Ekman and R. J. Davidson. *The nature of emotion: Fundamental questions.* Oxford University Press, 1994.

[7] F. Mairesse, M. A. Walker, M. R. Mehl, and R. K. Moore. Using linguistic cues for the automatic recognition of personality in conversation and text. *Journal of Artificial Intelligence Research*, 30(1):457–500, 2007.

[8] J. Oberlander and S. Nowson. Whose thumb is it anyway?: classifying author personality from weblog text. In *Proceedings of the COLING/ACL on Main conference poster sessions*, pages 627–634. Association for Computational Linguistics, 2006.

[9] J. Staiano, B. Lepri, N. Aharony, F. Pianesi, N. Sebe, and A. Pentland. Friends don't lie: inferring personality traits from social network structure. In *Proceedings of the 2012 ACM Conference on Ubiquitous Computing*, pages 321–330. ACM, 2012.

CrowdMM14 – 2014 International ACM Workshop on Crowdsourcing for Multimedia

Judith Redi
Delft University of Technology
Mekelweg 4
Delft, the Netherlands
j.a.redi@tudelft.nl

Mathias Lux
Klagenfurt University
Universitätsstraße 65-67
Klagenfurt, Austria
mlux@itec.aau.at

ABSTRACT

The power of crowds, leveraging a large number of human contributors and the capabilities of human computation, has enormous potential to address key challenges in the area of multimedia research. This power is, however, of difficult exploitation: challenges arise from the fact that a community of users or workers is a complex and dynamic system highly sensitive to changes in the form and the parameterization of their activities. Since 2012, the International ACM Workshop on Crowdsourcing for Multimedia *CrowdMM* has been the venue for collecting new insights on the effective deployment of crowdsourcing towards boosting Multimedia research. In its third edition, CrowdMM14 especially focuses on contributions that propose solutions for the key challenges that face widespread adoption of crowdsourcing paradigms in the multimedia research community. These include: identification of optimal crowd members (e.g., user expertise, worker reliability), providing effective explanations (i.e., good task design), controlling noise and quality in the results, designing incentive structures that do not breed cheating, adversarial environments, gathering necessary background information about crowd members without violating privacy, controlling descriptions of task.

Categories and Subject Descriptors

H.1.2 [**User/Machine Systems**]: [Human Factors, Human information processing]

Keywords

Crowdsourcing; Multimedia evaluation; Human Computation; Multimedia Annotation; Human Factors

1. INTRODUCTION

Crowdsourcing offers a time- and resource-efficient method for collecting large volumes of input data for system design and evaluation, making it possible to optimize multimedia systems more rapidly and to address human factors more effectively. Hence, it can be expected to exercise transformative impact on the field of multimedia in the coming years.

While the use of human computation is not new, i.e. the term "computer" originally described a human worker, technological advances have created new opportunities to leverage human effort in concert with automated methods to address limitations of current automation or to enhance current capabilities. The further enhancement of human intelligence attainable when contributions from multiple individuals are combined ("wisdom of the crowds") has just begun to give indications of greater potential for the multimedia field. We expect future multimedia computing will increasingly explore judicious use of humans and human computation to complement and extend existing methodologies.

On the other hand, at present crowdsourcing remains notoriously difficult to exploit effectively in multimedia settings, due to the volatile and dynamic nature of the crowd of workers which is addressed to complete research-related tasks. The aim of the 2014 International ACM Workshop on Crowdsourcing for Multimedia (CrowdMM14) is to introduce and explore novel approaches for exploiting crowdsourcing methodologies at their full potential in the full range of multimedia research topics of interest for ACM Multimedia 2014. The core topic of this workshop concentrates around one issue: *How to advance the use of crowdsourcing to the next level for the state-of-the-art in multimedia research?*

2. OBJECTIVE

The workshop focuses on advancing the state of the art of best practices for the use of crowdsourcing in multimedia research. A wealth of topics are addressed within the field of multimedia, cross-cutting all of the main conference areas. Contributions dealing with e.g. crowdsourcing-based identification and evaluation of multimedia quality of experience (Area: Multimedia HCI and QoE), visual and audio indexing via human computation or hybrid techniques (Area: Multimedia Search and Recommendation) or also crowdsourced log archival for forensics (Area: Multimedia Security, Privacy and Forensics), yet presenting a strong focus on crowdsourcing have been favored. Indeed, in its 2014 edition, CrowdMM put emphasis on on tackling the methodological challenges listed in section 3 of this paper. Crowdsourcing cannot be considered as a mature technology for multimedia research if the results it produces are not repeatable. To take crowdsourcing to the next level, it is necessary to determine best practices for test and incentive schemes

MM'14, November 3–7, 2014, Orlando, Florida, USA.
ACM 978-1-4503-3063-3/14/11.
http://dx.doi.org/10.1145/2647868.2647871.

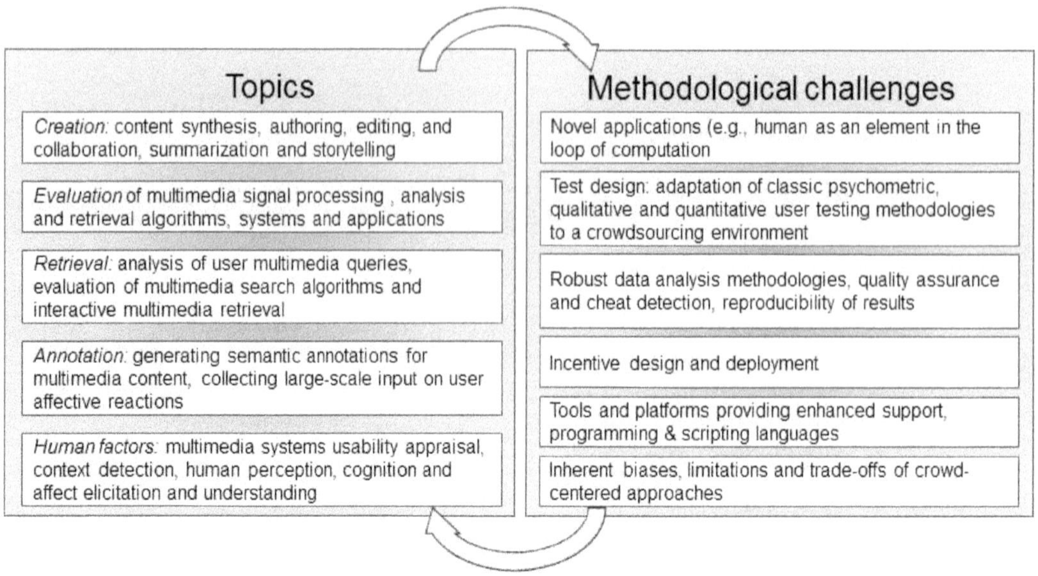

Figure 1: Topics and Methodological challenges addressed in CrowdMM14

design, as well as robust data analysis and quality control techniques. On the longer term (beyond CrowdMM14), our goal is to generate guidelines and recommendations for the use of crowdsourcing in multimedia, possibly also involving standardization bodies. To do so, it is necessary to focus on crowdsourcing not only as a mean for multimedia research, but also as an end, and this is the main purpose of CrowdMM14.

3. TOPICS

CrowdMM14 has a focus on theoretical, experimental, and methodological developments advancing state-of-the-art knowledge of crowdsourcing techniques for multimedia research. Submissions were encouraged to employ crowdsourcing, wisdom of the crowd, games with a purpose, or human computation in multimedia in the areas of research (topics), and propose innovative solutions with respect to the methodological challenges depicted in figure 1.

4. PROGRAM

The workshop program contained a combination of oral presentations, invited keynote presentations, a poster session for interactive presentation, and a panel discussion. Nhatvi Nguyen, CEO of Microworkers[1], one of today's prominent crowdsourcing platforms, joined CrowdMM14 as a keynote speaker, addressing insights into the daily work of a Crowdsourcing platform provider, from a technical as well as a legal and ethical point of view. CrowdMM14 also featured a "CrowdKeynote", during which all CrowdMM14 authors gave their view on the future and the Challenges that Crowdsourcing has still ahead.

CrowdMM received a total of 26 submissions (62% increase with respect to the 2013 edition), three of which short papers. Of these, 8 were accepted as oral presentations and 5 as poster presentations. All papers received at least three double blind reviews, and 3.4 reviews on average. The organizers are grateful to the Program Committee members for their efforts in reviewing and for their insightful comments.

5. ORGANIZERS & COMMITTEES

- Judith Redi, Dept. Intelligent Systems, Delft University of Technology, The Netherlands [2]
- Mathias Lux, Klagenfurt University, Austria [3]

In addition to the PC Members, the former workshop chairs are committed to the CrowdMM workshop and have agreed to form a steering committee to support integrity of the overall vision and goals. The steering committee contributed and will contribute in future CrowdMM editions in disseminating the workshop call for papers, reaching to the community in order to ensure that the workshop receives a large number of top quality submissions and recruiting leading members of the community as keynote and panelists. The CrowdMM14 steering committee was:

- Kuan-Ta Chen, Academia Sinica, Taiwan.
- Martha Larson, Delft University of Technology, The Netherlands
- Tobias Hoßfeld, University of Wuerzburg, Germany
- Wei-Ta Chu, National Chung Cheng University, Taiwan

[1] https://microworkers.com/

[2] http://www.mmi.tudelft.nl/~judith/

[3] http://www.itec.uni-klu.ac.at/~mlux/

EMASC14 — 1st International Workshop on Emerging Multimedia Applications and Services for Smart Cities

M. Anwar Hossain
King Saud University
Riyadh, KSA
mahossain@ksu.edu.sa

Abdulmotaleb El Saddik
University of Ottawa
Ontario, Canada
elsaddik@uottawa.ca

ABSTRACT
Smart city is the vision of future city - with increasingly instrumented, inter-connected and intelligent urban systems - to improve the quality of life in many aspects including public safety, healthcare, transportation, or energy. With the ever-increasing presence of multimodal sensors in the smart city infrastructure, multimedia plays an indispensable role. The proliferation of multimedia, sensors, pervasive devices, and infrastructures for realizing smart city has brought many challenges that are the core focus of EMASC workshop.

Categories and Subject Descriptors
A. General Literature; H.3.4 [Systems and Software]: Distributed systems; H.4.0 [General]; H.5.1 [Multimedia Information Systems]: Audio input/output, Video

General Terms
Design, Experimentation, Human Factors, Theory.

Keywords
Smart cities; multimedia; multimedia systems of systems; multimedia applications and services

1. INTRODUCTION
Smart cities embed sensor-rich, instrumented and interconnected infrastructure where new breeds of multimedia applications and services are emerging to fulfill the requirements of the residents. In such an interconnected environment, continuous steams of multimedia data are generated based on the multimodal sensors and socially connected people. These data streams are processed and analyzed to identify the needs of the residents, and to offer them required services to enhance their quality of life.

The opportunities and benefits of multimedia smart cities come with huge challenges. Dominant challenges include collaborative sensing and processing of multimedia data, multimedia service management, situation awareness and optimal decision making, integration of multimedia systems of systems, etc. The creation of effective and efficient multimedia services and applications will face these challenges. Thus, coordinated multi-disciplinary research is needed to address these challenges and reap the benefits of smart cities.

The EMASC 2014 workshop invited authors to submit papers covering the various research challenges. It received good responses from the authors as a first workshop and accordingly an interactive program was made possible to organize.

2. OBJECTIVES
This EMASC workshop brings together researchers and practitioners in multimedia, smart environment, multimodal sensing, service management, etc. to discuss about the challenges in creating multimedia services and applications for smart cities.

This workshop aimed to provide a forum of multi-disciplinary researchers and highlight the top research progress in the integration of multimedia for smart city applications and services.

3. TOPICS OF INTEREST
The EMASC 2014 workshop aims to report on the state-of-the-art techniques, methodologies, and emerging multimedia applications and services that help to realize smart cities.

Particular topics of interest include, but not limited to:

- Collaborative sensing, processing and aggregation of multimodal data
- Multimedia-driven situation awareness and decision support systems for smart city
- Mobile, anytime, anywhere sharing of multimedia data in smart city
- Smart multimedia 'systems of systems' in smart city
- Multimedia-enabled emergency response and event handling in smart city
- M2M sharing of multimedia data in smart city
- Multimedia IoT for smart city
- Multimedia service discovery, management and scheduling in smart city
- Crowd-sourcing in smart cities
- Cloud-based systems for smart cities
- Multimedia security and privacy for smart city applications

MM '14, Nov 03-07, 2014, Orlando, FL, USA.
ACM 978-1-4503-3063-3/14/11.
http://dx.doi.org/10.1145/2647868.2647872.

- Multimedia applications and services (education, health, transport etc.) in smart cities

4. EMASC PROGRAM

EMASC is a half-day fully-engaged workshop, held in Orlando, Florida, USA on November 7, 2014 in conjunction with 22nd ACM International Conference on Multimedia (ACM MM 2014).

There are total 8 presentations including two keynote speeches. The two keynote speakers are:

- Prof. Charles Hughes, Computer Science, University of Central Florida.
- Dr. Ben Amaba, Worldwide Executive, Dynamic Leadership and Innovation.

Besides, the authors of each accepted papers will have 20 min. to present their work and an extra 5 min. for question/answer.

5. ORGANIZERS

M. Anwar Hossain (General Co-chairs) is an Associate Professor in Software Engineering Department, CCIS, King Saud University, Riyadh, KSA. He received the B.Sc. Eng. degree in Computer Science and Engineering from Khulna University, Bangladesh. He obtained his master and Ph.D. degree from the University of Ottawa, Canada in 2005 and 2010, respectively. Dr. Hossain received IBM faculty award in 2011. His research interests include ambient intelligence, multimedia surveillance, sensor-cloud, smart cities, and cloud computing. He has authored and co-authored more than 60 publications including refereed journals, conference papers, and book chapters.

Abdulmotaleb El Saddik (General Co-chairs) is a Distinguished University Professor and University Research Chair in the School of Electrical Engineering and Computer Science at the University of Ottawa. He held regular and visiting positions in Canada, Spain, Saudi Arabia, UAE, Germany and China. He is an internationally-recognized scholar who has made strong contributions to the knowledge and understanding of multimedia computing, communications and applications. Prof. El Saddik is a Fellow of the IEEE (2009), for his contributions to interactive haptic audio visual systems. He was also elected Fellow of the Canadian Academy of Engineering (2010) and Fellow of the Engineering Institute of Canada (2010). He is the first Canadian in Computer Science & Engineering to receive the very prestigious Friedrich Wilhelm Bessel Award from the German Humboldt Foundation in 2007. He is the recipient of the Ontario Premier's Research Excellence Award (PREA), in 2004 and the National Capital Institute of Telecommunications (NCIT) New Professorship Incentive Award (2004). In 2008 he was appointed an IEEE Distinguished Lecturer, he also received the Professional of the Year Award, from the Canadian Lebanese Chamber of Commerce and Industry for Achievement in the Development of Canada. He has also received five Outstanding/Best Paper Awards. Most recently Dr. El Saddik has been the recipient of the 2010 Association of Computing Machinery (ACM) Distinguished Scientist Award, the 2011 Cátedra de Excelencia from Universidad Carlos III de Madrid, Spain and the 2010 IEEE Instrumentation and Measurement Society Technical Award, which is the highest award of IEEE Instrumentation and Measurement society, for his outstanding contributions to multimedia computing. He received the Faculty of Engineering's George S. Glinski Award for Excellence in Research for 2012. He also received the 2012 IEEE Ottawa Educator Award and the 2013 IEEE Canada Achievement Award: C.C. Gotlieb (Computer) Medal for important contributions to the field of computer engineering and science.

6. ACKNOWLEDGEMENTS

We would like to acknowledge the contributions made by the authors, the excellent review done by the PC members and the invited speakers for their keynote speech in EMASC workshop.

GeoMM 2014: The Third ACM Multimedia Workshop on Geotagging and Its Applications in Multimedia

Liangliang Cao
IBM Research
Yorktown Heights, NY, USA
liangliang.cao@us.ibm.com

Gerald Friedland
ICSI
Berkeley, CA, USA
fractor@icsi.berkeley.edu

Lexing Xie
Australian National University
Canberra, Australia
lexing.xie@anu.edu.au

ABSTRACT

The Third ACM Workshop on Geotagging and Its Applications in Multimedia(GeoMM'14), continues the workshops in 2012 and 2013, with the goal of building a forum for the presentation and synthesis of vision and insight from leading experts and practitioners on the developing directions of geotagging research related to multimedia. Following the success in previous years, the GeoMM workshop serves as a venue for the premier research in geotagging and multimedia, and continues to attract submissions from a diverse set of researchers, who address newly arising problems within this emerging field. Five regular papers are presented in this workshop, covering a number of novel applications and new methodologies. An invited paper is also presented to introduce the related MediaEval 2014 Placing task, which consists of 5 million geotagged photos and 25,000 geotagged videos. We believe this workshop will benefit more and more research works in the broad research field.

Categories and Subject Descriptors

I.5.4 [**Applications**]: Computer Vision

General Terms

Overview, Experiments

Keywords

Geo-tagged Multimedia; Location based Services; Overview

1. INTRODUCTION

In recent years, the rise of wide-spread use of GPS sensors and the increasing availability of open geographical databases has motivated a large volume of work on geotagging. The increase in the use of geotagging and improvements in geolocation support systems open up a new dimension for the description, organization and manipulation of multimedia data. This new dimension radically expands the usefulness of multimedia data both for daily users of the Internet and social networking sites as well as for experts in particular application scenarios.

The goal of this workshop is to bring together cutting-edge research in geotagging as well as novel applications related to geotagging. It will help facilitate in-depth discussions, share existing tools, and ultimately enhance the research efforts in this area. The workshop will serve as a forum for the presentation and synthesis of vision and insight from leading experts and practitioners on the developing directions of geotagging research related to multimedia.

Topics of interests include, but not limited to

- Collection and estimation of geotags
- Location estimation: inferring geolocation from visual and audio cues
- Mining unstructured web text (e.g., news, blogs) for location
- Knowledge discovery from open geographical databases (e.g., Google earth, GeoNames) and web photos
- Mining geotags from mobile devices and sensor network
- Applications of geotagging
- Photo and video annotation
- Business applications (e.g., geomarketing, targeted advertising etc.)
- Social networking
- Privacy and security issues
- Visualization of geotagged information
- 3D construction of world model
- Visualization of tourism, travel routes, and other spatial-temporal patterns

The call for papers attracted a number of submissions from both industry and academia institutions. We finally select five papers, which cover rich aspects of geomm, including profilling of business locations, capture-time classification, recommending photo-talking locations, urban computing, and inferring home locations. We are excited that a number of novel applications have been proposed and hope these work will make a big impact in the future.

MM'14, November 3–7, 2014, Orlando, Florida, USA.
ACM 978-1-4503-3063-3/14/11.
http://dx.doi.org/10.1145/2647868.2647873 .

In addition, we also invite a paper from the organizers of MediaEval 2014 Placing Task. The Placing task 2014 is a multimodal location estimation task with record-breaking 5 million geotagged photos and 25,000 geotagged videos. We would like to embrace the opportunity and challenge with this new event, and hope the datasets would be useful for many researchers in this field.

Finally, we are pround to host a number of keynote speakers who have done influential work in this field. Their talks will provide cutting edge overviews of the state of the art in this field.

We would like to send our warmest greetings and invite everyone who is interested in geomm to attend our workshop. After organizing this series of workshop for three years, we have witness the surge of this emerging area and we believe we will see more success in the future.

2. WORKSHOP ORGANIZERS

Liangliang Cao is a Research Staff Member in IBM T. J. Watson Research Center, and also an adjunct assistant professor at Columbia University. His research lies in the intersection of computer vision, multimedia and big data analytics. His work has won three prestigious visual recognition competitions, include ImageCLEF Medical Image Classification (2012, 2013), and ImageNet Large Scale Visual Recognition Challenge (2010). His contribution has been awarded the IBM Outstanding Accomplishment (2012), the Best Paper Award in the First International Workshop on Big Data Mining (2012), IBM Watson Emerging Leader in Multimedia and Signal Processing (2010), Facebook Fellowship Finalist (2010), and UIUC Computational Science and Engineering Fellowship (2009-2010). He has authored more than 40 papers in top conferences and journals, including ICCV, CVPR, ECCV, NIPS, ACM Multimedia, WWW, TPAMI, and PIEEE. He is a guest editor of ACM Transactions on Multimedia Computing, Communications (TOMCCAP) and Applications and also Computer Vision and Image Understanding (CVIU) Journal. He is a general chair of New York Area Multimedia and Vision Meeting in Greater in 2012 and 2013. Dr. Cao is an area chair of ACM Multimedia 2012 and IEEE WACV 2014. He fulfills review duties for more than 15 journals and various conferences.

Gerald Friedland is the Director of Audio and Multimedia Research at the International Computer Science Institute, a private non-profit lab affiliated with the University of California, Berkeley. His leads a group of currently 18 researchers that focus on acoustic techniques for video retrieval, multimodal location estimation, and the privacy implications of multimedia research. Dr. Friedland has published about 200 peer-reviewed articles in conferences, journals, and books and has authored a textbook on Multimedia Computing together with Dr. Ramesh Jain. More importantly, he has participated in MediaEval Placing since the beginning, has authored the inaugural Brave New Topic paper on Multimodal Location Estimation and has co-authored the book "Multimodal Location Estimation of Images and Videos" together with Jaeyoung Choi. He is the recipient of several research and industry recognitions, among them the European Academic Software Award and the Multimedia Entrepreneur Award by the German Federal Department of Economics. Most recently, he lead the team that won the ACM Multimedia Grand Challenge in 2009. Gerald Friedland is an associate editor for the ACM Transactions on Multimedia Computing, Communications, and Applications (TOMCCAP), IEEE Multimedia Magazine and regularly reviews for IEEE Transactions on Acoustics, Speech, and Language Processing, IEEE Transaction on Multimedia, IEEE Multimedia, SpringerâĂŹs Machine Vision and Application, and other journals. He has been involved in the organization of ACM Multimedia since 2009 and was program co-chair at IEEE ICME 2012. He is a senior member of IEEE and ACM and is also chairing the Special Interest Group on Audio and Speech Processing for Multimedia (SIGASP) which is part of the IEEE TC on Multimedia.

Lexing Xie is Senior Lecturer in the Research School of Computer Science at the Australian National University. She was research staff member at IBM T.J. Watson Research Center in New York from 2005 to 2010, and adjunct assistant professor at Columbia University 2007-2009. She received B.S. from Tsinghua University, Beijing, China, and M.S. and Ph.D. degrees from Columbia University, all in Electrical Engineering. Her research interests are in applied machine learning, multimedia, social media. Her recent projects are on multimedia content analysis, social media tracking and recommendation, visual semantics, large-scale image and video search. Lexing's research has received five best student paper and best paper awards between 2002 and 2011, and a Grand Challenge Multimodal Prize at ACM Multimedia 2012. She was the 2005 IBM Research Josef Raviv Memorial Postdoc fellow in Computer Science and Engineering. She currently serves an associate editor of IEEE Transactions on Multimedia, and ACM Transactions on Multimedia. Her service roles include the program and organizing committees of major multimedia, machine learning, web and social media conferences.

Acknowledgment

We would like to thank all authors who submitted contributions and the program committee members for their excellent work to review the papers. We are also very grateful for the invited keynote speakers for their presentations in the workshop.

Human-centered Event Understanding from Multimedia

Ansgar Scherp
Kiel University and Leibniz Information Center for Economics
Kiel, Germany
asc@informatik.uni-kiel.de

Vasileios Mezaris
Centre for Research and Technology Hellas
Thessaloniki, Greece
bmezaris@iti.gr

Bogdan Ionescu
University Politehnica of Bucharest
Bucharest, Romania
bionescu@alpha.imag.pub.ro

Francesco De Natale
University of Trento
Trento, Italy
francesco.denatale@unitn.it

ABSTRACT

This workshop focuses on the human-centered aspects of understanding events from multimedia content. This includes the notion of objects and their relation to events. The workshop brings together researchers from the different areas in multimedia and beyond that are interested in understanding the concept of events.

1. INTRODUCTION

Events are everywhere! We find them in life-log applications and emergency response systems as well as in domains like cultural heritage, news, sports, and surveillance. Thus, we can understand events as natural abstraction of human experience. The different applications and domains make use of different methods and approaches for detecting, representing, and using events. However, they share the common notion of considering events as important entities. Events are generally understood as perduring entities that unfold over time. They are occurrences in which humans participate and may be subject to discussions and interpretations by humans. In contrast, objects are enduring entities that unfold over space. While some consider objects as 4D entities, i. e., extending across time just as they do in space, others consider both events and objects as first class entities that require each other.[1]

[1] `http://www.slideshare.net/ascherp/slideshare-events-in-multimedia-theory-model-application-v07`, last accessed: July 11, 2014.

MM'14, Nov 03-07 2014, Orlando, FL, USA.
ACM 978-1-4503-3063-3/14/11.
http://dx.doi.org/10.1145/2647868.2647874.

2. WORKSHOP GOAL

The goal of this workshop is to present and discuss the different aspects and notions of events and objects. This includes methods for detecting activities and low-level events and objects from media content and other sensory data. It also targets solutions and approaches for detecting and modeling the relationships between events and objects. Finally, we invite submissions of novel applications that are based on the notion of events and objects and that make use of events and objects as first-class entities.

We bring together researchers from the different areas in multimedia and beyond that are interested in understanding the concept of events. We invite original work in the areas of event modeling, detection of events from multimedia data, processing of events, organization of multimedia data using events as unifying mechanism, and applications of these techniques.

3. WORKSHOP PROGRAMME

The workshop programme is organized into a keynote, a set of paper presentations, and a final discussion. The keynote is held by Ramesh Jain, University of California at Irvine, CA, USA with the title the "Objective Self".

The submissions accepted for the workshop are organized in two sessions[2]: A first set of papers deals with the detection of events in video. In this case, an event is most often defined as a complex interaction pattern that involves people and objects and is depicted in the video. In "Entity centric Feature Pooling for Complex Event Detection", the authors tackle the problem of detecting such events in YouTube-like videos. Their approach is based on understanding the spatial arrangement of people and objects that participate to an event. In "Skeleton-augmented Human Action Understanding by Learning with Progressively Refined Data", the authors focus on the human actors of the event, specifically

[2] `http://www.huevent14.uni-kiel.de/en/technical-programme`, last accessed: August 8, 2014.

on inferring skeletons that describe the human actions depicted in the video. In "Using Minute-by-Minute Match Report for Semantic Event Annotation in Soccer Video", the event-based analysis of video belonging to a very specific domain (soccer matches) is addressed. The soccer video is annotated using the match report; however, without assuming that perfect time synchronization exists between the video content and textual description of the match. Considering again a very specific but radically different domain, the authors of "Event Understanding in Endoscopic Surgery Videos" examine the segmentation of surgery video in subevents.

The second set of papers takes a somewhat different view on events: Instead of looking at events as short-term human actions or human-object interactions that are captured in video, they focus on broader personal and social events or on the user's interaction with the image / video content that relates to such events. The latter interaction can provide useful cues for the event-based organization of the media items. In "Concept-based image clustering and summarization of event-related image collections", the authors deal with the problem of summarizing image collections that correspond to a single event. To this end, they propose using trained visual concept detectors in combination with clustering methods. In "Sentiment Flow for Video Interestingness Prediction", the authors develop a method for predicting how interesting a video is, employing a mid-level sentiment representation for the video content. In "User Emotion Sensing in Search Process based on Chromatic Sensation", the authors propose a model for sensing the user's emotions by examining the colors (of photos, icons etc.) browsed or selected by the user. In "Investigating Human Factors in Forgery Detection Process", the authors deal with the difficult problem of detecting if an image is forged or not (which is a question that often arises when an image of an event such as a natural disaster or a war incident surfaces on the Web). They conduct a subjective evaluation to investigate human factors that are associated with this problem.

Finally, in the position paper titled "On the Personalization of Event-based Systems", the authors describe their position about personalization as a paradigm shift and discuss its relation to the event-based processing and organization of signals and digital content.

The keynote, author presentations, and position paper are used as kick-off for a final discussion about the different understandings of events and objects from the various fields. The questions discussed during the workshop include:

- How do the different works on events and objects relate to each other?
- How can they be harmonized and brought together under the roof of a common model?
- Should events and objects be considered first class entities?
- Which different understandings of relations between objects and events exist?

4. WORKSHOP HISTORY

The workshop finds its roots in earlier activities by some of the organizing members. For example, there have been three successful "Events in Multimedia" workshops which were held in conjunction with the previous editions of ACM Multimedia in Beijing, China (2009) [3], Florence, Italy (2010) [5], and Scottsdale, AZ, USA (2011) [2]. In those editions, the focus was on events only and not on an a human-centered approach of event understanding that also includes the notion of objects and their relation to events - as it is pursued in this workshop. The workshop on "Event-based Media Integration and Processing"[3] held last year at ACM Multimedia in Barcelona, Spain is also related but focused on events and their extraction from multimedia content. From these activities, also different special issues on the topic of events and objects in multimedia emerged [1, 4]. Finally, we released an extensive survey on modeling and indexing events in multimedia [6].

Acknowledgement.

We thank all presenters and participants at our workshops for their contributions and vivid discussions on the topic of events and objects in multimedia over the last years. In particular, we thank you all for the support in increasing the awareness and importance of the topic in our community.

5. REFERENCES

[1] V. Mezaris, A. Scherp, R. Jain, and M. S. Kankanhalli. Real-life events in multimedia: detection, representation, retrieval, and applications. *Multimedia Tools Appl.*, 70(1):1–6, 2014.

[2] V. Mezaris, A. Scherp, R. Jain, M. S. Kankanhalli, H. Zhou, J. Zhang, L. Wang, and Z. Zhang. Modeling and representing events in multimedia. In K. S. Candan, S. Panchanathan, B. Prabhakaran, H. Sundaram, W. chi Feng, and N. Sebe, editors, *Proceedings of the 19th International Conference on Multimedia 2011, Scottsdale, AZ, USA, November 28 - December 1, 2011*, pages 613–614. ACM, 2011.

[3] A. Scherp, R. Jain, and M. S. Kankanhalli. Events in multimedia. In W. Gao, Y. Rui, A. Hanjalic, C. Xu, E. G. Steinbach, A. El-Saddik, and M. X. Zhou, editors, *Proceedings of the 17th International Conference on Multimedia 2009, Vancouver, British Columbia, Canada, October 19-24, 2009*, pages 1147–1148. ACM, 2009.

[4] A. Scherp, R. Jain, and M. S. Kankanhalli. Introduction to the special issue of the multimedia tools and applications journal on events in multimedia. *Multimedia Tools Appl.*, 57(1):127–129, 2012.

[5] A. Scherp, R. Jain, M. S. Kankanhalli, and V. Mezaris. Modeling, detecting, and processing events in multimedia. In A. D. Bimbo, S.-F. Chang, and A. W. M. Smeulders, editors, *Proceedings of the 18th International Conference on Multimedia 2010, Firenze, Italy, October 25-29, 2010*, pages 1739–1740. ACM, 2010.

[6] A. Scherp and V. Mezaris. Survey on modeling and indexing events in multimedia. *Multimedia Tools Appl.*, 70(1):7–23, 2014.

[3] `http://ebmip.disi.unitn.it`, last accessed: July 11, 2014.

ImmersiveMe'14: 2nd ACM International Workshop on Immersive Media Experiences

Teresa Chambel
LaSIGE, Faculty of Sciences
University of Lisbon
Lisbon, Portugal
tc@di.fc.ul.pt

Paula Viana
Polytechnic of Porto and INESC TEC
Porto, Portugal
paula.viana@inesctec.pt

V. Michael Bove
MIT Media Lab
Cambridge, MA, USA
vmb@media.mit.edu

Sharon Strover
University of Texas at Austin
Austin, TX, USA
sharon.strover@austin.utexas.edu

Graham Thomas
BBC, UK
graham.thomas@bbc.co.uk

ABSTRACT
The 2nd ACM International Workshop on Immersive Media Experiences (ImmersiveMe'14) at ACM Multimedia aims at bringing together researchers, students, media producers, service providers and industry players in the emergent area of immersive media experiences, through the exploration of different scenarios, applications, and neighboring fields. This second edition, after a successful first edition at ACM Multimedia 2013, provides a platform for presenting on-going work, to consolidate and tie different research communities working on this engaging area, as well as to point directions for the future.

Categories and Subject Descriptors
H.5.1 [**Information Interfaces and Presentation**]: Multimedia Information Systems; I.2.10 [**Artificial Intelligence**]: Vision and Scene Understanding; H.3.3 [**Information Storage and Retrieval**]: Information Search and Retrieval

Keywords: Immersive media; perceptual immersion; multisensory interaction; participatory and affective media experiences; augmented reality and virtual environments.

1. INTRODUCTION
Immersive Media is related to aspects that have a direct impact on the viewers' experience and on their conscious feeling of being inside the virtual or surrounding world. Immersion may be determined by sensory modalities and surround effect as well as by participation and social immersion in the media chain, increasing the sense of belonging. It has an impact on the users and may benefit from personalized and context-aware environments and content. This interdisciplinary and transversal emerging field has the potential for strong impact on users' emotions, their sense of presence and engagement.

New approaches for capturing, producing, sharing and accessing information from users' perspectives and experiences, over the Internet, in social media, and through video on demand services offer tremendous opportunities for immersion, user participation and personalization. By using different media formats, including 3D content, panoramic displays, multiple views, as well as the possibility of delivering and accessing content through different communication methods, promote the development of a new participatory paradigm and enable new perceptual user experiences that provide more realistic, engaging and immersive involvement.

The workshop goal is to bring together researchers and practitioners in this field, and to foster discussion of ongoing work and future directions of related topics by providing a forum for focused exchanges on new ideas, developments, and results.

MM '14, Nov 03-07, 2014, Orlando, FL, USA.
ACM 978-1-4503-3063-3/14/11.
http://dx.doi.org/10.1145/2647868.2647875

2. TOPICS OF INTEREST
The workshop covers a broad set of topics related to the concept of Immersive Media Experiences in terms of 1) the user's perceptual experience; 2) the consumer's participation; 3) context-aware service personalization; 4) new media formats, including 3D, multiview and panoramic video and interaction approaches; 5) the integration of technology to make media more realistic, and production more efficient. Researchers were invited to contribute in the following areas:

- Perceptual Immersion and multisensory interaction (including smell, taste and touch)
- Audiovisual Immersion: 3D, panoramic, and holographic video, spatial and stereoscopic audio
- Augmented reality enhancing current perception of immersion
- Immersive TV, film and cinema
- Multisensory telecommunication
- Participatory media experiences including user generated content, collaborative scenarios and crowdsourcing
- Personalization and context-aware adaptation in immersive scenarios
- Enabling technologies and formats
- Immersive media applications
- Quality of experience in multiview environments
- Emotions and affective interaction for immersive media
- Social aspects in new media services
- Field trials and user studies of immersive media
- Design and evaluation of immersive media experiences

3. WORKSHOP CONTRIBUTIONS

This second edition of the ImmersiveMe workshop managed to attract a considerable number of high quality submissions from research teams around the world. Many of the papers presented at the workshop were motivated by real-life use cases and concrete application contexts, indicating practical relevance and applicability. These papers cover a broad number of relevant aspects that enable the creation and evaluation of immersive experiences, including synchronization of video streams captured from different viewing angles, multisensory interaction involving taste and smell, emotional computation, new applications of immersive storytelling concepts, virtual environments, games, and natural and immersive interaction. All these visions brought an interesting Immersive Media Experience to the workshop. The workshop was also enriched by an invited talk by Christopher Stapleton, an Experience Designer and Producer having projects with Disney, Universal Studios, Canon, IBM, Nickelodeon, Sanrio and the Wanda Group, where he presented his theories of immersion, imagination and innovation that can help define future design strategies for augmenting human experience.

4. WORKSHOP CHAIRS

Dr. Teresa Chambel is a professor at Faculty of Sciences, University of Lisbon (FCUL) in Portugal, and a senior researcher of the Human Computer Interaction and Multimedia group at the LaSIGE Lab. Her research interests include multimedia and hypermedia, with a special emphasis on video and hypervideo, human-computer interaction (HCI), creativity, immersion, visualization, accessibility, cognition and emotions, interactive TV, eLearning, digital talking books and digital art. Along with her students, she received the best paper award at EuroiTV'2011.

Dr. Paula Viana is a Coordinator Professor at the Polytechnic of Porto and a Senior Researcher at INESC Porto, a research institute with more than 25 years of research results in the area of Telecommunications and Multimedia Services. She has authored papers in the areas of Digital TV, Multimedia Information Systems and Content Management. Her long collaboration with broadcasters and Industries enables an integrated vision of both future research topics as well as new applications for finished research. She has been serving as an expert for the European Commission on the evaluation of research proposals and on the assessment of project results.

Dr. V. Michael Bove, Jr. holds a Ph.D. in Media Technology, from MIT, where he is head of the Object-Based Media Group at the Media Lab, and co-directs the Center for Future Storytelling and the consumer electronics working group CE2.0. He has authored papers on digital TV systems, video processing HW/SW design, multimedia, scene modeling, visual display technologies, and optics. He holds patents relating to video recording, hardcopy, iTV, and medical imaging. He is co-author with the late Stephen A. Benton of the book Holographic Imaging (Wiley, 2008). He is on the Board of Editors of the SMPTE Journal, served as associate editor of Optical Engineering and is a fellow of SPIE and of the Institute for Innovation,Creativity, and Capital. He was a founder of and technical advisor to WatchPoint Media, Inc. and served as technical advisor to OneLaptopPer Child.

Dr. Sharon Strover is the Philip G. Warner Regents Professor in Communication at the University of Texas where she teaches communications and telecommunications courses and directs the Telecommunications and Information Policy Institute. Her research investigates the relationship between economic outcomes, policy and investments in digital media programs; social media; the digital divide; rural broadband deployment; e-government; and market structure and policy issues for international audiovisual industries. She has worked with several government agencies on telecommunications policy matters. She recently stepped down from chairing her Department, to work on a national broadband infrastructure program with the federal government in Washington, D.C.

Prof. Graham Thomas leads Immersive & Interactive Content Section at BBC R&D. Whilst the current work in his section spans both audio and video, his background is in image processing, computer vision and their application to 3D virtual graphics. He was involved in a number of projects that have gone on to commercial success, e.g. free-d camera tracking system, retro-reflective chroma-key cloth, and sports graphics systems. Prior to 3D graphics, he worked on video compression, PAL coding, and motion estimation based on phase correlation (in his PhD), commercialized in a standards converter, which won an Emmy award and a Queen's Award to Industry. Graham holds over 20 patents and is a Visiting Professor at the University of Surrey.

5. PROGRAMME COMMITTEE

Adrian Cheok (City University London, UK)
Anthon Nijholt (Twente University, The Netherland)
Artur Pimenta Alves (Univ of Porto and INESC TEC, Portugal)
David Geerts (CUO Social Spaces, iMinds-KU Leuven, Belgium)
Fabien Gouyon (INESC TEC, Portugal)
George Lekakos (Athens Univ. of Econ. and Business, Greece)
João Magalhães (New University of Lisbon, Portugal)
Kostantinos Chorianopoulos (Ionian University, Greece)
Marc Cavazza, Teesside University, UK
Maria da Graça Pimentel (Universidade de São Paulo, Brazil)
Marian Ursu (University of York, UK)
Marianna Obrist (University of Sussex, UK)
Nelson Zagalo (University of Minho, Portugal)
Nimesha Ranasinghe (New York University Abu Dhabi)
Nuno Correia (New University of Lisbon, Portugal)
Omar A. Niamut (TNO, Delft, The Netherlands)
Pablo Cesar (CWI, The Netherlands)
Rene Kaiser (Joanneum Research, Graz, Austria)
Ryohei Nakatsu (National University of Singapore)
Santosh Basapur (Institute of Design, IIT, USA)
Teresa Andrade (University of Porto and INESC TEC, Portugal)
Teresa Romão (New University of Lisbon, Portugal)
Thibault Langlois (Lasige, Fac. Sciences, Univ. Lisbon, Portugal)

6. ACKNOWLEDGMENTS

This workshop was partially supported by: the Portuguese Foundation for Science and Technology through LaSIGE Strategic Project, ref. PEst-OE/EEI/UI0408/2014 and the ImTV project FCT/UTA-Est/MAI/0010/2009; and the Media, Arts and Technologies Project "NORTE-07-0124-FEDER-000061" funded by the North Portugal Regional Operational Programme (ON.2-O Novo Norte), under the National Strategic Reference Framework (NSRF), through the European Regional Development Fund (ERDF), and national funds, through the Portuguese funding agency, Fundação para a Ciência e a Tecnologia (FCT).

WISMM'14 – First ACM International Workshop on Internet-Scale Multimedia Management

Roger Zimmermann, Yi Yu
School of Computing, National University of Singapore, Singapore 117417
{rogerz,yuy}@comp.nus.edu.sg

ABSTRACT

Advanced technologies in consumer electronic products have enabled individual users to record, transmit and receive images and videos with mobile devices. Every day people create and consume massive amounts of multimedia information and data by engaging with various mobile Internet services. With a wide variety of multimedia information and data around us being aggregated over time, the Internet is getting increasingly information-centric. We are experiencing an age of increasing demands on how we host various people's online engagements and how to augment people's lives in the physical world with more personalized smart services. This workshop addresses a focused but broad research theme with an emphasis on how to manage and derive value from multimedia data in the social Internet landscape to facilitate the connections between users' physical world and their online activities.

Categories and Subject Descriptors

H.3.5 [**Information Storage and Retrieval**]: Online Information Services

Keywords

Location-based multimedia systems; geographic sensor information; social interactions; geo-social distribution; location recommendation; geographic popularity; multimedia content delivery; multimedia big data

1. BACKGROUND

We are witnessing unprecedented growth of multimedia information and data on the web, fostered by multimedia technology innovations and user engagement. One of the characteristics of multimedia information and data is that their scale is massive and requires a technological infrastructure that can accommodate rapid processing, large-scale storage, and flexible analysis of multi-structured data [1, 2, 3, 5]. For example, users like to search the web for goods to purchase or places to visit. Meanwhile, business owners may try to attract more customers with the help of advertising on various websites (*e.g.*, video advertising on YouTube, or banners on the online urban city guide Yelp). Clearly it is increasingly important to connect users' needs and businesses' advertisements via multimedia data and analytics, enabling users to easily find their desired goods or locations and enabling online information to reach the right clientele.

This workshop serves to engage researchers and practitioners who are interested in the scientific connection between the effective collection, analysis and use of multimedia data related to the user-centric physical world and their online activities. It is concerned with (i) data analytics between mobile users and their online behavior in the multimedia domain, (ii) bring together researchers, developers data engineers and scientists who work on different topics in the area of Internet-scale multimedia management, (iii) open a venue for encouraging interdisciplinary discussions in all relevant aspects of peoples' lives in the physical world, their online presence analytics, and a cohesive set of social multimedia data, (iv) collect novel methodologies adapted for the emerging research of Internet-scale multimedia management involving user physical actions and activities, user-centric multimedia content and data, and (v) formulate current and future research and technologies.

Topics of interest for research manuscripts may touch on several issues such as the following: (i) How can multimedia techniques provide user platforms with appealing aesthetics that elicit appropriate emotions to increase the success of commercial advertisement online activities?, (ii) How can multimedia communication technologies keep users engaged with the Internet on-the-go?, (iii) How can social media analytics techniques understand people's sentiments and characterize users' online activities?, and (iv) How can media management techniques accommodate large-scale databases and real-time processing for demand-aware user activities over the Internet?

2. MOTIVATION

This workshop has been motivated by our initial investigation of a piece of work on Foursquare data [4], *e.g.*, vast volumes of check-ins, venue photos, and venue comments are aggregated over time, which are potentially valuable multimedia sources about user physical activities and online sharing behavior in the era of big data. Driven by some questions we found in this study, we proposed this workshop.

The goal of the workshop is to provide a forum where the above and other related questions may be discussed in

MM'14, November 3–7, 2014, Orlando, Florida, USA.
ACM 978-1-4503-3063-3/14/11.
http://dx.doi.org/10.1145/2647868.2647876.

the wider context of Internet-scale multimedia management. As such, the aim of the workshop is also on promoting the methodological development of technologies, systems and applications of Internet-scale multimedia data analytics and management to satisfy the demands of various user-relevant value extractions of Internet multimedia and enabling users' diverse data managements [3, 5]. We hope that the event will provide a channel for Internet-scale multimedia management research to be exchanged to address multimedia technologies in terms of dealing with various user physical lives and online activities.

3. TOPICS OF INTEREST

This workshop is interested in research papers and posters with the goal of shaping and influencing the area of *Internet-scale multimedia management*, which is the science and technology relating to the collection, visualisation, analysis and presentation of multimedia data over the Internet to facilitate connections between users' physical world and online activities. This workshop includes, but is not limited to, the following topics:

- Massive user web behavior analytics for Internet multimedia management
- Location-aware multimedia analytics for online activities and management
- Real-world case studies of physical activity patterns from multimedia data analytics
- Mobile multimedia data traffic modeling and forecasting
- Visualization and interaction for massive music, image, and video data analytics
- Internet-scale multimedia content indexing and mining
- Applied mathematics and statistics of geographic data analytics for intelligent services
- Multimedia pattern recognition from integrated social events
- Fusing multiple sources, synchronizing metadata and integrating existing data sources and services into new demand-centric models (*e.g.*, advertising, security)
- Machine learning and natural language processing in user-centric multimedia big data
- Multimedia systems and applications targeting mobile users

4. FORMAT OF THE WORKSHOP

The workshop has been designed for a full day program on 7 November 2014. The call for papers attracted 18 full submissions and 6 short submissions from Italy, Singapore, Austria, Japan, China, Germany, France, Canada, United States, and Mexico. Each full paper was reviewed by at least three reviewers. From these submissions, we selected 6 full papers which will be organized in two sessions, and 7 short papers which will be presented in a poster session. Two invited talks are included from distinguished speakers:

- ***Storytelling with Big Multimedia Data***, by Ramesh Jain, University of California, Irvine, USA.
- ***Pushing Image Recognition in the Real-World – Towards Recognizing Millions of Entities***, by Xian-Sheng Hua, Microsoft Research, Redmond, USA.

5. PROGRAM COMMITTEE MEMBERS

The organizers would like to gratefully acknowledge the expertise and help of the TPC members of the workshop.

- Kiyoharu Aizawa (University of Tokyo, Japan)
- Michel Crucianu (CNAM, France)
- Shin'ichi Satoh (NII, Japan)
- Seon Ho Kim (USC, USA)
- Enhong Chen (USTC, China)
- Vincent Oria (NJIT, USA)
- Xian-Sheng Hua (Microsoft Research, USA)
- Lei Chen (HKUST, Hong Kong)
- Ichiro Ide (Nagoya University, Japan)
- Benoit Huet (Eurecom, France)
- Suhua Tang (UEC, Japan)
- Aaron Baughman (IBM, USA)
- Mustaq Ahmed (Google, USA)
- Toshihiko Yamasaki (University of Tokyo, Japan)
- Yi-Shin Chen (Nat'l Tsing Hua University, Taiwan)
- Luming Zhang (NUS, Singapore)
- J. Stephen Downie (UIUC, USA)

Acknowledgments

We are grateful to all the authors for submitting their contributions to this workshop. Without them this event would not have been possible.

Special thanks go to the additional reviewers, Yun Hao (UIUC, USA), Tao Chen (NUS, Singapore), and Tongwei Ren (Nanjing University, China).

This workshop has been partially supported by the Singapore National Research Foundation under its International Research Centre @ Singapore Funding Initiative and administered by the IDM Programme Office through the Centre of Social Media Innovations for Communities (COSMIC).

6. REFERENCES

[1] J. Anderson and L. Rainie. The Future of Big Data, the Pew Research Center's Internet & American Life Project Series, 2012.

[2] P. Norvig. Internet Scale Data Analysis. In 17th *ACM SIGKDD International Conference on Knowledge Discovery and Data Mining (KDD)*, pages 2–2, 2011.

[3] Y. Yu, S. Tang, and R. Zimmermann. Edge-based Locality Sensitive Hashing for Efficient Geo-fencing Application. In 21st *ACM SIGSPATIAL International Conference on Advances in Geographic Information Systems*, pages 576–579, 2013.

[4] Y. Yu, S. Tang, R. Zimmermann, and K. Aizawa. Empirical Observation of User Activities: Check-ins, Venue Photos and Tips in Foursquare. In *First ACM International Workshop on Internet-Scale Multimedia Management (ISMM)*, 2014.

[5] R. Zimmermann and Y. Yu. Social Interactions over Geographic-aware Multimedia Systems. In 21st *ACM International Conference on Multimedia*, pages 1115–1116, 2013.

3rd International Workshop on Socially-Aware Multimedia (SAM'14)

Pablo Cesar
CWI: Centrum Wiskunde & Informatica
Science Park 123, 1098 XG
Amsterdam, Netherlands
p.s.cesar@cwi.nl

David A. Shamma
Yahoo! Research
Santa Clara, CA, USA
aymans@acm.org

Matthew Cooper
FX Palo Alto Laboratory, Inc.
3174 Porter Drive, CA 94304
Palo Alto, USA
cooper@fxpal.com

Aisling Kelliher
Carnegie Mellon University
202c Margaret Morrison, PA 15213
Pittsburgh, USA
aislingk@andrew.cmu.edu

ABSTRACT
Multimedia social communication is becoming commonplace. Television is becoming smart and social; media sharing applications are transforming the way we converse and recall events and videoconferencing is a common application on our computers, phones, tablets and even televisions. The confluence of computer-mediated interaction, social networking, and multimedia content are radically reshaping social communications, bringing new challenges and opportunities.

This workshop, in its third edition, provides an opportunity to explore socially-aware multimedia, in which the social dimension of mediated interactions between people are considered to be as important as the characteristics of the media content. Even though this social dimension is implicitly addressed in some current solutions, further research is needed to better understand what makes multimedia socially-aware.

Categories and Subject Descriptors
H.1.2 [**Models and Principles**]: User/Machine Systems – *Human factors*. H.5.1 [**Information Interfaces and Presentation**]: Multimedia Information Systems – *Audio, Video*.

General Terms
Algorithms, Design, Experimentation, Human Factors

Keywords
Social Interaction, social communication, social media, communication, Information retrieval, micro-blogging

MM '14, Nov 03-07 2014, Orlando, FL, USA
ACM 978-1-4503-3063-3/14/11.
http://dx.doi.org/10.1145/2647868.2647877

1. INTRODUCTION
The goal of the workshop on socially-aware multimedia is to pave the way for future innovation by acting as a community-building event, where research challenges can be identified and classified.

Relevant insights can be found within a number of disciplines such as multimedia research, human-computer interaction, and sociology. In particular, multimedia research provides quantitative metrics regarding multimedia objects (e.g., precision and recall) and multimedia systems (e.g., delay, jitter). Human-Computer Interaction research incorporates both quantitative metrics and qualitative understanding regarding human perception (e.g., quality of experience); and sociology and communication science provide a better understanding about motivations and collective group behavior (e.g., conversational and interaction patterns, strength of interpersonal ties).

Nevertheless, we have yet to see a focus on how to measure, to formalize, and to consider social interactivity as a prime parameter for designing and developing multimedia systems and applications. For example, social media research is currently restricted to content curation, independent of the exchange of human conversations that happens around the media object. Acknowledging existing work, this workshop takes the field forward, by articulating the notion of socially aware-multimedia, focusing on the social interactions, on the shared activities, and on the group experiences.

2. CALL FOR PAPERS
The workshop on socially-aware multimedia provides a forum for researchers and practitioners to share novel and groundbreaking results. With special emphasis on innovative directions and on brave ideas, the final goal is to recognize an emergent inter-disciplinary area at the cross roads of multimedia research, social science, and human-computer interaction. In particular, we are interested in papers that focus on multimedia systems and applications, accounting for social interaction theories, metrics, and methodologies. We acknowledge the inter-disciplinary nature of the workshop, and encourage participation from different

research disciplines such as multimedia information retrieval, systems, and applications.

Topics include, but are not limited to:

- Applications of socially-aware multimedia
- Interactive end-to-end systems
- Multimedia modeling (in particular for social interaction and shared experiences)
- Socially-Aware multimedia content analysis and understanding
- Collaborative authoring of videos and multimedia sharing
- Social interaction theories and metrics
- Field trials and user studies of socially-aware multimedia applications
- Qualitative and quantitative evaluation of social participation
- Micro-Blogging and multimedia information retrieval
- Multimedia-Enabled social networking

3. PROGRAM

The International Workshop on Socially-Aware Multimedia (https://sites.google.com/site/sociallyawaremultimedia2014/) will be held in conjunction with the ACM International Multimedia Conference. It will take place on November 7th, 2014, in Orlando (FL), USA. The most pertinent contributions have been selected for inclusion in the workshop's agenda.

The workshop is organized primarily as a forum for discussion and knowledge exchange. Hence, its format is not restricted to paper presentations, but it includes interactive sessions, lead by invited speakers, in which discussion and knowledge exchange are encouraged. The workshop is structured as a working session, for encouraging interaction between the participants and for promoting discussions about socially-aware multimedia research.

As part of the program, there are four invited talks by:

- **Professor Tat-Seng Chua**: National University of Singapore
- **Dr. Munmun De Choudhury**: Georgia Tech
- **Professor Ramesh Jain**: University of California at Irvine
- **Dr. Aisling Kelliher**: Carnegie Mellon University.

The workshop includes as well two keynotes: "Visualizing Coordinated Communicative Behavior" by Dr. Karrie Karahalios and "Attention Rank: Using Social Media to Create Content in the New Information Landscape" by Dr. Mor Naaman.

Dr. Karrie Karahalios is an associate professor in computer science at the University of Illinois, Urbana-Champaign, where she heads the Social Spaces Group. Her work focuses on the interaction between people and the social cues they emit and perceive in face-to-face and mediated electronic spaces. Her work is informed by communication studies and visualizations of social communities. Of particular interest are interfaces for public online and physical gathering spaces such as twitter, chatrooms, cafes, parks, etc. Research projects range from studying tie strength between people to encouraging vocalization through visualization. A major theme in the work is to create interfaces that enable users to perceive conversational patterns that are present, but not obvious, in traditional communication interfaces. She received the Alfred P. Sloan Research Fellowship and the Faculty Early-Career Development Award from the US National Science Foundation (NSF CAREER) in the area of human-centered computing to better understand and visualize conversation dynamics.

Dr. Mor Naaman is an associate professor at Cornell Tech, and co-founder and Chief Scientist at Seen.co. Mor's research applies multidisciplinary methods to gain new insights about people and society from social media data, and to develop novel tools to make this data more accessible and usable in various settings. Previously, Mor worked as a research scientist at Yahoo! Research Berkeley, and received a Ph.D. in Computer Science from Stanford University. He is a recipient of a NSF Early Faculty CAREER Award, research awards from Google, Yahoo!, and Nokia, and three best paper awards. Find out more about Mor at http://mornaaman.com.

4. ORGANISERS

Dr. Pablo Cesar leads the Distributed and Interactive Systems group at CWI (The National Research Institute for Mathematics and Computer Science in the Netherlands). He has (co)-authored over 50 articles about multimedia systems and infrastructures, social media sharing, interactive media, multimedia content modelling, and user interaction. He has given tutorials about multimedia systems in prestigious conferences such as ACM Multimedia, CHI, and the WWW conference. http://homepages.cwi.nl/~garcia

Dr. David A. Shamma is a research scientist at Yahoo! Labs where he manages the HCI Research Group. He researches synchronous environments and connected experiences both online and in-the-world. Focusing on creative expression and sharing frameworks, he designs and prototypes systems for multimedia-mediated communication, as well as, develops targeted methods and metrics for understanding how people communicate online in small environments and at web scale. http://labs.yahoo.com/author/shamma/

Dr. Matthew Cooper is a senior research scientist in the multimedia analysis and visualization group at FX Palo Alto Laboratory (FXPAL). He has developed analysis techniques for indexing, retrieval, and management of digital music, text, photo, and video collections. He currently works on systems and interfaces for aggregation, annotation, and retrieval of web-distributed expository and presentation video. http://www.fxpal.com/people/matthew-cooper

Dr. Aisling Kelliher is an Associate Professor in the School of Design at Carnegie Mellon University, where she also holds an adjunct appointment in the Human-Computer Interaction Institute. She continues to serve as an adjunct professor at her former school - Arizona State University. Aisling leads the newly launched "Visible Process Lab" at CMU's School of Design. She is studying computational documentation, social curation, and the development of experiential media systems. http://www.andrew.cmu.edu/~aislingk/

5. ACKNOWLEDGMENTS

The workshop is supported by FX Palo Alto Laboratory.

Pablo Cesar would like to thank the funding from the Vconect project; European Community's Seventh Framework Programme (FP7/2007-2013) under grant agreement no. ICT-2011-287760.

We would like to thank the Technical Program Committee that helps shaping the program of the workshop.

Summary Abstract for the 3rd ACM International Workshop on Multimedia Analysis for Ecological Data

Concetto Spampinato
Dep. of Electrical, Electronics and Computer Engineering
University of Catania
95125 Catania, Italy
cspampin@dieei.unict.it

Vasileios Mezaris
Centre for Research and Technology Hellas
Informatics and Telematics Institute
Thermi 57001, Greece
bmezaris@iti.gr

Marco Cristani
Computer Science Department
University of Verona
37134 Verona, Italy
marco.cristani@univr.it

ABSTRACT

The 3rd ACM International Workshop on Multimedia Analysis for Ecological Data (MAED'14) is held as part of ACM Multimedia 2014.

MAED'14, following the previous two workshops of the MAED series (MAED'12 and MAED'13) held as part of, respectively, ACM Multimedia 2012 and ACM Multimedia 2013, is concerned with the processing, interpretation, and visualization of ecology-related multimedia content with the aim to support biologists in their investigations for analyzing and monitoring natural environments.

Categories and Subject Descriptors

H.1.0 [**Information Systems**]: Models and Principles

General Terms

Design, Human Factors, Management

Keywords

Multimedia Content Analysis; Fine-grained categorization; Animal and Plant Identification; Pollution Monitoring; Ecological Multimedia Data Retrieval

1. MOTIVATION

With the recent progress in digital cameras and sensors, as well as in network bandwidth and information storage capacities, the production of multimedia data has become an easy task. This has resulted in a huge amount of multimedia available on the web, in broadcast data streams, or in personal and professional databases. This explosion of multimedia data has created the urgent need for efficient organization, browsing and retrieval tools. It has also generated new possibilities for exploiting multimedia data in diverse and specialised applications that can significantly gain from the analysis and understanding of such data. Whilst a large number of multimedia analysis and understanding techniques have been developed specifically for investigating events and behaviours in human-centered applications, such as sports and surveillance, relatively little attention has been paid to the understanding of ecology-related multimedia content. On the other hand, ecology is nowadays being considered an interdisciplinary, collaborative and data-intensive science and as such discovering, integrating and analyzing heterogeneous data are of key important for researchers to address complex questions ranging from single particles to animals to the biosphere. This has led to a proliferation of multimedia data content in the last ten years: for instance, the Xeno-canto project[1] has recorded several thousands of bird sounds from all over the world; the Pl@ntNet project[2] has collected massive plant images for analyzing geographic distribution of plants in the Mediterranean area; the Fish4Knowledge project[3] has recorded many Terabytes of video data for monitoring Taiwanese coral reefs. The wide range of cameras continuously capturing birds nests, wolf, badger, fox and also the continuous collection of multimedia data for pollution monitoring are yet other important examples.

Despite the recent technology advances have enabled massive data collection, its analysis usually requires very time-consuming and expensive input by human observers. This analytical "bottleneck" greatly restricts the use of these technologies and demands for efficient organization, browsing and retrieval tools to enable proactive provision of analytical information. The automated analysis of such ecology-related multimedia data presents new challenges and the results are of great interest to the general public (e.g. considering mobile-based plant recognition applications for amateurs) as well as to domain experts. Examples of the latter include biologists working on understanding the natural environment, promoting its preservation, and studying the behaviour and interactions of the living organisms (insects, animals, etc.) that are part of it.

The goal of the 3rd ACM Workshop on Multimedia Analysis for Ecological Data[4] is to bring together the research community and to discuss the most recent progresses in multimedia data analysis in relation to the above challenges.

MM'14, November 3–7, 2014, Orlando, Florida, USA.
ACM 978-1-4503-3063-3/14/11.
http://dx.doi.org/10.1145/2647868.2647878.

[1]http://www.xeno-canto.org/
[2]http://www.plantnet-project.org/
[3]http://www.fish4knowledge.eu
[4]http://maed2014.dieei.unict.it

2. DESCRIPTION

The 3rd ACM International Workshop on Multimedia Analysis for Ecological Data aims at bringing together practitioners and researchers, both in multimedia and in ecology, to share ideas and experiences in designing and implementing novel multimedia analysis techniques and tools for ecological multimedia content. It includes six papers (selected among eleven submissions) describing methods for multimedia data processing with the goal to support researchers in their studies from underwater monitoring to solar radiation investigation.

In the paper of Palazzo and Murabito [5], a semi-supervised approach for fine-grained recognition is presented, which hits one of the most massive datasets in the multimedia-ecological field: we are talking about 20M of fish images, taken in an underwater scenario. This would certainly be one of the most intriguing challenge for verifying how fine-grained recognition systems are capable of doing their job, and identifying subtle differences among diverse species, whose image instances are taken in a noisy, real scenario.

From images to videosequences: in the paper of Katy *et al.* [3], underwater videos are taken into account, with the aim of recognizing fish species. Here, a whole processing chain is presented, from background subtraction to the recognition module, which turns out to be a very immediate help to researchers (even not scientists in the multimedia field) who have to face a common yet hard task.

From the sea to the mountains, Fedorov *et al.* [1] present a work on the identification of mountain peaks by edge-matching geo-tagged photographs and synthetic 360°panoramas created from coarse DEM (Digital Elevation Model) data. This will probably be intriguing since the diffusion of such applications on smartphones is nowadays increasing.

Flying from the mountains to the satellites, the work of Torres and Qiu [6] shows how a crowd-sourcing platform such as Geograph may help in the difficult task of image-based habitat classification, extending previous work and presenting interesting results on thousand of images. The main idea is that higher-level semantic features obtained by crowdsourcing can improve the limitations that visual features have for fine-grained visual categorization.

Nunnari and Fortuna turn from the earth to the sun [4], presenting a technique for identifying the hourly solar radiation, with the interesting possibility of applying the proposed technique for prediction.

Finally, Joly *et al.* [2] present a more general study on the performance of different identification systems, which can be seen as a function of the ordinariness or rarity of the categories in the dataset taken into account; in other words, the capacity to classify both the most and the less populated categories. This study is performed on three multimedia oriented life species datasets: PlantCLEF, BirdCLEF and FishCLEF.

3. CONCLUDING REMARKS

The ACM International Workshop on Multimedia Analysis for Ecological Data brings together practitioners and researchers, both in multimedia and in ecology, to share ideas and experiences for the analysis of multimedia content for natural environment monitoring. We hope that the selected papers will serve as valuable reference for the future research on this ground-breaking research area.

4. REFERENCES

[1] Fedorov, R., Fraternali, P., and Tagliasacchi, M. Mountain peak identification in visual content based on coarse digital elevation models. In *3rd ACM International Workshop on Multimedia Analysis for Ecological Data (MAED)* (New York, NY, USA, 2014), ACM.

[2] Joly, A., Goëau, H., Bonnet, P., Spampinato, C., Glotin, H., Rauber, A., Vellinga, W.-P., Fisher, R., and Müller, H. Are multimedia identification tools biodiversity-friendly ? In *3rd ACM International Workshop on Multimedia Analysis for Ecological Data (MAED)* (New York, NY, USA, 2014), ACM.

[3] Katy, B., Lingrand, D., and Precioso, F. Fish species recognition from video using svm classifier. In *3rd ACM International Workshop on Multimedia Analysis for Ecological Data (MAED)* (New York, NY, USA, 2014), ACM.

[4] Nunnari, S., and Fortuna, L. A typical day based approach to detrend solar radiation time series. In *3rd ACM International Workshop on Multimedia Analysis for Ecological Data (MAED)* (New York, NY, USA, 2014), ACM.

[5] Palazzo, S., and Murabito, F. Fish species identification in "real-life" underwater images. In *3rd ACM International Workshop on Multimedia Analysis for Ecological Data (MAED)* (New York, NY, USA, 2014), ACM.

[6] Torres, M., and Qiu, G. Crowd-sourcing applied to photograph-based automatic habitat classification. In *3rd ACM International Workshop on Multimedia Analysis for Ecological Data (MAED)* (New York, NY, USA, 2014), ACM.

PIVP 2014: First International Workshop on Perception Inspired Video Processing

Hari Kalva
Florida Atlantic University
777 Glades Road
Boca Raton, FL 33431, USA
hkalva@fau.edu

Homer Chen
National Taiwan University
1, Sec. 4, Roosevelt Road
Taipei 10617, Taiwan
homer@ntu.edu.tw

Gerardo Fernandez Escribano
University of Castilla La Mancha
Avenida de España s/n, 02071
Albacete, Spain
gerardo.fernandez@uclm.es

Velibor Adzic
Videopura
Delray Beach, FL, USA
velibor.adzic@videopura.com

ABSTRACT

This is a MM'14 Workshop Summary Abstract for PIVP'14 - 1st International Workshop on Perception Inspired Video Processing. Workshop provided a venue for researchers involved with perceptual video processing and coding to present their current work and to discuss future directions. The workshop program consisted of a keynote talk, oral presentations of full papers and interactive poster session for the short papers. All participants took part in the discussion panel at the end of workshop, exchanging ideas and suggestions for future work.

Categories and Subject Descriptors

H.5.1 [**Information Interfaces and Presentation**]: Multimedia Information Systems - *Evaluation/Methodology, Video*. I.2.10 [**Artificial Intelligence**]: Vision and Scene Understanding - *Motion, Perceptual reasoning, Video analysis*.

General Terms

Algorithms, Measurement, Performance, Design, Experimentation, Human Factors, Standardization, Theory.

Keywords

Multimedia; Video Coding; Perceptual Video; Human Vision.

INTRODUCTION

Video services are taking up increasingly large amount of Internet traffic today. For example, just two popular on-demand video services alone use up 49.4% of Internet downstream traffic during peak hours of 7:00 PM to 10:00 PM in the US [1]. Such on-demand video is being accessed from a range of consumer electronics devices such as TVs, DVRs, Blu-ray players, and mobile entertainment devices. Globally, consumer Internet video traffic will be 69% of all consumer Internet traffic in 2017, up from 57% in 2012. The sum of all forms of video (TV, video on demand, Internet, and P2P) will be in the range of 80 to 90 percent of global consumer traffic in the next three years [2]. The traditional approach to video compression based on hybrid coding (hybrid of motion compensation and transform coding) is being stretched to the limit and increasing the complexity of video encoders and decoders will not be sufficient to meet the continued bandwidth and storage demands placed by video services. As the amount of video increases, resources needed to process the video also increase. Processing tasks such as analytics and content understanding are especially resource intensive and have time critical applications. New approaches to video processing are needed to keep up with the service demands.

Video compression in its most commonly used form is designed to introduce imperceptible signal loss. As compression ratios increase, bitrate decreases, loss increases, and distortion becomes perceptible. In order to achieve compression that is close to optimal for a given distortion, a criterion has to be established to describe the quality of the reconstructed signal. Rate-distortion (RD) theory gives us a framework for modeling lossy compression [3]. In most of the cases RD models in modern video coding systems use mean squared error (MSE) and peak signal-to-noise ratio (PSNR) as a measure of distortion. There has been a significant amount of work dedicated to optimization of image and video coding based on the PSNR metric. Actually, it has been used as a distortion metric and a benchmark for most of the modern video coding standards, including the widely used codecs such as AVC/H.264 and HEVC [4, 5].

SIGNIFICANCE

Having in mind trends and current state-of-the-art in video coding, it is clear that novel approaches to video compression are needed in order to sustain growing demand for video content. One promising direction is exploration of perceptual and cognitive paradigms that haven't been fully utilized.

MM '14, Nov 03-07 2014, Orlando, FL, USA

ACM 978-1-4503-3063-3/14/11.

http://dx.doi.org/10.1145/2647868.2647879

Perceptual and cognitive factors affect how users acquire and process visual information, and an understanding of these factors and experiences offers opportunities to achieve the next big leap in video processing. In particular, many findings from areas such as Vision Science, Behavioral Sciences, and Neuroscience have strong implications for developing efficient, perceptually optimized video processing frameworks, algorithms, and applications

Perceptual methods for video coding can bring additional improvements in compression efficiency without affecting quality of experience [6, 7]. Another avenue of research is utilizing higher (cognitive) processing factors that are related to attention [8]. Combination of low level factors and high level processing gives promising results.

However, in order to fully exploit the possibilities of using perceptual and cognitive methods, we have to stay up to date with current developments in psychophysics and find ways to implement the findings from these studies. In this manner, PIVP workshop served as a perfect venue to present current research in both perception and cognitive inspired algorithms and methods and discuss ideas for future directions.

As another example of the workshop recognition and significance, outstanding workshop contributors are invited to submit an extended paper to the Special issue of Multimedia Tools and Applications.

TOPICS AND GOALS

The goal of this workshop is to bring together experts working on applying models, principles, and knowledge of human audio-visual perception and cognition to optimize video processing algorithms and applications.

Specific topics of interest in this workshop include:

- Perceptual video coding
- Quality of Experience
- Video analysis
- Perceptual models for video processing
- Influence of content on perception
- Influence of emotion on video perception
- Emotion detection in videos
- Neural correlates of video
- Influence of audio on video processing
- Datasets for perceptual video research.

ORGANIZING COMMITTEE

Hari Kalva, Florida Atlantic University, USA

Homer Chen, National Taiwan University, Taiwan

Velibor Adzic, Videopura, USA

Gerardo Fernandez, University of Castilla La Mancha, Spain

PROGRAM COMMITTEE

Ivan Bajic, Simon Fraser University

Alan Bovik, University of Texas at Austin

Damon Chandler, Oklahoma State University

Lai-Tee Cheok, Singapore Management University

Robert Cohen, Mitsubishi Electric Research Laboratories

Howard Hock, Florida Atlantic University

Patrick Le Callet, Universite de Nantes

King Ngan, Chinese University of Hong Kong

Adar Pelah, University of York

Vladimir Stankovic, University of Strathclyde

REFERENCES

[1] Sandvine global internet phenomena report 1Q 2013, http://www.sandvine.com/downloads/documents/Phenomena_1H_2013/Sandvine_Global_Internet_Phenomena_Report_1H_2013.pdf , May 2013..

[2] Cisco Visual Networking Index: Forecast and Methodology, 2012–2017, http://www.cisco.com/en/US/solutions/collateral/ns341/ns525/ns537/ns705/ns827/white_paper_c11-481360.pdf , May 2013.

[3] T. Berger, Rate-Distortion Theory, John Wiley & Sons, 1971.

[4] H. Kalva, "The H.264 Video Coding Standard," IEEE Multimedia, vol.13, no.4, pp.86-90, Oct.-Dec. 2006.

[5] G.J. Sullivan, J. Ohm, H. Woo-Jin, and T. Wiegand, "Overview of the High Efficiency Video Coding (HEVC) Standard," IEEE Transactions on Circuits and Systems for Video Technology, vol.22, no.12, pp.1649-1668, Dec. 2012.

[6] Velibor Adzic. 2012. What you see is what you should get. In Proceedings of the 20th ACM international conference on Multimedia (MM '12). ACM, New York, NY, USA, 1441-1444.

[7] P.-Y. Su, Y.-H. Huang, T.-S. Ou, and H. H. Chen, "Recent progress on prceptual video coding," in Proc. Visual Comm. Image Process., Nov. 2011.

[8] H. Hadizadeh, and I.V. Bajic, "Saliency-Aware Video Compression," IEEE Transactions on Image Processing , vol.23, no.1, pp.19,33, Jan. 2014.

Serious Games 2014: International Workshop on Serious Games

Wolfgang Effelsberg
Praktische Informatik IV
University of Mannheim
Mannheim, Germany
+49 621 181 2600
effelsberg@informatik.uni-mannheim.de

Stefan Göbel
KOM
TU Darmstadt
Darmstadt, Germany
+49 6151 16 6149
stefan.goebel@kom.tu-darmstadt.de

ABSTRACT
The ACM First International Workshop on Serious Games was held on November 7, 2014. It was co-located with ACM's International Conference on Multimedia in Orlando. The purpose of the workshop was to bring together researchers and practitioners working on the development and use of serious games. The rationale behind co-locating this workshop with ACM Multimedia was that games are indeed multimedia systems, involving 3D graphics, integrated audio processing, human factors for the input devices, and often also the real-time transmission of events over computer networks.

Categories and Subject Descriptors
[Applied Computing] Education, [Applied Computing] Health and Medical Sciences, [User/Machine Systems] Human Factors, [Computers and Education] Computer and Information Science Education

Keywords
Serious games, gamification, game development, elearning, games in health, games in education, games in culture

1. INTRODUCTION
Computer Games are very popular worldwide. The market volume has almost reached that of feature films. Serious games, however, are different from fun games: they have a serious purpose that is combined with the fun aspect for motivating the players. Examples for the serious purpose include education and training, fitness, health, marketing and many more. Thus, at this workshop, we had experts from both game development and the application areas, contributing their outstanding knowledge and innovative ideas. The authors of accepted papers were allowed to bring their games to the workshop for demonstration.

2. SCOPE
The workshop began with an invited talk on *The Five Most Important Research Issues in Effective Game Design* by Thomas Baranowski of Baylor College of Medicine in Houston, Texas. He is a professor for pediatrics with many years of experience in using games for childrens' health. Thomas Baranowski took the perspective of a behavioral scientist and gave recommendations for a successful game design from his large experience.

The invited talk was followed by three sessions of submitted and accepted papers: Serious Game Development, Serious Games in Health, and Serious Games in Education, Training and Culture. In the first session, Ralf Dörner and Ulrike Spierling presented a paper on *Serious Game Development as a Vehicle for Teaching Entertainment Technology and Interdisciplinary Teamwork*. They derived general advice on how game development can be used successfully in teaching. Luca Galli proposed rules how to employ game mechanics for serious games in his paper *Matching Game Mechanics and Human Computation Tasks in Games with a Purpose*. The interesting topic of *simulating players in a collaborative multiplayer serious game* was addressed by Viktor Wendel et al. They propose an approach to realistically simulate human player behavior in collaborative multiplayer serious games, taking learning, collaboration and teamwork into account. Laila Shoukry et al. use *learning analytics for serious games*. Learning analytics are a modern approach to evaluate teachware modules but they have not been used frequently for serious games before. The authors emphasize the importance of integrating logging software into the serious game in order to later analyze the learning behavior of the player.

In the second paper session, Andrea Ferracani et al. discuss the *design and implementation of a natural and immersive virtual interface for surgical safety checklist training*. Since operations are safety-critical for humans, the World Health Organization (WHO) has issued a safety checklist for surgeons, anesthesiologists and nurses to go through before they begin an operation, and the serious game of the authors helps them in performing this task. *Recent evidence on serious games in neurorehabilitation* is examined by Josef Wiemeyer. He analyzes more than 30 games in that context and concludes that a positive tendency can be observed for their effectiveness but the evidence is not yet convincing. John Preston takes a different approach at health games: He supports the development of serious *games for health in a big game jam* he holds every year, and in his paper he reports the interesting results of the most recent event.

In paper session 3, the application of games to education, training and culture was addressed. Michael Christel et al. presented *Lessons Learned from Testing a Children's Educational Game through Web Deployment*. They created four versions of a simple balance-fulcrum game, teaching the children about the importance of weight and its distance from the fulcrum, with different opportunities for socio-emotional learning added in. In their evaluation they reported interesting results about the use of the different versions; for example, the children stopped playing the game with

MM '14, Nov 03-07 2014, Orlando, FL, USA
ACM 978-1-4503-3063-3/14/11.
http://dx.doi.org/10.1145/2647868.2647880

the socio-emotional learning component earlier. In their paper *Games for Cultural Awareness* Jennifer Bohn et al. present a serious game for exchange students to learn about the culture of their host universities and their host countries. And Sandro Hardy et al. quantify *the challenge in an exercising game* where the user has to do specific training on a balance board; they interpret the degree of challenge they measure as a major indication for the motivation to keep playing.

Altogether the invited talk and the three papers sessions gave an excellent overview over the current state of the art in serious games.

3. ORGANIZERS OF THE WORKSHOP

This workshop was organized by Thomas Baranowski (Baylor College of Medicine, Houston, Texas), Mark Claypool (Worcester Polytechnic Institute, Worcester, Massachusetts), Ralf Dörner (University of Applied Sciences, Wiesbaden, Germany), Wolfgang Effelsberg (University of Mannheim, Germany), Stefan Göbel (Technische Universität Darmstadt, Germany), Florian 'Floyd' Mueller (Royal Melbourne Institute of Technology, Melbourne, Australia). They were also the chairs of the program committee.

4. PROGRAM COMITTEE

Jannicke Baalsrud Hauge, University of Bremen, Germany

Marc Cavazza, Teesside University, UK

Stefano A. Cerri, University of Montpellier II, France

Karin Coninx, Hasselt University, Belgium

Simon Egenfeldt-Nielsen, Serious Games Interactive, Denmark

Sara de Freitas, Serious Games Institute, University of Coventry, UK

Abdulmotaleb El Saddik, University of Ottawa, Canada

Henrik Hautop Lund, Technical University of Denmark, Denmark

Shamim Hossain, King Saud University, South Arabia

Wolfgang Huerst, University of Utrecht, Netherlands

Michael Kickmeier-Rust, TU Graz, Austria

Rainer Malaka, University of Bremen, Germany

Balthasar Manjón, Universidad Complutense Madrid, Spain

Timothy Marsh, James Cook University, Australia

Maic Masuch, Uni Duisburg-Essen, Germany

Robin Mellecker, University of Hong Kong, Hong Kong

Andre Miede, University of Applied Sciences Saarbrücken, Germany

Klara Nahrstedt, University of Illinois at Urbana-Champaign

Thomas Plagemann, University of Oslo, Norway,

Shervin Shirmohammadi, University of Ottawa, Canada

Ralf Steinmetz, Technische Universität Darmstadt, Germany

Erik Van der Spek, Eindhoven University of Technology, Netherlands

Steffen Walz, RMIT, Melbourne, Australia

Noah Wardrip-Fruin, University of California Santa Cruz, United States

Viktor Wendel, Technische Universität Darmstadt, Germany

Josef Wiemeyer, Technische Universität Darmstadt, Germany

Kevin Wong, Murdoch University, Australia

5. ACKNOWLEDGMENTS

We gratefully acknowledge the wonderful work the authors have done in writing and presenting their papers and demonstrations, and in the fruitful discussions during the workshop. We also acknowledge the great work the program committee did in reviewing all the papers; we have received at least three reviews for each paper, often five.

REFERENCES

You can find these papers in the workshop proceedings in ACM's Digital Library.

[1] Bohn, J., Eibl, M., Berger, A., Müller, S. 2014. Games for Cultural Awareness

[2] Christel, M., Stevens, S., Maher, B., Champer, M., Collier, S., Merchan Benavides, R. 2014. Lessons Learned from Testing a Children's Educational Game through Web Deployment

[3] Dörner, R., Spierling, U. 2014. Serious Game Development as a Vehicle for Teaching Entertainment Technology and Interdisciplinary Teamwork: Perspectives and Pitfalls

[4] Ferracani, A., Pezzatini, D., Del Bimbo, A. 2014. A Natural and Immersive Virtual Interface for the Surgical Safety Checklist Training

[5] Galli, L. 2014. Matching: Game Mechanics and Human Computation Tasks in Games with a Purpose

[6] Hardy, S., Kern, A., Dutz, T., Weber, Ch., Göbel, S., Steinmetz, R. 2014. What Makes a Game Challenging? An Approach to Quantify the Challenge of an Exergame for Balance Training

[7] Preston, J. 2014. Serious Game Development: Case Study of the 2013 CDC Games For Health Game Jam

[8] Shoukry, L., Göbel, S., Steinmetz, R. 2014. Learning Analytics and Serious Games: Trends and Considerations

[9] Wendel, V., Alef, J., Göbel, S., Steinmetz, R. 2014. A Method for Simulating Players in a Collaborative Multiplayer Serious Game

[10] Wiemeyer, J. 2014. Serious Games in Neurorehabilitation – A Review of Recent Evidence

Author Index

www.ingramcontent.com/pod-product-compliance
Ingram Content Group UK Ltd.
Pitfield, Milton Keynes, MK11 3LW, UK
UKHW051418290926
15471UKWH00009B/1671

9 781450 334266